THE NEW
JERUSALEM
BIBLE

Saints' Devotional Edition

THE NEW JERUSALEM
BIBLE

Introduction, Selections, and Commentary by

BERT GHEZZI

General Editor

HENRY WANSBROUGH

DARTON · LONGMAN + TODD

First published in Great Britain in 2002
by Darton, Longman and Todd Ltd
1 Spencer Court
140-142 Wandsworth High Street
London SW18 4JJ

First printed in the USA in 2002
by Doubleday, a division of Random House, Inc.
1540 Broadway, New York, New York 10036

Nilhi obstat   Anton Cowan
Imprimatur   Rt Rev John Crowley v.g.
BISHOP OF CENTRAL LONDON
Westminster, 4 September 1989

For Introduction, Selections, and Commentaries by Bert Ghezzi
Nihil obstat   Sister Lucy Vasquez, o.p., j.c.d.
Imprimatur   Most Reverend Norbert M. Dorsey, c.p., s.t.d.
BISHOP OF ORLANDO
Orlando, Florida, 24 August 2001

ISBN 0-232-52458-0

A catalogue record for this book is available from the British Library

Printed and bound in the USA

Contents

General Editor's Foreword

The Bible is not a book but a library, joining together dozens of writings, history, stories, poetry, and letters. The common factor between them is that they all speak to us of God, revealing his nature, his awesome sovereignty, and his tender love.

The Old Testament divides into three sections. The Histories (including the basic first five books, the great Law of Israel) show God's loving guidance and correction of Israel from nomad beginnings through all the trials and infidelities of the settled civilisation in Palestine. The Wisdom books (including the Psalms, the prayerbook of Israel) express the collective wisdom of Israel, drawn from God for the practical art of living. The prophetic writings gather the warnings and promises of God articulated by those special messengers who strove to keep Israel faithful for the centuries before Christ. By all these means God was forming his people, preparing them for the fulfilment of his purposes in Christ.

The New Testament divides into two sections. First are printed the four gospels, the record of the message of Good News brought by Jesus. Then are assembled the letters of Paul and the other apostolic figures to the nascent churches of Mediterranean Christianity, some written earlier than the gospels, instructing the early Christians and helping them solve their problems, but also providing a source of understanding and guidance for every Christian generation. The last book of the Bible, the Revelation to John, sums all up in the vision of deliverance from persecution and a glorious establishment of the reign of God in the New Jerusalem.

This standard Edition of *The New Jerusalem Bible* is based on the much larger Regular Edition first published in 1985. The translation follows the original Hebrew, Aramaic, and Greek texts. For the Old Testament the Hebrew (and infrequently Aramaic) provides the basic text, though this is supplemented where necessary by the Greek text established in the two centuries before Christ at Alexandria. Occasionally a double series of verse-numbers is given; this reflects a different numbering in the Hebrew and the Greek texts. The Greek version additionally provides the books called 'the Apocrypha', and also some supplements to other books (which are here printed in italics). In the New Testament italics are used exclusively to indicate quotations from elsewhere in the Bible. Gaps in the text are marked with ellipses (. . .); this indicates an unintelligible word or an incomplete sentence in the original, which scholars have not been able to fill out satisfactorily. Brackets in the Old Testament text show that the passage is considered a gloss, an addition or explanation later than the original text. The equal sign (=) indicates either a parallel passage within the same book, or simply 'equals'. Parallel lines (||) denote a parallel passage within another biblical book.

The word of many devoted scholars has contributed to this Bible: those who produced the parent *La Bible de Jérusalem* in 1956, the collaborators on the first English-language *The Jerusalem Bible* (1966), the revisers of *La Bible de Jérusalem* (1973), and those who combined to produce the Regular Edition of *The New Jerusalem Bible* in 1985. The grateful reader might spare a prayer of thanks and blessing on them all.

—Henry Wansbrough

Introduction to the Saints' Devotional Edition

The Saints and the Bible

In the Bible, God unfolds his wonderful plan for human beings. He wants to bring us into his divine family, adopting us as his sons and daughters, uniting us to himself, and making us holy by giving us the Holy Spirit. To help us along the way, the church, God's community on earth, has officially identified some people who have responded more fully than others to this divine plan. These men and women have loved God and others in a consistently extraordinary way, and we call them "saints." The church gives them to us as exemplars of the Christian life, so that by imitating them we too might become saints.

Exerting sheer human effort, however, does not make us saints. That's the exclusive work of the Holy Spirit, who draws us to Christ, claims us, transforms us, teaches us, guides us, corrects us, and enables us to do all things in love. We become saints by doing the right things in response to the Spirit. The church provides us direction and opportunities we need for growth in its teaching, liturgy, and practice.

Among these provisions for our holiness, the Bible holds a special place of importance. The saints tell us in their writings, for example, that in Scripture they found enlightenment for their minds and nourishment for their souls. Many also say that they met God in the Bible, for it is the Word of God and he is present in its pages.

As you will observe in this edition of the Bible, the saints steeped themselves in Scripture. You will see it in what they said, what they wrote, and above all in what they did, for in all things they concentrated on conforming to God's Word.

The saints have approached the Bible in a wide variety of ways, all of them instructive and spiritually stimulating for us. Here is a sampler of the saints' use of Scripture, which you will notice in greater detail as you read the selections in this Bible.

SAINTS STUDY SCRIPTURE

Regular Bible study is a basic means of growth, and saints have majored in it. All have avidly read Scripture. Monks like St. Bernard of Clairvaux and nuns like St. Teresa of Avila listened to the proclamation of the Word daily during Mass and the Liturgy of the Hours. Some like St. Jerome, St. Fulgentius of Ruspe, and St. Augustine studied the Bible professionally, preparing new translations, writing commentaries, and so making it more accessible for others. Scripture study also undergirded the writings of women saints like Jane de Chantal and Edith Stein. If we really want to grow in Christ, we will imitate the saints and make Bible study a part of our daily routine.

SAINTS MEMORIZE SCRIPTURE

Before the 1500s, when Bibles were scarce, saints committed Scripture to memory. St. Dominic, for example, held large portions of the Bible in his memory and used it as ready reference when he preached. Even when the invention of printing in the sixteenth century made more Bibles available, many saints continued the practice because it helped them mature in Christ. Memorizing Scripture is spiritually pragmatic. What better raw material could the Holy Spirit have to work with when he wants to inspire our thoughts?

SAINTS PRAY SCRIPTURE

The Bible is a source of Christian prayer, for there we meet the Word himself and can speak to God with his own inspired words. A preeminent example is Mary's Magnificat (see Lk 1:46–55). The Virgin drew from Scripture for every line of this prayer that celebrated her divine pregnancy. Many saints prayed the Psalms and other Bible texts several times a day at the Liturgy of the Hours. Some saints have prayed a single text so consistently that it became their life theme, as you will see in the case of St. Theresa of the Sacred Heart and St. Camillus de Lellis.

SAINTS USE SCRIPTURE IN SPIRITUAL WARFARE

Imitating Jesus' example in the desert (see Mt 4:1–11), saints have used God's Word to resist the devil. With Scripture, St. Anthony of Egypt sent demonic hordes scurrying through the desert. St. Lutgarde, whose knowledge of the Bible was somewhat limited because she did not understand Latin, nonetheless dismissed diabolical tormentors with verses from the Psalms. Quoting Scripture makes devils flee because the Bible contains God's own Word in human words. So like the saints, in times of trial or temptation, we can turn to the Bible for help.

SAINTS SEEK GUIDANCE IN SCRIPTURE

Saints have looked to the Bible for answers to questions that stumped them. In its pages they sought resolutions to dilemmas that seemed to block their way. When St. Thérèse of Lisieux, for example, was puzzled about her role in the body of Christ, she explored St. Paul's letters for direction. Her study pointed her to the simple path of service that she happily followed to sainthood. Experiences like St. Thérèse's show us that we can count on Scripture to guide us safely because we are not merely consulting an author who has some good ideas about life, but the Author of life himself.

God designed the Bible to communicate the truth to human beings, and saints have employed diverse means to spread his Word. Some gifted preachers like St. John Chrysostom and St. Vincent Ferrer held thousands spellbound with their exposition of Bible texts. Others like St. Clare of Assisi often simply shared Scripture one-on-one. In conversation and sermons, in letters and textbooks, in amphitheaters, on the street, and in homes, saints have announced the good news in the ways that best suited their character and their culture. Following their example, knowledge of Scripture will help us draw others to Christ and the church.

SAINTS APPLY SCRIPTURE

Saints do not read Scripture merely out of intellectual curiosity, or even just for inspiration. Above all, they are doers of the Word. When they think they have grasped the kernel of God's intent in a text, they strive to put it into practice. One line of Scripture sometimes triggers a dramatic turnaround as it did for St. Anthony, St. Augustine, and St. Alipius. Or a poignant verse might set a saint on a course for life. Jesus' words "I was hungry and you never gave me food" (Mt 25:42) caused St. Joan Delanoue to devote herself to care for destitute orphans. Or a saint may pray a particular text to help him get through daily nuisances, as St. John Cassian did with the verse from Psalm 70, "Come to my help, O God. Lord, hurry to my rescue."

Like the saints, we should read Scripture in order to acquire an ever-increasing understanding of God's Word. Like them, we should also pray Scripture in order to allow the Holy Spirit to take us into a deeper union with God. And finally like all the saints, we should become faithful doers of the Word, obeying what God says to us as we read the Bible.

To serve you in this most important quest, *The New Jerusalem Bible, Saints' Devotional Edition* is designed to help you grow in reading Scripture, praying with it, and applying it to your life.

Features of This Edition

THE BIBLE

The New Jerusalem Bible presents the complete text of the ancient canon of the Scriptures in a readable, modern translation of the Bible, which is based on the best scholarship and bears the imprimatur of the Roman Catholic Church.

READINGS

This Bible contains two hundred readings taken from the writings of the saints, one hundred for the Hebrew Scriptures of the Old Testament and one hundred for the New Testament. Each selection is located near the text it concerns. For your convenience in working your way through the Bible, the readings are numbered from 1 to 200. You will find a great diversity among the readings. They include commentaries, reflections, preaching, testimonies, poems, hymns, letters, and more. The readings are intended to draw you into the Scripture, so be sure to read the assigned text before you read the selection.

SAINTS ON SCRIPTURE

The Saints on Scripture is a mini-course on reading, praying, and applying God's Word. Based exclusively on the teaching and experience of the saints, the course's twenty units are located in two sections, the first following page 364 and the second following page 1180. You may choose to work your way systematically through the course from unit 1 to 20. Or you may read the units that interest you the most, as each is designed to stand alone. A listing of the Saints on Scripture appears on page xv.

BIOGRAPHICAL SKETCHES OF THE SAINTS AND INDEX OF THEIR READINGS

This *Saints' Devotional Edition* of the *New Jerusalem Bible* provides biographical sketches of the ninety saints whose selections appear in the text. Each mini-biography reports basic facts, includes the saint's feast day, and indexes the locations in the Bible where the saint's selections appear. The Biographical Sketches and Index is located at the back of the Bible beginning on page 1573.

THEMES

The list of themes presents the selections from the saints topically. It contains ninety-six subjects, alphabetically arranged from Almsgiving to Worship. Under each entry on the themes list, you will find the locations of Bible texts and the saints' readings that relate to them. Themes is located after Biographical Sketches on page 1589.

A CALENDAR OF SAINTS

Beginning on page 1593, you will find a calendar of saints. This list includes saints universally celebrated in the liturgy of the Roman Catholic Church, as well as saints especially honored in the English-speaking world.

PATRON SAINTS

A list of saints that the church has designated as patrons appears on page 1597. There you will find patrons for occupations, vocations, personal needs, countries, and other special concerns.

Saints on Scripture

THE NEW
JERUSALEM
BIBLE

THE NEW
JERUSALEM
BIBLE

THE OLD TESTAMENT

GENESIS

The creation of the world

1 In the beginning God created heaven and earth. ²Now the earth was a formless void, there was darkness over the deep, with a divine wind sweeping over the waters.

³God said, 'Let there be light,' and there was light. ⁴God saw that light was good, and God divided light from darkness. ⁵God called light 'day', and darkness he called 'night'. Evening came and morning came: the first day.

⁶God said, 'Let there be a vault through the middle of the waters to divide the waters in two.' And so it was. ⁷God made the vault, and it divided the waters under the vault from the waters above the vault. ⁸God called the vault 'heaven'. Evening came and morning came: the second day.

⁹God said, 'Let the waters under heaven come together into a single mass, and let dry land appear.' And so it was. ¹⁰God called the dry land 'earth' and the mass of waters 'seas', and God saw that it was good.

¹¹God said, 'Let the earth produce vegetation: seed-bearing plants, and fruit trees on earth, bearing fruit with their seed inside, each corresponding to its own species.' And so it was. ¹²The earth produced vegetation: the various kinds of seed-bearing plants and the fruit trees with seed inside, each corresponding to its own species. God saw that it was good. ¹³Evening came and morning came: the third day.

¹⁴God said, 'Let there be lights in the vault of heaven to divide day from night, and let them indicate festivals, days and years. ¹⁵Let them be lights in the vault of heaven to shine on the earth.' And so it was. ¹⁶God made the two great lights: the greater light to govern the day, the smaller light to govern the night, and the stars. ¹⁷God set them in the vault of heaven to shine on the earth, ¹⁸to govern the day and the night and to divide light from darkness. God saw that it was good. ¹⁹Evening came and morning came: the fourth day.

²⁰God said, 'Let the waters be alive with a swarm of living creatures, and let birds wing their way above the earth across the vault of heaven.' And so it was. ²¹God created great sea-monsters and all the creatures that glide and teem in the waters in their own species, and winged birds in their own species. God saw that it was good. ²²God blessed them, saying, 'Be fruitful, multiply, and fill the waters of the seas; and let the birds multiply on land.' ²³Evening came and morning came: the fifth day.

²⁴God said, 'Let the earth produce every kind of living creature in its own species: cattle, creeping things and wild animals of all kinds.' And so it was. ²⁵God made wild animals in their own species, and cattle in theirs, and every creature that crawls along the earth in its own species. God saw that it was good.

²⁶God said, 'Let us make man in our own image, in the likeness of ourselves, and let them be masters of the fish of the sea, the birds of heaven, the cattle, all the wild animals and all the creatures that creep along the ground.'

²⁷God created man in the image of himself,
   in the image of God he created him,
   male and female he created them.

²⁸God blessed them, saying to them, 'Be fruitful, multiply, fill the earth and subdue it. Be masters of the fish of the sea, the birds of

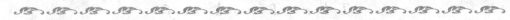

1 READ GENESIS 1:1–25.

In the beginning God created heaven and earth.—GENESIS 1:1

INVITATION TO LOVE

All your creatures, O Lord, invite me to love you. In every one of them I see a tongue that proclaims your goodness and greatness. The beauty of the heavens, the clearness of the sun and moon, the glistening of the stars, the brightness of the planets, the running streams of water, the greenness of the fields, the diversity of flowers, the variety of colors, and all that your divine goodness has ever made, O God of my heart and spouse of my soul, tells me that I should love you. Everything that I see invites me to your love, and blames me when I don't love you. I can't open my eyes without seeing preachers of your exalted wisdom. And I can't open my ears without hearing news of your goodness. For everything you have made tells me about you, O Lord. All created things show the love of the Creator.

Speaking of the creation, Scripture says a divine wind swept over the waters. It is as if it were the mind of some singular workman considering many ways to create an exquisite piece of art from a massive lump of gold. So God's divine love swept over all things, and with a sweet love still maintains, holds and governs them. Everything springs from the lively fountain of love. Love makes all that has being so beautiful, that if the eyes of our soul were not blinded by the scum of our passions and self-love, we would immediately see the Creator's love in everything.

ST. ROBERT SOUTHWELL, 1561–1595

YOU WILL FIND THE NEXT READING AT GENESIS 2.

heaven and all the living creatures that move on earth.' ²⁹God also said, 'Look, to you I give all the seed-bearing plants everywhere on the surface of the earth, and all the trees with seed-bearing fruit; this will be your food. ³⁰And to all the wild animals, all the birds of heaven and all the living creatures that creep along the ground, I give all the foliage of the plants as their food.' And so it was. ³¹God saw all he had made, and indeed it was very good. Evening came and morning came: the sixth day.

2 Thus heaven and earth were completed with all their array. ²On the seventh day God had completed the work he had been doing. He rested on the seventh day after all the work he had been doing. ³God blessed the seventh day and made it holy, because on that day he rested after all his work of creating.

⁴Such was the story of heaven and earth as they were created.

Paradise, and the test of free will

At the time when Yahweh God made earth and heaven ⁵there was as yet no wild bush on the earth nor had any wild plant yet sprung up, for Yahweh God had not sent rain on the earth, nor was there any man to till the soil. ⁶Instead, water flowed out of the ground and watered all the surface of the soil. ⁷Yahweh God shaped man from the soil of the ground and blew the breath of life into his nostrils, and man became a living being.

2   READ GENESIS 1:26–2:4.

God created man in the image of himself, . . . male and female he created them.

—GENESIS 1:27

TRUE TO GOD'S IMAGE

When the all-powerful, invisible, incomprehensible, and inestimable God formed us from clay, he ennobled us with the image of his own grandeur. What is there in common between us and God, between clay and spirit? For "God is spirit" (Jn 4:24). It is thus a great mark of esteem for us that God favored us with the image of his eternity and the likeness of his own life. Our greatness is our likeness to God, provided that we preserve it. . . .

As long as the soul makes good use of the virtues sown in her, she will be like God. God has taught us that we must return to him all the virtues that he gave us at our creation. He requires first of all that we love God with our whole heart (see Dt 6:5) for "he has loved us first" from the beginning, even before we existed (see 1 Jn 4:19). To love God therefore consists in renewing his image in us. That person loves God who keeps his commandments. Indeed, he says, "If you love me you will keep my commandments" (Jn 14:15). His commandment is mutual love, according to this word: "I give you a new commandment: love one another; you must love one another just as I have loved you" (Jn 13:34). And true love does not consist merely in talk but in "something active and genuine" (1 Jn 3:18). Hence, we must reflect for our God and Father the inviolate image of his holiness and he has said: "You must therefore be holy because I am holy" (Lv 11:45); with love, for he is love, and John has said: "God is love" (1 Jn 4:8); with tenderness and in truth for God is good and true.

ST. COLUMBAN, 542?–615

YOU WILL FIND THE NEXT READING AT GENESIS 3.

⁸Yahweh God planted a garden in Eden, which is in the east, and there he put the man he had fashioned. ⁹From the soil, Yahweh God caused to grow every kind of tree, enticing to look at and good to eat, with the tree of life in the middle of the garden, and the tree of the knowledge of good and evil.

¹⁰A river flowed from Eden to water the garden, and from there it divided to make four streams. ¹¹The first is named the Pishon, and this winds all through the land of Havilah where there is gold. ¹²The gold of this country is pure; bdellium and cornelian stone are found there. ¹³The second river is named the Gihon, and this winds all through the land of Cush. ¹⁴The third river is named the Tigris, and this flows to the east of Ashur. The fourth river is the Euphrates.

¹⁵Yahweh God took the man and settled him in the garden of Eden to cultivate and take care of it. ¹⁶Then Yahweh God gave the man this command, 'You are free to eat of all the trees in the garden. ¹⁷But of the tree of the knowledge of good and evil you are not to eat; for, the day you eat of that, you are doomed to die.'

¹⁸Yahweh God said, 'It is not right that the man should be alone. I shall make him a helper.' ¹⁹So from the soil Yahweh God fashioned all the wild animals and all the birds of

heaven. These he brought to the man to see what he would call them; each one was to bear the name the man would give it. ²⁰ The man gave names to all the cattle, all the birds of heaven and all the wild animals. But no helper suitable for the man was found for him. ²¹ Then, Yahweh God made the man fall into a deep sleep. And, while he was asleep, he took one of his ribs and closed the flesh up again forthwith. ²² Yahweh God fashioned the rib he had taken from the man into a woman, and brought her to the man. ²³ And the man said:

This one at last is bone of my bones
    and flesh of my flesh!
She is to be called Woman,
    because she was taken from Man.

²⁴ This is why a man leaves his father and mother and becomes attached to his wife, and they become one flesh.

²⁵ Now, both of them were naked, the man and his wife, but they felt no shame before each other.

The Fall

3 Now, the snake was the most subtle of all the wild animals that Yahweh God had made. It asked the woman, 'Did God really say you were not to eat from any of the trees in the garden?' ² The woman answered the snake, 'We may eat the fruit of the trees in the garden. ³ But of the fruit of the tree in the middle of the garden God said, "You must not eat it, nor touch it, under pain of death." ' ⁴ Then the snake said to the woman, 'No! You will not die! ⁵ God knows in fact that the day you eat it your eyes will be opened and you will be like gods, knowing good from evil.' ⁶ The woman saw that the tree was good to eat and pleasing to the eye, and that it was enticing for the wisdom that it could give. So she took some of its fruit and ate it. She also gave some to her husband who was with her, and he ate it. ⁷ Then the eyes of both of them were opened and they realised that they were naked. So they sewed fig-leaves together to make themselves loin-cloths.

⁸ The man and his wife heard the sound of Yahweh God walking in the garden in the cool of the day, and they hid from Yahweh God among the trees of the garden. ⁹ But Yahweh God called to the man. 'Where are you?' he asked. ¹⁰ 'I heard the sound of you in the garden,' he replied. 'I was afraid because I was naked, so I hid.' ¹¹ 'Who told you that you were naked?' he asked. 'Have you been eating from the tree I forbade you to eat?' ¹² The man replied, 'It was the woman you put with me; she gave me some fruit from the tree, and I ate it.' ¹³ Then Yahweh God said to the woman, 'Why did you do that?' The woman replied, 'The snake tempted me and I ate.'

¹⁴ Then Yahweh God said to the snake, 'Because you have done this,

Accursed be you
    of all animals wild and tame!
On your belly you will go
    and on dust you will feed
    as long as you live.
¹⁵ I shall put enmity
    between you and the woman,
    and between your offspring and hers;
    it[a] will bruise your head
    and you will strike its heel.'

¹⁶ To the woman he said:

I shall give you intense pain in
        childbearing,
    you will give birth to your children in
        pain.
    Your yearning will be for your husband,
    and he will dominate you.

¹⁷ To the man he said, 'Because you listened to the voice of your wife and ate from the tree of which I had forbidden you to eat,

Accursed be the soil because of you!
    Painfully will you get your food from it
    as long as you live.

3a Gk reads 'he', suggesting a personal saviour.

3 READ GENESIS 3:1–19.

Have you been eating from the tree I forbade you to eat?—GENESIS 3:11

UNDERSTANDING THE FALL

God placed man in Paradise . . . to till the immortal plants, by which is perhaps meant the divine conceptions, both the simpler and the more perfect. . . . And having honored him with the gift of free will, in order that he might obtain good as the result of his choice, God gave him a law, as material for his free will to act upon. This commandment specified those plants he might partake of, and one that he might not touch. This latter was the Tree of Knowledge. However, God did not forbid it because it was evil from the beginning when planted. Nor did God grudge it to men—let not the enemies of God wag their tongues in that direction, or imitate the serpent! But it would have been good if partaken of at the proper time.

For the Tree was, according to my theory, contemplation, which only those who have reached maturity of habit may safely undertake. But which is not good for those who are still somewhat simple and greedy, just as solid food is not good for those who are yet tender and have need of milk. But when through the devil's malice and the woman's caprice to which she succumbed . . . and which she pressed upon the man—alas for my weakness, for that of my first father was mine. He forgot the commandment that had been given him, and yielded to the deadly fruit. And for his sin he was banished at once from the Tree of Life, and from Paradise, and from God. He put on coats of skins, that is, perhaps, the coarser flesh, both mortal and full of conflict.

His own shame was the first thing that he learned, and he hid himself from God. Yet here too he makes a gain, that is, death and the cutting off of sin, in order that evil may not be immortal. Thus, his punishment is changed into a mercy, for it is in mercy, I am persuaded, that God inflicts punishment.   ST. GREGORY NAZIANZEN, 329?–390

YOU WILL FIND THE NEXT READING AT GENESIS 4.

18 It will yield you brambles and thistles,
   as you eat the produce of the land.
19 By the sweat of your face
   will you earn your food,
   until you return to the ground,
   as you were taken from it.
   For dust you are
   and to dust you shall return.'

20 The man named his wife 'Eve' because she was the mother of all those who live. 21 Yahweh God made tunics of skins for the man and his wife and clothed them. 22 Then Yahweh God said, 'Now that the man has become like one of us in knowing good from evil, he must not be allowed to reach out his hand and pick from the tree of life too, and eat and live for ever!' 23 So Yahweh God expelled him from the garden of Eden, to till the soil from which he had been taken. 24 He banished the man, and in front of the garden of Eden he posted the great winged creatures and the fiery flashing sword, to guard the way to the tree of life.

Cain and Abel

4 The man had intercourse with his wife Eve, and she conceived and gave birth to Cain. 'I have acquired a man with the help of Yahweh,' she said. ²She gave birth to a second child, Abel, the brother of Cain. Now Abel became a shepherd and kept flocks, while Cain tilled the soil. ³Time passed and Cain brought some of the produce of the soil as an offering for Yahweh, ⁴while Abel for his part brought the first-born of his flock and some of their fat as well. Yahweh looked with favour on Abel and his offering. ⁵But he did not look with favour on Cain and his offering, and Cain was very angry and downcast. ⁶Yahweh asked Cain, 'Why are you angry and downcast? ⁷If you are doing right, surely you ought to hold your head high! But if you are not doing right, Sin is crouching at the door hungry to get you. You can still master him.' ⁸Cain said to his brother Abel, 'Let us go out'; and while they were in the open country, Cain set on his brother Abel and killed him.

⁹Yahweh asked Cain, 'Where is your brother Abel?' 'I do not know,' he replied. 'Am I my brother's guardian?' ¹⁰'What have you done?' Yahweh asked. 'Listen! Your brother's blood is crying out to me from the ground. ¹¹Now be cursed and banned from the ground that has opened its mouth to receive your brother's blood at your hands. ¹²When you till the ground it will no longer yield up its strength to you. A restless wanderer you will be on earth.' ¹³Cain then said to Yahweh, 'My punishment is greater than I can bear. ¹⁴Look, today you drive me from the surface of the earth. I must hide from you, and be a restless wanderer on earth. Why, whoever comes across me will kill me!' ¹⁵'Very well, then,' Yahweh replied, 'whoever kills Cain will suffer a sevenfold vengeance.' So Yahweh put a mark on Cain, so that no one coming across him would kill him. ¹⁶Cain left Yahweh's presence and settled in the land of Nod, east of Eden.

The descendants of Cain

¹⁷Cain had intercourse with his wife, and she conceived and gave birth to Enoch. He became the founder of a city and gave the city the name of his son Enoch. ¹⁸Enoch fathered Irad, and Irad fathered Mehujael; Mehujael fathered Methushael, and Methushael fathered Lamech. ¹⁹Lamech married two women: the name of the first was Adah and the name of the second was Zillah. ²⁰Adah gave birth to Jabal: he was the ancestor of tent-dwelling herdsmen. ²¹His brother's name was Jubal: he was the ancestor of all who play the harp and the pipe. ²²As for Zillah, she gave birth to Tubal-Cain: he was the ancestor of all who work copper and iron. Tubal-Cain's sister was Naamah.

²³Lamech said to his wives:

Adah and Zillah, hear my voice,
wives of Lamech, listen to what I say:
I killed a man for wounding me,
a boy for striking me.
²⁴ Sevenfold vengeance for Cain,
but seventy-sevenfold for Lamech.

Seth and his descendants

²⁵Adam had intercourse with his wife, and she gave birth to a son whom she named Seth, 'because God has granted me other offspring', she said, 'in place of Abel, since Cain has killed him.' ²⁶A son was also born to Seth, and he named him Enosh. This man was the first to invoke the name Yahweh.

The patriarchs before the flood

5 This is the roll of Adam's descendants:
On the day that God created Adam he made him in the likeness of God. ²Male and female he created them. He blessed them and gave them the name Man, when they were created.

³When Adam was a hundred and thirty years old he fathered a son, in his likeness, after his image, and he called him Seth. ⁴Adam lived for eight hundred years after the birth of Seth and he fathered sons and daugh-

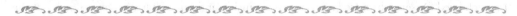

4 READ GENESIS 4:9–16.

So Yahweh put a mark on Cain, so that no one coming across him would kill him.

—GENESIS 4:15

GOD'S TENDER MERCY

God loves human beings, and loves them in no small measure. Don't say, "I have fornicated and committed adultery. I have done dreadful things not only once, but often. Will he ever forgive me?"

Listen to the psalmist: "How great is the abundance of your goodness, O Lord!" (see Ps 31:19). Your accumulated offenses do not surpass the abundance of God's mercies. Your wounds are not greater than the Physician's skill. Just give yourself up in faith. Tell the Physician your ailment. With David, say: "I will confess my sin to the Lord, and you forgave the wickedness of my heart"—and the same shall be done to you (see Ps 32:5).

My new catechumens, would you like to see the loving-kindness of God and the abundance of his long-suffering? Then hear about Adam. When Adam, God's first-formed man, sinned, could he not at once have killed him? But consider what the Lord does in his great love for Adam. He cast him out of Paradise because his sin made him unworthy to live there. However, God made him live close to Paradise so that, seeing from what and into what a state he had fallen, he might afterwards be saved by repentance.

Cain, the firstborn man murdered his brother. Yet after slaying his brother, to what is he condemned? "You shall become a restless wanderer on the earth" (see Gn 4:12). How great the offense, how light the sentence!

Brothers and sisters, make your heartfelt confession to the Lord. So you will both receive forgiveness for your former sins and also be counted worthy of the heavenly gift. You will thus inherit the heavenly kingdom with all the saints in Christ Jesus.   ST. CYRIL OF JERUSALEM, 315?–386

YOU WILL FIND THE NEXT READING AT GENESIS 19.

ters. ⁵In all, Adam lived for nine hundred and thirty years; then he died.

⁶When Seth was a hundred and five years old he fathered Enosh. ⁷After the birth of Enosh, Seth lived for eight hundred and seven years, and he fathered sons and daughters. ⁸In all, Seth lived for nine hundred and twelve years; then he died.

⁹When Enosh was ninety years old he fathered Kenan. ¹⁰After the birth of Kenan, Enosh lived for eight hundred and fifteen years and he fathered sons and daughters. ¹¹In all, Enosh lived for nine hundred and five years; then he died.

¹²When Kenan was seventy years old he fathered Mahalalel. ¹³After the birth of Mahalalel, Kenan lived for eight hundred and forty years and he fathered sons and daughters. ¹⁴In all, Kenan lived for nine hundred and ten years; then he died.

¹⁵When Mahalalel was sixty-five years old he fathered Jared. ¹⁶After the birth of Jared, Mahalalel lived for eight hundred and thirty years and he fathered sons and daughters. ¹⁷In

all, Mahalalel lived for eight hundred and ninety-five years; then he died.

¹⁸ When Jared was a hundred and sixty-two years old he fathered Enoch. ¹⁹ After the birth of Enoch, Jared lived for eight hundred years and he fathered sons and daughters. ²⁰ In all, Jared lived for nine hundred and sixty-two years; then he died.

²¹ When Enoch was sixty-five years old he fathered Methuselah. ²² Enoch walked with God. After the birth of Methuselah, Enoch lived for three hundred years and he fathered sons and daughters. ²³ In all, Enoch lived for three hundred and sixty-five years. ²⁴ Enoch walked with God, then was no more, because God took him.

²⁵ When Methuselah was a hundred and eighty-seven years old he fathered Lamech. ²⁶ After the birth of Lamech, Methuselah lived for seven hundred and eighty-two years and he fathered sons and daughters. ²⁷ In all, Methuselah lived for nine hundred and sixty-nine years; then he died.

²⁸ When Lamech was a hundred and eighty-two years old he fathered a son. ²⁹ He gave him the name Noah because, he said, 'Here is one who will give us, in the midst of our toil and the labouring of our hands, a consolation out of the very soil that Yahweh cursed.' ³⁰ After the birth of Noah, Lamech lived for five hundred and ninety-five years and fathered sons and daughters. ³¹ In all, Lamech lived for seven hundred and seventy-seven years; then he died.

³² When Noah was five hundred years old he fathered Shem, Ham and Japheth.

Sons of God and women

6 When people began being numerous on earth, and daughters had been born to them, ² the sons of God, looking at the women, saw how beautiful they were and married as many of them as they chose. ³ Yahweh said, 'My spirit cannot be indefinitely responsible for human beings, who are only flesh; let the time allowed each be a hundred and twenty years.' ⁴ The Nephilim were on earth in those days (and even afterwards) when the sons of God resorted to the women, and had children by them. These were the heroes of days gone by, men of renown.

The corruption of humanity

⁵ Yahweh saw that human wickedness was great on earth and that human hearts contrived nothing but wicked schemes all day long. ⁶ Yahweh regretted having made human beings on earth and was grieved at heart. ⁷ And Yahweh said, 'I shall rid the surface of the earth of the human beings whom I created—human and animal, the creeping things and the birds of heaven—for I regret having made them.' ⁸ But Noah won Yahweh's favour.

⁹ This is the story of Noah:

Noah was a good man, an upright man among his contemporaries, and he walked with God. ¹⁰ Noah fathered three sons, Shem, Ham and Japheth. ¹¹ God saw that the earth was corrupt and full of lawlessness. ¹² God looked at the earth: it was corrupt, for corrupt were the ways of all living things on earth.

Preparations for the flood

¹³ God said to Noah, 'I have decided that the end has come for all living things, for the earth is full of lawlessness because of human beings. So I am now about to destroy them and the earth. ¹⁴ Make yourself an ark out of resinous wood. Make it of reeds and caulk it with pitch inside and out. ¹⁵ This is how to make it: the length of the ark is to be three hundred cubits, its breadth fifty cubits, and its height thirty cubits. ¹⁶ Make a roof to the ark, building it up to a cubit higher. Put the entrance in the side of the ark, which is to be made with lower, second and third decks.

¹⁷ 'For my part I am going to send the flood, the waters, on earth, to destroy all living things having the breath of life under heaven; everything on earth is to perish. ¹⁸ But with you I shall establish my covenant and you will go aboard the ark, yourself, your sons, your wife, and your sons' wives along with you. ¹⁹ From all living creatures, from all living

things, you must take two of each kind aboard the ark, to save their lives with yours; they must be a male and a female. ²⁰Of every species of bird, of every kind of animal and of every kind of creature that creeps along the ground, two must go with you so that their lives may be saved. ²¹For your part, provide yourself with eatables of all kinds, and lay in a store of them, to serve as food for yourself and them.' ²²Noah did this; exactly as God commanded him, he did.

7 Yahweh said to Noah, 'Go aboard the ark, you and all your household, for you alone of your contemporaries do I see before me as an upright man. ²Of every clean animal you must take seven pairs, a male and its female; of the unclean animals you must take one pair, a male and its female ³(and of the birds of heaven, seven pairs, a male and its female), to preserve their species throughout the earth. ⁴For in seven days' time I shall make it rain on earth for forty days and forty nights, and I shall wipe every creature I have made off the face of the earth.' ⁵Noah did exactly as Yahweh commanded him.

⁶Noah was six hundred years old when the flood came, the waters over the earth.

⁷Noah with his sons, his wife, and his sons' wives boarded the ark to escape the waters of the flood. ⁸(Of the clean animals and the animals that are not clean, of the birds and all that creeps along the ground, ⁹one pair boarded the ark with Noah, one male and one female, as God had commanded Noah.) ¹⁰Seven days later the waters of the flood appeared on earth.

¹¹In the six hundredth year of Noah's life, in the second month, and on the seventeenth day of the month, that very day all the springs of the great deep burst through, and the sluices of heaven opened. ¹²And heavy rain fell on earth for forty days and forty nights.

¹³That very day Noah and his sons Shem, Ham and Japheth boarded the ark, with Noah's wife and the three wives of his sons, ¹⁴and with them every species of wild animal, every species of cattle, every species of creep-

ing things that creep along the ground, every species of bird, everything that flies, everything with wings. ¹⁵One pair of all that was alive and had the breath of life boarded the ark with Noah, ¹⁶and those that went aboard were a male and female of all that was alive, as God had commanded him.

Then Yahweh shut him in.

The flood

¹⁷The flood lasted forty days on earth. The waters swelled, lifting the ark until it floated off the ground. ¹⁸The waters rose, swelling higher above the ground, and the ark drifted away over the waters. ¹⁹The waters rose higher and higher above the ground until all the highest mountains under the whole of heaven were submerged. ²⁰The waters reached their peak fifteen cubits above the submerged mountains. ²¹And all living things that stirred on earth perished; birds, cattle, wild animals, all the creatures swarming over the earth, and all human beings. ²²Everything with the least breath of life in its nostrils, everything on dry land, died. ²³Every living thing on the face of the earth was wiped out, people, animals, creeping things and birds; they were wiped off the earth and only Noah was left, and those with him in the ark. ²⁴The waters maintained their level on earth for a hundred and fifty days.

The flood subsides

8 But God had Noah in mind, and all the wild animals and all the cattle that were with him in the ark. God sent a wind across the earth and the waters began to subside. ²The springs of the deep and the sluices of heaven were stopped up and the heavy rain from heaven was held back. ³Little by little, the waters ebbed from the earth. After a hundred and fifty days the waters fell, ⁴and in the seventh month, on the seventeenth day of the month, the ark came to rest on the mountains of Ararat. ⁵The waters gradually fell until the tenth month when, on the first day of the tenth month, the mountain tops appeared.

⁶At the end of forty days Noah opened the window he had made in the ark ⁷and released a raven, which flew back and forth as it waited for the waters to dry up on earth. ⁸He then released a dove, to see whether the waters were receding from the surface of the earth. ⁹But the dove, finding nowhere to perch, returned to him in the ark, for there was water over the whole surface of the earth; putting out his hand he took hold of it and brought it back into the ark with him. ¹⁰After waiting seven more days, he again released the dove from the ark. ¹¹In the evening, the dove came back to him and there in its beak was a freshly-picked olive leaf! So Noah realised that the waters were receding from the earth. ¹²After waiting seven more days, he released the dove, and now it returned to him no more.

¹³It was in the six hundred and first year of Noah's life, in the first month and on the first of the month, that the waters began drying out on earth. Noah lifted back the hatch of the ark and looked out. The surface of the ground was dry!

¹⁴In the second month, on the twenty-seventh day of the month, the earth was dry.

They disembark

¹⁵Then God said to Noah, ¹⁶'Come out of the ark, you, your wife, your sons, and your sons' wives with you. ¹⁷Bring out all the animals with you, all living things, the birds, the cattle and all the creeping things that creep along the ground, for them to swarm on earth, for them to breed and multiply on earth.' ¹⁸So Noah came out with his sons, his wife, and his sons' wives. ¹⁹And all the wild animals, all the cattle, all the birds and all the creeping things that creep along the ground, came out of the ark, one species after another.

²⁰Then Noah built an altar to Yahweh and, choosing from all the clean animals and all the clean birds he presented burnt offerings on the altar. ²¹Yahweh smelt the pleasing smell and said to himself, 'Never again will I curse the earth because of human beings, because their heart contrives evil from their infancy. Never

again will I strike down every living thing as I have done.

²²As long as earth endures:
  seed-time and harvest,
    cold and heat,
  summer and winter,
    day and night
    will never cease.'

The new world order

9God blessed Noah and his sons and said to them, 'Breed, multiply and fill the earth. ²Be the terror and the dread of all the animals on land and all the birds of heaven, of everything that moves on land and all the fish of the sea; they are placed in your hands. ³Every living thing that moves will be yours to eat, no less than the foliage of the plants. I give you everything, ⁴with this exception: you must not eat flesh with life, that is to say blood, in it. ⁵And I shall demand account of your life-blood, too. I shall demand it of every animal, and of man. Of man as regards his fellow-man, I shall demand account for human life.

⁶ He who sheds the blood of man,
    by man shall his blood be shed,
  for in the image of God
      was man created.
⁷ Be fruitful then and multiply,
    teem over the earth and subdue it!'

⁸God spoke as follows to Noah and his sons, ⁹'I am now establishing my covenant with you and with your descendants to come, ¹⁰and with every living creature that was with you: birds, cattle and every wild animal with you; everything that came out of the ark, every living thing on earth. ¹¹And I shall maintain my covenant with you: that never again shall all living things be destroyed by the waters of a flood, nor shall there ever again be a flood to devastate the earth.'

¹²'And this', God said, 'is the sign of the covenant which I now make between myself

and you and every living creature with you for all ages to come: 13 I now set my bow in the clouds and it will be the sign of the covenant between me and the earth. 14 When I gather the clouds over the earth and the bow appears in the clouds, 15 I shall recall the covenant between myself and you and every living creature, in a word all living things, and never again will the waters become a flood to destroy all living things. 16 When the bow is in the clouds I shall see it and call to mind the eternal covenant between God and every living creature on earth, that is, all living things.'

17 'That', God told Noah, 'is the sign of the covenant I have established between myself and all living things on earth.'

Noah and his sons

18 The sons of Noah who came out of the ark were Shem, Ham and Japheth—Ham being the father of Canaan. 19 These three were Noah's sons, and from these the whole earth was peopled.

20 Noah, a tiller of the soil, was the first to plant the vine. 21 He drank some of the wine, and while he was drunk, he lay uncovered in his tent. 22 Ham, father of Canaan, saw his father naked and told his two brothers outside. 23 Shem and Japheth took a cloak and they both put it over their shoulders, and walking backwards, covered their father's nakedness; they kept their faces turned away, and they did not look at their father naked. 24 When Noah awoke from his stupor he learned what his youngest son had done to him, 25 and said:

Accursed be Canaan,
   he shall be
his brothers' meanest slave.

26 He added:

Blessed be Yahweh, God of Shem,
   let Canaan be his slave!
27 May God make space for Japheth,
   may he live in the tents of Shem,
      and let Canaan be his slave!

28 After the flood Noah lived three hundred and fifty years. 29 In all, Noah's life lasted nine hundred and fifty years; then he died.

The peopling of the earth

10 These are the descendants of Noah's sons, Shem, Ham and Japheth, to whom sons were born after the flood:

2 Japheth's sons: Gomer, Magog, the Medes, Javan, Tubal, Meshech, Tiras. 3 Gomer's sons: Ashkenaz, Riphath, Togarmah. 4 Javan's sons: Elishah, Tarshish, the Kittim, the Dananites. 5 From these came the dispersal to the islands of the nations.

These were Japheth's sons, in their respective countries, each with its own language, by clan and nation.

6 Ham's sons: Cush, Mizraim, Put, Canaan. 7 Cush's sons: Seba, Havilah, Sabtah, Raamah, Sabteca. Raamah's sons: Sheba, Dedan.

8 Cush fathered Nimrod who was the first potentate on earth. 9 He was a mighty hunter in the eyes of Yahweh, hence the saying, 'Like Nimrod, a mighty hunter in the eyes of Yahweh'. 10 The mainstays of his empire were Babel, Erech and Accad, all of them in the land of Shinar. 11 From this country came Asshur, and he built Nineveh, Rehoboth-Ir, Calah, 12 and Resen between Nineveh and Calah (this being the capital).

13 Mizraim fathered the people of Lud, of Anam, Lehab, Naphtuh, 14 Pathros, Casluh and Caphtor, from which the Philistines came.

15 Canaan fathered Sidon, his first-born, then Heth, 16 and the Jebusites, the Amorites, Girgashites, 17 Hivites, Arkites, Sinites, 18 Arvadites, Zemarites and Hamathites. Later, the Canaanite clans spread out. 19 The Canaanite frontier stretched from Sidon all the way to Gerar near Gaza, and all the way to Sodom, Gomorrah, Admah and Zeboiim near Lesha.

20 These were Ham's sons, by clans and languages, by countries and nations.

21 Shem too fathered sons, being ancestor of all the sons of Eber and Japheth's elder brother.

22 Shem's sons: Elam, Asshur, Arpachshad, Lud, Aram. 23 Aram's sons: Uz, Hul, Gether and Mash.

24 Arpachshad fathered Shelah, and Shelah fathered Eber. 25 To Eber were born two sons: the first was called Peleg, because it was in his time that the earth was divided, and his brother was called Joktan. 26 Joktan fathered Almodad, Sheleph, Hazarmaveth, Jerah, 27 Hadoram, Uzal, Diklah, 28 Obal, Abima-El, Sheba, 29 Ophir, Havilah, Jobab; all these were sons of Joktan. 30 They occupied a stretch of country from Mesha all the way to Sephar, the eastern mountain range.

31 These were Shem's sons, by clans and languages, by countries and nations.

32 Such were the clans of Noah's descendants, listed by descent and nation. From them, other nations branched out on earth after the flood.

The tower of Babel

11 The whole world spoke the same language, with the same vocabulary. 2 Now, as people moved eastwards they found a valley in the land of Shinar where they settled. 3 They said to one another, 'Come, let us make bricks and bake them in the fire.' For stone they used bricks, and for mortar they used bitumen. 4 'Come,' they said, 'let us build ourselves a city and a tower with its top reaching heaven. Let us make a name for ourselves, so that we do not get scattered all over the world.'

5 Now Yahweh came down to see the city and the tower that the people had built. 6 'So they are all a single people with a single language!' said Yahweh. 'This is only the start of their undertakings! Now nothing they plan to do will be beyond them. 7 Come, let us go down and confuse their language there, so that they cannot understand one another.' 8 Yahweh scattered them thence all over the world, and they stopped building the city. 9 That is why it was called Babel, since there Yahweh confused the language of the whole world, and from there Yahweh scattered them all over the world.

The patriarchs after the flood

10 These are Shem's descendants:

When Shem was a hundred years old he fathered Arpachshad, two years after the flood. 11 After the birth of Arpachshad, Shem lived five hundred years and fathered sons and daughters.

12 When Arpachshad was thirty-five years old he fathered Shelah. 13 After the birth of Shelah, Arpachshad lived four hundred and three years and fathered sons and daughters.

14 When Shelah was thirty years old he fathered Eber. 15 After the birth of Eber, Shelah lived four hundred and three years and fathered sons and daughters.

16 When Eber was thirty-four years old he fathered Peleg. 17 After the birth of Peleg, Eber lived four hundred and thirty years and fathered sons and daughters.

18 When Peleg was thirty years old he fathered Reu. 19 After the birth of Reu, Peleg lived two hundred and nine years and fathered sons and daughters.

20 When Reu was thirty-two years old he fathered Serug. 21 After the birth of Serug, Reu lived two hundred and seven years and fathered sons and daughters.

22 When Serug was thirty years old he fathered Nahor. 23 After the birth of Nahor, Serug lived two hundred years and fathered sons and daughters.

24 When Nahor was twenty-nine years old he fathered Terah. 25 After the birth of Terah, Nahor lived a hundred and nineteen years and fathered sons and daughters.

26 When Terah was seventy years old he fathered Abram, Nahor and Haran.

The descendants of Terah

27 These are Terah's descendants:

Terah fathered Abram, Nahor and Haran. Haran fathered Lot. 28 Haran died in the presence of his father Terah in his native land, Ur of the Chaldaeans. 29 Abram and Nahor both married: Abram's wife was called Sarai, Nahor's wife was called Milcah daughter of

Haran, father of Milcah and Iscah. ³⁰ Sarai was barren, having no child.

³¹ Terah took his son Abram, his grandson Lot son of Haran, and his daughter-in-law the wife of Abram, and made them leave Ur of the Chaldaeans to go to the land of Canaan. But on arrival in Haran they settled there.

³² Terah's life lasted two hundred and five years; then he died at Haran.

The call of Abram

12 Yahweh said to Abram, 'Leave your country, your kindred and your father's house for a country which I shall show you; ² and I shall make you a great nation, I shall bless you and make your name famous; you are to be a blessing!

³ I shall bless those who bless you,
and shall curse those who curse you,
and all clans on earth
will bless themselves by you.'

⁴ So Abram went as Yahweh told him, and Lot went with him. Abram was seventy-five years old when he left Haran. ⁵ Abram took his wife Sarai, his nephew Lot, all the possessions they had amassed and the people they had acquired in Haran. They set off for the land of Canaan, and arrived there.

⁶ Abram passed through the country as far as the holy place at Shechem, the Oak of Moreh. The Canaanites were in the country at the time. ⁷ Yahweh appeared to Abram and said, 'I shall give this country to your progeny.' And there, Abram built an altar to Yahweh who had appeared to him. ⁸ From there he moved on to the mountainous district east of Bethel, where he pitched his tent, with Bethel to the west and Ai to the east. There he built an altar to Yahweh and invoked the name of Yahweh. ⁹ Then Abram made his way stage by stage to the Negeb.

Abram in Egypt[a]

¹⁰ There was a famine in the country, and Abram went down to Egypt to stay there for a time, since the famine in the country was severe. ¹¹ When he was about to enter Egypt, he said to his wife Sarai, 'Look, I know you are a beautiful woman. ¹² When the Egyptians see you they will say, "That is his wife," and they will kill me but leave you alive. ¹³ Therefore please tell them you are my sister, so that they may treat me well because of you and spare my life out of regard for you.' ¹⁴ When Abram arrived in Egypt the Egyptians did indeed see that the woman was very beautiful. ¹⁵ When Pharaoh's officials saw her they sang her praises to Pharaoh and the woman was taken into Pharaoh's household. ¹⁶ And Abram was very well treated because of her and received flocks, oxen, donkeys, men and women slaves, she-donkeys and camels. ¹⁷ But Yahweh inflicted severe plagues on Pharaoh and his household because of Abram's wife Sarai. ¹⁸ So Pharaoh summoned Abram and said, 'What is this you have done to me? Why did you not tell me she was your wife? ¹⁹ Why did you say, "She is my sister," so that I took her to be my wife? Now, here is your wife. Take her and go!' ²⁰ And Pharaoh gave his people orders about him; they sent him on his way with his wife and all his possessions.

Abram and Lot separate

13 From Egypt Abram returned to the Negeb with his wife and all he possessed, and Lot with him. ² Abram was very rich in livestock, silver and gold. ³ By stages he went from the Negeb to Bethel, where he had first pitched his tent, between Bethel and Ai, ⁴ at the place where he had formerly erected the altar. There Abram invoked the name of Yahweh.

⁵ Lot, who was travelling with Abram, had flocks and cattle of his own, and tents too. ⁶ The land was not sufficient to accommodate them both at once, for they had too many possessions to be able to live together. ⁷ Dispute broke out between the herdsmen of Abram's livestock and those of Lot. (The Canaanites

12a = 20; = 26:1–11.

and Perizzites were living in the country at the time.) [8]Accordingly Abram said to Lot, 'We do not want discord between us or between my herdsmen and yours, for we are kinsmen. [9]Is not the whole land open before you? Go in the opposite direction to me: if you take the left, I shall go right; if you take the right, I shall go left.'

[10]Looking round, Lot saw all the Jordan plain, irrigated everywhere—this was before Yahweh destroyed Sodom and Gomorrah—like the garden of Yahweh or the land of Egypt, as far as Zoar. [11]So Lot chose all the Jordan plain for himself and moved off eastwards. Thus they parted company: [12]Abram settled in the land of Canaan; Lot settled among the cities of the plain, pitching his tents on the outskirts of Sodom. [13]Now the people of Sodom were vicious and great sinners against Yahweh.

[14]Yahweh said to Abram after Lot had parted company from him, 'Look all round from where you are, to north and south, to east and west, [15]for all the land within sight I shall give to you and your descendants for ever. [16]I shall make your descendants like the dust on the ground; when people succeed in counting the specks of dust on the ground, then they will be able to count your descendants too! [17]On your feet! Travel the length and breadth of the country, for I mean to give it to you.'

[18]So Abram moved his tent and went to settle at the Oak of Mamre, at Hebron, and there he built an altar to Yahweh.

The campaign of the four great kings

14 When Amraphel king of Shinar, Arioch king of Ellasar, Chedor-Laomer king of Elam, and Tidal king of the Goiim, [2]made war on Bera king of Sodom, Birsha king of Gomorrah, Shinab king of Admah, Shemeber king of Zeboiim, and the king of Bela (that is, Zoar), [3]all the latter joined forces in the Valley of Siddim (now the Salt Sea). [4]For twelve years they had been under the yoke of Chedor-Laomer, but in the thirteenth year they revolted. [5]In the fourteenth year Chedor-Laomer arrived and the kings who had allied themselves with him. They defeated the Rephaim at Ashteroth-Carnaim, the Zuzim at Ham, the Emim in the Plain of Kiriathaim, [6]the Horites in the mountainous district of Seir near El-Paran, which is on the edge of the desert. [7]Wheeling round, they came to the Spring of Judgement (that is, Kadesh); they conquered all the territory of the Amalekites and also the Amorites who lived in Hazazon-Tamar. [8]Then the kings of Sodom, Gomorrah, Admah, Zeboiim and Bela (that is, Zoar) marched out and engaged them in the Valley of Siddim: [9]Chedor-Laomer king of Elam, Tidal king of the Goiim, Amraphel king of Shinar and Arioch king of Ellasar: four kings against five. [10]Now there were many bitumen wells in the Valley of Siddim, and in their flight the kings of Sodom and Gomorrah fell into them, while the rest fled into the hills. [11]The conquerors seized all the possessions of Sodom and Gomorrah, and all their provisions, and made off. [12]They also took Lot (the nephew of Abram) and his possessions and made off; he had been living at Sodom.

[13]A survivor came to tell Abram, and Aner the Hebrew, who was living at the Oak of the Amorite Mamre, the brother of Eshcol; these were allies of Abram. [14]When Abram heard that his kinsman had been taken captive, he mustered his retainers born in his own household, numbering three hundred and eighteen, and gave chase as far as Dan. [15]He and his retainers deployed against them under cover of dark, defeated them and pursued them as far as Hobah, north of Damascus. [16]He recaptured all the goods as well as his kinsman Lot and his possessions, together with the women and people.

Melchizedek

[17]When Abram returned from defeating Chedor-Laomer and the kings who had been on his side, the king of Sodom came to meet him in the Valley of Shaveh (that is, the Valley of the King). [18]Melchizedek king of Salem

brought bread and wine; he was a priest of God Most High. ¹⁹He pronounced this blessing:

Blessed be Abram by God Most High,
　Creator of heaven and earth.
And blessed be God Most High
　for putting your enemies into your
　　clutches.

²⁰And Abram gave him a tenth of everything.

²¹The king of Sodom said to Abram, 'Give me the people and take the possessions for yourself.' ²²But Abram replied to the king of Sodom, 'I swear by God Most High, Creator of heaven and earth: ²³not one thread, not one sandal strap, will I take of what is yours, for you to be able to say, "I made Abram rich." ²⁴For myself, nothing—except what the troops have used up, and the share due to the men who came with me, Eshcol, Aner and Mamre; let them take their share.'

The divine promises and covenant[a]

15 Some time later, the word of Yahweh came to Abram in a vision:

Do not be afraid, Abram!
I am your shield
and shall give you a very great reward.

²'Lord Yahweh,' Abram replied, 'what use are your gifts, as I am going on my way childless?...'[b] ³Since you have given me no offspring,' Abram continued, 'a member of my household will be my heir.' ⁴Then Yahweh's word came to him in reply, 'Such a one will not be your heir; no, your heir will be the issue of your own body.' ⁵Then taking him outside, he said, 'Look up at the sky and count the stars if you can. Just so will your descendants be,' he told him. ⁶Abram put his faith in Yahweh and this was reckoned to him as uprightness.

⁷He then said to him, 'I am Yahweh who brought you out of Ur of the Chaldaeans to give you this country as your possession.'

⁸'Lord Yahweh,' Abram replied, 'how can I know that I shall possess it?' ⁹He said to him, 'Bring me a three-year-old heifer, a three-year-old she-goat, a three-year-old ram, a turtledove and a young pigeon.' ¹⁰He brought him all these, split the animals down the middle and placed each half opposite the other; but the birds he did not divide. ¹¹And whenever birds of prey swooped down on the carcasses, Abram drove them off.

¹²Now, as the sun was on the point of setting, a trance fell on Abram, and a deep dark dread descended on him. ¹³Then Yahweh said to Abram, 'Know this for certain, that your descendants will be exiles in a land not their own, and be enslaved and oppressed for four hundred years. ¹⁴But I shall bring judgement on the nation that enslaves them and after this they will leave, with many possessions. ¹⁵For your part, you will join your ancestors in peace; you will be buried at a happy old age. ¹⁶In the fourth generation they will come back here, for until then the iniquity of the Amorites will not have reached its full extent.'

¹⁷When the sun had set and it was dark, there appeared a smoking firepot and a flaming torch passing between the animals' pieces. ¹⁸That day Yahweh made a covenant with Abram in these terms:

'To your descendants I give this country,
　from the River of Egypt to the Great
　　River,

the River Euphrates, ¹⁹the Kenites, the Kenizzites, the Kadmonites, ²⁰the Hittites, the Perizzites, the Rephaim, ²¹the Amorites, the Canaanites, the Girgashites, and the Jebusites.'

The birth of Ishmael[a]

16 Abram's wife Sarai had borne him no child, but she had an Egyptian slave-

---

15a = 17; 12:2–7.

15b The remainder of the v. is unintelligible.

16a = 21:8–19.

girl called Hagar. ²So Sarai said to Abram, 'Listen, now! Since Yahweh has kept me from having children, go to my slave-girl. Perhaps I shall get children through her.' And Abram took Sarai's advice.

³Thus, after Abram had lived in the land of Canaan for ten years, Sarai took Hagar her Egyptian slave-girl and gave her to Abram as his wife. ⁴He went to Hagar and she conceived. And once she knew she had conceived, her mistress counted for nothing in her eyes. ⁵Then Sarai said to Abram, 'This outrage done to me is your fault! It was I who put my slave-girl into your arms but, now she knows that she has conceived, I count for nothing in her eyes. Yahweh judge between me and you!' ⁶'Very well,' Abram said to Sarai, 'your slave-girl is at your disposal. Treat her as you think fit.' Sarai accordingly treated her so badly that she ran away from her.

⁷The angel of Yahweh found her by a spring in the desert, the spring on the road to Shur. ⁸He said, 'Hagar, slave-girl of Sarai, where have you come from, and where are you going?' 'I am running away from my mistress Sarai,' she replied. ⁹The angel of Yahweh said to her, 'Go back to your mistress and submit to her.' ¹⁰The angel of Yahweh further said to her, 'I shall make your descendants too numerous to be counted.' ¹¹Then the angel of Yahweh said to her:

> Now, you have conceived and will bear a
>   son,
>   and you shall name him Ishmael,
>   for Yahweh has heard your cries of
>   distress.
> ¹²A wild donkey of a man he will be,
>   his hand against every man, and every
>   man's hand against him,
>   living his life in defiance of all his
>   kinsmen.

¹³Hagar gave a name to Yahweh who had spoken to her, 'You are El Roi,' by which she meant, 'Did I not go on seeing here, after him who sees me?' ¹⁴This is why the well is called the well of Lahai Roi; it is between Kadesh and Bered.

¹⁵Hagar bore Abram a son, and Abram gave his son borne by Hagar the name Ishmael. ¹⁶Abram was eighty-six years old when Hagar bore him Ishmael.

The covenant and circumcision[a]

17 When Abram was ninety-nine years old Yahweh appeared to him and said, 'I am El Shaddai. Live in my presence, be perfect, ²and I shall grant a covenant between myself and you, and make you very numerous.' ³And Abram bowed to the ground.

God spoke to him as follows, ⁴'For my part, this is my covenant with you: you will become the father of many nations. ⁵And you are no longer to be called Abram; your name is to be Abraham, for I am making you father of many nations. ⁶I shall make you exceedingly fertile. I shall make you into nations, and your issue will be kings. ⁷And I shall maintain my covenant between myself and you, and your descendants after you, generation after generation, as a covenant in perpetuity, to be your God and the God of your descendants after you. ⁸And to you and to your descendants after you, I shall give the country where you are now immigrants, the entire land of Canaan, to own in perpetuity. And I shall be their God.'

⁹God further said to Abraham, 'You for your part must keep my covenant, you and your descendants after you, generation after generation. ¹⁰This is my covenant which you must keep between myself and you, and your descendants after you: every one of your males must be circumcised. ¹¹You must circumcise the flesh of your foreskin, and that will be the sign of the covenant between myself and you. ¹²As soon as he is eight days old, every one of your males, generation after generation, must be circumcised, including slaves born within the household or bought from a for-

17a = 15.

eigner not of your descent. ¹³Whether born within the household or bought, they must be circumcised. My covenant must be marked in your flesh as a covenant in perpetuity. ¹⁴The uncircumcised male, whose foreskin has not been circumcised—that person must be cut off from his people: he has broken my covenant.'

¹⁵Furthermore God said to Abraham, 'As regards your wife Sarai, you must not call her Sarai, but Sarah. ¹⁶I shall bless her and moreover give you a son by her. I shall bless her and she will become nations: kings of peoples will issue from her.' ¹⁷Abraham bowed to the ground, and he laughed,^b thinking to himself, 'Is a child to be born to a man one hundred years old, and will Sarah have a child at the age of ninety?' ¹⁸Abraham said to God, 'May Ishmael live in your presence! That will be enough!' ¹⁹But God replied, 'Yes, your wife Sarah will bear you a son whom you must name Isaac. And I shall maintain my covenant with him, a covenant in perpetuity, to be his God and the God of his descendants after him. ²⁰For Ishmael too I grant you your request. I hereby bless him and will make him fruitful and exceedingly numerous. He will be the father of twelve princes, and I shall make him into a great nation. ²¹But my covenant I shall maintain with Isaac, whom Sarah will bear you at this time next year.' ²²When he had finished speaking to Abraham, God went up from him.

²³Then Abraham took his son Ishmael, all the slaves born in his household or whom he had bought, in short all the males among the people of Abraham's household, and circumcised their foreskins that same day, as God had said to him. ²⁴Abraham was ninety-nine years old when his foreskin was circumcised. ²⁵Ishmael his son was thirteen years old when his foreskin was circumcised. ²⁶Abraham and his son Ishmael were circumcised on the very same day, ²⁷and all the men of his household, those born in the household and those bought from foreigners, were circumcised with him.

The apparition at Mamre

18 Yahweh appeared to him at the Oak of Mamre while he was sitting by the entrance of the tent during the hottest part of the day. ²He looked up, and there he saw three men standing near him. As soon as he saw them he ran from the entrance of the tent to greet them, and bowed to the ground. ³'My lord,' he said, 'if I find favour with you, please do not pass your servant by. ⁴Let me have a little water brought, and you can wash your feet and have a rest under the tree. ⁵Let me fetch a little bread and you can refresh yourselves before going further, now that you have come in your servant's direction.' They replied, 'Do as you say.'

⁶Abraham hurried to the tent and said to Sarah, 'Quick, knead three measures of best flour and make loaves.' ⁷Then, running to the herd, Abraham took a fine and tender calf and gave it to the servant, who hurried to prepare it. ⁸Then taking curds, milk and the calf which had been prepared, he laid all before them, and they ate while he remained standing near them under the tree.

⁹'Where is your wife Sarah?' they asked him. 'She is in the tent,' he replied. ¹⁰Then his guest said, 'I shall come back to you next year, and then your wife Sarah will have a son.' Sarah was listening at the entrance of the tent behind him. ¹¹Now Abraham and Sarah were old, well on in years, and Sarah had ceased to have her monthly periods. ¹²So Sarah laughed to herself, thinking, 'Now that I am past the age of childbearing, and my husband is an old man, is pleasure to come my way again?' ¹³But Yahweh asked Abraham, 'Why did Sarah laugh and say, "Am I really going to have a child now that I am old?" ¹⁴Nothing is impossible for Yahweh. I shall come back to you at the same time next year and Sarah will have a son.' ¹⁵Sarah said, 'I did not laugh,' lying because she

17*b* Play on the Hebr. Root 'laugh' in the name Isaac, which in fact means 'God will smile'.

was afraid. But he replied, 'Oh yes, you did laugh.'

Abraham intercedes for Sodom

16From there the men set out and arrived within sight of Sodom, with Abraham accompanying them to speed them on their way. 17Now Yahweh had wondered, 'Shall I conceal from Abraham what I am going to do, 18as Abraham will become a great and powerful nation and all nations on earth will bless themselves by him? 19For I have singled him out to command his sons and his family after him to keep the way of Yahweh by doing what is upright and just, so that Yahweh can carry out for Abraham what he has promised him.' 20Then Yahweh said, 'The outcry against Sodom and Gomorrah is so great and their sin is so grave, 21that I shall go down and see whether or not their actions are at all as the outcry reaching me would suggest. Then I shall know.'

22While the men left there and went to Sodom, Yahweh remained in Abraham's presence. 23Abraham stepped forward and said, 'Will you really destroy the upright with the guilty? 24Suppose there are fifty upright people in the city. Will you really destroy it? Will you not spare the place for the sake of the fifty upright in it? 25Do not think of doing such a thing: to put the upright to death with the guilty, so that upright and guilty fare alike! Is the judge of the whole world not to act justly?' 26Yahweh replied, 'If I find fifty upright people in the city of Sodom, I shall spare the whole place because of them.'

27Abraham spoke up and said, 'It is presumptuous of me to speak to the Lord, I who am dust and ashes: 28Suppose the fifty upright were five short? Would you destroy the whole city because of five?' 'No,' he replied, 'I shall not destroy it if I find forty-five there.' 29Abraham persisted and said, 'Suppose there are forty to be found there?' 'I shall not do it,' he replied, 'for the sake of the forty.'

30Abraham said, 'I hope the Lord will not be angry if I go on: Suppose there are only thirty to be found there?' 'I shall not do it,' he replied, 'if I find thirty there.' 31He said, 'It is presumptuous of me to speak to the Lord: Suppose there are only twenty there?' 'I shall not destroy it,' he replied, 'for the sake of the twenty.' 32He said, 'I trust my Lord will not be angry if I speak once more: perhaps there will only be ten.' 'I shall not destroy it,' he replied, 'for the sake of the ten.'

33When he had finished talking to Abraham Yahweh went away, and Abraham returned home.

The destruction of Sodom

19When the two angels reached Sodom in the evening, Lot was sitting at the gate of Sodom. As soon as Lot saw them, he stood up to greet them, and bowed to the ground. 2'My lords,' he said, 'please come down to your servant's house to stay the night and wash your feet. Then you can make an early start on your journey.' 'No,' they said, 'we shall spend the night in the square.' 3But he pressed them so much that they went home with him and entered his house. He prepared a meal for them, baking unleavened bread, and they had supper.

4They had not gone to bed when the house was surrounded by the townspeople, the men of Sodom both young and old, all the people without exception. 5Calling out to Lot they said, 'Where are the men who came to you tonight? Send them out to us so that we can have intercourse with them.'

6Lot came out to them at the door and, having shut the door behind him, 7said, 'Please, brothers, do not be wicked. 8Look, I have two daughters who are virgins. I am ready to send them out to you, for you to treat as you please, but do nothing to these men since they are now under the protection of my roof.' 9But they retorted, 'Stand back! This fellow came here as a foreigner, and now he wants to play the judge. Now we shall treat you worse than them.' Then they forced Lot back and moved forward to break down the door. 10But the men reached out, pulled Lot back into the

5 READ GENESIS 19.

Flee for your life. Do not look behind you.—GENESIS 19:17

AFFECTION FOR SIN

Although all the Israelites left Egypt in effect, not all of them left it in affection, and hence in the wilderness many of them regretted their lack of the onions and fleshpots of Egypt (see Nb 11:4–5). In like manner, there are penitents who leave sin in effect, but do not leave it in affection. They resolve never to sin again, but it is with a certain reluctance that they give up or abstain from the fatal delights of sin. Their heart renounces and shuns it but looks back at it just as Lot's wife looked back at Sodom.

They abstain from sin like sick men abstaining from melons. They don't eat them solely because the doctor warns them that they'll die if they do, but they begrudge giving them up, talk about them, would eat them if they could, want to smell them at least, and envy those who can eat them. In such a way weak, lazy penitents abstain regretfully for a while from sin. They would like very much to commit sins if they could do so without being damned. They speak about sin with a certain petulance and with liking for it and think those who commit sins are at peace with themselves. A man who had resolved to take vengeance on another will change his mind in the confessional but a little later you will find him among his friends talking delightedly about his quarrel and saying, "If it wasn't for the fear of God, I would do this or that". . . . Although he is out of Egypt in effect he is still there in appetite and in his longing for the garlic and onions on which he once glutted himself. He is like the woman who detests her illicit love affairs but still likes to be courted and pursued. Alas, all such people are in great peril!   ST. FRANCIS DE SALES, 1567–1622

YOU WILL FIND THE NEXT READING AT GENESIS 28.

house with them, and shut the door. ¹¹And they dazzled those who were at the door of the house, one and all, with a blinding light, so that they could not find the doorway.

¹²The men said to Lot, 'Have you anyone else here? Your sons, your daughters and all your people in the city, take them away, ¹³for we are about to destroy this place, since the outcry to Yahweh against those in it has grown so loud that Yahweh has sent us to destroy it.' ¹⁴So Lot went off and spoke to his future sons-in-law who were to marry his daughters. 'On your feet!' he said, 'Leave this place, for Yahweh is about to destroy the city.' But his sons-in-law thought he was joking.

¹⁵When dawn broke the angels urged Lot on, 'To your feet! Take your wife and your two daughters who are here, or you will be swept away in the punishment of the city.' ¹⁶And as he hesitated, the men seized his hand and the hands of his wife and his two daughters—Yahweh being merciful to him—and led him out and left him outside the city.

¹⁷When they had brought him outside, he was told, 'Flee for your life. Do not look behind you or stop anywhere on the plain. Flee to the hills or you will be swept away.' ¹⁸'Oh no, my lord!' Lot said to them, ¹⁹'You have already been very good to your servant and shown me even greater love by saving my life, but I cannot flee to the hills, or disaster will overtake me and I shall die. ²⁰That town over

there is near enough to flee to, and is small. Let me flee there—after all it is only a small place—and so survive.' 21 He replied, 'I grant you this favour too, and will not overthrow the town you speak of. 22 Hurry, flee to that one, for I cannot do anything until you reach it.' That is why the town is named Zoar.

23 The sun rose over the horizon just as Lot was entering Zoar. 24 Then Yahweh rained down on Sodom and Gomorrah brimstone and fire of his own sending. 25 He overthrew those cities and the whole plain, with all the people living in the cities and everything that grew there. 26 But Lot's wife looked back, and was turned into a pillar of salt.

27 Next morning, Abraham hurried to the place where he had stood before Yahweh, 28 and looking towards Sodom and Gomorrah and the whole area of the plain, he saw the smoke rising from the ground like smoke from a furnace.

29 Thus it was that, when God destroyed the cities of the plain, he did not forget Abraham and he rescued Lot from the midst of the overthrow, when he overthrew the cities where Lot was living.

The origin of the Moabites and the Ammonites[a]

30 After leaving Zoar Lot settled in the hill country with his two daughters, for he dared not stay at Zoar. He lived in a cave, he and his two daughters.

31 The elder said to the younger, 'Our father is an old man, and there is no one here to marry us in the normal way of the world. 32 Come on, let us ply our father with wine and sleep with him. In this way we can preserve the race by our father.' 33 That night they made their father drunk, and the elder slept with her father though he was unaware of her coming to bed or of her leaving. 34 The next day the elder said to the younger, 'Last night, I was the one who slept with our father. Let us make him drunk again tonight, and you go and sleep with him. In this way we can preserve the race by our father.' 35 They made their father drunk that night too, and the younger went and slept with him, though he was unaware of her coming to bed or of her leaving. 36 Both Lot's daughters thus became pregnant by their father. 37 The elder gave birth to a son whom she named Moab; and he is the ancestor of the Moabites of our own times. 38 The younger also gave birth to a son whom she named Ben-Ammi; and he is the ancestor of the Bene-Ammon of our own times.

Abraham at Gerar[a]

20 Abraham left there for the region of the Negeb, and settled between Kadesh and Shur. While staying in Gerar, 2 Abraham said of his wife Sarah, 'She is my sister,' and Abimelech the king of Gerar had Sarah brought to him. 3 But God visited Abimelech in a dream one night. 'You are to die,' he told him, 'because of the woman you have taken, for she is a married woman.' 4 Abimelech, however, had not gone near her; so he said, 'Lord, would you kill someone even if he is upright? 5 Did he not tell me himself, "She is my sister"? And she herself said, "He is my brother." I did this with a clear conscience and clean hands.' 6 'Yes, I know,' God replied in the dream, 'that you did this with a clear conscience and I myself prevented you from sinning against me. That was why I did not let you touch her. 7 Now send the man's wife back; for he is a prophet and can intercede on your behalf for your life. But understand that if you do not send her back, this means death for you and all yours.'

8 Early next morning, Abimelech summoned his full court and told them the whole story, at which the people were very much afraid. 9 Then summoning Abraham, Abimelech said to him, 'What have you done to us? What wrong have I done you, for you to bring such guilt on me and on my kingdom? You had no right to treat me like this.' 10 Abim-

19a Popular explanations of the name Moab as 'from my father' and of Ben Ammon as 'son of my kinsman.'

20a = 12:10–20; = 26:1–11.

elech then said to Abraham, 'What possessed you to do such a thing?' [11] 'Because', Abraham replied, 'I thought there would be no fear of God here and that I should be killed for the sake of my wife. [12] Anyway, she really is my sister, my father's daughter though not my mother's, besides being my wife. [13] So when God made me wander far from my father's home I said to her, "There is an act of love you can do me: everywhere we go, say of me that I am your brother." '

[14] Abimelech took sheep, cattle, men and women slaves, and presented them to Abraham, and gave him back his wife Sarah. [15] And Abimelech said, 'Look, my land is open to you. Settle wherever you please.' [16] To Sarah he said, 'Look, I am giving your brother a thousand pieces of silver. This will allay suspicions about you, as far as all the people round you are concerned; you have been completely vindicated.' [17] Abraham then interceded with God, and God healed Abimelech, his wife and his slave-girls, so that they could have children, [18] for Yahweh had made all the women of Abimelech's household barren on account of Sarah, Abraham's wife.

The birth of Isaac

21 Yahweh treated Sarah as he had said, and did what he had promised her. [2] Sarah conceived and bore Abraham a son in his old age, at the time God had promised. [3] Abraham named the son born to him Isaac, the son to whom Sarah had given birth. [4] Abraham circumcised his son Isaac when he was eight days old, as God had commanded him. [5] Abraham was a hundred years old when his son Isaac was born to him. [6] Sarah said:

> God has given me cause to laugh!
> All who hear about this will laugh
> with me!

[7] She added:

> Whoever would have told Abraham
> that Sarah would nurse children!
> Yet I have borne a son in his old age.

The dismissal of Hagar and Ishmael[a]

[8] The child grew and was weaned, and Abraham gave a great banquet on the day Isaac was weaned. [9] Now Sarah watched the son that Hagar the Egyptian had borne to Abraham, playing with her son Isaac. [10] 'Drive away that slave-girl and her son,' she said to Abraham, 'this slave-girl's son is not to share the inheritance with my son Isaac.' [11] This greatly distressed Abraham, because the slave-girl's child too was his son, [12] but God said to him, 'Do not distress yourself on account of the boy and your slave-girl. Do whatever Sarah says, for Isaac is the one through whom your name will be carried on. [13] But the slave-girl's son I shall also make into a great nation, for he too is your child.' [14] Early next morning, Abraham took some bread and a skin of water and, giving them to Hagar, put the child on her shoulder and sent her away.

She wandered off into the desert of Beersheba. [15] When the skin of water was finished she abandoned the child under a bush. [16] Then she went and sat down at a distance, about a bowshot away, thinking, 'I cannot bear to see the child die.' Sitting at a distance, she began to sob.

[17] God heard the boy crying, and the angel of God called to Hagar from heaven. 'What is wrong, Hagar?' he asked. 'Do not be afraid, for God has heard the boy's cry in his plight. [18] Go and pick the boy up and hold him safe, for I shall make him into a great nation.' [19] Then God opened Hagar's eyes and she saw a well, so she went and filled the skin with water and gave the boy a drink.

[20] God was with the boy. He grew up and made his home in the desert, and he became an archer. [21] He made his home in the desert of Paran, and his mother got him a wife from Egypt.

21a = 16.

Abraham and Abimelech at Beersheba[b]

22 About then, Abimelech and Phicol, the commander of his army, said to Abraham, 'Since God is with you in everything you do, 23 swear to me by God, here and now, that you will not act treacherously towards me or my kith and kin, but behave with the same faithful love to me and the land of which you are a guest as I have behaved to you.' 24 'Yes,' Abraham replied, 'I swear it.'

25 Abraham then reproached Abimelech about a well that Abimelech's servants had seized. 26 'I do not know who has done this,' Abimelech said. 'You yourself have never mentioned it to me and, for myself, I heard nothing of it till today.' 27 Abraham then took sheep and cattle and presented them to Abimelech, and the two of them made a covenant. 28 Abraham put seven lambs of the flock on one side. 29 'Why have you put these seven lambs on one side?' Abimelech asked Abraham. 30 He replied, 'You must accept these seven lambs from me as evidence that I have dug this well.' 31 This was why the place was called Beersheba: because there the two of them swore an oath.

32 After they had made a covenant at Beersheba, Abimelech and Phicol, the commander of his army, left and went back to Philistine territory. 33 And Abraham planted a tamarisk at Beersheba and there he invoked the name of Yahweh. 34 Abraham stayed for a long while in Philistine territory.

Abraham's sacrifice

22 It happened some time later that God put Abraham to the test. 'Abraham, Abraham!' he called. 'Here I am,' he replied. 2 God said, 'Take your son, your only son, your beloved Isaac, and go to the land of Moriah, where you are to offer him as a burnt offering on one of the mountains which I shall point out to you.'

3 Early next morning Abraham saddled his donkey and took with him two of his servants and his son Isaac. He chopped wood for the burnt offering and started on his journey to the place which God had indicated to him. 4 On the third day Abraham looked up and saw the place in the distance. 5 Then Abraham said to his servants, 'Stay here with the donkey. The boy and I are going over there; we shall worship and then come back to you.'

6 Abraham took the wood for the burnt offering, loaded it on Isaac, and carried in his own hands the fire and the knife. Then the two of them set out together. 7 Isaac spoke to his father Abraham. 'Father?' he said. 'Yes, my son,' he replied. 'Look,' he said, 'here are the fire and the wood, but where is the lamb for the burnt offering?' 8 Abraham replied, 'My son, God himself will provide the lamb for the burnt offering.' And the two of them went on together.

9 When they arrived at the place which God had indicated to him, Abraham built an altar there, and arranged the wood. Then he bound his son and put him on the altar on top of the wood. 10 Abraham stretched out his hand and took the knife to kill his son.

11 But the angel of Yahweh called to him from heaven. 'Abraham, Abraham!' he said. 'Here I am,' he replied. 12 'Do not raise your hand against the boy,' the angel said. 'Do not harm him, for now I know you fear God. You have not refused me your own beloved son.' 13 Then looking up, Abraham saw a ram caught by its horns in a bush. Abraham took the ram and offered it as a burnt offering in place of his son. 14 Abraham called this place 'Yahweh provides', and hence the saying today: 'On the mountain Yahweh provides.'

15 The angel of Yahweh called Abraham a second time from heaven. 16 'I swear by my own self, Yahweh declares, that because you have done this, because you have not refused me your own beloved son, 17 I will shower blessings on you and make your descendants as numerous as the stars of heaven and the

21b Fragments using two explanations of the name as 'Well of the Seven' and 'Well of the Oath'. The story is parallel with 26:15–33.

grains of sand on the seashore. Your descendants will gain possession of the gates of their enemies. ¹⁸All nations on earth will bless themselves by your descendants, because you have obeyed my command.'

¹⁹Abraham went back to his servants, and together they set out for Beersheba, and Abraham settled in Beersheba.

The descendants of Nahor

²⁰It happened some time later that Abraham received word that Milcah, too, had now borne sons to his brother Nahor: ²¹Uz his first-born, Buz his brother, Kemuel father of Aram, ²²Chesed, Hazo, Pildash, Jidlaph, Bethuel ²³(and Bethuel was the father of Rebekah). These were the eight children Milcah gave Nahor, Abraham's brother. ²⁴He had a concubine named Reumah, and she too had children: Tebah, Gaham, Tahash and Maacah.

The tomb of the patriarchs

23 The length of Sarah's life was a hundred and twenty-seven years. ²She died at Kiriath-Arba—now Hebron—in the land of Canaan, and Abraham proceeded to mourn and bewail her.

³Then rising from beside his dead, Abraham spoke to the Hittites, ⁴'I am a stranger resident here,' he said. 'Let me have a burial site of my own here, so that I can remove my dead for burial.' ⁵The Hittites replied to Abraham, ⁶'Please listen to us, my lord, we regard you as a prince of God; bury your dead in the best of our tombs; not one of us would refuse you his tomb for you to bury your dead.'

⁷At this, Abraham rose and bowed low to the local people, the Hittites, ⁸and pleaded with them as follows, 'If you consent to my removing my dead for burial, you must agree to intercede for me with Ephron son of Zohar, ⁹for him to let me have the cave he owns at Machpelah, which is on the edge of his field. Let him sell it to me in your presence at its full price, for a burial site of my own.' ¹⁰Now Ephron was sitting among the Hittites, and Ephron the Hittite answered Abraham in the hearing of the Hittites, of all the inhabitants of his town. ¹¹'No, my lord, listen to me,' he said. 'I give you the field and the cave in it; I make this gift in the presence of my kinsmen. Bury your dead.'

¹²Abraham bowed low to the local people ¹³and, in the hearing of the local people, replied to Ephron as follows, 'Be good enough to listen to me. I shall pay the price of the field; accept it from me and I shall bury my dead there.' ¹⁴Ephron replied to Abraham, ¹⁵'Please listen to me, my lord. What is a plot of land for four hundred shekels of silver between me and you? Bury your dead.' ¹⁶Abraham agreed to Ephron's terms, and Abraham weighed out for Ephron the silver he had stipulated in the hearing of the Hittites, namely four hundred shekels of silver, according to the current commercial rate.

¹⁷Thus Ephron's field at Machpelah, facing Mamre—the field and the cave in it and all the trees anywhere within the boundaries of the field—passed ¹⁸into Abraham's possession in the sight of the Hittites, of all the inhabitants of his town. ¹⁹And after this, Abraham buried his wife Sarah in the cave of the field of Machpelah, facing Mamre—now Hebron—in the land of Canaan. ²⁰And so the field and the cave in it passed from the Hittites into Abraham's possession as a burial site of his own.

The marriage of Isaac

24 By now Abraham was an old man, well on in years, and Yahweh had blessed Abraham in every way. ²Abraham said to the senior servant in his household, the steward of all his property, 'Place your hand under my thigh: ³I am going to make you swear by Yahweh, God of heaven and God of earth, that you will not choose a wife for my son from the daughters of the Canaanites among whom I live ⁴but will go to my native land and my own kinsfolk to choose a wife for my son Isaac.' ⁵The servant asked him, 'What if the girl does not want to follow me to this country? Should I then take your son back to the country from which you come?' ⁶Abraham replied, 'On no

account are you to take my son back there. 7 Yahweh, God of heaven and God of earth, who took me from my father's home, and from the land of my kinsfolk, and who promised me on oath, "I shall give this country to your descendants"—he will now send his angel ahead of you, so that you can get a wife for my son from there. 8 If then the girl refuses to follow you, you will be quit of this oath to me. Only do not take my son back there.' 9 And the servant placed his hand under the thigh of his master Abraham, and swore to him that he would do it.

10 The servant took ten of his master's camels and, carrying all kinds of gifts from his master, set out for the city of Nahor in Aram Naharaim. 11 In the evening, at the time when women come out to draw water, he made the camels kneel outside the town near the well. 12 And he said, 'Yahweh, God of my master Abraham, give me success today and show faithful love to my master Abraham. 13 While I stand by the spring as the young women from the town come out to draw water, 14 I shall say to one of the girls, "Please lower your pitcher and let me drink." And if she answers, "Drink, and I shall water your camels too," let her be the one you have decreed for your servant Isaac; by this I shall know you have shown faithful love to my master.'

15 He had not finished speaking when out came Rebekah—who was the daughter of Bethuel son of Milcah, the wife of Abraham's brother Nahor—with a pitcher on her shoulder. 16 The girl was very beautiful, and a virgin; no man had touched her. She went down to the spring, filled her pitcher and came up again. 17 Running towards her, the servant said, 'Please give me a sip of water from your pitcher.' 18 She replied, 'Drink, my lord,' and quickly lowered her pitcher on her arm and gave him a drink. 19 When she had finished letting him drink, she said, 'I shall draw water for your camels, too, until they have had enough.' 20 She quickly emptied her pitcher into the trough, and ran to the well again to

draw, and drew for all the camels. 21 All the while, the man stood watching her, not daring to speak, wondering whether Yahweh had made his journey successful or not.

22 When the camels had finished drinking, the man took a gold ring weighing half a shekel, and put it through her nose, and put two bracelets weighing ten gold shekels on her arms, 23 and said, 'Whose daughter are you? Please tell me. Is there room at your father's house for us to spend the night?' 24 She replied, 'I am the daughter of Bethuel, the son whom Milcah bore to Nahor.' 25 And she went on, 'We have plenty of straw and fodder, and room to spend the night.' 26 Then the man bowed down and worshipped Yahweh 27 saying, 'Blessed be Yahweh, God of my master Abraham, for not withholding his faithful love from my master. Yahweh has led me straight to the house of my master's brother.'

28 The girl ran to her mother's house to tell what had happened. 29 Now Rebekah had a brother called Laban, and Laban ran out to the man at the spring. 30 As soon as he had seen the ring and the bracelets his sister was wearing, and had heard his sister Rebekah saying, 'This is what the man said to me,' he went to the man and found him still standing by his camels at the spring. 31 He said to him, 'Come in, blessed of Yahweh, why stay out here when I have cleared the house and made room for the camels?' 32 The man went to the house, and Laban unloaded the camels. He provided straw and fodder for the camels and water for him and his companions to wash their feet.

33 They offered him food, but he said, 'I will eat nothing before I have said what I have to say.' Laban said, 'Speak.' 34 He said, 'I am Abraham's servant. 35 Yahweh has loaded my master with blessings, and Abraham is now very rich. He has given him flocks and herds, silver and gold, men and women slaves, camels and donkeys. 36 Sarah, my master's wife, bore my master a son in his old age, and he has made over all his property to him. 37 My master made me take this oath, "You are not to choose a wife for my son from the daughters of

the Canaanites in whose country I live. ³⁸Instead, you are to go to my father's home and to my own kinsfolk to choose a wife for my son." ³⁹I said to my master, "Suppose the girl will not agree to come with me?" ⁴⁰and his reply was, "Yahweh, in whose presence I have walked, will send his angel with you and make your journey successful, for you to choose a wife for my son from my own kinsfolk, from my father's house. ⁴¹Then you will be quit of my curse: if you go to my family and they refuse you, you will be quit of my curse." ⁴²Arriving today at the spring I said, "Yahweh, God of my master Abraham, please grant a successful outcome to the course I propose to take. ⁴³While I stand by the spring, if a girl comes out to draw water and I say to her, 'Please give me a little water to drink from your pitcher,' ⁴⁴if she replies, 'Drink by all means, and I shall draw water for your camels too,' let her be the girl whom Yahweh has decreed for my master's son." ⁴⁵I was still saying this in my mind when Rebekah came out, her pitcher on her shoulder. She came down to the spring and drew water. I said to her, "Please give me a drink." ⁴⁶Quickly she lowered her pitcher saying, "Drink, and I shall water your camels too." ⁴⁷I asked her, "Whose daughter are you?" She replied, "I am the daughter of Bethuel, whom Milcah bore to Nahor." Then I put this ring through her nose and these bracelets on her arms. ⁴⁸I bowed down and worshipped Yahweh, and I blessed Yahweh, God of my master Abraham, who had led me by a direct path to choose the daughter of my master's brother for his son. ⁴⁹Now tell me whether you are prepared to show constant and faithful love to my master; if not, say so, and I shall know what to do.'

⁵⁰Laban and Bethuel replied, 'This is from Yahweh; it is not for us to say yes or no to you. ⁵¹Rebekah is there before you. Take her and go; and let her become the wife of your master's son, as Yahweh has decreed.' ⁵²On hearing this, Abraham's servant bowed to the ground before Yahweh. ⁵³He brought out silver and gold ornaments and clothes which he gave to Rebekah; he also gave rich presents to her brother and to her mother.

⁵⁴They ate and drank, he and his companions, and spent the night there. Next morning when they were up, he said, 'Let me go back to my master.' ⁵⁵Rebekah's brother and mother replied, 'Let the girl stay with us for ten days or so; then she can go.' ⁵⁶But he replied, 'Do not delay me, since Yahweh has made my journey successful; let me leave and go back to my master.' ⁵⁷They replied, 'Let us call the girl and find out what she has to say.' ⁵⁸They called Rebekah and asked her, 'Will you go with this man?' She replied, 'I will.' ⁵⁹Accordingly they let their sister Rebekah go, with her nurse, and Abraham's servant and his men. ⁶⁰They blessed Rebekah and said to her:

Sister of ours, from you may there spring
thousands and tens of thousands!
May your descendants gain possession
of the gates of their enemies!

⁶¹And forthwith, Rebekah and her maids mounted the camels, and followed the man. The servant took Rebekah and departed.

⁶²Isaac meanwhile had come back from the well of Lahai Roi and was living in the Negeb. ⁶³While Isaac was out walking towards evening in the fields, he looked up and saw camels approaching. ⁶⁴And Rebekah looked up and saw Isaac. She jumped down from her camel, ⁶⁵and asked the servant, 'Who is that man walking through the fields towards us?' The servant replied, 'That is my master.' So she took her veil and covered herself up. ⁶⁶The servant told Isaac the whole story. ⁶⁷Then Isaac took her into his tent. He married Rebekah and made her his wife. And in his love for her, Isaac was consoled for the loss of his mother.

The descendants of Keturah

25 Abraham married another wife whose name was Keturah; ²and she bore him Zimram, Jokshan, Medan, Midian, Ishbak and Shuah. ³Jokshan was the father of Sheba and Dedan, and the descendants of Dedan

were the Asshurites, the Letushim and the Leummim. ⁴The descendants of Midian were Ephah, Epher, Hanoch, Abida and Eldaah. All these were sons of Keturah.

⁵Abraham left all his possessions to Isaac. ⁶To the sons of his concubines Abraham made grants during his lifetime, sending them away from his son Isaac eastward, to the Land of the East.

The death of Abraham

⁷The number of years Abraham lived was a hundred and seventy-five. ⁸When Abraham had breathed his last, dying at a happy ripe age, old and full of years, he was gathered to his people. ⁹His sons Isaac and Ishmael buried him in the cave of Machpelah facing Mamre, in the field of Ephron the Hittite son of Zohar. ¹⁰This was the field that Abraham had bought from the Hittites, and Abraham and his wife Sarah were buried there. ¹¹After Abraham's death, God blessed his son Isaac. Isaac settled near the well of Lahai Roi.

The descendants of Ishmael

¹²These are the descendants of Ishmael son of Abraham by Hagar, Sarah's Egyptian slave-girl. ¹³These are the names of the sons of Ishmael by name and line: Ishmael's first-born was Nebaioth; then Kedar, Adbeel, Mibsam, ¹⁴Mishma, Dumah, Massa, ¹⁵Hadad, Tema, Jetur, Naphish and Kedemah. ¹⁶These are the sons of Ishmael, and these are their names, according to their settlements and encampments, twelve chiefs of as many tribes.

¹⁷The number of years Ishmael lived was one hundred and thirty-seven. When he breathed his last and died, he was gathered to his people.

¹⁸He lived in the territory stretching from Havilah-by-Shur just outside Egypt on the way to Assyria, and he held his own against all his kinsmen.

The birth of Esau and Jacob

¹⁹This is the story of Isaac son of Abraham. Abraham fathered Isaac. ²⁰Isaac was forty years old when he married Rebekah the daughter of Bethuel the Aramaean of Paddan-Aram, and sister of Laban the Aramaean. ²¹Isaac prayed to Yahweh on behalf of his wife, for she was barren. Yahweh heard his prayer, and his wife Rebekah conceived. ²²But the children inside her struggled so much that she said, 'If this is the way of it, why go on living?' So she went to consult Yahweh, ²³and Yahweh said to her:

There are two nations in your womb,
 your issue will be two rival peoples.
One nation will have the mastery of the
  other,
 and the elder will serve the younger.

²⁴When the time came for her confinement, there were indeed twins in her womb. ²⁵The first to be born was red, altogether like a hairy cloak; so they named him Esau. ²⁶Then his brother was born, with his hand grasping Esau's heel; so they named him Jacob.ᵃ Isaac was sixty years old at the time of their birth. ²⁷When the boys grew up Esau became a skilled hunter, a man of the open country. Jacob on the other hand was a quiet man, staying at home among the tents. ²⁸Isaac preferred Esau, for he had a taste for wild game; but Rebekah preferred Jacob.

Esau gives up his birthright

²⁹Once, when Jacob was cooking a stew, Esau returned from the countryside exhausted. ³⁰Esau said to Jacob, 'Give me a mouthful of that red stuff there; I am exhausted'—hence the name given to him, Edom. ³¹Jacob said, 'First, give me your birthright in exchange.' ³²Esau said, 'Here I am, at death's door; what use is a birthright to me?' ³³Then Jacob said, 'First give me your oath'; he gave him his oath and sold his birthright to Jacob. ³⁴Then Jacob gave him some bread and lentil stew; he ate, drank, got up and went away. That was all Esau cared about his birthright.

25a Fragments full of word-play: Edom/Esau = red; Seir = hairy; Jacob = heel/supplant.

Isaac at Gerar[a]

26 There was a famine in the country—different from the previous famine which took place in the time of Abraham—and Isaac went to Abimelech, the Philistine king at Gerar. [2]Yahweh had appeared to him and said, 'Do not go down to Egypt; stay in the country which I shall point out to you. [3]Remain for the present in that country; I shall be with you and bless you, for I shall give all these countries to you and your descendants in fulfilment of the oath I swore to your father Abraham. [4]I shall make your descendants as numerous as the stars of heaven, and I shall give them all these countries, and all nations on earth will bless themselves by your descendants [5]in return for Abraham's obedience; for he kept my charge, my commandments, my statutes and my laws.' [6]So Isaac stayed at Gerar.

[7]When the people of the place asked him about his wife he replied, 'She is my sister,' for he was afraid to say, 'She is my wife,' thinking, 'The people of the place will kill me because of Rebekah, since she is beautiful.' [8]When he had been there some time, Abimelech the Philistine king happened to look out of the window and saw Isaac fondling his wife Rebekah. [9]Abimelech summoned Isaac and said to him, 'Surely she must be your wife! How could you have said, "She is my sister"?' Isaac replied, 'Because I thought I might be killed on her account.' [10]Abimelech said, 'What a thing to do to us! One of the people might easily have slept with your wife. We should have incurred guilt, thanks to you.' [11]Then Abimelech issued this order to all the people: 'Whoever touches this man or his wife will be put to death.'

[12]Isaac sowed his crops in that country, and that year he reaped a hundredfold. Yahweh blessed him [13]and the man became rich; he prospered more and more until he was very rich indeed. [14]He acquired flocks and herds and a large retinue. The Philistines began to envy him.

The wells between Gerar and Beersheba[b]

[15]The Philistines had blocked up all the wells dug by his father's servants—in the days of his father Abraham—filling them in with earth. [16]Then Abimelech said to Isaac, 'You must leave us, for you have become much more powerful than we are.' [17]So Isaac left; he pitched camp in the Valley of Gerar and there he stayed. [18]Isaac reopened the wells dug by the servants of his father Abraham and blocked up by the Philistines after Abraham's death, and he gave them the same names as his father had given them.

[19]But when Isaac's servants, digging in the valley, found a well of spring-water there, [20]the herdsmen of Gerar disputed it with Isaac's herdsmen, saying, 'That water is ours!' So Isaac named the well Esek, because they had disputed with him. [21]They dug another well, and there was a dispute over that one too; so he named it Sitnah. [22]Then he left there, and dug another well, and since there was no dispute over this one, he named it Rehoboth, saying, 'Now Yahweh has made room for us to thrive in the country.'

[23]From there he went up to Beersheba. [24]Yahweh appeared to him the same night and said:

I am the God of your father Abraham.
Do not be afraid, for I am with you.
I shall bless you and multiply your offspring
for my servant Abraham's sake.

[25]There he built an altar and invoked the name of Yahweh. There he pitched his tent, and there Isaac's servants sank a well.

The alliance with Abimelech[c]

[26]Abimelech came from Gerar to see him, with Ahuzzath his adviser and Phicol the commander of his army. [27]Isaac said to them,

26a = 12:10–20; = 20.
26b = 21:25–31.
26c = 21:22–33.

'Why do you come to me since you hate me, and have made me leave you?' ²⁸'It became clear to us that Yahweh was with you,' they replied, 'and so we thought, "It is time to have a treaty sworn between us, between us and you." So let us make a covenant with you: ²⁹that you will not do us any harm, since we never molested you but were unfailingly kind to you and let you go away in peace. Henceforth, Yahweh's blessing on you!' ³⁰He then made them a feast and they ate and drank.

³¹Early next morning, they exchanged oaths. Then Isaac bade them farewell and they left him as friends. ³²It happened, the same day, that Isaac's servants brought him news about the well they had been digging. 'We have found water!' they said to him. ³³So he called the well Sheba, and hence the town is named Beersheba to this day.

The Hittite wives of Esau

³⁴When Esau was forty years old he married Judith daughter of Beeri the Hittite, and Basemath daughter of Elon the Hittite. ³⁵These were a bitter disappointment to Isaac and Rebekah.

Jacob obtains Isaac's blessing by fraud

27 When Isaac had grown old, and his eyes were so weak that he could no longer see, he summoned his elder son Esau. 'Son!' he said, and Esau replied, 'Here I am.' ²He then said, 'Look, I am old and do not know when I may die. ³Now take your weapons, your quiver and bow; go out into the country and hunt me some game. ⁴Make me the kind of appetising dish I like and bring it to me to eat and I shall give you my special blessing before I die.'

⁵Rebekah was listening while Isaac was talking to his son Esau. So when Esau went into the country to hunt game for his father, ⁶Rebekah said to her son Jacob, 'I have just heard your father saying to your brother Esau, ⁷"Bring me some game and make an appetising dish for me to eat and then I shall bless you in Yahweh's presence before I die." ⁸Now, son,

listen to me and do as I tell you. ⁹Go to the flock and bring me back two good kids, so that I can make the kind of special dish your father likes. ¹⁰Then take it to your father for him to eat, so that he may bless you before he dies.'

¹¹Jacob said to his mother Rebekah, 'Look, my brother Esau is hairy, while I am smooth-skinned. ¹²If my father happens to touch me, he will see I am cheating him, and I shall bring a curse down on myself instead of a blessing.' ¹³But his mother replied, 'On me be the curse, my son! Just listen to me; go and fetch me the kids.' ¹⁴So he went to fetch them and brought them to his mother, and she made the kind of special dish his father liked. ¹⁵Rebekah took her elder son Esau's best clothes, which she had at home, and dressed her younger son Jacob in them, ¹⁶covering his arms and the smooth part of his neck with the skins of the kids. ¹⁷She then handed the special dish and the bread she had made to her son Jacob.

¹⁸He went to his father and said, 'Father!' 'Yes?' he replied. 'Which of my sons are you?' ¹⁹Jacob said to his father, 'I am Esau your first-born; I have done as you told me. Please sit up and eat some of the game I have brought and then give me your soul's blessing.' ²⁰Isaac said to his son, 'Son, how did you succeed so quickly?' He replied, 'Because Yahweh your God made things go well for me.' ²¹Isaac said to Jacob, 'Come closer, son, so that I can feel you and be sure whether you really are my son Esau or not.' ²²Jacob went closer to his father Isaac, who felt him and said, 'The voice is Jacob's voice but the arms are the arms of Esau!' ²³He did not recognise him since his arms were hairy like his brother Esau's, and so he blessed him. ²⁴He said, 'Are you really my son Esau?' And he replied, 'I am.' ²⁵Isaac said, 'Serve it to me, so that I can eat my son's game and give you my special blessing.' He served it to him and he ate; he offered him wine, and he drank. ²⁶His father Isaac said to him, 'Come closer, and kiss me, son.' ²⁷He went closer and kissed his father, who sniffed the smell of his clothes. Then he blessed him, saying:

Ah, the smell of my son
    is like the smell of a fertile field
    which Yahweh has blessed.
28 May God give you
    dew from heaven,
    and the richness of the earth,
    abundance of grain and wine!
29 Let peoples serve you
    and nations bow low before you!
Be master of your brothers;
    let your mother's other sons bow low
        before you!
Accursed be whoever curses you
    and blessed be whoever blesses you!

30 As soon as Isaac had finished blessing Jacob, and just as Jacob was leaving his father Isaac, his brother Esau returned from hunting. 31 He too made an appetising dish and brought it to his father, 'Father, please eat some of your son's game and then give me your special blessing.' 32 His father Isaac asked, 'Who are you?' 'I am your first-born son, Esau,' he replied. 33 At this Isaac was seized with a violent trembling and said, 'Who was it, then, that went hunting and brought me the game? I finished eating it just before you came; I blessed him, and now blessed he will remain!' 34 On hearing his father's words, Esau cried out loudly and bitterly and said to his father, 'Father, bless me too!' 35 But he replied, 'Your brother came by fraud and took your blessing.' 36 Esau said, 'His name should be Jacob right enough, for he has now supplanted me twice. First he took my birthright, and look, now he has gone and taken my blessing! But', he added, 'have you not kept a blessing for me?' 37 Isaac replied to Esau, 'I have already made him your master; I have given him all his brothers as servants, I have given him grain and wine to sustain him. So what can I do for you, son?' 38 Esau said to his father, 'Can you bless only once, father? Father, bless me too.' Isaac remained silent, and Esau began to weep aloud. 39 Then his father Isaac spoke again and said:

'Far from the richness of the earth
    and the dew of heaven above,
    your home will be.
40 By your sword you will live,
    and your brother will you serve.

But when you win your freedom, you will shake his yoke off your neck.'
41 Esau hated Jacob because of the blessing his father had given him, and Esau said to himself, 'The time to mourn for my father will soon be here. Then I shall kill my brother Jacob.' 42 When the words of Esau, her elder son, were repeated to Rebekah, she sent for her younger son Jacob and said to him, 'Look, your brother Esau means to take revenge and kill you. 43 Now, son, listen to me; go at once and take refuge with my brother Laban in Haran. 44 Stay with him a while, until your brother's fury cools, 45 until your brother's anger is diverted from you and he forgets what you have done to him. Then I shall send someone to bring you back. I do not want to lose you both on one day!'

Isaac sends Jacob to Laban

46 Rebekah said to Isaac, 'The Hittite women sicken me to death. If Jacob were to marry a Hittite woman like these, one of the local women, what would there be left in life for me?'

28 So Isaac summoned Jacob and blessed him; and he gave him this order: 'You are not to marry any of the Canaanite women. 2 Go off to Paddan-Aram, the home of Bethuel your mother's father, and there choose a wife for yourself from the daughters of Laban your mother's brother. 3 May El Shaddai bless you; may he make you fruitful and make you multiply so that you become a group of nations. 4 May he grant you the blessing of Abraham, you and your descendants after you, so that one day you may own the country where you are now living as a stranger—which God gave to Abraham.' 5 Then Isaac sent Jacob away, and Jacob went to Paddan-Aram, to

Laban son of Bethuel the Aramaean and brother of Rebekah the mother of Jacob and Esau.

Another marriage of Esau

6 When Esau saw that Isaac had blessed Jacob and sent him to Paddan-Aram to choose a wife there, and that in blessing him he had given him this order: 'You are not to choose a wife from the Canaanite women,' 7 and that, in obedience to his father and mother, Jacob had gone to Paddan-Aram, 8 Esau then realised how much his father Isaac disapproved of the Canaanite women. 9 So Esau went to Ishmael and chose for a wife, in addition to the wives he had, Mahalath daughter of Abraham's son Ishmael and sister of Nebaioth.

Jacob's dream

10 Jacob left Beersheba and set out for Haran. 11 When he had reached a certain place, he stopped there for the night, since the sun had set. Taking one of the stones of that place, he made it his pillow and lay down where he was. 12 He had a dream: there was a ladder, planted on the ground with its top reaching to heaven; and God's angels were going up and down on it. 13 And there was Yahweh, standing beside him and saying, 'I, Yahweh, am the God of Abraham your father, and the God of Isaac. The ground on which you are lying I shall give to you and your descendants. 14 Your descendants will be as plentiful as the dust on the ground; you will spread out to west and east, to north and south, and all clans on earth will bless themselves by you and your descendants. 15 Be sure, I am with you; I shall keep you safe wherever you go, and bring you back to this country, for I shall never desert you until I have done what I have promised you.' 16 Then Jacob awoke from his sleep and said, 'Truly, Yahweh is in this place and I did not know!' 17 He was afraid and said, 'How awe-inspiring this place is! This is nothing less than the abode of God, and this is the gate of heaven!' 18 Early next morning, Jacob took the stone he had used for his pillow, and set it up as a pillar, pouring oil over the top of it. 19 He named the place Bethel, but before that the town had been called Luz.

20 Jacob then made this vow, 'If God remains with me and keeps me safe on this journey I am making, if he gives me food to eat and clothes to wear, 21 and if I come home safe to my father's home, then Yahweh shall be my God. 22 This stone I have set up as a pillar is to be a house of God, and I shall faithfully pay you a tenth part of everything you give me.'

Jacob arrives at Laban's home

29 Continuing his journey, Jacob reached the Land of the Easterners. 2 And there, out in the open, he saw a well with three flocks of sheep lying beside it; this well was used for watering the flocks. Now the stone on the mouth of the well was a large one, 3 and only when all the flocks had collected there, did they roll the stone off the mouth of the well and water the sheep; then they would replace the stone over the mouth of the well. 4 Jacob said to the shepherds, 'Friends, where are you from?' They replied, 'We are from Haran.' 5 He asked them, 'Do you know Laban son of Nahor?' They replied, 'We do.' 6 Then he asked them, 'Is he well?' 'He is,' they replied, 'and here comes his daughter Rachel with the flock.' 7 Then he said, 'But it is still broad daylight, not the time to round up the animals. Why don't you water the sheep and take them back to graze?' 8 To which, they replied, 'We can't, until all the shepherds have assembled to roll the stone off the mouth of the well; then we can water the sheep.'

9 He was still talking to them, when Rachel arrived with her father's flock, for she was a shepherdess. 10 As soon as Jacob saw Rachel, his uncle Laban's daughter, with his uncle Laban's flock, he went up and, rolling the stone off the mouth of the well, watered his uncle Laban's sheep. 11 Jacob then kissed Rachel and burst into tears. 12 He told Rachel he was her father's kinsman and Rebekah's son, and she ran to tell her father. 13 As soon as he heard her speak of his sister's son Jacob,

6 READ GENESIS 28:12–22.

There was a ladder, planted on the ground with its top reaching to heaven.
—GENESIS 28:12

DEVOTED TO GOD

Consider Jacob's ladder, for it is a true picture of the devout life. The two sides between which we climb upward and to which the rungs are fastened represent prayer that calls down God's love and the sacraments that confer it. The rungs are various degrees of charity by which we advance from virtue to virtue, either descending by deeds of help and support for our neighbor or by contemplation ascending to a loving union with God.'

I ask you to regard attentively those who are on this ladder. They are either people with angelic hearts or angels in human bodies. They are not young, although they seem to be so because they are full of vigor and spiritual agility. They have wings to soar aloft to God in holy prayer and they also have feet to walk among people in a holy and lovable way of life. Their faces are beautiful and joyous because they accept all things meekly and mildly. Their legs, arms, and heads are uncovered because in their thoughts, affections, and deeds they have no purpose or motive but that of pleasing God. The rest of their body is clothed but only by a decent light robe, because they use the world and worldly things but do so in a most pure and proper way, taking of them only what is necessary for their condition. Such are devout persons.

Believe me . . . devotion is the delight of delights and queen of the virtues since it is the perfection of charity. If charity is milk, devotion is its cream. If it is a plant, devotion is its blossom. If it is a precious stone, devotion is its luster. If it is a rich ointment, devotion is its fragrance, yes the fragrance of sweetness that comforts people and rejoices angels.   ST. FRANCIS DE SALES, 1567–1622

YOU WILL FIND THE NEXT READING AT GENESIS 45.

Laban ran to greet him, embraced him, kissed him and took him to his house. Jacob told Laban everything that had happened, ¹⁴ and Laban said to him, 'You are indeed my bone and flesh!'

Jacob's two marriages

After Jacob had been staying with him for a month, ¹⁵ Laban said to Jacob, 'Just because you are my kinsman, why should you work for me for nothing? Tell me what wages you want.' ¹⁶ Now Laban had two daughters, the elder named Leah, and the younger Rachel. ¹⁷ Leah had lovely eyes, but Rachel was shapely and beautiful, ¹⁸ and Jacob had fallen in love with Rachel. So his answer was, 'I shall work for you for seven years in exchange for your younger daughter Rachel.' ¹⁹ Laban replied, 'It is better for me to give her to you than to a stranger; stay with me.'

²⁰ So Jacob worked for seven years for Rachel, and they seemed to him like a few days because he loved her so much. ²¹ Then Jacob said to Laban, 'Give me my wife, for my time is up and I should like to go to her.' ²² Laban gathered all the people of the place together, and gave a banquet. ²³ But when night came, he took his daughter Leah and

brought her to Jacob, and he slept with her. [24](Laban gave his slave-girl Zilpah to his daughter Leah as her slave.) [25]When morning came, it was Leah! So Jacob said to Laban, 'What have you done to me? Did I not work for you for Rachel? Why then have you tricked me?' [26]Laban replied, 'It is not the custom in our place to marry off the younger before the elder. [27]Finish this marriage week and I shall give you the other one too in return for your working for me for another seven years.' [28]Jacob agreed and, when he had finished the week, Laban gave him his daughter Rachel as his wife. [29](Laban gave his slave-girl Bilhah to his daughter Rachel as her slave.) [30]So Jacob slept with Rachel too, and he loved Rachel more than Leah. He worked for Laban for another seven years.

Jacob's children

[31]When Yahweh saw that Leah was unloved, he opened her womb, while Rachel remained barren. [32]Leah conceived and gave birth to a son whom she named Reuben, meaning 'Yahweh has seen my misery'; and she said, 'Now my husband will love me.' [33]Conceiving again, she gave birth to a son and said, 'Yahweh heard that I was unloved, and so he has given me this one too'; and she named him Simeon. [34]Again she conceived and gave birth to a son, and said, 'This time my husband will become attached to me, because I have borne him three sons.' Accordingly, she named him Levi. [35]Again she conceived and gave birth to a son, and said, 'Now I shall praise Yahweh!' Accordingly, she named him Judah. Then she had no more children.

30 Rachel, seeing that she herself gave Jacob no children, became jealous of her sister. And she said to Jacob, 'Give me children, or I shall die!' [2]This made Jacob angry with Rachel, and he retorted, 'Am I in the position of God, who has denied you motherhood?' [3]So she said, 'Here is my slave-girl, Bilhah. Sleep with her and let her give birth on my knees; through her, then, I too shall have children!' [4]So she gave him her slave-girl Bilhah as concubine. Jacob slept with her, [5]and Bilhah conceived and gave birth to a son by Jacob. [6]Then Rachel said, 'God has done me justice; yes, he has heard my prayer and given me a son.' Accordingly she named him Dan. [7]Again Rachel's slave-girl Bilhah conceived and gave birth to a second son by Jacob. [8]Then Rachel said, 'I have fought a fateful battle with my sister, and I have won!' So she named him Naphtali.

[9]Now Leah, seeing that she had ceased to bear children, took her slave-girl Zilpah and gave her to Jacob as concubine. [10]So Leah's slave-girl Zilpah gave birth to a son by Jacob. [11]Then Leah exclaimed, 'What good fortune!' So she named him Gad. [12]Leah's slave-girl Zilpah gave birth to a second son by Jacob. [13]Then Leah said, 'What blessedness! Women will call me blessed!' So she named him Asher.

[14]One day, at the time of the wheat harvest, Reuben found some mandrakes[a] in the field and brought them to his mother Leah. Rachel said to Leah, 'Please give me some of your son's mandrakes.' [15]Leah replied, 'Is it not enough to have taken my husband, without your taking my son's mandrakes as well?' So Rachel said, 'Very well, he can sleep with you tonight in return for your son's mandrakes.' [16]When Jacob came back from the fields that night, Leah went out to meet him and said, 'You must come to me, for I have hired you at the price of my son's mandrakes.' So he slept with her that night. [17]God heard Leah, and she conceived and gave birth to a fifth son by Jacob. [18]Then Leah said, 'God has given me my reward for giving my slave-girl to my husband.' So she named him Issachar. [19]Again Leah conceived and gave birth to a sixth son by Jacob, [20]and said, 'God has given me a fine gift; now my husband will bring me presents, for I have borne him six sons.' So she named him Zebulun. [21]Later she gave birth to a daughter and named her Dinah.

30a The Hebr. name is similar to 'love'; and it was considered an aphrodisiac by the ancients.

22 Then God remembered Rachel; he heard her and opened her womb. 23 She conceived and gave birth to a son, and said, 'God has taken away my disgrace!' 24 She named him Joseph, saying, 'May Yahweh add another son for me!'

How Jacob became rich

25 When Rachel had given birth to Joseph, Jacob said to Laban, 'Release me and let me go home to my own country. 26 Give me my wives for whom I have worked for you, and my children, and let me go. You are well aware how long I have worked for you.' 27 Laban replied, 'If I have done what pleases you . . . I have learnt by divination that Yahweh has blessed me because of you. 28 So name your wages,' he added, 'and I will pay.' 29 He replied, 'You know how hard I have worked for you, and how your stock has fared in my charge. 30 The little you had before I came has increased enormously, and Yahweh has blessed you wherever I have been. When am I to provide for my own household too?' 31 Laban said, 'How much am I to pay you?' Jacob replied, 'You need not pay me anything. I shall change my mind and go on tending your flock, if you do this one thing for me.

32 'Go through your entire flock today and remove every black animal among the sheep, and every speckled or spotted one among the goats. These will be my wages, 33 and my uprightness will answer for me later: when you come to check my wages, every goat I have that is not speckled or spotted, and every sheep that is not black will count as stolen by me.' 34 Laban replied, 'Good, just as you say.' 35 That same day he removed the striped and speckled he-goats and all the spotted and speckled she-goats, every one that had white on it, and all the black sheep, and entrusted these to his sons. 36 Then he put a three days' journey between himself and Jacob, while Jacob grazed the rest of Laban's flock.

37 Jacob then got fresh shoots from poplar, almond and plane trees, and peeled them in white strips, laying bare the white part of the shoots. 38 He set up the shoots he had peeled in front of the animals, in the troughs, in the water-holes where the animals came to drink. Since they mated when they came to drink, 39 the goats thus mated in front of the shoots and so the goats produced striped, spotted and speckled young. 40 The ewes, on the other hand, Jacob kept apart and made these face whatever was striped or black in Laban's flock. Thus he built up droves of his own which he did not put with Laban's flocks. 41 Furthermore, whenever the sturdier animals were mating, Jacob put the shoots where the animals could see them, in the troughs, so that they would mate in front of the shoots. 42 But when the animals were feeble, he did not put them there; so Laban got the feeble, and Jacob the sturdy. 43 Thus the man grew extremely rich, and came to own large flocks, men and women slaves, camels and donkeys.

Jacob's flight

31 Jacob learned that Laban's sons were saying, 'Jacob has taken everything that belonged to our father; it is at our father's expense that he has acquired all this wealth,' 2 and Jacob also saw that Laban's manner towards him was not as it had been in the past. 3 Yahweh said to Jacob, 'Go back to the land of your ancestors, where you were born, and I shall be with you.' 4 So Jacob had Rachel and Leah called to the fields where his flocks were, 5 and he said to them, 'I can see that your father's manner towards me is not as it was in the past, but the God of my father has been with me. 6 You yourselves know that I have worked for your father with all my might, 7 and that your father has tricked me, changing my wages ten times over, and yet God has not allowed him to harm me. 8 Whenever he said, "The spotted ones will be your wages," all the animals produced spotted young; whenever he said, "The striped ones will be your wages," all the animals produced striped young. 9 Thus God has reclaimed your father's livestock and given it to me. 10 Once, when the animals were on heat, I suddenly saw in a

dream that the he-goats covering the females were striped or spotted or piebald. [11] In the dream the angel of God called to me, "Jacob!" I said, "Here I am." [12] He said, "Now take note: all the he-goats covering the females are striped or spotted or piebald—for I too have noted all the things that Laban has been doing to you, [13] I am the God who appeared to you at Bethel, where you poured oil on a pillar and made a vow to me. On your feet, then, leave this country and return to the land of your birth."'

[14] In answer Rachel and Leah said to him, 'Are we still likely to inherit anything from our father's estate? [15] Does he not think of us as outsiders now? For not only has he sold us, but he has completely swallowed up the money he got for us. [16] All the wealth that God has reclaimed from our father belonged to us and our children in any case. So do whatever God has told you.'

[17] Forthwith, Jacob put his children and his wives on camels, [18] and drove off all his livestock—with all the possessions he had acquired, the livestock belonging to him which he had acquired in Paddan-Aram—to go to his father Isaac in Canaan. [19] Laban was away, shearing his sheep; Rachel in the meanwhile had appropriated the household idols belonging to her father, [20] and Jacob had outwitted Laban the Aramaean so that he would not be forewarned of his flight. [21] Thus he got away with all he had. He was soon across the River and heading for Mount Gilead.

Laban pursues Jacob

[22] Three days later Laban was told that Jacob had fled. [23] Taking his brothers with him, he pursued him for seven days and overtook him at Mount Gilead. [24] But God appeared to Laban the Aramaean in a dream that night and said to him, 'On no account say anything whatever to Jacob.' [25] Laban caught up with Jacob, who had pitched his tent in the hills; and Laban pitched camp on Mount Gilead.

[26] Laban said to Jacob, 'What do you mean by outwitting me and then carrying off my daughters like prisoners of war? [27] Why did you flee in secret, stealing away without letting me know, so that I could send you on your way rejoicing, with songs and the music of tambourines and harps? [28] You did not even let me kiss my sons and daughters. You have behaved like a fool. [29] It is in my power to harm you, but the God of your father said to me last night, "On no account say anything whatever to Jacob." [30] Now it may be you really went because you had such a longing for your father's house, but why did you steal my gods?'

[31] Jacob answered Laban, 'I was afraid, thinking you were going to snatch your daughters from me. [32] But whoever is found in possession of your gods shall not remain alive. In the presence of our brothers, examine for yourself what I have, and take what is yours.' Now Jacob did not know that Rachel had appropriated them. [33] Laban went into Jacob's tent, and then into Leah's tent and the tent of the two slave-girls, but he found nothing. He came out of Leah's tent and went into Rachel's. [34] Now Rachel had taken the household idols and put them inside a camel cushion, and was sitting on them. Laban went through everything in the tent but found nothing. [35] Then Rachel said to her father, 'Do not look angry, my lord, because I cannot rise in your presence, for I am as women are from time to time.' Laban searched but did not find the idols.

[36] Then Jacob lost his temper and took Laban to task. And Jacob said to Laban, 'What is my offence, what is my crime, for you to have hounded me like this? [37] You have gone through all my belongings; have you found anything belonging to your household? Produce it here in the presence of my brothers and yours, and let them decide between the two of us. [38] In all the twenty years I was under you, your ewes and your she-goats never miscarried, and I never ate rams from your flock. [39] Those mauled I never brought back to you, but bore the loss myself. You demanded compensation from me, whether the animal was

stolen in daylight or at night. ⁴⁰In the daytime the heat devoured me, and frost at night; I never had a good night's sleep. ⁴¹It was like this for the twenty years I spent in your household. Fourteen years I slaved for you for your two daughters, and six years for your flock, since you changed my wages ten times over. ⁴²If the God of my father, the God of Abraham, the Kinsman of Isaac, had not been with me, you would have sent me away empty-handed. But God saw my plight and my labours, and last night he delivered judgement.'

A treaty between Jacob and Laban

⁴³Laban replied to Jacob, 'These daughters are my daughters and these children are my children, this livestock is my livestock: everything you see belongs to me. But what can I do today about my daughters here or about the children they have borne? ⁴⁴So come, let us make a pact, you and me . . . ,ᵃ and let that serve as a witness between us.'

⁴⁵Jacob then took a stone and set it up as a memorial. ⁴⁶Jacob said to his kinsmen, 'Collect some stones,' and gathering some stones they made a cairn. They had a meal there, on the cairn, and ⁴⁷Laban called it Jegar-Sahadutha while Jacob called it Galeed. ⁴⁸Laban said, 'May this cairn be a witness between us today.' That is why he named it Galeed, ⁴⁹and also Mizpah, because he said, 'Let Yahweh act as watchman between us when we are no longer in sight of each other. ⁵⁰If you ill-treat my daughters or marry other women besides my daughters, even though no one be with us, remember: God is witness between us.' ⁵¹Then Laban said to Jacob, 'Here is this cairn I have thrown up between us, and here the pillar. ⁵²This cairn is a witness, and the pillar is a witness, that I am not to cross to your side of this cairn and you are not to cross to my side of this cairn and pillar, with hostile intent. ⁵³May the God of Abraham and the god of Nahor judge between us.' Then Jacob swore by the Kinsman of his father Isaac. ⁵⁴He offered a sacrifice on the mountain and in-

vited his kinsmen to the meal. They ate the meal, and passed the night on the mountain.

32 Early next morning, Laban kissed his grandchildren and daughters and blessed them. Then Laban left to return home. ²While Jacob was going on his way, angels of God encountered him, ³and on seeing them he said, 'This is God's camp,' and he named the place Mahanaim.

Jacob prepares for his meeting with Esau

⁴Jacob sent messengers ahead of him to his brother Esau in Seir, the open country of Edom, ⁵with these instructions, 'Say this to my lord Esau, "Here is the message of your servant Jacob: I have been staying with Laban and have been delayed there until now, ⁶and I own oxen, beasts of burden and flocks, and men and women slaves. I send news of this to my lord in the hope of winning your favour."'

⁷The messengers returned to Jacob and told him, 'We went to your brother Esau, and he is already on his way to meet you; there are four hundred men with him.'

⁸Jacob was greatly afraid and distressed. He divided the people with him, and the flocks and cattle, into two camps, ⁹thinking, 'If Esau comes to one of the camps and attacks it, the remaining camp may be able to escape.' ¹⁰Jacob said, 'God of my father Abraham, and God of my father Isaac, Yahweh who told me, "Go back to your native land and I will be good to you," ¹¹I am unworthy of all the faithful love and constancy you have shown your servant. I had only my staff when I crossed this Jordan, and now I have grown into two camps. ¹²I implore you, save me from my brother Esau's clutches, for I am afraid that he may come and attack me, mothers and children alike. ¹³Yet it was you who said, "I shall be very good to you, and make your descendants like the sand of the sea, which is too numerous to count."' ¹⁴Then Jacob passed that night there.

31a Some words have probably fallen out of the text at this point.

From what he had with him he chose a gift for his brother Esau: 15 two hundred she-goats and twenty he-goats, two hundred ewes and twenty rams, 16 thirty camels in milk with their calves, forty cows and ten bulls, twenty female donkeys and ten male. 17 He put them in the charge of his servants, in separate droves, and told his servants, 'Go ahead of me, leaving a space between each drove and the next.' 18 He gave the leading man this order: 'When my brother Esau meets you and asks, "Whose man are you? Where are you going? Whose are those animals that you are driving?" 19 you will answer, "Your servant Jacob's. They are a gift sent to my lord Esau. And Jacob himself is just behind us." ' 20 He gave the same order to the second and the third, and to all who were following the droves. 'That is what you must say to Esau when you find him. 21 And you must add, "Your servant Jacob himself is just behind us." ' For he thought, 'If I conciliate him by sending a gift in advance, perhaps he will be well inclined towards me when I face him.' 22 The gift went ahead of him, but he himself spent that night in the camp.

Jacob wrestles with God

23 That same night he got up and, taking his two wives, his two slave-girls and his eleven children, crossed the ford of the Jabbok. 24 After he had taken them across the stream, he sent all his possessions over too. 25 And Jacob was left alone.

Then someone wrestled with him until daybreak 26 who, seeing that he could not master him, struck him on the hip socket, and Jacob's hip was dislocated as he wrestled with him. 27 He said, 'Let me go, for day is breaking.' Jacob replied, 'I will not let you go unless you bless me.' 28 The other said, 'What is your name?' 'Jacob,' he replied. 29 He said, 'No longer are you to be called Jacob, but Israel[a] since you have shown your strength against God and men and have prevailed.' 30 Then Jacob asked, 'Please tell me your name.' He replied, 'Why do you ask my name?' With that, he blessed him there.

31 Jacob named the place Peniel, 'Because I have seen God face to face,' he said, 'and have survived.' 32 The sun rose as he passed Peniel, limping from his hip. 33 That is why to this day the Israelites do not eat the thigh sinew which is at the hip socket: because he had struck Jacob at the hip socket on the thigh sinew.

The meeting with Esau

33 Looking up, Jacob saw Esau coming and with him four hundred men. He then divided the children between Leah, Rachel and the two slave-girls. 2 He put the slave-girls and their children in front, with Leah and her children following, and Rachel and Joseph behind. 3 He himself went ahead of them and bowed to the ground seven times, until he reached his brother. 4 But Esau ran to meet him, took him in his arms, threw himself on his neck and wept as he kissed him. 5 Then looking up he saw the women and children. 'Who are these with you?' he asked. Jacob answered, 'The children whom God has bestowed on your servant.' 6 The slave-girls then came up with their children, and they all bowed low. 7 Then Leah too came up with her children, and they all bowed low. Finally Rachel and Joseph came up and bowed low.

8 Esau asked, 'What was the purpose of that whole camp I just met?' 'To win my lord's favour,' he replied. 9 'Brother, I have plenty,' Esau answered, 'keep what is yours.' 10 Jacob protested, 'No, if I have won your favour, please accept the gift I offer, for in fact I have come into your presence as into the presence of God, since you have received me kindly. 11 So accept the gift I have brought for you, since God has been generous to me and I have all I need.' And he urged him, and Esau accepted.

Jacob parts company with Esau

12 Esau said, 'Let us break camp and move off; I shall go beside you.' 13 But Jacob replied, 'As

32a = 35:10.

my lord knows, the children are weak, and the sheep and cows which have calved make it hard for me. If they are driven too hard, even for one day, the whole drove will die. ¹⁴May it please my lord to go on ahead of his servant. For my part, I shall move at a slower pace, to suit the flock I am driving and the children, until I join my lord in Seir.' ¹⁵Esau then said, 'At least let me leave you some of the people who are with me.' 'What for?' Jacob asked. 'Please indulge me, my lord!' ¹⁶So that day Esau turned back towards Seir, ¹⁷but Jacob made his way to Succoth, where he built himself a house and made shelters for his livestock; that is why the place was given the name of Succoth.

Jacob arrives at Shechem

¹⁸Jacob arrived safely at the town of Shechem in Canaanite territory, on his return from Paddan-Aram. He encamped opposite the town ¹⁹and for one hundred pieces of silver he bought from the sons of Hamor father of Shechem the piece of land on which he had pitched his tent. ²⁰There he erected an altar which he called 'El, God of Israel'.

The rape of Dinah

34 Dinah, who was Jacob's daughter by Leah, went out to visit some of the women of that region. ²Shechem son of Hamor the Hivite, headman of the region, saw her, seized her and forced her to sleep with him. ³He was captivated by Dinah daughter of Jacob; he fell in love with the girl and tried to win her heart. ⁴Accordingly Shechem said to his father Hamor, 'Get me this girl; I want to marry her.' ⁵Meanwhile, Jacob had heard how his daughter Dinah had been dishonoured, but since his sons were out in the countryside with his livestock, Jacob said nothing until they came back.

A matrimonial alliance with the Shechemites

⁶Hamor father of Shechem was visiting Jacob to discuss the matter with him, ⁷when Jacob's sons returned from the countryside and heard the news; the men were outraged and infuriated that Shechem had insulted Israel by sleeping with Jacob's daughter—a thing totally unacceptable. ⁸Hamor reasoned with them as follows, 'My son Shechem's heart is set on your daughter. Please allow her to marry him. ⁹Intermarry with us; give us your daughters and take our daughters for yourselves. ¹⁰We can live together, and the country will be open to you, for you to live in, and move about in, and acquire holdings.' ¹¹Then Shechem addressed the girl's father and brothers, 'Grant me this favour, and I will give you whatever you ask. ¹²Demand as high a bride-price from me as you please, and I will pay as much as you ask. Only let me marry the girl.'

¹³Jacob's sons gave Shechem and his father Hamor a crafty answer, speaking as they did because he had dishonoured their sister Dinah. ¹⁴'We cannot do this,' they said to them. 'To give our sister to an uncircumcised man would be a disgrace for us. ¹⁵We can agree only on one condition: that you become like us by circumcising all your males. ¹⁶Then we will give you our daughters, taking yours for ourselves; and we will stay with you to make one nation. ¹⁷But if you will not agree to our terms about being circumcised, we shall take our daughter and go.' ¹⁸Hamor and Shechem son of Hamor were pleased with what they heard. ¹⁹The young man did not hesitate about doing this, for he was deeply in love with Jacob's daughter. Moreover he was the most respected member of his entire family.

²⁰Hamor and his son Shechem went to the gate of their town and spoke to their fellow-townsmen as follows, ²¹'These men are friendly; let them settle in the region and move about freely in it; there is plenty of room here for them; we shall marry their daughters and give our daughters to them. ²²But these men will agree to settle with us and become a single nation only on this condition: that all our males be circumcised like them. ²³Will not the livestock they own, all their animals, become

ours? Then let us give our assent to this, so that they can settle with us.' 24 All the citizens of the town agreed to the proposal made by Hamor and his son Shechem, and all the males were circumcised.

The treacherous revenge of Simeon and Levi

25 Now on the third day, when the men were still in pain, Jacob's two sons Simeon and Levi, Dinah's brothers, each took his sword and advanced unopposed against the town and slaughtered all the males. 26 They killed Hamor and his son Shechem with the sword, removed Dinah from Shechem's house and came away. 27 When Jacob's other sons came on the slain, they pillaged the town in reprisal for the dishonouring of their sister. 28 They seized their flocks, cattle, donkeys, everything else in the town and in the countryside, 29 and all their possessions. They took all their children and wives captive and looted everything to be found in the houses.

30 Jacob said to Simeon and Levi, 'You have done me an ill turn by bringing me into bad odour with the people of the region, the Canaanites and the Perizzites. I have few men, whereas they will unite against me to defeat me and destroy me and my family.' 31 They retorted, 'Should our sister be treated like a whore?'

Jacob at Bethel

35 God said to Jacob, 'Move on, go to Bethel and settle there. Make an altar there for the God who appeared to you when you were fleeing from your brother Esau.'

2 Jacob said to his family and to all who were with him, 'Get rid of the foreign gods you have with you; cleanse yourselves, and change your clothes. 3 We must move on and go to Bethel. There I shall make an altar for the God who heard me when I was in distress, and gave me his help on the journey I made.' 4 They gave Jacob all the foreign gods in their possession, and the earrings that they were wearing. Jacob buried them under the oak tree near Shechem. 5 They broke camp; a divine terror struck the towns round about, and no one pursued the sons of Jacob.

6 When Jacob arrived at Luz in Canaan— that is, Bethel—and all the people with him, 7 he built an altar there and named the place El-Bethel, since it was there that God had appeared to him when he was fleeing from his brother. 8 Deborah, who had been Rebekah's nurse, died and was buried below Bethel, under the oak tree; so they named it the Oak of Tears.

9 God again appeared to Jacob on his return from Paddan-Aram, and blessed him. 10 God said to him, 'Your name is Jacob, but from now on you will be called not Jacob but Israel.ᵃ' Thus he came by the name Israel.

11 God said to him, 'I am El Shaddai. Be fruitful and multiply. A nation, indeed an assembly of nations, will descend from you, and kings will issue from your loins. 12 The country which I gave to Abraham and Isaac, I now give to you; and this country I shall give to your descendants after you.' 13 Then God went up from him.

14 Jacob raised a monument at the spot where he had spoken to him, a standing-stone, on which he made a libation and poured oil. 15 Jacob named the place Bethel where God had spoken to him.

The birth of Benjamin and the death of Rachel

16 They left Bethel, and while they were still some distance from Ephrath, Rachel went into labour, and her pains were severe. 17 When her labour was at its hardest, the midwife said to her, 'Do not worry, this is going to be another boy.' 18 At the moment when she breathed her last, for she was dying, she named him Ben-Oni. His father, however, named him Benjamin. 19 So Rachel died and was buried on the road to Ephrath, now Bethlehem. 20 Jacob raised a monument on her grave, that same monument of Rachel's Tomb which is there today.

35a = 32:29.

Reuben's incest

²¹ Israel left and pitched his tent beyond Migdal-Eder. ²² While Israel was living in that district, Reuben went and slept with Bilhah his father's concubine, and Israel found out.

The twelve sons of Jacob

The sons of Jacob were now twelve. ²³ The sons of Leah: Jacob's eldest son Reuben, then Simeon, Levi, Judah, Issachar and Zebulun. ²⁴ The sons of Rachel: Joseph and Benjamin. ²⁵ The sons of Bilhah, Rachel's slave-girl: Dan and Naphtali. ²⁶ The sons of Zilpah, Leah's slave-girl: Gad and Asher. These were the sons born to Jacob in Paddan-Aram.

The death of Isaac

²⁷ Jacob came home to his father Isaac at Mamre, at Kiriath-Arba—now Hebron—where Abraham and Isaac had stayed. ²⁸ Isaac was one hundred and eighty years old ²⁹ when he breathed his last. He died and was gathered to his people, an old man who had enjoyed his full span of life. His sons Esau and Jacob buried him.

Esau's wives and children in Canaan

36 These are the descendants of Esau, that is, Edom. ² Esau chose his wives from the women of Canaan: Adah daughter of Elon the Hittite, Oholibamah daughter of Anah, son of Zibeon the Horite, ³ Basemath daughter of Ishmael and sister of Nebaioth. ⁴ Adah bore Eliphaz to Esau, Basemath bore Reuel, ⁵ Oholibamah bore Jeush, Jalam and Korah. These were the sons of Esau born to him in Canaan.

Esau's migration

⁶ Esau took his wives, his sons and daughters, all the members of his household, his livestock, all his cattle and all the goods he had acquired in Canaan and left for Seir, away from his brother Jacob. ⁷ For they had acquired too much to live together. The land in which they were at that time could not support them both because of their livestock. ⁸ That is why Edom settled in the mountainous region of Seir. Esau is Edom.

Esau's descendants in Seir

⁹ These are the descendants of Esau, ancestor of Edom, in the mountainous region of Seir.

¹⁰ These are the names of Esau's sons: Eliphaz son of Esau's wife Adah, and Reuel son of Esau's wife Basemath. ¹¹ The sons of Eliphaz were: Teman, Omar, Zepho, Gatam and Kenaz. ¹² Eliphaz son of Esau had Timna for concubine and she bore him Amalek. These were the sons of Esau's wife Adah.

¹³ These were the sons of Reuel: Nahath, Zerah, Shammah and Mizzah. These were the sons of Esau's wife Basemath.

¹⁴ And these were the sons of Esau's wife Oholibamah daughter of Anah, son of Zibeon: she bore him Jeush, Jalam and Korah.

The chieftains of Edom

¹⁵ These are the chieftains of Esau.

The descendants of Eliphaz, Esau's eldest son: the chieftains of Teman, Omar, Zepho, Kenaz, ¹⁶ Gatam and Amalek. These are the chieftains of Eliphaz in Edom and are descended from Adah.

¹⁷ The descendants of Esau's son Reuel: the chieftains of Nahath, Zerah, Shammah and Mizzah. These are the chieftains of Reuel in Edom and are descended from Esau's wife Basemath.

¹⁸ The descendants of Esau's wife Oholibamah: the chieftains of Jeush, Jalam and Korah. These are the chieftains of Esau's wife Oholibamah daughter of Anah.

¹⁹ These were the sons of Esau—that is, Edom—and these are their chieftains.

The descendants of Seir the Horite

²⁰ These are the sons of Seir the Horite, natives of the country: Lotan, Shobal, Zibeon, Anah, ²¹ Dishon, Ezer and Dishan; these were the Horite chieftains descended from Seir, in

Edom. ²²The sons of Lotan were Hori and Hemam, and Lotan's sister was Timna. ²³These are the sons of Shobal: Alvan, Manahath, Ebal, Shepho and Onam. ²⁴These are the sons of Zibeon: Aiah, Anah—the Anah who found the hot springs in the desert while pasturing his father Zibeon's donkeys. ²⁵These are the children of Anah: Dishon, and Oholibamah daughter of Anah. ²⁶These are the sons of Dishon: Hemdan, Eshban, Ithran and Cheran. ²⁷These are the sons of Ezer: Bilhan, Zaavan and Akan. ²⁸These are the sons of Dishan: Uz and Aran.

²⁹These are the Horite chieftains: the chieftains of Lotan, Shobal, Zibeon, Anah, ³⁰Dishon, Ezer and Dishan. These are the chieftains of the Horites, by their clans, in Seir.

The kings of Edom

³¹These are the kings who reigned in Edom before an Israelite king. ³²In Edom reigned Bela son of Beor; his city was called Dinhabah. ³³Bela died and Jobab son of Zerah, from Bozrah, succeeded. ³⁴Jobab died and Husham from the land of the Temanites succeeded. ³⁵Husham died and Hadad son of Bedad succeeded; he defeated the Midianites in Moab, and his city was called Avith. ³⁶Hadad died and Samlah of Masrekah succeeded. ³⁷Samlah died and Shaul of Rehoboth-ha-Nahar succeeded. ³⁸Shaul died and Baal-Hanan son of Achbor succeeded. ³⁹Baal-Hanan died and Hadad succeeded; his city was called Pau and his wife's name was Mehetabel daughter of Matred, from Mezahab.

More chieftains of Edom

⁴⁰These are the names of the chieftains of Esau—according to their clans and localities: the chieftains of Timna, Alvah, Jetheth, ⁴¹Oholibamah, Elah, Pinon, ⁴²Kenaz, Teman, Mibzar, ⁴³Magdiel and Iram. These are the chieftains of Edom, as settled in the territory which they own. Esau was Edom's ancestor.

37 But Jacob settled in the land where his father had stayed, the land of Canaan.

Joseph and his brothers

²This is the story of Joseph.

Joseph was seventeen years old. As he was young, he was shepherding the flock with his brothers, with the sons of his father's wives, Bilhah and Zilpah; and Joseph brought his father bad reports about them.

³Jacob loved Joseph more than all his other sons, for he was the son of his old age, and he had a decorated tunic made for him. ⁴But his brothers, seeing how much more his father loved him than all his other sons, came to hate him so much that they could not say a civil word to him.

⁵Now Joseph had a dream, and he repeated it to his brothers, who then hated him more than ever. ⁶'Listen', he said, 'to the dream I had. ⁷We were binding sheaves in the field, when my sheaf suddenly rose and stood upright, and then your sheaves gathered round and bowed to my sheaf.' ⁸'So you want to be king over us,' his brothers retorted, 'you want to lord it over us?' And they hated him even more, on account of his dreams and of what he said. ⁹He had another dream which he recounted to his brothers. 'Look, I have had another dream,' he said. 'There were the sun, the moon and eleven stars, bowing down to me.' ¹⁰He told his father and brothers, and his father scolded him. 'A fine dream to have!' he said to him. 'Are all of us then, myself, your mother and your brothers, to come and bow to the ground before you?' ¹¹His brothers held it against him, but his father pondered the matter.

Joseph sold by his brothers

¹²His brothers went to pasture their father's flock at Shechem. ¹³Then Israel said to Joseph, 'Your brothers are with the flock at Shechem, aren't they? Come, I am going to send you to them.' 'I am ready,' he replied. ¹⁴He said to him, 'Go and see how your brothers and the flock are doing, and bring me word.' He sent him from the valley of Hebron, and Joseph arrived at Shechem.

¹⁵A man found him wandering in the countryside and asked him, 'What are you looking for?' ¹⁶'I am looking for my brothers,' he replied. 'Please tell me where they are pasturing their flock.' ¹⁷The man answered, 'They have moved on from here; indeed I heard them say, "Let us go to Dothan."' So Joseph went after his brothers and found them at Dothan.

¹⁸They saw him in the distance, and before he reached them they made a plot to kill him. ¹⁹'Here comes that dreamer,' they said to one another. ²⁰'Come on, let us kill him now and throw him down one of the storage-wells; we can say that some wild animal has devoured him. Then we shall see what becomes of his dreams.'

²¹But Reuben heard, and he saved him from their clutches. 'We must not take his life,' he said. ²²'Shed no blood,' said Reuben to them, 'throw him down that well out in the desert, but do not kill him yourselves'—intending to save him from them and to restore him to his father. ²³So, when Joseph reached his brothers, they pulled off his tunic, the decorated tunic which he was wearing, ²⁴and catching hold of him, threw him into the well. The well was empty, with no water in it. ²⁵They then sat down to eat.

Looking up, they saw a group of Ishmaelites who were coming from Gilead, their camels laden with gum tragacanth, balsam and resin, which they were taking to Egypt. ²⁶Then Judah said to his brothers, 'What do we gain by killing our brother and covering up his blood? ²⁷Come, let us sell him to the Ishmaelites, then we shall not have laid hands on him ourselves. After all, he is our brother, and our own flesh.' His brothers agreed.

²⁸Now some Midianite merchants were passing, and they pulled Joseph out of the well. They sold Joseph to the Ishmaelites for twenty shekels of silver, and these men took Joseph to Egypt. ²⁹When Reuben went back to the well, there was no sign of Joseph. Tearing his clothes, ³⁰he went back to his brothers.

'The boy has gone,' he said. 'What am I going to do?'

³¹They took Joseph's tunic and, slaughtering a goat, dipped the tunic in the blood. ³²Then they sent off the decorated tunic and had it taken to their father, with the message, 'This is what we have found. Do you recognise it as your son's tunic or not?' ³³He recognised it and cried, 'My son's tunic! A wild animal has devoured him! Joseph has been torn to pieces!' ³⁴Tearing his clothes and putting sackcloth round his waist, Jacob mourned his son for many days. ³⁵All his sons and daughters tried to comfort him, but he refused to be comforted. 'No,' he said, 'I will go down to Sheol in mourning and join my son.' Thus his father wept for him.

³⁶Meanwhile the Midianites had sold him in Egypt to Potiphar, one of Pharaoh's officials and commander of the guard.

The story of Judah and Tamar

38 It happened at about that time that Judah left his brothers, to go down and settle with a certain Adullamite called Hirah. ²There Judah saw the daughter of a Canaanite called Shua. He made her his wife and slept with her. ³She conceived and gave birth to a son whom she named Er. ⁴She conceived again and gave birth to a son whom she named Onan. ⁵Yet again she gave birth to a son whom she named Shelah. She was at Chezib when she gave birth to him.

⁶Judah took a wife for his first-born Er, and her name was Tamar. ⁷But Er, Judah's first-born, offended Yahweh, and Yahweh killed him. ⁸Then Judah said to Onan, 'Take your brother's wife, and do your duty as her brother-in-law, to maintain your brother's line.' ⁹But Onan, knowing that the line would not count as his, spilt his seed on the ground every time he slept with his brother's wife, to avoid providing offspring for his brother. ¹⁰What he did was offensive to Yahweh, who killed him too. ¹¹Then Judah said to his daughter-in-law Tamar, 'Go home as a widow to your father, until my son Shelah grows up,'

for he was thinking, 'He must not die like his brothers.' So Tamar went home to her father.

12 A long time passed, and then Shua's daughter, the wife of Judah, died. After Judah had been comforted he went up to Timnah for the shearing of his sheep, he and his friend Hirah the Adullamite. 13 When Tamar was told, 'Look, your father-in-law is going up to Timnah for the shearing of his sheep,' 14 she changed out of her widow's clothes, wrapped a veil around her to disguise herself, and sat down at the entrance to Enaim, which is on the way to Timnah; for she saw that, although Shelah was grown up, she had not been given to him as his wife.

15 Judah, seeing her, took her for a prostitute, since her face was veiled. 16 Going up to her on the road, he said, 'Here, let me sleep with you.' He did not know that she was his daughter-in-law. 'What will you give me for sleeping with you?' she asked. 17 'I will send you a kid from the flock,' he said. 'Agreed, if you give me a pledge until you send it,' she replied. 18 'What pledge shall I give you?' he asked. 'Your seal and cord and the staff you are holding,' she replied. He gave them to her and slept with her, and she conceived by him. 19 Then she got up and left him and, taking off her veil, resumed her widow's weeds.

20 Judah sent the kid by his friend the Adullamite, to recover the pledge from the woman. But he did not find her. 21 He enquired from the men of the place, 'Where is the prostitute who was by the roadside at Enaim?' 'There has been no prostitute there,' they answered. 22 So returning to Judah he said, 'I did not find her. What is more, the men of the place told me there had been no prostitute there.' 23 'Let her keep the things,' Judah said, 'or we shall become a laughing-stock. At least I sent her this kid, even though you did not find her.'

24 About three months later, Judah was told, 'Your daughter-in-law has played the harlot; furthermore, she is pregnant, as a result of her misconduct.' 'Bring her out,' Judah ordered, 'and let her be burnt alive!' 25 But as she was being led off, she sent word to her father-in-law, 'It was the owner of these who made me pregnant. Please verify', she said, 'whose seal and cord and staff these are.' 26 Judah recognised them and said, 'She was right and I was wrong, since I did not give her to my son Shelah.' He had no further intercourse with her.

27 When the time for her confinement came, there were twins in her womb! 28 During the delivery, one of them put out a hand, and the midwife caught it and tied a scarlet thread to it, indicating that this was the first to arrive. 29 Whereupon, he drew back his hand, and out came his brother. Then she said, 'What a breach you have opened for yourself!' So he was named Perez. 30 Then his brother came out with the scarlet thread on his hand, so he was named Zerah.

Joseph's early days in Egypt

39 Now Joseph had been taken down into Egypt. Potiphar the Egyptian, one of Pharaoh's officials and commander of the guard, bought him from the Ishmaelites who had taken him down there. 2 Yahweh was with Joseph, and everything he undertook was successful. He lodged in the house of his Egyptian master, 3 and when his master saw how Yahweh was with him and how Yahweh made everything he undertook successful, 4 he was pleased with Joseph and made him his personal attendant; and his master put him in charge of his household, entrusting him with all his possessions. 5 And from the time he put him in charge of his household and all his possessions, Yahweh blessed the Egyptian's household out of consideration for Joseph; Yahweh's blessing extended to all his possessions, both household and estate. 6 So he left Joseph to handle all his possessions, and with him there, concerned himself with nothing beyond the food he ate.

The attempt to seduce Joseph

Now Joseph was well built and handsome, 7 and it happened some time later that his master's wife cast her eyes on Joseph and said,

'Sleep with me.' ⁸But he refused. 'Look,' he said to his master's wife, 'with me here, my master does not concern himself with what happens in the house, having entrusted all his possessions to me. ⁹He himself wields no more authority in this house than I do. He has exempted nothing from me except yourself, because you are his wife. How could I do anything so wicked, and sin against God?' ¹⁰Although she spoke to Joseph day after day, he would not agree to sleep with her or be with her.

¹¹But one day when Joseph came into the house to do his work, and none of the men of the household happened to be indoors, ¹²she caught hold of him by his tunic and said, 'Sleep with me.' But he left the tunic in her hand, took to his heels and got out. ¹³When she saw that he had left the tunic in her hands as he ran out, ¹⁴she called her servants and said to them, 'Look at this! My husband brought in a Hebrew to make a fool of me! He burst in on me, but I screamed, ¹⁵and when he heard me scream, he left his tunic beside me and ran out of the house.'

¹⁶She kept his tunic by her until his master came home. ¹⁷Then she told him the same tale, 'The Hebrew slave you brought to us burst in on me to make a fool of me. ¹⁸But when I screamed, he left his tunic beside me and ran away.' ¹⁹When his master heard his wife say, 'This was how your slave treated me,' he became furious. ²⁰Joseph's master had him arrested and committed to the gaol where the king's prisoners were kept.

Joseph in gaol

And there in gaol he stayed. ²¹But Yahweh was with Joseph. He showed him faithful love and made him popular with the chief gaoler. ²²The chief gaoler put Joseph in charge of all the prisoners in the gaol, making him responsible for everything done there. ²³The chief gaoler did not bother about anything put in his charge, since Yahweh was with him, and Yahweh made everything he undertook successful.

Joseph interprets the dreams of Pharaoh's officials

40 It happened some time later that the king of Egypt's cup-bearer and his baker offended their master the king of Egypt. ²Pharaoh was angry with his two officials, the chief cup-bearer and the chief baker, ³and put them in custody in the house of the commander of the guard, in the gaol where Joseph was a prisoner. ⁴The commander of the guard assigned Joseph to them to attend to their wants, and they remained in custody for some time.

⁵Now both of them had dreams on the same night, each with its own meaning for the cup-bearer and the baker of the king of Egypt, who were prisoners in the gaol. ⁶When Joseph came to them in the morning, he saw that they looked gloomy, ⁷and he asked the two officials who were in custody with him in his master's house, 'Why these sad looks today?' ⁸They replied, 'We have each had a dream, but there is no one to interpret it.' 'Are not interpretations God's business?' Joseph asked them. 'Tell me about them.'

⁹So the chief cup-bearer described his dream to Joseph, telling him, 'In my dream there was a vine in front of me. ¹⁰On the vine were three branches; no sooner had it budded than it blossomed, and its clusters became ripe grapes. ¹¹I had Pharaoh's cup in my hand; I picked the grapes and squeezed them into Pharaoh's cup, and put the cup into Pharaoh's hand.' ¹²'This is what it means,' Joseph told him. 'The three branches are three days. ¹³In another three days Pharaoh will lift up your head by restoring you to your position. Then you will hand Pharaoh his cup, as you did before, when you were his cup-bearer. ¹⁴But be sure to remember me when things go well with you, and keep faith with me by kindly reminding Pharaoh about me, to get me out of this house. ¹⁵I was kidnapped from the land of the Hebrews in the first place, and even here I have done nothing to warrant being put in the dungeon.'

16 The chief baker, seeing that the interpretation had been favourable, said to Joseph, 'I too had a dream; there were three wicker trays on my head. 17 In the top tray there were all kinds of pastries for Pharaoh, such as a baker might make, and the birds were eating them off the tray on my head.' 18 Joseph replied as follows, 'This is what it means: the three trays are three days. 19 In another three days Pharaoh will lift up your head by hanging you on a gallows, and the birds will eat the flesh off your bones.'

20 And so it happened; the third day was Pharaoh's birthday and he gave a banquet for all his officials. Of his officials he lifted up the head of the chief cup-bearer and the chief baker, 21 the chief cup-bearer by restoring him to his cup-bearing, so that he again handed Pharaoh his cup; 22 and by hanging the chief baker, as Joseph had explained to them. 23 But the chief cup-bearer did not remember Joseph; he had forgotten him.

Pharaoh's dreams

41 Two years later it happened that Pharaoh had a dream: there he was, standing by the Nile, 2 and there, coming up from the Nile, were seven cows, sleek and fat, and they began to feed among the rushes. 3 And then seven other cows, wretched and lean, came up from the Nile, behind them; and these went over and stood beside the other cows on the bank of the Nile. 4 The wretched and lean cows ate the seven sleek and fat cows. Then Pharaoh woke up.

5 He fell asleep and dreamed a second time: there, growing on one stalk, were seven ears of grain, full and ripe. 6 And then sprouting up, behind them, came seven ears of grain, meagre and scorched by the east wind. 7 The scanty ears of grain swallowed the seven full and ripe ears of grain. Then Pharaoh woke up; it had been a dream.

8 In the morning Pharaoh, feeling disturbed, had all the magicians and wise men of Egypt summoned to him. Pharaoh told them his dream, but there was no one to interpret it for Pharaoh. 9 Then the chief cup-bearer addressed Pharaoh, 'Today, I recall having been at fault. 10 When Pharaoh was angry with his servants, he put myself and the chief baker in custody in the house of the commander of the guard. 11 We had a dream on the same night, he and I, and each man's dream had a meaning for himself. 12 There was a young Hebrew with us, one of the slaves belonging to the commander of the guard. We told our dreams to him and he interpreted them for us, telling each of us what his dream meant. 13 It turned out exactly according to his interpretation: I was restored to my position, but the other man was hanged.'

14 Then Pharaoh had Joseph summoned, and they hurried him from the dungeon. He shaved and changed his clothes, and presented himself before Pharaoh. 15 Pharaoh said to Joseph, 'I have had a dream, and there is no one to interpret it. But I have heard it said of you that you can interpret a dream the instant you hear it.' 16 'Not I,' Joseph replied to Pharaoh, 'God will give Pharaoh a favourable answer.'

17 So Pharaoh told Joseph, 'In my dream there I was, standing on the bank of the Nile. 18 And there were seven cows, fat and sleek, coming up out of the Nile, and they began to feed among the rushes. 19 And then seven other cows came up, behind them, starved, very wretched and lean; I have never seen such poor cows in all Egypt. 20 The lean and wretched cows ate up the first seven fat cows. 21 But when they had eaten them up, it was impossible to tell they had eaten them, for they looked as wretched as ever. Then I woke up. 22 And then again in my dream, there, growing on one stalk, were seven ears of grain, beautifully ripe; 23 but then sprouting up behind them came seven ears of grain, withered, meagre and scorched by the east wind. 24 Then the shrivelled ears of grain swallowed the seven ripe ears of grain. I have told the magicians, but no one has given me the answer.'

25 Joseph said to Pharaoh, 'Pharaoh's dreams are one and the same: God has re-

vealed to Pharaoh what he is going to do. 26 The seven fine cows are seven years and the seven ripe ears of grain are seven years; it is one and the same dream. 27 The seven gaunt and lean cows coming up behind them are seven years, as are the seven shrivelled ears of grain scorched by the east wind: there will be seven years of famine. 28 It is as I have told Pharaoh: God has revealed to Pharaoh what he is going to do. 29 Seven years are coming, bringing great plenty to the whole of Egypt, 30 but seven years of famine will follow them, when all the plenty in Egypt will be forgotten, and famine will exhaust the land. 31 The famine that is to follow will be so very severe that no one will remember what plenty the country used to enjoy. 32 The reason why Pharaoh had the same dream twice is that the event is already determined by God, and God will shortly bring it about.

33 'Pharaoh should now find someone intelligent and wise to govern Egypt. 34 Pharaoh should take action and appoint supervisors for the country, and impose a tax of one-fifth on Egypt during the seven years of plenty. 35 They will collect all the food produced during these good years that are coming, and store the grain under Pharaoh's authority, putting it in the towns and keeping it. 36 This food will form a reserve for the country against the seven years of famine which are coming on Egypt, so that the country will not be destroyed by the famine.'

Joseph's promotion

37 Pharaoh and all his ministers approved of what he had said. 38 Then Pharaoh asked his ministers, 'Can we find anyone else endowed with the spirit of God, like him?' 39 So Pharaoh said to Joseph, 'Since God has given you knowledge of all this, there can be no one as intelligent and wise as you. 40 You shall be my chancellor, and all my people shall respect your orders; only this throne shall set me above you.' 41 Pharaoh said to Joseph, 'I hereby make you governor of the whole of Egypt.' 42 Pharaoh took the ring from his hand and put it on Joseph's. He dressed him in robes of fine linen and put a gold chain round his neck. 43 He made him ride in the best chariot he had after his own, and they shouted '[Abrek!]' ahead of him. Thus he became governor of the whole of Egypt.

44 Pharaoh said to Joseph, 'Although I am Pharaoh, no one is to move hand or foot without your permission throughout Egypt.' 45 Pharaoh named Joseph Zaphenath-Paneah, and gave him Asenath daughter of Potiphera, priest of On, to be his wife. And Joseph began to journey all over Egypt.

46 Joseph was thirty years old when he entered the service of Pharaoh king of Egypt. After leaving Pharaoh's presence, Joseph travelled throughout the length and breadth of Egypt. 47 During the seven years of plenty, the soil yielded generously. 48 He collected all the food of the seven years while there was an abundance in Egypt, and stored the food in the towns, placing in each the food from the surrounding countryside. 49 Joseph gathered in grain like the sand of the sea, in such quantity that he gave up keeping count, since it was past accounting.

Joseph's sons

50 Before the year of famine came, two sons were born to Joseph: Asenath daughter of Potiphera, priest of On, bore him these. 51 Joseph named the first-born Manasseh, 'Because', he said, 'God has made me completely forget my hardships and my father's House.' 52 He named the second Ephraim, 'Because', he said, 'God has made me fruitful in the country of my misfortune.'

53 Then the seven years of plenty that there had been in Egypt came to an end, 54 and the seven years of famine set in, as Joseph had predicted. There was famine in every country, but throughout Egypt there was food. 55 But when all Egypt too began to feel the famine and the people appealed to Pharaoh for food, Pharaoh told all the Egyptians, 'Go to Joseph and do whatever he tells you.' 56 There was famine all over the world. Then Joseph opened all the

granaries and rationed out grain to the Egyptians, as the famine grew even worse in Egypt. ⁵⁷ People came to Egypt from all over the world to get supplies from Joseph, for the famine had grown severe throughout the world.

The first meeting between Joseph and his brothers

42 Jacob, seeing that there were supplies to be had in Egypt, said to his sons, 'Why do you keep staring at one another? ² I hear', he said, 'that there are supplies in Egypt. Go down and procure some for us there, so that we may survive and not die.' ³ So ten of Joseph's brothers went down to procure grain in Egypt. ⁴ But Jacob did not send Joseph's brother Benjamin with his brothers. 'Nothing must happen to him,' he thought.

⁵ Thus the sons of Israel were among the other people who came to get supplies, there being famine in Canaan. ⁶ It was Joseph, as the man in authority over the country, who allocated the rations to the entire population. So Joseph's brothers went and bowed down before him, their faces touching the ground. ⁷ As soon as Joseph saw his brothers he recognised them. But he did not make himself known to them, and he spoke harshly to them. 'Where have you come from?' he asked. 'From Canaan to get food,' they replied.

⁸ Now when Joseph recognised his brothers, but they did not recognise him, ⁹ Joseph remembered the dreams he had had about them, and said to them, 'You are spies. You have come to discover the country's weak points.' ¹⁰ 'No, my lord,' they said, 'your servants have come to get food. ¹¹ We are all sons of the same man. We are honest men, your servants are not spies.' ¹² 'Oh no,' he replied, 'you have come to discover the country's weak points.' ¹³ 'Your servants were twelve brothers,' they said, 'sons of the same man in Canaan, but the youngest is at present with our father, and the other one is no more.' ¹⁴ To which Joseph retorted, 'It is as I said, you are spies. ¹⁵ This is the test you are to undergo: as

sure as Pharaoh lives you shall not leave unless your youngest brother comes here. ¹⁶ Send one of your number to fetch your brother; you others will remain under arrest, so that your statements can be tested to see whether or not you are honest. If not, then as sure as Pharaoh lives you are spies.' ¹⁷ Whereupon, he put them all into custody for three days.

¹⁸ On the third day Joseph said to them, 'Do this and you will live, for I am a man who fears God. ¹⁹ If you are honest men, let one of your brothers be detained where you are imprisoned; the rest of you, go and take supplies home for your starving families. ²⁰ But you must bring your youngest brother back to me; in this way, what you have said will be verified, and you will not have to die!' And this is what they did. ²¹ And they said to one another, 'Clearly, we are being punished for what we did to our brother. We saw his deep misery when he pleaded with us, but we would not listen, and now this misery has come home to us.' ²² Reuben retorted to them, 'Did I not tell you not to wrong the boy? But you would not listen. Now comes the accounting.' ²³ They did not know that Joseph understood, because there was an interpreter between them. ²⁴ He turned away from them and wept. When he was able to speak to them again, he chose Simeon out of their number and had him bound while they looked on.

Jacob's sons return to Canaan

²⁵ Joseph gave the order to fill their panniers with grain, to put back each man's money in his sack, and to give them provisions for the journey. This was done for them. ²⁶ Then they loaded their supplies on their donkeys and went away. ²⁷ But when they camped for the night, one of them opened his sack to give his donkey some fodder and saw his money—there it was in the mouth of his sack. ²⁸ He said to his brothers, 'My money has been put back; here it is, in my sack!' Their hearts sank, and they looked at one another in panic, saying, 'What is this that God has done to us?'

29 Returning to their father Jacob in Canaan, they gave him a full report of what had happened to them, 30 'The man who is lord of the country spoke harshly to us, accusing us of spying on the country. 31 We told him, "We are honest men, we are not spies. 32 We were twelve brothers, sons of the same father. One of us is no more, and the youngest is at present with our father in Canaan." 33 But the man who is lord of the country said to us, "This is how I shall know whether you are honest: leave one of your brothers with me. Take supplies for your starving families and be gone, 34 but bring me back your youngest brother and then I shall know that you are not spies but honest men. Then I shall give your brother back to you and you will be free to move about the country." '

35 As they emptied their sacks, each discovered his bag of money in his sack. On seeing their bags of money they were afraid, and so was their father. 36 Then their father Jacob said to them, 'You are robbing me of my children; Joseph is no more; Simeon is no more; and now you want to take Benjamin. I bear the brunt of all this!'

37 Then Reuben said to his father, 'You may put my two sons to death if I do not bring him back to you. Put him in my care and I will bring him back to you.' 38 But he replied, 'My son is not going down with you, for now his brother is dead he is the only one left. If any harm came to him on the journey you are undertaking, you would send my white head down to Sheol with grief!'

Jacob's sons leave again with Benjamin

43 But the famine in the country grew worse, 2 and when they had finished eating the supplies which they had brought from Egypt their father said to them, 'Go back and get us a little food.' 3 'But', Judah replied, 'the man expressly warned us, "You will not be admitted to my presence unless your brother is with you." 4 If you are ready to send our brother with us, we will go down and get food for you. 5 But if you are not ready to send him, we will not go down, in view of the man's warning, "You will not be admitted to my presence unless your brother is with you." ' 6 Then Israel said, 'Why did you bring this misery on me by telling the man you had another brother?' 7 They replied, 'He kept questioning us about ourselves and our family, asking, "Is your father still alive?" and, "Have you another brother?" That is why we told him. How could we know he was going to say, "Bring your brother down here"?' 8 Judah then said to his father Israel, 'Send the boy with me, and let us be off and go, if we are to survive and not die, we, you, and our dependants. 9 I will go surety for him, and you can hold me responsible for him. If I do not bring him back to you and produce him before you, let me bear the blame all my life. 10 Indeed, if we had not wasted so much time we should have been there and back twice by now!'

11 Then their father Israel said to them, 'If it must be so, then do this: take some of the country's best products in your baggage and take them to the man as a gift: some balsam, some honey, gum tragacanth, resin, pistachio nuts and almonds. 12 Take double the amount of money with you and return the money put back in the mouths of your sacks; it may have been a mistake. 13 Take your brother, and go back to the man. 14 May El Shaddai move the man to be kind to you, and allow you to bring back your other brother and Benjamin. As for me, if I must be bereaved, bereaved I must be.'

The meeting with Joseph

15 The men took this gift; they took double the amount of money with them, and Benjamin. They set off, went down to Egypt and presented themselves before Joseph. 16 When Joseph saw Benjamin with them he said to his chamberlain, 'Take these men into the house. Slaughter a beast and prepare it, for these men are to eat with me at midday.' 17 The man did as Joseph had ordered, and took the men to Joseph's house.

¹⁸ The men were afraid at being taken to Joseph's house and said, 'We are being taken there because of the money replaced in our sacks the first time. They will set on us; they will fall on us and make slaves of us, and take our donkeys too.' ¹⁹ So they went up to Joseph's chamberlain and spoke to him at the entrance to the house. ²⁰ 'By your leave, sir,' they said, 'we came down once before to get supplies, ²¹ and when we reached camp and opened our sacks, there was each man's money in the mouth of his sack, to the full. But we have brought it back with us, ²² and we have brought more money with us for the supplies. We do not know who put our money in our sacks.' ²³ 'Set your minds at ease,' he replied, 'do not be afraid. Your God and the God of your father put treasure in your sacks for you. I received your money.' And he brought Simeon out to them.

²⁴ The man then took the men into Joseph's house. He offered them water to wash their feet, and gave their donkeys fodder. ²⁵ They arranged their gift while they waited for Joseph to come at midday, for they had heard they were to dine there.

²⁶ When Joseph arrived at the house they offered him the gift they had with them, bowing low before him. ²⁷ He greeted them pleasantly, asking, 'Is your father well, the old man you told me of? Is he still alive?' ²⁸ 'Your servant our father is well,' they replied, 'he is still alive,' and they bowed respectfully. ²⁹ Looking about, he saw his brother Benjamin, his mother's son. 'Is this your youngest brother', he asked, 'of whom you told me?' And he added, 'God be good to you, my son.' ³⁰ Joseph hurried out; so strong was the affection he felt for his brother that he wanted to cry. He went into his room and there he wept. ³¹ After washing his face he returned and, controlling himself, gave the order: 'Serve the meal.' ³² He was served separately; so were they, and so were the Egyptians who ate in his household, for the Egyptians could not take food with Hebrews; Egyptians have a horror of doing so. ³³ They were placed facing him in order of seniority, from the eldest to the youngest, and the men looked at one another in amazement. ³⁴ He had portions carried to them from his own dish, the portion for Benjamin being five times larger than any of the others. And they feasted with him and drank freely.

Joseph's cup in Benjamin's sack

44 Then Joseph instructed his chamberlain as follows: 'Fill these men's sacks with as much food as they can carry, and put each man's money in the mouth of his sack. ² And put my cup, the silver one, in the mouth of the youngest one's sack as well as the money for his rations.' He did as Joseph had instructed.

³ At daybreak, the men were sent off with their donkeys. ⁴ They had gone only a little way from the city, when Joseph said to his chamberlain, 'Away now and follow those men. When you catch up with them, say to them, "Why have you repaid good with evil? ⁵ Is this not what my lord uses for drinking and also for reading omens? What you have done is wrong." '

⁶ So when he caught up with them he repeated these words. ⁷ They asked him, 'What does my lord mean? Your servants would never think of doing such a thing. ⁸ Look, we brought you back the money we found in the mouths of our sacks, all the way from Canaan. Are we likely to have stolen silver or gold from your master's house? ⁹ Whichever of your servants is found to have it shall die, and the rest of us shall be slaves of my lord.' ¹⁰ 'Very well, then, it shall be as you say,' he replied, 'the one on whom it is found shall become my slave, but the rest of you can go free.' ¹¹ Each of them quickly lowered his sack to the ground, and each opened his own. ¹² He searched, beginning with the eldest and ending with the youngest, and found the cup in Benjamin's sack. ¹³ Then they tore their clothes, and when each man had reloaded his donkey they returned to the city.

¹⁴ When Judah and his brothers arrived at Joseph's house he was still there, so they fell on

the ground in front of him. 15 'What do you mean by doing this?' Joseph asked them. 'Did you not know that a man such as I am is a reader of omens?' 16 'What can we answer my lord?' Judah replied. 'What can we say? How can we clear ourselves? God himself has uncovered your servants' guilt. Here we are then, my lord's slaves, we no less than the one in whose possession the cup was found.' 17 'I could not think of doing such a thing,' he replied. 'The man in whose possession the cup was found shall be my slave, but you can go back unhindered to your father.'

Judah intervenes

18 At this, Judah went up to him and said, 'May it please my lord, let your servant have a word privately with my lord. Do not be angry with your servant, for you are like Pharaoh himself. 19 My lord questioned his servants, "Have you father or brother?" 20 And we said to my lord, "We have an old father, and a younger brother born of his old age. His brother is dead, so he is the only one by that mother now left, and his father loves him." 21 Then you said to your servants, "Bring him down to me, so that I can set eyes on him." 22 We replied to my lord, "The boy cannot leave his father. If he leaves him, his father will die." 23 But you said to your servants, "If your youngest brother does not come down with you, you will not be admitted to my presence again." 24 When we went back to your servant my father, we repeated to him what my lord had said. 25 So when our father said, "Go back and get us a little food," 26 we said, "We cannot go down. We shall go only if our youngest brother is with us for, unless our youngest brother is with us, we shall not be admitted to the man's presence." 27 So your servant our father said to us, "You know that my wife bore me two children. 28 When one of them left me, I supposed that he must have been torn to pieces, and I have never seen him since. 29 If you take this one from me too and any harm comes to him, you will send my white head down to Sheol with grief." 30 If I go to your servant my father now, and we do not have the boy with us, he will die as soon as he sees that the boy is not with us, for his heart is bound up with him; 31 and your servants will have sent your servant our father's white head down to Sheol with grief. 32 Now your servant went surety to my father for the boy. I said: "If I do not bring him back to you, let me bear the blame before my father all my life." 33 Let your servant stay, then, as my lord's slave in place of the boy, I implore you, and let the boy go back with his brothers. 34 How indeed could I go back to my father and not have the boy with me? I could not bear to see the misery that would overwhelm my father.'

Joseph makes himself known

45 Then Joseph could not control his feelings in front of all his retainers, and he exclaimed, 'Let everyone leave me.' No one therefore was present with him while Joseph made himself known to his brothers, 2 but he wept so loudly that all the Egyptians heard, and the news reached Pharaoh's palace.

3 Joseph said to his brothers, 'I am Joseph. Is my father really still alive?' His brothers could not answer him, they were so dumbfounded at seeing him. 4 Then Joseph said to his brothers, 'Come closer to me.' When they had come closer to him he said, 'I am your brother Joseph whom you sold into Egypt. 5 But now, do not grieve, do not reproach yourselves for having sold me here, since God sent me before you to preserve your lives. 6 For this is the second year there has been famine in the country, and there are still five years to come without ploughing or harvest. 7 God sent me before you to assure the survival of your race on earth and to save your lives by a great deliverance. 8 So it was not you who sent me here but God, and he has set me up as a father to Pharaoh, as lord of all his household and governor of the whole of Egypt.

9 'Return quickly to your father and tell him, "Your son Joseph says this: 'God has made me lord of all Egypt. Come down to me without delay. 10 You will live in the region of Goshen where you will be near me, you, your

7 READ GENESIS 45:1–15.

Do not reproach yourselves for having sold me here, since God sent me before you to preserve your lives.—GENESIS 45:5

DEFUSING ENVY

The holy Joseph is put before us as a pattern of chastity. Modesty shone forth from his manners and a certain loveliness that is found with chastity also radiated from him. Thus, his parents loved him more than their other children. But this love caused his brothers to make Joseph an object of envy that we must not ignore, because upon this the whole story turns. Yet, at the same time we learn that no desire to avenge his own sufferings swayed that just man. Joseph did not repay evil for evil.

How could Joseph have been worthy to be chosen before others if he had only loved those who loved him and had harmed those who harmed him? For many people behave that way. But it is wonderful if people do what the Savior taught and love their enemies (see Mt 5:44). And well may we wonder at Joseph who loved those who hurt him before the gospel came—who being injured, spared; being attacked, forgave; being sold, returned no evil, but repaid insult with favor. From the gospel we have been taught to do all this, but we cannot do it.

Let us also then learn that even the ancient patriarchs were subject to envy so that we may follow the example of how they patiently endured it. Remember that they were not men of another and higher nature than ours, but only more obedient; that they were not sinless, but repentant. But if the passion of envy scorched even some of our holy ancestors, how much more do we sinners need to take care so that it does not set fire to us? ST. AMBROSE, 339–397

YOU WILL FIND THE NEXT READING AT EXODUS 12.

children and your grandchildren, your flocks, your cattle and all your possessions. [11] There I shall provide for you—for there are five years of famine still to come—so that you, your household and all yours are not reduced to penury.' " [12] You can see with your own eyes, and my brother Benjamin can see too, that I am who I say I am. [13] Give my father a full report of all the honour I enjoy in Egypt, and of all you have seen; and quickly bring my father down here.'

[14] Then throwing his arms round the neck of his brother Benjamin he wept; and Benjamin wept on his shoulder. [15] He kissed all his brothers, weeping on each one. Only then were his brothers able to talk to him.

Pharaoh's invitation

[16] News reached Pharaoh's palace that Joseph's brothers had come, and Pharaoh was pleased to hear it, as were his servants. [17] Pharaoh told Joseph, 'Say to your brothers, "Do this: load your beasts and hurry away to Canaan. [18] Fetch your father and your families, and come back to me. I will give you the best territory in Egypt, where you will live off the fat of the land." [19] And you, for your part, give them this order: "Do this: take waggons from Egypt, for your little ones and your wives. Get your father and come. [20] Never mind about your property, for the best of all Egypt will be yours." '

The return to Canaan

21 Israel's sons did as they were told. Joseph gave them waggons as Pharaoh had ordered, and he gave them provisions for the journey. 22 To each and every one he gave new clothes, and to Benjamin three hundred shekels of silver and five changes of clothes. 23 And to his father he sent ten donkeys laden with the best that Egypt offered, and ten she-donkeys laden with grain, bread and food for his father's journey. 24 And so he sent his brothers on their way. His final words to them were, 'And let there be no upsets on the way!'

25 And so they left Egypt. When they reached their father Jacob in Canaan, 26 they gave him this report, 'Joseph is still alive. He is at this moment governor of all Egypt!' But he was as one stunned, for he did not believe them. 27 However, when they told him all Joseph had said to them, and when he saw the waggons that Joseph had sent to fetch him, the spirit of their father Jacob revived, 28 and Israel said, 'That is enough! My son Joseph is still alive. I must go and see him before I die.'

Jacob leaves for Egypt

46 So Israel set out with all his possessions. Arriving at Beersheba, he offered sacrifices to the God of his father Isaac. 2 God spoke to Israel in a vision at night, 'Jacob, Jacob,' he said. 'Here I am,' he replied. 3 'I am El, God of your father,' he said. 'Do not be afraid of going down to Egypt, for I will make you into a great nation there. 4 I shall go down to Egypt with you and I myself shall bring you back again, and Joseph's hand will close your eyes.' 5 So Jacob left Beersheba. Israel's sons conveyed their father Jacob, their little children and their wives in the waggons Pharaoh had sent to fetch him.

6 Taking their livestock and all that they had acquired in Canaan, they arrived in Egypt— Jacob and all his offspring. 7 With him to Egypt, he brought his sons and grandsons, his daughters and granddaughters—all his offspring.

Jacob's family[a]

8 These were the names of the Israelites, Jacob and his descendants, who arrived in Egypt:

Reuben, Jacob's first-born, 9 and the sons of Reuben: Hanoch, Pallu, Hezron and Carmi. 10 The sons of Simeon: Jemuel, Jamin, Ohad, Jachin, Zohar, and Shaul the son of the Canaanite woman. 11 The sons of Levi: Gershon, Kohath and Merari. 12 The sons of Judah: Er, Onan, Shelah, Perez, and Zerah (Er and Onan had died in Canaan), and Hezron and Hamul sons of Perez. 13 The sons of Issachar: Tola, Puvah, Jashub and Shimron. 14 The sons of Zebulun: Sered, Elon and Jahleel. 15 These were the sons that Leah had borne to Jacob in Paddan-Aram, besides his daughter Dinah; in all, his sons and daughters numbered thirty-three.

16 The sons of Gad: Ziphion, Haggi, Shuni, Ezbon, Eri, Arodi and Areli. 17 The sons of Asher: Jimnah, Jishvah, Jishvi, Beriah, with their sister Serah; the sons of Beriah: Heber and Malchiel. 18 These were the sons of Zilpah whom Laban gave to his daughter Leah; she bore these to Jacob—sixteen persons.

19 The sons of Rachel wife of Jacob: Joseph and Benjamin. 20 Born to Joseph in Egypt were: Manasseh and Ephraim sons of Asenath, daughter of Potiphera priest of On. 21 The sons of Benjamin: Bela, Becher, Ashbel, Gera, Naaman, Ehi, Rosh, Muppim, Huppim and Ard. 22 These were the sons that Rachel bore to Jacob—fourteen persons in all.

23 The sons of Dan: Hushim. 24 The sons of Naphtali: Jahzeel, Guni, Jezer and Shillem. 25 These were the sons of Bilhah whom Laban gave to his daughter Rachel; she bore these to Jacob—seven persons in all.

26 Altogether, the members of Jacob's family who arrived with him in Egypt—his own issue, not counting the wives of Jacob's sons— numbered sixty-six all told. 27 With Joseph's sons born to him in Egypt—two persons—the members of Jacob's family who went to Egypt totalled seventy.

46a ‖ Nb 26:5seq.

Joseph welcomes them

²⁸ Israel sent Judah ahead to Joseph, so that Judah might present himself to Joseph in Goshen. When they arrived in Goshen, ²⁹ Joseph had his chariot made ready and went up to Goshen to meet his father Israel. As soon as he appeared he threw his arms round his neck and for a long time wept on his shoulder. ³⁰ Israel said to Joseph, 'Now I can die, now that I have seen you in person and seen you still alive.'

³¹ Then Joseph said to his brothers and his father's family, 'I shall go back and break the news to Pharaoh. I shall tell him, "My brothers and my father's family who were in Canaan have come to me. ³² The men are shepherds and look after livestock, and they have brought their flocks and cattle and all their possessions." ³³ Thus, when Pharaoh summons you and asks, "What is your occupation?", ³⁴ you are to say, "Ever since our boyhood your servants have looked after livestock, we and our fathers before us," so that you can stay in the Goshen region—for the Egyptians have a horror of all shepherds.'

Pharaoh grants an audience

47 So Joseph went and told Pharaoh, 'My father and brothers have arrived from Canaan with their flocks and cattle and all their possessions. Here they are, in the region of Goshen.' ² He had taken five of his brothers, and he now presented them to Pharaoh. ³ Pharaoh asked his brothers, 'What is your occupation?' and they gave Pharaoh the answer, 'Your servants are shepherds, like our fathers before us.' ⁴ They went on to tell Pharaoh, 'We have come to stay in this country for the time being, since there is no pasturage for your servants' flocks, Canaan being stricken with famine. So now please allow your servants to settle in the region of Goshen.' ⁵ᵃ Then Pharaoh said to Joseph, ⁶ᵇ 'They may stay in the region of Goshen, and if you know of any capable men among them, put them in charge of my own livestock.'

Another version

⁵ᵇ Jacob and his sons went to Egypt where Joseph was. Pharaoh king of Egypt heard about this and said to Joseph, 'Your father and brothers have come to you. ⁶ᵃ The country of Egypt is open to you: settle your father and brothers in the best region.' ⁷ Joseph brought his father and presented him to Pharaoh. Jacob paid his respects to Pharaoh. ⁸ Pharaoh asked Jacob, 'How many years have you lived?' ⁹ Jacob said to Pharaoh, 'The years of my stay on earth add up to one hundred and thirty years. Few and unhappy my years have been, falling short of my ancestors' years in their stay on earth.' ¹⁰ Jacob then took leave of Pharaoh and withdrew from his presence. ¹¹ Joseph then settled his father and brothers, giving them land holdings in Egypt, in the best part of the country, the region of Rameses, as Pharaoh had ordered.

¹² Joseph provided his father, brothers and all his father's family with food, down to the least of them.

Joseph's agrarian policy

¹³ And on all the earth around there was now no food anywhere, for the famine had grown very severe, and Egypt and Canaan were both weak with hunger. ¹⁴ Joseph accumulated all the money to be found in Egypt and Canaan, in exchange for the supplies being handed out, and put the money in Pharaoh's palace.

¹⁵ When all the money in Egypt and Canaan was exhausted, all the Egyptians came to Joseph, pleading, 'Give us food, unless you want us to die before your eyes! For our money has come to an end.' ¹⁶ Joseph replied, 'Hand over your livestock and I shall issue you food in exchange for your livestock, if your money has come to an end.' ¹⁷ So they brought their livestock to Joseph, and Joseph gave them food in exchange for horses and livestock, whether sheep or cattle, and for donkeys. Thus he saw them through that year with food in exchange for all their livestock.

¹⁸ When that year was over, they came to

him the next year, and said to him, 'We cannot hide it from my lord: the truth is, our money has run out and the livestock is in my lord's possession. There is nothing left for my lord except our bodies and our land. ¹⁹ If we and our land are not to perish, take us and our land in exchange for food, and we with our land will become Pharaoh's serfs; only give us seed, so that we can survive and not die and the land not revert to desert!'

²⁰ Thus Joseph acquired all the land in Egypt for Pharaoh, since one by one the Egyptians sold their fields, so hard pressed were they by the famine; and the whole country passed into Pharaoh's possession, ²¹ while the people he reduced to serfdom from one end of Egypt to the other. ²² The only land he did not acquire belonged to the priests, for the priests received an allowance from Pharaoh and lived on the allowance that Pharaoh gave them. Hence they had no need to sell their land.

²³ Then Joseph said to the people, 'This is how we stand: I have bought you out, with your land, on Pharaoh's behalf. Here is seed for you to sow the land. ²⁴ But of the harvest you must give a fifth to Pharaoh. The other four-fifths you can have for sowing your fields, to provide food for yourselves and your households, and food for your children.' ²⁵ 'You have saved our lives!' they replied. 'If it please my lord, we will become serfs to Pharaoh.' ²⁶ So Joseph made a law, still in force today, as regards the soil of Egypt, that one-fifth should go to Pharaoh. Only the land of the priests did not go to Pharaoh.

Jacob's last wishes

²⁷ Thus Israel settled in Egypt, in the region of Goshen. They acquired property there; they were fruitful and grew very numerous. ²⁸ Jacob lived seventeen years in Egypt; thus Jacob's total age came to a hundred and forty-seven years. ²⁹ When Israel's time to die drew near he sent for his son Joseph and said to him,^a 'If you really love me, place your hand under my thigh as pledge that you will act with faithful love towards me: do not bury me

in Egypt! ³⁰ When I lie down with my ancestors, carry me out of Egypt and bury me in their tomb.' 'I shall do as you say,' he replied. ³¹ 'Swear to me,' he insisted. So he swore to him, and Israel sank back on the pillow.

Jacob adopts Joseph's two sons and blesses them

48 Some time later, Joseph was informed, 'Your father has been taken ill.' So he took with him his two sons Manasseh and Ephraim. ² When Jacob was told, 'Look, your son Joseph has come to you,' Israel, summoning his strength, sat up in bed. ³ 'El Shaddai appeared to me at Luz in Canaan,' Jacob told Joseph, 'and he blessed me, ⁴ saying to me, "I shall make you fruitful and numerous, and shall make you into an assembly of peoples and give this country to your descendants after you, to own in perpetuity." ⁵ Now your two sons, born to you in Egypt before I came to you in Egypt, shall be mine; Ephraim and Manasseh shall be as much mine as Reuben and Simeon. ⁶ But with regard to the children you have had since them, they shall be yours, and they shall be known by their brothers' names for the purpose of their inheritance.

⁷ 'When I was on my way from Paddan, to my sorrow death took your mother Rachel from me in Canaan, on the journey while only a short distance from Ephrath. I buried her there on the road to Ephrath—now Bethlehem.'

⁸ When Israel saw Joseph's two sons, he asked, 'Who are these?' ⁹ 'They are my sons, whom God has given me here,' Joseph told his father. 'Then bring them to me', he said, 'so that I may bless them.' ¹⁰ Now, Israel's eyes were dim with age, and he could not see. So Joseph made them come closer to him and he kissed and embraced them. ¹¹ Then Israel said to Joseph, 'I did not think I should ever see you again, and now God has let me see your children as well!' ¹² Then Joseph took them from his lap and bowed to the ground.

47a = 49:29–32; = 50:6.

¹³Then Joseph took the two of them, Ephraim with his right hand so that he should be on Israel's left, and Manasseh with his left hand, so that he should be on Israel's right, and brought them close to him. ¹⁴But Israel held out his right hand and laid it on the head of Ephraim, the younger, and his left on the head of Manasseh, crossing his hands—Manasseh was, in fact, the elder. ¹⁵Then he blessed Joseph saying:

May the God in whose presence my
        fathers Abraham and Isaac
        walked,
the God who has been my shepherd from
        my birth until this day,
¹⁶ the Angel who has saved me from all
        harm, bless these boys,
so that my name may live on in them, and
        the names of my ancestors
        Abraham and Isaac,
and they grow into teeming multitudes on
        earth!

¹⁷Joseph saw that his father was laying his right hand on the head of Ephraim, and this he thought was wrong, so he took his father's hand and tried to shift it from the head of Ephraim to the head of Manasseh. ¹⁸Joseph protested to his father, 'Not like that, father! This one is the elder; put your right hand on his head.' ¹⁹But his father refused. 'I know, my son, I know,' he said. 'He too shall become a people; he too will be great. But his younger brother will be greater, his offspring will be sufficient to constitute nations.' ²⁰So he blessed them that day, saying:

By you shall Israel bless itself, saying,
    'God make you like Ephraim and
        Manasseh!'

putting Ephraim before Manasseh. ²¹Then Israel said to Joseph, 'Now I am about to die. But God will be with you and take you back to the land of your ancestors. ²²As for me, I give you a Shechem[a] more than your brothers, the one I took from the Amorites with my sword and bow.'

Jacob's testament

49 Jacob called his sons and said, 'Gather round, so that I can tell you what is in store for you in the final days.

² Gather round, sons of Jacob, and listen;
    listen to Israel your father.

³ Reuben, you are my first-born,
    my vigour, and the first-fruit of my
        manhood,
    foremost in pride, foremost in strength,
⁴ uncontrolled as water: you will not be
        foremost,
    for you climbed into your father's bed,
    and so defiled my couch, to my sorrow.

⁵ Simeon and Levi are brothers
    in carrying out their malicious plans.
⁶ May my soul not enter their council
    nor my heart join their company,
    for in their rage they have killed men
    and hamstrung oxen at their whim.
⁷ Accursed be their rage for its
        ruthlessness,
    their wrath for its ferocity.
    I shall disperse them in Jacob,
    I shall scatter them through Israel.

⁸ Judah, your brothers will praise you:
    you grip your enemies by the neck,
    your father's sons will do you homage.
⁹ Judah is a lion's whelp;
    You stand over your prey, my son.
    Like a lion he crouches and lies down,
    a mighty lion: who dare rouse him?
¹⁰ The sceptre shall not pass from Judah,
    nor the ruler's staff from between his
        feet,
    until tribute be brought him
    and the peoples render him obedience.

48a *Shekem* = shoulder, but it is also the name of Joseph's burial-town.

11 He tethers his donkey to the vine,
   to its stock the foal of his she-donkey.
   He washes his clothes in wine,
   his robes in the blood of the grape.
12 His eyes are darkened with wine
   and his teeth are white with milk.

13 Zebulun will live by the seashore
   and be a sailor on board the ships,
   with Sidon on his flank.

14 Issachar is a strong donkey
   lying down among sheepfolds.

15 When he saw how good the resting-place
   and how pleasant the country,
   he bowed his shoulder to the load
   and became a slave to forced labour.

16 Dan will govern his people
   like any other of the tribes of Israel.
17 May Dan be a snake on the road,
   a viper on the path,
   who bites the horse on the hock
   so that its rider falls off backwards!

18 I long for your deliverance, Yahweh!

19 Gad will be raided by raiders,
   and he will raid at their heels.

20 Rich the food produced by Asher:
   he will furnish food fit for kings.

21 Naphtali is a swift hind
   bearing lovely fawns.

22 Joseph is a fruitful plant near a spring
   whose tendrils reach over the wall.
23 Archers in their hostility
   drew their bows and attacked him.
24 But their bows were broken by a mighty
          One,
   the sinews of their arms were snapped
   by the power of the Mighty One of Jacob,
   by the Name of the Stone of Israel,
25 the God of your father who assists you,

El Shaddai who blesses you:
   blessings of heaven above,
   blessings of the deep lying below,
   blessings of the breasts and womb,
26 blessings of the grain and flowers,
   blessings of the eternal mountains,
   bounty of the everlasting hills—
   may they descend on Joseph's head,
   on the crown of the one dedicated from
          among his brothers!

27 Benjamin is a ravening wolf,
   in the morning he devours the prey,
   in the evening he is still sharing out the
          spoil.'

28 All these make up the tribes of Israel,
twelve in number, and this is what their father
said to them as he bade them farewell, giving
each an appropriate blessing.

Jacob's last moments and death[a]

29 Then he gave them these instructions, 'I am
about to be gathered to my people. Bury me
with my ancestors, in the cave that is in the
field of Ephron the Hittite, 30 in the cave in the
field at Machpelah, facing Mamre, in Canaan,
which Abraham bought from Ephron the
Hittite as a burial site of his own. 31 There
Abraham and his wife Sarah were buried.
There Isaac and his wife Rebekah were
buried; and there I buried Leah—32 the field
and the cave in it which were bought from the
Hittites.'
33 When Jacob had finished giving his instructions to his sons, he drew his feet up into
the bed, and breathing his last was gathered to
his people.

Jacob's funeral

50 At this Joseph threw himself on his
father's face, covering it with tears
and kisses. 2 Then Joseph ordered the doctors
in his service to embalm his father. The doc-

49a = 47:29–31; = 50:6.

tors embalmed Israel, ³and it took them forty days, for embalming takes forty days to complete.

The Egyptians mourned him for seventy days. ⁴When the period of mourning for him was over, Joseph said to Pharaoh's household, 'If you have any affection for me, see that this message reaches Pharaoh's ears, ⁵"My father put me under oath, saying: I am about to die. In the tomb which I dug for myself in Canaan, that is where you are to bury me. So may I have leave to go up and bury my father, and then come back?" ' ⁶Pharaoh replied, 'Go up and bury your father, as he made you swear to do.'ᵃ

⁷Joseph went up to bury his father, and with him went all Pharaoh's officials, the dignitaries of his palace and all the dignitaries of Egypt, ⁸as well as all Joseph's family, his brothers and his father's family. The only people they left behind in Goshen were those unfit to travel, and their flocks and cattle. ⁹Chariots and horsemen went up with him too; it was a very large retinue.

¹⁰On arriving at Goren-ha-Atad, which is across the Jordan, they there held a long and solemn lamentation, and Joseph observed seven days' mourning for his father. ¹¹When the Canaanites, the local inhabitants, witnessed the mourning at Goren-ha-Atad, they said, 'This is a solemn act of mourning by the Egyptians,' which is why the place was given the name Abel-Mizraim—it is across the Jordan.

¹²His sons did what he had ordered them to do for him. ¹³His sons carried him to Canaan and buried him in the cave in the field at Machpelah, facing Mamre, which Abraham had bought from Ephron the Hittite as a burial site of his own. ¹⁴Then Joseph returned to Egypt with his brothers and all those who had come up with him to bury his father.

From the death of Jacob to the death of Joseph

¹⁵Seeing that their father was dead, Joseph's brothers said, 'What if Joseph intends to treat us as enemies and pay us back for all the wrong we did him?' ¹⁶So they sent this message to Joseph: 'Before your father died, he gave us this order: ¹⁷"You are to say to Joseph: Now please forgive the crime and faults of your brothers and all the wrong they did you." So now please forgive the crime of the servants of your father's God.' Joseph wept at the message they sent to him.

¹⁸Then his brothers went to him themselves and, throwing themselves at his feet, said, 'Take us as your slaves!' ¹⁹But Joseph replied, 'Do not be afraid; is it for me to put myself in God's place? ²⁰The evil you planned to do me has by God's design been turned to good, to bring about the present result: the survival of a numerous people. ²¹So there is no need to be afraid; I shall provide for you and your dependants.' In this way he reassured them by speaking affectionately to them.

²²So Joseph stayed in Egypt with his father's family; and Joseph lived a hundred and ten years. ²³Joseph saw the third generation of Ephraim's line, as also the children of Machir son of Manasseh, who were born on Joseph's lap. ²⁴At length Joseph said to his brothers, 'I am about to die; but God will be sure to remember you kindly and take you out of this country to the country which he promised on oath to Abraham, Isaac and Jacob.' ²⁵And Joseph put Israel's sons on oath, saying, 'When God remembers you with kindness, be sure to take my bones away from here.'

²⁶Joseph died at the age of a hundred and ten; he was embalmed and laid in a coffin in Egypt.

50a = 47:29–31; = 49:29–32.

EXODUS

The prosperity of the Hebrews in Egypt

1 These are the names of the Israelites who went with Jacob to Egypt, each of them went with his family: [2] Reuben, Simeon, Levi and Judah, [3] Issachar, Zebulun and Benjamin, [4] Dan and Naphtali, Gad and Asher. [5] In all, the descendants of Jacob numbered seventy persons. Joseph was in Egypt already. [6] Then Joseph died, and his brothers, and all that generation. [7] But the Israelites were fruitful and prolific; they became so numerous and powerful that eventually the whole land was full of them.

The Hebrews oppressed

[8] Then there came to power in Egypt a new king who had never heard of Joseph. [9] 'Look,' he said to his people, 'the Israelites are now more numerous and stronger than we are. [10] We must take precautions to stop them from increasing any further, or if war should break out, they might join the ranks of our enemies. They might take arms against us and then escape from the country.' [11] Accordingly they put taskmasters over the Israelites to wear them down by forced labour. In this way they built the store-cities of Pithom and Rameses for Pharaoh. [12] But the harder their lives were made, the more they increased and spread, until people came to fear the Israelites. [13] So the Egyptians gave them no mercy in the demands they made, [14] making their lives miserable with hard labour: with digging clay, making bricks, doing various kinds of fieldwork—all sorts of labour that they imposed on them without mercy.

[15] The king of Egypt then spoke to the Hebrew midwives, one of whom was called Shiphrah, and the other Puah. [16] 'When you attend Hebrew women in childbirth,' he said, 'look at the two stones. If it is a boy, kill him; if a girl, let her live.' [17] But the midwives were God-fearing women and did not obey the orders of the king of Egypt, but allowed the boys to live. [18] So the king of Egypt summoned the midwives and said to them, 'What do you mean by allowing the boys to live?' [19] The midwives said to Pharaoh, 'Hebrew women are not like Egyptian women, they are hardy and give birth before the midwife can get to them.' [20] For this, God was good to the midwives, and the people went on increasing and growing more powerful; [21] and since the midwives feared God, he gave them families of their own.

[22] Pharaoh then gave all his people this command: 'Throw every new-born boy into the river, but let all the girls live.'

The birth of Moses [a]

2 There was a man descended from Levi who had taken a woman of Levi as his wife. [2] She conceived and gave birth to a son and, seeing what a fine child he was, she kept him hidden for three months. [3] When she could hide him no longer, she got a papyrus basket for him; coating it with bitumen and pitch, she put the child inside and laid it among the reeds at the River's edge. [4] His sister took up position some distance away to see what would happen to him.

[5] Now Pharaoh's daughter went down to bathe in the river, while her maids walked along the riverside. Among the reeds she noticed the basket, and she sent her maid to fetch

2a Popular Hebr. Explanation of an Egyptian name.

it. ⁶She opened it and saw the child: the baby was crying. Feeling sorry for it, she said, 'This is one of the little Hebrews.' ⁷The child's sister then said to Pharaoh's daughter, 'Shall I go and find you a nurse among the Hebrew women to nurse the child for you?' ⁸'Yes,' said Pharaoh's daughter, and the girl went and called the child's own mother. ⁹Pharaoh's daughter said to her, 'Take this child away and nurse it for me. I shall pay you myself for doing so.' So the woman took the child away and nursed it. ¹⁰When the child grew up, she brought him to Pharaoh's daughter who treated him like a son; she named him Moses 'because', she said, 'I drew him out of the water.'

Moses escapes to Midian

¹¹It happened one day, when Moses was grown up, that he went to see his kinsmen. While he was watching their forced labour he also saw an Egyptian striking a Hebrew, one of his kinsmen. ¹²Looking this way and that and seeing no one in sight, he killed the Egyptian and hid him in the sand. ¹³On the following day he came back, and there were two Hebrews, fighting. He said to the man who was in the wrong, 'What do you mean by hitting your kinsman?' ¹⁴'And who appointed you', the man retorted, 'to be prince over us and judge? Do you intend to kill me as you killed the Egyptian?' Moses was frightened. 'Clearly that business has come to light,' he thought. ¹⁵When Pharaoh heard of the matter, he tried to put Moses to death, but Moses fled from Pharaoh. He went into Midianite territory and sat down beside a well.

¹⁶Now there was a priest of Midian with seven daughters. They used to come to draw water and fill the troughs to water their father's flock. ¹⁷Some shepherds came and drove them away, but Moses sprang to their help and watered their flock. ¹⁸When they returned to their father Reuel, he said to them, 'Why are you back so early today?' ¹⁹'An Egyptian protected us from the shepherds,' they said, 'and he even drew water for us and watered the flock.' ²⁰'And where is he?' he asked his daughters. 'Why did you leave the man there? Ask him to eat with us.' ²¹Moses agreed to stay on there with the man, who gave him his daughter Zipporah in marriage. ²²She gave birth to a son, whom he named Gershom 'because', he said, 'I am an alien in a foreign land.'

God remembers Israel

²³During this long period the king of Egypt died. The Israelites, groaning in their slavery, cried out for help and from the depths of their slavery their cry came up to God. ²⁴God heard their groaning; God remembered his covenant with Abraham, Isaac and Jacob. ²⁵God saw the Israelites and took note.

The burning bush[a]

3 Moses was looking after the flock of his father-in-law Jethro, the priest of Midian; he led it to the far side of the desert and came to Horeb, the mountain of God. ²The angel of Yahweh appeared to him in a flame blazing from the middle of a bush. Moses looked; there was the bush blazing, but the bush was not being burnt up. ³Moses said, 'I must go across and see this strange sight, and why the bush is not being burnt up.' ⁴When Yahweh saw him going across to look, God called to him from the middle of the bush. 'Moses, Moses!' he said. 'Here I am,' he answered. ⁵'Come no nearer,' he said. 'Take off your sandals, for the place where you are standing is holy ground. ⁶I am the God of your ancestors,' he said, 'the God of Abraham, the God of Isaac and the God of Jacob.' At this Moses covered his face, for he was afraid to look at God.

The mission of Moses

⁷Yahweh then said, 'I have indeed seen the misery of my people in Egypt. I have heard them crying for help on account of their taskmasters. Yes, I am well aware of their sufferings. ⁸And I have come down to rescue

3a = 6:2–13.

them from the clutches of the Egyptians and bring them up out of that country, to a country rich and broad, to a country flowing with milk and honey, to the home of the Canaanites, the Hittites, the Amorites, the Perizzites, the Hivites and the Jebusites. 9 Yes indeed, the Israelites' cry for help has reached me, and I have also seen the cruel way in which the Egyptians are oppressing them. 10 So now I am sending you to Pharaoh, for you to bring my people the Israelites out of Egypt.'

11 Moses said to God, 'Who am I to go to Pharaoh and bring the Israelites out of Egypt?' 12 'I shall be with you,' God said, 'and this is the sign by which you will know that I was the one who sent you. After you have led the people out of Egypt, you will worship God on this mountain.'

The divine name[b] revealed

13 Moses then said to God, 'Look, if I go to the Israelites and say to them, "The God of your ancestors has sent me to you," and they say to me, "What is his name?" what am I to tell them?' 14 God said to Moses, 'I am he who is.' And he said, 'This is what you are to say to the Israelites, "I am has sent me to you." ' 15 God further said to Moses, 'You are to tell the Israelites, "Yahweh, the God of your ancestors, the God of Abraham, the God of Isaac and the God of Jacob, has sent me to you." This is my name for all time, and thus I am to be invoked for all generations to come.

Moses instructed for his mission

16 'Go, gather the elders of Israel together and tell them, "Yahweh, the God of your ancestors, has appeared to me—the God of Abraham, of Isaac and of Jacob—and has indeed visited you and seen what is being done to you in Egypt, 17 and has said: I shall bring you out of the misery of Egypt to the country of the Canaanites, the Hittites, the Amorites, the Perizzites, the Hivites and the Jebusites, to a country flowing with milk and honey." 18 They will listen to your words, and you and the elders of Israel are to go to the king of Egypt and say to him, "Yahweh, the God of the Hebrews, has encountered us. So now please allow us to make a three-days' journey into the desert and sacrifice to Yahweh our God." 19 I am well aware that the king of Egypt will not let you go unless he is compelled by a mighty hand; 20 he will not let you go until I have stretched out my arm and struck Egypt with all the wonders I intend to work there.

The Egyptians to be plundered

21 'I shall ensure that the Egyptians are so much impressed with this people that when you go, you will not go empty-handed. 22 Every woman will ask her neighbour and the woman staying in her house for silver and golden jewellery, and clothing. In these you will dress your own sons and daughters, despoiling the Egyptians of them.'

Moses granted miraculous powers

4 Moses replied as follows, 'But suppose they will not believe me or listen to my words, and say to me, "Yahweh has not appeared to you"?' 2 Yahweh then said, 'What is that in your hand?' 'A staff,' he said. 3 'Throw it on the ground,' said Yahweh. Moses threw it on the ground; the staff turned into a snake and Moses recoiled from it. 4 Yahweh then said to Moses, 'Reach out your hand and catch it by the tail.' He reached out his hand, caught it, and in his hand it turned back into a staff. 5 'Thus they may believe that Yahweh, the God of their ancestors, the God of Abraham, the God of Isaac and the God of Jacob, has appeared to you.'

6 Next, Yahweh said to him, 'Put your hand inside your tunic.' He put his hand inside his tunic, then drew it out again: and his hand was diseased, white as snow. 7 Yahweh then said, 'Put your hand back inside your tunic.' He put his hand back inside his tunic and when he

3b 'Yahweh' may be some form of the verb 'to be'. God either refuses to give a name or reveals that he is the key to existence. The Gk understands it as a statement that God is Being itself.

drew it out, there it was restored, just like the rest of his flesh. 8 'Even so: should they not believe you nor be convinced by the first sign, the second sign will convince them; 9 but should they not be convinced by either of these two signs and refuse to listen to what you say, you are to take some water from the River and pour it on the ground, and the water you have taken from the River will turn to blood on the dry land.'

Aaron, the mouthpiece of Moses

10 Moses said to Yahweh, 'Please, my Lord, I have never been eloquent, even since you have spoken to your servant, for I am slow and hesitant of speech.' 11 'Who gave a person a mouth?' Yahweh said to him. 'Who makes a person dumb or deaf, gives sight or makes blind? Is it not I, Yahweh? 12 Now go, I shall help you speak and instruct you what to say.' 13 'Please, my Lord,' Moses replied, 'send anyone you decide to send!' 14 At this, Yahweh's anger kindled against Moses, and he said to him, 'There is your brother Aaron the Levite, is there not? I know that he is a good speaker. Here he comes to meet you. When he sees you, his heart will be full of joy. 15 You will speak to him and tell him what message to give. I shall help you speak, and him too, and instruct you what to do. 16 He will speak to the people in your place; he will be your mouthpiece, and you will be as the god inspiring him. 17 And take this staff in your hand; with this you will perform the signs.'

Moses leaves Midian and returns to Egypt

18 Moses went back to his father-in-law Jethro and said to him, 'Give me leave to return to my kinsmen in Egypt and see if they are still alive.' And Jethro said to Moses, 'Go in peace.' 19 Yahweh said to Moses in Midian, 'Go, return to Egypt, for all those who wanted to kill you are dead.' 20 So Moses took his wife and his son and, putting them on a donkey, started back for Egypt; and Moses took the staff of God in his hand. 21 Yahweh said to Moses, 'Think of the wonders I have given you power

to perform, once you are back in Egypt! You are to perform them before Pharaoh, but I myself shall make him obstinate, and he will not let the people go. 22 You will then say to Pharaoh, "This is what Yahweh says: Israel is my first-born son. 23 I told you: Let my son go and worship me; but since you refuse to let him go, well then! I shall put your first-born son to death." '

The son of Moses circumcised

24 On the journey, when he had halted for the night, Yahweh encountered him and tried to kill him. 25 Then Zipporah, taking up a flint, cut off her son's foreskin and with it touched his feet and said, 'You are my blood-bridegroom!' 26 So he let him go. She said, 'Blood-bridegroom' then, with reference to the circumcision.

Moses meets Aaron

27 Yahweh said to Aaron, 'Go into the desert to meet Moses.' So he went, and met him at the mountain of God and kissed him. 28 Moses then told Aaron all that Yahweh had said when sending him and all the signs he had ordered him to perform. 29 Moses and Aaron then went and gathered all the elders of the Israelites together, 30 and Aaron repeated everything that Yahweh had said to Moses, and in the sight of the people performed the signs. 31 The people were convinced, and they rejoiced that Yahweh had visited the Israelites and seen their misery, and they bowed to the ground in worship.

The first audience with Pharaoh

5 After this, Moses and Aaron went to Pharaoh and said to him, 'This is what Yahweh, God of Israel, says, "Let my people go, so that they can hold a feast in my honour in the desert." ' 2 'Who is Yahweh,' Pharaoh replied, 'for me to obey what he says and let Israel go? I know nothing of Yahweh, and I will not let Israel go.' 3 'The God of the Hebrews has encountered us,' they replied. 'Give us leave to make a three-days' journey into the desert and

sacrifice to Yahweh our God, or he will strike us with a plague or with the sword.' ⁴The king of Egypt said to them, 'Moses and Aaron, what do you mean by distracting the people from their work? Get back to your forced labour.' ⁵And Pharaoh said, 'Now that the people have grown to such numbers in the country, what do you mean by interrupting their forced labour?'

Instructions to the taskmasters

⁶That very day, Pharaoh gave the order to the people's taskmasters and their scribes, ⁷'Do not go on providing the people with straw for brickmaking as before; let them go and gather straw for themselves. ⁸But you will exact the same quantity of bricks from them as before, not reducing it at all, since they are lazy, and that is why their cry is, "Let us go and sacrifice to our God." ⁹Give these people more work to do, and see they do it instead of listening to lying speeches.'

¹⁰The people's taskmasters and scribes went out to speak to the people and said, 'Pharaoh says this, "I shall not provide you with any more straw. ¹¹Go and collect straw for yourselves where you can find it. But your output is not to be any less." ' ¹²So the people scattered all over Egypt to gather stubble for their straw. ¹³The taskmasters harassed them. 'You must complete your daily quota,' they said, 'just as when the straw was there.' ¹⁴And the Israelites' foremen whom Pharaoh's taskmasters had put in charge of them, were flogged and asked, 'Why have you not fulfilled your quota of bricks made today as before?'

The Hebrew scribes complain

¹⁵The Israelites' foremen went and appealed to Pharaoh. 'Why do you treat your servants like this?' they said. ¹⁶'No straw is provided for your servants, yet still the cry is, "Make bricks!" And now your servants are being flogged! ...' ¹⁷'You are lazy, lazy,' he retorted. 'That is why you say, "Let us go and sacrifice to Yahweh." ¹⁸Get back to your work at once.

You will not be provided with straw; all the same, you will deliver the quota of bricks.'

Recriminations of the people; prayer of Moses

¹⁹The Israelites' foremen saw they were in a difficult position on being told, 'You will not reduce your daily production of bricks.' ²⁰As they left Pharaoh's presence, they met Moses and Aaron who were standing in their way. ²¹'May Yahweh look down at you and judge!' they said to them. 'You have brought us into bad odour with Pharaoh and his officials; you have put a sword into their hand to kill us.' ²²Moses went back to Yahweh and said, 'Lord, why do you treat this people so harshly? Why did you send me? ²³Ever since I came to Pharaoh and spoke to him in your name, he has ill-treated this people, and you have done nothing at all about rescuing your people.'

6 Yahweh then said to Moses, 'Now you will see what I am going to do to Pharaoh. A mighty hand will force him to let them go, a mighty hand will force him to expel them from his country.'

Another account of the call of Moses ᵃ

²God spoke to Moses and said to him, 'I am Yahweh. ³To Abraham, Isaac and Jacob I appeared as El Shaddai, but I did not make my name Yahweh known to them. ⁴I also made my covenant with them to give them the land of Canaan, the country in which they were living as aliens. ⁵Furthermore, I have heard the groaning of the Israelites, enslaved by the Egyptians, and have remembered my covenant. ⁶So say to the Israelites, "I am Yahweh. I shall free you from the forced labour of the Egyptians; I shall rescue you from their slavery and I shall redeem you with outstretched arm and mighty acts of judgement. ⁷I shall take you as my people and I shall be your God. And you will know that I am Yahweh your God, who have freed you from the

6a = 3:1–4:23.

forced labour of the Egyptians. ⁸ Then I shall lead you into the country which I swore I would give to Abraham, Isaac and Jacob, and shall give it to you as your heritage, I, Yahweh." ' ⁹ And Moses repeated this to the Israelites, but they would not listen to Moses, so crushed was their spirit and so cruel their slavery.

¹⁰ Yahweh then said to Moses, ¹¹ 'Go to Pharaoh, king of Egypt, and tell him to let the Israelites leave his country.' ¹² But Moses spoke out in Yahweh's presence and said, 'The Israelites have not listened to me, so why should Pharaoh take any notice of a poor speaker like me?' ¹³ Yahweh spoke to Moses and Aaron and sent them to Pharaoh king of Egypt, to lead the Israelites out of Egypt.

The genealogy of Moses and Aaron

¹⁴ These were their heads of families:

The sons of Reuben, Israel's first-born: Hanoch, Pallu, Hezron and Carmi: these are the clans of Reuben.

¹⁵ The sons of Simeon: Jemuel, Jamin, Ohad, Jachin, Zohar, and Shaul son of the Canaanite woman: these are the clans of Simeon.

¹⁶ These were the names of the sons of Levi with their descendants: Gershon, Kohath and Merari. Levi lived for a hundred and thirty-seven years.

¹⁷ The sons of Gershon: Libni and Shimei, with their clans.

¹⁸ The sons of Kohath: Amram, Izhar, Hebron and Uzziel. Kohath lived for a hundred and thirty-three years.

¹⁹ The sons of Merari: Mahli and Mushi. These are the clans of Levi with their descendants.

²⁰ Amram married Jochebed, his aunt, who bore him Aaron and Moses. Amram lived for a hundred and thirty-seven years.

²¹ The sons of Izhar were: Korah, Nepheg and Zichri.

²² And the sons of Uzziel: Mishael, Elzaphan and Sithri.

²³ Aaron married Elisheba daughter of Amminadab and sister of Nahshon, and she bore him Nadab, Abihu, Eleazar and Ithamar.

²⁴ The sons of Korah: Assir, Elkanah and Abiasaph. These are the clans of the Korahites.

²⁵ Eleazar, son of Aaron, married one of Putiel's daughters who bore him Phinehas.

These were the Levitical heads of families, according to clan.

²⁶ It was to this Aaron and Moses that Yahweh said, 'Lead the Israelites out of Egypt in their armies.' ²⁷ It was they who spoke to Pharaoh, king of Egypt, to lead the Israelites out of Egypt—namely Moses and Aaron.

The narrative of Moses' call, continued

²⁸ Now the day when Yahweh spoke to Moses in Egypt, ²⁹ Yahweh said to Moses, 'Tell Pharaoh king of Egypt everything that I am going to say to you.' ³⁰ But Moses said to Yahweh's face, 'I am a poor speaker, so why should Pharaoh take any notice of me?'

7 Yahweh then said to Moses, 'Look, I have made you as a god for Pharaoh, and your brother Aaron is to be your prophet. ² You must say whatever I command you, and your brother Aaron will repeat to Pharaoh that he is to let the Israelites leave his country. ³ But I myself shall make Pharaoh stubborn and shall perform many a sign and wonder in Egypt. ⁴ Since Pharaoh will not listen to you, I shall lay my hand on Egypt and with great acts of judgement lead my armies, my people, the Israelites, out of Egypt. ⁵ And the Egyptians will know that I am Yahweh when I stretch out my hand against the Egyptians and lead the Israelites out of their country.'

⁶ Moses and Aaron did exactly as Yahweh had ordered. ⁷ Moses was eighty years old and Aaron eighty-three, when they spoke to Pharaoh.

The staff turned into a snake

⁸ Yahweh said to Moses and Aaron, ⁹ 'If Pharaoh says to you, "Display some marvel," you must say to Aaron, "Take your staff and throw

it down in front of Pharaoh, and let it turn into a serpent!" ' ¹⁰Moses and Aaron went to Pharaoh and did as Yahweh had ordered. Aaron threw down his staff in front of Pharaoh and his officials, and it turned into a serpent. ¹¹Then Pharaoh in his turn called for the sages and sorcerers, and by their spells the magicians of Egypt did the same. ¹²Each threw his staff down and these turned into serpents. But Aaron's staff swallowed up theirs. ¹³Pharaoh, however, remained obstinate and, as Yahweh had foretold, refused to listen to Moses and Aaron.

The first plague: the water turns to blood

¹⁴Yahweh then said to Moses, 'Pharaoh is adamant. He refuses to let the people go. ¹⁵Go to Pharaoh tomorrow morning as he makes his way to the water, confront him on the river bank and in your hand take the staff that turned into a snake. ¹⁶Say to him, "Yahweh, God of the Hebrews, sent me to say: Let my people go and worship in the desert. Up till now, you have refused to listen. ¹⁷This is what Yahweh says: You will know that I am Yahweh by this: with the staff that is in my hand I shall strike the waters of the River and they will turn to blood. ¹⁸The fish in the river will die, and the River will stink, and the Egyptians will not be able to drink the river water." '

¹⁹Yahweh said to Moses, 'Say to Aaron, "Take your staff and stretch out your hand over the waters of Egypt—over their rivers and canals, their marshland, and all their reservoirs—and they will turn to blood. There will be blood throughout the whole of Egypt, even in sticks and stones." ' ²⁰Moses and Aaron did as Yahweh ordered. He raised his staff and struck the waters of the River, with Pharaoh and his officials looking on, and all the water in the River turned to blood. ²¹The fish in the River died, and the River stank; and the Egyptians could no longer drink the River water. Throughout the whole of Egypt there was blood. ²²But by their spells the magicians of Egypt did the same; Pharaoh remained ob-

stinate and, as Yahweh had foretold, refused to listen to Moses and Aaron. ²³Pharaoh turned away and went back into his palace, taking no notice even of this. ²⁴And the Egyptians all dug holes along the river-bank in search of drinking water, since they could not drink the River water. ²⁵After Yahweh struck the River, seven days went by.

The second plague: the frogs

²⁶Then Yahweh said to Moses, 'Go to Pharaoh and say to him, "Yahweh says this: Let my people go and worship me. ²⁷If you refuse to let them go, I shall strike your whole territory with frogs. ²⁸The River will swarm with frogs; they will make their way into your palace, into your bedroom, onto your bed, into the houses of your officials and subjects, into your ovens, into your kneading bowls. ²⁹The frogs will actually clamber onto you, onto your subjects and onto all your officials." '

8 Yahweh then said to Moses, 'Say to Aaron, "Stretch out your hand with your staff, over the rivers, the canals and the marshland, and bring the frogs up over the land of Egypt." ' ²So Aaron stretched out his hand over the waters of Egypt, and the frogs came up and covered the land of Egypt. ³But by their spells the magicians did the same, bringing frogs over the land of Egypt.

⁴Pharaoh then summoned Moses and Aaron and said, 'Entreat Yahweh to take the frogs away from me and my subjects, and I promise to let the people go and sacrifice to Yahweh.' ⁵Moses said to Pharaoh, 'You are the one to gain by it: when would you like me to pray for you, your officials and your subjects, so as to rid you and your houses of the frogs so that they will be left only in the River?' ⁶'Tomorrow,' he said. Moses said, 'It shall be as you say, so that you will know that there is no one like Yahweh our God. ⁷The frogs will leave you, your houses, your officials and your subjects and will be left only in the River.' ⁸Moses and Aaron left Pharaoh's presence, and Moses pleaded with Yahweh about the frogs which

he had inflicted on Pharaoh. ⁹ Yahweh did as Moses asked, and in house and courtyard and field the frogs died. ¹⁰ They piled them up in heaps and the country stank. ¹¹ But once Pharaoh saw that there had been a respite, he became obstinate and, as Yahweh had foretold, refused to listen to them.

The third plague: the mosquitoes

¹² Yahweh then said to Moses, 'Say to Aaron, "Stretch out your staff and strike the dust of the earth, and it will turn into mosquitoes throughout the whole of Egypt." ' ¹³ Aaron stretched out his hand, with his staff, and struck the dust of the earth, and there were mosquitoes on man and beast; all the dust of the earth turned into mosquitoes throughout the whole of Egypt. ¹⁴ By their spells the magicians tried to produce mosquitoes in the same way but failed, and there were mosquitoes on man and beast. ¹⁵ So the magicians said to Pharaoh, 'This is the finger of God.' But Pharaoh was obstinate and, as Yahweh had foretold, refused to listen to them.

The fourth plague: the horseflies

¹⁶ Yahweh then said to Moses, 'Get up early in the morning and confront Pharaoh as he makes his way to the water. Say to him, "Yahweh says this: Let my people go and worship me. ¹⁷ But if you will not let my people go, I shall send horseflies on you, on your officials, your subjects and your houses. The Egyptians' houses will swarm with horseflies, and so will the very ground they stand on. ¹⁸ But I shall exempt the region of Goshen, where my people are living, that day; there will be no horseflies there, so that you will know that I am Yahweh, here in this country. ¹⁹ I shall make a distinction between my people and your people. This sign will take place tomorrow." ' ²⁰ Yahweh did this, and great swarms of horseflies found their way into Pharaoh's palace, into his officials' houses and all over Egypt; the country was ruined by the horseflies.

²¹ Pharaoh then summoned Moses and Aaron and said, 'Go and sacrifice to your God,

inside the country.' ²² 'That would never do,' Moses said, 'since what we sacrifice to Yahweh our God is outrageous to the Egyptians. If the Egyptians see us offering sacrifices which outrage them, won't they stone us? ²³ We shall make a three-days' journey into the desert to sacrifice to Yahweh our God, as he has ordered us.' ²⁴ Pharaoh said, 'I will let you go and sacrifice to Yahweh your God in the desert, provided you do not go very far. Pray for me.' ²⁵ 'The moment I leave you,' Moses said, 'I shall pray to Yahweh. Tomorrow morning the horseflies will leave Pharaoh, his officials and his subjects. But Pharaoh must stop trifling with us by not allowing the people to go and sacrifice to Yahweh.' ²⁶ Moses then left Pharaoh's presence and prayed to Yahweh, ²⁷ and Yahweh did as Moses asked; the horseflies left Pharaoh, his officials and his subjects; not one remained. ²⁸ But Pharaoh became obstinate this time too and did not let the people go.

The fifth plague: death of the Egyptians' livestock

9 Yahweh then said to Moses, 'Go to Pharaoh and say to him, "Yahweh, God of the Hebrews, says this: Let my people go and worship me. ² If you refuse to let them go and detain them any longer, ³ look, the hand of Yahweh will strike your livestock in the fields, horses, donkeys, camels, oxen and flocks with a deadly plague. ⁴ Yahweh will discriminate between the livestock of Israel and the livestock of Egypt: nothing of what belongs to the Israelites will die. ⁵ Yahweh has fixed the time. Tomorrow, he has said, Yahweh will do this in the country." ' ⁶ Next day Yahweh did this: all the Egyptians' livestock died, but nothing of the livestock owned by the Israelites died. ⁷ Pharaoh had enquiries made, and found that of the livestock owned by the Israelites not a single beast had died. But Pharaoh was obstinate and did not let the people go.

The sixth plague: the boils

⁸ Yahweh then said to Moses and Aaron, 'Take handfuls of soot from the kiln, and before

Pharaoh's eyes let Moses throw it in the air. ⁹ It will turn into fine dust over the whole of Egypt and produce boils breaking into sores on man and beast throughout the whole of Egypt.' ¹⁰ So they took soot from the kiln and stood in front of Pharaoh, and Moses threw it in the air, and on man and beast it brought out boils breaking into sores. ¹¹ And the magicians could not compete with Moses in the matter of the boils, for the magicians were covered with boils like all the other Egyptians. ¹² But Yahweh made Pharaoh stubborn and, as Yahweh had foretold to Moses, he did not listen to them.

The seventh plague: the hail

¹³ Yahweh then said to Moses, 'Get up early in the morning and confront Pharaoh. Say to him, "Yahweh, God of the Hebrews, says this: Let my people go and worship me. ¹⁴ For this time I am going to inflict all my plagues on you, on your officials and on your subjects, so that you will know that there is no one like me in the whole world. ¹⁵ Had I stretched out my hand to strike you and your subjects with pestilence, you would have been swept from the earth. ¹⁶ But I have let you survive for this reason: to display my power to you and to have my name talked of throughout the world. ¹⁷ Since you take a high hand with my people, refusing to let them go, ¹⁸ very well, at about this time tomorrow, I shall cause so severe a hail to fall as was never known in Egypt from the day of its foundation until now. ¹⁹ So now send word to have your livestock and everything else you own in the fields put under cover. On man or beast, all that happen to be in the fields and are not brought indoors, the hail will fall and they will die." '

²⁰ Those of Pharaoh's officials who respected what Yahweh said, brought their slaves and livestock indoors, ²¹ but those who did not take to heart what Yahweh said left their slaves and livestock in the fields.

²² Yahweh then said to Moses, 'Stretch out your hand towards heaven so that it hails throughout the whole of Egypt, on man and beast and on everything growing anywhere in Egypt.' ²³ Moses stretched out his staff towards heaven, and Yahweh thundered and rained down hail. Lightning struck the earth and Yahweh rained down hail on Egypt. ²⁴ And so there was hail, and lightning accompanied the hail, very severe, such as had never been known anywhere in Egypt since it first became a nation. ²⁵ All over Egypt the hail struck down everything in the fields, man and beast, and the hail beat down everything growing in the fields and shattered all the trees in the fields. ²⁶ The only place where there was no hail was in the Goshen region, where the Israelites lived.

²⁷ Pharaoh then sent for Moses and Aaron and said, 'This time, I have sinned. Yahweh is in the right; I and my subjects are in the wrong. ²⁸ Pray to Yahweh, for we cannot bear any more of this thunder and hail. I promise to let you go. You need stay no longer.' ²⁹ Moses said to him, 'The moment I leave the city I shall stretch out my hands to Yahweh. The thunder will stop, and there will be no more hail, so that you may know that the earth belongs to Yahweh. ³⁰ But as for you and your officials, I know very well that you still have no respect for Yahweh God.' ³¹ The flax and the barley were ruined, since the barley was in the ear and the flax in bud, ³² but the wheat and spelt were not destroyed, being late crops.

³³ Moses left Pharaoh and went out of the city. He stretched out his hands to Yahweh and the thunder and hail ceased and the rain stopped pouring down on the earth. ³⁴ When Pharaoh saw that rain and hail and thunder had stopped, he relapsed into sin, ³⁵ and he and his officials became obstinate again. Pharaoh was stubborn and, as Yahweh had foretold through Moses, refused to let the Israelites go.

The eighth plague: the locusts

10 Yahweh then said to Moses, 'Go to Pharaoh, for I have made him and his officials stubborn, to display these signs of mine among them; ² so that you can tell your sons and your grandsons how I made fools of the

Egyptians and what signs I performed among them, so that you would know that I am Yahweh.' [3] Moses and Aaron then went to Pharaoh and said to him, 'Yahweh, God of the Hebrews, says this, "How much longer will you refuse to submit to me? Let my people go and worship me. [4] Or, if you refuse to let my people go, tomorrow I shall send locusts into your country. [5] They will cover the surface of the soil so that the soil cannot be seen. They will devour the remainder of what has escaped, of what you have been left after the hail; they will devour all your trees growing in the fields; [6] they will fill your houses, all your officials' houses and all the Egyptians' houses—something your ancestors and your ancestors' ancestors have never seen from the day they first appeared on earth until now."' Then he turned on his heel and left Pharaoh's presence. [7] At which, Pharaoh's officials said to him, 'How much longer are we to be tricked by this fellow? Let the people go and worship Yahweh their God. Do you not finally realise that Egypt is on the brink of ruin?'

[8] So Moses and Aaron were brought back to Pharaoh who said to them, 'Go and worship Yahweh your God. But who are to go?' [9] Moses replied, 'We shall take our young men and our old men, we shall take our sons and daughters, our flocks and our herds, since we are going to hold a feast in Yahweh's honour.' [10] Pharaoh said, 'So I must let you go with your wives and children! May Yahweh preserve you! Plainly, you are up to no good! [11] Oh no! You men may go and worship Yahweh, since that was your original request.' With that, they were driven from Pharaoh's presence.

[12] Yahweh then said to Moses, 'Stretch out your hand over Egypt for the locusts. Let them invade Egypt and devour whatever is growing in the country, whatever the hail has left!' [13] Moses stretched his staff over Egypt, and over the country Yahweh sent an east wind which blew all that day and night. By morning, the east wind had brought the locusts. [14] The locusts invaded the whole of Egypt and settled all over Egypt, in great swarms; never had there been so many locusts before, nor would there be again. [15] They covered the surface of the ground till the land was devastated. They devoured whatever was growing in the fields and all the fruit on the trees that the hail had left. No green was left on tree or plant in the fields anywhere in Egypt.

[16] Pharaoh sent urgently for Moses and Aaron and said, 'I have sinned against Yahweh your God and against you. [17] Now forgive my sin, I implore you, just this once, and entreat Yahweh your God to turn this deadly thing away from me.' [18] When Moses left Pharaoh's presence he prayed to Yahweh, [19] and Yahweh changed the wind into a west wind, very strong, which carried the locusts away and swept them into the Sea of Reeds. There was not one locust left in the whole of Egypt. [20] But Yahweh made Pharaoh stubborn, and he did not let the Israelites go.

The ninth plague: the darkness

[21] Yahweh then said to Moses, 'Stretch out your hand towards heaven, and let darkness, darkness so thick that it can be felt, cover Egypt.' [22] So Moses stretched out his hand towards heaven, and for three days there was thick darkness over the whole of Egypt. [23] No one could see anyone else or move about for three days, but all the Israelites did have light where they were living.

[24] Pharaoh summoned Moses and said, 'Go and worship Yahweh, but your flocks and herds are to stay here. Your wives and children can go with you too.' [25] Moses said, 'But now you must give us sacrifices and burnt offerings to offer to Yahweh our God. [26] And our livestock will go with us too; not a hoof will be left behind; for we may need animals from these to worship Yahweh our God; for until we get there we ourselves cannot tell how we are to worship Yahweh.'

[27] But Yahweh made Pharaoh stubborn, and he refused to let them go. [28] Pharaoh said to Moses, 'Out of my sight! Be sure you never see my face again, for the next time you see my

face you die!' [29]Moses then said, 'You yourself have said it. I shall never see your face again.'

Announcement of the death of the first-born

11 Yahweh then said to Moses, 'I shall inflict one more plague on Pharaoh and Egypt, after which he will let you go away. When he lets you go, he will actually drive you out! [2]Now instruct the people that every man is to ask his neighbour, and every woman hers, for silver and golden jewellery.' [3]And Yahweh made the Egyptians impressed with the people, while Moses himself was a man of great importance in Egypt in the opinion of Pharaoh's officials and the people.

[4]Moses then said, 'Yahweh says this, "At midnight I shall pass through Egypt, [5]and all the first-born in Egypt will die, from the first-born of Pharaoh, heir to his throne, to the first-born of the slave-girl at the mill, and all the first-born of the livestock. [6]And throughout Egypt there will be great wailing, such as never was before, nor will be again. [7]But against the Israelites, whether man or beast, never a dog shall bark, so that you may know that Yahweh discriminates between Egypt and Israel. [8]Then all these officials of yours will come down to me and, bowing low before me, say: Go away, you and all the people who follow you! After which, I shall go." ' And, hot with anger, he left Pharaoh's presence.

[9]Yahweh then said to Moses, 'Pharaoh will not listen to you, so that more of my wonders may be displayed in Egypt.' [10]Moses and Aaron worked all these wonders in Pharaoh's presence, but Yahweh made Pharaoh stubborn, and he did not let the Israelites leave his country.

The Passover[a]

12 Yahweh said to Moses and Aaron in Egypt, [2]'This month must be the first of all the months for you, the first month of your year. [3]Speak to the whole community of Israel and say, "On the tenth day of this month each man must take an animal from the flock for his family: one animal for each household. [4]If the household is too small for the animal, he must join with his neighbour nearest to his house, depending on the number of persons. When you choose the animal, you will take into account what each can eat. [5]It must be an animal without blemish, a male one year old; you may choose it either from the sheep or from the goats. [6]You must keep it till the fourteenth day of the month when the whole assembly of the community of Israel will slaughter it at twilight. [7]Some of the blood must then be taken and put on both door-posts and the lintel of the houses where it is eaten. [8]That night, the flesh must be eaten, roasted over the fire; it must be eaten with unleavened bread and bitter herbs. [9]Do not eat any of it raw or boiled in water, but roasted over the fire, with the head, feet and entrails. [10]You must not leave any of it over till the morning: whatever is left till morning you must burn. [11]This is how you must eat it: with a belt round your waist, your sandals on your feet and your staff in your hand. You must eat it hurriedly: it is a Passover in Yahweh's honour. [12]That night, I shall go through Egypt and strike down all the first-born in Egypt, man and beast alike, and shall execute justice on all the gods of Egypt, I, Yahweh! [13]The blood will be a sign for you on the houses where you are. When I see the blood I shall pass over you, and you will escape the destructive plague when I strike Egypt. [14]This day must be commemorated by you, and you must keep it as a feast in Yahweh's honour. You must keep it as a feast-day for all generations; this is a decree for all time.

The feast of Unleavened Bread

[15]"For seven days you must eat unleavened bread. On the first day you must clean the leaven out of your houses, for anyone who eats leavened bread from the first to the seventh day must be outlawed from Israel. [16]On the first day you must hold a sacred assembly, and

12a Once a herdsmen's new year festival, the Passover receives a new meaning as the memorial of the exodus. The Feast of Unleavened Bread, an agricultural feast, is of separate origin.

8 READ EXODUS 12:1–14.

It is a Passover in Yahweh's honour. . . . You must keep it as a feast-day for all generations.—EXODUS 12:11, 14

THE EUCHARIST FORESHADOWED

From his last supper with his disciples, we know that Jesus said the old blessings over bread, wine, and the fruits of the earth, as they are prayed to this day. So he fulfilled one of the most sacred religious duties: the ceremonial Passover seder to commemorate deliverance from slavery in Egypt. . . .

Blessing and distributing bread and wine were part of the Passover rite. But here both receive an entirely new meaning. This is where the life of the church begins. . . . In the mouth of Christ, the old blessings become life-giving words (see Mt 26:26–28). The fruits of the earth become his body and blood, filled with his life. Visible creation, which he entered when he became a human being, is now united with him in a new, mysterious way. The things that serve to sustain human life are fundamentally transformed, and the people who partake of them are transformed too, drawn into the unity of life with Christ and filled with his divine life.

The Word's life-giving power is bound to the sacrifice. The Word became flesh in order to surrender the life he assumed, to offer himself and a creation redeemed by his sacrifice in praise to the Creator. Through the Lord's last supper, the Passover meal of the Old Covenant is converted into the Easter meal of the New Covenant: into the sacrifice on the cross at Golgotha and those joyous meals between Easter and Ascension when the disciples recognized the Lord in the breaking of the bread, and into the sacrifice of the Mass with Holy Communion.   ST. EDITH STEIN, 1891–1942

YOU WILL FIND THE NEXT READING AT EXODUS 14.

on the seventh day a sacred assembly. On those days no work may be done; you will prepare only what each requires to eat. ¹⁷ You must keep the feast of Unleavened Bread because it was on that same day that I brought your armies out of Egypt. You will keep that day, generation after generation; this is a decree for all time. ¹⁸ In the first month, from the evening of the fourteenth day until the evening of the twenty-first day, you must eat unleavened bread. ¹⁹ For seven days there may be no leaven in your houses, since anyone, either stranger or citizen of the country, who eats leavened bread will be outlawed from the community of Israel. ²⁰ You will eat nothing with leaven in it; wherever you live, you will eat unleavened bread." '

Injunctions relating to the Passover

²¹ Moses summoned all the elders of Israel and said to them, 'Go and choose a lamb or kid for your families, and kill the Passover victim. ²² Then take a bunch of hyssop, dip it in the blood that is in the basin, and with the blood from the basin touch the lintel and both door-posts; then let none of you venture out of the house till morning. ²³ Then, when Yahweh goes through Egypt to strike it, and sees the blood on the lintel and on both door-posts, he will pass over the door and not allow the De-

stroyer to enter your homes and strike. ²⁴ You will observe this as a decree binding you and your children for all time, ²⁵ and when you have entered the country which Yahweh will give you, as he has promised, you will observe this ritual. ²⁶ And when your children ask you, "What does this ritual mean?" ²⁷ you will tell them, "It is the Passover sacrifice in honour of Yahweh who passed over the houses of the Israelites in Egypt, and struck Egypt but spared our houses." ' And the people bowed in worship. ²⁸ The Israelites then went away and did as Yahweh had ordered Moses and Aaron.

The tenth plague: death of the first-born

²⁹ And at midnight Yahweh struck down all the first-born in Egypt from the first-born of Pharaoh, heir to his throne, to the first-born of the prisoner in the dungeon, and the first-born of all the livestock. ³⁰ Pharaoh and all his officials and all the Egyptians got up in the night, and there was great wailing in Egypt, for there was not a house without its dead. ³¹ It was still dark when Pharaoh summoned Moses and Aaron and said, 'Up, leave my subjects, you and the Israelites! Go and worship Yahweh as you have asked! ³² And take your flocks and herds as you have asked, and go! And bless me too!' ³³ The Egyptians urged the people on and hurried them out of the country because, they said, 'Otherwise we shall all be dead.' ³⁴ So the people carried off their dough still unleavened, their bowls wrapped in their cloaks, on their shoulders.

The Egyptians plundered

³⁵ The Israelites did as Moses had told them and asked the Egyptians for silver and golden jewellery, and clothing. ³⁶ Yahweh made the Egyptians so much impressed with the people that they gave them what they asked. So they despoiled the Egyptians.

Israel's departure

³⁷ The Israelites left Rameses for Succoth, about six hundred thousand on the march— men, that is, not counting their families. ³⁸ A mixed crowd of people went with them, and flocks and herds, quantities of livestock. ³⁹ And with the dough which they had brought from Egypt they baked unleavened cakes, because the dough had not risen, since they had been driven out of Egypt without time to linger or to prepare food for themselves. ⁴⁰ The time that the Israelites spent in Egypt was four hundred and thirty years. ⁴¹ And on the very day the four hundred and thirty years ended, all Yahweh's armies left Egypt. ⁴² The night when Yahweh kept vigil to bring them out of Egypt must be kept as a vigil in honour of Yahweh by all Israelites, for all generations.

Ordinances for the Passover

⁴³ Yahweh said to Moses and Aaron, 'This is the ritual for the Passover: no alien may eat it, ⁴⁴ but any slave bought for money may eat it, once you have circumcised him. ⁴⁵ No stranger and no hired servant may eat it. ⁴⁶ It must be eaten in one house alone; you will not take any of the meat out of the house; nor may you break any of its bones.

⁴⁷ 'The whole community of Israel must keep it. ⁴⁸ Should a stranger residing with you wish to keep the Passover in honour of Yahweh, all the males of his household must be circumcised: he will then be allowed to keep it and will count as a citizen of the country. But no uncircumcised person may eat it. ⁴⁹ The same law will apply to the citizen and the stranger resident among you.' ⁵⁰ The Israelites all did as Yahweh had ordered Moses and Aaron, ⁵¹ and that same day Yahweh brought the Israelites out of Egypt in their armies.

The first-born

13 Yahweh spoke to Moses and said, ² 'Consecrate all the first-born to me, the first birth from every womb, among the Israelites. Whether man or beast, it is mine.'

The feast of Unleavened Bread

³ Moses said to the people, 'Remember this day, on which you came out of Egypt, from the

place of slave-labour, for by the strength of his hand Yahweh brought you out of it; no leavened bread may be eaten. ⁴On this day, in the month of Abib, you are leaving, ⁵and when Yahweh has brought you into the country of the Canaanites, the Hittites, the Amorites, the Hivites and the Jebusites, flowing with milk and honey, which he swore to your ancestors that he would give you, then you must observe this rite in the same month. ⁶For seven days you will eat unleavened bread, and on the seventh day there must be a feast in Yahweh's honour. ⁷During these seven days unleavened bread may be eaten; no leavened bread may be seen among you, no leaven among you throughout your territory. ⁸And on that day you will explain to your son, "This is because of what Yahweh did for me when I came out of Egypt." ⁹This will serve as a sign on your hand would serve, or a reminder on your forehead, and in that way the law of Yahweh will be ever on your lips: for with a mighty hand Yahweh brought you out of Egypt. ¹⁰You shall observe this law at its appointed time, year by year.

The first-born

¹¹'When Yahweh has brought you into the Canaanites' country, as he swore to you and your ancestors that he would, and given it to you, ¹²to Yahweh you must make over whatever first issues from the womb, and every first-born cast by animals belonging to you: these males belong to Yahweh. ¹³But every first-born donkey you will redeem with a lamb or kid; if you do not redeem it, you must break its neck. All the human first-born, however, among your sons, you will redeem. ¹⁴And when your son asks you in days to come, "What does this mean?" you will tell him, "By the strength of his hand Yahweh brought us out of Egypt, out of the place of slave-labour. ¹⁵When Pharaoh stubbornly refused to let us go, Yahweh killed all the first-born in Egypt, of man and beast alike. This is why I sacrifice every male first issuing from the womb to Yahweh and redeem every first-born of my sons." ¹⁶This will serve as a sign on

your hand would serve, or a headband on your forehead, for by the strength of his hand Yahweh brought us out of Egypt.'

The departure of the Israelites

¹⁷When Pharaoh had let the people go, God did not let them take the road to the Philistines' territory, although that was the shortest, 'in case', God thought, 'the prospect of fighting makes the people change their minds and turn back to Egypt.' ¹⁸Instead, God led the people a roundabout way through the desert of the Sea of Reeds. The Israelites left Egypt fully armed. ¹⁹Moses took with him the bones of Joseph, since Joseph had put the Israelites on solemn oath with the words, 'It is sure that God will visit you,' he had said, 'and when that day comes you must take my bones away from here with you.'

²⁰They set out from Succoth and encamped at Etham, on the edge of the desert.

²¹Yahweh preceded them, by day in a pillar of cloud to show them the way, and by night in a pillar of fire to give them light, so that they could march by day and by night. ²²The pillar of cloud never left its place ahead of the people during the day, nor the pillar of fire during the night.

From Etham to the Sea of Reeds

14 Yahweh spoke to Moses and said, ²'Tell the Israelites to turn back and pitch camp in front of Pi-Hahiroth, between Migdol and the sea, facing Baal-Zephon. You must pitch your camp opposite this place, beside the sea, ³and then Pharaoh will think, "The Israelites are wandering to and fro in the countryside; the desert has closed in on them." ⁴I shall then make Pharaoh stubborn and he will set out in pursuit of them; and I shall win glory for myself at the expense of Pharaoh and his whole army, and then the Egyptians will know that I am Yahweh.' And the Israelites did this.

The Egyptians pursue the Israelites

⁵When Pharaoh king of Egypt was told that the people had fled, he and his officials

changed their attitude towards the people. 'What have we done,' they said, 'allowing Israel to leave our service?' 6 So Pharaoh had his chariot harnessed and set out with his troops, 7 taking six hundred of the best chariots and all the other chariots in Egypt, with officers in each. 8 Yahweh made Pharaoh king of Egypt stubborn, and he gave chase to the Israelites. The Israelites marched confidently away, 9 but the Egyptians, all Pharaoh's horses, his chariots, his horsemen and his army, gave chase and caught up with them where they lay encamped beside the sea near Pi-Hahiroth, facing Baal-Zephon. 10 As Pharaoh approached, the Israelites looked up—and there were the Egyptians in pursuit of them! The Israelites were terrified and cried out to Yahweh for help. 11 To Moses they said, 'Was it for lack of graves in Egypt, that you had to lead us out to die in the desert? What was the point of bringing us out of Egypt? 12 Did we not tell you as much in Egypt? Leave us alone, we said, we would rather work for the Egyptians! We prefer to work for the Egyptians than to die in the desert!' 13 Moses said to the people, 'Do not be afraid! Stand firm, and you will see what Yahweh will do to rescue you today: the Egyptians you see today you will never see again. 14 Yahweh will do the fighting for you; all you need to do is to keep calm.'

The miracle of the sea

15 Yahweh then said to Moses, 'Why cry out to me? Tell the Israelites to march on. 16 Your part is to raise your staff and stretch out your hand over the sea and divide it, so that the Israelites can walk through the sea on dry ground, 17 while I, for my part, shall make the Egyptians so stubborn that they will follow them, and I shall win glory for myself at the expense of Pharaoh and all his army, chariots and horsemen. 18 And when I have won glory for myself at the expense of Pharaoh and his chariots and horsemen, the Egyptians will know that I am Yahweh.'

19 Then the angel of God, who preceded the army of Israel, changed station and followed behind them. The pillar of cloud moved from their front and took position behind them. 20 It came between the army of the Egyptians and the army of Israel. The cloud was dark, and the night passed without the one drawing any closer to the other the whole night long. 21 Then Moses stretched out his hand over the sea, and Yahweh drove the sea back with a strong easterly wind all night and made the sea into dry land. The waters were divided 22 and the Israelites went on dry ground right through the sea, with walls of water to right and left of them. 23 The Egyptians gave chase, and all Pharaoh's horses, chariots and horsemen went into the sea after them. 24 In the morning watch, Yahweh looked down on the army of the Egyptians from the pillar of fire and cloud and threw the Egyptian army into confusion. 25 He so clogged their chariot wheels that they drove on only with difficulty, which made the Egyptians say, 'Let us flee from Israel, for Yahweh is fighting on their side against the Egyptians!' 26 Then Yahweh said to Moses, 'Stretch out your hand over the sea and let the waters flow back on the Egyptians and on their chariots and their horsemen.' 27 Moses stretched out his hand over the sea and, as day broke, the sea returned to its bed. The fleeing Egyptians ran straight into it, and Yahweh overthrew the Egyptians in the middle of the sea. 28 The returning waters washed right over the chariots and horsemen of Pharaoh's entire army, which had followed the Israelites into the sea; not a single one of them was left. 29 The Israelites, however, had marched through the sea on dry ground, with walls of water to right and left of them. 30 That day, Yahweh rescued Israel from the clutches of the Egyptians, and Israel saw the Egyptians lying dead on the sea-shore. 31 When Israel saw the mighty deed that Yahweh had performed against the Egyptians, the people revered Yahweh and put their faith in Yahweh and in Moses, his servant.

9 READ EXODUS 14:15–31.

That day, Yahweh rescued Israel from the clutches of the Egyptians.—EXODUS 14:30

SALVATION FOR ALL

The worship of demons has ceased; creation has been sanctified by the divine blood; altars and temples of idols have been overthrown; the knowledge of God has been implanted in men's minds; the co-essential Trinity, the uncreated divinity, one true God, Creator and Lord of all receives men's service; virtues are cultivated; the hope of resurrection has been granted through the resurrection of Christ; the demons shudder at those men who used to be under their subjection. And the marvel, indeed, is that all this has been successfully brought about through his cross and passion and death.

Throughout all the earth the gospel of the knowledge of God has been preached. No wars or weapons or armies were used to rout the enemy, but only a few, naked, poor, illiterate, persecuted and tormented men. With their lives in their hands, they preached him who was crucified in the flesh and died, and they became victors over the wise and powerful. For the omnipotent power of the cross accompanied them. Death itself, which once was man's worst terror, has been overthrown, and now that which was once the object of hate and loathing is preferred to life.

These are the achievements of Christ's presence. These are the tokens of his power. For it was not one people that he saved, as when through Moses he divided the sea and delivered Israel out of Egypt and the bondage of Pharaoh. No, rather he rescued all humankind from the corruption of death and the bitter tyranny of sin—not leading them by force to virtue, not overwhelming them with earth or burning them with fire, or ordering the sinners to be stoned, but persuading them by gentleness and long-suffering to choose virtue and vie with one another, and to find pleasure in the struggle to attain it. . . .

Hail! O Christ, the Word and Wisdom and Power of God, and God omnipotent! What can we helpless ones give you in return for all these good gifts?   ST. JOHN DAMASCENE, 675?–749?

YOU WILL FIND THE NEXT READING AT EXODUS 15.

Song of victory

15 It was then that Moses and the Israelites sang this song in Yahweh's honour:

I shall sing to Yahweh, for he has covered
    himself in glory,
        horse and rider he has thrown into the
            sea.
² Yah is my strength and my song,
    to him I owe my deliverance.

He is my God and I shall praise him,
    my father's God and I shall extol him.
³ Yahweh is a warrior;
    Yahweh is his name.
⁴ Pharaoh's chariots and army he has hurled
        into the sea
    the pick of his officers have been drowned
        in the Sea of Reeds.
⁵ The ocean has closed over them;
    they have sunk to the bottom like a
        stone.

6 Your right hand, Yahweh, wins glory by
 its strength,
 your right hand, Yahweh, shatters your
 foes,
7 and by your great majesty you fell your
 assailants;
 you unleash your fury, it consumes them
 like chaff.
8 A blast from your nostrils and the waters
 piled high;
 the waves stood firm as a dyke;
 the bed of the sea became firm ground.

9 The enemy said, 'I shall give chase and
 overtake,
 'I shall share out the spoil and glut myself
 on them,
 'I shall draw my sword, my hand will
 destroy them.'
10 You blew with your breath, the sea closed
 over them;
 they sank like lead in the terrible waters.
11 Yahweh, who is like you, majestic in
 sanctity,
 who like you among the holy ones,
 fearsome of deed, worker of wonders?
12 You stretched your right hand out, the
 earth swallowed them!
13 In your faithful love you led out the people
 you had redeemed,
 in your strength you have guided them to
 your holy dwelling.

14 Hearing of this, the peoples tremble;
 pangs seize on the people of Philistia;
15 the chieftains of Edom are dismayed,
 Moab's princes—panic has seized them,
 all the inhabitants of Canaan have melted
 away.
16 On them fall terror and dread;
 through the power of your arm they are
 still as stone
 while your people are passing, Yahweh,
 while the people you have purchased are
 passing.
17 You will bring them in and plant them
 on the mountain which is your heritage,

the place which you, Yahweh, have made
 your dwelling,
 the sanctuary, Yahweh, prepared by your
 own hands.
18   Yahweh will be king for ever and
 ever.

19 For when Pharaoh's cavalry, with his chariots and horsemen, had gone into the sea, Yahweh brought the waters of the sea back over them, though the Israelites went on dry ground right through the sea. 20 The prophetess Miriam, Aaron's sister, took up a tambourine, and all the women followed her with tambourines, dancing, 21 while Miriam took up from them the refrain:

Sing to Yahweh, for he has covered
 himself in glory,
 horse and rider he has thrown into
 the sea.

Marah

22 Moses led Israel away from the Sea of Reeds, and they entered the desert of Shur. They then travelled through the desert for three days without finding water. 23 When they reached Marah, they could not drink the Marah water because it was bitter; this is why the place was named Marah. 24 The people complained to Moses saying, 'What are we to drink?' 25 Moses appealed to Yahweh for help, and Yahweh showed him a piece of wood. When Moses threw it into the water, the water became sweet.

There he laid down a statute and law for
 them
 and there he put them to the test.

Then he said, 26 'If you listen carefully to the voice of Yahweh your God and do what he regards as right, if you pay attention to his commandments and keep all his laws, I shall never inflict on you any of the diseases that I inflicted on the Egyptians, for I am Yahweh your Healer.'

10 READ EXODUS 15.

You blew with your breath, the sea closed over them.—EXODUS 15:10

BAPTISM PREFIGURED

All flesh was corrupt by its iniquities. "My Spirit," says God, "shall not remain among men, because they are flesh" (see Gn 6:3). By this God shows that the grace of the Spirit is turned away by carnal impurity and the pollution of grave sin. However, God was willing to restore what was lacking. So he sent the flood and commanded Noah to go up into the ark. And as the flood subsided, after Noah had first dispatched a raven that did not return, he sent off a dove that returned with an olive twig (see Gn 8:6–11). You see the water, you see the wood [of the ark], you see the dove, and do you hesitate as to the mystery?

The water, then, is that in which the flesh is dipped, so that all carnal sin may be washed away. All wickedness is there buried. The wood is that on which the Lord Jesus was fastened when he suffered for us. As you have read in the New Testament, the Holy Spirit descended in the form of a dove, the Spirit who inspires in you peace of soul and tranquility of mind. The raven is the figure of sin, which goes forth and does not return, if you maintain righteousness in your thoughts and actions.

There is also a third testimony, as the Apostle teaches us: "Our ancestors all had the cloud over them and all passed through the sea. In the cloud and in the sea they were all baptised into Moses" (1 Co 10:1–2). And further, Moses himself says in his song: "You blew with your breath, the sea closed over them." You observe that even then holy Baptism was prefigured in that passage of the Hebrews, where the Egyptian perished and the Hebrew escaped. For what else are we daily taught in this sacrament but that guilt is swallowed up and error wiped away, but that virtue and innocence remain unharmed?   ST. AMBROSE, 339–397

YOU WILL FIND THE NEXT READING AT EXODUS 20.

27 So they came to Elim where there were twelve springs and seventy palm trees; and there they pitched camp beside the water.

The manna and the quails[a]

16 Setting out from Elim, the whole community of Israelites entered the desert of Sin, lying between Elim and Sinai—on the fifteenth day of the second month after they had left Egypt. 2 And the whole community of Israelites began complaining about Moses and Aaron in the desert 3 and said to them, 'Why did we not die at Yahweh's hand in Egypt, where we used to sit round the flesh pots and could eat to our heart's content! As it is, you have led us into this desert to starve this entire assembly to death!'

4 Yahweh then said to Moses, 'Look, I shall rain down bread for you from the heavens. Each day the people must go out and collect their ration for the day; I propose to test them in this way to see whether they will follow my law or not. 5 On the sixth day, however, when they prepare what they have brought in, this

16a ‖ Nb 11.

must be twice as much as they collect on ordinary days.'

⁶ Moses and Aaron then said to the whole community of Israelites, 'This evening you will know that it was Yahweh who brought you out of Egypt, ⁷ and tomorrow morning you will see the glory of Yahweh, for Yahweh has heard your complaints about him. What are we, that your complaint should be against us?' ⁸ Moses then said, 'This evening Yahweh will give you meat to eat, and tomorrow morning bread to your heart's content, for Yahweh has heard your complaints about him. What do we count for? Your complaints are not against us, but against Yahweh.'

⁹ Moses then said to Aaron, 'Say to the whole community of Israelites, "Approach Yahweh's presence, for he has heard your complaints." ' ¹⁰ As Aaron was speaking to the whole community of Israelites, they turned towards the desert, and there the glory of Yahweh appeared in the cloud. ¹¹ Yahweh then spoke to Moses and said, ¹² 'I have heard the Israelites' complaints. Speak to them as follows, "At twilight you will eat meat, and in the morning you will have bread to your heart's content, and then you will know that I am Yahweh your God." '

¹³ That evening, quails flew in and covered the camp, and next morning there was a layer of dew all round the camp. ¹⁴ When the layer of dew lifted, there on the surface of the desert was something fine and granular, as fine as hoarfrost on the ground. ¹⁵ As soon as the Israelites saw this, they said to one another, 'What is that ᵇ?' not knowing what it was. 'That', Moses told them, 'is the food which Yahweh has given you to eat. ¹⁶ These are Yahweh's orders: Each of you must collect as much as he needs to eat—a *homer* per head for each person in his tent.'

¹⁷ The Israelites did this. They collected it, some more, some less. ¹⁸ When they measured out what they had collected by the *homer,* no one who had collected more had too much, no one who had collected less had too little. Each had collected as much as he needed to eat.

¹⁹ Moses then said, 'No one may keep any of it for tomorrow.' ²⁰ But some of them took no notice of Moses and kept part of it for the following day, and it bred maggots and smelt foul; and Moses was angry with them. ²¹ Morning by morning they collected it, each man as much as he needed to eat, and once the sun grew hot, it melted away.

²² Now, on the sixth day they collected twice the amount of food: two *homer* per person, and all the leaders of the community came and told Moses this. ²³ Moses replied, 'This is what Yahweh said, "Tomorrow is a day of complete rest, a Sabbath sacred to Yahweh. Bake what you want to bake, boil what you want to boil; put aside what is left over, to be kept for tomorrow." ²⁴ So, as Moses ordered, they put it aside for the following day, and its smell was not foul nor were there maggots in it. ²⁵ 'Eat it today,' Moses said, 'for today is a Sabbath for Yahweh; you will find none in the fields today. ²⁶ For six days you will collect it, but on the seventh day, the Sabbath, there will be none.' ²⁷ On the seventh day some of the people went out to collect it, but they found none. ²⁸ Yahweh then said to Moses, 'How much longer will you refuse to obey my commandments and laws? ²⁹ Look, Yahweh has given you the Sabbath; this is why he gives you two days' food on the sixth day; each of you must stay in his place; on the seventh day no one may leave his home.' ³⁰ So on the seventh day the people rested.

³¹ The House of Israel named it 'manna'. It was like coriander seed; it was white and its taste was like that of wafers made with honey.

³² Moses then said, 'These are Yahweh's orders: Fill a *homer* with it and preserve it for your descendants, so that they can see the bread on which I fed you in the desert when I brought you out of Egypt.' ³³ Moses then said to Aaron, 'Take a jar and in it put a full *homer* of manna and store it in Yahweh's presence, to be kept for your descendants.' ³⁴ Accordingly,

16b Hebr. *Man hu.* Popular explanation of the name. Manna is an insect secretion found on tamarisks.

Aaron stored it in front of the Testimony, to be preserved, as Yahweh had ordered Moses.

[35] The Israelites ate manna for forty years, up to the time they reached inhabited country: they ate manna up to the time they reached the frontiers of Canaan. [36] A *homer* is one-tenth of an *ephah*.

The water from the rock[a]

17 The whole community of Israelites left the desert of Sin, travelling by stages as Yahweh ordered. They pitched camp at Rephidim where there was no water for the people to drink. [2] The people took issue with Moses for this and said, 'Give us water to drink.' Moses replied, 'Why take issue with me? Why do you put Yahweh to the test?' [3] But, tormented by thirst, the people complained to Moses. 'Why did you bring us out of Egypt,' they said, 'only to make us, our children and our livestock, die of thirst?' [4] Moses appealed to Yahweh for help. 'How am I to deal with this people?' he said. 'Any moment now they will stone me!' [5] Yahweh then said to Moses, 'Go on ahead of the people, taking some of the elders of Israel with you; in your hand take the staff with which you struck the River, and go. [6] I shall be waiting for you there on the rock (at Horeb). Strike the rock, and water will come out for the people to drink.' This was what Moses did, with the elders of Israel looking on. [7] He gave the place the names Massah and Meribah because of the Israelites' contentiousness and because they put Yahweh to the test by saying, 'Is Yahweh with us, or not?'

A battle against the Amalekites

[8] The Amalekites then came and attacked Israel at Rephidim. [9] Moses said to Joshua, 'Pick some men and tomorrow morning go out and engage Amalek. I, for my part, shall take my stand on the hilltop with the staff of God in my hand.' [10] Joshua did as Moses had told him and went out to engage Amalek, while Moses, Aaron and Hur went up to the top of the hill. [11] As long as Moses kept his arms raised, Israel had the advantage; when he let his arms fall, the advantage went to Amalek. [12] But Moses' arms grew heavy, so they took a stone and put it under him and on this he sat, with Aaron and Hur supporting his arms on each side.

Thus his arms remained unwavering till sunset, [13] and Joshua defeated Amalek, putting their people to the sword. [14] Yahweh then said to Moses, 'Write this down in a book to commemorate it, and repeat it over to Joshua, for I shall blot out all memory of Amalek under heaven.' [15] Moses then built an altar and named it Yahweh-Nissi [16] meaning, 'Lay hold of Yahweh's banner! Yahweh will be at war with Amalek generation after generation.'

The meeting of Jethro and Moses

18 Jethro, priest of Midian, Moses' father-in-law, had heard all about what God had done for Moses and for Israel his people: how Yahweh had brought Israel out of Egypt. [2] Jethro, Moses' father-in-law, then took back Zipporah, Moses' wife, whom Moses had sent home, [3] with her two sons; one of them was called Gershom because, he had said, 'I am an alien in a foreign land,' [4] and the other called Eliezer because 'My father's God is my help and has delivered me from Pharaoh's sword.'

[5] Then Jethro, Moses' father-in-law, with Moses' sons and wife, came to Moses in the desert where he was encamped, at the mountain of God. [6] 'Here is your father-in-law Jethro approaching', Moses was told, 'with your wife and her two sons.' [7] So Moses went out to greet his father-in-law, bowed low to him and kissed him; and when each had asked how the other was they went into the tent. [8] Moses then told his father-in-law all about what Yahweh had done to Pharaoh and the Egyptians for Israel's sake, and about all the hardships that they had encountered on the way, and how Yahweh had rescued them. [9] And Jethro was delighted at all Yahweh's

17a || Nb 20:1–13.

goodness to Israel in having rescued them from the clutches of the Egyptians. 10 'Blessed be Yahweh', Jethro exclaimed, 'for having rescued you from the clutches of the Egyptians and the clutches of Pharaoh, for having rescued the people from the grasp of the Egyptians! 11 Now I know that Yahweh is greater than all other gods . . .'

12 Jethro, Moses' father-in-law, then offered a burnt offering and other sacrifices to God; and Aaron and all the elders of Israel came and ate with Moses' father-in-law in the presence of God.

The appointment of judges[a]

13 On the following day, Moses took his seat to administer justice for the people, and the people were standing round him from morning till evening. 14 Seeing all he did for the people, Moses' father-in-law said to him, 'Why do you do this for the people, why sit here alone with the people standing round you from morning till evening?' 15 Moses replied to his father-in-law, 'Because the people come to me to consult God. 16 When they have a problem they come to me, and I give a ruling between the one and the other and make God's statutes and laws known to them.' 17 Moses' father-in-law then said to him, 'What you are doing is not right. 18 You will only tire yourself out, and the people with you too, for the work is too heavy for you. You cannot do it all yourself. 19 Now listen to the advice I am going to give you, and God be with you! Your task is to represent the people to God, to lay their cases before God, 20 and to teach them the statutes and laws, and show them the way they ought to follow and how they ought to behave. 21 At the same time, from the people at large choose capable and God-fearing men, men who are trustworthy and incorruptible, and put them in charge of them as heads of thousands, hundreds, fifties and tens, 22 and make them the people's permanent judges. They will refer all important matters to you, but all minor matters they will decide themselves, so making things easier for you by sharing the burden with you. 23 If you

do this—and may God so command you— you will be able to stand the strain, and all these people will go home satisfied.'

24 Moses took his father-in-law's advice and did just as he said. 25 Moses chose capable men from all Israel and put them in charge of the people as heads of thousands, hundreds, fifties and tens. 26 These acted as the people's permanent judges. They referred hard cases to Moses but decided minor matters themselves.

27 Moses then set his father-in-law on his way, and he travelled back to his own country.

The Israelites reach Sinai

19 Three months to the day after leaving Egypt, the Israelites reached the desert of Sinai. 2 Setting out from Rephidim, they reached the desert of Sinai and pitched camp in the desert; there, facing the mountain, Israel pitched camp.

Yahweh promises the covenant

3 Moses then went up to God, and Yahweh called to him from the mountain, saying, 'Say this to the House of Jacob! Tell the Israelites, 4 "You have seen for yourselves what I did to the Egyptians and how I carried you away on eagle's wings and brought you to me. 5 So now, if you are really prepared to obey me and keep my covenant, you, out of all peoples, shall be my personal possession, for the whole world is mine. 6 For me you shall be a kingdom of priests, a holy nation." Those are the words you are to say to the Israelites.' 7 So Moses went and summoned the people's elders and acquainted them with everything that Yahweh had bidden him, 8 and the people all replied with one accord, 'Whatever Yahweh has said, we will do.' Moses then reported to Yahweh what the people had said.

Preparing for the covenant

9 Yahweh then said to Moses, 'Look, I shall come to you in a dense cloud so that the people will hear when I speak to you and believe you

18a ‖ Dt 1:9–18.

ever after.' Moses then told Yahweh what the people had said.

¹⁰Yahweh then said to Moses, 'Go to the people and tell them to sanctify themselves today and tomorrow. They must wash their clothes ¹¹ and be ready for the day after tomorrow; for the day after tomorrow, in the sight of all the people, Yahweh will descend on Mount Sinai. ¹²You will mark out the limits of the mountain and say, "Take care not to go up the mountain or to touch the edge of it. Anyone who touches the mountain will be put to death. ¹³No one may lay a hand on him: he must be stoned or shot by arrow; whether man or beast, he shall not live." When the ram's horn sounds a long blast, they must go up the mountain.'

¹⁴So Moses came down from the mountain to the people; he made the people sanctify themselves and they washed their clothes. ¹⁵He then said to the people, 'Be ready for the day after tomorrow; do not touch a woman.'

The theophany on Sinai

¹⁶Now at daybreak two days later, there were peals of thunder and flashes of lightning, dense cloud on the mountain and a very loud trumpet blast; and, in the camp, all the people trembled. ¹⁷Then Moses led the people out of the camp to meet God; and they took their stand at the bottom of the mountain. ¹⁸Mount Sinai was entirely wrapped in smoke, because Yahweh had descended on it in the form of fire. The smoke rose like smoke from a furnace and the whole mountain shook violently. ¹⁹Louder and louder grew the trumpeting. Moses spoke, and God answered him in the thunder. ²⁰Yahweh descended on Mount Sinai, on the top of the mountain, and Yahweh called Moses to the top of the mountain; and Moses went up. ²¹Yahweh then said to Moses, 'Go down and warn the people not to break through to look at Yahweh, or many of them will perish. ²²Even the priests, who do have access to Yahweh, must sanctify themselves, or Yahweh may burst out against them.' ²³Moses said to Yahweh, 'The people cannot come up Mount Sinai, since you yourself warned us to

mark out the limits of the mountain and declare it sacred.' ²⁴Yahweh said, 'Away with you! Go down! Then come back bringing Aaron with you. But do not allow the priests and people to break through to come up to Yahweh, or he may burst out against them.' ²⁵So Moses went down to the people and spoke to them.

The Decalogue[a]

20 Then God spoke all these words. He said, ²'I am Yahweh your God who brought you out of Egypt, where you lived as slaves.

³'You shall have no other gods to rival me.

⁴'You shall not make yourself a carved image or any likeness of anything in heaven above or on earth beneath or in the waters under the earth.

⁵'You shall not bow down to them or serve them. For I, Yahweh your God, am a jealous God and I punish a parent's fault in the children, the grandchildren, and the great-grandchildren among those who hate me; ⁶but I act with faithful love towards thousands of those who love me and keep my commandments.

⁷'You shall not misuse the name of Yahweh your God, for Yahweh will not leave unpunished anyone who misuses his name.

⁸'Remember the Sabbath day and keep it holy. ⁹For six days you shall labour and do all your work, ¹⁰but the seventh day is a Sabbath for Yahweh your God. You shall do no work that day, neither you nor your son nor your daughter nor your servants, men or women, nor your animals nor the alien living with you. ¹¹For in six days Yahweh made the heavens, earth and sea and all that these contain, but on the seventh day he rested; that is why Yahweh has blessed the Sabbath day and made it sacred.

¹²'Honour your father and your mother so that you may live long in the land that Yahweh your God is giving you.

¹³'You shall not kill.

20a || Dt 5:6–22.

11 READ EXODUS 20:1–17.

You shall have no other gods to rival me.—EXODUS 20:3

HOW TO BE TRULY HOLY

In every race of human beings God inserts an understanding of righteousness, that is, what is always and universally just. Every race knows that such things as adultery, and fornication, and homicide are sinful. For example, though they all fornicate, they do not escape from the knowledge that they are acting unrighteously—with the exception of those possessed by an unclean spirit, those debased by wicked customs and sinful institutions, and those who have quenched their natural ideas. For we observe that such persons refuse to endure the same things they inflict on others. They also reproach each other for the evil acts that they commit.

Thus our Lord and Savior, Jesus Christ, spoke well when he summed up all righteousness in two commandments: "You shall love the Lord your God with all your heart, and with all your strength, and your neighbor as yourself" (see Lk 10:27). For the one who loves God with all his heart and who is filled with a God-fearing mind will reverence no other god. And the person who loves his neighbor as himself will wish for him the same good things that he wishes for himself—and no one will wish evil things for himself. So a person who loves his neighbor would pray and work that others may possess the same benefits as himself.

Therefore, since Scripture says all righteousness is divided into these two branches, whoever loves the Lord God with all his heart, and all his strength, and his neighbor as himself, would be a truly righteous person. ST. JUSTIN, 100?–165

YOU WILL FIND THE NEXT READING AT EXODUS 33.

14 'You shall not commit adultery.

15 'You shall not steal.

16 'You shall not give false evidence against your neighbour.

17 'You shall not set your heart on your neighbour's house. You shall not set your heart on your neighbour's spouse, or servant, man or woman, or ox, or donkey, or any of your neighbour's possessions.'

18 Seeing the thunder pealing, the lightning flashing, the trumpet blasting and the mountain smoking, the people were all terrified and kept their distance. 19 'Speak to us yourself,' they said to Moses, 'and we will obey; but do not let God speak to us, or we shall die.' 20 Moses said to the people, 'Do not be afraid; God has come to test you, so that your fear of him, being always in your mind, may keep you from sinning.' 21 So the people kept their distance while Moses approached the dark cloud where God was.

Law concerning the altar

22 Yahweh said to Moses, 'Tell the Israelites this, "You have seen for yourselves how I have spoken to you from heaven. 23 You must not make gods of silver to rival me, nor must you make yourselves gods of gold.

24 "You must make me an altar of earth on which to sacrifice your burnt offerings and communion sacrifices, your sheep and cattle. Wherever I choose to have my name remem-

bered, I shall come to you and bless you. 25 If you make me an altar of stone, do not build it of dressed stones; for if you use a chisel on it, you will profane it. 26 You must not go up to my altar by steps, in case you expose your nakedness on them." '

Laws concerning slaves

21 'These are the laws you must give them: 2 'When you buy a Hebrew slave, his service will last for six years. In the seventh year he will leave a free man without paying compensation. 3 If he came single, he will depart single; if he came married, his wife will depart with him. 4 If his master gives him a wife and she bears him sons or daughters, the wife and her children will belong to her master, and he will depart alone. 5 But if the slave says, "I love my master and my wife and children; I do not wish to be freed," 6 then his master will bring him before God and then, leading him to the door or the doorpost, his master will pierce his ear with an awl, and the slave will be permanently his. 7 If a man sells his daughter as a slave, she will not leave as male slaves do. 8 If she does not please her master who intended her for himself, he must let her be bought back: he has not the right to sell her to foreigners, for this would be a breach of faith with her. 9 If he intends her for his son, he must treat her as custom requires daughters to be treated. 10 If he takes another wife, he must not reduce the food, clothing or conjugal rights of the first one. 11 Should he deprive her of these three things she will leave a free woman, without paying compensation.

Homicide

12 'Anyone who by violence causes a death must be put to death. 13 If, however, he has not planned to do it but it comes from God by his hand, he can take refuge in a place which I shall appoint for you. 14 But should any person dare to kill another with deliberate planning, you will take that person even from my altar to be put to death.

15 'Anyone who strikes father or mother will be put to death. 16 Anyone who abducts a person—whether that person has since been sold or is still held—will be put to death. 17 Anyone who curses father or mother will be put to death.

Blows and wounds

18 'If people quarrel and one strikes the other a blow with stone or fist so that the injured party, though not dead, is confined to bed, 19 but later recovers and can go about, even with a stick, the one who struck the blow will have no liability, other than to compensate the injured party for the enforced inactivity and to take care of the injured party until the cure is complete.

20 'If someone beats his slave, male or female, and the slave dies at his hands, he must pay the penalty. 21 But should the slave survive for one or two days, he will pay no penalty because the slave is his by right of purchase.

22 'If people, when brawling, hurt a pregnant woman and she suffers a miscarriage but no further harm is done, the person responsible will pay compensation as fixed by the woman's master, paying as much as the judges decide. 23 If further harm is done, however, you will award life for life, 24 eye for eye, tooth for tooth, hand for hand, foot for foot, 25 burn for burn, wound for wound, stroke for stroke.

26 'If anyone strikes the eye of his slave, male or female, and destroys the use of it, he will give the slave his freedom to compensate for the eye. 27 If he knocks out the tooth of his slave, male or female, he will give the slave his freedom to compensate for the tooth.

28 'If an ox gores a man or woman to death, the ox will be stoned and its meat will not be eaten, but the owner of the ox will not be liable. 29 But if the ox has been in the habit of goring before, and if its owner has been warned but has not kept it under control, then should this ox kill a man or woman, it will be stoned and its owner put to death. 30 If a ransom is imposed on the owner, he will pay whatever is imposed, to redeem his life. 31 If the ox gores a boy or a girl, it will be treated in

accordance with this same rule. ³²If the ox gores a slave, male or female, its owner will pay the price—thirty shekels—to their master, and the ox will be stoned.

³³'If anyone leaves a pit uncovered, or digs a pit and does not cover it, and an ox, or donkey falls into it, ³⁴then the owner of the pit will make good the loss by compensating its owner, and the dead animal will be his. ³⁵If anyone's ox injures anyone else's ox causing its death, the owners will sell and share the money for it; they will also share the dead animal. ³⁶But if it is common knowledge that the ox has been in the habit of goring before, and its owner has not kept it under control, the owner will repay ox for ox, and will keep the dead animal.

Theft of animals

³⁷'If anyone steals an ox or a sheep and slaughters or sells it, he will pay back five beasts from the herd for the ox, and four animals from the flock for the sheep.'

22 'If a thief is caught breaking in and is struck a mortal blow, his blood may not be avenged, ²but if it happens after sunrise, his blood may be avenged. He will make full restitution; if he has not the means, he will be sold to pay for what he has stolen. ³If the stolen animal is found alive in his possession, be it ox, donkey or animal from the flock, he will pay back double.

Offences requiring compensation

⁴'If anyone puts his animals out to graze in a field or vineyard and lets them graze in someone else's field, he will make restitution for the part of the field that has been grazed on the basis of its yield. But if he has let the whole field be grazed, he will make restitution in proportion to the best crop of the field or vineyard.

⁵'If a fire breaks out, setting light to thorn bushes and burning stacks, standing corn or the field as a result, the person who started the fire will make full restitution.

⁶'If anyone entrusts money or goods to someone else's keeping and these are stolen from that person's house, the thief, if he can be discovered, will repay double. ⁷Should the thief not be discovered, the owner of the house will come into the presence of God, to declare that he has not laid hands on the other person's property.

⁸'In every case of law-breaking involving an ox, donkey, animal from the flock, clothing or lost property of any sort, the ownership of which is disputed, both parties will lay their case before God. The party whom God pronounces guilty will pay back double to the other.

⁹'If anyone entrusts a donkey, ox, animal from the flock or any other animal to someone else's keeping, and it dies or breaks a limb or is carried off without anyone seeing, ¹⁰an oath by Yahweh will decide between the two parties whether the keeper has laid hands on the other's property or not. The owner will take what remains, the keeper will not have to make good the loss. ¹¹Only if the animal has been stolen from him, will he make restitution to the owner. ¹²If it has been savaged by a wild animal, he must bring the savaged remains of the animal as evidence, and will then not have to make restitution.

¹³'If anyone borrows an animal from someone else, and it breaks a limb or dies in the owner's absence, he will make full restitution. ¹⁴But if the animal's owner has been present, he will not have to make good the loss. If the owner has hired it out, he will get the cost of its hire.

Violation of a virgin

¹⁵'If a man seduces a virgin who is not engaged to be married, he will pay her brideprice and make her his wife. ¹⁶If her father absolutely refuses to let him have her, he will pay a sum equivalent to the bride-price of a virgin.

Moral and religious laws

¹⁷'You will not allow a sorceress to live.
¹⁸'Anyone who has intercourse with an animal will be put to death.

19'Anyone who sacrifices to other gods will be put under the curse of destruction.

20'You will not molest or oppress aliens, for you yourselves were once aliens in Egypt. 21You will not ill-treat widows or orphans; 22if you ill-treat them in any way and they make an appeal to me for help, I shall certainly hear their appeal, 23my anger will be roused and I shall put you to the sword; then your own wives will be widows and your own children orphans.

24'If you lend money to any of my people, to anyone poor among you, you will not play the usurer with him: you will not demand interest from him.

25'If you take someone's cloak in pledge, you will return it to him at sunset. 26It is all the covering he has; it is the cloak he wraps his body in; what else will he sleep in? If he appeals to me, I shall listen. At least with me he will find compassion!

27'You will not revile God, nor curse your people's leader.

First-fruits and first-born

28'Do not be slow about making offerings from your abundance and your surplus. You will give me the first-born of your children; 29you will do the same with your flocks and herds. For the first seven days the first-born will stay with its mother; on the eighth day you will give it to me.

30'You must be people consecrated to me. You will not eat the meat of anything in the countryside savaged by wild animals; you will throw it to the dogs.'

Justice; duties towards enemies

23 'You will not spread false rumours. You will not lend support to the wicked by giving untrue evidence. 2You will not be led into wrong-doing by the majority nor, when giving evidence in a lawsuit, side with the majority to pervert the course of justice; 3nor will you show partiality to the poor in a lawsuit.

4'If you come on your enemy's ox or donkey straying, you will take it back to him. 5If you see the donkey of someone who hates you fallen under its load, do not stand back; you must go and help him with it.

6'You will not cheat the poor among you of their rights at law. 7Keep clear of fraud. Do not cause the death of the innocent or upright, and do not acquit the guilty. 8You will accept no bribes, for a bribe blinds the clear-sighted and is the ruin of the cause of the upright.

9'You will not oppress the alien; you know how an alien feels, for you yourselves were once aliens in Egypt.

The sabbatical year and the Sabbath

10'For six years you will sow your land and gather its produce, 11but in the seventh year you will let it lie fallow and forgo all produce from it, so that those of your people who are poor can take food from it and the wild animals eat what they have left. You will do the same with your vineyard and your olive grove.

12'For six days you will do your work, and on the seventh you will rest, so that your ox and your donkey may rest and the child of your slave-girl have a breathing space, and the alien too.

13'Take notice of everything I have told you and do not mention the name of any other god: let none ever be heard from your lips.

The great feasts

14'Three times a year you will hold a festival in my honour. 15You will observe the feast of Unleavened Bread. For seven days you will eat unleavened bread, as I have commanded you, at the appointed time in the month of Abib, for in that month you came out of Egypt. No one will appear before me empty-handed. 16You will also observe the feast of Harvest, of the first-fruits of your labours in sowing the fields, and the feast of Ingathering, at the end of the year, once you have brought the fruits of your labours in from the fields. 17Three times a year all your menfolk will appear before Lord Yahweh.

18'You will not offer the blood of my victim

with leavened bread, nor will the fat of my feast be kept till the following day.

19 'You will bring the best of the first-fruits of your soil to the house of Yahweh your God.

'You will not boil a kid in its mother's milk.

Promises and instructions for the entry into Canaan

20 'Look, I am sending an angel to precede you, to guard you as you go and bring you to the place that I have prepared. 21 Revere him and obey what he says. Do not defy him: he will not forgive any wrong-doing on your part, for my name is in him. 22 If, however, you obey what he says and do whatever I order, I shall be an enemy to your enemies and a foe to your foes. 23 My angel will precede you and lead you to the home of the Amorites, the Hittites, the Perizzites, the Canaanites, the Hivites and the Jebusites, whom I shall exterminate. 24 You will not bow down to their gods or worship them or observe their rites, but throw them down and smash their cultic stones. 25 You will worship Yahweh your God, and then I shall bless your food and water, and keep you free of sickness. 26 In your country no woman will miscarry, none be sterile, and I shall give you your full term of life.

27 'I shall send terror of myself ahead of you; I shall throw all the peoples you encounter into confusion, and make all your enemies take to their heels. 28 I shall send hornets ahead of you to drive Hivite, Canaanite and Hittite out before you. 29 I shall not drive them out ahead of you in a single year, or the land might become a desert where wild animals would multiply to your cost. 30 I shall drive them out little by little before you, until your numbers grow sufficient for you to take possession of the land. 31 And your frontiers I shall fix from the Sea of Reeds to the Sea of the Philistines, and from the desert to the River, for I shall put the inhabitants of the territory at your mercy, and you will drive them out before you. 32 You will make no pact with them or with their gods. 33 They may not stay in your country or they might make you sin against me, for you

would serve their gods, and that would be a snare for you!'

24 He then said to Moses, 'Come up to Yahweh, you and Aaron, Nadab and Abihu, and seventy of the elders of Israel and bow down at a distance. 2 Moses alone will approach Yahweh; the others will not approach, nor will the people come up with him.'

3 Moses went and told the people all Yahweh's words and all the laws, and all the people answered with one voice, 'All the words Yahweh has spoken we will carry out!' 4 Moses put all Yahweh's words into writing, and early next morning he built an altar at the foot of the mountain, with twelve standing-stones for the twelve tribes of Israel. 5 Then he sent certain young Israelites to offer burnt offerings and sacrifice bullocks to Yahweh as communion sacrifices. 6 Moses then took half the blood and put it into basins, and the other half he sprinkled on the altar. 7 Then, taking the Book of the Covenant, he read it to the listening people, who then said, 'We shall do everything that Yahweh has said; we shall obey.' 8 Moses then took the blood and sprinkled it over the people, saying, 'This is the blood of the covenant which Yahweh has made with you, entailing all these stipulations.'

9 Moses, Aaron, Nadab, Abihu and seventy elders of Israel then went up, 10 and they saw the God of Israel beneath whose feet there was what looked like a sapphire pavement pure as the heavens themselves, 11 but he did no harm to the Israelite notables; they actually gazed on God and then ate and drank.

Moses on the mountain

12 Yahweh said to Moses, 'Come up to me on the mountain. Stay there, and I will give you the stone tablets—the law and the commandment—which I have written for their instruction.' 13 Moses made ready, with Joshua his assistant, and they went up the mountain of God. 14 He said to the elders, 'Wait here for us until we come back to you. You have Aaron and Hur with you; if anyone has any matter to

settle, let him go to them.' ¹⁵Moses then went up the mountain.

Cloud covered the mountain. ¹⁶The glory of Yahweh rested on Mount Sinai and the cloud covered it for six days. On the seventh day Yahweh called to Moses from inside the cloud. ¹⁷To the watching Israelites, the glory of Yahweh looked like a devouring fire on the mountain top. ¹⁸Moses went right into the cloud and went on up the mountain. Moses stayed on the mountain for forty days and forty nights.

Contributions for the sanctuary

25 Yahweh spoke to Moses and said, ²'Tell the Israelites to set aside a contribution for me; you will accept a contribution from everyone whose heart prompts him to give it. ³And this is what you will accept from them: gold, silver and bronze; ⁴materials dyed violet-purple, red-purple and crimson, fine linen, goats' hair; ⁵rams' skins dyed red, fine leather, acacia wood; ⁶oil for the light, spices for the anointing oil and fragrant incense; ⁷cornelian and other stones to be set in the *ephod* and breastplate. ⁸Make me a sanctuary so that I can reside among them. ⁹You will make it all according to the design for the Dwelling and the design for its furnishings which I shall now show you.

The Dwelling and its furnishings; the ark[a]

¹⁰'You must make me an ark of acacia wood, two and a half cubits long, one and a half cubits wide and one and a half cubits high. ¹¹You will overlay it, inside and out, with pure gold and make a gold moulding all round it. ¹²You will cast four gold rings for it and fix them to its four supports: two rings on one side and two rings on the other. ¹³You will also make shafts of acacia wood and overlay them with gold ¹⁴and pass the shafts through the rings on the sides of the ark, by which to carry it. ¹⁵The shafts will stay in the rings of the ark and not be withdrawn. ¹⁶Inside the ark you will put the Testimony which I am about to give you.

¹⁷'You will also make a mercy-seat[b] of pure gold, two and a half cubits long and one and a half cubits wide, ¹⁸and you will model two great winged creatures of beaten gold, you will make them at the two ends of the mercy-seat. ¹⁹Model one of the winged creatures at one end and the other winged creature at the other end; you will model the winged creatures of a piece with the mercy-seat at either end. ²⁰The winged creatures must have their wings spread upwards, protecting the mercy-seat with their wings and facing each other, their faces being towards the mercy-seat. ²¹You will put the mercy-seat on the top of the ark, and inside the ark you will put the Testimony which I am about to give you. ²²There I shall come to meet you; from above the mercy-seat, from between the two winged creatures which are on the ark of the Testimony, I shall give you all my orders for the Israelites.

The table for the loaves of permanent offering

²³'You must also make a table of acacia wood, two cubits long, one cubit wide and one and a half cubits high. ²⁴You will overlay it with pure gold, and make a gold moulding all round it. ²⁵You will fit it with struts of a hand's breadth and make a gold moulding round the struts. ²⁶You will make four gold rings for it and fix the four rings at the four corners where the four legs are. ²⁷The rings must lie close to the struts to hold the shafts for carrying the table. ²⁸You must make the shafts of acacia wood and overlay them with gold. The table must be carried by these. ²⁹You must make dishes, cups, jars and libation bowls for it; you must make these of pure gold, ³⁰and on the table, in my presence, you will always put the loaves of permanent offering.

25a A wooden chest, symbol of God's presence, finally housed in the Temple. It disappeared in the destruction of 586 BC.

25b This covering of the ark is the place of God's appearing to Moses. The winged creatures correspond to Babylonian *karibu,* half-animal, half-human guards of the temples.

The lamp-stand

31 'You will also make a lamp-stand of pure gold; the lamp-stand must be of beaten gold, base and stem. Its cups, calyxes and petals, must be of a piece with it. 32 Six branches must spring from its sides: three of the lamp-stand's branches from one side, three of the lamp-stand's branches from the other. 33 The first branch must carry three cups shaped like almond blossoms, each with its calyx and petals; the second branch, too, must carry three cups shaped like almond blossoms, each with its calyx and bud, and similarly for all six branches springing from the lamp-stand. 34 The lamp-stand itself must carry four cups shaped like almond blossoms, each with its calyx and bud: 35 one calyx under the first two branches springing from the lamp-stand, one calyx under the next pair of branches and one calyx under the last pair of branches—thus for all six branches springing from the lamp-stand. 36 The calyxes and the branches will be of a piece with the lamp-stand, and the whole made from a single piece of pure gold, beaten out. 37 You will also make seven lamps for it and mount the lamps in such a way that they light up the space in front of it. 38 The snuffers and trays must be of pure gold. 39 You will use a talent of pure gold for the lamp-stand and all its accessories; 40 and see that you work to the design which was shown you on the mountain.'

The Dwelling; fabrics and hangings

26 'The Dwelling itself you will make with ten sheets of finely woven linen dyed violet-purple, red-purple and crimson. You will have them embroidered with great winged creatures. 2 The length of a single sheet is to be twenty-eight cubits, its width four cubits, all the sheets to be of the same size. 3 Five of the sheets are to be joined to one another, and the other five sheets are to be joined to one another. 4 You will make violet loops along the edge of the first sheet, at the end of the set, and do the same along the edge of the last sheet in the other set. 5 You will make fifty loops on the first sheet and fifty loops along the outer edge of the sheet of the second set, the loops corresponding to one another. 6 You will also make fifty gold clasps, and join the sheets together with the clasps. In this way the Dwelling will be a unified whole.

7 'You will make sheets of goats' hair to form a tent over the Dwelling; you will make eleven of these. 8 The length of a single sheet must be thirty cubits and its width four cubits, the eleven sheets to be all of the same size. 9 You will join five sheets together into one set, and six sheets into another; the sixth you will fold double over the front of the tent. 10 You will make fifty loops along the edge of the first sheet, at the end of the first set, and fifty loops along the edge of the sheet of the second set. 11 You will make fifty bronze clasps and insert the clasps into the loops, to draw the tent together and to make it a unified whole.

12 'Of the extra part of the sheets that overlap, half is to hang down the back of the Dwelling. 13 The extra cubit on either side along the length of the tent sheets must hang down the sides of the Dwelling on either side to cover it.

14 'And for the tent you will make a cover of rams' skins dyed red and a cover of fine leather over that.

The framework

15 'For the Dwelling you will make vertical frames of acacia wood. 16 Each frame must be ten cubits long and one and a half cubits wide. 17 Each frame must have twin tenons; that is how all the frames for the Dwelling must be made. 18 You will make frames for the Dwelling: twenty frames for the south side, to the south, 19 and make forty silver sockets under the twenty frames, two sockets under one frame for its two tenons, two sockets under the next frame for its two tenons; 20 and for the other side of the Dwelling, the north side, twenty frames 21 and forty silver sockets, two sockets under one frame, two sockets

under the next frame. ²²For the back of the Dwelling, on the west, you will make six frames, ²³and make two frames for the corners at the back of the Dwelling; ²⁴these must be coupled together at the bottom, and right up to the top, to the level of the first ring; this for the two frames that must form the two corners. ²⁵Thus there will be eight frames with their silver sockets: sixteen sockets; two sockets under one frame and two sockets under the next frame.

²⁶'You will make crossbars of acacia wood: five for the frames of the first side of the Dwelling, ²⁷five crossbars for the frames of the opposite side of the Dwelling, and five crossbars for the frames which form the back of the Dwelling, to the west. ²⁸The middle bar must join the frames from one end to the other, halfway up. ²⁹You will overlay the frames with gold, make gold rings for them, through which to place the crossbars, and overlay the crossbars with gold. ³⁰This is how you must erect the Dwelling, following the design shown you on the mountain.

The curtain

³¹'You will make a curtain of finely woven linen, dyed violet-purple, red-purple and crimson, and embroidered with great winged creatures, ³²and put it on four poles of acacia wood overlaid with gold, with golden hooks for them, set in four sockets of silver. ³³You will put the curtain below the clasps, so that inside behind the curtain, you can place the ark of the Testimony, and the curtain will mark the division for you between the Holy Place and the Holy of Holies. ³⁴You will put the mercy-seat on the ark of the Testimony in the Holy of Holies. ³⁵You will place the table outside the curtain, and the lamp-stand on the south side of the Dwelling, opposite the table; you will put the table on the north side. ³⁶For the entrance to the tent you will make a screen of finely woven linen embroidered with violet-purple, red-purple and crimson, ³⁷and for the screen you will make five poles of acacia wood and overlay them with gold, with

golden hooks, and for them you will cast five sockets of bronze.'

The altar of burnt offerings

27 'You will make the altar of acacia wood, five cubits long and five cubits wide; the altar will be square and three cubits high. ²At its four corners you will make horns, the horns must be of a piece with it, and you will overlay it with bronze. ³And for it you will make pans for taking away the fatty ashes, and shovels, sprinkling basins, hooks and fire pans; you will make all the altar accessories of bronze. ⁴You will also make a grating for it of bronze network, and on the four corners of the grating you will make four bronze rings. ⁵You will put it below the ledge of the altar, underneath, so that it comes halfway up the altar. ⁶You will make shafts for the altar, shafts of acacia wood and overlay them with bronze. ⁷The shafts will be passed through the rings in such a way that the shafts are on either side of the altar, for carrying it. ⁸You will make the altar hollow, out of boards; you will make it as you were shown on the mountain.

The court

⁹'Then you will make the court of the Dwelling. On the south side, the curtaining of the court must be of finely woven linen, one hundred cubits long (for the first side), ¹⁰its twenty poles and their twenty sockets being of bronze, and the poles' hooks and rods of silver. ¹¹So too for the north side, there must be a hundred cubits of curtaining, its twenty poles and their twenty sockets being of bronze, and the poles' hooks and rods of silver. ¹²Across the width of the court, on the west side, there must be fifty cubits of curtaining, with its ten poles and their ten sockets. ¹³The width of the court on the east side, facing the sunrise, must be fifty cubits, ¹⁴with fifteen cubits of curtaining on one side of the entrance, with its three poles and their three sockets, ¹⁵and on the other side of the entrance, fifteen cubits of curtaining, with its three poles and their three sockets; ¹⁶and for the gateway to the court

there must be a twenty-cubit screen of finely woven linen embroidered with violet-purple, red-purple and crimson, with its four poles and their four sockets. ¹⁷ All the poles round the court must be connected by silver rods; their hooks must be of silver and their sockets of bronze. ¹⁸ The length of the court must be one hundred cubits, its width fifty cubits and its height five cubits. All the curtaining must be made of finely woven linen, and their sockets of bronze. ¹⁹ All the accessories for general use in the Dwelling, all its pegs and all the pegs of the court, must be of bronze.

The oil for the lamps

²⁰ 'You will order the Israelites to bring you pure pounded olive oil for the light, and to keep a lamp burning all the time. ²¹ Aaron and his sons will tend it in the Tent of Meeting, outside the curtain hanging in front of the Testimony, from dusk to dawn, before Yahweh. This is a perpetual decree for all generations of Israelites.'

The priestly vestments

28 'From among the Israelites, summon your brother Aaron and his sons to be priests in my service: Aaron and Aaron's sons Nadab, Abihu, Eleazar and Ithamar. ² For your brother Aaron you will make sacred vestments to give dignity and magnificence. ³ You will instruct all the skilled men, whom I have endowed with skill, to make Aaron's vestments for his consecration to my priesthood. ⁴ These are the vestments which they must make: a pectoral, an *ephod*, a robe, an embroidered tunic, a turban and a belt. They must make sacred vestments for your brother Aaron and his sons, for them to be priests in my service. ⁵ They will use gold and violet material, red-purple and crimson, and finely woven linen.

The ephod^a

⁶ 'They will make the *ephod* of finely woven linen embroidered with gold, violet-purple, red-purple and crimson. ⁷ It will have two shoulder-straps joined to it; it will be joined to them by its two edges. ⁸ The waistband on the *ephod* to hold it in position must be of the same workmanship and be of a piece with it: of gold, violet-purple, red-purple and crimson materials and finely woven linen. ⁹ You will then take two cornelians and engrave them with the names of the sons of Israel, ¹⁰ six of their names on one stone, the remaining six names on the other, in the order of their birth. ¹¹ By the stone-carver's art—seal engraving— you will engrave the two stones with the names of the sons of Israel. You will have them mounted in gold settings ¹² and will put the two stones on the shoulder-straps of the *ephod*, to commemorate the sons of Israel. In this way Aaron will bear their names on his two shoulders, before Yahweh, as a reminder. ¹³ You will also make golden rosettes, ¹⁴ and two chains of pure gold twisted like cord, and will attach the cord-like chains to the rosettes.

The breastplate of judgement

¹⁵ 'You will make the breastplate of judgement of the same embroidered work as the *ephod*; you will make it of gold, violet-purple, red-purple and crimson materials and finely woven linen. ¹⁶ It must be square and doubled over, a span in length and a span in width. ¹⁷ In it you will set four rows of stones: a sard, topaz and emerald for the first row; ¹⁸ for the second row, a garnet, sapphire and diamond; ¹⁹ for the third row, a hyacinth, a ruby and an amethyst; ²⁰ and for the fourth row, a beryl, a cornelian and a jasper. These must be mounted in gold settings. ²¹ The stones will correspond to the names of the sons of Israel, twelve like their names, engraved like seals, each with the name of one of the twelve tribes. ²² For the breastplate you will make chains of pure gold twisted like cords, ²³ and on the breastplate you will make two gold rings, putting the two rings on the two outside edges of the breastplate ²⁴ and fastening the two gold cords to the

28a This can mean 1 a sort of pouch, 2 a priest's loin-cloth, 3 the high priest's breastplate.

two rings on the outside edges of the breast-plate. 25 The other two ends of the cords you will fasten to the two rosettes, putting these on the shoulder-straps of the *ephod,* on the front. 26 You will also make two gold rings and put them on the two edges of the breastplate, on the inner side, against the *ephod;* 27 and you will make two gold rings and put them low down on the front of the two shoulder-pieces of the *ephod,* close to the join, above the waist-band of the *ephod.* 28 The breastplate will be secured by a violet-purple cord passed through its rings and those of the *ephod,* so that the breastplate will sit above the waistband and not come apart from the *ephod.* 29 Thus Aaron will bear the names of the sons of Israel on the breastplate of judgement, on his heart, when he enters the sanctuary, as a reminder, before Yahweh, always. 30 To the breastplate of judgement you will add the *urim* and the *thummim,* and these will be on Aaron's heart when he goes into Yahweh's presence, and Aaron will bear the Israelites' judgement on his heart, in Yahweh's presence, always.

The robe

31 'You will make the robe of the *ephod* entirely of violet-purple. 32 In the centre it will have an opening for the head, the opening to have round it a border woven like the neck of a coat of mail, so that it will not get torn. 33 On its lower hem, you will make pomegranates of violet-purple, red-purple and crimson, and finely woven linen all round the hem, with golden bells between them all round: 34 a golden bell and then a pomegranate, alternately, all round the lower hem of the robe. 35 Aaron must wear it when he officiates, and the tinkling will be heard when he goes into the sanctuary into Yahweh's presence, or leaves it, and so he will not incur death.

The symbol of consecration

36 'You will make a flower of pure gold and on it, as you would engrave a seal, you will engrave, "Consecrated to Yahweh". 37 You will put it on a violet-purple cord; it will go on the turban; the front of the turban is the place where it must go. 38 This will go on Aaron's brow, and Aaron will thus take on himself the short-comings in the holy things consecrated by the Israelites, in all their holy offerings. It will be on his brow permanently, to make them acceptable to Yahweh. 39 The tunic you will weave of fine linen, and make a turban of fine linen, and an embroidered waistband.

The vestments of the priests

40 'For the sons of Aaron you will make tunics and waistbands. You will also make them head-dresses to give dignity and magnificence. 41 You will dress your brother Aaron and his sons in these; you will then anoint them, invest them and consecrate them to serve me in the priesthood. 42 You will also make them linen breeches reaching from waist to thigh, to cover their bare flesh. 43 Aaron and his sons will wear these when they go into the Tent of Meeting and when they approach the altar to serve in the sanctuary, as a precaution against incurring mortal guilt. This is a perpetual decree for Aaron and for his descendants after him.'

The consecration of Aaron and his sons; preparations

29 'This is what you will do to them, to consecrate them to my priesthood. Take one young bull and two rams without blemish; 2 also unleavened bread, unleavened cakes mixed with oil, and unleavened wafers spread with oil, made from fine wheat flour, 3 and put these into a basket and present them in the basket, at the same time as the bull and the two rams.

Their purification, clothing and anointing

4 'You will bring Aaron and his sons to the entrance of the Tent of Meeting and bathe them. 5 You will then take the vestments and dress Aaron in the tunic, the robe of the *ephod,* the *ephod,* and the breastplate, and tie the waistband of the *ephod* round his waist. 6 Then you will place the turban on his head, and on it put

the symbol of holy consecration. 7 You will then take the anointing oil and pour it on his head and so anoint him.

8 'Next, you will bring his sons and dress them in tunics, 9 and fasten waistbands round their waists and put the head-dresses on their heads. By perpetual decree the priesthood will be theirs. Then you will invest Aaron and his sons.

The offerings

10 'You will bring the bull in front of the Tent of Meeting, and Aaron and his sons will lay their hands on the bull's head. 11 You will then slaughter the bull before Yahweh at the entrance to the Tent of Meeting. 12 You will then take some of the bull's blood and with your finger put it on the horns of the altar. Next, pour out the rest of the blood at the foot of the altar. 13 And then take all the fat covering the entrails, the fatty mass over the liver, the two kidneys with their covering fat, and burn them on the altar. 14 But the young bull's flesh, its skin and its offal, you will burn outside the camp, for this is a sin offering.

15 'Next, you will take one of the rams, and Aaron and his sons will lay their hands on the ram's head. 16 You will then slaughter the ram, take its blood and pour it against the altar, all round. 17 Next, cut the ram into quarters, wash the entrails and legs and put them on the quarters and head. 18 Then burn the whole ram on the altar. This will be a burnt offering for Yahweh, a pleasing smell, a food offering burnt for Yahweh.

19 'Next, you will take the other ram, and Aaron and his sons will lay their hands on the ram's head. 20 You will then slaughter the ram, take some of its blood and put it on the lobe of Aaron's right ear, on the lobes of his sons' right ears, the thumbs of their right hands, and the big toes of their right feet, and pour the rest of the blood against the altar, all round. 21 You will then take some of the blood on the altar and some of the anointing oil, and sprinkle it on Aaron and his vestments and on his sons and on his sons' vestments: so that he and his

vestments will be consecrated and his sons too, and his sons' vestments.

The investiture of the priests

22 'You will then take the fatty parts of the ram: the tail, the fat covering the entrails, the fatty mass over the liver, the two kidneys with their covering fat and also the right thigh—for this is a ram of investiture— 23 and a loaf of bread, a cake of bread made with oil, and a wafer, from the basket of unleavened bread before Yahweh, 24 and put it all on the palms of Aaron and his sons, and make the gesture of offering before Yahweh. 25 Then you will take them back and burn them on the altar, on top of the burnt offering, as a smell pleasing before Yahweh, a food offering burnt for Yahweh.

26 'You will then take the forequarters of the ram of Aaron's investiture and with it make the gesture of offering before Yahweh; this will be your portion. 27 You will consecrate the forequarters that have been thus offered, as also the thigh that is set aside—what has been offered and what has been set aside from the ram of investiture of Aaron and his sons. 28 This, by perpetual decree, will be the portion that Aaron and his sons will receive from the Israelites, since it is the portion set aside, the portion set aside for Yahweh by the Israelites from their communion sacrifices: a portion set aside for Yahweh.

29 'Aaron's sacred vestments must pass to his sons after him, and they will wear them for their anointing and investiture. 30 Whichever of the sons of Aaron succeeds him in the priesthood and enters the Tent of Meeting to serve in the sanctuary, will wear them for seven days.

The sacred meal

31 'You will take the ram of investiture and cook its meat in a holy place. 32 Aaron and his sons will eat the meat of the ram and the bread which is in the basket, at the entrance to the Tent of Meeting. 33 They will eat what was used in making expiation for them at their in-

vesture and consecration. No unauthorised person may eat these; they are holy things. 34 If any of the meat from the investiture sacrifice, or the bread, should be left till morning, you will burn what is left. It may not be eaten; it is a holy thing. 35 This is what you will do for Aaron and his sons, implementing all the orders I have given you. You will take seven days over their investiture.

The consecration of the altar of burnt offerings

36 'On each of the days you will also offer a young bull as a sacrifice for sin, in expiation. You will offer a sin sacrifice for the altar when you make expiation for it; then you will consecrate it by anointing it. 37 For seven days you will make expiation for the altar, then you will consecrate it; it will then be especially holy, and whatever touches the altar will become holy.

The daily burnt offering

38 'This is what you must offer on the altar: two yearling male lambs each day in perpetuity. 39 The first lamb you will offer at dawn, and the second at twilight, 40 and with the first lamb, one-tenth of a measure of fine flour mixed with one-quarter of a *hin* of pounded olive oil and, for a libation, one-quarter of a *hin* of wine. 41 The second lamb you will offer at twilight, and do it with a similar cereal offering and libation as at dawn, as a pleasing smell, as an offering burnt for Yahweh, 42 a perpetual burnt offering for all your generations to come, at the entrance to the Tent of Meeting before Yahweh, where I shall meet you and speak to you.

43 'There I shall meet the Israelites in the place consecrated by my glory. 44 I shall consecrate the Tent of Meeting and the altar; I shall also consecrate Aaron and his sons, to be priests in my service. 45 And I shall live with the Israelites and be their God, 46 and they will know that I am Yahweh their God, who brought them out of Egypt to live among them: I, Yahweh their God.'

The altar of incense

30 'You will make an altar on which to burn incense; you will make it of acacia wood, 2 one cubit long, and one cubit wide—it must be square—and two cubits high; its horns must be of a piece with it. 3 You will overlay its top, its sides all round and its horns with pure gold and make a gold moulding to go all round. 4 You will make two gold rings for it below the moulding on its two opposite sides, to take the shafts used for carrying it. 5 You will make the shafts of acacia wood and overlay them with gold.

6 'You will put it in front of the curtain by the ark of Testimony, in front of the mercy-seat which is on the Testimony, where I shall meet you. 7 On it Aaron will burn fragrant incense each morning; when he trims the lamps, he will burn incense on it; 8 and when Aaron puts back the lamps at twilight, he will burn incense on it, incense perpetually before Yahweh for all your generations to come. 9 You will not offer unauthorised incense, or burnt offering, or cereal offering on it, and you will not pour any libation over it. 10 Once a year, Aaron will perform the rite of expiation on the horns of the altar; once a year, on the Day of Expiation, with the blood of the sacrifice for sin, he will make expiation for himself, for all your generations to come. It is especially holy for Yahweh.'

The poll tax

11 Yahweh then spoke to Moses and said, 12 'When you count the Israelites by census, each one of them must pay Yahweh a ransom for his life, to avoid any incidence of plague among them while you are holding the census. 13 Everyone subject to the census will pay half a shekel, reckoning by the sanctuary-shekel: twenty *gerah* to the shekel. This half-shekel will be set aside for Yahweh. 14 Everyone subject to the census, that is to say of twenty years and over, will pay the sum set aside for Yahweh. 15 The rich man must not give more, nor the poor man less, than half a shekel when he

pays the sum set aside for Yahweh in ransom for your lives. ¹⁶You will take the ransom money of the Israelites and apply it to the service of the Tent of Meeting, for it to be a reminder of the Israelites before Yahweh, as the ransom for your lives.'

The bronze basin

¹⁷Yahweh then spoke to Moses and said, ¹⁸'You will also make a bronze basin on its bronze stand, for washing. You will put it between the Tent of Meeting and the altar and put water in it, ¹⁹in which Aaron and his sons will wash their hands and feet. ²⁰Whenever they are to enter the Tent of Meeting, they will wash, to avoid incurring death; and whenever they approach the altar for their service, to burn an offering for Yahweh, ²¹they will wash their hands and feet, to avoid incurring death. This is a perpetual decree for him and his descendants for all their generations to come.'

The anointing oil

²²Yahweh spoke further to Moses and said, ²³'Take the finest spices: five hundred shekels of fresh myrrh, half as much (two hundred and fifty shekels) of fragrant cinnamon, two hundred and fifty shekels of scented reed, ²⁴five hundred shekels (reckoning by the sanctuary-shekel) of cassia, and one *hin* of olive oil. ²⁵You will make this into a holy anointing oil, such a blend as the perfumer might make; this will be a holy anointing oil. ²⁶With it you will anoint the Tent of Meeting and the ark of the Testimony, ²⁷the table and all its accessories, the lamp-stand and its accessories, the altar of incense, ²⁸the altar of burnt offerings and all its accessories, and the basin with its stand, ²⁹consecrating them, so that they will be especially holy and whatever touches them will become holy. ³⁰You will also anoint Aaron and his sons and consecrate them to be priests in my service. ³¹You will then speak to the Israelites and say, "This anointing oil will be holy for you for all your generations to come. ³²It must not be used for anointing the human body, nor may you make

any of the same mixture. It is a holy thing; you will regard it as holy. ³³Anyone who makes up the same oil or uses it on an unauthorised person will be outlawed from his people." '

The incense

³⁴Yahweh then said to Moses, 'Take sweet spices: storax, onycha, galbanum, sweet spices and pure frankincense in equal parts, ³⁵and compound an incense, such a blend as the perfumer might make, salted, pure, and holy. ³⁶You will grind some of this up very fine and put it in front of the Testimony in the Tent of Meeting, where I shall meet you. You will regard it as especially holy. ³⁷You may not make any incense of similar composition for your own use. You will regard it as holy, reserved for Yahweh. Anyone who makes up the same thing to use as perfume will be outlawed from his people.'

The craftsmen for the sanctuary

31 Yahweh then spoke to Moses and said, ²'Look, I have singled out Bezalel son of Uri, son of Hur, of the tribe of Judah, ³and have filled him with the spirit of God in wisdom, knowledge and skill in every kind of craft: ⁴in designing and carrying out work in gold and silver and bronze, ⁵in cutting stones to be set, in wood carving and in executing every kind of work. ⁶And to help him I have given him Oholiab son of Ahisamach, of the tribe of Dan, and have endowed the hearts of all the skilled men with the skill to make everything I have ordered you: ⁷the Tent of Meeting; the ark of the Testimony; the mercy-seat above it; and all the furniture of the tent; ⁸the table and all its accessories; the pure lamp-stand and all its equipment; the altar of incense; ⁹the altar of burnt offerings and all its accessories; the basin and its stand; ¹⁰the liturgical vestments, the sacred vestments for Aaron the priest, and the vestments for his sons, for their priestly functions; ¹¹the anointing oil and the fragrant incense for the sanctuary. They will do everything as I have ordered you.'

The Sabbath rest

[12] Yahweh then said to Moses, [13] 'Speak to the Israelites and say, "You will keep my Sabbaths properly, for this is a sign between myself and you for all your generations to come, so that you will know that it is I, Yahweh, who sanctify you. [14] You will keep the Sabbath, then; you will regard it as holy. Anyone who profanes it will be put to death; anyone who does any work on that day will be outlawed from his people. [15] Work must be done for six days, but the seventh day will be a day of complete rest, consecrated to Yahweh. Anyone who works on the Sabbath day will be put to death. [16] The Israelites will keep the Sabbath, observing the Sabbath for all their generations to come: this is an eternal covenant. [17] Between myself and the Israelites, this is a sign for ever, for in six days Yahweh made heaven and earth, but on the seventh day he rested and drew breath."'

The tablets of the Law committed to Moses

[18] When he had finished speaking to Moses on Mount Sinai, he gave him the two tablets of the Testimony, tablets of stone inscribed by the finger of God.

The golden calf [a]

32 When the people saw that Moses was a long time before coming down the mountain, they gathered round Aaron and said to him, 'Get to work, make us a god to go at our head; for that Moses, the man who brought us here from Egypt—we do not know what has become of him.' [2] Aaron replied, 'Strip off the gold rings in the ears of your wives and your sons and daughters, and bring them to me.' [3] The people all stripped off the gold rings from their ears and brought them to Aaron. [4] He received what they gave him, melted it down in a mould and with it made the statue of a calf. 'Israel,' the people shouted, 'here is your God who brought you here from Egypt!' [5] Observing this, Aaron built an altar before the statue and made this proclamation, 'Tomorrow will be a feast in Yahweh's honour.'

[6] Early next morning they sacrificed burnt offerings and brought communion sacrifices. The people then sat down to eat and drink, and afterwards got up to amuse themselves.

Moses forewarned by Yahweh

[7] Yahweh then said to Moses, 'Go down at once, for your people whom you brought here from Egypt have become corrupt. [8] They have quickly left the way which I ordered them to follow. They have cast themselves a metal calf, worshipped it and offered sacrifice to it, shouting, "Israel, here is your God who brought you here from Egypt!"' [9] Yahweh then said to Moses, 'I know these people; I know how obstinate they are! [10] So leave me now, so that my anger can blaze at them and I can put an end to them! I shall make a great nation out of you instead.'

The prayer of Moses

[11] Moses tried to pacify Yahweh his God. 'Yahweh,' he said, 'why should your anger blaze at your people, whom you have brought out of Egypt by your great power and mighty hand? [12] Why should the Egyptians say, "He brought them out with evil intention, to slaughter them in the mountains and wipe them off the face of the earth?" Give up your burning wrath; relent over this disaster intended for your people. [13] Remember your servants Abraham, Isaac and Jacob, to whom you swore by your very self and made this promise: "I shall make your offspring as numerous as the stars of heaven, and this whole country of which I have spoken, I shall give to your descendants, and it will be their heritage for ever."' [14] Yahweh then relented over the disaster which he had intended to inflict on his people.

Moses breaks the tablets of the Law

[15] Moses turned and came down the mountain with the two tablets of the Testimony in his

32a ‖ Dt 9:7seq.

hands, tablets inscribed on both sides, inscribed on the front and on the back. ¹⁶ The tablets were the work of God, and the writing on them was God's writing, engraved on the tablets.

¹⁷ When Joshua heard the noise of the people shouting, he said to Moses, 'There is the sound of battle in the camp!' ¹⁸ But he replied:

No song of victory is this sound,
no lament for defeat this sound;
but answering choruses I hear!

¹⁹ And there, as he approached the camp, he saw the calf and the groups dancing. Moses blazed with anger. He threw down the tablets he was holding, shattering them at the foot of the mountain. ²⁰ He seized the calf they had made and burned it, grinding it into powder which he scattered on the water, and made the Israelites drink it. ²¹ Moses then said to Aaron, 'What have these people done to you for you to have brought so great a sin on them?' ²² Aaron replied, 'My lord should not be so angry. You yourself know what a bad state these people are in! ²³ They said to me, "Make us a god to go at our head; for that Moses, the man who brought us here from Egypt—we do not know what has become of him." ²⁴ I then said to them, "Anyone with gold, strip it off!" They gave it to me. I threw it into the fire and out came this calf!'

The zeal of the Levites

²⁵ When Moses saw that the people were out of hand—for Aaron had let them get out of hand to the derision of their enemies all round them— ²⁶ Moses then stood at the gate of the camp and shouted, 'Who is for Yahweh? To me!' And all the Levites rallied round him. ²⁷ He said to them, 'Yahweh, God of Israel, says this, "Buckle on your sword, each of you, and go up and down the camp from gate to gate, every man of you slaughtering brother, friend and neighbour." ' ²⁸ The Levites did as Moses said, and of the people about three thousand men perished that day. ²⁹ 'Today', Moses said, 'you have consecrated yourselves to Yahweh, one at the cost of his son, another of his brother; and so he bestows a blessing on you today.'

Moses prays again

³⁰ On the following day Moses said to the people, 'You have committed a great sin. But now I shall go up to Yahweh: perhaps I can secure expiation for your sin.' ³¹ Moses then went back to Yahweh and said, 'Oh, this people has committed a great sin by making themselves a god of gold. ³² And yet, if it pleased you to forgive their sin . . . ! If not, please blot me out of the book you have written!' ³³ Yahweh said to Moses, 'Those who have sinned against me are the ones I shall blot out of my book. ³⁴ So now go and lead the people to the place I promised to you. My angel will indeed go at your head but, on the day of punishment, I shall punish them for their sin.' ³⁵ And Yahweh punished the people for having made the calf, the one Aaron had made.

The Israelites ordered to depart

33 Yahweh then said to Moses, 'Leave, move on from here, you and the people whom you have brought here from Egypt, to the country that I swore to Abraham, Isaac and Jacob that I would give to their descendants. ² I shall send an angel in front of you and drive out the Canaanites, the Amorites, the Hittites, the Perizzites, the Hivites and the Jebusites. ³ Move on towards a country flowing with milk and honey, but I myself shall not be going with you or I might annihilate you on the way, for you are an obstinate people.' ⁴ On hearing these stern words the people went into mourning and no one wore his ornaments.

⁵ Yahweh then said to Moses, 'Say to the Israelites, "You are an obstinate people. If I were to go with you even for a moment, I should annihilate you. So now take off your ornaments, and then I shall decide how to deal with you!" ' ⁶ So, from Mount Horeb onwards, the

Israelites stripped themselves of their ornaments.

The Tent

7 Moses used to take the Tent and pitch it outside the camp, far away from the camp. He called it the Tent of Meeting. Anyone who wanted to consult Yahweh would go out to the Tent of Meeting, outside the camp. 8 Whenever Moses went out to the Tent, the people would all stand up and every man would stand at the door of his tent and watch Moses until he went into the Tent. 9 And whenever Moses went into the Tent, the pillar of cloud would come down and station itself at the entrance to the Tent, while Yahweh spoke with Moses. 10 The people could all see the pillar of cloud stationed at the entrance to the Tent and the people would all stand up and bow low, each at the door of his tent. 11 Yahweh would talk to Moses face to face, as a man talks to his friend, and afterwards he would come back to the camp, but the young man who was his servant, Joshua son of Nun, never left the inside of the Tent.

Moses prays

12 Moses said to Yahweh, 'Look, you say to me, "Make the people move on," but you have not told me whom you are going to send with me, although you have said, "I know you by name and you enjoy my favour." 13 If indeed I enjoy your favour, please show me your ways, so that I understand you and continue to enjoy your favour; consider too that this nation is your people.' 14 Yahweh then said, 'I myself shall go with you and I shall give you rest.' 15 To which he said, 'If you do not come yourself, do not make us move on from here, 16 for how can it be known that I and my people enjoy your favour, if not by your coming with us? By this we shall be marked out, I and your people, from all the peoples on the face of the earth.' 17 Yahweh then said to Moses, 'Again I shall do what you have asked, because you enjoy my favour and because I know you by name.'

Moses on the mountain

18 He then said, 'Please show me your glory.' 19 Yahweh said, 'I shall make all my goodness pass before you, and before you I shall pronounce the name Yahweh; and I am gracious to those to whom I am gracious and I take pity on those on whom I take pity. 20 But my face', he said, 'you cannot see, for no human being can see me and survive.' 21 Then Yahweh said, 'Here is a place near me. You will stand on the rock, 22 and when my glory passes by, I shall put you in a cleft of the rock and shield you with my hand until I have gone past. 23 Then I shall take my hand away and you will see my back; but my face will not be seen.'

The covenant renewed; the tablets of the Law

34 Yahweh said to Moses, 'Cut two tablets of stone like the first ones and come up to me on the mountain, and I will write on the tablets the words that were on the first tablets, which you broke. 2 Be ready at dawn; at dawn come up Mount Sinai and wait for me there at the top of the mountain. 3 No one may come up with you, no one may be seen anywhere on the mountain; the flocks and herds may not even graze in front of this mountain.' 4 So he cut two tablets of stone like the first and, with the two tablets of stone in his hands, Moses went up Mount Sinai in the early morning as Yahweh had ordered. 5 And Yahweh descended in a cloud and stood with him there and pronounced the name Yahweh.

God appears

6 Then Yahweh passed before him and called out, 'Yahweh, Yahweh, God of tenderness and compassion, slow to anger, rich in faithful love and constancy, 7 maintaining his faithful love to thousands, forgiving fault, crime and sin, yet letting nothing go unchecked, and punishing the parent's fault in the children and in the grandchildren to the third and fourth generation!' 8 Moses immediately bowed to the ground in worship, 9 then he said, 'If indeed I

12 READ EXODUS 33:12–23.

Yahweh said, "I shall make all my goodness pass before you."—EXODUS 33:19

THE WAYS WE CONTEMPLATE GOD

We contemplate God in a variety of ways. For we not only discover God by admiring his incomprehensible essence . . . but we see him through the greatness of his creation, the consideration of his justice, and the aid of his daily providence. We see him: when with pure minds we contemplate what he has done with his saints in every generation; when with trembling heart we admire his power with which he governs, directs, and rules all things, or the vastness of his knowledge, and that eye of his from which no secrets of the heart can lie hid; . . . when in our wonder we think that the drops of rain, the days and hours of the ages, and all things past and future are present to his knowledge; when we gaze in unbounded admiration on that ineffable mercy of his, which with unwearied patience endures countless sins which are every moment being committed under his very eyes. . . .

We also contemplate God when we realize that he made us be born in such a way so that from our very cradles his grace and the knowledge of his law might be given to us. And that overcoming our enemy in us simply for the pleasure of his good will, he rewards us with eternal bliss and everlasting blessings; and lastly that he undertook the dispensation of his Incarnation for our salvation, and extended the marvels of his sacraments to all nations.

But there are numberless other considerations of this sort, . . . by which God is either seen by pure eyes or embraced. Certainly no one will preserve such considerations lastingly, if anything of carnal affections still survives in him, because "you can not," says the Lord, "see my face; for no human being shall see me and live," that is, live attached to this world and to earthly affections.

ST. JOHN CASSIAN, 360?–433?

YOU WILL FIND THE NEXT READING AT LEVITICUS 16.

do enjoy your favour, please, my Lord, come with us, although they are an obstinate people; and forgive our faults and sins, and adopt us as your heritage.'

The covenant

¹⁰He then said, 'Look, I am now making a covenant: I shall work such wonders at the head of your whole people as have never been worked in any other country or nation, and all the people round you will see what Yahweh can do, for what I shall do through you will be awe-inspiring. ¹¹Mark, then, what I command you today. I am going to drive out the Amorites, the Canaanites, the Hittites, the Perizzites, the Hivites and the Jebusites before you. ¹²Take care you make no pact with the inhabitants of the country which you are about to enter, or they will prove a snare in your community. ¹³You will tear down their altars, smash their cultic stones and cut down their sacred poles, ¹⁴for you will worship no other god, since Yahweh's name is the Jealous One; he is a jealous God. ¹⁵Make no pact with the inhabitants of the country or, when they prostitute themselves to their own gods and sacrifice to them, they will invite you and you will partake of their sacrifice, ¹⁶and then you

will choose wives for your sons from among their daughters, and their daughters, prostituting themselves to their own gods, will induce your sons to prostitute themselves to their gods.

¹⁷'You will not cast metal gods for yourself.

¹⁸'You will observe the feast of Unleavened Bread. For seven days you will eat unleavened bread, as I have commanded you, at the appointed time in the month of Abib, for in the month of Abib you came out of Egypt.

¹⁹'All that first issues from the womb belongs to me: every male, every first-born of flock or herd. ²⁰But the first-born donkey you will redeem with an animal from the flock; if you do not redeem it, you must break its neck. All the first-born of your sons you will redeem, and no one will appear before me empty-handed.

²¹'For six days you will labour, but on the seventh day you will rest; you will stop work even during ploughing and harvesting.

²²'You will observe the feast of Weeks, of the first-fruits of the wheat harvest, and the feast of Ingathering at the close of the year.

²³'Three times a year all your menfolk will appear before Lord Yahweh, God of Israel, ²⁴for I shall dispossess the nations before you and extend your frontiers, and no one will set his heart on your territory when you go away to appear before Yahweh your God three times a year.

²⁵'You will not offer the blood of my sacrificial victim with leavened bread, nor is the victim offered at the feast of Passover to be left until the following day.

²⁶'You will bring the best of the first-fruits of your soil to the house of Yahweh your God.

'You will not boil a kid in its mother's milk.'

²⁷Yahweh then said to Moses, 'Put these words in writing, for they are the terms of the covenant which I have made with you and with Israel.'

²⁸He stayed there with Yahweh for forty days and forty nights, eating and drinking nothing, and on the tablets he wrote the words of the covenant—the Ten Words.

Moses comes down from the mountain

²⁹When Moses came down from Mount Sinai with the two tablets of the Testimony in his hands, as he was coming down the mountain, Moses did not know that the skin of his face was radiant because he had been talking to him. ³⁰And when Aaron and all the Israelites saw Moses, the skin on his face was so radiant that they were afraid to go near him. ³¹But Moses called to them, and Aaron and all the leaders of the community rejoined him, and Moses talked to them, ³²after which all the Israelites came closer, and he passed on to them all the orders that Yahweh had given to him on Mount Sinai. ³³Once Moses had finished speaking to them, he put a veil over his face. ³⁴Whenever Moses went into Yahweh's presence to speak with him, he took the veil off until he came out. And when he came out, he would tell the Israelites what orders he had been given, ³⁵and the Israelites would see Moses' face radiant. Then Moses would put the veil back over his face until he went in to speak to him next time.

The Sabbath rest

35 Moses assembled the whole community of Israelites and said, 'These are the things Yahweh has ordered to be done: ²Work must be done for six days, but the seventh must be a holy day for you, a day of complete rest, in honour of Yahweh. Anyone who does any work on that day will be put to death. ³You will not light a fire on the Sabbath day in any of your homes.'

The materials are collected

⁴Moses spoke to the whole community of Israelites. 'This', he said, 'is what Yahweh has ordered: ⁵Set aside a contribution for Yahweh out of your possessions. Everyone whose heart prompts him to do so should bring a contribution for Yahweh: gold, silver and bronze; ⁶materials dyed violet-purple, red-purple and crimson, finely woven linen, goats' hair, ⁷rams' skins dyed red, fine leather, acacia wood, ⁸oil

for the light, spices for the anointing oil and for the fragrant incense; 9cornelian and other stones to be set in the *ephod* and breastplate. 10 And all those of you who have the skill must come and make everything that Yahweh has ordered: 11the Dwelling, its tent and its covering, its clasps and its frames, its crossbars, its pillars and its sockets; 12the ark, its shafts and all its accessories, the mercy-seat and the screening curtain; 13the table, its shafts and all its accessories, and the loaves of permanent offering; 14the lamp-stand for the light, its accessories, its lamps, and the oil for the light; 15the altar of incense and its shafts, the anointing oil, the fragrant incense, and the screen for the entrance, for the entrance of the tent; 16the altar of burnt offerings and its bronze grating, its shafts, and all its accessories; the basin and its stand; 17the curtaining for the court, its poles, its sockets, and the screen for the entrance to the court; 18the pegs for the Dwelling and the pegs for the court, and their cords; 19the liturgical vestments for service in the sanctuary—the sacred vestments for Aaron the priest, and the vestments for his sons, for their priestly functions.'

20 The whole community of Israelites then withdrew from Moses' presence. 21 And all those whose heart stirred them and all those whose spirit prompted them brought a contribution for Yahweh, for the work on the Tent of Meeting, for its general service and for the sacred vestments. 22 Men and women, they came, all those whose heart prompted them, bringing brooches, rings, bracelets, necklaces, golden objects of every kind—all those who had vowed gold to Yahweh, 23 while all those who happened to own violet-purple, red-purple or crimson materials, finely woven linen, goats' hair, rams' skins dyed red, or fine leather, brought that. 24 All those offering a contribution of silver or bronze brought their contribution for Yahweh and all who happened to own acacia wood, suitable for any of the work to be done, brought that. 25 All the skilled women set their hands to spinning, and brought what they had spun: violet-purple,

red-purple or crimson materials, and fine linen, 26 while all those women whose heart stirred them by virtue of their skill, spun goats' hair. 27 The leaders brought cornelians and other stones to be set in the *ephod* and breastplate, 28 and the spices and oil for the light, for the anointing oil and for the fragrant incense. 29 All those Israelites, men and women, whose heart prompted them to contribute to the entire work that Yahweh had ordered through Moses to be done, brought a contribution to Yahweh.

The craftsmen for the sanctuary

30 Moses then said to the Israelites, 'Look, Yahweh has singled out Bezalel son of Uri, son of Hur, of the tribe of Judah, 31 and has filled him with the spirit of God in wisdom, knowledge and skill in every kind of craft: 32 in designing and carrying out work in gold and silver and bronze, 33 in cutting stones to be set, in wood carving and in executing every kind of work. 34 And on him and on Oholiab son of Ahisamach, of the tribe of Dan, he has bestowed the gift of teaching, 35 and filled them with the skill to carry out every kind of work, that of the engraver, that of the embroiderer, that of the needleworker in violet-purple, red-purple and crimson materials and fine linen, that of the weaver, and indeed that of every kind of craftsman and designer.'

36 'Bezalel, Oholiab and all the men whom Yahweh has endowed with the skill and knowledge to know how to carry out all the work to be done on the sanctuary, will do exactly as Yahweh has ordered.'

A halt is called to the collection

2 Moses then summoned Bezalel, Oholiab and all the skilled men whose hearts Yahweh had endowed with skill, all whose heart stirred them to come forward and do the work. 3 From Moses they received everything that the Israelites had brought as contributions for carrying out the work of building the sanctuary, and, as they went on bringing their offer-

ings every morning, ⁴the skilled men who were doing all the work for the sanctuary, all left their particular work ⁵and said to Moses, 'The people are bringing more than is needed for the work Yahweh has ordered to be done.' ⁶Moses then gave the order and proclamation was made throughout the camp, 'No one, whether man or woman, must do anything more towards contributing for the sanctuary.' So the people were prevented from bringing any more, ⁷for the material to hand was enough, and more than enough, to complete all the work.

The Dwelling

⁸All the most skilled of the men doing the work made the Dwelling. Moses made it with ten sheets of finely woven linen, dyed violet-purple, red-purple and crimson and embroidered with great winged creatures. ⁹The length of a single sheet was twenty-eight cubits, its width four cubits, all the sheets being of the same size. ¹⁰He joined five of the sheets to one another, and the other five sheets to one another. ¹¹He made violet loops along the edge of the first sheet, at the end of the set, and did the same along the edge of the last sheet in the other set. ¹²He made fifty loops on the first sheet and fifty loops along the outer edge of the sheet of the second set, the loops corresponding to one another. ¹³He made fifty gold clasps and joined the sheets together with the clasps. In this way the Dwelling was a unified whole.

¹⁴Next he made sheets of goats' hair for the tent over the Dwelling; he made eleven of these. ¹⁵The length of a single sheet was thirty cubits and its width four cubits; the eleven sheets were all of the same size. ¹⁶He joined five sheets together into one set and six sheets into another. ¹⁷He made fifty loops along the edge of the last sheet of the first set, and fifty loops along the edge of the sheet of the second set. ¹⁸He made fifty bronze clasps, to draw the tent together and make it a unified whole. ¹⁹And for the tent he made a cover of rams' skins dyed red, and a cover of fine leather over that.

The framework

²⁰For the Dwelling he made vertical frames of acacia wood. ²¹Each frame was ten cubits long and one and a half cubits wide. ²²Each frame had twin tenons; this was how he made all the frames for the Dwelling. ²³He made frames for the Dwelling: twenty frames for the south side, to the south, ²⁴and made forty silver sockets under the twenty frames, two sockets under one frame for its two tenons, two sockets under the next frame for its two tenons; ²⁵and for the other side of the Dwelling, the north side, twenty frames ²⁶and forty silver sockets, two sockets under one frame, two sockets under the next frame. ²⁷For the back of the Dwelling, on the west, he made six frames. ²⁸He also made two frames for the corners at the back of the Dwelling; ²⁹these were coupled together at the bottom, staying so up to the top, to the level of the first ring; this he did with the two frames forming the two corners. ³⁰Thus there were eight frames with their sixteen silver sockets; two sockets under each frame. ³¹He made crossbars of acacia wood: five for the frames of the first side of the Dwelling, ³²five crossbars for the frames of the other side of the Dwelling and five crossbars for the frames which formed the back of the Dwelling, to the west. ³³He made the middle bar, to join the frames from one end to the other, halfway up. ³⁴He overlaid the frames with gold, made gold rings for them, through which to place the crossbars, and overlaid the crossbars with gold.

The curtain

³⁵He made a curtain of finely woven linen, dyed violet-purple, red-purple and crimson and embroidered with great winged creatures, ³⁶and for it he made four poles of acacia wood, overlaying them with gold, with golden hooks for them, for which he cast four sockets of silver. ³⁷For the entrance to the tent he made a screen of finely woven linen embroidered with violet-purple, red-purple and crimson, ³⁸as also the five columns for it and their

hooks; he overlaid their capitals and rods with gold, but their five sockets were of bronze.

The ark

37 Bezalel made the ark of acacia wood, two and a half cubits long, one and a half cubits wide and one and a half cubits high. ²He overlaid it, inside and out, with pure gold, and made a gold moulding all round it. ³He cast four gold rings for it at its four supports: two rings on one side and two rings on the other. ⁴He also made shafts of acacia wood and overlaid them with gold, ⁵and passed the shafts through the rings on the sides of the ark, by which to carry it. ⁶He also made a mercy-seat of pure gold, two and a half cubits long and one and a half cubits wide, ⁷and modelled two great winged creatures of beaten gold, putting them at the two ends of the mercy-seat, ⁸one winged creature at one end and the other winged creature at the other end, making the winged creatures of a piece with the mercy-seat at either end. ⁹The winged creatures had their wings spread upwards, protecting the ark with their wings and facing each other, their faces being towards the mercy-seat.

The table for the loaves of permanent offering

¹⁰He made the table of acacia wood, two cubits long, one cubit wide and one and a half cubits high, ¹¹and made a gold moulding all round it. ¹²He fitted it with struts a hand's breadth wide and made a gold moulding round the struts. ¹³He cast four gold rings for it and fixed the rings at the four corners where the four legs were. ¹⁴The rings lay close to the struts to hold the shafts for carrying the table. ¹⁵He made the shafts of acacia wood and overlaid them with gold; these were for carrying the table. ¹⁶He made the accessories which were to go on the table: its dishes, cups, jars and libation bowls, of pure gold.

The lamp-stand

¹⁷He also made the lamp-stand of pure gold, making the lamp-stand, base and stem, of beaten gold, its cups, calyxes and bud being of a piece with it. ¹⁸Six branches sprang from its sides: three of the lamp-stand's branches from one side, three of the lamp-stand's branches from the other. ¹⁹The first branch carried three cups shaped like almond blossoms, each with its calyx and bud; the second branch, too, carried three cups shaped like almond blossoms, each with its calyx and bud, and similarly all six branches springing from the lamp-stand. ²⁰The lamp-stand itself carried four cups shaped like almond blossoms, each with its calyx and bud: ²¹one calyx under the first two branches springing from the lamp-stand, one calyx under the next pair of branches and one calyx under the last pair of branches—thus for all six branches springing from the lamp-stand. ²²The calyxes and the branches were of a piece with the lamp-stand, and the whole was made from a single piece of pure gold, beaten out. ²³He also made its seven lamps, its snuffers and trays of pure gold. ²⁴He made the lamp-stand and all its accessories from a talent of pure gold.

The altar of incense; the anointing oil and incense

²⁵He made the altar of incense of acacia wood, one cubit long, and one cubit wide—it was square—and two cubits high, its horns were of a piece with it. ²⁶He overlaid its top, its sides all round and its horns with pure gold and made a moulding to go all round. ²⁷He made two gold rings for it below the moulding on its two opposite sides, to take the shafts used for carrying it. ²⁸He made the shafts of acacia wood and overlaid them with gold. ²⁹He also made the holy anointing oil and the fragrant incense, blending it as a perfumer would.

The altar of burnt offerings

38 He made the altar of burnt offerings of acacia wood, five cubits long and five cubits wide; it was square and three cubits high. ²At its four corners he made horns, the horns being of a piece with it, and overlaid it with bronze. ³He made all the altar accessories: the ash pans, shovels, sprinkling basins, hooks and fire pans; he made all the altar accessories of bronze. ⁴He also made a grating for the altar of bronze network, below its ledge, underneath, coming halfway up. ⁵He cast four rings for the four corners of the bronze grating to take the shafts. ⁶He made the shafts of acacia wood and overlaid them with bronze. ⁷He passed the shafts through the rings on the sides of the altar for carrying it. He made the altar hollow, out of boards.

The bronze basin

⁸He made the bronze basin and its bronze stand from the mirrors of the women who served at the entrance to the Tent of Meeting.

The court

⁹He made the court. On the south side, on the south, the curtaining of the court was of finely woven linen a hundred cubits long. ¹⁰Its twenty poles and their sockets being of bronze, and their hooks and rods of silver; ¹¹and on the north side, a hundred cubits of curtaining, its twenty poles and their twenty sockets being of bronze, and their hooks and rods of silver. ¹²On the west side there were fifty cubits of curtaining, with its ten poles and their ten sockets, the poles' hooks and rods being of silver; ¹³and on the east side on the east, there were fifty cubits. ¹⁴On the one side there were fifteen cubits of curtaining, with its three poles and their three sockets, ¹⁵and on the other side—either side of the gateway to the court—there were fifteen cubits of curtaining with its three poles and their three sockets. ¹⁶All the curtaining round the court was of finely woven linen, ¹⁷the sockets for the poles were of bronze, the poles' hooks and rods of silver, their capitals were overlaid with silver and all the poles of the court had silver rods. ¹⁸The screen for the gateway to the court was of finely woven linen embroidered with violet-purple, red-purple and crimson, twenty cubits long and five cubits high (all the way along) like the curtaining of the court, ¹⁹its four poles and their four sockets being of bronze, their hooks of silver, their capitals overlaid with silver, and their rods of silver. ²⁰All the pegs round the Dwelling and the court were of bronze.

The amount of metal used

²¹These are the accounts for the Dwelling—the Dwelling of the Testimony—drawn up by order of Moses, the work of Levites, produced by Ithamar son of Aaron, the priest.

²²Bezalel son of Uri, son of Hur, of the tribe of Judah, made everything that Yahweh ordered Moses to make, ²³his assistant being Oholiab son of Ahisamach, of the tribe of Dan, an engraver, embroiderer and needleworker in violet-purple, red-purple and crimson materials and fine linen.

²⁴The amount of gold used for the work, for the entire work for the sanctuary (the gold consecrated for the purpose) was twenty-nine talents and seven hundred and thirty shekels, reckoned by the sanctuary-shekel. ²⁵The silver from the census of the community was one hundred talents and one thousand seven hundred and seventy-five shekels, reckoned by the sanctuary-shekel, ²⁶one *beqa* per head, half a shekel reckoned by the sanctuary-shekel, for everyone of twenty years and over included in the census, for six hundred and three thousand five hundred and fifty persons. ²⁷A hundred talents of silver were used for casting the sockets for the sanctuary and the sockets for the curtain: a hundred sockets from a hundred talents, one talent per socket. ²⁸From the one thousand seven hundred and seventy-five shekels he made the hooks for the poles, overlaid their capitals and made the rods for them. ²⁹The bronze consecrated for the purpose amounted to seventy talents and two thousand four hundred shekels, ³⁰and from it he made the sockets for the entrance of the Tent of Meeting, the bronze altar, its bronze grating and all the altar accessories, ³¹the sockets all round the court, the sockets for the gateway to the court, all the pegs for the Dwelling and all the pegs round the court.

The vestments of the high priest

39 From the violet-purple, red-purple and crimson materials, they made the liturgical vestments for service in the sanctuary. They made the sacred vestments for Aaron, as Yahweh had ordered Moses.

The ephod

² They made the *ephod* of gold, of violet-purple, red-purple and crimson materials and finely woven linen. ³ They beat gold into thin plates and cut these into threads to work into the violet-purple, red-purple and crimson materials and the fine linen by needlework. ⁴ For the *ephod* they made shoulder-straps which were joined to it at its two edges. ⁵ The waistband on the *ephod* to hold it in position, was of a piece with it and of the same workmanship: of gold, violet-purple, red-purple and finely woven linen, as Yahweh had ordered Moses. ⁶ They worked the cornelians, mounted in gold setting, and engraved, like an engraved seal, with the names of the sons of Israel, ⁷ and put the stones on the shoulder-straps of the *ephod,* to commemorate the sons of Israel, as Yahweh had ordered Moses.

The breastplate of judgement

⁸ They made the breastplate of the same embroidered work as the *ephod*: of gold, violet-purple, red-purple and crimson materials and finely woven linen. ⁹ It was square and doubled over, a span in length and a span in width. ¹⁰ In it they set four rows of stones: a sard, a topaz and an emerald, for the first row; ¹¹ for the second row, a garnet, a sapphire and a diamond; ¹² for the third row, a hyacinth, a ruby and an amethyst; ¹³ and for the fourth row, a beryl, a cornelian and a jasper: mounted in gold settings, ¹⁴ the stones corresponding to the names of the sons of Israel, twelve like their names, engraved like seals, each with the name of one of the twelve tribes. ¹⁵ For the breastplate they made chains of pure gold twisted like cords, ¹⁶ and they made two gold rosettes and two gold rings, putting the two rings on the two outside edges of the breastplate ¹⁷ and fastening the two gold cords to the two rings on the outside edges of the breastplate. ¹⁸ The other two ends of the cords they fastened to the two rosettes, putting these on the shoulder-straps of the *ephod,* on the front. ¹⁹ They also made two gold rings and put them on the two outside edges of the breastplate, on the inner side, against the *ephod;* ²⁰ and they made two more gold rings and put them low down on the front of the two shoulder-straps of the *ephod,* close to the join, above the waistband of the *ephod.* ²¹ They secured the pectoral by a violet-purple cord passed through its rings and those of the *ephod,* so that the pectoral would sit above the waistband and not come apart from the *ephod,* as Yahweh had ordered Moses.

The robe

²² They made the robe of the *ephod* woven entirely of violet-purple. ²³ The opening in the centre of the robe was like the neck of a coat of mail; round the opening was a border, so that it would not get torn. ²⁴ On the lower hem of the robe, they made pomegranates of violet-purple, red-purple and crimson and finely woven linen, ²⁵ and made bells of pure gold, putting the bells between the pomegranates all round the lower hem of the robe: ²⁶ alternately, a bell and then a pomegranate, all round the lower hem of the robe of office, as Yahweh had ordered Moses.

The vestments of the priests

²⁷ They made the tunics of finely woven linen for Aaron and his sons, ²⁸ the turban of fine linen, the head-dresses of fine linen, the breeches of finely woven linen, ²⁹ the waistbands of finely woven linen embroidered with violet-purple, red-purple and crimson, as Yahweh had ordered Moses.

³⁰ They also made the flower—the symbol of holy consecration—of pure gold and on it, like an engraved seal, they engraved, 'Consecrated to Yahweh'. ³¹ They put it on a violet-

purple cord, to fasten it high up on the turban, as Yahweh had ordered Moses.

32 So all the work for the Dwelling, for the Tent of Meeting, was completed. They had done everything exactly as Yahweh had ordered Moses.

The finished work presented to Moses

33 They then brought Moses the Dwelling, the Tent and all its accessories: its clasps, frames, crossbars, poles and sockets; 34 the cover of rams' skins dyed red, the cover of fine leather and the screening curtain; 35 the ark of the Testimony and its shafts, and the mercy-seat; 36 the table, all its accessories and the loaves of permanent offering; 37 the lamp-stand of pure gold, its lamps—the array of lamps—and all its accessories, and the oil for the light; 38 the golden altar, the anointing oil, the fragrant incense and the screen for the entrance to the tent; 39 the bronze altar and its bronze grating, its shafts and all its accessories; the basin and its stand; 40 the curtaining for the court, its poles, its sockets, and the screen for the gateway to the court, its cords, its pegs and all the accessories for the service of the Dwelling, for the Tent of Meeting; 41 the liturgical vestments for officiating in the sanctuary—the sacred vestments for Aaron the priest, and the vestments for his sons—for the priestly functions. 42 The Israelites had done all the work exactly as Yahweh had ordered Moses.

43 Moses inspected all the work: they had indeed done it as Yahweh had ordered; and Moses blessed them.

The sanctuary erected and consecrated

40 Yahweh then spoke to Moses and said, 2 'On the first day of the first month, you will erect the Dwelling, the Tent of Meeting, 3 and place the ark of the Testimony in it and screen the ark with the curtain. 4 You will then bring in the table and arrange what has to be arranged on it. You will then bring in the lamp-stand and set up its lamps. 5 You will place the golden altar of incense in front of the ark of the Testimony, and place the screen at the entrance to the Dwelling. 6 You will place the altar of burnt offerings in front of the entrance to the Dwelling, the Tent of Meeting, 7 and you will place the basin between the Tent of Meeting and the altar, and fill it with water. 8 You will then set up the surrounding court and hang the screen at the gateway of the court. 9 Then, taking the anointing oil, you will anoint the Dwelling and everything inside, consecrating it and all its accessories; it will then be holy. 10 You will then anoint the altar of burnt offerings and all its accessories, consecrating the altar; the altar will then be especially holy. 11 You will then anoint the basin and its stand, and consecrate it. 12 You will then bring Aaron and his sons to the entrance of the Tent of Meeting, bathe them thoroughly 13 and then dress Aaron in the sacred vestments, and anoint and consecrate him, to serve me in the priesthood. 14 You will then bring his sons, dress them in tunics 15 and anoint them as you anointed their father, to serve me in the priesthood. Their anointing will confer an everlasting priesthood on them for all their generations to come.'

The divine commands are carried out

16 Moses did this; he did exactly as Yahweh had ordered him. 17 On the first day of the first month in the second year the Dwelling was erected. 18 Moses erected the Dwelling. He fixed its sockets, set up its frames, put its crossbars in position and set up its poles. 19 He spread the tent over the Dwelling and the covering for the tent over that, as Yahweh had ordered Moses. 20 He took the Testimony and put it in the ark, positioned the shafts on the ark and put the mercy-seat on top of the ark. 21 He brought the ark into the Dwelling and put the screening curtain in place, screening the ark of the Testimony, as Yahweh had ordered Moses. 22 He put the table inside the Tent of Meeting, against the side of the Dwelling, on the north, outside the curtain, 23 and on it arranged the loaves before Yahweh, as Yahweh had ordered Moses. 24 He put the lamp-stand inside the Tent of Meeting,

opposite the table, on the south side of the Dwelling, 25 and set up the lamps before Yahweh, as Yahweh had ordered Moses. 26 He put the golden altar inside the Tent of Meeting, in front of the curtain, 27 and on it burnt fragrant incense, as Yahweh had ordered Moses. 28 He then put the screen at the entrance to the Dwelling. 29 He put the altar of burnt offerings at the entrance to the Dwelling, to the Tent of Meeting, and on it offered the burnt offering and cereal offering, as Yahweh had ordered Moses. 30 He put the basin between the Tent of Meeting and the altar and put water in it for the ablutions, 31 where Moses, Aaron and his sons washed their hands and feet, 32 whenever they entered the Tent of Meeting or approached the altar they washed, as Yahweh had ordered Moses. 33 He then set up the court round the Dwelling and the altar and set up the screen at the gateway to the court. Thus Moses completed the work.

Yahweh takes possession of the sanctuary

34 The cloud then covered the Tent of Meeting and the glory of Yahweh filled the Dwelling. 35 Moses could not enter the Tent of Meeting, since the cloud stayed over it and the glory of Yahweh filled the Dwelling.

The cloud guides the Israelites

36 At every stage of their journey, whenever the cloud rose from the Dwelling, the Israelites would resume their march. 37 If the cloud did not rise, they would not resume their march until the day it did rise. 38 For Yahweh's cloud stayed over the Dwelling during the daytime and there was fire inside the cloud at night, for the whole House of Israel to see, at every stage of their journey.

LEVITICUS

The burnt offering

1 Yahweh summoned Moses and, speaking to him from the Tent of Meeting, said, ²'Speak to the Israelites; say to them, "When any of you brings an offering to Yahweh, he can offer an animal either from the herd or from the flock.

³"If his offering is to be a burnt offering from the herd, he must offer an unblemished male; he will offer it at the entrance to the Tent of Meeting, to make it acceptable to Yahweh. ⁴He must lay his hand on the victim's head, and it will be accepted as effectual for his expiation. ⁵He will then slaughter the bull before Yahweh, and the priests descended from Aaron will offer the blood. They will pour it all around the altar which stands at the entrance to the Tent of Meeting. ⁶He will then skin the victim and quarter it. ⁷The priests descended from Aaron will put a fire on the altar and arrange wood on the fire. ⁸The priests descended from Aaron will then arrange the quarters, the head and the fat on the wood on the fire on the altar. ⁹He will wash the entrails and shins in water, and the priest will burn it all on the altar as a burnt offering, food burnt as a smell pleasing to Yahweh.

¹⁰"If his offering is to be of an animal from the flock, of a lamb or a goat to be offered as a burnt offering, he must offer an unblemished male. ¹¹He will slaughter it on the north side of the altar, before Yahweh, and the priests descended from Aaron will pour the blood all around the altar. ¹²He will then quarter it, and the priest will arrange the quarters, the head and the fat on the wood on the fire on the altar. ¹³He will wash the entrails and shins in water,

and the priest will burn it all on the altar as a burnt offering, food burnt as a smell pleasing to Yahweh.

¹⁴"If his offering to Yahweh is to be a burnt offering of a bird, he must offer a turtledove or a young pigeon. ¹⁵The priest will offer it at the altar and wring off its head, which he will burn on the altar; its blood must then be squeezed out on the side of the altar. ¹⁶He will then remove the crop and the feathers and throw them on the eastern side of the altar, where the fatty ashes are put. ¹⁷He will then split it in half with a wing on each side, but without separating the two parts. The priest will then burn it on the altar, on the wood which is on the fire, as a burnt offering, food burnt as a smell pleasing to Yahweh." '

The cereal offering

2 ' "If anyone offers Yahweh a cereal offering, his offering must consist of wheaten flour on which he must pour wine and put incense. ²He will bring it to the priests descended from Aaron; he will take a handful of the wheaten flour, some of the oil and all the incense, and this the priest will burn on the altar as a memorial, as food burnt as a smell pleasing to Yahweh. ³The remainder of the cereal offering will revert to Aaron and his sons, an especially holy portion of the food burnt for Yahweh.

⁴"When you offer a cereal offering of dough baked in the oven, the wheaten flour must be prepared either in the form of unleavened cakes mixed with oil, or in the form of unleavened wafers spread with oil.

⁵"If your offering is a cereal offering cooked on the griddle, the wheaten flour mixed with oil must contain no leaven. ⁶You

will break it in pieces and pour oil over it. It is a cereal offering.

⁷"If your offering is a cereal offering cooked in the pan, the wheaten flour must be prepared with oil.

⁸"You will bring Yahweh the cereal offering thus prepared and present it to the priest; he will take it to the altar. ⁹And from the cereal offering the priest will take the memorial and burn it on the altar, food burnt as a smell pleasing to Yahweh. ¹⁰The remainder of the cereal offering will revert to Aaron and his descendants: it is especially holy since it is taken from the food burnt for Yahweh.

¹¹"None of the cereal offerings which you offer to Yahweh must be prepared with leaven, for you must never include leaven or honey in food burnt for Yahweh. ¹²You may offer them to Yahweh as an offering of first-fruits, but they will not make a pleasing smell if they are burnt on the altar. ¹³You will put salt in every cereal offering that you offer, and you will not fail to put the salt of the covenant of your God on your cereal offering; to every offering you will add an offering of salt to your God. ¹⁴If you offer Yahweh a cereal offering of first-fruits, you will offer it in the form of roasted ears of wheat or of bread made from ground wheat. ¹⁵You will add oil to it and put incense on it; it is a cereal offering; ¹⁶and from it the priest will burn the memorial with some bread and oil (and all the incense) as food burnt for Yahweh."'

The communion sacrifice

3 ' "If his sacrifice is a communion sacrifice, and if he offers an animal from the herd, be it male or female, whatever he offers before Yahweh must be unblemished. ²He will lay his hand on the victim's head and slaughter it at the entrance to the Tent of Meeting. The priests descended from Aaron will then pour the blood all around the altar. ³He will offer part of the communion sacrifice as food burnt for Yahweh: the fat covering the entrails, all the fat on the entrails, ⁴both kidneys, the fat on them and on the loins, the mass of fat which he

will remove from the liver and kidneys. ⁵The priests descended from Aaron will then burn this on the altar, in addition to the burnt offering, on the wood of the fire, food burnt as a smell pleasing to Yahweh.

⁶"If it is an animal from the flock which he offers as a communion sacrifice to Yahweh, be the animal that he offers male or female, it must be unblemished.

⁷"If he offers a sheep, he will offer it before Yahweh, ⁸he will lay his hand on the victim's head and slaughter it in front of the Tent of Meeting; the priests descended from Aaron will then pour its blood all around the altar. ⁹Of the communion sacrifice he will offer the following as food burnt for Yahweh: the fat, all the tail taken off near the base of the spine, the fat covering the entrails, all the fat on the entrails, ¹⁰both kidneys, the fat on them and on the loins, the mass of fat which he will remove from the liver and kidneys. ¹¹The priest will then burn this on the altar as food, as food burnt for Yahweh.

¹²"If his offering is a goat, he will offer it before Yahweh, ¹³he will lay his hand on the victim's head and slaughter it in front of the Tent of Meeting, and the descendants of Aaron will then pour its blood all around the altar. ¹⁴This is what he will then offer of it as food burnt for Yahweh: the fat covering the entrails, all the fat on the entrails, ¹⁵both kidneys, the fat on them and on the loins, the mass of fat which he will remove from the liver and kidneys. ¹⁶The priest will then burn these pieces on the altar as food burnt as a smell pleasing to Yahweh.

"All the fat belongs to Yahweh. ¹⁷This is a perpetual law for all your descendants, wherever you may live: that you will not eat either fat or blood."'

The sacrifice for sin:

4 Yahweh spoke to Moses and said: ²'Speak to the Israelites and say:

"If anyone sins inadvertently against any of Yahweh's commandments and does anything prohibited by them, ³if the one who sins is the anointed priest, thus making the people guilty, then for the sin which he has committed he must offer Yahweh a young bull, an unblemished animal from the herd, as a sacrifice for sin. 4 He will bring the bull before Yahweh at the entrance to the Tent of Meeting, will lay his hand on its head and slaughter it before Yahweh. 5 The anointed priest will then take some of the bull's blood and carry it into the Tent of Meeting. 6 He will then dip his finger in the blood and sprinkle it seven times in front of the sanctuary curtain, before Yahweh. 7 The priest will then put some of the blood on the horns of the altar of incense smoking before Yahweh in the Tent of Meeting, and will pour all the rest of the bull's blood at the foot of the altar of burnt offerings at the entrance to the Tent of Meeting.

8 "Of the bull offered as a sacrifice for sin, he will set aside all the fat: the fat covering the entrails, all the fat on the entrails, 9 both kidneys, the fat on them and on the loins, the mass of fat which he will remove from the liver and kidneys—10 exactly as was done with the portion set aside in the communion sacrifice—and the priest will burn these pieces on the altar of burnt offerings.

11 "The bull's skin and all its meat, its head, its shins, its entrails and its offal, 12 the whole bull he will then have carried out of the camp to a clean place, the place where the fatty ashes are thrown, and will burn it on a wood fire; it must be burnt where the ashes are thrown.

13 "If the whole community of Israel has sinned inadvertently and, without being aware of it has incurred guilt by doing something forbidden by Yahweh's commandments, 14 once the sin of which it is guilty has been discovered, the community must offer a young bull, an unblemished animal from the herd, as a sacrifice for sin, and bring it in front of the Tent of Meeting. 15 The elders of the community will then lay their hands on the bull's head before Yahweh, and the bull will be slaughtered before Yahweh.

16 "The anointed priest will then take some of the bull's blood into the Tent of Meeting. 17 He will then dip his finger in the blood and sprinkle it seven times in front of the curtain, before Yahweh. 18 He will then put some of the blood on the horns of the altar standing before Yahweh inside the Tent of Meeting, and then pour all the rest of the blood at the foot of the altar of burnt offerings at the entrance to the Tent of Meeting.

19 "He will then set aside all the fat from the animal and burn it on the altar. 20 He will then deal with the bull as he did with the bull in the sacrifice for sin. It will be dealt with in the same way; and once the priest has performed the rite of expiation for the people, they will be forgiven.

21 "He will then have the bull carried out of the camp and will burn it as he burned the first one. This is the sacrifice for the sin of the community.

22 "When a leader has sinned and inadvertently incurred guilt by doing something forbidden by the commandments of Yahweh his God 23 (or if the sin which he has committed is drawn to his attention), he must bring a he-goat as his offering, an unblemished male. 24 He will then lay his hand on the goat's head and slaughter it on the spot where the burnt offerings are slaughtered before Yahweh. This is a sacrifice for sin; 25 the priest will take some of the victim's blood on his finger and put it on the horns of the altar of burnt offerings. He will then pour the rest of its blood at the foot of the altar of burnt offerings 26 and burn all the fat on the altar, as with the fat in the communion sacrifice. This is how the priest must perform the rite of expiation for him to free him from his sin, and he will be forgiven.

27 "If one of the country people sins inadvertently and incurs guilt by doing something forbidden by Yahweh's commandments 28 (or if the sin which he has committed is drawn to his attention), he must bring a she-goat as his offering for the sin which he has committed, an unblemished female. 29 He will then lay his hand on the victim's head and slaughter it on the spot where the burnt offerings are slaughtered. 30 The priest will take some of its blood

on his finger and put it on the horns of the altar of burnt offerings. He will then pour all the rest of the blood at the foot of the altar. 31 He will then remove all the fat, as the fat was removed for the communion sacrifice, and the priest will burn it on the altar as a smell pleasing to Yahweh. This is how the priest must perform the rite of expiation for him, and he will be forgiven.

32 "If he wishes to bring a lamb as an offering for this kind of sacrifice, he must bring an unblemished female. 33 He will then lay his hand on the victim's head and slaughter it as a sacrifice for sin on the spot where the burnt offerings are slaughtered. 34 The priest will take some of the victim's blood on his finger and put it on the horns of the altar of burnt offerings. He will then pour all the rest of the blood at the foot of the altar. 35 He will then remove all the fat, as was done for the sheep in the communion sacrifice, and the priest will burn it as food burnt for Yahweh. This is how the priest must perform for him the rite of expiation for the sin which he has committed, and he will be forgiven."'

Some cases of sacrifice for sin

5 ' "If someone sins in any of these following cases:

"He should have come forward to give evidence when he heard the formal adjuration, having seen the incident or known the facts; but he has not spoken out, and so bears the consequences of his guilt;

2 "or someone touches something unclean, whatever it may be—the dead body of an unclean animal, wild or tame, or of one of the unclean reptiles—and without realising it becomes unclean, he becomes answerable for it;

3 "or he touches some human uncleanness, whatever it may be, contact with which makes him unclean; he does not notice it, then, realising it later, he becomes answerable for it;

4 "or someone lets slip an oath to do something either evil or good, in any of those matters on which someone may let slip an oath; he

does not notice it, then, realising it later, he becomes answerable for it;

5 "if he is answerable in any of those cases, he will have to confess the sin committed. 6 As a sacrifice of reparation for the sin committed, he will bring Yahweh a female from the flock (sheep or goat) as a sacrifice for sin; and the priest will perform the rite of expiation for him to free him from his sin.

Sins of private individuals (continued)

7 "If he cannot afford an animal from the flock as a sacrifice of reparation for the sin he has committed, he will bring Yahweh two turtledoves or two young pigeons—one as a sacrifice for sin and the other as a burnt offering. 8 He will bring them to the priest who will first offer the one intended for the sacrifice for sin. The priest will wring its neck but not remove the head. 9 He will sprinkle the side of the altar with the victim's blood, and then squeeze out the rest of the blood at the foot of the altar. This is a sacrifice for sin. 10 He will then offer the other bird as a burnt offering according to the ritual. This is how the priest must perform the rite of expiation for the person for the sin he has committed, and he will be forgiven.

11 "If he cannot afford two turtledoves or two young pigeons, he will bring a tenth of an *ephah* of wheaten flour as an offering for the sin committed; he must not mix oil with it or put incense on it, since this is a sacrifice for sin. 12 He will bring it to the priest, who will take a handful of it as a memorial, and burn this on the altar in addition to the offerings of food burnt for Yahweh. This is a sacrifice for sin. 13 This is how the priest must perform the rite of expiation for the person for the sin he has committed in any of those cases, and he will be forgiven. In this case, the priest has the same rights as in the case of a cereal offering."'

The sacrifice of reparation

14 Yahweh spoke to Moses and said:
15 'If someone is unfaithful and sins in-

advertently by infringing Yahweh's sacred rights, as a sacrifice of reparation he must bring Yahweh an unblemished ram from his flock, the value of which will be decided by you in silver shekels according to the rate of the sanctuary-shekel. [16] He will make amends for what his sin subtracted from the sacred rights, adding one-fifth to the value, and give it to the priest. The priest will then perform the rite of expiation for him with the ram for the sacrifice of reparation and he will be forgiven.

[17] 'If someone sins and without realising it does one of the things forbidden by Yahweh's commandments, he will answer for it and bear the consequences of his guilt. [18] As a sacrifice of reparation he must bring the priest an unblemished ram from his flock to the value which you decide, and the priest will perform the rite of expiation for him for the oversight unwittingly committed, and he will be forgiven. [19] This is a sacrifice of reparation; the man was certainly answerable to Yahweh.'

[20] Yahweh spoke to Moses and said:

[21] 'If someone sins and is unfaithful against Yahweh by deceiving his fellow-countryman over a deposit or a security, or by withholding something due to him or by exploiting him;

[22] 'or if he finds lost property and denies it;

'or if he perjures himself about anything that a human being may do criminally in such matters;

[23] 'if he sins and so becomes answerable, he must restore what he has taken or demanded in excess: the deposit confided to him, the lost property that he has found, [24] or any object about which he has perjured himself. He will add one-fifth to the principal and pay the whole to the person who held the property rights on the day when he incurred the guilt. [25] He will then bring Yahweh an unblemished ram from his flock to the value which you decide, to the priest as a sacrifice of reparation, [26] and the priest will perform the rite of expiation for him before Yahweh and he will be forgiven, whatever the act by which he incurred guilt.'

The ritual of the burnt offering

6 Yahweh spoke to Moses and said: [2] 'Give these orders to Aaron and his sons:

"This is the ritual for the burnt offering (that is, the burnt offering that stays on the altar brazier all night until morning and is consumed by the altar fire).

[3] "The priest will put on his linen tunic and put his linen drawers on to cover himself. He will then remove the fatty ashes of the burnt offering consumed by the altar fire and put them at the side of the altar. [4] He will then take off his clothes, put on others and carry the ashes to a clean place outside the camp.

[5] "The fire on the altar that consumes the burnt offering must not be allowed to go out. Every morning the priest will make it up with wood, arranging the burnt offering on it and burning the fat from the communion sacrifices. [6] The fire must always be burning on the altar; it must never go out.

The ritual of the cereal offering

[7] 'This is the ritual for the cereal offering:

"One of the descendants of Aaron will bring it into Yahweh's presence in front of the altar, [8] will take a handful of the wheaten flour (with the oil and all the incense which have been added to it) and burn the memorial on the altar as a smell pleasing to Yahweh; [9] and Aaron and his sons will eat the remainder in the form of unleavened loaves. They will eat it inside the holy place, in the court of the Tent of Meeting. [10] The portion I give them of the food burnt for me must not be baked with leaven; it is especially holy, like the sacrifice for sin and the sacrifice of reparation. [11] All male descendants of Aaron are entitled to eat this portion of the food burnt for Yahweh (this is a perpetual law for all your descendants) and anyone who touches it will become holy."'

[12] Yahweh spoke to Moses and said:

[13] 'This is the offering that Aaron and his sons must make to Yahweh on the day they are anointed: one-tenth of an *ephah* of wheaten flour as a perpetual cereal offering, half in the

morning and half in the evening. [14] It will be prepared on the griddle and mixed with oil; you will bring the paste as a cereal offering in several pieces, offering them as a smell pleasing to Yahweh. [15] When one of his sons is anointed priest to succeed him, he will do the same. This is a perpetual law.

'The entire cereal offering will be burnt for Yahweh. [16] Every cereal offering made by a priest will be a total sacrifice; none of it will be eaten.'

The ritual of the sacrifice for sin

[17] Yahweh spoke to Moses and said, [18] 'Speak to Aaron and his sons and say:

"This is the ritual for the sacrifice for sin:

"The victim must be slaughtered before Yahweh on the spot where the burnt offerings are slaughtered. It is especially holy. [19] The priest who offers this sacrifice will eat it. It will be eaten inside the holy place, in the court of the Tent of Meeting. [20] Everything touching the victim's meat will become holy, and if any of the blood splashes on clothing, the stain will be washed off inside the holy place. [21] The earthenware vessel in which the meat is cooked must be broken; if a bronze vessel has been used for the cooking, it must be scrubbed and thoroughly rinsed with water. [22] Any male who is a priest may eat the sacrifice. It is especially holy. [23] But no one may eat any of the victims offered for sin, the blood of which has been taken into the Tent of Meeting to make expiation inside the sanctuary. These must be burnt." '

The ritual of the sacrifice of reparation

7 ' "This is the ritual for the sacrifice of reparation:

"It is especially holy. [2] The victim must be slaughtered where the burnt offerings are slaughtered, and the priest will pour the blood all around the altar. [3] He will then offer all the fat: the tail, the fat covering the entrails, [4] both kidneys, the fat on them and on the loins, the mass of fat which he will remove from the liver and kidneys. [5] The priest will burn these pieces on the altar as food burnt for Yahweh. This is a sacrifice of reparation. [6] Every male who is a priest may eat it. It will be eaten inside the holy place; it is especially holy.

The rights of the priests

[7] "As with the sacrifice for sin, so with the sacrifice of reparation—the ritual is the same for both. The offering with which the priest performs the rite of expiation will revert to the priest. [8] The hide of the victim presented by someone to the priest to be offered as a burnt offering will revert to the priest. [9] Every cereal offering baked in the oven, every cereal offering cooked in the pan or on the griddle will revert to the priest who offers it. [10] Every cereal offering, mixed with oil or dry, will revert to all the descendants of Aaron without distinction.

The ritual of the communion sacrifice

[11] "This is the ritual for the communion sacrifice to be offered to Yahweh:

[12] "If this is offered as a sacrifice with praise, to the latter must be added an offering of unleavened cakes mixed with oil, unleavened wafers spread with oil, and wheaten flour in the form of cakes mixed with oil. [13] This offering, then, must be added to the cakes of leavened bread and to the communion sacrifice with praise. [14] One of the cakes of this offering must be presented as an offering to Yahweh; it will revert to the priest who pours out the blood of the communion sacrifice. [15] The meat of the victim will be eaten on the day the offering is made; nothing may be left until next morning.

[16] "If the victim is offered as a votive or a voluntary sacrifice, it must be eaten on the day it is offered, and the remainder may be eaten on the following day; [17] but on the third day whatever is left of the meat of the victim must be burnt.

General rules

[18] "If any of the meat of a victim offered as a communion sacrifice is eaten on the third day,

the person who has offered it will not be acceptable and will receive no credit for it. It will count as rotten meat, and the person who eats it will bear the consequences of the guilt.

¹⁹ "Meat that has touched anything unclean cannot be eaten; it must be burnt.

"Anyone clean may eat the meat, ²⁰ but anyone unclean who eats the meat of a communion sacrifice offered to Yahweh will be outlawed from his people. ²¹ Furthermore, if anyone touches anything unclean, human or animal, or any foul thing, and then eats the meat of a communion sacrifice offered to Yahweh, that individual will be outlawed from his people." '

²² Yahweh spoke to Moses and said, ²³ 'Speak to the Israelites and say:

"You may not eat the fat of ox, sheep or goat. ²⁴ The fat of an animal that has died a natural death or been savaged by beasts may be used for any other purpose, but you are not to eat it. ²⁵ Anyone who eats the fat of an animal offered as food burnt for Yahweh will be outlawed from his people.

²⁶ "Wherever you live, you will never eat blood, whether it be of bird or of beast. ²⁷ Anyone who eats any blood will be outlawed from his people." '

The priest's portion

²⁸ Yahweh spoke to Moses and said, ²⁹ 'Speak to the Israelites and say:

"Anyone who offers Yahweh a communion sacrifice must bring him part of his sacrifice as an offering. ³⁰ He must bring the food to be burnt for Yahweh, that is to say, the fat adhering to the forequarters, with his own hands. He will bring it, and also the forequarters, with which he will make the gesture of offering before Yahweh. ³¹ The priest will then burn the fat on the altar, and the forequarters will revert to Aaron and his descendants. ³² You will set aside the right thigh from your communion sacrifice and give it to the priest. ³³ The right thigh will be the portion of the descendant of Aaron who offers the blood and fat of the communion sacrifice. ³⁴ For I have

deprived the Israelites of the forequarter offered and the thigh presented in their communion sacrifices, and given them to the priest Aaron and his descendants; this is a perpetual law for the Israelites." '

Conclusion of the ritual of sacrifice

³⁵ Such was the portion of Aaron and his descendants in the food burnt for Yahweh, the day he presented them to Yahweh for them to become his priests. ³⁶ This was what Yahweh ordered the Israelites to give them on the day they were anointed: a perpetual law for all their descendants.

³⁷ Such was the ritual for burnt offering, cereal offering, sacrifice for sin, sacrifice of reparation, investiture sacrifice and communion sacrifice, ³⁸ which Yahweh laid down for Moses on Mount Sinai, the day he ordered the Israelites to make their offerings to Yahweh in the desert of Sinai.

Consecration rites for priests ᵃ

8 Yahweh spoke to Moses and said: ² 'Take Aaron and with him his sons, the vestments, the anointing oil, the bull for the sacrifice for sin, the two rams and the basket of unleavened bread. ³ Then call the whole community together at the entrance to the Tent of Meeting.'

⁴ Moses did as Yahweh ordered; the community gathered at the entrance to the Tent of Meeting, ⁵ and Moses said to them, 'This is what Yahweh has ordered to be done.'

⁶ He made Aaron and his sons come forward and washed them with water.

⁷ He then dressed him in the tunic, passed the waistband round his waist, vested him in the robe and put the *ephod* on him. He then put the waistband of the *ephod* round his waist, fastening it to him. ⁸ He put the breastplate on him, and placed the *urim* and *thummim* in it. ⁹ He put the turban on his head, and on the front of the turban, the golden flower;

8a ‖ Ex 28:1–29:35.

this was the symbol of holy consecration, which Yahweh had prescribed to Moses.

¹⁰ Moses then took the anointing oil and anointed the Dwelling and everything inside it, to consecrate them. ¹¹ He sprinkled the altar seven times and anointed the altar and its accessories, the basin and its stand, to consecrate them. ¹² He then poured some of the anointing oil on Aaron's head and anointed him to consecrate him.

¹³ Moses then made Aaron's sons come forward; he dressed them in tunics, passed the waistbands round their waists and put on their head-dresses, as Yahweh had ordered him.

¹⁴ He then had the bull for the sacrifice for sin brought forward. Aaron and his sons laid their hands on the victim's head ¹⁵ and Moses slaughtered it. He then took the blood and with his finger put some of it on the horns on the corners of the altar to purify the altar. He then poured the rest of the blood at the foot of the altar, which he consecrated by performing the rite of expiation over it. ¹⁶ He then took all the fat covering the entrails, the mass of fat over the liver, both kidneys and their fat; and he burnt this on the altar, ¹⁷ but the bull's skin, its meat and its offal he burnt outside the camp, as Yahweh had ordered Moses.

¹⁸ He then had the ram for the burnt offering brought forward. Aaron and his sons laid their hands on the ram's head ¹⁹ and Moses slaughtered it. He poured its blood all around the altar. ²⁰ He then quartered the ram and burned the head, the quarters and the fat. ²¹ He then washed the entrails and shins, and burnt the whole ram on the altar, as a burnt offering, offered to be a pleasing smell, as food burnt for Yahweh, as Yahweh had ordered Moses.

²² He then had the other ram brought forward, the ram for the investiture sacrifice. Aaron and his sons laid their hands on its head ²³ and Moses slaughtered it. He took some of its blood and put it on the lobe of Aaron's right ear, on the thumb of his right hand, and on the big toe of his right foot. ²⁴ He then made Aaron's sons come forward and he put some of the blood on the lobes of their right ears, on the thumbs of their right hands and on the big toes of their right feet. Next, Moses poured the rest of the blood all around the altar. ²⁵ He then took the fat: the tail, all the fat covering the entrails, the mass of fat over the liver, both kidneys and their fat, and the right thigh. ²⁶ From the basket of unleavened bread placed before Yahweh, he took an unleavened cake, a cake of bread made with oil, and a wafer; he placed these on the fat and the right thigh, ²⁷ and put it all into Aaron's hands and those of his sons, and made the gesture of offering before Yahweh. ²⁸ Moses then took them away from them and burned them on the altar, with the burnt offering. This was the investiture sacrifice, offered to be a pleasing smell, as food burnt for Yahweh. ²⁹ Moses then took the forequarter and made the gesture of offering before Yahweh. This was the portion of the ram of investiture that reverted to Moses, as Yahweh had ordered Moses.

³⁰ Moses then took some of the anointing oil and some of the blood that was on the altar and sprinkled Aaron and his vestments, and his sons and their vestments, with it. In this way he consecrated Aaron and his vestments and his sons and their vestments.

³¹ Moses then said to Aaron and his sons, 'Cook the meat at the entrance to the Tent of Meeting, and eat it there, as also the bread of the investiture sacrifice still in the basket of the investiture offerings, as I ordered, when I said, "Aaron and his sons must eat it." ³² What remains of the meat and bread you will burn. ³³ For seven days you will not leave the entrance to the Tent of Meeting, until the time of your investiture is complete; for your investiture will require seven days. ³⁴ Yahweh has ordered us to do as we have done today to perform the rite of expiation for you; ³⁵ hence, for seven days, day and night, you will remain at the entrance to the Tent of Meeting observing Yahweh's ritual; do this, and you will not incur death. For this was the order I received.' ³⁶ So Aaron and his sons did everything that Yahweh had ordered through Moses.

The priests assume their functions

9 On the eighth day Moses summoned Aaron and his sons and the elders of Israel; ²he said to Aaron, 'Take a calf to offer a sacrifice for sin, and a ram for a burnt offering, both without blemish, and bring them before Yahweh. ³Then say to the Israelites, "Take a goat to be offered as a sacrifice for sin, a calf and a lamb one year old (both without blemish) for a burnt offering, ⁴a bull and a ram for communion sacrifices to be slaughtered before Yahweh, and a cereal offering mixed with oil. For Yahweh will appear to you today." '

⁵They brought what Moses had ordered in front of the Tent of Meeting; then the whole community approached and stood before Yahweh. ⁶Moses then said, 'This is what Yahweh has ordered you to do, so that his glory may be visible to you.' ⁷Moses then addressed Aaron, 'Go to the altar and offer your sacrifice for sin and your burnt offering, and so perform the rite of expiation for yourself and your family. Then present the people's offering and perform the rite of expiation for them, as Yahweh has ordered.'

⁸Aaron went to the altar and slaughtered the calf as a sacrifice for his own sin. ⁹Aaron's sons then presented the blood to him; he dipped his finger in it and put some on the horns of the altar, and then poured the rest of the blood at the foot of the altar. ¹⁰The fat of the sacrifice for sin and the kidneys and the mass of fat over the liver he burned on the altar, as Yahweh had ordered Moses, ¹¹and the meat and the skin he burned outside the camp.

¹²He then slaughtered the burnt offering; Aaron's sons then handed him the blood, which he poured all around the altar. ¹³They then handed him the quartered victim and the head, and he burned these on the altar. ¹⁴He then washed the entrails and shins and burned them with the burnt offering on the altar.

¹⁵He then presented the people's offering. He took the goat for the people's sacrifice for sin, slaughtered it, and made a sacrifice for sin with it in the same way as with the first. ¹⁶He then had the burnt offering brought forward and proceeded according to the ritual. ¹⁷He then had the cereal offering brought forward, took a handful of it and burned it on the altar in addition to the morning burnt offering.

¹⁸Then he slaughtered the bull and the ram as a communion sacrifice for the people. Aaron's sons handed him the blood and he poured it all around the altar. ¹⁹The fat of the bull and the ram, the tail, the covering fat, the kidneys, the mass of fat over the liver, ²⁰he placed on the ribs and then burned on the altar. ²¹With the ribs and the right thigh Aaron made the gesture of offering as Yahweh had ordered Moses.

²²Aaron then raised his hands towards the people and blessed them. Having thus performed the sacrifice for sin, the burnt offering and the communion sacrifice, he came down ²³and entered the Tent of Meeting with Moses. Then they came out together to bless the people and the glory of Yahweh appeared to the entire people: ²⁴a flame leapt out from Yahweh's presence and consumed the burnt offering and fat on the altar. At this sight the entire people shouted for joy and fell on their faces.

Complementary legislation

10 Aaron's sons Nadab and Abihu each took his censer, put fire in it and incense on the fire, and presented unauthorised fire before Yahweh, which was not in accordance with his orders. ²At this a flame leapt out from Yahweh's presence and swallowed them up, and they perished before Yahweh. ³Moses then said to Aaron, 'That is what Yahweh meant when he said:

In those who are close to me I show my
  holiness,
and before all the people I show my glory.'

Aaron remained silent.

⁴Moses summoned Mishael and Elzaphan, sons of Aaron's uncle Uzziel, and said to them, 'Come here and take your brothers away from

the sanctuary, out of the camp.' ⁵They came and carried them away, still in their tunics, out of the camp, as Moses had said.

⁶Moses said to Aaron and his sons Eleazar and Ithamar, 'Do not disorder your hair or tear your clothes; or you may incur death and his retribution may overtake the whole community. No, it is for the entire House of Israel to lament your brothers who have been the victims of Yahweh's fire. ⁷To avoid incurring death, do not leave the entrance to the Tent of Meeting, for Yahweh's anointing oil is on you.' And they did as Moses said.

⁸Yahweh spoke to Aaron and said:

⁹'When you come to the Tent of Meeting, you and your sons with you, to avoid incurring death you may not drink wine or any other fermented liquor. This is a perpetual law for all your descendants. ¹⁰And so shall it be also when you separate the sacred from the profane, the unclean from the clean, ¹¹and when you teach the Israelites any of the decrees that Yahweh has pronounced for them through Moses.'

¹²Moses said to Aaron and his surviving sons, Eleazar and Ithamar, 'Take the cereal offering left over from the food burnt for Yahweh. Eat the unleavened part of it beside the altar, since it is especially holy. ¹³Eat it in the holy place, since it is the portion of the food burnt for Yahweh that is prescribed for you and your sons; this is the order I have received.

¹⁴'You, your sons and daughters with you, will eat in a clean place the forequarter offered and the thigh presented, for these have been given to you and your children as your due from the Israelites' communion sacrifices. ¹⁵The thigh presented and the forequarter offered, once the fat has been burnt, revert to you and your sons with you, after they have been presented before Yahweh with the gesture of offering, in virtue of a perpetual law as Yahweh has ordered.'

¹⁶Moses then enquired carefully about the goat offered as a sacrifice for sin, and found that they had burnt it. He was angry with Eleazar and Ithamar, Aaron's surviving sons, and said, ¹⁷'Why did you not eat this victim for sin in the holy place, since it is especially holy and was given to you to take away the community's guilt, by performing the rite of expiation for them before Yahweh? ¹⁸Since its blood was not taken inside the sanctuary, you should have eaten its meat there, as I ordered you.' ¹⁹Aaron said to Moses, 'Look, today they offered their sacrifice for sin and their burnt offering before Yahweh, and these disasters have befallen me. If I had eaten the sin offering today, would this have met with Yahweh's approval?' ²⁰And when Moses heard this, he was satisfied.

Clean and unclean animals [a]

11 Yahweh spoke to Moses and Aaron and said to them, ²'Speak to the Israelites and say:

"Of all animals living on land these are the creatures you may eat:

³"You may eat any animal that has a cloven hoof, divided into two parts, and that is a ruminant. ⁴The following, which either chew the cud or have a cloven hoof, are the ones that you may not eat: you will regard the camel as unclean, because though it is ruminant, it does not have a cloven hoof; ⁵you will regard the coney as unclean, because though it is ruminant, it does not have a cloven hoof; ⁶you will regard the hare as unclean, because though it is ruminant, it does not have a cloven hoof; ⁷you will regard the pig as unclean, because though it has a cloven hoof, divided into two parts, it is not a ruminant. ⁸You will not eat the meat of these or touch their dead bodies; you will regard them as unclean.

⁹"Of all that lives in water, these you may eat:

"Anything that has fins and scales, and lives in the water, whether in sea or river, you may eat. ¹⁰But anything in sea or river that does not have fins and scales, of all the small water-creatures and all the living things found there,

11a ‖ Dt 14:3–21.

you will regard as detestable. ¹¹You will regard them as detestable; you must not eat their meat and you will regard their carcasses as detestable. ¹²Anything that lives in water, but not having fins and scales, you will regard as detestable.

¹³"Of the birds these are the ones that you will regard as detestable; they may not be eaten, they are detestable for eating:

"The tawny vulture, the griffon, the osprey, ¹⁴the kite, the various kinds of buzzard, ¹⁵all kinds of raven, ¹⁶the ostrich, the screech owl, the seagull, the various kinds of hawk, ¹⁷horned owl, night owl, cormorant, barn owl, ¹⁸ibis, pelican, white vulture, ¹⁹stork, the various kinds of heron, the hoopoe and the bat.

²⁰"All winged insects moving on four feet you will regard as detestable for eating. ²¹Of all these winged insects you may eat only the following: those with the sort of legs above their feet which enable them to leap over the ground. ²²These are the ones you may eat: the various kinds of migratory locust, the various kinds of *solham* locust, *hargol* locust and *hagab* locust. ²³But all other winged insects on four feet you will regard as detestable for eating.

²⁴"By the following you will be made unclean. Anyone who touches the carcass of one will be unclean until evening. ²⁵Anyone who picks up their carcasses must wash his clothing and will be unclean until evening. ²⁶Animals that have hoofs, but not cloven, and that are not ruminant, you will regard as unclean; anyone who touches them will be unclean. ²⁷Those four-footed animals which walk on the flat of their paws you will regard as unclean; anyone who touches their carcasses will be unclean until evening, ²⁸and anyone who picks up their carcasses must wash his clothing and will be unclean until evening. You will regard them as unclean.

²⁹"Of the small creatures which crawl along the ground, these are the ones which you will regard as unclean: the mole, the rat, the various kinds of lizard: ³⁰gecko, *koah*, *letaah*, chameleon and *tinshamet*.

Rules on contact with things unclean

³¹"Of all the small creatures, these are the animals which you must regard as disgusting. Anyone who touches them when they are dead will be unclean until evening.

³²"Any object on which one of these creatures falls when it is dead becomes unclean: wooden utensil, clothing, skin, sacking, any utensil whatever. It must be immersed in water and will remain unclean until evening: then it will be clean. ³³If the creature falls into an earthenware vessel, the vessel must be broken; whatever the vessel contains is unclean. ³⁴Any edible food will be unclean if the water touches it; any drinkable liquid will be unclean, no matter what its container. ³⁵Anything on which the carcass of such a creature may fall will be unclean: be it oven or stove, it must be destroyed; for they are unclean and you will regard them as unclean ³⁶(although springs, wells and stretches of water will remain clean); anyone who touches one of their carcasses will be unclean. ³⁷If one of their carcasses falls on any kind of seed, the seed will remain clean; ³⁸but if the seed has been moistened and one of their carcasses falls on it, you will regard it as unclean.

³⁹"If one of the animals that you use as food dies, anyone who touches the carcass will be unclean until evening; ⁴⁰anyone who eats any of the carcass must wash his clothing and will remain unclean until evening; anyone who picks up the carcass must wash his clothing and will remain unclean until evening.

The religious aspect

⁴¹"Any creature that swarms on the ground is detestable for eating; it must not be eaten. ⁴²Anything that moves on its belly, anything that moves on four legs or more—in short all the creatures that swarm on the ground—you will not eat, since they are detestable. ⁴³Do not make yourselves detestable with all these swarming creatures; do not defile yourselves with them, do not be defiled by them. ⁴⁴For it is I, Yahweh, who am your God. You have

been sanctified and have become holy because I am holy: do not defile yourselves with all these creatures that swarm on the ground. 45 Yes, it is I, Yahweh, who brought you out of Egypt to be your God: you must therefore be holy because I am holy." '

Conclusion of rules concerning the clean and unclean

46 Such is the law concerning animals, birds, all living creatures that move in water and all creatures that swarm on the ground. 47 Its purpose is to distinguish the clean from the unclean, the creatures that may be eaten from those that may not be eaten.

Purification of a woman after childbirth

12 Yahweh spoke to Moses and said, 2 'Speak to the Israelites and say: "If a woman becomes pregnant and gives birth to a boy, she will be unclean for seven days as when in a state of pollution due to menstruation. 3 On the eighth day the child's foreskin must be circumcised, 4 and she will wait another thirty-three days for her blood to be purified. She will not touch anything consecrated nor go to the sanctuary until the time of her purification is over.

5 "If she gives birth to a girl, she will be unclean for two weeks, as during her monthly periods; and will wait another sixty-six days for her blood to be purified.

6 "When the period of her purification is over, for either boy or girl, she will bring the priest at the entrance to the Tent of Meeting a lamb one year old for a burnt offering, and a young pigeon or turtledove as a sacrifice for sin. 7 The priest must offer this before Yahweh, perform the rite of expiation for her, and she will be purified from her discharge of blood.

"Such is the law concerning a woman who gives birth to either a boy or a girl. 8 If she cannot afford a lamb, she must take two turtledoves or two young pigeons, one for the burnt offering and the other for the sacrifice for sin. The priest will perform the rite of expiation for her and she will be purified." '

Human skin-diseases

13 Yahweh said to Moses and Aaron, 2 'If a swelling or scab or spot appears on someone's skin, which could develop into a contagious skin-disease, that person must then be taken to the priest, either Aaron or one of his sons. 3 The priest will examine the disease on the skin. If the hair on the diseased part has turned white, or if the disease bites into the skin, the skin-disease is contagious, and after examination the priest will declare the person unclean. 4 But if there is a white spot on the skin without any visible depression of the skin or whitening of the hair, the priest will isolate the sick person for seven days. 5 On the seventh day he will examine the person, and if he observes that the disease persists though without spreading over the skin, he will isolate the person for a further seven days 6 and examine him again on the seventh. If he finds that the disease has faded and has not spread over the skin, the priest will declare the person clean. This was merely a scab. Once he has washed his clothing he will be clean.

7 'But if the scab spreads over the skin after the sick person has been examined by the priest and declared clean, then he will let himself be examined again by the priest. 8 After examining him and certifying the spread of the scab over the skin, the priest will declare him unclean: it is a contagious skin-disease.

9 'Someone who has a contagious skin-disease must be taken to the priest. 10 The priest will examine the sick person, and if he finds a whitish swelling with whitening of the hair and an ulcer forming on the skin, 11 this is a dormant skin-disease, and the priest will declare the person unclean. He will not isolate him; he is obviously unclean.

12 'But if the disease spreads all through the skin, if it covers the person entirely from head to foot so far as the priest can see, 13 the priest will then examine the sick person and, if he finds that the skin-disease covers his whole body, declare the sick person clean. Since it has all become white, he is clean. 14 But as soon as

an ulcer appears on him, he will be unclean.
¹⁵ After examining the ulcer, the priest will declare him unclean: the ulcer is unclean, it is contagious. ¹⁶ But if the ulcer becomes white again, the sick person will go to the priest; ¹⁷ the priest will examine him and if he finds that the disease has turned white, he will declare the sick person clean: he is clean.

¹⁸ 'When an ulcer appears on someone's skin, and then gets better, ¹⁹ and if then a white swelling or a reddish-white spot forms on the same place, the sick person will show himself to the priest. ²⁰ The priest will examine him, and if he finds a visible depression in the skin and a whitening of the hair, he will declare the person unclean: this is a case of contagious skin-disease breaking out in an ulcer. ²¹ But if on examination the priest finds neither white hair nor depression of the skin, but a fading of the affected part, he will isolate the sick person for seven days. ²² If the disease has then spread over the skin, he will declare the person unclean: this is a case of contagious skin-disease. ²³ But if the spot has stayed where it was and has not spread, it is the scar of the ulcer and the priest will declare the person clean.

²⁴ 'If someone has a burn on the skin and an abscess, a reddish-white or white spot, forms on the burn, ²⁵ the priest will then examine it. If he finds a whitening of the hair or a visible depression of the mark on the skin, a contagious disease has broken out in the burn. The priest will declare the sick person unclean: this is a contagious skin-disease. ²⁶ If on the other hand the priest on examination does not find white hair on the mark or depression of the skin, but a fading of the mark, the priest will isolate the person for seven days. ²⁷ He will examine the person on the seventh day and, if the disease has spread over the skin, he will declare the sick person unclean: this is a case of contagious skin-disease. ²⁸ If the mark has stayed where it was and has not spread over the skin, but has faded instead, it was only a swelling due to the burn. The priest will declare the person clean: it is merely a burn scar.

²⁹ 'If a man or a woman has a sore on the head or chin, ³⁰ the priest will examine the sore; and if he finds a depression visible in the skin, with the hair on it yellow and thin, he will declare the sick person unclean: this is tinea, that is to say, a contagious skin-disease of the head or chin. ³¹ If on examining this case of tinea the priest finds no visible depression in the skin and no yellow hair, he will isolate the person so affected for seven days. ³² He will examine the infected part on the seventh day, and if he finds that the tinea has not spread, that the hair on it is not yellow, and that there is no visible depression in the skin, ³³ the sick person will shave his hair off, all except the part affected with tinea, and the priest will again isolate him for seven days. ³⁴ He will examine the infected part on the seventh day, and if he finds that it has not spread over the skin, and that there is no visible depression of the skin, the priest will declare the sick person clean. After washing his clothes the person will be clean. ³⁵ But if after this purification the tinea does spread over the skin, ³⁶ the priest will examine the person; if he finds that the tinea has indeed spread over the skin, the sick person is unclean, and there is no need to verify whether the hair is yellow. ³⁷ Whereas if, so far as he can see, the tinea is arrested and dark hair is beginning to grow on it, the sick person is cured. He is clean, and the priest will declare him clean.

³⁸ 'If spots break out on the skin of a man or woman, and if these spots are white, ³⁹ the priest will examine them. If he finds that the spots are of a dull white, this is a rash that has broken out on the skin: the sick person is clean.

⁴⁰ 'If someone loses the hair of the scalp, this is baldness of the scalp but the person is clean. ⁴¹ If he loses hair off the front of the head, this is baldness of the forehead but the person is clean. ⁴² If, however, a reddish-white sore appears on scalp or forehead, a contagious skin-disease has broken out on the scalp or forehead. ⁴³ The priest will examine it, and if he finds a reddish-white swelling on scalp or forehead, looking like a contagious skin-disease, ⁴⁴ the person has such a disease: he is

unclean. The priest will declare him unclean; he has a contagious skin-disease of the head.

The law governing cases of contagious skin-diseases

45 'Anyone with a contagious skin-disease will wear torn clothing and disordered hair; and will cover the upper lip and shout, "Unclean, unclean." 46 As long as the disease lasts, such a person will be unclean and, being unclean, will live alone and live outside the camp.

Infections of clothing

47 'When a piece of clothing is infected with mould, be it woollen or linen clothing, 48 linen or woollen fabric or covering, or leather or anything made of leather, 49 if the spot on the clothing, leather, fabric, covering or object made of leather is a greenish or reddish colour, it is a disease to be shown to the priest. 50 The priest will examine the infection and isolate the object for seven days. 51 If on the seventh day he observes that the infection has spread on the clothing, fabric, covering, leather or object made of leather, whatever it may be, this is a contagious disease and the object is unclean. 52 He will burn this clothing, fabric, linen or woollen covering or leather object whatever it may be, on which the infection has appeared; for this is a contagious disease which must be destroyed by fire.

53 'But if on examination the priest finds that the infection has not spread on the clothing, fabric, covering, or leather object whatever it may be, 54 he will order the infected object to be washed and will isolate it again for a period of seven days. 55 After the washing, he will examine the infection and if he finds that there is no change in its appearance, even though it has not spread, the article is unclean. You will burn it; it is infected through and through.

56 'But if on examination the priest finds that the infection has diminished after washing, he will tear it out of the clothing, leather, fabric or covering. 57 But if the infection reappears on the same clothing, fabric, covering or leather object whatever it may be, this means that the infection is active; you will burn whatever is infected. 58 The clothing, fabric, covering or leather object whatever it may be, from which the infection disappears after being washed, will be clean after it has been washed a second time.

59 'Such is the law governing disease in a linen or woollen garment, a fabric or covering or leather object whatever it may be, when it is a question of declaring them clean or unclean.'

Purification from contagious skin-diseases

14 Yahweh spoke to Moses and said: 2 'This is the law to be applied on the day of the purification of someone who has suffered from a contagious skin-disease. Such a person will be taken to the priest, 3 and the priest will go outside the camp. If he finds on examination that the person has recovered from the disease, 4 he will order the following to be brought for his purification: two live birds that are clean, some cedar wood, scarlet material and hyssop. 5 He will then order one of the birds to be slaughtered in an earthenware pot over running water. 6 He will then take the live bird, the cedar wood, the scarlet material and the hyssop and dip all this (including the live bird) into the blood of the bird slaughtered over running water. 7 He will then sprinkle the person to be purified of the skin-disease seven times, and having declared the person clean, will set the live bird free to fly off into the countryside. 8 The person who is being purified will then wash all clothing, shave off all hair, and wash, and will then be clean. After this he will return to the camp, although he will remain outside his tent for seven days. 9 On the seventh day he will shave off all his hair—head, beard and eyebrows; he will shave off all his hair. After washing his clothing and his body he will be clean.

10 'On the eighth day he will take two unblemished lambs, an unblemished ewe one year old, three-tenths of wheaten flour mixed with oil for the cereal offering, and one *log* of oil. 11 The priest who is performing the purifi-

cation will place the person who is being purified, with all his offerings, at the entrance to the Tent of Meeting, before Yahweh. [12] He will then take one of the lambs and offer it as a sacrifice of reparation, as also the *log* of oil. With these he will make the gesture of offering before Yahweh. [13] He will then slaughter the lamb on that spot inside the holy place where the victims for the sacrifice for sin and for the burnt offering are slaughtered. This reparatory offering, like the sacrifice for sin, will revert to the priest: it is especially holy. [14] The priest will then take some blood of this sacrifice and put it on the lobe of the right ear, the thumb of the right hand, and the big toe of the right foot of the person who is being purified. [15] He will then take the *log* of oil and pour a little into the hollow of his left hand. [16] He will dip a finger of his right hand into the oil in the hollow of his left hand, and sprinkle the oil with his finger seven times before Yahweh. [17] He will then take some of the oil left in the hollow of his hand and put it on the lobe of the right ear, the thumb of the right hand, and the big toe of the right foot of the person being purified, in addition to the blood of the sacrifice of reparation. [18] The rest of the oil in the hollow of his hand he will put on the head of the person who is being purified. This is how the priest will perform the rite of expiation for such a person before Yahweh.

[19] 'The priest will then offer the sacrifice for sin, and perform the rite of expiation for uncleanness for the person who is being purified. After this, he will slaughter the burnt offering [20] and offer this and the cereal offering on the altar. So, when the priest has performed the rite of expiation for him the person will be clean.

[21] 'If he is poor and cannot afford all this, he need take only one lamb, the one for the sacrifice of reparation, and this will be presented with the gesture of offering to perform the rite of expiation for him. And for the cereal offering he will only take one-tenth of wheaten flour mixed with oil, and the *log* of oil, [22] and two turtledoves or two young pigeons, whichever he can afford, one for a sacrifice for sin and the other for the burnt offering. [23] He will bring these on the eighth day to the priest at the entrance to the Tent of Meeting before Yahweh, for his purification. [24] The priest will take the lamb for the sacrifice of reparation and the *log* of oil, and present them before Yahweh with the gesture of offering. [25] He will then slaughter the lamb for the sacrifice of reparation, take some of its blood and put it on the lobe of the right ear, the thumb of the right hand and the big toe of the right foot of the person who is being purified. [26] He will pour the oil into the hollow of his left hand, [27] and with his finger sprinkle the oil in the hollow of his left hand seven times before Yahweh. [28] He will then put some of the oil on the lobe of the right ear, the thumb of the right hand and the big toe of the right foot of the person who is being purified, as he did with the blood of the sacrifice of reparation. [29] The remainder of the oil in the hollow of his hand he will put on the head of the person who is being purified, thus performing the rite of expiation for him before Yahweh. [30] Of the two turtledoves or two young pigeons—whatever he has been able to afford—he will offer [31] a sacrifice for sin with one, and with the other a burnt offering with a cereal offering—whatever he has been able to afford. This is how the priest will perform before Yahweh the rite of expiation for the person who is being purified.

[32] 'Such is the law concerning someone with a contagious skin-disease who cannot afford the means of purification.'

Similar infections of houses

[33] Yahweh spoke to Moses and Aaron and said:

[34] 'When you reach Canaan, which I am giving you as your possession, if I infect a house with a disease in the country which you are to possess, [35] the owner will come and inform the priest and say, "I have seen something like a skin-disease in the house." [36] The priest will order the house to be emptied before he goes to examine the infection, or everything in the house will become unclean; after

which, the priest will go inside and examine the house; 37 and if on examination he finds the walls of the house pitted with reddish or greenish depressions which appear to be eating away the wall, 38 the priest will then go out of the house, to the door, and shut it up for seven days. 39 On the seventh day, the priest will come back and if on examination he finds that the infection has spread over the walls of the house, 40 he will order the infected stones to be removed and thrown into some unclean place outside the town. 41 He will then have all the inside of the house scraped, and the plaster that comes off will be emptied in an unclean place outside the town. 42 The stones will then be replaced with new ones and the house given a new coat of plaster.

43 'If the infection spreads again after the stones have been removed and the house scraped and replastered, 44 the priest will come and examine it. If he finds that the infection has spread, this means that there is a contagious disease in the house: it is unclean. 45 It must be pulled down and the stones, woodwork and all the plaster be taken to an unclean place outside the town.

46 'Anyone who enters the house while it is closed will be unclean until evening. 47 Anyone who sleeps there will wash his clothes. Anyone who eats there will wash his clothes. 48 But if the priest finds, when he comes to examine the infection, that it has not spread in the house since it was plastered, he will declare the house clean, for the infection is cured.

49 'As a sacrifice for the defilement of the house, he will take two birds, some cedar wood, scarlet material and hyssop. 50 He will slaughter one of the birds in an earthenware pot over running water. 51 He will then take the cedar wood, the hyssop, the scarlet material and the live bird, dip them into the blood of the slaughtered bird and into the running water and sprinkle the house seven times; 52 and after offering the sacrifice for the defilement of the house with the blood of the bird, the running water, the live bird, the cedar wood, the hyssop and the scarlet material, 53 he

will set the live bird free to fly out of the town into the countryside. Once the rite of expiation has been performed for the house in this way it will be clean.

54 'Such is the law governing all kinds of skin-disease and tinea, 55 diseases of clothing and houses, 56 swellings, scabs and spots. It defines the occasions when things are unclean and when clean. 57 Such is the law on skin-diseases.'

Sexual impurities

15 Yahweh spoke to Moses and Aaron and said:

2 'Speak to the Israelites and say to them:

"When a man has a discharge from his body, that discharge is unclean. 3 While the discharge continues, the nature of his uncleanness is as follows:

"Whether his body allows the discharge to flow or whether it retains it, he is unclean.

4 "Any bed the man lies on and anything he sits on will be unclean.

5 "Anyone who touches his bed must wash clothing and body and will be unclean until evening.

6 "Anyone who sits where the man has sat must wash clothing and body and will be unclean until evening.

7 "Anyone who touches the body of the man with the discharge must wash clothing and body and will be unclean until evening.

8 "If the man with the discharge spits on someone who is clean, that person must wash clothing and body and will be unclean until evening.

9 "Any saddle the man has ridden on will be unclean.

10 "All those who touch any object that has been under him will be unclean until evening.

"Anyone who picks up such an object must wash clothing and body and will be unclean until evening.

11 "All those whom the man with the discharge touches without having washed his hands must wash clothing and body and will be unclean until evening.

¹² "The earthenware vessel he touches must be broken and any wooden utensil must be rinsed.

¹³ "Once the man with the discharge is cured, he will allow seven days for his purification. He will wash his clothes and wash his body in running water and he will be clean. ¹⁴ On the eighth day he will take two turtledoves or two young pigeons and come before Yahweh at the entrance to the Tent of Meeting and give them to the priest. ¹⁵ The priest will offer one of them as a sacrifice for sin and the other as a burnt offering. And in this way the priest will perform the rite of expiation for him before Yahweh for his discharge.

¹⁶ "When a man has a seminal discharge, he must wash his whole body with water and will be unclean until evening. ¹⁷ Any clothing or leather touched by the seminal discharge must be washed and will be unclean until evening. ¹⁸ When a woman has had intercourse with a man, both of them must wash and will be unclean until evening.

¹⁹ "Whenever a woman has a discharge and the discharge from her body is of blood, she will remain in a state of menstrual pollution for seven days.

"Anyone who touches her will be unclean until evening.

²⁰ "Anything she lies on in this polluted state will be unclean; anything she sits on will be unclean.

²¹ "Anyone who touches her bed must wash clothing and body and will be unclean until evening.

²² "Anyone who touches anything she has sat on must wash clothing and body and will be unclean until evening. ²³ If there is anything on the bed or where she is sitting, anyone who touches it will be unclean until evening.

²⁴ "If a man goes so far as to sleep with her, he will contract her menstrual pollution and will be unclean for seven days. Any bed he lies on will be unclean.

²⁵ "If a woman has a prolonged discharge of blood outside the period, or if the period is prolonged, during the time this discharge lasts she will be in the same state of uncleanness as during her monthly periods. ²⁶ Any bed she lies on during the time this discharge lasts will be polluted in the same way as the bed she lies on during her monthly periods. Anything she sits on will be unclean as during her monthly periods. ²⁷ Anyone who touches it will be unclean and must wash clothing and body and will be unclean until evening.

²⁸ "Once she is cured of her discharge, she will allow seven days to go by; after that she will be clean. ²⁹ On the eighth day she will take two turtledoves or two young pigeons and bring them to the priest at the entrance to the Tent of Meeting. ³⁰ The priest will offer one of them as a sacrifice for sin and the other as a burnt offering. And in this way the priest will perform the rite of expiation for her before Yahweh for the discharge which made her unclean.

Conclusion of rules about impurities

³¹ "Hence you will warn the Israelites against contracting a state of uncleanness, rather than incurring death by defiling my Dwelling which is among them.

³² "Such is the law governing a man with a discharge or who is made unclean by a seminal discharge, ³³ a woman in a state of pollution due to menstruation, a man or a woman with a discharge, or a man who sleeps with a woman when she is unclean." '

The great Day of Expiation[a]

16 Yahweh spoke to Moses after the death of the two sons of Aaron who died when offering unauthorised fire. ² Yahweh spoke to Moses and said:

'Tell Aaron your brother that he may not enter the sanctuary inside the curtain in front of the mercy-seat on the ark whenever he chooses, in case he incurs death, for I appear in a cloud on the mercy-seat.

16a An important annual festival combining 1 a sacrifice of expiation by blood and 2 a primitive ritual of driving the bearer of sin away from the community.

3'This is how he must enter the sanctuary: with a young bull for a sacrifice for sin and a ram for a burnt offering. 4He will put on a tunic of consecrated linen, wear linen drawers on his body, a linen waistband round his waist, and a linen turban on his head. These are the sacred vestments he will put on after washing himself.

5'From the community of Israelites he will receive two he-goats for a sacrifice for sin and a ram for a burnt offering. 6After offering the bull as a sacrifice for his own sin and performing the rite of expiation for himself and his family, 7he will take the two he-goats and place them before Yahweh at the entrance to the Tent of Meeting. 8Aaron will then draw lots over the two goats, one lot to be for Yahweh and the other lot for Azazel. 9Aaron will then take the goat on which the lot "For Yahweh" has fallen, and offer it as a sacrifice for sin. 10But the goat on which the lot "For Azazel" has fallen, will be placed alive before Yahweh, for the rite of expiation to be performed with it, and for it then to be sent to Azazel in the desert.

11'Having offered the bull as a sacrifice for his own sin and performed the rite of expiation for himself and for his family, and slaughtered the bull as a sacrifice for sin, 12Aaron will then fill a censer with live coals from the altar before Yahweh, take two handfuls of finely ground aromatic incense and bring this inside the curtain. 13He will then put the incense on the fire before Yahweh, so that the cloud of incense hides the mercy-seat which is on the Testimony and he does not incur death. 14He will then take some of the bull's blood and sprinkle it with his finger on the eastern side of the mercy-seat. He will sprinkle some of the blood seven times with his finger in front of the mercy-seat.

15'He will then slaughter the goat for the sacrifice for the sin of the people, and take its blood inside the curtain, and with this blood do as he did with the blood of the bull, sprinkling it on the mercy-seat and in front of it. 16This is how he must perform the rite of ex-

piation for the sanctuary for the uncleanness of the Israelites, for their acts of rebellion and all their sins.

'And this is what he must do for the Tent of Meeting which remains with them, surrounded by their uncleanness. 17No one must be inside the Tent of Meeting, from the moment he enters to make expiation in the sanctuary until the time he comes out.

'When he has made expiation for himself, for his family, and for the whole community of Israel, 18he must come outside, go to the altar before Yahweh and perform the rite of expiation for it. He will take some of the bull's blood and some of the goat's blood and put it on the horns at the corners of the altar all around it, 19and sprinkle some of the blood on it seven times with his finger, thus purifying it and setting it apart from the uncleanness of the Israelites.

20'Once expiation for the sanctuary, the Tent of Meeting and the altar is complete, he will bring the goat which is still alive. 21Aaron will then lay both his hands on its head and over it confess all the guilt of the Israelites, all their acts of rebellion and all their sins. Having thus laid them on the goat's head, he will send it out into the desert under the charge of a man waiting ready, 22and the goat will bear all their guilt away into some desolate place.

'When he has sent the goat into the desert, 23Aaron will go back into the Tent of Meeting and take off the linen vestments which he wore to enter the sanctuary and leave them there. 24He will then wash his body inside the holy place, put on his vestments and come outside to offer his own and the people's burnt offering. He will perform the rite of expiation for himself and for the people, 25and burn the fat of the sacrifice for sin on the altar.

26'The man who led the goat away to Azazel will wash his clothes and body before entering the camp. 27The bull and the goat offered as a sacrifice for sin, the blood of which was taken into the sanctuary for the rite of expiation, must be taken outside the camp, where their skin, meat and offal are to be

13 READ LEVITICUS 16:1–22.

And the goat will bear all their guilt away into some desolate place.—LEVITICUS 16:22

THE LAMB OF GOD

Once a year on the greatest and most holy day of the year, on the Day of Atonement, the high priest stepped into the Holy of Holies before the face of the Lord to make "expiation for himself, for his family, and for the whole community of Israel" (verse 17). He sprinkled the throne of grace with the blood of a young bull and a goat . . . and in this way absolved himself and his house of "the unclean-ness of the Israelites, for their acts of rebellion and all their sins" (verse 16). No person was to be in the tent . . . when the high priest stepped into God's presence in this awesomely sacred place. . . . And even now he had to burn incense "so that the cloud of incense hides the mercy-seat . . . and he does not incur death" (verse 13). This solitary dialogue took place in deepest mystery.

The Day of Atonement is the Old Testament antecedent of Good Friday. The ram that is slaugh-tered for the sins of the people represents the spotless Lamb of God (so did, no doubt, that other, that was chosen by lot and burdened with the sins of the people—that was driven into the wilderness). And the high priest descended from Aaron foreshadows the eternal high priest. . . . [Christ] did not have to bring for himself an offering for sin because he was without sin. He did not have to await the hour prescribed by the Law, nor seek out the Holy of Holies in the temple. He stands always and everywhere, before the face of God; his own soul is the Holy of Holies. . . . He does not have to con-ceal himself from God by a protective cloud of incense. He gazes upon the uncovered face of the Eter-nal One and has nothing to fear. . . . And he unlocks the mystery of the high priest's realm.

ST. EDITH STEIN, 1891–1942

YOU WILL FIND THE NEXT READING AT LEVITICUS 26.

burnt. 28 The man who burns them will wash his clothes and body before entering the camp.

29 'This will be a perpetual law for you.

'On the tenth day of the seventh month you will fast and refrain from work, both citizen and resident alien; 30 for this is the day on which the rite of expiation will be performed for you to purify you, to purify you before Yahweh from all your sins. 31 It will be a sab-batical rest for you and you will fast. This is a perpetual law.

32 'The rite of expiation will be performed by the priest who has been anointed and in-stalled to officiate in succession to his father. He will put on the linen vestments, the sacred vestments, 33 and perform the rite of expiation for the holy sanctuary, the Tent of Meeting and the altar, and will then perform the rite of expiation for the priests and all the people of the community. 34 This will be a perpetual law for you; once a year the rite of expiation will be made for the Israelites for all their sins.'

And as Yahweh ordered Moses, so it was done.

Slaughtering and sacrifice

17 Yahweh spoke to Moses and said: 2 'Speak to Aaron and his sons and all the Israelites and say:

"This is the order that Yahweh has given:

³"Any man of the House of Israel who slaughters a bull, lamb or goat, whether inside the camp or outside it, ⁴without bringing it to the entrance to the Tent of Meeting to make an offering of it to Yahweh in front of his Dwelling, that man will be answerable for bloodshed; he has shed blood, and that man will be outlawed from his people. ⁵The purpose of this is that the Israelites should instead bring their sacrifices, which they would otherwise offer in the countryside, to Yahweh at the entrance to the Tent of Meeting, to the priest, and offer them as communion sacrifices to Yahweh; ⁶and the priest will sprinkle the blood on Yahweh's altar at the entrance to the Tent of Meeting and will burn the fat as a smell pleasing to Yahweh. ⁷No longer may they offer their sacrifices to the satyrs in whose service they used to prostitute themselves. This is a perpetual law for them and for their descendants."

⁸'You will also say to them, "Any member of the House of Israel or any resident alien who offers a burnt offering or sacrifice ⁹without bringing it to the entrance to the Tent of Meeting to offer it to Yahweh, will be outlawed from his people.

¹⁰"If any member of the House of Israel or any resident alien consumes blood of any kind, I shall set my face against that individual who consumes blood and shall outlaw him from his people. ¹¹For the life of the creature is in the blood, and I have given it to you for performing the rite of expiation on the altar for your lives, for blood is what expiates for a life. ¹²That is why I told the Israelites: None of you will consume blood, nor will any resident alien consume blood.

¹³"Anyone, whether Israelite or resident alien, who hunts and catches game, whether animal or bird, which it is lawful to eat, must pour out its blood and cover it with earth. ¹⁴For the life of every creature is its blood, and I have told the Israelites: You will not consume the blood of any creature, for the life of every creature is its blood, and anyone who consumes it will be outlawed.

¹⁵"Anyone, citizen or alien, who eats an animal that has died a natural death or been savaged, must wash clothing and body, and will be unclean until evening, but will then be clean. ¹⁶But anyone who does not wash clothing and body will bear the consequences of his guilt." '

Sexual prohibitions

18 Yahweh spoke to Moses and said: ²'Speak to the Israelites and say:

"I am Yahweh your God: ³You must not behave as they do in Egypt where you used to live; you must not behave as they do in Canaan where I am taking you, nor must you follow their laws. ⁴You must observe my customs and keep my laws, following them.

"I, Yahweh, am your God: ⁵hence you will keep my laws and my customs. Whoever complies with them will find life in them.

"I am Yahweh.

⁶"None of you will approach a woman who is closely related to him, to have intercourse with her. I am Yahweh.

⁷"You will not have intercourse with your father or your mother. She is your mother—you will not have intercourse with her.

⁸"You will not have intercourse with your father's wife; it is your father's sexual prerogative.

⁹"You will not have intercourse with your sister, whether she is your father's or your mother's daughter. Whether she was born in the same house or elsewhere, you will not have intercourse with her.

¹⁰"You will not have intercourse with your son's or your daughter's daughter; for their sexual privacy is your own.

¹¹"You will not have intercourse with the daughter of your father's wife, born to your father. She is your sister; you will not have intercourse with her.

¹²"You will not have intercourse with your father's sister; for she is your father's own flesh and blood.

¹³"You will not have intercourse with your mother's sister; for she is your mother's own flesh and blood.

14 "You will not have intercourse with your father's brother; you will not approach his wife. She is your aunt.

15 "You will not have intercourse with your daughter-in-law. She is your son's wife; you will not have intercourse with her.

16 "You will not have intercourse with your brother's wife; it is your brother's sexual prerogative.

17 "You will not have intercourse with a woman and her daughter; nor will you take her son's or her daughter's daughter, to have intercourse with them. They are your own flesh and blood; it would be incest.

18 "You will not take a woman and her sister into your harem at the same time, to have intercourse with the latter while the former is still alive.

19 "You will not approach and have intercourse with a woman who is in a state of menstrual pollution.

20 "Furthermore, you will not have intercourse with your fellow-citizen's wife; you would become unclean by doing so.

21 "You will not allow any of your children to be sacrificed to Molech,ª thus profaning the name of your God. I am Yahweh.

22 "You will not have intercourse with a man as you would with a woman. This is a hateful thing.

23 "You will not have intercourse with any kind of animal; you would become unclean by doing so. Nor will a woman offer herself to an animal, to have intercourse with it. This would be a violation of nature.

24 "Do not make yourselves unclean by any of these practices, for it was by such things that the nations that I am driving out before you made themselves unclean. 25 The country has become unclean; hence I am about to punish it for its guilt, and the country itself will vomit out its inhabitants.

26 "You, however, must keep my laws and customs and not do any of these hateful things: none of your citizens, none of your resident aliens. 27 For all these hateful things were done by the people who lived in the country before

you, and the country became unclean. 28 If you make it unclean, will it not vomit you out as it vomited out the nations there before you? 29 Yes, anyone who does any of these hateful things, whatever it may be, any person doing so, will be outlawed from his people; 30 so keep my rules and do not observe any of the hateful laws which were in force before you came; then you will not be made unclean by them. I am Yahweh your God." '

Moral and religious regulations

19 Yahweh spoke to Moses and said: 2 'Speak to the whole community of Israelites and say:

"Be holy, for I, Yahweh your God, am holy.

3 "Each of you will respect father and mother.

"And you will keep my Sabbaths; I am Yahweh your God.

4 "Do not turn to idols and do not cast metal gods for yourselves. I am Yahweh your God.

5 "If you offer a communion sacrifice to Yahweh, make it in such a way as to be acceptable. 6 It must be eaten the same day or the day after; whatever is left on the third day must be burnt. 7 If eaten on the third day it would be rotten food and not be acceptable. 8 Anyone who eats it must bear the consequences of this guilt, having profaned Yahweh's holiness; that person will be outlawed from his people.

9 "When you reap the harvest of your land, you will not reap to the very edges of the field, nor will you gather the gleanings of the harvest; 10 nor will you strip your vineyard bare, nor pick up the fallen grapes. You will leave them for the poor and the stranger. I am Yahweh your God.

11 "You will not steal, nor deal deceitfully or fraudulently with your fellow-citizen. 12 You will not swear by my name with intent to deceive and thus profane the name of your God. I am Yahweh. 13 You will not exploit or

18a A sacrifice by fire, Phoenician in origin, practised in Jerusalem right up to the Exile.

rob your fellow. You will not keep back the labourer's wage until next morning. ¹⁴ You will not curse the dumb or put an obstacle in the way of the blind, but will fear your God. I am Yahweh.

¹⁵ "You will not be unjust in administering justice. You will neither be partial to the poor nor overawed by the great, but will administer justice to your fellow-citizen justly. ¹⁶ You will not go about slandering your own family, nor will you put your neighbour's life in jeopardy. I am Yahweh. ¹⁷ You will not harbour hatred for your brother. You will reprove your fellow-countryman firmly and thus avoid burdening yourself with a sin. ¹⁸ You will not exact vengeance on, or bear any sort of grudge against, the members of your race, but will love your neighbour as yourself. I am Yahweh.

¹⁹ "You will keep my laws.

"You will not mate your cattle with those of another kind; you will not sow two kinds of grain in your field; you will not wear a garment made from two kinds of fabric.

²⁰ "If someone has intercourse with a woman who is the concubine slave of a man from whom she has not been redeemed and she has not been given her freedom, he will be liable for a fine, but they will not incur death, since she was not a free woman. ²¹ He will bring a sacrifice of reparation for Yahweh to the entrance of the Tent of Meeting. This will be a ram of reparation, ²² and with the ram of reparation the priest will perform the rite of expiation for him before Yahweh for the sin committed; and the sin he has committed will be forgiven.

²³ "Once you have entered the country and planted any kind of fruit tree, you will regard its fruit as uncircumcised. For three years you will count it as uncircumcised and it will not be eaten; ²⁴ in the fourth year, all its fruit will be consecrated to Yahweh in a feast of praise; ²⁵ and in the fifth year you may eat its fruit, so that it may yield you even more. I am Yahweh your God.

²⁶ "You will eat nothing with blood in it. You will not practise divination or magic.

²⁷ "You will not round off your hair at the edges or trim the edges of your beard. ²⁸ You will not gash your bodies when someone dies, and you will not tattoo yourselves. I am Yahweh.

²⁹ "Do not profane your daughter by making her a prostitute, or the country itself will become prostituted and filled with incest.

³⁰ "You will keep my Sabbaths and revere my sanctuary. I am Yahweh.

³¹ "Do not have recourse to the spirits of the dead or to magicians; they will defile you. I, Yahweh, am your God.

³² "You will stand up in the presence of grey hair, you will honour the person of the aged and fear your God. I am Yahweh.

³³ "If you have resident aliens in your country, you will not molest them. ³⁴ You will treat resident aliens as though they were native-born and love them as yourself—for you yourselves were once aliens in Egypt. I am Yahweh your God.

³⁵ "You will not be unjust in administering justice as regards measures of length, weight or capacity. ³⁶ You will have just scales, just weights, a just *ephah* and a just *hin*. I am Yahweh your God who brought you out of Egypt; ³⁷ hence you are to keep all my laws and all my customs and put them into practice. I am Yahweh." '

Penalties

20 Yahweh spoke to Moses and said: ² 'Say to the Israelites:

"Anyone, be he Israelite or alien resident in Israel, who gives any of his children to Molech, will be put to death. The people of the country must stone him, ³ and I shall set my face against that man and outlaw him from his people; for by giving a child of his to Molech he has defiled my sanctuary and profaned my holy name. ⁴ If the people of the country choose to close their eyes to the man's action when he gives a child of his to Molech, and do not put him to death, ⁵ I myself shall turn my face against that man and his clan. I shall outlaw them from their people, both him and all those after him who prostitute themselves by following Molech.

⁶ "If anyone has recourse to the spirits of the dead or to magicians, to prostitute himself by following them, I shall set my face against him and outlaw him from his people.

⁷ "Sanctify yourselves and be holy, for I am Yahweh your God.

⁸ "You will keep my laws and put them into practice, for it is I, Yahweh, who make you holy. ⁹ Hence:

"Anyone who curses father or mother will be put to death. Having cursed father or mother, the blood will be on that person's own head.

¹⁰ "The man who commits adultery with his neighbour's wife will be put to death, he and the woman.

¹¹ "The man who has intercourse with his father's wife has infringed his father's sexual prerogative. Both of them will be put to death; their blood will be on their own heads.

¹² "The man who has intercourse with his daughter-in-law: both of them will be put to death; they have violated nature, their blood will be on their own heads.

¹³ "The man who has intercourse with a man in the same way as with a woman: they have done a hateful thing together; they will be put to death; their blood will be on their own heads.

¹⁴ "The man who marries a woman and her mother: this is incest. They will be burnt alive, he and they; you will not tolerate incest.

¹⁵ "The man who has intercourse with an animal will be put to death; you will kill the animal too.

¹⁶ "The woman who approaches any animal to have intercourse with it: you will kill the woman and the animal. They will be put to death; their blood will be on their own heads.

¹⁷ "The man who marries his father's or his mother's daughter: if they have intercourse together, this is an outrage. They will be executed in public, for the man has had inter-

course with his sister; he will bear the consequences of his guilt.

¹⁸ "The man who has intercourse with a woman during her monthly periods and exposes her nakedness: he has laid bare the source of her blood, and she has exposed the source of her blood, and both of them will be outlawed from their people.

¹⁹ "You will not have intercourse with your mother's sister or your father's sister. Whoever does so, has had intercourse with a close relation; they will bear the consequences of their guilt.

²⁰ "The man who has intercourse with the wife of his paternal uncle has infringed his uncle's sexual prerogative; they will bear the consequences of their guilt and die childless.

²¹ "The man who marries his brother's wife: this is pollution; he has infringed his brother's sexual prerogative; they will die childless.

Concluding exhortation

²² "You will keep all my laws, all my decisions, and put them into practice, so that the country where I am taking you to live will not vomit you out. ²³ You will not follow the laws of the nations whom I am driving out before you; they practised all these things, which is why I detested them. ²⁴ As I have already told you, you will take possession of their soil, I myself shall give you possession of it, a country flowing with milk and honey.

"Since I, Yahweh your God, have set you apart from these peoples, ²⁵ you for your part will make a distinction between clean animals and unclean ones and between unclean birds and clean ones, and will not make yourselves detestable with any animal or bird or reptile, which I have set apart from you as unclean.

²⁶ "Be consecrated to me, for I, Yahweh, am holy, and I shall set you apart from all these peoples, for you to be mine.

²⁷ "Any man or woman of yours who is a necromancer or magician will be put to death; they will be stoned to death; their blood will be on their own heads." '

The holiness of the priesthood

21 Yahweh said to Moses:
'Speak to the priests descended from Aaron and say:

"None of them must make himself unclean by touching the corpse of one of his people, ²unless it be of one of his closest relations—father, mother, son, daughter, brother, ³or virgin sister, since she being unmarried is still his close relation: he can make himself unclean for her; ⁴but for a close female relation who is married he will not make himself unclean; he would profane himself.

⁵"They will not make tonsures on their heads, shave the edges of their beards, or gash their bodies. ⁶They will be consecrated to their God and will not profane the name of their God. For their function is to offer the food burnt for Yahweh, the food of their God, and so they must be holy.

⁷"They will not marry a woman profaned by prostitution, or one divorced by her husband, for the priest is consecrated to his God. ⁸"You will treat him as holy, for he offers the food of your God. For you, he will be a holy person, for I, Yahweh, who sanctify you, am holy.

⁹"If a priest's daughter profanes herself by prostitution, she profanes her father and will be burnt alive.

¹⁰"The priest who is pre-eminent over his brothers, on whose head the anointing oil has been poured, and who, robed in the sacred vestments, has received investiture, will not disorder his hair or tear his clothes; ¹¹he will not go near any corpse or make himself unclean even for his father or mother. ¹²He will not leave the holy place in such a way as to profane the sanctuary of his God; for he bears the consecration of the anointing oil of his God. I am Yahweh.

¹³"He will marry a woman who is still a virgin. ¹⁴He will not marry a woman who has been widowed or divorced or profaned by prostitution, but will marry a virgin from his own people: ¹⁵he must not make his own chil-

dren profane, for I, Yahweh, have sanctified him."'

¹⁶Yahweh spoke to Moses and said:

¹⁷'Speak to Aaron and say:

"None of your descendants, for all time, may come forward to offer the food of his God if he has any infirmity, ¹⁸for none may come forward if he has an infirmity, be he blind or lame, disfigured or deformed, ¹⁹or with an injured foot or arm, ²⁰a hunchback, someone with rickets or ophthalmia or the scab or running sores, or a eunuch. ²¹No descendant of the priest Aaron may come forward to offer the food burnt for Yahweh if he has any infirmity; if he has an infirmity, he will not come forward to offer the food of his God.

²²"He may eat the food of his God, things especially holy and things holy, ²³but he will not go near the curtain or approach the altar, since he has an infirmity and must not profane my holy things; for I, Yahweh, have sanctified them."'

²⁴And Moses promulgated this to Aaron, to his sons, and to all the Israelites.

Holiness in consuming sacred food

22 Yahweh spoke to Moses and said:
²'Speak to Aaron and his sons. They must be consecrated by the holy offerings of the Israelites and must not profane my holy name; for my sake they must sanctify it; I am Yahweh. ³Say to them:

"Any one of your descendants, for all time, who in a state of uncleanness approaches the holy offerings consecrated to Yahweh by the Israelites, will be outlawed from my presence. I am Yahweh.

⁴"Anyone of Aaron's line who is afflicted with a contagious skin-disease or a discharge will not eat holy things until he is clean. Anyone who touches anything made unclean by a dead body, or who has a seminal discharge, ⁵or who is made unclean by touching any kind of reptile or any one who has contaminated him with his own uncleanness, be it what it may, ⁶in short, anyone who has had any such contact will be unclean until evening, and must

not eat holy things until he has washed his body. 7 At sunset he will be clean and may then eat holy things, for these are his food.

8 "He must not eat an animal that has died a natural death or been savaged; he would contract uncleanness from it. I am Yahweh.

9 "They must keep my rules and not burden themselves with sin. If they profane them, they will incur death; I, Yahweh, have sanctified them.

10 "No lay person may eat anything holy; no guest or employee of a priest may eat anything holy. 11 But if the priest has acquired a slave by purchase, the slave may eat it like anyone born in his household; they will share his food.

12 "If a priest's daughter marries a layman, she will have no share in the holy things set aside, 13 but if she is widowed or divorced and, being childless, has had to return to her father's house as when she was young, she may share her father's food. No lay person may share it; 14 anyone who does eat a holy thing by inadvertence, will restore it to the priest with one-fifth added.

15 "They may not profane the holy offerings which the Israelites have set aside for Yahweh. 16 By eating these, they would burden them with guilt requiring a sacrifice of reparation; for I, Yahweh, have sanctified these offerings." '

17 Yahweh spoke to Moses and said:

18 'Speak to Aaron, to his sons, and to all the Israelites and say:

"Any member of the House of Israel or any alien resident in Israel who brings an offering either in payment of a vow or as a voluntary gift, and offers it as a burnt offering to Yahweh, 19 must, if he is to be acceptable, offer an unblemished male, be it bull or sheep or goat. 20 You will not offer anything with a blemish, for it would not make you acceptable.

21 "If anyone offers Yahweh a communion sacrifice, either to fulfil a vow or as a voluntary offering, the animal, be it from the herd or flock, must be perfect, if he is to be acceptable; it must be unblemished. 22 You will not offer Yahweh any animal which is blind, lame, mutilated, ulcerous, scabby or covered in sores. No part of such an animal will be offered on the altar as food burnt for Yahweh. 23 As a voluntary offering, you may offer a bull or a lamb that is underdeveloped or deformed; but such will not be acceptable in payment of a vow. 24 You will not offer Yahweh an animal if its testicles have been bruised, crushed, torn or cut off. You may not do that in your country, 25 and you may not accept any such from the hands of a stranger, to be offered as food for your God. Their deformity is a blemish, and they would not make you acceptable." '

26 Yahweh spoke to Moses and said:

27 'A calf, lamb, or kid will stay with its dam for seven days after being born. From the eighth day onwards, it will be acceptable as food burnt for Yahweh. 28 But no animal, whether cow or ewe, will be slaughtered on the same day as its young.

29 'If you offer Yahweh a sacrifice with praise, do it in the acceptable manner; 30 it must be eaten the same day; you will leave nothing over till next morning. I am Yahweh.

31 'You will keep my commands and put them into practice. I am Yahweh. 32 You will not profane my holy name—so that I may be honoured as holy among the Israelites, I, Yahweh, who make you holy, 33 I who brought you out of Egypt, to be your God, I, Yahweh.'

The ritual for the annual feasts

23 Yahweh spoke to Moses and said: 2 'Speak to the Israelites and say:

(The solemn festivals of Yahweh to which you will summon them are my sacred assemblies.)

"These are my solemn festivals:

The Sabbath

3 "You will work for six days, but the seventh will be a day of complete rest, a day for the sacred assembly on which you do no work at all. Wherever you live, this is a Sabbath for Yahweh.

4 "These are Yahweh's solemn festivals, the

sacred assemblies to which you will summon the Israelites on the appointed day:

The Passover and the feast of Unleavened Bread

5 "The fourteenth day of the first month, at twilight, is the Passover of Yahweh; 6 and the fifteenth day of the same month is the feast of Unleavened Bread for Yahweh. For seven days you will eat unleavened bread. 7 On the first day you will hold a sacred assembly; you will do no heavy work. 8 For seven days you will offer food burnt for Yahweh. On the seventh day there will be a sacred assembly; you will do no heavy work." '

The first sheaf

9 Yahweh spoke to Moses and said:

10 'Speak to the Israelites and say:

"When you enter the country which I am giving you and reap the harvest there, you will bring the priest the first sheaf of your harvest, 11 and he will present it to Yahweh with the gesture of offering, for you to be acceptable. The priest will make this offering on the day after the Sabbath, 12 and on the same day as you make this offering, you will offer Yahweh an unblemished lamb one year old as a burnt offering. 13 The cereal offering for that day will be two-tenths of wheaten flour mixed with oil, as food burnt as a smell pleasing to Yahweh. The libation will be a quarter of a *hin* of wine. 14 You will eat no bread, roasted ears of wheat or fresh produce before this day, before making the offering to your God. This is a perpetual law for all your descendants, wherever you live.

The feast of Weeks

15 "From the day after the Sabbath, the day on which you bring the sheaf of offering, you will count seven full weeks. 16 You will count fifty days, to the day after the seventh Sabbath, and then you will offer Yahweh a new cereal offering. 17 You will bring bread from your homes to present with the gesture of offering—two loaves, made of two-tenths of wheaten flour

baked with leaven; these are first-fruits for Yahweh. 18 In addition to the bread, you will offer seven unblemished lambs a year old, a young bull and two rams, as a burnt offering to Yahweh with a cereal offering and a libation, as food burnt as a smell pleasing to Yahweh. 19 You will also offer a goat as a sacrifice for sin, and two lambs a year old as communion sacrifice. 20 The priest will present them before Yahweh with the gesture of offering, in addition to the bread of the first-fruits. These, and the two lambs, are holy things for Yahweh, and will revert to the priest.

21 "On the same day, you will hold an assembly; for you this will be a sacred assembly; you will do no heavy work. This is a perpetual law for your descendants, wherever you live.

22 "When you reap the harvest in your country, you will not reap to the very edges of your field, nor will you gather the gleanings of the harvest. You will leave them for the poor and the stranger. I am Yahweh your God." '

23 Yahweh spoke to Moses and said:

24 'Speak to the Israelites and say:

"The first day of the seventh month[a] will be a day of rest for you, of remembrance and acclamation, a sacred assembly. 25 You will do no heavy work and you will offer food burnt for Yahweh." '

The Day of Expiation

26 Yahweh spoke to Moses and said:

27 'But the tenth day of this seventh month will be the Day of Expiation. You will hold a sacred assembly. You will fast and offer food burnt for Yahweh. 28 You will do no work that day, for it is the Day of Expiation, on which the rite of expiation will be performed for you before Yahweh your God. 29 Anyone who fails to fast that day will be outlawed from his people; 30 anyone who works that day I shall eliminate from his people. 31 No work will be done—this is a perpetual law for your descendants wherever you live. 32 It must be a day of

23a A Canaanite new-moon festival, but held now in one month only, the first of autumn.

complete rest for you. You will fast; on the evening of the ninth day of the month, from this evening till the following evening, you will rest completely.'

The feast of Shelters

33 Yahweh spoke to Moses and said:
   34 'Speak to the Israelites and say:
   "On the fifteenth day of this seventh month there will be the feast of Shelters for Yahweh, lasting for seven days. 35 The first day will be a day of sacred assembly; you will do no heavy work. 36 For seven days you will offer food burnt for Yahweh. On the eighth day you will hold a sacred assembly and you will offer food burnt for Yahweh. It is a day of solemn meeting; you will do no heavy work.

Conclusion of rules for festivals

37 "These are Yahweh's solemn festivals to which you will summon the Israelites, the sacred assemblies for the purpose of offering food burnt for Yahweh, consisting of burnt offerings, cereal offerings, sacrifices and libations, each on its appropriate day, 38 besides Yahweh's Sabbaths, and your presents and all your votive and voluntary gifts that you make to Yahweh.

Recapitulation on the feast of Shelters

39 "But on the fifteenth day of the seventh month, when you have gathered in the produce of the land, you will celebrate the feast of Yahweh for seven days. The first and eighth days will be days of rest. 40 On the first day you will take choice fruit, palm branches, boughs of leafy trees and flowering shrubs from the river bank, and for seven days enjoy yourselves before Yahweh your God. 41 You will celebrate a feast for Yahweh in this way for seven days every year. This is a perpetual law for your descendants.

   "You will keep this feast in the seventh month. 42 For seven days you will live in shelters: all the citizens of Israel will live in shelters, 43 so that your descendants may know

that I made the Israelites live in shelters when I brought them out of Egypt, I, Yahweh your God." '
   44 Moses then promulgated Yahweh's solemn festivals to the Israelites.

Complementary ritual prescriptions

24 Yahweh spoke to Moses and said: 2 'Order the Israelites to bring you crushed-olive oil for the lamp-stand, and keep a flame burning there continually. 3 Aaron will keep it permanently in trim from evening to morning, outside the curtain of the Testimony in the Tent of Meeting, before Yahweh. This is a perpetual decree for your descendants: 4 Aaron will keep the lamps permanently trimmed on the pure lamp-stand before Yahweh.
   5 'You will take wheaten flour and with it bake twelve loaves, each of two-tenths of an *ephah*. 6 You will then place them in two rows of six on the pure table before Yahweh 7 and put pure incense on each row, to make it food offered as a memorial, food burnt for Yahweh. 8 Every Sabbath they will be arranged before Yahweh. The Israelites will provide them as a permanent covenant. 9 They will belong to Aaron and his sons, who will eat them inside the holy place since, for him, they are an especially holy part of the food burnt for Yahweh. This is a permanent law.'

A case of blasphemy; the law of retaliation

10 There was a man whose mother was an Israelite woman and whose father was an Egyptian. He came out of his house and, in the camp, surrounded by the Israelites, he began to quarrel with a man who was an Israelite. 11 Now the son of the Israelite woman blasphemed the Name and cursed it. He was then taken to Moses (his mother's name was Shelomith daughter of Dibri, of the tribe of Dan). 12 He was then put under guard until Yahweh's will should be made clear to them.
   13 Yahweh spoke to Moses and said:
   14 'Take the man who pronounced the curse outside the camp. All those who heard him

must then lay their hands on his head, and the whole community must then stone him. 15 Then say to the Israelites:

"Anyone who curses his God will bear the consequences of his sin, 16 and anyone who blasphemes the name of Yahweh will be put to death; the whole community will stone him; be he alien or native-born, if he blasphemes the Name, he will be put to death.

17 "Anyone who strikes down any other human being will be put to death.

18 "Anyone who strikes down an animal will make restitution for it: a life for a life.

19 "Anyone who injures a neighbour shall receive the same in return, 20 broken limb for broken limb, eye for eye, tooth for tooth. As the injury inflicted, so will be the injury suffered. 21 Whoever strikes down an animal will make restitution for it, and whoever strikes down a human being will be put to death. 22 The sentence you pass will be the same, whether on native-born or on alien; for I am Yahweh your God." '

23 Moses having told the Israelites this, they took the man who had pronounced the curse out of the camp and stoned him. And so the Israelites carried out Yahweh's order to Moses.

The sabbatical year

25 Yahweh spoke to Moses on Mount Sinai and said:

2 'Speak to the Israelites and say to them:

"When you enter the country which I am giving you, the land must keep a Sabbath's rest for Yahweh. 3 For six years you will sow your field, for six years you will prune your vineyard and gather its produce. 4 But in the seventh year the land will have a sabbatical rest, a Sabbath for Yahweh. You will neither sow your field, nor prune your vineyard, 5 nor reap any grain which has grown of its own accord, nor gather the grapes from your untrimmed vine. It will be a year of rest for the land. 6 But what the land produces in its Sabbath will serve to feed you, your slave, male or female, your employee and your guest residing with you; 7 for your cattle too, and the wild animals

of your country, whatever it produces will serve as food.

The year of jubilee

8 "You will count seven weeks of years—seven times seven years, that is to say a period of seven weeks of years, forty-nine years. 9 And on the tenth day of the seventh month you will sound the trumpet; on the Day of Expiation you will sound the trumpet throughout the land. 10 You will declare this fiftieth year to be sacred and proclaim the liberation of all the country's inhabitants. You will keep this as a jubilee: each of you will return to his ancestral property, each to his own clan. 11 This fiftieth year will be a jubilee year for you; in it you will not sow, you will not harvest the grain that has come up on its own or in it gather grapes from your untrimmed vine. 12 The jubilee will be a holy thing for you; during it you will eat whatever the fields produce.

13 "In this year of jubilee, each of you will return to his ancestral property. 14 If you buy land from, or sell land to, your fellow-countryman, neither of you may exploit the other. 15 In buying from your fellow-countryman, you will take account of the number of years since the jubilee; the sale-price he fixes for you will depend on the number of productive years still to run. 16 The greater the number of years, the higher the price you will ask for it; the fewer the number of years, the greater the reduction; for what he is selling you is a certain number of harvests. 17 So you will not exploit one another, but fear your God, for I am Yahweh your God.

Divine guarantee for the sabbatical year

18 "Hence, you will put my laws and customs into practice; you will keep them and put them into practice, and you will live securely in the country. 19 The land will give its fruit, and you will eat your fill and live in security.

20 "In case you should ask: What shall we eat in this seventh year if we do not sow or harvest our produce? 21 I shall order my blessing to be on you in the sixth year, which will yield

you enough produce for three years. ²² You will have the old produce to eat while you are sowing in the eighth year, and even in the ninth year, you will be eating the old produce, while waiting for the harvest of that year.

Redemption of land

²³ "Land will not be sold absolutely, for the land belongs to me, and you are only strangers and guests of mine. ²⁴ You will allow a right of redemption over any ancestral property. ²⁵ If your brother becomes impoverished and sells off part of his ancestral property, his nearest male relative will come and exercise his family rights over what his brother has sold. ²⁶ The man who has no one to exercise this right may, once he has found the means to effect the redemption, ²⁷ calculate the number of years that the alienation would have lasted, repay to the purchaser the sum due for the time still to run, and so recover his ancestral property. ²⁸ If he cannot find the sum in compensation, the property sold will remain in the possession of the purchaser until the jubilee year. In the jubilee year, the latter will vacate it and return to his own ancestral property.

²⁹ "If anyone sells a dwelling house inside a walled town, he will have the right of redemption until the expiry of the year following the sale. His right of redemption is limited to the year; ³⁰ and if the redemption has not been effected by the end of the year, the house in the walled town will become the property of the purchaser and his descendants in perpetuity; he need not vacate it at the jubilee. ³¹ But houses in villages not enclosed by walls will be considered as situated in the open country; they carry the right of redemption, and the purchaser will vacate them at the jubilee.

³² "As regards the towns of the Levites, town houses forming part of their ancestral property will carry a perpetual right of redemption in their favour. ³³ If a Levite is the one to be affected by the right of redemption, at the jubilee he will vacate the purchased property and return to his own home, to the town in which he has a title to property. The

houses in the Levites' towns represent their ancestral property in Israel, ³⁴ and the arable land depending on these towns cannot be sold, being their ancestral property for ever.

Redemption of persons

³⁵ "If your brother becomes impoverished and cannot support himself in the community, you will assist him as you would a stranger or guest, so that he can go on living with you. ³⁶ Do not charge him interest on a loan, but fear your God, and let your brother live with you. ³⁷ You will not lend him money on interest or give him food to make a profit out of it. ³⁸ I am Yahweh your God who brought you out of Egypt to give you the land of Canaan and be your God.

³⁹ "If your brother becomes impoverished while with you and sells himself to you, you will not make him do the work of a slave; ⁴⁰ you will treat him like an employee or guest, and he will work for you until the jubilee year. ⁴¹ He will then leave you, both he and his children, and return to his clan and regain possession of his ancestral property. ⁴² For they are my servants whom I have brought out of Egypt, and they may not be bought and sold as slaves. ⁴³ You will not oppress your brother-Israelites harshly but will fear your God.

⁴⁴ "The male and female slaves you have will come from the nations round you; from these you may purchase male and female slaves. ⁴⁵ As slaves, you may also purchase the children of aliens resident among you, and also members of their families living with you who have been born on your soil; and they will become your property, ⁴⁶ and you may leave them as a legacy to your sons after you as their perpetual possession. These you may have for slaves; but you will not oppress your brother-Israelites.

⁴⁷ "If a stranger or guest living with you gets rich and your brother, in the course of dealings with him, becomes impoverished and sells himself to this stranger or guest, or to the descendant of a stranger's family, ⁴⁸ he will enjoy the right of redemption after being sold, and

one of his brothers may redeem him. ⁴⁹His paternal uncle, his uncle's son, or a member of his own family may redeem him; if he has the means, he may redeem himself. ⁵⁰By agreement with his purchaser, he will count the number of years between the year of sale and the jubilee year; his sale-price will be proportionate to the number of years, his time being valued as that of an employee. ⁵¹If there are still many years to run, in proportion to their number he will refund part of his sale-price as payment for his redemption. ⁵²And if there are only a few years still to run before the jubilee year, he will calculate with him what should be refunded for his redemption, in proportion to their number, ⁵³as though he were hired by the year. You will see to it that he is not harshly oppressed.

⁵⁴"If he has not been redeemed in any of these ways, he will go free in the jubilee year, both he and his children; ⁵⁵for the Israelites are my servants; they are my servants whom I brought out of Egypt. I am Yahweh your God." '

Summary: conclusion

26 ' "You will not make idols for yourselves; you will not erect statues or cultic stones, or erect carved stones in your country, for you to worship: for I, Yahweh, am your God. ²You will keep my Sabbaths and revere my sanctuary. I am Yahweh.

Blessings

³"If you live according to my laws, if you keep my commandments and put them into practice, ⁴I shall give you the rain you need at the right time; the soil will yield its produce and the trees of the countryside their fruit; ⁵you will thresh until vintage time and gather grapes until sowing time. You will eat your fill of bread and live secure in your land.

⁶"I shall give peace in the land, and you will go to sleep with no one to frighten you. I shall rid the land of beasts of prey. The sword will not pass through your land. ⁷You will pursue your enemies and they will fall before your sword; ⁸five of you pursuing a hundred of them, one hundred pursuing ten thousand; and your enemies will fall before your sword.

⁹"I shall turn towards you, I shall make you fertile and make your numbers grow, and I shall uphold my covenant with you.

¹⁰"Having eaten all you need of last year's harvest, you will throw out the old to make room for the new.

¹¹"I shall fix my home among you and never reject you. ¹²I shall live among you; I shall be your God and you will be my people, ¹³I, Yahweh your God, who brought you out of Egypt so that you should be their slaves no longer, and who broke the bonds of your yoke and made you walk with head held high.

Curses

¹⁴"But if you will not listen to me and do not put all these commandments into practice, ¹⁵if you reject my laws and detest my customs, and you break my covenant by not putting all my commandments into practice, ¹⁶this is how I shall treat you:

"I shall subject you to terror, consumption and fever, making you dim of sight and short of breath. You will sow your seed in vain, for your enemies will eat it. ¹⁷I shall turn against you and you will be defeated by your enemies. Your foes will have the mastery over you, and you will flee when no one is pursuing you.

¹⁸"And if, in spite of this, you will not listen to me, I shall punish you seven times over for your sins. ¹⁹I shall break your proud strength. I shall make the sky like iron for you, and your soil like bronze. ²⁰You will wear out your strength in vain, your land will not yield its produce, nor the trees of the country their fruit.

²¹"And if you go against me and will not listen to me, I shall heap seven times more plagues on you for your sins. ²²I shall send wild animals to attack you and rob you of your children, destroy your cattle and reduce your numbers until your roads are deserted.

²³"And if that does not reform you, and you

14 READ LEVITICUS 26:1–13.

I shall live among you; I shall be your God and you will be my people.—LEVITICUS 26:12

THE BLESSINGS OF HEAVEN

Who can measure the happiness of heaven, where no evil can touch us, no good will be out of reach; where life is to be one long laud extolling God, who will be all in all; where there will be no weariness to call for rest, no need to call for toil, no place for any energy but praise? Of this I am assured whenever I read or hear the sacred song: "How blessed are those who live in your house; they shall praise you continuously" (Ps 84:4). Every fiber and organ of our imperishable body will play its part in the praising of God. . . .

In heaven, all glory will be true glory, since no one could ever err in praising too little or too much. True honor will never be denied where due, never be given where undeserved, and, since none but the worthy are permitted there, no one will unworthily ambition glory. Perfect peace will reign, since nothing in ourselves or in any others could disturb this peace. The promised reward of virtue will be the best and the greatest of all possible prizes—the very Giver of virtue himself, for that is what the Prophet meant: "I shall be your God and you will be my people." God will be the source of every satisfaction, more than any heart can rightly crave, more than life and health, food and wealth, glory and honor, peace and every good—so that God, as St. Paul said, "may be all in all" (1 Co 15:28). He will be the consummation of all our desiring—the object of our unending vision, of our unlessening love, of our unwearying praise. And in this gift of vision, this response of love, this paean of praise, all alike will share, as all will share in everlasting life.   ST. AUGUSTINE, 354–430

YOU WILL FIND THE NEXT READING AT NUMBERS 20.

still go against me, 24 then I shall go against you and punish you another seven times over for your sins. 25 I shall bring the sword on you, which will avenge the covenant, and when you huddle inside your towns, I shall send pestilence among you, and you will fall into the enemy's clutches. 26 When I take away the bread which supports you, ten women will be able to bake your bread in one oven and will then dole your bread out by weight; you will eat but not be satisfied.

27 "And if, in spite of this, you will not listen to me but go against me, 28 I shall go against you in fury and punish you seven times over for your sins. 29 You will eat the flesh of your own sons, you will eat the flesh of your own daughters. 30 I shall destroy your high places and smash your incense-altars; I shall pile your corpses on the corpses of your foul idols and shall reject you. 31 I shall reduce your cities to ruins; I shall lay waste your sanctuary and refuse to inhale from you smells intended to please. 32 I shall make such a desolation of the country that your enemies who come to live there will be appalled by it. 33 And I shall scatter you among the nations. I shall unsheathe the sword against you, reducing your country to desert and your towns to ruins. 34 Then the country will indeed observe its Sabbaths, all the while it lies deserted, while you are in the

country of your enemies. Then indeed the country will rest and observe its Sabbaths. 35 And as it lies deserted it will rest, as it never did on your Sabbaths when you were living there. 36 I shall strike such fear into the hearts of those of you who survive in the countries of their enemies that the sound of a falling leaf will set them fleeing; they will flee as though fleeing from the sword, and fall when no one is pursuing. 37 They will stumble over one another as though fleeing before the sword, when no one is pursuing. You will be powerless to stand up to your enemies; 38 you will perish among the nations, and the land of your enemies will swallow you up. 39 Those of you who survive will pine away in their guilt in the countries of their enemies and, bearing the guilt of their ancestors too, will pine away like them.

40 "Then they shall admit their guilt and that of their ancestors and their infidelities against me, and further, their setting themselves against me.

41 "I in my turn will go against them and bring them into the land of their enemies. Then their uncircumcised hearts will grow humble and then they will accept the punishment for their guilt. 42 I shall remember my covenant with Jacob, I shall remember my covenant with Isaac and my covenant with Abraham; and I shall remember the country too.

43 "Abandoned, the country will keep its Sabbaths, as it lies deserted in their absence, and they will have to accept the punishment for their guilt, since they detested my customs and rejected my laws.

44 "Yet, in spite of all this, when they are in the land of their enemies, I shall not so utterly reject or detest them as to destroy them completely and break my covenant with them; for I am Yahweh their God. 45 For their sake I shall remember the covenant I made with those first generations that I brought out of Egypt while other nations watched, so that I should be their God, I, Yahweh." '

46 Such were the decrees, customs and laws

which Yahweh established between himself and the Israelites on Mount Sinai through Moses.

Tariffs and valuations

27 Yahweh spoke to Moses and said: 2 'Speak to the Israelites and say:

"If anyone vows the value of a person to Yahweh and wishes to discharge the vow:

3 "a man between twenty and sixty years of age will be valued at fifty silver shekels—the sanctuary-shekel; 4 a woman will be valued at thirty shekels;

5 "between five and twenty years, a boy will be valued at twenty shekels, a girl at ten shekels;

6 "between one month and five years, a boy will be valued at five silver shekels, a girl at three silver shekels;

7 "at sixty years and over, a man will be valued at fifteen shekels and a woman at ten shekels.

8 "If the person who made the vow cannot meet this valuation, he will present the person concerned to the priest, and the priest will set a value proportionate to the resources of the person who made the vow.

9 "In the case of an animal suitable for offering to Yahweh, any such animal given to Yahweh will be holy. 10 It cannot be exchanged or replaced, a good one instead of a bad one, or a bad one instead of a good one. If one animal is substituted for another, both of them will become holy. 11 In the case of an unclean animal unsuitable for offering to Yahweh, whatever it may be, it will be presented to the priest 12 and he will set a value on it, in relation to its worth. His valuation will be decisive; 13 but if the person wishes to redeem it, he will add one-fifth to the valuation.

14 "If a man consecrates his house to Yahweh, the priest will set a value on it, in relation to its worth. His valuation will be decisive. 15 If the man who has vowed his house wishes to redeem it, he will add one-fifth to the valuation, and it will revert to him.

16 "If a man consecrates one of the fields of

his ancestral property to Yahweh, its value will be calculated in terms of its yield, at the rate of fifty silver shekels to one *homer* of barley.

17 "If he consecrates the field during the jubilee year, he will abide by this valuation. 18 But if he consecrates it after the jubilee, the priest will calculate the price in terms of the number of years still to run until the next jubilee and the valuation will be reduced accordingly.

19 "If he wishes to redeem the field, he will add one-fifth to the valuation, and the field will revert to him. 20 If he does not redeem it but sells it to someone else, the right of redemption ceases; 21 when the purchaser has to vacate it at the jubilee year, it becomes consecrated to Yahweh, like a field vowed unconditionally; ownership of it passes to the priest.

22 "If he consecrates to Yahweh a field which he has bought, but which is not part of his ancestral property, 23 the priest will calculate the valuation in terms of the number of years still to run before the jubilee year; and the man will pay this sum the same day since it is consecrated to Yahweh. 24 In the jubilee year the field will revert to the vendor, the man to whose ancestral property the land belongs. 25 All your valuations will be made in sanctuary-shekels, at the rate of twenty *gerah* to the shekel.

Particular rules for the redemption

26 "The first-born of livestock is born to Yahweh; no one may consecrate it, whether it be cattle or sheep, for it belongs to Yahweh anyway. 27 But if it is an unclean animal, it may be redeemed at the valuation price with one-fifth added; if the animal is not redeemed, it will be sold at the valuation price.

28 "Nothing, however, that someone vows unconditionally to Yahweh may be redeemed, nothing he possesses, be it a human being or animal or field of his ancestral property. What is vowed unconditionally is especially holy and belongs to Yahweh. 29 A human being vowed unconditionally cannot be redeemed but will be put to death.

30 "All tithes on land, levied on the produce of the soil or on the fruit of trees, belong to Yahweh; they are consecrated to Yahweh. 31 If anyone wishes to redeem part of his tithe, he will add one-fifth to its value.

32 "In all tithes on herds or flocks, the tenth animal of all that pass under the herdsman's staff will be consecrated to Yahweh; 33 there will be no examining whether it is good or bad, and no substitution. If substitution takes place, the animal and its substitute will both become holy without possibility of redemption." '

34 Such were the orders which Yahweh gave Moses on Mount Sinai for the Israelites.

The Book of

NUMBERS

The census[a]

1 Yahweh spoke to Moses, in the desert of Sinai, in the Tent of Meeting, on the first day of the second month, in the second year after the exodus from Egypt, and said:

2 'Take a census of the whole community of Israelites by clans and families, taking a count of the names of all the males, head by head. 3 You and Aaron will register all those in Israel, twenty years of age and over, fit to bear arms, company by company; 4 you will have one man from each tribe, the head of his family, to help you.

The census officials

5 'These are the names of those who must help you:

For Reuben, Elizur son of Shedeur.

6 For Simeon, Shelumiel son of Zurishaddai.

7 For Judah, Nahshon son of Amminadab.

8 For Issachar, Nethanel son of Zuar.

9 For Zebulun, Eliab son of Helon.

10 Of the sons of Joseph: for Ephraim, Elishama son of Ammihud; for Manasseh, Gamaliel son of Pedahzur.

11 For Benjamin, Abidan son of Gideoni.

12 For Dan, Ahiezer son of Ammishaddai.

13 For Asher, Pagiel son of Ochran.

14 For Gad, Eliasaph son of Reuel.

15 For Naphtali, Ahira son of Enan.'

16 These were men of repute in the community; they were the leaders of their ancestral tribes, the heads of Israel's thousands.

17 Moses and Aaron took these men who had been named 18 and on the first day of the second month they mustered the whole community. The Israelites established their pedigrees by clans and families, and one by one the names of all men of twenty years and over were recorded. 19 As Yahweh had ordered, Moses registered them in the desert of Sinai.

Carrying out the census

20 Once the pedigrees of the descendants of Reuben, Israel's first-born, had been established by clans and families, the names of all the males of twenty years and over, fit to bear arms, were recorded one by one. 21 The total of these for the tribe of Reuben was forty-six thousand five hundred.

22 Once the pedigrees of Simeon's descendants had been established by clans and families, the names of all the males of twenty years and over, fit to bear arms, were recorded one by one. 23 The total of these for the tribe of Simeon was fifty-nine thousand three hundred.

24 Once the pedigrees of Gad's descendants had been established by clans and families, the names of all the males of twenty years and over, fit to bear arms, were recorded one by one. 25 The total of these for the tribe of Gad was forty-five thousand six hundred and fifty.

26 Once the pedigrees of Judah's descendants had been established by clans and families, the names of all the males of twenty years and over, fit to bear arms, were recorded one by one. 27 The total of these for the tribe of Judah was seventy-four thousand six hundred.

28 Once the pedigrees of Issachar's descendants had been established by clans and families, the names of all the males of twenty years

1a Israel is shown as a settled community, centred on the Levites. The numbers fit that period.

and over, fit to bear arms, were recorded one by one. ²⁹ The total of these for the tribe of Issachar was fifty-four thousand four hundred.

³⁰ Once the pedigrees of Zebulun's descendants had been established by clans and families, the names of all the males of twenty years and over, fit to bear arms, were recorded one by one. ³¹ The total of these for the tribe of Zebulun was fifty-seven thousand four hundred.

³² As regards the descendants of Joseph: once the pedigrees of Ephraim's descendants had been established by clans and families, the names of all the males of twenty years and over, fit to bear arms, were recorded one by one. ³³ The total of these for the tribe of Ephraim was forty thousand five hundred.

³⁴ Once the pedigrees of Manasseh's descendants had been established by clans and families, the names of all the males of twenty years and over, fit to bear arms, were recorded one by one. ³⁵ The total of these for the tribe of Manasseh was thirty-two thousand two hundred.

³⁶ Once the pedigrees of Benjamin's descendants had been established by clans and families, the names of all the males of twenty years and over, fit to bear arms, were recorded one by one. ³⁷ The total of these for the tribe of Benjamin was thirty-five thousand four hundred.

³⁸ Once the pedigrees of Dan's descendants had been established by clans and families, the names of all the males of twenty years and over, fit to bear arms, were recorded one by one. ³⁹ The total of these for the tribe of Dan was sixty-two thousand seven hundred.

⁴⁰ Once the pedigrees of Asher's descendants had been established by clans and families, the names of all the males of twenty years and over, fit to bear arms, were recorded one by one. ⁴¹ The total of these for the tribe of Asher was forty-one thousand five hundred.

⁴² Once the pedigrees of Naphtali's descendants had been established by clans and families, the names of all the males of twenty years

and over, fit to bear arms, were recorded one by one. ⁴³ The total of these for the tribe of Naphtali was fifty-three thousand four hundred.

⁴⁴ Such were the men registered by Moses, Aaron and the leaders of Israel, of whom there were twelve, each representing his family. ⁴⁵ All the Israelites of twenty years and over, fit to bear arms, were counted by families. ⁴⁶ Altogether, the total came to six hundred and three thousand five hundred and fifty.

⁴⁷ But the Levites and their tribes were not included in the count.

Statute for the Levites

⁴⁸ Yahweh spoke to Moses and said:

⁴⁹ 'Do not, however, take a census of the Levites, or register them with the other Israelites, ⁵⁰ but enrol the Levites to take charge of the Dwelling where the Testimony is and of all its furnishings and belongings. They must carry the Dwelling and all its furnishings; they must look after the Dwelling and pitch their camp round it. ⁵¹ Whenever the Dwelling is moved, the Levites will dismantle it; whenever the Dwelling stops for the night, the Levites will erect it. Any unauthorised person coming near it will be put to death. ⁵² The Israelites will pitch their tents, each in their own encampment and by their own standard, company by company, ⁵³ but the Levites will pitch their tents round the Dwelling where the Testimony is. In this way Retribution will be kept from falling on the whole community of Israelites, and the Levites will keep charge of the Dwelling of the Testimony.'

⁵⁴ The Israelites did exactly as Yahweh had ordered Moses. They did as he said.

Order of the tribes

2 Yahweh spoke to Moses and to Aaron and said:

² 'The Israelites must pitch their tents, each man by his own standard, under their family emblems. They must pitch their tents round the Dwelling where the Testimony is, some distance away.

3 'Encamped on the east side:

'Furthest towards the east, the standard of the camp of Judah, unit by unit. Leader of the Judahites: Nahshon son of Amminadab. 4 His company: seventy-four thousand six hundred men.

5 'Next to him:

'The tribe of Issachar. Leader of the Issacharites: Nethanel son of Zuar. 6 His company: fifty-four thousand four hundred men.

7 'The tribe of Zebulun. Leader of the Zebulunites: Eliab son of Helon. 8 His company: fifty-seven thousand four hundred men.

9 'The tribal forces in the camp of Judah number in all a hundred and eighty-six thousand four hundred. These will be the first to break camp.

10 'On the south side, the standard of the camp of Reuben, unit by unit. Leader of the Reubenites: Elizur son of Shedeur. 11 His company: forty-six thousand five hundred men.

12 'Next to him:

'The tribe of Simeon. Leader of the Simeonites: Shelumiel son of Zurishaddai. 13 His company: fifty-nine thousand three hundred men.

14 'The tribe of Gad. Leader of the Gadites: Eliasaph son of Reuel. 15 His company: forty-five thousand six hundred and fifty men.

16 'The tribal forces in the camp of Reuben number in all a hundred and fifty-one thousand four hundred and fifty. They will be second to break camp.

17 'Next, the Tent of Meeting will move, since the camp of the Levites is situated in the middle of the other camps. The order of movement will be the order of encampment, each man under his own standard.

18 'On the west side, the standard of the camp of Ephraim, unit by unit. Leader of the Ephraimites: Elishama son of Ammihud. 19 His company: forty thousand five hundred men.

20 'Next to him:

'The tribe of Manasseh. Leader of the Manassehites: Gamaliel son of Pedahzur. 21 His company: thirty-two thousand two hundred men.

22 'The tribe of Benjamin. Leader of the Benjaminites: Abidan son of Gideoni. 23 His company: thirty-five thousand four hundred men.

24 'The tribal forces in the camp of Ephraim number in all a hundred and eight thousand one hundred. They will be third to break camp.

25 'On the north side, the standard of the camp of Dan, unit by unit. Leader of the Danites: Ahiezer son of Ammishaddai. 26 His company: sixty-two thousand seven hundred men.

27 'Next to him:

'The tribe of Asher. Leader of the Asherites: Pagiel son of Ochran. 28 His company: forty-one thousand five hundred men.

29 'The tribe of Naphtali. Leader of the Naphtalites: Ahira son of Enan. 30 His company: fifty-three thousand four hundred men.

31 'The tribal forces in the camp of Dan number in all a hundred and fifty-seven thousand six hundred. They will be the last to break camp.

'All under their appropriate standards.'

32 Such was the tally of the Israelites when the census was taken by families. The full count of the entire camp, unit by unit, came to six hundred and three thousand five hundred and fifty. 33 But, as Yahweh had ordered Moses, the Levites were not included in the census of the Israelites.

34 The Israelites did exactly as Yahweh had ordered Moses. This was how they pitched camp, grouped by standards. This was how they broke camp, each man in his own clan, each man with his own family.

The tribe of Levi

3 These were the descendants of Aaron and Moses, at the time when Yahweh spoke to Moses on Mount Sinai.

2 These were the names of Aaron's sons: Nadab the eldest, then Abihu, Eleazar and Ithamar.

3 Such were the names of Aaron's sons,

priests anointed and invested with the powers of the priesthood. 4 Nadab and Abihu died in Yahweh's presence, in the desert of Sinai, when they offered unauthorised fire before Yahweh. They left no children and so it fell to Eleazar and Ithamar to exercise the priesthood under their father Aaron.

5 Yahweh spoke to Moses and said:

6 'Muster the tribe of Levi and put it at the disposal of the priest Aaron: they must be at his service. 7 They will undertake the duties incumbent on him and the whole community before the Tent of Meeting, in serving the Dwelling, 8 and they will be in charge of all the furnishings of the Tent of Meeting and undertake the duties incumbent on the Israelites in serving the Dwelling. 9 You will present the Levites to Aaron and his sons as men dedicated; they will be given to him by the Israelites.

10 'You will register Aaron and his sons, who will carry out their priestly duty. But any unauthorised person who comes near must be put to death.'

11 Yahweh spoke to Moses and said:

12 'Look, I myself have chosen the Levites from the Israelites instead of all the first-born, those who emerge first from the womb in Israel; the Levites therefore belong to me. 13 For every first-born belongs to me. On the day when I struck down all the first-born in Egypt, I consecrated all the first-born in Israel, human and animal, to be my own. They are mine, Yahweh's.'

14 Yahweh spoke to Moses in the desert of Sinai and said:

15 'You must take a census of Levi's descendants by families and clans; all the males of the age of one month and over will be counted.'

16 At Yahweh's word Moses took a census of them, as Yahweh had ordered. 17 These were the names of Levi's sons: Gershon, Kohath and Merari.

18 These were the names of Gershon's sons by their clans: Libni and Shimei; 19 Kohath's sons by their clans: Amram, Izhar, Hebron and Uzziel; 20 Merari's sons by their clans:

Mahli and Mushi. These were the clans of Levi, grouped by families.

21 From Gershon were descended the Libnite and Shimeite clans; these were the Gershonite clans. 22 Their full number, counting the males of one month and over, came to seven thousand five hundred. 23 The Gershonite clans pitched their camp behind the Dwelling, on the west side. 24 The leader of the House of Gershon was Eliasaph son of Lael. 25 As regards the Tent of Meeting, the Gershonites had charge of the Dwelling, the Tent and its covering, the screen for the entrance to the Tent of Meeting, 26 the curtaining of the court, the screen for the entrance to the court surrounding the Dwelling and the altar, and the cords required in dealing with all this.

27 From Kohath were descended the Amramite, Izharite, Hebronite and Uzzielite clans; these were the Kohathite clans. 28 Their full number, counting the males of one month and over, came to eight thousand three hundred. They were in charge of the sanctuary. 29 The Kohathite clans pitched their camp on the south side of the Dwelling. 30 The leader of the house of the Kohathite clans was Elizaphan son of Uzziel. 31 They were in charge of the ark, the table, the lamp-stand, the altars, the sacred vessels used in the liturgy, and the curtain with all its fittings.

32 The chief of the Levite leaders was Eleazar, son of Aaron the priest. He supervised the people responsible for the sanctuary.

33 From Merari were descended the Mahlite and Mushite clans; these were the Merarite clans. 34 Their full number, counting the males of one month and over, came to six thousand two hundred. 35 The leader of the House of the Merarite clans was Zuriel, son of Abihail. They pitched their camp on the north side of the Dwelling. 36 The Merarites were in charge of the framework of the Dwelling, with its crossbars, poles, sockets and all its accessories and fittings, 37 and also the poles round the court, with their sockets, pegs and cords.

38 Finally, on the east side, in front of the Dwelling, in front of the Tent of Meeting, to-

wards the east, was the camp of Moses and Aaron and his sons, who had charge of the sanctuary on behalf of the Israelites. Any unauthorised person coming near was to be put to death.

39 The total number of male Levites of the age of one month and over, whom Moses counted by clans as Yahweh had ordered, came to twenty-two thousand.

40 Yahweh said to Moses:

'Take a census of all the first-born of the Israelites, all the males from the age of one month and over; take a census of them by name. 41 You will then present the Levites to me, Yahweh, instead of Israel, and similarly the Levites' cattle instead of the first-born cattle of the Israelites.'

42 As Yahweh ordered, Moses took a census of all the first-born of the Israelites. 43 The total count, by name, of the first-born from the age of one month and over came to twenty-two thousand two hundred and seventy-three.

44 Yahweh then spoke to Moses and said:

45 'Take the Levites instead of all the first-born of the Israelites, and the Levites' cattle instead of their cattle; the Levites will be mine, Yahweh's. 46 For the ransom of the two hundred and seventy-three first-born of the Israelites in excess of the number of Levites, 47 you will take five shekels for each, by the sanctuary-shekel, at twenty *gerah* to the shekel; 48 you will then give this money to Aaron and his sons as the ransom for the extra number.'

49 Moses took the ransom money for the extra ones unransomed by the Levites; 50 he took the money for the first-born of the Israelites: one thousand three hundred and sixty-five shekels, by the sanctuary-shekel; 51 and Moses then handed over their ransom money to Aaron and his sons, at Yahweh's bidding, as Yahweh had ordered Moses.

The Levite clans

4 Yahweh spoke to Moses and said: 2 'Take a census by clans and families of the Levites descended from Kohath: 3 all the men

between thirty and fifty years of age and eligible for military service, who will have their duties in the Tent of Meeting.

4 'These are the duties of the Kohathites: looking after those things that are especially holy.

5 'When camp is broken, Aaron and his sons must come and take down the screening curtain, and cover the ark of the Testimony with it. 6 Over this, they will put a covering of fine leather, over which they will spread a cloth entirely of violet-purple. They will then fix the poles to the ark.

7 'Over the offertory table they will spread a violet cloth, and on it put the dishes, cups, bowls and libation jars; the bread of permanent offering will also be on it. 8 Over these they will spread a scarlet cloth and cover the whole with a covering of fine leather. They will then fix the poles to the table.

9 'They will then take a violet cloth and cover the lamp-stand, its lamps, snuffers, trays and all the oil jars used for it, 10 and will lay it and all its accessories in a covering of fine leather and put it on the litter.

11 'Over the golden altar they will spread a violet cloth, and cover that with a covering of fine leather. They will then fix the poles to it.

12 'They will then take all the other objects used in the service of the sanctuary, put them in a violet cloth, with a covering of fine leather, and put it all on the litter.

13 'When they have removed the ashes from the altar, they will spread a scarlet cloth over it, 14 and on this place all the objects used in the liturgy, the fire pans, hooks, scoops, sprinkling basins and all the altar accessories. Over this they will spread a covering of fine leather. They will then fix the poles to it.

15 'Once Aaron and his sons have finished covering the holy things and all their accessories at the breaking of camp, the Kohathites will come and carry them, but without touching any of the holy things on pain of death. Such is the load for the Kohathites in the Tent of Meeting. 16 But Eleazar, son of Aaron the priest, is responsible for looking after the oil

for the light, the fragrant incense, the daily cereal offering and the anointing oil, and for supervising the entire Dwelling and everything in it, the holy things and their accessories.'

¹⁷ Yahweh spoke to Moses and said:

¹⁸ 'You must not let the group of Kohathite clans be lost to the rest of the Levites. ¹⁹ But deal with them in this way, so that they may survive and not incur death by approaching those things that are especially holy. Aaron and his sons will go in and assign to each of them his task and load, ²⁰ in such a way that they have no need to incur the death penalty by going in and setting eyes on the holy things, even for an instant.'

²¹ Yahweh spoke to Moses and said:

²² 'Take a census of the Gershonites by families and clans, too: ²³ all the men between thirty and fifty years of age, eligible for military service, who will have their duties in the Tent of Meeting.

²⁴ 'These are the duties of the Gershonite clans, their functions and their loads. ²⁵ They will carry the curtaining of the Dwelling, the Tent of Meeting with its covering and the covering of fine leather that goes over it, the screen for the entrance to the Tent of Meeting, ²⁶ the curtaining of the court, the screen for the entrance to the court surrounding the Dwelling and the altar, the cords, all the accessories for worship, and all the necessary equipment.

'They will be responsible for these things. ²⁷ All the duties of the Gershonites, their functions and their loads, will be carried out under the direction of Aaron and his sons: you will see that they fulfil their charge. ²⁸ Such are the duties of the Gershonite clans in the Tent of Meeting. Their work will be supervised by Ithamar, son of Aaron the priest.

²⁹ 'You will take a census of the Merarites by clans and families. ³⁰ You will take a census of all the men between thirty and fifty years of age, eligible for military service, who will have their duties in the Tent of Meeting.

³¹ 'The load they carry and the duties incumbent on them in the Tent of Meeting will be as follows: the framework of the Dwelling, its cross-bars, poles and sockets, ³² the poles round the court with their sockets, pegs, cords and all their tackle. You will draw up a list of their names with the loads for which each is responsible.

³³ 'Such are the duties of the Merarite clans. All their duties in the Tent of Meeting will be supervised by Ithamar, son of Aaron the priest.'

Census of the Levites

³⁴ Moses, Aaron and the leaders of the community took a census of the Kohathites by clans and families: ³⁵ all the men between thirty and fifty years of age, eligible for military service, for duties in the Tent of Meeting. ³⁶ The number of men counted in their clans came to two thousand seven hundred and fifty. ³⁷ Such was the total number of men in the Kohathite clans who were eligible for duties in the Tent of Meeting and whom Moses and Aaron counted at Yahweh's bidding through Moses.

³⁸ A census was taken of the Gershonites by clans and families: ³⁹ all the men between thirty and fifty years of age, eligible for military service, for duties in the Tent of Meeting. ⁴⁰ The number of men counted in their clans and families came to two thousand six hundred and thirty. ⁴¹ Such was the total number of men in the Gershonite clans who were eligible for duties in the Tent of Meeting, and whom Moses and Aaron counted at Yahweh's bidding.

⁴² A census was taken of the Merarite clans by clans and families: ⁴³ all the men between thirty and fifty years of age, eligible for military service, for duties in the Tent of Meeting. ⁴⁴ The number of men counted in their clans came to three thousand two hundred. ⁴⁵ Such was the total number of men in the Merarite clans, whom Moses and Aaron counted at Yahweh's bidding through Moses.

⁴⁶ The total number of Levites whom Moses, Aaron and the leaders of Israel counted in their clans and families, ⁴⁷ all the men be-

tween thirty and fifty years of age, eligible for religious duties and for those of transporting the Tent of Meeting [48] came to eight thousand five hundred and eighty. [49] At Yahweh's bidding through Moses, a census was taken of them and each man was assigned his duty and load. And so the census was conducted by Moses as Yahweh had ordered him.

Expulsion of the unclean

5 Yahweh spoke to Moses and said: [2] 'Order the Israelites to expel from the camp all those suffering from a contagious skin-disease or from a discharge, or who have become unclean by touching a corpse. [3] Whether man or woman, you will expel them; you will expel them from the camp, so that they do not pollute their encampments, in the heart of which I dwell.'

[4] The Israelites did so: they expelled them from the camp. The Israelites did as Yahweh had told Moses.

Restitution

[5] Yahweh spoke to Moses and said, [6] 'Speak to the Israelites:

"If a man or woman commits any of the sins by which people break faith with Yahweh, that person incurs guilt.

[7] "The person must confess the sin committed and restore in full the amount owed, with one-fifth added. Payment is to be made to the person wronged.

[8] "If, however, the latter has no relation to whom restitution can be made, the restitution due to Yahweh reverts to the priest, apart from the ram of expiation with which the priest makes expiation for the guilty party. [9] For of everything the Israelites consecrate and bring to the priest he has a right to the portion set aside. [10] Whatever anyone consecrates is his own; whatever is given to the priest belongs to the priest." '

Cereal offering in cases of suspicion

[11] Yahweh spoke to Moses and said, [12] 'Speak to the Israelites and say:

"If anyone has a wife who goes astray and is unfaithful to him, [13] if some other man sleeps with the woman without the husband's knowledge, and she secretly makes herself unclean, without any witness against her, and without anyone catching her in the act; [14] if, then, a spirit of suspicion comes over the husband and makes him suspicious of the wife who has disgraced herself, or again if this spirit of suspicion comes over him and makes him suspicious of his wife even when she is innocent, [15] the man will bring his wife before the priest, and on her behalf make an offering of one-tenth of an *ephah* of barley meal. He will not pour oil over it or put incense on it, because this is a cereal offering for a case of suspicion, a memorial offering to recall guilt to mind.

[16] "The priest will then bring the woman forward and place her before Yahweh! [17] The priest will then take fresh water in an earthen jar, and on the water throw dust that he has taken from the floor of the Dwelling. [18] After he has placed the woman before Yahweh, he will unbind her hair and put the commemorative cereal offering (that is, the cereal offering for a case of suspicion) into her hands. In his own hands the priest will hold the water of bitterness and cursing.

[19] "The priest will then put the woman on oath. He will say to her: If it is not true that a man has slept with you, that you have gone astray and made yourself unclean while under your husband's authority, may this water of bitterness and cursing do you no harm. [20] But if it is true that you have gone astray while under your husband's authority, that you have made yourself unclean and that a man other than your husband has slept with you ... [21] Here the priest will impose an imprecatory oath on the woman. He will say to her: ... May Yahweh make you the object of your people's execration and curses, by making your sexual organs shrivel and your belly swell! [22] May this water of cursing entering your bowels, make your belly swell and your sexual organs shrivel! To which the woman will reply: Amen! Amen!

23 "Having written these curses on a scroll and washed them off in the water of bitterness, 24 the priest will make the woman drink the water of bitterness and cursing; when the water of cursing enters into her, it will become bitter.

25 "The priest will then take the cereal offering for a case of suspicion from the woman's hands, and hold it up before Yahweh with a gesture of offering, and so carry it up to the altar. 26 He will take a handful of it as a memorial and burn it on the altar.

"After this, he will make the woman drink the water. 27 After he has made her drink it, if it is true that she has made herself unclean and been unfaithful to her husband, the water of cursing then entering into her will indeed be bitter: her belly will swell and her sexual organs shrivel, and she will be an object of execration to her people. 28 But if she has not made herself unclean, but is clean, then she will go unscathed and will bear children.

29 "Such is the ritual in cases of suspicion, when a woman has gone astray and made herself unclean while under her husband's authority, 30 or when a spirit of suspicion has come over a man and made him suspicious of his wife. When a husband brings such a woman before Yahweh, the priest will apply this ritual to her in full. 31 The husband will be guiltless, but the woman will bear the consequences of her guilt." '

The nazirite

6 Yahweh spoke to Moses and said, 2 'Speak to the Israelites and say:
"If a man or a woman wishes to make a vow, the nazirite vow, to vow himself to Yahweh, 3 he will abstain from wine and fermented liquor, he will not drink vinegar derived from one or the other, he will not drink grape-juice or eat grapes, be they fresh or dried. 4 For the duration of his vow he will eat nothing that comes from the vine, not even juice of unripe grapes or skins of grapes. 5 As long as he is bound by his vow, no razor will touch his head; until the time for which he has vowed

himself to Yahweh is completed, he remains consecrated and will let his hair grow freely. 6 For the entire period of his vow to Yahweh, he will not go near a corpse, 7 he will not make himself unclean for his father or his mother, or his brother or his sister, should they die, since on his head he carries his vow to his God. 8 Throughout the whole of his vow he is a person consecrated to Yahweh.

9 "If anyone suddenly dies near him, making his vowed hair unclean, he will shave his head on the day he is purified, he will shave his head on the seventh day. 10 On the eighth day, he will bring two turtledoves or two young pigeons to the priest, at the entrance to the Tent of Meeting. 11 The priest will offer one as a sacrifice for sin, and the other as a burnt offering and will then perform for the person the rite of expiation for the pollution which he has contracted from the corpse. He will consecrate his head that same day; 12 he will vow himself to Yahweh for the period of his nazirate, and will bring a male yearling lamb as a sacrifice of reparation. The time already spent will not count, since his hair had become unclean.

13 "This is the ritual for the nazirite on the day when the period of his vow is completed. He will be led to the entrance of the Tent of Meeting, 14 bringing his offering to Yahweh: an unblemished male yearling lamb as a burnt offering, an unblemished yearling ewe lamb as a sacrifice for sin, an unblemished ram as a peace offering, 15 and a basket of unleavened loaves made of fine flour mixed with oil, and of unleavened wafers spread with oil, with the cereal offerings and libations appropriate to them. 16 The priest, having brought all this before Yahweh, will offer the nazirite's sin sacrifice and burnt offering. 17 The latter will then offer the ram as a communion sacrifice with the basket of unleavened bread, and the priest will offer the accompanying cereal offering and libation. 18 The nazirite will then shave off his vowed hair at the entrance to the Tent of Meeting and, taking the locks of his vowed head, he will put them in the fire of the communion sacrifice. 19 The priest will take the

shoulder of the ram, as soon as it is cooked, with an unleavened cake from the basket, and an unleavened wafer, and put them into the hands of the nazirite once he has shaved off his hair. ²⁰With these he will make the gesture of offering before Yahweh; as it is a holy thing, it reverts to the priest, in addition to the forequarter that has been presented and the thigh that has been set aside. After this, the nazirite may drink wine.

²¹"Such is the ritual for the nazirite. If, besides his hair, he has also vowed a personal offering to Yahweh, he will (apart from anything else that his means allow) fulfil the vow that he has made, in addition to what the ritual prescribes for his hair." '

The form of blessing

²²Yahweh spoke to Moses and said, ²³'Speak to Aaron and his sons and say:

"This is how you must bless the Israelites. You will say:

²⁴ May Yahweh bless you and keep you.
²⁵ May Yahweh let his face shine on you and
be gracious to you.
²⁶ May Yahweh show you his face and bring
you peace."

²⁷This is how they must call down my name on the Israelites, and then I shall bless them.'

Offering of wagons

7 On the day Moses finished erecting the Dwelling, he anointed and consecrated it and all its furniture, as well as the altar and all its equipment. When he had anointed and consecrated it all, ²the leaders of Israel made an offering; they were the heads of their families, the tribal leaders who had presided over the census. ³They brought their offering before Yahweh: six covered wagons and twelve oxen, one wagon for every two leaders and one ox each. They brought them in front of the Dwelling. ⁴Yahweh spoke to Moses and said, ⁵'Accept these from them, and let them be set apart for the service of the Tent of Meeting.

You will give them to the Levites, to each as his duties require.' ⁶Moses took the wagons and oxen, and gave them to the Levites. ⁷To the Gershonites he gave two wagons and four oxen for the duties they had to perform. ⁸To the Merarites he gave four wagons and eight oxen for the duties they had to perform under the direction of Ithamar, son of Aaron the priest. ⁹But to the Kohathites he gave none at all, because the sacred charge entrusted to them had to be carried on their shoulders.

Dedication offering

¹⁰The leaders then made an offering for the dedication of the altar, on the day it was anointed. They brought their offering before the altar, ¹¹and Yahweh said to Moses, 'Each day one of the leaders must bring his offering for the dedication of the altar.'

¹²On the first day an offering was brought by Nahshon son of Amminadab, of the tribe of Judah. ¹³His offering consisted of: one silver bowl weighing a hundred and thirty shekels, one silver sprinkling bowl weighing seventy shekels (sanctuary-shekels), both of them full of fine flour mixed with oil as a cereal offering, ¹⁴one golden bowl weighing ten shekels, full of incense, ¹⁵one young bull, one ram and one male yearling lamb as a burnt offering, ¹⁶one he-goat as a sacrifice for sin, ¹⁷and two bulls, five rams, five he-goats and five male yearling lambs as a communion sacrifice. Such was the offering of Nahshon son of Amminadab.

¹⁸On the second day an offering was brought by Nethanel son of Zuar, leader of Issachar. ¹⁹His offering consisted of: one silver bowl weighing a hundred and thirty shekels, one silver sprinkling bowl weighing seventy shekels (sanctuary-shekels), both of them full of fine flour mixed with oil as a cereal offering, ²⁰one golden bowl weighing ten shekels, full of incense, ²¹one young bull, one ram and one male yearling lamb as a burnt offering, ²²one he-goat as a sacrifice for sin, ²³and two bulls, five rams, five he-goats and five male yearling lambs as a communion sacrifice. Such was the offering of Nethanel son of Zuar.

24 On the third day an offering was brought by Eliab son of Helon, leader of the Zebulunites. 25 His offering consisted of: one silver bowl weighing a hundred and thirty shekels, one silver sprinkling bowl weighing seventy shekels (sanctuary-shekels), both of them full of fine flour mixed with oil as a cereal offering, 26 one golden bowl weighing ten shekels, full of incense, 27 one young bull, one ram and one male yearling lamb as a burnt offering, 28 one he-goat as a sacrifice for sin, 29 and two bulls, five rams, five he-goats and five male yearling lambs as a communion sacrifice. Such was the offering of Eliab son of Helon.

30 On the fourth day an offering was brought by Elizur son of Shedeur, leader of the Reubenites. 31 His offering consisted of: one silver bowl weighing a hundred and thirty shekels, one silver sprinkling bowl weighing seventy shekels (sanctuary-shekels), both of them full of fine flour mixed with oil as a cereal offering, 32 one golden bowl weighing ten shekels, full of incense, 33 one young bull, one ram and one male yearling lamb as a burnt offering, 34 one he-goat as a sacrifice for sin, 35 and two bulls, five rams, five he-goats and five male yearling lambs as a communion sacrifice. Such was the offering of Elizur son of Shedeur.

36 On the fifth day an offering was brought by Shelumiel son of Zurishaddai, leader of the Simeonites. 37 His offering consisted of: one silver bowl weighing a hundred and thirty shekels, one silver sprinkling bowl weighing seventy shekels (sanctuary-shekels), both of them full of fine flour mixed with oil as a cereal offering, 38 one golden bowl weighing ten shekels, full of incense, 39 one young bull, one ram and one male yearling lamb as a burnt offering, 40 one he-goat as a sacrifice for sin, 41 and two bulls, five rams, five he-goats and five male yearling lambs as a communion sacrifice. Such was the offering of Shelumiel son of Zurishaddai.

42 On the sixth day an offering was brought by Eliasaph son of Reuel, leader of the Gadites. 43 His offering consisted of: one silver bowl weighing a hundred and thirty shekels, one silver sprinkling bowl weighing seventy shekels (sanctuary-shekels), both of them full of fine flour mixed with oil as a cereal offering, 44 one golden bowl weighing ten shekels, full of incense, 45 one young bull, one ram and one male yearling lamb as a burnt offering, 46 one he-goat as a sacrifice for sin, 47 and two bulls, five rams, five he-goats and five male yearling lambs as a communion sacrifice. Such was the offering of Eliasaph son of Reuel.

48 On the seventh day an offering was brought by Elishama son of Ammihud, leader of the Ephraimites. 49 His offering consisted of: one silver bowl weighing a hundred and thirty shekels, one silver sprinkling bowl weighing seventy shekels (sanctuary-shekels), both of them full of fine flour mixed with oil as a cereal offering, 50 one golden bowl weighing ten shekels, full of incense, 51 one young bull, one ram and one male yearling lamb as a burnt offering, 52 one he-goat as a sacrifice for sin, 53 and two bulls, five rams, five he-goats and five male yearling lambs as a communion sacrifice. Such was the offering of Elishama son of Ammihud.

54 On the eighth day an offering was brought by Gamaliel son of Pedahzur, leader of the Manassehites. 55 His offering consisted of: one silver bowl weighing a hundred and thirty shekels, one silver sprinkling bowl weighing seventy shekels (sanctuary-shekels), both of them full of fine flour mixed with oil as a cereal offering, 56 one golden bowl weighing ten shekels, full of incense, 57 one young bull, one ram and one male yearling lamb as a burnt offering, 58 one he-goat as a sacrifice for sin, 59 and two bulls, five rams, five he-goats and five male yearling lambs as a communion sacrifice. Such was the offering of Gamaliel son of Pedahzur.

60 On the ninth day an offering was brought by Abidan son of Gideoni, leader of the Benjaminites. 61 His offering consisted of: one silver bowl weighing a hundred and thirty shekels, one sprinkling bowl weighing seventy shekels (sanctuary-shekels), both of them full

of fine flour mixed with oil as a cereal offering, 62 one golden bowl weighing ten shekels, full of incense, 63 one young bull, one ram and one male yearling lamb as a burnt offering, 64 one he-goat as a sacrifice for sin, 65 and two bulls, five rams, five he-goats and five male yearling lambs as a communion sacrifice. Such was the offering of Abidan son of Gideoni.

66 On the tenth day an offering was brought by Ahiezer son of Ammishaddai, leader of the Danites. 67 His offering consisted of: one silver bowl weighing a hundred and thirty shekels, one silver sprinkling bowl weighing seventy shekels (sanctuary-shekels), both of them full of fine flour mixed with oil as a cereal offering, 68 one golden bowl weighing ten shekels, full of incense, 69 one young bull, one ram and one male yearling lamb as a burnt offering, 70 one he-goat as a sacrifice for sin, 71 and two bulls, five rams, five he-goats and five male yearling lambs as a communion sacrifice. Such was the offering of Ahiezer son of Ammishaddai.

72 On the eleventh day an offering was brought by Pagiel son of Ochran, leader of the Asherites. 73 His offering consisted of: one silver bowl weighing a hundred and thirty shekels, one silver sprinkling bowl weighing seventy shekels (sanctuary-shekels), both of them full of fine flour mixed with oil as a cereal offering, 74 one golden bowl weighing ten shekels, full of incense, 75 one young bull, one ram and one male yearling lamb as a burnt offering, 76 one he-goat as a sacrifice for sin, 77 and two bulls, five rams, five he-goats and five male yearling lambs as a communion sacrifice. Such was the offering of Pagiel son of Ochran.

78 On the twelfth day an offering was brought by Ahira son of Enan, leader of the Naphtalites. 79 His offering consisted of: one silver bowl weighing a hundred and thirty shekels, one silver sprinkling bowl weighing seventy shekels (sanctuary-shekels), both of them full of fine flour mixed with oil as a cereal offering, 80 one golden bowl weighing ten shekels, full of incense, 81 one young bull, one ram and one male yearling lamb as a burnt offering, 82 one he-goat as a sacrifice for sin, 83 and two bulls, five rams, five he-goats and five male yearling lambs as a communion sacrifice. Such was the offering of Ahira son of Enan.

84 Such were the offerings made by the leaders of Israel for the dedication of the altar on the day it was anointed: twelve silver bowls, twelve silver sprinkling bowls, and twelve golden bowls. 85 Each silver bowl weighed a hundred and thirty shekels, and each sprinkling bowl seventy, the silver of these objects weighing in all two thousand four hundred sanctuary-shekels. 86 The twelve golden bowls full of incense each weighed ten shekels (sanctuary-shekels), the gold of these bowls weighing in all a hundred and twenty shekels.

87 The sum total of animals for the burnt offering: twelve bulls, twelve rams, twelve male yearling lambs, with their cereal offerings. For the sacrifice for sin, twelve he-goats. 88 The sum total of animals for the communion sacrifice: twenty-four bulls, sixty rams, sixty he-goats and sixty male yearling lambs.

Such were the offerings for the dedication of the altar, after it had been anointed.

89 When Moses went into the Tent of Meeting to speak with him, he heard the voice speaking to him from above the mercy-seat on the ark of the Testimony, from between the two great winged creatures. He then spoke to him.

The lamps for the lamp-stand

8 Yahweh spoke to Moses and said: 2 'Speak to Aaron and say, "When you set up the lamps, the seven lamps must throw their light towards the front of the lamp-stand."'

3 Aaron did this. He set up the lamps to the front of the lamp-stand, as Yahweh had ordered Moses. 4 This lamp-stand was worked in beaten gold, including its stem and its petals, which were also of beaten gold. This lamp-stand had been made according to the pattern Yahweh had shown to Moses.

The Levites are offered to Yahweh

⁵Yahweh spoke to Moses and said, ⁶'Separate the Levites from the Israelites and purify them. ⁷This is how you must purify them: you will sprinkle them with purifying water, and they will shave their bodies all over and wash their clothes. They will then be clean. ⁸They will then take a young bull, with the accompanying cereal offering of fine flour mixed with oil, and you will take a second young bull for a sacrifice for sin. ⁹You will then bring the Levites in front of the Tent of Meeting, and assemble the whole community of Israelites. ¹⁰Once you have brought the Levites before Yahweh, the Israelites will lay their hands on them. ¹¹Aaron will then offer the Levites, making the gesture of offering before Yahweh on behalf of the Israelites, admitting them to Yahweh's service.

¹²'The Levites will then lay their hands on the heads of the bulls, one of which you will offer as a sacrifice for sin, and the other as a burnt offering to Yahweh, to perform the rite of expiation for the Levites. ¹³Having brought the Levites before Aaron and his sons, you will present them to Yahweh with the gesture of offering. ¹⁴That is how you will set the Levites apart from the Israelites, for them to be mine. ¹⁵The Levites will then begin their ministry in the Tent of Meeting.

'You will purify them and offer them with the gesture of offering ¹⁶because, of the Israelites, they have been dedicated to me in place of all those who first emerge from the womb, instead of the first-born; of all the Israelites, I have taken them for my own. ¹⁷For all the first-born of the Israelites, whether human or animal, do indeed belong to me: the day I struck down all the first-born in Egypt, I consecrated them to myself, ¹⁸and now, in place of all the first-born of the Israelites, I have taken the Levites. ¹⁹Of the Israelites, I give the Levites to Aaron and his sons, as dedicated men, to minister in the Tent of Meeting on behalf of the Israelites and perform the rite of expiation for them, so that no disaster befalls the Israelites when the Israelites come close to the sanctuary.'

²⁰Moses, Aaron and the whole community of Israelites dealt with the Levites exactly as Yahweh had ordered Moses concerning them; this is what the Israelites did with them. ²¹The Levites purified themselves and washed their clothes, and Aaron presented them with the gesture of offering before Yahweh. He then performed the rite of expiation for them to purify them. ²²The Levites were then allowed to perform their ministry in the Tent of Meeting in the presence of Aaron and his sons. As Yahweh had ordered Moses concerning the Levites, so it was done with them.

The duration of their ministry

²³Yahweh spoke to Moses and said:

²⁴'This concerns the Levites. From the age of twenty-five onwards, the Levite will exercise his ministry and do duty in the Tent of Meeting. ²⁵After the age of fifty, he is no longer bound to the ministry; he will have no further duties; ²⁶but he will still help his brothers to assure the services in the Tent of Meeting, though he himself will no longer have any ministry. That is how you will act as regards the ministry of the Levites.'

Date of the Passover

9 Yahweh spoke to Moses, in the desert of Sinai, in the second year after the exodus from Egypt, in the first month, and said:

²'The Israelites must keep the Passover at its appointed time. ³The fourteenth day of this month, at twilight, is the time appointed for you to keep it. You will keep it with all the laws and customs proper to it.'

⁴Moses told the Israelites to keep the Passover. ⁵They kept it, in the desert of Sinai, in the first month, on the fourteenth day of the month, at twilight. The Israelites did everything as Yahweh had ordered Moses.

Individual cases

⁶It happened that some men had become unclean by touching a dead body; they could not

keep the Passover that day. They came the same day to Moses and Aaron, [7] and said, 'We have become unclean by touching a dead body. Why should we be excluded from bringing an offering to Yahweh at the proper time with the rest of the Israelites?' [8] Moses replied, 'Wait here until I hear what order Yahweh gives about you.'

[9] Yahweh spoke to Moses and said, [10] 'Speak to the Israelites and say:

"Any of you or your descendants who becomes unclean by touching a dead body, or is away on a long journey, can still keep a Passover for Yahweh. [11] Such persons will keep it in the second month, on the fourteenth day, at twilight. They will eat it with unleavened bread and bitter herbs; [12] nothing of it must be left over until morning, nor will they break any of its bones. They will keep it, following the entire Passover ritual. [13] But anyone who is clean, or who is not on a journey, but fails to keep the Passover, such a person will be outlawed from his people. For not having brought the offering to Yahweh at its appointed time, the person will bear the consequences of the sin.

[14] "A resident alien who keeps a Passover for Yahweh, will keep it in accordance with the ritual and customs of the Passover. You will have one law for alien and citizen alike." '

The cloud

[15] On the day the Dwelling was erected, the cloud covered the Dwelling, the Tent of the Testimony. From nightfall until morning it remained over the Dwelling looking like fire. [16] So the cloud covered it all the time, and at night it looked like fire.

[17] Whenever the cloud rose from the Tent, the Israelites broke camp, and wherever the cloud halted, there the Israelites pitched camp. [18] At Yahweh's order, the Israelites set out and, at Yahweh's order, the Israelites pitched camp. They remained in camp for as long as the cloud rested on the Dwelling. [19] If the cloud stayed for many days on the Dwelling, the Israelites performed their duty to Yahweh and

did not set out. [20] But if the cloud happened to stay for only a few days on the Dwelling, just as they had pitched camp at Yahweh's order, at Yahweh's order they set out. [21] If the cloud happened to remain only from evening to morning, they set out when it lifted the next morning. Or, if it stayed for a whole day and night, they set out only when it lifted. [22] Sometimes it stayed there for two days, a month, or a longer time; however long the cloud rested on the Dwelling, the Israelites remained in camp, and when it lifted they set out. [23] At Yahweh's order they pitched camp, and at Yahweh's order they set out. They performed their duty to Yahweh, as Yahweh had ordered through Moses.

The trumpets

10 Yahweh spoke to Moses and said: [2] 'Make yourself two trumpets; make them of beaten silver, so that you can use them for summoning the community, and for sounding the order to break camp. [3] Whenever they are sounded, the whole community must gather round you, at the entrance to the Tent of Meeting. [4] But if only one trumpet is sounded, then only the leaders, the heads of Israel's thousands, must gather round you.

[5] 'When the trumpet blast is accompanied by a battle cry,[a] the encampments pitched to the east will set out. [6] At the second blast accompanied by a battle cry, the encampments pitched to the south will set out. For breaking camp, the trumpet blast will be accompanied by a battle cry, [7] but for assembling the community the trumpets will be sounded without battle cry. [8] The Aaronite priests will sound the trumpets; this is a perpetual decree for you and your descendants.

[9] 'When in your country you go to war against an enemy who is oppressing you, you will sound trumpets with a battle cry, and Yahweh your God will remember you, and you will be delivered from your enemies. [10] At

---

10a Battle cry or cry of acclamation used also on royal occasions and in worship.

your festivals, solemnities and new-moon feasts, you will sound the trumpets over your burnt offerings and communion sacrifices, so that they recall you to the remembrance of your God. I am Yahweh your God.'

The order of march

¹¹ In the second year, in the second month, on the twentieth day of the month, the cloud rose from where the Dwelling of the Testimony was, ¹² and the Israelites set out, in marching order, from the desert of Sinai. The cloud came to rest in the desert of Paran.

¹³ These were the men who set out in the vanguard, at Yahweh's order through Moses: ¹⁴ first went the standard of the camp of the Judahites and their units, with Nahshon son of Amminadab commanding that contingent; ¹⁵ Nethanel son of Zuar commanding the tribal contingent of the Issacharites; ¹⁶ and Eliab son of Helon commanding the tribal contingent of the Zebulunites.

¹⁷ The Dwelling was then dismantled and the Gershonites and Merarites set out, carrying the Dwelling.

¹⁸ Then came the standard of the camp of the Reubenites and their units, with Elizur son of Shedeur commanding that contingent; ¹⁹ Shelumiel son of Zurishaddai commanding the tribal contingent of the Simeonites; ²⁰ and Eliasaph son of Reuel commanding the tribal contingent of the Gadites.

²¹ Then came the Kohathites carrying the sanctuary (the Dwelling was erected before they arrived).

²² Then came the standard of the camp of the Ephraimites and their units, with Elishama son of Ammihud commanding that contingent; ²³ Gamaliel son of Pedahzur commanding the tribal contingent of the Manassehites; ²⁴ and Abidan son of Gideoni commanding the tribal contingent of the Benjaminites.

²⁵ Last of all, the rearguard of all the camps, came the standard of the camp of the Danites and their units, with Ahiezer son of Ammishaddai commanding that contingent; ²⁶ Pagiel son of Ochran commanding the tribal contingent of the Asherites; ²⁷ and Ahira son of Enan commanding the tribal contingent of the Naphtalites.

²⁸ Such was the order of march for the Israelites, unit by unit. So they set out.

Moses' proposal to Hobab

²⁹ Moses said to Hobab son of Reuel the Midianite, his father-in-law, 'We are setting out for the country of which Yahweh has said: I shall give it to you. Come with us, and we will treat you well, for Yahweh has promised good things for Israel.' ³⁰ 'I will not come with you,' he replied, 'but shall go to my own country and kin.' ³¹ 'Do not leave us,' Moses said, 'for you know where we can camp in the desert, and so you will be our eyes. ³² If you come with us, we shall share with you whatever blessings Yahweh gives us.'

The departure

³³ They set out from Yahweh's mountain and travelled for three days, while the ark of the covenant of Yahweh preceded them on the three-day journey, searching out a place for them to halt.

³⁴ In the daytime, Yahweh's cloud was over them, once they had broken camp. ³⁵ Whenever the ark set out, Moses would say:

> Rise, Yahweh, may your enemies be
> scattered
> and those who hate you flee at your
> approach!

³⁶ And when it halted, he would say:

> Come back, Yahweh,
> to the countless thousands of Israel!

Taberah

11 Now the people began to complain, which was offensive to Yahweh's ears. When Yahweh heard, his anger was aroused and the fire of Yahweh broke out among them; it devoured one end of the camp. ² The people appealed to Moses who interceded with Yahweh and the fire died down. ³ So the place

was called Taberah, because the fire of Yahweh had broken out among them.

Kibroth-ha-Taavah; the people complain[a]

4 The rabble who had joined the people were feeling the pangs of hunger, and the Israelites began to weep again. 'Who will give us meat to eat?' they said. 5 'Think of the fish we used to eat free in Egypt, the cucumbers, melons, leeks, onions and garlic! 6 But now we are withering away; there is nothing wherever we look except this manna!'

7 The manna was like coriander seed and had the appearance of bdellium. 8 The people went round gathering it, and ground it in a mill or crushed it with a pestle; it was then cooked in a pot and made into pancakes. It tasted like cake made with oil. 9 When the dew fell on the camp at night-time, the manna fell with it.

The prayer of Moses

10 Moses heard the people weeping, each family at the door of its tent. Yahweh's anger was greatly aroused; Moses too found it disgraceful, 11 and he said to Yahweh:

'Why do you treat your servant so badly? In what respect have I failed to win your favour, for you to lay the burden of all these people on me? 12 Was it I who conceived all these people, was I their father, for you to say to me, "Carry them in your arms, like a foster-father carrying an unweaned child, to the country which I swore to give their fathers"? 13 Where am I to find meat to give all these people, pestering me with their tears and saying, "Give us meat to eat"? 14 I cannot carry all these people on my own; the weight is too much for me. 15 If this is how you mean to treat me, please kill me outright! If only I could win your favour and be spared the sight of my misery!'

Yahweh replies

16 Yahweh said to Moses, 'Collect me seventy of the elders of Israel, men you know to be the people's elders and scribes. Bring them to the Tent of Meeting, and let them stand beside you there. 17 I shall come down and talk to you there and shall take some of the spirit which is on you and put it on them. Then they will bear the burden of the people with you, and you will no longer have to bear it on your own.

18 'And say to the people, "Purify yourselves for tomorrow and you will have meat to eat, since you have wept in Yahweh's hearing, saying: Who will give us meat to eat? How happy we were in Egypt! Very well, Yahweh will give you meat to eat. 19 You will eat it not for one day, or two, or five, or ten or twenty, 20 but for a whole month, until it comes out of your nostrils and sickens you, since you have rejected Yahweh who is among you, and have wept before him saying: Why did we ever leave Egypt?"'

21 Moses said, 'The people round me number six hundred thousand foot soldiers, and you say, "I shall give them meat to eat for a whole month"! 22 If all the flocks and herds were slaughtered, would that be enough for them? If all the fish in the seas were collected, would that be enough for them?' 23 Yahweh said to Moses, 'Is the arm of Yahweh so short? You shall see whether the promise I have made to you comes true or not.'

The spirit given to the elders

24 Moses went out and told the people what Yahweh had said. Then he collected seventy of the people's elders and stationed them round the Tent. 25 Yahweh descended in the cloud. He spoke to him and took some of the spirit that was on him and put it on the seventy elders. When the spirit came on them they prophesied—but only once.

26 Two men had stayed back in the camp; one was called Eldad and the other Medad. The spirit came down on them; though they had not gone to the Tent, their names were enrolled among the rest. These began to prophesy in the camp. 27 A young man ran to tell Moses this. 'Look,' he said, 'Eldad and Medad are prophesying in the camp.' 28 Joshua son of

11a ‖ Ex 16.

Nun, who had served Moses since he was a boy, spoke up and said, 'My lord Moses, stop them!' ²⁹Moses replied, 'Are you jealous on my account? If only all Yahweh's people were prophets, and Yahweh had given them his spirit!' ³⁰Moses then went back to the camp with the elders of Israel.

The quails

³¹A wind, sent by Yahweh, started blowing from the sea bringing quails which it deposited on the camp. They lay for a distance of a day's march either side of the camp, two cubits thick on the ground. ³²The people were up all that day and night and all the next day collecting quails: the least gathered by anyone was ten *homer;* then they spread them out round the camp. ³³The meat was still between their teeth, not even chewed, when Yahweh's anger was aroused by the people. Yahweh struck them with a very great plague.

³⁴The name given to this place was Kibroth-ha-Taavah, because it was there that they buried the people who had indulged their greed.

³⁵From Kibroth-ha-Taavah the people set out for Hazeroth, and at Hazeroth they pitched camp.

Miriam and Aaron criticise Moses

12Miriam, and Aaron too, criticised Moses over the Cushite woman he had married. He had indeed married a Cushite woman. ²They said, 'Is Moses the only one through whom Yahweh has spoken? Has he not spoken through us too?' Yahweh heard this. ³Now Moses was extremely humble, the humblest man on earth.

God's answer

⁴Suddenly Yahweh said to Moses, Aaron and Miriam, 'Come out, all three of you, to the Tent of Meeting.' They went, all three of them, ⁵and Yahweh descended in a pillar of cloud and stood at the entrance of the Tent. He called Aaron and Miriam and they both came forward. ⁶Yahweh said:

Listen to my words!
 if there is a prophet among you,
I reveal myself to him in a vision,
 I speak to him in a dream.
⁷Not so with my servant Moses;
 to him my whole household is
  entrusted;
⁸to him I speak face to face,
 plainly and not in riddles,
 and he sees Yahweh's form.
How, then, could you dare
 to criticise my servant Moses?

⁹Yahweh's anger was aroused by them. He went away, ¹⁰and as soon as the cloud left the Tent, there was Miriam covered with a virulent skin-disease, white as snow! Aaron turned to look at her and saw that she had contracted a virulent skin-disease.

The prayer of Aaron and Moses

¹¹Aaron said to Moses:

'Oh, my Lord, please do not punish us for the sin we have been foolish enough to commit. ¹²Do not let her be like some monster with its flesh half eaten away when it leaves its mother's womb!'

¹³Moses pleaded with Yahweh. 'O God,' he said, 'I beg you, please heal her!'

¹⁴Yahweh then said to Moses, 'If her father had done no more than spit in her face, would she not be unclean for seven days? Have her shut out of the camp for seven days, and then have her brought in again.'

¹⁵Miriam was shut out of the camp for seven days. The people did not set out until she returned. ¹⁶Then the people moved on from Hazeroth and pitched camp in the desert of Paran.

The reconnaissance in Canaanᵃ

13Yahweh spoke to Moses and said, ²'Send out men, one from each tribe, to reconnoitre the land of Canaan which I am

13a ‖ Dt 1:20–29.

giving the Israelites. Each of them is to be a leading man of the tribe.'

³ At Yahweh's order, Moses sent them from the desert of Paran. All of them were leading men of Israel. ⁴ These were their names:

For the tribe of Reuben, Shammua son of Zaccur:

⁵ for the tribe of Simeon, Shaphat son of Hori;

⁶ for the tribe of Judah, Caleb son of Jephunneh;

⁷ for the tribe of Issachar, Igal son of Joseph;

⁸ for the tribe of Ephraim, Hoshea son of Nun;

⁹ for the tribe of Benjamin, Palti son of Raphu;

¹⁰ for the tribe of Zebulun, Gaddiel son of Sodi;

¹¹ for the tribe of Joseph, for the tribe of Manasseh, Gaddi son of Susi;

¹² for the tribe of Dan, Ammiel son of Gemalli;

¹³ for the tribe of Asher, Sethur son of Michael;

¹⁴ for the tribe of Naphtali, Nahbi son of Vophsi;

¹⁵ for the tribe of Gad, Geuel son of Machi.

¹⁶ Such were the names of the men whom Moses sent to reconnoitre the country. Moses then gave Hoshea son of Nun the name Joshua.

¹⁷ Moses sent them to reconnoitre the land of Canaan, 'Go up into the Negeb,' he said, 'then go up into the highlands. ¹⁸ See what sort of country it is, and what sort of people the inhabitants are, whether they are strong or weak, few or many, ¹⁹ what sort of land they live on, whether it is good or poor; what sort of towns they live in, whether they are open or fortified; ²⁰ what sort of land it is, fertile or barren, wooded or open. Be bold, and bring back some of the country's produce.'

It was the season for early grapes. ²¹ They went up and reconnoitred the country from the desert of Zin to Rehob, the Pass of Hamath. ²² They went up by way of the Negeb as far as Hebron, where Ahiman, Sheshai and Talmai, the Anakim, lived. (Hebron was founded seven years before Tanis in Egypt.) ²³ Reaching the Vale of Eshcol, there they lopped off a vine branch with a cluster of grapes, which two of them carried away on a pole, as well as pomegranates and figs. ²⁴ This place was called the Vale of Eshcol after the cluster which the Israelites cut there.

The expedition's report

²⁵ After forty days they returned from reconnoitring the country. ²⁶ Making their way to Moses, Aaron and the whole community of Israel, in the desert of Paran, at Kadesh, they made their report to them and the whole community, and displayed the country's produce.

²⁷ This was the report they gave: 'We made our way into the country where you sent us. It does indeed flow with milk and honey; here is what it produces. ²⁸ At the same time, its inhabitants are a powerful people; the towns are fortified and very big; yes, and we saw the Anakim there. ²⁹ The Amalekites occupy the Negeb area, the Hittites, Jebusites and Amorites the highlands, and the Canaanites the sea coast and the banks of the Jordan.'

³⁰ Caleb called the people round Moses to silence and then said, 'We must march in immediately and take it; we are certainly able to conquer it.' ³¹ But the men who had been with him said, 'We cannot attack these people; they are stronger than we are.' ³² And they began disparaging to the Israelites the country they had reconnoitred, saying, 'The country we have been to reconnoitre is a country that devours its inhabitants. All the people we saw there were of enormous size. ³³ We saw giants there too (the Anakim, descended from the Giants). We felt like grasshoppers, and so we seemed to them.'

The rebellion of Israel[a]

14 The whole community then cried out in dismay, and the people wept all that night. ² All the Israelites muttered at Moses

14a ‖ Dt 1:26–32.

and Aaron, and the whole community said to them, 'Would to God we had died in Egypt, or even that we had died in this desert! 3 Why has Yahweh brought us to this country, for us to perish by the sword and our wives and children to be seized as booty? Should we not do better to go back to Egypt?' 4 And they said to one another, 'Let us appoint a leader and go back to Egypt.'

5 At this, Moses and Aaron threw themselves on their faces in front of the whole assembled community of Israelites, 6 while Joshua son of Nun and Caleb son of Jephunneh, two of the men who had reconnoitred the country, tore their clothes 7 and addressed the whole community of Israelites as follows, 'The country we went to reconnoitre is a good country, an excellent country. 8 If Yahweh is pleased with us, he will lead us into this country and give it to us. It is a country flowing with milk and honey. 9 But do not rebel against Yahweh or be afraid of the people of the country, for we shall gobble them up. Their protecting shade has deserted them, while we have Yahweh on our side. Do not be afraid of them.'

Yahweh's anger; Moses intercedes[b]

10 The whole community was talking of stoning them, when the glory of Yahweh appeared to all the Israelites, inside the Tent of Meeting, 11 and Yahweh said to Moses:

'How much longer will these people treat me with contempt? How much longer will they refuse to trust me, in spite of all the signs I have displayed among them? 12 I shall strike them with pestilence and disown them. And of you I shall make a new nation, greater and mightier than they are.'

13 Moses said to Yahweh:

'Suppose the Egyptians hear about this— for by your power you brought these people out of their country—14 and tell the people living in this country. They have heard that you, Yahweh, are with this people, and that you, Yahweh, show yourself to them face to face; that your cloud stands over them and that you go before them in a pillar of cloud by day and a pillar of fire by night. 15 If you kill this people now as though it were one man, then the nations who have heard about you will say, 16 "Yahweh was not able to bring this people into the country which he had sworn to give them, and so he has slaughtered them in the desert." 17 No, my Lord! Now is the time to assert your power as you promised when you said, earlier, 18 "Yahweh, slow to anger and rich in faithful love, forgiving faults and transgression, and yet letting nothing go unchecked, punishing the parents' guilt in the children to the third and fourth generation." 19 In your most faithful love, please forgive this people's guilt, as you have done from Egypt until now.'

Pardon and punishment[c]

20 Yahweh said, 'I forgive them as you ask. 21 But—as I live, and as the glory of Yahweh fills the whole world—22 of all these people who have seen my glory and the signs that I worked in Egypt and in the desert, who have put me to the test ten times already and not obeyed my voice, 23 not one shall see the country which I promised to give their ancestors. Not one of those who have treated me contemptuously will see it. 24 However, since my servant Caleb is of another spirit and since he has obeyed me completely, I shall bring him into the country where he has been, and his descendants will own it 25 (the Amalekites and Canaanites occupy the plain). Tomorrow you will turn about and go back into the desert, in the direction of the Sea of Suph.'

26 Yahweh then spoke to Moses and Aaron and said:

27 'How much longer am I to endure this perverse community muttering against me? I have heard what the Israelites mutter against me. 28 Say to them, "As I live, Yahweh declares, I shall do to you what I have heard you saying. 29 In this desert your dead bodies will fall, all you who were counted in the census,

14b ‖ Ex 32:7–14; 34:6–7.   *14c* ‖ Dt 1:34–40.

from the age of twenty years and over who have muttered against me. ³⁰ I swear none of you will enter the country where I swore most solemnly to settle you, except Caleb son of Jephunneh, and Joshua son of Nun. ³¹ Your children, who you said would be seized as booty, will be the ones whom I shall bring in so that they get to know the country you disdained, ³²but, as for you, your dead bodies will fall in this desert ³³ and your children will be nomads in the desert for forty years, bearing the consequences of your faithlessness, until the last one of you lies dead in the desert. ³⁴ For forty days you reconnoitred the country. Each day will count as a year: for forty years you will bear the consequences of your guilt and learn what it means to reject me." ³⁵ I, Yahweh, have spoken: this is how I swear to treat this entire perverse community united against me. In this desert, to the last man, they shall die.'

³⁶ The men whom Moses had sent to reconnoitre the country and who on their return had incited the whole community of Israel to mutter about him by disparaging it, ³⁷ these men who had disparaged the country were all struck dead before Yahweh. ³⁸ Of the men who had gone to reconnoitre the country, only Joshua son of Nun and Caleb son of Jephunneh were left alive.

An abortive attempt by the Israelites

³⁹ When Moses told all the Israelites what had been said, the people set up a great outcry. ⁴⁰ Early next morning they set out for the heights of the hill country saying, 'Look, we will set out for the place about which Yahweh said that we have sinned.' ⁴¹ To which, Moses said, 'Why disobey Yahweh's order? No success will come of doing so. ⁴² Do not go, for Yahweh is not among you, and you will be defeated by your enemies. ⁴³ For the Amalekites and the Canaanites are ahead of you, and you will be put to the sword, since you have turned away from Yahweh, and Yahweh is not with you.' ⁴⁴ All the same, they presumptuously set off for the heights of the hill country. Neither the ark of the covenant of Yahweh nor Moses

left the camp. ⁴⁵ The Amalekites and Canaanites living in those highlands then came down, defeated them and harried them all the way to Hormah.

Cereal offerings to accompany sacrifices

15 Yahweh spoke to Moses and said, ² 'Speak to the Israelites and say:

"When you have arrived in the country where you are to live and which I am giving to you, ³ and you burn food as an offering to Yahweh either as a burnt offering or as a sacrifice, whether in payment of a vow, or as a voluntary gift, or on the occasion of one of your solemn feasts, from your herds and flocks as a smell pleasing to Yahweh: ⁴ the offerer will, as his personal gift to Yahweh, bring a cereal offering of one-tenth of an *ephah* of fine flour mixed with one-quarter of a *hin* of oil. ⁵ You will also make a libation of wine, one-quarter of a *hin* to each lamb, in addition to the burnt offering or sacrifice. ⁶ For a ram, you will make a cereal offering of two-tenths of an *ephah* of fine flour mixed with one-third of a *hin* of oil, ⁷ and a libation of one-third of a *hin* of wine as a smell pleasing to Yahweh. ⁸ If you offer a bull as a burnt offering or sacrifice, in payment of a vow or as a communion sacrifice for Yahweh, ⁹ in addition to the animal you will offer a cereal offering of three-tenths of an *ephah* of fine flour mixed with half a *hin* of oil, ¹⁰ and you will offer a libation of half a *hin* of wine, as food burnt as a smell pleasing to Yahweh. ¹¹ This will be done for every bull, every ram, every lamb or kid. ¹² Whatever the number of victims you intend to offer, you will do the same for each of them, however many there are.

¹³ "Every citizen of the country will act in this way whenever he offers food burnt as a smell pleasing to Yahweh; ¹⁴ and if an alien residing with you or with your descendants intends to offer food burnt as a smell pleasing to Yahweh, he will do as you do. ¹⁵ There will be one law for you, members of the community, and the resident alien alike, a law binding your descendants for ever: before Yahweh you

and the resident alien are no different.' ¹⁶One law, one statute, will apply for you and the resident alien." '

The first-fruits of bread

¹⁷Yahweh spoke to Moses and said, ¹⁸'Speak to the Israelites and say:

"When you have entered the country to which I am bringing you, ¹⁹you will set a portion aside for Yahweh when you eat that country's bread. ²⁰You will set one cake aside as the first-fruits of your dough; you will set this offering aside like the one set aside from your threshing. ²¹For all future generations you will set a portion of your dough aside for Yahweh.

Expiation for faults of inadvertence

²²"If through inadvertence you fail in any of these orders which Yahweh has given to Moses ²³(whatever orders Yahweh has given you or your descendants through Moses, from the day when Yahweh gave his orders), ²⁴this is what must be done:

"If it is an inadvertence on the part of the community, the community as a whole will offer a young bull as a burnt offering, as a smell pleasing to Yahweh, with the prescribed accompanying cereal offering and libation, and a he-goat as a sacrifice for sin. ²⁵The priest will perform the rite of expiation for the entire community of Israelites, and they will be forgiven, since it was an inadvertence. Once they have brought their offering as food burnt for Yahweh, and have presented their sacrifice for sin before Yahweh to make amends for their inadvertence, ²⁶the whole community of Israelites will be forgiven, as also the alien residing with them, since the entire people acted by inadvertence.

²⁷"If it is an individual who has sinned by inadvertence, he will offer a yearling kid as a sacrifice for sin. ²⁸The priest will perform the rite of expiation before Yahweh for the person who has gone astray owing to this sin of inadvertence and, expiation having been made for him, he will be forgiven; ²⁹whether he is an Israelite citizen or a resident alien, you will have one law for anyone who sins by inadvertence.

³⁰"But the individual who acts deliberately, be he citizen or alien, commits an outrage against Yahweh, and such a man will be outlawed from his people. ³¹Since he has treated Yahweh's word with contempt and has disobeyed his order, such a man will be outlawed absolutely and will bear the consequences of his guilt." '

Sabbath-breaking

³²While the Israelites were in the desert, a man was caught gathering wood on the Sabbath day. ³³Those who caught him gathering wood brought him before Moses, Aaron and the whole community. ³⁴He was kept in custody, because the penalty he should undergo had not yet been fixed. ³⁵Yahweh said to Moses, 'This man must be put to death. The whole community will stone him outside the camp.' ³⁶The whole community took him outside the camp and stoned him till he was dead, as Yahweh had ordered Moses.

Tassels on clothes

³⁷Yahweh spoke to Moses and said, ³⁸'Speak to the Israelites and tell them, for all generations to come, to put tassels on the hems of their clothes and work a violet thread into the tassel at the hem. ³⁹You will thus have a tassel, and the sight of it will remind you of all Yahweh's orders and how you are to put them into practice, and not follow the dictates of your own heart and eyes, which have led you to be unfaithful.

⁴⁰'This will remind you of all my orders; put them into practice, and you will be consecrated to your God. ⁴¹I, Yahweh your God, have brought you out of Egypt, to be your God, I, Yahweh your God.'

The rebellion of Korah, Dathan and Abiram

16 Now Korah son of Izhar, son of Kohath the Levite, and the Reubenites Dathan and Abiram sons of Eliab, and On son of Peleth were proud ²and rebelled against

Moses with two hundred and fifty Israelites who were leaders of the community, prominent at the solemn feasts, men of repute. ³These banded together against Moses and Aaron and said to them, 'You take too much on yourselves! The whole community, all its members, are consecrated, and Yahweh lives among them. Why set yourselves higher than Yahweh's community?'

⁴On hearing this, Moses threw himself on his face. ⁵Then he said to Korah and all in his party, 'Tomorrow morning Yahweh will reveal who is his, who the consecrated man whom he will allow to approach him. The one he allows to approach is the one whom he has chosen. ⁶This is what you must do: take the censers of Korah and all in his party, ⁷put fire in them and put incense in them before Yahweh tomorrow, and the one whom Yahweh chooses will be the consecrated man. Levites, you take too much on yourselves!'

⁸Moses then said to Korah, 'Now listen, you Levites! ⁹Is it not enough for you that the God of Israel has singled you out of the community of Israel, and called you to be near him, to serve in Yahweh's Dwelling and to represent the community by officiating on its behalf? ¹⁰He has called you to be near him, you and all your brother Levites with you, and now you want to be priests as well! ¹¹For which reason, you and all in your party have banded together against Yahweh himself: for what is Aaron, that you should mutter against him?'

¹²Moses then summoned Dathan and Abiram sons of Eliab. They replied, 'We will not come. ¹³Is it not enough for you to have brought us away from a country flowing with milk and honey to kill us in the desert, without your making yourself our absolute ruler? ¹⁴What is more, you have not brought us to a country flowing with milk and honey and you have not given us fields and vineyards for our heritage. Do you think you can hoodwink these people? We will not come.' ¹⁵Moses flew into a rage and said to Yahweh, 'Disregard their cereal offering! I have not taken so much

as a donkey from them, nor have I wronged any of them.'

The punishment

¹⁶Moses said to Korah, 'You and all your party, come before Yahweh tomorrow, you and they, and Aaron too. ¹⁷Each will take his censer, put incense in it, and bring his censer before Yahweh—two hundred and fifty censers. You and Aaron too will each bring his censer.' ¹⁸Each of them took his censer, put fire in it and placed incense on it, and stood at the entrance to the Tent of Meeting with Moses and Aaron. ¹⁹Then, Korah having assembled the whole community to confront them at the entrance to the Tent of Meeting, the glory of Yahweh appeared to the whole community.

²⁰Yahweh then spoke to Moses and Aaron. He said, ²¹'Get away from this community. I am going to destroy them here and now.' ²²They threw themselves on their faces and cried out, 'O God, God of the spirits that give life to every living thing, will you be angry with the whole community because one man has sinned?' ²³Yahweh then said to Moses, ²⁴'Speak to the community and say, "Stand well clear of Korah's tent." '

²⁵Moses stood up and went to Dathan and Abiram; the elders of Israel followed him. ²⁶He spoke to the community and said, 'Stand away, I tell you, from the tents of these sinners, and touch nothing that belongs to them, for fear that with all their sins you too will be swept away.' ²⁷So they moved away from Korah's tent.

Dathan and Abiram had come out and were standing at their tent doors, with their wives, their sons and their little ones. ²⁸Moses said, 'This is how you will know that Yahweh himself has sent me to perform all these tasks and that I am not doing them of my own accord. ²⁹If these people die a natural death such as people commonly die, then Yahweh has not sent me. ³⁰But if Yahweh does something utterly new, if the earth should open its mouth and swallow them and all their belongings, so that they go down alive to Sheol, then you will know that they held Yahweh in contempt.'

31 The moment he finished saying all this, the ground split apart under their feet, 32 the earth opened its mouth and swallowed them, their families, all Korah's people and all their property.

33 They went down alive to Sheol with all their belongings. The earth closed over them and they disappeared in the middle of the community. 34 At their cries, all the Israelites round them took to their heels, saying, 'We do not want the earth to swallow us too!'

35 Fire then shot out from Yahweh and consumed the two hundred and fifty men offering incense.

The censers

17 Yahweh then spoke to Moses and said, 2 'Tell Eleazar son of Aaron the priest to pick the censers out of the smouldering remains and scatter the fire from them away from here, 3 for these sinful censers have become sanctified at the price of human lives. Since they were brought before Yahweh and thus became consecrated, they must be hammered into sheets to cover the altar. They will be an object-lesson to the Israelites.'

4 The priest Eleazar took the bronze censers which had been carried by the men destroyed by the fire. They were hammered into sheets to cover the altar. 5 They are a reminder to the Israelites that no unauthorised person, no one not of Aaron's line, may approach and offer incense before Yahweh, on pain of suffering the fate of Korah and his party, as Yahweh had said through Moses.

Aaron intercedes

6 On the following day, the whole community of Israelites were muttering against Moses and Aaron and saying, 'You are responsible for killing Yahweh's people!' 7 Now, as the community was banding together against Moses and Aaron, they turned towards the Tent of Meeting, and there was the cloud covering it, and the glory of Yahweh appeared. 8 Moses

and Aaron then went to the front of the Tent of Meeting.

9 Yahweh spoke to Moses and said, 10 'Get away from this community. I am going to destroy them here and now.' They threw themselves on their faces. 11 Moses then said to Aaron, 'Take a censer, put fire in it from the altar, place incense on it and hurry to the community to perform the rite of expiation for them: for retribution has come from Yahweh, plague has broken out.' 12 Aaron took it as Moses said and ran into the middle of the community, but plague had already broken out among the people. He put in the incense and performed the rite of expiation for the people. 13 Then he stood between the living and the dead, and the plague stopped. 14 There were fourteen thousand seven hundred victims of the plague, apart from those who died because of Korah. 15 Aaron then went back to Moses at the entrance to the Tent of Meeting; the plague had been halted.

Aaron's branch

16 Yahweh spoke to Moses and said, 17 'Tell the Israelites to give you a branch for each of their families, one for each leader of each family: twelve branches. Write the name of each on his branch; 18 and on the branch of Levi write Aaron's name, since the head of the Levite families must have a branch too. 19 You will then put them inside the Tent of Meeting in front of the Testimony, where I make myself known to you. 20 The man whose branch sprouts will be the one I have chosen; this is how I shall put an end to the mutterings of the Israelites about you.'

21 Moses spoke to the Israelites, and all their leaders gave him one branch each, twelve branches in all for their families; Aaron's branch was among them. 22 Moses placed them before Yahweh in the Tent of the Testimony. 23 On the following day Moses went to the Tent of the Testimony and there, already sprouting, was Aaron's branch, representing the House of Levi; buds had formed, flowers had bloomed and almonds had al-

ready ripened. 24 Moses then brought out all the branches from before Yahweh to all the Israelites; they examined them and each one took back his own branch.

25 Yahweh then said to Moses, 'Put Aaron's branch back in front of the Testimony, where it will have its ritual place as a warning to the rebellious; thus you will rid me of their muttering for good, without their incurring death.' 26 Moses did as Yahweh had ordered. That is what he did.

Expiation: the function of the priesthood

27 The Israelites then said to Moses, 'We are lost! We are dead men! We are all dead men! 28 Anyone who approaches Yahweh's Dwelling with an offering will die. Are we to be doomed to the last man?'

18 Yahweh then said to Aaron: 'You, your sons and your ancestor's line with you will be answerable for offences against the sanctuary. You and your sons with you will be answerable for the offences of your priesthood. 2 You will admit your brothers of the branch of Levi, your ancestor's tribe, to join you and serve you, yourself and your sons, before the Tent of the Testimony. 3 They must be at your service and the service of the whole Tent. Provided they do not come near the sacred vessels or the altar, they will be in no more danger of death than you. 4 They must join you, they must take charge of the Tent of Meeting for the entire ministry of the Tent, and no unauthorised person will come near you. 5 You will take charge of the sanctuary and charge of the altar, and retribution will never again befall the Israelites. 6 Of the Israelites, I myself have chosen your brothers the Levites as a gift to you. As men dedicated, they will belong to Yahweh, to serve at the Tent of Meeting. 7 You and your sons will undertake the priestly duties in all that concerns the altar and all that lies behind the curtain. You will perform the liturgy, the duties of which I entrust to your priesthood. But an unauthorised person approaching will incur death.'

The priests' portion

8 Yahweh said to Aaron:

'I myself have put you in charge of everything set aside for me. Everything consecrated by the Israelites I give to you and your sons as your portion by perpetual decree. 9 Of the things especially holy, of the food offered, this is what will revert to you: every offering that the Israelites give back to me, whether it be a cereal offering, a sacrifice for sin or a sacrifice of reparation, is a thing especially holy and will revert to you and your sons. 10 You will eat the things especially holy. Every male may eat them. You will regard them as sacred.

11 'To you will revert also whatever is set aside from the offerings of the Israelites, whatever is held out with the gesture of offering; this I give to you and your sons and daughters, by perpetual decree. All members of your household may eat it unless they are unclean. 12 All the best of the oil, all the best of the new wine and wheat, these first-fruits offered by them to Yahweh I give to you. 13 All the first produce of the country brought by them to Yahweh will revert to you. All members of your household may eat it unless they are unclean. 14 Everything in Israel put under the curse of destruction will revert to you. 15 Every first-born of all creatures brought to Yahweh, human or animal, will revert to you, but you will have to redeem the first-born of man; you will also redeem the first-born of an unclean animal. 16 You will redeem it in the month in which it is born, valuing it at five shekels, at the sanctuary-shekel, which is twenty *gerah*. 17 But you will not redeem the first-born of cow, sheep and goat. They are holy: you will sprinkle their blood on the altar and burn the fat as food burnt to be a smell pleasing to Yahweh; 18 the meat will revert to you, as will the forequarter that has been presented with the gesture of offering, and the right thigh. 19 Everything the Israelites set aside for Yahweh from the holy things, I give to you and your sons and daughters, by perpetual decree. This is a covenant of salt for

ever before Yahweh, for you and your descendants too.'

The Levites' portion

20 Yahweh said to Aaron:

'You will have no heritage in their country, you will not have a portion like them; I shall be your portion and your heritage among the Israelites.

21 'Look, as heritage I give the Levites all the tithes collected in Israel, in return for their services, for the ministry they render in the Tent of Meeting. 22 The Israelites will no longer approach the Tent of Meeting, on pain of committing a deadly sin. 23 Levi will discharge the duties of the Tent of Meeting, and the Levites will bear the consequences of their own guilt. This is a perpetual decree binding all your descendants: the Levites will have no heritage among the Israelites, 24 for the tithe which the Israelites set aside for Yahweh is the heritage I have given the Levites. This is why I have told them that they will have no heritage among the Israelites.'

Tithes

25 Yahweh spoke to Moses and said, 26 'Speak to the Levites and say:

"When from the Israelites you receive the tithe which I have given you from them as your heritage, you will set a portion of this aside for Yahweh: a tithe of the tithe. 27 It will take the place of the portion set aside that is due from you, like the wheat from the threshing-floor and new wine from the press. 28 Thus you too will set a portion aside for Yahweh out of all the tithes you receive from the Israelites. You will give what you have set aside for Yahweh to the priest Aaron. 29 Out of all the gifts you receive, you will set a portion aside for Yahweh. Out of all these things, you will set aside the best, the sacred portion."

30 'You will say to them, "After you have set the best aside, the remainder will take the place, in the Levites' case, of the produce of the threshing-floor and wine-press. 31 You may consume this anywhere, you and the members of your households; this is your recompense for serving in the Tent of Meeting, 32 and you will not incur sin by doing so, once you have set aside the best; you will not be profaning the things consecrated by the Israelites and will not incur death." '

The ashes of the red heifer

19 Yahweh spoke to Moses and Aaron and said:

2 'This is a decree of the Law which Yahweh has prescribed. Tell the Israelites, they are to bring you a red heifer without fault or blemish that has never borne the yoke. 3 You will give it to the priest Eleazar. It will then be taken outside the camp and slaughtered in his presence. 4 The priest Eleazar will then take some of the victim's blood on his finger, and sprinkle this blood seven times towards the entrance to the Tent of Meeting. 5 The heifer will then be burnt while he looks on; its hide, flesh, blood and offal will be burnt. 6 The priest will then take some cedar wood, hyssop and scarlet material and throw them on the fire where the heifer is burning. 7 He will then wash his clothes and bathe himself; after which he will go back to the camp, though he will remain unclean until evening. 8 The man who has burnt the heifer will wash his clothes and bathe himself and will remain unclean until evening. 9 The man who gathers up the ashes of the heifer must be ritually clean; he will deposit them outside the camp, in a clean place. They will be kept for the ritual use of the Israelite community for making water for purification; it is a sacrifice for sin. 10 The man who has gathered up the ashes of the heifer will wash his clothes and remain unclean until evening. For the Israelites as for the resident alien, this will be a perpetual decree.

Cases of uncleanness

11 'Anyone who touches the corpse of anyone whatever will be unclean for seven days. 12 Such a person must be purified with these waters on the third and seventh day and will then be clean; otherwise he will not be clean.

¹³ Anyone who touches the corpse of anyone who has died and is not purified, defiles Yahweh's Dwelling; such a person will be outlawed from Israel, since the water for purification has not been sprinkled over him; he is unclean, and his uncleanness remains in him.

¹⁴ 'This is the law when someone dies in a tent. Anyone who goes into the tent, or anyone who is already in it, will be unclean for seven days, ¹⁵ and every open vessel with no cover tied over it will also be unclean.

¹⁶ 'Anyone in the open country who touches a murder victim, a corpse, human bones or a grave will be unclean for seven days.

The ritual of water for purification

¹⁷ 'For someone thus unclean, some of the ashes of the victim burnt as a sacrifice for sin will be taken and spring water must be poured over them, in a vessel. ¹⁸ Someone who is ritually clean will then take some hyssop and dip it in the water. This person will then sprinkle the tent, all the vessels and people who were there, and similarly anyone who has touched human bones, a murder victim, a corpse or a grave. ¹⁹ On the third and the seventh day the clean one will sprinkle the unclean, who on the seventh day will be clean. The latter will then wash his clothes and bathe in water, and in the evening he will be clean. ²⁰ Anyone who fails to be purified in this way will be outlawed from the community, and would defile Yahweh's sanctuary. Such a person is unclean, not having been sprinkled with the water for purification.

²¹ 'This will be a perpetual decree for them. The person who sprinkles the water for purification will wash his clothes, and anyone who touches the water for purification will be unclean until evening. ²² Anything that an unclean person touches will be unclean, and anyone who touches it will be unclean until evening.'

The waters of Meribah^a

20 The Israelites, the whole community, arrived in the first month at the desert of Zin. The people settled at Kadesh. There Miriam died and was buried.

² There was no water for the community, so they banded together against Moses and Aaron. ³ The people laid the blame on Moses. 'We would rather have died', they said, 'as our brothers died before Yahweh! ⁴ Why have you brought Yahweh's community into this desert, for us and our livestock to die here? ⁵ Why did you lead us out of Egypt, only to bring us to this wretched place? It is a place unfit for sowing, it has no figs, no vines, no pomegranates, and there is not even water to drink!'

⁶ Leaving the assembly, Moses and Aaron went to the entrance of the Tent of Meeting. They threw themselves on their faces, and the glory of Yahweh appeared to them. ⁷ Yahweh then spoke to Moses and said, ⁸ 'Take the branch and call the community together, you and your brother Aaron. Then, in full view of them, order this rock to release its water. You will release water from the rock for them and provide drink for the community and their livestock.'

⁹ Moses took up the branch from before Yahweh, as he had directed him. ¹⁰ Moses and Aaron then called the assembly together in front of the rock. He then said to them, 'Listen now, you rebels. Shall we make water gush from this rock for you?' ¹¹ Moses then raised his hand and struck the rock twice with the branch; water gushed out in abundance, and the community and their livestock drank.

The punishment of Moses and Aaron

¹² Yahweh then said to Moses and Aaron, 'Because you did not believe that I could assert my holiness before the Israelites' eyes, you will not lead this assembly into the country which I am giving them.'

¹³ These were the Waters of Meribah, where the Israelites laid the blame on Yahweh and where, by their means, he asserted his holiness.

20a ‖ Ex 17:1–7.

15 READ NUMBERS 20:1–11.

Moses then raised his hand and struck the rock twice with the branch; water gushed out in abundance.—NUMBERS 20:11

THE CROSS PREFIGURED

The most marvelous of all Christ's actions and miracles is his precious Cross. For no other thing has subdued death, expiated the sin of the first parent, despoiled Hades, bestowed the resurrection, granted the power to us of despising the present and even death itself, prepared the return to our former blessedness, opened the gates of Paradise, given our nature a seat at the right hand of God, and made us the children and heirs of God, save the Cross of our Lord Jesus Christ. . . .

The Tree of Life that was planted by God in Paradise pre-figured this precious Cross. For since death was by a tree, it was fitting that life and resurrection should be bestowed by a tree (see Gn 2, 3). Jacob . . . was the first to image the Cross, and when he blessed his sons with crossed hands (see Heb 11:21) he made most clearly the sign of the cross. Likewise also did Moses' rod, when it smote the sea in the figure of the Cross and saved Israel, while it overwhelmed Pharaoh in the depths; likewise also the hands stretched out crosswise and routing Amalek; and the bitter water made sweet by a tree, and the rock rent and pouring forth streams of water, and the rod that meant for Aaron the dignity of the high priesthood (see Ex 4); and the serpent lifted in triumph on a tree as though it were dead (see Nb 21:8–9), the tree bringing salvation to those who in faith saw their enemy dead, just as Christ was nailed to the tree in the flesh of sin which yet knew no sin. The mighty Moses cried, "You will see your life hanging on the tree before your eyes," and Isaiah likewise, "I have spread out my hands all the day unto a faithless and rebellious people" (see Is 65:2). But may we who worship this Cross obtain a part in Christ the crucified. Amen. ST. JOHN DAMASCENE, 675?–749?

YOU WILL FIND THE NEXT READING AT NUMBERS 24.

Edom refuses right of way

14 Moses sent messengers from Kadesh: 'To the king of Edom. Your brother Israel says this: You are aware of the great hardships we have encountered. 15 Our ancestors went down to Egypt and there we stayed for a long time. But the Egyptians treated us badly, as they had our ancestors. 16 When we appealed to Yahweh, he heard our cry and, sending an angel, brought us out of Egypt, and here we are, now, at Kadesh, a town on the borders of your territory. 17 We ask permission to pass through your country. We shall not go through the fields or vineyards; we shall not drink the water from the wells; we shall keep to the king's highway without turning to right or left until we have passed through your territory.' 18 To which, Edom replied, 'You will not pass through my country; if you do, I shall oppose you by force of arms.' 19 To which the Israelites replied, 'We shall keep to the high road; if I and my flocks drink any of your water, I am willing to pay for it. All I am asking is to pass through on foot.' 20 Edom replied: 'You shall not pass,' and Edom opposed them in great

numbers and great force. ²¹ At Edom's refusal to grant Israel passage through his territory, Israel turned away.

The death of Aaron

²² They set out from Kadesh, and the Israelites, the whole community, came to Mount Hor. ²³ Yahweh spoke to Moses and Aaron at Mount Hor, on the frontier of Edom, and said, ²⁴ 'Aaron is to be gathered to his people; he will not enter the country which I have given to the Israelites, since you both disobeyed my order at the Waters of Meribah. ²⁵ Take Aaron and his son Eleazar and bring them up Mount Hor. ²⁶ Then take Aaron's robes off him and dress his son Eleazar in them. Aaron will then be gathered to his people; that is where he will die.'

²⁷ Moses did as Yahweh ordered. With the whole community watching, they went up Mount Hor. ²⁸ Moses took Aaron's robes off him and dressed his son Eleazar in them, and there Aaron died, on the mountain-top. Moses and Eleazar then came back down the mountain. ²⁹ The whole community saw that Aaron had died, and for thirty days the whole House of Israel mourned for Aaron.

The capture of Hormah

21 The king of Arad, the Canaanite living in the Negeb, learned that Israel was coming by way of Atharim. He attacked Israel and took some prisoners. ² Israel then made this vow to Yahweh, 'If you deliver this people into my power, I shall curse their towns with destruction.' ³ Yahweh heard Israel's words and delivered the Canaanites into their power, and they destroyed them in accordance with their curse. Hence the place was given the name Hormah.

The bronze serpent

⁴ They left Mount Hor by the road to the Sea of Suph, to skirt round Edom. On the way the people lost patience. ⁵ They spoke against God and against Moses, 'Why did you bring us out of Egypt to die in the desert? For there is nei-

ther food nor water here; we are sick of this meagre diet.'

⁶ At this, God sent fiery serpents among the people; their bite brought death to many in Israel. ⁷ The people came and said to Moses, 'We have sinned by speaking against Yahweh and against you. Intercede for us with Yahweh to save us from these serpents.' Moses interceded for the people, ⁸ and Yahweh replied, 'Make a fiery serpent and raise it as a standard. Anyone who is bitten and looks at it will survive.' ⁹ Moses then made a serpent out of bronze and raised it as a standard, and anyone who was bitten by a serpent and looked at the bronze serpent survived.

By stages to Transjordan

¹⁰ The Israelites set out and camped at Oboth. ¹¹ Then they left Oboth and camped at Iye-Abarim, in the desert on the eastern border of Moab. ¹² They set out from there and camped in the gorge of the Zered. ¹³ They set out from there and camped on the other side of the Arnon.

This gorge in the desert begins in the territory of the Amorites. For the Arnon is the frontier of Moab, between the Moabites and the Amorites. ¹⁴ That is why it says in the Book of the Wars of Yahweh:

'. . . Waheb near Suphah and the gorges of the Arnon ¹⁵ and the slope of the ravine running down to the site of Ar and over against the frontier of Moab.'

¹⁶ And from there they went to Beer, that being the well in connection with which Yahweh had said to Moses, 'Call the people together and I will give them water.' ¹⁷ Then it was that Israel sang this song:

Spring up, well!
Sing out for the well,
¹⁸ sunk by the princes,
dug by the people's leaders
with the sceptre, with their staves!

—and from the desert to Mattanah, ¹⁹ and from Mattanah to Nahaliel, and from Nahaliel to Bamoth, [20] and from Bamoth to the valley that opens into the country of Moab, towards the heights of Pisgah overlooking the desert.

The conquest of Transjordan[a]

[21] Israel sent messengers to say to Sihon king of the Amorites, [22] 'I wish to pass through your country. We shall not stray into the fields or vineyards; we shall not drink the water from the wells; we shall keep to the king's highway until we have passed through your territory.'

[23] But Sihon would not give Israel leave to pass through his country. He assembled all his people, marched into the desert to meet Israel, and reached Jahaz, where he gave battle to Israel. [24] Israel defeated him by force of arms and conquered his country from the Arnon to the Jabbok, as far as the Ammonites, for Jazer marked the Ammonite frontier. [25] Israel took all these towns. Israel occupied all the Amorite towns, Heshbon and all its dependencies, [26] Heshbon being the capital of Sihon king of the Amorites, who had made war on the first king of Moab and captured all his territory as far as the Arnon. [27] Hence the poets say:

Come to Heshbon!
Let the city of Sihon
be rebuilt on firm foundations!

[28] For fire has burst from Heshbon[b]
a flame from the city of Sihon,
devouring Ar of Moab,
engulfing the heights of the Arnon.
[29] Oh, unhappy Moab!
People of Chemosh, you are lost!
He has resigned his sons as fugitives,
and his daughters as prisoners
to Sihon king of the Amorites.
[30] Their posterity has been destroyed
from Heshbon all the way to Dibon,
and we have lit a fire
all the way from Nophah to Medeba.

[31] Thus Israel occupied the Amorites' territory. [32] Moses then sent men to reconnoitre Jazer, and Israel took it and its dependencies, evicting the Amorites who lived there.

[33] They then turned and marched on Bashan. Og king of Bashan and all his people marched to meet them and give battle at Edrei. [34] Yahweh said to Moses, 'Do not be afraid of him, for I have put him, all his people and his country at your mercy. Treat him as you treated Sihon king of the Amorites, who lived in Heshbon.' [35] So they pressed their attack against him, his sons and all his people until there was no one left alive. And they took possession of his country.

22

The Israelites then set out and pitched their camp in the Plains of Moab, beyond the Jordan opposite Jericho.

The king of Moab appeals to Balaam

[2] Balak son of Zippor saw all that Israel had done to the Amorites, [3] and Moab was terrified of the people, because there were so many of them.

Moab was afraid of the Israelites; [4] he said to the elders of Midian, 'This horde will soon have cropped everything round us as closely as an ox crops grass in the countryside.'

Now Balak son of Zippor was king of Moab at the time. [5] He sent messengers to summon Balaam son of Beor, at Pethor on the River, in the territory of the Amawites, saying, 'Look, a people coming from Egypt has overrun the whole countryside; they have halted at my very door. [6] I beg you come and curse this people for me, for they are stronger than I am. We may then be able to defeat them and drive them out of the country. For this I know: anyone you bless is blessed, anyone you curse is accursed.'

[7] The elders of Moab and the elders of Midian set out, taking the fee for the divination with them. They found Balaam and gave him Balak's message. [8] He said to them, 'Stay the night here, and I will answer as Yahweh directs me.' So the chiefs of Moab stayed with

21a || Dt 2:26–36.   21b || Jr 48:45–46.

Balaam. ⁹God came to Balaam and said, 'Who are these men staying with you?' ¹⁰Balaam said to God, 'Balak son of Zippor, king of Moab, has sent me this message, ¹¹"Look, a people coming from Egypt has overrun the whole countryside. Come now and curse them for me; I may then be able to defeat them and drive them out." ' ¹²God said to Balaam, 'You are not to go with them. You are not to curse the people, for they are blessed.' ¹³In the morning Balaam got up and said to the chiefs sent by Balak, 'Go back to your country, for Yahweh will not let me go with you.' ¹⁴So the chiefs of Moab got up, went back to Balak and said, 'Balaam refuses to come with us.'

¹⁵And again Balak sent chiefs, more numerous and more renowned than the first. ¹⁶They came to Balaam and said, 'A message from Balak son of Zippor, "Now do not refuse to come to me. ¹⁷I will load you with honours and do whatever you say. I beg you come and curse this people for me." ' ¹⁸In reply, Balaam said to Balak's envoys, 'Even if Balak gave me his house full of silver and gold, I could not go against the order of Yahweh my God in anything, great or small. ¹⁹Now please stay the night here yourselves, and I will learn what else Yahweh has to tell me.' ²⁰God came to Balaam during the night and said to him, 'Have not these men come to summon you? Get up, go with them, but do only what I tell you to do.' ²¹Balaam got up and saddled his donkey and set out with the chiefs of Moab.

Balaam's donkey

²²His going kindled Yahweh's anger, and the angel of Yahweh took his stand on the road to bar his way. Balaam was riding his donkey and his two servants were with him. ²³Now the donkey saw the angel of Yahweh standing in the road with a drawn sword in his hand, and she turned off the road into the open country. Balaam then struck the donkey to turn her back onto the road. ²⁴The angel of Yahweh then went and stood on a narrow path among the vineyards, with a wall to the right and a wall to the left.

²⁵The donkey saw the angel of Yahweh and scraped against the wall, scraping Balaam's foot against it, so he struck her again. ²⁶The angel of Yahweh then moved and stood in a place so narrow that there was no room to pass either to right or left. ²⁷When the donkey saw the angel of Yahweh, she lay down under Balaam. Balaam flew into a rage and struck the donkey with his stick. ²⁸Yahweh then gave the donkey the power to talk, and she said to Balaam, 'What harm have I done you, for you to strike me three times like this?' ²⁹Balaam answered the donkey, 'Because you have been making a fool of me! If I had been carrying a sword, I should have killed you by now.' ³⁰The donkey said to Balaam, 'Am I not your donkey, and have I not been your mount all your life? Have I ever behaved like this with you before?' 'No,' he replied.

³¹Yahweh then opened Balaam's eyes and he saw the angel of Yahweh standing in the road with a drawn sword in his hand; and he bowed his head and threw himself on his face. ³²And the angel of Yahweh said to him, 'Why did you strike your donkey three times like that? I myself had come to bar your way; while I am here your road is blocked. ³³The donkey saw me and turned aside because of me three times. You are lucky she did turn aside, or I should have killed you by now, though I would have spared her.' ³⁴Balaam said to the angel of Yahweh, 'I have sinned. I did not know you were standing in the road to stop me. But if what I am doing displeases you, I will go home again.' ³⁵The angel of Yahweh said to Balaam, 'Go with these men, but say only what I tell you to say.' So Balaam went on with the chiefs sent by Balak.

Balaam and Balak

³⁶Balak learned that Balaam was coming and went out to meet him, in the direction of Ar in Moab, at the Arnon frontier on the country's furthest boundary. ³⁷Balak said to Balaam, 'Did I not send messengers to summon you? Why did you not come to me? Did you think,

perhaps, I could confer no honours on you?' 38 Balaam said to Balak, 'I have come to you after all. I suppose you know I cannot say anything on my own? The words God puts into my mouth are what I shall say.'

39 Balaam set out with Balak. They came to Kiriath-Huzoth. 40 Balak sacrificed oxen and sheep, and offered portions to Balaam and the chiefs who were with him. 41 Next morning Balak took Balaam and brought him up to Bamoth-Baal, from where he could see the edge of the camp.

23 Balaam said to Balak, 'Build me seven altars here and prepare me seven bulls and seven rams.' 2 Balak did as Balaam said and offered a burnt offering of one bull and one ram on each altar. 3 Balaam then said to Balak, 'Stand beside your burnt offerings while I go away. Perhaps Yahweh will come and meet me. If he does, I shall tell you whatever he reveals to me.' And he withdrew to a bare hill.

Balaam's prophecies

4 God came to meet Balaam, who said to him, 'I have prepared the seven altars and offered a burnt offering of one bull and one ram on each altar.' 5 Yahweh then put a prophecy into his mouth and said to him, 'Go back to Balak, and that is what you must say to him.' 6 So Balaam went back to him, and found him still standing beside his burnt offering, with all the chiefs of Moab. 7 He then declaimed his poem as follows:

Balak has brought me from Aram,
    the king of Moab from the hills of
        Kedem:
'Come and curse Jacob for me,
    come and denounce Israel!'
8 How shall I curse someone whom God has
        not cursed,
    how denounce someone God has not
        denounced?
9 Yes, from the top of the crags I see him,
    from the hills I descry him:

a people that dwells on its own,
    not to be reckoned among other nations!
10 Who can count the dust of Jacob?
    Who can number the cloud of Israel?
    May I die the death of the just,
    and may my future be like theirs!

11 Balak said to Balaam, 'What have you done to me? I brought you to curse my enemies, and you have heaped blessings on them!' 12 Balaam replied, 'Am I to depart from what Yahweh puts into my mouth?' 13 Balak then said, 'Please come somewhere else. From here you can see only the fringe of them, you cannot see them all. Curse them for me over there.' 14 He led him to the Lookouts' Field on the top of Pisgah. There he built seven altars and offered a burnt offering of one bull and one ram on each altar. 15 Balaam said to Balak, 'Stand here beside your burnt offerings while I wait over there.' 16 God came to meet Balaam, he put a prophecy into his mouth and said to him, 'Go back to Balak, and that is what you must say to him.' 17 So Balaam went to him and found him still standing beside his burnt offering and all the chiefs of Moab with him. 'What did Yahweh say?' Balak said to him. 18 Balaam then declaimed his poem, as follows:

Stand up, Balak, and listen,
    give ear to me, son of Zippor.
19 God is no human being that he should lie,
    no child of Adam to change his mind.
    Is it his to say and not to do,
    is it his to speak and not fulfil?
20 The charge laid on me is to bless,
    I shall bless, and I cannot reverse it.
21 I have perceived no guilt in Jacob,
    have seen no perversity in Israel.
    Yahweh his God is with him,
    and a royal acclamation to greet him.
22 God has brought him out of Egypt,
    is like the wild ox's horns to him.
23 There is no omen whatever against Jacob,
    no augury at all against Israel.
    Well may people say of Jacob,
    of Israel, 'What has God achieved?'

²⁴for here is a people like a lioness rising,
   poised like a lion to spring;
nor will he lie down till he has devoured
      his prey
and drunk the blood of his slain.

²⁵Balak said to Balaam, 'Very well! Do not
curse them. But at least do not bless them!'
²⁶Balaam retorted to Balak, 'Did I not tell
you? Whatever Yahweh says, I must do.'

²⁷Balak then said to Balaam, 'Come with
me now and I shall take you somewhere else.
From there perhaps it will please God to curse
them for me.' ²⁸So Balak led Balaam to the
summit of Peor, overlooking the wastelands.
²⁹Balaam then said to Balak, 'Build me seven
altars here and prepare me seven bulls and
seven rams.' ³⁰Balak did as Balaam said and
offered a burnt offering of one bull and one
ram on each altar.

24 Balaam then saw that it pleased Yahweh to bless Israel. He did not go as before to seek omens but turned towards the
desert. ²Raising his eyes Balaam saw Israel settled tribe by tribe; the spirit of God came on
him ³and he declaimed his poem, as follows:

The prophecy of Balaam son of Beor,
   the prophecy of the man with far-seeing
      eyes,
⁴   the prophecy of one who hears the
      words of God.
He sees what Shaddai makes him see,
receives the divine answer, and his eyes are
      opened.
⁵How fair your tents are, Jacob,
   how fair your dwellings, Israel,
⁶like valleys that stretch afar,
   like gardens by the banks of a river,
   like aloes planted by Yahweh,
   like cedars beside the waters!
⁷A hero arises from their stock,
   he reigns over countless peoples.
His king is greater than Agag,
   and his kingship held in honour.
⁸God has brought him out of Egypt,

is like the wild ox's horns to him.
He devours the corpses of his enemies,
   breaking their bones,
   piercing them with his arrows.
⁹He has crouched, he has lain down,
   like a lion, like a lioness;
who dare rouse him?
Blessed be those who bless you,
   and accursed be those who curse you!

¹⁰Balak flew into a rage with Balaam. He
struck his hands together and said to Balaam,
'I brought you to curse my enemies, and you
have insisted on blessing them three times
over! ¹¹So now go home as fast as your legs
can carry you. I promised to load you with
honours. Yahweh himself has deprived you of
them.' ¹²Balaam retorted to Balak, 'Did I not
tell the messengers you sent me, ¹³"Even if
Balak gave me his house full of gold and silver
I could not go against Yahweh's order and do
anything of my own accord, whether for good
or ill; whatever Yahweh says is what I shall
say"? ¹⁴Now that I am going back to my own
folk, let me warn you what this people will do
to your people, in days to come.' ¹⁵He then declaimed his poem, as follows:

The prophecy of Balaam son of Beor,
   the prophecy of the man with far-seeing
      eyes,
¹⁶the prophecy of one who hears the words
      of God,
of one who knows the knowledge of the
      Most High.
He sees what Shaddai makes him see,
receives the divine answer, and his eyes are
      opened.
¹⁷I see him—but not in the present.
I perceive him—but not close at hand:
a star is emerging from Jacob,
a sceptre is rising from Israel,
to strike the brow of Moab,
the skulls of all the children of Seth.ᵃ

24a The peoples mentioned will in fact be conquered by
David.

18 Edom too will be a conquered land,
　　Seir too will be a conquered land,
　　　when Israel exerts his strength,
19　　when Jacob tramples on his enemies
　　and destroys the last survivors of Ar.

20 Balaam then looked at Amalek and declaimed his poem, as follows:

　　Amalek, the earliest of nations!
　　　But his posterity will perish forever.

21 He then looked at the Kenites and declaimed his poem, as follows:

　　Your dwelling was firm, Kain,
　　　your nest perched high in the rock.
22 But the nest belongs to Beor;
　　how long will you be Asshur's captive?

23 He then declaimed his poem, as follows:

　　The Sea-people are gathering in the north,
24　　the vessels from the coasts of Kittim.
　　They will bear down on Asshur, bear
　　　　down on Eber;
　　he too will perish forever.

25 Balaam then got up, left and went home,
and Balak too went his way.

Israel at Peor

25 Israel settled at Shittim. The people gave themselves over to prostitution with Moabite women. 2 These invited them to the sacrifices of their gods, and the people ate and bowed down before their gods. 3 With Israel thus committed to the Baal of Peor, Yahweh's anger was aroused against them.

4 Yahweh said to Moses, 'Take all the leaders of the people. Impale them facing the sun, for Yahweh, to deflect his burning anger from Israel.' 5 Moses said to the judges of Israel, 'Each of you will put to death those of his people who have committed themselves to the Baal of Peor.'

6 One of the Israelites came along, bringing the Midianite woman into his family, under the very eyes of Moses and the whole community of Israelites as they were weeping at the entrance to the Tent of Meeting. 7 The priest Phinehas son of Eleazar, son of Aaron, on seeing this, stood up, left the assembly, seized a lance, 8 followed the Israelite into the alcove, and there ran them both through, the Israelite and the woman, through the stomach. Thus the plague which had struck the Israelites was arrested. 9 In the plague twenty-four thousand of them had died.

10 Yahweh then spoke and said, 11 'The priest Phinehas son of Eleazar, son of Aaron has deflected my wrath from the Israelites, he being the only one of them to have the same zeal as I have; for which reason, I did not make an end of the Israelites in my zeal. 12 For this reason I say: To him I grant my covenant of peace. 13 To him and his descendants after him, this covenant will assure the priesthood for ever. In reward for his zeal for his God, he will have the right to perform the ritual of expiation for the Israelites.'

14 The Israelite who had been killed (the one who was killed with the Midianite woman) was called Zimri son of Salu, leader of one of the Simeonite families. 15 The woman, the Midianite who was killed, was called Cozbi, daughter of Zur, chief of a clan, of a family, in Midian.

16 Yahweh then spoke to Moses and said, 17 'Harass the Midianites, strike them down, 18 for harassing you with their guile in the Peor affair and in the affair of their sister Cozbi, the daughter of a prince of Midian, the woman who was killed the day the plague came on account of the business of Peor.'

The census

26 After this plague, Yahweh spoke to Moses and to the priest Eleazar son of Aaron and said:

2 'Take a census of the whole community of Israelites, by families: all those of twenty years and over, fit to bear arms in Israel.'

3 So Moses and the priest Eleazar took a

16 READ NUMBERS 24:5–17.

A star is emerging from Jacob, a sceptre is rising from Israel.—NUMBERS 24:17

THE HEBREW SCRIPTURES PREDICT THE INCARNATION

The whole of inspired Scripture cries aloud concerning the unseemliness of the Cross and of the Word of God becoming man, as even its explicit words abundantly show. For prophets proclaimed beforehand concerning the wonder of the Virgin and the birth of her child, saying: "Lo, the Virgin shall be with child, and shall bring forth a Son, and they shall call his name Immanuel, which interpreted means 'God with us'" (see Is 7:14; Mt 1:23). And the great Moses . . . with reference to the Saviour's becoming man, having estimated what was said as important and assured of its truth, set it down in these words: "I see him—but not in the present. I perceive him—but not close at hand: a star is emerging from Jacob, a sceptre is rising from Israel, to strike the brow of Moab." And again: "How fair your tents are, Jacob, how fair your dwellings, Israel, like valleys that stretch afar, like gardens by the banks of a river, like aloes planted by Yahweh, like cedars beside the waters! A hero arises from their stock, he reigns over countless peoples" (verses 5–7).

Again Isaiah: "Before the child knows how to say father or mother, he shall take the power of Damascus and the spoils of Samaria before the king of Assyria" (see Is 8:4). That a man, then, shall appear is foretold in those words. But that he that is to come is Lord of all, they predict once more as follows: Behold the Lord "riding a swift cloud, is coming to Egypt. The false gods of Egypt totter before him" (Is 19:1). For from thence also it is that the Father calls him back, saying: "I called my son out of Egypt" (Hos 11:1). ST. ATHANASIUS, 297?–373

YOU WILL FIND THE NEXT READING AT DEUTERONOMY 6.

census of them on the Plains of Moab, near the Jordan by Jericho. They counted 4(as Yahweh had ordered Moses and the Israelites after leaving Egypt) men of twenty years and over:

5Reuben, the first-born of Israel. The sons of Reuben: for Hanoch, the Hanochite clan; for Pallu, the Palluite clan; 6for Hezron, the Hezronite clan; for Carmi, the Carmite clan. 7These were the Reubenite clans. They numbered forty-three thousand seven hundred and thirty men.

8The sons of Pallu: Eliab. 9The sons of Eliab: Nemuel, Dathan and Abiram. These two, Dathan and Abiram, men of repute in the community, were the ones who revolted against Moses and Aaron; they belonged to Korah's group when it revolted against Yahweh. 10The earth opened its mouth and swallowed them (with Korah when that group perished), when fire consumed the two hundred and fifty men. They were a sign. 11Korah's sons, however, did not perish.

12The sons of Simeon by clans: for Nemuel, the Nemuelite clan; for Jamin, the Jaminite clan; for Jachin, the Jachinite clan; 13for Zerah, the Zerahite clan; for Shaul, the Shaulite clan. 14These were the Simeonite clans. They numbered twenty-two thousand two hundred men.

15The sons of Gad by clans: for Zephon, the Zephonite clan; for Haggi, the Haggite clan; for Shuni, the Shunite clan; 16for Ozni, the

Oznite clan; for Eri, the Erite clan; ¹⁷for Arod, the Arodite clan; for Areli, the Arelite clan. ¹⁸These were the clans of the sons of Gad. They numbered forty thousand five hundred men.

¹⁹The sons of Judah: Er and Onan. Er and Onan died in the land of Canaan. ²⁰The other sons of Judah became clans: for Shelah, the Shelahite clan; for Perez, the Perezzite clan; for Zerah, the Zerahite clan. ²¹The sons of Perez were: for Hezron, the Hezronite clan; for Hamul, the Hamulite clan. ²²These were the clans of Judah. They numbered seventy-six thousand five hundred men.

²³The sons of Issachar by clans: for Tola, the Tolaite clan; for Puvah, the Puvahite clan; ²⁴for Jashub, the Jashubite clan; for Shimron, the Shimronite clan. ²⁵These were the clans of Issachar. They numbered sixty-four thousand three hundred men.

²⁶The sons of Zebulun by clans: for Sered, the Seredite clan; for Elon, the Elonite clan; for Jahleel, the Jahleelite clan. ²⁷These were the clans of Zebulun. They numbered sixty thousand five hundred men.

²⁸The sons of Joseph by clans: Manasseh and Ephraim.

²⁹The sons of Manasseh: for Machir, the Machirite clan; Machir fathered Gilead: for Gilead, the Gileadite clan. ³⁰These were the sons of Gilead: for Iezer, the Iezerite clan; for Helek, the Helekite clan; ³¹Asriel, the Asrielite clan; Shechem, the Shechemite clan; ³²Shemida, the Shemidaite clan; Hepher, the Hepherite clan. ³³Zelophehad son of Hepher had no sons, only daughters; the names of Zelophehad's daughters were Mahlah, Noah, Hoglah, Milcah and Tirzah. ³⁴These were the clans of Manasseh. They numbered fifty-two thousand seven hundred men.

³⁵These were the sons of Ephraim by clans: for Shuthelah, the Shuthelahite clan; for Becher, the Becherite clan; for Tahan, the Tahanite clan. ³⁶These were the sons of Shuthelah: for Eran, the Eranite clan. ³⁷These were the clans of Ephraim. They numbered thirty-two thousand five hundred men.

These were the sons of Joseph by clans.

³⁸The sons of Benjamin by clans: for Bela, the Belaite clan; for Ashbel, the Ashbelite clan; for Ahiram, the Ahiramite clan; ³⁹for Shephupham, the Shephuphamite clan; for Hupham, the Huphamite clan. ⁴⁰Bela's sons were Ard and Naaman; for Ard, the Ardite clan; for Naaman, the Naamanite clan. ⁴¹These were the sons of Benjamin by clans. They numbered forty-five thousand six hundred men.

⁴²These were the sons of Dan by clans: for Shuham, the Shuhamite clan. These were the sons of Dan by clans. ⁴³All the Shuhamite clans numbered sixty-four thousand four hundred men.

⁴⁴The sons of Asher by clans: for Imnah, the Imnahite clan; for Ishvi, the Ishvihite clan; for Beriah, the Beriahite clan. ⁴⁵For the sons of Beriah: for Heber, the Heberite clan; for Malchiel, the Malchielite clan. ⁴⁶The daughter of Asher was called Serah. ⁴⁷These were the clans of Asher. They numbered fifty-three thousand four hundred men.

⁴⁸The sons of Naphtali by clans: for Jahzeel, the Jahzeelite clan; for Guni, the Gunite clan; ⁴⁹for Jezer, the Jezerite clan; for Shillem, the Shillemite clan. ⁵⁰These were the clans of Naphtali as divided into clans. The sons of Naphtali numbered forty-five thousand four hundred men.

⁵¹Of the Israelites thus numbered, there were six hundred and one thousand seven hundred and thirty men.

⁵²Yahweh then spoke to Moses and said, ⁵³'The country must be shared out among these as a heritage, proportionately to the number of those inscribed. ⁵⁴To the large in number you will give a large area of land, to the small in number a small area; to each the heritage will be in proportion to the number registered. ⁵⁵The sharing out of the country must, however, be done by lot. Each will receive a heritage proportionate to the number of names in their patriarchal tribes; ⁵⁶the heritage of each tribe will be shared out by lot, depending on its larger or smaller numbers.'

Census of the Levites

⁵⁷These, by clans, are the Levites that were registered: for Gershon, the Gershonite clan; for Kohath, the Kohathite clan; for Merari, the Merarite clan. ⁵⁸These are the Levite clans: the Libnite clan, the Hebronite clan, the Mahlite clan, the Mushite clan, the Korahite clan.

Kohath fathered Amram. ⁵⁹Amram's wife was called Jokebed daughter of Levi, born to him in Egypt. To Amram she bore Aaron, Moses and Miriam their sister. ⁶⁰Aaron fathered Nadab and Abihu, Eleazar and Ithamar. ⁶¹Nadab and Abihu died when they brought unauthorised fire before Yahweh.

⁶²Altogether twenty-three thousand males of one month and over were registered. They were not registered with the Israelites, since they were given no heritage with the Israelites.

⁶³Such were the men registered by Moses and the priest Eleazar who took a census of the Israelites on the Plains of Moab near the Jordan by Jericho. ⁶⁴Not one of them was among those whom Moses and the priest Aaron had registered when they counted the Israelites in the desert of Sinai; ⁶⁵for Yahweh had told them that these were to die in the desert and that none of them would be left except Caleb son of Jephunneh and Joshua son of Nun.

The inheritance of daughters

27There then came forward the daughters of Zelophehad son of Hepher, son of Gilead, son of Machir, son of Manasseh; he belonged to the clans of Manasseh son of Joseph. His daughters' names were Mahlah, Noah, Hoglah, Milcah and Tirzah. ²They appeared before Moses, the priest Eleazar, the leaders and the whole community, at the entrance to the Tent of Meeting, and said, ³'Our father died in the desert. He was not a member of the party who banded together against Yahweh, Korah's party; it was for his own sin that he died without sons. ⁴Why should our father's name be lost to his clan? Since he had no son, give us some property like our father's kinsmen.'

⁵Moses took their case before Yahweh, ⁶and Yahweh spoke to Moses and said, ⁷'Zelophehad's daughters are right in what they say. You will indeed give them a property to be their heritage among their father's kinsmen; see that their father's heritage is passed on to them. ⁸Then speak to the Israelites and say, "If a man dies without sons, his heritage will pass to his daughter. ⁹If he has no daughter, the heritage will go to his brothers. ¹⁰If he has no brothers, his heritage will go to his father's brothers. ¹¹If his father has no brothers, his heritage will go to the member of his clan who is most nearly related; it will become his property. This will be a legal rule for the Israelites, as Yahweh has ordered Moses."'

Joshua the head of the community

¹²Yahweh said to Moses, 'Climb this mountain of the Abarim range, and look at the country which I have given to the Israelites. ¹³After you have seen it, you will be gathered to your people, as Aaron your brother was. ¹⁴For you both rebelled in the desert of Zin when the community disputed with me and when I ordered you to assert my holiness before their eyes by means of the water.' (These were the Waters of Meribah of Kadesh, in the desert of Zin.)

¹⁵Moses then said to Yahweh, ¹⁶'May it please Yahweh, God of the spirits that give life to all living creatures, to appoint a leader for this community, ¹⁷to be at their head in all their undertakings, a man who will lead them out and bring them in, so that Yahweh's community will not be like sheep without a shepherd.' ¹⁸Yahweh then said to Moses, 'Take Joshua son of Nun, a man in whom the spirit dwells, and lay your hand on him. ¹⁹Bring him before the priest Eleazar and the whole community and give him your orders in their presence, ²⁰conferring some of your own authority on him, so that the whole community of Israelites will obey him. ²¹He will present himself to the priest Eleazar who will consult

Yahweh on his behalf by means of the rite of the *urim;* at his command, they will go out and, at his command, they will come in, he and all the Israelites with him, the whole community.'

²² Moses did as Yahweh had ordered. He took Joshua, brought him before the priest Eleazar and the whole community, ²³ laid his hands on him and gave him his orders, as Yahweh had directed through Moses.

Regulations for sacrifices

28 Yahweh spoke to Moses and said, ² 'Give the Israelites this order: "Take care to bring me my offering, my sustenance in the form of food burnt as a smell pleasing to me, at the proper time."

³ 'You will then say to them: "This is the food which you will burn in offering to Yahweh:

"Every day, two unblemished yearling lambs as a perpetual burnt offering. ⁴ You will offer the first lamb in the morning and the second lamb at twilight, ⁵ with a cereal offering of one-tenth of an *ephah* of fine flour mixed with one-quarter of a *hin* of crushed-olive oil. ⁶ Such was the perpetual burnt offering made on Mount Sinai as a pleasing smell, as food burnt for Yahweh. ⁷ The accompanying libation will be of one-quarter of a *hin* for each lamb; the libation of fermented liquor for Yahweh will be poured inside the sanctuary. ⁸ The second lamb you will offer at twilight, offering it with the same cereal offering and the same libation as in the morning, as food burnt as a smell pleasing to Yahweh.

⁹ "On the Sabbath day, you will offer two unblemished yearling lambs and two-tenths of an *ephah* of fine flour as a cereal offering, mixed with oil, as well as the accompanying libation. ¹⁰ The Sabbath burnt offering will be offered every Sabbath in addition to the perpetual burnt offering, and the accompanying libation similarly.

¹¹ "At the beginning of each of your months you will offer a burnt offering to Yahweh: two young bulls, one ram and seven yearling lambs, without blemish; ¹² for each bull a cereal offering of three-tenths of an *ephah* of fine flour mixed with oil; for each ram, a cereal offering of two-tenths of fine flour mixed with oil; ¹³ for each lamb, a cereal offering of one-tenth of fine flour mixed with oil: as a burnt offering, as a pleasing smell, as food burnt for Yahweh. ¹⁴ The accompanying libations will be of half a *hin* of wine for a bull, one-third of a *hin* for a ram and one-quarter of a *hin* for a lamb. This will be the monthly burnt offering, month after month, every month of the year. ¹⁵ In addition to the perpetual burnt offering, a goat will be offered to Yahweh, as a sacrifice for sin, with its accompanying libation.

¹⁶ "The fourteenth day of the first month is the Passover of Yahweh, ¹⁷ and the fifteenth day of this month is a feast day. For seven days unleavened bread will be eaten. ¹⁸ On the first day there will be a sacred assembly; you will do no heavy work. ¹⁹ As food burnt as a burnt offering you will offer Yahweh two young bulls, a ram and seven yearling lambs, without blemish. ²⁰ The accompanying cereal offering of fine flour mixed with oil will be three-tenths of an *ephah* for a bull, two-tenths for a ram, ²¹ and one-tenth for each of the seven lambs. ²² There will also be a goat as a sacrifice for sin, for performing the rite of expiation for you. ²³ You will offer these in addition to the morning burnt offering, which is a perpetual burnt offering. ²⁴ You will do this every day for seven days. It is sustenance, food burnt as a smell pleasing to Yahweh, to be offered in addition to the perpetual burnt offering and its accompanying libation. ²⁵ On the seventh day you will hold a sacred assembly; you will do no heavy work.

²⁶ "On the day of the first-fruits, when you make your offering of new fruits to Yahweh at your feast of Weeks, you will hold a sacred assembly; you will do no heavy work. ²⁷ As a burnt offering as a smell pleasing to Yahweh, you will offer two young bulls, one ram and seven yearling lambs. ²⁸ The accompanying cereal offering of fine flour mixed with oil will

be three-tenths of an *ephah* for each bull, two-tenths for the ram, [29] and one-tenth for each of the seven lambs. [30] There will also be a goat as a sacrifice for sin, for performing the rite of expiation for you. [31] You will offer these in addition to the perpetual burnt offering and its accompanying cereal offering and libations." '

29 ' "In the seventh month, on the first day of the month, you will hold a sacred assembly; you will do no heavy work. For you this will be a day of Acclamations. [2] As a burnt offering, as a smell pleasing to Yahweh, you will offer one young bull, one ram and seven yearling lambs, without blemish. [3] The accompanying cereal offering of fine flour mixed with oil will be three-tenths of an *ephah* for the bull, two-tenths for the ram, [4] and one-tenth for each of the seven lambs. [5] There will also be a goat as a sacrifice for sin, for performing the rite of expiation for you. [6] This is in addition to the monthly burnt offering and its cereal offering, the perpetual burnt offering and its cereal offering, and the accompanying libations enjoined by law, as a pleasing smell, as food burnt for Yahweh.

[7] "On the tenth day of this seventh month, you will hold a sacred assembly; you will fast and do no work. [8] As a burnt offering for Yahweh, as a pleasing smell, you will offer one young bull, one ram and seven yearling lambs, which you will choose as being without blemish. [9] The accompanying cereal offering of fine flour mixed with oil will be three-tenths of an *ephah* for the bull, two-tenths for the ram, [10] and one-tenth for each of the seven lambs. [11] And a goat will be offered as a sacrifice for sin. This is in addition to the victim for sin at the feast of Expiation, to the perpetual burnt offering and its cereal offering, and their accompanying libations.

[12] "On the fifteenth day of the seventh month you will hold a sacred assembly; you will do no heavy work, and for seven days you will celebrate a feast for Yahweh. [13] As a burnt offering, as food burnt as a smell pleasing to Yahweh, you will offer thirteen young bulls,

two rams and fourteen yearling lambs, without blemish. [14] The accompanying cereal offering of fine flour mixed with oil will be three-tenths of an *ephah* for each of the thirteen bulls, two-tenths for each of the two rams, [15] and one-tenth for each of the fourteen lambs; [16] also one goat as a sacrifice for sin. This is in addition to the perpetual burnt offering and its cereal offering and libation.

[17] "On the second day: twelve young bulls, two rams and fourteen yearling lambs, without blemish; [18] the accompanying cereal offering and libations, as prescribed, in proportion to the number of bulls, rams and lambs; [19] also one goat as a sacrifice for sin. This is in addition to the perpetual burnt offering and its cereal offering and libations.

[20] "On the third day: eleven bulls, two rams and fourteen yearling lambs, without blemish; [21] the accompanying cereal offering and libations, as prescribed, in proportion to the number of bulls, rams and lambs; [22] also one goat as a sacrifice for sin. This is in addition to the perpetual burnt offering and its cereal offering and libations.

[23] "On the fourth day: ten bulls, two rams and fourteen yearling lambs, without blemish; [24] the accompanying cereal offering and libations, as prescribed, in proportion to the number of bulls, rams and lambs; [25] also one goat as a sacrifice for sin. This is in addition to the perpetual burnt offering and its cereal offering and libation.

[26] "On the fifth day: nine bulls, two rams and fourteen yearling lambs, without blemish; [27] the accompanying cereal offering and libations, as prescribed, in proportion to the number of bulls, rams and lambs; [28] also one goat as a sacrifice for sin. This is in addition to the perpetual burnt offering and its cereal offering and libation.

[29] "On the sixth day: eight bulls, two rams and fourteen yearling lambs, without blemish; [30] the accompanying cereal offering and libations, as prescribed, in proportion to the number of bulls, rams and lambs; [31] also one goat as a sacrifice for sin. This is in addition to the

perpetual burnt offering and its cereal offering and libations.

32 "On the seventh day: seven bulls, two rams and fourteen yearling lambs, without blemish; 33 the accompanying cereal offering and libations, as prescribed, in proportion to the number of bulls, rams and lambs; 34 also one goat as a sacrifice for sin. This is in addition to the perpetual burnt offering and its cereal offering and libation.

35 "On the eighth day you will hold an assembly; you will do no heavy work. 36 As a burnt offering, as food burnt as a smell pleasing to Yahweh, you will offer one bull, one ram and seven yearling lambs, without blemish; 37 the accompanying cereal offering and libations, as prescribed, in proportion to the number of bulls, rams and lambs; 38 also one goat as a sacrifice for sin. This is in addition to the perpetual burnt offering and its cereal offering and libation.

39 "This is what you are to do for Yahweh at your solemn feasts, over and above your votive offerings and your voluntary offerings, your burnt offerings, cereal offerings and libations, and your peace offerings." '

30 Moses told the Israelites exactly what Yahweh had ordered him.

Laws concerning vows

2 Moses spoke to the tribal leaders of the Israelites and said, 'This is what Yahweh has ordered:

3 "If a man makes a vow to Yahweh or a formal pledge under oath, he must not break his word: whatever he promises by word of mouth he must do.

4 "If a woman makes a vow to Yahweh or a formal pledge during her youth, while she is still in her father's house, 5 and if her father hears about this vow or pledge made by her and says nothing to her, her vow, whatever it may be, will be binding, and the pledge she has taken, whatever it may be, will be binding. 6 But if her father on the day he learns of it expresses his disapproval of it, then none of the

vows or pledges she has taken will be binding. Yahweh will not hold her to it, since her father has expressed his disapproval.

7 "If, being bound by vows or by a pledge voiced without due reflection, she then marries, 8 and if her husband hears of it but says nothing on the day he learns of it, her vows will be binding and the pledges she has taken will be binding. 9 But if on the day he learns of it he expresses his disapproval to her, this will annul the vow that she has made or the pledge that binds her, voiced without due reflection. Yahweh will not hold her to it.

10 "The vow of a widow or a divorced woman and all pledges taken by her are binding on her.

11 "If she has made a vow or taken a pledge under oath while in her husband's house, 12 and if when the husband learns of it he says nothing to her and does not express disapproval to her, then the vow, whatever it is, will be binding, and the pledge, whatever it is, will be binding. 13 But if the husband when he hears of it annuls it on the day he learns of it, no undertaking of hers, be it vow or pledge, will be binding. Since the husband has annulled it, Yahweh will not hold her to it.

14 "Every vow or oath that is binding on the wife may be endorsed or annulled by the husband.

15 "If by the following day the husband has said nothing to her, it means that he endorses her vow, whatever it may be, or her pledge, whatever it may be. He endorses them if he says nothing on the day he learns of them. 16 But if, having learnt of them, he annuls them later, he will bear the consequences for his wife's guilt." '

17 Such were the laws which Yahweh prescribed to Moses, concerning the relationship between a man and his wife, and between a father and his daughter while still young and living in her father's home.

The holy war against Midian

31 Yahweh spoke to Moses and said, 2 'Exact the full vengeance for the Is-

raelites on the Midianites. Afterwards you will be gathered to your people.'

3 Moses said to the people, 'Some of you are to take up arms for Yahweh's campaign against Midian, to carry out the vengeance of Yahweh on Midian. 4 You will put a thousand men in the field from each of the tribes of Israel.'

5 In this way Israel's thousands provided twelve thousand men equipped for war, one thousand from each tribe: 6 Moses put them in the field, one thousand from each tribe, with Phinehas, son of the priest Eleazar, to go with them carrying the sacred objects and the trumpets for the battle cry.

7 They made war on Midian, as Yahweh had ordered Moses, and put every male to death. 8 What is more, they killed the kings of Midian, Evi, Rekem, Zur, Hur and Reba, the five Midianite kings; they also put Balaam son of Beor to the sword. 9 The Israelites took the Midianite women and their little ones captive and carried off all their cattle, all their flocks and all their goods as booty. 10 They set fire to the towns where they lived and to all their encampments. 11 Then, taking all their booty, everything they had captured, human and animal, 12 they brought the captives, spoil and booty to Moses, the priest Eleazar and the whole community of Israelites at the camp on the Plains of Moab, near the Jordan by Jericho.

The slaughter of the women and purification of the booty

13 Moses, the priest Eleazar and all the leaders of the community went out of the camp to meet them. 14 Moses was enraged with the officers of the army, the commanders of the thousands and commanders of the hundreds, who had come back from this military expedition. 15 He said, 'Why have you spared the life of all the women? 16 They were the very ones who, on Balaam's advice, caused the Israelites to be unfaithful to Yahweh in the affair at Peor: hence the plague which struck Yahweh's community. 17 So kill all the male children and kill all the women who have ever slept with a man; 18 but spare the lives of the young girls who have never slept with a man, and keep them for yourselves. 19 As for you, bivouac outside the camp for seven days, everyone who has killed anyone or touched a corpse. Purify yourselves and your prisoners on the third and seventh days, 20 and purify all clothing, everything made of skin, everything woven of goat's hair and everything made of wood.'

21 The priest Eleazar said to the soldiers who had come back from the campaign, 'This is an article of the Law which Yahweh prescribed to Moses: 22 although gold, silver, bronze, iron, tin and lead, 23 everything that can withstand fire can be cleaned by being passed through fire, it must still be purified with water for purification. Whatever cannot resist fire you must pass through water.

24 'Wash your clothes on the seventh day and you will then be clean. You may then re-enter the camp.'

The allocation of the booty

25 Yahweh spoke to Moses and said:

26 'With the priest Eleazar and the heads of families in the community, take a count of the spoils and captives, human and animal. 27 You will then share out the spoil, half and half, between those who fought the campaign and the rest of the community. 28 From the share of the combatants who took part in the campaign, you will set aside one out of every five hundred persons, oxen, donkeys and sheep as Yahweh's portion. 29 You will take this from the half share coming to them and give it to the priest Eleazar as the portion set aside for Yahweh. 30 From the half coming to the Israelites, you will take one out of every fifty persons, oxen, donkeys, sheep, and all other animals, and give them to the Levites who are responsible for Yahweh's Dwelling.'

31 Moses and the priest Eleazar did as Yahweh had ordered Moses. 32 The spoils, the remainder of the booty captured by the soldiers, came to six hundred and seventy-five thousand sheep and goats, 33 seventy-two thousand head of cattle, 34 sixty-one thousand donkeys,

35 and in persons, women who had never slept with a man, thirty-two thousand in all. 36 Half was assigned to those who had taken part in the war, namely three hundred and thirty-seven thousand five hundred sheep and goats, 37 of which Yahweh's portion was six hundred and seventy-five, 38 thirty-six thousand head of cattle, of which Yahweh's portion was seventy-two, 39 thirty thousand five hundred donkeys, of which Yahweh's portion was sixty-one, 40 and sixteen thousand persons, of which Yahweh's portion was thirty-two. 41 Moses gave the priest Eleazar the portion set aside for Yahweh, as Yahweh had ordered Moses.

42 As for the half coming to the Israelites which Moses had separated from that of the combatants, 43 this half, the community's share, came to three hundred and thirty-seven thousand five hundred sheep and goats, 44 thirty-six thousand head of cattle, 45 thirty thousand five hundred donkeys 46 and sixteen thousand persons. 47 From this half, the Israelites' share, Moses took one out of every fifty, human and animal, and gave them to the Levites who were responsible for Yahweh's Dwelling, as Yahweh had ordered Moses.

The offerings

48 The officers of the thousands who had fought the campaign, the commanders of the thousands and commanders of the hundreds, came to Moses 49 and said, 'Your servants have numbered the soldiers under their command: none of our men is missing. 50 So, as an offering for Yahweh, we have brought what each of us has found in the way of gold ornaments, armlets and bracelets, rings, earrings and breastplates, to make expiation for ourselves before Yahweh.' 51 Moses and the priest Eleazar accepted this gold from them, all this jewellery. 52 This portion of gold given to Yahweh by the commanders of the thousands and commanders of the hundreds amounted to sixteen thousand seven hundred and fifty shekels.

53 Each of the soldiers took his own booty. 54 But Moses and the priest Eleazar, having accepted the gold from the commanders of the thousands and commanders of the hundreds, brought it into the Tent of Meeting, to be a reminder of the Israelites before Yahweh.

The allocation of Transjordan [a]

32 Now, the Reubenites and Gadites owned very large herds of cattle. Having seen that the territories of Jazer and Gilead formed an ideal region for raising stock, 2 the Gadites and Reubenites went to Moses, the priest Eleazar and the leaders of the community, and said to them, 3 'The territory of Ataroth, Dibon, Jazer, Nimrah, Heshbon, Elealeh, Sebam, Nebo and Beon, 4 which Yahweh has conquered before the advancing community of Israel, is ideal land for raising stock, and your servants are cattle breeders. 5 So', they said, 'if you approve, give your servants this land for us to own; do not make us cross the Jordan.'

6 Moses said to the Gadites and Reubenites, 'Do you intend your brothers to go into battle while you stay here? 7 Why are you discouraging the Israelites from crossing to the country which Yahweh has given them? 8 Your fathers behaved in the same way when I sent them from Kadesh-Barnea to see the country, 9 for, having gone as far as the Valley of Eshcol and seen the country, they discouraged the Israelites from entering the country which Yahweh had given them. 10 Hence Yahweh's anger was aroused that day and he swore this oath, 11 "No man of twenty years and over, who left Egypt, shall set eyes on the country which I promised on oath to Abraham, Isaac and Jacob . . . , for they have not followed me absolutely, 12 except for Caleb son of Jephunneh the Kenizzite, and Joshua son of Nun: these indeed have followed Yahweh absolutely." 13 Yahweh's anger being aroused by Israel, he made them wander in the desert for forty years, until the generation that offended Yahweh had all disappeared. 14 And now you rise up in your father's place, offshoot of sinful stock, to increase Yahweh's burning anger

32a ‖ Dt 3:12–20.

with Israel even more! ¹⁵ If you turn away from him, he will prolong the time spent in the desert, and you will bring about this entire people's ruin.'

¹⁶ They came to Moses and said, 'We should like to build sheepfolds here for our flocks and towns for our little ones. ¹⁷ We ourselves will take up arms and lead the Israelites until we have brought them to the place appointed for them, while our little ones stay in the fortified towns to be safe from the local inhabitants. ¹⁸ We will not return to our homes until every one of the Israelites has taken possession of his heritage. ¹⁹ For we shall have no heritage with them on the other bank of the Jordan or beyond, since our heritage has fallen to us here, east of the Jordan.'

²⁰ Moses said to them, 'If you do as you have said, if you are prepared to fight before Yahweh, ²¹ and if all those of you who bear arms cross the Jordan before Yahweh, until he has driven all his enemies out before him, ²² then, once the country has become subject to Yahweh, you may go back, and will have discharged your obligation to Yahweh and Israel, and Yahweh will consider this territory yours. ²³ But if you do not, you will sin against Yahweh, and be sure your sin will find you out. ²⁴ Build towns, then, for your little ones and folds for your flocks; but do what you have promised.'

²⁵ The Gadites and Reubenites said to Moses, 'Your servants will do as my lord directs. ²⁶ Our little ones, our wives, our flocks and all our livestock will stay in the towns of Gilead, ²⁷ but your servants, each armed for war, will cross in Yahweh's name and fight, as my lord says.'

²⁸ So Moses gave orders about them to the priest Eleazar, Joshua son of Nun, and the heads of families in the Israelite tribes. ²⁹ Moses said to them, 'If the Gadites and Reubenites, all those under arms, cross the Jordan with you to fight in Yahweh's name, then, once the country has become subject to you, you will give them the territory of Gilead as theirs. ³⁰ But if they will not cross with you

under arms, they will receive their domains in Canaan with the rest of you.'

³¹ To this, the Gadites and Reubenites replied, 'What Yahweh has said to your servants, we shall do. ³² Under arms, we shall cross in Yahweh's name into Canaan, so that ownership of our heritage on this side of the Jordan will be ours.' ³³ Moses then gave them—the Gadites, the Reubenites and the half-tribe of Manasseh son of Joseph—the kingdom of Sihon king of the Amorites and the kingdom of Og king of Bashan, the country and the towns within its territory, and the country's frontier-towns.

³⁴ The Gadites rebuilt Dibon, Ataroth, Aroer, ³⁵ Atroth-Shophan, Jazer, Jogbehah, ³⁶ Beth-Nimrah and Beth-Haran as fortified towns with folds for the flocks.

³⁷ The Reubenites rebuilt Heshbon, Elealeh, Kiriathaim, ³⁸ Nebo and Baal-Meon (the names of which were altered), and Sibmah, giving new names to the towns which they rebuilt.

³⁹ The descendants of Machir son of Manasseh went to Gilead. They conquered it and drove out the Amorites who were there. ⁴⁰ Moses gave Gilead to Machir son of Manasseh, and he settled there. ⁴¹ Jair son of Manasseh went and seized their encampments, renaming them the Encampments of Jair. ⁴² Nobah went and seized Kenat with its dependent townships, and called it Nobah after himself.

The stages of the Exodus

33 These were the stages of the journey made by the Israelites when they left Egypt in their companies under the leadership of Moses and Aaron. ² Moses recorded their starting-points in writing whenever they moved on at Yahweh's order. The stages, from one starting-point to another, were as follows:

³ They left Rameses in the first month. It was the fifteenth day of the first month, the day following the Passover, when the Israelites confidently set out, under the eyes of all Egypt. ⁴ The Egyptians were burying those of their

own people whom Yahweh had struck down, all the first-born; Yahweh had carried out his judgement on their gods.

⁵ The Israelites left Rameses and camped at Succoth. ⁶ Then they left Succoth and encamped at Etham which is on the edge of the desert. ⁷ They left Etham, turned back to Pi-Hahiroth, opposite Baal-Zephon, and encamped before Migdol. ⁸ They left Pi-Hahiroth, crossed the sea into the desert, and after marching for three days in the desert of Etham they encamped at Marah. ⁹ They left Marah and reached Elim. At Elim there were twelve springs of water and seventy palm trees; they encamped there. ¹⁰ They left Elim and encamped by the Sea of Reeds. ¹¹ They left the Sea of Reeds and encamped in the desert of Sin. ¹² They left the desert of Sin and encamped at Dophkah. ¹³ They left Dophkah and encamped at Alush. ¹⁴ They left Alush and encamped at Rephidim; the people found no drinking water there. ¹⁵ They left Rephidim and encamped in the desert of Sinai. ¹⁶ They left the desert of Sinai and encamped at Kibroth-ha-Taavah. ¹⁷ They left Kibroth-ha-Taavah and encamped at Hazeroth. ¹⁸ They left Hazeroth and encamped at Rithmah. ¹⁹ They left Rithmah and encamped at Rimmon-Perez. ²⁰ They left Rimmon-Perez and encamped at Libnah. ²¹ They left Libnah and encamped at Rissah. ²² They left Rissah and encamped at Kehelathah. ²³ They left Kehelathah and encamped at Mount Shepher. ²⁴ They left Mount Shepher and encamped at Haradah. ²⁵ They left Haradah and encamped at Makheloth. ²⁶ They left Makheloth and encamped at Tahath. ²⁷ They left Tahath and encamped at Terah. ²⁸ They left Terah and encamped at Mithkah. ²⁹ They left Mithkah and encamped at Hashmonah. ³⁰ They left Hashmonah and encamped at Moseroth. ³¹ They left Moseroth and encamped at Bene-Jaakan. ³² They left Bene-Jaakan and encamped at Hor-Gidgad. ³³ They left Hor-Gidgad and encamped at Jotbathah. ³⁴ They left Jotbathah and encamped at Abronah. ³⁵ They left Abronah and encamped

at Ezion-Geber. ³⁶ They left Ezion-Geber and encamped in the desert of Zin, that is, at Kadesh. ³⁷ They left Kadesh and encamped at Mount Hor, on the borders of the land of Edom. ³⁸ The priest Aaron went up Mount Hor on Yahweh's orders and died there in the fortieth year of the exodus of the Israelites from Egypt, in the fifth month, on the first day of the month. ³⁹ Aaron was a hundred and twenty-three years old when he died on Mount Hor. ⁴⁰ The king of Arad, the Canaanite who lived in the Negeb of Canaan, heard of the Israelites' arrival. ⁴¹ They left Mount Hor and encamped at Zalmonah. ⁴² They left Zalmonah and encamped at Punon. ⁴³ They left Punon and encamped at Oboth. ⁴⁴ They left Oboth and encamped in Moabite territory at Iye-Abarim. ⁴⁵ They left Iyim and encamped at Dibon-Gad. ⁴⁶ They left Dibon-Gad and encamped at Almon-Diblathaim. ⁴⁷ They left Almon-Diblathaim and encamped in the Abarim mountains facing Nebo. ⁴⁸ They left the Abarim mountains and encamped on the Plains of Moab, near the Jordan opposite Jericho. ⁴⁹ They encamped near the Jordan between Beth-ha-Jeshimoth and Abel-ha-Shittim, on the Plains of Moab.

The allocation of Canaan; God's order

⁵⁰ Yahweh spoke to Moses on the Plains of Moab, near the Jordan by Jericho, and said:

⁵¹ 'Speak to the Israelites and say:

"When you have crossed the Jordan into Canaan, ⁵² you will drive out all the local inhabitants before you. You will destroy all their painted images, you will destroy all their metal statues and you will demolish all their high places. ⁵³ You will take possession of the country and settle in it, for I have given you the country as your property. ⁵⁴ You will share it out by lot among your clans. To a large clan you will give a larger heritage, and to a smaller clan you will give a smaller heritage. Where the lot falls for each, that will be his. Your heritage will depend on the size of your tribe. ⁵⁵ If, however, you do not drive out the local inhabitants before you, the ones you allow to remain will be thorns in your eyes and thistles in your sides and will harass you in the country where you are living, 56and I shall treat you as I intended to treat them." '

The boundaries of Canaan

34 Yahweh spoke to Moses and said, 2'Give the Israelites this order. Say: "When you enter the country (Canaan), this will be the country which forms your heritage. This is Canaan as defined by its boundaries:

3"The southern part of your country will start from the desert of Zin, on the borders of Edom. Your southern boundary will start on the east at the end of the Salt Sea. 4It will then turn south towards the Ascent of the Scorpions and go by Zin to end in the south at Kadesh-Barnea. It will then run towards Hazar-Addar and pass through Azmon. 5From Azmon the boundary will turn towards the Torrent of Egypt and end at the Sea.

6"Your seaboard will be on the Great Sea; this will be your western boundary.

7"Your northern boundary will be as follows: you will draw a line from the Great Sea to Mount Hor, 8then from Mount Hor you will draw a line to the Pass of Hamath, and the boundary will end at Zedad. 9From there it will run on to Ziphron and end at Hazar-Enan. This will be your northern boundary.

10"You will then draw your eastern boundary from Hazar-Enan to Shepham. 11The boundary will run down from Shepham towards Riblah on the east side of Ain. Further down it will keep to the eastern shore of the Sea of Chinnereth. 12The frontier will then follow the Jordan and end at the Salt Sea.

"Such will be your country with the boundaries surrounding it." '

13Moses then gave the Israelites this order: 'This is the country, where your heritages will be assigned by lot, and which Yahweh has ordered to be given to the nine tribes and the half-tribe, 14for the tribe of the Reubenites with their families and the tribe of the Gadites with their families have already received their heritage; the half-tribe of Manasseh has also

received its heritage. 15These two tribes and the half-tribe have received their heritage on the other side of the Jordan by Jericho, to the east, towards the sunrise.'

The leaders in charge of the allocation

16Yahweh spoke to Moses and said:

17'Here are the names of the men who will divide the country up for you: the priest Eleazar and Joshua son of Nun, 18and you will take one leader from each tribe to divide the country up into heritages. 19Here are the names of these men:

'For the tribe of Judah, Caleb son of Jephunneh;

20'for the tribe of the Simeonites, Shemuel son of Ammihud;

21'for the tribe of Benjamin, Elidad son of Chislon;

22'for the tribe of the Danites, the leader Bukki son of Jogli;

23'for the sons of Joseph: for the tribe of Manasseh, the leader Hanniel son of Ephod;

24'for the tribe of the Ephraimites, the leader Kemuel son of Shiphtan;

25'for the tribe of the Zebulunites, the leader Elizaphan son of Parnach;

26'for the tribe of the Issacharites, the leader Paltiel son of Azzan;

27'for the tribe of the Asherites, the leader Ahihud son of Shelomi;

28'for the tribe of the Naphtalites, the leader Pedahel son of Ammihud.'

29These were the men whom Yahweh ordered to divide Canaan into heritages for the Israelites.

The portion of the Levites

35 Yahweh spoke to Moses on the Plains of Moab, near the Jordan by Jericho, and said:

2'Order the Israelites, from the heritage they possess, to give the Levites towns in which to live and pasture land round the towns. You will give these to the Levites. 3The towns must be their homes and the surrounding pasture land must be for their cattle, their possessions and all their animals. ⁴The pasture land surrounding the towns which you give to the Levites will extend, from the walls of the towns, for a thousand cubits all round.

⁵'Outside the town, measure two thousand cubits to the east, two thousand cubits to the south, two thousand cubits to the west and two thousand cubits to the north, the town lying in the centre; such will be the pasture lands of these towns. ⁶The towns you give to the Levites will be six cities of refuge, ceded by you as sanctuary for those who commit manslaughter; and you will give forty-two towns in addition. ⁷Altogether you will give the Levites forty-eight towns, with their pasture lands. ⁸Of the towns which you give from the Israelites' possessions, you will give more from those who have more, and less from those who have less. Each will give some of his towns to the Levites, in proportion to the heritage he himself has received.'

Cities of refuge

⁹Yahweh spoke to Moses and said:

¹⁰'Speak to the Israelites and say:

"Once you have crossed the Jordan into Canaan, ¹¹you will find towns, some of which you will make into cities of refuge where those who have accidentally committed manslaughter can take sanctuary. ¹²These towns will afford you refuge from the avenger of blood, so that the killer will not be put to death before standing trial before the community. ¹³Of the towns you give, six will serve you as cities of refuge: ¹⁴as cities of refuge, you will give three towns on the other side of the Jordan and will give three towns in Canaan. ¹⁵These six towns will serve as refuge for the Israelites, for the foreigner and for the resident alien, where anyone who has accidentally killed someone can take sanctuary.

¹⁶"But if he has struck the person with an iron object so as to cause death, he is a murderer. The murderer will be put to death. ¹⁷If he has struck him with a stone meant for killing, and has killed him, he is a murderer. The murderer will be put to death. ¹⁸Or if he

has struck him with a wooden instrument meant for killing, and has killed him, he is a murderer. The murderer will be put to death. ¹⁹The avenger of blood will put the murderer to death. Whenever he finds him, he will put him to death.

²⁰"If the killer has maliciously manhandled his victim, or thrown some lethal missile to strike him down, ²¹or out of enmity dealt him the death-blow with his fist, then he who struck the blow will be put to death; he is a murderer; the avenger of blood will put him to death whenever he finds him. ²²If, however, he has manhandled his victim by chance, without malice, or thrown some missile at him not meaning to hit him ²³or, without seeing him, dropped on him a stone meant for killing and so killed him, so long as he bore him no malice and wished him no harm, ²⁴then the community will decide in accordance with these rules between the one who struck the blow and the avenger of blood, ²⁵and will save the killer from the clutches of the avenger of blood. They will send him back to the city of refuge where he had taken sanctuary, and there he will stay until the death of the high priest who has been anointed with the holy oil. ²⁶Should the killer leave the bounds of the city of refuge in which he has taken sanctuary ²⁷and the avenger of blood encounter him outside the bounds of his city of refuge, the avenger of blood may kill him without fear of reprisal; ²⁸since the killer should stay in his city of refuge until the death of the high priest; only after the death of the high priest is he free to go back to his own piece of property. ²⁹Such will be the legal rule for you and your descendants, wherever you may live.

³⁰"In any case of homicide, the evidence of witnesses will determine whether the killer must be put to death; but a single witness is not enough to sustain a capital charge. ³¹You will not accept a ransom for the life of a murderer condemned to death; he must die. ³²Nor will you accept a ransom for anyone who, having taken sanctuary in his city or refuge, wishes to come back and live at home before the death

of the high priest. 33 Do not profane the country you live in. Blood profanes the country and, for the country, the only expiation for the blood shed in it is the blood of the man who shed it. 34 So do not defile the country which you live in and where I live; for I, Yahweh, live among the Israelites." '

A wife's inheritance

36 Then the heads of families of the clan descended from Gilead, son of Machir, son of Manasseh, one of the clans descended from Joseph, came forward and, addressing Moses and the leaders, the Israelite heads of families, 2 they said:

'Yahweh has ordered my lord to apportion the Israelites' heritages in the country by lot and my lord has been ordered by Yahweh to give the heritage of our brother Zelophehad to his daughters. 3 Now, if they marry someone from another Israelite tribe, their heritage will be alienated from our ancestral heritage. The heritage of the tribe to which they will then belong will be increased, and the heritage allotted to us will be diminished. 4 And when the jubilee for the Israelites comes round, these women's heritage will become part of the heritage of the tribe to which they then belong, and be alienated from the heritage of our ancestral tribe.'

5 At Yahweh's bidding, Moses gave the Israelites this order. He said:

'What the Josephite tribe says is true. 6 This is Yahweh's ruling for Zelophehad's daughters: "They may marry whom they please, providing they marry into a clan of their father's tribe. 7 But the heritages of Israelites are not to be transferred from tribe to tribe; each Israelite will stick to the heritage of his own tribe. 8 Any daughter who owns a heritage in an Israelite tribe will marry into a clan of her own paternal tribe, so that the Israelites may each preserve the heritage of his father. 9 No heritage may be transferred from one tribe to another; each Israelite tribe will stick to its own heritage." '

10 Zelophehad's daughters did as Yahweh had ordered Moses. 11 Mahlah, Tirzah, Hoglah, Milcah and Noah, daughters of Zelophehad, married the sons of their father's brothers. 12 Since they married into clans descended from Manasseh son of Joseph, their heritage reverted to the tribe of their father's clan.

Conclusion

13 Such were the commandments and laws that Yahweh prescribed for the Israelites through Moses on the Plains of Moab near the Jordan by Jericho.

DEUTERONOMY

The first discourse of Moses

1 These are the words which Moses addressed to all Israel beyond the Jordan, in the desert, in the Arabah facing Suph, between Paran and Tophel, Laban, Hazeroth and Dizahab. ² It is eleven days' journey from Horeb by way of Mount Seir to Kadesh-Barnea. ³ It was in the fortieth year, on the first day of the eleventh month, that Moses told the Israelites everything that Yahweh had ordered him to tell them.

⁴ He had defeated Sihon king of the Amorites, who lived at Heshbon, and Og king of Bashan, who lived at Ashtaroth and Edrei. ⁵ There, in Moab beyond the Jordan, Moses resolved to expound this Law. He said:

The final instructions at Horeb

⁶ 'Yahweh our God said to us at Horeb, "You have stayed long enough at this mountain. ⁷ Move on, continue your journey, go to the highlands of the Amorites, to all those who live in the Arabah, in the highlands, in the lowlands, in the Negeb and in the coastland; go into Canaan and to Lebanon as far as the great River Euphrates. ⁸ Look, that is the country I have given you; go and take possession of the country that Yahweh promised on oath to give to your ancestors, Abraham, Isaac and Jacob, and to their descendants after them."

⁹ 'At the same time, I told you,ᵃ "I cannot be responsible for you by myself. ¹⁰ Yahweh your God has increased your numbers, until you are now as numerous as the stars of heaven. ¹¹ And Yahweh your God is going to increase you a thousand times more, and bless you as he has promised you. ¹² So how can I cope by myself with the bitter burden that you are, and with your bickering? ¹³ From each of your tribes pick wise, shrewd and experienced men for me to make your leaders." ¹⁴ You replied, "Your plan is good." ¹⁵ So I took your tribal leaders, wise, experienced men, and appointed them to lead you, as captains of thousands, hundreds, fifties, tens, and as scribes for your tribes. ¹⁶ At that same time I told your judges, "You must give your brothers a fair hearing and see justice done between one person and his brother or the foreigner living with him. ¹⁷ You must be impartial in judgement and give an equal hearing to small and great alike. Do not be afraid of any human person, for the verdict is God's. Should a case be too difficult, bring it for me to hear. ¹⁸ And on that occasion I gave you instructions about everything you were to do."

Kadesh: the Israelites lose faithᵇ

¹⁹ 'So, as Yahweh our God had ordered, we left Horeb and made our way through that vast and terrible desert, which you saw on the way to the Amorite highlands, and arrived at Kadesh-Barnea. ²⁰ I then said, "You have now reached the Amorite highlands, which Yahweh our God has given us. ²¹ Look, Yahweh your God has given you this country. March in, take possession of it as Yahweh, the God of your ancestors, has said; do not be afraid or discouraged." ²² Then you all came to me and said, "Let us send men ahead of us to explore the country; they shall report to us which way we ought to take and what towns we shall come to." ²³ This seemed good advice to me and I selected twelve men from among you,

1a ‖ Ex 18:13–26.   *1b* ‖ Nb 13:1–14:9.

one from each tribe. 24 These men made towards the highlands and went up into them; they reached the Valley of Eshcol and reconnoitred it. 25 They collected some of the produce of the country and brought it down to us; and they made us this report, "Yahweh our God has given us a fine country." 26 You, however, refused to go up there and rebelled against the voice of Yahweh your God. 27 You muttered in your tents, saying, "Yahweh hates us, and that is why he has brought us out of Egypt, to put us into the Amorites' power and so destroy us. 28 What kind of place are we making for? Our brothers have discouraged us by saying that the people are stronger and taller than we are, the cities immense, with walls reaching to the sky. And we have seen Anakim[c] there too."

29 'And I said to you, "Do not take fright, do not be afraid of them. 30 Yahweh your God goes ahead of you and will be fighting on your side, just as you saw him act in Egypt. 31 You have seen him in the desert too: Yahweh your God continued to support you, as a man supports his son, all along the road you followed until you arrived here." 32 But for all this, you put no faith in Yahweh your God, 33 going ahead of you on the journey to find you a camping ground, by night in the fire to light your path, and in the cloud by day.

Yahweh's instructions at Kadesh[d]

34 'Yahweh heard what you were saying and in his anger swore this oath, 35 "Not one of these people, this perverse generation, will see the fine country I swore to give your ancestors, 36 except Caleb son of Jephunneh. He will see it. To him and to his children I shall give the land he has set foot on, for he has been perfectly obedient to Yahweh." 37 Yahweh was angry with me too, because of you. "You will not go in either," he said. 38 "Your assistant, Joshua son of Nun, will be the one to enter. Encourage him, since he is to bring Israel into possession of the country. 39 And your little ones too, who, you said, would be seized as booty, these children of yours who do not yet

know good from evil, they will go in; I shall give it to them and they will own it. 40 But, as regards yourselves, turn round, go back into the desert, towards the Sea of Suph."

41 'In reply, you then said to me, "We have sinned against Yahweh our God. We shall go up and fight just as Yahweh our God has ordered us." And each one of you buckled on his arms and equipped himself to march up into the highlands. 42 But Yahweh said to me, "Tell them this: Do not go up and fight. I am not with you. Do not let yourselves be defeated by your enemies." 43 So I told you, but you would not listen, and you rebelled against the voice of Yahweh; presumptuously you marched into the highlands. 44 The Amorites, who live in that country of hills, came swarming out against you like bees, pursued you and beat you from Seir to Hormah. 45 On your return, you wept in Yahweh's presence, but he would not listen to your cries or pay attention. 46 That was why you had to stay at Kadesh as long as you did.'

From Kadesh to the Arnon

2 'We then turned round and made for the desert, in the direction of the Sea of Suph, as Yahweh had ordered me. For many days we skirted Mount Seir. 2 Yahweh then said to me, 3 "You have gone far enough round this mountain; now turn north. 4 And give the people this order: You are about to pass through the territory of your kinsmen, the sons of Esau who live in Seir. They are afraid of you, and you will be well protected. 5 Do not provoke them, for I shall give you none of their land, no, not so much as a foot's length of it. I have given the highlands of Seir to Esau as his domain. 6 Pay them in money for what food you eat; and pay them in money for the water you drink. 7 Yahweh your God has blessed you in all you do; he has watched over your journeying through this vast desert. Yahweh your

1c According to legend, the Anakim and Rephaim are the original dwellers in Palestine, pictured as giants.

1d || Nb 14:21–35.

God has been with you these forty years and you have never been in want."

8 'So we passed beyond those relatives of ours, the children of Esau who live in Seir, by the road through the Arabah, Elath and Ezion-Geber; then, changing direction, we took the road towards the Plains of Moab. 9 Yahweh then said to me, "Do not attack Moab, do not provoke him to fight, for I shall give you none of his land, since I have given Ar to the children of Lot as their domain." 10 (At one time the Emim lived there, a great and numerous people, tall as the Anakim; 11 and, like the Anakim, they were considered to be Rephaim, though the Moabites call them Emim. 12 The Horites, too, lived in Seir at one time; these, however, were dispossessed and exterminated by the children of Esau who settled there in place of them, just as Israel has done in the country given to it by Yahweh as a heritage.) 13 "On your way, then! Cross the Wadi Zered!"

'And so we crossed the Wadi Zered. 14 From Kadesh-Barnea to the crossing of the Wadi Zered our wanderings had taken thirty-eight years; as a result of which, the entire generation of those of age to bear arms had been eliminated, as Yahweh had sworn to them. 15 Yahweh's hand had been against them, to eliminate them completely from the camp.

16 'When death had carried off from the people those of age to bear arms, to the last man, 17 Yahweh said this to me, 18 "You are now crossing Ar, the country of Moab, 19 and soon you will encounter the children of Ammon. Do not attack them, do not provoke them, for I shall give you none of the land belonging to the children of Ammon as your domain. I have given it to the children of Lot as theirs." 20 (This used also to be considered as Rephaim territory; at one time the Rephaim lived there, though the Ammonites call them Zamzummim, 21 a great and numerous people, and tall like the Anakim. Yahweh exterminated them for the Ammonites who dispossessed them and settled there in place of them, 22 just as he had done for the children of Esau who live in Seir, so that they dispossessed the Horites and settled there instead of them and are still there now. 23 It was the same with the Avvites who occupied encampments as far as Gaza: the Caphtorim, coming from Caphtor, exterminated them and settled there instead.) 24 "On your way! Break camp and cross the Wadi Arnon. See, I am putting Sihon the Amorite, king of Heshbon, at your mercy, and his country too. Set about the conquest; engage him in battle. 25 Today and henceforth, I shall fill the peoples under all heaven with fear and terror of you; whoever hears word of your approach will tremble and writhe in anguish because of you."

Conquest of the kingdom of Sihon [a]

26 'So, from the desert of Kedemoth I sent envoys to Sihon king of Heshbon with this peaceful message, 27 "I intend to cross your country. I shall go my way, straying neither to right nor to left. 28 I shall eat and pay for the food you choose to sell me, and I shall drink and pay for the water you let me have. I only want to march through, 29 just as the children of Esau who live in Seir permitted, as well as the Moabites who live in Ar, until I cross the Jordan into the country that Yahweh our God is giving us."

30 'But Sihon king of Heshbon would not give us leave to pass through his territory; Yahweh our God had made his spirit obstinate and his heart stubborn, to put him at your mercy, as he still is. 31 Yahweh said to me, "You see, I am starting to give you Sihon and his country. Begin the conquest by seizing his country." 32 Sihon marched out against us, he and all his people, to give battle at Jahaz. 33 And Yahweh our God handed him over to us: we defeated him and his sons and all his people. 34 We captured all his towns and laid all these towns under the curse of destruction: men, women and children, we left no survivors 35 except the livestock which we took as our booty, and the spoils of the captured

2a ‖ Nb 21:21–25.

towns. 36 From Aroer on the edge of the Arnon valley and from the town down in the valley, as far as Gilead, not one town was beyond our reach; Yahweh our God delivered them all to us. 37 You did not, however, go near the country of the Ammonites, or the region of the River Jabbok, or the towns in the highlands, or anywhere forbidden us by Yahweh our God.'

Conquest of the kingdom of Og[a]

3 'We then turned on Bashan and invaded that. And Og king of Bashan marched out against us, he and all his people, to give battle at Edrei. 2 Yahweh said to me, "Do not be afraid of him, for I have put him at your mercy, him, all his people and his country. You will treat him as you treated Sihon king of the Amorites who lived in Heshbon." 3 So, Yahweh our God put Og king of Bashan at our mercy too, with all his people. We beat him so thoroughly that nobody was left. 4 That was when we captured all his towns; there was not a town of theirs we did not take: sixty towns, the whole confederation of Argob, Og's kingdom in Bashan, 5 all of them fortresses defended by high walls and fortified with gates and bars, not to mention the Perizzite towns, which were very numerous. 6 We laid them under the curse of destruction as we had done Sihon king of Heshbon, laying all these towns under the curse of destruction: men, women and children— 7 but we seized the livestock and spoils of the towns as booty for ourselves.

8 'Thus, by then we had taken the country of the two Amorite kings beyond the Jordan, stretching from the Wadi Arnon to Mount Hermon 9 (the Sidonians call Hermon 'Sirion' and the Amorites call it 'Senir'): 10 all the towns of the tableland, all Gilead, and all Bashan as far as Salecah and Edrei, the capital cities of Og in Bashan. 11 (Og king of Bashan was the last survivor of the Rephaim; his bed was the iron bed that can be seen at Rabbah-of-the-Ammonites, nine cubits long and four wide, according to the human cubit.)

The partitioning of Transjordan[b]

12 'Then we took possession of this country, from Aroer on the Wadi Arnon. To the Reubenites and Gadites I gave half the highlands of Gilead with its towns. 13 To the half-tribe of Manasseh I gave the rest of Gilead and the whole of Bashan, Og's kingdom. (The whole confederation of Argob and the whole of Bashan is called the country of the Rephaim. 14 Since Jair son of Manasseh occupied the whole confederation of Argob as far as the frontiers of the Geshurites and Maacathites, after him Bashan is called the Encampments of Jair even today.) 15 To Machir I gave Gilead. 16 To the Reubenites and the Gadites I gave the region from Gilead to the Wadi Arnon, the middle of the ravine marking the boundary, and up as far as the Jabbok, the ravine marking the frontier of the Ammonites. 17 The Arabah and the Jordan serve as frontiers from Chinnereth down to the Sea of the Arabah (the Salt Sea), at the foot of the slopes of Pisgah on the east.

Further instructions from Moses

18 'I then gave you this order: "Yahweh your God has given you this country to be yours. Armed, every one of you fit to fight must go ahead of your brothers the Israelites. 19 Only your wives, your children and your flocks (you have many flocks, I know) must stay behind in the towns which I have given you, 20 until Yahweh has brought your brothers to rest as he has already brought you, and they too possess the territory which Yahweh your God is giving them on the other side of the Jordan; after that, you can go home, each to the domain I have given you." 21 I then gave Joshua this order, "You can see for yourself everything that Yahweh our God has done to these two kings; Yahweh will do the same to all the kingdoms through which you pass. 22 Do not be afraid of them: Yahweh your God himself is fighting for you."

3a ‖ Nb 21:33–35.   3b ‖ Nb 32.

23 'I then pleaded with Yahweh. 24 "My Lord Yahweh," I said, "now that you have begun to reveal your greatness and your power to your servant with works and mighty deeds no God in heaven or on earth can rival, 25 may I not go across and see this fine country on the other side of the Jordan, that fine upland country and the Lebanon?" 26 But, because of you, Yahweh was angry with me and would not listen. "Enough!" he said, "Do not mention this subject again! 27 Climb to the top of Pisgah; turn your eyes to the west, the north, the south, the east. Look well, for across this Jordan you shall not go. 28 Give Joshua your instructions; encourage him, strengthen him; for he will be the one to cross at the head of this people; he will be the one to bring them into possession of the country which you will see."

29 'We then stayed in the valley, close to Beth-Peor.'

The apostasy at Beth-Peor contrasted with true wisdom

4 'And now, Israel, listen to the laws and customs which I am teaching you today, so that, by observing them, you may survive to enter and take possession of the country which Yahweh, God of your ancestors, is giving you. 2 You must add nothing to what I command you, and take nothing from it, but keep the commandments of Yahweh your God just as I lay them down for you. 3 You can see for yourselves what Yahweh has done about the Baal of Peor; Yahweh your God has destroyed all those of you who followed the Baal of Peor; 4 but those of you who stayed faithful to Yahweh your God are all alive today. 5 Look: as Yahweh my God commanded me, I have taught you laws and customs, for you to observe in the country of which you are going to take possession. 6 Keep them, put them into practice, and other peoples will admire your wisdom and prudence. Once they know what all these laws are, they will exclaim, "No other people is as wise and prudent as this great nation!" 7 And indeed, what great nation has its gods as near as Yahweh our God is to us whenever we call to him? 8 And what great nation has laws and customs as upright as the entirety of this Law which I am laying down for you today?

The revelation at Horeb; its demands

9 'But take care, as you value your lives! Do not forget the things which you yourselves have seen, or let them slip from your heart as long as you live; teach them, rather, to your children and to your children's children. 10 The day you stood at Horeb in the presence of Yahweh your God, Yahweh said to me, "Summon the people to me; I want them to hear me speaking, so that they will learn to fear me all the days they live on earth, and teach this to their children." 11 So you came and stood at the foot of the mountain, and the mountain flamed to the very sky, a sky darkened by cloud, murky and thunderous. 12 Yahweh then spoke to you from the heart of the fire; you heard the sound of words but saw no shape; there was only a voice. 13 He revealed his covenant to you and commanded you to observe it, the Ten Words which he inscribed on two tablets of stone. 14 Yahweh then ordered me to teach you the laws and customs that you were to observe in the country into which you are about to cross, to take possession of it.

15 'Hence, be very careful what you do. Since you saw no shape that day at Horeb when Yahweh spoke to you from the heart of the fire, 16 see that you do not corrupt yourselves by making an image in the shape of anything whatever: be it statue of man or of woman, 17 or of any animal on the earth, or of any bird that flies in the heavens, 18 or of any reptile that crawls on the ground, or of any fish in the waters under the earth. 19 When you raise your eyes to heaven, when you see the sun, the moon, the stars—the entire array of heaven—do not be tempted to worship them and serve them. Yahweh your God has allotted these to all the other peoples under heaven, 20 but Yahweh has chosen you, bringing you out of the iron-foundry, Egypt, to be his own people, his own people as you still are today.

Of punishment to come, and of conversion

21 'Yahweh is angry with me because of you; he has sworn that I shall not cross the Jordan or enter the fine country which Yahweh your God is giving you as your heritage. 22 Yes, I am to die in this country; I shall not cross this Jordan; you will go over and take possession of that rich land. 23 Be careful not to forget the covenant which Yahweh your God has made with you, by sculpting an image or making a statue of anything, since Yahweh your God has forbidden this; 24 for Yahweh your God is a consuming fire, a jealous God.

25 'When you have fathered children and grandchildren and have grown old in the country, when you have grown corrupt and made some image, doing what Yahweh regards as wrong and so provoking his anger— 26 today I call heaven and earth to witness against you—you will quickly vanish from the country which you are crossing the Jordan to possess. Your days will not be prolonged there, for you will be utterly destroyed. 27 Yahweh will scatter you among the peoples, and only a small number of you will remain among the nations where Yahweh will have driven you. 28 There you will serve gods made by human hand, of wood and of stone, that cannot see or hear, eat or smell.

29 'If, however, from there you start searching once more for Yahweh your God, and if you search for him honestly and sincerely, you will find him. 30 You will suffer; everything I have said will befall you, but in the final days you will return to Yahweh your God and listen to his voice. 31 For Yahweh your God is a merciful God and will not desert or destroy you or forget the covenant which he made on oath with your ancestors.

The glory of having been chosen by God

32 'Put this question, then, to the ages that are past, that have gone before you, from when God created the human race on earth: Was there ever a word so majestic, from one end of heaven to the other? Was anything like it ever heard? 33 Did ever a people hear the voice of the living God speaking from the heart of the fire, as you have heard it, and remain alive? 34 Has it ever been known before that any god took action himself to bring one nation out of another one, by ordeals, signs, wonders, war with mighty hand and outstretched arm, by fearsome terrors—all of which things Yahweh your God has done for you before your eyes in Egypt?

35 'This he showed you, so that you might know that Yahweh is the true God and that there is no other. 36 To instruct you, he made you hear his voice from heaven, and on earth he let you see his great fire, and from the heart of the fire you heard his words. 37 Because he loved your ancestors and, after them, chose their descendants, he has brought you out of Egypt, displaying his presence and mighty power, 38 dispossessing for you nations who were larger and stronger than you, to make way for you and to give you their country as your heritage, as it still is today.

39 'Hence, grasp this today and meditate on it carefully: Yahweh is the true God, in heaven above as on earth beneath, he and no other. 40 Keep his laws and commandments as I give them to you today, so that you and your children after you may prosper and live long in the country that Yahweh your God is giving you for ever.'

The cities of refuge

41 Moses then set aside three towns in the east, beyond the Jordan, 42 to which any killer might flee who had accidentally, without any previous feud, killed his fellow; by taking refuge in one of these towns he could save his life. 43 These were, for the Reubenites, Bezer in the desert on the tableland; for the Gadites, Ramoth in Gilead; for the Manassehites, Golan in Bashan.

The second discourse of Moses

44 This is the Law which Moses presented to the Israelites. 45 These are the stipulations, the laws and the customs which Moses gave the Is-

raelites after they had left Egypt, ⁴⁶beyond the Jordan in the valley near Beth-Peor, in the country of Sihon the Amorite king who had lived at Heshbon. Moses and the Israelites had defeated him when they left Egypt, ⁴⁷and had taken possession of his country, as well as that of Og king of Bashan—two Amorite kings to the east beyond the Jordan, ⁴⁸from Aroer on the edge of the Arnon Valley, all the way to Mount Sion (that is, Hermon)— ⁴⁹and of the whole Arabah east of the Jordan as far as the Sea of the Arabah, at the foot of the slopes of Pisgah.

The Ten Commandments

5 Moses called all Israel together and said to them, 'Listen, Israel, to the laws and customs that I proclaim to you today. Learn them and take care to observe them.

²'Yahweh our God made a covenant with us at Horeb. ³Yahweh made this covenant not with our ancestors, but with us, with all of us alive here today. ⁴On the mountain, from the heart of the fire, Yahweh spoke to you face to face, ⁵while I stood between you and Yahweh to let you know what Yahweh was saying, since you were afraid of the fire and had not gone up the mountain. He said:

⁶' "I am Yahweh your God who brought you out of Egypt, out of the place of slave-labour.ᵃ

⁷' "You will have no gods other than me.

⁸' "You must not make yourselves any image or any likeness of anything in heaven above or on earth beneath or in the waters under the earth; ⁹you must not bow down to these gods or serve them. For I, Yahweh your God, am a jealous God and I punish the parents' fault in the children, the grandchildren and the great-grandchildren, among those who hate me; ¹⁰but I show faithful love to thousands, to those who love me and keep my commandments.

¹¹' "You must not misuse the name of Yahweh your God, for Yahweh will not leave unpunished anyone who uses his name for what is false.

¹²' "Observe the Sabbath day and keep it holy, as Yahweh your God has commanded you. ¹³Labour for six days, doing all your work, ¹⁴but the seventh day is a Sabbath for Yahweh your God. You must not do any work that day, neither you, nor your son, nor your daughter, nor your servants—male or female—nor your ox, nor your donkey, nor any of your animals, nor the foreigner who has made his home with you; ¹⁵so that your servants, male and female, may rest, as you do. Remember that you were once a slave in Egypt, and that Yahweh your God brought you out of there with mighty hand and outstretched arm; this is why Yahweh your God has commanded you to keep the Sabbath day.

¹⁶' "Honour your father and your mother, as Yahweh your God has commanded you, so that you may have long life and may prosper in the country which Yahweh your God is giving you.

¹⁷' "You must not kill.

¹⁸' "You must not commit adultery.

¹⁹' "You must not steal.

²⁰' "You must not give false evidence against your fellow.

²¹' "You must not set your heart on your neighbour's spouse, you must not set your heart on your neighbour's house, or field, or servant—man or woman—or ox, or donkey or any of your neighbour's possessions."

²²'These were the words Yahweh spoke to you when you were all assembled on the mountain. Thunderously, he spoke to you from the heart of the fire, in cloud and thick darkness. He added nothing, but wrote them on two tablets of stone which he gave to me.

Moses the mediator

²³'Now, having heard this voice coming out of the darkness, while the mountain was all on fire, you came to me, all of you, heads of tribes and elders, ²⁴and said, "Yahweh our God has shown us his glory and his greatness, and we

5a ‖ Ex 20:1–17.

have heard his voice from the heart of the fire. Today we have seen that God can speak with a human being and that person still live. 25 So why should we expose ourselves to death again? For this great fire might devour us if we go on listening to the voice of Yahweh our God, and then we should die. 26 For what creature of flesh could possibly live after hearing, as we have heard, the voice of the living God speaking from the heart of the fire? 27 Go nearer yourself and listen to everything that Yahweh our God may say, and then tell us everything that Yahweh our God has told you; we shall listen and put it into practice!"

28 'Yahweh heard what you were saying to me, and he then said to me, "I have heard what these people are saying. Everything they have said is well said. 29 If only their heart were always so, set on fearing me and on keeping my commandments, so that they and their children might prosper for ever! 30 Go and tell them to go back to their tents. 31 But you yourself stay here with me, and I shall tell you all the commandments, the laws and the customs which you are to teach them and which they are to observe in the country which I am giving them as their possession."

To love Yahweh is the essence of the Law

32 'Keep them and put them into practice: such is Yahweh's command to you. Stray neither to right nor to left. 33 Follow the whole way that Yahweh has marked for you, and you will survive to prosper and live long in the country which you are going to possess.'

6 'Such, then, are the commandments, the laws and the customs which Yahweh your God has instructed me to teach you, for you to observe in the country which you are on your way to possess. 2 And hence, if, throughout your lives, you fear Yahweh your God and keep all his laws and commandments, which I am laying down for you today, you will live long, you and your child and your grandchild. 3 Listen then, Israel, keep and observe what will make you prosperous and numerous, as

Yahweh, God of your ancestors, has promised you, in giving you a country flowing with milk and honey.

4 'Listen, Israel: Yahweh our God is the one, the only Yahweh. 5 You must love Yahweh your God with all your heart, with all your soul, with all your strength. 6 Let the words I enjoin on you today stay in your heart. 7 You shall tell them to your children, and keep on telling them, when you are sitting at home, when you are out and about, when you are lying down and when you are standing up; 8 you must fasten them on your hand as a sign and on your forehead as a headband; 9 you must write them on the doorposts of your house and on your gates.

10 'When Yahweh has brought you into the country which he swore to your ancestors Abraham, Isaac and Jacob that he would give you, with great and prosperous cities you have not built, 11 with houses full of good things you have not provided, with wells you have not dug, with vineyards and olive trees you have not planted, and then, when you have eaten as much as you want, 12 be careful you do not forget Yahweh who has brought you out of Egypt, out of the place of slave-labour. 13 Yahweh your God is the one you must fear, him alone you must serve, his is the name by which you must swear.

An appeal for loyalty

14 'Do not follow other gods, gods of the peoples round you, 15 for Yahweh your God among you is a jealous God; the wrath of Yahweh your God would blaze out against you, and he would wipe you off the face of the earth. 16 Do not put Yahweh your God to the test as you tested him at Massah. 17 Keep the commandments of Yahweh your God, and his instructions and laws which he has laid down for you, 18 and do what Yahweh regards as right and good, so that you may prosper and take possession of the fine country which Yahweh swore to give your ancestors, 19 driving out your enemies before you; such was Yahweh's promise.

17 READ DEUTERONOMY 6.

Let the words I enjoin on you today stay in your heart.—DEUTERONOMY 6:6

STANDING FIRM

Since we consist of soul and body, both are involved in staying on the path. As either may cause us to stumble, we must attend to both: Bodily purity, the protective abstinence from all shameful things and wicked acts. And purity of the soul, keeping true faith in God, neither adding to nor subtracting from it. Godliness is dimmed when the body is soiled and loses its integrity when falsehood enters the soul.

But our godliness maintains its beauty and integrity when the spirit sticks to the truth and the body keeps pure. What good is knowing the truth in words while polluting the body with evil deeds? What real good can purity produce if truth is not in the soul? These two rejoice with each other and unite as comrades-in-arms in the fight to bring us into God's presence.

So to protect our virtue, we cling to the rule of faith without changing it at all. And we must also obey the commandments of God, believing in him, fearing him as Lord, and loving him as Father. Correct behavior is produced by faith because, as Isaiah says, "If you will not take your stand on me you will not stand firm" (Is 7:9).

Further, faith itself is produced by truth, for faith must rest upon reality. When we believe in eternal realities, we hold to faith with confidence. Thus, since faith preserves our salvation, we must carefully sustain it by having a clear hold on reality.   ST. IRENAEUS OF LYONS, 130?–200?

YOU WILL FIND THE NEXT READING AT DEUTERONOMY 15.

20 'In times to come, when your child asks you, "What is the meaning of these instructions, laws and customs which Yahweh our God has laid down for you?" 21 you are to tell your child, "Once we were Pharaoh's slaves in Egypt, and Yahweh brought us out of Egypt by his mighty hand. 22 Before our eyes, Yahweh worked great and terrible signs and wonders against Egypt, against Pharaoh and his entire household. 23 And he brought us out of there, to lead us into the country which he had sworn to our ancestors that he would give us. 24 And Yahweh has commanded us to observe all these laws and to fear Yahweh our God, so as to be happy for ever and to survive, as we do to this day. 25 For us, right living will mean this: to keep and observe all these command-ments in obedience to Yahweh our God, as he has commanded us."'

Israel a people apart

7 'When Yahweh your God has brought you into the country which you are going to make your own, many nations will fall before you: Hittites, Girgashites, Amorites, Canaanites, Perizzites, Hivites and Jebusites, seven nations greater and stronger than yourselves. 2 Yahweh your God will put them at your mercy and you will conquer them. You must put them under the curse of destruction. You must not make any treaty with them or show them any pity. 3 You must not intermarry with them; you must not give a daughter of yours to a son of theirs, or take a daughter of theirs for a son of yours, 4 for your son would be seduced from following me into serving other gods; the wrath of Yahweh would blaze out against you and he would instantly destroy you. 5 Instead, treat them like this: tear down their altars, smash their standing-stones, cut down their sacred poles and burn their idols. 6 For you are a people consecrated to Yahweh your God; of all the peoples on earth, you have been chosen by Yahweh your God to be his own people.

God's election and his favour

7 'Yahweh set his heart on you and chose you not because you were the most numerous of all peoples—for indeed you were the smallest of all— 8 but because he loved you and meant to keep the oath which he swore to your ancestors: that was why Yahweh brought you out with his mighty hand and redeemed you from the place of slave-labour, from the power of Pharaoh king of Egypt. 9 From this you can see that Yahweh your God is the true God, the faithful God who, though he is true to his covenant and his faithful love for a thousand generations as regards those who love him and keep his commandments, 10 punishes in their own persons those that hate him. He destroys anyone who hates him, without delay; and it is in their own persons that he punishes them. 11 Hence, you must keep and observe the commandments, laws and customs which I am laying down for you today.

12 'Listen to these ordinances, be true to them and observe them, and in return Yahweh your God will be true to the covenant and love which he promised on oath to your ancestors. 13 He will love you and bless you and increase your numbers; he will bless the fruit of your body and the produce of your soil, your corn, your new wine, your oil, the issue of your cattle, the young of your flock, in the country which he swore to your ancestors that he would give you. 14 You will be the most blessed of all peoples. None of you, man or woman, will be sterile, no male or female of your beasts infertile. 15 Yahweh will deflect all illness from you; he will not afflict you with those evil plagues of Egypt which you have known, but will inflict them on all who hate you.

16 'So, devour all the peoples whom Yahweh your God puts at your mercy, show them no pity, do not serve their gods: or you will be ensnared.

The power of Yahweh

17 'You may say in your heart, "These nations outnumber me; how shall I be able to dispossess them?" 18 Do not be afraid of them: remember how Yahweh your God treated Pharaoh and all Egypt, 19 the great ordeals that you yourselves have seen, the signs and wonders, the mighty hand and outstretched arm with which Yahweh your God brought you out. This is how Yahweh your God will treat all the peoples whom you fear to face. 20 And what is more, Yahweh your God will send hornets to destroy those who are left and who hide from you.

21 'Do not be afraid of them, for Yahweh your God is among you, a great and terrible God. 22 Little by little, Yahweh your God will clear away these nations before you; you cannot destroy them all at once, or wild animals will breed and be disastrous for you. 23 But Yahweh your God will put them at your mercy, and disaster after disaster will overtake them until they are finally destroyed. 24 He will put their kings at your mercy and you will blot out their names under heaven; no one will be able to resist you—until you have destroyed them all.

25 'You must burn the statues of their gods, not coveting the gold and silver that covers them; take it and you will be caught in a snare: it is detestable to Yahweh your God. 26 You must not bring any detestable thing into your house: or you, like it, will come under the curse of destruction. You must regard them as unclean and loathsome, for they are under the curse of destruction.'

The ordeal in the desert

8 'You must keep and put into practice all the commandments which I enjoin on you

today, so that you may survive and increase in numbers and enter the country which Yahweh promised on oath to your ancestors, and make it your own. ²Remember the long road by which Yahweh your God led you for forty years in the desert, to humble you, to test you and know your inmost heart—whether you would keep his commandments or not. ³He humbled you, he made you feel hunger, he fed you with manna which neither you nor your ancestors had ever known, to make you understand that human beings live not on bread alone but on every word that comes from the mouth of Yahweh. ⁴The clothes on your back did not wear out and your feet were not swollen, all those forty years.

⁵'Learn from this that Yahweh your God was training you as a man trains his child, ⁶and keep the commandments of Yahweh your God, and so follow his ways and fear him.

The Promised Land and its temptations

⁷'But Yahweh your God is bringing you into a fine country, a land of streams and springs, of waters that well up from the deep in valleys and hills, ⁸a land of wheat and barley, of vines, of figs, of pomegranates, a land of olives, of oil, of honey, ⁹a land where you will eat bread without stint, where you will want nothing, a land where the stones are iron and where the hills may be quarried for copper. ¹⁰You will eat and have all you want and you will bless Yahweh your God in the fine country which he has given you.

¹¹'Be careful not to forget Yahweh your God, by neglecting his commandments, customs and laws which I am laying down for you today. ¹²When you have eaten all you want, when you have built fine houses to live in, ¹³when you have seen your flocks and herds increase, your silver and gold abound and all your possessions grow great, ¹⁴do not become proud of heart. Do not then forget Yahweh your God who brought you out of Egypt, out of the place of slave-labour, ¹⁵who guided you through this vast and dreadful desert, a land of fiery snakes, scorpions, thirst;

¹⁶who in this waterless place brought you water out of the flinty rock; who in this desert fed you with manna unknown to your ancestors, to humble you and test you and so make your future the happier.

¹⁷'Beware of thinking to yourself, "My own strength and the might of my own hand have given me the power to act like this." ¹⁸Remember Yahweh your God; he was the one who gave you the strength to act effectively like this, thus keeping then, as today, the covenant which he swore to your ancestors. ¹⁹Be sure: if you forget Yahweh your God, if you follow other gods, if you serve them and bow down to them—I testify to you today—you will perish. ²⁰Like the nations Yahweh is to destroy before you, so you yourselves will perish, for not having listened to the voice of Yahweh your God.'

Yahweh, not Israel, wins the victory

9 'Listen, Israel; today you are about to cross the Jordan, to go and dispossess nations greater and stronger than yourself, and cities immense, with walls reaching to the sky. ²A people great and tall, these Anakim, as you know; you have heard the saying: Who can stand up to the sons of Anak? ³Know then today that Yahweh your God himself will go ahead of you, destroying them like a devouring fire, and that he himself will subdue them before you so that you can dispossess and quickly make an end of them, as Yahweh has already said. ⁴Do not think to yourself, once Yahweh your God has driven them before you, "Yahweh has brought me into possession of this country because I am upright," when Yahweh is dispossessing these nations for you, because they do wrong. ⁵You are not going into their country to take possession because of any right behaviour or uprightness on your part; rather, it is because of their wickedness that Yahweh is dispossessing these nations for you, and also to keep the pact which he swore to your ancestors, Abraham, Isaac and Jacob. ⁶Be clear about this: Yahweh is not giving you possession of this fine country because of any

right conduct on your part, for you are an obstinate people.

Israel's conduct at Horeb; Moses intercedes[a]

7 'Remember; never forget how you provoked Yahweh your God in the desert. From the very day that you left Egypt until you arrived here, you have been rebels against Yahweh. 8 At Horeb, you provoked Yahweh, and Yahweh was so angry with you that he was ready to destroy you. 9 I had gone up the mountain to receive the stone tablets, the tablets of the covenant that Yahweh was making with you. I stayed forty days and forty nights on the mountain, with nothing to eat or drink. 10 Yahweh gave me the two stone tablets inscribed by the finger of God, exactly corresponding to what Yahweh had said to you on the mountain, from the heart of the fire, on the day of the Assembly. 11 After forty days and forty nights, having given me the two stone tablets, the tablets of the covenant, 12 Yahweh said to me, "Get up, go down quickly, for your people, whom you have brought out of Egypt, are corrupting one another. They have been quick to leave the way I marked out for them; they have cast themselves a metal idol." 13 Yahweh then said to me, "I have seen this people, and what an obstinate people they are! 14 Leave me, I am going to destroy them and wipe out their name under heaven; and I shall make you into a mightier and more numerous nation than they are!"

15 'I went back down the mountain, which was blazing with fire, and in my hands were the two tablets of the covenant. 16 When I looked, I saw that you had been sinning against Yahweh your God. You had cast yourselves a metal calf; you had been quick to leave the way marked out for you by Yahweh. 17 I seized the two tablets and with my two hands threw them down and broke them before your eyes. 18 Then I fell prostrate before Yahweh; as before, I spent forty days and forty nights with nothing to eat or drink, on account of all the sins which you had committed, by doing what was displeasing to Yahweh and thus arousing his anger. 19 For I was afraid of this anger, of the fury which so roused Yahweh against you that he was ready to destroy you. And, once again, Yahweh heard my prayer. 20 Yahweh was enraged with Aaron and was ready to destroy him too; I also pleaded for Aaron on that occasion. 21 That work of sin, the calf you had made, I took and burned and broke to pieces; having ground it to the finest dust, I threw its dust into the stream that comes down from the mountain.

Israel sins again; a prayer of Moses

22 'At Taberah too and at Massah and Kibroth-ha-Taavah, you provoked Yahweh. 23 And when Yahweh, meaning you to leave Kadesh-Barnea, said, "Go up and take possession of the country which I have given you," you rebelled against the command of Yahweh your God and would not believe him or listen to his voice. 24 You have been rebels against Yahweh from the day he first knew you.

25 'So I fell prostrate before Yahweh and lay there those forty days and forty nights, Yahweh having said that he was going to destroy you. 26 And I pleaded with Yahweh. "My Lord Yahweh," I said, "do not destroy your people, your heritage whom in your greatness you have redeemed, whom you have brought out of Egypt with your mighty hand. 27 Remember your servants, Abraham, Isaac, and Jacob; take no notice of this people's stubbornness, their wickedness, and their sin, 28 so that, in the country from which you have brought us, it may not be said, 'Yahweh was not able to bring them to the country which he had promised them. He hated them; that was why he brought them out—to slaughter them in the desert.' 29 But these are your people, your heritage, whom you yourself have brought out by your great power and your outstretched arm."'

The ark of the covenant; the choice of Levi

10 'Yahweh then said to me, "Cut two stone tablets like the first ones, and

9a ‖ Ex 32.

come up to me on the mountain. Make an ark of wood; ²on the tablets I shall inscribe the words that were on the first tablets, which you broke; put them in the ark." ³So I made an ark of acacia wood, cut two stone tablets like the first and went up the mountain with the two tablets in my hand. ⁴And he inscribed the tablets, as he had inscribed them before, with the Ten Words which Yahweh had said to you on the mountain, from the heart of the fire, on the day of the Assembly. Yahweh then gave them to me. ⁵I turned and came down from the mountain and put the tablets in the ark I had made, and there they stayed, as Yahweh had commanded me.

⁶'The Israelites left the wells of the Bene-Jaakan for Moserah, where Aaron died; he was buried there, and his son Eleazar succeeded him in the priesthood. ⁷From there, they set out for Gudgodah, and from Gudgodah for Jotbathah, an area rich in streams. ⁸Yahweh then set apart the tribe of Levi to carry the ark of Yahweh's covenant, to stand in the presence of Yahweh, to serve him and to bless in his name, as they still do today. ⁹This is why Levi has no share or heritage with his brothers: Yahweh is his heritage, as Yahweh your God then told him.

¹⁰'And, as before, I stayed on the mountain for forty days and forty nights. And again Yahweh heard my prayer and agreed not to destroy you. ¹¹And Yahweh said to me, "Be on your way at the head of this people, so that they can go and take possession of the country which I swore to their ancestors that I would give them."

Circumcision of the heart

¹²'And now, Israel, what does Yahweh your God ask of you? Only this: to fear Yahweh your God, to follow all his ways, to love him, to serve Yahweh your God with all your heart and all your soul, ¹³to keep the commandments and laws of Yahweh, which I am laying down for you today for your own good.

¹⁴'Look, to Yahweh your God belong heaven and the heaven of heavens, the earth and everything on it; ¹⁵yet it was on your ancestors, for love of them, that Yahweh set his heart to love them, and he chose their descendants after them, you yourselves, out of all nations, up to the present day. ¹⁶Circumcise your heart then and be obstinate no longer; ¹⁷for Yahweh your God is God of gods and Lord of lords, the great God, triumphant and terrible, free of favouritism, never to be bribed. ¹⁸He it is who sees justice done for the orphan and the widow, who loves the stranger and gives him food and clothing. ¹⁹(Love the stranger then, for you were once strangers in Egypt.) ²⁰Yahweh your God is the one whom you must fear and serve; to him you must hold firm; in his name take your oaths. ²¹Him you must praise, he is your God: for you he has done these great and terrible things which you have seen for yourselves; ²²and, although your ancestors numbered only seventy persons when they went down to Egypt, Yahweh your God has now made you as many as the stars of heaven.'

Israel's past experiences

11 'You must love Yahweh your God and always keep his observances, his laws, his customs, his commandments. ²You are the ones who have had the experience, not your children. They have not had the experience, they have not witnessed the lessons of Yahweh your God, his greatness, his mighty hand and his outstretched arm, ³the signs and the deeds which he performed in the heart of Egypt, against Pharaoh king of Egypt and his entire country, ⁴what he did to the armies of Egypt, to their horses and their chariots, by overwhelming them with the waters of the Sea of Reeds when they were pursuing you, and leaving no trace of them to this day; ⁵what he did for you in the desert, until you arrived here; ⁶what he did to Dathan and Abiram the sons of Eliab the Reubenite, when, with all Israel standing round, the earth opened its mouth and swallowed them, with their families, their tents and all their supporters. ⁷All these great deeds of Yahweh you have seen with your own eyes.

Promises and warnings

8'You must keep all the commandments which I enjoin on you today, so that you may have the strength to conquer the country into which you are about to cross, to take possession of it, 9and so that you may live long in the country which Yahweh promised on oath to bestow on your ancestors and their descendants, a country flowing with milk and honey.

10'For the country which you are about to enter and make your own is not like the country of Egypt from which you have come, where, having done your sowing, you had to water the seed by foot, as though in a vegetable garden. 11No, the country which you are about to enter and make your own, is a country of hills and valleys watered by the rain of heaven. 12Yahweh your God looks after this country, the eyes of Yahweh your God are always on it, from the beginning of the year to the end. 13Depend on it: if you faithfully obey the commandments I enjoin on you today, loving Yahweh your God and serving him with all your heart and all your soul, 14I shall give your country rain at the right time, rain in autumn, rain in spring, so that you can harvest your wheat, your new wine and your oil. 15I shall provide grass in the fields for your cattle, and you will eat to your heart's content. 16Beware of letting your heart be seduced: if you go astray, serve other gods and bow down to them, 17Yahweh's anger will be kindled against you, he will shut the heavens, there will be no more rain, the soil will not yield its produce and, in the fine country given you by Yahweh, you will quickly perish.

Conclusion

18'Let these words of mine remain in your heart and in your soul; fasten them on your hand as a sign and on your forehead as a headband. 19Teach them to your children, and keep on telling them, when you are sitting at home, when you are out and about, when you are lying down and when you are standing up. 20Write them on the doorposts of your house and on your gates, 21so that you and your children may live long in the country which Yahweh swore to your ancestors that he would give them for as long as there is a sky above the earth.

22'For if you faithfully keep and observe all these commandments that I enjoin on you today, loving Yahweh your God, following all his ways and holding fast to him, 23Yahweh will dispossess all these nations before you, and you will dispossess nations greater and more powerful than yourselves. 24Wherever the sole of your foot treads will be yours; your territory will run from the desert all the way to the Lebanon; and from the River, from the River Euphrates, as far as the Western Sea, will be your territory. 25No one will be able to resist you; Yahweh your God will make you feared and dreaded throughout the territory you tread, as he has promised you.

26'Today, look, I am offering you a blessing and a curse: 27a blessing, if you obey the commandments of Yahweh your God which I enjoin on you today; 28a curse, if you disobey the commandments of Yahweh your God and leave the way which today I have marked out for you, by following other gods hitherto unknown to you. 29And when Yahweh your God has brought you into the country which you are about to enter and make your own, you must set the blessing on Mount Gerizim and the curse on Mount Ebal. 30(These mountains, as everyone knows, are on the other side of the Jordan on the westward road, in the territory of the Canaanites who live in the Arabah, opposite Gilgal, near the Oak of Moreh.) 31For you are about to cross the Jordan, to enter and take possession of the country given you by Yahweh your God. You will possess it, you will live in it, 32and you must keep and observe all the laws and customs promulgated by me to you today.'

The deuteronomic code

12'Now, these are the laws and customs which you must keep in the country which Yahweh, God of your ancestors, is giving you as yours, and which you must observe every day that you live in that country.

The place of worship

2 'You must completely destroy all the places where the nations you dispossess have served their gods, on high mountains, on hills, under any spreading tree; 3 you must tear down their altars, smash their sacred stones, burn their sacred poles, hack to bits the statues of their gods and obliterate their name from that place.

4 'Not so must you behave towards Yahweh your God. 5 You must seek Yahweh your God in the place which he will choose from all your tribes, there to set his name and give it a home: that is where you must go. 6 That is where you must bring your burnt offerings and your sacrifices, your tithes and offerings held high, your votive offerings and your voluntary offerings, and the first-born of your herd and flock; 7 and that is where you must eat in the presence of Yahweh your God, rejoicing over your labours, you and your households, because Yahweh your God has blessed you.

8 'You must not behave as we are behaving here today, each of you doing what he himself sees fit, 9 since you have not yet come to the resting place and the heritage that Yahweh your God is going to give you. 10 You are about to cross the Jordan and live in the country given you by Yahweh your God as your heritage; he will grant you peace from all the enemies surrounding you, and you will live in safety. 11 To the place chosen by Yahweh your God as a home for his name, to that place you must bring all the things that I am laying down for you: your burnt offerings and your sacrifices, your tithes and offerings held high, and all the best of your possessions dedicated by you to Yahweh. 12 That is where you will rejoice in the presence of Yahweh your God, you and your sons and daughters, your serving men and women, and the Levite living in your community since he has no share or heritage of his own among you.

Sacrificial regulations

13 'Take care you do not offer your burnt offerings in all the sacred places you see; 14 only in the place that Yahweh chooses in one of your tribes may you offer your burnt offerings and do all the things which I have commanded you.

15 'This notwithstanding, and whenever you wish, you may slaughter and eat meat wherever you live—as much as the blessing of Yahweh affords you. Clean or unclean may eat it, as though it were gazelle or deer. 16 You will not, however, eat the blood, but will pour that like water on the ground.

17 'You must not eat the tithe of your wheat, of your new wine or of your oil, or the first-born of your herd or flock, or any of your votive offerings or voluntary offerings, or your offerings held high to Yahweh, at home. 18 You must eat these in the presence of Yahweh your God in the place Yahweh your God chooses and there alone, you, your son and your daughter, your serving man and serving woman, and the Levite living in your community, expressing your joy in all your labours in the presence of Yahweh your God. 19 As long as you live on your soil, be careful not to neglect the Levite.

20 'When Yahweh your God enlarges your territory as he has promised you, and you say, "I should like to eat meat," if you want to eat meat you may eat as much as you like. 21 If the place in which Yahweh your God chooses to set his name is too far away, you may slaughter any of your herd or flock that Yahweh has given you, as I have prescribed for you; you may eat as much of it as you please at home. 22 But you must eat it as you would gazelle or deer; clean and unclean may eat it together. 23 Take care, however, not to eat the blood, since blood is life, and you must not eat the life with the meat. 24 You must not eat it, but must pour it like water on the ground. 25 You must not eat it—so that you, and your children after you, may prosper, doing what is right in Yahweh's eyes. 26 But the holy things of yours and

the things which you have dedicated, you must go and take to the place chosen by Yahweh. ²⁷ The burnt offerings of meat and blood must be presented on the altar of Yahweh your God; whereas, in your sacrifices, the blood must be poured on the altar of Yahweh your God; the meat you yourselves may eat. ²⁸ Faithfully keep and obey all these orders which I am giving you, so that you and your children after you may prosper for ever, doing what is good and right in the eyes of Yahweh your God.

Against Canaanite cults

²⁹ 'When Yahweh your God has annihilated the nations confronting you, whom you are going to dispossess, and when you have dispossessed them and made your home in their country, ³⁰ beware of being entrapped into copying them, after they have been destroyed to make way for you, and do not enquire about their gods, saying, "How did these nations worship their gods? I am going to do the same too." ³¹ This is not the way to treat Yahweh your God. For in honour of their gods they have done everything detestable that Yahweh hates; yes, in honour of their gods, they even burn their own sons and daughters as sacrifices!'

13

'Whatever I am now commanding you, you must keep and observe, adding nothing to it, taking nothing away.

Against the enticements of idolatry

² 'If a prophet or a dreamer of dreams arises among you, offering you some sign or wonder, ³ and the sign or wonder comes about; and if he then says to you, "Let us follow other gods (hitherto unknown to you) and serve them," ⁴ you must not listen to that prophet's words or to that dreamer's dreams. Yahweh your God is testing you to know if you love Yahweh your God with all your heart and all your soul. ⁵ Yahweh your God is the one whom you must follow, him you must fear, his commandments you must keep, his voice you must obey, him

you must serve, to him you must hold fast. ⁶ That prophet or that dreamer of dreams must be put to death, since he has preached apostasy from Yahweh your God who brought you out of Egypt and redeemed you from the place of slave-labour; and he would have diverted you from the way in which Yahweh your God has commanded you to walk. You must banish this evil from among you.

⁷ 'If your brother, the son of your father or of your mother, or your son or daughter, or the spouse whom you embrace, or your most intimate friend, tries secretly to seduce you, saying, "Let us go and serve other gods," unknown to you or your ancestors before you, ⁸ gods of the peoples surrounding you, whether near you or far away, anywhere throughout the world, ⁹ you must not consent, you must not listen to him; you must show him no pity, you must not spare him or conceal his guilt. ¹⁰ No, you must kill him, your hand must strike the first blow in putting him to death and the hands of the rest of the people following. ¹¹ You must stone him to death, since he has tried to divert you from Yahweh your God who brought you out of Egypt, from the place of slave-labour. ¹² All Israel, hearing of this, will be afraid, and none of you will do such a wicked thing again.

¹³ 'If you hear that in one of the towns which Yahweh your God has given you for a home, ¹⁴ there are men, scoundrels from your own stock, who have led their fellow-citizens astray, saying, "Let us go and serve other gods," hitherto unknown to you, ¹⁵ it is your duty to look into the matter, examine it, and enquire most carefully. If it is proved and confirmed that such a hateful thing has taken place among you, ¹⁶ you must put the inhabitants of that town to the sword; you must lay it under the curse of destruction—the town and everything in it. ¹⁷ You must pile up all its loot in the public square and burn the town and all its loot, offering it all to Yahweh your God. It is to be a ruin for all time, and never rebuilt. ¹⁸ From what is thus put under the curse of destruction you must keep nothing back, so that

Yahweh may turn from the ferocity of his anger and show you mercy, and have pity on you and increase your numbers, as he swore he would to your ancestors, ¹⁹on condition that you listen to the voice of Yahweh your God by keeping all his commandments which I am enjoining on you today, and by doing what is right in the eyes of Yahweh your God.'

Against an idolatrous practice

14 'You are children of Yahweh your God. You must not gash yourselves or shave your foreheads for the dead. ²For you are a people consecrated to Yahweh your God, and Yahweh has chosen you to be his own people from all the peoples on the earth.

Clean and unclean animals^a

³'You must not eat anything disgusting. ⁴These are the animals you may eat: ox, sheep, goat, ⁵deer, gazelle, roebuck, ibex, antelope, oryx, mountain sheep. ⁶You may eat any animal that has a divided and cloven hoof and that is a ruminant. ⁷Of those, however, that are ruminants and of those that have a divided and cloven hoof you may not eat the following: the camel, the hare and the coney, which are ruminants but have no cloven hoof; you must class them as unclean. ⁸So also the pig, which though it has a cloven hoof is not a ruminant; you must class it as unclean. You must neither eat the meat of such animals nor touch their dead bodies.

⁹'Of whatever lives in water you may eat the following: you may eat anything that has fins and scales. ¹⁰But you must not eat anything without fins and scales: you must class it as unclean.

¹¹'You may eat all clean birds, ¹²but the following birds you must not eat: the tawny vulture, the griffon, the osprey, ¹³the kite and the several kinds of buzzard, ¹⁴all kinds of raven, ¹⁵the ostrich, the screech owl, the seagull, the several kinds of hawk, ¹⁶owl, barn owl, ibis, ¹⁷pelican, white vulture, cormorant, ¹⁸stork, the several kinds of heron, hoopoe and bat. ¹⁹You are to class all winged insects as unclean

and must not eat them. ²⁰You may eat any clean fowl.

²¹'You must not eat any animal that has died a natural death. You may give it to a resident foreigner to eat, or sell it to a foreigner. For you are a people consecrated to Yahweh your God.

'You must not boil a kid in its mother's milk.

The annual tithe

²²'Every year, you must take a tithe of what your fields produce from what you have sown ²³and, in the presence of Yahweh your God, in the place where he chooses to give his name a home, you must eat the tithe of your wheat, of your new wine and of your oil, and the first-born of your herd and flock; and by so doing, you will learn always to fear Yahweh your God.

²⁴'If the road is too long for you, if you cannot bring your tithe because the place in which Yahweh chooses to make a home for his name is too far away, when Yahweh your God has blessed you, ²⁵you must convert it into money and, with the money clasped in your hand, you must go to the place chosen by Yahweh your God; ²⁶there you may spend the money on whatever you like, oxen, sheep, wine, fermented liquor, anything you please. There you must eat in the presence of Yahweh your God and rejoice, you and your household. ²⁷Do not neglect the Levite living in your community, since he has no share or heritage of his own among you.

The third-year tithe

²⁸'At the end of every three years, you must take all the tithes of your harvests for that year and collect them in your community. ²⁹Then the Levite—since he has no share or heritage of his own among you—the foreigner, the orphan and the widow living in your community, will come and eat all they want. And so Yahweh your God will bless you in all the labours that you undertake.'

14a ‖ Lv 11:1.

The sabbatical year

15 'At the end of every seven years, you must grant remission. ²The nature of the remission is as follows: any creditor holding a personal pledge obtained from his fellow must release him from it; he must not exploit his fellow or his brother once the latter has appealed to Yahweh for remission. ³A foreigner you may exploit, but you must remit whatever claim you have on your brother. ⁴There must, then, be no poor among you. For Yahweh will grant you his blessing in the country which Yahweh your God is giving you to possess as your heritage, ⁵only if you pay careful attention to the voice of Yahweh your God, by keeping and practising all these commandments which I am enjoining on you today. ⁶If Yahweh your God blesses you as he has promised, you will be creditors to many nations but debtors to none; you will rule over many nations, and be ruled by none.

⁷'Is there anyone poor among you, one of your brothers, in any town of yours in the country which Yahweh your God is giving you? Do not harden your heart or close your hand against that poor brother of yours, ⁸but be open handed with him and lend him enough for his needs. ⁹Do not allow this mean thought in your heart, "The seventh year, the year of remission, is near," and scowl at your poor brother and give him nothing; he could appeal against you to Yahweh, and you would incur guilt! ¹⁰When you give to him, you must give with an open heart; for this, Yahweh your God will bless you in all your actions and in all your undertakings. ¹¹Of course, there will never cease to be poor people in the country, and that is why I am giving you this command: Always be open handed with your brother, and with anyone in your country who is in need and poor.

Slaves

¹²'If your fellow Hebrew, man or woman, sells himself to you, he can serve you for six years. In the seventh year you must set him free, ¹³and in setting him free you must not let him go empty handed. ¹⁴By way of present, you will load his shoulders with things from your flock, from your threshing-floor and from your winepress; as Yahweh your God has blessed you, so you must give to him. ¹⁵Remember that you were once a slave in Egypt and that Yahweh your God redeemed you; that is why I am giving you this order today.

¹⁶'But if he says to you, "I do not want to leave you," because he loves you and your household and is happy with you, ¹⁷you must take an awl and drive it through his ear into the door and he will be your servant for ever. You must do the same to a female slave.

¹⁸'Do not think it hard on you to have to give him his freedom; he is worth twice what a paid servant would cost you, and has served you for six years. And Yahweh your God will bless you in everything you do.

The first-born

¹⁹'You must consecrate every first-born male from your herd and flock to Yahweh your God. You must not put the first-born of your herd to work, or shear the first-born of your flock. ²⁰You must eat it, you and your household, each year, in the presence of Yahweh your God, in the place which Yahweh chooses. ²¹If it has any defect, if it is lame or blind—any serious defect—you must not sacrifice it to Yahweh your God. ²²You will eat it at home, unclean and clean together, as you would gazelle or deer; ²³only, you will not eat its blood, but pour that like water on the ground.'

The feasts: Passover and Unleavened Bread

16 'Observe the month of Abib and celebrate the Passover for Yahweh your God, because it was in the month of Abib that Yahweh your God brought you out of Egypt by night. ²You must sacrifice a Passover from your flock or herd for Yahweh your God in the place where Yahweh chooses to give his name a home. ³You must not eat leavened bread with this; for seven days you must eat it with unleavened bread—the bread of afflic-

18 READ DEUTERONOMY 15:1–11.

You must give with an open heart.—DEUTERONOMY 15:10

THE BENEFITS OF SERVING THE POOR

God permits the poor to exist in the world so that every person might have the means of atoning for his sins. If there were no poor, nobody would give alms and nobody would receive pardon. God could have made everyone rich, but he willed to help us through the misery of the poor. In this way, all may merit the grace of God—the poor by patience and the well-to-do by almsgiving. Truly, the want of the poor is of service to us.

If you correctly understand and diligently weigh the balance of your heart, you receive from the poor incomparably more than you give. Listen and see: a coin and a kingdom. What comparison is there . . . between the two? You give the poor a coin and you receive a kingdom from Christ; you provide a mouthful and you are given eternal life; you offer clothing and Christ grants you the forgiveness of your sins. . . . The wretchedness of the poor is the remedy of the rich, as our Lord said: "Give alms from what you have and, look, everything will be clean for you" (Lk 11:41).

In proportion to his means, each person should not come to church empty-handed. For if he wishes to receive, he must also give something. If he can, he should cover the poor with new clothing. If he cannot, he should give him old. If he feels unable to do this, he should offer a meal or welcome a stranger, give him a bed, and wash his feet.

There are two types of alms: the first is good, but the second is better. The first is that you feed the poor; the second is that you immediately pardon a brother or sister who has offended you. With the Lord's help, we must strive to practice both types of almsgiving.

ST. CAESARIUS OF ARLES, 470–543

YOU WILL FIND THE NEXT READING AT DEUTERONOMY 30.

tion—since you left Egypt in great haste; this is so that, as long as you live, you will remember the day you came out of Egypt. ⁴For seven days no leaven must be found in any house throughout your territory, nor must any of the meat that you sacrifice in the evening of the first day be kept overnight until the next day. ⁵You must sacrifice the Passover not in any of the towns given you by Yahweh your God, ⁶but in the place where Yahweh your God chooses to give his name a home; there you must sacrifice the Passover, in the evening at sunset, at the hour when you came out of Egypt. ⁷You will cook it and eat it in the place chosen by Yahweh your God, and in the morning you must return and go to your tents. ⁸For six days you will eat unleavened bread; on the seventh day there will be an assembly for Yahweh your God; and you must do no work.

Other feasts

⁹'You must count seven weeks, counting these seven weeks from the time you begin to put your sickle into the standing corn. ¹⁰You will then celebrate the feast of Weeks for Yahweh your God with the gift of a voluntary offering proportionate to the degree in which Yahweh

your God has blessed you. ¹¹ You must rejoice in the presence of Yahweh your God, in the place where Yahweh your God chooses to give his name a home, you, your son and your daughter, your serving men and women, the Levite living in your community, the foreigner, the orphan and the widow living among you. ¹² Remember that you were once a slave in Egypt, and carefully observe these laws.

¹³ 'You must celebrate the feast of Shelters for seven days, at the time when you gather in the produce of your threshing-floor and winepress. ¹⁴ You must rejoice at your feast, you, your son and your daughter, your serving men and women, the Levite, the foreigner, the orphan and the widow living in your community. ¹⁵ For seven days, you must celebrate the feast for Yahweh your God in the place chosen by Yahweh; for Yahweh your God will bless you in all your produce and in all your undertakings, so that you will have good reason to rejoice.

¹⁶ 'Three times a year all your menfolk must appear before Yahweh your God in the place chosen by him: at the feast of Unleavened Bread, at the feast of Weeks, at the feast of Shelters. No one must appear empty-handed before Yahweh, ¹⁷ but each must give what he can, in proportion to the blessing which Yahweh your God has bestowed on you.

Judges

¹⁸ 'You must appoint judges and scribes in each of the towns that Yahweh your God is giving you, for all your tribes; these are to mete out proper justice to the people. ¹⁹ You must not pervert the law; you must be impartial; you will take no bribes, for a bribe blinds the eyes of the wise and ruins the cause of the upright. ²⁰ Strict justice must be your ideal, so that you may live long in possession of the country given you by Yahweh your God.

Abuses in worship

²¹ 'You must not plant a sacred pole of any wood whatsoever beside the altar which you erect for Yahweh your God; ²² nor will you set up a standing-stone, a thing Yahweh your God would abhor.'

17 'To Yahweh your God you must sacrifice nothing from herd or flock that has any blemish or defect whatsoever, for Yahweh your God holds this detestable.

² 'If there is anyone, man or woman, among you in any of the towns given you by Yahweh your God, who does what is wrong in the eyes of Yahweh your God by violating his covenant, ³ who goes and serves other gods and worships them, or the sun or the moon or any of heaven's array—a thing I have forbidden— ⁴ and this person is denounced to you: if after careful enquiry it is found true and confirmed that this hateful thing has been done in Israel, ⁵ you must take the man or woman guilty of this evil deed outside your city gates, and there you must stone that man or woman to death. ⁶ A death sentence may be passed only on the word of two witnesses or three; and no one must be put to death on the word of one witness alone. ⁷ The witnesses' hands must strike the first blow in putting the condemned to death, the rest of the people following. You must banish this evil from among you.

Levitical judges

⁸ 'If a case comes before you which is too difficult for you, a case of murder, conflicting claims, damage to property—any kind of dispute—in your towns, you must make your way to the place chosen by Yahweh your God, ⁹ and approach the levitical priests and the judge then in office. They will hold an enquiry and let you know their sentence. ¹⁰ You must abide by the verdict which they give you in this place chosen by Yahweh, and you will take care to carry out all their instructions. ¹¹ You will abide by the decision which they give you and by the sentence which they pronounce, not deviating to right or to left from the verdict which they have given you. ¹² If anyone presumes to disobey either the priest

who is there in the service of Yahweh your God, or the judge, that person must die. You must banish this evil from Israel. ¹³And when the people hear of this they will all be afraid and not act presumptuously any more.

Kings

¹⁴'If, having reached the country given by Yahweh your God and having taken possession of it and, while living there, you think, "I should like to appoint a king to rule me—like all the surrounding nations," ¹⁵the king whom you appoint to rule you must be chosen by Yahweh your God; the appointment of a king must be made from your own brothers; on no account must you appoint as king some foreigner who is not a brother of yours.

¹⁶'He must not, however, acquire more and more horses, or send the people back to Egypt with a view to increasing his cavalry, since Yahweh has told you, "You must never go back that way again." ¹⁷Nor must he keep on acquiring more and more wives, for that could lead his heart astray. Nor must he acquire vast quantities of silver and gold. ¹⁸Once seated on his royal throne, and for his own use, he must write a copy of this Law on a scroll, at the dictation of the levitical priests. ¹⁹It must never leave him, and he must read it every day of his life and learn to fear Yahweh his God by keeping all the words of this Law and observing these rules, ²⁰so that he will not think himself superior to his brothers, and not deviate from these commandments either to right or to left. So doing, long will he occupy his throne, he and his sons, in Israel.'

The levitical priesthood

18 'The levitical priests, the whole tribe of Levi will be without share or heritage of their own in Israel; they will live on the foods offered to Yahweh and on his heritage. ²Levi will have no heritage of his own among his brothers; Yahweh will be his heritage, as he has promised him.

³'This is what is due to the priests from the people, from those who offer an ox or a sheep in sacrifice: the priest must be given the shoulder, the cheeks and the stomach. ⁴You must give him the first-fruits of your wheat, of your new wine and of your oil, as well as the first-fruits of your sheep-shearing. ⁵For Yahweh your God has chosen him from all your tribes to stand before Yahweh your God, to do the duties of the sacred ministry, and to bless in Yahweh's name—him and his sons for all time.

⁶'If a Levite living in one of your towns anywhere in Israel decides to move to the place chosen by Yahweh, ⁷he shall minister there in the name of Yahweh his God like all his fellow Levites who stand ministering there in the presence of Yahweh, ⁸eating equal shares with them—what he has from the sale of his patrimony notwithstanding.

Prophets

⁹'When you have entered the country given you by Yahweh your God, you must not learn to imitate the detestable practices of the nations there already. ¹⁰There must never be anyone among you who makes his son or daughter pass through the fire of sacrifice, who practises divination, who is soothsayer, augur or sorcerer, ¹¹weaver of spells, consulter of ghosts or mediums, or necromancer. ¹²For anyone who does these things is detestable to Yahweh your God; it is because of these detestable practices that Yahweh your God is driving out these nations before you.

¹³'You must be faultless in your relationship with Yahweh your God. ¹⁴For these nations whom you are going to dispossess have listened to soothsayers and mediums, but Yahweh your God does not permit you to do this. From among yourselves, from among your own brothers, ¹⁵Yahweh your God will raise up a prophet like me; you will listen to him. ¹⁶This is exactly what you asked Yahweh your God to do—at Horeb, on the day of the Assembly, when you said, "Never let me hear the voice of Yahweh my God or see this great fire again, or I shall die." ¹⁷Then Yahweh said to me, ¹⁸"What they have said is well said. From

their own brothers I shall raise up a prophet like yourself; ¹⁹I shall put my words into his mouth and he will tell them everything I command him. Anyone who refuses to listen to my words, spoken by him in my name, will have to render an account to me. ²⁰But the prophet who presumes to say something in my name which I have not commanded him to say, or who speaks in the name of other gods, that prophet must die."

²¹'You may be privately wondering, "How are we to tell that a prophecy does not come from Yahweh?" ²²When a prophet speaks in the name of Yahweh and the thing does not happen and the word is not fulfilled, then it has not been said by Yahweh. The prophet has spoken presumptuously. You have nothing to fear from him.'

Homicide and cities of refuge

19 'When Yahweh your God has annihilated the nations whose country Yahweh your God is going to give you, and you have dispossessed them and are living in their towns and in their houses, ²you must set aside three towns, centrally placed in the country which Yahweh your God is giving you for your own. ³You will keep the approaches to them in good order, dividing the area of the country which Yahweh your God is giving you as your heritage, into three parts, so that any killer can flee to these towns. ⁴Here is an example of how someone may save his life by fleeing to them.

'If anyone has struck his fellow accidentally, without any previous feud with him ⁵(for example, he goes with his fellow into the forest to cut wood; his arm swings the axe to fell a tree; the head slips off the handle and strikes his companion dead), that man may take refuge in one of these towns and save his life. ⁶It must not be allowed that the avenger of blood, in the heat of his anger, should pursue the killer and that the length of the road should help him to overtake and wound him fatally; for the man has not deserved to die, having had no previous feud with his victim.

⁷'Hence I am giving you this order: You must set aside three towns, ⁸and if Yahweh your God enlarges your territory, as he swore to your ancestors that he would, and gives you the whole country which he promised to give to your ancestors— ⁹provided that you keep and observe all the commandments which I am enjoining on you today, loving Yahweh your God and always following his ways— then, to those three towns you will add three more. ¹⁰In this way, innocent blood will not be shed in the country which Yahweh your God is going to give you as your heritage; otherwise you would incur blood-guilt.

¹¹'But if it happens that a man has a feud with his fellow and lies in wait for him and attacks him and fatally wounds him and he dies, and the man takes refuge in one of these towns, ¹²the elders of his own town must send there and have him taken and handed over to the avenger of blood, to be put to death. ¹³You must show him no pity. You must banish the shedding of innocent blood from Israel, and then you will prosper.

Boundaries

¹⁴'You must not displace your neighbour's boundary mark, positioned by men of old in the heritage soon to be yours, in the country which Yahweh your God is about to give you.

Witnesses

¹⁵'A single witness will not suffice to convict anyone of a crime or offence of any kind; whatever the misdemeanour, the evidence of two witnesses or three is required to sustain the charge.

¹⁶'If someone gives false evidence against anyone, laying a charge of apostasy, ¹⁷both parties to this dispute before Yahweh must appear before the priests and judges then in office. ¹⁸The judges will make a careful enquiry, and if it turns out that the witness is a liar and has made a false accusation against his brother, ¹⁹you must treat the witness as he would have treated his brother. You must banish this evil from among you. ²⁰The rest, hearing of this,

will be afraid and never again do such an evil thing among you. ²¹ You must show no pity.

Limits of retaliation

'Life for life, eye for eye, tooth for tooth, hand for hand, foot for foot.'

War and combatants

20 ¹'When you go to war against your enemies and see horses and chariots and an army greater than your own, you must not be afraid of them; Yahweh your God is with you, he who brought you out of Egypt. ² When you are about to join battle, the priest must come forward and address the people. ³ He must say to them, "Listen, Israel: today you are about to join battle with your enemies. Do not be faint hearted. Let there be no fear or trembling or alarm as you face them. ⁴ Yahweh your God is marching with you, to fight your enemies for you and make you victorious."

⁵'The scribes will then address the people, as follows:

"Has anyone built a new house and not yet dedicated it? Let him go home, in case he dies in battle and someone else performs the dedication.

⁶"Has anyone planted a vineyard and not yet enjoyed its fruit? Let him go home, in case he dies in battle and someone else enjoys its fruit.

⁷"Has anyone contracted to marry a girl and not yet married her? Let him go home, in case he dies in battle and someone else marries her."

⁸'Finally, the scribes will say to the people:

"Is anyone frightened or faint hearted? Let him go home, in case he makes his brothers faint hearted too!"

⁹'Then, when the scribes have finished speaking to the people, commanders will be appointed to lead them.

Captured towns

¹⁰'When you advance on a town to attack it, first offer it peace-terms. ¹¹ If it accepts these and opens its gates to you, all the people inside will owe you forced labour and work for you. ¹² But if it refuses peace and gives battle, you must besiege it. ¹³ Yahweh your God having handed it over to you, you will put the whole male population to the sword. ¹⁴ But the women, children, livestock and whatever the town contains by way of spoil, you may take for yourselves as booty. You will feed on the spoils of the enemies whom Yahweh your God has handed over to you.

¹⁵'That is how you will treat towns far away and not belonging to the nations near you. ¹⁶ But as regards the towns of those peoples whom Yahweh your God is giving you as your heritage, you must not spare the life of any living thing. ¹⁷ Instead, you must lay them under the curse of destruction: Hittites, Amorites, Canaanites, Perizzites, Hivites and Jebusites, as Yahweh your God has commanded, ¹⁸ so that they may not teach you to do all the detestable things which they do to honour their gods: in doing these, you would sin against Yahweh your God.

¹⁹'If, when attacking a town, you have to besiege it for a long time before you capture it, you must not destroy its trees by taking the axe to them: eat their fruit but do not cut them down. Is the tree in the fields human, that you should besiege it too? ²⁰ Any trees, however, which you know are not fruit trees, you may destroy and cut down and use to build siegeworks against the hostile town until it falls.'

The unidentified murderer

21 ¹'If, in the country which Yahweh your God gives you as your possession, a victim of murder is found lying in the open country and it is not known who has killed that person, ² your elders and scribes must measure the distance between the victim and the surrounding towns, ³ and establish which town is the nearest to the victim. The elders of that town must then take a heifer that has not yet been put to work or used as a draught animal under the yoke. ⁴ The elders of that town must bring the heifer down to a permanently flowing river, to a spot that has been neither

ploughed nor sown, and there by the river they must break the heifer's neck. ⁵ The priests, the sons of Levi, will then step forward, these being the men whom Yahweh your God has chosen to serve him and to bless in Yahweh's name, and it being their business to settle all cases of dispute or of violence. ⁶ All the elders of the town nearest to the victim of murder must then wash their hands in the stream, over the slaughtered heifer. ⁷ They must pronounce these words, "Our hands have not shed this blood and our eyes have seen nothing. ⁸ O Yahweh, forgive your people Israel whom you have redeemed, and let no innocent blood be shed among your people Israel. May this bloodshed be forgiven them!" ⁹ You must banish all shedding of innocent blood from among you, if you mean to do what is right in the eyes of Yahweh.

Women taken in war

¹⁰ 'When you go to war against your enemies and Yahweh your God delivers them into your power and you take prisoners, ¹¹ and among the prisoners you see a beautiful woman, and you fall in love with her, and you take her to be your wife ¹² and bring her home; she must shave her head and cut her nails, ¹³ and take off her prisoner's garb; she must stay inside your house and mourn her father and mother for a full month. You may then go to her and be a husband to her, and she will be your wife. ¹⁴ Should she cease to please you, you will let her go where she wishes, not selling her for money: you must not make any profit out of her, since you have exploited her.

Birthright

¹⁵ 'If a man has two wives, one loved and the other unloved, and the loved one and the unloved both bear him children, and if the first-born son is of the unloved wife, ¹⁶ when the man comes to bequeath his goods to his sons, he may not treat the son of the wife whom he loves as the first-born, at the expense of the son of the wife whom he does not love, the true first-born. ¹⁷ As his first-born he must

acknowledge the son of the wife whom he does not love, giving him a double share of his estate; this son being the first-fruit of his vigour, the right of the first-born is his.

The rebellious son

¹⁸ 'If a man has a stubborn and rebellious son who will not listen to the voice either of his father or of his mother and, even when they punish him, still will not pay attention to them, ¹⁹ his father and mother must take hold of him and bring him out to the elders of his town at the gate of that place. ²⁰ To the elders of his town, they will say, "This son of ours is stubborn and rebellious and will not listen to us; he is a wastrel and a drunkard." ²¹ All his fellow-citizens must then stone him to death. You must banish this evil from among you. All Israel, hearing of this, will be afraid.

Various rulings

²² 'If a man guilty of a capital offence is to be put to death, and you hang him from a tree, ²³ his body must not remain on the tree overnight; you must bury him the same day, since anyone hanged is a curse of God, and you must not bring pollution on the soil which Yahweh your God is giving you as your heritage.'

22 'If you see your brother's ox or one of his sheep straying, you must not disregard it: you must take it back to your brother. ² And if he is not close at hand or you do not know who he is, you must take it home with you and keep it by you until your brother comes to look for it; you will then return it to him.

³ 'You must do the same with his donkey, the same with his cloak, the same with anything that your brother loses and that you find; you must not disregard it.

⁴ 'If you see your brother's donkey or ox fall over on the road, you must not disregard it, but must help your brother get it on its feet again.

⁵ 'A woman must not dress like a man, nor a man like a woman; anyone who does this is detestable to Yahweh your God.

6'If, when out walking, you come across a bird's nest, in a tree or on the ground, with chicks or eggs and the mother bird sitting on the chicks or the eggs, you must not take the mother as well as the chicks. 7Let the mother go; the young you may take for yourself. Thus will you have prosperity and long life.

8'When you build a new house, you must give your roof a parapet; then your house will not incur blood-vengeance, should anyone fall off the top.

9'You must not sow any other crop in your vineyard, or the whole yield may become forfeit, both the crop you have sown and the yield of your vines.

10'You must not plough with ox and donkey together.

11'You must not wear clothing woven part of wool, part of linen.

12'You must make tassels for the four corners of the cloak in which you wrap yourself.

A young wife's reputation

13'If a man marries a woman, has sexual intercourse with her and then, turning against her, 14taxes her with misconduct and publicly defames her by saying, "I married this woman and when I had sexual intercourse with her I did not find evidence of her virginity," 15the girl's father and mother must take the evidence of her virginity and produce it before the elders of the town, at the gate. 16To the elders, the girl's father will say, "I gave this man my daughter for a wife and he has turned against her, 17and now he taxes her with misconduct, saying, I have found no evidence of virginity in your daughter. Here is the evidence of my daughter's virginity!" 18They must then display the cloth to the elders of the town. 19The elders of the town in question will have the man arrested and flogged, and fine him a hundred silver shekels for publicly defaming a virgin of Israel, and give this money to the girl's father. She will remain his wife; as long as he lives, he may not divorce her.

20'But if the accusation that the girl cannot show evidence of virginity is substantiated, 21she must be taken out, and at the door of her father's house her fellow-citizens must stone her to death for having committed an infamy in Israel by bringing disgrace on her father's family. You must banish this evil from among you.

Adultery and fornication

22'If a man is caught having sexual intercourse with another man's wife, both must be put to death: the man who has slept with her and the woman herself. You must banish this evil from Israel.

23'If a virgin is engaged to a man, and another man encounters her in the town and has sexual intercourse with her, 24you will take them both to the gate of the town in question and stone them to death: the girl, for not having called for help in the town; the man, for having exploited his fellow-citizen's wife. You must banish this evil from among you. 25But if the man ran into the betrothed girl in the open country and slept with her, having taken her by force, her ravisher alone must die; 26you must do nothing to the girl, she has not committed a capital offence. The case is like that of a man who attacks and kills his fellow: 27since he came across her in the open country, the betrothed girl may have called out, without anyone's coming to her rescue.

28'If a man meets a young virgin who is not betrothed and seizes her, sleeps with her and is caught in the act, 29her ravisher must give the girl's father fifty silver shekels; since he has exploited her, she must be his wife and, as long as he lives, he may not divorce her.'

23 'A man must not take his father's wife; he must not withdraw the skirt of his father's cloak from her.

Participation in public worship

2'A man whose testicles have been crushed or whose male member has been cut off must not be admitted to the assembly of Yahweh. 3No half-breed may be admitted to the assembly of Yahweh; not even his descendants to the tenth generation may be admitted to the assembly of Yahweh. ⁴No Ammonite or Moabite may be admitted to the assembly of Yahweh; not even his descendants to the tenth generation may be admitted to the assembly of Yahweh, and this is for all time; ⁵ since they did not come to meet you with food and drink when you were on your way out of Egypt, and even hired Balaam son of Beor to oppose you by cursing you, from Pethor in Aram Naharaim. ⁶ But Yahweh your God refused to listen to Balaam, and Yahweh your God turned the curse on you into a blessing, because Yahweh your God loved you. ⁷ Never, as long as you live, must you seek their welfare or their prosperity.

⁸ 'You must not regard the Edomite as detestable, for he is your brother; you must not regard the Egyptian as detestable, since you were once a foreigner in his country. ⁹ The third generation of children born to these may be admitted to the assembly of Yahweh.

Hygiene in camp

¹⁰ 'When you are in camp, at war with your enemies, you must avoid anything bad. ¹¹ If any one of you is unclean by reason of a nocturnal emission, he must leave and not come back into camp, ¹² but towards evening wash himself, and return to camp at sunset.

¹³ 'You must have a latrine outside the camp, and go out to this; ¹⁴ you must have a trowel in your equipment and, when you squat outside, you must scrape a hole with it, then turn round and cover up your excrement. ¹⁵ For Yahweh your God goes about the inside of your camp to guard you and put your enemies at your mercy. Your camp must therefore be a holy place; Yahweh must not see anything indecent there or he will desert you.

Miscellaneous

¹⁶ 'You must not allow a master to imprison a slave who has escaped from him and come to you. ¹⁷ Let him make his home with you and yours, wherever he pleases in whichever of your towns he prefers; you must not molest him.

¹⁸ 'There must be no sacred prostitute among the women of Israel, and no sacred prostitute among the men of Israel. ¹⁹ You must not bring the wages of a prostitute or the earnings of a 'dog'ᵃ to the house of Yahweh your God, whatever vow you may have made: both are detestable to Yahweh your God.

²⁰ 'You must not lend on interest to your brother, whether the loan be of money, of food, or of anything else that may earn interest. ²¹ You may demand interest on a loan to a foreigner, but you must not demand interest from your brother; so that Yahweh your God may bless you in all your labours, in the country which you are about to enter and make your own.

²² 'If you make a vow to Yahweh your God, you must not be slack about fulfilling it: Yahweh your God will certainly hold you answerable for it and you will incur guilt. ²³ If, however, you make no vow, you do not incur guilt. ²⁴ Whatever passes your lips you must keep to, and the vow that you have made to Yahweh, your generous God, you must fulfil.

²⁵ 'If you go into your neighbour's vineyard, you may eat as many grapes as you please, but you must not put any in your basket. ²⁶ If you go into your neighbour's standing corn, you may pick ears by hand, but you must not put a sickle into your neighbour's corn.'

Divorce

24 'Suppose a man has taken a wife and consummated the marriage; but she has not pleased him and he has found some impropriety of which to accuse her; he has therefore made out a writ of divorce for her and handed it to her and then dismissed her from his house; ² she leaves his home and goes away to become the wife of another man. ³ Then suppose this second man who has married her takes a dislike to her and makes out a writ of divorce for her and hands it to her and dismisses her from his house or if this other man who took her as his wife dies, ⁴ her first hus-

---

23a Contemptuous term for a male prostitute.

band, who has repudiated her, may not take her back as his wife now that she has been made unclean in this way. For that is detestable in Yahweh's eyes and you must not bring guilt on the country which Yahweh your God is giving you as your heritage.

Protection of the individual

5 'If a man is newly married, he must not join the army, nor must he be pestered at home; he must be left at home, free of all obligations for one year, to make his new wife happy.

6 'No one may take a mill or a millstone in pledge; that would be to take life itself in pledge.

7 'If anyone is caught, having kidnapped one of his brother-Israelites, whether he makes him his slave or sells him, that thief must die. You must banish this evil from among you.

8 'In a case of a virulent skin-disease, take care you faithfully observe and exactly carry out everything that the levitical priests direct you to do. You must keep and observe everything that I have commanded them. 9 Remember what Yahweh your God did to Miriam when you were on your way out of Egypt.

10 'If you are making your brother a loan on pledge, you must not go into his house and seize the pledge, whatever it may be. 11 You must stay outside, and the man to whom you are making the loan must bring the pledge out to you. 12 And if the man is poor, you must not go to bed with his pledge in your possession; 13 you must return it to him at sunset so that he can sleep in his cloak and bless you; and it will be an upright action on your part in God's view.

14 'You must not exploit a poor and needy wage-earner, be he one of your brothers or a foreigner resident in your community. 15 You must pay him his wages each day, not allowing the sun to set before you do, since he, being poor, needs them badly; otherwise he may appeal to Yahweh against you, and you would incur guilt.

16 'Parents may not be put to death for their children, nor children for parents, but each must be put to death for his own crime.

17 'You must not infringe the rights of the foreigner or the orphan; you must not take a widow's clothes in pledge. 18 Remember that you were once a slave in Egypt and that Yahweh your God redeemed you from that. That is why I am giving you this order.

19 'If, when reaping the harvest in your field, you overlook a sheaf in that field, do not go back for it. The foreigner, the orphan and the widow shall have it, so that Yahweh your God may bless you in all your undertakings.

20 'When you beat your olive tree, you must not go over the branches twice. The foreigner, the orphan and the widow shall have the rest.

21 'When you harvest your vineyard, you must not pick it over a second time. The foreigner, the orphan and the widow shall have the rest.

22 'Remember that you were once a slave in Egypt. That is why I am giving you this order.'

25 'If people fall out, they must go to court for judgement; the judges must declare the one who is right to be in the right, the one who is wrong to be in the wrong. 2 If the one who is in the wrong deserves a flogging, the judge must have him laid on the ground and flogged in his presence, the number of strokes proportionate to his offence. 3 He may impose forty strokes but no more; otherwise, by the infliction of more, serious injury may be caused and your brother be humiliated before you.

4 'You must not muzzle an ox when it is treading out the corn.

The levirate law

5 'If brothers live together and one of them dies childless, the dead man's wife may not marry a stranger outside the family. Her husband's brother must come to her and, exercising his duty as brother, make her his wife, 6 and the first son she bears must assume the dead

brother's name; by this means his name will not be obliterated from Israel. 7 But if the man declines to take his brother's wife, she must go to the elders at the gate and say, "I have no brother-in-law willing to perpetuate his brother's name in Israel; he declines to exercise his duty as brother in my favour." 8 The elders of the town must summon the man and talk to him. If, on appearing before them, he says, "I refuse to take her," 9 then the woman to whom he owes duty as brother must go up to him in the presence of the elders, take the sandal off his foot, spit in his face, and pronounce the following words, "This is what is done to the man who refuses to restore his brother's house," 10 and his family must henceforth be known in Israel as House of the Unshod.

Modesty in brawls

11 'If, when two men are fighting, the wife of one intervenes to protect her husband from the other's blows by reaching out and seizing the other by his private parts, 12 you must cut off her hand and show no pity.

Appendices

13 'You must not keep two different weights in your bag, one heavy, one light. 14 You must not keep two different measures in your house, one large, one small. 15 You must keep one weight, full and accurate, so that you may have long life in the country given you by Yahweh your God. 16 For anyone who does things of this kind and acts dishonestly is detestable to Yahweh your God.

17 'Remember how Amalek treated you when you were on your way out of Egypt. 18 He met you on your way and, after you had gone by, he fell on you from the rear and cut off the stragglers; when you were faint and weary, he had no fear of God. 19 When Yahweh your God has granted you peace from all the enemies surrounding you, in the country given you by Yahweh your God to own as your heritage, you must blot out the memory of Amalek under heaven. Do not forget.'

First-fruits

26 'When you have entered the country which Yahweh your God is giving you as heritage, when you have taken possession of it and are living in it, 2 you must set aside the first-fruits of all the produce of the soil raised by you in your country, given you by Yahweh your God. You must put these in a basket and go to the place where Yahweh your God chooses to give his name a home. 3 You will go to the priest then in office and say to him, "Today I declare to Yahweh my God that I have reached the country which Yahweh swore to our ancestors that he would give us."

4 'The priest will then take the basket from your hand and lay it before the altar of Yahweh your God. 5 In the presence of Yahweh your God, you will then pronounce these words:

"My father was a wandering Aramaean, who went down to Egypt with a small group of men, and stayed there, until he there became a great, powerful and numerous nation. 6 The Egyptians ill-treated us, they oppressed us and inflicted harsh slavery on us. 7 But we called on Yahweh, God of our ancestors. Yahweh heard our voice and saw our misery, our toil and our oppression; 8 and Yahweh brought us out of Egypt with mighty hand and outstretched arm, with great terror, and with signs and wonders. 9 He brought us here and has given us this country, a country flowing with milk and honey. 10 Hence, I now bring the first-fruits of the soil that you, Yahweh, have given me."

'You will then lay them before Yahweh your God, and prostrate yourself in the presence of Yahweh your God. 11 You must then rejoice in all the good things that Yahweh your God has bestowed on you and your family— you, the Levite and the foreigner living with you.

The third-year tithe

12 'In the third year, the tithing year, when you have finished taking the tithe of your whole

income and have given it to the Levite, the foreigner, the orphan and the widow so that, in your towns, they may eat to their heart's content, [13] in the presence of Yahweh your God, you must say:

"I have cleared my house of what was consecrated. Yes, I have given it to the Levite, the foreigner, the orphan and the widow, in accordance with all the commandments you have imposed on me, neither going beyond your commandments nor neglecting them. [14] When in mourning, I have not eaten any of it; when unclean, I have taken none of it away; I have given none of it for the dead. I have obeyed the voice of Yahweh my God and I have behaved in every way as you have commanded me. [15] Look down from your holy dwelling, from heaven, and bless your people Israel and the country which you have given us, as you swore to our ancestors, a country flowing with milk and honey." '

Israel, the people of Yahweh

[16] 'Yahweh your God commands you today to observe these laws and customs; you must keep and observe them with all your heart and with all your soul.

[17] 'Today you have obtained this declaration from Yahweh: that he will be your God, but only if you follow his ways, keep his statutes, his commandments, his customs, and listen to his voice. [18] And today Yahweh has obtained this declaration from you: that you will be his own people—as he has said—but only if you keep all his commandments; [19] then for praise and renown and honour, he will raise you higher than every other nation he has made, and you will be a people consecrated to Yahweh, as he has promised.'

The writing of the Law and religious ceremonies

27 Moses and the elders of Israel gave the people this command: 'Keep all the commandments which I am laying down for you today. [2] After you have crossed the Jordan into the country which Yahweh your God is giving you, you must set up tall stones, coat them with lime [3] and on them write all the words of this Law, when you have crossed and entered the country which Yahweh your God is giving you, a country flowing with milk and honey, as Yahweh, God of your ancestors, has promised you.

[4] 'When you have crossed the Jordan, you must erect these stones on Mount Ebal, as I command you today, and coat them with lime. [5] There, for Yahweh your God, you must build an altar of stones, on which no iron has been used. [6] You must build the altar of Yahweh your God of rough stones, and on this altar you will present burnt offerings to Yahweh your God, [7] and immolate communion sacrifices and eat them there, rejoicing in the presence of Yahweh your God. [8] On these stones you must write all the words of this Law; cut them carefully.'

[9] Moses and the levitical priests then said to all Israel: 'Be silent, Israel, and listen. Today you have become a people for Yahweh your God. [10] You must listen to the voice of Yahweh your God and observe the commandments and laws which I am laying down for you today.'

[11] That day Moses gave the people this order: [12] 'When you have crossed the Jordan, the following will stand on Mount Gerizim to bless the people: Simeon and Levi, Judah and Issachar, Joseph and Benjamin. [13] And the following will stand on Mount Ebal for the curse: Reuben, Gad and Asher, Zebulun, Dan and Naphtali. [14] The Levites will then speak, proclaiming loudly to all the Israelites:

[15] "Accursed be anyone who makes a carved or cast idol, a thing detestable to Yahweh, a workman's artefact, and sets it up in secret." And the people are all to respond by saying, Amen.

[16] "Accursed be anyone who treats father or mother dishonourably." And the people must all say, Amen.

[17] "Accursed be anyone who displaces a neighbour's boundary mark." And the people must all say, Amen.

18 "Accursed be anyone who leads the blind astray on the road." And the people must all say, Amen.

19 "Accursed be anyone who violates the rights of the foreigner, the orphan and the widow." And the people must all say, Amen.

20 "Accursed be anyone who has sexual intercourse with his father's wife and withdraws the skirt of his father's cloak from her." And the people must all say, Amen.

21 "Accursed be anyone who has sexual intercourse with any kind of animal." And the people must all say, Amen.

22 "Accursed be anyone who has sexual intercourse with his sister, the daughter of his father or of his mother." And the people must all say, Amen.

23 "Accursed be anyone who has sexual intercourse with his mother-in-law." And the people must all say, Amen.

24 "Accursed be anyone who secretly strikes down his neighbour." And the people must all say, Amen.

25 "Accursed be anyone who accepts a bribe to take an innocent life." And the people must all say, Amen.

26 "Accursed be anyone who does not make the words of this Law effective by putting them into practice." And the people must all say, Amen.'

Promised blessings

28 'But if you faithfully obey the voice of Yahweh your God, by keeping and observing all his commandments, which I am laying down for you today, Yahweh your God will raise you higher than every other nation in the world, 2 and all these blessings will befall and overtake you, for having obeyed the voice of Yahweh your God.

3 'You will be blessed in the town and blessed in the countryside; 4 blessed, the offspring of your body, the yield of your soil, the yield of your livestock, the young of your cattle and the increase of your flocks; 5 blessed, your basket and your kneading trough. 6 You will be blessed in coming home, and blessed in going out. 7 The enemies who attack you, Yahweh will defeat before your eyes; they will advance on you from one direction and flee from you in seven. 8 Yahweh will command blessedness to be with you, on your barns and on all your undertakings, and he will bless you in the country given you by Yahweh your God.

9 'From you Yahweh will make a people consecrated to himself, as he has sworn to you, if you keep the commandments of Yahweh your God and follow his ways. 10 The peoples of the world, seeing that you bear Yahweh's name, will all be afraid of you. 11 Yahweh will make you abound in possessions: in the offspring of your body, in the yield of your cattle and in the yield of your soil, in the country which he swore to your ancestors that he would give you. 12 For you Yahweh will open his treasury of rain, the heavens, to give your country its rain at the right time, and to bless all your labours. You will make many nations your subjects, yet you will be subject to none. 13 Yahweh will put you at the head, not at the tail; you will always be on top and never underneath, if you listen to the commandments of Yahweh your God, which I am laying down for you today, and then keep them and put them into practice, 14 not deviating to right or to left from any of the words which I am laying down for you today, by following other gods and serving them.

Curses

15 'But if you do not obey the voice of Yahweh your God, and do not keep and observe all his commandments and laws which I am laying down for you today then all these curses will befall and overtake you.

16 'You will be accursed in the town and accursed in the countryside; 17 accursed, your basket and your kneading trough; 18 accursed, the offspring of your body, the yield of your soil, the young of your cattle and the increase of your flock. 19 You will be accursed in coming home, and accursed in going out.

20 'Yahweh will send a curse on you, a spell, an imprecation on all your labours until you

have been destroyed and quickly perish, because of your perverse behaviour, for having deserted me. ²¹ Yahweh will fasten the plague on you, until it has exterminated you from the country which you are about to enter and make your own. ²² Yahweh will strike you down with consumption, fever, inflammation, burning fever, drought, wind-blast, mildew, and these will pursue you to your ruin. ²³ The heavens above you will be brass, the earth beneath you iron. ²⁴ Your country's rain Yahweh will turn into dust and sand; it will fall on you from the heavens until you perish. ²⁵ Yahweh will have you defeated by your enemies; you will advance on them from one direction and flee from them in seven; and you will be a terrifying object-lesson to all the kingdoms of the world. ²⁶ Your carcass will be carrion for all wild birds and all wild animals, with no one to scare them away.

²⁷ 'Yahweh will strike you down with Egyptian ulcers, with swellings in the groin, with scurvy and the itch, for which you will find no cure. ²⁸ Yahweh will strike you down with madness, blindness, distraction of mind, ²⁹ until you grope your way at noon like a blind man groping in the dark, and your steps will lead you nowhere.

'You will never be anything but exploited and plundered, with no one to save you. ³⁰ Get engaged to a woman, another man will have her; build a house, you will not live in it; plant a vineyard, you will not gather its first-fruits. ³¹ Your ox will be slaughtered before your eyes and you will eat none of it; your donkey will be carried off in front of you and not be returned to you; your sheep will be given to your enemies, and no one will come to your help. ³² Your sons and daughters will be handed over to another people, and every day you will wear your eyes out watching for them, while your hands are powerless. ³³ A nation hitherto unknown to you will eat the yield of your soil and of all your hard work. You will never be anything but exploited and crushed. ³⁴ You will be driven mad by the sights you will see. ³⁵ Yahweh will strike you down with foul ul-

cers on knee and leg, for which you will find no cure—from the sole of your foot to the top of your head.

³⁶ 'Yahweh will send away both you and the king whom you have appointed to rule you to a nation unknown either to you or to your ancestors, and there you will serve other gods, made of wood and stone. ³⁷ And you will be the astonishment, the byword, the laughing-stock of all the peoples where Yahweh is taking you.

³⁸ 'You will cast seed in plenty on the fields but harvest little, since the locust will devour it. ³⁹ You will plant and till your vineyards but not drink the wine or gather the grapes, since the grub will eat them up. ⁴⁰ You will grow olive trees throughout your territory but not anoint yourself with the oil, since your olive trees will be cut down. ⁴¹ You will father sons and daughters but they will not belong to you, since they will go into captivity. ⁴² All your trees and the whole yield of your soil will be the prey of insects.

⁴³ 'The foreigners living with you will rise higher and higher at your expense, while you yourself sink lower and lower. ⁴⁴ You will be subject to them, not they to you; they will be the ones at the head, and you the one at the tail.

⁴⁵ 'All these curses will befall you, pursue you and overtake you until you have been destroyed, for not having obeyed the voice of Yahweh your God by keeping his commandments and laws which he has laid down for you. ⁴⁶ They will be a sign and a wonder over you and your descendants for ever.

Of war and exile to come

⁴⁷ 'For not having joyfully and with happy heart served Yahweh your God, despite the abundance of everything, ⁴⁸ you will have to serve the enemy whom Yahweh will send against you, in hunger, thirst, lack of clothing and total privation. He will put an iron yoke on your neck, until he has destroyed you. ⁴⁹ Against you Yahweh will raise a distant nation from the ends of the earth like an eagle taking wing: a nation whose language you do

not understand, [50] a nation grim of face, with neither respect for the old, nor pity for the young. [51] He will eat the yield of your cattle and the yield of your soil until you have been destroyed; he will leave you neither wheat, nor wine, nor oil, nor the young of your cattle, nor increase of your flock, until he has made an end of you. [52] He will besiege you inside all your towns until your loftiest and most strongly fortified walls collapse, on which, throughout your country, you have relied. He will besiege you inside all the towns through-out your country, given you by Yahweh your God. [53] During the siege and in the distress to which your enemy will reduce you, you will eat the offspring of your own body, the flesh of the sons and daughters given you by Yahweh your God. [54] The gentlest and tenderest of your men will scowl at his brother, and at the wife whom he embraces, and at his remaining children, [55] not willing to give any of them any of his own children's flesh, which he is eating; because of the siege and the distress to which your enemy will reduce you in all your towns, he will have nothing left. [56] The most refined and fastidious of your women, so refined, so fastidious that she has never ventured to set the sole of her foot to the ground, will scowl at the husband whom she embraces, and at her son and daughter, and at the after-birth when it leaves her womb, and at the child to which she has given birth— [57] she will hide away and eat them, so complete will be the starvation re-sulting from the siege and the distress to which your enemy will reduce you in all your towns.

[58] 'If you do not keep and observe all the words of this Law, which are written in this book, in the fear of this glorious and awe-inspiring name: Yahweh your God, [59] Yahweh will strike you down with monstrous plagues, you and your descendants: with plagues griev-ous and lasting, diseases pernicious and en-during. [60] He will afflict you with all the mal-adies of Egypt which you used to dread, and they will fasten on you. [61] What is more, Yah-weh will afflict you with all the plagues and all the diseases not mentioned in the book of this Law, until you have been destroyed. [62] There will only be a small group of you left, you who were once as numerous as the stars of heaven.

'For not having obeyed the voice of Yahweh your God, [63] just as Yahweh used to delight in making you happy and in making your num-bers grow, so will he take delight in ruining you and destroying you. You will be torn from the country which you are about to enter and make your own. [64] Yahweh will scatter you throughout every people, from one end of the earth to the other; there you will serve other gods made of wood and stone, hitherto un-known either to you or to your ancestors. [65] Among these nations there will be no repose for you, no rest for the sole of your foot; there Yahweh will give you a quaking heart, weary eyes, halting breath. [66] Your life ahead of you will hang in doubt; you will be afraid day and night, uncertain of your life. [67] In the morning you will say, "How I wish it were evening!", and in the evening you will say, "How I wish it were morning!", such terror will grip your heart and such sights you will see! [68] Yahweh will send you back to Egypt, either by ship or by a road which I promised you would never see again. And there you will want to offer yourselves for sale to your enemies as serving men and women, but no one will buy you.'

The third discourse

[69] These are the words of the covenant which Yahweh ordered Moses to make with the Is-raelites in Moab, in addition to the covenant which he had made with them at Horeb.

Historical introduction

29 Moses called all Israel together and said to them:
'You have seen everything that Yahweh did before your eyes in Egypt, to Pharaoh, to his servants and to his whole country— [2] the great ordeals which you yourselves witnessed, those signs and the great wonders. [3] But until today Yahweh has not given you a heart to under-stand, eyes to see, or ears to hear.

4 'I have been leading you for forty years in the desert, yet the clothes which you have been wearing have not worn out, nor have the sandals on your feet. 5 You have had no bread to eat, you have had no wine or fermented liquor to drink, so that you would learn that I, Yahweh, am your God.

6 'When you reached this place, Sihon king of Heshbon and Og king of Bashan came out to do battle against us; we defeated them. 7 We conquered their country and gave it as heritage to Reuben, Gad and the half-tribe of Manasseh.

8 'Keep the words of this covenant, put them into practice, and you will thrive in everything you do.

The covenant in Moab

9 'All of you are standing here today in the presence of Yahweh your God: your tribal leaders, your elders, your scribes, all the men of Israel, 10 with your children and your wives (and the foreigner too who is in your camp, be he your wood-cutter or your water-carrier), 11 and you are about to pass into the covenant of Yahweh your God, sworn with imprecation, which he has made with you today, 12 and by which, today, he makes you a nation for himself and he himself becomes a God to you, as he has promised you, and as he swore to your ancestors Abraham, Isaac and Jacob. 13 Not only on your behalf am I today making this covenant and pronouncing this solemn curse, 14 not only on behalf of those standing here with us in the presence of Yahweh our God today, but also on behalf of those not here with us today.

15 'Yes, you know the people with whom we used to live in Egypt, and those through whose countries we have travelled—the nations through whom we have passed. 16 You have seen their abominations and their idols made of wood and stone, silver and gold, which were there.

17 'Let there be no man or woman of you, no clan or tribe, whose heart turns away from Yahweh your God today, to go and serve the gods of these nations. Among you let there be no root which bears poison or wormwood. 18 If, after hearing this imprecation, anyone, blessing himself, should say in his heart, "I shall do well enough if I follow the dictates of my heart; much water drives away thirst," 19 Yahweh will not pardon him. The wrath and jealousy of Yahweh will blaze against such a person; every curse written in this book will fall on him, and Yahweh will blot his name out under heaven. 20 Yahweh will single him out of all the tribes of Israel for misfortune, in accordance with all the curses of the covenant written in the book of this Law.

A threat of exile

21 'The future generation, that of your children coming after you, and the foreigner arriving from some far-away land, on seeing the plagues and diseases inflicted on this country by Yahweh, will exclaim, 22 "Sulphur! Salt!— The whole country is burning! No one will sow, nothing grow, no vegetation spring ever again! Devastation like that of Sodom and Gomorrah, Admah and Zeboiim, devastated by Yahweh in his furious wrath!" 23 And all the nations will exclaim, "Why has Yahweh treated this country like this? Why this great blaze of anger?"

24 'And people will say, "Because they deserted the covenant of Yahweh, God of their ancestors, the covenant which he made with them when he brought them out of Egypt; 25 because they went and served other gods and worshipped them, gods hitherto unknown to them, gods that were no part of their heritage from him: 26 this is why Yahweh's anger has blazed against this country, afflicting it with all the curses written in this book: 27 In anger, in fury, in fierce wrath, Yahweh has torn them from their own country and flung them into another country, where they are today." 28 Things hidden belong to Yahweh our God, but things revealed are ours and our children's for ever, so that we can put all the words of this Law into practice.'

Return from exile and conversion

30 'And when all these words have come true for you—the blessing and the curse, which I have offered you—if you meditate on them in your heart wherever among the nations Yahweh your God has driven you, ²if you return to Yahweh your God, if with all your heart and with all your soul you obey his voice, you and your children, in everything that I am laying down for you today, ³then Yahweh your God will bring back your captives, he will have pity on you and gather you back from all the peoples among whom Yahweh your God has scattered you. ⁴Should you have been banished to the very sky's end, Yahweh your God will gather you again even from there, will come there to reclaim you ⁵and bring you back to the country which belonged to your ancestors, so that you may possess it in your turn, and be made prosperous there and more numerous than your ancestors.

⁶'Yahweh your God will circumcise your heart and the heart of your descendants, so that you will love Yahweh your God with all your heart and soul, and so will live. ⁷Yahweh your God will make all these curses recoil on your foes and on your enemies who have persecuted you. ⁸And once again you will obey the voice of Yahweh your God and you will put all his commandments into practice, which I am laying down for you today. ⁹Yahweh your God will make you prosper in all your labours, in the offspring of your body, in the yield of your cattle and in the yield of your soil. For once again Yahweh will delight in your prosperity as he used to take delight in the prosperity of your ancestors, ¹⁰if you obey the voice of Yahweh your God, by keeping his commandments and decrees written in the book of this Law, and if you return to Yahweh your God with all your heart and soul.

¹¹'For this Law which I am laying down for you today is neither obscure for you nor beyond your reach. ¹²It is not in heaven, so that you need to wonder, "Who will go up to heaven for us and bring it down to us, so that we can hear and practise it?" ¹³Nor is it beyond the seas, so that you need to wonder, "Who will cross the seas for us and bring it back to us, so that we can hear and practise it?" ¹⁴No, the word is very near to you, it is in your mouth and in your heart for you to put into practice.

The two ways

¹⁵'Look, today I am offering you life and prosperity, death and disaster. ¹⁶If you obey the commandments of Yahweh your God, which I am laying down for you today, if you love Yahweh your God and follow his ways, if you keep his commandments, his laws and his customs, you will live and grow numerous, and Yahweh your God will bless you in the country which you are about to enter and make your own. ¹⁷But if your heart turns away, if you refuse to listen, if you let yourself be drawn into worshipping other gods and serving them, ¹⁸I tell you today, you will most certainly perish; you will not live for long in the country which you are crossing the Jordan to enter and possess. ¹⁹Today, I call heaven and earth to witness against you: I am offering you life or death, blessing or curse. Choose life, then, so that you and your descendants may live, ²⁰in the love of Yahweh your God, obeying his voice, holding fast to him; for in this your life consists, and on this depends the length of time that you stay in the country which Yahweh swore to your ancestors Abraham, Isaac and Jacob that he would give them.'

The commissioning of Joshua

31 Moses went and spoke to all Israel as follows, ²'Today, I am one hundred and twenty years old, and can no longer act as leader. Yahweh has told me, "You shall not cross this Jordan." ³Yahweh your God himself will lead you across, he himself will destroy and dispossess these nations confronting you; Joshua too will lead you across, as Yahweh has said. ⁴Yahweh will treat them as he has treated

19 READ DEUTERONOMY 30.

Look, today I am offering you life and prosperity, death and disaster.
—DEUTERONOMY 30:15

CHOOSE LIFE

The whole virtue of faith appears to consist in two things: first, we must believe most firmly what God promises is true. Secondly, we must be deeply convinced that what God threatens is not false.

Believe with your whole heart and mind that after good works you will obtain the reward promised. Similarly, believe without any hesitation whatever that if you have done evil you will suffer eternal punishment. Then you may know that your faith is entire, provided that you fulfill by deeds what you believe in your heart, and without delay turn away from evil to do good.

In turning away from evil you believe that there is punishment. In doing good you believe that you will attain to a reward. You must, however, realize that you derive no benefit from believing the one and doubting the other. It is profitable to turn away from evil only if one immediately does good. Likewise, it is advantageous to do good only if one completely turns away from evil. I mention this because there are many people who appear to give alms as the result of robbery and fraud, yet are unwilling to give up these evils. . . . If you wish to do good and evil at the same time, what can you gain from building up on one side and tearing down on the other, stealing from one person and clothing another? . . .

The whole virtue of faith . . . is to believe what God promises and what he threatens. So, if we want perfect faith to dwell in us, we must avoid evil out of fear of punishment and strive with all our might to do good out of desire for reward. Then we will not be obliged to endure everlasting punishment with unbelievers and the wicked, but will deserve to receive never-ending recompense together with the faithful who persevere in good works. ST. CAESARIUS OF ARLES, 470–543

YOU WILL FIND THE NEXT READING AT JOSHUA 2.

Sihon and Og the Amorite kings and their country—he destroyed them. ⁵Yahweh will put them at your mercy, and you will deal with them exactly as prescribed by the commandments which I have laid down for you. ⁶Be strong, stand firm, have no fear, do not be afraid of them, for Yahweh your God is going with you; he will not fail you or desert you.'

⁷Moses then summoned Joshua and, in the presence of all Israel, said to him, 'Be strong, stand firm; you will be the one to go with this people into the country which Yahweh has sworn to their ancestors that he would give them; you are to be the one who puts them into possession of it. ⁸Yahweh himself will lead you; he will be with you; he will not fail you or desert you. Have no fear, do not be alarmed.'

The ritual reading of the Law

⁹Moses committed this Law to writing and gave it to the priests, the sons of Levi, who carried the ark of Yahweh's covenant, and to all the elders of Israel. ¹⁰And Moses gave them this command, 'At the end of every seven

years, at the time fixed for the year of remission, at the feast of Shelters, ¹¹ when all Israel assembles in the presence of Yahweh your God in the place chosen by him, you must proclaim this Law in the hearing of all Israel. ¹²Call the people together, men, women, children, and the foreigner residing with you, so that, hearing it, they may learn to fear Yahweh your God and keep and observe all the words of this Law. ¹³Their children, who as yet do not know it, will hear it and learn to fear Yahweh your God, all the time you live in the country which you are crossing the Jordan to possess.'

Yahweh's instructions

¹⁴Yahweh said to Moses, 'And now the time is near when you must die. Summon Joshua and take your places at the Tent of Meeting, so that I can give him his orders.' Moses and Joshua went and took their places at the Tent of Meeting, ¹⁵and Yahweh showed himself at the Tent in a pillar of cloud; the pillar of cloud stood at the door of the Tent.

¹⁶Yahweh said to Moses, 'You will soon be sleeping with your ancestors, and this people is about to play the harlot by following the gods of the foreigners of the country, among whom they are going to live. They will desert me and break my covenant, which I have made with them. ¹⁷That very day, my anger will blaze against them; I shall desert them and hide my face from them. A host of disasters and misfortunes will overtake them to devour them, and when that day comes they will say, "If such disasters overtake me, surely Yahweh my God cannot be with me?" ¹⁸Yes indeed, I shall hide my face that day, on account of all the evil which they will have done by turning to other gods.

The song of witness

¹⁹'Now write down this song for you to use; teach it to the Israelites, put it into their mouths, for it to be a witness on my behalf against the Israelites: ²⁰against Israel, whom I am bringing into the country which I swore to his ancestors that I would give him, a country flowing with milk and honey: against Israel, who will eat to his heart's content and grow fat, and will then turn to other gods and serve them, despising me and breaking my covenant. ²¹When a host of disasters and misfortunes overtakes him, this song, like a witness, will give evidence against him, since his descendants will not have forgotten it. Yes, even today, before I have brought him to the country which I have promised him on oath, I know what plans he has in mind.' ²²So, that day, Moses wrote out this song and taught it to the Israelites.

²³To Joshua son of Nun, Yahweh gave this order, 'Be strong and stand firm, for you are to be the one to bring the Israelites into the country which I have promised them on oath, and I myself shall be with you.'

The Law placed beside the ark

²⁴When Moses had completely finished writing the words of this Law in a book, ²⁵he gave this command to the Levites who carried the ark of Yahweh's covenant: ²⁶'Take the book of this Law and put it beside the ark of the covenant of Yahweh your God. Let it lie there as evidence against you. ²⁷For I know how rebellious and stiff-necked you are. If today, while I am still alive and with you, you rebel against Yahweh, how much more will you rebel against him after my death!

Israel assembles to hear the song

²⁸'Gather all your tribal elders and scribes round me, so that I may be sure that they hear these words, as I call heaven and earth to witness against them. ²⁹For I know that after my death you are certain to grow corrupt; you will leave the way which I have marked out for you; in the final days disaster will befall you for having done what is evil in Yahweh's eyes, for having provoked his anger by your behaviour.'

³⁰In the hearing of the whole assembly of Israel, Moses then recited the words of this song to the end:

32 Listen, heavens, while I speak;
hear, earth, the words that I shall say!
[2] May my teaching fall like the rain,
may my word drop down like the dew,
like showers on the grass,
like light rain on the turf!
[3] For I shall proclaim the name of Yahweh.
Oh, tell the greatness of our God!

[4] He is the Rock, his work is perfect,
for all his ways are equitable.
A trustworthy God who does no wrong,
he is the Honest, the Upright One!
[5] They have acted perversely, those he
fathered without blemish,
a deceitful and underhand brood.
[6] Is this the return you make to Yahweh?
O people brainless and unwise!
Is this not your father, who gave you
being,
who made you, by whom you subsist?
[7] Think back on the days of old,
think over the years, down the ages.
Question your father, let him explain
to you,
your elders, and let them tell you!
[8] When the Most High gave the nations
each their heritage,
when he partitioned out the human
race,
he assigned the boundaries of nations
according to the number of the children
of God,
[9] but Yahweh's portion was his people,
Jacob was to be the measure of his
inheritance.

[10] In the desert he finds him,
in the howling expanses of the wastelands.
He protects him, rears him, guards him
as the pupil of his eye.
[11] Like an eagle watching its nest,
hovering over its young,
he spreads out his wings to hold him,
he supports him on his pinions.

[12] Yahweh alone is his guide;
no alien god for him!

[13] He gives him the heights of the land to
ride,
he feeds him on the yield of the
mountains,
he gives him honey from the rock to taste,
and oil from the flinty crag;
[14] curds from the cattle, milk from the flock,
and the richness of the pasture,
rams of Bashan's breed, and goats,
the richness of the wheat kernel;
the fermented blood of the grape for
drink.

[15] Jacob has eaten to his heart's content,
Jeshurun,[a] grown fat, has now lashed out.
(You have grown fat, gross, bloated.)
He has disowned the God who made him,
and dishonoured the Rock, his salvation,
[16] whose jealousy they aroused with
foreigners—
with things detestable they angered him.
[17] They sacrificed to demons who are not
God,
to gods hitherto unknown to them,
to newcomers of yesterday
whom their ancestors had never respected.
[18] (You forget the Rock who fathered you,
the God who made you, you no longer
remember.)
[19] Yahweh saw it and, in anger,
he spurned his sons and daughters.
[20] 'I shall hide my face from them,' he said,
'and see what will become of them.
For they are a deceitful brood,
children with no loyalty in them.
[21] They have roused me to jealousy with a
non-god,
they have exasperated me with their
idols.
In my turn I shall rouse them to jealousy
with a non-people,
I shall exasperate them with a stupid
nation.
[22] Yes, a fire has blazed from my anger,

32a A name for Israel (also in 33:5) of uncertain sense and
origin.

it will burn right down to the depths of
    Sheol;
it will devour the earth and all its produce,
it will set fire to the footings of the
    mountains.
23 I shall hurl disasters on them,
    on them I shall use up all my arrows.
24 They will be weakened by hunger,
    eaten away by plague and the bitter
        scourge.
    Against them I shall send the fang of wild
        animals
    and the poison of snakes that glide in the
        dust.
25 Outside, the sword bereaves,
    while inside terror will reign.
    Young man and girl alike will perish,
    suckling and greybeard both together.
26 I should crush them to dust, I said,
    I should wipe out all memory of them,
27 did I not fear the boasting of the enemy.'
    But do not let their foes be mistaken!
    Do not let them say, 'We have got the
        upper hand
    and Yahweh plays no part in this.'
28 What a short-sighted nation this is,
    how thoroughly imperceptive!
29 Were they wise, they would succeed,
    they would be able to read their destiny.
30 How else could one man rout a thousand,
    how could two put ten thousand to flight,
    were it not that their Rock has sold them,
    that Yahweh has delivered them up?

31 But their rock is not like our Rock;
    our enemies cannot pray for us!
32 For their vine springs from the stock of
    Sodom
    and from the groves of Gomorrah:
    their grapes are poisonous grapes,
    their clusters are bitter;
33 their wine is snakes' poison,
    the vipers' cruel venom.
34 But he, is he not safe with me,
    sealed inside my treasury?
35 Vengeance is mine, I will pay them back,
    for the time when they make a false step.

For the day of their ruin is close,
    doom is rushing towards them,
    for he will see to it that their power fails,
    that neither serf nor free man remains.
36 (For Yahweh will see his people righted,
    he will take pity on his servants.)
37 'Where are their gods then?' he will ask,
    'the rock where they sought refuge,
38 who ate the fat of their sacrifices
    and drank the wine of their libations?'
    Let these arise and help you,
    let these be the shelter above you!
39 See now that I, I am he,
    and beside me there is no other god.
    It is I who deal death and life;
    when I have struck, it is I who heal
    (no one can rescue anyone from me).

40 Yes, I raise my hand to heaven,
    and I say, 'As surely as I live for ever.
41 When I have whetted my flashing sword,
    I shall enforce justice,
    I shall return vengeance to my foes,
    I shall take vengeance on my foes.
42 I shall make my arrows drunk with blood,
    and my sword will feed on flesh:
    the blood of the wounded and the
        prisoners,
    the dishevelled heads of the enemy!'

43 Heavens, rejoice with him,
    let all the children of God pay him
        homage!
    Nations, rejoice with his people,
    let God's envoys tell of his power!
    For he will avenge the blood of his
        servants,
    he will return vengeance to my foes,
    he will repay those who hate him
    and purify his people's country.

44 Moses came with Joshua son of Nun and
recited all the words of this song in the people's hearing.

The Law, the source of life

45 When Moses had finished reciting these
words to all Israel, 46 he said to them, 'Take all

these words to heart; I intend them today to be evidence against you. You must order your children to keep and observe all the words of this Law. ⁴⁷ You must not think of this as empty words, for the Law is your life, and by its means you will live long in the country which you are crossing the Jordan to possess.'

Moses' death foretold

⁴⁸ Yahweh spoke to Moses that same day and said to him, ⁴⁹ 'Climb this mountain of the Abarim, Mount Nebo, in the country of Moab, opposite Jericho, and view the Canaan which I am giving to the Israelites as their domain. ⁵⁰ Die on the mountain you have climbed, and be gathered to your people, as your brother Aaron died on Mount Hor and was gathered to his people. ⁵¹ Because, with the other Israelites, you broke faith with me at the Waters of Meribah-Kadesh in the desert of Zin, because you did not make my holiness clear to the Israelites; ⁵² you may only see the country from outside; you cannot enter it—the country which I am giving to the Israelites.'

Moses blesses the tribes

33 This is the blessing that Moses, man of God, pronounced over the Israelites before he died. ² He said:

Yahweh came from Sinai,
from Seir he dawned on us,
from Mount Paran blazed forth.
For them he came, after the mustering at
        Kadesh,
from his zenith as far as the foothills.

³ You who love the ancestors!
Your holy ones are all at your command.
At your feet they fell,
under your guidance went swiftly on.

⁴ (Moses enjoined a law on us.)
The assembly of Jacob comes into its
        inheritance;
⁵ there was a king in Jeshurun
when the heads of the people foregathered
and the tribes of Israel were all assembled!

⁶ May Reuben survive and not die out,
survive though his men be few!

⁷ Of Judah he said this:
Listen, Yahweh, to the voice of Judah,
and bring him back to his people.
That his hands may defend his rights,
come to his help against his foes!

⁸ Of Levi he said:
To Levi, give your *urim,*
to your faithful one, your *thummim,*
having tested him at Massah,
having striven with him at the Waters of
        Meribah.
⁹ Of his father and mother, he says,
'I have not seen them.'
He does not acknowledge his brothers,
nor does he know his own children.
Yes, they have kept your word,
they hold firmly to your covenant.
¹⁰ They will teach your customs to Jacob,
and your Law to Israel.
They will put incense before you
and burnt offerings on your altar.
¹¹ Yahweh, bless his worthiness,
and accept the actions he performs.
Crush the loins of those who rise against
        him
and of his foes, so that they rise no more!

¹² Of Benjamin he said:
Beloved of Yahweh, he rests trustfully near
        him.
The Most High protects him day after day
and dwells between his hillsides.

¹³ Of Joseph he said:
His land is blessed by Yahweh.
For him the best of heaven's dew
and of the deep that lies below,
¹⁴ the best of what the sun makes grow,
of what springs with every month,
¹⁵ the first-fruits of the ancient mountains,
the best from the hills of old
¹⁶ the best of the land and all it holds,
the favour of him who dwells in the Bush.

May the hair grow thick on the head of
    Joseph,
on the brow of the consecrated one among
    his brothers!
¹⁷ First-born of the Bull, his the glory.
His horns are the wild ox's horns,
with which he gores the peoples
to the very ends of the earth.
Such are the myriads of Ephraim,
such are the thousands of Manasseh.

¹⁸ Of Zebulun he said:
Prosper, Zebulun, in your expeditions,
and you, Issachar, in your tents!
¹⁹ On the mountain where the people come
    to pray
they offer upright sacrifices,
for they taste the riches of the seas
and the treasures hidden in the sands.

²⁰ Of Gad he said:
Blessed be he who gives Gad space
    enough!
He lies there like a lioness;
he has savaged arm and face and head.
²¹ Then he took the first portion for
    himself,
saw that there was stored up for him a
    leader's share.
He has come at the head of the people,
has carried out the saving justice of
    Yahweh
and his judgements on Israel.

²² Of Dan he said:
Dan is a lion cub
leaping from Bashan.

²³ Of Naphtali he said:
Naphtali, sated with favours,
filled with the blessings of Yahweh:
the west and south are to be his domain.

²⁴ Of Asher he said:
Most blessed of the sons let Asher be!
Let him be the most privileged of his
    brothers

and let him bathe his feet in oil!
²⁵ Be your bolts of iron and of bronze
and your security as lasting as your days!

²⁶ No one is like the God of Jeshurun:
he rides the heavens to your rescue,
rides the clouds in his majesty!
²⁷ The God of old is your refuge,
his the eternal arm which here below
drives the enemy before you;
he it is who says, 'Destroy!'
²⁸ Israel rests trustfully.
The well-spring of Jacob is chosen out
for a land of corn and wine;
there heaven itself rains down dew.
²⁹ Blessed are you, O Israel!
Who is like you, O victorious people?
Yahweh is the shield that protects you
and the sword that leads you to triumph.
Your enemies will try to corrupt you,
but you yourself will trample on their
    backs.

The death of Moses

34 Then, leaving the Plains of Moab, Moses went up Mount Nebo, the peak of Pisgah opposite Jericho, and Yahweh showed him the whole country: Gilead as far as Dan, ² the whole of Naphtali, the country of Ephraim and Manasseh, the whole country of Judah as far as the Western Sea, ³ the Negeb, and the region of the Valley of Jericho, city of palm trees, as far as Zoar. ⁴ Yahweh said to him, 'This is the country which I promised on oath to give to Abraham, Isaac and Jacob, saying: I shall give it to your descendants. I have allowed you to see it for yourself, but you will not cross into it.'

⁵ There in the country of Moab, Moses, servant of Yahweh, died as Yahweh decreed; ⁶ he[a] buried him in the valley, in the country of Moab, opposite Beth-Peor; but to this day no one has ever found his grave. ⁷ Moses was a hundred and twenty years old when he died, his eye undimmed, his vigour unimpaired.

34a i.e. Yahweh, but Sam. and some Greek texts read 'they'.

⁸ The Israelites wept for Moses on the Plains of Moab for thirty days. The days of weeping for the mourning rites of Moses came to an end. ⁹ Joshua son of Nun was filled with the spirit of wisdom, for Moses had laid his hands on him, and him the Israelites obeyed, carrying out the order which Yahweh had given to Moses.

¹⁰ Since then, there has never been such a prophet in Israel as Moses, the man whom Yahweh knew face to face. ¹¹ What signs and wonders Yahweh caused him to perform in Egypt against Pharaoh, all his servants and his whole country! ¹² How mighty the hand and great the fear that Moses wielded in the eyes of all Israel!

The Book of
JOSHUA

The summons to enter the Promised Land

1 When Moses, servant of Yahweh, was dead, Yahweh spoke to Joshua son of Nun, Moses' adjutant. He said, ²'Moses my servant is dead; go now and cross this Jordan, you and this whole people, into the country which I am giving to them (the Israelites). ³Every place you tread with the soles of your feet I shall give you, as I declared to Moses that I would. ⁴From the desert and the Lebanon, to the Great River, the Euphrates (the entire country of the Hittites), and as far as the Great Sea to westward, is to be your territory. ⁵As long as you live, no one will be able to resist you; I shall be with you as I was with Moses; I shall not fail you or desert you.

God's help conditional on faithfulness to the Law

⁶'Be strong and stand firm, for you are the man to give this people possession of the land which I swore to their ancestors that I would give them. ⁷Only be strong and stand very firm and be careful to keep the whole Law which my servant Moses laid down for you. Do not swerve from this either to right or to left, and then you will succeed wherever you go. ⁸Have the book of this Law always on your lips; meditate on it day and night, so that you may carefully keep everything that is written in it. Then your undertakings will prosper, then you will have success. ⁹Have I not told you: Be strong and stand firm? Be fearless and undaunted, for go where you may, Yahweh your God is with you.'

Support from the Transjordanian tribes

¹⁰Joshua then gave the people's officials this instruction: ¹¹'Go through the camp and give the people this order, "Make provisions ready, for in three days' time you will cross this Jordan and go on to take possession of the land which Yahweh your God is giving you as your own." ' ¹²Joshua then said to the Reubenites and Gadites and the half-tribe of Manasseh, ¹³'Remember the order given you by Moses, servant of Yahweh: Yahweh your God, in bringing you to rest, has given you the land where we are. ¹⁴Your wives, your little ones and your cattle must stay in the country given you by Moses beyond the Jordan. But all you fighting men must cross in battle formation at the head of your brothers and help them, ¹⁵until Yahweh grants rest to your brothers and you alike, when they too have taken possession of the land which Yahweh your God is giving to them. Then you may go back and take possession of the land which belongs to you and which Moses, servant of Yahweh, has given you on the eastern side of the Jordan.' ¹⁶They answered Joshua, 'We will do whatever you order us, and wherever you send us we will go. ¹⁷We obeyed Moses in everything, and now we will obey you. Only may Yahweh your God be with you as he was with Moses! ¹⁸If anyone rebels against your orders or will not listen to your commands, let him be put to death. Only be strong and stand firm.'

Joshua's spies at Jericho

2 From Shittim, Joshua son of Nun secretly sent two men to reconnoitre. He said, 'Go and explore the country and Jericho.' They left; they went into the house of a prostitute called Rahab, to spend the night there. ² The king of Jericho was told, 'Some men have come here tonight from the Israelites, to reconnoitre the country.' ³ The king of Jericho then sent a message to Rahab, 'Send out the men who came to you and are lodging in your house, for they have come to reconnoitre the whole country.' ⁴ But the woman took the two men and hid them. 'It is true,' she said, 'the men did come to me, but I did not know where they came from. ⁵ When the city gate was about to be closed at nightfall, the men went out and I cannot say where they have gone. Follow them quickly and you will overtake them.'

⁶ She had taken them up to the roof and hidden them under some stalks of flax which she had laid out there. ⁷ The men hurried in pursuit of them towards the Jordan, as far as the fords, and the gate was shut once the pursuers had gone through.

The pact between Rahab and the spies

⁸ The two men had not yet settled down for the night when Rahab came up to them on the roof. ⁹ She said to them, 'I know that Yahweh has given you this country, that we are afraid of you and that everyone living in this country has been seized with terror at your approach; ¹⁰ for we have heard how Yahweh dried up the Sea of Reeds before you when you came out of Egypt and what you did to the two Amorite kings across the Jordan, Sihon and Og, whom you put under the curse of destruction. ¹¹ When we heard this, our hearts failed us, and now no one has any courage left to resist you, since Yahweh your God is God both in heaven above and on earth beneath. ¹² So, swear to me now by Yahweh, since I have been kind to you, ¹³ that you in your turn will be kind to my father's family; and give me a sure sign of this: that you will spare the lives of my father and mother, my brothers and sisters and all who belong to them, and will preserve us from death.'

¹⁴ The men replied, 'We pledge you our lives, provided that you say nothing about our mission. When Yahweh has given us the country, we shall treat you kindly and faithfully.' ¹⁵ She then let them down from the window on a rope, as her house was against the city wall and she actually lived in the wall. ¹⁶ 'Make for the hills,' she said, 'or you may run into your pursuers. Hide there for three days, until your pursuers have come back, and then go on your way.' ¹⁷ The men said, 'This is how we shall fulfil the oath which you have made us swear: ¹⁸ when we invade the country, you must tie this scarlet cord to the window from which you let us down, and collect your father, mother, brothers and entire family inside your house. ¹⁹ If anyone goes out of the doors of your house into the street, his blood will be on his own head and we shall not be to blame; but the blood of all staying inside the house with you will be on our heads if a hand is laid on any of them. ²⁰ But if you divulge our mission in the meanwhile, we shall be free of the oath which you have made us swear.' ²¹ She replied, 'Let it be as you say.' She let them go, and they left. She then tied the scarlet cord to the window.

The spies return

²² They left and made for the hills. They stayed there for three days, until their pursuers had gone home, having scoured the countryside without finding them. ²³ The two men then came down again from the hills, crossed over and, going to Joshua son of Nun, told him everything that had happened to them. ²⁴ To Joshua they said, 'Yahweh has put the whole country at our mercy, and its inhabitants are all panic-stricken at our approach.'

Before the crossing of the Jordan

3 Early in the morning, Joshua struck camp and set out from Shittim with all the Israelites. They went as far as the Jordan and there they camped before they crossed. ² Three days later, the officials went through the camp ³ and gave the people these instructions,

20 READ JOSHUA 2:1–21.

Swear to me now by Yahweh, since I have been kind to you, that you in your turn will be kind to my father's family.—JOSHUA 2:12–13

KINDNESS FOR KINDNESS

Because of her faith and hospitality, Rahab the harlot was saved. For when spies had been sent to Jericho by Joshua the son of Nun, the king of the land knew that they had come to spy on his country and sent men to capture them, so that when they were taken they might be put to death.

The hospitable Rahab received them and concealed them on the roof of her house under stalks of flax. Then when the men from the king appeared and said: "The men who were spying on our land came into your house; bring them out, for the king has ordered it," she replied, pointing in the opposite direction: "The men whom you are seeking did in fact come to my house; however, they left immediately and are continuing on their journey."

But to the spies she said: "I know for sure that the Lord God is giving you this land. . . . So when you have captured it, save me and my father's house." They said: "We will do as you requested. . . . Gather all your people under your roof and they will be saved. . . ." Then they gave her a sign, that she should hang from her house something scarlet in color. Thus, they clearly indicated beforehand that redemption would come through the blood of the Lord to all those who believe and hope in God. . . .

We should be especially mindful of the words that the Lord Jesus spoke when he taught clemency and long-suffering: "Be merciful, that you may obtain mercy. Forgive, that you may be forgiven. As you do, so shall it be done to you. As you give, so shall it be given to you. As you judge, so shall you be judged. As you are kind, so shall you be treated kindly. With what measure you measure, with the same shall it be measured to you" (see Mt 5:7; 6:14; 7:1, 12; Lk 6:31, 36–38).

ST. CLEMENT OF ROME, d. 100?

YOU WILL FIND THE NEXT READING AT JOSHUA 3.

'When you see the ark of the covenant of Yahweh your God being carried by the levitical priests, you will leave your position and follow it, ⁴ᵇ so that you may know which way to take, since you have never gone this way before. ⁴ᵃ Between you and the ark, however, keep a distance of about two thousand cubits: do not go near it.' ⁵ Joshua said to the people, 'Sanctify yourselves, since tomorrow Yahweh will work wonders among you.' ⁶ Joshua then said to the priests, 'Take up the ark of the covenant and cross at the head of the people.' They took up the ark of the covenant and moved to the head of the people.

Final instructions

⁷ Yahweh said to Joshua, 'This very day, I shall begin to make you great in the eyes of all Israel so that they will know that, as I was with Moses, so I shall be with you. ⁸ Now, give this order to the priests carrying the ark of the covenant, "When you have reached the brink

21 READ JOSHUA 3.

All Israel crossed on dry ground, until the whole nation had completed its crossing of the Jordan.—JOSHUA 3:17

BAPTIZED INTO NEW LIFE

Too long have you rolled in the mire; hasten . . . at the voice of Christ to my Jerusalem. For indeed the river of grace flows everywhere.

It does not rise in Palestine to disappear into some nearby sea. It spreads over the whole earth and flows into paradise, flowing in the opposite direction of those four rivers which come from paradise and bringing in things far more precious than those which come forth.

Those rivers carry perfumes, the fruit of the culture and germination of the earth. This river brings in human beings, begotten of the Holy Spirit.

Wherever you draw water, there also does this river flow; it is diverted throughout the whole earth, and it does not consume its water in those places into which it is divided. For it has a rich source, Christ, and flowing out from him it inundates the entire world.

This river is delightful and drinkable, attracting nothing that is salty and unpleasant. It is rendered sweet by the Spirit's coming, like the fount of Marah by the touch of the wood (see Ex 15:23–25). It can be crossed by those who are devout, but it is too deep for those who are worldly-minded and cannot even be approached by them.

Imitate Joshua the son of Nun. Bear the gospel, as he bore the ark. Leave behind the desert, that is, sin. Cross the Jordan, and hasten to the life according to the commands of Christ. Hurry to that land which brings forth fruits of joy; where—as promised—there flow milk and honey.

All these things constitute types for us; and they all prefigure truths which have now been revealed. ST. GREGORY OF NYSSA, 330?–395?

YOU WILL FIND THE NEXT READING AT JUDGES 3.

of the waters of the Jordan, you must halt in the Jordan itself." ' ⁹To the Israelites, Joshua then said, 'Come closer and hear the words of Yahweh your God.' ¹⁰Joshua said, 'By this, you are to know that the living God is with you and without a doubt will expel the Canaanites, the Hittites, the Hivites, Perizzites, Girgashites, Amorites and Jebusites before you. ¹¹Look, the ark of the covenant of the Lord of the whole earth is about to move into the Jordan at your head. ¹²Now choose twelve men from the tribes of Israel, one man from each tribe. ¹³As soon as the priests carrying the ark of Yahweh, Lord of the whole earth, have set the soles of their feet in the waters of the Jordan, the waters of the Jordan will be cut off; the upper waters flowing down will stop as a single mass.'

Crossing the Jordan

¹⁴Accordingly, when the people left their tents to cross the Jordan, the priests carried the ark

of the covenant ahead of the people. ¹⁵As soon as the bearers of the ark reached the Jordan and the feet of the priests carrying the ark touched the waters—the Jordan is in spate throughout the harvest season—¹⁶the upper waters stood still and formed a single mass over a great distance, at Adam, the town near Zarethan, while those flowing down to the Sea of the Arabah, the Salt Sea, were completely separated. The people crossed opposite Jericho. ¹⁷The priests carrying the ark of the covenant of Yahweh stood firm on dry ground in mid-Jordan, while all Israel crossed on dry ground, until the whole nation had completed its crossing of the Jordan.

The twelve memorial stones

4 When the whole nation had finished crossing the Jordan, Yahweh spoke to Joshua and said, ²'Choose twelve men from the people, one man from each tribe, and give them this order, ³"Here, from mid-Jordan, from the place where the priests' feet were standing, take twelve stones; carry them with you and set them down in the camp where you pass the night."' ⁴Joshua called the twelve men whom he had selected from the Israelites, one man from each tribe, ⁵and Joshua said to them, 'Go on ahead of the ark of Yahweh your God into mid-Jordan, and each of you take one stone on his shoulder, corresponding to the number of the tribes of Israel, ⁶to make this a sign among you; and when, in the future, your children ask you, "What do these stones mean for you?" ⁷you will then tell them, "The waters of the Jordan separated before the ark of the covenant of Yahweh; when it crossed the Jordan, the waters of the river separated. These stones are an everlasting reminder of this to the Israelites."' ⁸The Israelites did as Joshua ordered; they took twelve stones from mid-Jordan corresponding to the number of the tribes of Israel, as Yahweh had told Joshua; they carried them over to the camp and set them down there. ⁹Joshua then erected twelve stones in mid-Jordan, on the spot where the feet of the priests carrying the ark of the covenant had stood; and they are still there today.

The crossing ends

¹⁰The priests carrying the ark stood still in mid-Jordan, until everything had been done that Yahweh had ordered Joshua to tell the people (in accordance with everything that Moses had ordered Joshua); and the people hurried across. ¹¹When the people had finished crossing, the ark of Yahweh then crossed, with the priests, to the head of the people. ¹²The sons of Reuben, the sons of Gad and the half-tribe of Manasseh crossed in battle formation at the head of the Israelites, as Moses had told them. ¹³Some forty thousand warriors in arms, they crossed in Yahweh's presence, ready for battle, towards the plain of Jericho. ¹⁴That day, Yahweh made Joshua great in the eyes of all Israel, who respected him as they had respected Moses, as long as he lived. ¹⁵Yahweh said to Joshua, ¹⁶'Order the priests carrying the ark of the Testimony to come up out of the Jordan.' ¹⁷And Joshua gave the order to the priests, 'Come up, out of the Jordan!' ¹⁸Now, when the priests carrying the ark of the covenant of Yahweh came up out of mid-Jordan, no sooner had the soles of the priests' feet touched solid ground, than the waters of the Jordan returned to their bed and ran on, in spate as before.

Arrival at Gilgal

¹⁹It was the tenth day of the first month when the people came up from the Jordan and made their camp at Gilgal, on the eastern border of Jericho. ²⁰As regards those twelve stones, which they had taken from the Jordan, Joshua set them up at Gilgal. ²¹He then said to the Israelites, 'When, in the future, your children ask their fathers, "What are these stones?" ²²you will explain to your children, "Israel crossed this Jordan dry-shod. ²³For Yahweh your God dried up the waters of the Jordan in front of you until you had crossed, just as Yahweh your God did to the Sea of Reeds, which he dried up before us

until we had crossed it; ²⁴so that all the peoples of the earth may know how mighty the hand of Yahweh is, and always stand in awe of Yahweh your God.'' '

Terror of the peoples west of the Jordan

5 When all the kings of the Amorites living to westward across the Jordan, and all the kings of the Canaanites living on the seaboard, heard that Yahweh had dried up the waters of the Jordan before the Israelites until they had crossed, their hearts failed and they lost all courage to resist the Israelites.

Circumcision of the Hebrews at Gilgal

²At this time Yahweh said to Joshua, 'Make flint knives and circumcise the Israelites again (a second time). ³Joshua made flint knives and circumcised the Israelites on the Hill of Foreskins.

⁴The reason why Joshua circumcised them was this. All the males of the people who had come out of Egypt of age to bear arms had died in the desert on their journey after leaving Egypt. ⁵Now, all the people who came out had been circumcised; but none of those born in the desert, during the journey, after leaving Egypt, had been circumcised; ⁶for the Israelites walked the desert for forty years, until the whole nation had died out, that is, the men who had come out of Egypt of age to bear arms; they had not obeyed the voice of Yahweh, and Yahweh had sworn to them never to let them see the land which he had sworn to their ancestors that he would give us, a land flowing with milk and honey. ⁷But in place of these he set their sons, and these were the ones whom Joshua circumcised: they were uncircumcised because they had not been circumcised during the journey. ⁸When the circumcising of the whole nation was finished, they stayed resting in the camp till they were well again. ⁹Yahweh then said to Joshua, 'Today I have taken the shame of Egypt away from you.' Hence, the place has been called Gilgal*a* ever since.

Celebration of the Passover

¹⁰The Israelites pitched their camp at Gilgal and kept the Passover there on the fourteenth day of the month, at evening, in the plain of Jericho. ¹¹On the very next day after the Passover, they ate what the land produced, unleavened bread and roasted ears of corn. ¹²The manna stopped the day after they had eaten the produce of the land. The Israelites from that year onwards ate the produce of Canaan and had no more manna.

Prelude to the conquest of Jericho: a theophany

¹³Now when Joshua was near Jericho, he looked up and saw a man standing in front of him, grasping a naked sword. Joshua walked towards him and said to him, 'Are you on our side or on that of our enemies?' ¹⁴He replied, 'On neither side. I have come now as the captain of the army of Yahweh.' Joshua fell on his face to the ground, worshipping him, and said, 'What has my Lord to say to his servant?' ¹⁵The captain of the army of Yahweh answered Joshua, 'Take your sandals off your feet, for the place where you are standing is holy.' And Joshua did so.

Capture of Jericho*a*

6 Now, Jericho had shut and barricaded its gates (against the Israelites): no one came out and no one went in. ²Yahweh then said to Joshua, 'Look, I am putting Jericho, its picked troops and its king, at your mercy. ³All you warriors must march round the city (go right round the city once, doing the same on six successive days. ⁴Seven priests must carry seven ram's-horn trumpets in front of the ark. On the seventh day, you will go seven times round the city and the priests will blow their trumpets). ⁵When the ram's horn sounds (when

5a Word-play with *galloti* (= I have taken away). In fact Gilgal = circle, cf. 4:20.

6a The Hebr. text is longer than the Gk, which omits passages given here in parentheses.

you hear the sound of the trumpet), the entire people must utter a mighty war cry and the city wall will collapse then and there; the people will then go into the assault, each man straight ahead.'

⁶Joshua son of Nun summoned the priests and said to them, 'Take up the ark of the covenant, and let seven priests carry seven ram's-horn trumpets ahead of the ark of Yahweh.' ⁷To the people he then said, 'Forward! March round the city, and let the vanguard march ahead of the ark of Yahweh!' ⁸(Everything was done as Joshua had given orders to the people.) Seven priests, carrying seven ram's-horn trumpets ahead of Yahweh, moved forward blowing their trumpets; the ark of the covenant of Yahweh came behind them, ⁹the vanguard marched ahead of the priests, who blew their trumpets, the rearguard followed behind the ark; the men marched, the trumpets sounded.

¹⁰Joshua had given the people the following orders, 'Do not raise a war cry, do not let your voice be heard (not a word must pass your lips), until the day when I say, "Raise the war cry." That is when you must raise the war cry.'

¹¹He made the ark go round the city (going round it once), then they went back to camp, where they spent the night. ¹²Joshua got up early, and the priests took up the ark of Yahweh. ¹³Carrying the seven ram's-horn trumpets, the seven priests walked ahead of the ark of Yahweh, blowing their trumpets as they went, while the vanguard marched ahead of them and the rearguard behind the ark of Yahweh, and the march went on to the sound of the trumpet.

¹⁴They marched once round the city (on the second day) and went back to camp; and so on for six days. ¹⁵On the seventh day, they got up at dawn and marched (in the same manner) round the city seven times. (This was the only day when they marched round the city seven times.) ¹⁶At the seventh time, the priests blew their trumpets and Joshua said to the people, 'Raise the war cry, for Yahweh has given you the city!

Jericho placed under the curse of destruction

¹⁷'The city and everyone in it must be devoted to Yahweh under the curse of destruction; the life of Rahab the prostitute alone must be spared, with all those with her in her house, since she hid the messengers we sent. ¹⁸But beware of the curse of destruction, yourselves, for fear that, moved by greed, you take something lying under the curse; that would put the camp of Israel under the same curse and bring disaster on it. ¹⁹All the silver and all the gold, everything made of bronze or iron, will be consecrated to Yahweh and put in his treasury.'

²⁰The people raised the war cry, the trumpets sounded. When the people heard the sound of the trumpet, they raised a mighty war cry and the wall collapsed then and there. At once the people stormed the city, each man going straight forward; and they captured the city. ²¹They enforced the curse of destruction on everyone in the city: men and women, young and old, including the oxen, the sheep and the donkeys, slaughtering them all.

Rahab's house preserved

²²Joshua said to the two men who had reconnoitred the country, 'Go into the prostitute's house, and bring the woman out with all who belong to her, as you swore to her that you would.' ²³The young men who had been spies went and brought Rahab out, with her father and mother and brothers and all who belonged to her. They brought out all her clansmen too, and put them in a place of safety outside the camp of Israel.

²⁴They burned the city and everything inside it, except the silver, the gold and the things of bronze and iron; these they put into the treasury of Yahweh's house. ²⁵But Rahab the prostitute, her father's family and all who belonged to her, these Joshua spared. She is still living in Israel even today, for having hidden the messengers whom Joshua sent to reconnoitre Jericho.

A curse on anyone who rebuilds Jericho

26 At that time Joshua made them take this oath before Yahweh:

> Accursed before Yahweh be the man who
> rises up
> and rebuilds this city (Jericho)!
> On his first-born will he lay its
> foundations,
> on his youngest son set up its gates!

27 So Yahweh was with Joshua, whose fame spread throughout the country.

Violation of the curse of destruction

7 But the Israelites were unfaithful to the curse of destruction. Achan son of Carmi, son of Zabdi, son of Zerah, of the tribe of Judah, took something that fell under the curse of destruction, and the anger of Yahweh was aroused against the Israelites.

The sacrilege punished by a repulse at Ai

2 Now Joshua sent men from Jericho to Ai[a] (which is near Beth-Aven), to the east of Bethel, having said to them, 'Go up and reconnoitre the country.' They went up and reconnoitred Ai. 3 Coming back to Joshua, they said, 'There is no need for the whole people to go up; let some two or three thousand go and attack Ai. Spare the whole people such an effort; there are only a few of them!' 4 Of the people, some three thousand marched up, but these broke before the people of Ai, 5 who killed some thirty-six of them and pursued them from the town gate as far as Shebarim, and on the slope cut them to pieces. The hearts of the people melted away and turned to water.

Joshua's prayer

6 Joshua then tore his clothes and prostrated himself before the ark of Yahweh till nightfall; the elders of Israel did the same, and all poured dust on their heads. 7 And Joshua said, 'Alas, Lord Yahweh, why did you bother to bring this nation across the Jordan, if it was only to put us at the mercy of the Amorites and destroy us? If only we could have settled down on the other side of the Jordan! 8 Forgive me, Lord, but what can I say, now that Israel has turned tail on the enemy? 9 The Canaanites, all the inhabitants of the land, will hear of it; they will unite against us to wipe our name from the earth. And what will you do about your great Name then?'

Yahweh's answer

10 Yahweh said to Joshua, 'Stand up! Why are you lying prostrate like this? 11 Israel has sinned; they have violated the covenant which I imposed on them. They have gone so far as to take what was under the curse of destruction, they have even stolen it; they have actually hidden it; they have put it in their baggage. 12 That is why the Israelites cannot stand up to their foes, why they have turned tail on their enemies: because they have come under the curse of destruction themselves. Unless you get rid of the object among you which has been put under the curse of destruction, I shall be with you no longer.'

13 'Get up, sanctify the people and say, "Sanctify yourselves for tomorrow, since Yahweh, the God of Israel, declares: The curse of destruction has now fallen on you, Israel; you will not be able to stand up to your enemies, until you have rid yourselves of that object which has been put under the curse of destruction. 14 Tomorrow morning, therefore, you will come forward tribe by tribe, and then the tribe which Yahweh selects by lot will come forward clan by clan, and the clan which Yahweh selects by lot will come forward family by family, and the family which Yahweh selects by lot will come forward man by man. 15 And the man indicated by lot as regards the object which has been put under the curse of destruction will be delivered to the flames, he and

7a The word *ai* = ruin, and the site is a spectacular ruin.

all his possessions, for having violated the covenant with Yahweh and for having committed an infamy in Israel." '

The culprit discovered and punished

16 Joshua got up early; he made Israel come forward tribe by tribe, and the lot indicated the tribe of Judah. 17 He summoned the clans of Judah, and the lot indicated the clan of Zerah. He summoned the clan of Zerah, family by family, and the lot indicated Zabdi. 18 Joshua then summoned the family of Zabdi, man by man, and the lot indicated Achan son of Carmi, son of Zabdi, son of Zerah, of the tribe of Judah.

19 Joshua then said to Achan, 'My son, give glory to Yahweh, God of Israel, and confess; tell me what you have done and hide nothing from me.' 20 Achan replied to Joshua, 'Yes, I am the man who has sinned against Yahweh, God of Israel, and this is what I have done. 21 In the loot, I saw a fine robe from Shinar and two hundred shekels of silver and an ingot of gold weighing fifty shekels, I set my heart on them and I took them. They are hidden in the ground inside my tent, with the silver underneath.'

22 Joshua sent messengers; they ran to the tent, and the robe was indeed hidden in the tent, with the silver underneath. 23 They took the things out of the tent and, bringing them to Joshua and all the Israelites, laid them out before Yahweh.

24 Joshua then took Achan son of Zerah and led him up to the Vale of Achor, with the silver and the robe and the ingot of gold, his sons, his daughters, his oxen, his donkeys, his sheep, his goats, his tent and all his belongings. All Israel went with him.

25 Joshua said, 'Why have you brought misfortune on us? Today may Yahweh bring misfortune on you!' And all Israel stoned him to death (and they burned them and threw stones at them).

26 Over him, they raised a great mound of stones, which is still there today. Yahweh then relented from his fierce anger. That was why the place was called the Vale of Achor,[b] as it still is today.

The command given to Joshua

8 Yahweh then said to Joshua, 'Be fearless and undaunted. Take all your fighting men with you. Up! March against Ai. Look, I have put the king of Ai, his people, his town and his territory at your mercy. 2 You must treat Ai and its king as you treated Jericho and its king. The only booty you will take are the spoils and the cattle. Take up a concealed position by the town, to the rear of it.'

Joshua's stratagem to capture Ai

3 Joshua set out to march against Ai with all the fighting men. Joshua chose thirty thousand of the bravest and sent them out under cover of dark, 4 having given them these orders, 'Pay attention! You must take up a concealed position by the town, at the rear, not very far from the town, and be sure you all keep alert! 5 I, and the whole people with me, shall advance on the town, and when the people of Ai come out to engage us as they did the first time, we shall run away from them. 6 They will then give chase, and we shall draw them away from the town, since they will think, "They are running away from us as they did the first time." 7 You will then burst out of your concealed position and seize the town; Yahweh your God will put it at your mercy. 8 When you have captured the town, set fire to it, in obedience to Yahweh's command. Well then, these are my orders.'

9 Joshua sent them off, and they made their way to the place of ambush and took up position between Bethel and Ai, to the west of Ai. Joshua spent the night with the people, 10 then, getting up early next morning, reviewed the people and, with the elders of Israel, marched on Ai at their head. 11 All the warriors marching with him advanced on the front of the town and pitched camp north of Ai, with the valley between them and the town. 12 Joshua

7b Word-play with 'akar (= bring bad luck).

took about five thousand men and concealed these between Bethel and Ai, to the west of the town. 13 The people pitched the main camp to the north of the town and set up its ambush to the west of the town. Joshua went that night into the middle of the plain.

The capture of Ai

14 The king of Ai had seen this; the people of the town got up early and hurried out, so that he and all his people could engage Israel in battle on the slope facing the Arabah; but he did not know that an ambush had been laid for him to the rear of the town. 15 Joshua and all Israel pretended to be beaten by them and took to their heels along the road to the desert. 16 All the people in the town joined in the pursuit and, in pursuing Joshua, were drawn away from the town. 17 Not a man was left in Ai (nor in Bethel), who had not gone in pursuit of Israel; and in pursuing Israel they left the town undefended.

18 Yahweh then said to Joshua, 'Point the sabre in your hand at Ai; for I am about to put the town at your mercy.' Joshua pointed the sabre in his hand towards the town. 19 No sooner had he stretched out his hand than the men in ambush burst from their position, ran forward, entered the town, captured it and quickly set it on fire.

20 When the men of Ai looked back, they saw smoke rising from the town into the sky. None of them had the courage to run in any direction, for the people fleeing towards the desert turned back on their pursuers. 21 For, once Joshua and all Israel saw that the town had been seized by the men in ambush, and that smoke was rising from the town, they turned about and attacked the men of Ai. 22 The others came out from the town to engage them too, and the men of Ai were thus surrounded by Israelites, some on this side and some on that. The Israelites struck them down until not one was left alive and none to flee; 23 but the king of Ai was taken alive, and brought to Joshua. 24 When Israel had finished killing all the inhabitants of Ai in the open

ground, and in the desert where they had pursued them, and when every single one had fallen to the sword, all Israel returned to Ai and slaughtered its remaining population. 25 The number of those who fell that day, men and women together, was twelve thousand, all people of Ai.

The curse of destruction; the destruction of the town

26 Joshua did not draw back the hand with which he had pointed the sabre until he had subjected all the inhabitants of Ai to the curse of destruction. 27 For booty, Israel took only the cattle and the spoils of this town, in accordance with the order that Yahweh had given to Joshua. 28 Joshua then burned Ai, making it a ruin for evermore, a desolate place even today. 29 He hanged the king of Ai from a tree till evening; but at sunset Joshua ordered his body to be taken down from the tree. It was then thrown down at the entrance to the town gate and on top of it was raised a great mound of stones, which is still there today.

The altar of undressed stones on Mount Ebal

30 Joshua then built an altar to Yahweh, God of Israel, on Mount Ebal, 31 as Moses, servant of Yahweh, had ordered the Israelites, as is written in the law of Moses: an altar of undressed stones, on which no iron has been used. On this they presented burnt offerings to Yahweh and communion sacrifices as well.

The reading of the Law

32 There, Joshua wrote on the stones a copy of the Law of Moses, which Moses had written in the presence of the Israelites. 33 All Israel, with their elders, their officials and their judges, stood on either side of the ark, facing the levitical priests who were carrying the ark of the covenant of Yahweh, foreigners with the native-born, half of them on the upper slopes of Mount Gerizim, and half of them on the upper slopes of Mount Ebal, as Moses, servant of Yahweh, had originally ordered for the blessing of the people of Israel. 34 After this,

Joshua read all the words of the Law—the blessing and the cursing—exactly as it stands written in the Book of the Law. ³⁵ Of every word laid down by Moses, not one was left unread by Joshua in the presence of the whole assembly of Israel, including the women and children, and the foreigners living with them.

A coalition against Israel

9 Hearing these things, all the kings on this side of the Jordan, in the highlands and in the lowlands, all along the coast of the Great Sea towards the Lebanon, Hittites, Amorites, Canaanites, Perizzites, Hivites and Jebusites, with one consent ² formed a fighting alliance against Joshua and Israel.

The ruse of the Gibeonites

³ When the inhabitants of Gibeon learned how Joshua had treated Jericho and Ai, for their part, ⁴ they had recourse to a ruse. They provided themselves with supplies, and loaded their donkeys with old sacks and with old wineskins which had burst and been sewn up again. ⁵ They put on patched old sandals and worn-out clothes. The only bread they took with them to eat was dried up and crumbling. ⁶ They came to Joshua in the camp at Gilgal, and to him and the men of Israel they said, 'We come from a distant country, so make a treaty with us.' ⁷ The Israelites answered these Hivites, 'For all we know, you may live right among us. How then could we make a treaty with you?' ⁸ They said to Joshua, 'We are your servants.' 'But who are you?' Joshua asked them, 'and where do you come from?' ⁹ They said, 'Your servants have come from a country very far away, because of the fame of Yahweh your God; for we have heard of him and of all that he did in Egypt, ¹⁰ and of all that he did to the two Amorite kings who used to live on the other side of the Jordan: Sihon king of Heshbon, and Og king of Bashan, who used to live at Ashtaroth. ¹¹ Because of which, our elders and all the people of our country said to us, "Take provisions with you for the journey; go and meet them and say to them: We are your servants; so make a treaty with us." ¹² Here is our bread; it was warm when we took it from home to provide for our journey the day we set out to come to you, and now, you can see, it is dried up and crumbling. ¹³ These wineskins were new when we filled them; you can see, they have burst; and these clothes and sandals of ours are worn out from travelling such a long way.'

¹⁴ The leaders sampled some of the food they offered, but they did not ask Yahweh's orders. ¹⁵ Joshua made peace with them, and struck a treaty with them guaranteeing their lives, and the leaders of the community ratified it by oath.

¹⁶ Now it so happened that three days after the treaty had been made, it became known that they were a neighbouring people, living in Israel's region. ¹⁷ The Israelites set out from camp, arriving in their towns three days later. Their towns were Gibeon, Chephirah, Beeroth and Kiriath-Jearim. ¹⁸ The Israelites did not attack them, since the leaders of the community had sworn to them by Yahweh, God of Israel, but the whole community muttered against the leaders.

The Gibeonites' place in the community

¹⁹ The leaders, however, all said to the whole community, 'Since we have sworn an oath to them by Yahweh, God of Israel, we cannot touch them now. ²⁰ This is what we shall do with them: let them live, rather than bring retribution down on ourselves on account of the oath which we have sworn to them.' ²¹ And the leaders went on, 'Let them live, but let them be wood-cutters and water-carriers for the whole community.' Thus spoke the leaders. ²² Joshua sent for the Gibeonites and asked them, 'Why did you deceive us by saying, "We live very far away," when in fact you live right among us? ²³ From now on, you are accursed and will for ever be serfs, as wood-cutters and water-carriers in the house of my God.' ²⁴ Their answer to Joshua was, 'We did it because your servants had been rightly told that Yahweh your God had ordered his servant

Moses to give you the whole of this country and destroy all its inhabitants before you; also because, as you advanced on us, we feared very greatly for our lives. That was why we did this. 25 Now, as you see, we are at your mercy; do to us whatever you think good and right.' 26 What he did with them was this: he saved them from the hand of the Israelites, who did not kill them. 27 But that very day Joshua made them wood-cutters and water-carriers for the community and for the altar of Yahweh, at the place which he would eventually choose; and so they are today.

Five kings make war on Gibeon

10 Now, it happened that Adoni-Zedek king of Jerusalem, learned that Joshua had conquered Ai and put the town under the curse of destruction, treating Ai and its king as he had already treated Jericho and its king; and also that the inhabitants of Gibeon had made peace with Israel and were living with them. 2 There was consternation at this, since Gibeon was as important a town as any of the royal towns themselves (it was larger than Ai), while all its citizens were fighting men. 3 Consequently, Adoni-Zedek king of Jerusalem sent word to Hoham king of Hebron, Piram king of Jarmuth, Japhia king of Lachish, and Debir king of Eglon, 4 'Join me up here and help me to conquer Gibeon, since it has made peace with Joshua and the Israelites.' 5 The five Amorite kings joined forces and went up there, that is, the king of Jerusalem, the king of Hebron, the king of Jarmuth, the king of Lachish and the king of Eglon, they and all their armies; laying siege to Gibeon, they attacked it.

Joshua comes to the rescue of Gibeon

6 The men of Gibeon sent word to Joshua in the camp at Gilgal, 'Do not desert your servants; come up here quickly to save us and help us, since all the Amorite kings living in the highlands have allied themselves against us.' 7 Joshua came up from Gilgal, he, all the fighting men and all the bravest of his army.

8 Yahweh said to Joshua, 'Do not be afraid of these people; I have put them at your mercy; not one of them will put up any resistance.' 9 Having marched from Gilgal throughout the night, Joshua caught them unawares.

Aid from on high

10 Yahweh threw them into disorder at the sight of Israel, defeating them completely at Gibeon; furthermore, he pursued them by way of the Descent of Beth-Horon and harassed them as far as Azekah (and as far as Makkedah). 11 And as they fled from Israel down the Descent of Beth-Horon, Yahweh hurled huge hailstones from heaven on them all the way to Azekah, and they died. More of them died under the hailstones than under the swords of the Israelites. 12 Joshua then spoke to Yahweh, the day Yahweh delivered the Amorites to the Israelites. In the presence of Israel, Joshua said:

Sun, stand still over Gibeon,
and, moon, you too, over the Vale of
Aijalon!

13 And the sun stood still, and the moon halted, until the people had taken vengeance on their enemies.

Is this not written in the Book of the Just? The sun stood still in the middle of the sky and delayed its setting for almost a whole day. 14 There was never a day like that before or since, when Yahweh obeyed the voice of a man—for Yahweh was fighting for Israel. 15 Joshua, and all Israel with him, then went back to the camp at Gilgal.

The five kings in the cave at Makkedah

16 As regards the five kings, these had fled and hidden in the cave of Makkedah, 17 and news of this was brought to Joshua. 'The five kings have been found hiding in the cave at Makkedah.' 18 Joshua said, 'Roll great stones over the mouth of the cave and post men there to keep guard. 19 You yourselves, do not stay there doing nothing; pursue the enemy, cut off

their line of retreat and do not let them enter their towns, for Yahweh your God has put them at your mercy.'

²⁰ When Joshua and the Israelites had finished inflicting a very great defeat on them, to the point of destroying them, those who had escaped alive took refuge in their fortresses. ²¹ The people came back to Joshua's camp at Makkedah; they were all safe and sound, and no one dared to attempt anything against the Israelites.

²² Joshua then said, 'Clear the mouth of the cave and bring the five kings out to me.' ²³ They did so, and brought the five kings out of the cave to take them to him: the king of Jerusalem, the king of Hebron, the king of Jarmuth, the king of Lachish and the king of Eglon. ²⁴ When these kings had been brought out, Joshua assembled all the men of Israel and said to the chiefs of the warriors who had fought with him, 'Come forward and put your feet on the necks of these kings!' They came forward and put their feet on their necks. ²⁵ 'Be fearless and undaunted,' Joshua went on, 'be strong and stand firm, for this is how Yahweh will deal with all the enemies you fight.' ²⁶ With this, Joshua struck and killed them and had them hanged on five trees; they hung there till evening.

²⁷ At the hour of sunset, on Joshua's orders, they were taken down from the trees and thrown into the cave where they had been hiding. Great stones were laid over the mouth of the cave, and these are still there to this very day.

The conquest of the southern towns of Canaan

²⁸ The same day Joshua captured Makkedah, putting it and its king to the sword; he delivered them over to the curse of destruction, with every living creature there, and let no one escape, and he treated the king of Makkedah as he had treated the king of Jericho. ²⁹ Joshua, and all Israel with him, went on from Makkedah to Libnah and attacked it ³⁰ and Yahweh put this, too, and its king at Is-

rael's mercy; and Israel put every living creature there to the sword, and left none alive, and treated its king like the king of Jericho.

³¹ Joshua, and all Israel with him, went on from Libnah to Lachish and besieged it and attacked it. ³² Yahweh put Lachish at Israel's mercy, and Israel took it on the second day and put it and every living creature in it to the sword, as they had treated Libnah. ³³ Horam king of Gezer then marched up to help Lachish, but Joshua beat him and his people until not one was left alive.

³⁴ Joshua, and all Israel with him, went on from Lachish to Eglon. They besieged it and attacked it. ³⁵ The same day they took it and put it to the sword. That day he delivered over to the curse of destruction every living creature there, treating it as he had treated Lachish.

³⁶ Joshua, and all Israel with him, went on up from Eglon to Hebron. They attacked it, ³⁷ took it and put it to the sword, with its king, its dependencies and every living creature in it. As he had treated Eglon, so here, he left no one alive. He delivered it over to the curse of destruction, with every living creature in it.

³⁸ Joshua, and all Israel with him, then turned back on Debir and attacked it. ³⁹ He took it and its king and all the places belonging to it; they put them to the sword, and every living creature there they delivered over to the curse of destruction. He left no one alive. As he had treated Hebron, as he had treated Libnah and its king, so he treated Debir and its king.

The southern conquests recapitulated

⁴⁰ Thus Joshua subjugated the whole country: the highlands, the Negeb, the lowlands and watered foothills, and all their kings. He left not one survivor and put every living thing under the curse of destruction, as Yahweh, God of Israel, had commanded. ⁴¹ Joshua conquered them from Kadesh-Barnea to Gaza, and the whole region of Goshen as far as Gibeon. ⁴² All these kings and their territory Joshua captured in a single campaign, because

Yahweh, God of Israel, fought for Israel. ⁴³ And then Joshua, and all Israel with him, went back to the camp at Gilgal.

The conquest of the north

11 When Jabin king of Hazor heard about this, he sent word to Jobab king of Merom, to the king of Shimron, to the king of Achshaph ² and to the kings in the northern highlands, in the plain south of Chinneroth, and those in the lowlands and on the slopes of Dor to the west. ³ To eastward and to westward lived the Canaanites: in the highlands, the Amorites, Hittites, Perizzites and Jebusites; the Hivites, at the foot of Hermon in the area of Mizpah. ⁴ They set out with all their troops, a people as numerous as the sands of the sea, with a huge number of horses and chariots.

The victory at Merom

⁵ These kings, having all agreed on a meeting place, came and set up camp together at the Waters of Merom, to fight Israel. ⁶ Yahweh then said to Joshua, 'Do not be afraid of them, for by this time tomorrow I shall hand them all over, cut to pieces, to Israel; you will hamstring their horses and burn their chariots.' ⁷ With all his warriors Joshua caught them unawares near the Waters of Merom and fell on them. ⁸ Yahweh put them at Israel's mercy and they defeated them and pursued them as far as Sidon the Great, and as far as Misrephoth to the west, and as far as the Vale of Mizpah to the east; they harried them until not one of them was left alive. ⁹ Joshua treated them as Yahweh had told him; he hamstrung their horses and burned their chariots.

The capture of Hazor and of the other northern towns

¹⁰ Joshua then turned back and captured Hazor, putting its king to the sword. Hazor in olden days was the capital of all these kingdoms. ¹¹ In compliance with the curse of destruction, they put every living creature there to the sword. Not a living soul was left, and Hazor was burnt to the ground.

¹² All these royal cities and all their kings Joshua put to the sword in compliance with the curse of destruction, as Moses, servant of Yahweh, had ordered.

¹³ Yet of all these towns standing on their mounds, Israel burned none, apart from Hazor, burnt by Joshua. ¹⁴ All the spoils of these towns, including the livestock, the Israelites took as booty for themselves. But they put all the human beings to the sword till they had destroyed them completely; they did not leave a living soul.

The orders of Moses carried out by Joshua

¹⁵ What Yahweh had ordered his servant Moses, Moses in turn had ordered Joshua, and Joshua carried it out, leaving nothing undone of what Yahweh had ordered Moses. ¹⁶ In consequence, Joshua captured this entire country: the highlands, the whole Negeb and the whole of Goshen, the lowlands, the Arabah, the highlands and lowlands of Israel.

¹⁷ From Mount Halak, which rises towards Seir, to Baal-Gad in the Vale of Lebanon at the foot of Mount Hermon, he captured all their kings, struck them down and put them to death. ¹⁸ For many a day Joshua made war on all these kings; ¹⁹ no city had made peace with the Israelites except the Hivites who lived at Gibeon; all the rest had been captured in battle. ²⁰ For Yahweh had decided to harden the hearts of these men, so that they would engage Israel in battle and thus come under the curse of destruction and so receive no quarter but be exterminated, as Yahweh had ordered Moses.

Extermination of the Anakim

²¹ Joshua then went and wiped out the Anakim of the highlands, of Hebron, of Debir, of Anab, of all the highlands of Judah and of all the highlands of Israel; he delivered them and their towns over to the curse of destruction. ²² No Anakim were left in the territory of the Israelites, except at Gaza, Gath and Ashdod.

23 Joshua captured the entire country, just as Yahweh had told Moses, and he gave it as heritage to Israel, to be shared out between their tribes.

And the country had rest from warfare.

The kings conquered east of the Jordan

12 The kings of the country, whom the Israelites conquered and whose territory they took, on the further, eastern side of the Jordan, from the Wadi Arnon to Mount Hermon, with the entire Arabah to the east, were as follows:

2 Sihon king of the Amorites, who lived at Heshbon, ruled from Aroer which is on the edge of the Arnon Valley, including the bottom of the valley, half Gilead and as far as the Jabbok, the river forming the frontier with the Ammonites; 3 the eastern Arabah up to the Sea of Chinneroth, and as far as the Sea of the Arabah, or Salt Sea, on the eastern side, in the direction of Beth-Jeshimoth, and, in the south, the watered foothills of Mount Pisgah.

4 Og king of Bashan, one of the last of the Rephaim, who lived at Ashtaroth and Edrei, 5 ruled over Mount Hermon and Salecah, the whole of Bashan to the frontier of the Geshurites and Maacathites, and half Gilead to the frontier of Sihon king of Heshbon.

6 Moses, servant of Yahweh, and the Israelites conquered these, and Moses, servant of Yahweh, conferred their territory on the Reubenites, the Gadites and the half-tribe of Manasseh.

The kings conquered west of the Jordan

7 The kings of the country whom Joshua and the Israelites conquered on the nearer, western side of the Jordan, from Baal-Gad in the Vale of Lebanon to Mount Halak rising towards Seir, and whose heritage Joshua distributed to the tribes of Israel, dividing it up between them, were as follows:

8 In the highlands and the lowlands, in the Arabah and in the watered foothills, in the desert and in the Negeb, belonging to the Hittites, the Amorites, the Canaanites, the Perizzites, the Hivites and the Jebusites:

9 the king of Jericho, one;
the king of Ai near Bethel, one;
10 the king of Jerusalem, one;
the king of Hebron, one;
11 the king of Jarmuth, one;
the king of Lachish, one;
12 the king of Eglon, one;
the king of Gezer, one;
13 the king of Debir, one;
the king of Geder, one;
14 the king of Hormah, one;
the king of Arad, one;
15 the king of Libnah, one;
the king of Adullam, one;
16 the king of Makkedah, one;
the king of Bethel, one;
17 the king of Tappuah, one;
the king of Hepher, one;
18 the king of Aphek, one;
the king of Sharon, one;
19 the king of Merom, one;
the king of Hazor, one;
20 the king of Shimron Meron, one;
the king of Achshaph, one;
21 the king of Taanach, one;
the king of Megiddo, one;
22 the king of Kedesh, one;
the king of Jokneam in Carmel, one;
23 the king of Dor, on the Slopes of Dor, one;
the king of the nations in Galilee, one;
24 the king of Tirzah, one;
Total number of all these kings: thirty-one.

Lands remaining unconquered

13 Now Joshua had grown old and advanced in years. Yahweh said to him, 'You are now old and advanced in years, yet there is still a great deal of territory left to be taken possession of. 2 This is all the territory left:

'All the districts of the Philistines and the whole country of the Geshurites; 3 from the Shihor, facing Egypt, to the frontier of Ekron in the north, is reckoned as Canaanite territory. The five rulers of the Philistines have their seats at Gaza, Ashdod, Ashkelon, Gath and Ekron, respectively; the Avvites are in ⁴the south. The entire territory of the Canaanites, and Mearah which belongs to the Sidonians, as far as Aphekah and as far as the frontier of the Amorites; ⁵and then the country of the Gebalites with the entire Lebanon eastwards from Baal-Gad at the foot of Mount Hermon to the Pass of Hamath.

⁶'All who live in the highlands from the Lebanon to Misrephoth in the west—all the Sidonians—I myself shall dispossess before the Israelites. All you have to do is to distribute the territory as a heritage for the Israelites as I have ordered you. ⁷The time has come to divide this territory as a heritage between the nine tribes and the half-tribe of Manasseh: from the Jordan as far as the Great Sea in the west, you must give it them; the Great Sea will be their limit.'

The Transjordanian tribes

⁸As regards the other half-tribe of Manasseh, this and the Reubenites and Gadites had already received their heritage, given them by Moses on the further, eastern side of the Jordan, the one which Moses, servant of Yahweh, had already given them: ⁹The country onwards from Aroer on the edge of the Arnon Valley, with the town in the bottom of the valley and the entire tableland from Medeba to Dibon; ¹⁰all the towns of Sihon king of the Amorites, who had reigned in Heshbon, to the frontier of the Ammonites; ¹¹then Gilead and the territory of the Geshurites and Maacathites with the whole Hermon range and the whole of Bashan as far as Salecah; ¹²and in Bashan, the whole kingdom of Og, who had reigned in Ashtaroth and Edrei, and was the last of the survivors of the Rephaim. Moses had conquered and dispossessed these two kings. ¹³The Israelites did not, however, dispossess either the Geshurites or the Maacathites, hence Geshur and Maacah survive inside Israel even today.

¹⁴To the tribe of Levi alone no heritage was given; Yahweh, God of Israel, was his heritage, as he had told him.

The tribe of Reuben

¹⁵Moses had given the tribe of the sons of Reuben a share by clans. ¹⁶Thus, their territory was the entire tableland from Aroer on the edge of the Arnon Valley, with the town in the bottom of the valley, as far as Medeba, ¹⁷Heshbon with all the towns on the tableland: Dibon, Bamoth-Baal, Beth-Baal-Meon, ¹⁸Jahaz, Kedemoth, Mephaath, ¹⁹Kiriathaim, Sibmah and, in the highlands of the Arabah, Zereth-Shahar; ²⁰Beth-Peor, the watered foothills of Mount Pisgah, Beth-ha-Jeshimoth, ²¹all the towns on the tableland and the entire kingdom of Sihon king of the Amorites, who had reigned in Heshbon; he had been defeated by Moses, and with him the princes of Midian, Evi, Rekem, Zur, Hur and Reba, vassals of Sihon, formerly living in the country.

²²As regards Balaam son of Beor, the soothsayer, the Israelites had put him to the sword with those whom they had killed.

²³The boundary of the Reubenites was the Jordan and its territory.

Such was the heritage of the sons of Reuben, by clans, with the towns and villages belonging to them.

The tribe of Gad

²⁴Moses had given the tribe of Gad, the sons of Gad, a share by clans. ²⁵Their territory was Jazer, all the towns of Gilead, half the country of the Ammonites as far as Aroer facing Rabbah, ²⁶and from Heshbon to Ramath-Mizpeh and Betonim; from Mahanaim as far as the territory of Lo-Debar, ²⁷and in the valley: Beth-Haram, Beth-Nimrah, Succoth, and Zaphon—the rest of the kingdom of Sihon king of Heshbon—the Jordan and the territory running to the tip of the Sea of Chinneroth, on the further, eastern side of the Jordan.

²⁸Such was the heritage of the sons of Gad, by clans, with their towns and villages belonging to them.

The half-tribe of Manasseh

29 Moses had given the half-tribe of Manasseh a share by clans. 30 Their territory, starting from Mahanaim, was the whole of Bashan, the entire kingdom of Og king of Bashan, all the Encampments of Jair in Bashan: sixty towns. 31 Half of Gilead, with Ashtaroth, and Edrei, the royal cities of Og in Bashan, were allotted to the sons of Machir son of Manasseh, to half of the sons of Machir, by clans.

32 This was what Moses had conferred in heritage on the Plains of Moab on the further, eastern side of the Jordan opposite Jericho. 33 To the tribe of Levi, however, Moses gave no heritage; Yahweh, God of Israel, was his heritage, as he had told him.

The tribes west of the Jordan

14 This was what the Israelites received as their heritage in Canaan, which was given them as their heritage by the priest, Eleazar, and by Joshua son of Nun, with the heads of families of the tribes of Israel. 2 They received their heritage by lot, as Yahweh had ordered through Moses, as regards the nine tribes and the half-tribe. 3 For Moses himself had given the two-and-a-half tribes their heritage on the further side of the Jordan, although to the Levites he had given no heritage with them. 4 Since the sons of Joseph formed two tribes, Manasseh and Ephraim, no share in the country was given to the Levites, apart from some towns to live in, with their pasture lands for their livestock and their possessions. 5 The Israelites did as Yahweh had ordered Moses, and shared out the country.

Caleb's share

6 Some sons of Judah came to Joshua at Gilgal, and Caleb son of Jephunneh the Kenizzite said to him, 'You know what Yahweh said to Moses, man of God, at Kadesh-Barnea concerning you and me. 7 I was forty years old when Moses, servant of Yahweh, sent me from Kadesh-Barnea to reconnoitre this country, and I made him a completely honest report.

8 The brothers, however, who had gone up with me discouraged the people, whereas I myself scrupulously obeyed Yahweh my God. 9 That day Moses swore this oath, "Be sure of this, that the country your foot has trodden will be a heritage for you and your children for ever, since you have scrupulously obeyed Yahweh my God." 10 From then till now, Yahweh has kept me alive in observance of his promise. It is forty-five years since Yahweh said this to Moses—Israel was then going through the desert—and now I am eighty-five years old. 11 Today I am still as strong as the day when Moses sent me out on that errand; for fighting, for going and coming, I am as strong now as then. 12 It is time you gave me the highlands, of which Yahweh spoke to me that day. You heard that day that there were Anakim and large, fortified towns there; but if Yahweh is with me, I shall drive them out, as Yahweh has said.'

13 Joshua blessed Caleb son of Jephunneh and gave him Hebron as heritage. 14 And hence Hebron down to the present day has remained the heritage of Caleb son of Jephunneh the Kenizzite, since he had scrupulously obeyed Yahweh, God of Israel. 15 Hebron in olden days was called Kiriath-Arba. Arba had been the greatest of the Anakim.

And the country had rest from warfare.

The tribe of Judah

15 The portion falling to the tribe of the sons of Judah, by clans, was near the frontier of Edom, from the desert of Zin southwards to Kadesh in the south. 2 Their southern frontier began at the tip of the Salt Sea, at the southerly bay; 3 it proceeded south of the Ascent of Scorpions, crossed Zin and came up to Kadesh-Barnea from the south; past Hezron, it went on to Addar and turned towards Karka; 4 the frontier then went on to Azmon, came out at the Torrent of Egypt and reached as far as the sea. This is to be your southern frontier.

5 The eastern frontier was the Salt Sea as far as the mouth of the Jordan.

[6] The northern boundary began at the bay at the mouth of the Jordan. The boundary went up to Beth-Hoglah, passed north of Beth-ha-Arabah and went on to the Stone of Bohan son of Reuben. [7] The boundary then went on to Debir from the Vale of Achor and turned north towards the stone circle opposite the Ascent of Adummim, which is south of the Torrent; the boundary went on to the Waters of En-Shemesh and came out at En-Rogel. [8] It then went back up the Valley of Hinnom, coming from the south to the flank of the Jebusite—that is, Jerusalem—and climbed to the crest of the mountain barring the Valley of Hinnom to the west, at the northern end of the Valley of the Rephaim. [9] From the mountain top, the boundary curved round to the spring of the Waters of Nephtoah, went on to the towns of Mount Ephron and then turned towards Baalah—that is, Kiriath-Jearim. [10] From Baalah, the boundary curved westwards to the highlands of Seir, skirted the northern slope of Mount Jearim—that is, Chesalon—went down to Beth-Shemesh and through Timnah, [11] came out on the northern flank of Ekron, turned towards Shikkeron and, passing through the highlands of Baalah, came out at Jabneel, and reached as far as the sea.

[12] The western boundary was the Great Sea itself. Such was the frontier surrounding the sons of Judah, by clans.

The Calebites occupy the territory of Hebron

[13] Caleb son of Jephunneh was given a share within that of the sons of Judah, in accordance with Yahweh's order to Joshua: Kiriath-Arba, the town of the father of Anak—that is, Hebron. [14] Caleb drove out the three sons of Anak: Sheshai, Ahiman and Talmai, descended from Anak. [15] From there he marched on the inhabitants of Debir; Debir in olden days was called Kiriath-Sepher. [16] Caleb then said, 'To the man who attacks and takes Kiriath-Sepher, I shall give my daughter Achsah as wife.' [17] The man who captured it was Othniel son of Kenaz, brother of Caleb, who gave him his daughter Achsah as wife. [18] When she arrived, he urged her to ask her father for arable land, but when she alighted from the donkey and Caleb asked her, 'What is the matter?' [19] she said to him, 'Grant me a blessing! As the land you have given me is the Negeb, give me springs of water too!' So Caleb gave her what she wanted, the upper springs and the lower springs.

[20] Such was the heritage of the tribe of the sons of Judah, by clans.

Names of places owned by Judah

[21] Towns at the extremity of the tribe of the sons of Judah, near the frontier of Edom in the Negeb:

Kabzeel, Arad, Jagur, [22] Kinah, Dimon, Aroer, [23] Kedesh, Hazor-Ithnan, [24] Ziph, Telem, Bealoth, [25] Hazor-Hadattah, Kiriath-Hezron—that is, Hazor—[26] Amam, Shema, Moladah, [27] Hazar-Gaddah, Heshmon, Beth-Pelet, [28] Hazar-Shual, Beersheba and its dependencies, [29] Baalah, Iim, Ezem, [30] Eltolad, Chesil, Hormah, [31] Ziklag, Madmannah, Sansannah, [32] Lebaoth, Shilhim, Ain and Rimmon: in all, twenty-nine towns with their villages.

[33] In the lowlands:

Eshtaol, Zorah, Ashnah, [34] Zanoah, En-Gannim, Tappuah, Enam, [35] Jarmuth, Adullam, Socoh, Azekah, [36] Shaaraim, Aditaim, Ha-Gederah and Gederothaim: fourteen towns with their villages.

[37] Zenan, Hadashah, Migdal-Gad, [38] Dilean, Ha-Mizpeh, Jokteel, [39] Lachish, Bozkath, Eglon, [40] Cabbon, Lahmas, Chitlish, [41] Gederoth, Beth-Dagon, Naamah and Makkedah: sixteen towns with their villages.

[42] Libna, Ether, Asham, [43] Iphtah, Ashnah, Nezib, [44] Keilah, Achzib and Mareshah: nine towns with their villages.

[45] Ekron with its dependencies and its villages. [46] From Ekron to the sea, everything to the side of Ashdod, with its villages. [47] Ashdod with its dependencies and its villages; Gaza with its dependencies and its villages as far as

the Torrent of Egypt, the Great Sea forming the boundary.

48 In the highlands:

Shamir, Jattir, Socoh, 49 Dannah, Kiriath-Sepher, now Debir, 50 Anab, Eshtemoh, Anim, 51 Goshen, Holon and Giloh: eleven towns with their villages.

52 Arab, Dumah, Eshan, 53 Janum, Beth-Tappuah, Aphekah, 54 Humtah, Kiriath-Arba, now Hebron, and Zior: nine towns with their villages.

55 Maon, Carmel, Ziph, Juttah, 56 Jezreel, Jokdeam, Zanoah, 57 Ha-Kain, Gibeah and Timnah: ten towns with their villages.

58 Halhul, Beth-Zur, Gedor, 59 Maarath, Beth-Anoth and Eltekon: six towns with their villages.

Tekoa, Ephrathah, now Bethlehem, Peor, Etam, Kulon, Tatam, Sores, Carem, Gallim, Bether and Manach: eleven towns with their villages.

60 Kiriath-Baal, that is Kiriath-Jearim, and Rabbah: two towns with their villages.

61 In the desert:

Beth-Arabah, Middin, Secacah, 62 Nibshan, Salt Town and En-Gedi: six towns with their villages.

63 The Jebusites, however, who lived in Jerusalem, the sons of Judah were unable to dispossess, and the Jebusites still live in Jerusalem today, side by side with the sons of Judah.

The tribe of Ephraim

16 The portion of the sons of Joseph started on the east at the Jordan opposite Jericho (the Waters of Jericho) through the desert rising from Jericho into the highlands of Bethel; 2 from Bethel it went to Luz, and on towards the frontier of the Archites at Ataroth; 3 then passed downwards and westwards to the frontier of the Japhletites as far as the border of Lower Beth-Horon and on to Gezer, and reached as far as the sea.

4 Such was the heritage of the sons of Joseph, Manasseh and Ephraim.

5 As regards the territory of the sons of Ephraim, by clans, the frontier of their heritage ran from Ataroth-Arach to Upper Beth-Horon; 6 the frontier then reached as far as the sea . . . the Michmethath in the north, and the frontier turned east to Tanaath-Shiloh which it crossed in an easterly direction to Janoah; 7 it ran down to Ataroth and Naarah, touched Jericho and ended at the Jordan. 8 From Tappuah, the frontier ran westwards to the Torrent of Kanah and reached as far as the sea.

Such was the heritage of the tribe of the sons of Ephraim, by clans, 9 apart from the towns reserved for the sons of Ephraim inside the heritage of the sons of Manasseh, all these towns and their villages. 10 The Canaanites living in Gezer were not driven out; they have remained in Ephraim to the present day but are obliged to do forced labour.

The tribe of Manasseh

17 The portion of the tribe of Manasseh, who was in fact Joseph's first-born—went to Machir, Manasseh's first-born, father of Gilead, for he was a warrior; he had Gilead and Bashan. 2 The other sons of Manasseh had theirs, by clans: for the sons of Abiezer, for the sons of Helek, for the sons of Asriel, for the sons of Shechem, for the sons of Hepher, and for the sons of Shemida: these were the male children of Manasseh son of Joseph, by clans. 3 Zelophehad son of Hepher, son of Gilead, son of Machir, son of Manasseh, had no sons but only daughters, whose names were these: Mahlah, Noah, Hoglah, Milcah and Tirzah. 4 These approached the priest Eleazar, Joshua son of Nun and the leaders, and said, 'Yahweh ordered Moses to give us a heritage among our brothers.' In compliance with Yahweh's order, therefore, they were given a heritage among their father's brothers. 5 In this way ten portions fell to Manasseh, apart from Gilead and Bashan lying on the further side of the Jordan, 6 since Manasseh's daughters received a heritage as well as his sons. Gilead itself belonged to Manasseh's other sons.

7 On the side of Asher, the frontier of Ma-

nasseh was the Michmethath, which is opposite Shechem, and thence continued to the right to Jashib, which is at the spring of Tappuah. 8 The territory of Tappuah belonged to Manasseh, but Tappuah on Manasseh's border belonged to the sons of Ephraim. 9 The boundary went down to the Torrent of Kanah; south of the Torrent were the towns of Ephraim, excluding those owned by Ephraim among the towns of Manasseh; the boundary of Manasseh was north of the Torrent and reached as far as the sea. 10 The south belonged to Ephraim and the north to Manasseh and reached as far as the sea; they touched Asher to the north and Issachar to the east. 11 With Issachar and Asher, Manasseh shared Beth-Shean and its dependent towns, Ibleam and its dependent towns, the inhabitants of Dor and of its dependent towns, the inhabitants of Taanach and Megiddo and of their dependent towns: the Three of the Slopes. 12 But because the sons of Manasseh could not take possession of these towns, the Canaanites managed to live on in that territory. 13 When, however, the Israelites became stronger, they subjected the Canaanites to forced labour, though they never dispossessed them.

Land reclamation by the sons of Joseph

14 The sons of Joseph spoke as follows to Joshua, 'Why have you given me only one share, only one portion, as heritage, when I am a numerous people, since Yahweh has so blessed me?' 15 Joshua replied, 'If your people are so many, go up to the wooded area and clear space for yourselves in the area belonging to the Perizzites and Rephaim, since the highlands of Ephraim are too small for you.' 16 The sons of Joseph replied, 'The highlands are not enough for us, and what is more, all the Canaanites living on the land of the plain have iron chariots, so do those in Beth-Shean and its dependent towns, and those in the plain of Jezreel.' 17 Joshua said to the House of Joseph, to Ephraim and to Manasseh, 'You are a numerous people and your strength is great; you will not only have one share, 18 but a mountain

will be yours as well; even if it is a forest, you can clear it and its territories will be yours. And you will dispossess the Canaanites, although they have iron chariots and although they are strong.'

Seven other tribes

18 The whole community of the Israelites assembled at Shiloh, and the Tent of Meeting was set up there; the whole country had been subdued for them. 2 But among the Israelites there were still seven tribes left who had not received their heritage. 3 Joshua then said to the Israelites, 'How much more time are you going to waste before you go and take possession of the country which Yahweh, God of your ancestors, has given to you? 4 Choose three men from each tribe for me to send all over the country so that they can make a survey with a view to their inheritances and then come back to me. 5 They will divide the country into seven portions. Judah will remain in his territory in the south, and those of the House of Joseph will remain in their territory in the north. 6 You must survey the country in seven sections and bring your findings to me here, so that I can cast lots for you here, in the presence of Yahweh our God. 7 The Levites, however, will have no portion with the rest of you; the priesthood of Yahweh will be their heritage. As regards Gad and Reuben and the half-tribe of Manasseh, they have received their heritage on the further, eastern side of the Jordan, the one given them by Moses, servant of Yahweh.'

8 The men stood up and set off. To those who were to survey the country Joshua gave this order, 'Start out, then, go all over the country, survey it, and then come back to me; and I shall cast lots for you here, in the presence of Yahweh, at Shiloh.' 9 The men left, went all over the country and surveyed it by towns, in seven sections, writing down their findings in a book, and then went back to Joshua in the camp at Shiloh.

10 Joshua cast lots for them in Yahweh's presence at Shiloh, and there Joshua divided

the country between the Israelites, share by share.

The tribe of Benjamin

¹¹ A portion fell first to the tribe of the sons of Benjamin, by clans: the territory of their portion lay between the sons of Judah and the sons of Joseph. ¹² Their northern frontier began at the Jordan, went up the flank of Jericho to the north, climbed westwards through the highlands and came out at the desert of Beth-Aven. ¹³ Thence, the frontier went on to Luz, on the southern flank of Luz—now Bethel—and then down to Ataroth-Arach, on the mountain south of Lower Beth-Horon. ¹⁴ At this westerly point, the frontier curved round and turned south, from the mountain facing Beth-Horon from the south and came out at Kiriath-Baal, now Kiriath-Jearim, a town of the sons of Judah. That was the western side.

¹⁵ This was the south side: from the tip of Kiriath-Jearim, the frontier went to Gasin and came out near the spring of the Waters of Nephtoah, ¹⁶ it then went down to the edge of the mountain facing the Valley of Hinnom, in the Valley of the Rephaim to the north; it then went down into the Valley of Hinnom, past the southerly flank of the Jebusite, and went down to En-Rogel. ¹⁷ It then curved northwards, coming out at En-Shemesh, and came out at the stone circle opposite the Ascent of Adummim, then went down to the Stone of Bohan son of Reuben. ¹⁸ It then went on to Cheteph on the flank of Beth-ha-Arabah northwards, and went down into the Arabah; ¹⁹ the frontier then passed round the northern flank of Beth-Hoglah, and the frontier came out at the northern bay of the Salt Sea, at the southern end of the Jordan. Such was the southern frontier. ²⁰ The Jordan itself formed the frontier on the east.

Such was the heritage of the sons of Benjamin as defined by their frontier, by clans.

The towns of Benjamin

²¹ The towns of the tribe of the sons of Benjamin, by clans, were:

²² Jericho, Beth-Hoglah, Emek-Keziz; ²³ Beth-Arabah, Zemaraim, Bethel; Avvim, Parah, Ophrah; ²⁴ Chephar-Ammoni, Ophni, Geba: twelve towns and their villages.

²⁵ Gibeon, Ramah, Beeroth; ²⁶ Mizpeh, Chephirah, Mozah; ²⁷ Rekem, Irpeel, Taralah; ²⁸ Zela-ha-Eleph, the Jebusite—that is, Jerusalem—Gibeah and Kiriath: fourteen towns with their villages.

Such was the heritage of the sons of Benjamin, by clans.

The tribe of Simeon

19 The second lot to come out was for Simeon, for the tribe of the sons of Simeon, by clans; their heritage was within the heritage of the sons of Judah. ² As heritage, they received:

³ Beersheba, Shema, Moladah, ⁴ Hazar-Shual, Balah, Ezem, Eltolad, Bethul, Hormah, ⁵ Ziklag, Beth-ha-Marcaboth, Hazar-Susa, ⁶ Beth-Lebaoth and Sharuhen: thirteen towns and their villages.

⁷ Ain, Rimmon, Ether and Ashan: four towns and their villages, ⁸ with all the villages situated near these towns as far as Baalath-Beer and Ramah of the Negeb.

Such was the heritage of the tribe of the sons of Simeon, by clans. ⁹ The heritage of the sons of Simeon was taken out of the portion of the sons of Judah, because the share of the sons of Judah was too large for them; hence, the sons of Simeon received their heritage within the heritage of the sons of Judah.

The tribe of Zebulun

¹⁰ The third lot fell to the sons of Zebulun, by clans; the territory of their heritage stretched as far as Sadud; ¹¹ their frontier climbed westwards to Maraalah, touching Dabbesheth and the torrent facing Jokneam. ¹² From Sadud, the frontier turned east, towards the rising sun, as far as the frontier of Chisloth-Tabor; it came out at Dobrath and went up to Japhia. ¹³ Thence, it went east, towards the sunrise, to Gath-Hepher and Ittah-Kazin, came out at Rimmon and turned towards Neah. ¹⁴ The

northern frontier turned towards Hannathon and came to an end in the Valley of Iphtah-El; [15] with Kattath, Nahalal, Shimron, Iralah and Bethlehem: twelve towns with their villages.

[16] Such was the heritage of the sons of Zebulun, by clans: these towns with their villages.

The tribe of Issachar

[17] The fourth lot came out for Issachar, for the sons of Issachar, by clans. [18] Their territory stretched towards Jezreel and included Chesulloth, Shunem, [19] Hapharaim, Shion, Anaharath, [20] Dobrath, Kishion, Ebez, [21] Remeth, En-Gannim, En-Haddah and Beth-Pazzez. [22] Their frontier touched Tabor, Shahazimah and Beth-Shemesh, and the frontier came to an end at the Jordan: sixteen towns with their villages.

[23] Such was the heritage of the tribe of the sons of Issachar, by clans: the towns and their villages.

The tribe of Asher

[24] The fifth lot came out for the tribe of the sons of Asher, by clans. [25] Their territory included Helkath, Hali, Beten, Achshaph, [26] Alammelech, Amad and Mishal. [27] On the west, it touched Carmel and the course of the Libnath. On the side of the rising sun, it went as far as Beth-Dagon, touched Zebulun, the Valley of Iphtah-El on the north side, Beth-ha-Emek and Neiel, coming out with Cabul on the left, [28] with Abdon, Rehob, Hammon and Kanah as far as Sidon the Great. The frontier then turned towards Ramah, as far as the fortress-town of Tyre; [29] the frontier then went to Hosah and reached as far as the sea at Mahalab and Achzib, [30] with Acco, Aphek and Rehob: twenty-two towns with their villages.

[31] Such was the heritage of the tribe of the sons of Asher, by clans; these towns and their villages.

The tribe of Naphtali

[32] To the sons of Naphtali fell the sixth portion, to the sons of Naphtali, by clans. [33] Their frontier went from Heleph and the Oak of Zanaannim, with Adami-ha-Negeb and Jabneel, as far as Lakkum, and ended at the Jordan. [34] The westward boundary ran to Aznoth-Tabor and thence came out at Hukkok, marching with Zebulun in the south, Asher in the west and the Jordan in the east. [35] The fortified towns were Ziddim, Zer, Hammath, Rakkath, Chinnereth, [36] Adamah, Ramah, Hazor, [37] Kedesh, Edrei, En-Hazor, [38] Jiron, Migdal-El, Horem, Beth-Anath and Beth-Shemesh: nineteen towns and their villages.

[39] Such was the heritage of the sons of Naphtali, by clans: the towns and their villages.

The tribe of Dan

[40] To the tribe of the sons of Dan, by clans, fell the seventh portion. [41] The territory of their heritage comprised: Zorah, Eshtaol, Ir-Shemesh, [42] Shaalbim, Aijalon, Silatha, [43] Elon, Timnah, Ekron, [44] Eltekeh, Gibbethon, [45] Baalath, Azor, Bene-Berak and Gath-Rimmon; [46] and, by the sea, Jerakon with the territory facing Jaffa.

[47] The territory of the sons of Dan eluded them, however, and the sons of Dan consequently went up and attacked Leshem, captured it and put it to the sword. Having gained possession of it, they settled there and called Leshem, Dan, after Dan their ancestor.

[48] Such was the heritage of the tribe of the sons of Dan, by clans: these towns and their villages.

[49] Having finished dividing the country, frontier by frontier, the Israelites gave Joshua son of Nun a heritage among themselves; [50] at Yahweh's command, they gave him the town which he had asked for, Timnath-Serah in the highlands of Ephraim; he rebuilt the town and settled there.

[51] Such are the heritages which the priest Eleazar, Joshua son of Nun, and the heads of each family apportioned by lot between the tribes of Israel at Shiloh, in Yahweh's presence, at the door of the Tent of Meeting; and

thus the apportioning of the country was completed.

The cities of refuge

20 Yahweh said to Joshua, 2'Speak to the Israelites and say to them, "Choose yourselves the cities of refuge of which I spoke to you through Moses, 3to which anyone who has accidentally (unintentionally) killed someone else may flee, and which will serve you as refuge from the avenger of blood. 4(The killer must flee to one of these towns. He will stop at the entrance to the town gate and explain his case to the town elders. These will admit him to their town and assign him a place to live among them. 5If the avenger of blood pursues him, they must not hand the killer over to him, since he has killed his fellow unintentionally and was not motivated by long-standing hatred for him. 6He must stay in this town) until he is brought to trial before the community (until the death of the high priest then in office. Only then may the killer go back to his own town and to his own house in the town from which he has fled)." '

7For this purpose they designated Kedesh in Galilee, in the highlands of Naphtali, Shechem in the highlands of Ephraim, and Kiriath-Arba—now Hebron—in the highlands of Judah. 8On the other, eastern, side of the Jordan opposite Jericho, in the desert of the tableland, they chose Bezer of the tribe of Reuben, Ramoth in Gilead of the tribe of Gad, and Golan in Bashan of the tribe of Manasseh. 9Such were the towns designated for all the Israelites and for foreigners living among them, so that anyone who had accidentally killed someone could flee there and might escape the hand of the avenger of blood, until brought to trial before the community.

The levitical cities

21 The heads of families of the Levites then came to the priest, Eleazar, Joshua son of Nun and the heads of families of the tribes of Israel—2they were then at Shiloh in Canaan. They said to them, 'Through Moses, Yahweh ordered us to be given towns to live in, with their pasture lands for our livestock.' 3In compliance with Yahweh's order, the Israelites consequently and from their own heritage gave the Levites the following towns with their pasture lands:

4Lots were cast for the clans of the Kohathites: to those Levites who were sons of Aaron the priest, fell thirteen towns from the tribes of Judah, Simeon and Benjamin; 5to the other sons of Kohath, by clans, 6fell ten towns from the tribes of Ephraim, Dan, and the half-tribe of Manasseh. To the sons of Gershon, by clans, fell thirteen towns from the tribes of Issachar, Asher, Naphtali and the half-tribe of Manasseh in Bashan. 7To the sons of Merari, by clans, fell twelve towns from the tribes of Reuben, Gad and Zebulun.

8The Israelites assigned these towns and their pasture lands to the Levites by lot, as Yahweh had ordered through Moses.

The portion of the Kohathites

9From the tribe of Judah and the tribe of Simeon, they gave the towns named below. 10The first portion was for the sons of Aaron, belonging to the clans of the Kohathites, to the sons of Levi, since the first lot was theirs. 11They gave them Kiriath-Arba, Anak's father's town—now Hebron—in the highlands of Judah, with its surrounding pasture lands. 12The fields and villages of this town, however, they gave to Caleb son of Jephunneh as his property. 13To the sons of Aaron the priest they gave Hebron, a city of refuge for those who had killed, with its pasture lands, as well as Libnah with its pasture lands, 14Jattir with its pasture lands, Eshtemoa with its pasture lands, 15Holon with its pasture lands, Debir with its pasture lands, 16Ashan with its pasture lands, Juttah with its pasture lands, and Beth-Shemesh with its pasture lands: nine towns taken from these two tribes; 17and, from the tribe of Benjamin, Gibeon with its pasture lands, Geba with its pasture lands,

18 Anathoth with its pasture lands and Almon with its pasture lands: four towns.

19 Total number of towns for the priests, the sons of Aaron: thirteen towns with their pasture lands.

20 As regards the clans of the sons of Kohath, those Levites still left of the sons of Kohath, the towns of their lot were taken from the tribe of Ephraim. 21 They were given Shechem, a city of refuge for those who had killed, with its pasture lands, in the highlands of Ephraim, as well as Gezer with its pasture lands, 22 Kibzaim with its pasture lands, and Beth-Horon with its pasture lands: four towns; 23 from the tribe of Dan, Elteke with its pasture lands, Gibbethon with its pasture lands, 24 Aijalon with its pasture lands and Gath-Rimmon with its pasture lands: four towns; 25 and, from the half-tribe of Manasseh, Taanach with its pasture lands and Jibleam with its pasture lands: two towns.

26 In all: ten towns with their pasture lands for the remaining clans of the sons of Kohath.

The portion of the sons of Gershon

27 To the sons of Gershon, of the levitical clans, were given: from the half-tribe of Manasseh, Golan in Bashan, a city of refuge for those who had killed, with its pasture lands, and Ashtaroth with its pasture lands—two towns; 28 from the tribe of Issachar, Kishion with its pasture lands, Dobrath with its pasture lands, 29 Jarmuth with its pasture lands and En-Gannim with its pasture lands—four towns; 30 from the tribe of Asher, Mishal with its pasture lands, Abdon with its pasture lands, 31 Helkath with its pasture lands and Rehob with its pasture lands—four towns; 32 and, from the tribe of Naphtali, Kedesh in Galilee, a city of refuge for those who had killed, with its pasture lands, Hammoth-Dor with its pasture lands and Kartan with its pasture lands—three towns.

33 Total number of towns of the Gershonites, by clans: thirteen towns with their pasture lands.

The portion of the sons of Merari

34 To the clans of the sons of Merari, the remainder of the Levites, fell: from the tribe of Zebulun, Jokneam with its pasture lands, Kartah with its pasture lands, 35 Rimmon with its pasture lands and Nahalal with its pasture lands—four towns; 36 on the other side of the Jordan opposite Jericho, from the tribe of Reuben, Bezer in the desert, on the tableland, a city of refuge for those who had killed, with its pasture lands, Jahaz with its pasture lands, 37 Kedemoth with its pasture lands and Mephaath with its pasture lands—four towns; 38 and, from the tribe of Gad, Ramoth in Gilead, a city of refuge for those who had killed, with its pasture lands, Mahanaim with its pasture lands, 39 Heshbon with its pasture lands and Jazer with its pasture lands—four towns.

40 Total number of towns forming the lot of the sons of Merari by clans, of the remaining levitical clans: twelve towns.

41 The total number of towns for the Levites in Israelite territory was forty-eight towns with their pasture lands. 42 These towns consisted in each case of the town itself and the pasture land round it. This was the case with all the towns.

End of the distribution

43 This was how Yahweh gave the Israelites the entire country which he had sworn to give to their ancestors. They took possession of it and settled in it. 44 Yahweh granted them tranquillity on all their frontiers just as he had sworn to their ancestors and, of all their enemies, not one succeeded in resisting them. Yahweh put all their enemies at their mercy. 45 Of all the promises that Yahweh had made to the House of Israel, not one failed; all were fulfilled.

The Transjordanian tribes are sent home

22 Joshua then summoned the Reubenites, the Gadites and the half-tribe of

Manasseh ²and said to them, 'You have observed everything that Moses, servant of Yahweh, ordered you, and whenever I have given you an order you have listened to me. ³You have not deserted your brothers, from long ago until today, keeping the observance of the commandment of Yahweh your God. ⁴Now that Yahweh your God has granted your brothers the rest that he promised them, go back to your tents, to the country belonging to you which Moses, servant of Yahweh, gave you on the other side of the Jordan. ⁵But take great care to practise the commandments and the Law which Moses, servant of Yahweh, has given you: to love Yahweh your God, always to follow his paths, to keep his commandments, to be loyal to him and to serve him with all your heart and with all your soul.'

⁶Joshua blessed them and sent them away, and they went home to their tents.

⁷To one half of the tribe of Manasseh, Moses had given a territory in Bashan; to the other half, Joshua gave another among their brothers on the west bank of the Jordan. As Joshua sent them home to their tents, he blessed them ⁸and said to them, 'You are going back to your tents with great wealth, with a great deal of livestock, with silver and gold, bronze and iron and great quantities of clothing; share the spoils of your enemies with your brothers.'

An altar is built beside the Jordan

⁹The Reubenites, the Gadites and the half-tribe of Manasseh returned home, leaving the Israelites at Shiloh in Canaan, and made for Gilead, the territory which belonged to them as a result of Yahweh's order given through Moses. ¹⁰When they came to the stone circle by the Jordan, in Canaanite territory, the Reubenites, the Gadites and the half-tribe of Manasseh built an altar there beside the Jordan, a large, imposing altar.

¹¹This came to the ears of the Israelites. 'Look,' the word went round, 'the Reubenites, the Gadites and the half-tribe of Manasseh have built this altar on the Canaanite side, near the stone circle by the Jordan, on the Israelites' bank.'

¹²At this news, the whole community of the Israelites mustered at Shiloh, to march against them and make war on them.

Reproaches addressed to the eastern tribes

¹³The Israelites sent the priest Phinehas son of Eleazar to the Reubenites, the Gadites and the half-tribe of Manasseh, in Gilead, ¹⁴and with him ten leading men, one man from a leading family from each of the tribes of Israel, each of them being head of his family in the clans of Israel. ¹⁵Having reached the Reubenites, the Gadites and the half-tribe of Manasseh in Gilead, they said this:

¹⁶'The whole community of Israel says as follows, "What do you mean by this infidelity, which you have committed against the God of Israel by now repudiating your allegiance to Yahweh, and by building yourselves an altar with the intention now of rebelling against Yahweh? ¹⁷Was the crime which we committed at Peor so slight—although we have not managed to purify ourselves from that even now, in spite of the plague which has ravaged the community of Yahweh—¹⁸that you must now repudiate your allegiance to Yahweh? For since you are in rebellion against him today, tomorrow his anger will be aroused against the whole community of Israel. ¹⁹Is the country in which you have settled unclean? Then cross over into the country where Yahweh has settled, there where Yahweh's Dwelling now stands, and settle among us. But do not rebel against Yahweh or involve us in your rebellion by building a rival altar to the altar of Yahweh our God. ²⁰When Achan son of Zerah was unfaithful to the curse of destruction, did not the retribution come down on the whole community of Israel, although he was only one man? Did he not have to die for his crime?"'

The Transjordanian tribes justify their action

21 The Reubenites, the Gadites and the half-tribe of Manasseh spoke in their turn and answered the heads of the clans of Israel:

22 'The God of gods, Yahweh, the God of gods, Yahweh well knows, and let Israel know it too: if there has been rebellion or infidelity to Yahweh on our part, may he refuse to save us today! 23 And if we have built ourselves an altar with the intention of repudiating our allegiance to Yahweh and of presenting burnt offering and oblation or of offering communion sacrifices on it, may Yahweh himself call us to account for it! 24 The truth is, we have done this as a precaution: in the future, your descendants might say to ours, "What connection do you have with Yahweh, God of Israel? 25 Has not Yahweh set the frontier of the Jordan between us and you, you Reubenites and Gadites? You have no share in Yahweh." Thus, your descendants would be the cause of stopping ours from fearing Yahweh.

26 'So we said to each other, "Let us build this altar, not for burnt offerings or other sacrifices 27 but as a witness between us and you and between our descendants after us, attesting that we too have the right to worship Yahweh, in his presence, with our burnt offerings, our victims and our communion sacrifices. And so, in the future your descendants will not be able to say to ours: You have no share in Yahweh." 28 And we furthermore said, "If ever it were to happen that they did say this either to us or to our descendants in the future, we should reply: Look at this structure, Yahweh's altar, made by our ancestors not for burnt offerings or other sacrifices but as a witness between us and you." 29 Far be it from us to rebel against Yahweh or now to repudiate our allegiance to Yahweh by building an altar for burnt offerings or oblations or sacrifices, in rivalry with the altar of Yahweh our God that stands before his Dwelling!'

Peace restored

30 When the priest Phinehas, the leaders of the community and the heads of the clans of Israel who were with him, heard the words spoken by the Gadites, the Reubenites and the Manassehites, they approved of them. 31 The priest Phinehas son of Eleazar then said to the Reubenites, the Gadites and the Manassehites, 'Today, we can see that Yahweh is among us, since you have not been unfaithful to Yahweh in this matter; this means that you have spared the Israelites from Yahweh's avenging hand.'

32 The priest Phinehas son of Eleazar and the leaders left the Reubenites and the Gadites and went back from Gilead to Canaan and the Israelites, to whom they reported the answer. 33 The Israelites were pleased to hear this; the Israelites gave thanks to God and spoke no more of marching against them to make war on them and to ravage the country inhabited by the Reubenites and the Gadites. 34 The Reubenites and the Gadites called the altar . . . , 'Because', they said, 'it will be a witness between us that Yahweh is God.'

Joshua sums up his work

23 Now long after Yahweh had given Israel rest from all the enemies surrounding them—Joshua was old now, far advanced in years—2 Joshua summoned all Israel, their elders, leaders, judges and officials, and said to them, 'I myself am old, far advanced in years; 3 you for your part have witnessed all that Yahweh your God has done to all these nations for your sake; Yahweh your God himself has fought for you. 4 Look, these nations still remaining, and all the nations which I have exterminated from the Jordan all the way to the Great Sea in the west, I have allotted to you as the heritage for your tribes. 5 Yahweh your God will himself drive them out before you; he will dispossess them before you and you will take possession of their country, as Yahweh your God has promised you.

Rules of conduct when living among foreigners

6 'So be very firm about keeping and doing everything written in the Book of the Law of Moses, not swerving from that either to right or to left. 7 Never mix with the peoples who are still left beside you. Do not utter the names of their gods, do not swear by them, do not serve them and do not bow down to them. 8 On the contrary, you must be loyal to Yahweh your God as you have been till now. 9 Yahweh has dispossessed great and powerful nations before you, and no one so far has been able to resist you. 10 One man of you was able to rout a thousand of them, since Yahweh your God was himself fighting for you, as he had promised you. 11 Be very careful, as you value your life, to love Yahweh your God.

12 'But should you in any way relapse, if you make friends with the remnant of these nations still living beside you, if you intermarry with them, if you mix with them and they with you, 13 then know for certain that Yahweh your God will stop dispossessing these nations before you, and for you they will be a snare, a pitfall, thorns in your sides and thistles in your eyes, until you vanish from this fine country given you by Yahweh your God.

14 'Today, you see, I am going the way of all the earth. Acknowledge with all your heart and soul that of all the promises made to you by Yahweh your God, not one has failed: all have been fulfilled—not one has failed.

15 'As every promise made to you by Yahweh your God has been fulfilled for you, by the same token Yahweh will fulfil all his threats against you, even to exterminating you from this fine country given you by Yahweh your God.

16 'For if you violate the covenant which Yahweh your God has imposed on you, if you go and serve other gods and bow down to them, then Yahweh's anger will be roused against you and you will quickly vanish from the fine country which he has given you.'

The great assembly at Shechem

24 Joshua gathered all the tribes of Israel together at Shechem; he then summoned all the elders of Israel, its leaders, judges and officials, and they presented themselves in God's presence. 2 Joshua then said to all the people:

'Yahweh, the God of Israel, says this, "From time immemorial, your ancestors, Terah, father of Abraham and Nahor, lived beyond the River, and served other gods. 3 I then brought your ancestor Abraham from beyond the River and led him through the length and breadth of Canaan. I increased his descendants and I gave him Isaac. 4 To Isaac I gave Jacob and Esau. To Esau I gave possession of the mountainous country of Seir. Jacob and his sons went down into Egypt. 5 I then sent Moses and Aaron, and plagued Egypt with the wonders that I worked there; finally I brought you out. 6 I brought your ancestors out of Egypt, and you came to the Sea; the Egyptians pursued your ancestors with chariots and horsemen, to the Sea of Reeds. 7 They then called to Yahweh, and he spread a thick fog between you and the Egyptians, and made the sea go back on them and cover them. You saw with your own eyes what I did in Egypt. Then, for a long while, you lived in the desert. 8 I then brought you into the country of the Amorites, who used to live on the further side of the Jordan; they made war on you and I put them at your mercy; after which, you took possession of their country, since I destroyed them before you. 9 Next, Balak son of Zippor, king of Moab, rose to make war on Israel, and sent for Balaam son of Beor to come and curse you. 10 But I would not listen to Balaam; instead, he had to bless you, and I saved you from his power.

11 "You then crossed the Jordan and came to Jericho, but the inhabitants of Jericho made war on you: Amorites, Perizzites, Canaanites, Hittites, Girgashites, Hivites and Jebusites, and I put them all at your mercy. 12 I sent hornets ahead of you, which drove out the two

Amorite kings before you; this was not the work of your sword or of your bow. [13] And now I have given you a country for which you have not toiled, towns you have not built, although you live in them, vineyards and olive groves you have not planted, although you eat their fruit."

Israel chooses Yahweh

[14] 'So now, fear Yahweh and serve him truly and sincerely; banish the gods whom your ancestors served beyond the River and in Egypt, and serve Yahweh. [15] But if serving Yahweh seems a bad thing to you, today you must make up your minds whom you do mean to serve, whether the gods whom your ancestors served beyond the River, or the gods of the Amorites in whose country you are now living. As regards my family and me, we shall serve Yahweh.'

[16] The people replied, 'Far be it from us to desert Yahweh and to serve other gods! [17] Yahweh our God was the one who brought us and our ancestors here from Egypt, from the place of slave-labour, who worked those great wonders before our eyes and who kept us safe all along the way we travelled and among all the peoples through whom we passed. [18] And Yahweh has driven all the nations out for us, including the Amorites who used to live in the country. We too shall serve Yahweh, for he is our God.'

[19] Joshua then said to the people, 'You will not be able to serve Yahweh, since he is a holy God, he is a jealous God who will not tolerate either your misdeeds or your sins. [20] If you desert Yahweh and serve the foreigners' gods, he will turn and maltreat you anew and, in spite of having been good to you in the past, will destroy you.' [21] The people replied to Joshua, 'No! Yahweh is the one we mean to serve.' [22] Joshua then said to the people, 'You are witnesses to yourselves that you have chosen Yahweh, to serve him.' They replied, 'Witnesses we are!' [23] 'Then banish the foreign gods which you have with you and give your allegiance to Yahweh, God of Israel!' [24] The people replied to Joshua, 'Yahweh our God is the one whom we shall serve; his voice we shall obey!'

The covenant at Shechem

[25] That day Joshua made a covenant for the people; he laid down a statute and ordinance for them at Shechem. [26] Joshua wrote these words in the Book of the Law of God. He then took a large stone and set it up there, under the oak tree in Yahweh's sanctuary. [27] Joshua then said to all the people, 'Look, this stone will be a witness to us, since it has heard all the words that Yahweh has spoken to us: it will be a witness against you, in case you should deny your God.' [28] Joshua then dismissed the people, every one to his own heritage.

The death of Joshua

[29] After this, Joshua son of Nun, servant of Yahweh, died; he was a hundred and ten years old. [30] He was buried on the estate which he had received as his heritage, at Timnath-Serah which lies in the highlands of Ephraim, north of Mount Gaash. [31] Israel served Yahweh throughout the lifetime of Joshua and throughout the lifetime of those elders who outlived Joshua and had known all the deeds which Yahweh had done for the sake of Israel.

The bones of Joseph; the death of Eleazar

[32] As regards the bones of Joseph, which the Israelites had brought from Egypt, these were buried at Shechem in the plot of ground which Jacob had bought for a hundred pieces of silver from the sons of Hamor father of Shechem, and which had become the heritage of the sons of Joseph. [33] Eleazar son of Aaron then died and was buried at Gibeah, the town of his son Phinehas, which had been given to him in the highlands of Ephraim.

The Book of

JUDGES

The settlement of Judah, Simeon, Caleb and the Kenites

1 Now after Joshua's death, the Israelites consulted Yahweh, asking, 'Which of us is to march on the Canaanites first, to make war on them?' ² And Yahweh replied, 'Judah is to march on them first; I am delivering the country into his hands.' ³ Judah then said to his brother Simeon, 'March with me into the territory allotted to me; we shall make war on the Canaanites, and then I in my turn shall march into your territory with you.' And Simeon marched with him. ⁴ So Judah marched on them, and Yahweh delivered the Canaanites and Perizzites into their hands, and they defeated them at Bezek—ten thousand of them! ⁵ At Bezek they came upon Adoni-Bezek; they joined battle with him and defeated the Canaanites and Perizzites. ⁶ Adoni-Bezek took to flight, but they chased and captured him and cut off his thumbs and big toes. ⁷ Adoni-Bezek said, 'Seventy kings with their thumbs and big toes cut off used to pick up the crumbs under my table. As I did, God does to me.' He was taken to Jerusalem, and there he died. ⁸ (The sons of Judah attacked Jerusalem and took it: they put its people to the sword and set fire to the city.)

⁹ After this the sons of Judah went down to make war on the Canaanites who were living in the highlands, the Negeb and the lowlands. ¹⁰ Judah next marched on the Canaanites living in Hebron—the name of Hebron in olden days was Kiriath-Arba—and beat Sheshai, Ahiman and Talmai. ¹¹ From there, he marched on the inhabitants of Debir—the name of Debir in olden days was Kiriath-Sepher. ¹² Caleb said, 'To the man who con-

quers and captures Kiriath-Sepher, I shall give my daughter Achsah as wife.' ¹³ The man who captured it was Othniel son of Kenaz, younger brother of Caleb, who gave him his daughter Achsah as wife. ¹⁴ When she arrived, he urged her to ask her father for arable land, but when she alighted from the donkey and Caleb asked her, 'What is the matter?' ¹⁵ she said to him, 'Grant me a blessing! As the land you have given me is the Negeb, give me springs of water, too!' So Caleb gave her what she wanted: the upper springs and the lower springs.

¹⁶ The sons of Hobab the Kenite, father-in-law of Moses, marched up with the sons of Judah from the City of Palm Trees into the desert of Judah lying in the Negeb of Arad, where they went and settled among the people.

¹⁷ Judah then set out with his brother Simeon. They beat the Canaanites who lived in Zephath and delivered it over to the curse of destruction; hence the town was given the name of Hormah. ¹⁸ Judah then captured Gaza and its territory, Ashkelon and its territory, Ekron and its territory. ¹⁹ᵇ And Yahweh was with Judah, who made himself master of the highlands; ¹⁹ᵃ he could not, however, dispossess the inhabitants of the plain, since they had iron chariots.

²⁰ As Moses had directed, Hebron was given to Caleb, and he drove the three sons of Anak out of it. ²¹ As regards the Jebusites living in Jerusalem, the sons of Benjamin did not dispossess them, and the Jebusites have been living in Jerusalem with the sons of Benjamin ever since.

The capture of Bethel

²² Similarly, the House of Joseph marched on Bethel, and Yahweh was with them. ²³ The

House of Joseph made a reconnaissance of Bethel. (In olden days, the name of the town was Luz.) [24] The scouts saw a man coming out of the town and said to him, 'Show us how to get into the town and we shall show you faithful love.' [25] And when he had shown them a way into the town, they put the town to the sword but let the man and his whole clan go. [26] The man went off to the country of the Hittites and built a town which he called Luz; and that has been its name ever since.

The northern tribes

[27] Manasseh did not dispossess Beth-Shean and its dependencies, nor Taanach and its dependencies, nor the inhabitants of Dor and its dependencies, nor the inhabitants of Ibleam and its dependencies, nor the inhabitants of Megiddo and its dependencies; in those parts the Canaanites held their ground. [28] But when the Israelites became stronger, they subjected the Canaanites to forced labour, although they did not dispossess them. [29] Nor did Ephraim dispossess the Canaanites living in Gezer; thus, the Canaanites went on living in Gezer with him. [30] Zebulun did not dispossess the inhabitants of Kitron or of Nahalol. The Canaanites lived on with Zebulun but were subjected to forced labour. [31] Asher did not dispossess the inhabitants of Acco, nor those of Sidon, of Mahalab, of Achzib, of Helbah, of Aphek or of Rehob. [32] So the Asherites lived among the Canaanite inhabitants of the country, not having dispossessed them. [33] Naphtali did not dispossess the inhabitants of Beth-Shemesh or of Beth-Anath; they settled among the Canaanite inhabitants of the country, but the inhabitants of Beth-Shemesh and of Beth-Anath were subjected to forced labour for them. [34] The Amorites drove the Danites back into the highlands and would not let them come down into the plain. [35] The Amorites held their ground at Har-Heres and Shaalbim, but when the hand of the House of Joseph grew heavier, they were subjected to forced labour.

([36] The territory of the Edomites begins at the Ascent of Scorpions, runs to the Rock and continues on upwards.)

The Angel of Yahweh tells Israel of disasters to come

2 The Angel of Yahweh[a] went up from Gilgal to Bethel and said, 'I have brought you out of Egypt and led you into this country, which I promised on oath to your ancestors. I said, "I shall never break my covenant with you. [2] You for your part must make no covenant with the inhabitants of this country; you will destroy their altars." But you have not listened to my voice. What is the reason for this? [3] Very well, I now say this, "I am not going to drive these nations out before you. They will become your oppressors, and their gods will be a snare for you." ' [4] When the angel of Yahweh had spoken these words to all the Israelites, the people began to wail at the top of their voices. [5] And they called the place Bochim, and offered sacrifices to Yahweh there.

General reflections on the period of the Judges

[6] Joshua having dismissed the people, the Israelites then went away, each one to his own heritage, to occupy the country. [b][7] The people served Yahweh throughout the lifetime of Joshua and throughout the lifetime of those elders who outlived Joshua and had known all the great deeds which Yahweh had done for the sake of Israel. [8] Joshua son of Nun, servant of Yahweh, was a hundred and ten years old when he died. [9] He was buried on the estate which he had received as his heritage at Timnath-Heres in the highlands of Ephraim, north of Mount Gaash. [10] And when that whole generation had been gathered to its ancestors, another generation followed it which knew neither Yahweh nor the deeds which he had done for the sake of Israel.

2a An expression for Yahweh himself in visible form.

2b ‖ Jos 24:29–31.

Religious interpretation of the period of the Judges

[11] The Israelites then did what is evil in Yahweh's eyes and served the Baals. [12] They deserted Yahweh, God of their ancestors, who had brought them out of Egypt, and they followed other gods, from those of the surrounding peoples. They bowed down to these; they provoked Yahweh; [13] they deserted Yahweh to serve Baal and Astartes.[c] [14] Then Yahweh's anger grew hot against Israel. He handed them over to pillagers who plundered them; he delivered them to the enemies surrounding them, and they were no longer able to resist their enemies. [15] Whenever they mounted an expedition, Yahweh's hand was there to foil them, as Yahweh had told them and as Yahweh had sworn to them, so that they were in dire distress.

[16] Yahweh then appointed them judges, who rescued them from the hands of their plunderers. [17] But even to their judges they refused to listen. They prostituted themselves to other gods and bowed down before these. Very quickly they left the path which their ancestors had trodden in obedience to the orders of Yahweh; they did not follow their example. [18] When Yahweh appointed judges for them, Yahweh was with the judge and rescued them from the hands of their enemies as long as the judge lived, since Yahweh relented at their groans under their persecutors and oppressors. [19] But once the judge was dead, they relapsed into even worse corruption than their ancestors. They followed other gods; they served them and bowed before them and would not give up the practices and stubborn ways of their ancestors at all.

Why foreign nations survived in Canaan

[20] Yahweh's anger then blazed out against Israel, and he said, 'Since this people has broken the covenant which I laid down for their ancestors, since they have not listened to my voice, [21] in future I shall not drive before them any one of those nations which Joshua left when he died, [22] in order, by means of them, to put Israel to the test, to see whether or not they would tread the paths of Yahweh as once their ancestors had trodden them.' [23] Hence, Yahweh allowed these nations to remain; he did not hurry to drive them out, and did not deliver them into the hands of Joshua.

3 These are the nations which Yahweh allowed to remain, by their means to put all those Israelites to the test who had not experienced any of the Canaanite wars [2] (this was only to instruct the Israelites' descendants, to teach them the art of war, those at least who had not experienced it previously): [3] the five chiefs of the Philistines, all the Canaanites, the Sidonians, and the Hittites who lived in the range of the Lebanon, from the uplands of Baal-Hermon to the Pass of Hamath. [4] They were used to put Israel to the test and see if they would keep the orders which Yahweh had given their ancestors through Moses. [5] The Israelites lived among the Canaanites, Hittites and Amorites, the Perizzites, Hivites and Jebusites; [6] they married their daughters, they gave their own sons to their daughters and they served their gods.

Othniel

[7] The Israelites did what is evil in Yahweh's eyes. They forgot Yahweh their God and served Baals and Asherahs. [8] Then Yahweh's anger blazed out against Israel: he handed them over to Cushan-Rishathaim king of Edom, and the Israelites were enslaved to Cushan-Rishathaim for eight years.

[9] The Israelites then cried to Yahweh and Yahweh raised for the Israelites a deliverer who rescued them, Othniel son of Kenaz, Caleb's younger brother. [10] The spirit of Yahweh was on him; he became judge in Israel and set out for war. Yahweh delivered Cushan-Rishathaim king of Edom into his hands, and he triumphed over Cushan-

2c Canaanite deities, the male and female fertility gods. Astarte is also called Asherah.

Rishathaim. [11] The country then had peace for forty years. Othniel son of Kenaz then died.

Ehud

[12] Again the Israelites began doing what is evil in Yahweh's eyes, and Yahweh strengthened Eglon king of Moab against Israel, since they were doing what is evil in Yahweh's eyes. [13] Eglon in conjunction with the sons of Ammon and Amalek marched on Israel, beat them and captured the City of Palm Trees.[a] [14] The Israelites were enslaved to Eglon king of Moab for eighteen years.

[15] The Israelites then cried to Yahweh, and Yahweh raised a deliverer for them, Ehud son of Gera, a Benjaminite; he was left-handed. The Israelites appointed him to take their tribute to Eglon king of Moab. [16] Ehud made himself a dagger—it was double-edged and a foot long—and strapped it under his clothes on his right thigh. [17] He presented the tribute to Eglon king of Moab. This Eglon was a very fat man. [18] Having presented the tribute, Ehud sent away the men who had been carrying it; [19] but he himself, on reaching the Idols which are near Gilgal, went back and said, 'I have a secret message for you, O king.' The king commanded silence, and all his attendants withdrew. [20] Ehud went up to him; he was sitting in his private room upstairs, where it was cool. Ehud said to him, 'I have a message from God for you, O king.' The latter immediately rose from his seat. [21] Then Ehud, reaching with his left hand, drew the dagger he was carrying on his right thigh and thrust it into the king's belly. [22] The hilt too went in after the blade, and the fat closed over the blade, since Ehud did not pull the dagger out of his belly again. [23] Ehud went out through the privies, having shut and bolted the doors of the upstairs room behind him.

[24] When he had gone, the servants came back and looked; the doors of the upstairs room were bolted. They thought, 'He is probably covering his feet in the inner part of the cool room.' [25] They waited until they became embarrassed, but still he did not open the doors of the upstairs room. Eventually, they took the key and opened the door; and there lay their master, dead, on the ground.

[26] Meanwhile, Ehud had got away, passed the Idols and made good his escape to safety in Seirah. [27] Once there, he sounded the horn in the highlands of Ephraim, and the Israelites came down from the hills with him at their head. [28] And he said to them, 'Follow me, because Yahweh has delivered your enemy Moab into your hands.' So they followed him, seized the fords of the Jordan against Moab and allowed no one to cross. [29] On that occasion they beat the Moabites, some ten thousand men, all tough and seasoned fighters, and not one escaped. [30] That day Moab was humbled under the hand of Israel, and the country had peace for eighty years.

Shamgar

[31] After him came Shamgar son of Anath. He routed six hundred of the Philistines with an ox-goad; he too was a deliverer of Israel.

Deborah and Barak

4 Once Ehud was dead, the Israelites again began doing what is evil in Yahweh's eyes, [2] and Yahweh handed them over to Jabin king of Canaan, who reigned at Hazor. The commander of his army was Sisera, who lived in Harosheth-ha-Goiim.

[3] The Israelites then cried to Yahweh; for Jabin had nine hundred iron chariots and had cruelly oppressed the Israelites for twenty years.

[4] Deborah, a prophetess, wife of Lappidoth, was judging Israel at the time. [5] She used to sit under Deborah's Palm between Ramah and Bethel in the highlands of Ephraim, and the Israelites would come to her for justice. [6] She sent for Barak son of Abinoam from Kedesh in Naphtali, and said to him, 'Has not Yahweh, God of Israel, commanded, "Go! March to Mount Tabor and with you take ten thousand of the sons of Naphtali and the sons of

3a Jericho, well within the territory of Benjamin.

22 READ JUDGES 3:12–30.

The Israelites then cried to Yahweh, and Yahweh raised a deliverer for them.

—JUDGES 3:15

HOW GOD CALLS US

There are three kinds of calling. The first is from God, the second comes through human intervention, and the third is from compulsion.

A calling is from God when some inspiration takes possession of our heart, and even while we are asleep stirs in us a desire for eternal life . . . , and bids us follow God and cleave to his commandments with life-giving contrition. For example, Scripture says that the voice of the Lord called Abraham, when he said, "Leave your country, your kindred and your father's house" (Gn 12:1). . . .

The second kind of calling takes place when the example and advice of the saints stir us up and inflame us with the desire of salvation. . . . For example, we find in Holy Scripture that it was in this way through Moses that the children of Israel were delivered from the Egyptian bondage.

But the third kind of calling comes from compulsion. When we have been involved in the riches and pleasures of this life, trials suddenly come upon us, and strike us with the danger of death, the loss of our goods, or the death of loved ones. So finally we are involuntarily driven to turn to God whom we scorned to follow when we prospered. We often find instances of this compulsory call in Scripture, when we read that because of their sins the Lord delivered the Israelites to their enemies; and that because of their enemies' savage cruelty they turned and cried to Lord. For example, we read in Judges that "Yahweh raised a deliverer for them, Ehud son of Gera, a Benjamanite." The Psalms also speak of this calling: "Whenever he slaughtered them, they began to seek him, they turned back and looked eagerly for him, recalling that God was their rock, God the Most High, their redeemer" (Ps 78:34–35). And again: "They cried out to Yahweh in their distress; he rescued them from their plight" (Ps 107:19). And again: "They cry in anguish and Yahweh hears, and rescues them from all their troubles" (Ps 34:17).

ST. JOHN CASSIAN, 360?–433?

YOU WILL FIND THE NEXT READING AT RUTH 2.

Zebulun. [7]I shall entice Sisera, the commander of Jabin's army, to encounter you at the Torrent of Kishon with his chariots and troops; and I shall put him into your power"? ' [8]Barak replied, 'If you come with me, I shall go; if you will not come, I shall not go, for I do not know how to choose the day when the angel of Yahweh will grant me success.' [9]'I shall go with you then,' she said, 'but, the way you are going about it, the glory will not be yours; for Yahweh will deliver Sisera into the hands of a woman.' Deborah then stood up and went with Barak to Kedesh. [10]Barak summoned Zebulun and Naphtali. Ten thousand men marched behind him, and Deborah went with him.

Heber the Kenite

[11]Heber the Kenite had parted company with the tribe of Kain and with the sons of Hobab,

father-in-law of Moses; he had pitched his tent near the Oak of Zaanannim, not far from Kedesh.

Defeat of Sisera

¹²Sisera was informed that Barak son of Abinoam had encamped on Mount Tabor. ¹³Sisera summoned all his chariots—nine hundred iron chariots—and all the troops he had, from Harosheth-ha-Goiim to the Torrent of Kishon. ¹⁴Deborah said to Barak, 'Up! For today is the day when Yahweh has put Sisera into your power. Is not Yahweh marching at your head?' And Barak charged down from Mount Tabor with ten thousand men behind him. ¹⁵At Barak's advance, Yahweh struck terror into Sisera, all his chariots and his entire army. Sisera leapt down from his chariot and fled on foot. ¹⁶Barak pursued the chariots and the army as far as Harosheth-ha-Goiim. Sisera's whole army fell by the edge of the sword; not one man was spared.

Death of Sisera

¹⁷Sisera meanwhile fled on foot towards the tent of Jael, the wife of Heber the Kenite. For there was peace between Jabin king of Hazor and the family of Heber the Kenite. ¹⁸Jael came out to meet Sisera and said to him, 'Stay here, my lord, with me; do not be afraid!' He stayed with her in her tent, and she covered him with a rug. ¹⁹He said to her, 'Please give me a little water to drink, for I am thirsty.' She opened the skin of milk, gave him some to drink and covered him up again. ²⁰Then he said to her, 'Stand at the tent door, and if anyone comes and questions you—if he asks, "Is there a man here?" say, "No."' ²¹But Jael the wife of Heber took a tent-peg and picked up a mallet; she crept up softly to him and drove the peg into his temple right through to the ground. He was lying fast asleep, worn out; and so he died. ²²And now Barak came up in pursuit of Sisera. Jael went out to meet him and said, 'Come in, and I will show you the

man you are looking for.' He went into her tent; and there was Sisera dead, with the tent-peg through his temple.

Israel delivered

²³Thus God that day humbled Jabin king of Canaan before the Israelites. ²⁴And the Israelites bore down more and more heavily on that king of Canaan, Jabin, until he was utterly destroyed.

The song of Deborah and Barak

5 They sang a song that day, Deborah and Barak son of Abinoam, and the words were:

² That the warriors in Israel unbound their
    hair,
that the people came forward with a will,
bless Yahweh!

³ Listen, you kings! Give ear, you
    princes!
From me, from me comes a song for
    Yahweh.
I shall glorify Yahweh, God of Israel.

⁴ Yahweh, when you set out from Seir,
when you marched from the field of
    Edom,
the earth shook,
the heavens pelted,
the clouds pelted down water.
⁵ The mountains melted before Yahweh
    of Sinai,
before Yahweh, God of Israel.

⁶ In the days of Shamgar son of Anath,
in the days of Jael,
there were no more caravans;
those who went forth on their travels
took their way along by-paths.

⁷ The villages in Israel were no more,
they were no more
until you arose, O Deborah,
until you arose, mother of Israel!

8 They were choosing new gods
   when war was at the gates.
   Was there one shield, one spear to be
      found
   among the forty thousand men in
      Israel?

9 My heart is with the leaders of Israel,
   with the people who came forward with
      a will!
   Bless Yahweh!

10 You who ride white donkeys
   and sit on saddle-blankets as you ride,
   and you who go on foot,
11 sing—to the sound of the shepherds
   at the watering places!
   There they extol Yahweh's blessings,
   his saving acts for his villages in Israel!
   (Then Yahweh's people marched down to
      the gates.)

12 Awake, awake, Deborah!
   Awake, awake, declaim a song!
   Take heart, to your feet, Barak,
   capture your captors, son of Abinoam!

13 Then Israel marched down to the gates;
   like champions, Yahweh's people marched
      down to fight for him!

14 The princes of Ephraim are in the valley.
   Behind you, Benjamin is in your ranks.

   Captains have come down from Machir,
   those who wield the commander's staff,
      from Zebulun.
15 The princes of Issachar are with Deborah;
   Naphtali, with Barak, in the valley follows
      in hot pursuit.

   In the clans of Reuben
   there was much searching of heart.
16 Why did you stay among the sheepfolds,
   listening for the whistle, with the flocks?
   (In the clans of Reuben,
   there was much searching of heart.)

17 Gilead stayed on the other side of the
      Jordan,
   and why should Dan have stayed aboard
      ship?
   Asher remained beside the sea,
   peacefully living within his ports.

18 Zebulun is a people who have braved
      death,
   Naphtali too, on the high ground of the
      country.

19 The kings came and they fought,
   how they fought, those kings of Canaan,
   at Taanach, near the Waters of Megiddo,
   but no booty of silver did they take!

20 The stars fought from heaven,
   from their orbits they fought against
      Sisera.

21 The torrent of Kishon swept them away,
   the torrent of old, the torrent of Kishon.
   —March on, be strong my soul!

22 The horses' hooves then hammer the
      ground:
   galloping, galloping go his steeds.
23 'Curse Meroz,' said the Angel of Yahweh,
   'curse, curse the people living there
   for not having come to Yahweh's help,
   to Yahweh's help as warriors!'

24 Most blessed of women be Jael
   (the wife of Heber the Kenite);
   of tent-dwelling women, may she be most
      blessed!

25 He asked for water; she gave him milk;
   she offered him curds in a lordly dish.
26 She reached her hand out to seize the peg,
   her right hand to seize the workman's
      mallet.

   She hammered Sisera, she crushed his
      head,
   she pierced his temple and shattered it.

27 Between her feet, he crumpled, he fell,
     he lay;
 at her feet, he crumpled, he fell.
 Where he crumpled, there he fell,
     destroyed.

28 At the window, she leans and watches,
 Sisera's mother, through the lattice,
 'Why is his chariot so long coming?
 Why so delayed the hoof-beats from his
     chariot?'

29 The wisest of her ladies answers,
 and she to herself repeats,
30 'Are they not collecting and sharing out
     the spoil:
 a girl, two girls for each warrior;
 a booty of coloured and embroidered stuff
     for Sisera,
 one scarf, two embroidered scarves
     for me!'

31 So perish all your enemies, Yahweh!
 And let those who love you be like the sun
 when he emerges in all his strength!

And the country had peace for forty years.

Israel oppressed by the Midianites

6 The Israelites did what is evil in Yahweh's eyes, and for seven years Yahweh handed them over to Midian; 2 and Midian bore down heavily on Israel. To escape from the Midianites[a] the Israelites used the mountain clefts and the caves and shelters. 3 Whenever Israel sowed seed the Midianites would march up with Amalek and the sons of the East. They would march on Israel. 4 They would pitch camp on their territory and destroy the produce of the country as far as Gaza. They left Israel nothing to live on, not a sheep or an ox or a donkey, 5 for they came up as thick as locusts with their cattle and their tents; they and their camels were innumerable, they invaded the country to pillage it. 6 Thus, Midian brought Israel to great distress, and the Israelites cried to Yahweh.

A message from a prophet

7 When the Israelites cried to Yahweh because of Midian, 8 Yahweh sent a prophet to the Israelites. He said to them, 'This is what Yahweh, God of Israel, says, "It was I who brought you out of Egypt, and led you out of the place of slave-labour. 9 I rescued you from the power of the Egyptians and from the power of all who oppressed you. I drove them out before you and gave you their country to you. 10 And I said to you: I am Yahweh your God. You are not to fear the gods of the Amorites in whose country you are now living. But you have not listened to my voice."'

The Angel of Yahweh appears to Gideon

11 The Angel of Yahweh came and sat under the terebinth at Ophrah which belonged to Joash of Abiezer. Gideon his son was threshing wheat inside the wine-press, to keep it hidden from Midian, 12 and the Angel of Yahweh appeared to him and said, 'Yahweh is with you, valiant warrior!' 13 Gideon replied, 'Excuse me, my lord, but if Yahweh is with us, why is all this happening to us? And where are all his miracles which our ancestors used to tell us about when they said, "Did not Yahweh bring us out of Egypt?" But now Yahweh has deserted us; he has abandoned us to Midian.'

14 At this, Yahweh turned to him and said, 'Go in this strength of yours, and you will rescue Israel from the power of Midian. Am I not sending you myself?' 15 Gideon replied, 'Forgive me, my lord, but how can I deliver Israel? My clan is the weakest in Manasseh and I am the least important of my father's family.' 16 Yahweh replied, 'I shall be with you and you will crush Midian as though it were one man.' 17 Gideon said, 'If I have found favour in your sight, give me a sign that you are speaking to me. 18 Please do not go away from here until I come back to you, bringing you my offering and laying it before you.' And he replied, 'I shall stay until you come back.'

6a Nomads based in north-west Sinai, near the Amalekites.

19 Gideon went away, he prepared a young goat and from an *ephah* of flour he made unleavened cakes. He put the meat into a basket and the broth into a pot, then brought it all to him under the terebinth. As he approached, 20 the Angel of Yahweh said to him, 'Take the meat and unleavened cakes, put them on this rock and pour the broth over them.' Gideon did so. 21 The Angel of Yahweh then stretched out the tip of the staff which he was carrying, and touched the meat and unleavened cakes. Fire sprang from the rock and consumed the meat and unleavened cakes, and the Angel of Yahweh vanished before his eyes. 22 Gideon then knew that this was the Angel of Yahweh, and he said, 'Alas, my Lord Yahweh! Now I have seen the Angel of Yahweh face to face!' 23 Yahweh answered, 'Peace be with you; have no fear; you will not die.' 24 Gideon built an altar there to Yahweh and called it Yahweh-Peace. This altar stands in our own day at Ophrah of Abiezer.

Gideon against Baal

25 Now that night, Yahweh said to Gideon, 'Take your father's bull, the seven-year-old bull, and pull down the altar to Baal belonging to your father and cut down the sacred pole beside it. 26 Then, on top of this strong-point, build a proper altar to Yahweh your God. Then take the bull and burn it as a burnt offering on the wood of the sacred pole which you have cut down.' 27 Gideon then took ten of his servants and did as Yahweh had ordered him. But, being too frightened of his family and of the townspeople to do it in daylight, he did it at night. 28 Next morning, when the townspeople got up, they found that the altar to Baal had been destroyed, the sacred pole standing beside it had been cut down and the bull had been sacrificed as a burnt offering on the newly built altar. 29 'Who has done this?' they asked one another. They searched, made enquiries and declared, 'Gideon son of Joash has done it.' 30 The townspeople then said to Joash, 'Bring out your son; he must die for having destroyed Baal's altar and cut down the

sacred pole which stood beside it.' 31 To the people all crowding round him, Joash replied, 'Is it your job to plead for Baal? Is it your job to champion his cause? (Anyone who pleads for Baal must be put to death before dawn.) If he is a god, let him plead for himself, now that Gideon has destroyed his altar.' 32 That day, Gideon was given the name Jerubbaal, because, they said, 'Baal must plead against him, because he has destroyed his altar!'

The call to arms

33 All Midian and Amalek and the sons of the East joined forces and, having crossed the Jordan, pitched camp in the plain of Jezreel. 34 And the spirit of Yahweh clothed Gideon around; he sounded the horn and Abiezer rallied behind him. 35 He sent messengers throughout Manasseh, and Manasseh too rallied behind him; he sent messengers to Asher, Zebulun and Naphtali, and they marched out to meet him.

The sign of the fleece

36 Gideon said to God, 'If it is really you delivering Israel by means of me, as you have said, 37 look, I am going to put a woollen fleece on the threshing-floor; if there is dew only on the fleece and all the ground stays dry, then I shall know that you will deliver Israel by means of me, as you have said.' 38 And so it happened. Early next morning, Gideon got up, squeezed the fleece and wrung enough dew out of the fleece to fill a cup. 39 Gideon then said to God, 'Do not be angry with me if I speak just once more. Allow me to make the fleece-test just once more: let the fleece alone be dry and there be dew all over the ground!' 40 And God did so that night. The fleece alone stayed dry, and there was dew all over the ground.

Yahweh reduces the numbers of Gideon's army

7 Jerubbaal (that is, Gideon) got up very early, as did all the people who were with him; he pitched camp at En-Harod; the camp

of Midian was north of his, under the Hill of Moreh in the valley. ²Yahweh then said to Gideon, 'There are too many people with you for me to put Midian into their power; Israel might claim the credit for themselves at my expense: they might say, "My own hand has rescued me." ³So now make this proclamation to the people, "Anyone trembling with fear is to go back and watch from Mount Gilboa." ' Twenty-two thousand of the people went back, and ten thousand remained.

⁴Yahweh said to Gideon, 'There are still too many people. Take them down to the waterside and I shall sort them out for you there. If I say of someone, "He is to go with you," that man is to go with you. And if I say of anyone, "He is not to go with you," that man is not to go.' ⁵So Gideon took the people down to the waterside, and Yahweh said to him, 'All those who lap the water with their tongues, as a dog laps, put these on one side. And all those who kneel down to drink, put these on the other side.' ⁶The number of those who lapped with their hands to their mouth was three hundred; all the rest of the people had knelt to drink. ⁷Yahweh then said to Gideon, 'With the three hundred who lapped the water, I shall rescue you and put Midian into your power. Let the people as a whole disperse to their homes.' ⁸So they took the people's provisions and their horns, and then Gideon sent all the Israelites back to their tents, keeping only the three hundred. The camp of Midian was below his in the valley.

An omen of victory

⁹Now it happened, that same night, that Yahweh said to him, 'Get up and go down to the camp. I am putting it into your power. ¹⁰If, however, you are nervous about going down, go down to the camp with your servant Purah; ¹¹listen to what they are saying, and that will encourage you to go down to the camp.' So, with his servant Purah, he went down to the edge of the outposts of the camp.

¹²Midian, Amalek and all the sons of the East were deployed in the valley as thick as locusts; their camels were as innumerable as the sand on the seashore. ¹³Gideon got there just as a man was telling his comrade a dream; he was saying, 'This was the dream I had: a cake made of barley bread came rolling into the camp of Midian; it came to a tent, struck against it and turned it upside down.' ¹⁴His comrade replied, 'This can only be the sword of Gideon son of Joash the Israelite. God has put Midian and the whole camp into his power.' ¹⁵When Gideon heard the dream thus told and interpreted, he bowed in reverence; he then went back to the camp of Israel and said, 'On your feet, for Yahweh has put the camp of Midian into your power!'

The surprise attack

¹⁶Gideon then divided his three hundred men into three groups. To each he gave a horn and an empty pitcher, with a torch inside each pitcher. ¹⁷He said to them, 'Watch me, and do as I do. When I reach the edge of the camp, whatever I do, you must do also. ¹⁸I shall blow my horn, and so will all those who are with me; you too will then blow your horns all round the camp and shout, "For Yahweh and for Gideon!" '

¹⁹Gideon and his hundred companions reached the edge of the camp at the beginning of the middle watch, when the new sentries had just been posted; they blew their horns and smashed the pitchers in their hands. ²⁰The three groups blew their horns and smashed their pitchers; with their left hands they grasped the torches, with their right hands the horns for blowing them; and they shouted, 'The sword for Yahweh and for Gideon!' ²¹And they stood still, spaced out round the camp. The whole camp was thrown into confusion and the Midianites fled, shouting. ²²While the three hundred blew their horns, Yahweh made each man turn his sword against his comrade throughout the entire camp. They all fled as far as Beth-ha-Shittah in the direction of Zarethan, as far as the bank of Abel-Meholah opposite Tabbath.

The pursuit

23 The men of Israel mustered from Naphtali, Asher and all Manasseh, and pursued Midian. 24 Gideon sent messengers throughout the highlands of Ephraim to say, 'Come down to meet Midian, seize the water-points ahead of them as far as Beth-Barah and the Jordan.' All the men of Ephraim mustered and seized the water-points as far as Beth-Barah and the Jordan. 25 They captured the two Midianite chieftains, Oreb and Zeeb; they killed Oreb at Oreb's Rock and Zeeb at Zeeb's Winepress.[a] They pursued Midian; and they brought the heads of Oreb and Zeeb to Gideon on the other side of the Jordan.

The Ephraimites take offence

8 Now the men of Ephraim said to Gideon, 'What do you mean by treating us like this, not summoning us when you went to fight Midian?' And they reproached him bitterly. 2 He replied, 'What have I achieved, compared with you? Is not the gleaning of Ephraim's grapes better than the vintage of Abiezer? 3 God delivered Oreb and Zeeb, the chieftains of Midian, into your power. What was I able to do, in comparison with what you have done?' At these words, their anger with him died down.

Gideon pursues the enemy beyond the Jordan

4 Gideon reached the Jordan and crossed it, but he and his three hundred companions were exhausted with the pursuit. 5 So he said to the men of Succoth, 'Please give my followers some loaves of bread, since they are exhausted, and I am pursuing Zebah and Zalmunna the kings of Midian.' 6 The headmen of Succoth replied, 'Are the hands of Zebah and Zalmunna already in your grasp, that we should give bread to your army?' 7 'Very well,' retorted Gideon, 'when Yahweh has put Zebah and Zalmunna into my power, I shall tear your flesh off with desert-thorn and thistles.' 8 From there he went up to Penuel and asked the men of Penuel the same thing; they replied as those of Succoth had done. 9 And to those of Penuel he made a similar retort, 'When I return victorious, I shall destroy this tower.'

The defeat of Zebah and Zalmunna

10 Zebah and Zalmunna were in Karkor with their army, about fifteen thousand men, all that was left of the entire army of the sons of the East. Of men bearing arms, a hundred and twenty thousand had fallen. 11 Gideon approached them by the tent-dwellers' route, east of Nobah and Jogbehah, and attacked the army when it thought itself in safety. 12 Zebah and Zalmunna fled. He pursued them; he took the two kings of Midian prisoner— Zebah and Zalmunna—and the whole army he routed in panic.

Gideon's acts of vengeance

13 After the battle Gideon came back by the Ascent of Heres. 14 He caught a young man, one of the people of Succoth, and questioned him, and the latter wrote down the names of the headmen and elders of Succoth for him— seventy-seven men. 15 Gideon son of Joash then went to the people of Succoth and said, 'Here you see Zebah and Zalmunna, about whom you taunted me and said, "Are the hands of Zebah and Zalmunna already in your grasp, that we should give bread to your exhausted troops?" ' 16 He then seized the elders of the town and, taking desert-thorn and thistles, tore the men of Succoth to pieces. 17 He destroyed the tower of Penuel and slaughtered the townsmen. 18 He then said to Zebah and Zalmunna, 'The men you killed at Tabor— what were they like?' They replied, 'They looked like you. Every one of them carried himself like the son of a king.' 19 Gideon replied, 'They were my brothers, the sons of my own mother; as Yahweh lives, if you had spared their lives I would not kill you.' 20 To Jether his eldest son he said, 'Stand up and kill

7a Fragment explaining two place-names and independent of the main story.

them!' But the boy did not draw his sword; he dared not; he was still only a lad. 21 Zebah and Zalmunna then said, 'Stand up yourself, and strike us down; for as a man is, so is his strength.' Then Gideon stood up and killed Zebah and Zalmunna; and he took the crescents from round their camels' necks.

Latter days of Gideon

22 The men of Israel said to Gideon, 'Rule over us, you, your son and your grandson, since you have rescued us from the power of Midian.' 23 But Gideon replied, 'I will not rule you, neither will my son. Yahweh shall rule you.' 24 Gideon went on, however, 'Let me make you one request. Each of you give me one ring out of his booty'—for the vanquished had had gold rings, being Ishmaelites. 25 'We shall give them gladly,' they replied. So he spread out his cloak, and on it each of them threw a ring from his booty. 26 The weight of the gold rings which he had asked for amounted to seventeen hundred shekels of gold, besides the crescents and the earrings and purple garments worn by the kings of Midian, and besides the collars round their camels' necks. 27 From this Gideon made an *ephod*[a] and set it up in his town, in Ophrah. All Israel, following his example, prostituted themselves to it, and it was a snare for Gideon and his family.

28 Thus Midian was humbled before the Israelites. He did not raise his head again, and the country had peace for forty years, as long as Gideon lived. 29 So Jerubbaal son of Joash went to live at home. 30 Gideon had seventy sons begotten by him, for he had many wives. 31 His concubine, who lived in Shechem, also bore him a son, to whom he gave the name Abimelech. 32 Gideon son of Joash died after a happy old age and was buried in the tomb of Joash his father, at Ophrah of Abiezer.

Israel relapses into idolatry

33 After Gideon's death, the people of Israel again began to prostitute themselves to the Baals, taking Baal-Berith for their god. 34 The Israelites no longer remembered Yahweh their God, who had rescued them from all the enemies round them. 35 And to the family of Jerubbaal—Gideon—they showed no faithful gratitude for all the good which it had done for Israel.

The reign of Abimelech

9 Abimelech son of Jerubbaal confronted his mother's brothers at Shechem and, to them and to the whole clan of his maternal grandfather's family, he said, 2 'Please put this question to the leading men of Shechem: Which is better for you: to be ruled by seventy people—all Jerubbaal's sons—or to be ruled by one? Remember too that I am your own flesh and bone.' 3 His mother's brothers said all this on his behalf to all the leading men of Shechem, and their feelings swayed them to follow Abimelech, since they argued, 'He is our brother.' 4 So they gave him seventy shekels of silver from the temple of Baal-Berith, and with this Abimelech paid violent adventurers to follow him. 5 He then went to his father's house at Ophrah and put his brothers, Jerubbaal's seventy sons, to death on one and the same stone. Jotham, however, Jerubbaal's youngest son, escaped by going into hiding. 6 All the leading men of Shechem and all Beth-Millo then met and proclaimed Abimelech king at the oak of the cultic stone at Shechem.

Jotham's diatribe

7 News of this was brought to Jotham. He went and stood on the top of Mount Gerizim and shouted at the top of his voice:

> Hear me, leaders of Shechem,
> so that God may also hear you!

8 One day the trees went out
to anoint a king to rule them.
They said to the olive tree, 'Be our king!'

9 The olive tree replied,
'Must I forgo my oil

8a Here a cult-object, cf. Ex 28:6.

which gives honour to gods and men,
to stand and sway over the trees?'

¹⁰ Then the trees said to the fig tree,
'You come and be our king!'

¹¹ The fig tree replied,
'Must I forgo my sweetness,
forgo my excellent fruit,
to go and sway over the trees?'

¹² Then the trees said to the vine,
'You come and be our king!'

¹³ The vine replied,
'Must I forgo my wine
which cheers gods and men,
to go and sway over the trees?'

¹⁴ Then the trees all said to the thorn bush,
'You come and be our king!'

¹⁵ And the thorn bush replied to the trees,
'If you are anointing me in good faith to be
your king,
come and shelter in my shade.
But, if not, fire will come out of the thorn
bush
and devour the cedars of Lebanon.'

¹⁶'Now then, if you have acted in sincerity and good faith in making Abimelech king, if you have dealt honourably with Jerubbaal and his family, and have treated him as his actions deserved, ¹⁷my father having fought for you, risked his life and rescued you from the power of Midian, ¹⁸and you today having risen up against my father's family, murdered his sons—seventy of them on one and the same stone—and appointed Abimelech, his slave-girl's son, to rule the leading men of Shechem, because he is your brother!—¹⁹if, I say, you have acted in sincerity and good faith towards Jerubbaal and his family, then may Abimelech be your joy and may you be his! ²⁰If not, may fire come out of Abimelech and devour the leading men of Shechem and Beth-Millo, and fire come out of the leading men of Shechem and Beth-Millo to devour Abimelech!'

²¹ Jotham then took to his heels; he fled and made his way to Beer; and there he stayed, to be out of his brother Abimelech's reach.

Shechem revolts against Abimelech

²² Abimelech ruled Israel for three years. ²³ God then sent a spirit of discord between Abimelech and the leaders of Shechem, and the leaders of Shechem betrayed Abimelech. ²⁴ And this was so that the crime committed against Jerubbaal's seventy sons should be avenged, and their blood recoil on their brother Abimelech who had murdered them, and on those leaders of Shechem who had helped him to murder his brothers.

²⁵ The leaders of Shechem put men to ambush him on the mountain tops, and these robbed anyone travelling their way. Abimelech was told of this. ²⁶ Gaal son of Obed, with his brothers, happened to pass through Shechem and win the confidence of the leaders of Shechem. ²⁷ These went out into the countryside to harvest their vineyards; they trod the grapes and made merry and went into the temple of their god. They ate and drank there and cursed Abimelech. ²⁸ Gaal son of Obed said, 'Who is Abimelech, and what is Shechem, for us to be his slaves? Should not Jerubbaal's son and his lieutenant, Zebul, be serving the men of Hamor, father of Shechem? Why should we be his slaves? ²⁹ Who will put this people under my command, so that I can expel Abimelech? I should say to him, "Reinforce your army and come out!"' ³⁰ Zebul the governor of the town was told what Gaal son of Obed had said, and he was furious. ³¹ He sent messengers secretly to Abimelech to say, 'Look! Gaal son of Obed has come to Shechem with his brothers, and they are stirring up the town against you. ³²So, move under cover of dark, you and the men you have with you, and take up concealed positions in the countryside; ³³then in the morning at sunrise, break cover and rush on the town. When Gaal and his supporters come out

to meet you, treat them as occasion offers.' ³⁴ So Abimelech set off under cover of dark with all his own supporters and took up concealed positions over against Shechem, in four groups. ³⁵ As Gaal son of Obed was coming out and pausing at the entrance of the town gate, Abimelech and his supporters rose from their ambush. ³⁶ Gaal saw these men and said to Zebul, 'Look, there are men coming down from the tops of the mountains!' Zebul answered, 'You mistake the shadow of the mountains for men.' ³⁷ But Gaal insisted, 'Look, there are men coming down from the Navel of the Earth and another group is coming from the direction of the Diviners' Oak.' ³⁸ Zebul then said, 'Where are your mouthings now about "Who is Abimelech, for us to be his slaves?" Are not these the men you made light of? Sally out, then, and fight him.' ³⁹ Gaal sallied out at the head of the leaders of Shechem and engaged Abimelech. ⁴⁰ Abimelech drove Gaal off, who turned tail, many of his men falling dead before they could reach the gate. ⁴¹ Abimelech then stayed at Aruma, and Zebul expelled Gaal and his brothers and prevented them from living in Shechem.

Destruction of the town and citadel of Shechem

⁴² Next day, when the people went out into the countryside, Abimelech was told of this. ⁴³ He took his men, divided them into three groups and lay in wait in the fields. When he saw the people leaving the town, he bore down on them and slaughtered them. ⁴⁴ While Abimelech and his group rushed forward and took position at the entrance to the town gate, the two other groups fell on everyone in the fields and slaughtered them. ⁴⁵ All that day Abimelech attacked the town. He stormed it and slaughtered the people inside, razed the town and sowed it with salt. ⁴⁶ On hearing this, all the leading men inside Migdal-Shechem took refuge in the crypt of the temple of El-Berith. ⁴⁷ As soon as Abimelech heard that the leading men inside Migdal-Shechem had all gathered there, ⁴⁸ he went up Mount Zalmon with all

his men. Then taking an axe in his hands, he cut off the branch of a tree, picked it up and put it on his shoulder, and said to the men with him, 'Hurry and do what you have seen me do.' ⁴⁹ Each of his men similarly cut off a branch; then, following Abimelech, they piled the branches over the crypt and set it on fire over those who were inside; so that all the people in Migdal-Shechem died too, about a thousand men and women.

Siege of Thebez and death of Abimelech

⁵⁰ Abimelech then marched on Thebez, besieged it and captured it. ⁵¹ In the middle of the town there was a fortified tower in which all the men and women and all the leading men of the town took refuge. They locked the door behind them and climbed up to the roof of the tower. ⁵² Abimelech reached the tower and attacked it. As he was approaching the door of the tower to set it on fire, ⁵³ a woman threw down a millstone on his head and cracked his skull. ⁵⁴ He instantly called his young armour-bearer and said, 'Draw your sword and kill me, so that it will not be said of me that "A woman killed him".' His armour-bearer ran him through, and he died. ⁵⁵ When the men of Israel saw that Abimelech was dead, they dispersed to their homes.

⁵⁶ Thus God made to recoil on Abimelech the evil he had done his father by murdering his seventy brothers, ⁵⁷ and all the evil that the men of Shechem had done God made recoil on their heads too. And so the curse of Jotham son of Jerubbaal came true for them.

Tola

10 After Abimelech, Tola son of Puah, son of Dodo, rose to deliver Israel. He belonged to Issachar and lived at Shamir in the mountain country of Ephraim. ² He was judge in Israel for twenty-three years; he then died and was buried at Shamir.

Jair

³ After him rose Jair of Gilead, who judged Israel for twenty-two years. ⁴ He had thirty sons

who rode on thirty young donkeys and who owned thirty towns, still known today as the Encampments of Jair, in the territory of Gilead. ⁵Jair then died and was buried at Kamon.

Jephthah

⁶The Israelites again began doing what is evil in Yahweh's eyes. They served Baal and Astarte, and the gods of Aram and Sidon, the gods of Moab and those of the Ammonites and Philistines. They deserted Yahweh and served him no more. ⁷Yahweh's anger then grew hot against Israel and he gave them over into the power of the Philistines and the power of the Ammonites, ⁸who from that year onwards crushed and oppressed the Israelites for eighteen years—all those Israelites living on the other side of the Jordan in Amorite territory, in Gilead. ⁹Furthermore, the Ammonites would cross the Jordan and also make war on Judah, Benjamin and the House of Ephraim, so that Israel was in distress. ¹⁰The Israelites then cried to Yahweh and said, 'We have sinned against you, because we have turned from Yahweh our God to serve Baals.' ¹¹And Yahweh said to the Israelites, 'When Egyptians and Amorites, Ammonites and Philistines, ¹²when the Sidonians, Amalek and Midian oppressed you and you cried to me, did I not rescue you from their power? ¹³But it is you who have forsaken me and served other gods; and so I shall rescue you no more. ¹⁴Go and cry to the gods whom you have chosen. Let them rescue you in your time of trouble.' ¹⁵The Israelites replied to Yahweh, 'We have sinned. Treat us as you see fit, but please rescue us today.' ¹⁶They got rid of their foreign gods and served Yahweh, who could bear Israel's suffering no longer.

¹⁷The Ammonites gathered and pitched camp in Gilead. The Israelites rallied and pitched camp at Mizpah. ¹⁸The people, the chieftains of Gilead, then said to one another, 'Who will volunteer to attack the Ammonites? He shall be chief of all who live in Gilead!'

Jephthah lays down his terms

11 Jephthah the Gileadite was a valiant warrior. He was a prostitute's son. Gilead was Jephthah's father, ²but Gilead's wife also bore him sons, and the sons of this wife, when they grew up, drove Jephthah away, saying, 'No share of the paternal heritage for you, since you are a son of another woman.' ³Jephthah fled far from his brothers and settled in the territory of Tob. Jephthah enlisted a group of adventurers who used to go raiding with him.

⁴It was some time after this that the Ammonites made war on Israel. ⁵And when the Ammonites had attacked Israel, the elders of Gilead went to fetch Jephthah from the territory of Tob. ⁶'Come', they said, 'and be our commander, so that we can fight the Ammonites.' ⁷Jephthah replied to the elders of Gilead, 'Didn't you hate me and drive me out of my father's house? Why come to me now, when you are in trouble?' ⁸The elders of Gilead said to Jephthah, 'That is why we are turning to you now. Come with us; fight the Ammonites and be our chief, chief of all the people living in Gilead.' ⁹Jephthah then said to the elders of Gilead, 'If you bring me home to fight the Ammonites and Yahweh defeats them for me, I am to be your chief?' ¹⁰And the elders of Gilead then said to Jephthah, 'Yahweh be witness between us, if we do not do as you have said!' ¹¹So Jephthah set off with the elders of Gilead. The people put him at their head as chief and commander; and Jephthah repeated all his conditions at Mizpah in Yahweh's presence.

Jephthah negotiates with the Ammonites

¹²Jephthah sent messengers to the king of the Ammonites to say to him, 'What do you have against us, for you to come and make war on my country?' ¹³The king of the Ammonites replied to Jephthah's messengers, 'The reason is that when Israel came up from Egypt, they seized my country from the Arnon to the Jabbok and to the Jordan; so now restore it to me

peacefully.' ¹⁴Jephthah sent messengers back to the king of the Ammonites ¹⁵with this answer, 'Jephthah says this, "Israel seized neither the country of Moab nor the country of the Ammonites. ¹⁶When Israel came out of Egypt, they marched through the desert as far as the Sea of Reeds and, having reached Kadesh, ¹⁷Israel then sent messengers to the king of Edom to say: Please let me pass through your country, but the king of Edom would not listen. They sent similarly to the king of Moab, but he refused, and Israel remained at Kadesh; ¹⁸later, moving on through the desert and skirting the countries of Edom and Moab until arriving to the east of Moabite territory, the people camped on the other side of the Arnon but did not enter Moabite territory, the Arnon being the Moabite frontier. ¹⁹Israel then sent messengers to Sihon, king of the Amorites, ruling in Heshbon. Israel's message was: Please let me pass through your country to my destination. ²⁰But Sihon would not let Israel pass through his territory; he mustered his whole army; they encamped at Jahaz, and he then joined battle with Israel. ²¹Yahweh, God of Israel, delivered Sihon and his whole army into the power of Israel, who defeated them; as the result of which, Israel took possession of the entire territory of the Amorites living in that region. ²²Israel took possession of all the Amorite territory from the Arnon to the Jabbok and from the desert to the Jordan. ²³And now that Yahweh, God of Israel, has dispossessed the Amorites before his people Israel, do you think you can dispossess us? ²⁴Will you not keep as your possession whatever Chemosh, your god, has given you? And, just the same, we shall keep as ours whatever Yahweh our God has given us, to inherit from those who were before us! ²⁵Are you a better man than Balak son of Zippor, king of Moab? Did he pick a quarrel with Israel? Did he make war on them? ²⁶When Israel settled in Heshbon and its dependencies, and in Aroer and its dependencies, or in any of the towns on the banks of the Arnon (three hundred years ago), why did you not recover them then? ²⁷I for my part have done you no harm, but you are wronging me by making war on me. Let Yahweh the Judge give judgement today between the Israelites and the king of the Ammonites." ' ²⁸But the king of the Ammonites took no notice of the message that Jephthah sent him.

Jephthah's vow and his victory

²⁹The spirit of Yahweh was on Jephthah, who crossed Gilead and Manasseh, crossed by way of Mizpah in Gilead, and from Mizpah in Gilead crossed into Ammonite territory. ³⁰And Jephthah made a vow to Yahweh, 'If you deliver the Ammonites into my grasp, ³¹the first thing to come out of the doors of my house to meet me when I return in triumph from fighting the Ammonites shall belong to Yahweh, and I shall sacrifice it as a burnt offering.' ³²Jephthah crossed into Ammonite territory to attack them, and Yahweh delivered them into his grasp. ³³He beat them from Aroer to the border of Minnith (twenty towns) and to Abel-Keramim. It was a very severe defeat, and the Ammonites were humbled by the Israelites.

³⁴As Jephthah returned to his house at Mizpah, his daughter came out to meet him, dancing to the sound of tambourines. She was his only child; apart from her, he had neither son nor daughter. ³⁵When he saw her, he tore his clothes and exclaimed, 'Oh my daughter, what misery you have brought upon me! You have joined those who bring misery into my life! I have made a promise before Yahweh which I cannot retract.' ³⁶She replied, 'Father, you have made a promise to Yahweh; treat me as the promise that you have made requires, since Yahweh has granted you vengeance on your enemies the Ammonites.' ³⁷She then said to her father, 'Grant me this! Let me be free for two months. I shall go and wander in the mountains, and with my companions bewail my virginity.' ³⁸He replied, 'Go,' and let her go away for two months. So she went away with her companions and bewailed her virginity in the mountains. ³⁹When the two months

were over she went back to her father, and he treated her as the vow that he had uttered bound him. She had remained a virgin. And hence, the custom in Israel [40] for the daughters of Israel to leave home year by year and lament over the daughter of Jephthah the Gileadite for four days every year.

War between Ephraim and Gilead; the death of Jephthah

12 The men of Ephraim mobilised; they crossed the Jordan near Zaphon and said to Jephthah, 'Why did you go and make war on the Ammonites without asking us to go with you? We shall burn down your house over your head!' [2] Jephthah replied, 'My people and I were in serious conflict with the Ammonites. I summoned you, but you did not come to rescue me from them. [3] When I saw that no one was coming to rescue me, I took my life in my hands and marched against the Ammonites, and Yahweh handed them over to me. So why advance on me today to make war on me?' [4] Jephthah then mustered all the men of Gilead and made war on Ephraim, and the men of Gilead defeated Ephraim— since the latter used to say, 'You are only fugitives from Ephraim, you Gileadites in the heart of Ephraim and Manasseh.' [5] Gilead then cut Ephraim off from the fords of the Jordan, and whenever Ephraimite fugitives said, 'Let me cross,' the men of Gilead would ask, 'Are you an Ephraimite?' If he said, 'No,' [6] they then said, 'Very well, say Shibboleth.'[a] If anyone said, "Sibboleth", because he could not pronounce it, then they would seize him and kill him by the fords of the Jordan.

Forty-two thousand Ephraimites fell on this occasion.

[7] Jephthah judged Israel for six years. Jephthah the Gileadite then died and was buried in his town, in Gilead.

Ibzan

[8] After him, Ibzan of Bethlehem was judge in Israel. [9] He had thirty sons and thirty daughters. He gave his daughters in marriage outside his clan and brought in thirty brides from outside for his sons. He was judge in Israel for seven years. [10] Ibzan then died and was buried in Bethlehem.

Elon

[11] After him, Elon of Zebulun was judge in Israel. He was judge in Israel for ten years. [12] Elon of Zebulun then died and was buried at Aijalon in the territory of Zebulun.

Abdon

[13] After him, Abdon son of Hillel of Pirathon was judge in Israel. [14] He had forty sons and thirty grandsons who rode seventy young donkeys. He was judge in Israel for eight years. [15] Abdon son of Hillel of Pirathon then died and was buried at Pirathon in the territory of Ephraim, in the Amalekite highlands.

Samson

13 Again the Israelites began doing what is evil in Yahweh's eyes, and Yahweh delivered them into the power of the Philistines for forty years.

[2] There was a man of Zorah of the tribe of Dan, called Manoah. His wife was barren; she had borne no children. [3] The Angel of Yahweh appeared to this woman and said to her, 'You are barren and have had no child, but you are going to conceive and give birth to a son. [4] From now on, take great care. Drink no wine or fermented liquor, and eat nothing unclean. [5] For you are going to conceive and give birth to a son. No razor is to touch his head, for the boy is to be God's nazirite from his mother's womb; and he will start rescuing Israel from the power of the Philistines.' [6] The woman then went and told her husband, 'A man of God has just come to me, who looked like the Angel of God, so majestic was he. I did not ask him where he came from, and he did not tell me his name. [7] But he said to me, "You are going to conceive and will give birth to a son.

12a The word (='ear of corn') is chosen simply to show up local pronunciation.

From now on, drink no wine or fermented liquor, and eat nothing unclean. For the boy is to be God's nazirite from his mother's womb to his dying day." '

The Angel appears a second time

8 Manoah then pleaded with Yahweh and said, 'I beg you, Lord, let the man of God that you sent come to us again and instruct us what to do about the child when he is born.' 9 Yahweh heard Manoah's prayer, and the Angel of Yahweh visited the woman again while she was sitting in a field and when her husband Manoah was not with her. 10 The woman quickly ran and told her husband, 'Look,' she said, 'the man who came to me the other day has appeared to me again.' 11 Manoah got up, followed his wife, came to the man and said to him, 'Are you the man who spoke to this woman?' He replied, 'I am.' 12 Manoah then said, 'When your words come true, what will be the boy's way of life?' 13 The Angel of Yahweh replied to Manoah, 'From everything that I forbade this woman, let her abstain. 14 Let her swallow nothing that comes from the vine, let her drink no wine or fermented liquor, let her eat nothing unclean and let her obey all the orders that I have given her.' 15 Manoah then said to the Angel of Yahweh, 'Allow us to detain you while we prepare a kid for you'— 16b for Manoah did not know that this was the Angel of Yahweh. 16a The Angel of Yahweh said to Manoah, 'Even if you did detain me, I should not eat your food; but if you wish to prepare a burnt offering, offer it to Yahweh.' 17 Manoah then said to the Angel of Yahweh, 'What is your name, so that we may honour you when your words come true?' 18 The Angel of Yahweh replied, 'Why ask my name? It is a name of wonder.' 19 Manoah then took the kid and the oblation and offered it on the rock as a burnt offering to Yahweh the Wonderworker. Manoah and his wife looked on. 20 Now, as the flame rose heavenwards from the altar, the Angel of Yahweh ascended in this flame before the eyes of Manoah and his wife, and they fell face downwards on the ground. 21 After this, the Angel of Yahweh did not appear any more to Manoah and his wife, but Manoah understood that this had been the Angel of Yahweh. 22 And Manoah said to his wife, 'We are certain to die, because we have seen God.' 23 His wife replied, 'If Yahweh had meant to kill us, he would not have accepted a burnt offering and oblation from us, he would not have let us see all this and, at the same time, have told us such things.' 24 The woman gave birth to a son and called him Samson. The child grew, and Yahweh blessed him; 25 and the spirit of Yahweh began to stir him in the Camp of Dan, between Zorah and Eshtaol.

Samson marries

14 Samson went down to Timnah, and at Timnah he noticed a woman, a Philistine girl. 2 He went home again and told his father and mother this. 'At Timnah', he said, 'I noticed a woman, a Philistine girl. So now get her for me, to be my wife.' 3 His father and mother said to him, 'Is there no woman among your brothers' daughters or in our entire nation, for you to go and take a wife among these uncircumcised Philistines?' But Samson said to his father, 'Get that one for me; she is the one I am fond of.' 4 His father and mother did not know that all this came from Yahweh, who was seeking grounds for a quarrel with the Philistines, since at this time the Philistines dominated Israel.

5 Samson went down to Timnah and, as he reached the vineyards of Timnah, he saw a young lion coming roaring towards him. 6 The spirit of Yahweh seized on him and he tore the lion to pieces with his bare hands as though it were a kid; but he did not tell his father or mother what he had done. 7 He went down and talked to the woman, and he became fond of her. 8 Not long after this, Samson went back to marry her. He went out of his way to look at the carcass of the lion, and there was a swarm of bees in the lion's body, and honey. 9 He took up some honey in his hand and ate it as he went along. On returning to his father and

mother, he gave some to them, which they ate too, but he did not tell them that he had taken it from the lion's carcass. 10 His father then went down to the woman, and Samson made a feast there, as is the custom for young men. 11 And when the Philistines saw him, they chose thirty companions to stay with him.

Samson's riddle

12 Samson then said to them, 'Let me ask you a riddle. If you can give me the answer during the seven days of feasting, I shall give you thirty pieces of fine linen and thirty festal robes. 13 But if you cannot tell me the answer, then you in your turn must give me thirty pieces of fine linen and thirty festal robes.' 'Ask your riddle,' they replied, 'we are listening.' 14 So he said to them:

Out of the eater came what is eaten,
and out of the strong came what is sweet.

But three days went by and they could not solve the riddle.
15 On the fourth day they said to Samson's wife, 'Cajole your husband into explaining the riddle to us, or we shall burn you and your father's family to death. Did you invite us here to rob us?' 16 Samson's wife then went to him in tears and said, 'You only hate me, you do not love me. You have asked my fellow-countrymen a riddle and told not even me the answer.' He said to her, 'I have not told even my father or mother; why should I tell you?' 17 She wept on his neck for the seven days that their feasting lasted. She was so persistent that on the seventh day he told her the answer, and she told her fellow-countrymen.
18 So on the seventh day, before he went into the bedroom, the men of the town said to him:

What is sweeter than honey,
and what stronger than a lion?

He retorted:

If you had not ploughed with my heifer,
you would never have solved my riddle.

19 Then the spirit of Yahweh seized on him. He went down to Ashkelon, killed thirty men there, took what they wore and gave the festal robes to those who had answered the riddle, then burning with rage returned to his father's house. 20 Samson's wife was then given to the companion who had acted as his best man.

Samson burns the Philistines' harvest

15 Not long after this, at the time of the wheat harvest, Samson visited his wife, with a kid; he said, 'I wish to go to my wife in her room.' But her father would not let him enter. 2 'I felt sure', he said, 'that you had taken a real dislike to her, so I gave her to your companion. But would not her younger sister suit you better? Have her instead.' 3 But Samson answered them, 'I can get my revenge on the Philistines now only by doing them some damage.' 4 So Samson went off and caught three hundred foxes, then took torches and, turning the foxes tail to tail, put a torch between each pair of tails. 5 He lit the torches and set the foxes free in the Philistines' cornfields. In this way he burned both sheaves and standing corn, and the vines and olive trees as well.
6 The Philistines asked, 'Who has done this?' and received the answer, 'Samson, who married the Timnite's daughter; his father-in-law took the wife back again and gave her to his companion instead.' The Philistines then went and burned the woman and her father's family to death. 7 Samson said to them, 'If that is how you behave, I swear I will not rest till I have had my revenge on you.' 8 And he fell on them systematically and caused great havoc. Then he went down to the cave in the Rock of Etham and lived there.

The donkey's jawbone

9 The Philistines came up and encamped in Judah and made a foray against Lehi.
10 The men of Judah said to them, 'Why are you attacking us?' They replied, 'We have come to seize Samson and to treat him as he has treated us.' 11 Three thousand men of Judah then went down to the cave of the Rock

of Etham and said to him, 'Don't you know that the Philistines have us in their power? Now what have you done to us?' He replied, 'I have treated them only as they treated me.' ¹²They then said, 'We have come down to take you, to hand you over to the Philistines.' He said, 'Swear to me not to kill me yourselves.' ¹³They replied, 'No; we only want to bind you and hand you over to them; we certainly do not want to kill you.' They then bound him with two new ropes and brought him up from the Rock.

¹⁴As he was approaching Lehi, and the Philistines came running towards him with triumphant shouts, the spirit of Yahweh was on him; the ropes on his arms became like burnt strands of flax and the cords round his hands came untied. ¹⁵Coming across the fresh jawbone of a donkey, he reached out and snatched it up; and with it he slaughtered a thousand men. ¹⁶And Samson said:

With the jawbone of a donkey
    I have laid them in heaps,
with the jawbone of a donkey
    I have felled a thousand men.

¹⁷And with that he hurled the jawbone away; and that is why the place was called Ramath-Lehi.ᵃ ¹⁸And as he was very thirsty, he called on Yahweh and said, 'You yourself have worked this great deliverance by the hand of your servant; and now must I die of thirst and fall into the hands of the uncircumcised?' ¹⁹Then God opened a hollow in the ground, the hollow there is at Lehi, and water gushed out of it. Samson drank; his vigour returned and he revived. And therefore this spring was called En-ha-Kore;ᵇ it is still at Lehi today. ²⁰Samson was judge in Israel in the days of the Philistines for twenty years.

The gates of Gaza

16 Samson then went to Gaza and, seeing a prostitute there, went in to her. ²The men of Gaza being told, 'Samson has arrived,' surrounded the place and kept watch for him the whole night at the town gate. All that night they were going to make no move, thinking, 'Let us wait until daybreak, and then kill him.' ³Till midnight, however, Samson stayed in bed, and then at midnight he got up, seized the doors of the town gate and the two posts as well; he tore them up, bar and all, hoisted them on to his shoulders and carried them to the top of the hill overlooking Hebron.

Samson is betrayed by Delilah

⁴After this, he fell in love with a woman in the Vale of Sorek; she was called Delilah. ⁵The Philistine chiefs visited her and said, 'Cajole him and find out where his great strength comes from, and how we can master him, so that we can bind him and subdue him. In return we shall each give you eleven hundred silver shekels.'

⁶Delilah said to Samson, 'Please tell me where your great strength comes from, and what would be needed to bind and subdue you.' ⁷Samson replied, 'If I were bound with seven new bowstrings which had not yet been dried, I should lose my strength and become like any other man.' ⁸The Philistine chiefs brought Delilah seven new bowstrings which had not yet been dried and she took them and bound him with them. ⁹She had men concealed in her room, and she shouted, 'The Philistines are on you, Samson!' Then he snapped the bowstrings as a strand of tow snaps at a touch of the fire. So the secret of his strength remained unknown.

¹⁰Delilah then said to Samson, 'You have been laughing at me and telling me lies. But now please tell me what would be needed to bind you.' ¹¹He replied, 'If I were bound tightly with new ropes which have never been used, I should lose my strength and become like any other man.' ¹²Delilah then took new ropes and bound him with them, and she shouted, 'The Philistines are on you, Samson!'

15a Lit. 'hill of the jawbone'.

15b 'The Spring of the Caller', where Samson called on Yahweh.

She had men concealed in her room, but he snapped the ropes round his arms like thread.

¹³ Delilah then said to Samson, 'Up to now you have been laughing at me and telling me lies. Tell me what would be needed to bind you.' He replied, 'If you wove the seven locks of my hair into the warp of a cloth and beat them together tight with the reed, I should lose my strength and become like any other man.' ¹⁴ She lulled him to sleep, then wove the seven locks of his hair into the warp, beat them together tight with the reed and shouted, 'The Philistines are on you, Samson!' He woke from his sleep and pulled out both reed and warp. So the secret of his strength remained unknown.

¹⁵ Delilah said to him, 'How can you say that you love me, when your heart is not with me? Three times now you have laughed at me and have not told me where your great strength comes from.' ¹⁶ And day after day she pestered him with her talk, nagging him till he grew sick to death of it. ¹⁷ At last he confided everything to her; he said to her, 'A razor has never touched my head, because I have been God's nazirite from my mother's womb. If my head were shorn, then my power would leave me and I should lose my strength and become like any other man.' ¹⁸ Delilah then realized that he had really confided in her; she sent for the Philistine princes with the message, 'Come just once more: he has confided everything to me.' And the Philistine chiefs came to her with the money in their hands. ¹⁹ She lulled Samson to sleep in her lap, summoned a man and had him shear off the seven locks from his head. Thus for the first time she got control over him, and his strength left him. ²⁰ She cried, 'The Philistines are on you, Samson!' He awoke from sleep, thinking, 'I shall break free as I have done time after time and shake myself clear.' But he did not know that Yahweh had left him. ²¹ The Philistines seized him, put out his eyes and took him down to Gaza. They fettered him with a double chain of bronze and he spent his time turning the mill in the prison.

²² But his hair began to grow again when it had been cut off.

Samson's revenge and death

²³ The Philistine chiefs assembled to offer a great sacrifice to Dagon their god. And amid their festivities they said:

> Into our hands our god has delivered
> Samson our enemy.

²⁴ And as soon as the people saw their god, they acclaimed him, shouting his praises:

> Into our hands our god has delivered
> Samson our enemy,
> the man who laid our country waste
> and killed so many of us.

²⁵ And as their hearts were full of joy, they shouted, 'Summon Samson out to amuse us.' So Samson was summoned from prison, and he performed feats in front of them; then he was put to stand between the pillars. ²⁶ Samson then said to the boy who was leading him by the hand, 'Lead me where I can touch the pillars supporting the building, so that I can lean against them.' ²⁷ Now the building was crowded with men and women. All the Philistine chiefs were there, while about three thousand men and women were watching Samson's feats from the terrace. ²⁸ Samson called on Yahweh and cried out, 'Lord Yahweh, I beg you, remember me; give me strength again this once, O God, and let me be revenged on the Philistines at one blow for my two eyes.' ²⁹ And Samson took hold of the two central pillars supporting the building, and braced himself with his right arm round one and his left round the other; ³⁰ and he shouted, 'Let me die with the Philistines!' He then heaved with all his might, and the building fell on the chiefs and on all the people there. Those whom he brought to their death by his death outnumbered those whom he had done to death during his life. ³¹ His brothers and the whole of his father's family came down and

carried him away. They took him back and buried him between Zorah and Eshtaol in the tomb of Manoah his father. He had judged Israel for twenty years.

Micah's domestic shrine

17 In the highlands of Ephraim there was a man called Micayehu. [2] He said to his mother, 'The eleven hundred silver shekels which were taken from you and concerning which you uttered a curse, having said in my hearing . . .[a] Look, I have got that silver. I was the one who took it.' His mother said, 'May Yahweh bless my boy!' [3] He gave the eleven hundred shekels back to his mother, who said, 'I have indeed vowed to give this silver to Yahweh for my son, to have a statue carved and an idol cast in metal, but now I should like to give it back to you.' He, however, returned the money to his mother.

[4] His mother then took two hundred silver shekels and gave them to the metalworker. With them, he carved a statue (and cast an idol in metal) which was put in Micayehu's house. [5] This man Micah owned a shrine; he made an *ephod* and some domestic images, and installed one of his sons to be his priest. [6] In those days there was no king in Israel, and everyone did as he saw fit.

[7] There was a young man of Bethlehem in Judah, of the clan of Judah, who was a Levite and resided there as a stranger. [8] This man left the town of Bethlehem in Judah to settle wherever he could find a home. On his travels he came to the highlands of Ephraim and to Micah's house. [9] Micah asked him, 'Where do you come from?' The other replied, 'I am a Levite from Bethlehem in Judah. I am travelling, and am going to settle wherever I can find a home.' [10] Micah said to him, 'Stay here with me; be my father and priest and I shall give you ten silver shekels a year, and clothing and food.' [11] The Levite agreed to remain in the man's house, and the young man became like one of his sons to him. [12] Micah installed the Levite; the young man became Micah's priest and stayed in his house. [13] And Micah said, 'Now I know that Yahweh will treat me well, since I have this Levite as priest.'

The Danites in search of a territory

18 In those days there was no king in Israel.
Now in those days the tribe of Dan was in search of a territory to live in, for until then no territory had fallen to them among the tribes of Israel. [2] From their clan the Danites sent five brave men from Zorah and Eshtaol to reconnoitre the country and explore it. They said to them, 'Go and explore the country.' The five men came to the highlands of Ephraim, as far as Micah's house, and spent the night there. [3] When they were near Micah's house, they recognised the voice of the young Levite and, going nearer, said to him, 'Who brought you here? What are you doing here? What is keeping you here?' [4] He replied, 'Micah has made certain arrangements with me. He pays me a wage and I act as his priest.' [5] They replied, 'Then consult God, so that we may know whether the journey we are on will lead to success.' [6] The priest replied, 'Go in peace; Yahweh is watching over your journey.'

[7] The five men then left and, arriving at Laish, saw that the people living there had an untroubled existence, according to the customs of the Sidonians, peaceful and trusting, that there was no lack or shortage of any sort in the territory, that they were a long way away from the Sidonians and that they had no contact with the Aramaeans.

[8] They then went back to their brothers at Zorah and Eshtaol and, when the latter asked them, 'What have you to report?' [9] they said, 'Up! we must go against them, since we have looked at the country and it is excellent, though you take no action! Waste no time in setting out and taking possession of the country. [10] When you get there, you will find a trusting people. The country is wide, and God

17a The words of the curse are omitted lest even to quote them might have its effect.

has put it at your mercy. It is a place where there is no lack of anything on earth.'

The migration of the Danites

[11] From these places, consequently, from the clan of Danites at Zorah and Eshtaol, six hundred men set out equipped for war. [12] They went up and camped at Kiriath-Jearim in Judah; and for this reason the place is still called the Camp of Dan today. It lies to the west of Kiriath-Jearim. [13] From there they entered the highlands of Ephraim and came to Micah's house.

[14] The five men who had been to reconnoitre the country then spoke to their brothers. 'Do you know', they said, 'that in these houses there is an *ephod,* some domestic images, a carved statue and an idol cast in metal? So now work out what you have got to do!'

[15] So, turning off the road, they went to the young Levite's dwelling, to Micah's house, and greeted him peacefully. [16] While the six hundred men of the Danites, equipped for war, stood at the threshold of the gate, [17] the five who had been to reconnoitre the country went on into the house and took the carved statue, the *ephod,* the domestic images and the idol cast in metal; meanwhile the priest remained at the threshold of the gate with the six hundred men equipped for war. [18] These men, having entered Micah's house, took the carved statue, the *ephod,* the domestic images and the idol cast in metal. The priest, however, said, 'What are you doing?' [19] 'Be quiet,' they replied. 'Put your hand over your mouth and come with us, and become our father and priest. Are you better off as domestic priest to one man, or as priest to a tribe and clan in Israel?' [20] The priest was delighted; he took the *ephod,* the domestic images and the carved statue, and went off among the people.

[21] Resuming their original line of march, they set off, having put the women, children, livestock and baggage out in front. [22] They had gone some distance from Micah's house, when the people living in the houses near Micah's house raised the alarm and set off in pursuit of the Danites. [23] As they shouted after the Danites, the latter, turning about, said to Micah, 'What is the matter with you, that you are shouting like this?' [24] He replied, 'You have taken away my god, which I have had made, and the priest as well. You are going away, and what have I got left? And now you ask me, "What is the matter?"' [25] The Danites said, 'Let us hear no more from you, or quick-tempered men may set about you, and this might cost you your life and the lives of your family!' [26] So the Danites went on their way; and Micah, seeing that they were the stronger, turned and went home.

Capture of Laish; foundation of Dan and the sanctuary there

[27] So, having taken the god made by Micah, and the priest who had been his, the Danites marched on Laish, on a peaceful and trusting people. They put it to the sword and they burned down the town. [28] There was no one to come to the rescue, since it was a long way from Sidon and had no contact with the Aramaeans. It lay in the valley running towards Beth-Rehob. They rebuilt the town and settled in it [29] and called it Dan, from the name of Dan their ancestor who had been born to Israel; originally, however, the town had been called Laish. [30] The Danites erected the carved statue for themselves. Jonathan son of Gershom, son of Moses, and his sons after him were priests for the tribe of Dan till the day when the inhabitants of the country were carried away into exile. [31] The carved statue made by Micah they installed for their own use, and there it stayed as long as the house of God remained at Shiloh.

The Levite of Ephraim and his concubine

19 In those days, when there was no king in Israel, there was a man, a Levite, whose home was deep in the highlands of Ephraim. He took as concubine a woman from Bethlehem in Judah. [2] In a fit of anger his concubine left him and went back to her father's house at Bethlehem in Judah, and she

stayed there for some time—four months. [3] Her husband then set out after her, to appeal to her affections and fetch her back; he had his servant and two donkeys with him. As he was arriving at the house of the girl's father, the father saw him and came happily to meet him. [4] His father-in-law, the girl's father, kept him there; and he stayed with him for three days; they ate and drank and spent the nights there. [5] On the fourth day they got up early, and the Levite was preparing to leave when the girl's father said to his son-in-law, 'Have something to eat to gather strength; you can leave later.' [6] So they sat down and began eating and drinking, the two of them together; then the girl's father said to the young man, 'Please agree to spend tonight here too and enjoy yourself.' [7] And when the man got up to leave, the father-in-law pressed him again, and he spent another night there. [8] On the fifth day, the Levite got up early to leave, but the girl's father said to him, 'Please gather strength first!' So they stayed on until the sun began to go down, and the two men had a meal together. [9] The husband was getting up to leave with his concubine and his servant when his father-in-law, the girl's father, said, 'Look, day is fading into evening. Please spend the night here. Look, the day is nearly over. Spend the night here and enjoy yourself. Then, early tomorrow, you can leave on your journey and go back home.' [10] But the man, refusing to stay the night, got up and went on his way, until he arrived within sight of Jebus—that is, Jerusalem. He had with him two donkeys saddled, his concubine and his servant.

The crime of the men of Gibeah

[11] By the time they were near Jebus, the light was going fast. The servant said to his master, 'Come on, please, let us turn off into this Jebusite town and spend the night there.' [12] His master replied, 'We shall not turn off into a town of foreigners, of people who are not Israelites; we shall go on to Gibeah.' [13] He then said to his servant, 'Come on, we shall try to reach one or other of those places, either Gibeah or Ramah, and spend the night there.' [14] So they kept going and went on with their journey. As they approached Gibeah in Benjamin, the sun was setting. [15] So they turned that way to spend the night in Gibeah. Once inside, the Levite sat down in the town square, but no one offered to take them in for the night.

[16] Eventually, an old man came along at nightfall from his work in the fields. He too was from the highlands of Ephraim, although he was living in Gibeah; the people of the place, however, were Benjaminites. [17] Looking up, he saw the traveller in the town square. 'Where are you going?' said the old man, 'And where have you come from?' [18] 'We are on our way', the other replied, 'from Bethlehem in Judah to a place deep in the highlands of Ephraim. That is where I come from. I have been to Bethlehem in Judah and now I am going home, but no one has offered to take me into his house, [19] although we have straw and provender for our donkeys, and I also have bread and wine for myself, and this maidservant and the young man who is travelling with your servant; we are short of nothing.' [20] 'Welcome,' said the old man. 'I shall see that you have all you want. You cannot spend the night in the square.' [21] So he took him into his house and gave the donkeys provender. The travellers washed their feet, then ate and drank.

[22] While they were enjoying themselves, some townsmen, scoundrels, came crowding round the house; they battered on the door and said to the old man, master of the house, 'Send out the man who went into your house, we should like to have intercourse with him!' [23] The master of the house went out to them and said, 'No, brothers, please, do not be so wicked. Since this man is now under my roof, do not commit such an infamy. [24] Here is my daughter; she is a virgin; I shall bring her out to you. Ill-treat her, do what you please with her, but do not commit such an infamy against this man.' [25] But the men would not listen to him. So the Levite took hold of his concubine

and brought her out to them. They had intercourse with her and ill-treated her all night till morning; when dawn was breaking they let her go.

²⁶ At daybreak the girl came and fell on the threshold of her husband's host, and she stayed there until it was light. ²⁷ In the morning her husband got up and, opening the door of the house, was going out to continue his journey when he saw the woman, his concubine, lying at the door of the house with her hands on the threshold. ²⁸ 'Get up,' he said, 'we must leave!' There was no answer. He then loaded her on his donkey and began the journey home. ²⁹ Having reached his house, he took his knife, took hold of his concubine and cut her, limb by limb, into twelve pieces; he then sent her throughout the territory of Israel. ³⁰ He gave instructions to his messengers, 'This is what you are to say to all the Israelites, "Has anything like this been done since the day when the Israelites came out of Egypt until today? Take this to heart, discuss it; then give your verdict." ' And all who saw it declared, 'Never has such a thing been done or been seen since the Israelites came out of Egypt until today.'

The Israelites vow to avenge the crime at Gibeah

20 The Israelites then all turned out and, as one man, the entire community from Dan to Beersheba, including Gilead, assembled in Yahweh's presence at Mizpah. ² The leaders of the entire people, of all the tribes of Israel, were present at this assembly of God's people, four hundred thousand trained infantry. ³ The Benjaminites heard that the Israelites had gone up to Mizpah. The Israelites then said, 'Tell us how this crime was committed.' ⁴ The Levite, husband of the murdered woman, spoke in reply and said, ⁵ 'The men of Gibeah ganged up against me and, during the night, surrounded the house where I was lodging. They intended to murder me. They raped my concubine to death. ⁶ I then took my concubine, cut her up and sent her throughout

the entire territory of the heritage of Israel, since these men had committed a shameful act, an infamy, in Israel. ⁷ Now, all you Israelites, discuss the matter and give your decision here and now.'

⁸ The whole people stood up as one man and said, 'None of us will go home, none of us will go back to his house! ⁹ And this is what we are now going to do to Gibeah. We shall draw lots ¹⁰ and, throughout the tribes of Israel, select ten men out of a hundred, a hundred out of a thousand and a thousand out of ten thousand to collect food for the people, so that, on their arrival, the latter may treat Gibeah in Benjamin as this infamy perpetrated in Israel deserves.' ¹¹ Thus, as one man, all the men of Israel mustered against the town.

Obduracy of the Benjaminites

¹² The tribes of Israel sent messengers throughout the tribe of Benjamin to say, 'What is this crime which has been committed in your territory? ¹³ Now, give up these men, these scoundrels, living in Gibeah, so that we can put them to death and wipe out this evil from Israel.' The Benjaminites, however, would not listen to their brother Israelites.

The first engagements

¹⁴ The Benjaminites left their towns and mustered at Gibeah to fight the Israelites. ¹⁵ At the time, a count was made of the Benjaminites from the various towns: there were twenty-six thousand swordsmen; and the count excluded the inhabitants of Gibeah. ¹⁶ In this great army there were seven hundred first-rate left-handers, every man of whom could sling a stone at a hair and not miss it.

¹⁷ A count was also held of the men of Israel, excluding Benjamin: there were four hundred thousand men, all experienced swordsmen. ¹⁸ They moved off, up to Bethel, to consult God. The Israelites put the question, 'Which of us is to go first into battle against the Benjaminites?' And Yahweh replied, 'Judah is to go first.'

[275]

¹⁹In the morning, the Israelites moved off and pitched their camp over against Gibeah. ²⁰The men of Israel advanced to do battle with Benjamin; they drew up their battle line in front of Gibeah. ²¹But the Benjaminites sallied out from Gibeah and that day massacred twenty-two thousand Israelites. ²³The Israelites went and wept before Yahweh until evening; they then consulted Yahweh; they asked, 'Shall we join battle again with the sons of our brother Benjamin?' Yahweh replied, 'March against him!' ²²The army of the men of Israel then took fresh heart and again drew up their battle line in the same place as the day before. ²⁴This second day, the Israelites advanced against the Benjaminites, ²⁵and, this second day, Benjamin sallied out from Gibeah to meet them and massacred another eighteen thousand Israelites, all experienced swordsmen.

²⁶Then all the Israelites and the whole people went off to Bethel; they wept and sat in Yahweh's presence; they fasted all day till the evening and presented burnt offerings and communion sacrifices before Yahweh. ²⁷The Israelites then consulted Yahweh. In those days, the ark of the covenant of God was there, ²⁸and Phinehas son of Eleazer, son of Aaron was its minister at the time. They said, 'Ought I to go into battle against the sons of my brother Benjamin again, or should I stop?' Yahweh replied, 'March! For tomorrow I shall deliver him into your hands.'

Defeat of Benjamin

²⁹Israel then positioned troops in ambush all round Gibeah. ³⁰On the third day the Israelites marched against the Benjaminites and, as before, drew up their line in front of Gibeah. ³¹The Benjaminites sallied out to engage the people and let themselves be drawn away from the town. As before, they began by killing those of the people who were on the roads, one of which runs up to Bethel, and the other to Gibeah through open country: some thirty men of Israel. ³²The Benjaminites thought, 'We have beaten them, as we did the

first time,' but the Israelites had decided, 'We shall run away and draw them away from the town along the roads.'

³³All the Israelites then retreated and re-formed at Baal-Tamar, while the Israelite troops in ambush surged from their positions to the west of Gibeah. ³⁴Ten thousand picked men, chosen from the whole of Israel, launched their attack on Gibeah. The battle was fierce; and the others knew nothing of the disaster impending. ³⁵Yahweh defeated Benjamin before Israel and that day the Israelites killed twenty-five thousand one hundred men of Benjamin, all of them trained swordsmen.

³⁶The Benjaminites saw that they were beaten. The Israelites had given ground to Benjamin, since they were relying on the ambush which they had positioned close to Gibeah. ³⁷The troops in ambush threw themselves against Gibeah at top speed; fanning out, they put the whole town to the sword. ³⁸Now it had been agreed between the Israelites and those of the ambush that the latter should raise a smoke signal from the town, ³⁹whereupon the Israelites in the thick of the battle would turn about. Benjamin began by killing some of the Israelites, about thirty men, and thought, 'We have certainly beaten them, as we did in the first battle.' ⁴⁰But the signal, a column of smoke, began to rise from the town, and the Benjaminites looking back saw the whole town going up in flames to the sky. ⁴¹The Israelites then turned about, and the Benjaminites were seized with terror, for they saw that disaster had struck them.

⁴²They broke before the Israelite onslaught and made for the desert, but the fighters pressed them hard, while the others coming out of the town took and slaughtered them from the rear. ⁴³They hemmed in the Benjaminites, pursued them relentlessly, crushing them opposite Gibeah on the east. ⁴⁴Of Benjamin, eighteen thousand men fell, all of them brave men. ⁴⁵They then turned tail and fled into the desert, towards the Rock of Rimmon. Five thousand of them were picked off on the

roads, and the rest were relentlessly pursued as far as Gideon, two thousand of them being killed. ⁴⁶ The total number of Benjaminites who fell that day was twenty-five thousand swordsmen, all of them brave men. ⁴⁷ Six hundred men, however, turned tail and escaped into the desert, to the Rock of Rimmon, and there they stayed for four months.

⁴⁸ The men of Israel then went back to the Benjaminites, and put them to the sword—people, livestock and everything else that came their way in the town. And they fired all the towns involved.

Remorse of the Israelites

21 The men of Israel had sworn this oath at Mizpah, 'None of us is to give his daughter in marriage to Benjamin.' ² The people went to Bethel and stayed there until evening, sitting before God and raising their voices, made a great lament, ³ and exclaiming, 'Yahweh, God of Israel, why has this happened in Israel that a tribe should be missing from Israel today? ⁴ The next day the people got up early and built an altar there; they presented burnt offerings and communion sacrifices. ⁵ The Israelites then said, 'Out of all the tribes of Israel, who has not come to Yahweh, to the assembly?'—for they had sworn a solemn oath that anyone who did not come to Yahweh at Mizpah would certainly die.

⁶ Now the Israelites felt sorry about Benjamin their brother. 'Today', they said, 'a tribe has been amputated from Israel. ⁷ What shall we do to provide wives for those who are left, since we have sworn by Yahweh not to give them any of our own daughters in marriage?'

The girls of Jabesh given to the Benjaminites

⁸ They then asked, 'Out of the tribes of Israel, who is it that has not come to Yahweh at Mizpah?' It was discovered that no one from Jabesh in Gilead had come to the camp for the assembly; ⁹ for, a muster having been called of the people, none of the inhabitants of Jabesh in

Gilead was present. ¹⁰ The community then despatched twelve thousand of their bravest men there, with these orders: 'Go and slaughter all the inhabitants of Jabesh in Gilead, including the women and children. ¹¹ This is what you are to do. All males and all those women who have ever slept with a man, you will put under the curse of destruction, but the lives of the virgins you will spare.' And this they did. ¹² Among the inhabitants of Jabesh in Gilead they found four hundred young virgins who had never slept with a man, and brought them to the camp (to Shiloh in the territory of Canaan).

¹³ The whole community then sent messengers to offer peace to the Benjaminites who were at the Rock of Rimmon. ¹⁴ Benjamin then came home: they were given those of the women of Jabesh in Gilead whose lives had been spared, but there were not enough for all.

The rape of the daughters of Shiloh

¹⁵ The people felt sorry about Benjamin, Yahweh having made a breach in the tribes of Israel. ¹⁶ And the elders of the community said, 'What shall we do to provide wives for the survivors, since the women of Benjamin have been wiped out?' ¹⁷ They went on, 'How can we preserve a remnant for Benjamin so that a tribe may not be lost to Israel? ¹⁸ We cannot give them our own daughters in marriage'—for the Israelites had taken an oath, 'Accursed be the man who gives a wife to Benjamin!'

¹⁹ 'However,' they said, 'there is the feast of Yahweh, held every year at Shiloh.' (The town lies north of Bethel, east of the highway that runs from Bethel up to Shechem, and south of Lebonah.) ²⁰ So they told the Benjaminites to do as follows, 'Put yourselves in ambush in the vineyards. ²¹ Keep watch: when the girls of Shiloh come out in groups to dance, you then come out of the vineyards, each of you seize a wife from the girls of Shiloh and make for Benjaminite territory. ²² If their fathers or brothers come and complain to us, we shall

say, "Let us have them, since we could not take wives for everyone in the battle; and you could not give them to them, or you would then have been guilty."'

²³ The Benjaminites did this and, from the dancers whom they caught, took as many wives as there were men and then, setting off, went back to their heritage, rebuilt the towns and settled down in them.

²⁴ The Israelites then dispersed, each man to rejoin his tribe and clan, each leaving that place for his own heritage.

²⁵ In those days there was no king in Israel, and everyone did as he saw fit.

The Book of

RUTH

Naomi and Ruth

1 In the days when the Judges were governing, a famine occurred in the country and a certain man from Bethlehem of Judah went— he, his wife and his two sons—to live in the Plains of Moab. ²The man was called Elimelech, his wife Naomi and his two sons Mahlon and Chilion;ᵃ they were Ephrathites from Bethlehem of Judah. Going to the Plains of Moab, they settled there. ³Elimelech, Naomi's husband, died, and she and her two sons were left. ⁴These married Moabite women: one was called Orpah and the other Ruth. They lived there for about ten years. ⁵Mahlon and Chilion then both died too, and Naomi was thus bereft of her two sons and her husband. ⁶She then decided to come back from the Plains of Moab with her daughters-in-law, having heard in the Plains of Moab that God had visited his people and given them food. ⁷So, with her daughters-in-law, she left the place where she was living and they took the road back to Judah.

⁸Naomi said to her two daughters-in-law, 'Go back, each of you to your mother's house. ⁹May Yahweh show you faithful love, as you have done to those who have died and to me. Yahweh grant that you may each find happiness with a husband!' She then kissed them, but they began weeping loudly, ¹⁰and said, 'No, we shall go back with you to your people.' ¹¹'Go home, daughters,' Naomi replied. 'Why come with me? Have I any more sons in my womb to make husbands for you?ᵇ ¹²Go home, daughters, go, for I am now too old to marry again. Even if I said, "I still have a hope: I shall take a husband this very night and shall bear more sons," ¹³would you be prepared to

wait for them until they were grown up? Would you refuse to marry for their sake? No, daughters, I am bitterly sorry for your sakes that the hand of Yahweh should have been raised against me.' ¹⁴They started weeping loudly all over again; Orpah then kissed her mother-in-law and went back to her people. But Ruth stayed with her.

¹⁵Naomi then said, 'Look, your sister-in-law has gone back to her people and to her god. Go home, too; follow your sister-in-law.' ¹⁶But Ruth said, 'Do not press me to leave you and to stop going with you, for

> wherever you go, I shall go,
> wherever you live, I shall live.
> Your people will be my people,
> and your God will be my God.

¹⁷ Where you die, I shall die
> and there I shall be buried.
> Let Yahweh bring unnameable illsᶜ
>   on me
> and worse ills, too,
> if anything but death
> should part me from you!'

¹⁸Seeing that Ruth was determined to go with her, Naomi said no more.

¹⁹The two of them went on until they came to Bethlehem. Their arrival set the whole town astir, and the women said, 'Can this be

---

1a The names are chosen for their meanings: Mahlon = sickness, Chilion = passing away.

1b A dead husband's nearest male relative must marry the childless widow and father heirs to his name.

1c The disasters are not named because mere mention might bring their effect.

Naomi?' 20 To this she replied, 'Do not call me Naomi, call me Mara,*d* for Shaddai has made my lot bitter.

> 21 I departed full,
> and Yahweh has brought me home
>   empty.
> Why, then, call me Naomi,
> since Yahweh has pronounced
>   against me
> and Shaddai has made me wretched?'

22 This was how Naomi came home with her daughter-in-law, Ruth the Moabitess, on returning from the Plains of Moab. They arrived in Bethlehem at the beginning of the barley harvest.

Ruth in the fields of Boaz

2 Naomi had a kinsman on her husband's side, well-to-do and of Elimelech's clan. His name was Boaz. 2 Ruth the Moabitess said to Naomi, 'Let me go into the fields and glean ears of corn in the footsteps of some man who will look on me with favour.' She replied, 'Go, daughter.' 3 So she set out and went to glean in the fields behind the reapers. Chance led her to a plot of land belonging to Boaz of Elimelech's clan. 4 Boaz, as it happened, had just come from Bethlehem. 'Yahweh be with you!' he said to the reapers. 'Yahweh bless you!' they replied. 5 Boaz said to a servant of his who was in charge of the reapers, 'To whom does this young woman belong?' 6 And the servant in charge of the reapers replied, 'The girl is the Moabitess, the one who came back with Naomi from the Plains of Moab. 7 She said, "Please let me glean and pick up what falls from the sheaves behind the reapers." Thus she came, and here she stayed, with hardly a rest from morning until now.'

8 Boaz said to Ruth, 'Listen to me, daughter. You must not go gleaning in any other field. You must not go away from here. Stay close to my work-women. 9 Keep your eyes on whatever part of the field they are reaping and fol-low behind. I have forbidden my men to molest you. And if you are thirsty, go to the pitchers and drink what the servants have drawn.' 10 Ruth fell on her face, prostrated herself and said, 'How have I attracted your favour, for you to notice me, who am only a foreigner?' 11 Boaz replied, 'I have been told all about the way you have behaved to your mother-in-law since your husband's death, and how you left your own father and mother and the land where you were born to come to a people of whom you previously knew nothing. 12 May Yahweh repay you for what you have done, and may you be richly rewarded by Yahweh, the God of Israel, under whose wings you have come for refuge!' 13 She said, 'My lord, I hope you will always look on me with favour! You have comforted and encouraged me, though I am not even the equal of one of your work-women.'

14 When it was time to eat, Boaz said to her, 'Come and eat some of this bread and dip your piece in the vinegar.' Ruth sat down beside the reapers and Boaz made a heap of roasted grain for her; she ate till her hunger was satisfied, and she had some left over. 15 When she had got up to glean, Boaz gave orders to his work-people, 'Let her glean among the sheaves themselves. Do not molest her. 16 And be sure you pull a few ears of corn out of the bundles and drop them. Let her glean them, and do not scold her.' 17 So she gleaned in the field till evening. Then she beat out what she had gleaned and it came to about a bushel of barley.

18 Taking it with her, she went back to the town. Her mother-in-law saw what she had gleaned. Ruth also took out what she had kept after eating all she wanted, and gave that to her. 19 Her mother-in-law said, 'Where have you been gleaning today? Where have you been working? Blessed be the man who took notice of you!' Ruth told her mother-in-law in whose field she had been working. 'The name of the man with whom I have been working

1d Mara = the bitter one, Naomi = my sweetness.

23 READ RUTH 2.

Boaz gave orders to his work-people, "Let her glean among the sheaves themselves."

—RUTH 2:15

GIVING GENEROUSLY AND KINDLY

Give to your friend in such a way that you do not reproach him, or expect a reward. Do not wrinkle your brow, or turn aside your countenance or avert your eyes; but with a serene countenance, a cheerful aspect and pleasing speech, anticipate the request of him who is seeking a favor. Meet him with kindness, so that you may appear to be granting his request without being asked. The sensitive soul thinks nothing more worthy of a blush than to beg. Since, therefore, you and your friend ought to be of one heart and soul (see Ac 4:32), it is unjust, if there is not also but one purse. Let this law, therefore, be held in this respect among friends, namely, that they expend themselves and their goods for one another in such a way that he who gives preserves a cheerful aspect, and that he who receives does not lose confidence.

When Boaz observed the poverty of Ruth, the Moabite, he spoke to her as she was gathering ears of corn behind his reapers, consoled her and invited her to the table of his servants, and sparing in kindly fashion her embarrassment, he ordered his reapers to leave ears of corn even purposely so that she might collect them without shame. In the same way we ought the more adroitly to seek out the needs of our friends, anticipate their requests by good services, and observe such demeanor in our giving that the recipient, rather than the giver, appears to be bestowing the favor.

ST. AELRED OF RIEVAULX, 1110–1167

YOU WILL FIND THE NEXT READING AT RUTH 3.

today', she said, 'is Boaz.' 20 Naomi said to her daughter-in-law, 'May he be blessed by Yahweh who does not withhold his faithful love from living or dead! This man', Naomi added, 'is a close relation of ours. He is one of those who have the right of redemption over us.' 21 Ruth the Moabitess said to her mother-in-law, 'He also said, "Stay with my work-people until they have finished my whole harvest."' 22 Naomi said to Ruth, her daughter-in-law, 'It is better for you, daughter, to go with his work-women than to go to some other field where you might be ill-treated.' 23 So she stayed with Boaz's work-women, and gleaned until the barley and wheat harvests were finished. And she went on living with her mother-in-law.

Boaz's Promise

3 Her mother-in-law Naomi then said, 'Daughter, is it not my duty to see you happily settled? 2 And Boaz, the man with whose work-women you were, is he not our kinsman? Tonight he will be winnowing the barley on the threshing-floor. 3 So wash and perfume yourself, put on your cloak and go down to the threshing-floor. Don't let him recognise you while he is still eating and drinking. 4 But when he lies down, take note where he lies, then go and turn back the covering at his feet

24 READ RUTH 3.

I am your servant Ruth.—RUTH 3:9

THE REWARDS OF HUMILITY

There are various things that many people think are virtues but in reality are not such. I mean ecstasies or raptures, states of insensibility and impassibility, deific unions, levitations, transformations
and similar perfections. . . . Note well . . . that such perfections are not virtues. More correctly, they
are rewards God grants for virtues or slight indications of the happiness of the life to come. . . . They
are in no way necessary to serve and love God well and this should be our only intention. . . .

Let us gladly leave those supereminent favors to lofty souls. We do not deserve so high a rank in
God's service, and we should be more than happy to serve him in his kitchen or pantry or to be his
lackeys, porters, or chamberlains. Afterward if it seems good to him he may admit us to his cabinet
or private council. . . . The King of Glory does not reward his servants according to the offices they
hold but according to the love and humility with which they fulfill their offices. Saul sought his
father's asses and found the kingdom of Israel (see 1 S 9:1–17). Rebekah watered Abraham's camels
and became his son's wife (see Gn 24:1–67). Ruth gleaned after Boaz's reapers and lay down at his
feet, and then she was raised to his side and made his wife (see Rt 4:5–13).

Those high and elevated pretensions to extraordinary favors are very subject to illusions, decep-
tions, and deceit. . . . While blessing God for the supereminence of others, let us keep to our lower but
safer way. It is less excellent but better suited to our lack and littleness. If we conduct ourselves with
humility and good faith . . . , God will raise us up to heights that are truly great.

ST. FRANCIS DE SALES, 1567–1622

YOU WILL FIND THE NEXT READING AT 1 SAMUEL 3.

and lie down yourself. He will tell you what
to do.' ⁵Ruth said, 'I shall do everything you
tell me.'

⁶So she went down to the threshing-floor
and did everything her mother-in-law had
told her. ⁷When Boaz had finished eating and
drinking, he went off happily and lay down
beside the pile of barley. Ruth then quietly
went, turned back the covering at his feet and
lay down. ⁸In the middle of the night, he woke
up with a shock and looked about him; and
there lying at his feet was a woman. ⁹'Who are
you?' he said; and she replied, 'I am your servant Ruth. Spread the skirt of your cloak over

your servant for you have the right of redemption over me.' ¹⁰'May Yahweh bless you,
daughter,' he said, 'for this second act of faithful love of yours is greater than the first, since
you have not run after young men, poor or
rich. ¹¹Don't be afraid, daughter, I shall do
everything you ask, since the people at the gate
of my town all know that you are a woman of
great worth. ¹²But, though it is true that I have
the right of redemption over you, you have a
kinsman closer than myself. ¹³Stay here for
tonight and, in the morning, if he wishes to exercise his right over you, very well, let him redeem you. But if he does not wish to do so,

then as Yahweh lives, I shall redeem you. Lie here till morning.' ¹⁴So she lay at his feet till morning, but got up before the hour when one man can recognise another; and he thought, 'It must not be known that this woman came to the threshing-floor.' ¹⁵He then said, 'Let me have the cloak you are wearing, hold it out!' She held it out while he put six measures of barley into it and then loaded it on to her; and off she went to the town.

¹⁶When Ruth got home, her mother-in-law asked her, 'How did things go with you, daughter?' She then told her everything that the man had done for her. ¹⁷'He gave me these six measures of barley and said, "You must not go home empty-handed to your mother-in-law."' ¹⁸Naomi said, 'Do nothing, daughter, until you see how things have gone; I am sure he will not rest until he has settled the matter this very day.'

Boaz Marries Ruth

4 Boaz, meanwhile, had gone up to the gate and sat down, and the relative of whom he had spoken then came by. Boaz said to him, 'Here, my friend, come and sit down'; the man came and sat down. ²Boaz then picked out ten of the town's elders and said, 'Sit down here'; they sat down. ³Boaz then said to the man who had the right of redemption, 'Naomi, who has come back from the Plains of Moab, is selling the piece of land that belonged to our brother, Elimelech. ⁴I thought I should tell you about this and say, "Acquire it in the presence of the men who are sitting here and in the presence of the elders of my people. If you want to use your right of redemption, redeem it; if you do not, tell me so that I know, for I am the only person to redeem it besides yourself, and I myself come after you."' The man said, 'I am willing to redeem it.' ⁵Boaz then said, 'The day you acquire the field from Naomi, you also acquire Ruth the Moabitess, the wife of the man who has died, to perpetuate the dead man's name in his inheritance.' ⁶The man with the right of redemption then said, 'I cannot use my right of redemption without

jeopardising my own inheritance. Since I cannot use my right of redemption, exercise the right yourself.'

⁷Now, in former times, it was the custom in Israel to confirm a transaction in matters of redemption or inheritance by one of the parties taking off his sandal and giving it to the other.ᵃ This was how agreements were ratified in Israel. ⁸So, when the man with the right of redemption said to Boaz, 'Acquire it for yourself,' he took off his sandal.

⁹Boaz then said to the elders and all the people there, 'Today you are witnesses that from Naomi I acquire everything that used to belong to Elimelech, and everything that used to belong to Mahlon and Chilion ¹⁰and that I am also acquiring Ruth the Moabitess, Mahlon's widow, to be my wife, to perpetuate the dead man's name in his inheritance, so that the dead man's name will not be lost among his brothers and at the gate of his town. Today you are witnesses to this.' ¹¹All the people at the gate said, 'We are witnesses'; and the elders said, 'May Yahweh make the woman about to enter your family like Rachel and Leah who together built up the House of Israel.

Grow mighty in Ephrathah,
be renowned in Bethlehem!

¹²And through the children Yahweh will give you by this young woman, may your family be like the family of Perez, whom Tamar bore to Judah.'

¹³So Boaz took Ruth and she became his wife. And when they came together, Yahweh made her conceive and she bore a son. ¹⁴And the women said to Naomi, 'Blessed be Yahweh who has not left you today without anyone to redeem you. May his name be praised in Israel! ¹⁵The child will be a comfort to you and the prop of your old age, for he has been born to the daughter-in-law who

---

4a A distortion of the legislation given in Dt 25:9–10. To plant a sandal (or foot) on a field marks a claim to it. Here, taking off the sandal signifies renunciation of a claim.

loves you and is more to you than seven sons.' ¹⁶And Naomi, taking the child, held him to her breast; and she it was who looked after him.

¹⁷And the women of the neighbourhood gave him a name. 'A son', they said, 'has been born to Naomi,' and they called him Obed. This was the father of Jesse, the father of David.

The genealogy of David

¹⁸These are the descendants of Perez. Perez fathered Hezron, ¹⁹Hezron fathered Ram, Ram fathered Amminadab, ²⁰Amminadab fathered Nahshon, Nahshon fathered Salmon, ²¹Salmon fathered Boaz, Boaz fathered Obed, ²²Obed fathered Jesse, and Jesse fathered David.

The First Book of

SAMUEL

The pilgrimage to Shiloh

1 There was a man of Ramathaim, a Zuphite from the highlands of Ephraim whose name was Elkanah son of Jeroham, son of Elihu, son of Tohu, son of Zuph, an Ephraimite. ²He had two wives, one called Hannah, the other Peninnah; Peninnah had children but Hannah had none. ³Every year this man used to go up from his town to worship, and to sacrifice to Yahweh Sabaoth* at Shiloh. (The two sons of Eli, Hophni and Phinehas, were there as priests of Yahweh.)

⁴One day Elkanah offered a sacrifice. Now he used to give portions to Peninnah and to all her sons and daughters; ⁵to Hannah, however, he would give only one portion: for, although he loved Hannah more, Yahweh had made her barren. ⁶Furthermore, her rival would taunt and provoke her, because Yahweh had made her womb barren. ⁷And this went on year after year; every time they went up to the temple of Yahweh she used to taunt her. On that day she wept and would not eat anything; ⁸so her husband Elkanah said, 'Hannah, why are you crying? Why are you not eating anything? Why are you so sad? Am I not more to you than ten sons?'

Prayer of Hannah

⁹When they had finished eating in the room, Hannah got up and stood before Yahweh. Eli the priest was sitting on his seat by the doorpost of the temple of Yahweh. ¹⁰In the bitterness of her soul she prayed to Yahweh with many tears, ¹¹and she made this vow, 'Yahweh Sabaoth! Should you condescend to notice the humiliation of your servant and keep her in mind instead of disregarding your servant, and give her a boy, I will give him to Yahweh for the whole of his life and no razor shall ever touch his head.'

¹²While she went on praying to Yahweh, Eli was watching her mouth, ¹³for Hannah was speaking under her breath; her lips were moving but her voice could not be heard, and Eli thought that she was drunk. ¹⁴Eli said, 'How much longer are you going to stay drunk? Get rid of your wine.' ¹⁵'No, my lord,' Hannah replied, 'I am a woman in great trouble; I have not been drinking wine or strong drink—I am pouring out my soul before Yahweh. ¹⁶Do not take your servant for a worthless woman; all this time I have been speaking from the depth of my grief and my resentment.' ¹⁷Eli then replied, 'Go in peace, and may the God of Israel grant what you have asked of him.' ¹⁸To which she said, 'May your servant find favour in your sight.' With that, the woman went away; she began eating and was dejected no longer.

Birth and consecration of Samuel

¹⁹They got up early in the morning and, after worshipping Yahweh, set out and went home to Ramah. Elkanah lay with his wife Hannah, and Yahweh remembered her. ²⁰Hannah conceived and, in due course, gave birth to a son, whom she named Samuel,ᵇ 'since', she said, 'I asked Yahweh for him.' ²¹Elkanah, the husband, went up with all his family to offer the annual sacrifice to Yahweh and to fulfil his vow. ²²However, Hannah did not go up, hav-

1a A mysterious title stemming from the shrine at Shiloh and interpreted as 'Lord of armies'.

1b Samuel is derived from *shem-'el* (= the Name of God), but is here related to *sha'al* (= ask).

ing said to her husband, 'Not before the child has been weaned. Then I shall bring him and present him before Yahweh and he will stay there for ever.' ²³ Elkanah her husband then said to her, 'Do what you think fit; wait until you have weaned him. May Yahweh bring about what he has said.' So the woman stayed behind and nursed her child until she weaned him.

²⁴ When she had weaned him, she took him up with her, as well as a three-year-old bull, an *ephah* of flour and a skin of wine, and took him into the temple of Yahweh at Shiloh; the child was very young. ²⁵ They sacrificed the bull and led the child to Eli. ²⁶ She said, 'If you please, my lord! As you live, my lord, I am the woman who stood beside you here, praying to Yahweh. ²⁷ This is the child for which I was praying, and Yahweh has granted me what I asked of him. ²⁸ Now I make him over to Yahweh for the whole of his life. He is made over to Yahweh.' They then worshipped Yahweh there.

Song of Hannah

2 Hannah then prayed as follows:

My heart exults in Yahweh,
  in my God is my strength lifted up,
my mouth derides my foes,
  for I rejoice in your deliverance.

² There is no Holy One like Yahweh,
  (indeed, there is none but you)
no Rock like our God.

³ Do not keep talking so proudly,
  let no arrogance come from your mouth,
for Yahweh is a wise God,
  his to weigh up deeds.

⁴ The bow of the mighty has been broken
  but those who were tottering are now
    braced with strength.
⁵ The full fed are hiring themselves out for
    bread
  but the hungry need labour no more;
the barren woman bears sevenfold
  but the mother of many is left desolate.

⁶ Yahweh gives death and life,
  brings down to Sheol and draws up;
⁷ Yahweh makes poor and rich,
  he humbles and also exalts.

⁸ He raises the poor from the dust,
  he lifts the needy from the dunghill
to give them a place with princes,
  to assign them a seat of honour;
for to Yahweh belong the pillars of the
    earth,
  on these he has poised the world.

⁹ He safeguards the steps of his faithful
  but the wicked vanish in darkness
  (for human strength can win no victories).
¹⁰ Yahweh, his enemies are shattered,
  the Most High thunders in the heavens.

Yahweh judges the ends of the earth,
  he endows his king with power,
he raises up the strength of his Anointed.

¹¹ Elkanah then went home to Ramah, but the child stayed in Yahweh's service, in the presence of Eli the priest.

The sons of Eli

¹² Now the sons of Eli were scoundrels; they cared nothing for Yahweh ¹³ nor for what was due to the priests from the people. Whenever anyone offered a sacrifice, the priest's servant would come with a three-pronged fork in his hand while the meat was being cooked; ¹⁴ he would thrust this into cauldron or pan, or dish or pot, and the priest claimed for his own whatever the fork brought up. That was how they behaved with all the Israelites who came there to Shiloh. ¹⁵ The priest's servant would even come up before the fat had been burnt and say to the person who was making the sacrifice, 'Give the priest some meat for him to roast. He will not accept boiled meat from you, only raw.' ¹⁶ Then, if the person replied, 'Let the fat be burnt first, and then take for yourself whatever you choose,' he would retort, 'No! You must give it to me now or I shall

take it by force.' ¹⁷The young men's sin was very great in Yahweh's eyes, because they treated with contempt the offering made to Yahweh.

Samuel at Shiloh

¹⁸Samuel was in Yahweh's service, a child wearing a linen loincloth. ¹⁹His mother used to make him a little coat which she brought him each year when she came up with her husband to offer the yearly sacrifice. ²⁰Eli would bless Elkanah and his wife and say, 'May Yahweh grant you an heir by this woman in exchange for the one which she has made over to Yahweh,' and they would go home. ²¹Yahweh visited Hannah; she conceived and gave birth to three sons and two daughters. Meanwhile, the child Samuel grew up in Yahweh's presence.

More about the sons of Eli

²²Although very old, Eli heard about everything that his sons were doing to all Israel, ²³and said, 'Why are you behaving as all the people say you are? ²⁴No, my sons, what I hear reported by the people of Yahweh is not good. ²⁵If one person sins against another, God will be the arbiter, but if he sins against Yahweh, who will intercede for him?' But they did not listen to their father's words, for Yahweh was bent on killing them.

²⁶Meanwhile, the child Samuel went on growing in stature and in favour both with Yahweh and with people.

Punishment foretold

²⁷A man of God came to Eli and said to him, 'This is what Yahweh says, "Did I not reveal myself to your father's family when they were in Egypt as slaves in Pharaoh's household? ²⁸Did I not single him out of all the tribes of Israel to be my priest, to go up to my altar, to burn the offering, to carry the *ephod*ᵃ in my presence; and did I not grant all the burnt offerings made by the Israelites to your father's family? ²⁹Why do you trample on the offering and on the sacrifice which I have ordered for

my Dwelling, and honour your sons more than me, by growing fat on the best of the offerings of Israel, my people? ³⁰Whereas—this is what Yahweh, God of Israel, declares—I had promised that your family and your father's family would walk in my presence for ever, now, however—this is what Yahweh declares—nothing of the sort! Those who honour me I honour in my turn, and those who despise me will be an object of contempt. ³¹Be sure, the days are coming when I shall cut off your strength and the strength of your father's family, so that no one in your family will live to old age. ³²Beside the Dwelling, you will see all the benefits that I shall confer on Israel, but no one in your family will ever live to old age. ³³I shall keep one of you at my altar for his eyes to go blind and his soul to wither, but the bulk of your family will die by the sword.

³⁴'"What happens to your two sons Hophni and Phinehas will be a sign for you: on the same day both will die. ³⁵I shall raise myself a faithful priest, who will do as I intend and as I desire. I shall build him an enduring House and he will walk in the presence of my Anointed for ever. ³⁶The members of your House who survive will come and beg him on their knees for a silver coin and a loaf of bread and say: Please give me some priestly work, so that I can have a scrap of bread to eat."'

God calls Samuel

3 Now, the boy Samuel was serving Yahweh in the presence of Eli; in those days it was rare for Yahweh to speak; visions were uncommon. ²One day, it happened that Eli was lying down in his room. His eyes were beginning to grow dim; he could no longer see. ³The lamp of God had not yet gone out, and Samuel was lying in Yahweh's sanctuary, where the ark of God was, ⁴when Yahweh called, 'Samuel! Samuel!' He answered, 'Here I am,' ⁵and, running to Eli, he said, 'Here I am, as you called me.' Eli said, 'I did not call.

2a Not a garment as elsewhere, but a holder for the sacred lots.

25 READ 1 SAMUEL 3.

Speak, Yahweh; for your servant is listening.—1 SAMUEL 3:10

FOLLOWING CHRIST

Some men feel themselves called to high duties and works, to which others are not called. Why this is we do not know. . . . No one has any leave to take another's lower standard of holiness for his own. It is nothing to us what others are. If God calls us to greater renunciation of the world, and exacts a sacrifice of our hopes and fears, this is a mark of his love for us, this is a thing to be rejoiced in. . . .

We need not fear spiritual pride then, in following Christ's call, if we follow it as men in earnest. Earnestness has not time to compare itself with the state of other men; earnestness has too vivid a feeling of its own infirmities to be elated at itself. Earnestness is simply set on doing God's will. It simply says, "Speak, Lord for your servant is listening," "Lord, what would you have me do?"

Oh, that we had more of this spirit! Oh, that we could take that simple view of things, as to feel that the one thing which lies before us is to please God! What gain is it to please the world, to please the great, nay, even to please those whom we love compared with this? . . .

What can the world offer comparable with that insight into spiritual things, that keen faith, that heavenly peace, that high sanctity, that everlasting righteousness, that hope of glory, which they have who in sincerity love and follow our Lord Jesus Christ?

Let us beg and pray him day by day to reveal himself to our souls more fully; to quicken our senses; to give us sight and hearing, taste and touch of the world to come; so to work within us that we may sincerely say, "You shall guide me with your counsel, and after that receive me to glory" (see Ps 73:24).

VEN. JOHN HENRY NEWMAN, 1801–1890

YOU WILL FIND THE NEXT READING AT 1 SAMUEL 17.

Go back and lie down.' So he went and lay down. ⁶And again Yahweh called, 'Samuel! Samuel!' He got up and went to Eli and said, 'Here I am, as you called me.' He replied, 'I did not call, my son; go back and lie down.' ⁷As yet, Samuel had no knowledge of Yahweh and the word of Yahweh had not yet been revealed to him. ⁸Again Yahweh called, the third time. He got up and went to Eli and said, 'Here I am, as you called me.' Eli then understood that Yahweh was calling the child, ⁹and he said to Samuel, 'Go and lie down, and if someone calls say, "Speak, Yahweh; for your servant is listening." ' So Samuel went and lay down in his place.

¹⁰Yahweh then came and stood by, calling as he had done before, 'Samuel! Samuel!' Samuel answered, 'Speak, Yahweh; for your servant is listening.' ¹¹Yahweh then said to Samuel, 'I am going to do something in Israel which will make the ears of all who hear of it ring. ¹²I shall carry out that day against Eli everything that I have said about his family, from beginning to end. ¹³You are to tell him that I condemn his family for ever, since he is aware that his sons have been cursing God and yet has not corrected them. ¹⁴Therefore—I swear it to the family of Eli—no sacrifice or offering shall ever expiate the guilt of Eli's family.'

¹⁵Samuel lay where he was until morning and then opened the doors of Yahweh's temple. Samuel was afraid to tell Eli about the vision, ¹⁶but Eli called Samuel and said, 'Samuel, my son.' 'Here I am,' he replied. ¹⁷Eli asked, 'What message did he give you? Please do not hide it from me. May God bring unnameable ills on you and worse ones, too, if you hide from me anything of what he said to you.' ¹⁸Samuel then told him everything, hiding nothing from him. Eli said, 'He is Yahweh; let him do what he thinks good.'

¹⁹Samuel grew up. Yahweh was with him and did not let a single word fall to the ground of all that he had told him. ²⁰All Israel knew, from Dan to Beersheba, that Samuel was attested as a prophet of Yahweh. ²¹Yahweh continued to manifest himself at Shiloh, revealing himself to Samuel there, ¹and, for all Israel, the word of Samuel was as the word of Yahweh; since Eli was very old and his sons persisted in their wicked behaviour towards Yahweh.

Defeat of the Israelites and capture of the ark

It happened at that time that the Philistines mustered to make war on Israel and Israel went out to meet them in war, pitching camp near Ebenezer while the Philistines pitched camp at Aphek. ²The Philistines drew up their battle-line against Israel, the fighting was fierce, and Israel was beaten by the Philistines: about four thousand men in their ranks were killed on the field of battle. ³When the troops returned to camp, the elders of Israel said, 'Why has Yahweh caused us to be beaten by the Philistines today? Let us fetch the ark of our God from Shiloh so that, when it goes with us, it may save us from the clutches of our enemies.' ⁴So the troops sent to Shiloh and brought away the ark of Yahweh Sabaoth enthroned on the winged creatures; the two sons of Eli, Hophni and Phinehas, came with the ark. ⁵When the ark of Yahweh arrived in the camp, all Israel raised a great war cry so that the earth resounded. ⁶When the Philistines heard the noise of the war cry, they said, 'What

can this great war cry in the Hebrew camp mean?' And they realised that the ark of Yahweh had come into the camp. ⁷At this, the Philistines were afraid; for they said, 'God has come into the camp. Disaster!' they said. 'For nothing like this has ever happened before. ⁸Disaster! Who will rescue us from the clutches of this mighty God? This was the God who struck down Egypt with every kind of misfortune in the desert. ⁹But take courage and be men, Philistines, or you will become slaves to the Hebrews as they have been slaves to you. Be men and fight.' ¹⁰So the Philistines gave battle and Israel was defeated, each man fleeing to his tent. The slaughter was very great: on the Israelite side, thirty thousand foot soldiers fell. ¹¹The ark of God was captured too, and Hophni and Phinehas the two sons of Eli died.

Death of Eli

¹²A Benjaminite ran from the battle-line and reached Shiloh the same day, his clothes torn and dust on his head. ¹³When he arrived, Eli was sitting on his seat beside the gate watching the road, for his heart was trembling for the ark of God. The man came into the town and told the news, whereupon cries of anguish filled the town. ¹⁴Eli heard the sound and asked, 'What does this uproar mean?' The man hurried on and told Eli. ¹⁵Eli was ninety-eight years old; his gaze was fixed; he was blind. ¹⁶The man said to Eli, 'I have come from the camp. I escaped from the battle-line today.' 'My son,' said Eli, 'what happened?' ¹⁷The messenger replied, 'Israel has fled before the Philistines; the army has been utterly routed. What is worse, your two sons are dead and the ark of God has been captured.' ¹⁸When he mentioned the ark of God, Eli fell backwards off his seat by the gate and broke his neck and died, for he was old and heavy. He had been judge of Israel for forty years.

Death of the wife of Phinehas

¹⁹Now his daughter-in-law, the wife of Phinehas, was with child and near her time. When

she heard the news that the ark of God had been captured and that her father-in-law and husband were dead she crouched down and gave birth, for her labour pains had come on. 20 When she was at the point of death, the women at her side said, 'Do not be afraid; you have given birth to a son.' But she did not answer and took no notice. 21 She named the child Ichabod,ᵃ saying, 'The glory has gone from Israel,' alluding to the capture of the ark of God and to her father-in-law and husband. 22 She said, 'The glory has gone from Israel, because the ark of God has been captured.'

The ark brings disaster to the Philistines

5 When the Philistines had captured the ark of God, they took it from Ebenezer to Ashdod. 2 Taking the ark of God, the Philistines put it in the temple of Dagon, setting it down beside Dagon. 3 When the people of Ashdod got up the following morning and went to the temple of Dagon, there lay Dagon face down on the ground before the ark of Yahweh. They picked Dagon up and put him back in his place. 4 But when they got up on the following morning, there lay Dagon face down on the ground before the ark of Yahweh, and Dagon's head and two hands lay severed on the threshold; only the trunk of Dagon was left in its place. 5 This is why the priests of Dagon and the people frequenting Dagon's temple never step on Dagon's threshold in Ashdod, even today.

6 Yahweh oppressed the people of Ashdod; he ravaged them and afflicted them with tumours—Ashdod and its territory. When the people of Ashdod saw what was happening they said, 7 'The ark of the God of Israel must not stay here with us, for he is oppressing us and our god Dagon.' 8 So they summoned all the Philistine chiefs to them, and said, 'What shall we do with the ark of the God of Israel?' They decided, 'The ark of the God of Israel shall be taken away to Gath.' So they took the ark of the God of Israel to Gath. 9 But after they had taken it there, Yahweh oppressed

that town and a great panic broke out; afflicting the people of the town from highest to lowest, he brought them out in tumours too. 10 They then sent the ark of God to Ekron, but when it came to Ekron the Ekronites shouted, 'They have brought me the ark of the God of Israel to kill me and my people!' 11 They summoned all the Philistine chiefs and said, 'Send the ark of the God of Israel away; let it go back to where it belongs and not kill me and my people'—for there was mortal panic throughout the town; God was oppressing them. 12 The people who did not die were afflicted with tumours, and the wailing from the town rose to the sky.

Return of the ark

6 The ark of Yahweh was in Philistine territory for seven months. 2 The Philistines then called for their priests and diviners and asked, 'What shall we do with the ark of Yahweh? Tell us how to send it back to where it belongs.' 3 They replied, 'If you send the ark of the God of Israel away, you must certainly not send it away without a gift; you must pay him a guilt offering. You will then recover and will realise why he continually oppressed you.' 4 They then asked, 'What guilt offering ought we to pay him?' They replied, 'Corresponding to the number of Philistine chiefs: five golden tumours and five golden rats, since the same plague afflicted your chiefs as the rest of you. 5 So make models of your tumours and models of your rats ravaging the territory, and pay honour to the God of Israel. Then perhaps he will stop oppressing you, your gods and your country. 6 Why should you be as stubborn as Egypt and Pharaoh were? After he had brought disasters on them, did they not let the people leave? 7 Now, then, take and fit out a new cart, and two milch cows that have never borne the yoke. Then harness the cows to the cart and take their calves back to the byre. 8 Then take the ark of Yahweh, place it on the cart, and put the golden objects which you are

4a *Ei-kabod* = Where is the glory?

paying him as guilt offering in a box beside it; and then send it off on its own. ⁹Watch it; if it goes up the road to its own territory, towards Beth-Shemesh, then he was responsible for this great harm to us; but if not, we shall know that it was not his hand that struck us, and that this has happened to us by chance.'

¹⁰The people did this. They took two milch cows and harnessed them to the cart, shutting their calves in the byre. ¹¹They then put the ark of Yahweh on the cart, with the box and the golden rats and the models of their tumours.

¹²The cows made straight for Beth-Shemesh, keeping to the one road, lowing as they went and turning neither to right nor to left. The Philistine chiefs followed them as far as the boundaries of Beth-Shemesh.

The ark at Beth-Shemesh

¹³The people of Beth-Shemesh were reaping the wheat harvest in the plain when they looked up and saw the ark and went joyfully to meet it. ¹⁴When the cart came to the field of Joshua of Beth-Shemesh, it stopped. There was a large stone there, and they cut up the wood of the cart and offered the cows as a burnt offering to Yahweh. ¹⁵The Levites had taken down the ark of Yahweh and the box with it containing the golden objects and put these on the large stone. That day the people of Beth-Shemesh presented burnt offerings and made sacrifices to Yahweh. ¹⁶The five chiefs of the Philistines, having witnessed this, went back to Ekron the same day.

¹⁷The golden tumours paid by the Philistines as a guilt offering to Yahweh were as follows: one for Ashdod, one for Gaza, one for Ashkelon, one for Gath, one for Ekron; ¹⁸and golden rats to the number of all the Philistine towns, those of the five chiefs, from fortified towns down to open villages: still to this day the large stone in the field of Joshua of Beth-Shemesh, on which they put the ark of Yahweh, is a witness. ¹⁹Of the people of Beth-Shemesh the sons of Jeconiah had not rejoiced when they saw the ark of Yahweh, and Yahweh struck down seventy of them. The people mourned because Yahweh had struck them so fiercely.

The ark at Kiriath-Jearim

²⁰The people of Beth-Shemesh then said, 'Who can stand his ground before Yahweh, this holy God? To whom shall he go, so that we are rid of him?' ²¹So they sent messengers to the inhabitants of Kiriath-Jearim, to say, 'The Philistines have sent back the ark of Yahweh; come down and take it up to your town.'

7The men of Kiriath-Jearim came and, taking up the ark of Yahweh, brought it to the house of Abinadab on the hill, and consecrated his son Eleazar to guard the ark of Yahweh.

Samuel, judge and liberator

²From the day when the ark was installed at Kiriath-Jearim, a long time went by—twenty years—and the whole House of Israel longed for Yahweh. ³Samuel then spoke as follows to the whole House of Israel, 'If you are returning to Yahweh with all your heart, banish the foreign gods and Astartes which you now have, and set your heart on Yahweh and serve him alone; and he will deliver you from the power of the Philistines.' ⁴And the Israelites banished the Baals and Astartes and served Yahweh alone.

⁵Samuel then said, 'Muster all Israel at Mizpah and I shall plead with Yahweh for you.' ⁶So they mustered at Mizpah and drew water and poured it out before Yahweh. They fasted that day and declared, 'We have sinned against Yahweh.' And Samuel was judge over the Israelites at Mizpah.

⁷When the Philistines heard that the Israelites had mustered at Mizpah, the Philistine chiefs marched on Israel; and when the Israelites heard this, they were afraid of the Philistines. ⁸They said to Samuel, 'Do not stop calling on Yahweh our God to rescue us from the power of the Philistines.' ⁹Samuel took a

sucking lamb and presented it as a burnt offering to Yahweh, and he called on Yahweh on behalf of Israel and Yahweh heard him. [10] While Samuel was in the act of presenting burnt offering, the Philistines joined battle with Israel, but that day Yahweh thundered violently over the Philistines, threw them into panic and Israel defeated them. [11] The men of Israel sallied out from Mizpah in pursuit of the Philistines and beat them all the way to below Beth-Car. [12] Samuel then took a stone and erected it between Mizpah and the Tooth, and gave it the name Ebenezer,[a] saying, 'Yahweh helped us as far as this.'

[13] So the Philistines were humbled and no longer came into Israelite territory; Yahweh oppressed the Philistines throughout the life of Samuel. [14] The towns which the Philistines had taken from Israel were given back to Israel, from Ekron all the way to Gath, and Israel freed their territory from the power of the Philistines. There was peace, too, between Israel and the Amorites.

[15] Samuel was judge over Israel throughout his life. [16] Each year he went on circuit through Bethel and Gilgal and Mizpah and judged Israel in all these places. [17] He would then return to Ramah, since his home was there; there too he judged Israel. And there he built an altar to Yahweh.

The people ask for a king

8 When Samuel grew old, he appointed his sons as judges of Israel. [2] His eldest son was called Joel and his second one, Abijah; they were judges at Beersheba. [3] His sons did not follow his example but, seduced by the love of money, took bribes and gave biased verdicts. [4] The elders of Israel all assembled, went back to Samuel at Ramah, and said, [5] 'Look, you are old, and your sons are not following your example. So give us a king to judge us, like the other nations.' [6] Samuel thought that it was wrong of them to say, 'Let us have a king to judge us,' so he prayed to Yahweh. [7] But Yahweh said to Samuel, 'Obey the voice of the people in all that they say to you: it is not you

they have rejected [8] but me, not wishing me to reign over them any more. They are now doing to you exactly what they have done to me since the day I brought them out of Egypt until now, deserting me and serving other gods. [9] So, do what they ask; only, you must give them a solemn warning, and must tell them what the king who is to reign over them will do.'

Disadvantages of a monarchy

[10] Everything that Yahweh had said, Samuel then repeated to the people who were asking him for a king. [11] He said, 'This is what the king who is to reign over you will do. He will take your sons and direct them to his chariotry and cavalry, and they will run in front of his chariot. [12] He will use them as leaders of a thousand and leaders of fifty; he will make them plough his fields and gather in his harvest and make his weapons of war and the gear for his chariots. [13] He will take your daughters as perfumers, cooks and bakers. [14] He will take the best of your fields, your vineyards and your olive groves and give them to his officials. [15] He will tithe your crops and vineyards to provide for his courtiers and his officials. [16] He will take the best of your servants, men and women, of your oxen and your donkeys, and make them work for him. [17] He will tithe your flocks, and you yourselves will become his slaves. [18] When that day comes, you will cry aloud because of the king you have chosen for yourselves, but on that day Yahweh will not hear you.'

[19] The people, however, refused to listen to Samuel. They said, 'No! We are determined to have a king, [20] so that we can be like the other nations, with our own king to rule us and lead us and fight our battles.' [21] Samuel listened to all that the people had to say and repeated it in Yahweh's ear. [22] Yahweh then said to Samuel, 'Do as they ask and give them a king.' Samuel then said to the Israelites, 'Go home, each of you, to his own town.'

7a *Eben-ezer* = Stone of help.

Saul and his father's donkeys

9 Among the men of Benjamin was a man called Kish son of Abiel, son of Zeror, son of Becorath, son of Aphiah; a Benjaminite and a person of rank. ² He had a son called Saul, a handsome man in the prime of life. Of all the Israelites there was no one more handsome than he; he stood head and shoulders taller than anyone else.

³ Now since the donkeys belonging to Kish, Saul's father, had strayed, Kish said to his son Saul, 'My son, take one of the servants with you and be off; go and look for the donkeys.' ⁴ They went through the highlands of Ephraim, they went through the territory of Shalishah, and did not find them; they went through the territory of Shaalim but they were not there; they went through the territory of Benjamin and did not find them. ⁵ When they reached the territory of Zuph, Saul said to the servant who was with him, 'Come on, let us go back or my father will stop worrying over the donkeys and start being anxious about us.' ⁶ The servant, however, replied, 'Look, there is a man of God in this town, a man who is held in honour; everything he says comes true. Let us go there, then; perhaps he will be able to show us the way that we should take.' ⁷ Saul said to his servant, 'But if we do go, what can we take to the man? The food in our sacks is finished, and we have no present to offer the man of God. What else have we got?' ⁸ The servant spoke up again and said to Saul, 'Look, I happen to have a quarter of a silver shekel; I shall give that to the man of God, for him to tell us which way to go.' ¹⁰ Saul then said to his servant, 'Well said! Come on, let us go.' And they went off to the town where the man of God was.

Saul meets Samuel

¹¹ As they were going up the slope to the town they came across some girls going out to draw water, and said to them, 'Is the seer there?' ⁹ In Israel, in olden days, when anyone used to go to consult God, he would say, 'Come on, let us go to the seer,' for a man who is now called a 'prophet' used to be called a 'seer' in olden days. ¹² The girls replied, 'He is. He arrived a moment or two ahead of you. You had better hurry: he has just come to town because the people are having a sacrifice today on the high place. ¹³ You can catch him as soon as you go into the town, before he goes up to the high place for the meal. The people will not eat until he comes, since he must bless the sacrifice; after that, the guests will start eating. If you go up now, you will find him straight away.'

¹⁴ So they went up to the town and, as they were going through the gate, Samuel came out towards them on his way to the high place. ¹⁵ Now, Yahweh had given Samuel a revelation the day before Saul came, saying, ¹⁶ 'About this time tomorrow, I shall send you a man from the territory of Benjamin; you are to anoint him as prince of my people Israel, and he will save my people from the power of the Philistines; for I have seen the misery of my people and their cries of anguish have come to me.' ¹⁷ When Samuel saw Saul, Yahweh told him, 'That is the man of whom I said to you, "He is to govern my people."' ¹⁸ Saul accosted Samuel in the gateway and said, 'Tell me, please, where the seer's house is.' ¹⁹ Samuel replied to Saul, 'I am the seer. Go up ahead of me to the high place. You must eat with me today. Tomorrow, when I let you go, I shall tell you whatever is on your mind. ²⁰ As regards your donkeys, however, which strayed three days ago, do not worry about them; they have been found. And for whom is the whole wealth of Israel destined, if not for you and for all the members of your father's family?' ²¹ To this, Saul replied, 'Am I not a Benjaminite, from the smallest of the tribes of Israel? And is not my family the least of all the families of the tribe of Benjamin? Why are you saying a thing like this to me?'

²² Samuel then took Saul and his servant and brought them into the hall and gave them a place at the head of the guests, of whom there were about thirty. ²³ Samuel then said to

the cook, 'Serve the portion which I gave you and told you to put on one side.' ²⁴ The cook then picked up the leg and the tail and put it in front of Saul, saying, 'This is for you. This is what was left. Make a good meal . . .' That day, Saul ate with Samuel.

²⁵ They came down from the high place into the town. A bed was made for Saul on the roof and he lay down there.

Consecration of Saul

²⁶ At dawn, Samuel called to Saul on the roof, 'Get up, and I shall send you on your way.' Saul got up, and Samuel and he went outside together. ²⁷ They had walked as far as the end of the town when Samuel said to Saul, 'Tell the servant to go on ahead of us, but you stand still for a moment, so that I can make known to you the word of God.'

10 Samuel took a phial of oil and poured it on Saul's head; he then kissed him and said, 'Has not Yahweh anointed you as leader of his people Israel? You are the man who is to govern Yahweh's people and save them from the power of the enemies surrounding them. The sign for you that Yahweh has anointed you as prince of his heritage is this: ² after leaving me today, you will meet two men near the tomb of Rachel, on the frontier of Benjamin . . . and they will say to you, "The donkeys which you went looking for have been found, and your father has lost interest in the matter of the donkeys and is worrying about you and wondering, What am I to do about my son?" ³ Going on from there, you will come to the Oak of Tabor, where you will meet three men going up to God at Bethel; one will be carrying three kids, one three loaves of bread and the third a skin of wine. ⁴ They will greet you and give you two loaves of bread which you must accept from them. ⁵ After this, you will come to Gibeah of God (where the Philistine garrison is) and, when you are just outside the town, you will meet a group of prophets coming down from the high place, headed by lyre, tambourine, pipe and harp;

they will be in a state of ecstasy. ⁶ The spirit of Yahweh will then seize on you, and you will go into ecstasy with them, and be changed into another man. ⁷ When these signs have occurred, act as occasion serves, for God is with you. ⁸ You will then go down, ahead of me, to Gilgal, and I shall join you there to make burnt offerings and to offer communion sacrifices. You must wait seven days for me to come to you, and I shall then reveal to you what you must do.'

Return of Saul

⁹ As soon as he had turned his back to leave Samuel, God changed his heart. And all these signs occurred that very day . . . ¹⁰ From there, they came to Gibeah: and there was a group of prophets coming to meet him! The spirit of God seized on him and he fell into ecstasy with them. ¹¹ Seeing him prophesying with the prophets, all the people who had known him previously said to one another, 'What has come over the son of Kish? Is Saul one of the prophets too?' ¹² And one of the local people retorted, 'But who is their father?' Hence the origin of the proverb: Is Saul one of the prophets too?

¹³ When he came out of his ecstasy, he went into Gibeah. ¹⁴ Saul's uncle asked him and his servant, 'Where have you been?' 'Looking for the donkeys,' he replied, 'and when we could not find them anywhere, we went to Samuel.' ¹⁵ Saul's uncle said, 'Tell me please what Samuel said to you.' ¹⁶ Saul said to his uncle, 'He merely told us that the donkeys were already found,' but did not mention anything that Samuel had said about the kingship.

Saul is designated king by lot

¹⁷ Samuel summoned the people to Yahweh at Mizpah ¹⁸ and said to the Israelites, 'Yahweh, God of Israel, says this, "I brought Israel out of Egypt and delivered you from the power of the Egyptians and of all the kingdoms that were oppressing you." ¹⁹ But today you have rejected your God, him who saves you from all your difficulties and troubles; and you have

said, "No, you must set a king over us." Very well, take your positions before Yahweh, tribe by tribe and clan by clan.'

20 Samuel then made all the tribes of Israel come forward, and the lot indicated the tribe of Benjamin. 21 He then made the tribe of Benjamin come forward clan by clan, and the lot indicated the clan of Matri; he then made the clan of Matri come forward one by one, and the lot indicated Saul son of Kish, but when they looked for him, he was not to be found.

22 Again they consulted Yahweh, 'Has the man come here?' Yahweh replied, 'There he is, hiding among the baggage.' 23 So they ran and fetched him out and, as he stood among the people, he was head and shoulders taller than any of them. 24 Samuel then said to all the people, 'You have seen the man whom Yahweh has chosen, and that among the whole people he has no equal.' And all the people acclaimed him, shouting, 'Long live the king!'

25 Samuel then explained the king's constitutional position to the people and inscribed this in a book which he placed before Yahweh. Samuel then sent all the people away, everyone back to his home. 26 Saul too went home to Gibeah and with him went those strong men whose hearts God had touched. 27 But there were some scoundrels who said, 'How can this fellow save us?' These treated him with contempt and offered him no present.

Victory over the Ammonites

11 About a month later, Nahash the Ammonite marched up and laid siege to Jabesh in Gilead. All the men of Jabesh said to Nahash, 'Make a treaty with us and we will be your subjects.' 2 Nahash the Ammonite replied, 'I shall make a treaty with you only on this condition, that I put out all your right eyes, and I will make it a taunt to the whole of Israel.' 3 The elders of Jabesh said to him, 'Give us seven days' grace while we send messengers throughout the territory of Israel, and if no one comes to our help, we will come out to you.' 4 The messengers came to Gibeah of

Saul, and reported this to the people, and all the people wept aloud.

5 Now Saul was just then coming in from the fields behind his oxen, and he said, 'What is wrong? Why are the people weeping?' They explained to him what the men of Jabesh had said. 6 And the spirit of Yahweh seized on Saul when he heard these words, and he fell into a fury. 7 He took a yoke of oxen, cut them into pieces and sent these by messengers throughout the territory of Israel with these words, 'Anyone who will not march with Saul will have the same done to his oxen!' At this, a panic from Yahweh swept on the people and they marched out as one man. 8 Saul inspected them at Bezek; there were three hundred thousand of Israel and thirty thousand of Judah. 9 Then he said to the messengers who had come, 'This is what you are to say to the people of Jabesh in Gilead, "Tomorrow, by the time that the sun is hot, help will reach you." ' The messengers went and reported this to the people of Jabesh who were overjoyed; 10 they said to Nahash, 'Tomorrow we shall come out to you and you can do whatever you like to us.'

11 The next day, Saul disposed the army in three contingents, which burst into the middle of the camp during the dawn watch and slaughtered the Ammonites until high noon. The survivors were so scattered that no two of them were left together.

Saul is proclaimed king

12 The people then said to Samuel, 'Who said, "Must we have Saul reigning over us?" Hand the men over, for us to put them to death.' 13 'No one must be put to death today,' Saul said, 'for today Yahweh has intervened to rescue Israel.' 14 Samuel then said to the people, 'Let us now go to Gilgal and reaffirm the monarchy there.'

15 The people then all went to Gilgal. And there, at Gilgal, they proclaimed Saul king before Yahweh; they offered communion sacrifices before Yahweh, and there Saul and all the people of Israel gave themselves over to great rejoicing.

Samuel gives way to Saul

12 Samuel said to all Israel, 'I have faithfully done all that you asked of me, and have appointed you a king. ²In future, the king will lead you. As for me, I am old and grey, and in any case you have my sons. I have been your leader ever since I was young until today. ³Here I am. Bear witness against me before Yahweh and before his anointed. Whose ox have I taken? Whose donkey have I taken? Have I wronged or oppressed anyone? Have I taken a consideration from anyone for looking the other way? If so, I will make amends.' ⁴They said, 'You have neither wronged nor oppressed us nor accepted anything from anyone.' ⁵He said to them, 'Yahweh is your witness and his anointed is witness today that you have found nothing in my hands?' They replied, 'He is witness.'

⁶Samuel then said to the people, 'Yahweh is witness, he who raised up Moses and Aaron and who brought your ancestors out of Egypt. ⁷So now, stay where you are, while I plead with you before Yahweh and remind you of all the saving acts which he has done for you and for your ancestors. ⁸After Jacob had arrived in Egypt, the Egyptians oppressed them, and your ancestors cried to Yahweh. Yahweh then sent Moses and Aaron, who brought your ancestors out of Egypt and gave them a settled home here. ⁹They then forgot Yahweh their God and he sold them into the power of Sisera, general of the army of Hazor, and also into the power of the Philistines and of the king of Moab, who made war on them. ¹⁰They cried to Yahweh, "We have sinned," they said, "for we have deserted Yahweh and served the Baals and the Astartes. Rescue us now from the power of our enemies, and we will serve you." ¹¹Yahweh then sent Jerubbaal, Barak, Jephthah, and Samuel. He rescued you from the power of the enemies surrounding you, and you lived in security.

¹²'But when you saw Nahash, king of the Ammonites, marching on you, you said to me, "No, we must have a king to rule us"—although Yahweh your God is your king. ¹³So, here is the king whom you have chosen; Yahweh has appointed you a king. ¹⁴If you fear and serve Yahweh and obey his voice and do not rebel against his commands, and if both you and the king who rules you follow Yahweh your God, all will be well. ¹⁵But if you do not obey Yahweh's voice but rebel against his commands, Yahweh's hand will be against you and against your king.

¹⁶'Stay where you are and see the wonder which Yahweh will do before your eyes. ¹⁷Is it not now the wheat harvest? I shall call on Yahweh and he will send thunder and rain, so that you may clearly understand what a very wicked thing you have done, in Yahweh's eyes, by asking for a king.' ¹⁸Samuel then called on Yahweh, and Yahweh sent thunder and rain the same day, and all the people held Yahweh and Samuel in great awe. ¹⁹They all said to Samuel, 'Pray for your servants to Yahweh your God, to save us from death; for to all our sins we have added this wrong of asking for a king.'

²⁰Samuel said to the people, 'Do not be afraid. Although you have done all these wicked things, do not withdraw your allegiance from Yahweh. Instead, serve Yahweh with all your heart. ²¹Do not transfer your allegiance to useless idols which, being useless, are futile and cannot save anybody; ²²Yahweh, for the sake of his great name, will not desert his people, for it has pleased Yahweh to make you his people. ²³For my part, far be it from me to sin against Yahweh by ceasing to pray for you or to instruct you in the good and right way. ²⁴Fear none but Yahweh, and serve him faithfully with all your heart, bearing in mind the wonder which he has just performed. But, if you persist in wickedness, you and your king will perish.'

Revolt against the Philistines

13 Saul was . . . years old when he became king, and reigned over Israel for . . . years. ²Saul selected three thousand men of Israel; two thousand of them were with Saul at

Michmash and in the highlands of Bethel, and one thousand with Jonathan at Geba of Benjamin; the rest of the people Saul sent home, everyone to his tent.

3 Jonathan killed the Philistine governor stationed at Gibeah and the Philistines were informed that the Hebrews had risen in revolt. Saul had the trumpet sounded throughout the country, 4 and all Israel heard the news, 'Saul has killed the Philistine governor, and now Israel has antagonised the Philistines.' So all the people rallied behind Saul at Gilgal. 5 The Philistines mustered to make war on Israel, three thousand chariots, six thousand horses and a force as numerous as the sand on the seashore. They came up and pitched camp at Michmash, to the east of Beth-Aven. 6 When the Israelites saw that their plight was desperate, being so hard pressed, the people hid in caves, in holes, in crevices, in vaults, in wells. 7 Some also crossed the Jordan fords into the territory of Gad and Gilead.

Samuel breaks with Saul

Saul was still at Gilgal and all the people who followed him were trembling. 8 He waited for seven days, the period fixed by Samuel, but Samuel did not come to Gilgal, and the army, deserting Saul, began dispersing. 9 Saul then said, 'Bring me the burnt offering and the communion sacrifices.' And he presented the burnt offering. 10 Just as he had finished presenting the burnt offering, Samuel arrived, and Saul went out to meet and greet him. 11 Samuel said, 'What have you been doing?' Saul replied, 'I saw the army deserting me and dispersing, and you had not come at the time fixed, while the Philistines were mustering at Michmash. 12 So I thought: Now the Philistines are going to fall on me at Gilgal and I have not implored the favour of Yahweh. So I felt obliged to make the burnt offering myself.' 13 Samuel said to Saul, 'You have acted like a fool. You have not obeyed the order which Yahweh your God gave you. Otherwise, Yahweh would have confirmed your sovereignty over Israel for ever. 14 But now

your sovereignty will not last; Yahweh has discovered a man after his own heart and designated him as leader of his people, since you have not carried out what Yahweh ordered you.' 15 Samuel then got up and left Gilgal to continue his journey.

Those people remaining followed Saul as he went to join the warriors, and went from Gilgal to Geba of Benjamin. Saul reviewed the force that was with him; there were about six hundred men.

Preparations for battle

16 Saul, his son Jonathan, and the force that was with them took up their quarters in Geba of Benjamin while the Philistines camped at Michmash. 17 The raiding company sallied out of the Philistine camp in three groups: one group made for Ophrah in the territory of Shual; 18 one group made for Beth-Horon; and one group made for the high ground overlooking the Valley of the Hyenas, in the direction of the desert.

19 There was not a single blacksmith throughout the territory of Israel, the Philistines' reasoning being, 'We do not want the Hebrews making swords or spears.' 20 Hence, the Israelites were all in the habit of going down individually to the Philistines to sharpen their ploughshares, axes, mattocks and scythes. 21 The price was two-thirds of a shekel for ploughshares and axes, and one-third for sharpening mattocks and straightening goads. 22 So it was that on the day of the battle, no one in the army with Saul and Jonathan was equipped with either sword or spear; only Saul and his son Jonathan were so equipped.

23 A Philistine unit set out for the Pass of Michmash.

Jonathan attacks the outpost

14 One day, Jonathan son of Saul said to his armour-bearer, 'Come on, let us go across to the Philistine outpost over on the other side.' But he did not inform his father. 2 Saul was on the outskirts of Geba, sitting under the pomegranate tree that stands near

the threshing-floor; the force with him numbered about six hundred men. ³Ahijah son of Ahitub, brother of Ichabod, son of Phinehas, son of Eli, the priest of Yahweh at Shiloh, was carrying the *ephod.ᵃ* The force did not know that Jonathan had left.

⁴In the pass that Jonathan was trying to cross to reach the Philistine outpost, there is a rocky spur on one side and a rocky spur on the other; one is called Bozez, the other Seneh. ⁵The first spur stands to the north facing Michmash, the other to the south facing Geba. ⁶Jonathan said to his armour-bearer, 'Come on, let us go across to these uncircumcised people's outpost; perhaps Yahweh will do something for us, for Yahweh is free to grant deliverance through a few men, just as much as through many.' ⁷His armour-bearer replied, 'Do exactly as you think. I am with you; our hearts are as one.' ⁸Jonathan then said, 'Look, we will go across to these people and let ourselves be seen. ⁹If they say, "Do not move until we come to you," we shall stay where we are and not go up to them. ¹⁰But if they say, "Come up to us," we shall go up, for that will be the sign for us that Yahweh has given them into our power.'

¹¹When the two of them let themselves be seen by the Philistine outpost, the Philistines said, 'Look, the Hebrews are coming out of the holes where they have been hiding.' ¹²The men of the outpost then hailed Jonathan and his armour-bearer. 'Come up to us,' they said, 'we have something to tell you.' Jonathan then said to his armour-bearer, 'Follow me up; Yahweh has given them into the power of Israel.' ¹³Jonathan clambered up on hands and feet, with his armour-bearer behind him; the Philistines fell at Jonathan's onslaught, and his armour-bearer, coming behind, finished them off. ¹⁴This first killing made by Jonathan and his armour-bearer accounted for about twenty men . . .

Battle is engaged

¹⁵There was panic in the camp, in the field and throughout the army; outpost and raiding

company too were panic-stricken; the earth quaked: it was a panic from Yahweh. ¹⁶Saul's look-out men in Geba of Benjamin could see the camp scattering in all directions. ¹⁷Saul then said to the force that was with him, 'Call the roll and see who has left us.' So they called the roll, and Jonathan and his armour-bearer were missing.

¹⁸Saul then said to Ahijah, 'Bring the *ephod,'* since he was the man who carried the *ephod* in Israel. ¹⁹But while Saul was speaking to the priest, the turmoil in the Philistine camp grew worse and worse; and Saul said to the priest, 'Withdraw your hand.' ²⁰Saul and the whole force with him then formed up and advanced to where the fighting was going on: and there they all were, drawing their swords on one another in wild confusion. ²¹Those Hebrews who had earlier taken service with the Philistines and had accompanied them into camp, now defected to the Israelites who were with Saul and Jonathan. ²²Similarly, all those Israelites who had been hiding in the highlands of Ephraim, hearing that the Philistines were on the run, chased after them and joined in the fight. ²³That day Yahweh gave Israel the victory.

Jonathan violates Saul's prohibition

The fighting reached the other side of Beth-Horon. ²⁴As the men of Israel were hard pressed that day, Saul pronounced this imprecation over the people, 'A curse on anyone who eats food before evening, before I have taken revenge on my enemies!' So none of the people so much as tasted food.

²⁵Now there was a honeycomb out in the open. ²⁶The people came to the honeycomb, the honey was dripping out, but no one put a hand to his mouth, the people being in awe of the oath. ²⁷Jonathan, however, not having heard his father bind the people with the oath, reached with the end of the stick which he was carrying, thrust it into the honeycomb and put it to his mouth; whereupon his eyes grew

14a See note to 2:28.

brighter. 28 One of the people then spoke up. 'Your father', he said, 'has bound the people with this oath: "A curse on anyone who eats anything today." ' 29 'My father has brought trouble on the country,' Jonathan replied. 'See how much brighter my eyes are for having eaten this mouthful of honey. 30 By the same token, if the people had been allowed to eat some of the booty which they had captured from the enemy today, would not the defeat of the Philistines have been all the greater?'

The people commit a ritual fault

31 That day the Philistines were beaten from Michmash all the way to Aijalon, until the people were utterly exhausted. 32 The people flung themselves on the booty and, taking sheep, bullocks and calves, slaughtered them there on the ground and ate them with the blood. 33 Saul was informed, 'The people are sinning against Yahweh by eating with the blood!' He said, 'You have not kept faith! Roll me a large stone here!' 34 Saul then said, 'Scatter among the people and say, "Everyone is to bring his bullock or his sheep to me here." You will slaughter them here and eat, and not sin against Yahweh by eating with the blood.' Each individual brought what he happened to have that night, and they all slaughtered in the same place. 35 Saul built an altar to Yahweh; it was the first altar he had built to Yahweh.

Jonathan's guilt is discovered, but he is saved by the people

36 Saul said, 'Let us go down under cover of dark and plunder the Philistines until dawn; we shall not leave one of them alive.' 'Do whatever you think right,' they replied. But the priest said, 'Let us approach God here.' 37 Saul consulted God, 'Shall I go down and pursue the Philistines? Will you hand them over to Israel?' But he gave him no reply that day. 38 Saul then said, 'Come forward, all you leaders of the people; consider carefully where today's sin may lie; 39 for as Yahweh lives who gives victory to Israel, even if the sin lies with Jonathan my son, he shall be put to death.' But

not one out of all the people answered. 40 He then said to all Israel, 'Stand on one side, and I and Jonathan my son will stand on the other.' And the people replied to Saul, 'Do as you think right.' 41 Saul then said, 'Yahweh, God of Israel, why did you not answer your servant today? Yahweh, God of Israel, if the fault lies with me or with my son Jonathan, give *urim:* if the fault lies with your people Israel, give *thummim.*[b] Jonathan and Saul were indicated and the people went free. 42 Saul said, 'Cast the lot between me and my son Jonathan,' and Jonathan was indicated.

43 'I only tasted a mouthful of honey off the end of the stick which I was carrying. But I am ready to die.' 44 Saul said, 'May God bring unnameable ills on me, and worse ones too, if you do not die, Jonathan!' 45 But the people said to Saul, 'Must Jonathan die after winning this great victory for Israel? We will never allow that! As Yahweh lives, not one hair of his head shall fall to the ground, for his deeds today have been done with the help of God.' And so the people ransomed Jonathan and he was not put to death.

46 Saul decided not to pursue the Philistines, and the Philistines retired to their own territory.

Summary of Saul's reign

47 Saul consolidated his rule over Israel and made war on all his enemies on all fronts: on Moab, the Ammonites, Edom, the king of Zobah and the Philistines; whichever way he turned, he was victorious. 48 He did great deeds of valour; he defeated the Amalekites and delivered Israel from those who used to pillage him.

49 Saul's sons were: Jonathan, Ishvi and Malchishua. The names of his two daughters were: the elder, Merab, and the younger, Michal. 50 The name of Saul's wife was Ahinoam daughter of Ahimaaz. The name of his army commander was Abner son of Ner,

---

14b A simple yes/no answer is obtained by drawing one of the lots out of the *ephod.*

Saul's uncle. ⁵¹ Kish father of Saul, and Ner father of Abner were the sons of Abiel.

⁵² There was fierce warfare with the Philistines throughout Saul's life. Any strong or valiant man who caught Saul's eye, he recruited into his service.

Holy war against the Amalekites

15 Samuel said to Saul, 'I am the man whom Yahweh sent to anoint you as king of his people Israel, so now listen to the words of Yahweh. ²This is what Yahweh Sabaoth says, "I intend to punish what Amalek did to Israel—laying a trap for him on the way as he was coming up from Egypt. ³Now, go and crush Amalek; put him under the curse of destruction with all that he possesses. Do not spare him, but kill man and woman, babe and suckling, ox and sheep, camel and donkey." '

⁴Saul summoned the people and reviewed them at Telaim: two hundred thousand foot soldiers (and ten thousand men of Judah). ⁵Saul advanced on the town of Amalek and lay in ambush in the river bed. ⁶Saul said to the Kenites, 'Go away, leave your homes among the Amalekites, in case I destroy you with them—you acted with faithful love towards all the Israelites when they were coming up from Egypt.' So the Kenites moved away from the Amalekites.

⁷Saul then crushed the Amalekites, beginning at Havilah in the direction of Shur, which is to the east of Egypt. ⁸He took Agag king of the Amalekites alive and, executing the curse of destruction, put all the people to the sword. ⁹But Saul and the army spared Agag with the best of the sheep and cattle, the fatlings and lambs and all that was good. They did not want to consign these to the curse of destruction; they consigned only what was poor and worthless.

Saul is rejected by Yahweh

¹⁰The word of Yahweh came to Samuel, ¹¹'I regret having made Saul king, since he has broken his allegiance to me and not carried out my orders.' Samuel was appalled and cried to Yahweh all night long.

¹²In the morning, Samuel set off to find Saul. Samuel was told, 'Saul has been to Carmel, to raise himself a monument there, but now has turned about, moved on and gone down to Gilgal.' ¹³When Samuel reached Saul, Saul said, 'May you be blessed by Yahweh! I have carried out Yahweh's orders.' ¹⁴Samuel replied, 'Then what is this bleating of sheep in my ears and the lowing of cattle that I hear?' ¹⁵Saul said, 'They have been brought from Amalek, the people having spared the best of the sheep and cattle to sacrifice them to Yahweh, your God; the rest we have consigned to the curse of destruction.'

¹⁶Samuel then said to Saul, 'Stop! Let me tell you what Yahweh said to me last night.' He said, 'Go on.' ¹⁷Samuel said, 'Small as you may be in your own eyes, are you not the leader of the tribes of Israel? Yahweh has anointed you as king of Israel. ¹⁸When Yahweh sent you on a mission he said to you, "Go and put those sinners, the Amalekites, under the curse of destruction and make war on them until they are exterminated." ¹⁹Why then did you not obey Yahweh's voice? Why did you fall on the booty and do what is wrong in Yahweh's eyes?' ²⁰Saul replied to Samuel, 'But I did obey Yahweh's voice. I went on the mission which Yahweh gave me; I brought back Agag king of the Amalekites; I put Amalek under the curse of destruction; ²¹and from the booty the people have taken the best sheep and cattle of what was under the curse of destruction only to sacrifice them to Yahweh your God in Gilgal.' ²²To which, Samuel said:

> Is Yahweh pleased by burnt offerings and
>   sacrifices
> or by obedience to Yahweh's voice?
> Truly, obedience is better than sacrifice,
> submissiveness than the fat of rams.
> ²³ Rebellion is a sin of sorcery,
> presumption a crime of idolatry!

'Since you have rejected Yahweh's word, he has rejected you as king.'

Saul asks in vain for pardon

24 Saul then said to Samuel, 'I have sinned, having broken Yahweh's order and your instructions because I was afraid of the people and yielded to their demands. 25 Now, please forgive my sin and come back with me, so that I can worship Yahweh.' 26 Samuel said to Saul, 'I will not come back with you, since you have rejected Yahweh's word and Yahweh has rejected you as king of Israel.' 27 As Samuel turned away to leave, Saul caught at the hem of his cloak and it tore, 28 and Samuel said to him, 'Today Yahweh has torn the kingdom of Israel from you and given it to a neighbour of yours who is better than you.' 29 (The Glory of Israel, however, does not lie or go back on his word, not being human and liable to go back on his word.) 30 'I have sinned,' Saul said, 'but please still show me respect in front of my people's elders and in front of Israel, and come back with me, so that I can worship Yahweh your God.' 31 Samuel followed Saul back and Saul worshipped Yahweh.

Death of Agag and departure of Samuel

32 Samuel then said, 'Bring me Agag king of the Amalekites!' Agag came towards him unsteadily saying, 'Truly death is bitter!' 33 Samuel said:

As your sword has left women childless,
so will your mother be left childless among
women!

Samuel then butchered Agag before Yahweh at Gilgal.

34 Samuel left for Ramah, and Saul went up home to Gibeah of Saul. 35 Samuel did not see Saul again till his dying day. Samuel indeed mourned over Saul, but Yahweh regretted having made Saul king of Israel.

David is anointed by Samuel

16 Yahweh said to Samuel, 'How much longer do you mean to go on mourning over Saul, now that I myself have rejected him as ruler of Israel? Fill your horn with oil and go. I am sending you to Jesse of Bethlehem, for I have found myself a king from among his sons.' 2 Samuel replied, 'How can I go? When Saul hears of it he will kill me.' Yahweh then said, 'Take a heifer with you and say, "I have come to sacrifice to Yahweh." 3 Invite Jesse to the sacrifice, and I shall reveal to you what you must do; and you will anoint for me the one I indicate to you.'

4 Samuel did what Yahweh ordered and went to Bethlehem. The elders of the town came trembling to meet him and asked, 'Seer, is your coming favourable for us,' 5 'Yes,' he replied. 'I have come to sacrifice to Yahweh. Purify yourselves and come with me to the sacrifice.' He purified Jesse and his sons and invited them to the sacrifice.

6 When they arrived, he looked at Eliab and thought, 'This must be Yahweh's anointed now before him,' 7 but Yahweh said to Samuel, 'Take no notice of his appearance or his height, for I have rejected him; God does not see as human beings see; they look at appearances but Yahweh looks at the heart.' 8 Jesse then called Abinadab and presented him to Samuel, who said, 'Yahweh has not chosen this one either.' 9 Jesse then presented Shammah, but Samuel said, 'Yahweh has not chosen this one either.' 10 Jesse thus presented seven of his sons to Samuel, but Samuel said to Jesse, 'Yahweh has not chosen these.' 11 He then asked Jesse, 'Are these all the sons you have?' Jesse replied, 'There is still one left, the youngest; he is looking after the sheep.' Samuel then said to Jesse, 'Send for him, for we shall not sit down to eat until he arrives.' 12 Jesse had him sent for; he had ruddy cheeks, with fine eyes and an attractive appearance. Yahweh said, 'Get up and anoint him: he is the one!' 13 At this, Samuel took the horn of oil and anointed him, surrounded by his brothers; and the spirit of Yahweh seized on David from that day onwards. Samuel, for his part, set off and went to Ramah.

David enters Saul's service [a]

14 Now the spirit of Yahweh had withdrawn from Saul, and an evil spirit from Yahweh afflicted him with terrors. 15 Saul's servants said to him, 'An evil spirit from God is undoubtedly the cause of your terrors. 16 Let our lord give the order, and your servants who wait on you will look for a skilled harpist; when the evil spirit from God comes over you, he will play and it will do you good.' 17 Saul said to his attendants, 'Find me, please, a man who plays well, and bring him to me.' 18 One of the servants then spoke up and said, 'I have seen one of the sons of Jesse the Bethlehemite: he is a skilled player, a brave man and a fighter, well spoken, good-looking and Yahweh is with him.' 19 So Saul sent messengers to Jesse with the order, 'Send me your son David (who is with the sheep).' 20 Jesse took five loaves, a skin of wine and a kid, and sent them to Saul by his son David. 21 David went to Saul and entered his service; Saul became very fond of him and David became his armour-bearer. 22 Saul then sent a message to Jesse, 'Let David stay in my service, since he has won my favour.' 23 And whenever the spirit from God came over Saul, David would take a harp and play; Saul would then be soothed; it would do him good, and the evil spirit would leave him.

Goliath challenges the Israelite army

17 The Philistines mustered their troops for war; they assembled at Socoh in Judah and pitched camp between Socoh and Azekah, in Ephes-Dammim. 2 Saul and the Israelites also mustered, pitching camp in the Valley of the Terebinth, and drew up their battle-line opposite the Philistines. 3 The Philistines occupied the high ground on one side and the Israelites occupied the high ground on the other side, with the valley between them.

4 A champion stepped out from the Philistine ranks; his name was Goliath, from Gath; he was six cubits and one span tall. 5 On his head was a bronze helmet and he wore a breastplate of scale-armour; the breastplate weighed five thousand shekels of bronze. 6 He had bronze greaves on his legs and a bronze scimitar slung across his shoulders. 7 The shaft of his spear was like a weaver's beam, and the head of his spear weighed six hundred shekels of iron. A shield-bearer walked in front of him.

8 Taking position in front of the Israelite lines, he shouted, 'Why have you come out to range yourselves for battle? Am I not a Philistine and are you not Saul's lackeys? Choose a man and let him come down to me. 9 If he can fight it out with me and kill me, we will be your servants; but if I can beat him and kill him, you become our servants and serve us.' 10 The Philistine then said, 'I challenge the ranks of Israel today. Give me a man and we will fight it out!' 11 When Saul and all Israel heard what the Philistine said, they were dismayed and terrified.

David arrives in the camp

12 David was the son of an Ephrathite from Bethlehem of Judah whose name was Jesse; Jesse had eight sons and, by Saul's time, he was old and well on in years. 13 Jesse's eldest three sons followed Saul to the war. The names of the three sons who went to the war were: the eldest Eliab, the second Abinadab and the third Shammah. 14 David was the youngest; the eldest three followed Saul. 15 David alternated between serving Saul and looking after his father's sheep at Bethlehem. 16 Morning and evening, the Philistine advanced, presenting himself thus for forty days. 17 Jesse said to his son David, 'Take your brothers this *ephah* of roasted grain and these ten loaves, and hurry to the camp, to your brothers. 18 And take these ten cheeses to their commanding officer; find out how your brothers are and bring some token back from them; 19 they are with

16a There are two separate versions of David's early association with Saul: 1 David is a court musician; 2 He is a shepherd visiting his brothers. In this part of David's story there is a series of doublets: 18:11 = 19:8–10; 18:17–19 = 18:20–27; 19:1–7 = 20:1–42; 24 = 26; 21:11–16 = 27:1–12.

Saul and all the men of Israel in the Valley of the Terebinth, fighting the Philistines.'

20 David got up early in the morning and, leaving the sheep with someone to guard them, took up his load and went off as Jesse had ordered; he reached the encampment just as the troops were leaving to take up battle stations and shouting the war cry. 21 Israel and the Philistines drew up their lines facing one another. 22 David left his bundle in charge of the baggage guard and, running to the battle-line, went and asked his brothers how they were.

23 While he was talking to them, the champion (Goliath, the Philistine from Gath) came up from the Philistine ranks and made his usual speech, which David heard. 24 As soon as the Israelites saw this man, they all ran away from him and were terrified. 25 The Israelites said, 'You saw that man who just came up? He comes to challenge Israel. The king will lavish riches on the man who kills him, he will give him his daughter in marriage and exempt his father's family from all taxes in Israel.'

26 David asked the men who were standing near him, 'What would be the reward for killing this Philistine and saving Israel from disgrace? Who is this uncircumcised Philistine, to challenge the armies of the living God?' 27 The people told him what they had been saying, 'That would be the reward for killing him,' they said. 28 His eldest brother Eliab heard David talking to the men and grew angry with him. 'Why have you come down here?' he said. 'Whom have you left in charge of those few sheep in the desert? I know how impudent and artful you are; you have come to watch the battle!' 29 David retorted, 'What have I done? May I not even speak?' 30 And he turned away from him to someone else and asked the same question, to which the people replied as before. 31 David's words were noted, however, and reported to Saul, who sent for him.

David volunteers to accept the challenge

32 David said to Saul, 'Let no one be discouraged on his account; your servant will go and fight this Philistine.' 33 Saul said to David, 'You cannot go and fight the Philistine; you are only a boy and he has been a warrior since his youth.'

34 David said to Saul, 'Your servant used to look after the sheep for his father and whenever a lion or a bear came and took a sheep from the flock, 35 I used to follow it up, lay into it and snatch the sheep out of its jaws. If it turned on me, I would seize it by the beard and batter it to death. 36 Your servant has killed both lion and bear, and this uncircumcised Philistine will end up like one of them for having challenged the armies of the living God.' 37 'Yahweh,' David went on, 'who delivered me from the claws of lion and bear, will deliver me from the clutches of this Philistine.' Then Saul said to David, 'Go, and Yahweh be with you!'

38 Saul dressed David in his own armour; he put a bronze helmet on his head, dressed him in a breastplate 39 and buckled his own sword over David's armour. David tried to walk but, not being used to them, said to Saul, 'I cannot walk in these; I am not used to them.' So they took them off again.

David and Goliath

40 He took his stick in his hand, selected five smooth stones from the river bed and put them in his shepherd's bag, in his pouch; then, sling in hand, he walked towards the Philistine. 41 The Philistine, preceded by his shield-bearer, came nearer and nearer to David. 42 When the Philistine looked David up and down, what he saw filled him with scorn, because David was only a lad, with ruddy cheeks and an attractive appearance. 43 The Philistine said to David, 'Am I a dog for you to come after me with sticks?' And the Philistine cursed David by his gods. 44 The Philistine said to David, 'Come over here and I will give your flesh to the birds of the air and the wild beasts!' 45 David retorted to the Philistine, 'You come to me with sword, spear and scimitar, but I come to you in the name of Yahweh Sabaoth, God of the armies of Israel, whom you have

26   READ 1 SAMUEL 17:32–58.

I come to you in the name of Yahweh Sabaoth.—1 SAMUEL 17:45

THE POWER OF GOD'S NAME

The Liturgy of the Hours chooses this reading from St. Gregory of Nyssa about the name of Jesus as a comment on David's use of God's name in his conquest of Goliath:

No one has known Christ better than Paul, nor surpassed him in the careful example he gave of what anyone should be who bears Christ's name. . . .

Paul teaches us the power of Christ's name when he calls him the power and the wisdom of God, our peace, the unapproachable light where God dwells, our expiation and redemption, our great high priest, our paschal sacrifice, our propitiation; when he declares him to be the radiance of God's glory, the very pattern of his nature, the creator of all ages, our spiritual food and drink, the rock and the water, the bedrock of our faith, the cornerstone, the visible image of the invisible God. He goes on to speak of him as the mighty God, the head of his body, the Church, the firstborn of the new creation, the firstfruits of those who have fallen asleep, the firstborn of the dead, the eldest of many brothers: he tells us that Christ is the mediator between God and man, the only-begotten Son crowned with glory and honor, the Lord of glory, the beginning of all things, the king of justice and of peace, the king of the whole universe, ruling a realm that has no limits.

Paul calls Christ by many other titles too numerous to recall here. Their cumulative force will give some conception of the marvelous content of the name "Christ," revealing to us his inexpressible majesty, insofar as our minds and thoughts can comprehend it. Since, by the goodness of God, we who are called "Christians" have been granted the honor of sharing this name, the greatest, the highest, the most sublime of all names, it follows that each of the titles that express its meaning should be clearly reflected in us. If we are not to lie when we call ourselves "Christians," we must bear witness to it by our way of living.   ST. GREGORY OF NYSSA, 330?–395?

YOU WILL FIND THE NEXT READING AT 1 SAMUEL 26.

challenged. ⁴⁶ Today, Yahweh will deliver you into my hand; I shall kill you, I shall cut off your head; today, I shall give your corpse and the corpses of the Philistine army to the birds of the air and the wild beasts, so that the whole world may know that there is a God in Israel, ⁴⁷ and this whole assembly know that Yahweh does not give victory by means of sword and spear—for Yahweh is lord of the battle and he will deliver you into our power.'

⁴⁸ No sooner had the Philistine started forward to confront David than David darted out of the lines and ran to meet the Philistine. ⁴⁹ Putting his hand in his bag, he took out a stone, slung it and struck the Philistine on the forehead; the stone penetrated his forehead and he fell face downwards on the ground. ⁵⁰ Thus David triumphed over the Philistine with a sling and a stone; he hit the Philistine and killed him, though he had

no sword in his hand. ⁵¹ David ran and stood over the Philistine, seized his sword, pulled it from the scabbard, despatched him and cut off his head.

When the Philistines saw that their champion was dead, they fled. ⁵² The men of Israel and of Judah started forward, shouting their war cry, and pursued the Philistines as far as the approaches of Gath and the gates of Ekron. The Philistine dead lay all along the road from Shaaraim as far as Gath and Ekron. ⁵³ Turning back from their ferocious pursuit of the Philistines, the Israelites plundered their camp. ⁵⁴ And David took the Philistine's head and brought it to Jerusalem; his weapons, however, he put in his own tent.

David the conqueror of Goliath is presented to Saul

⁵⁵ When Saul saw David going to engage the Philistine he said to Abner, the army commander, 'Abner, whose son is that boy?' 'On your life, O king,' Abner replied, 'I do not know.' ⁵⁶ The king said, 'Find out whose son the lad is.'

⁵⁷ When David came back after killing the Philistine, Abner took him and brought him before Saul with the Philistine's head in his hand. ⁵⁸ Saul asked him, 'Whose son are you, young man?' David replied, 'The son of your servant Jesse of Bethlehem.'

18 When David had finished talking to Saul, Jonathan felt an instant affection for David; Jonathan loved him like his very self; ² Saul engaged him that very day and would not let him go home to his father. ³ Jonathan made a pact with David, since he loved him like his very self; ⁴ Jonathan took off the cloak which he was wearing and gave it to David, and his armour too, even including his sword, his bow and his belt. ⁵ Wherever David was sent on a mission by Saul, he was successful, and Saul put him in command of the fighting men; all the people respected him and so did Saul's staff.

Saul starts being jealous

⁶ On their return, when David was coming back from killing the Philistine, the women came out of all the towns of Israel singing and dancing to meet King Saul, with tambourines, sistrums and cries of joy; ⁷ and as they danced the women sang:

Saul has killed his thousands,
and David his tens of thousands.

⁸ Saul was very angry; the incident displeased him. 'They have given David the tens of thousands,' he said, 'but me only the thousands; what more can he have, except the throne?' ⁹ And Saul watched David jealously from that day onwards.

¹⁰ The following day, an evil spirit from God seized on Saul and he fell into a frenzy while he was indoors. David played the harp as on other occasions; Saul had a spear in his hand. ¹¹ Saul brandished the spear; he said, 'I will pin David to the wall!' David evaded him twice.

¹² Saul feared David, since Yahweh was with him and had withdrawn from Saul. ¹³ So Saul removed him from his presence and appointed him commander of a thousand; he led the people on campaign. ¹⁴ In all his expeditions, David was successful and Yahweh was with him. ¹⁵ And Saul, seeing how very successful he was, was afraid of him. ¹⁶ All Israel and Judah loved David, however, since he was their leader on campaign.

David's marriage

¹⁷ Saul said to David, 'This is my elder daughter Merab; I shall give her to you in marriage; but you must serve me bravely and fight Yahweh's wars.' Saul thought, 'Better than strike the blow myself, let the Philistines do it!' ¹⁸ David replied to Saul, 'Who am I and what is my lineage—and my father's family—in Israel, for me to become the king's son-in-law?' ¹⁹ When the time came for Merab daughter of Saul to be given to David, she was given to Adriel of Meholah instead.

20 Now Michal daughter of Saul fell in love with David. When Saul heard this he was pleased. 21 He thought, 'Yes, I shall give her to him; she can be the snare for him, so that the Philistines will get him.' (On two occasions, Saul told David, 'Today, you shall be my son-in-law.') 22 Saul gave instructions to his servants, 'Have a private word with David and say, "Look, the king is fond of you and all his servants love you—why not be the king's son-in-law?"' 23 Saul's servants repeated these words in David's ear, to which David replied, 'Do you think that becoming the king's son-in-law is a trivial matter; I have neither wealth nor position.' 24 Saul's servants then reported back, 'This is what David said.' 25 Saul replied, 'Tell David this, "The king desires no bride-price except one hundred Philistine foreskins, in vengeance on the king's enemies."' Saul was counting on getting David killed by the Philistines.

26 When his servants repeated this to David, David thought it would be a fine thing to be the king's son-in-law. And no time was lost 27 before David got up to go, he and his men, and killed two hundred of the Philistines. David brought their foreskins back and counted them out before the king, so that he could be the king's son-in-law. Saul then gave him his daughter Michal in marriage.

28 Saul could not but see that Yahweh was with David, and that the whole House of Israel loved him; 29 Saul became more afraid of David than ever, and became his inveterate enemy. 30 The Philistine chiefs kept mounting their campaigns but, whenever they did so, David proved more successful than any of Saul's staff; consequently he gained great renown.

Jonathan intercedes for David

19 Saul let his son Jonathan and all his servants know of his intention to kill David. But Jonathan, Saul's son, held David in great affection; 2 and Jonathan warned David, 'My father Saul is looking for a way to kill you, so be on your guard tomorrow morning; go into hiding, stay out of sight. 3 I shall go out and keep my father company in the countryside where you will be, and shall talk to my father about you; I shall see what the situation is and then tell you.'

4 Jonathan spoke highly of David to Saul his father and said, 'The king should not harm his servant David; far from harming you, what he has done has been greatly to your advantage. 5 He took his life in his hands, he killed the Philistine, and Yahweh brought about a great victory for all Israel. You saw for yourself. How pleased you were! Why then sin against innocent blood by killing David for no reason?' 6 Saul was impressed by Jonathan's words. Saul swore, 'As Yahweh lives, I will not kill him.' 7 Jonathan called David and told him all this. Jonathan then brought him to Saul, and David remained in attendance as before.

Saul's attempt on David's life

8 War broke out again and David sallied out to fight the Philistines; he inflicted a great defeat on them and they fled before him. 9 An evil spirit from Yahweh came over Saul while he was sitting in his house with his spear in his hand; David was playing the harp. 10 Saul tried to pin David to the wall with his spear, but he avoided Saul's thrust and the spear stuck in the wall. David fled and made good his escape.

David is saved by Michal

That same night 11 Saul sent agents to watch David's house, intending to kill him in the morning. But Michal, David's wife, warned him, 'If you do not escape tonight, you will be a dead man tomorrow!' 12 Michal then let David down through the window, and he made off, took to flight and so escaped.

13 Michal then took a domestic image, laid it on the bed, put a tress of goats' hair at the head of the bed and put a cover over it. 14 When Saul sent the agents to arrest David, she said, 'He is ill.' 15 Saul sent the agents back to see David, with the words, 'Bring him to me on

his bed, for me to kill him!' 16 So in the agents went, and there in bed was the image, with the tress of goats' hair on its head! 17 Saul then said to Michal, 'Why have you deceived me like this and let my enemy go, and so make his escape?' Michal replied to Saul, 'He said, "Let me go, or I shall kill you!"'

Saul and David at Ramah with Samuel

18 David, having fled and made his escape, went to Samuel at Ramah and told him exactly how Saul had treated him; he and Samuel went and lived in the huts. 19 Word was brought to Saul, 'David is in the huts at Ramah.' 20 Saul accordingly sent agents to capture David; when they saw the community of prophets prophesying, and Samuel there as their leader, the spirit of God came over Saul's agents, and they too fell into frenzy. 21 When Saul was told of this, he sent other agents, and they too fell into frenzy; Saul then sent a third group of agents, and they fell into frenzy too.

22 He then went to Ramah himself and, arriving at the large storage-well at Seku, asked, 'Where are Samuel and David?' And someone said, 'Why, they are in the huts at Ramah!' 23 Making his way from there to the huts at Ramah, the spirit of God came over him too, and he went along in a frenzy until he arrived at the huts at Ramah. 24 He too stripped off his clothes and he too fell into a frenzy in Samuel's presence, then collapsed naked on the ground for the rest of that day and all night. Hence the saying: Is Saul one of the prophets too?

Jonathan helps David to escape

20 Fleeing from the huts at Ramah, David went and confronted Jonathan, 'What have I done, what is my guilt, how have I wronged your father, for him to want to take my life?' 2 He replied, 'You must not think that! You are not going to die. My father, you see, does nothing, important or unimportant, without confiding in me, so why should my father hide this from me? It is not true.' 3 In reply, David swore, 'Your father knows very well that I enjoy your favour, and thinks,

"Jonathan must not know about this or he will be upset." But, as Yahweh lives and as you yourself live, there is only a step between me and death.'

4 At which, Jonathan said to David, 'Whatever you think best, I will certainly do for you.' 5 David replied, 'Look, tomorrow is New Moon and I ought to sit at table with the king, but you must let me go and hide in the countryside until the evening. 6 If your father notices my absence, you must say, "David insistently asked me for permission to hurry over to Bethlehem, his home town, because they are holding the annual sacrifice there for the whole clan." 7 If he says, "Very well," your servant is safe, but if he flies into a rage, you may be sure that he has some evil plan. 8 Show your servant faithful love, since you have bound your servant to you by a pact in Yahweh's name. But if I am guilty, then kill me yourself—why take me to your father?' 9 Jonathan replied, 'Perish the thought! If I knew for sure that my father was determined to do you a mischief, would I not have told you?' 10 David then said to Jonathan, 'Who will let me know if your father gives you a harsh answer?'

11 Jonathan then said to David, 'Come on, let us go out into the country,' and the pair of them went out into the country. 12 Jonathan then said to David, 'By Yahweh, God of Israel! I shall sound my father this time tomorrow; if all is well for David and I do not then send and inform you, 13 may Yahweh bring unnameable ills to Jonathan and worse ones too! If my father intends to do you a mischief, I shall tell you so and let you get away, so that you can be safe. And may Yahweh be with you as he used to be with my father! 14 If I am still alive, show your servant faithful love; if I die, 15 never withdraw your faithful love from my family. When Yahweh has exterminated every enemy of David's from the face of the earth, 16 do not let Jonathan's name be exterminated with Saul's family, or may Yahweh call David to account!' 17 Jonathan then renewed his oath to David, since he loved him like his very soul.

¹⁸ Jonathan then said to David, 'Tomorrow is New Moon; your absence will be noticed, since your place will be empty. ¹⁹ The day after tomorrow your absence will be very marked, and you must go to the place where you hid on the day of the deed, and stay beside that mound. ²⁰ For my part, the day after tomorrow I shall shoot three arrows in that direction, as though at a target. ²¹ I shall then send a servant to go and find the arrows. If I say to him, "The arrows are this side of you, get them," come out, since all will be well for you and nothing the matter, as sure as Yahweh lives. ²² But if I say to him, "The arrows are ahead of you," then be off, for Yahweh himself will be sending you away. ²³ And as regards the agreement we made, you and I, why, Yahweh is witness between us for ever.'

²⁴ So David hid in the country; New Moon came and the king sat down to his meal. ²⁵ He sat in his usual place with his back to the wall, Jonathan sat facing him and Abner sat next to Saul; but David's place was empty. ²⁶ Saul said nothing that day, thinking, 'It is sheer chance; he is unclean.' ²⁷ On the day after New Moon, the second day, David's place was still empty. ²⁸ Saul said to his son Jonathan, 'Why did not the son of Jesse come to the meal either yesterday or today?' ²⁹ Jonathan answered Saul, 'David insistently asked me for permission to go to Bethlehem. "Please let me go," he said, "for we are holding the clan sacrifice in the town and my brothers have ordered me to attend. So now, if I enjoy your favour, let me get away and see my brothers." That is why he has not come to the king's table.'

³⁰ Saul flew into a rage with Jonathan and said, 'Son of a rebellious slut! Don't I know that you side with the son of Jesse to your own shame and your mother's dishonour? ³¹ As long as the son of Jesse lives on earth, neither you nor your royal rights are secure. Now have him fetched and brought to me; he deserves to die.' ³² Jonathan retorted to his father Saul, 'Why should he die? What has he done?' ³³ But Saul brandished his spear at him to strike him, and Jonathan realised that his father was determined that David should die. ³⁴ Hot with anger, Jonathan got up from the table and ate nothing on the second day of the month, being upset about David—and because his father had insulted him.

³⁵ Next morning, Jonathan went out into the country at the time agreed with David, taking a young servant with him. ³⁶ He said to his servant, 'Run and find the arrows which I am going to shoot,' and the servant ran while Jonathan shot an arrow ahead of him. ³⁷ When the servant reached the spot to which Jonathan had shot the arrow, Jonathan shouted after him, 'Is not the arrow ahead of you?' ³⁸ Again Jonathan shouted after the servant, 'Quick! Hurry, do not stand around.' Jonathan's servant picked up the arrow and brought it back to his master. ³⁹ The servant suspected nothing; only Jonathan and David knew what was meant.

⁴⁰ Jonathan then gave his weapons to his servant and said, 'Go and carry them to the town.' ⁴¹ As soon as the servant had gone, David stood up beside the mound, threw himself to the ground, prostrating himself three times. They then embraced each other, both weeping copiously. ⁴² Jonathan then said to David, 'Go in peace. And as regards the oath that both of us have sworn by the name of Yahweh, may Yahweh be witness between you and me, between your descendants and mine for ever.'

21 David then got up and left, and Jonathan went back to the town.

David and the priest at Nob

² David then went to Nob, to Ahimelech the priest. Ahimelech came out trembling to meet David and said, 'Why are you alone? Why is nobody with you?' ³ David replied to Ahimelech the priest, 'The king has given me an order and said to me, "Do not let anyone know anything about the mission on which I am sending you, or about the order which I have given you." I have arranged to meet the guards at such and such a place. ⁴ Meanwhile,

if you have five loaves of bread to hand, give them to me, or whatever there is.' ⁵The priest replied to David, 'I have no ordinary bread to hand; there are only consecrated loaves of per-manent offering—provided that the men have kept themselves from women?'

⁶David replied to the priest, 'Certainly, women have been forbidden to us, as always when I set off on a campaign. The men's things are clean. Though this is a profane journey, they are certainly clean today as far as their things are concerned.' ⁷The priest then gave him what had been consecrated, for the only bread there was the loaves of permanent offering, which is taken out of Yahweh's pres-ence, to be replaced by warm bread on the day when it is removed.

⁸Now one of Saul's servants happened to be there that day, detained in Yahweh's presence; his name was Doeg the Edomite and he was the strongest of Saul's shepherds.

⁹David then said to Ahimelech, 'Have you no spear or sword here to hand? I did not bring either my sword or my weapons with me, because the king's business was urgent.' ¹⁰The priest replied, 'The sword of Goliath the Philistine whom you killed in the Valley of the Terebinth is here, wrapped in a piece of clothing behind the *ephod;*ᵃ if you care to take it, do so, for that is the only one here.' David said, 'There is nothing like that one; give it to me.'

David with the Philistines

¹¹David journeyed on and that day fled out of Saul's reach, going to Achish king of Gath. ¹²Achish's servants said to him, 'Is not this David, the king of the country? Was it not of him that they sang as they danced:

Saul has killed his thousands,
and David his tens of thousands?'

¹³David pondered on these words and be-came very frightened of Achish king of Gath. ¹⁴When their eyes were on him, he played the madman and, when they held him, he feigned

lunacy. He drummed his feet on the doors of the gate and let his spittle run down his beard.

¹⁵Achish said to his servants, 'You can see that this man is mad. Why bring him to me? ¹⁶Have I not enough madmen, without your bringing me this one to weary me with his an-tics? Is he to join my household?'

David the outlaw

22 David left there and took refuge in the Cave of Adullam; his brothers and his father's whole family heard this and joined him there. ²All those in distress, all those in debt, all those who had a grievance, gathered round him and he became their leader. There were about four hundred men with him.

³From there David went to Mizpah in Moab and said to the king of Moab, 'Allow my father and mother to stay with you until I know what God intends to do for me.' ⁴He left them with the king of Moab and there they stayed all the time that David was in the stronghold.

⁵The prophet Gad, however, said to David, 'Do not stay in the stronghold; leave and make your way into the territory of Judah.' David then left and went to the forest of Hereth.

Massacre of the priests of Nob

⁶When Saul heard that David and the men with him had been discovered, Saul was at Gibeah, seated under the tamarisk on the high place, spear in hand, with all his staff standing round him. ⁷'Listen, Benjaminites!' said Saul to them, 'Is the son of Jesse going to give you all fields and vineyards and make all of you commanders of thousands and commanders of hundreds ⁸that you all conspire against me? No one warned me when my son made a pact with the son of Jesse; none of you felt sorry for me or warned me when my son incited my servant to become my enemy, as he is now.'

⁹Then, up spoke Doeg the Edomite, who was in command of Saul's staff, 'I saw the son

21a Here either the container of the sacred lots or some ob-ject used in worship.

of Jesse coming to Nob, to Ahimelech son of Ahitub. ¹⁰That man consulted Yahweh on his behalf, gave him provisions and also the sword of Goliath the Philistine.' ¹¹The king then sent for the priest Ahimelech son of Ahitub and his whole family, the priests of Nob; they all came to the king.

¹²Saul said, 'Now listen, son of Ahitub!' He replied, 'Here I am, my lord.' ¹³'Why have you conspired against me,' said Saul, 'you and the son of Jesse, giving him bread and a sword and consulting God on his behalf, for him to rebel against me as is now the case?' ¹⁴Ahimelech replied to the king, 'Of all those in your service, who is more loyal than David son-in-law to the king, captain of your bodyguard, honoured in your household? ¹⁵Was today the first time I ever consulted God on his behalf? Indeed it was not! The king has no grounds for bringing any charge against his servant or against his whole family, for your servant knew nothing whatever about all this.' ¹⁶The king retorted, 'You must die, Ahimelech, you and your whole family.'

¹⁷The king said to the scouts who were standing round him, 'Forward! and put the priests of Yahweh to death, for they too are on David's side, they knew that he was escaping, yet did not warn me of it.' The king's professional soldiers, however, would not lift a hand to strike the priests of Yahweh. ¹⁸The king then said to Doeg, 'Forward, you! Fall on the priests!' Doeg the Edomite stepped forward and fell on the priests, himself that day killing eighty-five men who wore the linen *ephod*. ¹⁹Nob, the town of the priests, Saul put to the sword: men and women, children and infants, cattle, donkeys and sheep.

²⁰One son of Ahimelech son of Ahitub alone escaped. His name was Abiathar, and he fled away to join David. ²¹When Abiathar told David that Saul had slaughtered the priests of Yahweh, ²²David said to Abiathar, 'I knew, that day when Doeg the Edomite was there, that he would be sure to inform Saul. I am responsible for the death of all your kinsmen. ²³Stay with me, do not be afraid, for he

who seeks your life seeks mine; you will be safe with me.'

David at Keilah

23 News was then brought to David, 'The Philistines are besieging Keilah and plundering the threshing-floors'. ²David consulted Yahweh, 'Shall I go and fight these Philistines?' Yahweh replied to David, 'Go and fight the Philistines and save Keilah.' ³But David's men said to him, 'We are already afraid here in Judah; how much more, then, if we go to Keilah to fight the Philistine troops!' ⁴So David consulted Yahweh again and Yahweh replied, 'Be on your way; go down to Keilah, since I shall give the Philistines into your power.' ⁵So David and his men went to Keilah and fought the Philistines and carried off their cattle and inflicted a great defeat on them. Thus David saved the inhabitants of Keilah. ⁶When Abiathar son of Ahimelech took refuge with David, he went down to Keilah with the *ephod* in his hand.

⁷When word was brought to Saul that David had gone to Keilah he said, 'God has delivered him into my power: he has trapped himself by going into a town with gates and bars.' ⁸Saul called all the people to arms, to go down to Keilah and besiege David and his men. ⁹David, however, was aware that Saul was plotting evil against him, and said to Abiathar the priest, 'Bring the *ephod*.' ¹⁰David said, 'Yahweh, God of Israel, your servant has heard that Saul is preparing to come to Keilah and destroy the town because of me. ¹¹Will Saul come down as your servant has heard? Yahweh, God of Israel, I beg you, let your servant know.' Yahweh replied, 'He will come down.' ¹²David then went on to ask, 'Will the notables of Keilah hand me and my men over to Saul?' Yahweh replied, 'They will hand you over.' ¹³At this, David made off with his men, about six hundred in number; they left Keilah and went where they could. When Saul was told that David had escaped from Keilah, he abandoned the expedition.

¹⁴David stayed in the desert, in the strong-

holds; he stayed in the mountains, in the desert of Ziph; Saul kept looking for him day after day, but God did not deliver him into his power.

David at Horesh; visit from Jonathan

[15] David was aware that Saul had mounted an expedition to take his life. David was then at Horesh in the desert of Ziph. [16] Jonathan son of Saul set off and went to David at Horesh and encouraged him in the name of God. [17] 'Do not be afraid,' he said, 'for my father Saul's hand will not reach you. You are to reign over Israel, and I shall be second to you. Saul my father is himself aware of this.' [18] And the two made a pact before Yahweh. David stayed at Horesh and Jonathan went home.

David has a narrow escape from Saul

[19] Some men from Ziph then went up to Saul at Gibeah and said, 'Look, David is hiding among us in the strongholds at Horesh, on the Hill of Hachilah to the south of the wastelands. [20] Now whenever you wish to go down, my lord king, do so; we shall make it our task to hand him over to the king.' [21] Saul replied, 'May you be blessed by Yahweh for sympathising with me. [22] Go and make doubly sure, find out exactly what place he frequents, for I have been told that he is very cunning. [23] Take careful note of all the hiding places where he lurks, and come back to me when you are certain. I shall then come with you and, if he is in the country, I shall track him down through every clan in Judah!'

[24] Setting off they went to Ziph ahead of Saul. Meanwhile, David and his men were in the desert of Maon, in the plain to the south of the wastelands. [25] When Saul and his men set out in search, David was told and went down to the gorge running through the desert of Maon. [26] Saul and his men proceeded along one side of the mountain, David and his men along the other. David was hurrying to escape from Saul, while Saul and his men were trying to cross over to David and his men's side, to capture them, [27] when a messenger came to Saul and said, 'Come at once, the Philistines have invaded the country.' [28] So Saul broke off his pursuit of David and went to oppose the Philistines. That is why the place is called the Gorge of Separations.

David spares Saul

24 From there David went up and installed himself in the strongholds of En-Gedi. [2] Once Saul was back from pursuing the Philistines, he was told, 'David is now in the desert of En-Gedi.' [3] Saul thereupon took three thousand men selected from all Israel and went in search of David and his men east of the Rocks of the Mountain Goats. [4] He came to the sheepfolds along the route, where there was a cave, and went in to cover his feet. Now David and his men were sitting in the recesses of the cave; [5] David's men said to him, 'Today is the day of which Yahweh said to you, "I shall deliver your enemy into your power; do what you like with him." ' David got up and, unobserved, cut off the border of Saul's cloak. [6] Afterwards David reproached himself for having cut off the border of Saul's cloak. [7] He said to his men, 'Yahweh preserve me from doing such a thing to my lord as to raise my hand against him, since he is Yahweh's anointed.' [8] By these words David restrained his men and would not let them attack Saul.

[9] Saul then left the cave and went on his way. After this, David too left the cave and called after Saul, 'My lord king!' Saul looked behind him and David, bowing to the ground, prostrated himself. [10] David then said to Saul, 'Why do you listen to people who say, "David intends your ruin"? [11] This very day you have seen for yourself how Yahweh put you in my power in the cave and how, refusing to kill you, I spared you saying, "I will not raise my hand against my lord, since he is Yahweh's anointed." [12] Look, father, look at the border of your cloak in my hand. Since, although I cut the border off your cloak, I did not kill you, surely you realise that I intend neither mischief nor crime. I have not wronged you, and yet you hunt me down to take my life. [13] May

Yahweh be judge between me and you, and may Yahweh avenge me on you; but I shall never lay a hand on you! ¹⁴(As the old proverb says: Wickedness comes out of wicked people, but I shall never lay a hand on you!) ¹⁵On whose trail is the king of Israel campaigning? Whom are you pursuing? On the trail of a dead dog, of a flea! ¹⁶May Yahweh be the judge and decide between me and you; may he examine and defend my cause and give judgement for me by rescuing me from your clutches!'

¹⁷When David had finished saying this to Saul, Saul said, 'Is that your voice, my son David?' And Saul began to weep aloud. ¹⁸'You are upright and I am not,' he said to David, 'since you have behaved well to me, whereas I have behaved badly to you. ¹⁹And today you have shown how well you have behaved to me, since Yahweh had put me in your power but you did not kill me. ²⁰When a man comes on his enemy, does he let him go unmolested? May Yahweh reward you for the good you have done me today! ²¹Now I know that you will indeed reign and that the sovereignty in Israel will pass into your hands. ²²Now swear to me by Yahweh that you will not suppress my descendants once I am gone, or blot my name out of my family.' ²³This David swore to Saul, and Saul went home while David and his men went back to the stronghold.

Death of Samuel; story of Nabal and Abigail

25 Samuel died and all Israel assembled to mourn for him. They buried him at his home in Ramah.

David then set off and went down to the desert of Maon.

²Now, there was a man in Maon whose business was at Carmel; the man was very rich: he owned three thousand sheep and a thousand goats. He was then at Carmel, having his sheep shorn. ³The man's name was Nabal and his wife's Abigail. She was a woman of intelligence and beauty, but the man was miserly and churlish. He was a Calebite.

⁴When David heard in the desert that Nabal was at his sheepshearing, ⁵he sent ten men off, having said to them, 'Go up to Carmel, visit Nabal and greet him from me. ⁶And this is what you are to say to my brother, "Peace to you, peace to your family, peace to all that is yours! ⁷I hear that you now have the shearers; your shepherds were with us recently: we did not molest them, nor did they lose anything all the while they were at Carmel. ⁸Ask your young men and they will tell you. I hope that you will give the men a welcome, coming as we do on a festival. Whatever you have to hand please give to your servants and to your son David." '

⁹David's men went and said all this to Nabal for David, and waited. ¹⁰Nabal retorted to the men in David's service, 'Who is David? Who is the son of Jesse? ¹¹There are many servants nowadays who run away from their masters. Am I to take my bread and my wine and the meat that I have slaughtered for my shearers and give it to men who come from I know not where?' ¹²David's men turned on their heels and went back, and on their arrival told him exactly what had been said. ¹³David then said to his men, 'Every man buckle on his sword!' And they buckled on their swords, and David buckled on his too; about four hundred followed David while two hundred stayed with the baggage.

¹⁴Now one of the young men told Abigail, Nabal's wife. He said, 'David sent messengers from the desert to greet our master, but he flared up at them. ¹⁵Now, these men were very good to us; they did not molest us and we lost nothing all the time we had anything to do with them while we were out in the country. ¹⁶Night and day, they were like a rampart to us, all the time we were with them, minding the sheep. ¹⁷So now make up your mind what you should do, for the ruin of our master and his whole family is a certainty, and he is such a brute that no one can say a word to him.'

¹⁸Abigail hastily took two hundred loaves, two skins of wine, five sheep ready prepared,

five measures of roasted grain, a hundred bunches of raisins and two hundred cakes of figs and loaded them on donkeys. ¹⁹ She said to her servants, 'Go on ahead, I shall follow you'—but she did not tell her husband Nabal.

²⁰ As she was riding her donkey down behind a fold in the mountain, David and his men happened to be coming down in her direction; and she met them. ²¹ Now, David had decided, 'It was a waste of time my guarding all this man's property in the desert so that he lost nothing at all! He has repaid me bad for good. ²² May God bring unnameable ills on David and worse ones, too, if by morning I leave a single manjack alive of all who belong to him!' ²³ As soon as Abigail saw David, she quickly dismounted from the donkey and, falling on her face in front of David, prostrated herself on the ground. ²⁴ She fell at his feet and said, 'Let me take the blame, my lord. Let your servant speak in your ear; listen to what your servant has to say! ²⁵ My lord, please pay no attention to this brute Nabal ᵃ for his nature is like his name; "Brute" is his name and brutal he is. But I, your servant, did not see the men whom my lord sent. ²⁶ And now, my lord, as Yahweh lives and as your soul lives, by Yahweh who kept you from the crime of bloodshed and from taking vengeance with your own hand, may your enemies and all those ill-disposed towards you become like Nabal. ²⁷ As for the present which your servant has brought my lord, I should like this to be given to the men in your service. ²⁸ Please forgive your servant for any offence I have given you, for Yahweh will certainly assure you of a lasting dynasty, since you are fighting Yahweh's battles and no fault has been found in you throughout your life. ²⁹ Should anyone set out to hunt you down and try to kill you, your life will be kept close in the wallet of life with Yahweh your God, while your enemies' lives he will fling out of the pouch of the sling. ³⁰ Once Yahweh has done for you all the good things which he has said he will do for you, and made you ruler of Israel, ³¹ you must have no anxiety, my lord, no remorse, over having

wantonly shed blood, over having taken a revenge. When Yahweh has done well by you, then remember your servant.'

³² David said to Abigail, 'Blessed be Yahweh, God of Israel, who sent you to meet me today! ³³ Blessed be your wisdom and blessed you yourself for today having restrained me from the crime of bloodshed and from exacting revenge! ³⁴ But as Yahweh, God of Israel, lives, who prevented me from harming you, had you not hurried out to meet me, I swear Nabal would not have had a single manjack left alive by morning!' ³⁵ David then accepted what she had brought him and said, 'Go home in peace; yes, I have listened to you and have pardoned you.'

³⁶ Abigail returned to Nabal. He was holding a feast, a princely feast, in his house; Nabal was in high spirits, and as he was very drunk she told him nothing at all till it was daylight. ³⁷ In the morning, when Nabal's wine had left him and his wife told him everything that had happened, his heart died within him and he became like a stone. ³⁸ About ten days later Yahweh struck Nabal, and he died.

³⁹ When David heard that Nabal was dead, he said, 'Blessed be Yahweh for having defended my cause over the insult which I received from Nabal, and for having restrained his servant from doing wrong! Yahweh has made Nabal's wickedness rebound on his own head!'

⁴⁰ David then sent Abigail an offer of marriage. When the men in David's service came to Abigail at Carmel, they said, 'David has sent us to take you to him, to be his wife.' ⁴¹ She stood up, then prostrated herself on the ground. 'Consider your servant a slave', she said, 'to wash the feet of my lord's servants.' ⁴² Quickly Abigail stood up again and mounted a donkey; followed by five of her servant-girls, she followed David's messengers and became his wife.

⁴³ David had also married Ahinoam of Jezreel and he kept them both as wives. ⁴⁴ Saul

25a Nabal = fool.

had given his daughter Michal, David's wife, to Palti son of Laish, from Gallim.

David spares Saul

26 Some men from Ziph went to Saul at Gibeah and said, 'Look, David is hiding on the Hill of Hachilah on the edge of the wastelands!' ²So Saul set off and went down to the desert of Ziph, accompanied by three thousand picked men of Israel, to search for David in the desert of Ziph. ³Saul pitched camp on the Hill of Hachilah, which is on the edge of the wastelands near the road. David was then living in the desert and saw that Saul had come after him into the desert. ⁴Accordingly, David sent out spies and learned that Saul had indeed arrived. ⁵Setting off, David went to the place where Saul had pitched camp. He saw the place where Saul and Abner son of Ner, commander of his army, had bedded down. Saul had bedded down inside the camp with the troops bivouacking round him.

⁶Speaking to Ahimelech the Hittite and Abishai son of Zeruiah and brother of Joab, David said, 'Who will come down with me to the camp, to Saul?' Abishai answered, 'I will go down with you.' ⁷So in the dark David and Abishai made their way towards the force, where they found Saul lying asleep inside the camp, his spear stuck in the ground beside his head, with Abner and the troops lying round him.

⁸Abishai then said to David, 'Today God has put your enemy in your power; so now let me pin him to the ground with his own spear. Just one stroke! I shall not need to strike him twice.' ⁹David said to Abishai, 'Do not kill him, for who could raise his hand against Yahweh's anointed and go unpunished? ¹⁰As Yahweh lives,' David said, 'Yahweh himself will strike him down: either the day will come for him to die, or he will go into battle and perish then. ¹¹Yahweh forbid that I should raise my hand against Yahweh's anointed! But now let us take the spear beside his head and the pitcher of water, and let us go away.'

¹²David took the spear and the pitcher of water from beside Saul's head, and they made off. No one saw, no one knew, no one woke up; they were all asleep, because a torpor from Yahweh had fallen on them.

¹³David crossed to the other side and halted on the top of the mountain a long way off; there was a wide space between them. ¹⁴David then called out to the troops and to Abner son of Ner, 'Abner, why don't you answer?' Abner replied, 'Who is that calling?' ¹⁵David said to Abner, 'Are you not a man? Who is your equal in Israel? Why, then, did you not guard the king your lord? One of the people came to kill the king your lord. ¹⁶What you did was not well done. As Yahweh lives, you all deserve to die since you did not guard your lord, Yahweh's anointed. Look where the king's spear is now, and the pitcher of water which was beside his head!'

¹⁷Recognising David's voice, Saul said, 'Is that your voice, my son David?' David replied, 'It is my voice, my lord king. ¹⁸Why is my lord pursuing his servant?' he said. 'What have I done? What crime have I committed? ¹⁹May my lord king now listen to his servant's words: if Yahweh has incited you against me, may he be appeased with an offering; but if human beings have done it, may they be accursed before Yahweh, since they have as effectively banished me today from sharing in Yahweh's heritage as if they had said, "Go and serve other gods!" ²⁰So I pray now that my blood shall not be shed on soil remote from Yahweh's presence, when the king of Israel has mounted an expedition to take my life, as one might hunt a partridge in the mountains!'

²¹Saul replied, 'I have done wrong! Come back, my son David; I shall never harm you again, since today you have shown respect for my life. Yes, I have behaved like a fool, I have been profoundly in the wrong.' ²²In reply, David said, 'Here is the king's spear. Let one of the men come across and get it. ²³May Yahweh reward each as each has been upright and loyal. Today Yahweh put you in my power but I would not raise my hand against Yahweh's anointed. ²⁴As today I set great value by your

27 READ 1 SAMUEL 26:2–25.

Come back, my son David; I shall never harm you again, since today you have shown respect for my life.—1 SAMUEL 26:21

LOVING THOSE WHO HATE YOU

The distinguishing mark of those who strive after perfection is that they love the sinner, detesting only his sins; that when they avenge wrongdoing they do so, not with the cruelty of hatred, but with justice administered with moderation. . . . The just men of old did not mete out punishment for wrongdoing, except when and to the extent that they were divinely authorized to do so. So let no one think that he can put to death or condemn whomever he wishes or punish the guilty in whatever way he may decide. . . .

King Saul had conceived a bitter enmity against David and, extremely unmindful of all that David had done for him, persecuted him with an intense hatred. When however David had Saul securely in his power and could have done to him whatever he wished, he chose to spare his life rather than kill him. He was not ordered by God to kill him, but neither was he forbidden to do so.

On the contrary, God had revealed to David that he could with impunity do to Saul whatever he wished. This freedom David used to show mercy to Saul. Tell me, I ask you, who was it that he feared, when he refused to slay Saul? We cannot say that it was Saul himself whom he feared, since he already held Saul in his power. Neither can we say that it was God, since it was God who had delivered Saul into his hands.

If, therefore, it was neither the difficulty of the act nor fear that was the reason for his unwillingness to kill Saul, we can only conclude that the reason was his love for his enemy. Behold, then, how David the warrior-king obeyed the precept that we have received from Christ, that we love our enemies" (see Mt 5:44).   ST. AUGUSTINE, 354–430

YOU WILL FIND THE NEXT READING AT 2 SAMUEL 7.

life, so may Yahweh set great value by my life and deliver me from every tribulation!'

²⁵ Saul then said, 'May you be blessed, my son David! In what you undertake, you will certainly succeed.' David then went on his way and Saul returned home.

David takes refuge at Gath

27 'One of these days,' David thought, 'I shall perish at the hand of Saul. The best thing that I can do is to get away into the country of the Philistines; then Saul will give up tracking me through the length and breadth of Israel and I shall be safe from him.' ² So David set off and went over, he and his six hundred men, to Achish son of Maoch, king of Gath. ³ He settled at Gath with Achish, he and his men, each with his family and David with his two wives, Ahinoam of Jezreel and Abigail widow of Nabal of Carmel. ⁴ When news reached Saul that David had fled to Gath, he stopped searching for him.

David as vassal of the Philistines

⁵David said to Achish, 'If I have won your favour, let me be given a place in one of the outlying towns, where I can live. Why should your servant live in the royal city with you?' ⁶That very day Achish gave him Ziklag; and this is why Ziklag has been the property of the kings of Judah to the present day. ⁷The time that David stayed in Philistine territory amounted to a year and four months.

⁸David and his men went out on raids against the Geshurites, Girzites and Amalekites, for these are the tribes inhabiting the region which, from Telam, goes in the direction of Shur, as far as Egypt. ⁹David laid the countryside waste and left neither man nor woman alive; he carried off the sheep and cattle, the donkeys, camels and clothing, and then came back again to Achish. ¹⁰Achish would ask, 'Where did you go raiding today?' David would reply, 'Against the Negeb of Judah,' or 'the Negeb of Jerahmeel,' or 'the Negeb of the Kenites.' ¹¹David spared neither man nor woman to bring back alive to Gath, 'in case', as he thought, 'they inform on us and say, "David did such and such." ' This was the way David conducted his raids all the time he stayed in Philistine territory. ¹²Achish trusted David. 'He has made himself detested by his own people Israel,' he thought, 'and so will be my servant for ever.'

The Philistines go to war with Israel

28 It then happened that the Philistines mustered their forces for war, to fight Israel, and Achish said to David, 'It is understood that you and your men go into battle with me.' ²David said to Achish, 'In that case, you will soon see what your servant can do.' Achish replied to David, 'Right, I shall appoint you as my permanent bodyguard.'

Saul and the witch of En-Dor

³Now Samuel was dead, and all Israel had mourned him and buried him at Ramah, his own town. Saul had expelled the necromancers and wizards from the country.

⁴Meanwhile the Philistines had mustered and had come and pitched camp at Shunem. Saul mustered all Israel and they encamped at Gilboa. ⁵When Saul saw the Philistine camp, he was afraid and his heart trembled violently. ⁶Saul consulted Yahweh, but Yahweh gave him no answer, either by dream, divination or prophet. ⁷Saul then said to his servants, 'Find a necromancer for me, so that I can go and consult her.' His servants replied, 'There is a necromancer at En-Dor.'

⁸And so Saul, disguising himself and changing his clothes, set out accompanied by two men; their visit to the woman took place at night. 'Disclose the future to me', he said, 'by means of a ghost. Conjure up the one I shall name to you.' ⁹The woman replied, 'Look, you know what Saul has done, how he has outlawed necromancers and wizards from the country; why are you setting a trap for my life, then, to have me killed?' ¹⁰But Saul swore to her by Yahweh, 'As Yahweh lives,' he said, 'no blame shall attach to you for this business.' ¹¹The woman asked, 'Whom shall I conjure up for you?' He replied, 'Conjure up Samuel.'

¹²The woman then saw Samuel and, giving a great cry, she said to Saul, 'Why have you deceived me? You are Saul!' ¹³The king said, 'Do not be afraid! What do you see?' The woman replied to Saul, 'I see a ghost rising from the earth.' ¹⁴'What is he like?' he asked. She replied, 'It is an old man coming up; he is wrapped in a cloak.' Saul then knew that it was Samuel and, bowing to the ground, prostrated himself.

¹⁵Samuel said to Saul, 'Why have you disturbed my rest by conjuring me up?' Saul replied, 'I am in great distress; the Philistines are waging war on me, and God has abandoned me and no longer answers me either by prophet or by dream; and so I have summoned you to tell me what I ought to do.' ¹⁶Samuel said, 'Why consult me, when Yahweh has abandoned you and has become your enemy? ¹⁷Yahweh has treated you as he foretold

through me; he has snatched the sovereignty from your hand and given it to your neighbour, David, 18 because you disobeyed Yahweh's voice and did not execute his fierce anger against Amalek. That is why Yahweh is treating you like this today. 19 What is more, Yahweh will deliver Israel and you too, into the power of the Philistines. Tomorrow you and your sons will be with me; and Yahweh will hand over the army of Israel into the power of the Philistines.'

20 Immediately Saul fell full length on the ground. He was terrified by what Samuel had said and was also weak from having eaten nothing all that day and night. 21 The woman went to Saul and, seeing his terror, said, 'Look, your servant has obeyed your order; I have taken my life in my hands and obeyed the command which you gave me. 22 Now please, you in your turn listen to what your servant has to say. Let me offer you a piece of bread. Eat something and get some strength for your journey.' 23 But he refused. 'I will not eat,' he said. His servants however pressed him, and so did the woman. Allowing himself to be persuaded by them, he got up from the ground and sat on the bed. 24 The woman owned a fattened calf which she quickly slaughtered, and she took some flour and kneaded it and with it baked some unleavened cakes 25 which she served to Saul and his servants; they ate, and then set off and left the same night.

David is sent away by the Philistine leaders

29 The Philistines mustered all their forces at Aphek while the Israelites pitched camp near the spring in Jezreel. 2 The Philistine commanders marched past with their hundreds and their thousands, and David and his men brought up the rear with Achish. 3 The Philistine chiefs asked, 'What are these Hebrews doing?' Achish replied to them, 'Why, this is David the servant of Saul, king of Israel, who has been with me for the last year or two. I have had no fault to find with him from the day he gave himself up to me until the present time.' 4 But the Philistine chiefs were angry with him. 'Send the man back,' they said, 'make him go back to the place which you assigned to him. He cannot go into battle with us, in case he turns on us once battle is joined. Would there be a better way for the man to regain his master's favour than with the heads of these men here? 5 Is not this the David of whom they sang as they danced:

Saul has killed his thousands,
and David his tens of thousands'?

6 So Achish called David and said, 'As Yahweh lives, you are loyal, and I am quite content with all your doings in our campaigning together, since I have found no fault with you from the day you came to me until the present time. But you are not acceptable to the chiefs. 7 So go home, in peace, rather than antagonise them.'

8 'But what have I done,' David asked Achish, 'what fault have you had to find with your servant from the day I entered your service to the present time, for me not to be allowed to go and fight the enemies of my lord the king?' 9 In reply, Achish said to David, 'In my opinion, it is true, you are as good as an angel of God; but the Philistine chiefs have said, "He must not go into battle with us." 10 So get up early tomorrow morning, with your master's servants who came with you, and go to the place which I assigned to you. Do not harbour resentment, since personally I have no fault to find with you. Get up early tomorrow morning and, as soon as it is light, be off.'

11 So David and his men got up early to leave at dawn and go back to Philistine territory. And the Philistines marched on Jezreel.

Reprisals against the Amalekites

30 Now by the time David and his men reached Ziklag three days later, the Amalekites had raided the Negeb and Ziklag; they had sacked Ziklag and burnt it down. 2 They had taken the women prisoner, and

everyone who was there, both small and great. They had not killed anyone, but had carried them off and gone away. ³ When David and his men arrived, they found the town burnt down and their wives and sons and daughters taken captive. ⁴ Then David and the people with him wept aloud till they were too weak to weep any more. ⁵ David's two wives had been captured: Ahinoam of Jezreel and Abigail widow of Nabal of Carmel.

⁶ David was in great trouble, since the people were talking of stoning him; the people all felt very bitter, each man for his own sons and daughters. But David took courage from Yahweh his God. ⁷ To the priest Abiathar son of Ahimelech, David said, 'Bring me the *ephod*.' Abiathar brought the *ephod* to David. ⁸ David then consulted Yahweh, 'Shall I go in pursuit of these raiders? Will I overtake them?' The answer was, 'Go in pursuit; you will certainly overtake them and rescue the captives.' ⁹ David accordingly set off with the six hundred men who were with him and reached the torrent of Besor. ¹⁰ David then continued the pursuit with four hundred men, two hundred staying behind who were too exhausted to cross the torrent of Besor.

¹¹ Out in the country they found an Egyptian and brought him to David. They gave him some bread to eat and some water to drink; ¹² they also gave him a piece of fig cake and two bunches of raisins; he ate these and his spirits revived—he had had nothing to eat or drink for three days and three nights. ¹³ David then said to him, 'Whose man are you and where do you come from?' He replied, 'I am a young Egyptian, the slave of an Amalekite; my master abandoned me because I fell sick three days ago. ¹⁴ We raided the Negeb of the Cherethites, and the Negeb of Judah, and the Negeb of Caleb too, and we burnt Ziklag down.' ¹⁵ David said, 'Will you guide me to these raiders?' He replied, 'Swear to me by God not to kill me or hand me over to my master, and I will guide you to these raiders.'

¹⁶ He guided him to them, and there they were, scattered over the whole countryside, eating, drinking and celebrating, on account of the enormous booty which they had brought back from the territory of the Philistines and the territory of Judah. ¹⁷ David slaughtered them from dawn until the evening of the following day. No one escaped, except four hundred young men who mounted camels and fled. ¹⁸ He rescued everything that the Amalekites had taken—David also rescued his two wives. ¹⁹ Nothing of theirs was lost, whether small or great, from the booty or sons and daughters—everything that had been taken from them; David recovered everything. ²⁰ They captured the flocks and herds as well and drove them in front of him. 'This is David's booty,' they shouted.

²¹ When David reached the two hundred men who had been too exhausted to follow him and whom he had left at the torrent of Besor, they came out to meet David and the party accompanying him; David approached with his party and greeted them. ²² But all the rogues and scoundrels among the men who had gone with David began saying, 'Since they did not go with us, we shall not give them any of the booty which we have rescued, except that each of them can have his wife and children. Let them take them away and be off.' ²³ But David said, 'Do not behave like this, brothers, with what Yahweh has given us; he has protected us and has handed over to us the raiders who attacked us. ²⁴ Who would agree with you on this? No:

As the share of the man who goes into
    battle,
so is the share of the man who stays with
    the baggage.

They will share alike.' ²⁵ And from that day on, he made that a rule and custom for Israel, which obtains to the present day.

²⁶ When David reached Ziklag, he sent parts of the booty to the elders of Judah, town by town, with this message, 'Here is a present for you, taken from the booty of Yahweh's enemies':

27 to those in Bethel,
  to those in Ramoth of the Negeb,
28 to those in Jattir,
  to those in Aroer,
  to those in Siphmoth,
  to those in Eshtemoa,
29 to those in Carmel,
  to those in the towns of Jerahmeel,
  to those in the towns of the Kenites,
30 to those in Hormah,
  to those in Borashan,
  to those in Athach,
31 to those in Hebron

and to all the places which David and his men had frequented.

Battle of Mount Gilboa and death of Saul

31 The Philistines gave battle to Israel, and the Israelites, fleeing from the Philistines, fell and were slaughtered on Mount Gilboa. 2 The Philistines bore down on Saul and his sons, and they killed Jonathan, Abinadab and Malchishua, Saul's sons. 3 The fighting grew fiercer round Saul; the archers came upon him, and he was severely wounded 4 by the archers. Saul then said to his armour-bearer, 'Draw your sword and run me through with it; I do not want these uncircumcised men to come and make fun of me.'

But his armour-bearer was very much afraid and would not do it. So Saul took his own sword and fell on it. 5 His armour-bearer, seeing that Saul was dead, fell on his sword too and died with him. 6 Thus died Saul, his three sons and his armour-bearer, together on the same day. 7 When the Israelites who were on the other side of the Jordan saw that the Israelites had been routed and that Saul and his sons were dead, they abandoned their towns and fled. The Philistines then came and occupied them.

8 When the Philistines came on the following day to strip the dead, they found Saul and his three sons lying on Mount Gilboa. 9 They cut off his head and, stripping him of his armour, had these carried round the territory of the Philistines to proclaim the good news to their idols and their people. 10 They put his armour in the temple of Astarte; and his body they fastened to the walls of Beth-Shean.

11 When the inhabitants of Jabesh in Gilead heard what the Philistines had done to Saul, 12 the warriors all set out and, having marched all night, took the bodies of Saul and his sons off the walls of Beth-Shean; they brought them to Jabesh and burned them there. 13 They then took their bones and buried them under the tamarisk of Jabesh, and fasted for seven days.

The Second Book of

SAMUEL

David learns of Saul's death

1 Saul was dead and David, returning after his victory over the Amalekites, had been at Ziklag for two days. ²On the third day, a man arrived from Saul's camp with his clothes torn and earth on his head. When he came to David, he fell to the ground and prostrated himself. ³David asked him, 'Where have you come from?' 'I have escaped from the Israelite camp,' he said. ⁴David said, 'What has happened? Tell me.' He replied, 'The people fled from the battle, and many of them have fallen and are dead. Saul and his son Jonathan are dead too.'

⁵Then David asked the young man who brought the news, 'How do you know that Saul and his son Jonathan are dead?' ⁶The young man replied, 'I happened to be on Mount Gilboa, and there was Saul, leaning on his spear, with the chariots and the cavalry bearing down on him. ⁷Glancing behind him and seeing me, he shouted to me. I replied, "Here I am!" ⁸He said, "Who are you?" I replied, "I am an Amalekite." ⁹He then said, "Come here and kill me. My head is swimming, although I still have all my strength." ¹⁰So I went over to him and killed him, because I knew that once he fell he could not survive. I then took the crown which he had on his head and the bracelet on his arm, and have brought them here to my lord.'

¹¹David then took hold of his clothes and tore them, and all the men with him did the same. ¹²They mourned and wept and fasted until the evening for Saul and his son Jonathan, for the people of Yahweh and for the House of Israel, because they had fallen by the sword.

¹³David said to the young man who had brought the news, 'Where are you from?' He replied, 'I am the son of a resident foreigner, an Amalekite.' ¹⁴David said, 'How was it that you were not afraid to lift your hand to destroy Yahweh's anointed?' ¹⁵Then David called one of the young men. 'Come here,' he said, 'strike him down.' The man struck him and he died. ¹⁶David said, 'Your blood be on your own head. You convicted yourself out of your own mouth by saying, "I killed Yahweh's anointed."'

David's elegy over Saul and Jonathan

¹⁷David sang the following lament over Saul and his son Jonathan ¹⁸(it is for teaching archery to the children of Judah; it is written in the Book of the Just):ᵃ

¹⁹ Does the splendour of Israel
   lie dead on your heights?
   How did the heroes fall?

²⁰ Do not speak of it in Gath,
   nor broadcast it in the streets of
      Ashkelon,
   for fear the daughters of the Philistines
      rejoice,
   for fear the daughters of the
      uncircumcised gloat.

²¹ You mountains of Gilboa,
   no dew, no rain fall on you,
   O treacherous fields
   where the heroes' shield lies
      dishonoured!

1a Poetry from this book is quoted elsewhere too in the Bible.

Not greased with oil, the shield of Saul,
22 but with the blood of wounded men, the
fat of warriors!
The bow of Jonathan never turned back,
the sword of Saul never came home
unsated!

23 Saul and Jonathan, beloved and
handsome,
were divided neither in life, nor in
death.
Swifter than eagles were they,
stronger than lions.

24 O daughters of Israel, weep for Saul
who gave you scarlet and fine linen to
wear,
who pinned golden jewellery
on your dresses!

25 How did the heroes fall
in the thick of the battle?

Jonathan, by your dying I too am
stricken,
26 I am desolate for you, Jonathan my
brother.
Very dear you were to me,
your love more wonderful to me
than the love of a woman.

27 How did the heroes fall
and the weapons of war succumb!

David consecrated king at Hebron

2 After this David consulted Yahweh, asking, 'Shall I go up to one of the towns of
Judah?' Yahweh replied, 'Go up!' 'Which one
shall I go to?' David asked. 'To Hebron,' was
the reply. 2 So David went up, with his two
wives Ahinoam of Jezreel and Abigail widow
of Nabal of Carmel. 3 In addition David
brought up the men who were with him, each
with his family, and they settled in the towns
of Hebron. 4 The men of Judah came, and
there they anointed David as king of the
House of Judah.

David's message to the people of Jabesh

They told David that the people of Jabesh in
Gilead had given Saul burial, 5 so David sent
messengers to the people of Jabesh in Gilead.
'May you be blessed by Yahweh,' he said, 'for
showing this faithful love to Saul your lord,
and for burying him. 6 And now may Yahweh
show faithful love and constancy towards you!
I too shall treat you well because you have
done this. 7 And now take courage and be men
of valour. Saul your lord is dead, but the
House of Judah has anointed me to be their
king.'

Abner imposes Ishbaal as king of Israel

8 Abner son of Ner, Saul's army commander,
had taken Ishbaal son of Saul and brought
him over to Mahanaim. 9 He had made him
king of Gilead, of the Asherites, of Jezreel, of
Ephraim, of Benjamin and indeed of all Israel.
10 Ishbaal son of Saul was forty years old when
he became king of Israel, and he reigned for
two years. Only the House of Judah supported
David. 11 The length of David's reign over
Judah in Hebron was seven years and six
months.

War between Israel and Judah; the battle
of Gibeon

12 Abner son of Ner, with the retainers of Ishbaal son of Saul, marched out from Mahanaim
to Gibeon. 13 Joab son of Zeruiah, with David's
retainers, also took the field, encountering
them at the pool of Gibeon. There they halted,
one party on one side of the pool, and the other
opposite.

14 Abner then said to Joab, 'Let the men
come forward and fight it out between us!'
Joab replied, 'Let them come forward.' 15 So
they came forward and were numbered off,
twelve from Benjamin for Ishbaal son of Saul,
and twelve of David's retainers. 16 Each caught
his opponent by the head and drove his sword
into his side; and thus they all fell together.
Hence the place was called the Field of Sides;
it is at Gibeon.

¹⁷ That day a very fierce battle took place, and Abner and the men of Israel were beaten by David's retainers. ¹⁸ The three sons of Zeruiah were there, Joab, Abishai, and Asahel. Now Asahel could run like a wild gazelle. ¹⁹ Asahel chased Abner, not swerving to the right or left from pursuing him. ²⁰ Abner turned and said, 'Asahel, is that you?' He replied, 'It is.' ²¹ Abner said, 'Turn to your right or your left, catch one of the men and take his spoil!' But Asahel would not break off the pursuit. ²² Again Abner spoke to Asahel, 'Stop following me, unless you want me to strike you to the ground; and then how could I look your brother Joab in the face?' ²³ But he refused to be diverted, so Abner struck him in the belly with the butt of his spear so that the shaft came out through his back; and he fell at his feet and died on the spot. On coming to the place where Asahel had fallen and died, everyone halted.

²⁴ Joab and Abishai took up the pursuit of Abner and at sunset reached the Hill of Ammah, which is to the east of Giah on the road through the desert of Gibeon. ²⁵ The Benjaminites gathered in close formation behind Abner and halted on the top of a hill. ²⁶ Abner called out to Joab, 'Is the sword to go on devouring for ever? Surely you see that this can only end in bitterness? How long will it be before you order those people to stop pursuing their brothers?' ²⁷ Joab replied, 'As Yahweh lives, if you had not spoken, these men would not have given up the pursuit of their brothers until morning.' ²⁸ Joab then sounded the trumpet and all the troops halted; they pursued Israel no further and fought no more.

²⁹ All that night Abner and his men made their way through the Arabah; they crossed the Jordan and, marching throughout the morning, came to Mahanaim. ³⁰ Joab, having stopped pursuing Abner, mustered the whole contingent; David's retainers had lost nineteen men in addition to Asahel, ³¹ but had killed three hundred and sixty of Benjamin, Abner's men. ³² They took up Asahel and buried him in his father's tomb, which is at Bethlehem.

Joab and his men then marched throughout the night, reaching Hebron at daybreak.

3 So the war dragged on between the House of Saul and the House of David, but David grew steadily stronger and the House of Saul steadily weaker.

The sons born to David at Hebron

² The sons born to David at Hebron were: his first-born Amnon, by Ahinoam of Jezreel; ³ his second Chileab, by Abigail widow of Nabal of Carmel; the third Absalom son of Maacah, daughter of Talmai king of Geshur; ⁴ the fourth Adonijah son of Haggith; the fifth Shephatiah son of Abital; ⁵ the sixth Ithream, by David's wife, Eglah. These were born to David at Hebron.

The rift between Abner and Ishbaal

⁶ This is what took place during the war between the House of Saul and the House of David. Abner took complete control in the House of Saul. ⁷ Now, there was a concubine of Saul's called Rizpah daughter of Aiah, and Abner took her. Ishbaal said to Abner, 'Why have you slept with my father's concubine?' ⁸ At these words of Ishbaal, Abner flew into a rage. 'Am I a dog's head?' he shouted. 'Here am I, full of faithful love towards the House of Saul your father, his brothers and his friends, not leaving you to the hands of David, and now you find fault with me over a woman! ⁹ May God bring unnameable ills on Abner, and worse ones, too, if I do not bring about what Yahweh has sworn to David: ¹⁰ to take the sovereignty from the House of Saul, and establish David's throne over Israel as well as Judah, from Dan to Beersheba!' ¹¹ Ishbaal dared not say a single word to Abner in reply, as he was afraid of him.

Abner negotiates with David

¹² Abner sent messengers on his own behalf to say to David, '. . . and furthermore, come to an agreement with me and I will give you my support to win all Israel over to you.' ¹³ 'Very

well,' David said, 'I will come to an agreement with you. I impose one condition however; you will not be admitted to my presence unless you bring me Michal, Saul's daughter, when you come to see me.' ¹⁴David then sent messengers to say to Ishbaal son of Saul, 'Give me back my wife Michal, whom I acquired for a hundred foreskins of the Philistines.' ¹⁵So Ishbaal sent for her to be taken from her husband Paltiel son of Laish. ¹⁶Her husband set off with her and followed her, weeping as he went, as far as Bahurim; but Abner said to him, 'Go back!' and he went.

¹⁷Now Abner conferred with the elders of Israel. 'For a long time now,' he said, 'you have wanted David as your king. ¹⁸Now you must take action, since Yahweh has said of David, "By the hand of my servant David I shall deliver my people Israel from the clutches of the Philistines and all their enemies."' ¹⁹Abner also spoke to the men of Benjamin and then went to Hebron to tell David everything that had been agreed by Israel and the House of Benjamin.

²⁰Abner, accompanied by twenty men, came to David at Hebron, and David held a feast for Abner and the men who were with him. ²¹Abner then said to David, 'I must get up and go. I am going to rally all Israel to my lord the king, so that they will make an alliance with you, and you will reign over all that you desire.' So David allowed Abner to go, and he went unmolested.

The murder of Abner

²²David's retainers were just then coming back with Joab from a raid, bringing a great quantity of booty with them. Abner was no longer with David at Hebron, since David had allowed him to go, and he had gone unmolested. ²³When Joab and the whole company with him had arrived, Joab was told, 'Abner son of Ner has been to the king, and the king has allowed Abner to go away unmolested.' ²⁴Joab then went to the king and said, 'What have you done? Abner comes to you and you let him go away and now he has gone—why?

²⁵You know Abner son of Ner! He came to trick you, to discover your every move, to find out what you are doing.'

²⁶Joab left David's presence and sent messengers after Abner and these, unknown to David, brought him back from the storage-well at Sirah. ²⁷When Abner reached Hebron, Joab took him aside in the town-gate, as if to have a quiet word with him, and there struck him a mortal blow in the belly to avenge the blood of his brother Asahel. ²⁸Afterwards, when David heard of this, he said, 'I and my kingdom are for ever innocent before Yahweh of the blood of Abner son of Ner; ²⁹may it fall on the head of Joab and on all his family! May the House of Joab never be free of men afflicted with haemorrhage or a virulent skin-disease, whose strength is in the distaff, who fall by the sword, who lack food.' ³⁰(Joab and his brother Abishai had murdered Abner because he killed their brother Asahel at the battle of Gibeon.) ³¹David then said to Joab and the whole company with him, 'Tear your clothes, put on sackcloth, and mourn over Abner,' and King David walked behind the bier. ³²They buried Abner at Hebron, and the king wept aloud on his grave, and the people all wept too. ³³The king made this lament over Abner:

Should Abner have died as a brute dies?
³⁴ Your hands were not tied, your feet not chained;
you fell as a man falls at the hands of criminals.

And all the people wept for him louder than ever.

³⁵The people then all tried to persuade David to have some food while it was still daylight, but David swore this oath, 'May God bring unnameable ills on me, and worse ills, too, if I taste bread or anything whatever until the sun is down!' ³⁶All the people took note of this and it pleased them; indeed, everything the king did pleased the people. ³⁷That day, all the people and all Israel understood that the

king had had no part in the murder of Abner son of Ner.

³⁸The king said to his retainers, 'Do you not realise that a prince, a great man, has fallen in Israel today? ³⁹I, though anointed king, am weak at present, and these men, the sons of Zeruiah, are too strong for me. May Yahweh repay the criminal as his crime deserves!'

The murder of Ishbaal

4 When Saul's son heard that Abner had died at Hebron, his heart failed him, and all Israel was alarmed. ²Now, Saul's son had two freebooting chieftains; one was called Baanah, the other Rechab. They were the sons of Rimmon of Beeroth, and Benjaminites— for Beeroth is regarded as belonging to Benjamin. ³The people of Beeroth had taken refuge in Gittaim, where they have remained to this day as resident foreigners.

⁴Jonathan son of Saul had a son with crippled feet. He was five years old when the news about Saul and Jonathan came from Jezreel. His nurse picked him up and fled but, as she hurried away, he fell and was lamed. His name was Meribbaal.

⁵The sons of Rimmon of Beeroth, Rechab and Baanah, set out; they came to Ishbaal's house at the hottest part of the day when he was taking his midday rest. ⁶The woman who kept the door had been cleaning wheat and had drowsed off to sleep. ⁷Rechab and his brother Baanah stole past her and entered the house, where he was lying on his bed in his bedroom. They struck him and killed him, then cut off his head and, taking the head with them, travelled all night by way of the Arabah. ⁸They brought Ishbaal's head to David at Hebron. 'Here', they said to the king, 'is the head of Ishbaal son of Saul, your enemy, who meant to take your life. Yahweh has avenged my lord the king today on Saul and on his offspring.'

⁹But David answered Rechab and his brother Baanah, the sons of Rimmon, by saying, 'As Yahweh lives, who has rescued me from every danger, ¹⁰when someone told me,

"Saul is dead!" supposing himself to be bringing me good news, I seized and put him to death at Ziklag, and that was how I rewarded him for his news! ¹¹How much more when bandits have killed an upright man in his house, and on his bed! Am I not to demand an account of his blood from you, and rid the earth of you?' ¹²David then gave an order to the men, who put them to death, cut off their hands and feet, and hung them up beside the pool of Hebron. Ishbaal's head they took and buried in Abner's grave at Hebron.

David is anointed king of Israel

5 All the tribes of Israel then came to David at Hebron and said, 'Look, we are your own flesh and bone. ²In days past when Saul was our king, it was you who led Israel on its campaigns, and to you it was that Yahweh promised, "You are to shepherd my people Israel and be leader of Israel." ' ³So all the elders of Israel came to the king at Hebron, and King David made a pact with them in Yahweh's presence at Hebron, and they anointed David as king of Israel.

⁴David was thirty years old when he became king, and he reigned for forty years. ⁵In Hebron he reigned over Judah for seven years and six months; then he reigned in Jerusalem over all Israel and Judah for thirty-three years.

The capture of Jerusalem

⁶The king and his men then marched on Jerusalem, on the Jebusites living in the territory. These said to David, 'You will not get in here. The blind and the lame will hold you off.' (That is to say: David will never get in here.) ⁷But David captured the citadel of Zion, that is, the City of David. ⁸That day, David said, 'Whoever gets up the tunnel and kills a Jebusite . . .'ᵃ As for the blind and the lame, David hated them with his whole being. (Hence the saying: the blind and the lame may not enter the Temple.) ⁹David went to live in

5a The sentence breaks off. The tunnel, a secret passage from the spring to the interior of the city, still exists.

the citadel and called it the City of David. David then built a wall round it, from the Millo inwards. [10] David grew stronger and stronger, and Yahweh, God of Sabaoth, was with him.

[11] Hiram king of Tyre sent envoys to David, with cedar wood, carpenters and stone-cutters, who built David a palace. [12] David then knew that Yahweh had confirmed him as king of Israel and, for the sake of his people Israel, had extended his sovereignty.

The sons born to David in Jerusalem

[13] After coming from Hebron, David took other concubines and wives in Jerusalem, and sons and daughters were born to him. [14] These are the names of those born to him in Jerusalem: Shammua, Shobab, Nathan, Solomon, [15] Ibhar, Elishua, Nepheg, Japhia, [16] Elishama, Eliada, Eliphelet.

Victory over the Philistines

[17] When the Philistines heard that David had been anointed as king of Israel, they all went up to seek him out. On hearing this, David went down to the stronghold. [18] When the Philistines arrived, they deployed in the Valley of the Rephaim. [19] David consulted Yahweh and asked, 'Shall I attack the Philistines? Will you deliver them into my power?' Yahweh replied to David, 'Attack! I shall certainly deliver the Philistines into your power.' [20] Accordingly, David went to Baal-Perazim and there David defeated them. He said, 'Yahweh has made a breach in my enemies for me, as though they had been breached by a flood.' This is why the place was given the name Baal Perazim. [21] They had left their gods behind them there, and David and his men carried them off.

[22] Again the Philistines invaded and deployed in the Valley of the Rephaim. [23] David consulted Yahweh, who replied, 'Do not attack them from the front; go round to their rear and engage them opposite the balsam trees. [24] When you hear the sound of footsteps in the tops of the balsam trees, advance, for that will be Yahweh going out ahead of you to defeat the Philistine army.' [25] David did as Yahweh had ordered and beat the Philistines from Gibeon to the Pass of Gezer.

The ark in Jerusalem

6 David again mustered all the picked troops of Israel, thirty thousand men. [2] Setting off with the whole force then with him, David went to Baalah of Judah, from there to bring up the ark of God, who bears the title 'Yahweh Sabaoth, enthroned on the winged creatures'. [3] They transported the ark of God on a new cart and brought it out of Abinadab's house which is on the hill. Uzzah and Ahio, the sons of Abinadab, drove the cart, [4] Uzzah walked alongside the ark of God and Ahio went in front. [5] David and the whole House of Israel danced before Yahweh with all their might, singing to the accompaniment of harps, lyres, tambourines, sistrums and cymbals. [6] When they came to Nacon's threshing-floor, Uzzah reached his hand out to the ark of God and steadied it, as the oxen were making it tilt. [7] This roused Yahweh's anger against Uzzah, and for this crime God struck him down on the spot, and there he died beside the ark of God. [8] David resented Yahweh's having broken out against Uzzah, and the place was given the name Perez-Uzzah,[a] which it still has today.

[9] That day David felt afraid of Yahweh. 'How can the ark of Yahweh come to be with me?' he said. [10] So David decided not to take the ark of Yahweh with him into the city of David but diverted it to the house of Obed-Edom of Gath. [11] The ark of Yahweh remained in the house of Obed-Edom of Gath for three months, and Yahweh blessed Obed-Edom and his whole family.

[12] King David was informed that Yahweh had blessed Obed-Edom's family and everything belonging to him on account of the ark of God. David accordingly went and, amid great rejoicing, brought the ark of God up

6a 'Uzzah's Breach', a popular explanation of the name.

from Obed-Edom's house to the City of David. ¹³When the bearers of the ark of Yahweh had gone six paces, he sacrificed an ox and a fat sheep. ¹⁴And David danced whirling round before Yahweh with all his might, wearing a linen loincloth. ¹⁵Thus with war cries and blasts on the horn, David and the entire House of Israel brought up the ark of Yahweh. ¹⁶Now as the ark of Yahweh entered the City of David, Michal daughter of Saul was watching from the window and when she saw King David leaping and whirling round before Yahweh, the sight of him filled her with contempt. ¹⁷They brought the ark of Yahweh in and put it in position, inside the tent which David had erected for it; and David presented burnt offerings and communion sacrifices in Yahweh's presence. ¹⁸And when David had finished presenting burnt offerings, he blessed the people in the name of Yahweh Sabaoth. ¹⁹To all the people, to the whole multitude of Israelites, men and women, he then distributed to each a loaf of bread, a portion of dates and a raisin cake. Then the people all went back to their homes.

²⁰As David was coming back to bless his household, Michal daughter of Saul came out to meet him. 'Much honour the king of Israel has won today,' she said, 'making an exhibition of himself under the eyes of his servant-maids, making an exhibition of himself like a buffoon!' ²¹David replied to Michal, 'I was dancing for Yahweh, not for them. As Yahweh lives, who chose me in preference to your father and his whole family to make me leader of Israel, Yahweh's people, I shall dance before Yahweh and ²²lower myself even further than that. In your eyes I may be base, but by the maids you speak of, by them, I shall be held in honour!' ²³And to the day of her death, Michal, daughter of Saul, had no children.

Nathan's prophecy

7 Once the king had settled into his palace and Yahweh had granted him rest from all the enemies surrounding him, ²the king said to the prophet Nathan, 'Look, I am living in a cedar-wood palace, while the ark of God is under awnings.' ³Nathan said to the king, 'Go and do whatever you have in mind, for Yahweh is with you.'

⁴But that very night, the word of Yahweh came to Nathan:

⁵'Go and tell my servant David, "Yahweh says this: Are you to build me a temple for me to live in? ⁶I have never lived in a house from the day when I brought the Israelites out of Egypt until today, but have kept travelling with a tent for shelter. ⁷In all my travels with all the Israelites, did I say to any of the judges of Israel, whom I had commanded to shepherd my people Israel: Why do you not build me a cedar-wood temple?" ⁸This is what you must say to my servant David, "Yahweh Sabaoth says this: I took you from the pasture, from following the sheep, to be leader of my people Israel; ⁹I have been with you wherever you went; I have got rid of all your enemies for you. I am going to make your fame as great as the fame of the greatest on earth. ¹⁰I am going to provide a place for my people Israel; I shall plant them there, and there they will live and never be disturbed again; nor will they be oppressed by the wicked any more, as they were in former times ¹¹ever since the time when I instituted judges to govern my people Israel; and I shall grant you rest from all your enemies. Yahweh furthermore tells you that he will make you a dynasty. ¹²And when your days are over and you fall asleep with your ancestors, I shall appoint your heir, your own son to succeed you (and I shall make his sovereignty secure. ¹³He will build a temple for my name)ᵃ and I shall make his royal throne secure for ever. ¹⁴I shall be a father to him and he a son to me; if he does wrong, I shall punish him with a rod such as men use, with blows such as mankind gives. ¹⁵But my faithful love will never be withdrawn from him as I withdrew it from Saul, whom I removed from before you. ¹⁶Your dynasty and your sovereignty

7a The words in parentheses were probably added during Solomon's reign.

28 READ 2 SAMUEL 7:18–29.

Who am I, Lord Yahweh, and what is my lineage, for you to have led me as far as this?—2 SAMUEL 7:18

THANKING A MARVELOUS GOD

Like David—and borrowing some of the great patriarch's words—St Patrick expresses profound thanks to God for allowing him to participate in extending divine mercy to so many people:

. . . I am never weary of giving thanks to my God, who has kept me safe "in the day of my trial" (see Ps 95:9). In such a way that today I may in full confidence offer him a sacrifice of my soul as a "living victim" to Christ my Lord (see Rm 12:1). For it is he who "has defended me from all my afflictions" (see Ps 34:7), so that I may say to him, "Who am I, Lord," or what is my calling, that you have appeared to me in such divine power? So that today, among the gentiles, I may praise you ceaselessly and magnify your name, wherever I may be. And this, not merely in good times, but also in distress. So that whatever will come my way, whether good or bad, I may accept it calmly, and always give thanks to God, who has ever shown me how I should believe in him unfailing without end. And he has heard and helped me, so that I, for all my ignorance, should "in these latter days" (see Ac 2:17) dare to undertake this work that is so holy and so wonderful.

Thus in some small way, I may come to imitate those whom long ago the Lord foretold would announce the gospel, "as a sign to all the gentiles before the world comes to its end" (see Mt 24:14). This is what we have seen, thus has it been fulfilled. Mark it well, we testify that the gospel has been preached as far as any man has gone. ST. PATRICK, 389–461

YOU WILL FIND THE NEXT READING AT 2 SAMUEL 12.

will ever stand firm before me and your throne be for ever secure." '

¹⁷Nathan related all these words and this whole revelation to David.

David's prayer

¹⁸King David then went in, sat down in Yahweh's presence and said:

'Who am I, Lord Yahweh, and what is my lineage, for you to have led me as far as this? ¹⁹Yet, to you, Lord Yahweh, this seemed too little, and now you extend your promises for your servant's family into the distant future. Such is human destiny, Lord Yahweh. ²⁰What more can David say to you, since you, Lord Yahweh, know all about your servant? ²¹Because of your promise and since you were so inclined, you have had the generosity to reveal this to your servant. ²²That is why you are great, Lord Yahweh; there is no one like you, no God but you alone, as everything that we have heard confirms. ²³Is there another people on earth like your people, like Israel, whom a god proceeded to redeem, to make them his people and to make a name for himself by performing great and terrible things on their behalf, by driving out nations and their gods before his people?—²⁴for you constituted your people Israel your own people for ever and you, Yahweh, became their God.

25 'Now, Yahweh God, may the promise which you have made for your servant and for his family stand firm forever as you have said, 26 so that your name will be exalted for ever and people will say, "Israel's God is Yahweh Sabaoth." Your servant David's dynasty will be secure before you, 27 since you, Yahweh Sabaoth, the God of Israel, have disclosed to your servant, "I am going to build you a dynasty." Hence, your servant has ventured to offer this prayer to you. 28 Yes, Lord Yahweh, you are God indeed, your words are true and you have made this generous promise to your servant. 29 What is more, you have deigned to bless your servant's dynasty, so that it may remain for ever before you; for you, Lord Yahweh, have spoken; and may your servant's dynasty be blessed with your blessing for ever.'

David's wars

8 After this, David defeated the Philistines and subdued them. From the grip of the Philistines he wrested . . . 2 He also defeated the Moabites and, making them lie on the ground, measured them off by the line; he measured out two lines to be put to death and one full line to have their lives spared. The Moabites became David's subjects and paid him tribute.

3 David defeated Hadadezer son of Rehob, king of Zobah, when the latter mounted an expedition to extend his power over the River. 4 David captured one thousand seven hundred charioteers and twenty thousand foot soldiers from him; David hamstrung all the chariot teams, keeping only a hundred of them. 5 The Aramaeans of Damascus came to the help of Hadadezer king of Zobah, but David killed twenty-two thousand of the Aramaeans. 6 David then imposed governors on Aram of Damascus, and the Aramaeans became David's subjects and paid him tribute. Wherever David went, Yahweh gave him victory. 7 David took the golden shields carried by Hadadezer's guards and brought them to Jerusalem. 8 From Betah and Berothai, towns belonging to Hadadezer, King David captured a great quantity of bronze.

9 When Tou king of Hamath heard that David had defeated Hadadezer's entire army, 10 he sent his son Hadoram to King David to greet him and to congratulate him on having made war on Hadadezer and on having defeated him, since Hadadezer was at war with Tou. Hadoram brought with him objects made of silver, gold and bronze, 11 which King David also consecrated to Yahweh, as he had already consecrated the silver and gold taken from all the nations which he had subjugated—12 from Aram, Moab, the Ammonites, the Philistines and Amalek; and from the spoil of Hadadezer son of Rehob, king of Zobah.

13 David became famous when he came home from defeating the Edomites in the Valley of Salt—eighteen thousand of them. 14 He imposed governors on Edom and all the Edomites became David's subjects. Wherever David went, Yahweh gave him victory.

The administration of the kingdom[a]

15 David ruled over all Israel, administering law and justice to all his people. 16 Joab son of Zeruiah was in command of the army; Jehoshaphat son of Ahilud was herald; 17 Zadok and Abiathar son of Ahimelech, son of Ahitub, were priests; Seraiah was secretary; 18 Benaiah son of Jehoiada was in command of the Cherethites and Pelethites; David's sons were priests.

David's kindness to Jonathan's son

9 David asked, 'Is there anyone belonging to Saul's family left, to whom I might show faithful love for Jonathan's sake?' 2 Now Saul's family had a servant whose name was Ziba. When he had been summoned to David, the king said, 'Are you Ziba?' 'At your service,' he replied. 3 The king said, 'Is there no one left, belonging to Saul's family, for me to treat with God's own faithful love?' Ziba said to the king, 'There is still one of Jonathan's sons. He

8a = 20:23–26.

has crippled feet.' ⁴The king asked 'Where is he?' Ziba replied, 'He is living in the household of Machir son of Ammiel, at Lo-Debar.' ⁵So King David sent for him to be fetched from the house of Machir son of Ammiel at Lo-Debar.

⁶On entering David's presence, Meribbaal son of Jonathan, son of Saul, fell on his face and prostrated himself. David said, 'Meribbaal!' He replied, 'Here I am, at your service.' ⁷David then said, 'Do not be afraid; I will indeed treat you with faithful love for your father Jonathan's sake. I shall restore all your grandfather Saul's estates to you, and you will always eat at my table.' ⁸Meribbaal prostrated himself and said, 'Who is your servant, for you to show favour to a dead dog like me?'

⁹The king then summoned Saul's servant Ziba and said, 'Everything belonging to Saul and his family, I give to your master's son. ¹⁰You must work the land for him, you and your sons and your slaves; you must harvest the produce to provide food for your master's family to eat. But Meribbaal, your master's son, will always take his own meals at my table.' Now, Ziba had fifteen sons and twenty slaves. ¹¹Ziba said to the king, 'Your servant will do everything my lord the king has ordered his servant.'

So Meribbaal ate at David's table like one of the king's sons. ¹²Meribbaal had a young son whose name was Micha. All the people living in Ziba's household entered Meribbaal's service. ¹³Meribbaal lived in Jerusalem, since he always ate at the king's table. He was crippled in both feet.

David's ambassadors are insulted

10 After this, when the king of the Ammonites died and his son Hanun succeeded him, ²David thought, 'I shall show Hanun son of Nahash the same faithful love as his father showed me.' And David sent his representatives to offer him condolences over his father. But, when David's representatives reached the Ammonites' country, ³the Ammonite princes said to Hanun their master, 'Do you really think David means to honour your father when he sends you messengers with sympathy? On the contrary, the reason why David has sent his representatives to you is to explore the city, to reconnoitre and so overthrow it.' ⁴Whereupon Hanun seized David's representatives, shaved off half their beards, cut their clothes off halfway up, at their buttocks, and sent them away. ⁵When David was told, he sent someone to meet them, since the men were overcome with shame. 'Stay in Jericho', the king said, 'until your beards have grown again, and come back then.'

The first Ammonite campaign

⁶When the Ammonites realised that they had antagonised David, they sent agents to hire twenty thousand foot soldiers from the Aramaeans of Beth-Rehob and the Aramaeans of Zobah, one thousand men from the king of Maacah and twelve thousand men from the prince of Tob. ⁷When David heard this, he sent Joab with the whole army, the champions. ⁸The Ammonites marched out and drew up their line of battle at the city gate, while the Aramaeans of Zobah and of Rehob and the men of Tob and Maacah kept their distance in the open country. ⁹Joab, seeing that he had to fight on two fronts, to his front and to his rear, chose the best of Israel's picked men and drew them up in line facing the Aramaeans. ¹⁰He entrusted the rest of the army to his brother Abishai, and drew them up in line facing the Ammonites. ¹¹'If the Aramaeans prove too strong for me,' he said, 'you must come to my help; if the Ammonites prove too strong for you, I shall come to yours. ¹²Be brave! Let us acquit ourselves like men for the sake of our people and for the cities of our God. And let Yahweh do as he thinks right!' ¹³Joab and the force with him joined battle with the Aramaeans, who fled at his onslaught. ¹⁴When the Ammonites saw that the Aramaeans had fled, they too fled from Abishai and withdrew into the city. Hence, Joab broke off his campaign against the Ammonites and returned to Jerusalem.

Victory over the Aramaeans

15 The Aramaeans, realising that Israel had got the better of them, concentrated their forces. 16 Hadadezer sent messengers and mobilised the Aramaeans living on the other side of the river; and these arrived at Helam, with Shobach the commander of Hadadezer's army, at their head. 17 David, being informed of this, mustered all Israel, crossed the Jordan and arrived at Helam. The Aramaeans drew up in line facing David and engaged him. 18 But the Aramaeans fled from Israel, and David killed seven hundred of their chariot teams and forty thousand men; he also cut down Shobach the commander of their army, who died there. 19 When all Hadadezer's vassal kings saw that Israel had got the better of them, they made peace with the Israelites and became their subjects. The Aramaeans were afraid to give any more help to the Ammonites.

The second Ammonite campaign; David's sin

11 At the turn of the year, at the time when kings go campaigning, David sent Joab and with him his guards and all Israel. They massacred the Ammonites and laid siege to Rabbah-of-the-Ammonites. David, however, remained in Jerusalem.

2 It happened towards evening when David had got up from resting and was strolling on the palace roof, that from the roof he saw a woman bathing; the woman was very beautiful. 3 David made enquiries about this woman and was told, 'Why, that is Bathsheba daughter of Eliam and wife of Uriah the Hittite.' 4 David then sent messengers to fetch her. She came to him, and he lay with her, just after she had purified herself from her period. She then went home again. 5 The woman conceived and sent word to David, 'I am pregnant.'

6 David then sent word to Joab, 'Send me Uriah the Hittite,' whereupon Joab sent Uriah to David. 7 When Uriah reached him, David asked how Joab was and how the army was and how the war was going. 8 David then said to Uriah, 'Go down to your house and wash your feet.' Uriah left the palace and was followed by a present from the king's table. 9 Uriah, however, slept at the palace gate with all his master's bodyguard and did not go down to his house.

10 This was reported to David; 'Uriah', they said 'has not gone down to his house.' So David asked Uriah, 'Haven't you just arrived from the journey? Why didn't you go down to your house?' 11 To which Uriah replied, 'The ark, Israel and Judah are lodged in huts; my master Joab and my lord's guards are camping in the open. Am I to go to my house, then, and eat and drink and sleep with my wife? As Yahweh lives, and as you yourself live, I shall do no such thing!' 12 David then said to Uriah, 'Stay on here today; tomorrow I shall send you off.' So Uriah stayed that day in Jerusalem. 13 The next day, David invited him to eat and drink in his presence and made him drunk. In the evening, Uriah went out and bedded down with his master's bodyguard, but did not go down to his house.

14 Next morning David wrote a letter to Joab and sent it by Uriah. 15 In the letter he wrote, 'Put Uriah out in front where the fighting is fiercest and then fall back, so that he gets wounded and killed.' 16 Joab, then besieging the city, stationed Uriah at a point where he knew that there would be tough fighters. 17 The people of the city sallied out and engaged Joab; there were casualties in the army, among David's guards, and Uriah the Hittite was killed as well.

18 Joab sent David a full account of the battle. 19 To the messenger he gave this order: 'When you have finished telling the king all about the battle, 20 if the king's anger is aroused and he says, "Why did you go near the town to give battle? Didn't you know that they would shoot from the ramparts? 21 Who killed Abimelech son of Jerubbaal? Wasn't it a woman who dropped a millstone on him from the ramparts, causing his death at Thebez? Why did you go near the ramparts?" you are to say, "Your servant Uriah the Hittite is dead too." '

29 READ 2 SAMUEL 12:1–14.

David said to Nathan, "I have sinned against Yahweh."—2 SAMUEL 12:13

RECOVERING FROM SIN

How many sins each of us commits from one hour to the next! And yet among ordinary men and women who would think there is any obligation to admit to these sins? But King David, great and powerful though he was, could not for even the briefest moment endure to keep hidden within himself the consciousness of his crime, confessing his guilt to the Lord without delay and with intense sorrow (see Ps 51). . . .

So great was the sorrow of his inmost heart that the Lord was moved to say to him through Nathan: "Yahweh, for his part, forgives your sin; you are not to die." The readiness with which God pardoned him is a clear indication of the depth of the king's repentance, which wiped away the offense of so great a crime.

Others, when reproved . . . because of their sins, only aggravate their guilt when they seek to deny or excuse it. . . . Holy people, however, who strive to fight the good fight to the end . . . , may happen to fall like other people. Should they commit sin more by reason of the frailty of their nature than by reason of any desire to sin, they rise up to continue the race with even greater eagerness and, under the stimulus of sorrow, to gain even greater victories. So their sin is not to be regarded as an obstacle to their progress but rather as an incentive to hasten it.

These saintly people, should they happen to fall into sin, do not . . . relax their efforts in the fight but carry on the contest unremittingly or even . . . receive greater grace to bring them to victory. How much more, then, should we refrain from judging because of one fall into sin those who are striving earnestly to lead a holy life, since he is blessed who has been able to recover himself after a fall; for resurrection also after death is the reward of the blessed.   ST. AMBROSE, 340?–397

YOU WILL FIND THE NEXT READING AT 1 KINGS 17.

²²So the messenger set off and, on his arrival, told David everything that Joab had instructed him to say. David flew into a rage with Joab and said to the messenger, 'Why did you go near the ramparts? Who killed Abimelech son of Jerubbaal? Wasn't it a woman who dropped a millstone on him from the ramparts, causing his death at Thebez? Why did you go near the ramparts?' ²³The messenger replied to David, 'Their men had won an initial advantage and then came out to engage us in the open. We then drove them back into the gateway, ²⁴but the archers shot at your retainers from the ramparts; some of the king's retainers lost their lives, and your servant Uriah the Hittite is dead too.'

²⁵David then said to the messenger, 'Say this to Joab, "Do not take the matter to heart; the sword devours now one and now another. Attack the town in greater force and destroy it." That will encourage him.' ²⁶When Uriah's wife heard that her husband Uriah was dead, she mourned for her husband. ²⁷When the period of mourning was over, David sent to have

her brought to his house; she became his wife and bore him a son. But what David had done displeased Yahweh.

David is rebuked by Nathan; his repentance

12 Yahweh sent the prophet Nathan to David. He came to him and said:

In the same town were two men,
  one rich, the other poor.
² The rich man had flocks and herds
  in great abundance;
³ the poor man had nothing but a ewe
    lamb,
only a single little one which he had
    bought.
He fostered it and it grew up with him
    and his children,
eating his bread, drinking from his cup,
sleeping in his arms; it was like a daughter
    to him.
⁴ When a traveller came to stay, the rich
    man
would not take anything from his own
    flock or herd
to provide for the wayfarer who had come
    to him.
Instead, he stole the poor man's lamb
and prepared that for his guest.

⁵ David flew into a great rage with the man. 'As Yahweh lives,' he said to Nathan 'the man who did this deserves to die. ⁶ For doing such a thing and for having shown no pity, he shall make fourfold restitution for the lamb.'

⁷ Nathan then said to David, 'You are the man! Yahweh, God of Israel, says this, "I anointed you king of Israel, I saved you from Saul's clutches, ⁸ I gave you your master's household and your master's wives into your arms, I gave you the House of Israel and the House of Judah; and, if this is still too little, I shall give you other things as well. ⁹ Why did you show contempt for Yahweh, by doing what displeases him? You put Uriah the Hittite to the sword, you took his wife to be your wife, causing his death by the sword of the Ammonites. ¹⁰ For this, your household will never be free of the sword, since you showed contempt for me and took the wife of Uriah the Hittite, to make her your wife."

¹¹ 'Yahweh says this, "Out of your own household I shall raise misfortune for you. Before your very eyes I shall take your wives and give them to your neighbour, who will lie with your wives in broad daylight. ¹² You have worked in secret, but I shall work this for all Israel to see, in broad daylight." '

¹³ David said to Nathan, 'I have sinned against Yahweh.' Nathan then said to David, 'Yahweh, for his part, forgives your sin; you are not to die. ¹⁴ But, since you have outraged Yahweh by doing this, the child born to you will die.' ¹⁵ And Nathan went home.

Death of Bathsheba's child; birth of Solomon

Yahweh struck the child which Uriah's wife had borne to David and it fell gravely ill. ¹⁶ David pleaded with Yahweh for the child; he kept a strict fast and went home and spent the night lying on the ground, covered with sacking. ¹⁷ The officials of his household stood round him, intending to get him off the ground, but he refused, nor would he take food with them. ¹⁸ On the seventh day the child died. David's retinue were afraid to tell him that the child was dead. 'Even when the child was alive', they thought, 'we reasoned with him and he would not listen to us. How can we tell him that the child is dead? He will do something desperate.' ¹⁹ David, however, noticed that his retinue were whispering among themselves, and realised that the child was dead. 'Is the child dead?' he asked the officers. They replied, 'He is dead.'

²⁰ David got off the ground, bathed and anointed himself and put on fresh clothes. Then he went into Yahweh's sanctuary and prostrated himself. On returning to his house, he asked to be served with food and ate it. ²¹ His retinue said, 'Why are you acting like this? When the child was alive, you fasted and wept; now that the child is dead, you get up and take food!' ²² 'When the child was alive',

he replied, 'I fasted and wept because I kept thinking, "Who knows? Perhaps Yahweh will take pity on me and the child will live." 23 But now that he is dead, why should I fast? Can I bring him back again? I shall go to him but he cannot come back to me.'

24 David consoled his wife Bathsheba. He went to her and slept with her. She conceived and gave birth to a son, whom she called Solomon. Yahweh loved him 25 and made this known by means of the prophet Nathan, who named him Jedidiah, as Yahweh had instructed.

Capture of Rabbah

26 Joab assaulted Rabbah-of-the-Ammonites and captured the royal town. 27 He then sent messengers to tell David, 'I have assaulted Rabbah and captured the water supply. 28 So now muster the rest of the army, lay siege to the town and take it, or I will take it and the town will be called after me!' 29 So David mustered the whole army and marched on Rabbah; he assaulted the town and captured it. 30 He took the crown off Milcom's head; it weighed one talent of gold, and in it was set a precious stone which went on David's head instead. He carried off great quantities of booty from the town.' 31 And he expelled its inhabitants, setting them to work with saws, iron picks and iron axes, employing them at brickmaking. He treated all the Ammonite towns in the same way. David and the whole army returned to Jerusalem.

Amnon violates his sister Tamar

13 After this, the following events took place. Absalom son of David had a beautiful sister whose name was Tamar; Amnon son of David fell in love with her. 2 Amnon was so obsessed with his sister Tamar that it made him ill, since she was a virgin and Amnon thought it impossible to do anything to her. 3 But Amnon had a friend called Jonadab son of Shimeah, David's brother, and Jonadab was a very shrewd man. 4 'Son of the king,' he said, 'tell me why, morning after morning, you look so worn? Won't you tell me?' Amnon replied, 'I am in love with Tamar, my brother Absalom's sister.' 5 Then Jonadab said, 'Take to your bed, pretend to be ill and, when your father comes to visit you, say, "Please let my sister Tamar come and give me something to eat; let her prepare the food where I can see. What she gives me I shall eat." ' 6 So Amnon lay down and pretended to be ill. The king then came to visit him and Amnon said to the king, 'Please let my sister Tamar come and make a cake or two where I can watch. What she gives me, I shall eat.' 7 David then sent word to Tamar at the palace, 'Go to your brother Amnon's house and prepare some food for him.' 8 Tamar went to the house of her brother Amnon who was lying there in bed. She took dough and kneaded it, and she made some cakes while he watched, and baked the cakes. 9 She then took the pan and dished them up in front of him, but he refused to eat. Amnon said, 'Let everyone leave me!' So everyone withdrew. 10 Amnon then said to Tamar, 'Bring the food to the inner room, so that I can eat what you give me.' So Tamar took the cakes which she had made and brought them to her brother Amnon in the inner room. 11 And as she was offering the food to him, he caught hold of her and said, 'Come to bed with me, sister!' 12 She replied, 'No, brother! Do not force me! This is no way to behave in Israel. Do not do anything so disgraceful! 13 Wherever should I go? I should be marked with this shame, while you would become disgraced in Israel. Why not go and speak to the king? He will not refuse to give me to you.' 14 But he would not listen to her; he overpowered her and raped her.

15 Amnon was then seized with extreme hatred for her; the hatred he now felt for her was greater than his earlier love. 'Get up and go!' he said. 16 She said, 'No, brother! To send me away would be worse than the other wrong you have done me!' But he would not listen to her. 17 He called his personal servant. 'Rid me of this woman!' he said. 'Throw her out and bolt the door behind her!' 18 (She was wearing

a magnificent dress, for this was what the king's unmarried daughters wore in days gone by.) So the servant put her out and bolted the door behind her.

19 Tamar put dust on her head, tore the magnificent dress which she was wearing, laid her hand on her head, and went away, crying aloud as she went.

20 Her brother Absalom said to her, 'Has Amnon your brother been with you? Sister, be quiet; he is your brother; do not take the matter to heart!' Tamar, however, went back to her brother Absalom's house inconsolable.

21 When King David heard the whole story, he was very angry; but he had no wish to harm his son Amnon, whom he loved because he was his first-born. 22 Absalom, however, would not so much as speak to Amnon, since he hated Amnon for having raped his sister Tamar.

Absalom kills Amnon and flees

23 Two years later, when Absalom had the sheep-shearers at Baal-Hazor, which is near Ephraim, he invited all the king's sons. 24 Absalom went to the king and said, 'Now sir, your servant has the sheep-shearers. Will the king and his retinue be pleased to come with your servant?' 25 'No, my son,' the king replied, 'we must not all come and be a burden to you.' And though Absalom was insistent, he would not go but dismissed him. 26 Absalom persisted, 'Then at least let my brother Amnon come with us.' The king said, 'Why should he go with you?' 27 On Absalom's insistence, however, he let Amnon and all the king's sons to go with him.

Absalom prepared a royal banquet 28 and then gave this order to the servants, 'Listen carefully; when Amnon's heart is merry with wine and I say, "Strike Amnon down", then kill him. Don't be afraid. Have I not myself given you the order? Use your strength and show your mettle!' 29 Absalom's servants treated Amnon as Absalom had ordered. The king's sons all leapt to their feet, mounted their mules and fled.

30 While they were on the road, word reached David, 'Absalom has killed all the king's sons; not one of them is left.' 31 The king stood up, tore his clothes and threw himself on the ground. All his officers tore their clothes too. 32 Jonadab son of Shimeah, David's brother, then spoke up and said, 'Do not let my lord take to heart the report that all the young men, the king's sons, have been killed, since only Amnon is dead: for Absalom has been promising himself to do this since the day when Amnon raped his sister Tamar. 33 So my lord the king must not imagine that all the king's sons are dead; only Amnon is dead 34 and Absalom has fled.'

The man on sentry duty looked up and saw a large troop coming along the road from Bahurim. The sentry came to tell the king, 'I have seen some people coming down the Bahurim road on the mountainside.' 35 Jonadab then said to the king, 'These are the king's sons arriving: what your servant said is exactly what happened.' 36 He had scarcely finished speaking when the king's sons arrived and wept aloud; the king and all his retinue wept aloud too. 37 Absalom had gone to Talmai son of Ammihud, king of Geshur. The king mourned for his son every day.

Joab negotiates Absalom's return

38 When Absalom had gone to Geshur, he stayed there for three years. 39 Once the king was consoled over Amnon's death, his anger against Absalom subsided.

14 Now, Joab son of Zeruiah observed that the king was favourably inclined to Absalom. 2 Joab therefore sent to Tekoa for a wise woman. 'Pretend to be in mourning,' he said. 'Dress yourself in mourning, do not perfume yourself; act like a woman who has long been mourning for the dead. 3 Then go to the king and say this to him.' And Joab put the words into her mouth which she was to say.

4 So the woman of Tekoa went to the king and, falling on her face to the ground, prostrated herself. 'Help, my lord king!' she said. 5 The king said, 'What is the matter?'

'As you see,' she replied, 'I am a widow; my husband is dead. ⁶Your servant had two sons and out in the fields, where there was no one to intervene, they had a quarrel. And one of them struck the other one and killed him. ⁷And now the whole clan has risen against your servant. "Give up the man who killed his brother," they say, "so that we can put him to death, to atone for the life of the brother whom he has murdered; and thus we shall destroy the heir as well." By this means, they will extinguish the ember still left to me, leaving my husband neither name nor survivor on the face of the earth.' ⁸Then the king said to the woman, 'Go home; I myself shall give orders about your case.' ⁹The woman of Tekoa said to the king, 'My lord king! May the guilt be on me and on my family; the king and his throne are innocent of it.' ¹⁰'Bring me the man who threatened you,' the king replied, 'and he shall never hurt you again.' ¹¹She then said, 'Let the king be pleased to pronounce the name of Yahweh your God, so that the avenger of blood may not do greater harm and destroy my son.' 'As Yahweh lives,' he said, 'not one of your son's hairs shall fall to the ground!'

¹²Then the woman said, 'Permit your servant to say something else to my lord the king.' 'Go on,' he said. ¹³The woman said, 'Why then has the king, who by giving this verdict has condemned himself, conceived the idea, against God's people's interests, of not bringing home the son whom he has banished? ¹⁴We are all mortal; we are like water spilt on the ground, which cannot be gathered up again, nor does God raise up a corpse; let the king therefore make plans for his banished son not to remain far away from him in exile. ¹⁵'Now, the reason why I came to speak about this to my lord the king is that I was being intimidated, and your servant thought, "I shall speak to the king; perhaps the king will do what his servant asks. ¹⁶Surely the king will consent to save his servant from the clutches of the man who is trying to cut both me and my son off from God's heritage. ¹⁷Let a word from my lord the king, restore the peace!" your servant thought, "for my lord the king is like the Angel of God in understanding good and evil." May Yahweh your God be with you!'

¹⁸Replying to the woman, the king said, 'Now do not evade the question which I am going to ask you.' The woman said, 'Let my lord the king ask his question.' ¹⁹'Is not Joab's hand behind you in all this?' the king asked. The woman replied, 'As you live, my lord king, I cannot escape what my lord the king says, either to right or to left. Yes, it was your servant Joab who gave me my orders; he put all these words into your servant's mouth. ²⁰Your servant Joab did this to approach the matter indirectly, but my lord has the wisdom of the Angel of God; he knows everything that happens on earth!'

²¹The king then said to Joab, 'Very well, the suit is granted. Go and bring the young man Absalom back.' ²²Joab fell on his face to the ground, prostrated himself and blessed the king. 'My lord king,' Joab said, 'today your servant knows that he has won your favour, since the king has done what his servant asked.' ²³Joab then set off, went to Geshur, and brought Absalom back to Jerusalem. ²⁴The king, however, said, 'Let him retire to his own house; he is not to appear in my presence.' So Absalom retired to his own house and was not received by the king.

Some details about Absalom

²⁵In all Israel there was no one more praised for his beauty than Absalom; from the sole of his foot to the crown of his head, he could not be faulted. ²⁶When he cut his hair—he shaved it once a year because his hair got too heavy—he would weigh the hair: two hundred shekels, king's weight. ²⁷To Absalom were born three sons and one daughter called Tamar; she was a beautiful woman.

Absalom obtains his pardon

²⁸Absalom lived in Jerusalem for two years without being received by the king. ²⁹Absalom then summoned Joab, intending to send

him to the king, but Joab would not come to him. He sent for him a second time, but still he would not come. ³⁰ At this, Absalom said to his retainers, 'Look, Joab's field is next to mine and he has barley in it; go and set it on fire.' Absalom's retainers set fire to the field. ³¹ Joab then stirred himself, went to Absalom in his house and asked, 'Why have your retainers set my field on fire?' ³² Absalom replied to Joab, 'Look, I sent word to you: Come here, so that I can send you to the king to say, "Why come back from Geshur? Better for me to have been there still!" Now I want to be received by the king, and if I am guilty, let him put me to death!' ³³ Joab went to the king and told him this. He then summoned Absalom, who prostrated himself with his face to the ground before the king. And the king kissed Absalom.

Absalom's intrigues

15 After this, Absalom procured a chariot and horses, with fifty men to run ahead of him. ² He would get up early and stand beside the road leading to the city gate; and whenever a man with some lawsuit had to come before the king's tribunal, Absalom would call out to him and ask, 'Which town are you from?' If he answered, 'Your servant is from one of the tribes of Israel,' ³ then Absalom would say, 'Look, your case is sound and just, but not one of the king's deputies will listen to you.' ⁴ Absalom would say, 'Oh, who will appoint me judge in the land? Then anyone with a lawsuit or a plea could come to me and I should see he had justice!' ⁵ And whenever anyone came up to him to prostrate himself, he would stretch out his hand, draw him to him and kiss him. ⁶ Absalom acted like this with every Israelite who appealed to the king's tribunal, and so Absalom won the Israelites' hearts.

Absalom's rebellion

⁷ When four years had gone by, Absalom said to the king, 'Allow me to go to Hebron and fulfil the vow which I have made to Yahweh; ⁸ for, when I was in Geshur, in Aram, your ser-

vant made this vow, "If Yahweh brings me back to Jerusalem, I shall pay my devotions to Yahweh in Hebron." ' ⁹ The king said to him, 'Go in peace.' So he set off and went to Hebron.

¹⁰ Absalom sent couriers throughout the tribes of Israel to say, 'When you hear the trumpet sound, you are to say, "Absalom is king at Hebron!" ' ¹¹ With Absalom went two hundred men from Jerusalem; they had been invited and had gone in all innocence, unaware of what was going on. ¹² Absalom sent for Ahithophel the Gilonite, David's counsellor, from Giloh his town, and had him with him while offering the sacrifices. The conspiracy grew in strength, since Absalom's supporters grew in number.

David's flight

¹³ A messenger came and told David, 'The men of Israel have shifted their allegiance to Absalom.' ¹⁴ David said to all his retinue then with him in Jerusalem, 'Up, let us flee, or we shall not escape from Absalom! Leave as quickly as you can, in case he mounts a sudden attack, overcomes us and puts the city to the sword.' ¹⁵ The king's retinue replied, 'Whatever my lord the king decides, we are at your service.' ¹⁶ The king set out on foot with his whole household, leaving ten concubines to look after the palace. ¹⁷ The king set out on foot with everyone following, and they halted at the last house. ¹⁸ All his officers stood at his side. All the Cherethites and all the Pelethites, with Ittai and all the six hundred Gittites who had come in his retinue from Gath, marched past the king. ¹⁹ The king said to Ittai the Gittite, 'You, why are you coming with us? Go back and stay with the king, for you are a foreigner, indeed an exile from your homeland. ²⁰ You arrived only yesterday; should I take you wandering with us today, when I do not know myself where I am going? Go back, take your fellow countrymen with you, and may Yahweh show you mercy and faithful love!' ²¹ Ittai replied to the king, 'As Yahweh lives, and as my lord the king lives, wherever my

lord the king may be, for death or life, your servant will be there too.' ²²David then said to Ittai, 'Go ahead, march past!' And Ittai of Gath marched past with all his men and with all his children too. ²³The entire population was weeping aloud as the king stood in the bed of the Kidron and everyone marched past him, making for the desert.

The ark is left in Jerusalem

²⁴Zadok was there too, and all the Levites with him, carrying the ark of God. They set the ark of God down beside Abiathar until everyone had finished marching out of the town. ²⁵The king then said to Zadok, 'Take the ark of God back into the city. Should I win Yahweh's favour, he will bring me back and allow me to see it and its tent once more. ²⁶But should he say, "You displease me," here I am: let him treat me as he sees fit.' ²⁷The king said to Zadok the priest, 'Look, you and Abiathar go back quietly into the city, with your two sons, your own son Ahimaaz and Jonathan son of Abiathar. ²⁸You see, I shall wait in the passes of the desert plain until word comes from you bringing me news.' ²⁹So Zadok and Abiathar took the ark of God back to Jerusalem and stayed there.

Hushai is briefed to work for David

³⁰David then made his way up the Mount of Olives, weeping as he went, his head covered and his feet bare. And all the people with him had their heads covered and made their way up, weeping as they went. ³¹David was then informed that Ahithophel was among the conspirators with Absalom. David said, 'I beg you, Yahweh, turn Ahithophel's advice to folly.'

³²As David reached the summit, where God is worshipped, he saw Hushai the Archite, his friend, coming to meet him with his tunic torn and with earth on his head. ³³David said, 'If you go along with me, you will be a burden to me. ³⁴But if you go back to the city and say to Absalom, "I am at your service, my lord king; once I was in your father's service,

but now I shall serve you," you will be able to thwart Ahithophel's advice for me. ³⁵Surely the priests Zadok and Abiathar will be with you? Anything you hear from the palace you must report to the priests Zadok and Abiathar. ³⁶You see, their two sons are there with them, Zadok's son Ahimaaz, and Abiathar's son Jonathan; through these, you will send me word of everything you hear.' ³⁷Hushai, David's friend, entered the city just as Absalom was reaching Jerusalem.

David and Ziba

16 When David had passed a little beyond the summit, Meribbaal's retainer, Ziba, met him with a pair of donkeys, saddled and laden with two hundred loaves of bread, a hundred bunches of raisins, a hundred of the season's fruits, and a skin of wine. ²The king said to Ziba, 'What are you going to do with that?' 'The donkeys', Ziba replied, 'are for the king's family to ride, the bread and the fruit for the soldiers to eat, the wine is for drinking by those who get exhausted in the desert.' ³The king asked 'And where is your master's son?' Ziba replied to the king, 'Why, he has stayed in Jerusalem because, he says, "Today, the House of Israel will give me back my father's kingdom."' ⁴Then the king said to Ziba, 'Everything owned by Meribbaal is yours.' Ziba said, 'I prostrate myself! May I be worthy of your favour, my lord king!'

Shimei curses David

⁵As David was reaching Bahurim, out came a man of the same clan as Saul's family. His name was Shimei son of Gera and, as he came, he uttered curse after curse ⁶and threw stones at David and at all King David's retinue, even though the whole army and all the champions formed an escort round the king on either side. ⁷The words of his curse were these, 'Off with you, off with you, man of blood, scoundrel! ⁸Yahweh has paid you back for all the spilt blood of the House of Saul whose sovereignty you have usurped; and Yahweh has transferred the sovereign power to Absalom

your son. Now your wickedness has overtaken you, man of blood that you are.' [9]Abishai son of Zeruiah said to the king, 'Why should this dead dog curse my lord the king? Let me go over and cut his head off.' [10]But the king replied, 'What concern is my business to you, sons of Zeruiah? Let him curse! If Yahweh has said to him, "Curse David!" what right has anyone to say, "Why have you done so?"' [11]David said to Abishai and all his retinue, 'Why, the son sprung from my own body is now seeking my life; all the more reason for this Benjaminite to do so! Let him curse on, if Yahweh has told him to! [12]Perhaps Yahweh will look on my wretchedness and will repay me with good for his curses today.' [13]So David and his men went on their way, and Shimei kept pace with him along the opposite mountainside, cursing as he went, throwing stones and flinging dust. [14]The king and all the people who were with him arrived exhausted at . . .[a] . . . and there they drew breath.

Hushai ingratiates himself with Absalom

[15]Absalom entered Jerusalem with all the men of Israel; with him was Ahithophel. [16]When Hushai the Archite, David's friend, reached Absalom, Hushai said to Absalom, 'Long live the king! Long live the king!' [17]Absalom said to Hushai, 'Is this your faithful love for your friend? Why didn't you go away with your friend?' [18]Hushai replied to Absalom, 'No, the man whom Yahweh and this people and all the men of Israel have chosen, he is the man for me, and with him will I stay! [19]Besides, whom should I serve, if not his son? As I served your father, so shall I serve you.'

Absalom and David's concubines

[20]Absalom said to Ahithophel, 'Think carefully. What shall we do?' [21]Ahithophel replied to Absalom, 'Go to your father's concubines whom he left to look after the palace; then all Israel will hear that you have thoroughly antagonised your father, and the resolution of all your supporters will be strengthened.' [22]So a tent was pitched for Absalom on the flat roof

and, with all Israel watching, Absalom went to his father's concubines. [23]At the time, whatever advice Ahithophel gave was treated like a decision obtained from God; as by David, so by Absalom, was all Ahithophel's advice regarded.

Hushai thwarts Ahithophel's plans

17 Ahithophel said to Absalom, 'Let me choose twelve thousand men and set off this very night in pursuit of David. [2]I shall fall on him while he is tired and dispirited; I shall strike terror into him, and all the people who are with him will run away. I shall kill only the king, [3]and I shall then bring all the people back to you, like a bride returning to her husband. You seek the life of one individual only; the people as a whole will have peace.' [4]The suggestion seemed a good one to Absalom and all the elders of Israel.

[5]Then Absalom said, 'Now call Hushai the Archite, for us to hear what he too has to say.' [6]When Hushai had come to Absalom, Absalom said, 'This is what Ahithophel says. Are we to do as he suggests? If not, suggest something yourself.' [7]Hushai said to Absalom, 'On this occasion the advice given by Ahithophel is not good. [8]You know', Hushai went on, 'that your father and his men are great fighters and that they are now as angry as a wild bear robbed of her cubs. Your father is a man of war: he will not let the army rest during the night. [9]At this moment he is concealed in some hollow or other place. If at the outset there are casualties among our troops, word will go round that the army supporting Absalom has met with disaster. [10]And then even the valiant, the truly lion-hearted, will be demoralised; for all Israel knows that your father is a champion and that the men with him are valiant. [11]For my part, I offer this advice: Summon all Israel, from Dan to Beersheba, to rally to you, as numerous as the sand on the seashore, and you take the field in person with them. [12]We shall reach him wherever he is to be found; we shall

_16a_ A place-name is missing.

fall on him as the dew falls on the ground, and not leave him or any one of the men with him. ¹³ Should he retire into a town, all Israel will bring ropes to that town, and we shall drag it into the river-bed until not a pebble of it is to be found.' ¹⁴ Then Absalom and all the people of Israel said, 'Hushai the Arkite's advice is better than Ahithophel's,' Yahweh having resolved to thwart Ahithophel's shrewd advice and so bring disaster on Absalom.

¹⁵ Hushai then told the priests Zadok and Abiathar, 'Ahithophel gave such and such advice to Absalom and the elders of Israel, but I advised so and so. ¹⁶ Send with all speed to David and say, "Do not camp in the desert passes tonight, but get through them as fast as you can, or the king and his whole army may be annihilated."'

David is warned and crosses the Jordan

¹⁷ Jonathan and Ahimaaz were posted at the Fuller's Spring; a servant-girl was to go and warn them and they in turn were to warn King David, since they could not give themselves away by coming into the city themselves. ¹⁸ A young man saw them nonetheless and told Absalom. The pair of them, however, made off quickly, reaching the house of a man in Bahurim. In his courtyard was a storage-well and they got down into it. ¹⁹ The woman took a piece of canvas and, spreading it over the mouth of the storage-well, scattered crushed grain on it so that nothing showed.

²⁰ When Absalom's servants reached the woman at the house, they said, 'Where are Ahimaaz and Jonathan?' The woman said, 'They have gone further on, towards the water.' They searched but, having found nothing, went back to Jerusalem.

²¹ When they had gone, the men climbed out of the storage-well and went to warn King David. 'Set out!' they told David. 'Cross the water quickly, for Ahithophel has given such and such advice against you!' ²² So David and all the troops with him set off and crossed the Jordan. By dawn no one was left, all had crossed the Jordan.

²³ When Ahithophel saw that his advice had not been followed, he saddled his donkey and set off and went home to his own town. Then, having set his house in order, he hanged himself. He was buried in his father's tomb.

Absalom crosses the Jordan; David at Mahanaim

²⁴ David had reached Mahanaim by the time that Absalom crossed the Jordan with all the men of Israel. ²⁵ Absalom had put Amasa in command of the army in place of Joab. This Amasa was the son of a man called Ithra the Ishmaelite, who had married Abigail, daughter of Jesse and sister of Zeruiah, mother of Joab. ²⁶ Israel and Absalom pitched their camp in the territory of Gilead.

²⁷ When David reached Mahanaim, Shobi son of Nahash from Rabbah-of-the-Ammonites, Machir son of Ammiel from Lo-Debar, and Barzillai the Gileadite from Rogelim ²⁸ brought bedding, rugs, bowls and crockery; and wheat, barley, meal, roasted grain, beans, lentils, ²⁹ honey, curds and cows' cheese and sheep's cheese, which they presented to David and the people with him for them to eat. 'The army', they said, 'must have been hungry, tired and thirsty in the desert.'

Defeat of Absalom's party

18 David reviewed the troops who were with him and appointed commanders of thousands and commanders of hundreds to lead them. ² David divided the army into three groups, one under the command of Joab, another under the command of Abishai son of Zeruiah and brother of Joab, and the third under the command of Ittai the Gittite. David then said to the troops, 'I shall take the field in person with you.' ³ But the troops replied, 'You are not to take the field. No one will bother about us if we run away, they will not even bother about us if half of us are killed, but you are ten thousand times more valuable. So it is better if you stay inside the town, in case we need reinforcements.' ⁴ David said, 'I will do what you think best.' And the king stood be-

side the gate as the troops marched out by their hundreds and their thousands. ⁵The king gave orders to Joab, Abishai and Ittai, 'For my sake, treat young Absalom gently!' And the troops all heard the king give all the commanders these orders about Absalom. ⁶So the troops marched out into the open to engage Israel, and the battle took place in the Forest of Ephraim. ⁷There, the army of Israel was beaten by David's retainers; it was a great defeat that day, with twenty thousand casualties. ⁸The fighting spread throughout the region and that day the forest claimed more victims than the sword.

Death of Absalom

⁹Absalom happened to run into some of David's guards. Absalom was riding his mule and the mule passed under the thick branches of a great oak. Absalom's head got caught in the oak and he was left hanging between heaven and earth, while the mule he was riding went on. ¹⁰Someone saw this and reported to Joab, 'I have just seen Absalom hanging from an oak.' ¹¹Joab said to the man who had informed him, 'If you saw him, why did you not strike him to the ground then and there? I would have made it my business to give you ten silver shekels and a belt!' ¹²The man replied to Joab, 'Even if I could feel the weight of a thousand silver shekels in my hand, I would not lift my hand against the king's son. In our own hearing, the king gave you and Abishai and Ittai these orders, "For my sake, spare young Absalom." ¹³Even if I had deceived myself, nothing stays hidden from the king and you would have dissociated yourself from me.' ¹⁴Joab then said, 'I cannot waste time arguing with you!' And, taking three darts in his hand, he planted them in Absalom's heart, while he was still alive, deep in the oak-tree. ¹⁵Ten soldiers, Joab's armour-bearers, then came in close, struck Absalom and killed him.

¹⁶Joab then had the trumpet sounded, and the troops left off pursuing Israel, since Joab held the troops back. ¹⁷They took Absalom, flung him into a deep pit in the forest and raised a huge cairn over him. All the Israelites had fled, dispersing to their homes.

¹⁸Now, during his lifetime, Absalom had made and erected a pillar to himself, which is in the Valley of the King. 'I have no son', he said, 'to preserve the memory of my name.' He gave his own name to the pillar, and today it is still called Absalom's Monument.

The news is brought to David

¹⁹Ahimaaz son of Zadok said, 'Let me run and tell the king the good news that Yahweh has vindicated his cause by ridding him of his enemies.' ²⁰But Joab said, 'Today you would be no bearer of good news, some other day you may be; but today you would not be bringing good news, since the king's son is dead.' ²¹Joab then said to the Cushite, 'Go and tell the king what you have seen.' The Cushite prostrated himself to Joab and ran off. ²²But Ahimaaz son of Zadok persisted. 'Come what may,' he said to Joab, 'please let me run after the Cushite.' 'My son,' Joab said, 'why run? You will get no reward for your news.' ²³But he replied, 'Come what may, let me run!' and Joab said 'Run, then!' So Ahimaaz ran off along the road through the Plain, outrunning the Cushite.

²⁴David was sitting between the two gates. The sentry, having gone up to the roof of the gate, looked out from the ramparts and saw a man running alone. ²⁵The sentry called down to the king and told him. The king said, 'If he is alone, he is bringing good news.' ²⁶As the man drew steadily nearer, the lookout man saw another man running, and the sentry above the gate shouted, 'Here comes another man, running alone!' David said, 'He too is a bearer of good news.' ²⁷The sentry said, 'I recognise the way the first man runs; Ahimaaz son of Zadok runs like that.' 'He is a good man', said the king, 'and comes with good news.'

²⁸Ahimaaz went up to the king. 'All hail!' he said, prostrating himself on the ground before the king. 'Blessed be Yahweh your God',

he said, 'who has handed over the men who rebelled against my lord the king!' ²⁹'Is all well with young Absalom?' the king asked. Ahimaaz replied, 'I saw a great commotion when Joab, the king's servant, sent your servant off, but I do not know what it was.' ³⁰The king said, 'Go and stand over there.' He stood to one side and waited.

³¹Then the Cushite arrived. 'Good news for my lord the king!' the Cushite shouted. 'Today Yahweh has vindicated your cause, by ridding you of all who had risen up against you.' ³²'Is all well with young Absalom?' the king asked the Cushite. 'May the enemies of my lord the king', the Cushite answered, 'and all who rise up to harm you, share the fate of that young man!'

David mourns for Absalom

19 The king shuddered. He went up to the room over the gate and burst into tears; and, as he wept, he kept saying, 'Oh, my son Absalom! My son! My son Absalom! If only I had died instead of you! Oh, Absalom my son, my son!' ²Word was brought to Joab, 'The king is weeping and mourning for Absalom.' ³And for the entire army that day, victory was turned to mourning, the troops having learnt that the king was grieving for his son. ⁴And that day the troops came furtively back into town, like troops creeping shamefacedly away when deserting in battle. ⁵The king had covered his face and kept crying aloud, 'My son Absalom! Oh, Absalom my son, my son!'

⁶Joab went inside to the king and said, 'Today you have made all your servants feel ashamed—today, when they have saved your life, the lives of your sons and daughters, the lives of your wives and the lives of your concubines!—because you love those who hate you and hate those who love you. ⁷Today you have made it plain that commanders and soldiers mean nothing to you—for today I can see that you would be content if we were all dead, provided that Absalom was alive! ⁸Now get up, come out and reassure your soldiers; for if you do not come out, I swear by Yahweh, not one

man will stay with you tonight; and this will be a worse misfortune for you than anything that has happened to you from your youth until now!' ⁹The king got up and took his seat at the gate. An announcement was made to the whole army: 'The king is sitting at the gate.' And the whole army assembled in front of the king.

Preparations for David's return

¹⁰Israel had fled, dispersing to their homes. Throughout the tribes of Israel all was dissension and people began saying, 'The king, having freed us from the clutches of our enemies, having saved us from the clutches of the Philistines, has himself had to flee the country to escape from Absalom; ¹¹and now Absalom, whom we had anointed to reign over us, has died in battle. Why does no one suggest that the king should be brought back?'

¹²bWhat was being said throughout Israel reached the king. ¹²ªKing David then sent word to the priests Zadok and Abiathar, 'Say to the elders of Judah, "Why should you be the last to bring the king home? ¹³You are my brothers, you are my own flesh and bone: why should you be the last to bring the king back?" ¹⁴And say to Amasa, "Are you not my own flesh and bone? May God bring unnameable ills on me and worse ills, too, if you do not become my permanent army commander instead of Joab!" ' ¹⁵Thus he rallied the hearts of the men of Judah to a man and, as a result, they sent word to the king, 'Come back, you and all who serve you.'

Episodes connected with David's return: Shimei

¹⁶So the king started home and reached the Jordan. Judah, coming to meet the king to escort him across the Jordan, had arrived at Gilgal. ¹⁷Shimei son of Gera, the Benjaminite of Bahurim, hurried down with the men of Judah to meet King David. ¹⁸With him were a thousand men from Benjamin. Ziba, servant of the House of Saul, with his fifteen sons and twenty servants, arrived at the Jordan before

the king ¹⁹and worked manfully ferrying the king's family across and doing whatever he required.

While the king was crossing the Jordan, Shimei son of Gera fell at the king's feet ²⁰and said to the king, 'I hope my lord does not regard me as guilty of a crime! Forget about the wrong your servant did on the day my lord the king left Jerusalem. Let my lord not hold my guilt against me. ²¹For your servant is aware of having sinned, and that is why I have come today—the first member of the whole House of Joseph to come down to meet my lord the king.'

²²At this, Abishai son of Zeruiah spoke up and said, 'Does Shimei not deserve death for having cursed Yahweh's anointed?' ²³To which David replied, 'What concern is my business to you, sons of Zeruiah, that you should oppose my wishes today? Could anyone be put to death in Israel today? Today I know for sure that I am king of Israel?' ²⁴'Your life is spared,' the king said. And the king gave him his oath.

Meribbaal

²⁵Meribbaal son of Saul also went down to meet the king. He had not cared for his feet or hands, he had not trimmed his moustache or washed his clothes from the day of the king's departure till the day of his peaceful return. ²⁶When he arrived from Jerusalem to greet the king, the king asked him, 'Why did you not come with me, Meribbaal?' ²⁷'My lord king,' he replied, 'my retainer deceived me. Your servant said to him, "Saddle the donkey for me to ride, so that I can go with the king," your servant being lame. ²⁸He has slandered your servant to my lord the king. My lord the king, however, is like the Angel of God, so do as you think right. ²⁹My father's entire family deserved no better than death from my lord the king, and yet you admitted your servant to the ranks of those who eat at your table. What right have I to make any further appeal to the king?' ³⁰The king said, 'You need say no more. I rule that you and Ziba divide the prop-

erty between you.' ³¹'Let him take it all,' Meribbaal said to the king, 'since my lord the king has come back home in peace!'

Barzillai

³²Barzillai the Gileadite had come down from Rogelim and accompanied the king towards the Jordan, intending to take leave of him at the Jordan. ³³Barzillai was a man of great age; he was eighty years old. He had kept the king in provisions during his stay at Mahanaim, being a very wealthy man. ³⁴'Come with me', the king said to Barzillai, 'and I will provide for you at my side in Jerusalem.' ³⁵Barzillai replied to the king, 'How many years have I left to live, for me to go up to Jerusalem with the king? ³⁶I am now eighty years old; can I tell the good from the bad? Has your servant any taste for his food and drink? Can I still hear the voices of men and women singers? Why should your servant be a further burden to my lord the king? ³⁷Your servant will go a little way across the Jordan with the king; but why should the king reward me so generously for that? ³⁸Please allow your servant to go home again, so that I can die in my own town near the grave of my father and mother. But here is your servant Chimham; let him go with my lord the king; treat him as you think right.' ³⁹The king said, 'Let Chimham come along with me then; I shall do whatever you wish for him, and anything you request I shall do for your sake.' ⁴⁰The people then all crossed the Jordan, and the king, having crossed, kissed Barzillai and blessed him, and the latter went home.

Judah and Israel dispute over the king

⁴¹The king went on to Gilgal and Chimham went with him. All the people of Judah accompanied the king, and also half the people of Israel. ⁴²All the men of Israel then came to the king. 'Why', they asked the king, 'have our brothers, the men of Judah, carried you off and brought the king and his family across the Jordan, and all David's men with him?' ⁴³All the men of Judah retorted to the men of Israel,

'Because the king is more closely related to us. Why do you take offence at this? Have we been eating at the king's expense? Have we taken any position for ourselves?' ⁴⁴The men of Israel replied to the men of Judah, 'We have ten shares in the king and, what is more, we are your elder brothers, so why have you slighted us? Were we not the first to suggest bringing back our king?' The men of Judah's words were even more intemperate than those of the men of Israel.

Sheba's revolt

20 Now there happened to be a scoundrel there called Sheba son of Bichri, a Benjaminite, who sounded the trumpet and shouted:

> We have no share in David,
> we have no heritage in the son of Jesse.
> Every man to his tents, O Israel!

²At this all the men of Israel deserted David and followed Sheba son of Bichri. But the men of Judah stuck close to their king, from the Jordan all the way to Jerusalem. ³David returned to his palace in Jerusalem. The king took the ten concubines, whom he had left to look after the palace, and put them under guard. He provided for their upkeep but never went near them again; they were shut away until the day they died, widows, as it were, of a living man.

Assassination of Amasa

⁴The king said to Amasa, 'Summon me the men of Judah and be here yourself within three days.' ⁵Amasa went off to summon Judah, but he took longer than the time fixed by David. ⁶David then said to Abishai, 'Sheba son of Bichri is now in a position to do us more damage even than Absalom. Take your master's retainers and be after him, before he can reach any fortified towns and elude us.' ⁷Joab, the Cherethites, the Pelethites and all the champions took the field under Abishai, setting off from Jerusalem in pursuit of Sheba

son of Bichri. ⁸They were near the great stone at Gibeon when Amasa met them, coming the other way. Joab was wearing his uniform, over which he had buckled on a sword hanging from his waist in its scabbard; the sword came out and fell. ⁹Joab said to Amasa, 'Are you well, brother?' and, with his right hand, took Amasa by the beard to kiss him. ¹⁰Amasa paid no attention to the sword, which Joab had now picked up, and Joab struck him with it in the belly, spilling his entrails all over the ground. He did not need to strike a second blow; and Amasa died, while Joab and Abishai hurried on in pursuit of Sheba son of Bichri.

¹¹One of Joab's men stood on guard beside Amasa, shouting, 'Whoever is on Joab's side, whoever is for David, follow Joab!' ¹²Amasa meanwhile lay wallowing in his blood in the middle of the road. Seeing that everyone was stopping, the man dragged Amasa off the road into the field and threw a cloak over him, having realised that everyone passing would stop. ¹³Once Amasa had been taken off the road, the men all carried on, following Joab in pursuit of Sheba son of Bichri.

End of the revolt

¹⁴Sheba crossed all the tribes of Israel as far as Abel Beth-Maacah, and the Bichrites all . . . They formed up and followed him. ¹⁵Laying siege to him in Abel Beth-Maacah, they threw up a ramp against the outer wall of the town, ¹⁶while the whole army accompanying Joab undermined the wall to bring it down. A quick-witted woman shouted from the town, 'Listen! ¹⁷Listen! Say to Joab, "Come here, I want to speak to you." ' He came forward, and the woman said, 'Are you Joab?' 'I am', he replied. She said, 'Listen to what your servant says.' 'I am listening,' he replied. ¹⁸She then spoke as follows, 'In olden days people used to say, "Abel and Dan are where you should enquire ¹⁹whether a tradition established by the faithful of Israel has finally died out." And yet you are trying to destroy a town, a metropolis of Israel. Why do you want to devour Yahweh's heritage?' ²⁰'The last thing I want to

do', said Joab, 'is either to devour or to destroy. 21 This is not the issue; a man from the highlands of Ephraim, called Sheba son of Bichri, has revolted against the king, against David. Hand that one man over and I will raise the siege of the town.' 'Very well,' the woman said to Joab, 'his head will be thrown over the wall to you.' 22 The woman went and spoke to all the people as her wisdom dictated. They cut off the head of Sheba son of Bichri and threw it down to Joab. He had the trumpet sounded and they withdrew from the town and all went home, while Joab himself went back to the king in Jerusalem.

David's principal officials a

23 Joab commanded the whole army; Benaiah son of Jehoiada commanded the Cherethites and Pelethites; 24 Adoram was in charge of forced labour; Jehoshaphat son of Ahilud was herald; 25 Shiya was secretary; Zadok and Abiathar were priests; 26 also: Ira the Jairite was David's priest.

The great famine and the execution of Saul's descendants a

21 In the days of David there was a famine which lasted for three years on end. David consulted Yahweh, and Yahweh said, 'Saul and his family have incurred blood-guilt, by putting the Gibeonites to death.' 2 Then the king summoned the Gibeonites and said—now, the Gibeonites were not Israelites, but were a remnant of the Amorites, to whom the Israelites had bound themselves by oath; Saul, however, in his zeal for the Israelites and for Judah, had done his best to exterminate them—hence David said to the Gibeonites, 3 'What can I do for you? How can I make amends, so that you will call a blessing down on Yahweh's heritage?' 4 The Gibeonites replied, 'Our quarrel with Saul and his family cannot be settled for silver or gold, nor by putting to death one man in Israel.' David said, 'Say what you want and I will do it for you.' 5 Then they replied to the king, 'The man who

dismembered us and planned to annihilate us, so that we should not exist anywhere in Israelite territory—6 we want seven of his descendants handed over to us; and we shall dismember them before Yahweh at Gibeon on Yahweh's hill.' 'I shall hand them over,' said the king. 7 The king, however, spared Meribbaal son of Jonathan, son of Saul, on account of the oath by Yahweh binding them together, binding David and Jonathan son of Saul. 8 The king took the two sons born to Saul by Rizpah daughter of Aiah: Armoni and Meribbaal; and the five sons borne by Merab daughter of Saul to Adriel son of Barzillai, of Meholah. 9 He handed these over to the Gibeonites who dismembered them before Yahweh on the hill. The seven of them perished together; they were put to death in the first days of the harvest, at the beginning of the barley harvest.

10 Rizpah daughter of Aiah, wearing sacking and spreading some out for herself on the rock, from the beginning of the barley harvest until the rain fell on them from heaven, kept the birds of the sky away from them in the daytime, and the wild animals away at night. 11 David was told of what Saul's concubine, Rizpah daughter of Aiah, had done.

12 David went and recovered the bones of Saul and his son Jonathan from the notables of Jabesh in Gilead. The latter had stolen them from the square in Beth-Shean, where the Philistines had hung them, when the Philistines had defeated Saul at Gilboa. 13 David fetched the bones of Saul and his son Jonathan. The bones of the men who had been dismembered were collected 14 and these, with the bones of Saul and his son Jonathan, were buried in the territory of Benjamin, at Zela, in the tomb of Saul's father, Kish. The king's orders were carried out to the letter and after that, God took pity on the country.

20a = 8:16–18.

21a Chh. 21–24 interrupt the succession narrative with 6 appendices in balancing pairs: famine and plague (21:1–14; 24), military exploits (21:15–22; 23:8–39), hymns of David (22; 23:1–7).

Various exploits against the Philistines

15 Once again the Philistines made war on Israel. David went down with his retainers; they fought the Philistines and David began to tire. 16 There was a champion, one of the sons of Rapha. His spear weighed three hundred shekels of bronze; he was wearing a new sword and was confident of killing David. 17 Abishai son of Zeruiah came to his rescue, however, attacking the Philistine and killing him. Then it was that David's men swore the following oath to him, 'You are never to go into battle with us again, in case you should extinguish the lamp of Israel!'

18 After this, war with the Philistines broke out again at Gob. This was when Sibbecai of Hushah killed Saph, one of the sons of Rapha.

19 Again, war with the Philistines broke out at Gob, and Elhanan son of Jair, of Bethlehem, killed Goliath of Gath, the shaft of whose spear was like a weaver's beam.

20 There was further warfare at Gath, where there was a man of huge stature with six fingers on each hand and six toes on each foot, twenty-four in all. He too was a son of Rapha. 21 When he defied Israel, Jonathan son of Shimea, brother of David cut him down.

22 These four were sons of Rapha in Gath and fell at the hands of David and his retainers.

A hymn of victory[a]

22 David addressed the words of this song to Yahweh, when Yahweh had delivered him from the clutches of all his enemies and from the clutches of Saul. 2 He said:

Yahweh is my rock and my fortress,
3 my deliverer is my God.
I take refuge in him, my rock,
my shield, my saving strength,
my stronghold, my place of refuge.

My Saviour, you have saved me from
violence;
4 I call to Yahweh, who is worthy of praise,
and I am saved from my foes.

5 With Death's breakers closing in on me,
Belial's torrents ready to swallow me,
6 Sheol's snares on every side of me,
Death's traps lying ahead of me,

7 I called to Yahweh in my anguish,
I cried for help to my God,
from his Temple he heard my voice,
my cry came to his ears!

8 Then the earth quaked and rocked,
the heavens' foundations shuddered,
they quaked at his blazing anger.
9 Smoke rose from his nostrils,
from his mouth devouring fire
(coals were kindled at it).

10 He parted the heavens and came down,
a storm-cloud underneath his feet;
11 riding one of the winged creatures, he
flew,
soaring on the wings of the wind.

12 He wrapped himself in darkness,
his pavilion dark waters and dense
cloud.
13 A brightness lit up before him,
hail and blazing fire.

14 Yahweh thundered from the heavens,
the Most High made his voice heard.
15 He shot his arrows and scattered them,
his lightning flashed and routed them.

16 The very springs of ocean were exposed,
the world's foundations were laid bare,
at the roaring of Yahweh,
at the blast of breath from his nostrils!

17 He reached down from on high, snatched
me up,
pulled me from the watery depths,
18 rescued me from my mighty foe,
from my enemies who were stronger
than I.

22a = Ps 18.

19 They assailed me on my day of disaster,
  but Yahweh was there to support me,
20 he freed me, set me at large,
  he rescued me, because he loves me.

21 Yahweh rewards me for my uprightness,
  as my hands are pure so he repays me,
22 since I have kept the ways of Yahweh,
  and not fallen away from my God.

23 His judgements are all before me,
  his statutes I have not put away from me;
24 I am blameless before him,
  I keep myself clear of evil.

25 Hence Yahweh repaid me for acting
    uprightly
  because he could see I was pure.
26 Faithful you are to the faithful,
  blameless with the blameless,

27 sincere to the sincere
  but cunning to the crafty,
28 you save a people that is humble
  and humiliate those with haughty
    looks.

29 Yahweh, you yourself are my lamp,
  my God lights up my darkness;
30 with you I storm the rampart
  with my God I can scale any wall.

31 This God, his way is blameless;
  the word of Yahweh is refined in the
    furnace,
  for he alone is the shield
  of all who take refuge in him.

32 For who is God but Yahweh,
  who is a rock but our God:
33 this God who girds me with strength,
  who makes my way free from blame,

34 who makes me as swift as a deer
  and sets me firmly on the heights,
35 who trains my hands for battle
  my arms to bend a bow of bronze.

36 You give me your invincible shield,
  you never cease to listen to me,
37 you give me the strides of a giant,
  give me ankles that never weaken—

38 I pursue my enemies and exterminate
    them,
  not turning back till they are annihilated;
39 I strike them down, and they cannot rise,
  they fall, they are under my feet.

40 You have girded me with strength for the
    fight,
  bent down my assailants beneath me,
41 made my enemies retreat before me;
  and those who hate me I destroy.

42 They cry out, there is no one to save,
  to Yahweh, but no answer comes.
43 I crumble them like the dust of the
    squares,
  trample them like the mud of the
    streets.

44 You free me from the quarrels of my
    people,
  you place me at the head of the nations,
  a people I did not know are now my
    servants,

45 foreigners come wooing my favour,
  no sooner do they hear than they
    obey me,
46 foreigners grow faint of heart,
  they come trembling out of their
    fastnesses.

47 Life to Yahweh! Blessed be my rock!
  Exalted be the God of my salvation,
48 the God who gives me vengeance
  and crushes the peoples under me,

49 who takes me away from my enemies.
  You lift me high above those who attack
    me,
  you deliver me from the man of
    violence.

50 For this I will praise you, Yahweh, among
the nations,
and sing praise to your name.
51 He saves his king, time after time,
displays faithful love for his anointed,
for David and his heirs for ever.

Last words of David

23 These are the last words of David:

Thus speaks David son of Jesse,
thus speaks the man raised to eminence,
the anointed of the God of Jacob,
the singer of the songs of Israel:

2 The spirit of Yahweh speaks through me,
his word is on my tongue;
3 the God of Jacob has spoken,
the Rock of Israel has said to me:

He whose rule is upright on earth,
who rules in the fear of God,
4 is like the morning light at sunrise
(on a cloudless morning)
making the grass of the earth sparkle after
rain.

5 Yes, my House stands firm with God:
he has made an eternal covenant
with me,
all in order, well assured;
does he not bring to fruition my every
victory and desire?

6 But men of Belial he rejects like
thorns,
for these are never taken up in the
hand:
7 no one touches them
except with a pitchfork or spear-shaft,
and then only to burn them to nothing!

David's champions

8 These are the names of David's champions:
Ishbaal the Hachmonite leader of the Three; it
was he who brandished his spear over eight
hundred men whom he had killed at one time.

9 Next, there was Eleazar son of Dodo, the
Ahohite, one of the three champions. He was
with David at Pas-Dammim when the Philistines mustered for battle there and the men of
Israel had disbanded. 10 But he stood his
ground and cut down the Philistines until his
hand was so stiff that he could not let go of the
sword. Yahweh brought about a great victory
that day, and the people rallied behind him, although only to plunder. 11 Next, there was
Shamma son of Elah, the Hararite. The Philistines had mustered at Lehi. There was a field
full of lentils there; the people fled from the
Philistines, 12 but he took his stand in the middle of the field, held it, and cut down the Philistines; and Yahweh brought about a great victory.

13 Three members of the Thirty went down
at the beginning of the harvest and came to
David at the Cave of Adullam while a company of Philistines was encamped in the Valley of the Rephaim. 14 David was then in
the stronghold, and there was a Philistine garrison in Bethlehem. 15 Longingly David said,
'If only someone would fetch me a drink of
water from the well that stands by the gate at
Bethlehem!' 16 At this, the three champions,
forcing their way through the Philistine camp,
drew water from the well that stands by the
gate of Bethlehem and, taking it away, presented it to David. He, however, would not
drink any of it, but poured it out as a libation
to Yahweh. 17 'Yahweh preserve me', he said,
'from doing such a thing! This is the blood of
men who went at risk of their lives.' That was
why he would not drink. Such were the deeds
of these three champions.

18 Abishai, brother of Joab and son of
Zeruiah, was leader of the Thirty. It was he
who brandished his spear over three hundred
men whom he had killed, winning himself a
name among the Thirty. 19 He was a most illustrious member of the Thirty and became
their captain, but he was not equal to the
Three.

20 Benaiah of Kabzeel was the son of Jehoiada and hero of many exploits. He it was

who slaughtered two formidable Moabites and, one snowy day, climbed down and slaughtered the lion in the storage-well. [21] He also slaughtered an Egyptian of great stature. The Egyptian was armed with a spear, but he took him on with a staff, tore the spear from the Egyptian's hand and killed the man with it. [22] Such were the exploits of Benaiah son of Jehoiada, winning him a name among the thirty champions. [23] He was a most illustrious member of the Thirty, but he was not equal to the Three. David put him in command of his bodyguard.

[24] Asahel brother of Joab was one of the
    Thirty;
    Elhanan son of Dodo, of Bethlehem;
[25] Shammah of Harod;
    Elika of Harod;
[26] Helez of Beth-Pelet;
    Ira son of Ikkesh, of Tekoa;
[27] Abiezer of Anathoth;
    Sibbecai of Hushah;
[28] Zalmon of Ahoh;
    Maharai of Netophah;
[29] Heled son of Baanah, of Netophah;
    Ittai son of Ribai, of Gibeah in
        Benjamin;
[30] Benaiah of Pirathon;
    Hiddai of the Torrents of Gaash;
[31] Abibaal of Beth-ha-Arabah;
    Azmaveth of Bahurim;
[32] Eliahba of Shaalbon;
    Jashen of Gimzo;
    Jonathan [33] son of Shammah, of Harar;
    Ahiam son of Sharar, of Harar;
[34] Eliphelet son of Ahasbai, of Beth-
        Maacah;
    Eliam son of Ahithophel, of Gilo;
[35] Hezro of Carmel;
    Paarai of Arab;
[36] Igal son of Nathan, of Zobah;
    Bani the Gadite;
[37] Zelek the Ammonite;
    Naharai of Beeroth squire to Joab, son of
        Zeruiah;
[38] Ira of Jattir;

Gareb of Jattir;
[39] Uriah the Hittite—

thirty-seven in all.

The census

24 Again, Yahweh's anger was aroused against Israel, and he incited David against them. 'Go,' he said, 'take a census of Israel and Judah.' [2] The king said to Joab and the senior army officers who were with him, 'Now, go through all the tribes of Israel from Dan to Beersheba, and take a census of the people; I wish to know the size of the population.' [3] Joab said to the king, 'May Yahweh your God multiply the people a hundred times—however many there are—while my lord the king still has eyes to see it, but why should my lord the king be set on this?' [4] The king nonetheless enforced his order on Joab and the senior officers, and Joab and the senior officers left the king's presence, to take a census of the people of Israel.

[5] They crossed the Jordan and made a start with Aroer and the town in the middle of the valley, then moved on to the Gadites and to Jazer. [6] They then went to Gilead and the territory of the Hittites, to Kadesh; they then went to Dan and from Dan cut across to Sidon. [7] They then went to the fortress of Tyre and to all the towns of the Hittites and Canaanites ending up in the Negeb of Judah at Beersheba. [8] Having travelled throughout the country, after nine months and twenty days they returned to Jerusalem.

[9] Joab gave the king the census results for the people; Israel had eight hundred thousand fighting men who could wield a sword, and Judah five hundred thousand.

The pestilence; God's forgiveness

[10] But afterwards David's heart misgave him for having taken a census of the people. David then said to Yahweh, 'I have committed a grave sin by doing this. But now, Yahweh, I beg you to forgive your servant for this fault, for I have acted very foolishly.' [11] When, how-

ever, David got up next morning, the following message had come from Yahweh to the prophet Gad, David's seer, 12'Go and say to David, "Yahweh says this: I offer you three things; choose which one of them I am to inflict on you."' 13So Gad went to David and said, 'Which do you prefer: to have three years of famine befall your country; to flee for three months before a pursuing army; or to have three days of epidemic in your country? Now think, and decide how I am to answer him who sends me.' 14David said to Gad, 'I am very apprehensive . . . Better to fall into Yahweh's hands, since his mercies are great, than to fall into the hands of men!' 15So David chose the epidemic.

It was the time of the wheat harvest. So Yahweh unleashed an epidemic on Israel from that morning until the time determined; plague ravaged the people and, of the people from Dan to Beersheba, seventy thousand died. 16But when the angel stretched his hand towards Jerusalem to destroy it, Yahweh felt sorry about the calamity and said to the angel who was destroying the people, 'Enough now! Hold your hand!' The angel of Yahweh was standing by the threshing-floor of Araunah the Jebusite. 17When David saw the angel who was ravaging the people, he said to Yahweh, 'I was the one who sinned. I was the one who acted wrongly. But these, the flock, what have they done? Let your hand lie heavy on me and on my family!'

The building of an altar

18Gad went to David that day and said, 'Go up and raise an altar to Yahweh on the threshing-floor of Araunah the Jebusite.' 19So, at Gad's bidding, David went up, as Yahweh had ordered. 20When Araunah looked up and saw the king and his retinue advancing towards him—Araunah was threshing the wheat—Araunah came forward and prostrated himself on the ground at the king's feet. 21'Why has my lord the king come to his servant?' Araunah asked. David replied, 'To buy the threshing-floor from you, to build an altar to Yahweh, so that the plague may be lifted from the people.' 22Araunah said to David, 'Let my lord the king take it and make what offerings he thinks fit. Here are the oxen for the burnt offering, the threshing-sleds and the oxen's yokes for the wood. 23My lord the king's servant will give the king everything. And', Araunah said to the king, 'may Yahweh your God accept what you offer!'

24'No,' said the king to Araunah, 'I shall give you a price for it; I will not offer Yahweh my God burnt offerings which have cost me nothing.' David bought the threshing-floor and the oxen for fifty shekels of silver. 25David built an altar to Yahweh and offered burnt offerings and communion sacrifices. Yahweh then took pity on the country and the plague was lifted from Israel.

Last days of David and activities of Adonijah

1 King David was now a very old man, and though wrapped in bedclothes he could not keep warm. ²So his servants said to him, 'Let us find a young girl for my lord the king, to wait on the king and look after him; she will lie close beside you and this will keep my lord the king warm.' ³Having searched for a beautiful girl throughout the territory of Israel, they found Abishag of Shunem and brought her to the king. ⁴The girl was very beautiful. She looked after the king and waited on him but the king did not have intercourse with her. ⁵Now Adonijah son of Haggith was growing pretentious and saying, 'I shall be king!' Accordingly, he procured a chariot and team with fifty guards to run ahead of him. ⁶Never once in his life had his father crossed him by saying, 'Why are you behaving like that?' He was very handsome too; his mother had given birth to him after Absalom. ⁷He conferred with Joab son of Zeruiah and with the priest Abiathar, who both rallied to Adonijah's cause; ⁸but neither Zadok the priest, nor Benaiah son of Jehoiada, nor the prophet Nathan, nor Shimei and Rei, nor David's champions, supported Adonijah.

⁹One day when Adonijah was sacrificing sheep, oxen and fattened calves at the Sliding Stone which is beside the Fuller's Spring, he invited all his brothers, the royal princes, and all the men of Judah in the king's service; ¹⁰but he did not invite the prophet Nathan, or Benaiah, or the champions, or his brother Solomon.

The intrigues of Nathan and Bathsheba

¹¹Nathan then said to Bathsheba, Solomon's mother, 'Have you not heard that, unknown to our lord David, Adonijah son of Haggith has become king? ¹²Well, this is my advice to you if you want to save your own life and the life of your son Solomon. ¹³Go straight in to King David and say, "My lord king, did you not make your servant this promise on oath: Your son Solomon is to be king after me; he is the one who is to sit on my throne? How is it, then, that Adonijah is king?" ¹⁴And while you are still there talking to the king, I shall come in after you and confirm what you say.'

¹⁵So Bathsheba went to the king in his room (he was very old and Abishag of Shunem was in attendance on him). ¹⁶She knelt, prostrated herself before the king, and the king said, 'What do you want?' ¹⁷'My lord,' she replied, 'you swore to your servant by Yahweh your God, "Your son Solomon is to be king after me; he is the one who is to sit on my throne." ¹⁸And now here is Adonijah king, and you, my lord king, knowing nothing about it! ¹⁹He has sacrificed quantities of oxen, fattened calves and sheep, and invited all the royal princes, the priest Abiathar, and Joab the army commander; but he has not invited your servant Solomon. ²⁰Yet you are the man, my lord king, to whom all Israel looks, to tell them who is to succeed my lord the king. ²¹And when my lord the king falls asleep with his ancestors, Solomon and I shall be made to suffer for this.'

²²She was still speaking to the king when the prophet Nathan came in. ²³The king was told, 'The prophet Nathan is here'; and he came into the king's presence and prostrated himself on his face before the king. ²⁴'My lord king,' said Nathan, 'is this, then, your decree, "Adonijah is to be king after me; he is the one who is to sit on my throne"? ²⁵For he has gone

down today and sacrificed quantities of oxen, fattened calves and sheep, and invited all the royal princes, the army commanders, and the priest Abiathar; and they are there now, eating and drinking in his presence and shouting, "Long live King Adonijah!" 26 He has not, however, invited me your servant, Zadok the priest, Benaiah son of Jehoiada, or your servant Solomon. 27 Can it be that this is done with my lord the king's approval and that you have not told those loyal to you who is to succeed to the throne of my lord the king?'

Solomon is consecrated king on David's nomination

28 King David then spoke. 'Call Bathsheba to me,' he said. And she came into the king's presence and stood before him. 29 Then the king swore this oath, 'As Yahweh lives, who has delivered me from all adversity, 30 just as I swore to you by Yahweh, God of Israel, that your son Solomon should be king after me and take my place on my throne, so I shall bring it about this very day.' 31 Bathsheba knelt down, prostrated herself on her face before the king and said, 'May my lord King David live for ever!' 32 Then King David said, 'Summon Zadok the priest, the prophet Nathan and Benaiah son of Jehoiada.' So they came into the king's presence. 33 'Take the royal guard with you,' said the king, 'mount my son Solomon on my own mule and escort him down to Gihon. 34 There Zadok the priest and the prophet Nathan are to anoint him king of Israel; then sound the trumpet and shout, "Long live King Solomon!" 35 Then you are to escort him back, and he is then to assume my throne and be king in place of me, for he is the man whom I have appointed as ruler of Israel and of Judah.' 36 Benaiah son of Jehoiada answered the king. 'Amen!' he said. 'And may Yahweh, God of my lord the king, confirm it! 37 As Yahweh has been with my lord the king, so may he be with Solomon and make his throne even greater than the throne of my lord King David!'

38 Zadok the priest, the prophet Nathan,

Benaiah son of Jehoiada, and the Cherethites and Pelethites then went down; they mounted Solomon on King David's mule and escorted him to Gihon. 39 Zadok the priest took the horn of oil from the Tent and anointed Solomon. They sounded the trumpet and all the people shouted, 'Long live King Solomon!' 40 The people all escorted him back, with pipes playing and loud rejoicing and shouts to split the earth.

Adonijah is afraid

41 Adonijah and his guests, who had by then finished their meal, all heard the noise. Joab too heard the sound of the trumpet and said, 'What is that noise of uproar in the city?' 42 While he was still speaking, Jonathan son of Abiathar the priest arrived. 'Come in,' Adonijah said, 'you are an honest man, so you must be bringing good news.' 43 'The truth is,' Jonathan answered, 'our lord King David has made Solomon king. 44 With him, the king sent Zadok the priest, the prophet Nathan, Benaiah son of Jehoiada and the Cherethites and Pelethites; they mounted him on the king's mule, 45 and Zadok the priest and the prophet Nathan have anointed him king at Gihon; and they have gone back again with shouts of joy and the city is now in an uproar; that was the noise you heard. 46 What is more, Solomon is seated on the royal throne. 47 And further, the king's officers have been to congratulate our lord King David with the words, "May your God make the name of Solomon more glorious than yours, and his throne more exalted than your own!" And the king bowed down on his bed, 48 and then said, "Blessed be Yahweh, God of Israel, for setting one of my own sons on the throne while I am still alive to see it!" '

49 At this, all Adonijah's guests, taking fright, got up and made off in their several directions. 50 Adonijah, in terror of Solomon, got up and ran off to cling to the horns of the altar. 51 Solomon was told, 'You should know that Adonijah is terrified of King Solomon and is now clinging to the horns of the altar, say-

ing, "Let King Solomon first swear to me that he will not have his servant executed." '
⁵²'Should he bear himself honourably,' Solomon answered, 'not one hair of his shall fall to the ground; but if he proves difficult, he shall die.' ⁵³King Solomon then sent for him to be brought down from the altar; he came and threw himself prostrate before King Solomon; Solomon said to him, 'Go to your house.'

David's testament; his death

2 As David's life drew to its close he laid this charge on his son Solomon, ²'I am going the way of all the earth. Be strong and show yourself a man. ³Observe the injunctions of Yahweh your God, following his ways and keeping his laws, his commandments, his ordinances and his decrees, as stands written in the Law of Moses, so that you may be successful in everything you do and undertake, ⁴and that Yahweh may fulfil the promise which he made me, "If your sons are careful how they behave, and walk loyally before me with all their heart and soul, you will never want for a man on the throne of Israel."

⁵'You know too what Joab son of Zeruiah did to me, and what he did to the two commanders of the army of Israel, Abner son of Ner and Amasa son of Jether; how he murdered them, shedding the blood of war in time of peace and staining the belt round my waist and the sandals on my feet with the blood of war. ⁶You will be wise not to let his grey head go down to Sheol in peace. ⁷As regards the sons of Barzillai of Gilead, treat them with faithful love, let them be among those who eat at your table, for they were as kind to me when I was fleeing from your brother Absalom. ⁸You also have with you Shimei son of Gera, the Benjaminite from Bahurim. He called down a terrible curse on me the day I left for Mahanaim, but he came down to meet me at the Jordan and I swore to him by Yahweh that I would not put him to death. ⁹But you, you must not let him go unpunished; you are a wise man and will know how to deal with him, to bring his grey head down to Sheol in blood.'

¹⁰So David fell asleep with his ancestors and was buried in the City of David. ¹¹David was king of Israel for a period of forty years: he reigned at Hebron for seven years, and in Jerusalem for thirty-three.

The death of Adonijah

¹²Solomon then sat on the throne of David, and his sovereignty was securely established.

¹³Adonijah son of Haggith went to Bathsheba mother of Solomon. 'Do you bring peace?' she asked. He replied, 'Yes, peace.' ¹⁴Then he said, 'I have something to say to you.' 'Say on,' she replied. ¹⁵'You know', he said, 'that the kingdom should have come to me, and that all Israel expected me to be king; but the crown eluded me and fell to my brother, since it came to him from Yahweh. ¹⁶Now I have one request to make you; do not refuse me.' 'Go on,' she said. ¹⁷He went on, 'Please ask King Solomon—for he will not refuse you—to give me Abishag of Shunem in marriage.' ¹⁸'Very well,' Bathsheba replied, 'I shall speak to the king about you.' ¹⁹So Bathsheba went to King Solomon to speak to him about Adonijah; the king got up to meet her and bowed before her; he then sat down on his throne; a seat was brought for the king's mother, and she sat down on his right. ²⁰She said, 'I have one small request to make you; do not refuse me.' 'Mother,' the king replied, 'make your request, for I shall not refuse you.' ²¹'Let Abishag of Shunem', she said, 'be given in marriage to your brother Adonijah.' ²²King Solomon replied to his mother, 'And why do you request Abishag of Shunem for Adonijah? You might as well request the kingdom for him, since he is my elder brother and Abiathar the priest and Joab son of Zeruiah are on his side.' ²³And King Solomon swore by Yahweh: 'May God bring unnameable ills on me, and worse ills, too,' he said, 'if Adonijah does not pay for these words of his with his life! ²⁴As Yahweh lives who has set me securely on the throne of my father David, and who, as he promised, has given him a dynasty, Adonijah shall be put to death this very day.' ²⁵And

King Solomon commissioned Benaiah son of Jehoiada to strike him down, and that was how he died.

The fate of Abiathar and Joab

26 As for Abiathar the priest, the king said to him, 'Go to Anathoth to your estate. You deserve to die, but I am not going to put you to death now, since you carried the ark of Yahweh in the presence of my father David and shared all my father's hardships.' 27 Solomon deprived Abiathar of the priesthood of Yahweh, thus fulfilling the prophecy which Yahweh had uttered against the House of Eli at Shiloh.

28 When the news reached Joab—for Joab had lent his support to Adonijah, though he had not supported Absalom—he fled to the Tent of Yahweh and clung to the horns of the altar. 29 King Solomon was told, 'Joab has fled to the Tent of Yahweh; he is there beside the altar.' On this, Solomon sent word to Joab, 'What reason did you have for fleeing to the altar?' Joab replied, 'I was afraid of you and fled to Yahweh.' Solomon then sent Benaiah son of Jehoiada. 'Go', he said, 'and strike him down.' 30 Accordingly Benaiah went to the Tent of Yahweh. 'By order of the king,' he said, 'come out!' 'No,' he said, 'I will die here.' So Benaiah brought word back to the king, 'This is what Joab said, and the answer he gave me.' 31 'Do as he says,' the king replied. 'Strike him down and bury him, and so rid me and my family today of the innocent blood which Joab has shed. 32 Yahweh will bring his blood down on his own head, because he struck down two more upright and better men than he, and, without my father David's knowledge, put to the sword Abner son of Ner, commander of the army of Israel, and Amasa son of Jether, commander of the army of Judah. 33 May their blood come down on the head of Joab and his descendants for ever, but may David, his descendants, his dynasty, his throne, have peace for ever from Yahweh.' 34 Whereupon Benaiah son of Jehoiada went out, struck Joab down and put him to death; he was buried at his home in the desert. 35 In his place as head of the army the king appointed Benaiah son of Jehoiada and, in place of Abiathar, the priest Zadok.

The disobedience and death of Shimei

36 The king had Shimei summoned to him. 'Build yourself a house in Jerusalem,' he told him. 'You are to live there; do not leave it to go anywhere at all. 37 The day you go out and cross the ravine of the Kidron, be sure you will certainly die. Your blood will be on your own head.' 38 'That is a fair demand,' Shimei replied to the king, 'your servant will do as my lord the king orders.' And for a long time Shimei lived in Jerusalem.

39 But when three years had gone by, it happened that two of Shimei's slaves ran away to Achish son of Maacah, king of Gath; Shimei was told, 'Your slaves are in Gath.' 40 On this, Shimei got up and saddled his donkey and went to Achish at Gath to find his slaves. He went off and brought his slaves back from Gath. 41 Solomon was informed that Shimei had left Jerusalem for Gath and come back again.

42 The king had Shimei summoned to him. 'Did I not make you swear by Yahweh,' he said, 'and did I not warn you, "The day you leave to go anywhere at all, be sure you will certainly die"? To which you replied, "That is a fair demand." 43 Why did you not keep the oath to Yahweh and the order which I imposed on you?' 44 The king then said to Shimei, 'You know well all the evil you did to my father David. Yahweh is about to bring your wickedness down on your own head. 45 But may King Solomon be blessed, and may the throne of David be kept secure before Yahweh for ever!' 46 The king gave orders to Benaiah son of Jehoiada; he went out and struck Shimei down; and that was how he died. And now the kingdom was securely in Solomon's hands.

Solomon the sage

3 Solomon became the son-in-law of Pharaoh king of Egypt; he married Pharaoh's

daughter, and took her to the City of David until he could complete the building of his palace, the Temple of Yahweh and the ramparts of Jerusalem. ²The people, however, were still sacrificing on the high places, because at that time a dwelling-place for the name of Yahweh had not yet been built. ³Solomon loved Yahweh: he followed the precepts of his father David, except that he offered sacrifice and incense on the high places.

Solomon's dream at Gibeon

⁴The king went to Gibeon to sacrifice there, since that was the principal high place—Solomon presented a thousand burnt offerings on that altar. ⁵At Gibeon Yahweh appeared to Solomon in a dream during the night. God said, 'Ask what you would like me to give you.' ⁶Solomon replied, 'You showed most faithful love to your servant David, my father, when he lived his life before you in faithfulness and uprightness and integrity of heart; you have continued this most faithful love to him by allowing a son of his to sit on his throne today. ⁷Now, Yahweh my God, you have made your servant king in succession to David my father. But I am a very young man, unskilled in leadership. ⁸And here is your servant, surrounded with your people whom you have chosen, a people so numerous that its number cannot be counted or reckoned. ⁹So give your servant a heart to understand how to govern your people, how to discern between good and evil, for how could one otherwise govern such a great people as yours?' ¹⁰It pleased Yahweh that Solomon should have asked for this. ¹¹'Since you have asked for this,' God said, 'and not asked for long life for yourself or riches or the lives of your enemies but have asked for a discerning judgement for yourself, ¹²here and now I do what you ask. I give you a heart wise and shrewd as no one has had before and no one will have after you. ¹³What you have not asked I shall give you too: such riches and glory as no other king can match. ¹⁴And I shall give you a long life, if you follow my ways, keeping my laws and com-

mandments, as your father David followed them.' ¹⁵Then Solomon woke up; it had been a dream. He returned to Jerusalem and stood before the ark of the covenant of Yahweh; he presented burnt offerings and communion sacrifices and held a banquet for all those in his service.

The judgement of Solomon

¹⁶Later two prostitutes came to the king and stood before him. ¹⁷'If it please you, my lord,' one of the women said, 'this woman and I live in the same house, and while she was in the house I gave birth to a child. ¹⁸Now it happened on the third day after my delivery that this woman also gave birth to a child. We were alone together; there was no one else in the house with us; just the two of us in the house. ¹⁹Now one night this woman's son died; she overlaid him. ²⁰And in the middle of the night she got up and took my son from beside me while your servant was asleep; she took him in her arms and put her own dead son in mine. ²¹When I got up to suckle my child, there he was, dead. But in the morning I looked at him carefully, and he was not the child I had borne at all.' ²²Then the other woman spoke. 'That is not true! My son is the live one, yours is the dead one'; and the first retorted, 'That is not true! Your son is the dead one, mine is the live one.' And so they wrangled before the king. ²³'This one says,' the king observed, ' "My son is the one who is alive; your son is dead," while the other says, "That is not true! Your son is the dead one, mine is the live one." ²⁴Bring me a sword,' said the king; and a sword was brought into the king's presence. ²⁵'Cut the living child in two,' the king said, 'and give half to one, half to the other.' ²⁶At this the woman who was the mother of the living child addressed the king, for she felt acutely for her son. 'I beg you, my lord,' she said, 'let them give her the live child; on no account let them kill him!' But the other said, 'He shall belong to neither of us. Cut him in half!' ²⁷Then the king gave his decision. 'Give the live child to the first woman,' he said, 'and do not kill him.

She is his mother.' ²⁸ All Israel came to hear of the judgement which the king had pronounced and held the king in awe, recognising that he possessed divine wisdom for dispensing justice.

Solomon's high officials

4 King Solomon was king of all Israel, ²and these were his high officials:

Azariah son of Zadok, priest;
³ Elihaph and Ahijah sons of Shisha,
secretaries;
Jehoshaphat son of Ahilud, herald.
⁴ (Benaiah son of Jehoiada, commander of
the army.
Zadok and Abiathar, priests);
⁵ Azariah son of Nathan, chief
administrator;
Zabud son of Nathan, Friend of the
King;
⁶ Ahishar, master of the palace;
Eliab son of Joab, commander of the army;
Adoram son of Abda, in charge of forced
labour.

Solomon's administrators

⁷ Solomon had twelve administrators for all Israel who saw to the provisioning of the king and his household; each had to provide for one month in the year.

⁸ These are their names:
Son of Hur, in the mountain country of Ephraim.
⁹ Son of Deker, in Makaz, Shaalbim, Beth-Shemesh, Aijalon, Beth-Hanan.
¹⁰ Son of Hesed, in Arubboth; his district was Socoh and the whole territory of Hepher.
¹¹ Son of Abinadab, all the Slopes of Dor. Tabaath Solomon's daughter was his wife.
¹² Baana son of Ahilud, in Taanach and Megiddo as far as the other side of Jokmeam, and all Beth-Shean below Jezreel, from Beth-Shean as far as Abel-Meholah by Zarethan.
¹³ Son of Geber, in Ramoth-Gilead: his district was the Encampments of Jair son of Manasseh, which are in Gilead; he had the region

of Argob, which is in Bashan: sixty fortified towns, walled and with bolts of bronze.
¹⁴ Ahinadab son of Iddo, in Mahanaim.
¹⁵ Ahimaaz in Naphtali; he too married a daughter of Solomon, Basemath.
¹⁶ Baana son of Hushai, in Asher and in the highlands.
¹⁷ Jehoshaphat son of Paruah, in Issachar.
¹⁸ Shimei son of Ela, in Benjamin.
¹⁹ Geber son of Uri, in the territory of Gad, the territory of Sihon king of the Amorites and of Og king of Bashan.

In addition, there was one administrator in the country.

5 ⁷ These ᵃ administrators provided the food for Solomon and for all those who were admitted by him to the royal table, each for the period of a month; they ensured that nothing was wanting. ⁸ They also provided the barley and straw for the horses and draught animals, where required, each according to the quota demanded of him. ² The daily provisions for Solomon were: thirty measures of fine flour and sixty measures of meal, ³ten fattened oxen, twenty free-grazing oxen, one hundred sheep, besides deer and gazelles, roebucks and fattened poultry. ⁴ For he was master of all Transeuphrates—of all the kings of Transeuphrates from Tiphsah to Gaza—and he enjoyed peace on all his frontiers. ⁵ Judah and Israel lived in security, everyone under his vine and his fig tree, from Dan to Beersheba, throughout the lifetime of Solomon.

4 ²⁰ Judah and Israel were numerous, as numerous as the sand on the sea-shore; they ate and drank and were happy.

5 ¹ Solomon was overlord of all the kingdoms from the River ᵇ to the territory of the Philistines and the Egyptian border. They brought tribute and served him all his life long. ⁶ And Solomon had four thousand stalls

5a This edition follows the order of the Gk, as more logical.
5b The Euphrates.

of horses for his chariots and twelve thousand cavalrymen.

Solomon's fame

⁹God gave Solomon immense wisdom and understanding, and a heart as vast as the sand on the sea-shore. ¹⁰The wisdom of Solomon surpassed the wisdom of all the sons of the East and all the wisdom of Egypt. ¹¹He was wiser than anyone else, wiser than Ethan the Ezrahite, than the sons of Mahol, Heman, Calcol and Darda; his fame spread to all the surrounding nations. ¹²He composed three thousand proverbs, and his songs numbered a thousand and five. ¹³He could discourse on plants from the cedar in Lebanon to the hyssop growing on the wall; and he could discourse on animals and birds and reptiles and fish. ¹⁴Men from all nations came to hear Solomon's wisdom, and he received gifts from all the kings in the world, who had heard of his wisdom.

Preparations for building the Temple

¹⁵Hiram king of Tyre sent an embassy to Solomon, having learnt that he had been anointed king in succession to his father and because Hiram had always been a friend of David. ¹⁶And Solomon sent this message to Hiram, ¹⁷'You are aware that my father David was unable to build a temple for the name of Yahweh his God, on account of the wars waged on him from every side, until Yahweh put his enemies under the soles of his feet. ¹⁸But now Yahweh my God has given me peace on every side: not one enemy, no calamities. ¹⁹I propose, then, to build a temple for the name of Yahweh my God, in accordance with what Yahweh told my father David, "Your son whom I shall place on your throne to succeed you will be the man to build a temple for my name." ²⁰So now have cedars of Lebanon cut down for me; my servants will work with your servants, and I shall pay for the hire of your servants at whatever rate you fix. As you know, we have no one as skilled in felling trees as the Sidonians.' ²¹When Hiram heard what

Solomon had said, he was delighted. 'Now blessed be Yahweh,' he said, 'who has given David a wise son to rule over this great people!' ²²And Hiram sent word to Solomon, 'I have received your message. For my part, I shall supply you with all you require in the way of cedar wood and juniper. ²³Your servants will bring these down from Lebanon to the sea, and I shall have them towed by sea to any place you name; I shall discharge them there, and you will take them over. For your part, you will see to the provisioning of my household as I desire.' ²⁴So Hiram provided Solomon with all the cedar wood and juniper he wanted ²⁵while Solomon gave Hiram twenty thousand *kor* of wheat to feed his household, and twenty thousand *kor* of pure oil. Solomon gave Hiram this every year. ²⁶Yahweh gave Solomon wisdom as he had promised him; good relations persisted between Solomon and Hiram, and the two of them concluded a treaty.

²⁷King Solomon raised a levy throughout Israel for forced labour: the levy numbered thirty thousand men. ²⁸He sent these to Lebanon in relays, ten thousand a month; they spent one month in Lebanon and two months at home. Adoram was in charge of the forced labour. ²⁹Solomon also had seventy thousand porters and eighty thousand quarrymen in the mountains, ³⁰as well as the administrators, officials who supervised the work, three thousand three hundred of them in charge of the men employed in the work. ³¹At the king's orders they quarried huge stones, special stones for the laying of the temple foundations, dressed stones. ³²Solomon's workmen and Hiram's workmen and the Giblites cut and assembled the wood and stone for the building of the Temple.

The Temple building

6In the four hundred and eightieth year after the Israelites came out of Egypt, in the fourth year of Solomon's reign over Israel, in the month of Ziv, which is the second month, he began building the Temple of Yahweh.

² The temple which King Solomon built for Yahweh was sixty cubits long, twenty cubits wide and twenty-five high. ³ The portico in front of the Hekal of the Temple was twenty cubits long across the width of the Temple and ten cubits wide along the length of the Temple. ⁴ He made windows for the Temple with frames and latticework. ⁵ He also built an annex against the Temple wall, right round the Hekal and Debir. He built lateral storeys all round; ⁶ the lowest lateral storey was five cubits wide, the middle one six cubits, and the third seven cubits, for he had made the outside of the Temple wall correspondingly stepped back all round, so that the annex was not attached to the Temple walls. ⁷ (The building of the Temple was done with quarry-dressed stone; no sound of hammer or pick or any iron tool was to be heard in the Temple while it was being built.) ⁸ The entrance to the lowest storey was at the right-hand corner of the Temple; access to the middle storey was by a spiral staircase, and so from the middle storey to the third. ⁹ Having finished building the Temple, he roofed the Temple with a coffered ceiling of cedar wood. ¹⁰ Round the outside of the Temple he then built the annex which was five cubits high and was joined to the Temple by cedar-wood beams. ¹¹ And the word of Yahweh came to Solomon, ¹² 'With regard to this temple which you are now building, if you follow my statutes and obey my ordinances and faithfully follow my commandments, I shall fulfil the promise which I made about you to your father David. ¹³ And I shall make my home among the Israelites and never forsake Israel my people.'

¹⁴ Solomon finished building the Temple.

Interior furnishings; the Holy of Holies

¹⁵ He lined the inside of the Temple walls with panels of cedar wood—panelling them on the inside from the floor of the Temple to the beams of the ceiling—and laid the floor of the Temple with juniper planks. ¹⁶ The twenty cubits measured from the end of the Temple he built of cedar planks from the floor to the beams, and this part was reserved as the Debir, the Holy of Holies. ¹⁷ The Temple measured forty cubits—the Hekal—in front of the Debir. ¹⁸ There was cedar wood round the inside of the Temple, ornamentally carved with gourds and rosettes; all was cedar wood, with no stone showing. ¹⁹ In the inner part of the Temple he designed a Debir, to contain the ark of the covenant of Yahweh. ²⁰ The Debir was twenty cubits long, twenty cubits wide, and twenty high, and he overlaid it on the inside with pure gold. He made an altar of cedar wood ²¹ in front of the Debir and overlaid it with gold. ²² He overlaid the whole Temple with gold, the whole Temple entirely.

The great winged creatures

²³ In the Debir he made two great winged creatures of wild-olive wood . . . It was ten cubits high. ²⁴ One winged creature's wing was five cubits long and the other wing five cubits: ten cubits from wing tip to wing tip. ²⁵ The other winged creature also measured ten cubits; both had the same measurements and the same shape. ²⁶ The height of one was the same as the other's. ²⁷ He placed them in the middle of the inner chamber; their wings were spread out so that the wing of one touched one of the walls and the wing of the other touched the other wall, while their wings met in the middle of the chamber wing to wing. ²⁸ And he overlaid them with gold. ²⁹ All round the Temple walls he carved figures of winged creatures, palm trees and rosettes, both inside and outside. ³⁰ He overlaid the floor of the Temple with gold, both inside and outside.

The doors; the court

³¹ He made the door of the Debir with uprights of wild-olive wood, and door jambs with five indented sections, ³² and the two leaves of wild-olive wood. He carved figures of great winged creatures, palm trees and rosettes which he overlaid with gold, and he gilded winged creatures and palm trees. ³³ Similarly, he made uprights of wild-olive wood for the door of the Hekal, and door

jambs with four indented sections, 34 and the two leaves of juniper: one leaf had two ribs binding it, and the other had two ribs binding it. 35 He carved winged creatures, palm trees and rosettes, which he overlaid with gold laid evenly over the carvings.

36 He built the wall of the inner court in three courses of dressed stone and one course of cedar beams.

The date

37 In the fourth year, in the month of Ziv, the foundations of the Temple were laid; 38 in the eleventh year, in the month of Bul—that is, the eighth month—the Temple was completed exactly as it had been planned and designed. Solomon took seven years to build it.

Solomon's palace

7 As regards his palace, Solomon spent thirteen years on it before the building was completed. 2 He built the House of the Forest of Lebanon, a hundred cubits long, fifty cubits wide, and thirty cubits high, on four rows of cedar-wood pillars, 3 with lengths of cedar wood laid horizontally on the pillars. The upper part was panelled with cedar right down to the tie-beams on forty-five pillars, fifteen in each row. 4 There were three rows of window-frames, with the windows corresponding to one another at three levels. 5 All the doorways and windows were rectangular, with the windows corresponding to one another at three levels. 6 He also made the Colonnade, fifty cubits long and thirty cubits broad, with a cornice in front. 7 He also made the Hall of the Throne where he used to dispense justice, that is, the Hall of Justice; it was panelled in cedar from floor to beams. 8 His own living quarters, in the other court and inwards from the Hall, were of the same construction. And there was a house similar to this Hall for Pharaoh's daughter whom he had taken in marriage.

9 All these buildings were of special stones cut to measure, trimmed on the inner and outer sides with the saw, from the foundations to the coping— 10 the foundations were of special stones, huge stones, of ten and eight cubits, 11 and, above these, special stones, cut to measure, and cedar wood— 12 and, on the outside, the great court had three courses of dressed stone round it and one course of cedar beams; so also had the inner court of the Temple of Yahweh and the vestibule of the Temple.

Hiram, the bronzeworker

13 King Solomon sent for Hiram of Tyre; 14 he was the son of a widow of the tribe of Naphtali, but his father had been a Tyrian, a bronzeworker. He was a highly intelligent craftsman, skilled in all types of bronzework. He came to King Solomon and did all this work for him.

The bronze pillars

15 He cast the two bronze pillars; the height of one pillar was eighteen cubits, and a cord twelve cubits long gave the measurement of its girth; so also was the second pillar. 16 He made two capitals of cast bronze for the tops of the pillars; the height of one capital was five cubits, and the height of the other five cubits. 17 He made two sets of filigree to cover the moulding of the two capitals surmounting the pillars, one filigree for one capital and one filigree for the other. 18 He also made pomegranates: two rows of them round each filigree, 19b four hundred in all, 20 applied on the raised moulding behind the filigree; there were two hundred pomegranates round one capital and the same round the other capital. 19a The capitals surrounding the pillars were lily-shaped. 21 He erected the pillars in front of the portico of the Temple, he erected the right-hand pillar and named it Jachin; he erected the left-hand pillar and named it Boaz. 22 Thus, the work on the pillars was completed.

The bronze Sea

23 He made the Sea of cast metal, ten cubits from rim to rim, circular in shape and five cubits high; a cord thirty cubits long gave the measurement of its girth. 24 Under its rim and

completely encircling it were gourds surrounding the Sea; over a length of thirty cubits
the gourds were in two rows, of one and the
same casting with the rest. 25 It rested on
twelve oxen, three facing north, three facing
west, three facing south, three facing east; on
these, their hindquarters all turned inwards,
stood the Sea. 26 It was a hand's breadth in
thickness, and its rim was shaped like the rim
of a cup, lily-shaped. It could hold two thousand measures.

The wheeled stands and the bronze basins

27 He made the ten bronze stands; each stand
was four cubits long, four cubits wide, and
three high. 28 They were designed as follows;
they had an undercarriage and crosspieces to
the undercarriage. 29 On the crosspieces of the
undercarriage were lions and bulls and
winged creatures, and on top of the undercarriage was a support; under the lions and oxen
there were scrolls in the style of . . . 30 Each
stand had four bronze wheels with bronze
axles; its four feet had shoulderings under the
basin, and the shoulderings were cast . . . 31 Its
mouth measured one and a half cubits from
where the shoulderings met to the top; its
mouth was round like a stand for a vessel, and
on the mouth there were engravings too; the
crosspieces, however, were rectangular and
not round. 32 The four wheels were under the
crosspieces. The axles of the wheels were inside the stands; the height of the wheels was
one and a half cubits. 33 The wheels were designed like chariot wheels: their axles, felloes,
spokes and naves had all been cast. 34 There
were four shoulderings at the four corners of
each stand: the stand and the shoulderings
were all of a piece. 35 At the top of the stand
there was a support, circular in shape and half
a cubit high; and on top of the stand there
were lugs. The crosspieces were of a piece
with the stand. 36 On the bands he engraved
winged creatures and lions and palm leaves
. . . and scrolls right round. 37 He made the ten
stands like this: the same casting and the same
measurements for all.

38 He made ten bronze basins; each basin
held forty measures and each basin measured
four cubits, one basin to each of the ten stands.
39 He arranged the stands, five on the right-
hand side of the Temple, five on the left-hand
side of the Temple; the Sea he placed on the
right-hand side of the Temple, to the south
east.

The utensils; summary

40 Hiram made the ash containers, the scoops
and the sprinkling bowls. He finished all the
work that he did for King Solomon on the
Temple of Yahweh:

41 Two pillars; the two mouldings of the
capitals surrounding the pillars; the two sets of
filigree to cover the two mouldings of the capitals surmounting the pillars; 42 the four hundred pomegranates for the two sets of filigree—two rows of pomegranates for each set
of filigree;
43 the ten stands and the ten basins on the
stands;
44 the one Sea and the twelve oxen beneath
the Sea;
45 the ash containers, the scoops, and
sprinkling bowls.
   All these objects made by Hiram for King
Solomon for the Temple of Yahweh were of
burnished bronze. 46 He made them by the
process of sand casting, in the plain of the Jordan between Succoth and Zarethan. 47 There
were so many of them, that the weight of the
bronze was never calculated.
   48 Solomon made all the objects designed
for the Temple of Yahweh: the golden altar
and the gold table for the loaves of permanent
offering; 49 the lamp-stands, five on the right
and five on the left in front of the Debir, of
pure gold; the floral work, the lamps, the
tongs, of gold; 50 the basins, the snuffers,
the sprinkling bowls, the incense ladles and
the pans, of real gold; the door panels—for the
inner shrine—that is, the Holy of Holies—
and for the Hekal, of gold.
   51 Thus all the work done by King Solomon
for the Temple of Yahweh was completed, and

Solomon brought in the gifts which his father David had consecrated; and he had the silver, the gold and the utensils put into the treasuries of the Temple of Yahweh.

The ark is brought into the Temple

8 Solomon then summoned the elders of Israel to Jerusalem to bring the ark of the covenant of Yahweh up from the City of David, that is, Zion. ² All the men of Israel assembled round King Solomon in the month of Ethanim, at the time of the feast (that is, the seventh month). ³ When all the elders of Israel had arrived, the priests took up the ark ⁴ and the Tent of Meeting and all the sacred utensils which were in the Tent. ⁵ King Solomon and all Israel, present with him before the ark, sacrificed countless, innumerable sheep and oxen. ⁶ The priests brought the ark of the covenant of Yahweh to its place, in the Debir of the Temple, that is, in the Holy of Holies, under the wings of the winged creatures ⁷ for the winged creatures spread their wings over the place where the ark stood, forming a canopy over the ark and its shafts. ⁸ These were so long, however, that the ends of the shafts could be seen from the Holy Place in front of the Debir, though they could not be seen from outside. They are still there today. ⁹ There was nothing in the ark except the two stone tablets which Moses had placed in it at Horeb, the tablets of the covenant which Yahweh made with the Israelites when they came out of Egypt.

Yahweh takes possession of his Temple

¹⁰ Now when the priests came out of the Holy Place, the cloud filled the Temple of Yahweh, ¹¹ and because of the cloud the priests could not stay and perform their duties. For the glory of Yahweh filled the Temple of Yahweh. ¹² Then Solomon said:

Yahweh has chosen to dwell in thick cloud.
¹³ I have built you a princely dwelling, a residence for you for ever.

Solomon addresses the people

¹⁴ The king then turned round and blessed the whole assembly of Israel, while the whole assembly of Israel stood. ¹⁵ He said, 'Blessed be Yahweh, God of Israel, who has carried out by his hand what he promised with his mouth to my father David, when he said, ¹⁶ "From the day I brought my people Israel out of Egypt I chose no city, in any of the tribes of Israel, to have a temple built where my name should be; but I did choose David to rule my people Israel." ¹⁷ My father David had set his heart on building a temple for the name of Yahweh, God of Israel, ¹⁸ but Yahweh said to my father David, "You have set your heart on building a temple for my name, and in this you have done well; ¹⁹ and yet, you are not the man to build the temple; but your son, yet to be born to you, will be the one to build the temple for my name." ²⁰ Yahweh has kept the promise which he made: I have succeeded my father David and am seated on the throne of Israel, as Yahweh promised; I have built the temple for the name of Yahweh, God of Israel, ²¹ and in it I have made a place for the ark containing the covenant of Yahweh which he made with our ancestors when he brought them out of Egypt.'

Solomon's prayer for himself

²² Then, in the presence of the whole assembly of Israel, Solomon stood facing the altar of Yahweh and, stretching out his hands towards heaven, ²³ said, 'Yahweh, God of Israel, there is no god like you in heaven above or on earth beneath, as loyal to the covenant and faithful in love to your servants as long as they walk wholeheartedly in your way. ²⁴ You have kept the promise you made to your servant, my father David, as you promised him you would. Today you have carried it out by your power. ²⁵ And now, Yahweh, God of Israel, keep the promise which you made to your servant David when you said, "You will never lack for a man to sit before me on the throne of Israel, provided that your sons are careful how they

behave, walking before me as you yourself have done." 26 So now, God of Israel, let the words come true which you spoke to your servant, my father David. 27 Yet will God really live with human beings on earth? Why, the heavens, the highest of the heavens, cannot contain you. How much less this temple built by me! 28 Even so, listen favourably to the prayer and entreaty of your servant, Yahweh my God; listen to the cry and to the prayer which your servant makes to you today: 29 day and night may your eyes watch over this temple, over this place of which you have said, "My name will be there." Listen to the prayer which your servant offers in this place.

Solomon's prayer for the people

30 'Listen to the entreaty of your servant and of your people Israel; whenever they pray in this place, listen from the place where you reside in heaven; and when you hear, forgive.

31 'If someone has wronged his neighbour and a curse is laid on him to make him swear an oath here before your altar in this Temple, 32 then listen from the place where you reside in heaven and do justice between your servants: condemning the guilty one by making him suffer for his conduct, and acquitting the upright by rewarding him as his uprightness deserves.

33 'When your people Israel are defeated by the enemy because they have sinned against you, but then return to you and acknowledge your name, and pray and seek your favours in this Temple, 34 then listen from the place where you reside in heaven; forgive the sin of your people Israel, and bring them back to the country which you gave to their ancestors.

35 'When the heavens are shut and there is no rain because they have sinned against you, if they pray in this place and praise your name and, having been humbled by you, desist from their sin, 36 then listen from the place where you reside in heaven and forgive the sin of your servant and your people Israel—for you are constantly showing them the good way which they must follow—and send rain on your country, which you have given to your people as their heritage.

37 'Should there be famine in the country, or pestilence, wind-blast or mildew, locust or caterpillar; should their enemy lay siege to one of their gates; should there be any plague or any disease: 38 whatever be the prayer or entreaty of any individual aware of a particular affliction: when that person stretches out the hands towards this Temple, 39 then listen from heaven where you reside; forgive and, since you know what is in the heart, deal with each as their conduct deserves—for you alone know what is in every human heart—40 so that they may reverence you throughout their lives in the country which you gave to our ancestors.

Supplementary section

41 'Even the foreigner, not belonging to your people Israel but coming from a distant country, attracted by your name— 42 for they too will hear of your name, of your mighty hand and outstretched arm—if a foreigner comes and prays in this Temple, 43 listen from heaven where you reside, and grant all that the foreigner asks of you, so that all the peoples of the earth may acknowledge your name and, like your people Israel, revere you and know that this Temple, which I have built, bears your name.

44 'If your people go out to war against the enemy, on whatever missions you send them, and they pray to Yahweh, turning towards the city which you have chosen and towards the Temple which I have built for your name, 45 then listen from heaven to their prayer and their entreaty, and uphold their cause.

46 'When they sin against you—for there is no one who does not sin—and you are angry with them and abandon them to the enemy, and their captors carry them off to a hostile country, be it far away or near, 47 if they come to their senses in the country to which they have been taken as captives and repent and entreat you in the country of their captors, saying, "We have sinned, we have acted per-

versely and wickedly," 48 and turn back to you with all their heart and soul in the country of the enemies who have taken them captive, and pray to you, turning towards the country which you gave to their ancestors, towards the city which you have chosen and towards the Temple which I have built for your name, 49 listen to their prayer and their entreaty from the place where you reside in heaven, uphold their case, 50 forgive your people for having sinned against you and for all the crimes against you of which they have been guilty, and allow them to arouse the pity of their captors so that these may have pity on them: 51 for they are your people and your heritage whom you brought out of Egypt, that iron foundry!

Conclusion of the prayer and blessing of the people

52 'May your eyes be open to the entreaty of your servant and the entreaty of your people Israel, to listen to them, whatever they ask of you. 53 For you it was who set them apart from all the peoples of the earth to be your heritage, as you declared through your servant Moses when you brought our ancestors out of Egypt, Lord Yahweh.'

54 When Solomon had finished offering to Yahweh this whole prayer and entreaty, he rose from where he was kneeling with hands stretched out towards heaven before the altar of Yahweh, 55 and stood upright. And in a loud voice he blessed the whole assembly of Israel. 56 'Blessed be Yahweh,' he said, 'who has granted rest to his people Israel, keeping all his promises. Of all the promises of good that he made through his servant Moses, not one has failed. 57 May Yahweh our God be with us, as he was with our ancestors; may he never desert us or cast us off. 58 May he turn our hearts towards him so that we may follow all his ways and keep the commandments and laws and ordinances which he gave to our ancestors. 59 May these words of mine, of my entreaty before Yahweh, be present with Yahweh our God day and night, that he may uphold the cause of his servant and the cause of Israel his

people, as each day requires, 60 so that all the peoples of the earth may come to know that Yahweh is God indeed and that there is no other. 61 May your hearts be wholly with Yahweh our God, following his laws and keeping his commandments as at this present day.'

The sacrifices on the feast of Dedication

62 The king and all Israel with him offered sacrifice before Yahweh. 63 Solomon offered a communion sacrifice of twenty-two thousand oxen and a hundred and twenty thousand sheep to Yahweh; and thus the king and all the Israelites dedicated the Temple of Yahweh. 64 On the same day the king consecrated the middle part of the court in front of the Temple of Yahweh; for that was where he presented the burnt offerings, oblations and fatty parts of the communion sacrifices, since the bronze altar which stood before Yahweh was too small to hold the burnt offering, oblation and the fatty parts of the communion sacrifice. 65 And then Solomon and with him all Israel from the Pass of Hamath to the Torrent of Egypt—a great assembly—celebrated the feast before Yahweh our God for seven days. 66 On the eighth day he dismissed the people, who bade farewell to the king and went home joyful and happy of heart over all the goodness which Yahweh had shown to his servant and his people Israel.

Yahweh appears a second time

9 When Solomon had finished building the Temple of Yahweh, the royal palace and everything else which Solomon had wanted to do, 2 Yahweh appeared to Solomon a second time, as he had appeared to him at Gibeon. 3 Yahweh said to him, 'I have heard your prayer and the entreaty which you have before me. I consecrate this temple which you have built: I place my name there for ever; my eyes and my heart will be there always. 4 For your part, if you walk before me in innocence of heart and in honesty, like your father David, if you do everything that I command and keep my laws and my ordinances, 5 I shall make

your royal throne secure over Israel for ever, as I promised your father David when I said, "You will never lack for a man on the throne of Israel." 6 But if you turn away from me, either you or your descendants, and instead of keeping my commandments and laws which I have laid down for you, you go and serve other gods and worship them, 7 then I shall banish Israel from the country which I have given them, and shall disown this Temple which I have consecrated for my name, and Israel will be a proverb and a byword among all peoples. 8 As for this once-exalted Temple, everyone who passes by will be appalled, and they will whistle and say, "Why has Yahweh treated this country and this Temple like this?" 9 And the answer will be, "Because they deserted Yahweh their God who brought their ancestors out of Egypt, and they adopted other gods and worshipped and served them; that is why Yahweh has brought all these disasters on them." '

The bargain with Hiram

10 At the end of the twenty years that it took Solomon to erect the two buildings, the Temple of Yahweh and the royal palace 11 (Hiram king of Tyre had provided Solomon with all the cedar wood, juniper wood and gold that he wanted), King Solomon gave Hiram twenty towns in the territory of Galilee. 12 But when Hiram came from Tyre to view the towns that Solomon had given him, he was not pleased with them. 13 He said, 'What kind of towns are these you have given me, brother?' And to this day they are known as 'cabul-land'. 14 Hiram sent the king one hundred and twenty talents of gold.

Forced labour for Solomon's building programme

15 This is an account of the forced labour levied by King Solomon for building the Temple of Yahweh, his own palace, the Millo and the fortifications of Jerusalem, Hazor, Megiddo, Gezer 16 (Pharaoh king of Egypt mounted an expedition, captured Gezer, burnt it down and massacred the Canaanites living there; he then gave the town as a dowry to his daughter, Solomon's wife, 17 and Solomon rebuilt Gezer), Lower Beth-Horon, 18 Baalath, Tamar in the desert, inside the country, 19 all Solomon's storage towns owned by Solomon, all the towns for his chariots and horses, and whatever Solomon was pleased to build in Jerusalem, in the Lebanon and in all the countries under his rule. 20 All those who survived of the Amorite, Hittite, Perizzite, Hivite and Jebusite peoples, who were not Israelites— 21 their descendants still remaining in the country on whom the Israelites had not been able to enforce the curse of destruction—these Solomon levied as forced labourers, as is still the case today. 22 Solomon did not, however, impose forced labour on the Israelites; for they were soldiers, his officials, his administrators, his officers and his chariot and cavalry commanders. 23 There were five hundred and fifty officials in charge of the foremen over Solomon's work, who supervised the people employed on the work.

24 After Pharaoh's daughter had moved from the City of David up to the palace which he had built for her, he then built the Millo.

25 Three times a year Solomon presented burnt offerings and communion sacrifices on the altar which he had built for Yahweh and set his burnt offerings smoking before Yahweh.

Thus he completed the Temple.

Solomon as ship-owner

26 King Solomon equipped a fleet at Ezion-Geber, which is near Elath on the shores of the Red Sea, in Edom. 27 For this fleet Hiram sent men of his, experienced sailors, to serve with those in Solomon's service. 28 They went to Ophir and took on four hundred and twenty talents of gold, which they brought back to Solomon.

The queen of Sheba visits Solomon

10 The queen of Sheba heard of Solomon's fame and came to test him with difficult questions. 2 She arrived in Jerusalem with a

very large retinue, with camels laden with spices and an immense quantity of gold and precious stones. Having reached Solomon, she discussed with him everything that she had in mind, ³and Solomon had an answer for all her questions; not one of them was too obscure for the king to answer for her. ⁴When the queen of Sheba saw how very wise Solomon was, the palace which he had built, ⁵the food at his table, the accommodation for his officials, the organisation of his staff and the way they were dressed, his cupbearers, and the burnt offerings which he presented in the Temple of Yahweh, it left her breathless, ⁶and she said to the king, 'The report I heard in my own country about your wisdom in handling your affairs was true then! ⁷Until I came and saw for myself, I did not believe the reports, but clearly I was told less than half: for wisdom and prosperity, you surpass what was reported to me. ⁸How fortunate your wives are! How fortunate these courtiers of yours, continually in attendance on you and listening to your wisdom! ⁹Blessed be Yahweh your God who has shown you his favour by setting you on the throne of Israel! Because of Yahweh's everlasting love for Israel, he has made you king to administer law and justice.' ¹⁰And she presented the king with a hundred and twenty talents of gold and great quantities of spices and precious stones; no such wealth of spices ever came again as those which the queen of Sheba gave to King Solomon. ¹¹Similarly, Hiram's fleet, which brought the gold from Ophir, also brought back great cargoes of *almug* timber and precious stones. ¹²Of the *almug* timber the king made supports for the Temple of Yahweh and for the royal palace, and harps and lyres for the musicians; no more of this *almug* timber has since come or been seen to this day. ¹³And King Solomon, in his turn, presented the queen of Sheba with everything that she expressed a wish for, besides those presents which he gave her with a munificence worthy of King Solomon. After which, she went home to her own country, she and her servants.

Solomon's wealth

¹⁴The weight of gold received annually by Solomon amounted to six hundred and sixty-six talents of gold, ¹⁵besides what tolls and foreign trade, as well as everything the Arab kings and the provincial governors brought in. ¹⁶King Solomon made two hundred great shields of beaten gold, six hundred shekels of gold going into one shield; ¹⁷also three hundred small shields of beaten gold, three *mina* of gold going into one shield; and the king put these into the House of the Forest of Lebanon. ¹⁸The king also made a great ivory throne which he overlaid with refined gold. ¹⁹The throne had six steps, a back with a rounded top, and arms on each side of the seat; two lions stood beside the arms, ²⁰and twelve lions stood on each side of the six steps. Nothing like it has ever been made in any other kingdom.

²¹All King Solomon's drinking vessels were of gold, and all the plate in the House of the Forest of Lebanon was of pure gold; silver was little thought of in Solomon's days, ²²since the king had a fleet of Tarshish[a] at sea with Hiram's fleet, and once every three years the fleet of Tarshish would come back laden with gold and silver, ivory, apes and baboons. ²³For riches and for wisdom, King Solomon surpassed all kings on earth, ²⁴and the whole world consulted Solomon to hear the wisdom which God had implanted in his heart; ²⁵and everyone would bring a present with him: things made of silver, things made of gold, robes, armour, spices, horses and mules; and this went on year after year.

Solomon's chariots and cavalry

²⁶Solomon then built up a force of chariots and cavalry; he had one thousand four hundred chariots and twelve thousand horses, these he stationed in the chariot towns and near the king in Jerusalem. ²⁷In Jerusalem the

---

10a Meaning uncertain, perhaps a place-name. Or 'refinery ships', so ships for carrying metal.

Saints on Scripture

1 EXPERIENCING THE POWER OF GOD'S WORD

BL. HUMBERT OF ROMANS, 1200?–1277

So it is with the word that goes from my mouth: it will not return to me unfulfilled or before having carried out my good pleasure and having achieved what it was sent to do ISAIAH 55:11

In 1254, Humbert of Romans became the fifth master-general of the Dominicans. His massive book, *On the Formation of Preachers,* mined the Bible for texts that applied to preachers and interpreted them in ways that gave his brothers a new enthusiasm for their work. Following is a selection from this book that piles up Scripture references declaring the power of God's Word:

THERE ARE many people whose spirits are in their bodies like corpses in their tombs. And, just as God will, at the end of time, raise up dead bodies by his word, so he now gives life to dead spirits by the power of his word. "The hour is coming—indeed it is already here—when the dead will hear the voice of the Son of God, and all who hear it will live" (Jn 5:25).

Again, there are many who, spiritually, have nothing to live on. But it is the word of God which sustains man's spiritual life. "Human beings live not on bread alone but on every word that comes from the mouth of God" (Mt 4:4). . . .

Again, there are many who have no perception in spiritual matters and lead an entirely animal life. But the word of God enables them to move on into a spiritual life. So it says, "The words I have spoken to you are spirit and they are life" (Jn 6:63). They are called "spirit and life" because of their effect, which is to instill a spiritual life into people.

Again, there are many who, in the darkness of this world, do not know how to hold to the right path. But the word of God is like a torch by night, showing them the right way. "Your word is a lamp for my feet, a light on my path" (Ps 119:105).

Again, there are some medicines which work against some kinds of sickness, but not against them all. But the word of God works against every kind of spiritual sickness. "Your word is all powerful, Lord, it cures everything" (see Ws 18:15, 16:12).

Again, there are people whose hearts are harder than rock. The word of God sometimes breaks this hardness. "Is my word not . . . like a hammer shattering a rock?" (Jr 23:29).

Again, there are people whose piety and compunction and devotion towards God are quite dried up. "My soul is like soil with no water before you" (see Ps 143:6). But the word of the Lord sometimes melts them. "When he sends his word it thaws them" (Ps 147:18).

Again, there are many people in whom charity has grown cold. But the word of the Lord rekindles it. "Is my word not like fire?" (Jr 23:29), setting things ablaze, that is.

Again, there are many who are in great need of help against the temptations of the devil. But the word of God is a sword with which a man can defend himself against them, as we can see from the Lord, who defended himself against temptation with sacred words (see Mt 4:4–11). "And the sword of the Spirit, that is, the word of God" (Ep 6:17).

Again, the word of God is like powerful soap which is strong enough to wash the filth out of dirty linen. "You are clean already, by means of the word that I have spoken to you" (Jn 15:3). . . .

Again, there are many who are a long way from being saints. But the word of God makes them saints. "Consecrate them in the truth; your word is truth" (Jn 17:17). . . .

And these are not the only useful results with which the word of God benefits men. There are many others too. This is why it says, "The word of God is full of power" (see Qo 8:4), which refers to the many different kinds of effectiveness that it has, like a precious stone which is good for many different purposes.

2 READING SCRIPTURE: ESSENTIAL FOR CHRISTIAN LIVING ST. JOHN CHRYSOSTOM, 347–407

St. John Chrysostom says that laypeople must read Scripture more regularly than monks because Bible study corrects the bad effects of life's circumstances on our spirituality:

I AM ALWAYS encouraging you to pay attention not only to what is said here in church, but also, when you are at home, to continue constantly in the practice of reading the divine Scriptures. . . . For let not anyone say to me those silly, contemptible words, "I'm stuck at the courthouse all day." "I'm tied up with political affairs." "I'm in an apprentice program." "I've got a wife." "I'm raising kids." "I'm responsible for a household." "I'm a businessman." "Reading the Bible isn't my thing. That's for those who are set apart, for those who have made the mountaintops their home, who have a way of life without interruptions."

What are you saying, man? It's not your business to pay attention to the Bible because you are distracted by thousands of concerns? Then Bible reading belongs more to you than to the monks! For they do not make as much use of the help of the divine Scriptures as those who always have a great many things to do. . . . But you are always standing in the line of battle and are constantly being hit, so you need more medicine. For not only does your spouse irritate you, but your son annoys you, and a servant makes you lose your temper. An enemy schemes against you, a friend envies you, a neighbor insults you, a colleague trips you up. Often a lawsuit impends, poverty distresses, loss of possessions brings sorrow. At one moment success puffs you up; at another, failure deflates you. Numerous powerful inducements to anger and anxiety, to discouragement and grief, to vanity and loss of sense surround us on every side. A thousand missiles rain down from every direction. And so we constantly need the whole range of equipment supplied by Scripture. . . .

Since many things of this kind besiege our soul, we need the divine medicines, so that we might treat the wounds we already have, and so that we might check beforehand the wounds that are not yet, but are going to be, from afar extinguishing the missiles of the devil and repelling them through the constant reading of the divine Scriptures. For it is not possible, not possible for anyone to be saved who does not constantly have the benefit of spiritual reading.

PURSUING GOD IN SCRIPTURE: PRACTICAL ADVICE ON READING THE BIBLE BL. ALPHONSUS DE OROZCO, 1500–1591

Bl. Alphonsus, a great Spanish mystic and spiritual director, urges us to take a disciplined approach to reading Scripture:

ST. AUGUSTINE gave to reading the function of seeking the treasure. Meditation, she said, will find it, prayer digs for it with all its might, and contemplation sets it forth in clear light. The holy doctor bases this on those words of the gospel: "Everyone who searches finds; everyone who knocks will have the door opened" (Mt 7:8). So that seeking God is part of holy reading, just as worldly reading . . . leads to losing him. . . . If, then, you want to find the Lord of mercy, read learned and spiritual doctors, for St. Lipsianus says: "As in prayer we speak with God, in reading our God speaks to us. . . ."

We owe much to those who in what they wrote enlightened our understanding. . . .But the book which not only speaks to the understanding but also awakens the will to the love of God should be held in high esteem. Hardly ever should we allow it to leave our hands. It should be read with the mind in repose, doing violence to oneself to pay attention, and casting aside every other thought.

Do not go jumping about from one book to another. . . . For we enjoy variety in what we read, but perseverance in reading is what brings us profit. You should always pick out certain passages from what you have read and fix them in your mind. . . . Always have a definite time each day for reading, just as you should have for prayer and contemplation.

3 SCRIPTURE LEADS US TO ETERNAL LIFE

ST. BONAVENTURE, 1218–1274

St. Bonaventure also taught that Scripture is our road to everlasting union with God:

THE END or fruit of Holy Scripture is not something restricted, but the fullness of eternal happiness. These writings which contain "the message of eternal life" (Jn 6:63) were written, not only that we might believe in, but also that we might possess that everlasting life in which we shall see, and love, and be fulfilled of all we desire. Then we shall really know that "love of Christ, which is beyond knowledge," and thus "be filled with the utter fullness of God" (Ep 3:19). This is the fullness to which the divine Scriptures would lead us, as is truly said in the words of the Apostle quoted above. Such, then, must be our goal and our intent in studying and in teaching the Scriptures, and also in hearing them.

And that we attain this fruit and end rightly, by the straight road of Scripture itself, we must begin at the beginning. That is, we must reach out in a spirit of pure faith to the Father of all light, and kneeling in our hearts, ask him to give us, through his Son and in the Holy Spirit, the true knowledge of Jesus Christ, and together with knowledge, love for him. By knowing and loving Christ, by being confirmed in faith and "planted in love" (Ep 3:17), we can know the breadth, length, and depth of Scripture, and, through such knowledge, attain unto the all-surpassing knowledge and measureless love which is the Blessed Trinity. To this do the saints' desires tend. This is the final state, replete with all that is true and good.

Lord Jesus Christ, pierce my soul with your love so that I may always long for you alone, who are the bread of angels and the fulfillment of the soul's deepest desires. May my heart always hunger and feed upon you, so that my soul may be filled with the sweetness of your presence. May my soul thirst for you, who are the source of life, wisdom, knowledge, light and all the riches of God the Father. May I always seek and find you, think upon you, speak to you and do all things for the honour and glory of your holy name. Be always my only hope, my peace, my refuge and my help in whom my heart is rooted so that I may never be separated from you. ST. BONAVENTURE

UNDERSTANDING SCRIPTURE THROUGH FAITH IN CHRIST

ST. BONAVENTURE, 1218–1274

Franciscan theologian St. Bonaventure taught that without faith in Christ you cannot understand Scripture:

THE SCRIPTURE originated, not in human research, but in divine revelation coming from the "Father of all light—from whom every fatherhood, in heaven or on earth, takes its name" (Jm 1:17, Ep 3:15); from whom, through his Son Jesus Christ, the Holy Spirit flows into our souls. By this Spirit, who apportions his gifts and distributes "them at will to each individual" (1 Co 12:11), faith is given and through faith "we have Christ dwelling" in our hearts (see Ep 3:17). It is from such knowledge of Jesus Christ first of all that the firmness of our understanding of Scripture comes.

So, no one can penetrate its meaning unless he has first had infused into him faith in Jesus Christ as the lamp, the door, and also the foundation of the entire Scripture: for "as long as we are . . . exiled from the Lord" (2 Co 5:6), faith is, as regards every supernatural illumination, the foundation that supports us, the lamp that guides us, and the door that leads us in. It is by faith, moreover, that the wisdom given us by God must be measured, so that you "never pride yourself on being better than you really are." Instead you should "think of yourself dispassionately, recognising that God has given to each one his measure of faith" (Rm 12:3).

4 THE INEXHAUSTIBLE RICHNESS OF GOD'S WORD

ST. EPHREM, 306?–373?

"Do you understand what you are reading?" He replied, "How could I, unless I have someone to guide me?" ACTS 8:30–31

St. Ephrem encourages us to appreciate the inexhaustible, kaleidoscopic treasury of God's Word:

WHO IS CAPABLE of grasping all the riches of a single one of your words, O Lord? What we grasp is much less than what we leave behind, just like thirsty people who drink from a spring. The perspectives of your Word are many, just as the perspectives of those who study it are many.

The Lord has colored his Word with many kinds of beauty, so that everyone who scrutinizes it can contemplate what he loves. And he has hidden all treasures in his word so that each of us might find a treasure in what we ponder. His word is a tree of life, which on every side holds out blessed fruits to you. It is like that rock opened in the desert, which becomes a spiritual drink for all people everywhere: "All ate the same spiritual food and all drank the same spiritual drink" (1 Co 10:3–4).

Let him who discovers one of the riches of his Word not think that there is nothing else in the word of God but what he has found. Let him rather realize that he has been able to discover only one thing among many others. Enriched by the Word, let him not think that the Word is thus impoverished. Incapable of exhausting its riches, let him give thanks for its greatness.

Rejoice because you are satisfied, but do not grieve because Scripture is greater than you. The thirsty person is glad to drink, but does not grieve at his inability to deplete the spring. It is much more important that the spring quench your thirst than that your thirst deplete the spring. If your thirst is slaked without doing harm to the spring, you can drink again whenever you are thirsty. On the contrary, if you dry up the spring, your victory will become your misfortune.

Give thanks for what you have received and do not grumble about what remains unused. What you have grasped and taken away is your part, but what remains is your inheritance. Through perseverance, therefore, receive at other moments what through weakness you have been unable to receive immediately. Do not be impudent either to wish to take at one gulp what cannot be grasped in one attempt, or to draw away from what you could receive little by little.

WE NEED A GUIDE TO THE BIBLE ST. JEROME, 341?–420

The great Bible scholar-saint Jerome advises us that to interpret Scripture correctly, we must have a guide:

I N THE APOCALYPSE a book is shown sealed with seven seals, which if you hand to an educated person saying, "Read this," he will answer, "I can't because it's sealed." Today many people claim to be educated, yet the Scriptures are a sealed book to them, one which they cannot open except through him who has the key of David, "he that opens and no one shuts; and shuts and no one opens" (see Rv 3:7).

In the Acts of the Apostles, Philip asked the holy eunuch who was reading Isaiah, "Do you understand what you are reading?" He answered: "How could I, unless I have someone to guide me?" (Ac 8:30–31). Yet although he had the book in his hand and took the words of the Lord into his mind, and even had them on his tongue and pronounced them with his lips, he still did not know the one he unknowingly worshiped in the book. Then Philip came and showed him Jesus, who was concealed beneath the letter. What a wonderful teacher! In the same hour the eunuch both believed and was baptized. He became one of the faithful and a saint. He was no longer a pupil, but a master.

I have touched on this instance to convince you that you can make no progress in the holy Scriptures unless you have a guide to show you the way.

5 SCRIPTURE AND TRADITION

ST. VINCENT OF LÉRINS, D. 450?

Think back on the days of old,
think over the years, down the ages.
Question your father, let him explain to you,
your elders, and let them tell you! DEUTERONOMY 32:7

St. Vincent, a fifth-century monk and scholar, set out to devise a general rule to distinguish Christian truth from heresy. So he studied Scripture, the fathers of the church, and the general councils. He summarized his findings in a little book, the *Commonitory or Reminder*. In the following selection from that book, he reminds us that in order to interpret Scripture correctly we need the guidance of the church. We must understand the Bible in the context of the living Tradition, which the Holy Spirit communicates to us in the doctrine, life, and worship of the church.

I HAVE OFTEN inquired most earnestly and attentively from very many experts in sanctity and learning, how and by what definite and universal rule I might distinguish the truth of the Catholic faith from the falsity of heretical perversion. And I have always received answer of this kind from almost all of them—that whether I or anyone else wished to detect the frauds of newly rising heretics, to avoid their snares, and to remain secure and whole in the sound faith, one ought with the Lord's help to fortify one's faith in a twofold manner: first, by the authority of the divine law, and secondly, by the tradition of the Catholic Church.

Here perhaps someone will ask, "Since the canon of Scripture is complete and is in itself sufficient and more than sufficient on all points, what need is there to join to it the authority of ecclesiastical interpretation?" The answer of course is that, owing to the very depth of Holy Scripture itself, all do not receive it in one and the same sense. But one in one way and another in another interpret the declarations of the same writer, so that it seems possible to elicit from it as many opinions as there are men. For Novatian expounds it one way, ... Donatus, another, ... and quite lately

Nestorius another. So it is most necessary on account of the great intricacies of such various errors that the rule for the interpretation of the Prophets and Apostles should be laid down in accordance with the standard of the ecclesiastical and Catholic understanding of them.

Also in the Catholic Church itself we take great care that we hold that which has been believed everywhere, always, by all. For that is truly and properly *Catholic,* as the very force and meaning of the word show, which comprehends everything almost universally. And we shall observe this rule if we follow universality, antiquity, consent. We shall follow universality if we confess that one faith to be true which the whole church throughout the world confesses; antiquity, if we in no wise depart from those interpretations which it is plain that our ancestors and fathers proclaimed; consent, if in antiquity itself we eagerly follow the definitions and beliefs of all, or certainly nearly all, priests and doctors alike.

For today's Catholic, the first places to look for guidance in interpreting Scripture are the *Catechism of the Catholic Church,* articles 1 to 141, and *Dei Verbum,* Vatican Council II's Dogmatic Constitution on Divine Revelation. Among many reliable books that offer an introduction to a Catholic understanding of the Bible, the following are especially practical and popular: Kevin Perrotta, *Your One-Stop Guide to the Bible*; George Martin, *Reading Scripture as the Word of God;* and Jerome Kodell, *The Catholic Bible Study Handbook.*

6 UNDERSTANDING THE SPIRITUAL SENSE OF SCRIPTURE

ST. BEDE, THE VENERABLE, 673–735

The words I have spoken to you are spirit and they are life. JOHN 6:63

Venerable Bede, a lifelong student of Scripture and the fathers of the church, came to understand the Bible as a gateway into the deeper world of the Spirit. He regarded the spiritual sense of Scripture as vital, even more important than the literal grammatical meaning of the text. And he developed a method of interpreting the Bible spiritually, which he described in the following passage:

THE WHOLE SERIES of divine Scripture is interpreted in a fourfold way. In all holy books we should ascertain what everlasting truths are intimated there, what deeds are narrated, what future events are foretold and what commands or counsels are contained there. . . . The word of the heavenly oracle can be received in either a historical, or allegorical, a tropological (that is, moral) or even an anagogical sense.

It is history when something is recorded clearly as it was literally said or done. For example, the people of Israel saved from Egypt is reported to have made a tabernacle of the Lord in the wilderness.

It is allegory when the presence of Christ or the sacraments are designated by mystical words or events. For example, when Isaiah says "A shoot will spring from the stock of Jesse, a new shoot will grow from his roots" (Is 11:1), he means the Virgin Mary shall be born of the root of David and Christ shall be born out of her stock. This may be illustrated also with regard to events. For example, the people saved from slavery in Egypt through the blood of the Lamb signifies the church freed by the passion of Christ from the domination of the devil.

It is tropology, that is, a moral manner of speaking, when appearing in either literal or figurative language, it appertains to moral instruction and correction. For example, as when John gives the warning, "Little children, let us not love in word or speech, but in deed and in truth" (1 Jn 3:18, RSV); in figures as when Solomon says "At all times, dress in white and keep your head well scented" (Qo 9:8), which is to be interpreted, at all times let your work be clean and let not charity depart from your heart.

It is anagogy, that is, a form of speech looking to higher things which discusses, either in plain or mystical words, future rewards and in what the future life of heaven consists. For example, in plain words, "Blessed are the pure in heart: they shall see God" (Mt 5:8). But in mystical words, "Blessed are those who will have washed their robes clean, so that they will have the right to feed on the tree of life and can come through the gates into the city" (Rv 22:14), which means blessed are they who cleanse their thoughts and actions so that they may have the power to see the Lord Christ, who says "I am the Way; I am Truth and Life" (Jn 14:6) and they who through the teaching and example of the preceding fathers enter into the kingdom of heaven.

I pray you, noble Jesus, that as you have graciously granted me joyfully to drink the words of your knowledge, so you will also of your goodness grant me to come at length to yourself, the fount of all wisdom, and to dwell in your presence forever. ST. BEDE

7 PUTTING GOD'S WORD INTO PRACTICE

ST. AUGUSTINE, 354–430

Everyone who listens to these words of mine and acts on them will be like a sensible man who built his house on rock. MATTHEW 7:24

M Y BROTHERS, let me tell you plainly that you are deceiving yourself if you hear the Word without the intention of putting into practice what you hear. Try to realize that if it is a good thing to hear the Word, it is much better to put it into practice. If you do not listen to it, you neglect hearing it and you will not build anything. If you listen to it and fail to act accordingly, you will be constructing a ruin.

In this regard, the Lord makes a suggestion by means of a very exact comparison. He tells us: "Everyone who listens to these words of mine and acts on them will be like a sensible man who built his house on rock. Rain came down, floods rose, gales blew and hurled themselves against that house, and it did not fall" (Mt 7:24–25). Why did it not fall? Because "it was founded on rock." So, to listen and to put into practice is to build on rock. And by the mere fact of listening we are already in the process of building.

"But everyone," our Lord continues, "who listens to these words of mine and does not act on them will be like a stupid man who built" also. But what did he build? He "built his house." But because he did not put into practice what he heard, this did not do him any good, for he "built on sand" (Mt 7:26). He, then, builds on sand who listens but fails to act. And he builds on rock who listens and puts into practice. But he who refuses to listen builds neither on sand nor on rock. And note what follows: "Rain came down, floods rose, gales blew and struck that house, and it fell; and what a fall it had!" (Mt 7:27).

Someone might say to me: "What is the use of listening if there is no intention of acting upon what one hears? For if I listen without putting into practice I shall construct a ruin. Is it not safer to refrain from listening to anything?"

The Lord did not want to consider this attitude in his comparison, but he has given us what is necessary to determine its value. In this world, there are constant rains, winds, torrents. If you build neither on rock nor on sand, since you refuse to listen, it means you will be without any protection. Rain comes, torrents come: will you then be secure when you are carried away for want of shelter? Reflect carefully, therefore, on the decision you will make. You will not be secure—as you might imagine you are—because you have failed to listen. Being without protection and having no shelter of any kind, you will of necessity be cast down, carried away, submerged. If it is a bad thing to build on sand, it is just as bad not to build anything. So we can conclude that there is nothing better than to build on rock. It is bad to refuse to listen, and it is just as bad to listen but to refuse to act. "You must do what the Word tells you and not just listen to it and deceive yourselves" (Jm 1:22).

8 SCRIPTURE AS A MIRROR OF THE SOUL

The saints urge us to regard Scripture as a mirror of our souls. Looking into it we can see ourselves as we are and compare our conduct to God's standards. And where we see that we do not measure up, we can ask him for the grace to change.

ST. GREGORY THE GREAT, 540?–604

Anyone who listens to the Word and takes no action is like someone who looks at his own features in a mirror and, once he has seen what he looks like, goes off and immediately forgets it. JAMES 1:23–24

THE HOLY SCRIPTURE is put before the eyes of our mind like a mirror in which we can view the condition of our soul. In it we can see what are our unsightly traits and what are our attractive qualities. By it we judge how we are growing and still how far we are from reaching our full stature.

Scripture tells of the achievements of the saints and stirs up the hearts of us weaklings to follow them. By remembering their victorious deeds, it strengthens our weakness that we may strive against sin. And so by the words of Scripture, it happens that our soul trembles less at the battle because we see how many brave people before us have conquered their enemies.

Sometimes Scripture shows us not only how the saints fought bravely, but also how they fell, so that we may see by the example of the mighty not only what weapons we must take if we want to conquer, but also what snares we must keep clear of, if we want to avoid falling.

For example, here is Job on the one hand, waxing nobler under trial, and on the other hand, David tired and failing utterly (see 2 S 11). And so the glory of the great strengthens our hope and their backsliding stirs us up to stay watchful and lowly. The one cheering us with gladness, the other putting us on our guard through fear. Therefore, the soul of the person who hears these things may by the one gain sure and certain hope and by the other fearfulness and watchfulness, and so neither be rashly puffed up, nor hopelessly cast down, nor may faint under the weight of dread because the example of him who triumphed stirs up her trustfulness.

ST. NORBERT, 1080–1134

But anyone who looks steadily at the perfect law of freedom and keeps to it—not listening and forgetting, but putting it into practice—will be blessed in every undertaking. JAMES 1:25

NEVER BE TIRED of studying these writings where you find a short exhortation to remain faithful in serving God. For the word of God is fiery. It is inflamed with the fire of the Holy Spirit. It consumes vices and promotes virtue. It bestows wisdom on well-disposed people and provides for them heavenly food.

Therefore, Christ said, "Blessed are they who hear the word of God and keep it" (see Lk 11:28). So, Mary, by listening attentively to the word of God, chose the best part that Martha, busy with her activities, couldn't obtain (see Lk 10:38–42). Listen cheerfully to the word of God, keep it judiciously and observe it faithfully. Thus at the end of time you may rejoice to hear Christ's consoling words: "Come, you whom my Father has blessed, take as your heritage the kingdom prepared for you since the foundation of the world" (Mt 25:34).

ST. CLARE OF ASSISI, 1193–1253

For [Wisdom] is a reflection of the eternal light, untarnished mirror of God's active power, and image of his goodness. WISDOM 7:26

[The Son] is the reflection of God's glory and bears the impress of God's own being. HEBREWS 1:3

LOOK INTO that mirror daily. . . . Always study your face in it, so that within and without you may adorn and clothe and gird yourself with all manner of virtue. So by God's grace you can contemplate blessed poverty, holy humility and sacred charity, which are reflected in that mirror.

9 FINDING HER WAY IN SCRIPTURE

ST. THÉRÈSE OF LISIEUX, 1873–1897

Your word is a lamp for my feet, a light on my path. PSALM 119:105

At key moments in her life, St. Thérèse of Lisieux (1873–1897), perhaps the most popular and influential saint of our time, turned to the Bible for direction. In *The Story of a Soul,* her auto-biography, she describes numerous occasions when she found a Scripture text that cleared her mind and adjusted the course of her life. Millions have benefited from Thérèse's teaching about her "little way" of doing everything with love. She formulated this simple approach by reflecting on Scripture and acting on it.

Even before she articulated her little way Thérèse did everything out of love. For example, she tells how as a novice she volunteered to escort a sick and irritable sister from prayers to dinner. Daily she endured a barrage of complaints, but performed her service with kindness and a smile. Without being asked, Thérèse always cut the sister's bread for her, a little loving act that ultimately won the sick nun's trust and affection.

The real test of Thérèse's little way, however, came when she had to love a sister that she did not like:

FORMERLY ONE of our nuns managed to irritate me whatever she did or said. The devil was mixed up in it, for it was certainly he who made me see so many disagreeable traits in her. As I did not want to give way to my natural dislike for her, I told myself that charity should not only be a matter of feeling but should show itself in deeds. So I set myself to do for this sister just what I should have done for someone I loved most dearly. Every time I met her, I prayed for her and offered God all her virtues and her merits. I was sure this would greatly delight Jesus, for every artist likes to have his works praised and the divine Artist of souls is pleased when we do not halt outside the exterior of the sanctuary where He has chosen to dwell but go inside and admire its beauty.

I did not remain content with praying a lot for this nun who caused me so much disturbance. I tried to do as many things for her as I could, and whenever I was tempted to speak unpleasantly to her, I made myself give her a pleasant smile and tried to change the subject. *The Imitation [of Christ]* says: "It is more profitable to leave to everyone his way of thinking than to give way to contentious discourses."

When I was violently tempted by the devil and if I could slip away without her seeing my inner struggle, I would flee like a soldier deserting the battlefield. And after all this she asked me one day with a beaming face: "Sister Thérèse, will you please tell me what attracts you so much to me? You give me such a charming smile whenever we meet." Ah! It was Jesus hidden in the depth of her soul who attracted me, Jesus who makes the bitterest things sweet.

Thérèse had found the way of true discipleship, following Jesus who taught us by word and example to lay down our lives for our friends (Jn 15:13).

10 PATTERNING THEIR LIVES ON SCRIPTURE

Our modern culture persuades us that pleasing ourselves, coming out on top, having more stuff—all of these self-centered attitudes—will make us happy. But the message of Scripture as applied by the saints dramatically contradicts that spurious notion. Real joy comes not from aggrandizing ourselves, but from selflessly giving of ourselves to others.

ST. JOAN DELANOUE, 1666–1736

I was hungry and you never gave me food. MATTHEW 25:42

WHEN JOAN DELANOUE was twenty-five years old, she inherited her merchant father's shop and the family home. Soon the devout, somewhat scrupulous young woman became a petty money-grubber. She opened her shop on Sundays, unheard of in France of her day. She even bought food just before meal times so that at other times she could truthfully tell beggars there was no food in the house.

In 1693 a wandering visionary named Frances Souchet brought Joan messages she claimed came from God. The woman's visits disturbed Joan and provoked her to repentance. During Lent that year on the advice of a priest, she began to close her shop on Sundays and to fast three days a week. At Pentecost Mrs. Souchet came around with more divine communications. In one of the visionary's messages Joan heard Christ's words, "I was hungry and you never gave me food." An immediate change came over her, and on the spot she renounced her greed. As a sign of her dramatic conversion, Joan gave Mrs. Souchet her loveliest dress.

Joan left her business and money behind. Embracing poverty herself and over-coming opposition and hardships, she served the poor for the rest of her life. In a short time Joan attracted a number of women to serve alongside her, and in 1704 she founded the Sisters of Saint Anne, a community devoted to caring for orphans and the elderly.

ST. CAMILLUS DE LELLIS, 1550–1614

[I was] sick and you visited me. MATTHEW 25:36

ST. CAMILLUS WAS A GIANT for his times, standing six feet, six inches tall. He also became a spiritual giant through his unselfish service of the sick.

At seventeen Camillus went to fight against the Turks, and while at war his leg became infected with a serious disease that remained with him for life. He rebelled as a youth, so addicted to gambling that it nearly destroyed him. By age twenty-four he had literally lost his shirt to this risky indulgence. At twenty-five, however, he responded to a friar's preaching with radical repentance. He turned his life to Christ and wanted to become a Capuchin. But the order refused to admit him because of his diseased leg. So Camillus went to work at a hospital for the incurably sick in Rome where he had spent some time when his leg was first infected. There he devoted himself entirely to the care of the sick.

Soon Camillus surrounded himself with other young men who were committed to serve the sick. He organized a religious order, the Ministers of the Sick, which founded and staffed hospitals throughout Italy. Sick and in pain most of the time himself, Camillus served tirelessly and without complaint. His brothers reported that the saying of Christ, "I was sick and you visited me," seems to have been engraved on his heart. Daily he used to repeat those words as he encouraged his colleagues to love the sick without thought of themselves.

king made silver as common as stones, and cedar wood as plentiful as sycamore in the lowlands. ²⁸Solomon's horses were imported from Muzur and Cilicia. The king's dealers acquired them from Cilicia at the prevailing price. ²⁹A chariot was imported from Egypt for six hundred silver shekels and a horse from Cilicia for a hundred and fifty. They also supplied the Hittite and Aramaean kings, who all used them as middlemen.

Solomon's wives

11 King Solomon loved many foreign women: not only Pharaoh's daughter but Moabites, Edomites, Sidonians and Hittites, ²from those peoples of whom Yahweh had said to the Israelites, 'You are not to go among them nor they among you, or they will be sure to sway your hearts to their own gods.' But Solomon was deeply attached to them. ³He had seven hundred wives of royal rank and three hundred concubines. ⁴When Solomon grew old his wives swayed his heart to other gods; and his heart was not wholly with Yahweh his God as his father David's had been. ⁵Solomon became a follower of Astarte, the goddess of the Sidonians, and of Milcom, the Ammonite abomination. ⁶He did what was displeasing to Yahweh, and was not a wholehearted follower of Yahweh, as his father David had been. ⁷Then it was that Solomon built a high place for Chemosh, the abomination of Moab, on the mountain to the east of Jerusalem, and to Milcom, the abomination of the Ammonites. ⁸He did the same for all his foreign wives, who offered incense and sacrifice to their gods.

⁹Yahweh was angry with Solomon because his heart had turned away from Yahweh, God of Israel, who had twice appeared to him ¹⁰and had forbidden him to follow other gods; but he did not carry out Yahweh's order. ¹¹Yahweh therefore said to Solomon, 'Since you have behaved like this and have not kept my covenant or the laws which I laid down for you, I shall tear the kingdom away from you and give it to one of your servants. ¹²For your father David's sake, however, I shall not do this during your lifetime, but shall tear it out of your son's hands. ¹³Even so, I shall not tear the whole kingdom from him. For the sake of my servant David, and for the sake of Jerusalem which I have chosen, I shall leave your son one tribe.'

Solomon's foreign enemies

¹⁴Yahweh raised an enemy against Solomon, Hadad the Edomite, of the kingly stock of Edom. ¹⁵After David had crushed Edom, Joab the army commander had gone to bury the dead and had slaughtered the entire male population of Edom ¹⁶(Joab stayed there with all Israel for six months until he had exterminated the entire male population of Edom), ¹⁷but Hadad with a number of Edomites in his father's service had fled to Egypt. Hadad had been only a boy at the time. ¹⁸They set out from Midian, and on reaching Paran, took a number of men from Paran with them and went on to Egypt, to Pharaoh the king of Egypt, who provided him with a house, undertook to maintain him, and assigned him an estate. ¹⁹Hadad became a great favourite of Pharaoh who gave him his own wife's sister in marriage, the sister of the Great Lady Tahpenes. ²⁰The sister of Tahpenes bore him his son Genubath whom Tahpenes brought up in Pharaoh's palace, Genubath living in Pharaoh's palace with Pharaoh's own children. ²¹But when news reached Hadad in Egypt that David had fallen asleep with his ancestors and that Joab the army commander was dead, he said to Pharaoh, 'Give me leave to go that I may return to my own country.' ²²'What do you lack here with me,' Pharaoh said, 'for you to want to go back to your country?' 'Nothing,' he replied, 'but please let me go.' ²⁵ᵇHence the harm which Hadad caused: he loathed Israel and ruled Edom.

²³God raised a second enemy against Solomon, Rezon son of Eliada. He had fled from his master, Hadadezer king of Zobah. ²⁴A number of men having rallied to him, he became leader of a marauding band (which

was then massacred by David). Rezon captured Damascus and settled there and became king of Damascus. 25a He was hostile to Israel as long as Solomon lived.

The revolt of Jeroboam

26 Jeroboam was the son of Nebat, an Ephraimite from Zeredah; the name of his mother, a widow, was Zeruah; he was in Solomon's service but revolted against the king. 27 This is the account of his revolt.

Solomon was building the Millo and closing the breach in the City of David his father. 28 Now this Jeroboam was a man of great energy; Solomon, noticing how the young man set about his work, put him in charge of all the forced labour of the House of Joseph. 29 One day when Jeroboam had gone out of Jerusalem, the prophet Ahijah of Shiloh accosted him on the road. Ahijah was wearing a new cloak; the two of them were in the open country by themselves. 30 Ahijah took the new cloak which he was wearing and tore it into twelve strips, 31 saying to Jeroboam: 'Take ten strips for yourself, for Yahweh, God of Israel, says this, "I am going to tear the kingdom from Solomon's hand and give ten tribes to you. 32 He will keep one tribe for the sake of my servant David and for the sake of Jerusalem, the city which I have chosen out of all the tribes of Israel; 33 for he has forsaken me to worship Astarte the goddess of the Sidonians, Chemosh the god of Moab, Milcom the god of the Ammonites; he has not followed my ways by doing what I regard as right, or by keeping my laws and ordinances as his father David did. 34 But it is not from his hands that I will take the kingdom, since I have made him a prince for as long as he lives, for the sake of my servant David who kept my commandments and laws. 35 I shall, however, take the kingdom from the hand of his son, and I shall give it to you, that is, the ten tribes. 36 I shall give one tribe to his son, so that my servant David may always have a lamp in my presence in Jerusalem, the city which I have chosen as a dwelling-place for my name. 37 You nonethe-

less I shall appoint to rule over as much as you wish, and you will be king of Israel. 38 If you listen to all my orders and follow my ways, by doing what I regard as right and by keeping my laws and commandments as my servant David did, then I shall be with you and shall build you as enduring a dynasty as the one which I built for David. I shall give Israel to you, 39 and I shall humble the descendants of David, but not for ever." '

40 Solomon tried to kill Jeroboam but he made off and fled to Egypt, to Shishak king of Egypt, and he remained in Egypt until Solomon's death.

The end of the reign of Solomon

41 The rest of the history of Solomon, his entire career, his wisdom, is this not recorded in the Book of the Annals of Solomon? 42 Solomon's reign in Jerusalem over all Israel lasted forty years. 43 When Solomon fell asleep with his ancestors, he was buried in the City of David his father; his son Rehoboam succeeded him.

The assembly at Shechem

12 Rehoboam then went to Shechem, all Israel having come to Shechem to proclaim him king. 2 (As soon as Jeroboam son of Nebat heard the news—he was still in Egypt, where he had taken refuge from King Solomon—he returned from Egypt. 3 They now sent for him, and Jeroboam and the whole assembly of Israel came.) And they spoke as follows to Rehoboam, 4 'Your father laid a cruel yoke on us; if you will lighten your father's cruel slavery, that heavy yoke which he imposed on us, we are willing to serve you.' 5 He said to them, 'Go away for three days and then come back to me.' And the people went away.

6 King Rehoboam then consulted the elders who had been in attendance on his father Solomon while he was alive, and said, 'How do you advise me to answer this people?' 7 They replied, 'If you become the servant of this people today, and submit to them and give them a fair reply, then they will remain your servants

for ever.' ⁸But he rejected the advice given him by the elders and consulted the young men in attendance on him, who had grown up with him. ⁹He said, 'How do you advise us to answer these people who have been saying, "Lighten the yoke which your father imposed on us!"? ' ¹⁰The young men who had grown up with him replied, 'This is the way to answer these people who have been saying, "Your father made our yoke heavy, you must lighten it for us!" This is the right thing to say to them, "My little finger is thicker than my father's loins. ¹¹Although my father laid a heavy yoke on you, I shall make it heavier still. My father controlled you with the whip, but I shall apply a spiked lash!" '

¹²On the third day Jeroboam and all the people came to Rehoboam in obedience to the king's instruction: 'Come back to me in three days' time.' ¹³And the king gave the people a harsh answer, rejecting the advice given him by the elders ¹⁴and speaking to them as the young men had recommended, 'My father made your yoke heavy, I shall make it heavier still! My father controlled you with the whip, but I shall apply a spiked lash!'

¹⁵Thus the king refused to listen to the people, and this was brought about by Yahweh to fulfil the promise which he had made through Ahijah of Shiloh to Jeroboam son of Nebat. ¹⁶When all Israel saw that the king refused to listen to them, the people answered the king thus:

What share have we in David?
——No heritage in the son of Jesse!
Away to your tents, Israel!
Now look after your own House,
David!

So Israel went home again. ¹⁷Rehoboam, however, reigned over those Israelites who lived in the towns of Judah. ¹⁸When King Rehoboam sent Adoram, who was in charge of forced labour, all Israel stoned him to death, while King Rehoboam managed to mount his chariot and escape to Jerusalem. ¹⁹And Israel has remained in rebellion against the House of David from that day to this.

The political schism

²⁰When all Israel heard that Jeroboam had returned, they summoned him to the assembly and made him king of all Israel; no one remained loyal to the House of David, except the tribe of Judah.

²¹When Rehoboam reached Jerusalem he mustered the whole House of Judah and the tribe of Benjamin, a hundred and eighty thousand picked warriors, to fight the House of Israel and win back the kingdom for Rehoboam son of Solomon. ²²But the word of Yahweh came to Shemaiah, man of God, ²³'Say this to Rehoboam son of Solomon, king of Judah, to the whole House of Judah, to Benjamin and to the rest of the people, ²⁴"Yahweh says this: Do not go and make war on your brothers, the Israelites; let everyone go home, for this is my doing." ' They obeyed the command of Yahweh and turned back in accordance with his word.

²⁵Jeroboam fortified Shechem in the mountain country of Ephraim and made that his residence. Then, leaving there, he fortified Penuel.

The religious schism

²⁶Jeroboam thought to himself, 'As things are, the kingdom will revert to the House of David. ²⁷If this people continues to go up to the Temple of Yahweh in Jerusalem to offer sacrifices, the people's heart will turn back again to their lord, Rehoboam king of Judah, and they will put me to death.' ²⁸So the king thought this over and then made two golden calves; he said to the people, 'You have been going up to Jerusalem long enough. Here is your God, Israel, who brought you out of Egypt!' ²⁹He set one up at Bethel, ³⁰and the people went in procession in front of the other one all the way to Dan. In Israel this gave rise to sin, for the people went to Bethel to worship the one, and all the way to Dan to worship the other. ³¹He set up shrines on the high places

and appointed priests from ordinary families, who were not of levitical descent. 32 Jeroboam also instituted a feast in the eighth month, on the fifteenth of the month, like the feast kept in Judah, when he offered sacrifices on the altar. This he did at Bethel, offering sacrifices to the calves which he had made and, at Bethel, installing the priests of the high places which he had set up. 33 On the fifteenth of the eighth month, the month which he had chosen deliberately, he offered sacrifices on the altar which he had made at Bethel; he instituted a feast for the Israelites and himself went up to the altar to burn the sacrifice.

The condemnation of the altar in Bethel

13 There came to Bethel at Yahweh's command a man of God from Judah, just as Jeroboam was standing by the altar to offer the sacrifice, 2 and at Yahweh's command this man denounced the altar. 'Altar, altar,' he said, 'Yahweh says this, "A son is to be born to the House of David, Josiah by name, and on you he will slaughter the priests of the high places who have offered sacrifice on you, and on you he will burn human bones."' 3 At the same time he gave a sign. 'This is the sign', he said, 'that Yahweh has spoken, "This altar will burst apart and the ashes which are on it will be spilt."' 4 When the king heard how the man of God denounced the altar of Bethel, he stretched out his hand from the altar, saying, 'Seize him!' But the hand he stretched out against the man withered, and he could not draw it back, 5 and the altar burst apart and the ashes from the altar were spilt, in accordance with the sign given by the man of God at Yahweh's command. 6 The king said to the man of God, 'I beg you to placate Yahweh your God, and so restore me the use of my hand.' The man of God placated Yahweh; the king's hand was restored as it had been before. 7 The king then said to the man of God, 'Come home with me and refresh yourself, and I shall give you a present,' 8 but the man of God replied to the king, 'Were you to give me half your palace, I would not go with you. I will eat and drink nothing here, 9 for I have had Yahweh's order, "You are to eat or drink nothing, nor to return by the way you came."' 10 And he left by another road and did not return by the way he had come to Bethel.

The man of God and the prophet

11 Now there was an old prophet living in Bethel, and his sons came to tell him all that the man of God had done in Bethel that day; and the words which he had said to the king, they told these to their father too. 12 'Which road did he take?' their father asked. His sons showed him the road which the man of God who came from Judah had taken. 13 'Saddle the donkey for me,' he said to his sons; they saddled the donkey for him and he mounted. 14 He followed the man of God and found him sitting under a terebinth. 'Are you the man of God', he said, 'who came from Judah?' 'I am,' he replied. 15 'Come home with me,' he said, 'and take some food.' 16 'I cannot go back with you,' he answered, 'or eat or drink anything here, 17 for I have received Yahweh's order, "You are to eat or drink nothing there, nor to return by the way you came."' 18 'I too am a prophet like you,' the other replied, 'and an angel told me this by Yahweh's command, "Bring him back with you to your house to eat and drink."' He was lying to him. 19 The man of God went back with him; he ate and drank at his house.

20 As they were sitting at table a word of Yahweh came to the prophet who had brought him back, 21 and he addressed the man of God who came from Judah. 'Yahweh says this,' he said. '"Since you have defied Yahweh's command and not obeyed the orders which Yahweh your God gave you, 22 but have come back and eaten and drunk where he forbade you to eat and drink, your corpse will never reach the tomb of your ancestors."' 23 After he had eaten and drunk, the prophet saddled the donkey for him, and he turned about and went away. 24 A lion met him on the road and killed him; his corpse lay stretched out on the road; the donkey stood there beside

it; the lion stood by the corpse too. ²⁵ People going by saw the corpse lying on the road and the lion standing by the corpse, and went and spoke about it in the town where the old prophet lived. ²⁶ When the prophet who had made the man turn back heard about it, he said, 'That is the man of God who defied Yahweh's command! Yahweh has handed him over to the lion, which has mauled and killed him, just as Yahweh had foretold it would.' ²⁷ He said to his sons, 'Saddle the donkey for me,' and they saddled it. ²⁸ He set off and found the man's corpse lying on the road with the donkey and the lion standing beside the corpse; the lion had neither eaten the corpse nor mauled the donkey. ²⁹ The prophet lifted the corpse of the man of God and put it on the donkey and brought it back to the town where he lived to hold mourning for him and bury him. ³⁰ He laid the corpse in his own tomb, and they raised the mourning cry for him, 'Alas, my brother!' ³¹ After burying him, the prophet said to his sons, 'When I die, bury me in the same tomb as the man of God, lay my bones beside his. ³² For the word he uttered at Yahweh's command against the altar of Bethel and against all the shrines of the high places in the towns of Samaria will certainly come true.'

³³ Jeroboam did not give up his wicked ways after this incident, but went on appointing priests for the high places from the common people. He consecrated as priests of the high places any who wished to be. ³⁴ Such conduct made the House of Jeroboam a sinful House, and caused its ruin and extinction from the face of the earth.

Continuation of the reign of Jeroboam I (931–910)

14 At that time Abijah, Jeroboam's son, fell sick, ² and Jeroboam said to his wife, 'Come, please disguise yourself so that no one will recognise you as Jeroboam's wife, and go to Shiloh; the prophet Ahijah is there, the man who said I was to be king of this people. ³ Go to him, and take ten loaves and some savoury food and a jar of honey; he will tell you what

will happen to the child.' ⁴ Jeroboam's wife did this: she set out, went to Shiloh and came to Ahijah's house. ⁵ Now Ahijah could not see, his eyes were fixed with age, but Yahweh had told him, 'Jeroboam's wife is now on her way to ask you for a prophecy about her son, as he is sick. You will tell her such and such. When she comes, she will pretend to be some other woman.' ⁶ So when Ahijah heard her footsteps at the door, he called, 'Come in, wife of Jeroboam; why pretend to be someone else? I have bad news for you. ⁷ Go and tell Jeroboam, "Yahweh, God of Israel, says this: I raised you from the people and made you leader of my people Israel; ⁸ I tore the kingdom from the House of David and gave it to you. But you have not been like my servant David who kept my commandments and followed me with all his heart, doing only what I regard as right; ⁹ you have done more evil than all your predecessors, you have gone and made yourself other gods, idols of cast metal, provoking my anger, and you have turned your back on me. ¹⁰ For this I shall bring disaster on the House of Jeroboam, I shall wipe out every manjack of the family of Jeroboam, fettered or free in Israel, I shall sweep away the House of Jeroboam as a man sweeps dung away till none is left. ¹¹ Those of Jeroboam's family who die in the city, the dogs will eat; and those who die in the open country, the birds of the air will eat, for Yahweh has spoken." ¹² Now get up and go home; at the moment your feet enter the town, the child will die. ¹³ All Israel will mourn for him, and bury him; and he alone of Jeroboam's family will have a proper burial, for in him alone of the House of Jeroboam can Yahweh, God of Israel, find anything good. ¹⁴ Yahweh will set a king over Israel, who will put an end to the House of Jeroboam. ¹⁵ Yahweh will make Israel shake, till it quivers like a reed in the water; he will uproot Israel from this prosperous land which he gave to their ancestors and scatter them beyond the River for provoking Yahweh to anger by making their sacred poles. ¹⁶ He will abandon Israel for the sins which Jeroboam has committed and made Israel commit.' 17 Jeroboam's wife rose and left. She arrived at Tirzah, and when she crossed the threshold of the palace, the child was already dead. 18 They buried him, and all Israel mourned for him, just as Yahweh had foretold through his servant Ahijah the prophet.

19 The rest of the history of Jeroboam, what wars he waged, how he governed, this is recorded in the Book of the Annals of the Kings of Israel. 20 Jeroboam's reign lasted twenty-two years. Then he fell asleep with his ancestors; his son Nadab succeeded him.

The reign of Rehoboam (931–913)

21 In Judah, Rehoboam son of Solomon became king; he was forty-one years old when he came to the throne and he reigned for seventeen years in Jerusalem, the city which Yahweh had chosen out of all the tribes of Israel, to give his name a home there. His mother's name was Naamah, the Ammonite. 22 He did what is displeasing to Yahweh, arousing his resentment more than his ancestors by all the sins which they had committed; 23 they had built themselves high places, and had set up pillars and sacred poles on every high hill and under every spreading tree. 24 There were even male sacred prostitutes in the country. He copied all the shameful practices of the nations whom Yahweh had dispossessed for the Israelites.

25 And so it happened that in the fifth year of King Rehoboam, Shishak king of Egypt advanced on Jerusalem 26 and carried off all the treasures of the Temple of Yahweh and the treasures of the royal palace; he took everything away, including all the golden shields which Solomon had made. 27 To replace those King Rehoboam made bronze shields, entrusting them to the commanders of the guard who guarded the king's palace gate. 28 Whenever the king went to the Temple of Yahweh, the guards would carry them, returning them to the guardroom afterwards.

29 The rest of the history of Rehoboam, his entire career, is this not recorded in the Book of the Annals of the Kings of Judah? 30 War-fare between Rehoboam and Jeroboam went on throughout the period. 31 When Rehoboam fell asleep with his ancestors, he was buried in the City of David; his son Abijam succeeded him.

The reign of Abijam in Judah (913–911)

15 In the eighteenth year of King Jeroboam son of Nebat, Abijam became king of Judah 2 and reigned for three years in Jerusalem. His mother's name was Maacah descendant of Absalom. 3 In everything he followed the sinful example of his father before him; his heart was not wholly with Yahweh his God, as the heart of David his ancestor had been. 4 However, for David's sake, Yahweh his God gave him a lamp in Jerusalem, with a son to succeed him, so keeping Jerusalem secure; 5 for David had done what Yahweh regarded as right and had never in all his life disobeyed whatever he commanded him (except in the matter of Uriah the Hittite).*a*

7 The rest of the history of Abijam, his entire career, is this not recorded in the Book of the Annals of the Kings of Judah? Abijam and Jeroboam made war on each other. 8 When Abijam fell asleep with his ancestors, he was buried in the City of David; his son Asa succeeded him.

The reign of Asa in Judah (911–870)

9 In the twentieth year of Jeroboam king of Israel, Asa became king of Judah 10 and reigned for forty-one years in Jerusalem. His mother's name was Maacah descendant of Absalom. 11 Asa did what Yahweh regards as right, as his ancestor David had done. 12 He drove the male prostitutes out of the country and got rid of all the idols which his ancestors had made. 13 He even deprived his grandmother Maacah of the dignity of Great Lady for having made an obscenity for Asherah; Asa cut down her obscenity and burnt it in the ravine of the Kidron. 14 Though the high places were not abolished, Asa's heart was loyal to Yahweh throughout

15a v. 6 is omitted as in some Gk texts; it doubles 14:30.

his life. ¹⁵He deposited his father's and his own dedicated gifts of silver, gold and sacred vessels in the Temple of Yahweh.

¹⁶Asa and Baasha king of Israel were at war with each other throughout their reigns. ¹⁷Baasha king of Israel marched on Judah and fortified Ramah to blockade Asa king of Judah. ¹⁸Asa then took all the remaining silver and gold left in the treasuries of the Temple of Yahweh and the royal palace. Entrusting this to his servants, King Asa sent them with the following message to Ben-Hadad son of Tabrimmon, son of Hezion, the king of Aram who lived in Damascus, ¹⁹'Let us make an alliance between myself and yourself, between my father and your father! Look, I have sent you a gift of silver and gold. Come, break off your alliance with Baasha king of Israel, which will make him withdraw from me.' ²⁰Ben-Hadad listened favourably to King Asa, and sent the generals of his armies to attack the towns of Israel; he ravaged Ijon, Dan, Abel-Beth-Maacah, all Chinneroth, and the whole territory of Naphtali. ²¹When Baasha heard this he gave up fortifying Ramah and retired to Tirzah. ²²King Asa then summoned all Judah, no one was exempt; they took away the stones and timber with which Baasha had been fortifying Ramah, and King Asa used them to fortify Geba of Benjamin and Mizpah.

²³The rest of the history of Asa, all his valour, his entire career, is this not recorded in the Book of the Annals of the Kings of Judah? In his old age, however, he contracted a disease of his feet. ²⁴When Asa fell asleep with his ancestors, he was buried with his ancestors in the City of his ancestor David; his son Jehoshaphat succeeded him.

The reign of Nadab in Israel (910–909)

²⁵Nadab son of Jeroboam became king of Israel in the second year of Asa king of Judah, and he reigned over Israel for two years. ²⁶He did what is displeasing to Yahweh; he copied his father's example and the sin into which he had led Israel. ²⁷Baasha son of Ahijah, of the House of Issachar, plotted against him and murdered him at Gibbethon, a Philistine town which Nadab and all Israel were besieging. ²⁸Baasha killed Nadab and succeeded him in the third year of Asa king of Judah. ²⁹No sooner was he king than he butchered the entire House of Jeroboam, not sparing a soul, and put an end to it, just as Yahweh had foretold through his servant Ahijah of Shiloh, ³⁰because of the sins which he had committed and into which he had led Israel, and because he had provoked the anger of Yahweh, God of Israel.

³¹The rest of the history of Nadab, his entire career, is this not recorded in ³²the Book of the Annals of the Kings of Israel?

The reign of Baasha in Israel (909–886)

³³In the third year of Asa king of Judah, Baasha son of Ahijah became king of Israel at Tirzah for twenty-four years. ³⁴He did what is displeasing to Yahweh; he copied the example of Jeroboam and the sin into which he had led Israel.

16 The word of Yahweh came to Jehu son of Hanani against Baasha: ²'I raised you from the dust and made you leader of my people Israel, but you have followed Jeroboam's example and led my people Israel into sins which provoke my anger. ³Now I shall sweep away Baasha and his House; I shall make your House like the House of Jeroboam son of Nebat. ⁴Those of Baasha's family who die in the city, the dogs will eat; and those who die in the open country, the birds of the air will eat.'

⁵The rest of the history of Baasha, his career, his valour, is this not recorded in the Book of the Annals of the Kings of Israel? ⁶When Baasha fell asleep with his ancestors, he was buried in Tirzah; his son Elah succeeded him.

⁷Furthermore, the word of Yahweh was delivered through the prophet Jehu son of Hanani against Baasha and his House, first because of the many ways in which he had dis-

pleased Yahweh, provoking him to anger by his actions and becoming like the House of Jeroboam; secondly because he had destroyed that House.

The reign of Elah in Israel (886–885)

⁸ In the twenty-sixth year of Asa king of Judah, Elah son of Baasha became king of Israel at Tirzah, for two years. ⁹ Zimri, one of his officers, captain of half his chariotry, plotted against him. While he was at Tirzah, drinking himself senseless in the house of Arza who was master of the palace in Tirzah, ¹⁰ Zimri came in, struck him down and killed him in the twenty-seventh year of Asa king of Judah, and succeeded him. ¹¹ On his accession, as soon as he was seated on the throne, he butchered Baasha's entire family, not leaving him one manjack of them alive, neither relative nor friend. ¹² Zimri destroyed the whole House of Baasha, in accordance with the word which Yahweh had spoken against Baasha through the prophet Jehu, ¹³ because of all the sins of Baasha and his son Elah into which they had led Israel, provoking the anger of Yahweh, God of Israel, with their worthless idols.

¹⁴ The history of Elah, his entire career, is this not recorded in the Book of the Annals of the Kings of Israel?

The reign of Zimri in Israel (885)

¹⁵ In the twenty-seventh year of Asa king of Judah, Zimri became king for seven days, at Tirzah. The people were then encamped in front of Gibbethon, a Philistine town. ¹⁶ When news reached the camp of how Zimri had not only plotted against but actually killed the king, all Israel proclaimed the army commander Omri as king of Israel in the camp that very day. ¹⁷ Omri, and all Israel with him, raised the siege of Gibbethon and laid siege to Tirzah. ¹⁸ When Zimri saw that the town had been captured, he went into the keep of the royal palace, burned the palace over his own head, and died. ¹⁹ This was because of the sin which he had committed in doing what is displeasing to Yahweh, by copying the example of Jeroboam and the sin into which he had led Israel.

²⁰ The rest of the history of Zimri and of his conspiracy, is this not recorded in the Book of the Annals of the Kings of Israel?

²¹ The people of Israel then split into two factions: one half following Tibni son of Ginath to make him king, the other half following Omri. ²² But the faction of Omri proved stronger than that of Tibni son of Ginath; thus Tibni lost his life and Omri became king.

The reign of Omri in Israel (885–874)

²³ In the thirty-first year of Asa king of Judah, Omri became king of Israel and reigned for twelve years. He reigned for six years at Tirzah. ²⁴ Then for two talents of silver he bought the hill of Samaria from Shemer and on it built a town which he named Samaria after Shemer who had owned the hill. ²⁵ Omri did what is displeasing to Yahweh, and was worse than all his predecessors. ²⁶ In every way he copied the example of Jeroboam son of Nebat and the sins into which he had led Israel, provoking the anger of Yahweh, God of Israel, with their worthless idols.

²⁷ The rest of the history of Omri, his career, his valour, is this not recorded in the Book of the Annals of the Kings of Israel? ²⁸ When Omri fell asleep with his ancestors, he was buried in Samaria; his son Ahab succeeded him.

Introduction to the reign of Ahab (874–853)

²⁹ Ahab son of Omri became king of Israel in the thirty-eighth year of Asa king of Judah, and reigned over Israel for twenty-two years in Samaria. ³⁰ Ahab son of Omri did what is displeasing to Yahweh, and was worse than all his predecessors. ³¹ The least that he did was to follow the sinful example of Jeroboam son of Nebat: he married Jezebel daughter of Ethbaal, king of the Sidonians, and then proceeded to serve Baal and worship him. ³² He erected an altar to him in the temple of Baal which he built in Samaria. ³³ Ahab also put up a sacred pole and committed other crimes as

well, provoking the anger of Yahweh, God of Israel, more than all the kings of Israel his predecessors. 34 It was in his time that Hiel of Bethel rebuilt Jericho. Laying its foundations cost him his eldest son Abiram and erecting its gates cost him his youngest son Segub, just as Yahweh had foretold through Joshua son of Nun.ª

Elijah foretells the drought

17 Elijah the Tishbite, of Tishbe in Gilead, said to Ahab, 'By the life of Yahweh, God of Israel, whom I serve, there will be neither dew nor rain these coming years unless I give the word.'

In the ravine of the Cherith

2 The word of Yahweh came to him, 3 'Go away from here, go east and hide by the torrent of Cherith, east of the Jordan. 4 You can drink from the stream, and I have ordered the ravens to bring you food there.' 5 So he set out and did as Yahweh had said; he went and stayed by the torrent of Cherith, east of the Jordan. 6 The ravens brought him bread in the morning and meat in the evening, and he quenched his thirst at the stream.

At Zarephath; the miracle of the flour and the oilª

7 But after a while the stream dried up, for the country had had no rain. 8 And then the word of Yahweh came to him, 9 'Up and go to Zarephath in Sidonia, and stay there. I have ordered a widow there to give you food.' 10 So he went off to Sidon. And when he reached the city gate, there was a widow gathering sticks. Addressing her he said, 'Please bring a little water in a pitcher for me to drink.' 11 She was on her way to fetch it when he called after her. 'Please', he said, 'bring me a scrap of bread in your hand.' 12 'As Yahweh your God lives,' she replied, 'I have no baked bread, but only a handful of meal in a jar and a little oil in a jug; I am just gathering a stick or two to go and prepare this for myself and my son to eat, and

then we shall die.' 13 But Elijah said to her, 'Do not be afraid, go and do as you have said; but first make a little scone of it for me and bring it to me, and then make some for yourself and for your son. 14 For Yahweh, God of Israel, says this:

> Jar of meal shall not be spent,
> jug of oil shall not be emptied,
> before the day when Yahweh sends
> rain on the face of the earth.'

15 The woman went and did as Elijah told her and they ate the food, she, himself and her son. 16 The jar of meal was not spent nor the jug of oil emptied, just as Yahweh had foretold through Elijah.

The widow's son raised to lifeᵇ

17 It happened after this that the son of the mistress of the house fell sick; his illness was so severe that in the end he expired. 18 And the woman said to Elijah, 'What quarrel have you with me, man of God? Have you come here to bring my sins home to me and to kill my son?' 19 'Give me your son,' he said and, taking him from her lap, he carried him to the upper room where he was staying and laid him on his bed. 20 He cried out to Yahweh, 'Yahweh my God, by killing her son do you mean to bring grief even to the widow who is looking after me?' 21 He stretched himself on the child three times and cried out to Yahweh, 'Yahweh my God, may the soul of this child, I beg you, come into him again!' 22 Yahweh heard Elijah's prayer and the child's soul came back into his body and he revived. 23 Elijah took the child, brought him down from the upper room into the house, and gave him to his mother. 'Look,' Elijah said, 'your son is alive.' 24 And the woman replied, 'Now I know you are a man of God and the word of Yahweh in your mouth is truth itself.'

16a Jos 6:26.
17a ‖ 2 K 4:1–7.
17b ‖ 2 K 4:18–37.

30 READ 1 KINGS 17.

"Please," he said, "bring me a scrap of bread in your hand."—1 KINGS 17:11

HONORING THE POOR

Help is humiliating when it appeals to men from below, taking heed only of their material wants. It humiliates when there is no reciprocity. When you give a poor man nothing but bread or clothes, there is no likelihood of his ever giving you anything in return.

But help honors when it appeals to him from above. It respects him when it deals with his soul, with his religious, moral and political education, and with all that emancipates him from his passions. Help honors when, to the bread that nourishes, it adds the visit that consoles, advice that enlightens, the friendly handshake that lifts up flagging courage. It esteems the poor man when it treats him with respect, not only as an equal, but as a superior, since he is suffering what perhaps we are incapable of suffering. After all, he is the messenger of God to us, sent to prove our justice and our charity, and to save us by our works.

Help then becomes honorable, because it may become mutual. Every person who gives a kind word, good advice, a consolation today, may tomorrow need a kind word, advice, or consolation. The hand that you clasp clasps yours in return. That indigent family whom you love loves you in return, and will have largely acquitted themselves towards you when they shall have prayed for you....

Those who know the road to the poor man's house, whose feet have swept the dust from his stairs, never knock at his door without a sentiment of respect. They know that in accepting bread from their hand, as he takes the light from God, the poor man honors them; they know that the theater and every other place of entertainment can be paid for, but that nothing in this world can pay for two tears of joy in the eyes of a poor mother, nor the grasp of an honest man's hand when one has enabled him to wait till he gets work. BL. FREDERIC OZANAM, 1813–1853

YOU WILL FIND THE NEXT READING AT 1 KINGS 18.

Elijah and Obadiah

18 A long time went by, and the word of Yahweh came to Elijah in the third year, 'Go, present yourself to Ahab, and I will send rain on the country.' [2] So Elijah set off to present himself to Ahab.

As the famine was particularly severe in Samaria, [3] Ahab summoned Obadiah, the master of the palace—Obadiah held Yahweh in great reverence: [4] when Jezebel was butchering the prophets of Yahweh, Obadiah took a hundred of them and hid them, fifty at a time, in a cave, and kept them provided with food and water— [5] and Ahab said to Obadiah, 'Come along, we must scour the country, all the springs and all the ravines in the hope of finding grass to keep horses and mules alive, or we shall have to slaughter some of our stock.' [6] They divided the country for the purpose of their survey; Ahab went one way by himself and Obadiah went another way by himself. [7] While Obadiah was on his way, whom should he meet but Elijah. Recognising him he fell on his face and said, 'So it is you, my lord Elijah!' ⁸'Yes,' he replied, 'go and tell your master, "Elijah is here."' ⁹But Obadiah said, 'What sin have I committed, for you to put your servant into Ahab's power and cause my death? ¹⁰As Yahweh your God lives, there is no nation or kingdom where my master has not sent in search of you; and when they said, "He is not there," he made the kingdom or nation swear an oath that they did not know where you were. ¹¹And now you say to me, "Go and tell your master: Elijah is here." ¹²But as soon as I leave you, the spirit of Yahweh will carry you away and I shall not know where; I shall go and tell Ahab; he will not be able to find you, and then he will kill me. Yet from his youth your servant has revered Yahweh. ¹³Has no one told my lord what I did when Jezebel butchered the prophets of Yahweh, how I hid a hundred of them in a cave, fifty at a time, and kept them provided with food and water? ¹⁴And now you say to me, "Go and tell your master: Elijah is here." Why, he will kill me!' ¹⁵Elijah replied, 'As Yahweh Sabaoth lives, whom I serve, I shall present myself to him today!'

Elijah and Ahab

¹⁶Obadiah went to find Ahab and tell him the news, and Ahab then went to find Elijah. ¹⁷When he saw Elijah, Ahab said, 'So there you are, you scourge of Israel!' ¹⁸'Not I,' he replied, 'I am not the scourge of Israel, you and your family are; because you have deserted Yahweh and followed Baal. ¹⁹Now give orders for all Israel to gather round me on Mount Carmel, and also the four hundred prophets of Baal who eat at Jezebel's table.'

The sacrifice on Carmel

²⁰Ahab called all Israel together and assembled the prophets on Mount Carmel. ²¹Elijah stepped out in front of all the people. 'How long', he said, 'do you mean to hobble first on one leg then on the other? If Yahweh is God, follow him; if Baal, follow him.' But the people had nothing to say. ²²Elijah then said to them, 'I, I alone, am left as a prophet of Yahweh, while the prophets of Baal are four hundred and fifty. ²³Let two bulls be given us; let them choose one for themselves, dismember it but not set fire to it. I in my turn shall prepare the other bull, but not set fire to it. ²⁴You must call on the name of your god, and I shall call on the name of Yahweh; the god who answers with fire, is God indeed.' The people all answered, 'Agreed!' ²⁵Elijah then said to the prophets of Baal, 'Choose one bull and begin, for there are more of you. Call on the name of your god but light no fire.' ²⁶They took the bull and prepared it, and from morning to midday they called on the name of Baal. 'O Baal, answer us!' they cried, but there was no voice, no answer, as they performed their hobbling dance round the altar which they had made. ²⁷Midday came, and Elijah mocked them. 'Call louder,' he said, 'for he is a god: he is preoccupied or he is busy, or he has gone on a journey; perhaps he is asleep and needs to be woken up!' ²⁸So they shouted louder and gashed themselves, as their custom was, with swords and spears until the blood flowed down them. ²⁹Midday passed, and they ranted on until the time when the offering is presented; but there was no voice, no answer, no sign of attention.

³⁰Then Elijah said to all the people, 'Come over to me,' and all the people came over to him. He repaired Yahweh's altar which had been torn down. ³¹Elijah took twelve stones, corresponding to the number of tribes of the sons of Jacob, to whom the word of Yahweh had come, 'Israel is to be your name,' ³²and built an altar in the name of Yahweh. Round the altar he dug a trench of a size to hold two measures of seed. ³³He then arranged the wood, dismembered the bull, and laid it on the wood. ³⁴Then he said, 'Fill four jars with water and pour it on the burnt offering and on the wood.' They did this. He said, 'Do it a second time;' they did it a second time. He said, 'Do it a third time;' they did it a third time. ³⁵The water flowed round the altar until even the trench itself was full of water. ³⁶At the

31   READ 1 KINGS 18:16–40.

Then Yahweh's fire fell and consumed the burnt offering and the wood and licked up the water in the trench.—1 KINGS 18:38

BAPTIZED IN WATER AND THE SPIRIT

Since Christ made us for incorruption, and we transgressed his saving command, he condemned us to the corruption of death in order that our evil should not be immortal. And when in his compassion he stooped to his servants and became like us, he redeemed us from corruption through his own passion. He caused the fountain of remission to well forth for us out of his holy and immaculate side: water for our regeneration and the washing away of sin and corruption; and blood to drink as the pledge of life eternal (see Jn 19:34). And he laid on us the command to be born again of water and of the Spirit (see Jn 3:5), the Holy Spirit drawing near to the water through prayer and invocation. For since human nature is twofold, consisting of soul and body, he gave us a twofold purification of water and of the Spirit. The Spirit renews that part in us that is made in his image and likeness. And the water by the grace of the Spirit cleanses the body from sin and delivers it from corruption. The water expresses the image of death, but the Spirit offers the guarantee of life.

For from the beginning the Spirit of God moved upon the face of the waters (see Gn 1:2) and the Scripture witnesses that water has the power of purification (see Lv 15:10). In the time of Noah God washed away the sin of the world by water (see Gn 6:17). . . . Elijah manifested the grace of the Spirit mingled with the water when he burned the holocaust by pouring on water. And almost everything is purified by water according to the law: for the things of sight are symbols of the things of thought. The regeneration, however, takes place in the spirit: for by the Spirit faith has the power of making us sons of God, creatures as we are, and of leading us into our original blessedness.

ST. JOHN DAMASCENE, 675?–749?

YOU WILL FIND THE NEXT READING AT 1 KINGS 21.

time when the offering is presented, Elijah the prophet stepped forward. 'Yahweh, God of Abraham, Isaac and Israel,' he said, 'let them know today that you are God in Israel, and that I am your servant, that I have done all these things at your command. ³⁷ Answer me, Yahweh, answer me, so that this people may know that you, Yahweh, are God and are winning back their hearts.'

³⁸ Then Yahweh's fire fell and consumed the burnt offering and the wood and licked up the water in the trench. ³⁹ When all the people saw this they fell on their faces. 'Yahweh is God,' they cried, 'Yahweh is God!' ⁴⁰ Elijah said, 'Seize the prophets of Baal: do not let one of them escape.' They seized them, and Elijah took them down to the Kishon, and there he slaughtered them.

The drought ends

⁴¹ Elijah said to Ahab, 'Go back now, eat and drink; for I hear the approaching sound of rain.' ⁴² While Ahab went back to eat and drink, Elijah climbed to the top of Carmel and

bowed down to the ground, putting his face between his knees. ⁴³'Now go up', he told his servant, 'and look out to sea.' He went up and looked. 'There is nothing at all,' he said. Seven times Elijah told him to go back. ⁴⁴The seventh time, the servant said, 'Now there is a cloud, small as a man's hand, rising from the sea.' Elijah said, 'Go and say to Ahab, "Harness the chariot and go down before the rain stops you." ' ⁴⁵And with that the sky grew dark with cloud and storm, and rain fell in torrents. Ahab mounted his chariot and made for Jezreel. ⁴⁶But the hand of Yahweh had come on Elijah and, hitching up his clothes, he ran ahead of Ahab all the way to Jezreel.

The journey to Horeb

19 When Ahab told Jezebel everything that Elijah had done, and how he had put all the prophets to the sword, ²Jezebel sent a messenger to Elijah to say, 'May the gods bring unnameable ills on me and worse ills too, if by this time tomorrow I have not made your life like one of theirs!' ³He was afraid and fled for his life. He came to Beersheba, a town of Judah, where he left his servant. ⁴He himself went on into the desert, a day's journey, and sitting under a furze bush wished he were dead. 'Yahweh,' he said, 'I have had enough. Take my life; I am no better than my ancestors.' ⁵Then he lay down and went to sleep. Then all of a sudden an angel touched him and said, 'Get up and eat.' ⁶He looked round, and there at his head was a scone baked on hot stones, and a jar of water. He ate and drank and then lay down again. ⁷But the angel of Yahweh came back a second time and touched him and said, 'Get up and eat, or the journey will be too long for you.' ⁸So he got up and ate and drank, and strengthened by that food he walked for forty days and forty nights until he reached Horeb, God's mountain.

The encounter with God

⁹There he went into a cave and spent the night there. Then the word of Yahweh came to him saying, 'What are you doing here, Elijah?'

¹⁰He replied, 'I am full of jealous zeal for Yahweh Sabaoth, because the Israelites have abandoned your covenant, have torn down your altars and put your prophets to the sword. I am the only one left, and now they want to kill me.' ¹¹Then he was told, 'Go out and stand on the mountain before Yahweh.' For at that moment Yahweh was going by. A mighty hurricane split the mountains and shattered the rocks before Yahweh. But Yahweh was not in the hurricane. And after the hurricane, an earthquake. But Yahweh was not in the earthquake. ¹²And after the earthquake, fire. But Yahweh was not in the fire. And after the fire, a light murmuring sound. ¹³And when Elijah heard this, he covered his face with his cloak and went out and stood at the entrance of the cave. Then a voice came to him, which said, 'What are you doing here, Elijah?' ¹⁴He replied, 'I am full of jealous zeal for Yahweh, God Sabaoth, because the Israelites have abandoned your covenant, have torn down your altars and put your prophets to the sword. I am the only one left and now they want to kill me.' ¹⁵'Go,' Yahweh said, 'go back by the same way to the desert of Damascus. You must go and anoint Hazael as king of Aram. ¹⁶You must anoint Jehu son of Nimshi as king of Israel, and anoint Elisha son of Shaphat, of Abel-Meholah, as prophet to succeed you. ¹⁷Anyone who escapes the sword of Hazael will be put to death by Jehu; and anyone who escapes the sword of Jehu will be put to death by Elisha. ¹⁸But I shall spare seven thousand in Israel; all the knees that have not bent before Baal, all the mouths that have not kissed him.'

The call of Elisha

¹⁹Leaving there, he came on Elisha son of Shaphat as he was ploughing behind twelve yoke of oxen, he himself being with the twelfth. Elijah passed near to him and threw his cloak over him. ²⁰Elisha left his oxen and ran after Elijah. 'Let me kiss my father and mother, then I will follow you,' he said. Elijah answered, 'Go, go back; for have I done any-

thing to you?' 21 Elisha turned away, took a yoke of oxen and slaughtered them. He used the oxen's tackle for cooking the meat, which he gave the people to eat. He then rose and, following Elijah, became his servant.

The siege of Samaria

20 Ben-Hadad king of Aram mustered his whole army—thirty-two kings were with him, and horses and chariots—and marched on Samaria, to besiege it and take it by assault. 2 He sent messengers into the city to Ahab king of Israel to tell him, 'Ben-Hadad says this, 3 "Your silver and gold are mine. Your wives and children remain yours." ' 4 The king of Israel replied, 'As you command, my lord king. Myself and all I have are yours.'

5 The messengers came again, this time they said, 'Ben-Hadad says this, "I have already sent you an order to hand over your silver and your gold, your wives and your children; 6 but I swear, this time tomorrow, I shall send my servants to ransack your house and your servants' houses and lay hands on everything that they value and take it away." '

7 The king of Israel summoned all the elders of the country and said, 'You can see clearly how this man intends to ruin us. He has already demanded my wives and my children, although I have not refused him my silver and gold.' 8 All the elders and all the people said, 'Take no notice. Do not consent.' 9 So he gave this answer to Ben-Hadad's messengers, 'Say to my lord the king, "All you first required of your servant I will do, but this I cannot do." ' And the messengers went back with the answer.

10 Ben-Hadad then sent him the following message, 'May the gods bring unnameable ills on me and worse ills too, if there is enough dust in Samaria for each of my followers to have a handful!' 11 But the king of Israel returned this answer, 'Say: the man who puts on his armour is not the one to boast, but the man who takes it off.' 12 When Ben-Hadad heard this message—he was under the awnings drinking with the kings—he gave orders to his servants, 'Take up position!' And they took up their positions against the city.

Victory for Israel

13 A prophet then arrived, looking for Ahab king of Israel. 'Yahweh says this,' he said. ' "You have seen this huge army? This very day I shall deliver it into your hands, and you will know that I am Yahweh." ' 14 'By whose means?' Ahab asked. The prophet replied, 'Yahweh says this, "By means of the guards of the district governors." ' 'Who will co-ordinate the attack?' Ahab asked. 'You will,' the prophet replied.

15 So Ahab inspected the guards of the district governors: there were two hundred and thirty-two. After these he reviewed the army, all the Israelites: there were seven thousand. 16 They made a sortie at midday, when Ben-Hadad was drinking himself senseless under the awnings, he and the thirty-two kings who were allies. 17 The guards of the district governors led the sortie. A report was made to Ben-Hadad: 'Some men have come out of Samaria.' 18 He said, 'If they have come out for peace, take them alive; if they have come out for war, take them alive too.' 19 So they made a sortie from the city, the district governors' guards and behind them the army, 20 and each struck down his man. Aram took to flight and Israel pursued; Ben-Hadad king of Aram escaped on horseback. 21 The king of Israel then advanced, capturing horses and chariots and inflicting a great defeat on Aram.

Respite

22 The prophet then went to the king of Israel and said, 'Now is the time to be resolute and think carefully about what you should do, for at the turn of the year the king of Aram will march against you.'

23 The servants of the king of Aram said to him, 'Their gods are gods of the mountains; that is why they have proved stronger than we are. But if we fight them on level ground, we shall certainly beat them. 24 This is what you must do: remove all these kings from their

commands and appoint professional soldiers in their place. ²⁵ You, for your part, must recruit an army as large as the one which deserted you, with as many horses and as many chariots; then if we fight them on level ground, we shall certainly beat them.' He listened to their advice and acted accordingly.

The victory of Aphek

²⁶ At the turn of the year, Ben-Hadad mustered the Aramaeans and marched on Aphek to fight Israel. ²⁷ The Israelites were already mobilised and provisioned, and marched out to meet them. Encamped opposite them, the Israelites looked like two herds of goats, whereas the Aramaeans filled the countryside. ²⁸ The man of God then went to the king of Israel and said, 'Yahweh says this, "Since Aram has said that Yahweh is a god of the mountains and not a god of the plains, I shall put the whole of this huge army into your power, and you will know that I am Yahweh." ' ²⁹ For seven days they were encamped opposite each other. On the seventh day battle was joined and the Israelites slaughtered the Aramaeans, a hundred thousand foot soldiers in one day. ³⁰ The rest fled to Aphek, into the citadel, but the city walls collapsed on twenty-seven thousand of the survivors.

Now Ben-Hadad had fled and taken refuge in an inner room inside the citadel. ³¹ 'Look,' his servants said to him, 'we have heard that the kings of Israel are faithful and kind kings. Let us put sackcloth round our waists and cords round our heads and go out to the king of Israel; perhaps he will spare your life.' ³² So they wrapped sackcloth round their waists and put cords round their heads and went to the king of Israel, and said, 'Your servant Ben-Hadad says, "Spare my life." ' ³³ 'So he is still alive?' he replied. 'He is my brother.' The men took this for a good omen and quickly seized on his words. 'Yes,' they said, 'Ben-Hadad is your brother.' Ahab said, 'Go and fetch him.' Then Ben-Hadad came out to him and Ahab made him get up into his chariot. ³⁴ Ben-Hadad said, 'I shall restore the towns which my father took from your father and you may set up a trading quarter for yourself in Damascus as my father did in Samaria.' 'With a treaty,' Ahab said, 'I shall set you free.' Granting him a treaty, Ahab let him go.

A prophet condemns Ahab's policy

³⁵ At Yahweh's command a member of the brotherhood of prophets said to a companion of his, 'Strike me,' but the man refused to strike him. ³⁶ So he said to him, 'Since you have disobeyed Yahweh's order, the very moment you leave me a lion will kill you.' And no sooner had he left him than he met a lion, which killed him. ³⁷ The prophet then went to find another man and said, 'Strike me,' and the man struck him and wounded him. ³⁸ The prophet then went and stood waiting for the king on the road, disguising himself with a bandage over his eyes. ³⁹ As the king passed, he called out to him, 'Your servant was making his way to where the fight was thickest when someone left the fighting to bring a man to me, and said, "Guard this man; if he is found missing, your life will pay for his, or else you will have to pay one talent of silver." ⁴⁰ But your servant was busy with one thing and another, the man disappeared.' The king of Israel said, 'That is your sentence then. You have pronounced it yourself.' ⁴¹ At this the man quickly pulled off the bandage over his eyes, and the king of Israel recognised him as one of the prophets. ⁴² He said to the king, 'Yahweh says this, "Since you have let the man escape who was under my curse of destruction, your life will pay for his, your people for his people." ' ⁴³ And the king of Israel went home, gloomy and out of temper, back to Samaria.

Naboth refuses to hand over his vineyard

21 This is what happened next: Naboth of Jezreel had a vineyard close by the palace of Ahab king of Samaria, ² and Ahab said to Naboth, 'Give me your vineyard to be my vegetable garden, since it adjoins my palace; I will give you a better vineyard for it

or, if you prefer, I will give you its value in money.' ³Naboth, however, said to Ahab, 'Yahweh forbid that I should give you my ancestral heritage!'

Ahab and Jezebel

⁴Ahab went home gloomy and out of temper at the words of Naboth of Jezreel, 'I will not give you my heritage from my ancestors.' He lay down on his bed and turned his face away and refused to eat. ⁵His wife Jezebel came to him. 'Why are you so dispirited,' she said, 'that you refuse to eat?' ⁶He said, 'I have been talking to Naboth of Jezreel. I said, "Give me your vineyard either for money or, if you prefer, for another vineyard in exchange." But he said, "I will not give you my vineyard."' ⁷Then his wife Jezebel said, 'Some king of Israel you make! Get up, eat and take heart; I myself shall get you the vineyard of Naboth the Jezreelite.'

Naboth is murdered

⁸So she wrote a letter in Ahab's name and sealed it with his seal, sending the letter to the elders and notables of the city where Naboth lived. ⁹In the letter, she wrote, 'Proclaim a fast, and put Naboth in a prominent place among the people. ¹⁰There confront him with a couple of scoundrels who will accuse him as follows, "You have cursed God and the king." Then take him outside and stone him to death.'

¹¹The men of Naboth's city, the elders and notables living in his city, did what Jezebel ordered, as was written in the letter which she had sent him. ¹²They proclaimed a fast and put Naboth in a prominent place among the people. ¹³The two scoundrels then came and confronted him, and the scoundrels then publicly accused Naboth as follows, 'Naboth has cursed God and the king.' He was then taken outside the city and stoned to death. ¹⁴They then sent word to Jezebel, 'Naboth has been stoned to death.' ¹⁵When Jezebel heard that Naboth had been stoned to death, she said to Ahab, 'Get up! Take possession of the vine-

yard which Naboth of Jezreel refused to sell you, for Naboth is no longer alive, he is dead.' ¹⁶When Ahab heard that Naboth was dead, he got up to go down to the vineyard of Naboth of Jezreel and take possession of it.

Elijah pronounces God's sentence

¹⁷Then the word of Yahweh came to Elijah the Tishbite, ¹⁸'Up! Go down to meet Ahab king of Israel, in Samaria. You will find him in Naboth's vineyard; he has gone down to take possession of it. ¹⁹You are to say this to him, "Yahweh says this: You have committed murder and now you usurp as well. For this—and Yahweh says this—in the place where the dogs licked the blood of Naboth, the dogs will lick your blood too." 'ᵃ ²⁰Ahab said to Elijah, 'So you have caught me, O my enemy!' Elijah answered, 'I have caught you! For your double dealing, and since you have done what is displeasing to Yahweh, ²¹I shall now bring disaster down on you; I shall sweep away your descendants and wipe out every manjack of the House of Ahab, fettered or free in Israel. ²²I shall treat your House as I treated the house of Jeroboam son of Nebat and of Baasha son of Ahijah, for provoking my anger and leading Israel into sin. ²³(Against Jezebel too Yahweh spoke these words, "The dogs will eat Jezebel in the Field of Jezreel.") ²⁴Those of Ahab's family who die in the city, the dogs will eat; and those who die in the open country, the birds of the air will eat.'

²⁵And indeed there never was anyone like Ahab for double dealing and for doing what is displeasing to Yahweh, urged on by Jezebel his wife. ²⁶He behaved in the most abominable way, adhering to idols, just as the Amorites had, whom Yahweh had dispossessed for the Israelites.

Ahab repents

²⁷When Ahab heard these words, he tore his garments and put sackcloth next to his skin and fasted; he slept in the sackcloth; he walked

21a ‖ 2 K 9:25–26.

32 READ 1 KINGS 21.

Against Jezebel too Yahweh spoke these words, "The dogs will eat Jezebel in the Field of Jezreel."—1 KINGS 21:23

DOUBLE JEOPARDY

Don't dream that we are to be held less guilty when we find that we have not been alone in sin. Just the opposite. Collaborating with others in sin adds to our punishment. The serpent was more heavily punished than Eve, and Eve more heavily than Adam. And Jezebel suffered more than Ahab, who took the vineyard of Naboth. She had planned the whole affair and opened the way for her husband's crime. So if you cause someone to fall, you shall suffer more grievously than the person you have ruined. For a person to commit sin himself is less wicked than to lead others into sin.

So if we see others sinning we must do more than refuse to help them. We must draw them out of the pit of destruction so that we do not suffer as their accomplices. May we never forget that terrible judgment seat, the river of fire, the chains that can never be unlocked, the darkness that cannot be pierced, the sound of teeth gnashing, the deadly worm. But you protest that God is good. Are then all these things idle words?

Is there no punishment for the rich man who ignored Lazarus (Lk 16:20–26)? Are those who denied Christ the necessities of life not to depart from him into everlasting fire, prepared for the devil and his angels (Mt 25:41–46)? The servant that had no compassion on his fellow who owed him a small sum, shall he or shall he not be delivered to the tormentors (Mt 18:23–25)? Scripture says concerning those that commit adultery that their worm never dies and their fire is never quenched (Mk 9:8). Is that not true?   ST. JOHN CHRYSOSTOM, 347–407

YOU WILL FIND THE NEXT READING AT 2 KINGS 6.

with slow steps. ²⁸Then the word of Yahweh came to Elijah the Tishbite, ²⁹'Have you seen how Ahab has humbled himself before me? Since he has humbled himself before me, I shall not bring the disaster in his days; I shall bring the disaster down on his House in his son's days.'*b*

Ahab plans a campaign against Ramoth in Gilead

22 There was a lull of three years, with no fighting between Aram and Israel. ²Then, in the third year, Jehoshaphat king of Judah paid a visit to the king of Israel. ³The king of Israel said to his officers, 'You are aware that Ramoth in Gilead belongs to us? And yet we do nothing to wrest it away from the king of Aram.' ⁴He said to Jehoshaphat, 'Will you come with me to attack Ramoth in Gilead?' Jehoshaphat replied to the king of Israel, 'I will be as you, my men as yours, my horses as yours.'

The spurious prophets predict success

⁵Jehoshaphat, however, said to the king of Israel, 'First, please enquire what the word of

21b See 2 K 9–10.

[381]

Yahweh is.' ⁶The king of Israel then called the prophets together, about four hundred of them. 'Should I go and attack Ramoth in Gilead,' he asked, 'or should I hold back?' 'Go ahead,' they replied, 'for Yahweh has already given it to the king.' ⁷Jehoshaphat, however, said, 'Is there no other prophet of Yahweh here, so that we can enquire through him?' ⁸The king of Israel said to Jehoshaphat, 'There is one more man through whom we can consult Yahweh, but I hate him because he never has a favourable prophecy for me, only unfavourable ones; he is Micaiah son of Imlah.' 'I hope the king's words are unjustified,' said Jehoshaphat. ⁹The king of Israel then summoned a court official and said, 'Bring Micaiah son of Imlah immediately.'

¹⁰The king of Israel and Jehoshaphat king of Judah were sitting each on his throne, wearing their robes, in an open space just outside the gate of Samaria, with all the prophets in a state of ecstasy before them. ¹¹Zedekiah son of Kenaanah, who had made himself some iron horns, said, 'Yahweh says, "With horns like these you will gore the Aramaeans till you make an end of them."' ¹²And all the prophets cried ecstatically in the same vein, saying, 'March on Ramoth in Gilead! Success is sure, for Yahweh has already given it to the king!'

The prophet Micaiah predicts defeat

¹³The messenger who had gone to summon Micaiah said to him, 'Look here, what the prophets are saying is uniformly favourable to the king. I hope you will say the same as they do and speak favourably.' ¹⁴Micaiah said, 'As Yahweh lives, I shall speak as Yahweh tells me!' ¹⁵When he came to the king, the king said, 'Micaiah, should we go and attack Ramoth in Gilead, or should we hold back?' He replied, 'Go ahead! Success is sure, for Yahweh has already given it to the king!' ¹⁶The king then said, 'How often must I put you on oath to tell me nothing but the truth in the name of Yahweh?' ¹⁷Then he spoke out:

I saw all Israel scattered on the mountains like sheep without a shepherd.
And Yahweh said, 'These have no master, let them all go safely home!'

¹⁸At this the king of Israel said to Jehoshaphat, 'Did I not tell you that he never gives me favourable prophecies, but only unfavourable ones?' ¹⁹Micaiah went on, 'Now listen to the word of Yahweh. I saw Yahweh seated on his throne with the whole array of heaven standing by him, on his right and on his left. ²⁰Yahweh said, "Who will entice Ahab into marching to his death at Ramoth in Gilead?" At which some answered one way, and some another. ²¹A spirit then came forward and stood before Yahweh and said, "I will entice him." ²²"How?" Yahweh asked. He replied, "I shall go and be a deceptive spirit in the mouths of all his prophets." Yahweh said, "You will succeed in enticing him. Go and do it." ²³And now, you see, Yahweh has put a deceptive spirit into the mouths of all your prophets here, for in fact Yahweh has pronounced disaster on you.'

²⁴Zedekiah son of Chenaanah then came up, struck Micaiah on the cheek and said, 'Which way did Yahweh's spirit leave me, to speak to you?' ²⁵'That is what you will find out,' Micaiah retorted, 'the day you go from room to room, trying to hide.' ²⁶The king of Israel said, 'Seize Micaiah and hand him over to Amon, governor of the city, and Joash, the king's son, ²⁷and say, "These are the king's orders: Put this man in prison and feed him on nothing but bread and water until I am safely home."' ²⁸Micaiah said, 'If you ever do get home safely, Yahweh has not spoken through me.'

Ahab falls at Ramoth in Gilead

²⁹The king of Israel and Jehoshaphat king of Judah marched on Ramoth in Gilead. ³⁰The king of Israel said to Jehoshaphat, 'I shall disguise myself to go into battle, but you put on your robes.' So the king of Israel disguised himself and went into battle. ³¹Now, the king

of Aram had given his chariot commanders the following order, 'Do not attack anyone of whatever rank, except the king of Israel.' 32So, when the chariot commanders saw Jehoshaphat, they thought, 'That is obviously the king of Israel,' and surrounded him to attack. But when Jehoshaphat shouted his war cry 33the chariot commanders, realising that he was not the king of Israel, broke off their pursuit.

34Someone, however, drawing his bow without any special aim, shot the king of Israel between the joints of his armour. 'Turn about!' said the king to his charioteer. 'Get me out of the fighting; I am collapsing.' 35But the battle grew fiercer as the day went on and the king had to be held upright in his chariot facing the Aramaeans, the blood from the wound running into the bottom of the chariot, until in the evening he died. 36At sundown a shout ran through the ranks, 'Every man back to his town, every man back to his country!' 37The king is dead.' He was taken to Samaria and in Samaria the king was buried. 38They washed the chariot at the Pool of Samaria; the dogs licked up the blood, and the prostitutes washed in it, in accordance with the word which Yahweh had spoken.

The end of the reign of Ahab

39The rest of the history of Ahab, his entire career, the ivory house he erected, all the towns he built, is this not recorded in the Book of the Annals of the Kings of Israel? 40When Ahab fell asleep with his ancestors, his son Ahaziah succeeded him.

The reign of Jehoshaphat in Judah (870–848)

41Jehoshaphat son of Asa became king of Judah in the fourth year of Ahab king of Israel. 42Jehoshaphat was thirty-five years old when he came to the throne, and he reigned for twenty-five years in Jerusalem. His mother's name was Azubah daughter of Shilhi. 43In every way he followed the example of his father Asa undeviatingly, doing what is pleasing to Yahweh. 44The high places, however, were not abolished; the people still offered sacrifice and incense on the high places. 45Jehoshaphat was at peace with the king of Israel.

46The rest of the history of Jehoshaphat, the valour he showed, the wars he waged, is this not recorded in the Book of the Annals of the Kings of Judah? 47The few male sacred prostitutes left over from the days of his father Asa, he expelled from the country. 48At the time, Edom had no king, and King 49Jehoshaphat built ships of Tarshish to go to Ophir for gold, but they never made the voyage since the ships were wrecked at Ezion-Geber. 50Ahaziah son of Ahab then proposed to Jehoshaphat, 'Let my men go to sea with yours.' But Jehoshaphat would not agree. 51When Jehoshaphat fell asleep with his ancestors he was buried in the City of his ancestor, David; his son Jehoram succeeded him.

King Ahaziah of Israel (853–852) and the prophet Elijah

52Ahaziah son of Ahab became king of Israel in Samaria in the seventeenth year of Jehoshaphat king of Judah, and reigned over Israel for two years. 53He did what is displeasing to Yahweh, by following the example of his father and mother, and of Jeroboam son of Nebat who had led Israel into sin. 54He served Baal and worshipped him, and provoked the anger of Yahweh God of Israel just as his father had done.

The Second Book of the

KINGS

1 After Ahab's death Moab rebelled against Israel.

2 Ahaziah had fallen from the balcony of his upper room in Samaria, and was lying ill; so he sent messengers, saying to them, 'Go and consult Baal-Zebub[a] god of Ekron and ask whether I shall recover from my illness.' 3 But the angel of Yahweh said to Elijah the Tishbite, 'Up! Go and intercept the king of Samaria's messengers. Say to them, "Is there no God in Israel, for you to go and consult Baal-Zebub god of Ekron? 4 Yahweh says this: You will never leave the bed you have got into; you are certainly going to die." ' And Elijah set out.

5 The messengers returned to the king, who said, 'Why have you come back?' 6 'A man came to meet us,' they answered. 'He said, "Go back to the king who sent you and tell him: Yahweh says this: Is there no God in Israel, for you to go and consult Baal-Zebub god of Ekron? For this, you will never leave the bed you have got into; you are certainly going to die." '

7 He said, 'This man who met you and said all this, what was he like?' 8 'A man wearing a hair cloak', they answered, 'and a leather loincloth.' 'It was Elijah the Tishbite,' he said.

9 He then sent a captain of fifty soldiers with his fifty men to Elijah, whom they found sitting on top of a hill; the captain went up to him and said, 'Man of God, the king says, "Come down." ' 10 Elijah answered the captain, 'If I am a man of God, may fire fall from heaven and destroy both you and your fifty men.' And fire fell from heaven and destroyed him and his fifty men. 11 The king sent a second captain of fifty to him, again with fifty men, and he too went up and said, 'Man of God, this is the king's order, "Come down at once." ' 12 Elijah answered them, 'If I am a man of God, may fire fall from heaven and destroy both you and your fifty men.' And lightning fell from heaven and destroyed him and his fifty men. 13 The king then sent a third captain of fifty to him, with another fifty men. The third captain of fifty came up to Elijah, fell on his knees before him and pleaded with him. 'Man of God,' he said, 'may my life and the lives of these fifty servants of yours count for something in your eyes. 14 Fire has fallen from heaven and destroyed two captains of fifties and their companies, but this time may my life count for something in your eyes!' 15 The angel of Yahweh said to Elijah, 'Go down with him; do not be afraid of him.' He rose and accompanied him down to the king, 16 and said to him, 'Yahweh says this, "Since you sent messengers to consult Baal-Zebub god of Ekron, you will never leave the bed you have got into; you are certainly going to die." '

17 And, in accordance with the word of Yahweh which Elijah had uttered, he died. Since he had no son, his brother Jehoram succeeded him, in the second year of Jehoram son of Jehoshaphat, king of Judah. 18 The rest of the history of Ahaziah, and his career, is this not recorded in the Book of the Annals of the Kings of Israel?

Elijah is taken up to heaven and Elisha succeeds him

2 This is what happened when Yahweh took Elijah up to heaven in the whirlwind: Elijah and Elisha set out from Gilgal, 2 and Elijah

---

1a A mocking pun (= Baal of Flies). The god's real name was Baal-Zebul (= Baal the Prince).

said to Elisha, 'You stay here, for Yahweh is only sending me to Bethel.' But Elisha replied, 'As Yahweh lives and as you yourself live, I will not leave you!' and they went down to Bethel. 3 The brotherhood of prophets living at Bethel came out to meet Elisha and said, 'Do you know that Yahweh will carry your lord and master away today?' 'Yes, I know,' he said, 'be quiet.' 4 Elijah said, 'Elisha, you stay here, Yahweh is only sending me to Jericho.' But he replied, 'As Yahweh lives and as you yourself live, I will not leave you!' and they went on to Jericho. 5 The brotherhood of prophets living at Jericho went up to Elisha and said, 'Do you know that Yahweh will carry your lord and master away today?' 'Yes, I know,' he said, 'be quiet.' 6 Elijah said, 'Elisha, you stay here, Yahweh is only sending me to the Jordan.' But he replied, 'As Yahweh lives and as you yourself live, I will not leave you!' And they went on together.

7 Fifty of the brotherhood of prophets followed them, halting some distance away as the two of them stood beside the Jordan. 8 Elijah took his cloak, rolled it up and struck the water; and the water divided to left and right, and the two of them crossed over dry-shod. 9 When they had crossed, Elijah said to Elisha, 'Make your request. What can I do for you before I am snatched away from you?' Elisha answered, 'Let me inherit a double share of your spirit.' 10 'Your request is difficult,' Elijah said. 'If you see me while I am being snatched away from you, it will be as you ask; if not, it will not be so.' 11 Now as they walked on, talking as they went, a chariot of fire appeared and horses of fire coming between the two of them; and Elijah went up to heaven in the whirlwind. 12 Elisha saw it, and shouted, 'My father! My father! Chariot of Israel and its chargers!' Then he lost sight of him, and taking hold of his own clothes he tore them in half. 13 He picked up Elijah's cloak which had fallen, and went back and stood on the bank of the Jordan.

14 He took Elijah's cloak and struck the water. 'Where is Yahweh, the God of Elijah?'

he cried. As he struck the water it divided to right and left, and Elisha crossed over. 15 The brotherhood of prophets saw him in the distance, and said, 'The spirit of Elijah has come to rest on Elisha'; they went to meet him and bowed to the ground before him. 16 'Look,' they said, 'your servants have fifty strong men with them, let them go and look for your master; the Spirit of Yahweh may have taken him up and thrown him down on a mountain or into a valley.' 'Send no one,' he replied. 17 But they so shamed him with their insistence that he consented. So they sent fifty men who searched for three days without finding him. 18 They then came back to Elisha who had stayed in Jericho; he said, 'Didn't I tell you not to go?'

Two miracles of Elisha

19 The people of the city said to Elisha, 'The city is pleasant to live in, as my lord indeed can see, but the water is foul and the country suffers from miscarriages.' 20 'Bring me a new bowl,' he said, 'and put some salt in it.' They brought it to him. 21 Then he went to the source of the water, threw salt into it and said, 'Yahweh says this, "I make this water wholesome: neither death nor miscarriage shall come from it any more." ' 22 And the water became wholesome, as it is today, exactly as Elisha had said it would.

23 From there he went up to Bethel, and while he was on the road, some small boys came out of the town and jeered at him. 'Hurry up, baldy!' they shouted. 'Come on up, baldy!' 24 He turned round and looked at them; and he cursed them in the name of Yahweh. And two bears came out of the forest and savaged forty-two of the boys. 25 From there he went on to Mount Carmel and then returned to Samaria.

Introduction to the reign of Jehoram in Israel (852–841)

3 Jehoram son of Ahab became king of Israel in Samaria in the eighteenth year of Jehoshaphat king of Judah, and reigned for

twelve years. [2] He did what is displeasing to Yahweh, though not like his father and mother, for he did away with the pillar to Baal which his father had made. [3] Nonetheless, he continued to practise the sins into which Jeroboam son of Nebat had led Israel and did not give them up.

The expedition of Israel and Judah against Moab

[4] Mesha king of Moab was a sheep-breeder and used to pay the king of Israel in tribute a hundred thousand lambs and a hundred thousand rams with their wool. [5] But when Ahab died, the king of Moab rebelled against the king of Israel.

[6] At once King Jehoram left Samaria and mustered all Israel. [7] After this he sent word to the king of Judah, 'The king of Moab has rebelled against me. Will you go to war with me against Moab?' 'I will,' he replied. 'I will be as you, my men as yours, my horses as yours,' [8] and added, 'Which way are we to attack?' 'Through the desert of Edom,' the other answered.

[9] So they set out, the king of Israel, the king of Judah and the king of Edom. They carried out a flanking movement for seven days, until there was no water left for the troops or for the beasts of their baggage train. [10] 'Alas!' the king of Israel exclaimed, 'Yahweh has summoned us three kings, only to put us into the power of Moab.' [11] But the king of Judah said, 'Is there no prophet of Yahweh here for us to consult Yahweh through him?' One of the king of Israel's servants answered, 'Elisha son of Shaphat is here, who used to pour water on the hands of Elijah.' [12] 'The word of Yahweh is with him,' the king of Judah said. So the king of Israel, the king of Judah and the king of Edom went to consult him. [13] But Elisha said to the king of Israel, 'What business have you with me? Go to your father's and your mother's prophets.' 'No,' the king of Israel answered, 'Yahweh is the one who has summoned us three kings, only to put us into the power of Moab.' Elisha replied, [14] 'By the life of Yahweh Sabaoth whom I serve, if I did not respect the king of Judah, I would take no notice of you, nor so much as look at you. [15] Now bring me someone who can play the lyre.' And as the musician played, the hand of Yahweh came on him [16] and he said, 'Yahweh says this, "Dig in this valley ditch after ditch," [17] for Yahweh says, "You will see no wind, you will see no rain, but this valley will become full of water, and you and your troops and your baggage animals will drink." [18] But this is only a trifle in Yahweh's eyes, for he will put Moab itself into your power. [19] You will storm every fortified town, fell every productive tree, block every water-hole, ruin all the best fields with stones.' [20] Next morning at the time when the oblation was being offered, water came from the direction of Edom, and the whole terrain was flooded.

[21] When the Moabites learned that the kings were advancing to fight them, all those of an age to bear arms were mobilised; they took up position on the frontier. [22] In the morning when they got up, the sun was shining on the water; and in the distance the Moabites saw the water as red as blood. [23] 'This is blood!' they said. 'The kings must have fought among themselves and killed one another. So now for the booty, Moab!' [24] But when they reached the Israelite camp, the Israelites launched their attack and the Moabites fled before them, and as they advanced they cut the Moabites to pieces. [25] They laid the towns in ruins, and each man threw a stone into all the best fields to fill them up, and they blocked every water-hole and felled every productive tree. In the end, there was only Kir-Hareseth left, which the slingers surrounded and bombarded. [26] When the king of Moab saw that the battle had turned against him, he mustered seven hundred swordsmen in the hope of breaking a way out and going to the king of Aram, but he failed. [27] Then he took his eldest son who was to succeed him and offered him as a sacrifice on the city wall. Alarmed at this, the Israelites withdrew and retired to their own territory.

The widow's oil[a]

4 The wife of a member of the prophetic brotherhood appealed to Elisha. 'Your servant my husband is dead,' she said, 'and you know how your servant revered Yahweh. A creditor has now come to take my two children and make them his slaves.' ²Elisha said, 'What can I do for you? Tell me, what have you got in the house?' 'Your servant has nothing in the house,' she replied, 'except a flask of oil.' ³Then he said, 'Go outside and borrow jars from all your neighbours, empty jars and not too few. ⁴When you come back, shut the door on yourself and your sons, and pour the oil into all these jars, putting each aside when it is full.' ⁵So she left him; and she shut the door on herself and her sons; they passed her the jars and she went on pouring. ⁶When the jars were full, she said to her son, 'Pass me another jar.' 'There are no more,' he replied. Then the oil stopped flowing. ⁷She went and told the man of God, who said, 'Go and sell the oil and redeem your pledge; you and your children can live on the remainder.'

The woman of Shunem and her son

⁸One day as Elisha was on his way to Shunem, a woman of rank who lived there pressed him to stay and eat there. After this he always broke his journey for a meal when he passed that way. ⁹She said to her husband, 'Look, I am sure the man who is constantly passing our way must be a holy man of God. ¹⁰Let us build him a small walled room, and put him a bed in it, and a table and chair and lamp; whenever he comes to us he can rest there.' ¹¹One day when he came, he retired to the upper room and lay down. ¹²He said to his servant Gehazi, 'Call our Shunammite.' He called her and when she appeared, Elisha said, ¹³'Tell her this: "Look, you have gone to all this trouble for us, what can we do for you? Is there anything you would like said for you to the king or to the commander of the army?"' But she replied, 'I live with my own people about me.' ¹⁴'What can I do for you then?' he asked. Ge-

hazi replied, 'Well, she has no son and her husband is old.' ¹⁵Elisha said, 'Call her.' The servant called her and she stood at the door. ¹⁶'This time next year', he said, 'you will hold a son in your arms.' But she said, 'No, my lord, do not deceive your servant.' ¹⁷But the woman did conceive, and she gave birth to a son at the time that Elisha had said she would.

¹⁸The child grew up; one day he went to his father who was with the reapers, ¹⁹and exclaimed to his father, 'Oh, my head! My head!' The father told a servant to carry him to his mother.[b] ²⁰He lifted him up and took him to his mother, and the boy lay on her lap until midday, when he died. ²¹She went upstairs, laid him on the bed of the man of God, shut the door on him and went out. ²²She called her husband and said, 'Send me one of the servants with a donkey. I must hurry to the man of God and back.' ²³'Why go to him today?' he asked. 'It is not New Moon or Sabbath.' But she replied, 'Never mind.' ²⁴She had the donkey saddled and said to her servant, 'Lead on, go! Do not draw rein until I give the order.' ²⁵She set off and made her way to the man of God at Mount Carmel. When the man of God saw her in the distance, he said to his servant Gehazi, 'Look, here comes our Shunammite! ²⁶Now run and meet her and ask her, "Are you well? Is your husband well? Your child well?"' 'Yes,' she replied. ²⁷When she came to the man of God there on the mountain, she took hold of his feet. Gehazi stepped forward to push her away, but the man of God said, 'Leave her; there is bitterness in her soul and Yahweh has hidden it from me, he has not told me.' ²⁸She said, 'Did I ask my lord for a son? Did I not say: Don't deceive me?'

²⁹Elisha said to Gehazi, 'Hitch up your clothes, take my staff in your hand and go. If you meet anyone, do not greet him; if anyone greets you, do not answer him. You are to stretch out my staff over the child.' ³⁰But the child's mother said, 'As Yahweh lives and as you yourself live, I will not leave you.' Then he

4a ‖ 1 K 17:8–15.   *4b* ‖ 1 K 17:17–24.

stood up and followed her. ³¹ Gehazi had gone ahead of them and had stretched out the staff over the child, but there was no sound or response. He went back to meet Elisha and told him. 'The child has not woken up,' he said. ³² Elisha then went to the house, and there on his bed lay the child, dead. ³³ He went in and shut the door on the two of them and prayed to Yahweh. ³⁴ Then he climbed on to the bed and stretched himself on top of the child, putting his mouth on his mouth, his eyes to his eyes, and his hands on his hands, and as he lowered himself on to him, the child's flesh grew warm. ³⁵ Then he got up and walked to and fro inside the house, and then climbed on to the bed again and lowered himself on to the child seven times in all; then the child sneezed and opened his eyes. ³⁶ He then summoned Gehazi. 'Call our Shunammite,' he said. He called her. When she came to him, he said, 'Pick up your son.' ³⁷ She went in and, falling at his feet, prostrated herself on the floor and then picked up her son and went out.

The poisoned soup

³⁸ Elisha went back to Gilgal while there was famine in the country. As the brotherhood of prophets were sitting with him, he said to his servant, 'Put the large pot on the fire and cook some soup for the brotherhood.' ³⁹ One of them went into the fields to gather herbs and came on some wild vine, off which he gathered enough gourds to fill his lap. On his return, he cut them up into the pot of soup; they did not know what they were. ⁴⁰ They then poured the soup out for the men to eat, but they had no sooner tasted the soup than they cried, 'Man of God, there is death in the pot!' And they could not eat it. ⁴¹ 'Bring some meal then,' Elisha said. This he threw into the pot, and said, 'Pour out, for the company to eat!' And there was nothing harmful in the pot.

The multiplication of loaves

⁴² A man came from Baal-Shalishah, bringing the man of God bread from the first-fruits, twenty barley loaves and fresh grain still in the husk. 'Give it to the company to eat,' Elisha said. ⁴³ But his servant replied, 'How can I serve this to a hundred men?' 'Give it to the company to eat,' he insisted, 'for Yahweh says this, "They will eat and have some left over."' ⁴⁴ He served them; they ate and had some left over, as Yahweh had said.

Naaman is healed

5 Naaman, army commander to the king of Aram, was a man who enjoyed his master's respect and favour, since through him Yahweh had granted victory to the Aramaeans. ² But the man suffered from a virulent skin-disease. Now, on one of their raids into Israelite territory, the Aramaeans had carried off a little girl, who became a servant of Naaman's wife. ³ She said to her mistress, 'If only my master would approach the prophet of Samaria! He would cure him of his skin-disease.' ⁴ Naaman went and told his master. 'This and this', he reported, 'is what the girl from Israel has said.' ⁵ 'Go by all means,' said the king of Aram, 'I shall send a letter to the king of Israel.' So Naaman left, taking with him ten talents of silver, six thousand shekels of gold and ten festal robes. ⁶ He presented the letter to the king of Israel. It read, 'With this letter, I am sending my servant Naaman to you for you to cure him of his skin-disease.' ⁷ When the king of Israel read the letter, he tore his clothes. 'Am I a god to give death and life,' he said, 'for him to send a man to me and ask me to cure him of his skin-disease? Listen to this and take note of it and see how he intends to pick a quarrel with me.'

⁸ When Elisha heard that the king of Israel had torn his clothes, he sent word to the king, 'Why have you torn your clothes? Let him come to me, and he will find there is a prophet in Israel.' ⁹ So Naaman came with his team and chariot and drew up at the door of Elisha's house. ¹⁰ And Elisha sent him a messenger to say, 'Go and bathe seven times in the Jordan, and your flesh will become clean once more.' ¹¹ But Naaman was indignant and went off, saying, 'Here was I, thinking he would be sure

to come out to me, and stand there, and call on the name of Yahweh his God, and wave his hand over the spot and cure the part that was diseased. ¹²Surely, Abana and Parpar, the rivers of Damascus, are better than any water in Israel? Could I not bathe in them and become clean?' And he turned round and went off in a rage. ¹³But his servants approached him and said, 'Father, if the prophet had asked you to do something difficult, would you not have done it? All the more reason, then, when he says to you, "Bathe, and you will become clean."' ¹⁴So he went down and immersed himself seven times in the Jordan, as Elisha had told him to do. And his flesh became clean once more like the flesh of a little child.

¹⁵Returning to Elisha with his whole escort, he went in and, presenting himself, said, 'Now I know that there is no God anywhere on earth except in Israel. Now, please, accept a present from your servant.' ¹⁶But Elisha replied, 'As Yahweh lives, whom I serve, I will accept nothing.' Naaman pressed him to accept, but he refused. ¹⁷Then Naaman said, 'Since your answer is "No," allow your servant to be given as much earth as two mules may carry, since your servant will no longer make burnt offerings or sacrifice to any god except Yahweh. ¹⁸Only—and may Yahweh forgive your servant for this—when my master goes to the temple of Rimmon to worship there, he leans on my arm, and I bow down in the temple of Rimmon when he does; may Yahweh forgive your servant for doing this!' ¹⁹'Go in peace,' Elisha replied.

²⁰Naaman had gone a small distance, when Gehazi, Elisha's servant, said to himself, 'My master has let this Aramaean Naaman off lightly, by not accepting what he offered. As Yahweh lives, I will run after him and get something out of him.' ²¹So Gehazi set off in pursuit of Naaman. When Naaman saw him running after him, he jumped down from his chariot to meet him. 'Is all well?' he asked. ²²'All is well,' he said. 'My master has sent me to say, "This very moment two young men of the prophetic brotherhood have arrived from the highlands of Ephraim. Be kind enough to give them a talent of silver and two festal robes."' ²³'Please accept two talents,' Naaman replied, and pressed him, tying up the two talents of silver in two bags with the two festal robes and consigning them to two of his servants who carried them ahead of Gehazi. ²⁴When he reached Ophel, he took these from them and put them away in the house. He then dismissed the men, who went away.

²⁵He, for his part, went and presented himself to his master. Elisha said, 'Gehazi, where have you been?' 'Your servant has not been anywhere,' he replied. ²⁶But Elisha said to him, 'Was not my heart present there when someone left his chariot to meet you? Now you have taken the money, you can buy gardens with it, and olive groves, sheep and oxen, male and female slaves. ²⁷But Naaman's disease of the skin will cling to you and your descendants for ever.' And Gehazi left his presence white as snow from skin-disease.

The axe lost and found

6 The brotherhood of prophets said to Elisha, 'Look, the place where we are living with you is too small for us. ²Let us go to the Jordan, then, and each of us cut a beam there, and we will make our living quarters there.' He replied, 'Go.' ³'Be good enough to go with your servants,' one of them said. 'I will go,' he replied, ⁴and went with them. On reaching the Jordan they began cutting down timber. ⁵But, as one of them was felling his beam, the iron axehead fell into the water. 'Alas, my lord,' he exclaimed, 'and it was a borrowed one too!' ⁶'Where did it fall?' the man of God asked; and he showed him the spot. Then, cutting a stick, Elisha threw it in at that point and made the iron axehead float. ⁷'Lift it out,' he said; and the man stretched out his hand and took it.

Elisha captures an armed band of Aramaeans

⁸The king of Aram was at war with Israel. He conferred with his officers and said, 'You must attack at such and such a place.' ⁹Elisha, how-

[389]

33 READ 2 KINGS 6:1–7; EXODUS 4:1–5.

Then, cutting a stick, Elisha threw it in . . . and made the iron axehead float.

—2 KINGS 6:6

THE MIRACLE OF THE EUCHARIST

Perhaps you will say, "I see bread and wine, how is it that you assert that I receive the Body of Christ?" Let us prove that this is not what nature made, but what the blessing consecrated. The power of blessing is greater than that of nature because by blessing nature itself is changed.

Moses was holding a rod, he cast it down and it became a serpent. Again, he took hold of the tail of the serpent and it returned to the nature of a rod. By virtue of the prophetic office there were two changes in the nature both of the serpent and of the rod. Again, in Elisha's time, one of the sons of the prophets lost the head from his axe, which sank in the Jordan. He asked Elisha's aid, and the prophet cast in a piece of wood and the iron swam. This, too, we clearly recognize as having happened contrary to nature.

We observe, then, that grace has more power than nature. Yet so far we have only spoken of the grace of a prophet's blessing. But if the blessing of man had such power as to change nature, what are we to say of that divine consecration where the very words of the Lord and Savior operate? The Lord Jesus Himself proclaims: "This is my Body" (see Mt 26:26). Before the blessing of the heavenly words another nature is spoken of, after the consecration the Body is signified. He himself speaks of his Blood. Before the consecration it has another name, after it is called Blood. And you say, *Amen,* that is, *It is true.* Let the heart within confess what the mouth utters, let the soul feel what the voice speaks.

ST. AMBROSE, 340?–397

YOU WILL FIND THE NEXT READING AT TOBIT 12.

ever, sent word to the king of Israel, 'Be on your guard about such and such a place, because the Aramaeans are going to attack it.' [10] The king of Israel accordingly sent men to the place which Elisha had named. And he kept warning the king, and the king stayed on the alert; and this happened more than once or twice.

[11] The king of Aram grew very much disturbed over this. He summoned his officers, and said, 'Tell me which of you is betraying us to the king of Israel.' [12] 'No one, my lord king,' one of his officers replied. 'It is Elisha, the prophet in Israel. The words you utter in your bedchamber, he reveals to the king of Israel.' [13] 'Go and find out where he is,' the king said, 'so that I can send people to capture him.' Word was brought to him, 'He is now in Dothan.' [14] So he sent horses and chariots there, and a large force; and these, arriving during the night, surrounded the town.

[15] Next day, Elisha got up early and went out; and there surrounding the town was an armed force with horses and chariots. 'Oh, my lord,' his servant said, 'what are we to do?' [16] 'Do not be afraid,' he replied, 'for there are more on our side than on theirs.' [17] And Elisha prayed. 'Yahweh,' he said, 'open his eyes and

make him see.' Yahweh opened the servant's eyes, and he saw the mountain covered in fiery horses and chariots surrounding Elisha.

18 As the Aramaeans came down towards him, Elisha prayed to Yahweh, 'I beg you to strike these people sun-blind.' And, at Elisha's word, he struck them sun-blind. 19 Then Elisha said to them, 'This is not the road, nor is this the town. Follow me; I shall lead you to the man you are looking for.' But he led them to Samaria. 20 As they entered Samaria, Elisha said, 'Yahweh, open these people's eyes, and let them see.' Yahweh opened their eyes and they saw; they were inside Samaria.

21 When the king of Israel saw them, he said to Elisha, 'Shall I kill them, father?' 22 'Do not kill them,' he replied. 'Do you kill your own prisoners with sword and bow? Offer them food and water, so that they can eat and drink, and then let them go back to their master.' 23 So the king provided a great feast for them; and when they had eaten and drunk, he sent them off and they went back to their master. Aramaean raiding parties never invaded the territory of Israel again.

Samaria besieged; the famine

24 It happened after this that Ben-Hadad king of Aram, mustering his whole army, marched on and laid siege to Samaria. 25 In Samaria there was great famine, and so strict was the siege that the head of a donkey sold for eighty shekels of silver, and one quarter-*kab* of wild onions for five shekels of silver.

26 Now as the king was passing along the city wall, a woman shouted, 'Help, my lord king!' 27 'If Yahweh does not help you,' he retorted, 'where can I find help for you? From the threshing-floor? From the winepress?' 28 Then the king asked, 'What is the matter?' 'This woman here', she answered, 'said to me, "Give up your son; we will eat him today, and eat my son tomorrow." 29 So we cooked my son and ate him. Next day, I said to her, "Give up your son for us to eat." But she has hidden her son.' 30 On hearing the woman's words, the king tore his clothes; the king was walking on the wall, and the people saw that underneath he was wearing sackcloth next his body. 31 'May God bring unnameable ills on me, and worse ills, too,' he said, 'if the head of Elisha son of Shaphat remains on his shoulders today!'

Elisha foretells imminent relief

32 Elisha was sitting in his house, and the elders were sitting with him. The king sent a messenger ahead but, before the man arrived, Elisha had said to the elders, 'Do you see how this son of a murderer has given orders to cut off my head? Look, when the messenger comes, shut the door; hold the door against him. Isn't that the sound of his master's step behind him?' 33 He was still actually speaking, when the king arrived and said, 'This misery plainly comes from Yahweh. Why should I still trust in Yahweh?'

7 'Listen to the word of Yahweh,' Elisha said. 'Yahweh says this, "By this time tomorrow a measure of finest flour will sell for one shekel, and two measures of barley for one shekel, at the gate of Samaria." ' 2 The equerry on whose arm the king was leaning retorted to Elisha, 'Even if Yahweh made windows in the sky, could this word come true?' 'You will see it with your own eyes,' Elisha replied, 'though you will eat none of it.'

The Aramaean camp is found abandoned

3 Now at the entrance to the gate—for they were afflicted with virulent skin-disease—there were four men and they debated among themselves, 'Why sit here waiting for death? 4 If we decide to go into the city, what with the famine in it, we shall die there; if we stay where we are, we shall die just the same. Come on, let us go over to the Aramaean camp; if they spare our lives, we live; if they kill us, well, then we die.' 5 So at dusk they set out and made for the Aramaean camp, but when they reached the confines of the camp there was not a soul there. 6 For Yahweh had caused the Aramaeans in their camp to hear a noise of chariots and

horses, the noise of a great army; and they had said to one another, 'Listen! The king of Israel has hired the Hittite and Egyptian kings against us, to attack us.' 7 So in the dusk they had made off and fled, abandoning their tents, their horses and their donkeys; leaving the camp just as it was, they had fled for their lives. 8 The men with skin-disease, then, reached the confines of the camp. They went into one of the tents and ate and drank, and from it carried off silver and gold and clothing; these they took and hid. Then they came back and, entering another tent, looted it too, and took and hid their booty.

The siege at an end; the famine ceases

9 Then they said to one another, 'We are doing wrong. This is a day of good news, yet we are holding our tongues! If we wait till morning, we shall certainly be punished. Come on, let us go and take the news to the palace.' 10 Off they went and shouted out to the guards on the city gate, 'We have been to the Aramaean camp. There was not a soul there, no sound of anyone, only tethered horses and tethered donkeys, and their tents just as they were.' 11 The gatekeepers shouted the news, which was reported inside the palace.

12 The king got up while it was still dark and said to his officers, 'I can tell you what the Aramaeans have done to us. They know we are starving, so they have left the camp to hide in the open country. "They will come out of the city," they think, "we shall catch them alive and get into the city." ' 13 One of his officers replied, 'Five of the surviving horses still left us had better be taken—they would die in any case like all the rest. Let us send them and see.' 14 So they took two chariot teams and the king sent them after the Aramaean army, saying, 'Go and see.' 15 They followed them as far as the Jordan, finding the whole way strewn with clothes and gear which the Aramaeans had thrown away in their panic. The scouts returned and informed the king.

16 Then the people went out and plundered the Aramaean camp: a measure of finest flour sold for one shekel, and two measures of barley for one shekel, as Yahweh had promised they would. 17 The king had detailed the equerry, on whose arm he leaned, as commander of the guard on the gate, but the people trampled on him in the gateway and he died, as the man of God had foretold when the king had come down to him. 18 (What Elisha had said to the king came true, 'Two measures of barley will sell for one shekel, and a measure of finest flour for one shekel, by this time tomorrow at the gate of Samaria.' 19 And the equerry in question had replied to the man of God, 'Even if Yahweh made windows in the sky, could this word come true?' 'You will see it with your own eyes,' Elisha had answered, 'though you will eat none of it.' 20 And that was what happened to him: for the people trampled on him in the gateway and he died.)

Epilogue to the story of the woman of Shunem

8 Elisha had said to the woman whose son he had raised to life, 'Move away with your family, and live where you can in some foreign country, for Yahweh has called up a famine—it is already coming on the country—for seven years.' 2 The woman hurried to do what the man of God had told her: she set out, she and her family, and for seven years she lived in Philistine territory. 3 When the seven years were over, the woman returned from Philistine territory and went to lodge a claim with the king for her house and land.

4 Now the king was talking to Gehazi, the servant of the man of God. 'Tell me', he was saying, 'all about the marvels which Elisha did.' 5 Gehazi was just telling the king how Elisha had raised the dead child to life, when the woman whose son Elisha had raised lodged her claim with the king for her house and land. 'My lord king,' Gehazi said, 'this is the very woman, and that is her son whom Elisha raised to life.' 6 The king questioned the woman, who told him the story. The king then delegated one of the officials to her with this order, 'See that all her property is restored

to her, and all the revenue from her land from the day she left the country until now.'

Elisha and Hazael of Damascus

7 Elisha went to Damascus. Ben-Hadad king of Aram was ill, and was told, 'The man of God has come all the way to us.' 8 Then the king said to Hazael, 'Take a present with you and go and meet the man of God; consult Yahweh through him, and find out if I shall recover from my illness.'

9 So Hazael went to meet Elisha, taking with him as a present the best that Damascus could offer, a load for forty camels. He arrived and, presenting himself, said, 'Your son Ben-Hadad king of Aram has sent me to ask you, "Shall I recover from my illness?"' 10 Elisha replied, 'Go and tell him, "You might recover," though Yahweh has shown me that he will certainly die.' 11 Then the face of the man of God went rigid, and his look grew strangely fixed, and he wept. 12 'Why', Hazael asked, 'does my lord weep?' 'Because I know', Elisha replied, 'what harm you will do to the Israelites: you will burn down their fortresses, put their picked warriors to the sword, dash their little children to pieces, disembowel their pregnant women.' 13 'But what is your servant?' Hazael said. 'How could this dog achieve anything so great?' 'In a vision from Yahweh,' Elisha replied, 'I have seen you king of Aram.'

14 Leaving Elisha, Hazael went back to his master who asked, 'What did Elisha say to you?' He replied, 'He told me that you might recover.' 15 Next day he took a blanket, soaked it in water, and spread it over his face. So died Ben-Hadad, and Hazael succeeded him.

The reign of Jehoram in Judah (848–841)

16 In the fifth year of Jehoram son of Ahab, king of Israel, Jehoram son of Jehoshaphat became king of Judah. 17 He was thirty-two years old when he came to the throne, and he reigned for eight years in Jerusalem. 18 He followed the example of the kings of Israel as the House of Ahab were doing; he had married one of Ahab's daughters; and he did what is displeasing to Yahweh. 19 But Yahweh was unwilling to destroy Judah, because of his servant David, and was faithful to the promise which he had made him to leave him a lamp for ever in his presence.

20 In his time Edom threw off the domination of Judah and set up a king for itself. 21 Jehoram crossed to Zair, and with him all the chariots . . . Under cover of dark, he and his chariot commanders broke through the Edomites surrounding him; the people fled to their tents. 22 Even so, Edom threw off the domination of Judah, remaining free to the present day. Libnah also revolted at that time.

23 The rest of the history of Jehoram, his entire career, is this not recorded in the Book of the Annals of the Kings of Judah? 24 Then Jehoram fell asleep with his ancestors and was buried with them in the City of David; his son Ahaziah succeeded him.

The reign of Ahaziah in Judah (841)

25 In the twelfth year of Jehoram son of Ahab, king of Israel, Ahaziah son of Jehoram, king of Judah, became king. 26 Ahaziah was twenty-two years old when he came to the throne, and he reigned for one year in Jerusalem. His mother's name was Athaliah granddaughter of Omri king of Israel. 27 He followed the example of the House of Ahab and did what is displeasing to Yahweh, as the House of Ahab were doing, to whom he was related by marriage.

28 He went with Jehoram son of Ahab to make war on Hazael king of Aram at Ramoth in Gilead, but the Aramaeans wounded Jehoram. 29 King Jehoram returned to Jezreel to recover from the wounds which he had received at Ramah, fighting against Hazael king of Aram. Ahaziah son of Jehoram, king of Judah, went down to Jezreel to visit Jehoram son of Ahab because he was ailing.

A disciple of Elisha anoints Jehu king

9 The prophet Elisha summoned a member of the prophetic brotherhood to him, 'Hitch up your clothes, take this flask of oil,

and go to Ramoth in Gilead. ²When you arrive there, look for Jehuson of Jehoshaphat, son of Nimshi. Then, when you find him, tell him to get up and leave his companions, and take him into an inner room. ³Take the flask of oil then and pour it over his head, and say, "Yahweh says this: I have anointed you king of Israel." Then open the door and flee as fast as you can.'

⁴The young man left for Ramoth in Gilead ⁵and when he arrived, found the senior officers of the army sitting together. 'I have a message for you, commander,' he said. 'For which of us?' asked Jehu. 'For you, commander,' he answered. ⁶Jehu then got up and went into the house. And the young man poured the oil on his head, saying, 'Yahweh, God of Israel, says this, "I have anointed you king of Yahweh's people, of Israel. ⁷You will strike down the family of Ahab your master, and I shall avenge the blood of my servants the prophets and all of Yahweh's servants, on Jezebel ⁸and on the whole family of Ahab. I shall destroy every manjack of Ahab's family, fettered or free in Israel. ⁹I shall make the House of Ahab like the House of Jeroboam son of Nebat and of Baasha son of Ahijah. ¹⁰As for Jezebel, the dogs will eat her in the field of Jezreel; no one will bury her." ' With this, he opened the door and made his escape.

Jehu proclaimed king

¹¹Jehu came out to his master's officers. 'Is all well?' they asked him. 'Why did this madman come to you?' 'You know the fellow and how he talks,' he answered. ¹²'Evasion!' they cried, 'Come on, tell us.' He replied, 'He said this and that to me. He said, "Yahweh says this: I have anointed you king of Israel." ' ¹³Whereupon they all took their cloaks and spread them under him on the bare steps; they sounded the trumpet and shouted, 'Jehu is king!'

Jehu prepares to usurp power

¹⁴Jehu son of Jehoshaphat, son of Nimshi plotted against Jehoram. (At the time, Jehoram,

with all Israel, was holding Ramoth in Gilead against an attack by Hazael king of Aram, ¹⁵but King Jehoram had gone back to Jezreel to recover from the wounds which he had received from the Aramaeans while he was fighting against Hazael king of Aram.) 'If you agree,' Jehu said, 'let no one leave the town to go and take the news to Jezreel.' ¹⁶Jehu then mounted his chariot and left for Jezreel; Jehoram had taken to his bed there, and Ahaziah king of Judah had gone down to visit him.

¹⁷The lookout posted on the tower of Jezreel saw Jehu's troop approaching. 'I can see a body of men,' he shouted. Jehoram gave the order: 'Have a horseman sent to meet them and ask, "Is all well?" ' ¹⁸The horseman went to meet Jehu and said, 'The king says, "Is all well?" ' 'What has it to do with you whether all is well?' Jehu replied. 'Fall in behind me.' The lookout reported, 'The messenger has reached them and is not coming back.' ¹⁹The king sent a second horseman who reached them and said, 'The king says, "Is all well?" ' 'What has it to do with you whether all is well?' Jehu replied. 'Fall in behind me.' ²⁰The lookout reported, 'He has reached them and is not coming back. The manner of driving is like that of Jehu son of Nimshi: he drives like a madman.' ²¹'Harness!' Jehoram cried; and they harnessed his chariot. Then Jehoram king of Israel and Ahaziah king of Judah, each in his chariot, set out to meet Jehu. They reached him in the field of Naboth of Jezreel.

The assassination of Jehoram

²²As soon as Jehoram saw Jehu he asked, 'Is all well, Jehu?' 'What a question!' he replied, 'when all the while the prostitutions and countless sorceries of your mother Jezebel go on.' ²³At this, Jehoram wheeled and fled, saying to Ahaziah, 'Treason, Ahaziah!' ²⁴But Jehu had drawn his bow; he struck Jehoram between the shoulder-blades, the arrow went through the king's heart, and he sank down in his chariot. ²⁵'Pick him up,' Jehu said to Bidkar, his equerry, 'and throw him into the field of Naboth of Jezreel. Remember how, when

you and I manned a chariot together behind Ahab his father, Yahweh pronounced this sentence against him,ᵃ 26 "This I swear. Yesterday I saw the blood of Naboth and the blood of his sons—Yahweh says this. And in this same field I shall requite you—Yahweh says this." So pick him up, and throw him into the field, as Yahweh declared should happen!'

The assassination of Ahaziah

27 When Ahaziah king of Judah saw this, he fled along the Beth-ha-Gan road, but Jehu went in pursuit of him. 'Strike him down too,' he said. And they wounded him in his chariot at the slope of Gur, which is near Ibleam, and he took refuge in Megiddo, where he died. 28 His servants carried him in a chariot to Jerusalem and buried him in his tomb in the City of David. 29 Ahaziah had become king of Judah in the eleventh year of Jehoram son of Ahab.

The assassination of Jezebel

30 When Jehu went back to Jezreel, Jezebel was told. She made up her eyes with mascara, adorned her head and appeared at the window. 31 As Jehu came through the gateway she said, 'How did Zimri get on after killing his master?' 32 Jehu looked up to the window and said, 'Who is on my side? Who?' And two or three officials looked down at him. 33 'Throw her down,' he said. They threw her down and her blood spattered the walls and the horses; and Jehu rode over her. 34 He went in and ate and drank, then said, 'See to this accursed woman, and give her burial; after all, she was a king's daughter.' 35 But when they went to bury her, they found nothing but her skull, feet and hands. 36 They came back and told Jehu, who said, 'This is the word of Yahweh which he spoke through his servant Elijah the Tishbite, "The dogs will eat the flesh of Jezebel in the field of Jezreel; 37 the corpse of Jezebel will be like dung spread on the fields, so that no one will be able to say: This was Jezebel." '

The massacre of the royal family of Israel

10 There were seventy of Ahab's sons in Samaria. Jehu sent to Samaria, to the authorities of the city, to the elders and to the guardians of Ahab's children. He said, 2 'Now, when this letter reaches you, you have your master's sons with you; you also have chariots and horses, a fortified city and weapons. 3 See which of your master's sons is the best and worthiest, put him on his father's throne and fight for your master's dynasty!' 4 They were utterly terrified. 'We have seen how the two kings could not stand up to him,' they said, 'so how could we?' 5 Consequently the master of the palace, the governor of the city, the elders and the guardians sent word to Jehu, 'We are your servants. We shall do whatever you order us. We shall not proclaim a king; act as you think best.'

6 Jehu then wrote them a second letter. He said, 'If you are for me and if you are prepared to accept orders from me, take the heads of the men of your master's family and come to me at Jezreel by this time tomorrow.' (There were seventy of Ahab's sons being educated there by the leading men of the city.) 7 When this letter reached them, they took the king's sons and butchered all seventy of them, put their heads in baskets and sent them to him at Jezreel.

8 The messenger came and told Jehu, 'They have brought the heads of the king's sons.' 'Leave them in two heaps at the entrance to the gate until morning,' he replied. 9 When morning came, he went out and, standing, said to all the people, 'No guilt attaches to you! I did indeed plot against my master and have killed him; but what about all these? Who struck them? 10 Know, then, that nothing will fail to be fulfilled of the prophecy uttered by Yahweh against the House of Ahab; Yahweh has done what he said through his servant Elijah.' 11 Jehu then killed every member of the House of Ahab surviving in Jezreel, all his

9a ‖ 1 K 21:19.

leading men, his close friends, his priests; he did not leave a single one alive.

The massacre of the princes of Judah

¹²Jehu then set out for Samaria. As he was on his way, at Beth-Eked of the Shepherds, ¹³he met the brothers of Ahaziah king of Judah. 'Who are you?' he asked. 'We are Ahaziah's brothers,' they replied, 'and we are on our way to pay our respects to the king's sons and the queen mother's sons.' ¹⁴'Take them alive,' he said. They took them alive, and he slaughtered them at the storage-well of Beth-Eked, forty-two of them; he did not spare a single one.

Jehu and Jehonadab

¹⁵Leaving there, he came on Jehonadab son of Rechab who was on his way to meet him. He greeted him and said, 'Is your heart true to mine, as my heart is to yours?' Jehonadab replied, 'Yes.' 'If so,' Jehu said, 'give me your hand.' Jehonadab gave him his hand, and Jehu took him up beside him in his chariot. ¹⁶'Come with me,' he said, 'and witness my zeal for Yahweh,' and took him along in his chariot. ¹⁷When he entered Samaria, he killed all the survivors of Ahab's family there; he destroyed it, as Yahweh had told Elijah it would happen.

The destruction of Baal's adherents and temple

¹⁸Then Jehu assembled all the people. 'Ahab did Baal some small service,' he said, 'but Jehu will do him a great one. ¹⁹Now call me all the prophets of Baal and all his priests. Not one is to be absent: I have a great sacrifice to offer to Baal. If anyone is absent, he will forfeit his life.' This was a trick on Jehu's part to destroy the devotees of Baal. ²⁰'Summon a sacred assembly for Baal,' he commanded; and they summoned it. ²¹Jehu sent messengers throughout Israel, and all the devotees of Baal arrived, not a man was left who did not attend. They crowded into the temple of Baal until it was full from wall to wall. ²²Jehu then said to the keeper of the wardrobe, 'Bring out vestments for all the devotees of Baal'; he brought out the vestments for them. ²³Jehu then went into the temple of Baal with Jehonadab son of Rechab and said to Baal's devotees, 'Make quite sure that there are no devotees of Yahweh in here with you, but only devotees of Baal.' ²⁴He then proceeded to present sacrifices and burnt offerings.

Now Jehu had stationed eighty of his men outside, having said, 'Whoever lets one of the people go whom I am now putting within your clutches, will pay for it with his life.' ²⁵When he had finished making the burnt offering, he gave the order to the guards and equerries, 'Go in, strike them down! Let no one out!' The guards and equerries went in, putting everyone to the sword all the way to the sanctuary of Baal's temple. ²⁶They took the sacred pole out of Baal's temple and burned it. ²⁷They demolished Baal's image and demolished Baal's temple too, making it into a latrine, which it still is today.

The reign of Jehu in Israel (841–814)

²⁸Thus Jehu rid Israel of Baal. ²⁹Even so, Jehu did not give up the sins into which Jeroboam son of Nebat had led Israel, the golden calves of Bethel and Dan. ³⁰Yahweh said to Jehu, 'Since you have done well in carrying out what pleases me, and have done everything I required to be done to the House of Ahab, your sons will occupy the throne of Israel down to the fourth generation.' ³¹Jehu, however, did not faithfully and wholeheartedly follow the law of Yahweh, God of Israel; he did not give up the sins into which Jeroboam son of Nebat had led Israel.

³²At that time Yahweh began to whittle Israel down, and Hazael defeated the Israelites throughout the territory east of the Jordan: ³³the whole territory of Gilead—of the Gadites, the Reubenites and the Manassehites—from Aroer on the River Arnon: Gilead and Bashan.

³⁴The rest of the history of Jehu, his entire career, all his prowess, is this not recorded in

the Book of the Annals of the Kings of Israel? ³⁵ Then he fell asleep with his ancestors and was buried in Samaria; his son Jehoahaz succeeded him. ³⁶ Jehu's reign over Israel in Samaria lasted twenty-eight years.

Athaliah (841–835)

11 When Athaliah mother of Ahaziah learned that her son was dead, she promptly murdered all those of royal stock.

² But Jehosheba, daughter of King Jehoram and sister of Ahaziah, surreptitiously rescued Jehoash son of Ahaziah from among the princes who were to be murdered, and put him with his nurse in the sleeping quarters; in this way she hid him from Athaliah, and he was not killed. ³ He stayed, hidden with her in the Temple of Yahweh for six years, while Athaliah governed the country.

⁴ In the seventh year, Jehoiada sent for the regimental commanders of the Carians and the guards, and had them brought to him in the Temple of Yahweh. He made a pact with them, put them on oath, then showed them the king's son. He gave them this order, ⁵ 'This is what you must do: a third of you who come on duty on the Sabbath must mount guard at the royal palace,ᵃ ⁷ and your two other sections who come off duty on the Sabbath and mount guard at the Temple of Yahweh ⁸ must surround the king, each man with his weapons in his hand; anyone forcing his way through the ranks is to be killed. And you will escort the king as he leaves and as he comes in.'

⁹ The regimental commanders did everything as Jehoiada the priest had ordered, and each one brought his men, those coming on duty on the Sabbath and those going off duty on the Sabbath, and reported to Jehoiada the priest. ¹⁰ The priest then issued the regimental commanders with King David's spears and shields, which were kept in the Temple of Yahweh. ¹¹ The guards then took position, each man with his weapons in his hand, from the south corner of the Temple to the north corner of the Temple, all round the altar and the Temple. ¹² Then Jehoiada brought the king's son out—crowned him and gave him a copy of the covenant; and they made him king and anointed him, and they clapped their hands and shouted, 'Long live the king!'

¹³ On hearing the people shouting, Athaliah joined the people in the Temple of Yahweh. ¹⁴ When she looked, there stood the king on a dais, as the custom was, with the officers and trumpeters at the king's side, and all the people of the country rejoicing and blowing the trumpets; then Athaliah tore her clothes and shouted, 'Treason, treason!' ¹⁵ Jehoiada the priest then gave the orders to the commanders in charge of the troops, 'Take her out under guard and put to death anyone who follows her.' 'For', the priest had already said, 'she must not be killed inside the Temple of Yahweh.' ¹⁶ They seized her, and when she reached the horses' entry to the palace, she was killed there.

¹⁷ Jehoiada made a covenant between Yahweh, the king and the people that they would remain Yahweh's people; and another one between the king and the people. ¹⁸ All the people of the country then went to the temple of Baal and demolished it; they smashed its altars and its images and killed Mattan the priest of Baal in front of the altars.

The priest made arrangements for the security of the Temple of Yahweh. ¹⁹ He then took the regimental commanders, the Carians, the guards and all the people of the country, and they escorted the king down from the Temple of Yahweh, entering the palace through the Gate of the Guards. Jehoash took his seat on the throne of the kings. ²⁰ All the people of the country were delighted; the city, however, made no move. And Athaliah was put to death inside the palace.

The reign of Jehoash in Judah (835–796)

12 Jehoash was seven years old when he came to the throne. ² Jehoash became king in the seventh year of Jehu, and reigned for forty years in Jerusalem. His mother's

---

11a v. 6 is omitted as a confused gloss.

name was Zibiah of Beersheba. ³All his life Jehoash did what Yahweh regards as right, having been instructed by Jehoiada the priest. ⁴The high places, however, were not abolished, and the people still offered sacrifices and incense on the high places.

⁵Jehoash said to the priests, 'All the money from the sacred revenues brought to the Temple of Yahweh, the money from personal taxes, and all the money voluntarily offered to the Temple— ⁶the priests are to receive this individually from people of their acquaintance and will carry out all the repairs to the Temple which need to be made.' ⁷Now in the twenty-third year of King Jehoash the priests had done no repairs to the Temple; ⁸so King Jehoash summoned Jehoiada the priest and the other priests. 'Why are you not repairing the Temple?' he asked. 'You are no longer to accept money from people of your acquaintance but are to hand it over for the Temple repairs.' ⁹The priests agreed to accept no money from the people and no longer to be responsible for repairs to the Temple.

¹⁰Jehoiada the priest took a chest, bored a hole in the lid and placed it beside the pillar, to the right of the entry to the Temple of Yahweh; in it the priests who guarded the threshold put all the money which was given for the Temple of Yahweh. ¹¹Whenever they saw that there was a great deal of money in the chest, the king's secretary would come, and they would empty it out and reckon the money then in the Temple of Yahweh. ¹²Once checked, they paid this money over to the masters of works attached to the Temple of Yahweh, and these in turn spent it on carpenters and builders working on the Temple of Yahweh, ¹³on masons and stonecutters, and on buying timber and dressed stone to be used for repairs to the Temple of Yahweh; in short, for all the costs of the Temple repairs. ¹⁴But no silver basins, knives, sprinkling bowls, trumpets or gold or silver objects were made for the Temple of Yahweh out of the money presented, ¹⁵which was all given to the masters of works for repairing the Temple of Yahweh.

¹⁶No accounts were kept with the men to whom the money was paid over to be spent on the workmen, since they were honest in their work. ¹⁷Money offered in expiation of an offence or of a sin was not given to the Temple of Yahweh; that was for the priests.

¹⁸At that time Hazael king of Aram went to war against Gath, and captured it; he then prepared to attack Jerusalem. ¹⁹Jehoash king of Judah took all the sacred offerings dedicated by his ancestors, the kings of Judah, Jehoshaphat, Jehoram and Ahaziah, with those which he himself had dedicated, and all the gold which was to be found in the treasuries of the Temple of Yahweh and of the palace; he sent it all to Hazael king of Aram, who retired from Jerusalem.

²⁰The rest of the history of Joash, his entire career, is this not recorded in the Book of the Annals of the Kings of Judah? ²¹His own retainers rebelled and hatched a plot; they murdered Joash in the palace of the Millo . . . ²²Jozacar son of Shimeath and Jehozabad son of Shomer were the retainers who struck the blows from which he died. He was buried with his ancestors in the City of David; his son Amaziah succeeded him.

The reign of Jehoahaz in Israel (814–798)

13 In the twenty-third year of Joash son of Ahaziah, king of Judah, Jehoahaz son of Jehu became king of Israel in Samaria. He reigned for seventeen years. ²He did what is displeasing to Yahweh and copied the sin into which Jeroboam son of Nebat had led Israel; he did not give it up.

³This aroused Yahweh's anger against the Israelites, and he delivered them without respite into the power of Hazael king of Aram and of Ben-Hadad son of Hazael. ⁴Jehoahaz, however, tried to placate Yahweh, and Yahweh heard him, for he had seen the oppression which the king of Aram was inflicting on Israel. ⁵Yahweh gave Israel a saviour who freed them from the grip of Aram, and the Israelites lived in their tents as in the past. ⁶But they did not give up the sin into which Jeroboam had

led Israel; they persisted in it, and even the sacred pole stayed standing in Samaria. ⁷Of Jehoahaz's army Yahweh left only fifty horsemen, ten chariots and ten thousand foot soldiers. The king of Aram had destroyed them, making them like dust trampled under foot.

⁸The rest of the history of Jehoahaz, his entire career, his prowess, is this not recorded in the Book of the Annals of the Kings of Israel? ⁹Then Jehoahaz fell asleep with his ancestors, and was buried in Samaria; his son Joash succeeded him.

The reign of Jehoash in Israel (798–783)

¹⁰In the thirty-seventh year of Joash king of Judah, Jehoash son of Jehoahaz, became king of Israel in Samaria. He reigned for sixteen years. ¹¹He did what is displeasing to Yahweh, he did not give up the sin into which Jeroboam son of Nebat had led Israel; he persisted in it.

¹²The rest of the history of Joash, his entire career, his prowess, how he waged war on Amaziah king of Judah, is this not recorded in the Book of the Annals of the Kings of Israel? ¹³Then Joash fell asleep with his ancestors, and Jeroboam ascended his throne. Joash was buried in Samaria with the kings of Israel.

The death of Elisha

¹⁴When Elisha had fallen ill of the illness of which he was to die, Joash king of Israel went down to him and shedding tears over him said, 'Father! Father! Chariot of Israel and its chargers!' ¹⁵Elisha said to him, 'Bring bow and arrows,' and he sent for a bow and arrows. ¹⁶Then Elisha said to the king, 'Draw the bow,' and he drew it. Elisha put his hands over the hands of the king, ¹⁷then he said, 'Open the window towards the east,' and he opened it. Then Elisha said, 'Shoot!' And he shot. Elisha said, 'Arrow of victory over Aram! You will defeat Aram at Aphek—completely.' ¹⁸Elisha said, 'Take the arrows,' and he took them. Then he said to the king, 'Strike the ground,' and he struck it three times, then

stopped. ¹⁹At this the man of God grew angry with him. 'You should have struck half a dozen times,' he said, 'and you would have beaten Aram completely; now you will beat Aram only three times.'

²⁰Elisha died and was buried. Bands of Moabites were making incursions into the country every year. ²¹Some people happened to be carrying a man out for burial; at the sight of one of these bands, they flung the man into the tomb of Elisha and made off. The man had no sooner touched the bones of Elisha than he came to life and stood up on his feet.

Victory over the Aramaeans

²²Hazael king of Aram had oppressed the Israelites throughout the lifetime of Jehoahaz, ²³but Yahweh was kind and took pity on them. Because of the covenant which he had made with Abraham, Isaac and Jacob, he relented towards them; he had no wish to destroy them, he did not cast them out of his presence. ²⁴Hazael king of Aram died, and his son Ben-Hadad succeeded him. ²⁵From Ben-Hadad son of Hazael, Jehoash son of Jehoahaz recaptured the towns which Hazael had seized from his father Jehoahaz by force of arms. Joash defeated him three times and recovered the Israelite towns.

The reign of Amaziah in Judah (796–781)

14 In the second year of Joash son of Jehoahaz, king of Israel, Amaziah son of Joash became king of Judah. ²He was twenty-five years old when he came to the throne, and he reigned for twenty-nine years in Jerusalem. His mother's name was Jehoaddin of Jerusalem. ³He did what Yahweh regards as right, though not like his ancestor David; he imitated his father Joash in all respects. ⁴The high places, however, were not abolished, and the people still offered sacrifices and incense on the high places.

⁵Once the kingdom was firmly under his control, he killed those of his retainers who

had murdered the king his father. ⁶But he did not put the murderers' sons to death, in accordance with what is written in the Book of Moses, where Yahweh has commanded: *'Parents may not be put to death for their children, nor children for parents, but each must be put to death for his own crime.'*^a

⁷It was he who slaughtered the Edomites in the Valley of Salt, ten thousand of them, and captured the Rock; he gave it the name Joktheel, which it bears to the present day.

⁸Amaziah then sent messengers to Jehoash son of Jehoahaz, king of Israel, saying, 'Come and make a trial of strength!' ⁹Jehoash king of Israel sent back word to Amaziah king of Judah, 'The thistle of Lebanon sent a message to the cedar of Lebanon, saying, "Give my son your daughter in marriage"; but a wild animal of the Lebanon ran over the thistle and squashed it. ¹⁰You have conquered Edom and now aspire to even greater glory. Stay where you belong! Why provoke disaster, to your own and Judah's ruin?'

¹¹But Amaziah would not listen, so Jehoash king of Israel marched to the attack. And at Beth-Shemesh, which belongs to Judah, he and Amaziah king of Judah made their trial of strength. ¹²Judah was defeated by Israel, and everyone fled to his tent. ¹³The king of Judah, Amaziah son of Jehoash, son of Ahaziah, was taken prisoner at Beth-Shemesh by Jehoash king of Israel who led him off to Jerusalem, where he demolished four hundred cubits of the city wall between the Ephraim Gate and the Corner Gate; ¹⁴all the gold and silver, and all the vessels to be found in the Temple of Yahweh and in the palace treasury, and hostages besides, he then took back with him to Samaria.

¹⁵The rest of the history of Jehoash, his entire career, his prowess, how he waged war on Amaziah king of Judah, is this not recorded in the Book of the Annals of the Kings of Israel? ¹⁶Then Joash fell asleep with his ancestors, and was buried in Samaria with the kings of Israel; his son Jeroboam succeeded him.

¹⁷Amaziah son of Joash, king of Judah, lived for fifteen years after the death of Jehoash son of Jehoahaz, king of Israel.

¹⁸The rest of the history of Amaziah, is this not recorded in the Book of the Annals of the Kings of Judah? ¹⁹A plot having been hatched against him in Jerusalem, he fled to Lachish; but he was followed to Lachish where he was murdered. ²⁰He was then transported by horse and buried in Jerusalem with his ancestors in the City of David. ²¹All the people of Judah then chose Uzziah, who was sixteen years old, and made him king in succession to his father Amaziah. ²²It was he who rebuilt Elath, recovering it for Judah, after the king had fallen asleep with his ancestors.

The reign of Jeroboam II in Israel (783–743)

²³In the fifteenth year of Amaziah son of Joash, king of Judah, Jeroboam son of Joash became king of Israel in Samaria. He reigned for forty-one years. ²⁴He did what is displeasing to Yahweh and did not give up any of the sins into which Jeroboam son of Nebat had led Israel.

²⁵It was he who recovered the territory of Israel from the Pass of Hamath to the Sea of the Arabah, in accordance with the word which Yahweh, God of Israel, had spoken through his servant Jonah son of Amittai, the prophet from Gath-Hepher. ²⁶For Yahweh had seen how very bitter the affliction of Israel was, with no one, either fettered or free, to come to Israel's help. ²⁷But Yahweh had resolved not to blot out the name of Israel under heaven; he rescued them by means of Jeroboam son of Joash.

²⁸The rest of the history of Jeroboam, his entire career, his prowess, what wars he waged, how he brought Damascus and Hamath back to their allegiance to Judah and Israel, is this not recorded in the Book of the Annals of the Kings of Israel? ²⁹Then Jeroboam fell asleep with his ancestors and was buried in Samaria with the kings of Israel; his son Zechariah succeeded him.

14a Dt 24:16.

The reign of Uzziah in Judah (781–740)

15 In the seventeenth year of Jeroboam king of Israel, Uzziah son of Amaziah became king of Judah. ²He was sixteen years old when he came to the throne, and he reigned for fifty-two years in Jerusalem. His mother's name was Jecoliah of Jerusalem. ³He did what Yahweh regards as right, just as his father Amaziah had done. ⁴The high places, however, were not abolished, and the people still offered sacrifices and incense on the high places.

⁵But Yahweh struck the king, and he was afflicted with a virulent skin-disease till his dying day. He lived confined to his room, while Jotham the king's son, who was master of the palace, governed the country.

⁶The rest of the history of Uzziah, his entire career, is this not recorded in the Book of the Annals of the Kings of Judah? ⁷Then Uzziah fell asleep with his ancestors and was buried in the City of David; his son Jotham then succeeded him.

The reign of Zechariah in Israel (743)

⁸In the thirty-eighth year of Uzziah king of Judah, Zechariah son of Jeroboam became king of Israel in Samaria for six months. ⁹He did what is displeasing to Yahweh, as his fathers had done; he did not give up the sins into which Jeroboam son of Nebat had led Israel.

Shallum son of Jabesh plotted against him, murdered him at Ibleam, ¹⁰and succeeded him.

¹¹The rest of the history of Zechariah is recorded in the Book of the Annals of the Kings of Israel. ¹²This was the word which Yahweh had spoken to Jehu, 'Your sons will sit on the throne of Israel to the fourth generation.' And so it turned out.

The reign of Shallum in Israel (743)

¹³Shallum son of Jabesh became king in the thirty-ninth year of Uzziah king of Judah and reigned for one month in Samaria.

¹⁴Then Menahem son of Gadi marched from Tirzah, entered Samaria, murdered Shallum son of Jabesh there and succeeded him.

¹⁵The rest of the history of Shallum, and the plot he hatched, is recorded in the Book of the Annals of the Kings of Israel. ¹⁶Menahem then sacked Tappuah—killing all who were in it—and its territory from Tirzah onwards, because it had not opened its gates to him; he sacked the town and disembowelled all the pregnant women.

The reign of Menahem in Israel (743–738)

¹⁷In the thirty-ninth year of Uzziah king of Judah, Menahem son of Gadi became king of Israel. He reigned for ten years in Samaria. ¹⁸He did what is displeasing to Yahweh, he did not give up the sins into which Jeroboam son of Nebat had led Israel.

In his days ¹⁹Pul[a] king of Assyria invaded the country. Menahem gave Pul a thousand talents of silver in return for his support in strengthening his hold on the royal power. ²⁰Menahem levied this sum from Israel, from all the men of rank, at the rate of fifty shekels a head, to be given to the king of Assyria, who then withdrew and did not stay in the country.

²¹The rest of the history of Menahem, his entire career, is this not recorded in the Book of the Annals of the Kings of Israel? ²²Then Menahem fell asleep with his ancestors; his son Pekahiah succeeded him.

The reign of Pekahiah in Israel (738–737)

²³In the fiftieth year of Uzziah king of Judah, Pekahiah son of Menahem became king of Israel in Samaria. He reigned for two years. ²⁴He did what is displeasing to Yahweh; he did not give up the sins into which Jeroboam son of Nebat had led Israel.

²⁵Pekah son of Remaliah, his equerry, plotted against him and assassinated him in the

15a Name taken by Tiglath-Pileser III of Assyria when he assumed power also in Babylon.

palace keep . . .[b] He had fifty Gileadites with him. He killed the king and succeeded him.

²⁶ The rest of the history of Pekahiah, his entire career, is recorded in the Book of the Annals of the Kings of Israel.

The reign of Pekah in Israel (737–732)

²⁷ In the fifty-second year of Uzziah king of Judah, Pekah son of Remaliah became king of Israel in Samaria. He reigned for twenty years. ²⁸ He did what is displeasing to Yahweh; he did not give up the sins into which Jeroboam son of Nebat had led Israel.

²⁹ In the days of Pekah king of Israel, Tiglath-Pileser king of Assyria came and captured Ijon, Abel-Beth-Maacah, Janoah, Kedesh, Hazor, Gilead and Galilee—the whole territory of Naphtali and deported the population to Assyria. ³⁰ Hoshea son of Elah hatched a plot against Pekah son of Remaliah; he murdered the king and succeeded him.

³¹ The rest of the history of Pekah, his entire career, is recorded in the Book of the Annals of the Kings of Israel.

The reign of Jotham in Judah (740–736)

³² In the second year of Pekah son of Remaliah, king of Israel, Jotham son of Uzziah became king of Judah. ³³ He was twenty-five years old when he came to the throne, and he reigned for sixteen years in Jerusalem. His mother's name was Jerusha daughter of Zadok. ³⁴ He did what Yahweh regards as right, just as his father Uzziah had done. ³⁵ The high places, however, were not abolished, and the people still offered sacrifices and incense on the high places.

It was he who built the Upper Gate of the Temple of Yahweh.

³⁶ The rest of the history of Jotham, his entire career, is this not recorded in the Book of the Annals of the Kings of Judah? ³⁷ At that time Yahweh began sending Razon king of Aram and Pekah son of Remaliah against Judah. ³⁸ Then Jotham fell asleep with his ancestors and was buried in the City of David, his ancestor; his son Ahaz succeeded him.

The reign of Ahaz in Judah (736–716)

16 In the seventeenth year of Pekah son of Remaliah, Ahaz son of Jotham became king of Judah. ²Ahaz was twenty years old when he came to the throne, and he reigned for sixteen years in Jerusalem. He did not do what Yahweh his God regards as right, as his ancestor David had done. ³ He followed the example of the kings of Israel, even causing his son to pass through the fire of sacrifice, also copying the disgusting practices of the nations whom Yahweh had dispossessed for the Israelites. ⁴ He offered sacrifices and incense on the high places, on the hills and under every luxuriant tree.

⁵ Then it was that Razon king of Aram and Pekah son of Remaliah, king of Israel, launched their campaign against Jerusalem. They besieged it but could not reduce it. ⁶(At that time, the king of Edom recovered Elath for Edom; he drove the Judaeans out of Elath, and the Edomites occupied it and have been there ever since.) ⁷ Ahaz then sent messengers to Tiglath-Pileser king of Assyria to say, 'I am your servant and your son. Come and rescue me from the king of Aram and the king of Israel who are making war on me.' ⁸ And Ahaz took what silver and gold was to be found in the Temple of Yahweh and in the palace treasury, and sent this as a present to the king of Assyria. ⁹ The king of Assyria granted his request and, marching on Damascus, captured it; he deported its population to Kir and put Razon to death.

¹⁰ When King Ahaz went to Damascus to meet Tiglath-Pileser king of Assyria, he saw the altar which was in Damascus. King Ahaz then sent a picture and model of the altar, with details of its construction, to Uriah the priest. ¹¹ Uriah the priest constructed the altar; all the instructions sent by King Ahaz from Damascus were carried out by Uriah the priest before King Ahaz returned from Damascus. ¹² When the king arrived from Damascus, he inspected

15b Hebr. adds 'Argob and Arieh', a gloss on 'Gileadites'.

the altar, he approached it and ascended it. ¹³ And on the altar he made his burnt offering and his oblation; he poured out his libation and sprinkled the blood of his communion sacrifices. ¹⁴ The altar which used to stand before Yahweh he removed from the front of the Temple, where it had stood between the new altar and the Temple of Yahweh, and placed it at the north side of the new altar. ¹⁵ King Ahaz gave this order to Uriah the priest, 'In future you will present the morning burnt offering, the evening oblation, the king's burnt offering and oblation, the burnt offering, the oblation and the libations of all the people of the country on the large altar; on it you will pour out all the blood of the burnt offerings and sacrifices. As regards the bronze altar, I shall see to that.' ¹⁶ Uriah the priest did everything that King Ahaz had ordered.

¹⁷ King Ahaz broke up the wheeled stands; removed the crosspieces and the basins from them, and took the bronze Sea off the oxen supporting it, and rested it on the stone pavement. ¹⁸ And from the Temple of Yahweh, in deference to the king of Assyria, he removed the dais for the throne which had been built inside, and the royal entrance on the outside.

¹⁹ The rest of the history of Ahaz, his entire career, is this not recorded in the Book of the Annals of the Kings of Judah? ²⁰ Then Ahaz fell asleep with his ancestors and was buried in the City of David; his son Hezekiah succeeded him.

The reign of Hoshea in Israel (732–724)

17 In the twelfth year of Ahaz king of Judah, Hoshea son of Elah became king of Israel in Samaria, and reigned for nine years. ² He did what is displeasing to Yahweh, though not like the preceding kings of Israel.

³ Shalmaneser king of Assyria made war on Hoshea who submitted to him and paid him tribute. ⁴ But the king of Assyria discovered that Hoshea was playing a double game with him; he had sent messengers to Sais, to the king of Egypt, and had not, as in previous years, handed over the tribute to the king of Assyria. For this the king of Assyria imprisoned him in chains.

The fall of Samaria (721)

⁵ The king of Assyria invaded the whole country and, coming to Samaria, laid siege to it for three years. ⁶ In the ninth year of Hoshea the king of Assyria captured Samaria and deported the Israelites to Assyria. He settled them in Halah on the Habor, a river of Gozan, and in the cities of the Medes.

Observations on the fall of the Northern Kingdom

⁷ This happened because the Israelites had sinned against Yahweh their God who had brought them out of Egypt, out of the grip of Pharaoh king of Egypt. They worshipped other gods, ⁸ they followed the practices of the nations which Yahweh had dispossessed for them. ⁹ The Israelites spoke slightingly of Yahweh their God. They built themselves high places wherever they lived, from watchtower to fortified town. ¹⁰ They set up pillars and sacred poles for themselves on every high hill and under every luxuriant tree. ¹¹ They sacrificed on all the high places like the nations which Yahweh had expelled for them, and did wicked things there, provoking Yahweh's anger. ¹² They served idols, although Yahweh had told them, 'This you must not do.'

¹³ And yet through all the prophets and the seers, Yahweh had given Israel and Judah this warning, 'Turn from your wicked ways and keep my commandments and my laws in accordance with the entire Law which I laid down for your fathers and delivered to them through my servants the prophets.' ¹⁴ But they would not listen, they were as stubborn as their ancestors, who had no faith in Yahweh their God. ¹⁵ They despised his laws and the covenant which he had made with their ancestors and the warnings which he had given them. Pursuing futility, they themselves be-

came futile through copying the nations round them, although Yahweh had ordered them not to act as they did. ⁱ⁶They rejected all the commandments of Yahweh their God and cast themselves metal idols, two calves; they made themselves sacred poles, they worshipped the whole array of heaven, and they served Baal. ¹⁷They caused their sons and daughters to pass through the fire of sacrifice, also they practised divination and sorcery, they sold themselves to doing what displeases Yahweh, provoking his anger. ¹⁸Because of which, Yahweh became enraged with Israel and thrust them away from him. The tribe of Judah was the only one left.

¹⁹Judah did not keep the commandments of Yahweh their God either but copied the practices which Israel had introduced. ²⁰Yahweh rejected the whole race of Israel; he brought them low, delivering them into the hands of marauders, until at length he thrust them away from him. ²¹And indeed he had torn Israel away from the House of David, and they had made Jeroboam son of Nebat king; Jeroboam had drawn Israel away from Yahweh and led them into a great sin. ²²The Israelites copied the sin which Jeroboam had committed; they did not give it up, ²³until at length Yahweh thrust Israel away from him, as he had foretold through all his servants the prophets; he deported the Israelites from their own country to Assyria, where they have been ever since.

The origin of the Samaritans

²⁴The king of Assyria brought people from Babylon, Cuthah, Avva, Hamath and Sepharvaim, and settled them in the towns of Samaria to replace the Israelites; these took possession of Samaria and lived in its towns. ²⁵When they first came to live there, they did not worship Yahweh; hence, Yahweh set lions on them, which killed a number of them. ²⁶Consequently, the king of Assyria was informed as follows, 'The nations whom you deported and settled in the towns of Samaria do not know how to worship the local god, and

he has set lions on them; and now these are killing them because they do not know how to worship the local god.' ²⁷So the king of Assyria gave this order, 'Send back one of the priests whom I deported from there; let him go and live there and teach them how to worship the local god.' ²⁸Accordingly, one of the priests who had been deported from Samaria came to live in Bethel; he taught them how to worship Yahweh.

²⁹Each nationality made gods of its own and put them in the shrines on the high places built by the Samaritans; each nationality did this in the towns where it lived. ³⁰The people from Babylon had made a Succoth-Benoth, the people from Cuthah a Nergal, the people from Hamath an Ashima, ³¹the Avvites a Nibhaz and a Tartak; while the Sepharvites caused their children to pass through the fire of sacrifice to Adrammelech and Anammelech, gods of Sepharvaim. ³²They worshipped Yahweh as well, and they appointed priests out of their own number for the high places, and these officiated in the shrines on the high places. ³³They worshipped Yahweh and served their own gods at the same time, with the rites of the countries from which they had been deported. ³⁴They still follow their old rites even now.

They did not worship Yahweh and did not conform to his statutes or ritual, or the law or the commandments, which Yahweh had laid down for the sons of Jacob to whom he gave the name Israel. ³⁵Yahweh had made a covenant with them and had given them this command, 'You are not to worship alien gods, you are not to bow down to them or serve them or offer them sacrifices. ³⁶You are to bow down and offer sacrifice only to Yahweh who brought you out of Egypt with great power and outstretched arm. ³⁷You are to observe the statutes and ritual, the law and the commandments which he has given you in writing and to which you are always to conform; you are not to worship alien gods. ³⁸Do not forget the covenant which I have made with you, and do not venerate alien gods.

39 But venerate Yahweh your God, and he will deliver you from the clutches of all your enemies.' 40 But they would not listen and still followed their old rites.

41 These nationalities, then, worshipped Yahweh and served their idols as well, as did their children; and their children's children still behave today as their ancestors behaved in the past.

Introduction to the reign of Hezekiah (716–687)

18 In the third year of Hoshea son of Elah, king of Israel, Hezekiah son of Ahaz became king of Judah. 2 He was twenty-five years old when he came to the throne, and he reigned for twenty-nine years in Jerusalem. His mother's name was Abijah daughter of Zechariah. 3 He did what Yahweh regards as right, just as his ancestor David had done. 4 He abolished the high places, broke the pillars, cut down the sacred poles and smashed the bronze serpent which Moses had made; for up to that time the Israelites had offered sacrifices to it; it was called Nehushtan.

5 He put his trust in Yahweh, God of Israel. No king of Judah after him could be compared with him—nor any of those before him. 6 He was devoted to Yahweh, never turning from him, but keeping the commandments which Yahweh had laid down for Moses. 7 And so Yahweh was with him, and he was successful in all that he undertook. He rebelled against the king of Assyria and refused to serve him. 8 He beat the Philistines back to Gaza, laying their territory waste from watchtower to fortified town.

The fall of Samaria; recapitulation

9 In the fourth year of Hezekiah, which was the seventh year of Hoshea son of Elah, king of Israel, Shalmaneser king of Assyria marched on Samaria and laid siege to it. 10 He captured it after three years. Samaria fell in the sixth year of Hezekiah, which was the ninth year of Hoshea king of Israel. 11 The king of Assyria deported the Israelites to Assyria and settled them in Halah on the Habor, a river of Gozan, and in the cities of the Medes. 12 This happened because they had not obeyed the voice of Yahweh their God and had broken his covenant, everything that Moses servant of Yahweh had laid down. They neither listened to it nor put it into practice.

Sennacherib's invasion[a]

13 In the fourteenth year of King Hezekiah, Sennacherib king of Assyria advanced on all the fortified towns of Judah and captured them. 14 Then Hezekiah king of Judah sent this message to the king of Assyria at Lachish, 'I have been at fault. Call off the attack, and I will submit to whatever you impose on me.' The king of Assyria exacted three hundred talents of silver and thirty talents of gold from Hezekiah king of Judah, 15 and Hezekiah gave him all the silver in the Temple of Yahweh and in the palace treasury. 16 At which time, Hezekiah stripped the facing from the leaves and jambs of the doors of the Temple of Yahweh, which an earlier king of Judah had put on, and gave it to the king of Assyria.

The embassy of the cupbearer-in-chief

17 From Lachish the king of Assyria sent the cupbearer-in-chief with a large force to King Hezekiah in Jerusalem. He marched on Jerusalem and, on his arrival, took up position near the conduit of the upper pool which is on the road to the Fuller's Field. 18 He summoned the king. The master of the palace, Eliakim son of Hilkiah, Shebnah the secretary and the herald Joah son of Asaph went out to him. 19 The cupbearer-in-chief said to them, 'Say to Hezekiah, "The great king, the king of Assyria, says this: What makes you so confident? 20 Do you think empty words are as good as strategy and military strength? Who are you relying on, to dare to rebel against me?

18a The whole of 18:13–20:19 is repeated with minor variations in Is 36–39.

²¹There you are, relying on that broken reed Egypt, which pricks and pierces the hand of whoever leans on it. That is what Pharaoh king of Egypt is like to all who rely on him. ²²You may say to me: We rely on Yahweh our God. But have his high places and altars not been suppressed by Hezekiah who told Judah and Jerusalem: Here, in Jerusalem, is the altar before which you must worship? ²³Very well, then, make a wager with my lord the king of Assyria: I will give you two thousand horses if you can find horsemen to ride them. ²⁴How could you repel a single one of the least of my master's soldiers? And yet you have relied on Egypt for chariots and horsemen. ²⁵And lastly, have I marched on this place to lay it waste without warrant from Yahweh? Yahweh himself said to me: March on this country and lay it waste." '

²⁶Eliakim, Shebnah and Joah said to the cupbearer-in-chief, 'Please speak to your servants in Aramaic, for we understand it; do not speak to us in the Judaean language within earshot of the people on the ramparts.' ²⁷But the cupbearer-in-chief said, 'Do you think my lord sent me here to say these things to your master or to you? On the contrary, it was to the people sitting on the ramparts who, like you, are doomed to eat their own dung and drink their own urine.'

²⁸The cupbearer-in-chief then drew himself up and shouted loudly in the Judaean language, 'Listen to the word of the great king, the king of Assyria. ²⁹The king says this, "Do not let Hezekiah delude you. He will be powerless to save you from my clutches. ³⁰Do not let Hezekiah persuade you to rely on Yahweh by saying: Yahweh is sure to save us; this city will not fall into the king of Assyria's clutches. ³¹Do not listen to Hezekiah, for the king of Assyria says this: Make peace with me, surrender to me, and every one of you will be free to eat the fruit of his own vine and of his own fig tree and to drink the water of his own storage-well ³²until I come and take you away to a country like your own, a land of corn and good wine, a land of bread and vineyards, a land of oil and honey: and so you will survive and not die. Do not listen to Hezekiah; he is deluding you when he says: Yahweh will save us. ³³Has any god of any nation been able to save his country from the king of Assyria's clutches? ³⁴Where are the gods of Hamath and Arpad? Where are the gods of Sepharvaim and Hena and Ivvah? Where are the local gods of Samaria? Did they save Samaria from my clutches? ³⁵Of all the local gods, which ones have saved their countries from my clutches, for Yahweh to be able to save Jerusalem from my clutches?" '

³⁶The people, however, kept quiet and said nothing in reply, since the king had given the order, 'You are not to answer him.' ³⁷The master of the palace, Eliakim son of Hilkiah, Shebnah the secretary and the herald Joah son of Asaph, with their clothes torn, went to Hezekiah and reported what the cupbearer-in-chief had said.

The prophet Isaiah is consulted

19 On hearing this, King Hezekiah tore his clothes, put on sackcloth and went to the Temple of Yahweh. ²He sent Eliakim master of the palace, Shebnah the secretary and the elders of the priests, wearing sackcloth, to the prophet Isaiah son of Amoz. ³They said to him, 'This is what Hezekiah says, "Today is a day of suffering, of punishment, of disgrace. Children come to birth, and there is no strength to bring them forth. ⁴May Yahweh your God hear the words of the cupbearer-in-chief whom his master, the king of Assyria, has sent to insult the living God, and may Yahweh your God punish the words he has heard. Offer your prayer for the remnant still remaining." '

⁵King Hezekiah's ministers went to Isaiah, ⁶and Isaiah said to them, 'Say to your master, "Yahweh says this: Do not be afraid of the words which you have heard or the blasphemies which the king of Assyria's minions have uttered against me. ⁷Look, I am going to put a spirit in him and, on the strength of a rumour, he will go back to his own country, and

in that country I shall make him fall by the sword." '

The cupbearer returns to his master

8 The cupbearer turned about and rejoined the king of Assyria, who was then attacking Libnah, as the cupbearer had learnt that the king had already left Lachish 9 on hearing that Tirhakah king of Cush was on his way to attack him.

Sennacherib's letter to Hezekiah

10 Sennacherib again sent messengers to Hezekiah, saying, 'Tell Hezekiah king of Judah this, "Do not let your God on whom you are relying deceive you with the promise: Jerusalem will not fall into the king of Assyria's clutches. 11 You have learnt by now what the kings of Assyria have done to all the other countries, devoting them to destruction. Are you likely to be saved? 12 Did the gods of the nations whom my ancestors devastated save them—Gozan, Haran, Rezeph and the Edenites who were in Tel Basar? 13 Where is the king of Hamath, the king of Arpad, the king of Lair, of Sepharvaim, of Hena, of Ivvah?" '

14 Hezekiah took the letter from the messengers' hands and read it; he then went up to the Temple of Yahweh and spread it out before Yahweh. 15 Hezekiah said this prayer in the presence of Yahweh, 'Yahweh Sabaoth, God of Israel, enthroned on the winged creatures, you alone are God of all the kingdoms of the world, you made heaven and earth. 16 Give ear, Yahweh, and listen; open your eyes, Yahweh, and see! Hear the words of Sennacherib, who has sent to insult the living God. 17 It is true, Yahweh, that the kings of Assyria have destroyed the nations, 18 they have thrown their gods on the fire, for these were not gods but human artefacts—wood and stone—and hence they have destroyed them. 19 But now, Yahweh our God, save us from his clutches, I beg you, and let all the kingdoms of the world know that you alone are God, Yahweh.'

Isaiah intervenes

20 Isaiah son of Amoz then sent the following message to Hezekiah, 'Yahweh, God of Israel, says this, "I have heard the prayer which you have addressed to me about Sennacherib king of Assyria." 21 Here is the pronouncement which Yahweh has made about him:

"She despises you, she scorns you,
  the virgin daughter of Zion;
she tosses her head at you,
  the daughter of Jerusalem!
22 Whom have you insulted, whom have you
      blasphemed?
  Against whom raised your voice
  and lifted your haughty eyes?
  Against the Holy One of Israel!
23 Through your envoys you have insulted
      the Lord,
  thinking: With my many chariots
  I have climbed the mountain-tops,
  the utmost peaks of Lebanon.
  I have felled
  its mighty cedars,
  its finest cypresses,
  have reached its furthest recesses,
  its forest garden.
24 Yes, I have dug
  and drunk of foreign waters;
  under the soles of my feet
  I have dried up all Egypt's rivers.

25 "Do you hear? Long ago
  I prepared this,
  from days of old I actually planned it,
  now I carry it out.
  You were to lay walled cities
  in heaps of ruins;
26 that was why their inhabitants,
  feeble of hand,
  were dismayed and discomfited,
  were weak as grass,
  were frail as plants,
  were like grass of housetop and
      meadow
  under the east wind.

27 But whether you stand up or you sit down,
    whether you go out or you come in, I
        know it.
28 Because you have raved against me,
    and your arrogance has reached my ears,
    I shall put a hook through your nostrils
    and a muzzle on your lips,
    and make you return by the road
    by which you came.

A sign for Hezekiah

29 "And this will be the sign for you:

    this year will be eaten the self-sown grain,
    next year what sprouts in the fallow;
    but in the third year sow and reap,
    plant vineyards and eat their fruit.
30 The surviving remnant of the House of
        Judah will bring forth
    new roots below and fruits above;
31 for a remnant will issue from Jerusalem,
    and survivors from Mount Zion.
    Yahweh Sabaoth's jealous love will
        accomplish this.

32 "This, then, is what Yahweh says about the
king of Assyria:

    "He will not enter this city,
    will shoot no arrow at it,
    confront it with no shield,
    throw up no earthwork against it.
33 By the road by which he came, by that he
        will return;
    he will not enter this city, declares
        Yahweh.
34 I shall protect this city and save it
    for my sake and my servant David's
        sake."'

Sennacherib is punished

35 That same night the angel of Yahweh went
out and struck down a hundred and eighty-
five thousand men in the Assyrian camp. In
the early morning when it was time to get up,
there they lay, so many corpses.
    36 Sennacherib struck camp and left; he re-
turned home and stayed in Nineveh. 37 One
day when he was worshipping in the temple of
his god Nisroch, his sons Adrammelech and
Sharezer struck him down with the sword
and escaped into the territory of Ararat. His
son Esarhaddon succeeded him.

The illness and cure of Hezekiah

20 About then Hezekiah fell ill and was at
the point of death. The prophet Isaiah
son of Amoz came and said to him, 'Yahweh
says this, "Put your affairs in order, for you are
going to die, you will not live." ' 2 Hezekiah
turned his face to the wall and addressed this
prayer to Yahweh, 3 'Ah, Yahweh, remember,
I beg you, that I have behaved faithfully
and with sincerity of heart in your presence
and done what you regard as right.' And
Hezekiah shed many tears.
    4 Isaiah had not left the middle court, before
the word of Yahweh came to him, 5 'Go back
and say to Hezekiah, prince of my people,
"Yahweh, the God of your ancestor David,
says this: I have heard your prayer and seen
your tears. I shall cure you: in three days' time
you will go up to the Temple of Yahweh. 6 I
shall add fifteen years to your life. I shall save
you and this city from the king of Assyria's
clutches and defend this city for my sake and
my servant David's sake."'
    7 'Bring a fig poultice,' Isaiah said; they
brought one, applied it to the ulcer, and the
king recovered.
    8 Hezekiah said to Isaiah, 'What is the sign
to tell me that Yahweh will cure me and that I
shall be going up to the Temple of Yahweh in
three days' time?' 9 'Here', Isaiah replied, 'is
the sign from Yahweh that he will do what he
has said; would you like the shadow to go forward ten steps, or to go back ten steps?' 10 'It is
easy for the shadow to lengthen ten steps,'
Hezekiah replied. 'No, I would rather the
shadow went back ten steps.' 11 The prophet
Isaiah then called on Yahweh, who made
the shadow cast by the declining sun on
the steps—the steps to Ahaz's roof-room—go
back ten steps.

The Babylonian embassy

¹² At that time the king of Babylon, Merodach-Baladan son of Baladan, sent letters and a gift to Hezekiah, for he had heard of his illness and his recovery. ¹³ Hezekiah was delighted at this and showed the ambassadors his entire treasury, the silver, gold, spices, precious oil, his armoury too, and everything to be seen in his storehouses. There was nothing in his palace or in his whole domain that Hezekiah did not show them.

¹⁴ The prophet Isaiah then came to King Hezekiah and asked him, 'What have these men said, and where have they come from?' Hezekiah answered, 'They have come from a distant country, from Babylon.' ¹⁵ Isaiah said, 'What have they seen in your palace?' 'They have seen everything in my palace,' Hezekiah answered. 'There is nothing in my storehouses that I have not shown them.'

¹⁶ Then Isaiah said to Hezekiah, 'Listen to the word of Yahweh, ¹⁷ "The days are coming when everything in your palace, everything that your ancestors have amassed until now, will be carried off to Babylon. Not a thing will be left," Yahweh says. ¹⁸ "Sons sprung from you, sons fathered by you, will be abducted to be eunuchs in the palace of the king of Babylon." ' ¹⁹ Hezekiah said to Isaiah, 'This word of Yahweh that you announce is reassuring,' for he was thinking, 'And why not? So long as there is peace and security during my lifetime.'

The end of the reign of Hezekiah

²⁰ The rest of the history of Hezekiah, all his prowess, how he constructed the pool and the conduit to bring water into the city, is this not recorded in the Book of the Annals of the Kings of Judah? ²¹ Then Hezekiah fell asleep with his ancestors; his son Manasseh succeeded him.

The reign of Manasseh in Judah (687–642)

21 Manasseh was twelve years old when he came to the throne and he reigned for fifty-five years in Jerusalem. His mother's name was Hephzibah. ² He did what is displeasing to Yahweh, copying the disgusting practices of the nations whom Yahweh had dispossessed for the Israelites.

³ He rebuilt the high places which his father Hezekiah had destroyed, he set up altars to Baal and made a sacred pole as Ahab king of Israel had done, he worshipped the whole array of heaven and served it. ⁴ He built altars in the Temple of Yahweh of which Yahweh had said, 'Jerusalem is where I shall put my name.' ⁵ He built altars to the whole array of heaven in the two courts of the Temple of Yahweh. ⁶ He caused his son to pass through the fire of sacrifice, he also practised soothsaying and divination and set up mediums and spirit guides. He did very many more things displeasing to Yahweh, thus provoking his anger. ⁷ He had an image of Asherah carved and placed it inside the Temple of which Yahweh had said to David and his son Solomon, 'In this Temple and in Jerusalem, the city which I have chosen out of all the tribes of Israel, I shall put my Name for ever. ⁸ Nor shall I ever again set Israel's footsteps wandering outside the country which I gave to their ancestors, provided they are careful to observe all I have commanded them as laid down in the whole Law which my servant Moses prescribed for them.' ⁹ But they would not listen, and Manasseh misled them into doing worse things than the nations whom Yahweh had destroyed for the Israelites.

¹⁰ Then Yahweh spoke through his servants the prophets as follows, ¹¹ 'Since Manasseh king of Judah has done these shameful deeds, doing more wicked deeds than anything which the Amorites did before him, and has led Judah too into sin with his idols, ¹² Yahweh, God of Israel, says this, "Look, I shall bring such disaster on Jerusalem and Judah as will make the ears of all who hear of it tingle. ¹³ Over Jerusalem I shall stretch the same measuring line as over Samaria, the same plumb-rule as for the House of Ahab; I shall scour Jerusalem as someone scours a dish and, having scoured it, turns it upside down.

¹⁴ I shall cast away the remnant of my heritage, delivering them into the clutches of their enemies and making them the prey and booty of all their enemies, ¹⁵ because they have done what is displeasing to me and have provoked my anger from the day their ancestors came out of Egypt until now." '

¹⁶ Manasseh shed innocent blood, too, in such great quantity that he flooded Jerusalem from one end to the other, besides the sins into which he led Judah by doing what is displeasing to Yahweh.

¹⁷ The rest of the history of Manasseh, his entire career, the sins he committed, is this not recorded in the Book of the Annals of the Kings of Judah? ¹⁸ Then Manasseh fell asleep with his ancestors and was buried in the garden of his palace, the Garden of Uzza; his son Amon succeeded him.

The reign of Amon in Judah (642–640)

¹⁹ Amon was twenty-two years old when he came to the throne, and he reigned for two years in Jerusalem. His mother's name was Meshullemeth daughter of Haruz, of Jotbah. ²⁰ He did what is displeasing to Yahweh, as Manasseh his father had done. ²¹ In every respect he followed the example of his father, serving the idols which his father had served, and worshipping them. ²² He abandoned Yahweh, God of his ancestors; he did not follow the way of Yahweh.

²³ Amon's retinue plotted against the king and killed him in his own palace. ²⁴ The people of the country, however, slaughtered all those who had plotted against King Amon and proclaimed his son Josiah as his successor.

²⁵ The rest of the history of Amon, his entire career, is this not recorded in the Book of the Annals of the Kings of Judah? ²⁶ He was buried in his father's tomb in the Garden of Uzza; his son Josiah succeeded him.

Introduction to the reign of Josiah (640–609)

22 Josiah was eight years old when he came to the throne, and he reigned for thirty-one years in Jerusalem. His mother's

name was Jedidah daughter of Adaiah, of Bozkath. ² He did what Yahweh regards as right, and in every respect followed the example of his ancestor David, not deviating from it to right or left.

The Book of the Law discovered

³ In the eighteenth year of King Josiah, the king sent the secretary Shaphan son of Azaliah, son of Meshullam to the Temple of Yahweh. ⁴ 'Go to Hilkiah the high priest,' he told him, 'and tell him to melt down the silver contributed to the Temple of Yahweh and collected by the guardians of the threshold from the people. ⁵ He is to hand it over to the masters of works attached to the Temple of Yahweh, for them to pay it over to men working on the Temple of Yahweh, to repair the damaged parts of the Temple: ⁶ to the carpenters, builders and masons, and for buying timber and dressed stone for the Temple repairs.' ⁷ The latter were not required to render account of the money handed over to them, since they were conscientious in their work.

⁸ The high priest Hilkiah said to Shaphan the secretary, 'I have found the Book of the Law in the Temple of Yahweh.' And Hilkiah gave the book to Shaphan, who read it. ⁹ Shaphan the secretary went to the king, reporting furthermore to him as follows, 'Your servants have melted down the silver which was in the Temple and have handed it over to the masters of works attached to the Temple of Yahweh.' ¹⁰ Then Shaphan the secretary informed the king, 'The priest Hilkiah has given me a book'; and Shaphan read it aloud in the king's presence.

The prophetess Huldah consulted

¹¹ On hearing the words of the Book of the Law he tore his clothes. ¹² Then the king gave the following order to the priest Hilkiah, Ahikam son of Shaphan, Achbor son of Micaiah, Shaphan the secretary and Asaiah the king's minister: ¹³ 'Go and consult Yahweh on behalf of me and the people about the words of the book that has been discovered; for Yah-

weh's furious wrath has been kindled against us because our ancestors disobeyed the word of Yahweh by not doing what this book says they ought to have done.'

¹⁴ The priest Hilkiah, Ahikam, Achbor, Shaphan and Asaiah went to the prophetess Huldah wife of Shallum son of Tikvah, son of Harhas the keeper of the wardrobe; she lived in Jerusalem in the new town. They put the matter to her, ¹⁵ and she replied, 'Yahweh, God of Israel, says this, "To the man who sent you to me say this: ¹⁶ Yahweh says this: I am going to bring disaster on this place and the people who live in it—all the words of the book read by the king of Judah. ¹⁷ Because they have abandoned me and sacrificed to other gods, so as to provoke my anger by their every action, my wrath is kindled against this place, and nothing can stop it. ¹⁸ As for the king of Judah who sent you to consult Yahweh, say this to him: As regards the words you have heard . . . ¹⁹ But since your heart has been touched and you have humbled yourself before Yahweh on hearing what I have decreed against this place and the people who live in it, how they will become an object of horror and cursing, and have torn your clothes and wept before me, I too have heard—Yahweh says this. ²⁰ So look, when I gather you to your ancestors, you will be gathered into your grave in peace; you will not live to see the great disaster that I am going to bring on this place." ' They took this answer to the king.

The solemn reading of the Law and renewal of the covenant

23 The king then had all the elders of Judah and of Jerusalem summoned to him, ² and the king went up to the Temple of Yahweh with all the people of Judah and all the inhabitants of Jerusalem, priests, prophets and the whole populace, high and low. In their hearing he read out the entire contents of the Book of the Covenant discovered in the Temple of Yahweh. ³ The king then, standing on the dais, bound himself by the covenant before Yahweh, to follow Yahweh, to keep his commandments, decrees and laws with all his heart and soul, and to carry out the terms of the covenant as written in this book. All the people pledged their allegiance to the covenant.

Religious reform in Judah

⁴ The king ordered Hilkiah with the priest next in rank and the guardians of the threshold to remove all the cult objects which had been made for Baal, Asherah and the whole array of heaven; he burnt them outside Jerusalem in the fields of the Kidron and had the ashes taken to Bethel. ⁵ He exterminated the spurious priests whom the kings of Judah had appointed and who offered sacrifice on the high places, in the towns of Judah and the neighbourhood of Jerusalem; also those who offered sacrifice to Baal, to the sun, the moon, the constellations and the whole array of heaven. ⁶ And from the Temple of Yahweh he took the sacred pole outside Jerusalem to the Kidron valley and in the Kidron valley he burnt it, reducing it to ashes and throwing its ashes on the common burial-ground. ⁷ He pulled down the house of the sacred male prostitutes which was in the Temple of Yahweh and where the women wove veils for Asherah.

⁸ He brought all the priests in from the towns of Judah, and from Geba to Beersheba he rendered unsanctified the high places where these priests had offered sacrifice. He pulled down the High Place of the Gates, which stood at the gate of Joshua, the governor of the city, to the left of the entry to the city. ⁹ The priests of the high places, however, did not officiate at the altar of Yahweh in Jerusalem, although they did share the unleavened bread of their brother-priests. ¹⁰ He rendered unsanctified Tophet in the Valley of Ben-Hinnom, so that no one could pass his son or daughter through the fire of sacrifice to Molech. ¹¹ He destroyed the horses which the kings of Judah had dedicated to the sun at the entrance to the Temple of Yahweh, near the apartment of Nathan-Melech the official, in

the precincts, and he burned the solar chariot. 12 The king pulled down altars which the kings of Judah had built on the roof and those which Manasseh had built in the two courts of the Temple of Yahweh, and broke them to pieces on the spot, throwing their rubble into the Kidron valley. 13 The king rendered unsanctified the high places facing Jerusalem, to the south of the Mount of Olives, which Solomon king of Israel had built for Astarte the Sidonian abomination, for Chemosh the Moabite abomination, and for Milcom the Ammonite abomination. 14 He also smashed the sacred pillars, cut down the sacred poles, and covered with human bones the places where they had stood.

The reform is extended to the former Northern Kingdom

15 As for the altar which was at Bethel, the high place built by Jeroboam son of Nebat who had led Israel into sin, he demolished this altar and this high place as well, in the same way, breaking up its stones and reducing them to powder. The sacred pole he burned.

16 On looking round, Josiah saw the tombs there on the hillside; he had the bones fetched from the tombs and burned them on the altar. This he rendered unsanctified, in accordance with the word of Yahweh which the man of God had proclaimed when Jeroboam was standing by the altar at the time of the feast. On looking round, Josiah caught sight of the tomb of the man of God who had foretold these things. 17 'What is that monument I see?' he asked. The townspeople replied, 'It is the tomb of the man of God who came from Judah and foretold what you have done to the altar.' 18 'Let him rest,' the king said, 'and let no one disturb his bones.' So they left his bones untouched, with the bones of the prophet who came from Samaria.

19 Josiah also destroyed all the shrines on the high places which were in the towns of Samaria and which the kings of Israel had built to provoke Yahweh's anger; he treated these places exactly as he had treated the one at Bethel. 20 All the priests of the high places who were there he slaughtered on the altars, and on those altars burned human bones. Then he returned to Jerusalem.

The Passover

21 The king gave this order to the whole people: 'Celebrate a Passover to Yahweh your God, as prescribed in this Book of the Covenant.' 22 No Passover like this had ever been celebrated since the days when the judges ruled Israel, nor throughout the entire period of the kings of Israel and the kings of Judah. 23 The eighteenth year of King Josiah was the only time when such a Passover was celebrated in Yahweh's honour in Jerusalem.

Final comments on the religious reform

24 What is more, the spirit-guides and mediums, the household gods and idols, and all the abominations to be seen in the country of Judah and in Jerusalem, were swept away by Josiah to give effect to the words of the Law written in the book found by the priest Hilkiah in the Temple of Yahweh. 25 No king before him turned to Yahweh as he did, with all his heart, all his soul, all his strength, in perfect loyalty to the Law of Moses; nor did any king like him arise again.

26 Yet Yahweh did not renounce the heat of his great anger which had been aroused against Judah by all the provocations which Manasseh had caused him. 27 Yahweh said, 'I shall thrust Judah away from me too, as I have already thrust Israel; I shall cast off Jerusalem, this city which I have chosen, and the Temple of which I have said: My Name shall be there.'

The end of the reign of Josiah

28 The rest of the history of Josiah, his entire career, is this not recorded in the Book of the Annals of the Kings of Judah? 29 In his times, Pharaoh Necho king of Egypt was advancing to meet the king of Assyria at the River Euphrates, and King Josiah went to intercept him; but Necho killed him at Megiddo in the first encounter. 30 His retainers

carried his body from Megiddo by chariot; they brought him to Jerusalem and buried him in his own tomb. The people of the country then took Jehoahaz son of Josiah and anointed him, proclaiming him king in succession to his father.

The reign of Jehoahaz in Judah (609)

31 Jehoahaz was twenty-three years old when he came to the throne, and he reigned for three months in Jerusalem. His mother's name was Hamutal daughter of Jeremiah, of Libnah. 32 He did what is displeasing to Yahweh, just as his ancestors had done.

33 Pharaoh Necho put him in chains at Riblah in Hamath, to prevent his reigning any longer in Jerusalem, and imposed a levy of a hundred talents of silver and ten talents of gold on the country. 34 Pharaoh Necho then made Eliakim son of Josiah king in succession to Josiah his father, and changed his name to Jehoiakim. Carrying off Jehoahaz, he took him to Egypt, where he died.

35 Jehoiakim paid over the silver and gold to Pharaoh, but first had to tax the people of the country before he could raise the sum which Pharaoh demanded: he levied the silver and gold to be paid over to Pharaoh Necho from each according to his means.

The reign of Jehoiakim in Judah (609–598)

36 Jehoiakim was twenty-five years old when he came to the throne, and he reigned for eleven years in Jerusalem. His mother's name was Zebidah daughter of Pedaiah of Rumah. 37 He did what is displeasing to Yahweh, just as his ancestors had done.

24 In his times, Nebuchadnezzar king of Babylon invaded, and Jehoiakim became his vassal for three years, but then rebelled against him a second time. 2 So he sent armed bands of Chaldaeans, Aramaeans, Moabites and Ammonites against him; he sent these against Judah to destroy it, in accordance with the word which Yahweh had spoken through his servants the prophets. 3 It was en-

tirely due to Yahweh's anger that this happened to Judah; he had resolved to thrust them away from him because of Manasseh's sins and all that he had done, 4 and also because of the innocent blood which he had shed, flooding Jerusalem with innocent blood. Yahweh would not forgive.

5 The rest of the history of Jehoiakim, his entire career, is this not recorded in the Book of the Annals of the Kings of Judah? 6 Then Jehoiakim fell asleep with his ancestors; his son Jehoiachin succeeded him.

7 The king of Egypt did not leave his own country again, because the king of Babylon had conquered everywhere belonging to the king of Egypt, from the Torrent of Egypt to the River Euphrates.

Introduction to the reign of Jehoiachin (598–597)

8 Jehoiachin was eighteen years old when he came to the throne, and he reigned for three months in Jerusalem. His mother's name was Nehushta daughter of Elnathan of Jerusalem. 9 He did what is displeasing to Yahweh, just as his father had done.

The first deportation

10 At that time the troops of Nebuchadnezzar king of Babylon advanced on Jerusalem, and the city was besieged. 11 Nebuchadnezzar king of Babylon advanced on the city and his generals laid siege to it. 12 Jehoiachin king of Judah—he, his mother, his retinue, his nobles and his officials—then surrendered to the king of Babylon, and the king of Babylon took them prisoner in the eighth year of his reign. 13 The latter carried off all the treasures of the Temple of Yahweh and the treasures of the palace and broke up all the golden furnishings which Solomon king of Israel had made for the sanctuary of Yahweh, as Yahweh had foretold. 14 He carried all Jerusalem off into exile, all the nobles and all the notables, ten thousand of these were exiled, with all the blacksmiths and metalworkers; only the poorest people in the country were left behind. 15 He

deported Jehoiachin to Babylon, as also the king's mother, his officials and the nobility of the country; he made them all leave Jerusalem for exile in Babylon. ¹⁶All the men of distinction, seven thousand of them, the blacksmiths and metalworkers, one thousand of them, all the men capable of bearing arms, were led off into exile in Babylon by the king of Babylon.

¹⁷The king of Babylon deposed Jehoiachin in favour of his paternal uncle Mattaniah, whose name he changed to Zedekiah.

Introduction to the reign of Zedekiah in Judah (598–587) ª

¹⁸Zedekiah was twenty-one years old when he came to the throne, and he reigned for eleven years in Jerusalem. His mother's name was Hamital daughter of Jeremiah, of Libnah. ¹⁹He did what is displeasing to Yahweh, just as Jehoiakim had done. ²⁰It was entirely due to Yahweh's anger that this happened to Jerusalem and Judah. It resulted in his casting them from his presence. Zedekiah rebelled against the king of Babylon.

The siege of Jerusalem

25 In the ninth year of his reign, in the tenth month, on the tenth day of the month, Nebuchadnezzar king of Babylon advanced on Jerusalem with his entire army; he pitched camp in front of the city and threw up earthworks round it. ²The city lay under siege till the eleventh year of King Zedekiah. ³In the fourth month, on the ninth day of the month, when famine was raging in the city and there was no food for the populace, ⁴a breach was made in the city wall. The king then made his escape under cover of dark, with all the fighting men, by way of the gate between the two walls, which is near the king's garden—the Chaldaeans had surrounded the city—and made his way towards the Arabah. ⁵The Chaldaean troops pursued the king and caught up with him in the Plains of Jericho, where all his troops deserted. ⁶The Chaldaeans captured the king and took him to the king of Babylon at Riblah, who passed sen-

tence on him. ⁷He had Zedekiah's sons slaughtered before his eyes, then put out Zedekiah's eyes and, loading him with chains, carried him off to Babylon.

The sack of Jerusalem; the second deportation

⁸In the fifth month, on the seventh day of the month—it was in the nineteenth year of Nebuchadnezzar king of Babylon—Nebuzaradan commander of the guard, a member of the king of Babylon's staff, entered Jerusalem. ⁹He burned down the Temple of Yahweh, the royal palace and all the houses in Jerusalem. ¹⁰The Chaldaean troops who accompanied the commander of the guard demolished the walls surrounding Jerusalem. ¹¹Nebuzaradan commander of the guard deported the remainder of the population left in the city, the deserters who had gone over to the king of Babylon, and the rest of the common people. ¹²But the commander of the guard left some of the poor country people behind as vineyard workers and ploughmen.

¹³The Chaldaeans broke up the bronze pillars from the Temple of Yahweh, the wheeled stands and the bronze Sea, which were in the Temple of Yahweh, and took the bronze away to Babylon. ¹⁴They also took the ash containers, the scoops, the knives, the incense boats, and all the bronze furnishings used in worship. ¹⁵The commander of the guard also took the censers and the sprinkling bowls, everything made of gold and everything made of silver. ¹⁶As regards the two pillars, the one Sea and the wheeled stands, which Solomon had made for the Temple of Yahweh, there was no reckoning the weight of bronze in all these objects. ¹⁷The height of one pillar was eighteen cubits, and on it stood a capital of bronze, the height of the capital being five cubits; round the capital were filigree and pomegranates, all in bronze. So also for the second pillar.

¹⁸The commander of the guard took prisoner Seraiah the chief priest, Zephaniah the

24a ‖ Jr 52.

priest next in rank, and the three guardians of the threshold. ¹⁹ In the city he took prisoner an official who was in command of the fighting men, five of the king's personal friends who were discovered in the city, the secretary to the army commander, responsible for military conscription, and sixty men of distinction discovered in the city. ²⁰ Nebuzaradan commander of the guard took these men and brought them to the king of Babylon at Riblah, ²¹ and at Riblah in the territory of Hamath the king of Babylon had them put to death. Thus Judah was deported from its country.

Gedaliah governor of Judah

²² For the people remaining in the country of Judah whom Nebuchadnezzar king of Babylon had left behind, he appointed Gedaliah son of Ahikam, son of Shaphan as governor. ²³ When the military leaders and their men all heard that the king of Babylon had appointed Gedaliah as governor, they went to him at Mizpah: Ishmael son of Nethaniah, Johanan son of Kareah, Seraiah son of Tanhumeth the Netophathite, Jaazaniah the Maacathite, they and their men. ²⁴ To them and to their men

Gedaliah swore an oath. 'Do not be afraid of the Chaldaeans,' he said, 'stay in the country, serve the king of Babylon, and all will go well with you.'

²⁵ But in the seventh month, Ishmael son of Nethaniah, son of Elishama, who was of royal descent, and ten men with him, came and murdered Gedaliah, as well as the Judaeans and Chaldaeans who were with him at Mizpah. ²⁶ Then all the people, high and low, with the military leaders, set off and went to Egypt, being afraid of the Chaldaeans.

King Jehoiachin pardoned

²⁷ In the thirty-seventh year of the exile of Jehoiachin king of Judah, in the twelfth month, on the twenty-seventh day of the month, Evil-Merodach king of Babylon, in the year he came to the throne, pardoned Jehoiachin king of Judah and released him from prison. ²⁸ He treated him with kindness and allotted him a seat above those of the other kings who were with him in Babylon. ²⁹ So Jehoiachin laid aside his prisoner's garb, and for the rest of his life always ate at the king's table. ³⁰ And his upkeep was permanently ensured by the king, day after day, for the rest of his life.

The First Book of

CHRONICLES

The origin of the three ethnic groups

1 Adam, Seth, Enosh, ²Kenan, Mahalalel, Jared, ³Enoch, Methuselah, Lamech, ⁴Noah, Shem, Ham and Japheth.

The Japhethites

⁵Sons of Japheth: Gomer, Magog, the Medes, Javan, Tubal, Meshech, Tiras.

⁶Sons of Gomer: Ashkenaz, Riphath, Togarmah. ⁷Sons of Javan: Elishah, Tarshish, the Kittim, the Dananites.

The Hamites

⁸Sons of Ham: Cush, Mizraim, Put, Canaan.

⁹Sons of Cush: Seba, Havilah, Sabta, Raama, Sabeteca. Sons of Raamah: Sheba, Dedan. ¹⁰Cush fathered Nimrod, the first mighty warrior on earth.

¹¹Mizraim fathered the people of Lud, of Anam, of Lehab, of Naphtuh, ¹²of Pathros, Casluh and Caphtor, from which the Philistines came. ¹³Canaan fathered Sidon, his first-born, then Heth, ¹⁴and the Jebusites, the Amorites, Girgashites, ¹⁵Hivites, Arkites, Sinites, ¹⁶Arvadites, Zemarites, Hamathites.

The Semites

¹⁷Sons of Shem: Elam, Asshur, Arpachshad, Lud, Aram.

Sons of Aram: Uz, Hul, Gether and Meshech.

¹⁸Arpachshad fathered Shelah, and Shelah fathered Eber. ¹⁹To Eber were born two sons; the first was called Peleg, because it was in his time that the earth was divided into districts, and his brother was called Joktan.

²⁰Joktan fathered Almodad, Sheleph, Hazarmaveth, Jerah, ²¹Hadoram, Uzal, Diklah, ²²Ebal, Abimael, Sheba, ²³Ophir, Havilah, Jobab; all these are sons of Joktan.

From Shem to Abraham

²⁴Arpachshad, Shelah, ²⁵Eber, Peleg, Reu, ²⁶Serug, Nahor, Terah, ²⁷Abram, that is, Abraham. ²⁸Sons of Abraham: Isaac and Ishmael. ²⁹These are their descendants:

The Ishmaelites

The first-born of Ishmael, Nebaioth; then Kedar, Adbeel, Mibsam, ³⁰Mishma, Dumah, Massa, Hada, Tema, ³¹Jetur, Naphish and Kedemah. These are the sons of Ishmael.

³²Sons of Keturah, Abraham's concubine: she gave birth to Zimran, Jokshan, Medan, Midian, Ishbak, and Shuah. Sons of Jokshan: Sheba and Dedan. ³³Sons of Midian: Ephah, Epher, Hanoch, Abida, Eldaah. All these are sons of Keturah.

Isaac and Esau

³⁴Abraham fathered Isaac. Sons of Isaac: Esau and Israel.

³⁵Sons of Esau: Eliphaz, Reuel, Jeush, Jalam and Korah. ³⁶Sons of Eliphaz: Teman, Omar, Zephi, Gatam, Kenaz, Timna, Amalek. ³⁷Sons of Reuel: Nahath, Zerah, Shammah, Mizzah.

Seir

³⁸Sons of Seir: Lotan, Shobal, Zibeon, Anah, Dishon, Ezer, Dishan. ³⁹Sons of Lotan: Hori and Homam. Sister of Lotan: Timma. ⁴⁰Sons of Shobal: Alian, Manahath, Ebal, Shephi, Onam. Sons of Zibeon: Aiah and Anah. ⁴¹Son of Anah: Dishon. Sons of Dishon: Hamran, Eshban, Ithran, Cheran. ⁴²Sons of Ezer: Bil-

han, Zaavan, Jaakan. Sons of Dishan: Uz and Aran.

The kings of Edom

43 These are the kings who ruled in Edom before an Israelite king ruled: Bela son of Beor; his city was called Dinhabah. 44 Bela died and Jobab son of Zerah, from Bozrah, succeeded. 45 Jobab died and Husham from the territory of the Temanites succeeded. 46 Husham died and Hada son of Bedad succeeded; he defeated the Midianites in Moab, and his city was called Avith. 47 Hadad died and Samlah of Masrekah succeeded. 48 Samlah died and Shaul of Rehoboth-ha-Nahar succeeded. 49 Shaul died and Baal-Hanan son of Achbor succeeded. 50 Baal-Hanan died and Hadad succeeded. His city was called Pai; his wife's name was Mehetabel daughter of Matred, daughter of Mezahab.

The chiefs of Edom

51 Hadad died, and then there were chiefs in Edom: Chief Timna, Chief Aliah, Chief Jetheth, 52 Chief Oholibamah, Chief Elah, Chief Pinon, 53 Chief Kenaz, Chief Teman, Chief Mibzar, 54 Chief Magdiel, Chief Iram. These were the chiefs of Edom.

The sons of Israel

2 These are the sons of Israel: Reuben, Simeon, Levi, Judah, Issachar, and Zebulun. 2 Dan, Joseph, and Benjamin, Naphtali, Gad, and Asher.

The descendants of Judah

3 Sons of Judah: Er, Onan and Shelah. These three were born to him by Bath-shua the Canaanite woman. Er, Judah's first-born, displeased Yahweh who put him to death. 4 Tamar, Judah's daughter-in-law, bore him Perez and Zerah. Judah had five sons in all.

5 Sons of Perez: Hezron and Hamul.

6 Sons of Zerah: Zimri, Ethan, Heman, Calcol and Dara, five in all.

7 Sons of Carmi: Achar, who brought trouble on Israel by being unfaithful to the curse of destruction.

8 Sons of Ethan: Azariah.

The ancestors of David

9 Sons of Hezron: there were born to him Jerahmeel, Ram, Chelubai.

10 Ram fathered Amminadab, Amminadab fathered Nahshon chief of the sons of Judah, 11 Nahshon fathered Salma, Salma fathered Boaz. 12 Boaz fathered Obed, Obed fathered Jesse. 13 Jesse fathered Eliab, his first-born, Abinadab second, Shimea third, 14 Nethanel fourth, Raddai fifth, 15 Ozem sixth, David seventh. 16 Their sisters were Zeruiah and Abigail. Sons of Zeruiah: Abishai, Joab and Asahel: three. 17 Abigail gave birth to Amasa; father of Amasa was Jether the Ishmaelite.

Caleb

18 Caleb son of Hezron fathered Jerioth by Azubah his wife; these are her sons: Jesher, Shobab and Ardon. 19 Azubah died, and Caleb married Ephrath, who bore him Hur. 20 Hur fathered Uri, Uri fathered Bezalel.

21 Afterwards, Hezron married the daughter of Machir, father of Gilead; he married her when he was sixty years old and she bore him Segub. 22 Segub fathered Jair who held twenty-three towns in the territory of Gilead. 23 From them, however, Geshur and Aram took the Encampments of Jair and Kenath with its dependencies: sixty towns. All these used to belong to the sons of Machir father of Gilead.

24 After Hezron's death, Caleb married Ephrathah, wife of Hezron his father, who bore him Ashhur father of Tekoa.

Jerahmeel

25 Jerahmeel, Hezron's eldest son, fathered Hezron, his first-born, Ram, Bunah, Oren, Ozem, Ahijah. 26 Jerahmeel had another wife called Atarah; she was the mother of Onam.

27 Sons of Ram, Jerahmeel's first-born: Maaz, Jamin and Eker.

28 Sons of Onam: Shammai and Jada. Sons

of Shammai: Nadab and Abishur. ²⁹ Abishur's wife was called Abihail; she bore him Ahban and Molid. ³⁰ Sons of Nadab: Seled and Ephraim. Seled died leaving no son. ³¹ Son of Ephraim: Ishi; son of Ishi: Sheshan; son of Sheshan: Ahlai. ³² Sons of Jada, Shammai's brother: Jether and Jonathan. Jether died leaving no sons. ³³ Sons of Jonathan: Peleth and Zaza.

These were the sons of Jerahmeel.

³⁴ Sheshan had no sons, only daughters. He had an Egyptian slave Jarha ³⁵ to whom Sheshan gave his daughter in marriage. She bore him Attai. ³⁶ Attai fathered Nathan, Nathan fathered Zabad, ³⁷ Zabad fathered Ephlal, Ephlal fathered Obed, ³⁸ Obed fathered Jehu, Jehu fathered Azariah, ³⁹ Azariah fathered Helez, Helez fathered Eleasah, ⁴⁰ Eleasah fathered Sismai, Sismai fathered Shallum, ⁴¹ Shallum fathered Jekamiah, Jekamiah fathered Elishama.

Caleb

⁴² Sons of Caleb, Jerahmeel's brother: Mesha, his first-born, who fathered Ziph. His son was Mareshah, father of Hebron. ⁴³ Sons of Hebron: Korah, Tappuah, Rekem and Shema. ⁴⁴ Shema fathered Raham, father of Jorkeam. Rekem fathered Shammai. ⁴⁵ Shammai's son was Maon, and Maon fathered Beth-Zur.

⁴⁶ Ephah, Caleb's concubine, gave birth to Haran, Moza and Gazez. Haran fathered Gazez.

⁴⁷ Sons of Jahdai: Regem, Jotham, Geshan, Pelet, Ephah and Shaaph.

⁴⁸ Maacah, Caleb's concubine, gave birth to Sheber and Tirhanah. ⁴⁹ She gave birth to Shaaph, who fathered Madmannah, and Sheva, who fathered Machbenah and Gibea.

The daughter of Caleb was Achsah.

⁵⁰ These were the sons of Caleb.

Hur

Sons of Hur, the first-born of Ephrathah: Shobal fathered Kiriath-Jearim; ⁵¹ Salma fathered Bethlehem; Hareph fathered Beth-Gader. ⁵² Shobal, father of Kiriath-Jearim, had sons: Haroeh, that is, half of the Manahathites, ⁵³ and the clans of Kiriath-Jearim: the Ithrites, Puthites, Shumathites and Mishraites. Their descendants are the people of Zorah and Eshtaol.

⁵⁴ Sons of Salma: Bethlehem, the Netophathites, Atroth Beth-Joab, half of the Manahathites, the Zorathites, ⁵⁵ the Sophrite clans living at Jabez, the Tirathites, the Shimeathites, the Sucathites. They were the Kenites descended from Hammath, father of the House of Rechab.

The sons of David

3 These are the sons of David who were born to him in Hebron: the first-born Amnon, by Ahinoam of Jezreel; second, Daniel, by Abigail of Carmel; ² third, Absalom son of Maacah, daughter of Talmai king of Geshur; fourth, Adonijah son of Haggith; ³ fifth, Shephatiah by Abital, sixth, Ithream by his wife Eglah. ⁴ Six, therefore, were born to him in Hebron, where he reigned for three years and six months.

He reigned for thirty-three years in Jerusalem. ⁵ These are the sons who were born to him in Jerusalem: Shimea, Shobab, Nathan, Solomon, the four of them children of Bath-Shua daughter of Ammiel; ⁶ Ibhar, Elishama, Eliphelet, ⁷ Nogah, Nepheg, Japhia, ⁸ Elishama, Eliada, Eliphelet: nine.

⁹ All these were sons of David, not counting the sons of the concubines. Tamar was their sister.

The kings of Judah

¹⁰ Sons of Solomon: Rehoboam; Abijah his son, Asa his son, Jehoshaphat his son, ¹¹ Joram his son, Ahaziah his son, Joash his son, ¹² Amaziah his son, Azariah his son, Jotham his son, ¹³ Ahaz his son, Hezekiah his son, Manasseh his son, ¹⁴ Amon his son, Josiah his son. ¹⁵ Sons of Josiah: Johanan, the first-born, Jehoiakim second, Zedekiah third, Shallum fourth. ¹⁶ The sons of Jehoiakim: Jeconiah his son, Zedekiah his son.

The royal line after the exile

17 Sons of Jeconiah the captive: Shealtiel his son, 18 then Malchiram, Pedaiah, Shenazzar, Jechamiah, Hoshama, Nedabiah. 19 Sons of Pedaiah: Zerubbabel and Shimei. Sons of Zerubbabel: Meshullam and Hananiah; Shelomith was their sister. 20 Sons of Meshullam: Hashubah, Ohel, Berechiah, Hasadiah, Jushab-Hesed: five. 21 Sons of Hananiah: Pelatiah; Jeshaiah his son, Rephaiah his son, Arnan his son, Obadiah his son, Shecaniah his son. 22 Sons of Shecaniah: Shemaiah, Hattush, Igal, Bariah, Neariah, Shaphat: six. 23 Sons of Neariah: Elioenai, Hizkiah, Azrikam: three. 24 Sons of Elioenai: Hodaviah, Eliashib, Pelaiah, Akkub, Johanan, Delaiah, Anani: seven.

Judah; Shobal

4 Sons of Judah: Perez, Hezron, Carmi, Hur, Shobal. 2 Reaiah son of Shobal fathered Jahath, and Jahath fathered Ahumai and Lahad. These are the Zoreathite clans.

Hur

3 These are Abi-Etam, Jezreel, Ishma, and Idbash, whose sister was called Hazzelelponi.

4 Penuel fathered Gedor, and Ezer fathered Hushah.

These were the sons of Hur, first-born of Ephrathah and father of Bethlehem.

Ashhur

5 Ashhur, father of Tekoa, had two wives: Helah and Naarah.

6 Naarah bore him Ahuzzam, Hepher, the Timnites, and the Ahashtarites—these were the sons of Naarah.

7 Sons of Helah: Zereth, Zohar, Ethnan.

8 Koz fathered Anub, Hazzobebah and the clans of Aharhel son of Harum. 9 Jabez was better known than his brothers. His mother gave him the name Jabez, 'because', she said, 'in distress I gave birth to him.' 10 Jabez called on the God of Israel. 'If you truly bless me,' he said, 'you will extend my lands, your hand will be with me, you will keep harm away and my distress will cease.' God granted him what he had asked.

Caleb

11 Chelub, Shuhah's brother, fathered Mehir, who fathered Eshton. 12 Eshton fathered Bethrapha, Paseah and Tehinnah father of Irnahash. These were the men of Recab.

13 Sons of Kenaz: Othniel and Seraiah. Sons of Othniel: Hathath and Meonothai; 14 Meonothai fathered Ophrah. Seraiah fathered Joab, father of Geharashim—for they were craftsmen.

15 Sons of Caleb son of Jephunneh: Iru, Elah and Naam. Sons of Elah: Kenaz.

16 Sons of Jehallelel: Ziph, Ziphah, Tiria, Asarel.

17 Sons of Ezrah: Jether, Mered, Epher, Jalon. She conceived Miriam, Shammai, and Ishbah, the father of Eshtemoa, 18 whose Judaean wife gave birth to Jered father of Gedor, Heber father of Soco, and Jekuthiel, father of Zanoah. These were the sons of Bithiah the daughter of Pharaoh whom Mered had married.

19 The sons of Hodiah's wife, sister of Naham father of Keilah the Garmite and of Eshtemoa the Maacathite . . .

20 Sons of Shimon: Amnon, Rinnah, Ben-Hanan, Tilon.

Sons of Ishi: Zoheth and Ben-Zoheth.

Shelah

21 Sons of Shelah son of Judah: Er father of Lecah, Laadah father of Mareshah, and the clans of linenworkers at Beth-Ashbea, 22 Jokim, the men of Cozeba, Joash and Saraph where Moab found wives and then returned to Bethlehem. (These are old traditions.) 23 These were potters and lived at Netaim and Gederah; they resided there, working for the king.

Simeon

24 Sons of Simeon: Nemuel, Jamin, Jarib, Zerah, Saul; 25 Shallum was his son, Mibsam his son, Mishma his son. 26 The sons of Mishma:

Hammuel his son, Zaccur his son, Shimei his son. ²⁷Shimei had sixteen sons and six daughters, but his brothers did not have many children, and the sum of their clans did not multiply as the sons of Judah did.

²⁸They lived in Beersheba, Moladah and Hazar-Shual, ²⁹Bilhah, Ezem and Tolad, ³⁰Bethuel, Hormah and Ziklag, ³¹Beth-Marcaboth, Hazar-Susim, Beth-Biri, Shaaraim. ³²These were their towns until the reign of David. Their settlements were: Etam, Ain, Rimmon, Tochen and Ashan, five towns, ³³and all the dependencies surrounding these towns as far as Baalath. That was where they lived and they had an official genealogy. ³⁴Meshobab, Jamlech, Joshah son of Amaziah, ³⁵Joel, Jehu son of Joshibiah, son of Seraiah, son of Asiel, ³⁶Elioenai, Jaakobah, Jeshohaiah, Asaiah, Adiel, Jesimiel, Benaiah, ³⁷Ziza, Ben-Shiphi, Ben-Allon, Ben-Jedaiah, Ben-Shimri, Ben-Shemaiah— ³⁸these above named were princes in their clans in their ancestral home. Their numbers increased enormously. ³⁹In search of pasture for their flocks, they spread from the Pass of Gerar to the eastern end of the valley, ⁴⁰where they found good, fat pasture; the land was broad, untroubled, peaceful. Hamites had been living there before them.

⁴¹These Simeonites, recorded by name, arrived there in the time of Hezekiah king of Judah; they overran their tents and the dwellings which they found there. They put them under a curse of destruction still in force today and settled in their place, since there was pasturage for their flocks.

⁴²Five hundred of them, of the Simeonites, went to Mount Seir, their leaders being Pelatiah, Neariah, Rephaiah, and Uzziel, the sons of Ishi. ⁴³They defeated the surviving fugitives of Amalek and still live there today.

Reuben

5 Sons of Reuben, first-born of Israel. He was indeed the first-born but, when he defiled his father's bed, his birthright was given to the sons of Joseph son of Israel, and he was no longer reckoned as the eldest son.

²Although Judah grew greater than his brothers and a leader came from him, the birthright was Joseph's.

³Sons of Reuben, first-born of Israel: Henoch, Pallu, Hezron, Carmi.

Joel

⁴Sons of Joel: Shemaiah his son, Gog his son, Shimei his son, ⁵Micah his son, Reaiah his son, Baal his son. ⁶Beerah his son, whom Tiglath-Pileser king of Assyria carried off into exile, was the chief of the Reubenites.

⁷His brothers, by families, were grouped according to relationship. Jeiel was first, then Zechariah ⁸and Bela son of Azaz, son of Shema, son of Joel.

Territory of Reuben

It was Reuben who lived in Aroer and his territory extended as far as Nebo and Baal-Meon. ⁹To eastward, what he occupied extended to the edge of the desert and the River Euphrates, for they had many herds in Gilead. ¹⁰In the time of Saul, they made war on the Hagrites, whom they defeated and who were then living in their tents throughout the eastern front of Gilead.

Gad

¹¹Next to them, in Bashan as far as Salecah, lived the sons of Gad. ¹²Joel was the first, Shapham the second, then Janai and Shaphat in Bashan.

¹³Their brothers, by families, were Michael, Meshullam, Sheba, Jorai, Jacan, Zia, Eber: seven. ¹⁴These were the sons of Abihail: Ben-Huri, Ben-Jaroah, Ben-Gilead, Ben-Michael, Ben-Jeshishai, Ben-Jahdo, Ben-Buz. ¹⁵Ahi son of Abdiel, son of Guni, was the head of their families. ¹⁶They inhabited Gilead, Bashan and its dependencies, as well as all the pasture lands of Sharon on their extremities. ¹⁷In the time of Jotham king of Judah and in the time of Jeroboam king of Israel, all of them were included in the official genealogy.

18 The sons of Reuben, the Gadites and the half-tribe of Manasseh had warriors, men armed with shield and sword who could handle the bow and were trained for war, to the number of forty-four thousand seven hundred and sixty fit for service. 19 They made war on the Hagrites, on Jetur, Naphish and Nodab. 20 God came to their help, and the Hagrites and all their allies fell into their hands, for they called on God as they fought, and because they put their trust in him he heard their prayer. 21 Of their livestock they carried off fifty thousand camels, two hundred and fifty thousand sheep, two thousand donkeys and a hundred thousand people. 22 Because the war was of God, the slaughter was great. They continued to live in their territory until the exile.

The half-tribe of Manasseh

23 The sons of the half-tribe of Manasseh lived in the territory between Bashan and Baal-Hermon, Senir and Mount Hermon.

They were numerous. 24 These were the heads of their families: Epher, Ishi, Eliel, Azriel, Jeremiah, Hodaviah, Jahdiel—stout fighting men, men of renown, heads of their families.

25 But since they were unfaithful to the God of their ancestors and prostituted themselves to the gods of the peoples of the country whom God had destroyed before them, 26 the God of Israel roused the hostility of Pul, king of Assyria, that is the wrath of Tiglath-Pileser, king of Assyria who deported them—the Reubenites, the Gadites and the half-tribe of Manasseh—taking them off to Halah, Habor, Hara and the river of Gozan. They are still there today.

The lineage of the high priests

27 Sons of Levi: Gershom, Kohath and Merari. 28 Sons of Kohath: Amram, Izhar, Hebron, Uzziel. 29 Children of Amram: Aaron, Moses and Miriam. Sons of Aaron: Nadab and Abihu, Eleazar and Ithamar.

30 Eleazar fathered Phinehas, Phinehas fathered Abishua, 31 Abishua fathered Bukki,

Bukki fathered Uzzi. 32 Uzzi fathered Zerahiah, Zerahiah fathered Meraioth. 33 Meraioth fathered Amariah, Amariah fathered Ahitub, 34 Ahitub fathered Zadok, Zadok fathered Ahimaaz. 35 Ahimaaz fathered Azariah, Azariah fathered Johanan. 36 Johanan fathered Azariah. He it was who officiated as priest in the Temple which Solomon built in Jerusalem. 37 Azariah fathered Amariah, Amariah fathered Ahitub, 38 Ahitub fathered Zadok, Zadok fathered Shallum, 39 Shallum fathered Hilkiah, Hilkiah fathered Azariah, 40 Azariah fathered Seraiah, Seraiah fathered Jehozadak, 41 and Jehozadak went into exile when, at the hands of Nebuchadnezzar, Yahweh exiled Judah and Jerusalem.

The line of Levi

6 Sons of Levi: Gershom, Kohath and Merari. 2 These are the names of the sons of Gershom: Libni and Shimei. 3 Sons of Kohath: Amram, Izhar, Hebron, Uzziel. 4 Sons of Merari: Mahli and Mushi.

These are the levitical clans according to their father.

5 Of Gershom: Libni his son, Jahath his son, Zimmah his son, 6 Joah his son, Iddo his son, Zerah his son, Jeatherai his son.

7 Sons of Kohath: Amminadab his son, Korah his son, Assir his son, 8 Elkanah his son, Ebiasaph his son, Assir his son. 9 Tahath his son, Uriel his son, Uzziah his son, Shaul his son. 10 Sons of Elkanah: Amasai and Ahimoth. 11 Elkanah his son, Zophai his son, Nahath his son, 12 Eliab his son, Jeroham his son, Elkanah his son. 13 Sons of Elkanah: Samuel his firstborn, the second Abijah.

14 Sons of Merari: Mahli, Libni his son, 15 Shimei his son, Haggiah his son, Asaiah his son.

The singers

16 These are the men whom David nominated to lead the singing in the Temple of Yahweh after the ark had come to rest there. 17 They were responsible for the singing before the Dwelling, the Tent of Meeting, until Solomon

had built the Temple of Yahweh in Jerusalem and then continued their customary duties.

¹⁸These were the persons in office, with their sons:

Of the sons of Kohath: Heman the singer, son of Joel, son of Samuel, ¹⁹son of Elkanah, son of Jeroham, son of Eliel, son of Toah, ²⁰son of Zuph, son of Elkanah, son of Mahath, son of Amasai, ²¹son of Elkanah, son of Joel, son of Azariah, son of Zephaniah, ²²son of Tahath, son of Assir, son of Ebiasaph, son of Korah, ²³son of Izhar, son of Kohath, son of Levi, son of Israel.

²⁴His brother Asaph stood on his right: Asaph son of Berechiah, son of Shimea, ²⁵son of Michael, son of Baaseiah, son of Malchijah, ²⁶son of Ethni, son of Zerah, son of Adaiah, ²⁷son of Ethan, son of Zimmah, son of Shimei, ²⁸son of Jahath, son of Gershom, son of Levi.

²⁹On the left, the sons of Merari: Ethan son of Kishi, son of Abdi, son of Malluch, ³⁰son of Hashabiah, son of Amaziah, son of Hilkiah, ³¹son of Amzi, son of Bani, son of Shemer, ³²son of Mahli, son of Mushi, son of Merari, son of Levi.

The other Levites

³³Their brother Levites were dedicated for all the other duties of the Dwelling, the Temple of God, ³⁴but Aaron and his sons burned the offerings on the altar of burnt offering and on the altar of incense; they were entirely responsible for the most holy things and for the ritual of expiation for Israel, in accordance with all that Moses, servant of God, had commanded.

³⁵These were the sons of Aaron: Eleazar his son, Phinehas his son, Abishua his son, ³⁶Bukki his son, Uzzi his son, Zerahiah his son, ³⁷Meraioth his son, Amariah his son, Ahitub his son, ³⁸Zadok his son, Ahimaaz his son.

Towns of the Aaronites

³⁹These were their places of settlement within their prescribed territory:

The sons of Aaron of the Kohathite clan— for to these the first lot fell— ⁴⁰were given Hebron in the territory of Judah with its sur-rounding pasture lands. ⁴¹But the open country of the town and its dependencies were given to Caleb son of Jephunneh. ⁴²The sons of Aaron were also given the cities of refuge, Hebron, Libnah with its pasture lands, Jattir, Eshtemoa with its pasture lands. ⁴³Hilen with its pasture lands, Debir with its pasture lands, ⁴⁴Ashan with its pasture lands and Beth-Shemesh with its pasture lands; ⁴⁵and, from the tribe of Benjamin, Geba with its pasture lands, Alemeth with its pasture lands and Anathoth with its pasture lands. In all, the towns distributed among their clans numbered thirteen.

Towns of the other Levites

⁴⁶The remaining sons of Kohath were allotted ten towns from the clans of the tribe, that is, from the half-tribe of Manasseh. ⁴⁷The sons of Gershom and their clans were allotted thirteen towns from the tribe of Issachar, from the tribe of Asher, from the tribe of Naphtali and from the tribe of Manasseh in Bashan. ⁴⁸The sons of Merari and their clans were allotted twelve towns from the tribe of Reuben, from the tribe of Gad and from the tribe of Zebulun. ⁴⁹The Israelites gave these towns with their pasture lands to the Levites. ⁵⁰From the tribe of the sons of Judah, from the tribe of the sons of Simeon and from the tribe of the sons of Benjamin, they also allotted them those towns to which they gave their names.

⁵¹Towns from the tribe of Ephraim were also assigned to the territory of some clans of the sons of Kohath. ⁵²They were given the cities of refuge: Shechem in the highlands of Ephraim with its pasture lands, Gezer and its pasture lands, ⁵³Jokmeam with its pasture lands, Beth-Horon with its pasture lands, ⁵⁴Aijalon with its pasture lands and Gath-Rimmon with its pasture lands ⁵⁵and from the half-tribe of Manasseh, Aner with its pasture lands and Bileam with its pasture lands. So much was given to the remaining families of the sons of Kohath.

⁵⁶From the half-tribe of Manasseh, the sons of Gershom according to family were given

Golan in Bashan with its pasture lands and Ashtaroth with its pasture lands; ⁵⁷from the tribe of Issachar, Kedesh with its pasture lands, Daberath with its pasture lands, ⁵⁸Ramoth with its pasture lands and Anem with its pasture lands; ⁵⁹from the tribe of Asher: Mashal with its pasture lands, Abdon with its pasture lands. ⁶⁰Hukok with its pasture lands and Rehob with its pasture lands; ⁶¹from the tribe of Naphtali, Kedesh in Galilee with its pasture lands, Hammon with its pasture lands and Kiriataim with its pasture lands.

⁶²To the remainder of the sons of Merari: from the tribe of Zebulun, Rimmon with its pasture lands and Tabor with its pasture lands; ⁶³in Transjordan, near Jericho, east of the Jordan, from the tribe of Reuben: Bezer in the desert with its pasture lands, Jahzah with its pasture lands, ⁶⁴Kedemoth with its pasture lands and Mephaath with its pasture lands; ⁶⁵from the tribe of Gad: Ramoth in Gilead with its pasture lands, Mahanaim with its pasture lands, ⁶⁶Heshbon with its pasture lands and Jazer with its pasture lands.

Issachar

7 For the sons of Issachar: Tola, Puah, Jashub, Shimron: four.

²Sons of Tola: Uzzi, Rephaiah, Jeriel, Jahmai, Ibsam, Shemuel, heads of their families of Tola. In the time of David, these numbered twenty-two thousand six hundred stout fighting men, grouped according to their kinship.

³Sons of Uzzi: Izrahiah. Sons of Izrahiah: Michael, Obadiah, Joel, Isshiah. In all five chiefs, ⁴responsible for fighting companies amounting to thirty-six thousand troops, according to relationship and family, for they had many women and children. ⁵They had kinsmen belonging to all the clans of Issachar, eighty-seven thousand stout fighting men, all belonging to one related group.

Benjamin

⁶Sons of Benjamin: Bela, Becher, Jediael: three.

⁷Sons of Bela: Ezbon, Uzzi, Uzziel, Jerimoth and Iri: five, chiefs of families and warriors. Their official genealogy included twenty-two thousand and thirty-four members.

⁸Sons of Becher: Zemirah, Joash, Eliezar, Elioenai, Omri, Jeremoth, Abijah, Anathoth, Alemeth, all these were the sons of Becher. ⁹The official genealogy of the descendants of the chiefs of their families included twenty thousand two hundred warriors.

¹⁰Sons of Jediael: Bilhan. Sons of Bilhan: Jeush, Benjamin, Ehud, Chenaanah, Zethan, Tarshish, Ahishahar. ¹¹All these sons of Jediael, became heads of families, stout fighting men, numbering seventeen thousand two hundred men fit for active service.

Naphtali

¹²Shuppim and Huppim. Son of Ir: Hushim; his son: Aher.

¹³Sons of Naphtali: Jahziel, Guni, Jezer, Shallum.

These were the sons of Bilhah.

Manasseh

¹⁴Sons of Manasseh: Asriel, born of his Aramaean concubine. She gave birth to Machir, father of Gilead. ¹⁵Machir took a wife for Huppim and Shuppim. His sister's name was Maacah.

The name of the second son was Zelophehad. Zelophehad had daughters.

¹⁶Maacah the wife of Machir gave birth to a son whom she called Peresh. His brother was called Sheresh and his sons Ulam and Rakem.

¹⁷Sons of Ulam: Bedan. These were the sons of Gilead son of Machir, son of Manasseh.

¹⁸His sister Hammoleketh gave birth to Ishod, Abiezer and Mahlah.

¹⁹Shemida had sons: Ahian, Shechem, Likhi and Aniam.

Ephraim

²⁰Sons of Ephraim: Shuthelah, Bered his son, Tahath his son, Eleadah his son, Tahath his son, ²¹Zabad his son, Shuthelah his son and

Ezer and Elead whom the men of Gath, natives of the country, killed when they came down to raid their cattle. ²²Their father Ephraim mourned for a long time and his brothers came to comfort him. ²³He had intercourse with his wife, who conceived and gave birth to a son whom he called Beriah because his house was in misfortune. ²⁴He had a daughter, Sheerah, who built Upper and Lower Beth-Horon and Uzzen-Sheerah.

²⁵Rephah was his son, Shuthelah his son, Tahan his son, ²⁶Ladan his son, Ammihud his son, Elishama his son, ²⁷Nun his son, Joshua his son.

²⁸They had lands and settlements in Bethel and its dependencies from Naaran on the east to Gezer and its dependencies on the west, as well as Shechem and its dependencies as far as Ayyah and its dependencies. ²⁹Beth-Shean with its dependencies, Taanach and its dependencies, Megiddo and its dependencies and Dor with its dependencies were in the hands of the sons of Manasseh. There lived the sons of Joseph son of Israel.

Asher

³⁰Sons of Asher: Imnah, Ishvah, Ishvi, Beriah; their sister Serah.

³¹Sons of Beriah: Heber and Malchiel. He fathered Birzaith. ³²Heber fathered Japhlet, Shomer, Hotham and their sister Shua. ³³Sons of Japhlet: Pasach, Bimhal and Ashvath. These were the sons of Japhlet. ³⁴Sons of Shomer his brother: Rohgah, Hubbah and Aram. ³⁵Sons of Helem his brother: Zophah, Imna, Shelesh and Amal. ³⁶Sons of Zophah: Suah, Harnepher, Shual, Beri and Imrah. ³⁷Bezer, Hod, Shamma, Shilshah, Ithran and Beerah. ³⁸Sons of Ithran: Jephunneh, Pispa, Ara.

³⁹Sons of Ulla: Arah, Hanniel, Rizia.

⁴⁰All these were the sons of Asher, heads of families, picked men, warriors and senior princes. They were registered in fighting companies to the number of twenty-six thousand men.

The line of Benjamin

8 Benjamin was father of Bela, his first-born, Ashbel second, Ahiram third, ²Nohah fourth, Rapha fifth. ³Bela had sons: Addar, Gera father of Ehud, ⁴Abishua, Naaman, Ahoah, ⁵Gera, Shephuphan and Huram.

In Geba

⁶These are the sons of Ehud. They were heads of families of the inhabitants of Geba and led them into exile at Manahath: ⁷Naaman, Ahijah and Gera. It was he who led them into exile; he became the father of Uzza and Ahihud.

In Moab

⁸Shaharaim had children in the Plains of Moab after he had dismissed his wives, Hushim and Baara. ⁹By his new wife he had sons: Jobab, Zibia, Mesha, Malcam, ¹⁰Jeuz, Sachia, Mirmah. These were his sons, heads of families.

In Ono and Lud

¹¹By Hushim he had sons: Abitub and Elpaal. ¹²The sons of Elpaal were Eber, Misham and Shemed, who built Ono and Lud and its dependencies.

In Aijalon

¹³Beriah and Shema were the chiefs of the families who lived at Aijalon; they routed the inhabitants of Gath.

¹⁴His brother was Shashak.

In Jerusalem

Jeremoth, ¹⁵Zebadiah, Arad, Eder, ¹⁶Michael, Ishpah, Joha were the sons of Beriah.

¹⁷Zebadiah, Meshullam, Hizki, Haber, ¹⁸Ishmerai, Izliah, Jobab were the sons of Elpaal.

¹⁹Jakim, Zichri, Zabdi, ²⁰Elienai, Zillethai, Eliel, ²¹Adaiah, Beraiah, Shimrath were the sons of Shimei.

²²Ishpan, Eber, Eliel, ²³Abdon, Zichri,

Hanan, 24 Hananiah, Elam, Anthothijah, 25 Iphdeiah, Penuel were the sons of Shashak.

26 Shamsherai, Shehariah, Athaliah, 27 Jaareshaiah, Elijah, Zichri were the sons of Jeroham.

28 These were chiefs of families according to their relationship. They lived in Jerusalem.

In Gibeon

29 At Gibeon lived Jeiel the father of Gibeon, whose wife was called Maacah. 30 His first-born son was Abdon, then Zur, Kish, Baal, Ner, Nadab, 31 Gedor, Ahio, Zecher 32 and Mikloth. Mikloth fathered Shimeah. But they, unlike their brothers, lived at Jerusalem with their brothers.

Saul and his family

33 Ner fathered Kish, Kish fathered Saul, Saul fathered Jonathan, Malchishua, Abinadab and Eshbaal. 34 Son of Jonathan: Meribbaal. Meribbaal fathered Micah. 35 Sons of Micah: Pithon, Melech, Tarea, Ahaz. 36 Ahaz fathered Jehoaddah, Jehoaddah fathered Alemeth, Azmaveth and Zimri. Zimri fathered Moza, 37 Moza fathered Binea, Raphah his son, Eleasah his son and Azel his son. 38 Azel had six sons, whose names were these: Azrikam, his first-born, then Ishmael, Sheariah, Obadiah, Hanan. All these were sons of Azel.

39 Sons of Eshek his brother: Ulam, his first-born, Jeush second, Eliphelet third.

40 The sons of Ulam were warriors—archers. They had as many as a hundred and fifty sons and grandsons.

All these belonged to the sons of Benjamin.

Jerusalem, the holy city of Israel

9 Thus, all Israel's official genealogies had been entered in the records of the kings of Israel and Judah before they were deported to Babylon for their infidelity.

2 Now the first citizens to return to their property in their cities were the Israelites, the priests, the Levites and the temple slaves. 3 In Jerusalem, there settled Judaeans, Benjaminites, Ephraimites and Manassehites.

4 Uthai son of Ammihud, son of Omri, son of Imri, son of Bani, one of the sons of Perez son of Judah. 5 Of the descendants of Shelah: Asaiah, the first-born, and his sons. 6 Of the sons of Zerah: Jeuel. And six hundred and ninety of their kinsmen.

7 And of the sons of Benjamin: Sallu son of Meshullam, son of Hodaviah, son of Hassenuah; 8 Ibneiah son of Jeroham; Elah son of Uzzi, son of Michri; and Meshullam son of Shephatiah, son of Reuel, son of Ibnijah. 9 Their kinsmen, according to their relationship, numbered nine hundred and fifty-six. All these men were chiefs of their families.

10 Of the priests there were Jedaiah, Jehoiarib, Jachin, 11 Azariah son of Hilkiah, son of Meshullam, son of Zadok, son of Meraioth, son of Ahitub, the chief of the Temple of God; 12 Adaiah son of Jeroham, son of Pashhur, son of Malchijah; and Maasai son of Adiel, son of Jahzerah, son of Meshullam, son of Meshillemith, son of Immer. 13 Their kinsmen, heads of families, numbered one thousand seven hundred and sixty—men expert in the ministerial service of the Temple of God.

14 Of the Levites there were Shemaiah son of Hasshub, son of Azrikam, son of Hashabiah of the sons of Merari, 15 Bakbakar, Heresh, Galai, Mattaniah son of Mica, son of Zichri, son of Asaph. 16 Obadiah son of Shemaiah, son of Galal, son of Jeduthun and Berechiah son of Asa, son of Elkanah, who lived in the dependencies of the Netophathites.

17 The gatekeepers were Shallum, Akkub, Talmon, Ahiman and their kinsmen. Shallum was the chief 18 and is still gatekeeper of the King's Gate to the east. They were the gatekeepers of the camps of the sons of Levi.

19 Shallum son of Kore, son of Ebiasaph, son of Korah, and his brothers belonging to his family, the Korahites, were also in charge of the ministerial service as doorkeepers of the Tent, as their ancestors had been keepers of the entrance to the camp of Yahweh. 20 Formerly, Phinehas son of Eleazar had been in charge of them—Yahweh be with him! 21 Zechariah son of Meshelemiah was gate-

keeper at the door of the Tent of Meeting. ²² All the keepers of the gate at the thresholds were picked men; there were two hundred and twelve of them. They were grouped by relationship in their various villages. These were confirmed in office by David and Samuel the seer because of their dependability. ²³ They and their sons continued in charge as guards of the gates of the Temple of Yahweh, the house of the Tent. ²⁴ The gatekeepers were assigned to the four sides, east, west, north and south, ²⁵ and their brothers in their villages were required to assist them from time to time for a week, ²⁶ since the four head gatekeepers were permanently on duty.

They were Levites and were in charge of the accommodation and supplies of the Temple of God. ²⁷ They spent the night in the precincts of the Temple of God, their duties being to guard it and open it every morning. ²⁸ Some of them were in charge of the implements of worship, having to count them when they took them out and when they put them away. ²⁹ Others of them were put in charge of the implements, of all the objects in the sanctuary and of the flour, the wine, the oil, the incense and the perfume. ³⁰ Members of the priestly caste, however, mixed the ointment for the perfume.

³¹ One of the Levites, Mattithiah—he was the first-born of Shallum the Korahite—had regular charge of baking operations. ³² Some of their kinsmen the Kohathites were responsible for the loaves to be set out in rows Sabbath by Sabbath.

³³ In addition, there were the singers, the heads of the levitical families, who were accommodated in the Temple, free of other responsibilities because they were on duty day and night.

³⁴ Such were the chiefs of the levitical families, according to their relationship; these lived in Jerusalem.

The ancestors of Saul

³⁵ Jeiel father of Gibeon lived at Gibeon and his wife was called Maacah. ³⁶ His first-born son was Abdon, then Zur, Kish, Baal, Ner, Nadab, ³⁷ Gedor, Ahio, Zechariah and Mikloth. ³⁸ Mikloth fathered Shimeam. But they, unlike their brothers, lived at Jerusalem with their brothers.

³⁹ Ner fathered Kish, Kish fathered Saul, Saul fathered Jonathan, Malchishua, Abinadab and Eshbaal. ⁴⁰ Son of Jonathan: Meribbaal. Meribbaal fathered Micah. ⁴¹ Sons of Micah: Pithon, Melech, Tahrea. ⁴² Ahaz fathered Jarah, Jarah fathered Alemeth, Azmaveth and Zimri; Zimri fathered Moza, ⁴³ Moza fathered Binea, Rephaiah his son, Eleasah his son and Azel his son. ⁴⁴ Azel had six sons; their names were these: Azrikam his first-born, Ishmael, Sheariah, Obadiah, Hanan. These were the sons of Azel.

Death of Saul

10 The Philistines gave battle to Israel and the Israelites, fleeing from the Philistines, fell and were slaughtered on Mount Gilboa. ² The Philistines bore down on Saul and his sons, and they killed Jonathan, Abinadab and Malchishua, Saul's sons. ³ The fighting grew fiercer round Saul; the archers came upon him, and he was wounded by the archers. ⁴ Saul then said to his armour-bearer, 'Draw your sword and run me through with it. I do not want these uncircumcised men to come and make fun of me.' But his armour-bearer was very much afraid and would not do it. So Saul took his own sword and fell on it. ⁵ His armour-bearer, seeing that Saul was dead, fell on his sword too and died with him. ⁶ Thus died Saul, his three sons and his entire household together. ⁷ When all the Israelites who were in the valley saw that the Israelites had been routed and that Saul and his sons were dead, they abandoned their towns and fled. The Philistines then came and occupied them.

⁸ When the Philistines came on the following day to strip the dead, they found Saul and his sons lying on Mount Gilboa. ⁹ They stripped him and, taking his head and his armour, had these carried round the territory of

the Philistines to proclaim the good news to their idols and their people. ¹⁰ They placed his armour in the temple of their gods and nailed his head up in the temple of Dagon.

¹¹ When all the inhabitants of Jabesh in Gilead heard everything that the Philistines had done to Saul, ¹² the warriors all set out and took the bodies of Saul and his sons away; they brought them to Jabesh and buried their bones under the tamarisk of Jabesh and fasted for seven days.

¹³ Thus died Saul in the infidelity of which he had been guilty towards Yahweh, in that he had not obeyed the word of Yahweh and because he had consulted a necromancer for guidance. ¹⁴ He had not consulted Yahweh, who therefore caused his death and transferred the monarchy to David son of Jesse.

David is anointed as king of Israel

11 All Israel then rallied to David at Hebron and said, 'Look, we are your own flesh and bone. ² In days past when Saul was king, it was you who led Israel on its campaigns, and Yahweh your God promised you, "You are to shepherd my people Israel and be leader of my people Israel." ' ³ So all the elders of Israel came to the king at Hebron, and David made a pact with them in Yahweh's presence at Hebron, and they anointed David as king of Israel, in accordance with the word of Yahweh through Samuel.

The capture of Jerusalem

⁴ David and all Israel then marched on Jerusalem (that is to say, Jebus); the inhabitants of the territory were the Jebusites. ⁵ The inhabitants of Jebus said to David, 'You will not get in here.' But David captured the citadel of Zion, that is, the City of David. ⁶ David said, 'The first man to kill a Jebusite will be made army commander and chief.' Joab son of Zeruiah was the first man to go up, and was made commander of the army. ⁷ David went to live in the citadel, and that is how it came to be called the City of David. ⁸ He then built a wall round the city, all round, beginning from the Millo, and Joab restored the rest of the city. ⁹ Thus David grew stronger and stronger, for Yahweh Sabaoth was with him.

David's champions

¹⁰ These are David's principal champions who joined forces with him in his kingdom, with all Israel, to make him king in accordance with the word of Yahweh concerning Israel. ¹¹ This is the roll of David's champions: Jashobeam son of Hachmoni, head of the Three; he it was who brandished his spear over three hundred men whom he had killed at one time.

¹² Next, there was Eleazar son of Dodo, the Ahohite, one of the three champions. ¹³ He was with David at Pas-Dammim when the Philistines mustered for battle there. There was a field full of barley there; and the people fled from the Philistines. ¹⁴ And they took their stand in the middle of the field, held it and cut down the Philistines; and Yahweh brought about a great victory.

¹⁵ Three members of the Thirty went down to David at the rock near the Cave of Adullam while a company of Philistines was encamped in the Valley of the Rephaim. ¹⁶ David was then in the stronghold and there was a Philistine garrison in Bethlehem. ¹⁷ Longingly, David said, 'If only someone would fetch me a drink of water from the well that stands by the gate at Bethlehem!' ¹⁸ At this the three champions, forcing their way through the Philistine camp, drew water from the well that stands by the gate of Bethlehem and, bringing it away, presented it to David. David, however, would not drink any of it, but poured it out as a libation to Yahweh. ¹⁹ 'God preserve me', he said, 'from doing such a thing! Am I to drink these men's blood? For at the risk of their lives they brought it.' And so he would not drink. Such were the deeds of the three champions.

²⁰ Abishai, brother of Joab, was leader of the Thirty. He it was who brandished his spear over three hundred men whom he had killed,

winning himself a name among the Thirty. 21 He was a most illustrious member of the Thirty and became their captain, but he was not equal to the Three.

22 Benaiah son of Jehoiada from Kabzeel was the hero of many exploits; he it was who slaughtered two formidable Moabites and, one snowy day, climbed down and slaughtered the lion in the storage-well. 23 He also slaughtered an Egyptian, a man who was seven and a half feet tall. The Egyptian was armed with a spear in his hand like a weaver's beam, but he took him on with a staff, tore the spear from the Egyptian's hand and killed the man with it. 24 Such were the exploits of Benaiah son of Jehoiada, winning him a name among the thirty champions. 25 He was a most illustrious member of the Thirty, but he was not equal to the Three. David put him in command of his bodyguard.

26 The military champions were:

Asahel brother of Joab;
Elhanan son of Dodo, of Bethlehem;
27 Shammoth of Haror;
Helez the Pelonite;
28 Ira son of Ikkesh, of Tekoa;
Abiezer of Anathoth;
29 Sibbecai of Hushah;
Ilai of Ahoh;
30 Maharai of Netophah;
Heled son of Baanah, of Netophah.
31 Ithai son of Ribai, of Gibeah in Benjamin.
Benaiah of Pirathon;
32 Hurai of the Torrents of Gaash;
Abiel of Beth-ha-Arabah;
33 Azmaveth of Bahurim;
Eliahba of Shaalbon;
34 the sons of Hashem of Gizon;
Jonathan son of Shagee, of Harar;
35 Ahiam son of Sachar, of Harar;
Eliphelet son of Ur;
36 Hepher of Mecherah;
Ahijah the Pelonite;
37 Hezro of Carmel;
Naarai son of Ezbai;
38 Joel brother of Nathan;

Mibhar son of Hagri;
39 Zelek the Ammonite;
Naharai of Beeroth, armour-bearer to Joab son of Zeruiah;
40 Ira of Jattir;
Gareb of Jattir;
41 Uriah the Hittite;
Zabad son of Ahlai;
42 Adina son of Shiza the Reubenite, chief of the Reubenites and commander of the Thirty;
43 Hanan son of Maacah;
Joshaphat the Mithnite;
44 Uzzia of Ashteroth;
Shama and Jeiel sons of Hotham of Aroer;
45 Jediael son of Shimri, and Joha his brother, the Tizite;
46 Eliel the Mahavite;
Jeribai and Joshaviah sons of Elnaam;
Ithmah the Moabite;
47 Eliel, Obed, and Jaasiel of Zobah.

Early defections to David

12 These are the men who rallied to David at Ziklag while he was still being kept away from Saul son of Kish; they were among the champions, the warriors. 2 They were equipped with bows and could sling stones or shoot arrows from the bow with either right hand or left.

Of Saul's fellow-tribesmen from Benjamin: 3 Ahiezer the leader, and Joash, sons of Hassemar of Gibeah, Jeziel and Peleth, sons of Azmaveth, Berachah and Jehu of Anathoth, 4 Ishmaiah of Gibeon, one of the champions in the Thirty and commander of the Thirty, 5 Jeremiah, Jahaziel, Johanan and Jozabed of Gederoth, 6 Eluzai, Jerimoth, Bealiah, Shemariah, Shephatiah of Hariph, 7 Elkanah, Isshiah, Azarel, Joezer and Jashobeam the Korahites, 8 Joelah, Zebadiah, sons of Jeroham of Gedor.

9 From the Gadites, some good, capable fighting men defected and came to David at the stronghold in the desert—all skilled with shield and spear, fierce as lions and nimble as mountain gazelles. 10 Ezer was the leader,

Obadiah second, Eliab third, ¹¹Mishmannah fourth, Jeremiah fifth, ¹²Attai sixth, Eliel seventh, ¹³Johanan eighth, Elzabad ninth, ¹⁴Jeremiah tenth, Machbannai eleventh. ¹⁵These Gadites were the leaders of the troops, the least of them a match for a hundred men and the greatest a match for a thousand. ¹⁶These were the men who once crossed the Jordan in the first month, when it had overflowed its banks and had driven out all the lowlanders to east and west.

¹⁷Some of the Benjaminites and Judahites also joined David at the stronghold. ¹⁸When David came forward to meet them, he responded to them by saying, 'If you have come to me with peaceful intent to help me, you will find me a good friend. But if it is to betray me to my enemies, seeing that I have done nothing wrong, may the God of our ancestors take note and condemn you.'

¹⁹Then the Spirit invested Amasai the leader of the Thirty:

'We are your men, David; with you, son of Jesse!
Peace be with you, peace be with you;
        peace be with those who help you!
For your God has helped you!'

And David accepted them, including them among his more senior officers.

²⁰Some Manassehites also defected to David as he was setting out with the Philistines to fight Saul. But he did not help the Philistines because, after consultation, their chiefs sent him away, saying, 'He will defect to his master Saul and it will cost us our heads!' ²¹He was on his way to Ziklag when these Manassehites deserted to him: Adnah, Jozabad, Jediael, Michael, Jozabad, Elihu, Zillethai, chiefs of thousands in Manasseh. ²²They helped David and his band, since they were all men of standing and became officers in the army.

²³Indeed reinforcements reached David day after day, so that his camp grew into a camp of prodigious size.

The warriors who assured David's kingship

²⁴These are the numbers of fully armed men who joined David at Hebron to transfer Saul's kingdom to him in accordance with the order of Yahweh:

²⁵Judahites carrying shield and spear: six thousand eight hundred fully armed warriors;

²⁶Simeonites; seven thousand one hundred champions valiant in war;

²⁷Levites: four thousand six hundred, ²⁸in addition to Jehoiada, in command of the Aaronites, with three thousand seven hundred of these, ²⁹Zadok, a young and valiant champion, and twenty-two commanders of his family;

³⁰Benjaminites: three thousand kinsmen of Saul, most of them hitherto in the service of the House of Saul;

³¹Ephraimites: twenty thousand eight hundred valiant champions, men famous in their families;

³²of the half-tribe of Manasseh: eighteen thousand men assigned by name to go and proclaim David king;

³³Issacharites, sound judges of the times when Israel should take action, and the way to do it: two hundred chiefs and all their kinsmen under their command;

³⁴Zebulunites: fifty thousand men fit for service, marshalled for battle, with warlike weapons of every kind, staunch-hearted auxiliaries;

³⁵Naphtalites: a thousand commanders, and with them thirty-seven thousand men armed with shield and spear;

³⁶Danites: twenty-eight thousand six hundred men marshalled for battle;

³⁷Asherites: forty thousand men fit for service, marshalled for battle;

³⁸from Transjordan: a hundred and twenty thousand men of Reuben, Gad and the half-tribe of Manasseh, with warlike weapons of every kind.

³⁹All these warriors in battle array came to David at Hebron with the firm determination of making David king of all Israel; and the rest

of Israel, too, was of one mind in wanting to make David king. ⁴⁰For three days they stayed there with David, eating and drinking, their fellow-tribesmen having made preparations for them; ⁴¹their neighbours too, from as far away as Issachar and Zebulun and Naphtali, came bringing food on donkeys, camels, mules and oxen—supplies of flour, fig cakes, bunches of raisins, wine, oil, quantities of oxen and sheep—for there was joy in Israel.

The ark brought back from Kiriath-Jearim

13 David conferred with the commanders of the thousands and the hundreds, in fact with all the leaders. ²Then, to the whole assembly of Israel, David said, 'If this has your approval, and if Yahweh our God wills it so, we shall send messengers to the rest of our brothers throughout the territories of Israel, and also to the priests and Levites in their towns and pasture lands, bidding them join us. ³And then we will go and recover the ark of our God, for in the days of Saul we neglected to do it.'

⁴The whole assembly agreed to this, because all the people thought that this was the right thing to do. ⁵So David summoned all Israel from the Shihor of Egypt to the Pass of Hamath, to bring the ark of God from Kiriath-Jearim. ⁶David and all Israel then went up to Baalah, to Kiriath-Jearim in Judah, from there to bring up the ark of God, which bears the title 'Yahweh enthroned on the winged creatures'. ⁷They transported the ark of God out of Abinadab's house on a new cart. Uzzah and Ahio drove the cart. ⁸David and all Israel danced before God with all their might, singing to the accompaniment of harps, lyres, tambourines, cymbals and trumpets. ⁹When they came to the threshing-floor of the Javelin, Uzzah reached out his hand to steady the ark, as the oxen were making it tilt. ¹⁰This roused Yahweh's anger against Uzzah, and he struck him down because he had laid his hand on the ark, and there he died before God. ¹¹David resented Yahweh's having broken out against Uzzah, and the place was

given the name Perez-Uzzah, which it still has today.

¹²That day David felt afraid of God. 'How can I bring the ark of God to be with me?' he said. ¹³So David did not take the ark with him into the City of David but had it put in the house of Obed-Edom of Gath. ¹⁴The ark of God remained with Obed-Edom, in his house, for three months, and Yahweh blessed Obed-Edom's family and everything that belonged to him.

David in Jerusalem, his palace, his children

14 Hiram king of Tyre sent envoys to David, with cedar wood, stone-cutters and carpenters, to build him a palace. ²David then knew that Yahweh had confirmed him as king of Israel and, for the sake of his people, had extended his sovereignty.

³David took more wives in Jerusalem and fathered more sons and daughters. ⁴These are the names of the children born to him in Jerusalem: Shammua, Shobab, Nathan, Solomon, ⁵Ibhar, Elishua, Elpelet, ⁶Nogah, Nepheg, Japhia, ⁷Elishama, Beeliada, Eliphelet.

Victories over the Philistines

⁸When the Philistines heard that David had been anointed as king of all Israel, they all invaded to seek him out. On hearing this, David marched out towards them. ⁹When the Philistines arrived, they deployed in the Valley of the Rephaim. ¹⁰David consulted God and asked, 'Shall I attack the Philistines? Will you deliver them into my power?' Yahweh replied to him, 'Attack! I shall deliver them into your power.' ¹¹Accordingly, they went up to Baal-Perazim and there David defeated them. David said, 'Through me God has made a breach in my enemies, as though they had been breached by a flood.' This is why the place was given the name Baal-Perazim. ¹²They had left their gods behind there, and David ordered them to be burnt.

¹³Again the Philistines deployed in the valley. ¹⁴David again consulted God, and God

replied, 'Do not attack them from the front; go round and engage them opposite the balsam trees. ¹⁵ When you hear the sound of footsteps in the tops of the balsam trees, launch your attack, for that will be God going out ahead of you to defeat the Philistine army.' ¹⁶ David did as God had ordered, and they beat the Philistine army from Gibeon to Gezer.

¹⁷ David's fame then spread to every country, and Yahweh made him feared by every nation.

Preparations for moving the ark

15 After he had put up buildings for himself in the City of David, he prepared a place for the ark of God and pitched a tent for it. ² David then said, 'No one but the Levites should carry the ark of God, since Yahweh has chosen them to carry the ark of Yahweh and to minister to him for ever.'

³ David then summoned all Israel to Jerusalem, to move the ark of Yahweh to the place which he had prepared for it. ⁴ David also called the sons of Aaron and the Levites together: ⁵ of the sons of Kohath: Uriel the chief and his hundred and twenty kinsmen; ⁶ of the sons of Merari: Asaiah the chief and his two hundred and twenty kinsmen; ⁷ of the sons of Gershom: Joel the chief and his hundred and thirty kinsmen; ⁸ of the sons of Elizaphan: Shemaiah the chief and his two hundred kinsmen; ⁹ of the sons of Hebron: Eliel the chief and eighty kinsmen; ¹⁰ of the sons of Uzziel: Amminadab the chief and his hundred and twelve kinsmen.

¹¹ David then sent for the priests Zadok and Abiathar, and the Levites Uriel, Asaiah, Joel, Shemaiah, Eliel and Amminadab. ¹² To them he said, 'You are the heads of the levitical families. Sanctify yourselves, you and your kinsmen, so that you can move the ark of Yahweh, God of Israel, to the place which I have prepared for it. ¹³ Because you were not there the first time, Yahweh our God broke out at us because we did not handle it properly.' ¹⁴ So the priests and the Levites sanctified themselves, to move the ark of Yahweh, God of Israel,

¹⁵ and the Levites carried the ark of God with the shafts on their shoulders, as Moses had ordered in accordance with the word of Yahweh.

¹⁶ David also told the heads of the Levites to appoint their kinsmen as singers with the accompaniment of musical instruments, lyres, harps, and cymbals to play joyfully. ¹⁷ The Levites then appointed Heman son of Joel, Asaph son of Berechiah, one of his brothers, Ethan son of Kushaiah, one of their Merarite kinsmen; ¹⁸ and with them their kinsmen of the second rank: Zechariah, Uzziel, Shemiramoth, Jehiel, Unni, Eliab, Benaiah, Maaseiah, Mattithiah, Eliphelehu, Mikneiah, and Obed-Edom and Jehiel the gatekeepers. ¹⁹ The singers, Heman, Asaph and Ethan, were to play the bronze cymbals. ²⁰ Zechariah, Uzziel, Shemiramoth, Jehiel, Unni, Eliab, Maaseiah and Benaiah were to play the lyre. ²¹ Mattithiah, Eliphelehu, Mikneiah, Obed-Edom, Jehiel and Azaziah, giving the beat, were to play the harp. ²² Chenaniah, the levitical director of transport was in charge of the transport, being skilful at it. ²³ Berechiah and Elkanah were gatekeepers for the ark. ²⁴ The priests Shebaniah, Joshaphat, Nethanel, Amasai, Zechariah, Benaiah and Eliezer blew trumpets before the ark of God, while Obed-Edom and Jehiah were also gatekeepers for the ark.

The ark is brought to Jerusalem

²⁵ David, the elders of Israel and the commanders of the thousands accordingly went, amid great rejoicing, to bring the ark of the covenant of Yahweh up from Obed-Edom's house, ²⁶ and since God was helping the Levites who carried the ark of the covenant of Yahweh, they sacrificed seven bulls and seven rams. ²⁷ David, all the Levites who carried the ark, the singers and Chenaniah, director of transport, wore cloaks of fine linen. David also wore a linen *ephod*. ²⁸ Thus, with war-cries and the sounding of the horn, the trumpets and the cymbals, and the music of lyres and harps, all Israel transported the ark of the covenant of Yahweh. ²⁹ Now, as the ark of the

covenant of Yahweh entered the City of David, Michal daughter of Saul was watching from the window and, when she saw King David dancing and playing, the sight of him filled her with contempt.

16 They brought the ark of God in and put it inside the tent which David had erected for it, and brought burnt offerings and made communion sacrifices in God's presence. ² And when David had finished making burnt offerings and communion sacrifices, he blessed the people in the name of Yahweh. ³ To all the Israelites, both men and women, to each, he then distributed a loaf of bread, a portion of meat and a raisin cake.

The service of the Levites before the ark

⁴ He appointed some of the Levites as ministers before the ark of Yahweh, to extol, glorify and praise Yahweh, God of Israel; ⁵ first Asaph, second Zechariah, then Uzziel, Shemiramoth, Jehiel, Mattithiah, Eliab, Benaiah, Obed-Edom and Jeiel, who played the lyre and harp, while Asaph played the cymbals. ⁶ The priests Benaiah and Jahaziel continually blew the trumpet before the ark of the covenant of God. ⁷ On that day, David was the first to assign to Asaph and his kinsmen the giving of thanks to Yahweh:

⁸ Give thanks to Yahweh, call his name aloud,
  proclaim his deeds to the peoples.
⁹ Chant to him, play to him,
  sing about all his wonders!

¹⁰ Take pride in his holy name,
  let your heart rejoice, you seekers of Yahweh!
¹¹ Seek out Yahweh, seek his strength,
  continually seek out his presence!

¹² Remember what wonders he has done,
  what miracles, what rulings he has given,
¹³ you offspring of Israel his servant,
  you children of Jacob his chosen one!

¹⁴ For he is Yahweh our God,
  his authority extends throughout the world.
¹⁵ For ever remember his covenant,
  the pact imposed for a thousand generations,
¹⁶ which he concluded with Abraham,
  which was sworn by him to Isaac,

¹⁷ since he confirmed it as a law for Jacob,
  as an eternal covenant for Israel,
¹⁸ saying, 'I will give you the country;
  Canaan is the measure of your inheritance,

¹⁹ 'though you are few in number,
  only a few strangers there!'

²⁰ As they wandered from nation to nation,
  from this kingdom to that people,
²¹ he would not let anyone oppress them
  and on their account he admonished kings,
²² 'You are not to touch my anointed ones,
  my prophets are not to be harmed!'

²³ Sing to Yahweh, all the earth,
  day after day proclaim his salvation!
²⁴ Declare his glory among the nations,
  his marvels to every people!

²⁵ Great is Yahweh, worthy of all praise,
  more awesome than any of the gods.
²⁶ Nothingness, all the gods of the nations.

  Yahweh it was who made the heavens,
²⁷ in his presence are splendour and majesty,
  in his sanctuary strength and joy.

²⁸ Give Yahweh his due, families of peoples,
  give Yahweh his due of glory and power,
²⁹ give Yahweh the glory due to his name!

  Bring an offering and enter his courts,
  bow down to Yahweh in his sacred court,
³⁰ tremble before him, all the earth!

  The world is firm, it cannot be moved,
³¹ let the heavens rejoice and earth be glad!
  Say among the nations, 'Yahweh is king!'

32 Let the sea thunder and all it holds,
the countryside exult and everything that
is in it,
33 and all the trees of the forest cry out for joy
at Yahweh's approach, for he is coming to
judge the earth.

34 Give thanks to Yahweh, for he is good,
for his faithful love lasts for ever!

35 Say, 'Save us, God of our salvation,
gather us together and free us from the
nations,
so that we may give thanks to your holy
name—
to be extolled whenever you are praised!'

36 Blessed be Yahweh, God of Israel,
from everlasting to everlasting!

To which all the people said, 'Amen, Alleluia!'

37 There before the ark of the covenant of
Yahweh David left Asaph and his kinsmen to
maintain a permanent ministry before the ark
as each day's ritual required, 38 and also Obed-
Edom with his sixty-eight kinsmen. Obed-
Edom son of Jeduthun, and Hosah were gatekeepers.

39 Zadok the priest and the priests, his kinsmen, he left before the dwelling of Yahweh on
the high place at Gibeon 40 to bring burnt offerings to Yahweh unfailingly, morning and
evening, on the altar of burnt offering, and to
carry out all that is written in the Law of Yahweh laid down for Israel. 41 With them were
Heman and Jeduthun and the rest of those
who were chosen and assigned by name to
give thanks to Yahweh, 'for his faithful love
lasts for ever'. 42 With them were Heman and
Jeduthun to play trumpets and cymbals, as
well as instruments for accompanying sacred
song. The sons of Jeduthun were in charge of
the gates.
43 Then all the people went back to their
homes, and David went back to bless his
household.

Nathan's prophecy

17 It happened, once David had settled
into his palace, that David said to the
prophet Nathan, 'Here am I living in a cedar-
wood palace, while the ark of the covenant of
Yahweh is under awnings.' 2 Nathan said to
David, 'Do whatever you have in mind, for
God is with you.'
3 But that very night the word of God came
to Nathan, as follows:
4 'Go and tell my servant David, "Yahweh
says this: You must not build a temple for me
to live in. 5 I have never lived in a house from
the day when I brought Israel out until today,
but have kept travelling from tent to tent and
from shelter to shelter. 6 In all my travels with
all Israel, did I say to any of the judges of Israel, whom I had commanded to shepherd my
people: Why do you not build me a cedar-
wood temple? 7 This is what you must say to
my servant David: Yahweh Sabaoth says this: I
took you from the pasture, from following the
sheep, to be leader of my people Israel. 8 I have
been with you wherever you went; I have got
rid of all your enemies for you. I am going to
make your fame like that of the greatest men
on earth. 9 I am going to provide a place for my
people Israel; I shall plant them there and
there they will live and never be disturbed
again; nor will they be oppressed by the
wicked as they were in former times 10 ever
since I instituted judges to govern my people
Israel; I shall subdue all your enemies. Yahweh moreover tells you that he will build you
a dynasty. 11 And when your days are over and
you have gone to join your ancestors, I shall
appoint your heir—who will be one of your
sons—to succeed you, and I shall make his
sovereignty secure. 12 He will build a temple
for me and I shall make his throne secure for
ever. 13 I shall be his father and he will be my
son, and I shall not withdraw my favour from
him, as I withdrew it from your predecessor.
14 I shall set him over my temple and kingdom for ever and his throne will be for ever
secure." '

15 Nathan related all these words and this whole revelation to David.

David's prayer

16 King David then went in, sat down in Yahweh's presence and said:

'Who am I, Yahweh God, and what is my lineage, that you have led me as far as this? 17 Yet, to you, O God, this seemed too little, and now you extend your promises for your servant's family into the distant future, making me see as it were a whole succession of men, and it is Yahweh God himself who raises it up. 18 What more can David reply to you for the honour you have given to your servant? You yourself have singled out your servant. 19 For your servant, and since you were so inclined, you have had the generosity to reveal all this greatness to come. 20 Yahweh, there is no one like you, no God but you alone, as everything that we have heard confirms. 21 Is there another people on earth like your people Israel, whom a god has proceeded to redeem, to make them his people and to make them famous and do for them great and terrible deeds, by driving out nations before your people, whom you redeemed from Egypt?— 22 for you made your people Israel your own people for ever and you, Yahweh, became their God.

23 'Now, Yahweh, may the promise which you have made for your servant and as regards his family hold good for ever, and do as you have said. 24 May it hold good, so your name will be exalted for ever and people will say, "Israel's God is Yahweh Sabaoth; he is God for Israel." Your servant David's dynasty will be secure before you 25 since you, my God, have disclosed to your servant that you are going to build him a dynasty. Hence, your servant has ventured to offer this prayer to you. 26 Yes, Yahweh, you are God indeed, and you have made this generous promise to your servant. 27 What is more, you have deigned to bless your servant's dynasty, so that it may remain for ever before you; and since you, Yahweh, have blessed it, blessed will it be for ever.'

David's wars

18 After this David defeated the Philistines and subdued them. From the grip of the Philistines he wrested Gath and its dependencies. 2 He also defeated the Moabites; the Moabites became David's subjects and paid him tribute.

3 David also defeated Hadadezer king of Zobah, which lies in the direction of Hamath, when the latter mounted an expedition to assert his rule on the River Euphrates. 4 David captured one thousand chariots, seven thousand charioteers and twenty thousand foot soldiers from him; David hamstrung all the chariot teams, keeping only a hundred of them. 5 The Aramaeans of Damascus came to the help of Hadadezer king of Zobah, but David killed twenty-two thousand of the Aramaeans. 6 David then imposed governors in Aram of Damascus, and the Aramaeans became David's subjects and paid him tribute. Wherever David went, Yahweh gave him victory. 7 David took the golden shields carried by Hadadezer's guards and brought them to Jerusalem. 8 From Tibhath and from Cun, towns belonging to Hadadezer, David captured a great quantity of bronze, with which Solomon made the bronze Sea, the pillars and the bronze implements.

9 When Tou king of Hamath heard that David had defeated the entire army of Hadadezer king of Zobah, 10 he sent his son Hadoram to King David to greet him and to congratulate him on having made war on Hadadezer and on having defeated him, since Hadadezer was at war with Tou. He also sent all sorts of objects made of gold, silver and bronze, 11 which King David also consecrated to Yahweh, as well as the silver and gold which he had levied from all the nations, from Edom, Moab, the Ammonites, the Philistines and Amalek.

12 Abishai son of Zeruiah defeated the Edomites in the Valley of Salt—eighteen thousand of them. 13 He stationed garrisons in Edom, and all the Edomites became David's

subjects. Wherever David went, Yahweh gave him victory.

The administration of the kingdom

¹⁴David ruled over all Israel, administering law and justice to all his people. ¹⁵Joab son of Zeruiah was in command of the army; Jehoshaphat son of Ahilud was herald; ¹⁶Zadok son of Ahitub and Abiathar son of Ahimelech were priests; Shusha was secretary; ¹⁷Benaiah son of Jehoiada was in command of the Cherethites and Pelethites; David's sons took first place after the king.

David's ambassadors are insulted

19 After this, when Nahash king of the Ammonites died and his son Hanun succeeded him, ²David thought, 'I shall show Hanun son of Nahash the same faithful love as his father showed me.' And David sent representatives to offer him condolences over his father. But when David's representatives reached Hanun in the Ammonites' country to present these condolences, ³the Ammonite leaders said to Hanun, 'Do you really think David means to honour your father when he sends you messengers with sympathy? On the contrary, the reason why his representatives have come to you is to explore, overthrow and reconnoitre the country.' ⁴Whereupon Hanun seized David's representatives, shaved them, cut their clothes off half-way up, right by their buttocks, and sent them away. ⁵As soon as David was told how the men had been treated, he sent someone to meet them, since the men were overcome with shame. 'Stay in Jericho,' the king said, 'until your beards have grown, and come back then.'

The first Ammonite campaign

⁶When the Ammonites realised that they had antagonised David, Hanun and the Ammonites sent a thousand talents of silver to hire chariots and cavalry from the Aramaeans of Upper Mesopotamia, of Maacah and of Zobah. ⁷They hired thirty-two thousand chariots and the king of Maacah with his people, who came and encamped before Medeba, while the Ammonites, having left their towns and mustered, were advancing to the war. ⁸When David heard this, he sent Joab with the whole army, the champions. ⁹The Ammonites marched out and drew up their line of battle at the city gate, while the kings who had come kept their distance in the open country. ¹⁰Joab, seeing that he had to fight on two fronts, to his front and to his rear, chose the best of Israel's picked men and drew them up in line facing the Aramaeans. ¹¹He entrusted the rest of the army to his brother Abishai, and drew them up in line facing the Ammonites. ¹²'If the Aramaeans prove too strong for me,' he said, 'you must come to my help; if the Ammonites prove too strong for you, I shall come to yours. ¹³Be brave and let us fight valiantly, for the sake of our people and for the cities of our God! And let Yahweh dispose as he thinks fit!' ¹⁴Joab and the force with him joined battle with the Aramaeans, who fled at his onslaught. ¹⁵When the Ammonites saw that the Aramaeans had fled, they too fled from his brother Abishai and withdrew into the city. Joab then returned to Jerusalem.

Victory over the Aramaeans

¹⁶The Aramaeans, realising that Israel had got the better of them, sent messengers and mobilised the Aramaeans living on the other side of the River, with Shophach, commander of Hadadezer's army, at their head. ¹⁷David, being informed of this, mustered all Israel, crossed the Jordan, made contact with them and took up position near them. David drew up his line of battle facing the Aramaeans, who then engaged him. ¹⁸But the Aramaeans fled from Israel, and David killed seven thousand of their chariot teams and forty thousand men; and also Shophach, the commander of the army. ¹⁹When Hadadezer's vassals saw that Israel had got the better of them, they made peace with David and became his subjects. The Aramaeans were unwilling to give any more help to the Ammonites.

The second Ammonite campaign

20 At the turn of the year, at the time when kings go campaigning, Joab led out the troops and, having ravaged the Ammonites' territory, proceeded to lay siege to Rabbah. David, however, remained in Jerusalem. Joab reduced Rabbah and dismantled it. ² David took the crown off Milcom's head and found that it weighed a talent of gold, and in it was set a precious stone which went on David's head instead. He carried off great quantities of booty from the city. ³ And he expelled its inhabitants, setting them to work with saws, iron picks and axes. David treated all the Ammonite towns in the same way. David and all the people then returned to Jerusalem.

Various exploits against the Philistines

⁴ After this war broke out with the Philistines at Gezer. This was when Sibbecai of Hushah killed Sippai, one of the Rephaim, and the Philistines were subdued.

⁵ Again, war with the Philistines broke out, and Elhanan son of Jair killed Lahmi brother of Goliath of Gath, the shaft of whose spear was like a weaver's beam.

⁶ There was further warfare at Gath, where there was a man of huge stature with six fingers on each hand and six toes on each foot, twenty-four in all. He too was a son of Rapha. ⁷ When he defied Israel, Jonathan son of Shimea, brother of David cut him down.

⁸ These men were sons of Rapha in Gath and fell at the hands of David and his guards.

The census

21 Satan took his stand against Israel and incited David to take a census of Israel. ² David said to Joab and the people's princes, 'Go, and take a census of Israel, from Beersheba to Dan, then bring it back to me and let me know the total.' ³ Joab replied, 'May Yahweh multiply his people to a hundred times what they are today! But my lord king, are they not all my lord's servants in any case? Why should my lord insist on this? Why

should he involve Israel in guilt?' ⁴ But the king enforced his order on Joab, and Joab set out, travelled throughout all Israel, and then returned to Jerusalem. ⁵ Joab gave David the census results for the people: all Israel had eleven hundred thousand men who could wield a sword; Judah had four hundred and seventy thousand men who could wield a sword. ⁶ Joab had found the king's command so distasteful that he did not include Levi and Benjamin.

The pestilence; God's forgiveness

⁷ God looked with displeasure on this and punished Israel in consequence. ⁸ David then said to God, 'I have committed a grave sin by doing this. But now I beg you to forgive your servant for this fault, for I have acted very foolishly.' ⁹ Yahweh then spoke to Gad, David's seer, ¹⁰ 'Go and say to David, "Yahweh says this: I offer you three things; choose which one of them I am to inflict on you."' ¹¹ So Gad went to David and said, 'Yahweh says this, ¹² "Take your choice between three years of famine; or three months of disaster at the hands of your enemies, with your enemies' sword overtaking you; or three days of Yahweh's sword, an epidemic in the country, while the angel of Yahweh wreaks havoc throughout the territory of Israel." Now decide how I am to answer him who sends me.' ¹³ David said to Gad, 'I am very apprehensive. Better for me to fall into Yahweh's hand, since his mercies are very great, than for me to fall into the hands of human enemies.'

¹⁴ So Yahweh unleashed an epidemic on Israel, and seventy thousand Israelites succumbed. ¹⁵ Next, God sent the angel to Jerusalem to destroy it, but as he was about to destroy it, Yahweh looked down and felt sorry about the calamity; and he said to the destroying angel, 'Enough now! Hold your hand!' The angel of Yahweh was standing by the threshing-floor of Ornan the Jebusite. ¹⁶ David, raising his eyes, saw the angel of Yahweh standing between earth and heaven, a drawn sword in his hand stretched out to-

wards Jerusalem. David and the elders then put on sackcloth and fell on their faces, ¹⁷and David said to God, 'Did I not order the people to be counted? I was the one who sinned and actually committed the wrong. But these, the flock, what have they done? Yahweh my God, let your hand lie heavy on me and on my family; but spare your people from the plague!'

The altar is built

¹⁸The angel of Yahweh then ordered Gad to tell David that David should go up and erect an altar to Yahweh on the threshing-floor of Ornan the Jebusite. ¹⁹So, at Gad's bidding, given in Yahweh's name, David went up. ²⁰Ornan had turned round and seen the angel, and he and his four sons with him had hidden. ²¹When David arrived Ornan was threshing wheat. He looked up and saw David and came off the threshing-floor and prostrated himself on the ground at David's feet. ²²David then said to Ornan, 'Let me have the site of the threshing-floor, so that I can build an altar to Yahweh on it; let me have it at the full price— so that the plague may be lifted from the people.' Ornan said to David, ²³'Take it, and let my lord the king do what he thinks fit. Look, I shall give you the oxen for burnt offerings, the threshing-sleds for the wood and the wheat for the oblation. I shall give everything.'

²⁴'No,' said King David to Ornan, 'I insist on buying it at the full price. I will not offer Yahweh what belongs to you or bring burnt offerings which have cost me nothing.' ²⁵So David gave Ornan six hundred shekels of gold by weight for the site.

²⁶There David built an altar to Yahweh and brought burnt offerings and peace offerings. He called on Yahweh, and Yahweh answered him with fire from heaven on the altar of burnt offering. ²⁷Then Yahweh ordered the angel to sheathe his sword. ²⁸Whereupon, seeing that Yahweh had answered him on the threshing-floor of Ornan the Jebusite, David offered sacrifice there. ²⁹The Dwelling which Moses had made in the desert and the altar of burnt offering were at that time on the high place at Gibeon, ³⁰but David could not go there to consult God because he was terrified of the angel's sword.

22 David then said, 'This is to be the house of Yahweh God and this the altar of burnt offering for Israel.'

Preparations for the building of the Temple

²David then gave orders for all foreigners in Israel to be rounded up, and appointed quarrymen to cut dressed stone for building the house of God. ³David also prepared great quantities of iron to make nails for the leaves of the doors and for the clamps, and more bronze than could be weighed, ⁴as well as innumerable cedar-wood logs, as the Sidonians and Tyrians had brought cedar logs to David in great quantities.

⁵David then said, 'My son Solomon is young and immature, and the house to be built for Yahweh must be superlatively fine, the most famous and splendid in any country. I shall now make the preparations for it.' And so, before he died, David made ample preparations. ⁶He then summoned his son Solomon and commanded him to build a house for Yahweh, God of Israel. ⁷'My son,' David said to Solomon, 'my heart was set on building a house for the name of Yahweh my God. ⁸But the word of Yahweh came to me, "You have shed much blood and fought great wars; it is not for you to build a house for my name, since you have shed much blood in my sight on earth. ⁹Look, a son will be born to you. He will be a man of peace, and I shall give him peace from his enemies on all sides; for Solomon is to be his name,ᵃ and in his days I shall give Israel peace and tranquillity. ¹⁰He must build a house for my name; he will be my son and I shall be his father, and I shall make the throne of his kingdom secure over Israel for ever." ¹¹Now, my son, may Yahweh be with you and give you success in building a house for Yahweh your God, as he has prom-

22a The name is here derived from *shalom* = peace.

ised about you. 12 And especially, may Yahweh give you discretion and discernment, may he give you his orders for Israel, so that you may observe the Law of Yahweh your God. 13 Success will be yours, only if you observe the statutes and ordinances which Yahweh gave Moses as regulations for Israel. Be strong and stand fast, be fearless, be dauntless. 14 Now, poor as I am, I have set aside for the house of Yahweh a hundred thousand talents of gold, a million talents of silver and more bronze and iron than can be weighed, there being so much. I have also provided timber and stone, to which you may add more. 15 Furthermore, you have a large number of workmen, quarrymen, masons, carpenters and all sorts of craftsmen for every kind of work, 16 while your gold and silver, bronze and iron will be beyond reckoning. Set to work, then, and may Yahweh be with you!'

17 David then commanded all the leaders of Israel to help his son Solomon. 18 'Has not Yahweh your God been with you and given you peace on all sides, having put the inhabitants of the country into my power and the country now having been subdued for Yahweh and his people? 19 So now devote heart and soul to searching for Yahweh your God. Set to and build the sanctuary of Yahweh God, so that you can bring the ark of the covenant of Yahweh and the holy vessels of God into the house built for the name of Yahweh.'

The orders and functions of the Levites

23 When David had become old and full of days, he made his son Solomon king of Israel, 2 and then summoned all the leaders of Israel, with the priests and Levites.

3 A census was taken of those Levites thirty years old and upwards. On a count of heads, they numbered thirty-eight thousand men; 4 twenty-four thousand were responsible for the service of the House of Yahweh, six thousand were officials and judges, 5 four thousand were gatekeepers and four thousand praised Yahweh on the instruments which David had made for praising him.

6 David then divided the Levites into classes: Gershon, Kohath and Merari.

7 Of the Gershonites there were Ladan and Shimei. 8 Sons of Ladan: Jehiel first, Zetham, Joel; three in all. 9 Sons of Shimei: Shelomoth, Haziel, Haran; three in all. These are the heads of families of Ladan. 10 Sons of Shimei: Jahath, Zina, Jeush, Beriah; these were the sons of Shimei; four in all. 11 Jahath was the eldest, Zizah the second, then Jeush and Beriah, who had not many children and were reckoned as one family.

12 Sons of Kohath: Amram, Izhar, Hebron, Uzziel; four in all. 13 Sons of Amram: Aaron and Moses. Aaron was set apart to consecrate the things that were especially holy, he and his sons for ever, to burn incense in the presence of Yahweh, to serve him and to bless in his name for ever. 14 Moses, man of God, and his sons were reckoned with the tribe of Levi. 15 Sons of Moses: Gershom and Eliezer. 16 Sons of Gershom: Shebuel, the first. 17 Of the sons of Eliezer, Rehabiah was the first. Eliezer had no other sons, but the sons of Rehabiah were very numerous. 18 Sons of Izhar: Shelomith, the first. 19 Sons of Hebron: Jeriah first, Amariah second, Jahaziel third, Jekameam fourth. 20 Sons of Uzziel: Micah first, Isshiah second.

21 Sons of Merari: Mahli and Mushi. Sons of Mahli: Eleazar and Kish. 22 Eleazar died without sons, but he did have daughters, whom their cousins, the sons of Kish, married. 23 Sons of Mushi: Mahli, Eder, Jeremoth: three in all.

24 These were the sons of Levi by their families, the heads of families, and those registered by name, individually; whoever was twenty years old or upwards had his function in the service of the Temple of Yahweh.

25 For David said, 'Since Yahweh, God of Israel, has given rest to his people Israel and has taken up residence in Jerusalem for ever, 26 the Levites need no longer carry the Dwelling or any of the objects required for its service.' 27 For, according to the last words of David, the Levites who had been registered were of twenty years and upwards. 28 Their duty now is to help the sons of Aaron in the

service of the House of Yahweh, in the care of the courts and rooms, the purification of all the holy things, the work for the service of the House of God, 29 the loaves of permanent offering, the flour for the oblation, the wafers of unleavened bread, the pan-baked materials, the unmixed materials and all measures of volume and length. 30 Furthermore, they have to be present every morning to give thanks and praise to Yahweh, and also in the evening, 31 and at the bringing of every burnt offering to Yahweh on Sabbath, New Moon or solemn feast, appearing regularly before Yahweh in accordance with the numbers required of them. 32 In serving the Temple of Yahweh they observe the ritual of the Tent of Meeting, the ritual of the sanctuary and the ritual of their kinsmen, the sons of Aaron.'

The classification of the priests

24 Orders of the sons of Aaron: Sons of Aaron: Nadab, Abihu, Eleazar, Ithamar. 2 Nadab and Abihu died in their father's lifetime leaving no children, so Eleazar and Ithamar filled the office of priest. 3 With Zadok of the sons of Eleazar, and Ahimelech of the sons of Ithamar, David allocated them according to the classification of their duties. 4 Since the sons of Eleazar were found to have more headmen than the sons of Ithamar, they allocated sixteen heads of families to the sons of Eleazar and eight heads of families to the sons of Ithamar. 5 They allocated them by lot, both alike, there being religious officials and officials of God among the sons of Eleazar, as among the sons of Ithamar. 6 The levitical scribe Shemaiah son of Nethanel, recorded them in the presence of the king, the leaders, Zadok the priest, Ahimelech son of Abiathar and the heads of the priestly and levitical families, so that two families were selected for Eleazar for each one selected for Ithamar.

7 The first lot fell to Jehoiarib, the second to Jedaiah, 8 the third to Harim, the fourth to Seorim, 9 the fifth to Malchijah, the sixth to Mijamin, 10 the seventh to Hakkoz, the eighth to Abijah, 11 the ninth to Jeshua, the tenth to Shecaniah, 12 the eleventh to Eliashib, the twelfth to Jakim, 13 the thirteenth to Huppah, the fourteenth to Ishbaal, 14 the fifteenth to Bilgah, the sixteenth to Immer, 15 the seventeenth to Hezir, the eighteenth to Happizzez, 16 the nineteenth to Pethahiah, the twentieth to Jehezkel, 17 the twenty-first to Jachin, the twenty-second to Gamul, 18 the twenty-third to Delaiah and the twenty-fourth to Maaziah.

19 These were their classifications for their duties when they entered the House of Yahweh in accordance with their prescriptions laid down by Aaron their ancestor as Yahweh, God of Israel, had commanded him.

20 As regards the rest of the sons of Levi:

Of the sons of Amram: Shubael. Of the sons of Shubael: Jehdeiah. 21 As regards Rehabiah, of the sons of Rehabiah: Isshiah, the first one. 22 Of the sons of Izhar: Shelomoth; of the sons of Shelomoth: Jahath. 23 Of the sons of Hebron: Jeriah the first, Amariah the second, Jahaziel the third, Jekameam the fourth. 24 The son of Uzziel was Micah; of the sons of Micah: Shamir. 25 The brother of Micah was Isshiah; of the sons of Isshiah, Zechariah. 26 The sons of Merari were Mahli and Mushi; of his sons: Jaaziah his son. 27 The sons of Merari by his son Jaaziah were Shoham, Zaccur and Ibri. 28 Of Mahli, there was Eleazar who had no sons, 29 and Kish; and of the sons of Kish: Jerahmeel. 30 The sons of Mushi were Mahli, Eder and Jerimoth.

These were the Levites according to families. 31 Like their kinsmen, the sons of Aaron, these heads of families, senior and junior alike, also drew lots in the presence of King David, Zadok, Ahimelech, and the heads of the priestly and levitical families.

The cantors

25 For the liturgy, David and the religious officials selected the sons of Asaph, of Heman and of Jeduthun, who were to prophesy to the accompaniment of harps, lyres and cymbals. The list of ministrants for this service was as follows:

2 Of the sons of Asaph: Zaccur, Joseph,

Nethaniah, Asharelah; the sons of Asaph were under the direction of Asaph who prophesied at the king's direction.

³Of Jeduthun there were the sons of Jeduthun: Gedaliah, Zeri, Jeshaiah, Hashabiah and Mattithiah, six, under the direction of their father Jeduthun who, with the harp, prophesied when thanks and praise were to be given to Yahweh.

⁴Of Heman there were the sons of Heman: Bukkiah, Mattaniah, Uzziel, Shebuel, Jerimoth, Hananiah, Hanani, Eliathah, Giddalti, Romamti-Ezer, Joshbekashah, Mallothi, Hothir, Mahazioth. ⁵All these were sons of Heman, the king's seer; at God's word they blew the horn. God gave Heman fourteen sons and three daughters. ⁶Under the king's direction all these had the duty of singing to the accompaniment of cymbal, lyre and harp for the liturgy of the house of God under the direction of their fathers.

Asaph, Jeduthun and Heman, ⁷trained in the songs of Yahweh, with their brothers, numbered two hundred and eighty-eight, all expert. ⁸Junior and senior, master and pupil alike, they drew lots for their term of duty. ⁹The first to whom the lot fell was the Asaphite, Joseph. The second was Gedaliah, who with his sons and brothers made twelve. ¹⁰The third was Zaccur, who with his sons and brothers made twelve. ¹¹The fourth was Izri, who with his sons and brothers made twelve. ¹²The fifth was Nethaniah, who with his sons and brothers made twelve. ¹³The sixth was Bukkiah, who with his sons and brothers made twelve. ¹⁴The seventh was Jesharelah, who with his sons and brothers made twelve. ¹⁵The eighth was Jeshaiah, who with his sons and brothers made twelve. ¹⁶The ninth was Mattaniah, who with his sons and brothers made twelve. ¹⁷The tenth was Shimei, who with his sons and brothers made twelve. ¹⁸The eleventh was Azarel, who with his sons and brothers made twelve. ¹⁹The twelfth was Hashabiah, who with his sons and brothers made twelve. ²⁰The thirteenth was Shubael, who with his sons and brothers made

twelve. ²¹The fourteenth was Mattithiah, who with his sons and brothers made twelve. ²²The fifteenth was Jeremoth, who with his sons and brothers made twelve. ²³The sixteenth was Hananiah, who with his sons and brothers made twelve. ²⁴The seventeenth was Joshbekashah, who with his sons and brothers made twelve. ²⁵The eighteenth was Hanani, who with his sons and brothers made twelve. ²⁶The nineteenth was Mallothi, who with his sons and brothers made twelve. ²⁷The twentieth was Eliathah, who with his sons and brothers made twelve. ²⁸The twenty-first was Hothir, who with his sons and brothers made twelve. ²⁹The twenty-second was Giddalti, who with his sons and brothers made twelve. ³⁰The twenty-third was Mahazioth, who with his sons and brothers made twelve. ³¹The twenty-fourth was Romamti-Ezer, who with his sons and brothers made twelve.

The gatekeepers

26 As regards the orders of the gatekeepers:

Of the Korahites there was Meshelemiah son of Kore, one of the sons of Ebiasaph, ²and Meshelemiah's sons: Zechariah the first-born, Jediael the second, Zebadiah the third, Jathniel the fourth, ³Elam the fifth, Jehohanan the sixth, Elioenai the seventh.

⁴Obed-Edom's sons were: Shemaiah the first-born, Jehozabad the second, Joah the third, Sacar the fourth, Nethanel the fifth, ⁵Ammiel the sixth, Issachar the seventh, Peullethai the eighth; God had indeed blessed him. ⁶His son Shemaiah also had sons who wielded authority in their family, because they were men of outstanding quality. ⁷The sons of Shemaiah were: Othni, Rephael, Obed and Elzabad, whose brothers Elihu and Semachiah were outstanding men. ⁸All these were sons of Obed-Edom, who with their sons and brothers were men of standing, well fitted for their task. Obed-Edom had sixty-two.

⁹Meshelemiah had eighteen outstanding sons and brothers.

¹⁰Hosah, one of the sons of Merari, had

sons: Shimri was the first, for although he was not the first-born his father had made him the chief. ¹¹ Hilkiah was the second, Tebaliah the third, Zechariah the fourth: Hosah had thirteen sons and brothers in all.

¹² These orders of gatekeepers, allocated according to their headmen, had duties, just like their brothers, of serving in the house of Yahweh. ¹³ Similarly, they drew lots for each gate, whether their families were large or small. ¹⁴ For the eastern one, the lot fell to Shelemiah; and when they drew lots for Zechariah his son, a shrewd counsellor, his lot came out for the north. ¹⁵ To Obed-Edom went the south, and to his sons the storehouses. ¹⁶ To Shuppim and Hosah went the west with the Gate of the Felled Tree-trunk on the upper road. The corresponding guards were as follows: ¹⁷ for the east gate, six per day; for the north gate, four per day; for the south gate, four per day; for the storehouses, two each; ¹⁸ for the Parbar at the west gate, four by the road and two for the Parbar. ¹⁹ These were the orders of the gatekeepers of the sons of Korah and the sons of Merari.

Other levitical duties

²⁰ The Levites, their brothers, who were responsible for the treasures of the house of God and for the treasures of consecrated gifts, ²¹ were the sons of Ladan and belonged to the Gershonites—the heads of the families of Ladan were descended from Ladan the Gershonite—that is to say, the Jehielites. ²² The sons of the Jehielites, Zetham and Joel his brother, were responsible for the treasures of the house of Yahweh.

²³ Over the Amramites, Izharites, Hebronites, and Uzzielites ²⁴ was Shebuel son of Gershom, son of Moses, who was governor of the treasures; ²⁵ and his brothers of the line of Eliezer were Rehabiah his son, Jeshaiah his son, Joram his son, Zichri his son and Shelomoth his son. ²⁶ This Shelomoth and his kinsmen were responsible for all the consecrated treasures dedicated by King David, by the heads of families, by the commanders of the thousands and hundreds and by the commanders of the army, ²⁷ who had dedicated a part of the spoils of war to the service of the house of Yahweh, ²⁸ and also for all that Samuel the seer, Saul son of Kish, Abner son of Ner and Joab son of Zeruiah had dedicated. In fact, whatever was dedicated was the responsibility of Shelomoth and his kinsmen.

²⁹ Of the Izharites, Chananiah and his sons were assigned to secular duties for Israel as officials and judges.

³⁰ Of the Hebronites, Hashabiah and his kinsmen, one thousand seven hundred outstanding men were in charge of Israel west of Jordan in everything pertaining to Yahweh and to the service of the king. ³¹ Of the Hebronites, Jerijah was the head. In the fortieth year of David's reign research was done on the lineage and relationships of the Hebronites, and men of outstanding quality from among them were found at Jazer in Gilead. ³² There were twenty-seven hundred outstanding men, heads of families, whom King David put in charge of the Reubenites, the Gadites and the half-tribe of Manasseh in all matters pertaining to God and the king.

Military and civil organisation

27 The Israelites listed according to heads of families, commanders of thousands and hundreds, with their officials in the king's service who dealt with all matters affecting the companies on monthly duty, month by month throughout the year, each company consisting of twenty-four thousand men:

² The commander of the first company detailed for the first month was Jashobeam son of Zabdiel, whose company consisted of twenty-four thousand men. ³ He belonged to the family of Perez and was the senior military officer of all those detailed for the first month.

⁴ The commander of the company for the second month was Dodai the Ahohite, whose company consisted of twenty-four thousand men.

⁵ The officer commanding the third body of

men for the third month was Benaiah son of Jehoiada, the chief priest, whose company consisted of twenty-four thousand men. ⁶This was the Benaiah who was an important member of the Thirty and his company. His son was Ammizabad.

⁷The fourth for the fourth month was Asahel brother of Joab, and his son Zebadiah after him, whose company consisted of twenty-four thousand men.

⁸The fifth officer commanding for the fifth month was Shamhuth the Zerahite, whose company consisted of twenty-four thousand men.

⁹The sixth for the sixth month was Ira son of Ikkesh of Tekoa, whose company consisted of twenty-four thousand men.

¹⁰The seventh for the seventh month was Helez the Pelonite, one of the Ephraimites, whose company consisted of twenty-four thousand men.

¹¹The eighth for the eighth month was Sibbecai of Hushah, a Zerahite, whose company consisted of twenty-four thousand men.

¹²The ninth for the ninth month was Abiezer of Anathoth, a Benjaminite, whose company consisted of twenty-four thousand men.

¹³The tenth for the tenth month was Maharai of Netophah, a Zerahite, whose company consisted of twenty-four thousand men.

¹⁴The eleventh for the eleventh month was Benaiah of Pirathon, an Ephraimite, whose company consisted of twenty-four thousand men.

¹⁵The twelfth for the twelfth month was Heldai of Netophah, of Othniel, whose company consisted of twenty-four thousand men.

List of tribal chiefs

¹⁶Responsible for the tribes of Israel were chief Eliezer son of Zichri for the Reubenites, Shephatiah son of Maacah for the Simeonites, ¹⁷Hashabiah son of Kemuel for the Levites, Zadok for the Aaronites, ¹⁸Elihu, one of David's brothers, for Judah, Omri son of Michael for Issachar, ¹⁹Ishmaiah son of Oba-

diah for Zebulun, Jerimoth son of Azriel for Naphtali, ²⁰Hoshea son of Azaziah for the Ephraimites, Joel son of Pedaiah for the half-tribe of Manasseh, ²¹Iddo son of Zechariah for the half-tribe of Manasseh in Gilead, Jaasiel son of Abner for Benjamin, ²²and Azarel son of Jeroham for Dan.

These were the tribal chiefs of Israel.

The uncompleted census

²³Now in the census David did not include those who were twenty years old and under, since Yahweh had promised to make Israel as numerous as the stars of heaven. ²⁴Joab son of Zeruiah began the count but never finished. This is why retribution came upon Israel, and the number did not come up to that recorded in the annals of King David.

²⁵Overseer of the king's supplies: Azmaveth son of Adiel. Overseer of supplies in the countryside, towns, villages and fortresses: Jonathan son of Uzziah. ²⁶Overseer of the farmers who tilled the land: Ezri son of Chelub. ²⁷Overseer of vineyards: Shimei of Ramah. Overseer of those in the vineyards who looked after the wine cellars: Zabdi of Shepham. ²⁸Overseer of olive and sycamore trees in the Shephelah: Baal-Hanan of Geder. Overseer of oil supplies: Joash. ²⁹Overseer of cattle at pasture in the plains of Sharon: Shitrai of Sharon. Overseer of cattle in the valleys: Shaphat son of Adlai. ³⁰Overseer of camels: Obil the Ishmaelite. ³¹Overseer of donkeys: Jehdeiah of Meranoth. Overseer of flocks: Jaziz the Hagrite.

All the above supervised the property belonging to King David.

The king's personal advisers

³²Jonathan, David's uncle, a councillor, wise man and scribe, and Jehiel son of Hachmoni took care of the king's sons. ³³Ahitophel was the king's counsellor and Hushai, the Archite, was Friend of the King. ³⁴Jehoiada son of Benaiah and Abiathar succeeded Ahitophel—Joab was commander of the king's army.

David's instructions for the Temple

28 David then summoned to Jerusalem all the officials of Israel—the tribal chiefs, the senior officials in the royal service, the commanders of the thousands, the commanders of the hundreds and the overseers of all the property and livestock belonging to the king and to his sons—including the court officials, the champions and all the men of standing. ²King David then rose to his feet and said:

'My brothers and my people, listen to me. I have set my heart on building a settled home for the ark of the covenant of Yahweh, for the footstool for our God, but when I was ready to build it, ³God said to me, "You must not build a house for my name, for you have been a man of war and have shed blood."

⁴'Even so, out of my entire family, it was I whom Yahweh, God of Israel, chose to reign over Israel for ever. Having chosen Judah as leader, and my family out of the House of Judah, it pleased him out of all my father's sons to make me king of all Israel. ⁵Out of all my sons—for Yahweh has given me many—he has chosen my son Solomon to sit on Yahweh's sovereign throne over Israel. ⁶Furthermore, he has told me, "Solomon your son is the man to build my house and my courts, for I have chosen him to be my son and I shall be his father. ⁷I shall make his sovereignty secure for ever if he sturdily carries out my commandments and ordinances as he does now."

⁸'So now in the sight of all Israel, the assembly of Yahweh, and in the hearing of our God, I charge you to observe and adhere strictly to all the commandments of Yahweh your God, so that you may retain possession of this fine country and leave it to your sons after you as a heritage for ever.

⁹'And you, Solomon my son, know the God of your father and serve him with an undivided heart and willing mind; for Yahweh scrutinises all hearts and understands whatever plans they may devise. If you seek him, he will let you find him; but forsake him and he will cast you off for ever. ¹⁰So, since Yahweh has chosen you to build a house for his sanctuary, go resolutely to work!'

¹¹David then gave his son Solomon the plans for the portico, the plans for the buildings, its storehouses, its upper rooms, its inner rooms and the room for the throne of mercy ¹²as well as the plans for everything that he had in mind: for the courts of the house of Yahweh, for all the surrounding rooms, for the treasuries of the house of God and for the sacred treasuries, ¹³for the orders of priests and Levites, for all the duties to be carried out in the service of the house of Yahweh, and for all the liturgical objects to be used in the house of Yahweh; ¹⁴for the gold bullion, for all the golden liturgical objects of various uses; for the silver bullion, for all the silver liturgical objects of various uses; ¹⁵for the gold bullion for the golden lamp-stands and for their lamps, and for the silver bullion for the silver lamp-stands and their lights, depending on the function of each lamp-stand; ¹⁶for the gold bullion for each of the tables for the loaves of permanent offering and the silver for the silver tables; ¹⁷for the pure gold for the forks, the bowls and the jars, for the gold bullion for each of the golden basins and for the silver bullion for each of the silver basins; ¹⁸and for the refined gold bullion for the altar of incense; also for the gold for the model of the chariot and of the great winged creatures which cover the ark of the covenant of Yahweh with wings outspread— ¹⁹all this was in the document conveying Yahweh's instructions, by which he revealed the pattern of what was to be done.

²⁰David then said to his son Solomon, 'Be resolute and courageous in your work, do not be afraid or disheartened, because Yahweh God, my God, is with you. He will not fail you or forsake you before you have finished all the work to be done for the house of Yahweh. ²¹And besides, there are the orders of priests and Levites for whatever is needed in connection with the house of God, and you have at your disposal every kind of craftsman for

whatever has to be done, as well as the officials and all the people entirely at your command.'

The voluntary offerings

29 David then addressed the whole assembly, 'Solomon my son, whom Yahweh has specifically chosen, is young and immature, and the work is great; this palace is not for any human being but for Yahweh God. ²With all the resources I can command, for the house of my God I have provided gold for what must be made of gold, silver for what must be made of silver, bronze for what must be made of bronze, iron for what must be made of iron, wood for what must be made of wood, as well as cornelian for inlay work, slabs of multi-coloured mosaic, every kind of precious stone and quantities of alabaster. ³Furthermore, because my affections are set on the house of my God, I have also given what gold and silver I personally own for the house of my God, over and above everything which I have already provided for the holy Temple—⁴that is to say, three thousand talents of gold of Ophir, and seven thousand talents of refined silver for overlaying the walls of the buildings, ⁵the gold being for what must be made of gold, and the silver for what must be made of silver: and for whatever the craftsmen must make. Who, then, is willing to devote himself to Yahweh's service today?'

⁶At this, the heads of families, the tribal chiefs of Israel, the commanders of the thousands and the hundreds and those who managed the king's affairs, ⁷volunteered a gift of five thousand talents and ten thousand darics of gold, ten thousand talents of silver, eighteen thousand talents of bronze and a hundred thousand talents of iron, ⁸while those who owned precious stones presented them to the treasury of the house of Yahweh in the custody of Jehiel the Gershonite. ⁹The people rejoiced at what these had given so readily, since they had presented their freewill offerings wholeheartedly to Yahweh. King David too was filled with joy.

David's thanksgiving

¹⁰Hence, in the presence of the whole assembly David blessed Yahweh. David said:

'May you be blessed, Yahweh, God of Israel our ancestor, for ever and for ever! ¹¹Yours, Yahweh, is the greatness, the power, the splendour, length of days and glory, everything in heaven and on earth is yours. Yours is the sovereignty, Yahweh; you are exalted, supreme over all. ¹²Wealth and riches come from you, you are ruler of all, in your hand lie strength and power, and you bestow greatness and might on whomsoever you please. ¹³So now, our God, we give thanks to you and praise your majestic name, ¹⁴for who am I and what is my people, for us to be able to volunteer offerings like this?—since everything has come from you and we have given you only what you bestowed in the first place, ¹⁵and we are guests before you, and passing visitors as were all our ancestors, our days on earth fleeting as a shadow and without hope. ¹⁶Yahweh our God, all this wealth, which we have provided to build a house for your holy name, has come from you and all belongs to you.

¹⁷'Knowing, my God, how you examine our motives and how you delight in integrity, with integrity of motive I have willingly given all this and have been overjoyed to see your people, now present here, willingly offering their gifts to you. ¹⁸Yahweh, God of Abraham, Isaac and Israel our ancestors, watch over this for ever, shape the purpose of your people's heart and direct their hearts to you, ¹⁹and give an undivided heart to Solomon my son to keep your commandments, your decrees and your statutes, to put them all into effect and to build the palace for which I have made provision.'

²⁰David then addressed the whole assembly: 'Now bless Yahweh your God!' And the whole assembly blessed Yahweh, God of their ancestors, bowing down in homage to Yahweh, and to the king.

Accession of Solomon and the end of the reign of David

21 On the day following this, they slaughtered sacrifices and brought burnt offerings to Yahweh on behalf of Israel—a thousand bulls, a thousand rams, a thousand lambs with their libations, as well as many other sacrifices— 22 and they ate and drank that day in Yahweh's presence with great joy. They then made Solomon son of David king a second time, anointing him as leader for Yahweh, and Zadok as priest. 23 Solomon took his seat on Yahweh's throne, to reign in succession to David his father. He prospered, and all Israel obeyed him. 24 All the chiefs, all the leading citizens and all King David's other sons pledged allegiance to King Solomon. 25 Yahweh made Solomon exceedingly powerful, as all Israel could see, and gave him a reign of such splendour as no previous king of Israel ever had.

26 David son of Jesse was king of all Israel. 27 He was king of Israel for a period of forty years; he reigned at Hebron for seven years, and in Jerusalem for thirty-three. 28 He died at a good old age, full of days, riches and honour. Then his son Solomon succeeded him. 29 The history of King David, from first to last, is all written down in the records of Samuel the seer, the records of Nathan the prophet and the records of Gad the seer, 30 with his entire reign, his mighty deeds and the times which he, Israel and all the kings of other countries, had experienced.

The Second Book of

CHRONICLES

God confers wisdom on Solomon

1 Solomon son of David then made himself secure over his kingdom. Yahweh his God was with him, making him more and more powerful. ²Solomon then spoke to all Israel, to the commanders of thousands and of hundreds, to the judges and to every leader in all Israel, the heads of families. ³Solomon, and the whole assembly with him, then went to the high place at Gibeon, where God's Tent of Meeting was, which Moses, servant of God, had made in the desert. ⁴The ark of the covenant, however, David had brought from Kiriath-Jearim to the place which he had prepared for it, having pitched a tent for it in Jerusalem. ⁵The bronze altar which Bezalel son of Uri, son of Hur, had made was there, in front of Yahweh's Dwelling, where Solomon and the assembly consulted him. ⁶There Solomon presented a burnt offering before Yahweh on the bronze altar of the Tent of Meeting, making on it one thousand burnt offerings.

⁷That night God appeared to Solomon and said, 'Ask what you would like me to give you.' ⁸Solomon replied to God, 'You showed most faithful love to David my father, and you have made me king in succession to him. ⁹Yahweh God, the promise you made to David my father has now been fulfilled, since you have made me king over a people as numerous as the dust of the earth. ¹⁰Therefore give me wisdom and knowledge to act as leader of this people, for how otherwise could such a great people as yours be governed?'

¹¹'Since that is what you want,' God said to Solomon, 'since you have asked, not for riches, treasure, honour, the lives of your enemies, or even for a long life, but for wisdom and knowledge to govern my people of whom I have made you king, ¹²therefore wisdom and knowledge are granted you. I give you riches too, and treasure, and honour such as no king had before you and none will have after you.'

¹³So Solomon came away from the high place at Gibeon, from the Tent of Meeting, to Jerusalem and reigned over Israel.

¹⁴Solomon then built up a force of chariots and cavalry; he had one thousand four hundred chariots and twelve thousand horses; these he kept in the chariot towns and near the king at Jerusalem. ¹⁵In Jerusalem the king made silver and gold as common as stones, and cedar wood as plentiful as sycamore in the lowlands. ¹⁶Solomon's horses were imported from Muzur and Cilicia. The king's dealers acquired them in Cilicia at the prevailing price. ¹⁷A chariot was imported from Egypt for six hundred silver shekels and a horse from Cilicia for a hundred and fifty. They also supplied the Hittite and Aramaean kings, who all used them as middlemen.

The final preparations; Huram of Tyre

¹⁸Solomon then gave the order to build a house for the name of Yahweh and a palace in which to reign.

2 And Solomon allocated seventy thousand men to be porters and eighty thousand to quarry in the hills and three thousand six hundred overseers for them. ²And Solomon sent this message to Huram king of Tyre, 'Do as you did for my father David when you sent him cedars for him to build himself a palace to live in. ³You see, I am building a house for the

name of Yahweh my God, to acknowledge his holiness so that perfumed incense may be burnt before him, the loaves of permanent offering be perpetually laid out and the burnt offerings be made morning and evening, on the Sabbaths, New Moons and solemn festivals of Yahweh our God, as prescribed to Israel for ever; 4and the house which I am building must be large, for our God is greater than all gods; 5even so, who would not find it an impossible task to build a house for him, when the heavens and the heavens of the heavens cannot contain him? And who am I to build a house for him except to burn incense before him? 6So now send me a man skilled at working in gold, silver, bronze, iron, scarlet, crimson and violet materials, and who knows the art of engraving too; he is to work with my skilled men in Judah and Jerusalem, whom my father David has provided. 7Also send me cedar, juniper and *algum* trunks from the Lebanon, for I know that your servants know the art of felling timber in the Lebanon. And, my servants will work with your servants 8in preparing a vast quantity of timber for me, since the house which I intend to build is to be of a size to marvel at. 9Furthermore, for the upkeep of the woodcutters whom you employ to cut the timber, I shall provide twenty thousand *kor* of wheat, twenty thousand *kor* of barley, twenty thousand *bat* of wine and twenty thousand *bat* of oil.'

10In a letter sent to King Solomon, Huram king of Tyre replied, 'Because Yahweh loves his people he has made you their king!' 11Huram went on to say, 'Praised be Yahweh, God of Israel, who made heaven and earth and has given King David a wise son, endowed with discretion and discernment, to build a house for Yahweh and a palace in which to reign!— 12I am now sending you a skilled and intelligent man, Huram-Abi 13the son of a Danite woman by a Tyrian father. He knows the arts of working in gold, silver, bronze, iron, stone, wood, scarlet, violet, fine linen and crimson materials, and is competent to carry out any kind of engraving and to exe-

cute any design which may be entrusted to him, in collaboration with your skilled men and those of my lord David, your father.

14'So now let my lord send his servants the wheat, barley, oil and wine as promised 15and we will fell all the wood you need from Lebanon, and bring it to you in rafts by sea to Jaffa; and it will be your responsibility to transport it to Jerusalem.'

16Solomon then took a census of all the aliens resident in Israel similar to the census which his father David had taken; it was found that there were a hundred and fifty-three thousand six hundred. 17He impressed seventy thousand of them as porters, eighty thousand as quarrymen in the hills and three thousand six hundred as overseers to make sure the people worked.

Solomon builds the Temple

3 Solomon then began building the house of Yahweh in Jerusalem on Mount Moriah where David his father had had a vision—on the site which David had prepared—on the threshing-floor of Ornan the Jebusite. 2He began building it on the second day of the second month of the fourth year of his reign. 3These are the dimensions which Solomon fixed for the structure of the house of God: its length in cubits, according to the old standard, was sixty cubits and its width twenty cubits; 4and the portico in front of the house was the full width of the house, that is, twenty cubits, and its height was a hundred and twenty cubits; on the inside he overlaid it with pure gold. 5The Great Hall he lined with juniper, which he overlaid with fine gold and ornamented with palm trees and festoons, 6and he decorated the hall beautifully with precious stones and with gold from Parvaim, 7overlaying the hall, its beams and its thresholds, its walls and its doors, with gold and engraving the walls with great winged creatures.

8He also made the Holy of Holies, the length of which corresponded to the width of the Great Hall, being twenty cubits, with a width of twenty cubits, and this he overlaid with fine gold weighing six hundred talents, 9while the weight of the gold nails was fifty shekels. He also overlaid the upper rooms with gold. 10In the Holy of Holies he modelled two winged creatures of wrought metal work and overlaid them with gold. 11The total span of their wings was twenty cubits; one wing, being five cubits long, touched the wall of the house and the other wing, being five cubits long, touched the wing of the other winged creature; 12while one wing of the other, five cubits long, touched the other wall of the house and the other wing, five cubits long, touched the wing of the other winged creature. 13The spread of these creatures' wings was twenty cubits. They stood in an upright position, with their faces towards the Hall.

14He also made the Curtain of violet, scarlet, crimson and fine linen, working a design of winged creatures on it.

15In front of the Hall he made two pillars thirty-five cubits high, and on the top of each a capital measuring five cubits. 16He made festoons, in the Debir, to go at the tops of the pillars, and made a hundred pomegranates to go on the festoons. 17He erected the pillars in front of the Temple, one on the right, the other on the left; the one on the right he called Jachin and the one on the left, Boaz.

4 He made a bronze altar, twenty cubits long, twenty cubits wide and ten cubits high. 2He made the Sea of cast metal, ten cubits from rim to rim, circular in shape and five cubits high; a cord thirty cubits long gave the measurement of its girth. 3Under it and completely encircling it were things like oxen, ten to the cubit round the entire Sea; the oxen were in two rows, of one and the same casting with the rest. 4It rested on twelve oxen, three facing north, three facing west, three facing south, three facing east; on these, their hindquarters all turned inwards, stood the Sea. 5It was a hand's breadth in thickness, and its rim was shaped like the rim of a cup—lily-shaped. It could hold three thousand *bat*.

6He made ten basins, putting five on the right and five on the left, for washing in; the things to be offered as burnt offerings were to be rinsed in these, but the Sea was for the priests to wash in. 7He made the ten golden lamp-stands according to the pattern and placed them in the Hekal, five on the right and five on the left. 8He made ten tables which he set up in the Hekal, five on the right and five on the left. He also made a hundred golden sprinkling bowls.

9He made the court of the priests and the great court with its gates and plated the gates with bronze. 10The Sea he placed on the right-hand side of the Temple, to the south-east.

11Huram made the ash containers, the scoops and the sprinkling bowls. Thus Huram completed all the work done for King Solomon for the Temple of God: 12the two pillars; the mouldings of the capitals surmounting the two pillars; the two sets of filigree to cover the two mouldings of the capitals surmounting the pillars; 13the four hundred pomegranates for the two sets of filigree—two rows of pomegranates for each set of filigree; 14the ten stands and the ten basins on the stands; 15the one Sea and the twelve oxen beneath it; 16the ash containers, scoops and forks.

All these utensils made by Huram-Abi for King Solomon for the Temple of Yahweh were of burnished bronze. 17The King made them by the process of sand casting, in the plain of the Jordan between Succoth and Zeredah. 18There was such an enormous quantity of them that the weight of the bronze could not be calculated.

19Solomon made all the objects designed for the Temple of God, as well as the golden altar and the tables for the loaves of permanent offering; 20the lamp-stands with their lamps to burn, as prescribed, in front of the Debir, of pure gold; 21the floral work, the lamps, the tongs, of gold (and it was pure gold); 22the snuffers, the sprinkling bowls, incense ladles and the pans, of real gold; and the entrance to the Temple, the inner doors (for the Holy of Holies) and the doors of the Temple itself, that is of the Hekal, were also made of gold.

5 Thus all the work done by Solomon for the Temple of Yahweh was completed, and Solomon brought in the gifts which his father David had consecrated; and he had the silver, the gold and all the utensils put into the treasuries of the Temple of God.

The ark is brought to the Temple

2 Solomon then assembled the elders of Israel to Jerusalem, all the tribal chiefs, the princes of the families of Israel, to bring the ark of the covenant of Yahweh up from the City of David, that is, Zion. 3 All the men of Israel assembled round the king at the time of the feast, that is, in the seventh month. 4 When all the elders of Israel had arrived, the Levites took up the ark; 5 they brought up the ark and the Tent of Meeting and all the sacred utensils which were in the Tent; the levitical priests brought them up.

6 King Solomon and the whole assembly of Israel present with him before the ark sacrificed countless, innumerable sheep and oxen. 7 The priests brought the ark of the covenant of Yahweh to its place, in the Debir of the Temple, that is, in the Holy of Holies, under the wings of the winged creatures; 8 for they spread their wings over the place where the ark stood, forming a canopy over the ark and its shafts. 9 The shafts were so long, however, that the ends of the shafts of the ark could be seen in front of the Holy Place in front of the Debir, though they could not be seen from outside. They are still there today. 10 There was nothing in the ark except the two tablets which Moses had placed in it at Horeb, when Yahweh made a covenant with the Israelites when they came out of Egypt.

The Lord takes possession of his Temple

11 Now when the priests came out of the Holy Place—for all the priests present had sanctified themselves regardless of the orders to which they belonged, 12 and all the levitical singers, Asaph, Heman and Jeduthun with their sons and brothers, dressed in linen, were standing to the east of the altar with cymbals, lyres and harps and with them one hundred and twenty priests blowing the trumpets, 13 and the harmony between trumpeters and singers was such that only one melody could be heard as they praised and gave thanks to Yahweh—and the singing began, to the accompaniment of trumpets, cymbals and musical instruments, and they praised Yahweh 'for he is good, for his faithful love is everlasting'—then the Temple was filled with the cloud of the glory of Yahweh, 14 and because of the cloud the priests could not stay and perform their duties. For the glory of Yahweh filled the Temple of God.

6 Then Solomon said:

Yahweh has chosen to dwell in thick
    cloud,
2 and I have built you a princely
    dwelling,
a residence for you for ever.

Solomon addresses the people

3 Then the king turned round and blessed the whole assembly of Israel, while the whole assembly of Israel stood. 4 He said, 'Blessed be Yahweh, God of Israel, who has carried out by his hand what he promised verbally to my father David, when he said, 5 "From the day I brought my people out of Egypt I chose no city, in any of the tribes of Israel, to have a temple built where my name should be, nor did I choose anyone to be prince of my people Israel; 6 but I did choose Jerusalem for my name to be there, and I did choose David to rule my people Israel." 7 My father David had set his heart on building a temple for the name of Yahweh, God of Israel, 8 but Yahweh said to my father David, "You have set your heart on building a temple for my name, and in this you have done well; 9 and yet, you are not the man to build the temple; but your son, yet to be born to you, will

be the one to build the temple for my name." [10]Yahweh has kept the promise which he made: I have succeeded my father David and am seated on the throne of Israel, as Yahweh promised; I have built the temple for the name of Yahweh, God of Israel, [11]and I have placed in it the ark containing the covenant of Yahweh, which he made with the Israelites.'

Solomon's prayer for himself

[12]Then in the presence of the whole assembly of Israel, he stood facing the altar of Yahweh and stretched out his hands— [13]for Solomon had made a bronze platform, five cubits long, five cubits wide and five cubits high, which he had placed in the middle of the court and on which he was standing; he knelt down in front of the whole assembly of Israel, stretched out his hands to heaven— [14]and said, 'Yahweh, God of Israel, there is no god like you in heaven or on earth, you who are loyal to the covenant and show faithful love to your servants as long as they walk wholeheartedly in your way. [15]You have kept it with your servant, my father David, as you promised him you would. What you promised verbally today you have carried out by your hand. [16]And now, Yahweh, God of Israel, keep the promise which you made to your servant David when you said, "You will never lack for a man to sit in my presence before me on the throne of Israel, provided that your sons are careful how they behave, following my law as you yourself have done." [17]So now, God of Israel, let the words come true which you spoke to your servant, my father David. [18]Yet will God really live with the people on earth? Why, the heavens and the heavens of the heavens cannot contain you! How much less this temple built by me! [19]Even so, listen favourably to the prayer and entreaty of your servant, Yahweh my God; listen to the cry and to the prayer which your servant makes to you: [20]Day and night, may your eyes watch over this temple, over this place in which you have promised to put your name. Listen to the prayer which your servant offers in this place.

Solomon's prayer for the people

[21]'Listen to the entreaties of your servant and of your people Israel; whenever they pray in this place, listen from the place where you reside in heaven; and when you hear, forgive.

[22]'If someone has wronged his neighbour and a curse is laid on him to make him swear here before your altar in this Temple, [23]then listen from heaven and do justice between your servants, paying back the guilty one by making him suffer for his conduct, and acquitting the upright by rewarding him as his uprightness deserves.

[24]'If your people Israel are defeated by the enemy because they have sinned against you, but then return to you and acknowledge your name, and pray and seek your favour in this temple, [25]then listen from heaven; forgive the sin of your people Israel, and bring them back to the country which you gave to them and their ancestors.

[26]'When the heavens are shut and there is no rain because they have sinned against you, if they pray in this place and praise your name and, having been humbled by you, desist from their sin, [27]then listen from heaven and forgive the sin of your servant and of your people Israel—for you are constantly showing them the good way which they must follow—and send rain on your country, which you have given to your people as their heritage.

[28]'Should there be famine in the country, or pestilence, wind-blast or mildew, locust or caterpillar; should their enemy lay siege to their territory; should there be any plague or any disease; [29]whatever be the prayer or entreaty of any individual, or of all your people Israel, each being aware of his own affliction and pain; when he stretches out his hands towards this Temple, [30]then listen from heaven where you reside; forgive and, since you know what is in his heart, deal with each as his conduct deserves—for you alone know what is in the human heart— [31]so that they may revere

you by following your directions, which you gave to our ancestors, throughout their lives on earth.

³²'Even the foreigner, not belonging to your people Israel but coming from a distant country, attracted by your great name, your mighty hand and outstretched arm, if he comes and prays in this Temple, ³³then listen from heaven where you reside, and grant all that the foreigner asks of you, so that all the peoples of the earth may acknowledge your name and, like your people Israel, revere you, and know that this Temple, which I have built, bears your name.

³⁴'If your people go out to war against their enemies, on whatever mission you send them, and they pray to you, turning towards this city which you have chosen and towards the Temple which I have built for your name, ³⁵then listen from heaven to their prayer and their entreaty, and uphold their cause.

³⁶'When they sin against you—for there is no one who does not sin—and you are angry with them and abandon them to the enemy, and their captors carry them off to a country be it far away or near, ³⁷if they come to their senses in the country to which they have been taken as captives and pray to you once again in the country of their captivity, saying, "We have sinned, we have acted wrongly and wickedly," ³⁸and turn back to you with all their heart and soul in the country of their captivity to which they have been carried away as captives, and pray, turning towards the country which you gave to their ancestors, towards the city you have chosen, and towards the Temple which I have built for your name, ³⁹then listen from heaven where you reside, hear their prayer and entreaties, uphold their cause and forgive your people for having sinned against you.

Conclusion of the prayer

⁴⁰'Now, O my God, may your eyes be open and your ears attentive to prayer offered in this place. ⁴¹And now

Yahweh God, go up to your resting-place,
  you and your fortress, the Ark!
Let your priests, Yahweh God, be robed in
  salvation,
  let your faithful rejoice in what is good!
⁴² Yahweh God, do not rebuff your
  Anointed—
remember the faithful love of your servant
  David!'

The dedication

7 When Solomon had finished his prayer, fire came down from heaven and consumed the burnt offering and the sacrifices; and the glory of Yahweh filled the Temple. ²The priests could not enter the Temple of Yahweh, because the glory of Yahweh filled the Temple of Yahweh. ³When all the Israelites saw the fire come down and the glory of Yahweh resting on the Temple, they bowed down on the pavement with their faces to the earth, worshipping and praising Yahweh with 'For he is good, for his faithful love lasts for ever!'

⁴Then the king and all the people offered sacrifices before Yahweh. ⁵King Solomon offered a sacrifice of twenty-two thousand oxen and a hundred and twenty thousand sheep; and thus the king and all the people dedicated the Temple of God. ⁶The priests stood in their places, as did the Levites with Yahweh's musical instruments which King David had provided, to render 'Give thanks to Yahweh, for his faithful love lasts for ever!' whenever David offered praise to their accompaniment. Opposite them, the priests blew trumpets, while all Israel stood.

⁷Solomon also consecrated the middle part of the court in front of the Temple of Yahweh; for that was where he presented the burnt offerings and the fatty parts of the communion sacrifices, since the bronze altar which Solomon had made could not hold the burnt offering, the oblation and the fatty parts. ⁸And then Solomon and with him all Israel from the Pass of Hamath to the Torrent of Egypt—a very great assembly—celebrated the feast for

seven days. ⁹On the eighth day they held the assembly, for they had devoted seven days to the dedication of the altar and seven days to the feast. ¹⁰On the twenty-third day of the seventh month Solomon dismissed the people to their homes, rejoicing and happy of heart over the goodness which Yahweh had shown to David, to Solomon and to his people Israel.

Yahweh appears and gives a warning

¹¹ Thus Solomon finished the Temple of Yahweh and the royal palace, and he successfully concluded everything that he was of a mind to do in the Temple of Yahweh and in his own palace. ¹² Then Yahweh appeared to Solomon in the night and said, 'I have heard your prayer and have chosen this place for myself as a house of sacrifice. ¹³If I shut the heavens so that there is no rain, or if I command the locusts to devour the country, or if I send pestilence among my people, ¹⁴if my people who bear my name humble themselves, and pray and seek my presence and turn from their wicked ways, then I will listen from heaven and forgive their sins and restore their country. ¹⁵Now and for the future my eyes are open and my ears attentive to prayer offered in this place, ¹⁶for now I have chosen and consecrated this Temple, for my name to be there for ever; my eyes and my heart will constantly be there. ¹⁷And if, for your part, you walk before me as your father David did, and do everything that I have commanded you to do, and keep my laws and my ordinances, ¹⁸I shall make your royal throne secure, as I covenanted with your father David when I said: You will never lack for a male to rule in Israel. ¹⁹But if you turn away and forsake my laws and commandments which I have laid down for you, and go and serve other gods and worship them, ²⁰then I shall uproot them from the country which I have given them, and shall disown this Temple which I have consecrated for my name and make it a proverb and a byword among all the peoples. ²¹And at this once-exalted Temple, everyone who passes by will be appalled, and will say,

"Why has Yahweh treated this country and this Temple like this?" ²²And the answer will be, "Because they deserted Yahweh, the God of their ancestors, who brought them out of Egypt, and adopted other gods and worshipped and served them; that is why he has brought all these disasters on them."'

Conclusion: The completion of the building programme

8 At the end of the twenty years which it took Solomon to build the Temple of Yahweh and his own palace, ²and to rebuild the towns which Huram had given him and settle them with Israelites, ³Solomon mounted an expedition against Hamath-Zobah and captured it. ⁴He also fortified Tadmor in the desert and all the storage towns which he had built in Hamath. ⁵He also built Upper Beth-Horon and Lower Beth-Horon as fortified towns with walls and gates and bars, ⁶also Baalath and all Solomon's storage towns, all the towns for his chariots and horses, and everything which Solomon was pleased to build in Jerusalem, in the Lebanon and throughout the territory under his rule. ⁷All those who survived of the Hittite, Amorite, Perizzite, Hivite and Jebusite peoples, who did not belong to Israel—⁸those of their descendants still remaining in the country, whom the Israelites had not exterminated, these Solomon levied for forced labour, as is still the case today. ⁹Solomon did not, however, impose forced labour on the Israelites for his work—for they were soldiers, his senior officers and his chariot and cavalry commanders. ¹⁰There were two hundred and fifty of King Solomon's officials in charge of the foremen who supervised the people.

¹¹Solomon moved Pharaoh's daughter up from the City of David to the palace which he had built for her. 'I must not be responsible', he said, 'for a woman living in the palace of David king of Israel, for these buildings to which the ark of Yahweh has come are sacred.'

¹²Thereafter, Solomon made burnt offerings to Yahweh on the altar of Yahweh which

he had built in front of the portico, 13 in accordance with the regular prescriptions for burnt sacrifice as commanded by Moses, on the Sabbaths, New Moons and the three annual feasts; the feast of Unleavened Bread, the feast of Weeks and the feast of Shelters. 14 Following the prescriptions of his father David, he assigned the orders of priests to their duties and the Levites to their tasks of praise and of assisting the priests in accordance with day-to-day requirements; as also the gatekeepers in their various orders to each gate—for such was the command of David, man of God. 15 Nor was there deviation on any point from the king's command as regards the priests, the Levites or even the storehouses.

16 Thus, all the work was over which Solomon had put in hand when the Temple of Yahweh was founded until it was finished. The Temple of Yahweh was complete in every detail.

Solomon in his glory

17 Solomon then mounted an expedition to Ezion-Geber and Elath on the sea-coast of Edom. 18 Huram sent him ships through his agents, as well as experienced sailors, who went to Ophir with men in Solomon's service, where they took on four hundred and fifty talents of gold, which they brought back to King Solomon.

9 The queen of Sheba heard of Solomon's fame and came to Jerusalem to test Solomon with difficult questions, with a very large retinue with camels laden with spices and an immense quantity of gold and precious stones. Having reached Solomon, she discussed everything that she had in mind with him, 2 and Solomon had an answer for all her questions; not one of them was too obscure for Solomon to answer for her. 3 When the queen of Sheba saw how wise Solomon was, the palace which he had built, 4 the food at his table, the accommodation for his officials, the organisation of his staff and the way they were dressed, his cupbearers and the way they were dressed, and the burnt offerings, which he made in the Temple of Yahweh, it left her breathless, 5 and she said to the king, 'The report I heard in my own country about you and about your wisdom in handling your affairs was true, then! 6 Until I came and saw for myself, I did not believe the reports, but clearly I was told less than half about the true extent of your wisdom. You surpass what was reported to me. 7 How fortunate your people are! How fortunate your courtiers, continually in attendance on you and listening to your wisdom! 8 Blessed be Yahweh your God. Because your God loved Israel and meant to keep it secure for ever, he has made you its king to administer law and justice.' 9 And she presented the king with a hundred and twenty talents of gold and great quantities of spices and precious stones. There never were such spices as those which the queen of Sheba gave to King Solomon. 10 Similarly, the men employed by Huram and the men employed by Solomon, who brought the gold from Ophir, also brought back *algum* wood and precious stones. 11 Of the *algum* wood the king made steps for the Temple of Yahweh and for the royal palace, and harps and lyres for the musicians, the like of which had never before been seen in Judah. 12 And King Solomon, in his turn, presented the queen of Sheba with everything that she expressed a wish for, besides what he gave her in exchange for what she had brought to the king. After which, she went home to her own country, she and her servants.

13 The weight of the gold received annually by Solomon amounted to six hundred and sixty-six talents of gold, 14 besides what tolls and foreign trade brought in; all the Arab kings and the provincial governors also brought gold and silver to Solomon. 15 King Solomon made two hundred great shields of beaten gold, six hundred shekels of beaten gold going into one shield; 16 also three hundred small shields of beaten gold, three hundred shekels of gold going into one shield; and the king put these into the House of the Forest

of Lebanon. ¹⁷The king also made a great
ivory throne which he overlaid with refined
gold. ¹⁸The throne had six steps with a golden
foot-rest attached to the throne, and arms on
each side of the seat and two lions standing beside the arms, ¹⁹and twelve lions stood on either side of the six steps. Nothing like it had
ever been made in any other kingdom.

²⁰All King Solomon's drinking vessels
were of gold, and all the plate in the House of
the Forest of Lebanon was of pure gold; silver
was little thought of in Solomon's days, ²¹since
the king's ships went to Tarshish with
Huram's employees, and once every three
years the merchantmen would come back
laden with gold and silver, ivory, apes and baboons. ²²For riches and for wisdom, King Solomon surpassed all kings on earth, ²³and all
the kings in the world consulted Solomon to
hear the wisdom which God had implanted in
his heart, ²⁴and everyone would bring a present with him: objects of silver and of gold,
robes, armour, spices, horses and mules; and
this went on year after year.

²⁵Solomon also had four thousand stalls for
horses and chariots, and twelve thousand cavalrymen; these he stationed in the chariot
towns and near the king in Jerusalem. ²⁶He
was overlord of all the kings from the River to
the territory of the Philistines and the Egyptian border. ²⁷In Jerusalem the king made silver as common as stones, and cedar wood
as plentiful as sycamore in the Lowlands.
²⁸Horses were imported for Solomon from
Muzur and all the other countries too.

The death of Solomon

²⁹The rest of the history of Solomon, from
first to last, is this not all written down in the
records of Nathan the prophet, in the Prophecy of Ahijah of Shiloh, and in the Vision of
Iddo the seer concerning Jeroboam son of
Nebat? ³⁰Solomon reigned in Jerusalem over
all Israel for forty years. ³¹When Solomon fell
asleep with his ancestors, he was buried in the
City of his father David; Rehoboam his son
succeeded him.

The schism

10Rehoboam then went to Shechem, all
Israel having come to Shechem to pro-
claim him king. ²As soon as Jeroboam son of
Nebat heard the news—he was in Egypt,
where he had taken refuge from King Solomon—he returned from Egypt. ³They now
sent for him, so Jeroboam and all Israel came
and spoke as follows to Rehoboam, ⁴'Your father laid a cruel yoke on us; if you will lighten
your father's cruel slavery, that heavy yoke
which he imposed on us, we are willing to
serve you.' ⁵He said to them, 'Come back to
me in three days' time.' And the people went
away.

⁶King Rehoboam then consulted the elders,
who had been in attendance on his father
Solomon while he was alive, and said, 'How
do you advise me to answer this people?'
⁷They replied, 'If you are fair to these people,
pleasant to them and give them a fair reply,
they will remain your servants for ever.' ⁸But
he rejected the advice given him by the elders
and consulted the young men in attendance on
him, who had grown up with him. ⁹He said,
'How do you advise us to answer these people
who have been saying, "Lighten the yoke
which your father imposed on us"?' ¹⁰The
young men who had grown up with him
replied, 'This is the way to answer the people
who have been saying, "Your father made our
yoke heavy, you must lighten it for us!" This is
the right thing to say to them, "My little finger
is thicker than my father's loins! ¹¹Although
my father laid a heavy yoke on you, I shall
make it heavier still! My father controlled you
with the whip, but I shall apply a spiked
lash!"' ¹²On the third day, Jeroboam and all
the people came to Rehoboam in obedience to
the king's instructions, 'Come back to me in
three days' time.' ¹³And the king gave them a
harsh answer. King Rehoboam, rejecting the
advice of the elders, ¹⁴spoke to them as the
young men had recommended, 'My father
made your yoke heavy, but I shall add to it. My
father controlled you with the whip, but I shall

apply a spiked lash.' ¹⁵Thus the king refused to listen to the people, and this was brought about by God, so that Yahweh might fulfil the promise which he had made through Ahijah of Shiloh to Jeroboam son of Nebat. ¹⁶When all Israel saw that the king refused to listen to them, the people answered the king thus:

What share have we in David?
—no heritage in the son of Jesse!
Each of you, to your tents, Israel!
Now look to your own house, David!

So Israel went home again. ¹⁷Rehoboam, however, reigned over those Israelites who lived in the towns of Judah. ¹⁸When King Rehoboam sent Adoram who was in charge of forced labour, the Israelites stoned him to death, while King Rehoboam managed to mount his chariot and escape to Jerusalem. ¹⁹And Israel has remained in rebellion against the House of David from that day to this.

11 When Rehoboam reached Jerusalem, he mustered a hundred and eighty thousand picked warriors of the House of Judah and Benjamin to fight Israel and win back the kingdom for Rehoboam. ²But the word of Yahweh came to Shemaiah, man of God, ³'Say this to Rehoboam son of Solomon, king of Judah, and to all Israel in Judah and Benjamin, ⁴"Yahweh says this: Do not go and make war on your brothers; let everyone go home, for this is my doing." ' They obeyed Yahweh's command and went back instead of marching against Jeroboam.

⁵Rehoboam, residing in Jerusalem, fortified a number of towns for the defence of Judah. ⁶He built Bethlehem, Etam, Tekoa, ⁷Beth-Zur, Soco, Adullam, ⁸Gath, Mareshah, Ziph, ⁹Adoraim, Lachish, Azekah, ¹⁰Zorah, Aijalon, Hebron, these being the fortified towns in Judah and Benjamin. ¹¹He equipped these fortresses, stationing commanders in them, with supplies of food, oil and wine, ¹²and shields and spears in each of these towns, making them extremely strong and thus retaining control of Judah and Benjamin.

The priests and Levites migrate to Judah

¹³The priests and the Levites from all over Israel left their districts to put themselves at his disposal. ¹⁴The Levites, indeed, abandoned their pasture lands and their holdings and came to Judah and Jerusalem because Jeroboam and his sons had excluded them from the priesthood of Yahweh. ¹⁵Jeroboam had appointed his own priests for the high places dedicated to the satyrs and calves which he had made. ¹⁶And those members of all the tribes of Israel who were determined to seek Yahweh, God of Israel, followed those priests and Levites to Jerusalem to sacrifice to Yahweh, God of their ancestors. ¹⁷These added strength to the kingdom of Judah and gave their support to Rehoboam son of Solomon for three years. For three years they remained loyal to David and Solomon.

Rehoboam's family

¹⁸Rehoboam married Mahalath daughter of Jerimoth, son of David, and of Abihail daughter of Eliab son of Jesse, ¹⁹and she bore him sons: Jeush, Shemariah and Zaham. ²⁰After her, he married Maacah daughter of Absalom, who bore him Abijah, Attai, Ziza and Shelomith. ²¹Rehoboam loved Maacah daughter of Absalom, more than all his other wives and concubines. He had in fact a total of eighteen wives and sixty concubines and fathered twenty-eight sons and sixty daughters. ²²Rehoboam named Abijah son of Maacah as head, hence leader, of his brothers, with a view to making him king, ²³and acted wisely by distributing his sons throughout the territories of Judah and Benjamin, some in each fortified town, where he provided plenty of food for them and found them wives.

Rehoboam's unfaithfulness

12 When Rehoboam had consolidated the kingdom and become strong, he, and all Israel with him, abandoned the Law of Yahweh; ²and thus it happened that in the fifth year of King Rehoboam, Shishak king of

Egypt marched on Jerusalem, because they had been unfaithful to Yahweh, ³with twelve hundred chariots and sixty thousand cavalry and countless hordes of Libyans, Sukkiim and Cushites who came from Egypt with him. ⁴They captured the fortified towns of Judah and reached Jerusalem. ⁵The prophet Shemaiah then came to Rehoboam and the generals of Judah, who had fallen back on Jerusalem before Shishak's advance, and said to them, 'Yahweh says this, "You have abandoned me and so I have abandoned you into Shishak's clutches." ' ⁶At this, the Israelite generals and the king humbled themselves and said, 'Yahweh is just!' ⁷When Yahweh saw that they had humbled themselves, the word of Yahweh came to Shemaiah as follows, 'They have humbled themselves. I shall not destroy them but shall grant them some degree of deliverance. My retribution will not be poured out on Jerusalem by means of Shishak; ⁸they are nonetheless to become his slaves, so that they may learn the difference between serving me and serving kings of other countries.'

⁹So Shishak king of Egypt advanced on Jerusalem and carried off the treasures of the Temple and the treasures of the royal palace. He took everything away, including the golden shields which Solomon had made. ¹⁰To replace these, King Rehoboam made bronze shields, entrusting them to the commanders of the guard who guarded the king's palace gate. ¹¹Whenever the king went to the Temple of Yahweh, the guards would come out carrying them, returning them to the guardroom afterwards.

Summary of the reign

¹²Because King Rehoboam had humbled himself, the retribution of Yahweh turned away from him so as not to destroy him completely; and there were also some good features in Judah. ¹³Thus he was able to strengthen his position in Jerusalem and continue as king; for Rehoboam was forty-one years old when he came to the throne and remained king for seventeen years in Jerusalem,

the city chosen by Yahweh from all the tribes of Israel to put his name there. His mother's name was Naamah the Ammonite. ¹⁴But he did wrong in not setting his heart on seeking Yahweh.

¹⁵The history of Rehoboam, from first to last, is this not all written down in the records of Shemaiah the prophet and of Iddo the seer? Warfare between Rehoboam and Jeroboam went on throughout the period. ¹⁶When Rehoboam fell asleep with his ancestors, he was buried in the City of David; his son Abijah succeeded him.

War breaks out

13 In the eighteenth year of King Jeroboam, Abijah became king of Judah ²and reigned for three years in Jerusalem. His mother's name was Micaiah daughter of Uriel of Gibeah. When war broke out between Abijah and Jeroboam, ³Abijah took the field with an army of four hundred thousand picked warriors, while Jeroboam took the field against him with eight hundred thousand picked warriors.

Abijah addresses the Israelites

⁴Abijah took position on Mount Zemaraim, in the highlands of Ephraim. 'Jeroboam and all Israel,' he cried, 'listen to me! ⁵Do you not know that Yahweh, God of Israel, has given eternal sovereignty of Israel to David and his sons by an inviolable covenant? ⁶Yet Jeroboam son of Nebat, the slave of Solomon son of David, rose in revolt against his master. ⁷Worthless men, scoundrels, rallied to him, proving too strong for Rehoboam son of Solomon, as Rehoboam was then inexperienced and timid and unable to resist them. ⁸And now you propose to resist Yahweh's sovereignty as exercised by the sons of David because there is a great number of you and you have the golden calves that Jeroboam made you for gods! ⁹Have you not driven out the priests of Yahweh, the sons of Aaron and the Levites, to make priests of your own like the peoples of foreign countries? Anyone who

comes with a bull and seven rams to get himself consecrated can become priest of these gods that are no gods. ¹⁰But for our part, our God is Yahweh, and we have not abandoned him; our priests are sons of Aaron who minister to Yahweh, and those who serve are Levites; ¹¹morning after morning, evening after evening, they present burnt offerings and perfumed incense to Yahweh, they put the bread of permanent offering on the clean table and nightly light the lamps on the golden lamp-stand; for we keep the decree of Yahweh our God, although you have abandoned him. ¹²See how God is with us, at our head, and his priests with trumpets to sound the alarm against you! Israelites, do not make war on Yahweh, God of your ancestors, for you will not succeed.'

The battle

¹³Now Jeroboam had sent a party round to ambush them from the rear; thus the main force confronted Judah and the ambush lay to their rear. ¹⁴And when Judah looked round, they found themselves being attacked from front and rear. They called on Yahweh, the priests sounded the trumpets, ¹⁵and the men of Judah raised the war cry and, as they raised the cry, God routed Jeroboam and all Israel before Abijah and Judah. ¹⁶So the Israelites fled before Judah, because God had given Judah the upper hand, ¹⁷and Abijah and his army inflicted a great slaughter on them: five hundred thousand of Israel's picked men fell, killed. ¹⁸So the Israelites were humbled on that occasion, while the Judaeans won, since they had relied on Yahweh, God of their ancestors.

The end of the reign of Abijah

¹⁹Abijah pursued Jeroboam, taking from him the towns of Bethel with its dependencies, Jeshanah with its dependencies and Ephron with its dependencies, ²⁰nor did Jeroboam regain strength during Abijah's lifetime. Eventually Yahweh struck him and he died, ²¹but Abijah grew stronger than ever; he married

fourteen wives and fathered twenty-two sons and sixteen daughters. ²²The rest of the history of Abijah, his conduct and his sayings, are recorded in the *midrash* of the prophet Iddo. ²³When Abijah fell asleep with his ancestors, he was buried in the City of David; his son Asa succeeded him.

Peace under Asa

In his time the country was at peace for ten years.

14 Asa did what Yahweh his God regards as good and right. ²He abolished the foreign altars and the high places, broke the pillars, cut down the sacred poles, ³and urged Judah to seek Yahweh, God of their ancestors, and to observe the law and commandment. ⁴Because he abolished the high places and incense altars through the towns of Judah, the kingdom under him was undisturbed. ⁵He rebuilt the fortified towns of Judah, since the country was at peace and free of war during those years, because Yahweh had granted him peace.

⁶'Let us rebuild these towns,' he told Judah, 'let us surround them with wall and tower, with gate and bar while the country is still ours, for we have sought Yahweh our God and he has sought us and given us peace all around.' They built and prospered.

⁷Asa had an army of three hundred thousand men of Judah armed with shields and spears and two hundred and eighty thousand men of Benjamin armed with shields and bows, all of them outstanding soldiers.

Invasion by Zerah

⁸Zerah the Cushite took the field against them with an army a million strong and three hundred chariots, and penetrated to Mareshah. ⁹Asa took the field against him and the battle-lines were drawn up in the Valley of Zephathah, at Mareshah. ¹⁰Asa then called on Yahweh his God and said, 'Yahweh, numbers and strength make no difference to you when you give your help. Help us, Yahweh

our God, for, relying on you, we are confronting this horde in your name. Yahweh, you are our God. Human strength cannot prevail against you!'

¹¹ Yahweh routed the Cushites before Asa and Judah. The Cushites fled, ¹² and Asa pursued them with his army as far as Gerar. So many of the Cushites fell that they were unable to survive. They were cut to pieces by Yahweh and his army.

They carried off a great deal of booty, ¹³ they destroyed all the towns round Gerar— for a panic from Yahweh had seized the towns—and plundered all the towns since they were full of loot. ¹⁴ They also routed the cattle-owners and carried off great numbers of sheep and camels; then they returned to Jerusalem.

Azariah's sermon and the reform

15 The spirit of God then came on Azariah son of Oded; ² he went out to meet Asa and said, 'Listen to me, Asa, and all you in Judah and in Benjamin: Yahweh will be with you so long as you are with him. If you seek him, he will let you find him; but if you desert him, he will desert you. ³ For a long time Israel did not have the true God or a teacher-priest or a law, ⁴ but when in their distress they turned to Yahweh, God of Israel, and sought him, he let them find him. ⁵ In those times there was no security for people as they went about their business, but great unrest affecting the inhabitants of all countries, ⁶ nation being crushed by nation and city by city, since God caused confusion among them by every kind of distress. ⁷ So be strong, do not be discouraged, for your deeds will be rewarded.'

Asa's religious reforms

⁸ When Asa heard these words and the prophecy, he took courage and removed the abominable idols throughout the land of Judah and Benjamin as well as from the towns which he had captured in the highlands of Ephraim, and repaired the altar of Yahweh which stood in front of the portico of Yahweh. ⁹ He sum-

moned all Judah and Benjamin as well as those Ephraimites, Manassehites and Simeonites who had settled with them—for a great many people from Israel had gone over to Asa when they saw that Yahweh his God was with him. ¹⁰ They assembled in Jerusalem in the third month of the fifteenth year of Asa's reign, ¹¹ that day sacrificing to Yahweh seven hundred oxen and seven thousand sheep from the booty which they had brought back. ¹² They then made a covenant to seek Yahweh, God of their ancestors, with all their heart and soul; ¹³ anyone who would not seek Yahweh, God of Israel, was to be put to death, whether high or low, man or woman. ¹⁴ They pledged their oath to Yahweh in ringing tones, with shouts of joy, to the sound of trumpet and horn; ¹⁵ all Judah rejoiced over the oath, for they had sworn it wholeheartedly, and sought him so earnestly that he allowed them to find him; Yahweh gave them peace all round.

¹⁶ King Asa even deprived his mother Maacah of the dignity of Great Lady for having made an obscenity for Asherah; Asa cut down her obscenity, smashed it and burnt it in the ravine of the Kidron. ¹⁷ Though the high places were not abolished in Israel, Asa's heart was loyal throughout his life. ¹⁸ He deposited his father's and his own dedicated gifts of silver, gold and sacred vessels, in the Temple of Yahweh.

¹⁹ Up to the thirty-fifth year of Asa's reign there was no war.

War with Israel

16 In the thirty-sixth year of Asa's reign, Baasha king of Israel marched on Judah and fortified Ramah to block the communications of Asa king of Judah. ² Asa then took silver and gold from the treasuries of the Temple of Yahweh and the royal palace and sent this with the following message to Ben-Hadad king of Aram, who lived in Damascus, ³ 'Let us make an alliance between me and you, between my father and your father! Look, I have sent you silver and gold. Come, break off your alliance with Baasha king of Israel, which will

make him withdraw from me.' ⁴Ben-Hadad listened favourably to King Asa and sent the generals of his armies to attack the towns of Israel; he ravaged Ijon, Dan, Abel-Maim and all the storage towns of Naphtali. ⁵When Baasha heard this he gave up fortifying Ramah, abandoning this work. ⁶King Asa then had all Judah carry away the stones and timber with which Baasha had been fortifying Ramah, and used them to fortify Geba and Mizpah.

⁷Then it was that Hanani the seer came to Asa king of Judah and said, 'Because you relied on the king of Aram and not on Yahweh your God, the king of Aram's army will slip through your fingers. ⁸Did not the Cushites and Libyans form a vast army with great numbers of chariots and cavalry? Even so, because you relied on Yahweh, he gave you the upper hand; ⁹for Yahweh's eyes rove to and fro across the whole world to support those whose hearts are loyal to him. You have acted like a fool in this respect; hence, from now on you will have wars.' ¹⁰Enraged with the seer, Asa had him put in the stocks in prison, being angry with him over this; at the same time Asa ill-treated some of the people too.

The end of the reign of Asa

¹¹The history of Asa, from first to last, is recorded in the Book of the Kings of Judah and Israel. ¹²In the thirty-ninth year of his reign, Asa contracted a disease in his feet, which became very severe; in his illness, however, he consulted not Yahweh but the doctors. ¹³Asa then fell asleep with his ancestors, dying in the forty-first year of his reign. ¹⁴He was buried in the tomb which he had ordered to be cut for him in the City of David. He was laid in the burial chamber which was filled with perfume blended from all sorts of oils, and a very great funeral fire was made for him.

Jehoshaphat's military policy

17 When his son Jehoshaphat succeeded him, he made himself stronger against Israel ²by stationing troops in all the fortified towns in Judah and by garrisoning Judah and the towns of Ephraim which his father Asa had captured.

His devotion to religion

³Yahweh was with Jehoshaphat because he followed the example of his father's earlier days and did not have recourse to Baal, ⁴but sought Yahweh, the God of his father, following his commandments and not behaving as Israel did. ⁵Because of this, Yahweh put him in secure control of the kingdom, while all Judah gave Jehoshaphat presents until ample riches and honour were his. ⁶He was so enthusiastic about obeying Yahweh that once again he abolished the high places and sacred poles in Judah.

⁷In the third year of his reign he sent his leading men—Ben-Hail, Obadiah, Zechariah, Nethanel and Micaiah, to give instruction in the towns of Judah. ⁸With them went the Levites: Shemaiah, Nethaniah, Zebadiah, Asahel, Shemiramoth, Jehonathan, Adonijah and Tobijah, the Levites; Elishama and Jehoram the priests went with them. ⁹They gave instruction in Judah, having with them the book of the Law of Yahweh, and went round all the towns of Judah instructing the people.

¹⁰A panic from Yahweh seized all the kings of the countries surrounding Judah, as a result of which they did not make war on Jehoshaphat. ¹¹Some of the Philistines brought Jehoshaphat presents and a load of silver and the Arabs brought him seven thousand seven hundred rams and seven thousand seven hundred he-goats.

¹²Jehoshaphat became more and more powerful. He built fortresses and storage towns in Judah.

The army

¹³He accumulated ample supplies in the towns of Judah.

He also had warriors, outstanding men, in Jerusalem. ¹⁴According to family, this is how they were classified:

Over the commanders of the thousands of

Judah was General Adnah, who had three hundred thousand outstanding men;

15 Under him was General Jehohanan, who had two hundred and eighty thousand;

16 Under him was Amasiah son of Zichri, who had volunteered for Yahweh and who had two hundred thousand outstanding men;

17 That outstanding soldier, Eliada, represented Benjamin, and he had two hundred thousand men armed with bow and shield;

18 And under him Jehozabad, who had one hundred and eighty thousand equipped for war.

19 These were in attendance on the king, apart from those whom the king had stationed in the fortified towns all over Judah.

His alliance with Ahab and the intervention of the prophets

18 Although Jehoshaphat enjoyed great wealth and honour, he allied himself by marriage to Ahab. 2 After some years he paid a visit to Ahab in Samaria. Ahab slaughtered an immense number of sheep and oxen for him and his retinue, to induce him to attack Ramoth-Gilead. 3 Ahab king of Israel then said to Jehoshaphat king of Judah, 'Will you come with me to Ramoth-Gilead?' He replied, 'I will share in battle with you, my men with yours.'

The spurious prophets predict success

4 Jehoshaphat, however, said to the king of Israel, 'First, please consult the word of Yahweh.' 5 So the king of Israel called the prophets together, four hundred of them. 'Should we go and attack Ramoth-Gilead,' he asked, 'or should I hold back?' 'March,' they replied, 'for God will deliver it into the king's power.' 6 Jehoshaphat, however, said, 'Is there no other prophet of Yahweh here, for us to consult?' 7 The king of Israel answered Jehoshaphat, 'There is one more man through whom we can consult Yahweh, but I hate him because he never has a favourable prophecy for me, always unfavourable ones; he is Micaiah son of Imlah.' 'The king should not say such things,'

said Jehoshaphat. 8 The king of Israel then summoned a court official and said, 'Bring Micaiah son of Imlah immediately.'

9 The king of Israel and Jehoshaphat king of Judah were sitting each on his throne, wearing their robes; in an open space just outside the gate of Samaria, with all the prophets prophesying before them, 10 Zedekiah son of Chenaanah, who had made himself some iron horns, said, 'Yahweh says, "With horns like these, you will gore the Aramaeans till you make an end of them."' 11 And all the prophets prophesied in the same vein, saying, 'March on Ramoth-Gilead! Success is sure, for Yahweh has already given it to the king!'

The prophet Micaiah predicts defeat

12 The messenger who had gone to summon Micaiah said to him, 'Look! What the prophets are saying is uniformly favourable to the king. So I hope you will say the same as they do and speak favourably.' 13 Micaiah said, 'As Yahweh lives, I shall speak exactly as Yahweh tells me!' 14 When he came to the king, the king said, 'Micaiah, should we march to attack Ramoth-Gilead, or should I hold back?' He replied, 'Go and conquer, Yahweh will deliver them into your power!' 15 The king went on, 'How often must I put you on oath to tell me nothing but the truth in the name of Yahweh?' 16 Then he spoke out.

> I saw all Israel scattered on the mountains like sheep without a shepherd.
> And Yahweh said, 'These have no master, let them all go peacefully home!'

17 At this the king of Israel said to Jehoshaphat, 'Did I not tell you that he never gives me favourable prophecies, but only unfavourable ones?' 18 Micaiah went on, 'Now listen to the word of Yahweh. I saw Yahweh seated on his throne with the whole array of heaven standing on his right and on his left. 19 Yahweh said, "Who will entice Ahab king of Israel into marching to his death at Ramoth-Gilead?" At which some answered one way, and some another. 20 A spirit then

came forward and stood before Yahweh and said, "I will entice him." "How?" Yahweh asked. ²¹He replied, "I shall go and be a deceptive spirit in the mouths of all his prophets." Yahweh said, "You will succeed in enticing him. Go and do it." ²²And now, you see, Yahweh has put a deceptive spirit into the mouths of your prophets here, for in fact Yahweh has pronounced disaster on you.'

²³Zedekiah son of Chenaanah then came up, struck Micaiah on the cheek and said, 'Which way did Yahweh's spirit leave me, to speak to you?' ²⁴'That is what you will find out,' Micaiah retorted, 'the day you go from room to room, trying to hide.' ²⁵The king of Israel said, 'Seize Micaiah and hand him over to Amon governor of the city, and Joash the king's son, ²⁶and say, "These are the king's orders: Put this man in prison and feed him on nothing but bread and water until I am safely home." ' ²⁷Micaiah said, 'If you ever do get home safely, Yahweh has not spoken through me.'

The battle

²⁸The king of Israel and Jehoshaphat king of Judah marched on Ramoth-Gilead. ²⁹The king of Israel said to Jehoshaphat, 'I shall disguise myself to go into battle, but you put on your robes.' So the king of Israel disguised himself, and they went into battle. ³⁰Now, the king of Aram had given his chariot commanders the following order, 'Do not attack anyone of whatever rank, except the king of Israel.' ³¹So, when the chariot commanders saw Jehoshaphat, they thought, 'That is the king of Israel,' and surrounded him to attack. But when Jehoshaphat shouted his war cry, Yahweh came to his help, God drew them away from him, ³²for the chariot commanders, realising that he was not the king of Israel, broke off their pursuit.

³³Someone, however, drawing his bow without any special aim, shot the king of Israel between the joints of his armour. 'Turn about!' he said to his charioteer. 'Get me out of the fighting; I am collapsing.' ³⁴But the battle

grew fiercer as the day went on, and the king of Israel had to be held upright in his chariot facing the Aramaeans until the evening, and at sunset he died.

Jehoshaphat is rebuked by a prophet

19 Jehoshaphat king of Judah returned home safely, however, to Jerusalem. ²Jehu son of Hanani the seer went to meet him and said to King Jehoshaphat, 'Should a man give help to the wicked? Should you love those who hate Yahweh and so bring his retribution on yourself? ³All the same, there are good things to your credit, since you have removed the sacred poles from the country and have set your heart on seeking God.'

His judicial reforms

⁴Jehoshaphat resided in Jerusalem but regularly went on progress among the people, from Beersheba to the highlands of Ephraim, to convert them to Yahweh, God of their ancestors. ⁵He also appointed judges in the country in every one of the fortified towns of Judah, ⁶saying to the judges, 'Be careful what you do, since you are judging not by any human power but in the name of Yahweh, who will be with you when you pronounce sentence. ⁷This being so, let fear of Yahweh govern you; be careful what you do, for Yahweh our God will not tolerate malpractice, partiality or the taking of bribes.'

⁸Jehoshaphat also appointed some of the Levites, priests and heads of Israelite families in Jerusalem to settle disputes. They lived in Jerusalem ⁹and Jehoshaphat gave them the following charge: 'In fear of Yahweh and with conscientious integrity, this is how you are to act: ¹⁰whatever case your brothers living in other towns refer to you, whether involving blood feuds or law and commandment, statutes and judgements, you are to instruct them in such manner that they do not incur guilt before Yahweh and that you and your brothers do not incur his anger. If you act thus, you will not incur guilt. ¹¹Amariah the chief priest himself will be your president in all reli-

gious cases, and Zebadiah son of Ishmael, leader of the House of Judah, in all civil oncs, while the Levites will act as officers of the court. Be firm, put this into practice and may Yahweh protect the right!'

A holy war

20 Some time later, the Moabites and Ammonites, and with them the Meunites, advanced to war against Jehoshaphat. ²Jehoshaphat received the following intelligence, 'A vast horde is advancing on you from the other side of the Sea, from Edom; they are already at Hazazon-Tamar, that is, En-Gedi.'

³Jehoshaphat was alarmed and resolved to have recourse to Yahweh; he proclaimed a fast throughout all Judah. ⁴So Judah assembled to seek help from Yahweh; to seek Yahweh they came from every town in Judah.

⁵Then, standing in the Temple of Yahweh in front of the new court among the assembled people of Judah and Jerusalem, Jehoshaphat ⁶said, 'Yahweh, God of our ancestors, are you not God in heaven, and do you not rule all the kingdoms of the nations? Your power and might are such that no one can resist you. ⁷Did not you, our God, dispossess the inhabitants of this country for your people Israel and give it to the descendants of Abraham, your friend, for ever? ⁸They have lived in it and built you a sanctuary there for your name, ⁹saying, "If disaster, war, flood, pestilence or famine befall us, and we stand in front of this Temple, before you—for your name is in this Temple—and cry to you in our distress, then you will listen and rescue us."

¹⁰'Now see, the Ammonites and Moabites and the people of Mount Seir, whom you would not allow Israel to invade when they came out of Egypt—on the contrary, Israel avoided them, and did not destroy them—¹¹see how they reward us, by coming to drive us out of your possession which you allotted to us! ¹²Our God, will you not pass sentence on them, since we are helpless against this vast horde about to attack us? Because we do not know what to do, we look to you.'

¹³All Judah, including their families, wives and children, were standing before Yahweh, ¹⁴when, in the middle of the assembly, the spirit of Yahweh came on Jahaziel son of Zechariah, son of Benaiah, son of Jeiel, son of Mattaniah the Levite, a member of the clan of Asaph, ¹⁵who then cried, 'Listen, all Judah and you citizens of Jerusalem, and you, King Jehoshaphat! Yahweh says this to you, "Do not be afraid, do not be daunted by this vast horde, for the war is not your affair but God's. ¹⁶Go down against them tomorrow; they are coming up by the Slope of Ziz and you will encounter them at the end of the ravine near the desert of Jeruel. ¹⁷You will not need to fight in this battle. Take up your position, stand firm, and see what salvation Yahweh has in store for you. Judah and Jerusalem, be fearless, be dauntless; march out against them tomorrow and Yahweh will be with you."'

¹⁸Jehoshaphat bowed his head, his face to the ground, and all Judah and the citizens of Jerusalem fell down before Yahweh to worship Yahweh. ¹⁹Then the Levites—both the Kohathites and Korahites—stood up to praise Yahweh, God of Israel, at the top of their voices.

²⁰Early next morning they prepared to set out for the desert of Tekoa. As they were setting out, Jehoshaphat stood up and said, 'Listen to me, Judah and you citizens of Jerusalem! Believe in Yahweh your God and you will be secure; believe in his prophets and you will be successful.' ²¹Then, having conferred with the people, he appointed singers who were to praise Yahweh and go out ahead of the army in sacred vestments, singing

Praise Yahweh,
for his faithful love endures for ever!

²²The moment they began their shouts of praise, Yahweh sprang an ambush on the Ammonites, Moabites and the people of Mount Seir who were invading Judah, and that was the end of them, ²³for the Ammonites and Moabites turned on the people of Mount Seir,

and put them under the curse of destruction and then, having finished off the people of Seir, set to work slaughtering one another.

²⁴When Judah reached the point overlooking the desert and looked towards the horde, there were nothing but corpses lying on the ground; no one escaped. ²⁵When Jehoshaphat arrived to take the booty, they found quantities of cattle and innumerable possessions, clothes and valuables, which they seized for themselves; it was impossible to carry it, and it took them three days to collect it. ²⁶On the fourth day they assembled in the Valley of Beracah, where they blessed Yahweh—hence the place was given the name Valley of Beracah, which it still has today. ²⁷Then all the men of Judah and Jerusalem returned joyfully to Jerusalem with Jehoshaphat at their head as Yahweh had given them cause to rejoice over their enemies. ²⁸To the sound of lyre, harp and trumpet they came to Jerusalem, to the Temple of Yahweh, ²⁹and a panic from Yahweh seized all the neighbouring kings when they heard how Yahweh had fought against the enemies of Israel. ³⁰And henceforth Jehoshaphat's reign was undisturbed, for his God gave him peace all round.

The end of the reign of Jehoshaphat

³¹So Jehoshaphat reigned over Judah. He was thirty-five years old when he came to the throne and he reigned for twenty-five years in Jerusalem. His mother's name was Azubah daughter of Shilhi. ³²He followed the example of his father Asa undeviatingly, doing what Yahweh regards as right. ³³The high places, however, were not abolished; the people had still not set their hearts on the God of their ancestors. ³⁴The rest of the history of Jehoshaphat, from first to last, is written down in the records of Jehu son of Hanani, which are quoted in the Book of the Kings of Israel.

³⁵Afterwards, Jehoshaphat formed a partnership with Ahaziah king of Israel, which was very wrong of him. ³⁶He joined him in building some ships to go to Tarshish; they built them at Ezion-Geber. ³⁷Eliezer son of Dodavahu of Mareshah then prophesied against Jehoshaphat as follows, 'Because you have become Ahaziah's partner, Yahweh has wrecked your efforts.' The ships were wrecked and were never fit to sail for Tarshish.

21 Then Jehoshaphat fell asleep with his ancestors and was buried with them in the city of David; his son Jehoram succeeded him.

Accession of Jehoram; he massacres his brothers

²Jehoram's brothers, sons of Jehoshaphat, were Azariah, Jehiel, Zechariah, Azariahu, Michael and Shephatiah—all of them sons of Jehoshaphat king of Israel. ³Their father had lavishly given them presents of silver, gold and other valuables as well as fortified towns in Judah; but the throne he bequeathed to Jehoram since he was the first-born. ⁴Jehoram, having taken control of his father's kingdom and secured his own position, put all his brothers to the sword and some officials of Israel too.

⁵Jehoram was thirty-two years old when he came to the throne, and he reigned for eight years in Jerusalem. ⁶He followed the example of the kings of Israel as the House of Ahab were doing, he having married one of Ahab's daughters; and he did what is displeasing to Yahweh. ⁷But Yahweh would not destroy the House of David, because of the covenant which he had made with David, promising to provide him and his sons with a lamp for ever.

The disasters of his reign

⁸In his time Edom threw off the domination of Judah and set up a king for itself. ⁹Jehoram crossed the frontier, and with him his commanders and all his chariots. Under cover of dark, he and his chariot commanders broke through the Edomites surrounding him. ¹⁰Thus Edom threw off the domination of Judah and has remained free to the present day. Libnah revolted against him at the same

time, because he had abandoned Yahweh, God of his ancestors. 11 What is more, he set up high places in the highlands of Judah, leading the citizens of Jerusalem and the people of Judah into apostasy.

12 Something written by the prophet Elijah then came into his hands. It said, 'Yahweh, God of your ancestor David, says this, "Since you have not followed the example of your father Jehoshaphat or of Asa king of Judah, 13 but have followed the example of the kings of Israel and have led Judah and the citizens of Jerusalem into apostasy, just as the House of Ahab has led Israel into apostasy, and have even murdered your brothers, your own family, who were better men than you, 14 Yahweh is going to afflict your people, your sons, your wives and all your property with a great calamity, 15 and you yourself with a severe disease affecting your bowels, as a result of which disease, continuing day after day, you will suffer protrusion of your bowels." '

16 Yahweh then roused the hostility of the Philistines and of the Arabs living near the Cushites against Jehoram. 17 They invaded Judah, forcing their way into it and carrying off all the property to be found in the king's palace, as well as his sons and his wives, so that he was left no sons at all except his youngest son Jehoahaz. 18 And after all this, Yahweh afflicted him with an incurable disease of the bowels; 19 in due time, after about two years, his bowels protruded as a result of his disease and he died in acute pain. His people did not make a funeral pyre for him, as they had for his ancestors.

20 He was thirty-two years old when he came to the throne and he reigned for eight years in Jerusalem. He passed away unlamented and was buried in the City of David, though not in the tombs of the kings.

Reign of Ahaziah

22 The inhabitants of Jerusalem then made his youngest son Ahaziah king in succession to him, since the marauders who had attacked the camp with the Arabs had killed all the older ones. That was why Ahaziah son of Jehoram, king of Judah became king. 2 Ahaziah was forty-two years old when he came to the throne and he reigned for one year in Jerusalem. His mother's name was Athaliah, descendant of Omri. 3 He too followed the example of the House of Ahab, for his mother being his adviser brought about his condemnation. 4 He did what is displeasing to Yahweh as the House of Ahab did, for they were his advisers after his father's death, to his undoing. 5 He followed their advice and went with Jehoram son of Ahab, king of Israel, to make war on Hazael king of Aram at Ramoth-Gilead. But the Aramaeans wounded Jehoram, 6 who returned to Jezreel to recover from the wounds which he had received at Ramoth, fighting against Hazael king of Aram. Ahaziah son of Jehoram, king of Judah, went down to Jezreel to visit Jehoram son of Ahab because he was ailing. 7 Through this visit to Jehoram God brought ruin on Ahaziah. On his arrival he went out with Jehoram to meet Jehu son of Nimshi whom Yahweh had anointed to make an end of the House of Ahab. 8 While Jehu was executing sentence on the House of Ahab and came across the officers of Judah and Ahaziah's nephews who were in attendance on Ahaziah, he killed them, 9 and then went in search of Ahaziah. The latter was captured while hiding in Samaria, and taken to Jehu who put him to death. But they gave him burial because, they said, 'He was the grandson of Jehoshaphat who sought Yahweh with all his heart.'

As a result, there was no member of Ahaziah's family left who was strong enough to rule the kingdom.

Athaliah massacres the royal family of Judah

10 When Athaliah mother of Ahaziah learned that her son was dead, she promptly did away with all the royal stock of the House of Judah. 11 But Jehosheba the king's daughter, surreptitiously rescued Joash son of Ahaziah from among the chiefs who were to be murdered,

and put him with his nurse in the sleeping quarters; in this way Jehosheba daughter of King Joram and wife of Jehoiada the priest—she was the sister of Ahaziah—hid him from Athaliah, and he was not put to death. ¹²He stayed hidden with them in the Temple of God for six years while Athaliah governed the country.

Accession of Joash and death of Athaliah

23 In the seventh year Jehoiada decided to take action and made a pact with the regimental commanders, Azariah son of Jeroham, Ishmael son of Jehohanan, Azariah son of Obed, Maaseiah son of Adaiah and Elishaphat son of Zichri. ²These went all over Judah, gathering the Levites from all the towns of Judah, and the heads of the Israelite families, who then came to Jerusalem, ³and the whole assembly made a pact with the king in the Temple of God. Jehoiada said to them, 'Look, the king's son is now to be king, as Yahweh has promised of the sons of David! ⁴This is what you must do: a third of you priests and Levites who come on duty on the Sabbath must guard the gates, ⁵a third the royal palace, a third the Foundation Gate, while the people must all stay in the courts of the Temple of Yahweh. ⁶No one must enter the Temple of Yahweh except the priests and the ministering Levites; they may come in because they are consecrated. But the people must all observe Yahweh's regulations. ⁷The Levites must surround the king, each man with his weapons in his hands; anyone who enters the Temple must be killed. And you will escort the king when he comes in and when he leaves.'

⁸The Levites and all Judah did everything as Jehoiada the priest had ordered, and each one brought his men, those coming on duty on the Sabbath and those going off duty on the Sabbath, for Jehoiada the priest had not released any of the divisions from duty. ⁹Jehoiada the priest then issued the regimental commanders with King David's spears and large and small shields, which were kept in the Temple of God. ¹⁰He then positioned all the people, each man with his weapon in his hand, from the south side of the Temple to the north side of the Temple, close to the altar and the Temple, to form a circle round the king. ¹¹Then they brought the king's son out, crowned him, gave him a copy of the covenant and made him king. When Jehoiada and his sons had anointed him, they shouted, 'Long live the king!'

¹²On hearing the people shouting as they ran to acclaim the king, Athaliah joined the people in the Temple of Yahweh. ¹³When she looked, there stood the king on his dais by the entrance, with the officers and trumpeters at the king's side, and all the people of the country rejoicing and blowing the trumpets, and the singers with their musical instruments leading the hymns of praise. Then Athaliah tore her clothes and shouted, 'Treason, treason!' ¹⁴Jehoiada the priest then gave the order to the regimental commanders in charge of the troops, 'Take her out between the ranks and put to the sword anyone who follows her.' For the priest had already said, 'Do not kill her inside the Temple of Yahweh.' ¹⁵So they made way for her, and when she reached the entrance to the Horses' Gate of the palace, they killed her there.

Jehoiada's reform

¹⁶Jehoiada made a covenant between himself, all the people and the king to remain Yahweh's people. ¹⁷All the people then went to the temple of Baal and demolished it; they smashed its altars and its images and killed Mattan the priest of Baal in front of the altars.

¹⁸Jehoiada entrusted the security of the Temple of Yahweh to the priests and Levites, whom David had put in charge of the Temple of Yahweh to present the burnt offerings of Yahweh as laid down in the Law of Moses, with joy and song as ordained by David. ¹⁹He also appointed gatekeepers for the gates of the Temple of Yahweh, so that no one who was unclean might enter for any purpose at all.

²⁰He then took the regimental commanders, the nobles, the government officials and

all the people of the land and he escorted the king down from the Temple of Yahweh. Entering the palace through the Upper Gate, they placed the king on the royal throne. 21 All the people of the land were delighted, and the city made no move after Athaliah had been put to death.

24 Joash was seven years old when he came to the throne and he reigned for forty years in Jerusalem. His mother's name was Zibiah of Beersheba. 2 Joash did what Yahweh regards as right throughout the lifetime of Jehoiada the priest. 3 Jehoiada found him two wives and he fathered several sons and daughters.

Joash repairs the Temple

4 Later, Joash made up his mind to repair the Temple of Yahweh. 5 Calling the priests and the Levites together, he said, 'Go out to the towns of Judah and collect money from all Israel for annual repairs to the Temple of Yahweh. Do this quickly.' But the Levites were in no hurry, 6 so the king summoned Jehoiada the chief priest and said, 'Why have you not insisted on the Levites' bringing in the tax from Judah and Jerusalem for the Tent of Witness, as imposed by Moses servant of Yahweh and the community of Israel?'— 7 Athaliah and her sons, whom she corrupted, despoiled the Temple of God and even assigned all the sacred revenues of the Temple of Yahweh to Baal. 8 So, at the king's order, a chest was made and put outside the gate of the Temple of Yahweh, 9 and a proclamation was issued throughout Judah and Jerusalem that the tax, which Moses servant of God had imposed on Israel in the desert, was to be brought to Yahweh. 10 Then all the officials and all the people gladly brought in their contributions, depositing them in the chest until the payment was complete.

11 Whenever the chest was brought by the Levites for royal inspection and found to contain a large sum of money, the king's secretary and the chief priest's representative would come and empty the chest and then have it returned to its place. This was done day after day and a great deal of money was collected. 12 The king and Jehoiada handed it over to the foreman attached to the Temple of Yahweh, and the hired masons and carpenters set about repairing the Temple of Yahweh; and iron-workers and bronze-workers laboured to repair the Temple of Yahweh. 13 The workmen got on with the task—the repair work made good progress at their hands—until they had restored the Temple of God to its former state and reconditioned it. 14 When they had finished, they brought the balance of the money to the king and Jehoiada, and with this vessels were made for the Temple of Yahweh, vessels for the liturgy and for the burnt offerings, bowls and other gold and silver vessels. And the perpetual burnt offering was offered in the Temple of Yahweh throughout Jehoiada's lifetime.

15 But Jehoiada, growing old, had his fill of days and died. He died at the age of a hundred and thirty years, 16 and was buried with the kings in the City of David because he had served Israel and God and his Temple well.

Joash's decline and death

17 After Jehoiada's death the officials of Judah came to pay court to the king, and the king listened to their advice, 18 and they abandoned the Temple of Yahweh, God of their ancestors, for the worship of sacred poles and idols. Judah and Jerusalem incurred wrath because of this guilt of theirs. 19 He sent their prophets to lead them back to Yahweh; these put the case against them, but they would not listen. 20 The spirit of God then invested Zechariah son of Jehoiada the priest. He stood up before the people and said, 'God says this, "Why transgress Yahweh's commands to your certain ruin? For if you abandon Yahweh, he will abandon you." ' 21 They then plotted against him and, at the king's order, stoned him in the court of the Temple of Yahweh. 22 Thus King Joash, forgetful of the devotion which Jehoiada father of Zechariah had displayed on

his behalf, murdered his son, who cried out as he died, 'Yahweh will see this and avenge it!' 23 At the turn of the year, the Aramaean army made war on Joash. When they reached Judah and Jerusalem, they massacred all the nation's government officials and sent all their booty to the king of Damascus. 24 Although the invading Aramaean army was only a small body of men, Yahweh allowed them to defeat a very large army because they had abandoned Yahweh, God of their ancestors; thus they executed judgement on Joash.

After they had retired—for they left him seriously wounded— 25 his own retainers plotted against him to avenge the blood of the son of Jehoiada the priest and murdered him in his bed. When he died he was buried in the City of David, but not in the tombs of the kings. 26 These were the conspirators: Zabad son of Shimeath the Ammonite and Jehozabad son of Shimrith the Moabite. 27 As regards his sons, the heavy tribute imposed on him, and the restoration of the Temple of God, this is recorded in the Commentary on the Book of the Kings. His son Amaziah succeeded him.

Accession of Amaziah

25 Amaziah was twenty-five years old when he came to the throne and he reigned for twenty-nine years in Jerusalem. His mother's name was Jehoaddan of Jerusalem. 2 He did what Yahweh regards as right, though not wholeheartedly. 3 Once the kingdom was firmly under his control, he killed those of his retainers who had murdered the king his father. 4 But he did not put their sons to death; this was in accordance with what is written in the Law, in the book of Moses, where Yahweh had commanded, 'Parents may not be put to death for children, nor children for parents, but each must be put to death for his own crime.' [a]

His victorious campaign against Edom

5 Amaziah summoned Judah and organised all Judah and Benjamin by families under commanders of thousands and commanders of hundreds. He also made a register of those who were twenty years old and upwards, and found there were three hundred thousand picked men, ready for service and capable of wielding spear and shield. 6 Furthermore, he hired a hundred thousand tough fighting men from Israel for a hundred talents of silver. 7 A man of God then came to him and said, 'My lord king, do not let the Israelite troops march with you, for Yahweh is not with Israel or with any of the Ephraimites. 8 For however valiantly you act in war, God will bring you down before the enemy, for God has the power to uphold or to throw down.' 9 Amaziah said to the man of God, 'But what about the hundred talents which I have paid for the Israelite troops?' 'Yahweh can give you far more than that,' said the man of God. 10 At this, Amaziah dismissed the troops who had come to him from Ephraim and sent them home again. They were furious with Judah and went home in a great rage.

11 Amaziah then, coming to a decision, led out his own troops and, having reached the Valley of Salt, struck down ten thousand Seirites. 12 The men of Judah captured ten thousand more alive and, taking them to the summit of the Rock, threw them off the summit of the Rock so that they were all dashed to pieces. 13 Meanwhile, the troops whom Amaziah had dismissed and not allowed to go into battle with him rased the towns of Judah, from Samaria to Beth-Horon, killing three thousand of their inhabitants and capturing great quantities of plunder.

14 On returning from his slaughter of the Edomites, Amaziah brought the gods of the Seirites with him; he set these up as his gods, bowing down before them and burning incense to them. 15 Yahweh's anger was aroused by Amaziah and he sent him a prophet, who said to him, 'Why do you consult those people's gods when they could not save their own people from your clutches?' 16 He was still speaking when Amaziah interrupted

25a ‖ Dt 24:16.

him. 'Have we appointed you a royal counsellor? Stop, as you value your life!' So the prophet stopped, and then said, 'I know that God has decided to destroy you for having done this and for not listening to my advice.'

His disastrous campaign against Israel

¹⁷ After consultation, Amaziah king of Judah then sent a message to Joash son of Jehoahaz son of Jehu, king of Israel, saying, 'Come and make a trial of strength!' ¹⁸ Joash king of Israel sent back word to Amaziah king of Judah, 'The thistle of Lebanon sent a message to the cedar of Lebanon, saying, "Give my son your daughter in marriage"; but a wild animal of the Lebanon ran over the thistle and squashed it. ¹⁹ "Look at me, the conqueror of Edom," you say, and now aspire to even greater glory. But stay where you belong! Why challenge disaster, to your own and Judah's ruin?'

²⁰ But Amaziah would not listen, for this was an act of God to deliver them up for having consulted the gods of Edom. ²¹ So Joash king of Israel marched to the attack. And at Beth-Shemesh, which belongs to Judah, he and Amaziah king of Judah made their trial of strength. ²² Judah was defeated by Israel, and everyone fled to his tent. ²³ The king of Judah, Amaziah son of Joash, son of Ahaziah, was taken prisoner at Beth-Shemesh by Joash king of Israel who led him off to Jerusalem, where he demolished four hundred cubits of the city wall between the Ephraim Gate and the Corner Gate; ²⁴ he then took back with him to Samaria all the gold and silver, and all the vessels to be found in the Temple of God in the care of Obed-Edom, the treasures in the palace, and hostages besides.

His death

²⁵ Amaziah son of Joash, king of Judah, lived for fifteen years after the death of Joash son of Jehoahaz, king of Israel.

²⁶ The rest of the history of Amaziah, from first to last, is this not recorded in the Book of the Kings of Judah and Israel? ²⁷ Some time after Amaziah had defected from Yahweh, a plot having been hatched against him in Jerusalem, he fled to Lachish where he was murdered. ²⁸ He was then transported by horse and buried with his ancestors in the city of David.

Accession of Uzziah

26 All the people then chose Uzziah, who was sixteen years old, and made him king in succession to his father Amaziah. ²It was he who rebuilt Elath, recovering it for Judah, after the king had fallen asleep with his ancestors. ³Uzziah was sixteen years old when he came to the throne and he reigned for fifty-two years in Jerusalem. His mother's name was Jecoliah of Jerusalem. ⁴He did what is pleasing to Yahweh, just as his father Amaziah had done; ⁵he consulted God throughout the lifetime of Zechariah, who instructed him in the fear of God. And as long as he consulted Yahweh, God gave him success.

His military strength

⁶He went on campaign against the Philistines, demolished the walls of Gath, the walls of Jabneh and the walls of Ashdod, and built towns in the area of Ashdod and elsewhere in Philistine territory. ⁷God helped him against the Philistines, the Arabs living at Gur-Baal and the Meunites. ⁸The Meunites paid tribute to Uzziah and his fame spread as far as the frontier of Egypt, since he kept growing stronger and stronger.

⁹Uzziah built towers in Jerusalem, at the Corner Gate, at the Valley Gate and at the Angle, and fortified them. ¹⁰He built towers in the desert too, and dug many storage-wells, for he had large herds in the lowlands and on the tableland, and farmers and vine dressers in the hills and fertile lands: for he loved the land.

¹¹Uzziah had a trained army ready to go on campaign, organised in companies manned as detailed by the scribe Jeiel and the staff-officer Maaseiah, and commanded by Hananiah one of the king's generals. ¹²The heads of families of the military champions numbered in all two

thousand six hundred. ¹³Under them was an army of three hundred and seven thousand five hundred men ready for war, a powerful force to support the king against the enemy. ¹⁴Uzziah provided shields, spears, helmets, armour, bows and sling-stones for the entire army. ¹⁵He also erected expertly contrived devices for the towers and angles of Jerusalem from which to shoot arrows and drop large stones. His fame spread far and wide, for he was miraculously helped to become strong.

He is struck with a virulent skin-disease for his pride

¹⁶But once he was strong, his arrogance was such that it led to his downfall; he was unfaithful to Yahweh his God by entering the Temple of Yahweh to burn incense on the altar of incense. ¹⁷Azariah the priest with eight brave priests of Yahweh followed him in; ¹⁸confronting King Uzziah, they said to him, 'Uzziah, you are not allowed to burn incense to Yahweh; only the Aaronite priests consecrated for the purpose may burn incense. Leave the sanctuary, for you have been unfaithful and will have no honour from Yahweh God.' ¹⁹Uzziah, censer in hand to burn incense, flew into a rage. But while he was raging at the priests, a virulent skin-disease broke out on his forehead in the presence of the priests, in the Temple of Yahweh, there by the altar of incense. ²⁰When Azariah the chief priest and all the other priests turned towards him, there was skin-disease on his forehead and they hurried him outside, and he himself was equally anxious to get out, because Yahweh had struck him.

²¹King Uzziah was afflicted with skin-disease till his dying day. Because of this, he lived confined to his room and was excluded from the Temple of Yahweh, while Jotham his son, who was master of the palace, governed the people of the country.

²²The rest of the history of Uzziah, from first to last, has been written by the prophet Isaiah son of Amoz. ²³Then Uzziah fell asleep with his ancestors and was buried with them in the field beside the burial ground of the kings since, it was reasoned, he was afflicted with virulent skin-disease. His son Jotham then succeeded him.

The reign of Jotham

27 Jotham was twenty-five years old when he came to the throne and he reigned for sixteen years in Jerusalem. His mother's name was Jerushah daughter of Zadok. ²He did what Yahweh regards as right, just as his father Uzziah had done. Only he did not enter Yahweh's sanctuary. But the people continued to do wrong.

³It was he who built the Upper Gate of the Temple of Yahweh and carried out considerable work on the wall of the Ophel. ⁴He also built towns in the highlands of Judah and built forts and towers in the wooded areas.

⁵He also went to war against the king of the Ammonites and defeated them; and the Ammonites had to give him a hundred talents of silver, ten thousand *kor* of wheat and ten thousand of barley that year. And the Ammonites paid him the same amount, the second and third years afterwards. ⁶Jotham became powerful because he kept an unswerving course before Yahweh his God.

⁷The rest of the history of Jotham, all his wars and his policy, are recorded in the Book of the Kings of Israel and Judah. ⁸He was twenty-five years old when he came to the throne and he reigned for sixteen years in Jerusalem. ⁹Then Jotham fell asleep with his ancestors, and was buried in the City of David; his son Ahaz succeeded him.

Accession of Ahaz: his idolatry

28 Ahaz was twenty years old when he came to the throne and he reigned for sixteen years in Jerusalem. He did not do what Yahweh regards as right, as his ancestor David had done. ²He followed the example of the kings of Israel, even having images cast for the Baals; ³he burned incense in the Valley of Ben-Hinnom, caused his sons to pass through the fire of sacrifice, copying the disgusting prac-

tices of the nations whom Yahweh had dispossessed for the Israelites. ⁴He offered sacrifices and incense on the high places, on the hills and under every green tree.

The Syro-Ephraimite War

⁵So Yahweh his God put him at the mercy of the king of Aram, who defeated him and took large numbers of captives, carrying them off to Damascus. He also put him at the mercy of the king of Israel, who inflicted heavy casualties on him. ⁶In a single day, Pekah son of Remaliah killed a hundred and twenty thousand in Judah, all of them prominent men, because they had abandoned Yahweh, God of their ancestors. ⁷Zichri, an Ephraimite champion, killed Maaseiah the king's son, Azrikam the controller of the household and Elkanah the king's second-in-command. ⁸Of their brothers, the Israelites took two hundred thousand captive including wives, sons, daughters; they also took quantities of booty, carrying everything off to Samaria.

The Israelites obey the prophet Oded

⁹Now there was a prophet of Yahweh there by the name of Oded, who went out to meet the troops returning to Samaria and said, 'Look, because Yahweh, God of your ancestors, was angry with Judah, he put them at your mercy, but you have slaughtered them with such fury as reached to heaven, ¹⁰and now you propose to reduce the children of Judah and Jerusalem to being your male and female slaves! Have you not yourselves committed sins against Yahweh your God? ¹¹Now listen to me: release the captives you have taken from your brothers, for the fierce anger of Yahweh hangs over you.'

¹²Some of the Ephraimite chieftains—Azariah son of Jehohanan, Berechaiah son of Meshillemoth, Jehizkiah son of Shallum and Amasa son of Hadlai—then protested to those returning from the war ¹³and said to them, 'You must not bring the captives here, for we have already sinned against Yahweh and you

propose to add to our sin and guilt, although our guilt is already great, and fierce anger is hanging over Israel.' ¹⁴So in the presence of the officials and whole assembly, the soldiers gave up the captives and the booty. ¹⁵Men nominated for the purpose then took charge of the captives. From the booty they clothed all those of them who were naked; they gave them clothing and sandals, provided them with food and drink, mounted on donkeys all those who were infirm and took them back to Jericho, the city of palm trees, to their brothers. Then they returned to Samaria.

Ahaz appeals to Assyria; his apostasy

¹⁶This was when King Ahaz sent asking the king of Assyria to come to his assistance.

¹⁷The Edomites again invaded, defeated Judah, and carried off captives, ¹⁸while the Philistines raided the towns in the lowlands and in the Negeb of Judah, capturing Beth-Shemesh, Aijalon, Gederoth, Soco and its dependencies, Timnah and its dependencies and Gimzo and its dependencies, and settled there. ¹⁹For Yahweh brought Judah low because of Ahaz king of Israel, since he behaved without restraint in Judah and had been unfaithful to Yahweh. ²⁰Tiglath-Pileser king of Assyria attacked and besieged him; but he could not overpower him. ²¹Although Ahaz robbed the Temple of Yahweh and the palaces of the king and princes and gave the proceeds to the king of Assyria, he received no help from him.

²²During the time when he was under siege he disobeyed Yahweh even more grossly, this King Ahaz. ²³For he offered sacrifices to the gods of Damascus who had defeated him. 'Since the gods of the kings of Aram', he thought, 'have supported them, I shall sacrifice to them, and perhaps they will help me.' But they proved to be his and all Israel's downfall.

²⁴Ahaz then collected the equipment of the Temple of God, broke up the equipment of the Temple of God, sealed the doors of the Temple of Yahweh and put his own altars in every corner of Jerusalem; ²⁵he set up high

places in every town of Judah to burn incense to other gods, thus provoking the anger of Yahweh, God of his ancestors.

²⁶ The rest of his history, his whole policy, from first to last, is recorded in the Book of the Kings of Judah and Israel. ²⁷ Then Ahaz fell asleep with his ancestors and was buried in the City, in Jerusalem, though he was not taken to the tombs of the kings of Israel. His son Hezekiah succeeded him.

Accession of Hezekiah

29 Hezekiah was twenty-five years old when he came to the throne and he reigned for twenty-nine years in Jerusalem. His mother's name was Abijah daughter of Zechariah. ² He did what Yahweh regards as right, just as his ancestor David had done.

The purification of the Temple

³ In the first month of the first year of his reign, he opened the doors of the Temple of Yahweh, having repaired them. ⁴ He then brought in the priests and the Levites, assembled them in the eastern square, ⁵ and said to them,

'Listen to me, Levites! First sanctify yourselves, then sanctify the Temple of Yahweh, God of your ancestors, and remove the filth from the sanctuary. ⁶ Our ancestors were unfaithful, and did what is displeasing to Yahweh our God. They abandoned him, turned their faces away from Yahweh's home and turned their backs on him. ⁷ They even closed the doors of the portico, put out the lamps and stopped burning incense and making burnt offerings in the sanctuary of the God of Israel. ⁸ This was why Yahweh's anger fell on Judah and Jerusalem and he made them an object of terror, astonishment and derision, as you can see for yourselves. ⁹ Yes, our ancestors were put to the sword, and our sons, our daughters and our wives were taken captive because of this. ¹⁰ I am now determined to make a covenant with Yahweh, God of Israel, so that his fierce anger may turn away from us. ¹¹ Now, my sons, do not be remiss, for Yahweh

has chosen you to stand in his presence and serve him by conducting his worship and offering him incense.'

¹² The Levites set about it—Mahath son of Amasai and Joel son of Azariah, from the Kohathites; Kish son of Abdi and Azariah son of Jehallel, from the Merarites; Joah son of Zimmah and Eden son of Joah, from the Gershonites; ¹³ Shimri and Jeuel, of the sons of Elizaphan; Zechariah and Mattaniah of the sons of Asaph; ¹⁴ Jehiel and Shimei of the sons of Heman; Shemaiah and Uzziel of the sons of Jeduthun— ¹⁵ and gathered their brothers together; they sanctified themselves, and in obedience to the king's order, in accordance with the words of Yahweh, they came to purify the Temple of Yahweh.

¹⁶ The priests went into the inner part of the Temple of Yahweh to purify it. They brought all the unclean things which they found in Yahweh's sanctuary, out into the court of the Temple of Yahweh, where the Levites collected them and took them out to the Kidron Valley. ¹⁷ They began sanctifying on the first day of the first month, and by the eighth day of the month had reached Yahweh's portico; thus they took eight days to sanctify the Temple of Yahweh, and by the sixteenth day of the first month everything was finished.

The sacrifice of expiation

¹⁸ They then waited on King Hezekiah and said, 'We have purified the whole Temple of Yahweh, the altar of burnt offering with all its equipment and the table for the loaves of permanent offering with all their equipment. ¹⁹ We have also got ready and sanctified all the equipment which King Ahaz in his infidelity had removed during his reign. It is all ready in front of Yahweh's altar.'

²⁰ King Hezekiah lost no time but called the officials of the city together and went up to the Temple of Yahweh. ²¹ They brought seven bulls, seven rams, seven lambs and seven goats as a sin sacrifice for the royal house, for the sanctuary and for Judah, and he ordered the Aaronite priests to offer them on Yahweh's

altar. ²²So they slaughtered the bulls and the priests took the blood and sprinkled it over the altar. They then slaughtered the rams and sprinkled the blood over the altar; and they slaughtered the lambs and sprinkled the blood over the altar. ²³Then they brought the goats, the sacrifice for sin, before the king and the assembly who laid their hands on them. ²⁴The priests slaughtered them and made a sacrifice for sin with their blood at the altar to expiate for all Israel, since the king had ordered the burnt offering and the sacrifice for sin on behalf of all Israel.

²⁵He positioned the Levites in the Temple of Yahweh with cymbals, lyres and harps, in accordance with the ordinance of David, of Gad the king's seer and of Nathan the prophet, for such was Yahweh's order conveyed through his prophets. ²⁶When the Levites stood with David's musical instruments, and the priests with the trumpets, ²⁷Hezekiah ordered the burnt offering to be presented on the altar. And as the burnt offering began, the hymns of Yahweh began too, and the trumpets sounded, to the accompaniment of the instruments of David king of Israel, ²⁸while the whole congregation worshipped, the singers singing and the trumpeters sounding the trumpets, continuously until the burnt offering was over.

The cult begins again

²⁹When the burnt offering was finished, the king and all those present with him fell to their knees and worshipped. ³⁰Then King Hezekiah and the officials told the Levites to sing praise to Yahweh in the words of David and Asaph the seer; and joyfully they sang their praises, then knelt in worship.

³¹Hezekiah spoke again, 'Now that you have consecrated yourselves to Yahweh, come forward and bring thanksgiving sacrifices to the Temple of Yahweh.' Then the congregation brought thanksgiving sacrifices and those who were generous brought burnt offerings. ³²The number of burnt offerings brought by the congregation was seventy bulls, a hundred rams and two hundred lambs, all as burnt offerings for Yahweh. ³³The consecrated gifts amounted to six hundred bulls and three thousand sheep. ³⁴The priests were too few, however, and were unable to dismember all the burnt offerings, so their brothers, the Levites, helped them until the work was finished and the priests had sanctified themselves; for the Levites had been more conscientious about sanctifying themselves than the priests had. ³⁵In addition to the abundance of burnt offerings, there were also the fatty pieces for communion sacrifices and the libations for the burnt offerings.

And so the liturgy of Yahweh's Temple was restored, ³⁶and Hezekiah and all the people rejoiced over what God had provided for the people, since everything had happened so suddenly.

Preparations for the Passover

30 Hezekiah sent messengers to all Israel and Judah, and also wrote letters to Ephraim and Manasseh, bidding them come to the Temple of Yahweh in Jerusalem to celebrate the Passover in honour of Yahweh, God of Israel. ²For the king and his officials and the whole congregation in Jerusalem had agreed to celebrate the Passover in the second month, ³having been unable to celebrate it at the proper time, since the priests had not purified themselves in sufficient number, and the people were not assembled in Jerusalem. ⁴And since this arrangement seemed fitting to the king and the whole congregation, ⁵they resolved to send a proclamation throughout Israel, from Dan to Beersheba, calling on the people to come to Jerusalem and celebrate a Passover in honour of Yahweh, God of Israel, since they had not celebrated it in a body as prescribed. ⁶So, by order of the king, courtiers set out with letters from the king and his officials for every part of Israel and Judah, saying, 'Israelites, return to Yahweh, God of Abraham, Isaac and Israel, and he will return to those of you who are left and have escaped the grasp of the kings of Assyria. ⁷Do not be like

your fathers and brothers who were unfaithful to Yahweh, God of their ancestors; he brought them to ruin, as you can see. ⁸Do not be stubborn like your ancestors. Submit to Yahweh, come to his sanctuary which he has consecrated for ever, and serve Yahweh your God, so that his fierce anger may turn away from you. ⁹For if you return to Yahweh, your brothers and your sons will be treated mercifully by their captors and be allowed to return to this country; for Yahweh your God is gracious and merciful and will not turn his face away from you, if you return to him.'

¹⁰The courtiers went from town to town through the territory of Ephraim and Manasseh and as far as Zebulon but the people laughed and scoffed at them; ¹¹even so, some people from Asher and Manasseh and Zebulon were humble enough to come to Jerusalem, ¹²while in Judah the hand of God was also at work inspiring a unanimous desire to obey the order of the king and the officials in accordance with the word of Yahweh.

The Passover and feast of Unleavened Bread

¹³A huge crowd assembled in Jerusalem to celebrate the feast of Unleavened Bread in the second month. An immense crowd ¹⁴set to work removing the altars then in Jerusalem; they also removed all the incense altars and threw them into the Kidron Valley. ¹⁵They then slaughtered the Passover victims on the fourteenth day of the second month. Ashamed of themselves, the priests and Levites had in the meanwhile sanctified themselves and brought burnt offerings to the Temple of Yahweh, ¹⁶so they now stood in their positions prescribed in the Law of Moses man of God, the priests sprinkling the blood handed to them by the Levites. ¹⁷Since many people in the congregation had not sanctified themselves, the Levites took care of the slaughter of the Passover victims to consecrate them to Yahweh for all who were not clean. ¹⁸For a great many people, especially from Ephraim, Manasseh, Issachar and Zebulon, had not purified themselves, since they did not eat the Passover as prescribed. But Hezekiah prayed for them as follows, 'May Yahweh in his goodness pardon ¹⁹everyone whose heart is set on seeking God, Yahweh, God of his ancestors, even if he has not been purified as holy things demand.' ²⁰Yahweh listened to Hezekiah and left the people unharmed.

²¹Amid great rejoicing, the Israelites present in Jerusalem celebrated the feast of Unleavened Bread for seven days, while day after day the Levites and the priests praised Yahweh with all their might. ²²Hezekiah then encouraged all the Levites who had such understanding of Yahweh.

Having finished the seven-day festival, during which they sacrificed communion sacrifices and praised Yahweh, God of their ancestors, ²³the whole congregation decided to celebrate for a further seven days. So they joyfully celebrated for another seven days, ²⁴Hezekiah king of Judah contributing a thousand bulls and seven thousand sheep for the congregation, and the officials another thousand bulls and ten thousand sheep. And a large number of priests sanctified themselves. ²⁵The whole congregation of Judah, the priests, the Levites, the whole congregation coming from Israel and the foreigners coming from the territory of Israel as well as those resident in Judah, rejoiced. ²⁶There was great rejoicing in Jerusalem, for since the days of Solomon son of David, king of Israel, nothing comparable had ever occurred in Jerusalem. ²⁷The levitical priests then stood up and blessed the people and their voice was heard, and their prayer reached his holy dwelling in heaven.

The purification of the country

31 When all this was complete, all Israel present went out to the towns of Judah, broke the pillars, cut down the sacred poles, wrecked the high places and the altars, and did away with them entirely throughout Judah, Benjamin, Ephraim, and Manasseh. Then all the Israelites returned to their towns, everyone to his property.

The reorganisation of the priests and Levites

[2] Hezekiah re-established the priestly and levitical orders, each man in his proper order according to his duties, whether priest or Levite, to bring burnt offerings and communion sacrifices, to serve and to give thanks and praise within the gates of Yahweh's camp. [3] He also established a king's portion from his possessions for the morning and evening burnt offerings, and the burnt offerings for the Sabbaths, New Moons and festivals, as laid down in the Law of Yahweh. [4] He furthermore requested the people living in Jerusalem to present the portion for the priests and Levites so that they might devote themselves to the Law of Yahweh. [5] As soon as the order had been promulgated, the Israelites provided the first fruits of grain, new wine, olive oil, honey and every other kind of agricultural produce in abundance; they brought in an abundant tithe of everything. [6] The Israelites and Judaeans living in the towns of Judah also brought in the tithe of cattle and sheep, and the tithe of sacred gifts consecrated to Yahweh their God, laying them in heaps. [7] They began accumulating the heaps in the third month and had finished them by the seventh. [8] When Hezekiah and the officials came to inspect the heaps they praised Yahweh and his people Israel.

[9] While Hezekiah was questioning the priests and Levites about the heaps, [10] Azariah, the chief priest, of the family of Zadok, replied as follows, 'Since they began bringing the contributions to the Temple of Yahweh,' he said, 'we have had enough to eat and quantities left over, for Yahweh has blessed his people; this mass of stuff is left.' [11] Hezekiah then ordered them to have storerooms prepared in the Temple of Yahweh and, when they had got them ready, [12] they conscientiously brought in the contributions, tithes and consecrated gifts, Conaniah the Levite was put in charge of them, with Shimei his brother as his assistant, [13] and with Jehiel, Azaziah, Nahath, Asahel, Jeremith, Jozabad, Eliel, Ismachiah, Mahath,

and Benaiah as overseers under Conaniah and his brother Shimei, by order of King Hezekiah and of Azariah, the chief of the Temple of God. [14] Kore son of Jimnah the Levite, keeper of the eastern gate, was made responsible for the voluntary offerings to God and for providing the portion set aside for Yahweh and the most holy gifts. [15] Supporting him loyally in the priestly towns were Eden, Miniamin, Jeshua, Shemaiah, Amariah and Shechaniah, who made the distributions to their brothers in their various orders, whether high or low, [16] irrespective of their official genealogy, to the males of thirty years and upwards—to each one who attended the Temple of Yahweh to fulfil his daily obligations—for the performance of their duties appropriate to their orders: [17] the priests being registered according to family and the Levites of twenty years and upwards according to their duties within their orders. [18] And the official genealogy included all their household, their wives, their sons and their daughters, throughout the community, since these men were obliged to keep sanctifying themselves anew. [19] The Aaronite priests who lived on the pasture lands belonging to their towns, had men named in every town to distribute portions to every male among the priests and to everyone included in the official genealogy of the Levites.

[20] Hezekiah did this throughout all Judah. He did what Yahweh his God regards as good and right and loyal. [21] Everything that he undertook, whether in the service of the Temple of God or in connection with the law or the commandments, he did in absolute devotion to his God, and so succeeded.

Sennacherib's invasion

32 After these loyal actions, Sennacherib king of Assyria advanced and invaded Judah, and laid siege to the fortified towns, intending to demolish them. [2] Hezekiah, realising that Sennacherib's advance was the preliminary to an attack on Jerusalem, [3] consulted his officers and warriors about sealing off the waters of the springs outside the city, and they

supported him. ⁴ So a large number of people were called out to block all the springs and cut off the watercourse flowing through the country. 'Why', they said, 'should the kings of Assyria find plenty of water when they arrive?'

⁵ Acting with determination, he also repaired all the damaged parts of the wall, built towers on it, constructed a second wall on the outer side, strengthened the Millo of the City of David and made quantities of missiles and shields. ⁶ He then appointed generals to command the people, summoned them to him in the square by the city gate and spoke as follows to encourage them, ⁷ 'Be strong and brave; do not be afraid or tremble when you face the king of Assyria and the whole horde he brings with him, for there are more on our side than on his. ⁸ He has only human strength, but we have Yahweh our God to help us and fight our battles.' The people took heart at the words of Hezekiah king of Judah.

Sennacherib's blasphemous ultimatum and downfall

⁹ Next, Sennacherib king of Assyria, who was then besieging Lachish with all his forces, sent his representatives to Jerusalem, to Hezekiah king of Judah, and all Judah at Jerusalem, with the following message, ¹⁰ 'Sennacherib king of Assyria says this, "What gives you the confidence to remain in the fortress of Jerusalem? ¹¹ Isn't Hezekiah deluding you, only to condemn you to die of famine and thirst, when he says: Yahweh our God will save us from the King of Assyria's clutches? ¹² Isn't Hezekiah the very man who has suppressed his high places and altars, and given the order to Judah and to Jerusalem: You must worship before one altar and on that alone offer incense? ¹³ Don't you know what I and my ancestors have done to all the peoples of the other countries? Have the national gods of those countries had the slightest success in saving their countries from my clutches? ¹⁴ Of all the gods of those nations whom my ancestors devoted to destruction, which one has been able to save his people from my clutches, for your

god to be able to save you from my clutches? ¹⁵ Do not let Hezekiah mislead you. Do not let him delude you like this. Do not believe him, for no god of any nation or kingdom has been able to save his people from me or from my ancestors' clutches. No more will your god be able to save you from my clutches." ' ¹⁶ And his representatives said a great deal more, maligning Yahweh God, and his servant Hezekiah.

¹⁷ He also wrote a letter to insult Yahweh, God of Israel, maligning him as follows, 'Just as the national gods of the other countries could not save their peoples from my clutches, so Hezekiah's god cannot save his people from my clutches.' ¹⁸ They then shouted loudly in the Judaean language to the people of Jerusalem on the ramparts to frighten and confuse them, in the hope of capturing the city, ¹⁹ maligning the God of Jerusalem as though he were one of the man-made gods of other peoples in the world.

²⁰ Then King Hezekiah and the prophet Isaiah son of Amoz prayed and cried out to Heaven about this, ²¹ and Yahweh sent an angel who destroyed every warrior, commander and officer in the king of Assyria's camp. So he had to retire shamefacedly to his own country and when he went into the temple of his god, some of his own sons there struck him down with the sword. ²² So Yahweh saved Hezekiah and the inhabitants of Jerusalem from the clutches of Sennacherib king of Assyria and of everyone else, and gave them peace on every side. ²³ Many people then brought gifts to Yahweh in Jerusalem and valuable presents to Hezekiah king of Judah; from then on, all the other nations held him in high esteem.

The closing years of Hezekiah's reign

²⁴ About then Hezekiah fell ill and was at the point of death. He prayed to Yahweh, who heard him and granted him a sign. ²⁵ But Hezekiah made no return for the benefit which he had received; he became proud and brought retribution on himself and on Judah and Jerusalem. ²⁶ Then, however, Hezekiah

did humble himself in his pride, and so did the inhabitants of Jerusalem; as a result of which, Yahweh's retribution did not overtake them during Hezekiah's lifetime.

27 Hezekiah enjoyed immense riches and honour. He built himself treasuries for gold, silver, precious stones, spices, jewels and every kind of desirable object, 28 as well as store-houses for his returns of grain, new wine and olive oil, and stalls for all kinds of cattle and pens for the flocks. 29 He also provided himself with donkeys in addition to his immense wealth of flocks and herds, since God had made him immensely wealthy.

30 It was Hezekiah who stopped the upper outlet of the waters of Gihon and directed them straight down on the west side of the City of David. Hezekiah succeeded in all that he undertook, 31 although when the envoys were sent to him by the rulers of Babylon to enquire about the extraordinary thing which had taken place in the country, God left him alone to test him and discover what lay in his heart.

32 The rest of the history of Hezekiah, and his deeds of faithful love, are recorded in the Vision of the prophet Isaiah son of Amoz, in the Book of the Kings of Judah and Israel. 33 Then Hezekiah fell asleep with his ancestors and was buried in the upper section of the tombs of the sons of David. All Judah and the inhabitants of Jerusalem paid him honours at his death. His son Manasseh succeeded him.

Manasseh undoes the work of Hezekiah

33 Manasseh was twelve years old when he came to the throne, and he reigned for fifty-five years in Jerusalem. 2 He did what is displeasing to Yahweh, copying the disgusting practices of the nations whom Yahweh had dispossessed for the Israelites.

3 He rebuilt the high places which his father Hezekiah had demolished, he set up altars to Baal and made sacred poles, he worshipped the whole array of heaven and served it. 4 He built altars in the Temple of Yahweh, of which Yahweh had said, 'My name will be in Jerusalem for ever.' 5 He built altars to the whole array of heaven in the two courts of the Temple of Yahweh. 6 He caused his sons to pass through the fire of sacrifice in the Valley of Ben-Hinnom. He practised soothsaying, divination and sorcery, and had dealings with mediums and spirit-guides. He did very many more things displeasing to Yahweh, thus provoking his anger. 7 He put a sculpted image, an idol which he had had made, inside the Temple of which God had said to David and his son Solomon, 'In this Temple and in Jerusalem, the city which I have chosen out of all the tribes of Israel, I shall put my name for ever. 8 Nor shall I ever again remove Israel's foot from the soil on which I established your ancestors on condition that they were careful to observe all I commanded them as laid down in the whole Law, the statutes and the ordinances, given through Moses.' 9 But Manasseh misled Judah and the inhabitants of Jerusalem into doing worse things than the nations which Yahweh had destroyed for the Israelites. 10 When Yahweh spoke to Manasseh and his people, they would not listen.

Manasseh's captivity and conversion

11 Yahweh then brought down on them the generals of the king of Assyria's army who captured Manasseh with hooks, put him in chains and took him to Babylon. 12 While in his distress, he placated Yahweh his God by genuinely humbling himself before the God of his ancestors. 13 When he prayed to him, he was moved by his entreaty, heard his supplication and brought him back to Jerusalem to his kingdom. Manasseh realised then that Yahweh is God.

14 Afterwards, he rebuilt the outer wall of the City of David, to the west of Gihon, in the valley, up to the Fish Gate and round the Ophel, and made it very much higher. And he stationed military governors in all the fortified towns of Judah.

15 He also removed the foreign gods and the idol from the Temple of Yahweh, as well as all the altars which he had built on the mountain of the Temple of Yahweh and in Jerusalem,

and threw them out of the city. ¹⁶He repaired the altar of Yahweh and offered communion sacrifices and thanksgiving offerings on it, and commanded Judah to serve Yahweh, God of Israel. ¹⁷The people, however, went on sacrificing at the high places, although only to Yahweh their God.

¹⁸The rest of the history of Manasseh, his prayer to his God, and the prophecies of the seers who spoke to him in the name of Yahweh, God of Israel, can be found in the Annals of the Kings of Israel. ¹⁹His prayer and how God was moved by his entreaty, all his sins, his infidelity, the sites where he built high places and set up sacred poles and idols before humbling himself, are set down in the records of Hozai. ²⁰Then Manasseh fell asleep with his ancestors and was buried in the garden of his palace. His son Amon succeeded him.

The obduracy of Amon

²¹Amon was twenty-two years old when he came to the throne, and he reigned for two years in Jerusalem. ²²He did what is displeasing to Yahweh, as his father Manasseh had done, for Amon sacrificed to all the images which his father Manasseh had made, and served them. ²³He did not humble himself before Yahweh as his father Manasseh had done; on the contrary, Amon wilfully added to his guilt. ²⁴His retinue plotted against him and killed him in his own palace. ²⁵The people of the country, however, slaughtered all those who had plotted against King Amon and proclaimed his son Josiah as his successor.

Accession of Josiah

34 Josiah was eight years old when he came to the throne, and he reigned for thirty-one years in Jerusalem. ²He did what is pleasing to Yahweh, and followed the example of his ancestor David, not deviating from it to right or to left.

The first reforms

³In the eighth year of his reign, when he was still a youth, he began to seek the God of his ancestor David. In the twelfth year he began to purge Judah and Jerusalem of the high places, the sacred poles and the sculpted and cast images. ⁴He superintended the smashing of the altars of Baal, he broke up the incense altars standing above them, he shattered the sacred poles and the sculpted and cast images and reduced them to powder, scattering the powder on the graves of those who had sacrificed to them. ⁵He burned the bones of their priests on their altars and so purified Judah and Jerusalem. ⁶In the towns of Manasseh, Ephraim and Simeon, as far as Naphtali, and round their open spaces, ⁷he smashed the altars and sacred poles, reduced the sculpted images to powder and broke up all the incense altars throughout the territory of Israel. Then he returned to Jerusalem.

Work on the Temple

⁸In the eighteenth year of his reign, after purging the country and the Temple, he commissioned Shaphan son of Azaliah, Maaseiah governor of the city and the herald Joah son of Joahaz, to repair the Temple of Yahweh his God. ⁹When they came to the high priest Hilkiah, they handed over the money contributed to the Temple of God and collected by the levitical guardians of the threshold from Manasseh and Ephraim, from all the rest of Israel, from all Judah and Benjamin, and from the inhabitants of Jerusalem. ¹⁰They handed it over to the masters of works attached to the Temple of Yahweh, and these gave it to the men working on the Temple of Yahweh to repair and restore the Temple; ¹¹they gave it to the craftsmen and builders for buying dressed stone and timber for beams, to underpin the buildings which the kings of Judah had allowed to fall into decay.

¹²The men were conscientious in doing their work; their foremen were Jahath and Obadiah, Levites descended from Merari, and Zechariah and Meshullam, descended from Kohath, who supervised. The Levites—all of whom were skilled instrumentalists—¹³were in charge of the carriers and supervised all the

workmen at their various jobs, while some of the Levites acted as secretaries, book-keepers and gatekeepers.

The Book of the Law discovered

¹⁴While bringing out the money contributed to the Temple of Yahweh, the priest Hilkiah found the book of the Law of Yahweh given through Moses. ¹⁵Hilkiah then said to Shaphan the secretary, 'I have found the Book of the Law in the Temple of Yahweh.' And Hilkiah gave the book to Shaphan. ¹⁶Shaphan took the book to the king, reporting furthermore to him as follows, 'Your servants have done everything entrusted to them. ¹⁷They have melted down the silver which was in the Temple of Yahweh and have handed it over to the supervisors and the masters of works.' ¹⁸Shaphan the secretary also informed the king, 'The priest Hilkiah has given me a book'; and Shaphan read extracts from it in the king's presence.

¹⁹On hearing the words of the Law, the king tore his clothes. ²⁰Then the king gave the following order to Hilkiah, Ahikam son of Shaphan, Abdon son of Micah, Shaphan the secretary and Asaiah the king's minister, ²¹'Go and consult Yahweh on behalf of me and of those left in Israel and Judah about the words of the book that has been discovered: for Yahweh's furious wrath has been pouring down on us because our ancestors did not obey the word of Yahweh by doing what this book says they ought to have done.'

Huldah the prophetess is consulted

²²Hilkiah and those whom the king had designated went to the prophetess Huldah wife of Shallum, son of Tokhath, son of Hasrah, the keeper of the wardrobe; she lived in Jerusalem in the new town. They spoke to her about this, ²³and she replied, 'Yahweh, God of Israel, says this, "To the man who sent you to me reply: ²⁴Yahweh says this: I am going to bring disaster on this place and the people who live in it—all the curses set down in the book read in

the king of Judah's presence. ²⁵Because they have abandoned me and burnt incense to other gods, so as to provoke my anger by their every action, my wrath is about to be poured down on this place, and nothing can stop it. ²⁶As for the king of Judah who sent you to consult Yahweh, say this to him: Yahweh, God of Israel, says this: The words you have heard . . . ²⁷But since your heart has been touched and you have humbled yourself before God on hearing what he has decreed against this place and the people who live in it, have torn your clothes and wept before me, I too have heard"—Yahweh says this. ²⁸"Look, when I gather you to your ancestors, you will be gathered into your grave in peace; you will not live to see the great disaster that I am going to bring on this place and on the people who live in it."' They took this answer to the king.

The renewal of the covenant

²⁹The king then had all the elders of Judah and of Jerusalem summoned, ³⁰and the king went up to the temple of Yahweh, with all the men of Judah and all the inhabitants of Jerusalem, priests, Levites and all the people, high and low. In their hearing he read out the entire contents of the Book of the Covenant discovered in the Temple of Yahweh. ³¹The king then, standing on the dais, bound himself by the covenant before Yahweh, to follow Yahweh, to keep his commandments, decrees and laws with all his heart and soul and to carry out the terms of the covenant as written in this book. ³²He made all those present in Jerusalem and Benjamin pledge their allegiance to it.

The citizens of Jerusalem took action in keeping with the covenant of God, the God of their ancestors, ³³while Josiah removed all the abominations throughout the territories belonging to the Israelites and required all inhabitants of Israel to serve Yahweh their God; throughout his lifetime they did not deviate from following Yahweh, God of their ancestors.

Preparations for the Passover

35 Josiah then celebrated a Passover to Yahweh in Jerusalem. The Passover victims were slaughtered on the fourteenth day of the first month.

²He assigned the priests to their posts, encouraging them to do their duty in the Temple of Yahweh. ³Then he said to the Levites, who had understanding for all Israel and were consecrated to Yahweh, 'Put the sacred ark in the Temple built by Solomon son of David, king of Israel. You need not carry it about on your shoulders any more. Now serve Yahweh your God and Israel his people! ⁴Prepare yourselves by families according to your orders, as laid down in the decree of David king of Israel and that of Solomon his son, ⁵and take up positions in the sanctuary corresponding to the family divisions of your brothers the laity, so that there are Levites for each family division. ⁶Slaughter the Passover, sanctify yourselves and prepare it so that your brothers can observe it in the way the word of Yahweh through Moses requires.'

⁷For the laity Josiah provided small livestock, that is, lambs and young goats—everything for the Passover offerings for all who attended—to the number of thirty thousand, as well as three thousand bullocks; these were from the king's own possessions. ⁸His officials also made voluntary contributions for the people, the priests and the Levites; and Hilkiah, Zechariah and Jehiel, the chiefs of the Temple of God, gave two thousand six hundred lambs and three hundred bullocks to the priests for the Passover offerings; ⁹while Conaniah, Shemaiah, Nethanel his brother, Hashabiah, Jeiel and Jozabad, the head Levites, provided five thousand lambs and five hundred bullocks as Passover offerings for the Levites.

The celebration of the Passover

¹⁰So the service was arranged, the priests stood in their places and the Levites in their orders as the king had commanded. ¹¹Then they slaughtered the Passover victims and while the priests sprinkled the blood as they received it from the Levites, the latter did the skinning. ¹²Next they put the burnt offering aside for presentation to the family divisions of the laity, so that they could offer it to Yahweh in the way prescribed in the Book of Moses; they did the same with the bullocks. ¹³They roasted the Passover victim over an open fire in accordance with the regulation and boiled the consecrated offerings in pots, kettles and pans, which they then distributed to all the laity as quickly as they could.

¹⁴Afterwards they provided for themselves and the priests, since the Aaronite priests were kept busy till nightfall making the burnt offerings and offering the fat; that was why the Levites prepared the Passover for themselves and for the Aaronite priests. ¹⁵The Asaphite singers were at their places, in accordance with the command of David and Asaph, Heman and Jeduthun the king's seer; so were the gatekeepers at each gate. Because they could not leave their duties, their brothers the Levites prepared the Passover for them.

¹⁶So the whole service of Yahweh was arranged that day to celebrate the Passover and to bring burnt offerings on the altar of Yahweh, in accordance with King Josiah's command. ¹⁷On that occasion the Israelites who were present celebrated the Passover and the feast of Unleavened Bread for seven days. ¹⁸No Passover like this one had ever been celebrated in Israel since the days of the prophet Samuel, nor had any of the kings of Israel ever celebrated a Passover like the one celebrated by Josiah, the priests, the Levites, all Judah and Israel who were present, and the inhabitants of Jerusalem.

Death of Josiah

¹⁹This Passover was celebrated in the eighteenth year of Josiah's reign.

²⁰After all this, when Josiah had provided for the Temple, Necho king of Egypt advanced to give battle at Carchemish on the Euphrates and Josiah went to intercept him. ²¹Necho however sent him messengers to say,

'Why be concerned about me, king of Judah? I have not come today to attack you; my quarrel is with another dynasty. God has commanded me to move quickly, so keep well clear of the god who is with me!' 22 But Josiah was not to be deflected from his determination to fight him, and would not listen to Necho's words, which came from the mouth of God. He gave battle in the plain of Megiddo. 23 The archers shot King Josiah. The king then said to his retainers, 'Take me away; I am badly wounded.' 24 So his retainers lifted him out of his own chariot, transferred him to one which he had in reserve and brought him to Jerusalem, where he died and was buried in the tombs of his ancestors. All Judah and Jerusalem held mourning for Josiah. 25 Jeremiah composed a lament for Josiah and all the male and female singers to this day lament Josiah in their dirges; they have made it a rule in Israel; they are recorded in the Lamentations.

26 The rest of the history of Josiah, his deeds of faithful love conforming to what is prescribed in the Law of Yahweh, 27 his history from first to last, are recorded in the Book of the Kings of Israel and Judah.

Jehoahaz

36 The people of the land then took Jehoahaz son of Josiah and proclaimed him king of Jerusalem in succession to his father. 2 Jehoahaz was twenty-three years old when he came to the throne, and he reigned for three months in Jerusalem. 3 The king of Egypt deposed him in Jerusalem and imposed a levy of a hundred talents of silver and one talent of gold on the country. 4 The king of Egypt then made his brother Eliakim king of Judah and Jerusalem, and changed his name to Jehoiakim. Carrying off his brother Jehoahaz, Necho took him to Egypt.

Jehoiakim

5 Jehoiakim was twenty-five years old when he came to the throne, and he reigned for eleven years in Jerusalem. He did what is displeasing to Yahweh his God. 6 Nebuchadnezzar king of Babylon attacked him, loaded him with chains and took him to Babylon. 7 To Babylon Nebuchadnezzar also took some of the objects belonging to the Temple of Yahweh and put them in his palace in Babylon. 8 The rest of the history of Jehoiakim, the shameful things that he did and what happened to him in consequence, these are recorded in the Book of the Kings of Israel and Judah. His son Jehoiachin succeeded him.

Jehoiachin

9 Jehoiachin was eighteen years old when he came to the throne, and he reigned for three months and ten days in Jerusalem. He did what is displeasing to Yahweh. 10 At the turn of the year, King Nebuchadnezzar sent for him and had him taken to Babylon, with the valuables belonging to the Temple of Yahweh, and made his brother Zedekiah king of Judah and Jerusalem.

Zedekiah

11 Zedekiah was twenty-one years old when he came to the throne, and he reigned for eleven years in Jerusalem. 12 He did what is displeasing to Yahweh his God. He did not listen humbly to the prophet Jeremiah who spoke for Yahweh. 13 Furthermore, he rebelled against King Nebuchadnezzar who had made him swear allegiance to him by God. He became stubborn, and obstinately refused to return to Yahweh, God of Israel.

The nation

14 Furthermore, all the leaders of Judah, the priests and the people too, added infidelity to infidelity, copying all the shameful practices of the nations and defiling the Temple of Yahweh which he himself had consecrated in Jerusalem. 15 Yahweh, God of their ancestors, continuously sent them word through his messengers because he felt sorry for his people and his dwelling, 16 but they ridiculed the messengers of God, they despised his words, they laughed at his prophets, until Yahweh's wrath

with his people became so fierce that there was no further remedy.

Ruin

17 So against them he summoned the king of the Chaldaeans and he put their young men to the sword within the very building of their Temple, not sparing young man or girl, or the old and infirm; he put them all at his mercy. 18 All the things belonging to the Temple of God, whether large or small, the treasures of the Temple of Yahweh, the treasures of the king and his officials, everything he took to Babylon. 19 He burned down the temple of God, demolished the walls of Jerusalem, burned all its palaces to the ground and destroyed everything of value in it. 20 And those who had escaped the sword he deported to Babylon, where they were enslaved by him and his descendants until the rise of the king-dom of Persia, 21 to fulfil Yahweh's prophecy through Jeremiah: *Until the country has paid off its Sabbaths, it will lie fallow for all the days of its desolation—until the seventy years are complete.*[a]

A new hope

22 In the first year of Cyrus king of Persia—to fulfil the word of Yahweh through Jere-miah—Yahweh roused the spirit of Cyrus king of Persia to issue a proclamation and to have it publicly displayed throughout his kingdom: 23 'Cyrus king of Persia says this, "Yahweh, the God of Heaven, has given me all the kingdoms of the earth and has appointed me to build him a Temple in Jerusalem, which is in Judah. Whoever there is among you of all his people, may his God be with him! Let him go up."'

36a A combination of Lv 26:34–35 and Jr 25:11; 29:10.

The Book of

EZRA

The return of the exiles

1 In the first year of Cyrus king of Persia—
to fulfil the word of Yahweh spoken
through Jeremiah[a]—Yahweh roused the
spirit of Cyrus king of Persia to issue a proclamation and to have it publicly displayed
throughout his kingdom:

2 'Cyrus king of Persia says this, "Yahweh,
the God of heaven, has given me all the
kingdoms of the earth and has appointed
me to build him a Temple in Jerusalem, in
Judah. 3 Whoever among you belongs to the
full tally of his people, may his God be with
him! Let him go up to Jerusalem, in Judah,
and build the Temple of Yahweh, God of
Israel, who is the God in Jerusalem. 4 And
let each survivor, wherever he lives, be
helped by the people of his locality with silver, gold, equipment and riding beasts, as
well as voluntary offerings for the Temple
of God which is in Jerusalem." '

5 Then the heads of families of Judah and of
Benjamin, the priests and the Levites, in fact
all whose spirit had been roused by God, prepared to go and rebuild the Temple of Yahweh in Jerusalem; 6 and all their neighbours
gave them every kind of help: silver, gold,
equipment, riding beasts and valuable presents, in addition to their voluntary offerings.
7 Furthermore, King Cyrus handed over
the articles belonging to the Temple of Yahweh which Nebuchadnezzar had carried
away from Jerusalem and put in the temple of
his god. 8 Cyrus king of Persia handed them
over to Mithredath the treasurer who checked
them out to Sheshbazzar the prince of Judah.
9 The inventory was as follows: thirty gold

dishes; one thousand silver dishes, twenty-
nine repaired; 10 thirty gold bowls; a thousand
silver bowls, four hundred and ten damaged;
one thousand other articles. 11 In all, five thousand four hundred articles of gold and silver.
Sheshbazzar took all these with him when he
led the exiles back from Babylon to Jerusalem.

List of the first exiles to return

2 These were the people of the province who
returned[a] from the captivity of the Exile,
those whom Nebuchadnezzar king of Babylon had deported to Babylon, and who returned to Jerusalem and Judah, each to his
own town. 2 They were the ones who arrived
with Zerubbabel, Jeshua, Nehemiah, Seraiah,
Reelaiah, Nahamani, Mordecai, Bilshan, Mis-
par, Bigvai, Rehum and Baanah.

The number of the men of the people of the
country of Israel: 3 sons of Parosh, two thousand one hundred and seventy-two; 4 sons of
Shephatiah, three hundred and seventy-two;
5 sons of Arah, seven hundred and seventy-
five; 6 sons of Pahath-Moab, that is to say the
sons of Jeshua and Joab, two thousand eight
hundred and twelve; 7 sons of Elam, one thousand two hundred and fifty-four; 8 sons of
Zattu, nine hundred and forty-five; 9 sons
of Zaccai, seven hundred and sixty; 10 sons of
Bani, six hundred and forty-two; 11 sons of
Bebai, six hundred and twenty-three; 12 sons
of Azgad, one thousand two hundred and
twenty-two; 13 sons of Adonikam, six hundred
and sixty-six; 14 sons of Bigvai, two thousand
and fifty-six; 15 sons of Adin, four hundred
and fifty-four; 16 sons of Ater, that is to say of
Hezekiah, ninety-eight; 17 sons of Bezai, three

1a Jr 25:11–12; 29:10.   2a ‖ Ne 7:6–72.

hundred and twenty-three; ¹⁸sons of Jorah, one hundred and twelve; ¹⁹sons of Hashum, two hundred and twenty-three; ²⁰sons of Gibbar, ninety-five; ²¹sons of Bethlehem, one hundred and twenty-three; ²²men of Netophah, fifty-six; ²³men of Anathoth, one hundred and twenty-eight; ²⁴sons of Azmaveth, forty-two; ²⁵sons of Kiriath-Jearim, Chephirah and Beeroth, seven hundred and forty-three; ²⁶sons of Ramah and Geba, six hundred and twenty-one; ²⁷men of Michmas, one hundred and twenty-two; ²⁸men of Bethel and Ai, two hundred and twenty-three; ²⁹sons of Nebo, fifty-two; ³⁰of Magbish, one hundred and fifty-six; ³¹sons of the other Elam, one thousand two hundred and fifty-four; ³²sons of Harim, three hundred and twenty; ³³sons of Lod, Hadid and Ono, seven hundred and twenty-five; ³⁴sons of Jericho, three hundred and forty-five; ³⁵sons of Senaah, three thousand six hundred and thirty.

³⁶The priests: sons of Jedaiah, of the House of Jeshua, nine hundred and seventy-three; ³⁷sons of Immer, one thousand and fifty-two; ³⁸sons of Pashhur, one thousand two hundred and forty-seven; ³⁹sons of Harim, one thousand and seventeen.

⁴⁰The Levites: sons of Jeshua and Kadmiel, of the line of Hodaviah, seventy-four.

⁴¹The singers: sons of Asaph, one hundred and twenty-eight.

⁴²The sons of the gatekeepers: sons of Shallum, sons of Ater, sons of Talmon, sons of Akkub, sons of Hatita, sons of Shobai: in all, one hundred and thirty-nine.

⁴³The temple slaves: sons of Ziha, sons of Hasupha, sons of Tabbaoth, ⁴⁴sons of Keros, sons of Siaha, sons of Padon, ⁴⁵sons of Lebanah, sons of Hagabah, sons of Akkub, ⁴⁶sons of Hagab, sons of Shamlai, sons of Hanan, ⁴⁷sons of Giddel, sons of Gahar, sons of Reaiah, ⁴⁸sons of Rezin, sons of Nekoda, sons of Gazzam, ⁴⁹sons of Uzza, sons of Paseah, sons of Besai, ⁵⁰sons of Asnah, sons of the Meunites, sons of the Nephisites, ⁵¹sons of Bakbuk, sons of Hakupha, sons of Harhur, ⁵²sons of Bazluth, sons of Mehida, sons of

Harsha, ⁵³sons of Barkos, sons of Sisera, sons of Temah, ⁵⁴sons of Neziah, sons of Hatipha.

⁵⁵The sons of Solomon's slaves: sons of Sotai, sons of Hassophereth, sons of Peruda, ⁵⁶sons of Jaalah, sons of Darkon, sons of Giddel, ⁵⁷sons of Shephatiah, sons of Hattil, sons of Pochereth-ha-Zebaim, sons of Ami. ⁵⁸The total of the temple slaves and the sons of Solomon's slaves: three hundred and ninety-two.

⁵⁹The following, who came from Tel-Melah, Tel-Harsha, Cherub, Addan and Immer, could not prove that their families and ancestry were of Israelite origin: ⁶⁰the sons of Delaiah, the sons of Tobiah, the sons of Nekoda: six hundred and fifty-two. ⁶¹And among the sons of the priests: the sons of Habaiah, the sons of Hakkoz, the sons of Barzillai—who had married one of the daughters of Barzillai the Gileadite, whose name he adopted. ⁶²These had looked for their entries in the official genealogies but were not to be found there, and were hence disqualified from the priesthood. ⁶³Consequently, His Excellency forbade them to eat any of the consecrated food until a priest appeared who could consult *urim* and *thummim*.

⁶⁴The whole assembly numbered forty-two thousand, three hundred and sixty people, ⁶⁵not counting their male and female slaves to the number of seven thousand three hundred and thirty-seven. They also had two hundred male and female singers. ⁶⁶Their horses numbered seven hundred and thirty-six, their mules two hundred and forty-five, ⁶⁷their camels four hundred and thirty-five and their donkeys six thousand seven hundred and twenty.

⁶⁸When they arrived at the Temple of Yahweh in Jerusalem, a certain number of heads of families made voluntary offerings for the Temple of God, for its rebuilding on its site. ⁶⁹In accordance with their means they gave sixty-one thousand gold drachmas, five thousand silver minas and one hundred priestly robes to the sacred treasury.

⁷⁰The priests, the Levites and some of the

people settled in Jerusalem; the singers, the gatekeepers and the temple slaves in their appropriate towns; and all the other Israelites in their own towns.

Resumption of the sacrificial liturgy

3 When the seventh month came after the Israelites had been resettled in their towns, the people gathered as one person in Jerusalem. [2] Then Jeshua son of Jozadak, with his brother priests, and Zerubbabel son of Shealtiel, with his brothers, set about rebuilding the altar of the God of Israel, to offer burnt offerings on it as prescribed in the Law of Moses man of God. [3] They erected the altar on its old site, despite their fear of the people of the country, and on it they presented burnt offerings to Yahweh, burnt offerings morning and evening; [4] they celebrated the feast of Shelters as prescribed,[a] offering daily the number of burnt offerings required from day to day, [5] and in addition presented the continual burnt offerings prescribed for the Sabbaths, for the New Moons and for all the festivals sacred to Yahweh, as well as those voluntary offerings made by individuals to Yahweh. [6] From the first day of the seventh month they began presenting burnt offerings to Yahweh, though the foundations of the Temple of Yahweh had not yet been laid.

[7] They also contributed money for the masons and carpenters, and food, drink and oil for the Sidonians and Tyrians for bringing cedar wood from Lebanon by sea to Jaffa, for which Cyrus king of Persia had given permission. [8] It was in the second month of the second year after their arrival at the Temple of God in Jerusalem that Zerubbabel son of Shealtiel and Jeshua son of Jozadak, with the rest of their brothers, the priests, the Levites and all the people who had returned to Jerusalem from captivity, began the work by appointing some of the Levites who were twenty years old or more to superintend the work on the Temple of Yahweh. [9] The Levites, Jeshua, his sons and his brothers, with Kadmiel, Binnui and his sons, the sons of Hodaviah, agreed to su-

perintend the men working on the Temple of God. [10] When the builders had laid the foundations of the Temple of Yahweh, the priests in their robes stood forward with trumpets, and the Levites, the sons of Asaph, with cymbals, to praise Yahweh according to the ordinances of David king of Israel. [11] They chanted praise and thanksgiving to Yahweh because for Israel, they said, 'he is good, and everlasting in his faithful love.' Then all the people raised a mighty shout of praise to Yahweh, since the foundations of the Temple of Yahweh had now been laid. [12] Many of the older priests, Levites and heads of families, who had seen the first temple, wept very loudly when the foundations of this one were laid before their eyes, but many others shouted aloud for joy, [13] so that nobody could distinguish the noise of the joyful shout from the noise of the people's weeping; for the people shouted so loudly that the noise could be heard far away.

Opposition from the Samaritans: their tactics under Cyrus

4 When the enemies of Judah and Benjamin heard that the exiles were building the Temple of Yahweh, God of Israel, [2] they came to Zerubbabel and Jeshua and the heads of families and said, 'Let us help you build, for we resort to your God as you do and we have been sacrificing to him since the time of Esarhaddon king of Assyria, who brought us here.' [3] Zerubbabel, Jeshua, and the other heads of Israelite families replied, 'It is out of the question that you should join us in building a Temple for our God. We shall build for Yahweh, God of Israel, on our own, as King Cyrus king of Persia has commanded us.' [4] The people of the country then set about demoralising the people of Judah and deterring them from building; [5] they also bribed counsellors against them to frustrate their purpose throughout the lifetime of Cyrus king of Persia right on into the reign of Darius king of Persia.

3a Ex 23:14.

*Samaritan tactics under Xerxes and
Artaxerxes*[a]

⁶In the reign of Xerxes, at the beginning of his
reign, they drew up an accusation against the
inhabitants of Judah and Jerusalem.

⁷In the days of Artaxerxes, Mithredath,
Tabeel and their other associates wrote to
Artaxerxes king of Persia against Jerusalem;
the text of the letter was written in Aramaic
writing and dialect.

⁸Then Rehum the governor and Shimshai
the secretary wrote a letter to King Artaxerxes, denouncing Jerusalem as follows:

⁹'From Rehum the governor and Shimshai
the secretary and their other associates, the
judges, the legates, the Persian officials, the
people of Uruk, Babylon and Susa—that is,
the Elamites— ¹⁰and the other peoples
whom the great and illustrious Ashurbani-
pal deported and settled in the towns of
Samaria and in the rest of Transeuphrates.'

¹¹This is the text of the letter which they sent
him:

'To King Artaxerxes, from your servants
the people of Transeuphrates:
¹²'May the king now please be informed
that the Jews, who have come up from you
to us, have arrived in Jerusalem and are rebuilding the rebellious and evil city; they
have begun rebuilding the walls and are
laying the foundations; ¹³and now the king
should be informed that once this city is rebuilt and the walls are restored, they will
refuse to pay tribute, tax or toll, thus the
king will incur a loss; ¹⁴and now, because
we eat the palace salt, it is not proper for us
to see this affront offered to the king; we
therefore send this information to the king
¹⁵so that a search may be made in the
archives of your ancestors: in which
archives you will find and learn that this
city is a rebellious city, the bane of kings and
provinces, and that sedition has been stirred
up there from ancient times; that is why this

city was destroyed. ¹⁶We inform the king
that if this city is rebuilt and its walls are restored, you will soon have no territories left
in Transeuphrates.'

¹⁷The king sent this reply:

'To Rehum the governor, to Shimshai the
secretary, and to their other associates resident in Samaria and elsewhere in Transeuphrates: Greetings!
¹⁸'And now, the document which you
sent us has been accurately translated for
me, ¹⁹and by my orders search has been
made, and it has been found that this city
has rebelled against the kings in the past
and that revolt and sedition have been contrived in it; ²⁰and that powerful kings have
reigned in Jerusalem, governing the whole
of Transeuphrates and exacting tribute, tax
and toll; ²¹now give orders for these men to
cease work; this city is not to be rebuilt until
I give the order. ²²Beware of acting negligently in this matter. Why should the harm
grow, to endanger the king?'

²³As soon as the text of King Artaxerxes'
document had been read to Rehum the governor, Shimshai the secretary and their associates, they hurried to the Jews in Jerusalem and
stopped their work by force of arms.

The rebuilding of the Temple (520–515 BC)

²⁴Work on the Temple of God in Jerusalem
then ceased, and was discontinued until the
second year of the reign of Darius King of
Persia.

5 When the prophets Haggai and Zechariah
son of Iddo prophesied to the Jews who
were in Judah and Jerusalem in the name of
the God of Israel who was over them, ²Zerub-
babel son of Shealtiel and Jeshua son of
Jozadak began rebuilding the Temple of God
in Jerusalem; with them were the prophets of
God, supporting them.

4a The passage 4:6–6:18 is written in Aramaic.

³It was then that Tattenai governor of Transeuphrates, Shethar-Bozenai and their associates came to them and asked, 'Who gave you the order to rebuild this Temple and complete this structure? ⁴What are the names of the men putting up this building?' ⁵But the eyes of their God were watching over the elders of the Jews, so they were not forced to stop until a report could reach Darius and an official reply about the matter could be received from him.

The governor's letter to King Darius

⁶A copy of the letter which Tattenai, governor of Transeuphrates, Shethar-Bozenai and his associates, the officials in Transeuphrates, sent to King Darius. ⁷They sent him a report which ran as follows:

'To King Darius, hearty greetings!

⁸'The king should be informed that we went to the province of Judah, to the Temple of the great God, which is being rebuilt with large stones; beams are being embedded in the walls; the work is being carried out energetically and is making good progress. ⁹Questioning these elders, we asked them, "Who gave you permission to rebuild this Temple and complete this structure?" ¹⁰We also asked them their names, to inform you, so that we could record the names of the men who were their leaders.

¹¹'They gave us the following answer, "We are the servants of the God of heaven and earth; we are rebuilding the Temple built many years ago, which a great king of Israel had built and completed. ¹²But because our ancestors angered the God of heaven, he handed them over to Nebuchadnezzar the Chaldaean king of Babylon who destroyed this Temple and deported the people to Babylon. ¹³In the first year of Cyrus king of Babylon, however, King Cyrus issued an official order that this Temple of God should be rebuilt; ¹⁴furthermore, those gold and silver articles be-

longing to the Temple of God, which Nebuchadnezzar had removed from the temple in Jerusalem and brought to the temple of Babylon, King Cyrus in turn removed from the temple of Babylon and handed back to a certain Sheshbazzar whom he had appointed governor. ¹⁵He said to him, 'Take these articles; go and return them to the Temple which is in Jerusalem and let the Temple of God be rebuilt on its original site;' ¹⁶this Sheshbazzar then came and laid the foundations of the Temple of God in Jerusalem, and it has been under construction ever since, and is not yet finished."

¹⁷'Hence, if it please the king, let search be made in the royal treasuries in Babylon, to find out if it is true that an official order was issued by King Cyrus for this temple of God in Jerusalem to be rebuilt; and let the king's decision on this matter be sent to us.'

King Darius replies

6 Then, on the order of King Darius, search was made in the archives deposited in the treasuries in Babylon ²and a scroll was found in the fortress of Ecbatana, which ran as follows:

'Memorandum.

³'In the first year of King Cyrus, King Cyrus issued this order:

"Temple of God in Jerusalem.

"The Temple is to be rebuilt as a place of offering sacrifice and its foundations retained. Its height is to be sixty cubits, its width sixty cubits, ⁴with three layers of large stones and one layer of timber. The cost is to be met by the royal treasury. ⁵Furthermore, the gold and silver articles belonging to the Temple of God which Nebuchadnezzar took from the Temple in Jerusalem and brought to Babylon are to be given back and returned to the temple in Jerusalem, each to its proper place, and deposited in the Temple of God."

⁶'Hence, Tattenai governor of Transeuphrates, Shethar-Bozenai and your asso-

ciates, the officials of Transeuphrates, keep away from there! ⁷Leave the governor of the Jews and the elders of the Jews alone, to get on with their work on that Temple of God; they are permitted to rebuild that Temple of God on that site. ⁸And herewith are my instructions as to how you will assist these elders of the Jews in the rebuilding of that Temple of God: the cost is to be paid in full to these men from the royal revenue, that is, from the taxes of Transeuphrates, and without interruption. ⁹And whatever is required—young bulls, rams, lambs for burnt offerings to the God of heaven, wheat, salt, wine, oil, as the priests in Jerusalem request—is to be given them day by day without fail, ¹⁰so that they may offer sacrifices acceptable to the God of heaven and pray for the life of the king and his sons. ¹¹Furthermore I have issued an instruction that if anyone disobeys this order, a beam is to be torn from his house, he is to be impaled on it and his house is to be reduced to a rubbish-heap for his offence; ¹²and may the God who has caused his name to live there overthrow the king of any people who dares to defy this and destroy that Temple of God in Jerusalem! I, Darius, have issued this order. Let it be punctiliously obeyed!'

The Temple is completed

¹³Tattenai governor of Transeuphrates, Shethar-Bozenai and their associates punctiliously obeyed the instructions sent by King Darius; ¹⁴and the elders of the Jews made good progress over their building, thanks to the prophetic activity of the prophet Haggai and Zechariah son of Iddo, completing the reconstruction in accordance with the command of the God of Israel and the order of Cyrus and of Darius. ¹⁵This Temple was completed on the twenty-third day of the month of Adar, in the sixth year of the reign of King Darius. ¹⁶The Israelites—the priests, the Levites and the remainder of the exiles—joyfully celebrated the dedication of this Temple of God;

¹⁷for the dedication of this Temple of God they offered one hundred bulls, two hundred rams, four hundred lambs and, as a sin offering for all Israel, twelve he-goats, corresponding to the number of the tribes of Israel. ¹⁸Then they installed the priests in their orders and the Levites in their positions for the ministry of the Temple of God in Jerusalem, as prescribed in the Book of Moses.

The Passover of 515 BC

¹⁹The exiles celebrated the Passover on the fourteenth day of the first month. ²⁰The Levites, as one man, had purified themselves; all were pure, so they sacrificed the Passover for all the exiles, for their brothers the priests and for themselves. ²¹So the Israelites who had returned from exile and all those who had renounced the filthy practices of the people of the country to join them in resorting to Yahweh, God of Israel, ate the Passover. ²²For seven days they joyfully celebrated the feast of Unleavened Bread, for Yahweh had given them cause to rejoice, having moved the heart of the king of Assyria in their favour to support them in their work on the Temple of God, the God of Israel.

The mission and personality of Ezra

7 After these events, in the reign of Artaxerxes king of Persia, Ezra son of Seraiah, son of Azariah, son of Hilkiah, ²son of Shallum, son of Zadok, son of Ahitub, ³son of Amariah, son of Azariah, son of Meraioth, ⁴son of Zerahiah, son of Uzzi, son of Bukki, ⁵son of Abishua, son of Phinehas, son of Eleazar, son of the chief priest Aaron— ⁶this Ezra came up from Babylon. He was a scribe versed in the Law of Moses, which Yahweh, God of Israel, had given. The king gave him everything that he asked for, since the hand of Yahweh his God was over him. ⁷A number of Israelites, priests, Levites, singers, gatekeepers and temple slaves went up to Jerusalem in the seventh year of the reign of King Artaxerxes. ⁸Ezra arrived in Jerusalem in the fifth month, in the seventh year of the king's reign; ⁹for he

had ordered the departure from Babylon on the first day of the first month, and he arrived in Jerusalem on the first day of the fifth month, since the kindly hand of his God was over him. ¹⁰For Ezra had devoted himself to studying the Law of Yahweh so as to put into practice and teach its statutes and rulings.

The order of Artaxerxes

¹¹This is the text of the document which King Artaxerxes gave to Ezra, the priest-scribe, a student of matters pertaining to Yahweh's commandments and statutes relating to Israel:

¹²'Artaxerxes, king of kings, to the priest Ezra, Secretary of the Law of the God of heaven: greetings!

¹³'Now here are my orders. All members of the people of Israel in my kingdom, including their priests and Levites, who freely choose to go to Jerusalem, may go with you, ¹⁴for you are being sent by the king and his seven counsellors to investigate how the Law of your God, in which you are expert, is being applied in Judah and Jerusalem, ¹⁵and to transport the silver and gold which the king and his counsellors have voluntarily offered to the God of Israel who resides in Jerusalem, ¹⁶as well as all the silver and gold which you receive throughout the province of Babylon and the voluntary offerings freely contributed by the people and the priests for the Temple of their God in Jerusalem.

¹⁷'This money you will punctiliously use for the purchase of bulls, rams, lambs and the materials for the oblations and libations which go with them, offering these on the altar of the Temple of your God in Jerusalem, ¹⁸and using the remainder of the silver and gold in accordance with the will of your God as you and your brothers may think fit.

¹⁹'You will deliver the articles which have been given you for the ministry of the Temple of your God, to the God of Jerusalem, ²⁰and whatever else is needed and you are obliged to supply for the Temple of your God, you will supply from the royal treasury.

²¹'I, King Artaxerxes, have issued the following instruction to all the treasurers of Transeuphrates: Whatever the priest Ezra, Secretary of the Law of the God of heaven, may request of you is to be punctiliously complied with: ²²up to one hundred talents of silver, one hundred *kor* of wheat, one hundred *bat* of wine, one hundred *bat* of oil, and unlimited salt. ²³Whatever the God of heaven demands for the Temple of the God of heaven must be diligently provided; why should retribution come on the realm of the king and of his sons? ²⁴You are further informed that it is against the law to impose tribute, tax or toll on any of the priests, Levites, singers, gatekeepers, temple slaves or other servants of this temple of God.

²⁵'And you, Ezra, by virtue of the wisdom of your God, which you possess, are to appoint magistrates and scribes to administer justice for the whole people of Transeuphrates, that is, for all who know the Law of your God; and you are to teach it to those who do not know it. ²⁶And on anyone who will not comply with the Law of your God and the Law of the king let sentence be swiftly executed, whether it be death, banishment, fine or imprisonment.'

Ezra's journey from Babylonia to Palestine

²⁷Blessed be Yahweh, God of our ancestors, who moved the king's heart in this way to restore the beauty of the Temple of Yahweh in Jerusalem, ²⁸won for me the faithful love of the king, his counsellors and all the most powerful of the king's officials! Taking heart since the hand of Yahweh my God was over me, I assembled those Israelite heads of families who were to go with me.

8 These, with their genealogies, were the heads of families who set out from Babylon with me in the reign of King Artaxerxes:

2 Of the sons of Phinehas: Gershom; of the sons of Ithamar: Daniel; of the sons of David: Hattush ³son of Shechaniah; of the sons of Parosh: Zechariah, and with him a hundred and fifty males officially registered; ⁴of the sons of Pahath-Moab: Elioenai son of Zerahiah, and with him two hundred males; ⁵of the sons of Zattu: Shechaniah son of Jahaziel, and with him three hundred males; ⁶of the sons of Adin: Ebed son of Jonathan, and with him fifty males; ⁷of the sons of Elam: Jeshaiah son of Athaliah, and with him seventy males; ⁸of the sons of Shephatiah: Zebadiah son of Michael, and with him eighty males; ⁹of the sons of Joab: Obadiah son of Jehiel, and with him two hundred and eighteen males; ¹⁰of the sons of Bani: Shelomith son of Josiphiah, and with him a hundred and sixty males; ¹¹of the sons of Bebai: Zechariah son of Bebai, and with him twenty-eight males; ¹²of the sons of Azgad: Johanan son of Hakkatan, and with him a hundred and ten males; ¹³of the sons of Adonikam: the younger sons, whose names are: Eliphelet, Jeiel and Shemaiah, and with them sixty males; ¹⁴and of the sons of Bigvai: Uthai son of Zabud, and with him seventy males.

¹⁵I assembled them near the canal which runs to Ahava, where we camped for three days. I noticed laymen and priests, but I could not discover any Levites there. ¹⁶I then sent for Eliezer, Ariel, Shemaiah, Elnathan, Jarib, Elnathan, Nathan, Zechariah and Meshullam, judicious men, ¹⁷and sent them to Iddo, the leading man of a place called Casiphia; I told them what they were to say to Iddo and his kinsmen, living at the place called Casiphia, that is, to provide us with people to serve the Temple of our God. ¹⁸And because the hand of God was good to us, they sent us a wise man of the sons of Mahli son of Levi, son of Israel, a certain Sherebiah with his sons and kinsmen: eighteen men; ¹⁹also Hashabiah and with him his brother Jeshaiah of the sons of Merari with his kinsmen and sons: twenty men; ²⁰and two hundred and twenty temple slaves—descendants of the temple slaves whom David and the princes had assigned to serve the Levites— all of them designated by name.

²¹There, beside the Ahava Canal, I then proclaimed a fast, to humble ourselves before our God and to pray to him for a successful journey for us, our dependants and all our belongings. ²²For I should have been ashamed to ask the king for a company of cavalry to protect us from hostile people on our road, as we had already said to the king, 'The hand of our God is over all who seek him for their protection, but his mighty retribution befalls all those who forsake him.' ²³So we fasted and pleaded with our God about this, and he heard us.

²⁴I next chose twelve of the leading priests, and also Sherebiah and Hashabiah with ten of their kinsmen. ²⁵To them I weighed out the silver, the gold and the utensils, the contributions which the king, his counsellors, his notables and all the Israelites there present had made for the Temple of our God. ²⁶To them I weighed out and handed over six hundred and fifty talents of silver, one hundred utensils of silver valued at two talents, one hundred talents of gold, ²⁷twenty golden bowls valued at a thousand darics and two utensils of fine burnished copper as precious as gold. ²⁸I said to them, 'You are consecrated to Yahweh; these utensils are consecrated too; the silver and gold are a voluntary offering to Yahweh, God of your ancestors. ²⁹Guard them carefully until you weigh them out to the leading priests, the Levites, and the heads of families of Israel in Jerusalem in the rooms of the Temple of Yahweh.' ³⁰The priests and Levites then took charge of the silver, the gold and the utensils thus weighed, to bring them to Jerusalem to the Temple of our God.

³¹On the twelfth day of the first month we left the Ahava Canal to make our way to Jerusalem; the hand of our God was over us and protected us from enemies and surprise attacks on our way. ³²When we arrived in Jerusalem, we rested for three days. ³³On the fourth day the silver, the gold and the utensils were weighed in the Temple of our God and

handed over to the priest Meremoth son of Uriah and, with him, Eleazar son of Phinehas; with them were the Levites Jozabad son of Jeshua and Noadiah son of Binnui. ³⁴ By number and weight all was there. The total weight was recorded at the same time.

³⁵ When the exiles arrived from their captivity, they offered burnt offerings to the God of Israel—twelve bulls on behalf of all Israel, ninety-six rams, seventy-two lambs, and as a sin offering twelve he-goats: the whole of this as a burnt offering to Yahweh.

³⁶ They also delivered the king's instructions to the king's satraps and the governors of Transeuphrates, who then supported the people and the Temple of God.

The marriages with foreigners dissolved

9 Once this was done, the officials approached me to say, 'The people of Israel, the priests and the Levites, have not renounced the disgusting practices of the people of the country—the Canaanites, the Hittites, the Perizzites, the Jebusites, the Moabites, the Egyptians and the Amorites— ² since they and their sons have married some of their women, as a result of which the holy race has been contaminated by the people of the country. The officials and leaders have been the worst offenders in this act of infidelity.' ³ On hearing this, I tore my clothes and my cloak; I pulled hair from my head and beard and sat down in horror. ⁴ All who trembled at the words of the God of Israel gathered round me, when faced with the infidelity of the exiles, while I went on sitting there in horror until the evening sacrifice. ⁵ At the evening sacrifice I came out of my stupor and, falling on my knees in my torn clothes and cloak, stretched out my hands to Yahweh my God, ⁶ and said:

'My God, I am ashamed, I blush to lift my face to you, my God. For our iniquities have increased, until they are higher than our heads, and our guilt has risen as high as heaven. ⁷ From the days of our ancestors until now we have been deeply guilty and, because of our iniquities, we, our kings and our priests, have been handed over to the kings of other countries, to the sword, to captivity, to pillage, to shame, as is the case today. ⁸ And now, for a brief moment, the favour of Yahweh our God has allowed a remnant of us to escape and given us a stable home in his holy place, so that our God can raise our spirits and revive us a little in our slavery. ⁹ For we are slaves; but God has not forgotten us in our slavery; he has extended his faithful love to us even under the kings of Persia and revived us to rebuild the Temple of our God, restore its ruins and provide us with a refuge in Judah and in Jerusalem. ¹⁰ But now, our God, what can we say after this? For we have abandoned your commandments, ¹¹ which you gave through your servants the prophets in these terms, "The country which you are about to possess is a polluted country, polluted by the people of the country and their disgusting practices, which have filled it with their filth from end to end. ¹² Hence you are not to give your daughters in marriage to their sons, or let their daughters marry your sons, or ever concern yourselves about peace or good relations with them, if you want to grow stronger, to live off the fat of the land and bequeath it to your sons for ever."

¹³ 'After all that has befallen us because of our evil deeds and our deep guilt—though you, our God, have punished us less than our iniquities deserved and have allowed us to escape like this— ¹⁴ are we to break your commandments again and intermarry with people with these disgusting practices? Would you not be enraged with us to the point of destroying us, leaving neither remnant nor survivor? ¹⁵ Yahweh, God of Israel, you are upright. We survive only as the remnant we are today. We come before you in our guilt; because of it we cannot stand in your presence.'

10 While Ezra, weeping and prostrating himself in front of the Temple of God, was praying and making confession, a very large crowd of men, women and children of Israel gathered round him, the people weep-

ing bitterly. ²Then Shechaniah son of Jehiel, one of the sons of Elam, spoke up and said to Ezra, 'We have been unfaithful to our God by marrying foreign women from the people of the country. But, in spite of this, there is still some hope for Israel. ³We will make a covenant with our God to send away all the foreign wives and their children in obedience to the advice of my lord and of those who tremble at the commandment of our God. Let us act in accordance with the Law. ⁴Go ahead, do your duty; we support you. Be brave, take action!' ⁵Then Ezra stood up and put the leading priests and Levites and all Israel on oath to do what had been said. They took the oath. ⁶Ezra then left his place in front of the Temple of God and went to the room of Jehohanan son of Eliashib, where he spent the night without eating food or drinking water, because he was still mourning over the exiles' infidelity.

⁷A proclamation was issued throughout Judah and Jerusalem that all the exiles were to assemble in Jerusalem, ⁸and that anyone who failed within three days to answer the summons of the officials and elders was to forfeit all his possessions and himself be excluded from the community of the exiles. ⁹As a result, all the men of Judah and Benjamin assembled in Jerusalem within the three days; it was the twentieth day of the ninth month. All the people sat down in the square in front of the Temple of God, trembling because of the matter in hand and because of the heavy rain. ¹⁰The priest Ezra then stood up and said to them, 'You have been unfaithful and have married foreign wives, thus adding to Israel's guilt. ¹¹So now give thanks to Yahweh, God of your ancestors, and do his will by holding aloof from the people of the country and from foreign wives.' ¹²In ringing tones, the whole assembly answered, 'Yes, our duty is to do as you say. ¹³But there are many people here and it is the rainy season; we cannot stay out in the open; besides, this is not something that can be dealt with in one or two days, since many of us have been unfaithful over this. ¹⁴Let our offi-

cials deputise for the whole community, and all the people in our towns who have married foreign wives can come at stated times, accompanied by elders and judges from each town, until our God's fierce anger over this is turned away from us.' ¹⁵Only Jonathan son of Asahel and Jahzeiah son of Tikvah, supported by Meshullam and Shabbethai the Levite, were opposed to this. ¹⁶The exiles did as had been proposed. And the priest Ezra selected the family heads of the various families, all of them by name, who began their sittings on the first day of the tenth month to look into the matter. ¹⁷And by the first day of the first month they had dealt with all the men who had married foreign women.

The list of the guilty

¹⁸Among the priests who were found to have married foreign wives were:

of the sons of Jeshua son of Jozadak and his brothers: Maaseiah, Eliezer, Jarib and Gedaliah, ¹⁹who agreed to send their wives away; their guilt offering was a ram from the flock for their guilt;

²⁰of the sons of Immer: Hanani and Zebadiah;

²¹of the sons of Harim: Maaseiah, Elijah, Shemaiah, Jehiel and Uzziah;

²²of the sons of Pashhur: Elioenai, Maaseiah, Ishmael, Nethanel, Jozabad and Elasah;

²³of the Levites: Jozabad, Shimei, Kelaiah—that is, Kelita—Pethahiah, Judah, and Eliezer;

²⁴of the singers: Eliashib and Zaccur;

of the gatekeepers: Shallum, Telem and Uri;

²⁵and of the Israelites:

of the sons of Parosh: Ramiah, Izziah, Malchijah, Mijamin, Eleazar, Malchijah and Benaiah;

²⁶of the sons of Elam: Mattaniah, Zechariah, Jehiel, Abdi, Jeremoth and Elijah;

²⁷of the sons of Zattu: Elioenai, Eliashib, Mattaniah, Jeremoth, Zabad and Aziza;

²⁸of the sons of Bebai: Jehohanan, Hananiah, Zabbai, Atlai;

29 of the sons of Bigvai: Meshullam, Malluch, Jedaiah, Jashub, Sheal, Jeremoth;

30 of the sons of Pahath-Moab: Adna, Chelal, Benaiah, Maaseiah, Mattaniah, Bezalel, Binnui and Manasseh;

31 of the sons of Harim: Eliezer, Isshijah, Malchijah, Shemaiah, Shimeon, 32 Benjamin, Malluch, Shemariah;

33 of the sons of Hashum: Mattenai, Mattattah, Zabad, Eliphelet, Jeremai, Manasseh, Shimei;

34 of the sons of Bani: Maadai, Amram, Uel, 35 Benaiah, Bediah, Jeluhi, 36 Vaniah, Meremoth, Eliashib, 37 Mattaniah, Mattenai and Jaasau;

38 of the sons of Binnui: Shimei, 39 Shelemiah, Nathan and Adaiah;

40 of the sons of Zaccai: Shashai, Sharai, 41 Azarel, Shelemiah, Shemariah, 42 Shallum, Amariah, Joseph;

43 of the sons of Nebo: Jeiel, Mattithiah, Zabad, Zebina, Jaddai, Joel, Benaiah.

44 All these had married foreign wives but sent them away with their children.

The Book of

NEHEMIAH

Nehemiah's call: his mission to Judah

1 The words of Nehemiah son of Hacaliah.
It happened in the month of Chislev, in the
twentieth year, while I was in the citadel of
Susa, ²that Hanani, one of my brothers, arrived with some men from Judah. I asked
them about the Jews—those who had escaped
and those who survived from the captivity—
and about Jerusalem. ³They replied, 'The survivors remaining there in the province since
the captivity are in a very bad and demoralised
condition: the walls of Jerusalem are in ruins
and its gates have been burnt down.' ⁴On
hearing this I sat down and wept; for some
days I mourned, fasting and praying before
the God of heaven.

⁵I said, 'Yahweh, God of heaven—the great
and awe-inspiring God who keeps a covenant
of faithful love with those who love him and
obey his commandments— ⁶let your ear be attentive and your eyes open, to listen to your
servant's prayer, which I now offer to you day
and night on behalf of your servants the Israelites. I admit the sins of the Israelites, which
we have committed against you. Both I and my
father's House have sinned; ⁷we have acted
very wickedly towards you by not keeping the
commandments, laws and rulings which you
enjoined on your servant Moses.*ᵃ* ⁸Remember,
I beg you, the promise which you solemnly
made to your servant Moses, "If you are unfaithful, I shall scatter you among the peoples;
⁹but if you come back to me and keep my commandments and practise them, even though
those who have been banished are at the very
sky's end, I shall gather them from there and
bring them back to the place which I have chosen as a dwelling-place for my name." ¹⁰Since

they are your servants, your people, whom you
have redeemed with your mighty power and
strong hand, ¹¹O Lord, let your ear now be attentive to your servant's prayer and to the
prayer of your servants who want to revere
your name. I beg you let your servant be successful today and win this man's compassion.'

At the time I was cupbearer to the king.

2 In the month of Nisan, in the twentieth
year of King Artaxerxes, since I was in
charge of the wine, I took the wine and offered it to the king. Now, he had never seen
me looking depressed before. ²So the king
said to me, 'Why are you looking depressed?
You are not sick! This must be a sadness of the
heart.' Thoroughly alarmed by this, ³I said to
the king, 'May the king live for ever! How can
I not look depressed when the city where the
tombs of my ancestors are lies in ruins and its
gates have been burnt down?' ⁴The king then
said to me, 'What would you like me to do?'
Praying to the God of heaven, ⁵I said to the
king, 'If the king approves and your servant
enjoys your favour, send me to Judah, to the
city of the tombs of my ancestors, so that I can
rebuild it.' ⁶The king—with the queen sitting
beside him—said, 'How long will your journey take, and when will you come back?'
Once I had given him a definite time, the king
approved my mission.

⁷I then said to the king, 'If the king approves, may I be given orders for the governors of Transeuphrates to let me pass through
on my way to Judah? ⁸Also an order for
Asaph, keeper of the king's forest, to supply
me with timber for the beams of the gates of

1a Dt 30:1–4.

the citadel of the Temple, for the city walls and for the house which I am to occupy?' These the king granted me because the kindly hand of my God was over me.

⁹ When I reached the governors of Transeuphrates, I gave them the king's orders. The king had sent an escort of army officers and cavalry along with me.

¹⁰ When Sanballat the Horonite and Tobiah the official of Ammon heard about this, they were exceedingly displeased that someone had come to promote the welfare of the Israelites.

The decision to rebuild the walls of Jerusalem

¹¹ And so I reached Jerusalem. After I had been there three days, ¹² I got up during the night with a few other men—I had not told anyone what my God had inspired me to do for Jerusalem—taking no animal with me other than my own mount. ¹³ Under cover of dark I went out through the Valley Gate towards the Dragon's Fountain as far as the Dung Gate, and examined the wall of Jerusalem where it was broken down and its gates burnt out. ¹⁴ I then crossed to the Fountain Gate and the King's Pool, but it was impassable to my mount. ¹⁵ So I went up the Valley in the dark, examining the wall; I then went in again through the Valley Gate, coming back ¹⁶ without the officials knowing where I had gone or what I had been doing. So far I had said nothing to the Jews: neither to the priests, the nobles, the officials nor any other persons involved in the undertaking.

¹⁷ I then said to them, 'You see what a sorry state we are in: Jerusalem is in ruins and its gates have been burnt down. Come on, we must rebuild the walls of Jerusalem and put an end to our humiliating position!' ¹⁸ And I told them how the kindly hand of my God had been over me, and the words which the king had said to me. At this they said, 'Let us start building at once!' and they set their hands to the good work.

¹⁹ When Sanballat the Horonite, Tobiah the official of Ammon, and Geshem the Arab heard about this, they laughed at us and jeered. They said, 'What is this you are doing? Are you going to revolt against the king?' ²⁰ But I gave them this answer, 'The God of heaven will grant us success and we, his servants, mean to start building; as for you, you have neither share nor right nor memorial in Jerusalem.'

How the walls were rebuilt

3 Eliashib the high priest with his brother priests then set to work and rebuilt the Sheep Gate; they made the framework, hung its doors, fixed its bolts and bars and proceeded as far as the Tower of the Hundred and the Tower of Hananel. ² The men of Jericho built next to him; Zaccur son of Imri built next to them. ³ The sons of Ha-Senaah rebuilt the Fish Gate; they made the framework, hung its doors and fixed its bolts and bars. ⁴ Meremoth son of Uriah, son of Hakkoz, carried out repairs next to them; Meshullam son of Berechiah, son of Meshezabel, carried out repairs next to him; and Zadok son of Baana carried out repairs next to him. ⁵ The men of Tekoa carried out repairs next to him, though their nobles would not demean themselves to help their masters. ⁶ Joiada son of Paseah and Meshullam son of Besodeiah repaired the gate of the New Quarter; they made the framework, hung its doors and fixed its bolts and bars. ⁷ Next to them repairs were carried out by Melatiah of Gibeon, Jadon of Meronoth, and the men of Gibeon and Mizpah, for the sake of the governor of Transeuphrates. ⁸ Next to them repairs were carried out by Uzziel son of Harhaiah, a member of the metal-workers' guild, and next to him repairs were carried out by Hananiah of the perfumers' guild. These renovated the wall of Jerusalem as far as the Broad Wall.

⁹ Next to them repairs were carried out by Rephaiah son of Hur, who was head of one half of the district of Jerusalem. ¹⁰ Next to them Jedaiah son of Harumaph carried out repairs opposite his own house; next to him repairs were carried out by Hattush son of

Hashabneiah. ¹¹Malchijah son of Harim and Hasshub son of Pahath-Moab repaired another section as far as the Furnace Tower. ¹²Next to them repairs were carried out by Shallum son of Hallohesh, head of the other half of the district of Jerusalem, by him and his sons. ¹³Hanun and the inhabitants of Zanoah repaired the Valley Gate: they rebuilt it, hung its doors and fixed its bolts and bars; they also repaired a thousand cubits of wall up to the Dung Gate. ¹⁴Malchijah son of Rechab, head of the district of Beth-ha-Cherem, repaired the Dung Gate; he rebuilt it, hung its doors and fixed its bolts and bars.

¹⁵Shallum son of Col-Hozeh, head of the district of Mizpah, repaired the Fountain Gate; he rebuilt it, roofed it, hung its doors and fixed its bolts and bars. He also rebuilt the wall of the Pool of Siloah, adjoining the king's garden, as far as the steps going down from the City of David. ¹⁶After him, Nehemiah son of Azbuk, head of half the district of Beth-Zur, carried out repairs from a point opposite the Davidic Tombs to the artificial pool and the House of the Champions. ¹⁷After him, repairs were carried out by the Levites: Rehum son of Bani; and next to him Hashabiah, head of one half of the district of Keilah, carried out repairs for his own district. ¹⁸After him, repairs were carried out by their brothers: Binnui son of Henadad, head of the other half of the district of Keilah. ¹⁹Next to him, Ezer son of Jeshua, headman of Mizpah, repaired another section in front of the ascent to the armoury at the Angle.

²⁰After him, Baruch son of Zabbai repaired another section from the Angle to the door of the house of Eliashib the high priest. ²¹After him, Meremoth son of Uriah, son of Hakkoz, repaired another section from the door of Eliashib's house as far as the end of Eliashib's house. ²²And after him repairs were carried out by the priests who lived in the district. ²³After them repairs were carried out by Benjamin and Hasshub, opposite their own house. After them repairs were carried out by Azariah son of Maaseiah, son of Ananiah, be-

side his own house. ²⁴After him, Binnui son of Henadad repaired another section from Azariah's house as far as the Angle at the corner. ²⁵After him, Palal son of Uzai carried out repairs in front of the Angle and the tower projecting from the king's Upper Palace by the Court of the Guard; and after him, Pedaiah son of Parosh carried out the repairs ²⁶to a point by the Water Gate to the east and the projecting tower. ²⁷After him, the men of Tekoa repaired another section from in front of the great projecting tower as far as the wall of Ophel.

²⁸From the Horse Gate onwards repairs were carried out by the priests, each in front of his own house. ²⁹After them repairs were carried out by Zadok son of Immer in front of his house, and after him repairs were carried out by Shemaiah son of Shechaniah, keeper of the East Gate. ³⁰After him Hananiah son of Shelemiah and Hanun sixth son of Zalaph repaired another section, after whom repairs were carried out by Meshullam son of Berechiah in front of his room. ³¹After him Malchijah, of the metal-workers' guild, repaired as far as the Hall of the temple slaves and merchants, in front of the Muster Gate, as far as the upper room at the corner. ³²And between the upper room at the corner and the Sheep Gate repairs were carried out by the goldsmiths and the merchants.

The effect on the Jews' opponents

³³When Sanballat heard that we were rebuilding the wall, he became furiously angry. ³⁴He ridiculed the Jews and in front of his kinsmen and the aristocracy of Samaria he exclaimed, 'What are these pathetic Jews doing...? Are they going to give up? Or offer sacrifices? Or complete the work in a day? Can they put new life into stones taken from rubbish heaps and even charred?' ³⁵And beside him Tobiah of Ammon remarked, 'If a jackal were to jump on what they are building, it would knock their stone wall down!' ³⁶Listen, our God, for we are despised! Make their sneers fall back on their own heads! Send

them as booty to a land of captivity! ³⁷ Do not pardon their wickedness, may their sin never be erased before you, for they have insulted the builders to their face!

³⁸ Meanwhile we were rebuilding the wall, which was soon joined up all the way round to mid-height; the people put their hearts into the work.

4 When Sanballat, Tobiah, the Arabs, the Ammonites and the Ashdodites heard that repairs to the walls of Jerusalem were going forward—that the gaps were beginning to fill up—they became very angry, ² and they all plotted to come and attack Jerusalem and upset my plans.

³ We, however, prayed to our God and organised a guard day and night to protect the city from them. ⁴ But in Judah the saying went, 'The strength of the carrier falters, the rubbish heap is so vast that by ourselves we cannot rebuild the wall!' ⁵ And our opponents said, 'They will never know or see a thing, until we are in there among them, and then we shall massacre them and put a stop to the work.'

⁶ Now when the Jews who lived near them had warned us ten times over, 'They are coming up against us from every place they live in,' ⁷ men took up position in the space behind the wall at those points where it was lowest, and I organised the people by families with their swords, spears and bows. ⁸ Aware of their anxiety, I then addressed the nobles, the officials and the rest of the people, 'Do not be afraid of them. Remember the great and awe-inspiring Lord and fight for your kinsmen, your sons, your daughters, your wives and your homes.' ⁹ Once our enemies heard that we were forewarned and that God had thwarted their plan, they withdrew and we all went back to the wall, each one to his work.

¹⁰ From then on, half my own retainers went on working, while the other half stood by, armed with spears, shields, bows and armour to protect the whole House of Judah as they rebuilt the wall. ¹¹ The carriers were armed, working with one hand and holding a

spear in the other. ¹² Each builder had his sword strapped to his side as he built. Beside me stood a trumpeter. ¹³ I then said to the nobles, the officials and the rest of the people, 'The work is great and widely spread out, and we are deployed along the wall some way from one another. ¹⁴ Rally to us wherever you hear the trumpet sounding; our God will fight for us.' ¹⁵ And so we went on with the work from break of day until the stars came out. ¹⁶ At the same time I also told the people, 'Let every man, with his attendant, spend the night inside Jerusalem; we shall spend the night on guard and the day at work.' ¹⁷ Neither I, nor my brothers, nor my attendants, nor my bodyguards, ever took off our clothes; each one kept his spear in his right hand.

The social problems of Nehemiah;
he vindicates his administration

5 There was a great outcry from the people, and from their wives, against their brother Jews. ² Some said, 'We are having to pledge our sons and daughters to get enough grain to eat and keep us alive.' ³ Others said, 'We are having to mortgage our fields, our vineyards and our houses to get grain because of the shortage.' ⁴ Still others said, 'We have had to borrow money on our fields and our vineyards to pay the royal tax; ⁵ and though we belong to the same race as our brothers, and our children are as good as theirs, we shall have to sell our sons and our daughters into slavery; some of our daughters have been sold into slavery already. We can do nothing about it, since our fields and our vineyards now belong to others.'

⁶ When I heard their complaints and these words I was very angry. ⁷ Having turned the matter over in my mind, I reprimanded the nobles and the officials as follows, 'Each of you is imposing a burden on his brother.' Summoning a great assembly to deal with them, ⁸ I said to them, 'To the best of our power, we have redeemed our brother Jews who were forced to sell themselves to foreigners, and now you in turn are selling your brothers, for them to be bought back by us!' They were

silent and could find nothing to say. 9'What you are doing', I went on, 'is wrong. Do you not want to walk in the fear of our God and escape the sneers of the nations, our enemies? 10I too, with my brothers and retainers, have lent them money and grain. Let us cancel these pledges. 11This very day return them their fields, their vineyards, their olive groves and their houses, and cancel the claim on the money, grain, new wine and olive oil, which you have lent them.' 12'We shall make restitution,' they replied, 'we shall claim nothing more from them; we shall do as you say.' Summoning the priests, I then made them swear to do as they had promised. 13Then, shaking out the fold of my garment, I said, 'May God thus shake out of house and possessions anyone who does not make good this promise; may he be shaken out thus and left empty!' And the whole assembly answered, 'Amen' and praised Yahweh. And the people kept this promise.

14What is more, from the time when the king appointed me to be their governor in Judah, from the twentieth to the thirty-second year of King Artaxerxes, for twelve years, neither I nor my brothers ever levied the governor's subsistence allowance, 15whereas the former governors, my predecessors, had been a burden on the people, from whom they took forty silver shekels a day for food and wine, while their attendants oppressed the people too. But I, fearing God, never did this. 16Also, not acquiring any land, I concentrated on the work of this wall and all my attendants joined in the work together, too.

17Furthermore, magistrates and officials to the number of a hundred and fifty ate at my table, not to mention those who came to us from the surrounding nations. 18Every day, one ox, six fine sheep, as well as poultry, were prepared for me; every ten days, skins of wine were brought in bulk. But even so, I never claimed the governor's subsistence allowance, since the people already had burden enough to bear.

19To my credit, my God, remember all I have done for this people.

The intrigues of Nehemiah's enemies; the wall is finished

6 When Sanballat, Tobiah, Geshem the Arab and our other enemies heard that I had rebuilt the wall and that not a single gap was left—though at that time I had not fixed the doors to the gates— 2Sanballat and Geshem sent me this message, 'Come and meet us at Ha-Chephirim in the Vale of Ono.' But they had evil designs on me. 3So I sent messengers to them to say, 'I am engaged in a great undertaking, so I cannot come down. Why should the work stop while I leave it and come down to you?' 4Four times they sent me the same invitation and I made them the same reply. 5The fifth time, with the same purpose in mind, Sanballat sent me his servant bearing an open letter. 6It ran, 'There is a rumour among the nations—and Gashmu confirms it—that you and the Jews are thinking of rebelling, which is why you are rebuilding the wall, and you intend to become their king; 7and that you have even briefed prophets to acclaim you in Jerusalem with the cry, "There is a king in Judah!" Now, these rumours are going to reach the king; so you had better come and discuss them with us.' 8To this I sent him the following reply, 'As regards what you say, nothing of the sort has occurred; it is a figment of your own imagination.' 9For they were all trying to terrorise us, thinking, 'They will become demoralised over the work and it will not get finished.' But my morale rose even higher.

10Then, when I went to visit Shemaiah son of Delaiah, son of Mehetabel, since he was prevented from coming to me, he said:

We must gather at the Temple of God,
inside the sanctuary itself;
we must shut the sanctuary doors,
for they are coming to kill you,
they are coming to kill you tonight!

11But I retorted, 'Should a man like me run away? Would a man like me go into the Temple to save his life? I shall not go in!' 12I realised that God had not sent him to say this, but that he had produced this prophecy for me because Tobiah was paying him [13] to terrorise me into doing as he said and committing a sin, so that they would have grounds for blackening my reputation and blaming me.

[14] Remember Tobiah, my God, for what he did; and Noadiah the prophetess, and the other prophets who tried to terrorise me.

[15] The wall was finished within fifty-two days, on the twenty-fifth of Elul. [16] When all our enemies heard about it and all the surrounding nations saw it, they thought it a wonderful thing, because they realised that this work had been accomplished by the power of our God.

[17] During this same period, the nobles of Judah kept sending letter after letter to Tobiah, and letters from Tobiah kept arriving for them; [18] for he had many sworn to his interest in Judah, since he was son-in-law to Shecaniah son of Arah, and his son Jehohanan had married the daughter of Meshullam son of Berechiah. [19] They even cried up his good deeds in my presence, and they reported what I said back to him. And Tobiah kept sending letters to terrorise me.

7 Now, when the wall had been rebuilt and I had hung the doors, the gatekeepers (the singers and the Levites) were then appointed. [2] I entrusted the administration of Jerusalem to my brother Hanani, and to Hananiah the commander of the citadel, for he was a more trustworthy, God-fearing man than many others. [3] I said to them, 'The gates of Jerusalem must not be opened until the sun gets hot; and the doors must be shut and barred before it begins to go down. Detail guards from the residents of Jerusalem, each to his post, in front of his own house.'

The repopulation of Jerusalem

[4] The city was large and spacious but the population was small, and the houses had not been rebuilt. [5] My God then inspired me to assemble the nobles, the officials and the people for the purpose of taking a census by families. I discovered the genealogical register of those who had returned in the first group, and there I found entered:

List of the first exiles to return [a]

[6] These are the people of the province who returned from the captivity of the Exile, those whom Nebuchadnezzar king of Babylon had deported, and who returned to Jerusalem and Judah, each to his own town. [7] They were the ones who arrived with Zerubbabel, Jeshua, Nehemiah, Azariah, Raamiah, Nahamani, Mordecai, Bilshan, Mispereth, Bigvai, Nehum, Baanah.

The number of the men of the people of Israel: [8] sons of Parosh, two thousand one hundred and seventy-two; [9] sons of Shephatiah, three hundred and seventy-two; [10] sons of Arah, six hundred and fifty-two; [11] sons of Pahath-Moab, that is to say sons of Jeshua and Joab, two thousand eight hundred and eighteen; [12] sons of Elam, one thousand two hundred and fifty-four; [13] sons of Zattu, eight hundred and forty-five; [14] sons of Zaccai, seven hundred and sixty; [15] sons of Binnui, six hundred and forty-eight; [16] sons of Bebai, six hundred and twenty-eight; [17] sons of Azgad, two thousand three hundred and twenty-two; [18] sons of Adonikam, six hundred and sixty-seven; [19] sons of Bigvai, two thousand and sixty-seven; [20] sons of Adin, six hundred and fifty-five; [21] sons of Ater, that is to say of Hezekiah, ninety-eight; [22] sons of Hashum, three hundred and twenty-eight; [23] sons of Bezai, three hundred and twenty-four; [24] sons of Hariph, one hundred and twelve; [25] sons of Gibeon, ninety-five; [26] men of Bethlehem and Netophah, one hundred and eighty-eight; [27] men of Anathoth, one hundred and twenty-eight; [28] men of Beth-Azmaveth, forty-two; [29] men of Kiriath-Jearim, Chephirah and Beeroth, seven hundred and forty-three; [30] men of Ramah and Geba, six hundred and twenty-

7a ‖ Ezr 2:1–70.

one; 31 men of Michmas, one hundred and twenty-two; 32 men of Bethel and Ai, one hundred and twenty-three; 33 men of the other Nebo, fifty-two; 34 sons of the other Elam, one thousand two hundred and fifty-four; 35 sons of Harim, three hundred and twenty; 36 sons of Jericho, three hundred and forty-five; 37 sons of Lod, Hadid and Ono, seven hundred and twenty-one; 38 sons of Senaah, three thousand nine hundred and thirty.

39 The priests: sons of Jedaiah, of the House of Jeshua, nine hundred and seventy-three; 40 sons of Immer, one thousand and fifty-two; 41 sons of Pashhur, one thousand two hundred and forty-seven; 42 sons of Harim, one thousand and seventeen.

43 The Levites: sons of Jeshua, of Kadmiel, of the sons of Hodiah, seventy-four.

44 The singers: sons of Asaph, one hundred and forty-eight.

45 The gatekeepers: sons of Shallum, sons of Ater, sons of Talmon, sons of Akkub, sons of Hatita, sons of Shobai, one hundred and thirty-eight.

46 The temple slaves: sons of Ziha, sons of Hasupha, sons of Tabbaoth, 47 sons of Keros, sons of Sia, sons of Padon, 48 sons of Lebana, sons of Hagaba, sons of Shalmai, 49 sons of Hanan, sons of Giddel, sons of Gahar, 50 sons of Reaiah, sons of Rezin, sons of Nekoda, 51 sons of Gazzam, sons of Uzza, sons of Paseah, 52 sons of Besai, sons of the Meunites, sons of the Nephusites, 53 sons of Bakbuk, sons of Hakupha, sons of Harhur, 54 sons of Bazlith, sons of Mehida, sons of Harsha, 55 sons of Barkos, sons of Sisera, sons of Temah, 56 sons of Nezaiah, sons of Hatipha.

57 The sons of Solomon's slaves: sons of Sotai, sons of Sophereth, sons of Perida, 58 sons of Jaala, sons of Darkon, sons of Giddel, 59 sons of Shephatiah, sons of Hattil, sons of Pochereth-ha-Zebaim, sons of Amon. 60 The total of the temple slaves and the sons of Solomon's slaves: three hundred and ninety-two.

61 The following, who came from Tel-Melah, Tel-Harsha, Cherub, Addon and Immer, could not prove that their families and ancestry were of Israelite origin: 62 the sons of Delaiah, the sons of Tobiah, the sons of Nekoda: six hundred and forty-two. 63 And among the priests: the sons of Hobaiah, the sons of Hakkoz, the sons of Barzillai—who had married one of the daughters of Barzillai the Gileadite, whose name he adopted. 64 These had looked for their entries in the official genealogies but were not to be found there, and were hence disqualified from the priesthood. 65 Consequently, His Excellency forbade them to eat any of the consecrated food until a priest appeared who could consult *urim* and *thummim.*

66 The whole assembly numbered forty-two thousand three hundred and sixty people, 67 not counting their slaves and maidservants to the number of seven thousand three hundred and thirty-seven. They also had two hundred and forty-five male and female singers. 68 They had four hundred and thirty-five camels and six thousand seven hundred and twenty donkeys.

69 A certain number of heads of families contributed to the work. His Excellency contributed one thousand gold drachmas, fifty bowls, and thirty priestly robes to the fund. 70 And heads of families gave twenty thousand gold drachmas and two thousand two hundred silver minas to the work fund. 71 The gifts made by the rest of the people amounted to twenty thousand gold drachmas, two thousand silver minas, and sixty-seven priestly robes.

72 The priests, the Levites and some of the people lived in Jerusalem and thereabouts; the singers, the gatekeepers, and the temple slaves in their appropriate towns; and all the other Israelites, in their own towns.

Judaism is born; Ezra reads the Law;
the feast of Shelters

Now when the seventh month came round—the Israelites being in their towns—

8 all the people gathered as one man in the square in front of the Water Gate, and asked the scribe Ezra to bring the Book of the

Law of Moses which Yahweh had prescribed for Israel. ²Accordingly, on the first day of the seventh month, the priest Ezra brought the Law before the assembly, consisting of men, women and all those old enough to understand. ³In the square in front of the Water Gate, in the presence of the men and women, and of those old enough to understand, he read from the book from dawn till noon; all the people listened attentively to the Book of the Law.

⁴The scribe Ezra stood on a wooden dais erected for the purpose; beside him stood, on his right, Mattithiah, Shema, Anaiah, Uriah, Hilkiah and Maaseiah; on his left, Pedaiah, Mishael, Malchijah, Hashum, Hashbaddanah, Zechariah, and Meshullam. ⁵In full view of all the people—since he stood higher than them all—Ezra opened the book; and when he opened it, all the people stood up. ⁶Then Ezra blessed Yahweh, the great God, and all the people raised their hands and answered, 'Amen! Amen!'; then they bowed down and, face to the ground, prostrated themselves before Yahweh. ⁷And Jeshua, Bani, Sherebiah, Jamin, Akkub, Shabbethai, Hodiah, Maaseiah, Kelita, Azariah, Jozabab, Hanan, Pelaiah, who were Levites, explained the Law to the people, while the people all kept their places. ⁸Ezra read from the book of the Law of God, translating and giving the sense; so the reading was understood.

⁹Then His Excellency Nehemiah and the priest-scribe Ezra and the Levites who were instructing the people said to all the people, 'Today is sacred to Yahweh your God. Do not be mournful, do not weep.' For the people were all in tears as they listened to the words of the Law.

¹⁰He then said, 'You may go; eat what is rich, drink what is sweet and send a helping to the man who has nothing prepared. For today is sacred to our Lord. Do not be sad: the joy of Yahweh is your stronghold.' ¹¹And the Levites calmed all the people down, saying, 'Keep quiet; this is a sacred day. Do not be sad.' ¹²Then all the people went off to eat and drink and give helpings away and enjoy themselves to the full, since they had understood the meaning of what had been proclaimed to them.

¹³On the second day, the heads of families of the whole people, and the priests and Levites, gathered round the scribe Ezra to study the words of the Law. ¹⁴And written in the Law that Yahweh had prescribed through Moses[a] they found that the Israelites were to live in shelters during the feast of the seventh month. ¹⁵So they issued a proclamation and had it circulated in all their towns and in Jerusalem: 'Go into the hills and bring branches of olive, pine, myrtle, palm and other leafy trees to make shelters, as it says in the book.' ¹⁶The people went out; they brought branches and made shelters for themselves, each man on his roof, in their courtyards, in the precincts of the Temple of God, in the square of the Water Gate and in the square of the Ephraim Gate. ¹⁷The whole assembly, all who had returned from the captivity, put up shelters and lived in them; this the Israelites had not done from the days of Joshua son of Nun till that day, and there was very great merrymaking.

¹⁸Each day, from the first day to the last one, Ezra read from the Book of the Law of God. They celebrated the feast for seven days; on the eighth day, as prescribed, they held a solemn assembly.

The ceremony of expiation

9 On the twenty-fourth day of this month the Israelites, in sackcloth and with dust on their heads, assembled for a fast. ²Then those of Israelite stock who had severed relations with all foreigners stood up and confessed their sins and the iniquities of their ancestors. ³Standing, each man in his place, they read from the Book of the Law of Yahweh their God for one quarter of the day; for another quarter they confessed their sins and worshipped Yahweh their God. ⁴On the Levites'

8a Lv 23:33–43.

platform stood Jeshua, Binnui, Kadmiel, Shebaniah, Bunni, Sherebiah, Bani and Chenani, calling to Yahweh their God in ringing tones. ⁵ The Levites, Jeshua, Kadmiel, Bani, Hashabneiah, Sherebiah, Hodiah, Shebaniah and Pethahiah said, 'Stand up and bless Yahweh your God!

> 'Blessed are you, Yahweh our God
> from everlasting to everlasting,
> and blessed be your glorious name,
> surpassing all blessing and praise!

⁶ 'You, Yahweh, are the one, only Yahweh,
> you have created the heavens,
> the heaven of heavens and all their array,
> the earth and all it bears,
> the seas and all they hold.
> To all of them you give life,
> and the array of heaven worships you.

⁷ 'You are Yahweh God,
> who chose Abram,
> brought him out of Ur in Chaldaea
> and changed his name to Abraham.
⁸ Finding his heart was faithful to you,
> you made a covenant with him,
> to give the country of the Canaanites,
> the Hittites, the Amorites,
> the Perizzites, the Jebusites and the
> Girgashites
> to him and his descendants.
> And you have made good your promises,
> for you are upright.

⁹ 'You saw the distress of our ancestors in
> Egypt,
> you heard their cry by the Sea of Reeds.
¹⁰ You displayed signs and wonders against
> Pharaoh,
> against all his servants and all the people of
> his land;
> for you knew how arrogantly they treated
> them.
> You won a reputation which you keep to
> this day.
¹¹ You opened up the sea in front of them:

they walked on dry ground right through
> the sea.
> Into the depths you hurled their pursuers
> like a stone into the raging waters.
¹² With a pillar of cloud you led them by day,
> with a pillar of fire by night:
> to light the way ahead of them
> by which they were to go.
¹³ You came down on Mount Sinai
> and spoke with them from heaven;
> you gave them right rules, reliable laws,
> good statutes and commandments;
¹⁴ you revealed your holy Sabbath to them;
> you laid down commandments, statutes
> and law for them
> through your servant Moses.
¹⁵ For their hunger you gave them bread
> from heaven,
> for their thirst you brought them water
> out of a rock,
> and you told them to go in and take
> possession of the country
> which you had sworn to give them.

¹⁶ 'But they and our ancestors acted
> arrogantly,
> grew obstinate and flouted your
> commands.
¹⁷ They refused to obey,
> forgetful of the wonders which you had
> worked for them;
> they grew obstinate
> and made up their minds to return
> to their slavery in Egypt.
> But because you are a forgiving God,
> gracious and compassionate,
> patient and rich in faithful love,
> you did not abandon them!

¹⁸ 'Even when they cast themselves a calf out
> of molten metal
> and said, "This is your God
> who brought you up from Egypt!"
> and committed monstrous impieties,
¹⁹ you, in your great compassion,
> did not abandon them in the desert:
> the pillar of cloud did not leave them,

leading them on their path by day,
nor the pillar of fire by night,
lighting the way ahead of them
by which they were to go.
20 You gave them your good spirit to instruct
them,
you did not withhold your manna from
their mouths,
you gave them water for their thirst.
21 For forty years you cared for them in the
desert,
so that they went short of nothing,
their clothes did not wear out,
nor were their feet swollen.

22 'You gave them kingdoms and peoples,
allotting them these as frontier lands;
they occupied the country of Sihon king of
Heshbon,
and the country of Og king of Bashan.
23 You gave them as many children
as there are stars in the sky,
and brought them into the country
which you had promised their ancestors
that they would enter and possess.
24 The children entered
and took possession of the country
and before them you subdued
the country's inhabitants, the Canaanites,
whom you put at their mercy,
with their kings and the peoples of the
country,
for them to treat as they pleased;
25 they captured fortified towns
and a fertile countryside,
they took possession of houses
stocked with all kinds of goods,
of storage-wells ready-hewn, of vineyards,
olive groves
and fruit trees in profusion;
so they ate, were full, grew fat
and revelled in your great goodness.

26 'But they grew disobedient, rebelled
against you
and thrust your law behind their
backs;

they slaughtered your prophets
who had reproved them
to bring them back to you,
and committed monstrous impieties.
27 So you put them at the mercy of their
enemies
who oppressed them.
But when they were being oppressed and
called to you,
you heard them from heaven
and because of your great compassion
you gave them deliverers
who rescued them from their oppressors'
clutches.
28 But once at peace again,
again they did what was wrong before
you;
so you put them at the mercy of their
enemies
who then became their rulers.
When they called to you again,
you heard them from heaven
and, because of your compassion, rescued
them many times.
29 You warned them, to bring them back to
your law,
but they became arrogant,
did not obey your commandments
and sinned against your rules,
in whose observance is life;
they turned a stubborn shoulder,
were obstinate, and disobeyed.
30 You were patient with them for many
years
and warned them by your spirit
through your prophets,
but they would not listen;
so you put them at the mercy of the people
of the country.
31 But, because of your great compassion,
you did not destroy them completely
nor abandon them,
for you are a gracious, compassionate God.
32 Now, our God—the great God,
the Mighty and Awe-inspiring One,
maintaining the covenant and your
faithful love—

count as no small thing this misery
which has befallen us, our kings, our
        princes,
our priests, our prophets, and all your
        people
from the times of the Assyrian kings
to the present day.
33 You have been upright
in all that has happened to us,
for you acted faithfully,
while we did wrong.
34 Our kings, our princes, our priests
and our ancestors did not keep your law
or pay attention to your commandments
        and obligations
which you imposed upon them.
35 Even in their own kingdom,
despite your great goodness
which you bestowed on them,
despite the wide and fertile country
which you had lavished on them,
they did not serve you
or renounce their evil deeds.
36 See, we are slaves today,
slaves in the country which you gave to
        our ancestors
for them to eat the good things it
        produces.
37 Its abundant produce goes to the kings
whom, for our sins, you have set over us,
who rule over our persons
and over our cattle as they please.
We are in great distress.'

*A record of the promises made by
the community*

10 In view of all this we make a firm agreement, in writing. Our princes, our Levites, our priests and the rest of the people
have put their names to the document under
seal.

2 On the sealed document were the names
of: Nehemiah, son of Hacaliah, and Zedekiah;
3 Seraiah, Azariah, Jeremiah, 4 Pashhur, Amariah, Malchijah, 5 Hattush, Shebaniah, Malluch, 6 Harim, Meremoth, Obadiah, 7 Daniel,
Ginnethon, Baruch, 8 Meshullam, Abijah, Mijamin, 9 Maaziah, Bilgai, Shemaiah: these
were the priests.

10 The Levites were: Jeshua son of Azaniah,
Binnui of the sons of Henadad, Kadmiel,
11 and their kinsmen Shebaniah, Hodaviah,
Kelita, Pelaiah, Hanan, 12 Mica, Rehob,
Hashabiah, 13 Zaccur, Sherebiah, Shebaniah,
14 Hodiah, Bani, Chenani.

15 The leaders of the people were: Parosh,
Pahath-Moab, Elam, Zattu, Bani, 16 Bunni,
Azgad, Bebai, 17 Adonijah, Bigvai, Adin,
18 Ater, Hezekiah, Azzur, 19 Hodiah, Hashum,
Bezai, 20 Hariph, Anathoth, Nebai, 21 Magpi-
ash, Meshullam, Hezir, 22 Meshezabel, Zadok,
Jaddua, 23 Pelatiah, Hanan, Anaiah, 24 Hoshea,
Hananiah, Hasshub, 25 Hallohesh, Pilha,
Shobek, 26 Rehum, Hashabnah, Maaseiah,
27 Ahijah, Hanan, Anan, 28 Malluch, Harim,
Baanah.

29 And the rest of the people, the priests, the
Levites, the gatekeepers, the singers, the temple slaves and all those who had severed relations with the people of the country to adhere
to the law of God, as also their wives, their
sons, their daughters, that is, all those who had
reached the age of discretion, 30 have joined
their esteemed brothers in a solemn oath to
follow the law of God given through Moses,
servant of God, and to observe and practise all
the commandments of Yahweh our Lord,
with his rules and his statutes.

31 We will not give our daughters in marriage to the peoples of the country, nor allow
their daughters to marry our sons.

32 If the people of the country bring goods
or foodstuff of any kind to sell on the Sabbath
day, we will buy nothing from them on Sabbath or holy day.

In the seventh year, we will forgo the produce of the soil and the exaction of all debts.

33 We recognise the following obligations:
to give one-third of a shekel yearly for the
service of the Temple of our God: 34 for the
loaves of permanent offering, for the perpetual oblation, for the perpetual burnt offering,
for the sacrifices on Sabbaths, on New Moons
and on festivals, for the consecrated gifts, the

sin offerings to expiate for Israel, in short, for the whole work of the Temple of our God;[a]

[36] and further, to bring yearly to the Temple of our God the first-fruits of our soil and the first-fruits of all our orchards, [37] also the first-born of our sons and of our cattle, as the law prescribes, the first-born of our herds and flocks should be taken to the Temple of our God for the priests officiating in the Temple of our God. [38] Furthermore, we shall bring the best of our dough, of every kind of fruit, of the new wine and of the oil to the priests, to the storerooms of the Temple of our God, and the tithe on our soil to the Levites—the Levites will themselves collect the tithes from all the towns of our religion. [39] An Aaronite priest will accompany the Levites when they collect the tithes, and the Levites will bring a tenth part [40a,b] of the tithes to the Temple of our God, into the treasury storerooms; for these rooms are where the Israelites and the Levites are to bring the contributions of corn, wine and oil, and where the vessels of the sanctuary are, and the officiating priests, the gatekeepers and the singers.

[35] Furthermore, as regards deliveries of wood for burning on the altar of our God as the law prescribes, we have arranged, by drawing lots, how these deliveries are to be made at the Temple of our God by the priests, the Levites and the people by families, at stated times every year.

[40c] We will no longer neglect the Temple of our God.

Nehemiah's method of repopulating Jerusalem

11 Now the leaders of the people took up residence in Jerusalem; so the rest of the people drew lots: one man in ten was to come and live in Jerusalem, the holy city, while the other nine were to stay in the towns outside. [2] The people praised all those who volunteered to live in Jerusalem.

[3] In the towns of Judah each man lived on his own property, but these are the provincial leaders, the Israelites, the priests, the Levites, the temple slaves and the descendants of Solomon's slaves, who made their homes in Jerusalem:

The Jewish population at Jerusalem

[4] Of the sons of Judah and the sons of Benjamin who made their homes in Jerusalem there were:

Of the sons of Judah: Athaiah son of Uzziah, son of Zechariah, son of Amariah, son of Shephatiah, son of Mehalalel, of the descendants of Perez; [5] and Maaseiah son of Baruch, son of Col-Hozeh, son of Hazaiah, son of Adaiah, son of Joiarib, son of Zechariah, descendant of Shelah. [6] The total number of the descendants of Perez living in Jerusalem was four hundred and sixty-eight outstanding people.

[7] These are the sons of Benjamin: Sallu son of Meshullam, son of Joed, son of Pedaiah, son of Kolaiah, son of Maaseiah, son of Ithiel, son of Jeshaiah, [8] and his brothers Gabbai and Sallai; nine hundred and twenty-eight.

[9] Joel son of Zichri was their chief, and Judah son of Hassenuah was second in command of the city.

[10] Of the priests there were Jedaiah son of Joiakim, son of [11] Seraiah, son of Hilkiah, son of Meshullam, son of Zadok, son of Meraioth, son of Ahitub, the chief of the Temple of God, [12] and their kinsmen who performed the Temple liturgy: eight hundred and twenty-two; Adaiah son of Jeroham, son of Pelaliah, son of Amzi, son of Zechariah, son of Pashhur, son of Malchijah, [13] and his kinsfolk, heads of families: two hundred and forty-two; and Amashai son of Azarel, son of Ahzai, son of Meshillemoth, son of Immer, [14] and his kinsfolk, outstanding people: one hundred and twenty-eight.

Their chief was Zabdiel son of Haggadol.

[15] Of the Levites there were Shemaiah son of Hasshub, son of Azrikam, son of Hashabiah, son of Bunni; [16] Shabbethai and Jozabad, the levitical leaders responsible for

10a v. 35 is found after v. 40b.

work outside the Temple of God; 17 Mattaniah son of Mica, son of Zabdi, son of Asaph, who led the praises and intoned the thanksgiving associated with the prayer, Bakbukiah being his junior colleague; and Obadiah son of Shammua, son of Galal, son of Jeduthun. 18 The total number of Levites in the holy city was two hundred and eighty-four.

Supplementary notes

19 The gatekeepers: Akkub, Talmon and their kinsmen, who kept watch at the gates: one hundred and seventy-two.[a]

21 The temple slaves lived on Ophel; Ziha and Gishpa were in charge of the temple slaves. 22 The official in charge of the Levites in Jerusalem was Uzzi son of Bani, son of Hashabiah, son of Mattaniah, son of Mica, of the sons of Asaph, who led the singing in the liturgy of the Temple of God; 23 for the singers were under royal orders, with regulations laying down what was required of them day by day. 24 Petahiah son of Meshezabel, of the sons of Zerah son of Judah, was the king's minister for all matters connected with the people.

The Jewish population outside Jerusalem

20 The rest of Israel, including the priests and Levites, made their homes throughout the towns of Judah, each man on his own inheritance, 25 and in the villages near their lands. Some of the sons of Judah made their homes in Kiriath-Arba and its dependencies, Dibon and its dependencies, Jekabzeel and its dependencies, 26 Jeshua, Moladah, Beth-Pelet, 27 Hazar-Shual, Beersheba and its dependencies, 28 Ziklag, Meconah and its dependencies, 29 En-Rimmon, Zorah, Jarmuth, 30 Zanoah, Adullam and their villages, Lachish and its lands, and Azekah and its dependencies; thus, they settled from Beersheba as far as the Valley of Hinnom.

31 And some Benjaminites made their homes in Geba, Michmash, Aija, Bethel and its dependencies, 32 Anathoth, Nob, Ananiah, 33 Hazor, Ramah, Gittaim, 34 Hadid, Zeboim, Neballat, 35 Lod, Ono and the Valley of Craftsmen.

36 Some levitical groups lived in Judah, some in Benjamin.

Priests and Levites who returned under Zerubbabel and Jeshua

12 These are the priests and the Levites who came back with Zerubbabel son of Shealtiel, and Jeshua:

2 Seraiah, Jeremiah, Ezra, 3 Amariah, Malluch, Hattush, Shecaniah, Rehum, Meremoth, 4 Iddo, Ginnethoi, Abijah, 5 Mijamin, Maadiah, Bilgah, 6 Shemaiah, and Joiarib, Jedaiah, 7 Sallu, Amok, Hilkiah, Jedaiah—these were the heads of the priests and their kinsmen in the days of Jeshua.

8 The Levites were Jeshua, Binnui, Kadmiel, Sherebiah, Judah, Mattaniah—this last, with his brothers, was in charge of the songs of praise, 9 while Bakbukiah and Unno, their colleagues, formed the alternate choir to theirs.

Genealogical list of high priests

10 Jeshua fathered Joiakim, Joiakim fathered Eliashib, Eliashib fathered Joiada, 11 Joiada fathered Johanan, and Johanan fathered Jaddua.

Priests and Levites in the time of the High Priest Joiakim

12 In the days of Joiakim the heads of the priestly families were: family of Seraiah, Meraiah; of Jeremiah, Hananiah; 13 of Ezra, Meshullam; of Amariah, Jehohanan; 14 of Malluch, Jonathan; of Shebaniah, Joseph; 15 of Harim, Adna; of Meremoth, Helkai; 16 of Iddo, Zechariah; of Ginnethon, Meshullam; 17 of Abijah, Zichri; of Minjamin, . . . ; of Moadiah, Piltai; 18 of Bilgah, Shammua; of Shemaiah, Jehonathan; 19 and of Jojarib, Mattenai; of Jedaiah, Uzzi; 20 of Sallai, Kallai; of Amok, Eber; 21 of Hilkiah, Hashabiah; of Jedaiah, Nethanel.

22 In the time of Eliashib, Joiada, Johanan

11a v. 20 is transposed to follow v. 24.

and Jaddua, the heads of the families of priests were registered in the Book of Chronicles, up to the reign of Darius the Persian.

23 The Levites who were heads of families were registered in the Book of Chronicles up to the time of Johanan, grandson of Eliashib. 24 The heads of the Levites were Hashabiah, Sherebiah, Jeshua, Binnui, Kadmiel, while their brothers who formed an alternate choir for the hymns of praise and thanksgiving, as David, man of God, had prescribed, section corresponding to section, 25 were Mattaniah, Bakbukiah and Obadiah. Meshullam, Talmon and Akkub were the gatekeepers guarding the stores at the gates. 26 These lived in the days of Joiakim son of Jeshua, son of Jozadak, and in the days of Nehemiah the governor and of Ezra the priest-scribe.

The dedication of the wall of Jerusalem

27 At the dedication of the wall of Jerusalem the Levites were sent for, wherever they lived, to come to Jerusalem and joyfully perform the dedication with hymns of thanksgiving and songs to the accompaniment of cymbals, lyres and harps. 28 Accordingly, the levitical singers assembled from the district round Jerusalem, from the villages of the Netophathites, 29 from Beth-Gilgal and from their farms at Geba and Azmaveth—for the singers had built themselves villages all round Jerusalem. 30 When the priests and Levites had purified themselves, they then purified the people, the gates and the wall.

31 I then made the leaders of Judah come on to the top of the wall and appointed two large choirs. One made its way along the top of the wall, to the right, towards the Dung Gate; 32 bringing up the rear were Hoshaiah and half the leaders of Judah, 33 and also Azariah, Ezra, Meshullam, 34 Judah, Benjamin, Shemaiah and Jeremiah, 35 of the priests, with trumpets; then Zechariah son of Jonathan, son of Shemaiah, son of Mattaniah, son of Micaiah, son of Zaccur, son of Asaph, 36 with his kinsmen, Shemaiah, Azarel, Milalai, Gilalai, Maai,

Nethanel, Juda, Hanani, with the musical instruments of David, man of God. The scribe Ezra walked at their head. 37 At the Fountain Gate they went straight on up the steps of the City of David, along the top of the rampart by the stairway of the wall, above the Palace of David as far as the Water Gate, on the east.

38 The other choir made its way to the left; I and half the leaders of the people followed them along the top of the wall from the Tower of the Furnaces to the Broad Wall, 39 from the Ephraim Gate, the Fish Gate, the Tower of Hananel and the Tower of the Hundred as far as the Sheep Gate, and they came to a halt at the Prison Gate.

40 The two choirs then took their places in the Temple of God. But I had half the magistrates with me 41 as well as the priests, Eliakim, Maaseiah, Miniamin, Micaiah, Elioenai, Zechariah, Hananiah with the trumpets, 42 and Maaseiah, Shemaiah, Eleazar, Uzzi, Jehohanan, Malchijah, Elam and Ezer. The singers sang loudly under the direction of Jezrahiah. 43 There were great sacrifices offered that day and the people rejoiced, God having given them good cause for rejoicing; the women and children rejoiced too, and the joy of Jerusalem could be heard from far away.

A golden age

44 For the rooms intended for the treasures, contributions, first-fruits and tithes, supervisors were then appointed whose business it was to collect in them those portions from the town lands awarded by the Law to the priests and Levites. For Judah rejoiced in the officiating priests and Levites, 45 since they—with the singers and gatekeepers—performed the liturgy of their God and the rites of purification as ordained by David and his son Solomon. 46 For from ancient times, from the days of David and Asaph, they had been the leaders in rendering hymns of praise and thanksgiving to God. 47 In the days of Zerubbabel and Nehemiah, all Israel supplied regular daily portions for the singers and gatekeep-

ers, and gave the dedicated contributions to the Levites; and the Levites gave the dedicated contributions to the Aaronites.

13 At that time they were reading to the people from the Book of Moses, when they found this written in it, *'No Ammonite or Moabite is to be admitted* to the assembly of God, *and this is for all time,* 2*since they did not come to meet* the Israelites *with bread and water, and even hired Balaam to oppose* them *by cursing* them; *but* our *God turned the curse into a blessing.'* [a] 3 Having heard the Law, they excluded all foreigners from Israel.

The second mission of Nehemiah

4 Earlier, Eliashib the priest, who was in charge of the rooms of the Temple of our God, and who was close to Tobiah, 5 had provided him with a large room where they previously used to store the meal offerings, incense, utensils, tithes of corn, wine and oil, that is, the part of the Levites, singers and gatekeepers, and the contributions for the priests. 6 While all this was going on I was away from Jerusalem, for in the thirty-second year of Artaxerxes king of Babylon I had gone to see the king. But after some time I asked the king for permission to leave, 7 and returned to Jerusalem, where I learned about the crime which Eliashib had committed for Tobiah's benefit, by providing him with a room in the courts of the Temple of God. 8 I was extremely displeased and threw all Tobiah's household goods out of the room and into the street. 9 I then gave orders for the room to be purified, and had the utensils of the Temple of God, the meal offerings and the incense, all replaced.

10 I also learned that the Levites had not been receiving their allocations, as a result of which the Levites and singers who performed the liturgy had all withdrawn to their farms. 11 I then reprimanded the officials. 'Why is the Temple of God deserted?' I asked. And I collected them together again and brought them back to their posts; 12 and all Judah then delivered the tithe of corn, wine and oil to the storehouses. 13 As supervisors of the storehouses I appointed Shelemiah the priest, Zadok the scribe, Pedaiah one of the Levites and, as their assistant, Hanan son of Zaccur, son of Mattaniah, since they were considered reliable people; their duty was to make the distributions to their kinsmen.

14 Remember me for this, my God, and do not blot out the good deeds which I have done for the Temple of my God and its observances!

15 At the same time I saw people in Judah treading the winepress, bringing in sacks of grain and loading donkeys on the Sabbath; they were also bringing wine, grapes, figs and every kind of merchandise into Jerusalem on the Sabbath day. So I forbade them to sell the food. 16 Tyrians living there were bringing in fish and every kind of merchandise which they were selling to the Judaeans on the Sabbath in Jerusalem itself. 17 So I also reprimanded the leading men of Judah, saying to them, 'What a wicked way to behave, profaning the Sabbath day! 18 Was this not exactly what your ancestors did, with the result that our God brought all this misery down on us and on this city? And now you are adding to the wrath hanging over Israel by profaning the Sabbath yourselves!' 19 So when the gates of Jerusalem were getting dark at the approach of the Sabbath, I gave orders for the doors to be shut and directed that they were not to be opened again until the Sabbath was over. I stationed some of my attendants at the gates to make sure that no merchandise was brought in on the Sabbath day. 20 So the traders and dealers in goods of all kinds spent the night outside Jerusalem once or twice, 21 until I reprimanded them. I said to them, 'Why are you spending the night in front of the wall? Do it again, and I shall use force on you.' After this, they did not come on the Sabbath. 22 I then ordered the Levites to purify themselves and act as guards at the gates, so that the Sabbath day might be kept holy.

13a Dt 23:4–6.

Remember this also to my credit, have pity on me in the greatness of your faithful love.

²³ At that time too, I saw Jews who had married wives from Ashdod, Ammon and Moab; ²⁴ as regards their children, half of them spoke the language of Ashdod or the language of one of the other peoples, but could no longer speak the language of Judah. ²⁵ I reprimanded them, I cursed them, I struck several of them and tore out their hair and adjured them by God, 'You are not to give your daughters in marriage to their sons or let their daughters marry your sons, or marry them yourselves! ²⁶ Was it not because of women like these that Solomon king of Israel sinned? Although among many nations there was no king like him and he was loved by his God, and God made him king of all Israel, even then foreign women led him into sinning! ²⁷ Were you obedient when you committed this very grave crime: breaking faith with our God by marrying foreign wives?'

²⁸ One of the sons of Jehoiada, son of Eliashib the high priest, was a son-in-law of Sanballat the Horonite; I drove him from my presence.

²⁹ Remember them, my God, for having defiled the priesthood and the covenant of the priests and Levites!

³⁰ And so I purged them of everything foreign; I drew up regulations for the priests and Levites, defining each man's duty, ³¹ as well as for the deliveries of wood at the proper times, and for the first-fruits.

Remember this, my God, to my credit!

The Book of

TOBIT

1 The tale of Tobit son of Tobiel, son of Ananiel, son of Aduel, son of Gabael, of the lineage of Asiel and tribe of Naphtali. ² In the days of Shalmaneser king of Assyria, he was exiled from Thisbe, which is south of Kedesh-Naphtali in Upper Galilee, above Hazor, some distance to the west, north of Shephat.

Tobit the exile

³ I, Tobit, have walked in paths of truth and in good works all the days of my life. I have given much in alms to my brothers and fellow country-folk, exiled like me to Nineveh in the country of Assyria. ⁴ In my young days, when I was still at home in the land of Israel, the whole tribe of Naphtali my ancestor broke away from the House of David and from Jerusalem, though this was the city chosen out of all the tribes of Israel for their sacrifices; here, the Temple—God's dwelling-place—had been built and hallowed for all generations to come. ⁵ All my brothers and the House of Naphtali sacrificed on every hill-top in Galilee to the calf that Jeroboam king of Israel had made at Dan.

⁶ Often I was quite alone in making the pilgrimage to Jerusalem, fulfilling the Law that binds all Israel perpetually. I would hurry to Jerusalem with the first yield of fruits and beasts, the tithe of cattle and the sheep's first shearings. ⁷ I would give these to the priests, the sons of Aaron, for the altar. To the Levites ministering at Jerusalem I would give my tithe of wine and corn, olives, pomegranates and other fruits. Six years in succession I took the second tithe in money and went and paid it annually at Jerusalem. ⁸ I gave the third to orphans and widows and to the strangers who live among the Israelites; I brought it them as a gift every three years. When we ate, we obeyed both the ordinances of the law of Moses and the exhortations of Deborah the mother of our ancestor Ananiel; for my father had died and left me an orphan. ⁹ When I came to man's estate, I married a woman from our kinsfolk whose name was Anna; she bore me a son whom I called Tobias.

¹⁰ When the banishment into Assyria came, I was taken away and went to Nineveh. All my brothers and the people of my race ate the food of the heathen, ¹¹ but for my part I was careful not to eat the food of the heathen. ¹² And because I had kept faith with my God with my whole heart, ¹³ the Most High granted me the favour of Shalmaneser, and I became the king's purveyor. ¹⁴ Until his death I used to travel to Media, where I transacted business on his behalf, and I deposited sacks of silver worth ten talents with Gabael the brother of Gabrias at Rhages in Media.

¹⁵ On the death of Shalmaneser his son Sennacherib succeeded; the roads into Media were barred, and I could no longer go there. ¹⁶ In the days of Shalmaneser I had often given alms to the people of my race; ¹⁷ I gave my bread to the hungry and clothes to those who lacked them; and I buried, when I saw them, the bodies of my country-folk thrown over the walls of Nineveh.

¹⁸ I also buried those who were killed by Sennacherib. When Sennacherib was beating a disorderly retreat from Judaea after the King of heaven had punished his blasphemies, he killed a great number of Israelites in his rage. So I stole their bodies to bury them; Sennacherib looked for them and could not find them. ¹⁹ A Ninevite went and told the king it was I who had buried them secretly.

When I knew that the king had been told about me and saw myself being hunted by men who would put me to death, I was afraid and fled. 20 All my goods were seized; they were all confiscated by the treasury; nothing was left me but my wife Anna and my son Tobias.

21 Less than forty days after this, the king was murdered by his two sons, who then fled to the mountains of Ararat. His son Esarhaddon succeeded. Ahikar the son of my brother Anael, was appointed chancellor of the exchequer for the kingdom and given the main ordering of affairs. 22 Ahikar then interceded for me and I was allowed to return to Nineveh, since Ahikar had been chief cupbearer, keeper of the signet, administrator and treasurer under Sennacherib king of Assyria, and Esarhaddon had kept him in office. He was a relation of mine; he was my nephew.

Tobit blinded

2 In the reign of Esarhaddon, therefore, I returned home, and my wife Anna was restored to me with my son Tobias. At our feast of Pentecost (the feast of Weeks) there was a good dinner. I took my place for the meal; 2 the table was brought to me and various dishes were brought. I then said to my son Tobias, 'Go, my child, and seek out some poor, loyal-hearted man among our brothers exiled in Nineveh, and bring him to share my meal. I will wait until you come back, my child.' 3 So Tobias went out to look for some poor man among our brothers, but he came back again and said, 'Father!' I replied, 'What is it, my child?' He went on, 'Father, one of our nation has just been murdered; he has been strangled and then thrown down in the market place; he is there still.' 4 I sprang up at once, left my meal untouched, took the man from the market place and laid him in one of my rooms, waiting until sunset to bury him. 5 I came in again and washed myself and ate my bread in sorrow, 6 remembering the words of the prophet Amos concerning Bethel:

I shall turn your festivals into mourning and all your singing into lamentation.[a]

7 And I wept. When the sun was down, I went and dug a grave and buried him. 8 My neighbours laughed and said, 'See! He is not afraid any more.' (You must remember that a price had been set on my head earlier for this very thing.) 'Once before he had to flee, yet here he is, beginning to bury the dead again.' 9 That night I took a bath; then I went into the courtyard and lay down by the courtyard wall. Since it was hot I left my face uncovered. 10 I did not know that there were sparrows in the wall above my head; their hot droppings fell into my eyes. This caused white spots to form, which I went to have treated by the doctors. But the more ointments they tried me with, the more the spots blinded me, and in the end, I became completely blind. I remained without sight four years; all my brothers were distressed on my behalf; and Ahikar provided for my upkeep for two years, until he left for Elymais.

11 My wife Anna then undertook woman's work; she would spin wool and take cloth to weave; 12 she used to deliver whatever had been ordered from her and then receive payment. Now on the seventh day of the month of Dystros, she finished a piece of work and delivered it to her customers. They paid her all that was due, and into the bargain presented her with a kid for a meal. 13 When the kid came into my house, it began to bleat. I called to my wife and said, 'Where does this creature come from? Suppose it has been stolen! Let the owners have it back; we have no right to eat stolen goods'. 14 She said, 'No, it was a present given me over and above my wages.' I did not believe her, and told her to give it back to the owners (I felt deeply ashamed of her). To which, she replied, 'What about your own alms? What about your own good works? Everyone knows what return you have had for them.'

2a Am 8:10.

3 Then, sad at heart, I sighed and wept, and began this prayer of lamentation:

2 You are just, O Lord,
　and just are all your works.
　All your ways are grace and truth,
　and you are the Judge of the world.

3 Therefore, Lord,
　remember me, look on me.
　Do not punish me for my sins
　or for my needless faults
　or those of my ancestors.

4 For we have sinned against you
　and broken your commandments;
　and you have given us over to be
　　　　plundered,
　to captivity and death,
　to be the talk, the laughing-stock and
　　　　scorn
　of all the nations among whom you have
　　　　dispersed us.

5 And now all your decrees are true
　when you deal with me as my faults
　　　　deserve,
　and those of my ancestors.
　For we have neither kept your
　　　　commandments
　nor walked in truth before you.

6 So now, do with me as you will;
　be pleased to take my life from me;
　so that I may be delivered from earth
　and become earth again.
　Better death than life for me,
　for I have endured groundless insult
　and am in deepest sorrow.

　Lord, be pleased
　to deliver me from this affliction.
　Let me go away to my everlasting home;
　do not turn your face from me, O Lord.
　Better death for me than life prolonged
　in the face of unrelenting misery:
　I can no longer bear to listen to insults.

Sarah

7 It chanced on the same day that Sarah the daughter of Raguel, who lived in Media at Ecbatana, also heard insults from one of her father's maids. 8 For she had been given in marriage seven times, and Asmodeus, the worst of demons, had killed her bridegrooms one after another before ever they had slept with her as man with wife. The servant-girl said, 'Yes, you kill your bridegrooms yourself. That makes seven already to whom you have been given, and you have not once been in luck yet. 9 Just because your bridegrooms have died, that is no reason for punishing us. Go and join them, and may we be spared the sight of any child of yours!' 10 That day, she grieved, she sobbed, and she went up to her father's room intending to hang herself. But then she thought, 'Suppose they were to blame my father! They would say, "You had an only daughter whom you loved, and now she has hanged herself for grief." I cannot cause my father a sorrow which would bring down his old age to the dwelling of the dead. I should do better not to hang myself, but to beg the Lord to let me die and not live to hear any more insults.' 11 And at this, by the window, with outstretched arms she said this prayer:

　You are blessed, O God of mercy!
　May your name be blessed for ever,
　and may all things you have made
　bless you everlastingly.

12 And now I turn my face
　and I raise my eyes to you.
13 Let your word deliver me from earth;
　I can hear myself insulted no longer.

14 O Lord, you know
　that I have remained pure;
　no man has touched me;
15 I have not dishonoured your name
　or my father's name
　in this land of exile.

I am my father's only daughter,
he has no other child as heir;
he has no brother at his side,
nor has he any kinsman left
for whom I ought to keep myself.

I have lost seven husbands already;
why should I live any longer?
If it does not please you to take my life,
then look on me with pity;
I can no longer bear to hear myself
defamed.

16 This time the prayer of each of them found favour before the glory of God, 17 and Raphael was sent to bring remedy to them both. He was to take the white spots from the eyes of Tobit, so that he might see God's light with his own eyes; and he was to give Sarah the daughter of Raguel as bride to Tobias son of Tobit, and to rid her of Asmodeus, that worst of demons. For it was to Tobias before all other suitors that she belonged by right. Tobit was coming back from the courtyard into the house at the same moment as Sarah the daughter of Raguel was coming down from the upper room.

Tobias

4 The same day Tobit remembered the silver that he had left with Gabael at Rhages in Media 2 and thought, 'I have come to the point of praying for death; I should do well to call my son Tobias and tell him about the money before I die.' 3 He summoned his son Tobias and told him, 'When I die, give me an honourable burial. Honour your mother, and never abandon her all the days of your life. Do all that she wants, and give her no reason for sorrow. 4 Remember, my child, all the risks she ran for your sake when you were in her womb. And when she dies, bury her at my side in the same grave.

5 'My child, be faithful to the Lord all your days. Never entertain the will to sin or to transgress his laws. Do good works all the days of your life, never follow ways that are not upright; 6 for if you act in truthfulness, you will be successful in all your actions, as everyone is who practises what is upright.

7 'Set aside part of your goods for almsgiving. Never turn your face from the poor and God will never turn his from you. 8 Measure your alms by what you have; if you have much, give more; if you have little, do not be afraid to give less in alms. 9 So doing, you will lay up for yourself a great treasure for the day of necessity. 10 For almsgiving delivers from death and saves people from passing down to darkness. 11 Almsgiving is a most effective offering for all those who do it in the presence of the Most High.

12 'My child, avoid all loose conduct. Choose a wife of your father's stock. Do not take a foreign wife outside your father's tribe, because we are the children of the prophets. Remember Noah, Abraham, Isaac and Jacob, our ancestors from the beginning. All of them took wives from their own kindred, and they were blessed in their children, and their race will inherit the earth. 13 You, too, my child, must love your own brothers; never presume to despise your brothers, the sons and daughters of your people; choose your wife from among them. For pride brings ruin and much worry; idleness causes need and poverty, for the mother of famine is idleness.

14 'Do not keep back until next day the wages of those who work for you; pay them at once. If you serve God you will be rewarded. Be careful, my child, in all you do, well-disciplined in all your behaviour. 15 Do to no one what you would not want done to you. Do not drink wine to the point of drunkenness; do not let excess be your travelling companion.

16 'Give your bread to those who are hungry, and your clothes to those who lack clothing. Of whatever you own in plenty, devote a proportion to almsgiving; and when you give alms, do it ungrudgingly. 17 Be generous with bread and wine on the graves of upright people, but not for the sinner.

18 'Ask advice of every wise person; never scorn any profitable advice. 19 Bless the Lord

God in everything; beg him to guide your ways and bring your paths and purposes to their end. For wisdom is not the property of every nation; their desire for what is good is conferred by the Lord. At his will he lifts up or he casts down to the depths of the dwelling of the dead. So now, my child, remember these precepts and never let them fade from your heart.

20 'Now, my child, I must tell you I have left ten talents of silver with Gabael son of Gabrias, at Rhages in Media. 21 Do not be afraid, my child, if we have grown poor. You have great wealth if you fear God, if you shun every kind of sin and if you do what is pleasing to the Lord your God.'

Raphael

5 Tobias then replied to his father Tobit, 'Father, I shall do everything you have told me. 2 But how am I to recover the silver from him? He does not know me, nor I him. What token am I to give him for him to believe me and hand the silver over to me? And besides, I do not know what roads to take for this journey into Media.' 3 Then Tobit answered his son Tobias, 'Each of us set his signature to a note which I cut in two, so that each could keep half of it. I took one piece, and put the other with the silver. To think it was twenty years ago I left this silver in his keeping! And now, my child, find a trustworthy travelling companion—we shall pay him for his time until you arrive back—and then go and collect the silver from Gabael.'

4 Tobias went out to look for a man who knew the way to go with him to Media. Outside he found Raphael the angel standing facing him, though he did not guess he was an angel of God. 5 He said, 'Where do you come from, friend?' The angel replied, 'I am one of your brother Israelites; I have come to these parts to look for work.' Tobias asked, 'Do you know the road to Media?' 6 The other replied, 'Certainly I do, I have been there many times; I have knowledge and experience of all the ways. I have often been to Media and stayed with Gabael one of our kinsmen who lives at Rhages in Media. It usually takes two full days to get from Ecbatana to Rhages; Rhages lies in the mountains, and Ecbatana is in the middle of the plain.' 7 Tobias said, 'Wait for me, friend, while I go and tell my father; I need you to come with me; I shall pay you for your time.' 8 The other replied, 'Good, I shall wait; but do not be long.'

9 Tobias went in and told his father that he had found one of their brother Israelites. And the father said, 'Fetch him in; I want to find out about his family and tribe. I must see if he is going to be a reliable companion for you, my child.' So Tobias went out and called him, 'Friend,' he said, 'my father wants you.'

10 The angel came into the house; Tobit greeted him, and the other answered, wishing him happiness in plenty. Tobit replied, 'Can I ever be happy again? I am a blind man; I no longer see the light of heaven; I am sunk in darkness like the dead who see the light no more. I am a man buried alive; I hear people speak but cannot see them.' The angel said, 'Take comfort; before long God will heal you. Take comfort.' Tobit said, 'My son Tobias wishes to go to Media. Will you join him as his guide? Brother, I will pay you.' He replied, 'I am willing to go with him; I know all the ways; I have often been to Media, I have crossed all its plains and mountains, and I know all its roads.' 11 Tobit said, 'Brother, what family and what tribe do you belong to? Will you tell me, brother?' 12 'What does my tribe matter to you?' the angel said. Tobit said, 'I want to be quite sure whose son you are and what your name is.' 13 The angel said, 'I am Azarias, son of the great Ananias, one of your kinsmen.' 14 'Welcome and greetings, brother! Do not be offended at my wanting to know the name of your family; I find you are my kinsman of a good and honourable line. I know Ananias and Nathan, the two sons of the great Shemaiah. They used to go to Jerusalem with me; we have worshipped together there and they have never strayed from the right path. Your brothers are worthy men; you come of good stock; welcome.'

15 He went on, 'I engage you at a drachma a day, with the same expenses as my own son's. Complete the journey with my son 16 and I shall go beyond the agreed wage.' The angel replied, 'I shall complete the journey with him. Do not be afraid. On the journey outward all will be well; on the journey back all will be well; the road is safe.' 17 Tobit said, 'Blessings on you, brother!' Then he turned to his son. 'My child', he said, 'prepare what you need for the journey, and set off with your brother. May God in heaven protect you abroad and bring you both back to me safe and sound! May his angel go with you and protect you, my child!'

Tobias left the house to set out and kissed his father and mother. Tobit said, 'A happy journey!' 18 His mother burst into tears and said to Tobit, 'Why must you send my child away? Is he not the staff of our hands, as he goes about before us? 19 Surely money is not the only thing that matters? Surely it is not as precious as our child? 20 The way of life God had already given us was good enough.' 21 He said, 'Do not think such thoughts. Going away and coming back, all will be well with our child. You will see for yourself when he comes back safe and sound! Do not think such thoughts; do not worry on their account, my sister. 22 A good angel will go with him; he will have a good journey and come back to us well and happy.'

6 And she dried her tears.

The fish

2 The boy left with the angel, and the dog followed behind. The two walked on, and when the first evening came they camped beside the Tigris. 3 The boy had gone down to the river to wash his feet, when a great fish leapt out of the water and tried to swallow his foot. The boy gave a shout 4 and the angel said, 'Catch the fish; do not let it go.' The boy mastered the fish and pulled it onto the bank. 5 The angel said, 'Cut it open; take out gall, heart and liver; set these aside and throw the entrails away, for gall and heart and liver have curative properties.' 6 The boy cut the fish open and took out gall and heart and liver. He fried part of the fish for his meal and kept some for salting. Then they walked on again together until they were nearly in Media.

7 Then the boy asked the angel this question, 'Brother Azarias, what can the fish's heart, liver and gall cure?' 8 He replied, 'You burn the fish's heart and liver, and their smoke is used in the case of a man or woman plagued by a demon or evil spirit; any such affliction disappears for good, leaving no trace. 9 As regards the gall, this is used as an eye ointment for anyone having white spots on his eyes; after using it, you have only to blow on the spots to cure them.'

10 They entered Media and had nearly reached Ecbatana 11 when Raphael said to the boy, 'Brother Tobias.' 'Yes?' he replied. The angel went on, 'Tonight we are to stay with Raguel, who is a kinsman of yours. He has a daughter called Sarah, 12 but apart from Sarah he has no other son or daughter. Now you are her next of kin; she belongs to you before anyone else and you may claim her father's inheritance. She is a thoughtful, courageous and very lovely girl, and her father loves her dearly. 13 You have the right to marry her. Listen, brother; this very evening I shall speak about the girl to her father and arrange for her to be betrothed to you, and when we come back from Rhages we can celebrate the marriage. I assure you, Raguel has no right whatever to refuse you or to betroth her to anyone else. That would be asking for death, as prescribed in the Book of Moses, once he is aware that kinship gives you the pre-eminent right to marry his daughter. So listen, brother. This very evening we shall speak about the girl and ask for her hand in marriage. When we come back from Rhages we shall fetch her and take her home with us.'

14 Tobias replied to Raphael, 'Brother Azarias, I have been told that she has already been given in marriage seven times and that

each time her bridegroom has died in the bridal room. He died the same night as he entered her room; and I have heard people say it was a demon that killed them, ¹⁵and this makes me afraid. To her the demon does no harm because he loves her, but as soon as a man tries to approach her, he kills him. I am my father's only son, and I have no wish to die. I do not want my father and mother to grieve over me for the rest of their lives; they have no other son to bury them.' ¹⁶The angel said, 'Have you forgotten your father's advice? After all, he urged you to choose a wife from your father's family. Listen then, brother. Do not worry about the demon; take her. This very evening, I promise, she will be given you as your wife. ¹⁷Then once you are in the bridal room, take the heart and liver of the fish and lay a little of it on the burning incense. The reek will rise, ¹⁸the demon will smell it and flee, and there is no danger that he will ever be found near the girl again. Then, before you sleep together, first stand up, both of you, and pray. Ask the Lord of heaven to grant you his grace and protection. Do not be afraid; she was destined for you from the beginning, and you are the one to save her. She will follow you, and I pledge my word she will give you children who will be like brothers to you. Do not worry.' And when Tobias heard Raphael say this, when he understood that Sarah was his sister, a kinswoman of his father's family, he fell so deeply in love with her that he could no longer call his heart his own.

Raguel

7 As they entered Ecbatana, Tobias said, 'Brother Azarias, take me at once to our brother Raguel's.' And he showed him the way to the house of Raguel, whom they found sitting beside his courtyard door. They greeted him first, and he replied, 'Welcome and greetings, brothers.' And he took them into his house. ²He said to his wife Edna, 'How like my brother Tobit this young man is!' ³Edna asked them where they came from; they said, 'We are sons of Naphtali exiled in Nineveh.'

⁴'Do you know our brother Tobit?' 'Yes.' 'How is he?' ⁵'He is alive and well.' And Tobias added, 'He is my father.' ⁶Raguel leapt to his feet and kissed him and wept. ⁷Then, finding words, he said, 'Blessings on you, child! You are the son of a noble father. How sad it is that someone so bright and full of good deeds should have gone blind!' He fell on the neck of his kinsman Tobias and wept. ⁸And his wife Edna wept for him, and so did his daughter Sarah. ⁹Raguel killed a ram from the flock, and they gave them a warm welcome.

They washed and bathed and sat down to table. Then Tobias said to Raphael, 'Brother Azarias, will you ask Raguel to give me my sister Sarah?' ¹⁰Raguel overheard the words, and said to the young man, 'Eat and drink, and make the most of your evening; no one else has the right to take my daughter Sarah— no one but you, my brother. In any case even I am not at liberty to give her to anyone else, since you are her next of kin. However, my boy, I must be frank with you: ¹¹I have tried to find a husband for her seven times among our kinsmen, and all of them have died the first evening, on going to her room. But for the present, my boy, eat and drink; the Lord will grant you his grace and peace.' Tobias spoke out, 'I will not hear of eating and drinking till you have come to a decision about me.' Raguel answered, 'Very well. Since, by the prescription of the Book of Moses she is given to you, Heaven itself decrees she shall be yours. I therefore entrust your sister to you. From now on you are her brother and she is your sister. She is given to you from today for ever. The Lord of heaven favour you tonight, my child, and grant you his grace and peace.' ¹²Raguel called for his daughter Sarah, took her by the hand and gave her to Tobias with these words, 'I entrust her to you; the law and the ruling recorded in the Book of Moses assign her to you as your wife. Take her; bring her home safe and sound to your father's house. The God of heaven grant you a good journey in peace.' ¹³Then he turned to her mother and asked her to fetch him writing paper. He drew up the marriage contract, and so he gave his daughter as bride to Tobias according to the ordinance of the Law of Moses.

¹⁴ After this they began to eat and drink. ¹⁵ Raguel called his wife Edna and said, 'My sister, prepare the second room and take her there.' ¹⁶ She went and made the bed in this room as he had ordered, and took her daughter to it. She wept over her, then wiped away her tears and said, 'Courage, daughter! May the Lord of heaven turn your grief to joy! Courage, daughter!' And she went out.

The grave

8 When they had finished eating and drinking and it seemed time to go to bed, the young man was taken from the dining room to the bedroom. ² Tobias remembered Raphael's advice; he went to his bag, took the fish's heart and liver out of it and put some on the burning incense. ³ The reek of the fish distressed the demon, who fled through the air to Egypt. Raphael pursued him there, shackled him and strangled him forthwith.

⁴ The parents meanwhile had gone out and shut the door behind them. Tobias rose from the bed, and said to Sarah, 'Get up, my sister! You and I must pray and petition our Lord to win his grace and his protection.' ⁵ She stood up, and they began praying for protection, and this was how he began:

> You are blessed, O God of our fathers;
> blessed too is your name
> for ever and ever.
> Let the heavens bless you
> and all things you have made
> for evermore.

⁶ You it was who created Adam,
> you who created Eve his wife
> to be his help and support;
> and from these two the human race was
>   born.
> You it was who said,
> *'It is not right that the man should be alone;*
> *let us make him a helper like him.'* ᵃ

⁷ And so I take my sister
> not for any lustful motive,
> but I do it in singleness of heart.
> Be kind enough to have pity on her and
>   on me
> and bring us to old age together.

⁸ And together they said, 'Amen, Amen,' ⁹ and lay down for the night.

But Raguel rose and called his servants, who came and helped him dig a grave. ¹⁰ He had thought, 'Heaven grant he does not die! We should be overwhelmed with ridicule and shame.' ¹¹ When the grave was ready, Raguel went back to the house, called his wife ¹² and said, 'Will you send a maid to the room to see if Tobias is still alive? For if he is dead, we may be able to bury him without anyone else knowing.' ¹³ They sent the maid, lit the lamp, opened the door and the maid went in. She found the two fast asleep together; ¹⁴ she came out again and whispered, 'He is not dead; all is well.' ¹⁵ Then Raguel blessed the God of heaven with these words:

> You are blessed, my God,
> with every blessing that is pure;
> may you be blessed for evermore!

¹⁶ You are blessed for having made me glad.
> What I feared has not happened,
> instead you have shown us
> your boundless mercy.

¹⁷ You are blessed for taking pity
> on this only son, this only daughter.
> Grant them, Master, your mercy and your
>   protection;
> let them live out their lives
> in happiness and in mercy.

¹⁸ And he made his servants fill the grave in before dawn broke.

¹⁹ He told his wife to make an ovenful of bread; he went to his flock, brought back two

8a Gn 2:18.

oxen and four sheep and gave orders for them to be cooked; and preparations began. ²⁰ He called Tobias and said, 'I will not hear of your leaving here for a fortnight. You are to stay where you are, eating and drinking, with me. You will make my daughter happy again after all her troubles. ²¹ After that, take away a half of all I have, and take her safe and sound back to your father. When my wife and I are dead you shall have the other half. Courage, my boy! I am your father, and Edna is your mother. We are your parents in future, as we are your sister's. Courage, my son!'

The wedding feast

9 Then Tobias turned to Raphael. ² 'Brother Azarias,' he said, 'take four servants and two camels and leave for Rhages. ³ Go to Gabael's house, give him the receipt and see about the money; then invite him to come with you to my wedding feast. ⁴ You know that my father must be counting the days and that I cannot lose a single one without worrying him. ⁵ You see what Raguel has pledged himself to do; I am bound by his oath.' So Raphael left for Rhages in Media with the four servants and two camels. They stayed with Gabael, and Raphael showed him the receipt. He told him about the marriage of Tobias son of Tobit and gave him his invitation to the wedding feast. Gabael started counting out the sacks to him—the seals were intact—and they loaded them on to the camels. ⁶ Early in the morning they set off together for the feast, and reached Raguel's house where they found Tobias dining. He rose to greet Gabael, who burst into tears and blessed him with the words, 'Excellent son of a father beyond reproach, just and generous in his dealings! The Lord give heaven's blessing to you, to your wife, to your wife's father and mother! Blessed be God for granting me the sight of this living image of my cousin Tobit!'

10 Every day, meanwhile, Tobit kept reckoning the days required for the journey there and the journey back. The full number

went by, and still his son had not come. ² Then he thought, 'I hope he has not been delayed there! I hope Gabael is not dead, so that no one will give him the silver.' ³ And he began to worry. ⁴ His wife Anna kept saying, 'My son is dead! He is no longer among the living!' And she began to weep and mourn over her son. She kept saying, ⁵ 'Alas! I should never have let you leave me, my child, you, the light of my eyes.' ⁶ And Tobit would reply, 'Hush, my sister! Do not worry. All is well with him. Something has happened there to delay them. His companion is someone we can trust, one of our kinsmen at that. Do not lose heart, my sister. ⁷ He will soon be here.' But all she would say was, 'Leave me alone; do not try to deceive me. My child is dead.' And every day she would go abruptly out to watch the road by which her son had left. She trusted no eyes but her own. Once the sun had set she would come home again, only to weep and moan all night, unable to sleep.

After the fourteen days of feasting that Raguel had sworn to keep for his daughter's marriage, Tobias came to him and said, 'Let me go now; my father and mother must have lost all hope of seeing me again. So I beg you, father, to let me return to my father's house; I have told you the plight he was in when I left him.' ⁸ Raguel said to Tobias, 'Stay, my son, stay with me. I shall send messengers to your father Tobit to give him news of you.' ⁹ But Tobias pressed him, 'No, I beg you to let me go back to my father's house.' ¹⁰ Without more ado, Raguel committed Sarah his bride into his keeping. He gave Tobias half his wealth, slaves, men and women, oxen and sheep, donkeys and camels, clothes and money and household things. ¹¹ And so he let them leave happily. To Tobias he said these parting words, 'Good health, my son, and a happy journey! May the Lord of heaven be gracious to you and to your wife Sarah! I hope to see your children before I die.' ¹² To his daughter Sarah he said, 'Go now to your father-in-law's house, since henceforward they are as much your parents as those who gave you life. Go in peace, my daughter, I hope to hear nothing but good of you, as long as I live.' He said goodbye to them and let them go.

Edna in her turn said to Tobias, 'Dear son and brother, may it please the Lord to bring you back again! I hope to live long enough to see the children of you and my daughter Sarah before I die. In the sight of the Lord I give my daughter into your keeping. Never make her unhappy as long as you live. Go in peace, my son. Henceforward I am your mother and Sarah is your sister. May we all live happily for the rest of our lives!' And she kissed them both and saw them set out happily.

¹³Tobias left Raguel's house with his mind at ease. In his gladness he blessed the Lord of heaven and earth, the King of all that is, for the happy issue of his travels. He gave this blessing to Raguel and his wife Edna, 'May it be my happiness to honour you for the rest of my life!'

Tobit's sight restored

11 They were nearly at Kaserin, opposite Nineveh, ²when Raphael said, 'You know the plight in which we left your father; ³let us go on ahead of your wife and prepare the house ourselves while she travels behind with the others.' ⁴They went on together (Raphael warned Tobias to take the gall with him) and the dog followed them.

⁵Anna was sitting, watching the road by which her son would come. ⁶She was sure at once it must be he and said to the father, 'Here comes your son, with his companion.'

⁷Raphael said to Tobias before he reached his father, 'I give you my word that your father's eyes will open. ⁸You must put the fish's gall to his eyes; the medicine will smart and will draw a filmy white skin off his eyes. And your father will no more be blind but will be able to see the light.'

⁹The mother ran forward and threw her arms round her son's neck. 'Now I can die,' she said, 'I have seen you again.' And she wept. ¹⁰Tobit rose to his feet and stumbled across the courtyard through the door. Tobias came on towards him ¹¹(he had the fish's gall in his hand). He blew into his eyes and said, steadying him, 'Take courage, father!' With this he applied the medicine, left it there a while, ¹²then with both hands peeled away a filmy skin from the corners of his eyes. ¹³Then his father fell on his neck ¹⁴and wept. He exclaimed, 'I can see you, my son, the light of my eyes!' And he said:

Blessed be God!
Blessed be his great name!
Blessed be all his holy angels!
Blessed be his great name
for evermore!

¹⁵ For, having afflicted me,
he has had pity on me
and now I see my son Tobias!

Tobias went indoors, joyfully blessing God at the top of his voice. Then he told his father everything; how his journey had been successful and he had brought the silver back; how he had married Sarah the daughter of Raguel; how she was following him now, close behind, and could not be far from the gates of Nineveh.

¹⁶Tobit set off to the gates of Nineveh to meet his daughter-in-law, giving joyful praise to God as he went. When the people of Nineveh saw him walking without a guide and stepping forward as briskly as of old, they were astonished. ¹⁷Tobit described to them how God had taken pity on him and had opened his eyes. Then Tobit met Sarah the bride of his son Tobias, and blessed her in these words. 'Welcome, daughter! Blessed be your God for sending you to us, my daughter. Blessings on your father, blessings on my son Tobias, blessings on yourself, my daughter. Welcome now to your own house in joyfulness and in blessedness. Come in, my daughter.' That day brought joy to the Jews of Nineveh, ¹⁸and his cousins Ahikar and Nadab came to share in Tobit's happiness.

The revelation

12 When the wedding feast was over, Tobit called his son Tobias and said, 'My son, you ought to think about paying the amount due to your fellow traveller; give him more than the figure agreed on.' 2 'Father,' he replied, 'how much am I to give him for his help? Even if I give him half the goods he brought back with me, I shall not be the loser. 3 He has brought me back safe and sound, he has cured my wife, he has brought the money back too, and now he has cured you as well. How much am I to give him for all this?' 4 Tobit said, 'He has richly earned half what he brought back'. 5 So Tobias called his companion and said, 'Take half of what you brought back, in payment for all you have done, and go in peace.'

6 Then Raphael took them both aside and said, 'Bless God, utter his praise before all the living for the favour he has shown you. Bless and extol his name. Proclaim before all people the deeds of God as they deserve, and never tire of giving him thanks. 7 It is right to keep the secret of a king, yet right to reveal and publish the works of God as they deserve. Do what is good, and no evil can befall you.

8 'Prayer with fasting and alms with uprightness are better than riches with iniquity. Better to practise almsgiving than to hoard up gold. 9 Almsgiving saves from death and purges every kind of sin. Those who give alms have their fill of days; 10 those who commit sin and do evil bring harm on themselves.

11 'I am going to tell you the whole truth, hiding nothing from you. I have already told you that it is right to keep the secret of a king, yet right too to reveal in a worthy way the words of God. 12 So you must know that when you and Sarah were at prayer, it was I who offered your supplications before the glory of the Lord and who read them; so too when you were burying the dead. 13 When you did not hesitate to get up and leave the table to go and bury a dead man, I was sent to test your faith, 14 and at the same time God sent me to heal you and your daughter-in-law Sarah. 15 I am Raphael, one of the seven angels who stand ever ready to enter the presence of the glory of the Lord.'

16 They were both overwhelmed with awe; they fell on their faces in terror. 17 But the angel said, 'Do not be afraid; peace be with you. Bless God for ever. 18 As far as I was concerned, when I was with you, my presence was not by any decision of mine, but by the will of God; he is the one whom you must bless as long as you live, he the one that you must praise. 19 You thought you saw me eating, but that was appearance and no more. 20 Now bless the Lord on earth and give thanks to God. I am about to return to him who sent me from above. Write down all that has happened.' And he rose in the air. 21 When they stood up again, he was no longer visible. They praised God with hymns; they thanked him for having performed such wonders; had not an angel of God appeared to them?

Zion

13 And he said:

Blessed be God who lives for ever,
 for his reign endures throughout all ages!
2 For he both punishes and pardons;
 he sends people down to the depths of the
  underworld
 and draws them up from utter
  Destruction;
 no one can escape his hand.
3 Declare his praise before the nations,
 you who are the children of Israel!
 For if he has scattered you among them,
4 there too he has shown you his greatness.
 Extol him before all the living;
 he is our Lord
 and he is our God;
 he is our Father,
 and he is God for ever and ever.

5 Though he punishes you for your
  iniquities,
 he will take pity on you all;

he will gather you from every nation
wherever you have been scattered.
6 If you return to him
with all your heart and all your soul,
behaving honestly towards him,
then he will return to you
and hide his face from you no longer.
Consider how well he has treated you;
loudly give him thanks.
Bless the Lord of justice
and extol the King of the ages.

I for my part sing his praise
in the country of my exile;
I make his power and greatness known
to a nation that has sinned.
Sinners, return to him;
let your conduct be upright before him;
perhaps he will be gracious to you
and take pity on you.
7 I for my part extol God
and my soul rejoices
in the King of heaven.
Let his greatness 8 be on every tongue,
his praises be sung in Jerusalem.

9 Jerusalem, Holy City,
God has scourged you for what you have
done
but will still take pity on the children of
the upright.
10 Thank the Lord as he deserves
and bless the King of the ages,
that your Temple may be rebuilt with joy
within you;
within you he may comfort every exile,
and within you he may love all those who
are distressed,
for all generations to come.

11 A bright light will shine
over all the regions of the earth;
many nations will come from far away,
from all the ends of the earth,
to dwell close to the holy name of the Lord
God,
with gifts in their hands for the King of
heaven.

Within you, generation after generation
will proclaim their joy,
and the name of her who is Elect will
endure
through the generations to come.

12 Cursed be any who affront you,
cursed be any who destroy you,
who throw down your walls,
who rase your towers,
who burn your houses!
Eternally blessed be he who rebuilds you!
13 Then you will exult, and rejoice
over the children of the upright,
for they will all have been gathered in
and will bless the Lord of the ages.

14 Blessed are those who love you,
blessed those who rejoice over your
peace,
blessed those who have mourned
over all your punishment!
For they will soon rejoice within you,
witness all your blessedness in days to
come.
15 My soul blesses the Lord, the great
King
16 because Jerusalem will be built anew
and his house for ever and ever.

What bliss, if one of my family be left
to see your glory and praise the King of
heaven!
The gates of Jerusalem will be built
of sapphire and of emerald,
and all your walls of precious stone,
the towers of Jerusalem will be built of
gold
and their battlements of pure gold.
17 The streets of Jerusalem will be paved
with ruby and with stones from Ophir;
the gates of Jerusalem will resound
with songs of exultation;
and all her houses will say,
'Alleluia! Blessed be the God of Israel.'
Within you they will bless the holy name
for ever and ever.

34 READ TOBIT 12.

Prayer with fasting and alms with uprightness are better than riches with iniquity.

—TOBIT 12:8

PRAYER WITH GOOD WORKS

Through prayer and almsgiving, Tobit and Sarah received God's mercy for their son Tobias and healing of Tobit's blindness. In this chapter, Raphael, God's messenger, prescribes prayer, fasting, and almsgiving as fundamental means of grace. In the following instruction, St. Cyprian of Carthage proclaims the effectiveness of these spiritual disciplines:

The Lord taught us to pray not only in words, but also in actions. He prayed frequently himself and showed us by example what we must do. As Scripture says: "In the morning . . . he got up and left the house and went off to a lonely place and prayed there" (Mk 1:35). But if the sinless one prayed, how much more ought sinners to pray.

When we stand praying, we ought to be watchful and earnest with our whole heart, intent on our prayers. Let all carnal and worldly thoughts pass away. Don't let the soul think on anything except the object of its prayer. Thus the priest prepares the minds of the people by saying, "Lift up your hearts," so that upon the people's response, "We have lifted them up to the Lord," he may be reminded himself to think of nothing but the Lord.

Moreover, those who pray should not come to the Lord with fruitless or naked prayers. Petition is ineffectual when it is a barren entreaty that implores God. For as every tree that bears no fruit is cut down and cast into the fire, so also assuredly words that do not bear fruit cannot deserve anything of God because they are not fruitful in any good action. Thus Scripture instructs us, saying, "Prayer is good with fasting and almsgiving." For he who will reward us on judgment day for our works and alms will even in this life listen mercifully to those who come to him in prayer combined with good works. ST. CYPRIAN OF CARTHAGE, 200?–258

YOU WILL FIND THE NEXT READING AT 2 MACCABEES 7.

14 The end of the hymns of Tobit.

Nineveh

Tobit died when he was a hundred and twelve years old and received an honourable burial in Nineveh. [2] He had been sixty-two when he went blind; and after his cure, he lived in comfort, practising almsgiving and continually praising God and extolling his greatness.

[3] When he was at the point of death he summoned his son Tobias and gave him these instructions, [4] 'My son, take your children and hurry away to Media, since I believe the word of God pronounced over Nineveh by Nahum. Everything will come true, everything happen that the emissaries of God, the prophets of Israel, have predicted against Assyria and Nineveh; not one of their words will prove empty. It will all take place in due time. You will be

safer in Media than in Assyria or in Babylonia. Since I for my part know and believe that everything God has said will come true; so it will be, and not a word of the prophecies will fail.

'A census will be taken of our brothers living in the land of Israel and they will be exiled far from their own fair country. The entire territory of Israel will become a desert, and Samaria and Jerusalem will become a desert, and the house of God, for a time, will be laid waste and burnt. ⁵Then once again God will take pity on them and bring them back to the land of Israel. They will rebuild his house, although it will be less beautiful than the first, until the time is fulfilled. But after this, all will return from captivity and rebuild Jerusalem in all her glory, and the house of God will be rebuilt within her as the prophets of Israel have foretold. ⁶And all the people of the whole earth will be converted and will reverence God with all sincerity. All will renounce their false gods who have led them astray into error, ⁷and will bless the God of ages in uprightness. All the Israelites spared in those days will remember God in sincerity of heart. They will come and gather in Jerusalem and thereafter dwell securely in the land of Abraham, which will be theirs. And those who sincerely love God will rejoice. And those who commit sin and wickedness will vanish from the earth.

⁸'And now, my children, I lay this duty on you; serve God sincerely, and do what is pleasing to him. And lay on your children the obligation to behave uprightly, to give alms, to keep God in mind and to bless his name always, sincerely and with all their might.

⁹'So then, my son, leave Nineveh, do not stay here. ¹⁰As soon as you have buried your mother next to me, go the same day, whenever it may be, and do not linger in this country where I see wickedness and perfidy unashamedly triumphant. Consider, my child, all the things done by Nadab to his foster-father Ahikar. Was not Ahikar forced to go underground, though still a living man? But God made the criminal pay for his outrage before his victim's eyes, since Ahikar came back to the light of day, while Nadab went down to everlasting darkness in punishment for plotting against Ahikar's life. Because of his good works Ahikar escaped the deadly snare Nadab had laid for him, and Nadab fell into it to his own ruin. ¹¹So, my children, you see what comes of almsgiving, and what wickedness leads to, I mean to death. But now breath fails me.'

They laid him back on his bed; he died and was buried with honour.

¹²When his mother died, Tobias buried her beside his father. Then he left for Media with his wife and children. He lived in Ecbatana with Raguel, his father-in-law. ¹³He treated the ageing parents of his wife with every care and respect, and later buried them in Ecbatana in Media. Tobias inherited the patrimony of Raguel besides that of his father Tobit. ¹⁴Much honoured, he lived to the age of a hundred and seventeen years. ¹⁵Before he died he witnessed the ruin of Nineveh. He saw the Ninevites taken prisoner and deported to Media by Cyaxares king of Media. He blessed God for everything he inflicted on the Ninevites and Assyrians. Before his death he had the opportunity of rejoicing over the fate of Nineveh, and he blessed the Lord God for ever and ever. Amen.

JUDITH

Nebuchadnezzar and Arphaxad

1 It was the twelfth year of Nebuchadnezzar who reigned over the Assyrians in the great city of Nineveh. Arphaxad was then reigning over the Medes in Ecbatana. ²He surrounded this city with walls of dressed stones three cubits thick and six cubits long, making the rampart seventy cubits high and fifty cubits wide. ³At the gates he placed towers one hundred cubits high and, at the foundations, sixty cubits wide, ⁴the gates themselves being seventy cubits high and forty wide to allow his forces to march out in a body and his infantry to parade freely.

⁵About this time King Nebuchadnezzar gave battle to King Arphaxad in the great plain lying in the territory of Ragae. ⁶Supporting him were all the peoples from the highlands, all from the Euphrates and Tigris and Hydaspes, and those from the plains who were subject to Arioch, king of the Elymaeans. Thus many nations had mustered to take part in the battle of the Cheleoudites.

⁷Nebuchadnezzar king of the Assyrians sent a message to all the inhabitants of Persia, to all the inhabitants of the western countries, Cilicia, Damascus, Lebanon, Anti-Lebanon, to all those along the coast, ⁸to the peoples of Carmel, Gilead, Upper Galilee, the great plain of Esdraelon, ⁹to the people of Samaria and its outlying towns, to those beyond Jordan, as far away as Jerusalem, Bethany, Chelous, Kadesh, the river of Egypt, Tahpanhes, Rameses and the whole territory of Goshen, ¹⁰beyond Tanis too and Memphis, and to all the inhabitants of Egypt as far as the frontiers of Ethiopia. ¹¹But the inhabitants of these countries ignored the summons of Nebuchadnezzar king of the Assyrians and did not rally to him to make war. They were not afraid of him, since in their view he appeared isolated. Hence they sent his ambassadors back with nothing achieved and in disgrace. ¹²Nebuchadnezzar was furious with all these countries. He swore by his throne and kingdom to take revenge on all the territories of Cilicia, Damascus and Syria, of the Moabites and of the Ammonites, of Judaea and Egypt as far as the limits of the two seas, and to ravage them with the sword.

The campaign against Arphaxad

¹³In the seventeenth year, he gave battle with his whole army to King Arphaxad and in this battle defeated him. He routed Arphaxad's entire army and all his cavalry and chariots; ¹⁴he occupied his towns and advanced on Ecbatana; he seized its towers and plundered its market places, reducing its former magnificence to a mockery. ¹⁵He later captured Arphaxad in the mountains of Ragae and, thrusting him through with his spears, destroyed him once and for all.

¹⁶He then retired with his troops and all who had joined forces with him: a vast horde of armed men. Then he and his army gave themselves up to carefree feasting for a hundred and twenty days.

The campaign in the west

2 In the eighteenth year, on the twenty-second day of the first month, a rumour ran through the palace that Nebuchadnezzar king of the Assyrians was to have his revenge on all the countries, as he had threatened. ²Summoning his general staff and senior officers, he held a secret conference with them, and with his own lips pronounced utter destruction on the entire area. ³It was then decreed that everyone should be put to death who had not answered the king's appeal.

⁴When the council was over, Nebuchadnezzar king of the Assyrians sent for Holofernes, general-in-chief of his armies and subordinate only to himself. He said to him, ⁵'Thus speaks the Great King, lord of the whole world, "Go; take men of proven valour, about a hundred and twenty thousand foot soldiers and a strong company of horse with twelve thousand cavalrymen; ⁶then advance against all the western lands, since these people have disregarded my call. ⁷Bid them have earth and water ready, because in my rage I am about to march on them; the feet of my soldiers will cover the whole face of the earth, and I shall plunder it. ⁸Their wounded will fill the valleys and the torrents, and rivers, blocked with their dead, will overflow. ⁹I shall lead them captive to the ends of the earth. ¹⁰Now go! Begin by conquering this whole region for me. If they surrender to you, hold them for me until the time comes to punish them. ¹¹But if they resist, look on no one with clemency, hand them over to slaughter and plunder throughout the territory entrusted to you. ¹²For by my life and by the living power of my kingdom I have spoken. All this I shall do by my power. ¹³And you, neglect none of your master's commands, act strictly according to my orders without further delay." '

¹⁴Leaving the presence of his sovereign, Holofernes immediately summoned all the marshals, generals and officers of the Assyrian army ¹⁵and detailed the picked troops as his master had ordered, about a hundred and twenty thousand men and a further twelve thousand mounted archers. ¹⁶He organised these in the normal battle formation. ¹⁷He then secured vast numbers of camels, donkeys and mules to carry the baggage, and innumerable sheep, oxen and goats for food supplies. ¹⁸Every man received full rations and a generous sum of gold and silver from the king's purse.

¹⁹He then set out for the campaign with his whole army, in advance of King Nebuchadnezzar, to overwhelm the whole western region with his chariots, his horsemen and his picked body of foot. ²⁰A motley gathering followed in his rear, as numerous as locusts or the grains of sand on the ground; there was no counting their multitude.

The stages of Holofernes' advance

²¹Thus they set out from Nineveh and marched for three days towards the Plain of Bectileth. From Bectileth they went on to pitch camp near the mountains that lie to the north of Upper Cilicia. ²²From there Holofernes advanced into the highlands with his whole army, infantry, horsemen, chariots. ²³He cut his way through Put and Lud, carried away captive all the sons of Rassis and sons of Ishmael living on the verge of the desert south of Cheleon, ²⁴marched along the Euphrates, crossed Mesopotamia, rased all the fortified towns controlling the Wadi Abron and reached the sea. ²⁵Next he attacked the territories of Cilicia, butchering all who offered him resistance, advanced on the southern frontiers of Japheth, facing Arabia, ²⁶completely encircled the Midianites, burned their tents and plundered their sheep-folds, ²⁷made his way down to the Damascus plain at the time of the wheat harvest, set fire to the fields, destroyed the flocks and herds, sacked the towns, laid the countryside waste and put all the young men to the sword. ²⁸Fear and trembling seized all the coastal peoples; those of Sidon and Tyre, those of Sur, Ocina and Jamnia. The populations of Azotos and Ascalon were panic-stricken.

3 They therefore sent envoys to him to sue for peace, to say, ²'We are servants of the great King Nebuchadnezzar; we lie prostrate before you. Treat us as you think fit. ³Our cattle-farms, all our land, all our wheat fields, our flocks and herds, all the sheep-folds in our encampments are at your disposal. Do with them as you please. ⁴Our towns and their inhabitants too are at your service; go and

treat them as you think fit.' ⁵These men came to Holofernes and delivered the message as above.

⁶He then made his way down to the coast with his army and stationed garrisons in all the fortified towns, levying outstanding men there as auxiliaries. ⁷The people of these cities and of all the other towns in the neighbourhood welcomed him, wearing garlands and dancing to the sound of tambourines. ⁸But he demolished their shrines and cut down their sacred trees, carrying out his commission to destroy all local gods so that the nations should worship Nebuchadnezzar alone and people of every language and nationality should hail him as a god.

⁹Thus he reached the edge of Esdraelon, in the neighbourhood of Dothan, a village facing the great ridge of Judaea. ¹⁰He pitched camp between Geba and Scythopolis and stayed there a full month to re-provision his forces.

Judaea on the alert

4 When the Israelites living in Judaea heard how Holofernes, general-in-chief of Nebuchadnezzar king of the Assyrians, had treated the various nations, plundering their temples and destroying them, ²they were thoroughly alarmed at his approach and trembled for Jerusalem and the Temple of the Lord their God. ³They had returned from captivity only a short time before, and the resettlement of the people in Judaea and the reconsecration of the sacred furnishings, of the altar, and of the Temple, which had been profaned, were of recent date.

⁴They therefore alerted the whole of Samaria, Kona, Beth-Horon, Belmain, Jericho, Choba, Aesora and the Salem valley. ⁵They occupied the summits of the highest mountains and fortified the villages on them; they laid in supplies for the coming war, as the fields had just been harvested. ⁶Joakim the high priest, resident in Jerusalem at the time, wrote to the inhabitants of Bethulia and of Betomesthaim, two towns facing Esdraelon, towards the plain of Dothan. ⁷He ordered

them to occupy the mountain passes, the only means of access to Judaea, for there it would be easy for them to halt an attacking force, the narrowness of the approach not allowing men to advance more than two abreast. ⁸The Israelites carried out the orders of Joakim the high priest and of the people's Council of Elders in session at Jerusalem.

A nation at prayer

⁹All the men of Israel cried most fervently to God and humbled themselves before him. ¹⁰They, their wives, their children, their cattle, all their resident aliens, hired or slave, wrapped sackcloth round their loins. ¹¹All the Israelites in Jerusalem, including women and children, lay prostrate in front of the Temple, and with ashes on their heads stretched out their hands before the Lord. ¹²They draped the altar itself in sackcloth and fervently joined together in begging the God of Israel not to let their children be carried off, their wives distributed as booty, the towns of their heritage destroyed, the Temple profaned and desecrated for the heathen to gloat over. ¹³The Lord heard them and looked kindly on their distress.

The people fasted for many days throughout Judaea as well as in Jerusalem before the sanctuary of the Lord Almighty. ¹⁴Joakim the high priest and all who stood before the Lord, the Lord's priests and ministers, wore sackcloth round their loins as they offered the perpetual burnt offering and the votive and voluntary offerings of the people. ¹⁵With ashes on their turbans they earnestly called on the Lord to look kindly on the House of Israel.

A council of war in Holofernes' camp

5 Holofernes, general-in-chief of the Assyrian army, received the intelligence that the Israelites were preparing for war, that they had closed the mountain passes, fortified all the high peaks and laid obstructions in the plains. ²Holofernes was furious. He summoned all the princes of Moab, all the generals

of Ammon and all the satraps of the coastal regions. [3]'Men of Canaan,' he said, 'tell me: what people is this that occupies the hill-country? What towns does it inhabit? How large is its army? What are the sources of its power and strength? Who is the king who rules it and commands its army? [4]Why have they disdained to wait on me, as all the western peoples have?'

[5]Achior, leader of all the Ammonites, replied, 'May my lord be pleased to listen to what your servant is going to say. I shall give you the facts about these mountain folk whose home lies close to you. You will hear no lie from the mouth of your servant. [6]These people are descended from the Chaldaeans. [7]They once came to live in Mesopotamia, because they did not want to follow the gods of their ancestors who lived in Chaldaea. [8]They abandoned the way of their ancestors to worship the God of heaven, the God they learnt to acknowledge. Banished from the presence of their own gods, they fled to Mesopotamia where they lived for a long time. [9]When God told them to leave their home and set out for Canaan, they settled there and accumulated gold and silver and great herds of cattle. [10]Next, famine having overwhelmed the land of Canaan, they went down to Egypt where they stayed till they were well nourished. There they became a great multitude, a race beyond counting. [11]But the king of Egypt turned against them and exploited them by forcing them to make bricks; he degraded them, reducing them to slavery. [12]They cried to their God, who struck the entire land of Egypt with incurable plagues, and the Egyptians expelled them. [13]God dried up the Red Sea before them [14]and led them forward by way of Sinai and Kadesh-Barnea. Having driven off all the inhabitants of the desert, [15]they settled in the land of the Amorites and in their strength exterminated the entire population of Heshbon. Then, having crossed the Jordan, they took possession of all the hill-country, [16]driving out the Canaanites before them and the Perizzites, Jebusites, She-

chemites and all the Girgashites, and lived there for many years. [17]All the while they did not sin before their God, prosperity was theirs, for they have a God who hates wickedness. [18]But when they turned from the path he had marked out for them some were exterminated in a series of battles, others were taken captive to a foreign land. The Temple of their God was rased to the ground and their towns were seized by their enemies. [19]Then having turned once again to their God, they came back from the places to which they had been dispersed and scattered, regained possession of Jerusalem, where they have their Temple, and reoccupied the hill-country which had been left deserted. [20]So, now, master and lord, if this people has committed any fault, if they have sinned against their God, let us first be sure that they really have this reason to fail, then advance and attack them. [21]But if their nation is guiltless, my lord would do better to abstain, for fear that their Lord and God should protect them. We should then become the laughing-stock of the whole world.'

[22]When Achior had ended this speech, all the people crowding round the tent began protesting. Holofernes' own senior officers, as well as all the coastal peoples and the Moabites, threatened to tear him limb from limb. [23]'Why should we be afraid of the Israelites? They are a weak and powerless people, quite unable to stand a stiff attack. [24]Forward! Advance! Your army, Holofernes our master, will swallow them in one mouthful!'

Achior handed over to the Israelites

6 When the uproar of those crowding round the council had subsided, Holofernes, general-in-chief of the Assyrian army, reprimanded Achior in front of the whole crowd of foreigners and Ammonites. [2]'Achior, who do you think you are, you and the Ephraimite mercenaries, playing the prophet like this with us today, and trying to dissuade us from making war on the people of Israel? You claim their God will protect them. And who is God

if not Nebuchadnezzar? He himself will display his power and wipe them off the face of the earth, and their God will certainly not save them. ³But we, his servants, shall destroy them as easily as a single individual. They can never resist the strength of our cavalry. ⁴We shall burn them all. Their mountains will be drunk with their blood and their plains filled with their corpses. Far from being able to resist us, every one of them will die; thus says King Nebuchadnezzar, lord of the whole world. For he has spoken, and his words will not prove empty. ⁵As for you, Achior, you Ammonite mercenary, who in a rash moment said these words, you will not see my face again until the day when I have taken my revenge on this brood from Egypt. ⁶And then the swords of my soldiers and the spears of my officers will pierce your sides. You will fall among their wounded, the moment I turn on Israel. ⁷My servants will now take you into the hill-country and leave you near one of the towns in the passes; ⁸you will not die, until you share their ruin. ⁹No need to look so sad if you cherish the secret hope that they will not be captured! I have spoken; none of my words will prove idle.'

¹⁰Holofernes having commanded his tent-orderlies to seize Achior, to take him to Bethulia and to hand him over to the Israelites, ¹¹the orderlies took him, escorted him out of the camp and across the plain, and then, making for the hill-country, reached the springs below Bethulia. ¹²As soon as the men of the town sighted them, they snatched up their weapons, left the town and made for the mountain tops, while all the slingers pelted them with stones to prevent them from coming up. ¹³However, they managed to take cover at the foot of the slope, where they bound Achior and left him lying at the bottom of the mountain and returned to their master.

¹⁴The Israelites then came down from their town, stopped by him, unbound him and took him to Bethulia, where they brought him before the chief men of the town, ¹⁵who at that time were Uzziah son of Micah of the tribe of Simeon, Chabris son of Gothoniel and Charmis son of Melchiel. ¹⁶These summoned all the elders of the town. The young men and the women also hurried to the assembly. Achior was made to stand with all the people surrounding him, and Uzziah questioned him about what had happened. ¹⁷He answered by telling them what had been said at Holofernes' council, and what he himself had said in the presence of the Assyrian leaders, and how Holofernes had bragged of what he would do to the House of Israel. ¹⁸At this the people fell to the ground and worshipped God. ¹⁹'Lord God of heaven,' they cried, 'take notice of their arrogance and have pity on the humiliation of our race. Look kindly today on those who are consecrated to you.' ²⁰They then spoke reassuringly to Achior and praised him warmly. ²¹After the assembly Uzziah took him home and gave a banquet for the elders; all that night they called on the God of Israel for help.

The campaign against Israel

7 The following day Holofernes issued orders to his whole army and to the whole host of auxiliaries who had joined him, to break camp and march on Bethulia, to occupy the mountain passes and so open the campaign against the Israelites. ²The troops broke camp that same day. The actual fighting force numbered one hundred and twenty thousand infantry and twelve thousand cavalry, not to mention the baggage train with the vast number of men on foot concerned with that. ³They penetrated the valley in the neighbourhood of Bethulia, near the spring, and deployed on a wide front from Dothan to Balbaim and, in depth, from Bethulia to Cyamon, which faces Esdraelon. ⁴When the Israelites saw this horde, they were all appalled and said to each other, 'Now they will lick the whole country clean. Not even the loftiest peaks, the gorges or the hills will be able to stand the weight of them.' ⁵Each man snatched up his arms; they lit beacons on their towers and spent the whole night on watch.

⁶On the second day Holofernes deployed his entire cavalry in sight of the Israelites in Bethulia. ⁷He reconnoitred the slopes leading up to the town, located the water-points, seized them and posted pickets over them and returned to the main body. ⁸The chieftains of the sons of Esau, all the leaders of the Moabites and the generals of the coastal district then came to him and said, ⁹'If our master will be pleased to listen to us, his forces will not sustain a single wound. ¹⁰These Israelites do not rely so much on their spears as on the height of the mountains where they live. And admittedly it is not at all easy to scale these heights of theirs.

¹¹'This being the case, master, avoid engaging them in a pitched battle and then you will not lose a single man. ¹²Stay in camp, keep all your troops there too, while your servants seize the spring which rises at the foot of the mountain, ¹³since that is what provides the population of Bethulia with their water supply. Thirst will then force them to surrender their town. Meanwhile, we and our men will climb the nearest mountain tops and form advance posts there to prevent anyone from leaving the town. ¹⁴Hunger will waste them, with their wives and children, and before the sword can reach them they will already be lying in the streets outside their houses. ¹⁵And you will make them pay dearly for their defiance and their refusal to meet you peaceably.'

¹⁶Their words pleased Holofernes as well as all his officers, and he decided to do as they suggested. ¹⁷Accordingly, a troop of Moabites moved forward with a further five thousand Assyrians. They penetrated the valley and seized the Israelites' waterpoints and springs. ¹⁸Meanwhile the Edomites and Ammonites went and took up positions in the highlands opposite Dothan, sending some of their men to the south-east opposite Egrebel near Chous on the Wadi Mochmur. The rest of the Assyrian army took up positions in the plain, covering every inch of the ground; their tents and equipment made an immense encampment, so vast were their numbers.

¹⁹The Israelites called on the Lord their God, dispirited because the enemy had surrounded them and cut all line of retreat. ²⁰For thirty-four days the Assyrian army, infantry, chariots, cavalrymen, had them surrounded. Every water-jar the inhabitants of Bethulia had was empty, ²¹their storage-wells were drying up; on no day could a man drink his fill, since their water was rationed. ²²Their little children pined away, the women and young men grew weak with thirst; they collapsed in the streets and gateways of the town; they had no strength left.

²³Young men, women, children, the whole people thronged clamouring round Uzziah and the chief men of the town, shouting in the presence of the assembled elders, ²⁴'May God be judge between you and us! For you have done us great harm, by not suing for peace with the Assyrians. ²⁵And now there is no one to help us. God has delivered us into their hands to be prostrated before them in thirst and utter helplessness. ²⁶Call them in at once; hand the whole town over to be sacked by Holofernes' men and all his army. ²⁷After all, we should be much better off as their booty than we are now; no doubt we shall be enslaved, but at least we shall be alive and not see our little ones dying before our eyes or our wives and children perishing. ²⁸By heaven and earth and by our God, the Lord of our fathers, who is punishing us for our sins and the sins of our ancestors, we implore you to take this course now, today.' ²⁹Bitter lamentations rose from the whole assembly, and they all cried loudly to the Lord God.

³⁰Then Uzziah spoke to them, 'Take heart, brothers! Let us hold out five days more. By then the Lord our God will take pity on us, for he will not desert us altogether. ³¹At the end of this time, if no help is forthcoming, I shall do as you have said.' ³²With that he dismissed the people to their various quarters. The men went to man the walls and towers of the town, sending the women and children home. The town was full of despondency.

Description of Judith

8 Judith was informed at the time of what had happened. She was the daughter of Merari son of Ox, son of Joseph, son of Oziel, son of Elkiah, son of Ananias, son of Gideon, son of Raphaim, son of Ahitub, son of Elijah, son of Hilkiah, son of Eliab, son of Nathanael, son of Salamiel, son of Sarasadai, son of Israel. ² Her husband Manasseh, of her own tribe and family, had died at the time of the barley harvest. ³ He was supervising the men as they bound up the sheaves in the field when he caught sunstroke and had to take to his bed. He died in Bethulia, his home town, and was buried with his ancestors in the field that lies between Dothan and Balamon. ⁴ As a widow, Judith stayed inside her home for three years and four months. ⁵ She had had an upper room built for herself on the roof. She wore sackcloth next to the skin and dressed in widow's weeds. ⁶ She fasted every day of her widowhood except for the Sabbath eve, the Sabbath itself, the eve of New Moon, the feast of New Moon and the joyful festivals of the House of Israel. ⁷ Now she was very beautiful, charming to see. Her husband Manasseh had left her gold and silver, menservants and maidservants, herds and land; and she lived among all her possessions ⁸ without anyone finding a word to say against her, so devoutly did she fear God.

Judith and the elders

⁹ Hearing how the water shortage had demoralised the people and how they had complained bitterly to the headman of the town, and being also told what Uzziah had said to them and how he had given them his oath to surrender the town to the Assyrians in five days' time, ¹⁰ Judith immediately sent the serving-woman who ran her household to summon Chabris and Charmis, two elders of the town. ¹¹ When these came in she said:

'Listen to me, leaders of the people of Bethulia. You were wrong to speak to the people as you did today and to bind yourself by oath, in defiance of God, to surrender the town to our enemies if the Lord did not come to your help within a set number of days. ¹² Who are you, to put God to the test today, you, of all people, to set yourselves above him? ¹³ You put the Lord Almighty to the test! You do not understand anything, and never will. ¹⁴ If you cannot sound the depths of the human heart or unravel the arguments of the human mind, how can you fathom the God who made all things, or sound his mind or unravel his purposes? No, brothers, do not provoke the anger of the Lord our God. ¹⁵ Although it may not be his will to help us within the next five days, he has the power to protect us for as many days as he pleases, just as he has the power to destroy us before our enemies. ¹⁶ But you have no right to demand guarantees where the designs of the Lord our God are concerned. For God is not to be threatened as a human being is, nor is he, like a mere human, to be cajoled. ¹⁷ Rather, as we wait patiently for him to save, let us plead with him to help us. He will hear our voice if such is his good pleasure.

¹⁸ 'And indeed of recent times and still today there is not one tribe of ours, or family, or village, or town that has worshipped gods made by human hand, as once was done, ¹⁹ which was the reason why our ancestors were delivered over to sword and sack, and perished in misery at the hands of our enemies. ²⁰ We for our part acknowledge no other God but him; and so we may hope he will not look on us disdainfully or desert our nation.

²¹ 'If indeed they capture us, as you expect, then all Judaea will be captured too, and our holy places plundered, and we shall answer with our blood for their profanation. ²² The slaughter of our brothers, the captivity of our country, the unpeopling of our heritage, will recoil on our own heads among the nations whose slaves we shall become, and our new masters will look down on us as an outrage and a disgrace; ²³ for our surrender will not reinstate us in their favour; no, the Lord our God will make it a thing to be ashamed of.

24So now, brothers, let us set an example to our brothers, since their lives depend on us, and the sanctuary—Temple and altar—rests on us.

25'All this being so, let us rather give thanks to the Lord our God who, as he tested our ancestors, is now testing us. 26Remember how he treated Abraham, all the ordeals of Isaac, all that happened to Jacob in Syrian Mesopotamia while he kept the sheep of Laban, his mother's brother. 27For as these ordeals were intended by him to search their hearts, so now this is not vengeance that God is exacting on us, but a warning inflicted by the Lord on those who are near his heart.'

28Uzziah replied, 'Everything you have just said comes from an honest heart and no one will contradict a word of it. 29Not that today is the first time your wisdom has been displayed; from your earliest years all the people have known how shrewd you are and of how sound a heart. 30But, parched with thirst, the people forced us to act as we had promised them and to bind ourselves by an inviolable oath. 31You are a devout woman; pray to the Lord, then, to send us a downpour to fill our storage-wells, so that our faintness may pass.'

32Judith replied, 'Listen to me, I intend to do something, the memory of which will be handed down to the children of our race from age to age. 33Tonight you must be at the gate of the town. I shall make my way out with my attendant. Before the time fixed by you for surrendering the town to our enemies, the Lord will make use of me to rescue Israel. 34You must not ask what I intend to do; I shall not tell you until I have done it.' 35Uzziah and the chief men said, 'Go in peace. May the Lord show you a way to take revenge on our enemies.' 36And leaving the upper room they went back to their posts.

Judith's prayer

9 Judith threw herself face to the ground, scattered ashes on her head, undressed as far as the sackcloth she was wearing and cried loudly to the Lord. At the same time in Jerusalem the evening incense was being offered in the Temple of God. Judith said:

2 Lord, God of my ancestor Simeon,
you armed him with a sword to take
vengeance on the foreigners
who had undone a virgin's belt to her
shame,
laid bare her thigh to her confusion,
violated her womb to her dishonour,
since, though you said, 'This must not be,'
they did it.
3 For this you handed their leaders over to
slaughter,
and their bed, defiled by their treachery,
was itself betrayed in blood.
You struck the slaves with the chieftains
and the chieftains with their retainers.
4 You left their wives to be carried off,
their daughters to be taken captive,
and their spoils to be shared out
among the sons you loved,
who had been so zealous for you,
had loathed the stain put on their blood
and called on you for help.

O God, my God,
now hear this widow too;
5 for you have made the past,
and what is happening now, and what will
follow.
What is, what will be, you have planned;
what has been, you designed.
6 Your purposes stood forward;
'See, here we are!' they said.
For all your ways are prepared
and your judgements delivered with
foreknowledge.
7 See the Assyrians, with their army
abounding
glorying in their horses and their riders,
exulting in the strength of their infantry.
Trust as they may in shield and spear,
in bow and sling,
in you they have not recognised the Lord,
the breaker of battle-lines;
8 yours alone is the title of Lord.

Break their violence with your might,
in your anger bring down their strength.
For they plan to profane your holy places,
to defile the tabernacle, the resting place of
    your glorious name,
and to hack down the horn of your altar.
9 Observe their arrogance,
send your fury on their heads,
give the strength I have in mind
to this widow's hand.
10 By guile of my lips
strike down slave with master,
and master with retainer.
Break their pride
by a woman's hand.

11 Your strength does not lie in numbers,
nor your might in strong men;
since you are the God of the humble,
the help of the oppressed,
the support of the weak,
the refuge of the forsaken,
the Saviour of the despairing.
12 Please, please, God of my father,
God of the heritage of Israel,
Master of heaven and earth,
Creator of the waters,
King of your whole creation,
hear my prayer.
13 Give me a beguiling tongue
to wound and kill
those who have formed such cruel designs
against your covenant,
against your holy dwelling-place,
against Mount Zion,
against the house belonging to your sons.
14 And demonstrate to every nation, every
    tribe,
that you are the Lord, God of all power, all
    might,
and that the race of Israel has no protector
    but you.

Judith goes to the camp of Holofernes

10 Thus Judith called on the God of Israel. When she had finished praying, 2 she got up from the floor, summoned her maid and went down into the rooms which she used on Sabbath days and festivals. 3 There she removed the sackcloth she was wearing and taking off her widow's dress, she washed all over, anointed herself plentifully with perfumes, dressed her hair, wrapped a turban round it and put on the robe of joy she used to wear when her husband Manasseh was alive. 4 She put sandals on her feet, put on her necklaces, bracelets, rings, earrings and all her jewellery, and made herself beautiful enough to beguile the eye of any man who saw her. 5 Then she handed her maid a skin of wine and a flask of oil, filled a bag with barley girdle-cakes, cakes of dried fruit and pure loaves, and wrapping all these provisions up gave them to her as well. 6 They then went out, making for the town gate of Bethulia. There they found Uzziah waiting with the two elders of the town, Chabris and Charmis. 7 When they saw Judith, her face so changed and her clothes so different, they were lost in admiration of her beauty. They said to her:

8 May the God of our ancestors keep you in
    his favour!
May he crown your designs with success
to the glory of the children of Israel,
to the greater glory of Jerusalem!

9 Judith worshipped God, and then she said, 'Have the town gate opened for me so that I can go out and fulfil all the wishes you expressed to me.' They did as she asked and gave orders to the young men to open the gate for her. 10 This done, Judith went out accompanied by her maid, while the men of the town watched her all the way down the mountain and across the valley, until they lost sight of her.

11 As the women were making straight through the valley, an advance unit of Assyrians intercepted them, 12 and, seizing Judith, began to question her. 'Which side are you on? Where do you come from? Where are you going?' 'I am a daughter of the Hebrews,' she replied, 'and I am fleeing from them since they

will soon be your prey. ¹³I am on my way to see Holofernes, the general of your army, to give him trustworthy information. I shall show him the road to take if he wants to capture all the hill-country without losing one man or one life.' ¹⁴As the men listened to what she was saying, they stared in astonishment at the sight of such a beautiful woman. ¹⁵'It will prove the saving of you,' they said to her, 'coming down to see our master of your own accord. You had better go to his tent; some of our men will escort you and hand you over to him. ¹⁶Once you are in his presence do not be afraid. Tell him what you have just told us and you will be well treated.' ¹⁷They then detailed a hundred of their men as escort for herself and her attendant, and these led them to the tent of Holofernes.

¹⁸News of her coming had already spread through the tents, and there was a general stir in the camp. She was still outside the tent of Holofernes waiting to be announced, when a crowd began forming round her. ¹⁹They were immediately impressed by her beauty and impressed with the Israelites because of her. 'Who could despise a people who have women like this?' they kept saying. 'Better not leave one of them alive; let any go and they could twist the whole world round their fingers!'

²⁰The bodyguard and adjutants of Holofernes then came out and led Judith into the tent. ²¹Holofernes was resting on his bed under a canopy of purple and gold studded with emeralds and precious stones. ²²The men announced her and he came out to the entrance to the tent, with silver torches carried before him.

²³When Judith confronted the general and his adjutant, the beauty of her face astonished them all. She fell on her face and did homage to him, but his servants raised her from the ground.

The first meeting of Judith with Holofernes

11 'Courage, woman,' Holofernes said, 'do not be afraid. I have never hurt anyone who chose to serve Nebuchadnezzar, king of the whole world. ²Even now, if your nation of mountain dwellers had not insulted me, I would not have raised a spear against them. This was their fault, not mine. ³But tell me, why have you fled from them and come to us? ... Anyhow, this will prove the saving of you. Courage! You will live through this night, and many after. ⁴No one will hurt you. On the contrary, you will be treated as well as any who serve my lord King Nebuchadnezzar.'

⁵Judith said, 'Please listen favourably to what your slave has to say. Permit your servant to speak in your presence, I shall speak no word of a lie to my lord tonight. ⁶You have only to follow your servant's advice and God will bring your work to a successful conclusion; in what my lord undertakes he will not fail. ⁷Long life to Nebuchadnezzar, king of the whole world, who has sent you to set every living soul to rights; may his power endure! Since, thanks to you, he is served not only by human beings, but because of your might the wild animals themselves, the cattle, and the birds of the air are to live in the service of Nebuchadnezzar and his whole House.

⁸'We have indeed heard of your genius and adroitness of mind. It is known everywhere in the world that throughout the empire you have no rival for ability, wealth of experience and brilliance in waging war. ⁹We have also heard what Achior said in his speech to your council. The men of Bethulia having spared him, he has told them everything that he said to you. ¹⁰Now, master and lord, do not disregard what he said; keep it in your mind, since it is true; our nation will not be punished, the sword will indeed have no power over them, unless they sin against their God. ¹¹But as it is, my lord need expect no repulse or setback, since death is about to fall on their heads, for sin has gained a hold over them, provoking the anger of their God each time that they commit it. ¹²As they are short of food and their water is giving out, they have resolved to fall back on their cattle and decided to make use of all the things that God has, by his laws,

forbidden them to eat. ¹³Not only have they made up their minds to eat the first-fruits of corn and the tithes of wine and oil, though these have been consecrated by them and set apart for the priests who serve in Jerusalem in the presence of our God, and may not lawfully even be handled by ordinary people, ¹⁴but they have sent men to Jerusalem—where the inhabitants are doing much the same—to bring them back authorisation from the Council of Elders. ¹⁵Now this will be the outcome: when the permission arrives and they act on it, that very day they will be delivered over to you for destruction.

¹⁶'When I, your servant, came to know all this, I fled from them. God has sent me to do things with you at which the world will be astonished when it hears. ¹⁷Your servant is a devout woman; she honours the God of heaven day and night. I therefore propose, my lord, to stay with you. I, your servant, shall go out every night into the valley and pray to God to let me know when they have committed their sin. ¹⁸I shall then come and tell you, so that you can march out with your whole army; and none of them will be able to resist you. ¹⁹I shall be your guide right across Judaea until you reach Jerusalem; there I shall enthrone you in the very middle of the city. And then you can round them up like shepherd-less sheep, with never a dog daring to bark at you. Foreknowledge tells me this; this has been foretold to me and I have been sent to reveal it to you.'

²⁰Her words pleased Holofernes, and all his adjutants. Full of admiration at her wisdom they exclaimed, ²¹'There is no woman like her from one end of the earth to the other, so lovely of face and so wise of speech!' ²²Holofernes said, 'God has done well to send you ahead of the others. Strength will be ours, and ruin theirs who have insulted my lord. ²³As for you, you are as beautiful as you are eloquent; if you do as you have promised, your God shall be my God, and you yourself shall make your home in the palace of King Nebuchadnezzar and be famous throughout the world.'

12With that he had her brought in to where his silver dinner service was already laid, and had his own food served to her and his own wine poured out for her. ²But Judith said, 'I would rather not eat this, in case I incur some fault. What I have brought will be enough for me.' ³'Suppose your provisions run out,' Holofernes asked, 'how could we get more of the same sort? We have no one belonging to your race here.' ⁴'May your soul live, my lord,' Judith answered, 'the Lord will have used me to accomplish his plan, before your servant has finished these provisions.' ⁵Holofernes' adjutants then took her to a tent where she slept until midnight. A little before the morning watch, she got up. ⁶She had already sent this request to Holofernes, 'Let my lord kindly give orders for your servant to be allowed to go out and pray,' ⁷and Holofernes had ordered his guards not to prevent her. She stayed in the camp for three days; she went out each night to the valley of Bethulia and washed at the spring where the picket had been posted. ⁸As she went she prayed to the Lord God of Israel to guide her in her plan to relieve the children of her people. ⁹Having purified herself, she would return and stay in her tent until her meal was brought her in the evening.

Judith at the banquet of Holofernes

¹⁰On the fourth day Holofernes gave a banquet, inviting only his own staff and none of the other officers. ¹¹He said to Bagoas, the officer in charge of his personal affairs, 'Go and persuade that Hebrew woman you are looking after to come and join us and eat and drink in our company. ¹²We shall be disgraced if we let a woman like this go without seducing her. If we do not seduce her, everyone will laugh at us!' ¹³Bagoas then left Holofernes and went to see Judith. 'Would this young and lovely woman condescend to come to my lord?' he asked. 'She will occupy the seat of honour opposite him, drink the joyful wine with us and be treated today like one of the Assyrian ladies who stand in the palace of Nebuchadnezzar.'

14 'Who am I', Judith replied, 'to resist my lord? I shall not hesitate to do whatever he wishes, and doing this will be my joy to my dying day.'

15 So she got up and put on her dress and all her feminine adornments. Her maid preceded her, and on the floor in front of Holofernes spread the fleece which Bagoas had given Judith for her daily use to lie on as she ate.

16 Judith came in and took her place. The heart of Holofernes was ravished at the sight; his very soul was stirred. He was seized with a violent desire to sleep with her; and indeed since the first day he saw her, he had been waiting for an opportunity to seduce her. 17 'Drink then!' Holofernes said. 'Enjoy yourself with us!' 18 'I am delighted to do so, my lord, for since my birth I have never felt my life more worthwhile than today.' 19 She took what her maid had prepared, and ate and drank facing him. 20 Holofernes was so enchanted with her that he drank far more wine than he had drunk on any other day in his life.

13 It grew late and his staff hurried away. Bagoas closed the tent from the outside, having shown out those who still lingered in his lord's presence. They went to their beds wearied with too much drinking, 2 and Judith was left alone in the tent with Holofernes who had collapsed wine-sodden on his bed. 3 Judith then told her maid to stay just outside the bedroom and wait for her to come out, as she did every morning. She had let it be understood she would be going out to her prayers and had also spoken of her intention to Bagoas.

4 By now everyone had left Holofernes, and no one, either important or unimportant, was left in the bedroom. Standing beside the bed, Judith murmured to herself:

Lord God, to whom all strength belongs,
prosper what my hands are now to do
for the greater glory of Jerusalem;
5 now is the time to recover your heritage
and to further my plans
to crush the enemies arrayed against us.

6 With that she went up to the bedpost by Holofernes' head and took down his scimitar; 7 coming closer to the bed she caught him by the hair and said, 'Make me strong today, Lord God of Israel!' 8 Twice she struck at his neck with all her might, and cut off his head. 9 She then rolled his body off the bed and pulled down the canopy from the bedposts. After which, she went out and gave the head of Holofernes to her maid 10 who put it in her food bag. The two then left the camp together, as they always did when they went to pray. Once they were out of the camp, they skirted the ravine, climbed the slope to Bethulia and made for the gates.

Judith brings the head of Holofernes to Bethulia

11 From a distance, Judith shouted to the guards on the gates, 'Open the gate! Open! For the Lord our God is with us still, displaying his strength in Israel and his might against our enemies, as he has done today!' 12 Hearing her voice, the townsmen hurried down to the town gate and summoned the elders. 13 Everyone, great and small, came running down, since her arrival was unexpected. They threw the gate open, welcomed the women, lit a fire to see by and crowded round them. 14 Then Judith raised her voice and said, 'Praise God! Praise him! Praise the God who has not withdrawn his mercy from the House of Israel, but has shattered our enemies by my hand tonight!' 15 She pulled the head out of the bag and held it for them to see. 'This is the head of Holofernes, general-in-chief of the Assyrian army; here is the canopy under which he lay drunk! The Lord has struck him down by the hand of a woman! 16 Glory to the Lord who has protected me in the course I took! My face seduced him, only to his own undoing; he committed no sin with me to shame me or disgrace me.'

17 Overcome with emotion, the people all prostrated themselves and worshipped God, exclaiming with one voice, 'Blessings on you, our God, for confounding your people's enemies today!' 18 Uzziah then said to Judith:

May you be blessed, my daughter, by God
    Most High,
beyond all women on earth;
and blessed be the Lord God,
Creator of heaven and earth,
who guided you to cut off the head
of the leader of our enemies!
19 The trust which you have shown
    will not pass from human hearts,
as they commemorate
    the power of God for evermore.
20 God grant you may be always held in
    honour
and rewarded with blessings,
since you did not consider your own life
when our nation was brought to its knees,
but warded off our ruin,
    walking in the right path before our God.

And the people all said, 'Amen! Amen!'

The Jews attack the Assyrian camp

14 Judith said, 'Listen to me, brothers. Take this head and hang it on your battlements. 2 When morning comes and the sun is up, let every man take his arms and every able-bodied man leave the town. Appoint a leader for them, as if you meant to march down to the plain against the Assyrian advanced post. But you must not do this. 3 The Assyrians will gather up their equipment, make for their camp and wake up their commanders; they in turn will rush to the tent of Holofernes and not be able to find him. They will then be seized with panic and flee at your advance. 4 All you and the others who live in the territory of Israel will have to do is to give chase and slaughter them as they retreat.

5 'But before you do this, call me Achior the Ammonite, for him to see and identify the man who held the House of Israel in contempt, the man who sent him to us as someone already doomed to die.' 6 So they had Achior brought from Uzziah's house. No sooner had he arrived and seen the head of Holofernes held by a member of the people's assembly than he fell on his face in a faint. 7 They lifted

him up. He then threw himself at Judith's feet and, prostrate before her, exclaimed:

May you be blessed in all the tents of
    Judah
and in every nation;
those who hear your name
    will be seized with dread!

8 'Now tell me everything that you have done in these past few days.' And surrounded by the people, Judith told him everything she had done from the day she left Bethulia to the moment when she was speaking. 9 When she came to the end, the people cheered at the top of their voices until the town echoed. 10 Achior, recognising all that the God of Israel had done, believed ardently in him and, accepting circumcision, was permanently incorporated into the House of Israel.

11 At daybreak they hung the head of Holofernes on the ramparts. Every man took his arms and they all went out in groups to the slopes of the mountain. 12 Seeing this, the Assyrians sent word to their leaders, who in turn reported to the generals, the captains of thousands and all the other officers; 13 and these in their turn reported to the tent of Holofernes. 'Rouse our master,' they said to his majordomo, 'these slaves have dared to march down on us to attack—and to be wiped out to a man!' 14 Bagoas went inside and struck the curtain dividing the tent, thinking that Holofernes was sleeping with Judith. 15 But as no one seemed to hear, he drew the curtain and went into the bedroom, to find him thrown down dead on the threshold, with his head cut off. 16 He gave a great shout, wept, sobbed, shrieked and rent his clothes. 17 He then went into the tent which Judith had occupied and could not find her either. Then, rushing out to the men, he shouted, 18 'The slaves have rebelled! A single Hebrew woman has brought shame on the House of Nebuchadnezzar. Holofernes is lying dead on the ground, without his head!' 19 When they heard this, the leaders of the

Assyrian army tore their tunics in consternation, and the camp rang with their wild cries and their shouting.

15 When the men who were still in their tents heard the news they were appalled. ²Panic-stricken and trembling, no two of them could keep together, the rout was complete, with one accord they fled along every track across the plain or through the mountains. ³The men who had been bivouacking in the mountains round Bethulia were fleeing too. Then all the Israelite warriors charged down on them. ⁴Uzziah sent messengers to Betomasthaim, Bebai, Choba, Kola, throughout the whole territory of Israel, to inform them of what had happened and to urge them all to hurl themselves on the enemy and annihilate them. ⁵As soon as the Israelites heard the news, they fell on them as one man and massacred them all the way to Choba. The men of Jerusalem and the entire mountain country also rallied to them, once they had been informed of the events in the enemy camp. Then the men of Gilead and Galilee attacked them on the flank and struck at them fiercely till they neared Damascus and its territory. ⁶All the other inhabitants of Bethulia fell on the Assyrian camp and looted it to their great profit. ⁷The Israelites returning from the slaughter seized what was left. The hamlets and villages of the mountain country and the plain also captured a great deal of booty, since there were vast stores of it.

Thanksgiving

⁸Joakim the high priest and the entire Council of Elders of Israel, who were in Jerusalem, came to gaze on the benefits that the Lord had lavished on Israel and to see Judith and congratulate her. ⁹On coming to her house, they blessed her with one accord, saying:

> You are the glory of Jerusalem!
> You are the great pride of Israel!
> You are the highest honour of our race!

¹⁰ By doing all this with your own hand
  you have deserved well of Israel,
  and God has approved what you have
      done.
  May you be blessed by the Lord Almighty
  in all the days to come!

And the people all said, 'Amen!'

¹¹The people looted the camp for thirty days. They gave Judith the tent of Holofernes, all his silver plate, his divans, his drinking bowls and all his furniture. She took this, loaded her mule, harnessed her carts and heaped the things into them. ¹²All the women of Israel, hurrying to see her, formed choirs of dancers in her honour. Judith took wands of vine-leaves in her hand and distributed them to the women who accompanied her; ¹³she and her companions put on wreaths of olive. Then she took her place at the head of the procession and led the women as they danced. All the men of Israel, armed and garlanded, followed them, singing hymns. ¹⁴With all Israel round her, Judith broke into this song of thanksgiving and the whole people sang this hymn:

16 Break into song for my God, to the
    tambourine,
  sing in honour of the Lord, to the cymbal,
  let psalm and canticle mingle for him,
  extol his name, invoke it!
² For the Lord is a God who breaks battle-
    lines;
  he has pitched his camp in the middle of
    his people
  to deliver me from the hands of my
    oppressors.

³ Assyria came down from the mountains of
    the north,
  came with tens of thousands of his army.
  Their multitude blocked the ravines,
  their horses covered the hills.
⁴ He threatened to burn up my country,
  destroy my young men with the sword,
  dash my sucklings to the ground,

make prey of my little ones,
carry off my maidens;
5 but the Lord Almighty has thwarted
them
by a woman's hand.

6 For their hero did not fall at the young
men's hands,
it was not the sons of Titans struck him
down,
no proud giants made that attack,
but Judith, the daughter of Merari,
who disarmed him with the beauty of her
face.
7 She laid aside her widow's dress
to raise up those who were oppressed in
Israel;
she anointed her face with perfume,
8 bound her hair under a turban,
put on a linen gown to seduce him.
9 Her sandal ravished his eye,
her beauty took his soul prisoner
and the scimitar cut through his neck!

10 The Persians trembled at her boldness,
the Medes were daunted by her daring.
11 These were struck with fear when my
lowly ones raised the war cry,
these were seized with terror when my
weak ones shouted,
and when they raised their voices these
gave ground.
12 The children of mere girls ran them
through,
pierced them like the offspring of
deserters.
They perished in the battle of my Lord!

13 I shall sing a new song to my God.
Lord, you are great, you are glorious,
wonderfully strong, unconquerable.
14 May your whole creation serve you!
For you spoke and things came into
being,
you sent your breath and they were put
together,
and no one can resist your voice.

15 Should mountains be tossed from their
foundations
to mingle with the waves,
should rocks melt
like wax before your face,
to those who fear you,
you would still be merciful.

16 A little thing indeed
is a sweetly smelling sacrifice,
still less the fat
burned for you in burnt offering;
but whoever fears the Lord
is great for ever.

17 Woe to the nations
who rise against my race!
The Lord Almighty
will punish them on judgement day.
He will send fire and worms in their
flesh
and they will weep with pain for
evermore.

18 When they reached Jerusalem they fell on their faces before God and, once the people had been purified, they presented their burnt offerings, voluntary offerings and gifts. 19 All Holofernes' property given her by the people, and the canopy she herself had stripped from his bed, Judith vowed to God as a dedicated offering. 20 For three months the people gave themselves up to rejoicings in front of the Temple in Jerusalem, where Judith stayed with them.

Judith lives to old age; her death

21 When this was over, everyone returned home. Judith went back to Bethulia and lived on her property; as long as she lived, she enjoyed a great reputation throughout the country. 22 She had many suitors, but all her days, from the time her husband Manasseh died and was gathered to his people, she never gave herself to another man. 23 Her fame spread more and more, the older she grew in her husband's house; she lived to the age of one hundred and

five. She emancipated her maid, then died in Bethulia and was buried in the cave where Manasseh her husband lay. 24 The House of Israel mourned her for seven days. Before her death she had distributed her property among her own relations and those of her husband Manasseh.

25 Never again during the lifetime of Judith, nor indeed for a long time after her death, did anyone trouble the Israelites.

Mordecai's dream[a]

1 [a]*In the second year of the reign of the Great King, Ahasuerus, on the first day of Nisan, a dream came to Mordecai son of Jair, son of Shimei, son of Kish, of the tribe of Benjamin,* [b]*a Jew living at Susa and holding high office at the royal court.* [c]*He was one of the captives whom Nebuchadnezzar king of Babylon had deported from Jerusalem with Jeconiah king of Judah.*

[d]*This was his dream. There were cries and noise, thunder and earthquakes, and disorder over the whole earth.* [e]*Then two great dragons came forward, each ready for the fray, and set up a great roar.* [f]*At the sound of them every nation made ready to wage war against the nation of the just.* [g]*A day of darkness and gloom, of affliction and distress, oppression and great disturbance on earth!* [h]*The entire upright nation was thrown into consternation at the fear of the evils awaiting it and prepared for death, crying out to God.* [i]*Then from its cry, as from a little spring, there grew a great river, a flood of water.* [k]*Light came as the sun rose, and the humble were raised up and devoured the mighty.*

[l]*On awakening from this dream and vision of God's designs, Mordecai thought deeply about the matter, trying his best all day to discover what its meaning might be.*

A plot against the king

[m]*Mordecai was lodging at court with Bigthan and Teresh, two of the king's eunuchs who guarded the palace.* [n]*Having got wind of their plotting and gained knowledge of their designs, he discovered that they were preparing to assassinate King Ahasuerus, and he warned the king against them.* [o]*The king gave orders for the two officers to be tortured; they confessed and were executed.*

[p]*He then had these events entered in his Record Book, while Mordecai himself also wrote an account of them.* [q]*The king then appointed Mordecai to an office at court and rewarded him with presents.* [r]*But Haman son of Hammedatha, the Agagite, who enjoyed high favour with the king, determined to injure Mordecai in revenge for the affair of the king's two officers.*

Ahasuerus' banquet

1 It was in the days of Ahasuerus, the Ahasuerus whose empire stretched from India to Ethiopia and comprised one hundred and twenty-seven provinces. [2] In those days, when King Ahasuerus was sitting on his royal throne in the citadel of Susa, [3] in the third year of his reign, he gave a banquet at his court for all his officers-of-state and ministers, Persian and Median army-commanders, nobles and provincial governors. [4] Thus he displayed the riches and splendour of his empire and the pomp and glory of his majesty; the festivities went on for a long time, a hundred and eighty days.

[5] When this period was over, for seven days the king gave a banquet for all the people living in the citadel of Susa, to high and low alike, on the esplanade in the gardens of the royal palace. [6] There were white and violet hangings fastened with cords of fine linen and purple thread to silver rings on marble columns, couches of gold and silver on a pavement of porphyry, marble, mother-of-pearl and precious stones. [7] For drinking there were golden cups of various design and plenty of wine provided by the king with royal liberal-

1a Passages printed in italics are contained only in the LXX version.

ity. ⁸The royal edict did not, however, make drinking obligatory, the king having instructed the officials of his household to treat each guest according to the guest's own wishes.

Disgrace of Queen Vashti

⁹Queen Vashti, for her part, gave a banquet for the women in the royal palace of King Ahasuerus. ¹⁰On the seventh day, when the king was merry with wine, he commanded Mehuman, Biztha, Harbona, Bigtha, Abagtha, Zethar and Carkas, the seven officers in attendance on the person of King Ahasuerus, ¹¹to bring Queen Vashti before the king, crowned with her royal diadem, in order to display her beauty to the people and the officers-of-state, since she was very beautiful. ¹²But Queen Vashti refused to come at the king's command delivered by the officers. The king was very angry at this and his rage grew hot. ¹³Addressing himself to the wise men who were versed in the law—it being the practice to refer matters affecting the king to expert lawyers and jurists— ¹⁴he summoned Carshena, Shethar, Admatha, Tarshish, Meres, Marsena and Memucan, seven Persian and Median officers-of-state who had privileged access to the royal presence and occupied the leading positions in the kingdom. ¹⁵'According to law,' he said, 'what is to be done to Queen Vashti for not obeying the command of King Ahasuerus delivered by the officers?' ¹⁶In the presence of the king and the officers-of-state, Memucan replied, 'Queen Vashti has wronged not only the king but also all the officers-of-state and all the peoples inhabiting the provinces of King Ahasuerus. ¹⁷The queen's conduct will soon become known to all the women, who will adopt a contemptuous attitude towards their own husbands. They will say, "King Ahasuerus himself commanded Queen Vashti to appear before him and she did not come." ¹⁸Before the day is out, the wives of the Persian and Median officers-of-state will be telling every one of the king's officers-of-state what they have heard about the queen's behaviour;

and that will mean contempt and anger all round. ¹⁹If it is the king's pleasure, let him issue a royal edict, to be irrevocably incorporated into the laws of the Persians and Medes, to the effect that Vashti is never to appear again before King Ahasuerus, and let the king confer her royal dignity on a worthier woman. ²⁰Let this edict issued by the king be proclaimed throughout his empire—which is great—and all the women will henceforth bow to the authority of their husbands, both high and low alike.'

²¹This speech pleased the king and the officers-of-state, and the king did as Memucan advised. ²²He sent letters to all the provinces of the kingdom, to each province in its own script and to each nation in its own language, ensuring that every husband should be master in his own house.

Esther becomes queen

2 Some time after this, when the king's wrath had subsided, Ahasuerus remembered Vashti, how she had behaved, and the measures taken against her. ²The king's gentlemen-in-waiting said, 'A search should be made on the king's behalf for beautiful young virgins, ³and the king appoint commissioners throughout the provinces of his realm to bring all these beautiful young virgins to the citadel of Susa, to the harem under the authority of Hegai the king's eunuch, custodian of the women. Here he will give them whatever they need for enhancing their beauty, ⁴and the girl who pleases the king can take Vashti's place as queen.' This advice pleased the king and he acted on it.

⁵Now in the citadel of Susa there lived a Jew called Mordecai son of Jair, son of Shimei, son of Kish, of the tribe of Benjamin, ⁶who had been deported from Jerusalem among the captives taken away with Jeconiah king of Judah by Nebuchadnezzar king of Babylon, ⁷and was now bringing up a certain Hadassah, otherwise called Esther, his uncle's daughter, who had lost both father and mother; the girl had a good figure and a beau-

tiful face, and on the death of her parents Mordecai had adopted her as his daughter.

8 On the promulgation of the royal command and edict a great number of girls were brought to the citadel of Susa where they were entrusted to Hegai. Esther, too, was taken to the king's palace and entrusted to Hegai, the custodian of the women. 9 The girl pleased him and won his favour. Not only did he quickly provide her with all she needed for her dressing room and her meals, but he gave her seven special maids from the king's household and transferred her and her maids to the best part of the harem. 10 Esther had not divulged her race or parentage, since Mordecai had forbidden her to do so. 11 Mordecai walked up and down in front of the courtyard of the harem all day and every day, to learn how Esther was and how she was being treated.

12 Each girl had to appear in turn before King Ahasuerus after a delay of twelve months fixed by the regulations for the women; this preparatory period was occupied as follows: six months with oil of myrrh, and six months with spices and lotions commonly used for feminine beauty treatment. 13 When each girl went to the king, she was given whatever she wanted to take with her, since she then moved from the harem into the royal household. 14 She went there in the evening, and the following morning returned to another harem entrusted to the care of Shaashgaz, the king's officer, custodian of the concubines. She did not go to the king any more, unless he was particularly pleased with her and had her summoned by name.

15 But when it was the turn of Esther the daughter of Abihail, whose nephew Mordecai had adopted her as his own daughter, to go into the king's presence, she did not ask for anything beyond what had been assigned her by Hegai, the king's officer, custodian of the women. Esther won the approval of all who saw her. 16 She was brought to King Ahasuerus in his royal apartments in the tenth month, which is called Tebeth, in the seventh

year of his reign; 17 and the king liked Esther better than any of the other women; none of the other girls found so much favour and approval with him. So he set the royal diadem on her head and proclaimed her queen instead of Vashti.

18 The king then gave a great banquet, Esther's banquet, for all his officers-of-state and ministers, decreed a holiday for all the provinces and distributed largesse with royal prodigality.

Mordecai and Haman

19 When Esther, like the other girls, had been transferred to the second harem, 20 she did not divulge her parentage or race, in obedience to the orders of Mordecai, whose instructions she continued to follow as when she had been under his care. 21 At this time Mordecai was attached to the Chancellery and two malcontents, Bigthan and Teresh, officers in the king's service as Guards of the Threshold, plotted to assassinate King Ahasuerus. 22 Mordecai came to hear of this and informed Queen Esther, who in turn, on Mordecai's authority, told the king. 23 The matter was investigated and proved to be true. The two conspirators were sent to the gallows, and the incident was recorded in the Annals, in the royal presence.

3 Shortly afterwards, King Ahasuerus singled out Haman son of Hammedatha, a native of Agag, for promotion. He raised him in rank, granting him precedence over all his colleagues, the other officers-of-state, 2 and all the royal officials employed at the Chancellery used to bow low and prostrate themselves whenever Haman appeared—such was the king's command. Mordecai refused either to bow or to prostrate himself. 3 'Why do you flout the royal command?' the officials of the Chancellery asked Mordecai. 4 Day after day they asked him this, but he took no notice of them. In the end they reported the matter to Haman, to see whether Mordecai would persist in his attitude, since he had told them that

he was a Jew. 6 Haman could see for himself that Mordecai did not bow or prostrate himself in his presence; he became furiously angry. 6 And, on being told what race Mordecai belonged to, he thought it beneath him merely to get rid of Mordecai, but made up his mind to wipe out all the members of Mordecai's race, the Jews, living in Ahasuerus' entire empire.

The decree of extermination against the Jews

7 In the first month, that is the month of Nisan, of the twelfth year of King Ahasuerus, the *pur* [a] (that is, the lot) was cast in Haman's presence, to determine the day and the month. The lot falling on the twelfth month, which is Adar, 8 Haman said to King Ahasuerus, 'There is a certain unassimilated nation scattered among the other nations throughout the provinces of your realm; their laws are different from those of all the other nations, and the royal laws they ignore; hence it is not in the king's interests to tolerate them. 9 If their destruction be signed, so please the king, I am ready to pay ten thousand talents of silver to the king's receivers, to be credited to the royal treasury.'

10 The king then took his signet ring off his hand and gave it to Haman son of Hammedatha, the persecutor of the Jews. 11 'Keep the money,' he said, 'and you can have the people too; do what you like with them.'

12 The royal scribes were therefore summoned for the thirteenth day of the first month, when they wrote out the orders addressed by Haman to the king's satraps, to the governors ruling each province and to the principal officials of each people, to each province in its own script and to each people in its own language. The edict was signed in the name of King Ahasuerus and sealed with his ring, 13 and letters were sent by runners to every province of the realm, ordering the destruction, slaughter and annihilation of all Jews, young and old, including women and children, on the same day—the thirteenth day of the twelfth month, which is Adar—and the seizing of their possessions.

13a *The text of the letter was as follows:*

'The Great King, Ahasuerus, to the governors of the hundred and twenty-seven provinces stretching from India to Ethiopia, and to their subordinate district commissioners:

13b 'Being placed in authority over many nations and ruling the whole world, I have resolved never to be carried away by the insolence of power, but always to rule with moderation and clemency, so as to assure for my subjects a life ever free from storms and, offering my kingdom the benefits of civilisation and free transit from end to end, to restore that peace which all men desire. 13c In consultation with our advisers as to how this aim is to be effected, we have been informed by one of them, eminent among us for prudence and well proved for his unfailing devotion and unshakeable trustworthiness, and in rank second only to our majesty, Haman by name, 13d that there is, mingled among all the tribes of the earth, a certain ill-disposed people, opposed by its laws to every other nation and continually defying the royal ordinances, in such a way as to obstruct that form of government assured by us to the general good.

13e 'Considering therefore that this people, unique of its kind, is in complete opposition to all humanity from which it differs by its outlandish laws, that it is hostile to our interests and that it commits the most heinous crimes, to the point of endangering the stability of the realm:

13f 'We command that those persons designated to you in the letters written by Haman, who was appointed to watch over our interests and is a second father to us, be all destroyed, root and branch, including women and children, by the swords of their enemies, without any pity or mercy, on the fourteenth day of the twelfth month, Adar, of the present year, 13g so that, these past and present malcontents being in one day forcibly thrown down to Hades, our

3a From this the name of the feast on which the book is read, Purim, is derived. It is a joyful feast, characterised by banquets.

government may henceforward enjoy perpetual stability and peace.'

¹⁴Copies of this decree, to be promulgated as law in each province, were published to the various peoples, so that each might be ready for the day aforementioned. ¹⁵At the king's command, the runners set out with all speed; the decree was first promulgated in the citadel of Susa.

While the king and Haman gave themselves up to feasting and drinking, consternation reigned in the city of Susa.

Mordecai and Esther try to avert the danger

4 When Mordecai learned what had happened, he tore his garments and put on sackcloth and ashes. Then he walked into the centre of the city, wailing loudly and bitterly, ²until he arrived in front of the Chancellery, which no one clothed in sackcloth was allowed to enter. ³And in every province, no sooner had the royal command and edict arrived, than among the Jews there was great mourning, fasting, weeping and wailing, and many lay on sackcloth and ashes.

⁴When Queen Esther's maids and officers came and told her, she was overcome with grief. She sent clothes for Mordecai to put on instead of his sackcloth, but he refused them. ⁵Esther then summoned Hathach, an officer whom the king had appointed to wait on her, and ordered him to go to Mordecai and enquire what the matter was and why he was acting in this way.

⁶Hathach went out to Mordecai in the city square in front of the Chancellery, ⁷and Mordecai told him what had happened to him personally, and also about the sum of money which Haman had offered to pay into the royal treasury to procure the destruction of the Jews. ⁸He also gave him a copy of the edict of extermination published in Susa for him to show Esther for her information, with the message that she was to go to the king and implore his favour and plead with him for the race to which she belonged. ⁸ᵃ'Remember your humbler circumstances,' he said, 'when you were fed by my hand. Since Haman, the second person in the realm, has petitioned the king for our deaths, ⁸ᵇinvoke the Lord, speak to the king for us and save us from death!'

⁹Hathach came back and told Esther what Mordecai had said; ¹⁰and she replied with the following message for Mordecai, ¹¹'Royal officials and people living in the provinces alike all know that for anyone, man or woman, who approaches the king in the private apartments without having been summoned there, there is only one law: he must die, unless the king, by pointing his golden sceptre towards him, grants him his life. And I have not been summoned to the king for the last thirty days.'

¹²These words of Esther were reported to Mordecai, ¹³who sent back the following reply, 'Do not suppose that, because you are in the king's palace, you are going to be the one Jew to escape. ¹⁴No; if you persist in remaining silent at such a time, relief and deliverance will come to the Jews from another quarter, but both you and your father's whole family will perish. Who knows? Perhaps you have come to the throne for just such a time as this.'

¹⁵Whereupon Esther sent this reply to Mordecai, ¹⁶'Go and assemble all the Jews now in Susa and fast for me. Do not eat or drink day or night for three days. For my part, I and my waiting-women shall keep the same fast, after which I shall go to the king in spite of the law; and if I perish, I perish.' ¹⁷Mordecai went away and carried out Esther's instructions.

Mordecai's prayer

¹⁷ᵃ*Then calling to mind all the wonderful works of the Lord, he offered this prayer:*

¹⁷ᵇ*Lord, Lord, Almighty King,*
    everything is subject to your power,
    and there is no one who can withstand you
    in your determination to save Israel.

¹⁷ᶜ*You have made heaven and earth,*
    and all the marvels that are under heaven.

You are the Master of the universe
and no one can resist you, Lord.

^{17d}*You know all things,*
you, Lord, know
that neither pride, self-esteem nor vainglory
prompted me to do what I have done:
to refuse to prostrate myself
before proud Haman.
Gladly would I have kissed the soles of his
feet,
had this assured the safety of Israel.

^{17e}*But what I have done, I have done,*
rather than place the glory of a man
above the glory of God;
and I shall not prostrate myself to anyone
except, Lord, to you,
and, in so doing, I shall not be acting in pride.

^{17f}*And now, Lord God,*
King, God of Abraham
spare your people!
For our ruin is being plotted,
there are plans to destroy your ancient
heritage.
^{17g}*Do not overlook your inheritance,*
which you redeemed from Egypt to be yours.
^{17h}*Hear my supplication,*
have mercy on your heritage,
and turn our grief into rejoicing,
so that we may live, Lord, to hymn your
name.
Do not suffer the mouths
of those who praise you to perish.

¹⁷ⁱ*And all Israel cried out with all their might,*
since death was staring them in the face.

Esther's prayer

^{17k}*Queen Esther also took refuge with the Lord in*
the mortal peril which had overtaken her. She
took off her sumptuous robes and put on sorrow-
ful mourning. Instead of expensive perfumes, she
covered her head with ashes and dung. She morti-
fied her body severely, and the former scenes of her
happiness and elegance were now littered with

tresses torn from her hair. She besought the Lord
God of Israel in these words:

^{17l}*My Lord, our King, the Only One,*
come to my help, for I am alone
and have no helper but you
and am about to take my life in my hands.

^{17m}*I have been taught from infancy*
in the bosom of my family
that you, Lord, have chosen
Israel out of all the nations
and our ancestors out of all before them,
to be your heritage for ever;
and that you have treated them as you
promised.

¹⁷ⁿ*But we have sinned against you*
and you have handed us over to our enemies
for paying honour to their gods.
Lord, you are upright.

^{17o}*But they are not satisfied*
with the bitterness of our slavery:
they have pledged themselves to their idols
to abolish the decree that your own lips have
uttered,
to blot out your heritage,
to stop the mouths of those who praise you,
to quench your altar and the glory of your
House,
^{17p}*and instead to open the mouths of the*
heathen,
to sing the praise of worthless idols
and for ever to idolise a king of flesh.

^{17q}*Do not yield your sceptre, Lord,*
to what does not exist.
Never let our ruin be matter for laughter.
Turn these plots against their authors,
and make an example
of the man who leads the attack on us.
^{17r}*Remember, Lord; reveal yourself*
in the time of our distress.

As for me, give me courage,
King of gods and Master of all powers!

17s *Put persuasive words into my mouth*
  when I face the lion;
  change his feeling into hatred for our enemy,
  so that he may meet his end,
  and all those like him!

17t *As for ourselves, save us by your hand,*
  and come to my help, for I am alone
  and have no one but you, Lord.
17u *You have knowledge of all things,*
  and you know that I hate honours from the
    godless,
  that I loathe the bed of the uncircumcised,
  of any foreigner whatever.
17w *You know I am under constraint,*
  that I loathe the symbol of my high position
  bound round my brow when I appear at
    court;
  I loathe it as if it were a filthy rag
  and do not wear it on my days of leisure.
17x *Your servant has not eaten at Haman's table,*
  nor taken pleasure in the royal banquets,
  nor drunk the wine of libations.
17y *Nor has your servant found pleasure*
  from the day of her promotion until now
  except in you, Lord, God of Abraham.
17z *O God, whose strength prevails over all,*
  listen to the voice of the desperate,
  save us from the hand of the wicked,
  and free me from my fear!

Esther intrudes on the royal presence

5 1a *On the third day, when she had finished praying, she took off her suppliant's mourning attire and dressed herself in her full splendour. Radiant as she then appeared, she invoked God who watches over all people and saves them. With her, she took two ladies-in-waiting. With a delicate air she leaned on one, while the other accompanied her carrying her train.* 1b *Rosy with the full flush of her beauty, her face radiated joy and love: but her heart shrank with fear.* 1c *Having passed through door after door, she found herself in the presence of the king. He was sitting on his royal throne, dressed in all his robes of state, glittering with gold and precious stones—a formidable sight.* 1d *He looked up, afire with majesty and,*

blazing with anger, saw her. The queen sank to the floor. As she fainted, the colour drained from her face and her head fell against the lady-in-waiting beside her. 1e *But God changed the king's heart, inducing a milder spirit. He sprang from his throne in alarm and took her in his arms until she recovered, comforting her with soothing words.* 1f *'What is the matter, Esther?' he said. 'I am your brother. Take heart, you are not going to die; our order applies only to ordinary people. Come to me.'* 2 *And raising his golden sceptre he laid it on Esther's neck, embraced her and said, 'Speak to me.'* 2a *'Sire,' she said, 'to me you looked like one of God's angels, and my heart was moved with fear of your majesty. For you are a figure of wonder, my lord, and your face is full of graciousness.'* 2b *But as she spoke she fell down in a faint. The king grew more agitated, and his courtiers all set about reviving her.* 3 'What is the matter, Queen Esther?' the king said. 'Tell me what you want; even if it is half my kingdom, I grant it you.' 4 'Would it please the king,' Esther replied, 'to come with Haman today to the banquet I have prepared for him?' 5 The king said, 'Tell Haman to come at once, so that Esther may have her wish.'

6 So the king and Haman came to the banquet that Esther had prepared and, during the banquet, the king again said to Esther, 'Tell me your request; I grant it to you. Tell me what you want; even if it is half my kingdom, it is yours for the asking.' 7 'What do I want, what is my request?' Esther replied. 8 'If I have found favour in the king's eyes, and if it is his pleasure to grant what I ask and to agree to my request, let the king and Haman come to the banquet I intend to give them tomorrow, and then I shall do as the king says.'

9 Haman left full of joy and high spirits that day; but when he saw Mordecai at the Chancellery, neither standing up nor stirring at his approach, he felt a gust of anger. 10 He restrained himself, however. Returning home, he sent for his friends and Zeresh his wife 11 and held forth to them about his dazzling wealth, his many children, how the king had raised him to a position of honour and pro-

moted him over the heads of the king's offi-cers-of-state and ministers. ¹²'What is more,' he added, 'Queen Esther has just invited me and the king—no one else except me—to a banquet she was giving, and better still she has invited me and the king again tomorrow. ¹³But what do I care about all this when all the while I see Mordecai the Jew sitting there at the Chancellery?' ¹⁴'Have a fifty-cubit gal-lows run up,' said Zeresh his wife and all his friends, 'and in the morning ask the king to have Mordecai hanged on it. Then you can go with the king to the banquet, without a care in the world!' Delighted with this advice, Haman had the gallows erected.

The discomfiture of Haman

6 That night the king could not sleep; he called for the Record Book, or Annals, to be brought and read to him. ²They contained an account of how Mordecai had denounced Bigthan and Teresh, two of the king's eunuchs serving as Guards of the Threshold, who had plotted to assassinate King Ahasuerus. ³'And what honour and dignity', the king asked, 'was conferred on Mordecai for this?' 'Noth-ing has been done for him,' the gentlemen-in-waiting replied. ⁴The king then said, 'Who is outside in the antechamber?' Haman had, that very moment, entered the outer ante-chamber of the private apartments, to ask the king to have Mordecai hanged on the gallows which he had just put up for the purpose. ⁵So the king's gentlemen-in-waiting replied, 'It is Haman out in the antechamber.' 'Bring him in,' the king said, ⁶and, as soon as Haman came in, went on to ask, 'What is the right way to treat a man whom the king wishes to honour?' 'Whom', thought Haman, 'would the king wish to honour, if not me?' ⁷So he replied, 'If the king wishes to honour some-one, ⁸royal robes should be brought from the king's wardrobe, and a horse from the king's stable, sporting a royal diadem on its head. ⁹The robes and horse should be entrusted to one of the noblest of the king's officers-of-state, who should then array the man whom

the king wishes to honour and lead him on horseback through the city square, proclaim-ing before him: "This is the way a man shall be treated whom the king wishes to honour."' ¹⁰'Hurry,' the king said to Haman, 'take the robes and the horse, and do everything you have just said to Mordecai the Jew, who works at the Chancellery. On no account leave out anything that you have mentioned.'

¹¹So taking the robes and the horse, Haman arrayed Mordecai and led him on horseback through the city square, proclaiming before him: 'This is the way a man shall be treated whom the king wishes to honour.' ¹²After this Mordecai returned to the Chancellery, while Haman went hurrying home in dejection and covering his face. ¹³He told his wife Zeresh and all his friends what had just happened. His wife Zeresh and his friends said, 'You are beginning to fall, and Mordecai to rise; if he is Jewish, you will never get the better of him. With him against you, your fall is certain.'

Haman at Esther's banquet

¹⁴While they were still talking, the king's offi-cers arrived in a hurry to escort Haman to the banquet that Esther was giving.

7 The king and Haman went to Queen Es-ther's banquet, ²and this second day, dur-ing the banquet, the king again said to Esther, 'Tell me your request, Queen Esther. I grant it to you. Whatever you want; even if it is half my kingdom, it is yours for the asking.' ³'If I have found favour in your eyes, O king,' Queen Esther replied, 'and if it please your majesty, grant me my life—that is my request; and the lives of my people—that is what I want. ⁴For we have been handed over, my people and I, to destruction, slaughter and an-nihilation; had we merely been sold as slaves and servant-girls, I should not have said any-thing; but in the present case, it will be beyond the persecutor's means to make good the loss that the king is about to sustain.' ⁵King Ahas-uerus interrupted Queen Esther, 'Who is this man?' he exclaimed. 'Where is the man who

has thought of doing such a thing?' ⁶Esther replied, 'The persecutor, the enemy? Why, this wretch Haman!' Haman quaked with terror in the presence of the king and queen. ⁷In a rage the king got up from the banquet and went into the palace garden; while Haman, realising that the king was determined on his ruin, stayed behind to beg Queen Esther for his life.

⁸When the king came back from the palace garden into the banqueting hall, he found Haman sprawled across the couch where Esther was reclining. 'What!' the king exclaimed. 'Is he going to rape the queen in my own palace?' The words were scarcely out of his mouth than a veil was thrown over Haman's face. ⁹In the royal presence, Harbona, one of the officers, said, 'There is that fifty-cubit gallows, too, which Haman ran up for Mordecai, who spoke up to the king's great advantage. It is all ready at his house.' 'Hang him on it,' said the king. ¹⁰So Haman was hanged on the gallows which he had erected for Mordecai, and the king's wrath subsided.

The royal favour passes to the Jews

8 That same day King Ahasuerus gave Queen Esther the house of Haman, the persecutor of the Jews. Mordecai was presented to the king, Esther having revealed their mutual relationship. ²The king, who had recovered his signet ring from Haman, took it off and gave it to Mordecai, while Esther gave Mordecai charge of Haman's house.

³Esther again went to speak to the king. She fell at his feet, weeping and imploring his favour, to frustrate the malice that Haman the Agagite had been plotting against the Jews. ⁴The king held out the golden sceptre to her, whereupon Esther stood up and faced him. ⁵'If such is the king's good pleasure,' she said, 'and if I have found favour before him, if my petition seems proper to him and if I myself am pleasing to his eyes, may he be pleased to issue a written revocation of the letters which Haman son of Hammedatha, the Agagite, has had written, ordering the destruction of the Jews throughout the royal provinces. ⁶For how can I look on, while my people suffer what is proposed for them? How can I bear to witness the extermination of my relatives?'

⁷King Ahasuerus said to Queen Esther and to Mordecai the Jew, 'I for my part have given Esther Haman's house, and have had him hanged on the gallows for planning to destroy the Jews. ⁸You, for your part, write what you please as regards the Jews, in the king's name, and seal it with the king's signet; for any edict written in the king's name and sealed with his signet is irrevocable.' ⁹The royal scribes were summoned at once—it was the third month, the month of Sivan, on the twenty-third day—and at Mordecai's dictation an order was written to the Jews, the satraps, governors and principal officials of the provinces stretching from India to Ethiopia, a hundred and twenty-seven provinces, to each province in its own script, and to each people in its own language, and to the Jews in their own script and language. ¹⁰These letters, written in the name of King Ahasuerus and sealed with the king's signet, were carried by couriers mounted on horses from the king's own stud-farms. ¹¹In them the king granted the Jews, in whatever city they lived, the right to assemble in self-defence, with permission to destroy, slaughter and annihilate any armed force of any people or province that might attack them, together with their women and children, and to plunder their possessions, ¹²with effect from the same day throughout the provinces of King Ahasuerus—the thirteenth day of the twelfth month, which is Adar.

The decree of rehabilitation

¹²ᵃ The text of the letter was as follows:

¹²ᵇ 'The Great King, Ahasuerus, to the satraps of the hundred and twenty-seven provinces which stretch from India to Ethiopia, to the provincial governors and to all our loyal subjects, greeting:

¹²ᶜ 'Many people, repeatedly honoured by the extreme bounty of their benefactors, only

grow the more arrogant. It is not enough for them to seek our subjects' injury, but unable as they are to support the weight of their own surfeit they turn to scheming against their benefactors themselves. 12d Not content with banishing gratitude from the human heart, but elated by the plaudits of people unacquainted with goodness, notwithstanding that all is for ever under the eye of God, they expect to escape his justice, so hostile to the wicked. 12e Thus it has often happened to those placed in authority that, having entrusted friends with the conduct of affairs and allowed themselves to be influenced by them, they find themselves sharing with these the guilt of innocent blood and involved in irremediable misfortunes, 12f the upright intentions of rulers having been misled by false arguments of the evilly disposed. 12g This may be seen without recourse to the history of earlier times to which we have referred; you have only to look at what is before you, at the crimes perpetrated by a plague of unworthy officials. 12h For the future, we shall exert our efforts to assure the tranquillity and peace of the realm for all, 12i by adopting new policies and by always judging matters that are brought to our notice in the most equitable spirit.

12k 'Thus Haman son of Hammedatha, a Macedonian, without a drop of Persian blood and far removed from our goodness, enjoyed our hospitality 12l and was treated by us with the benevolence which we show to every nation, even to the extent of being proclaimed our 'father' and being accorded universally the prostration of respect as second in dignity to the royal throne. 12m But he, unable to keep within his own high rank, schemed to deprive us of our realm and of our life. 12n Furthermore, by tortuous wiles and arguments, he would have had us destroy Mordecai, our saviour and constant benefactor, with Esther the blameless partner of our majesty, and their whole nation besides. 12o He thought by these means to leave us without support and so to transfer the Persian empire to the Macedonians.

12p 'But we find that the Jews, marked out for annihilation by this arch-scoundrel, are not

criminals: they are in fact governed by the most just of laws. 12q They are children of the Most High, the great and living God to whom we and our ancestors owe the continuing prosperity of our realm. 12r You will therefore do well not to act on the letters sent by Haman son of Hammedatha, since their author has been hanged at the gates of Susa with his whole household: a fitting punishment, which God, Master of the Universe, has speedily inflicted on him. 12s Put up copies of this letter everywhere, allow the Jews to observe their own customs without fear, and come to their help against anyone who attacks them on the day originally chosen for their maltreatment, that is, the thirteenth day of the twelfth month, which is Adar. 12t For the all-powerful God has made this day a day of joy and not of ruin for the chosen people. 12u You, for your part, among your solemn festivals celebrate this as a special day with every kind of feasting, so that now and in the future, for you and for Persians of good will, it may commemorate your rescue, and for your enemies may stand as a reminder of their ruin.

12v 'Every city and, more generally, every country, which does not follow these instructions, will be mercilessly devastated with fire and sword, and made not only inaccessible to human beings but hateful to wild animals and even birds for ever.'

13 Copies of this edict, to be promulgated as law in each province, were published to the various peoples, so that the Jews could be ready on the day stated to avenge themselves on their enemies. 14 The couriers, mounted on the king's horses, set out in great haste and urgency at the king's command. The edict was also published in the citadel of Susa. 15 Mordecai left the royal presence in a princely gown of violet and white, with a great golden crown and a cloak of fine linen and purple. The city of Susa shouted for joy. 16 For the Jews there was light and gladness, joy and honour. 17 In every province and in every city, wherever the king's command and decree arrived, there was

joy and gladness among the Jews, with feasting and holiday-making. Of the country's population many became Jews, since now the Jews were feared.

The great Day of Purim

9 The king's command and decree came into force on the thirteenth day of the twelfth month, Adar, and the day on which the enemies of the Jews had hoped to crush them produced the very opposite effect: the Jews it was who crushed their enemies. ²In their towns throughout the provinces of King Ahasuerus, the Jews assembled to strike at those who had planned to injure them. No one resisted them, since the various peoples were now all afraid of them. ³Provincial officers-of-state, satraps, governors and royal officials, all supported the Jews for fear of Mordecai. ⁴And indeed Mordecai was a power in the palace and his fame was spreading through all the provinces; Mordecai was steadily growing more powerful.

⁵So the Jews struck down all their enemies with the sword, with resulting slaughter and destruction, and worked their will on their opponents. ⁶In the citadel of Susa alone, the Jews put to death and slaughtered five hundred men, ⁷notably Parshandatha, Dalphon, Aspatha, ⁸Poratha, Adalia, Aridatha, ⁹Parmashtha, Arisai, Aridai and Jezatha, ¹⁰the ten sons of Haman son of Hammedatha, the persecutor of the Jews. But they took no plunder.

¹¹The number of those killed in the citadel of Susa was reported to the king that same day. ¹²The king said to Queen Esther, 'In the citadel of Susa the Jews have killed five hundred men and also the ten sons of Haman. What must they have done in the other provinces of the realm? Tell me your request; I grant it to you. Tell me what else you would like; it is yours for the asking.' ¹³'If such is the king's pleasure,' Esther replied, 'let the Jews of Susa be allowed to enforce today's decree tomorrow as well. And as for the ten sons of Haman, let their bodies be hanged on the gallows.' ¹⁴Whereupon, the king having given

the order, the edict was promulgated in Susa and the ten sons of Haman were hanged. ¹⁵Thus the Jews of Susa reassembled on the fourteenth day of the month of Adar and killed three hundred men in the city. But they took no plunder.

¹⁶The other Jews who lived in the king's provinces also assembled to defend their lives and rid themselves of their enemies. They slaughtered seventy-five thousand of their opponents. But they took no plunder. ¹⁷This was on the thirteenth day of the month of Adar. On the fourteenth day they rested and made it a day of feasting and gladness. ¹⁸But for the Jews of Susa, who had assembled on the thirteenth and fourteenth days, the fifteenth was the day they rested, making that a day of feasting and gladness. ¹⁹This is why Jewish country people, those who live in undefended villages, keep the fourteenth day of the month of Adar as a day of gladness, feasting and holiday-making, and the exchanging of presents with one another, ¹⁹ᵃ*whereas for those who live in cities the day of rejoicing and exchanging presents with their neighbours is the fifteenth day of Adar.*

The official institution of the feast of Purim

²⁰Mordecai committed these events to writing. Then he sent letters to all the Jews living in the provinces of King Ahasuerus, both near and far, ²¹enjoining them to celebrate the fourteenth and fifteenth days of the month of Adar every year, ²²as the days on which the Jews had rid themselves of their enemies, and the month in which their sorrow had been turned into gladness, and mourning into a holiday. He therefore told them to keep these as days of festivity and gladness when they were to exchange presents and make gifts to the poor.

²³Once having begun, the Jews continued observing these practices, Mordecai having written them an account ²⁴of how Haman son of Hammedatha, the Agagite, the persecutor of all the Jews, had plotted their destruction

and had cast the *pur,* that is, the lot, for their overthrow and ruin; ²⁵but how, when he went back to the king to ask him to order the hanging of Mordecai, the wicked scheme which he had devised against the Jews recoiled on his own head, and both he and his sons were hanged on the gallows; ²⁶and that, hence, these days were called Purim, from the word *pur.* And so, because of what was written in this letter, and because of what they had seen for themselves and of what had happened to them, ²⁷the Jews willingly bound themselves, their descendants and all who should join them, to celebrate these two days without fail, in the manner prescribed and at the time appointed, year after year. ²⁸Thus commemorated and celebrated from generation to generation, in every family, in every province, in every city, these days of Purim will never be abrogated among the Jews, nor will their memory perish from their race.

²⁹Queen Esther, the daughter of Abihail, wrote with full authority to ratify this second letter, ³⁰and sent letters to all the Jews of the hundred and twenty-seven provinces of the realm of Ahasuerus, in terms of peace and loyalty ³¹enjoining them to observe these days of Purim at the appointed time, as Mordecai the Jew had recommended, and in the manner prescribed for themselves and their descendants, with additional ordinances for fasts and lamentations. ³²The ordinance of Esther fixed the law of Purim, which was then recorded in a book.

Praise of Mordecai

10King Ahasuerus put not only the mainland under tribute but the Mediterranean islands as well. ²All his feats of power and valour, and the account of the high honour to which he raised Mordecai: all this is recorded in the Book of the Annals of the Kings of Media and Persia.

³And Mordecai the Jew was next in rank to King Ahasuerus. He was a man held in respect among the Jews, esteemed by thousands of his brothers, a man who sought the good of his people and cared for the welfare of his entire race.

³ᵃ*And Mordecai said, 'All this is God's doing.* ³ᵇ*I remember the dream I had about these matters, nothing of which has failed to come true:* ³ᶜ*the little spring that became a river, the light that shone, the sun, the flood of water. Esther is the river—she whom the king married and made queen.* ³ᵈ*The two dragons are Haman and myself.* ³ᵉ*The nations are those that banded together to blot out the name of Jew.* ³ᶠ*The single nation, mine, is Israel, those who cried out to God and were saved. Yes, the Lord has saved his people, the Lord has delivered us from all these evils, God has worked such signs and great wonders as have never occurred among the nations.*

³ᵍ*'Two destinies he appointed, one for his own people, one for the nations at large.* ³ʰ*And these two destinies were worked out at the hour and time and day laid down by God, involving all the nations.* ³ⁱ*In this way God has remembered his people and vindicated his heritage;* ³ᵏ*and for them these days, the fourteenth and fifteenth of the month of Adar, are to be days of assembly, of joy and of gladness before God, through all generations and for ever among his people Israel.'*

Note to the Greek translation of the book

³ˡ*In the fourth year of the reign of Ptolemy and Cleopatra, Dositheus, who affirmed that he was a priest and Levite, and Ptolemy his son brought the foregoing letter concerning Purim. They vouched for its authenticity, the translation having been made by Lysimachus son of Ptolemy, a member of the Jerusalem community.*

The First Book of

MACCABEES

Alexander and his successors

1 Alexander of Macedon son of Philip had come from the land of Kittim*a* and defeated Darius king of the Persians and Medes, whom he succeeded as ruler, at first of Hellas. [2] He undertook many campaigns, gained possession of many fortresses, and put the local kings to death. [3] So he advanced to the ends of the earth, plundering nation after nation; the earth grew silent before him, and his ambitious heart swelled with pride. [4] He assembled very powerful forces and subdued provinces, nations and princes, and they became his tributaries. [5] But the time came when Alexander took to his bed, in the knowledge that he was dying. [6] He summoned his officers, noblemen who had been brought up with him from his youth, and divided his kingdom among them while he was still alive. [7] Alexander had reigned twelve years when he died. [8] Each of his officers established himself in his own region. [9] All assumed crowns after his death, they and their heirs after them for many years, bringing increasing evils on the world.

Antiochus Epiphanes: Israel infected with Hellenism

[10] From these there grew a wicked offshoot, Antiochus Epiphanes son of King Antiochus; once a hostage in Rome, he became king in the 107th year*b* of the kingdom of the Greeks. [11] It was then that there emerged from Israel a set of renegades who led many people astray. 'Come,' they said, 'let us ally ourselves with the gentiles surrounding us, for since we separated ourselves from them many misfortunes have overtaken us.' [12] This proposal proved acceptable, [13] and a number of the people eagerly approached the king, who authorised them to practise the gentiles' observances. [14] So they built a gymnasium in Jerusalem, such as the gentiles have, [15] disguised their circumcision, and abandoned the holy covenant, submitting to gentile rule as willing slaves of impiety.

First Egyptian campaign and pillage of the Temple

[16] Once Antiochus had seen his authority established, he determined to make himself king of Egypt and the ruler of both kingdoms. [17] He invaded Egypt in massive strength, with chariots and elephants (and cavalry) and a large fleet. [18] He engaged Ptolemy king of Egypt in battle, and Ptolemy turned back and fled before his advance, leaving many casualties. [19] The fortified cities of Egypt were captured, and Antiochus plundered the country. [20] After his conquest of Egypt, in the year 143, Antiochus turned about and advanced on Israel and Jerusalem in massive strength.*c* [21] Insolently breaking into the sanctuary, he removed the golden altar and the lamp-stand for the light with all its fittings, [22] together with the table for the loaves of permanent offering, the libation vessels, the cups, the golden censers, the veil, the crowns, and the golden decoration on the front of the Temple, which he stripped of everything. [23] He made off with the silver and gold and precious vessels; he discovered the secret treasures and seized them

1a Term extended from inhabitants of Kition to all Cypriots and then to all Greeks.

1b Dates in the text of 1–2 M are of the era starting with the foundation of Antioch in 312 BC.

1c ‖ 2 M 5:11–16.

²⁴and, removing all these, he went back to his own country, having shed much blood and uttered words of extreme arrogance.

²⁵There was deep mourning for Israel throughout the country:

²⁶ Rulers and elders groaned;
girls and young men wasted away;
the women's beauty suffered a change;
²⁷ every bridegroom took up a dirge,
the bride sat grief-stricken on her
marriage-bed.
²⁸ The earth quaked because of its
inhabitants
and the whole House of Jacob was clothed
with shame.

Intervention of the Mysarch and construction of the Acra

²⁹Two years later the king sent the Mysarch through the cities of Judah. He came to Jerusalem with an impressive force, ³⁰and addressing them with what appeared to be peaceful words, he gained their confidence; then suddenly he fell on the city, dealing it a terrible blow, and destroying many of the people of Israel. ³¹He pillaged the city and set it on fire, tore down its houses and encircling wall, ³²took the women and children captive and commandeered the cattle. ³³They then rebuilt the City of David with a great strong wall and strong towers and made this their Citadel. ³⁴There they installed a brood of sinners, of renegades, who fortified themselves inside it, ³⁵storing arms and provisions, and depositing there the loot they had collected from Jerusalem; they were to prove a great trouble.

³⁶ It became an ambush for the sanctuary,
an evil adversary for Israel at all times.
³⁷ They shed innocent blood all round the
sanctuary
and defiled the sanctuary itself.
³⁸ The citizens of Jerusalem fled because of
them,
she became a dwelling-place of strangers;
estranged from her own offspring,

her children forsook her.
³⁹ Her sanctuary became as forsaken as a
desert,
her feasts were turned into mourning,
her Sabbaths into a mockery,
her honour into reproach.
⁴⁰ Her dishonour now fully matched her
former glory,
her greatness was turned into grief.

Installation of gentile cults

⁴¹The king then issued a proclamation to his whole kingdom that all were to become a single people, each nation renouncing its particular customs. ⁴²All the gentiles conformed to the king's decree, ⁴³and many Israelites chose to accept his religion, sacrificing to idols and profaning the Sabbath. ⁴⁴The king also sent edicts by messenger to Jerusalem and the towns of Judah, directing them to adopt customs foreign to the country, ⁴⁵banning burnt offerings, sacrifices and libations from the sanctuary, profaning Sabbaths and feasts, ⁴⁶defiling the sanctuary and everything holy, ⁴⁷building altars, shrines and temples for idols, sacrificing pigs and unclean beasts, ⁴⁸leaving their sons uncircumcised, and prostituting themselves to all kinds of impurity and abomination, ⁴⁹so that they should forget the Law and revoke all observance of it. ⁵⁰Anyone not obeying the king's command was to be put to death. ⁵¹Writing in such terms to every part of his kingdom, the king appointed inspectors for the whole people and directed all the towns of Judah to offer sacrifice city by city. ⁵²Many of the people—that is, every apostate from the Law—rallied to them and so committed evil in the country, ⁵³forcing Israel into hiding in any possible place of refuge.

⁵⁴On the fifteenth day of Chislev in the year 145 the king built the appalling abomination[d] on top of the altar of burnt offering; and altars were built in the surrounding towns of Judah

1d An idolatrous altar erected on the Jewish altar of burnt offering.

55 and incense offered at the doors of houses and in the streets. 56 Any books of the Law that came to light were torn up and burned. 57 Whenever anyone was discovered possessing a copy of the covenant or practising the Law, the king's decree sentenced him to death. 58 Month after month they took harsh action against any offenders they discovered in the towns of Israel. 59 On the twenty-fifth day of each month, sacrifice was offered on the altar erected on top of the altar of burnt offering. 60 Women who had had their children circumcised were put to death according to the edict 61 with their babies hung round their necks, and the members of their household and those who had performed the circumcision were executed with them.

62 Yet there were many in Israel who stood firm and found the courage to refuse unclean food. 63 They chose death rather than contamination by such fare or profanation of the holy covenant, and they were executed. 64 It was a truly dreadful retribution that visited Israel.

Mattathias and his sons

2 About then, Mattathias son of John, son of Simeon, a priest of the line of Joarib, left Jerusalem and settled in Modein. 2 He had five sons, John known as Gaddi, 3 Simon called Thassi, 4 Judas called Maccabaeus, 5 Eleazar, called Avaran, and Jonathan called Apphus. 6 When he saw the blasphemies being committed in Judah and Jerusalem, 7 he said, 'Alas that I should have been born to witness the ruin of my people and the ruin of the Holy City, and to sit by while she is delivered over to her enemies, and the sanctuary into the hand of foreigners.

8 'Her Temple has become like someone of
no repute,
9 the vessels that were her glory have been
carried off as booty,
her babies have been slaughtered in her
streets,
her young men by the enemy's sword.
10 Is there a nation that has not claimed
a share of her royal prerogatives,
that has not taken some of her spoils?
11 All her ornaments have been snatched
from her,
her former freedom has become slavery.
12 See how the Holy Place, our beauty, our
glory,
is now laid waste,
see how the gentiles have profaned it!
13 What have we left to live for?'

14 Mattathias and his sons tore their garments, put on sackcloth, and observed deep mourning.

The ordeal of the sacrifice at Modein

15 The king's commissioners who were enforcing the apostasy came to the town of Modein for the sacrifices. 16 Many Israelites gathered round them, but Mattathias and his sons drew apart. 17 The king's commissioners then addressed Mattathias as follows, 'You are a respected leader, a great man in this town; you have sons and brothers to support you. 18 Be the first to step forward and conform to the king's decree, as all the nations have done, and the leaders of Judah and the survivors in Jerusalem; you and your sons shall be reckoned among the Friends of the King, you and your sons will be honoured with gold and silver and many presents.' 19 Raising his voice, Mattathias retorted, 'Even if every nation living in the king's dominions obeys him, each forsaking its ancestral religion to conform to his decrees, 20 I, my sons and my brothers will still follow the covenant of our ancestors. 21 May Heaven preserve us from forsaking the Law and its observances. 22 As for the king's orders, we will not follow them: we shall not swerve from our own religion either to right or to left.' 23 As he finished speaking, a Jew came forward in the sight of all to offer sacrifice on the altar in Modein as the royal edict required. 24 When Mattathias saw this, he was fired with zeal; stirred to the depth of his being, he gave vent to his legitimate anger, threw himself on the man and slaughtered him on the altar.

²⁵ At the same time he killed the king's commissioner who was there to enforce the sacrifice, and tore down the altar. ²⁶ In his zeal for the Law he acted as Phinehas had against Zimri son of Salu.ª ²⁷ Then Mattathias went through the town, shouting at the top of his voice, 'Let everyone who has any zeal for the Law and takes his stand on the covenant come out and follow me.' ²⁸ Then he fled with his sons into the hills, leaving all their possessions behind in the town.

The ordeal of the Sabbath in the desert

²⁹ Many people who were concerned for virtue and justice went down to the desert and stayed there, ³⁰ taking with them their sons, their wives and their cattle, so oppressive had their sufferings become. ³¹ Word was brought to the royal officials and forces stationed in Jerusalem, in the City of David, that those who had repudiated the king's edict had gone down to the hiding places in the desert. ³² A strong detachment went after them, and when it came up with them ranged itself against them in battle formation, preparing to attack them on the Sabbath day, ³³ and said, 'Enough of this! Come out and do as the king orders and you will be spared.' ³⁴ The others, however, replied, 'We refuse to come out, and we will not obey the king's orders and profane the Sabbath day.' ³⁵ The royal forces at once went into action, ³⁶ but the others offered no opposition; not a stone was thrown, there was no barricading of the hiding places. ³⁷ They only said, 'Let us all die innocent; let heaven and earth bear witness that you are massacring us with no pretence of justice.' ³⁸ The attack was pressed home on the Sabbath itself, and they were slaughtered, with their wives and children and cattle, to the number of one thousand persons.

The activity of Mattathias and his associates

³⁹ When the news reached Mattathias and his friends, they mourned them bitterly ⁴⁰ and said to one another, 'If we all do as our brothers have done, and refuse to fight the gentiles

for our lives and institutions, they will only destroy us the sooner from the earth.' ⁴¹ So then and there they came to this decision, 'If anyone attacks us on the Sabbath day, whoever he may be, we shall resist him; we must not all be killed, as our brothers were in the hiding places.'

⁴² Soon they were joined by the Hasidaean party,ᵇ stout fighting men of Israel, each one a volunteer on the side of the Law. ⁴³ All the refugees from the persecution rallied to them, giving them added support. ⁴⁴ They organised themselves into an armed force, striking down the sinners in their anger, and the renegades in their fury, and those who escaped them fled to the gentiles for safety. ⁴⁵ Mattathias and his friends made a tour, overthrowing the altars ⁴⁶ and forcibly circumcising all the boys they found uncircumcised in the territories of Israel. ⁴⁷ They hunted down the upstarts and managed their campaign to good effect. ⁴⁸ They wrested the Law out of the control of the gentiles and the kings and reduced the sinners to impotence.

The testament and death of Mattathias

⁴⁹ As the days of Mattathias were drawing to a close, he said to his sons, 'Arrogance and outrage are now in the ascendant; it is a period of turmoil and bitter hatred. ⁵⁰ This is the time, my children, for you to have a burning zeal for the Law and to give your lives for the covenant of our ancestors.

⁵¹ Remember the deeds performed by our
    ancestors, each in his generation,
and you will win great honour and
    everlasting renown.
⁵² Was not Abraham tested and found
    faithful,
was that not considered as justifying him?
⁵³ Joseph in the time of his distress
    maintained the Law,

2a Nb 25:6–15.

2b lit. 'the devout'. They soon split into two groups, the Pharisees and the Essenes.

and so became lord of Egypt.

54 Phinehas, our father, in return for his
burning zeal,
received the covenant of everlasting
priesthood.

55 Joshua, for carrying out his task,
became judge of Israel.

56 Caleb, for his testimony before the
assembled people,
received an inheritance in the land.

57 David for his generous heart
inherited the throne of an everlasting
kingdom.

58 Elijah for his consuming fervour for the
Law
was caught up to heaven itself.

59 Hananiah, Azariah and Mishael, for their
fidelity,
were saved from the flame.

60 Daniel for his singleness of heart
was rescued from the lion's jaws.

61 Know then that, generation after
generation,
no one who hopes in him will be
overcome.

62 Do not fear the threats of the sinner,
all his brave show must come to the
dunghill and the worms.

63 Exalted today, tomorrow he is nowhere to
be found,
for he has returned to the dust he came
from
and his scheming is brought to nothing.

64 My children, be resolute and courageous
for the Law,
for it will bring you glory.

65 'Here is your brother Simeon, I know he
is a man of sound judgement. Listen to him all
your lives; let him take your father's place.
66 Judas Maccabaeus, strong and brave from
his youth, let him be your general and conduct
the war against the gentiles. 67 The rest of you
are to enrol in your ranks all those who keep
the Law, and to assure the vengeance of your
people. 68 Pay back the gentiles to the full, and
hold fast to the ordinance of the Law.' 69 Then
he blessed them and was joined to his ancestors. 70 He died in the year 146 and was buried
in his ancestral tomb at Modein, and all Israel
mourned him deeply.

The eulogy of Judas Maccabaeus

3 His son, Judas, known as Maccabaeus, then
took his place. 2 All his brothers, and all
who had attached themselves to his father,
supported him, and they fought for Israel with
a will.

3 He extended the fame of his people.
Like a giant, he put on the breastplate
and buckled on his war harness;
he engaged in battle after battle,
protecting the ranks with his sword.

4 He was like a lion in his exploits,
like a young lion roaring over its prey.

5 He pursued and tracked down the
renegades,
he consigned those who troubled his
people to the flames.

6 The renegades quailed with the terror he
inspired,
all evil-doers were utterly confounded,
and deliverance went forward under his
leadership.

7 He brought bitterness to many a king
and rejoicing to Jacob by his deeds,
his memory is blessed for ever and ever.

8 He went through the towns of Judah
eliminating the irreligious from them,
and diverted the Retribution from Israel.

9 His name resounded to the ends of the
earth,
he rallied those who were on the point of
perishing.

Initial successes of Judas [a]

10 Next, Apollonius mustered the gentiles and
a large force from Samaria to make war on Israel. 11 When Judas learned of it, he went out
to meet him and routed and killed him. Many
fell wounded, and the survivors took to flight.

3a ‖ 2 M 8.

12 Their spoils were seized and the sword of Apollonius was taken by Judas, who used it to fight with throughout his life. 13 On hearing that Judas had raised a mixed force of believers and seasoned fighters, 14 Seron, commander of the Syrian troops, said, 'I shall make a name for myself and gain honour in the kingdom if I fight Judas and those supporters of his who are so contemptuous of the king's orders.' 15 He therefore launched another expedition, with a strong army of unbelievers to support him in taking revenge on the Israelites. 16 He had nearly reached the descent of Beth-Horon when Judas went out to confront him with a handful of men. 17 But as soon as these saw the force advancing to meet them, they said to Judas, 'How can we, few as we are, engage such overwhelming numbers? We are exhausted as it is, not having had anything to eat today.' 18 'It is easy', Judas answered, 'for a great number to be defeated by a few; indeed, in the sight of Heaven, deliverance, whether by many or by few, is all one; 19 for victory in war does not depend on the size of the fighting force: Heaven accords the strength. 20 They are coming against us in full-blown insolence and lawlessness to destroy us, our wives and our children, and to plunder us; 21 but we are fighting for our lives and our laws, 22 and he will crush them before our eyes; do not be afraid of them.' 23 When he had finished speaking, he made a sudden sally against Seron and his force and overwhelmed them. 24 Judas pursued them down from Beth-Horon as far as the plain. About eight hundred of their men fell, and the rest took refuge in the country of the Philistines. 25 Judas and his brothers began to be feared, and alarm seized the surrounding peoples. 26 His name even reached the king's ears, and among the nations there was talk of Judas and his battles.

Antiochus prepares to invade Persia and Judaea; regency of Lysias

27 The news of these events infuriated Antiochus, and he ordered mobilisation of all the forces in his kingdom, a very powerful army.

28 Opening his treasury, he distributed a year's pay to his troops, telling them to be prepared for any eventuality. 29 He then found that the money in his coffers had run short and that the tribute of the province had decreased, as a result of the dissension and disaster brought on the country by his own abrogation of laws that had been in force from antiquity. 30 He began to fear that, as had happened more than once, he would not have enough to cover the expenses and the lavish bounties he had previously been accustomed to make on a larger scale than his predecessors on the throne. 31 In this grave quandary he resolved to invade Persia, there to levy tribute on the provinces and so accumulate substantial funds. 32 He therefore left Lysias, a nobleman and member of the royal family, to manage the royal affairs between the River Euphrates and the Egyptian frontier, 33 making him responsible for the education of his son Antiochus, until he should come back. 34 To him Antiochus made over half his forces, with the elephants, giving him instructions about what he wanted done, particularly with regard to the inhabitants of Judaea and Jerusalem, 35 against whom he was to send a force, to crush and destroy the power of Israel and the remnant of Jerusalem, to wipe out their very memory from the place, 36 to settle foreigners in all parts of their territory and to distribute their land into lots. 37 The king took the remaining half of his troops with him and set out from Antioch, the capital of his kingdom, in the year 147; he crossed the River Euphrates and made his way through the Upper Provinces.

Gorgias and Nicanor lead the Syrian army into Judaea

38 Lysias chose Ptolemy son of Dorymenes, with Nicanor and Gorgias, influential men from among the Friends of the King, 39 and, under their command, despatched forty thousand foot and seven thousand horse to invade the land of Judah and devastate it, as the king had ordered. 40 The entire force set out and reached the neighbourhood of Emmaus in the

lowlands, where they pitched camp. 41 The local merchants, hearing the news of this, arrived at the camp, bringing with them a large amount of gold and silver, and fetters as well, proposing to buy the Israelites as slaves; they were accompanied by a company from Idumaea and the Philistine country. 42 Judas and his brothers saw that the situation was going from bad to worse and that armies were camping in their territory; they were also well aware that the king had ordered the people's total destruction. 43 So they said to each other, 'Let us restore the ruins of our people and fight for our people and our sanctuary.' 44 The Assembly was summoned, to prepare for war, to offer prayer and to implore compassion and mercy.

45 Jerusalem was as empty as a desert,
none of her children to go in and out.
The sanctuary was trodden underfoot,
men of an alien race held the Citadel,
which had become a lodging for gentiles.
There was no more rejoicing for Jacob,
the flute and lyre were mute.

The Jews muster at Mizpah

46 After mustering, they made their way to Mizpah, opposite Jerusalem, since Mizpah was traditionally a place of prayer for Israel. 47 That day they fasted and put on sackcloth, covering their heads with ashes and tearing their garments. 48 For the guidance that the gentiles would have sought from the images of their false gods, they opened the Book of the Law. 49 They also brought out the priestly vestments, with first-fruits and tithes, and marshalled the Nazirites who had completed the period of their vow. 50 Then, raising their voices to Heaven, they cried, 'What shall we do with these people, and where are we to take them? 51 Your holy place has been trampled underfoot and defiled, your priests mourn in their humiliation, 52 and now the gentiles are in alliance to destroy us: you know what they have in mind for us. 53 How can we stand up and face them if you do not come to our aid?'

54 Then they sounded the trumpets and raised a great shout.

55 Next, Judas appointed leaders for the people, to command a thousand, a hundred, fifty or ten men. 56 Those who were in the middle of building a house, or were about to be married, or were planting a vineyard, or were afraid, he told to go home again, as the Law allowed. 57 The column then marched off and took up a position south of Emmaus. 58 'Stand to your arms,' Judas told them, 'acquit yourselves bravely, in the morning be ready to fight these gentiles massed against us to destroy us and our sanctuary. 59 Better for us to die in battle than to watch the ruin of our nation and our Holy Place. 60 Whatever be the will of Heaven, he will perform it.'

The battle of Emmaus

4 Gorgias took with him five thousand foot and a thousand picked cavalry, and the force moved off by night 2 with the object of attacking the Jewish position and dealing them an unexpected blow; the men from the Citadel were there to guide him. 3 Judas got wind of it and himself moved off with his fighters to strike at the royal army at Emmaus, 4 while its fighting troops were still dispersed outside the camp. 5 Hence, when Gorgias reached Judas' camp, he found no one and began looking for the Jews in the mountains. 'For', he said, 'we have got them on the run.' 6 First light found Judas in the plain with three thousand men, although these lacked the armour and swords they would have wished. 7 They could now see the gentile encampment with its strong fortifications and cavalry surrounding it, clearly people who understood warfare.

8 Judas said to his men, 'Do not be afraid of their numbers, and do not flinch at their attack. 9 Remember how our ancestors were delivered at the Red Sea when Pharaoh was pursuing them in force. 10 And now let us call on Heaven: if he cares for us, he will remember his covenant with our ancestors and will destroy this army confronting us today; 11 then

all the nations will know for certain that there is One who ransoms and saves Israel.'

12 The foreigners looked up and, seeing the Jews advancing against them, 13 came out of the camp to join battle. Judas' men sounded the trumpet 14 and engaged them. The gentiles were defeated and fled towards the plain 15 and all the stragglers fell by the sword. The pursuit continued as far as Gezer and the plains of Idumaea, Azotus and Jamnia, and the enemy lost about three thousand men.

16 Breaking off the pursuit, Judas returned with his men 17 and said to the people, 'Never mind the booty, for we have another battle ahead of us. 18 Gorgias and his troops are still near us in the mountains. First stand up to our enemies and fight them, and then you can safely collect the booty.' 19 The words were hardly out of Judas' mouth, when a detachment came into view, peering down from the mountain. 20 Observing that their own troops had been routed and that the camp had been fired—since the smoke, which they could see, attested the fact— 21 they were panic-stricken at the sight; and when, furthermore, they saw Judas' troops drawn up for battle on the plain, 22 they all fled into Philistine territory. 23 Judas then turned back to plunder the camp, and a large sum in gold and silver, with violet and sea-purple stuffs, and many other valuables were carried off. 24 On their return, the Jews chanted praises to Heaven, singing, 'He is kind and his love is everlasting!' 25 That day had seen a remarkable deliverance in Israel. 26 Those of the foreigners who had escaped came and gave Lysias an account of all that had happened. 27 The news shocked and dismayed him, for affairs in Israel had not gone as he intended, and the result was quite the opposite to what the king had ordered.

First campaign of Lysias [a]

28 The next year he mobilised sixty thousand picked troops and five thousand cavalry with the intention of finishing off the Jews. 29 They advanced into Idumaea and made their base at Beth-Zur, where Judas met them with ten thousand men. 30 When he saw their military strength he offered this prayer, 'Blessed are you, Saviour of Israel, who shattered the mighty warrior's attack at the hand of your servant David, and delivered the Philistine camp into the hands of Jonathan son of Saul, and his armour-bearer. 31 Crush this expedition in the same way at the hands of your people Israel; let their troops and cavalry bring them nothing but shame. 32 Sow panic in their ranks, confound the confidence they put in their numbers and send them reeling in defeat. 33 Overthrow them by the sword of those who love you, and all who acknowledge your name will sing your praises.' 34 The two forces engaged, and five thousand men of Lysias' troops fell in hand-to-hand fighting. 35 Seeing the rout of his army and the courage of Judas' troops and their readiness to live or die nobly, Lysias withdrew to Antioch, where he recruited mercenaries for a further invasion of Judaea in even greater strength.

Purification and dedication of the Temple [b]

36 Judas and his brothers then said, 'Now that our enemies have been defeated, let us go up to purify the sanctuary and dedicate it.' 37 So they marshalled the whole army, and went up to Mount Zion. 38 There they found the sanctuary deserted, the altar desecrated, the gates burnt down, and vegetation growing in the courts as it might in a wood or on some mountain, while the storerooms were in ruins. 39 They tore their garments and mourned bitterly, putting dust on their heads. 40 They prostrated themselves on the ground, and when the trumpets gave the signal they cried aloud to Heaven.

41 Judas then ordered his men to keep the Citadel garrison engaged until he had purified the sanctuary. 42 Next, he selected priests who were blameless and zealous for the Law 43 to purify the sanctuary and remove the stones of the 'Pollution' to some unclean place. 44 They discussed what should be done

4a ‖ 2 M 11:1–12.   4b ‖ 2 M 10:1–8.

about the altar of burnt offering which had been profaned, ⁴⁵and very properly decided to pull it down, rather than later be embarrassed about it since it had been defiled by the gentiles. They therefore demolished it ⁴⁶and deposited the stones in a suitable place on the hill of the Dwelling to await the appearance of a prophet who should give a ruling about them. ⁴⁷They took unhewn stones, as the Law prescribed, and built a new altar on the lines of the old one. ⁴⁸They restored the Holy Place and the interior of the Dwelling, and purified the courts. ⁴⁹They made new sacred vessels, and brought the lamp-stand, the altar of incense, and the table into the Temple. ⁵⁰They burned incense on the altar and lit the lamps on the lamp-stand, and these shone inside the Temple. ⁵¹They placed the loaves on the table and hung the curtains and completed all the tasks they had undertaken.

⁵²On the twenty-fifth of the ninth month, Chislev, in the year 148 they rose at dawn ⁵³and offered a lawful sacrifice on the new altar of burnt offering which they had made. ⁵⁴The altar was dedicated, to the sound of hymns, zithers, lyres and cymbals, at the same time of year and on the same day on which the gentiles had originally profaned it. ⁵⁵The whole people fell prostrate in adoration and then praised Heaven who had granted them success. ⁵⁶For eight days they celebrated the dedication of the altar, joyfully offering burnt offerings, communion and thanksgiving sacrifices. ⁵⁷They ornamented the front of the Temple with crowns and bosses of gold, renovated the gates and storerooms, providing the latter with doors. ⁵⁸There was no end to the rejoicing among the people, since the disgrace inflicted by the gentiles had been effaced. ⁵⁹Judas, with his brothers and the whole assembly of Israel, made it a law that the days of the dedication of the altar should be celebrated yearly at the proper season, for eight days beginning on the twenty-fifth of the month of Chislev, with rejoicing and gladness.ᶜ

⁶⁰They then proceeded to build high walls with strong towers round Mount Zion, to prevent the gentiles from coming and riding roughshod over it as in the past. ⁶¹Judas stationed a garrison there to guard it; he also fortified Beth-Zur, so that the people would have a fortress confronting Idumaea.

The expedition against the Idumaeans and Ammonites

5 When the surrounding nations heard that the altar had been rebuilt and the sanctuary restored to what it had been before, they became very angry ²and decided to destroy the descendants of Jacob living among them; they began to murder and evict our people.

³Judas made war on the sons of Esau in Idumaea,ᵃ in the region of Acrabattene where they were besieging the Israelites. He dealt them a serious blow, drove them off and despoiled them. ⁴He also remembered the wickedness of the sons of Baean, who were a menace and a trap for the people with their ambushes on the roads. ⁵Having blockaded them in their town and besieged them, he put them under the curse of destruction; he then set fire to their towers and burned them down with everyone inside. ⁶Next, he crossed over to the Ammonites where he found a strong fighting force and a numerous people, commanded by Timotheus. ⁷He fought many battles with them, defeated them and cut them to pieces. ⁸Having captured Jazer and its dependent villages, he retired to Judaea.

Preliminaries to campaigns in Galilee and Gilead

⁹Next, the gentiles of Gilead banded together to destroy the Israelites living in their territory. The latter, however, took refuge in the fortress of Dathema, ¹⁰and sent the following letter to Judas and his brothers:

'The gentiles round us have banded themselves together against us to destroy us, ¹¹and they are preparing to storm the

4c The Feast of Hanukkah, a feast of lights.

5a ‖ 2 M 10:15–23.

fortress in which we have taken refuge; Timotheus is in command of their forces. [12]Come at once and rescue us from their clutches, for we have already suffered great losses. [13]All our countrymen living in Tobias' country have been killed, their women and children have been taken into captivity, their property has been seized, and about a thousand men have been destroyed there.'

[14]While the letter was being read, other messengers arrived from Galilee with their garments torn, bearing similar news, [15]'The people of Ptolemais, Tyre and Sidon have joined forces with the whole of gentile Galilee to destroy us!'

[16]When Judas and the people heard this, they held a great assembly to decide what should be done for their oppressed countrymen who were under attack from their enemies. [17]Judas said to his brother Simon, 'Pick your men and go and relieve your countrymen in Galilee, while my brother Jonathan and I make our way into Gilead.' [18]He left Joseph son of Zechariah and the people's leader Azariah with the remainder of the army in Judaea to keep guard, and gave them these orders, [19]'You are to be responsible for our people. Do not engage the gentiles until we return.' [20]Simon was allotted three thousand men for the expedition into Galilee, Judas eight thousand for Gilead.

The expeditions in Galilee and Gilead

[21]Simon advanced into Galilee, engaged the gentiles in several battles and swept all before him; [22]he pursued them to the gate of Ptolemais, and they lost about three thousand men, whose spoils he collected. [23]With him, he took away the Jews of Galilee and Arbatta, with their wives and children and all their possessions, and brought them into Judaea with great rejoicing.

[24]Meanwhile Judas Maccabaeus and his brother Jonathan crossed the Jordan[b] and made a three-days' march through the desert, [25]where they encountered the Nabataeans,[c]

who gave them a friendly reception and told them everything that had been happening to their brothers in Gilead, [26]many of whom, they said, were shut up in Bozrah and Bosor, Alema, Chaspho, Maked and Carnaim, all large fortified towns. [27]Others were blockaded in the other towns of Gilead, and the enemy planned to attack and capture these strongholds the very next day, and destroy all the people inside them on one day.

[28]Judas and his army at once turned off by the desert road to Bozrah. He took the town and, having put all the males to the sword and collected the booty, burned it down. [29]When night came, he left the place, and they continued their march until they reached the fortress. [30]In the light of dawn they looked, and there was an innumerable horde, setting up ladders and engines to capture the fortress; the assault was just beginning. [31]When Judas saw that the attack had begun and that the war cry was rising to heaven from the city, mingled with trumpet calls and a great clamour, [32]he said to the men of his army, 'Into battle today for your brothers!' [33]Dividing them into three commands, he advanced on the enemy's rear, with trumpets sounding and prayers shouted aloud. [34]The troops of Timotheus, recognising that this was Maccabaeus, fled before his advance; Maccabaeus dealt them a crushing defeat; about eight thousand of their men fell that day. [35]Then, wheeling on Alema, he attacked and captured it and, having killed all the males and collected the booty, burned the place down. [36]From there he moved on and took Chaspho, Maked, Bosor and the remaining towns of Gilead. [37]After these events, Timotheus mustered another force and pitched camp opposite Raphon, on the far side of the stream-bed. [38]Judas sent men to reconnoitre the camp, and these reported back as follows, 'With him are massed all the gentiles surrounding us, making a very

5b ‖ 2 M 12:10–31.

5c An Arab people, centred on Petra and controlling the trade routes for 200 years.

numerous army, ³⁹ with Arab mercenaries as auxiliaries; they are encamped on the far side of the stream-bed, and ready to launch an attack on you.' Judas then advanced to engage them, ⁴⁰ and was approaching the watercourse with his troops when Timotheus told the commanders of his army, 'If he crosses first we shall not be able to resist him, because he will have a great advantage over us; ⁴¹ but if he is afraid and camps on the other side of the stream, we shall cross over to him and the advantage will then be ours.'

⁴² As soon as Judas reached the watercourse, he posted people's scribes along it, giving them this order: 'Do not let anyone pitch his tent; all are to go into battle!' ⁴³ He was himself the first across to the enemy side, with all the people following. He defeated all the opposing gentiles, who threw down their arms and ran for refuge in the sanctuary of Carnaim. ⁴⁴ The Jews first captured the town and then burned down the temple with everyone inside. And so Carnaim was overthrown, and the enemy could offer no further resistance to Judas.

⁴⁵ Next, Judas assembled all the Israelites living in Gilead, from the least to the greatest, with their wives, children and belongings, an enormous muster, to take them to Judaea. ⁴⁶ They reached Ephron, a large town straddling the road and strongly fortified. As it was impossible to by-pass it either to right or to left, there was nothing for it but to march straight through. ⁴⁷ But the people of the town denied them passage and barricaded the gates with stones. ⁴⁸ Judas sent them a conciliatory message in these terms, 'We want to pass through your territory to reach our own; no one will do you any harm, we only want to go through on foot.' But they would not open up for him. ⁴⁹ So Judas sent an order down the column for everyone to halt where he stood. ⁵⁰ The fighting men took up their positions; Judas attacked the town all day and night, and the town fell to him. ⁵¹ He put all the males to the sword, rased the town to the ground, plundered it and marched through the town square over the bodies of the dead. ⁵² They then crossed the Jordan into the Great Plain, opposite Beth-Shean, ⁵³ Judas all the time rallying the stragglers and encouraging the people the whole way until they reached Judaea. ⁵⁴ They climbed Mount Zion in joy and gladness and presented burnt offerings because they had returned safe and sound without having lost a single man.

Reversal at Jamnia

⁵⁵ While Judas and Jonathan were in Gilead and Simon his brother in Galilee outside Ptolemais, ⁵⁶ Joseph son of Zechariah, and Azariah, who were in command of the army, heard of their valiant deeds and of the battles they had been fighting, ⁵⁷ and said, 'Let us make a name for ourselves too and go and fight the nations around us.' ⁵⁸ So they issued orders to the men under their command and marched on Jamnia. ⁵⁹ Gorgias and his men came out of the town and gave battle. ⁶⁰ Joseph and Azariah were routed and pursued as far as the frontiers of Judaea. That day about two thousand Israelites lost their lives. ⁶¹ Our people thus met with a great reverse, because they had not listened to Judas and his brothers, thinking that they would do something equally valiant. ⁶² They were not, however, of the same breed of men as those to whom the deliverance of Israel was entrusted.

Successes in Idumaea and Philistia

⁶³ The noble Judas and his brothers, however, were held in high honour throughout Israel and among all the nations wherever their name was heard, ⁶⁴ and people thronged round to acclaim them. ⁶⁵ Judas marched out with his brothers to fight the Edomites in the country towards the south; he stormed Hebron and its dependent villages, threw down its fortifications and burned down its encircling towers. ⁶⁶ Leaving there, he made for the country of the Philistines and passed through Marisa. ⁶⁷ Among the fallen in that day's fighting were some priests who sought to prove their courage there by joining in the battle, a

foolhardy venture. [68]Judas next turned on Azotus, which belonged to the Philistines; he overthrew their altars, burned the statues of their gods and, having pillaged their towns, withdrew to Judaea.

The last days of Antiochus Epiphanes [a]

6 King Antiochus, meanwhile, was making his way through the Upper Provinces; he had heard that in Persia there was a city called Elymais, renowned for its riches, its silver and gold, [2]and its very wealthy temple containing golden armour, breastplates and weapons, left there by Alexander son of Philip, the king of Macedon, the first to reign over the Greeks. [3]He therefore went and attempted to take the city and pillage it, but without success, the citizens having been forewarned. [4]They resisted him by force of arms. He was routed, and began retreating, very gloomily, towards Babylon. [5]But, while he was still in Persia, news reached him that the armies which had invaded Judaea had been routed, [6]and that Lysias in particular had advanced in massive strength, only to be forced to turn and flee before the Jews; that the latter were now stronger than ever, thanks to the arms, supplies and abundant spoils acquired from the armies they had cut to pieces, [7]and that they had pulled down the abomination which he had erected on the altar in Jerusalem, had encircled the sanctuary with high walls as in the past, and had fortified Beth-Zur, one of his cities. [8]When the king heard this news he was amazed and profoundly shaken; he threw himself on his bed and fell sick with grief, since things had not turned out for him as he had planned. [9]And there he remained for many days, subject to deep and recurrent fits of melancholy, until he realised that he was dying. [10]Then, summoning all his Friends, he said to them, 'Sleep evades my eyes, and my heart is cowed by anxiety. [11]I have been wondering how I could have come to such a pitch of distress, so great a flood as that which now engulfs me—I who was so generous and well-loved in my heyday. [12]But now I recall how wrongly I acted in Jerusalem when I seized all the vessels of silver and gold there and ordered the extermination of the inhabitants of Judah for no reason at all. [13]This, I am convinced, is why these misfortunes have overtaken me, and why I am dying of melancholy in a foreign land.'

The accession of Antiochus V

[14]He summoned Philip, one of his Friends, and made him regent of the whole kingdom. [15]He entrusted him with his diadem, his robe and his signet, on the understanding that he was to educate his son Antiochus and train him for the throne. [16]King Antiochus then died, in the year 149. [17]Lysias, learning that the king was dead, established on the throne in succession to him his son Antiochus, whom he had brought up from childhood—and styled him Eupator.

The siege of the Citadel of Jerusalem by Judas Maccabaeus

[18]The people in the Citadel at the time were blockading Israel round the sanctuary and were taking every opportunity to harm them and to support the gentiles. [19]Judas decided that they must be destroyed, and he mobilised the whole people to besiege them. [20]They assembled and laid siege to the Citadel in the year 150, building batteries and siege-engines. [21]But some of the besieged broke through the blockade, and to these a number of renegades from Israel attached themselves. [22]They made their way to the king and said, 'How much longer are you going to wait before you see justice done and avenge our fellows? [23]We were content to serve your father, to comply with his orders, and to obey his edicts. [24]As a result our own people will have nothing to do with us; what is more, they have killed all those of us they could catch, and looted our family property. [25]Nor is it on us alone that their blows have fallen, but on all your territories. [26]At this moment, they are laying siege to

6a ‖ 2 M 1:11–17; 9.

the Citadel of Jerusalem, to capture it, and they have fortified the sanctuary and Beth-Zur. 27 Unless you forestall them at once, they will go on to even bigger things, and then you will never be able to control them.'

Campaign of Antiochus V and Lysias; the battle of Beth-Zechariah

28 The king was furious when he heard this and summoned all his Friends, the generals of his forces and the marshals of horse. 29 He recruited mercenaries from other kingdoms and the Mediterranean islands. 30 His forces numbered a hundred thousand foot soldiers, twenty thousand cavalry and thirty-two elephants with experience of battle conditions. 31 They advanced through Idumaea and besieged Beth-Zur, pressing the attack for days on end; they also constructed siege-engines, but the defenders made a sortie and set these on fire, putting up a brave resistance.

32 At this, Judas left the Citadel and pitched camp at Beth-Zechariah opposite the royal encampment. 33 The king rose at daybreak and marched his army at top speed down the road to Beth-Zechariah, where his forces took up their battle formations and sounded the trumpets. 34 The elephants were given a syrup of grapes and mulberries to prepare them for the battle. 35 These animals were distributed among the phalanxes, to each elephant being allocated a thousand men dressed in coats of mail with bronze helmets on their heads; five hundred picked horsemen were also assigned to each beast. 36 The horsemen anticipated every move their elephant made; wherever it went they went with it, never quitting it. 37 On each elephant, to protect it, was a stout wooden tower, kept in position by girths, each with its three combatants, as well as its mahout. 38 The remainder of the cavalry was stationed on one or other of the two flanks of the army, to harass the enemy and cover the phalanxes.

39 When the sun glinted on the bronze and golden shields, the mountains caught the glint and gleamed like fiery torches. 40 One part of the royal army was deployed on the upper slopes of the mountain and the other in the valley below; they advanced in solid, well-disciplined formation. 41 Everyone trembled at the noise made by this vast multitude, the thunder of the troops on the march and the clanking of their armour, for it was an immense and mighty army. 42 Judas and his army advanced to give battle, and six hundred of the king's army were killed. 43 Eleazar, called Avaran, noticing that one of the elephants was royally caparisoned and was also taller than all the others, and supposing that the king was mounted on it, 44 sacrificed himself to save his people and win an imperishable name. 45 Boldly charging towards the creature through the thick of the phalanx, dealing death to right and left, so that the enemy scattered on either side at his onslaught, 46 he darted in under the elephant, thrust at it from underneath, and killed it. The beast collapsed on top of him, and he died on the spot. 47 The Jews however realising how strong the king was and how ferocious his army, retreated ahead of them.

The capture of Beth-Zur and siege of Mount Zion by the Syrians

48 The royal army moved up to encounter them outside Jerusalem, and the king began to blockade Judaea and Mount Zion. 49 He granted peace terms to the people of Beth-Zur, who evacuated the town; it lacked store of provisions to withstand a siege, since the land was enjoying a sabbatical year. 50 Having occupied Beth-Zur, the king stationed a garrison there to hold it. 51 He besieged the sanctuary for a long time, erecting batteries and siege-engines, flame-throwers and ballistas, scorpions to discharge arrows, and catapults. 52 The defenders countered these by constructing their own engines and were thus able to prolong their resistance. 53 But they had no food in their stores since it was the seventh year, and because those who had taken refuge in Judaea from the gentiles had eaten up the last of their reserves. 54 Only a few men were left in the

Holy Place, owing to the severity of the famine; the rest had dispersed and gone home.

The king grants the Jews religious freedom

55 Meanwhile Philip, whom King Antiochus before his death had appointed to train his son Antiochus for the throne, 56 had returned from Persia and Media with the forces that had accompanied the king, and was planning to seize control of affairs. 57 On hearing this, Lysias at once decided to leave,[b] and said to the king, the generals of the army and the men, 'We are growing weaker every day, we are short of food, and the place we are besieging is well fortified; moreover the affairs of the kingdom demand our attention. 58 Let us offer the hand of friendship to these men and make peace with them and with their whole nation. 59 Let us grant them permission to follow their own customs as before, since it is our abolition of these customs that has provoked them into acting like this.' 60 The king and his commanders approved this argument, and he offered the Jews peace terms, which they accepted. 61 The king and the generals ratified the treaty by oath, and the besieged accordingly left the fortress. 62 The king then entered Mount Zion, but on seeing how impregnable the place was, he broke the oath he had sworn and gave orders for the encircling wall to be demolished. 63 He then hurriedly withdrew, making off for Antioch, where he found Philip already master of the city. Antiochus gave battle and captured the city by force of arms.

Demetrius I becomes king, and sends Bacchides and Alcimus to Judaea[a]

7 In the year 151, Demetrius son of Seleucus left Rome and arrived with a few men at a town on the coast, where he inaugurated his reign. 2 It so happened that, as he was entering the royal residence of his ancestors, the army captured Antiochus and Lysias, and intended to bring them to him. 3 On hearing this, he said, 'Keep them out of my sight.' 4 The army put them to death, and Demetrius ascended his throne. 5 Next, all those Israelites without law or piety, led by Alcimus, whose ambition was to become high priest, 6 approached the king and denounced our people to him. 'Judas and his brothers', they said, 'have killed all your friends, and he has driven us out of our country. 7 Send someone now whom you can trust; let him go and see the wholesale ruin Judas has brought on us and on the king's dominions, and let him punish the wretches and all who assist them.'

8 The king chose Bacchides, one of the Friends of the King, governor of Transeuphrates, an important personage in the kingdom and loyal to the king. 9 He sent him with the godless Alcimus, whom he confirmed in the high priesthood, with orders to exact retribution from the Israelites. 10 So they set out with a large force and, on reaching Judaea, sent emissaries to Judas and his brothers with proposals peaceable yet treacherous. 11 The latter, however, did not put any faith in their words, aware that they had come with a large force. 12 Nevertheless, a commission of scribes presented themselves before Alcimus and Bacchides, to sue for just terms. 13 The first among the Israelites to ask them for peace terms were the Hasidaeans, 14 who reasoned thus, 'This is a priest of Aaron's line who has come with the armed forces; he will not wrong us.' 15 He did in fact discuss peace terms with them and gave them his oath, 'We shall not attempt to injure you or your friends.' 16 They believed him, but he arrested sixty of them and put them to death on one day, fulfilling the words of scripture: 17 *They have scattered the bodies of your faithful, and shed their blood all round Jerusalem, leaving no one to bury them!*[b] 18 At this, fear and dread gripped the whole people. 'There is no truth or virtue in them,' they said, 'they have broken their agreement and their sworn oath.'

19 Bacchides then left Jerusalem and encamped at Beth-Zeth, and from there sent and arrested many of the men who had deserted

6b ‖ 2 M 11:13–33.   7a ‖ 2 M 14:1–10.   7b ‖ Ps 79:2–3.

him and a few of our people too; he had them killed and thrown down the great well. ²⁰ He then put Alcimus in charge of the province, leaving an army with him to support him; Bacchides himself returned to the king. ²¹ Alcimus continued his struggle to become high priest, ²² and all who were disturbing the peace of their own people rallied to him, and, having won control of Judaea, did much harm in Israel. ²³ Seeing that all the wrongs done to the Israelites by Alcimus and his supporters exceeded what the gentiles had done, ²⁴ Judas went right round the whole territory of Judaea to take vengeance on those who had deserted him and to prevent their free movement about the country.

Nicanor in Judaea and battle of Caphar-Salama

²⁵ When Alcimus saw how strong Judas and his supporters had grown and realised that he was powerless to resist them, he went back to the king, to whom he made malicious accusations against them. ²⁶ The king sent Nicanor, one of his generals ranking as Illustrious and a bitter enemy of Israel, with orders to exterminate the people. ²⁷ Reaching Jerusalem with a large force, Nicanor sent a friendly, yet treacherous, message to Judas and his brothers, as follows: ²⁸ 'Let us have no fighting between you and me; I shall come with a small escort for a peaceful meeting with you.' ²⁹ He met Judas and they exchanged friendly greetings; the enemy, however, had made preparations to abduct Judas. ³⁰ When Judas became aware of Nicanor's treacherous purpose in coming to see him, he took fright and refused any further meeting. ³¹ Nicanor then realised that his plan had been discovered, and took the field against Judas, to give battle near Caphar-Salama. ³² About five hundred of Nicanor's men fell; the rest took refuge in the City of David.

Threats against the Temple

³³ After these events Nicanor went up to Mount Zion. Some of the priests came out of the Holy Place with some elders, to give him a friendly welcome and show him the burnt offering being presented for the king. ³⁴ But he ridiculed them, laughed at them, defiled them and used insolent language, swearing in his rage, ³⁵ 'Unless Judas is handed over to me this time with his army, as soon as I am safely back, I promise you, I shall burn this building down!' ³⁶ Then he went off in a fury. At this, the priests went in again, and stood weeping in front of the altar and the Temple, saying, ³⁷ 'You have chosen this house to be called by your name, to be a house of prayer and petition for your people. ³⁸ Take vengeance on this man and on his army, and let them fall by the sword; remember their blasphemies and give them no respite.'

The 'Day of Nicanor' at Adasa

³⁹ Nicanor left Jerusalem and encamped at Beth-Horon, where he was joined by an army from Syria. ⁴⁰ Judas, meanwhile, camped at Adasa with three thousand men, and offered this prayer, ⁴¹ 'When the king's envoys blasphemed, your angel went out and struck down one hundred and eighty-five thousand of his men. ⁴² In the same way let us see you crush this army today, so that everyone else may know that this man has spoken blasphemously against your sanctuary: pass judgement on him as his wickedness deserves!'

⁴³ The armies met in battle on the thirteenth of the month Adar,ᶜ and Nicanor's army was crushed, he himself being the first to fall in the battle. ⁴⁴ When Nicanor's soldiers saw him fall, they threw down their arms and fled. ⁴⁵ The Jews pursued them a day's journey, from Adasa to the approaches of Gezer; they sounded their trumpets in warning as they followed them, ⁴⁶ and people came out of all the surrounding Judaean villages to encircle the fugitives, who then turned back on their own men. All fell by the sword, not one being left alive. ⁴⁷ Having collected the spoils and booty, they cut off Nicanor's head and the

7c ‖ 2 M 15:25–36.

right hand he had stretched out in a display of insolence; these were taken and displayed within sight of Jerusalem. ⁴⁸ The people were overjoyed and kept that day as a great holiday: ⁴⁹ indeed they decided to celebrate it annually on the thirteenth of Adar. ⁵⁰ For a short while Judaea enjoyed peace.

A eulogy of the Romans

8 Now Judas had heard of the reputation of the Romans: how strong they were, and how well disposed towards any who made common cause with them, making a treaty of friendship with anyone who approached them. ² (And, indeed, they were extremely powerful.) He had been told of their wars and of their prowess among the Gauls, whom they had conquered and put under tribute; ³ and of all they had done in the province of Spain to gain possession of the silver and gold mines there, ⁴ making themselves masters of the whole country by their determination and perseverance, despite its great distance from their own; of the kings who came from the ends of the earth to attack them, only to be crushed by them and overwhelmed with disaster, and of others who paid them annual tribute; ⁵ Philip, Perseus king of the Kittim, and others who had dared to make war on them, had been defeated and reduced to subjection, ⁶ while Antiochus the Great, king of Asia, who had advanced to attack them with a hundred and twenty elephants, cavalry, chariots and a very large army, had also suffered defeat at their hands; ⁷ they had taken him alive and imposed on him and his successors, on agreed terms, the payment of an enormous tribute, the surrender of hostages, and the cession ⁸ of the Indian territory, with Media, Lydia, and some of their best provinces, which they took from him and gave to King Eumenes. ⁹ Judas had also heard how, when the Greeks planned an expedition to destroy the Romans, ¹⁰ the latter had got wind of it and, sending a single general against them, had fought a campaign in which they inflicted heavy casualties, carried their women and children away into captivity, pillaged their goods, subdued their country, tore down their fortresses and reduced them to a slavery lasting to the present day; ¹¹ and how they had destroyed and subjugated all the other kingdoms and islands that resisted them.

¹² But where their friends and those who relied on them were concerned, they had always stood by their friendship. They had subdued kings far and near, and all who heard their name went in terror of them. ¹³ One man, if they determined to help him and advance him to a throne, would certainly occupy it, while another, if they so determined, would find himself deposed; their influence was paramount. ¹⁴ In spite of all this, no single one of them had assumed a crown or put on the purple for his own aggrandisement. ¹⁵ They had set up a senate, where three hundred and twenty councillors deliberated daily, constantly debating how best to regulate public affairs. ¹⁶ They entrusted their government to one man for a year at a time, with absolute power over their whole empire, and this man was obeyed by all without envy or jealousy.

The alliance between the Jews and Romans

¹⁷ Having chosen Eupolemus son of John, of the family of Accos, and Jason son of Eleazar, Judas sent them to Rome to make a treaty of friendship and alliance with these people, ¹⁸ in the hope of being rid of the yoke, for they could see that Greek rule was reducing Israel to slavery. ¹⁹ The envoys made the lengthy journey to Rome and presented themselves before the Senate with their formal proposal: ²⁰ 'Judas Maccabaeus and his brothers, with the Jewish people, have sent us to you to conclude a treaty of alliance and peace with you, and to enrol ourselves as your allies and friends.'

²¹ The proposal met with the approval of the senators. ²² Here is a copy of the rescript which they engraved on bronze tablets and sent to Jerusalem to be kept there by the Jews as a record of peace and alliance:

23 'Good fortune attend the Romans and the Jewish nation by sea and land for ever; may sword or enemy be far from them!

24 'If war comes first to Rome or any of her allies throughout her dominions, 25 the Jewish nation will take action as her ally, as occasion may require, and do it whole-heartedly. 26 They will not give or supply to the enemy any grain, arms, money or ships: thus has Rome decided, and they are to honour their obligations without guarantees. 27 In the same way, if war comes first to the Jewish nation, the Romans will support them energetically as occasion may offer, 28 and the aggressor will not be furnished with grain, arms, money or ships: such is the Roman decision, and they will honour these obligations without treachery. 29 Such are the articles under which the Romans have concluded their treaty with the Jewish people. 30 If, later, either party should decide to make any addition or deletion, they will be free to do so, and any such addition or deletion will be binding.

31 'As regards the wrongs done to them by King Demetrius, we have written to him in these terms: Why have you made your yoke lie heavy on our friends and allies the Jews? 32 If they appeal against you again, we shall uphold their rights and make war on you by sea and land.'

Battle of Beer-Zaith and death of Judas Maccabaeus

9 Demetrius, hearing that Nicanor and his army had fallen in battle, sent Bacchides and Alcimus a second time into Judaea, and with them the right wing of his army. 2 They took the road to Galilee and besieged Mesaloth in Arbela, and captured it, putting many people to death. 3 In the first month of the year 152, they encamped outside Jerusalem; 4 they then moved on, making their way to Beer-Zaith with twenty thousand foot and two thousand horse. 5 Judas lay in camp at Elasa, with three thousand picked men. 6 When they saw the huge size of the enemy forces they were terrified, and many slipped out of the camp, until no more than eight hundred of the force were left. 7 With battle now inevitable, Judas realised that his army had melted away; he was aghast, for he had no time to rally them. 8 Yet, dismayed as he was, he said to those who were left, 'Up! Let us face the enemy; we may yet have the strength to fight them.' 9 His men tried to dissuade him, declaring, 'We have no strength for anything but to escape with our lives this time; then we can come back with our brothers to fight them; by ourselves we are too few.' 10 Judas retorted, 'That I should do such a thing as run away from them! If our time has come, at least let us die like men for our countrymen, and leave nothing to tarnish our reputation.'

11 The army marched out of camp and drew up, facing the enemy. The cavalry was drawn up in two squadrons; the slingers and archers marched in the van of the army, and all the best fighters were put in the front rank; 12 Bacchides was on the right wing. The phalanx advanced from between the two squadrons, sounding the trumpets; the men on Judas' side also blew their trumpets, 13 and the earth shook with the noise of the armies. The engagement lasted from morning until evening.

14 Judas saw that Bacchides and the main strength of his army lay on the right; all the stout-hearted rallied to him, 15 and they crushed the right wing, pursuing them as far as the Azara Hills. 16 But when the Syrians on the left wing saw that the right had been broken, they turned and followed hot on the heels of Judas and his men to take them in the rear. 17 The fight became desperate, and there were many casualties on both sides. 18 Judas himself fell, and the remnant fled.

The funeral of Judas Maccabaeus

19 Jonathan and Simon took up their brother Judas and buried him in his ancestral tomb at Modein. 20 All Israel wept and mourned him deeply and for many days they repeated this dirge. 21 'What a downfall for the strong man, the man who kept Israel safe!' 22 The other deeds of Judas, the battles he fought, the ex-

ploits he performed, and all his titles to greatness have not been recorded; but they were
very many.

The triumph of the Greek party; Jonathan leads the resistance

23 After the death of Judas, the renegades came
out of hiding throughout Israel and all the
evil-doers reappeared. 24 At that time there
was a severe famine, and the country went
over to their side. 25 Bacchides deliberately
chose the enemies of religion to administer the
country. 26 These traced and searched out the
friends of Judas and brought them before Bacchides, who ill-treated and mocked them. 27 A
terrible oppression began in Israel; there had
been nothing like it since the disappearance of
prophecy among them.

28 The friends of Judas then all united in
saying to Jonathan, 29 'Since your brother
Judas died, there has been no one like him to
head the resistance against our enemies, people like Bacchides and others who hate our nation. 30 Accordingly, we have today chosen you
to take his place as our ruler and leader and to
fight our campaigns.' 31 Whereupon, Jonathan
took command, in succession to his brother
Judas.

Jonathan in the desert of Tekoa; bloody encounters round Medeba

32 Bacchides, when he heard the news, made
plans to kill Jonathan. 33 But this became
known to Jonathan, his brother Simon and all
his supporters, and they took refuge in the
desert of Tekoa, camping by the water-supply
at Asphar storage-well. 34 (Bacchides came to
know of this on the Sabbath day, and he too
crossed the Jordan with his entire army.)

35 Jonathan sent his brother, who was one of
his commanders, to ask his friends the
Nabataeans to store their considerable baggage for them. 36 The sons of Amrai, however,
those of Medeba, intercepted them, captured
John and everything he had and made off with
their prize. 37 Later, Jonathan and his brother
Simon were told that the sons of Amrai were

celebrating an important wedding, and were
escorting the bride, a daughter of one of the
great notables of Canaan, from Nabata with a
large retinue. 38 Remembering the bloody end
of their brother John, they went up and hid
under cover of the mountain. 39 As they were
keeping watch, a noisy procession came into
sight with a great deal of baggage, and the
bridegroom, with his groomsmen and his
family, came out to meet it with tambourines
and a band, and rich, warlike display. 40 The
Jews rushed down on them from their ambush and killed them, inflicting heavy casualties; the survivors escaped to the mountain,
leaving their entire baggage train to be captured. 41 Thus, *the wedding was turned into
mourning and the music of their band into
lamentation.*[a] 42 Having in this way avenged in
full the blood of their brother, they returned to
the marshes of the Jordan.

Crossing the Jordan

43 As soon as Bacchides heard this, he came on
the Sabbath day with a considerable force to
the steep banks of the Jordan. 44 Jonathan said
to his men, 'Up! Let us fight for our lives, for
today it is not as in the old days. 45 You can see,
we shall have to fight on our front and to our
rear; we have the waters of the Jordan on one
side, the marsh and scrub on the other, and we
have no line of withdrawal. 46 This is the moment to call on Heaven, to deliver you from the
clutches of your enemies.' 47 The engagement
was begun by Jonathan, who aimed a blow at
Bacchides, but the Syrian disengaged himself
and withdrew, 48 where-upon Jonathan and
his men leapt into the Jordan and swam to the
other bank; the enemy did not, however, cross
the Jordan in pursuit. 49 That day, Bacchides
lost about a thousand men.

Bacchides builds fortifications; the death of Alcimus

50 Bacchides went back to Jerusalem and
began fortifying some of the Judaean towns:

9a Am 8:10.

the fortresses of Jericho, Emmaus, Beth-Horon, Bethel, Timnath, Pharathon and Tephon, with high walls and barred gates, 51 and stationed a garrison in each of them to harass Israel. 52 He also fortified the town of Beth-Zur, Gezer and the Citadel, and placed troops in them with supplies of provisions. 53 He took the sons of the leading men of the country as hostages, and had them placed under guard in the Citadel of Jerusalem.

54 In the year 153, in the second month, Alcimus ordered the demolition of the wall of the inner court of the sanctuary, destroying the work of the prophets. Alcimus had just begun the demolition 55 when he suffered a stroke, and his work was interrupted. His mouth became obstructed, and his paralysis made him incapable of speaking at all or giving directions to his household; 56 it was not long before he died in great agony. 57 On the death of Alcimus, Bacchides went back to the king, and Judaea was left in peace for two years.

The siege of Beth-Bassi

58 The renegades then all agreed on a plan. 'Now is the time,' they said, 'while Jonathan and his supporters are living in peace and are full of confidence, for us to bring back Bacchides, and he will arrest the lot of them in one night.' 59 So they went to him and reached an understanding. 60 Bacchides at once set out with a large force, and sent secret instructions to all his allies in Judaea to seize Jonathan and his supporters. But they were unable to do this because their plan became known, 61 and Jonathan and his men arrested some fifty of the men of the country who were ringleaders in the plot, and put them to death.

62 Jonathan and Simon then retired with their partisans to Beth-Bassi in the desert; they rebuilt the ruinous parts of the place and fortified it. 63 When Bacchides heard this, he mustered his whole force and notified his adherents in Judaea. 64 He then proceeded to lay siege to Beth-Bassi, the fighting was protracted, and he constructed siege-engines. 65 Jonathan, however, leaving his brother Si-

mon in the town, broke out into the countryside with a handful of men. 66 He launched a blow at Odomera and his brothers, and at the sons of Phasiron in their encampment; whereupon, these too came into the struggle, joining forces with him. 67 Simon and his people, meanwhile, made a sortie from the town and set fire to the siege-engines. 68 Taking the offensive against Bacchides, they defeated him. He was greatly disconcerted to find that his plan and his assault had come to nothing, 69 and vented his anger on those renegades who had induced him to enter the country, putting many of them to death; he then decided to take his own troops home. 70 Discovering this, Jonathan sent envoys to negotiate peace terms and the release of prisoners with him. 71 Bacchides agreed to this, accepting his proposals and swearing never to seek occasion to harm him for the rest of his life. 72 Having surrendered to Jonathan those prisoners he had earlier taken in Judaea, he turned about and withdrew to his own country, and never again came near their frontiers. 73 The sword no longer hung over Israel, and Jonathan settled in Michmash, where he began to judge the people and to rid Israel of the godless.

Alexander Balas competes for Jonathan's support and appoints him high priest

10 In the year 160, Alexander, son of Antiochus Epiphanes, raised an army and occupied Ptolemais. He was well received, and there inaugurated his reign. 2 On hearing this, King Demetrius assembled a very large army and marched off to do battle with him. 3 Demetrius furthermore sent Jonathan a most conciliatory letter, promising to promote him in rank, 4 for, as he said, 'We had better move first to come to terms with these people before he makes common cause with Alexander against us; 5 he will not have forgotten all the wrongs we inflicted on him and his brothers, and on his nation.' 6 He even authorised him to raise an army, to manufacture arms, and to describe himself as his ally, and ordered

the hostages in the Citadel to be surrendered to him.

⁷Jonathan went straight to Jerusalem and read the letter in the hearing of the whole people and of the men in the Citadel. ⁸They were terrified when they heard that the king had given him authority to raise an army. ⁹The men in the Citadel surrendered the hostages to Jonathan, who handed them back to their parents. ¹⁰Jonathan then took up residence in Jerusalem and began the rebuilding and restoration of the city. ¹¹He ordered those responsible for the work to build the walls and the defences round Mount Zion of squared stone blocks to make them stronger, and this was done. ¹²The foreigners in the fortresses built by Bacchides abandoned them, ¹³one after another leaving his post to go back to his own country. ¹⁴Only at Beth-Zur were a few left of those who had forsaken the Law and the precepts, since this was their refuge.

¹⁵King Alexander heard of all the promises Demetrius had sent to Jonathan, and he was also given an account of the battles and exploits of this man and his brothers and of the hardships they had endured. ¹⁶'Shall we ever find another man like him?' he exclaimed. 'We must make him our friend and ally!' ¹⁷He therefore wrote him a letter, addressing him in these terms:

¹⁸'King Alexander to his brother Jonathan, greetings.

¹⁹'You have been brought to our notice as a strong man of action and as someone who deserves to be our friend. ²⁰Accordingly, we have today appointed you high priest of your nation, with the title of "Friend of the King"'—he also sent him a purple robe and a golden crown—'and you are to study our interests and maintain friendly relations with us.'

²¹Jonathan put on the sacred vestments in the seventh month of the year 160, on the feast of Shelters; he then set about raising troops and manufacturing arms in quantity.

A letter from Demetrius I to Jonathan

²²Demetrius was displeased when he heard what had happened. ²³'What have we been doing,' he said, 'for Alexander to forestall us in winning the friendship of the Jews and so improving his own position? ²⁴I too shall address an appeal to them, offering them advancement and riches as an inducement to support me.' ²⁵And he wrote to them as follows:

'King Demetrius to the Jewish nation, greetings.

²⁶'We have heard how you have kept your agreement with us and have maintained friendly relations with us and have not gone over to our enemies, and it has given us great satisfaction. ²⁷If you now continue to keep faith with us, we shall make you a handsome return for what you do on our behalf. ²⁸We shall accord you many exemptions and grant you privileges.

²⁹'Henceforth I release you and exempt all the Jews from the tribute, the salt dues and the crown levies, ³⁰and whereas I am entitled to one-third of the grain and one-half of the fruit of the trees, I release from this levy, from today and for the future, Judaea and the three districts annexed to it from Samaria-Galilee, from this day henceforth in perpetuity. ³¹Jerusalem will be sacred and exempt, with its territory, from tithes and dues. ³²I relinquish control of the Citadel in Jerusalem and make it over to the high priest, so that he may man it with a garrison of his own choosing. ³³Every Jewish person taken from Judaea into captivity in any part of my kingdom I set free without ransom, and decree that all will be exempt from taxes, even on their livestock. ³⁴All festivals, Sabbaths, New Moons and days of special observance, and the three days before and three days after a festival, will be days of exemption and quittance for all the Jews in my kingdom, ³⁵and no one will have the right to exact payment from,

or to molest, any of them for any matter whatsoever.

36 'Jews will be enrolled in the king's forces to the number of thirty thousand men and receive maintenance on the same scale as the rest of the king's forces. 37 Some of them will be stationed in the king's major fortresses, and from among others appointments will be made to positions of trust in the kingdom. Their officers and commanders will be appointed from their own number and will live under their own laws, as the king has prescribed for Judaea.

38 'As regards the three districts annexed to Judaea from the province of Samaria, these will be integrated into Judaea and considered as coming under one governor, obeying the high priest's authority and no other. 39 Ptolemais and the land thereto pertaining I present to the sanctuary in Jerusalem, to meet the necessary expenses of public worship. 40 And I make a personal grant of fifteen thousand silver shekels annually chargeable to the royal revenue from appropriate places. 41 And the entire surplus, which has not been paid in by the officials as in previous years, will henceforth be paid over by them for work on the Temple. 42 In addition, the sum of five thousand silver shekels, levied annually on the profits of the sanctuary, as shown in the annual accounts, is also relinquished as the perquisite of the priests who perform the liturgy. 43 Anyone who takes refuge in the Temple in Jerusalem or any of its precincts, when in debt to the royal exchequer or otherwise, will be discharged in full possession of all the goods he owns in my kingdom. 44 As regards the building and restoration of the sanctuary, the expense of the work will be met from the royal exchequer. 45 The reconstruction of the walls of Jerusalem and the fortification of the perimeter will also be a charge on the royal exchequer, as also the reconstruction of other city walls in Judaea.'

Jonathan rejects Demetrius' offers; death of Demetrius

46 When Jonathan and the people heard these proposals, they put no faith in them and refused to accept them, remembering what great wrongs Demetrius had done to Israel and how cruelly he had oppressed them. 47 They decided in favour of Alexander, since he seemed to offer the better inducements of the two, and they became his constant allies. 48 King Alexander now mustered large forces and advanced against Demetrius. 49 The two kings met in battle. Demetrius' army was defeated, and Alexander pursued him energetically. 50 He continued the battle with vigour until sunset. And that day Demetrius was killed.

Alexander's marriage with Cleopatra; Jonathan as commander-in-chief and governor-general

51 Alexander sent ambassadors to Ptolemy king of Egypt, with this message:

52 'Since I have returned to my kingdom, have ascended the throne of my ancestors, have gained control by crushing Demetrius, and so recovered our country— 53 for I fought him and we crushed both him and his army, and I now occupy his royal throne— 54 let us now make a treaty of friendship. Give me your daughter in marriage: as your son-in-law, I shall give you, and her, presents which are worthy of you.'

55 King Ptolemy replied as follows:

'Happy the day when you returned to the land of your ancestors and ascended their royal throne! 56 I shall at once do for you what your letter proposes; but meet me at Ptolemais, so that we can see one another, and I shall become your father-in-law, as you have asked.'

57 Ptolemy left Egypt with his daughter Cleopatra and reached Ptolemais in the year 162. 58 King Alexander went to meet him, and

Ptolemy gave him the hand of his daughter Cleopatra and celebrated her wedding in Ptolemais with great magnificence, as kings do. ⁵⁹ King Alexander then wrote to Jonathan to come and meet him. ⁶⁰ Jonathan made his way in state to Ptolemais and met the two kings; he gave them and their friends silver and gold, and many gifts, and made a favourable impression on them. ⁶¹ A number of scoundrels, the pest of Israel, combined to denounce him, but the king paid no attention to them. ⁶² In fact, the king commanded that Jonathan should be divested of his own garments and clothed in the purple, which was done. ⁶³ The king then seated him by his side and said to his officers, 'Escort him into the centre of the city and proclaim that no one is to bring charges against him on any count; no one is to molest him for any reason.' ⁶⁴ And so, when his accusers saw the honour done him by this proclamation, and Jonathan himself invested in the purple, they all fled. ⁶⁵ The king did him the honour of enrolling him among the First Friends, and appointed him commander-in-chief and governor-general. ⁶⁶ Jonathan then returned to Jerusalem in peace and gladness.

Demetrius II; Apollonius, governor of Coele-Syria, defeated by Jonathan

⁶⁷ In the year 165, Demetrius son of Demetrius came from Crete to the land of his ancestors. ⁶⁸ When King Alexander heard of it he was plunged into gloom, and retired to Antioch. ⁶⁹ Demetrius confirmed Apollonius as governor of Coele-Syria; the latter assembled a large force, encamped at Jamnia and sent the following message to Jonathan the high priest:

⁷⁰ 'You are entirely alone in rising against us, and now I find myself ridiculed and reproached on your account. Why do you use your authority to our disadvantage in the mountains? ⁷¹ If you are so confident in your forces, come down now to meet us on the plain and let us take each other's measure there; on my side I have the strength of

the towns. ⁷² Ask and learn who I am and who the others supporting us are. You will hear that you cannot stand up to us, since your ancestors were twice routed on their own ground, ⁷³ nor will you now be able to withstand the cavalry or so great an army on the plain, where there is neither rock, nor stone, nor refuge of any kind.'

⁷⁴ On hearing Apollonius' words, Jonathan's spirit was roused; he picked ten thousand men and left Jerusalem, and his brother Simon joined him with reinforcements. ⁷⁵ He drew up his forces outside Joppa, the citizens having shut him out, since Apollonius had a garrison in Joppa. When they began the attack, ⁷⁶ the citizens took fright and opened the gates, and Jonathan occupied Joppa. ⁷⁷ Hearing this, Apollonius marshalled three thousand cavalry and a large army and made his way to Azotus as though intending to march through, while in fact pressing on into the plain, since he had a great number of cavalry on which he was relying. ⁷⁸ Jonathan pursued him as far as Azotus, where the armies joined battle. ⁷⁹ Now, Apollonius had left a thousand horsemen in concealment behind them. ⁸⁰ Jonathan knew of this enemy position behind him; the horsemen surrounded his army, firing their arrows into his men from morning till evening. ⁸¹ But the troops stood firm, as Jonathan had ordered. Once the cavalry was exhausted, ⁸² Simon sent his own troops into attack against the phalanx, which he cut to pieces and routed. ⁸³ The cavalry scattered over the plain and fled to Azotus, where they took sanctuary in Beth-Dagon, the temple of their idol. ⁸⁴ Jonathan, however, set fire to Azotus and the surrounding towns, plundered them, and burned down the temple of Dagon, with all the fugitives who had crowded into it. ⁸⁵ The enemy losses, counting those who fell by the sword and those burnt to death, totalled about eight thousand men. ⁸⁶ Jonathan then left and pitched camp outside Ascalon, where the citizens came out to meet him with great ceremony. ⁸⁷ Jonathan then re-

turned to Jerusalem with his followers, laden with booty. 88 In the event, when King Alexander heard what had happened, he awarded Jonathan further honours: 89 he sent him the golden brooch, of the kind customarily presented to the King's Cousins, and gave him proprietary rights over Ekron and the land adjoining it.

Ptolemy VI supports Demetrius II but dies, as does Alexander Balas

11 The king of Egypt then assembled an army as numerous as the sands of the seashore, with many ships, and set out to take possession of Alexander's kingdom by a ruse and add it to his own kingdom. 2 He set off for Syria with protestations of peace, and the people of the towns opened their gates to him and came out to meet him, since King Alexander's orders were to welcome him, Ptolemy being his father-in-law. 3 On entering the towns, however, Ptolemy quartered troops as a garrison in each one. 4 When he reached Azotus he was shown the burnt-out temple of Dagon, with Azotus and its suburbs in ruins, corpses scattered here and there, and the charred remains of those whom Jonathan had burnt to death in the battle, piled into heaps along his route. 5 They explained to the king what Jonathan had done, hoping for his disapproval; but the king said nothing. 6 Jonathan went in state to meet the king at Joppa, where they greeted each other and spent the night. 7 Jonathan accompanied the king as far as the river called Eleutherus, and then returned to Jerusalem. 8 King Ptolemy for his part occupied the coastal towns as far as Seleucia on the coast, all the while maturing his wicked designs against Alexander. 9 He sent envoys to King Demetrius to say, 'Come and let us make a treaty; I shall give you my daughter, whom Alexander now has, and you shall rule your father's kingdom. 10 I regret having given my daughter to that man, since he has tried to kill me.' 11 He made this accusation because he coveted his kingdom. 12 Having carried off his daughter and bestowed her on Demetrius, he broke with Alexander, and their enmity became open. 13 Ptolemy next entered Antioch and assumed the crown of Asia; he now wore on his head the two crowns of Egypt and Asia. 14 King Alexander was in Cilicia at the time, since the people of those parts had risen in revolt, 15 but when he heard the news, he advanced on his rival to give battle, while Ptolemy for his part also took the field, met him with a strong force and routed him. 16 Alexander fled to Arabia for refuge, and King Ptolemy reigned supreme. 17 Zabdiel the Arab cut off Alexander's head and sent it to Ptolemy. 18 Three days later King Ptolemy died, and the Egyptian garrisons in the strongholds were killed by the local inhabitants. 19 So Demetrius became king in the year 167.

Early relations between Demetrius and Jonathan

20 At the same time, Jonathan mustered the men of Judaea for an assault on the Citadel of Jerusalem, and they set up numerous siege-engines against it. 21 But some renegades who hated their nation made their way to the king and told him that Jonathan was besieging the Citadel. 22 The king was angered by the news. No sooner had he been informed than he set out and came to Ptolemais. He wrote to Jonathan, telling him to raise the siege and to meet him for a conference in Ptolemais as soon as possible. 23 When Jonathan heard this, he gave orders for the siege to continue; he then selected a deputation from the elders of Israel and the priests, and took the deliberate risk 24 of himself taking silver and gold, clothing and numerous other presents, and going to Ptolemais to face the king, whose favour he succeeded in winning; 25 and although one or two renegades of his nation brought charges against him, 26 the king treated him as his predecessors had treated him, and promoted him in the presence of all his friends. 27 He confirmed him in the high priesthood and whatever other distinctions he already held, and had him ranked among the First Friends. 28 Jonathan asked the king to exempt Judaea

and the three Samaritan districts from taxation, promising him three hundred talents in return. 29 The king consented, and wrote Jonathan a rescript covering the whole matter, in these terms:

A new charter favouring the Jews

30 'King Demetrius to Jonathan his brother, and to the Jewish nation, greetings.

31 'We have written to Lasthenes our cousin concerning you, and now send you this copy of our rescript for your own information:

32 "King Demetrius to his father Lasthenes, greetings.

33 "The nation of the Jews is our ally; they fulfil their obligations to us, and in view of their goodwill towards us we have decided to show them our bounty. 34 We confirm them in their possession of the territory of Judaea and the three districts of Aphairema, Lydda and Ramathaim; these were annexed to Judaea from Samaritan territory, with all their dependencies, in favour of all who offer sacrifice in Jerusalem, instead of the royal dues which the king formerly received from them every year, from the yield of the soil and the fruit crops. 35 As regards our other rights over the tithes and taxes due to us, over the salt marshes, and the crown taxes due to us, as from today we release them from them all. 36 None of these grants will be revoked henceforth or anywhere. 37 You will make yourself responsible for having a copy of this made, to be given to Jonathan and displayed on the holy mountain in a conspicuous place." '

Demetrius II rescued by Jonathan's troops at Antioch

38 When King Demetrius saw that the country was at peace under his rule and that no resistance was offered him, he dismissed his forces, and sent all the men home, except for the foreign troops that he had recruited in the foreign island, thus incurring the enmity of the veter-

ans who had served his ancestors. 39 Now Trypho, one of Alexander's former supporters, noting that all the troops were muttering against Demetrius, went to see Iamleku, the Arab who was bringing up Antiochus, Alexander's young son, 40 and repeatedly urged him to let him have the boy, so that he might succeed his father as king; he told him of Demetrius' decision and of the resentment it had aroused among his troops. He spent a long time there. 41 Jonathan, meanwhile, sent to ask King Demetrius to withdraw the garrisons from the Citadel in Jerusalem and from the other fortresses, since they were constantly fighting Israel. 42 Demetrius sent word back to Jonathan, 'Not only will I do this for you and for your nation, but I shall heap honours on you and your nation if I find a favourable opportunity. 43 For the present, you would do well to send me reinforcements, since all my troops have deserted.' 44 Jonathan sent three thousand experienced soldiers to him in Antioch; when they reached the king, he was delighted at their arrival. 45 The citizens crowded together in the centre of the city, to the number of some hundred and twenty thousand, intending to kill the king. 46 The king took refuge in the palace, while the citizens occupied the thoroughfares of the city and began to attack. 47 The king then called on the Jews for help; and these all rallied round him, then fanned out through the city, and that day killed about a hundred thousand of its inhabitants. 48 They fired the city, seizing a great deal of plunder at the same time, and secured the king's safety. 49 When the citizens saw that the Jews had the city at their mercy, their courage failed them, and they made an abject appeal to the king, 50 'Give us the right hand of peace, and let the Jews stop their fight against us and the city.' 51 They threw down their arms and made peace. The Jews were covered in glory, in the eyes of the king and of everyone else in his kingdom. Having won renown in his kingdom, they returned to Jerusalem laden with booty. 52 Thus, King Demetrius sat all the more securely on his royal throne, and the country was quiet under his government. [53] But he gave the lie to all the promises he had made, and changed his attitude to Jonathan, giving nothing in return for the services Jonathan had rendered him, but thwarting him at every turn.

Jonathan opposes Demetrius II; Simon retakes Beth-Zur; the Hazor incident

[54] After this, Trypho came back with the little boy Antiochus, who became king and was crowned. [55] All the troops that Demetrius had summarily dismissed rallied to Antiochus, and made war on Demetrius, who turned tail and fled. [56] Trypho captured the elephants and seized Antioch.

[57] Young Antiochus then wrote as follows to Jonathan: 'I confirm you in the high priesthood and set you over the four districts and appoint you one of the Friends of the King.' [58] He sent him a service of gold plate, and granted him the right to drink from gold vessels, and to wear the purple and the golden brooch. [59] He appointed his brother Simon commander-in-chief of the region from the Ladder of Tyre to the frontiers of Egypt. [60] Jonathan then set out and made a progress through Transeuphrates and its towns, and the entire Syrian army rallied to his support. He came to Ascalon and was received in state by the inhabitants. [61] From there he proceeded to Gaza, but the people of Gaza shut him out, so he laid siege to it, burning down its suburbs and plundering them. [62] The people of Gaza then pleaded with Jonathan, and he made peace with them; but he took the sons of their chief men as hostages and sent them away to Jerusalem. He then travelled through the country as far as Damascus.

[63] Jonathan now learned that Demetrius' generals had arrived at Kadesh in Galilee with a large army, intending to remove him from office, [64] and went to engage them, leaving his brother Simon inside the country. [65] Simon laid siege to Beth-Zur, attacking it day after day, and blockading the inhabitants [66] till they sued for peace, which he granted them, though

he expelled them from the town and occupied it, stationing a garrison there. [67] Jonathan and his army, meanwhile, having pitched camp by the Lake of Gennesar, rose early, and by morning were already in the plain of Hazor. [68] The foreigners' army advanced to fight them on the plain, having first positioned an ambush for him in the mountains. While the main body was advancing directly towards the Jews, [69] the troops in ambush broke cover and attacked first. [70] All the men with Jonathan fled; no one was left, except Mattathias son of Absalom and Judas son of Chalphi, the generals of his army. [71] At this, Jonathan tore his garments, put dust on his head, and prayed. [72] Then he returned to the fight and routed the enemy, who fled. [73] When the fugitives from his own forces saw this, they came back to him and joined in the pursuit as far as Kadesh where the enemy encampment was, and there they themselves pitched camp. [74] About three thousand of the foreign troops fell that day. Jonathan then returned to Jerusalem.

Jonathan's relations with Rome and Sparta

12 When Jonathan saw that circumstances were working in his favour, he sent a select mission to Rome to confirm and renew his treaty of friendship with the Romans. [2] He also sent letters to the same effect to the Spartans and to other places. [3] The envoys made their way to Rome, entered the Senate and said, 'Jonathan the high priest and the Jewish nation have sent us to renew your treaty of friendship and alliance with them as before.' [4] The Senate gave them letters to the authorities of each place, to procure their safe conduct to Judaea.

[5] The following is the copy of the letter Jonathan wrote to the Spartans:

[6] 'Jonathan the high priest, the senate of the nation, the priests and the rest of the Jewish people to the Spartans their brothers, greetings.

[7] 'In the past, a letter was sent to Onias, the high priest, from Areios, one of your

kings, stating that you are indeed our brothers, as the copy subjoined attests. 8 Onias received the envoy with honour, and accepted the letter, in which a clear declaration was made of friendship and alliance. 9 For our part, though we have no need of these, having the consolation of the holy books in our possession, 10 we venture to send to renew our fraternal friendship with you, so that we may not become strangers to you, a long time having elapsed since you last wrote to us. 11 We, for our part, on every occasion, at our festivals and on other appointed days, unfailingly remember you in the sacrifices we offer and in our prayers, as it is right and fitting to remember brothers. 12 We rejoice in your renown.

13 'We ourselves, however, have had many trials and many wars, the neighbouring kings making war on us. 14 We were unwilling to trouble you or our other allies and friends during these wars, 15 since we have the support of Heaven to help us, thanks to which we have been delivered from our enemies, and they are the ones who have been brought low. 16 We have therefore chosen Numenius son of Antiochus, and Antipater son of Jason, and sent them to the Romans to renew our former treaty of friendship and alliance, 17 and we have ordered them also to visit you, to greet you and deliver you this letter of ours concerning the renewal of our brotherhood; 18 we shall be grateful for an answer to it.'

19 The following is the copy of the letter sent to Onias:

20 'Areios king of the Spartans, to Onias the high priest, greetings.

21 'It has been discovered in records regarding the Spartans and Jews that they are brothers, and of the race of Abraham. 22 Now that this has come to our knowledge, we shall be obliged if you will send us news of your welfare. 23 Our own message to you is this: your flocks and your posses-sions are ours, and ours are yours, and we are instructing our envoys to give you a message to this effect.'

Jonathan in Coele-Syria; Simon in Philistia

24 Jonathan learned that Demetrius' generals had returned with a larger army than before to make war on him. 25 He therefore left Jerusalem and went to engage them in the area of Hamath, not giving them the time to invade his own territory. 26 He sent spies into their camp, who told him on their return that the enemy were taking up positions for a night attack on the Jews. 27 At sunset, Jonathan ordered his men to keep watch with their weapons at hand, in readiness to fight at any time during the night, and posted advance guards all round the camp. 28 On learning that Jonathan and his men were ready to fight, the enemy took fright and, with quaking hearts, lit fires in their bivouac and decamped. 29 Jonathan and his men, watching the glow of the fires, were unaware of their withdrawal until morning, 30 and although Jonathan pursued them, he failed to overtake them, for they had already crossed the river Eleutherus. 31 So Jonathan wheeled round on the Arabs called Zabadaeans, beat them and plundered them; 32 then, breaking camp, he went to Damascus, thus crossing the whole province. 33 Simon, meanwhile, had also set out and had penetrated as far as Ascalon and the neighbouring towns. He then turned on Joppa and moved quickly to occupy it, 34 for he had heard of their intention to hand over this strong point to the supporters of Demetrius; he stationed a garrison there to hold it.

Building work in Jerusalem

35 Jonathan, on his return, called a meeting of the elders of the people and decided with them to build fortresses in Judaea 36 and to heighten the walls of Jerusalem and erect a high barrier between the Citadel and the city, to cut the former off from the city and isolate it, to prevent the occupants from buying or selling. 37 Rebuilding the city was a co-operative effort:

part of the wall over the eastern ravine had fallen down; he restored the quarter called Chaphenatha. 38 Simon, meanwhile, rebuilt Adida in the lowlands, fortifying it, and erecting gates with bolts.

Jonathan falls into the hands of his enemies

39 Trypho's ambition was to become king of Asia, assume the crown, and overpower King Antiochus. 40 He was apprehensive that Jonathan might not allow him to do this, and might even make war on him, so he set out and came to Beth-Shean, in the hopes of finding some pretext for having him arrested and put to death. 41 Jonathan went out to intercept him, with forty thousand picked men in battle order, and arrived at Beth-Shean. 42 When Trypho saw him there with a large force, he hesitated to make any move against him. 43 He even received him with honour, commended him to all his friends, gave him presents and ordered his friends and his troops to obey him as they would himself. 44 He said to Jonathan, 'Why have you given all these people so much trouble, when there is no threat of war between us? 45 Send them back home; pick yourself a few men as your bodyguard, and come with me to Ptolemais, which I am going to hand over to you, with the other fortresses and the remaining troops and all the officials; after which, I shall take the road for home. This was my purpose in coming here.' 46 Jonathan trusted him and did as he said; he dismissed his forces, who went back to Judaea. 47 With him he retained three thousand men, of whom he left two thousand in Galilee, while a thousand accompanied him. 48 But as soon as Jonathan had entered Ptolemais, the people of Ptolemais closed the gates, seized him, and put all those who had entered with him to the sword. 49 Trypho sent troops and cavalry into Galilee and the Great Plain to destroy all Jonathan's supporters. 50 These, concluding that he had been taken and had perished with his companions, encouraged one another, marching with closed ranks and ready to give battle, 51 and when their pursuers saw that they would fight for their lives, they turned back. 52 All reached Judaea safe and sound, and there they lamented Jonathan and his companions, being very frightened indeed; all Israel was plunged into mourning. 53 The surrounding nations were all now looking for ways of destroying them: 'They have no leader,' they said, 'no ally; we have only to attack them now, and we shall blot out their very memory from all peoples.'

Simon takes command

13 Simon heard that Trypho had collected a large army to invade and devastate Judaea, 2 and when he saw how the people were quaking with fear, he went up to Jerusalem, called the people together, 3 and exhorted them thus, 'You know yourselves how much I and my brothers and my father's family have done for the laws and the sanctuary; you know what wars and hardships we have experienced. 4 That is why my brothers are all dead, for Israel's sake, and I am the only one left. 5 Far be it from me, then, to be sparing of my own life in any time of oppression, for I am not worth more than my brothers. 6 Rather will I avenge my nation and the sanctuary and your wives and children, now that the foreigners are all united in malice to destroy us.' 7 The people's spirit rekindled as they listened to his words, 8 and they shouted back at him, 'You are our leader in place of Judas and your brother Jonathan. 9 Fight our battles for us, and we will do whatever you tell us.' 10 So he assembled all the fighting men and hurried on with completing the walls of Jerusalem, fortifying the whole perimeter. 11 He sent a considerable force to Joppa under Jonathan son of Absalom who drove out the inhabitants and remained there in occupation.

Simon repels Trypho from Judaea

12 Trypho now left Ptolemais with a large army to invade Judaea, taking Jonathan with him under guard. 13 Simon pitched camp in Adida, facing the plain. 14 When Trypho

learned that Simon had taken the place of his brother Jonathan and that he intended to join battle with him, he sent envoys to him with this message, ¹⁵'Your brother Jonathan was in debt to the royal exchequer for the offices he held; that is why we are detaining him. ¹⁶If you send a hundred talents of silver and two of his sons as hostages, to make sure that on his release he does not revolt against us, we shall release him.' ¹⁷Although Simon was aware that the message was a ruse, he sent for the money and the boys for fear of incurring great hostility from the people, ¹⁸who would have said that Jonathan had died because Simon would not send Trypho the money and the children. ¹⁹He therefore sent both the boys and the hundred talents, but Trypho broke his word and did not release Jonathan. ²⁰Next, Trypho set about the invasion and devastation of the country; he made a detour along the Adora road, but Simon and his army confronted him wherever he attempted to go. ²¹The men in the Citadel kept sending messengers to Trypho, urging him to get through to them by way of the desert and send them supplies. ²²Trypho organised his entire cavalry to go, but that night it snowed so heavily that he could not get through for the snow, so he left there and moved off into Gilead. ²³As he approached Baskama he killed Jonathan, who was buried there. ²⁴Trypho turned back and regained his own country.

Jonathan is buried in the mausoleum built by Simon at Modein

²⁵Simon sent and recovered the bones of his brother Jonathan, and buried him in Modein, the town of his ancestors. ²⁶All Israel kept solemn mourning for him and long bewailed him. ²⁷Over the tomb of his father and brothers, Simon raised a monument high enough to catch the eye, using dressed stone back and front. ²⁸He erected seven pyramids facing each other, for his father and mother and his four brothers, ²⁹surrounding them with a structure consisting of tall columns surmounted by trophies of arms to their everlast-ing memory and, beside the trophies of arms, ships sculpted on a scale to be seen by all who sail the sea. ³⁰Such was the monument he constructed at Modein, and it is still there today.

The favours of Demetrius II to Simon

³¹Now Trypho, betraying the trust of young King Antiochus, put him to death. ³²He usurped his throne, assuming the crown of Asia, and brought great havoc on the country. ³³Simon built up the fortresses of Judaea, surrounding them with high towers, great walls and gates with bolts, and stocked these fortresses with food. ³⁴He also sent a delegation to King Demetrius, to get him to grant the province a remission, since all Trypho did was to despoil. ³⁵King Demetrius replied to his request in a letter framed as follows:

³⁶'King Demetrius to Simon, high priest and Friend of Kings, and to the elders and nation of the Jews, greetings.

³⁷'It has pleased us to accept the golden crown and the palm you have sent us, and we are disposed to make a general peace with you, and to write to the officials to grant you remissions. ³⁸Everything that we have decreed concerning you remains in force, and the fortresses you have built may remain in your hands. ³⁹We pardon all offences, unwitting or intentional, hitherto committed, and remit the crown tax you now owe us; and whatever other taxes were levied in Jerusalem are no longer to be levied. ⁴⁰If any of you are suitable for enrolment in our bodyguard, let them be enrolled, and let there be peace between us.'

⁴¹The gentile yoke was thus lifted from Israel in the year 170, ⁴²when our people began engrossing their documents and contracts: 'In the first year of Simon, eminent high priest, commander-in-chief and ethnarch of the Jews'.

The capture of Gezer by Simon

⁴³About that time Simon laid siege to Gezer, surrounding it with his troops. He constructed

a mobile tower, brought it up to the city, opened a breach in one of the bastions and took it. 44 The men in the mobile tower sprang out into the city, where great confusion ensued. 45 The citizens, accompanied by their wives and children, mounted the ramparts with their garments torn and loudly implored Simon to make peace with them: 46 'Treat us', they said, 'not as our wickedness deserves, but as your mercy prompts you.' 47 Simon came to terms with them and stopped the fighting; but he expelled them from the city, purified the houses which contained idols, and then made his entry with songs of praise. 48 He banished all impurity from it, settled in it people who observed the Law, and having fortified it, built a residence there for himself.

Simon occupies the Citadel in Jerusalem

49 The occupants of the Citadel in Jerusalem, prevented as they were from coming out and going into the countryside to buy and sell, were in desperate need of food, and numbers of them were being carried off by starvation. 50 They begged Simon to make peace with them, and he granted this, though he expelled them and purified the Citadel from its pollutions. 51 The Jews made their entry on the twenty-third day of the second month in the year 171, with acclamations and carrying palms, to the sound of lyres, cymbals and harps, chanting hymns and canticles, since a great enemy had been crushed and thrown out of Israel. Simon made it a day of annual rejoicing. 52 He fortified the Temple hill on the Citadel side, and took up residence there with his men. 53 Since his son John had come to manhood, Simon appointed him general-in-chief, with his residence in Gezer.

Eulogy of Simon

14 In the year 172, King Demetrius assembled his forces and marched into Media to raise help for the fight against Trypho. 2 When Arsaces king of Persia and Media heard that Demetrius had entered his territory, he sent one of his generals to capture him

alive. 3 The general defeated the army of Demetrius, seized him and brought him to Arsaces, who imprisoned him. 4 The country was at peace throughout the days of Simon.

He sought the good of his nation
 and they were well pleased with his
  authority,
 as with his magnificence, throughout his
  life.
5 To crown his titles to glory,
 he took Joppa and made it a harbour,
 gaining access to the Mediterranean Isles.
6 He enlarged the frontiers of his nation,
 keeping his mastery over the homeland,
7 resettling a host of captives.
He conquered Gezer, Beth-Zur and the
  Citadel,
 ridding them of every impurity,
 and no one could resist him.
8 The people farmed their land in peace;
 the land gave its produce,
 the trees of the plain their fruit.
9 The elders sat at ease in the squares,
 all their talk was of their prosperity;
 the young men wore splendid armour.
10 He kept the towns supplied with
  provisions
 and furnished with fortifications,
 until his fame resounded to the ends of the
  earth.
11 He established peace in the land,
 and Israel knew great joy.
12 Each man sat under his own vine and his
  own fig tree,
 and there was no one to make them afraid.
13 No enemy was left in the land to fight
  them,
 the very kings of those times had been
  crushed.
14 He encouraged the afflicted members of
  his people,
 suppressing every wicked man and
  renegade.
He strove to observe the Law,
15 and gave new splendour to the Temple,
 enriching it with many sacred vessels.

Renewal of the alliances with Sparta and with Rome

16 When it became known in Rome and as far as Sparta that Jonathan was dead, people were deeply grieved. 17 But as soon as they heard that his brother Simon had succeeded him as high priest and was master of the country and the cities in it, 18 they wrote to him on bronze tablets to renew the treaty of friendship and alliance which they had made with his brothers, Judas and Jonathan, 19 and the document was read out before the assembly in Jerusalem.

20 This is the copy of the letter sent by the Spartans:

'The rulers and the city of Sparta, to Simon the high priest and to the elders and priests and the rest of the people of the Jews, greetings.

21 'The ambassadors whom you sent to our people have informed us of your glory and prosperity, and we are delighted with their visit. 22 We have recorded their declarations in the minutes of our public assemblies, as follows, "Numenius son of Antiochus, and Antipater son of Jason, ambassadors of the Jews, came to us to renew their friendship with us. 23 And it was the people's pleasure to receive these personages with honour and to deposit a copy of their statements in the public archives, so that the people of Sparta might preserve a record of them. A copy was also made for Simon the high priest."'

24 After this, Simon sent Numenius to Rome as the bearer of a large golden shield weighing a thousand *mina,* to confirm the alliance with them.

Official honours decreed for Simon

25 When these events were reported to our people, they said, 'What mark of appreciation shall we give to Simon and his sons? 26 He stood firm, he and his brothers and his father's house: he fought off the enemies of Israel and secured its freedom.' So they recorded an inscription on bronze tablets and set it up on pillars on Mount Zion. 27 This is a copy of the text:

'The eighteenth of Elul, in the year 172, being the third year of Simon, eminent high priest:

28 'In Asaramel, in the Grand Assembly of priests and people, of princes of the nation and of elders of the country:

'We are acquainted with the matters following:

29 'When there was almost incessant fighting in the country Simon, son of Mattathias, a priest of the line of Joarib, and his brothers courted danger and withstood their nation's enemies to safeguard the integrity of their sanctuary and of the Law, and so brought their nation great glory;

30 'For when, Jonathan having rallied his nation and become its high priest and having then been gathered to his ancestors, 31 the enemy planned to invade the country, intending to devastate their territory and to lay hands on their sanctuary, 32 Simon next came forward to fight for his nation: spending much of his personal wealth on arming his nation's fighting men and on providing their pay; 33 fortifying the towns of Judaea, as well as Beth-Zur on the Judaean frontier where the enemy arsenal had formerly been, and stationing in it a garrison of Jewish soldiers; 34 fortifying Joppa on the coast, and Gezer on the borders of Azotus, a place formerly inhabited by the enemy, founding a Jewish colony there, and providing the settlers with everything they needed to set them on their feet;

35 'In consequence of which, the people, aware of Simon's loyalty and of the glory which he was determined to win for his nation, have made him their ethnarch and high priest, for all his services and for the integrity and loyalty which he has shown towards his nation, and for having by every means sought to enhance his people's power;

36 'It has fallen to him in his time to expel the foreigners from his country, including those in the City of David in Jerusalem, who had converted it into a citadel for their own use, from which they would sally out to defile the surroundings of the sanctuary and to violate its sacred character; 37 to station Jewish soldiers there instead for the security of the country and the city; and to heighten the walls of Jerusalem;

38 'And since King Demetrius has heard that the Romans call the Jews their friends, allies and brothers, 39 and that they have given an honourable reception to Simon's ambassadors, and, furthermore, 40 that the Jews and priests are happy that Simon should, pending the advent of a genuine prophet, be their ethnarch and high priest for life 41 therefore he has confirmed him in the high-priestly office, has raised him to the rank of Friend and has showered great honours on him, also confirming him as their commander-in-chief, 42 with the right to appoint officials to oversee the fabric of the sanctuary and to administer the country, munitions and fortresses; 43 he is to have personal charge of the sanctuary, and to be obeyed by all; all official documents in the country must be drawn up in his name; and he may assume the purple and may wear golden ornaments;

44 'Furthermore, it is against the law for any member of the public or of the priesthood to contravene any of these enactments or to contest his decisions, or to convene a meeting anywhere in the country without his permission, or to assume the purple or wear the golden brooch; 45 and anyone acting contrary to, or rejecting any article of, these enactments is liable to punishment;

46 'And since the people have unanimously agreed to grant Simon the right to act as aforesaid, and 47 since Simon, for his part, has given his assent, and has consented to assume the high-priestly office and to be commander-in-chief and ethnarch of the Jews and their priests, and to preside over all:

48 'So, be it now enacted: that this record be inscribed on bronze tablets and be erected at some conspicuous place within the precincts of the Temple, 49 and that copies be deposited in the Treasury for Simon and his descendants.'

Letter of Antiochus VII and siege of Dora

15 Antiochus son of King Demetrius addressed a letter from the Mediterranean Isles to Simon, priest and ethnarch of the Jews, and to the whole nation; 2 this was how it read:

'King Antiochus to Simon, high priest and ethnarch, and to the Jewish nation, greetings.

3 'Whereas certain scoundrels have seized control of the kingdom of our fathers, and I propose to claim back the kingdom so that I may re-establish it as it was before, and whereas I have accordingly recruited very large forces and fitted out warships, 4 intending to make a landing in the country and to hunt down the men who have ruined it and laid waste many towns in my kingdom;

5 'I now, therefore, confirm in your favour all remissions of taxes granted to you by the kings my predecessors, as well as the waiving of whatever presents they may have conceded. 6 I hereby authorise you to mint your own coinage as legal tender for your own country. 7 I declare Jerusalem and the sanctuary to be free; all the arms you have manufactured and the fortresses you have built and now occupy may remain yours. 8 All debts to the royal treasury, present or future, are cancelled henceforth in perpetuity. 9 Furthermore, when we have won back our kingdom, we shall bestow such great honour on yourself, your nation and the sanctuary as will make your glory known throughout the world.'

10 Antiochus invaded the land of his ancestors in the year 174 and, since the troops all

rallied to him, Trypho was left with few supporters. ¹¹Antiochus pursued the usurper, who took refuge in Dora on the coast, ¹²knowing that misfortunes were piling up on him and that his troops had deserted him. ¹³Antiochus pitched camp outside Dora with a hundred and twenty thousand fighting men and eight thousand cavalry. ¹⁴He laid siege to the city while the ships closed in from the sea, so that he had the city under attack from land and sea, and allowed no one to go in or come out.

The ambassadors return from Rome to Judaea; the alliance with Rome proclaimed

¹⁵Numenius and his companions, meanwhile, arrived from Rome, bringing letters addressed to various kings and states, in the following terms:

¹⁶'Lucius, consul of the Romans, to King Ptolemy, greetings.

¹⁷'The Jewish ambassadors have come to us as our friends and allies to renew our original friendship and alliance in the name of the high priest Simon and the Jewish people. ¹⁸They have brought a golden shield worth a thousand *mina*. ¹⁹Accordingly, we have seen fit to write to various kings and states, warning them neither to molest the Jewish people nor to attack either them or their towns or their country, nor to ally themselves with any such aggressors. ²⁰We have seen fit to accept the shield from them. ²¹If, therefore, any scoundrels have fled their country to take refuge with you, hand them over to Simon the high priest, to be punished by him according to their law.'

²²The consul sent the same letter to King Demetrius, to Attalus, Ariarathes and Arsaces, ²³and to all states, including Sampsames, the Spartans, Delos, Myndos, Sicyon, Caria, Samos, Pamphylia, Lycia, Halicarnassus, Rhodes, Phaselis, Cos, Side, Arados, Gortyn, Cyprus and Cyrene. ²⁴They also drew up a copy for Simon the high priest.

Antiochus VII, besieging Dora, becomes hostile to Simon and sends him a reprimand

²⁵Antiochus, meanwhile, from his positions on the outskirts of Dora, was continually throwing detachments against the town. He constructed siege-engines, and blockaded Trypho, preventing movement in or out. ²⁶Simon sent him two thousand picked men to support him in the fight, with silver and gold and plenty of equipment. ²⁷But Antiochus would not accept them; instead, he repudiated all his previous agreements with Simon and completely changed his attitude to him. ²⁸He sent him Athenobius, one of his Friends, to confer with him and say, 'You are now occupying Joppa and Gezer and the Citadel in Jerusalem, which are towns in my kingdom. ²⁹You have laid waste their territory and done immense harm to the country; and you have seized control of many places properly in my kingdom. ³⁰Either now surrender the towns you have taken and the taxes from the places you have seized outside the frontiers of Judaea, ³¹or else pay me five hundred talents of silver in compensation for them and for the destruction you have done, and another five hundred talents for the taxes from the towns; otherwise we shall come and make war on you.' ³²When the King's Friend, Athenobius, reached Jerusalem and saw Simon's magnificence, his cabinet of gold and silver plate and the state he kept, he was dumbfounded. He delivered the king's message, ³³but Simon gave him this answer, 'We have not taken foreign territory or any alien property but have occupied our ancestral heritage, for some time unjustly wrested from us by our enemies; ³⁴now that we have a favourable opportunity, we are merely recovering our ancestral heritage. ³⁵As regards Joppa and Gezer, which you claim, these were towns that did great harm to our people and laid waste our country; we are prepared to give a hundred talents for them.' Without so much as a word in answer, ³⁶the envoy went back to the king in a rage and reported on

Simon's answer and his magnificence, and on everything he had seen, at which the king fell into a fury.

Cendebaeus, governor of the coastal region, harasses Judaea

37 Trypho now boarded a ship and escaped to Orthosia. 38 The king appointed Cendebaeus military governor of the coastal region and allotted him a force of infantry and cavalry. 39 He ordered him to deploy his men facing Judaea, and instructed him to rebuild Kedron and fortify its gates, and to make war on our people, while the king himself went in pursuit of Trypho. 40 Cendebaeus arrived at Jamnia and began to provoke our people forthwith, invading Judaea, taking prisoners, and massacring. 41 Having rebuilt Kedron, he stationed cavalry and troops there to make sorties and patrol the roads of Judaea, as the king had ordered.

The victory of Simon's sons over Cendebaeus

16 John then went up from Gezer and reported to his father Simon what Cendebaeus was busy doing. 2 At this, Simon summoned his two elder sons, Judas and John, and said to them, 'My brothers and I, and my father's House, have fought the enemies of Israel from our youth until today, and many a time we have been successful in rescuing Israel. 3 But now I am an old man, while you, by the mercy of Heaven, are the right age; take the place of my brother and myself, go out and fight for our nation, and may Heaven's aid be with you.' 4 He then selected twenty thousand of the country's fighting men and cavalry, and these marched against Cendebaeus, spending the night at Modein. 5 Making an early start, they marched into the plain, to find a large army opposing them, both infantry and cavalry; there was, however, a stream-bed in between. 6 John drew up facing them, he and his army and, seeing that the men were afraid to cross the stream-bed, crossed over first himself. When his men saw this, they too crossed after him. 7 He divided his army into two, with

the cavalry in the centre and the infantry on either flank, as the opposing cavalry was very numerous. 8 The trumpets rang out; Cendebaeus and his army were put to flight, many of them falling mortally wounded and the rest of them fleeing to the fortress. 9 Then it was that Judas, John's brother, was wounded, but John pursued them until Cendebaeus reached Kedron, which he had rebuilt. 10 Their flight took them as far as the towers in the countryside of Azotus, and John burnt these down. The enemy losses amounted to ten thousand men; John returned safely to Judaea.

Simon's tragic death at Dok; his son John succeeds him

11 Ptolemy son of Abubos had been appointed general in command of the Plain of Jericho; he owned a great deal of silver and gold, 12 and was the high priest's son-in-law. 13 His ambition was fired; he hoped to make himself master of the whole country and therefore treacherously began to plot the destruction of Simon and his sons. 14 Simon, who was inspecting the towns up and down the country and attending to their administration, had come down to Jericho with his sons Mattathias and Judas, in the year 172, in the eleventh month, the month of Shebat. 15 The son of Abubos lured them into a small fortress called Dok, which he had built, where he offered them a great banquet, having previously hidden men in the place. 16 When Simon and his sons were drunk, Ptolemy and his men reached for their weapons, rushed on Simon in the banqueting hall and killed him with his two sons and some of his servants. 17 He thus committed a great act of treachery and rendered evil for good.

18 Ptolemy wrote a report of the affair and sent it to the king, in the expectation of being sent reinforcements and of having the cities and the province made over to him. 19 He also sent people to Gezer to murder John, and sent written orders to the military commanders to come to him so that he could give them silver, gold and presents; 20 and he also sent others to

seize control of Jerusalem and the Temple mount. ²¹ But someone had been too quick for him and had already informed John in Gezer that his father and brothers had perished, adding, 'He is sending someone to kill you too!' ²² Overcome as John was by the news, he arrested the men who had come to kill him and put them to death, being forewarned of their murderous design. ²³ The rest of John's acts, the battles he fought and the exploits he performed, the city walls he built, and all his other achievements, ²⁴ from the day he succeeded his father as high priest, are recorded in the annals of his pontificate.

The Second Book of

MACCABEES

First letter to the Jews of Egypt

1 'To their brothers, the Jews living in Egypt, from their brothers, the Jews in Jerusalem and Judaea, greetings and untroubled peace.

2 'May God prosper you, remembering his covenant with Abraham, Isaac and Jacob, his faithful servants. 3 May he give you all a heart to worship him and to do his will with a generous mind and a willing spirit. 4 May he open your hearts to his Law and his precepts, and give you peace. 5 May he hear your prayers and be reconciled with you, and not abandon you in time of evil. 6 Such is our prayer for you.

7 'During the reign of Demetrius, in the year 169, we Jews wrote to you as follows, "In the extremity of trouble that befell us in the years after Jason and his associates had betrayed the Holy Land and the kingdom, 8 burning down the Temple gateway and shedding innocent blood, we prayed to the Lord and were then heard. And we then offered a sacrifice, with wheat-flour, we lit the lamps and we set out the loaves."

9 'And we now recommend you too to keep the feast of Shelters in the month of Chislev, in the year one hundred and eighty-eight.'

Second letter to the Jews of Egypt

10 'The people of Jerusalem and of Judaea, the senate and Judas, to Aristobulus, tutor to King Ptolemy and one of the family of the anointed priests, and to the Jews in Egypt, greetings and good health.

Thanksgiving for the punishment of Antiochus

11 'Since we have been rescued by God from great danger, we give him great thanks for championing our cause against the king, 12 for he it was who carried off those who had taken up arms against the Holy City. 13 For when their leader reached Persia with his seemingly irresistible army, he was cut to pieces in the temple of Nanaea, as the result of a ruse employed by the priests who served that goddess. 14 On the pretext of marrying Nanaea, Antiochus came to the place with his friends, intending to take its many treasures as a dowry. 15 The priests of Nanaea had put these on display, and he for his part had entered the temple precincts with only a small retinue. As soon as Antiochus had gone inside the temple, the priests shut him in, 16 opened a trap-door hidden in the ceiling and struck the leader down by hurling stones like thunderbolts. They then cut him into pieces and threw his head to those who were waiting outside. 17 Blessed in all things be our God, who has delivered the sacrilegious over to death!

The miraculous preservation of the sacred fire

18 'As we shall be celebrating the purification of the Temple on the twenty-fifth of Chislev, we consider it proper to notify you, so that you too may celebrate it, as you do the feast of Shelters and the fire that appeared when Nehemiah, the builder of the Temple and the altar, offered sacrifice. 19 For when our ancestors were being deported to Persia, the devout priests of the time took some of the fire from the altar and hid it secretly in a hole like a dry well, where they concealed it in such a way that the place was unknown to anyone. 20 When some years had elapsed, in God's good time, Nehemiah, commissioned by the king of Persia, sent the descendants of the

priests who had hidden the fire to look for it. When they reported that in fact they had found not fire but a thick liquid, Nehemiah ordered them to draw some out and bring it back. ²¹When they had done this, Nehemiah ordered the priests to pour this liquid over the sacrificial materials, that is, the wood and what lay on it. ²²When this had been done, and when in due course the sun, which had previously been clouded over, shone out, a great fire flared up, to the astonishment of all. ²³While the sacrifice was being burned, the priests offered prayer, Jonathan intoning with all the priests, and the rest responding with Nehemiah. ²⁴The prayer took this form, "Lord, Lord God, Creator of all things, awesome, strong, just, merciful, the only king and benefactor, ²⁵the only provider, who alone are just, almighty and everlasting, the deliverer of Israel from every evil, who made our fathers your chosen ones and sanctified them, ²⁶accept this sacrifice on behalf of all your people Israel, and protect your heritage and consecrate it. ²⁷Bring together those of us who are dispersed, set free those in slavery among the heathen, look favourably on those held in contempt or abhorrence, and let the heathen know that you are our God. ²⁸Punish those who oppress us and affront us by their insolence, ²⁹and plant your people firmly in your Holy Place, as Moses promised."

³⁰'The priests then chanted hymns accompanied by the harp. ³¹When the sacrifice had been burnt, Nehemiah ordered the remaining liquid to be poured over large stones, ³²and when this was done a flame flared up, to be absorbed in a corresponding blaze of light from the altar. ³³When the matter became known and the king of the Persians heard that, in the place where the exiled priests had hidden the fire, a liquid had appeared, with which Nehemiah and his people had purified the sacrificial offerings, ³⁴the king, after verifying the facts, had the place enclosed and pronounced sacred. ³⁵To the people on whom the king bestowed it, he granted a part of the considerable revenue he derived from it. ³⁶Nehemiah and

his people termed this stuff "nephtar", which means "purification", but it is commonly called "naphta".

Jeremiah conceals the tent, ark and altar

2 'It is on record that the prophet Jeremiah ordered the deportees to take the fire, as we have described, ²and how, having given them the Law, the prophet warned the deportees never to forget the Lord's precepts, nor to let their thoughts be tempted by the sight of gold and silver statues or the finery adorning them. ³Among other similar admonitions, he urged them not to let the Law depart from their hearts.

⁴'The same document also describes how the prophet, warned by an oracle, gave orders for the tent and the ark to go with him, when he set out for the mountain which Moses had climbed to survey God's heritage. ⁵On his arrival, Jeremiah found a cave-dwelling, into which he put the tent, the ark and the altar of incense, afterwards blocking up the entrance. ⁶Some of his companions went back later to mark out the path but were unable to find it. ⁷When Jeremiah learned this, he reproached them, "The place is to remain unknown", he said, "until God gathers his people together again and shows them his mercy. ⁸Then the Lord will bring these things once more to light, and the glory of the Lord will be seen, and so will the cloud, as it was revealed in the time of Moses[a] and when Solomon[b] prayed that the holy place might be gloriously hallowed."

⁹'It was also recorded how Solomon in his wisdom offered the sacrifice of the dedication and completion of the sanctuary. ¹⁰As Moses had prayed to the Lord and fire had come down from heaven and burned up the sacrifice, so Solomon also prayed, and the fire from above consumed the burnt offerings. ¹¹Moses[c] had said, "Because the sacrifice for sin had not been eaten, it was burnt instead." ¹²Solomon[d] similarly observed the eight-day festival.

2a Ex 24:16.   2b 1 K 8:10–11.
2c Lv 10:16–17.   2d 1 K 8:65–66.

Nehemiah's library

13 'In addition to the above, it was also recorded, both in these writings and in the *Memoirs of Nehemiah,* how Nehemiah founded a library and made a collection of the books dealing with the kings and the prophets, the writings of David and the letters of the kings on the subject of offerings. 14 Similarly, Judas made a complete collection of the books dispersed in the late war, and these we still have. 15 If you need any of them, send someone to fetch them.

An invitation to the dedication

16 'Since we are about to celebrate the purification, we now write, requesting you to observe the same days. 17 God, who has saved his whole people, conferring heritage, kingdom, priesthood and sanctification on all of us, 18 as he has promised in the Law, will surely, as our hope is in him, be swift to show us mercy and gather us together from everywhere under heaven to the holy place, since he has rescued us from great evils and has purified it.'

Preface

19 The story of Judas Maccabaeus and his brothers, the purification of the great Temple, the dedication of the altar, 20 together with the wars against Antiochus Epiphanes and his son Eupator, 21 and the celestial manifestations that came to hearten the brave champions of Judaism, so that, few though they were, they pillaged the whole country, routed the barbarian hordes, 22 recovered the sanctuary renowned the whole world over, liberated the city and re-established the laws by then all but abolished, the Lord showing his favour by all his gracious help to them— 23 all this, already related in five books by Jason of Cyrene, we shall attempt to condense into a single work. 24 Considering the spate of figures and the difficulty encountered, because of the mass of material, by those who wish to immerse themselves in historical records, 25 we have aimed at providing diversion for those who merely want something to read, a saving of labour for those who enjoy committing things to memory, and profit for each and all. 26 For us who have undertaken the drudgery of this abridgement, it has been no easy task but a matter of sweat and midnight oil, 27 comparable to the exacting task of someone organising a banquet, whose aim is to satisfy a variety of tastes. Nevertheless, for the sake of rendering a general service, we remain glad to endure this drudgery, 28 leaving accuracy of detail to the historian, and concentrating our effort on tracing the outlines in this condensed version. 29 Just as the architect of a new house is responsible for the construction as a whole, while the man undertaking the ceramic painting has to take into consideration only the decorative requirements, so, I think, it is with us. 30 To make the subject his own, to explore its by-ways, to be meticulous about details, is the business of the original historian, 31 but the person making the adaptation must be allowed to aim at conciseness of expression and to forgo any exhaustive treatment of his subject.

32 So now let us begin our narrative, without adding any more to what has been said above; there would be no sense in expanding the preface to the history and curtailing the history itself.

The arrival of Heliodorus in Jerusalem

3 While the holy city was inhabited in all peace and the laws were observed as perfectly as possible, owing to the piety of Onias the high priest and his hatred of wickedness, 2 it came about that the kings themselves honoured the holy place and enhanced the glory of the Temple with the most splendid offerings, 3 even to the extent that Seleucus king of Asia defrayed from his own revenues all the expenses arising out of the sacrificial liturgy. 4 But a certain Simon, of the tribe of Bilgah, on being appointed administrator of the Temple, came into conflict with the high priest over the regulation of the city markets. 5 Unable to get the better of Onias, he went off to Apollonius,

son of Thraseos, who was at that time commander-in-chief of Coele-Syria and Phoenicia, [6] and made out to him that the Treasury in Jerusalem was groaning with untold wealth, that the amount contributed was incalculable and out of all proportion to expenditure on the sacrifice, but that it could all be brought under the control of the king. [7] Apollonius met the king and told him about the wealth that had been disclosed to him; whereupon the king selected Heliodorus, his chancellor, and sent him with instructions to effect the removal of the reported wealth. [8] Heliodorus lost no time in setting out, ostensibly to inspect the towns of Coele-Syria and Phoenicia, but in fact to accomplish the king's purpose. [9] On his arrival in Jerusalem, and after a hospitable reception from the high priest and the city, he announced what had been disclosed, thus revealing the reason for his presence, and asked if this was indeed the true situation. [10] The high priest explained that there were funds set aside for widows and orphans, [11] with some belonging to Hyrcanus son of Tobias, a man occupying a very exalted position, and that the whole sum, in contrast to what the evil Simon had alleged, amounted to four hundred talents of silver and two hundred of gold. [12] He also added that it was entirely out of the question that an injustice should be done to those who had put their trust in the sanctity of the place and in the inviolable majesty of a Temple venerated throughout the entire world.

Consternation in Jerusalem

[13] But Heliodorus, because of his instructions from the king, peremptorily insisted that the funds must be confiscated for the royal exchequer. [14] Fixing a day for the purpose, he went in to draw up an inventory of the funds. There was no little consternation throughout the city; [15] the priests in their sacred vestments prostrated themselves before the altar and prayed to Heaven, to the Author of the law governing deposits, to preserve these funds intact for the depositors. [16] The appearance of the high priest was enough to pierce the heart

of the beholder, his expression and his altered colour betraying the anguish of his soul; [17] the man was so overwhelmed by fear and bodily trembling that those who saw him could not possibly mistake the distress he was suffering. [18] People rushed headlong from the houses, intent on making public supplication because of the indignity threatening the holy place. [19] Women thronged the streets swathed in sackcloth below their breasts; girls secluded indoors came running, some to the doorways, some to the city walls, while others leaned out of the windows, [20] all stretching out their hands to Heaven in entreaty. [21] It was pitiful to see the people crowding together to prostrate themselves, and the foreboding of the high priest in his deep anguish. [22] While they were calling on the all-powerful Lord to preserve the deposits intact for the depositors, in full security, [23] Heliodorus set about his appointed task.

The punishment of Heliodorus

[24] He had already arrived with his bodyguard near the Treasury, when the Sovereign of spirits and of every power caused so great an apparition that all who had dared to accompany Heliodorus were dumbfounded at the power of God and reduced to abject terror. [25] Before their eyes appeared a horse richly caparisoned and carrying a fearsome rider. Rearing violently, it struck at Heliodorus with its forefeet. The rider was seen to be accoutred entirely in gold. [26] Two other young men of outstanding strength and radiant beauty, magnificently apparelled, appeared to him at the same time and, taking their stand on each side of him, flogged him unremittingly, inflicting stroke after stroke. [27] Suddenly Heliodorus fell to the ground, enveloped in thick darkness. His men came to his rescue and placed him in a litter, [28] this man who but a moment before had made his way into the Treasury, as we said above, with a great retinue and his whole bodyguard; and as they carried him away, powerless to help himself, they openly acknowledged the sovereign power of God.

29 While Heliodorus lay prostrate under the divine visitation, speechless and bereft of all hope of deliverance, 30 the Jews blessed the Lord who had miraculously glorified his own holy place. And the Temple, which a little while before had been filled with terror and commotion, now overflowed with joy and gladness at the manifestation of the almighty Lord. 31 Some of Heliodorus' companions quickly begged Onias to entreat the Most High to grant the man his life, lying as he did at the very point of death.

32 The high priest, afraid that the king might suspect the Jews of some foul play concerning Heliodorus, did indeed offer a sacrifice for the man's recovery. 33 And while the high priest was performing the rite of expiation, the same young men again appeared to Heliodorus, wearing the same apparel and, standing beside him, said, 'Be very grateful to Onias the high priest, since it is for his sake that the Lord has granted you your life. 34 As for you, who have been scourged by Heaven, you must proclaim to everyone the grandeur of God's power.' So saying, they vanished.

The conversion of Heliodorus

35 Heliodorus offered sacrifice to the Lord and made most solemn vows to the preserver of his life, and then took courteous leave of Onias and marched his forces back to the king. 36 He openly testified to everyone about the works of the supreme God which he had seen with his own eyes. 37 When the king asked Heliodorus what sort of man would be the right person to send to Jerusalem on a second occasion, he replied, 38 'If you have some enemy or anyone disloyal to the state, send him there, and you will get him back well flogged, if he survives at all, since some peculiarly divine power attaches to the holy place. 39 He who has his dwelling in heaven watches over the place and defends it, and he strikes down and destroys those who come to harm it.' 40 This was the outcome of the affair of Heliodorus and the preservation of the Treasury.

The misdeeds of Simon, administrator of the Temple

4 The Simon mentioned above as the informer against the funds and against his country began slandering Onias, insinuating that the latter had been responsible for the assault on Heliodorus and himself had contrived this misfortune. 2 Simon now had the effrontery to name this benefactor of the city, this protector of his compatriots, this zealot for the laws, as an enemy of the public good. 3 This hostility reached such proportions that murders were actually committed by some of Simon's agents, 4 and at this point Onias, recognising how mischievous this rivalry was, and aware that Apollonius son of Menestheus, the general commanding Coele-Syria and Phoenicia, was encouraging Simon in his malice, 5 went to see the king, not to play the accuser of his fellow-citizens, but having the public and private welfare of the entire people at heart. 6 He saw that, without some intervention by the king, an orderly administration would no longer be possible, nor would Simon put a stop to his folly.

Jason, the high priest, introduces Hellenism

7 When Seleucus had departed this life and Antiochus styled Epiphanes had succeeded to the kingdom, Jason, brother of Onias, usurped the high priesthood: 8 he approached the king with a promise of three hundred and sixty talents of silver, with eighty talents to come from some other source of revenue. 9 He further committed himself to paying another hundred and fifty, if the king would empower him to set up a gymnasium and youth centre, and to register the Antiochists of Jerusalem. 10 When the king gave his assent, Jason, as soon as he had seized power, imposed the Greek way of life on his fellow-countrymen. 11 He suppressed the liberties which the kings had graciously granted to the Jews at the instance of John, father of that Eupolemus who was later to be sent on an embassy to negotiate a treaty of friendship and alliance with the Romans

and, overthrowing the lawful institutions, introduced new usages contrary to the Law. ¹²He went so far as to found a gymnasium at the very foot of the Citadel, and to fit out the noblest of his young men in the petasos. ¹³Godless wretch that he was and no true high priest, Jason set no bounds to his impiety; indeed the hellenising process reached such a pitch ¹⁴that the priests ceased to show any interest in serving the altar; but, scorning the Temple and neglecting the sacrifices, they would hurry, on the stroke of the gong, to take part in the distribution, forbidden by the Law, of the oil on the exercise ground; ¹⁵setting no store by the honours of their fatherland, they esteemed hellenic glories best of all. ¹⁶But all this brought its own retribution; the very people whose way of life they envied, whom they sought to resemble in everything, proved to be their enemies and executioners. ¹⁷It is no small thing to violate the divine laws, as the period that followed will demonstrate.

¹⁸On the occasion of the quadrennial games at Tyre in the presence of the king, ¹⁹the vile Jason sent an embassy of Antiochists from Jerusalem, taking with them three hundred silver drachmas for the sacrifice to Hercules. But even those who brought the money did not think it would be right to spend it on the sacrifice and decided to reserve it for some other item of expenditure; ²⁰and so what the sender had intended for the sacrifice to Hercules was in fact applied, at the suggestion of those who brought it, to the construction of triremes.

Antiochus Epiphanes is acclaimed in Jerusalem

²¹Apollonius son of Menestheus had been sent to Egypt to attend the wedding of King Philometor. Antiochus, having learnt that the latter had become hostile to his affairs, began thinking about his own safety: that was why he had come to Joppa. He then moved to Jerusalem, ²²where he was given a magnificent welcome by Jason and the city, and escorted in by torchlight with acclamation. After which, he marched his army into Phoenicia.

Menelaus becomes high priest

²³When three years had passed, Jason sent Menelaus, brother of the Simon mentioned above, to convey the money to the king and to complete negotiations on various essential matters. ²⁴But Menelaus, on being presented to the king, flattered him by his own appearance of authority, and so secured the high priesthood for himself, outbidding Jason by three hundred talents of silver. ²⁵He returned with the royal mandate, bringing nothing worthy of the high priesthood and supported only by the fury of a cruel tyrant and the rage of a savage beast. ²⁶Thus Jason, who had supplanted his own brother, was in turn supplanted by a third, and obliged to take refuge in Ammanitis. ²⁷As for Menelaus, he secured the office, but defaulted altogether on the sums promised to the king, ²⁸although Sostratus, the commandant of the Citadel, whose business it was to collect the revenue, kept demanding payment. The pair of them in consequence were summoned before the king, ²⁹Menelaus leaving his brother Lysimachus as deputy high priest, while Sostratus left Crates, the commander of the Cypriots, to act for him.

The murder of Onias

³⁰While all this was going on, it happened that the people of Tarsus and Mallus revolted, because their towns had been given as a present to Antiochis, the king's concubine. ³¹The king therefore hurried off to settle the affair, leaving Andronicus, one of his dignitaries, to act as his deputy. ³²Thinking he had found a favourable opportunity, Menelaus abstracted a number of golden vessels from the Temple and presented them to Andronicus, and managed to sell others to Tyre and the surrounding cities. ³³On receiving clear evidence to this effect, Onias retired to a place of sanctuary at Daphne near Antioch and then taxed him with it. ³⁴Menelaus then had a quiet word with Andronicus, urging him to get rid of Onias. Andronicus sought out Onias and, resorting to the trick of offering him his

right hand on oath, succeeded in persuading him, despite the latter's lingering suspicions, to leave sanctuary; whereupon, in defiance of all justice, he immediately put him to death. ³⁵ The result was that not only Jews but many people of other nationalities were appalled and outraged by the unjust murder of this man.

³⁶ On the king's return from the region of Cilicia, the Jews of the capital, and those Greeks who shared their hatred of the crime, appealed to him about the unjustified murder of Onias. ³⁷ Antiochus was profoundly grieved and filled with pity, and he wept for the prudence and moderation of the dead man. ³⁸ Burning with indignation, he immediately stripped Andronicus of the purple, tore his garments off him and, parading him through the length of the city, rid the world of the assassin on the very spot where he had laid impious hands on Onias, the Lord dealing out to him the punishment he deserved.

Lysimachus killed in an insurrection

³⁹ Now Lysimachus with the connivance of Menelaus had committed many sacrilegious thefts in the city, and when the facts became widely known, the populace rose against Lysimachus, who had already disposed of many pieces of gold plate. ⁴⁰ The infuriated mob was becoming menacing, and Lysimachus armed nearly three thousand men and took aggressive action; the troops were led by a certain Auranus, a man advanced in years and no less in folly. ⁴¹ Recognising this act of aggression as the work of Lysimachus, some snatched up stones, others cudgels, while others scooped up handfuls of ashes lying at hand, and all hurled everything indiscriminately at Lysimachus' men, ⁴² to such effect that they wounded many of them, even killing a few, and routed them all; the sacrilegious thief himself they killed near the Treasury.

Menelaus buys his acquittal

⁴³ As a result of this, legal proceedings were taken against Menelaus. ⁴⁴ When the king came down to Tyre, three men deputed by the Senate pleaded their case before him. ⁴⁵ Menelaus, seeing the case had gone against him, promised a substantial sum to Ptolemy son of Dorymenes if he would influence the king in his favour. ⁴⁶ Ptolemy then took the king aside into a colonnade, as though for a breath of fresh air, and persuaded him to change his mind; ⁴⁷ the king then dismissed the charges against Menelaus, the cause of all this evil, while he condemned to death the other poor wretches who, had they pleaded even before Scythians, would have been let off scot-free. ⁴⁸ No time was lost in carrying out this unjust punishment on those who had championed the cause of the city, the townships and the sacred vessels. ⁴⁹ Some Tyrians even were so outraged by the crime that they provided sumptuously for their funeral, ⁵⁰ while, as a result of the greed of the powerful, Menelaus remained in power, growing more wicked than ever and establishing himself as the chief enemy of his fellow-citizens.

Second Egyptian campaign

5 At about this time, Antiochus was preparing for his second attack on Egypt. ² It then happened that all over the city for nearly forty days there were apparitions of horsemen galloping through the air in cloth of gold, troops of lancers fully armed, ³ squadrons of cavalry in order of battle, attacks and charges this way and that, a flourish of shields, a forest of pikes, a brandishing of swords, a hurling of missiles, a glittering of golden accoutrements and armour of all kinds. ⁴ So everyone prayed that this manifestation might prove a good omen.

Jason's insurrection; counteraction by Antiochus Epiphanes

⁵ Then, on the strength of a false report that Antiochus was dead, Jason took at least a thousand men and launched an unexpected attack on the city. When the walls had been breached and the city was finally on the point of being taken, Menelaus took refuge in the Citadel. ⁶ Jason, however, made a pitiless

slaughter of his fellow-citizens, oblivious of the fact that success against his own countrymen was the greatest of disasters, but rather picturing himself as winning trophies from some enemy, and not from his fellow-countrymen. [7]Even so, he did not manage to seize power; and, in the end, his machinations brought him nothing but shame, and he took refuge once more in Ammanitis. [8]His career of wickedness was thus brought to a halt: imprisoned by Aretas, the Arab despot, escaping from his town, hunted by everyone, detested for having overthrown the laws, abhorred as the butcher of his country and his countrymen, he drifted to Egypt. [9]He who had exiled so many from their fatherland, himself perished on foreign soil, having travelled to Sparta, hoping that, for kinship's sake, he might find harbour there. [10]So many carcasses he had thrust out to lie unburied; now he himself had none to mourn him, no funeral rites, no place in the tomb of his ancestors.

[11]When the king came to hear of what had happened, he concluded that Judaea was in revolt. He therefore marched from Egypt, raging like a wild beast, and began by storming the city. [12]He then ordered his soldiers to cut down without mercy everyone they encountered, and to butcher all who took refuge in their houses. [13]It was a massacre of young and old, a slaughter of women and children, a butchery of young girls and infants. [14]There were eighty thousand victims in the course of those three days, forty thousand dying by violence and as many again being sold into slavery.

Pillage of the Temple[a]

[15]Not content with this, he had the audacity to enter the holiest Temple in the entire world, with Menelaus, that traitor to the laws and to his country, as his guide; [16]with impure hands he seized the sacred vessels; with impious hands he seized the offerings presented by other kings for the aggrandisement, glory and dignity of the holy place.

[17]Holding so high an opinion of himself,

Antiochus did not realise that the Lord was temporarily angry at the sins of the inhabitants of the city, hence his unconcern for the holy place. [18]Had they not been entangled in many sins, Antiochus too, like Heliodorus when King Seleucus sent him to inspect the Treasury, would have been flogged the moment he arrived and checked in his presumption. [19]The Lord, however, had not chosen the people for the sake of the holy place, but the holy place for the sake of the people; [20]and so the holy place itself, having shared the disasters that befell the people, in due course also shared their good fortune; having been abandoned by the Almighty in his anger, once the great Sovereign was placated it was reinstated in all its glory.

[21]Antiochus, having extracted eighteen hundred talents from the Temple, hurried back to Antioch; in his pride he would have undertaken to make the dry land navigable and the sea passable on foot, so high his arrogance soared. [22]But he left officials behind to plague the nation: in Jerusalem, Philip, a Phrygian by race, and by nature more barbarous than the man who appointed him; [23]on Mount Gerizim, Andronicus; and, besides these, Menelaus, who lorded it over his countrymen worse than all the others.

Activities of Apollonius the Mysarch

In his rooted hostility to the Jews, [24]the king also sent the Mysarch Apollonius at the head of an army twenty-two thousand strong, with orders to put to death all men in their prime and to sell the women and children. [25]Arriving in Jerusalem and posing as a man of peace, this man waited until the holy day of the Sabbath and then, taking advantage of the Jews as they rested from work, ordered his men to parade fully armed; [26]all those who came out to watch he put to the sword; then, rushing into the city with his armed troops, he cut down an immense number of people.

[27]Judas, also known as Maccabaeus, how-

5a ‖ 1 M 1:20–24.

ever, with about nine others, withdrew into the desert. He lived like the wild animals in the hills with his companions, eating nothing but wild plants to avoid contracting defilement.

Gentile cults imposed[a]

6 Shortly afterwards, the king sent Gerontes the Athenian to force the Jews to violate their ancestral customs and live no longer by the laws of God; 2 and to profane the Temple in Jerusalem and dedicate it to Olympian Zeus, and the one on Mount Gerizim to Zeus, Patron of Strangers, as the inhabitants of the latter place had requested. 3 The advent of these evils was painfully hard for all the people to bear. 4 The Temple was filled with revelling and debauchery by the gentiles, who took their pleasure with prostitutes and had intercourse with women in the sacred precincts, introducing other indecencies besides. 5 The altar of sacrifice was loaded with victims proscribed by the law as profane. 6 No one might either keep the Sabbath or observe the traditional feasts, or so much as admit to being a Jew. 7 People were driven by harsh compulsion to take part in the monthly ritual meal commemorating the king's birthday; and when a feast of Dionysus occurred, they were forced to wear ivy wreaths and walk in the Dionysiac procession. 8 A decree was issued at the instance of the people of Ptolemais for the neighbouring Greek cities, enforcing the same conduct on the Jews there, obliging them to share in the sacrificial meals, 9 and ordering the execution of those who would not voluntarily conform to Greek customs. So it became clear that disaster was imminent.

10 For example, two women were charged with having circumcised their children. They were paraded publicly round the town, with their babies hung at their breasts, and then hurled over the city wall. 11 Other people, who had assembled in some near-by caves to keep the seventh day without attracting attention, were denounced to Philip, and were then all burnt to death together, since their consciences would not allow them to defend themselves, out of respect for the holiness of the day.

Providential significance of the persecution

12 Now, I urge anyone who may read this book not to be dismayed at these calamities, but to reflect that such visitations are intended not to destroy our race but to discipline it. 13 Indeed, when evil-doers are not left for long to their own devices but incur swift retribution, it is a sign of great benevolence. 14 In the case of other nations, the Master waits patiently for them to attain the full measure of their sins before he punishes them, but with us he has decided to deal differently, 15 rather than have to punish us later, when our sins come to full measure. 16 And so he never entirely withdraws his mercy from us; he may discipline us by some disaster, but he does not desert his own people. 17 Let this be said simply by way of reminder; we must return to our story without more ado.

The martyrdom of Eleazar

18 Eleazar, one of the foremost teachers of the Law, a man already advanced in years and of most noble appearance, had his mouth forced open, to make him eat a piece of pork. 19 But he, resolving to die with honour rather than to live disgraced, walked of his own accord to the torture of the wheel, 20 having spat the stuff out, as befits those with the courage to reject what is not lawful to taste, rather than live. 21 The people supervising the ritual meal, forbidden by the Law, because of the length of time for which they had known him, took him aside and privately urged him to have meat brought of a kind he could properly use, prepared by himself, and only pretend to eat the portions of sacrificial meat as prescribed by the king; 22 this action would enable him to escape death, by availing himself of an act of kindness prompted by their long friendship. 23 But having taken a noble decision worthy of his years and the dignity of his great age and the well-

6a ‖ 1 M 1:45–51, 60–61; 2:32–38.

earned distinction of his grey hairs, worthy too of his impeccable conduct from boyhood, and above all of the holy legislation established by God himself, he answered accordingly, telling them to send him at once to Hades. 24 'Pretence', he said, 'does not befit our time of life; many young people would suppose that Eleazar at the age of ninety had conformed to the foreigners' way of life 25 and, because I had played this part for the sake of a paltry brief spell of life, might themselves be led astray on my account; I should only bring defilement and disgrace on my old age. 26 Even though for the moment I avoid execution by man, I can never, living or dead, elude the grasp of the Almighty. 27 Therefore if I am man enough to quit this life here and now, I shall prove myself worthy of my old age, 28 and I shall have left the young a noble example of how to make a good death, eagerly and generously, for the venerable and holy laws.'

So saying, he walked straight to the wheel, 29 while those who were escorting him, recently so well disposed towards him, turned against him after this declaration, which they regarded as sheer madness. 30 He for his part, just before he died under the blows, gave a sigh and said, 'The Lord whose knowledge is holy sees clearly that, though I might have escaped death, from awe of him I gladly endure these agonies of body under the lash, and that in my soul I am glad to suffer.'

31 This was how he died, leaving his death as an example of nobility and a record of virtue not only for the young but for the greater part of the nation.

The martyrdom of the seven brothers

7 It also happened that seven brothers were arrested with their mother. The king tried to force them to taste some pork, which the Law forbids, by torturing them with whips and scourges. 2 One of them, acting as spokesman for the others, said, 'What are you trying to find out from us? We are prepared to die rather than break the laws of our ancestors.' 3 The king, in a fury, ordered pans and caul-drons to be heated over a fire. 4 As soon as these were red-hot, he commanded that their spokesman should have his tongue cut out, his head scalped and his extremities cut off, while the other brothers and his mother looked on. 5 When he had been rendered completely helpless, the king gave orders for him to be brought, still breathing, to the fire and fried alive in a pan. As the smoke from the pan drifted about, his mother and the rest encouraged one another to die nobly, with such words as these, 6 'The Lord God is watching and certainly feels sorry for us, as Moses declared in his song, which clearly states that "he will take pity on his servants." '

7 When the first had left the world in this way, they brought the second forward to be tortured. After stripping the skin from his head, hair and all, they asked him, 'Will you eat some pork, before your body is tortured limb by limb?' 8 Replying in his ancestral tongue, he said, 'No!' So he too was put to the torture in his turn. 9 With his last breath he exclaimed, 'Cruel brute, you may discharge us from this present life, but the King of the world will raise us up, since we die for his laws, to live again for ever.'

10 After him, they tortured the third, who on being asked for his tongue promptly thrust it out and boldly held out his hands, 11 courageously saying, 'Heaven gave me these limbs; for the sake of his laws I have no concern for them; from him I hope to receive them again.' 12 The king and his attendants were astounded at the young man's courage and his utter indifference to suffering.

13 When this one was dead they subjected the fourth to the same torments and tortures. 14 When he neared his end he cried, 'Ours is the better choice, to meet death at men's hands, yet relying on God's promise that we shall be raised up by him; whereas for you there can be no resurrection to new life.'

15 Next they brought forward the fifth and began torturing him. 16 But he looked at the king and said, 'You have power over human beings, mortal as you are, and can act as you

35 READ 2 MACCABEES 7.

She watched the death of seven sons in the course of a single day, and bravely endured it because of her hopes in the Lord.—2 MACCABEES 7:20

LOVE STRONGER THAN DEATH

There stood the noble and high-minded lads, the gallant sons of a noble mother, the glorious champions of the truth. There they stood with one longing and one aim, looking to one road to life, even to receive death for God's sake. There they stood, brothers in both soul and body, only covetous of each other's death. O what a mystery! They snatched at agony as at treasure and periled themselves for the teaching of the law with no more fear for what was before them than regret for what they would leave behind. They dreaded only that a brother might unwillingly be spared from the torment of the conflict to gain a disastrous victory.

There stood the brave and noble mother, burning with love of her children and of God with her heart rent as few human hearts are torn. She agonized less over the tortures that her children suffered than she did over fear that they might shrink from them. Her anxiety was for the living rather than for the dead. The living were still contending, the dead had safely left the field. She was concerned for her living sons as she did not know how God would receive them. But she knew that God had joined her dead sons to himself.   ST. GREGORY NAZIANZEN, 329?–390

YOU WILL FIND THE NEXT READING AT JOB 1.

please. But do not think that our race has been deserted by God. [17]Only wait, and you will see in your turn how his mighty power will torment you and your descendants.'

[18]After him, they led out the sixth, and his dying words were these, 'Do not delude yourself: we are suffering like this through our own fault, having sinned against our own God; hence, appalling things have befallen us— [19]but do not think you yourself will go unpunished for attempting to make war on God.'

[20]But the mother was especially admirable and worthy of honourable remembrance, for she watched the death of seven sons in the course of a single day, and bravely endured it because of her hopes in the Lord. [21]Indeed she encouraged each of them in their ancestral tongue; filled with noble conviction, she reinforced her womanly argument with manly courage, saying to them, [22]'I do not know how you appeared in my womb; it was not I who endowed you with breath and life, I had not the shaping of your every part. [23]And hence, the Creator of the world, who made everyone and ordained the origin of all things, will in his mercy give you back breath and life, since for the sake of his laws you have no concern for yourselves.'

[24]Antiochus thought he was being ridiculed, suspecting insult in the tone of her voice; and as the youngest was still alive he appealed to him not with mere words but with promises on oath to make him both rich and happy if he would abandon the traditions of his ancestors; he would make him his Friend and entrust him with public office. [25]The young man took no notice at all, and so the

king then appealed to the mother, urging her to advise the youth to save his life. 26 After a great deal of urging on his part she agreed to try persuasion on her son. 27 Bending over him, she fooled the cruel tyrant with these words, uttered in their ancestral tongue, 'My son, have pity on me; I carried you nine months in my womb and suckled you three years, fed you and reared you to the age you are now, and provided for you. 28 I implore you, my child, look at the earth and sky and everything in them, and consider how God made them out of what did not exist, and that human beings come into being in the same way. 29 Do not fear this executioner, but prove yourself worthy of your brothers and accept death, so that I may receive you back with them in the day of mercy.'

30 She had hardly finished, when the young man said, 'What are you all waiting for? I will not comply with the king's ordinance; I obey the ordinance of the Law given to our ancestors through Moses. 31 As for you, who have contrived every kind of evil against the Hebrews, you will certainly not escape the hands of God. 32 We are suffering for our own sins; 33 and if, to punish and discipline us, our living Lord is briefly angry with us, he will be reconciled with us in due course. 34 But you, unholy wretch and wickedest of villains, what cause have you for pride, nourishing vain hopes and raising your hand against his servants?— 35 for you have not yet escaped the judgement of God the almighty, the all-seeing. 36 Our brothers, having endured brief pain, for the sake of ever-flowing life have died for the covenant of God, while you, by God's judgement, will have to pay the just penalty for your arrogance. 37 I too, like my brothers, surrender my body and life for the laws of my ancestors, begging God quickly to take pity on our nation, and by trials and afflictions to bring you to confess that he alone is God, 38 so that with my brothers and myself there may be an end to the wrath of the Almighty, rightly let loose on our whole nation.'

39 The king fell into a rage and treated this one more cruelly than the others, for he was himself smarting from the young man's scorn. 40 And so the last brother met his end undefiled and with perfect trust in the Lord. 41 The mother was the last to die, after her sons.

42 But let this be sufficient account of the ritual meals and monstrous tortures.

Judas Maccabaeus and the resistance

8 Judas, otherwise known as Maccabaeus, and his companions made their way secretly among the villages, rallying their fellow-countrymen; they recruited those who remained loyal to Judaism and assembled about six thousand. 2 They called on the Lord to have regard for the people oppressed on all sides, to take pity on the Temple profaned by the godless, 3 to have mercy on the city now being destroyed and levelled to the ground, to hear the blood of the victims that cried aloud to him, 4 to remember too the criminal slaughter of innocent babies and to avenge the blasphemies perpetrated against his name. 5 As soon as Maccabaeus had an organised force, he at once proved invincible to the foreigners, the Lord's anger having turned into compassion. 6 Making surprise attacks on towns and villages, he fired them; he captured favourable positions and inflicted very heavy losses on the enemy, 7 generally availing himself of the cover of night for such enterprises. The fame of his valour spread far and wide.

Campaign of Nicanor and Gorgias a

8 When Philip saw Judas was making steady progress and winning more and more frequent successes, he wrote to Ptolemy, the general officer commanding Coele-Syria and Phoenicia, asking for reinforcements in the royal interest. 9 Ptolemy chose Nicanor son of Patroclus, one of the king's First Friends, and sent him without delay at the head of an international force of at least twenty thousand men to exterminate the entire Jewish race. As his associate he appointed Gorgias, a professional

8a ‖ 1 M 3:38–4:25.

general of wide military experience. ¹⁰Nicanor for his part proposed, by the sale of Jewish prisoners of war, to raise the two thousand talents of tribute money owed by the king to the Romans. ¹¹He lost no time in sending the seaboard towns an invitation to come and buy Jewish manpower, promising delivery of ninety head for one talent; but he did not reckon on the judgement from the Almighty that was soon to overtake him.

¹²When news reached Judas of Nicanor's advance, he warned his men of the enemy's approach, ¹³whereupon the cowardly ones and those who lacked confidence in the justice of God took to their heels and ran away. ¹⁴The rest sold all their remaining possessions, at the same time praying the Lord to deliver them from the godless Nicanor, who had sold them even in advance of any encounter— ¹⁵if not for their own sakes, then at least out of consideration for the covenants made with their ancestors, and because they themselves bore his sacred and majestic name.

¹⁶Maccabaeus marshalled his men, who numbered about six thousand, and exhorted them not to be dismayed at the enemy or discouraged at the vast horde of gentiles wickedly advancing against them, but to fight bravely, ¹⁷keeping before their eyes the outrage committed by them against the holy place and the infamous and scornful treatment inflicted on the city, not to mention the destruction of their traditional way of life. ¹⁸'They may put their trust in their weapons and their exploits,' he said, 'but our confidence is in almighty God, who is able with a single nod to overthrow both those marching on us and the whole world with them.' ¹⁹He reminded them of the occasions on which their ancestors had received help: that time when, under Sennacherib, a hundred and eighty-five thousand men had perished;[b] ²⁰that time in Babylonia when in the battle with the Galatians the Jewish combatants numbered only eight thousand, with four thousand Macedonians, yet when the Macedonians were hard pressed, the eight thousand had destroyed a hundred and twenty thousand, thanks to the help they had received from Heaven, and had taken great booty as a result.

²¹Having so roused their courage by these words that they were ready to die for the laws and their country, he then divided his army into four, ²²putting his brothers, Simon, Joseph and Jonathan in command of one division each, and assigning them fifteen hundred men apiece. ²³Next, he ordered Esdrias to read the Holy Book aloud and gave them their watchword 'Help from God'. Then, putting himself at the head of the first division, he attacked Nicanor. ²⁴With the Almighty for their ally they slaughtered over nine thousand of the enemy, wounded and crippled the greater part of Nicanor's army and put them all to flight. ²⁵The money of their prospective purchasers fell into their hands. After pursuing them for a good while, they turned back, since time was pressing: ²⁶it was the eve of the Sabbath, and for that reason they did not prolong their pursuit. ²⁷They collected the enemy's weapons and stripped them of their spoils, and because of the Sabbath even more heartily blessed and praised the Lord, who had saved them and who had chosen that day for the first manifestation of his compassion. ²⁸When the Sabbath was over, they distributed some of the booty among the victims of the persecution and the widows and orphans; the rest they divided among themselves and their children. ²⁹They then joined in public supplication, imploring the merciful Lord to be fully reconciled with his servants.

The defeat of Timotheus and Bacchides

³⁰They also challenged the forces of Timotheus and Bacchides and destroyed over twenty thousand of them, gaining possession of several high fortresses. They divided their enormous booty into two equal shares, one for themselves, the other for the victims of the persecution and the orphans and widows, not forgetting the aged. ³¹They carefully collected

8b 2 K 19:35. The next incident is non-biblical.

the enemy's weapons and stored them in suitable places. The rest of the spoils they took to Jerusalem. [32] They killed the tribal chieftain on Timotheus' staff, an extremely wicked man who had done great harm to the Jews. [33] In the course of their victory celebrations in Jerusalem, they burned the men who had fired the Holy Gates; with Callisthenes they had taken refuge in one small house; so these received a fitting reward for their sacrilege.

The flight and testimony of Nicanor

[34] The triple-dyed scoundrel Nicanor, who had brought the thousand merchants to buy the Jews, [35] finding himself with the Lord's help humbled by men he had himself reckoned as of very little account, stripped off his robes of state, and made his way across country unaccompanied, like a runaway slave, reaching Antioch by a singular stroke of fortune, since his army had been destroyed. [36] Thus the man who had promised the Romans to make good their tribute money by selling the prisoners from Jerusalem, bore witness that the Jews had a defender and that they were in consequence invulnerable, since they followed the laws which that defender had ordained.

The last days of Antiochus Epiphanes [a]

9 At about the same time, Antiochus was beating a disorderly retreat from Persia. [2] He had entered the city called Persepolis, planning to rob the temple and occupy the city; but the population at once sprang to arms to defend themselves, with the result that Antiochus was routed by the inhabitants and forced to beat a humiliating retreat. [3] On his arrival in Ecbatana he learned what had happened to Nicanor and to Timotheus' forces. [4] Flying into a passion, he resolved to make the Jews pay for the disgrace inflicted by those who had routed him, and with this in mind he ordered his charioteer to drive without stopping and get the journey over. But the sentence of Heaven was already hanging over him. In his pride, he had said, 'When I reach Jerusalem, I shall turn it into a mass grave for the Jews.' [5] But the all-seeing Lord, the God of Israel, struck him with an incurable and unseen complaint. The words were hardly out of his mouth when he was seized with an incurable pain in his bowels and with excruciating internal torture; [6] and this was only right, since he had inflicted many barbaric tortures on the bowels of others. [7] Even so, he in no way diminished his arrogance; still bursting with pride, breathing fire in his wrath against the Jews, he was in the act of ordering an even keener pace when the chariot gave a sudden lurch and out he fell and, in this serious fall, was dragged along, every joint of his body wrenched out of place. [8] He who only a little while before had thought in his superhuman boastfulness he could command the waves of the sea, he who had imagined he could weigh mountain peaks in a balance, found himself flat on the ground and then being carried in a litter, a visible demonstration to all of the power of God, [9] in that the very eyes of this godless man teemed with worms and his flesh rotted away while he lingered on in agonising pain, and the stench of his decay sickened the whole army. [10] A short while before, he had thought to grasp the stars of heaven; now no one could bring himself to act as his bearer, for the stench was intolerable.

[11] Then and there, as a consequence, in his shattered state, he began to shed his excessive pride and come to his senses under the divine lash, spasms of pain overtaking him. [12] His stench being unbearable even to himself, he exclaimed, 'It is right to submit to God; no mortal should aspire to equality with the Godhead.' [13] The wretch began to pray to the Master, who would never take pity on him now, declaring [14] that the holy city, towards which he had been speeding to rase it to the ground and turn it into a mass grave, should be declared free; [15] as for the Jews, whom he had considered as not even worth burying, so much carrion to be thrown out with their chil-

9a ‖ 1 M 6:1–16.

dren for birds and beasts to prey on, he would give them all equal rights with the Athenians; ¹⁶the holy Temple which he had once plundered he would now adorn with the finest offerings; he would restore all the sacred vessels many times over; he would defray from his personal revenue the expenses incurred for the sacrifices; ¹⁷and, to crown all, he would himself turn Jew and visit every inhabited place, proclaiming the power of God.

Antiochus writes to the Jews

¹⁸Finding no respite at all from his suffering, God's just sentence having overtaken him, he abandoned all hope for himself and wrote the Jews the letter transcribed below, which takes the form of an appeal in these terms:

¹⁹'To the excellent Jews, to the citizens, Antiochus, king and commander-in-chief, sends hearty greetings, wishing them all health and prosperity.

²⁰'If you and your children are well and your affairs as you would wish, we are profoundly thankful. ²¹For my part, I cherish affectionate memories of you.

'On my return from the country of Persia I fell seriously ill, and thought it necessary to make provision for the common security of all. ²²Not that I despair of my condition, for I have great hope of shaking off the malady, ²³but considering how my father, whenever he was making an expedition into the uplands, would designate his successor ²⁴so that, in case of any unforeseen event or disquieting rumour, the people of the provinces might know to whom he had left the conduct of affairs, and thus remain undisturbed; ²⁵furthermore, being well aware that the sovereigns on our frontiers and the neighbours of our realm are watching for opportunities and waiting to see what will happen, I have designated as king my son Antiochus, whom I have more than once entrusted and commended to most of you when I was setting out for the upland satrapies; a transcript of my letter to

him is appended hereto. ²⁶I therefore urge and require you, being mindful of the benefits both public and personal received from me, that you each persist in those sentiments of goodwill that you harbour towards me. ²⁷I am confident that he will pursue my own policy with benevolence and humanity, and will prove accommodating to your interests.'

²⁸And so this murderer and blasphemer, having endured sufferings as terrible as those which he had made others endure, met his pitiable fate, and ended his life in the mountains far from his home. ²⁹His comrade Philip brought back his body, and then, fearing Antiochus' son, withdrew to Egypt, to the court of Ptolemy Philometor.

The purification of the Temple ^a

10 Maccabaeus and his companions, under the Lord's guidance, restored the Temple and the city, ²and pulled down the altars erected by the foreigners in the market place, as well as the shrines. ³They purified the sanctuary and built another altar; then, striking fire from flints and using this fire, they offered the first sacrifice for two years, burning incense, lighting the lamps and setting out the loaves. ⁴When they had done this, prostrating themselves on the ground, they implored the Lord never again to let them fall into such adversity, but if they should ever sin, to correct them with moderation and not to deliver them over to blasphemous and barbarous nations. ⁵This day of the purification of the Temple fell on the very day on which the Temple had been profaned by the foreigners, the twenty-fifth of the same month, Chislev. ⁶They kept eight festal days with rejoicing, in the manner of the feast of Shelters, remembering how, not long before at the time of the feast of Shelters, they had been living in the mountains and caverns like wild beasts. ⁷Then, carrying thyrsuses, leafy boughs and palms, they offered

10a ‖ 1 M 4:36–61.

hymns to him who had brought the cleansing of his own holy place to a happy outcome. [8] They also decreed by public edict, ratified by vote, that the whole Jewish nation should celebrate those same days every year.

Reign of Antiochus V: early years

[9] Such were the circumstances attending the death of Antiochus styled Epiphanes. [10] Our task now is to unfold the history of Antiochus Eupator, son of that godless man, and briefly to relate the evil effects of the wars. [11] On coming to the throne, this prince put at the head of affairs a certain Lysias, the general officer commanding Coele-Syria and Phoenicia, [12] whereas Ptolemy, known as Macron, and the first person to govern the Jews justly, had done his best to govern them peacefully to make up for the wrongs inflicted on them in the past. [13] Denounced, in consequence, to Eupator by the Friends of the King, he heard himself called traitor at every turn: for having abandoned Cyprus, which had been entrusted to him by Philometer, for having gone over to Antiochus Epiphanes, and for having shed no lustre on his illustrious office: he committed suicide by poisoning himself.

Gorgias and the Idumaean fortresses

[14] Gorgias now became general of the area; he maintained a force of mercenaries and a continual state of war with the Jews.[b] [15] At the same time, the Idumaeans, who controlled important fortresses, were harassing the Jews, welcoming outlaws from Jerusalem and endeavouring to maintain a state of war. [16] Maccabaeus and his men, after making public supplication to God, entreating him to support them, began operations against the Idumaean fortresses. [17] Vigorously pressing home their attack, they seized possession of these vantage points, beating off all who fought on the ramparts; they slaughtered all who fell into their hands, accounting for no fewer than twenty thousand. [18] Nine thousand at least took refuge in two exceptionally strong towers with everything they needed to withstand a siege,

[19] whereupon, Maccabaeus left Simon and Joseph, with Zacchaeus and his forces, in sufficient numbers to besiege them, and himself went off to other places requiring his attention. [20] But Simon's men were greedy for money and allowed themselves to be bribed by some of the men in the towers; accepting seventy thousand drachmas, they let a number of them escape. [21] When Maccabaeus was told what had happened, he summoned the people's commanders and accused the offenders of having sold their brothers for money by releasing their enemies to fight them. [22] Having executed them as traitors, he at once proceeded to capture both towers. [23] Successful in all that he undertook by force of arms, in these two fortresses he slaughtered more than twenty thousand men.

Judas defeats Timotheus and captures Gezer

[24] Timotheus, who had been beaten by the Jews once before, now assembled an enormous force of mercenaries, mustering cavalry from Asia in considerable numbers, and soon appeared in Judaea, expecting to conquer it by force of arms. [25] At his approach, Maccabaeus and his men made their supplications to God, sprinkling earth on their heads and putting sackcloth round their waists. [26] Prostrating themselves on the terrace before the altar, they begged him to support them and to show himself the enemy of their enemies, the adversary of their adversaries, as the Law clearly states.

[27] After these prayers, they armed themselves and advanced a fair distance from the city, halting when they were close to the enemy. [28] As the first light of dawn began to spread, the two sides joined battle, the one having as their pledge of success and victory not only their own valour but their recourse to the Lord, the other making their own ardour their mainstay in the fight. [29] When the battle was at its height, the enemy saw five magnificent men appear from heaven on horses with golden bridles and put themselves at the head

10b ‖ 1 M 5:1–8.

of the Jews; 30 surrounding Maccabaeus and screening him with their own armour, they kept him unscathed, while they rained arrows and thunderbolts on the enemy until, blinded and confused, they scattered in complete disorder. 31 Twenty thousand five hundred infantry and six hundred cavalry were slaughtered. 32 Timotheus himself fled to a strongly guarded citadel called Gezer, where Chaereas was in command. 33 For four days Maccabaeus and his men eagerly besieged the fortress, 34 while the defenders, confident in the security of the place, hurled fearful blasphemies and godless insults at them. 35 At daybreak on the fifth day, twenty young men of Maccabaeus' forces, fired with indignation at the blasphemies, manfully assaulted the wall, with wild courage cutting down everyone they encountered. 36 Others, in a similar scaling operation, took the defenders in the rear, and set fire to the towers, lighting pyres on which they burned the blasphemers alive. The first, meanwhile, breaking open the gates, let the rest of the army in and, at their head, captured the town. 37 Timotheus had hidden in a storage-well, but they killed him, with his brother Chaereas, and Apollophanes. 38 When all this was over, with hymns and thanksgiving they blessed the Lord, who had shown such great kindness to Israel and given them the victory.

The first campaign of Lysias [a]

11 Almost immediately afterwards, Lysias, the king's tutor and cousin, chief minister of the realm, much disturbed at the turn of events, 2 mustered about eighty thousand foot soldiers and his entire cavalry and advanced against the Jews, intending to make the city a place for Greeks to live in, 3 to levy a tax on the Temple as on other national shrines, and to put the office of high priest up for sale every year; 4 he took no account at all of the power of God, being sublimely confident in his tens of thousands of infantrymen, his thousands of cavalry, and his eighty elephants.

5 Invading Judaea, he approached Beth-Zur, a fortified position about twenty miles from Jerusalem, and began to subject it to strong pressure. 6 When Maccabaeus and his men learned that Lysias was besieging the fortresses, they and the populace with them begged the Lord with lamentation and tears to send a good angel to save Israel. 7 Maccabaeus himself was the first to take up his weapons, and he urged the rest to risk their lives with him in support of their brothers; so they sallied out resolutely, as one man. 8 They were still near Jerusalem when a rider attired in white appeared at their head, brandishing golden weapons. 9 With one accord they all blessed the God of mercy, and found themselves filled with such courage that they were ready to lay low not men only but the fiercest beasts and walls of iron. 10 They advanced in battle order with the aid of their celestial ally, the Lord having had mercy on them. 11 Charging like lions on the enemy, they laid low eleven thousand of the infantry and sixteen hundred horsemen, and routed all the rest. 12 Of those, the majority got away, wounded and weaponless. Lysias himself escaped only by ignominious flight.

Lysias makes peace with the Jews; four letters concerning the treaty [b]

13 Now Lysias was not lacking in intelligence and, as he reflected on the reverse he had just suffered, he realised that the Hebrews were invincible because the mighty God fought for them. He therefore sent them a delegation 14 to persuade them to accept reasonable terms all round, and promised to compel the king to become their friend. 15 Maccabaeus, thinking only of the common good, agreed to all that Lysias proposed, and whatever Maccabaeus submitted to Lysias in writing concerning the Jews was granted by the king.

16 Here is the text of the letter Lysias wrote to the Jews:

'Lysias to the Jewish people, greetings.

17 'John and Absalom, your envoys, have

11a ‖ 1 M 4:26–35.   11b ‖ 1 M 6:57.

delivered to me the communication transcribed below, requesting me to approve its provisions. ¹⁸ Anything requiring the king's attention I have put before him; whatever was possible, I have granted. ¹⁹ Provided you maintain your goodwill towards the interests of the State, I shall do my best in the future to promote your well-being. ²⁰ As regards the details, I have given orders for your envoys and my own officials to discuss these with you. ²¹ May you prosper.

'The twenty-fourth day of Dioscorus, in the year one hundred and forty-eight.'

²² The king's letter ran as follows:

'King Antiochus to his brother Lysias, greetings.

²³ 'Now that our father has taken his place among the gods, our will is that the subjects of the realm be left undisturbed to attend to their own affairs. ²⁴ We understand that the Jews do not approve our father's policy, the adoption of Greek customs, but prefer their own way of life and ask to be allowed to observe their own laws. ²⁵ Accordingly, since we intend this people to be free from vexation like any other, our ruling is that the Temple be restored to them and that they conduct their affairs according to the customs of their ancestors.

²⁶ 'It will therefore be your concern to send them a mission of friendship, so that on learning our policy they may have confidence and happily go about their business.'

²⁷ The king's letter to the Jewish nation was in these terms:

'King Antiochus to the Jewish Senate and the rest of the Jews, greetings.

²⁸ 'If you are well, that is as we would wish; we ourselves are in good health.

²⁹ 'Menelaus informs us that you wish to return home and attend to your own affairs. ³⁰ Accordingly, all those who return before the thirtieth day of Xanthicus may rest assured that they have nothing to fear.

³¹ The Jews may make use of their own kind of food and their own laws as formerly, and none of them is to be molested in any way for any unwitting offences. ³² I am in fact sending Menelaus to set your minds at rest. ³³ Farewell.

'The fifteenth day of Xanthicus in the year one hundred and forty-eight.'

³⁴ The Romans also sent the Jews a letter, which read as follows:

'Quintus Memmius, Titus Manilius, Manius Sergius, legates of the Romans, to the people of the Jews, greetings.

³⁵ 'Whatever Lysias, the king's Cousin, has granted you we also approve. ³⁶ As for the matters he decided to refer to the king, consider them carefully and send someone without delay, if we are to interpret them to your advantage, because we are leaving for Antioch. ³⁷ Lose no time, therefore, in sending us those who can tell us what your intentions are. ³⁸ Farewell.

'The fifteenth day of Dioscorus in the year one hundred and forty-eight.'

Incidents at Joppa and Jamnia

12 These agreements once concluded, Lysias returned to the king and the Jews went back to their farming. ² Among the local generals, Timotheus and Apollonius son of Gennaeus, as also Hieronymus and Demophon, and Nicanor the Cypriarch as well, would not allow the Jews to live in peace and quiet.

³ The people of Joppa committed a particularly wicked crime: they invited the Jews living among them to go aboard some boats they had lying ready, taking their wives and children. There was no hint of any intention to harm them; ⁴ there had been a public vote by the citizens, and the Jews accepted, as well they might, being peaceable people with no reason to suspect anything. But once out in the open sea they were all sent to the bottom, a company of at least two hundred.

⁵ When Judas heard of the cruel fate of his countrymen, he issued his orders to his men ⁶ and after invoking God, the just judge, he attacked his brothers' murderers. Under cover of dark he set fire to the port, burned the boats and put to the sword everyone who had taken refuge there. ⁷ As the town gates were closed, he withdrew, intending to come back and wipe out the whole community of Joppa. ⁸ But hearing that the people of Jamnia were planning to treat their resident Jews in the same way, ⁹ he made a night attack on the Jamnites and fired the port with its fleet; the glow of the flames was seen as far off as Jerusalem, thirty miles away.

The expedition in Gilead [a]

¹⁰ When they had left the town barely a mile behind them in their advance on Timotheus, Judas was attacked by an Arab force of at least five thousand foot soldiers, with five hundred cavalry. ¹¹ A fierce engagement followed, and with God's help Judas' men won the day; the defeated nomads begged Judas to offer them the right hand of friendship, and promised to surrender their herds and make themselves generally useful to him. ¹² Realising that they might indeed prove valuable in many ways, Judas consented to make peace with them and after an exchange of pledges the Arabs withdrew to their tents.

¹³ Judas also attacked a certain fortified town, closed by ramparts and inhabited by a medley of races; its name was Caspin. ¹⁴ Confident in the strength of their walls and their stock of provisions, the besieged adopted an insolent attitude to Judas and his men, reinforcing their insults with blasphemies and profanity. ¹⁵ But Judas and his men invoked the great Sovereign of the world who without battering-ram or siege-engine had overthrown Jericho in the days of Joshua; they then made a fierce assault on the wall. ¹⁶ By God's will, having captured the town, they made such indescribable slaughter that the nearby lake, a quarter of a mile across, seemed filled to overflowing with blood.

The battle of the Carnaim [b]

¹⁷ Ninety-five miles further on from there, they reached the Charax, in the country of Jews known as Tubians. ¹⁸ They did not find Timotheus himself in that neighbourhood; he had already left the district, having achieved nothing apart from leaving a very strong garrison at one point. ¹⁹ Dositheus and Sosipater, two of the Maccabaean generals, marched out and destroyed the force Timotheus had left behind in the fortress, amounting to more than ten thousand men. ²⁰ Maccabaeus himself divided his army into cohorts to which he assigned commanders, and then hurried in pursuit of Timotheus, whose troops numbered one hundred and twenty thousand infantry and two thousand five hundred cavalry. ²¹ Timotheus' first move on learning of Judas' advance was to send away the women and children and the rest of the baggage train to the place called the Carnaim, since it was an impregnable position, difficult of access owing to the narrowness of all the approaches. ²² Judas' cohort came into sight first. The enemy, seized with fright and panic-stricken by the manifestation of the All-seeing, began to flee, one running this way, one running that, often wounding one another in consequence and running on the points of one another's swords. ²³ Judas pursued them with a will, cutting the sinners to pieces and killing something like thirty thousand men. ²⁴ Timotheus himself, having fallen into the hands of Dositheus and Sosipater and their men, very craftily pleaded with them to let him go with his life, on the grounds that he had the relatives and even the brothers of many of them in his power, and that these could otherwise expect short shrift. ²⁵ When at long last he convinced them that he would honour his promise and return these people safe and sound, they let him go for the sake of saving their brothers.

²⁶ Reaching the Carnaim and the Atar-

12a ‖ 1 M 5:24–54.   12b ‖ 1 M 5:37–44.

gateion, Judas slaughtered twenty-five thousand men.

The return by way of Ephron and Scythopolis

27 Having defeated and destroyed them, he led his army against Ephron, a fortified town, where Lysanias was living. Stalwart young men drawn up outside the walls offered vigorous resistance, while inside there were quantities of war-engines and missiles in reserve. 28 But the Jews, having invoked the Sovereign who by his power shatters enemies' defences, gained control of the town and cut down nearly twenty-five thousand of the people inside. 29 Moving off from there, they pressed on to Scythopolis, 30 seventy-five miles from Jerusalem. But as the Jews who had settled there assured Judas that the people of Scythopolis had always treated them well and had been particularly kind to them when times were at their worst, 31 he and his men thanked them and urged them to extend the same friendship to his race in the future.

They reached Jerusalem shortly before the feast of Weeks.

The campaign against Gorgias

32 After Pentecost, as it is called, they marched against Gorgias, the general commanding Idumaea. 33 He came out at the head of three thousand infantry and four hundred cavalry; 34 in the course of the ensuing battle a few Jews lost their lives.

35 A man called Dositheus, a horseman of the Tubian contingent, a valiant man, overpowered Gorgias and, gripping him by the cloak, was forcibly dragging him along, intending to take the accursed man alive, but one of the Thracian cavalry, hurling himself on Dositheus, slashed his shoulder, and Gorgias escaped to Marisa. 36 Meanwhile, since Esdrias and his men had been fighting for a long time and were exhausted, Judas called on the Lord to show himself their ally and leader in battle.

37 Then, chanting the battle cry and hymns at the top of his voice in his ancestral tongue, by a surprise attack he routed Gorgias' troops.

The sacrifice for the fallen

38 Judas then rallied his army and moved on to the town of Adullam where, as it was the seventh day of the week, they purified themselves according to custom and kept the Sabbath. 39 Next day, they came to find Judas (since the necessity was by now urgent) to have the bodies of the fallen taken up and laid to rest among their relatives in their ancestral tombs. 40 But when they found on each of the dead men, under their tunics, objects dedicated to the idols of Jamnia, which the Law prohibits to Jews, it became clear to everyone that this was why these men had lost their lives. 41 All then blessed the ways of the Lord, the upright judge who brings hidden things to light, 42 and gave themselves to prayer, begging that the sin committed might be completely forgiven. Next, the valiant Judas urged the soldiers to keep themselves free from all sin, having seen with their own eyes the effects of the sin of those who had fallen; 43 after this he took a collection from them individually, amounting to nearly two thousand drachmas, and sent it to Jerusalem to have a sacrifice for sin offered, an action altogether fine and noble, prompted by his belief in the resurrection. 44 For had he not expected the fallen to rise again, it would have been superfluous and foolish to pray for the dead, 45 whereas if he had in view the splendid recompense reserved for those who make a pious end, the thought was holy and devout. Hence, he had this expiatory sacrifice offered for the dead, so that they might be released from their sin.

The campaign of Antiochus V and Lysias; horrible death of Menelaus

13 In the year one hundred and forty-nine, Judas and his men discovered that Antiochus Eupator was advancing in force against Judaea, 2 and with him Lysias his tutor and chief minister; he had moreover a Greek force of one hundred and ten thousand infantry,

five thousand three hundred cavalry, twenty-two elephants, and three hundred chariots fitted with scythes.

3 Menelaus, too, joined them and very craftily kept urging Antiochus on, not for the welfare of his own country but in the hope of being restored to office. 4 But the King of kings stirred up the anger of Antiochus against the guilty wretch, and when Lysias made it clear to the king that Menelaus was the cause of all the troubles, Antiochus gave orders for him to be taken to Beroea and there put to death by the local method of execution. 5 In that place there is a tower fifty cubits high, full of ash, with an internal lip all round overhanging the ashes. 6 If anyone is convicted of sacrilegious theft or of some other heinous crime, he is taken up to the top and pushed over to perish. 7 In such a manner was the renegade fated to die; Menelaus had not even the privilege of burial. 8 Deserved justice, this; since he had committed many sins against the altar, the fire and ashes of which were holy, it was in ashes that he met his death.

The prayers and success of the Jews near Modein

9 The king, then, was advancing, his mind filled with barbarous designs, to give the Jews a demonstration of far worse things than anything that had happened under his father. 10 When Judas heard of this, he ordered the people day and night to call on the Lord as never before, to come to the help of those who were in peril of being deprived of the Law, their fatherland and the holy Temple, 11 and not to allow the people, just when they were beginning to breathe again, to fall into the power of ill-famed foreigners. 12 When they had all, with one voice, obeyed his instructions and had made their petitions to the merciful Lord, weeping, fasting and prostrating themselves for three days continuously, Judas spoke words of encouragement and told them to keep close to him. 13 After separate consultation with the elders, he resolved not to wait for the king's army to invade Judaea and take pos-

session of the city, but to march out and settle the whole matter with the Lord's help.

14 Having thus committed the outcome to the Creator of the world, and having exhorted his soldiers to fight bravely to the death for the laws, the Temple, the city, their country and their way of life, he encamped his army near Modein. 15 Giving his men the password 'Victory from God', he made a night attack on the king's pavilion with a picked band of the bravest young men. Inside the camp he destroyed about two thousand, and his men cut down the largest of the elephants with its mahout; 16 having eventually filled the camp with terror and confusion, they successfully withdrew, 17 just as dawn was breaking. This was achieved, thanks to the protection which the Lord granted Judas.

Antiochus V negotiates with the Jews[a]

18 The king, having had a taste of Jewish daring, now tried to capture their positions by trickery. 19 He advanced on Beth-Zur, a strong fortress of the Jews, but was checked, overcome and so repulsed.

20 Judas supplied the garrison with what they needed, 21 but Rhodocus, of the Jewish army, supplied the enemy with secret information; the man was identified, arrested, and dealt with. 22 A second time, the king parleyed with the garrison of Beth-Zur; he offered and accepted pledges of friendship, retired, then attacked Judas and his men, but lost the battle. 23 He was then told that Philip, left in charge of affairs, had rebelled in Antioch. He was stunned by this, opened negotiations with the Jews, came to an agreement, and swore to abide by all reasonable conditions. Agreement reached, he offered a sacrifice, honoured the Temple, and made generous gifts to the holy place.

24 He received Maccabaeus kindly and, leaving Hegemonides to exercise command from Ptolemais to the territory of the Gerrenians, 25 went to Ptolemais. The inhabitants of

13a ‖ 1 M 6:48–63.

the place disapproved of the treaty; they complained furiously and wanted to annul its provisions. 26 Lysias mounted the rostrum and made a convincing defence of the provisions which convinced and calmed them and won their goodwill. He then withdrew to Antioch.

So much for the episode of the king's offensive and retreat.

Alcimus the high priest intervenes

14 ᵃ Three years after this, Judas and his men learned that Demetrius son of Seleucus had landed at the port of Tripolis with a strong army and a fleet, 2 and that he had occupied the country and had killed Antiochus and his tutor Lysias. 3 A certain Alcimus, a former high priest, had wilfully incurred defilement at the time of the insurrection; realising that whichever way he turned there was no security for him, nor any further access to the holy altar, 4 he went to King Demetrius in about the year one hundred and fifty-one and presented him with a golden crown and a palm, together with the traditional olive branches from the Temple; there, for that day, he let the matter rest.

5 Presently he found an opportunity to further his mad plan. When Demetrius called him into his council and questioned him about the dispositions and intentions of the Jews, he replied, 6 'Those Jews called Hasidaeans, who are led by Judas Maccabaeus, are war-mongers and rebels who are preventing the kingdom from finding stability. 7 That is why, after being deprived of my hereditary dignity—I mean the high priesthood—I have come here now, 8 first out of genuine concern for the king's interests, and secondly, out of a regard for our own fellow-citizens, because the irresponsible behaviour of those I have mentioned has brought no slight misery on our entire race. 9 When your majesty has taken note of all these points, may it please you to make provision for the welfare of our country and our oppressed nation, as befits the gracious benevolence you extend to all; 10 for, as long as Judas remains alive, the State will never enjoy peace.'

11 No sooner had he spoken thus than the rest of the King's Friends, who were hostile to Judas' activities, stoked Demetrius' anger. 12 The latter at once selected Nicanor, then commander of the elephants, promoted him to the command of Judaea and despatched him 13 with instructions to dispose of Judas, disperse his followers and instal Alcimus as high priest of the greatest of temples. 14 The foreigners in Judaea, who had fled before Judas, flocked to join Nicanor, thinking that the misfortunes and troubles of the Jews would be to their own advantage.

Nicanor makes friends with Judas

15 When the Jews heard that Nicanor was coming and that the foreigners were about to attack, they sprinkled dust over themselves and made supplication to him who had established his people for ever and who never failed to support his own heritage by direct manifestations. 16 On their leader's orders, they at once left the place where they were and confronted the enemy at the village of Dessau. 17 Simon, brother of Judas, engaged Nicanor but, owing to the sudden arrival of the enemy, suffered a slight reverse. 18 Nicanor, however, had heard how brave Judas and his men were and how resolutely they always fought for their country, and he did not dare allow bloodshed to decide the issue. 19 And so he sent Posidonius, Theodotus and Mattathias to offer the Jews pledges of friendship and to accept theirs.

20 After careful consideration of his terms, the leader communicated them to his troops, and since they were all clearly of one mind they agreed to the treaty. 21 A day was fixed on which the respective leaders were to meet as individuals. A litter came out from either side and seats were set up. 22 Judas had posted armed men in strategic positions, in case of a sudden treacherous move by the enemy. The leaders held their conference and reached agreement. 23 Nicanor took up residence in

14a ‖ 1 M 7.

Jerusalem and did nothing out of place there; indeed, he sent away the crowds that had flocked to join him. 24 He kept Judas constantly with him, becoming deeply attached to him 25 and encouraged him to marry and have children. Judas married, settled down and led a normal life.

Alcimus rekindles hostilities, and Nicanor threatens the Temple

26 When Alcimus saw how friendly the two men had become, he went to Demetrius with a copy of the treaty they had signed and told him that Nicanor was harbouring thoughts against the interests of the State, and was planning that Judas, an enemy of the realm, should fill the next vacancy among the Friends of the King.

27 The king flew into a rage; roused by the slanders of this villain, he wrote to Nicanor, telling him of his strong displeasure at these agreements and ordering him immediately to send Maccabaeus to Antioch in chains. 28 When the letter reached Nicanor, he was very much upset, for he disliked the prospect of breaking an agreement with a man who had done nothing wrong. 29 Since, however, there was no way of opposing the king, he waited for an opportunity to carry out the order by a stratagem. 30 Maccabaeus began to notice that Nicanor was treating him more sharply and that his manner of speaking to him was more abrupt than it had been, and he concluded that such sharpness could have no very good motive. He therefore collected a considerable number of his followers and got away from Nicanor. 31 The latter, realising that the man had well and truly outmanoeuvred him, went to the greatest and holiest of Temples when the priests were offering the customary sacrifices, and ordered them to surrender Judas. 32 When they protested on oath that they did not know where the wanted man could be, 33 he stretched out his right hand towards the Temple and swore this oath, 'If you do not hand Judas over to me as prisoner, I shall rase this dwelling of God to the ground, I shall demolish the altar, and on this very spot I shall erect a splendid temple to Dionysus.' 34 With these words he left them. The priests stretched out their hands to heaven, calling on him who has at all times done battle for our nation; this was their prayer: 35 'O Lord in need of nothing, it has pleased you that the Temple where you dwell should be here with us. 36 Now, therefore, holy Lord of all holiness, preserve for ever from all profanation this House, so newly purified.'

The death of Razis

37 Now, a man called Razis, one of the elders of Jerusalem, was denounced to Nicanor. He was a man who loved his countrymen and stood high in their esteem, and he was known as the father of the Jews because of his kindness. 38 In the earlier days of the insurrection he had been convicted of Judaism, and he had risked both life and limb for Judaism with the utmost zeal. 39 Nicanor, by way of demonstrating the enmity he had for the Jews, sent over five hundred soldiers to arrest him, 40 reckoning that if he eliminated this man he would be dealing them a severe blow. 41 When the troops were on the point of capturing the tower and were forcing the outer door and calling for fire to set the doors alight, Razis, finding himself completely surrounded, fell on his own sword, 42 nobly resolving to die rather than fall into the clutches of these villains and suffer outrages unworthy of his noble birth. 43 But in the heat of conflict he missed his thrust, and while the troops swarmed in through the doorways, he ran nimbly upstairs to the parapet and manfully threw himself down among the troops. 44 But, as they immediately drew back, he fell into the middle of the empty space. 45 Still breathing, and blazing with anger, he struggled to his feet, blood spurting in all directions, and despite his terrible wounds ran right through the crowd; then, taking his stand on a steep rock, 46 although he had now lost every drop of blood, he tore out his entrails and taking them in both hands flung them down on the crowd, calling on the Master of

his life and spirit to give them back to him one day. Thus he died.

Nicanor's blasphemies

15 Nicanor heard that Judas and his men were in the neighbourhood of Samaria, so he decided to attack them, at no risk to himself, on the day of rest. ² Those Jews who had been compelled to follow him, said, 'Do not massacre them in such a savage, barbarous way. Respect the day on which the All-seeing has conferred a special holiness.' ³ At this the triple-dyed scoundrel asked if there were in heaven a sovereign who had ordered the keeping of the Sabbath day. ⁴ When they answered, 'The living Lord himself, the Heavenly Sovereign, has ordered the observance of the seventh day,' ⁵ he retorted, 'And I, as sovereign on earth, order you to take up arms and do the king's business.' For all that, he did not manage to carry out his wicked plan.

Judas harangues his men; his dream

⁶ While Nicanor, in his unlimited boastfulness and pride, was planning to erect a general trophy with the spoils taken from Judas and his men, ⁷ Maccabaeus remained firm in his confident conviction that the Lord would stand by him. ⁸ He urged his men not to be dismayed by the foreigners' attacks but, keeping in mind the help that had come to them from Heaven in the past, to be confident that this time too victory would be theirs with the help of the Almighty. ⁹ He put fresh heart into them by citing the Law and the Prophets and, by stirring up memories of the battles they had already won, he filled them with new enthusiasm. ¹⁰ Having thus aroused their courage, he ended his exhortation by demonstrating the treachery of the foreigners and how they had violated their oaths.

¹¹ Having armed each one of them not so much with the safety given by shield and lance as with that confidence which springs from noble language, he encouraged them all by describing to them a convincing dream—a vision, as it were. ¹² What he had seen was this:

Onias, the former high priest, that paragon of men, modest of bearing and gentle of manners, suitably eloquent and trained from boyhood in the practice of every virtue—Onias was stretching out his hands and praying for the whole Jewish community. ¹³ Next, there appeared a man equally remarkable for his great age and dignity and invested with a marvellous and impressive air of majesty. ¹⁴ Onias began to speak: 'This is a man', he said, 'who loves his brothers and prays much for the people and the holy city—Jeremiah, the prophet of God.' ¹⁵ Jeremiah then stretched out his right hand and presented Judas with a golden sword, saying as he gave it, ¹⁶ 'Take this holy sword as a gift from God; with it you will shatter the enemy.'

The disposition of the combatants

¹⁷ Encouraged by the noble words of Judas, which had the power to inspire valour and give the young the spirit of mature men, they decided not to entrench themselves in a camp, but bravely to take the offensive and, in hand-to-hand fighting, to commit the result to the fortune of war, since the city, their holy religion and the Temple were in danger. ¹⁸ Their concern for their wives and children, their brothers and relatives, had shrunk to minute importance; their chief and greatest fear was for the consecrated Temple. ¹⁹ Those left behind in the city felt a similar anxiety, alarmed as they were about the forthcoming encounter in the open country. ²⁰ Everyone now awaited the coming issue. The enemy had already concentrated their forces and stood formed up in order of battle, with the elephants drawn up in a strategic position and the cavalry disposed on the wings. ²¹ Maccabaeus took note of these masses confronting him, the glittering array of armour and the fierce aspect of the elephants; then, raising his hands to heaven, he called on the Lord who works miracles, in the knowledge that it is not by force of arms but as he sees fit to decide, that victory is granted by him to such as deserve it. ²² His prayer was worded thus: 'You, Master, sent your angel in the days

of Hezekiah king of Judaea, and he destroyed no less than one hundred and eighty-five thousand of Sennacherib's army; 23 now, once again, Sovereign of heaven, send a good angel before us to spread terror and dismay. 24 May these men be struck down by the might of your arm, since they have come with blasphemy on their lips to attack your holy people.' And on these words he finished.

The defeat and death of Nicanor[a]

25 Nicanor and his men advanced to the sound of trumpets and war songs, 26 but the men of Judas closed with the enemy uttering invocations and prayers. 27 Fighting with their hands and praying to God in their hearts, they cut down at least thirty-five thousand men and were greatly cheered by this manifestation of God. 28 When the engagement was over and they were withdrawing in triumph, they recognised Nicanor, lying dead in full armour. 29 With shouting and confusion all around, they blessed the sovereign Master in their ancestral tongue. 30 He who, as protagonist, had devoted himself, body and soul, to his fellow-citizens, and had preserved the love he felt even in youth for those of his own race, gave orders for Nicanor's head to be cut off, with his arm up to the shoulder, and taken to Jerusalem. 31 When he arrived there himself, he called his countrymen together, stationed the priests in front of the altar and then sent for the people from the Citadel. 32 He showed them the head of the abominable Nicanor, and

the hand which this infamous man had stretched out so insolently against the holy House of the Almighty. 33 Then, cutting out godless Nicanor's tongue, he gave orders for it to be fed piecemeal to the birds, and for the salary of his folly to be hung up in front of the Temple. 34 At this, everyone sent blessings heavenwards to the glorious Lord, saying, 'Blessed be he who has preserved his holy place from pollution!'

35 He hung Nicanor's head from the Citadel, a clear and evident sign to all of the help of the Lord. 36 They all decreed by public vote never to let that day go by unobserved, but to celebrate the thirteenth day of the twelfth month, called Adar in Aramaic, the eve of what is called the Day of Mordecai.

Compiler's epilogue

37 So ends the episode of Nicanor, and as, since then, the city has remained in the possession of the Hebrews, I shall bring my own work to an end here too. 38 If it is well composed and to the point, that is just what I wanted. If it is worthless and mediocre, that is all I could manage. 39 Just as it is injurious to drink wine by itself, or again water alone, whereas wine mixed with water is pleasant and produces a delightful sense of well-being, so skill in presenting the incidents is what delights the understanding of those who read the book. And here I close.

15a ‖ 1 M 7:43–50.

The Book of

JOB

Satan tests Job

1 There was once a man in the land of Uz called Job: a sound and honest man who feared God and shunned evil. ² Seven sons and three daughters were born to him. ³ And he owned seven thousand sheep, three thousand camels, five hundred yoke of oxen and five hundred she-donkeys, and many servants besides. This man was the most prosperous of all the Sons of the East. ⁴ It was the custom of his sons to hold banquets in one another's houses in turn, and to invite their three sisters to eat and drink with them. ⁵ Once each series of banquets was over, Job would send for them to come and be purified, and at dawn on the following day he would make a burnt offering for each of them. 'Perhaps', Job would say, 'my sons have sinned and in their heart blasphemed.' So that was what Job used to do each time.

⁶ One day when the sons of God*ᵃ* came to attend on Yahweh, among them came Satan. ⁷ So Yahweh said to Satan, 'Where have you been?' 'Prowling about on earth,' he answered, 'roaming around there.' ⁸ So Yahweh asked him, 'Did you pay any attention to my servant Job? There is no one like him on the earth: a sound and honest man who fears God and shuns evil.' ⁹ 'Yes,' Satan said, 'but Job is not God-fearing for nothing, is he? ¹⁰ Have you not put a wall round him and his house and all his domain? You have blessed all he undertakes, and his flocks throng the countryside. ¹¹ But stretch out your hand and lay a finger on his possessions: then, I warrant you, he will curse you to your face.' ¹² 'Very well,' Yahweh said to Satan, 'all he has is in your power. But keep your hands off his person.' So Satan left the presence of Yahweh.

¹³ On the day when Job's sons and daughters were eating and drinking in their eldest brother's house, ¹⁴ a messenger came to Job. 'Your oxen', he said, 'were at the plough, with the donkeys grazing at their side, ¹⁵ when the Sabaeans swept down on them and carried them off, and put the servants to the sword: I alone have escaped to tell you.' ¹⁶ He had not finished speaking when another messenger arrived. 'The fire of God', he said, 'has fallen from heaven and burnt the sheep and shepherds to ashes: I alone have escaped to tell you.' ¹⁷ He had not finished speaking when another messenger arrived. 'The Chaldaeans,' he said, 'three bands of them, have raided the camels and made off with them, and put the servants to the sword: I alone have escaped to tell you.' ¹⁸ He had not finished speaking when another messenger arrived. 'Your sons and daughters', he said, 'were eating and drinking at their eldest brother's house, ¹⁹ when suddenly from the desert a gale sprang up, and it battered all four corners of the house which fell in on the young people. They are dead: I alone have escaped to tell you.'

²⁰ Then Job stood up, tore his robe and shaved his head. Then, falling to the ground, he prostrated himself ²¹ and said:

> Naked I came from my mother's womb,
> naked I shall return again.
> Yahweh gave, Yahweh has taken back.
> Blessed be the name of Yahweh!

²² In all this misfortune Job committed no sin, and he did not reproach God.

1a God's court and council, the angels. These include Satan, 'the accuser', who is responsible for testing human beings in their faithfulness to God. He is later identified with the spirit of evil.

36 READ JOB 1.

In all this misfortune Job committed no sin, and he did not reproach God.—JOB 1:22

ACCEPTING SUFFERING

After having lost all his goods and all his children, Job got up, tore up his garments, shaved his head, and fell to the ground in adoration. These expressions of grief testify that he felt the pain of this blow. But the fact that he fell to the ground in adoration clearly shows that even in pain he did not rebel against the decision of the One who struck him. . . . He said: "Naked I came from my mother's womb, naked I shall return again." In other words: "I have lost what I would have to abandon after having received it. Therefore what have I lost that was my own?" Seeing that he had lost everything by the Lord's hand, in order to stay patient he remembered the time when he did not yet have what he had just lost. That thought toned down the pain of his grief.

Knowing that Satan did not have the power to test him without God's permission, he did not say: "Yahweh gave, but the devil has taken away," but "Yahweh gave, Yahweh has taken back." Maybe he would have had something to complain about if the enemy had taken the good that the Creator had given. But since he who has taken is none other than he who gave, he has only taken back his own property and not taken away ours. If we have received from his goodness those possessions we enjoy in this life, why do we complain if he judges it wise to take them away from us?

Job concludes by praising his Judge with these words: "Blessed be the name of Yahweh!" Though caught in the throes of a trial, this man sings a hymn of praise to the Lord.

ST. GREGORY THE GREAT, 540?–604

YOU WILL FIND THE NEXT READING AT JOB 7.

2 Another day, the sons of God came to attend on Yahweh and Satan came with them too. ²So Yahweh said to Satan, 'Where have you been?' 'Prowling about on earth,' he answered, 'roaming around there.' ³So Yahweh asked him, 'Did you pay any attention to my servant Job? There is no one like him on the earth: a sound and honest man who fears God and shuns evil. He persists in his integrity still; you achieved nothing by provoking me to ruin him.' ⁴'Skin after skin!'ᵃ Satan replied. 'Someone will give away all he has to save his life. ⁵But stretch out your hand and lay a finger on his bone and flesh; I warrant you, he will curse you to your face.' ⁶'Very well,' Yahweh said to Satan, 'he is in your power. But spare his life.' ⁷So Satan left the presence of Yahweh.

He struck Job down with malignant ulcers from the sole of his foot to the top of his head. ⁸Job took a piece of pot to scrape himself, and went and sat among the ashes. ⁹Then his wife said to him, 'Why persist in this integrity of yours? Curse God and die.' ¹⁰'That is how a fool of a woman talks,' Job replied. 'If we take happiness from God's hand, must we not take sorrow too?' And in all this misfortune Job uttered no sinful word.

¹¹The news of all the disasters that had

2a Proverb, meaning perhaps that physical hurt is worse than progressive loss of goods.

fallen on Job came to the ears of three of his friends. Each of them set out from home— Eliphaz of Teman, Bildad of Shuah and Zophar of Naamath—and by common consent they decided to go and offer him sympathy and consolation. [12] Looking at him from a distance, they could not recognise him; they wept aloud and tore their robes and threw dust over their heads. [13] They sat there on the ground beside him for seven days and seven nights. To Job they spoke never a word, for they saw how much he was suffering.

Job curses the day of his birth

3 In the end it was Job who broke the silence and cursed the day of his birth. [2] This is what he said:

[3] Perish the day on which I was born
  and the night that told of a boy
    conceived.
[4] May that day be darkness,
  may God on high have no thought for it,
  may no light shine on it.
[5] May murk and shadow dark as death
    claim it for their own,
  clouds hang over it,
  eclipse swoop down on it.
[6] See! Let obscurity seize on it,
  from the days of the year let it be
    excluded,
  into the reckoning of the months not
    find its way.
[7] And may that night be sterile,
  devoid of any cries of joy!
[8] Let it be cursed by those who curse certain
    days[a]
  and are ready to rouse Leviathan.
[9] Dark be the stars of its morning,
  let it wait in vain for light
  and never see the opening eyes of dawn.
[10] Since it would not shut the doors of the
    womb on me
  to hide sorrow from my eyes.
[11] Why was I not still-born,
  or why did I not perish as I left the
    womb?

[12] Why were there knees to receive me,
  breasts for me to suck?
[13] Now I should be lying in peace,
  wrapped in a restful slumber,
[14] with the kings and high viziers of
    earth
  who have built their dwellings in
    desolate places,
[15] or with princes who have quantities of
    gold
  and silver cramming their tombs;
[16] or, put away like an abortive child, I
    should not have existed,
  like little ones that never see the
    light.
[17] Down there, the wicked bustle no
    more,
  there the weary rest.
[18] Prisoners, all left in peace,
  hear no more the shouts of the
    oppressor.
[19] High and low are there together,
  and the slave is free of his master.
[20] Why give light to a man of grief?
  Why give life to those bitter of heart,
[21] who long for a death that never comes,
  and hunt for it more than for buried
    treasure?
[22] They would be glad to see the grave-
    mound
  and shout with joy if they reached
    the tomb.
[23] Why give light to one who does not see
    his way,
  whom God shuts in all alone?

[24] My only food is sighs,
  and my groans pour out like
    water.
[25] Whatever I fear comes true,
  whatever I dread befalls me.
[26] For me, there is no calm, no
    peace;
  my torments banish rest.

3a Sorcerers. Leviathan is the monster of primeval chaos, always lurking to engulf order.

Confidence in God

4 Eliphaz of Teman spoke next. He said:

2 If we say something to you, will you bear
with us?
Who in any case could refrain from
speaking now?
3 You have schooled many others,
giving strength to feeble hands;
4 your words supported any who wavered
and strengthened every failing knee.
5 And now your turn has come, and you lose
patience,
at the first touch on yourself you are
overwhelmed!
6 Does not your piety give you confidence,
and your integrity of life give you
hope?
7 Can you recall anyone guiltless that
perished?
Where then have the honest been wiped
out?
8 I speak from experience: those who plough
iniquity
and sow disaster, reap just that.
9 Under the breath of God, they perish:
a blast of his anger, and they are
destroyed;
10 the lion's roars, his savage growls,
like the fangs of a lion cub, are broken
off.
11 The lion dies for lack of prey
and the lioness's whelps are dispersed.
12 I have received a secret revelation,
a whisper has come to my ears;
13 by night when dreams confuse the mind
and slumber lies heavy on everyone,
14 a shiver of horror ran through me
and filled all my bones with fright.
15 A breath slid over my face,
the hairs of my body bristled.
16 Someone stood there—I did not know his
face,
but the form stayed there before my
eyes.
Silence—then I heard a voice,

17 'Can a mortal seem upright to God,
would anybody seem pure in the
presence of his Maker?
18 God cannot rely even on his own
servants,
even with his angels he finds fault.
19 What then of those who live in houses of
clay,
who are founded on dust?
20 They are crushed as easily as a moth,
between morning and evening they are
ground to powder.
They vanish for ever, with no one to
bring them back.
21 Their tent-peg is snatched from them,
and they die devoid of wisdom.'

5 Make your appeal then. Will you find an
answer?
To which of the holy ones will you
turn?
2 Resentment kills the senseless,
and anger brings death to the fool.
3 I have seen the senseless taking root,
when a curse fell suddenly on his
house.
4 His children are deprived of prop and stay,
ruined at the gate, and no one to defend
them;
5 their harvest goes to feed the hungry,
God snatches it from their mouths,
and covetous people thirst for their
possessions.
6 No, misery does not grow out of the soil,
nor sorrow spring from the ground.
7 It is people who breed trouble for
themselves
as surely as eagles fly to the height.
8 If I were you, I should appeal to God
and lay my case before him.
9 His works are great, past all reckoning,
marvels beyond all counting.
10 He sends down rain to the earth,
pours down water on the fields.
11 If his will is to raise up the downcast,
or exalt the afflicted to the heights of
prosperity,

12 he frustrates the plans of the artful
    so that they cannot succeed in their
        intrigues.
13 He traps the crafty in the snare of their
        own trickery,
    throws the plans of the cunning into
        disarray.
14 In daylight they come up against
        darkness,
    and grope their way as if noon were
        night.
15 He rescues the bankrupt from their jaws,
    and the needy from the grasp of the
        mighty.
16 Hope springs afresh for the weak,
    and wickedness must shut its mouth.

17 Blessed are those whom God corrects!
    Do not then scorn the lesson of
        Shaddai![a]
18 For he who wounds is he who soothes the
        sore,
    and the hand that hurts is the hand that
        heals.
19 Six times he will deliver you from sorrow,
    and the seventh time, evil will not touch
        you.
20 In time of famine, he will save you from
        death,
    and in wartime from the stroke of the
        sword.
21 You will be safe from the lash of the
        tongue,
    unafraid at the approach of the
        despoiler.
22 You will laugh at drought and frost,
    and have no fear of the beasts of the
        earth.
23 You will have a pact with the stones of the
        field,
    and live in amity with wild beasts.
24 You will know that your tent is secure,
    and your sheepfold unharmed when
        you inspect it.
25 You will see your descendants multiply,
    your offspring grow like the grass in the
        fields.

26 At a ripe age you will go to the grave,
    like a wheatsheaf stacked in due season.
27 All this we have observed and it is so!
    Heed it, you will be the wiser for it!

Only the sufferer knows his own grief

6 Job spoke next. He said:

2 If only my misery could be weighed,
    and all my ills be put together on the
        scales!
3 But they outweigh the sands of the seas:
    what wonder then if my words are
        wild?
4 The arrows of Shaddai stick fast in me,
    my spirit absorbs their poison,
    God's terrors stand paraded against me.
5 Does a wild donkey bray when it has
        grass,
    or an ox low when its fodder is within
        reach?
6 Is not food insipid, eaten without salt,
    is there any taste in egg-white?
7 But the very things my appetite revolts at
    are now my diet in sickness.
8 Will no one hear my prayer,
    will not God himself grant my hope?
9 May it please God to crush me,
    to give his hand free play and do away
        with me!
10 This thought, at least, would give me
        comfort
    (a thrill of joy in unrelenting pain),
    that I never rebelled against the Holy
        One's decrees.
11 But have I the strength to go on waiting?
    And why be patient, when doomed to
        such an end?
12 Is mine the strength of stone,
    is my flesh made of bronze?
13 Can I support myself on nothing?
    Has not all help deserted me?
14 Refuse faithful love to your neighbour
    and you forsake the fear of Shaddai.

5a A name of God in patriarchal times, the dramatic setting
of the dialogues.

¹⁵ Like the torrent, my brothers have proved deceptive,
  as fleeting torrents they flow:
¹⁶ the ice makes their waters turgid
  when, above them, the snow melts,
¹⁷ but, come the burning summer, they run dry,
  they vanish in the heat of the sun.
¹⁸ Caravans leave the trail to find them,
  go deep into wastelands, and are lost.
¹⁹ The caravans of Tema look to them,
  and on them Sheba's convoys build their hopes.
²⁰ Their trust brings only embarrassment,
  they reach them only to be thwarted.

²¹ And this is how you now treat me,
  terrified at the sight of me, you take fright.
²² Have I said to you, 'Give me something,
  make some present for me at your own cost,
²³ snatch me from the grasp of an oppressor,
  ransom me from the grip of a violent man'?
²⁴ Put me right, and I shall say no more;
  show me where I have been at fault.
²⁵ Fair comment can be borne without resentment,
  but what are your strictures aimed at?
²⁶ Do you think mere words deserve censure,
  desperate speech that the wind blows away?
²⁷ Soon you will be haggling over the price of an orphan,
  and selling your friend at bargain price!
²⁸ Come, I beg you, look at me:
  man to man, I shall not lie.
²⁹ Relent then, no harm is done;
  relent then, since I am upright.
³⁰ Is evil to be found on my lips?
  Can I not recognise misfortune when I taste it?

7 Is not human life on earth just conscript service?
  Do we not live a hireling's life?

² Like a slave, sighing for the shade,
  or a hireling with no thought but for his wages,
³ I have months of futility assigned to me,
  nights of suffering to be my lot.
⁴ Lying in bed I wonder, 'When will it be day?'
  No sooner up than, 'When will evening come?'
  And crazy thoughts obsess me till twilight falls.
⁵ Vermin and loathsome scabs cover my body;
  my skin is cracked and oozes pus.
⁶ Swifter than a weaver's shuttle my days have passed,
  and vanished, leaving no hope behind.
⁷ Remember that my life is but a breath,
  and that my eyes will never again see joy.
⁸ The eye that once saw me will look on me no more,
  your eyes will turn my way, and I shall not be there.
⁹ A cloud dissolves and is gone,
  so no one who goes down to Sheol ever comes up again,
¹⁰ ever comes home again,
  and his house knows that person no more.
¹¹ That is why I cannot keep quiet:
  in my anguish of spirit I shall speak,
  in my bitterness of soul I shall complain.
¹² Am I the Sea,^a or some sea monster,
  that you should keep me under guard?
¹³ If I say, 'My bed will comfort me,
  my couch will lighten my complaints,'
¹⁴ you then frighten me with dreams
  and terrify me with visions,
¹⁵ so that strangling would seem welcome in comparison,
  yes, death preferable to what I suffer.

7a In Babylonian myths the Sea was a goddess, held back from sweeping civilisation away.

37 READ JOB 7.

What are human beings that you should take them so seriously?—JOB 7:17

WEIGHED DOWN BY SELF-WILL

Each one wants to make his own law when he prefers his own will to the common, eternal law. He seeks to imitate his Creator in a perverse way, so that as God is for himself his own law and depends on himself alone, so does man want to govern himself and make his own will his law. This heavy and unbearable yoke weighs on all Adam's sons, alas, making our necks curve and bend down so that our life seems to draw near hell (see Ps 88:3). . . .

The soul struggling under this load laments saying: "Why have you set me against you, and I am become a burden for myself?" (see verse 20, KJV). By the words "I am become a burden for myself" is shown that he himself is his own law and that nobody but himself did that. But what he said previously, speaking to God: "Why have you set me against you?" means that he has not escaped God's law. It is proper to God's eternally just law that he who does not want to accept its sweet rule will be the slave of his own will as a penance; he who casts away the pleasant yoke and light load of charity (see Mt 11:30) will have to bear unwillingly the unbearable burden of his own will. By a mysterious and just measure the eternal law has set its fugitive against himself yet retaining him captive, for he can neither escape the law of justice which he deserves nor remain with God in his light, rest, and glory, because he is subject to power and banished from happiness.

O Lord, my God, "Why do you not take away my sin, and wherefore do you not remove my evil" (see verse 21), that delivered from the heavy load of self-will, I may breathe under charity's light burden . . . ? ST. BERNARD OF CLAIRVAUX, 1090?–1153

YOU WILL FIND THE NEXT READING AT JOB 12.

16 I am wasting away, my life is not unending;
  leave me then, for my days are but a
    breath.
17 What are human beings that you should
    take them so seriously,
  subjecting them to your scrutiny,
18 that morning after morning you should
    examine them
  and at every instant test them?
19 Will you never take your eyes off me
  long enough for me to swallow my
    spittle?
20 Suppose I have sinned, what have I done
    to you,
  you tireless watcher of humanity?

Why do you choose me as your
    target?
  Why should I be a burden to you?
21 Can you not tolerate my sin,
  not overlook my fault?
  For soon I shall be lying in the dust,
    you will look for me and I shall be
      no more.

The unswerving course of God's justice

8 Bildad of Shuah spoke next. He said:

2 How much longer are you going to talk
    like this
  and go blustering on in this way?

3 Can God deflect the course of right
  or Shaddai falsify justice?
4 If your sons sinned against him,
  he has punished them for their wrong-
    doing.
6a You for your part, if you are pure and
    honest,
5   must now seek God, plead with
      Shaddai.
6b Forthwith his light will shine on you and
    he will restore
  an upright man's house to prosperity.
7 Your former state will seem as nothing
    to you,
  so great will your future be.

8 Question the generation that has passed,
  meditate on the experience of its
    ancestors—
9 for we children of yesterday, we know
    nothing,
  our life on earth passes like a shadow—
10 but they will teach you, they will tell you,
  and their thought is expressed in these
    sayings,
11 'Can papyrus flourish except in marshes?
  Without water can the rushes grow?
12 Even when green and before being cut,
  fastest of all plants they wither.
13 Such is the fate of all who forget God;
  so perishes the hope of the godless.
14 His hope is nothing but gossamer,
  his confidence a spider's web.
15 Let him lean on his house, it will not stand
    firm;
  cling to it, it will not hold.
16 Like some lush plant in the sunlight,
  he sent his young shoots sprouting over
    the garden;
17 but his roots were twined in a heap of
    stones,
  he drew his life among the rocks.
18 Snatch him from his bed,
  and it denies it ever saw him.
19 Now he rots on the roadside,
  and others are springing up in
    the soil.

20 Believe me, God neither spurns anyone of
    integrity,
  nor lends his aid to the evil.
21 Once again laughter may fill your mouth
  and cries of joy break from your lips.
22 Your enemies will be covered with shame
  and the tent of the wicked will vanish!'

God's justice is above all law

9 Job spoke next. He said:

2 Indeed, I know it is as you say:
  how could anyone claim to be upright
    before God?
3 Anyone trying to argue matters with him,
  could not give him one answer in a
    thousand.
4 Among the wisest and the hardiest,
  who then can successfully defy him?
5 He moves the mountains, though they do
    not know it;
  he throws them down when he is angry.
6 He shakes the earth, and moves it from its
    place,
  making all its pillars tremble.
7 The sun, at his command, forbears to rise,
  and on the stars he sets a seal.
8 He and no other has stretched out the
    heavens
  and trampled on the back of the Sea.
9 He has made the Bear and Orion,
  the Pleiades and the Mansions of the
    South.
10 The works he does are great and
    unfathomable,
  and his marvels cannot be counted.
11 If he passes me, I do not see him;
  he slips by, imperceptible to me.
12 If he snatches his prey, who is going to stop
    him
  or dare to ask, 'What are you doing?'
13 God does not renounce his anger:
  beneath him, Rahab's[a] minions still lie
    prostrate.

9a Another name for the Sea as monster of chaos, also used
of the Red Sea.

¹⁴ And here am I, proposing to defend
myself
and select my arguments against him!
¹⁵ Even if I am upright, what point is there
in answering him?
I can only plead for mercy with my
judge!
¹⁶ And if he deigned to answer my citation,
I cannot believe he would listen to what
I said,
¹⁷ he who crushes me for one hair,
who, for no reason, wounds and
wounds again,
¹⁸ not even letting me regain my breath,
with so much bitterness he fills me!
¹⁹ Shall I try force? Look how strong he is!
Or go to court? But who will summon
him?
²⁰ If I prove myself upright, his mouth may
condemn me,
even if I am innocent, he may
pronounce me perverse.
²¹ But am I innocent? I am no longer sure,
and life itself I despise!
²² It is all one, and hence I boldly say:
he destroys innocent and guilty alike.
²³ When a sudden deadly scourge descends,
he laughs at the plight of the innocent.
²⁴ When a country falls into the power of the
wicked,
he veils the faces of its judges.
Or if not he, who else?
²⁵ My days pass: more swiftly than a runner
they flee away with never a glimpse of
happiness,
²⁶ they skim past like a reed canoe,
like an eagle swooping on its prey.
²⁷ If I decide to stifle my complaining,
change countenance, and wear a
smiling face,
²⁸ fear seizes me at the thought of all my
woes,
for I know you do not regard me as
innocent.
²⁹ And if I have done wrong,
why should I put myself to useless
trouble?

³⁰ If I wash myself in melted snow,
clean my hands with soda,
³¹ you will only plunge me into the dung,
till my clothes themselves recoil from
me!
³² For he is not human like me: impossible
for me to answer him
or appear alongside him in court.
³³ There is no arbiter between us,
to lay his hand on both,
³⁴ to stay his rod from me,
or keep away his daunting terrors.
³⁵ Nonetheless, unafraid of him, I shall
speak:
since I do not see myself like that
at all!

10 Since I have lost all taste for life,
I shall give free rein to my complaining;
I shall let my embittered soul speak out.
² I shall say to God, 'Do not condemn me,
tell me what your case is against me.
³ Is it right for you to attack me,
in contempt for what you yourself have
made,
thus abetting the schemes of the
wicked?
⁴ Are your eyes mere human eyes,
do you see as human beings see?
⁵ Are you mortal like human beings?
do your years pass as human days
pass?
⁶ You, who enquire into my faults
and investigate my sins,
⁷ you know very well that I am innocent,
and that no one can rescue me from
your grasp.
⁸ Your hands having shaped and created
me,
now you change your mind and mean
to destroy me!
⁹ Having made me, remember, as though
of clay,
now you mean to turn me back into
dust!
¹⁰ Did you not pour me out like milk,
and then let me thicken like curds,

11 clothe me with skin and flesh,
    and weave me of bone and sinew?
12 In your love you gave me life,
    and in your care watched over my every
        breath.
13 Yet, all the while, you had a secret plan:
    I know that you were biding your time
14 to see if I should sin
    and then not acquit me of my faults.
15 Woe to me, if I am guilty;
    even if I am upright, I dare not lift my
        head,
    so overwhelmed with shame and drunk
        with pain am I!
16 Proud as a lion, you hunt me down,
    multiplying your exploits at my
        expense,
17 attacking me again and again,
    your fury against me ever increasing,
    your troops assailing me, wave after
        wave.
18 Why did you bring me out of the womb?
    I should have perished then, unseen by
        any eye,
19 a being that had never been,
    to be carried from womb to grave.
20 The days of my life are few enough:
    turn your eyes away, leave me a little joy,
21 before I go to the place of no return,
    to the land of darkness and shadow
        dark as death,
22 where dimness and disorder hold sway,
    and light itself is like dead of night.

Job must acknowledge God's wisdom

11 Zophar of Naamath spoke next. He
    said:

2 Is babbling to go without an answer?
    Is wordiness a proof of uprightness?
3 Do you think your talking strikes people
        dumb,
    will you jeer with no one to refute you?
4 These were your words, 'My conduct is
        pure,
    in your eyes I am free of blame!'

5 Will no one let God speak,
    open his lips and give you answer,
6 show you the secrets of wisdom
    which put all cleverness to shame?
    Then you would realise that God is
        calling you to account for your sin.
7 Can you claim to fathom the depth of
        God,
    can you reach the limit of Shaddai?
8 It is higher than the heavens: what can you
        do?
    It is deeper than Sheol: what can you
        know?
9 It would be longer to measure than the
        earth
    and broader than the sea.
10 If he intervenes to close or convoke the
        assembly,
    who is to prevent him?
11 He knows how deceptive human beings
        are,
    and he sees their misdeeds too, and
        marks them well.
12 Hence empty-headed people would do
        well to study sense
    and people who behave like wild
        donkeys to let themselves be
        tamed.
13 Come, reconsider your attitude,
    stretch out your hands towards him!
14 If you repudiate the sin which you have
        doubtless committed
    and do not allow wickedness to live on
        in your tents,
15 you will be able to raise an unsullied face,
    unwavering and free from fear,
16 for you will forget about your misery,
    thinking of it only as a flood that passed
        long ago.
17 Then begins an existence more radiant
        than noon,
    and the very darkness will be bright as
        morning.
18 Confident because there is hope;
    after your troubles, you will sleep
        secure.

¹⁹ When you lie down to rest, no one will
trouble you,
and many will seek your favour.
²⁰ But as for the wicked, their eyes are weary,
there is no refuge for them;
their only hope is to breathe their last.

*God's wisdom is best seen in the awesome
works of his omnipotence*

12 Job spoke next. He said:

² Doubtless, you are the voice of the people,
and when you die, wisdom will die with
you!
³ But I have a brain, as well as you,
I am in no way inferior to you,
and who, in any case, does not know all
that?
⁴ Anyone becomes a laughing-stock to his
friends
if he cries to God and expects an
answer.
People laugh at anyone who has
integrity and is upright.
⁵ 'Add insult to injury,' think the
prosperous,
'strike the fellow now that he is
staggering!'
⁶ And yet the tents of brigands are left in
peace:
those who provoke God dwell secure
and so does anyone who makes a god of
his fist!
⁷ You have only to ask the cattle, for them to
instruct you,
and the birds of the sky, for them to
inform you.
⁸ The creeping things of earth will give you
lessons,
and the fish of the sea provide you an
explanation:
⁹ there is not one such creature but will
know
that the hand of God has arranged
things like this!
¹⁰ In his hand is the soul of every living thing
and the breath of every human being!

¹¹ Can the ear not distinguish the value of
what is said,
just as the palate can tell one food from
another?
¹² Wisdom is found in the old,
and discretion comes with great age.
¹³ But in him there is wisdom, and power too,
and good counsel no less than
discretion.
¹⁴ What he destroys, no one can rebuild;
whom he imprisons, no one can release.
¹⁵ Is there a drought? He has withheld the
waters.
Do they play havoc on earth? He has let
them loose.
¹⁶ In him is strength, in him resourcefulness,
beguiler and beguiled alike are his.
¹⁷ He robs a country's counsellors of their
wits,
turns judges into fools.
¹⁸ He undoes the belts of kings
and knots a rope round their waists.
¹⁹ He makes priests walk barefoot,
and overthrows the powers that are
established.
²⁰ He strikes the most assured of speakers
dumb
and robs old people of their discretion.
²¹ He pours contempt on the nobly born,
and unbuckles the belt of the strong.
²² He unveils the depths of darkness,
brings shadow dark as death to the
light.
²³ He builds nations up, then ruins them,
he makes peoples expand, then
suppresses them.
²⁴ He strips a country's leaders of their
judgement,
and leaves them to wander in a trackless
waste,
²⁵ to grope about in unlit darkness,
lurching to and fro as though drunk.

13 I have seen all this with my own
eyes,
heard with my own ears and
understood.

38 READ JOB 12.

In his hand is the soul of every living thing.—JOB 12:10

WISDOM'S FOLLY

Sometimes even a person who singleheartedly devotes himself to good works is exposed to mockery. His conduct should excite admiration, but it only provokes abuse. Then, whereas praise would have put him in danger of turning outward, these affronts compel him to enter within himself and attach himself all the more firmly to God, as he finds nothing outside in which he can rest in peace.

Therefore he puts all his hope in his Creator and, in the midst of ridicule, he seeks only him who knows the hearts of men. His distressed heart approaches God in proportion as he becomes a stranger to the esteem of others. Therefore he pours himself out in prayer and, feeling himself persecuted from without, he sees divine things become more and more evident to his eyes.

The wisdom of the world teaches its disciples to seek high places of honor, to rejoice in attaining vain acquisition of worldly glory, to return with interest the evils that others bring upon us; when possible, to give way to no person's opposition; but when this is not possible to hide the malice we cannot execute under an appearance of affability and peace.

Very different is the wisdom of the saints. They never seek to appear other than they are and their words show what is in their hearts. They love truth for its own sake and avoid lying. They do good without expecting a return. They would rather suffer evil than bring it on others. They do not seek to avenge a wrong. They account outrages received for love and truth as a gain.

This simplicity of the just is laughed at because the wise people of the world regard the virtue of the upright heart as folly. But this simplicity of conscience, which the impious judge mean and despicable, is precisely what renders the virtue of the righteous agreeable to God.

ST. GREGORY THE GREAT, 540?–604

YOU WILL FIND THE NEXT READING AT JOB 21.

2 Whatever you know, I know too;
   I am in no way inferior to you.
3 But my words are intended for Shaddai;
   I mean to remonstrate with God.
4 As for you, you are only charlatans,
   all worthless as doctors!
5 Will no one teach you to be quiet
   —the only wisdom that becomes you!
6 Kindly listen to my accusation
   and give your attention to the way I
   shall plead.

7 Do you mean to defend God by
      prevarication
   and by dishonest argument,
8 and, taking his side like this,
   appoint yourselves as his advocates?
9 How would you fare, if he were to
      scrutinise you?
   Can he be duped as mortals are
      duped?
10 He would inflict a harsh rebuke on you
   for your covert partiality.

11 Does his majesty not affright you?
  Does his terror not overcome you?
12 Your received ideas are maxims of ash,
  your retorts, retorts of clay.
13 Be quiet! Kindly let me do the talking,
  happen to me what may.
14 I am putting my flesh between my teeth,
  I am taking my life in my hands;
15 let him kill me if he will; I have no other
  hope
  than to justify my conduct in his eyes.
16 And this is what will save me,
  for the wicked would not dare to
  appear before him.

17 Listen carefully to my words,
  and pay attention to what I am going to
  say.
18 You see, I shall proceed by form of law,
  knowing that I am upright.
19 Who wants to contest my case?
  In advance, I agree to be silenced and to
  die!
20 Only grant me two concessions,
  and then I shall not hide away from
  your face:
21 remove your hand, which lies so heavy on
  me,
  no longer make me cower from your
  terror.
22 Then call me forward and I shall answer,
  or rather, I shall speak and you will
  answer.
23 How many faults and crimes have I
  committed?
  Tell me what my misdeed has been,
  what my sin?
24 Why do you hide your face
  and look on me as your enemy?
25 Do you want to intimidate a wind-blown
  leaf,
  do you want to pursue a dry straw?
26 You who lay bitter allegations against me
  and tax me with the faults of my youth
27 and have put my feet in the stocks;
  you examine my every step
  and measure my footprints one by one!

28 For his part, he crumbles away like rotten
  wood,
  or like a moth-eaten garment,
14 a human being, born of woman,
  whose life is short but full
  of trouble.
2 Like a flower, such a one blossoms and
  withers,
  fleeting as a shadow, transient.
3 And this is the creature on whom you fix
  your gaze,
  and bring to judgement before you!
4 But will anyone produce the pure from
  what is impure?
  No one can!
5 Since his days are measured out,
  since his tale of months depends on you,
  since you assign him bounds he cannot
  pass,
6 turn your eyes from him, leave him alone,
  like a hired labourer, to finish his day in
  peace.
7 There is always hope for a tree:
  when felled, it can start its life again;
  its shoots continue to sprout.
8 Its roots may have grown old in the
  earth,
  its stump rotting in the ground,
9 but let it scent the water, and it buds,
  and puts out branches like a plant
  newly set.
10 But a human being? He dies, and dead he
  remains,
  breathes his last, and then where is he?
11 The waters of the sea will vanish,
  the rivers stop flowing and run dry:
12 a human being, once laid to rest, will never
  rise again,
  the heavens will wear out before he
  wakes up,
  or before he is roused from his sleep.

13 Will no one hide me in Sheol,
  and shelter me there till your anger is
  past,
  fixing a certain day for calling me to
  mind—

14 can the dead come back to life?—
　　day after day of my service, I should be
　　　　waiting
　　for my relief to come.
15 Then you would call, and I should answer,
　　you would want to see once more what
　　　　you have made.
16 Whereas now you count every step I take,
　　you would then stop spying on my sin;
17 you would seal up my crime in a bag,
　　and put a cover over my fault.

18 Alas! Just as, eventually, the mountain falls
　　　　down,
　　the rock moves from its place,
19 water wears away the stones,
　　the cloudburst erodes the soil;
　　so you destroy whatever hope a person
　　　　has.
20 You crush him once for all, and he is gone;
　　first you disfigure him, then you dismiss
　　　　him.
21 His children may rise to honours—he does
　　　　not know it;
　　they may come down in the world—he
　　　　does not care.
22 He feels no pangs, except for his own
　　　　body,
　　makes no lament, except for his own self.

Job's own words condemn him

15 Eliphaz of Teman spoke next. He said:

2 Does anyone wise respond with windy
　　　　arguments,
　　or feed on an east wind?
3 Or make a defence with ineffectual words
　　and speeches good for nothing?
4 You do worse: you suppress reverence,
　　you discredit discussion before God.
5 Your very fault incites you to speak like
　　　　this,
　　hence you adopt this language of
　　　　cunning.
6 Your own mouth condemns you, and
　　　　not I;
　　your own lips bear witness against you.

7 Are you the first-born of the human race,
　　brought into the world before the hills?
8 Have you been a listener at God's council,
　　or established a monopoly of wisdom?
9 What knowledge do you have that we
　　　　have not,
　　what understanding that is not ours
　　　　too?
10 One of us is an old, grey-headed man
　　loaded with more years than your
　　　　father!
11 Can you ignore these divine consolations
　　and the moderate tone of our words?
12 How passion carries you away!
　　And how you roll your eyes,
13 when you vent your anger on God
　　and speeches come tripping off your
　　　　tongue!
14 How can anyone be pure,
　　anyone born of woman be upright?
15 God cannot rely even on his holy ones,
　　to him, even the heavens seem impure.
16 How much more, this hateful, corrupt
　　　　thing,
　　humanity, which soaks up wickedness
　　　　like water!
17 Listen to me, I have a lesson for you:
　　I am going to impart my own
　　　　experience
18 and the tradition of the sages
　　who have remained faithful to their
　　　　ancestors,
19 to whom alone the land was given—
　　no foreigner included among them.
20 The life of the wicked is unceasing
　　　　torment,
　　the years allotted to the tyrant are
　　　　numbered.
21 A cry of panic echoes in his ear;
　　when all is peace, his destroyer swoops
　　　　down on him.
22 No more can he count on escaping from
　　　　the dark,
　　but knows that he is destined for the
　　　　sword,
23 marked down as meat for the vulture.
　　He knows that his ruin is at hand.

²⁴ The hour of darkness terrifies him,
  distress and anguish assail him
  as when a king is poised for the
    assault.
²⁵ He raised his hand against God,
  boldly he defied Shaddai!
²⁶ Head lowered, he charged him,
  with his massively bossed shield.
²⁷ His face had grown full and fat,
  and his thighs too heavy with flesh.
²⁸ He had occupied the towns he had
    destroyed,
  with their uninhabited houses
  about to fall into ruins;
²⁹ but no great profit to him, his luck will not
    hold,
  he will cast his shadow over the country
    no longer,
³⁰   (he will not escape the dark).
  A flame will scorch his young shoots,
  the wind will carry off his blossom.
³¹ Let him not trust in his great height
  or delusion will be his.
³² His palm trees will wither before their
    time
  and his branches never again be green.
³³ Like the vine, he will shake off his unripe
    fruit,
  like the olive tree, shed his blossom.
³⁴ Yes, sterile is the spawn of the sinner,
  and fire consumes the tents of the venal.
³⁵ Whoever conceives malice, breeds disaster,
  bears as offspring only a false hope.

Human injustice and divine justice

16 Job spoke next. He said:

² How often have I heard all this before!
  What sorry comforters you are!
³ 'When will these windy arguments be
    over?'
  or again, 'What sickness drives you to
    defend yourself?'
⁴ Oh yes! I too could talk as you do,
  if you were in my place;
  I could overwhelm you with speeches,
  shaking my head over you,

⁵ and speak words of encouragement,
  and then have no more to say.
⁶ When I speak, my suffering does not stop;
  if I say nothing, is it in any way
    reduced?
⁷ And now it is driving me to distraction;
  you have struck my whole
    acquaintanceship with horror,
⁸ now it rounds on me, my slanderer has
    now turned witness,
  he appears against me, accusing me face
    to face;
⁹ his anger tears and hounds me
  with gnashing teeth.
  My enemies look daggers at me,
¹⁰   and open gaping jaws.
  Their sneers strike like slaps in the face;
  and they all set on me at once.
¹¹ Yes, God has handed me over to the
    godless,
  and cast me into the hands of the
    wicked.

¹² I was living at peace, until he made me
    totter,
  taking me by the neck to shatter me.
  He has set me up as his target:
¹³   he shoots his arrows at me from all sides,
  pitilessly pierces my loins,
  and pours my gall out on the ground.
¹⁴ Breach after breach he drives through me,
  charging on me like a warrior.
¹⁵ I have sewn sackcloth over my skin,
  thrown my forehead in the dust.
¹⁶ My face is red with tears,
  and shadow dark as death covers my
    eyelids.
¹⁷ Nonetheless, my hands are free of
    violence,
  and my prayer is pure.
¹⁸ Cover not my blood, O earth,
  and let my cry mount without cease!
¹⁹ Henceforth I have a witness in heaven,
  my defender is there on high.
²⁰ Interpreter of my thoughts there with
    God,
  before whom flow my tears,

21 let my anguish plead the cause of a man at
grips with God,
just as a man might defend his fellow.
22 For the years of my life are numbered,
and I am leaving by the road of no
return.

17

My breathing is growing weaker
and the gravediggers are gathering
for me.
2 Scoffers are my only companions,
their harshness haunts my nights.
3 So you must go bail for me to yourself,
for which of them cares to clap his hand
on mine?
4 For you have shut their hearts to reason,
hence not a hand is lifted.
5 Just so is a man who invites his friends to
share his property
while the eyes of his own children
languish.

6 I have become a byword among
foreigners,
and a creature on whose face to spit,
7 since I am nearly blind with grief
and my limbs are reduced to a
shadow.
8 Any honest person is appalled at the
sight,
the innocent is indignant at the sinner.
9 Anyone upright grows stronger step by
step:
and anyone whose hands are clean
grows ever in vigour!

10 Come on then, all of you, back to the
attack!
I shall not find one wise man among
you!

11 My days are over, so are my plans,
my heart-strings are broken;
12 yet they would have me believe that night
is day,
that light to dispel the darkness is at
hand,

13 when all I want, in fact, is to dwell in
Sheol
and in that darkness there to make my
bed!
14 To the tomb, I cry, 'You are my father!'—
to the worm, 'You are my mother—
you, my sister!'
15 Where then is my hope?
Who can see any happiness for me?
16 unless they come down to Sheol with me,
all of us sinking into the dust
together?

The inevitable fate of the wicked

18

Bildad of Shuah spoke next. He said:

2 What prevents you others from saying
something?
Think—for it is our turn to speak!
3 Why do you regard us as animals,
considering us no more than brutes?
4 Tear yourself to pieces if you will,
but the world, for all your rage, will not
turn to desert,
the rocks will not shift from their
places.
5 The light of the wicked must certainly be
put out,
the lamp that gives him light cease to
shine.
6 In his tent the light is dimmed,
the lamp that shone on him is snuffed.
7 His vigorous stride loses its power,
his own designs falter.
8 For into the net his own feet carry him,
he walks into the snares.
9 A spring grips him by the heel,
a trap snaps shut, and he is caught.
10 Hidden in the ground is a snare to catch
him,
pitfalls lie across his path.
11 Terrors threaten him from all sides
following him step by step.
12 Hunger becomes his companion,
by his side Disaster stands.
13 Disease devours his skin,
Death's First-Born gnaws his limbs.

14 He will be torn from the shelter of his tent,
  and you will drag him to the King of
    Terrors.ᵃ
15 You can live in the tent, since it is no
    longer his,
  and brimstone will be scattered on his
    sheepfold.
16 Below, his roots dry out
  and his branches are blasted above.
17 His memory fades from the land,
  his name is forgotten in the countryside.
18 Driven from the light into the darkness,
  he is banished from the world,
19 without issue or posterity among his own
    people
  or a single survivor where he used to
    live.
20 His end appals the west
  and fills the east with terror.
21 Such indeed is the fate of the places where
    wickedness dwells—
  the home of everyone who knows not
    God.

Faith at its height in total desertion

19 Job spoke next. He said:

2 How much longer are you going to
    torment me
  and crush me by your speeches?
3 You have insulted me ten times already:
  have you no shame at maltreating me?
4 Even if I had gone astray,
  my error would still be my own affair.
5 But, whereas you take this superior
    attitude
  and claim that my disgrace is my own
    fault,
6 I tell you that God has wronged me
  and enveloped me in his net.
7 If I protest against such violence, I am not
    heard,
  if I appeal against it, judgement is never
    given.
8 He has built an impassable wall across my
    path
  and covered my way with darkness.

9 He has deprived me of my glory
  and taken the crown from my head.
10 He assails me from all directions to make
    me vanish;
  he uproots my hope as he might
    a tree.
11 Inflamed with anger against me,
  he regards me as his foe.
12 His troops have come in force,
  directing their line of advance towards
    me,
  they are now encamped round
    my tent.

13 He has alienated my brothers from me,
  my relatives take care to avoid me,
14 my intimate friends have gone away
  and the guests in my house have
    forgotten me.
15 My slave-girls regard me as an intruder,
  a stranger as far as they are concerned.
16 My servant does not answer when I call
    him,
  I am obliged to beg favours from him!
17 My breath is unbearable to my wife,
  my stench to my own brothers.
18 Even the children look down on me,
  whenever I stand up, they start jeering
    at me.
19 All my dearest friends recoil from me in
    horror:
  those I loved best have turned against
    me.
20 My flesh is rotting under my skin,
  my bones are sticking out like teeth.
21 Pity me, pity me, my friends,
  since I have been struck by the hand of
    God.
22 Must you persecute me just as God does,
  and give my body no peace?

23 Will no one let my words be recorded,
  inscribed on some monument
24 with iron chisel and engraving tool,
  cut into the rock for ever?

18a Figures of oriental mythology.

25 I know that I have a living Defender[a]
and that he will rise up last, on the dust
of the earth.
26 After my awakening, he will set me close
to him,
and from my flesh I shall look on God.
27 He whom I shall see will take my part:
my eyes will be gazing on no stranger.
My heart sinks within me.
28 When you say, 'How can we confound
him?
What pretext can we discover against
him?'
29 You yourselves had best beware the sword,
since the wrath bursts into flame at
wicked deeds
and then you will learn that there is
indeed a judgement!

The course of justice admits of no exception

20 Zophar of Naamath spoke next. He
said:

2 My thoughts urge me to reply to this,
and hence the impatience that grips me.
3 I have put up with prating that outrages
me
and now my mind inspires me with an
answer.
4 Do you not know, that since time began
and human beings were set on the
earth,
5 the triumph of the wicked has always been
brief,
and the sinner's gladness has never
lasted long?
6 Towering to the sky he may have been,
his head touching the clouds;
7 but he vanishes, like a phantom, once for
all,
while those who used to see him, ask,
'Where is he?'
8 Like a dream that leaves no trace he takes
his flight,
like a vision in the night he flies away.
9 The eye accustomed to see him sees him
no more,

his home will never set eyes on him
again.
10 His sons will have to reimburse the poor
and his children pay back his riches.
11 His bones used to be full of youthful
vigour:
and there it lies, in the dust with him,
now!
12 Evil was sweet to his mouth,
he would shelter it under his tongue;
13 cultivating it carefully,
he would let it linger on his palate.
14 Such food goes bad in his belly,
working inside him like the poison of a
viper.
15 Now he has to vomit up the wealth that he
has swallowed,
God makes him disgorge it.
16 He used to suck vipers' venom,
and the tongue of the adder kills him.
17 No more will he know the streams of oil
or the torrents of honey and cream.
18 When he gives back his winnings, his
cheerfulness will fade,
and the satisfied air he had when
business was thriving.
19 Since he once destroyed the huts of the
poor,
plundering houses instead of building
them up,
20 since his avarice could never be satisfied,
now all his hoarding will not save him;
21 since nothing could escape his greed,
his prosperity will not last.
22 When he has everything he needs, want
will seize him,
and misery will light on him with all its
force.
23 On him God looses all his burning
wrath,
hurling against his flesh a hail of
arrows.

19a Technical term for the closest relative, the avenger of
blood. Having no belief in life after death, Job yet bursts the
bounds of his belief and asserts that he will somehow see his
vindication by God himself. 'Rise up' is a technical term for
the action of defendant or judge.

²⁴ If he escapes the weapons of iron,
the bow of bronze will transfix him.
²⁵ Out of his back sticks an arrow,
from his gall a shining point.
The terrors advance on him,
²⁶ all the hidden darknesses are waiting to
carry him off.
A fire unlit by human hand devours him,
and consumes what is left in his tent.
²⁷ The heavens lay bare his iniquity,
and the earth rises up against him.
²⁸ The income of his house pours away,
like the torrents, on the day of
retribution.
²⁹ Such is the fate God reserves for the
wicked,
the inheritance he assigns to the
accursed!

Facts give the lie

21 Job spoke next. He said:

² Listen carefully to my words;
let this be the consolation you allow me.
³ Permit me to speak in my turn;
you may jeer when I have spoken.
⁴ Is my complaint just about a fellow-
mortal?
I have good grounds to be perturbed!
⁵ Give your attention to me; you will be
dumbfounded
and will place your hand over your
mouth.
⁶ I myself am appalled at the very thought,
and my flesh creeps.
⁷ Why do the wicked still live on,
their power increasing with their age?
⁸ They see their posterity assured,
and their offspring secure before their
eyes.
⁹ The peace of their houses has nothing to
fear,
the rod that God wields is not for them.
¹⁰ No mishap with their bull at breeding-
time,
nor miscarriage with their cow at
calving.

¹¹ They let their infants frisk like lambs,
their children dance like deer.
¹² They sing to the tambourine and harp,
and rejoice to the sound of the pipe.
¹³ They end their lives in happiness
and go down in peace to Sheol.
¹⁴ Yet these are the ones who say to God, 'Go
away!
We do not want to learn your ways.
¹⁵ What is the point of our serving Shaddai?
What should we gain from praying to
him?'
¹⁶ Surely they have won their own
prosperity,
since God is kept so far from their
plans?
¹⁷ Do we often see the light of the wicked
put out,
or disaster overtake him,
or the retribution of God destroy his
possessions,
¹⁸ or the wind blow him away like a straw,
or a whirlwind carry him off like chaff?
¹⁹ So God is storing up punishment for his
children?
But the wicked himself should be
punished, and should know it!
²⁰ He himself should witness his own ruin,
and himself drink the anger of Shaddai.
²¹ Once he is gone, what joy can he gain
from his family,
once the number of his months has been
cut off?
²² But who can teach wisdom to God,
to him who is judge of those on high?
²³ And again: one person dies in the fullness
of strength,
in all possible happiness and ease,
²⁴ thighs padded with fat
and the marrow in the bones good and
moist.
²⁵ Another dies in bitterness of heart,
never having tasted happiness.
²⁶ They lie together down in the dust
and the worms soon cover them both.

39   READ JOB 21:7–34.

Do we often see the light of the wicked put out, or disaster overtake him?—JOB 21:17

WHY BAD THINGS HAPPEN TO GOOD PEOPLE

Perhaps you wonder, "Why are the wicked joyous? Why do they live in luxury? Why don't they have to strive like I do?"

The reason is that they who have not signed up to strive for the crown are not required to undergo the labors of the contest. Those who haven't gone down to the track don't smear themselves with oil, nor get covered with dust. Trouble comes only to those on their way to glory. The perfumed spectators prefer to watch, not to join in the struggle, nor to endure the sun, the heat, the dust, and the rain.

So those who have devoted themselves to pleasures, luxury, robbery, gain or honors are spectators rather than combatants. They have the profit of labor but not the fruits of virtue. They love their ease. By cunning and wickedness they heap up riches. But they will pay the penalty of their iniquity, though it be late in coming. Their rest will be in hell, yours in paradise. Thus, Job said beautifully that "watch is kept at his tomb" (verse 32), for they cannot have the calm of quiet rest that he enjoys who shall rise again.   ST. AMBROSE, 339–397

YOU WILL FIND THE NEXT READING AT PSALM 19.

27 Oh, I know what is in your minds,
     what you so spitefully think about me!
28 'What has become of the great lord's
          house,' you say,
     'where is the tent where the wicked
          used to live?'
29 Have you never questioned people who
          travel,
     do you not understand the testimony
          they give:
30 on the day of disaster, the wicked is
          spared,
     on the day of retribution, he is kept
          safe?
31 And who is there then to reproach him for
          his deeds
     and to pay him back for the things he
          has done?
32 He is carried away to the cemetery,
     and a watch is kept at his tomb.
33 The clods of the ravine lie easy on him,
     and the whole population walk behind.

34 So what sense is there in your empty
          consolation?
     your answers are the left-overs of
          infidelity!

*Admission of guilt leads to reconciliation
with God*

22 Eliphaz of Teman spoke next. He said:

2 Can a human being contribute anything to
          God,
     when even someone intelligent can
          benefit only himself?
3 Does Shaddai derive any benefit from
          your uprightness,
     or profit from your blameless conduct?
4 Do you think he is punishing you for your
          piety
     and bringing you to justice for that?
5 No, for your great wickedness, more
          likely,
     for your unlimited sins!

[629]

6 You have exacted unearned pledges from
your brothers,
stripped people naked of their clothes,
7 failed to give water to the thirsty
and refused bread to the hungry;
8 handed the land over to a strong man,
for some favoured person to move in,
9 sent widows away empty-handed
and crushed the arms of orphans.
10 No wonder, then, if snares are all around
you,
and sudden terrors make you afraid;
11 if light has turned to darkness, so that you
cannot see,
and you have been submerged in the
flood.
12 Does not God live high in the heavens,
does he not see the zenith of the
stars?
13 And because he is up there, you have said,
'What does God know?
Can he judge through the dark
cloud?
14 The clouds, to him, are an impenetrable
veil,
as he goes his way on the rim of the
heavens.'
15 And will you still follow the ancient
trail
trodden by the wicked,
16 those who were borne off before their
time,
whose foundations were swamped by a
flood,
17 for having said to God, 'Go away!
What can Shaddai do to us?'
18 Yet he himself had filled their houses with
good things,
although excluded from the plans of the
wicked!
19 At such a spectacle, the upright rejoice,
and the innocent deride them:
20 'See how our enemies have been
destroyed!
See how their wealth has perished in
the flames!'

21 Well then! Make peace with him, be
reconciled,
and all your happiness will be restored
to you.
22 Welcome the teaching from his lips,
and keep his words close to your
heart.
23 If you return, humbled, to Shaddai
and drive wickedness far from your
tent,
24 if you lay your gold down on the dust,
Ophir down among the pebbles of the
torrent,
25 Shaddai will be bars of gold to you
and silver piled in heaps.
26 Then Shaddai will be all your delight,
and you will lift your face to God.
27 You will pray, and he will hear;
and you will be able to fulfil your vows.
28 Whatever you undertake will go well,
and light will shine on your path;
29 for he casts down the pride of the
arrogant,
but he saves those of downcast eyes.
30 He rescues anyone who is innocent;
have your hands clean, and you will be
saved.

God is far off, and evil triumphant

23 Job spoke next. He said:

2 My lament is still rebellious;
despite my groans, his hand is just as
heavy.
3 Will no one help me to know
how to travel to his dwelling?
4 I should set out my case to him,
advancing any number of grievances.
5 Then I could learn his defence, every word
of it,
taking note of everything he said to me.
6 Would he put all his strength into this
debate with me?
No, he would only have to give his
attention to me,
7 to recognise his opponent as upright
and so I should win my case for ever.

8 If I go to the east, he is not there;
   or to the west, I still cannot see him.
9 If I seek him in the north, he is not to be
      found,
   invisible as ever, if I turn to the south.
10 And yet he knows every step I take!
   Let him test me in the crucible: I shall
      come out pure gold.
11 My footsteps have followed close in his,
   I have walked in his way without
      swerving;
12 I have not neglected the commandment of
      his lips,
   in my heart I have cherished the words
      of his mouth.
13 But once he has made up his mind, who
      can change it?
   Whatever he plans, that he carries out.
14 No doubt, then, but he will carry out my
      sentence,
   like so many other decrees that he has
      made.
15 That is why I am full of fear before him,
   and the more I think, the greater grows
      my dread of him.
16 God has undermined my courage,
   Shaddai has filled me with fear.
17 The darkness having failed to destroy me,
   I am plunged back into obscurity by
      him!

24 Why does Shaddai not make known
      the times he has fixed;
   why do his faithful never see his Days?ᵃ
2 The wicked move boundary-marks
      away,
   they carry off flock and shepherd.
3 They drive away the orphan's donkey,
   as security, they seize the widow's ox.
4 The needy have to keep out of the way,
   poor country people have to keep out of
      sight.
5 Like wild desert donkeys, they go out to
      work,
   searching from dawn for food,
   and at evening for something on which
      to feed their children.

6 They go harvesting in the field of some
      scoundrel,
   they go pilfering in the vineyards of the
      wicked.
10 They go about naked, lacking clothes,
   and starving while they carry the
      sheaves.
11 Two little walls, their shelter at high noon;
   parched with thirst, they have to tread
      the winepress.
7 They spend the night naked, lacking
      clothes,
   with no covering against the cold.
8 Mountain rainstorms cut them through,
   unsheltered, they hug the rocks.
9 The orphan child is torn from the breast,
   the child of the poor is exacted as
      security.
12 From the towns come the groans of the
      dying
   and the gasp of the wounded crying for
      help.
   Yet God remains deaf to prayer!

13 In contrast, there are those who reject the
      light:
   who know nothing of its ways
   and who do not frequent its paths.
14 When all is dark the murderer leaves his
      bed
   to kill the poor and needy.
   During the night the thief goes on the
      prowl,
16a   breaking into houses while the darkness
      lasts.
15 The eye of the adulterer watches for
      twilight,
   'No one will see me,' he mutters
   as he masks his face.
16b In the daytime they keep out of sight,
   these people who do not want to know
      the light.
17 For all of them, morning is a time of
      shadow dark as death,

24a i.e., his Days of Retribution, as the Day of Yahweh in
prophetic writings.

since that is when they know what
fear is.[b]

25 Is this not so? Who can prove me a liar
or show that my words have no
substance?

A hymn to God's omnipotence

25 Bildad of Shuah spoke next. He said:

2 What sovereignty, what awe, is his
who creates peace on his heights!
3 Who can count his armies?
Against whom does his lightning not
surge forth?
4 Could anyone think God regards him as
virtuous,
the child of woman as pure!
5 Why, the very moon lacks lustre,
the very stars seem impure to him!
6 How much less a human, this maggot,
the child of man, this worm![a]

26 5 The Shadows[a] tremble underneath
the earth,
the waters and their denizens are
afraid.
6 Before his eyes, Sheol is bare,
Perdition itself is uncovered.
7 He it was who spread the North above the
void
and poised the earth on nothingness.
8 He fastens up the waters in his clouds,
without the clouds giving way under
their weight.
9 He covers the face of the full moon,
spreading his cloud across it.
10 He has traced a ring on the surface of the
waters,
at the boundary between light and dark.
11 The pillars of the heavens tremble,
awe-struck at his threats.
12 By his power, he has whipped up the Sea,
by his skill, he has crushed Rahab.
13 His breath has made the heavens
luminous,
his hand transfixed the Fleeing Serpent.

14 This is only a fraction of what he has done
and all we catch of it is the feeblest echo.
But who can conceive the thunder of his
power?

Bildad's rhetoric is beside the point

26 Job spoke next. He said:

2 To one so weak, what a help you are,
for the arm that is powerless, what a
rescuer!
3 What excellent advice you give the
unlearned,
you are never at a loss for a helpful
suggestion!
4 For whom are these words of yours
intended
and whence comes that wit you are now
displaying?

*Job reaffirms his innocence while
acknowledging God's power*

27 And Job continued his solemn dis-
course. He said:

2 I swear by the living God who denies me
justice,
by Shaddai who has filled me with
bitterness,
3 that as long as a shred of life is left in me,
and the breath of God breathes in my
nostrils,
4 my lips will never speak evil
nor my tongue utter any lie.
5 Far from admitting you to be in the right,
I shall maintain my integrity to my
dying day.
6 I take my stand on my uprightness, I shall
not stir:
in my heart I need not be ashamed of
my days.

24b vv. 18–24 are conjecturally placed after 27:23. The text is
corrupt.

25a 26:1–4 are conjecturally placed after 26:14. They belong
to Job's speech.

26a i.e., the powerless dead.

7 Let my enemy meet the fate of the
     wicked,
   my adversary, the lot of the evil-doer!
8 For what hope does the godless have when
     he prays
   and raises his soul to God?
9 Is God likely to hear his cries
   when disaster descends on him?
10 Did he make Shaddai all his delight,
   calling on him at every turn?
11 But I am showing you the way that God
     works,
   making no secret of Shaddai's designs.
12 And if you had all understood them for
     yourselves,
   you would not have wasted your breath
     in empty words.

Discourse of Zophar; the fate of the wicked

13 This is the fate that God assigns to the
     wicked,
   the inheritance that the violent receive
     from Shaddai.
14 Though he have many children, it is but
     for the sword;
   his descendants will never have enough
     to eat.
15 Plague will bury those he leaves behind
     him,
   and their widows will have no chance to
     mourn them.
16 Though he amass silver like dust
   and gather fine clothes like clay,
17 let him gather!—some good man will
     wear them,
   while his silver is shared among the
     upright.
18 All he has built himself is a spider's web,
   made himself a watchman's shack.
19 He goes to bed rich, but never again:
   he wakes to find it has all gone.
20 Terror assails him in broad daylight,
   and at night a whirlwind sweeps him
     off.
21 An east wind picks him up and drags him
     away,
   snatching him up from his homestead.

22 Pitilessly he is turned into a target,
   and forced to flee from the hands that
     menace him.
23 His downfall is greeted with applause,
   he is hissed wherever he goes.

24 18acb He is no more than a straw
       floating on the water,
   his estate is accursed throughout the
     land,
   nobody goes near his vineyard.
19 As drought and heat make snow
     disappear,
   so does Sheol anyone who has sinned.
20 The womb that shaped him forgets him
   and his name is recalled no longer.
   Thus wickedness is blasted as a tree is
     struck.
21 He used to ill-treat the childless woman
   and show no kindness to the widow.
22 But he who lays mighty hold on tyrants
   rises up to take away a life that seemed
     secure.
23 He let him build his hopes on false
     security,
   but kept his eyes on every step he took.
24 He had his time of glory, now he vanishes,
   wilting like the saltwort once it is
     picked,
   and withering like an ear of corn.

Wisdom is beyond human reach

28 Silver has its mines,
   and gold a place for refining.
2 Iron is extracted from the earth,
   the smelted rocks yield copper.
3 Man makes an end of darkness,
   to the utmost limit he digs
   the black rock in shadow dark as death.
4 Foreigners bore into ravines
   in unfrequented places,
   swinging suspended far from human
     beings.
5 That earth from which bread comes
   is ravaged underground by fire.
6 There, the rocks have veins of sapphire
   and their dust contains gold.

7 That is a path unknown to birds of prey,
  unseen by the eye of any vulture;
8 a path not trodden by the lordly beasts,
  where no lion ever walked.
9 Man attacks the flint,
  upturning mountains by their roots.
10 He cuts canals through the rock,
  on the watch for anything precious.
11 He explores the sources of rivers,
  bringing hidden things to light.
12 But where does Wisdom come from?
  Where is Intelligence to be found?

13 No human being knows the way to her,
  she is not to be found on earth where
    they live.
14 'She is not in me,' says the Abyss;
  'Nor here,' replies the Sea.
15 She cannot be bought with solid gold,
  nor paid for with any weight of silver,
16 nor valued against gold of Ophir,
  precious agate or sapphire.
17 Neither gold nor glass compares with her,
  for her, a vase of fine gold would be no
    exchange,
18 let alone coral or crystal:
    better go fishing for Wisdom than for
      pearls!
19 Topaz from Cush is worthless in
    comparison,
  and gold, even refined, is valueless.
20 But where does Wisdom come from?
  Where is Intelligence to be found?
21 She cannot be seen by any living
    creature,
  she is hidden from the birds of the sky.
22 Perdition and Death both say,
  'We have heard only rumours of her.'
23 God alone understands her path
  and knows where she is to be found.
24 (For he sees to the remotest parts of the
    earth,
  and observes all that lies under heaven.)
25 When he willed to give weight to the
    wind
  and measured out the waters with a
    gauge,

26 when he imposed a law on the rain
  and mapped a route for thunderclaps to
    follow,
27 then he saw and evaluated her,
  looked her through and through,
    assessing her.
28 Then he said to human beings,
  'Wisdom?—that is fear of the Lord;
  Intelligence?—avoidance of evil.'

Job's complaints and apologia

29 And Job continued his solemn discourse. He said:

2 Will no one bring back to me the months
    that have gone,
  and the days when God was my
    guardian,
3 when his lamp shone over my head,
  and his light was my guide in the
    darkness?
4 Shall I ever see my days of harvest
    again
  when God protected my tent;
5 when Shaddai still dwelt with me,
  and my children were around me;
6 when my feet were bathed in milk,
  and streams of oil poured from the
    rocks?
7 When I went out to the gate of the city,
  when I took my seat in the square,
8 as soon as I appeared, the young men
    stepped aside,
  and the old men rose to their feet.
9 Men of note broke off their speeches,
  and put their hands over their
    mouths;
10 the voices of rulers were silenced,
  and their tongues stayed still in their
    mouths.
21 They*a* waited anxiously to hear me,
  and listened in silence to what I had to
    say.
22 When I had finished, no one contradicted,

29a vv. 21–25 are inserted here because they follow on better
from v. 10 and lead up to v. 11.

my words dropping on them, one
by one.

²³ They waited for me as though for rain,
open-mouthed as though for a late
shower.

²⁴ If I smiled at them, it was too good to be
true,
they watched my face for the least sign
of favour.

²⁵ As their chief, I told them which course to
take,
like a king living among his troops,
and I led them wherever I chose.

¹¹ On hearing me, people congratulated me,
on seeing me, people deferred to me,

¹² because I freed the poor in distress
and the orphan who had no helper.

¹³ The dying man's blessing rested on me
and I gave the widow's heart cause to
rejoice.

¹⁴ Uprightness I wore as a garment,
fair judgement was my cloak and my
turban.

¹⁵ I was eyes for the blind,
and feet for the lame.

¹⁶ Who but me was father of the poor?
The stranger's case had a hearing from
me.

¹⁷ I used to break the fangs of the wicked,
and snatch their prey from their
jaws.

¹⁸ And I used to say, 'I shall die in honour,
after days as numerous as the sand.

¹⁹ My roots can reach the water,
the dews of night settle on my leaves.

²⁰ My glory will be for ever new
and the bow in my hand for ever
strong.'

30 And now I am the laughing-stock
of people who are younger than
I am
and whose parents I would have disdained
to put with the dogs guarding my
flock.

² And what use to me was the strength of
their hands?—
enfeebled as they were,

³ worn out by want and hunger,
for they used to gnaw the roots of the
thirsty ground—
that place of gloom, ruin and
desolation—

⁴ they used to pick saltwort among the
scrub,
making their meals off roots of broom.

⁵ Outlawed from human company,
which raised hue and cry against them,
as against thieves,

⁶ they made their homes in the sides of
ravines,
in holes in the earth or in clefts of rock.

⁷ You could hear them braying from the
bushes
as they huddled together in the thistles.

⁸ Children of scoundrels, worse, nameless
people,
the very outcasts of society!

⁹ And these are the ones who now make up
songs about me
and use me as a byword!

¹⁰ Filled with disgust, they keep their
distance,
on seeing me, they spit without
restraint.

¹¹ And since God has loosened my bowstring and afflicted me,
they too throw off the bridle in my
presence.

¹² Their brats surge forward on my right,
to see when I am having a little peace,
and advance on me with threatening
strides.

¹³ They cut off all means of escape
seizing the chance to destroy me, and no
one stops them.

¹⁴ They move in, as if through a wide breach,
and I go tumbling beneath the rubble.

¹⁵ Terror rounds on me,
my confidence is dispersed as though by
the wind,
my hope of safety vanishes like a cloud.

16 And now the life in me trickles away,
days of grief have gripped me.
17 At night-time sickness saps my bones
I am gnawed by wounds that never
sleep.
18 Violently, he has caught me by my clothes,
has gripped me by the collar of my coat.
19 He has thrown me into the mud;
I am no more than dust and ashes.

20 I cry to you, and you give me no answer;
I stand before you, but you take no
notice.
21 You have grown cruel to me,
and your strong hand torments me
unmercifully.
22 You carry me away astride the wind
and blow me to pieces in a tempest.
23 Yes, I know that you are taking me
towards death,
to the common meeting-place of all the
living.

24 Yet have I ever laid a hand on the poor
when they cried out for justice in
calamity?
25 Have I not wept for those whose life is
hard,
felt pity for the penniless?
26 I hoped for happiness, but sorrow came;
I looked for light, but there was
darkness.
27 My stomach seethes, is never still,
days of suffering have struck me.
28 Sombre I go, yet no one comforts me,
and if I rise in the council, I rise to weep.
29 I have become brother to the jackal
and companion to the ostrich.
30 My skin has turned black on me,
my bones are burnt with fever.
31 My harp is tuned to dirges,
my pipe to the voice of mourners.

Job's apologia

31 I had made an agreement with my eyes
not to linger on any virgin.
2 Now what portion does God allot from
above,

what fate does Shaddai apportion from
his heaven—
3 if not the disasters appropriate to the
wicked
and the calamities fit for evil-doers?
4 But surely he sees how I behave,
does he not count all my steps?
5 Have I been a fellow-traveller with
falsehood,
or hastened my steps towards deceit?
6 Let him weigh me on accurate scales:
then he, God, will recognise my
integrity!
7 If my feet have wandered from the
rightful path,
or if my eyes have led my heart astray,
or if my hands are smirched with any
stain,
8 let someone else eat what I have sown
and let my young shoots all be rooted
out.
9 If my heart has been seduced by a woman,
or if I have lurked at my neighbour's
door,
10 let my wife go and grind for someone else,
let others have intercourse with her!
11 For I would have committed a sin of lust,
a crime punishable by the law,
12 a fire, indeed, burning all to Perdition,
which would have devoured my whole
revenue.
13 If I have ever infringed the rights of
slave
or slave-girl in legal actions against
me—
14 what shall I do, when God stands up?
What shall I say, when he holds his
assize?
15 Did he not create them in the womb
like me,
the same God forming us in the womb?
38 If my land cries for vengeance against me
and its furrows weep in concert,
39 if I have eaten its produce without paying,
and caused the death of its owners,
40a let brambles grow instead of wheat,
rank weeds instead of barley!

¹⁶ Have I been insensible to the needs of the
poor,
or let a widow's eyes grow dim?
¹⁷ Have I eaten my bit of bread on my own
without sharing it with the orphan?
¹⁸ I, whom God has fostered father-like from
childhood,
and guided since I left my mother's
womb,
¹⁹ have I ever seen a wretch in need of
clothing,
or the poor with nothing to wear,
²⁰ without his having cause to bless me from
his heart,
as he felt the warmth of the fleece from
my lambs?
²¹ Have I raised my hand against an orphan,
presuming on my credit at the gate?
²² If so, let my shoulder fall from its socket,
let my arm break off at the elbow!
²³ For the terror of God would fall on me
and I could not then stand my ground
before his majesty.

²⁴ Have I put my faith in gold,
saying to fine gold, 'Ah, my security'?
²⁵ Have I ever gloated over my great
wealth,
or the riches that my hands have won?
²⁶ Or has the sight of the sun in its glory,
or the glow of the moon as it walked
the sky,
²⁷ secretly stolen my heart,
so that I blew them a kiss?
²⁸ That too would be a criminal offence,
to have denied the supreme God.
²⁹ Have I rejoiced at my enemy's misfortune,
or exulted when disaster overtook
him?—
³⁰ I, who would not allow my tongue to sin
or to lay his life under a curse.
³¹ The people of my tent, did they not say,
'Will anyone name a person whom he
has not filled with meat?'
³² No stranger ever had to sleep outside,
my door was always open to the
traveller.

³³ Have I ever concealed my transgression
from others
or kept my fault a secret in my
breast?
³⁴ Have I ever stood in fear of common
gossip,
or dreaded any family's contempt,
and so kept quiet, not venturing out of
doors?
³⁵ Will no one give me a hearing?
I have said my last word; now let
Shaddai reply!
When my adversary has drafted his writ
against me
³⁶ I shall wear it on my shoulder,
and bind it round my head like a royal
turban.
³⁷ I shall give him an account of my every
step
and go as boldly as a prince to meet
him.

^{40b} End of the words of Job.

Elihu joins the discussion

32 These three men stopped arguing with
Job, because he was convinced of his uprightness. ² But Elihu son of Barachel the
Buzite, of the clan of Ram, became very angry.
He fumed with rage against Job for thinking
that he was right and God was wrong; ³ and he
was equally angry with the three friends for
giving up the argument and thus putting God
in the wrong. ⁴ While they and Job were talking, Elihu had waited, because they were older
than he was; ⁵ but when he saw that the three
men had not another word to say in answer,
his anger burst out. ⁶ And Elihu son of
Barachel the Buzite began to speak. He said:

Prologue

I am still young,
and you are old,
so I was shy and hesitant
to tell you what I know.
⁷ I thought, 'Age ought to speak,
advancing years will convey wisdom.'

8 There is, you see, a spirit residing in
    humanity,
    the breath of God conferring
      intelligence.
9 Great age does not give wisdom,
    nor seniority fair judgement.
10 And so I ask you for a hearing;
    now it is my turn to tell what I know.
11 Up to now, I was hanging on your
    words,
    I paid attention to your arguments
    as each of you chose his words.
12 I paid very close attention;
    and I see that none of you has
      confounded Job,
    not one of you has refuted what he says.
13 So do not say, 'We have found wisdom;
    our teaching is divine and not human.'
14 I am not going to follow the same line of
    argument;
    my reply to Job will be couched in
      different terms.

15 They are nonplussed for an answer,
    words have failed them.
16 I have been waiting. Since they do not
    speak,
    since they have given up the argument,
17 now I shall have my say,
    my turn has come to say what I know.
18 For I am full of words
    and forced to speak by a spirit within
      me;
19 within me, it feels like new wine seeking a
    vent,
    bursting out of new wine-skins.
20 To gain relief, I must speak,
    I must open my lips and reply.
21 I shall not take anyone's side,
    I shall not flatter anyone.
22 I do not know how to flatter—
    or my Creator would make short work
      of me.

Job's presumption

33 So, Job, please listen to my words
    and attend to all I have to say.

2 Now as I open my mouth,
    and my tongue shapes words against
      my palate,
3 I shall utter words of wisdom from the
    heart,
    my lips will speak in all sincerity.
5 Refute me, if you can.
    Prepare yourself, take up your position!
6 Look, I am your equal, not some god,
    like you I was moulded out of clay.
4 God's was the spirit that made me,
    Shaddai's the breath that gave me life.
7 No fear of me, therefore, need affright
    you,
    my hand will not lie heavy over you.
8 How could you say in my hearing—
    for the sound of your words did not
      escape me—
9 'I am clean, and sinless,
    I am pure, without fault.
10 But he keeps inventing excuses against me
    and regards me as his enemy.
11 He puts me in the stocks,
    he watches my every path'?
12 In saying so, I tell you, you are wrong:
    for God is greater than any human
      being.
13 Why then quarrel with him
    for not replying to you, word for
      word?
14 God speaks first in one way,
    and then in another, although we do not
      realise it.
15 In dreams and in night-visions,
    when slumber has settled on humanity
    and people are asleep in bed,
16 he speaks in someone's ear,
    frightens him with apparitions
17 to turn him from what he is doing
    and to put an end to his pride.
18 And thus he preserves his soul from the
    abyss,
    his life from passing down the Canal.
19 Or again, he corrects by the sufferings of
    the sick-bed,
    when someone's bones tremble
      continuously

20 and the thought of food revolts him,
  however tasty it is,
21 and his flesh rots away while you
  watch it
  and the bones beneath begin to show,
22 and his soul is drawing nearer to the
  abyss
  and his life to the dwelling of the
  dead.
23 Then, if there is an Angel near him,
  a Mediator, one in a thousand,
  to remind him where his duty lies,
24 to take pity on him and to say,
  'Spare him from going down to the
  abyss:
  I have found the ransom for his life,'
25 his flesh will recover its childhood
  freshness,
  he will return to the days of his youth.
26 He will pray to God who has restored him
  to favour,
  and will come into his presence with
  joy.
  He will tell others how he has received
  saving justice
27 and sing this hymn before his
  companions,
  'I sinned and left the path of right,
  but God has not punished me as my sin
  deserved.
28 He has spared my soul from going down
  to the abyss
  and is making my life see the light.'
29 All this is what God keeps doing
  again and yet again for human beings,
30 to snatch souls back from the abyss
  and to make the light of the living still
  shine.
31 Pay attention, Job, listen to me:
  keep quiet, I have more to say.
32 If you have anything to say, refute me,
  speak out, for I would gladly accept that
  you are upright.
33 If not, then listen to me:
  keep quiet, and I will teach you
  wisdom.

The three sages have failed to justify God

34

Elihu continued his speech. He said:
2 And now, you sages, listen to what I say,
  lend me your ears, you learned men.
3 The ear distinguishes the value of what is
  said,
  just as the palate can tell one food from
  another.
4 Let us consider together God's ruling
  and decide what we all mean by good.
5 Job has been saying, 'I am upright
  and God denies me fair judgement.
6 My judge is treating me cruelly,
  my wound is incurable, for no fault of
  mine.'
7 Can anyone else exist like Job,
  who laps up mockery like water,
8 who consorts with evil-doers
  and marches in step with the wicked?
9 Did he not say, 'No one derives any benefit
  from enjoying the society of God'?

10 Listen to me then, like intelligent people.
  Far be evil from God
  or injustice from Shaddai!
11 For he pays people back for what they do,
  treating each as his own conduct
  deserves.
12 Be sure of it: God never does wrong,
  Shaddai does not pervert what is just.
13 Did someone else entrust the world to his
  care
  was he given charge of the universe by
  someone else?
14 If he were to recall his spirit,
  to concentrate his breath back in
  himself,
15 all flesh would instantly perish
  and all people would return to dust.
16 If you have any intelligence, listen to this,
  lend your ear to the sound of my words.
17 Could an enemy of fair judgement ever
  govern?
  Would you dare condemn the Upright
  One, the Almighty,

18 who says to a king, 'You are a scoundrel!'
and to nobles, 'You are wicked!',
19 who is unimpressed by princes
and makes no distinction between rich
and poor,
since all alike have been made by him?
20 They die suddenly, at dead of night,
they perish—these great ones—and
disappear:
it costs him no effort to remove a tyrant.
21 For his eyes keep watch on human ways,
and he observes every step.
22 No darkness, no shadow dark as death
where wrong-doers can hide!
23 He serves no writ on anyone,
no summons to appear before God's
court:
24 he breaks the powerful without enquiry
and sets up others in their places.
25 He knows the sort of things they do!
He overthrows them at night, to be
trampled on.
26 He beats them like criminals
chained up for all to see,
27 since they have turned their backs
on him,
having understood so little of his
ways
28 as to make the cries of the weak rise to
him
and let him hear the appeal of the
afflicted.

29 But if he is still silent and no one can move
him,
if he veils his face, so that no one can see
him,
he is taking pity on nations and
individuals,
30 is setting some wrong-doer free from
the meshes of affliction.
31 When such a one says to God,
'I was misled, I shall not do wrong any
more;
32 although I have sinned, instruct me;
although I did wrong, I will not do it
again,'

33 in your opinion, should he punish such a
one—
you who have rejected his decisions?
This is for you to decide—not for
me!—
so kindly enlighten us!
34 Ordinary sensible people, however, will
say to me,
and so will any sage who has been
listening to me,
35 'Job's words are spoken without any
knowledge,
what he says shows no intelligence.
36 Kindly examine him thoroughly,
since his answers imply that he is a
criminal.
37 For to his sin he now adds rebellion,
bringing law to an end among us
and heaping abuse on God.'

God's transcendence

35 Elihu continued his speech. He said:

2 Do you think you can prove yourself
upright
and establish your uprightness before
God
3 by daring to say to him, 'What does it
matter to you,
or how does it benefit me, whether I
have sinned or not?'
4 Very well, I shall tell you
and your friends as well.

5 Take a look at the skies and see,
observe how high the clouds are above
you.
6 If you sin, how can you affect him?
If you heap up crimes, what effect has it
on him?
7 If you are upright, what do you give him,
what benefit does he receive at your
hands?
8 Your wickedness affects only your
fellows,
your uprightness, other human
beings.

9 They too groan under the weight of
    oppression,
      they cry for help under the tyranny of
      the mighty,
10 but none of them thinks of saying, 'Where
    is God, my Maker,
      who makes glad songs ring out at night,
11 who has made us more intelligent than
    wild animals
      wiser than birds in the sky?'
12 Cry they may, but get no answer,
      to be spared from the arrogance of the
      wicked.
13 Of course God does not listen to
    trivialities,
      Shaddai pays no attention to them.
14 And how much less when you say, 'I
    cannot see him,
      my case is open and I am waiting for
      him.'
15 Or, 'His anger never punishes,
      he does not seem aware of human
      rebellion.'
16 Hence, when Job speaks, he talks
    nonsense,
      ignorantly babbling on and on.

The real meaning of Job's sufferings

36 Elihu went on speaking. He said:

2 Be patient a little longer while I explain,
    for I have more to say on God's behalf.
3 I shall range far afield for my arguments
    to prove my Maker just.
4 I guarantee, nothing I shall say will be
    untrue:
    you have a man of sound learning here.
5 God does not reject anyone whose heart is
    pure
6   or let the sinner live on in all his power.
  He does accord fair judgement to the
    afflicted;
7   he does uphold what the upright
    deserve.
  When he raises kings to thrones,
    if they grow proud of their unending
    rule,

8 then he fetters them with chains,
    they are caught in the bonds of
    affliction.
9 He shows them the import of their deeds,
    of the sins of pride they have
    committed.
10 In their ears he sounds a warning,
    ordering them to turn back from doing
    wrong.
11 If they take notice and obey him,
    the rest of their days are prosperous
    and the years pass pleasantly.
12 If not, they go down the Canal
    and perish in their stupidity.
13 The stubborn, who cherish their anger
    and do not cry for help when he chains
    them,
14 die in the bloom of youth
    or live among the male prostitutes of
    the temple.
15 But God saves the afflicted by his
    affliction,
    warning him in his misery.
16 You, too, he would like to snatch from
    torment.
  While you were enjoying boundless
    abundance,
    with rich food piled high on your table,
17 you did not bring the wicked to trial
    and did not give fair judgement to the
    orphan.
18 Beware of being led astray by abundance,
    of being corrupted by expensive
    presents.
19 Take the powerful to law, not merely the
    penniless,
    those whose arm is strong, not merely
    the weak.
20 Do not crush people you do not know
    to install your relations in their place.
21 Avoid any tendency to wrong-doing,
    for this is why affliction is testing you
    now.

Hymn to God's omnipotence

22 See, God is sublime in his strength
    and who can teach lessons as he does?

23 Who has even told him which course to
take,
or dared to say to him, 'You have done
wrong'?

24 Consider, rather, how you may praise his
work,
a theme that many have sung.

25 This is something that everyone can see,
gazing, as we do, from afar.

26 Yes, the greatness of God exceeds our
knowledge,
the number of his years is past counting.

27 It is he who makes the raindrops small
and pulverises the rain into mist.

28 And the clouds then pour this out,
sending it streaming down on the
human race.

31 By these means, he sustains the peoples,
giving them plenty to eat.

29 And who can fathom how he spreads the
clouds,
or why such crashes thunder from his
tent?

30 He spreads a mist before him
and covers the tops of the mountains.

32 He gathers up the lightning in his hands,
assigning it the mark where to strike.

33 His crashing gives warning of its coming,
anger flashes out against iniquity.

37 At this, my very heart quakes
and leaps out of its place.

2 Listen, oh listen, to the blast of his voice
and the sound that issues from his
mouth.

3 His lightning is hurled across the heaven,
it strikes to the extremities of earth.

4 After it comes a roaring sound,
God thunders with majestic voice.
He does not check his thunderbolts
until his voice resounds no more.

5 Yes, certainly God shows us marvels
and does great deeds that we cannot
understand.

6 When he says to the snow, 'Fall on the
earth!'
to the showers, 'Now rain hard!'

7 he brings all human activity to a standstill,
for everyone to acknowledge his work.

8 The animals go back to their dens
and take shelter in their lairs.

9 The storm wind comes from the Mansion
of the South,
and the north winds usher in the cold.

10 At the breath of God, ice comes next,
the surface of the waters hardens over.

11 He weighs the clouds down with moisture,
and the storm clouds radiate his
lightning.

12 He himself guides their wheeling motion
presiding over their seasonal changes.
They carry out his orders to the letter
all over this earthly world.

13 Whether to punish earth's peoples
or as a work of faithful love, he
despatches them.

14 Listen to this, Job, without flinching
and reflect on the marvellous works of
God.

15 Do you know how God controls them
or how his clouds make the lightning
flash?

16 Do you know how he balances the
clouds—
a miracle of consummate skill?

17 When your clothes are hot to your body
and the earth lies still under the south
wind,

18 can you, like him, stretch out the sky,
tempered like a mirror of cast metal?

19 Teach me what we should say to him:
but better discuss no further, since we
are in the dark.

20 Does he take note when I speak?
When human beings give orders, does
he take it in?

21 There are times when the light vanishes,
behind darkening clouds;
then comes the wind, sweeping them
away,

22 and brightness spreads from the
north.
God is clothed in fearful splendour:

23 he, Shaddai, is far beyond our reach.

Supreme in power, in equity,
    excelling in saving justice, yet no
      oppressor—
24 no wonder then that people fear him:
    everyone thoughtful holds him in awe!

Job must bow to the Creator's wisdom

38 Then from the heart of the tempest
    Yahweh gave Job his answer. He said:

2 Who is this, obscuring my intentions
    with his ignorant words?
3 Brace yourself like a fighter;
    I am going to ask the questions, and you
      are to inform me!
4 Where were you when I laid the earth's
      foundations?
    Tell me, since you are so well-informed!
5 Who decided its dimensions, do you
      know?
    Or who stretched the measuring line
      across it?
6 What supports its pillars at their bases?
    Who laid its cornerstone
7 to the joyful concert of the morning stars
    and unanimous acclaim of the sons of
      God?
8 Who pent up the sea behind closed
      doors
    when it leapt tumultuous from the
      womb,
9 when I wrapped it in a robe of mist
    and made black clouds its swaddling
      bands;
10 when I cut out the place I had decreed
      for it
    and imposed gates and a bolt?
11 'Come so far,' I said, 'and no further;
    here your proud waves must break!'

12 Have you ever in your life given orders to
      the morning
    or sent the dawn to its post,
13 to grasp the earth by its edges
    and shake the wicked out of it?
14 She turns it as red as a clay seal,
    she tints it as though it were a dress,
15 stealing the light from evil-doers
    and breaking the arm raised to strike.
16 Have you been right down to the sources
      of the sea
    and walked about at the bottom of the
      Abyss?
17 Have you been shown the gates of
      Death,
    have you seen the janitors of the
      Shadow dark as death?
18 Have you an inkling of the extent of the
      earth?
    Tell me all about it if you have!
19 Which is the way to the home of the Light,
    and where does darkness live?—
20 You could then show them the way to
      their proper places,
    you could put them on the path home
      again!
21 If you do know, you must have been born
      when they were,
    you must be very old by now!

22 Have you visited the place where the snow
      is stored?
    Have you seen the stores of hail,
23 which I keep for times of distress,
    for days of battle and war?
24 From which direction does the lightning
      fork,
    where in the world does the east wind
      blow itself out?
25 Who bores a channel for the downpour
    or clears the way for the rolling
      thunder
26 so that rain may fall on lands where no one
      lives,
    and the deserts void of human dwelling,
27 to meet the needs of the lonely wastes
    and make grass sprout on the thirsty
      ground?
28 Has the rain a father?
    Who begets the dewdrops?
29 What womb brings forth the ice,
    who gives birth to the frost of heaven,
30 when the waters grow hard as stone
    and the surface of the deep congeals?

³¹ Can you fasten the harness of the Pleiades,
    or untie Orion's bands?
³² Can you guide the Crown season by season
    and show the Bear and its cubs which
    way to go?
³³ Have you grasped the celestial laws?
    Could you make their writ run on the
    earth?
³⁴ Can your voice carry as far as the clouds
    and make the pent-up waters do your
    bidding?
³⁵ Will lightning flashes come at your
    command
    and answer, 'Here we are'?
³⁶ Who endowed the ibis with wisdom
    and gave the cock his intelligence?
³⁷ Whose skill details every cloud
    and tilts the water-skins of heaven
³⁸ until the dust solidifies
    and the cracks in the ground close up?

³⁹ Do you go hunting prey for the lioness;
    do you satisfy the hunger of young
    lions
⁴⁰ where they crouch in their den,
    waiting eagerly in the bushes?
⁴¹ Who makes provision for the raven
    when his little ones cry out to God
    craning their necks in search of food?

39

Do you know when mountain goats
    give birth?
    Have you ever watched deer in
    labour?
² Have you ever counted the months that
    they carry their young?
    Do you know when they give birth?
³ They crouch to drop their young,
    they get rid of their burdens
⁴ and the calves, having grown big and
    strong,
    go off into the desert and never come
    back to them.
⁵ Who has given the wild donkey his
    freedom,
    who has undone the harness of the
    brayer?

⁶ I have given him the wastelands as his
    home,
    the salt plain as his habitat.
⁷ He scorns the turmoil of the town,
    obeys no donkey-man's shouts.
⁸ The mountains are the pastures that he
    ranges
    in quest of anything green.
⁹ Is the wild ox willing to serve you
    or spend a night beside your manger?
¹⁰ If you tie a rope round his neck
    will he harrow the furrows for you?
¹¹ Can you rely on his massive strength
    and leave him to do your heavy work?
¹² Can you depend on him to come home
    and pile your grain on your threshing-
    floor?

¹³ Can the wing of the ostrich be compared
    with the plumage of stork or falcon?
¹⁴ She leaves her eggs on the ground
    with only earth to warm them;
¹⁵ forgetting that a foot may tread on them
    or a wild animal crush them.
¹⁶ Cruel to her chicks as if they were not
    hers,
    little she cares if her labour goes for
    nothing.
¹⁷ God, you see, has deprived her of wisdom
    and given her no share of intelligence.
¹⁸ Yet, if she bestirs herself to use her height,
    she can make fools of horse and rider
    too.

¹⁹ Are you the one who makes the horse so
    brave
    and covers his neck with flowing
    mane?
²⁰ Do you make him leap like a grasshopper?
    His haughty neighing inspires terror.
²¹ Exultantly he paws the soil of the valley,
    and charges the battle-line in all his
    strength.
²² He laughs at fear; he is afraid of nothing,
    he recoils before no sword.
²³ On his back the quiver rattles,
    the flashing spear and javelin.

²⁴ Trembling with impatience, he eats up the miles;
  when the trumpet sounds, there is no holding him.
²⁵ At each trumpet blast he neighs exultantly.
  He scents the battle from afar,
  the thundering of the commanders and the war cry.

²⁶ Is it your wisdom that sets the hawk flying
  when he spreads his wings to travel south?
²⁷ Does the eagle soar at your command
  to make her eyrie in the heights?
²⁸ She spends her nights among the crags
  with a needle of rock as her fortress,
²⁹ from which she watches for prey,
  fixing it with her far-ranging eye.
³⁰ Even her young drink blood;
  where anyone has been killed, she is there.

40

Still speaking to Job, Yahweh said:

² Is Yahweh's opponent going to give way?
  Has God's critic thought up an answer?

³ Job replied to Yahweh:

⁴ My words have been frivolous: what can I reply?
  I had better lay my hand over my mouth.
⁵ I have spoken once, I shall not speak again;
  I have spoken twice, I have nothing more to say.

God is master of the forces of evil

⁶ Yahweh gave Job his answer from the heart of the tempest. He said:

⁷ Brace yourself like a fighter,
  I am going to ask the questions, and you are to inform me!
⁸ Do you really want to reverse my judgement,
  put me in the wrong and yourself in the right?

⁹ Has your arm the strength of God's,
  can your voice thunder as loud?
¹⁰ Come on, display your majesty and grandeur,
  robe yourself in splendour and glory.
¹¹ Let the fury of your anger burst forth,
  humble the haughty at a glance!
¹² At a glance, bring down all the proud,
  strike down the wicked where they stand.
¹³ Bury the lot of them in the ground,
  shut them, every one, in the Dungeon.
¹⁴ And I shall be the first to pay you homage,
  since your own right hand is strong enough to save you.

Behemoth[a]

¹⁵ But look at Behemoth, my creature, just as you are!
  He feeds on greenstuff like the ox,
¹⁶ but what strength he has in his loins,
  what power in his stomach muscles!
¹⁷ His tail is as stiff as a cedar,
  the sinews of his thighs are tightly knit.
¹⁸ His bones are bronze tubes,
  his frame like forged iron.
¹⁹ He is the first of the works of God.
  His Maker threatened him with the sword,
²⁰ forbidding him the mountain regions
  and all the wild animals that play there.
²¹ Under the lotus he lies,
  he hides among the reeds in the swamps.
²² The leaves of the lotus give him shade,
  the willows by the stream shelter him.
²³ If the river overflows, he does not worry:
  Jordan might come up to his mouth, but he would not care.
²⁴ Who is going to catch him by the eyes
  or put poles through his nose?

40a Lit. 'the Beast', sometimes a mythical buffalo, but here the hippopotamus.

Leviathan[b]

25 Leviathan, too! Can you catch him with a
       fish-hook
    or hold his tongue down with a rope?
26 Can you put a cane through his nostrils
    or pierce his jaw with a hook?
27 Will he plead lengthily with you,
    addressing you in diffident tones?
28 Will he strike a bargain with you
    to become your slave for life?
29 Will you make a pet of him, like a bird,
    keep him on a lead to amuse your little
       girls?
30 Is he to be sold by the fishing guild
    and then retailed by merchants?
31 Riddle his hide with darts?
    Or his head with fishing spears?
32 You have only to lay a finger on him
    never to forget the struggle or risk it
       again!

41 Any hope you might have would be
       futile,
    the mere sight of him would
       overwhelm you.
2 When roused, he grows ferocious,
    who could ever stand up to him?
3 Who has ever attacked him with
       impunity?
    No one beneath all heaven!
4 Next I will talk of his limbs
    and describe his matchless strength—
5 who can undo the front of his tunic
    or pierce the double armour of his
       breastplate?
6 Who dare open the gates of his mouth?
    Terror reigns round his teeth!
7 His back is like rows of shields,
    sealed with a stone seal,
8 touching each other so close
    that no breath could pass between,
9 sticking to one another
    making an impervious whole.
10 His sneezes radiate light,
    his eyes are like the eyelashes of the
       dawn.

11 From his mouth come fiery torches,
    sparks of fire fly out of it.
12 His nostrils belch smoke
    like a cauldron boiling on the fire.
13 His breath could kindle coals,
    flame issues from his mouth.
14 His strength resides in his neck,
    violence leaps before him as he goes.
17 When he stands up, the waves take fright
    and the billows of the sea retreat.
15 The strips of his flesh are jointed together,
    firmly set in and immovable.
16 His heart is as hard as rock
    unyielding as the lower millstone.
18 Sword may strike but will not stick in
       him,
    no more will spear, javelin or lance.
19 Iron means no more to him than straw,
    nor bronze than rotten wood.
20 No arrow can make him flee,
    a sling-stone tickles him like hay.
21 Club seems to him like straw,
    he laughs at the whirring javelin.
22 He has sharp potsherds underneath,
    and moves across the slime like a
       harrow.
23 He makes the depths seethe like a
       cauldron,
    he makes the sea fume like a scent
       burner.
24 Behind him he leaves a glittering wake—
    a white fleece seems to float on the
       deeps.
25 He has no equal on earth,
    being created without fear.
26 He looks the haughtiest in the eye;
    of all the lordly beasts he is king.

Job's final answer

42 This was the answer Job gave to Yah-
       weh:

2 I know that you are all-powerful:
    what you conceive, you can perform.

40b Properly the monster of chaos, see 26:13, but here described as a crocodile.

3 I was the man who misrepresented your
    intentions
  with my ignorant words.
  You have told me about great works that I
    cannot understand,
    about marvels which are beyond me, of
      which I know nothing.
4 (Listen, please, and let me speak:
  I am going to ask the questions, and you
    are to inform me.)
5 Before, I knew you only by hearsay
  but now, having seen you with my own
    eyes,
6 I retract what I have said,
  and repent in dust and ashes.

Yahweh rebukes the three sages

7 When Yahweh had finished saying this to
Job, he said to Eliphaz of Teman, 'I burn with
anger against you and your two friends, for
not having spoken correctly about me as my
servant Job has done. 8 So now find seven bullocks and seven rams, and take them back
with you to my servant Job and make a burnt
offering for yourselves, while Job, my servant,
offers prayers for you. I shall show him favour
and shall not inflict my displeasure on you for
not having spoken about me correctly, as my
servant Job has done.' 9 Eliphaz of Teman, Bildad of Shuah and Zophar of Naamath went
away to do as Yahweh had ordered, and Yahweh listened to Job with favour.

Yahweh restores Job's fortunes

10 And Yahweh restored Job's condition, while
Job was interceding for his friends. More than
that, Yahweh gave him double what he had
before. 11 And all his brothers and all his sisters
and all his friends of former times came to see
him. Over dinner in his house, they showed
their sympathy and comforted him for all the
evils Yahweh had inflicted on him. Each of
them gave him a silver coin, and each a gold
ring. 12 Yahweh blessed Job's latter condition
even more than his former one. He came to
own fourteen thousand sheep, six thousand
camels, a thousand yoke of oxen and a thousand she-donkeys. 13 He had seven sons and
three daughters; 14 his first daughter he called
'Turtledove', the second 'Cassia' and the third
'Mascara'. 15 Throughout the land there were
no women as beautiful as the daughters of Job.
And their father gave them inheritance rights
like their brothers.

16 After this, Job lived for another one hundred and forty years, and saw his children and
his children's children to the fourth generation. 17 Then, old and full of days, Job died.

The Book of
PSALMS

1 How blessed is anyone who rejects the
advice of the wicked
and does not take a stand in the path that
sinners tread,
nor a seat in company with cynics,
2 but who delights in the law of Yahweh
· and murmurs his law day and night.

3 Such a one is like a tree planted near
streams;
it bears fruit in season
and its leaves never wither,
and every project succeeds.
4 How different the wicked, how different!

Just like chaff blown around by the wind
5 the wicked will not stand firm at the
Judgement
nor sinners in the gathering of the upright.
6 For Yahweh watches over the path of the
upright,
but the path of the wicked is doomed.

2 Why this uproar among the nations,
this impotent muttering of the peoples?
2 Kings of the earth take up position,
princes plot together
against Yahweh and his anointed,
3 'Now let us break their fetters!
Now let us throw off their bonds!'

4 He who is enthroned in the heavens
laughs,
Yahweh makes a mockery of them,
5 then in his anger rebukes them,
in his rage he strikes them with terror.

6 'I myself have anointed my king
on Zion my holy mountain.'

7 I will proclaim the decree of Yahweh:
He said to me, 'You are my son,
today have I fathered you.
8 Ask of me, and I shall give you the nations
as your birthright,
the whole wide world as your possession.
9 With an iron sceptre you will break them,
shatter them like so many pots.'

10 So now, you kings, come to your senses,
you earthly rulers, learn your lesson!
11 In fear be submissive to Yahweh;
12 with trembling kiss his feet,
lest he be angry and your way come to
nothing,
for his fury flares up in a moment.

How blessed are all who take refuge in
him!

3 *Psalm of David, when he was fleeing
from his son Absalom[a]*
1 Yahweh, how countless are my enemies,
how countless those who rise up against
me,
2 how countless those who say of me,
'No salvation for him from his God!' *Pause*

3 But you, Yahweh, the shield at my side,
my glory, you hold my head high.

1a The Book of Psalms is divided into five 'books', or groups
of individual psalms.

3a Many psalms have brief descriptions in the Masoretic
Text (Hebrew). Where this occurs, the Hebrew verse numbering begins with the description, and the English verses are
one less than the Hebrew.

⁴ I cry out to Yahweh;
he answers from his holy mountain. *Pause*

⁵ As for me, if I lie down and sleep,
I shall awake, for Yahweh sustains me.
⁶ I have no fear of people in their thousands
upon thousands,
who range themselves against me
wherever I turn.

⁷ Arise, Yahweh, rescue me, my God!
You strike all my foes across the face,
you break the teeth of the wicked.
⁸ In Yahweh is salvation,
on your people, your blessing! *Pause*

4 *For the choirmaster:*
For strings; psalm of David
¹ When I call, answer me, God, upholder of
my right.
In my distress you have set me at large;
take pity on me and hear my prayer!

² Children of men, how long will you be
heavy of heart,
why love what is vain and chase after
illusions? *Pause*
³ Realise that Yahweh performs wonders for
his faithful,
Yahweh listens when I call to him.

⁴ Be careful not to sin,
speak in your hearts, and on your beds
keep silence. *Pause*

⁵ Loyally offer sacrifices, and trust in
Yahweh.
⁶ Many keep saying, 'Who will put
happiness before our eyes?'
Let the light of your face shine on us.

Yahweh, ⁷ to my heart you are a richer joy
than all their corn and new wine.

⁸ In peace I lie down and at once fall asleep,
for it is you and none other, Yahweh, who
make me rest secure.

5 *For the choirmaster: For flutes;*
psalm of David
¹ Give ear to my words, Yahweh,
spare a thought for my sighing.
² Listen to my cry for help,
my King and my God!

To you I pray, ³ Yahweh.
At daybreak you hear my voice;
at daybreak I lay my case before you
and fix my eyes on you.

⁴ You are not a God who takes pleasure in
evil,
no sinner can be your guest.
⁵ Boasters cannot stand their ground
under your gaze.

You hate evil-doers,
⁶ liars you destroy;
the violent and deceitful
Yahweh detests.

⁷ But, so great is your faithful love,
I may come into your house,
and before your holy temple
bow down in reverence of you.

⁸ In your saving justice, Yahweh,
lead me,
because of those who lie in wait
for me;
make your way plain before me.

⁹ Not a word from their lips can be
trusted,
through and through they are
destruction,
their throats are wide-open graves,
their tongues seductive.

¹⁰ Lay the guilt on them, God,
make their intrigues their own
downfall;
for their countless offences, thrust them
from you,
since they have rebelled against you.

11 But joy for all who take refuge in you,
  endless songs of gladness!
 You shelter them, they rejoice in you,
  those who love your name.

12 It is you who bless the upright, Yahweh,
  you surround them with favour as with a
   shield.

6 ᵃ *For the choirmaster: For strings, for
   the octachord; psalm of David*
1 Yahweh, let your rebuke to me not be in
   anger,
  your punishment not in the heat of wrath.
2 Have pity on me, Yahweh, for I am fading
   away.
 Heal me, Yahweh, my bones are shaken,
3 my spirit is shaken to its very depths.
 But you, Yahweh . . . how long?

4 Yahweh, relent and save my life
  rescue me because of your faithful love,
5 for in death there is no remembrance of
   you;
  who could sing your praises in Sheol?

6 I am worn out with groaning,
  every night I drench my pillow
  and soak my bed with tears.
7 My eyes waste away with vexation.
  Arrogance from all my foes!
8 Away from me, all evil-doers!

 For Yahweh has heard the sound of my
   weeping,
9 Yahweh has heard my pleading.
 Yahweh will accept my prayer.
10 Let all my enemies be put to confusion,
   shaken to their depths,
  let them retreat in sudden confusion.

7 *Lament of David, which he sang
   to Yahweh about Cush the Benjaminite*
1 Yahweh my God, I take refuge in you,
  save me from all my pursuers and rescue
   me,
2 or he will savage me like a lion,
  carry me off with no one to rescue me.

3 Yahweh my God, if I have done this:
  if injustice has stained my hands,
4 if I have repaid my ally with treachery
  or spared one who attacked me
   unprovoked,
5 may an enemy hunt me down and catch
   me,
  may he trample my life into the ground
  and crush my vital parts into the dust.

Pause

6 Arise, Yahweh, in your anger,
 rise up against the arrogance of
   my foes.
  Awake, my God,
  you demand judgement.
7 Let the assembly of nations gather round
   you;
  return above it on high!
8 (Yahweh judges the nations.)

 Judge me, Yahweh, as my uprightness
  and my integrity deserve.
9 Put an end to the malice of the
   wicked,
  make the upright stand firm,
 you who discern hearts and minds,
  God the upright.

10 God is a shield that protects me,
  saving the honest of heart.
11 God is an upright judge,
   slow to anger,
    but a God at all times threatening
12   for those who will not repent.

 Let the enemy whet his sword,
 draw his bow and make ready;
13 but he is making ready instruments of
   death for himself
  and tipping his arrows with fire;
14 look at him: pregnant with malice,
  conceiving spite, he gives birth to
   treachery.

6a The first of the seven Penitential Psalms (6; 32; 38; 51; 102; 130; 142).

[650]

9-10^a

*For the choirmaster: On
oboe and harp; psalm of David*

¹⁵ He digs a trap, scoops it out,
  but he falls into the snare he made himself.
¹⁶ His spite recoils on his own head,
  his brutality falls back on his own skull.

¹⁷ I thank Yahweh for his saving justice.
  I sing to the name of the Most High.

8

*For the choirmaster:
On the . . . of Gath;^a psalm of David*

¹ Yahweh our Lord,
  how majestic is your name throughout the
    world!

Whoever keeps singing of your majesty
    higher than the heavens,
² even through the mouths of children, or of
    babes in arms,
  you make him a fortress, firm against your
    foes,
  to subdue the enemy and the rebel.

³ I look up at your heavens, shaped by your
    fingers,
  at the moon and the stars you set firm—
⁴ what are human beings that you spare a
    thought for them,
  or the child of Adam that you care for
    him?

⁵ Yet you have made him little less than a
    god,
  you have crowned him with glory and
    beauty,
⁶ made him lord of the works of your
    hands,
  put all things under his feet,

⁷ sheep and cattle, all of them,
  and even the wild beasts,
⁸ birds in the sky, fish in the sea,
  when he makes his way across the
    ocean.

⁹ Yahweh our Lord,
  how majestic your name throughout the
    world!

ALEPH ¹ I thank you, Yahweh, with my whole
    heart,
  I recount all your wonders,

² I rejoice and delight in you,
  I sing to your name, Most High.

BET ³ My enemies are in retreat,
  they stumble and perish at your presence,
⁴ for you have given fair judgement in my
    favour,
  seated on your throne as upright judge.

GIMEL ⁵ You have rebuked the nations,
    destroyed the wicked,
  blotted out their name for ever and ever;
⁶ the enemy is wiped out—mere ruins for
    ever—
  you have annihilated their cities, their
    memory has perished.

HE See, ⁷ Yahweh is enthroned for ever,
  keeping his throne firm for judgement;
⁸ he will himself judge the world in
    uprightness,
  will give a true verdict on the nations.

WAW ⁹ May Yahweh be a stronghold for the
    oppressed,
  a stronghold in times of trouble!
¹⁰ Those who revere your name can rely on
    you,
  you never desert those who seek you,
    Yahweh.

ZAIN ¹¹ Sing to Yahweh who dwells in Zion,
  tell the nations his mighty deeds,
¹² for the avenger of blood does not forget
    them,
  he does not ignore the cry of the
    afflicted.

8a Perhaps on the harp or on a melody of Gath, i.e. Philistine.

9-10a One poem with initial letters in alphabetical order,
though in our corrupt text some are missing.

HET ¹³Have pity on me, Yahweh, see my affliction,
pull me back from the gates of death,
¹⁴ that I may recount all your praises at the gates of the daughter of Zion
and rejoice in your salvation.

TET ¹⁵The nations have fallen into the trap they made,
their feet caught in the snare they laid.
¹⁶ Yahweh has made himself known, given judgement,
he has ensnared the wicked in the work of their own hands.
Muted music Pause

YOD ¹⁷May the wicked turn away to Sheol,
all the nations forgetful of God.
KAPH ¹⁸For the needy is not forgotten for ever,
not for ever does the hope of the poor come to nothing.

¹⁹ Arise, Yahweh; human strength shall not prevail.
The nations shall stand trial before you.
²⁰ Strike them with terror, Yahweh;
the nations shall know that they are no more than human! *Pause*

10 LAMED ¹ Why, Yahweh, do you keep so distant,
stay hidden in times of trouble?
² In his pride the wicked hunts down the weak,
who is caught in the schemes he devises.
(MEM) ³The wicked is proud of his inmost desires,
by his blasphemies the grasping spurns Yahweh,
(NUN) ⁴the wicked in his arrogance does not look very far;
'There is no God,' is his only thought.

⁵ In all circumstances his step is assured;
your judgements are above his head.
His rivals? He scoffs at them all.

⁶ He says in his heart, 'I shall never be shaken,'
free of trouble himself, ⁷he wishes it on others.

(SAMEK)
PE His speech is full of lies and browbeating,
under his tongue lurk spite and wickedness.
⁸ In the undergrowth he lies in ambush,
in his hiding-place he murders the innocent.

AIN He watches intently for the downtrodden,
⁹ lurking unseen like a lion in his lair,
lurking to pounce on the poor;
he pounces on him and drags him off in his net.

(ZADE)
¹⁰ He keeps watch, crouching down low,
the poor wretch falls into his clutches;
¹¹ he says in his heart, 'God forgets,
he has turned away his face to avoid seeing the end.'

QOPH ¹²Rise, Yahweh! God, raise your hand,
do not forget the afflicted!
¹³ Why should the wicked spurn God,
assuring himself you will never follow it up?

RESH ¹⁴You have seen for yourself the trouble and vexation,
you watch so as to take it in hand.
The oppressed relies on you;
you are the only recourse of the orphan.

SHIN ¹⁵Break the arm of the wicked and evil,
seek out wickedness till there is none left to be found.
¹⁶ Yahweh is king for ever and ever,
the heathen has vanished from his country.

TAW [17] Yahweh, you listen to the laments of
the poor,
you give them courage, you grant them a
hearing,
[18] to give judgement for the orphaned and
exploited,
so that earthborn humans may strike
terror no more.

11 [a]
For the choirmaster:
Of David

[1] In Yahweh I have found refuge.
How can you say to me,
'Bird, flee to your mountain?

[2] 'For look, the wicked are drawing their
bows,
fitting their arrows to the string
to shoot honest men from the shadows.
[3] If the foundations fall to ruin, what can
the upright do?'

[4] Yahweh in his holy temple!
Yahweh, his throne is in heaven;
his eyes watch over the world,
his gaze scrutinises the children of Adam.

[5] Yahweh examines the upright and the
wicked,
the lover of violence he detests.
[6] He will rain down red-hot coals,
fire and sulphur on the wicked,
a scorching wind will be their lot.

[7] For Yahweh is upright and loves
uprightness,
the honest will ever see his face.

12
For the choirmaster:
On the octachord; psalm of David

[1] Help, Yahweh! No one loyal is left,
the faithful have vanished from among the
children of Adam.
[2] Friend tells lies to friend,
and, smooth-tongued, speaks from an
insincere heart.

[3] May Yahweh cut away every smooth lip,
every boastful tongue,

[4] those who say, 'In our tongue lies our
strength,
our lips are our allies; who can master us?'
[5] 'For the poor who are plundered, the
needy who groan,
now will I act,' says Yahweh,
'I will grant salvation to those who sigh
for it.'

[6] Yahweh's promises are promises
unalloyed,
natural silver which comes from the earth
seven times refined.

[7] You, Yahweh, will watch over them,
you will protect them from that brood for
ever.
[8] The wicked will scatter in every direction,
as the height of depravity among the
children of Adam.

13
For the choirmaster:
Psalm of David

[1] How long, Yahweh, will you forget me?
For ever?
How long will you turn away your face
from me?
[2] How long must I nurse rebellion in my
soul,
sorrow in my heart day and night?
How long is the enemy to domineer over
me?
[3] Look down, answer me, Yahweh my God!
Give light to my eyes or I shall fall into the
sleep of death.

[4] Or my foe will boast, 'I have overpowered
him,'
and my enemy have the joy of seeing me
stumble.
[5] As for me, I trust in your faithful love,
Yahweh.
Let my heart delight in your saving help,

11a In this edition the Hebr. numbering of the Pss is used.
From Ps 10 to Ps 147 the chap. numbers are one more than in
the Gk and Vulgate.

6 let me sing to Yahweh for his generosity
    to me,
  let me sing to the name of Yahweh the
    Most High!

14[a]

For the choirmaster:
Of David

1 The fool has said in his heart,
  'There is no God.'
  Their deeds are corrupt and vile,
    not one of them does right.

2 Yahweh looks down from heaven
    at the children of Adam.
  To see if a single one is wise,
    a single one seeks God.

3 All have turned away,
    all alike turned sour,
  not one of them does right,
    not a single one.

4 Are they not aware, all these evil-doers?
    They are devouring my people,
    this is the bread they eat,
    and they never call to Yahweh.

5 They will be gripped with fear,
    where there is no need for fear,
  for God takes the side of the upright;
6 you may mock the plans of the poor,
    but Yahweh is their refuge.

7 Who will bring from Zion salvation for
    Israel?
  When Yahweh brings his people home,
  what joy for Jacob, what happiness for
    Israel!

15

Psalm of David

1 Yahweh, who can find a home in your tent,
  who can dwell on your holy mountain?

2 Whoever lives blamelessly,
  who acts uprightly,
  who speaks the truth from the heart,
3 who keeps the tongue under control,

who does not wrong a comrade,
  who casts no discredit on a neighbour,
4 who looks with scorn on the vile,
  but honours those who fear Yahweh,

who stands by an oath at any cost,
5 who asks no interest on loans,
  who takes no bribe to harm the innocent.
  No one who so acts can ever be shaken.

16

In a quiet voice:
Of David

1 Protect me, O God, in you is my refuge.

2 To Yahweh I say, 'You are my Lord,
  my happiness is in none 3 of the sacred
    spirits of the earth.'

They only take advantage of all who love
    them.
4 People flock to their teeming idols.
  Never shall I pour libations to them!
  Never take their names on my lips.

5 My birthright, my cup is Yahweh;
  you, you alone, hold my lot secure.
6 The measuring-line marks out for me a
    delightful place,
  my birthright is all I could wish.

7 I bless Yahweh who is my counsellor,
  even at night my heart instructs me.
8 I keep Yahweh before me always,
  for with him at my right hand, nothing
    can shake me.

9 So my heart rejoices, my soul delights,
  my body too will rest secure,
10 for you will not abandon me to Sheol,
  you cannot allow your faithful servant to
    see the abyss.
11 You will teach me the path of life,
  unbounded joy in your presence,
  at your right hand delight for ever.

14a Almost identical with Ps 53 except that the proper name
'Yahweh' here occurs for 'God'.

17
Prayer of David

1 Listen, Yahweh, to an upright cause,
    pay attention to my cry,
lend an ear to my prayer,
    my lips free from deceit.
2 From your presence will issue my
        vindication,
    your eyes fixed on what is right.

3 You probe my heart, examine me at night,
you test me by fire and find no evil.
I have not sinned with my mouth 4 as most
    people do.

I have treasured the word from your lips,
5 my steps never stray from the paths you
        lay down,
from your tracks; so my feet never
        stumble.
6 I call upon you, God, for you answer me;
turn your ear to me, hear what I say.
7 Show the evidence of your faithful love,
saviour of those who hope in your strength
        against attack.

8 Guard me as the pupil of an eye,
    shelter me in the shadow of your wings
9 from the presence of the wicked who
        would maltreat me;
deadly enemies are closing in on me.
10 Engrossed in themselves
    they are mouthing arrogant words.
11 They are advancing against me, now they
        are closing in,
watching for the chance to hurl me to the
        ground,
12 like a lion preparing to pounce,
    like a young lion crouching in ambush.

13 Arise, Yahweh, confront him and bring
        him down,
with your sword save my life from the
        wicked,
14 Yahweh, from mortals, by your hand,
from mortals whose part in life is in this
        world.

You fill their bellies from your store,
their children will have all they desire,
and leave their surplus to their children.
15 But I in my uprightness will see your face,
and when I awake I shall be filled with the
        vision of you.

18
a *For the choirmaster: Of David, the
    servant of Yahweh, who addressed
the words of this song to Yahweh when Yahweh had
    delivered him from all his enemies and
    from the clutches of Saul. He said:*
1 I love you, Yahweh, my strength
    (my Saviour, you have saved me from
        violence).

2 Yahweh is my rock and my fortress,
    my deliverer is my God.
I take refuge in him, my rock,
my shield, my saving strength,
my stronghold, my place of refuge.

3 I call to Yahweh who is worthy of praise,
    and I am saved from my foes.

4 With Death's breakers closing in
        on me,
Belial's torrents ready to swallow me,
5 Sheol's snares every side of me,
Death's traps lying ahead of me,

6 I called to Yahweh in my anguish,
I cried for help to my God;
from his Temple he heard my voice,
my cry came to his ears.

7 Then the earth quaked and rocked,
the mountains' foundations shuddered,
they quaked at his blazing anger.
8 Smoke rose from his nostrils,
from his mouth devouring fire
(coals were kindled at it).

9 He parted the heavens and came down,
a storm-cloud underneath his feet;

18a ‖ 2 S 22.

[655]

¹⁰ riding one of the winged creatures, he
      flew,
  soaring on the wings of the wind.

¹¹ His covering he made the darkness,
  his pavilion dark waters and dense
      cloud.
¹² A brightness lit up before him,
  hail and blazing fire.

¹³ Yahweh thundered from the heavens,
  the Most High made his voice heard.
¹⁴ He shot his arrows and scattered them,
  he hurled his lightning and routed
      them.

¹⁵ The very springs of ocean were exposed,
  the world's foundations were laid bare,
  at your roaring, Yahweh,
  at the blast of breath from your nostrils!

¹⁶ He reached down from on high, snatched
      me up,
  pulled me from the watery depths,
¹⁷ rescued me from my mighty foe,
  from my enemies who were stronger
      than I.

¹⁸ They assailed me on my day of disaster
  but Yahweh was there to support me;
¹⁹ he freed me, set me at large,
  he rescued me because he loves me.

²⁰ Yahweh rewards me for my uprightness,
  as my hands are pure, so he repays me,
²¹ since I have kept the ways of Yahweh,
  and not fallen away from my God.

²² His judgements are all before me,
  his statutes I have not put away from me.
²³ I am blameless before him,
  I keep myself clear of evil.

²⁴ So Yahweh repaid me for acting uprightly
  because he could see I was pure.
²⁵ You are faithful to the faithful,
  blameless with the blameless,

²⁶ sincere to the sincere,
  but cunning to the crafty,
²⁷ you save a people that is humble
  and humiliate those with haughty looks.

²⁸ Yahweh, you yourself are my lamp,
  my God lights up my darkness;
²⁹ with you I storm the rampart,
  with my God I can scale any wall.

³⁰ This God, his way is blameless;
  the word of Yahweh is refined in the
      furnace,
  for he alone is the shield
  of all who take refuge in him.

³¹ For who is God but Yahweh,
  who is a rock but our God?
³² This God who girds me with strength,
  who makes my way free from blame,

³³ who makes me as swift as a deer
  and sets me firmly on the heights,
³⁴ who trains my hands for battle,
  my arms to bend a bow of bronze.

³⁵ You give me your invincible shield
  (your right hand upholds me)
  you never cease to listen to me,
³⁶ you give me the strides of a giant,
  give me ankles that never weaken.

³⁷ I pursue my enemies and overtake them,
  not turning back till they are annihilated;
³⁸ I strike them down and they cannot rise,
  they fall, they are under my feet.

³⁹ You have girded me with strength for the
      fight,
  bent down my assailants beneath me,
⁴⁰ made my enemies retreat before me;
  and those who hate me I destroy.

⁴¹ They cry out, there is no one to save;
  to Yahweh, but no answer comes.
⁴² I crumble them like dust before the wind,
  trample them like the mud of the streets.

43 You free me from the quarrels of my
people,
you place me at the head of the nations,
a people I did not know are now my
servants;

44 foreigners come wooing my favour,
no sooner do they hear than they obey me;
45 foreigners grow faint of heart,
they come trembling out of their
fastnesses.

46 Life to Yahweh! Blessed be my rock!
Exalted be the God of my salvation,
47 the God who gives me vengeance,
and subjects whole peoples to me,

48 who rescues me from my raging enemies.
You lift me high above those who attack
me,
you deliver me from the man of violence.

49 For this I will praise you, Yahweh, among
the nations,
and sing praise to your name.

50 He saves his king time after time,
displays his faithful love for his anointed,
for David and his heirs for ever.

19

For the choirmaster:
Psalm of David

1 The heavens declare the glory of God,
the vault of heaven proclaims his
handiwork,
2 day discourses of it to day,
night to night hands on the knowledge.

3 No utterance at all, no speech,
not a sound to be heard,
4 but from the entire earth the design stands
out,
this message reaches the whole world.

High above, he pitched a tent for the sun,
5 who comes forth from his pavilion like a
bridegroom,
delights like a champion in the course to
be run.

6 Rising on the one horizon
he runs his circuit to the other,
and nothing can escape his heat.

7 The Law of Yahweh is perfect,
refreshment to the soul;
the decree of Yahweh is trustworthy,
wisdom for the simple.

8 The precepts of Yahweh are honest,
joy for the heart;
the commandment of Yahweh is
pure,
light for the eyes.

9 The fear of Yahweh is pure,
lasting for ever;
the judgements of Yahweh are true,
upright, every one,

10 more desirable than gold,
even than the finest gold;
his words are sweeter than honey,
that drips from the comb.

11 Thus your servant is formed by them;
observing them brings great reward.
12 But who can detect his own failings?
Wash away my hidden faults.

13 And from pride preserve your servant,
never let it be my master.
So shall I be above reproach,
free from grave sin.

14 May the words of my mouth always
find favour,
and the whispering of my heart,
in your presence, Yahweh,
my rock, my redeemer.

20

For the choirmaster:
Psalm of David

1 May Yahweh answer you in time of
trouble,
may the name of the God of Jacob protect
you!

40 READ PSALM 19.

The heavens declare the glory of God.—PSALM 19:1

NO EXCUSES

What else, O Lord, are all your creatures but flaming firebrands with which you have enkindled my frozen heart, disposing it to love you? Every morning, O my soul, at the gate of your house you find the whole world—birds, animals, the fields and the heavens at your service, so that in the name of all creation you might freely offer your love to the Creator.

A wonderful noise of all his creatures invites you to this divine love. They declare to you his majesty with plain speeches. "The heavens declare the glory of God, the vault of heaven proclaims his handiwork." Their voices are heard in all languages, so no one has an excuse for not loving him.

The heavens, O Lord, standing securely in their peace, reveal your glory. They tell us what our heavenly rest will be like because you allow us to see such beauty. O my God, how rich you are to be served by such wonderful lamps as the stars! Who but you could have made such a beautiful brightness, such diverse forces, such contrary motions, without erring in any one point? O lumpish heart of mine, how is it that seeing such excellence and greatness does not lift you up to those heavenly places?

If I turn my eyes to my own little world and study myself, I find great cause to love you. I realize that you created everything for my service and benefit. If I open my ears I shall hear the Psalmist who says to me, "In myself I discover your wonderful science because knowing myself reveals your infinite wisdom" (see Ps 8). So Isaiah says to sinners, "Rebels, turn to your heart for in yourselves you shall see who is your God" (see Is 46:8). ST. ROBERT SOUTHWELL, 1561–1595

YOU WILL FIND THE NEXT READING AT PSALM 22.

2 May he send you help from the sanctuary,
   give you support from Zion!
3 May he remember all your sacrifices
   and delight in your burnt offerings! *Pause*
4 May he grant you your heart's desire
   and crown all your plans with success!

5 So that with joy we can hail your victory
   and draw up our ranks in the name of
      our God.

May Yahweh grant all your petitions.

6 Now I know that pYahweh
   gives victory to his anointed.
   He will respond from his holy heavens

with great deeds of victory from his right
   hand.

7 Some call on chariots, some on horses,
   but we on the name of Yahweh our God.
8 They will crumple and fall,
   while we stand upright and firm.

9 Yahweh, save the king,
   answer us when we call.

21
For the choirmaster:
Psalm of David

1 Yahweh, the king rejoices in your power;
   How your saving help fills him with joy!

2 You have granted him his heart's desire,
   not denied him the prayer of his lips.
                                        Pause

3 For you come to meet him with blessings
      of prosperity,
   put a crown of pure gold on his head.
4 He has asked for life, you have given it
      him,
   length of days for ever and ever.

5 Great his glory through your saving help;
   you invest him with splendour and
      majesty.
6 You confer on him everlasting blessings,
   you gladden him with the joy of your
      presence.
7 For the king puts his trust in Yahweh;
   the faithful love of the Most High will
      keep him from falling.

8 Your hand will reach all your enemies,
   your right hand all who hate you.
9 You will hurl them into a blazing furnace
   on the day when you appear;
   Yahweh will engulf them in his anger,
   and fire will devour them.
10 You will purge the earth of their
      descendants,
   the human race of their posterity.

11 They have devised evil against you
   but, plot as they may, they will not
      succeed,
12 since you will make them turn tail,
   by shooting your arrows in their faces.

13 Rise, Yahweh, in your power!
   We will sing and make music in honour of
      your strength.

22 *For the choirmaster: To 'the Doe
    of the Dawn'; psalm of David*
1 My God, my God, why have you forsaken
   me?
   The words of my groaning do nothing to
      save me.

2 My God, I call by day but you do not
      answer,
   at night, but I find no respite.

3 Yet you, the Holy One,
   who make your home in the praises of
      Israel,
4 in you our ancestors put their trust,
   they trusted and you set them free.
5 To you they called for help and were
      delivered;
   in you they trusted and were not put to
      shame.

6 But I am a worm, less than human,
   scorn of mankind, contempt of the people;
7 all who see me jeer at me,
   they sneer and wag their heads,
8 'He trusted himself to Yahweh, let
      Yahweh set him free!
   Let him deliver him, as he took such
      delight in him.'

9 It was you who drew me from the womb
   and soothed me on my mother's breast.
10 On you was I cast from my birth,
   from the womb I have belonged to you.
11 Do not hold aloof, for trouble is upon me,
   and no one to help me!

12 Many bulls are encircling me,
   wild bulls of Bashan closing in on me.
13 Lions ravening and roaring
   open their jaws at me.

14 My strength is trickling away,
   my bones are all disjointed,
   my heart has turned to wax,
   melting inside me.
15 My mouth is dry as earthenware,
   my tongue sticks to my jaw.
   You lay me down in the dust of death.

16 A pack of dogs surrounds me,
   a gang of villains closing in on me
   as if to hack off my hands and my feet.
17 I can count every one of my bones,
   while they look on and gloat;

¹⁸ they divide my garments among them
and cast lots for my clothing.

¹⁹ Yahweh, do not hold aloof!
My strength, come quickly to my help,
²⁰ rescue my soul from the sword,
the one life I have from the grasp of the
dog!
²¹ Save me from the lion's mouth,
my poor life from the wild bulls' horns!

²² I shall proclaim your name to my brothers,
praise you in full assembly:
²³ 'You who fear Yahweh, praise him!
All the race of Jacob, honour him!
Revere him, all the race of Israel!'

²⁴ For he has not despised
nor disregarded the poverty of the poor,
has not turned away his face,
but has listened to the cry for help.

²⁵ Of you is my praise in the thronged
assembly,
I will perform my vows before all who
fear him.
²⁶ The poor will eat and be filled,
those who seek Yahweh will praise him,
'May your heart live for ever.'

²⁷ The whole wide world will remember and
return to Yahweh,
all the families of nations bow down
before him.
²⁸ For to Yahweh, ruler of the nations,
belongs kingly power!
²⁹ All who prosper on earth will bow before
him,
all who go down to the dust will do
reverence before him.
And those who are dead, ³⁰ their
descendants will serve him,
will proclaim his name to generations
³¹ still to come;
and these will tell of his saving justice to a
people yet unborn:
he has fulfilled it.

23
Psalm of David

¹ Yahweh is my shepherd, I lack nothing.
² In grassy meadows he lets me lie.

By tranquil streams he leads me
³ to restore my spirit.
He guides me in paths of saving justice
as befits his name.

⁴ Even were I to walk in a ravine as dark as
death
I should fear no danger, for you are at my
side.
Your staff and your crook are there to
soothe me.

⁵ You prepare a table for me
under the eyes of my enemies;
you anoint my head with oil;
my cup brims over.

⁶ Kindness and faithful love pursue me
every day of my life.
I make my home in the house of Yahweh
for all time to come.

24
Psalm of David

¹ To Yahweh belong the earth and all it
contains,
the world and all who live there;
² it is he who laid its foundations on the seas,
on the flowing waters fixed it firm.

³ Who shall go up to the mountain of
Yahweh?
Who shall take a stand in his holy place?

⁴ The clean of hands and pure of heart,
whose heart is not set on vanities,
who does not swear an oath in order to
deceive.

⁵ Such a one will receive blessing from
Yahweh,
saving justice from the God of his
salvation.

41   READ PSALM 22.

My God, my God, why have you forsaken me?—PSALM 22:1

ABANDONED BY GOD?

For more than forty years, St. Jane de Chantal suffered from depression. Like Jesus himself, who prayed this verse from the cross (see Mt 27:46), she sometimes felt abandoned by God. But also like the Lord, who agonized with fear of the cross and yet obeyed his Father, Jane consistently obeyed God even when she felt least like doing it. She expressed both her pain and commitment in this letter to her mentor, St. Francis de Sales:

I live in dread, not because of harm to myself, but because I fear to displease God. Oh, how far away his help seems! Thinking of this I spent last night in great bitterness and could utter no other words than these, "My God, my God, why have you forsaken me?" At daybreak God gave me a little light in the highest part of my soul, yet only there. But it was almost imperceptible, nor did the rest of my soul and its faculties share the enjoyment, which lasted only about the time of half a Hail Mary. Then trouble rushed back upon me with a mighty force, and all was darkness. Although worn down by this sense of abandonment, in utter dryness, I said, "Do, Lord, whatever is pleasing to you, I wish it. Annihilate me, I am content. Overwhelm me, I most sincerely desire it. Tear out, cut, burn, do just as you please, I am yours." God has shown me that he does not make much account of faith that comes of sentiment and emotions. This is why, though against my inclination, I never wish for sensible devotion. I do not desire it. God is enough for me. Enduring my absolute misery, I hope in him, and I trust he will continue to support me so that his will may be accomplished in me.

ST. JANE DE CHANTAL, 1572–1641

YOU WILL FIND THE NEXT READING AT PSALM 50.

6 Such is the people that seeks him,
  that seeks your presence, God of Jacob.
                                        Pause

7 Gates, lift high your heads,
  raise high the ancient gateways,
  and the king of glory shall enter!

8 Who is he, this king of glory?
  It is Yahweh, strong and valiant,
  Yahweh valiant in battle.

9 Gates, lift high your heads,
  raise high the ancient gateways,
  and the king of glory shall enter!

10 Who is he, this king of glory?
   Yahweh Sabaoth,
   he is the king of glory.   *Pause*

25   *Of David*

ALEPH ¹ADORATION I offer, Yahweh,
   ² to you, my God.

BET BUT in my trust in you do not put me to shame,
        let not my enemies gloat over me.

GIMEL ³CALLING to you, none shall ever be
        put to shame,

but shame is theirs who groundlessly
  break faith.

DALET 4 DIRECT me in your ways, Yahweh,
  and teach me your paths.

HE 5 ENCOURAGE me to walk in your truth and
    teach me
  since you are the God who saves me.

(WAW) FOR my hope is in you all day long—
7c such is your generosity, Yahweh.

ZAIN 6 GOODNESS and faithful love have been
    yours for ever,
  Yahweh, do not forget them.

HET 7 HOLD not my youthful sins against
    me,
  but remember me as your faithful love
    dictates.

TET 8 INTEGRITY and generosity are marks of
    Yahweh
  for he brings sinners back to the path.

YOD 9 JUDICIOUSLY he guides the humble,
  instructing the poor in his way.

KAPH 10 KINDNESS unfailing and constancy
    mark all Yahweh's paths,
  for those who keep his covenant and his
    decrees.

LAMED 11 LET my sin, great though it is, be
    forgiven,
  Yahweh, for the sake of your name.

MEM 12 MEN who respect Yahweh, what of
    them?
  He teaches them the way they must
    choose.

NUN 13 NEIGHBOURS to happiness will they
    live,
  and their children inherit the land.

SAMEK 14 ONLY those who fear Yahweh have
    his secret
  and his covenant, for their understanding.

AIN 15 PERMANENTLY my eyes are on
    Yahweh,
  for he will free my feet from the snare.

PE 16 QUICK, turn to me, pity me,
  alone and wretched as I am!

ZADE 17 RELIEVE the distress of my heart,
  bring me out of my constraint.

(QOPH) 18 SPARE a glance for my misery and
    pain,
  take all my sins away.

RESH 19 TAKE note how countless are my
    enemies,
  how violent their hatred for me.

SHIN 20 UNLESS you guard me and rescue me
  I shall be put to shame, for you are my
    refuge.

TAW 21 VIRTUE and integrity be my
    protection,
  for my hope, Yahweh, is in you.

22 Ransom Israel, O God,
  from all its troubles.

26   *Of David*

1 Yahweh, be my judge!
  I go on my way in innocence,
  my trust in Yahweh never wavers.

2 Probe me, Yahweh, examine me,
  Test my heart and my mind in the fire.
3 For your faithful love is before my eyes,
  and I live my life by your truth.

4 No sitting with wastrels for me,
  no travelling with hypocrites;
5 I hate the company of sinners,
  I refuse to sit down with the wicked.

6 I will wash my hands in innocence
  and join the procession round your altar,
    Yahweh,
7 to make heard the sound of thanksgiving,
  to proclaim all your wonders.
8 Yahweh, I love the beauty of your house
  and the place where your glory dwells.

9 Do not couple me with sinners,
  nor my life with men of violence,
10 whose hands are stained with guilt,
  their right hands heavy with bribes.

11 In innocence I will go on my way;
  ransom me, take pity on me.
12 I take my stand on the right path;
  I will bless you, Yahweh, in the assemblies.

27

Of David

1 Yahweh is my light and my salvation,
  whom should I fear?
  Yahweh is the fortress of my life,
  whom should I dread?

2 When the wicked advance against me
    to eat me up,
  they, my opponents, my enemies,
  are the ones who stumble and fall.

3 Though an army pitch camp against me,
    my heart will not fear,
  though war break out against me,
  my trust will never be shaken.

4 One thing I ask of Yahweh,
    one thing I seek:
  to dwell in Yahweh's house
    all the days of my life,
  to enjoy the sweetness of Yahweh,
    to seek out his temple.

5 For he hides me away under his roof
    on the day of evil,
  he folds me in the recesses of his tent,
    sets me high on a rock.

6 Now my head is held high
    above the enemies who surround me;
  in his tent I will offer
    sacrifices of acclaim.

  I will sing, I will make music for Yahweh.

7 Yahweh, hear my voice as I cry,
    pity me, answer me!

8 Of you my heart has said,
    'Seek his face!'
  Your face, Yahweh, I seek;
9   do not turn away from me.

  Do not thrust aside your servant in
      anger,
    without you I am helpless.
  Never leave me, never forsake me,
    God, my Saviour.
10 Though my father and mother
      forsake me,
  Yahweh will gather me up.

11 Yahweh, teach me your way,
  lead me on the path of integrity
    because of my enemies;
12 do not abandon me to the will of my
      foes—
  false witnesses have risen against me,
    and are breathing out violence.

13 This I believe: I shall see the goodness of
      Yahweh,
    in the land of the living.
14 Put your hope in Yahweh, be strong, let
      your heart be bold,
    put your hope in Yahweh.

28

Of David

1 To you, Yahweh, I cry,
    my rock, do not be deaf to me!
  If you stay silent
    I shall be like those who sink into
      oblivion.

2 Hear the sound of my prayer
    when I call upon you,
  when I raise my hands, Yahweh,
    towards your Holy of Holies.

3 Do not drag me away with the wicked,
    with evil-doers,
  who talk to their partners of peace
    with treachery in their hearts.

4 Repay them as their deeds deserve,
  as befits their treacherous actions;
as befits their handiwork repay them,
  let their deserts fall back on themselves.

5 They do not comprehend the deeds of
    Yahweh,
  the work of his hands.
May he pull them down and not rebuild
    them!

6 Blessed be Yahweh
  for he hears the sound of my prayer.

7 Yahweh is my strength and my shield,
  in him my heart trusts.
I have been helped; my body has recovered
    its vigour,
  with all my heart I thank him.

8 Yahweh is the strength of his people,
  a safe refuge for his anointed.
9 Save your people, bless your heritage,
  shepherd them and carry them for ever!

29

Psalm of David

1 Give Yahweh his due, sons of God,
  give Yahweh his due of glory and strength,
2 give Yahweh the glory due to his name,
  adore Yahweh in the splendour of
    holiness.

3 Yahweh's voice over the waters, the God of
    glory thunders;
  Yahweh over countless waters,
4 Yahweh's voice in power, Yahweh's voice
    in splendour;

5 Yahweh's voice shatters cedars,
  Yahweh shatters cedars of Lebanon,
6 he makes Lebanon skip like a calf,
  Sirion like a young wild ox.

7 Yahweh's voice carves out lightning-shafts,
8 Yahweh's voice convulses the desert,
  Yahweh convulses the desert of Kadesh,

9 Yahweh's voice convulses terebinths,
  strips forests bare.

In his palace all cry, 'Glory!'
10 Yahweh was enthroned for the flood,
  Yahweh is enthroned as king for ever.
11 Yahweh will give strength to his people,
  Yahweh blesses his people with peace.

30

*Psalm of David; canticle for the
Dedication of the House*

1 I praise you to the heights, Yahweh, for
    you have raised me up,
  you have not let my foes make merry
    over me.
2 Yahweh, my God, I cried to you for help
    and you healed me.
3 Yahweh, you have lifted me out of Sheol,
  from among those who sink into oblivion
    you have given me life.

4 Make music for Yahweh, all you who are
    faithful to him,
  praise his unforgettable holiness.
5 His anger lasts but a moment, his favour
    through life;
  In the evening come tears, but with dawn
    cries of joy.

6   Carefree, I used to think,
    'Nothing can ever shake me!'
7 Your favour, Yahweh, set me on
    impregnable heights,
  but you turned away your face and I was
    terrified.

8   To you, Yahweh, I call,
    to my God I cry for mercy.
9 What point is there in my death, my going
    down to the abyss?
  Can the dust praise you or proclaim your
    faithfulness?

10 Listen, Yahweh, take pity on me,
  Yahweh, be my help!
11 You have turned my mourning into
    dancing,

you have stripped off my sackcloth and
   clothed me with joy.
12 So my heart will sing to you unceasingly,
   Yahweh, my God, I shall praise you for
      ever.

31

For the choirmaster:
Psalm of David

1 In you, Yahweh, I have taken refuge,
   let me never be put to shame,
   in your saving justice deliver me,
      rescue me,
2 turn your ear to me, make haste.

Be for me a rock-fastness,
   a fortified citadel to save me.
3 You are my rock, my rampart;
   true to your name, lead me and guide me!

4 Draw me out of the net they have spread
      for me,
   for you are my refuge;
5 to your hands I commit my spirit,
   by you have I been redeemed.

God of truth, 6 you hate
   worshippers of ineffectual idols;
   but my trust is in Yahweh:
7 I will delight and rejoice in your faithful
      love!

You, who have seen my misery,
   and witnessed the miseries of my soul,
8 have not handed me over to the enemy,
   but have given me freedom to roam at
      large.

9 Take pity on me, Yahweh,
   for I am in trouble.
   Vexation is gnawing away my eyes,
   my soul deep within me.

10 For my life is worn out with sorrow,
   and my years with sighs.
   My strength gives way under my
      misery,
   and my bones are all wasted away.

11 The sheer number of my enemies
   makes me contemptible,
   loathsome to my neighbours,
   and my friends shrink from me in
      horror.

When people see me in the street
   they take to their heels.
12 I have no more place in their hearts than a
      corpse,
   or something lost.

13 All I hear is slander
   —terror wherever I turn—
   as they plot together against me,
   scheming to take my life.

14 But my trust is in you, Yahweh;
   I say, 'You are my God,'
15 every moment of my life is in your hands,
      rescue me
   from the clutches of my foes who
      pursue me;
16 let your face shine on your servant,
   save me in your faithful love.

17 I call on you, Yahweh, so let disgrace fall
      not on me,
   but on the wicked.
   Let them go down to Sheol in silence,
18   muzzles on their lying mouths,
   which speak arrogantly against the
      upright
   in pride and contempt.

19 Yahweh, what quantities of good
      things
   you have in store for those who fear
      you,
   and bestow on those who make you their
      refuge,
   for all humanity to see.

20 Safe in your presence you hide them,
   far from human plotting,
   shielding them in your tent,
   far from contentious tongues.

21 Blessed be Yahweh who works for me
miracles of his faithful love
(in a fortified city)!
22 In a state of terror I cried,
'I have been cut off from your sight!'
Yet you heard my plea for help
when I cried out to you.

23 Love Yahweh, all his faithful:
Yahweh protects his loyal servants,
but he repays the arrogant
with interest.
24 Be brave, take heart,
all who put your hope in Yahweh.

32

Of David; poem

1 How blessed are those whose offence is
forgiven,
whose sin blotted out.
2 How blessed are those to whom Yahweh
imputes no guilt,
whose spirit harbours no deceit.

3 I said not a word, but my bones wasted
away
from groaning all the day;
4 day and night
your hand lay heavy upon me;
my heart grew parched as stubble
in summer drought.   *Pause*

5 I made my sin known to you,
did not conceal my guilt.
I said, 'I shall confess
my offence to Yahweh.'
And you, for your part, took away my
guilt,
forgave my sin.   *Pause*

6 That is why each of your faithful ones
prays to you
in time of distress.
Even if great floods overflow,
they will never reach your faithful.
7 You are a refuge for me,
you guard me in trouble,

with songs of deliverance you surround
me.   *Pause*
8 I shall instruct you and teach you the way
to go;
I shall not take my eyes off you.

9 Do not be like horse or mule;
they do not understand bridle or bit;
if you advance to master them,
there is no means of getting them to come
near.

10 Countless troubles are in store for the
wicked,
but one who trusts in Yahweh is enfolded
in his faithful love.

11 Rejoice in Yahweh,
exult all you upright,
shout for joy, you honest of heart.

33

Shout for joy, you upright;
praise comes well from the honest.
2 Give thanks to Yahweh on the lyre,
play for him on the ten-stringed lyre.
3 Sing to him a new song,
make sweet music for your cry of victory.

4 The word of Yahweh is straightforward,
all he does springs from his constancy.
5 He loves uprightness and justice;
the faithful love of Yahweh fills the
earth.
6 By the word of Yahweh the heavens were
made,
by the breath of his mouth all their array.
7 He collects the waters of the sea like a
dam,
he stores away the abyss in his treasure-
house.

8 Let the whole earth fear Yahweh,
let all who dwell in the world revere him;
9 for, the moment he spoke, it was so,
no sooner had he commanded, than there
it stood!

10 Yahweh thwarts the plans of nations,
  frustrates the counsels of peoples;
11 but Yahweh's own plan stands firm for
    ever,
  his heart's counsel from age to age.
12 How blessed the nation whose God is
    Yahweh,
  the people he has chosen as his heritage.

13 From heaven Yahweh looks down,
  he sees all the children of Adam,
14 from the place where he sits he watches
  all who dwell on the earth;
15 he alone moulds their hearts,
  he understands all they do.

16 A large army will not keep a king safe,
  nor his strength save a warrior's life;
17 it is delusion to rely on a horse for safety,
  for all its power it cannot save.

18 But see how Yahweh watches over those
    who fear him,
  those who rely on his faithful love,
19 to rescue them from death
  and keep them alive in famine.

20 We are waiting for Yahweh;
  he is our help and our shield,
21 for in him our heart rejoices,
  in his holy name we trust.
22 Yahweh, let your faithful love rest on us,
  as our hope has rested in you.

34

*Of David, when he had feigned
insanity before Abimelech, and
Abimelech sent him away*

ALEPH 1 I will bless Yahweh at all times,
  his praise continually on my lips.
BET 2 I will praise Yahweh from my heart;
  let the humble hear and rejoice.

GIMEL 3 Proclaim with me the greatness of
    Yahweh,
  let us acclaim his name together.
DALET 4 I seek Yahweh and he answers me,
  frees me from all my fears.

HE 5 Fix your gaze on Yahweh and your face
    will grow bright,
  you will never hang your head in shame.
ZAIN 6 A pauper calls out and Yahweh
    hears,
  saves him from all his troubles.

HET 7 The angel of Yahweh encamps
  around those who fear him, and rescues
    them.
TET 8 Taste and see that Yahweh is good.
  How blessed are those who take refuge in
    him.

YOD 9 Fear Yahweh, you his holy ones;
  those who fear him lack for nothing.
KAPH 10 Young lions may go needy and
    hungry,
  but those who seek Yahweh lack nothing
    good.

LAMED 11 Come, my children, listen to me,
  I will teach you the fear of Yahweh.
MEM 12 Who among you delights in life,
  longs for time to enjoy prosperity?

NUN 13 Guard your tongue from evil,
  your lips from any breath of deceit.
SAMEK 14 Turn away from evil and do
    good,
  seek peace and pursue it.

AIN 15 The eyes of Yahweh are on the
    upright,
  his ear turned to their cry.
PE 16 But Yahweh's face is set against those
    who do evil,
  to cut off the memory of them from the
    earth.

ZADE 17 They cry in anguish and Yahweh
    hears,
  and rescues them from all their
    troubles.
QOPH 18 Yahweh is near to the broken-
    hearted,
  he helps those whose spirit is crushed.

RESH ¹⁹Though hardships without number
beset the upright,
Yahweh brings rescue from them all.
SHIN ²⁰Yahweh takes care of all their bones,
not one of them will be broken.

TAW ²¹But to the wicked evil brings death,
those who hate the upright will pay the
penalty.
²²Yahweh ransoms the lives of those who
serve him,
and there will be no penalty for those who
take refuge in him.

35

Of David

¹Accuse my accusers, Yahweh,
attack my attackers.
²Grasp your buckler and shield,
up, and help me.
³Brandish spear and pike
to confront my pursuers,
give me the assurance, 'I am your Saviour.'

⁴Shame and humiliation on those
who are out to kill me!
Defeat and repulse in dismay
on those who plot my downfall.

⁵May they be like chaff before the wind,
with the angel of Yahweh to chase
them.
⁶May their way be dark and slippery,
with the angel of Yahweh to hound
them.

⁷Unprovoked they laid their snare for me,
unprovoked dug a trap to kill me.
⁸Ruin comes upon them unawares;
the snare they have laid will catch them,
and into their own trap they will fall.

⁹Then I shall delight in Yahweh,
rejoice that he has saved me.
¹⁰My very bones will all exclaim,
Yahweh, who can compare with you
in rescuing the poor from the oppressor;
the needy from the exploiter?

¹¹False witnesses come forward against me
asking me questions I cannot answer,
they cross-examine me, ¹²repay my
kindness with cruelty,
make my life barren.

¹³But I, when they were ill, had worn
sackcloth,
and mortified myself with fasting,
praying ever anew in my heart,
¹⁴as if for a friend or brother; I had
wandered restless,
as if mourning a mother,
so bowed had I been in sorrow.

¹⁵When I stumble they gather in glee,
gather around me;
strangers I never even knew
tear me apart incessantly.
¹⁶If I fall they surround me,
grinding their teeth at me.

¹⁷How much longer, Lord, will you
look on?
Rescue me from their onslaughts,
from young lions rescue the one life that
I have.

¹⁸I will give you thanks in the great
assembly
praise you where the people gather.

¹⁹Let not my lying enemies
gloat over me;
those who hate me unprovoked
look askance at me.

²⁰They have no greeting of peace
to the peace-loving people of the land;
they think up deceptive speeches.
²¹Their mouths wide open to accuse me,
they say, 'Come on now, we saw you.'

²²You saw it, Yahweh, do not stay silent;
Lord, do not stand aloof from me.
²³Up, awake, to my defence,
my God and my Lord, to my cause.

24 In your saving justice give judgement for
   me, Yahweh my God,
   and do not let them gloat over me.

25 Do not let them think, 'Just as we hoped,'
   nor, 'Now we have swallowed him up.'
26 Shame and dismay on them all
   who gloat over my misfortunes.
   Let all who profit at my expense
   be covered with shame and disgrace.

27 But let all who delight in my uprightness
   shout for joy and gladness;
   let them constantly say,
   'Great is Yahweh,
   who delights to see his servant in peace.'

28 And my tongue shall recount your saving
   justice,
   all day long sing your praise.

36 a
For the choirmaster:
Of the servant of Yahweh; of David

1 Sin is the oracle of the wicked
   in the depths of his heart;
   there is no fear of God
   before his eyes.

2 He sees himself with too flattering an eye
   to detect and detest his guilt;
3 all he says is malicious and deceitful,
   he has turned his back on wisdom.

To get his way 4 he hatches malicious plots
   even in his bed;
   once set on his evil course
   no wickedness is too much for him.

5 Yahweh, your faithful love is in the
   heavens,
   your constancy reaches to the clouds,
6 your saving justice is like towering
   mountains,
   your judgements like the mighty deep.

Yahweh, you support both man and beast;
7 how precious, God, is your faithful love.

So the children of Adam
take refuge in the shadow of your wings.

8 They feast on the bounty of your house,
   you let them drink from your delicious
   streams;
9 in you is the source of life,
   by your light we see the light.

10 Maintain your faithful love to those who
   acknowledge you,
   and your saving justice to the honest of
   heart.

11 Do not let the foot of the arrogant
   overtake me
   or wicked hands drive me away.

12 There they have fallen, the evil-doers,
   flung down, never to rise again.

37
Of David

ALEPH 1 Do not get heated about the wicked
   or envy those who do wrong.
2 Quick as the grass they wither,
   fading like the green of the fields.

BET 3 Put your trust in Yahweh and do right,
   make your home in the land and live
   secure.
4 Make Yahweh your joy
   and he will give you your heart's desires.

GIMEL 5 Commit your destiny to Yahweh,
   be confident in him, and he will act,
6 making your uprightness clear as daylight,
   and the justice of your cause as the noon.

DALET 7 Stay quiet before Yahweh, wait
   longingly for him,
   do not get heated over someone who is
   making a fortune,
   succeeding by devious means.

36a The two parts of the Ps in different rhythms may have
existed separately.

HE ⁸Refrain from anger, leave rage aside,
    do not get heated—it can do no good;
  ⁹for evil-doers will be annihilated,
    while those who hope in Yahweh shall
        have the land for their own.

WAW ¹⁰A little while and the wicked will be
      no more,
    however well you search for the place, the
      wicked will not be there;
  ¹¹but the poor will have the land for their
      own,
    to enjoy untroubled peace.

ZAIN ¹²The wicked plots against the upright
    and gnashes his teeth at him,
  ¹³but Yahweh only laughs at his efforts,
    knowing that his end is in sight.

HET ¹⁴Though the wicked draw his sword
    and bend his bow to slaughter the honest
    and bring down the poor and the needy,
  ¹⁵his sword will pierce his own heart,
    and his bow will be shattered.

TET ¹⁶What little the upright possesses
    outweighs all the wealth of the wicked;
  ¹⁷for the weapons of the wicked shall be
      shattered,
    while Yahweh supports the upright.

YOD ¹⁸The lives of the just are in Yahweh's
      care,
    their birthright will endure for ever;
  ¹⁹they will not be put to shame when bad
      times come,
    in time of famine they will have plenty.

KAPH ²⁰The wicked, enemies of Yahweh,
      will be destroyed,
    they will vanish like the green of the
      pasture,
    they will vanish in smoke.

LAMED ²¹The wicked borrows and will not
      repay,
    but the upright is generous in giving;

²²those he blesses will have the land for their
    own,
    and those he curses be annihilated.

MEM ²³Yahweh guides a strong man's steps
    and keeps them firm;
    and takes pleasure in him.
  ²⁴When he trips he is not thrown
      sprawling,
    since Yahweh supports him by the
      hand.

NUN ²⁵Now I am old, but ever since my
      youth
    I never saw an upright person
      abandoned,
    or the descendants of the upright forced to
      beg their bread.
  ²⁶The upright is always compassionate,
      always lending,
    so his descendants reap a blessing.

SAMEK ²⁷Turn your back on evil and do
      good,
    you will have a home for ever,
  ²⁸for Yahweh loves justice
    and will not forsake his faithful.

AIN Evil-doers will perish eternally,
    the descendants of the wicked be
      annihilated,
  ²⁹but the upright shall have the land for
      their own,
    there they shall live for ever.

PE ³⁰Wisdom comes from the lips of the
      upright,
    and his tongue speaks what is right;
  ³¹the law of his God is in his heart,
    his foot will never slip.

ZADE ³²The wicked keeps a close eye on the
      upright,
    looking out for a chance to kill him;
  ³³Yahweh will never abandon him to the
      clutches of the wicked,
    nor let him be condemned if he is tried.

QOPH ³⁴ Put your hope in Yahweh, keep to his path,
he will raise you up to make the land your own;
you will look on while the wicked are annihilated.

RESH ³⁵ I have seen the wicked exultant,
towering like a cedar of Lebanon.
³⁶ When next I passed he was gone,
I searched for him and he was nowhere to be found.

SHIN ³⁷ Observe the innocent, consider the honest,
for the lover of peace will not lack children.
³⁸ But the wicked will all be destroyed together,
and their children annihilated.

TAW ³⁹ The upright have Yahweh for their Saviour,
their refuge in times of trouble;
⁴⁰ Yahweh helps them and rescues them,
he will rescue them from the wicked,
and save them because they take refuge in him.

38

Psalm of David;
in commemoration

¹ Yahweh, do not correct me in anger,
do not discipline me in wrath.
² For your arrows have pierced deep into me,
your hand has pressed down upon me.
³ Your indignation has left no part of me unscathed,
my sin has left no health in my bones.

⁴ My sins stand higher than my head,
they weigh on me as an unbearable weight.
⁵ I have stinking, festering wounds,
thanks to my folly.
⁶ I am twisted and bent double,
I spend my days in gloom.

⁷ My loins burn with fever,
no part of me is unscathed.
⁸ Numbed and utterly crushed
I groan in distress of heart.

⁹ Lord, all my longing is known to you,
my sighing no secret from you,
¹⁰ my heart is throbbing, my strength has failed,
the light has gone out of my eyes.

¹¹ Friends and companions shun my disease,
even the dearest of them keep their distance.
¹² Those with designs on my life lay snares,
those who wish me ill speak of violence
and hatch treachery all day long.

¹³ But I hear nothing, as though I were deaf,
as though dumb, saying not a word.
¹⁴ I am like the one who, hearing nothing,
has no sharp answer to make.

¹⁵ For in you, Yahweh, I put my hope,
you, Lord my God, will give answer.
¹⁶ I said, 'Never let them gloat over me,
do not let them take advantage of me if my foot slips.'

¹⁷ There is no escape for me from falling,
no relief from my misery.
¹⁸ But I make no secret of my guilt,
I am anxious at the thought of my sin.

¹⁹ There is no numbering those who oppose me without cause,
no counting those who hate me unprovoked,
²⁰ repaying me evil for good,
slandering me for trying to do them good.

²¹ Yahweh, do not desert me,
my God, do not stand aloof from me.
²² Come quickly to my help,
Lord, my Saviour!

39

For the choirmaster: For Jeduthun;
psalm of David

1 I said, 'I will watch how I behave
    so that I do not sin by my tongue.
I will keep a muzzle on my mouth
    as long as any sinner is near.'
2 I stayed dumb, silent, speechless,
    but the sinner's prosperity redoubled my
        torment.

3 My heart had been smouldering within
        me,
    but at the thought of this it flared up
    and the words came bursting out,
4 'Yahweh, let me know my fate,
    how much longer I have to live.
Show me just how frail I am.

5 'Look, you have given me but a hand's
        breadth or two of life,
    the length of my life is as nothing to you.
Every human being that stands on earth is
        a mere puff of wind,
6 every human being that walks only a
        shadow;
    a mere puff of wind is the wealth stored
        away—
no knowing who will profit from it.'

7 So now, Lord, what am I to hope for?
    My hope is in you.
8 Save me from all my sins,
    do not make me the butt of fools.
9 I keep silence, I speak no more
    since you yourself have been at work.

10 Take your scourge away from me.
    I am worn out by the blows you deal me.
11 You correct human beings by punishing
        sin,
    like a moth you eat away all their
        desires—
a human being is a mere puff of wind.

12 Yahweh, hear my prayer,
    listen to my cry for help,
    do not remain deaf to my weeping.

For I am a stranger in your house,
    a nomad like all my ancestors.
13 Turn away your gaze that I may breathe
        freely
    before I depart and am no more!

40

For the choirmaster:
Psalm of David

1 I waited, I waited for Yahweh,
    then he stooped to me
    and heard my cry for help.

2 He pulled me up from the seething chasm,
    from the mud of the mire.
He set my feet on rock,
    and made my footsteps firm.

3 He put a fresh song in my mouth,
    praise of our God.
Many will be awestruck at the sight,
    and will put their trust in Yahweh.

4 How blessed are those
    who put their trust in Yahweh,
who have not sided with rebels
    and those who have gone astray in
        falsehood.

5 How much you have done,
    Yahweh, my God—
your wonders, your plans for us—
    you have no equal.
I will proclaim and speak of them;
    they are beyond number.

6 You wanted no sacrifice or cereal offering,
    but you gave me an open ear,
you did not ask for burnt offering or
        sacrifice for sin;
7   then I said, 'Here I am, I am coming.'
In the scroll of the book it is written of me,
8   my delight is to do your will;
your law, my God,
    is deep in my heart.

9 I proclaimed the saving justice of Yahweh
    in the great assembly.
See, I will not hold my tongue,
    as you well know.

¹⁰ I have not kept your saving justice locked
    in the depths of my heart,
  but have spoken of your constancy and
    saving help.
  I have made no secret of your faithful and
    steadfast love,
    in the great assembly.

¹¹ You, Yahweh, have not withheld
    your tenderness from me;
  your faithful and steadfast love
    will always guard me.

¹² For troubles surround me,
    until they are beyond number;
  my sins have overtaken me;
    I cannot see my way.
  They outnumber the hairs of my head,
    and my heart fails me.

¹³ Be pleased, Yahweh, to rescue me,^a
    Yahweh, come quickly and help me!
¹⁴ Shame and dismay to all
    who seek to take my life.

  Back with them, let them be humiliated
    who delight in my misfortunes.
¹⁵ Let them be aghast with shame,
    those who say to me, 'Aha, aha!'

¹⁶ But joy and happiness in you
    to all who seek you!
  Let them ceaselessly cry, 'Great is Yahweh'
    who love your saving power.

¹⁷ Poor and needy as I am,
    the Lord has me in mind.
  You, my helper, my Saviour,
    my God, do not delay.

41

For the choirmaster:
Psalm of David

¹ Blessed is anyone who cares for the poor
    and the weak;
  in time of trouble Yahweh rescues him.
² Yahweh protects him, gives him life and
    happiness on earth.

  Do not abandon him to his enemies'
    pleasure!
³ Yahweh sustains him on his bed of
    sickness;
  you transform altogether the bed where
    he lies sick.

⁴ For my part I said, 'Yahweh, take pity on
    me!
  Cure me for I have sinned against you.'
⁵ My enemies speak to me only of
    disaster,
  'When will he die and his name
    disappear?'
⁶ When people come to see me their talk is
    hollow,
  when they get out they spread the news
    with spite in their hearts.

⁷ All who hate me whisper together about
    me
  and reckon I deserve the misery I
    suffer.
⁸ 'A fatal sickness has a grip on him;
  now that he is down, he will never get up
    again.'
⁹ Even my trusted friend on whom I
    relied,
  who shared my table, takes advantage of
    me.

¹⁰ But you, Yahweh, take pity on me!
  Put me on my feet and I will give them
    their due.
¹¹ This will convince me that you delight
    in me,
  if my enemy no longer exults over me.
¹² Then you will keep me unscathed,
  and set me in your presence for ever.

¹³ Blessed be Yahweh, the God of Israel,
    from eternity to eternity.
    Amen, Amen.^a

40a vv. 13–17 recur in Ps 70.

41a A doxology closes each book of the Psalter: Pss 72, 89, 106, 150.

42-43

For the choirmaster:
Poem of the sons of Korah

¹ As a deer yearns
  for running streams,
so I yearn
  for you, my God.

² I thirst for God,
  the living God;
when shall I go to see
  the face of God?

³ I have no food but tears
  day and night,
as all day long I am taunted,
  'Where is your God?'

⁴ This I remember
  as I pour out my heart,
how I used to pass under the roof of the
      Most High
  used to go to the house of God,
among cries of joy and praise,
  the sound of the feast.

⁵ Why be so downcast,
  why all these sighs?
Hope in God! I will praise him still,
  my Saviour, ⁶my God.

When I am downcast
  I think of you:
from the land of Jordan and Hermon,
  I think of you, humble mountain.

⁷ Deep is calling to deep
  by the roar of your cataracts,
all your waves and breakers
  have rolled over me.

⁸ In the daytime God sends his faithful love,
  and even at night;
the song it inspires in me
  is a prayer to my living God.

⁹ I shall say to God, my rock,
  'Why have you forgotten me?
Why must I go around in mourning,
  harrassed by the enemy?'

¹⁰ With death in my bones,
  my enemies taunt me,
all day long they ask me,
  'Where is your God?'

¹¹ Why so downcast,
  why all these sighs?
Hope in God! I will praise him still,
  my Saviour, my God.

43

¹ Judge me, God, defend my cause
  against a people who have no faithful
      love;
from those who are treacherous and
      unjust,
  rescue me.

² For you are the God of my strength;
  why abandon me?
Why must I go around in mourning,
  harrassed by the enemy?

³ Send out your light and your truth;
  they shall be my guide,
to lead me to your holy mountain
  to the place where you dwell.

⁴ Then I shall go to the altar of God,
  to the God of my joy.
I will rejoice and praise you on the harp,
  O God, my God.

⁵ Why so downcast,
  why all these sighs?
Hope in God! I will praise him still,
  my Saviour, my God.

44

For the choirmaster:
Poem of the sons of Korah

¹ God, we have heard for ourselves,
  our ancestors have told us,
of the deeds you did in their days,
  in days of old, ²by your hand.

To establish them in the land you drove
    out nations,
to make room for them you harried
    peoples.
3 It was not their own sword that won the
    land,
nor their own arms which made them
    victorious,
but your hand it was and your arm,
and the light of your presence, for you
    loved them.

4 You are my king, my God,
  who decreed Jacob's victories;
5 through you we conquered our opponents,
  in your name we trampled down those
    who rose up against us.

6 For my trust was not in my bow,
  my victory was not won by my sword;
7 it was you who saved us from our
    opponents,
you who put to shame those who hate us.
8 Our boast was always of God,
  we praised your name without ceasing.
                         Pause

9 Yet now you have abandoned and
    humiliated us,
you no longer take the field with our
    armies,
10 you leave us to fall back before the enemy,
  those who hate us plunder us at will.

11 You hand us over like sheep for slaughter,
  you scatter us among the nations,
12 you sell your people for a trifle
  and make no profit on the sale.

13 You make us the butt of our neighbours,
  the mockery and scorn of those around us,
14 you make us a by-word among nations,
  other peoples shake their heads over us.

15 All day long I brood on my disgrace,
  the shame written clear on my face,
16 from the sound of insult and abuse,
  from the sight of hatred and vengefulness.

17 All this has befallen us though we had not
    forgotten you,
nor been disloyal to your covenant,
18 our hearts never turning away,
  our feet never straying from your path.
19 Yet you have crushed us in the place where
    jackals live,
and immersed us in shadow dark as
    death.

20 Had we forgotten the name of our God
  and stretched out our hands to a foreign
    god,
21 would not God have found this out,
  for he knows the secrets of the heart?
22 For your sake we are being massacred all
    day long,
treated as sheep to be slaughtered.

23 Wake, Lord! Why are you asleep?
  Awake! Do not abandon us for good.
24 Why do you turn your face away,
  forgetting that we are poor and harrassed?

25 For we are bowed down to the dust,
  and lie prone on the ground.
26 Arise! Come to our help!
  Ransom us, as your faithful love demands.

45 *For the choirmaster: Tune: 'Lilies . . .';*
    poem of the sons of Korah, love song
1 My heart is stirred by a noble theme,
  I address my poem to the king,
  my tongue the pen of an expert scribe.

2 Of all men you are the most handsome,
  gracefulness is a dew upon your lips,
  for God has blessed you for ever.

3 Warrior, strap your sword at your side,
  in your majesty and splendour advance,
4   ride on
  in the cause of truth, gentleness and
    uprightness.

Stretch the bowstring tight, lending terror
  to your right hand.

5 Your arrows are sharp, nations lie at your
    mercy,
  the king's enemies lose heart.

6 Your throne is from God, for ever and ever,
  the sceptre of your kingship a sceptre of
    justice,
7 you love uprightness and detest evil.

  This is why God, your God, has anointed
    you
  with oil of gladness, as none of your rivals,
8 your robes all myrrh and aloes.

  From palaces of ivory, harps bring you joy,
9 in your retinue are daughters of kings,
  the consort at your right hand in gold of
    Ophir.

10 Listen, my daughter, attend to my words
    and hear;
  forget your own nation and your ancestral
    home,
11 then the king will fall in love with your
    beauty;
  he is your lord, bow down before him.
12 The daughter of Tyre will court your
    favour with gifts,
  and the richest of peoples 13 with jewels set
    in gold.

  Clothed 14 in brocade, the king's daughter
    is led within
  to the king with the maidens of her
    retinue;
  her companions are brought to her,
15 they enter the king's palace with joy and
    rejoicing.
16 Instead of your ancestors you will have
    sons;
  you will make them rulers over the whole
    world.

17 I will make your name endure from
    generation to generation,
  so nations will sing your praise for ever
    and ever.

46

For the choirmaster:
Of the sons of Korah; for oboe; song
1 God is both refuge and strength for us,
  a help always ready in trouble;
2 so we shall not be afraid though the earth
    be in turmoil,
  though mountains tumble into the depths
    of the sea,
3 and its waters roar and seethe,
  and the mountains totter as it heaves.

  (Yahweh Sabaoth is with us,
    our citadel, the God of Jacob.)   *Pause*

4 There is a river whose streams bring joy to
    God's city,
  it sanctifies the dwelling of the Most High.
5 God is in the city, it cannot fall;
  at break of day God comes to its rescue.
6 Nations are in uproar, kingdoms are
    tumbling,
  when he raises his voice the earth crumbles
    away.

7   Yahweh Sabaoth is with us,
      our citadel, the God of Jacob.   *Pause*

8 Come, consider the wonders of Yahweh,
  the astounding deeds he has done on the
    earth;
9 he puts an end to wars over the whole
    wide world,
  he breaks the bow, he snaps the spear,
  shields he burns in the fire.
10 'Be still and acknowledge that I am God,
  supreme over nations, supreme over the
    world.'

11   Yahweh Sabaoth is with us,
      our citadel, the God of Jacob.   *Pause*

47

For the choirmaster:
Psalm of the sons of Korah
1 Clap your hands, all peoples,
  acclaim God with shouts of joy.

2 For Yahweh, the Most High, is glorious,
  the great king over all the earth.

3 He brings peoples under our yoke
   and nations under our feet.

4 He chooses for us our birthright,
   the pride of Jacob whom he loves.   *Pause*

5 God goes up to shouts of acclaim,
   Yahweh to a fanfare on the ram's horn.

6 Let the music sound for our God, let it
      sound,
   let the music sound for our king, let it
      sound.

7 For he is king of the whole world;
   learn the music, let it sound for God!
8 God reigns over the nations,
   seated on his holy throne.

9 The leaders of the nations rally
   to the people of the God of Abraham.
   The shields of the earth belong to God,
   who is exalted on high.

48
*Song;
psalm of the sons of Korah*
1 Great is Yahweh and most worthy of
      praise
   in the city of our God,
   the holy mountain, 2 towering in beauty,
   the joy of the whole world:

   Mount Zion in the heart of the north,
      the settlement of the great king;
3 God himself among its palaces
      has proved himself its bulwark.

4 For look, kings made alliance,
      together they advanced;
5 without a second glance, when they saw,
      they panicked and fled away.

6 Trembling seized them on the spot,
      pains like those of a woman in labour;
7 it was the east wind,
      that wrecker of ships from Tarshish.

8 What we had heard we saw for ourselves
      in the city of our God,
   in the city of Yahweh Sabaoth,
      which God has established for ever.
                                        Pause

9 We reflect on your faithful love, God,
      in your temple!
10 Both your name and your praise, God,
      are over the whole wide world.

   Your right hand is full of saving justice,
11   Mount Zion rejoices,
   the daughters of Judah delight
      because of your saving justice.

12 Go round Zion, walk right through her,
      count her bastions,
13 admire her walls,
      examine her palaces,
   to tell future generations
14   that such is God;
   our God for ever and ever,
      he is our guide!

49
*For the choirmaster:
Psalm of the sons of Korah*
1 Hear this, all nations,
   listen, all who dwell on earth,
2 people high and low,
   rich and poor alike!

3 My lips have wisdom to utter,
   my heart good sense to whisper.
4 I listen carefully to a proverb,
   I set my riddle to the music of the harp.

5 Why should I be afraid in times of
      trouble?
   Malice dogs me and hems me in.
6 They trust in their wealth,
   and boast of the profusion of their riches.

7 But no one can ever redeem himself
   or pay his own ransom to God,
8 the price for himself is too high;
   it can never be 9 that he will live on for ever
   and avoid the sight of the abyss.

¹⁰ For he will see the wise also die
no less than the fool and the brute,
and leave their wealth behind for
others.

¹¹ For ever no home but their tombs,
their dwelling-place age after age,
though they gave their name to whole
territories.

¹² In prosperity people lose their good
sense,
they become no better than dumb animals.
¹³ So they go on in their self-assurance,
right up to the end they are content with
their lot.   *Pause*

¹⁴ They are penned in Sheol like sheep,
Death will lead them to pasture,
and those who are honest will rule over
them.

In the morning all trace of them will be
gone,
Sheol will be their home.
¹⁵ But my soul God will ransom
from the clutches of Sheol, and will snatch
me up.   *Pause*

¹⁶ Do not be overawed when someone gets
rich,
and lives in ever greater splendour;
¹⁷ when he dies he will take nothing with
him,
his wealth will not go down with him.

¹⁸ Though he pampered himself while he
lived
—and people praise you for looking after
yourself—
¹⁹ he will go to join the ranks of his
ancestors,
who will never again see the light.

²⁰ In prosperity people lose their good
sense,
they become no better than dumb animals.

50   *Psalm of Asaph*

¹ The God of gods, Yahweh, is speaking,
from east to west he summons the earth.
² From Zion, perfection of beauty, he shines
forth;
³ he is coming, our God, and will not be
silent.

Devouring fire ahead of him,
raging tempest around him,
⁴ he summons the heavens from on high,
and the earth to judge his people.

⁵ 'Gather to me my faithful,
who sealed my covenant by sacrifice.'
⁶ The heavens proclaim his saving justice,
'God himself is judge.'   *Pause*

⁷ 'Listen, my people, I am speaking,
Israel, I am giving evidence against you,
I, God, your God.

⁸ 'It is not with your sacrifices that I find
fault,
those burnt offerings constantly before me;
⁹ I will not accept any bull from your
homes,
nor a single goat from your folds.

¹⁰ 'For all forest creatures are mine already,
the animals on the mountains in their
thousands.
¹¹ I know every bird in the air,
whatever moves in the fields is mine.

¹² 'If I am hungry I shall not tell you,
since the world and all it holds is mine.
¹³ Am I to eat the flesh of bulls
or drink the blood of goats?

¹⁴ 'Let thanksgiving be your sacrifice
to God,
fulfil the vows you make to the Most
High;
¹⁵ then if you call to me in time of trouble
I will rescue you and you will honour me.'

42 READ PSALM 50:1–15.

Let thanksgiving be your sacrifice to God.—PSALM 50:14

THIRST FOR LOVE

I long for no other treasure but love, for it alone can make us pleasing to God. Jesus has shown us the only path which leads to this divine furnace of love. It is the complete abandonment of a baby sleeping without a fear in its father's arms. . . . In his name the prophet Isaiah reveals that on the last day the Lord "shall feed his flock like a shepherd: He shall gather together the lambs with his arm, and shall take them up in his bosom" (see Is 40:11). . . .

If people who are as weak and imperfect as I am only felt what I feel, not one of them would despair of scaling the summit of the mountain of love. Jesus does not demand great deeds. All He wants is self-surrender and gratitude. "I will not accept any bull from your homes, nor a single goat from your folds. For all forest creatures are mine already, the animals on the mountains in their thousands. I know every bird in the air, whatever moves in the fields is mine. If I am hungry I shall not tell you, since the world and all it holds is mine. Am I to eat the flesh of bulls and drink the blood of goats? Let thanksgiving be your sacrifice to God" (Ps 50:9–14).

That is all Jesus asks from us. He needs nothing from us except our love. God, who declares he has no need to tell us he is hungry, does not hesitate to *beg* a drop of water from the woman of Samaria (see Jn 4:7) . . . He was thirsty! But when he said: "Give me something to drink," the Creator of the universe was asking for the love of the poor thing he had created. He was thirsty for love! And now more than ever Jesus thirsts. From the worldly he meets with only ingratitude and indifference, and even among his disciples . . . very few . . . surrender fully to the tenderness of his infinite love.

St. Thérèse of Lisieux, 1873–1897

YOU WILL FIND THE NEXT READING AT PSALM 51.

16 But to the wicked, God says:

'What right have you to recite my statutes,
to take my covenant on your lips,
17 when you detest my teaching,
and thrust my words behind you?

18 'You make friends with a thief as soon as
you see one,
you feel at home with adulterers,
19 your conversation is devoted to
wickedness,
and your tongue to inventing lies.

20 'You sit there, slandering your own
brother,
you malign your own mother's son.
21 You do this, and am I to say nothing?
Do you think that I am really like you?
I charge you, indict you to your face.

22 'Think it out, you who forget God,
or I will tear you apart without hope of a
rescuer.
23 Honour to me is a sacrifice of
thanksgiving;
to the upright I will show God's salvation.'

51

*For the choirmaster: Of David, when
the prophet Nathan had come to him
because he had gone to Bathsheba*

1 Have mercy on me, O God, in your
faithful love,
in your great tenderness wipe away my
offences;
2 wash me clean from my guilt,
purify me from my sin.

3 For I am well aware of my offences,
my sin is constantly in mind.
4 Against you, you alone, I have sinned,
I have done what you see to be wrong,

that you may show your saving justice
when you pass sentence,
and your victory may appear when you
give judgement,
5 remember, I was born guilty,
a sinner from the moment of conception.

6 But you delight in sincerity of heart,
and in secret you teach me wisdom.
7 Purify me with hyssop till I am clean,
wash me till I am whiter than snow.

8 Let me hear the sound of joy and
gladness,
and the bones you have crushed will
dance.
9 Turn away your face from my sins,
and wipe away all my guilt.

10 God, create in me a clean heart,
renew within me a resolute spirit,
11 do not thrust me away from your presence,
do not take away from me your spirit of
holiness.

12 Give me back the joy of your salvation,
sustain in me a generous spirit.
13 I shall teach the wicked your paths,
and sinners will return to you.

14 Deliver me from bloodshed, God, God of
my salvation,

and my tongue will acclaim your saving
justice.
15 Lord, open my lips,
and my mouth will speak out your
praise.

16 Sacrifice gives you no pleasure,
burnt offering you do not desire.
17 Sacrifice to God is a broken spirit,
a broken, contrite heart you never scorn.

18 In your graciousness do good to Zion,
rebuild the walls of Jerusalem.
19 Then you will delight in upright sacrifices,
—burnt offerings and whole oblations—
and young bulls will be offered on your
altar.

52

*For the choirmaster: Poem of David,
when Doeg the Edomite went and
warned Saul, 'David has gone
to Abimelech's house'*

1 Why take pride in being wicked,
you champion in villainy,
all day long 2 plotting crime?
Your tongue is razor-sharp,
you artist in perfidy.

3 You prefer evil to good,
lying to uprightness.   *Pause*
4 You revel in destructive talk,
treacherous tongue!

5 That is why God will crush you,
destroy you once and for all,
snatch you from your tent,
uproot you from the land of the living.
                                         Pause

6 The upright will be awestruck as they
see it,
they will mock him,
7 'So much for someone who would not
place
his reliance in God,
but relied on his own great wealth,
and made himself strong by crime.'

43 READ PSALM 51.

Wash me clean from my guilt, purify me from my sin.—PSALM 51:2

FIGHTING IMPERFECTIONS

What a pity it is to see souls who perceive themselves still subject to many imperfections after striving to be devout for a while and then begin to be dissatisfied, disturbed, and discouraged. [They] almost let their hearts give in to a temptation to give up everything and go back to their old way of life. On the other hand, are not those souls also in extreme danger who by an opposite temptation think themselves cleansed of every imperfection on the very first day of their purgation, regard themselves as perfect before they have scarcely begun, and try to fly without wings? . . . They are in great peril of a relapse on being too soon out of the physician's care. . . . Instead, we should follow the example of the psalmist David. Although already washed and cleansed, he asked to be washed and cleansed still more and more (see Ps 51:2).

The work of purging the soul neither can nor should end except with our life itself. We must not be disturbed at our imperfections, since for us perfection consists in fighting against them. How can we fight against them unless we see them, or overcome them unless we face them? Our victory does not consist in being unconscious of them but in not consenting to them. And not to consent to them is to be displeased with them. To practice humility it is absolutely necessary for us at times to suffer wounds in this spiritual warfare, but we are never vanquished unless we lose our life or our courage. Imperfections and venial sins cannot deprive us of spiritual life. It is lost only by mortal sin. Therefore it only remains for us not to lose courage. . . . Fortunately for us, in this war we are always victorious provided that we are willing to fight. ST. FRANCIS DE SALES, 1567–1622

YOU WILL FIND THE NEXT READING AT PSALM 63.

8 But I, like a flourishing olive tree
   in the house of God,
put my trust in God's faithful love,
   for ever and ever.

9 I shall praise you for ever
   for what you have done,
and shall trust in your name, so full of
      goodness,
   in the presence of your faithful.

53 ^a^ *For the choirmaster: In sickness;*
                poem of David
1 The fool has said in his heart,
   'There is no God!'

They are corrupt, vile and unjust,
   not one of them does right.

2 God looks down from heaven
   at the children of Adam,
to see if a single one is wise,
   a single one seeks God.

3 All have proved faithless,
   all alike turned sour,
not one of them does right,
   not a single one.

53a Almost identical with Ps 14 except that the name 'Yahweh' is not used.

4 Are they not aware, these evil-doers?
  They are devouring my people;
this is the bread they eat,
  and they never call upon God.

5 They will be gripped with fear,
  just where there is no need for fear,
for God scatters the bones of him who
    besieges you;
  they are mocked because God rejects
    them.

6 Who will bring from Zion salvation for
    Israel?
When God brings his people home,
  what joy for Jacob, what happiness for
    Israel!

54 *For the choirmaster: On stringed
instruments; poem of David; when the
Ziphites went to Saul and said, 'Is not David hiding
with us?'*

1 God, save me by your name,
  in your power vindicate me.
2 God, hear my prayer,
  listen to the words I speak.

3 Arrogant men are attacking me,
  bullies hounding me to death,
no room in their thoughts for God. *Pause*

4 But now God is coming to my help,
  the Lord, among those who sustain me.
5 May their wickedness recoil on those who
    lie in wait for me.
Yahweh, in your constancy destroy them.

6 How gladly will I offer you sacrifice,
  and praise your name, for it is good,
7 for it has rescued me from all my troubles,
  and my eye has feasted on my enemies.

55 *For the choirmaster: For strings;
poem of David*

1 God, hear my prayer,
  do not hide away from my plea,
2 give me a hearing, answer me,
  my troubles give me no peace.

I shudder 3 at the enemy's shouts,
  at the outcry of the wicked;
they heap up charges against me,
  in their anger bring hostile accusations
    against me.

4 My heart writhes within me,
  the terrors of death come upon me,
5 fear and trembling overwhelm me,
  and shuddering grips me.

6 And I say,
'Who will give me wings like a dove,
  to fly away and find rest?'
7 How far I would escape,
  and make a nest in the desert! *Pause*

8 I would soon find a refuge
  from the storm of abuse,
from the 9 destructive tempest, Lord,
  from the flood of their tongues.

For I see violence
  and strife in the city,
10 day and night they make their rounds
  along the city walls,

Inside live malice and mischief,
11   inside lives destruction,
tyranny and treachery never absent
  from its central square.

12 Were it an enemy who insulted me,
    that I could bear;
if an opponent pitted himself against me,
    I could turn away from him.

13 But you, a person of my own rank,
    a comrade and dear friend,
14 to whom I was bound by intimate
    friendship
  in the house of God!

May they recoil in disorder,
15   may death descend on them,
may they go down alive to Sheol,
  since evil shares their home with them.

16 For my part, I appeal to God,
  and Yahweh saves me;
17 evening, morning, noon,
  I complain and I groan.

He hears my cry,
18 he ransoms me and gives me peace
  from the feud against me,
  for they are taking me to law.

19 But God will listen and will humble
    them,
  he who has been enthroned from the
    beginning;
  no change of heart for them,
  for they do not fear God.

20 They attack those at peace with them,
  going back on their oaths;
21 though their mouth is smoother than
    butter,
  enmity is in their hearts;
  their words more soothing than oil,
  yet sharpened like swords.

22 Unload your burden onto Yahweh
  and he will sustain you;
  never will he allow
  the upright to stumble.

23 You, God, will thrust them down
  to the abyss of destruction,
  men bloodthirsty and deceptive,
  before half their days are spent.

For my part, I put my trust in you.

56 *For the choirmaster: Tune: 'The
  oppression of distant princes'; of David;
  in a quiet voice; when the Philistines seized
    him in Gath*
1 Take pity on me, God, as they harry me,
  pressing their attacks home all day.
2 Those who harry me lie in wait for me all
    day,
  countless are those who attack me from
    the heights.

3 When I am afraid, I put my trust in you,
4 in God, whose word I praise,
  in God I put my trust and have no fear,
  what power has human strength over me?

5 All day long they carp at my words,
  their only thought is to harm me,
6 they gather together, lie in wait and spy on
    my movements,
  as though determined to take my life.

7 Because of this crime reject them,
  in your anger, God, strike down the
    nations.
8 You yourself have counted up my
    sorrows,
  collect my tears in your wineskin.
9 Then my enemies will turn back
  on the day when I call.

This I know, that God is on my side.
10 In God whose word I praise,
  in Yahweh whose word I praise,
11 in God I put my trust and have no fear;
  what can mortal man do to me?

12 I am bound by the vows I have made,
    God,
  I will pay you the debt of thanks,
13 for you have saved my life from death
  to walk in the presence of God,
  in the light of the living.

57 *For the choirmaster: Tune: 'Do not
  destroy'; of David; in a quiet voice;
  when he escaped from Saul in the cave*
1 Take pity on me, God, take pity on me,
  for in you I take refuge,
  in the shadow of your wings I take refuge,
  until the destruction is past.

2 I call to God the Most High,
  to God who has done everything for me;
3 may he send from heaven and save me,
  and check those who harry me;   *Pause*
  may God send his faithful love and his
    constancy.

4 I lie surrounded by lions,
  greedy for human prey,
  their teeth are spears and arrows,
  their tongue a sharp sword.

5 Be exalted above the heavens, God!
    Your glory over all the earth!
6 They laid a snare in my path
  —I was bowed with care—
  they dug a pit ahead of me,
  but fell in it themselves.   *Pause*

7 My heart is ready, God,
    my heart is ready;
  I will sing, and make music for you.
8   Awake, my glory,
  awake, lyre and harp,
    that I may awake the Dawn.

9 I will praise you among the peoples,
    Lord,
  I will make music for you among
    nations,
10 for your faithful love towers to heaven,
  your constancy to the clouds.
11 Be exalted above the heavens, God!
    Your glory over all the earth!

58 *For the choirmaster: Tune: 'Do not destroy'; of David; in a quiet voice*
1 Divine as you are, do you truly give
    upright verdicts?
  do you judge fairly the children of
    Adam?
2 No! You devise injustice in your
    hearts,
  and with your hands you administer
    tyranny on the earth.

3 Since the womb they have gone astray,
    the wicked,
  on the wrong path since their birth, with
    their unjust verdicts.
4 They are poisonous as any snake,
  deaf as an adder that blocks its ears
5 so as not to hear the magician's music,
  however skilful his spells.

6 God, break the teeth in their mouths,
  snap off the fangs of these young lions,
    Yahweh.
7 May they drain away like water running
    to waste,
  may they wither like trampled grass,
8 like the slug that melts as it moves
  or a still-born child that never sees
    the sun.

9 Before they sprout thorns like the
    bramble,
  green or burnt up, may retribution whirl
    them away.
10 The upright will rejoice to see vengeance
    done,
  and will bathe his feet in the blood of the
    wicked.
11 'So', people will say, 'the upright does have
    a reward;
  there is a God to dispense justice on
    earth.'

59 *For the choirmaster: Tune: 'Do not destroy'; of David; in a quiet voice; when Saul sent men to watch David's house in order to have him killed*
1 Rescue me from my enemies, my God,
  be my stronghold from my assailants,
2 rescue me from evil-doers,
  from men of violence save me.

3 Look at them, lurking to ambush me,
  violent men are attacking me,
  for no fault, no sin of mine, Yahweh, 4 for
    no guilt,
  they come running to take up position.

  Wake up, stand by me and keep watch,
5 Yahweh, God of Sabaoth, God of Israel,
  rise up, to punish all the nations,
  show no mercy to all these malicious
    traitors.   *Pause*

6   Back they come at nightfall,
    snarling like curs,
    prowling through the town.

7 Look how they rant in speech
  with swords on their lips,
  'Who is there to hear us?'

8 For your part, Yahweh, you laugh at
    them,
  you make mockery of all nations.
9 My strength, I keep my eyes fixed
    on you.

For my stronghold is God,
10 the God who loves me faithfully is coming
    to meet me,
  God will let me feast my eyes on those
    who lie in wait for me.

11 Do not annihilate them, or my people may
    forget;
  shake them in your power, bring them
    low,
    Lord, our shield.

12 Sin is in their mouths, sin on their lips,
  so let them be trapped in their pride
  for the curses and lies that they utter.

13 Destroy them in your anger, destroy them
    till they are no more,
  and let it be known that God is Master
  in Jacob and the whole wide world. *Pause*

14   Back they come at nightfall,
    snarling like curs,
    prowling through the town,
15 scavenging for something to eat,
  growling unless they have their fill.

16 And so I will sing of your strength,
  in the morning acclaim your faithful
    love;
  you have been a stronghold for me,
  a refuge when I was in trouble.

17 My strength, I will make music for you,
  for my stronghold is God,
  the God who loves me faithfully.

60

*For the choirmaster: To the tune
'The decree is a lily'; in a quiet voice;
of David; to be learnt; when he was at war
with Aram-Naharaim and Aram-Zobah,
and Joab marched back to destroy twelve thousand
Edomites in the Valley of Salt*[a]

1 God, you have rejected us, broken us,
  you were angry, come back to us!
2 You made the earth tremble, split it open;
  now mend the rifts, it is tottering still.

3 You have forced your people to drink a
    bitter draught,
  forced us to drink a wine that made us
    reel.
4 You gave a signal to those who fear you
  to let them escape out of range of the bow.
                                    Pause

5 To rescue those you love,
  save with your right hand and answer us.

6 God has spoken from his sanctuary,
  'In triumph I will divide up Shechem,
  and share out the Valley of Succoth.

7 'Mine is Gilead, mine Manasseh,
  Ephraim the helmet on my head,
  Judah my commander's baton,

8 'Moab a bowl for me to wash in,
  on Edom I plant my sandal.
  Now try shouting "Victory!" over me,
    Philistia!'

9 Who will lead me against a fortified city,
  who will guide me into Edom,
10 if not you, the God who has rejected us?
  God, you no longer march with our armies.

11 Bring us help in our time of crisis,
  any human help is worthless.
12 With God we shall do deeds of valour,
  he will trample down our enemies.

60a The verse numbers in the English are two less than the
Massoretic Text (Hebrew). The description is two verses
long.

61

For the choirmaster: For strings;
of David

1 God, hear my cry,
   listen to my prayer.
2 From the end of the earth I call to you
   with fainting heart.
   Lead me to the high rock that stands far
      out of my reach.

3 For you are my refuge,
   a strong tower against the enemy.
4 Let me stay in your tent for ever,
   taking refuge in the shelter of your
      wings!
5 For you, God, accept my vows,
   you grant me the heritage of those who
      fear your name.

6 Let the king live on and on,
   let his years continue age after age.
7 May his throne be always in God's
      presence,
   your faithful love and constancy watch
      over him.

8 Then I shall always sing to your
      name,
   day after day fulfilling my vows.

62

For the choirmaster . . . : Jeduthun;
psalm of David

1 In God alone there is rest for my soul,
   from him comes my safety;
2 he alone is my rock, my safety,
   my stronghold so that I stand
      unshaken.

3 How much longer will you set on a
      victim,
   all together, intent on murder,
   like a rampart already leaning over,
   a wall already damaged?
4 Trickery is their only plan,
   deception their only pleasure,
   with lies on their lips they pronounce a
      blessing,
   with a curse in their hearts.   *Pause*

5 Rest in God alone, my soul!
   He is the source of my hope.
6 He alone is my rock, my safety,
   my stronghold, so that I stand
      unwavering.
7 In God is my safety and my glory,
   the rock of my strength.

In God is my refuge; 8 trust in him,
   you people, at all times.
Pour out your hearts to him,
   God is a refuge for us.   *Pause*

9 Ordinary people are a mere puff of wind,
   important people a delusion;
set both on the scales together,
   and they are lighter than a puff of wind.

10 Put no trust in extortion,
   no empty hopes in robbery;
however much wealth may multiply,
   do not set your heart on it.

11 Once God has spoken,
   twice have I heard this:
Strength belongs to God,
12   to you, Lord, faithful love;
   and you repay everyone as their deeds
      deserve.

63

Psalm of David; when he was in
the desert of Judah

1 God, you are my God, I pine for you;
   my heart thirsts for you,
   my body longs for you,
   as a land parched, dreary and waterless.
2 Thus I have gazed on you in the sanctuary,
   seeing your power and your glory.

3 Better your faithful love than life itself;
   my lips will praise you.
4 Thus I will bless you all my life,
   in your name lift up my hands.
5 All my longings fulfilled as with fat and
      rich foods,
   a song of joy on my lips and praise in my
      mouth.

44 READ PSALM 63.

Better your faithful love than life itself.—PSALM 63:3

KNOWING AND LOVING GOD

The wise soul does not merely care to know God superficially, but strives to know him in truth and to learn his goodness and worth. To such a soul God is not only good, but the Highest Good. Thus knowing him, she loves him wholly because of his goodness, and loving him she desires to possess him. And then God, the Highest Good, gives himself to the soul, and she feels his presence and tastes his sweetness, and enjoys him with great delight.

Then as the soul partakes of the Highest Love, he touches her and she falls in love with her Beloved. She wants to hold him fast, and embraces him, presses him to her, and joins herself to God. And God draws her to himself with a great sweetness of love. The power of love transforms the lover into the loved, and the loved into the lover. The soul, inflamed by God's love, by the power of love is united to God, her Beloved. Just as heated iron receives in itself the heat and color and power and strength and form of fire, and is made, as it were, entirely fire, so it is with the soul that is united to God by the perfect grace of divine love. Such a soul is made, as it were, divine. She is transformed into God, not changed in her own substance, but wholly transformed in her life so that by God's love she becomes divinized.

Do you realize what good things that knowing God brings us? In the way of God, the person who wants to possess God must first know him, and then God's love that transforms the lover into the loved will follow. BL. ANGELA OF FOLIGNO, 1248?–1309

YOU WILL FIND THE NEXT READING AT PSALM 72.

6 On my bed when I think of you,
   I muse on you in the watches of the night,
7 for you have always been my help;
   in the shadow of your wings I rejoice;
8 my heart clings to you,
   your right hand supports me.

9 May those who are hounding me to
      death
   go down to the depths of the earth,
10 given over to the blade of the sword,
   and left as food for jackals.
11 Then the king shall rejoice in God,
   all who swear by him shall gain
      recognition,
   for the mouths of liars shall be silenced.

64 *For the choirmaster:*
   Psalm of David
1 Listen, God, to my voice as I plead,
   protect my life from fear of the enemy;
2 hide me from the league of the wicked,
   from the gang of evil-doers.

3 They sharpen their tongues like a sword,
   aim their arrows of poisonous abuse,
4 shoot at the innocent from cover,
   shoot suddenly, with nothing to fear.

5 They support each other in their evil
      designs,
   they discuss how to lay their snares.
   'Who will see us?' they say,

6 'or will penetrate our secrets?'
He will do that, he who penetrates human
nature to its depths,
the depths of the heart.

7 God has shot them with his arrow,
sudden were their wounds.
8 He brings them down because of their
tongue,
and all who see them shake their heads.

9 Everyone will be awestruck,
proclaim what God has done,
and understand why he has done it.

10 The upright will rejoice in Yahweh,
will take refuge in him,
and all the honest will praise him.

65

For the choirmaster:
Psalm of David; song
1 Praise is rightfully yours,
God, in Zion.
Vows to you shall be fulfilled,
2   for you answer prayer.

All humanity must come to you
3   with its sinful deeds.
Our faults overwhelm us,
but you blot them out.

4 How blessed those whom you choose
and invite to dwell in your courts.
We shall be filled with the good things of
your house,
of your holy temple.

5 You respond to us with the marvels of
your saving justice,
God our Saviour,
hope of the whole wide world,
even the distant islands.

6 By your strength you hold the mountains
steady,
being clothed in power,
7 you calm the turmoil of the seas,
the turmoil of their waves.

The nations are in uproar,
in panic those who live at the ends of
the earth;
8 your miracles bring shouts of joy
to the gateways of morning and evening.

9 You visit the earth and make it fruitful,
you fill it with riches;
the river of God brims over with water,
you provide the grain.

To that end
10 you water its furrows abundantly, level its
ridges,
soften it with showers and bless its shoots.

11 You crown the year with your generosity,
richness seeps from your tracks,
12 the pastures of the desert grow moist,
the hillsides are wrapped in joy,
13 the meadows are covered with flocks,
the valleys clothed with wheat;
they shout and sing for joy.

66

For the choirmaster:
Song; psalm
1 Acclaim God, all the earth,
2 sing psalms to the glory of his name,
glorify him with your praises,
3 say to God, 'How awesome you are!

'Your achievements are the measure of
your power,
your enemies woo your favour,
4 all the earth bows down before you,
sings psalms to you, sings psalms to your
name.'   *Pause*

5 Come and see the marvels of God,
his awesome deeds for the children of
Adam:
6 he changed the sea into dry land,
they crossed the river on foot.

So let us rejoice in him,
7 who rules for ever by his power;
his eyes keep watch on the nations
to forestall rebellion against him.   *Pause*

⁸ Nations, bless our God,
 let the sound of his praise be heard;
⁹ he brings us to life
 and keeps our feet from stumbling.

¹⁰ God, you have put us to the test,
 refined us like silver,
¹¹ let us fall into the net;
 you have put a heavy strain on our backs,
¹² let men ride over our heads;
 but now the ordeal by fire and water is
 over,
 you have led us out to breathe again.

¹³ I bring burnt offerings to your house,
 I fulfil to you my vows,
¹⁴ the vows that rose to my lips,
 that I pronounced when I was in trouble.

¹⁵ I will offer you rich burnt offerings,
 with the smoke of burning rams.
 I will sacrifice to you bullocks and goats.
 Pause

¹⁶ Come and listen, all who fear God,
 while I tell what he has done for me.

¹⁷ To him I cried aloud,
 high praise was on my tongue.
¹⁸ Had I been aware of guilt in my heart,
 the Lord would not have listened,
¹⁹ but in fact God did listen,
 attentive to the sound of my prayer.

²⁰ Blessed be God
 who has not turned away my prayer,
 nor his own faithful love from me.

67

For the choirmaster: For strings;
psalm; song

¹ May God show kindness and bless us,
 and make his face shine on us. *Pause*
² Then the earth will acknowledge your
 ways,
 and all nations your power to save.

³ Let the nations praise you, God,
 let all the nations praise you.

⁴ Let the nations rejoice and sing for joy,
 for you judge the world with justice,
 you judge the peoples with fairness,
 you guide the nations on earth. *Pause*

⁵ Let the nations praise you, God,
 let all the nations praise you.

⁶ The earth has yielded its produce;
 God, our God has blessed us.
⁷ May God continue to bless us,
 and be revered by the whole wide world.

68

For the choirmaster:
Psalm of David; song

¹ Let God arise, let his enemies scatter,
 let his opponents flee before him.
² You disperse them like smoke;
 as wax melts in the presence of a fire,
 so the wicked melt at the presence of God.

³ The upright rejoice in the presence of God,
 delighted and crying out for joy.
⁴ Sing to God, play music to his name,
 build a road for the Rider of the Clouds,
 rejoice in Yahweh, dance before him.

⁵ Father of orphans, defender of widows,
 such is God in his holy dwelling.
⁶ God gives the lonely a home to live in,
 leads prisoners out into prosperity,
 but rebels must live in the bare wastelands.

⁷ God, when you set out at the head of your
 people,
 when you strode over the desert, ⁸the
 earth rocked, *Pause*
 the heavens pelted down rain at the
 presence of God,
 at the presence of God, the God of Israel.

⁹ God, you rained down a shower of
 blessings,
 when your heritage was weary you gave it
 strength.
¹⁰ Your family found a home, which you
 in your generosity provided for the
 humble.

11 The Lord gave a command,
the good news of a countless army.
12 The chieftains of the army are in flight, in
flight,
and the fair one at home is sharing out the
spoils.

13 While you are at ease in the sheepfolds,
the wings of the Dove*a* are being covered
with silver,
and her feathers with a sheen of green
gold;
14 when Shaddai scatters the chieftains,
through her it snows*b* on the Dark
Mountain.

15 A mountain of God, the mountain of
Bashan!
a haughty mountain, the mountain of
Bashan!
16 Why be envious, haughty mountains,
of the mountain God has chosen for his
dwelling?
There God will dwell for ever.

17 The chariots of God are thousand upon
thousand;
God has come from Sinai to the sanctuary.
18 You have climbed the heights, taken
captives,
you have taken men as tribute, even rebels
that Yahweh God might have a dwelling-
place.

19 Blessed be the Lord day after day,
he carries us along, God our Saviour.
Pause

20 This God of ours is a God who saves;
from Lord Yahweh comes escape from
death;
21 but God smashes the head of his enemies,
the long-haired skull of the prowling
criminal.

22 The Lord has said, 'I will bring them back
from Bashan,

I will bring them back from the depths of
the sea,
23 so that you may bathe your feet in blood,
and the tongues of your dogs feast on your
enemies.'

24 Your processions, God, are for all to see,
the processions of my God, of my king, to
the sanctuary;
25 singers ahead, musicians behind,
in the middle come girls, beating their
drums.

26 In choirs they bless God,
Yahweh, since the foundation of Israel.

27 Benjamin was there, the youngest in
front,
the princes of Judah in bright-coloured
robes,
the princes of Zebulun, the princes of
Naphtali.

28 Take command, my God, as befits your
power,
the power, God, which you have wielded
for us,
29 from your temple high above Jerusalem.
Kings will come to you bearing tribute.

30 Rebuke the Beast of the Reeds,
that herd of bulls, that people of calves,
who bow down with ingots of silver.
Scatter the people who delight in war.
31 From Egypt nobles will come,
Ethiopia will stretch out its hands to God.

32 Kingdoms of the earth, sing to God,
play for 33 the Rider of the Heavens, the
primeval heavens. *Pause*
There he speaks, with a voice of power!
34 Acknowledge the power of God.

68a Two obscure vv., referring perhaps to Jg 5; some tribes
missed Israel's glorious victory.

68b Perhaps the salt sown on devastated Shechem after the
victory.

Over Israel his splendour, in the clouds his
power.
35 Awesome is God in his sanctuary.
He, the God of Israel,
gives strength and power to his people.

Blessed be God.

69

*For the choirmaster: Tune:
'Lilies . . .'; of David*

1 Save me, God, for the waters
have closed in on my very being.

2 I am sinking in the deepest swamp
and there is no firm ground.
I have stepped into deep water
and the waves are washing over me.

3 I am exhausted with calling out, my throat
is hoarse,
my eyes are worn out with searching for
my God.

4 More numerous than the hairs of my head
are those who hate me without reason.
Those who seek to get rid of me are
powerful,
my treacherous enemies.
(Must I give back what I have never
stolen?)

5 God, you know how foolish I am,
my offences are not hidden from you.

6 Those who hope in you must not be made
fools of,
Yahweh Sabaoth, because of me!
Those who seek you must not be
disgraced,
God of Israel, because of me!

7 It is for you I bear insults,
my face is covered with shame,
8 I am estranged from my brothers,
alienated from my own mother's sons;
9 for I am eaten up with zeal for your house,
and insults directed against you fall
on me.

10 I mortify myself with fasting,
and find myself insulted for it,
11 I dress myself in sackcloth
and become their laughing-stock,
12 the gossip of people sitting at the gate,
and the theme of drunkards' songs.

13 And so, I pray to you, Yahweh,
at the time of your favour;
in your faithful love answer me,
in the constancy of your saving power.

14 Rescue me from the mire before I sink in;
so I shall be saved from those who
hate me,
from the watery depths.
15 Let not the waves wash over me,
nor the deep swallow me up,
nor the pit close its mouth on me.

16 Answer me, Yahweh, for your faithful
love is generous;
in your tenderness turn towards me;
17 do not turn away from your servant,
be quick to answer me, for I am in trouble.
18 Come to my side, redeem me,
ransom me because of my enemies.

19 You know well the insults,
the shame and disgrace I endure.
Every one of my oppressors is known
to you.
20 Insult has broken my heart past cure.
I hoped for sympathy, but in vain,
for consolers—not one to be found.

21 To eat they gave me poison,
to drink, vinegar when I was thirsty.
22 May their own table prove a trap for them,
and their abundance a snare;
23 may their eyes grow so dim that they
cannot see,
all their muscles lose their strength.

24 Vent your fury on them,
let your burning anger overtake them.
25 Reduce their encampment to ruin,
and leave their tents untenanted,

26 for hounding someone you had already
stricken,
for redoubling the pain of one you had
wounded.

27 Charge them with crime after crime,
exclude them from your saving justice,
28 erase them from the book of life,
do not enrol them among the upright.

29 For myself, wounded wretch that I am,
by your saving power raise me up!
30 I will praise God's name in song,
I will extol him by thanksgiving,
31 for this will please Yahweh more than
an ox,
than a bullock horned and hoofed.

32 The humble have seen and are glad.
Let your courage revive, you who
seek God.
33 For God listens to the poor,
he has never scorned his captive
people.
34 Let heaven and earth and seas,
and all that stirs in them, acclaim him!

35 For God will save Zion,
and rebuild the cities of Judah,
and people will live there on their own
land;
36 the descendants of his servants will
inherit it,
and those who love his name will dwell
there.

70 ᵃ *For the choirmaster: Of David;*
in commemoration
1 Be pleased, God, to rescue me,
Yahweh, come quickly and help me!
2 Shame and dismay to those
who seek my life!

Back with them! Let them be humiliated
who delight in my misfortunes.
3 Let them shrink away covered with
shame,
those who say to me, 'Aha, aha!'

4 But joy and happiness in you
to all who seek you.
Let them ceaselessly cry, 'God is great',
who love your saving power.

5 Poor and needy as I am,
God, come quickly to me!
Yahweh, my helper, my Saviour,
do not delay!

71 In you, Yahweh, I take refuge,
I shall never be put to shame.
2 In your saving justice rescue me,
deliver me,
listen to me and save me.

3 Be a sheltering rock for me,
always accessible;
you have determined to save me,
for you are my rock, my fortress.
4 My God, rescue me from the clutches of
the wicked,
from the grasp of the rogue and the
ruthless.

5 For you are my hope, Lord,
my trust, Yahweh, since boyhood.
6 On you I have relied since my birth,
since my mother's womb you have been
my portion,
the constant theme of my praise.

7 Many were bewildered at me,
but you are my sure refuge.
8 My mouth is full of your praises,
filled with your splendour all day long.

9 Do not reject me in my old age,
nor desert me when my strength is failing,
10 for my enemies are discussing me,
those with designs on my life are plotting
together.

11 'Hound him down, for God has deserted
him!

70a = 40:13–17.

Seize him, there is no one to rescue him.'
¹² God, do not stand aloof,
my God, come quickly to help me.

¹³ Shame and ruin
on those who slander me,
may those intent on harming me
be covered with insult and infamy.

¹⁴ As for me, my hope will never fade,
I will praise you more and more.
¹⁵ My lips shall proclaim your saving
justice,
your saving power all day long.

¹⁶ I will come in the power of Yahweh
to tell of your justice, yours alone.
¹⁷ God, you have taught me from boyhood,
and I am still proclaiming your marvels.

¹⁸ Now that I am old and grey-haired,
God, do not desert me,
till I have proclaimed your strength
to generations still to come,
your power ¹⁹ and justice to the skies.

You have done great things,
God, who is like you?
²⁰ You have shown me much misery and
hardship,
but you will give me life again,
You will raise me up again from the
depths of the earth,
²¹ prolong my old age, and comfort me
again.

²² For my part, I will thank you on the lyre
for your constancy, my God.
I will play the harp in your honour,
Holy One of Israel.

²³ My lips sing for joy as I play to you,
because you have redeemed me,
²⁴ and all day long my tongue muses on
your saving justice.
Shame and disgrace on those intent to
harm me!

72

Of Solomon

¹ God, endow the king with your own fair
judgement,
the son of the king with your own
saving justice,
² that he may rule your people with justice,
and your poor with fair judgement.

³ Mountains and hills,
bring peace to the people!
With justice ⁴ he will judge the poor of the
people,
he will save the children of the needy
and crush their oppressors.

⁵ In the sight of the sun and the moon he
will endure,
age after age.
⁶ He will come down like rain on mown
grass,
like showers moistening the land.

⁷ In his days uprightness shall flourish,
and peace in plenty till the moon is no
more.
⁸ His empire shall stretch from sea to sea,
from the river to the limits of the earth.

⁹ The Beast will cower before him,
his enemies lick the dust;
¹⁰ the kings of Tarshish and the islands
will pay him tribute.

The kings of Sheba and Saba
will offer gifts;
¹¹ all kings will do him homage,
all nations become his servants.

¹² For he rescues the needy who calls to him,
and the poor who has no one to help.
¹³ He has pity on the weak and the needy,
and saves the needy from death.

¹⁴ From oppression and violence he redeems
their lives,
their blood is precious in his sight.

45   READ PSALM 72.

God, endow the king with your own fair judgement, the son of the king with your own saving justice.—PSALM 72:1

JESUS, JUDGE AND SAVIOR

David begs the Father, "O God, commit your judgment to the king, and your justice to the king's son, . . ." He means: Do not judge us in your own majesty, O God, but entrust this office to your Son, our Lord, in your stead. Delegate to him the work of judging, and let him be my judge who has been my redeemer. Not because I am unaware of either your probity or your mercy do I ask this, most loving Father, for you are . . . most righteous and gentle by your very nature. . . .

But I dread to appear in the light of your truth, I am afraid in its presence, for you have not experienced my weakness or the wretchedness and toil to which I have been subject since infancy. Appoint rather as my judge, most merciful Father, him who has shared my experience of hunger, cold, sadness, and distress. Appoint him who has known from within the wretchedness and limitations of the human lot, who has endured the crafty attacks and deceits of evil, who has known what it is to be tempted and to suffer in every way. On these very grounds, remembering his own temptations and sufferings, he will graciously aid those who are tempted, for he has learned mercy from the things he suffered. He knows of what I am made. From his own sharing in them he knows my frailty and the wild, tempestuous waves of this sea on which we are shipwrecked. This is why I willingly submit to his judgment and embrace his sentence, since for me, his most wretched and unworthy servant, he was judged and sentenced to death. He allowed himself to be condemned to crucifixion rather than condemn me to hell. And so I will not reject him as judge whom I have as redeemer.

ST. THOMAS OF VILLANOVA, 1488–1555

YOU WILL FIND THE NEXT READING AT PSALM 80.

15 (Long may he live; may the gold of Sheba
    be given him!)
  Prayer will be offered for him constantly,
    and blessings invoked on him all day.

16 May wheat abound in the land,
    waving on the heights of the hills,
  like Lebanon with its fruits and flowers at
    their best,
  like the grasses of the earth.

17 May his name be blessed for ever,
    and endure in the sight of the sun.

In him shall be blessed every race in the
    world,
  and all nations call him blessed.

18 Blessed be Yahweh, the God of Israel,
    who alone works wonders;
19 blessed for ever his glorious name.
  May the whole world be filled with his
    glory!
  Amen! Amen!

20 End of the prayers of David, son of
    Jesse.

BOOK THREE: PSALMS 73–89

73

Psalm of Asaph

¹ Indeed God is good to Israel,
the Lord to those who are pure of heart.

² My feet were on the point of stumbling,
a little more and I had slipped,
³ envying the arrogant as I did,
and seeing the prosperity of the wicked.

⁴ For them no such thing as pain,
untroubled, their comfortable portliness;
⁵ exempt from the cares which are the
human lot,
they have no part in Adam's afflictions.

⁶ So pride is a necklace to them,
violence the garment they wear.
⁷ From their fat oozes out malice,
their hearts drip with cunning.

⁸ Cynically they advocate evil,
loftily they advocate force.
⁹ Their mouth claims heaven for
themselves,
and their tongue is never still on earth.

¹⁰ That is why my people turn to them,
and enjoy the waters of plenty,
¹¹ saying, 'How can God know?
What knowledge can the Most High
have?'
¹² That is what the wicked are like,
piling up wealth without any worries.

¹³ Was it useless, then, to have kept my own
heart clean,
to have washed my hands in innocence?

¹⁴ When I was under a hail of blows all day
long,
and punished every morning,
¹⁵ had I said, 'I shall talk like them,'
I should have betrayed your children's
race.

¹⁶ So I set myself to understand this:
how difficult I found it!
¹⁷ Until I went into the sanctuaries of
the gods
and understood what was destined to
become of them.
¹⁸ You place them on a slippery slope
and drive them down into chaos.

¹⁹ How sudden their hideous destruction!
They are swept away, annihilated by
terror!
²⁰ Like a dream upon waking, Lord,
when you awake, you dismiss their image.

²¹ My heart grew embittered,
my affections dried up,
²² I was stupid and uncomprehending,
a clumsy animal in your presence.

²³ Even so, I stayed in your presence,
you grasped me by the right hand;
²⁴ you will guide me with advice,
and will draw me in the wake of your
glory.

²⁵ Who else is there for me in heaven?
And, with you, I lack nothing on earth.
²⁶ My heart and my flesh are pining away:
my heart's rock, my portion, God for ever!

²⁷ Truly, those who abandon you will perish;
you destroy those who adulterously desert
you,
²⁸ whereas my happiness is to be near God.
I have made the Lord Yahweh my refuge,
to tell of all your works.

74

Poem of Asaph

¹ God, why have you finally rejected us,
your anger blazing against the flock you
used to pasture?
² Remember the people you took to yourself
long ago,
your own tribe which you redeemed,
and this Mount Zion where you came to
live.

3 Come up to these endless ruins!
The enemy have sacked everything in the
sanctuary;
4 your opponents made uproar in the place
of assemblies,
they fixed their emblems over the
entrance,
emblems 5 never known before.

Their axes deep in the wood, 6 hacking at
the panels,
they battered them down with axe and
pick;
7 they set fire to your sanctuary,
profanely rased to the ground the
dwelling-place of your name.

8 They said to themselves, 'Let us crush
them at one stroke!'
They burned down every sacred shrine in
the land.
9 We see no signs, no prophet any more,
and none of us knows how long it will last.

10 How much longer, God, will the enemy
blaspheme?
Is the enemy to insult your name for
ever?
11 Why hold back your hand,
keep your right hand hidden in the folds
of your robe?

12 Yet, God, my king from the first,
author of saving acts throughout the earth,
13 by your power you split the sea in two,
and smashed the heads of the monsters on
the waters.

14 You crushed Leviathan's[a] heads,
gave him as food to the wild animals.
15 You released the springs and brooks,
and turned primordial rivers into dry land.

16 Yours is the day and yours the night,
you caused sun and light to exist,
17 you fixed all the boundaries of the earth,
you created summer and winter.

18 Remember, Yahweh, the enemy's
blasphemy,
a foolish people insults your name.
19 Do not surrender your turtledove to the
beast;
do not forget for ever the life of your
oppressed people.

20 Look to the covenant!
All the hiding-places of the land are full,
haunts of violence.
21 Do not let the downtrodden retreat in
confusion,
give the poor and needy cause to praise
your name.

22 Arise, God, champion your own cause,
remember how fools blaspheme you all
day long!
23 Do not forget the shouting of your
enemies,
the ever-mounting uproar of your
adversaries.

75 *For the choirmaster: Tune: 'Do not
destroy'; psalm of Asaph; song*
1 We give thanks to you, God, we give
thanks to you,
as we call upon your name, as we recount
your wonders.

2 'At the appointed time
I myself shall dispense justice.
3 The earth quakes and all its inhabitants;
it is I who hold its pillars firm.   *Pause*

4 'I said to the boastful, "Do not boast!"
to the wicked, "Do not flaunt your
strength!
5 Do not flaunt your strength so proudly,
do not talk with that arrogant stance." '

6 No longer from east to west,
no longer in the mountainous desert,

74a Properly a mythical monster of chaos, it stands here for
the evil power of Egypt.

⁷ is God judging in uprightness,
  bringing some down, raising others.
⁸ Yahweh is holding a cup
  filled with a heady blend of wine;
  he will pour it, they will drink it to the
    dregs,
  all the wicked on earth will drink it.

⁹ But I shall speak out for ever,
  shall make music for the God of Jacob.
¹⁰ I shall break down all the strength of the
    wicked,
  and the strength of the upright will rise
    high.

76 *For the choirmaster: For strings;*
   psalm of Asaph; song
¹ God is acknowledged in Judah,
  his name is great in Israel,
² his tent is pitched in Salem,
  his dwelling is in Zion;
³ there he has broken the lightning-flashes
    of the bow,
  shield and sword and war.   *Pause*

⁴ Radiant you are, and renowned
  for the mountains of booty ⁵taken from
    them.
  Heroes are now sleeping their last sleep,
  the warriors' arms have failed them;
⁶ at your reproof, God of Jacob,
  chariot and horse stand stunned.

⁷ You, you alone, strike terror! Who can
    hold his ground
  in your presence when your anger strikes?
⁸ From heaven your verdicts thunder,
  the earth is silent with dread
⁹ when God takes his stand to give
    judgement,
  to save all the humble of the earth.   *Pause*

¹⁰ Human anger serves only to praise you,
  the survivors of your anger will huddle
    round you.
¹¹ Make and fulfil your vows to Yahweh
    your God,

let those who surround him make
    offerings to the Awesome One.
¹² He cuts short the breath of princes,
  strikes terror in earthly kings.

77 *For the choirmaster . . . ; Jeduthun;*
   psalm of Asaph
¹ I cry to God in distress,
  I cry to God and he hears me.

² In the day of my distress I sought the
    Lord;
  all night I tirelessly stretched out my
    hands,
  my heart refused to be consoled.
³ I sigh as I think of God,
  my spirit faints away as I ponder on him.
                                   Pause

⁴ You kept me from closing my eyes,
  I was too distraught to speak;
⁵ I thought of former times,
  years long past ⁶I recalled;
  through the night I ponder in my heart,
  as I reflect, my spirit asks this question:

⁷ Is the Lord's rejection final?
  Will he never show favour again?
⁸ Is his faithful love gone for ever?
  Has his Word come to an end for all
    time?
⁹ Does God forget to show mercy?
  In anger does he shut off his tenderness?
                                   Pause

¹⁰ And I said, 'This is what wounds me,
  the right hand of the Most High has lost its
    strength.'
¹¹ Remembering Yahweh's great deeds,
  remembering your wonders in the past,
¹² I reflect on all that you did,
  I ponder all your great deeds.

¹³ God, your ways are holy!
  What god is as great as our God?
¹⁴ You are the God who does marvellous
    deeds,

brought nations to acknowledge your
power,
15 with your own arm redeeming your
people,
the children of Jacob and Joseph.   *Pause*

16 When the waters saw you, God,
when the waters saw you they writhed in
anguish,
the very depths shook with fear.
17 The clouds pelted down water,
the sky thundered,
your arrows shot back and forth.

18 The rolling of your thunder was heard,
your lightning-flashes lit up the world,
the earth shuddered and shook.
19 Your way led over the sea,
your path over the countless waters,
and none could trace your footsteps.

20 You guided your people like a flock
by the hand of Moses and Aaron.

78

Psalm of Asaph

1 My people, listen to my teaching,
pay attention to what I say.
2 I will speak to you in poetry,
unfold the mysteries of the past.

3 What we have heard and know,
what our ancestors have told us
4 we shall not conceal from their
descendants,
but will tell to a generation still to come:

the praises of Yahweh, his power,
the wonderful deeds he has done.
5 He instituted a witness in Jacob,
he established a law in Israel,

he commanded our ancestors
to hand it down to their descendants,
6 that a generation still to come might
know it,
children yet to be born.

They should be sure to tell their own
children,
7 and should put their trust in God,
never forgetting God's great deeds,
always keeping his commands,

8 and not, like their ancestors,
be a stubborn and rebellious generation,
a generation weak of purpose,
their spirit fickle towards God.

9 The archer sons of Ephraim
turned tail when the time came for
fighting;
10 they failed to keep God's covenant,
they refused to follow his Law;

11 they had forgotten his great deeds,
the marvels he had shown them;
12 he did marvels in the sight of their
ancestors
in Egypt, in the plains of Tanis.

13 He split the sea and brought them
through,
made the waters stand up like a dam;
14 he led them with a cloud by day,
and all the night with the light of a fire;

15 he split rocks in the desert,
let them drink as though from the limitless
depths;
16 he brought forth streams from a rock,
made waters flow down in torrents.

17 But they only sinned against him more
than ever,
defying the Most High in barren country;
18 they deliberately challenged God
by demanding food to their hearts'
content.

19 They insulted God by saying,
'Can God make a banquet in the desert?
20 True, when he struck the rock,
waters gushed out and flowed in torrents;
but what of bread? Can he give that,
can he provide meat for his people?'

21 When he heard them Yahweh vented his
        anger,
    fire blazed against Jacob,
    his anger mounted against Israel,
22 because they had no faith in God,
    no trust in his power to save.

23 Even so he gave orders to the skies above,
    he opened the sluice-gates of heaven;
24 he rained down manna to feed them,
    he gave them the wheat of heaven;
25 mere mortals ate the bread of the Mighty,
    he sent them as much food as they could
        want.

26 He roused an east wind in the heavens,
    despatched a south wind by his strength;
27 he rained down meat on them like dust,
    birds thick as sand on the seashore,
28 tumbling into the middle of his camp,
    all around his dwelling-place.

29 They ate as much food as they wanted,
    he satisfied all their cravings;
30 but their cravings were still upon them,
    the food was still in their mouths,
31 when the wrath of God attacked them,
    slaughtering their strongest men,
    laying low the flower of Israel.

32 Despite all this, they went on sinning,
    they put no faith in his marvels.
33 He made their days vanish in mist,
    their years in sudden ruin.

34 Whenever he slaughtered them, they
        began to seek him,
    they turned back and looked eagerly for
        him,
35 recalling that God was their rock,
    God the Most High, their redeemer.

36 They tried to hoodwink him with their
        mouths,
    their tongues were deceitful towards him;
37 their hearts were not loyal to him,
    they were not faithful to his covenant.

38 But in his compassion he forgave their
        guilt
    instead of killing them,
    time and again repressing his anger
    instead of rousing his full wrath,
39 remembering they were creatures of
        flesh,
    a breath of wind that passes, never to
        return.

40 How often they defied him in the desert!
    How often they grieved him in the
        wastelands!
41 Repeatedly they challenged God,
    provoking the Holy One of Israel,
42 not remembering his hand,
    the time when he saved them from the
        oppressor,
43 he who did his signs in Egypt,
    his miracles in the plains of Tanis,
44 turning their rivers to blood,
    their streams so that they had nothing to
        drink.

45 He sent horseflies to eat them up,
    and frogs to devastate them,
46 consigning their crops to the caterpillar,
    the fruit of their hard work to the locust;

47 he killed their vines with hail,
    their sycamore trees with frost,
48 delivering up their cattle to hail,
    and their flocks to thunderbolts.

49 He loosed against them the full heat of his
        anger,
    fury, rage and destruction,
    a detachment of destroying angels;
50 he gave free course to his anger.

    He did not exempt their own selves from
        death,
    delivering up their lives to the plague.
51 He struck all the first-born in Egypt,
    the flower of the youth in the tents
        of Ham.

52 He brought out his people like sheep,
   guiding them like a flock in the desert,
53 leading them safe and unafraid,
   while the sea engulfed their enemies.

54 He brought them to his holy land,
   the hill-country won by his right hand;
55 he dispossessed nations before them,
   measured out a heritage for each of them,
   and settled the tribes of Israel in their
       tents.

56 But still they challenged the Most High
       God and defied him,
   refusing to keep his decrees;
57 as perverse and treacherous as their
       ancestors,
   they gave way like a faulty bow,
58 provoking him with their high places,
   rousing his jealousy with their idols.

59 God listened and vented his wrath,
   he totally rejected Israel;
60 he forsook his dwelling in Shiloh,
   the tent where he used to dwell on the
       earth.

61 He abandoned his power to captivity,
   his splendour to the enemy's clutches;
62 he gave up his people to the sword,
   he vented his wrath on his own heritage.

63 Fire devoured their young men,
   their young girls had no wedding-song;
64 their priests fell by the sword
   and their widows sang no dirge.

65 The Lord arose as though he had been
       asleep,
   like a strong man fighting-mad with wine,
66 he struck his enemies on the rump,
   and put them to everlasting shame.

67 Rejecting the tents of Joseph,
   passing over the tribe of Ephraim,
68 he chose the tribe of Judah,
   his well-loved mountain of Zion;

69 he built his sanctuary like high hills,
   like the earth set it firm for ever.

70 He chose David to be his servant,
   took him from the sheepfold,
71 took him from tending ewes
   to pasture his servant Jacob,
   and Israel his heritage.
72 He pastured them with unblemished
       heart,
   with a sensitive hand he led them.

79   *Psalm of Asaph*

1 God, the pagans have invaded your
       heritage,
   they have defiled your holy temple,
   they have laid Jerusalem in ruins,
2 they have left the corpses of your servants
   as food for the birds of the air,
   the bodies of your faithful for the wild
       beasts.

3 Around Jerusalem they have shed blood
       like water,
   leaving no one to bury them.
4 We are the scorn of our neighbours,
   the butt and laughing-stock of those
       around us.
5 How long will you be angry, Yahweh? For
       ever?
   Is your jealousy to go on smouldering like
       a fire?

6 Pour out your anger on the nations
   who do not acknowledge you,
   and on the kingdoms
   that do not call on your name;
7 for they have devoured Jacob
   and devastated his home.

8 Do not count against us the guilt of former
       generations,
   in your tenderness come quickly to
       meet us,
   for we are utterly weakened;
9 help us, God our Saviour,

for the glory of your name;
Yahweh, wipe away our sins,
rescue us for the sake of your name.

10 Why should the nations ask,
'Where is their God?'
Let us see the nations suffer vengeance
for shedding your servants' blood.
11 May the groans of the captive reach you,
by your great strength save those who are
condemned to death!
12 Repay our neighbours sevenfold
for the insults they have levelled at you,
Lord.
13 And we, your people, the flock that you
pasture,
will thank you for ever,
will recite your praises from age to age.

80
For the choirmaster: Tune: 'The decrees are lilies'; psalm of Asaph

1 Shepherd of Israel, listen,
you who lead Joseph like a flock,
enthroned on the winged creatures, shine
forth
2 over Ephraim, Benjamin and Manasseh;
rouse your valour
and come to our help.

3 God, bring us back,
let your face shine on us and we shall be
safe.

4 Yahweh, God Sabaoth, how long
will you flare up at your people's prayer?
5 You have made tears their food,
threefold tears their drink.
6 You let our neighbours quarrel over us,
our enemies mock us.

7 God Sabaoth, bring us back,
let your face shine on us and we shall be
safe.

8 You brought a vine out of Egypt,
to plant it you drove out nations;
9 you cleared a space for it,
it took root and filled the whole country.

10 The mountains were covered with its
shade,
and the cedars of God with its branches,
11 its boughs stretched as far as the sea,
its shoots as far as the River.

12 Why have you broken down its fences?
Every passer-by plucks its grapes,
13 boars from the forest tear at it,
wild beasts feed on it.

14 God Sabaoth, come back, we pray,
look down from heaven and see,
visit this vine;
15 protect what your own hand has planted.
16 They have thrown it on the fire like dung,
the frown of your rebuke will destroy
them.

17 May your hand protect those at your side,
the child of Adam you have strengthened
for yourself!
18 Never again will we turn away from you,
give us life and we will call upon your
name.

19 God Sabaoth, bring us back,
let your face shine on us and we shall be
safe.

81
For the choirmaster: On the . . . of Gath; of Asaph

1 Sing for joy to God our strength,
shout in triumph to the God of Jacob.

2 Strike up the music, beat the tambourine,
play the melodious harp and the lyre;
3 blow the trumpet for the new month,
for the full moon, for our feast day!

4 For Israel has this statute,
a decision of the God of Jacob,
5 a decree he imposed on Joseph,
when he went to war against Egypt.

I heard a voice unknown to me,
6 'I freed his shoulder from the burden,

46 READ PSALM 80.

God, bring us back, let your face shine on us and we shall be safe.—PSALM 80:3

GOD WITH US

When God saw the world overwhelmed with fear, he put his love into operation to recall the world to himself; his grace, to invite the world to come to him; and his affection, to embrace it. At the time of the flood . . . he calls Noah to generate a new world, encourages him with gentle words, gives him his intimate trust. . . . Then God calls Abraham. . . . He goes with him on his way, . . . snatches him from injustices, consoles him in his hospitality and astonishes him with an unhoped-for birth, so that . . . drawn by the great sweetness of the divine love, he learns to love God and no longer to fear him. . . .

Later God consoles the fleeing Jacob with dreams. When he comes back, God challenges him to combat and, in the battle, he clasps Jacob in his arms so that he might love the Father of battles and no longer fear him. Then God calls Moses and speaks to him with a father's love, to invite him to deliver his people.

In all these events, the flame of divine love enkindled the human heart, the rapture of the love of God was infused into the tenderest feelings of human beings; and they, wounded in soul, began to long to see God with the eyes of their flesh. . . .

Love does not accept not seeing what it loves. Did not all the saints take little account of all they obtained if they did not see God? . . . So the Psalmist says: "Let your face shine on us and we shall be safe" (Ps 80:3). Is this not why the heathens made themselves idols? Even at the heart of error, they saw with their eyes what they adored. . . .

Let no one, therefore, think that God was wrong to come to men through a man. He took flesh among us that we might see him.   ST. PETER CHRYSOLOGUS, 406–450?

YOU WILL FIND THE NEXT READING AT PSALM 84.

his hands were able to lay aside the
    labourer's basket.
7 You cried out in your distress, so I rescued
    you.

'Hidden in the storm, I answered you,
I tested you at the waters of Meribah.
                                                    Pause
8 Listen, my people, while I give you
    warning;
Israel, if only you would listen to me!

9 'You shall have no strange gods,
    shall worship no alien god.
10 I, Yahweh, am your God,
    who brought you here from Egypt,
    you have only to open your mouth for me
        to fill it.

11 'My people would not listen to me,
    Israel would have none of me.
12 So I left them to their stubborn selves,
    to follow their own devices.

13 'If only my people would listen to me,
   if only Israel would walk in my ways,
14 at one stroke I would subdue their
      enemies,
   turn my hand against their opponents.

15 'Those who hate Yahweh would woo his
      favour,
   though their doom was sealed for ever,
16 while I would feed him on pure wheat,
   would give you your fill of honey from the
      rock.'

82 *Psalm of Asaph*

1 God takes his stand in the divine assembly,
   surrounded by the gods he gives
      judgement.

2 'How much longer will you give unjust
      judgements
   and uphold the prestige of the wicked?
3 Let the weak and the orphan have justice,
   be fair to the wretched and the destitute.
                                    Pause

4 'Rescue the weak and the needy,
   save them from the clutches of the wicked.

5 'Ignorant and uncomprehending, they
      wander in darkness,
   while the foundations of the world are
      tottering.
6 I had thought, "Are you gods,
   are all of you sons of the Most High?"
7 No! you will die as human beings do,
   as one man, princes, you will fall.'
8 Arise, God, judge the world,
   for all nations belong to you.

83 *Song; psalm of Asaph*

1 God, do not remain silent,
   do not stay quiet or unmoved, God!
2 See how your enemies are in uproar,
   how those who hate you are rearing their
      heads.

3 They are laying plans against your people,
   conspiring against those you cherish;
4 they say, 'Come, let us annihilate them as a
      nation,
   the name of Israel shall be remembered no
      more!'

5 They conspire with a single mind,
   they conclude an alliance against you,
6 the tents of Edom and the Ishmaelites,
   Moab and the Hagrites,
7 Gebal, Ammon, Amalek,
   Philistia and the Tyrians;
8 even Assyria has joined them
   to reinforce the children of Lot.   *Pause*

9 Treat them like Midian and Sisera,
   like Jabin at the river Kishon;
10 wiped out at En-Dor,
   they served to manure the ground.
11 Treat their leaders like Oreb and Zeeb,
   all their commanders like Zebah and
      Zalmunna,
12 for they said, 'Let us take for ourselves
   God's settlements.'

13 My God, treat them like thistledown,
   like chaff at the mercy of the wind.
14 As fire devours a forest,
   as a flame sets mountains ablaze,
15 so drive them away with your tempest,
   by your whirlwind fill them with terror.
16 Shame written all over their faces,
   let them seek your name, Yahweh!
17 Dishonour and terror be always theirs,
   death also and destruction.
18 Let them know that you alone bear the
      name of Yahweh,
   Most High over all the earth.

84 *For the choirmaster: On the . . . of Gath; psalm of the sons of Korah*

1 How lovely are your dwelling-places,
   Yahweh Sabaoth.
2 My whole being yearns and pines
   for Yahweh's courts,
   My heart and my body cry out for joy
      to the living God.

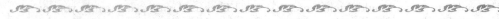

47 READ PSALM 84.

They make their way from height to height, God shows himself to them in Zion.

—PSALM 84:7

MAKING SPIRITUAL PROGRESS

You should always remember that in our spiritual life it is not how it has begun that matters, but its progress and its end. Judas began well but ended badly, and St. Paul ended well though he was wrong at the beginning. The attainment of perfection depends on unswerving perseverance in acquiring every virtue. In the way that leads to God we slip back if we are not advancing because no man can ever remain stationary. And the blessed, as the Holy Spirit said in Psalm 84, will go from height to height.

Now the best means to that end is to keep the goodness and mercy of God towards us continually in mind. And to have also a constant dread so that we do not become unworthy and forfeit them. So we must be faithful in daily practices of prayer, meditation, self-examination, spiritual reading. We must also make daily efforts in charity, mortification, humility and simplicity.

Let our Lord lead you. He will direct everything through you. Trust yourself to him and, in imitation of him, be humble and gentle and faithful in all you do. You will see that it will all go well.

ST. VINCENT DE PAUL, 1581–1660

YOU WILL FIND THE NEXT READING AT PSALM 103.

3 Even the sparrow has found a home,
  the swallow a nest to place its young:
your altars, Yahweh Sabaoth,
   my King and my God.

4 How blessed are those who live in your
     house;
   they shall praise you continually. *Pause*
5 Blessed those who find their strength in
     you,
   whose hearts are set on pilgrimage.

6 As they pass through the Valley of the
     Balsam,
  they make there a water-hole,
  and—a further blessing—early rain fills it.
7 They make their way from height to
     height,
  God shows himself to them in Zion.

8 Yahweh, God Sabaoth, hear my prayer,
  listen, God of Jacob.
9 God, our shield, look,
  and see the face of your anointed.

10 Better one day in your courts
     than a thousand at my own devices,
  to stand on the threshold of God's
     house
  than to live in the tents of the wicked.

11 For Yahweh God is a rampart and
     shield,
  he gives grace and glory;
  Yahweh refuses nothing good
     to those whose life is blameless.

12 Yahweh Sabaoth,
  blessed is he who trusts in you.

85

*For the choirmaster: Psalm of the
sons of Korah*

1 Yahweh, you are gracious to your land,
  you bring back the captives of Jacob,
2 you take away the guilt of your people,
  you blot out all their sin.   *Pause*

3 You retract all your anger,
  you renounce the heat of your fury.

4 Bring us back, God our Saviour,
  appease your indignation against us!
5 Will you be angry with us for ever?
  Will you prolong your wrath age after age?

6 Will you not give us life again,
  for your people to rejoice in you?
7 Show us, Lord, your faithful love,
  grant us your saving help.

8 I am listening. What is God's message?
  Yahweh's message is peace
  for his people, for his faithful,
  if only they renounce their folly.
9 His saving help is near for those who
        fear him,
  his glory will dwell in our land.

10 Faithful Love and Loyalty join together,
  Saving Justice and Peace embrace.
11 Loyalty will spring up from the earth,
  and Justice will lean down from heaven.

12 Yahweh will himself give prosperity,
  and our soil will yield its harvest.
13 Justice will walk before him,
  treading out a path.

86

Prayer of David

1 Listen to me, Yahweh, answer me,
  for I am poor and needy.
2 Guard me, for I am faithful,
  save your servant who relies on you.

  You are my God, 3 take pity on me, Lord,
  for to you I cry all the day.
4 Fill your servant's heart with joy, Lord,
  for to you I raise up my heart.

5 Lord, you are kind and forgiving,
  rich in faithful love for all who call
        upon you.
6 Yahweh, hear my prayer,
  listen to the sound of my pleading.

7 In my day of distress I call upon you,
  because you answer me, Lord;
8 among the gods there is none to compare
        with you,
  no great deeds to compare with yours.

9 All nations will come and adore you, Lord,
  and give glory to your name.
10 For you are great and do marvellous deeds,
  you, God, and none other.

11 Teach me, Yahweh, your ways,
  that I may not stray from your loyalty;
  let my heart's one aim be to fear your
        name.

12 I thank you with all my heart, Lord
        my God,
  I will glorify your name for ever,
13 for your faithful love for me is so great
  that you have rescued me from the depths
        of Sheol.

14 Arrogant men, God, are rising up
        against me,
  a brutal gang is after my life,
  in their scheme of things you have no
        place.

15 But you, Lord, God of tenderness and
        mercy,
  slow to anger, rich in faithful love and
        loyalty,
16 turn to me and pity me.

  Give to your servant your strength,
  to the child of your servant your saving
        help,
17 give me a sign of your kindness.

18 My enemies will see to their shame
  that you, Yahweh, help and console me.

87
Psalm of the sons of Korah; song

¹ With its foundations on the holy
       mountains,
² Yahweh loves his city,
  he prefers the gates of Zion
  to any dwelling-place in Jacob.

³ He speaks of glory for you,
  city of God,   *Pause*

⁴ 'I number Rahab and Babylon
  among those that acknowledge me;
  look at Tyre, Philistia, Ethiopia,
  so and so was born there.'

⁵ But of Zion it will be said,
  'Every one was born there,'
  her guarantee is the Most High.

⁶ Yahweh in his register of peoples
  will note against each, 'Born there', *Pause*
⁷ princes no less than native-born;
  all make their home in you.

88
*Song; psalm of the sons of Korah;
in sickness; in suffering; poem for Heman
the native-born*

¹ Yahweh, God of my salvation,
  when I cry out to you in the night,
² may my prayer reach your presence,
  hear my cry for help.

³ For I am filled with misery,
  my life is on the brink of Sheol;
⁴ already numbered among those who sink
       into oblivion,
  I am as one bereft of strength,
⁵ left alone among the dead,
  like the slaughtered lying in the grave,
  whom you remember no more,
  cut off as they are from your protection.

⁶ You have plunged me to the bottom of the
       grave,
  in the darkness, in the depths;
⁷ weighted down by your anger,
  kept low by your waves.   *Pause*

⁸ You have deprived me of my friends,
  made me repulsive to them,
  imprisoned, with no escape;
⁹ my eyes are worn out with suffering.
  I call to you, Yahweh, all day,
  I stretch out my hands to you.

¹⁰ Do you work wonders for the dead,
  can shadows rise up to praise you? *Pause*

¹¹ Do they speak in the grave of your faithful
     love,
  of your constancy in the place of
     perdition?
¹² Are your wonders known in the
     darkness,
  your saving justice in the land of
     oblivion?

¹³ But, for my part, I cry to you, Yahweh,
  every morning my prayer comes before
     you;
¹⁴ why, Yahweh, do you rebuff me,
  turn your face away from me?

¹⁵ Wretched and close to death since
     childhood,
  I have borne your terrors—I am finished!
¹⁶ Your anger has overwhelmed me,
  your terrors annihilated me.

¹⁷ They flood around me all day long,
  close in on me all at once.
¹⁸ You have deprived me of friends and
     companions,
  and all that I know is the dark.

89
Poem for Ethan the native-born

¹ I shall sing the faithful love of Yahweh for
     ever,
  from age to age my lips shall declare your
     constancy,
² for you have said: love is built to last for
     ever,
  you have fixed your constancy firm in the
     heavens.

3 'I have made a covenant with my
      Chosen One,
   sworn an oath to my servant David:
4 I have made your dynasty firm for ever,
   built your throne stable age after age.'
                                    Pause

5 The heavens praise your wonders,
      Yahweh,
   your constancy in the gathering of your
      faithful.
6 Who in the skies can compare with
      Yahweh?
   Who among the sons of god can rival
      him?

7 God, awesome in the assembly of holy
      ones,
   great and dreaded among all who
      surround him,
8 Yahweh, God Sabaoth, who is like you?
   Mighty Yahweh, your constancy is all
      round you!

9 You control the pride of the ocean,
   when its waves ride high you calm them.
10 You split Rahab*a* in two like a corpse,
   scattered your enemies with your mighty
      arm.

11 Yours are the heavens and yours the earth,
   the world and all it holds, you founded
      them;
12 you created the north and the south,
   Tabor and Hermon hail your name with
      joy.

13 Yours is a strong arm,
   mighty your hand, your right hand raised
      high;
14 Saving Justice and Fair Judgement the
      foundations of your throne,
   Faithful Love and Constancy march
      before you.

15 How blessed the nation that learns to
   acclaim you!

They will live, Yahweh, in the light of
      your presence.
16 In your name they rejoice all day long,
   by your saving justice they are raised up.

17 You are the flower of their strength,
   by your favour our strength is
      triumphant;
18 for to Yahweh belongs our shield,
   to the Holy One of Israel our king.

19 Once you spoke in a vision,
   to your faithful you said:
   'I have given strength to a warrior,
   I have raised up a man chosen from my
      people.

20 'I have found David my servant,
   and anointed him with my holy oil.
21 My hand will always be with him,
   my arm will make him strong.

22 'No enemy will be able to outwit him,
   no wicked man overcome him;
23 I shall crush his enemies before him,
   strike his opponents dead.

24 'My constancy and faithful love will be
      with him,
   in my name his strength will be
      triumphant.
25 I shall establish his power over the sea,
   his dominion over the rivers.

26 'He will cry to me, "You are my father,
   my God, the rock of my salvation!"
27 So I shall make him my first-born,
   the highest of earthly kings.

28 'I shall maintain my faithful love for
      him always,
   my covenant with him will stay firm.
29 I have established his dynasty for ever,
   his throne to be as lasting as the
      heavens.

89a Usually the sea as a monster of chaos, subdued at creation; or Egypt subdued at the exodus.

30 'Should his descendants desert my law,
and not keep to my rulings,
31 should they violate my statutes,
and not observe my commandments,

32 'then I shall punish their offences with
the rod,
their guilt with the whip,
33 but I shall never withdraw from him
my faithful love,
I shall not belie my constancy.

34 'I shall not violate my covenant,
I shall not withdraw the word once
spoken.
35 I have sworn by my holiness, once and
for all,
never will I break faith with David.

36 'His dynasty shall endure for ever,
his throne like the sun before me,
37 as the moon is established for ever,
a faithful witness in the skies.'   *Pause*

38 Yet you yourself—you have spurned
and rejected,
and have vented your wrath on your
anointed,
39 you have repudiated the covenant with
your servant,
dishonoured his crown in the dust.

40 You have pierced all his defences,
and laid his strongholds in ruins,
41 everyone passing by plunders him,
he has become the butt of his
neighbours.

42 You have raised high the right hand of
his opponents,
have made all his enemies happy;
43 you have snapped off his sword on a
rock,
and failed to support him in battle.

44 You have stripped him of his splendid
sceptre,
and toppled his throne to the ground.

45 You have aged him before his time,
enveloped him in shame.   *Pause*

46 How long, Yahweh, will you remain
hidden? For ever?
Is your anger to go on smouldering like
a fire?
47 Remember me; how long have I left?
For what pointless end did you create all
the children of Adam?
48 Who can live and never see death?
Who can save himself from the clutches of
Sheol?   *Pause*

49 Lord, what of those pledges of your
faithful love?
You made an oath to David by your
constancy.
50 Do not forget the insults to your servant;
I take to heart the taunts of the nations,
51 which your enemies have levelled,
Yahweh,
have levelled at the footsteps of your
anointed!

52 Blessed be Yahweh for ever.
Amen, Amen.

BOOK FOUR: PSALMS 90–106

90   *Prayer of Moses, man of God*

1 Lord, you have been our refuge
from age to age.
2 Before the mountains were born,
before the earth and the world came to
birth,
from eternity to eternity you are God.

3 You bring human beings to the dust,
by saying, 'Return, children of Adam.'
4 A thousand years are to you
like a yesterday which has passed,
like a watch of the night.

5 You flood them with sleep
—in the morning they will be like
growing grass:

6 in the morning it is blossoming and
       growing,
    by evening it is withered and dry.

7 For we have been destroyed by your
       wrath,
    dismayed by your anger.
8 You have taken note of our guilty deeds,
    our secrets in the full light of your
       presence.

9 All our days pass under your wrath,
    our lives are over like a sigh.
10 The span of our life is seventy years—
    eighty for those who are strong—
    but their whole extent is anxiety and
       trouble,
    they are over in a moment and we are
       gone.

11 Who feels the power of your anger,
    or who that fears you, your wrath?

12 Teach us to count up the days that are ours,
    and we shall come to the heart of wisdom.
13 Come back, Yahweh! How long must we
       wait?
    Take pity on your servants.

14 Each morning fill us with your faithful
       love,
    we shall sing and be happy all our days;
15 let our joy be as long as the time that you
       afflicted us,
    the years when we experienced disaster.

16 Show your servants the deeds you do,
    let their children enjoy your splendour!
17 May the sweetness of the Lord be upon us,
    to confirm the work we have done!

91
You who live in the secret place of
       Elyon,
    spend your nights in the shelter of
       Shaddai,
2 saying to Yahweh, 'My refuge, my fortress,
    my God in whom I trust!'

3 He rescues you from the snare
    of the fowler set on destruction;
4 he covers you with his pinions,
    you find shelter under his wings.
    His constancy is shield and protection.

5 You need not fear the terrors of night,
    the arrow that flies in the daytime,
6 the plague that stalks in the darkness,
    the scourge that wreaks havoc at high
       noon.

7 Though a thousand fall at your side,
    ten thousand at your right hand,
    you yourself will remain unscathed.
8 You have only to keep your eyes open
    to see how the wicked are repaid,
9 you who say, 'Yahweh my refuge!'
    and make Elyon your fortress.

10 No disaster can overtake you,
    no plague come near your tent;
11 he has given his angels orders about you
    to guard you wherever you go.

12 They will carry you in their arms
    in case you trip over a stone.
13 You will walk upon wild beast and adder,
    you will trample young lions and snakes.

14 'Since he clings to me I rescue him,
    I raise him high, since he acknowledges
       my name.
15 He calls to me and I answer him:
    in distress I am at his side,
    I rescue him and bring him honour.
16 I shall satisfy him with long life,
    and grant him to see my salvation.'

92
Psalm; song for the Sabbath

1 It is good to give thanks to Yahweh,
    to make music for your name, Most High,
2 to proclaim your faithful love at daybreak,
    and your constancy all through the night,
3 on the lyre, the ten-stringed lyre,
    to the murmur of the harp.

4 You have brought me joy, Yahweh, by
    your deeds,
at the work of your hands I cry out,
5 'How great are your works, Yahweh,
immensely deep your thoughts!'
6 Stupid people cannot realise this,
fools do not grasp it.

7 The wicked may sprout like weeds,
and every evil-doer flourish,
but only to be eternally destroyed;
8 whereas you are supreme for ever,
    Yahweh.

9 Look how your enemies perish,
how all evil-doers are scattered!
10 You give me the strength of the wild ox,
you anoint me with fresh oil;
11 I caught sight of the ambush against me,
overheard the plans of the wicked.

12 The upright will flourish like the palm
    tree,
will grow like a cedar of Lebanon.
13 Planted in the house of Yahweh,
they will flourish in the courts of our God.

14 In old age they will still bear fruit,
will remain fresh and green,
15 to proclaim Yahweh's integrity;
my rock, in whom no fault can be found.

93 Yahweh is king, robed in majesty,
robed is Yahweh and girded with
    power.

2 The world is indeed set firm, it can never
    be shaken;
your throne is set firm from of old,
from all eternity you exist.

3 The rivers lift up, Yahweh,
the rivers lift up their voices,
the rivers lift up their thunder.

4 Greater than the voice of many waters,
more majestic than the breakers of the sea,
Yahweh is majestic in the heights.

5 Your decrees stand firm, unshakeable,
holiness is the beauty of your house,
Yahweh, for all time to come.

94 God of vengeance, Yahweh,
God of vengeance, shine forth!
2 Arise, judge of the world,
give back the proud what they deserve!

3 How long are the wicked, Yahweh,
how long are the wicked to triumph?
4 They bluster and boast,
they flaunt themselves, all the evil-doers.

5 They crush your people, Yahweh,
they oppress your heritage,
6 they murder the widow and the stranger,
bring the orphan to a violent death.

7 They say, 'Yahweh is not looking,
the God of Jacob is taking no notice.'
8 Take notice yourselves, you coarsest of
    people!
Fools, when will you learn some sense?

9 Shall he who implanted the ear not hear,
he who fashioned the eye not see?
10 Shall he who instructs nations not punish?
Yahweh, the teacher of all people,
11 knows human plans and how insipid
    they are.

12 How blessed are those you instruct,
    Yahweh,
whom you teach by means of your law,
13 to give them respite in evil times,
till a pit is dug for the wicked.

14 Yahweh will not abandon his people,
he will not desert his heritage;
15 for judgement will again become saving
    justice,
and in its wake all upright hearts will
    follow.

16 Who rises up on my side against the
    wicked?

Who stands firm on my side against all
    evil-doers?
17 If Yahweh did not come to my help,
    I should soon find myself dwelling in the
        silence.

18 I need only say, 'I am slipping,'
    for your faithful love, Yahweh, to support
        me;
19 however great the anxiety of my heart,
    your consolations soothe me.

20 Are you partner to a destructive court,
    that gives disorder the status of law?
21 They make an attack on the life of the
        upright,
    and condemn innocent blood.

22 No! Yahweh is a stronghold to me,
    my God is my rock of refuge.
23 He turns back their guilt on themselves,
    annihilates them for their wickedness,
    he annihilates them, Yahweh our God.

95 Come, let us cry out with joy to
        Yahweh,
    acclaim the rock of our salvation.
2 Let us come into his presence with
        thanksgiving,
    acclaim him with music.

3 For Yahweh is a great God,
    a king greater than all the gods.
4 In his power are the depths of the earth,
    the peaks of the mountains are his;
5 the sea belongs to him, for he made it,
    and the dry land, moulded by his hands.

6 Come, let us bow low and do reverence;
    kneel before Yahweh who made us!
7 For he is our God,
    and we the people of his sheepfold,
    the flock of his hand.

If only you would listen to him today!
8 Do not harden your hearts as at Meribah,
    as at the time of Massah in the desert,[a]

9 when your ancestors challenged me,
    put me to the test, and saw what I
        could do!

10 For forty years that generation
        sickened me,
    and I said, 'Always fickle hearts;
    they cannot grasp my ways.'
11 Then in my anger I swore
    they would never enter my place of rest.

96 Sing a new song to Yahweh!
    Sing to Yahweh, all the earth!
2 Sing to Yahweh, bless his name!

Proclaim his salvation day after day,
3 declare his glory among the nations,
    his marvels to every people!

4 Great is Yahweh, worthy of all praise,
    more awesome than any of the gods.
5 All the gods of the nations are idols!

It was Yahweh who made the heavens;
6 in his presence are splendour and majesty,
    in his sanctuary power and beauty.

7 Give to Yahweh, families of nations,
    give to Yahweh glory and power,
8 give to Yahweh the glory due to his
        name!

Bring an offering and enter his courts,
9 adore Yahweh in the splendour of his
        holiness.
    Tremble before him, all the earth.

10 Say among the nations, 'Yahweh is king.'
    The world is set firm, it cannot be moved.
    He will judge the nations with justice.

11 Let the heavens rejoice and earth be
        glad!
    Let the sea thunder, and all it holds!

95a Incidents during the desert journey: *Meribah* = dispute,
Massah = temptation.

¹² Let the countryside exult, and all that
is in it,
and all the trees of the forest cry out for joy,

¹³ at Yahweh's approach, for he is coming,
coming to judge the earth;
he will judge the world with saving
justice,
and the nations with constancy.

97 Yahweh is king! Let earth rejoice,
the many isles be glad!
² Cloud, black cloud enfolds him,
saving justice and judgement the
foundations of his throne.

³ Fire goes before him,
sets ablaze his enemies all around;
⁴ his lightning-flashes light up the world,
the earth sees it and quakes.

⁵ The mountains melt like wax,
before the Lord of all the earth.
⁶ The heavens proclaim his saving justice,
all nations see his glory.

⁷ Shame on all who serve images,
who pride themselves on their idols;
bow down to him, all you gods!

⁸ Zion hears and is glad,
the daughters of Judah exult,
because of your judgements, Yahweh.

⁹ For you are Yahweh,
Most High over all the earth,
far transcending all gods.

¹⁰ Yahweh loves those who hate evil,
he keeps safe his faithful,
rescues them from the clutches of the
wicked.

¹¹ Light dawns for the upright,
and joy for honest hearts.
¹² Rejoice in Yahweh, you who are upright,
praise his unforgettable holiness.

98 *Psalm*

¹ Sing a new song to Yahweh,
for he has performed wonders,
his saving power is in his right hand
and his holy arm.

² Yahweh has made known his saving
power,
revealed his saving justice for the nations
to see,
³ mindful of his faithful love and his
constancy
to the House of Israel.

The whole wide world has seen
the saving power of our God.
⁴ Acclaim Yahweh, all the earth,
burst into shouts of joy!

⁵ Play to Yahweh on the harp,
to the sound of instruments;
⁶ to the sound of trumpet and horn,
acclaim the presence of the King.

⁷ Let the sea thunder, and all that it holds,
the world and all who live in it.
⁸ Let the rivers clap their hands,
and the mountains shout for joy together,

⁹ at Yahweh's approach, for he is coming
to judge the earth;
he will judge the world with saving justice
and the nations with fairness.

99 Yahweh is king, the peoples tremble;
he is enthroned on the winged
creatures, the earth shivers;
² Yahweh is great in Zion.

He is supreme over all nations;
³ let them praise your name, great and
awesome;
holy is he ⁴ and mighty!

You are a king who loves justice,
you established honesty, justice and
uprightness;
in Jacob it is you who are active.

5 Exalt Yahweh our God,
  bow down at his footstool;
    holy is he!

6 Moses and Aaron are among his priests,
    and Samuel,
  calling on his name; they called on
      Yahweh
  and he answered them.

7 He spoke with them in the pillar of fire,
  they obeyed his decrees, the Law he gave
    them.

8 Yahweh our God, you answered them,
  you were a God of forgiveness to them,
    but punished them for their sins.

9   Exalt Yahweh our God,
  bow down at his holy mountain;
    holy is Yahweh our God!

100 *Psalm for thanksgiving*

1 Acclaim Yahweh, all the earth,
2 serve Yahweh with gladness,
  come into his presence with songs of joy!

3 Be sure that Yahweh is God,
  he made us, we belong to him,
  his people, the flock of his sheepfold.

4 Come within his gates giving thanks,
  to his courts singing praise,
  give thanks to him and bless his name!

5 For Yahweh is good,
  his faithful love is everlasting,
  his constancy from age to age.

101 *Psalm of David*

1 I will sing of faithful love and judgement;
  to you, Yahweh, will I make music.
2 I will go forward in the path of the
    blameless;
  when will you come to me?

I will live in purity of heart,
  in my house,
3 I will not set before my eyes
  anything sordid.

I hate those who act crookedly;
  this has no attraction for me.
4 Let the perverse of heart keep away
    from me;
  the wicked I disregard.

5 One who secretly slanders a comrade,
  I reduce to silence;
  haughty looks, proud heart,
    these I cannot abide.

6 I look to the faithful of the land
  to be my companions,
  only he who walks in the path of the
      blameless
  shall be my servant.

7 There is no room in my house
  for anyone who practises deceit;
  no liar will stand his ground
  where I can see him.

8 Morning after morning I reduce to silence
  all the wicked in the land,
  banishing from the city of Yahweh
  all evil-doers.

102 *[a]Prayer of someone afflicted, who in misfortune pours out sorrows before Yahweh*

1   Yahweh, hear my prayer,
  let my cry for help reach you.
2   Do not turn away your face from me
  when I am in trouble;
  bend down and listen to me,
  when I call, be quick to answer me!

3   For my days are vanishing like smoke,
  my bones burning like an oven;

102a Two poems: vv. 1–11 + 23–27 form a personal lament,
vv. 12–22 a prayer for pity.

4 like grass struck by blight, my heart is
    withering,
    I forget to eat my meals.
5 From the effort of voicing my groans
    my bones stick out through my skin.

6 I am like a desert-owl in the wastes,
    a screech-owl among ruins,
7 I keep vigil and moan
    like a lone bird on a roof.
8 All day long my enemies taunt me,
    those who once praised me now use me
    as a curse.

9 Ashes are the food that I eat,
    my drink is mingled with tears,
10 because of your fury and anger,
    since you have raised me up only to cast
    me away;
11 my days are like a fading shadow,
    I am withering up like grass.

12 But you, Yahweh, are enthroned for ever,
    each generation in turn remembers you.
13 Rise up, take pity on Zion!
    the time has come to have mercy on her,
    the moment has come;
14 for your servants love her very stones,
    are moved to pity by her dust.

15 Then will the nations revere the name of
    Yahweh,
    and all the kings of the earth your glory;
16 when Yahweh builds Zion anew,
    he will be seen in his glory;
17 he will turn to hear the prayer of the
    destitute,
    and will not treat their prayer with
    scorn.

18 This shall be put on record for a future
    generation,
    and a people yet to be born shall praise
    God:
19 Yahweh has leaned down from the heights
    of his sanctuary,
    has looked down from heaven to earth,

20 to listen to the sighing of the captive,
    and set free those condemned to death,
21 to proclaim the name of Yahweh in Zion,
    his praise in Jerusalem;
22 nations will gather together,
    and kingdoms to worship Yahweh.

23 In my journeying my strength has
    failed on the way;
24 let me know the short time I have left.
    Do not take me away before half my
    days are done,
    for your years run on from age to age.

25 Long ago you laid earth's foundations,
    the heavens are the work of your hands.
26 They pass away but you remain;
    they all wear out like a garment,
    like outworn clothes you change them;
27 but you never alter, and your years
    never end.

28 The children of those who serve you
    will dwell secure,
    and their descendants live on in your
    presence.

103   *Of David*

1 Bless Yahweh, my soul,
    from the depths of my being, his holy
    name;
2 bless Yahweh, my soul,
    never forget all his acts of kindness.

3 He forgives all your offences,
    cures all your diseases,
4 he redeems your life from the abyss,
    crowns you with faithful love and
    tenderness;
5 he contents you with good things all your
    life,
    renews your youth like an eagle's.

6 Yahweh acts with uprightness,
    with justice to all who are oppressed;
7 he revealed to Moses his ways,
    his great deeds to the children of Israel.

48 READ PSALM 103.

He . . . renews your youth like an eagle's.—PSALM 103:5

CAPTURED BY CHRIST

You remember that I have compared the Savior to that eagle about which Psalm 103 says, he "renews your youth like an eagle's." There are many points of likeness. The eagle rises above the ground, wings his way aloft, and soars skyward. Similarly, the Savior rose from the grave, ascended to the exalted mansions of paradise, and entered the heights of heaven. In this way the Savior is aptly likened to an eagle.

But what can we make of the fact that the eagle is a bird of prey and often a robber? Even in this the Savior is like the eagle. He bore off his prey when he carried off from the jaws of hell the humanity that he had swooped to take to himself. Yes, he was like an eagle when he led captive to a higher home those he had delivered from the mastery of another lord, the devil. As Psalm 68 prophesied of him, "You have climbed the heights, taken captives, you have taken men as tribute" (verse 18).

Oh how nobly the Psalmist paints the triumph of the Lord! We know that in the past when kings marched in triumph that the procession of prisoners walked before the chariot of their conqueror. But the Lord enters the heavens not following after, but amid a most glorious band of captives. That band are not led before his chariot, but themselves bear up their savior.

ST. MAXIMUS OF TURIN, 380?–467

YOU WILL FIND THE NEXT READING AT PSALM 116.

8 Yahweh is tenderness and pity,
  slow to anger and rich in faithful love;
9 his indignation does not last for ever,
  nor his resentment remain for all time;
10 he does not treat us as our sins deserve,
  nor repay us as befits our offences.

11 As the height of heaven above earth,
  so strong is his faithful love for those who
    fear him.
12 As the distance of east from west,
  so far from us does he put our faults.

13 As tenderly as a father treats his children,
  so Yahweh treats those who fear him;
14 he knows of what we are made,
  he remembers that we are dust.

15 As for a human person—his days are like
    grass,
  he blooms like the wild flowers;
16 as soon as the wind blows he is gone,
  never to be seen there again.

17 But Yahweh's faithful love for those who
    fear him
  is from eternity and for ever;
  and his saving justice to their children's
    children;
18 as long as they keep his covenant,
  and carefully obey his precepts.

19 Yahweh has fixed his throne in
    heaven,
  his sovereign power rules over all.

20 Bless Yahweh, all his angels,
  mighty warriors who fulfil his
      commands,
  attentive to the sound of his words.

21 Bless Yahweh, all his armies,
  servants who fulfil his wishes.
22 Bless Yahweh, all his works,
  in every place where he rules.
  Bless Yahweh, my soul.

104

Bless Yahweh, my soul,
Yahweh, my God, how great
      you are!
Clothed in majesty and splendour,
2 wearing the light as a robe!

You stretch out the heavens like a tent,
3 build your palace on the waters above,
  making the clouds your chariot,
  gliding on the wings of the wind,
4 appointing the winds your messengers,
  flames of fire your servants.

5 You fixed the earth on its foundations,
  for ever and ever it shall not be shaken;
6 you covered it with the deep like a
      garment,
  the waters overtopping the mountains.

7 At your reproof the waters fled,
  at the voice of your thunder they sped
      away,
8 flowing over mountains, down valleys,
  to the place you had fixed for them;
9 you made a limit they were not to
      cross,
  they were not to return and cover the
      earth.

10 In the ravines you opened up springs,
  running down between the mountains,
11 supplying water for all the wild beasts;
  the wild asses quench their thirst,
12 on their banks the birds of the air make
      their nests,
  they sing among the leaves.

13 From your high halls you water the
      mountains,
  satisfying the earth with the fruit of your
      works:
14 for cattle you make the grass grow,
  and for people the plants they need,
  to bring forth food from the earth,
15 and wine to cheer people's hearts,
  oil to make their faces glow,
  food to make them sturdy of heart.

16 The trees of Yahweh drink their fill,
  the cedars of Lebanon which he sowed;
17 there the birds build their nests,
  on the highest branches the stork makes its
      home;
18 for the wild goats there are the mountains,
  in the crags the coneys find refuge.

19 He made the moon to mark the seasons,
  the sun knows when to set.
20 You bring on darkness, and night falls,
  when all the forest beasts roam around;
21 young lions roar for their prey,
  asking God for their food.

22 The sun rises and away they steal,
  back to their lairs to lie down,
23 and man goes out to work,
  to labour till evening falls.

24 How countless are your works, Yahweh,
  all of them made so wisely!
  The earth is full of your creatures.

25 Then there is the sea, with its vast
      expanses
  teeming with countless creatures,
  creatures both great and small;
26 there ships pass to and fro,
  and Leviathan whom you made to sport
      with.

27 They all depend upon you,
  to feed them when they need it.
28 You provide the food they gather,
  your open hand gives them their fill.

29 Turn away your face and they panic;
   take back their breath and they die
   and revert to dust.
30 Send out your breath and life begins;
   you renew the face of the earth.

31 Glory to Yahweh for ever!
   May Yahweh find joy in his creatures!
32 At his glance the earth trembles,
   at his touch the mountains pour forth
      smoke.

33 I shall sing to Yahweh all my life,
   make music for my God as long as
      I live.
34 May my musings be pleasing to him,
   for Yahweh gives me joy.
35 May sinners vanish from the earth,
   and the wicked exist no more!

Bless Yahweh, my soul.

105 Alleluia!

1 Give thanks to Yahweh, call on his
      name,
   proclaim his deeds to the peoples!
2 Sing to him, make music for him,
   recount all his wonders!
3 Glory in his holy name,
   let the hearts that seek Yahweh rejoice!

4 Seek Yahweh and his strength,
   tirelessly seek his presence!
5 Remember the marvels he has done,
   his wonders, the judgements he has
      spoken.
6 Stock of Abraham, his servant,
   children of Jacob whom he chose!
7 He is Yahweh our God,
   his judgements touch the whole world.

8 He remembers his covenant for ever,
   the promise he laid down for a thousand
      generations,
9 which he concluded with Abraham,
   the oath he swore to Isaac.

10 He established it as a statute for Jacob,
   an everlasting covenant with Israel,
11 saying, 'To you I give a land,
   Canaan, your allotted birthright.'

12 When they were insignificant in numbers,
   a handful of strangers in the land,
13 wandering from country to country,
   from one kingdom and nation to another,

14 he allowed no one to oppress them;
   for their sake he instructed kings,
15 'Do not touch my anointed ones,
   to my prophets you may do no harm.'

16 He called down famine on the land,
   he took away their food supply;
17 he sent a man ahead of them,
   Joseph, sold as a slave.

18 So his feet were weighed down with
      shackles,
   his neck was put in irons.
19 In due time his prophecy was fulfilled,
   the word of Yahweh proved him true.

20 The king sent orders to release him,
   the ruler of nations set him free;
21 he put him in charge of his household,
   the ruler of all he possessed,

22 to instruct his princes as he saw fit,
   to teach his counsellors wisdom.
23 Then Israel migrated to Egypt,
   Jacob settled in the country of Ham.

24 He made his people increase in numbers,
   he gave them more strength than their
      enemies,
25 whose heart he turned to hate his own
      people,
   to double-cross his servants.

26 He sent his servant Moses,
   and Aaron, the man of his choice.
27 They worked there the wonders he
      commanded,
   marvels in the country of Ham.

28 Darkness he sent, and darkness fell,
  but that nation defied his orders.
29 He turned their rivers to blood,
  and killed all the fish in them.

30 Their country was overrun with frogs,
  even in the royal apartments;
31 at his word came flies,
  and mosquitoes throughout the country.

32 He gave them hail as their rain,
  flames of fire in their land;
33 he blasted their vine and their fig tree,
  and shattered the trees of the country.

34 At his word came locusts,
  hoppers beyond all counting;
35 they devoured every green thing in the land,
  devoured all the produce of the soil.

36 He struck all the first-born in their land,
  the flower of all their manhood;
37 he led Israel out with silver and gold;
  in their tribes there was none who stumbled.

38 Egypt was glad at their leaving,
  for terror of Israel had seized them.
39 He spread out a cloud to cover them,
  and fire to light up the night.

40 They asked and he brought them quails,
  food from heaven to their hearts' content;
41 he opened a rock, the waters gushed out,
  and flowed in dry ground as a river.

42 Faithful to his sacred promise,
  given to his servant Abraham,
43 he led out his people with rejoicing,
  his chosen ones with shouts of joy.

44 He gave them the territories of nations,
  they reaped the fruit of other people's labours,
45 on condition that they kept his statutes,
  and remained obedient to his laws.

106 Alleluia!

Give thanks to Yahweh, for he is good,
  his faithful love is everlasting!
2 Who can recount all Yahweh's triumphs,
  who can fully voice his praise?

3 How blessed are those who keep to what is just,
  whose conduct is always upright!
4 Remember me, Yahweh,
  in your love for your people.

Come near to me with your saving power,
5 let me share the happiness of your chosen ones,
  let me share the joy of your people,
  the pride of your heritage.

6 Like our ancestors, we have sinned,
  we have acted wickedly, guiltily;
7 our ancestors in Egypt never grasped
  the meaning of your wonders.

They did not bear in mind your countless acts of love,
  at the Sea of Reeds they defied the Most High;
8 but for the sake of his name he saved them,
  to make known his mighty power.

9 At his rebuke the Sea of Reeds dried up,
  he let them pass through the deep as though it were desert,
10 so he saved them from their opponents' clutches,
  rescued them from the clutches of their enemies.

11 The waters enveloped their enemies,
  not one of whom was left.
12 Then they believed what he had said,
  and sang his praises.

13 But they soon forgot his achievements,
  they did not even wait for his plans;

¹⁴ they were overwhelmed with greed in the
wastelands,
in the solitary wastes they challenged
God.

¹⁵ He gave them all they asked for,
but struck them with a deep wasting
sickness;
¹⁶ in the camp they grew jealous of Moses,
and of Aaron, Yahweh's holy one.

¹⁷ The earth opened and swallowed up
Dathan,
closed in on Abiram's faction;
¹⁸ fire flamed out against their faction,
the renegades were engulfed in flames.

¹⁹ At Horeb they made a calf,
bowed low before cast metal;
²⁰ they exchanged their glory
for the image of a grass-eating bull.

²¹ They forgot the God who was saving
them,
who had done great deeds in Egypt,
²² such wonders in the land of Ham,
such awesome deeds at the Sea of Reeds.

²³ He thought of putting an end to them,
had not Moses, his chosen one,
taken a stand in the breach and confronted
him,
to turn his anger away from destroying
them.

²⁴ They counted a desirable land for
nothing,
they put no trust in his promise;
²⁵ they stayed in their tents and grumbled,
they would not listen to Yahweh's
voice.

²⁶ So he lifted his hand against them,
to strike them down in the desert,
²⁷ to strike down their descendants among
the nations,
to scatter them all over the world.

²⁸ They committed themselves to serve
Baal-Peor,
and ate sacrifices made to lifeless gods.
²⁹ They so provoked him by their actions
that a plague broke out among them.

³⁰ Then up stood Phinehas to intervene,
and the plague was checked;
³¹ for this he is the example of uprightness,
from age to age for ever.

³² At the waters of Meribah they so angered
Yahweh,
that Moses suffered on their account,
³³ for they had embittered his spirit,
and he spoke without due thought.

³⁴ They did not destroy the nations,
as Yahweh had told them to do,
³⁵ but intermarried with them,
and adopted their ways.

³⁶ They worshipped those nations' false gods,
till they found themselves entrapped,
³⁷ and sacrificed their own sons
and their daughters to demons.

³⁸ Innocent blood they shed,
the blood of their sons and daughters;
offering them to the idols of Canaan,
they polluted the country with blood.

³⁹ They defiled themselves by such actions,
their behaviour was that of a harlot.
⁴⁰ Yahweh's anger blazed out at his people,
his own heritage filled him with disgust.

⁴¹ He handed them over to the nations,
and their opponents became their masters;
⁴² their enemies lorded it over them,
crushing them under their rule.

⁴³ Time and again he rescued them,
but they still defied him deliberately,
and sank ever deeper in their guilt;
⁴⁴ even so he took pity on their distress,
as soon as he heard them cry out.

45 Bearing his covenant with them in mind,
  he relented in his boundless and faithful
    love;
46 he ensured that they received compassion,
  in their treatment by all their captors.

47 Save us, Yahweh our God,
  gather us from among the nations,
  that we may give thanks to your holy
    name,
  and may glory in praising you.

48 Blessed be Yahweh, the God of Israel,
  from all eternity and for ever!
  Let all the people say, 'Amen'.

BOOK FIVE: PSALMS 107–150

107 Alleluia!

1 Give thanks to Yahweh for he is good,
  his faithful love lasts for ever.

2 So let them say whom Yahweh redeemed,
  whom he redeemed from the power of
    their enemies,
3 bringing them back from foreign lands,
  from east and west, north and south.

4 They were wandering in the desert, in the
    wastelands,
  could find no way to an inhabited city;
5 they were hungry and thirsty,
  their life was ebbing away.

6 They cried out to Yahweh in their distress,
  he rescued them from their plight,
7 he set them on the road,
  straight to an inhabited city.

8 Let them thank Yahweh for his faithful
    love,
  for his wonders for the children of
    Adam!
9 He has fed the hungry to their hearts'
    content,
  filled the starving with good things.

10 Sojourners in gloom and shadow dark as
    death,
  fettered in misery and chains,
11 for defying the orders of Yahweh,
  for scorning the plan of the Most High—
12 he subdued their spirit by hard labour;
  if they fell there was no one to help.

13 They cried out to Yahweh in their distress,
  he rescued them from their plight,
14 he brought them out from gloom and
    shadow dark as death,
  and shattered their chains.

15 Let them thank Yahweh for his faithful
    love,
  for his wonders for the children of Adam!
16 He broke open gates of bronze
  and smashed iron bars.

17 Fools for their rebellious ways,
  wretched because of their sins,
18 finding all food repugnant,
  brought close to the gates of death—

19 they cried out to Yahweh in their distress;
  he rescued them from their plight,
20 he sent out his word and cured them,
  and rescued their life from the abyss.

21 Let them thank Yahweh for his faithful
    love,
  for his wonders for the children of Adam!
22 Let them offer thanksgiving sacrifices,
  and recount with shouts of joy what he has
    done!

23 Voyagers on the sea in ships,
  plying their trade on the great ocean,
24 have seen the works of Yahweh,
  his wonders in the deep.

25 By his word he raised a storm-wind,
  lashing up towering waves.
26 Up to the sky then down to the depths!
  Their stomachs were turned to water;
27 they staggered and reeled like drunkards,
  and all their skill went under.

28 They cried out to Yahweh in their distress,
    he rescued them from their plight,
29 he reduced the storm to a calm,
    and all the waters subsided,
30 and he brought them, overjoyed at the
        stillness,
    to the port where they were bound.

31 Let them thank Yahweh for his faithful
        love,
    for his wonders for the children of Adam!
32 Let them extol him in the assembly of the
        people,
    and praise him in the council of elders.

33 He has turned rivers into desert,
    bubbling springs into arid ground,
34 fertile country into salt-flats,
    because the people living there were evil.

35 But he has turned desert into stretches of
        water,
    arid ground into bubbling springs,
36 and has given the hungry a home,
    where they have built themselves a city.

37 There they sow fields and plant vines,
    and reap a harvest of their produce.
38 He blesses them and their numbers
        increase,
    he keeps their cattle at full strength.

39 Their numbers had fallen, they had grown
        weak,
    under pressure of disaster and hardship;
40 he covered princes in contempt,
    left them to wander in trackless wastes.

41 But the needy he raises from their misery,
    makes their families as numerous as sheep.
42 At the sight the honest rejoice,
    and the wicked have nothing to say.

43 Who is wise? Such a one should take this
        to heart,
    and come to understand Yahweh's faithful
        love.

108 [a]
Song; psalm of David

1 My heart is ready, God,
    I will sing and make music;
    come, my glory!
2 Awake, lyre and harp,
    I will awake the Dawn!

3 I will praise you among the peoples,
        Yahweh,
    I will play to you among nations,
4 for your faithful love towers to heaven,
    and your constancy to the clouds.

5 Be exalted above the heavens, God.
    Your glory over the whole earth!

6 To rescue those you love,
    save with your right hand and answer us.

7 God has spoken from his sanctuary,
    'In triumph I will divide up Shechem,
    and share out the Valley of Succoth.

8 'Mine is Gilead, mine Manasseh,
    Ephraim the helmet on my head,
    Judah my commander's baton,

9 'Moab a bowl for me to wash in,
    on Edom I plant my sandal,
    over Philistia I cry victory.'

10 Who will lead me against a fortified
        city,
    who will guide me into Edom,
11 if not you, the God who has rejected us?
    God, you no longer march with our
        armies.

12 Bring us help in our time of crisis,
    any human assistance is worthless.
13 With God we shall do deeds of
        valour,
    he will trample down our enemies.

108a = 57:7–11 + 60:5–12.

109

For the choirmaster:
Psalm of David

1 God whom I praise, do not be silent!
2 Wicked and deceiving words
    are being said about me,
    false accusations are cast in my teeth.
3 Words of hate fly all around me,
    though I give no cause for hostility.

4 In return for my friendship they
      denounce me,
    and all I can do is pray!
5 They repay my kindness with evil,
    and friendship with hatred.

6 'Set up a wicked man against him
    as accuser to stand on his right.
7 At his trial may he emerge as guilty,
    even his prayer construed as a crime!

8 'May his life be cut short,
    someone else take over his office,
9 his children be orphaned,
    his wife be widowed.

10 'May his children wander perpetually,
    beggars, driven from the ruins of their
      house,
11 a creditor seize all his goods,
    and strangers make off with his
      earnings.

12 'May there be none left faithful enough to
      show him love,
    no one take pity on his orphans,
13 the line of his descendants cut off,
    his name wiped out in one generation.

14 'May Yahweh never forget the crimes of
      his ancestors,
    and his mother's sins not be wiped out;
15 may Yahweh keep these constantly in
      mind,
    to cut off the remembrance of them from
      the earth.'

16 He had no thought of being loyal,
    but hounded the poor and the needy
    and the broken-hearted to their death.

17 He had a taste for cursing; let it recoil on
      him!
    No taste for blessing; let it never come his
      way!
18 Cursing has been the uniform he wore;
    let it soak into him like water,
    like oil right into his bones.
19 Let it be as a robe which envelops him
      completely,
    a sash which he always wears.

20 Let this be the salary Yahweh pays
    the accusers who blacken my name.
21 Yahweh, treat them as your name
      demands;
    as your faithful love is generous, deliver
      me.

22 Poor and needy as I am,
    my wounds go right to the heart;
23 I am passing away like a fading shadow,
    they have shaken me off like a locust.

24 My knees are weak from lack of food,
    my body lean for lack of fat.
25 I have become the butt of their taunts,
    they shake their heads at the sight of me.

26 Help me, Yahweh my God,
    save me as your faithful love demands.
27 Let them know that yours is the saving
      hand,
    that this, Yahweh, is your work.

28 Let them curse, provided that you bless;
    let their attacks bring shame to them and
      joy to your servant!
29 Let my accusers be clothed in disgrace,
    enveloped in a cloak of shame.

30 With generous thanks to Yahweh on my
      lips,
    I shall praise him before all the people,
31 for he stands at the side of the poor,
    to save their lives from those who sit in
      judgement on them.

110

Psalm of David

1 Yahweh declared to my Lord, 'Take your
    seat at my right hand,
till I have made your enemies your
    footstool.'

2 Yahweh will stretch out the sceptre of your
    power;
from Zion you will rule your foes all
    around you.

3 Royal[a] dignity has been yours from the day
    of your birth,
sacred honour from the womb, from the
    dawn of your youth.

4 Yahweh has sworn an oath he will never
    retract,
you are a priest for ever of the order of
    Melchizedek.

5 At your right hand, Lord,
    he shatters kings when his anger breaks
    out.
6 He judges nations, heaping up corpses,
    he breaks heads over the whole wide
    world.
7 He drinks from a stream as he goes,
    and therefore he holds his head high.

111

Alleluia!

ALEPH I give thanks to Yahweh with all my
        heart,
BET   in the meeting-place of honest people, in
        the assembly.
GIMEL 2 Great are the deeds of Yahweh,
DALET to be pondered by all who delight in
        them.

HE   3 Full of splendour and majesty his
        work,
WAW   his saving justice stands firm for ever.
ZAIN   4 He gives us a memorial of his great
        deeds;
HET   Yahweh is mercy and tenderness.

TET   5 He gives food to those who fear him,
YOD   he keeps his covenant ever in mind.
KAPH   6 His works show his people his
        power
LAMED in giving them the birthright of the
        nations.

MEM   7 The works of his hands are fidelity
        and justice,
NUN   all his precepts are trustworthy,
SAMEK 8 established for ever and ever,
AIN   accomplished in fidelity and honesty.

PE   9 Deliverance he sends to his people,
ZADE   his covenant he imposes for ever;
QOPH   holy and awesome his name.
RESH   10 The root of wisdom is fear of
        Yahweh;
SHIN   those who attain it are wise.
TAW   His praise will continue for ever.

112

Alleluia!

ALEPH How blessed is anyone who fears
        Yahweh,
BET   who delights in his commandments!
GIMEL 2 His descendants shall be powerful on
        earth,
DALET the race of the honest shall receive
        blessings:

HE   3 Riches and wealth for his family;
WAW   his uprightness stands firm for ever.
ZAIN   4 For the honest he shines as a lamp in
        the dark,
HET   generous, tender-hearted, and upright.

TET   5 All goes well for one who lends
        generously,
YOD   who is honest in all his dealing;
KAPH   6 for all time to come he will not
        stumble,
LAMED for all time to come the upright will
        be remembered.

110a *Conjectural translation of a textually corrupt and ob-*
scure v.

MEM ⁷Bad news holds no fears for him,
NUN firm is his heart, trusting in Yahweh.
SAMEK ⁸His heart held steady, he has no
fears,
AIN till he can gloat over his enemies.

PE ⁹To the needy he gives without stint,
ZADE his uprightness stands firm for ever;
QOPH his reputation is founded on strength.

RESH ¹⁰The wicked are vexed at the sight,
SHIN they grind their teeth and waste away.
TAW The desires of the wicked will be
frustrated.

113 Alleluia!

Praise, servants of Yahweh,
praise the name of Yahweh.

² Blessed be the name of Yahweh,
henceforth and for ever.
³ From the rising of the sun to its setting,
praised be the name of Yahweh!

⁴ Supreme over all nations is Yahweh,
supreme over the heavens his glory.
⁵ Who is like Yahweh our God?
His throne is set on high,
⁶ but he stoops to look down on heaven and
earth.

⁷ He raises the poor from the dust,
he lifts the needy from the dunghill,
⁸ to give them a place among princes,
among princes of his people.
⁹ He lets the barren woman be seated at
home,
the happy mother of sons.

114 ªAlleluia!

¹ When Israel came out of Egypt,
the House of Jacob from a people of
foreign speech,
² Judah became his sanctuary,
and Israel his domain.

³ The sea fled at the sight,
the Jordan turned back,
⁴ the mountains skipped like rams,
the hills like sheep.

⁵ Sea, what makes you flee?
Jordan, why turn back?
⁶ Why skip like rams, you mountains?
Why like sheep, you hills?

⁷ Tremble, earth, at the coming of the
Lord,
at the coming of the God of Jacob,
⁸ who turns rock into pool,
flint into fountain.

115 ªNot to us, Yahweh, not to us,
but to your name give the glory,
for your faithful love and your constancy!
² Why should the nations ask, 'Where is
their God?'

³ Our God is in heaven,
he creates whatever he chooses.
⁴ They have idols of silver and gold,
made by human hands.

⁵ These have mouths but say nothing,
have eyes but see nothing,
⁶ have ears but hear nothing,
have noses but smell nothing.

⁷ They have hands but cannot feel,
have feet but cannot walk,
no sound comes from their throats.
⁸ Their makers will end up like them,
and all who rely on them.

⁹ House of Israel, rely on Yahweh;
he is their help and their shield.
¹⁰ House of Aaron, rely on Yahweh;
he is their help and their shield.
¹¹ You who fear Yahweh, rely on
Yahweh;
he is their help and their shield.

114a Ps 113A in Vulgate   *115a* Ps 113B in Vulgate

12 Yahweh will keep us in mind, he will
         bless,
    he will bless the House of Israel,
    he will bless the House of Aaron,
13 he will bless those who fear Yahweh,
    small and great alike.

14 May Yahweh add to your numbers,
    yours and your children's too!
15 May you be blessed by Yahweh,
    who made heaven and earth.

16 Heaven belongs to Yahweh,
    but earth he has given to the children of
         Adam.

17 The dead cannot praise Yahweh,
    those who sink into silence,
18 but we, the living, shall bless Yahweh,
    henceforth and for ever.

116 ªAlleluia!

1 I am filled with love when Yahweh
         listens
    to the sound of my prayer,
2 when he bends down to hear me,
    as I call.

3 The bonds of death were all round me,
    the snares of Sheol held me fast;
    distress and anguish held me in their grip,
4   I called on the name of Yahweh.

    Deliver me, Yahweh, I beg you.

5 Yahweh is merciful and upright,
    our God is tenderness.
6 Yahweh looks after the simple,
    when I was brought low he gave me
         strength.

7 My heart, be at peace once again,
    for Yahweh has treated you generously.
8 He has rescued me from death, my eyes
         from tears,
    and my feet from stumbling.

9 I shall pass my life in the presence of
         Yahweh,
    in the land of the living.

10 My trust does not fail even when I say,
    'I am completely wretched.'
11 In my terror I said,
    'No human being can be relied on.'
12 What return can I make to Yahweh
    for his generosity to me?
13 I shall take up the cup of salvation
    and call on the name of Yahweh.

14 I shall fulfil my vows to Yahweh,
    witnessed by all his people.

15 Costly in Yahweh's sight
    is the death of his faithful.

16 I beg you, Yahweh! I am your servant,
    I am your servant and my mother was
         your servant;
    you have undone my fetters.
17 I shall offer you a sacrifice of thanksgiving
    and call on the name of Yahweh.

18 I shall fulfil my vows to Yahweh,
    witnessed by all his people,
19 in the courts of the house of Yahweh,
    in your very heart, Jerusalem.

117 Alleluia!

1 Praise Yahweh, all nations,
    extol him, all peoples,
2 for his faithful love is strong
    and his constancy never-ending.

118 Alleluia!

1 Give thanks to Yahweh for he is good,
    for his faithful love endures for ever.

2 Let the House of Israel say,
    'His faithful love endures for ever.'

116a Pss 114–115 in Vulgate

49 READ PSALM 116.

What return can I make to Yahweh for all his generosity to me?—PSALM 116:12

GRATITUDE FOR THE NEW CREATION

What shall I render to the Lord for all these gifts? . . . Faith certainly bids me love him all the more whom I regard as that much greater than I, for he not only gives me myself, he also gives me himself. . . .

God is not unjust when he claims for himself his works and gifts. Why would not an artifact love its artist, if it is able to do so? Why would it not love him all it can, since it can do nothing except by his gift? In addition, the fact that man was made out of nothing, gratuitously . . . renders the debt of love clearer and proves the divine exaction more just. Besides, how much did the benefit increase when God, multiplying his mercy, saved men and beasts? I am speaking of us who exchanged our glory for the likeness of a calf that eats grass (see Ps 106:20), who have become by sin like irrational beasts (see Ps 49:20).

If I owe all for having been created, what can I add for being remade in this way? It was less easy to remake me than to make me. It is written not only about me but of every created being: "He spoke and they were made" (see Ps 148:5). But he who made me by a single word, in remaking me had to speak many words, work miracles, suffer hardships, and not only hardships but even unjust treatment. "What return can I make to Yahweh for all his generosity to me?"

In his first work he gave me myself; in his second he gave me himself. Given, and regiven, I owe myself twice over. What can I give God in return for himself? Even if I could give him myself a thousand times, what am I to God?   ST. BERNARD OF CLAIRVAUX, 1090?–1153

YOU WILL FIND THE NEXT READING AT PSALM 118.

³ Let the House of Aaron say,
  'His faithful love endures for ever.'
⁴ Let those who fear Yahweh say,
  'His faithful love endures for ever.'

⁵ In my distress I called to Yahweh,
  he heard me and brought me relief.
⁶ With Yahweh on my side I fear nothing;
  what can human beings do to me?
⁷ With Yahweh on my side as my help,
  I gloat over my enemies.

⁸ It is better to take refuge in Yahweh
  than to rely on human beings;

⁹ better to take refuge in Yahweh
  than to rely on princes.

¹⁰ Nations were swarming around me,
   in the name of Yahweh I cut them down;
¹¹ they swarmed around me, pressing
                  upon me,
   in the name of Yahweh I cut them down.
¹² They swarmed around me like bees,
   they flared up like a brushwood fire,
   in the name of Yahweh I cut them down.

¹³ I was pushed hard, to make me fall,
   but Yahweh came to my help.

50 READ PSALM 118.

Though Yahweh punished me sternly, he has not abandoned me to death.—PSALM 118:18

MAKING THE MOST OF SICKNESS

Many are the wiles of the devil. If he is not able to disturb the soul by means of poverty, he suggests riches as an attraction. If he has not won the victory by insults and disgrace, he suggests praise and glory. Overcome by health, he makes the body ill. Not having been able to seduce it through pleasures, he tries to overthrow it by involuntary sufferings. He joins to this, very severe illness, to disturb the faint-hearted in their love of God. But he also destroys the body by very violent fevers and weighs it down with intolerable thirst. If, being a sinner, you undergo all these things, remind yourself of the punishment to come, the everlasting fire and the sufferings inflicted by justice, and do not be discouraged here and now.

Rejoice that God visits you and keep this blessed saying on your lips: "Though Yahweh has punished me sternly, he has not abandoned me to death." You were iron, but fire has burnt the rust off you. If you are righteous and fall ill, you will go from strength to strength. Are you gold? You will pass through fire purged. Have you been give a thorn in the flesh? (see 2 Co 12:7). Exult, and see who else was treated like that; it is an honor to have the same sufferings as Paul. . . . By virtue offer holy words in a loud voice. For it is said: "For myself, wounded wretch that I am, by your saving power raise me up!" (Ps 69:29). By this share of wretchedness you will be made perfect. For he said: "Yahweh listens when I call to him" (Ps 4:3). So open your mouth wide to be taught by these exercises of the soul, seeing that we are under the eyes of our enemy.   ST. SYNCLETICA, d. 400?

YOU WILL FIND THE NEXT READING AT PSALM 139.

14 Yahweh is my strength and my song,
he has been my Saviour.

15 Shouts of joy and salvation,
in the tents of the upright,
'Yahweh's right hand is triumphant,
16 Yahweh's right hand is victorious,
Yahweh's right hand is triumphant!'

17 I shall not die, I shall live
to recount the great deeds of Yahweh.
18 Though Yahweh punished me sternly,
he has not abandoned me to death.

19 Open for me the gates of saving justice,
I shall go in and thank Yahweh.

20 This is the gate of Yahweh,
where the upright go in.
21 I thank you for hearing me,
and making yourself my Saviour.

22 The stone which the builders rejected
has become the cornerstone;
23 This is Yahweh's doing,
and we marvel at it.
24 This is the day which Yahweh has made,
a day for us to rejoice and be glad.

25 We beg you, Yahweh, save us,
we beg you, Yahweh, give us victory!
26 Blessed in the name of Yahweh is he who
is coming!

We bless you from the house of Yahweh.
27 Yahweh is God,
  he gives us light.

Link your processions, branches in
    hand,
  up to the horns of the altar.
28 You are my God, I thank you,
  all praise to you, my God.
I thank you for hearing me,
  and making yourself my Saviour.

29 Give thanks to Yahweh for he is good,
  for his faithful love endures for ever.

119

ALEPH 1 How blessed are those
    whose way is blameless,
  who walk in the Law of Yahweh!
2 Blessed are those who observe his
    instructions,
  who seek him with all their hearts,
3 and, doing no evil,
  who walk in his ways.
4 You lay down your precepts
  to be carefully kept.
5 May my ways be steady
  in doing your will.
6 Then I shall not be shamed,
  if my gaze is fixed on your
    commandments.
7 I thank you with a sincere heart
  for teaching me your upright judgements.
8 I shall do your will;
  do not ever abandon me wholly.

BET 9 How can a young man keep his way
    spotless?
  By keeping your words.
10 With all my heart I seek you,
  do not let me stray from your
    commandments.
11 In my heart I treasure your promises,
  to avoid sinning against you.
12 Blessed are you, Yahweh,
  teach me your will!
13 With my lips I have repeated
  all the judgements you have given.

14 In the way of your instructions lies my joy,
  a joy beyond all wealth.
15 I will ponder your precepts
  and fix my gaze on your paths.
16 I find my delight in your will,
  I do not forget your words.

GIMEL 17 Be generous to your servant and I
    shall live,
  and shall keep your words.
18 Open my eyes and I shall fix my gaze
  on the wonders of your Law.
19 Wayfarer though I am on the earth,
  do not hide your commandments from me.
20 My heart is pining away with longing
  at all times for your judgements.
21 You have rebuked the arrogant, the
    accursed,
  who stray from your commandments.
22 Set me free from taunts and contempt
  since I observe your instructions.
23 Though princes sit plotting against me,
  your servant keeps pondering your will.
24 Your instructions are my delight,
  your wishes my counsellors.

DALET 25 Down in the dust I lie prostrate;
  true to your word, revive me.
26 I tell you my ways and you answer me;
  teach me your wishes.
27 Show me the way of your precepts,
  that I may reflect on your wonders.
28 I am melting away for grief;
  true to your word, raise me up.
29 Keep me far from the way of deceit,
  grant me the grace of your Law.
30 I have chosen the way of constancy,
  I have moulded myself to your
    judgements.
31 I cling to your instructions,
  Yahweh, do not disappoint me.
32 I run the way of your commandments,
  for you have given me freedom of heart.

HE 33 Teach me, Yahweh, the way of your
    will,
  and I will observe it.

34 Give me understanding and I will observe
   your Law,
   and keep it wholeheartedly.
35 Guide me in the way of your
   commandments,
   for my delight is there.
36 Bend my heart to your instructions,
   not to selfish gain.
37 Avert my eyes from pointless images,
   by your word give me life.
38 Keep your promise to your servant
   so that all may hold you in awe.
39 Avert the taunts that I dread,
   for your judgements are generous.
40 See how I yearn for your precepts;
   in your saving justice give me life.

WAW 41 Let your faithful love come to me,
   Yahweh,
   true to your promise, save me!
42 Give me an answer to the taunts against me,
   since I rely on your word.
43 Do not deprive me of that faithful word,
   since my hope lies in your judgements.
44 I shall keep your Law without fail
   for ever and ever.
45 I shall live in all freedom
   because I have sought your precepts.
46 I shall speak of your instructions before
   kings
   and will not be shamed.
47 Your commandments fill me with delight,
   I love them dearly.
48 I stretch out my hands to your
   commandments that I love,
   and I ponder your judgements.

ZAIN 49 Keep in mind your promise to your
   servant
   on which I have built my hope.
50 It is my comfort in distress,
   that your promise gives me life.
51 Endlessly the arrogant have jeered at me,
   but I have not swerved from your Law.
52 I have kept your age-old judgements in
   mind,
   Yahweh, and I am comforted.

53 Fury grips me when I see the wicked
   who abandon your Law.
54 Your judgements are my song
   where I live in exile.
55 All night, Yahweh, I hold your name in
   mind,
   I keep your Law.
56 This is what it means to me,
   observing your precepts.

HET 57 My task, I have said, Yahweh,
   is to keep your word.
58 Wholeheartedly I entreat your favour;
   true to your promise, take pity on me!
59 I have reflected on my ways,
   and I turn my steps to your instructions.
60 I hurry without delay
   to keep your commandments.
61 Though caught in the snares of the
   wicked,
   I do not forget your Law.
62 At midnight I rise to praise you
   for your upright judgements.
63 I am a friend to all who fear you
   and keep your precepts.
64 Your faithful love fills the earth,
   Yahweh, teach me your judgements.

TET 65 You have been generous to your
   servant, Yahweh,
   true to your promise.
66 Teach me judgement and knowledge,
   for I rely on your commandments.
67 Before I was punished I used to go astray,
   but now I keep to your promise.
68 You are generous and act generously,
   teach me your will.
69 The arrogant blacken me with lies
   though I wholeheartedly observe your
   precepts.
70 Their hearts are gross like rich fat,
   but my delight is in your Law.
71 It was good for me that I had to suffer,
   the better to learn your judgements.
72 The Law you have uttered is more
   precious to me
   than all the wealth in the world.

YOD 73 Your hands have made me and held
me firm,
give me understanding and I shall learn
your commandments.
74 Those who fear you rejoice at the sight of
me
since I put my hope in your word.
75 I know, Yahweh, that your judgements are
upright,
and in punishing me you show your
constancy.
76 Your faithful love must be my consolation,
as you have promised your servant.
77 Treat me with tenderness and I shall live,
for your Law is my delight.
78 Let the arrogant who tell lies against me
be shamed,
while I ponder your precepts.
79 Let those who fear you rally to me,
those who understand your instructions.
80 My heart shall be faultless towards your
will;
then I shall not be ashamed.

KAPH 81 I shall wear myself out for your
salvation,
for your word is my hope.
82 My eyes, too, are worn out waiting for
your promise,
when will you have pity on me?
83 For I am like a smoked wineskin,
but I do not forget your will.
84 How long has your servant to live?
When will you bring my persecutors to
judgement?
85 The arrogant have dug pitfalls for me
in defiance of your Law.
86 All your commandments show
constancy.
Help me when they pursue me
dishonestly.
87 They have almost annihilated me on
earth,
but I have not deserted your precepts.
88 True to your faithful love, give me life,
and I shall keep the instructions you
have laid down.

LAMED 89 For ever, Yahweh, your word
is planted firm in heaven.
90 Your constancy endures from age to age;
you established the earth and it stands
firm.
91 Through your judgements all stands firm
to this day,
for all creation is your servant.
92 Had your Law not been my delight,
I would have perished in my misery.
93 I shall never forget your precepts,
for by them you have given me life.
94 I am yours, save me,
for I seek your precepts.
95 The wicked may hope to destroy me,
but all my thought is of your instructions.
96 I have seen that all perfection is finite,
but your commandment has no limit.

MEM 97 How I love your Law!
I ponder it all day long.
98 You make me wiser than my enemies
by your commandment which is mine for
ever.
99 I am wiser than all my teachers
because I ponder your instructions.
100 I have more understanding than the
aged
because I keep your precepts.
101 I restrain my foot from evil paths
to keep your word.
102 I do not turn aside from your judgements,
because you yourself have instructed me.
103 How pleasant your promise to my palate,
sweeter than honey in my mouth!
104 From your precepts I learn wisdom,
so I hate all deceptive ways.

NUN 105 Your word is a lamp for my feet,
a light on my path.
106 I have sworn—and shall maintain it—
to keep your upright judgements.
107 I am utterly wretched, Yahweh;
true to your promise, give me life.
108 Accept, Yahweh, the tribute from my
mouth,
and teach me your judgements.

¹⁰⁹My life is in your hands perpetually,
  I do not forget your Law.
¹¹⁰The wicked have laid out a snare for me,
  but I have not strayed from your precepts.
¹¹¹Your instructions are my eternal heritage,
  they are the joy of my heart.
¹¹²I devote myself to obeying your statutes,
  their recompense is eternal.

SAMEK ¹¹³I hate a divided heart,
  I love your Law.
¹¹⁴You are my refuge and shield,
  I put my hope in your word.
¹¹⁵Leave me alone, you wicked,
  I shall observe the commandments of my
    God.
¹¹⁶True to your word, support me and I shall
    live;
  do not disappoint me of my hope.
¹¹⁷Uphold me and I shall be saved,
  my gaze fixed on your will.
¹¹⁸You shake off all who stray from your will;
  deceit fills their horizon.
¹¹⁹In your sight all the wicked of the earth
    are like rust,
  so I love your instructions.
¹²⁰My whole body trembles before you,
  your judgements fill me with fear.

AIN ¹²¹All my conduct has been just and
    upright,
  do not hand me over to my oppressors.
¹²²Guarantee the well-being of your servant,
  do not let the proud oppress me.
¹²³My eyes are languishing for your
    salvation
  and for the saving justice you have
    promised.
¹²⁴Show your faithful love to your servant,
  teach me your judgements.
¹²⁵Your servant am I; give me understanding
  and I shall know your instructions.
¹²⁶It is time to take action, Yahweh,
  your Law is being broken.
¹²⁷So I love your commandments
  more than gold, purest gold.
¹²⁸So I rule my life by your precepts,
  I hate all deceptive paths.

PE ¹²⁹Wonderful are your instructions,
  so I observe them.
¹³⁰As your word unfolds it gives light,
  and even the simple understand.
¹³¹I open wide my mouth,
  panting eagerly for your commandments.
¹³²Turn to me, pity me;
  those who love your name deserve it.
¹³³Keep my steps firm in your promise;
  that no evil may triumph over me.
¹³⁴Rescue me from human oppression,
  and I will observe your precepts.
¹³⁵Let your face shine on your servant,
  teach me your will.
¹³⁶My eyes stream with tears
  because your Law is disregarded.

ZADE ¹³⁷You are upright, Yahweh,
  and your judgements are honest.
¹³⁸You impose uprightness as a witness to
    yourself,
  it is constancy itself.
¹³⁹My zeal is burning me up
  because my oppressors forget your word.
¹⁴⁰Your promise is well tested,
  your servant holds it dear.
¹⁴¹Puny and despised as I am,
  I do not forget your precepts.
¹⁴²Your saving justice is for ever just,
  and your Law is trustworthy.
¹⁴³Though anguish and distress grip me
  your commandments are my delight.
¹⁴⁴Your instructions are upright for ever,
  give me understanding and I shall live.

QOPH ¹⁴⁵I call with all my heart; answer me,
    Yahweh,
  and I will observe your judgements.
¹⁴⁶I call to you; save me,
  and I will keep your instructions.
¹⁴⁷I am awake before dawn to cry for help,
  I put my hope in your word.
¹⁴⁸My eyes are awake before each watch of
    the night,
  to ponder your promise.
¹⁴⁹In your faithful love, Yahweh, listen to my
    voice,
  let your judgements give me life.

¹⁵⁰My pursuers are coming closer to their
wicked designs,
and further from your Law.
¹⁵¹You are close to me, Yahweh,
and all your commandments are true.
¹⁵²Long have I known that your instructions
were laid down to last for ever.

RESH ¹⁵³Look at my suffering and rescue me,
for I do not forget your Law.
¹⁵⁴Plead my cause and defend me;
as you promised, give me life.
¹⁵⁵Salvation is far from the wicked,
for they do not seek your will.
¹⁵⁶Your kindnesses to me are countless,
Yahweh;
true to your judgements, give me life.
¹⁵⁷Though my enemies and oppressors are
countless,
I do not turn aside from your instructions.
¹⁵⁸The sight of these renegades appals me;
they do not observe your promise.
¹⁵⁹See how I love your precepts;
true to your faithful love, give me life.
¹⁶⁰Faithfulness is the essence of your word,
your upright judgements hold good for
ever.

SHIN ¹⁶¹Though princes hound me
unprovoked,
what fills me with awe is your word.
¹⁶²I rejoice in your promise
like one who finds a vast treasure.
¹⁶³Falsehood I hate and detest,
my love is for your Law.
¹⁶⁴Seven times a day I praise you
for your upright judgements.
¹⁶⁵Great peace for those who love your Law;
no stumbling-blocks for them!
¹⁶⁶I am waiting for your salvation,
Yahweh,
I fulfil your commandments.
¹⁶⁷I observe your instructions,
I love them dearly.
¹⁶⁸I observe your precepts, your
judgements,
for all my ways are before you.

TAW ¹⁶⁹May my cry approach your presence,
Yahweh;
by your word give me understanding.
¹⁷⁰May my prayer come into your presence,
rescue me as you have promised.
¹⁷¹May my lips proclaim your praise,
for you teach me your will.
¹⁷²May my tongue recite your promise,
for all your commandments are upright.
¹⁷³May your hand be there to help me,
since I have chosen your precepts.
¹⁷⁴I long for your salvation, Yahweh,
your Law is my delight.
¹⁷⁵May I live only to praise you,
may your judgements be my help.
¹⁷⁶I am wandering like a lost sheep,
come and look for your servant,

for I have not forgotten your
commandments.

120 *Song of Ascents* ^a

¹ To Yahweh when I am in trouble
I call and he answers me.
² Yahweh, save me from lying lips
and a treacherous tongue!

³ What will he repay you, what more,
treacherous tongue?
⁴ War-arrows made sharp
over red-hot charcoal.

⁵ How wretched I am, living in Meshech,
dwelling in the tents of Kedar!

⁶ Too long have I lived
among people who hate peace.
⁷ When I speak of peace
they are all for war!

121 *Song of Ascents*

¹ I lift up my eyes to the mountains;
where is my help to come from?

120a The Songs of Ascents (Pss 120–134) were sung by pilgrims on their way up to Jerusalem.

2 My help comes from Yahweh
   who made heaven and earth.
3 May he save your foot from stumbling;
   may he, your guardian, not fall asleep!
4 You see—he neither sleeps nor slumbers,
   the guardian of Israel.

5 Yahweh is your guardian, your shade,
   Yahweh, at your right hand.
6 By day the sun will not strike you,
   nor the moon by night.

7 Yahweh guards you from all harm
   Yahweh guards your life,
8 Yahweh guards your comings and goings,
   henceforth and for ever.

122 *Song of Ascents; of David*

1 I rejoiced that they said to me,
   'Let us go to the house of Yahweh.'
2 At last our feet are standing
   at your gates, Jerusalem!

3 Jerusalem, built as a city,
   in one united whole,
4 there the tribes go up,
   the tribes of Yahweh,
   a sign for Israel to give thanks
   to the name of Yahweh.
5 For there are set the thrones of judgement,
   the thrones of the house of David.

6 Pray for the peace of Jerusalem,
   prosperity for your homes!
7 Peace within your walls,
   prosperity in your palaces!

8 For love of my brothers and my friends
   I will say, 'Peace upon you!'
9 For love of the house of Yahweh our God
   I will pray for your well-being.

123 *Song of Ascents*

1 I lift up my eyes to you
   who are enthroned in heaven.

2 Just as the eyes of slaves
   are on their masters' hand,

or the eyes of a slave-girl
   on the hand of her mistress,
so our eyes are on Yahweh our God,
   for him to take pity on us.

3 Have pity on us, Yahweh, have pity,
   for we have had our full share of scorn,
4 more than our share
   of jeers from the complacent.

(Scorn is for the proud.)

124 *Song of Ascents; of David*

1 If Yahweh had not been on our side
   —let Israel repeat it—
2 if Yahweh had not been on our side
   when people attacked us,
3 they would have swallowed us alive
   in the heat of their anger.

4 Then water was washing us away,
   a torrent running right over us;
5 running right over us then
   were turbulent waters.

6 Blessed be Yahweh for not letting us fall
   a prey to their teeth!
7 We escaped like a bird
   from the fowlers' net.

The net was broken
   and we escaped;
8 our help is in the name of Yahweh,
   who made heaven and earth.

125 *Song of Ascents*

1 Whoever trusts in Yahweh is like Mount
   Zion:
   unshakeable, it stands for ever.
2 Jerusalem! The mountains encircle her:
   so Yahweh encircles his people,
   henceforth and for ever.

3 The sceptre of the wicked will not come to
      rest
      over the heritage of the upright;
  or the upright might set
      their own hands to evil.

4 Do good, Yahweh, to those who are
      good,
      to the sincere at heart.
5 But the crooked, the twisted, turn them
      away,
      Yahweh, with evil-doers.

Peace to Israel!

126   *Song of Ascents*

1 When Yahweh brought back Zion's
      captives
      we lived in a dream;
2 then our mouths filled with laughter,
      and our lips with song.

Then the nations kept saying, 'What
      great deeds
      Yahweh has done for them!'
3 Yes, Yahweh did great deeds for us,
      and we were overjoyed.

4 Bring back, Yahweh, our people from
      captivity
      like torrents in the Negeb!
5 Those who sow in tears
      sing as they reap.

6 He went off, went off weeping,
      carrying the seed.
  He comes back, comes back singing,
      bringing in his sheaves.

127   *Song of Ascents;*
             of Solomon

1 If Yahweh does not build a house
  in vain do its builders toil.
  If Yahweh does not guard a city
  in vain does its guard keep watch.

2 In vain you get up earlier,
  and put off going to bed,
  sweating to make a living,
  since it is he who provides for his
      beloved as they sleep.

3 Sons are a birthright from Yahweh,
  children are a reward from him.
4 Like arrows in a warrior's hand
  are the sons you father when young.

5 How blessed is the man
  who has filled his quiver with them;
  in dispute with his enemies at the
      city gate
  he will not be worsted.

128   *Song of Ascents*

1 How blessed are all who fear Yahweh,
      who walk in his ways!

2 Your own labours will yield you a
      living,
      happy and prosperous will you be.
3 Your wife a fruitful vine
      in the inner places of your house.
  Your children round your table
      like shoots of an olive tree.

4 Such are the blessings that fall
      on those who fear Yahweh.
5 May Yahweh bless you from Zion!
  May you see Jerusalem prosper
      all the days of your life,
6 and live to see your children's children!

Peace to Israel!

129   *Song of Ascents*

1 Often as men have attacked me since I was
      young
      —let Israel repeat it—
2 often as men have attacked me since I was
      young,
      they have never overcome me.

3 On my back ploughmen have set to
work,
making long furrows,
4 but Yahweh the upright has shattered
the yoke of the wicked.

5 Let all who hate Zion
be thrown back in confusion,
6 let them be like grass on a roof,
dried up before it is cut,
7 never to fill the reaper's arm
nor the binder's lap.
8 And no passer-by will say,
'The blessing of Yahweh be on you!

'We bless you in the name of Yahweh.'

130 *Song of Ascents*

1 From the depths I call to you, Yahweh:
2 Lord, hear my cry.
Listen attentively
to the sound of my pleading!

3 If you kept a record of our sins,
Lord, who could stand their ground?
4 But with you is forgiveness,
that you may be revered.

5 I rely, my whole being relies,
Yahweh, on your promise.
6 My whole being hopes in the Lord,
more than watchmen for daybreak;
more than watchmen for daybreak
7 let Israel hope in Yahweh.

For with Yahweh is faithful love,
with him generous ransom;
8 and he will ransom Israel
from all its sins.

131 *Song of Ascents*

1 Yahweh, my heart is not haughty,
I do not set my sights too high.
I have taken no part in great affairs,
in wonders beyond my scope.

2 No, I hold myself in quiet and silence,
like a little child in its mother's arms,
like a little child, so I keep myself.
3 Let Israel hope in Yahweh
henceforth and for ever.

132 *Song of Ascents*

1 Yahweh, remember David
and all the hardships he endured,
2 the oath he swore to Yahweh,
his vow to the Mighty One of Jacob:

3 'I will not enter tent or house,
will not climb into bed,
4 will not allow myself to sleep,
not even to close my eyes,
5 till I have found a place for Yahweh,
a dwelling for the Mighty One of Jacob!'

6 Listen, we heard of it in Ephrathah,
we found it at Forest-Fields.
7 Let us go into his dwelling-place,
and worship at his footstool.

8 Go up, Yahweh, to your resting-place,
you and the ark of your strength.
9 Your priests are robed in saving justice,
your faithful are shouting for joy.
10 For the sake of your servant David,
do not reject your anointed.

11 Yahweh has sworn to David,
and will always remain true to his word,
'I promise that I will set
a son of yours upon your throne.
12 If your sons observe my covenant
and the instructions I have taught
them,
their sons too for evermore
will occupy your throne.'

13 For Yahweh has chosen Zion,
he has desired it as a home.
14 'Here shall I rest for evermore,
here shall I make my home as I have
wished.

15 'I shall generously bless her produce,
    give her needy their fill of food,
16 I shall clothe her priests with salvation,
    and her faithful will sing aloud for joy.

17 'There I shall raise up a line of
        descendants for David,
    light a lamp for my anointed;
18 I shall clothe his enemies with shame,
    while his own crown shall flourish.'

133
Song of Ascents

1 How good, how delightful it is
    to live as brothers all together!

2 It is like a fine oil on the head,
    running down the beard,
    running down Aaron's beard,
    onto the collar of his robes.

3 It is like the dew of Hermon
    falling on the heights of Zion;
    for there Yahweh bestows his blessing,
    everlasting life.

134
Song of Ascents

1 Come, bless Yahweh,
    all you who serve Yahweh,
    serving in the house of Yahweh,
    in the courts of the house of our
        God.
    Through the night watches
2 stretch out your hands towards the
        sanctuary
    and bless Yahweh.

3 May Yahweh bless you from Zion,
    he who made heaven and earth!

135
a Alleluia!

Praise the name of Yahweh,
    you who serve Yahweh, praise him,
2 serving in the house of Yahweh,
    in the courts of the house of our God.

3 Praise Yahweh, for Yahweh is good,
    make music for his name—it brings joy—
4 for Yahweh has chosen Jacob for himself,
    Israel as his own possession.

5 For I know that Yahweh is great,
    our Lord is above all gods.
6 Yahweh does whatever he pleases
    in heaven, on earth,
    in the waters and all the depths.

7 He summons up clouds from the borders
        of earth,
    sends rain with lightning-flashes,
    and brings the wind out of his storehouse.

8 He struck the first-born in Egypt,
    man and beast alike,
9 he sent signs and wonders into the heart of
        Egypt,
    against Pharaoh and all his officials.

10 He struck down many nations,
    he slaughtered mighty kings,
11 Sihon king of the Amorites,
    and Og king of Bashan,
    and all the kingdoms of Canaan.
12 He gave their land as a birthright,
    a birthright to his people Israel.

13 Yahweh, your name endures for ever,
    Yahweh, your memory is fresh from age to
        age.
14 For Yahweh vindicates his people,
    feels compassion for his servants.

15 The idols of the nations are silver and gold,
    made by human hands.
16 These have mouths but say nothing,
    have eyes but see nothing,
17 have ears but hear nothing,
    and they have no breath in their mouths.
18 Their makers will end up like them,
    everyone who relies on them.

135a Composed entirely of fragments or reminiscences of other Pss.

¹⁹ House of Israel, bless Yahweh,
House of Aaron, bless Yahweh,
²⁰ House of Levi, bless Yahweh,
you who fear Yahweh, bless Yahweh.

²¹ Blessed be Yahweh from Zion,
he who dwells in Jerusalem!

136 Alleluia!

¹ Give thanks to Yahweh for he is good,
for his faithful love endures for ever.
² Give thanks to the God of gods,
for his faithful love endures for ever.
³ Give thanks to the Lord of lords,
for his faithful love endures for ever.

⁴ He alone works wonders,
for his faithful love endures for ever.
⁵ In wisdom he made the heavens,
for his faithful love endures for ever.
⁶ He set the earth firm on the waters,
for his faithful love endures for ever.

⁷ He made the great lights,
for his faithful love endures for ever.
⁸ The sun to rule the day,
for his faithful love endures for ever.
⁹ Moon and stars to rule the night,
for his faithful love endures for ever.

¹⁰ He struck down the first-born of Egypt,
for his faithful love endures for ever.
¹¹ He brought Israel out from among them,
for his faithful love endures for ever.
¹² With mighty hand and outstretched arm,
for his faithful love endures for ever.

¹³ He split the Sea of Reeds in two,
for his faithful love endures for ever.
¹⁴ Let Israel pass through the middle,
for his faithful love endures for ever.
¹⁵ And drowned Pharaoh and all his army,
for his faithful love endures for ever.

¹⁶ He led his people through the desert,
for his faithful love endures for ever.

¹⁷ He struck down mighty kings,
for his faithful love endures for ever.
¹⁸ Slaughtered famous kings,
for his faithful love endures for ever.
¹⁹ Sihon king of the Amorites,
for his faithful love endures for ever.
²⁰ And Og king of Bashan,
for his faithful love endures for ever.

²¹ He gave their land as a birthright,
for his faithful love endures for ever.
²² A birthright to his servant Israel,
for his faithful love endures for ever.
²³ He kept us in mind when we were
humbled,
for his faithful love endures for ever.
²⁴ And rescued us from our enemies,
for his faithful love endures for ever.

²⁵ He provides food for all living creatures,
for his faithful love endures for ever.
²⁶ Give thanks to the God of heaven,
for his faithful love endures for ever.

137 By the rivers of Babylon
we sat and wept
at the memory of Zion.
² On the poplars there
we had hung up our harps.

³ For there our gaolers had asked us
to sing them a song,
our captors to make merry,
'Sing us one of the songs of Zion.'

⁴ How could we sing a song of Yahweh
on alien soil?
⁵ If I forget you, Jerusalem,
may my right hand wither!

⁶ May my tongue remain stuck to my palate
if I do not keep you in mind,
if I do not count Jerusalem
the greatest of my joys.

⁷ Remember, Yahweh, to the Edomites' cost,
the day of Jerusalem,

how they said, 'Down with it! Rase it to
  the ground!'

8 Daughter of Babel, doomed to destruction,
  a blessing on anyone
  who treats you as you treated us,
9 a blessing on anyone who seizes your
  babies
  and shatters them against a rock!

138

Of David

1 I thank you, Yahweh, with all my heart,
  for you have listened to the cry I uttered.
  In the presence of angels I sing to you,
2 I bow down before your holy Temple.

I praise your name for your faithful love
    and your constancy;
  your promises surpass even your fame.
3 You heard me on the day when I called,
  and you gave new strength to my heart.

4 All the kings of the earth give thanks to
    you, Yahweh,
  when they hear the promises you make;
5 they sing of Yahweh's ways,
  'Great is the glory of Yahweh!'
6 Sublime as he is, Yahweh looks on the
    humble,
  the proud he picks out from afar.

7 Though I live surrounded by trouble
  you give me life—to my enemies' fury!
  You stretch out your right hand and save
    me,
8 Yahweh will do all things for me.
  Yahweh, your faithful love endures for
    ever,
  do not abandon what you have made.

139

For the choirmaster:
Psalm of David

1 Yahweh, you examine me and know me,
2 you know when I sit, when I rise,
  you understand my thoughts from afar.
3 You watch when I walk or lie down,
  you know every detail of my conduct.

4 A word is not yet on my tongue
  before you, Yahweh, know all about it.
5 You fence me in, behind and in front,
  you have laid your hand upon me.
6 Such amazing knowledge is beyond me,
  a height to which I cannot attain.

7 Where shall I go to escape your spirit?
  Where shall I flee from your presence?
8 If I scale the heavens you are there,
  if I lie flat in Sheol, there you are.

9 If I speed away on the wings of the
    dawn,
  if I dwell beyond the ocean,
10 even there your hand will be guiding me,
  your right hand holding me fast.

11 I will say, 'Let the darkness cover me,
  and the night wrap itself around me,'
12 even darkness to you is not dark,
  and night is as clear as the day.

13 You created my inmost self,
  knit me together in my mother's womb.
14 For so many marvels I thank you;
  a wonder am I, and all your works are
    wonders.

You knew me through and through,
15 my being held no secrets from you,
  when I was being formed in secret,
  textured in the depths of the earth.

16 Your eyes could see my embryo.
  In your book all my days were inscribed,
  every one that was fixed is there.

17 How hard for me to grasp your
    thoughts,
  how many, God, there are!
18 If I count them, they are more than the
    grains of sand;
  if I come to an end, I am still with you.

19 If only, God, you would kill the wicked!—
  Men of violence, keep away from me!—

51 READ PSALM 139.

Yahweh, you examine me and know me, . . . you know every detail of my conduct.
—PSALM 139:1, 3

LIVING IN GOD'S PRESENCE

How happy should we be if every morning our eyes were open to this truth—the invisible presence of God—if we saw by faith, with the eyes of our soul everywhere within and without us the three persons of the adorable Trinity with their divine attributes! What would be the dangers and events of this life to us in his presence to whom earth and hell are subjected? We know that when anything most excellent and admirable attracts our sight, the mind is lost in it, and the attention so absorbed that it is difficult for us to draw away from it. Every feeling and thought is taken up by the object so admirable.

What is most striking in this is that when we sin, we not only sin in the presence of God, but in God himself, for since he is the source of motion and life, it follows that the sinner uses the concurrence of God himself to offend and sin against him, turning the means of life: health, time, the powers of nature and space to this horrid perversion and abuse against their almighty giver. . . . What a deep thought that God himself is the very life of our being. He dwells in the soul of each one of us as in his own element.

Oh, my God, my blindness has been truly great—to have thought of you so little through my life, though living wholly in you. Every word I have uttered has been known to you; every action seen by you, every secret thought before you. Yet, I have thought, acted and spoken as if you neither heard nor saw me—without respect or love for you or remembrance that the soul you have given me was formed only for you and has the power of enjoying you at every moment of my life.

ST. ELIZABETH ANN SETON, 1774–1821

YOU WILL FIND THE NEXT READING AT PROVERBS 4.

20 those who speak blasphemously about you,
and take no account of your thoughts.

21 Yahweh, do I not hate those who
hate you,
and loathe those who defy you?
22 My hate for them has no limits,
I regard them as my own enemies.

23 God, examine me and know my heart,
test me and know my concerns.
24 Make sure that I am not on my way to
ruin,
and guide me on the road of eternity.

140 *For the choirmaster:*
Psalm of David
1 Rescue me, Yahweh, from evil men,
protect me from violent men,
2 whose heart is bent on malice,
day after day they harbour strife;
3 their tongues as barbed as a serpent's,
viper's venom behind their lips. *Pause*

4 Keep me, Yahweh, from the clutches of
the wicked,
protect me from violent men,
who are bent on making me stumble,
5b laying out snares where I walk,

⁵ᵇ in their arrogance hiding pitfall and
noose
⁵ᶜ to trap me as I pass. *Pause*

⁶ I said to Yahweh, 'You are my God.'
Listen, Yahweh, to the sound of my
prayer.
⁷ Yahweh my Lord, my saving strength,
you shield my head when battle comes.
⁸ Yahweh, do not grant the wicked their
wishes,
do not let their plots succeed. *Pause*

Do not let my attackers ⁹prevail,
but let them be overwhelmed by their
own malice.
¹⁰ May red-hot embers rain down on them,
may they be flung into the mire once
and for all.
¹¹ May the slanderer find no rest anywhere,
may evil hunt down violent men
implacably.

¹² I know that Yahweh will give judgement
for the wretched,
justice for the needy.
¹³ The upright shall praise your name,
the honest dwell in your presence.

141 *Psalm of David*

¹ Yahweh, I am calling, hurry to me,
listen to my voice when I call to you.
² May my prayer be like incense in your
presence,
my uplifted hands like the evening
sacrifice.

³ Yahweh, mount a guard over my
mouth,
a guard at the door of my lips.
⁴ Check any impulse to speak evil,
to share the foul deeds of evil-doers.

I shall not sample their delights!
⁵ May the upright correct me with a
friend's rebuke;

but the wicked shall never anoint my head
with oil,
for that would make me party to their
crimes.

⁶ They are delivered into the power of the
rock, their judge,
those who took pleasure in hearing me say,
⁷ 'Like a shattered millstone on the ground
our bones are scattered at the mouth of
Sheol.'

⁸ To you, Yahweh, I turn my eyes,
in you I take refuge, do not leave me
unprotected.
⁹ Save me from the traps that are set for me,
the snares of evil-doers.

¹⁰ Let the wicked fall each into his own net,
while I pass on my way.

142 *Psalm of David; when he was in the cave; prayer*

¹ To Yahweh I cry out with my plea.
To Yahweh I cry out with entreaty.
² I pour out my worry in his presence,
in his presence I unfold my troubles.
³ However faint my spirit;
you are watching over my path.

On the road I have to travel
they have hidden a trap for me.
⁴ Look on my right and see—
there is no one who recognises me.
All refuge is denied me,
no one cares whether I live or die.

⁵ I cry out to you, Yahweh,
I affirm, 'You are my refuge,
my share in the land of the living!'
⁶ Listen to my calling,
for I am miserably weak.

Rescue me from my persecutors,
for they are too strong for me.
⁷ Lead me out of prison
that I may praise your name.
The upright gather round me
because of your generosity to me.

143 *Psalm of David*

1 Yahweh, hear my prayer,
  listen to my pleading;
  in your constancy answer me,
  in your saving justice;
2 do not put your servant on trial,
  for no one living can be found guiltless at
      your tribunal.

3 An enemy is in deadly pursuit,
  crushing me into the ground,
  forcing me to live in darkness,
  like those long dead.
4 My spirit is faint,
  and within me my heart is numb with fear.

5 I recall the days of old,
  reflecting on all your deeds,
  I ponder the works of your hands.
6 I stretch out my hands to you,
  my heart like a land thirsty for you. *Pause*

7 Answer me quickly, Yahweh,
  my spirit is worn out;
  do not turn away your face from me,
  or I shall be like those who sink into
      oblivion.

8 Let dawn bring news of your faithful love,
  for I place my trust in you;
  show me the road I must travel
  for you to relieve my heart.

9 Rescue me from my enemies, Yahweh,
  since in you I find protection.
10 Teach me to do your will,
  for you are my God.
  May your generous spirit lead me
  on even ground.

11 Yahweh, for the sake of your name,
  in your saving justice give me life,
  rescue me from distress.
12 In your faithful love annihilate my
      enemies,
  destroy all those who oppress me,
  for I am your servant.

144 [a] *Of David*

1 Blessed be Yahweh, my rock,
  who trains my hands for war
  and my fingers for battle,
2 my faithful love, my bastion,
  my citadel, my Saviour;
  I shelter behind him, my shield,
  he makes the peoples submit to me.

3 Yahweh, what is a human being for you
      to notice,
  a child of Adam for you to think about?
4 Human life, a mere puff of wind,
  days as fleeting as a shadow.

5 Yahweh, part the heavens and come
      down,
  touch the mountains, make them
      smoke.
6 Scatter them with continuous lightning-
      flashes,
  rout them with a volley of your arrows.

7 Stretch down your hand from above,
  save me, rescue me from deep waters,
  from the clutches of foreigners,
8 whose every word is worthless,
  whose right hand is raised in perjury.

9 God, I sing to you a new song,
  I play to you on the ten-stringed lyre,
10 for you give kings their victories,
  you rescue your servant David.

From the sword of evil 11 save me,
  rescue me from the clutches of foreigners
  whose every word is worthless,
  whose right hand testifies to falsehood.

12 May our sons be like plants
      growing tall from their earliest days,
  our daughters like pillars
      carved fit for a palace,

144a After prayers for help (vv. 1–11) drawn from other Pss,
vv. 12–15 envisage messianic blessings.

13 our barns filled to overflowing
    with every kind of crop,
the sheep in our pastures be numbered
    in thousands and tens of thousands,

14 our cattle well fed,
    free of raids and pillage,
    free of outcry in our streets.

15 How blessed the nation of whom this is
    true,
blessed the nation whose God is Yahweh!

145 *Hymn of Praise; of David*

ALEPH ¹I shall praise you to the heights, God
    my King,
I shall bless your name for ever and ever.
BET ²Day after day I shall bless you,
    I shall praise your name for ever and
    ever.
GIMEL ³Great is Yahweh and worthy of all
    praise,
his greatness beyond all reckoning.

DALET ⁴Each age will praise your deeds to the
    next,
proclaiming your mighty works.
HE ⁵Your renown is the splendour of your
    glory,
I will ponder the story of your wonders.

WAW ⁶They will speak of your awesome
    power,
and I shall recount your greatness.
ZAIN ⁷They will bring out the memory of
    your great generosity,
and joyfully acclaim your saving justice.

HET ⁸Yahweh is tenderness and pity,
    slow to anger, full of faithful love.
TET ⁹Yahweh is generous to all,
    his tenderness embraces all his creatures.

YOD ¹⁰All your creatures shall thank you,
    Yahweh,
and your faithful shall bless you.

KAPH ¹¹They shall speak of the glory of your
    kingship
and tell of your might,

LAMED ¹²making known your mighty deeds
    to the children of Adam,
the glory and majesty of your kingship.
MEM ¹³Your kingship is a kingship for
    ever,
your reign lasts from age to age.

(NUN) Yahweh is trustworthy in all his
    words,
and upright in all his deeds.
SAMEK ¹⁴Yahweh supports all who
    stumble,
lifts up those who are bowed down.

AIN ¹⁵All look to you in hope
    and you feed them with the food of the
    season.
PE ¹⁶And, with generous hand,
    you satisfy the desires of every living
    creature.

ZADE ¹⁷Upright in all that he does,
    Yahweh acts only in faithful love.
QOPH ¹⁸He is close to all who call upon him,
    all who call on him from the heart.

RESH ¹⁹He fulfils the desires of all who fear
    him,
he hears their cry and he saves them.
SHIN ²⁰Yahweh guards all who love him,
    but all the wicked he destroys.

TAW ²¹My mouth shall always praise
    Yahweh,
let every creature bless his holy name
for ever and ever.

146 Alleluia!

Praise Yahweh, my soul!
² I will praise Yahweh all my life,
I will make music to my God as long as I
    live.

³ Do not put your trust in princes,
in any child of Adam, who has no power
to save.
⁴ When his spirit goes forth he returns to
the earth,
on that very day all his plans come to
nothing.

⁵ How blessed is he who has Jacob's God to
help him,
his hope is in Yahweh his God,
⁶ who made heaven and earth,
the sea and all that is in them.

He keeps faith for ever,
⁷ gives justice to the oppressed,
gives food to the hungry;
Yahweh sets prisoners free.

⁸ Yahweh gives sight to the blind,
lifts up those who are bowed down.
⁹ Yahweh protects the stranger,
he sustains the orphan and the widow.

8c Yahweh loves the upright,
9c but he frustrates the wicked.
¹⁰ Yahweh reigns for ever,
your God, Zion, from age to age.

147 ªAlleluia!

¹ Praise Yahweh—it is good to sing psalms
to our God—how pleasant to praise him.
² Yahweh, Builder of Jerusalem!
He gathers together the exiles of Israel,
³ healing the broken-hearted
and binding up their wounds;
⁴ he counts out the number of the stars,
and gives each one of them a name.

⁵ Our Lord is great, all-powerful,
his wisdom beyond all telling.
⁶ Yahweh sustains the poor,
and humbles the wicked to the ground.

⁷ Sing to Yahweh in thanksgiving,
play the harp for our God.

⁸ He veils the sky with clouds,
and provides the earth with rain,
makes grass grow on the hills
and plants for people to use,
⁹ gives fodder to cattle
and to young ravens when they cry.

¹⁰ He takes no delight in the power of
horses,
no pleasure in human sturdiness;
¹¹ his pleasure is in those who fear him,
in those who hope in his faithful love.

¹² Praise Yahweh, Jerusalem,
Zion, praise your God.

¹³ For he gives strength to the bars of your
gates,
he blesses your children within you,
¹⁴ he maintains the peace of your
frontiers,
gives you your fill of finest wheat.

¹⁵ He sends his word to the earth,
his command runs quickly,
¹⁶ he spreads the snow like flax,
strews hoarfrost like ashes,

¹⁷ he sends ice-crystals like breadcrumbs,
and who can withstand that cold?
¹⁸ When he sends his word it thaws them,
when he makes his wind blow, the waters
are unstopped.

¹⁹ He reveals his word to Jacob,
his statutes and judgements to Israel.
²⁰ For no other nation has he done this,
no other has known his judgements.

148 Alleluia!

Praise Yahweh from the heavens,
praise him in the heights.
² Praise him, all his angels,
praise him, all his host!

147a Pss 146–147 in Vulgate

³ Praise him, sun and moon,
   praise him, all shining stars,
⁴ praise him, highest heavens,
   praise him, waters above the heavens.

⁵ Let them praise the name of Yahweh
   at whose command they were made;
⁶ he established them for ever and ever
   by an unchanging decree.

⁷ Praise Yahweh from the earth,
   sea-monsters and all the depths,
⁸ fire and hail, snow and mist,
   storm-winds that obey his word,
⁹ mountains and every hill,
   orchards and every cedar,
¹⁰ wild animals and all cattle,
   reptiles and winged birds,

¹¹ kings of the earth and all nations,
   princes and all judges on earth,
¹² young men and girls,
   old people and children together.

¹³ Let them praise the name of Yahweh,
   for his name alone is sublime,
   his splendour transcends earth and heaven.
¹⁴ For he heightens the strength of his
      people,
   to the praise of all his faithful,
   the children of Israel, the people close to
      him.

149 Alleluia!

Sing a new song to Yahweh:
   his praise in the assembly of the faithful!
² Israel shall rejoice in its Maker,
   the children of Zion delight in their king;
³ they shall dance in praise of his name,
   play to him on tambourines and harp!

⁴ For Yahweh loves his people,
   he will crown the humble with salvation.
⁵ The faithful exult in glory,
   shout for joy as they worship him,
⁶ praising God to the heights with their
      voices,
   a two-edged sword in their hands,

⁷ to wreak vengeance on the nations,
   punishment on the peoples,
⁸ to load their kings with chains
   and their nobles with iron fetters,
⁹ to execute on them the judgement
      passed—
   to the honour of all his faithful.

150 Alleluia!

Praise God in his holy place,
   praise him in the heavenly vault of his
      power,
² praise him for his mighty deeds,
   praise him for all his greatness.

³ Praise him with fanfare of trumpet,
   praise him with harp and lyre,
⁴ praise him with tambourines and dancing,
   praise him with strings and pipes,
⁵ praise him with the clamour of cymbals,
   praise him with triumphant cymbals,
⁶ Let everything that breathes praise
      Yahweh.

Alleluia!

THE PROVERBS

The Book of

Title and purpose of the book

1 The proverbs of Solomon son of David, king of Israel:

2 for learning what wisdom and discipline are,
> for understanding words of deep meaning,

3 for acquiring a disciplined insight,
> uprightness, justice and fair dealing;

4 for teaching sound judgement to the simple,
> and knowledge and reflection to the young;

6 for perceiving the meaning of proverbs and obscure sayings,
> the sayings of the sages and their riddles.

5 Let the wise listen and learn yet more,
> and a person of discernment will acquire the art of guidance.

7 The fear of Yahweh is the beginning of knowledge;
> fools spurn wisdom and discipline.

The sage speaks: avoid bad company

8 Listen, my child, to your father's instruction,
> do not reject your mother's teaching:

9 they will be a crown of grace for your head,
> a circlet for your neck.

10 My child, if sinners try to seduce you,
> do not go with them.

11 If they say, 'Come with us:
> let us lie in ambush to shed blood;
> if we plan an ambush for the innocent without provocation,

12 we can swallow them alive, like Sheol,
> and whole, like those who sink into oblivion.

13 We shall find treasures of every sort,
> we shall fill our houses with plunder;

14 throw in your lot with us:
> one purse between us all.'

15 My child, do not follow them in their way,
> keep your steps out of their path

16 *for their feet hasten to evil,*
> *they are quick to shed blood;*[a]

17 for the net is spread in vain
> if any winged creature can see it.

18 It is for their own blood such people lie in wait,
> their ambush is against their own selves!

19 Such are the paths of all who seek dishonest gain:
> which robs of their lives all who take it for their own.

Wisdom speaks: a warning to the heedless

20 Wisdom calls aloud in the streets,
> she raises her voice in the public squares;

21 she calls out at the street corners,
> she delivers her message at the city gates.

22 'You simple people, how much longer will you cling
> to your simple ways?
> How much longer will mockers revel in their mocking
> and fools go on hating knowledge?

1a A quotation of Is 59:7, absent from the best Gk MSS.

23 Pay attention to my warning.
　　To you I will pour out my heart
　　and tell you what I have to say.
24 Since I have called and you have
　　　refused me,
　　since I have beckoned and no one has
　　　taken notice,
25 since you have ignored all my advice
　　and rejected all my warnings,
26 I, for my part, shall laugh at your
　　　distress,
　　I shall jeer when terror befalls you,
27 when terror befalls you, like a storm,
　　when your distress arrives, like a
　　　whirlwind,
　　when ordeal and anguish bear down on
　　　you.
28 Then they will call me, but I shall not
　　　answer,
　　they will look eagerly for me and will
　　　not find me.
29 They have hated knowledge,
　　they have not chosen the fear of
　　　Yahweh,
30 they have taken no notice of my advice,
　　they have spurned all my warnings:
31 so they will have to eat the fruits of their
　　　own ways of life,
　　and choke themselves with their own
　　　scheming.
32 For the errors of the simple lead to their
　　　death,
　　the complacency of fools works their
　　　own ruin;
33 but whoever listens to me may live secure,
　　will have quiet, fearing no mischance.'

Wisdom, a safeguard against bad company

2 My child, if you take my words to heart,
　if you set store by my commandments,
2 tuning your ear to wisdom,
　　tuning your heart to understanding,
3 yes, if your plea is for clear perception,
　　if you cry out for understanding,
4 if you look for it as though for silver,
　　search for it as though for buried
　　　treasure,

5 then you will understand what the fear of
　　　Yahweh is,
　　and discover the knowledge of God.
6 For Yahweh himself is giver of wisdom,
　　from his mouth issue knowledge and
　　　understanding.
7 He reserves his advice for the honest,
　　a shield to those whose ways are sound;
8 he stands guard over the paths of equity,
　　he keeps watch over the way of those
　　　faithful to him.
9 Then you will understand uprightness,
　　equity and fair dealing,
　　the paths that lead to happiness.
10 When wisdom comes into your heart
　　and knowledge fills your soul with
　　　delight,
11 then prudence will be there to watch over
　　　you,
　　and understanding will be your
　　　guardian
12 to keep you from the way that is evil,
　　from those whose speech is deceitful,
13 from those who leave the paths of honesty
　　to walk the roads of darkness:
14 those who find their joy in doing wrong,
　　and their delight in deceitfulness,
15 whose tracks are twisted,
　　and the paths that they tread crooked.
16 To keep you, too, from the woman who
　　　belongs to another,[a]
　　from the stranger, with her wheedling
　　　words;
17 she has left the partner of her younger days,
　　she has forgotten the covenant of her
　　　God;
18 her house is tilting towards Death,
　　down to the Shades go her paths.
19 Of those who go to her not one returns,
　　they never regain the paths of life.

20 Thus you will tread the way of good
　　　people,
　　persisting in the paths of the upright.

2a Adultery, besides its literal meaning, also symbolises desertion of Yahweh, Israel's spouse.

²¹ For the land will be for the honest to
live in,
the innocent will have it for their
home;
²² while the wicked will be cut off from the
land,
and the faithless rooted out of it.

How to acquire wisdom

3 My child, do not forget my teaching,
let your heart keep my principles,
² since they will increase your length
of days,
your years of life and your well-being.

³ Let faithful love and constancy never
leave you:
tie them round your neck,
write them on the tablet of your
heart.
⁴ Thus you will find favour and success
in the sight of God and of people.
⁵ Trust wholeheartedly in Yahweh,
put no faith in your own perception;
⁶ acknowledge him in every course you
take,
and he will see that your paths are
smooth.
⁷ Do not congratulate yourself on your own
wisdom,
fear Yahweh and turn your back on
evil:
⁸ health-giving, this, to your body,
relief to your bones.

⁹ Honour Yahweh with what goods you
have
and with the first-fruits of all your
produce;
¹⁰ then your barns will be filled with corn,
your vats overflowing with new wine.

¹¹ My child, do not scorn correction from
Yahweh,
do not resent his reproof;
¹² for Yahweh reproves those he loves,
as a father the child whom he loves.

The joys of wisdom

¹³ Blessed are those who have discovered
wisdom,
those who have acquired
understanding!
¹⁴ Gaining her is more rewarding than silver,
her yield is more valuable than gold.
¹⁵ She is beyond the price of pearls,
nothing you could covet is her equal.
¹⁶ In her right hand is length of days;
in her left hand, riches and honour.
¹⁷ Her ways are filled with delight,
her paths all lead to contentment.
¹⁸ She is a tree of life for those who hold
her fast,
those who cling to her live happy lives.

¹⁹ In wisdom, Yahweh laid the earth's
foundations,
in understanding he spread out the
heavens.
²⁰ Through his knowledge the depths were
cleft open,
and the clouds distil the dew.

²¹ My child, hold to sound advice and
prudence,
never let them out of sight;
²² they will give life to your soul
and beauty to your neck.
²³ You will go on your way in safety,
your feet will not stumble.
²⁴ When you go to bed, you will not be
afraid;
once in bed, your sleep will be sweet.
²⁵ Have no fear either of sudden terror
or of attack mounted by wicked men,
²⁶ since Yahweh will be your guarantor,
he will keep your steps from the snare.

²⁷ Refuse no kindness to those who have a
right to it,
if it is in your power to perform it.
²⁸ Do not say to your neighbour, 'Go away!
Come another time!
I will give it you tomorrow,' if you can
do it now.

²⁹ Do not plot harm against your neighbour
  who is living unsuspecting beside you.
³⁰ Do not pick a groundless quarrel with
  anyone
  who has done you no harm.
³¹ Do not envy the man of violence,
  never model your conduct on his;
³² for the wilful wrong-doer is abhorrent to
  Yahweh,
  who confides only in the honest.
³³ Yahweh's curse lies on the house of the
  wicked,
  but he blesses the home of the upright.
³⁴ He mocks those who mock,
  but accords his favour to the humble.
³⁵ Glory is the portion of the wise,
  all that fools inherit is contempt.

On choosing wisdom

4 Listen, my children, to a father's
  instruction;
  pay attention, and learn what
  understanding is.
² What I am offering you is sound doctrine:
  do not forsake my teaching.
³ I too was once a child with a father,
  in my mother's eyes a tender child,
  unique.
⁴ This was what he used to teach me,
  'Let your heart treasure what I have to
  say,
  keep my principles and you will live;
⁵ acquire wisdom, acquire understanding,
  never forget her, never deviate from my
  words.
⁶ Do not desert her, she will keep you safe;
  love her, she will watch over you.
⁷ The first principle of wisdom is: acquire
  wisdom;
  at the cost of all you have, acquire
  understanding!
⁸ Hold her close, and she will make you
  great;
  embrace her, and she will be your pride;
⁹ she will provide a graceful garland for
  your head,
  bestow a crown of honour on you.'

¹⁰ Listen, my child, take my words to
  heart,
  and the years of your life will be
  multiplied.
¹¹ I have educated you in the ways of
  wisdom,
  I have guided you along the path of
  honesty.
¹² When you walk, your going will be
  unhindered,
  if you run, you will not stumble.
¹³ Hold fast to discipline, never let her go,
  keep your eyes on her, she is your life.
¹⁴ Do not follow the path of the wicked,
  do not walk the way that the evil go.
¹⁵ Avoid it, do not take it,
  turn your back on it, pass it by.
¹⁶ For they cannot sleep unless they have first
  done wrong,
  they miss their sleep if they have not
  made someone stumble;
¹⁷ for the bread of wickedness is what
  they eat,
  and the wine of violence is what they
  drink.
¹⁸ The path of the upright is like the light
  of dawn,
  its brightness growing to the fullness
  of day;
¹⁹ the way of the wicked is as dark as night,
  they cannot tell the obstacles they
  stumble over.

²⁰ My child, pay attention to what I am
  telling you,
  listen carefully to my words;
²¹ do not let them out of your sight,
  keep them deep in your heart.
²² For they are life to those who find them
  and health to all humanity.
²³ More than all else, keep watch over your
  heart,
  since here are the wellsprings of life.
²⁴ Turn your back on the mouth that
  misleads,
  keep your distance from lips that
  deceive.

52 READ PROVERBS 4.

More than all else, keep watch over your heart, since here are the wellsprings of life.
—PROVERBS 4:23

THE GIFT OF FEAR

Since grace has been given to us to flee from superstitious error, to be joined to the truth, and to serve the living God, . . . let us reflect on God and things divine in a way that corresponds to this gift. Let us begin at the most fitting point, as Solomon declared: "The first principle of wisdom is: acquire wisdom." And he tells what this is: the beginning of wisdom is fear of the Lord (see Pr 1:7). . . .

We must be grounded, purified and enlightened by fear, and thus be raised to the height. For where fear is, there is keeping of the commandments. Where there is keeping of the commandments, there is purifying of the flesh, that cloud that covers the soul and prevents it from seeing the Divine Ray. Where there is purifying there is illumination, and illumination satisfies the desire of those who long for that which surpasses all greatness.

So we must purify ourselves first, and then approach this converse with the Pure. Otherwise . . . like the Centurion, we would seek for healing, but would not through a praiseworthy fear receive the Healer into our house (see Mt 8:5–13). As long as each one of us is still uncleansed, let him speak like the Centurion: "I am not worthy to have you under my roof" (Mt 8:8). But when he shall have looked upon Jesus, though he be little like Zacchaeus, and climb up the sycamore tree by mortifying his members which are upon the earth, then he shall receive the Word, and it shall be said to him, "Today salvation has come to this house" (Lk 19:9). Then let him lay hold of the salvation, and bring forth fruit more perfectly, scattering and pouring forth rightly that which, like a publican, he wrongly gathered. . . . So let us purify ourselves, and receive the elementary initiation of the Word, that we may do ourselves the utmost good, making ourselves godlike, and receiving the Word at his coming; and also holding him fast and showing him to others.   ST. GREGORY NAZIANZEN, 329?–390

YOU WILL FIND THE NEXT READING AT PROVERBS 6.

25 Let your eyes be fixed ahead,
  your gaze be straight before you.
26 Let the path you tread be level
  and all your ways be firm.
27 Turn neither to right nor to left,
  keep your foot clear of evil.

Against adultery; where the wise man's love should be

5 My son, pay attention to my wisdom,
  listen carefully to what I know;

2 so that you may preserve discretion
  and your lips may guard knowledge.
  Take no notice of a loose-living woman,
3 for the lips of the adulteress drip with
    honey,
  her palate is more unctuous than oil,
4 but in the end she is bitter as
    wormwood,
  sharp as a two-edged sword.
5 Her feet go down to death,
  Sheol the goal of her steps;

6 far from following the path of life,
  her course is uncertain and she does not
    know it.
7 And now, son, listen to me,
  never deviate from what I say:
8 set your course as far from her as possible,
  go nowhere near the door of her house,
9 or she will hand over your honour to
    others,
  the years of your life to a man without
    pity,
10 and strangers will batten on your property,
  and your produce go to the house of a
    stranger,
11 and, at your ending,
  your body and flesh having been
    consumed,
  you will groan 12 and exclaim,
  'Alas, I hated discipline,
  my heart spurned all correction;
13 I would not attend to the voice of my
    masters,
  I would not listen to those who tried to
    teach me.
14 Now I have come to nearly every kind of
    misery,
  in the assembly and in the community.'
15 Drink the water from your own storage-
    well,
  fresh water from your own spring.
16 Even if your fountains overflow outside,
  your streams of water in the public
    squares:
17 let them be for you alone,
  and not for strangers with you.
18 May your fountain-head be blessed!

  Find joy with the wife you married in
    your youth,
19   fair as a hind, graceful as a fawn:
  hers the breasts that ever fill you with
    delight,
  hers the love that ever holds you
    captive.
20 Why be seduced, my son, by someone
    else's wife,

and fondle the breast of a woman who
  belongs to another?
21 For the eyes of Yahweh observe human
    ways,
  and survey all human paths.
22 The wicked is snared in his own misdeeds,
  is caught in the meshes of his own sin.
23 For want of discipline, he dies,
  led astray by his own excessive folly.

On surety rashly offered

6 My child, if you have gone surety for your
    neighbour,
  if you have guaranteed the bond of a
    stranger,
2 if you have committed yourself with your
    lips,
  if through words of yours you have
    been entrapped,
3 do this, my child, to extricate yourself—
  since you have put yourself in the power
    of your neighbour:
  go, humble yourself, plead with your
    neighbour,
4 give your eyes no sleep,
  your eyelids no rest,
5 break free like a gazelle from the trap,
  like a bird from the fowler's clutches.

The idler and the ant

6 Idler, go to the ant;
  ponder her ways and grow wise:
7 no one gives her orders,
  no overseer, no master,
8 yet all through the summer she gets her
    food ready,
  and gathers her supplies at harvest
    time.
9 How long do you intend to lie there, idler?
  When are you going to rise from your
    sleep?
10 A little sleep, a little drowsiness,
  a little folding of the arms to lie back,
11 and poverty comes like a vagrant
  and, like a beggar, dearth.ᵃ

6a = 24:33–34.

Portrait of a scoundrel

12 A scoundrel, a vicious man,
  he goes with a leer on his lips,
13 winking his eye, shuffling his foot,
  beckoning with his finger.
14 Trickery in his heart, always scheming
    evil,
  he sows dissension.
15 Disaster will overtake him sharply for this,
  suddenly, irretrievably, he will be
    broken.

Seven things abhorrent to God

16 There are six things that Yahweh hates,
  seven that he abhors:
17 a haughty look, a lying tongue,
  hands that shed innocent blood,
18 a heart that weaves wicked plots,
  feet that hurry to do evil,
19 a false witness who lies with every
    breath,
  and one who sows dissension among
    brothers.

More fatherly advice

20 Keep your father's precept, my child,
  do not spurn your mother's teaching.
21 Bind them ever to your heart,
  tie them round your neck.
22 While you are active, they will guide you,
  when you fall asleep, they will watch
    over you,
  when you wake up, they will converse
    with you.

23 For the precept is a lamp,
  the teaching is a light;
  correction and discipline are the way to
    life,
24 preserving you from the woman of bad
    character,
  from the wheedling talk of a woman
    who belongs to another.
25 Do not covet her beauty in your heart
  or let her captivate you with the play of
    her eyes;

26 a prostitute can be bought for a hunk of
    bread,
  but a married woman aims to snare a
    precious life.
27 Can a man carry fire inside his shirt
  without setting his clothes alight?
28 Can you walk on red-hot coals
  without burning your feet?
29 Just so, the man who makes love to his
    neighbour's wife:
  no one who touches her will get off
    unpunished.
30 People attach but little blame to a thief
  who steals only to satisfy his hunger;
31 yet even he, if caught, will have to repay
    sevenfold
  and hand over all his family resources.
32 But the adulterer has no sense;
  he works his own destruction.
33 All he will get is blows and contempt,
  and dishonour never to be blotted out.
34 For jealousy inflames the husband
  who will show no mercy when the day
    comes for revenge;
35 he will not consider any compensation;
  lavish what gifts you may, he will not be
    placated.

7 My child, keep my words,
  and treasure my precepts,
2 keep my precepts and you will live,
  keep my teaching as the apple of your
    eye.
3 Bind these to your fingers,
  write them on the tablet of your heart.
4 Say to Wisdom, 'You are my sister!'
  Call Understanding your relation,
5 to save yourself from the woman that
    belongs to another,
  from the stranger, with her seductive
    words.

6 While I was at the window of my house,
  I was looking out through the lattice
7 and I saw, among the callow youths,
  I noticed among the lads,
  one boy who had no sense.

53   READ PROVERBS 6:16–35.

Can a man carry fire inside his shirt without setting his clothes alight?—PROVERBS 6:27

PRACTICING CHASTITY

In the following letter to his brother, St. Leonard prescribes a practical approach to living chastely:

To speak quite frankly, my dear brother, I believe you are under a delusion. You seem to have got into your head the silly notion that it is impossible for you to live chastely. With this false principle fixed in your mind, at each temptation you immediately give up.

True, without God's grace we cannot live a chaste life. But it is also true that God gives his grace to those who try their best. "From the man who does what lies in him God withholds not grace" (see Ps 84:11).

So when temptation comes, turn straight to God, and he will help you. He said so, clearly: "Seek and you shall receive" (see Mt 7:7). With God's help you will keep from sin.

Impress, then, on yourself this great truth. Even if all hell's devils came against you to tempt you, you won't sin unless you want to—provided that you trust not in your own powers, but in the assistance of God. He doesn't refuse help to those who ask it with a lively faith.

This is the only way to get clear of the labyrinth you are in. Of course, you must avoid dangerous occasions and keep guard over your eyes. Try it, and you will see the good results. Meanwhile, I recommend you to God, that he may give you the true spirit of penance and mortification without which it is no easy thing to triumph over so degrading a vice. May God bless you.

ST. LEONARD OF PORT MAURICE, 1676–1751

YOU WILL FIND THE NEXT READING AT PROVERBS 8.

⁸ Going along the lane, near the corner
　　where she lives,
　　he reaches the path to her house,
⁹ at twilight when day is declining,
　　at dead of night and in the dark.
¹⁰ And look, a woman is coming to meet him,
　　dressed like a prostitute, false of heart.
¹¹ She is loud and brazen;
　　her feet cannot rest at home.
¹² Once in the street, once in the square,
　　she lurks at every corner.
¹³ She catches hold of him, she kisses him,
　　the bold-faced creature says to him,
¹⁴ 'I had to offer a communion sacrifice,
　　I have discharged my vows today;

¹⁵ that is why I came out to meet you,
　　to look for you, and now I have
　　found you.
¹⁶ I have spread coverlets over my divan,
　　embroidered stuff, Egyptian material,
¹⁷ I have sprinkled my bed with myrrh,
　　with aloes and cinnamon.
¹⁸ Come on, we'll make love as much as we
　　like, till morning.
　　Let us enjoy the delights of love!
¹⁹ For my husband is not at home,
　　he has gone on a very long journey,
²⁰ taking his moneybags with him;
　　he will not be back till the moon
　　is full.'

21 With her persistent coaxing she overcomes
    him,
      lures him on with her wheedling patter.
22 Forthwith he follows her,
      like an ox on its way to the
        slaughterhouse,
      like a madman on his way to the stocks,
23 until an arrow pierces him to the liver,
      like the bird that dashes into the net
      without realising that its life is at stake.
24 And now, son, listen to me,
      pay attention to the words I have
        to say:
25 do not let your heart stray into her ways,
      or wander into her paths;
26 she has done so many to death,
      and the strongest have all been her
        victims.
27 Her house is the way to Sheol,
      the descent to the courts of death.

Wisdom speaks again

8 Is not Wisdom calling?
    Is not Understanding raising her
      voice?
2 On the heights overlooking the road,
    at the crossways, she takes her stand;
3 by the gates, at the entrance to the city,
    on the access-roads, she cries out,
4 'I am calling to you, all people,
    my words are addressed to all
      humanity.
5 Simpletons, learn how to behave,
    fools, come to your senses.
6 Listen, I have something important to tell
      you,
    when I speak, my words are right.
7 My mouth proclaims the truth,
    for evil is abhorrent to my lips.
8 All the words from my mouth are upright,
    nothing false there, nothing crooked,
9 everything plain, if you can understand,
    straight, if you have acquired
      knowledge.
10 Accept my discipline rather than silver,
    and knowledge of me in preference to
      finest gold.

11 For Wisdom is more precious than jewels,
    and nothing else is so worthy of desire.

Wisdom sings her own praises; wisdom, the guide of kings

12 'I, Wisdom, share house with Discretion,
    I am mistress of the art of thought.
13 (Fear of Yahweh means hatred of evil.)
    I hate pride and arrogance,
      wicked behaviour and a lying mouth.
14 To me belong good advice and prudence,
    I am perception: power is mine!
15 By me monarchs rule
    and princes decree what is right;
16 by me rulers govern,
    so do nobles, the lawful authorities.
17 I love those who love me;
    whoever searches eagerly for me
      finds me.
18 With me are riches and honour,
    lasting wealth and saving justice.
19 The fruit I give is better than gold, even
      the finest,
    the return I make is better than pure
      silver.
20 I walk in the way of uprightness
    in the path of justice,
21 to endow my friends with my wealth
    and to fill their treasuries.

Wisdom as Creator [a]

22 'Yahweh created me, first-fruits of his
      fashioning,
    before the oldest of his works.
23 From everlasting, I was firmly set,
    from the beginning, before the earth
      came into being.
24 The deep was not, when I was born,
    nor were the springs with their
      abounding waters.
25 Before the mountains were settled,
    before the hills, I came to birth;

8a Wisdom's creation by God was on a different plane to all
his other works. Wisdom almost seems to be a distinct per-
sonality, sharing in God's activity, and his agent in the world.
The concept given here will be used in the NT to express
Christ's relationship to his Father.

54 READ PROVERBS 8:22–31.

I was beside the master craftsman, . . . at play everywhere on his earth, delighting to be with the children of men.—PROVERBS 8:30–31

DELIGHTING IN GOD'S PRESENCE

O my Lord and my Good! I cannot say this without tears and great delight of soul that you, Lord, should wish to be with us, and are with us in the Sacrament. . . . If our faults do not impede us, we may rejoice in you and you will take your delight in us, since you say your delight is to be with the children of men. O my Lord! What is this? Whenever I hear these words they are a great comfort to me, as they were even when I had gone far astray. Is it possible, Lord, that there can be a soul which reaches a state in which you grant it such graces and favors and can realize that you take your delight in it, and yet offends you again? Even after you have shown it so many favors and such signal marks of love that it cannot doubt them since it sees your works so clearly? Yes, there is indeed such a soul—there is myself. And I have done this not once, but often. May it please your goodness, Lord, that I may be alone in my ingratitude, that I may be the only one to have committed so great a wrong and been so excessively ungrateful. Yet even from me some good has been brought forth by your infinite goodness, and, the greater have been my sins, the more has the great blessing of your mercies shone forth in me. How many reasons have I for singing of them for ever!

ST. TERESA OF AVILA, 1515–1582

YOU WILL FIND THE NEXT READING AT PROVERBS 16.

26 before he had made the earth, the
   countryside,
   and the first elements of the world.
27 When he fixed the heavens firm, I was
   there,
   when he drew a circle on the surface of
   the deep,
28 when he thickened the clouds above,
   when the sources of the deep began to
   swell,
29 when he assigned the sea its boundaries
   —and the waters will not encroach on
   the shore—
   when he traced the foundations of the
   earth,
30 I was beside the master craftsman,
   delighting him day after day,
   ever at play in his presence,

31 at play everywhere on his earth,
   delighting to be with the children of
   men.

The supreme invitation

32 'And now, my children, listen to me.
   Happy are those who keep my ways.
33 Listen to instruction and become wise,
   do not reject it.
34 Blessed, whoever listens to me,
   who day after day keeps watch at my
   gates
   to guard my portals.
35 For whoever finds me finds life,
   and obtains the favour of Yahweh;
36 but whoever misses me harms himself,
   all who hate me are in love with
   death.'

Wisdom as hostess

9 Wisdom has built herself a house,
  she has hewn her seven pillars,
2 she has slaughtered her beasts, drawn her
    wine,
  she has laid her table.
3 She has despatched her maidservants
  and proclaimed from the heights above
    the city,
4 'Who is simple? Let him come this way.'
  To the fool she says,
5 'Come and eat my bread,
  drink the wine which I have drawn!
6 Leave foolishness behind and you will
    live,
  go forwards in the ways of perception.'

Against cynics

7 Reprove a mocker and you attract
    contempt,
  rebuke the wicked and you attract
    dishonour.
8 Do not rebuke the mocker, he will hate
    you.
  Rebuke the wise and he will love you
    for it.
9 Be open with the wise, he grows wiser still,
  teach the upright, he will gain yet more.
10 The first principle of wisdom is the fear of
    Yahweh,
  What God's holy ones know—this is
    understanding.
11 For by me your days will be multiplied,
  and your years of life increased.
12 Are you wise? You are wise to your own
    good.
  A mocker? The burden is yours alone.

A silly woman apes Wisdom

13 A silly woman acts on impulse,
  is foolish and knows nothing.
14 She sits at the door of her house,
  on a throne high up in the city,
15 calling to the passers-by,
  who are walking straight past on their
    way,

16 'Who is simple? Turn aside, come over
    here.'
  To the fool she says,
17 'Stolen waters are sweet,
  and bread tastes better when eaten in
    secret.'
18 But the fool does not know that this is
    where the Shades are
  and that her guests are already in the
    vales of Sheol.

The Proverbs of Solomon

10 The proverbs of Solomon.

  A wise child is a father's joy,[a]
  a foolish child a mother's grief.

2 Treasures wickedly come by give no
    benefit,
  but uprightness brings delivery from
    death.[b]

3 Yahweh does not let the upright go
    hungry,
  but he thwarts the greed of the wicked.

4 A slack hand brings poverty,
  but the hand of the diligent brings
    wealth.

5 Reaping at harvest-time is the mark of the
    prudent,
  sleeping at harvest-time is the sign of
    the worthless.

6 Blessings are on the head of the upright,
  but the mouth of the godless is a cover
    for violence.

7 The upright is remembered with blessings,
  the name of the wicked rots away.

8 The wise of heart takes orders,
  but a gabbling fool heads for ruin.

10a = 15:20. *10b* = 11:4.

9 Anyone whose ways are honourable walks
secure,
but whoever follows crooked ways is
soon unmasked.

10 A wink of the eye brings trouble,
a bold rebuke brings peace.

11 The mouth of the upright is a life-giving
fountain,
but the mouth of the godless is a cover
for violence.

12 Hatred provokes disputes,
but love excuses all offences.

13 On the lips of the discerning is found
wisdom,
on the back of a fool, the stick.

14 Wise people store up knowledge,
but the mouth of a fool makes ruin
imminent.

15 The wealth of the rich is their stronghold,^{c}
poverty is the undoing of the weak.

16 The wage of the upright affords life,
but sin is all the wicked earns.

17 Whoever abides by discipline, walks
towards life,
whoever ignores correction goes astray.

18 Liars' lips are a cover for hatred,
whoever utters slander is a fool.

19 A flood of words is never without fault;
whoever controls the lips is wise.

20 The tongue of the upright is purest silver,
the heart of the wicked is of trumpery
value.

21 The lips of the upright nourish many
peoples,
but fools die for want of sense.

22 The blessing of Yahweh is what brings
riches,
to this, hard toil has nothing to add.

23 A fool takes pleasure in doing wrong,
the intelligent in cultivating wisdom.

24 What the wicked fears overtakes him,
what the upright desires comes to him
as a present.

25 When the storm is over, the wicked is no
more,
but the upright stands firm for ever.

26 As vinegar to the teeth, smoke to the eyes,
so the sluggard to the one who sends
him.

27 The fear of Yahweh adds length to life,
the years of the wicked will be cut
short.

28 The hope of the upright is joy,
the expectations of the wicked come to
nothing.

29 The way of Yahweh is a rampart for the
honest,
for evil-doers nothing but ruin.

30 The upright will never have to give way,
but the land will offer no home for the
wicked.

31 The mouth of the upright utters wisdom,
the tongue that deceives will be cut off.

32 The lips of the upright know about
kindness,
the mouth of the wicked about deceit.

11 A false balance is abhorrent to
Yahweh,
a just weight is pleasing to him.

10c = 18:11.

² Pride comes first; disgrace soon follows;
    with the humble is wisdom found.

³ The honest have their own honesty for
    guidance,
  the treacherous are ruined by their own
    perfidy.

⁴ In the day of retribution riches will be
    useless,
  but uprightness delivers from death.*a*

⁵ The uprightness of the good makes their
    way straight,
  the wicked fall by their own
    wickedness.

⁶ Their uprightness sets the honest free,
  the treacherous are imprisoned by their
    own desires.

⁷ The hope of the wicked perishes with
    death,
  hope placed in riches comes to
    nothing.

⁸ The upright escapes affliction,
  the wicked incurs it instead.

⁹ Through his mouth the godless is the ruin
    of his neighbour,
  but by knowledge the upright are
    safeguarded.

¹⁰ When the upright prosper the city rejoices,
  when the wicked are ruined there is a
    shout of joy.

¹¹ A city is raised on the blessing of the
    honest,
  and demolished by the mouth of the
    wicked.

¹² Whoever looks down on a neighbour lacks
    good sense;
  the intelligent keeps a check on the
    tongue.

¹³ A tittle-tattler lets secrets out,
  the trustworthy keeps things hidden.

¹⁴ For want of leadership a people perishes,
  safety lies in many advisers.

¹⁵ Whoever goes bail for a stranger does
    himself harm,
  anyone who shuns going surety is safe.

¹⁶ A gracious woman acquires honour,
  violent people acquire wealth.

¹⁷ Faithful love brings its own reward,
  the inflexible injure their own selves.

¹⁸ Disappointment crowns the labours of the
    wicked,
  whoever sows uprightness reaps a solid
    reward.

¹⁹ Whoever establishes uprightness is on the
    way to life,
  whoever pursues evil, on the way to
    death.

²⁰ Tortuous hearts are abhorrent to Yahweh,
  dear to him, those whose ways are
    blameless.

²¹ Be sure of it, the wicked will not go
    unpunished,
  but the race of the upright will come to
    no harm.

²² A golden ring in the snout of a pig
  is a lovely woman who lacks discretion.

²³ The hope of the upright is nothing but
    good,
  the expectation of the wicked is
    retribution.

²⁴ One scatters money around, yet only adds
    to his wealth,
  another is excessively mean, but only
    grows the poorer.

11a = 10:2.

25 The soul who blesses will prosper,
   whoever satisfies others will also be
      satisfied.

26 The people's curse is on those who hoard
      the wheat,
   their blessing on the head of those who
      sell it.

27 Whoever strives for good obtains favour,
   whoever looks for evil will get an evil
      return.

28 Whoever trusts in riches will have a fall,
   the upright will flourish like the
      leaves.

29 Whoever misgoverns a house inherits the
      wind,
   and the fool becomes slave to the wise.

30 The fruit of the upright is a tree of life:
   the sage captivates souls.

31 If here on earth the upright gets due
      reward,
   how much more the wicked and the
      sinner!

12 Whoever loves discipline, loves
      knowledge,
   stupid are those who hate correction.

2 The honest obtains Yahweh's favour,
   the schemer incurs his condemnation.

3 No one is made secure by wickedness,
   but nothing shakes the roots of the
      upright.

4 A capable wife, her husband's crown,
   a shameless wife, a cancer in his
      bones.

5 The plans of the upright are honest,
   the intrigues of the wicked are full of
      deceit.

6 The words of the wicked are snares to
      shed blood,
   what the honest say keeps them safe.

7 Once thrown down, the wicked are no
      more,
   but the house of the upright stands
      firm.

8 A person is praised for prudence,
   anyone of tortuous heart incurs
      contempt.

9 Better a common fellow who has a slave
   than someone who gives himself airs
      and has nothing to eat.

10 The upright has compassion on his
      animals,
   but the heart of the wicked is ruthless.

11 Whoever works his land shall have bread
      and to spare,
   but no one who chases fantasies has any
      sense.[a]

12 The godless delights in the snare of the
      wicked,
   but the root of the upright bears fruit.

13 In the sin of the lips lies a disastrous trap,
   but the upright finds a way out of
      misfortune.

14 Abundance of good things is the fruit of
      the lips;
   labour brings its own return.

15 Fools think the way they go is straight,
   the wise listens to advice.

16 The fool shows anger straightaway,
   the discreet conceals dislike.

17 To tell the truth is to further justice,
   a false witness is nothing but deceit.

12a = 28:19.

¹⁸ Thoughtless words can wound like a
sword,
but the tongue of the wise brings
healing.

¹⁹ Sincere lips endure for ever,
the lying tongue lasts only a moment.

²⁰ Deceit is in the heart of the schemer,
joy with those who give counsels of
peace.

²¹ No harm can come to the upright,
but the wicked are swamped by
misfortunes.

²² Lying lips are abhorrent to Yahweh;
dear to him those who make truth their
way of life.

²³ The discreet keeps knowledge hidden,
the heart of fools proclaims their folly.

²⁴ For the diligent hand, authority;
for the slack hand, forced labour.

²⁵ Worry makes a heart heavy,
a kindly word makes it glad.

²⁶ The upright shows the way to a friend;
the way of the wicked leads them astray.

²⁷ The idle has no game to roast;
diligence is anyone's most precious
possession.

²⁸ In the way of uprightness is life,
the ways of the vengeful lead to death.

13 A wise child listens to a father's
discipline,
a cynic will not listen to reproof.

² The fruit of the mouth provides a good
meal,
but the soul of the treacherous feeds on
violence.

³ A guard on the mouth makes life secure,
whoever talks too much is lost.

⁴ The idler hungers but has no food;
hard workers get their fill.

⁵ The upright hates a lying word,
but the wicked slanders and defames.

⁶ Uprightness stands guard over one whose
way is honest,
sin causes the ruin of the wicked.

⁷ There are some who, on nothing, pretend
to be rich,
some, with great wealth, pretend to be
poor.

⁸ The ransom for life is a person's wealth;
but the poor will not hear the reproof.

⁹ The light of the upright is joyful,
the lamp of the wicked goes out.

¹⁰ Insolence breeds only disputes,
wisdom lies with those who take advice.

¹¹ A sudden fortune will dwindle away,
accumulation little by little is the way to
riches.

¹² Hope deferred makes the heart sick,
desire fulfilled is a tree of life.

¹³ Contempt for the word is self-destructive,
respect for the commandment wins
salvation.

¹⁴ The teaching of the wise is a life-giving
fountain
for eluding the snares of death.ᵃ

¹⁵ Good sense wins favour,
but the way of the treacherous is
hard.

13a = 14:27.

[759]

16 Anyone of discretion acts by the light of
      knowledge,
   the fool parades his folly.

17 A bad messenger falls into misfortune,
   a trusty messenger brings healing.

18 Whoever rejects discipline wins poverty
      and scorn;
   for anyone who accepts correction:
      honour.

19 Desire fulfilled is sweet to the soul;
   fools are loth to turn—from evil.

20 Whoever walks with the wise becomes
      wise,
   whoever mixes with fools will be
      ruined.

21 Evil will pursue the sinner,
   but good will reward the upright.

22 The good bequeaths a heritage to
      children's children,
   the wealth of the sinner is stored away
      for the upright.

23 Though the farms of the poor yield much
      food,
   some perish for lack of justice.

24 Whoever fails to use the stick hates his
      child;
   whoever is free with correction loves
      him.

25 The upright eats to the full,
   the belly of the wicked goes empty.

14 Wisdom builds herself a house;
     with her own hands Folly pulls it
     down.

2 Whoever keeps to an honest course fears
      Yahweh,
   whoever deserts his paths shows
      contempt for him.

3 Pride sprouts in the mouth of the fool,
   the lips of the wise keep them safe.

4 No oxen, empty manger;
   strong bull, much cash.

5 The truthful witness tells no lies,
   the false witness lies with every
      breath.

6 In vain the mocker looks for wisdom,
   knowledge comes easy to the intelligent.

7 Keep well clear of the fool,
   you will not find wise lips there.

8 With people of discretion, wisdom keeps
      a watch over their conduct,
   but the folly of fools leads them astray.

9 Fools mock at the sacrifice for sin,
   but favour resides among the honest.

10 The heart knows its own grief best,
   nor can a stranger share its joy.

11 The house of the wicked will be destroyed,
   the tent of the honest will prosper.

12 There are ways that some think straight,
   but they lead in the end to death.*

13 Even in laughter the heart finds sadness,
   and joy makes way for sorrow.

14 The miscreant will reap the reward of his
      conduct,
   and the good the reward of his deeds.

15 The simpleton believes any message,
   a person of discretion treads a careful
      path.

16 The wise fears evil and avoids it,
   the fool is insolent and conceited.

14a = 16:25.

¹⁷ A quick-tempered person commits rash
    acts,
  but a schemer is detestable.

¹⁸ Simpletons have folly for their portion,
  people of discretion knowledge for their
    crown.

¹⁹ The evil bow down before the good,
  the wicked, at the gates of the upright.

²⁰ The poor is detestable even to a friend,
  but many are they who love someone
    rich.

²¹ One who despises the needy is at fault,
  one who takes pity on the poor is
    blessed.

²² Plan evil—isn't this to go astray?
  Those who plan for good can earn
    faithful love and constancy.

²³ Hard work always yields its profit,
  idle talk brings only want.

²⁴ The crown of the wise is their riches;
  the folly of fools is folly.

²⁵ A truthful witness saves lives,
  whoever utters lies is a deceiver.

²⁶ In the fear of Yahweh is powerful security;
  for his children he is a refuge.

²⁷ The fear of Yahweh is a life-giving spring
  for eluding the snares of death.ᵇ

²⁸ Large population, monarch's glory;
  dwindling population, ruler's ruin.

²⁹ Mastery of temper is high proof of
    intelligence,
  a quick temper makes folly worse than
    ever.

³⁰ The life of the body is a tranquil heart,
  but envy is a cancer in the bones.

³¹ To oppress the weak insults the Creator,
  kindness to the needy honours the
    Creator.

³² For evil-doing, the wicked will be flung
    headlong,
  but in integrity the upright will find
    refuge.

³³ Wisdom resides in an understanding
    heart;
  she is not to be found in the hearts of
    fools.

³⁴ Uprightness makes a nation great,
  by sin whole races are disgraced.

³⁵ A king shows favour to a wise minister,
  but anger to one who shames him.

15 A mild answer turns away wrath,
   sharp words stir up anger.

² The tongue of the wise makes knowledge
    welcome,
  the mouth of a fool spews folly.

³ The eyes of Yahweh are everywhere:
  observing the wicked and the good.

⁴ The tongue that soothes is a tree of life;
  the perverse tongue, a breaker of
    hearts.

⁵ Only a fool spurns a father's discipline,
  whoever accepts correction is
    discreet.

⁶ In the house of the upright there is no lack
    of treasure,
  the earnings of the wicked are fraught
    with anxiety.

⁷ The lips of the wise spread knowledge,
  not so the hearts of fools.

14b = 13:14.

⁸ The sacrifice of the wicked is abhorrent to
   Yahweh,
  dear to him is the prayer of the honest.

⁹ The conduct of the wicked is abhorrent to
   Yahweh,
  but he loves the person whose goal is
   uprightness.

¹⁰ Correction is severe for one who leaves
   the way;
  whoever hates being reprimanded
   will die.

¹¹ Sheol and Perdition lie open to Yahweh;
  how much more the human heart!

¹² The mocker does not care to be
   reprimanded,
  and will not choose the wise as
   companions.

¹³ Glad heart means happy face,
  where the heart is sad the spirit is
   broken.

¹⁴ The heart of the wise seeks knowledge,
  a fool's mouth feeds on folly.

¹⁵ For the poor every day is evil,
  for the joyous heart it is always festival
   time.

¹⁶ Better to have little and with it fear of
   Yahweh
  than immense wealth and with it
   anxiety.

¹⁷ Better a dish of herbs when love is there
  than a fattened ox and hatred to go
   with it.

¹⁸ The hot-headed provokes disputes,
  the equable allays dissension.

¹⁹ The way of the lazy is like a thorny hedge,
  the path of the honest is a broad
   highway.

²⁰ A wise child is a father's joy;ᵃ
  only a brute despises his mother.

²¹ Folly appeals to someone without sense,
  a person of understanding goes straight
   forward.

²² Without deliberation plans come to
   nothing.
  Plans succeed where counsellors are
   many.

²³ Anyone who has a ready answer has joy
   too:
  how satisfying is the apt reply!

²⁴ For the prudent, the path of life leads
   upwards
  thus avoiding Sheol below.

²⁵ Yahweh pulls down the house of the
   proud,
  but he keeps the widow's boundaries
   intact.

²⁶ Wicked scheming is abhorrent to
   Yahweh,
  but words that are kind are pure.

²⁷ Craving for dishonest gain brings trouble
   on a house,
  hatred of bribery earns life.

²⁸ The heart of the upright reflects before
   answering,
  the mouth of the wicked spews out
   wickedness.

²⁹ Yahweh keeps his distance from the
   wicked,
  but he listens to the prayers of the
   upright.

³⁰ A kindly glance gives joy to the heart,
  good news lends strength to the bones.

15a = 10:1.

³¹ The ear attentive to wholesome correction
finds itself at home in the company of
the wise.

³² Whoever rejects correction lacks self-
respect,
whoever accepts reproof grows in
understanding.

³³ The fear of Yahweh is a school of wisdom,
before there can be glory, there must be
humility.ᵇ

16 A human heart makes the plans,
Yahweh gives the answer.

² A person's own acts seem right to the
doer,
but Yahweh is the weigher of souls.

³ Commend what you do to Yahweh,
and what you plan will be achieved.

⁴ Yahweh made everything for its own
purpose,
yes, even the wicked for the day of
disaster.

⁵ Every arrogant heart is abhorrent to
Yahweh:
be sure this will not go unpunished.

⁶ By faithful love and constancy sin is
expiated;
by fear of Yahweh evil is avoided.

⁷ Let Yahweh be pleased with someone's
way of life
and he makes that person's very
enemies into friends.

⁸ Better have little and with it uprightness
than great revenues with injustice.

⁹ The human heart may plan a course,
but it is Yahweh who makes the steps
secure.

¹⁰ The lips of the king utter prophecies,
he keeps faith when he speaks in
judgement.

¹¹ The balances and scales belong to Yahweh,
all the weights in the bag are of his
making.

¹² Evil-doing is abhorrent to kings,
since uprightness is a throne's
foundation.

¹³ Upright lips are welcome to a king,
he loves someone of honest words.

¹⁴ The king's wrath is the herald of death,
but the wise will appease it.

¹⁵ When the king's face brightens it spells
life,
his favour is like the rain in spring.

¹⁶ Better gain wisdom than gold,
choose understanding in preference to
silver.

¹⁷ To turn from evil is the way of the
honest;
whoever watches the path keeps life
safe.

¹⁸ Pride goes before destruction,
a haughty spirit before a fall.

¹⁹ Better be humble with the poor
than share the booty with the proud.

²⁰ Whoever listens closely to the word finds
happiness;
whoever trusts Yahweh is blessed.

²¹ The wise of heart is acclaimed as
intelligent,
sweetness of speech increases
knowledge.

15b = 18:12.

²² Shrewdness is a fountain of life for its
        possessor,
   the folly of fools is their own
        punishment.

²³ The heart of the wise lends shrewdness to
        speech
   and makes words more persuasive.

²⁴ Kindly words are a honeycomb,
   sweet to the taste, wholesome to the
        body.

²⁵ There is a way that some think straight,
   but it leads in the end to death.ᵃ

²⁶ A worker's appetite works on his behalf,
   for his hunger urges him on.

²⁷ A worthless person concocts evil,
   such a one's talk is like a scorching
        fire.

²⁸ A troublemaker sows strife,
   a slanderer divides friend from
        friend.

²⁹ The violent lures his neighbour astray
   and leads him by a way that is not
        good.

³⁰ Whoever narrows the eyes to think up
        tricks
   and purses the lips has already done
        wrong.

³¹ White hairs are a crown of honour,
   they are found in the ways of
        uprightness.

³² Better an equable person than a hero,
   someone with self-mastery than one
        who takes a city.

³³ In the fold of the garment the lot is
        thrown,
   but from Yahweh comes the decision.

17 Better a mouthful of dry bread with
        peace
   than a house filled with quarrelsome
        sacrifices.

² A shrewd servant comes off better than an
        unworthy child,
   he will share the inheritance with the
        brothers.

³ A furnace for silver, a foundry for gold,ᵃ
   but Yahweh for the testing of hearts!

⁴ An evil-doer pays heed to malicious talk,
   a liar listens to a slanderous tongue.

⁵ To mock the poor is to insult the
        Creator,
   no one who laughs at distress will go
        unpunished.

⁶ The crown of the aged is their children's
        children;
   the children's glory is their father.

⁷ Fine words do not become the foolish,
   false words become a prince still less.

⁸ A gift works like a talisman for one who
        holds it:
   it brings prosperity at every turn.

⁹ Whoever covers an offence promotes
        love,
   whoever again raises the matter divides
        friends.

¹⁰ A reproof makes more impression on a
        person of understanding
   than a hundred strokes on a fool.

¹¹ The wicked person thinks of nothing but
        rebellion,
   but a cruel messenger will be sent to
        such a one.

16a = 14:12.   17a = 27:21.

55 READ PROVERBS 16.

The human heart may plan a course, but it is Yahweh who makes the steps secure.
—PROVERBS 16:9

SHAPED BY GOD'S WILL

Since Scripture says God made everything for its own purpose, the day must come when the work will conform to and agree with its Maker. It is therefore necessary for our souls to reach a similar state in which, just as God willed everything to exist for himself, we wish that neither ourselves nor other beings to have been nor to be except for his will alone; [and] not for our pleasure. The satisfaction of our wants . . . delights us less than to see his will done in us and for us, which we implore every day in prayer saying ". . . your will be done on earth, as in heaven. . . ." O pure and sacred love! O sweet and pleasant affection! O pure and sinless intention of the will, all the more sinless and pure since it frees us from the taint of selfish vanity, all the more sweet and pleasant, for all that is found in it is divine. It is deifying to go through such an experience.

As a drop of water seems to disappear completely in a big quantity of wine, even assuming the wine's taste and color; just as red, molten iron becomes so much like fire it seems to lose its primary state; just as the air on a sunny day seems transformed into sunshine instead of being lit up; so it is necessary for the saints that all human feelings melt in a mysterious way and flow into the will of God. Otherwise how will God be all in all if something human survives in man? (see 1 Co 15:28). No doubt, the substance remains though under another form, another glory, another power. . . . I do not think that can take place until the word is fulfilled: *"You must love the Lord your God with all your heart, with all your soul,* with all your mind *and with all your strength"* (Mk 12:30).

ST. BERNARD OF CLAIRVAUX, 1090?–1153

YOU WILL FIND THE NEXT READING AT ECCLESIASTES 1.

12 Rather come on a bear robbed of her cubs
    than on a fool in his folly.

13 Disaster will never be far from the
    house
    of one who returns evil for good.

14 As well unleash a flood as start a dispute;
    desist before the quarrel breaks out.

15 To absolve the guilty and condemn the
    upright,
    both alike are abhorrent to Yahweh.

16 What good is money in the hand of a fool?
    To buy wisdom with it? The desire is
    not there.

17 A friend is a friend at all times,
    it is for adversity that a brother is
    born.

18 Whoever offers guarantees lacks sense
    and goes surety for a neighbour.

19 The double-dealer loves sin,
    the proud courts ruin.

20 The tortuous of heart finds no happiness,
   the perverse of speech falls into misery.

21 He who fathers a stupid child does so to
      his sorrow,
   the father of a fool knows no joy.

22 A glad heart is excellent medicine,
   a depressed spirit wastes the bones
      away.

23 Under cover of his cloak a bad man takes
      a gift
   to pervert the course of justice.

24 The intelligent has wisdom there before
      him,
   but the eyes of a fool range to the ends
      of the earth.

25 A foolish child is a father's sorrow,
   and the grief of her who gave the child
      birth.

26 To fine the upright is indeed a crime,
   to strike the noble is an injustice.

27 Whoever can control the tongue knows
      what knowledge is,
   someone of understanding keeps a cool
      temper.

28 If the fool holds his tongue, he may pass
      for wise;
   if he seals his lips, he may pass for
      intelligent.

18 Whoever lives alone follows private
      whims,
   and is angered by advice of any kind.

2 A fool takes no pleasure in understanding
   but only in airing an opinion.

3 When wickedness comes, indignity comes
      too,
   and, with contempt, dishonour.

4 Deep waters, such are human words:
   a gushing stream, the utterance of
      wisdom.

5 It is not good to show partiality for the
      wicked
   and so to deprive the upright when
      giving judgement.

6 The lips of a fool go to the law-courts
   with a mouth that pleads for a beating.

7 The mouth of the fool works its owner's
      ruin,
   the lips of a fool are a snare for their
      owner's life.

8 The words of a slanderer are tasty morsels
   that go right down into the belly.[a]

9 Whoever is idle at work
   is blood-brother to the destroyer.

10 The name of Yahweh is a strong tower;
   the upright runs to it and is secure.

11 The wealth of the rich forms a
      stronghold,[b]
   a high wall, as the rich supposes.

12 The human heart is haughty until
      destruction comes,
   before there can be glory there must be
      humility.[c]

13 To retort without first listening
   is both foolish and embarrassing.

14 Sickness the human spirit can endure,
   but when the spirit is broken, who can
      bear this?

15 The heart of the intelligent acquires
      learning,
   the ears of the wise search for
      knowledge.

18a = 26:22.   18b = 10:15.   18c = 15:33.

¹⁶ A present will open all doors
    and win access to the great.

¹⁷ The first to plead is adjudged to be
    upright,
    until the next comes and cross-examines
    him.

¹⁸ The lot puts an end to disputes
    and decides between men of power.

¹⁹ A brother offended is worse than a
    fortified city,
    and quarrels are like the locks of
    a keep.

²⁰ From the fruit of the mouth is a stomach
    filled,
    it is the yield of the lips that gives
    contentment.

²¹ Death and life are in the gift of the tongue,
    those who indulge it must eat the fruit
    it yields.

²² He who finds a wife finds happiness,
    receiving a mark of favour from
    Yahweh.

²³ The language of the poor is entreaty,
    the answer of the rich harshness.

²⁴ There are friends who point the way
    to ruin,
    others are closer than a brother.

19 Better the poor living an honest life
    than the adept at double-talk who is
    a fool.

² Where knowledge is wanting, zeal is not
    good;
    whoever goes too quickly stumbles.

³ Folly leads conduct astray,
    yet it is against Yahweh that the heart
    rages.

⁴ Wealth multiplies friends,
    but the one friend the poor has is taken
    away.

⁵ The false witness will not go unpunished,^a
    no one who utters lies will go free.

⁶ The nobleman has many to court his
    favour,
    to a giver of gifts, everyone is friend.

⁷ The poor man's brothers hate him, every
    one;
    his friends—how much the more do
    these desert him!

He goes in search of words, but there are
    none to be had.^b

⁸ Whoever acquires sense wins profit
    from it,
    whoever treasures understanding finds
    happiness.

⁹ The false witness will not go unpunished,^c
    whoever utters lies will be destroyed.

¹⁰ It is not fitting for a fool to live in luxury,
    still less for a slave to govern princes.

¹¹ Good sense makes for self-control,
    and for pride in overlooking an offence.

¹² Like the roaring of a lion, the anger of a
    king,
    but like dew on the grass his favour.

¹³ A foolish child is a disaster for the father,
    the bickerings of a wife are like an ever-
    dripping gutter.

¹⁴ From fathers comes inheritance of house
    and wealth,
    from Yahweh a wife who is discreet.

19a = 19:9.
19b A fragment, probably lacking the first line.
19c = 19:5.

¹⁵ Idleness lulls to sleep,
  the feckless soul will go hungry.

¹⁶ Keeping the commandment is self-
      preservation,
  but whoever despises these ways
      will die.

¹⁷ Whoever is kind to the poor is lending to
      Yahweh
  who will repay him the kindness done.

¹⁸ While there is hope for him, chastise your
      child,
  but do not get so angry as to kill him.

¹⁹ The violent lays himself open to a penalty;
  spare him, and you aggravate his
      crime.

²⁰ Listen to advice, accept correction,
  to be the wiser in the time to come.

²¹ Many are the plans in the human heart,
  but the purpose of Yahweh—that
      stands firm.

²² Faithful love is what people look for in a
      person;
  they prefer the poor to a liar.

²³ The fear of Yahweh leads to life,
  it brings food and shelter, without fear
      of evil.

²⁴ Into the dish the idler dips his hand,
  but bring it back to his mouth he
      cannot.ᵈ

²⁵ Strike a cynic, and simpletons will be more
      wary;
  reprove the intelligent and he will
      understand your meaning.

²⁶ He who ill-treats his father and drives out
      his mother
  is a child both worthless and depraved.

²⁷ Give up listening to instruction, my child,
  if you mean to stray from words of
      knowledge.

²⁸ A perjured witness holds the law in scorn;
  the mouth of the wicked feasts on
      evil-doing.

²⁹ Punishments were made for mockers,
  and beating for the backs of fools.

20 Wine is reckless, liquor rowdy;
  unwise is anyone whom it seduces.

² Like the roaring of a lion is the fury of a
      king;
  whoever provokes him sins against
      himself.

³ It is praiseworthy to stop short of a
      law-suit;
  only a fool flies into a rage.

⁴ In autumn the idler does not plough,
  at harvest time he looks—nothing
      there!

⁵ The resources of the human heart are like
      deep waters:
  an understanding person has only to
      draw on them.

⁶ Many describe themselves as people of
      faithful love,
  but who can find someone really to be
      trusted?

⁷ The upright whose ways are blameless—
  blessed the children who come after!

⁸ A king enthroned on the judgement seat
  with one look scatters all that is evil.

⁹ Who can say, 'I have cleansed my heart,
  I am purified of my sin'?

19d = 26:15.

10 One weight here, another there; here one
measure, there another:
both alike are abhorrent to Yahweh.

11 A young man's character appears in what
he does,
if his behaviour is pure and straight.

12 Ear that hears, eye that sees,
Yahweh has made both of these.

13 Do not love sleep or you will know
poverty;
keep your eyes open and have your fill
of food.

14 'No good, no good!' says the buyer,
but he goes off congratulating himself.

15 There are gold and jewels of every type,
but a priceless ornament is speech
informed by knowledge.

16 Take the man's clothes! He has gone
surety for a stranger.
Take a pledge from him to the profit of
persons unknown![a]

17 Bread is sweet when it is got by fraud,
but later the mouth is full of grit.

18 Plans are matured by consultation;
take wise advice when waging war.

19 The bearer of gossip lets out secrets;
do not mingle with chatterers.

20 Whoever curses father or mother
will have his lamp put out in the
deepest darkness.

21 Property quickly come by at first
will not be blessed in the end.

22 Do not say, 'I shall repay evil';
put your hope in Yahweh and he will
keep you safe.

23 One weight here, another there: this is
abhorrent to Yahweh,
false scales are not good.

24 Yahweh guides the steps of the powerful:
but who can comprehend human
ways?

25 Anyone is trapped who cries 'Dedicated!'
and begins to reflect only after the vow.

26 A wise king winnows the wicked
and makes the wheel pass over them.

27 The human spirit is the lamp of
Yahweh—
searching the deepest self.

28 Faithful love and loyalty mount guard
over the king,
his throne is founded on saving
justice.

29 The pride of the young is their strength,
the ornament of the old, grey hairs.

30 Wounding strokes are good medicine for
evil,
blows have an effect on the inmost
self.

21 Like flowing water is a king's heart in
Yahweh's hand;
he directs it wherever he pleases.

2 All actions are straight in the doer's own
eyes,
but it is Yahweh who weighs hearts.

3 To do what is upright and just
is more pleasing to Yahweh than
sacrifice.

4 Haughty eye, proud heart,
lamp of the wicked, nothing but sin.

20a = 27:13.

5 The hardworking is thoughtful, and all is
  gain;
 too much haste, and all that comes of it
  is want.

6 To make a fortune with the help of a lying
  tongue:
 such is the idle fantasy of those who
  look for death.

7 The violence of the wicked proves their
  ruin,
 for they refuse to do what is right.

8 The way of the felon is devious,
 the conduct of the innocent straight.

9 Better the corner of a roof to live on
 than a house shared with a quarrelsome
  woman.[a]

10 The soul of the wicked is intent on evil,
 to such a person no neighbour can ever
  do right.

11 When a cynic is punished, simpletons
  grow wiser,
 but someone of understanding acquires
  knowledge by instruction.

12 The Upright One watches the house of the
  wicked;
 he hurls the wicked to destruction.

13 Whoever refuses to listen to the cry of
  the weak,
 will in turn plead and not be heard.

14 Anger is mollified by a covert gift,
 raging fury by a present under cover of
  the cloak.

15 Doing what is right fills the upright
  with joy,
 but evil-doers with terror.

16 Whoever strays far from the way of
  prudence
 will rest in the assembly of shadows.

17 Pleasure-lovers stay poor,
 no one will grow rich who loves wine
  and good living.

18 The wicked is a ransom for the upright;
 and the law-breaker for the honest.

19 Better to live in a desert land
 than with a quarrelsome and irritable
  woman.

20 The wise has valuables and oil at home,
 but a fool soon runs through both.

21 Whoever pursues uprightness and faithful
  love
 will find life, uprightness and honour.

22 A sage can scale a garrisoned city
 and shatter the rampart on which it
  relied.

23 Watch kept over mouth and tongue
 keeps the watcher safe from disaster.

24 Insolent, haughty—the name is 'Cynic';
 overweening pride marks such
  behaviour.

25 The idler's desires are the death of him,
 since his hands will do no work.

26 All day long the godless is racked by
  desire,
 the upright gives without ever refusing.

27 The sacrifice of the wicked is abhorrent,
 above all if it is offered for bad motives.

28 The false witness will perish,
 but no one who knows how to listen
  will ever be silenced.

29 The wicked man's strength shows on his
  face,
 but the honest it is whose steps are firm.

21a = 25:24.

30 No wisdom, no understanding,
    no advice is worth anything before
      Yahweh.

31 Fit out the cavalry for the day of battle,
    but the victory is Yahweh's.

22 Fame is preferable to great wealth,
    favour, to silver and gold.

2 Rich and poor rub shoulders,
    Yahweh has made them both.

3 The discreet sees danger and takes shelter,
    simpletons go ahead and pay the
      penalty.ª

4 The reward of humility is the fear of
      Yahweh,
    and riches, honour and life.

5 Thorns and snares line the path of the
      wilful,
    whoever values life will stay at a
      distance.

6 Give a lad a training suitable to his
      character
    and, even when old, he will not go back
      on it.

7 The rich lords it over the poor,
    the borrower is the lender's slave.

8 Whoever sows injustice reaps disaster,
    and the rod of such anger will
      disappear.

9 A kindly eye will earn a blessing,
    such a person shares out food with the
      poor.

10 Expel the mocker and strife goes too,
    law-suits and dislike die down.

11 Whoever loves the pure of heart
    and is gracious of speech has the king
      for a friend.

12 Yahweh's eyes protect knowledge,
    but he confounds deceitful speeches.

13 'There is a lion outside,' says the idler,
    'I shall be killed in the street!'

14 The mouth of an adulterous woman is a
      deep pit,
    into it falls the man whom Yahweh
      rebukes.

15 Folly is anchored in the heart of a youth,
    the whip of instruction will rid him
      of it.

16 Harsh treatment enriches the poor,
    but a gift impoverishes the rich.

Sayings of the sages

17 Give ear, listen to the sayings of the sages,
    and apply your heart to what I know,
18 for it will be a delight to keep them deep
      within you
    to have them all ready on your lips.
19 So that your trust may be in Yahweh,
    it is you whom I wish to instruct today.

20 Have I not written for you thirty chapters
    of advice and knowledge,
21 to make you know the certainty of true
      sayings,
    so that you can return with sound
      answers to those who sent you?

22 Do not despoil the weak, for he is weak,
    and do not oppress the poor at the gate,
23 for Yahweh takes up their cause,
    and extorts the life of their extortioners.

24 Do not make friends with one who gives
      way to anger,
    make no one quick-tempered a
      companion of yours,
25 for fear you learn such behaviour
    and in it find a snare for yourself.

22a = 27:12.

26 Do not be one of those who go guarantor,
   who go surety for debts:
27 if you have no means of paying
   your bed will be taken from under you.

28 Do not displace the ancient boundary-
     stone[b]
   set by your ancestors.

29 You see someone alert at his business?
   His aim will be to serve kings;
   not for him the service of the obscure.

23 If you take your seat at a great man's
       table,
   take careful note of what you have
     before you;
2 if you have a big appetite
   put a knife to your throat.
3 Do not hanker for his delicacies,
   for they are deceptive food.

4 Do not wear yourself out in quest of
     wealth,
   stop applying your mind to this.
5 Fix your gaze on it, and it is there no
     longer,
   for it is able to sprout wings
   like an eagle that flies off to the sky.

6 Do not eat the food of anyone whose eye is
     jealous,
   do not hanker for his delicacies.
7 For what he is really thinking about is
     himself:
   'Eat and drink,' he tells you, but his
     heart is not with you.
8 You will spit out whatever you have eaten
   and find your compliments wasted.

9 Do not waste words on a fool,
   who will not appreciate the shrewdness
     of your remarks.

10 Do not displace the ancient boundary-
     stone,[a]
   or encroach on orphans' lands,

11 for they have a powerful avenger,
   and he will take up their cause against
     you.

12 Apply your heart to discipline,
   and your ears to instructive sayings.

13 Do not be chary of correcting a child,
   a stroke of the cane is not likely to be
     fatal.
14 Give him a stroke of the cane,
   you will save his soul from Sheol.
15 My child, if your heart is wise,
   then my own heart is glad,
16 and my inmost self rejoices
   when from your lips come honest
     words.

17 Do not let your heart be envious of sinners
   but remain steady every day in the fear
     of Yahweh;
18 for there is a future,
   and your hope will not come to nothing.

19 Listen, my child, and be wise,
   and guide your heart in the way.

20 Do not be one of those forever tippling
     wine
   nor one of those who gorge themselves
     with meat;
21 for the drunkard and glutton impoverish
     themselves,
   and sleepiness is clothed in rags.

22 Listen to your father from whom you are
     sprung,
   do not despise your mother in her
     old age.
23 Purchase truth—never sell it—
   wisdom, discipline, and discernment.
24 The father of the upright will rejoice
     indeed,
   he who fathers a wise child will have
     joy of it.

22b = 23:10.   23a = 22:28.

25 Your father and mother will be happy,
   and she who bore you joyful.

26 My child, pay attention to me,
   let your eyes take pleasure in my way:
27 a prostitute is a deep pit,
   a narrow well, the woman who belongs
      to another.
28 Yes, like a brigand, she lies in wait,
   increasing the number of law-breakers.

29 For whom is pity, for whom contempt,
   for whom is strife, for whom complaint,
   for whom blows struck at random,
   for whom the clouded eye?
30 For those who linger over wine too long,
   ever on the look-out for the blended
      liquors.
31 Do not gaze at wine, how red it is,
   how it sparkles in the cup!
   How smoothly it slips down the
      throat!
32 In the end its bite is like a serpent's,
   its sting as sharp as an adder's.
33 Your eyes will see peculiar things,
   you will talk nonsense from your heart.
34 You will be like someone sleeping in
      mid-ocean,
   like one asleep at the mast-head.
35 'Struck me, have they? But I'm not hurt.
   Beaten me? I don't feel anything.
   When shall I wake up? . . .
   I'll ask for more of it!'

24 Do not be envious of the wicked
   or wish for their company,
2 for their hearts are scheming violence,
   their lips talking mischief.

3 By wisdom a house is built,
   by understanding it is made strong;
4 by knowledge its storerooms are filled
   with riches of every kind, rare and
      desirable.

5 The wise is mighty in power,
   strength is reinforced by science;

6 for it is by strategy that you wage war,
   and victory depends on having many
      counsellors.

7 For a fool wisdom is an inaccessible
      fortress:
   at the city gate he does not open his
      mouth.

8 Anyone intent on evil-doing
   is known as a master in cunning.

9 Folly dreams of nothing but sin,
   the mocker is abhorrent.

10 If you lose heart when things go wrong,
   your strength is not worth much.

11 Save those being dragged towards death,
   but can you rescue those on their way to
      execution?
12 If you say, 'But look, we did not know,'
   will the Weigher of the heart pay no
      attention?
   Will not the Guardian of your soul be
      aware
   and repay you as your deeds deserve?

13 Eat honey, my child, since it is good;
   honey that drips from the comb is sweet
      to the taste:
14 and so, for sure, will wisdom be to your
      soul:
   find it and you will have a future
   and your hope will not be cut short.

15 Do not lurk, wicked man, round the
      upright man's dwelling,
   do not despoil his house.
16 For though the upright falls seven times,
   he gets up again;
   the wicked are the ones who stumble in
      adversity.

17 Should your enemy fall, do not rejoice,
   when he stumbles do not let your heart
      exult:

[773]

18 for fear that Yahweh will be displeased at
the sight
and turn his anger away from him.

19 Do not be indignant about the wicked,
do not be envious of the evil,
20 for there is no future for the evil,
the lamp of the wicked will go out.

21 Fear Yahweh, my child, and fear the king;
do not ally yourself with innovators;
22 for suddenly disaster will loom for them,
and who knows what ruin will seize
them and their friends?

Further selections from the sages

23 The following are also taken from the sages:

To show partiality in judgement is not
good.

24 Whoever tells the wicked, 'You are
upright,'
peoples curse him, nations revile him;
25 but those who correct him, come out of it
well,
on them will come a happy blessing.

26 Whoever returns an honest answer,
plants a kiss on the lips.

27 Plan what you want on the open ground,
make your preparation in the field;
then go and build your house.

28 Do not bear witness lightly against your
neighbour,
nor deceive with your lips.

29 Do not say, 'I will treat my neighbour as
my neighbour treated me;
I will repay everyone what each has
earned.'

30 By the idler's field I was passing,
by the vineyard of a man who had no
sense,

31 there it all lay, deep in thorns,
entirely overgrown with weeds,
and its stone wall broken down.
32 And as I gazed I pondered,
I drew this lesson from the sight,
33 'A little sleep, a little drowsiness,
a little folding of the arms to lie back
34 and poverty comes like a vagrant,
and, like a beggar, dearth.'[a]

More proverbs of Solomon

25 Here are some more of Solomon's proverbs, transcribed at the court of Hezekiah king of Judah:

2 To conceal a matter, this is the glory of
God,
to sift it thoroughly, the glory of kings.
3 The heavens for height and the earth for
depth,
unfathomable, as are the hearts of
kings.

4 From silver remove the dross
and it emerges wholly purified;
5 from the king's presence remove the
wicked
and on uprightness his throne is
founded.

6 In the presence of the king do not give
yourself airs,
do not take a place among the great;
7 better to be invited, 'Come up here',
than be humiliated in the presence of
the prince.

8 What your eyes have witnessed
do not produce too quickly at the trial,
for what are you to do at the end
should your neighbour confute you?

9 Have the quarrel out with your neighbour,
but do not disclose another's secret,
10 for fear your listener put you to shame,
and the loss of repute be irremediable.

24a = 6:10–11.

11 Like apples of gold inlaid with silver
    is a word that is aptly spoken.
12 A golden ring, an ornament of finest gold,
    is a wise rebuke to an attentive ear.

13 The coolness of snow in harvest time,
    such is a trustworthy messenger to those
        who send him:
    he revives the soul of his master.

14 Clouds and wind, but no rain:
    such is anyone whose promises are
        princely but never kept.

15 With patience a judge may be cajoled:
    a soft tongue breaks bones.

16 Eat to your satisfaction what honey you
        may find,
    but not to excess or you will bring it up
        again.

17 Do not set foot too often in your
        neighbour's house,
    for fear the neighbour tire of you and
        come to hate you.

18 A mace, a sword, a piercing arrow,
    such is anyone who bears false witness
        against a companion.

19 Decaying tooth, lame foot,
    such is the fickle when trusted in time
        of trouble:
20   as well take off your coat in bitter
        weather.

    You are pouring vinegar on a wound
        when you sing songs to a sorrowing
        heart.

21 If your enemy is hungry, give him
        something to eat;
    if thirsty, something to drink.
22 By this you will be heaping red-hot coals
        on his head,
    and Yahweh will reward you.

23 The north wind begets the rain,
    and a backbiting tongue, black looks.

24 Better the corner of a roof to live on
    than a house shared with a quarrelsome
        woman.[a]

25 Cold water to a thirsty throat;
    such is good news from a distant
        land.

26 A churned-up spring, a fountain
        fouled;
    such is the upright person trembling
        before the wicked.

27 It is not good to eat too much honey,
    nor to seek for glory on top of glory.

28 An open town, and without defences:
    such is anyone who lacks self-control.

26

Snow no more befits the summer, nor
    rain the harvest-time,
    than honours befit a fool.

2 As the sparrow escapes, and the swallow
        flies away,
    so the undeserved curse will never hit
        its mark.

3 A whip for the horse, a bridle for the
        donkey,
    and for the backs of fools, a stick.

4 Do not answer a fool in the terms of his
        folly
    for fear you grow like him yourself.

5 Answer a fool in the terms of his folly
    for fear he imagine himself wise.

6 He wounds himself, he takes violence for
        his drink,
    who sends a message by a fool.

25a = 21:9.

7 Unreliable as the legs of the lame,
   so is a proverb in the mouth of fools.

8 As well tie the stone to the sling
   as pay honour to a fool.

9 A thorn branch in a drunkard's hand,
   such is a proverb in the mouth of fools.

10 An archer wounding everyone,
    such is he who hires the passing fool
      and drunkard.

11 As a dog returns to its vomit,
    so a fool reverts to his folly.

12 You see someone who thinks himself
      wise?
    More to be hoped for from a fool than
      from him!

13 'A wild beast on the road!' says the idler,
    'a lion in the streets!'

14 The door turns on its hinges,
    the idler on his bed.

15 Into the dish the idler dips his hand,
    but is too tired to bring it back to his
      mouth.ᵃ

16 The idler thinks himself wiser
    than seven people who answer with
      discretion.

17 He takes a stray dog by the ears,
    who meddles in someone else's
      quarrel.

18 Like a madman hurling firebrands,
    arrows and death,
19 so is anyone who lies to a companion
    and then says, 'Aren't I amusing?'

20 No wood, and the fire goes out;
    no slanderer, and quarrelling dies
      down.

21 Charcoal for live embers, wood for fire,
    and the quarrelsome for kindling strife.

22 The words of a slanderer are tasty morsels
    that go right down into the belly.ᵇ

23 Base silver-plate on top of clay:
    such are fervent lips and a wicked heart.
24 Whoever hates may hide it in speech,
    but deep within lies treachery;
25 do not trust such a person's pretty
      speeches,
    since in the heart lurk seven
      abominations.
26 Hatred may disguise itself with guile,
    to reveal its wickedness later in the
      assembly.

27 Whoever digs a pit falls into it,
    the stone comes back on him that
      rolls it.

28 The lying tongue hates its victims,
    the wheedling mouth causes ruin.

27 Do not congratulate yourself about
      tomorrow,
   since you do not know what today will
      bring forth.

2 Let someone else sing your praises, but not
      your own mouth,
   a stranger, but not your own lips.

3 Heavy is the stone, weighty is the sand;
   heavier than both—a grudge borne by a
      fool.

4 Cruel is wrath, overwhelming is anger;
   but jealousy, who can withstand that?

5 Better open reproof
   than feigned love.

6 Trustworthy are blows from a friend,
   deceitful are kisses from a foe.

26a = 19:24.   26b = 18:8.

7 The gorged throat revolts at honey,
   the hungry throat finds all bitterness
      sweet.

8 Like a bird that strays from its nest,
   so is anyone who strays away from
      home.

9 Oil and perfume gladden the heart,
   and the sweetness of friendship rather
      than self-reliance.

10 Do not give up your friend or your father's
      friend;
   when trouble comes, do not go off to
      your brother's house,
   better a near neighbour than a distant
      brother.

11 Learn to be wise, my child, and gladden
      my heart,
   that I may have an answer for anyone
      who insults me.

12 The discreet sees danger and takes
      shelter,
   simpletons go ahead and pay the
      penalty.*a*

13 Take the man's clothes! He has gone
      surety for a stranger.
   Take a pledge from him, for persons
      unknown.*b*

14 Whoever at dawn loudly blesses his
      neighbour—
   it will be reckoned to him as a curse.

15 The dripping of a gutter on a rainy day
   and a quarrelsome woman are alike;
16 whoever can restrain her, can restrain the
      wind,
   and take a firm hold on grease.

17 Iron is sharpened by iron,
   one person is sharpened by contact with
      another.

18 Whoever tends the fig tree eats its figs,
   whoever looks after his master will be
      honoured.

19 As water reflects face back to face,
   so one human heart reflects another.

20 Sheol and Perdition are never satisfied,
   insatiable, too, are human eyes.

21 A furnace for silver, a foundry for gold:
   a person is worth what his reputation is
      worth.

22 Pound a fool in a mortar,
   among grain with a pestle,
      his folly will not leave him.

23 Know your flocks' condition well,
   take good care of your herds;
24 for riches do not last for ever,
   crowns do not hand themselves on from
      age to age.
25 The grass once gone, the aftergrowth
      appearing,
   the hay gathered in from the
      mountains,
26 you should have lambs to clothe you,
   goats to buy you a field,
27 goat's milk sufficient to feed you,
   to feed your household and provide for
      your serving girls.

28 The wicked flees when no one is
      pursuing,
   the upright is bold as a lion.

2 A country in revolt throws up many
      leaders:
   with one person wise and experienced,
      you have stability.

3 The wicked oppresses the weak:
   here is a devastating rain—and
      farewell, bread!

27a = 22:3.   27b = 20:16.

⁴ Those who forsake the law sing the praises
of the wicked,
those who observe the law are angered
by them.

⁵ The wicked do not know what justice
means,
those who seek Yahweh understand
everything.

⁶ Better someone poor living an honest life
than someone of devious ways however
rich.

⁷ An intelligent child is one who keeps the
Law;
an associate of profligates brings shame
on his father.

⁸ Whoever increases wealth by usury and
interest
amasses it for someone else who will
bestow it on the poor.

⁹ Whoever refuses to listen to the Law,
such a one's very prayer is an
abomination.

¹⁰ Whoever seduces the honest to evil ways
will fall into his own pit.
The blameless are the heirs to happiness.

¹¹ The rich may think himself wise,
but the intelligent poor will unmask
him.

¹² When the upright triumph, there is great
exultation:
when the wicked are in the ascendant,
people take cover.ᵃ

¹³ No one who conceals his sins will prosper,
whoever confesses and renounces them
will find mercy.

¹⁴ Blessed the person who is never without
fear,
whoever hardens his heart will fall into
distress.

¹⁵ Like a roaring lion or a springing bear
is a wicked ruler of a powerless people.

¹⁶ An unenlightened ruler is rich in rapacity,
one who hates greed will lengthen his
days.

¹⁷ A man guilty of murder will flee till he
reaches his tomb:
let no one halt him!

¹⁸ Whoever lives an honest life will be safe,
whoever wavers between two ways falls
down in one of them.

¹⁹ Whoever works his land shall have bread
and to spare,
but no one who chases fantasies has any
sense.ᵇ

²⁰ A trustworthy person will be
overwhelmed with blessings,
but no one who tries to get rich quickly
will go unpunished.

²¹ It is not good to show partiality,
but people will do wrong for a
mouthful of bread.

²² The person of greedy eye chases after
wealth,
not knowing that want will be the
result.

²³ Anyone who reproves another
will enjoy more favour in the end than
the flatterer.

²⁴ Whoever robs father and mother saying,
'Nothing wrong in that!'
is comrade for a brigand.

²⁵ The covetous provokes disputes,
whoever trusts in Yahweh will
prosper.

28a = 28:28.   28b = 12:11.

26 Whoever trusts his own wit is a fool,
  anyone whose ways are wise will be
    safe.

27 No one who gives to the poor will ever go
    short,
  but whoever closes his eyes will have
    curses in plenty.
28 When the wicked are in the ascendant,
    people take cover,[c]
  but when they perish, the upright
    multiply.

29 Whoever is stiff-necked under reproof
  will be suddenly and irremediably
    broken.

2 When the upright are on the increase, the
    people rejoice;
  when the wicked are in power, the
    people groan.

3 The lover of Wisdom makes his father
    glad,
  but the patron of prostitutes fritters his
    wealth away.

4 A king gives a country stability by justice,
  an extortioner brings it to ruin.

5 Whoever flatters his companion
  spreads a net for his feet.

6 In the sin of the wicked lies a snare,
  but the upright exults and rejoices.

7 The upright understands the cause of the
    weak,
  the wicked has not the wit to
    understand it.

8 Scoffers set a city in ferment,
  but the wise moderate anger.

9 Let someone wise argue with a fool,
  anger and good humour alike will be
    wasted.

10 The bloodthirsty hate the honest,
  but the upright seek them out.

11 The fool blurts out every angry feeling,
  but the wise subdues and restrains
    them.

12 When a ruler listens to false reports,
  all his ministers will be scoundrels.

13 Poor and oppressor are found together,
  Yahweh gives light to the eyes of both.

14 The king who judges the weak with
    equity
  sees his throne set firm for ever.

15 The stick and the reprimand bestow
    wisdom,
  a young man left to himself brings
    shame on his mother.

16 When the wicked are on the increase, sin
    multiplies,
  but the upright will witness their
    downfall.

17 Correct your child, and he will give you
    peace of mind;
  he will delight your soul.

18 Where there is no vision the people get out
    of hand;
  happy are they who keep the law.

19 Not by words is a slave corrected:
  even if he understands, he will take no
    notice.

20 You see someone too ready of speech?
  There is more to be hoped for from a
    fool!

21 If a slave is pampered from childhood,
  he will prove ungrateful in the end.

28c = 28:12.

[779]

22 The hot-head provokes disputes,
   someone in a rage commits all sorts
   of sins.

23 Pride brings humiliation,
   whoever humbles himself will win
   honour.

24 To hear the curse and disclose nothing
   is to share with the thief and to hate
   oneself.

25 To be afraid of human beings is a snare,
   whoever trusts in Yahweh is secure.

26 Many people seek a ruler's favour,
   but the rights of each come from
   Yahweh.

27 Abhorrent to the upright is the sinful,
   abhorrent to the wicked is one whose
   way is straight.

The sayings of Agur

30 The sayings of Agur son of Jakeh, of Massa.ᵃ Prophecy of this man for Ithiel, for Ithiel and for Ucal.

2 I am myself the stupidest of people,
   bereft of human intelligence,
3 I have not learnt wisdom,
   and I lack the knowledge of the holy
   ones.
4 Who has mounted to the heavens, then
   come down again?
   Who has gathered the wind in the clasp
   of his hand?
   Who has wrapped the waters in his cloak?
   Who has set all the ends of the earth
   firm?
   What is his name?
   What is his child's name?
   Do you know?

5 Every word of God is unalloyed,
   a shield to those who take refuge in
   him.

6 To his words make no addition,
   lest he reprove you
   and account you a liar.

7 Two things I beg of you,
   do not grudge me them before I die:
8 keep falsehood and lies far from me,
   give me neither poverty nor riches,
   grant me only my share of food,
9 for fear that, surrounded by plenty, I
   should fall away
   and say, 'Yahweh—who is Yahweh?'
   or else, in destitution, take to stealing
   and profane the name of my God.

10 Do not blacken a slave's name to his
    master,
    lest he curse you, and you suffer for it.

11 There is a breed of person that curses his
    father
    and does not bless his mother;
12 a breed that, laying claim to purity,
    has not yet been cleansed of its filth;
13 a breed haughty of eye,
    with disdain in every glance;
14 a breed with swords for teeth,
    with knives for jaws,
    devouring the oppressed from the earth
    and the needy from the land.

15 The leech has two daughters: 'Give! Give!'
    There are three insatiable things,
    four, indeed, that never say, 'Enough!'
16 Sheol, the barren womb,
    earth which can never have its fill of
    water,
    fire which never says, 'Enough!'

17 The eye which looks jeeringly on a father,
    and scorns the obedience due to a
    mother,
    will be pecked out by the ravens of the
    valley,
    and eaten by the vultures.

30a In northern Arabia, home also of Lemuel (31:1). The wisdom of eastern sages was proverbial.

¹⁸ There are three things beyond my
        comprehension,
    four, indeed, that I do not understand:
¹⁹ the way of an eagle through the skies,
    the way of a snake over the rock,
    the way of a ship in mid-ocean,
    the way of a man with a girl.

²⁰ This is how an adulteress behaves:
    she eats, then wipes her mouth and says,
    'I have done nothing wrong!'

²¹ There are three things at which the earth
        trembles,
    four, indeed, which it cannot endure:
²² a slave become king,
    a brute gorged with food,
²³ a hateful woman wed at last,
    a servant girl inheriting from her
        mistress.

²⁴ There are four creatures little on the
        earth,
    though they are wisest of the wise:
²⁵ ants, a race with no strength,
    yet in the summer they make sure of
        their food;
²⁶ the coneys, a race without defences,
    yet they make their home in the rocks;
²⁷ locusts, which have no king,
    yet they all march in good order;
²⁸ lizards, which you can catch in your
        hand,
    yet they frequent the palaces of kings.

²⁹ There are three things of stately tread,
    four, indeed, of stately walk:
³⁰ the lion, bravest of beasts,
    he will draw back from nothing;
³¹ a vigorous cock, a he-goat,
    and the king when he harangues his
        people.

³² If you have been foolish enough to fly into
        a passion
    and now have second thoughts, lay your
        hand on your lips.

³³ For by churning the milk you produce
        butter,
    by wringing the nose you produce
        blood,
    and by whipping up anger you produce
        strife.

The sayings of Lemuel

31 ¹ The sayings of Lemuel king of Massa,
    taught him by his mother:

² What, my son! What, son of my womb!
    What, son of my vows!
³ Do not expend your energy on women
    nor your wealth on those who ruin
        kings.

⁴ Not for kings, O Lemuel,
    not for kings the drinking of wine,
    not for princes the love of liquor,
⁵ for fear that in liquor they forget what
        they have decreed
    and pervert the course of justice against
        all the poor.

⁶ Procure strong drink for someone about to
        die,
    wine for him whose heart is heavy:
⁷ let him drink and forget his misfortune,
    and remember his misery no more.

⁸ Make your views heard, on behalf of the
        dumb,
    on behalf of all the unwanted;
⁹ make your views heard, pronounce an
        upright verdict,
    defend the cause of the poor and the
        wretched.

The truly capable woman

ALEPH ¹⁰ The truly capable woman—who
        can find her?
    She is far beyond the price of pearls.

BET ¹¹ Her husband's heart has confidence in
        her,
    from her he will derive no little profit.

GIMEL ¹²Advantage and not hurt she brings him
    all the days of her life.

DALET ¹³She selects wool and flax,
    she does her work with eager hands.

HE ¹⁴She is like those merchant vessels,
    bringing her food from far away.

WAW ¹⁵She gets up while it is still dark
    giving her household their food,
    giving orders to her serving girls.

ZAIN ¹⁶She sets her mind on a field, then she buys it;
    with what her hands have earned she plants a vineyard.

HET ¹⁷She puts her back into her work
    and shows how strong her arms can be.

TET ¹⁸She knows that her affairs are going well;
    her lamp does not go out at night.

YOD ¹⁹She sets her hands to the distaff,
    her fingers grasp the spindle.

KAPH ²⁰She holds out her hands to the poor,
    she opens her arms to the needy.

LAMED ²¹Snow may come, she has no fears for her household,
    with all her servants warmly clothed.

MEM ²²She makes her own quilts,
    she is dressed in fine linen and purple.

NUN ²³Her husband is respected at the city gates,
    taking his seat among the elders of the land.

SAMEK ²⁴She weaves materials and sells them,
    she supplies the merchant with sashes.

AIN ²⁵She is clothed in strength and dignity,
    she can laugh at the day to come.

PE ²⁶When she opens her mouth, she does so wisely;
    on her tongue is kindly instruction.

ZADE ²⁷She keeps good watch on the conduct of her household,
    no bread of idleness for her.

QOPH ²⁸Her children stand up and proclaim her blessed,
    her husband, too, sings her praises:

RESH ²⁹'Many women have done admirable things,
    but you surpass them all!'

SHIN ³⁰Charm is deceitful, and beauty empty;
    the woman who fears Yahweh is the one to praise.

TAW ³¹Give her a share in what her hands have worked for,
    and let her works tell her praises at the city gates.

ECCLESIASTES

1 Composition of Qoheleth son of David, king in Jerusalem.

Part One: Prologue

2 Sheer futility, Qoheleth says. Sheer futility: everything is futile! 3 What profit can we show for all our toil, toiling under the sun? 4 A generation goes, a generation comes, yet the earth stands firm for ever. 5 The sun rises, the sun sets; then to its place it speeds and there it rises. 6 Southward goes the wind, then turns to the north; it turns and turns again; then back to its circling goes the wind. 7 Into the sea go all the rivers, and yet the sea is never filled, and still to their goal the rivers go. 8 All things are wearisome. No one can say that eyes have not had enough of seeing, ears their fill of hearing.

9 What was, will be again,
   what has been done, will be done again,
   and there is nothing new under the sun!

10 Take anything which people acclaim as being new: it existed in the centuries preceding us. 11 No memory remains of the past, and so it will be for the centuries to come—they will not be remembered by their successors.

Life of Solomon

12 I, Qoheleth, have reigned over Israel in Jerusalem. 13 Wisely I have applied myself to investigation and exploration of everything that happens under heaven. What a wearisome task God has given humanity to keep us busy! 14 I have seen everything that is done under the sun: how futile it all is, mere chasing after the wind!

15 What is twisted cannot be straightened,
   what is not there cannot be counted.

16 I thought to myself: I have acquired a greater stock of wisdom than anyone before me in Jerusalem. I myself have mastered every kind of wisdom and science. 17 I have applied myself to understanding philosophy and science, stupidity and folly, and I now realise that all this too is chasing after the wind.

18 Much wisdom, much grief;
   the more knowledge, the more sorrow.

2 I thought to myself, 'Very well, I will try pleasure and see what enjoyment has to offer.' And this was futile too. 2 This laughter, I reflected, is a madness, this pleasure no use at all. 3 I decided to hand my body over to drinking wine, my mind still guiding me in wisdom; I resolved to embrace folly, to discover the best way for people to spend their days under the sun. 4 I worked on a grand scale: built myself palaces, planted vineyards; 5 made myself gardens and orchards, planting every kind of fruit tree in them; 6 had pools made for watering the young trees of my plantations. 7 I bought slaves, male and female, had homeborn slaves as well; herds and flocks I had too, more than anyone in Jerusalem before me. 8 I amassed silver and gold, the treasures of kings and provinces; acquired singers, men and women, and every human luxury, chest upon chest of it. 9 So I grew great, greater than anyone in Jerusalem before me; nor did my wisdom leave me. 10 I denied my eyes nothing that they desired, refused my heart no pleasure, for I found all my hard work a pleasure, such was the return for all my efforts. 11 I then reflected on all that my hands had achieved and all the effort I had put into its achieving. What futility it all was, what chasing after the

56 READ ECCLESIASTES 1:1–9; 2:1–26.

Sheer futility. . . . Sheer futility: everything is futile!—ECCLESIASTES 1:2

THE FUTILITY OF SELF-INDULGENCE

The writer of Ecclesiastes signed himself "Qoheleth," or "the Preacher." As a literary device he identified himself with Solomon, using the name of Israel's great sage to authorize his wisdom. The older translation of his opening—"Vanity of vanities; all is vanity"—does not stab our conscience as sharply as the freshly translated cry, "Sheer futility." St. John Chrysostom, the foremost preacher of the eastern church, drives the point home:

While Solomon was given up to the lust of the world, he regarded it a great and noble pursuit. So he devoted his attention to it. He built magnificent palaces, he horded gold, he assembled choirs of singers and all sorts of servants to attend to the luxury of his meals. He looked for gratification in the charm of gardens and beautiful bodies. In short, he dedicated himself to all kinds of pleasure and recreation.

But when he came to his senses and could look out from that dark pit to the light of true wisdom, he spoke that high saying, so worthy of heaven: "Sheer futility; everything is futile." And you, too, if you will ever shake yourself loose from your debasing habits, will shout this cry, and an even higher cry as you repent of your extravagant indulgences.

The ages that preceded Solomon had not left him so precious an inheritance of wisdom as we have received from those preceding us. The old law did not forbid those indulgences, nor declare foolish the enjoyment of idle luxuries. And yet we can see how low, how worthless such things are. As for us, we are called to a higher life. We ascend to a nobler standpoint, and brace ourselves in a hardier school. And for no other reason than that we are called to strive for a truly spiritual life.

ST. JOHN CHRYSOSTOM, 347–407

YOU WILL FIND THE NEXT READING AT ECCLESIASTES 3.

wind! There is nothing to be gained under the sun.

¹²My reflections then turned to wisdom, stupidity and folly. For instance, what can the successor of a king do? What has been done already. ¹³More is to be gained from wisdom than from folly, just as one gains more from light than from darkness; this, of course, I see:

¹⁴ The wise have their eyes open,
  the fool walks in the dark.

No doubt! But I know, too, that one fate awaits them both. ¹⁵'Since the fool's fate', I thought to myself, 'will be my fate too, what is the point of my having been wise?' I realised that this too is futile. ¹⁶For there is no lasting memory for the wise or the fool, and in the days to come both will be forgotten; the wise, no less than the fool, must die. ¹⁷Life I have come to hate, for what is done under the sun disgusts me, since all is futility and chasing after the wind. ¹⁸All I have toiled for under the sun and now bequeath to my successor I have come to hate; ¹⁹who knows whether he will be wise or a fool? Yet he will be master of all the work into which I have put my efforts and wisdom under the sun. That is futile too. ²⁰I have come to despair of all the efforts I have expended under the sun. ²¹For here is one who has laboured wisely, skilfully and successfully and must leave what is his own to someone who has not toiled for it at all. This is futile too, and grossly unjust; ²²for what does he gain for all the toil and strain that he has undergone under the sun— ²³since his days are full of sorrow, his work is full of stress and even at night he has no peace of mind? This is futile too.

²⁴There is no happiness except in eating and drinking, and in enjoying one's achievements; and I see that this too comes from God's hand; ²⁵for who would get anything to eat or drink, unless all this came from him? ²⁶Wisdom, knowledge and joy, God gives to those who please him, but on the sinner he lays the task of gathering and storing up for someone else who is pleasing to him. This too is futility and chasing after the wind.

Death

3 There is a season for everything, a time for every occupation under heaven:

² A time for giving birth,
   a time for dying;
   a time for planting,
   a time for uprooting what has been
      planted.
³ A time for killing,
   a time for healing;
   a time for knocking down,
   a time for building.
⁴ A time for tears,
   a time for laughter;
   a time for mourning,
   a time for dancing.
⁵ A time for throwing stones away,
   a time for gathering them;
   a time for embracing,

a time to refrain from embracing.
⁶ A time for searching,
   a time for losing;
   a time for keeping,
   a time for discarding.
⁷ A time for tearing,
   a time for sewing;
   a time for keeping silent,
   a time for speaking.
⁸ A time for loving,
   a time for hating;
   a time for war,
   a time for peace.

⁹What do people gain from the efforts they make? ¹⁰I contemplate the task that God gives humanity to labour at. ¹¹All that he does is apt for its time; but although he has given us an awareness of the passage of time, we can grasp neither the beginning nor the end of what God does.

¹²I know there is no happiness for a human being except in pleasure and enjoyment through life. ¹³And when we eat and drink and find happiness in all our achievements, this is a gift from God.

¹⁴I know that whatever God does will be for ever.

To this there is nothing to add,
   from this there is nothing to subtract,
   and the way God acts inspires dread.

¹⁵ What is, has been already,
   what will be, is already;
   God seeks out anyone who is persecuted.

¹⁶ Again I observe under the sun:
   crime is where justice should be,
   the criminal is where the upright
      should be.

¹⁷And I think to myself: the upright and the criminal will both be judged by God, since there is a time for every thing and every action here.

¹⁸I think to myself: where human beings are concerned, this is so that God can test them

57 READ ECCLESIASTES 3:1–11.

A time for giving birth, a time for dying.—ECCLESIASTES 3:2

TIMELY BIRTH, TIMELY DEATH

I believe that a birth is right and not out of its time when—as Isaiah says—someone has conceived out of the fear of God, and through the birth pains of the soul generates his own salvation. For in a certain sense we are our own parents when through the good disposition of our soul and complete freedom of our will we form, generate and bring ourselves to the Light.

We do this by the fact that we bring God into ourselves, having become children of God, children of virtue, and children of the Most High. On the other hand, we bring ourselves into the world out of due time and form ourselves in an imperfect and immature manner when we have not been molded in the pattern of Christ (see Rm 8:29). For it is necessary that the man of God be without reproach and perfect.

If the manner in which we are born at the right time is evident, equally clear to all is the way we die at the opportune moment. And in the eyes of St. Paul, every moment was opportune for a good death. For he cries out, *"For your sake we are being massacred all day long"* (Rm 8:36; see Ps 44:22). And we bear within ourselves the very sentence of death.

The manner in which Paul dies each day is not obscure. He never lives in sin. He always mortifies his flesh and bears within himself the mortification of the body of Christ because he is always crucified with Christ. He never lives for himself but always has Christ living in him. In my opinion this is the timely and favorable death that leads to true life.   St. GREGORY OF NYSSA, 330?–395?

YOU WILL FIND THE NEXT READING AT SONG OF SONGS 1.

and show them that they are animals. ¹⁹For the fate of human and the fate of animal is the same: as the one dies, so the other dies; both have the selfsame breath. Human is in no way better off than animal—since all is futile.

²⁰ Everything goes to the same place,
everything comes from the dust,
everything returns to the dust.

²¹ Who knows if the human spirit mounts upward or if the animal spirit goes downward to the earth?

²²I see there is no contentment for a human being except happiness in achievement; such is the lot of a human being. No one can tell us what will happen after we are gone.

Society

4 Then again, I contemplate all the oppression that is committed under the sun. Take for instance the tears of the oppressed. No one to comfort them! The power their oppressors wield. No one to comfort them! ²So, rather than the living who still have lives to live, I congratulate the dead who have already met death; ³happier than both of these are those who are yet unborn and have not seen the evil things that are done under the sun. ⁴I see that all effort and all achievement spring from mu-

tual jealousy. This too is futility and chasing after the wind.

⁵ The fool folds his arms
  and eats his own flesh away.

⁶ Better one hand full of repose
  than two hands full of achievements
  to chase after the wind.

⁷ And something else futile I observe under the sun: ⁸a person is quite alone—no child, no brother; and yet there is no end to his efforts, his eyes can never have their fill of riches. For whom, then, do I work so hard and grudge myself pleasure? This too is futile, a sorry business.

⁹ Better two than one alone, since thus their work is really rewarding. ¹⁰If one should fall, the other helps him up; but what of the person with no one to help him up when he falls? ¹¹Again: if two sleep together they keep warm, but how can anyone keep warm alone? ¹²Where one alone would be overcome, two will put up resistance; and a threefold cord is not quickly broken.

¹³ Better a youngster poor and wise
  than a monarch old and silly
  who will no longer take advice—
¹⁴ even though stepping from prison to the
    throne,
  even though born a beggar in that
    kingdom.

¹⁵I observe that all who live and move under the sun support the young newcomer who takes over. ¹⁶He takes his place at the head of innumerable subjects; but his successors will not think the more kindly of him for that. This too is futile and chasing after the wind. ¹⁷Watch your step when you go to the House of God: drawing near to listen is better than the offering of a sacrifice by fools, though they do not know that they are doing wrong.

5 Be in no hurry to speak; do not hastily declare yourself before God; for God is in heaven, you on earth. Be sparing, then, of speech:

² From too much worrying comes illusion,
  from too much talking, the accents of folly.

³If you make a vow to God, discharge it without delay, for God has no love for fools. Discharge your vow. ⁴Better a vow unmade than made and not discharged. ⁵Do not allow your mouth to make a sinner of you, and do not say to the messenger that it was a mistake. Why give God occasion to be angry with you and ruin all the work that you have done?

⁶ From too many illusions
  come futility and too much talk.

Therefore, fear God.
⁷If in a province you see the poor oppressed, fair judgement and justice violated, do not be surprised, for over every official there watches a higher official, and over these, higher officials still. ⁸But what the land yields is for the benefit of all, a king is served by the fields.

Money

⁹ No one who loves money ever has enough,
  no one who loves luxury has any income;

this, too, is futile.

¹⁰ Where goods abound, parasites abound:

where is the owner's profit, apart from feasting his eyes?
¹¹The labourer's sleep is sweet, whether he has eaten little or much, but the surfeit of the rich will not let him sleep at all. ¹²Something grossly unjust I observe under the sun: riches stored and turning to loss for their owner. ¹³An unlucky venture, and those riches are lost; a son is born to him, and he has nothing to leave him. ¹⁴Naked from his mother's womb he came; as naked as he came

will he depart; not one of his achievements can he take with him. ¹⁵ And something else grossly unjust: that as he came, so must he go; what profit can he show after toiling to earn the wind, ¹⁶ as he spends the rest of his days in darkness, mourning, many sorrows, sickness and exasperation.

¹⁷ So my conclusion is this: true happiness lies in eating and drinking and enjoying whatever has been achieved under the sun, throughout the life given by God: for this is the lot of humanity. ¹⁸ And whenever God gives someone riches and property, with the ability to enjoy them and to find contentment in work, this is a gift from God. ¹⁹ For such a person will hardly notice the passing of time, so long as God keeps his heart occupied with joy.

6 I see another evil under the sun, which goes hard with people: ² suppose someone has received from God riches, property, honours—nothing at all left to wish for; but God does not give the chance to enjoy them, and some stranger enjoys them. This is futile, and grievous suffering too. ³ Or take someone who has had a hundred children and lived for many years, and, having reached old age, has never enjoyed the good things of life and has not even got a tomb; it seems to me, a still-born child is happier.

⁴ In futility it came, into darkness it departs,
and in darkness will its name be buried.

⁵ It has never so much as seen or known the sun; all the same, it will rest more easily than that person, ⁶ who would never have known the good things of life, even by living a thousand years twice over. Do we not all go to the same place in the end?

⁷ All toil is for the mouth,
yet the appetite is never satisfied.

⁸ What advantage has the wise over the
fool?
And what of the pauper who knows how
to behave in society?

⁹ Better the object seen than the sting of
desire:
for the latter too is futile and chasing after
the wind.

¹⁰ What has been is already defined—we
know what people are:
They cannot bring to justice one who is
stronger than themselves.

¹¹ The more we say, the more futile it is: what good can we derive from it? ¹² And who knows what is best for someone during life, during the days of futile life which are spent like a shadow? Who can tell anyone what will happen after him under the sun?

Part Two: Prologue

7 Better a good name than costly oil,
the day of death than the day of birth.
² Better go to the house of mourning
than to the house of feasting;
for to this end everyone comes,
let the living take this to heart.
³ Better sadness than laughter:
a joyful heart may be concealed behind sad
looks.
⁴ The heart of the wise is in the house of
mourning,
the heart of fools in the house of gaiety.
⁵ Better attend to the reprimand of the
wise
than listen to a song sung by a fool.
⁶ For like the crackling of thorns under the
cauldron
is the laughter of fools:
and that too is futile.
⁷ But being oppressed drives a sage mad,
and a present corrupts the heart.

Warnings

⁸ Better the end of a matter than its
beginning,
better patience than ambition.

⁹ Do not be too easily exasperated, for exasperation dwells in the heart of fools. ¹⁰ Do

not ask why the past was better than the present, for this is not a question prompted by wisdom.

11 Wisdom is as good as a legacy,
profitable to those who enjoy the light of
the sun.
12 For as money protects, so does wisdom,
and the advantage of knowledge is this:
that wisdom bestows life on those who
possess her.
13 Consider God's creation:
who, for instance, can straighten what
God has bent?
14 When things are going well, enjoy
yourself,
and when they are going badly, consider
this:
God has designed the one no less than the
other
so that we should take nothing for
granted.
15 In my futile life, I have seen everything:
the upright person perishing in
uprightness
and the wicked person surviving in
wickedness.
16 Do not be upright to excess
and do not make yourself unduly wise:
why should you destroy yourself?
17 Do not be wicked to excess,
and do not be a fool:
why die before your time?
18 It is wise to hold on to one and not let go
of the other,
since the godfearing will find both.

19 Wisdom makes the wise stronger than a dozen governors in a city.
20 No one on earth is sufficiently upright to do good without ever sinning.
21 Again, do not listen to all that people say, then you will not hear your servant abusing you.
22 For often, as you very well know, you have abused others.
23 Thanks to wisdom, I have found all this

to be true; I resolved to be wise, but this was beyond my reach!

24 The past is out of reach,
buried deep—who can discover it?

25 But I have reached the point where, having learnt, explored and investigated wisdom and reflection, I recognise evil as being a form of madness, and folly as something stupid.

26 And I find woman more bitter than
Death,
she is a snare,
her heart is a net, and her arms are
chains.
The man who is pleasing to God eludes
her,
but the sinner is captured by her.
27 This is what I think, says Qoheleth,
having examined one thing after another
to draw some conclusion,
28 which I am still looking for, although
unsuccessfully:
one man in a thousand, I may find,
but a woman better than other women—
never.
29 This alone is my conclusion:
God has created man straightforward,
and human artifices are human inventions.

8 Who compares with the sage?
Who else knows how to explain things?
Wisdom lights up the face,
enlivening a grim expression.
2 Obey the king's command and, because of
the divine promise,
3 be in no hurry to depart from it;
do not be obstinate in a bad cause,
since the king will do as he likes in any
case.
4 Since the word of a king is sovereign,
what is the point of saying, 'Why do that?'
5 One who obeys the command will come to
no harm;
the heart of the sage knows the right
moment and verdict,

⁶ for there is a right moment and verdict for
    everything;
but misfortune lies heavy upon anyone
⁷ who does not know what the outcome will
    be,
no one is going to say how things will turn
    out.
⁸ No one can control the wind and stop it
    from blowing,
no one can control the day of death.
From war there is no escape,
no more can wickedness save the person
    who commits it.

⁹ I have seen all this to be so, having carefully studied everything taking place under
the sun, while one person tyrannises over another to the former's detriment.

¹⁰ And again, I have observed the wicked
carried to their graves, and people leaving the
holy place and, once out in the city, forgetting
how the wicked used to behave; how futile this
is too!

¹¹ Because the sentence on the evil-doer is
not carried out on the instant, people's hearts
are full of desire to do wrong. ¹² The sinner
who does wrong a hundred times lives on. But
this too I know, that there is good in store for
people who fear God, because they fear him,
¹³ but there is no good in store for the wicked
because he does not fear God, and so, like a
shadow, he will not prolong his days. ¹⁴ Another futile thing that happens on earth: upright people being treated as though they were
wicked and wicked people being treated as
though they were upright. To me this is one
more example of futility.

¹⁵ And therefore I praise joy, since human
happiness lies only in eating and drinking and
in taking pleasure; this comes from what
someone achieves during the days of life that
God gives under the sun.

¹⁶ Having applied myself to acquiring wisdom and to observing the activity taking place
in the world—for day and night our eyes
enjoy no rest— ¹⁷ I have scrutinised God's
whole creation: you cannot get to the bottom

of everything taking place under the sun; you
may wear yourself out in the search, but you
will never find it. Not even a sage can get to
the bottom of it, even if he says that he has
done so.

Destiny

9 Yes, I have applied myself to all this and experienced all this to be so: that is to say, that
the upright and the wise, with their activities,
are in the hands of God.

We do not understand either love or hate,
    where we are concerned, both of them are
        ² futile.
And for all of us is reserved a common
    fate,
for the upright and for the wicked,
for the good and for the bad;
whether we are ritually pure or not,
whether we offer sacrifice or not:
it is the same for the good and for the
        sinner,
for someone who takes a vow, as for
        someone who fears to do so.

³ This is another evil among those occur-
ring under the sun: that there should be the
same fate for everyone. The human heart,
however, is full of wickedness; folly lurks in
our hearts throughout our lives, until we end
among the dead.

⁴ But there is hope for someone still linked
    to the rest of the living:
better be a live dog than a dead lion.

⁵ The living are at least aware that they are
going to die, but the dead know nothing whatever. No more wages for them, since their
memory is forgotten. ⁶ Their love, their hate,
their jealousy, have perished long since, and
they will never have any further part in what
goes on under the sun.

⁷ So, eat your bread in joy,
    drink your wine with a glad heart,

since God has already approved your
  actions.
⁸ At all times, dress in white
  and keep your head well scented.
⁹ Spend your life with the woman you love,
  all the days of futile life God gives you
      under the sun,
  throughout your futile days,
  since this is your lot in life
  and in the effort you expend under the
      sun.
¹⁰ Whatever work you find to do,
  do it with all your might,
  for there is neither achievement, nor
      planning, nor science,
  nor wisdom in Sheol where you are going.
¹¹ Another thing I have observed under the
      sun:
  that the race is not won by the speediest,
  nor the battle by the champions;
  it is not the wise who get food,
  nor the intelligent wealth,
  nor the learned favour:
  chance and mischance befall them all.
¹² We do not know when our time will
      come:
  like fish caught in the treacherous net,
  like birds caught in the snare,
  just so are we all trapped by misfortune
  when it suddenly overtakes us.

Wisdom and folly

¹³ Here is another example of the wisdom I
have acquired under the sun and it strikes me
as important:
  ¹⁴ There was once a small town, with only a
few inhabitants; a mighty king made war on
it, laying siege to it and building great siege-
works round it. ¹⁵ But there was in that town a
poverty-stricken sage who by his wisdom
saved the town. No one remembered this poor
man afterwards. ¹⁶ So I say:

  Wisdom is more effective than brute force,
  but the wisdom of a poor man is not
      valued:
  no one listens to what he has to say.

¹⁷ The calm words of the wise make themselves heard above the shouts of someone commanding an army of fools.

¹⁸ Wisdom is worth more than weapons of
      war,
  but a single sin undoes a deal of good.

10 One dead fly can spoil the scent-
      maker's oil:
  a grain of stupidity outweighs wisdom and
      glory.

² The sage's heart leads him aright,
  the fool's leads him astray.

³ A fool walks down the road, he has no
      wit—
  and everyone remarks, 'How silly he is!'

⁴ If the anger of the ruler rises against you,
do not leave your post; composure mitigates
grave offences.
  ⁵ One evil I observe under the sun: the sort
of misjudgement to which rulers are prone—
⁶ folly promoted to the top and the rich taking
the lowest place. ⁷ I see slaves riding on horses
and princes on foot like slaves.

⁸ He who digs a pit falls into it,
  he who undermines a wall gets bitten by a
      snake,
⁹ he who quarries stones gets hurt by them,
  he who chops wood takes a risk from it.

¹⁰ If, for want of sharpening, the blade is
blunt, you have to work twice as hard; but it is
the outcome that makes wisdom rewarding.

¹¹ If, for want of charming, the snake bites,
  the snake-charmer gets nothing out of it.

¹² The sayings of a sage give pleasure,
  what a fool says procures his own ruin:
¹³ his words have their origin in stupidity
  and their ending in treacherous folly.
¹⁴ A fool talks a great deal,

but none of us in fact can tell the future;
what will happen after us, who can tell?

¹⁵ A fool finds hard work very tiring,
he cannot even find his own way into
town.

¹⁶ Woe to you, country with a lad for king,
and where princes start feasting in the
morning!
¹⁷ Happy the land whose king is nobly born,
where princes eat at a respectable hour
to keep themselves strong and not merely
to revel!

¹⁸ Thanks to idleness, the roof-tree gives
way,
thanks to carelessness, the house lets in the
rain.

¹⁹ We give parties to enjoy ourselves,
wine makes us cheerful
and money has an answer for everything.

²⁰ Do not abuse the king, even in thought,
do not abuse a rich man, even in your
bedroom,
for a bird of the air might carry the news,
a winged messenger might repeat what
you have said.

11

Cast your bread on the water,
eventually you will recover it.
² Offer a share to seven or to eight people,
you can never tell what disaster may occur.
³ When clouds are full of rain,
they will shed it on the earth.
If a tree falls, whether south or north,
where it falls, there it will lie.
⁴ Keep watching the wind and you will
never sow,
keep staring at the clouds and you will
never reap.
⁵ You do not understand how the wind
blows,
or how the embryo grows in a woman's
womb:

no more can you understand the work of
God, the Creator of all.
⁶ In the morning, sow your seed,
until evening, do not cease from labour,
for of any two things you do not know
which will succeed,
or which of the two is the better.

Old age

⁷ How sweet light is,
how delightful it is to see the sun!
⁸ However many years you live,
enjoy them all,
but remember, the days of darkness will be
many:
futility awaits you at the end.

⁹ Young man, enjoy yourself while you are
young,
make the most of the days of your
youth,
follow the prompting and desire of heart
and eye,
but remember, God will call you to
account for everything.
¹⁰ Rid your heart of indignation,
keep your body clear of suffering,
though youth and the age of black hair are
both futile.

12

Remember your Creator while you are
still young,
before the bad days come,
before the years come which, you will say,
give you no pleasure;
² before the sun and the light grow dim
and the moon and stars,
before the clouds return after the rain;
³ the time when your watchmen become
shaky,
when strong men are bent double,
when the women, one by one, quit
grinding,
and, as they look out of the window, find
their sight growing dim.
⁴ When the street-door is kept shut,
when the sound of grinding fades away,

when the first cry of a bird wakes
    you up,
when all the singing has stopped;
⁵ when going uphill is an ordeal
and you are frightened at every step you
    take—
yet the almond tree is in flower
and the grasshopper is weighed down
and the caper-bush loses its tang;
while you are on the way to your
    everlasting home
and the mourners are assembling in the
    street;
⁶ before the silver thread snaps,
or the golden bowl is cracked,
or the pitcher shattered at the fountain,
or the pulley broken at the well-head:
⁷ the dust returns to the earth from which it
    came,
and the spirit returns to God who gave it.

⁸ Sheer futility, Qoheleth says, everything is
futile.

Epilogue *ᵃ*

⁹ Besides being a sage, Qoheleth taught the people what he himself knew, having weighed, studied and emended many proverbs. ¹⁰ Qoheleth took pains to write in an attractive style and by it to convey truths.

¹¹ The sayings of a sage are like goads, like pegs positioned by shepherds: the same shepherd finds a use for both.

¹² Furthermore, my child, you must realise that writing books involves endless hard work, and that much study wearies the body.

¹³ To sum up the whole matter: fear God and keep his commandments, for that is the duty of everyone. ¹⁴ For God will call all our deeds to judgement, all that is hidden, be it good or bad.

12a Not by the same hand as the rest. Perhaps by a disciple with a similar cast of mind.

The Song of

SONGS

1 Solomon's Song of Songs.

BELOVED: ² Let him kiss me with the kisses of
his mouth,
for your love-making is sweeter than wine;
³ delicate is the fragrance of your perfume,
your name is an oil poured out,
and that is why girls love you.

⁴ Draw me in your footsteps, let us run.
The king has brought me into his rooms;
you will be our joy and our gladness.
We shall praise your love more than
wine;
how right it is to love you.

BELOVED: ⁵ I am black but lovely, daughters of
Jerusalem,
like the tents of Kedar,
like the pavilions of Salmah.
⁶ Take no notice of my dark colouring,
it is the sun that has burnt me.
My mother's sons turned their anger
on me,
they made me look after the vineyards.
My own vineyard I had not looked after!

⁷ Tell me then, sweetheart,
where will you lead your flock to graze,
where will you rest it at noon?
That I may no more wander like a
vagabond
beside the flocks of your companions.

CHORUS: ⁸ If you do not know this, O loveliest
of women,
follow the tracks of the flock,
and take your kids to graze
close by the shepherds' tents.

LOVER: ⁹ I compare you, my love,
to my mare harnessed to Pharaoh's chariot.
¹⁰ Your cheeks show fair between their
pendants
and your neck within its necklaces.
¹¹ We shall make you golden earrings
and beads of silver.

DUO: ¹²—While the king rests in his own
room
my nard yields its perfume.
¹³ My love is a sachet of myrrh
lying between my breasts.
¹⁴ My love is a cluster of henna flowers
among the vines of En-Gedi.ᵃ

¹⁵ —How beautiful you are, my beloved,
how beautiful you are!
Your eyes are doves.
¹⁶ —How beautiful you are, my love,
and how you delight me!
Our bed is the greensward.

¹⁷ —The beams of our house are cedar trees,
its panelling the cypress.

2 —I am the rose of Sharon,
the lily of the valleys.

² —As a lily among the thistles,
so is my beloved among girls.

³ —As an apple tree among the trees of the
wood,
so is my love among young men.
In his delightful shade I sit,
and his fruit is sweet to my taste.

1a A fertile oasis of vines and palms on the desolate west
shore of the Dead Sea.

58 READ THE SONG OF SONGS 1:1–4.

Draw me in your footsteps, let us run.—SONG OF SONGS 1:4

DRAWN TO JESUS

Jesus said: "No one can come to me unless drawn by the Father who sent me" (Jn 6:44). . . . And that, no doubt, is why the Holy Spirit, long before the birth of Jesus, dictated this prophetic prayer: "Draw me in your footsteps, let us run." When we ask to be drawn, we are wanting to be closely united with the object which has won our heart. If fire and iron could reason and if the iron said to the fire: "Draw me," that would prove its wish to be so identified with the fire as to share its very substance. Well, that is just what my prayer is. I ask Jesus to draw me into the flames of his love and to unite me so closely to him that he lives and acts in me. I feel that the more the fire of love encompasses my heart, the more I shall say: "Draw me," and the more will those souls who are near to mine (see verse 3, Douay) "run swiftly in the sweet odour of the Beloved." Yes, they will run and we shall run together, for souls on fire cannot stay still. Like Mary, they may sit at the feet of Jesus, listening to his gentle yet exciting words. They seem to give him nothing, yet they give much more than Martha who is anxious "about many things. . . ."

This lesson has been understood by all the saints, perhaps especially by those who have illumined the world with the teaching of the gospels. Was it not in prayer that St. Paul, St. Augustine, St. Thomas Aquinas, St. John of the Cross, St. Teresa, and so many other friends of God found that wonderful knowledge which has enraptured the greatest intellects? Archimedes said: "Give me a fulcrum and with a lever I will move the world." What he could not get, the saints have been given. The Almighty has given them a fulcrum: himself, himself alone. For a lever they have that prayer which burns with the fire of love. Thus they have moved the world, and it is with this lever that those still battling in the world move it and will go on moving it till the end of time.

ST. THÉRÈSE OF LISIEUX, 1873–1897

YOU WILL FIND THE NEXT READING AT SONG OF SONGS 3.

4 He has taken me to his cellar,
and his banner over me is love.
5 Feed me with raisin cakes,
restore me with apples,
for I am sick with love.

6 His left arm is under my head,
his right embraces me.

7 —I charge you,
daughters of Jerusalem,
by all gazelles and wild does,
do not rouse, do not wake my
beloved
before she pleases.

BELOVED: 8 I hear my love.
See how he comes
leaping on the mountains,
bounding over the hills.
9 My love is like a gazelle,
like a young stag.

See where he stands
behind our wall.
He looks in at the window,
he peers through the opening.

10 My love lifts up his voice,
he says to me,
'Come then, my beloved,
my lovely one, come.
11 For see, winter is past,
the rains are over and gone.

12 'Flowers are appearing on the earth.
The season of glad songs has come,
the cooing of the turtledove is heard in our
     land.
13 The fig tree is forming its first figs
and the blossoming vines give out their
          fragrance.
Come then, my beloved,
my lovely one, come.

14 'My dove, hiding in the clefts of the rock,
in the coverts of the cliff,
show me your face,
let me hear your voice;
for your voice is sweet
and your face is lovely.'
15 Catch the foxes for us,
the little foxes
that make havoc of the vineyards,
for our vineyards are in fruit.

16 My love is mine and I am his.
He pastures his flock among the lilies.

17 Before the day-breeze rises,
before the shadows flee, return!
Be, my love, like a gazelle, like a young
          stag,
on the mountains of Bether.

3 On my bed at night I sought
the man who is my sweetheart:
I sought but could not find him!
2 So I shall get up and go through the city;
in the streets and in the squares,

I shall seek my sweetheart.
I sought but could not find him!

3 I came upon the watchmen—
those who go on their rounds in the city:
'Have you seen my sweetheart?'

4 Barely had I passed them
when I found my sweetheart.
I caught him, would not let him go,
not till I had brought him
to my mother's house,
to the room where she conceived me!

LOVER: 5 I charge you,
daughters of Jerusalem,
by gazelles and wild does,
do not rouse, do not wake my beloved
before she pleases.

POET: 6 What is this coming up from the
          desert
like a column of smoke,
breathing of myrrh and frankincense
and every exotic perfume?
7 Here comes Solomon's litter.
Around it are sixty champions,
the flower of the warriors of Israel;
8 all of them skilled swordsmen,
expert in war.
Each man has his sword at his side,
against alarms by night.

9 King Solomon
has had a palanquin made
of wood from Lebanon.
10 He has had the posts made of silver,
the canopy of gold,
the seat of purple;
the centre is inlaid with ebony.

11 Daughters of Zion,
come and see King Solomon,
wearing the diadem with which his
          mother crowned him
on his wedding day,
on the day of his heart's joy.

59 READ THE SONG OF SONGS 3:1–4.

On my bed at night I sought the man who is my sweetheart.—SONG OF SONGS 3:1

THE WAYS OF SEEKING GOD

Traditionally, the church has read the erotic imagery of the Song of Songs as a type of our union with God. So we should not be jarred by the passage's tenderness or by words like "sweetheart." The compiler of St. Gertrude's Revelations *says she understood this selection as a model for seeking God:*

By the opening words of the passage, she understood the first way of seeking God—by the praises and blessings that we offer him in the quietness of contemplation. So the words, "I sought but could not find him," follow immediately because the soul, imprisoned in the flesh, cannot praise God perfectly.

In the words, "in the streets and in the squares I shall seek my sweetheart," she understood the second manner of seeking God. They express the thanksgiving the soul offers God for all his gifts. "I sought but could not find him" is added because we cannot praise God adequately.

By the words, "I came upon the watchmen," she understands the justice and mercy of God that cause the soul to compare her unworthiness to the benefits that God has given her. Then by her grief and repentance for her faults she begins to seek his mercy, saying, "Have you seen my sweetheart?"

And finally, having no faith in her own merits, she turns with humble confidence to the divine mercy. By fervent prayers and the inspiration of grace, she at last finds him whom her heart seeks. She feels her heart deeply moved by all the sweetness of the divine mercy and many other indescribable graces. For this grace communicates to the body as well as to the mind a marvelous glory and brightness. ST. GERTRUDE THE GREAT, 1256–1302

YOU WILL FIND THE NEXT READING AT WISDOM 3.

4 LOVER: How beautiful you are, my beloved,
how beautiful you are!
Your eyes are doves,
behind your veil;
your hair is like a flock of goats
surging down Mount Gilead.
2 Your teeth, a flock of sheep to be shorn
when they come up from the washing.
Each one has its twin,
not one unpaired with another.
3 Your lips are a scarlet thread
and your words enchanting.
Your cheeks, behind your veil,
are halves of pomegranate.
4 Your neck is the Tower of David
built on layers,
hung round with a thousand
bucklers,
and each the shield of a hero.
5 Your two breasts are two fawns,
twins of a gazelle,
that feed among the lilies.

6 Before the day-breeze rises,
before the shadows flee,
I shall go to the mountain of myrrh,
to the hill of frankincense.

7 You are wholly beautiful, my beloved,
  and without a blemish.
8 Come from Lebanon, my promised bride,
  come from Lebanon, come on your way.
  Look down from the heights of Amanus,
  from the crests of Senir and Hermon,
  the haunt of lions,
  the mountains of leopards.

9 You ravish my heart,
  my sister, my promised bride,
  you ravish my heart
  with a single one of your glances,
  with a single link of your necklace.
10 What spells lie in your love,
  my sister, my promised bride!
  How delicious is your love, more delicious
      than wine!
  How fragrant your perfumes,
  more fragrant than all spices!
11 Your lips, my promised bride,
  distil wild honey.
  Honey and milk
  are under your tongue;
  and the scent of your garments
  is like the scent of Lebanon.

12 She is a garden enclosed,
  my sister, my promised bride;
  a garden enclosed,
  a sealed fountain.
13 Your shoots form an orchard of
      pomegranate trees,
  bearing most exquisite fruit:
14 nard and saffron,
  calamus and cinnamon,
  with all the incense-bearing trees;
  myrrh and aloes,
  with the subtlest odours.
15 Fountain of the garden,
  well of living water,
  streams flowing down from Lebanon!

BELOVED: 16 Awake, north wind,
  come, wind of the south!
  Breathe over my garden,
  to spread its sweet smell around.

Let my love come into his garden,
  let him taste its most exquisite fruits.

5 LOVER: I come into my garden,
  my sister, my promised bride,
  I pick my myrrh and balsam,
  I eat my honey and my honeycomb,
  I drink my wine and my milk.

POET: Eat, friends, and drink,
  drink deep, my dearest friends.

BELOVED: 2 I sleep, but my heart is awake.
  I hear my love knocking.
  'Open to me, my sister, my beloved,
  my dove, my perfect one,
  for my head is wet with dew,
  my hair with the drops of night.'

3 —'I have taken off my tunic,
  am I to put it on again?
  I have washed my feet,
  am I to dirty them again?'
4 My love thrust his hand
  through the hole in the door;
  I trembled to the core of my being.
5 Then I got up
  to open to my love,
  myrrh ran off my hands,
  pure myrrh off my fingers,
  on to the handle of the bolt.

6 I opened to my love,
  but he had turned and gone.
  My soul failed at his flight,
  I sought but could not find him,
  I called, but he did not answer.

7 The watchmen met me,
  those who go on their rounds in the city.
  They beat me, they wounded me,
  they took my cloak away from me:
  those guardians of the ramparts!

8 I charge you,
  daughters of Jerusalem,
  if you should find my love,

what are you to tell him?
—That I am sick with love!

CHORUS: 9 What makes your lover better than
    other lovers,
O loveliest of women?
What makes your lover better than other
    lovers,
to put us under such an oath?

BELOVED: 10 My love is fresh and ruddy,
to be known among ten thousand.
11 His head is golden, purest gold,
his locks are palm fronds
and black as the raven.
12 His eyes are like doves
beside the water-courses,
bathing themselves in milk,
perching on a fountain-rim.
13 His cheeks are beds of spices,
banks sweetly scented.
His lips are lilies,
distilling pure myrrh.
14 His hands are golden, rounded,
set with jewels of Tarshish.
His belly a block of ivory
covered with sapphires.
15 His legs are alabaster columns
set in sockets of pure gold.
His appearance is that of Lebanon,
unrivalled as the cedars.
16 His conversation is sweetness itself,
he is altogether lovable.
Such is my love, such is my friend,
O daughters of Jerusalem.

6 CHORUS: Where did your lover go,
O loveliest of women?
Which way did your lover turn
so that we can help you seek him?

BELOVED: 2 My love went down to his garden,
to the beds of spices,
to pasture his flock on the grass
and gather lilies.

3 I belong to my love, and my love to me.
He pastures his flock among the lilies.

LOVER: 4 You are fair as Tirzah,ᵃ my beloved,
enchanting as Jerusalem,
formidable as an army!
5 Turn your eyes away from me,
they take me by assault!
Your hair is like a flock of goats
surging down the slopes of Gilead.
6 Your teeth are like a flock of ewes
as they come up from being washed.
Each one has its twin,
not one unpaired with another.
7 Your cheeks, behind your veil,
are halves of pomegranate.
8 There are sixty queens
and eighty concubines
(and countless girls).
9 My dove is my only one,
perfect and mine.
She is the darling of her mother,
the favourite of the one who bore her.
Girls have seen her and proclaimed her
    blessed,
queens and concubines have sung her
    praises,
10 'Who is this arising like the dawn,
fair as the moon,
resplendent as the sun,
formidable as an army?'

11 I went down to the nut orchard
to see the fresh shoots in the valley,
to see if the vines were budding
and the pomegranate trees in flower.
12 Before I knew . . . my desire had
    hurled me
onto the chariots of Amminadib!ᵇ

7 CHORUS: Come back, come back, girl from
    Shulam,ᵃ
come back, come back, where we can look
    at you!

6a Early capital of the northern kingdom. The name means
'agreeable, pleasant'.

6b Perhaps a mythical figure who rides around on a chariot
interfering in love-affairs.

7a Obscure; it may also be a name derived from Solomon,
'she who belongs to Solomon'.

Why are you looking at the girl from
    Shulam,
dancing between two lines of dancers?

LOVER: ²How beautiful are your feet in their
    sandals,
O prince's daughter!
The curve of your thighs is like the curve
    of a necklace,
work of a master hand.
³ Your navel is a bowl well rounded
    with no lack of wine,
your belly a heap of wheat
surrounded with lilies.
⁴ Your two breasts are two fawns,
    twins of a gazelle.
⁵ Your neck is an ivory tower.
Your eyes, the pools of Heshbon,
by the gate of Bath-Rabbim.
Your nose, the Tower of Lebanon,
sentinel facing Damascus.
⁶ Your head is held high like Carmel,
    and its hair is as dark as purple;
a king is held captive in your tresses.

⁷ How beautiful you are, how charming,
    my love, my delight!
⁸ In stature like the palm tree,
    its fruit-clusters your breasts.
⁹ I have decided, 'I shall climb the palm
    tree,
I shall seize its clusters of dates!'
May your breasts be clusters of grapes,
your breath sweet-scented as apples,
¹⁰ and your palate like sweet wine.

BELOVED: Flowing down the throat of my
    love,
as it runs on the lips of those who sleep.
¹¹ I belong to my love,
    and his desire is for me.

¹² Come, my love,
    let us go to the fields.
We will spend the night in the villages,
¹³ and in the early morning we will go to the
    vineyards.

We will see if the vines are budding,
    if their blossoms are opening,
if the pomegranate trees are in flower.
Then I shall give you
the gift of my love.
¹⁴ The mandrakes yield their fragrance,
    the most exquisite fruits are at our doors;
the new as well as the old,
I have stored them for you, my love.

8 Ah, why are you not my brother,
   nursed at my mother's breast!
Then if I met you out of doors, I could
    kiss you
without people thinking ill of me.
² I should lead you, I should take you into
    my mother's house, and you
    would teach me!
I should give you spiced wine to drink,
juice of my pomegranates.
³ His left arm is under my head
    and his right embraces me.

LOVER: ⁴I charge you,
    daughters of Jerusalem,
do not rouse, do not wake my beloved,
before she pleases!

⁵ Who is this coming up from the desert
    leaning on her lover?

I awakened you under the apple tree,
    where your mother conceived you,
where she who bore you conceived you.

BELOVED: ⁶Set me like a seal on your heart,
    like a seal on your arm.
For love is strong as Death,
passion as relentless as Sheol.
The flash of it is a flash of fire,
a flame of Yahweh himself.
⁷ Love no flood can quench,
    no torrents drown.
Were a man to offer all his family
    wealth
to buy love,
contempt is all that he would gain.

shekels of silver. ¹²But I tend my own vineyard myself. You, Solomon, may have your thousand shekels, and those who oversee its produce their two hundred.

Final additions

¹³You who dwell in the gardens, my companions listen for your voice; let me hear it.

¹⁴Haste away, my love,
be like a gazelle,
a young stag,
on the spice-laden mountains.

Two epigrams

⁸Our sister is little: her breasts are not yet formed. What shall we do for our sister on the day she is spoken for? ⁹If she is a rampart, on the crest we shall build a battlement of silver; if she is a door, we shall board her up with planks of cedar.

¹⁰I am a wall, and my breasts represent its towers. And under their eyes I have found true peace.

¹¹Solomon had a vineyard at Baal-Hamon. He entrusted it to overseers, and each one was to pay him the value of its produce, a thousand

On seeking God and rejecting evil

1 Love uprightness you who are rulers on
     earth,
  be properly disposed towards the Lord
  and seek him in simplicity of heart;
² for he will be found by those who do not
     put him to the test,
  revealing himself to those who do not
     mistrust him.
³ Perverse thoughts, however, separate
     people from God,
  and power, when put to the test,
     confounds the stupid.
⁴ Wisdom will never enter the soul of a
     wrong-doer,
  nor dwell in a body enslaved to sin;
⁵ for the holy spirit of instruction flees
     deceitfulness,
  recoils from unintelligent thoughts,
  is thwarted by the onset of vice.

⁶ Wisdom is a spirit friendly to humanity,
  though she will not let a blasphemer's
     words go unpunished;
  since God observes the very soul
  and accurately surveys the heart,
  listening to every word.
⁷ For the spirit of the Lord fills the world,
  and that which holds everything together
     knows every word said.
⁸ No one who speaks what is wrong will go
     undetected,
  nor will avenging Justice pass by such
     a one.
⁹ For the schemes of the godless will be
     examined,
  and a report of his words will reach the
     Lord

to convict him of his crimes.
¹⁰ There is a jealous ear that overhears
     everything,
  not even a murmur of complaint
     escapes it.
¹¹ So beware of uttering frivolous
     complaints,
  restrain your tongue from finding fault;
  even what is said in secret has
     repercussions,
  and a lying mouth deals death to the soul.

¹² Do not court death by the errors of your
     ways,
  nor invite destruction through the work of
     your hands.
¹³ For God did not make Death,
  he takes no pleasure in destroying the
     living.
¹⁴ To exist—for this he created all things;
  the creatures of the world have health in
     them,
  in them is no fatal poison,
  and Hades has no power over the world:
¹⁵ for uprightness is immortal.

Life as the godless see it

¹⁶ But the godless call for Death with deed
     and word,
  counting him friend, they wear themselves
     out for him;
  with him they make a pact,
  worthy as they are to belong to him.

2 And this is the false argument they use,
  'Our life is short and dreary,
  there is no remedy when our end comes,
  no one is known to have come back from
     Hades.

2 We came into being by chance
and afterwards shall be as though we had
never been.
The breath in our nostrils is a puff of
smoke,
reason a spark from the beating of our
hearts;
3 extinguish this and the body turns to ashes,
and the spirit melts away like the yielding
air.
4 In time, our name will be forgotten,
nobody will remember what we have
done;
our life will pass away like wisps of cloud,
dissolving like the mist
that the sun's rays drive away
and that its heat dispels.
5 For our days are the passing of a shadow,
our end is without return,
the seal is affixed and nobody comes back.

6 'Come then, let us enjoy the good things of
today,
let us use created things with the zest of
youth:
7 take our fill of the dearest wines and
perfumes,
on no account forgo the flowers of spring
8 but crown ourselves with rosebuds before
they wither,
9 no meadow excluded from our orgy;
let us leave the signs of our revelry
everywhere,
since this is our portion, this our lot!
10 'As for the upright man who is poor, let us
oppress him;
let us not spare the widow,
nor respect old age, white-haired with
many years.
11 Let our might be the yardstick of right,
since weakness argues its own futility.
12 Let us lay traps for the upright man, since
he annoys us
and opposes our way of life,
reproaches us for our sins against the Law,
and accuses us of sins against our
upbringing.

13 He claims to have knowledge of God,
and calls himself a child of the Lord.
14 We see him as a reproof to our way of
thinking,
the very sight of him weighs our spirits
down;
15 for his kind of life is not like other
people's,
and his ways are quite different.
16 In his opinion we are counterfeit;
he avoids our ways as he would filth;
he proclaims the final end of the upright as
blessed
and boasts of having God for his father.
17 Let us see if what he says is true,
and test him to see what sort of end he will
have.
18 For if the upright man is God's son, God
will help him
and rescue him from the clutches of his
enemies.
19 Let us test him with cruelty and with
torture,
and thus explore this gentleness of his
and put his patience to the test.
20 Let us condemn him to a shameful death
since God will rescue him—or so he
claims.'

Error of the godless

21 This is the way they reason, but they are
misled,
since their malice makes them blind.
22 They do not know the hidden things of
God,
they do not hope for the reward of
holiness,
they do not believe in a reward for
blameless souls.
23 For God created human beings to be
immortal,
he made them as an image of his own
nature;
24 Death came into the world only through
the Devil's envy,
as those who belong to him find to their
cost.

Destinies of the good and bad compared

3 But the souls of the upright are in the
hands of God,
and no torment can touch them.
2 To the unenlightened, they appeared to
die,
their departure was regarded as disaster,
3 their leaving us like annihilation;
but they are at peace.
4 If, as it seemed to us, they suffered
punishment,
their hope was rich with immortality;
5 slight was their correction, great will their
blessings be.
God was putting them to the test
and has proved them worthy to be with
him;
6 he has tested them like gold in a furnace,
and accepted them as a perfect burnt
offering.
7 At their time of visitation, they will shine
out;
as sparks run through the stubble, so will
they.
8 They will judge nations, rule over
peoples,
and the Lord will be their king for ever.
9 Those who trust in him will understand
the truth,
those who are faithful will live with him in
love;
for grace and mercy await his holy ones,
and he intervenes on behalf of his chosen.

10 But the godless will be duly punished for
their reasoning,
for having neglected the upright and
deserted the Lord.
11 Yes, wretched are they who scorn wisdom
and discipline:
their hope is void,
their toil unavailing,
their achievements unprofitable;
12 their wives are reckless,
their children depraved,
their descendants accursed.

Better be sterile than have godless children

13 Blessed the sterile woman if she be
blameless,
and has not known an unlawful bed,
for she will have fruit at the visitation of
souls.
14 Blessed, too, the eunuch whose hand
commits no crime,
and who harbours no resentment against
the Lord:
a special favour will be granted to him for
his loyalty,
a most desirable portion in the temple of
the Lord.
15 For the fruit of honest labours is glorious,
and the root of understanding does not
decay.
16 But the children of adulterers will not
reach maturity,
the offspring of an unlawful bed will
disappear.
17 Even if they live long, they will count for
nothing,
their old age will go unhonoured at the
last;
18 while if they die early, they have neither
hope
nor comfort on the day of judgement,
19 for the end of a race of evil-doers is harsh.

4 Better to have no children yet to have
virtue,
since immortality perpetuates its memory;
for God and human beings both
recognise it.
2 Present, we imitate it,
absent, we long for it;
crowned, it holds triumph through
eternity,
having striven for untainted prizes and
emerged the victor.
3 But the offspring of the godless come to
nothing, however prolific,
sprung from a bastard stock, they will
never strike deep roots,
never put down firm foundations.

60 READ WISDOM 3:1–12.

If, as it seemed to us, they suffered punishment, their hope was rich with immortality.

—WISDOM 3:4

GOD'S INSCRUTABLE JUSTICE

We are schooled to bear misfortune calmly, for good and bad men without distinction have to bear it; and we set no great store by prosperity, since bad and good men alike may come to enjoy it. So it is that, even in these temporal vicissitudes where God's justice is not apparent, divine revelation must save us from confusion.

We cannot know, for example, what secret decree of God's justice makes this good man poor and that man rich; . . . Here we have an irreligious man in excellent health, there a holy man wasting away to a shadow with disease. . . .

It would be intelligible if there were only some consistency in the seeming senselessness of these arrangements. . . . But not only are the good sometimes unfortunate and the wicked fortunate—a seeming injustice—but, as often as not, bad luck befalls bad men and good luck good men. . . .

Accordingly, even though we cannot understand what kind of divine judgment can positively or even permissively will such inequalities—since God is omnipotent, all-wise, all-just, and in no way weak, rash, or unfair—it is still good for our souls to learn to attach no importance to the good or ill fortune which we see visited without distinction upon the good and the bad. We learn, too, to seek the good things that are meant for the good, and to avoid at all costs the evil things that are fit for the bad.

When, however, we come to that judgment of God the proper name of which is "judgment day" . . . it will be shown plainly how just is that divine decree which makes practically all of God's judgments lie beyond the present understanding of men's minds, even though devout men may know by faith that God's hidden judgments are most surely just. ST. AUGUSTINE, 354–430

YOU WILL FIND THE NEXT READING AT WISDOM 7.

4 They may branch out for a time,
  but, on unsteady foundations, they will be
    rocked by the wind
  and uprooted by the force of the storm;
5 their branches, yet unformed, will be
      snapped off,
  their fruit be useless,
  too unripe to eat,
  fit for nothing.
6 For children begotten of unlawful bed

witness, when put on trial, to their parents'
  wickedness.

The premature death of the upright

7 The upright, though he die before his
    time, will find rest.
8 Length of days is not what makes age
    honourable,
  nor number of years the true measure of
    life;

[805]

9 understanding, this is grey hairs,
untarnished life, this is ripe old age.
10 Having won God's favour, he has been
loved
and, as he was living among sinners, has
been taken away.
11 He has been carried off so that evil may
not warp his understanding
or deceitfulness seduce his soul;
12 for the fascination of evil throws good
things into the shade,
and the whirlwind of desire corrupts a
simple heart.
13 Having come to perfection so soon, he has
lived long;
14 his soul being pleasing to the Lord,
he has hurried away from the wickedness
around him.

Yet people look on, uncomprehending;
and it does not enter their heads
15 that grace and mercy await his
chosen ones
and that he intervenes on behalf of his holy
ones.
16 The upright who dies condemns the
godless who survive,
and youth quickly perfected condemns
the lengthy old age of the wicked.
17 These people see the end of the wise
without understanding what the Lord has
in store
or why he has taken such a one to
safety;
18 they look on and sneer,
but the Lord will laugh at them.
19 Soon they will be corpses without
honour,
objects of horror among the dead
for ever.
For he will shatter them and fling them
headlong and dumbfounded.
He will shake them from their
foundations;
they will be utterly laid waste,
a prey to grief,
and their memory will perish.

The godless called to judgement

20 When the count of their sins has been
drawn up, in terror they will
come,
and their crimes, confronting them, will
accuse them.

5 Then the upright will stand up boldly
to face those who had oppressed him
and had thought so little of his sufferings.
2 And, seeing him, they will be seized with
terrible fear,
amazed that he should have been so
unexpectedly saved.
3 Stricken with remorse, they will say to one
another
with groans and labouring breath,
4 'This is the one whom we used to mock,
making him the butt of our insults, fools
that we were!
His life we regarded as madness,
his ending as without honour.
5 How has he come to be counted as one of
the children of God
and to have his lot among the holy ones?
6 Clearly we have strayed from the way of
truth;
the light of justice has not shone for us,
the sun has not risen for us.
7 We have left no path of lawlessness or ruin
unexplored,
we have crossed deserts where there was
no track,
but the way of the Lord is one we have
never known.
8 What good has arrogance been to us?
What has been the purpose of our riches
and boastfulness?
9 All those things have passed like a
shadow,
passed like a fleeting rumour.
10 Like a ship that cuts through heaving
waves—
leaving no trace to show where it has
passed,
no wake from its keel in the waves.

11 Or like a bird flying through the air—
   leaving no proof of its passing;
   it whips the light air with the stroke of its
      pinions,
   tears it apart in its whirring rush,
   drives its way onward with sweeping
      wing,
   and afterwards no sign is seen of its
      passage.
12 Or like an arrow shot at a mark,
   the pierced air closing so quickly on itself,
   there is no knowing which way the arrow
      has passed.
13 So with us: scarcely born, we disappear;
   of virtue not a trace have we to show,
   we have spent ourselves in our own
      wickedness!'

14 For the hope of the godless is like chaff
      carried on the wind,
   like fine spray driven by the storm;
   it disperses like smoke before the wind,
   goes away like the memory of a one-day
      guest.

*Glorious destiny of the upright and
punishment of the godless*

15 But the upright live for ever,
   their recompense is with the Lord,
   and the Most High takes care of them.
16 So they will receive the glorious crown
   and the diadem of beauty from the Lord's
      hand;
   for he will shelter them with his right
      hand
   and with his arm he will shield them.

17 For armour he will take his jealous love,
   he will arm creation to punish his enemies;
18 he will put on justice as a breastplate,
   and for helmet wear his forthright
      judgement;
19 he will take up invincible holiness for
      shield,
20 of his pitiless wrath he will forge a sword,
   and the universe will march with him to
      fight the reckless.

21 Bolts truly aimed, the shafts of lightning
      will leap,
   and from the clouds, as from a full-drawn
      bow, fly to their mark;
22 and the catapult will hurl hailstones
      charged with fury.
   The waters of the sea will rage against
      them,
   the rivers engulf them without pity,
23 a mighty gale will rise against them
   and winnow them like a hurricane.
   Thus wickedness will lay the whole earth
      waste
   and evil-doing bring down the thrones of
      the mighty.

Kings should seek Wisdom

6 Listen then, kings, and understand;
  rulers of remotest lands, take warning;
2 hear this, you who govern great
      populations,
   taking pride in your hosts of subject
      nations!
3 For sovereignty is given to you by the
      Lord
   and power by the Most High,
   who will himself probe your acts and
      scrutinise your intentions.

4 If therefore, as servants of his kingdom,
      you have not ruled justly
   nor observed the law,
   nor followed the will of God,
5 he will fall on you swiftly and terribly.
   On the highly placed a ruthless judgement
      falls;
6 the lowly are pardoned, out of pity,
   but the mighty will be mightily tormented.
7 For the Lord of all does not cower before
      anyone,
   he does not stand in awe of greatness,
   since he himself has made small and great
   and provides for all alike;
8 but a searching trial awaits those who
      wield power.
9 So, monarchs, my words are meant for
      you,

so that you may learn wisdom and not fall
   into error;
10 for those who in holiness observe holy
      things will be adjudged holy,
and, accepting instruction from them, will
      find their defence in them.
11 Set your heart, therefore, on what I have to
      say,
listen with a will, and you will be
      instructed.

Wisdom sought is Wisdom found

12 Wisdom is brilliant, she never fades.
By those who love her, she is readily seen,
by those who seek her, she is readily found.
13 She anticipates those who desire her by
      making herself known first.
14 Whoever gets up early to seek her will
      have no trouble
but will find her sitting at the door.
15 Meditating on her is understanding in its
      perfect form,
and anyone keeping awake for her will
      soon be free from care.
16 For she herself searches everywhere for
      those who are worthy of her,
benevolently appearing to them on their
      ways,
anticipating their every thought.
17 For Wisdom begins with the sincere desire
      for instruction,
care for instruction means loving her,
18 loving her means keeping her laws,
attention to her laws guarantees
      incorruptibility,
19 and incorruptibility brings us near
      to God;
20 the desire for Wisdom thus leads to
      sovereignty.
21 If then thrones and sceptres delight you,
      monarchs of the nations,
honour Wisdom, so that you may reign for
      ever.

Solomon proposes to describe Wisdom

22 What Wisdom is and how she was born, I
      shall now explain;

I shall hide no mysteries from you,
but shall follow her steps from the outset
      of her origin,
setting out what we know of her in full
      light,
without departing from the truth.
23 Blighting envy is no companion for me,
for envy has nothing in common with
      Wisdom.
24 In the greatest number of the wise lies the
      world's salvation,
in a sagacious king the stability of a people.
25 Learn, therefore, from my words; the gain
      will be yours.

Solomon a man like other men

7 I too am mortal like everyone else,
   a descendant of the first man formed from
      the earth.
I was modelled in flesh inside a mother's
      womb,
2 where, for ten months, in blood I acquired
      substance—
the result of virile seed and pleasure,
      sleep's companion.
3 I too, when I was born, drew in the
      common air,
I fell on the same ground that bears
      us all,
and crying was the first sound I made, like
      everyone else.
4 I was nurtured in swaddling clothes, with
      every care.
5 No king has known any other beginning
      of existence;
6 for there is only one way into life, and one
      way out of it.

Solomon's respect for Wisdom

7 And so I prayed,[a] and understanding was
      given me;
I entreated, and the spirit of Wisdom came
      to me.
8 I esteemed her more than sceptres and
      thrones;

7a cf. 1 K 3:4–14.

compared with her, I held riches as
  nothing.
⁹ I reckoned no precious stone to be her
  equal,
for compared with her, all gold is a pinch
  of sand,
and beside her, silver ranks as mud.
¹⁰ I loved her more than health or
  beauty,
preferred her to the light,
since her radiance never sleeps.
¹¹ In her company all good things came
  to me,
and at her hands incalculable wealth.
¹² All these delighted me, since Wisdom
  brings them,
though I did not then realise that she was
  their mother.
¹³ What I learned diligently, I shall pass on
  liberally,
I shall not conceal how rich she is.
¹⁴ For she is to human beings an
  inexhaustible treasure,
and those who acquire this win God's
  friendship,
commended to him by the gifts of
  instruction.

His appeal for divine inspiration

¹⁵ May God grant me to speak as he would
  wish
and conceive thoughts worthy of the gifts
  I have received,
since he is both guide to Wisdom and
  director of sages;
¹⁶ for we are in his hand, yes, ourselves and
  our sayings,
and all intellectual and all practical
  knowledge.
¹⁷ He it was who gave me sure knowledge
  of what exists,
to understand the structure of the world
  and the action of the elements,
¹⁸ the beginning, end and middle of the
  times,
the alternation of the solstices and the
  succession of the seasons,

¹⁹ the cycles of the year and the position of
  the stars,
²⁰ the natures of animals and the instincts of
  wild beasts,
the powers of spirits and human mental
  processes,
the varieties of plants and the medical
  properties of roots.
²¹ And now I understand everything, hidden
  or visible,
for Wisdom, the designer of all things, has
  instructed me.

Eulogy of Wisdom

²² For within her is a spirit[b]
  intelligent, holy,
unique, manifold, subtle,
mobile, incisive, unsullied,
lucid, invulnerable, benevolent, shrewd,
²³ irresistible, beneficent, friendly to human
  beings,
steadfast, dependable, unperturbed,
almighty, all-surveying,
penetrating all intelligent, pure and most
  subtle spirits.
²⁴ For Wisdom is quicker to move than any
  motion;
she is so pure, she pervades and permeates
  all things.
²⁵ She is a breath of the power of God,
pure emanation of the glory of the
  Almighty;
so nothing impure can find its way into
  her.
²⁶ For she is a reflection of the eternal light,
untarnished mirror of God's active power,
and image of his goodness.

²⁷ Although she is alone, she can do
  everything;
herself unchanging, she renews the
  world,

7b The peak of OT writing on Wisdom (cf. Jb 28; Pr 8:22). The twenty-one qualities show Wisdom originating and participating in God, inseparable from him but working in the world.

and, generation after generation, passing
into holy souls,
she makes them into God's friends and
prophets;
28 for God loves only those who dwell with
Wisdom.
29 She is indeed more splendid than the sun,
she outshines all the constellations;
compared with light, she takes first place,
30 for light must yield to night,
but against Wisdom evil cannot prevail.

8 Strongly she reaches from one end of the
world to the other
and she governs the whole world for its
good.

Solomon's love for Wisdom

2 Wisdom I loved and searched for from my
youth;
I resolved to have her as my bride,
I fell in love with her beauty.
3 She enhances her noble birth by sharing
God's life,
for the Master of All has always loved her.
4 Indeed, she shares the secrets of God's
knowledge,
and she chooses what he will do.
5 If in this life wealth is a desirable
possession,
what is more wealthy than Wisdom whose
work is everywhere?
6 Or if it be the intellect that is at work,
who, more than she, designs whatever
exists?
7 Or if it be uprightness you love,
why, virtues are the fruit of her labours,
since it is she who teaches temperance and
prudence,
justice and fortitude;
nothing in life is more useful for human
beings.
8 Or if you are eager for wide experience,
she knows the past, she forecasts the
future;
she knows how to turn maxims, and solve
riddles;

she has foreknowledge of signs and
wonders,
and of the unfolding of the ages and the
times.

Wisdom indispensable to rulers

9 I therefore determined to take her to share
my life,
knowing that she would be my counsellor
in prosperity
and comfort me in cares and sorrow.
10 'Thanks to her, I shall be admired by the
masses
and honoured, though young, by the
elders.
11 I shall be reckoned shrewd as a judge,
and the great will be amazed at me.
12 They will wait on my silences,
and pay attention when I speak;
if I speak at some length, they will lay
their hand on their lips.
13 By means of her, immortality will be mine,
I shall leave an everlasting memory to my
successors.
14 I shall govern peoples, and nations will be
subject to me;
15 at the sound of my name fearsome despots
will be afraid;
I shall show myself kind to the people and
valiant in battle.

16 'When I go home I shall take my ease with
her,
for nothing is bitter in her company,
when life is shared with her there is no
pain,
nothing but pleasure and joy.'

Solomon prepares to ask for Wisdom

17 Having meditated on all this,
and having come to the conclusion
that immortality resides in kinship with
Wisdom,
18 noble contentment in her friendship,
inexhaustible riches in her activities,
understanding in cultivating her society,
and renown in conversing with her,

61 READ WISDOM 7:7–8:1.

And so I prayed, . . . and the spirit of Wisdom came to me.—WISDOM 7:7

HOW WE ACQUIRE WISDOM

The door to wisdom is a yearning for it and a powerful desire. Hence the Psalm: "You have only to open your mouth for me to fill it" (Ps 81:10). That is the road by which wisdom comes within me . . . and likewise charity. . . .

The manner in which such wisdom is obtained is clearly seen from authority and through examples. As to the former, the Book of Wisdom reads: "For Wisdom begins with the sincere desire for instruction, care for instruction means loving her, loving her means keeping her laws, attention to her laws guarantees incorruptibility, and incorruptibility brings us near to God" (Ws 6:17–19).

But discipline is twofold: scholastic and personal, the latter concerning ethics. And scholastic discipline without personal discipline is insufficient for wisdom. For a person becomes wise not merely by listening: he must also conform. Hence the Psalm on wisdom reads: "Teach me goodness and discipline and knowledge" (see Ps 119:66). . . . So it is through goodness and discipline that knowledge dwells within us. A sick man is not healed by listening to a physician: he must follow the physician's prescription. . . .

The eager desire for discipline gives birth to love. So the proper attention to discipline is love. For if you love discipline, you love virtue in yourself and in others and in its Source. Discipline, however, need not be servile. It may be free, so that it loves the one who imposes it, and acts out of love, not out of fear (see 1 Jn 4:18). If you are poor as a result of discipline, you must love poverty. And the same applies to the other perfections. But love is the observance of the laws. . . . When you keep the law, you are sanctified and filled with the Holy Spirit; and in this you are drawn away from any love that is not God.　　　　　　　　　　　　　　　　　　　　　　　　　ST. BONAVENTURE, 1218–1274

YOU WILL FIND THE NEXT READING AT WISDOM 11.

I went all ways, seeking how to get her.
19 I was a boy of happy disposition,
　　I had received a good soul as my lot,
20 or rather, being good, I had entered an
　　　　undefiled body;
21 but, realising that I could never possess
　　　　Wisdom unless God gave her
　　　　to me,
　　—a sign of intelligence in itself, to know
　　　　in whose gift she lay—
　　I prayed to the Lord and entreated him,
　　and with all my heart I said:

Solomon's prayer[a] for Wisdom

9 'God of our ancestors, Lord of mercy,
　　who by your word have made the
　　　　universe,
2 and in your wisdom have fitted human
　　　　beings
　　to rule the creatures that you have made,
3 to govern the world in holiness and saving
　　　　justice

9a cf. 1 K 3:6–9.

[811]

and in honesty of soul to dispense fair
     judgement,
4 grant me Wisdom, consort of your throne,
   and do not reject me from the number of
     your children.
5 For I am your servant, son of your serving
     maid,
   a feeble man, with little time to live,
   with small understanding of justice and
     the laws.
6 Indeed, were anyone perfect among the
     sons of men,
   if he lacked the Wisdom that comes from
     you, he would still count for
     nothing.

7 'You have chosen me to be king over your
     people,
   to be judge of your sons and daughters.
8 You have bidden me build a temple on
     your holy mountain,
   and an altar in the city where you have
     pitched your tent,
   a copy of the holy Tent which you
     prepared at the beginning.
9 With you is Wisdom, she who knows your
     works,
   she who was present when you made the
     world;
   she understands what is pleasing in your
     eyes
   and what agrees with your
     commandments.
10 Despatch her from the holy heavens,
   send her forth from your throne of glory
   to help me and to toil with me
   and teach me what is pleasing to you;
11 since she knows and understands
     everything
   she will guide me prudently in my actions
   and will protect me with her glory.
12 Then all I do will be acceptable,
   I shall govern your people justly
   and be worthy of my father's throne.

13 'What human being indeed can know the
     intentions of God?

And who can comprehend the will of the
     Lord?
14 For the reasoning of mortals is inadequate,
   our attitudes of mind unstable;
15 for a perishable body presses down the soul,
   and this tent of clay weighs down the
     mind with its many cares.
16 It is hard enough for us to work out what
     is on earth,
   laborious to know what lies within our
     reach;
   who, then, can discover what is in the
     heavens?
17 And who could ever have known your
     will, had you not given Wisdom
   and sent your holy Spirit from above?
18 Thus have the paths of those on earth been
     straightened
   and people have been taught what pleases
     you,
   and have been saved, by Wisdom.'

From Adam to Moses[a]

10 It was Wisdom who protected the first
     man to be fashioned,
   the father of the world, who had been
     created all alone,
   she it was who rescued him from his fall
2 and gave him the strength to subjugate all
     things.
3 But when in his wrath a wicked man
     deserted her,
   he perished in his fratricidal fury.

4 When because of him the earth was
     drowned, it was Wisdom again
     who saved it,
   piloting the upright man on valueless
     timber.
5 Again, when, concurring in wickedness,
     the nations had been thrown into
     confusion,
   she singled out the upright man, preserved
     him blameless before God

10a v. 1 Adam, v. 3 Cain, v. 4 Noah, v. 5 Abraham, v. 6 Lot,
v. 10 Jacob, v. 13 Joseph.

and fortified him against pity for his child.

⁶ She it was who, while the godless perished,
    saved the upright man
as he fled from the fire raining down on
    the Five Cities,

⁷ in witness against whose evil ways
a desolate land still smokes,
where plants bear fruit that never ripens
and where, monument to an unbelieving
    soul, there stands a pillar of salt.

⁸ For, by ignoring the path of Wisdom,
not only did they suffer the loss of not
    knowing the good,
but they left the world a memorial to their
    folly,
so that their offences could not pass
    unnoticed.

⁹ But Wisdom delivered her servants from
    their ordeals.

¹⁰ The upright man, fleeing from the anger
    of his brother,
was led by her along straight paths.
She showed him the kingdom of God
and taught him the knowledge of holy
    things.
She brought him success in his labours
and gave him full return for all his
    efforts;

¹¹ she stood by him against grasping and
    oppressive men
and she made him rich.

¹² She preserved him from his enemies
and saved him from the traps they set for
    him.
In an arduous struggle she awarded him
    the prize,
to teach him that piety is stronger than all.

¹³ She did not forsake the upright man when
    he was sold,
but snatched him away from sin;

¹⁴ she accompanied him down into the pit,
nor did she abandon him in his chains
until she had brought him the sceptre of a
    kingdom
and authority over his despotic masters,

thus exposing as liars those who had
    traduced him,
and giving him honour everlasting.

The Exodus

¹⁵ It was Wisdom who delivered a holy
    people,
a blameless race, from a nation of
    oppressors.

¹⁶ She entered the soul of a servant of the
    Lord,
and withstood fearsome kings with
    wonders and signs.

¹⁷ To the holy people she gave the wages of
    their labours;
she guided them by a marvellous road,
herself their shelter by day—
and their starlight through the night.

¹⁸ She brought them across the Red Sea,
leading them through an immensity of
    water,

¹⁹ whereas she drowned their enemies,
then spat them out from the depths of the
    abyss.

²⁰ So the upright despoiled the godless;
Lord, they extolled your holy name,
and with one accord praised your
    protecting hand;

²¹ for Wisdom opened the mouths of the
    dumb
and made eloquent the tongues of babes.

11 She made their actions successful, by
    means of a holy prophet.

² They journeyed through an unpeopled
    desert
and pitched their tents in inaccessible
    places.

³ They stood firm against their enemies,
fought off their foes.

First antithesis: miracle of the water

⁴ On you they called when they were thirsty,
and from the rocky cliff water was given
    them,
from hard stone a remedy for their
    thirst.

5 Thus, what had served to punish their
enemies
became a benefit for them in their
difficulties.
6 Whereas their enemies had only the ever-
flowing source
of a river fouled with mingled blood and
mud,
7 to punish them for their decree of
infanticide,
you gave your people, against all hope,
water in abundance,
8 once you had shown by the thirst that they
were experiencing
how severely you were punishing their
enemies.
9 From their own ordeals, which were only
loving correction,
they realised how an angry sentence was
tormenting the godless;
10 for you had tested your own as a father
admonishes,
but the others you had punished as a
pitiless king condemns,
11 and, whether far or near, they were
equally afflicted.
12 For a double sorrow seized on them,
and a groaning at the memory of the past;
13 when they learned that the punishments
they were receiving
were beneficial to the others, they realised
it was the Lord,
14 while for the man whom long before they
had exposed and later mockingly
rebuffed,
they felt only admiration when all was
done,
having suffered a thirst so different from
that of the upright.

God's forbearance with Egypt

15 For their foolish and wicked notions
which led them astray
into worshipping mindless reptiles and
contemptible beetles,
you sent a horde of mindless animals to
punish them

16 and to teach them that the agent of sin is
the agent of punishment.
17 And indeed your all-powerful hand which
created
the world from formless matter, did not
lack means
to unleash a horde of bears or savage lions
on them
18 or unknown beasts, newly created, full of
rage,
breathing out fire,
or puffing out stinking smoke,
or flashing fearful sparks from their eyes,
19 beasts able not only to destroy them, being
so savage,
but even to strike them dead by their
terrifying appearance.
20 However, without these, one breath could
have blown them over,
pursued by Justice,
whirled away by the breath of your
power.
You, however, ordered all things by
measure, number and weight.

This forbearance explained

21 For your great power is always at your
service,
and who can withstand the might of your
arm?
22 The whole world, for you, can no more
than tip a balance,
like a drop of morning dew falling on the
ground.
23 Yet you are merciful to all, because you are
almighty,
you overlook people's sins, so that they can
repent.
24 Yes, you love everything that exists,
and nothing that you have made disgusts
you,
since, if you had hated something, you
would not have made it.
25 And how could a thing subsist, had you
not willed it?
Or how be preserved, if not called forth by
you?

62 READ WISDOM 11:21–12:2.

You overlook people's sins, so that they can repent.—WISDOM 11:23

GOD'S LOVE FOR SINNERS

Consider God's patience in waiting for sinners to return to him. Ah, sinners! Who could ever bear what God has endured from you? If you had offended your best friends or your parents to the degree that you have offended God, they surely would have sought revenge. When you insulted the Lord, he was able to chastise you. You repeated the insult, and he did not punish your guilt, but preserved your life and sustained it. He pretended not to see the injuries you offered him so that you might return to your senses and stop offending him. "You overlook people's sins, so that they can repent."

But how, O Lord, is it that you cannot see a single sin and that you silently endure so many? "Your eyes are too pure to rest on evil, you cannot look on at oppression. Why do you look on at those who play the traitor, why say nothing while the wicked swallows someone more upright than himself?" (Hab 1:13). You see the vindictive prefer their own honor to yours. You see the unjust, instead of restoring what they have stolen continuing to steal; the unchaste, instead of being ashamed of their impurities bragging about them; the scandalous, not content with their own sins trying to draw others into rebellion against you. You see all this and hold your peace and do not inflict vengeance.

God waits for sinners that they may one day repent, and that after their repentance, he may pardon and forgive them. "As I live—declares the Lord Yahweh—I do not take pleasure in the death of the wicked but in the conversion of the wicked who changes his ways and saves his life" (Ezk 33:11).

ST. ALPHONSUS LIGUORI, 1696–1787

YOU WILL FIND THE NEXT READING AT WISDOM 13.

26 No, you spare all, since all is yours, Lord,
    lover of life!

12 For your imperishable spirit is in
    everything!
2 And thus, gradually, you correct those
    who offend;
you admonish and remind them of how
    they have sinned,
so that they may abstain from evil and
    trust in you, Lord.

God's forbearance with Canaan

3 The ancient inhabitants of your holy
    land
4 you hated for their loathsome practices,
their acts of sorcery, and unholy rites.
5 Those ruthless murderers of children,
those eaters of entrails at feasts of human
    flesh and of blood,
those initiates of secret brotherhoods,
6 those murderous parents of defenceless
    beings,
you determined to destroy at our
    ancestors' hands,
7 so that this land, dearer to you than any
    other,
might receive a worthy colony of God's
    children.

8 Even so, since these were human, you
    treated them leniently,

sending hornets as forerunners of your
army,
to exterminate them little by little.
⁹ Not that you were unable to hand the
godless over to the upright in
pitched battle
or destroy them at once by savage beasts or
one harsh word;
¹⁰ but, by carrying out your sentences
gradually, you gave them a chance
to repent,
although you knew that they were
inherently evil,
innately wicked,
¹¹ and fixed in their cast of mind;
for they were a race accursed from the
beginning.

This forbearance explained

Nor was it from awe of anyone that you let
their sins go unpunished.
¹² For who is there to ask, 'What have you
done?'
Or who is there to disagree with your
sentence?
Who to arraign you for destroying
nations which you have
created?
Who to confront you by championing the
wicked?
¹³ For there is no god, other than you, who
cares for every one,
to whom you have to prove that your
sentences have been just.
¹⁴ No more could any king or despot
challenge you over those whom
you have punished.
¹⁵ For, being upright yourself, you rule the
universe uprightly,
and hold it as incompatible with your
power
to condemn anyone who has not deserved
to be punished.
¹⁶ For your strength is the basis of your
saving justice,
and your sovereignty over all makes you
lenient to all.

¹⁷ You show your strength when people will
not believe in your absolute power,
and you confound any insolence in those
who do know it.
¹⁸ But you, controlling your strength, are
mild in judgement, and govern us
with great lenience,
for you have only to will, and your power
is there.

God's lessons for Israel

¹⁹ By acting thus, you have taught your
people
that the upright must be kindly to his
fellows,
and you have given your children the good
hope
that after sins you will grant repentance.
²⁰ For, if with such care and indulgence you
have punished
your children's enemies, though doomed
to death,
and have given them time and place to be
rid of their wickedness,
²¹ with what exact attention have you not
judged your children,
to whose ancestors, by oaths and
covenants, you made such
generous promises?
²² Thus, you instruct us, when you punish
our enemies in moderation,
that we should reflect on your kindness
when we judge,
and, when we are judged, we should look
for mercy.

Progressive punishment of the Egyptians

²³ And this is why people leading foolish and
wicked lives
were tortured by you with their own
abominations;
²⁴ for they had strayed too far on the paths of
error
by taking the vilest and most despicable of
animals for gods,
being deluded like silly little children.
²⁵ So, as to children with no sense,

you gave them a sentence making fools
of them.
26 Those, however, who would not take
warning from a mocking
reproof
were soon to endure a sentence worthy
of God.
27 The creatures that made them suffer and
against which they protested,
those very creatures that they had taken
for gods and by which they were
punished they saw in their true
light;
and he whom hitherto they had refused to
know, they realised was true God.
And this is why the final condemnation
fell on them.

Indictment of idolatry: the deification of nature

13 Yes, naturally stupid are all who are
unaware of God,
and who, from good things seen, have not
been able to discover Him-who-is,
or, by studying the works, have not
recognised the Artificer.
2 Fire, however, or wind, or the swift air,
the sphere of the stars, impetuous water,
heaven's lamps,
are what they have held to be the gods
who govern the world.

3 If, charmed by their beauty, they have
taken these for gods,
let them know how much the Master of
these excels them,
since he was the very source of beauty that
created them.
4 And if they have been impressed by their
power and energy,
let them deduce from these how much
mightier is he that has formed
them,
5 since through the grandeur and beauty of
the creatures
we may, by analogy, contemplate their
Author.

6 Small blame, however, attaches to them,
for perhaps they go astray
only in their search for God and their
eagerness to find him;
7 familiar with his works, they investigate
them
and fall victim to appearances, seeing so
much beauty.
8 But even so, they have no excuse:
9 if they are capable of acquiring enough
knowledge
to be able to investigate the world,
how have they been so slow to find its
Master?

The cult of idols

10 But wretched are they, with their hopes set
on dead things,
who have given the title of gods to human
artefacts,
gold or silver, skilfully worked,
figures of animals,
or useless stone, carved by some hand long
ago.

11 Take a woodcutter. He fells a suitable tree,
neatly strips off the bark all over
and then with admirable skill
works the wood into an object useful in
daily life.
12 The bits left over from his work
he uses for cooking his food, then eats his
fill.
13 There is still a good-for-nothing bit left
over,
a gnarled and knotted billet:
he takes it and whittles it with the
concentration of his leisure hours,
he shapes it with the skill of experience,
he gives it a human shape
14 or perhaps he makes it into some vile
animal,
smears it with ochre, paints its surface red,
coats over all its blemishes.
15 He next makes a worthy home for it,
lets it into the wall, fixes it with an iron
clamp.

63 READ WISDOM 13:1–9.

Through the grandeur and beauty of the creatures we may, by analogy, contemplate their Author.—WISDOM 13:5

THE REASONABLENESS OF FAITH

By the greatness of his works and the beauty of the things that he has made we rightly discern the Creator of worlds. The Creator of great things is supreme in greatness, of beautiful things, supreme in beauty. Since the work transcends our thoughts, the Maker must transcend all thought. Thus heaven and air and earth and seas are fair. Fair also the whole universe. . . . But if our thought can estimate this beauty of the universe by a natural instinct . . . must we not recognize the Lord of this universal beauty as himself most beautiful amid all the beauty that surrounds him? We must confess that God is most beautiful, and that with a beauty which, though it transcend our comprehension, forces itself upon our perception.

Thus my mind, full of these results which by its own reflection and the teaching of Scripture it had attained, rested with assurance, as on some peaceful watch-tower, upon that glorious conclusion. It recognized that its true nature made it capable of one homage to its Creator, and of none other. . . . That is, the homage of conviction that his is a greatness too vast for our comprehension but not for our faith. For a reasonable faith is akin to reason and accepts its aid, even though that same reason cannot cope with the vastness of eternal Omnipotence.

Beneath all these thoughts lay an instinctive hope . . . in the reward of some perfect blessedness to be earned by devotion to God and upright living. . . . For true faith in God would pass unrewarded, if the soul be destroyed by death. . . . Even unaided reason pleaded that it was unworthy of God to usher man into an existence that has some share of his thought and wisdom, only to await the sentence of life withdrawn and of eternal death. . . . For, on the only rational theory of creation, its purpose was that things non-existent should come into being, not that things existing should cease to be.

ST. HILARY OF POITIERS, 315?–368?

YOU WILL FIND THE NEXT READING AT ECCLESIASTICUS 1.

16 Thus he makes sure that it will not fall
    down—
   being well aware that it cannot help
    itself,
   since it is only an image, and needs to be
    helped.
17 And yet, if he wishes to pray for his goods,
    for his marriage, for his children,
   he does not blush to harangue this lifeless
    thing—

for health, he invokes what is weak,
18 for life, he pleads with what is dead,
   for help, he goes begging to total
    inexperience,
   for a journey, what cannot even use its
    feet,
19 for profit, an undertaking, and success in
    pursuing his craft,
   he asks skill from something whose hands
    have no skill whatever.

14 Or someone else, taking ship to cross
the wild waves,
loudly invokes a piece of wood[a] frailer
than the vessel that bears him.
2 Agreed, the ship is the product of a
craving for gain,
its building embodies the wisdom of the
shipwright;
3 but your providence, Father, is what
steers it,
you having opened a pathway even
through the sea,
and a safe way over the waves,
4 showing that you can save, whatever
happens,
so that, even without experience, someone
may put to sea.
5 It is not your will that the works of your
Wisdom should be sterile,
so people entrust their lives to the smallest
piece of wood,
cross the waves on a raft, yet are kept safe
and sound.
6 Why, in the beginning, when the proud
giants were perishing,
the hope of the world took refuge on a raft
and, steered by your hand, preserved the
seed of a new generation for the
ages to come.

7 For blessed is the wood which serves the
cause of uprightness
8 but accursed the man-made idol, yes, it
and its maker,
he for having made it, and it because,
though perishable, it has been
called god.
9 For God holds the godless and his
godlessness in equal hatred;
10 both work and workman will alike be
punished.
11 Hence even the idols of the nations will
have a visitation
since, in God's creation, they have become
an abomination,
a scandal for human souls,
a snare for the feet of the foolish.

Origin of the cult of idols

12 The idea of making idols was the origin of
fornication,
their discovery corrupted life.
13 They did not exist at the beginning, they
will not exist for ever;
14 human vanity brought them into the
world,
and a quick end is therefore reserved for
them.
15 A father afflicted by untimely mourning
has an image made of his child so soon
carried off,[b]
and now pays divine honours to what
yesterday was only a corpse,
handing on mysteries and ceremonies to
his people;
16 time passes, the custom hardens and is
observed as law.
17 Rulers were the ones who ordered that
statues should be worshipped:
people who could not honour them in
person, because they lived too far
away,
would have a portrait made of their
distant countenance,
to have an image that they could see of the
king whom they honoured;
meaning, by such zeal, to flatter the absent
as if he were present.
18 Even people who did not know him
were stimulated into spreading his cult by
the artist's enthusiasm;
19 for the latter, doubtless wishing to please
his ruler,
exerted all his skill to surpass the reality,
20 and the crowd, attracted by the beauty of
the work,
mistook for a god someone whom recently
they had honoured as a man.
21 And this became a snare for life:
that people, whether enslaved by
misfortune or by tyranny,

14a A ship's figurehead.
14b The Gk custom of giving the dead divine rank.

[819]

should have conferred the ineffable Name
    on sticks and stones.

The consequences of idolatry

22 It is not enough, however, for them to
    have such misconceptions about
    God;
  for, living in the fierce warfare of
    ignorance,
  they call these terrible evils peace.
23 With their child-murdering rites, their
    occult mysteries,
  or their frenzied orgies with outlandish
    customs,
24 they no longer retain any purity in their
    lives or their marriages,
  one treacherously murdering another or
    wronging him by adultery.
25 Everywhere a welter of blood and murder,
    theft and fraud,
  corruption, treachery, riot, perjury,
26 disturbance of decent people, forgetfulness
    of favours,
  pollution of souls, sins against nature,
  disorder in marriage, adultery and
    debauchery.
27 For the worship of idols with no name
  is the beginning, cause, and end of every
    evil.
28 For these people either carry their
    merrymaking to the point of
    frenzy,
  or they prophesy what is not true, or they
    live wicked lives,
  or they perjure themselves without
    hesitation;
29 since they put their trust in lifeless
    idols
  they do not reckon their false oaths can
    harm them.

30 But they will be justly punished for this
    double crime:
  for degrading the concept of God by
    adhering to idols;
  and for wickedly perjuring themselves in
    contempt for what is holy.

31 For it is not the power of the things by
    which they swear
  but the punishment reserved for sinners
  that always follows the offences of wicked
    people.

Israel not idolatrous

15 But you, our God, are kind and true,
  slow to anger, governing the universe
    with mercy.
2 Even if we sin, we are yours, since we
    acknowledge your power,
  but we will not sin, knowing we count as
    yours.
3 To know you is indeed the perfect
    virtue,
  and to know your power is the root of
    immortality.
4 We have not been duped by inventions of
    misapplied human skill,
  or by the sterile work of painters,
  by figures daubed with assorted colours,
5 the sight of which sets fools yearning
  and hankering for the lifeless form of an
    unbreathing image.
6 Lovers of evil and worthy of such hopes
  are those who make them, those who want
    them and those who worship
    them.

The makers of idols are fools

7 Take a potter, now, laboriously working
    the soft earth,
  shaping each object for us to use.
  Out of the self-same clay,
  he models vessels intended for a noble use
  and those for a contrary purpose, all alike:
  but which of these two uses each will have
  is for the potter himself to decide.
8 Then—ill-spent effort!—from the same
    clay he models a futile god,
  although so recently made out of earth
    himself
  and shortly to return to what he was taken
    from,
  when asked to give back the soul that has
    been lent to him.

⁹ Even so, he does not worry about having
    to die
or about the shortness of his life,
but strives to outdo the goldsmiths and
    silversmiths,
imitates the bronzeworkers,
and prides himself on modelling
    counterfeits.
¹⁰ Ashes, his heart;
more vile than earth, his hope;
more wretched than clay, his life!
¹¹ For he has misconceived the One who has
    modelled him,
who breathed an active soul into him
and inspired a living spirit.
¹² What is more, he looks on this life of ours
    as a kind of game,
and our time here like a fair, full of
    bargains.
'However foul the means,' he says, 'a man
    must make a living.'
¹³ He, more than any other, knows he is
    sinning,
he who from one earthy stuff makes both
    brittle pots and idols.

The folly of the Egyptians: their indiscriminate idolatry

¹⁴ But most foolish, more pitiable even than
    the soul of a little child,
are the enemies who once played the
    tyrant with your people,
¹⁵ and have taken all the idols of the heathen
    for gods;
these can use neither their eyes for
    seeing
nor their nostrils for breathing the air
nor their ears for hearing
nor the fingers on their hands for
    handling
nor their feet for walking.
¹⁶ They have been made, you see, by a
    human being,
modelled by a being whose own breath is
    borrowed.
No man can model a god to resemble
    himself;

¹⁷ subject to death, his impious hands can
    produce
only something dead.
He himself is worthier than the things he
    worships;
he will at least have lived, but never
    they.
¹⁸ And they worship even the most
    loathsome of animals,
worse than the rest in their degree of
    stupidity,
¹⁹ without a trace of beauty—if that is what
    is attractive in animals—
and excluded from God's praises and
    blessing.

Second antithesis: frogs and quails

16 Thus they were appropriately
    punished by similar creatures
and tormented by swarms of vermin.
² In contrast to this punishment, you did
    your people a kindness
and, to satisfy their sharp appetite,
provided quails—a luscious rarity—for
    them to eat.
³ Thus the Egyptians,
at the repulsive sight of the creatures sent
    against them,
were to find that, though they longed for
    food,
they had lost their natural appetite;
whereas your own people, after a short
    privation,
were to have a rare relish for their
    portion.
⁴ Inevitable that relentless want should seize
    on the former oppressors;
enough for your people to be shown
how their enemies were being tortured.

Third antithesis: locusts and bronze serpent

⁵ Even when the fearful rage of wild
    animals overtook them
and they were perishing from the bites of
    writhing snakes,
your retribution did not continue to the
    end.

⁶ Affliction struck them briefly, by way of
  warning,
and they had a saving token*a* to remind
  them of the commandment of
  your Law,
⁷ for whoever turned to it was saved, not by
  what he looked at,
but by you, the Saviour of all.
⁸ And by such means you proved to our
  enemies
that you are the one who delivers from
  every evil;
⁹ for them, the bites of locusts and flies
  proved fatal
and no remedy could be found to save
  their lives,
since they deserved to be punished by such
  creatures.

¹⁰ But your children,
not even the fangs of poisonous snakes
  could bring them down;
for your mercy came to their help and
  cured them.
¹¹ One sting—how quickly healed!—
to remind them of your pronouncements
rather than that, by sinking into deep
  forgetfulness,
they should be cut off from your kindness.
¹² No herb, no poultice cured them,
but your all-healing word, Lord.

¹³ Yes, you are the one with power over life
  and death,
bringing to the gates of Hades and back
  again.
¹⁴ A human being out of malice may put to
  death,
but cannot bring the departed spirit back
or free the soul that Hades has once
  received.

Fourth antithesis: hail and manna

¹⁵ It is not possible to escape your hand.
¹⁶ The godless who refused to acknowledge
  you
were scourged by the strength of your arm,

pursued by no ordinary rains, hail and
  unrelenting downpours,
and consumed by fire.
¹⁷ Even more wonderful, in the water—
  which quenches all—
the fire*b* raged fiercer than ever;
for the elements fight for the upright.
¹⁸ At one moment, the fire would die down,
to avoid consuming the animals sent
  against the godless
and to make clear to them by that sight,
  that the sentence of God was
  pursuing them;
¹⁹ at another, in the very heart of the water, it
  would burn more fiercely than fire
to ruin the produce of a wicked land.
²⁰ How differently with your people! You
  gave them the food of angels,
from heaven untiringly providing them
  bread already prepared,
containing every delight, to satisfy every
  taste.
²¹ And the substance you gave
showed your sweetness towards your
  children,
for, conforming to the taste of whoever
  ate it,
it transformed itself into what each eater
  wished.
²² Snow and ice endured the fire, without
  melting;
this was to show them that, to destroy the
  harvests of their enemies,
fire would burn even in hail and flare in
  falling rain,
²³ whereas, on the other hand, it would even
  forget its own strength
in the service of feeding the upright.

²⁴ For the creation, being at the service of
  you, its Creator,
tautens to punish the wicked
and slackens for the benefit of those who
  trust in you.

16a The bronze snake, Nb 21:4–9.

16b cf. the lightning of Ex 9:24.

25 And this is why, by changing into all things,
    it obediently served your all-nourishing
        bounty,
  conforming to the wishes of those who
        were in need;
26 so that your beloved children, Lord, might
        learn
  that the various crops are not what provide
        nourishment,
  but your word which preserves all who
        believe in you.
27 For that which fire could not destroy
  melted in the heat of a single fleeting
        sunbeam,
28 to show that, to give you thanks, we must
      rise before the sun
  and meet you at the dawning of the day;
29 whereas the hope of the ungrateful melts
       like winter frost
  and flows away like water running to
       waste.

Fifth antithesis: darkness and pillar of fire[a]

17 Yes, your judgements are great and
      impenetrable,
  which is why uninstructed souls have gone
       astray.
2 While the wicked supposed they had a
      holy nation in their power,
  they themselves lay prisoners of the dark,
      in the fetters of long night,
  confined under their own roofs, banished
      from eternal providence.
3 While they thought to remain unnoticed
      with their secret sins,
  curtained by dark forgetfulness,
  they were scattered in fearful dismay,
  terrified by apparitions.
4 The hiding place sheltering them could
      not ward off their fear;
  terrifying noises echoed round them;
  and gloomy, grim-faced spectres haunted
      them.
5 No fire had power enough to give them
      light,
  nor could the brightly blazing stars
  illuminate that dreadful night.

6 The only light for them was a great,
      spontaneous blaze—
  a fearful sight to see!
  And in their terror, once that sight had
      vanished,
  they thought what they had seen more
      terrible than ever.
7 Their magical illusions were powerless
      now,
  and their claims to intelligence were
      ignominiously confounded;
8 for those who promised to drive out fears
      and disorders from sick souls
  were now themselves sick with ludicrous
      fright.
9 Even when there was nothing frightful to
      scare them,
  the vermin creeping past and the hissing
      of reptiles filled them with
      panic;
10 they died convulsed with fright,
  refusing even to look at empty air, which
      cannot be eluded anyhow!
11 Wickedness is confessedly very cowardly,
      and it condemns itself;
  under pressure from conscience it always
      assumes the worst.
12 Fear, indeed, is nothing other
  than the failure of the help offered by
      reason;
13 the less you rely within yourself on this,
  the more alarming it is not to know the
      cause of your suffering.
14 And they, all locked in the same sleep,
  while that darkness lasted—which was in
      fact quite powerless
  and had issued from the depths of equally
      powerless Hades—
15 were now chased by monstrous
      spectres,
  now paralysed by the fainting of their
      souls;
  for a sudden, unexpected terror had
      attacked them.

17a cf. Ex 10:21–23. It is here supposed that darkness came
on some while light continued for others.

16 And thus, whoever it might be that fell
    there
stayed clamped to the spot in this prison
    without bars.
17 Whether he was ploughman or
    shepherd,
or somebody at work in the desert,
he was still overtaken and suffered the
    inevitable fate,
for all had been bound by the one same
    chain of darkness.
18 The soughing of the wind,
the tuneful noise of birds in the spreading
    branches,
the measured beat of water in its powerful
    course,
the headlong din of rocks cascading down,
19 the unseen course of bounding animals,
the roaring of the most savage of wild
    beasts,
the echo rebounding from the clefts in the
    mountains,
all held them paralysed with fear.
20 For the whole world shone with the light
    of day
and, unhindered, went about its work;
21 over them alone there spread a heavy
    darkness,
image of the dark that would receive
    them.
But heavier than the darkness was the
    burden they were to themselves.

18 For your holy ones, however, there was
    a very great light.
The Egyptians, who could hear them but
    not see them,
called them fortunate because they had not
    suffered too;
2 they thanked them for doing no injury in
    return for previous wrongs
and asked forgiveness for their past ill-
    will.
3 In contrast to the darkness, you gave your
    people a pillar of blazing fire
to guide them on their unknown journey,
a mild sun for their ambitious migration.

4 But well those others deserved to be
    deprived of light
and imprisoned in darkness,
for they had kept in captivity your children,
by whom the incorruptible light of the
    Law was to be given to the world.

*Sixth antithesis: night of bereavement and
night of deliverance*

5 As they had resolved to kill the infants of
    the holy ones,
and as of those exposed only one child had
    been saved,
you punished them by carrying off their
    horde of children
and by destroying them all in the wild
    water.
6 That night had been known in advance to
    our ancestors,
so that, well knowing him in whom they
    had put their trust, they would be
    sure of his promises.
7 Your people thus were waiting
both for the rescue of the upright and for
    the ruin of the enemy;
8 for by the very vengeance that you exacted
    on our adversaries,
you glorified us by calling us to you.
9 So the holy children of the good offered
    sacrifice in secret
and with one accord enacted this holy law:
that the holy ones should share good
    things and dangers alike;
and forthwith they chanted the hymns of
    the ancestors.

10 In echo came the discordant cries of their
    enemies,
and the pitiful wails of people mourning
    for their children
could be heard from far away.
11 One and the same punishment had struck
    slave and master alike,
and now commoner and king had the
    same sufferings to endure.
12 Struck by the same death, all had
    innumerable dead.

There were not enough living left to bury
    them,
for, at one stroke, the flower of their
    offspring had perished.
13 Those whose spells had made them
        completely incredulous,
when faced with the destruction of their
    first-born,
acknowledged this people to be child of
    God.

14 When peaceful silence lay over all,
    and night had run the half of her swift
        course,
15 down from the heavens, from the royal
        throne,
leapt your all-powerful Word
like a pitiless warrior into the heart of a
    land doomed to destruction.
Carrying your unambiguous command
    like a sharp sword,
16 it stood, and filled the universe with death;
though standing on the earth, it touched
    the sky.
17 Immediately, dreams and gruesome
        visions
overwhelmed them with terror,
unexpected fears assailed them.
18 Hurled down, some here, some there, half
    dead,
they were able to say why they were dying;
19 for the dreams that had troubled them
had warned them why beforehand,
so that they should not perish without
    knowing why they were being
        afflicted.

Threat of annihilation in the desert

20 Experience of death, however, touched the
        upright too,
and a great many were struck down in the
        desert.
But the Retribution did not last long,
21 for a blameless man hurried to their
        defence.
Wielding the weapons of his sacred office,
prayer and expiating incense,

he confronted Retribution and put an end
    to the plague,
thus showing that he was your servant.
22 He overcame Hostility, not by physical
        strength,
nor by force of arms;
but by word he prevailed over the
        Punisher,
by recalling the oaths made to the Fathers,
    and the covenants.
23 Already the corpses lay piled in heaps,
when he interposed and beat Retribution
        back
and cut off its approach to the living.
24 For the whole world was on his flowing
        robe,
the glorious names of the Fathers
        engraved on the four rows of
        stones,
and your Majesty on the diadem on his
        head.
25 From these the Destroyer recoiled, he was
        afraid of these.
This one experience of Retribution was
    enough.

Seventh antithesis: the Red Sea

19 But the godless were assailed by
        merciless anger to the very end,
for he knew beforehand what they
        would do,
2 how, after letting his people leave and
        hastening their departure,
they would change their minds and give
        chase.
3 They were actually still conducting their
        mourning rites
and lamenting at the tombs of their
        dead,
when another mad scheme came into their
        heads
and they set out to pursue, as though
        runaways,
the people whom they had expelled and
        begged to go.
4 A well-deserved fate urged them to this
        extreme

and made them forget what had already
    happened,
so that they would add to their torments
the one punishment outstanding
⁵ and, while your people were experiencing
    a journey
contrary to all expectations,
would themselves meet an extraordinary
    death.

⁶ For the whole creation, submissive to your
    commands,
had its very nature re-created,
so that your children should be preserved
    from harm.
⁷ Overshadowing the camp there was the
    cloud;
where there had been water, dry land was
    seen to rise;
the Red Sea became an unimpeded way,
the tempestuous waves, a green plain;
⁸ sheltered by your hand, the whole nation
    passed across,
gazing at these amazing prodigies.
⁹ They were like horses at pasture,
they skipped like lambs,
singing your praises, Lord, their deliverer.
¹⁰ For they still remembered the events of
    their exile,
how the land had bred mosquitoes instead
    of animals
and the River had disgorged millions of
    frogs instead of fish.
¹¹ Later they were to see a new way for birds
    to come into being,
when, goaded by greed, they demanded
    something tasty,
¹² and quails came up out of the sea to satisfy
    them.

Egypt guiltier than Sodom

¹³ On the sinners, however, punishments
    rained down
not without violent thunder as early
    warning;
and they suffered what their own crimes
    had justly deserved

since they had shown such bitter hatred to
    foreigners.
¹⁴ Others, indeed, had failed to welcome
    strangers who came to them,
but the Egyptians had enslaved their own
    guests and benefactors.
¹⁵ The sinners, moreover, will certainly be
    punished for it,
since they gave the foreigners a hostile
    welcome;
¹⁶ but the latter, having given a festive
    reception
to people who already shared the same
    rights as themselves,
later overwhelmed them with terrible
    labours.
¹⁷ Hence they were struck with blindness,
like the sinners at the gate of the upright,
when, yawning darkness all around them,
each had to grope his way through his own
    door.

A new harmony in nature

¹⁸ A new attuning of the elements
    occurred,
as on a harp the notes may change their
    rhythm,
though all the while preserving the same
    tone;
and this is just what happened:
¹⁹ land animals became aquatic,
swimming ones took to the land,
²⁰ fire reinforced its strength in water,
and water forgot the power of
    extinguishing it;
²¹ flames, on the other hand, did not char the
    flesh
of delicate animals that ventured into
    them;
nor did they melt the heavenly food
resembling ice and as easily melted.

Conclusion

²² Yes, Lord, in every way you have made
    your people great and glorious;
you have never failed to help them at any
    time or place.

The Book of
ECCLESIASTICUS

Translator's foreword

[1] The Law, the Prophets, [2] and the other writers succeeding them have passed on to us great lessons, [3] in consequence of which Israel must be commended for learning and wisdom. [4] Furthermore, it is a duty, not only to acquire learning by reading, [5] but also, once having acquired it, to make oneself of use to people outside [6] by what one can say or write. [7] My grandfather Jesus, having long devoted himself to the reading [8] of the Law, [9] the Prophets [10] and other books of the Fathers [11] and having become very learned in them, [12] himself decided to write something on the subjects of learning and wisdom, [13] so that people who wanted to learn might, by themselves accepting these disciplines, [14] learn how better to live according to the Law.

[15] You are therefore asked [16] to read this book [17] with good will and attention [18] and to show indulgence [19] in those places where, notwithstanding our efforts at interpretation, we may seem [20] to have failed to give an adequate rendering of this or that expression; [21] the fact is that there is no equivalent [22] for things originally written in Hebrew when it is a question of translating them into another language; [23] what is more, [24] the Law itself, the Prophets [25] and the other books [26] differ considerably in translation from what appears in the original text.

[27] It was in the thirty-eighth year of the late King Euergetes[a] [28] that, coming to Egypt and spending some time here, [29] and finding life here consistent with a high degree of wisdom, [30] I became convinced of an immediate duty to apply myself in my turn with pains and diligence to the translation of the book that follows; [31] and I spent much time and learning on it [32] in the course of this period, [33] to complete the work and to publish the book [34] for the benefit of those too who, domiciled abroad, wish to study, [35] to reform their behaviour, and to live as the Law requires.

The origin of wisdom

1 All wisdom comes from the Lord,
   she is with him for ever.
[2] The sands of the sea, the drops
      of rain,
   the days of eternity—who can count
      them?
[3] The height of the sky, the breadth of the
      earth,
   the depth of the abyss—who can
      explore them?
[4] Wisdom was created before
      everything,
   prudent understanding subsists from
      remotest ages.
[6] For whom has the root of wisdom ever
      been uncovered?
   Her resourceful ways, who knows
      them?
[8] One only is wise, terrible indeed,
[9]   seated on his throne, the Lord.
   It was he who created, inspected and
      weighed her up,
   and then poured her out on all his
      works—
[10] as much to each living creature as he
      chose—
   bestowing her on those who
      love him.

Foreword a Ptolemy VII Euergetes Physcon (170–117 BC). So the date is 132 BC.

The fear of God

11 The fear of the Lord is glory and pride,
    happiness and a crown of joyfulness.
12 The fear of the Lord gladdens the heart,
    giving happiness, joy and long life.
13 For those who fear the Lord, all will end
        well:
    on their dying day they will be blessed.
14 The basis of wisdom is to fear the Lord;
    she was created with the faithful in
        their mothers' womb;
15 she has made a home in the human race,
        an age-old foundation,
    and to their descendants will she
        faithfully cling.
16 The fullness of wisdom is to fear the
        Lord;
    she intoxicates them with her fruits;
17 she fills their entire house with treasures
    and their storerooms with her produce.
18 The crown of wisdom is to fear the Lord:
    she makes peace and health flourish.
19 The Lord has seen and assessed her,
    he has showered down knowledge and
        intelligence,
    he has exalted the renown of those who
        possess her.
20 The root of wisdom is to fear the Lord,
    and her branches are long life.

Patience and self-control

22 The rage of the wicked cannot put him in
        the right,
    for the weight of his rage is his
        downfall.
23 A patient person puts up with things until
        the right time comes:
    but his joy will break out in the end.
24 Till the time comes he keeps his thoughts
        to himself,
    and many a lip will affirm how wise
        he is.

Wisdom and uprightness

25 Wisdom's treasures contain the maxims
        of knowledge,

the sinner, however, holds piety in
        abhorrence.
26 If you desire wisdom, keep the
        commandments,
    and the Lord will bestow it on you.
27 For the fear of the Lord is wisdom and
        instruction,
    and what pleases him is faithfulness and
        gentleness.
28 Do not stand out against fear of the Lord,
    do not practise it with a double
        heart.
29 Do not act a part in public,
    keep watch over your lips.
30 Do not grow too high and mighty, for fear
        you fall
    and cover yourself in disgrace;
    for the Lord would then reveal your
        secrets
    and overthrow you before the whole
        community
    for not having practised fear of the Lord
    and for having a heart full of deceit.

The fear of God in time of ordeal

2 My child, if you aspire to serve the Lord,
    prepare yourself for an ordeal.
2 Be sincere of heart, be steadfast,
    and do not be alarmed when disaster
        comes.
3 Cling to him and do not leave him,
    so that you may be honoured at the end
        of your days.
4 Whatever happens to you, accept it,
    and in the uncertainties of your humble
        state, be patient,
5 since gold is tested in the fire,
    and the chosen in the furnace of
        humiliation.
6 Trust him and he will uphold you,
    follow a straight path and hope in him.
7 You who fear the Lord, wait for his
        mercy;
    do not turn aside, for fear you fall.
8 You who fear the Lord, trust him,
    and you will not be robbed of your
        reward.

64 READ ECCLESIASTICUS 1.

Wisdom's treasuries contain the maxims of knowledge, the sinner, however, holds piety in abhorrence.—ECCLESIASTICUS 1:25

TRUE VALUES

Some people are careless about their true life and greedy for things that pass away. But they either do not understand eternal realities or, if they understand them, they assign them little value. They feel no sorrow, nor do they know how to take wise advice. Forgetting the heavenly possessions that they have lost, they think themselves happy with what they have. They don't lift their eyes to the light of truth for which they were created. No keen desire ever makes them cast a longing look toward the everlasting fatherland. They rejoice in the blindness that they are suffering, as though it were glorious daylight.

However, while the elect use the things that pass away, they regard them as having no permanent value. They strive to reach the true end for which they were created. Since nothing outside of God satisfies them, they find rest in hoping for and contemplating their Maker. They long to take their place among the citizens above, and although still physically in the world, each of them in mind and heart ascends above it. They are grieved over the hardships of the exile they are enduring, but rouse themselves by the constant pricking of their love to look to their fatherland above. The farther along they get on the wise course that they have chosen, the deeper grows their sorrow that they have not yet attained the enduring realities. ST. GREGORY THE GREAT, 540?–604

YOU WILL FIND THE NEXT READING AT ECCLESIASTICUS 3.

⁹ You who fear the Lord, hope for those
  good gifts of his,
    everlasting joy and mercy.
¹⁰ Look at the generations of old and see:
    who ever trusted in the Lord and was
      put to shame?
    Or who ever, steadfastly fearing him, was
      forsaken?
      Or who ever called to him and was
        ignored?
¹¹ For the Lord is compassionate and
    merciful,
      he forgives sins and saves in the time of
        distress.
¹² Woe to faint hearts and listless hands,
    and to the sinner who treads two
      paths.

¹³ Woe to the listless heart that has no faith,
    for such will have no protection.
¹⁴ Woe to you who have lost the strength to
    endure;
      what will you do at the Lord's
        visitation?
¹⁵ Those who fear the Lord do not disdain
    his words,
      and those who love him keep his ways.
¹⁶ Those who fear the Lord do their best to
    please him,
      and those who love him will find
        satisfaction in the Law.
¹⁷ Those who fear the Lord keep their hearts
    prepared
      and humble themselves in his
        presence.

18 Let us fall into the hands of the Lord, not
into any human clutches;
for as his majesty is, so too is his
mercy.

Duties towards parents

3 Children, listen to me for I am your
father:
do what I tell you, and so be safe;
2 for the Lord honours the father above his
children
and upholds the rights of a mother over
her sons.
3 Whoever respects a father expiates sins,
4 whoever honours a mother is like
someone amassing a fortune.
5 Whoever respects a father will in turn be
happy with children,
the day he prays for help, he will be
heard.
6 Long life comes to anyone who honours a
father,
whoever obeys the Lord makes a
mother happy.
7 Such a one serves parents as well as the
Lord.
8 Respect your father in deed as well as
word,
so that blessing may come on you from
him;
9 since a father's blessing makes his
children's house firm,
while a mother's curse tears up its
foundations.
10 Do not make a boast of disgrace
overtaking your father,
your father's disgrace reflects no honour
on you;
11 for a person's own honour derives from
the respect shown to his father,
and a mother held in dishonour is a
reproach to her children.
12 My child, support your father in his old
age,
do not grieve him during his life.
13 Even if his mind should fail, show him
sympathy,

do not despise him in your health and
strength;
14 for kindness to a father will not be
forgotten
but will serve as reparation for your sins.
15 On your own day of ordeal God will
remember you:
like frost in sunshine, your sins will
melt away.
16 Whoever deserts a father is no better than
a blasphemer,
and whoever distresses a mother is
accursed of the Lord.

Humility

17 My child, be gentle in carrying out your
business,
and you will be better loved than a
lavish giver.
18 The greater you are, the more humbly you
should behave,
and then you will find favour with the
Lord;
20 for great though the power of the Lord is,
he accepts the homage of the humble.
21 Do not try to understand things that are
too difficult for you,
or try to discover what is beyond your
powers.
22 Concentrate on what has been assigned
you,
you have no need to worry over
mysteries.
23 Do not meddle with matters that are
beyond you;
what you have been taught already
exceeds the scope of the human
mind.
24 For many have been misled by their own
notions,
wicked presumption having warped
their judgement.

Pride

26 A stubborn heart will come to a bad end,
and whoever dallies with danger will
perish in it.

27 A stubborn heart is weighed down with
   troubles,
      the sinner heaps sin on sin.
28 For the disease of the proud there is no
   cure,
      since an evil growth has taken root
         there.
29 The heart of the sensible will reflect on
   parables,
      an attentive ear is the sage's dream.

Charity to the poor

30 Water puts out a blazing fire,
      almsgiving expiates sins.
31 Whoever gives favours in return is
   mindful of the future;
      at the moment of falling, such a person
         will find support.

4 My child, do not refuse the poor a
   livelihood,
      do not tantalise the needy.
2 Do not add to the sufferings of the
   hungry,
      do not bait anyone in distress.
3 Do not aggravate a heart already angry,
      nor keep the destitute waiting for your
         alms.
4 Do not repulse a hard-pressed beggar,
      nor turn your face from the poor.
5 Do not avert your eyes from the needy,
      give no one occasion to curse you;
6 for if someone curses you in distress,
      his Maker will give ear to the
         imprecation.
7 Gain the love of the community,
      in the presence of the great bow your
         head.
8 To the poor lend an ear,
      and courteously return the greeting.
9 Save the oppressed from the hand of the
   oppressor,
      and do not be mean-spirited in your
         judgements.
10 Be like a father to the fatherless
      and as good as a husband to their
         mothers.

And you will be like a child to the Most
   High,
      who will love you more than your own
         mother does.

Wisdom as educator

11 Wisdom brings up her own children
      and cares for those who seek her.
12 Whoever loves her loves life,
      those who seek her early will be filled
         with joy.
13 Whoever possesses her will inherit
   honour,
      and wherever he walks the Lord
         will bless him.
14 Those who serve her minister to the
   Holy One,
      and the Lord loves those who
         love her.
15 Whoever obeys her rules the nations,
      whoever pays attention to her dwells
         secure.
16 If he trusts himself to her he will inherit
   her,
      and his descendants will remain in
         possession of her;
17 for though she takes him at first through
   winding ways,
      bringing fear and faintness on him,
   trying him out with her discipline till she
      can trust him,
      and testing him with her ordeals,
18 she then comes back to him on the straight
   road, makes him happy
      and reveals her secrets to him.
19 If he goes astray, however, she abandons
   him
      and leaves him to his own destruction.

Modesty and deference to others

20 Take circumstances into account and
   beware of evil,
      and have no cause to be ashamed of
         yourself;
21 for there is a shame that leads to sin
      and a shame that is honourable and
         gracious.

65 READ ECCLESIASTICUS 3:30–4:10.

Water puts out a blazing fire, almsgiving expiates sins.—ECCLESIASTICUS 3:30

MERCY CURES OUR SINFULNESS

Many and great . . . are the divine blessings by which the large and abundant mercy of God the Father and Christ has both worked and is always working for our salvation. . . . Christ humbled himself that he might cure our wounds; he served that he might draw those to liberty who were held in bondage. . . .

But even more, what providence and what great clemency are constituted by the fact that we are provided for by a plan of salvation ensuring that more abundant care is taken for preserving us after we are already redeemed. For when the Lord had come and healed the wounds which Adam had borne, and had cured the old poisons of the serpent, he gave a law to the sound man, and bade him sin no more, lest something more serious happen to him in his sinning.

Let us . . . acknowledge the saving gift of divine mercy by cleaning and purging our sins. Let us, who cannot be without some wound of conscience, heal our wounds with spiritual remedies.

The remedies for propitiating God are given in the words of God himself; divine instructions have taught what sinners ought to do, that God is satisfied by just works, that sins are cleansed by the merits of mercy. As Ecclesiasticus declares, "almsgiving expiates sins."

"Therefore . . . let us whose fear is inclined toward God, and whose minds, after spurning and trampling the world underfoot, are turned to heavenly and divine things, offer obedience with full faith, devoted minds, and continual good works in order to deserve well of the Lord. Let us give Christ earthly garments that we may receive heavenly clothing. Let us give worldly food and drink that together with Abraham and Isaac and Jacob we may come to the heavenly banquet.

ST. CYPRIAN OF CARTHAGE, 200?–258

YOU WILL FIND THE NEXT READING AT ECCLESIASTICUS 6.

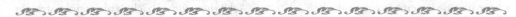

22 Do not be too severe on yourself,
   do not let shame lead you to ruin.
23 Do not refrain from speaking when it will
   do good,
   and do not hide your wisdom;
24 for your wisdom is made known by what
   you say,
   your erudition by the words you
   utter.
25 Do not contradict the truth,
   rather blush for your own ignorance.

26 Do not be ashamed to confess your sins,
   do not struggle against the current of
   the river.
27 Do not grovel to the foolish,
   do not show partiality to the influential.
28 Fight to the death for truth,
   and the Lord God will war on your side.
29 Do not be bold of tongue,
   yet idle and slack in deed;
30 do not be like a lion at home,
   or cowardly towards your servants.

31 Do not let your hands be outstretched to
    receive,
  yet tight-fisted when the time comes to
    give back.

Wealth and presumption

5 Do not put your confidence in your
    money
  or say, 'With this I am self-sufficient.'
2 Do not be led by your appetites and energy
  to follow the passions of your heart.
3 And do not say, 'Who has authority over
    me?'
  for the Lord will certainly give you your
    deserts.
4 Do not say, 'I have sinned, but what harm
    has befallen me?'
  for the Lord's forbearance is long.
5 Do not be so sure of forgiveness
  that you add sin to sin.
6 And do not say, 'His compassion is great,
  he will forgive me my many sins';
  for with him are both mercy and
    retribution,
  and his anger does not pass from
    sinners.
7 Do not delay your return to the Lord,
  do not put it off day after day;
  for suddenly the Lord's wrath will blaze
    out,
  and on the day of punishment you will
    be utterly destroyed.
8 Do not set your heart on ill-gotten gains,
  they will be of no use to you on the day
    of disaster.

Straightforwardness and self-possession

9 Do not winnow in every wind,
  or walk along every by-way
  (as the double-talking sinner does).
10 Be steady in your convictions,
  and be a person of your word.
11 Be quick to listen,
  and deliberate in giving an answer.
12 If you understand the matter, give your
    neighbour an answer,
  if not, keep your hand over your mouth.

13 Both honour and disgrace come from
    talking,
  the tongue is its owner's downfall.
14 Do not get a name for scandal-mongering,
  do not set traps with your tongue;
  for as shame lies in store for the thief,
  so harsh condemnation awaits the
    deceitful.
15 Avoid offences in great as in small matters,
  and do not exchange friendship for
    enmity,

6 for a bad name will earn you shame and
    reproach,
  as happens to the double-talking
    sinner.
2 Do not get carried aloft on the wings of
    passion,
  for fear your strength tear itself apart
    like a bull,
3 and you devour your own foliage and
    destroy your own fruit
  and end by making yourself like a piece
    of dried-up wood.
4 An evil temper destroys the person who
    has it
  and makes him the laughing-stock of
    his enemies.

Friendship

5 A kindly turn of speech attracts new
    friends,
  a courteous tongue invites many a
    friendly response.
6 Let your acquaintances be many,
  but for advisers choose one out of a
    thousand.
7 If you want to make a friend, take him on
    trial,
  and do not be in a hurry to trust him;
8 for one kind of friend is so only when it
    suits him
  but will not stand by you in your day of
    trouble.
9 Another kind of friend will fall out with
    you
  and to your dismay make your quarrel
    public,

66 READ ECCLESIASTICUS 6:5–17.

A loyal friend is the elixir of life.—ECCLESIASTICUS 6:16

THE JOY OF FRIENDSHIP

Scarcely any happiness whatever can exist among mankind without friendship, and a man is to be compared to a beast if he has no one to rejoice with him in adversity, no one to whom to unburden his mind if any annoyance crosses his path or with whom to share some unusually sublime or illuminating inspiration. "What of the person with no one to help him up when he falls?" (Qo 4:10). . . .

But what happiness, what security, what joy to have someone to whom you dare to speak on terms of equality as to another self; one to whom you need have no fear to confess your failings; one to whom you can unblushingly make known what progress you have made in the spiritual life; one to whom you can entrust all the secrets of your heart and before whom you can place all your plans! What, therefore, is more pleasant than so to unite to oneself the spirit of another and of two to form one. No boasting is thereafter to be feared, no suspicion to be dreaded, no correction . . . to cause pain, no praise . . . to bring a charge of adulation. . . . "A friend," says the Sage, "is the elixir of life." . . . For elixir is not more powerful or more efficacious for our wounds in all our temporal needs than the possession of a friend who meets every misfortune joyfully, so that, as the Apostle says, shoulder to shoulder they bear one another's burdens (see Ga 6:2). . . .

And . . . friendship is a stage bordering upon that perfection which consists in the love and knowledge of God, so that man from being a friend of his fellowman becomes the friend of God, according to the words of the Savior in the Gospel: "I will not now call you servants, but my friends." (See Jn 15:15).

ST. AELRED OF RIEVAULX, 1110–1167

YOU WILL FIND THE NEXT READING AT ECCLESIASTICUS 10.

10 and a third kind of friend will share your
table,
but not stand by you in your day of
trouble:
11 when you are doing well he will be your
second self,
ordering your servants about;
12 but, if disaster befalls you, he will recoil
from you
and keep out of your way.
13 Keep well clear of your enemies,
and be wary of your friends.
14 A loyal friend is a powerful defence:
whoever finds one has indeed found a
treasure.

15 A loyal friend is something beyond
price,
there is no measuring his worth.
16 A loyal friend is the elixir of life,
and those who fear the Lord will
find one.
17 Whoever fears the Lord makes true
friends,
for as a person is, so is his friend too.

Apprenticeship to wisdom

18 My child, from your earliest youth choose
instruction,
and till your hair is white you will keep
finding wisdom.

¹⁹ Like ploughman and sower, cultivate her
  and wait for her fine harvest,
   for in tilling her you will toil a little while,
    but very soon you will be eating her
     crops.
²⁰ How very harsh she is to the
    undisciplined!
   The senseless does not stay with her for
    long:
²¹ she will weigh as heavily on the senseless
    as a touchstone
   and such a person will lose no time in
    throwing her off;
²² for Wisdom is true to her name,
   she is not accessible to many.
²³ Listen, my child, and take my advice,
   do not reject my counsel:
²⁴ put your feet into her fetters,
   and your neck into her collar;
²⁵ offer your shoulder to her burden,
   do not be impatient of her bonds;
²⁶ court her with all your soul,
   and with all your might keep in her
    ways;
²⁷ search for her, track her down: she will
    reveal herself;
   once you hold her, do not let her go.
²⁸ For in the end you will find rest in her
   and she will take the form of joy for you:
²⁹ her fetters you will find a mighty defence,
   her collars, a precious necklace.
³⁰ Her yoke will be a golden ornament,
   and her bonds be purple ribbons;
³¹ you will wear her like a robe of honour,
   you will put her on like a crown of joy.
³² If you wish it, my child, you can be taught;
   apply yourself, and you will become
    intelligent.
³³ If you love listening, you will learn,
   if you pay attention, you will become
    wise.
³⁴ Attend the gathering of elders;
   if there is a wise man there, attach
    yourself to him.
³⁵ Listen willingly to any discourse coming
    from God,
   do not let wise proverbs escape you.

³⁶ If you see a man of understanding, visit
    him early,
   let your feet wear out his doorstep.
³⁷ Reflect on the injunctions of the Lord,
   busy yourself at all times with his
    commandments.
  He will strengthen your mind,
   and the wisdom you desire will be
    granted you.

Miscellaneous advice

7 Do no evil, and evil will not befall
    you;
² shun wrong, and it will avoid you.
³ My child, do not sow in the furrows of
    wickedness,
   for fear you have to reap them seven
    times over.
⁴ Do not ask the Lord for the highest place,
   or the king for a seat of honour.
⁵ Do not parade your uprightness before the
    Lord,
   or your wisdom before the king.
⁶ Do not scheme to be appointed judge,
   for fear you should not be strong
    enough to stamp out injustice,
  for fear of being swayed by someone
    influential
   and so of risking the loss of your
    integrity.
⁷ Do not wrong the general body of
    citizens
   and so lower yourself in popular esteem.
⁸ Do not be drawn to sin twice over,
   for you will not go unpunished even
    once.
⁹ Do not say, 'God will be impressed by my
    numerous offerings;
   when I sacrifice to God Most High, he
    is bound to accept.'

¹⁰ Do not be hesitant in prayer;
   do not neglect to give alms.

¹¹ Do not laugh at someone who is sad of
    heart,
   for he who brings low can lift up high.

12 Do not make up lies against your brother,
   nor against a friend either.
13 Mind you tell no lies,
   for no good can come of it.

14 Do not talk too much at the gathering of
   elders,
   and do not repeat yourself at your
   prayers.

15 Do not shirk tiring jobs
   or farm work, ordained by the Most
   High.

16 Do not swell the ranks of sinners,
   remember that the retribution will not
   delay.
17 Be very humble,
   since the recompense for the godless is
   fire and worms.
18 Do not barter a friend away for the sake of
   profit,
   nor a true brother for the gold of Ophir.
19 Do not turn against a wise and good wife;
   her gracious presence is worth more
   than gold.
20 Do not ill-treat a slave who is an honest
   worker,
   or a wage-earner who is devoted to you.
21 Love an intelligent slave with all your
   heart,
   and do not deny such a slave his
   freedom.

Children

22 Have you cattle? Look after them;
   if they are making you a profit, keep
   them.
23 Have you children? Educate them,
   from childhood make them bow the
   neck.
24 Have you daughters? Take care of their
   bodies,
   but do not be over-indulgent.
25 Marry a daughter off, and you have
   finished a great work;
   but give her to a man of sense.

26 Have you a wife to your liking? Do not
   turn her out;
   but if you do not love her, never trust
   her.

Parents

27 With all your heart honour your father,
   never forget the birthpangs of your
   mother.
28 Remember that you owe your birth to
   them;
   how can you repay them for what they
   have done for you?

Priests

29 With all your soul, fear the Lord
   and revere his priests.
30 With all your might love him who made
   you,
   and do not abandon his ministers.
31 Fear the Lord and honour the priest
   and give him the portion enjoined on
   you:
   first-fruits, sacrifice of reparation,
   shoulder-gift,
   sanctification sacrifice, first-fruits of the
   holy things.

The poor and afflicted

32 And also give generously to the poor,
   so that your blessing may lack nothing.
33 Let your generosity extend to all the
   living,
   do not withhold it even from the
   dead.
34 Do not turn your back on those who weep,
   but share the grief of the grief-stricken.
35 Do not shrink from visiting the sick;
   in this way you will make yourself
   loved.
36 In everything you do, remember your end,
   and you will never sin.

Prudence and commonsense

8 Do not try conclusions with anyone
   influential,
   in case you later fall into his clutches.

2 Do not quarrel with anyone rich,
  in case he puts his weight against you;
for gold has destroyed many,
  and has swayed the hearts of kings.

3 Do not argue with anyone argumentative,
  do not pile wood on that fire.
4 Do not joke with anyone uncouth,
  for fear of hearing your ancestors
    insulted.

5 Do not revile a repentant sinner;
  remember that we all are guilty.
6 Do not despise anyone in old age;
  after all, some of us too are growing old.
7 Do not gloat over anyone's death;
  remember that we all have to die.

Tradition

8 Do not scorn the discourse of the wise,
  but make yourself familiar with their
    maxims,
  since from these you will learn the
    theory
  and the art of serving the great.
9 Do not dismiss what the old people have to
    say,
  for they too were taught by their
    parents;
  from them you will learn how to think,
  and the art of the timely answer.

Prudence

10 Do not kindle the coals of the sinner,
  in case you scorch yourself in his
    blaze.
11 Refuse to be provoked by the insolent,
  for fear that such a one try to trap you
    in your words.

12 Do not lend to anyone who is stronger
    than you are—
  if you do lend, resign yourself to loss.

13 Do not stand surety beyond your means;
  if you do stand surety, be prepared to
    pay up.

14 Do not go to law with a judge,
  since judgement will be given in his
    favour.

15 Do not go travelling with a rash man,
  for fear he becomes burdensome
    to you;
he will act as the whim takes him,
  and you will both be ruined by his
    folly.
16 Do not argue with a quick-tempered man,
  do not go with him where there are no
    other people,
since blood counts for nothing in his eyes,
  and where no help is to be had, he will
    strike you down.

17 Do not ask a fool for advice,
  since a fool will not be able to keep a
    confidence.
18 In a stranger's presence do nothing that
    should be kept secret,
  since you cannot tell what use the
    stranger will make of it.
19 Do not open your heart to all comers,
  nor lay claim to their good offices.

Women

9 Do not be jealous of the wife you love,
  do not teach her lessons in how to
    harm you.
2 Do not put yourself in a woman's hands
  or she may come to dominate you
    completely.
3 Do not keep company with a prostitute,
  in case you get entangled in her snares.
4 Do not dally with a singing girl,
  in case you get caught by her wiles.
5 Do not stare at a pretty girl,
  in case you and she incur the same
    punishment.
6 Do not give your heart to whores,
  or you will ruin your inheritance.
7 Keep your eyes to yourself in the streets of
    a town,
  do not prowl about its unfrequented
    quarters.

8 Turn your eyes away from a handsome
woman,
do not stare at a beauty belonging to
someone else.
Because of a woman's beauty, many have
been undone;
this makes passion flare up like a fire.
9 Never sit down with a married woman,
or sit at table with her drinking wine,
in case you let your heart succumb to her
and you lose all self-control and slide to
disaster.

Relations with people

10 Do not desert an old friend;
the new one will not be his match.
New friend, new wine;
when it grows old, you drink it with
pleasure.
11 Do not envy the sinner his success;
you do not know how that will end.
12 Do not take pleasure in what pleases the
godless;
remember they will not go unpunished
here below.

13 Keep your distance from the man who has
the power to put to death,
and you will not be haunted by the fear
of dying.
If you do approach him, make no false
move,
or he may take your life.
Realise that you are treading among trip-
lines,
that you are strolling on the
battlements.
14 Cultivate your neighbours to the best of
your ability,
and consult with the wise.
15 For conversation seek the intelligent,
let all your discussions bear on the law
of the Most High.
16 Have the upright for your table
companions,
and let your pride be in fearing the Lord.

17 Work from skilled hands will earn its
praise,
but a leader of the people must be
skilful in words.
18 A chatterbox is a terror to his town,
a loose talker is detested.

Government

10 A sagacious ruler educates his people,
and he makes his subjects
understand order.
2 As the magistrate is, so will his officials be,
as the governor is, so will be the
inhabitants of his city.
3 An undisciplined king will be the ruin of
his people,
a city owes its prosperity to the
intelligence of its leading men.
4 The government of the earth is in the
hands of the Lord,
he sets the right leader over it at the
right time.
5 Human success is in the hands of the Lord.
He invests the scribe with honour.

Against pride

6 Do not resent your neighbour's every
offence,
and never act in a fit of passion.

7 Pride is hateful to God and humanity,
and injustice is abhorrent to both.

8 Sovereignty passes from nation to nation
because of injustice, arrogance and
money.

9 What has dust and ashes to pride itself on?
Even in life its entrails are repellent.
10 A long illness makes a fool of the doctor;
a king today is a corpse tomorrow.
11 For in death the portion of all alike will be
insects, wild animals and worms.

12 The first stage of pride is to desert the Lord
and to turn one's heart away from one's
Maker.

67 READ ECCLESIASTICUS 10:6–18.

The first stage of pride is to desert the Lord and to turn one's heart away from one's Maker.—ECCLESIASTICUS 10:12

PRIDE, THE BEGINNING OF ALL SIN

Our first parents only fell openly into the sin of disobedience because, secretly, they had begun to be guilty. Actually, their bad deed could not have been done had not bad will preceded it; what is more, the root of their bad will was nothing else than pride. For "pride is the beginning of all sin" (see Si 10:13). And what is pride but an appetite for inordinate exaltation?

Now, exaltation is inordinate when the soul cuts itself off from the very Source to which it should keep close and somehow makes itself and becomes an end to itself. This takes place when the soul becomes inordinately pleased with itself, and such self-pleasing occurs when the soul falls away from the unchangeable Good which ought to please the soul far more than the soul can please itself. Now, this falling away is the soul's own doing, for, if the will had merely remained firm in the love of that higher immutable Good which lighted its mind into knowledge and warmed its will into love, it would not have turned away in search of satisfaction in itself and, by so doing, have lost that light and warmth.

And thus Eve would not have believed that the serpent's lie was true, nor would Adam have preferred the will of his wife to the will of God nor have supposed that his transgression of God's command was venial when he refused to abandon the partner of his life even in a partnership of sin.

ST. AUGUSTINE, 354–430

YOU WILL FIND THE NEXT READING AT ECCLESIASTICUS 17.

13 Since the first stage of pride is sin,
  whoever clings to it will pour forth
    filth.
  This is why the Lord inflicts unexpected
    punishments
  on such people, utterly destroying them.
14 The Lord has turned mighty princes off
    their thrones
  and seated the humble there instead.
15 The Lord has plucked up the proud by the
    roots,
  and planted the lowly in their place.
16 The Lord has overthrown the lands of the
    nations
  and destroyed them to the very
    foundations of the earth.

17 Sometimes he has taken them away and
    destroyed them,
  and blotted out their memory from the
    earth.
18 Pride was not created for human
    beings,
  nor furious rage for those born of
    woman.

Persons deserving honour

19 What race deserves honour? The human
    race.
  What race deserves honour? Those who
    fear the Lord.
  What race deserves contempt? The
    human race.

What race deserves contempt? Those
who break the Law.

20 A leader is honoured by his brothers,
and those who fear the Lord are
honoured by him.

22 The rich, the noble, the poor,
let them pride themselves on fearing the
Lord.

23 It is not right to despise one who is poor
but intelligent,
and it is not good to honour one who is
a sinner.

24 Magnate, magistrate, potentate, all are to
be honoured,
but none is greater than the one who
fears the Lord.

25 A wise slave will have free men waiting on
him,
and the enlightened will not complain.

Frankness and humility

26 Do not try to be smart when you do your
work,
do not put on airs when you are in
difficulties.

27 Better the hardworking who has plenty of
everything,
than the pretentious at a loss for a meal.

28 My child, be modest in your self-esteem,
and value yourself at your proper
worth.

29 Who can justify one who inflicts injuries
on himself,
or respect one who is full of self-
contempt?

30 The poor is honoured for wit,
and the rich for wealth.

31 Honoured in poverty, how much the more
in wealth!
Dishonoured in wealth, how much the
more in poverty!

The deceptiveness of appearances

11 Wisdom enables the poor to stand
erect,
and gives to the poor a place with the
great.

2 Do not praise anyone for good looks,
nor dislike anyone for mere appearance.

3 Small among winged creatures is the bee
but her produce is the sweetest of the
sweet.

4 Do not grow proud when people honour
you;
for the works of the Lord are wonderful
but hidden from human beings.

5 Many monarchs have been made to sit on
the ground,
and the person nobody thought of has
worn the crown.

6 Many influential people have been utterly
disgraced,
and prominent people have fallen into
the power of others.

Deliberation and reflection

7 Do not find fault before making thorough
enquiry;
first reflect, then give a reprimand.

8 Listen before you answer,
and do not interrupt a speech before it is
finished.

9 Do not wrangle about something that does
not concern you,
do not interfere in the quarrels of
sinners.

10 My child, do not take on a great amount of
business;
if you multiply your interests, you are
bound to suffer for it;
hurry as fast as you can, yet you will never
arrive,
nor will you escape by running away.

11 Some people work very hard at top speed,
only to find themselves falling further
behind.

Trust in God alone

12 Or there is the slow kind of person,
needing help,
poor in possessions and rich in poverty;

and the Lord turns a favourable eye on
  him,
  lifts him out of his wretched condition,
¹³ and enables him to hold his head high,
  thus causing general astonishment.
¹⁴ Good and bad, life and death,
  poverty and wealth, all come from the
  Lord.
¹⁷ To the devout the Lord's gift remains
  constant,
  and his favour will be there to lead
  them for ever.
¹⁸ Others grow rich by pinching and
  scraping,
  and here is the reward they receive for it:
¹⁹ although they say, 'Now I can sit back
  and enjoy the benefit of what I have got,'
  they do not know how long this will last;
  they will have to leave their goods to
  others and die.
²⁰ Stick to your job, work hard at it
  and grow old at your work.
²¹ Do not admire the achievements of
  sinners,
  trust the Lord and mind your own
  business;
  since it is a trifle in the eyes of the Lord,
  in a moment, suddenly to make the
  poor rich.
²² The blessing of the Lord is the reward of
  the devout,
  in a moment God brings his blessing to
  flower.
²³ Do not say, 'What are my needs,
  how much shall I have in the future?'
²⁴ And do not say, 'I am self-sufficient,
  what disaster can affect me now?'
²⁵ In prosperous times, disasters are forgotten
  and in times of disaster, no one
  remembers prosperity.
²⁶ Yet it is a trifle for the Lord on the day
  someone dies
  to repay him as his conduct deserves.
²⁷ A moment's adversity, and pleasures are
  forgotten;
  in a person's last hour his deeds will
  stand revealed.

²⁸ Call no one fortunate before his death;
  it is by his end that someone will be
  known.

Distrust the wicked

²⁹ Do not bring everyone home with you,
  for many are the traps of the crafty.
³⁰ Like a captive partridge in a cage, so is the
  heart of the proud:
  like a spy he watches for your downfall,
³¹ ever on the look-out, turning good into
  bad
  and finding fault with what is
  praiseworthy.
³² A hearthful of glowing coals starts from a
  single spark,
  and the sinner lurks for the chance to
  spill blood.
³³ Beware of a scoundrel and his evil
  contrivances,
  in case he puts a smear on you for
  ever.
³⁴ Give a home to a stranger and he will
  start trouble
  and estrange you from your own family.

Rules for doing good

12 If you mean to do a kindness, choose
  the right person,
  then your good deeds will not be
  wasted.
² Do good to someone devout, and you will
  be rewarded,
  if not by that person, then certainly by
  the Most High.
³ No good will come to one who persists in
  evil,
  or who refuses to give alms.
⁴ Give to the devout,
  do not go to the help of a sinner.
⁵ Do good to the humble,
  give nothing to the godless.
  Refuse him bread, do not give him any,
  it might make him stronger than you
  are;
  then you would be repaid evil twice over
  for all the good you had done him.

6 For the Most High himself detests sinners,
    and will repay the wicked with what
        they deserve.
7 Give to the good,
    and do not go to the help of a sinner.

True and false friends

8 In prosperity you cannot always tell a true
        friend,
    but in adversity you cannot mistake an
        enemy.
9 When someone is doing well that person's
        enemies are sad,
    when someone is doing badly, even a
        friend will keep at a distance.
10 Do not ever trust an enemy;
    as bronze tarnishes, so does an enemy's
        malice.
11 Even if he behaves humbly and comes
        bowing and scraping,
    maintain your reserve and be on your
        guard against him.
    Behave towards him as if you were
        polishing a mirror,
    you will find that his tarnish cannot last.
12 Do not stand him beside you
    in case he thrusts you out and takes
        your place.
    Do not seat him on your right,
        or he will be after your position,
    and then you will remember what I have
        said
    and sadly admit that I was right.
13 Who feels sorry for a snake-charmer bitten
        by a snake,
    or for those who take risks with savage
        animals?—
14 just so for one who consorts with a
        sinner,
    and becomes an accomplice in
        his sins.
15 He will stay with you for a while,
    but if you once give way he will press
        his advantage.
16 An enemy may have sweetness on his lips,
    and in his heart a scheme to throw you
        into the ditch.

An enemy may have tears in his eyes,
    but if he gets a chance there can never
        be too much blood for him.
17 If you meet with misfortune, you will find
        him there before you,
    and, pretending to help you, he will trip
        you up.
18 He will wag his head and clap his hands,
    he will whisper a lot and his expression
        will change.

Mix with your equals

13 Whoever touches pitch will be
        defiled,
    and anyone who associates with the
        proud will come
        to be like them.
2 Do not try to carry a burden too heavy for
        you,
    do not associate with someone more
        powerful and wealthy than
        yourself.
    Why put the clay pot next to the iron
        cauldron?
    It will only break when they bang
        against each other.
3 The rich does wrong and takes a high line;
    the poor is wronged and has to beg for
        pardon.
4 If you are useful the rich will exploit you,
    if you go bankrupt he will desert you.
5 Are you well off?—he will live with you,
    he will clean you out without a single
        qualm.
6 Does he need you?—he will hoodwink
        you,
    smile at you and raise your hopes;
    he will speak politely to you
        and say, 'Is there anything you need?'
7 He will make you feel small at his dinner
        parties
    and, having cleaned you out two or
        three times over,
    will end by laughing at you.
    Afterwards, when he sees you, he will
        avoid you
    and shake his head about you.

⁸ Take care you are not hoodwinked
  and thus humiliated through your own
    stupidity.
⁹ When an influential person invites you,
    show reluctance,
  and he will press his invitation all the
    more.
¹⁰ Do not thrust yourself forward, in case you
    are pushed aside,
  but do not stand aloof, or you will be
    overlooked.
¹¹ Do not affect to treat him as an equal,
  do not trust his flow of words;
  since all this talking is expressly meant to
    test you,
  under cover of geniality he will be
    weighing you up.

¹² Pitiless is anyone who retails gossip;
  he will not spare you either blows or
    chains.
¹³ Be wary, take very great care,
  because you are walking with your own
    downfall.

¹⁵ Every living thing loves its own sort,
  and every man his fellow.
¹⁶ Every creature mixes with its kind,
  and human beings stick to their own
    sort.
¹⁷ How can wolf and lamb agree?—
  Just so with sinner and devout.
¹⁸ What peace can there be between hyena
    and dog?
  And what peace between rich and
    poor?
¹⁹ Wild desert donkeys are the prey of lions;
  so too, the poor is the quarry of the rich.
²⁰ The proud thinks humility abhorrent;
  so too, the rich abominates the poor.
²¹ When the rich stumbles he is supported by
    friends;
  when the poor falls, his friends push
    him away.
²² When the rich slips, there are many hands
    to catch him,
  if he talks nonsense he is congratulated.

The poor slips, and is blamed for it,
  he may talk good sense, but no room is
    made for him.
²³ The rich speaks and everyone stops
    talking,
  and then they praise his discourse to the
    skies.
  The poor speaks and people say, 'Who is
    this?'
  and if he stumbles, they trip him up yet
    more.

²⁴ Wealth is good where there is no sin,
  poverty is evil, the godless say.

²⁵ The heart moulds a person's expression
  whether for better or worse.
²⁶ Happy heart, cheerful expression;
  but wearisome work, inventing
    proverbs.

True happiness

14 Blessed is anyone who has not sinned
    in speech
  and who needs feel no remorse
    for sins.
² Blessed is anyone whose conscience
    brings no reproach
  and who has never given up hope.

Envy and greed

³ Wealth is not the right thing for the
    niggardly,
  and what use are possessions to the
    covetous?
⁴ Whoever hoards by stinting himself is
    hoarding for others,
  and others will live sumptuously on his
    riches.

⁵ If someone is mean to himself, whom does
    he benefit?
  He does not even enjoy what is
    his own.
⁶ No one is meaner than the person who
    is mean to himself,
  this is how his wickedness repays him.

7 If he does any good, he does it
    unintentionally,
  and in the end he himself reveals his
    wickedness.
8 Wicked the person who has an envious
    eye,
  averting his face, and careless of others'
    lives.

9 The eye of the grasping is not content with
    what he has,
  greed shrivels up the soul.

10 The miser is grudging of bread,
  there is famine at his table.

11 My child, treat yourself as well as you can
    afford,
  and bring worthy offerings to the
    Lord.
12 Remember that death will not delay,
  and that you have never seen Sheol's
    contract.
13 Be kind to your friend before you die,
  treat him as generously as you can
    afford.
14 Do not refuse yourself the good things of
    today,
  do not let your share of what is lawfully
    desired pass you by.
15 Will you not have to leave your fortune to
    another,
  and the fruit of your labour to be
    divided by lot?
16 Give and receive, enjoy yourself—
  there are no pleasures to be found in
    Sheol.
17 Like clothes, every body will wear out,
  the age-old law is, 'Everyone must die.'
18 Like foliage growing on a bushy tree,
  some leaves falling, others growing,
  so are the generations of flesh and
    blood:
  one dies, another is born.
19 Every achievement rots away and
    perishes,
  and with it goes its author.

The happiness of the sage

20 Blessed is anyone who meditates on
    wisdom,
  and reasons with intelligence,
21 who studies her ways in his heart,
  and ponders her secrets.
22 He pursues her like a hunter,
  and lies in wait by her path;
23 he peeps in at her windows,
  and listens at her doors;
24 he lodges close to her house,
  and fixes his peg in her walls;
25 he pitches his tent at her side,
  and lodges in an excellent lodging;
26 he sets his children in her shade,
  and camps beneath her branches;
27 he is sheltered by her from the heat,
  and in her glory he makes his home.

15 Whoever fears the Lord will act like
    this,
  and whoever grasps the Law will obtain
    wisdom.
2 She will come to meet him like a
    mother,
  and receive him like a virgin bride.
3 She will give him the bread of
    understanding to eat,
  and the water of wisdom to drink.
4 He will lean on her and will not fall,
  he will rely on her and not be put to
    shame.
5 She will raise him high above his
    neighbours,
  and in full assembly she will open his
    mouth.
6 He will find happiness and a crown
    of joy,
  he will inherit an everlasting name.
7 Fools will not gain possession of her,
  nor will sinners set eyes on her.
8 She stands remote from pride,
  and liars cannot call her to mind.
9 Praise is unseemly in a sinner's mouth,
  since it has not been put there by the
    Lord.

10 For praise should be uttered only in
    wisdom,
    and the Lord himself then prompts it.

Freedom of choice

11 Do not say, 'The Lord was responsible for
    my sinning,'
    for he does not do what he hates.
12 Do not say, 'It was he who led me
    astray,'
    for he has no use for a sinner.
13 The Lord hates all that is foul,
    and no one who fears him will love it
    either.
14 He himself made human beings in the
    beginning,
    and then left them free to make their
    own decisions.
15 If you choose, you will keep the
    commandments
    and so be faithful to his will.
16 He has set fire and water before you;
    put out your hand to whichever you
    prefer.
17 A human being has life and death before
    him;
    whichever he prefers will be given him.
18 For vast is the wisdom of the Lord;
    he is almighty and all-seeing.
19 His eyes are on those who fear him,
    he notes every human action.
20 He never commanded anyone to be
    godless,
    he has given no one permission to sin.

The fate of the obstinate

16 Do not long for a brood of worthless
    children,
    and do not take pleasure in godless
    sons.
2 However many you have, take no pleasure
    in them,
    unless the fear of the Lord lives among
    them.
3 Do not count on their having long life,
    do not put too much faith in their
    number;

for better have one than a thousand,
    better die childless than have children
    who are godless.
4 One person of sense can populate a city,
    but a race of lawless people will be
    destroyed.
5 My eyes have seen many such things,
    my ears have heard things even more
    impressive.
6 Fire is kindled in a sinful society,
    Retribution blazes in a rebellious
    nation.
7 God did not pardon the giants of old
    who, confident in their strength, had
    rebelled.
8 He did not spare the people with whom
    Lot lived;
    he abhorred them, rather, for their
    pride.
9 He was pitiless to the nation of
    perdition—
    those people who gloried in their sins—
10 as also to the six hundred thousand men
    on the march,
    who had banded together in their
    obstinacy.
11 And had there been only one man
    stubborn,
    it would have been amazing had he
    escaped unpunished,
    since mercy and wrath alike belong to the
    Lord
    who is mighty to forgive and to pour
    out wrath.
12 As great as his mercy, so is his severity;
    he judges each person as his deeds
    deserve:
13 the sinner will not escape with his ill-
    gotten gains
    nor the patience of the devout go for
    nothing.
14 He takes note of every charitable action,
    and everyone is treated as he deserves.

Certainty of retribution

17 Do not say, 'I shall hide from the Lord;
    who is going to remember me up there?

I shall not be noticed among so many
    people;
    what am I in the immensity of
        creation?'
18 For see, the sky and the heavens above the
        sky,
    the abyss and the earth shake at his
        visitation.
19 The mountains and earth's foundations
        alike
    quail and tremble when he looks at
        them.
20 But to all this no one gives thought.
    Who keeps his movements in mind?
21 The storm wind itself is invisible,
    and most of what he does goes
        undetected.
22 'Who will report whether justice has been
        done?
    Who will be watching? The covenant is
        remote!'
23 Such are the thoughts of the person of
        little sense,
    stupid, misguided, cherishing his folly.

Human beings in the creation

24 Listen to me, my child, and learn
        knowledge,
    and give your whole mind to my words.
25 I shall expound discipline methodically
    and proclaim knowledge with
        precision.

26 When God created his works in the
        beginning,
    he assigned them their places as soon as
        they were made.
27 He determined his works for all time,
    from their origins to their distant
        generations.
    They know neither hunger nor weariness,
    and they never desert their duties.
28 Not one has ever got in the way of another,
    and they will never disobey his word.
29 And afterwards the Lord looked at the
        earth,
    and filled it with his good things.

30 He covered its surface with every kind of
        animal,
    and to it they will return.

17 The Lord fashioned human beings
        from the earth,
    to consign them back to it.
2 He gave them so many days and so much
        time,
    he gave them authority over everything
        on earth.
3 He clothed them in strength, like
        himself,
    and made them in his own image.
4 He filled all living things with dread of
        human beings,
    making them masters over beasts and
        birds.
6 He made them a tongue, eyes and ears,
    and gave them a heart to think with.
7 He filled them with knowledge and
        intelligence,
    and showed them what was good and
        what evil.
8 He put his own light in their hearts
    to show them the magnificence of his
        works,
10 so that they would praise his holy name
    as they told of his magnificent works.
11 He set knowledge before them,
    he endowed them with the law of life.
12 He established an eternal covenant with
        them,
    and revealed his judgements to
        them.
13 Their eyes saw the majesty of his
        glory,
    and their ears heard the glory of
        his voice.
14 He said to them, 'Beware of all wrong-
        doing';
    he gave each a commandment
        concerning his neighbour.

The divine judge

15 Their ways are always under his eye,
    they cannot be hidden from his sight.

68 READ ECCLESIASTICUS 17.

The Lord fashioned human beings from the earth, to consign them back to it.
— ECCLESIASTICUS 17:1

MAKING THE MOST OF TIME

Let the soul, brothers, practice wisdom daily with respect to this material body of ours. When we come to our beds in the evening let it say to our members:

"O legs, how much power have you to stand up and move before you die and become motionless? Will you not now willingly stand up for your Lord?"

"Oh hands, the time is coming when you shall be unable to move, and when you shall never be clasped in each other again. Why then, before you come to that hour, do you not stretch yourselves out to the Lord?"

"O body, before we are separated and you are placed in the ground to decay, rise up boldly to worship the Lord without resistance. Bear me up so that I might give thanks to God with a good will, before you seek to lie down and take your rest. And if you listen to me, we shall enjoy happiness together, inheriting God's blessing. But if you don't listen to me, then cursed am I that I have ever been chained to you, for on your account I—a wretched thing—shall be condemned."

Now, if you do this daily and consecrate yourselves, you shall become real temples of God. And since God dwells in you, the cunning and wiles of Satan shall not be able to harm you.

ST. PACHOMIUS, 292?–346

YOU WILL FIND THE NEXT READING AT ECCLESIASTICUS 18.

17 Over each nation he has set a governor,
  but Israel is the Lord's own portion.
19 Their actions are all as plain as the sun to
    him,
  and his eyes rest constantly on their
    conduct.
20 Their iniquities are not hidden from him,
  all their sins are before the Lord.
22 Almsgiving is like a signet ring to him,
  he cherishes generosity like the pupil of
    an eye.
23 One day he will rise and reward them,
  he will repay their deserts on their own
    heads.
24 But to those who repent he permits return,
  and he encourages those who have lost
    hope.

Exhortation to repentance

25 Return to the Lord and renounce your
    sins,
  plead before his face, stop offending
    him.
26 Come back to the Most High, turn away
    from iniquity
  and hold all that is foul in abhorrence.
27 Who is going to praise the Most High in
    Sheol
  if we do not glorify him while we are
    alive?
28 The dead can praise no more than those
    who do not exist,
  only those with life and health can
    praise the Lord.

29 How great is the mercy of the Lord,
   his pardon for those who turn to him!
30 For we cannot have everything,
   human beings are not immortal.
31 What is brighter than the sun? And yet it
   fades.
   Flesh and blood think of nothing but
   evil.
32 He surveys the armies of the lofty sky,
   and all of us are only dust and ashes.

The greatness of God

18 He who lives for ever has created the
   sum of things.
2   The Lord alone will be found just.
4 He has given no one the power to
   proclaim his works to the end,
   and who can fathom his magnificent
   deeds?
5 Who can assess his magnificent strength,
   and who can go further and tell all of
   his mercies?
6 Nothing can be added to them, nothing
   subtracted,
   it is impossible to fathom the marvels of
   the Lord.
7 When someone finishes he is only
   beginning,
   and when he stops he is as puzzled as
   ever.

The nothingness of human beings

8 What is a human being, what purpose
   does he serve?
   What is good and what is bad for him?
9 The length of his life: a hundred years at
   most.
10 Like a drop of water from the sea, or a
   grain of sand,
   such are these few years compared with
   eternity.
11 This is why the Lord is patient with them
   and pours out his mercy on them.
12 He sees and recognises how wretched their
   end is,
   and so he makes his forgiveness the
   greater.

13 Human compassion extends to
   neighbours,
   but the Lord's compassion extends to
   everyone;
   rebuking, correcting and teaching,
   bringing them back as a shepherd
   brings his flock.
14 He has compassion on those who accept
   correction,
   and who fervently search for his
   judgements.

The art of giving

15 My child, do not temper your favours with
   blame
   nor any of your gifts with words that
   hurt.
16 Does not dew relieve the heat?
   In the same way a word is worth more
   than a gift.
17 Why surely, a word is better than a good
   present,
   but a generous person is ready with both.
18 A fool will offer nothing but insult,
   and a grudging gift makes the eyes
   smart.

Reflection and foresight

19 Learn before you speak,
   take care of yourself before you fall ill.
20 Examine yourself before judgement
   comes,
   and on the day of visitation you will be
   acquitted.
21 Humble yourself before you fall ill,
   repent as soon as the sin is committed.
22 Let nothing prevent your discharging a
   vow in good time,
   and do not wait till death to set matters
   right.
23 Prepare yourself before making a vow,
   and do not be like someone who tempts
   the Lord.
24 Bear in mind the retribution of the last
   days,
   the time of vengeance when God averts
   his face.

69 READ ECCLESIASTICUS 18.

The wise will be cautious in everything, in sinful times will take care not to offend.

—ECCLESIASTICUS 18:27

THE WAY OF WISDOM

The Son of God said to the spouse [St. Bridget]: "What is true wisdom that comes from God? It consists not in the simplicity of the poor, nor in the merit of the learned, but in a truly Christian life. The true lover of wisdom is the one who each day learns to die well; who frequently reflects upon the state in which he may be found at the hour of death; who remembers the judgment that follows it, when all that he has done will be reviewed and no fault will remain unpunished."

"The truly wise person, dead to the vanities of the world, contents himself with the necessaries of life, abstains from excesses, and applies himself as much as possible to give to God proofs of his love. … When he considers seriously the inconstancy and falseness of the world, may he not rejoice to have avoided sin by renouncing his own will for that of God? Is it not also a great advantage for him to have preserved his soul from the miseries that sin produces, and to have made it beautiful by loving God? And to have strengthened it by disdaining things that pass away and attaching himself to those that endure forever?"

"True wisdom, then, consists in works, not in great talents that the world admires. For the wise in the world's estimation—those that follow its maxims—are the foolish who disregard the will of God and don't know how to control their passions. And the spiritually blind, so much the more culpable, as they know that all that captivates them here below is of very short duration, and that the joys of heaven that they despise will last forever through all eternity."

ST. BRIDGET OF SWEDEN, 1303–1373

YOU WILL FIND THE NEXT READING AT ECCLESIASTICUS 31.

²⁵ In a time of plenty remember times of famine,
  think of poverty and want when you are rich.

²⁶ The time slips by between dawn and dusk,
  everything passes quickly for the Lord.

²⁷ The wise will be cautious in everything,
  in sinful times will take care not to offend.

²⁸ Every person of sense recognises wisdom,
  and will respect anyone who has found her.

²⁹ Those who understand sayings have toiled for their wisdom
  and have poured out accurate maxims.

Self-control

³⁰ Do not be governed by your passions,
  restrain your desires.

³¹ If you allow yourself to satisfy your desires,
  this will make you the laughing-stock of your enemies.

³² Do not indulge in luxurious living,
  do not get involved in such society.

33 Do not beggar yourself by banqueting on
credit
when there is nothing in your pocket.

19

A drunken workman will never grow
rich,
and one who makes light of small
matters will gradually sink.
2 Wine and women corrupt intelligent
men,
the customer of whores loses all sense
of shame.
3 Grubs and worms will have him as their
legacy,
and the man who knows no shame will
lose his life.

Against loose talk

4 Being too ready to trust shows shallowness
of mind,
and sinning harms the sinner.
5 Taking pleasure in evil earns
condemnation;
6 by hating gossip one avoids evil.
7 Never repeat what you are told
and you will come to no harm;
8 whether to friend or foe, do not talk
about it,
unless it would be sinful not to, do not
reveal it;
9 you would be heard out, then mistrusted,
and in due course you would be hated.
10 Have you heard something? Let it die
with you.
Courage! It will not burst you!
11 A fool will suffer birthpangs over a piece
of news,
like a woman labouring with child.
12 Like an arrow stuck in the flesh of the
thigh,
so is a piece of news inside a fool.

Do not trust everything you hear

13 Question your friend, he may have done
nothing at all;
and if he has done anything, he will not
do it again.

14 Question your neighbour, he may have
said nothing at all;
and if he has said anything, he will not
say it again.
15 Question your friend, for slander is very
common,
do not believe all you hear.
16 People sometimes make a slip, without
meaning what they say;
and which of us has never sinned by
speech?
17 Question your neighbour before you
threaten him,
and defer to the Law of the Most
High.

True and false wisdom

20 Wisdom consists entirely in fearing the
Lord,
and wisdom is entirely constituted by
the fulfilling of the Law.
22 Being learned in evil, however, is not
wisdom,
there is no prudence in the advice of
sinners.
23 There is a cleverness that is detestable;
whoever has no wisdom is a fool.
24 Better be short of sense and full of
fear,
than abound in shrewdness and
violate the Law.
25 There is a wickedness which is scrupulous
but nonetheless dishonest,
and there are those who misuse
kindness to win their case.
26 There is the person who will walk bowed
down with grief,
when inwardly this is nothing but
deceit:
27 he hides his face and pretends to be
deaf,
if he is not unmasked, he will take
advantage of you.
28 There is the person who is prevented from
sinning by lack of strength,
yet he will do wrong when he gets the
chance.

²⁹ You can tell a person by his appearance,
  you can tell a thinker by the look on his
    face.
³⁰ The way a person dresses, the way he
    laughs,
  the way he walks, tell you what he is.

Silence and speech

20 There is the rebuke that is untimely,
  and there is the person who keeps
    quiet, and he is the shrewd one.
² But how much better to rebuke than to
    fume!
³   The person who acknowledges a fault
    wards off punishment.

⁴ Like a eunuch trying to take a girl's
    virginity
  is someone who tries to impose justice
    by force.

⁵ There is the person who keeps quiet and is
    considered wise,
  another incurs hatred for talking too
    much.

⁶ There is the person who keeps quiet, not
    knowing how to answer,
  another keeps quiet, knowing when to
    speak.

⁷ The wise will keep quiet till the right
    moment,
  but a garrulous fool will always
    misjudge it.

⁸ Someone who talks too much will earn
    dislike,
  and someone who usurps authority will
    earn hatred.

Paradoxes

⁹ There is the person who finds misfortune
    a boon,
  and the piece of luck that turns to loss.

¹⁰ There is the gift that affords you no profit,
  and the gift that repays you double.

¹¹ There is the honour that leads to
    humiliation,
  and there are people in a low state who
    raise their heads.

¹² There is the person who buys much for
    little,
  yet pays for it seven times over.

¹³ The wise wins love with words,
  while fools may shower favours in vain.

¹⁴ The gift of the stupid will bring you no
    advantage,
  his eyes look for seven times as much in
    return.

¹⁵ He gives little and reviles much,
  he opens his mouth like the town
    crier,
  he lends today and demands payment
    tomorrow;
  he is a detestable fellow.

¹⁶ The fool will say, 'I have no friends,
  I get no gratitude for my good deeds;
¹⁷ those who eat my bread have malicious
    tongues.'
  How often he will be laughed at, and by
    how many!

Inappropriate talk

¹⁸ Better a slip on the pavement than a slip of
    the tongue;
  this is how ruin takes the wicked by
    surprise.

¹⁹ A coarse-grained person is like an
    indiscreet story
  endlessly retold by the ignorant.

²⁰ A maxim is rejected when coming from a
    fool,
  since the fool does not utter it on the apt
    occasion.

²¹ There is a person who is prevented from
    sinning by poverty;
  no qualms of conscience disturb that
    person's rest.

22 There is a person who courts destruction
    out of false shame,
  courts destruction for the sake of a fool's
    opinion.

23 There is a person who out of false shame
    makes promises to a friend,
  and so makes an enemy for nothing.

Lying

24 Lying is an ugly blot on anyone,
  and ever on the lips of the
    undisciplined.

25 A thief is preferable to an inveterate
    liar,
  but both are heading for ruin.

26 Lying is an abominable habit,
  the liar's disgrace lasts for ever.

Wisdom

27 The wise gains advancement by words,
  the shrewd wins favour from the
    great.

28 Whoever tills the soil will have a full
    harvest,
  whoever wins favour from the great
    will secure pardon for offences.

29 Presents and gifts blind the eyes of the
    wise
  and stifle rebukes like a muzzle on the
    mouth.

30 Wisdom concealed, and treasure
    undiscovered,
  what use is either of these?
31 Better one who conceals his folly
  than one who conceals his wisdom.*a*

Various sins

21 My child, have you sinned? Do so no
    more,
  and ask forgiveness for your previous
    faults.

2 Flee from sin as from a snake,
  if you approach it, it will bite you;
  its teeth are lion's teeth,
    they take human life away.
3 All law-breaking is like a two-edged
    sword,
  the wounds it inflicts are beyond cure.

4 Terror and violence make havoc of riches,
  similarly, desolation overtakes the
    houses of the proud.
5 A plea from the mouth of the poor goes
    straight to the ear of God,
  whose judgement comes without
    delay.

6 Whoever resents reproof walks in the
    sinner's footsteps;
  whoever fears the Lord is repentant of
    heart.

7 The glib speaker is known far and wide,
  but the wary detects every slip.

8 To build your house with other people's
    money
  is like collecting stones for your own
    tomb.

9 A meeting of the lawless is like a heap of
    tow:
  they will end in a blazing fire.

10 The sinner's road is smoothly paved,
  but it ends at the pit of Sheol.

The wise and the foolish

11 Whoever keeps the Law will master his
    instincts;
  the fear of the Lord is made perfect in
    wisdom.

12 No one who lacks aptitude can be taught,
  but certain aptitudes give rise to
    bitterness.

20a = 41:14–15.

¹³ The sage's knowledge is as rich as the
abyss
and his advice is like a living spring.
¹⁴ The heart of a fool is like a broken jar,
it will not hold any knowledge.
¹⁵ If the educated hears a wise saying,
he praises it and caps it with another;
if a debauchee hears it, he does not
like it
and tosses it behind his back.

¹⁶ The talk of a fool is like a load on a
journey,
but it is a pleasure to listen to the
intelligent.
¹⁷ The utterance of the shrewd will be
eagerly awaited in the assembly,
what he says will be given serious
consideration.

¹⁸ The wisdom of a fool is like the wreckage
of a house,
the knowledge of a dolt is incoherent
talk.

¹⁹ To the senseless fellow instruction is like
fetters on the feet,
like manacles on the right hand.

²⁰ A fool laughs at the top of his voice,
but the intelligent quietly smiles.

²¹ To the shrewd instruction is like a golden
ornament,
like a bracelet on the right arm.

²² The step of a fool goes straight into a
house,
but a person of much experience makes
a respectful approach;
²³ the stupid peeps inside through the
door,
a well-bred person waits outside.
²⁴ Listening at doors is a sign of bad
upbringing,
the perceptive would be ashamed to
do so.

²⁵ The lips of gossips repeat the words of
others,
the words of the wise are carefully
weighed.

²⁶ The heart of fools is in their mouth,
but the mouth of the wise is in their
heart.
²⁷ When the godless curses Satan,
he is cursing himself.
²⁸ The scandal-monger sullies himself
and earns the hatred of the
neighbourhood.

The idler

22 An idler is like a stone covered in
filth,
everyone whistles at his disgrace.
² An idler is like a lump of dung,
anyone picking it up shakes it off his
hand.

Degenerate children

³ It is a disgrace to have fathered a badly
brought-up son,
but the birth of any daughter is a loss;
⁴ a sensible daughter will find a husband,
but a shameless one is a grief to her
father.
⁵ A brazen daughter puts father and mother
to shame,
and will be disowned by both.

⁶ An untimely remonstrance is like music at
a funeral,
but a thrashing and correction are
wisdom at all times.

Wisdom and folly

⁹ Teaching a fool is like gluing bits of
pottery together—
you are rousing someone who is
besotted with sleep.
¹⁰ You might as well talk to someone sound
asleep;
when you have finished the fool will
say, 'What's up?'

11 Shed tears for the dead, who has left the
   light behind;
   shed tears for the fool, who has left his
   wits behind.
   Shed quieter tears for the dead who is at
   rest,
   for the fool life is worse than death.
12 Mourning for the dead lasts seven days,
   for the foolish and ungodly all the days
   of their lives.
13 Do not waste many words on the stupid,
   do not go near a dolt.

   Beware of him, or you will have trouble
   and be soiled by contact with him;
   keep away from him, and you will have
   peace of mind
   and not be exasperated by his folly.

14 What is heavier than lead,
   and what is its name if not 'fool'?
15 Sand and salt and a lump of iron
   are a lighter burden than a dolt.

16 A tie-beam bonded into a building
   will not be dislodged by an earthquake;
   so too, a heart resolved after due reflection
   will not flinch at the critical moment.

17 A heart founded on intelligent reflection
   is like a stucco decoration on a smooth
   wall.

18 Pebbles placed on top of a wall
   will not stand up to the wind;
   no more can the heart of a fool frightened
   at his own thoughts
   stand up to fear.

Friendship

19 Prick an eye and you will draw a tear,
   prick a heart and you reveal its feelings.

20 Throw stones at birds and you scare them
   away,
   reproach a friend and you destroy a
   friendship.

21 If you have drawn your sword on a
   friend,
   do not despair; there is a way back.
22 If you have opened your mouth against
   your friend,
   do not worry; there is hope for
   reconciliation;
   but insult, arrogance, betrayal of secrets,
   and the stab in the back—
   in these cases any friend is lost.

23 Win your neighbour's confidence when he
   is poor,
   so that you may enjoy his later good
   fortune with him;
   stand by him in times of trouble,
   in order to have your share when he
   comes into a legacy.

24 Fire is heralded by the reek of the furnace
   and smoke,
   so too, bloodshed by insults.

25 I shall not be ashamed to shelter a friend
   nor shall I hide away from him,
26 and if evil comes to me through him,
   everyone who hears about it will beware
   of him.

Vigilance

27 Who will set a guard on my mouth,
   and an efficient seal on my lips,
   to keep me from falling,
   and my tongue from causing my
   ruin?

23 Lord, father and master of my life,
   do not abandon me to their whims,
   do not let me fall because of them.
2 Who will lay whips to my thoughts,
   and the discipline of wisdom to my
   heart,
   to be merciless to my errors
   and not let my sins go unchecked,
3 for fear my errors should multiply
   and my sins then abound

and I fall before my adversaries,
and my enemy gloat over me?
⁴ Lord, father and God of my life,
do not let my eyes be proud,
⁵ turn envy away from me,
⁶ do not let lechery and lust grip me,
do not leave me a prey to shameless
desire.

Swearing

⁷ Children, listen to what I teach,
no one who keeps it will be caught out.
⁸ The sinner is ensnared by his own lips,
both the abusive and the proud are
tripped by them.
⁹ Do not get into the habit of swearing,
do not make a habit of naming the Holy
One;
¹⁰ for just as a slave who is constantly
overseen
will never be without bruises,
so someone who is always swearing and
uttering the Name
will not be exempt from sin.
¹¹ A man for ever swearing is full of iniquity,
and the scourge will not depart from
his house.
If he offends, his sin will be on him,
if he did it unheedingly, he has doubly
sinned;
if he swears a false oath, he will not be
treated as innocent,
for his house will be filled with
calamities.

Foul language

¹² One way of talking is like death,
let it not be found in the heritage of
Jacob
since devout people have nothing to do
with that:
they will not wallow in sin.
¹³ Do not get into the habit of using coarse
and foul language
since this involves sinful words.
¹⁴ Remember your father and mother
when you are sitting with the great,

for fear you forget yourself in their
presence
and behave like a fool,
and then wish you had not been born
and curse the day of your birth.
¹⁵ No one in the habit of using shameful
language
will break himself of it as long as he
lives.

Lechery

¹⁶ There are two types of people who commit
sin after sin
and a third who attracts retribution—
¹⁷ desire, blazing like a furnace,
will not die down until it has been
sated—
the man who lusts after members of his
own family
is not going to stop until he is quite
burnt out;
every food is sweet to the promiscuous,
and he will not desist until he dies;
¹⁸ and the man who sins against the marriage
bed
and says to himself, 'Who can see me?
There is darkness all round me, the walls
hide me,
no one can see me, why should I worry?
The Most High will not remember my
sins.'
¹⁹ What he fears are human eyes,
he does not realise that the eyes of the
Lord
are ten thousand times brighter than the
sun,
observing every aspect of human
behaviour,
seeing into the most secret corners.
²⁰ All things were known to him before they
were created,
and are still, now that they are
finished.
²¹ This man will be punished in view of the
whole town,
and will be seized when he least
expects it.

The adulteress

22 Similarly the woman unfaithful to her
    husband,
    who provides him with an heir by
       another man:
23 first, she has disobeyed the Law of the
       Most High;
    secondly, she has been false to her
       husband;
    and thirdly, she has gone whoring in
       adultery
24   and conceived children by another
       man.
    She will be led before the assembly,
       an enquiry will be held about her
       children.
25 Her children will strike no root,
    her branches will bear no fruit.
26 She will leave an accursed memory behind
       her,
    her shame will never be wiped out.
27 And those who survive her will
       recognise
    that nothing is better than fearing the
       Lord,
    and nothing sweeter than adherence to
       the Lord's commandments.

Discourse of Wisdom

24 Wisdom[a] speaks her own praises,
    in the midst of her people she glories
       in herself.
 2 She opens her mouth in the assembly of
       the Most High,
    she glories in herself in the presence of
       the Mighty One:
 3 'I came forth from the mouth of the Most
       High,
    and I covered the earth like mist.
 4 I had my tent in the heights,
    and my throne was a pillar of
       cloud.
 5 Alone, I have made the circuit of the
       heavens
    and walked through the depths of the
       abyss.

 6 Over the waves of the sea and over the
       whole earth,
    and over every people and nation I have
       held sway.
 7 Among all these I searched for rest,
    and looked to see in whose territory I
       might pitch camp.
 8 Then the Creator of all things instructed
       me
    and he who created me fixed a place for
       my tent.
    He said, "Pitch your tent in Jacob,
       make Israel your inheritance."
 9 From eternity, in the beginning, he created
       me,
    and for eternity I shall remain.
10 In the holy tent I ministered before him
    and thus became established in Zion.
11 In the beloved city he has given me rest,
    and in Jerusalem I wield my authority.
12 I have taken root in a privileged people,
    in the Lord's property, in his
       inheritance.
13 I have grown tall as a cedar on Lebanon,
    as a cypress on Mount Hermon;
14 I have grown tall as a palm in En-Gedi,
    as the rose bushes of Jericho;
    as a fine olive in the plain,
    as a plane tree, I have grown tall.
15 Like cinnamon and acanthus, I have
       yielded a perfume,
    like choice myrrh, have breathed out a
       scent,
    like galbanum, onycha, labdanum,
    like the smoke of incense in the tent.
16 I have spread my branches like a terebinth,
    and my branches are glorious and
       graceful.
17 I am like a vine putting out graceful
       shoots,
    my blossoms bear the fruit of glory and
       wealth.

24a A high point: personified Wisdom shares God's throne
(the cloud) but also chooses Israel for an inheritance and
more specifically serves in the Temple. Sira then identifies
Wisdom with the Law.

19 Approach me, you who desire me,
 and take your fill of my fruits,
20 for memories of me are sweeter than
  honey,
 inheriting me is sweeter than the
  honeycomb.
21 They who eat me will hunger for more,
 they who drink me will thirst for
  more.
22 No one who obeys me will ever have to
  blush,
 no one who acts as I dictate will ever
  sin.'

Wisdom and the Law

23 All this is no other than the Book of the
  Covenant of the Most High God,
 the Law that Moses enjoined on us,
 an inheritance for the communities of
  Jacob.
25 This is what makes wisdom brim over like
  the Pishon,
 like the Tigris in the season of fruit,
26 what makes intelligence overflow like the
  Euphrates,
 like the Jordan at harvest time;
27 and makes discipline flow like the Nile,
 like the Gihon when the grapes are
  harvested.
28 The first man did not finish discovering
  about her,
 nor has the most recent tracked her
  down;
29 for her thoughts are wider than the sea,
 and her designs more profound than
  the abyss.
30 And I, like a conduit from a river,
 like a watercourse running into a
  garden,
31 I said, 'I am going to water my orchard,
 I intend to irrigate my flower beds.'
 And see, my conduit has grown into a
  river,
 and my river has grown into a sea.
32 Making discipline shine forth from
  daybreak,
 I shall send its light far and wide.

33 I shall pour out teaching like prophecy,
 as a legacy to all future generations.
34 And note, I have been working not merely
  for myself,
 but for all who are seeking wisdom.

Proverbs

25 There are three things my soul
  delights in,
 and which are delightful to God and to
  all people:
 concord between brothers, friendship
  between neighbours,
 and a wife and husband who live
  happily together.

2 There are three sorts of people my soul
  hates,
 and whose existence I consider an
  outrage:
 the poor swollen with pride, the rich who
  is a liar
 and an adulterous old man who has no
  sense.

The aged

3 If you have gathered nothing in your
  youth,
 how can you discover anything in your
  old age?
4 How fine a thing: sound judgement with
  grey hairs,
 and for greybeards to know how to
  advise!
5 How fine a thing: wisdom in the aged,
 and considered advice coming from
  people of distinction!
6 The crown of the aged is ripe experience,
 their glory, the fear of the Lord.

Numerical proverbs

7 There are nine things I can think of which
  strike me as happy,
 and a tenth which is now on my tongue:
 the man who can be proud of his children,
 he who lives to see the downfall of his
  enemies;

8 happy is he who keeps house with a
    sensible wife;
  he who does not toil with ox and
    donkey;[a]
  he who has never sinned with his tongue;
  he who does not serve a man less
    worthy than himself;
9 happy is he who has acquired good
    sense
  and can find attentive ears for what he
    has to say;
10 how great is he who has acquired
    wisdom;
  but unsurpassed is one who fears the
    Lord.
11 The fear of the Lord surpasses
    everything;
  what can compare with someone who
    has mastered that?

Women

13 Any wound rather than a wound of the
    heart!
  Any spite rather than the spite of
    woman!
14 Any evil rather than an evil caused by an
    enemy!
  Any vengeance rather than the
    vengeance of a foe!
15 There is no poison worse than the poison
    of a snake,
  there is no fury worse than the fury of
    an enemy.
16 I would sooner keep house with a lion or a
    dragon
  than keep house with a spiteful wife.

17 A woman's spite changes her appearance
  and makes her face as grim as a
    bear's.
18 When her husband goes out to dinner
    with his neighbours,
  he cannot help heaving bitter sighs.

19 No spite can approach the spite of a
    woman,
  may a sinner's lot be hers!

20 Like the climbing of a sandhill for elderly
    feet,
  such is a garrulous wife for a quiet
    husband.
21 Do not be taken in by a woman's beauty,
  never lose your head over a woman.
22 Bad temper, insolence and shame hold
    sway
  where the wife supports the husband.
23 Low spirits, gloomy face, stricken heart:
  such is a spiteful wife.
  Slack hands and sagging knees:
  such is the wife who does not make her
    husband happy.

24 Sin began with a woman,
  and thanks to her we must all die.

25 Do not let water find a leak,
  nor a spiteful woman give free rein to
    her tongue.
26 If she will not do as you tell her,
  get rid of her.

26 How blessed is the husband of a really
    good wife;
  the number of his days will be doubled.
2 A perfect wife is the joy of her husband,
  he will live out the years of his life in
    peace.
3 A good wife is the best of portions,
  reserved for those who fear the Lord;
4 rich or poor, their hearts will be glad,
  their faces cheerful, whatever the
    season.

5 There are three things that I dread,
  and a fourth which terrifies me:
  slander by a whole town, the gathering of
    a mob,
  and a false accusation—these are all
    worse than death;
6 but a woman jealous of a woman means
    heartbreak and sorrow,
  and all this is the scourge of the tongue.

25a Such an uneven team is prohibited by Dt 22:10.

7 A bad wife is a badly fitting ox-yoke,
  trying to master her is like grasping a
   scorpion.
8 A drunken wife will goad anyone to fury,
  she cannot conceal her own
   degradation.

9 A woman's wantonness shows in her
   wide-eyed look,
  her eyelashes leave no doubt.
10 Keep a headstrong daughter under firm
   control,
  or, feeling free, she will take advantage
   of it.
11 Keep a strict watch on her shameless eye,
  do not be surprised if she disgraces you.
12 Like a thirsty traveller she will open her
   mouth
  and drink any water she comes across;
  she will sit down in front of every tent-peg
  and open her quiver to any arrow.

13 The grace of a wife will charm her
   husband,
  her understanding will make him the
   stronger.
14 A silent wife is a gift from the Lord,
  no price can be put on a well-trained
   character.
15 A modest wife is a boon twice over,
  a chaste character cannot be over-
   valued.
16 Like the sun rising over the mountains of
   the Lord,
  such is the beauty of a good wife in a
   well-run house.
17 Like a lamp shining on the sacred lamp-
   stand,
  such is a beautiful face on a well-
   proportioned body.
18 Like golden pillars on a silver base,
  such are shapely legs on firm-set heels.

Depressing things

28 There are two things which grieve my
   heart
  and a third arouses my anger:

a warrior wasting away through poverty,
  the intelligent treated with contempt,
someone turning back from virtue to sin—
  the Lord marks out such a person for a
   violent death.

Commerce

29 It is difficult for a merchant to avoid doing
   wrong
  and for a trader not to incur sin.

27 Many have sinned for the sake of
   profit,
  one who hopes to be rich must turn a
   blind eye.
2 A peg will stick in the joint between two
   stones,
  and sin will wedge itself between selling
   and buying.
3 Whoever does not firmly hold to the fear
   of the Lord,
  his house will soon be overthrown.

Speech

4 In a shaken sieve the rubbish is left
   behind,
  so too the defects of a person appear in
   speech.
5 The kiln tests the work of the potter,
  the test of a person is in conversation.
6 The orchard where the tree grows is
   judged by its fruit,
  similarly words betray what a person
   feels.
7 Do not praise anyone who has not yet
   spoken,
  since this is where people are tested.

Virtue

8 If you pursue virtue, you will attain it
  and put it on like a festal gown.
9 Birds consort with their kind,
  truth comes home to those who
   practise it.
10 The lion lies in wait for its prey,
  so does sin for those who do
   wrong.

11 The conversation of the devout is wisdom
      at all times,
   but the fool is as changeable as the
      moon.

12 When visiting stupid people, choose the
      right moment,
   but among the thoughtful take your
      time.

13 The conversation of fools is disgusting,
   raucous their laughter in their sinful
      pleasures.

14 The talk of hard-swearing people makes
      your hair stand on end,
   their brawling makes you stop your
      ears.

15 A quarrel between the proud leads to
      bloodshed,
   and their insults are embarrassing to
      hear.

Secrets

16 A betrayer of secrets forfeits all trust
   and will never find the kind of friend
      he wants.
17 Be fond of a friend and keep faith with
      him,
   but if you have betrayed his secrets, do
      not go after him any more;
18 for, as one destroys a person by killing
      him,
   so you have killed your neighbour's
      friendship,
19 and as you let a bird slip through your
      fingers,
   so you have let your friend go, and will
      not catch him.
20 Do not go after him—he is far away,
   he has fled like a gazelle from the
      snare.
21 For a wound can be bandaged and abuse
      forgiven,
   but for the betrayer of a secret there is
      no hope.

Hypocrisy

22 Someone with a sly wink is plotting
      mischief,
   no one can dissuade him from it.
23 Honey-tongued to your face,
   he is lost in admiration at your words;
      but behind your back he has other things
         to say,
      and turns your words into a stumbling-
         block.
24 I have found many things to hate, but
      nothing as much as him,
   and the Lord hates him too.

25 Whoever throws a stone in the air, throws
      it on to his own head;
   a treacherous blow cuts both ways.
26 The man who digs a pit falls into it,
   whoever sets a snare will be caught
      by it.
27 On anyone who does evil, evil will recoil,
   without his knowing where it comes
      from.

28 Sarcasm and abuse are the mark of the
      arrogant,
   but vengeance lies in wait like a lion for
      such a one.
29 The trap will close on all who rejoice in
      the downfall of the devout,
   and pain will eat them up before they
      die.

Resentment

30 Resentment and anger, these are foul
      things too,
   and a sinner is a master at them both.

28 Whoever exacts vengeance will
      experience the vengeance of the
         Lord,
   who keeps strict account of sin.
2 Pardon your neighbour any wrongs done
      to you,
   and when you pray, your sins will be
      forgiven.

3 If anyone nurses anger against another,
  can one then demand compassion from
    the Lord?
4 Showing no pity for someone like oneself,
  can one then plead for one's own sins?
5 Mere creature of flesh, yet cherishing
    resentment!—
  who will forgive one for sinning?
6 Remember the last things, and stop hating,
  corruption and death, and be faithful to
    the commandments.
7 Remember the commandments, and do
    not bear your fellow ill-will,
  remember the covenant of the Most
    High, and ignore the offence.

Quarrels

8 Avoid quarrelling and you will sin less;
  for the hot-tempered provokes
    quarrels,
9 a sinner sows trouble between friends,
  introducing discord among the
    peaceful.
10 The way a fire burns depends on its
    fuel,
  a quarrel spreads in proportion to its
    violence;
  a man's rage depends on his strength,
    his fury grows fiercer in proportion to
    his wealth.
11 A sudden quarrel kindles fire,
  a hasty dispute leads to bloodshed.
12 Blow on a spark and up it flares,
  spit on it and out it goes;
  both are the effects of your mouth.

The tongue

13 A curse on the scandal-monger and
    double-talker,
  such a person has ruined many who
    lived in concord.
14 That third tongue has shattered the peace
    of many
  and driven them from nation to nation;
  it has pulled down fortified cities,
    and overthrown the houses of the
    great.

15 The third tongue has had upright wives
    divorced,
  depriving them of reward for their hard
    work.
16 No one who listens to it will ever know
    peace of mind,
  will ever live in peace again.
17 A stroke of the whip raises a weal,
  but a stroke of the tongue breaks
    bones.
18 Many have fallen by the edge of the
    sword,
  but many more have fallen by the
    tongue.
19 Blessed is anyone who has been sheltered
    from it,
  and has not experienced its fury,
  who has not dragged its yoke about,
  or been bound in its chains;
20 for its yoke is an iron yoke,
  its chains are bronze chains;
21 the death it inflicts is a miserable death,
  Sheol is preferable to it.
22 It cannot gain a hold over the devout,
  they are not burnt by its flames.
23 Those who desert the Lord will fall
    into it,
  it will flare up inextinguishably among
    them,
  it will be let loose against them like a lion,
  it will tear them like a leopard.
24 Be sure you put a thorn-hedge round your
    property,
  lock away your silver and gold;
25 then make scales and weights for your
    words,
  and put a door with bolts across your
    mouth.
26 Take care you take no false step through it,
  in case you fall a prey to him who lies in
    wait.

Loans

29 Making your neighbour a loan is an act
    of mercy,
  to lend him a helping hand is to keep
    the commandments.

2 Lend to your neighbour in his time of
  need,
  and in your turn repay your neighbour
  on time.
3 Be as good as your word and keep faith
  with him,
  and you will find your needs met every
  time.
4 Many treat a loan as a windfall,
  and embarrass those who have come to
  their rescue.
5 Until he gets something, a man will kiss
  his neighbour's hand,
  and refer diffidently to his wealth;
  but when the loan falls due, he puts this
  off,
  he repays with offhand words,
  and pleads the inconvenience of the
  time.
6 Even if he can be made to pay, his creditor
  will recover barely half,
  and consider even that a windfall.
  But otherwise he will be cheated of his
  money,
  and undeservedly gain himself an
  enemy;
  the man will pay him back in curses and
  abuse,
  and with insults instead of honour.
7 Many, not out of malice, refuse to
  lend;
  they are merely anxious not to be
  cheated for nothing.

Almsgiving

8 Nevertheless, be patient with those who
  are badly off,
  do not keep them waiting on your
  generosity.
9 In obedience to the commandment, help
  the poor;
  do not turn the poor away empty-
  handed in their need.
10 Spend your money on your brother or
  your friend,
  do not leave it under a stone to rust
  away.

11 Use your wealth as the Most High has
  decreed;
  you will find that more profitable than
  gold.
12 Stock your store-rooms with almsgiving;
  this will save you from all misfortune.
13 Better than sturdy shield or weighty
  spear,
  this will fight for you against the enemy.

Guarantees

14 A good man will go surety for his
  neighbour;
  only a shameless wretch would desert
  him.
15 Do not forget the favour your guarantor
  has done you;
  he has given his life for you.
16 A sinner is careless of his guarantor's
  prosperity,
  the ungrateful forgets his deliverer.
17 Going surety has ruined many who were
  prosperous,
  tossing them about in a heavy sea.
18 It has driven the powerful from home
  to wander among foreign nations.
19 A wicked man in a hurry to stand
  guarantor
  in the hope of profit, is hurrying to be
  sentenced.
20 Come to your neighbour's help as far as
  you can,
  but take care not to fall into the same
  plight.

Staying in other people's houses

21 The first thing in life is water, and bread,
  and clothing,
  and a house for the sake of privacy.
22 Better the life of the poor under a roof of
  planks,
  than lavish fare in somebody else's
  house.
23 Whether you have little or much, be
  content with it,
  and you will not hear your household
  complaining.

24 It is a miserable life, going from house to
house;
wherever you stay, you dare not open
your mouth,
25 you do not belong, you receive no thanks
for the drink you pour out
and hear embittering words into the
bargain:
26 'Come along, stranger, lay the table,
what have you got ready? give me
something to eat!'
27 'Go away, stranger, make room for
someone important;
my brother is coming to stay, I need the
house.'
28 It is hard for the reasonable
to be begrudged hospitality
to be shamed like a debtor.

Bringing up children

30 Whoever loves his son will beat him
frequently
so that in after years the son may be his
comfort.

2 Whoever is strict with his son will reap the
benefit,
and be able to boast of him to his
acquaintances.

3 Whoever educates his son will be the envy
of his enemy,
and will be proud of him among his
friends.

4 Even when the father dies, he might well
not be dead,
since he leaves his likeness behind him.

5 In life he has had the joy of his company,
dying, he has no anxieties.
6 He leaves an avenger against his enemies
and a rewarder of favours for his
friends.

7 Whoever coddles his son will bandage his
wounds,
his heart will turn over at every cry.

8 A badly broken-in horse turns out
stubborn,
a son left to himself turns out
headstrong.
9 Pamper your child and he will terrorise
you,
play along with him and he will bring
you sorrow.

10 Do not laugh with him, or one day you
will weep with him
and end up gnashing your teeth.
11 While he is young, do not allow him his
freedom
and do not wink at his mistakes.
12 Bend his neck in youth,
bruise his ribs while he is a child,
or else he will grow stubborn and
disobedient,
and hurt you very deeply.
13 Be strict with your son, and persevere with
him,
or you will rue his insolence.

Health

14 Better be poor if healthy and fit
than rich if tormented in body.
15 Health and strength are better than any
gold,
a robust body than untold wealth.
16 No riches can outweigh bodily health,
no enjoyment surpass a cheerful heart.
17 Better death than a wretched life,
and everlasting rest than chronic illness.
18 Good things lavished on a closed mouth
are like food offerings put on a grave.
19 What use is an offering to an idol
which can neither eat nor smell?
How describe someone pursued by the
Lord's displeasure?
20   He looks and sighs
like a eunuch embracing a pretty girl—
how he sighs!

Happiness

21 Do not abandon yourself to sorrow,
do not torment yourself with brooding.

²² Gladness of heart is life to anyone,
  joy is what gives length of days.
²³ Give your cares the slip, console your heart,
  chase sorrow far away;
 for sorrow has been the ruin of many,
  and is no use to anybody.
²⁴ Jealousy and anger shorten your days,
  and worry brings premature old age.
²⁵ A genial heart makes a good trencherman,
  someone who enjoys a good meal.

Riches

31 The sleeplessness brought by wealth
   makes a person lose weight,
 the worry it causes drives away sleep.
² The worries of the daytime prevent you
   from sleeping,
  like a serious illness, they keep sleep at
   bay.
³ The rich for ever toils, piling up money,
  and then, leaving off, he is gorged with
   luxuries;
⁴ the poor for ever toils, barely making a
   living,
  and then, leaving off, is poorer than
   ever.

⁵ No one who loves money can easily avoid
   sinning,
  whoever pursues profit will be
   corrupted by it.
⁶ Gold has been the ruin of many;
  their coming destruction was self-
   evident,
⁷ since it is a snare for those who sacrifice to
   it
  and stupid people all get caught in it.
⁸ Happy the rich who is found to be
   blameless
  and does not go chasing after gold.
⁹ Who is he, so that we can congratulate
   him,
  for he has achieved marvels among his
   fellows?
¹⁰ Who has been through this test and
   emerged perfect?
  He may well be proud of that!

Who has had the chance to sin and has not
   sinned,
  had the chance to do wrong and has not
   done it?
¹¹ His fortune will be firmly based
  and the assembly will acclaim his
   generosity.

Dinner parties

¹² If you are sitting down to a lavish table,
  do not display your greed,
  do not say, 'What a lot to eat!'
¹³ Remember, it is bad to have a greedy eye.
  Is any creature more wicked than
   the eye?
  —That is why it is always weeping!
¹⁴ Do not reach out for anything your host
   has his eye on,
  do not jostle him at the dish.
¹⁵ Judge your fellow-guest's needs by your
   own,
  be thoughtful in every way.
¹⁶ Eat what is offered you like a well
   brought-up person,
  do not wolf your food or you will earn
   dislike.
¹⁷ For politeness' sake be the first to stop;
  do not act the glutton, or you will give
   offence,
¹⁸ and if you are sitting with a large party,
  do not help yourself before the others do.
¹⁹ A little is quite enough for a well-bred
   person;
  his breathing is easy when he lies in bed.
²⁰ A moderate diet ensures sound sleep,
  one gets up early, in the best of spirits.
  Sleeplessness, biliousness and gripe
  are what the glutton has to endure.
²¹ If you are forced to eat too much,
  get up, go and vomit, and you will feel
   better.
²² Listen to me, my child, do not disregard
   me,
  eventually you will see the force of my
   words.
  Be moderate in all your activities
  and illness will never overtake you.

70 READ ECCLESIASTICUS 31:1–11.

No one who loves money can easily avoid sinning.—ECCLESIASTICUS 31:5

POSSESSIONS NEVER SATISFY

Oh you who accumulate possessions and hoard them and never feel satisfied, wake up and learn so that you don't fall into evil, thinking that you are headed for paradise and possibly ending up in hell.

How hard you have to work to acquire so many possessions! You sweat a lot. You lose sleep. You are always worrying and troubled. You are always going over the sea or across the land, never staying at home. And what does all this get you except constant aggravation? You are never happy because your greed cannot be satisfied. It is never content and would never say, "Enough!" It always craves more and more.

If you acquire many possessions, you get them only with much sweat, aggravation and sorrow. And when in the end you must leave them, you suffer more aggravation, sorrow and distress. It is a no-win situation. I know of an old man who had a lot of money. To protect his cash from thieves he treated it as a cat does her kittens—he hid it one day here, the next day there. Now he buried it in the barn, now he put it in the wheat, now among the beans. He moved it so many times that finally he could not remember where he had put it. He roamed around looking for it and crying. When someone asked why he was crying, he was ashamed to answer. He was grieving because he feared that he would never find it. And he died with his fists clenched, angrily regretting his loss.

So what does accumulating possessions bring you except grief?

ST. BERNARDINO OF SIENA, 1380–1444

YOU WILL FIND THE NEXT READING AT ISAIAH 1.

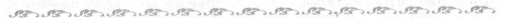

23 People praise the person who keeps a
    splendid table,
  and their opinion of his munificence is
    sound.
24 But a niggardly host provokes universal
    resentment
  and people will retail instances of his
    meanness.

Wine

25 Do not play the valiant at your wine,
  for wine has been the undoing of many.
26 The furnace proves the temper of steel,
  and wine proves hearts in the drinking
    bouts of braggarts.

27 Wine gives life
    if drunk in moderation.
  What is life worth without wine?
    It came into being to make people happy.
28 Drunk at the right time and in the right
    amount,
  wine makes for a glad heart and a
    cheerful mind.
29 Bitterness of soul comes of wine drunk to
    excess
  out of temper or bravado.
30 Drunkenness excites the stupid to a fury to
    his own harm,
  it reduces his strength while leading to
    blows.

³¹ Do not provoke your fellow-guest at a
wine feast,
    do not make fun of him when he is
enjoying himself,
  do not take him to task
    or annoy him by reclaiming money
owed.

Banquets

32 Have they made you the presider? Do
not let it go to your head,
  behave like everyone else in the party,
  see that they are happy and then sit
down yourself.
² Having discharged your duties, take your
place
  so that your joy may be through theirs,
  and you may receive the crown for your
competence.
³ Speak, old man—it is proper that you
should—
  but with discretion: do not spoil the
music.
⁴ If someone is singing, do not ramble on
  and do not play the sage at the wrong
moment.
⁵ An amber seal on a precious stone,
  such is a concert of music at a wine feast.
⁶ An emerald seal in a golden setting,
  such are strains of music with a vintage
wine.

⁷ Speak, young man, when you must,
  but twice at most, and then only if
questioned.
⁸ Keep to the point, say much in few words;
  give the impression of knowing but not
wanting to speak.
⁹ Among eminent people do not behave as
though you were their equal;
  do not make frivolous remarks when
someone else is speaking.
¹⁰ Lightning comes before the thunder,
  favour goes ahead of a modest person.
¹¹ Leave in good time, do not bring up the
rear,
  and hurry home without loitering.

¹² There amuse yourself, and do what you
have a mind to,
  but do not sin by arrogant talk.
¹³ And for all this bless your Creator,
  who intoxicates you with his favours.

The fear of God

¹⁴ Whoever fears the Lord will accept his
correction;
  those who look for him will win his
favour.
¹⁵ Whoever seeks the Law will be nourished
by it,
  the hypocrite will find it a stumblingblock.
¹⁶ Those who fear the Lord win his approval,
  their good deeds shining like a light.

¹⁷ The sinner waves reproof aside,
  he finds an excuse for headstrong
behaviour.
¹⁸ A sensible person never scorns a warning;
  foreigners and the proud do not know
about fear.

¹⁹ Never act without reflection,
  and you will not regret your actions.
²⁰ Do not venture on a rough road,
  for fear of stumbling over the stones.
²¹ Do not be over-confident on an even
road
²²   and beware of your own children.
²³ Watch yourself in everything you do;
  this is also the way to keep the
commandments.
²⁴ Anyone who trusts in the Law obeys its
precepts,
  no one who has confidence in the Lord
will come to harm.

33 No evil will befall one who fears the
Lord,
  such a one will be rescued even in the
ordeal.
² No one who hates the Law is wise,
  one who is hypocritical about it is like a
storm-tossed ship.

³ An intelligent person will put faith in the
Law,
for such a one the Law is as dependable
as a prophecy.

⁴ Prepare what you have to say and you will
get a hearing,
marshal your information before you
answer.
⁵ The feelings of a fool are like a cart-wheel,
a fool's thought revolves like a turning
axle.
⁶ A rutting stallion is like a sarcastic
friend;
he neighs, whoever rides him.

Inequality

⁷ Why is one day better than another,
though the sun gives the same daylight
throughout the year?
⁸ They have been differentiated in the mind
of the Lord,
who has diversified the seasons and
feasts;
⁹ some he has made more important and has
hallowed,
others he has made ordinary days.
¹⁰ Human beings come from the ground,
Adam himself was formed out of
earth;
¹¹ in the fullness of his wisdom
the Lord has made distinctions between
them,
and diversified their conditions.
¹² Some of them he has blessed,
hallowing and setting them near him;
others he has cursed and humiliated
by degrading them from their positions.
¹³ Like clay in the hands of the potter
to mould as it pleases him,
so are human beings in the hands of their
Maker
to reward as he judges right.
¹⁴ Opposite evil stands good,
opposite death, life;
so too opposite the devout stands the
sinner.

¹⁵ Contemplate all the works of the Most
High,
you will find they go in pairs, by
opposites.

¹⁶ Although the last to come, I have kept my
eyes open
like a man picking up what the grape-
pickers have left.
¹⁷ By the blessing of the Lord I have come in
first,
and like a true grape-picker have filled
my winepress.
¹⁸ And note, I have not been working merely
for myself,
but for all who seek instruction.

¹⁹ Listen to me, important public figures,
presidents of the assembly, give ear!

Independence

²⁰ Neither to son nor wife, brother nor
friend,
give power over yourself during your
own lifetime.
And do not give your property to anyone
else,
in case you regret it and have to ask for
it back.
²¹ As long as you live and there is breath in
your body,
do not yield power over yourself to
anyone;
²² better for your children to come begging
to you,
than for you to have to go begging to
them.
²³ In all you do be the master,
and leave a reputation unstained.
²⁴ The day your life draws to a close,
at the hour of death, then distribute
your heritage.

Slaves

²⁵ Fodder, the stick and burdens for a
donkey,
bread, discipline and work for a slave.

²⁶ Work your slave hard, and you will have
    peace of mind,
      leave his hands idle, and he will be
      asking for his freedom.
²⁷ Yoke and harness will bow the neck,
    for a bad servant, torments and the
    rack.
²⁸ Set him to work, so that he will not be idle;
    idleness teaches every kind of mischief.
²⁹ Keep him at his duties, where he should
    be,
      if he is disobedient, clap him in irons.
³⁰ But do not be over-exacting with anyone,
    and do nothing contrary to justice.

³¹ You have only one slave? Treat him like
    yourself,
      since you have acquired him with
      blood.
³² You have only one slave? Treat him as a
    brother,
      since you need him as you need
      yourself.
³³ If you ill-treat him and he runs away,
    which way will you go to look for him?

Dreams

34 Vain and deceptive hopes are for the
    foolish,
    and dreams lend wings to fools.
² As well clutch at shadows and chase the
    wind
    as put any faith in dreams.
³ Dreams are no different from mirrors;
    confronting a face, the reflection of that
    face.
⁴ What can be cleansed by uncleanness,
    what can be verified by falsehood?
⁵ Divinations, auguries and dreams are
    nonsense,
    like the fantasies of a pregnant woman.
⁶ Unless sent as emissaries from the Most
    High,
    do not give them a thought;
⁷ for dreams have led many astray,
    and those who relied on them have
    come to grief.

⁸ Fulfilling the Law requires no such
    falsehood,
    and wisdom is perfected in veracity.

Travelling

⁹ A much travelled man knows many
    things,
    and a man of great experience will talk
    sound sense.
¹⁰ Someone who has never had his trials
    knows little;
    but the travelled man is master of every
    situation.
¹¹ I have seen many things on my travels,
    I have understood more than I can put
    into words.
¹² I have often been in danger of death,
    but I have been spared, and this is why:
¹³ the spirit of those who fear the Lord can
    survive,
    for their hope is in someone with power
    to save them.
¹⁴ No one who fears the Lord need ever
    hesitate,
    or ever be daunted, since the Lord is his
    hope.
¹⁵ Happy the soul of one who fears the
    Lord.
    On whom does he rely? Who supports
    him?
¹⁶ The eyes of the Lord watch over those
    who love him,
    he is their powerful protection and their
    strong support,
    their screen from the desert wind, their
    shelter from the midday sun,
    a guard against stumbling, an assurance
    against a fall.
¹⁷ He revives the spirit and brightens the
    eyes,
    he gives health, life and blessing.

Sacrifices

¹⁸ The sacrifice of an offering unjustly
    acquired is a mockery;
    the gifts of the impious are
    unacceptable.

19 The Most High takes no pleasure in
    offerings from the godless,
  multiplying sacrifices will not gain
    pardon for sin.
20 Offering sacrifice from the property of
    the poor
  is as bad as slaughtering a son before
    his father's eyes.
21 A meagre diet is the very life of the
    poor,
  to deprive them of it is to commit
    murder.
22 To take away a fellow-man's livelihood is
    to kill him,
  to deprive an employee of his wages is
    to shed blood.
23 If one person builds while another pulls
    down,
  what will they get out of it but trouble?
24 If one person prays and another calls down
    a curse,
  to which one's voice is the Master going
    to listen?
25 If someone washes after touching a corpse,
    and then touches it again,
  what is the good of his washing?
26 Just so with someone who fasts for sin,
    and then goes and commits it again.
  Who is going to hear that person's prayer?
  What is the good of the self-abasement?

The Law and sacrifices

35 One who keeps the Law multiplies
    offerings;
  one who follows the commandments
    offers communion sacrifices.
2 Proof of gratitude is an offering of fine
    flour,
  almsgiving a sacrifice of praise.
3 To abandon wickedness is what pleases the
    Lord,
  to give up wrong-doing is an expiatory
    sacrifice.
4 Do not appear empty-handed in the Lord's
    presence;
  for all these things are due under the
    commandment.

5 The offering of the upright graces the
    altar,
  and its savour rises before the Most
    High.
6 The sacrifice of the upright is acceptable,
  its memorial will not be forgotten.
7 Honour the Lord with generosity,
  do not stint the first-fruits you bring.
8 Add a smiling face to all your gifts,
  and be cheerful as you dedicate your
    tithes.
9 Give to the Most High as he has given to
    you,
  as generously as your means can afford;
10 for the Lord is a good rewarder,
  he will reward you seven times over.

Divine justice

11 Do not try to bribe him with presents, he
    will not accept them,
  do not put your faith in wrongly
    motivated sacrifices;
12 for the Lord is a judge
  who is utterly impartial.
13 He never shows partiality to the detriment
    of the poor,
  he listens to the plea of the injured
    party.
14 He does not ignore the orphan's
    supplication,
  nor the widow's as she pours out her
    complaint.
15 Do the widow's tears not run down her
    cheeks,
  as she accuses the man who is the cause
    of them?
16 Whoever wholeheartedly serves God will
    be accepted,
  his petitions will carry to the clouds.
17 The prayer of the humble pierces the
    clouds:
  and until it does, he is not to be
    consoled,
18 nor will he desist until the Most High
    takes notice of him,
  acquits the upright and delivers
    judgement.

¹⁹ And the Lord will not be slow,
nor will he be dilatory on their behalf,
²⁰ until he has crushed the loins of the
merciless
and exacted vengeance on the nations,
²¹ until he has eliminated the hordes of the
arrogant
and broken the sceptres of the wicked,
²² until he has repaid all people as their deeds
deserve
and human actions as their intentions
merit,
²³ until he has judged the case of his people
and made them rejoice in his mercy.
²⁴ Mercy is welcome in time of trouble,
like rain clouds in time of drought.

*Prayer for the deliverance and restoration
of Israel*

36 Take pity on us, Master, Lord of the
universe, look at us,
spread fear of yourself throughout all
other nations.
² Raise your hand against the foreign
nations
and let them see your might.
³ As, in their sight, you have proved yourself
holy to us,
so now, in our sight, prove yourself
great to them.
⁴ Let them acknowledge you, just as we
have acknowledged
that there is no God but you, Lord.
⁵ Send new portents, do fresh wonders,
win glory for your hand and your right
arm.
⁶ Rouse your fury, pour out your rage,
destroy the opponent, annihilate the
enemy.
⁷ Hasten the day, remember the oath,
and let people tell of your mighty
deeds.
⁸ Let fiery wrath swallow up the survivor,
and destruction overtake those who
oppress your people.
⁹ Crush the heads of hostile rulers
who say, 'There is no one else but us!'

¹⁰ Gather together all the tribes of Jacob,
restore them their heritage as at the
beginning.
¹¹ Take pity, Lord, on the people called by
your name,
on Israel whom you have made your
first-born.
¹² Have compassion on your holy city,
on Jerusalem, the place where you
rest.
¹³ Fill Zion with your praises
and your sanctuary with your glory.
¹⁴ Vindicate those whom you created first,
fulfil what has been prophesied in your
name.
¹⁵ Give those who wait for you their reward,
let your prophets be proved true.
¹⁶ Grant, Lord, the prayer of your servants,
in the terms of Aaron's blessing on your
people,
¹⁷ so that all the earth's inhabitants may
acknowledge
that you are the Lord, the everlasting
God.

Discrimination

¹⁸ The stomach takes in all kinds of food,
but some foods are better than others.
¹⁹ As the palate discerns the flavour of game,
so a shrewd listener detects lying words.
²⁰ A perverse character causes depression in
others;
it needs experience to know how to
repay such a one.

Choosing a wife

²¹ A woman will accept any husband,
but some daughters are better than
others.
²² A woman's beauty delights the beholder,
a man likes nothing better.
²³ If her tongue is kind and gentle,
her husband is the happiest of men.
²⁴ The man who takes a wife has the
makings of a fortune,
a helper to match himself, a pillar of
support.

25 When property has no fence, it is open to
   plunder,
  when a man has no wife, he is aimless
   and querulous.
26 Will anyone trust an armed thief
  who flits from town to town?
27 So it is with the man who has no nest,
  and lodges wherever night overtakes
   him.

False friends

37 Any friend will say, 'I am your friend
   too,'
  but some friends are friends only in
   name.
2 Is it not a deadly sorrow
  when a comrade or a friend turns
   enemy?
3 O evil inclination, why were you created,
  to cover the earth with deceit?
4 One kind of comrade congratulates a
   friend in prosperity
  but in time of trouble appears on the
   other side.
5 One kind of comrade genuinely feels for a
   friend
  and when it comes to a fight, springs to
   arms.
6 Do not forget the genuine friend,
  do not push him out of mind once you
   are rich.

Advisers

7 Any adviser will offer advice,
  but some are governed by self-interest.
8 Beware of someone who offers advice;
  first find out what he wants himself—
  since his advice coincides with his own
   interest—
  in case he has designs on you
9 and tells you, 'You are on the right road,'
  but stands well clear to see what will
   happen to you.
10 Do not consult anyone who looks at you
   askance,
  conceal your plans from people jealous
   of you.

11 Do not consult a woman about her
   rival,
  or a coward about war,
  a merchant about prices,
   or a buyer about selling,
  anyone mean about gratitude,
   or anyone selfish about kindness,
  a lazy fellow about any sort of work,
   or a casual worker about finishing
   a job,
  an idle servant about a major
   undertaking—
  do not rely on these for any advice.
12 But have constant recourse to some devout
   person,
  whom you know to be a keeper of the
   commandments,
  whose soul matches your own,
  and who, if you go wrong, will be
   sympathetic.
13 Finally, stick to the advice your own heart
   gives you,
  no one can be truer to you than that;
14 since a person's soul often gives a clearer
   warning
  than seven watchmen perched on a
   watchtower.
15 And besides all this beg the Most High
  to guide your steps into the truth.

True and false wisdom

16 Reason should be the basis for every
   activity,
  reflection must come before any
   undertaking.
17 Thoughts are rooted in the heart,
  and this sends out four branches:
18 good and evil, life and death,
  and mistress of them always is the
   tongue.
19 One kind of person is clever at teaching
   others,
  yet is no good whatever to himself;
20 another, very eloquent, is detested
  and ends by starving to death,
21 not having won the favour of the Lord,
  and being destitute of all wisdom.

22 Another considers himself wise
 and proclaims his intellectual
 conclusions as certainties.
23 But the truly wise instructs his people
 and his intellectual conclusions are
 certainties.
24 The wise is showered with blessings,
 and all who see him will call him happy.
25 Human life lasts a number of days,
 but the days of Israel are beyond
 counting.
26 The wise will earn confidence among the
 people,
 his name will live for ever.

Moderation

27 During your life, my child, see what suits
 your constitution,
 do not give it what you find disagrees
 with it;
28 for not everything is good for everybody,
 nor does everybody like everything.
29 Do not be insatiable for any delicacy,
 do not be greedy for food,
30 for over-eating leads to illness
 and excess leads to liver-attacks.
31 Many people have died from over-eating;
 control yourself, and so prolong your
 life.

Medicine and illness

38 Treat the doctor with the honour that
 is his due,
 in consideration of his services;
 for he too has been created by the
 Lord.
2 Healing itself comes from the Most
 High,
 like a gift received from a king.
3 The doctor's learning keeps his head high,
 and the great regard him with awe.
4 The Lord has brought forth medicinal
 herbs from the ground,
 and no one sensible will despise them.
5 Did not a piece of wood once sweeten the
 water,
 thus giving proof of its power?ª

6 He has also given some people knowledge,
 so that they may draw credit from his
 mighty works.
7 He uses these for healing and relieving
 pain;
 the druggist makes up a mixture from
 them.
8 Thus, there is no end to his activities;
 thanks to him, well-being exists
 throughout the world.

9 My child, when you are ill, do not rebel,
 but pray to the Lord and he will heal
 you.
10 Renounce your faults, keep your hands
 unsoiled,
 and cleanse your heart from all sin.
11 Offer incense and a memorial of fine flour,
 make as rich an offering as you can
 afford.
12 Then let the doctor take over—the Lord
 created him too—
 do not let him leave you, for you need
 him.
13 There are times when good health
 depends on doctors.
14 For they, in their turn, will pray the
 Lord
 to grant them the grace to relieve
 and to heal, and so prolong your life.
15 Whoever sins in the eyes of his Maker,
 let such a one come under the care of
 the doctor!

Mourning

16 My child, shed tears over the dead,
 lament for the dead to show your
 sorrow,
 then bury the body with due ceremony
 and do not fail to honour the grave.
17 Weep bitterly, beat your breast,
 observe the mourning the dead deserves
 for a day or two, to avoid censorious
 comment,
 and then be comforted in your sorrow;

38a Ex 15:23–25.

¹⁸ for grief can lead to death,
    a grief-stricken heart loses all energy.
¹⁹ In affliction sorrow persists,
    a life of grief is hard to bear.
²⁰ Do not abandon your heart to grief,
    drive it away, bear your own end in
       mind.
²¹ Do not forget, there is no coming back;
    you cannot help the dead, and you will
       harm yourself.
²² 'Remember my doom, since it will be
       yours too;
    I yesterday, you today!'
²³ Once the dead are laid to rest, let their
       memory rest,
    do not fret for them, once their spirit
       departs.

Trades and crafts

²⁴ Leisure gives the scribe the chance to
       acquire wisdom;
    a man with few commitments can grow
       wise.
²⁵ How can the ploughman become wise,
    whose sole ambition is to wield the
       goad,
    driving his oxen, engrossed in their work,
    his conversation limited to bullocks,
²⁶ his thoughts absorbed in the furrows he
       traces
    and his long evenings spent in fattening
       heifers?
²⁷ Similarly with all workmen and
       craftsmen,
    toiling day and night;
    those who engrave seals,
    for ever trying to think of a new design,
    concentrating on catching a good likeness
    and staying up late to get the work
       done.
²⁸ Similarly with the blacksmith sitting by
       his anvil;
    he considers what to do with the pig-
       iron,
    the breath of the fire scorches his skin,
    as he contends with the heat of the
       furnace;

the noise of the hammer deafens him,
    his eyes are fixed on the pattern;
he concentrates on getting the job done
       well
    and stays up late to apply the finishing
       touches.
²⁹ Similarly with the potter, sitting at his
       work,
    turning the wheel with his feet;
constantly on the alert over his work,
    each flick of the finger premeditated;
³⁰ he pummels the clay with his arm,
    and with his feet he kneads it;
he concentrates on applying the glaze right
    and stays up late to clean the kiln.
³¹ All these people rely on their hands
    and each is skilled at his own craft.
³² A town could not be inhabited without
       them,
    there would be no settling, no
       travelling.
³³ But you will not find them in the
       parliament,
    they do not hold high rank in the
       assembly.
They do not sit on the judicial bench,
    and they do not meditate on the Law.
³⁴ They are not remarkable for their culture
       or judgement,
    nor are they found frequenting the
       philosophers.
They sustain the structure of the world,
    and their prayer is concerned with their
       trade.

The scribe

39 Not so with one who concentrates his
       mind
    and his meditation on the Law of the
       Most High.
He researches into the wisdom of all the
       Ancients,
    he occupies his time with the
       prophecies.
² He preserves the discourses of famous men,
    he is at home with the niceties of
       parables.

3 He researches into the hidden sense of
  proverbs,
  he ponders the obscurities of parables.
4 He enters the service of princes,
  he is seen in the presence of rulers.
  He travels in foreign countries,
  he has experienced human good and
  human evil.
5 At dawn and with all his heart
  he turns to the Lord his Creator;
  he pleads in the presence of the Most
  High,
  he opens his mouth in prayer
  and makes entreaty for his sins.
6 If such be the will of the great Lord,
  he will be filled with the spirit of
  intelligence,
  he will shower forth words of wisdom,
  and in prayer give thanks to the Lord.
7 He will grow upright in purpose and
  learning,
  he will ponder the Lord's hidden
  mysteries.
8 He will display the instruction he has
  received,
  taking his pride in the Law of the
  Lord's covenant.
9 Many will praise his intelligence
  and it will never be forgotten.
  His memory will not disappear,
  generation after generation his name
  will live.
10 Nations will proclaim his wisdom,
  the assembly will celebrate his
  praises.ᵃ
11 If he lives long, his name will be more
  glorious than a thousand others,
  and if he dies, that will satisfy him just
  as well.

Invitation to praise God

12 And here are some more of my reflections:
  yes, I am as full as the moon at the full!
13 Listen to me, devout children, and
  blossom
  like the rose that grows on the bank of a
  watercourse.

14 Give off a sweet smell like incense,
  flower like the lily, spread your
  fragrance abroad,
  sing a song of praise
  blessing the Lord for all his works.
15 Declare the greatness of his name,
  proclaim his praise
  with song and with lyre,
  and this is how you must sing his
  praises:
16 'How wonderful, the actions of the
  Lord!
  Whatever he orders is done at the
  proper time!'
  You must not say, 'What is this? Why is
  that?'
  There is a proper time for every
  question.
17 At his word, the water stops and piles up
  high,
  at his voice, the watery reservoirs take
  shape,
18 at his command, whatever he wants is
  done,
  no one can stop him, if he intends to
  save.
19 He can see whatever human beings are
  doing,
  nothing can be hidden from his eye;
20 his gaze stretches from eternity to
  eternity,
  and nothing can astonish him.
21 You must not say, 'What is this? Why is
  that?'
  for everything has been made for a
  purpose.

22 As his blessing covers the dry land like a
  river
  and soaks it like a flood,
23 so retribution is his legacy to the nations,
  just as he has turned fresh waters to salt.
24 His ways are as smooth for the devout,
  as they are full of obstacles for the
  wicked.

39a = 44:15.

²⁵ Good things were created from the
  beginning for good people,
  as bad ones were for sinners.
²⁶ The prime needs of human beings for
  living
  are water and fire, iron and salt,
  wheat-flour, milk and honey,
  the juice of the grape, oil and clothing.
²⁷ All these are good for those who are good,
  but turn out bad for sinners.

²⁸ Some winds have been created for
  punishing,
  in his fury, he uses them as scourges;
  on the day of doom, they unleash their
  violence
  and appease the wrath of their Creator.
²⁹ Fire and hail, famine and death,
  have all been created for punishing.
³⁰ Wild animals' fangs, scorpions, vipers,
  the avenging sword for the ruin of the
  godless:
³¹ all of them exult in discharging his orders,
  ready on earth whenever the need arises
  and, when their time comes, not falling
  short of his word.

³² That is why I was determined from the
  outset,
  why I have pondered and why I have
  written,
³³ 'The works of the Lord are all good,
  when the time is right, he gives
  whatever is needed.
³⁴ You must not say, "This is worse than
  that,"
  for, sooner or later, everything proves
  its worth.
³⁵ So now, sing with all your heart and
  voice,
  and bless the name of the Lord!'

Human wretchedness

40 A hard lot has been created for human
  beings,
  a heavy yoke lies on the children of
  Adam

from the day they come out of their
  mother's womb,
  till the day they return to the mother of
  them all.
² What fills them with foreboding and their
  hearts with fear
  is dread of the day of death.
³ From the one who sits on a glorious throne
  to the wretch in dust and ashes,
⁴ from the one who wears purple and a
  crown
  to the one dressed in sacking,
  all is fury and jealousy, turmoil and unrest,
  fear of death, rivalry, strife.
⁵ And even at night while he rests on his
  bed
  his sleep only gives a new twist to his
  worries:
⁶ scarcely has he lain down to rest,
  when in his sleep, as if in broad
  daylight,
  he is troubled with nightmares,
  like one who has escaped from a battle,
⁷ and at the moment of rescue he wakes up,
  amazed that there was nothing to be
  afraid of!
⁸ For all creatures, human and animal—
  and seven times more for sinners—
⁹ there is death and blood and strife and the
  sword,
  disasters, famine, affliction, plague.
¹⁰ These things were all created for the
  wicked,
  and the Flood came because of them.
¹¹ All that comes from the earth returns to
  the earth,[a]
  and what comes from the water returns
  to the sea.

Various maxims

¹² All bribery and injustice will be blotted out,
  but good faith will stand for ever.
¹³ Ill-gotten wealth will vanish like a torrent,
  like the single thunder-clap that heralds
  rain.

40a = 41:10.

14 When he opens his hand, he rejoices,
   by the same token, sinners come to
      ruin.
15 The sprigs of the godless will not make
      many branches,
   tainted roots find only hard rock.
16 The reed that grows by every lake and
      river's edge
   is the first plant to be uprooted.
17 Charity is a very paradise of blessing
   and almsgiving endures for ever.
18 For a person of private means and one
      who works hard, life is pleasant,
   better off than either, one who finds a
      treasure.
19 Children and the founding of a city
      perpetuate a name:
   more esteemed than either, a perfect
      wife.
20 Wine and music cheer the heart;
   better than either, the love of wisdom.
21 Flute and harp add sweetness to a song;
   better than either, a melodious voice.
22 The eye longs for grace and beauty;
   better than either, the green of spring
      corn.
23 Friend or comrade—it is always well met;
   better than either, a wife and husband.
24 Brothers and allies are good in times of
      trouble;
   better than either, almsgiving to the
      rescue.
25 Gold and silver will steady your feet;
   more esteemed than either, good advice.
26 Money and strength make a confident
      heart;
   better than either, the fear of the Lord.
   With fear of the Lord, nothing is lacking:
      no need to seek for other help.
27 Fear of the Lord is a paradise of blessing,
   a better protection than the highest
      reputation.

Sponging

28 My child, do not live by sponging off
      others,
   better be dead than be a sponger.

29 A life spent in eyeing someone else's
      table
   cannot be accounted a life at all.
   Other people's food defiles the gullet;
   a wise, well-brought-up person will
      beware of doing this.
30 What a sponger says may sound very
      sweet
   but in his belly there burns a fire.

Death

41 O death, how bitter it is to remember
      you
   for someone peacefully living with his
      possessions,
   for someone with no worries and
      everything going well
   and who can still enjoy his food!

2 O death, your sentence is welcome
   to one in want, whose strength is
      failing,
   to one worn out with age and a thousand
      worries,
   resentful and impatient!

3 Do not dread death's sentence;
   remember those who came before you
      and those who will come after.
4 This is the sentence passed on all living
      creatures by the Lord,
   so why object to what seems good to the
      Most High?
   Whether your life lasts ten or a hundred or
      a thousand years,
   its length will not be held against you in
      Sheol.

The fate of the wicked

5 Hateful brats, such are the children of
      sinners,
   who foregather in the haunts of the
      godless.
6 The inheritance of sinners' children is
      doomed to perish,
   their posterity will endure lasting
      reproach.

⁷ A godless father will be blamed by his
children
for the reproach he has brought on
them.
⁸ A bad outlook for you, godless people,
who have forsaken the Law of God
Most High.
⁹ When you were born, you were born to be
accursed,
and when you die, that curse will be
your portion.
¹⁰ All that comes from the earth returns to
the earth,ᵃ
so too the wicked proceed from curse to
destruction.
¹¹ Mourning concerns only the bodies of the
dead,
but the worthless name of sinners will
be blotted out.

¹² Be careful of your reputation, for it will
last you longer
than a thousand great hoards of
gold.
¹³ A good life lasts a certain number of
days,
but a good reputation lasts for
ever.

Sense of shame

¹⁴ Keep my instructions and be at peace, my
children.
Wisdomᵇ hidden away and treasure
undisplayed,
what use is either of these?
¹⁵ Better someone who hides his folly
than one who hides his wisdom.
¹⁶ Preserve a sense of shame in the following
matters,
for not every kind of shame is right to
harbour,
nor is every situation correctly
appraised by all.
¹⁷ Be ashamed, before father and mother, of
depraved behaviour,
and before prince or potentate of telling
lies;

¹⁸ of wrong-doing before judge or
magistrate,
and of impiety before the assembly of
the people;
¹⁹ of sharp practice before your companion
and your friend,
and of theft before the neighbourhood
you live in.
²⁰ Before the truth and covenant of God,
be ashamed of leaning elbows on the
table,
²¹ of being ungracious when giving or
receiving,
of ignoring those who greet you,
²² of gazing at a loose woman,
of repulsing your fellow-countryman,
²³ of misappropriating another's portion or
gift,
of paying court to another man's wife,
²⁴ of making advances to his servant-girl
—do not go near her bed—
²⁵ of saying disagreeable things to friends
—do not follow up a gift with a taunt—
²⁶ of repeating everything you hear
and of betraying confidences.
²⁷ Then you will know what true shame is,
and you will find yourself in everyone's
graces.

42 The following things you should not
be ashamed of,
and do not sin from fear of what others
think:
² of the Law of the Most High or of the
covenant,
of a verdict that acquits the godless,
³ of keeping accounts with a travelling
companion,
of settling property on your friends,
⁴ of being accurate over scales and weights,
of making small and large profits,
⁵ of gaining from commercial transactions,
of disciplining your children strictly,
of lashing a wicked slave till you draw
blood.

41a = 40:11.   *41b* = 20:30–31.

6 With an interfering wife, it is as well to
use your seal,
and where there are many hands, lock
things up.
7 Whatever stores you issue, do it by
number and weight,
spendings and takings, put everything
in writing.
8 Do not be ashamed to correct a stupid
person or a fool,
or an old dotard who bickers with
young people.
Then you will show yourself really
educated
and win the approval of everyone.

Worries of a father with a daughter

9 Unknown to her, a daughter keeps her
father awake,
the worry she gives him drives away his
sleep:
in her youth, in case she never marries,
married, in case she should be
disliked,
10 as a virgin, in case she should be defiled
and found with child in her father's
house,
having a husband, in case she goes astray,
married, in case she should be sterile!
11 Your daughter is headstrong? Keep a
sharp look-out
that she does not make you the
laughing-stock of your enemies,
the talk of the town, the object of common
gossip,
and put you to public shame.

Women

12 Do not stare at any man for his good
looks,
do not sit down with women;
13 for moth comes out of clothes,
and woman's spite out of woman.
14 Better a man's spite than a woman's
kindness:
women give rise to shame and
reproach.

God's glory in nature

15 Next, I shall remind you of the works of
the Lord,
and tell of what I have seen.
By the words of the Lord his works come
into being
and all creation obeys his will.
16 The shining sun looks down on all things,
and the work of the Lord is full of his
glory.
17 The Lord has not granted the Holy Ones
the power
to tell of all his marvels
which the Almighty Lord has solidly
constructed
for the universe to stand firm in his
glory.
18 He has fathomed both the abyss and the
human heart
and seen into their devious ways;
for the Most High knows all there is to
know
and sees the signs of the times.
19 He declares what is past and what
will be,
and reveals the trend of hidden
things.
20 Not a thought escapes him,
not a single word is hidden from him.
21 He has embellished the magnificent works
of his wisdom,
he is from everlasting to everlasting,
nothing can be added to him, nothing
taken away,
he needs no one's advice.
22 How lovely, all his works,
how dazzling to the eye!
23 They all live and last for ever,
and, whatever the circumstances, all
obey.
24 All things go in pairs, by opposites,
he has not made anything imperfect:
25 one thing complements the excellence of
another.
Who could ever grow tired of gazing at
his glory?

The sun

43
¹ Pride of the heights, a clear vault of the
  sky—
   such is the beauty of the heavens, a
     glorious sight.
² The sun, as he emerges, proclaims at his
   rising,
   'How wonderful a thing, the work of
     the Most High!'
³ At his zenith, he parches the ground,
   who can withstand his blaze?
⁴ We have to blow the furnace to produce
   any heat,
   the sun burns the mountains three times
     as much;
   breathing out blasts of fire,
     flashing his rays, he dazzles the eyes.
⁵ Great is the Lord who created him
   and whose word speeds him on his
     course.

The moon

⁶ And then the moon, ever punctual
   to mark the times, an everlasting sign:
⁷ It is the moon that signals the feasts,
   a luminary that wanes after being full.
⁸ The month derives its name from hers,
   she waxes wonderfully in her phases,
   banner of the hosts on high,
     shining in the vault of heaven.

The stars

⁹ The glory of the stars makes the beauty of
   the sky,
   a brilliant adornment of the Lord on
     High.
¹⁰ At the words of the Holy One they stand
   as he decrees,
   and never grow slack at their watch.

The rainbow

¹¹ See the rainbow and praise its Maker,
   so superbly beautiful in its splendour.
¹² Across the sky it forms a glorious arc
   drawn by the hands of the Most
     High.

The wonders of nature

¹³ By his command he sends the snow,
   he speeds the lightning by his
     command.
¹⁴ In the same way, his treasuries open
   and the clouds fly out like birds.
¹⁵ His great power solidifies the clouds,
   then pulverises them into hail.
¹⁷ᵃ At the roar of his thunder, the earth
     writhes in labour,
¹⁶   at the sight of him, the mountains
       quake.
   At his will the south wind blows,
¹⁷ᵇ   or the storm from the north and the
       whirlwind.
¹⁸ He sprinkles snow like birds alighting,
   it comes down like locusts settling.
   The eye marvels at the beauty of its
     whiteness,
   and the mind is amazed at its
     falling.
¹⁹ Over the earth, like salt, he also
     pours hoarfrost,
   which, when it freezes, bristles like
     thorns.
²⁰ The cold wind blows from the north,
   and ice forms on the water;
   it forms on every piece of standing
     water,
   covering it like a breastplate.
²¹ The wind swallows up the mountains
     and scorches the desert,
   like a fire it consumes the vegetation.
²² But cloud brings swift healing,
   and dew brings joy after the heat.
²³ By his own resourcefulness he has tamed
     the abyss,
   and planted it with islands.
²⁴ Those who sail the sea tell of its
     dangers,
   their accounts fill our ears with
     amazement:
²⁵ for there too exist strange and wonderful
     works,
   animals of every kind and huge sea
     creatures.

26 Thanks to God, his messenger reaches
port,
everything works out according to his
word.
27 We could say much more and still fall
short;
to put it concisely, 'He is all.'
28 Where shall we find sufficient power to
glorify him,
since he is the Great One, above all his
works,
29 the awe-inspiring Lord, stupendously
great,
and wonderful in his power?
30 Exalt the Lord in your praises
as high as you may—still he surpasses
you.
Exert all your strength when you exalt him,
do not grow tired—you will never
come to the end.
31 Who has ever seen him to describe him?
Who can glorify him as he deserves?
32 Many mysteries remain even greater than
these,
for we have seen only a few of his
works,
33 the Lord himself having created all things
and given wisdom to those who are
devout.

God's glory in history

44 Next let us praise illustrious men,
our ancestors in their successive
generations.
2 The Lord has created an abundance of
glory,
and displayed his greatness from earliest
times.
3 Some wielded authority as kings
and were renowned for their strength;
others were intelligent advisers
and uttered prophetic sayings.
4 Others directed the people by their advice,
by their understanding of the popular
mind,
and by the wise words of their teaching;

5 others composed musical melodies
and set down ballads;
6 others were rich and powerful,
living peacefully in their homes.
7 All these were honoured by their
contemporaries
and were the glory of their day.
8 Some of them left a name behind them,
so that their praises are still sung.
9 While others have left no memory,
and disappeared as though they had not
existed.
They are now as though they had never
been,
and so too, their children after them.
10 But here is a list of illustrious men
whose good works have not been
forgotten.
11 In their descendants they find
a rich inheritance, their posterity.
12 Their descendants stand by the
commandments
and, thanks to them, so do their
children's children.
13 Their offspring will last for ever,
their glory will not fade.
14 Their bodies have been buried in
peace,
and their name lives on for all
generations.
15 The peoples will proclaim their wisdom,
the assembly will celebrate their
praises.[a]

Enoch

16 Enoch pleased the Lord and was
transferred to heaven,
an example for the conversion of all
generations.

Noah

17 Noah was found perfectly upright,
in the time of retribution he became the
heir:

44a = 39:10.

because of him a remnant was preserved
    for the earth
    at the coming of the Flood.
18 Everlasting covenants were made with him
    that never again should every living
        creature perish by flood.

Abraham

19 Abraham, the great ancestor of a host of
    nations,
    no one was ever his equal in glory.
20 He observed the Law of the Most High,
    and entered into a covenant with him.
He confirmed the covenant in his own
    flesh,
    and proved himself faithful under
        ordeal.
21 The Lord therefore promised him on oath
    to bless the nations through his
        descendants,
to multiply him like the dust on the
    ground,
    to exalt his descendants like the stars,
and to give them the land as their heritage,
    from one sea to the other,
from the River to the ends of the earth.

Isaac and Jacob

22 To Isaac too, for the sake of Abraham his
    father,
    he assured 23 the blessing of all humanity;
        he caused the covenant to rest on the
            head of Jacob.
He confirmed him in his blessings
    and gave him the land as his
        inheritance;
he divided it into portions,
    and shared it out among the twelve
        tribes.

Moses

45 From Jacob's stock he produced a
        generous man
    who found favour in the eyes of all
        humanity,
beloved by God and people,
    Moses, of blessed memory.

2 He made him the equal of the holy ones in
    glory
    and made him strong, to the terror of
        his enemies.
3 By the word of Moses, he made prodigies
    cease
    and raised him high in the respect of
        kings;
he gave him commandments for his
    people,
    and showed him something of his
        glory.
4 For his loyalty and gentleness he
    sanctified him,
    choosing him alone out of all human
        beings;
5 he allowed him to hear his voice,
    and led him into the darkness;
6 he gave him the commandments face to
    face,
    the law of life and knowledge,
to teach Jacob his ordinances
    and Israel his decrees.

Aaron

He raised up Aaron, a holy man like
    Moses,
    his brother, of the tribe of Levi.
7 He made an everlasting covenant with
    him,
    and gave him the priesthood of the
        people.
He adorned him with impressive
    vestments,
    he dressed him in a robe of glory.
8 He clothed him in glorious perfection
    and invested him with rich
        ornaments,
    the breeches, the long robe, the *ephod*.
9 To surround the robe he gave him
    pomegranates,
    and many gold bells all round
to chime at every step,
    for their sound to be heard in the
        Temple
    as a reminder to the children of his
        people;

¹⁰ and a sacred vestment of gold and
 aquamarine
and scarlet, the work of an embroiderer;
the pectoral of judgement, the *urim* and
 thummim,
 of plaited crimson, the work of a
 craftsman;
¹¹ precious stones cut like seals
 mounted in gold, the work of a jeweller,
as a reminder with their engraved
 inscriptions
 of the number of the tribes of Israel;
¹² and a golden diadem on his turban,
 engraved with the seal of consecration;
superb ornamentation, magnificent work,
 adornment to delight the eye.
¹³ There had never been such lovely things
 before him,
 and no one else has ever put them on,
but only his own sons,
 and his descendants for all time.
¹⁴ His sacrifices were to be burnt entirely,
 twice each day and for ever.
¹⁵ Moses consecrated him
 and anointed him with holy oil;
and this was an everlasting covenant for
 him,
 and for his descendants as long as the
 heavens endure,
that he should preside over worship, act as
 priest,
 and bless the people in the name of the
 Lord.
¹⁶ He chose him out of all the living
 to offer sacrifices to the Lord,
incense and perfume as a memorial
 to make expiation for the people.
¹⁷ He entrusted him with his
 commandments,
 committed to him the statutes of the
 Law
for him to teach Jacob his decrees
 and enlighten Israel on his Law.
¹⁸ Others plotted against him,
 they were jealous of him in the desert,
Dathan and Abiram and their men,
 Korah and his crew in fury and rage.

¹⁹ The Lord saw it and was displeased,
 his raging fury made an end of them;
he worked miracles on them,
 consuming them by his flaming fire.
²⁰ And he added to Aaron's glory,
 he gave him an inheritance;
he allotted him the offerings of the first-
 fruits,
 before all else, as much bread as he
 could want.
²¹ Thus they eat the sacrifices of the Lord
 which he gave to him and his
 posterity.
²² But of the people's territory he
 inherits nothing,
he alone of all the people has no
 share,
 'For I myself am your share and
 heritage.'

Phinehas

²³ Phinehas son of Eleazar is third in glory
 because of his zeal in the fear of the
 Lord,
because he stood firm when the people
 revolted,
 with a staunch and courageous heart;
 and in this way made expiation for
 Israel.
²⁴ Hence a covenant of peace was sealed with
 him,
 making him governor of both sanctuary
 and people,
and securing to him and his descendants
 the high priestly dignity for ever.
²⁵ There was also a covenant with David
 son of Jesse, of the tribe of Judah,
a royal succession by exclusively linear
 descent,
 but the succession of Aaron passes to all
 his descendants.
²⁶ May God endow your hearts with wisdom
 to judge his people uprightly,
so that the virtues of your ancestors may
 never fade,
 and their glory may pass to all their
 descendants!

Joshua

46 Mighty in war was Joshua son of Nun,
successor to Moses in the prophetic
office,
who well deserved his name,[a]
and was a great saviour of the chosen
people,
wreaking vengeance on the enemies who
opposed him,
and so bringing Israel into its
inheritance.
2 How splendid he was when, arms uplifted,
he brandished his sword against cities!
3 Who had ever shown such determination
as his?
He himself led the battles of the Lord.
4 Was not the sun held back by his hand,
and one day drawn out into two?
5 He called on the Most High, the Mighty
One,
while pressing the enemies from all
directions,
and the great Lord answered him
with hard and violent hailstones.
6 He fell on that enemy nation,
and at the Descent destroyed all
resistance
to make the nations acknowledge his
warlike prowess
and that he was waging war on behalf
of the Lord.

Caleb

7 For he was a follower of the Mighty One,
in the time of Moses showing his
devotion,
he and Caleb son of Jephunneh,
by opposing the whole community,
by preventing the people from sinning,
and by silencing the mutters of
rebellion.
8 Hence these two alone were preserved
out of six hundred thousand men on the
march,
and brought into their inheritance,
into a land where milk and honey flow.

9 And the Lord conferred strength on Caleb
too,
which stayed by him into old age,
so that he could invest the highlands of the
country
which his descendants kept as their
inheritance,
10 so that every Israelite might see
that it is good to follow the Lord.

The Judges

11 The Judges too, each when he was
called,
all men whose hearts were never
disloyal,
who never turned their backs on the
Lord—
may their memory be blessed!
12 May their bones flourish again from the
tomb,
and may the names of those illustrious
men
be worthily borne by their sons!

Samuel

13 Samuel was the beloved of his Lord;
prophet of the Lord, he instituted the
kingdom,
and anointed rulers over his people.
14 By the Law of the Lord he judged the
assembly,
and the Lord watched over Jacob.
15 By his loyalty he was recognised as a
prophet,
by his words he was known to be a
trustworthy seer.
16 He called on the Lord, the Mighty One,
when his enemies pressed in from all
directions,
by offering a sucking lamb.
17 And the Lord thundered from heaven,
and made his voice heard in a rolling
peal;
18 he massacred the leaders of the enemy,
and all the rulers of the Philistines.

46a Yehoshua' (= Joshua) means 'Yahweh saves'.

¹⁹ Before the time of his everlasting rest
    he bore witness to the Lord and his
        anointed,
'Of no property, not even a pair of sandals,
    have I ever deprived a soul.'
    Nor did anyone accuse him.
²⁰ And, having fallen asleep, he prophesied
        again,
    warning the king of his end;
he spoke from the depths of the earth in
        prophecy,
    to blot out the wickedness of the
        people.

Nathan

47 After him arose Nathan,
    to prophesy in the time of David.

David

² As the fat is set apart from the communion
        sacrifice,
    so was David chosen out of the
        Israelites.
³ He played with lions as though with kids,
    and with bears as though with lambs.
⁴ While still a boy, did he not slay the giant
    and take away the people's shame,
by hurling a stone from his sling
    and cutting short the boasting of
        Goliath?
⁵ For he called on the Lord Most High,
    who gave strength to his right arm
to put a mighty warrior to death
    and assert the strength of his own
        people.
⁶ Hence they gave him credit for ten
        thousand,
    and praised him while they blessed the
        Lord,
    by offering him a crown of glory.
⁷ For he destroyed the enemies on every
        front,
    he annihilated his foes, the Philistines,
    and crushed their strength for ever.
⁸ In all his activities he gave thanks
    to the Holy One Most High in words of
        glory;

he put all his heart into his songs
    out of love for his Creator.
⁹ He placed singers before the altar,
    melodiously to sing;
¹⁰ he gave the feasts their splendour,
    the festivals their solemn pomp,
causing the Lord's holy name to be praised
    and the sanctuary to resound from
        dawn.
¹¹ The Lord took away his sins,
    making his strength ever greater;
he gave him a royal covenant,
    and a glorious throne in Israel.

Solomon

¹² A wise son succeeded him,
    who lived content, thanks to him.
¹³ Solomon reigned in a time of peace,
    and God gave him peace all round
so that he could raise a house to his name
    and prepare an everlasting sanctuary.
¹⁴ How wise you were despite your youth,
    like a river, brimming over with
        intelligence!
¹⁵ Your mind ranged the earth,
    you filled it with mysterious sayings.
¹⁶ Your name reached the distant islands,
    and you were loved for your peace.ᵃ
¹⁷ Your songs, your proverbs, your sayings
    and your answers were the wonder of
        the world.
¹⁸ In the name of the Lord God,
    of him who is called the God of Israel,
you amassed gold like so much tin,
    and made silver as common as lead.
¹⁹ You abandoned your body to women,
    you became the slave of your appetites.
²⁰ You stained your honour,
    you profaned your stock,
so bringing retribution on your children
    and affliction for your folly:
²¹ the empire split in two,
    from Ephraim arose a rebel kingdom.
²² But the Lord never goes back on his mercy,
    never cancels any of his words,

47a Solomon means 'man of peace'.

will neither deny offspring to his elect
    nor stamp out the line of the man who
      loved him.
And hence, he has granted a remnant to
    Jacob
    and to David a root sprung from him.

Rehoboam

23 Solomon rested with his ancestors,
    leaving one of his stock as his successor,
the stupidest member of the nation,
    brainless Rehoboam, who drove the
      people to rebel.

Jeroboam

24 Next, Jeroboam son of Nebat, who made
    Israel sin,
    and set Ephraim on the way of evil;
from then on their sins multiplied so
    excessively
    as to drive them out of their country;
25 for they tried out every kind of
    wickedness,
    until vengeance overtook them.

Elijah

48 Then the prophet Elijah arose like a
    fire,
    his word flaring like a torch.
2 It was he who brought famine on them
    and decimated them in his zeal.
3 By the word of the Lord he shut up the
    heavens,
    three times also he brought down fire.
4 How glorious you were in your miracles,
    Elijah!
    Has anyone reason to boast as you
      have?—
5 rousing a corpse from death,
    from Sheol, by the word of the Most
      High;
6 dragging kings down to destruction,
    and high dignitaries from their beds;
7 hearing a rebuke on Sinai
    and decrees of punishment on Horeb;
8 anointing kings as avengers,
    and prophets to succeed you;

9 taken up in the whirlwind of fire,
    in a chariot with fiery horses;
10 designated in the prophecies of doom
    to allay God's wrath before the fury
      breaks,
    to turn the hearts of fathers towards their
      children,[a]
    and to restore the tribes of Jacob.
11 Blessed, those who will see you,
    and those who have fallen asleep in
      love;
    for we too shall certainly have life.

Elisha

12 Such was Elijah, who was enveloped in a
    whirlwind;
    and Elisha was filled with his spirit;
throughout his life no ruler could shake
    him,
    and no one could subdue him.
13 No task was too hard for him,
    and even in death his body prophesied.
14 In his lifetime he performed wonders,
    and in death his works were
      marvellous.

Infidelity and punishment

15 Despite all this the people did not repent,
    nor did they give up their sins,
    until they were herded out of their country
    and scattered all over the earth;
16 only a few of the people were left,
    with a ruler of the House of David.
    Some of them did what pleased the Lord,
    others piled sin on sin.

Hezekiah

17 Hezekiah fortified his city,
    and laid on a water-supply inside it;
    with iron he tunnelled through the rock
    and constructed storage-tanks.
18 In his days Sennacherib invaded
    and sent Rabshakeh;
    he lifted his hand against Zion,
    and boasted loudly in his arrogance.

48a Ml 3:24.

¹⁹ Then their hearts and hands trembled,
    they felt the pangs of a woman in labour,
²⁰ but they called on the merciful Lord,
    stretching out their hands towards him.
  Swiftly the Holy One heard them from
      heaven
    and delivered them by the agency of
      Isaiah;
²¹ he struck the camp of the Assyrians
    and his Angel annihilated them.

Isaiah

²² For Hezekiah did what is pleasing to the
      Lord,
    and was steadfast*b* in the ways of David
      his father,
  enjoined on him by the prophet Isaiah,
    a great man trustworthy in his vision.
²³ In his days the sun moved back;
    he prolonged the life of the king.
²⁴ In the power of the spirit he saw the last
      things,
    he comforted the mourners of Zion,
²⁵ he revealed the future to the end of time,
    and hidden things long before they
      happened.

Josiah

49 The memory of Josiah is like blended
      incense
  prepared by the perfumer's art;
  it is as sweet as honey to all mouths,
    and like music at a wine feast.
² He took the right course, of converting the
      people,
    he rooted out the iniquitous
      abominations,
³ he set his heart on the Lord,
    in godless times he upheld the cause of
      religion.

The last kings and prophets

⁴ Apart from David, Hezekiah and Josiah,
    they all heaped wrong on wrong,
  they abandoned the Law of the Most
      High:
    the kings of Judah disappeared;

⁵ for they handed their power over to others
    and their honour to a foreign nation.
⁶ The holy, chosen city was burnt down,
    her streets were left deserted,
⁷ as Jeremiah had predicted; for they had ill-
      treated him,
    though consecrated a prophet in his
      mother's womb,
  to tear up and afflict *and destroy,*
    but also *to build up and to plant.*^a
⁸ Ezekiel saw a vision of glory
    which God showed to him
      above the chariot of the great winged
      creatures,
⁹ for he mentioned the enemies in the
      downpour
    to the advantage of those who follow
      the right way.
¹⁰ As for the twelve prophets,
    may their bones flower again from the
      tomb,
  since they have comforted Jacob
    and redeemed him in faith and hope.

Zerubbabel and Joshua

¹¹ How shall we extol Zerubbabel?
    He was like a signet ring on the right
      hand,
¹² so too was Joshua son of Jozadak;
    they who in their days built the Temple
  and raised a sanctuary sacred to the Lord,
    destined to everlasting glory.

Nehemiah

¹³ Great too is the memory of Nehemiah,
    who rebuilt our walls which lay in
      ruins,
  erected the bolted gates
    and rebuilt our houses.

Retrospect

¹⁴ No one else has ever been created on earth
      to equal Enoch,
    for he was taken up from earth.

48*b* Word-play on 'Hezekiah' (= Yahweh makes strong).
49*a* Jr 1:10.

15 And no one else ever born has been like
	Joseph,
	the leader of his brothers, the prop of
		his people;
	his bones received a visitation.
16 Shem and Seth were the most honoured of
		men,
	but above every living creature is Adam.

Simonª the high priest

50 It was the High Priest Simon son of
	Onias
	who repaired the Temple during his
		lifetime
	and in his day fortified the sanctuary.
2 He laid the foundations of double depth,
	the high buttresses of the Temple
		precincts.
3 In his day the pool was excavated,
	a reservoir as huge as the sea.
4 Anxious to save the people from ruin,
	he fortified the city against siege.
5 How splendid he was with the people
		thronging round him,
	when he emerged from the curtained
		shrine,
6 like the morning star among the clouds,
	like the moon at the full,
7 like the sun shining on the Temple of the
		Most High,
	like the rainbow gleaming against
		brilliant clouds,
8 like a rose in springtime,
	like a lily by a spring,
	like a branch of the incense tree in
		summer,
9 	like fire and incense in the censer,
	like a massive golden vessel
		encrusted with every kind of precious
			stone,
10 like an olive tree loaded with fruit,
	like a cypress soaring to the clouds;
11 when he took his ceremonial robe
	and put on his magnificent ornaments,
	when he went up to the holy altar
	and filled the sanctuary precincts with
		his grandeur;

12 when he received the portions from the
		hands of the priests,
	himself standing by the altar hearth,
	crowned with the circle of his brothers,
		as a cedar of Lebanon is by its foliage,
	as though surrounded by the trunks of
		palm trees.
13 	When all the sons of Aaron in their
		glory,
	with the offerings of the Lord in their
		hands,
	stood before the whole assembly of
		Israel,
14 while he completed the rites at the altars,
	nobly presenting the offerings to the
		Almighty, Most High!
15 He would reach out his hand to the cup
	and pour a libation of wine,
	pouring it at the foot of the altar,
	a fragrance pleasing to the Most High,
		King of All;
16 then the sons of Aaron would shout
	and blow their metal trumpets,
	making a mighty sound ring out
	as a reminder before the Most High;
17 and immediately the people all together
	would fall on their faces to the ground,
	in adoration of their Lord,
	the Almighty, God Most High,
18 and with the cantors chanting their hymns
		of praise.
	Sweet was the melody of all these voices,
19 as the people pleaded with the Lord Most
		High
	and prayed in the presence of the
		Merciful,
	until the service of the Lord was completed
	and the ceremony at an end.
20 Then he would come down and raise his
		hands
	over the whole assembly of the
		Israelites,
	to give them the Lord's blessing from his
		lips,
	being privileged to pronounce his name;

50a Simon II, son of Onias III, high priest c. 220–195 BC.

21 and once again the people would bow low
   to receive the blessing of the Most High.

Exhortation

22 And now bless the God of all things,
   the doer of great deeds everywhere,
who has exalted our days from the womb
   and has acted mercifully towards us.
23 May he grant us cheerful hearts
   and bring peace in our time,
   in Israel for ages on ages.
24 May his mercy be faithfully with us,
   may he redeem us in our own times!

Numerical proverb

25 There are two nations that my soul detests,
   the third is not a nation at all:
26 the inhabitants of Mount Seir, the
     Philistines,
   and the stupid people living at Shechem.

Conclusion

27 Instruction in wisdom and knowledge
   is what has been written in this book
by Jesus son of Sira Eleazar of Jerusalem,
   who has poured a rain of wisdom from his
     heart.
28 Blessed is he who devotes his time to these
   and grows wise by taking them to heart!
29 If he practises them he will be strong
     enough for anything,
   since the light of the Lord is his path.

Hymn of thanksgiving

51 I shall give thanks to you, Lord and
     King,
   and praise you, God my Saviour,
   I give thanks to your name;
2 for you have been my guard and support
   and redeemed my body from
     destruction,
from the snare of the lying tongue,
   from lips that fabricate falsehood;
in the presence of my assailants, you were
     on my side;
you have been my support, you have
     redeemed me,

3 true to your abounding kindness
   —and the greatness of your name—you
     liberated me
from the fangs of those seeking to devour
     me,
   from the clutches of those seeking my
     life,
   from the many ordeals which I have
     endured,
4 from the stifling heat which hemmed me in,
   from the heart of a fire which I had not
     kindled,
5 from deep in the belly of Sheol,
6   treacherous denunciations to the king.
My soul has been close to death,
   my life had gone down to the brink of
     Sheol.
7 I was completely surrounded, there was no
     one to help me;
   I looked for someone to help me, there
     was no one.
8 Then I remembered your mercy, Lord,
   and your deeds from earliest times,
how you deliver those who wait for you
     patiently,
   and save them from the clutches of their
     enemies.
9 And I sent up my plea from the earth,
   I begged to be delivered from death.
10 I called on the Lord, the father of my Lord,
   'Do not desert me in the days of ordeal,
   in the days of the proud, when we are
     helpless.
I shall praise your name unceasingly
   and gratefully sing its praises.'
11 And my plea was heard,
   for you saved me from destruction,
   you delivered me from that time of evil.
12 And therefore I shall thank you and praise
     you,
   and bless the name of the Lord.

Poem on the quest for wisdom

13 When I was still a youth, before I went
     travelling,
   in my prayers I asked outright for
     wisdom.

14 Outside the sanctuary I would pray for
  her,
   and to the last I shall continue to seek
   her.
15 From her blossoming to the ripening of
  her grape
   my heart has taken its delight in her.
  My foot has pursued a straight path,
   I have sought her ever since my youth.
16 By bowing my ear a little, I have received
  her,
   and have found much instruction.
17 Thanks to her I have advanced;
   glory be to him who has given me
   wisdom!
18 For I was determined to put her into
  practice,
   have earnestly pursued the good, and
   shall not be put to shame.
19 My soul has fought to possess her,
   I have been scrupulous in keeping the
   Law;
  I have stretched out my hands to heaven
   and bewailed how little I knew of her;
20 I have directed my soul towards her,
   and in purity I have found her;
  having my heart fixed on her from the
  outset,
   I shall never be deserted;

21 my very core having yearned to discover
  her,
   I have now acquired a good possession.
22 In reward the Lord has given me a tongue
   with which I shall sing his praises.
23 Come close to me, you ignorant,
   take your place in my school.
24 Why complain about lacking these things
   when your souls are so thirsty for
   them?
25 I have opened my mouth, I have said:
   'Buy her without money,
26 put your necks under her yoke,
   let your souls receive instruction,
   she is near, within your reach.'
27 See for yourselves: how slight my efforts
  have been
   to win so much peace.
28 Buy instruction with a large sum of silver,
   thanks to her you will gain much gold.
29 May your souls rejoice in the mercy of the
  Lord,
   may you never be ashamed of praising
   him.
30 Do your work before the appointed time
   and at the appointed time he will give
   you your reward.

(Subscript:) Wisdom of Jesus, son of Sira.

Title

1 The vision of Isaiah son of Amoz concerning Judah and Jerusalem, which he received in the reigns of Uzziah, Jotham, Ahaz and Hezekiah kings of Judah.

Against an ungrateful people

2 Listen, you heavens; earth, attend, for
    Yahweh is speaking,
'I have reared children and brought them
    up,
but they have rebelled against me.
3 The ox knows its owner and the donkey
    its master's crib;
Israel does not know, my people do not
    understand.'
4 Disaster, sinful nation, people weighed
    down with guilt,
race of wrong-doers, perverted children!
They have abandoned Yahweh, despised
    the Holy One of Israel,
they have turned away from him.
5 Where shall I strike you next, if you persist
    in treason?
The whole head is sick, the whole heart is
    diseased,
6 from the sole of the foot to the head there
    is nothing healthy:
only wounds, bruises and open sores
not dressed, not bandaged, not soothed
    with ointment,
7 your country a desolation, your towns
    burnt down,
your soil, foreigners lay it waste before
    your eyes,
a desolation like devastation by foreigners.
8 The daughter of Zion is left like a shanty
    in a vineyard,

like a shed in a cucumber field, like a city
    besieged.
9 Had Yahweh Sabaoth not left us a few
    survivors,
we should be like Sodom, we should be
    the same as Gomorrah.

Against hypocrisy

10 Hear what Yahweh says, you rulers of
    Sodom;
listen to what our God teaches, you people
    of Gomorrah.
11 'What are your endless sacrifices to me?'
    says Yahweh.
'I am sick of burnt offerings of rams
and the fat of calves.
I take no pleasure in the blood
of bulls and lambs and goats.
12 When you come and present yourselves
    before me,
who has asked you to trample through my
    courts?
13 Bring no more futile cereal offerings,
the smoke from them fills me with disgust.
New Moons, Sabbaths, assemblies—I
    cannot endure solemnity
    combined with guilt.
14 Your New Moons and your meetings I
    utterly detest;
to me they are a burden I am tired of
    bearing.
15 When you stretch out your hands I turn
    my eyes away.
You may multiply your prayers, I shall not
    be listening.
Your hands are covered in blood,
16 wash, make yourselves clean.
Take your wrong-doing out of my sight.

Cease doing evil. ¹⁷Learn to do good,
search for justice, discipline the violent,
be just to the orphan, plead for the widow.

¹⁸ 'Come, let us talk this over,' says Yahweh.
'Though your sins are like scarlet,
they shall be white as snow;
though they are red as crimson, they shall
be like wool.
¹⁹ If you are willing to obey, you shall eat the
good things of the earth.
²⁰ But if you refuse and rebel, the sword shall
eat you instead—
for Yahweh's mouth has spoken.'

Lament for Jerusalem

²¹ The faithful city,
what a harlot*ᵃ* she has become!
Zion, once full of fair judgement,
where saving justice used to dwell,
but now assassins!

²² Your silver has turned into dross,
your wine is watered.
²³ Your princes are rebels,
accomplices of brigands.

All of them greedy for presents
and eager for bribes,
they show no justice to the orphan,
and the widow's cause never reaches them.

²⁴ Hence, the Lord Yahweh Sabaoth,
the Mighty One of Israel, says this,
'Disaster, I shall get the better of my
enemies,
I shall avenge myself on my foes.

²⁵ 'I shall turn my hand against you,
I shall purge your dross as though with
potash,
I shall remove all your alloy.

²⁶ 'And I shall restore your judges as at first,
your counsellors as in bygone days,
after which you will be called City of
Saving Justice,
Faithful City.'

²⁷ Zion will be redeemed by fair judgement,
and those who return, by saving justice.
²⁸ Rebels and sinners alike will be destroyed,
and those who abandon Yahweh will
perish.

Against sacred trees

²⁹ How ashamed you will be of the
terebinths
which gave you such delight;
and how you will blush for the gardens
which you chose!
³⁰ For you will be like a terebinth with faded
leaves,
like a garden without water;
³¹ the strong will become like tinder, his
work like the spark;
both will go up in flames together,
with no one to put them out.

Everlasting peace

2 The vision of Isaiah son of Amoz, concerning Judah and Jerusalem.

² It will happen in the final days
that the mountain of Yahweh's house
will rise higher than the mountains
and tower above the heights.
Then all the nations will stream to it,
³ many peoples will come to it and say,
'Come, let us go up to the mountain of
Yahweh,
to the house of the God of Jacob
that he may teach us his ways
so that we may walk in his paths.'
For the Law will issue from Zion
and the word of Yahweh from
Jerusalem.

⁴ Then he will judge between the nations
and arbitrate between many peoples.
They will hammer their swords into
ploughshares
and their spears into sickles.

1a Prostitution is a frequent figure for unfaithfulness to
Yahweh.

71 READ ISAIAH 1:1–20.

Take your wrong-doing out of my sight. Cease doing evil. Learn to do good.
—ISAIAH 1:16–17

THE GRACE OF REPENTANCE

Let us attend to what is good, pleasing, and acceptable in the sight of him who formed us. Let us look steadfastly to the blood of Christ, and see how precious that blood is to God, which, having been shed for our salvation, has set the grace of repentance before the whole world. Let us turn to every age that has passed, and learn that, from generation to generation, the Lord has granted a grace of repentance to all who would be converted to him. Noah preached repentance, and as many as listened to him were saved. Jonah proclaimed destruction to the Ninevites. But they, repented of their sins, propitiated God by prayer, and obtained salvation. . . .

By the Holy Spirit the ministers of God's grace have spoken of repentance. And the Lord of all things has himself declared with an oath regarding it, "As I live, says the Lord, I desire not the death of the sinner, but rather his repentance" adding, moreover, this gracious declaration: "Repent O house of Israel, of your iniquity" (see Ezk 33:11). . . .

And as he says through Isaiah: "Wash, make yourselves clean. Take your wrong-doing out of my sight. Cease doing evil. Learn to do good, search for justice, discipline the violent, be just to the orphan, plead for the widow. 'Come, let us talk this over,' says Yahweh, 'Though your sins are like scarlet, they shall be white as snow. . . . If you are willing to obey, you shall eat the good things of the earth. But if you refuse and rebel, the sword shall eat you instead.' " By his almighty will God has declared these things because he wants all of his beloved to share in the grace of repentance.

Therefore, let us yield obedience to his excellent and glorious will. Let us implore his mercy and loving kindness and forsake all fruitless efforts, strife and envy, which leads to death. And let us turn and have recourse to his compassion.
ST. CLEMENT OF ROME, d. 100?

YOU WILL FIND THE NEXT READING AT ISAIAH 5.

Nation will not lift sword against nation,
no longer will they learn how to make war.[a]

⁵ House of Jacob, come, let us walk in
Yahweh's light.

The brilliance of Yahweh's majesty

⁶ You have rejected your people, the House
of Jacob,
for it has long been full of sorcerers
like the Philistines,

and is overrun with foreigners.
⁷ The country is full of silver and gold and
treasures unlimited,
the country is full of horses, its chariots are
unlimited;
⁸ the country is full of idols.
They bow down before the work of their
hands,
before what their own fingers have made.

2a || Mi 4:1–3.

9 Human nature has been humbled,
     humankind brought low:
 do not raise them again!
10 Go into the rock, hide in the dust,
   in terror of Yahweh, at the brilliance of
       his majesty,
   when he arises to make the earth
       quake.

11 Human pride will lower its eyes,
   human arrogance will be humbled,
   and Yahweh alone will be exalted, on
       that day.
12 That will be a day for Yahweh Sabaoth,
   for all who are majestic and haughty,
   for all who are proud, to be brought low,
13 for all the cedars of Lebanon, high and
       proud,
   and for all the oaks of Bashan;
14 for all the high mountains
   and for all the proud hills;
15 for every lofty tower
   and for every towering wall;
16 for all the ships of Tarshish
   and for everything held precious.

17 Human pride will be humbled,
   human arrogance brought low,
   and Yahweh alone will be exalted, on
       that day.

18 When the idols all disappear,
19 they will go into the caverns of the rocks
   and into the fissures of the earth
   in terror of Yahweh, at the brilliance of his
       majesty,
   when he arises to make the earth quake.

20 That day, people will fling to moles and
bats the silver idols and golden idols which
have been made for them to worship,

21 and go into the crevices of the rocks
   and the clefts in the cliffs,
   in terror of Yahweh, at the brilliance of his
       majesty,
   when he arises to make the earth quake.

22 Have no more to do with humankind,
   which has only the breath in its nostrils.
   How much is this worth?

Anarchy in Jerusalem

3 Now the Lord Yahweh Sabaoth
   is about to deprive Jerusalem and Judah
   of resources and provisions—
   all reserves of food, all reserves of water—
2 of hero, warrior, judge, prophet,
   diviner, elder, 3 captain, dignitary,
   counsellor, architect, soothsayer.
4 'I shall give them boys for princes,
   raw lads to rule over them.'
5 People will be ill-treated by one another,
   each by his neighbour;
   the young will insult the aged,
   and the low, the respected.
6 Yes, a man will catch hold of his brother
   in their father's house, to say,
   'You have a cloak, so you be leader,
   and rule this heap of ruins.'
7 And, that day, the other will protest,
   'I am no healer;
   in my house there is neither food nor
       clothing;
   do not make me leader of the people.'
8 For Jerusalem has collapsed
   and Judah has fallen,
   because their words and deeds affront
       Yahweh
   and insult his glorious gaze.
9 Their complacency bears witness against
       them,
   they parade their sin like Sodom;
   they do not conceal it, all the worse for
       them,
   for they have hatched their own downfall.
10 Say, 'Blessed the upright,
   for he will feed on the fruit of his deeds;
11 woe to the wicked, it will go ill with him,
   for he will be treated as his actions
       deserve.'
12 O my people, their oppressors pillage them
   and extortioners rule over them!
   O my people, your rulers mislead you
   and efface the paths you ought to follow!

¹³ Yahweh has risen to accuse,
is standing to pass judgement on the
people.
¹⁴ Yahweh is about to try
the elders and the princes of his people,
'You are the ones who have ravaged the
vineyard,
the spoils of the poor are in your
houses.
¹⁵ By what right do you crush my
people
and grind the faces of the poor?'
says the Lord Yahweh Sabaoth.

The women of Jerusalem

¹⁶ Yahweh says:

Because Zion's daughters are proud
and walk with heads held high
and enticing eyes—with mincing steps
they go,
jingling the bangles on their feet—
¹⁷ the Lord will give Zion's daughters
scabby heads,
Yahweh will lay their foreheads bare.

¹⁸ That day the Lord will take away the
ornamental chains, medallions, crescents,
¹⁹ pendants, bracelets, trinkets, ²⁰ diadems, an-
kle-chains, necklaces, scent bottles, amulets,
²¹ finger-rings, nose-rings, ²² party dresses,
cloaks, scarves, purses, ²³ mirrors, linen
clothes, turbans and mantillas.

²⁴ Then, instead of perfume, a stink;
instead of belt, a rope,
instead of hair elaborately dressed, a
shaven scalp,
instead of gorgeous clothes, sacking round
the waist,
and brand marks instead of beauty.

Misery in Jerusalem

²⁵ Your men will fall by the sword,
your warriors in battle,
²⁶ and her gates will moan and mourn;
she will sit on the ground, deserted.

4 That day, seven women will catch hold of
one man and say, 'We will eat our own
food, and wear our own clothing, but just let
us bear your name. Take our disgrace away.'

Yahweh's seedling

² That day, Yahweh's seedling will turn to
beauty and glory,
what the earth brings forth will turn to the
pride and ornament
of Israel's survivors.
³ Those who are left in Zion and remain in
Jerusalem
will be called holy,
all those in Jerusalem noted down to live.
⁴ When the Lord has washed away
the filth of Zion's daughters
and with the wind of judgement and the
wind of burning cleansed
Jerusalem of the blood shed in her,
⁵ Yahweh will create,
over every house on Mount Zion
and over those who assemble there,
a cloud by day,
and by night smoke with the brightness of
a flaring fire.
For over all will be the Glory as canopy
⁶ and tent
to give shade by day from the heat,
refuge and shelter from the storm and the
rain.

The song of the vineyard

5 Let me sing my beloved
the song of my friend for his vineyard.

My beloved had a vineyard
on a fertile hillside.
² He dug it, cleared it of stones,
and planted it with red grapes.
In the middle he built a tower,
he hewed a press there too.
He expected it to yield fine grapes:
wild grapes were all it yielded.

³ And now, citizens of Jerusalem and people
of Judah,

I ask you to judge between me and my
vineyard.
⁴ What more could I have done for my
vineyard
that I have not done?
Why, when I expected it to yield fine
grapes,
has it yielded wild ones?

⁵ Very well, I shall tell you what I am going
to do to my vineyard:
I shall take away its hedge, for it to be
grazed on,
and knock down its wall, for it to be
trampled on.
⁶ I shall let it go to waste, unpruned,
undug,
overgrown by brambles and thorn-bushes,
and I shall command the clouds to rain no
rain on it.
⁷ Now, the vineyard of Yahweh Sabaoth is
the House of Israel,
and the people of Judah the plant he
cherished.
He expected fair judgement, but found
injustice,
uprightness, but found cries of distress.

Curses

⁸ Woe to those who add house to house
and join field to field
until there is nowhere left
and they are the sole inhabitants of the
country.
⁹ Yahweh Sabaoth has sworn this in my
hearing,
'Many houses will be brought to ruin,
great and fine ones left untenanted;
¹⁰ for ten acres of vineyard will yield only
one barrel,
and ten bushel of seed will yield only one
bushel.'

¹¹ Woe to those who get up early to go after
strong drink,
and stay up late at night inflamed with
wine.

¹² Nothing but harp and lyre, tambourine
and pipe,
and wine for their drinking bouts.

Never a thought for the works of Yahweh,
never a glance for what his hands have
done.
¹³ That is why my people is in exile, for want
of perception;
her dignitaries starving, her populace
parched with thirst.
¹⁴ That is why Sheol opens wide its throat
and gapes with measureless jaw
and down go her noblemen and populace
and her loud revellers merry to the last!

¹⁵ Human nature has been humbled,
humankind brought low,ᵃ
and the eyes of the proud have been
humbled.
¹⁶ Yahweh Sabaoth is the more respected for
his judgement,
God the Holy One has displayed his
holiness by his justice!
¹⁷ Now the lambs will graze in their old
pastures,
and the fields laid waste by fat cattle will
feed the kids.

¹⁸ Woe to those who drag guilt along by the
reins of duplicity,
drag along sin as though with a cart rope;
¹⁹ to those who say, 'Why doesn't he do his
work quickly
so that we can see it;
why doesn't the Holy One of Israel's
design hurry up and come true
so that we can experience it?'

²⁰ Woe to those who call what is bad, good,
and what is good, bad,
who substitute darkness for light and light
for darkness,
who substitute bitter for sweet and sweet
for bitter.

5a The refrain of the poem in 2:6–22; perhaps vv. 14–16 belong there.

72 READ ISAIAH 5:8–14.

Never a thought for the works of Yahweh, never a glance for what his hands have done.—ISAIAH 5:12

MIRRORS OF GOD

Woe to you who give "never a thought for the works of Yahweh, never a glance for what his hands have done," says Isaiah. We often recognize an artist from his works even though we have never seen him. For example, the statues of the excellent sculptor Phydias were so distinctive that many people felt they knew him even though they had never met him.

O Creator of all things, what image reveals you more plainly than I? What skillful artist could paint anything that could even approximate the wonderful beauty of the brightness of the sky and flowers of the field? I see your omnipotence, my God, in all creatures as though they were mirrors. Your majesty shines forth from every one of them, and as our eyes behold them we come to know your goodness. And if we perceive the order, harmony, and concord of this world, what excuse can we give for not being lifted up and wholly fixed on God? If we were not deaf to the creation's lovely music, it would make us forget all things and absorb us into the divine life.

Just as an arrow does not hover in the air but flies toward the target, so our thoughts must not hover over earthly things but fly to God. Rise up, therefore, O my soul, open your eyes and awake. And if your sight is so dim that you cannot make out the divine power that is at work in the world, at least look at his creatures that reveal who he is. As Jesus himself said to the spiritually blind, "if you refuse to believe in me, at least believe in the work I do" (Jn 10:38).

ST. ROBERT SOUTHWELL, 1561–1595

YOU WILL FIND THE NEXT READING AT ISAIAH 42.

²¹ Woe to those who think themselves
  wise
and believe themselves enlightened.

²² Woe to those whose might lies in wine
  bibbing,
their heroism in mixing strong
  drinks,
²³ who acquit the guilty for a bribe
and deny justice to the upright.
²⁴ Yes, as the flame devours the stubble,
as the straw flares up and disappears,
their root will be like decay
and their shoot be carried off like
  dust,

for having rejected the law of Yahweh
  Sabaoth,
for having despised the word of the Holy
  One of Israel.

Yahweh's anger

²⁵ This is why Yahweh's anger has blazed out
  against his people;
and he has raised his hand against them to
  strike them;
why the mountains have shuddered
and why corpses are lying like dung in the
  streets.
After all this, his anger is not spent.
No, his hand is still raised!

Yahweh summons the invaders

26 He hoists a signal for a distant nation,
    he whistles them up from the ends of
        the earth;
    and see how swift, how fleet they
        come!

27 None of them tired, none of them
        stumbling,
    none of them asleep or drowsy,
    none of them with belt unfastened,
    none of them with broken sandal-strap.

28 Their arrows are sharpened,
    their bows all strung,
    their horses' hoofs you would think were
        flint
    and their wheels, a whirlwind!

29 Their roar is like that of a lioness,
    like fierce young lions they roar,
    growling they seize their prey
    and carry it off, with no one to prevent it,

30 growling at it, that day,
    like the growling of the sea.
    Only look at the country: darkness and
        distress,
    and the light turned to darkness by the
        clouds.

The call of Isaiah

6 In the year of King Uzziah's death I saw the Lord seated on a high and lofty throne; his train filled the sanctuary. 2 Above him stood seraphs, each one with six wings: two to cover its face, two to cover its feet and two for flying; 3 and they were shouting these words to each other:

Holy, holy, holy is Yahweh Sabaoth.
His glory fills the whole earth.

4 The door-posts shook at the sound of their shouting, and the Temple was full of smoke.
5 Then I said:

'Woe is me! I am lost,
for I am a man of unclean lips
and I live among a people of unclean lips,
and my eyes have seen the King, Yahweh
    Sabaoth.'

6 Then one of the seraphs flew to me, holding in its hand a live coal which it had taken from the altar with a pair of tongs. 7 With this it touched my mouth and said:

'Look, this has touched your lips,
your guilt has been removed
and your sin forgiven.'

8 I then heard the voice of the Lord saying:

'Whom shall I send? Who will go for us?'

And I said, 'Here am I, send me.' 9 He said:

'Go, and say to this people,
"Listen and listen, but never understand!
Look and look, but never perceive!"
10 Make this people's heart coarse,
    make their ears dull, shut their eyes tight,
    or they will use their eyes to see,
    use their ears to hear,
    use their heart to understand,
    and change their ways and be healed.'

11 I then said, 'Until when, Lord?' He replied, 'Until towns are in ruins and deserted, houses untenanted and a great desolation reigns in the land, 12 and Yahweh has driven the people away and the country is totally abandoned. 13 And suppose one-tenth of them are left in it, that will be stripped again, like the terebinth, like the oak, cut back to the stock; their stock is a holy seed.'

Isaiah intervenes

7 In the reign of Ahaz son of Jotham, son of Uzziah king of Judah, Razon king of Aram advanced on Jerusalem with Pekah son of Remaliah king of Israel, to attack it; but he was unable to attack it. 2 The House of

David was informed: 'Aram has halted in Ephraimite territory.' At this, his heart and his people's hearts shook like forest trees shaking in the wind.

3 Yahweh then said to Isaiah, 'Go out with your son Shear-Jashub,[a] and meet Ahaz at the end of the conduit of the upper pool, on the road to the Fuller's Field, 4 and say to him, "Pay attention and keep calm. Do not be frightened or demoralised by these two smouldering sticks of firewood, by the fierce anger of Razon, Aram and the son of Remaliah, 5 or because Aram, Ephraim and the son of Remaliah have been plotting against you and saying: 6 Let us mount an attack on Judah, destroy it, force it onto our side and install the son of Tabeel there as king.

7 "Lord Yahweh says this:

This will not happen, it will never occur,
8 for the head of Aram is Damascus,
and the head of Damascus is Razon;
another sixty-five years,
and Ephraim will cease to be a people.
9 The head of Ephraim is Samaria,
and the head of Samaria is the son of
    Remaliah.
If you will not take your stand on me
you will not stand firm." '

Isaiah intervenes again

10 Yahweh spoke to Ahaz again and said:

11 Ask Yahweh your God for a sign,
either in the depths of Sheol or in the
    heights above.

12 But Ahaz said, 'I will not ask. I will not put
    Yahweh to the test.'
13 He then said:

Listen now, House of David:
are you not satisfied with trying human
    patience
that you should try my God's patience too?
14 The Lord will give you a sign in any case:
It is this: the young woman[b] is with child

and will give birth to a son
whom she will call Immanuel.
15 On curds and honey will he feed
until he knows how to refuse the bad
and choose the good.
16 Before the child knows how to refuse the
    bad and choose the good,
the lands whose two kings are frightening
    you will be deserted.
17 Yahweh will bring times for you,
your people and your ancestral House,
such as have not been seen
since Ephraim broke away from Judah
    (the king of Assyria).

Prediction of an invasion

18 When that day comes,
Yahweh will whistle up mosquitoes
from the distant streams of Egypt
and bees from the land of Assyria,
19 and they will all come and settle
on the streams in the gullies, in the holes in
    the rocks,
on all the thorn-bushes and on all the
    water-points.
20 That day the Lord will shave,
with a razor hired from the other side of
    the River
(with the king of Assyria),
the head and the hair of the leg,
and take off the beard, too.
21 When that day comes, each man will raise
one heifer and two sheep,
22 and because of the abundant milk they give
(on curds will he feed)
all who are left in the country
will feed on curds and honey.
23 When that day comes, wherever there
    used to be a thousand vines
worth a thousand pieces of silver,
all will be brambles and thorn-bushes;

7a The name means 'a remnant will return'.

7b Perhaps Ahaz's wife, about to give birth to Hezekiah, but Isaiah sees it as symbolic of the fulfilment of royal messianic prophecies. For 'young woman' Gk reads 'virgin', interpreted by Mt of Mary.

24 to be ventured into only with arrows and
    bow,
for the country will be nothing but
    brambles and thorn-bushes.
25 No more will you venture
on any hillside formerly under the hoe
for fear of the brambles and thorn-bushes;
it will be fit only for pasturing the cattle,
a tramping-ground for sheep.

The birth of a son to Isaiah

8 Yahweh said to me, 'Take a large tablet and
on it with an ordinary stylus write,
"Maher-Shalal-Hash-Baz". 2 And take reliable witnesses, the priest Uriah and Zechariah son of Jeberechiah.'

3 I then had intercourse with the prophetess, who then conceived and gave birth to a son.[a] Yahweh said to me, 'Call him Maher-Shalal-Hash-Baz, 4 for before the child knows how to say "mother" or "father", the wealth of Damascus and the booty of Samaria will be carried away while the king of Assyria looks on.'

Shiloah and the Euphrates

5 Yahweh spoke to me again and said, 6 'Since this people has rejected the waters of Shiloah which flow smoothly, and has trembled before Razon and the son of Remaliah, 7 now, against it, the Lord will bring the mighty, swelling waters of the River (the king of Assyria and all his glory); the River will flood up all its channels and overflow all its banks; 8 it will flow into Judah, flooding everything and passing on; it will reach right up to the neck, and the spreading of its wings will cover the whole extent of your country, Immanuel!

9 Realise this, peoples, and be afraid,
listen, all members of far-off nations!
Arm yourselves yet be afraid!
Arm yourselves yet be afraid!
10 Devise plans as you may: they will come to
    nothing!
Make what pronouncements you like; it
    will not come about!
For God is with us!'

Isaiah's mission

11 For this was how Yahweh spoke to me
    when his hand seized hold of me
and he taught me not to follow the path of
    this people, saying,
12 'Do not call conspiracy all that this people
    calls conspiracy;
do not dread what they dread, have no
    fear of that.
13 Yahweh Sabaoth is the one you will
    proclaim holy,
him you will dread, him you will fear.
14 He will be a sanctuary, a stumbling-stone,
a rock to trip up the two Houses of
    Israel;
a snare and a trap for the inhabitants of
    Jerusalem,
15 over which many of them will stumble,
    fall and be broken,
be ensnared and made captive.
16 Bind up the testimony, seal the instruction
in the heart of my disciples.'
17 My trust is in Yahweh who hides his face
    from the House of Jacob;
I put my hope in him.
18 Look, I and the children whom Yahweh
    has given me
shall become signs and portents in Israel
    on behalf of Yahweh Sabaoth who
    dwells on Mount Zion.
19 And should people say to you,
'Go and consult ghosts and wizards that
    whisper and mutter'—
a people should certainly consult its gods
and the dead on behalf of the living!
20 As regards instruction and testimony,
without doubt this is how they will talk,
and hence there will be no dawn for
    them.

Wandering in darkness

21 Oppressed and starving he will wander the
    country;

8a His name means 'Speedy-spoil-quick-booty', a prediction of the destruction of Damascus and Samaria in 722 BC.

and, once starving, he will become
    frenzied
and curse his king and his God; turning
    his gaze upward,
22 then down to earth, there will be only
    anguish,
gloom, the confusion of night, swirling
    darkness.
23 For is not everything dark as night for a
    country in distress?

Deliverance

As the past humbled the land of Zebulun and
the land of Naphtali, so the future will glorify
the Way of the Sea, beyond the Jordan, the territory of the nations.

9 The people that walked in darkness have
    seen a great light;
on the inhabitants of a country in shadow
    dark as death light has blazed
    forth.
2 You have enlarged the nation, you have
    increased its joy;
they rejoice before you as people rejoice at
    harvest time,
as they exult when they are dividing the
    spoils.

3 For the yoke that weighed on it, the bar
    across its shoulders,
the rod of its oppressor,
these you have broken as on the day of
    Midian.

4 For all the footgear clanking over the
    ground
and all the clothing rolled in blood,
will be burnt, will be food for the flames.

5 For a son has been born for us,
a son has been given to us,
and dominion has been laid on his
    shoulders;
and this is the name he has been given,
'Wonder-Counsellor, Mighty-God,
Eternal-Father, Prince-of-Peace'

6 to extend his dominion in boundless peace,
over the throne of David and over his
    kingdom
to make it secure and sustain it
in fair judgement and integrity.
From this time onwards and for ever,
the jealous love of Yahweh Sabaoth will do
    this.

The ordeals of the Northern Kingdom

7 The Lord has launched a word at Jacob
and it has fallen on Israel;
8 and the people will all soon know it,
Ephraim and the inhabitants of Samaria,
who say in the pride of their arrogant
    hearts,
9 'The bricks have fallen down but we shall
    rebuild with dressed stone;
the sycamores have been felled but we
    shall replace them with cedars.'
10 But, against them, Yahweh has raised their
    foe Razon,
he has whipped up their enemies,
11 Aram to the east, Philistines to the west,
to devour Israel with gaping jaws.
After all this, his anger is not spent.
No, his hand is still raised!

12 But the people would not come back to
    him who struck them,
they would not seek out Yahweh Sabaoth;
13 hence Yahweh has topped and tailed
    Israel,
cutting off palm and reed in a single day.
14 (The 'top' is the elder and the man of rank;
the 'tail' is the prophet teaching lies.)
15 This people's leaders have led them
    astray,
and those who are led by them are
    swallowed up.
16 Hence the Lord will no longer take
    delight in their young people,
or pity on their orphans and widows,
since all of them are godless and evil,
and everything they say is madness.
After all this, his anger is not spent.
No, his hand is still raised!

17 Yes, wickedness has been burning like a
  fire,
  devouring bramble and thorn-bush,
  setting the forest thickets ablaze—
  up they go in billowing smoke!
18 The country has been set on fire
  by the fury of Yahweh Sabaoth,
  and the people are like food for the flames.
  No one spares a thought for his brother.
19 They have sliced to the right and are still
  hungry,
  they have eaten to the left and are not
  satisfied;
  each devours the flesh of his own arm.
20 Manasseh devours Ephraim, Ephraim
  Manasseh,
  together they turn against Judah.
  After all this, his anger is not spent.
  No, his hand is still raised!

10 Woe to those who enact unjust decrees,
  who compose oppressive legislation
2 to deny justice to the weak
  and to cheat the humblest of my people of
  fair judgement,
  to make widows their prey
  and to rob the orphan.
3 What will you do on the day of
  punishment,
  when disaster comes from far away?
  To whom will you run for help
  and where will you leave your riches,
4 to avoid squatting among the captives
  or falling among the slain?
  After all this, his anger is not spent.
  No, his hand is still raised!

Against the king of Assyria

5 Woe to Assyria, rod of my anger,
  the club in their hands is my fury!
6 I was sending him against a godless
  nation,
  commissioning him against the people
  who enraged me,
  to pillage and plunder at will
  and trample on them like the mud in the
  streets.

7 But this was not his intention
  nor did his heart plan it so,
  for he dreamed of putting an end to
  them,
  of liquidating nations without number!
8 For he thought, 'Are not my officers all
  kings?
9 Is not Calno like Carchemish,
  Hamath like Arpad,
  Samaria like Damascus?
10 As my hand has found the kingdoms of
  the false gods,
  where there were more images than in
  Jerusalem and Samaria,
11 as I have treated Samaria and her false
  gods
  shall I not treat Jerusalem and her statues
  too?'

12 When the Lord has completed all his
work on Mount Zion and in Jerusalem, he will
punish the fruit of the king of Assyria's boastful heart and the insolence of his haughty
looks.

13 For he thinks:

  'By the strength of my own arm I have
  done this
  and by my own wisdom: how intelligent I
  have been!
  I have abolished the frontiers between
  peoples,
  I have plundered their treasures,
  like a hero, I have subjugated their
  inhabitants.
14 My hand has found, as though a bird's
  nest,
  the riches of the peoples.
  Like someone collecting deserted eggs,
  I have collected the whole world
  while no one has fluttered a wing
  or opened a beak to squawk.'

15 Does the axe claim more credit than the
  man who wields it,
  or the saw more strength than the man
  who handles it?

As though a staff controlled those who
    raise it,
or the club could raise what is not made of
    wood!
16 That is why Yahweh Sabaoth is going to
    inflict
leanness on his stout men,
and beneath his glory kindle a fever
    burning like a fire.
17 The light of Israel will become a fire
and its Holy One a flame
burning and devouring
his thorn-bushes and brambles in a day.
18 He will consume his luxuriant forest and
    productive ground,
he will ravage body and soul:
it will be like a consumptive wasting away;
19 and what remain of the trees of his forest
will be so few that a child could write their
    number.

The little remnant

20 When that day comes,
the remnant of Israel and the survivors of
    the House of Jacob
will stop relying on the man who strikes
    them
and will truly rely on Yahweh,
the Holy One of Israel.
21 A remnant will return, the remnant of
    Jacob,
to the mighty God.
22 Israel, though your people are like the
    sand of the sea,
only a remnant of them will return:
a destruction has been decreed
which will make justice overflow,
23 for, throughout the country,
the Lord Yahweh Sabaoth will enforce the
    destruction now decreed.

Trust in God

24 That is why the Lord Yahweh Sabaoth says
this:

My people who live in Zion,
do not be afraid of Assyria!

He may strike you with the rod,
he may raise the club against you
(on the way from Egypt),
25 but in a very short time
the retribution will come to an end,
and my anger will destroy them.
26 Yahweh Sabaoth will brandish a whip
    at him
as he struck Midian at Oreb's Rock,
will brandish his rod at the Sea
as he raised it on the way from Egypt.
27 When that day comes,
his burden will fall from your shoulder,
and his yoke from your neck,
and the yoke will be destroyed . . .

The invasion

28 He has reached Aiath,
he has moved on to Migron,
he has left his baggage train at Michmash.
29 They have passed through the defile,
they have bivouacked at Geba.
Ramah quaked, Gibeah of Saul has fled.
30 Cry your loudest, Bath-Gallim!
Pay attention, Laish!
Answer her, Anathoth!
31 Madmenah has run away,
the inhabitants of Gebim have taken cover.
32 This very day, as he halts at Nob,
he will shake his fist at the mountain of
    the daughter of Zion,
the hill of Jerusalem.
33 See how the Lord Yahweh Sabaoth
    violently lops off the foliage!
The ones standing highest are cut down,
    the proudest are laid low!
34 The forest thickets fall beneath the axe,
and the Lebanon falls to the blows of a
    Mighty One.

The descendant of David

11 A shoot will spring from the stock of
    Jesse,
a new shoot will grow from his roots.
2 On him will rest the spirit of Yahweh,
the spirit of wisdom and insight,
the spirit of counsel and power,

the spirit of knowledge and fear of
    Yahweh:
3 his inspiration will lie in fearing Yahweh.
  His judgement will not be by appearances,
  his verdict not given on hearsay.
4 He will judge the weak with integrity
  and give fair sentence for the humblest in
    the land.
  He will strike the country with the rod of
    his mouth
  and with the breath of his lips bring death
    to the wicked.
5 Uprightness will be the belt around his
    waist,
  and constancy the belt about his hips.

6 The wolf will live with the lamb,
  the panther lie down with the kid,
  calf, lion and fat-stock beast together,
  with a little boy to lead them.
7 The cow and the bear will graze,
  their young will lie down together.
  The lion will eat hay like the ox.
8 The infant will play over the den of the
    adder;
  the baby will put his hand into the viper's
    lair.
9 No hurt, no harm will be done
  on all my holy mountain,
  for the country will be full of knowledge
    of Yahweh
  as the waters cover the sea.

Return from the dispersion

10 That day, the root of Jesse, standing as a
    signal for the peoples,
  will be sought out by the nations and its
    home will be glorious.
11 When that day comes,
  the Lord will raise his hand a second time
  to ransom the remnant of his people,
  those still left, from Assyria, from Egypt,
  from Pathros, Cush and Elam,
  from Shinar, Hamath and the islands of
    the Sea.
12 He will hoist a signal for the nations
  and assemble the outcasts of Israel;

he will gather the scattered people of
    Judah
  from the four corners of the earth.
13 Then Ephraim's jealousy will cease
  and Judah's enemies be suppressed;
  Ephraim will no longer be jealous of
    Judah
  nor Judah any longer hostile to Ephraim,
14 but together they will swoop on the
    Philistines' back, to the west,
  and together pillage the people of the
    east.
  Edom and Moab will be subject to their
    sway
  and the Ammonites will obey them.
15 Then Yahweh will dry up the gulf of the
    Sea of Egypt,
  he will raise his hand against the River
  with the heat of his breath.
  He will divide it into seven streams
  for them to cross dry-shod.
16 And there will be a highway for the
    remnant of his people
  for those still left, from Assyria,
  as there was for Israel
  when he came out of Egypt.

Psalm

12 And, that day, you will say:
  'I praise you, Yahweh, you have been
    angry with me
  but your anger is now appeased and you
    have comforted me.
2 Look, he is the God of my salvation:
  I shall have faith and not be afraid,
  for Yahweh is my strength and my song,
  he has been my salvation.'[a]

3 Joyfully you will draw water
  from the springs of salvation
4 and, that day, you will say,
  'Praise Yahweh, invoke his name.[b]
  Proclaim his deeds to the people,
  declare his name sublime.

12a ‖ Ex 15:2.   *12b* ‖ Ps 105:1.

⁵ Sing of Yahweh, for his works are
    majestic,
make them known throughout the world.
⁶ Cry and shout for joy, you who live in
    Zion,
For the Holy One of Israel is among you
    in his greatness.'

Against Babylon

13 Proclamation about Babylon, seen by
    Isaiah son of Amoz.

² On a bare hill hoist a signal,
    shout for them,
    beckon them to come
    to the Nobles' Gate.
³ I have issued orders
    to my sacred warriors,
    I have summoned my heroes to serve my
    anger,
    my proud champions.
⁴ The noise of a great crowd in the
    mountains,
    like an immense people,
    the tumultuous sound of kingdoms,
    of nations mustering:
    it is Yahweh Sabaoth
    marshalling the troops for battle.
⁵ They come from a distant country, from
    the far horizons,
    Yahweh and the instruments of his fury
    to lay the whole country waste.
⁶ Howl! For the Day of Yahweh is near,
    coming like devastation from Shaddai.
⁷ This is why all hands fall limp,
    why all the men are losing heart;
⁸ they are panic-stricken,
    seized with pains and convulsions;
    they writhe like a woman in labour,
    they look at one another appalled,
    with feverish faces.
⁹ Look, the Day of Yahweh is coming,
    merciless, with wrath and burning anger,
    to reduce the country to a desert
    and root out the sinners from it.
¹⁰ For in the sky the stars and Orion
    will shed their light no longer,

the sun will be dark when it rises,
    and the moon will no longer give its
    light.
¹¹ I am going to punish the world for its
    wickedness
    and the wicked for their guilt,
    and put an end to the pride of the arrogant
    and humble the haughtiness of despots.
¹² I shall make people scarcer than pure gold,
    human life scarcer than the gold of Ophir.
¹³ This is why I am going to shake the
    heavens,
    why the earth will reel on its foundations,
    under the wrath of Yahweh Sabaoth,
    the day when his anger ignites.
¹⁴ Then like a hunted gazelle, like sheep that
    nobody gathers in,
    everyone will head back to his people,
    everyone will flee to his native land.
¹⁵ All those who are found will be stabbed,
    all those captured will fall by the sword,
¹⁶ their babies dashed to pieces before their
    eyes,
    their houses plundered, their wives raped.
¹⁷ Look, against them I am stirring up the
    Medes
    who care nothing for silver,
    who set no value by gold.
¹⁸ Bows will annihilate the young men,
    they will have no pity for the fruit of the
    womb,
    or mercy in their eyes for children.
¹⁹ And Babylon, that pearl of kingdoms,
    that splendid jewel of the Chaldaeans,
    will, like Sodom and Gomorrah,
    be overthrown by God.
²⁰ Never again will anyone live there or
    reside there
    for all generations to come.
    Never again will the Arab pitch his tent
    there,
    or the shepherds bring their flocks to rest.
²¹ But beasts of the desert will make their
    haunt there
    and owls fill their houses,
    there ostriches will settle their home,
    there goats will dance.

22 Hyenas will howl in its towers,
  jackals in its delightful palaces,
  for its doom is about to come
  and its days will not last long.

The end of the Exile

14 Yahweh will have pity on Jacob, he will choose Israel once more and resettle them on their native soil. Foreigners will join them, attaching themselves to the House of Jacob. 2 Peoples will take them and escort them home, and the House of Israel will take them as slaves, men and women on Yahweh's soil. They will enslave those who enslaved them and will master their oppressors.

The death of the king of Babylon

3 When that day comes, and Yahweh gives you rest from your suffering and torment and the grim servitude to which you have been subjected, 4 you will recite this satire on the king of Babylon and say:

  'How did the tyrant end?
  How did his arrogance end?
5 Yahweh has broken the staff of the
      wicked,
  the sceptre of rulers,
6 furiously lashing peoples
  with continual blows,
  angrily hammering nations,
  pursuing without respite.
7 The whole world is at rest and calm,
  shouts of joy resounding,
8 the cypresses, the cedars of Lebanon,
  rejoice aloud at your fate,
  "Now that you have been laid low,
  no one comes up to fell us."

9 'On your account, Sheol below
  is astir to greet your arrival.
  He has roused the ghosts to greet you,
  all the rulers of the world.
  He has made all the kings of the nations
  get up from their thrones.
10 They will all greet you with the words,
  "So, you too are now as weak as we are!

You, too, have become like us.
11 Your pride has been flung down to Sheol
  with the music of your lyres;
  under you a mattress of maggots,
  over you a blanket of worms.
12 How did you come to fall from the
      heavens,
  Daystar, son of Dawn?
  How did you come to be thrown to the
      ground,
  conqueror of nations?
13 You who used to think to yourself:
  I shall scale the heavens;
  higher than the stars of God
  I shall set my throne.
  I shall sit on the Mount of Assembly
  far away to the north.
14 I shall climb high above the clouds,
  I shall rival the Most High."
15 Now you have been flung down to Sheol,
  into the depths of the abyss!

16 'When they see you, they will scrutinise
      you
  and consider what you have become,
  "Is this the man who
      made the world tremble,
  who overthrew kingdoms?
17 He made the world a desert,
  he levelled cities
  and never freed his prisoners to go home."
18 All other kings of nations, all of them,
  lie honourably, each in his own tomb;
19 but you have been thrown away, unburied,
  like a loathsome branch,
  covered with heaps of the slain pierced by
      the sword
  who fall on the rocks of the abyss
  like trampled carrion.

20 'You will not rejoin them in the grave,
  for you have brought your country to ruin
  and destroyed your people.
  The offspring of the wicked
  leave no name behind them.
21 Make ready to slaughter his sons
  for the guilt of their father!

Never again must they rise to conquer the
world
and cover the face of the earth with their
cities.

22 'I will rise against them, declares Yahweh
Sabaoth, and deprive Babylon of name, remnant, offspring and posterity, declares Yahweh. 23 I shall turn it into the haunt of hedge-
hogs, a swamp. I shall sweep it with the broom
of destruction, declares Yahweh Sabaoth.'

Against Assyria

24 Yahweh Sabaoth has sworn it,
'Yes, what I have planned will take place,
what I have decided will be so:

25 'I shall break Assyria in my country,
I shall trample on him on my mountains.
Then his yoke will slip off them,
his burden will slip from their shoulders.'

26 This is the decision taken in defiance of
the whole world;
this, the hand outstretched in defiance of
all nations.

27 Once Yahweh Sabaoth has decided, who
will stop him?
Once he stretches out his hand, who can
withdraw it?

Against the Philistines

28 In the year Ahaz died came this proclamation:

29 All Philistia, do not rejoice
because the rod which used to beat you is
now broken,
for the serpent stock will produce a viper,
its offspring will be a flying dragon.

30 While the first-born of the poor are
grazing
and the destitute are resting in safety,
I shall make your stock die of hunger
and then slaughter what remains of you.

31 Howl, gate! Shriek, city!
Totter, all Philistia!
For a smoke is coming from the north,
and there are no deserters in those
battalions.

32 What reply will be given then
to the messengers of that nation?—
That Yahweh founded Zion
and there the poor of his people will find
refuge.

On Moab [a]

15 Proclamation about Moab:

Laid waste in a night,
Ar-Moab lies silent;
Laid waste in a night,
Kir-Moab lies silent.
2 The daughter of Dibon has climbed
to the high places to weep;
on Nebo and in Medeba
Moab laments.

Every head shaven,
every beard cut off,
3 they wear sackcloth in their streets;
on their roofs and in their squares,
everyone is lamenting
and collapsing in tears.

4 Heshbon and Elealeh are crying out in
distress,
their voices can be heard as far as Jahaz.
That is why the warriors of Moab are
shivering,
his soul trembles at the sound.
5 His heart cries out in distress for Moab,
whose fugitives are already at Zoar,
nearly at Eglath-Shelishiyah.

They climb the slope of Luhith, [b]
weeping as they go;
on the road to Horonaim
they utter heart-rending cries.

15a cf. Jr 48.   15b ‖ Jr 48:5.

⁶ The Waters of Nimrim
have become a waste land,
the grass dried up, the plants withered
away,
nothing green any more.

⁷ That is why they are carrying
what they could save of their stores
across the Ravine of the Willows.

⁸ For the cry for help re-echoes
round the territory of Moab;
their wailing, right to Eglaim,
to Beer-Elim, their wailing;

⁹ Dimon's waters are swollen with blood,
and I have worse in store for Dimon:
a lion for those of Moab who survive,
for those left on its soil.

The Moabites' petition

16 Send the lamb to the ruler of the
land,
from Sela by the desert,
to the mountain of the daughter of
Zion,
² for soon, like a fluttered bird,
like nestlings cast out,
will be the women of Moab at the fords of
the Arnon.

³ Hold a council, make a decision.
At noon spread your shadow
as if it were night.
Hide those who have been driven out,
do not betray the fugitive,
⁴ let those who have been driven out of
Moab
come and live with you;
be their refuge in the face of the
devastator.
Once the oppression is past,
and the devastation has stopped
and those now trampling on the country
have gone away,
⁵ the throne will be made secure in faithful
love,

and on it will sit in constancy within the
tent of David
a judge seeking fair judgement and
pursuing uprightness.

⁶ We have heard about Moab's pride,
about how very proud it is,
about its arrogance, its pride, its rage,
its bravado, which will come to
nothing!

Moab's lament

⁷ And so Moab is wailing for Moab,
wailing, every one of them.
For the raisin cakes of Kir-Hareseth[a]
you mourn, stricken with grief.
⁸ For Heshbon's vineyards are
withering,
the vine of Sibmah
whose red grapes used to overcome
the overlords of the nations.
It used to reach to Jazer,
had wound its way into the desert,
its shoots grew so numerous
they spread across the sea.
⁹ And so I weep, as Jazer weeps,
for the vine of Sibmah.
I water you with my tears,
Heshbon and Elealeh.
For over your harvest and vintage
the cheering has died away;
¹⁰ joy and gladness
have vanished from the orchards.
No more revelry in the vineyards,
no more happy shouting;
no more the treader treads wine in the
presses,
the cheering has ceased.
¹¹ That is why my whole being
quivers like harp strings for Moab,
my very heart, for Kir-Heres.
¹² Moab will be seen,
wearing itself out on the high places
and going to its temple to pray,
but it will accomplish nothing.

16a ‖ Jr 48:29–30.

[907]

¹³Such was the word which Yahweh spoke about Moab in the past. ¹⁴And now Yahweh has spoken in these terms, 'Within three years, as a hired worker reckons them, the glory of Moab will be humbled, despite its teeming population. It will be reduced to nothing, an insignificant remnant.'

Against Damascus and Israel

17 Proclamation about Damascus:

Damascus will soon cease to be a city,
it will become a heap of ruins.
² Its towns, abandoned for ever,
will be pastures for flocks;
there they will rest with no one to disturb them.
³ Ephraim will be stripped of its defences
and Damascus of its sovereignty;
and the remnant of Aram will be treated
like the glory of the Israelites—
declares Yahweh Sabaoth.

⁴ When that day comes, Jacob's glory will diminish,
from being fat he will grow lean;
⁵ as when a reaper gathers in the standing corn,
harvesting the ears of corn with his arm,
or when they glean the ears in the Valley of Rephaim,
⁶ nothing will remain but pickings,
as when an olive tree is beaten;
two or three berries left on the topmost bough,
four or five berries on the branches of the tree—
declares Yahweh, God of Israel.

⁷That day, a man will look to his Creator and his eyes will turn to the Holy One of Israel. ⁸He will no longer look to altars, his own handiwork, or to what his own fingers have made: the sacred poles and incense-altars.

⁹ That day, its cities of refuge will be abandoned

as were the woods and heaths
at the Israelites' advance:
there will be desolation.
¹⁰ Since you have forgotten the God of your salvation,
and failed to keep the Rock, your refuge, in mind,
you plant pleasure-gardens,
you sow exotic seeds;
¹¹ the day you plant them, you get them to sprout,
and, next morning, your seedlings are in flower;
but the harvest will vanish on the day of disease
and incurable pain.

¹² Disaster! The thunder of vast hordes,
a thunder like the thunder of the seas,
the roar of nations roaring like the roar of mighty floods,
¹³ of nations roaring like the roar of ocean!
He rebukes them and far away they flee,
driven like chaff on the mountains before the wind,
like an eddy of dust before the storm.
¹⁴ At evening all is terror,
by morning all have disappeared.
Such will be the lot of those who plunder us,
such, the fate of our despoilers.

Against Cush

18 Disaster! Land of the whirring locust
beyond the rivers of Cush,
² who send ambassadors by sea,
in little reed-boats across the waters!
Go, swift messengers
to a nation tall and bronzed,
to a people feared far and near,
a mighty and masterful nation
whose country is criss-crossed with rivers.
³ All you who inhabit the world,
you who people the earth,
when the signal is hoisted on the mountains, you will see,

when the ram's-horn is sounded, you will
hear.
⁴ For this is what Yahweh has told me,
'I shall sit here quietly looking down,
like the burning heat in the daytime,
like a dewy mist in the heat of harvest.'
⁵ For, before the harvest, once the flowering
is over
and blossom turns into ripening grape,
the branches will be cut off with pruning
knives,
and the shoots taken off, cut away.
⁶ All has been abandoned
to the mountain birds of prey
and the wild animals:
the birds of prey will summer on them,
and all the wild animals winter on them.

⁷ Then, an offering will be brought to Yahweh Sabaoth on behalf of a people tall and
bronzed, on behalf of a people feared far and
near, on behalf of a mighty and masterful nation whose country is criss-crossed with rivers:
to the place where the name of Yahweh
Sabaoth resides, Mount Zion.

Against Egypt

19 Proclamation about Egypt:

Look! Yahweh, riding a swift cloud,
is coming to Egypt.
The false gods of Egypt totter before him
and Egypt's heart quails within her.
² I shall stir up Egypt against Egypt,
they will fight one another,
brother against brother, friend against
friend,
city against city, kingdom against
kingdom.
³ Egypt's spirit will fail within her
and I shall confound her deliberations.
They will consult false gods and wizards,
ghosts and sorcerers.
⁴ And I shall hand Egypt over
to the clutches of a cruel master,
a ruthless king will rule them—
declares Yahweh Sabaoth.

⁵ The waters will ebb from the sea,
the river will dry up and run low,
⁶ the streams will become foul,
the rivers of Egypt sink and dry up.
Rush and reed will turn black,
⁷ the Nile-plants on the banks of the Nile;
all the vegetation of the Nile,
will wither, blow away and be no more.
⁸ The fishermen will groan, it will be
mourning
for all who cast hook in the Nile;
those who spread nets on the waters will
lose heart.
⁹ The workers of carded flax
and the weavers of white cloth
will be confounded,
¹⁰ the weavers dismayed,
all the workmen dejected.
¹¹ Yes, the princes of Zoan are fools,
Pharaoh's wisest councillors make up a
stupid council.
How dare you say to Pharaoh,
'I am descended from sages, I am
descended from bygone kings'?
¹² Where are these sages of yours?
Let them tell you, so that all may know,
the plans Yahweh Sabaoth has made
against Egypt!
¹³ The princes of Zoan are fools,
the princes of Noph, self-deceivers,
the top men of her provinces
have led Egypt astray.
¹⁴ Yahweh has infused them
with a giddy spirit;
they have led Egypt astray in all she
undertakes
like a drunkard straying about as he
vomits.
¹⁵ Nowadays no one does for Egypt
what top and tail, palm and reed used
to do.

The conversion of Egypt

¹⁶ That day Egypt will be like women, trembling and terrified at the threatening hand of
Yahweh Sabaoth, when he raises it against
her. ¹⁷ The land of Judah will become Egypt's

shame; whenever she is reminded of it, she will be terrified, because of the plan which Yahweh Sabaoth has laid against her. ¹⁸ That day in Egypt there will be five towns speaking the language of Canaan and pledging themselves to Yahweh Sabaoth; one of them will be called City of the Sun. ¹⁹ That day there will be an altar dedicated to Yahweh in the centre of Egypt and, close to the frontier, a pillar dedicated to Yahweh, ²⁰ and this will be a sign and a witness to Yahweh Sabaoth in Egypt. When they cry to Yahweh for help because of oppressors, he will send them a Saviour and leader to deliver them. ²¹ Yahweh will reveal himself to Egypt, and the Egyptians will acknowledge Yahweh that day and will offer sacrifices and cereal offerings, and will make vows to Yahweh and perform them. ²² And if Yahweh strikes Egypt, having struck he will heal, and they will turn to Yahweh who will hear their prayers and heal them. ²³ That day there will be a highway from Egypt to Assyria. Assyria will have access to Egypt and Egypt have access to Assyria. Egypt will serve with Assyria.

²⁴ That day Israel will make a third with Egypt and Assyria, a blessing at the centre of the world, ²⁵ and Yahweh Sabaoth will bless them in the words, 'Blessed be my people Egypt, Assyria my creation, and Israel my heritage.'

Relating to the capture of Ashdod

20 The year the general-in-chief, sent by Sargon king of Assyria, came to Ashdod and stormed and captured it ² at that time Yahweh spoke through Isaiah son of Amoz and said, 'Go, undo the sackcloth round your waist and take the sandals off your feet.' And he did so, and walked about, naked and barefoot. ³ Yahweh then said, 'As my servant Isaiah has been walking about naked and barefoot for the last three years as a sign and portent for Egypt and Cush, ⁴ so the king of Assyria will lead the captives of Egypt and the exiles of Cush, young and old, naked and barefoot, their buttocks bared, to the shame of Egypt. ⁵ Then they will be afraid and ashamed of

Cush their hope and Egypt their pride, ⁶ and the inhabitants of this coast will say on that day, "Look what has happened to our hope, to those to whom we fled for help, to escape from the king of Assyria. How are we going to escape?" '

The fall of Babylon

21 Proclamation about the coastal desert:

As whirlwinds sweeping over the Negeb,
he comes from the desert, from a fearsome country.
² A harsh vision has been shown me,
'The traitor betrays and the despoiler despoils.
Advance, Elam, lay siege, Media!'
I have cut short all groaning.
³ This is why my loins are racked with pain,
why I am seized with pangs like the pangs of a woman in labour;
I am too distressed to hear, too afraid to look.
⁴ My heart is bewildered, dread overwhelms me,
the twilight I longed for has become my horror.
⁵ They lay the table, spread the cloth,
they eat, they drink.
Up, princes, grease the shield!

⁶ For this is what the Lord has told me,
'Go, post a look-out, let him report what he sees.
⁷ He will see cavalry, horsemen two by two,
men mounted on donkeys, men mounted on camels;
let him watch alertly, be very alert indeed!'
⁸ Then the look-out shouted,
'On the watchtower, Lord,
I stay all day
and at my post
I stand all night.
⁹ Now the cavalry is coming, horsemen two by two.'
He shouted again and said,
'Babylon has fallen, has fallen,

and all the images of her gods he has
        shattered to the ground!'
10 You whom I have threshed, grain of my
        threshing-floor,
    what I have heard from Yahweh Sabaoth,
        God of Israel,
    I am telling you now.

On Edom

11 Proclamation about Dumah:

    From Seir, someone shouts to me,
    'Watchman, what time of night?
    Watchman, what time of night?'

12 The watchman answers,
    'Morning is coming, then night again.
    If you want to ask, ask!
    Come back! Come here!'

Against the Arabs

13 Proclamation about the wastelands:

    In the thickets, on the wastelands, you
        spend the night,
    you caravans of Dedanites.
14 Bring water for the thirsty!
    The inhabitants of Tema went
    with bread to greet the fugitive.
15 For these have fled before the sword,
    the naked sword and the bent bow,
    the press of battle.

16 For this is what the Lord has told me,
'In one year's time as a hired worker reck-
ons it, all the glory of Kedar will be finished
17 and, of the valiant archers, the Kedarites,
hardly any will be left, for Yahweh, God of Israel, has spoken.'

Against rejoicing in Jerusalem

22 Prophecy on the Valley of Vision:

    Now what is the matter with you
    for you all to be up on the housetops,
2 full of excitement, boisterous town, joyful
        city?

Your slain have not fallen to the sword
nor died in battle.
3 Your leaders have all fled together,
    captured without a bow between them,
    all who could be found have been captured
        at a blow,
    far though they had fled.
4 That is why I said, 'Turn your eyes away
        from me,
    let me weep bitterly;
    do not try to comfort me
    over the ruin of the daughter of my people.'

5 For this is a day of rout, panic and
        confusion,
    the work of the Lord Yahweh Sabaoth
    in the Valley of Vision.
    The wall is sapped,
    cries for help ring out to the mountains.
6 Elam has picked up his quiver,
    with manned chariots and horsemen, and
        Kir has bared his shield.
7 Your fairest valleys are full of chariots
    and the horsemen take up positions at the
        gates;
8 thus falls the defence of Judah.

    That day you turned your gaze
    to the weapons in the House of the Forest.
9 You saw how many breaches there were in
        the City of David.
    You collected the waters of the lower pool.
10 You surveyed the houses in Jerusalem
    and pulled houses down to strengthen the
        wall.
11 Between the two walls you made a
        reservoir
    for the waters of the old pool.
    But you did not look to the Creator of
        these things,
    you did not look to the One who fashioned
        them long ago.

12 That day the Lord Yahweh Sabaoth called
        on you
    to weep and mourn,
    to shave your heads, to put on sackcloth.

13 But instead there is joy and merriment,
    killing of oxen, slaughtering of sheep,
    eating of meat, drinking of wine,
    'Let us eat and drink,
    for tomorrow we shall be dead.'
14 Then Yahweh Sabaoth revealed this to my
        ears,
    'This guilt will never be forgiven you,
            until you are dead,'
    says the Lord Yahweh Sabaoth.

Against Shebna

15 The Lord Yahweh Sabaoth says this:

    Go and find that steward,
    Shebna, the master of the palace:
16 'What do you own here, who gave you the
        right
    for you to hew yourself a tomb here?'
    He is hewing himself a tomb,
    is digging a resting-place for himself in the
        rock.
17 But Yahweh will throw you away, strong
        as you are,
    will grasp you in his grip,
18 will screw you up into a ball,
    a ball thrown into a vast space.
    There you will die, with your splendid
        chariots,
    disgrace to your master's palace!
19 I shall hound you from your office,
    I shall snatch you from your post
20 and, when that day comes,
    I shall summon my servant
    Eliakim son of Hilkiah.
21 I shall dress him in your tunic,
    I shall put your sash round his waist,
    I shall invest him with your authority;
    and he will be a father
    to the inhabitants of Jerusalem
    and to the House of Judah.
22 I shall place the key of David's palace on
        his shoulder;
    when he opens, no one will close,
    when he closes, no one will open.
23 I shall drive him like a nail into a firm
        place;

and he will become a throne of glory for
        his family.

24 'On him will depend all the glory of his
family, the descendants and offspring, all
the vessels of small capacity too, from cups
to pitchers. 25 That day, declares Yahweh
Sabaoth, the nail driven into a firm place will
give way, will be torn out and fall. And the
whole load hanging on it will be lost. For Yahweh has spoken.'

Against Tyre

23 Proclamation about Tyre:

    Howl, ships of Tarshish, for all has been
        destroyed—
    no more houses, no way of getting in:
    the news has reached them from Kittim.
2 Be struck dumb, inhabitants of the coast,
    you merchants of Sidon,
    whose messengers cross the sea
3 to the wide ocean.
    The grain of the Canal, the harvest of the
        Nile,
    formed her revenue.
    She was the market for the nations.
4 Blush, Sidon (citadel of the seas),
    for this is what the sea has said,
    'I have felt no birth-pangs, never given
        birth,
    never reared boys nor brought up
        girls.'

5 When the news reaches Egypt,
    they will tremble to hear Tyre's fate.
6 Cross to Tarshish, howl, inhabitants of
        the coast.

7 Is this your proud city
    founded far back in the past,
    whose steps led her far afield
    to found her colonies?
8 Who took this decision
    against Tyre, who used to hand out
        crowns,
    whose traders were princes,

whose merchants, men honoured in the
city?
9 Yahweh Sabaoth took this decision
to wither the pride of all beauty
and humiliate those honoured in the city.
10 Cultivate your country like the Delta,
daughter of Tarshish,
for your marine docks are no more.
11 He has raised his hand against the sea,
he has shaken kingdoms,
Yahweh has ordained the destruction
of the fortresses of Canaan.

12 He has said, 'Exult no more,
ill-treated virgin daughter of Sidon!
Get up, cross to Kittim,
no respite for you there, either.'
13 Look at the land of the Chaldaeans,
a people who used not to exist!
Assyria assigned it to the creatures of the
wilds;
they raised their siege-towers against it,
demolished its bastions,
reduced it to ruin.
14 Howl, ships of Tarshish, for your fortress
has been destroyed.

15 When that day comes, Tyre will be forgotten for seventy years, the length of one
king's life. But when the seventy years are
over, Tyre will become like the whore in the
song:

16 'Take your harp, walk the town,
whore whom men have forgotten!
Play sweetly, song after song,
to make them remember you.'

17 At the end of the seventy years Yahweh
will visit Tyre. She will receive her pay again
and play the whore with all the kingdoms of
the world on the surface of the earth. 18 But
her profits and wages will be dedicated to
Yahweh. They will not be stored or hoarded,
but her profits will go to those who live in
Yahweh's presence, for them to have as much
food as they want and splendid clothes.

Yahweh's judgement

24 See how Yahweh lays the earth
waste,
makes it a desert, buckles its surface,
scatters its inhabitants,
2 priest and people alike, master and slave,
mistress and maid, seller and buyer,
lender and borrower, creditor and
debtor.
3 Ravaged, ravaged the earth will be,
despoiled, despoiled,
for Yahweh has uttered this word.
4 The earth is mourning, pining away,
the pick of earth's people are withering
away.
5 The earth is defiled
by the feet of its inhabitants,
for they have transgressed the laws,
violated the decree, broken the everlasting
covenant.
6 That is why the curse has consumed the
earth
and its inhabitants pay the penalty,
that is why the inhabitants of the earth
have been burnt up
and few people are left.

Song about the ruined city

7 The new wine is mourning, the vine is
withering away,
the once merry-hearted are sighing.
8 The cheerful sound of tambourines is
silent,
the sound of revelling is over,
the cheerful sound of the harp is silent.
9 No more will they sing over their wine,
liquor will taste bitter to the drinker.
10 The city of nothingness is in ruins,
every house is shut, no one can enter.
11 People shout in the streets to try to get
wine;
all joy has vanished,
happiness has been banished from the
country.
12 Nothing but rubble in the city,
the gate has collapsed in ruins.

13 For at the heart of earth's life, among the
      peoples,
    it is as at the beating of the olive trees,
    as at the gleaning of the grapes
    when the grape harvest is over.
14 They raise their voices, shouting for joy,
    in Yahweh's honour they shout from the
      west.
15 'Yes, in the east, give glory to Yahweh,
    in the islands of the sea, to the name of
      Yahweh, God of Israel!'
16 We have heard psalms from the remotest
      parts of earth,
    'Glory to the Upright One!'

The last battle

    But I thought, 'What an ordeal,
    what an ordeal! What misery for me!'
    The traitors have betrayed,
    the traitors have acted most treacherously.
17 Fear, the pit and the snare for you,
    inhabitants of the city!
18 And whoever flees from the cry of fear
    will fall into the pit,
    and whoever climbs out of the pit
    will be caught in the snare.ᵃ
    Yes, the sluice-gates above are open,
    the foundations of the earth are quaking.
19 A cracking, the earth cracks open,
    a jolting, the earth gives a jolt,
    a lurching, the earth lurches backwards
      and forwards.
20 The earth will reel to and fro like a
      drunkard,
    it will be shaken like a shanty;
    so heavy will be its sin on it,
    it will fall, never to rise again.
21 When that day comes, Yahweh will punish
    the armies of the sky above
    and on earth the kings of the earth;
22 they will be herded together,
    herded together like prisoners in a
      dungeon
    and shut up in gaol,
    and, after long years, punished.
23 The moon will be confused and the sun
      ashamed,

for Yahweh Sabaoth is king
on Mount Zion and in Jerusalem,
and the Glory will radiate on their
      elders.

A hymn of thanksgiving

25 Yahweh, you are my God,
    I shall praise you to the heights, I shall
      praise your name;
    for you have accomplished marvels,
    plans long-conceived, faithfully, firmly.
2 For you have made the town a heap of
      stones,
    the fortified city a ruin.
    The foreigners' citadel is a city no longer,
    it will never be rebuilt.
3 Hence mighty peoples will honour you,
    the city of pitiless nations hold you in awe;
4 For you have been a refuge for the weak,
    a refuge for the needy in distress,
    a shelter from the storm,
    shade from the heat;
    for the breath of the pitiless
    is like a winter storm.
5 Like heat in a dry land
    you calm the foreigners' tumult;
    as heat under the shadow of a cloud,
    so the song of the pitiless dies away.

The divine banquet

6 On this mountain, for all peoples,
    Yahweh Sabaoth is preparing
    a banquet of rich food, a banquet of fine
      wines,
    of succulent food, of well-strained
      wines.
7 On this mountain, he has destroyed
    the veil which used to veil all peoples,
    the pall enveloping all nations;
8 he has destroyed death for ever.
    Lord Yahweh has wiped away the tears
      from every cheek;
    he has taken his people's shame away
      everywhere on earth,
    for Yahweh has spoken.

24a ‖ Jr 48:43–44.

9 And on that day, it will be said,
  'Look, this is our God,
  in him we put our hope that he should
      save us,
  this is Yahweh, we put our hope in him.
  Let us exult and rejoice since he has saved
      us.'
10 For Yahweh's hand will rest on this
      mountain,
  and Moab will be trodden under his feet
  as straw is trodden into the dung-heap.
11 He may stretch his hands wide on the
      mountain
  like a swimmer stretching out his hands to
      swim.
  But he will humble his pride
  despite what his hands may attempt.
12 And the impregnable fortress of your walls,
  he has overthrown, laid low,
  flung to the ground, in the dust.

A hymn of thanksgiving

26 That day, this song will be sung in
      Judah:

  'We have a fortress city,
  the walls and ramparts provide safety.
2 Open the gates! Let the upright nation
      come in,
  the nation that keeps faith!
3 This is the plan decreed: you will
      guarantee peace,
  the peace entrusted to you.
4 Trust in Yahweh for ever,
  for Yahweh is a rock for ever.
5 He has brought low the dwellers on the
      heights,
  the lofty citadel;
  he lays it low, brings it to the ground,
  flings it down in the dust.
6 It will be trodden under foot,
  by the feet of the needy, the steps of the
      weak.'

A psalm

7 The path of the Upright One is honesty;
  you smooth the honest way of the upright.

8 Following the path of your judgements,
  Yahweh, we set our hopes in you,
  your name, your memory are all our soul
      desires.
9 At night my soul longs for you
  and my spirit within me seeks you out;
  for when your judgements appear on earth
  the inhabitants of the world learn what
      saving justice is.
10 If pity is shown to the wicked
  without his learning what saving justice is,
  he will act wrongly in the land of right
      conduct
  and not see the majesty of Yahweh.
11 Yahweh, your hand is raised but they do
      not see!
  The antagonists of your people will look
      and grow pale;
  with your fiery wrath you will devour
      your enemies.

12 Yahweh, you will grant us peace,
  having completed all our undertakings
      for us.
13 Yahweh our God, other lords than you
      have ruled us
  but, loyal to you alone, we invoke your
      name.
14 The dead will not come back to life,
  the shadows will not rise again,
  for you have punished them, annihilated
      them,
  wiping out their very memory.
15 You have made the nation larger, Yahweh,
  made the nation larger and won yourself
      glory,
  you have rolled back the frontiers of the
      country.

16 Yahweh, in distress they had recourse to
      you,
  they expended themselves in prayer,
  since your punishment was on them.
17 As a pregnant woman near her time of
      delivery
  writhes and cries out in her pangs,
  so have we been, Yahweh, in your eyes:

18 we have been pregnant, we have writhed,
but we have given birth only to wind:
we have not given salvation to the earth,
no inhabitants for the world have been
brought to birth.
19 Your dead will come back to life, your
corpses will rise again.
Wake up and sing, you dwellers in the
dust,
for your dew will be a radiant dew,
but the earth will give birth to the shades.

The Lord's judgement

20 Go, my people, go to your private room,
shut yourselves in.
Hide yourselves a little while
until the retribution has passed.

21 For see, Yahweh emerges from his
dwelling
to punish the inhabitants of earth for their
guilt;
and the earth will reveal the blood shed
on it
and no longer hide its slain.

27 That day Yahweh will punish,
with his unyielding sword, massive
and strong,
Leviathan*ᵃ* the fleeing serpent,
Leviathan the coiling serpent;
he will kill that dragon that lives in
the sea.

Yahweh's vineyard

2 That day,
sing of the splendid vineyard!
3 I, Yahweh, am its guardian,
from time to time I water it;
so that no harm befall it,
I guard it night and day.

4 —I do not have a wall.
Who can reduce me to brambles and
thorn-bushes?
—I shall make war and trample on it
and at the same time burn it.

5 Or should they beg for my protection,
let them make their peace with me,
peace let them make with me.

Pardon and punishment

6 In days to come, Jacob will take root,
Israel will bud and blossom
and the surface of the world be one vast
harvest.
7 Has he struck him as he was struck by
those who struck him?
Has he murdered him as he was murdered
by those who murdered him?
8 By expelling, by excluding him, you have
executed a sentence,
he has blown him away with a breath as
rough as the east wind.
9 For that is how Jacob's guilt will be
forgiven,
such will be the result of renouncing
his sin,
when all the altar-stones have been
smashed to pieces
like lumps of chalk,
when the sacred poles and incense-altars
stand no longer.
10 For the fortified city is abandoned now,
deserted, forsaken as a desert
where calves browse, where they lie down,
destroying its branches.
11 When boughs go dry, they get burnt,
women come and use them for firewood.
Now, this is a people that does not
understand,
and so its Maker will not take pity on it,
he who formed it will not show it any
mercy.

The Israelites return

12 When that day comes,
Yahweh will start his threshing
from the course of the River to the Torrent
of Egypt,
and you will be gathered one by one,
Israelites!

27a A mythical monster of primeval chaos.

[916]

13 When that day comes,
   the great ram's-horn will be sounded,
   and those lost in Assyria will come,
   and those banished to Egypt,
   and they will worship Yahweh
   on the holy mountain, in Jerusalem.

Against Samaria

28 Woe to the haughty crown of
      Ephraim's drunkards,
   to the fading flower of its proud splendour
   sited at the head of the lush valley,
   to those prostrated by wine!
2 See, a strong and mighty man in the
      Lord's service,
   like a storm of hail, a destroying tempest,
   like immense flood-waters overflowing,
   with his hand he throws them to the
      ground.
3 They will be trampled underfoot,
   the haughty crown of Ephraim's
      drunkards,
4 and the faded flower of its proud
      splendour
   sited at the head of the lush valley.
   Like a fig ripe before summer comes:
   whoever spots it forthwith picks and
      swallows it.

5 That day Yahweh Sabaoth
   will be a crown of splendour
   and a proud diadem
   for the remnant of his people,
6 a spirit of fair judgement
   for him who sits in judgement,
   and the strength of those who repel the
      assault on the gate.

Against false prophets

7 These too have been confused by wine,
   have gone astray owing to liquor.
   Priest and prophet have become confused
      by liquor,
   are sodden with wine, have strayed owing
      to liquor,
   have become confused in their visions,
   have strayed in their decisions.

8 Yes, every table is covered in filthy vomit,
   not one is clean!

9 'Whom does he think he is lecturing?
   Whom does he think his message is for?
   Babies just weaned?
   Babies just taken from the breast?
10 With his
   "Sav lasav, sav lasav,
   kav lakav, kav lakav,
   zeer sham, zeer sham!" '

11 Now, with stammering lips
   and in a foreign language,
   he will talk to this nation.
12 He used to say to them, 'Here you can rest!
   Here you can let the weary rest!
   Here all is quiet.'
   But they refused to listen.
13 Now Yahweh is going to say this to them,
   'Sav lasav, sav lasav,
   kav lakav, kav lakav,
   zeer sham, zeer sham.'
   So that when they walk they will fall over
      backwards
   and so be broken, trapped and taken
      captive.

Against evil counsellors

14 Hence listen to Yahweh's word, you
      insolent men,
   rulers of this people in Jerusalem.
15 Because you have said, 'We have made a
      treaty with Death
   and have struck a pact with Sheol.
   When the scourging flood comes over,
   it will not touch us,
   for we have made lies our refuge
   and hidden under falsehood.'
16 So the Lord Yahweh says this,
   'Now I shall lay a stone in Zion,
   a granite stone, a precious corner-stone,
   a firm foundation-stone:
   no one who relies on this will stumble.
17 And I will make fair judgement the
      measure,
   and uprightness the plumb-line.'

But hail will sweep away the refuge of lies
and floods wash away the hiding-place;
18 your treaty with Death will be broken
and your pact with Sheol will not hold.
When the scourging flood comes over,
you will be trodden down by it;
19 every time it comes over, it will seize
on you,
for it will come over, morning after
morning,
day by day and night by night.
Nothing but fear will make you
understand what you hear.
20 For the bed is too short to stretch in,
the blanket too narrow for covering.
21 Yes, as on Mount Perazim, Yahweh will
rise,
as in the Valley of Gibeon, he will storm
to do his work, his mysterious work,
to do his deed, his extraordinary deed.
22 Stop scoffing, then,
or your bonds will be tightened further,
for I have heard it: it has been irrevocably
decided
as regards the whole country
by the Lord Yahweh Sabaoth.

A parable

23 Listen closely to my words,
be attentive, understand what I am saying.
24 Does the ploughman plough all day to
sow,
breaking up and harrowing his ground?
25 Once he has levelled its surface,
does he not scatter fennel, sow cummin?
Then he puts in wheat, millet, barley
and, round the edges, spelt,
26 for his God has taught him this rule and
instructed him.
27 Fennel must not be crushed with a sledge,
nor cart-wheels driven over cummin;
fennel must be beaten with a stick,
and cummin with a flail.
28 When you are threshing wheat,
you do not waste time crushing it;
you get the horse and cart-wheel moving,
but you do not grind it fine.

29 All this is a gift from Yahweh Sabaoth,
marvellous advice leading to great
achievements.

On Jerusalem

29 Woe, Ariel,[a] Ariel,
city where David encamped.
Let year after year pass,
let the feasts make their full round,
2 then I shall inflict trouble on Ariel,
and there will be sighing and sobbing,
and I shall make it truly Ariel.
3 I shall encamp all round you,
I shall lay siege to you
and mount siege-works against you.
4 You will be laid low, will speak from the
underworld,
your words will rise like a murmur from
the dust.
Your voice from the earth will be like a
ghost's,
it will whisper as though coming from the
dust.

5 The horde of your enemies will be like
fine dust,
the horde of the warriors like flying
chaff.
And suddenly, in an instant,
6 you will be visited by Yahweh Sabaoth
with thunder, earthquake, mighty din,
hurricane, tempest, flame of devouring
fire.
7 It will be like a dream, like a vision at
night:
the horde of all the nations at war with
Ariel,
all those fighting, besieging and
troubling it.
8 It will be like the dream of a hungry man:
he eats, then wakes up with an empty
belly;
or like the dream of a thirsty man:
he drinks, then wakes up exhausted with a
parched throat.

29a Symbolic name for Jerusalem (=? lion of God).

So will it be with the horde of all the
  nations
making war on Mount Zion.

9 Be stupefied and stunned,
  go blind, unseeing,
  drunk but not on wine,
  staggering but not through liquor.
10 For Yahweh has infused you with a spirit
    of lethargy,
  he has closed your eyes (the prophets),
  he has veiled your heads (the seers).

11 For to you every vision has become like
the words of a sealed book. You give it to
someone able to read and say, 'Read that.' He
replies, 'I cannot, because it is sealed.' 12 You
then give the book to someone who cannot
read, and say, 'Read that.' He replies, 'I cannot
read.'

Prophecy

13 The Lord then said:

  Because this people approaches me only in
    words,
  honours me only with lip-service
  while their hearts are far from me,
  and reverence for me, as far as they are
    concerned,
  is nothing but human commandment, a
    lesson memorised,
14 very well, I shall have to go on
  astounding this people with prodigies and
    wonders:
  for the wisdom of its wise men is doomed,
  the understanding of any who understand
    will vanish.

The triumph of right

15 Woe to those who burrow down
  to conceal their plans from Yahweh,
  who scheme in the dark
  and say, 'Who can see us? Who knows
    who we are?'
16 How perverse you are!
  Is the potter no better than the clay?

Something that was made, can it say of its
    maker,
  'He did not make me'?
  Or a pot say of the potter,
  'He does not know his job'?
17 Is it not true that in a very short time
  the Lebanon will become productive
    ground,
  so productive you might take it for a
    forest?
18 That day the deaf
  will hear the words of the book
  and, delivered from shadow and darkness,
  the eyes of the blind will see.
19 The lowly will find ever more joy in
    Yahweh
  and the poorest of people will delight in
    the Holy One of Israel;
20 for the tyrant will be no more, the scoffer
    has vanished
  and all those on the look-out for evil have
    been destroyed:
21 those who incriminate others by their
    words,
  those who lay traps for the arbitrator at the
    gate
  and groundlessly deprive the upright of
    fair judgement.
22 That is why Yahweh, God of the House of
    Jacob,
  Abraham's redeemer, says this,
  'No longer shall Jacob be disappointed,
  no more shall his face grow pale,
23 for when he sees his children,
  my creatures, home again with him,
  he will acknowledge my name as holy,
  he will acknowledge the Holy One of
    Jacob to be holy
  and will hold the God of Israel in awe.
24 Erring spirits will learn to understand
  and murmurers accept instruction.'

Against the embassy to Egypt

30 Woe to the rebellious children—
    declares Yahweh—
  who make plans which do not come
    from me

and make alliances not inspired by me,
and so add sin to sin!
2 They are leaving for Egypt,
without consulting me,
to take refuge in Pharaoh's protection,
to shelter in Egypt's shadow.
3 Pharaoh's protection will be your
shame,
the shelter of Egypt's shadow your
confounding.
4 For his princes have gone to Zoan
and his messengers have reached
Hanes.
5 Everyone has been disappointed
by a people who cannot help,
who bring neither aid nor profit,
only disappointment and confusion.

Another prophecy against an embassy

6 Proclamation about the beasts of the Negeb:

Into the land of distress and of anguish,
of lioness and roaring lion,
of viper and flying dragon,
they bear their riches on donkeys' backs,
their treasures on camels' humps,
to a nation that cannot help:
7 Egypt, whose help is vain and futile;
and so I call her 'Rahab*a*-the-collapsed'.

Testament

8 Now go, inscribe this on a tablet,
write it on a scroll,
so that it may serve for time to come
for ever and for ever.
9 This is a rebellious people, they are lying
children,
children who will not listen to Yahweh's
Law.
10 To the seers they say, 'See nothing!'
To the prophets, 'Do not prophesy the
truth to us;
tell us flattering things; have illusory
visions;
11 turn aside from the way, leave the
path,
rid us of the Holy One of Israel.'

12 So the Holy One of Israel says this,
'Since you have rejected this word
and put your trust in fraud and
disloyalty
and rely on these,
13 for you this guilt will prove to be
a breach opening up,
a bulge at the top of a wall
which suddenly and all at once comes
crashing down.
14 He will shatter it like an earthenware pot,
ruthlessly knocking it to pieces,
so that of the fragments not one shard can
be found
with which to take up fire from the hearth
or scoop water from the storage-well.'

15 For Lord Yahweh, the Holy One of Israel,
says this,
'Your salvation lay in conversion and
tranquillity,
your strength in serenity and trust
and you would have none of it.
16 "No," you said, "we shall flee on horses."
And so flee you will!
And again, "We shall ride on swift ones."
And so your pursuers will be swift!
17 A thousand will quake at the threat of one
and when five threaten you will flee,
until what is left of you will be
like a flagstaff on a mountain top,
like a signal on a hill.'

God will forgive

18 But Yahweh is waiting to be gracious to
you,
the Exalted One, to take pity on you,
for Yahweh is a God of fair judgement;
blessed are all who hope in him.

19 Yes, people of Zion living in Jerusalem,
you will weep no more.
He will be gracious to you when your cry
for help rings out;
as soon as he hears it, he will answer you.

30a = Egypt.

20 When the Lord has given you the bread of
        suffering and the water of distress,
    he who is your teacher will hide no longer,
    and you will see your teacher with your
        own eyes.
21 Your ears will hear these words behind
        you,
    'This is the way, keep to it,'
    whether you turn to right or left.
22 You will hold unclean the silverplating of
        your idols
    and the goldplating of your images.
    You will throw them away like the
        polluted things they are,
    shouting after them, 'Good riddance!'
23 He will send rain for the seed you sow in
        the ground,
    and the bread that the ground provides
        will be rich and nourishing.
    That day, your cattle will graze in wide
        pastures.
24 Oxen and donkeys that work the land
    will eat for fodder wild sorrel,
    spread by the shovel-load and fork-load.
25 On every lofty mountain, on every high
        hill
    there will be streams and water-courses,
        on the day of the great slaughter
    when the strongholds fall.
26 Then moonlight will be bright as sunlight
    and sunlight itself be seven times brighter
    —like the light of seven days in one—
    on the day Yahweh dresses his people's
        wound
    and heals the scars of the blows they have
        received.

Against Assyria

27 See, the name of Yahweh comes from
        afar,
    blazing his anger, heavy his threat.
    His lips are brimming over with fury,
    his tongue is like a devouring fire.
28 His breath is like a river in spate
    coming up to the neck,
    to sift the nations with the sieve of
        destruction,

to harness the peoples in a bridle, that will
        lead them astray.
29 Your song will be like that on a festal
        night,
    and there will be joy in your hearts
    as when to the sound of the flute people
        make a pilgrimage
    to the mountain of Yahweh, the Rock of
        Israel.
30 Yahweh will make his majestic voice
        ring out,
    he will show the weight of his arm
    in the heat of his anger, with a devouring
        fire,
    with thunderbolt, downpour and
        hailstones.
31 Yes, at Yahweh's voice Assyria will be
        terrified,
    he will strike him with his rod;
32 each time he goes by, will fall the
        punishing rod
    that Yahweh will lay on him,
    to the sound of tambourines and harps,
    in the battles which he will wage against
        him with uplifted hand.
33 Yes, Topheth[b] has been ready for a long
        time now,
    that too is ready for the king,
    deep and wide his pyre,
    fire and wood in plenty.
    Yahweh's breath, like a stream of
        brimstone,
    will set fire to it.

Against the Egyptian alliance

31 Woe to those going down to Egypt
        for help,
    who put their trust in horses,
    who rely on the quantity of chariots,
    and on great strength of cavalrymen,
    but do not look to the Holy One of Israel
    or consult Yahweh.
2 Yet he too is wise and can bring disaster
    and he will not go back on his word;
    he will rise against the breed of evil-doers

30b The rubbish-dump of Jerusalem.

and against those who protect wrong-
doers.

3 The Egyptian is human, not divine,
his horses are flesh, not spirit;
Yahweh will stretch out his hand:
the protector will stumble,
the protected will fall
and all will perish together.

Against Assyria

4 Yes, this is what Yahweh has said to me:
As a lion or lion cub
growls over its prey,
when scores of shepherds
are summoned to drive it off,
without being frightened by their shouting
or cowed by the noise they make,
just so will Yahweh Sabaoth descend
to fight for Mount Zion and for its hill.
5 Like hovering birds,
so will Yahweh Sabaoth protect Jerusalem;
by protecting it, he will save it,
by supporting it, he will deliver it.
6 Come back to the one whom the Israelites
have so deeply betrayed!
7 For, that day, each of you will throw away
the false gods of silver and the false gods of
gold
which your own sinful hands have made.
8 Assyria will fall by the sword, not that of a
man,
will be devoured by the sword, of no
human being,
he will flee before the sword
and his young warriors will be enslaved.
9 In his terror he will abandon his rock,
and his panic-stricken officers desert the
standard—
declares Yahweh, whose fire is in Zion,
whose furnace, in Jerusalem.

A good king

32 There will be a king who reigns
uprightly
and princes who rule with fair judgement;
2 each will be like a shelter from the wind,
a refuge from the storm,

like streams on arid ground,
like the shade of a solid rock in a desolate
land.
3 The eyes of seers will no longer be closed,
the ears of hearers will be alert,
4 the heart of the hasty will learn to think
things over,
and the tongue of stammerers will speak
promptly and clearly.
5 The fool will no longer be called generous,
nor the rascal be styled bountiful.

Niggard and noble

6 For the fool speaks folly
and his heart is set on villainy;
he is godless in his actions
and his words ascribe error to Yahweh;
he starves the hungry of their food
and refuses drink to the thirsty.
7 Everything to do with the rascal is evil,
he devises infamous plans
to ruin the poor with lying words
even when the needy has right on his
side;
8 but the noble person plans only noble
things,
noble his every move.

Against the women of Jerusalem

9 Stand up, you haughty women, listen to
my words;
you over-confident daughters, pay
attention to what I say.

10 Within one year and a few days
you will tremble, you over-confident
women;
grape-harvesting will be finished,
gathering will never happen again.

11 Shudder, you haughty women,
tremble, you over-confident women;
strip, undress, put sackcloth round your
waists.

12 Beat your breasts for the pleasant fields,
for the fruitful vine,

13 for my people's soil where the bramble-
bush will be growing
and for all the happy houses, for the
rejoicing city.

14 For the citadel will be abandoned
and the thronged city deserted,
Ophel[a] and the Keep will be denuded for
ever,
the playground of wild donkeys
and the pasture of flocks,

Outpouring of the spirit

15 until the spirit is poured out on us from
above,
and the desert becomes an orchard,
and an orchard that seems like a forest.

16 Fair judgement will fix its home in the
desert,
and uprightness live in this orchard,
17 and the product of uprightness will be
peace,
the effect of uprightness being quiet and
security for ever.

18 My people will live in a peaceful home,
in peaceful houses, tranquil dwellings.
19 And should the forest be totally
destroyed
and the city gravely humiliated,
20 you will be happy to sow wherever there is
water
and to let the ox and donkey roam free.

The expected deliverance

33 Woe to you, destroying though not
yourself destroyed,
betraying though not yourself betrayed;
when you have finished destroying, you
will be destroyed,
when you have stopped betraying, you will
be betrayed.
2 Yahweh, show us your mercy,
we hope in you.
Be our arm every morning
and our salvation in time of distress.

3 At the sound of tumult the peoples flee,
when you stand up the nations scatter.
4 Your spoil is gathered in as a grasshopper
gathers in,
like a swarm of locusts people descend
on it.
5 Yahweh is exalted, for he is enthroned
above,
he has filled Zion with fair judgement and
saving justice.

6 You can count on this all your days:
wisdom and knowledge are the riches that
save,
the fear of Yahweh is his treasure.

7 Look, Ariel is lamenting in the streets,
the ambassadors of peace are weeping
bitterly.
8 The highways are deserted,
no travellers any more on the roads.
Agreements are broken, witnesses held in
contempt,
there is respect for no one.
9 The land pines away in mourning,
the Lebanon is withering with shame,
Sharon has become like the wasteland,
Bashan and Carmel are shuddering.
10 'Now I shall stand up,' says Yahweh,
'now I shall rise, now draw myself up.
11 You conceive chaff, you give birth to straw:
like fire, my breath will devour you.
12 The peoples will be burnt up as though by
quicklime,
like cut thorns they will be burnt on the
fire.
13 You who are far away, listen to what I
have done,
and you who are near, realise my strength.'
14 The sinners in Zion are panic-stricken
and fear seizes on the godless,
'Which of us can survive the devouring
fire,
which of us survive everlasting burning?'

32a The hill of the earliest city of Jerusalem; the keep is presumably a great tower.

15 The one who acts uprightly and speaks
    honestly,
who scorns to get rich by extortion,
who rejects bribes out of hand,
who refuses to listen to plans involving
    bloodshed
and shuts his eyes rather than countenance
    crime:
16 such a man will live on the heights,
the craggy rocks will be his refuge,
he will be fed, he will not want for water.

The return to Jerusalem

17 Your eyes will gaze on the king in his
    beauty,
they will look on a country stretching far
    and wide.
18 Your heart will meditate on past terrors,
'Where is the man who did the counting?
Where is the man who did the weighing?
Where is the man who counted off the
    towers?'
19 No more will you see that insolent
    people,
that people of unintelligible speech,
of barbarous and meaningless tongue.
20 Gaze at Zion, city of our feasts;
your eyes will see Jerusalem
as a home that is secure,
a tent not to be moved,
none of its tent-pegs ever to be pulled out,
none of its guy-ropes ever to be broken.

21 There it is that Yahweh shows us his
    power,
like a place of rivers and very wide canals
on which will row no galley,
over which will pass no majestic ship.
22 (For Yahweh is our judge, Yahweh our
    lawgiver,
Yahweh is our king and our Saviour.)
23 Your tackle has given way,
it cannot support the mast,
it cannot hoist the pennon.
And so there is much booty to be shared
    out;
the lame fall to plundering,

24 and no one living there will say, 'I am
    sickly';
the people living there will find their guilt
    forgiven.

The sentence on Edom

34 Come near and listen, you nations,
pay attention, you peoples.
Let the earth and its contents listen,
the world and its entire population.
2 For Yahweh is angry with all the nations,
enraged with all their hordes.
He has vowed them to destruction,
handed them over to slaughter.
3 Their dead will be thrown away,
the stench will rise from their corpses,
the mountains will run with their blood,
4 the entire array of heaven will fall apart.
The heavens will be rolled up like a scroll
and all their array will fade away,
as fade the leaves falling from the vine,
as fade those falling from the fig tree.

5 For my sword has drunk deep in the
    heavens:
see how it now falls on Edom,
on the people vowed to destruction,
to punish them.
6 Yahweh's sword is gorged with blood,
it is greasy with fat,
with the blood of lambs and goats,
with the fat of the kidneys of rams.
For Yahweh has a sacrifice in Bozrah,
a great slaughter in the land of Edom.
7 The wild oxen will fall with them,
the bullocks with the bulls;
their land will be drenched with blood
and their dust will be greasy with fat.
8 For this will be Yahweh's day of
    vengeance,
the year of retribution in Zion's lawsuit.

9 Its streams will turn into pitch,
its dust into brimstone,
its country will turn into blazing pitch.
10 Never quenched night or day,
its smoke rising for ever,

it will lie waste age after age,
no one will travel through it for ever and
ever.
11 It will be the haunt of pelican and
hedgehog,
the owl and the raven will live there;
over it Yahweh will stretch the measuring
line of chaos
and the plumb-line of emptiness.

12 There will be no more nobles
to proclaim the royal authority;
there will be an end of all its princes.
13 Brambles will grow in its bastions,
nettles and thorn-bushes in its fortresses,
it will be the lair of jackals,
an enclosure for ostriches.
14 Wild cats will meet hyenas there,
satyr will call to satyr,
there Lilith too will lurk
and find somewhere to rest.
15 The snake will nest and lay eggs there,
will hatch and gather its young into the
shade;
and there the vultures will assemble,
each one with its mate.
16 Search in Yahweh's book, and read,
not one of these will be missing,
not one of them lacking a mate;
for thus his mouth has ordained it,
and his spirit has brought them together.
17 He has thrown the lot for each,
his hand has measured out their share;
they will possess it for ever,
and live there age after age.

The triumph of Jerusalem

35 Let the desert and the dry lands be
glad,
let the wasteland rejoice and bloom;
like the asphodel, 2 let it burst into flower,
let it rejoice and sing for joy.
The glory of Lebanon is bestowed on it,
the splendour of Carmel and Sharon;
then they will see the glory of Yahweh,
the splendour of our God.
3 Strengthen all weary hands,

steady all trembling knees
4 and say to the faint-hearted,
'Be strong! Do not be afraid.
Here is your God,
vengeance is coming,
divine retribution;
he is coming to save you.'

5 Then the eyes of the blind will be opened,
the ears of the deaf unsealed,
6 then the lame will leap like a deer
and the tongue of the dumb sing for joy;
for water will gush in the desert
and streams in the wastelands,
7 the parched ground will become a marsh
and the thirsty land springs of water;
the lairs where the jackals used to live
will become plots of reed and papyrus.

8 And through it will run a road for them
and a highway
which will be called the Sacred Way;
the unclean will not be allowed to use it;
He will be the one to use this road,
the fool will not stray along it.
9 No lion will be there,
no ferocious beast set foot on it,
nothing of the sort be found;
it will be used by the redeemed.
10 For those whom Yahweh has ransomed
will return,
they will come to Zion shouting for joy,
their heads crowned with joy unending;
rejoicing and gladness will escort them
and sorrow and sighing will take flight.

Sennacherib's invasion[a]

36 In the fourteenth year of King Hezekiah, Sennacherib king of Assyria advanced on all the fortified towns of Judah
and captured them. 2 From Lachish the king
of Assyria sent the cupbearer-in-chief with a
large force to King Hezekiah in Jerusalem.
The cupbearer-in-chief took up position near

36a chh. 36–39 form a historical appendix, reproducing the
story of Isaiah given in 2 K 18:13,17–20:19.

the conduit of the upper pool on the road to the Fuller's Field. ³The master of the palace, Eliakim son of Hilkiah, Shebna the secretary and the herald Joah son of Asaph went out to him. ⁴The cupbearer-in-chief said to them, 'Say to Hezekiah, "The great king, the king of Assyria, says this: What makes you so confident? ⁵Do you think empty words are as good as strategy and military strength? Who are you relying on, to dare to rebel against me? ⁶There you are, relying on that broken reed, Egypt, which pricks and pierces the hand of the person who leans on it. That is what Pharaoh king of Egypt is like to all who rely on him. ⁷You may say to me: We rely on Yahweh our God. But haven't his high places and altars been suppressed by Hezekiah, who told Judah and Jerusalem: This is the altar before which you must worship? ⁸Very well, then, make a wager with my lord the king of Assyria: I will give you two thousand horses if you can find horsemen to ride them. ⁹How could you repulse a single one of the least of my master's soldiers? And yet you have relied on Egypt for chariots and horsemen. ¹⁰And lastly, have I marched on this country to lay it waste without warrant from Yahweh? Yahweh himself said to me: March on this country and lay it waste."'

¹¹Eliakim, Shebna and Joah said to the cupbearer-in-chief, 'Please speak to your servants in Aramaic, for we understand it; do not speak to us in the Judaean language within earshot of the people on the ramparts.' ¹²But the cupbearer-in-chief said, 'Do you think my lord sent me here to say these things to your master or to you? On the contrary, it was to the people sitting on the ramparts who, like you, are doomed to eat their own dung and drink their own urine.'

¹³The cupbearer-in-chief then drew himself up and shouted loudly in the Judaean language, 'Listen to the words of the great king, the king of Assyria. ¹⁴The king says this, "Do not let Hezekiah delude you! He will be powerless to save you. ¹⁵Do not let Hezekiah persuade you to rely on Yahweh by saying: Yah-

weh is sure to save us; this city will not fall into the king of Assyria's clutches. ¹⁶Do not listen to Hezekiah, for the king of Assyria says this: Make peace with me, ¹⁷surrender to me, and every one of you will be free to eat the fruit of his own vine and of his own fig tree and to drink the water of his own storage-well until I come and take you away to a country like your own, a land of corn and good wine, a land of bread and vineyards. ¹⁸Do not let Hezekiah delude you by saying: Yahweh will save us. Has any god of any nation been able to save his country from the king of Assyria's clutches? ¹⁹Where are the gods of Hamath and Arpad? Where are the gods of Sepharvaim? Where are the national gods of Samaria? Did they save Samaria from my clutches? ²⁰Of all the national gods, which ones have saved their countries from my clutches, that Yahweh should be able to save Jerusalem from my clutches?"'

²¹They, however, kept quiet and said nothing in reply, since the king had given the order, 'You are not to answer him.' ²²The master of the palace, Eliakim son of Hilkiah, Shebna the secretary and the herald Joah son of Asaph, with their clothes torn, went to Hezekiah and reported what the cupbearer-in-chief had said.

The prophet Isaiah is consulted

37On hearing this, King Hezekiah tore his clothes, put on sackcloth and went to the Temple of Yahweh. ²He sent Eliakim master of the palace, Shebna the secretary and the elders of the priests, wearing sackcloth, to the prophet Isaiah son of Amoz. ³They said to him, 'This is what Hezekiah says, "Today is a day of suffering, of punishment, of disgrace. Children come to birth and there is no strength to bring them forth. ⁴May Yahweh your God hear the words of the cupbearer-in-chief whom his master, the king of Assyria, has sent to insult the living God, and may Yahweh your God punish the words he has heard! Offer your prayer for the remnant still left."'

5 When King Hezekiah's ministers came to Isaiah, 6 he said to them, 'Say to your master, "Yahweh says this: Do not be afraid of the words which you have heard or the blasphemies which the king of Assyria's minions have uttered against me. 7 Look, I am going to put a spirit in him and, on the strength of a rumour, he will go back to his own country, and in that country I shall make him fall by the sword."'

The cupbearer returns to his master

8 The cupbearer turned about and rejoined the king of Assyria, who was then attacking Libnah, the cupbearer having learnt that the king had already left Lachish 9 on hearing that Tirhakah king of Cush was on his way to attack him.

Second account of Sennacherib's activities

Sennacherib again sent messengers to Hezekiah, saying, 10 'Tell Hezekiah king of Judah this, "Do not let your God on whom you are relying deceive you with the promise: Jerusalem will not fall into the king of Assyria's clutches. 11 You have learnt by now what the kings of Assyria have done to all the other countries, putting them under the curse of destruction. Are you likely to be saved? 12 Did the gods of the nations whom my ancestors devastated save them—Gozan, Haran, Rezeph and the Edenites who were in Tel Basar? 13 Where is the king of Hamath, the king of Arpad, the king of Lair, of Sepharvaim, of Hena, of Ivvah?"'

14 Hezekiah took the letter from the messengers' hands and read it; he then went up to the Temple of Yahweh and spread it out before Yahweh. 15 Hezekiah said this prayer in the presence of Yahweh, 16 'Yahweh Sabaoth, God of Israel, enthroned on the winged creatures, you alone are God of all the kingdoms of the world, you made heaven and earth. 17 Give ear, Yahweh, and listen; open your eyes, Yahweh, and see! Hear the words of Sennacherib, who has sent to insult the living God. 18 It is true, Yahweh, that the kings of Assyria have destroyed all the nations (and their countries); 19 they have thrown their gods on the fire, for these were not gods but human artefacts—wood and stone—and hence they have destroyed them. 20 But now, Yahweh our God, save us from his clutches, I beg you, and let all the kingdoms of the world know that you alone are God, Yahweh.'

Isaiah intervenes

21 Isaiah son of Amoz then sent the following message to Hezekiah, 'Yahweh, God of Israel, says this, "In answer to the prayer which you have addressed to me about Sennacherib king of Assyria. 22 Here is the pronouncement which Yahweh has made about him:

> She despises you, she scorns you,
>   the virgin daughter of Zion;
> she tosses her head at you,
>   the daughter of Jerusalem!
> 23 Whom have you insulted, whom did you
>   blaspheme?
>   Against whom raised your voice
> and lifted your haughty eyes?
>   Against the Holy One of Israel.
> 24 Through your minions you have insulted
>   the Lord,
>   thinking: With my many chariots
> I have climbed the mountain-tops,
>   the utmost peaks of Lebanon.
> I have felled its mighty cedars,
>   its finest cypresses,
> have reached its furthest peak,
>   its forest garden.
> 25 Yes, I have dug and drunk
>   of foreign waters;
> under the soles of my feet
>   I have dried up all Egypt's rivers.
>
> 26 Do you hear? Long ago
>   I prepared this,
> from days of old I actually planned it,
>   now I carry it out.
> You were to lay walled cities
>   in heaps of ruins;
> 27 that was why their inhabitants,

feeble of hand,
were dismayed and discomfited,
were weak as grass,
were frail as plants,
were like grass of housetop and meadow
under the east wind.
²⁸ But whether you stand up or sit down,
whether you go out or come in, I know it
(and how you rave against me).
²⁹ Because you have raved against me
and your arrogance has reached my ears,
I shall put a hook through your nostrils
and a muzzle on your lips,
and make you return by the road
by which you came.

A sign for Hezekiah

³⁰ And this will be the sign for you:
This year will be eaten the self-sown
grain,
next year what sprouts in the fallow;
but in the third year sow and reap,
plant vineyards and eat their fruit.
³¹ The surviving remnant of the House of
Judah will bring forth
new roots below and fruits above;
³² for a remnant will issue from Jerusalem,
and survivors from Mount Zion.
Yahweh Sabaoth's jealous love will
accomplish this." '

A prophecy on Assyria

³³ 'This, then, is what Yahweh says about the
king of Assyria:

He will not enter this city,
will shoot no arrow at it,
confront it with no shield,
throw up no earthwork against it.
³⁴ By the road by which he came, by that he
will return;
he will not enter this city, declares
Yahweh.
³⁵ I shall protect this city and save it
for my sake and my servant David's
sake.'

Sennacherib is punished

³⁶ That same night the angel of Yahweh went
out and struck down a hundred and eighty-
five thousand men in the Assyrian camp. In
the early morning when it was time to get up,
there they lay, so many corpses.

³⁷ Sennacherib struck camp and left; he returned home and stayed in Nineveh. ³⁸ One
day when he was worshipping in the temple of
his god Nisroch, his sons Adrammelech and
Sharezer struck him down with the sword
and escaped into the territory of Ararat. His
son Esarhaddon succeeded him.

The illness and cure of Hezekiah

38 About then, Hezekiah fell ill and was at
the point of death. The prophet Isaiah
son of Amoz came and said to him, 'Yahweh
says this, "Put your affairs in order, for you are
going to die, you will not live." ' ² Hezekiah
turned his face to the wall and addressed this
prayer to Yahweh, ³ 'Ah, Yahweh, remember,
I beg you, that I have behaved faithfully
and with sincerity of heart in your presence
and done what you regard as right.' And
Hezekiah shed many tears.

⁴ Then the word of Yahweh came to Isaiah,
⁵ 'Go and say to Hezekiah, "Yahweh, the God
of your ancestor David, says this: I have heard
your prayer and seen your tears. I shall cure
you: in three days' time you will go up to the
Temple of Yahweh. I shall add fifteen years to
your life. ⁶ I shall save you and this city from
the king of Assyria's clutches and defend this
city for my sake and my servant David's
sake." '

²¹ 'Bring a fig poultice,' Isaiah said, 'apply it
to the ulcer and he will recover.' ²² Hezekiah
said, 'What is the sign to tell me that I shall be
going up to the Temple of Yahweh?' ᵃ ⁷ 'Here',
Isaiah replied, 'is the sign from Yahweh that
he will do what he has said. ⁸ Look, I shall
make the shadow cast by the declining sun on

38a vv. 21–22 were misplaced when the canticle of Hezekiah
was inserted. They are here restored.

the steps—the steps to Ahaz's roof-room—go back ten steps.' And the sun went back the ten steps by which it had declined.

The canticle of Hezekiah

9 Canticle of Hezekiah king of Judah after his illness and recovery.

10 I thought: In the noon of my life
I am to depart.
At the gates of Sheol I shall be held
for the rest of my days.
11 I thought: I shall never see Yahweh
again
in the land of the living,
I shall never see again a single one
of those who live on earth.
12 My home has been pulled up, and thrown
away
like a shepherd's tent;
like a weaver, I have rolled up my life,
he has cut me from the loom.
From dawn to dark, you have been
making an end of me;
13 till daybreak, I cried for help;
like a lion, he has crushed all my bones,
from dawn to dark, you have been making
an end of me.
14 I twitter like a swallow,
I moan like a dove,
my eyes have grown dim from looking up.
Lord, I am overwhelmed, come to my
help.
15 How can I speak and what can I say to
him?
He is the one to act.
I must eke out the rest of my years
in bitterness of soul.

16 The Lord is over them; they live,
and everything in them lives by his
spirit.
You will cure me. Restore me to life.
17 At once, my bitterness turns to well-being.
For you have preserved my soul
from the pit of nothingness,
you have thrust all my sins behind you.

18 For Sheol cannot praise you,
nor Death celebrate you;
those who go down to the pit
can hope no longer in your constancy.
19 The living, the living are the ones who
praise you,
as I do today.
Fathers tell their sons
about your constancy.
20 Yahweh, come to my help
and we will make our harps resound
all the days of our life
in the Temple of Yahweh.

The Babylonian embassy

39 At that time, the king of Babylon, Merodach-Baladan son of Baladan, sent letters and a gift to Hezekiah, for he had heard of his illness and his recovery. 2 Hezekiah was delighted at this and showed the ambassadors his entire treasury, the silver, gold, spices, precious oil, his armoury too, and everything to be seen in his storehouses. There was nothing in his palace or in his whole domain that Hezekiah did not show them.

3 The prophet Isaiah then came to King Hezekiah and asked him, 'What have these men said, and where have they come to you from?' Hezekiah answered, 'They have come from a distant country, from Babylon.' 4 Isaiah said, 'What have they seen in your palace?' 'They have seen everything in my palace,' Hezekiah answered. 'There is nothing in my storehouses that I have not shown them.'

5 Then Isaiah said to Hezekiah, 'Listen to the word of Yahweh Sabaoth, 6 "The days are coming when everything in your palace, everything that your ancestors have amassed until now, will be carried off to Babylon. Not a thing will be left," Yahweh says. 7 "Sons sprung from you, sons begotten by you, will be abducted to be eunuchs in the palace of the king of Babylon." ' 8 Hezekiah said to Isaiah, 'This word of Yahweh that you announce is reassuring,' for he was thinking, 'There is going to be peace and security during my lifetime.'

Prediction of deliverance

40 ¹'Console my people, console them,'
says your God.
² 'Speak to the heart of Jerusalem
and cry to her
that her period of service is ended,
that her guilt has been atoned for,
that, from the hand of Yahweh, she has
received
double punishment for all her sins.'

³ A voice cries, 'Prepare in the desert
a way for Yahweh.
Make a straight highway for our God
across the wastelands.
⁴ Let every valley be filled in,
every mountain and hill be levelled,
every cliff become a plateau,
every escarpment a plain;
⁵ then the glory of Yahweh will be revealed
and all humanity will see it together,
for the mouth of Yahweh has spoken.'

⁶ A voice said, 'Cry aloud!' and I said,
'What shall I cry?'
—'All humanity is grass
and all its beauty like the wild flower's.
⁷ The grass withers, the flower fades
when the breath of Yahweh blows on
them.
(The grass is surely the people.)
⁸ The grass withers, the flower fades,
but the word of our God remains for ever.'

⁹ Go up on a high mountain,
messenger of Zion.
Shout as loud as you can,
messenger of Jerusalem!
Shout fearlessly,
say to the towns of Judah,
'Here is your God.'

¹⁰ Here is Lord Yahweh coming with power,
his arm maintains his authority,
his reward is with him
and his prize precedes him.ᵃ

¹¹ He is like a shepherd feeding his flock,
gathering lambs in his arms,
holding them against his breast
and leading to their rest the mother ewes.

The majesty of God

¹² Who was it measured the water of the sea
in the hollow of his hand
and calculated the heavens to the nearest
inch,
gauged the dust of the earth to the nearest
bushel,
weighed the mountains in scales,
the hills in a balance?
¹³ Who directed the spirit of Yahweh,
what counsellor could have instructed
him?
¹⁴ Whom has he consulted to enlighten him,
to instruct him in the path of judgement,
to teach him knowledge
and show him how to understand?
¹⁵ See, the nations are like a drop in a bucket,
they count as a grain of dust on the scales.
See, coasts and islands weigh no more than
fine powder.
¹⁶ The Lebanon is not enough for the
burning fires
nor its animals enough for the burnt
offering.
¹⁷ All the nations are as nothing before him,
for him they count as nothingness and
emptiness.
¹⁸ To whom can you compare God?
What image can you contrive of him?

¹⁹ The craftsman casts an idol,
a goldsmith overlays it with gold
and casts silver chains for it.
²⁰ Someone too poor to afford a sacrifice
chooses a piece of wood that will not rot;
he then seeks out a skilled craftsman
to set up an idol that will not totter.
²¹ Did you not know,
had you not heard?

40a = 62:11.

[930]

Was it not told you from the beginning?
Have you not understood how the earth
was set on its foundations?
22 He who sits enthroned above the circle of
the earth,
the inhabitants of which are like
grasshoppers,
stretches out the heavens like a cloth,
spreads them out like a tent to live in.
23 He reduces princes to nothing,
the rulers of the world to mere emptiness.
24 Scarcely are they planted, scarcely sown,
scarcely has their stem taken root in the
soil,
than he blows on them and they wither
and the storm carries them away like
chaff.
25 'To whom can you compare me,
or who is my equal?' says the Holy One.
26 Lift your eyes and look:
he who created these things
leads out their army in order,
summoning each of them by name.
So mighty is his power, so great his
strength,
that not one fails to answer.
27 How can you say, Jacob, how can you
repeat, Israel,
'My way is hidden from Yahweh,
my rights are ignored by my God'?
28 Did you not know? Had you not heard?
Yahweh is the everlasting God,
he created the remotest parts of the
earth.
He does not grow tired or weary,
his understanding is beyond fathoming.
29 He gives strength to the weary,
he strengthens the powerless.
30 Youths grow tired and weary,
the young stumble and fall,
31 but those who hope in Yahweh will regain
their strength,
they will sprout wings like eagles,
though they run they will not grow
weary,
though they walk they will never tire.

Cyrus, the instrument of Yahweh

41 Coasts and islands, fall silent
before me,
and let the peoples renew their strength,
let them come forward and speak;
let us assemble for judgement.
2 'Who has raised from the east
him whom saving justice summons in its
train,
him to whom Yahweh delivers up the
nations
and subjects kings,
him who reduces them to dust with his
sword,
and to driven stubble with his bow,
3 him who pursues them and advances
unhindered,
his feet scarcely touching the road?
4 Who has acted thus, who has done this?
He who calls each generation from the
beginning:
I, Yahweh, who am the first
and till the last I shall still be there.'
5 The coasts and islands have seen and taken
fright,
the remotest parts of earth are trembling:
they are approaching, they are here!
6 People help one another,
they say to each other, 'Take heart!'
7 The woodworker encourages the smelter,
the polisher encourages the hammerer,
saying of the soldering, 'It is sound';
and he fastens it with nails
to keep it steady.

Israel, chosen and protected by Yahweh

8 But you, Israel, my servant,
Jacob whom I have chosen,
descendant of Abraham my friend,
9 whom I have taken to myself, from the
remotest parts of the earth
and summoned from countries far away,
to whom I have said, 'You are my servant,
I have chosen you, I have not rejected you,'
10 do not be afraid, for I am with you;
do not be alarmed, for I am your God.

I give you strength, truly I help you,
truly I hold you firm with my saving right
hand.
11 Look, all those who rage against you
will be put to shame and humiliated;
those who picked quarrels with you
will be reduced to nothing and will
perish.
12 You will look for them but will not find
them,
those who used to fight you;
they will be destroyed and brought to
nothing,
those who made war on you.
13 For I, Yahweh, your God,
I grasp you by your right hand;
I tell you, 'Do not be afraid,
I shall help you.'
14 Do not be afraid, Jacob, you worm!
You little handful of Israel!
I shall help you, declares Yahweh;
your redeemer[a] is the Holy One of Israel.
15 Look, I am making you into a threshing-
sledge,
new, with double teeth;
you will thresh and beat the mountains to
dust
and reduce the hills to straw.
16 You will winnow them and the wind will
carry them off,
the gale will scatter them;
whereas you will rejoice in Yahweh,
will glory in the Holy One of Israel.
17 The oppressed and needy search for water,
and there is none,
their tongue is parched with thirst.
I, Yahweh, shall answer them,
I, the God of Israel, shall not abandon
them.
18 I shall open up rivers on barren heights
and water-holes down in the ravines;
I shall turn the desert into a lake
and dry ground into springs of water.
19 I shall plant the desert with cedar trees,
acacias, myrtles and olives;
in the wastelands I shall put cypress trees,
plane trees and box trees side by side;

20 so that people may see and know,
so that they may all observe and
understand
that the hand of Yahweh has done this,
that the Holy One of Israel has created it.

The fatuity of idols

21 'Present your case,' says Yahweh,
'Produce your arguments,' says Jacob's
king.
22 'Let them produce and reveal to us
what is going to happen.
What happened in the past?
Reveal it so that we can consider it
and know what the outcome will be.
Or tell us about the future,
23 reveal what is to happen next,
and then we shall know that you are
gods.
At least, do something, be it good
or bad,
so that we may feel alarm and fear.
24 Look, you are less than nothingness,
and what you do is less than nothing;
to choose you is an outrage.'
25 I have raised him from the north and he
has come,
from the east he has been summoned by
name.
He tramples on rulers like mud,
like a potter treading clay.
26 Who revealed this from the beginning for
us to know,
and in the past for us to say, 'That is
right'?
No one in fact revealed it, no one
proclaimed it,
no one has heard you speak.
27 First-fruits of Zion, look, here they
come!
I send a messenger to Jerusalem,
28 and I look—no one,
not a single counsellor among them
who, if I asked, could give an answer.

41a The go'el, the closest relative, defender and avenger of blood, often used of Yahweh in the Pss.

29 Taken altogether they are nothingness,
what they do is nothing,
their statues, wind and emptiness.

First song of the servant

42 Here is my servant[a] whom I uphold,
my chosen one in whom my soul
delights.
I have sent my spirit upon him,
he will bring fair judgement to the
nations.
2 He does not cry out or raise his voice,
his voice is not heard in the street;
3 he does not break the crushed reed
or snuff the faltering wick.
Faithfully he presents fair judgement;
4 he will not grow faint, he will not be
crushed
until he has established fair judgement on
earth,
and the coasts and islands are waiting for
his instruction.
5 Thus says God, Yahweh,
who created the heavens and spread them
out,
who hammered into shape the earth and
what comes from it,
who gave breath to the people on it,
and spirit to those who walk on it:
6 I, Yahweh, have called you in saving
justice,
I have grasped you by the hand and
shaped you;
I have made you a covenant of the
people
and light to the nations,
7 to open the eyes of the blind,
to free captives from prison,
and those who live in darkness from the
dungeon.
8 I am Yahweh, that is my name!
I shall not yield my glory to another,
nor my honour to idols.
9 See how the former predictions have come
true.
Fresh things I now reveal;
before they appear I tell you of them.

Song of victory

10 Sing a new song to Yahweh!
Let his praise be sung from remotest parts
of the earth
by those who sail the sea and by everything
in it,
by the coasts and islands and those who
inhabit them.
11 Let the desert and its cities raise their
voices,
the encampments where Kedar lives.
Let the inhabitants of the Rock cry aloud
for joy
and shout from the mountain tops.
12 Let them give glory to Yahweh
and, in the coasts and islands, let them
voice his praise.
13 Yahweh advances like a hero,
like a warrior he rouses his fire.
He shouts, he raises the war cry,
he shows his might against his foes.
14 'From long ago I have been silent,
I have kept quiet, held myself in
check,
groaning like a woman in labour,
panting and gasping for air.
15 I shall ravage mountain and hill,
shall wither all their vegetation;
I shall turn the torrents into firm
ground
and dry up the marshes.
16 I shall lead the blind by a road they do not
know,
by paths they do not know I shall conduct
them.
I shall turn the darkness into light before
them
and the quagmires into solid ground.
This I shall do—without fail.'
17 Those who trust in idols will recoil,
they will blush for shame, who say to
metal images,
'You are our gods.'

42a The first of the four Songs of the Servant (42:1–9;
49:1–6; 50:4–11; 52:13–53:12).

73 READ ISAIAH 42:1–17.

I shall lead the blind by a road they do not know, by paths they do not know I shall conduct them.—ISAIAH 42:16

REFLECTIONS OF DIVINE GOODNESS

If we study attentively the history of the creation of our race, we shall find that man was made in the image of God, so that his ways also might be an imitation of the ways of his Maker. The natural, real and highest dignity we can attain is that the goodness of the divine nature should be reflected in us as in a mirror. As a means of reaching this dignity, we are daily offered the grace of our Savior. For as in the first Adam all men are fallen, so in the Second Adam can all men be raised up again (see 1 Co 15:22).

Our restoration from the consequences of Adam's fall is sheer mercy of God and nothing else. We should not have loved him unless he first loved us (see 1 Jn 4:19) and scattered the darkness of our ignorance by the light of his truth. This the Lord promised by the mouth of Isaiah when he said, "I shall lead the blind by a road they do not know, by paths they do not know I shall conduct them. I shall turn the darkness into light before them and the quagmires into solid ground. This I shall do—without fail."

And we know from the Apostle John how God fulfilled his promise. "We are well aware also that the Son of God has come, and has given us understanding so that we may know the One who is true. We are in the One who is true as we are in his Son, Jesus Christ" (1 Jn 5:20). Therefore, because of the great love by which he has loved us, God renews his likeness in us. More importantly, so that he might find in us the reflection of his goodness, he who works all in all allows us to work along with himself. Thus he lights candles in our dark minds and kindles in us the fire of his love in order to make us love not only himself but also whatever he loves. ST. LEO THE GREAT, d. 461

YOU WILL FIND THE NEXT READING AT ISAIAH 49.

Israel's blindness

18 Listen, you deaf!
Look and see, you blind!
19 Who so blind as my servant,
so deaf as the messenger I send?
(Who so blind as the friend I have taken to
myself,
so deaf as Yahweh's servant?)
20 You have seen many things but not
observed them;
your ears are open but you do not hear.

21 Yahweh wished, because of his saving
justice,
to make the Law great and glorious.
22 Yet here is a people pillaged and plundered,
all of them shut up in caves,
imprisoned in dungeons.
They have been pillaged, with no one to
rescue them,
plundered, with no one to say, 'Give it
back!'
23 Which of you will listen to this,
who pay attention and listen in future?

²⁴ Who surrendered Jacob to the plunderer
and Israel to the pillagers?
Was it not Yahweh, against whom we had
sinned,
in whose ways they would not walk
and whose Law they would not obey?
²⁵ On him he poured out his blazing anger
and the fury of war;
it enveloped him in flames and yet he did
not understand;
it burned him up, but he did not learn a
lesson.

God, Israel's protector and liberator

43 And now, thus says Yahweh,
he who created you, Jacob,
who formed you, Israel:
Do not be afraid, for I have redeemed you;
I have called you by your name, you are
mine.
² Should you pass through the waters, I shall
be with you;
or through rivers, they will not swallow
you up.
Should you walk through fire, you will not
suffer,
and the flame will not burn you.
³ For I am Yahweh, your God,
the Holy One of Israel, your Saviour.
I have given Egypt for your ransom,
Cush and Seba in exchange for you.
⁴ Since I regard you as precious,
since you are honoured and I love you,
I therefore give people in exchange for
you,
and nations in return for your life.
⁵ Do not be afraid, for I am with you.
I shall bring your offspring from the east,
and gather you from the west.
⁶ To the north I shall say, 'Give them up!'
and to the south, 'Do not hold them back!'
Bring back my sons from far away,
and my daughters from the remotest part
of the earth,
⁷ everyone who bears my name,
whom I have created for my glory,
whom I have formed, whom I have made.

Yahweh alone is God

⁸ Bring forward the people that is blind, yet
has eyes,
that is deaf and yet has ears.
⁹ Let all the nations assemble,
let the peoples gather here!
Which of them has proclaimed this
and revealed things to us in the past?
Let them bring their witnesses to justify
themselves,
let others hear and say, 'It is true.'
¹⁰ You yourselves are my witnesses, declares
Yahweh,
and the servant whom I have chosen,
so that you may know and believe me
and understand that it is I.
No god was formed before me,
nor will be after me.
¹¹ I, I am Yahweh,
and there is no other Saviour but me.
¹² I have revealed, have saved, and have
proclaimed,
not some foreigner among you.
You are my witnesses, declares Yahweh,

I am God, ¹³ yes, from eternity I am.
No one can deliver from my hand;
when I act, who can thwart me?

Against Babylon

¹⁴ Thus says Yahweh,
your redeemer, the Holy One of Israel:
For your sake I have sent to Babylon,
I shall knock down all the prison bars,
and the Chaldaeans' shouts of joy will
change to lamentations.
¹⁵ I am Yahweh, your Holy One,
the Creator of Israel, your king.

Miracles of the new Exodus

¹⁶ Thus says Yahweh,
who made a way through the sea,
a path in the raging waters,
¹⁷ who led out chariot and horse
together with an army of picked troops:
they lay down never to rise again,

they were snuffed out, put out like a
wick.
18 No need to remember past events,
no need to think about what was done
before.
19 Look, I am doing something new,
now it emerges; can you not see it?
Yes, I am making a road in the desert
and rivers in wastelands.
20 The wild animals will honour me,
the jackals and the ostriches,
for bestowing water in the desert
and rivers on the wastelands
for my people, my chosen one, to drink.
21 The people I have shaped for myself
will broadcast my praises.

Israel's ingratitude

22 But, Jacob, you have not invoked me;
no, Israel, you have grown weary of me.
23 You have not brought me lambs as your
burnt offerings
and have not honoured me with your
sacrifices.
I have not subjected you to cereal
offering,
I have not wearied you by demanding
incense.
24 You have not bought expensive reed
for me
or sated me with the fat of your sacrifices.
Instead by your sins you have treated me
like a slave,
you have wearied me with your crimes,
25 I, I it is who blot out your acts of revolt for
my own sake
and shall not call your sins to mind.
26 Remind me, and we will judge this
together;
state your own case and justify yourself.
27 Your first ancestor sinned,
your interpreters revolted against me.
28 That is why I deposed the chief men of my
sanctuary,
why I put Jacob under the curse of
destruction
and subjected Israel to insult.

The blessing in store for Israel

44 And now listen, Jacob my servant,
Israel whom I have chosen.
2 Thus says Yahweh who made you,
who formed you in the womb; he will
help you.
Do not be afraid, Jacob my servant,
Jeshurun^a whom I have chosen.
3 For I shall pour out water on the thirsty
soil
and streams on the dry ground.
I shall pour out my spirit on your
descendants,
my blessing on your offspring,
4 and they will spring up among the grass,
like willows on the banks of a stream.
5 One person will say, 'I belong to Yahweh,'
another will call himself by Jacob's name.
On his hand another will write 'Yahweh's'
and be surnamed 'Israel'.

There is only one God

6 Thus says Yahweh, Israel's king,
Yahweh Sabaoth, his redeemer:
I am the first and I am the last;
there is no God except me.
7 Who is like me? Let him call out,
let him affirm it and convince me it is so;
let him say what has been happening
since I instituted an eternal people,
and predict to them what will happen
next!
8 Have no fear, do not be afraid:
have I not told you and revealed it long
ago?
You are my witnesses.
Is there any God except me?
There is no Rock; I know of none.

The fatuity of idols

9 The makers of idols are all nothingness; the
works they delight in serve no purpose. And
these are the witness against them: they see

44a Rare poetic name of Israel, perhaps meaning 'the upright one'.

nothing, they know nothing; and so they will be put to shame. ¹⁰Who ever fashioned a god or cast an image without hope of gain? ¹¹Watch how all its devotees will be put to shame, and the men who made it too, who are only human. Let them all assemble, let them stand forward and feel both fear and shame!

¹²The blacksmith makes an axe over the charcoal, beats it into shape with a hammer, works on it with his strong arm. Then he feels hungry and his strength deserts him; having drunk no water, he is exhausted.

¹³The wood carver *b* takes his measurements, outlines the image with chalk, executes it with the chisel, following the outline with a compass. He makes it look like a human being, with human standards of beauty, so that it can reside in a house. ¹⁴He has cut down cedars, has selected an oak and a terebinth which he has grown for himself among the trees in the forest and has planted a pine tree which the rain has nourished. ¹⁵Once it is suitable to burn, he takes some of it to warm himself; having kindled it, he bakes bread. But he also makes a god and worships it; he makes an idol from it and bows down before it. ¹⁶Half of it he burns on the fire, over this half he roasts meat, eats it and is replete; at the same time he warms himself and says, 'Ah, how warm I am, watching the flames!' ¹⁷With the remainder he makes a god, his idol, bows down before it, worships it and prays to it. 'Save me,' he says, 'for you are my god.'

¹⁸They know nothing, they understand nothing, since their eyes are incapable of seeing and their hearts of reflecting. ¹⁹Not one of them looks into his heart, not one of them has the knowledge and wit to think, 'I burned half of it on the fire and cooked food over the embers. Am I right to make something disgusting out of what is left? Am I right to bow down before a block of wood?'

²⁰He hankers after ashes, his deluded heart has led him astray; he will not save himself, he will not think, 'What I have in my hand is nothing but a lie!'

Loyalty to Yahweh

²¹ Remember these things, Jacob,
  and Israel, since you are my servant.
 I formed you, you are my servant;
  Israel, I shall not forget you.
²² I have dispelled your acts of revolt like a
    cloud
  and your sins like a mist.
  Come back to me, for I have redeemed
    you.
²³ Heavens, shout for joy, for Yahweh has
    acted!
  Underworld, shout aloud!
  Shout for joy, you mountains,
  forests and all your trees!
  For Yahweh has redeemed Jacob
  and displayed his glory in Israel.

God, Creator of the world and lord of history

²⁴ Thus says Yahweh, your redeemer,
  he who formed you in the womb:
  I, Yahweh, have made all things,
  I alone spread out the heavens.
  When I hammered the earth into shape,
    who was with me?
²⁵ I, who foil the omens of soothsayers
  and make fools of diviners,
  who confound sages
  turning their knowledge into folly,
²⁶ who confirm the word of my servant
  and make the plans of my envoys succeed;
  who say to Jerusalem, 'You will be
    inhabited,'
  and to the towns of Judah, 'You will be
    rebuilt
  and I shall restore the ruins of Jerusalem';
²⁷ who say to the ocean, 'Dry up!
  I shall make your rivers run dry';
²⁸ who say to Cyrus, 'My shepherd.'
  He will perform my entire will
  by saying to Jerusalem, 'You will be
    rebuilt,'
  and to the Temple, 'You will be
    refounded.'

44b ‖ Ws 13:11–16.

Cyrus, the instrument of God

45 Thus says Yahweh to his anointed
one,
to Cyrus whom, he says, I have grasped by
his right hand,
to make the nations bow before him
and to disarm kings,
to open gateways before him
so that their gates be closed no more:
2 I myself shall go before you,
I shall level the heights,
I shall shatter the bronze gateways,
I shall smash the iron bars.
3 I shall give you secret treasures
and hidden hoards of wealth,
so that you will know that I am Yahweh,
who call you by your name,
the God of Israel.
4 It is for the sake of my servant Jacob
and of Israel my chosen one,
that I have called you by your name,
have given you a title though you do not
know me.
5 I am Yahweh, and there is no other,
there is no other God except me.
Though you do not know me, I have
armed you
6 so that it may be known from east to west
that there is no one except me.
I am Yahweh, and there is no other,
7 I form the light and I create the darkness,
I make well-being, and I create disaster,
I, Yahweh, do all these things.

Prayer

8 Rain down, you heavens, from above,
and let the clouds pour down saving
justice,
let the earth open up and blossom with
salvation,
and let justice sprout with it;
I, Yahweh, have created it!

The supreme power of Yahweh

9 Woe to anyone who argues with his
Maker,
one earthenware pot among many!
Does the clay say to its potter, 'What are
you doing?
Your work has no hands!'
10 Woe to anyone who asks a father, 'Why
are you begetting?'
and a woman, 'Why are you giving
birth?'
11 Thus says Yahweh,
the Holy One of Israel and his Maker:
I am asked for signs regarding my sons,
I am given orders about the work I do.
12 It was I who made the earth
and I created human beings on it,
mine were the hands that spread out the
heavens
and I have given the orders to all their
array.
13 I myself have raised him in saving justice
and I shall make all paths level for him.
He will rebuild my city
and bring my exiles home
without ransom or indemnity,
says Yahweh Sabaoth.

The conversion of the nations

14 Thus says Yahweh:
The produce of Egypt, the commerce of
Cush
and the men of Seba, tall of stature,
will come over to you and belong
to you.
They will follow you, walking in
chains,
they will bow before you,
they will pray to you,
'With you alone is God, and there is no
other!
The gods do not exist.'
15 Truly, you are a God who conceals
himself,
God of Israel, Saviour!
16 They are shamed and humbled, every
one of them,
humiliated they go, the makers of idols.
17 Israel will be saved by Yahweh,
saved everlastingly.

You will never be ashamed or humiliated
for ever and ever.

¹⁸ For thus says Yahweh, the Creator of the
heavens—
he is God, who shaped the earth and
made it,
who set it firm;
he did not create it to be chaos,
he formed it to be lived in:
I am Yahweh, and there is no other.

¹⁹ I have not spoken in secret,
in some dark corner of the underworld.
I did not say, 'Offspring of Jacob,
search for me in chaos!'
I am Yahweh: I proclaim saving
justice,
I say what is true.

God, lord of the whole universe

²⁰ Assemble, come, all of you gather round,
survivors of the nations.
They have no knowledge, those who
parade their wooden idols
and pray to a god
that cannot save.

²¹ Speak up, present your case,
let them put their heads together!
Who foretold this in the past,
who revealed it long ago?
Was it not I, Yahweh?
There is no other god except me,
no saving God, no Saviour except me!

²² Turn to me and you will be saved,
all you ends of the earth,
for I am God, and there is no other.

²³ By my own self I swear it;
what comes from my mouth is saving
justice,
it is an irrevocable word:
All shall bend the knee to me,
by me every tongue shall swear,

²⁴ saying, 'In Yahweh alone
are saving justice and strength,'
until all those who used to rage at him
come to him in shame.

²⁵ In Yahweh the whole race of Israel
finds justice and glory.

The fall of Babylon

46 Bel^a is crouching, Nebo cowering,
their idols are being put on animals,
on beasts of burden,
the loads you have been carrying
are a burden to a weary beast.

² They are cowering and crouching
together,
no one can save this burden,
they themselves have gone into captivity.

³ Listen to me, House of Jacob,
all who remain of the House of Israel,
whom I have carried since the womb,
whom I have supported since you were
conceived.

⁴ Until your old age I shall be the same,
until your hair is grey I shall carry you.
As I have done, so I shall support you,
I myself shall carry and shall save you.

⁵ With whom can you compare me,
equate me,
to whom can you liken me, making equals
of us?

⁶ They lavish gold from their purses
and weigh out silver on the scales.
They engage a goldsmith to make a god,
then bow low and actually adore!

⁷ They lift it on their shoulders and carry it,
and put it down where it is meant to stand,
so that it never moves from the spot.
You may cry out to it in distress, it never
replies,
it never saves anyone in trouble.

⁸ Remember this and stand firm;
rebels, look into your hearts.

⁹ Remember the things that happened long
ago,
for I am God, and there is no other;
I am God, and there is none like me.

¹⁰ From the beginning I revealed the future,
in advance, what has not yet occurred.
I say: My purpose will come about,
I shall do whatever I please;

46a Bel and Nebo are Babylonian chief gods, of the sky and
wisdom respectively.

11 I call a bird of prey from the east,
  my man predestined, from a distant land.
  What I have said, I shall do,
  what I have planned, I shall perform.
12 Listen to me, you hard-hearted people
  far removed from saving justice:
13 I am bringing my justice nearer,
  it is not far away,
  my salvation will not delay.
  I shall place my salvation in Zion
  and my glory in Israel.

Lament for Babylon

47 Step down! Sit in the dust,
  virgin daughter of Babylon.
  Sit on the ground, no throne,
  daughter of the Chaldaeans,
  for never again will you be called
  tender and delicate.
2 Take the grinding mill, crush up the
    meal.
  Remove your veil,
  tie up your skirt, bare your legs,
  cross the rivers.
3 Let your nakedness be displayed
  and your shame exposed.
  I am going to take vengeance
  and no one will stand in my way.

4 Our redeemer, Yahweh Sabaoth is his
    name,
  the Holy One of Israel, says:
5 Sit in silence, bury yourself in darkness,
  daughter of the Chaldaeans,
  for never again will you be called
  the mistress of kingdoms.
6 Being angry with my people,
  I rejected my heritage,
  surrendering them into your clutches.
  You showed them no mercy,
  you made your yoke very heavy on the
    aged.
7 You thought, 'I shall be a queen for ever.'
  You did not reflect on these matters
  or think about the future.
8 Now listen to this, voluptuous woman,
  lolling at ease

and thinking to yourself,
  'I am the only one who matters.
  I shall never be widowed,
  never know bereavement.'
9 Yet both these things will befall you,
  suddenly, in one day.
  Bereavement and widowhood
  will suddenly befall you
  in spite of all your witchcraft
  and the potency of your spells.
10 Confident in your wickedness,
  you thought, 'No one can see me.'
  Your wishes and your knowledge
  were what deluded you,
  as you thought to yourself,
  'I am the only one who matters.'
11 Hence, disaster will befall you
  which you will not know how to charm
    away,
  calamity overtake you
  which you will not be able to avert,
  ruination will suddenly befall you,
  such as you have never known.
12 Keep to your spells then,
  and all your sorceries,
  at which you have worked so hard since
    you were young.
  Perhaps you will succeed,
  perhaps you will strike terror!
13 You have had many tiring consultations:
  let the astrologers come forward now and
    save you,
  the star-gazers
  who announce month by month
  what will happen to you next.
14 Look, they are like wisps of straw,
  the fire will burn them up.
  They will not save their lives
  from the power of the flame.
  No embers these, for keeping warm,
  no fire to sit beside!
15 Such will your wizards prove to be
    for you,
  for whom you have worked so hard since
    you were young;
  each wandering his own way,
  none of them can save you.

Yahweh has foretold everything

48 Listen to this, House of Jacob,
you who are called by the name of
Israel
and issued from the waters of Judah,
who swear by the name of Yahweh
and invoke the God of Israel,
though not in good faith or uprightness;
² for they call themselves after the holy city
and rely on the God of Israel,
Yahweh Sabaoth is his name.
³ Things now past I revealed long ago,
they issued from my mouth, I proclaimed
them;
suddenly I acted and they happened.
⁴ For I knew you to be obstinate,
your neck an iron sinew
and your forehead bronze.
⁵ As I told you about it long before,
before it happened I revealed it to you,
so that you could not say, 'My statue did it,
my idol, my metal image, ordained this.'
⁶ You have heard and seen all this,
why won't you admit it?
Now I am going to reveal new things
to you,
secrets that you do not know;
⁷ they have just been created, not long ago,
and until today you have heard nothing
about them,
so that you cannot say, 'Yes, I knew about
this.'
⁸ No, you have not heard, you have not
known,
for a long time your ear has not been
attentive,
for I knew how treacherous you were;
you have been called a rebel since the
womb.
⁹ For the sake of my name I shall defer my
anger,
for the sake of my honour I shall be
patient with you, rather than
destroy you.
¹⁰ Look, I have purchased you, but not for
silver,

I have chosen you out of the cauldron of
affliction.
¹¹ For my sake and my sake only shall I act,
for why should my name be profaned?
I will not yield my glory to another.

Yahweh has chosen Cyrus

¹² Listen to me, Jacob,
Israel whom I have called:
I, and none else, am the first,
I am also the last.
¹³ My hand laid the foundations of earth
and my right hand spread out the heavens.
I summon them
and they all present themselves together.
¹⁴ Assemble, all of you, and listen;
which of them has revealed this?
Yahweh loves him; he will do his
pleasure
on Babylon and the race of the
Chaldaeans;
¹⁵ I, I have spoken, yes, I have summoned
him,
I have brought him, and he will succeed.

Israel's destiny

¹⁶ Come near and listen to this:
from the first, I never spoke obscurely;
when it happened, I was there,
and now Lord Yahweh has sent me with
his spirit.
¹⁷ Thus says Yahweh, your redeemer, the
Holy One of Israel:
I am Yahweh your God and teach you for
your own good,
I lead you in the way you ought to go.
¹⁸ If only you had listened to my
commandments!
Your prosperity would have been like a
river
and your saving justice like the waves of
the sea.
¹⁹ Your descendants would have been
numbered like the sand,
your offspring as many as its grains.
Their name would never be cancelled or
blotted out from my presence.

The end of the Exile

20 Come out from Babylon! Flee from the
    Chaldaeans!
  Declare this with cries of joy, proclaim it,
  carry it to the remotest parts of earth,
  say, 'Yahweh has redeemed his servant
    Jacob.'
21 Those he led through the arid country
    never went thirsty;
  he made water flow for them from the
    rock,
  he split the rock and out streamed the
    water.
22 There is no peace, says Yahweh, for the
    wicked.

Second song of the servant

49 Coasts and islands, listen to me,
  pay attention, distant peoples.
  Yahweh called me when I was in the
    womb,
  before my birth he had pronounced my
    name.
2 He made my mouth like a sharp sword,
  he hid me in the shadow of his hand.
  He made me into a sharpened arrow
  and concealed me in his quiver.
3 He said to me, 'Israel, you are my servant,
  through whom I shall manifest my glory.'
4 But I said, 'My toil has been futile,
  I have exhausted myself for nothing, to no
    purpose.'
  Yet all the while my cause was with
    Yahweh
  and my reward with my God.
5 And now Yahweh has spoken,
  who formed me in the womb to be his
    servant,
  to bring Jacob back to him
  and to re-unite Israel to him;
  —I shall be honoured in Yahweh's eyes,
  and my God has been my strength.—
6 He said, 'It is not enough for you to be my
    servant,
  to restore the tribes of Jacob and bring
    back the survivors of Israel;

  I shall make you a light to the nations
  so that my salvation may reach the
    remotest parts of earth.'
7 Thus says Yahweh,
  the redeemer, the Holy One of Israel,
  to the one who is despised, detested by the
    nation,
  to the slave of despots:
  Kings will stand up when they see,
  princes will see and bow low,
  because of Yahweh who is faithful,
  the Holy One of Israel who has chosen
    you.

The joyful homecoming

8 Thus says Yahweh:
  At the time of my favour I have answered
    you,
  on the day of salvation I have helped you.
  I have formed you and have appointed you
  to be the covenant for a people,
  to restore the land,
  to return ravaged properties,
9 to say to prisoners, 'Come out,'
  to those who are in darkness,
    'Show yourselves.'
  Along the roadway they will graze,
  and any bare height will be their
    pasture.
10 They will never hunger or thirst,
  scorching wind and sun will never plague
    them;
  for he who pities them will lead them,
  will guide them to springs of water.
11 I shall turn all my mountains into a road
  and my highways will be raised aloft.
12 Look! Here they come from far away,
  look, these from the north and the west,
  those from the land of Sinim.ᵃ

13 Shout for joy, you heavens; earth, exult!
  Mountains, break into joyful cries!
  For Yahweh has consoled his people,
  is taking pity on his afflicted ones.

49a Syene in Egypt, modern Aswan, where there was a large
Jewish colony.

74 READ ISAIAH 49.

Look, I have engraved you on the palms of my hands.—ISAIAH 49:16

CONFIDENT OF GOD'S CARE

To strengthen us in the holy virtue of confidence our kind and lovable savior assumes the most loving titles possible. He calls himself, and really is, our friend, our advocate, our shepherd, our brother, our father, our soul, our life, and the spouse of our souls. And he styles us as his sheep, his brothers and sisters, his children, his portion and inheritance, his soul and his heart.

He assures us in Scripture that his care for us is unceasing (see Ws 12:13), and that he himself will always carry us in his heart (see Is 46:3). Again he promises that even though a mother should forget her child, he will never forget us—that he has us written on his hands so as to have us ever in his sight. And whoever touches us touches the apple of his eye (see Zc 2:12).

He tells us that his Father loves us as he, our Lord, loves him, and that he loves us as the Father loves him (see Jn 17:26; 15:9); that he desires that we should be with him in the heart of the eternal Father and seated with him on his throne (see Rv 3:21)—in a word, that we should be one with him, and perfectly united with him and his Father (see Jn 17:23).

And he also promises us that in the event of our having displeased him, if we return to him with humility, sorrow, confidence in his goodness and the resolve to abandon sin, he will receive us with an embrace, forget all our offenses and clothe us with the robe of his grace and love (see Lk 15:21).

After this who will not have confidence, and abandon himself entirely to the care of such a friend, brother, father, and spouse who knows what is best for us and in his extreme goodness leads us to our true end, supreme happiness?　　　　　　　　　　　　　　　　　ST. JOHN EUDES, 1601–1680

YOU WILL FIND THE NEXT READING AT ISAIAH 53.

¹⁴ Zion was saying, 'Yahweh has abandoned
　　me,
　the Lord has forgotten me.'
¹⁵ Can a woman forget her baby at the
　　breast,
　feel no pity for the child she has borne?
　Even if these were to forget,
　I shall not forget you.
¹⁶ Look, I have engraved you on the palms of
　　my hands,
　your ramparts are ever before me.
¹⁷ Your rebuilders are hurrying,
　your destroyers and despoilers will soon go
　　away.

¹⁸ Raise your eyes and look around you:
　all are assembling, coming to you.^b
　By my life, declares Yahweh,
　you will put them all on like jewels,
　like a bride, you will fasten them on.
¹⁹ For your desolate places and your ruins
　and your devastated country
　from now on will be too cramped for your
　　inhabitants,
　and your devourers will be far away.
²⁰ Once more they will say in your hearing,
　the children of whom you were bereft,

49b = 60:4.

[943]

'The place is too cramped for me,
make room for me to live.'
21 Then you will think to yourself,
'Who has borne me these?
I was bereft and barren,
exiled, turned out of my home;
who has reared these?
I was left all alone,
so where have these come from?'

22 Thus says Lord Yahweh:
Look, I am beckoning to the nations
and hoisting a signal to the peoples:
they will bring your sons in their arms
and your daughters will be carried on their
shoulders.
23 Kings will be your foster-fathers
and their princesses, your foster-mothers.
They will fall prostrate before you, faces to
the ground,
and lick the dust at your feet.
And you will know that I am Yahweh;
those who hope in me will not be
disappointed.
24 Can the body be snatched from the
warrior,
can the tyrant's captive be set free?
25 But thus says Yahweh:
The warrior's captive will indeed be
snatched away
and the tyrant's booty will indeed be set
free;
I myself shall fight those who fight you
and I myself shall save your children.
26 I shall make your oppressors eat their own
flesh,
they will be as drunk on their own blood
as on new wine.
And all humanity will know
that I am Yahweh, your Saviour,
your redeemer, the Mighty One of Jacob.

Israel's punishment

50 Thus says Yahweh:
Where is your mother's writ of
divorce
by which I repudiated her?

Or to which of my creditors
have I sold you?
Look, you have been sold for your own
misdeeds,
your mother was repudiated for your acts
of rebellion.
2 Why was there no one there when I came?
Why did no one answer when I called?
Is my hand too short to redeem?
Have I not strength to save?
Look, with a threat I can dry the sea,
and turn rivers to desert;
the fish in them go rotten for want of
water
and die of thirst.
3 I dress the heavens in black,
I cover them in sackcloth.

Third song of the servant

4 Lord Yahweh has given me a disciple's
tongue,
for me to know how to give a word of
comfort to the weary.
Morning by morning he makes my ear
alert
to listen like a disciple.
5 Lord Yahweh has opened my ear
and I have not resisted,
I have not turned away.
6 I have offered my back to those who
struck me,
my cheeks to those who plucked my beard;
I have not turned my face away
from insult and spitting.
7 Lord Yahweh comes to my help,
this is why insult has not touched me,
this is why I have set my face like flint
and know that I shall not be put to shame.
8 He who grants me saving justice is near!
Who will bring a case against me?
Let us appear in court together!
Who has a case against me?
Let him approach me!
9 Look, Lord Yahweh is coming to my help!
Who dares condemn me?
Look at them, all falling apart
like moth-eaten clothes!

10 Which of you fears Yahweh
   and listens to his servant's voice?
   Which of you walks in darkness
   and sees no light?
   Let him trust in the name of Yahweh
   and lean on his God!
11 Look, all you who light a fire
   and arm yourselves with firebrands,
   walk by the light of your fire
   and the firebrands you have kindled!
   This is what you will get from me:
   you will lie down in torment!

The blessings in store for the chosen people

51 Listen to me, you who pursue saving
      justice,
   you who seek Yahweh.
   Consider the rock from which you were
      hewn,
   the quarry from which you were dug.
2 Consider Abraham your father
   and Sarah who gave you birth.
   When I called him he was the only one
   but I blessed him and made him
      numerous.
3 Yes, Yahweh has pity on Zion,
   has pity on all her ruins;
   he will turn her desert into an Eden
   and her wastelands into the garden of
      Yahweh.
   Joy and gladness will be found in her,
   thanksgiving and the sound of music.

God's reign of saving justice

4 Pay attention to me, my people,
   listen to me, my nation,
   for a law will come from me,
   and I shall make my saving justice the
      light of peoples.
5 My justice is suddenly approaching,
   my salvation appears,
   my arm is about to judge the peoples.
   The coasts and islands will put their hope
      in me
   and put their trust in my arm.
6 Raise your eyes to the heavens,
   look down at the earth;

for the heavens will vanish like smoke,
   the earth wear out like clothing
   and its inhabitants die like vermin,
   but my salvation will last for ever
   and my saving justice remain inviolable.

7 Listen to me, you who know what saving
      justice means,
   a people who take my laws to heart:
   do not fear people's taunts,
   do not be alarmed by their insults,
8 for the moth will eat them like clothing,
   the grub will devour them like wool,
   but my saving justice will last for ever
   and my salvation for all generations.

The awakening of Yahweh

9 Awake, awake! Clothe yourself in
      strength,
   arm of Yahweh.
   Awake, as in the olden days,
   generations long ago!
   Was it not you who split Rahab[a] in half,
   who pierced the Dragon through?
10 Was it not you who dried up the sea,
   the waters of the great Abyss;
   who made the sea-bed into a road
   for the redeemed to go across?
11 This is why those whom Yahweh has
      ransomed will return,
   they will enter Zion shouting for joy,
   their heads crowned with a joy unending;
   joy and gladness will escort them
   and sorrow and sighing will take flight.

Yahweh, the consoler

12 I, I am your consoler.
   Why then should you be afraid
   of mortal human beings, of a child
      of man,
   whose fate is that of the grass?
13 You forget about Yahweh your Creator
   who spread out the heavens and laid the
      earth's foundations;

51a Creation is represented as a triumph over the monsters
of chaos, especially the sea.

you have never stopped trembling all day
   long
before the fury of the oppressor
when he was bent on destruction.
Where is the oppressor's fury now?
14 The despairing captive is soon to be set
   free;
he will not die in the dungeon,
nor will his food run out.
15 I am Yahweh your God who stirs up the
   sea, making its waves roar—
Yahweh Sabaoth is my name.
16 I put my words into your mouth,
I hid you in the shadow of my hand,
to spread out the heavens and lay the
   earth's foundations
and say to Zion, 'You are my people.'

The awakening of Jerusalem

17 Awake, awake!
To your feet, Jerusalem!
You who from Yahweh's hand
have drunk the cup of his wrath.
The chalice, the stupefying cup,
you have drained to the dregs.
18 There is no one to guide her
of all the children she has borne,
no one to grasp her hand
of all the children she has reared.
19 Double disaster has befallen you—
who is there to sympathise?
Pillage and ruin, famine and sword—
who is there to console you?
20 Your children are lying helpless
at the end of every street
like an antelope trapped in a net;
they are filled to the brim with Yahweh's
   wrath,
with the rebuke of your God.
21 So listen to this, afflicted one,
drunk, though not with wine.
22 Thus says your Lord Yahweh,
your God, defender of your people:
Look, I am taking
the stupefying cup from your hand,
the chalice, the cup of my wrath,
you will not have to drink again.

23 I shall hand it to your tormentors
who used to say to you,
'On the ground! So that we can walk over
   you!'
And you would flatten your back like the
   ground,
like a street for them to walk on.

The liberation of Jerusalem

52 Awake, awake!
Clothe yourself in strength, Zion.
Put on your finest clothes,
Jerusalem, Holy City;
for the uncircumcised and the unclean
will enter you no more.
2 Shake off your dust; get up,
captive Jerusalem!
The chains have fallen from your neck,
captive daughter of Jerusalem!
3 For Yahweh says this,
'You were sold for nothing;
you will be redeemed without money.'
4 For the Lord Yahweh says this,
'Long ago my people went to Egypt and
   settled there as aliens;
finally Assyria oppressed them for no
   reason.
5 So now what is to be done,'
declares Yahweh,
'since my people have been carried off for
   nothing,
their masters howl in triumph,'
declares Yahweh,
'and my name is held in contempt all day,
   every day?
6 Because of this my people will know my
   name,
because of this they will know when the
   day comes,
that it is I saying, Here I am!'

A prediction of salvation

7 How beautiful on the mountains,
are the feet of the messenger announcing
   peace,
of the messenger of good news,
who proclaims salvation

and says to Zion,
'Your God is king!'
8 The voices of your watchmen!
Now they raise their voices,
shouting for joy together,
for with their own eyes they have seen
Yahweh returning to Zion.
9 Break into shouts together,
shouts of joy, you ruins of Jerusalem;
for Yahweh has consoled his people,
he has redeemed Jerusalem.
10 Yahweh has bared his holy arm
for all the nations to see,
and all the ends of the earth
have seen the salvation of our God.
11 Go away, go away, leave that place,
do not touch anything unclean.
Get out of her, purify yourselves,
you who carry Yahweh's vessels!
12 For you are not to hurry away,
you are not to leave like fugitives.
No, Yahweh marches at your head
and the God of Israel is your rearguard.

Fourth song of the servant

13 Look, my servant will prosper,
will grow great, will rise to great
heights.

14 As many people were aghast at him
—he was so inhumanly disfigured
that he no longer looked like a man—
15 so many nations will be astonished
and kings will stay tight-lipped before
him,
seeing what had never been told them,
learning what they had not heard before.

53 Who has given credence to what we
have heard?
And who has seen in it a revelation of
Yahweh's arm?
2 Like a sapling he grew up before him,
like a root in arid ground.
He had no form or charm to attract us,
no beauty to win our hearts;
3 he was despised, the lowest of men,

a man of sorrows, familiar with suffering,
one from whom, as it were, we averted our
gaze,
despised, for whom we had no regard.
4 Yet ours were the sufferings he was
bearing,
ours the sorrows he was carrying,
while we thought of him as someone being
punished
and struck with affliction by God;
5 whereas he was being wounded for our
rebellions,
crushed because of our guilt;
the punishment reconciling us fell on him,
and we have been healed by his bruises.
6 We had all gone astray like sheep,
each taking his own way,
and Yahweh brought the acts of rebellion
of all of us to bear on him.
7 Ill-treated and afflicted,
he never opened his mouth,
like a lamb led to the slaughter-house,
like a sheep dumb before its shearers
he never opened his mouth.

8 Forcibly, after sentence, he was taken.
Which of his contemporaries was
concerned
at his having been cut off from the land of
the living,
at his having been struck dead for his
people's rebellion?
9 He was given a grave with the wicked,
and his tomb is with the rich,
although he had done no violence,
had spoken no deceit.

10 It was Yahweh's good pleasure to crush
him with pain;
if he gives his life as a sin offering,
he will see his offspring and prolong his
life,
and through him Yahweh's good pleasure
will be done.

11 After the ordeal he has endured,
he will see the light and be content.

75 READ ISAIAH 53.

He was bearing the sin of many and interceding for the rebellious.—ISAIAH 53:12

THE POWER OF THE CROSS

Let us not be ashamed of the cross of our Savior, but rather glory in it. For the message of the cross is to Jews a stumbling block and to gentiles foolishness, but to us salvation. And to them who are perishing it is foolishness, but to us who are being saved it is the power of God (see 1 Co 1:18, 23). For it was not a mere man who died for us, . . . but the Son of God, God made man. Further, if the lamb under Moses drove the Destroyer far away (see Ex 12:23), how much more so did the Lamb of God, who takes away the sin of the world, deliver us from our sins? (see Jn 1:29). The blood of a silly sheep gave salvation. And shall not the blood of the Only-Begotten much rather save?

If any disbelieve the power of the Crucified, let him ask the devils. If any believes not words, let him believe what he sees. Many have been crucified throughout the world, but by none of these are the devils scared. But when they see even the sign of the cross of Christ, who was crucified for us, they shudder. For those men died for their own sins, but Christ for the sins of others. For, as Peter declared, he had done nothing wrong, neither had he spoken any deceit (see 1 P 2:22). However, it is not Peter alone who says this, for then we might suspect that he was partial to his Teacher. But it is Isaiah who says it, who was not indeed present with him in the flesh, but in the Spirit saw his coming in the flesh (see Is 53:9).

Yet why now bring the prophet only as a witness? Take for a witness Pilate himself, who sentenced him, saying, "I find no fault in this man" (see Lk 23:14). . . . There is yet another witness of the sinlessness of Jesus—the robber, the first man admitted into Paradise—who rebuked his fellow and said, "We are paying for what we did. But this man has done nothing wrong" (Lk 23:41). . . .

ST. CYRIL OF JERUSALEM, 315?–386

YOU WILL FIND THE NEXT READING AT ISAIAH 60.

By his knowledge, the upright one, my
    servant will justify many
by taking their guilt on himself.

12 Hence I shall give him a portion with the
    many,
and he will share the booty with the
    mighty,
for having exposed himself to death
and for being counted as one of the
    rebellious,
whereas he was bearing the sin of many
and interceding for the rebellious.

Jerusalem restored to Yahweh's favour

54 Shout for joy, barren one who has
    borne no children!
Break into cries and shouts of joy, you who
    were never in labour!
For the children of the forsaken one are
    more in number
than the children of the wedded wife, says
    Yahweh.
2 Widen the space of your tent,
extend the curtains of your home, do not
    hold back!

Lengthen your ropes, make your tent-pegs
    firm,
3 for you will burst out to right and to left,
    your race will dispossess the nations
    and repopulate deserted towns.
4 Do not fear, you will not be put to shame
    again,
    do not worry, you will not be disgraced
    again;
    for you will forget the shame of your
    youth
    and no longer remember the dishonour of
    your widowhood.
5 For your Creator is your husband,
    Yahweh Sabaoth is his name,
    the Holy One of Israel is your redeemer,
    he is called God of the whole world.
6 Yes, Yahweh has called you back
    like a forsaken, grief-stricken wife,
    like the repudiated wife of his youth,
    says your God.
7 I did forsake you for a brief moment,
    but in great compassion I shall take you
    back.
8 In a flood of anger, for a moment
    I hid my face from you.
    But in everlasting love I have taken pity
    on you,
    says Yahweh, your redeemer.
9 For me it will be as in the days of Noah
    when I swore that Noah's waters
    should never flood the world again.
    So now I swear never to be angry with you
    and never to rebuke you again.
10 For the mountains may go away
    and the hills may totter,
    but my faithful love will never leave you,
    my covenant of peace will never totter,
    says Yahweh who takes pity on you.

The new Jerusalem

11 Unhappy creature, storm-tossed, unpitied,
    look, I shall lay your stones on agates
    and your foundations on sapphires.
12 I shall make your battlements rubies,
    your gateways firestone
    and your entire wall precious stones.

13 All your children will be taught by
    Yahweh
    and great will be your children's
    prosperity.
14 In saving justice you will be made firm,
    free from oppression: you will have
    nothing to fear;
    free from terror: it will not approach you.
15 Should anyone attack you, that will not be
    my doing,
    and whoever does attack you, for your
    sake will fall.
16 I created the smith
    who blows on the charcoal-fire
    to produce a weapon for his use;
    I also created the destroyer
    to ruin it.
17 No weapon forged against you will
    succeed.
    Any voice raised against you in court you
    will refute.
    Such is the lot of the servants of Yahweh,
    the saving justice I assure them,
    declares Yahweh.

Final invitation

55 Oh, come to the water all you who are
    thirsty;
    though you have no money, come!
    Buy and eat; come, buy wine and milk
    without money, free!
2 Why spend money on what cannot
    nourish
    and your wages on what fails to satisfy?
    Listen carefully to me,
    and you will have good things to eat
    and rich food to enjoy.
3 Pay attention, come to me;
    listen, and you will live.

    I shall make an everlasting covenant with
    you
    in fulfilment of the favours promised to
    David.
4 Look, I have made him a witness to
    peoples,
    a leader and lawgiver to peoples.

⁵ Look, you will summon a nation
         unknown to you,
a nation unknown to you will hurry to you
for the sake of Yahweh your God,
because the Holy One of Israel has
         glorified you.

⁶ Seek out Yahweh while he is still to be
         found,
call to him while he is still near.
⁷ Let the wicked abandon his way
and the evil one his thoughts.
Let him turn back to Yahweh who will
         take pity on him,
to our God, for he is rich in forgiveness;
⁸ for my thoughts are not your thoughts
and your ways are not my ways,
declares Yahweh.
⁹ For the heavens are as high above earth
as my ways are above your ways,
my thoughts above your thoughts.
¹⁰ For, as the rain and the snow come down
         from the sky
and do not return before having watered
         the earth,
fertilising it and making it germinate
to provide seed for the sower and food to
         eat,
¹¹ so it is with the word that goes from my
         mouth:
it will not return to me unfulfilled
or before having carried out my good
         pleasure
and having achieved what it was sent
         to do.

Conclusion

¹² Yes, you will go out with joy
and be led away in safety.
Mountains and hills will break into joyful
         cries before you
and all the trees of the countryside clap
         their hands.
¹³ Cypress will grow instead of thorns,
myrtle instead of nettles.
And this will be fame for Yahweh,
an eternal monument never to be effaced.

Promises to foreigners

56 Thus says Yahweh:
Make fair judgement your concern,
         act with justice,
for soon my salvation will come
and my saving justice be manifest.
² Blessed is anyone who does this,
anyone who clings to it,
observing the Sabbath, not profaning it,
and abstaining from every evil deed.
³ No foreigner adhering to Yahweh should
         say,
'Yahweh will utterly exclude me from his
         people.'
No eunuch should say,
'Look, I am a dried-up tree.'
⁴ For Yahweh says this: To the eunuchs who
         observe my Sabbaths
and choose to do my good pleasure
and cling to my covenant,
⁵ I shall give them in my house and within
         my walls
a monument and a name better than sons
         and daughters;
I shall give them an everlasting
         name
that will never be effaced.
⁶ As for foreigners who adhere to Yahweh
         to serve him,
to love Yahweh's name and become his
         servants,
all who observe the Sabbath, not profaning
         it,
and cling to my covenant:
⁷ these I shall lead to my holy mountain
and make them joyful in my house of
         prayer.
Their burnt offerings and sacrifices will be
         accepted on my altar,
for my house will be called a house of
         prayer for all peoples.

⁸ Lord Yahweh who gathers the exiles of
         Israel declares:
There are others I shall gather besides
         those already gathered.

9 Come and gorge, all you wild beasts,
all you beasts of the forest!

The unworthiness of the nation's leaders

10 Its watchmen are all blind,
they know nothing.
Dumb watchdogs all, unable to bark,
they dream, lie down, and love to sleep.
11 Greedy dogs, never satisfied, such are the
shepherds,
who understand nothing;
they all go their own way,
each to the last man after his own
interest.
12 'Come, let me fetch wine;
we will get drunk on strong drink,
tomorrow will be just as wonderful as
today
and even more so!'

57 The upright person perishes
and no one cares.
The faithful is taken off
and no one takes it to heart.
Yes, because of the evil times
the upright is taken off;
2 he will enter peace,
and those who follow the right way
will find rest on their beds.

Against idolatry

3 But you, you children of a witch, come
here,
adulterous race prostituting yourselves!
4 At whom are you jeering,
at whom are you making faces
and sticking out your tongue?
Are you not the spawn of rebellion,
a lying race?
5 Lusting among the terebinths,
and under every spreading tree,
sacrificing children in the ravines,
below the clefts in the rocks.
6 The smooth stones of the ravines will be
your portion,
yes, these will be your lot.
To these you have poured libations,

have brought your cereal offering.
Can all this appease me?
7 On a mountain high and lofty
you have put your bed.
Thither, too, you have climbed
to offer sacrifice.
8 Behind door and doorpost
you have set your reminder.
Yes, far from me, you exposed yourself,
climbed on to your bed,
and made the most of it.
You struck a profitable bargain
with those whose bed you love,
whoring with them often,
with your eyes on the sacred symbol.
9 You went to Molech[a] with oil,
you were prodigal with your perfumes;
you sent your envoys far afield,
down to Sheol itself.
10 Though tired by so much travelling,
you never said, 'It is no use.'
Finding your strength revive,
you never gave up.
11 Who was it you dreaded, and feared,
that you should betray me,
no longer remember me
and not spare a thought for me?
Was I not silent for a long time?
So you cannot have been afraid of me.
12 Now I shall expose this uprightness of
yours,
and little good it did you.
13 When you cry for help,
let those thronging round you save you!
The wind will carry them all away,
one puff will take them off.
But whoever trusts in me will inherit the
country,
he will own my holy mountain.

Salvation for the weak

14 Then it will be said:
Level up, level up, clear the way,
remove the obstacle from my people's way,

57a 'The King', a Semitic deity to whom children were sacrificed.

¹⁵ for thus says the High and Exalted One
who lives eternally
and whose name is holy,
'I live in the holy heights
but I am with the contrite and humble,
to revive the spirit of the humble,
to revive the heart of the contrite.

¹⁶ 'For I do not want to be forever accusing
nor always to be angry,
or the spirit would fail under my
onslaught,
the souls that I myself have made.

¹⁷ 'Angered by his wicked cupidity,
I hid and struck him in anger,
but he rebelliously went the way of his
choice.
¹⁸ 'I saw how he behaved, but I shall heal
him,
I shall lead him, fill him with consolation,
him and those who mourn for him,
¹⁹ bringing praise to their lips.
Peace, peace to far and near, Yahweh says,
and I shall heal him.'
²⁰ The wicked, however, are like the restless
sea
that cannot be still,
whose waters throw up mud and dirt.
²¹ 'No peace', says Yahweh, 'for the wicked.'

Fasting pleasing to God

58 Shout for all you are worth, do not
hold back,
raise your voice like a trumpet.
To my people proclaim their rebellious
acts,
to the House of Jacob, their sins.
² They seek for me day after day,
they long to know my ways,
like a nation that has acted uprightly
and not forsaken the law of its God.
They ask me for laws that are upright,
they long to be near God:
³ 'Why have we fasted, if you do not see,
why mortify ourselves if you never
notice?'

Look, you seek your own pleasure on your
fastdays
and you exploit all your workmen;
⁴ look, the only purpose of your fasting is to
quarrel and squabble
and strike viciously with your fist.
Fasting like yours today
will never make your voice heard on high.
⁵ Is that the sort of fast that pleases me,
a day when a person inflicts pain on
himself?
Hanging your head like a reed,
spreading out sackcloth and ashes?
Is that what you call fasting,
a day acceptable to Yahweh?
⁶ Is not this the sort of fast that pleases me:
to break unjust fetters,
to undo the thongs of the yoke.
to let the oppressed go free,
and to break all yokes?
⁷ Is it not sharing your food with the
hungry,
and sheltering the homeless poor;
if you see someone lacking clothes, to
clothe him,
and not to turn away from your own kin?
⁸ Then your light will blaze out like the
dawn
and your wound be quickly healed over.
Saving justice will go ahead of you
and Yahweh's glory come behind you.
⁹ Then you will cry for help and Yahweh
will answer;
you will call and he will say, 'I am here.'
If you do away with the yoke,
the clenched fist and malicious words,
¹⁰ if you deprive yourself for the hungry
and satisfy the needs of the afflicted,
your light will rise in the darkness,
and your darkest hour will be like noon.
¹¹ Yahweh will always guide you,
will satisfy your needs in the scorched
land;
he will give strength to your bones
and you will be like a watered garden,
like a flowing spring
whose waters never run dry.

12 Your ancient ruins will be rebuilt;
you will build on age-old foundations.
You will be called 'Breach-mender',
'Restorer of streets to be lived in'.

The Sabbath

13 If you refrain from breaking the Sabbath,
from taking your own pleasure on my holy
day,
if you call the Sabbath 'Delightful',
and the day sacred to Yahweh
'Honourable',
if you honour it by abstaining from travel,
from seeking your own pleasure and from
too much talk,
14 then you will find true happiness in
Yahweh,
and I shall lead you in triumph over the
heights of the land.
I shall feed you on the heritage of your
father Jacob,
for the mouth of Yahweh has spoken.

Penitential psalm

59 No, the arm of Yahweh is not too short
to save,
nor his ear too dull to hear,
2 but your guilty deeds have made a gulf
between you and your God.
Your sins have made him hide his face
from you
so as not to hear you,
3 since your hands are stained with blood
and your fingers with guilt;
your lips utter lies,
your tongues murmur wickedness.
4 No one makes upright accusations
or pleads sincerely.
All rely on empty words, utter falsehood,
conceive trouble and give birth to evil.

5 They are hatching adders' eggs
and weaving a spider's web;
eat one of their eggs and you die,
crush one and a viper emerges.
6 Their webs are useless for clothing,
their deeds are useless for wearing;

their deeds are deeds of guilt,
violence fills their hands.
7 Their feet run to do evil;
they are quick to shed innocent blood.
Their thoughts are thoughts of guilt,
wherever they go there is havoc and ruin.
8 They do not know the way of peace,
there is no fair judgement in their course,
they have made their own crooked paths,
and no one treading them knows any
peace.
9 Thus fair judgement is remote from us
nor can uprightness overtake us.
We looked for light and all is darkness,
for brightness and we walk in gloom.
10 Like the blind we feel our way along walls,
we grope our way like people without
eyes.
We stumble as though noon were twilight,
among the robust we are like the dead.
11 We growl, all of us, like bears,
like doves we make no sound but
moaning,
waiting for the fair judgement that never
comes,
for salvation, but that is far away.

12 How often we have rebelled against you
and our sins bear witness against us.
Our rebellious acts are indeed with us,
we are well aware of our guilt:
13 rebellion and denial of Yahweh,
turning our back on our God,
talking violence and revolt,
murmuring lies in our heart.
14 Fair judgement is driven away
and saving justice stands aloof,
for good faith has stumbled in the street
and sincerity cannot enter.
15 Good faith has vanished;
anyone abstaining from evil is victimised.

Yahweh saw this and was displeased
that there was no fair judgement.
16 He saw there was no one
and wondered there was no one to
intervene.

So he made his own arm his mainstay,
his own saving justice his support.

¹⁷ He put on saving justice like a breastplate,
on his head the helmet of salvation.
He put on the clothes of vengeance like a
tunic
and wrapped himself in jealousy like a
cloak.

¹⁸ To each he repays his due,
retribution to his enemies, reprisals on his
foes,
to the coasts and islands he will repay their
due.

¹⁹ From the west, Yahweh's name will be
feared,
and from the east, his glory,
for he will come like a pent-up stream
impelled by the breath of Yahweh.

²⁰ Then for Zion will come a redeemer,
for those who stop rebelling in Jacob,
declares Yahweh.

Prophecy

²¹ 'For my part, this is my covenant with them,
says Yahweh. My spirit with which I endowed
you, and my words that I have put in your
mouth, will not leave your mouth, or the
mouths of your children, or the mouths of
your children's children, says Yahweh, henceforth and for ever.'

The splendour of Jerusalem

60 Arise, shine out, for your light has
come,
and the glory of Yahweh has risen on you.

² Look! though night still covers the earth
and darkness the peoples,
on you Yahweh is rising
and over you his glory can be seen.

³ The nations will come to your light
and kings to your dawning brightness.

⁴ Lift up your eyes and look around:
all are assembling and coming towards
you,^a
your sons coming from far away
and your daughters being carried on the
hip.

⁵ At this sight you will grow radiant,
your heart will throb and dilate,
since the riches of the sea will flow to you,
the wealth of the nations come to you;

⁶ camels in throngs will fill your streets,
the young camels of Midian and Ephah;
everyone in Saba will come,
bringing gold and incense
and proclaiming Yahweh's praises.

⁷ All the flocks of Kedar will gather inside
you,
the rams of Nebaioth will be at your
service
as acceptable victims on my altar,
and I shall glorify my glorious house.

⁸ Who are these flying like a cloud,
like doves to their dovecote?

⁹ Why, the coasts and islands put their hope
in me
and the vessels of Tarshish take the lead
in bringing your children from far away,
and their silver and gold with them,
for the sake of the name of Yahweh your
God,
of the Holy One of Israel who has made
you glorious.

¹⁰ Foreigners will rebuild your walls
and their kings will serve you.
For though I struck you in anger,
in mercy I have pitied you.

¹¹ Your gates will always be open,
never closed, either day or night,
for the riches of the nations to be brought
you
and their kings to be let in.

¹² For the nation and kingdom that will not
serve you will perish,
and the nations will be utterly destroyed.

¹³ The glory of the Lebanon will come to you,
cypress, plane-tree, box-tree, one and all,
to adorn the site of my sanctuary,
for me to honour the place where I stand.

60a = 49:18.

76 READ ISAIAH 60:1–11.

The nations will come to your light and kings to your dawning brightness.—ISAIAH 60:3

THE DAWN OF OUR HOPE

From very early times the church has regarded Isaiah 60 as a prophecy of Christ's manifestation to the world and has read it in the liturgy for the Epiphany. With this text in mind, St. Leo the Great preached the following sermon on that great feast:

The Word made flesh was pleased to reveal himself by degrees to those for whom he had come. When Jesus was born he was manifested to those who would believe, but hidden from his enemies. At that time the heavens declared the glory of God when angels appeared to tell the shepherds the good news of a Savior's birth. Now the guiding star leads the wise men to worship him, so that from the rising to the setting of the sun the birth of the true king might be known everywhere. And so that through those wise men the kingdoms of the east might learn the great truth, and the Roman Empire remain no more in darkness.

We recognize in the wise men who came to worship Christ the first fruits of that revelation to the gentiles by which we also are called and enlightened. Therefore, let us keep this feast with grateful hearts, thankfully remembering this dawn of our blessed hope. For from that worship the wise men paid to the newborn Christ we date our becoming heirs of God and coheirs with Christ. Thus, let us reverence this sacred day on which the Author of our salvation was manifested. As the wise men fell down and worshiped him in the manger, so let us fall down and worship him enthroned almighty in heaven. As they opened their treasures and presented him mystic and symbolic gifts, so let us strive to open our hearts to him and from them present him a worthy offering.

ST. LEO THE GREAT, d. 461

YOU WILL FIND THE NEXT READING AT JEREMIAH 4.

14 Your oppressors' children will humbly
approach you,
at your feet all who despised you will fall
addressing you as 'City of Yahweh',
'Zion of the Holy One of Israel'.
15 Instead of your being forsaken and hated,
avoided by everyone,
I will make you an object of eternal
pride,
a source of joy from age to age.
16 You will suck the milk of nations,
you will suck the wealth of kings,

and you will know that I, Yahweh, am
your Saviour,
that your redeemer is the Mighty One of
Jacob.
17 For bronze I shall bring gold
and for iron I shall bring silver,
and for wood, bronze,
and for stone, iron;
I shall make Peace your administration
and Saving Justice your government.
18 Violence will no longer be heard of in your
country,

nor devastation and ruin within your
frontiers.
You will call your walls 'Salvation'
and your gates 'Praise'.

19 No more will the sun give you daylight,
nor moonlight shine on you,
but Yahweh will be your everlasting
light,
your God will be your splendour.
20 Your sun will set no more
nor will your moon wane,
for Yahweh will be your everlasting light
and your days of mourning will be over.
21 Your people, all of them upright,
will possess the country for ever,
the shoot I myself have planted,
my handiwork, for my own glory.
22 The smallest will grow into a thousand,
the weakest one into a mighty nation.
When the time is ripe, I, Yahweh,
shall quickly bring it about.

A prophet's mission

61 The spirit of Lord Yahweh is on me
for Yahweh has anointed me.
He has sent me to bring the news to the
afflicted,
to soothe the broken-hearted,
2 to proclaim liberty to captives,
release to those in prison,
to proclaim a year of favour from Yahweh
and a day of vengeance for our God,
to comfort all who mourn
3 (to give to Zion's mourners),
to give them for ashes a garland,
for mourning-dress, the oil of gladness,
for despondency, festal attire;
and they will be called 'terebinths of
saving justice',
planted by Yahweh to glorify him.
4 They will rebuild the ancient ruins,
they will raise what has long lain waste,
they will restore the ruined cities,
all that has lain waste for ages past.
5 Strangers will come forward to feed your
flocks,

foreigners be your ploughmen and
vinedressers;
6 but you will be called 'priests of Yahweh'
and be addressed as 'ministers of our God'.
You will feed on the wealth of nations,
you will supplant them in their glory.
7 To make up for your shame, you will
receive double;
instead of disgrace, shouts of joy will be
their lot;
yes, they will have a double portion in
their country
and everlasting joy will be theirs.
8 For I am Yahweh: I love fair judgement,
I hate robbery and wrong-doing,
and I shall reward them faithfully
and make an everlasting covenant with
them.
9 Their race will be famous throughout the
nations
and their offspring throughout the
peoples.
All who see them will admit
that they are a race whom Yahweh has
blessed.

Thanksgiving

10 I exult for joy in Yahweh,
my soul rejoices in my God,
for he has clothed me in garments of
salvation,
he has wrapped me in a cloak of saving
justice,
like a bridegroom wearing his garland,
like a bride adorned in her jewels.
11 For as the earth sends up its shoots
and a garden makes seeds sprout,
so Lord Yahweh makes saving justice and
praise
spring up in the sight of all nations.

The splendour of Jerusalem

62 About Zion I will not be silent,
about Jerusalem I shall not rest
until saving justice dawns for her like a
bright light
and her salvation like a blazing torch.

2 The nations will then see your saving
justice,
and all kings your glory,
and you will be called a new name
which Yahweh's mouth will reveal.
3 You will be a crown of splendour in
Yahweh's hand,
a princely diadem in the hand of your
God.
4 No more will you be known as 'Forsaken'
or your country be known as 'Desolation';
instead, you will be called 'My Delight is
in her'
and your country 'The Wedded';
for Yahweh will take delight in you
and your country will have its wedding.
5 Like a young man marrying a virgin,
your rebuilder will wed you,
and as the bridegroom rejoices in his
bride,
so will your God rejoice in you.

6 On your walls, Jerusalem, I have posted
watchmen;
they will never fall silent, day or night.
No peace for you, as you keep Yahweh's
attention!
7 And give him no peace either
until he restores Jerusalem
and makes her the pride of the world!
8 Yahweh has sworn by his right hand
and by his mighty arm:
Never again shall I give your grain
to feed your enemies.
Never again will foreigners drink the wine
for which you have toiled.
9 No, the reapers will eat it and praise
Yahweh,
the harvesters will drink it in my sacred
courts!

Conclusion

10 Pass through, pass through the gates.
Clear a way for my people!
Level up, level up the highway,
remove the stones!
Hoist a signal to the peoples!

11 This is what Yahweh has proclaimed
to the remotest part of earth:
Say to the daughter of Zion, 'Look, your
salvation is coming;
with him comes his reward, his
achievement precedes him!'[a]

12 They will be called 'The Holy People',
'Yahweh's Redeemed',
while you will be called 'Sought-after',
'City-not-forsaken'.

Judgement of the nations

63 Who is this coming from Edom,
from Bozrah in crimson garments,
so magnificently dressed,
marching so full of strength?
—It is I, whose word is saving justice,
whose power is to save.
2 —Why are your garments red,
your clothes like someone treading the
winepress?
3 —I have trodden the winepress alone;
of my people, not one was with me.
So I trod them down in my anger,
I trampled on them in my wrath.
Their blood squirted over my garments
and all my clothes are stained.
4 For I have decided on a day of
vengeance,
my year of retribution has come.
5 I looked: there was no one to help me;
I was appalled but could find no
supporter!
Then my own arm came to my rescue
and my own fury supported me.
6 I crushed the peoples in my anger,
I shattered them in my fury
and sent their blood streaming to the
ground.

Meditation on the history of Israel

7 I shall recount Yahweh's acts of faithful
love,
Yahweh's praises,

62a = 40:10.

in return for all that Yahweh has done
    for us,
for his great kindness to the House of
    Israel,
for all that he has done in his mercy,
for the abundance of his acts of faithful
    love.

8 For he said, 'Truly they are my people,
children who will not betray me,'
and he became their Saviour.
9 In all their troubles,
    it was no messenger or angel
but his presence that saved them.
In his love and pity
he himself redeemed them,
lifted them up and carried them
throughout the days of old.
10 But they rebelled
and vexed his holy Spirit.
Then he became their enemy
and himself waged war on them.
11 But he called the past to mind,
Moses his servant.
Where is he who saved them from the sea,
the Shepherd of his flock?
Where was he who put
his holy Spirit among them,
12 whose glorious arm led the way
by Moses' right hand?
Who divided the waters before them
to win himself everlasting renown,
13 who led them through the depths
as easily as a horse through the desert?
They stumbled as little
14 as cattle going down to the plain.
Yahweh's Spirit led them to rest.
This was how you guided your people
to win yourself glorious renown.

15 Look down from heaven and see
from your holy and glorious dwelling.
Where is your zeal and your might?
Are your deepest feelings,
your mercy to me, to be restrained?
16 After all, you are our Father.
If Abraham will not own us,

if Israel will not acknowledge us,
you, Yahweh, are our Father,
'Our Redeemer' is your name from
    of old.
17 Why, Yahweh, do you let us wander from
    your ways
and let our hearts grow too hard to fear
    you?
Return, for the sake of your servants,
the tribes of your heritage.
18 Your holy people have owned it for so
    short a time,
our enemies have trampled on your
    sanctuary.
19 We have long been like those you do not
    rule,
people who do not bear your name.

Oh, that you would tear the heavens open
    and come down
—in your presence the mountains would
    quake,
64 as fire sets brushwood alight,
    as fire makes water boil—
to make your name known to your
    foes;
the nations would tremble at your
    presence,
2 at the unexpected miracles you would do.
(Oh, that you would come down,
in your presence the mountains would
    quake!)

3 Never has anyone heard,
no ear has heard, no eye has seen
any god but you act like this
for the sake of those who trust him.
4 You come to meet those
who are happy to act uprightly;
keeping your ways reminds them of you.
Yes, you have been angry and we have
    been sinners;
now we persist in your ways and we shall
    be saved.
5 We have all been like unclean things
and our upright deeds like filthy rags.
We wither, all of us, like leaves,

and all our misdeeds carry us off like the
    wind.
6 There is no one to invoke your name,
    to rouse himself to hold fast to you,
    for you have hidden your face from us
    and given us up to the power of our
        misdeeds.
7 And yet, Yahweh, you are our Father;
    we the clay and you our potter,
    all of us are the work of your hands.
8 Yahweh, do not let your anger go too far
    and do not remember guilt for ever.
    Look, please, we are all your people;
9 your holy cities have become a desert,
    Zion has become a desert,
    Jerusalem a wasteland.
10 Our holy and glorious Temple,
    in which our ancestors used to praise you,
    has been burnt to the ground;
    all our delight lies in ruins.
11 Yahweh, can you restrain yourself at all
        this?
    Will you stay silent and afflict us beyond
        endurance?

The coming judgement

65 I have let myself be approached by
        those who did not consult me,
    I have let myself be found by those who
        did not seek me.
    I said, 'Here I am, here I am!'
    to a nation that did not invoke my name.
2 Each day I stretched out my hands
    to a rebellious people
    who follow a way which is not good,
    as the fancy takes them;
3 a people constantly provoking me to my
        face
    by sacrificing in gardens,
    burning incense on bricks,
4 living in tombs,
    spending the night in dark corners,
    eating the meat of pigs,
    putting unclean foods on their plates.
5 'Keep your distance,' they say,
    'do not touch me, lest my sanctity come
        near you!'

Such words are like stifling smoke
    to me,
    an ever-burning fire.
6 Look, it is inscribed before me:
    I shall not be silent until I have repaid
        them,
    repaid them in full,
7 punished your guilt and your ancestors'
        guilt together,
    Yahweh declares.
    For having burnt incense on the
        mountains
    and insulted me on the hills,
    I shall pay them back in full for what they
        have done.

8 Yahweh says this:
    As when a bunch of grapes is found still to
        have juice in it,
    people say, 'Do not destroy it,
    for it contains a blessing,'
    so I shall act for my servants' sake,
    I shall not destroy them all.
9 I shall produce descendants from Jacob
    and heirs to my mountains from Judah,
    my chosen ones will own them
    and my servants will live there.
10 Sharon will be a pasture for flocks,
    the Valley of Achor a feeding ground for
        cattle,
    for those of my people who have sought
        me.
11 But as for those of you who abandon
        Yahweh,
    who forget my holy mountain,
    who lay the table for Gad,*a*
    who fill cups of mixed wine for Meni,
12 you I shall destine to the sword
    and all of you will stoop to be slaughtered,
    because I called and you would not
        answer,
    I spoke and you would not listen;
    you have done what I consider evil,
    you chose to do what displeases me.

65a Gad is the Aramaean god of luck, Meni an unknown
god, possibly of fate.

¹³ Therefore Lord Yahweh says this:
   You will see my servants eating
   while you go hungry;
   you will see my servants drinking
   while you go thirsty;
   you will see my servants rejoicing
   while you are put to shame;
¹⁴ you will hear my servants shouting for joy
   of heart,
   while you shriek for sorrow of heart
   and howl with a broken spirit.
¹⁵ And you will leave your name behind as a
   curse for my chosen ones,
   'May Lord Yahweh strike you dead!'
   But to his servants he will give another
   name.
¹⁶ Whoever blesses himself on earth will
   bless himself by the God of
   truth,
   and whoever swears an oath on earth
   will swear by the God of truth,
   for past troubles will be forgotten
   and hidden from my eyes.
¹⁷ For look, I am going to create new
   heavens and a new earth,
   and the past will not be remembered
   and will come no more to mind.
¹⁸ Rather be joyful, be glad for ever
   at what I am creating,
   for look, I am creating Jerusalem to be
   'Joy'
   and my people to be 'Gladness'.
¹⁹ I shall be joyful in Jerusalem
   and I shall rejoice in my people.
   No more will the sound of weeping be
   heard there,
   nor the sound of a shriek;
²⁰ never again will there be an infant there
   who lives only a few days,
   nor an old man who does not run his full
   course;
   for the youngest will die at a hundred,
   and at a hundred the sinner will be
   accursed.
²¹ They will build houses and live in them,
   they will plant vineyards and eat their
   fruit.

²² They will not build for others to live in,
   or plant for others to eat;
   for the days of my people will be like the
   days of a tree,
   and my chosen ones will themselves use
   what they have made.
²³ They will not toil in vain,
   nor bear children destined to disaster,
   for they are the race of Yahweh's blessed
   ones
   and so are their offspring.
²⁴ Thus, before they call I shall answer,
   before they stop speaking I shall have
   heard.
²⁵ The wolf and the young lamb will feed
   together,
   the lion will eat hay like the ox,
   and dust be the serpent's food.
   No hurt, no harm will be done
   *on all my holy mountain,*ᵇ
   Yahweh says.

Prophecy on the Temple

66 Thus says Yahweh:
   With heaven my throne
   and earth my footstool,
   what house could you build me,
   what place for me to rest,
² when all these things were made by me
   and all belong to me?—declares
   Yahweh.
   But my eyes are drawn to the person
   of humbled and contrite spirit,
   who trembles at my word.

³ Some slaughter a bull, some kill a human
   being,
   some sacrifice a lamb, some strangle a dog,
   some present an offering of pig's blood,
   some burn memorial incense, a revolting
   blessing;
   all these people have chosen their own
   ways
   and take delight in their disgusting
   practices.

65b = 11:7, 9.

4 I too take delight in making fools of them,
  I shall bring what they most fear down on
        them
  because I have called and no one would
        answer,
  I spoke and no one listened.
  They have done what I regard as evil,
  have chosen what displeases me.

Judgement on Jerusalem

5 Listen to the word of Yahweh,
  you who tremble at his word.
  Your brothers, who hate and reject you
  because of my name, have said,
  'Let Yahweh show his glory,
  let us witness your joy!'
  But they will be put to shame.

6 Listen! An uproar from the city!
  A voice from the Temple!
  The voice of Yahweh
  bringing retribution on his enemies.

7 Before being in labour she has given
        birth.
  Before the birth pangs came, she has
        been delivered of a child.

8 Who ever heard of such a thing,
  who ever saw anything like this?
  Can a country be born in one day?
  Can a nation be brought forth all at
        once?
  For Zion, scarcely in labour, has brought
        forth her children!

9 Shall I open the womb and not bring to
        birth?
  says Yahweh.
  Shall I, who bring to birth, close the
        womb?
  says your God.

10 Rejoice with Jerusalem,
  be glad for her, all you who love her!
  Rejoice, rejoice with her,
  all you who mourned her!

11 So that you may be suckled and satisfied
  from her consoling breast,
  so that you may drink deep with delight
  from her generous nipple.

12 For Yahweh says this:
  Look, I am going to send peace
  flowing over her like a river,
  and like a stream in spate
  the glory of the nations.

  You will be suckled, carried on her hip
  and fondled in her lap.
13 As a mother comforts a child,
  so I shall comfort you;
  you will be comforted in Jerusalem.

14 At the sight your heart will rejoice,
  and your limbs regain vigour like the
        grass.
  To his servants Yahweh will reveal his
        hand,
  but to his enemies his fury.

15 For see how Yahweh comes in fire,
  his chariots like the whirlwind,
  to assuage his anger with burning,
  his rebukes with flaming fire.

16 For by fire will Yahweh execute fair
        judgement,
  and by his sword, on all people;
  and Yahweh's victims will be many.
17 As for those who sanctify themselves
  and purify themselves to enter the
        gardens,
  following the one in the centre,
  who eat the flesh of pigs, revolting things
        and rats:
  their deeds and their thoughts will perish
        together,
  declares Yahweh.

An eschatological discourse

18 I am coming to gather every nation and
every language. They will come to witness my
glory. 19 I shall give them a sign and send some
of their survivors to the nations: to Tarshish,

Put, Lud, Meshech, Tubal and Javan,ᵃ to the distant coasts and islands that have never heard of me or seen my glory. They will proclaim my glory to the nations, ²⁰ and from all the nations they will bring all your brothers as an offering to Yahweh, on horses, in chariots, in litters, on mules and on camels, to my holy mountain, Jerusalem, Yahweh says, like Israelites bringing offerings in clean vessels to Yahweh's house. ²¹ And some of them I shall make into priests and Levites, Yahweh says.

²² For as the new heavens and the new earth I am making will endure before me, declares Yahweh, so will your race and your name endure.

²³ From New Moon to New Moon,
    from Sabbath to Sabbath,
all humanity will come and bow
    in my presence, Yahweh says.
²⁴ And on their way out they will see
    the corpses of those
who rebelled against me;
    for their worm will never die
nor their fire be put out,
    and they will be held in horror by all
        humanity.

66a Possible identifications: Spain, Lybia, Lydia, Phrygia, Cilicia, or Greece.

JEREMIAH

1 The words of Jeremiah son of Hilkiah, one of the priests living at Anathoth in the territory of Benjamin. ²The word of Yahweh came to him in the days of Josiah son of Amon, king of Judah, in the thirteenth year of his reign; ³then in the days of Jehoiakim son of Josiah, king of Judah, until the end of the eleventh year of Zedekiah son of Josiah, king of Judah, until the deportation of Jerusalem, in the fifth month.

The call of Jeremiah

⁴The word of Yahweh came to me, saying:

⁵ 'Before I formed you in the womb I knew
      you;
   before you came to birth I consecrated you;
   I appointed you as prophet to the nations.'

⁶I then said, 'Ah, ah, ah, Lord Yahweh; you see, I do not know how to speak: I am only a child!'

⁷ But Yahweh replied,
   'Do not say, "I am only a child,"
   for you must go to all to whom I send you
   and say whatever I command you.
⁸ Do not be afraid of confronting them,
   for I am with you to rescue you,
   Yahweh declares.'

⁹Then Yahweh stretched out his hand and touched my mouth, and Yahweh said to me:

   'There! I have put my words into your
      mouth.
¹⁰ Look, today I have set you
   over the nations and kingdoms,
   to uproot and to knock down,
   to destroy and to overthrow,
   to build and to plant.'

¹¹The word of Yahweh came to me, asking, 'Jeremiah, what do you see?' I answered, 'I see a branch of the Watchful Tree.' ¹²Then Yahweh said, 'Well seen, for I am watching over my word to perform it.'

¹³A second time the word of Yahweh came to me, asking, 'What do you see?' I answered, 'I see a cooking pot on the boil, with its mouth tilting from the north.' ¹⁴Then Yahweh said:

   'From the north disaster will come boiling
      over
   on all who live in the country,
¹⁵ for I am now summoning
   all the families of the kingdoms of the
      north,
   Yahweh declares.
   They will come, and each will set his
      throne
   in front of the gates of Jerusalem,
   all round, against its walls
   and against all the towns of Judah.
¹⁶ I shall pronounce my judgements on
      them
   because of all their wickedness,
   since they have abandoned me,
   offering incense to other gods
   and worshipping what their own hands
      have made.

¹⁷ 'As for you, prepare yourself for action.
   Stand up and tell them
   all I command you.
   Have no fear of them
   and in their presence I will make you
      fearless.

18 For look, today I have made you
   into a fortified city,
   a pillar of iron,
   a wall of bronze
   to stand against the whole country:
   the kings of Judah, its princes,
   its priests and the people of the country.
19 They will fight against you
   but will not overcome you,
   for I am with you,
   Yahweh declares,
   to rescue you.'

The earliest preaching of Jeremiah:
the infidelity of Israel

2 The word of Yahweh came to me, saying,
  2 'Go and shout this in Jerusalem's ears:

   'Yahweh says this:
   "I remember your faithful love,
   the affection of your bridal days,
   when you followed me through the
         desert,
   through a land unsown.
3 Israel was sacred to Yahweh;
   the first-fruits of his harvest;
   all who ate this incurred guilt,
   disaster befell them,
   Yahweh declares." '
4 Listen to Yahweh's word, House of Jacob
   and all the families of the House of Israel.
5 Yahweh says this,
   'What did your ancestors find wrong
         in me
   for them to have deserted me so far
   as to follow Futility
   and become futile themselves?
6 They never said, "Where is Yahweh,
   who brought us out of Egypt
   and led us through the desert,
   through a land of plains and ravines,
   through a land of drought, of shadow dark
         as death,
   a land through which no one passes
   and where no human being lives?"
7 I brought you to a country of plenty,
   to enjoy its produce and good things;

but when you entered you defiled my
      country
   and made my heritage loathsome.
8 The priests never asked, "Where is
      Yahweh?"
   Those skilled in the Law did not know
      me,
   the shepherds too rebelled against me
   and the prophets prophesied by Baal
   and followed the Useless Ones.
9 So I must state my case against you once
      more,
   Yahweh declares,
   and state my case against your children's
      children:
10 Cross to the isles of the Kittim[a] and look,
   send to Kedar and carefully observe,
   see if anything like this has happened
      before!
11 Does a nation change its gods?
   —and these are not gods at all!
   Yet my people have exchanged their Glory
   for the Useless One!
12 You heavens, stand aghast at this,
   horrified, utterly appalled,
   Yahweh declares.
13 For my people have committed two
      crimes:
   they have abandoned me,
   the fountain of living water,
   and dug water-tanks for themselves,
   cracked water-tanks
   that hold no water.

14 'Is Israel a slave?
   Was he born into serfdom,
   for him to be preyed on like this?
15 Lions have roared at him,
   they have made their voices heard.
   They have left this country a desert,
   his towns lie burnt and uninhabited.
16 The people of Noph and Tahpanhes[b]
   have shaved your skull!

2a i.e. the Greeks. Kedar is a nomadic Arab tribe, so 'Go east
or west'.

2b Noph and Tahpanhes are towns in the Egyptian Delta.

17 Have you not brought this on yourself,
by abandoning Yahweh your God,
when he was guiding you on your way?
18 What is the good of going to Egypt now
to drink the water of the Nile?
What is the good of going to Assyria
to drink the water of the River?
19 Your wickedness will bring its own
punishment,
your infidelities will bring you to book,
so give thought and see
how evil and bitter it is
to abandon Yahweh your God
and not to stand in awe of me,
the Lord Yahweh Sabaoth declares.

20 'It is long ago now since you broke your
yoke,
burst your bonds
and said, "I will not serve!"
Yet on every high hill
and under every green tree
you have sprawled and played the whore.
21 Yet I had planted you, a red vine
of completely sound stock.
How is it you have turned into seedlings
of a vine that is alien to me?
22 Even though you scrub yourself with
soda
and put in quantities of soap,
the stain of your guilt would still be visible
to me,
the Lord Yahweh declares.
23 How dare you say, "I am not defiled,
I have not run after the Baals?"
Look at your behaviour in the Valley,
realise what you have done.
24 A wild she-donkey, at home in the desert,
snuffing the breeze in desire;
who can control her when she is on heat?
Males need not trouble to look for her,
they will find her in her month.
25 Beware! Your own foot will go unshod,
your own throat grow dry!
But you said, "It is no use! No!
For I love the Strangers
and they are the ones I shall follow."

26 'Like a thief ashamed at being caught,
so will the House of Israel be:
they, their kings, their chief men,
their priests and their prophets,
27 who say to a piece of wood, "You are my
father,"
and to a stone, "You gave birth to me."
For they turn to me their backs,
never their faces;
yet when trouble comes they shout,
"Get up! Save us!"
28 Where are your gods you made for
yourself?
Let them get up if they can save you
when trouble comes!
For you have as many gods
as you have towns, Judah!ᶜ
29 Why make out a case against me?
You have all rebelled against me,
Yahweh declares.
30 In vain I have struck your children,
they have not accepted correction;
your own sword has devoured your
prophets
like a marauding lion.
31 Now you of this generation, listen to what
Yahweh says:
Have I been a desert for Israel,
or a land of gloom?
Why do my people say,
"We are our own masters,
we will come to you no more"?
32 Does a girl forget her ornaments,
a bride her sash?
And yet my people have forgotten me,
days beyond number.

33 'How well you set your course
in pursuit of love!
And so you have schooled your ways
to wicked deeds.
34 The very skirts of your robe are stained
with the blood of the poor,
of innocent men you never caught
breaking and entering!

2c = 11:13.

And in spite of all this,

³⁵ you say, "I am innocent,
    let his anger turn from me!"
Now I pass sentence on you
    for saying, "I have not sinned."

³⁶ 'How frivolously you undertake
    a change of course!
But you will be disappointed by Egypt
    just as you were by Assyria.
³⁷ You will have to leave there too
    with your hands on your head,
for Yahweh has rejected those that you
        rely on,
you will come to no good with them.'

Conversion

3 'If a man divorces his wife
    and she leaves him
    and becomes someone else's,
has he the right to go back to her?
Has not that piece of land
    been totally polluted?
And you, having played the whore with
        many lovers,
you claim the right to come back to me!
    Yahweh demands.

² 'Lift your eyes to the bare heights and
        look!
Where have you not offered your sex!
You waited by the roadside for them
    like an Arab in the desert.
You have polluted the country
    with your prostitution and your vices:
³ this is why the showers have been
        withheld,
    the late rains have not come.

'But you maintained a prostitute's bold
        front,
    with no trace of a blush.
⁴ From now on, do not cry out at me, "My
        father!
My beloved ever since I was young!
⁵ Will he keep up his anger for ever,
    maintain his wrath to the end?"

You say this but still go on sinning,
    being so obstinate.'

The Northern Kingdom urged to repent

⁶ In the days of King Josiah, Yahweh said to me, 'Have you seen what disloyal Israel has done? How she has made her way up every high hill and to every green tree, and played the whore there? ⁷ I thought, "After doing all this she will come back to me." But she did not come back. Her faithless sister Judah saw this. ⁸ She also saw that I had repudiated disloyal Israel for all her adulteries and given her her divorce papers. Her faithless sister Judah, however, was not afraid: she too went and played the whore. ⁹ And with her shameless whoring, she polluted the country; she committed adultery with stones and pieces of wood. ¹⁰ Worse than all this: Judah, her faithless sister, has come back to me not in sincerity, but only in pretence, Yahweh declares.'

¹¹ And Yahweh said to me, 'Disloyal Israel is upright, compared with faithless Judah. ¹² So go and shout words towards the north, and say:

"Come back, disloyal Israel,
    Yahweh declares,
I shall frown on you no more,
    since I am merciful,
    Yahweh declares.
I shall not keep my anger for ever.
¹³ Only acknowledge your guilt:
how you have rebelled against Yahweh
        your God,
how you have prostituted yourself with the
        Strangers
under every green tree
and have not listened to my voice,
    Yahweh declares.

Zion in the messianic age

¹⁴ "Come back, disloyal children, Yahweh declares, for I alone am your Master, and I will take you, one from a town, two from a family, and bring you to Zion. ¹⁵ I shall give you shepherds after my own heart, who will pasture

you wisely and discreetly. ¹⁶ Then, when you have increased and grown numerous in the country, Yahweh declares, no one will ever again say: The ark of the covenant of Yahweh! It will not enter their minds, they will not remember it or miss it, nor will another one be made. ¹⁷ When that time comes, Jerusalem will be called: The Throne of Yahweh, and all the nations will converge on her, on Yahweh's name, on Jerusalem, and will no longer follow their own stubborn and wicked inclinations.

¹⁸ "When those days come, the House of Judah will join the House of Israel; together they will come from the land of the north to the country I gave your ancestors as their heritage."

Continuation of the poem on conversion

¹⁹ 'And I was thinking:
How am I to rank you as my children?
I shall give you a country of delights,
the fairest heritage of all the nations!
I thought: You will call me Father
and will never cease to follow me.
²⁰ But like a woman betraying her lover,
House of Israel, you have betrayed me,'
Yahweh declares.

²¹ A noise is heard on the bare heights:
the weeping and entreaty of the Israelites,
for they have gone wildly astray,
have forgotten Yahweh their God.
²² 'Come back, disloyal sons,
I want to cure your disloyalty.'
'We are here, we are coming to you,
for you are Yahweh our God.
²³ The hills are a delusion after all,
so is the tumult of the mountains.
Yahweh our God is, after all,
the saving of Israel.
²⁴ Shame has devoured what our ancestors
worked for
ever since we were young,
their flocks and herds, their sons and their
daughters.
²⁵ Let us lie down in our shame,
let our confusion cover us,

for we have sinned against Yahweh our
God,
we and our ancestors, from our youth until
today,
and have not listened to the voice of
Yahweh our God.'

4 'If you come back, Israel,
Yahweh declares,
if you come back to me,
if you take your Horrors out of my
sight,
if you go roving no more,
² if you swear, "As Yahweh lives!"
truthfully, justly, uprightly,
then the nations will bless themselves by
him
and glory in him.

³ 'For Yahweh says this
to the men of Judah and Jerusalem,
"Clear the ground that lies neglected,
do not sow among thorns.
⁴ Circumcise yourselves for Yahweh,
apply circumcision to your hearts,
men of Judah and inhabitants of
Jerusalem,
or my wrath will leap out like a fire
and burn with no one to quench it,
in return for the wickedness of your
deeds." 'ᵃ

Invasion from the north

⁵ Announce it in Judah,
proclaim it in Jerusalem, say,
'Sound the trumpet in the countryside,
shout the message aloud:
Mobilise!
Take to the fortified towns!ᵇ
⁶ Signpost the way to Zion!
Run! Do not delay!
For I am bringing disaster from the
north,
an immense calamity.
⁷ The lion is up from his thicket,

4a = 21:12. 4b = 8:14.

77 READ JEREMIAH 4:1–4.

Circumcise yourselves for Yahweh, apply circumcision to your hearts.—JEREMIAH 4:4

CIRCUMCISE YOUR HEART

Law and covenant have been entirely changed. God changed the first pact with Adam, and gave a new one to Noah. He gave another to Abraham, and changed this to give a new one to Moses. When the covenant with Moses was no longer observed, he gave another pact in this last age, a pact never again to be changed. . . .

All these covenants were different from each other. Moreover, the circumcision that is approved by the giver of those covenants is the kind of circumcision spoken of by Jeremiah: *Circumcise your hearts.* . . . He promised a new covenant, different from the first, though the giver of both is one and the same. This is the covenant that he promised: *All shall know me from the least to the greatest* (see Jr 31:34). In this covenant there is no longer any circumcision of the flesh, any seal upon the people. . . .

God is truthful and his commandments are most trustworthy. Every covenant proved firm and trustworthy in its own time, and those who have been circumcised in heart are brought to life and receive a second circumcision beside the true Jordan, the waters of baptism that bring forgiveness of sins.

Jesus, son of Nun, renewed the people's circumcision with a stone knife when he had crossed the Jordan with the Israelites. Jesus, our Savior, renews the circumcision of the heart for the nations who have believed in him and are washed by baptism: circumcision *by the sword of his word, sharper than a two-edged sword* (see Heb 4:12).

Jesus, son of Nun, led the people across the Jordan into the promised land. Jesus, our Savior, has promised the land of the living to all who have crossed the true Jordan, have believed, and are circumcised in heart.

Blessed, then, are those who are circumcised in heart, and have been reborn in water through the second circumcision. They will receive their inheritance with Abraham, the faithful leader and father of all nations, for his faith was credited to him for righteousness" (see Gn 15:6).

ST. APHRAATES OF PERSIA, d. 345?

YOU WILL FIND THE NEXT READING AT JEREMIAH 8.

the destroyer of nations is on his way,
he has come from his home
to reduce your land to a desert;
your towns will be in ruins, uninhabited.
⁸ So wrap yourselves in sackcloth,
lament and wail,
since Yahweh's burning anger
has not turned away from us.

⁹ 'That day,' Yahweh declares,
'the king's heart will fail him,
the princes' hearts will fail them too,
the priests will stand aghast,
the prophets stupefied.'
¹⁰ Then I said, 'Ah, Lord Yahweh,
how sadly you deceived this people and
Jerusalem

when you used to say, "You will have
    peace,"
whereas the sword is now at our throats!
¹¹ When that time comes, this will be said
to this people and to Jerusalem:
The scorching wind from the desert
    heights
comes towards the daughter of my people
—and not to winnow or to cleanse!
¹² A gale of wind comes to me from over
    there.
Now I myself shall pass sentence on them!'

¹³ Look, he is advancing like the clouds,
his chariots like a hurricane,
his horses swifter than eagles.
Disaster for us! We are lost!
¹⁴ Wash your heart clean of wickedness,
    Jerusalem,
and so be saved.
How long will you go on harbouring
your pernicious thoughts?
¹⁵ For a voice from Dan shouts the news,
proclaims disaster from the highlands of
    Ephraim.
¹⁶ Report it to the nations,
proclaim it to Jerusalem,
'Enemies are coming from a distant
    country,
shouting their war cry against the towns of
    Judah;
¹⁷ they surround her like watchmen round a
    field
because she has rebelled against me',
Yahweh declares.
¹⁸ 'Your own behaviour and actions
have brought this on yourself.
Your wickedness, how bitter,
has stabbed you to the heart!'

¹⁹ In the pit of my stomach how great my
    agony!
Walls of my heart!
My heart is throbbing!
I cannot keep quiet,
for I have heard the trumpet call,
the battle cry.

²⁰ Ruin on ruin is the news:
the whole land is laid waste,
my tents are suddenly destroyed,
in one moment all that sheltered me.
²¹ How long must I see the standard
and hear the trumpet call?

²² 'This is because my people are stupid,
they do not know me,
they are slow-witted children,
they have no understanding,
they are clever enough at doing wrong,
but do not know how to do right.'

²³ I looked to the earth—it was a formless
    waste;
to the heavens, and their light had gone.
²⁴ I looked to the mountains—they were
    quaking
and all the hills rocking to and fro.
²⁵ I looked—there was no one at all,
the very birds of heaven had all fled.
²⁶ I looked—the fruitful land was a desert,
all its towns in ruins
before Yahweh,
before his burning anger.
²⁷ Yes, Yahweh has said this,
'The whole country will be laid waste,
though I shall not annihilate it completely.
²⁸ For this, the earth will go into mourning
and the heavens above grow dark.
For I have spoken, I have decided,
I shall not change my mind or go back
    on it.'

²⁹ At the din of horseman and archer
the entire city takes to flight:
some plunge into the thickets,
others scale the rocks;
every town is abandoned,
not a single person is left there.
³⁰ And, once despoiled, what are you going
    to do?
You may dress yourself in scarlet,
put on ornaments of gold,
enlarge your eyes with paint
but you make yourself pretty in vain.

Your former lovers disdain you,
your life is what they are seeking.
31 Yes, I hear screams like those of a woman
    in labour,
anguish like that of a woman giving birth
    to her first child;
they are the screams of the daughter of
    Zion, gasping,
hands outstretched,
'Unhappy me! I am dying,
the murderers have killed me!'

Reasons for the invasion

5 Rove the streets of Jerusalem,
  now look and enquire,
see in her squares
if you can find an individual,
one individual who does right
and seeks the truth,
and I will pardon her,
Yahweh says.
2 Although they say, 'As Yahweh lives,'
they are, in fact, swearing a false oath.
3 Yahweh, do your eyes not look for truth?
You have struck them; they have not
    felt it.
You have annihilated them, for they
    ignored the lesson.
They have set their faces harder than rock,
they have refused to repent.
4 I thought, 'These are only the poor!
They behave stupidly
since they do not know Yahweh's way
or the ruling of their God.
5 I shall approach the great men
and speak to them,
for these will know Yahweh's way
and the ruling of their God.'
But these, too, have broken the yoke,
have burst the bonds.
6 And so, a lion from the forest will
    slaughter them,
a wolf from the plains will despoil them,
a leopard will be lurking round their
    towns:
anyone who goes out will be torn to
    pieces—

because of their many crimes,
their countless infidelities.
7 'Why should I pardon you?
Your sons have abandoned me,
to swear by gods that are not gods at all.
I fed them full, and they became
    adulterers,
they hurried to the brothel.
8 They are well-fed, roving stallions,
each neighing for his neighbour's wife.
9 Shall I fail to punish this,
Yahweh demands,
or on such a nation
to exact vengeance?ᵃ
10 Scale her terraces! Destroy!
But do not annihilate her completely!
Strip off her branches,
for Yahweh does not own them!
11 How treacherously they have treated me,
the House of Israel and the House of
    Judah!
Yahweh declares.

12 'They have denied Yahweh,
they have said, "He is nothing;
no evil will overtake us,
we shall not see sword or famine.
13 And the prophets? Nothing but wind;
the word is not in them;
let those very things happen to them!" '
14 Because of this,
Yahweh, God Sabaoth, says this,
'Since you have said such things,
now I shall make my words
a fire in your mouth,
and make this people wood,
for the fire to devour.
15 Now I shall bring on you
a nation from afar, House of Israel,
Yahweh declares,
an enduring nation,
an ancient nation,
a nation whose language you do not
    know,

5a = 5:29; 9:8.

nor can you grasp what they say.

16 Their quiver a gaping tomb,
they are all of them fighters.

17 They will devour your harvest and your
food,
devour your sons and daughters,
devour your flocks and herds,
devour your vines and fig trees,
and demolish your fortified towns
in which you trust—with the sword!'

Lesson to be drawn from the punishment

18 'Yet even in those days, Yahweh declares, I shall not annihilate you completely.

19 'And when you ask, "Why has Yahweh our God done all this to us?" you will give them this answer, "As you abandon me to serve alien gods in your own country, so you must serve aliens in a country not your own."

In a time of famine (?)

20 'Announce this in the House of Jacob,
proclaim it in Judah, and say,

21 "Now listen to this,
stupid, brainless people
who have eyes and do not see,
who have ears and do not hear!

22 Have you no fear of me?
Yahweh demands.
Will you not tremble before me
who set the sand as limit to the sea,
as an everlasting barrier it cannot pass?
Its waves may toss but not prevail,
they may roar but cannot pass beyond.

23 But this people
has a rebellious, unruly heart;
they have rebelled and gone!

24 Nor do they say to themselves:
Now we ought to fear Yahweh our
God
who gives the rain, of autumn
and of spring, at the right season,
and reserves us
the weeks appointed for harvest.

25 Your misdeeds have upset all this,
your sins have deprived you of these
blessings."

Resumption of the theme of the invasion

26 Yes, there are wicked men among my
people
who watch like fowlers on the alert;
they set traps
and they catch human beings.

27 Like a cage full of birds
so are their houses full of loot;
they have grown rich and powerful
because of it,

28 they are fat, they are sleek,
in wickedness they go to any lengths:
they have no respect for rights,
for orphans' rights, and yet they succeed!
They have not upheld the cause of the
needy.

29 Shall I fail to punish this,
Yahweh demands,
or on such a nation
to exact vengeance?[b]

30 Horrible, disgusting things
are happening in the land:

31 the prophets prophesy falsely
and the priests exploit the people.
And my people love it!
But when the end comes, what will you
do?

More about the invasion

6 Flee in a body, Benjaminites,
right away from Jerusalem!
Sound the trumpet in Tekoa![a]
Light the beacon on Beth-ha-Cherem!
For disaster lowers from the north,
an immense calamity.

2 Beautiful, delicate as she is,
I shall destroy the daughter of Zion!

3 Shepherds are advancing on her
with their flocks.
They have pitched their tents all round
her,
each grazes his part.

4 Prepare for holy war against her!

5b = 5:9; 9:8.

6a Both towns are south, but in sight, of Jerusalem.

To arms! We shall attack at noon!
Disaster for us! The light is fading,
the evening shadows lengthen.
⁵ To arms! We shall attack at night
and destroy her palaces.
⁶ For Yahweh Sabaoth says this,
'Cut down trees,
throw up an earthwork outside Jerusalem:
this is the city to be punished,
with nothing but oppression in her.
⁷ As a well keeps its water fresh
so she keeps her wickedness fresh.
Violence and ruin are what you hear
in her,
wounds and blows always forced on my
attention.
⁸ Reform, Jerusalem,
or I shall turn my attention away from you
and reduce you to a desert,
a land without people.'
⁹ Yahweh Sabaoth says this,
'They will glean, glean what is left of
Israel
like a vine.
Like a grape-picker, pass your hand again
over the branches!'
¹⁰ To whom should I speak, whom warn,
for them to hear?
Look, their ears are uncircumcised,
they cannot listen.
Look, for them Yahweh's word is
something to sneer at,
they have no taste for it.
¹¹ So I am full of Yahweh's wrath,
I am weary of holding it in.
Then pour it on the children in the streets,
and on the bands of youths as well,
for husband and wife will both be taken,
the greybeard and the man weighed down
with years.
¹² Their houses will pass to other men,
so will their fields and wives.
Yes, I shall stretch my hand
over those living in this country,
Yahweh declares.
¹³ For, from the least to greatest,
they are all greedy for gain;

prophet no less than priest,
all of them practise fraud.
¹⁴ Without concern they dress my people's
wound,
saying, 'Peace! Peace!'
whereas there is no peace.
¹⁵ They should be ashamed of their
loathsome deeds.
Not they! They feel no shame,
they do not even know how to blush.
And so as others fall, they too will fall,
will be thrown down when I come and
punish them,
Yahweh says.ᵇ

¹⁶ Yahweh says this,
'Stand at the crossroads and look,
ask for the ancient paths:
which was the good way? Take it
and you will find rest for yourselves.
But they have said, "We will not take it."
¹⁷ I posted look-outs on your behalf:
Listen to the sound of the trumpet!
But they said, "We will not listen."
¹⁸ Then hear, you nations,
and know, assembly,
what is going to happen to them!
¹⁹ Listen, earth!
Watch, I shall bring disaster
on this people:
it is the fruit of the way they think,
since they have not listened to my words
nor to my law, but have rejected it.
²⁰ What do I care about incense
imported from Sheba,
or fragrant cane
from a distant country?
Your burnt offerings are not acceptable,
your sacrifices do not please me.'
²¹ And so, Yahweh says this,
'In front of this people I shall now lay
obstacles
for them to stumble over;
father and son alike,
neighbour and friend will perish.'

6b = 8:10–12.

²² Yahweh says this,
'Look, a people is coming from the land of
the north,
from the far ends of the earth a great
nation is rising;
²³ they are armed with bow and spear,
they are cruel and pitiless;
their noise is like the roaring of the sea;
they are riding horses,
they are ready to fight against you as one
man,
against you, daughter of Zion.^c
²⁴ We have heard the news,
our hands fall limp,
anguish has gripped us,
pain like that of a woman in labour.
²⁵ Do not go out into the countryside,
do not venture onto the roads,
for the enemy's sword is there,
terror on every side.
²⁶ Put on sackcloth, daughter of my
people,
roll in ashes;
mourn as for an only son,
a very bitter dirge.
For on us suddenly
the destroyer is coming.

²⁷ 'I have appointed you as tester of my
people,
to learn and to test how they behave.
²⁸ All of them are total rebels
peddlers of slander,
hard as bronze and iron,
all agents of corruption.
²⁹ The bellows blast away
to make the fire burn away the lead.
In vain the smelter does his work,
for the dross is not purged out.
³⁰ "Silver-reject", men call them,
and indeed Yahweh has rejected them!'

True worship

7 The word that came to Jeremiah from
Yahweh, saying, ² 'Stand at the gate of the
Temple of Yahweh and there proclaim this
message. Say, "Listen to the word of Yahweh,
all you of Judah who come in by these gates to
worship Yahweh. ³ Yahweh Sabaoth, the God
of Israel, says this: Amend your behaviour and
your actions and I will let you stay in this
place. ⁴ Do not put your faith in delusive
words, such as: This is Yahweh's sanctuary,
Yahweh's sanctuary, Yahweh's sanctuary!
⁵ But if you really amend your behaviour and
your actions, if you really treat one another
fairly, ⁶ if you do not exploit the stranger, the
orphan and the widow, if you do not shed innocent blood in this place and if you do not follow other gods, to your own ruin, ⁷ then I shall
let you stay in this place, in the country I gave
for ever to your ancestors of old. ⁸ Look, you
are putting your faith in delusive, worthless
words! ⁹ Steal, would you, murder, commit
adultery, perjure yourselves, burn incense to
Baal, follow other gods of whom you know
nothing? — ¹⁰ and then come and stand before
me in this Temple that bears my name, saying:
Now we are safe to go on doing all these loathsome things! ¹¹ Do you look on this Temple
that bears my name as a den of bandits? I, at
any rate, can see straight, Yahweh declares.

¹² "Now go to the place which used to be
mine at Shiloh, where I once gave my name a
home; see what I have done to it because of the
wickedness of my people Israel! ¹³ And now,
since you have done all these things, Yahweh
declares, and refused to listen when I spoke so
urgently, so persistently, or to answer when I
called you, ¹⁴ I shall treat this Temple that
bears my name, and in which you put your
heart, the place that I gave you and your ancestors, just as I treated Shiloh, ¹⁵ and I shall
drive you out of my sight, as I did all your
kinsfolk, the whole race of Ephraim."

¹⁶ 'You, for your part, must not intercede for
this people, nor raise either plea or prayer on
their behalf; do not plead with me, for I will
not listen to you. ¹⁷ Can you not see what they
are doing in the towns of Judah and in the
streets of Jerusalem? ¹⁸ The children collect
the wood, the fathers light the fire, the women

6c = 50:41–43.

knead the dough, to make cakes for the Queen of Heaven;[a] and, to spite me, they pour libations to alien gods. ¹⁹Is it really me they spite, Yahweh demands, is it not in fact themselves, to their own confusion? ²⁰So, Lord Yahweh says this, "My anger, my wrath will be poured down on this place, on man and beast, on the trees of the countryside and the fruits of the soil; it will burn, and not be quenched."

²¹'Yahweh Sabaoth, the God of Israel, says this, "Add your burnt offerings to your sacrifices and eat all the meat. ²²For when I brought your ancestors out of Egypt, I said nothing to them, gave them no orders, about burnt offerings or sacrifices. ²³My one command to them was this: Listen to my voice, then I will be your God and you shall be my people. In everything, follow the way that I mark out for you, and you shall prosper. ²⁴But they did not listen, they did not pay attention; they followed their own devices, their own stubborn and wicked inclinations, and got worse rather than better. ²⁵From the day your ancestors left Egypt until today, I have sent you all my servants the prophets, persistently sending them day after day. ²⁶But they have not listened to me, have not paid attention; they have deliberately resisted, behaving worse than their ancestors. ²⁷So you will tell them all this, but they will not listen to you; you will call them, but they will not answer you." ²⁸Then you are to say to them, "This is the nation that will neither listen to the voice of Yahweh its God nor take correction. Sincerity is no more, it has vanished from their mouths.

²⁹"Cut off your tresses, throw them away!
  On the bare heights raise a dirge,
  for Yahweh has rejected, has abandoned,
  a brood that enrages him!"

³⁰'Yes, the people of Judah have done what displeases me, Yahweh declares. They have set up their Horrors in the Temple that bears my name, to defile it, ³¹and have built the high places of Topheth[b] in the Valley of Ben-Hinnom, to burn their sons and daughters: a thing I never ordered, that had never entered my thoughts.[c] ³²So now the days are coming, Yahweh declares, when people will no longer say Topheth or Valley of Ben-Hinnom, but Valley of Slaughter. Topheth will become a burial ground, for lack of other space; ³³the corpses of this people will be food for the birds of the sky and the animals of earth, and there will be no one to drive them off. ³⁴I shall silence the shouts of rejoicing and mirth and the voices of bridegroom and bride, in the towns of Judah and the streets of Jerusalem, for the country will be reduced to desert.'

8 'When that time comes, Yahweh declares, the bones of the kings of Judah, the bones of its chief men, the bones of the priests, the bones of the prophets and the bones of the inhabitants of Jerusalem, will be taken from their tombs. ²They will be spread out before the sun, the moon, the whole array of heaven, whom they have loved and served, followed, consulted and worshipped. They will not be gathered or reburied but will be left lying on the surface like dung.[a] ³And death will seem preferable to life to all the survivors of this wicked race, wherever I have driven them, Yahweh Sabaoth declares.

Threats, laments, advice Israel's perversity

⁴'You are to tell them, "Yahweh says this:
  If someone falls, can he not stand up
    again?
  If people stray, can they not turn back?
⁵Why does this people persist in acts of
    infidelity,
  why does Jerusalem persist in continuous
    infidelity?
  They cling to illusion,
  they refuse to turn back.

7a Mesopotamian goddess of fertility.

7b The rubbish-dump of Jerusalem, where children were also sacrificed.

7c = 32:34–35.

8a = 25:33.

⁶ I have listened attentively:
they have never said anything like that.
Not one repents of wickedness
saying: What have I done?
Each one keeps returning to the course
like a horse charging into battle.
⁷ Even the stork in the sky
knows the appropriate season;
turtledove, swallow and crane
observe their time of migration.
But my people do not know
Yahweh's laws!" '

The Law as administered by the priests

⁸ How can you say, 'We are wise,
since we have Yahweh's Law?'
Look how it has been falsified
by the lying pen of the scribes!
⁹ The wise are put to shame,
alarmed, caught out
because they have rejected Yahweh's word.
What price their wisdom now?

Repetition of an earlier threat ᵇ

¹⁰ So I shall give their wives to other men,
their fields to new masters,
for, from the least to greatest,
they are all greedy for gain;
prophet no less than priest,
all of them practise fraud.
¹¹ Without concern they dress
the wound of the daughter of my people,
saying, 'Peace! Peace!'
whereas there is no peace.
¹² They should be ashamed of their
loathsome deeds.
Not they! They feel no shame,
they do not even know how to blush.
And so as others fall, they too will fall,
will be thrown down when the time for
punishing them comes,
Yahweh says.

Threats against Judah the Vine

¹³ I shall put an end to them, Yahweh
declares,
no more grapes on the vine,

no more figs on the fig tree
only withered leaves:
I have found them people to trample on
them!
¹⁴ Why are we sitting still?
Mobilise!
Take to the fortified towns ᶜ
and there fall silent,
since Yahweh our God means to
silence us
by giving us poisoned water to drink
because we have sinned against him.
¹⁵ We are hoping for peace—no good
came of it!
For the time of healing—nothing but
terror! ᵈ
¹⁶ From Dan you can hear
the snorting of his horses;
at the neighing of his stallions
the whole country quakes;
they are coming to devour the country and
its contents,
the town and those that live in it.
¹⁷ Yes, now I am sending you
poisonous snakes
against which no charm exists;
and they will bite you,
Yahweh declares.

A lament of the prophet during a famine

¹⁸ Incurable sorrow overtakes me,
my heart fails me.
¹⁹ Hark, from the daughter of my people the
cry for help,
ringing far and wide throughout the
land!
'Is Yahweh no longer in Zion,
her King no longer there?'
(Why have they provoked me with their
idols,
with their futile foreign gods?)
²⁰ 'Harvest is over, summer at an end,
and we have not been saved!'

8b A duplicate of 6:12–15, absent in the Gk text.
8c = 4:5.
8d = 14:19.

78 READ JEREMIAH 8:4–7.

If someone falls, can he not stand up again?—JEREMIAH 8:4

SURE-FOOTED SINNERS

A sinner who repents learns to be prudent. He is like an ass that, once he has fallen in a spot, afterwards looks more carefully where he sets his foot. For fear of punishment he takes care not to fall into those sins again or into any others.

O great idiot who keeps on sinning! Why don't you consider what the ass teaches you about saving your soul? The ass doesn't fall again, but you always do. If you would only turn to God with love, you would learn much about prudence.

O children, don't you know that when you are learning to write with a pen you make blots? And you who want to ride a horse, don't you know you will never learn unless you fall sometimes?

Now I want to ask older people about this. Old man and old woman, are you there?

"Yes."

Tell me, have you fallen into sin over and over again?

"Yes."

Well, have you returned to God?

"Yes."

See, you would never have learned what sin is unless you had tried it. Scripture says "In the old is prudence" (see Jb 12:12), and do you know why? Because they have experience. They have fallen often, and so they walk more gingerly. They think about how they had better set their feet. As they see death approaching, they thank God that they have had time to turn to him. And they do not trust themselves not to fall, but always ask God to help them not to fall again.

ST. BERNARDINO OF SIENA, 1380–1444

YOU WILL FIND THE NEXT READING AT JEREMIAH 10.

21 The wound of the daughter of my people
      wounds me too,
  all looks dark to me, terror grips me.
22 Is there no balm in Gilead any more?
  Is no doctor there?
  Then why is there no progress
  in the cure of the daughter of my people?
23 Who will turn my head into a fountain,
  and my eyes into a spring of tears,
  that I can weep day and night
  over the slain of the daughter of my
      people?

The moral corruption of Judah

9 Who will find me a wayfarer's shelter
  in the desert,
  for me to quit my people,
  and leave them far behind?
  For all of them are adulterers,
  a conspiracy of traitors.
2 They bend their tongues like a bow;
  not truth but falsehood
  holds sway in the land;
  yes, they go from crime to crime,

but me they do not know,
Yahweh declares.
3 Let each be on his guard against his
friend;
do not trust a brother,
for every brother aims but to supplant,
and every friend is a peddler of slander.
4 Each one cheats his friend,
never telling the truth;
they have trained their tongues to lie
and devote all their energies to doing
wrong.
5 You live in a world of bad faith!
Out of bad faith, they refuse to know me,
Yahweh declares.
6 And, so, Yahweh Sabaoth declares,
now I shall purge them and test them,
no other way to treat the daughter of my
people!
7 Their tongue is a deadly arrow,
their words are in bad faith;
with his mouth each wishes his neighbour
peace,
while in his heart plotting a trap for
him.
8 Shall I fail to punish them for this,
Yahweh demands,
or on such a nation
fail to exact vengeance?*a*

Sorrow in Zion

9 I raise the wail and lament for the
mountains,
the dirge for the desert pastures,
for they have been burnt: no one passes
there,
the sound of flocks is heard no more.
Birds of the sky and animals,
all have fled, all are gone.
10 I shall make Jerusalem a heap of ruins,
a lair for jackals,
and the towns of Judah
an uninhabited wasteland.

11 Who is wise enough to understand this?
To whom has Yahweh's mouth spoken to explain it?

Why is the country annihilated,
burnt like the desert where no one passes?

12 Yahweh says, 'This is because they have
forsaken my Law which I gave them and have
not listened to my voice or followed it, 13 but
have followed their own stubborn hearts, have
followed the Baals as their ancestors taught
them.' 14 So Yahweh Sabaoth, the God of Israel, says this, 'Now I shall give this people
wormwood to eat and poisoned water to
drink.*b* 15 I shall scatter them among nations
unknown to their ancestors or to them; and I
shall pursue them with the sword until I have
annihilated them.'

16 Yahweh Sabaoth says this,
'Prepare to call for the mourning
women!
Send for those who are best at it!
17 Let them lose no time in raising the
lament over us!
Let our eyes rain tears,
our eyelids run with weeping!
18 A lament makes itself heard in Zion,
"What ruin is ours,
what utter shame!
For we must leave the country,
our homes have been knocked down!" '
19 Now listen, you women, to Yahweh's
word,
let your ears take in the word his own
mouth speaks.
Teach your daughters how to wail
and teach one another this dirge,
20 'Death has climbed in at our windows,
and made its way into our palaces;
it has cut down the children in the
street,
the young people in the squares—
21 Speak! Yahweh declares this—
human corpses are strewn
like dung in the open field,
like sheaves left by the reaper,
with no one to gather them.'

9a = 5:9, 29.   9b = 23:15.

True wisdom

22 Yahweh says this,
'Let the sage not boast of wisdom,
  nor the valiant of valour,
  nor the wealthy of riches!
23 But let anyone who wants to boast, boast
    of this:
  of understanding and knowing me.
For I am Yahweh, who acts with faithful
    love,
  justice, and uprightness on earth;
  yes, these are what please me,'
Yahweh declares.

Circumcision, a false guarantee

24 'Look, the days are coming, Yahweh declares, when I shall punish all who are circumcised only in the flesh: 25 Egypt, Judah, Edom, the Ammonites, Moab, and all the men with shaven temples who live in the desert. For all those nations, and the whole House of Israel too, are uncircumcised at heart.'

Idols and the true God

10 Listen, House of Israel, to the word that Yahweh addresses to you. Yahweh says this:

2 'Do not learn the ways of the nations
  or take alarm at the heavenly signs,
  alarmed though the nations may be at
    them.
3 Yes, the customs of the peoples are quite
    futile:
  wood, nothing more, cut out of a forest,
  worked with a blade by a carver's hand,
4 then embellished with silver and gold,
  then fastened with hammer and nails
  to keep it from moving.
5 Like scarecrows in a melon patch, they
    cannot talk,
  they have to be carried, since they cannot
    walk.
Have no fear of them: they can do no
    harm
  —nor any good either!'

6 Yahweh, there is no one like you,
  so great you are,
  so great your mighty name.
7 Who would not revere you, King of
    nations?
  Yes, this is your due.
Since of all the wise among the nations,
  and in all their kingdoms,
  there is not a single one like you.

8 All of them are brutish and stupid:
  the Futile Ones' teaching is but wood,
9 silver leaf imported from Tarshish
  and gold from Ophir,
  the work of carver or goldsmith;
  then dressed up in violet and purple,
  all the work of skilled men.
10 But Yahweh is the true God.
He is the living God,
  the everlasting King.
The earth quakes when he is wrathful,
  the nations cannot endure his fury.

11 'Tell them this, "The gods who did not make the heavens and the earth will vanish from the earth and from under these heavens." '

12 By his power he made the earth,
  by his wisdom set the world firm,
  but his discernment spread out the
    heavens.
13 When he thunders
  there is a roaring of waters in heaven;
  he raises clouds from the remotest parts of
    the earth,
  makes the lightning flash for the
    downpour,
  and brings the wind from his storehouse.
14 At this all people stand stupefied,
    uncomprehending,
  every goldsmith blushes for his idols;
  his castings are but delusion,
  with no breath in them.
15 They are futile, a laughable production;
  when the time comes for them to be
    punished, they will vanish.

79 READ JEREMIAH 10:1–16.

Every goldsmith blushes for his idols; his castings are but delusion, with no breath in them.—JEREMIAH 10:14

PLEASING GOD

We do not honor with numerous sacrifices and garlands of flowers such deities as men have formed and set in shrines and called *gods* because we see that these are soulless and dead. They do not have the form of God (for we do not consider that God has such a form as some say that they imitate to his honor), but have the names and forms of those wicked demons that have appeared. For why do we need to tell you who already know into what forms the craftsmen, carving and cutting, casting and hammering, fashion the materials? . . .

But we have received by tradition that God does not need any material offerings because he himself is the provider of all things. And . . . we are convinced that he accepts only those who imitate the excellent qualities that reside in him—temperance, justice, generosity, and all virtues peculiar to a God who is called by no proper name. . . . In the beginning, out of his goodness and for our sake, he created all things from unformed matter. If we by our works show ourselves worthy of this, his design, we are deemed worthy . . . of reigning in company with him, freed from corruption and suffering.

For as in the beginning he created us when we were not, so do we consider that, similarly those who choose to do what is pleasing to him are, because of their choice, deemed worthy of incorruption and of fellowship with him. For the coming into being at first was not in our own power; and in order that we may use the rationality he has given us to choose to please him, he both persuades us and leads us to faith. ST. JUSTIN, 100?–165

YOU WILL FIND THE NEXT READING AT JEREMIAH 16.

16 The Heritage of Jacob is not like these,
  for he is the maker of everything,
  and Israel is the tribe that is his heritage.
  His name is Yahweh Sabaoth.[a]

Punic in the country

17 Pick up your pack from the ground,
  you the besieged!
18 For Yahweh says this,
  'Now I shall throw out
  the inhabitants of the country,
  this time,
  and bring distress on them,
  so that they may find me!'

19 Disaster is on me! What a wound!
  My injury is incurable!
  And I used to think,
  'If this is the worst, I can bear it!'
20 But now my tent is destroyed,
  all my ropes are snapped,
  my sons have left me and are no more;
  no one is left to put my tent up again
  or to hang the side-cloths.
21 The shepherds are the ones who have been
    stupid:
  they have not searched for Yahweh.

10a = 51:15–19.

[979]

This is why they have not prospered
and why their whole flock has been
    dispersed.
22 Listen! A terrible noise!
A mighty uproar from the land of the
    north
to reduce the towns of Judah
to desert, to a lair for jackals!

23 I know, Yahweh,
no one's course is in his control,
nor is it in anyone's power, as he goes his
    way,
to guide his own steps.
24 Correct me, Yahweh, but with
    moderation,
not in your anger, or you will reduce me to
    nothing.

25 Pour out your anger on the nations
who do not acknowledge you,
and on the families
that do not call on your name,
for they have devoured Jacob,
have devoured and made an end of him
and reduced his home to desolation.

Jeremiah and observance of the covenant

11 The word that came to Jeremiah from
Yahweh, 2 'Hear the terms of this
covenant; tell them to the people of Judah and
to the inhabitants of Jerusalem. 3 Tell them,
"Yahweh, God of Israel, says this: Cursed be
anyone who will not listen to the terms of this
covenant 4 which I ordained for your ancestors
when I brought them out of Egypt, out of that
iron-foundry. Listen to my voice, I told them,
carry out all my orders, then you will be my
people and I shall be your God, 5 so that I may
fulfil the oath I swore to your ancestors, that I
may give them a country flowing with milk
and honey, as is the case today." ' I replied, 'So
be it, Yahweh!' 6 Then Yahweh said to me,
'Proclaim all these terms in the towns of Judah
and in the streets of Jerusalem, saying, "Listen
to the terms of this covenant and obey them.
7 For when I brought your ancestors out of

Egypt, I solemnly warned them, and have persistently warned them until today, saying: Listen to my voice. 8 But they did not listen, did
not pay attention; instead, each followed his
own stubborn and wicked inclinations. And
against them, in consequence, I put into action
the words of this covenant which I had ordered them to obey and which they had not
obeyed." '

9 Yahweh said to me, 'Plainly there is conspiracy among the people of Judah and the citizens of Jerusalem. 10 They have reverted to
the sins of their ancestors who refused to listen
to my words: they too are following other gods
and serving them. The House of Israel and the
House of Judah have broken my covenant
which I made with their ancestors. 11 And so,
Yahweh says this, "I shall now bring a disaster
on them which they cannot escape; they will
call to me for help, but I shall not listen to
them. 12 The towns of Judah and the citizens
of Jerusalem will then go and call for help to
the gods to whom they burn incense, but these
will be no help at all to them in their time of
distress!

13 "For you have as many gods
as you have towns, Judah!ª
You have built as many altars to Shame,
as many incense altars to Baal,
as Jerusalem has streets!

14 "You, for your part, must not intercede
for this people, nor raise either plea or prayer
on their behalf, for I will not listen when their
distress forces them to call to me for help."

Rebuke to the frequenters of the Temple

15 'What is my beloved doing in my house?
She has achieved her wicked plans.
Can vows and consecrated meat
turn disaster from you
for you to be so happy?
16 "Green olive-tree covered in fine fruit",
was Yahweh's name for you.

11a = 2:28.

With a shattering noise
he has set fire to it,
its branches are broken.'

17 And Yahweh Sabaoth, who planted you, has decreed disaster for you because of the evil the House of Israel and the House of Judah have done, provoking me by burning incense to Baal.

Jeremiah persecuted at Anathoth

18 Yahweh informed me and I knew it; you then revealed their scheming to me. 19 I for my part was like a trustful lamb being led to the slaughterhouse, not knowing the schemes they were plotting against me, 'Let us destroy the tree in its strength, let us cut him off from the land of the living, so that his name may no longer be remembered!'

20 Yahweh Sabaoth, whose judgement is
upright,
tester of motives and thoughts,
I shall see your vengeance on them,
for I have revealed my cause to you.*b*

21 Against the people of Anathoth who are determined to kill me and say to me, 'Do not prophesy in the name of Yahweh or you will die at our hands!' 22 Yahweh says this, 'I am about to punish them. Their young people will die by the sword, their sons and daughters by famine. 23 Not one will be left when I bring disaster on the people of Anathoth, when the year for punishing them comes.'

The prosperity of the wicked

12 Your uprightness is too great, Yahweh, for me to dispute with you.
But I should like to discuss some points of
justice with you:
Why is it that the way of the wicked
prospers?
Why do all treacherous people thrive?
2 You plant them, they take root,
they flourish, yes, and bear fruit.
You are on their lips,

yet far from their heart.
3 You know me, Yahweh, you see me,
you probe my heart, which is close to
yours.
Drag them off like sheep for the
slaughterhouse,
reserve them for the day of butchery.

4 (How long will the land be in mourning, and the grass wither all over the countryside? The animals and birds are dying as a result of the wickedness of the inhabitants.)

For they say,
'God does not see our fate.'

5 'If you find it exhausting to race against
me on foot,
how will you compete against horses?
In a country at peace you feel secure,
but how will you fare in the thickets of the
Jordan?

6 'For even your brothers and your own family will betray you. They will pursue you in full cry. (Put no faith in them when they speak you fair!')

Yahweh laments his ravaged inheritance

7 I have abandoned my house,
left my heritage,
I have delivered what I dearly loved
into the clutches of its enemies.
8 To me, my heritage has behaved
like a lion in the forest,
it roared at me ferociously:
so I now hate it.
9 I see my heritage as a brightly-coloured
bird of prey
attacked by birds of prey on every side!
Go, assemble all the wild animals,
make them come and dine!
10 Many shepherds have laid my vineyard
waste,
have trampled over my plot of land,

11b = 20:12.

the plot of land which was my joy,
reducing my favourite estate
to a deserted wilderness.
11 They have made it a waste;
wasted, it mourns before me.
The whole country has been devastated
and no one takes it to heart.
12 The devastators have arrived
on all the bare heights of the desert
(for Yahweh wields a devouring sword);
from one end of the country to the other,
there is no peace for any living thing.
13 Wheat they have sown, thorns they reap:
they have worn themselves out, to no
profit.
They are disappointed in their harvests,
because of Yahweh's burning anger.

The neighbouring peoples: their judgement and salvation

14 Yahweh says this, 'As regards all my evil neighbours who have laid hands on the heritage I granted my people Israel, look, I shall uproot them from their soil, (though I shall uproot the House of Judah from among them). 15 But having uprooted them, I shall take pity on them again and bring them back each to its own heritage, each to its own country, 16 and if they carefully learn my people's ways and swear by my name, "As Yahweh lives", as they have taught my people to swear by Baal, then they will be re-established among my people. 17 But if any nation refuses to listen, I shall uproot it for ever and destroy it, Yahweh declares.'

The useless waistcloth[a]

13 Yahweh said this to me, 'Go and buy a linen waistcloth and put it round your waist. But do not dip it in water.' 2 And so, as Yahweh had ordered, I bought a waistcloth and put it round my waist. 3 A second time the word of Yahweh came to me, 4 'Take the waistcloth that you have bought and are wearing round your waist. Up, go to the Euphrates and hide it there in a hole in the rock.' 5 So I went and hid it by the Euphrates as Yahweh had ordered me. 6 A long time later, Yahweh said to me, 'Up, go to the Euphrates and fetch the waistcloth I ordered you to hide there.' 7 So I went to the Euphrates, and I searched, and I took the waistcloth from the place where I had hidden it. And there was the waistcloth ruined, no use for anything. 8 Then the word of Yahweh was addressed to me as follows, 9 'Yahweh says this, "In the same way I shall ruin the pride of Judah, the immense pride of Jerusalem. 10 This evil people, these people who refuse to listen to my words, who follow their own stubborn inclinations and run after other gods, serving and worshipping them— this people will become like this waistcloth, no good for anything. 11 For just as a waistcloth clings to a man's waist, so I made the whole House of Israel and the whole House of Judah cling to me, Yahweh declares, to be my people, my glory, my honour and my pride. But they have not listened."

The wine jugs smashed together

12 'You will also say this to them, "Yahweh, God of Israel, says this: Any jug can be filled with wine." And if they answer you, "Do you think we do not know that any jug can be filled with wine?" 13 you are to say, "Yahweh says this: Look, I shall fill all the inhabitants of this country, the kings who occupy the throne of David, the priests, the prophets and all the citizens of Jerusalem, with drunkenness. 14 Then I shall smash them one against the other, parents and children all together, Yahweh declares. Mercilessly, relentlessly, pitilessly, I shall destroy them." '

A vision of exile

15 Listen and pay attention, do not be
proud:
Yahweh is speaking!
16 Give glory to Yahweh your God
before the darkness comes,
before your feet stumble

13a The Euphrates is probably symbolised by the river Parah near Jr's home.

on the darkened mountains.
You hope for light,
but he will turn it to shadow dark as
death,
will change it to blackness.
17 If you do not listen to this warning,
I shall weep in secret for your pride;
my eyes will weep bitterly
and stream with tears,
for Yahweh's flock is being led into
captivity.

Jehoiachin threatened

18 Tell the king and the queen mother,
'Sit in a lower place,
since your glorious crown
has fallen from your head.
19 The towns of the Negeb are shut off
with no one to give access to them.
All Judah has been deported,
deported wholesale.'

An admonition to impenitent Jerusalem

20 Raise your eyes and look at these
now coming from the north.
Where is the flock once entrusted to you,
the flock which was your pride?
21 What will you say when they come and
punish you,
you yourself having taught them?
Against you, in the lead, will come your
friends.
Then will not anguish grip you
as it grips a woman in labour?
22 And should you ask yourself,
'Why is all this happening to me?'
it is because of your great guilt
that your skirts have been pulled up
and you have been manhandled.
23 Can the Ethiopian change his skin,
or the leopard his spots?
And you, can you do right,
being so accustomed to wrong?
24 'I shall scatter you like chaff
on the desert wind.
25 This is your share, the part allotted you,
from me, Yahweh declares,

because you have forgotten me
and put your trust in Delusion.
26 I am the one who pulls your skirts up over
your face
to let your shame be seen.
27 Oh! Your adulteries, your shrieks of
pleasure,
your vile prostitution!
On the hills, in the fields,
I have seen your Horrors.
Jerusalem, disaster is coming for you!
How much longer till you are made
clean?'

The great drought

14 The word of Yahweh that came to Jeremiah on the occasion of the drought.

2 'Judah is in mourning,
her towns are pining,
sinking to the ground;
a cry goes up from Jerusalem.
3 The nobles send their servants for
water,
they come to the water-tanks,
find no water,
and return with their pitchers empty.
Dismayed and bewildered,
they cover their heads.
4 Because the soil is all cracked
since the country has had no rain;
the farmers are dismayed,
they cover their heads.
5 Even the doe in the countryside
giving birth abandons her young,
for there is no grass;
6 the wild donkeys standing on the bare
heights
gasp for air like jackals:
their eyes grow dim
for lack of pasture.'

7 Although our sins witness against us,
Yahweh, for your name's sake,
intervene!
Yes, our acts of infidelity have been
many,

we have sinned against you!

8 Yahweh, hope of Israel,
its Saviour in time of distress,
why are you like a stranger in this
country,
like a traveller staying only for one
night?

9 Why are you like someone bemused,
like a warrior who has no power to
rescue?
And yet, Yahweh, you are among us,
we are called by your name.
Do not desert us!

10 Yahweh says this about this people, 'They take such pleasure in darting hither and thither, they cannot restrain their feet! But Yahweh takes pleasure in them no longer; now he will keep their guilt in mind and punish their sins.'

11 Yahweh then said to me, 'Do not intercede for this people or their welfare. 12 If they fast, I will not listen to their plea; if they offer burnt offerings and cereal offerings I will not accept them. Rather, I shall make an end of them by sword, famine and plague.'

13 'Ah, Lord Yahweh,' I answered, 'here are the prophets telling them, "You will not see the sword, famine will not touch you; I promise you true peace in this place."'

14 Then Yahweh said to me, 'The prophets are prophesying lies in my name; I have not sent them, I gave them no orders, I never spoke to them. Delusive visions, hollow predictions, daydreams of their own, that is what they prophesy to you. 15 Therefore, Yahweh says this: The prophets who prophesy in my name when I have not sent them, and tell you there will be no sword or famine in this country, these same prophets will meet their end by sword and famine. 16 And as for the people to whom they prophesy, they will be tossed into the streets of Jerusalem, victims of famine and the sword, with not a soul to bury them: neither them nor their wives, nor their sons, nor their daughters. I shall pour their own wickedness down on them.

17 'So say this word to them:
May my eyes shed tears
night and day, unceasingly,
since the daughter of my people has
sustained a fearsome wound,
a crippling injury.

18 If I go into the countryside,
there lie those killed by the sword;
if I go into the city,
I see people tortured with hunger;
even prophets and priests
roam the country at their wits' end.'

19 Have you rejected Judah altogether?
Does your very soul revolt at Zion?
Why have you struck us down without
hope of cure?
We were hoping for peace—no good came
of it!
For the moment of cure—nothing but
terror!ᵃ

20 Yahweh, we acknowledge our wickedness
and our ancestors' guilt:
we have indeed sinned against you.

21 For your name's sake do not reject us,
do not dishonour the throne of your glory.
Remember us; do not break your covenant
with us.

22 Can any of the nations' Futile Ones make
it rain?
Can the heavens of their own accord give
showers?
Are you not the one, Yahweh our God?
In you is our hope,
since you make all these things.

15 Yahweh said to me, 'Even if Moses and Samuel pleaded before me, I could not sympathise with this people! Drive them out of my sight; away with them! 2 And if they ask you, "Where shall we go?" tell them this, "Yahweh says this:

Those for the plague, to the plague;
those for the sword, to the sword;

14a = 8:15.

those for famine, to famine;
those for captivity, to captivity!ª

3 "I shall consign them to four kinds of thing, Yahweh declares: the sword to kill, the dogs to drag away, the birds of heaven and wild animals of earth to devour and to destroy. 4 I shall make them an object of horror to all the kingdoms of the earth, because of Manasseh son of Hezekiah, king of Judah, and what he did in Jerusalem." '

The horrors of war

5 Who is there to pity you, Jerusalem,
who to grieve for you,
who to go out of his way
and ask how you are?
6 'You yourself have rejected me, Yahweh
declares,
you have turned your back on me;
so I have stretched my hand over you and
destroyed you.
Tired of relenting,
7 I have winnowed them with a winnow
at the country's gates.
They have been bereft, I have destroyed
my people,
but they refuse to leave their ways.
8 I have made their widows outnumber
the sand of the sea.
On the mother of young warriors
I bring the destroyer in broad daylight.
Suddenly I bring
anguish and terror down on her.
9 The mother of seven sons grows faint
and gasps for breath.
It is still day, but already her sun has set,
she is dismayed and distracted;
and the rest of them I shall consign to the
sword,
to their enemies, Yahweh declares.'

The call b of Jeremiah renewed

10 A disaster for me, mother, that you bore me
to be a man of strife and dissension for the
whole country.
I neither lend nor borrow,

yet all of them curse me.
11 Have I not genuinely done my best to
serve you, Yahweh?
Have I not interceded with you
in time of disaster and distress!
12 'Can iron break the iron of the north and
the bronze?
13 Your wealth and your treasures
I shall hand over to plunder, without
repayment,
because of all your sins, throughout your
territory.
14 I shall enslave you to your enemies
in a country which you do not know,
for my anger has kindled a fire
that will burn you up.' c

15 Yahweh, you know!
Remember me, take care of me,
and avenge me on my persecutors.
However long your anger endures, do not
snatch me away.
Realise that I suffer insult for your sake.
16 When your words came, I devoured them:
your word was my delight
and the joy of my heart;
for I was called by your Name,
Yahweh, God Sabaoth.
17 I never sat in the company of scoffers
amusing myself;
with your hands on me I held myself aloof,
since you had filled me with indignation.
18 Why is my suffering continual,
my wound incurable, refusing to be
healed?
Truly, for me you are a deceptive stream
with uncertain waters!

19 To which Yahweh replied,
'If you repent, I shall restore you
to plead before me.

15a = 43:11.

15b The 'confessions of Jr' (11:18–12:5; 15:10–21; 17:14–18; 18:18–23; 20:7–18) show Jr in a dialogue of astounding intimacy with Yahweh.

15c = 17:3–4.

If you distinguish between the precious
and the base,
you shall be as my own mouth.
They will come back to you,
but you must not go back to them.
20 As far as these people are concerned, I
shall make you
a fortified wall of bronze.
They will fight against you
but will not overcome you,
because I am with you
to save you and rescue you,
Yahweh declares.
21 I shall rescue you from the clutches of the
wicked
and redeem you from the grasp of the
violent.'

The prophet's life is itself symbolic

16 The word of Yahweh was addressed to
me as follows:
2 'You are not to marry or have sons and
daughters in this place. 3 For Yahweh says this
regarding the sons and daughters to be born in
this place, about the mothers who give birth to
them, and about the fathers who beget them in
this land, 4 "They will die of deadly diseases,
unlamented and unburied; they will be like
dung spread on the ground; they will meet
their end by sword and famine, and their
corpses will be food for the birds of the sky and
the beasts of earth."

5 'Yes, Yahweh says this, "Go into no house
where there is mourning, do not go and
lament or grieve with them; for I have withdrawn my peace from this people, Yahweh declares, and faithful love and pity too. 6 High or
low, they will die in this country, without burial or lament; there will be no gashing, no
shaving of the head for them. 7 No bread will
be broken for the mourner to comfort him for
the dead; no cup of consolation will be offered
him for his father or his mother.

8 "And do not enter a house where there is
feasting, to sit with them and eat and drink.
9 For Yahweh Sabaoth, the God of Israel, says
this: In this place, before your eyes, in your
own days, I will silence the shouts of rejoicing
and mirth and the voices of bridegroom and
bride.

10 "When you tell these people this and they
ask you: Why has Yahweh decreed such complete and total disaster for us? What have we
done wrong? What sin have we committed
against Yahweh our God? 11 then you are to
answer: It is because your ancestors abandoned me, Yahweh declares, and followed
other gods, and served and worshipped them.
They abandoned me and did not keep my
Law. 12 And you for your part have behaved
even worse than your ancestors. Look, each of
you follows his own stubborn and wicked inclinations, without listening to me. 13 And so, I
shall eject you from this country into a country
unknown to you or to your ancestors, and
there you can serve other gods, day and night,
for I shall show you no more favour."

The return of the scattered Israelites

14 'Look, the days are coming, Yahweh declares, when people will no longer say, "As
Yahweh lives who brought the Israelites out of
Egypt!" 15 but, "As Yahweh lives who brought
the Israelites back from the land of the north
and all the countries to which he had driven
them." I shall bring them back to the very soil
I gave their ancestors.'[a]

The invasion foretold

16 'Watch, I shall send for many fishermen,
Yahweh declares, and these will fish them up;
next, I shall send for many huntsmen, and
these will hunt them out of every mountain,
every hill, and out of the holes in the rocks.
17 For my eyes watch all their ways, these are
not hidden from me, and their guilt does not
escape my gaze. 18 I shall requite their guilt
and their sin twice over, since they have polluted my country with the carcasses of their
Horrors, and filled my heritage with their
Abominations.'[b]

16a = 23:7–8.

16b The Horrors and Abominations are idols.

80 READ JEREMIAH 16:14–21.

To you the nations will come from the remotest parts of the earth.—JEREMIAH 16:19

FISHERS OF PEOPLE

. . . I would be glad to pour out my soul even to the point of death, if the Lord would so grant it me, because I am so much in God's debt. For he gave me such great grace, that many people through me were reborn to God, and afterward confirmed and brought to perfection. And so then a clergy was ordained for them everywhere, to care for this people freshly brought alive in their faith. They are those whom the Lord has chosen "from the remotest parts of the earth," just as before he had promised by his prophets: "To you the nations will come from the remotest parts of the earth, and say, ". . . Can human beings make their own gods? These are not gods at all!" And again: "I shall make you a light to the nations so that my salvation may reach the remotest parts of earth" (Is 49:6).

And there I want to "await his promise," for he never deceives, as he promises in the gospel: ". . . Many will come from east and west and sit down with Abraham and Isaac and Jacob" (Mt 8:11); just as we believe that the faithful will come from the whole world.

So, therefore it is our duty to fish well and with loving care, just as the Lord urges and teaches us: "Come after me and I will make you fishers of people" (Mt 4:19). And again through the prophets, "Look, I send fishers and many hunters, says God" (see Jr 16:16) and so forth. Because of this, it was vital that we let down our nets so that a "vast crowd and multitude" (see Lk 16:16) might be taken for God. Also that everywhere there might be priests who might baptize and teach a needy and willing people.   ST. PATRICK, 389–461

YOU WILL FIND THE NEXT READING AT JEREMIAH 17.

The conversion of the nations

19 Yahweh, my strength, my stronghold,
  my refuge in time of distress!
  To you the nations will come
  from the remotest parts of the earth and
    say,
  'Our fathers inherited nothing but
    Delusion,
  Futility of no use whatever.
20 Can human beings make their own
    gods?
  These are not gods at all!'
21 'Now listen, I will make them
    acknowledge,
  this time I will make them acknowledge

my hand and my might;
  and then they will know that Yahweh
    is my name.'

Judah's contaminated worship

17 'The sin of Judah is written with
    an iron pen,
  engraved with a diamond point
  on the tablet of the heart
  and on the horns of their altars,
2 while their children remember
  their altars and their sacred pole
  beside the green trees, on the lofty
    hills.
3 My mountain on the plain,
  your wealth and all your treasures

I shall hand over to be plundered,
because of the sin of your high places
throughout your territory.
⁴ You will have to relinquish your heritage
which I gave you;
I will enslave you to your enemies
in a country which you do not know,
for my fiery anger kindled by you
will burn for ever.'ᵃ

A group of wisdom sayings

⁵ Yahweh says this,
'Accursed be anyone who trusts in human
beings,
who relies on human strength
and whose heart turns from Yahweh.
⁶ Such a person is like scrub in the
wastelands:
when good comes, it does not affect him
since he lives in the parched places of the
desert,
uninhabited, salt land.

⁷ 'Blessed is anyone who trusts in Yahweh,
with Yahweh to rely on.
⁸ Such a person is like a tree by the
waterside
that thrusts its roots to the stream:
when the heat comes it has nothing to fear,
its foliage stays green;
untroubled in a year of drought,
it never stops bearing fruit.

⁹ 'The heart is more devious than any other
thing,
and is depraved; who can pierce its secrets?
¹⁰ I, Yahweh, search the heart,
test the motives,
to give each person what his conduct
and his actions deserve.

¹¹ 'The partridge will hatch eggs it has not
laid.
No different is the person who gets riches
unjustly:
his days half done, they will desert him
and he prove a fool after all.'

Confidence in the Temple and in Yahweh

¹² A glorious throne, sublime from the
beginning,
such is our Holy Place.
¹³ Yahweh, hope of Israel,
all who abandon you will be put to
shame,
those who turn from you will be
registered in the underworld,
since they have abandoned Yahweh, the
fountain of living water.

A prayer for vengeance

¹⁴ Heal me, Yahweh, and I shall be healed,
save me, and I shall be saved,
for you are my praise.
¹⁵ Look, they keep saying to me,
'Where is Yahweh's word? Let it come
true then!'
¹⁶ Yet I have never urged you to send
disaster,
I never desired the fatal day,
this you know;
what came from my lips was not concealed
from you.
¹⁷ Do not be a terror to me,
you, my refuge in time of disaster.
¹⁸ Let my persecutors be confounded,
not me,
let them, not me, be terrified.
On them bring the day of disaster,
destroy them, destroy them twice over!

Observance of the Sabbath

¹⁹ Yahweh said this to me, 'Go and stand at the
Gate of the Sons of the People by which the
kings of Judah go in and out—and at all the
gates of Jerusalem. ²⁰ Say to them, "Listen to
the word of Yahweh, you kings of Judah, all
you people of Judah too, and all you inhabitants of Jerusalem who pass through the gates.
²¹ Yahweh says this: As you value your lives,
on no account carry a burden on the Sabbath
day or bring it in through the gates of Jerusa-

17a = 15:13–14.

81 READ JEREMIAH 17.

Heal me, Yahweh, and I shall be healed, save me, and I shall be saved.—JEREMIAH 17:14

THE SPIRITUAL LIFE

Let us lean on the unshakable rock which is Christ, as Scripture says, "He set my feet on rock, and made my footsteps firm" (Ps 40:2). Once we are settled and fortified, let us begin contemplating: we will see what he tells us and how we will respond to the things for which he reproaches us.

Indeed . . . the first degree of contemplation is to consider without ceasing what the Lord wants. . . . In many things we all offend him; our lack of simplicity clashes with the rectitude of his will, and this prevents us from . . . attaching ourselves to him. Therefore, we must humble ourselves . . . by saying: "Heal me, Yahweh, and I shall be healed, save me, and I shall be saved. . . ."

When the eye of our heart is purified by such thoughts, we will . . . no longer consider what God's will is for us but what his will is in itself. God wills life, and there is nothing more useful or advantageous than to accept his will. That is why we should see to it that the energy we expend in trying to preserve our life be diverted into striving . . . to avoid ever deviating from the path that leads to life.

Then . . . by following the guidance of the Holy Spirit who scrutinizes the very depths of God, we should reflect on how kind the Lord is and how good in himself. We should ask with the Prophet to see the will of the Lord, and ask him to make us visit no longer our heart but his temple (see Ps 27:4). . . .

These two points summarize the content of the entire spiritual life: at the sight of ourselves we are troubled and contrite for our salvation, while in the contemplation of God we are at peace and the joy of the Holy Spirit consoles us. On the one side, fear and humility; on the other, hope and love.

ST. BERNARD OF CLAIRVAUX, 1090?–1153

YOU WILL FIND THE NEXT READING AT JEREMIAH 31.

lem. ²² Bring no burden out of your houses on the Sabbath day, and do no work. Keep the Sabbath day holy, as I ordered your ancestors. ²³ They would not hear, would not pay attention; they deliberately refused to listen or accept instruction. ²⁴ But if you listen carefully to me, Yahweh declares, and bring no burden in through the gates of this city on the Sabbath day, if you keep the Sabbath holy and do no work on that day, ²⁵ then, through the gates of this city, kings and princes occupying the throne of David will continue to make their entry, riding in chariots or on horseback, they, their chief men, the people of Judah and the inhabitants of Jerusalem. And this city will be inhabited for ever. ²⁶ They will come from the towns of Judah, from the districts round Jerusalem, from the territory of Benjamin, from the lowlands, from the highlands, from the Negeb, to offer burnt offering and sacrifice, and cereal offering and incense, to offer thanksgiving sacrifices in the Temple of Yahweh. ²⁷ But if you do not listen to me to keep the Sabbath day holy, and to refrain from entering the gates of Jerusalem with burdens on the Sabbath day, then I shall set fire to its gates; fire will devour the palaces of Jerusalem and not be quenched."'

Jeremiah visits the potter

18 The word that came to Jeremiah from Yahweh as follows, ²'Get up and make your way down to the potter's house, and there I shall tell you what I have to say.' ³So I went down to the potter's house; and there he was, working at the wheel. ⁴But the vessel he was making came out wrong, as may happen with clay when a potter is at work. So he began again and shaped it into another vessel, as he thought fit. ⁵Then the word of Yahweh came to me as follows, ⁶'House of Israel, can I not do to you what this potter does? Yahweh demands. Yes, like clay in the potter's hand, so you are in mine, House of Israel. ⁷Sometimes I announce that I shall uproot, break down and destroy a certain nation or kingdom, ⁸but should the nation I have threatened abandon its wickedness, I then change my mind about the disaster which I had intended to inflict on it. ⁹Sometimes I announce that I shall build up and plant a certain nation or kingdom, ¹⁰but should that nation do what displeases me and refuse to listen to my voice, I then change my mind about the good which I was intending to confer on it. ¹¹So now, say this to the people of Judah and the inhabitants of Jerusalem, "Yahweh says this: Listen, I am preparing a disaster for you, I am working out a plan against you. So now, each one of you, turn back from your evil ways, amend your conduct and actions." ¹²They, however, will say, "It is no use! We shall follow our own plans; each of us will act on his own wicked inclinations."'

About Israel's repudiation of Yahweh

¹³ Therefore, Yahweh says this,
'Ask, please, among the nations
if anyone has heard anything like this.
The Virgin of Israel
has done a very horrible thing.
¹⁴ Does the snow of Lebanon
ever leave the rocks of its slopes?
Do the rivers of foreign lands,
their cold flowing waters, ever run dry?
¹⁵ And yet my people have forgotten me!

They burn incense to a Nothing!
They have been made to stumble in their
ways,
the ancient paths,
to walk in paths,
on an unmade road,
¹⁶ to make their country an object of
horror,
everlastingly derided:
every passer-by will be appalled at it
and shake his head.
¹⁷ Like the east wind, I shall scatter them
before the enemy.
I shall show them my back, not my face,
the day they are ruined.'

A plot against Jeremiah

¹⁸'Come on,' they said, 'let us concoct a plot against Jeremiah, for the Law will not perish for lack of priests, nor advice for lack of wise men, nor the word for lack of prophets. Come on, let us slander him and pay no attention to anything he says.'

¹⁹ Pay attention to me, Yahweh,
hear what my adversaries are saying.
²⁰ Should evil be returned for good?
Now they are digging a pit for me.
Remember how I pleaded before you
and spoke good of them,
to turn your retribution away from
them.
²¹ So, hand their sons over to famine,
abandon them to the edge of the sword.
Let their wives become
childless and widowed.
Let their husbands die of plague,
their young men be cut down by the sword
in battle.
²² Let cries re-echo from their houses
as you bring raiders suddenly on them.
For they have dug a pit to catch me,
they have laid snares to trap my feet.
²³ But you, Yahweh, know
all about their murderous plot against me.
Do not forgive their guilt,
do not efface their sin from your sight.

Let them be hurled down before you,
deal with them while you are angry!

*The broken jug and the altercation
with Pashhur*

19 Then Yahweh said to Jeremiah, 'Go and buy a potter's earthenware jug. Take some of the people's elders and some of the senior priests with you. ²Go out towards the Valley of Ben-Hinnom, just outside the Gate of the Potsherds. There proclaim the words I shall say to you. ³You must say, "Kings of Judah, inhabitants of Jerusalem! Listen to the word of Yahweh! Yahweh Sabaoth, the God of Israel, says this: I am about to bring such a disaster on this place that the ears of every one who hears of it will ring. ⁴For they have abandoned me and have made this place unrecognisable, and offered incense here to other gods which neither they nor their ancestors nor the kings of Judah ever knew before. They have filled this place with the blood of the innocent; ⁵for they have built high places for Baal to burn their sons as burnt offerings to Baal, a thing I never ordered, never mentioned, that had never entered my thoughts. ⁶So now the days are coming, Yahweh declares, when people will no longer call this place Topheth, or Valley of Ben-Hinnom, but Valley of Slaughter. ⁷Because of this place, I shall empty Judah and Jerusalem of sound advice; I shall make them fall by the sword before their enemies, by the hand of those determined to kill them; I shall give their corpses as food to the birds of the sky and the animals of earth. ⁸And I shall make this city an object of horror and derision; every passer-by will be appalled at it and whistle at the sight of all the wounds it has sustained. ⁹I shall make them eat the flesh of their own sons and daughters: they will eat one another during the siege, in the shortage to which their enemies, and those determined to kill them, will reduce them."

¹⁰'You must break this jug in front of the men who are with you, ¹¹and say to them, "Yahweh Sabaoth says this: I am going to break this people and this city just as one breaks a potter's pot, so that it can never be mended again.

"Topheth will become a burial ground, for lack of other burial space. ¹²That is how I shall treat this place, Yahweh declares, and its inhabitants, by making this city like Topheth. ¹³The houses of Jerusalem and those of the kings of Judah, all the houses on the roofs of which they offered incense to the whole array of heaven and poured libations to other gods, will be unclean, like this place Topheth." '

¹⁴Jeremiah then came back from Topheth where Yahweh had sent him to prophesy, and stood in the court of the Temple of Yahweh and said to all the people, ¹⁵'Yahweh Sabaoth, the God of Israel, says this, "Yes, on this city, and on all the towns belonging to it, I shall bring all the disaster which I had decreed for it, since they have stubbornly refused to listen to my words." '

20 Now the priest Pashhur son of Immer, who was the chief of police in the Temple of Yahweh, heard Jeremiah making this prophecy. ²Pashhur struck the prophet Jeremiah and then put him in the stocks, in the Upper Benjamin Gate leading into the Temple of Yahweh. ³Next day, Pashhur had Jeremiah taken out of the stocks; Jeremiah then said to him, 'Not Pashhur but Terror-on-every-Side is Yahweh's name for you. ⁴For Yahweh says this, "I am going to hand you over to terror, you and all your friends; they will fall by the sword of their enemies, your own eyes will see it. The whole of Judah, too, I shall hand over to the king of Babylon; he will carry them off captive to Babylon and put them to the sword. ⁵And all the wealth of this city, all its stores, all its valuables, all the treasures of the kings of Judah, I shall hand over to their enemies who will plunder them, round them up and carry them off to Babylon. ⁶As for you, Pashhur, and your whole household, you will go into captivity; you will go to Babylon; there you will die, and there be buried, you and all your friends to whom you have prophesied lies." '

Selections from the 'Confessions' of Jeremiah

7 You have seduced me, Yahweh, and I have
  let myself be seduced;
you have overpowered me: you were the
  stronger.
I am a laughing-stock all day long,
they all make fun of me.
8 For whenever I speak, I have to howl
and proclaim, 'Violence and ruin!'
For me, Yahweh's word has been the cause
of insult and derision all day long.
9 I would say to myself, 'I will not think
  about him,
I will not speak in his name any more,'
but then there seemed to be a fire burning
  in my heart,
imprisoned in my bones.
The effort to restrain it wearied me,
I could not do it.
10 I heard so many disparaging me,
'Terror on every side!
Denounce him! Let us denounce him!'
All those who were on good terms with me
watched for my downfall,
'Perhaps he will be seduced into error.
Then we shall get the better of him
and take our revenge!'
11 But Yahweh is at my side like a mighty
  hero;
my opponents will stumble, vanquished,
confounded by their failure;
everlasting, unforgettable disgrace will be
  theirs.
12 Yahweh Sabaoth, you[a] who test the
  upright,
observer of motives and thoughts, I shall
  see your vengeance on them,
for I have revealed my cause to you.
13 Sing to Yahweh,
praise Yahweh,
for he has delivered the soul of one in need
from the clutches of evil doers.

14 A curse on the day when I was born!
May the day my mother bore me be
  unblessed!
15 A curse on the man who brought my
  father the news,
'A son, a boy has been born to you!'
making him overjoyed.
16 May this man be like the towns
that Yahweh overthrew without mercy;
may he hear the warning-cry at dawn
and the shout of battle at high noon,
17 for not killing me in the womb;
my mother would have been my grave
and her womb pregnant for ever.
18 Why ever did I come out of the womb
to see toil and sorrow
and end my days in shame?

Jeremiah answers the envoys of Zedekiah

21 The word that came to Jeremiah from Yahweh when King Zedekiah sent Pashhur[a] son of Malchiah to him, with the priest Zephaniah son of Maaseiah, to say this, 2 'Please consult Yahweh for us, since Nebuchadnezzar king of Babylon is making war on us: perhaps Yahweh will work one of his many miracles for us and force him to withdraw.' 3 Jeremiah said to them, 'Take this answer to Zedekiah, 4 "Yahweh, God of Israel, says this: I shall bring back the weapons of war which you are now carrying, and with which you are fighting the king of Babylon and the Chaldaeans now besieging you; from outside the walls, I shall stack them in the centre of this city. 5 And I shall fight against you myself with outstretched hand and mighty arm, in anger, fury and great wrath. 6 I shall strike down the inhabitants of this city, human and animal; they will die of a great plague. 7 Then, Yahweh declares, I shall deliver Zedekiah king of Judah, his officials, the people and those of this city who have escaped the plague, the sword, or the famine, into the clutches of Nebuchadnezzar king of Babylon, into the clutches of their enemies and into the clutches of those determined to kill them; mercilessly,

20a = 11:20.

21a Not to be confused with the Pashhur of ch. 20, a different person.

relentlessly, pitilessly, he will put them to the sword."

8 'And you must say to this people, "Yahweh says this: Look, I offer you a choice between the way of life and the way of death. 9 Anyone who stays in this city will die by sword, by famine, or by plague; but anyone who leaves it and surrenders to the Chaldaeans now besieging you will live; he will escape with his life.[b] 10 For I am determined on disaster, and not prosperity, for this city, Yahweh declares. It will be handed over to the king of Babylon, and he will burn it down."'

Address to the royal family of Judah

11 To the royal House of Judah. Listen to the word of Yahweh, 12 House of David! Yahweh says this:

> Each morning give fair judgement,
> rescue anyone who has been wronged
> from the hands of his oppressor,
> or else my wrath will leap out like a fire,
> it will burn and no one will be able to
>   quench it,
> because of the wickedness of your
>   actions.[c]
> 13 My quarrel is with you, resident of the
>   valley,
> Rock-in-the-Plain,
> Yahweh declares,
> with you that say, 'Who would dare attack
>   us and enter our lairs?'
> 14 I shall punish you as your actions
>   deserve,
> Yahweh declares,
> I shall set fire to its forest
> and it will devour all around it.

22 Yahweh said this, 'Go down to the palace of the king of Judah and there say this word, 2 "Listen to the word of Yahweh, king of Judah now occupying the throne of David, you, your officials and your people who go through these gates. 3 Yahweh says this: Act uprightly and justly; rescue from the hands of the oppressor anyone who has been wronged, do not exploit or ill-treat the stranger, the orphan, the widow; shed no innocent blood in this place. 4 For if you are scrupulous in obeying this command, then kings occupying the throne of David will continue to make their entry through the gates of this palace riding in chariots or on horseback, they, their officials and their people. 5 But if you do not listen to these words, then I swear by myself, Yahweh declares, this palace shall become a ruin!

6 "Yes, this is what Yahweh says about the palace of the king of Judah:

> You are like Gilead to me,
> like a peak of Lebanon.
> All the same, I will reduce you to a
>   desert,
> to uninhabited towns.
> 7 I dedicate men to destroy you,
> each man with his weapons;
> they will cut down your finest cedars
> and throw them on the fire.

8 "And when many nations pass this city, they will say to one another: Why has Yahweh treated this great city like this? 9 And the answer will be: Because they abandoned the covenant of Yahweh their God to worship other gods and serve them."'

Prophecies against various kings: against Jehoahaz

10 Do not weep for the man who is dead,
     do not raise the dirge for him.
> Weep rather for the one who has gone
>   away,
> since he will never come back,
> never see his native land again.

11 For this is what Yahweh has said about Shallum son of Josiah, king of Judah, who succeeded Josiah his father and was forced to leave this place, 'He will never come back to it 12 but will die in the place to which he has been

21b = 38:2.   *21c* = 4:4.

taken captive; and he will never see this country again.

Against Jehoiakim

13 'Disaster for the man who builds his house
      without uprightness,
    his upstairs rooms without fair judgement,
    who makes his fellow-man work for
      nothing,
    without paying him his wages,
14 who says, "I shall build myself a spacious
      palace
    with airy upstairs rooms,"
    who makes windows in it,
    panels it with cedar, and paints it
      vermilion.
15 Are you more of a king
    because of your passion for cedar?
    Did your father go hungry or thirsty?
    But he did what is just and upright,
    so all went well for him.
16 He used to examine the cases of poor and
      needy,
    then all went well.
    Is not that what it means to know me?
      Yahweh demands.
17 You on the other hand have eyes and heart
    for nothing but your own interests,
    for shedding innocent blood
    and perpetrating violence and oppression.'

18 That is why Yahweh says this about Jehoiakim son of Josiah, king of Judah:

    'No lamenting for him,
    "My poor brother! My poor sister!"
    No lamenting for him,
    "His poor lordship! His poor majesty!"
19 He will have a donkey's funeral
    —dragged away and thrown
    out of the gates of Jerusalem.'

Against Jehoiachin

20 'Climb the Lebanon range and shriek,
    raise your voice in Bashan,
    shriek from the Abarim,
    for all your lovers have been ruined!
21 I spoke to you in your prosperity,
    but you said, "I will not listen!"
    From your youth this has been how you
      behaved,
    refusing to listen to my voice.
22 The wind will shepherd all your
      shepherds away
    and your lovers will go into captivity.
    Then you will blush deep with shame
    at the thought of all your wickedness.
23 You who have made the Lebanon your
      home
    and made your nest among the cedars,
    how you will groan when anguish
      overtakes you,
    pangs like those of a woman in
      labour!

24 'As I live, Yahweh declares, even if Coniah[a] son of Jehoiakim, king of Judah, were the signet ring on my right hand, I would still wrench you off! 25 I shall hand you over to those determined to kill you, to those you dread, to Nebuchadnezzar king of Babylon, to the Chaldaeans. 26 I shall hurl you and the mother who bore you into another country; you were not born there but you will both die there. 27 They will not return to the country to which they desperately long to return.'

28 Is he a shoddy broken pot,
    this man Coniah,
    a crock that no one wants?
    Why are he and his offspring ejected,
    hurled into a country
    they know nothing of?
29 O land, land, land,
    listen to the word of Yahweh!
30 Yahweh says this,
    'List this man as: Childless;
    a man who made a failure of his life,
    since none of his offspring will
      succeed
    in occupying the throne of David,
    or ruling in Judah again.'

22a Alternative name for Jeconiah.

Messianic prophecies; the future king

23 ¹'Disaster for the shepherds who lose and scatter the sheep of my pasture, Yahweh declares. ²This, therefore, is what Yahweh, God of Israel, says about the shepherds who shepherd my people, "You have scattered my flock, you have driven them away and have not taken care of them. Right, I shall take care of you for your misdeeds, Yahweh declares! ³But the remnant of my flock I myself shall gather from all the countries where I have driven them, and bring them back to their folds; they will be fruitful and increase in numbers. ⁴For them I shall raise up shepherds to shepherd them and pasture them. No fear, no terror for them any more; not one shall be lost, Yahweh declares!

⁵ Look, the days are coming, Yahweh
        declares,
    when I shall raise an upright Branch for
        David;
    he will reign as king and be wise,
    doing what is just and upright in the
        country.
⁶ In his days Judah will triumph
    and Israel live in safety.
    And this is the name ᵃ he will be called,
    'Yahweh-is-our-Saving-Justice.' "

⁷'So, look, the days are coming, Yahweh declares, when people will no longer say, "As Yahweh lives who brought the Israelites out of Egypt," ⁸but, "As Yahweh lives who led back and brought home the offspring of the House of Israel from the land of the north and all the countries to which he had driven them, to live on their own soil." ᵇ

A tract against the false prophets

⁹On the prophets.

    My heart is broken within me,
    I tremble in all my bones;
    I am like a drunken man,
    like a man overcome with wine,

because of Yahweh and his holy words:
¹⁰ 'For the country is full of adulterers;
    yes, because of a curse, the country is in
        mourning
    and the pasturage in the desert has
        dried up;
    they are prompt to do wrong,
    make no effort to do right.
¹¹ Yes, even prophet and priest are godless,
    I have detected their wickedness in my
        own House,
    Yahweh declares.
¹² Because of this, their way will prove
    treacherous going for them;
    in the darkness where they are driven,
    there they will fall.
    For I shall bring disaster on them,
    when the year for punishing them comes,
    Yahweh declares.

¹³ 'In the prophets of Samaria
    I have seen insanity:
    they prophesied in the name of Baal
    and led my people Israel astray.
¹⁴ But in the prophets of Jerusalem
    I have seen something horrible:
    adultery, persistent lying,
    such abetting of the wicked
    that no one renounces his wickedness.
    To me they are all like Sodom
    and its inhabitants are like Gomorrah.
¹⁵ So this is what Yahweh Sabaoth says about
        the prophets,
    "Now I shall give them wormwood to eat
    and make them drink poisoned water, ᶜ
    since from the prophets of Jerusalem
    godlessness has spread throughout the
        land."

¹⁶ 'Yahweh Sabaoth says this,
    "Do not listen to what those prophets
        prophesy to you;
    they are deluding you,

23a This messianic title contrasts with Zedekiah (= Yahweh my Saving Justice), cf. 33:15–16.

23b = 16:14–15.   23c = 9:14.

they retail visions of their own,
and not what comes from Yahweh's
mouth.
17 To those who despise me, they keep
saying:
Yahweh has spoken: you will have peace!
and to all who follow their own stubborn
inclinations:
No disaster will touch you."

18 But who has been present in Yahweh's
council and seen, and heard his word? Who
has paid attention to his word and listened
to it?

19 Look, Yahweh's hurricane, his wrath,
bursts out,
a fearsome hurricane,
to burst on the heads of the wicked;
20 Yahweh's anger will not withdraw
until he has performed, has carried out,
what he has in mind.
In the final days, you will understand this
clearly,[d]
21 'I did not send these prophets,
yet they ran!
I did not speak to them,
yet they prophesied!
22 Had they been present in my council,
they could have proclaimed my words to
my people
and turned them from their evil way
and from the wickedness of their deeds!

23 'Am I a God when near, Yahweh
demands,
and not a God when far away?
24 Can anyone hide somewhere secret
without my seeing him? Yahweh
demands.
Do I not fill heaven and earth?
Yahweh demands.

25 'I have heard what the prophets say who
make their lying prophecies in my name. "I
have had a dream," they say, "I have had a
dream!" 26 How long are there to be those
among the prophets who prophesy lies and are
in fact prophets of their own delusions?
27 They are doing their best, by means of the
dreams that they keep telling each other, to
make my people forget my name, just as their
ancestors forgot my name in favour of Baal.
28 Let the prophet who has had a dream tell it
for a dream! And let him who receives a word
from me, deliver my word accurately!

'What have straw and wheat in common?
Yahweh demands.
29 Is my word not like fire,
Yahweh demands,
is it not like a hammer shattering a
rock?

30 'So, then, I have a quarrel with the
prophets, Yahweh declares, that steal my
words from one another. 31 I have a quarrel
with the prophets, Yahweh declares, who wag
their tongues to utter prophecies. 32 I have a
quarrel with the prophets who make prophecies out of lying dreams, Yahweh declares,
who recount them, and lead my people astray
by their lies and their bragging. I certainly
never sent them or commissioned them, and
they serve no good purpose for this people,
Yahweh declares.

33 'And when this people, or a prophet, or a
priest, asks you, "What is Yahweh's burden?"
you must answer, "You are the burden, and I
shall get rid of you, Yahweh declares!"

34 'As for the prophet, the priest, or anyone
else, who says, "Yahweh's burden", I shall
punish that man, and his household too.
35 This is what you must say to one another,
among yourselves, "What answer has Yahweh
given?" or "What has Yahweh said?" 36 But
stop using the expression "Yahweh's burden",
for what each man says will be his own responsibility. And you twist the words of the
living God, of Yahweh Sabaoth, our God.
37 This is the way to speak to a prophet, "What
answer has Yahweh given?" or "What has

23d = 30:23–24.

Yahweh said?" ³⁸But if you say, "Yahweh's burden", then Yahweh says this, "Since you use the expression 'Yahweh's burden', when I have warned you to stop saying, 'Yahweh's burden', ³⁹believe me, I shall pick you up and fling you from my presence, you and the city I gave to you and to your ancestors. ⁴⁰I shall bring down everlasting shame on you, everlasting and unforgettable disgrace." '

The two baskets of figs [a]

24 Yahweh gave me a vision: set out in front of the Temple of Yahweh were two baskets of figs. This was after Nebuchadnezzar king of Babylon had led Jeconiah son of Jehoiakim, king of Judah, away into exile from Jerusalem, with the chief men of Judah, the blacksmiths and metalworkers, and had taken them to Babylon. ²One basket contained excellent figs, like those that ripen first; the other contained very bad figs, so bad they were uneatable. ³Yahweh said to me, 'What do you see, Jeremiah?' 'Figs,' I answered, 'the good ones excellent, the bad ones very bad, so bad as to be uneatable.' ⁴Then the word of Yahweh was addressed to me, ⁵'Yahweh, the God of Israel, says this, "As these figs are good, so I mean to concern myself with the welfare of the exiles of Judah whom I have sent from this place to the country of the Chaldaeans. ⁶My eyes will watch over them for their good, to bring them back to this country, to build them up and not to break them down, to plant them and not to uproot them. ⁷I shall give them a heart to acknowledge that I am Yahweh. They will be my people and I shall be their God, for they will return to me with all their heart. ⁸As for the bad figs, the figs so bad as to be uneatable—yes, Yahweh says this— that is how I shall treat Zedekiah king of Judah, his chief men and what is left of Jerusalem, those who remain in this country and those living in Egypt. ⁹I shall make them an object of horror, a disaster, to all the kingdoms of the earth, a thing of shame, a byword, a laughing-stock, a curse, wherever I shall drive them. ¹⁰Sword, famine and plague I shall send

against them until they have vanished from the soil I gave to them and to their ancestors." '

Babylon; the scourge of Yahweh

25 The word that was addressed to Jeremiah about all the people of Judah in the fourth year of Jehoiakim son of Josiah, king of Judah (that is to say the first year of Nebuchadnezzar king of Babylon). ²The prophet Jeremiah proclaimed it before all the people of Judah and all the inhabitants of Jerusalem:

³'For twenty-three years, from the thirteenth year of Josiah son of Amon, king of Judah, until today, the word of Yahweh has been addressed to me and I have never tired of speaking to you (but you have not listened. ⁴Furthermore, Yahweh has untiringly sent you all his servants the prophets, but you have not listened or paid attention). ⁵The message was this, "Turn back, each one of you, from your evil behaviour and your evil actions, and you will go on living on the soil Yahweh long ago gave to you and your ancestors for ever. ⁶(And do not follow other gods to serve and worship them, do not provoke me with things you yourselves have made, and then I shall not harm you.) ⁷But you have not listened to me (Yahweh declares, so that you have now provoked me with things you yourselves have made, and thus harmed yourselves)."

⁸'So—this is what Yahweh Sabaoth says, "Since you have not listened to my words, ⁹I shall now send for all the families of the north (Yahweh declares, that is, for Nebuchadnezzar king of Babylon, my servant) and bring them down on this country and its inhabitants (and on all these surrounding nations); I shall curse them with utter destruction and make them an object of horror, of scorn, and ruin them for ever. ¹⁰From them I shall banish the shouts of rejoicing and mirth, the voices of bridegroom and bride, the sound of the handmill and the light of the lamp; ¹¹and this whole country will be reduced to ruin and des-

24a ‖ Ezk 11:14–21.

olation, and these nations will be enslaved to the king of Babylon for seventy years. ¹²(But when the seventy years are over, I shall punish the king of Babylon and that nation, Yahweh declares, for the wrong they have done, that is, the country of the Chaldaeans, and make it desolate for ever), ¹³and against that country I shall perform all the words with which I have threatened it, that is, everything written in this book." '

The vision of the cup

What Jeremiah prophesied against all the nations.

¹⁴('For these in their turn are to be enslaved to powerful nations and great kings, and I shall pay them back as their deeds and handiwork deserve.')

¹⁵For Yahweh, the God of Israel, said this to me, 'Take this cup of the wine of wrath and make all the nations to whom I send you drink it; ¹⁶they will drink and reel and lose their wits, because of the sword I am sending among them.' ¹⁷I took the cup from Yahweh's hand and made all the nations to whom Yahweh sent me drink it ¹⁸(Jerusalem and the towns of Judah, its kings and its chief men, to make them a ruin, an object of horror and derision and a curse, as is the case today): ¹⁹Pharaoh king of Egypt, his officials, his chief men and all his people, ²⁰with the whole conglomeration of peoples there (all the kings of the country of Uz); all the kings of the country of the Philistines, Ashkelon, Gaza, Ekron and what is still left of Ashdod; ²¹Edom, Moab and the Ammonites; ²²(all) the kings of Tyre, (all) the kings of Sidon, the kings of the island across the sea; ²³Dedan, Tema, Buz, all the people with shaven temples; ²⁴all the kings of Arabia (and all the kings of the conglomeration of peoples) who live in the desert ²⁵(all the kings of Zimri), all the kings of Elam, and all the kings of Media; ²⁶all the kings of the north, near and far, one after another: in short, all the kingdoms on the face of the earth. (As for the king of Sheshak, he will drink last of all.)

²⁷'You will say to them, "Yahweh Sabaoth, the God of Israel, says this: Drink! Get drunk! Vomit! Fall, never to rise again, before the sword that I am sending among you!" ²⁸If they refuse to take the cup from your hand and drink, you will say to them, "Yahweh Sabaoth says this: You must drink! ²⁹Look, for a start, I am bringing disaster on the city that bears my name, so are you likely to go unpunished? You certainly will not go unpunished, for next I shall summon a sword against all the inhabitants of the land, Yahweh declares."

³⁰'For your part, you are to prophesy all these words to them. Say to them:

"Yahweh roars from on high,
he thunders from his holy dwelling-place,
loudly he roars at his own fold,
shouts aloud like those who tread the grape
at all the inhabitants of the land.
³¹ The noise resounds to the remotest parts of the earth.
For Yahweh is indicting the nations,
arraigning all humanity for judgement;
the wicked he assigns to the sword,
Yahweh declares.
³² Yahweh Sabaoth says this:
Look, disaster is spreading
from nation to nation,
a mighty tempest is rising
from the far ends of the earth.

³³"Those slaughtered by Yahweh that day will be scattered across the world from end to end. No dirge will be raised for them; no one will gather them or bury them; they will stay lying on the surface like dung.ᵃ

³⁴ "Howl, shepherds, shriek,
roll on the ground, you lords of the flock,
for your days have come to be slaughtered and to be scattered,
and like a choice vase you will fall.

25a = 8:2.

35 No refuge then for the shepherds,
    no escape for the lords of the flock!
36 Listen! A shriek from the shepherds,
    a howl from the lords of the flock!
    For Yahweh has laid their pasture waste,
37 the peaceful sheepfolds are reduced to
        silence
    owing to Yahweh's furious anger.
38 The lion has left his lair
    and their country is a wasteland now,
    owing to the devastating fury,
    owing to his furious anger." '

Arrest and trial of Jeremiah

26 At the beginning of the reign of Jehoiakim son of Josiah, king of Judah,
this word came to Jeremiah from Yahweh,
2 'Yahweh says this, "Stand in the court of the
Temple of Yahweh. To all the people from the
towns of Judah who come to worship in the
Temple of Yahweh you will say everything I
have ordered you to say, not omitting one syl-
lable. 3 Perhaps they will listen and each turn
from his evil way: if so, I shall relent and not
bring the disaster on them which I intend because of their misdeeds." 4 Say to them, "Yahweh says this: If you will not listen to me and
follow my Law which I have given you, 5 and
pay attention to the words of my servants the
prophets whom I have never tired of sending
to you, although you never have paid attention, 6 I shall treat this Temple as I treated
Shiloh, and make this city a curse for all the
nations of the world." '

7 The priests and prophets and all the people heard Jeremiah say these words in the
Temple of Yahweh. 8 When Jeremiah had finished saying everything that Yahweh had ordered him to say to all the people, the priests
and prophets and all the people seized hold of
him and said, 'You will die for this! 9 Why
have you made this prophecy in Yahweh's
name, "This Temple will become like Shiloh,
and this city become an uninhabited ruin"?'
And the people all crowded in on Jeremiah in
the Temple of Yahweh. 10 Hearing of this, the
chief men of Judah came up from the royal

palace to the Temple of Yahweh and took
their seats at the entry of the New Gate of the
Temple of Yahweh.

11 The priests and prophets then said to the
chief men and all the people, 'This man deserves to die, since he has prophesied against
this city, as you have heard with your own
ears.' 12 Jeremiah, however, replied to all the
chief men and all the people as follows, 'Yahweh himself sent me to prophesy against this
Temple and this city all the things you have
heard. 13 So now amend your behaviour and
actions, listen to the voice of Yahweh your
God, and Yahweh will relent about the disaster that he has decreed for you. 14 For myself, I
am, as you see, in your hands. Do whatever
you please or think right with me. 15 But be
sure of this, that if you put me to death, you
will be bringing innocent blood on yourselves,
on this city and on its inhabitants, since Yahweh has truly sent me to you to say all this for
you to hear.'

16 The chief men and all the people then
said to the priests and prophets, 'This man
does not deserve to die: he has spoken to us in
the name of Yahweh our God.' 17 And some of
the country's elders rose to address all the assembled people. 18 'Micah of Moresheth,' they
said, 'who prophesied in the days of Hezekiah
king of Judah, had this to say to all the people
of Judah, "Yahweh Sabaoth says this:

*Zion will become ploughland,
Jerusalem a heap of rubble
and the Temple Mount a wooded height."* [a]

19 'Did Hezekiah king of Judah and all
Judah put him to death for this? Did they not
rather, fearing Yahweh, plead with him, to
such effect that Yahweh relented about the
disaster which he had decreed for them? Are
we now to burden our souls with such a
crime?'

20 There was another man, too, who used to
prophesy in Yahweh's name, Uriah son of

26a = Mi 3:12.

Shemaiah, from Kiriath-Jearim. He prophesied exactly the same things against this city and this country as Jeremiah. ²¹ When King Jehoiakim with all his officers and all the chief men heard what he said, the king was determined to put him to death. On hearing this, Uriah took fright and, fleeing, escaped to Egypt. ²² King Jehoiakim, however, sent Elnathan son of Achbor to Egypt with others, ²³ who brought Uriah back from Egypt and took him to King Jehoiakim, who had him put to the sword and his body thrown into the common burial ground. ²⁴ But Jeremiah had a protector in Ahikam son of Shaphan, so he was not handed over to the people to be put to death.

The symbolic yoke and the message to neighbouring kings

27 (At the beginning of the reign of Zedekiah son of Josiah, king of Judah, this word came to Jeremiah from Yahweh:) ² Yahweh said this to me, 'Make yourself thongs and yokes and put them on your neck. ³ Then send them to the king of Edom, the king of Moab, the king of the Ammonites, the king of Tyre, and the king of Sidon, through their envoys accredited to Zedekiah king of Judah in Jerusalem. ⁴ Give them the following message for their masters, "Yahweh Sabaoth, God of Israel, says this: You must tell your masters this: ⁵ I by my great power and outstretched arm made the earth, the human beings and the animals that are on earth, and I give them to whom I please. ⁶ For the present, I have handed all these countries over to Nebuchadnezzar king of Babylon, my servant; I have even put the wild animals at his service. ⁷ (All the nations will serve him, his son and his grandson, until the time for his own country comes in its turn, when mighty nations and great kings will enslave him.) ⁸ Any nation or kingdom that will not serve Nebuchadnezzar king of Babylon and will not bow its neck to the yoke of the king of Babylon, I shall punish that nation with sword, famine and plague, Yahweh declares, until I have destroyed it by

his hand. ⁹ For your own part, do not listen to your prophets, your diviners, dreamers, magicians and sorcerers, who tell you: You will not be enslaved by the king of Babylon. ¹⁰ They prophesy lies to you, the result of which will be that you will be banished from your soil, that I shall drive you out, and you will perish. ¹¹ The nation, however, that is prepared to bend its neck to the yoke of the king of Babylon and serve him, I shall leave in peace on its own soil, Yahweh declares, to farm it and stay on it." '

¹² To Zedekiah king of Judah I spoke in exactly the same terms. 'Bend your necks', I told him, 'to the yoke of the king of Babylon; serve him and his people and you will survive. ¹³ (Why so anxious to die, you and your people, by sword, famine and plague, with which Yahweh has threatened the nation refusing to serve the king of Babylon?) ¹⁴ Do not listen to the words the prophets say to you, "You will not be enslaved by the king of Babylon." They prophesy lies to you. ¹⁵ Since I have not sent them, Yahweh declares, they prophesy untruths to you in my name. The result will be that I shall drive you out, you will perish, and so will the prophets who prophesy to you.'

¹⁶ I also spoke to the priests and to all this people as follows, 'Yahweh says this, "Do not listen to the words of your prophets who prophesy to you as follows: Look, the vessels of the Temple of Yahweh will very shortly be brought back from Babylon. They prophesy lies to you. ¹⁷ (Do not listen to them; serve the king of Babylon and you will survive. Why should this city become a ruin?) ¹⁸ If they are real prophets, if Yahweh's word is really with them, they ought now to be pleading with Yahweh Sabaoth that the remaining vessels in the Temple of Yahweh, in the palace of the king of Judah and elsewhere in Jerusalem, do not go to Babylon too! ¹⁹ For this is what Yahweh Sabaoth says about (the pillars, the Sea, the stands and) the other vessels still remaining in this city, ²⁰ those not carried off by Nebuchadnezzar king of Babylon when he took Jeconiah son of Jehoiakim, king of Judah, into exile from Jerusalem to Babylon (with all the

leading men of Judah and Jerusalem). ²¹ Yes, this is what Yahweh Sabaoth, God of Israel, says about the vessels still remaining in the Temple of Yahweh, in the palace of the king of Judah and elsewhere in Jerusalem: ²² They will be carried off to Babylon (and stay there until the day I punish them), Yahweh declares. (Then I shall bring them back and restore them to this place.)" '

The dispute with Hananiah

28 That same year, at the beginning of the reign of Zedekiah king of Judah, in the fifth month of the fourth year, the prophet Hananiah son of Azzur, a Gibeonite, spoke as follows to Jeremiah in the Temple of Yahweh in the presence of the priests and of all the people, ² 'Yahweh Sabaoth, the God of Israel, says this, "I have broken the yoke of the king of Babylon. ³ In exactly two years' time I shall bring back all the vessels of the Temple of Yahweh which Nebuchadnezzar king of Babylon took away from here and carried off to Babylon. ⁴ And I shall also bring back Jeconiah son of Jehoiakim, king of Judah and all the exiles of Judah who have gone to Babylon, Yahweh declares, for I shall break the yoke of the king of Babylon." '

⁵ The prophet Jeremiah then replied to the prophet Hananiah in front of the priests and all the people present in the Temple of Yahweh. ⁶ 'So be it!' the prophet Jeremiah said, 'May Yahweh do so! May he fulfil the words that you have prophesied and bring all the vessels of the Temple of Yahweh and all the exiles back to this place from Babylon. ⁷ Listen carefully, however, to this word that I am now going to say for you and all the people to hear: ⁸ From remote times, the prophets who preceded you and me prophesied war, disaster and plague for many countries and for great kingdoms; ⁹ the prophet who prophesies peace can be recognised as one truly sent by Yahweh only when his word comes true.'

¹⁰ The prophet Hananiah then snatched the yoke off the neck of the prophet Jeremiah and broke it. ¹¹ In front of all the people Hananiah then said, 'Yahweh says this, "This is how, in exactly two years' time, I shall break the yoke of Nebuchadnezzar king of Babylon and take it off the necks of all the nations." ' At this, the prophet Jeremiah went away.

¹² After the prophet Hananiah had broken the yoke he had snatched off the prophet Jeremiah's neck, the word of Yahweh came to Jeremiah, ¹³ 'Go to Hananiah and tell him this, "Yahweh says this: You have broken the wooden yokes only to make iron yokes to replace them! ¹⁴ For Yahweh Sabaoth, the God of Israel, says this: An iron yoke is what I now lay on the necks of all these nations to enslave them to Nebuchadnezzar king of Babylon. (They will be enslaved to him; I have even given him the wild animals.)" '

¹⁵ The prophet Jeremiah said to the prophet Hananiah, 'Listen carefully, Hananiah: Yahweh has not sent you; and thanks to you this people is now relying on what is false. ¹⁶ And so, Yahweh says this, "I am going to send you off the face of the earth: you will die this year (since you have preached rebellion against Yahweh)." '

¹⁷ The prophet Hananiah died the same year, in the seventh month.

The letter to the exiles

29 This is the text of the letter that the prophet Jeremiah sent from Jerusalem to those who were left of the elders in exile, to the priests, the prophets and all the people whom Nebuchadnezzar had deported from Jerusalem to Babylon. ² This was after King Jeconiah had left Jerusalem with the queen mother, the eunuchs, the chief men of Judah and Jerusalem, and the blacksmiths and metalworkers. ³ The letter was entrusted to Elasah son of Shaphan and to Gemariah son of Hilkiah, whom Zedekiah king of Judah had sent to Babylon, to Nebuchadnezzar king of Babylon. The letter said:

⁴ 'Yahweh Sabaoth, the God of Israel, says this to all the exiles deported from Jerusalem to Babylon: ⁵ Build houses, settle down;

plant gardens and eat what they produce; 6marry and have sons and daughters; choose wives for your sons, find husbands for your daughters so that these can bear sons and daughters in their turn; you must increase there and not decrease. 7Work for the good of the city to which I have exiled you; pray to Yahweh on its behalf, since on its welfare yours depends. 8For Yahweh Sabaoth, the God of Israel, says this: Do not be deceived by the prophets who are with you or by your diviners; do not listen to the dreams you have, 9since they prophesy lies to you in my name. I have not sent them, Yahweh declares. 10For Yahweh says this: When the seventy years granted to Babylon are over, I shall intervene on your behalf and fulfil my favourable promise to you by bringing you back to this place. 11Yes, I know what plans I have in mind for you, Yahweh declares, plans for peace, not for disaster, to give you a future and a hope. 12When you call to me and come and pray to me, I shall listen to you. 13When you search for me, you will find me; when you search wholeheartedly for me, 14I shall let you find me (Yahweh declares. I shall restore your fortunes and gather you in from all the nations and wherever I have driven you, Yahweh declares. I shall bring you back to the place from which I exiled you).

15'Since you say: Yahweh has raised up prophets for us in Babylon— 16this is what Yahweh says about the king now occupying the throne of David and all the people living in this city, your brothers who did not go with you into exile: 17Yahweh Sabaoth says this: I am now going to send them sword, famine and plague; I shall make them like rotten figs, so bad as to be uneatable. 18I shall pursue them with sword, famine and plague. I shall make them an object of terror to all the kingdoms of the earth, a curse, a thing of horror, scorn and derision to all the nations where I have driven them, 19because they have refused to

listen to my words, Yahweh declares, although I have persistently sent them all my servants the prophets; but they would not listen, Yahweh declares. 20But all you exiles, whom I have sent from Jerusalem to Babylon, listen to Yahweh's word!

21'This is what Yahweh Sabaoth, God of Israel, says about Ahab son of Kolaiah, and Zedekiah son of Maaseiah, who prophesy lies to you in my name: I shall hand them over now to Nebuchadnezzar king of Babylon who will put them to death before your very eyes. 22This curse, based on their fate, will be used by all the exiles of Judah in Babylon: May Yahweh treat you like Zedekiah and Ahab, roasted alive by the king of Babylon, 23because they have done a scandalous thing in Israel, committing adultery with their neighbour's wives and speaking lying words in my name without orders from me. I know all the same and am witness to it, Yahweh declares.'

Prophecy against Shemaiah

24'And to Shemaiah of Nehelam you will speak as follows: 25Yahweh Sabaoth, God of Israel, says this: Since you, on your own initiative, have sent a letter to all the people in Jerusalem, to the priest Zephaniah son of Maaseiah (and to all the priests), saying: 26Yahweh has appointed you priest in place of the priest Jehoiada to keep order in the Temple of Yahweh, to put any crazy fellow posing as a prophet in the stocks and collar, 27why then have you not disciplined Jeremiah of Anathoth, now posing as a prophet to you? 28Why, he has even sent us a message in Babylon, saying: It will be a long time. Build houses, settle down; plant gardens and eat what they produce.' . . .

29(Now, after the priest Zephaniah had read this letter to the prophet Jeremiah), 30the word of Yahweh came then to Jeremiah as follows, 31'Send this message to all the exiles, "This is what Yahweh says about Shemaiah of

Nehelam: Since Shemaiah has prophesied to you without my sending him, and since he has caused you to rely on what is false ³²for that reason, Yahweh declares, I shall punish Shemaiah of Nehelam and his descendants; no male member of his family will survive among this people to see the happiness that I will bestow on my people (Yahweh declares, since he has preached rebellion against Yahweh)." '

Promise of recovery for Israel

30 The word which came to Jeremiah from Yahweh, as follows, ²'Yahweh, God of Israel, says this, "Write for yourself in a book all the words I have spoken to you. ³For look, the days are coming, Yahweh declares, when I shall bring back the captives of my people Israel (and Judah), Yahweh says. I shall make them come back and take possession of the country I gave to their ancestors." '

⁴These are the words Yahweh spoke about Israel (and Judah):

⁵ Yahweh says this:
We have heard a cry of panic,
of terror, not of peace.
⁶ Now ask and see:
can a man bear children?
Then why do I see each man
with his hands on his loins like a woman
in labour?
Why has every face grown pale?
⁷ Disaster! This is the great day,
no other like it:
a time of distress for Jacob,
though he will be saved from it.

⁸(That day, Yahweh Sabaoth declares, I shall break the yoke now on your neck and snap your chains; and foreigners will enslave you no more, ⁹but Israel and Judah will serve Yahweh their God, and David their king whom I shall raise up for them.)

¹⁰ So do not be afraid, my servant Jacob,
Yahweh declares,
Israel, do not be alarmed:

for look, I shall rescue you from distant
countries
and your descendants from the country
where they are captive.
Jacob will return and be at peace,
secure, with no one to trouble him.
¹¹ For I am with you to save you,
Yahweh declares,
I shall make an end of all the nations
where I have driven you,
but I shall not make an end of you,
only discipline you in moderation,
not to let you go quite unpunished.ᵃ

¹² Yes, Yahweh says this:
Your wound is incurable,
your injury past healing.
¹³ There is no one to plead your cause;
for an ulcer there are remedies,
but for you no cure at all.
¹⁴ All your lovers have forgotten you,
they look for you no more.
Yes, I have struck you as an enemy strikes,
with cruel punishment
(because of your great guilt and countless
sins).
¹⁵ Why cry out because of your wound?
Your pain is incurable!
Because of your great guilt and countless
sins,
I have treated you like this.
¹⁶ But all those who devoured you will be
devoured,
all your enemies, all, go into captivity,
those who despoiled you will be despoiled,
and all who pillaged you be pillaged.
¹⁷ For I shall restore you to health
and heal your wounds, Yahweh declares,
you who used to be called 'Outcast',
'Zion for whom no one cares'.

¹⁸ Yahweh says this:
Look, I shall restore the tents of Jacob
and take pity on his dwellings:
the town will be rebuilt on its mound,

30a = 46:27–28.

the stronghold where it ought to stand.

19 From them will come thanksgiving
and shouts of joy.
I shall make them increase, they will not
decrease;
I shall make them honoured, no more to
be humbled.

20 Their sons will be as once they were,
their community fixed firmly before me,
and I shall punish all their oppressors.

21 Their prince will be one of their own,
their ruler come from their own people,
and I shall permit him to approach me
freely;
for who, otherwise, would be so bold
as to approach me, Yahweh demands?

22 You will be my people and I shall be your
God.

23 Look, Yahweh's hurricane, his wrath,
bursts out,
a roaring hurricane,
to burst on the heads of the wicked;

24 Yahweh's burning anger will not turn
aside
until he has performed, has carried out,
what he has in mind.
In the final days, you will understand this.*b*

31 When that time comes, Yahweh declares, I shall be the God of all the families of Israel, and they will be my people.

2 Yahweh says this:
They have found pardon in the desert,
those who have survived the sword.
Israel is marching to his rest.

3 Yahweh has appeared to me from afar;
I have loved you with an everlasting love
and so I still maintain my faithful love for
you.

4 I shall build you once more, yes, you will
be rebuilt,
Virgin of Israel!
Once more in your best attire,
and with your tambourines,
you will go out dancing gaily.

5 Once more you will plant vineyards
on the mountains of Samaria
(those who plant will themselves enjoy the
fruit).

6 Yes, a day will come when the watchmen
shout
on the mountains of Ephraim,
'Up! Let us go up to Zion,
to Yahweh our God!'

7 For Yahweh says this:
Shout with joy for Jacob!
Hail the chief of nations!
Proclaim! Praise! Shout,
'Yahweh has saved his people,
the remnant of Israel!'

8 Watch, I shall bring them back
from the land of the north
and gather them in from the far ends of
the earth.
With them, the blind and the lame,
women with child, women in labour,
all together: a mighty throng will return
here!

9 In tears they will return,
in prayer I shall lead them.
I shall guide them to streams of water,
by a smooth path where they will not
stumble.
For I am a father to Israel,
and Ephraim is my first-born son.

10 Listen, nations, to the word of Yahweh.
On the farthest coasts and islands proclaim
it, say,
'He who scattered Israel is gathering him,
will guard him as a shepherd guarding his
flock.'

11 For Yahweh has ransomed Jacob,
rescued him from a hand stronger than his
own.

12 They will come, shouting for joy on the
heights of Zion,
thronging towards Yahweh's lavish gifts,

30b = 23:19–20.

82 READ JEREMIAH 31:1–4, 31–38.

Look, the days are coming, Yahweh declares, when I shall make a new covenant with the House of Israel.—JEREMIAH 31:31

CHRIST IS THE NEW COVENANT

St. Justin explains Christianity to Trypho, a Jew:

We have not trusted in any other God (for there is no other), but in him in whom you also have trusted, the God of Abraham, and of Isaac, and of Jacob. But we do not trust through Moses or through the law. . . . But I have read that there shall be a final law, and a final supreme covenant that all who are seeking the inheritance of God must observe. For the law promulgated on Horeb is now old, and belongs to yourselves alone; but this is for all universally. . . . An eternal and final law, that is, Christ, has been given to us, and the covenant is trustworthy, after which there shall be no law, no commandment, no ordinance. Have you not read in Isaiah: ". . . a law shall go forth from me, and my judgment shall be for a light to the nations" (see Is 51:4–5). And Jeremiah also speaks of this new covenant: "Look, the days are coming, Yahweh declares, when I shall make a new covenant with the House of Israel (and the House of Judah), but not like the covenant I made with their ancestors the day I took them by the hand to bring them out of Egypt." If, therefore, God proclaimed a new covenant . . . , and this a light of the nations, we see that people approach God, leaving their idols and other unrighteousness through the name of him who was crucified, Jesus Christ, and abide by their confession even unto death, and maintain piety. Moreover, by the works and by the attendant miracles, all may understand that he is the new law, and the new covenant, and the expectation of those who out of every people wait for the good things of God. For the true spiritual Israel, and descendants of Judah, Jacob, Isaac, and Abraham . . . are we who have been led to God through this crucified Christ.

ST. JUSTIN, 100?–165

YOU WILL FIND THE NEXT READING AT JEREMIAH 33.

for wheat, new wine and oil,
sheep and cattle;
they will be like a well-watered garden,
they will sorrow no more.
13 The young girl will then take pleasure in
the dance,
and young men and old alike;
I shall change their mourning into
gladness,
comfort them, give them joy after their
troubles;
14 I shall refresh my priests with rich food,

and my people will gorge themselves on
my lavish gifts,
Yahweh declares.

15 Yahweh says this:
A voice is heard in Ramah,
lamenting and weeping bitterly:
it is Rachel[a] weeping for her children,
refusing to be comforted for her children,
because they are no more.

31a Ancestor of the deported tribe of Benjamin.

16 Yahweh says this:
Stop your lamenting
dry your eyes,
for your labour will have a reward,
Yahweh declares,
and they will return from the enemy's
country.
17 There is hope for your future after all,
Yahweh declares,
your children will return to their
homeland.
18 I have indeed heard Ephraim's grieving,
'You flogged me, I took a flogging,
like a young, untrained bull.
Bring me back, let me come back,
for you are Yahweh my God!
19 For, since I turned away, I have repented;
having understood, I beat my breast.
I was deeply ashamed, I blushed,
aware of the disgrace incurred when I was
young.'
20 Is Ephraim, then, so dear a son to me,
a child so favoured,
that whenever I mention him
I remember him lovingly still?
That is why I yearn for him,
why I must take pity on him,
Yahweh declares.

21 Set up your signposts,
raise yourself landmarks,
fix your mind on the road,
the way by which you went.
Come home, Virgin of Israel,
come home to these towns of yours.
22 How long will you hesitate,
rebellious daughter?
For Yahweh is creating something new on
earth:
the Woman sets out to find her Husband
again.

Promise of restoration to Judah

23 Yahweh Sabaoth, the God of Israel, says this,
'In the country of Judah and in its towns, they
will use these words once more, when I bring
their captives home:

"Yahweh bless you,
home of saving justice,
holy mountain!"

24 'And in this country, Judah and all its towns,
the ploughmen and those who wander with
their flocks, will live together, 25 for I shall give
the weary all they need and satisfy all those
whose strength has gone.'

26 At this, I awoke and saw
that my sleep had been sweet to me.

Israel and Judah

27 'Look, the days are coming, Yahweh declares, when I shall sow the House of Israel
and the House of Judah with the seed both of
people and of cattle. 28 And as I once watched
over them to uproot, to knock down, to overthrow, destroy and bring disaster, so now I
shall watch over them to build and to plant,
Yahweh declares.

Individual retribution

29 'In those days people will no longer say:

"The fathers have eaten unripe grapes;
the children's teeth are set on edge."*b*

30 But each will die for his own guilt. Everyone who eats unripe grapes will have his own
teeth set on edge.

The new covenant

31 'Look, the days are coming, Yahweh declares, when I shall make a new covenant with
the House of Israel (and the House of Judah),
32 but not like the covenant I made with their
ancestors the day I took them by the hand to
bring them out of Egypt, a covenant which
they broke, even though I was their Master,
Yahweh declares. 33 No, this is the covenant I
shall make with the House of Israel when
those days have come, Yahweh declares.
Within them I shall plant my Law, writing it

31b ‖ Ezk 18:2.

on their hearts. Then I shall be their God and they will be my people. ³⁴ There will be no further need for everyone to teach neighbour or brother, saying, "Learn to know Yahweh!" No, they will all know me, from the least to the greatest, Yahweh declares, since I shall forgive their guilt and never more call their sin to mind.'

Israel will endure

³⁵ Yahweh who provides the sun to shine by
    day,
  who regulates moon and stars to shine by
    night,
  who stirs the sea, making its waves
    roar,
  he whose name is Yahweh Sabaoth, says
    this,
³⁶ 'Were this established order ever to pass
    away
  before me, Yahweh declares,
  then the race of Israel would also
    cease
  being a nation for ever before me!'
³⁷ Yahweh says this,
  'Were the heavens above ever to be
    measured,
  the foundations of the earth below ever to
    be fathomed,
  then I too would reject the whole race of
    Israel
  for all that they have done, Yahweh
    declares.'

Jerusalem magnificently rebuilt

³⁸ 'Look, the days are coming, Yahweh declares, when the City will be rebuilt for Yahweh, from the Tower of Hananel to the Corner Gate. ³⁹ Then once again the measuring line will stretch straight to the Hill of Gareb, turning then to Goah. ⁴⁰ And the whole valley, with its corpses and ashes, and all the ground beside the ravine of the Kidron as far as the corner of the Horse Gate, eastwards, will be consecrated to Yahweh. It will never be destroyed or demolished again.

Jeremiah buys a field in token of future prosperity

32 The word that came to Jeremiah from Yahweh in the tenth year of Zedekiah king of Judah, which was the eighteenth year of Nebuchadnezzar. ² The army of the king of Babylon was then besieging Jerusalem, and the prophet Jeremiah was confined in the Court of the Guard in the king of Judah's palace, ³ where Zedekiah king of Judah had confined him, saying, 'Why do you keep prophesying like this, "Yahweh says this: I am going to hand this city over to the king of Babylon and he will capture it; ⁴ and Zedekiah king of Judah will not escape the clutches of the Chaldaeans, but will certainly be handed over to the king of Babylon, speak to him personally and see him face to face. ⁵ He will take Zedekiah away to Babylon and there he will stay (until I attend to him, Yahweh declares. If you fight the Chaldaeans you will not succeed!)"'

⁶ Jeremiah said, 'The word of Yahweh has been addressed to me as follows, ⁷ "Look, Hanamel the son of your uncle Shallum will come to you and say: Buy my field at Anathoth, for you have the right of redemption to purchase it." ⁸ And, as Yahweh had said, my cousin Hanamel came to me, in the Court of the Guard and said, "Buy my field at Anathoth in the territory of Benjamin, for you have the right of inheritance and right of redemption; buy it." I knew then that this was Yahweh's order. ⁹ Accordingly, I bought the field from my cousin Hanamel of Anathoth and weighed him out the money: seventeen silver shekels. ¹⁰ I drew up the deeds and sealed it, called in witnesses and weighed out the money on the scales. ¹¹ I then took both the sealed deed of purchase (with its stipulations and clauses) and its open copy ¹² and handed over the deed of purchase to Baruch son of Neriah, son of Mahseiah, in the presence of my cousin Hanamel, of the witnesses who had signed the deed of purchase, and of all the Judaeans who then happened to be in the Court

of the Guard. [13]In their presence I gave Baruch this order, [14]"Yahweh Sabaoth, God of Israel, says this: Take these deeds, the sealed deed of purchase and its open copy, and put them in an earthenware pot, so that they may be preserved for a long time. [15]For Yahweh Sabaoth, God of Israel, says this: Houses, fields and vineyards will again be bought in this country."

[16]'After I had entrusted the deed of purchase to Baruch son of Neriah, I prayed to Yahweh as follows, [17]"Ah, Lord Yahweh, you made the heavens and the earth by your great power and outstretched arm. To you nothing is impossible. [18]You show faithful love to thousands but repay the fathers' guilt in full to their children after them. Great and mighty God, whose name is Yahweh Sabaoth, [19]great in purpose, mighty in deed, whose eyes are open on all human ways, rewarding every individual as that person's ways and actions deserve! [20]You performed signs and wonders in Egypt, as you still do in Israel and among humanity today. You have won the name for yourself which is yours today. [21]You brought your people Israel out of Egypt with signs and wonders, with mighty hand and outstretched arm and fearsome terror. [22]Then you gave them this country which you had promised on oath to their ancestors, a country flowing with milk and honey. [23]They then entered it, taking possession of it, but they would not listen to your voice nor follow your Law: they would do nothing you ordered them to do; and so you made this total disaster befall them. [24]Look! The earthworks are already in place to take the city and, by means of sword, famine and plague, the city is now within the clutches of the Chaldaeans attacking it. What you said has now come true, as you see. [25]Yet you yourself, Lord Yahweh, told me: Buy the field, pay for it, have it witnessed although the city is already in the Chaldaeans' clutches."'

[26]The word of Yahweh was addressed to me as follows, [27]'Look, I am Yahweh, God of all humanity. Is anything impossible to me?

[28]'So, Yahweh says this, "I shall hand this

city over to the Chaldaeans and to Nebuchadnezzar king of Babylon, and he will capture it; [29]the Chaldaeans attacking this city will enter it, fire it and burn it to the ground, with the houses on whose roofs incense has been offered to Baal and libations poured to other gods, to provoke my anger. [30]For the people of Israel and Judah alike have done nothing but what displeases me since they were young. (The people of Israel in fact have done nothing but provoke my anger by their actions, Yahweh declares.) [31]Yes, from the day when this city was built until today, it has been such cause of anger and wrath to me that I mean to remove it from my sight, [32]on account of all the wickedness the people of Israel and the people of Judah have done to provoke my anger; they, their kings, their chief men, their priests, their prophets, the people of Judah and the inhabitants of Jerusalem. [33]They turned to me their backs, never their faces; and though I taught them so urgently, so untiringly, they would not listen and accept correction. [34]Instead, they set up their Horrors in the Temple that bears my name to defile it, [35]and built the high places of Baal in the Valley of Ben-Hinnom, to burn their sons and daughters alive in honour of Molech:[a] a thing I have never ordered, that had never entered my thoughts—that they would cause Judah to sin by anything so loathsome!

[36]"So now, this is what Yahweh, God of Israel, says about this city of which you now say: By means of sword, famine and plague, it is already within the king of Babylon's clutches: [37]Look, I shall gather them in from all the countries where I have driven them in my anger, my fury and great wrath. I shall bring them back to this place and make them live in safety. [38]Then they will be my people, and I shall be their God. [39]I shall give them singleness of heart and singleness of conduct so that they will always fear me, for their own good and that of their children after them. [40]I shall make an everlasting covenant with them,

32a = 7:30–31.

never to cease in my efforts for their welfare, and I shall put respect for me in their hearts, so that they will never turn away from me again. ⁴¹ My joy will lie in them and in doing them good, and I shall plant them firmly in this country, with all my heart and soul. ⁴² For Yahweh says this: Just as I have brought this complete and total disaster on this people, so I shall bring them all the good things I have promised them. ⁴³ Fields will again be bought in this country of which you now say: It is a wasteland without human or animal, already in the clutches of the Chaldaeans. ⁴⁴ People will buy fields, pay money, draw up deeds, seal them and have them witnessed in the territory of Benjamin, in the districts round Jerusalem, in the towns of Judah, of the highlands, of the lowlands and of the Negeb. For I shall bring back their captives, Yahweh declares." '

Another promise of recovery

33 Jeremiah was still confined to the Court of the Guard when the word of Yahweh came to him a second time, as follows, ² 'Yahweh who made the earth, who formed it and set it firm—Yahweh is his name—says this, ³ "Call to me and I will answer you; I will tell you great secrets of which you know nothing. ⁴ For this is what Yahweh, God of Israel, says about the houses of this city and the palaces of the kings of Judah which are about to be destroyed by means of the earthworks and the sword; ⁵ about those now fighting the Chaldaeans, only to fill the city with corpses, those whom I have slaughtered in my furious anger, those whose wickedness has made me hide my face from this city: ⁶ Look, I shall bring them remedy and cure; I shall cure them and reveal a new order of peace and loyalty to them. ⁷ I shall bring back the captives of Judah and the captives of Israel and shall rebuild them as before. ⁸ I shall cleanse them of all their guilt, by which they have offended me, I shall forgive all their guilty actions, by which they have offended me and rebelled against me. ⁹ And, for me, Jerusalem will become a name of joy and praise and pride for all the nations on earth to

see; when they hear of all the prosperity that I shall give, they will be seized with fear and trembling at all the prosperity and the peace that I provide for it."

¹⁰ 'Yahweh says this, "In this place of which you now say: It is a ruin, without human or animal, in the towns of Judah and desolate streets of Jerusalem where there is neither human nor animal, once more will be heard ¹¹ shouts of rejoicing and mirth, the voices of bridegroom and bride, and the singing of those who bring thanksgiving sacrifices to the Temple of Yahweh: Give thanks to Yahweh Sabaoth, for Yahweh is good, for his faithful love is everlasting. For I shall bring back the country's captives, as before, Yahweh says."

¹² 'Yahweh Sabaoth says this, "In this ruinous place, without human or animal, in all its towns, once again there will be pastures for the shepherds to rest their flocks. ¹³ In the towns of the highlands, of the lowlands and the Negeb, in the territory of Benjamin, in the districts round Jerusalem and in the towns of Judah, once again the flocks shall pass under the hand of someone who counts them, Yahweh says.

The institutions of the future

¹⁴ "Look, the days are coming, Yahweh declares, when I shall fulfil the promise of happiness I made to the House of Israel and the House of Judah:

¹⁵ In those days and at that time,
  I shall make an upright Branch grow for David,
  who will do what is just and upright in the country.
¹⁶ In those days Judah will triumph
  and Israel live in safety.
  And this is the name the city will be called:
  Yahweh-is-our-Saving-Justice." ᵃ

¹⁷ 'For Yahweh says this, "David will never lack a male descendant to occupy the throne of the House of Israel, ¹⁸ nor will the levitical

33a = 23:5–6.

83 READ JEREMIAH 33:1–18.

I shall make an upright Branch grow for David, who will do what is just and upright in the country.—JEREMIAH 33:15

ANTICIPATING THE INCARNATION

When the Lord came to earth he did not make some spectacular use of the sun, moon, stars, fire or air because he came not to make a display but to heal those who were suffering. Someone putting on a show would simply appear and dazzle us. But for one seeking to heal and teach, the way is to give himself to those in need and to appear in a form that they can relate to. . . .

Now nothing in creation had gone astray with regard to their notions of God except human beings. Neither sun, nor moon, nor heaven, nor the stars, nor water, nor air had swerved from their order. But knowing their Creator and Sovereign, the Word, they remain as they were made. But human beings alone, having rejected what was good, devised things of nought instead of the truth. They have ascribed the honor due to God . . . to stone images of demons and men.

The Divine Goodness could not overlook so grave a matter. Because men could not identify the Lord as ordering and guiding the whole universe, he took to himself a part of the whole—his human body—and united himself to it so that they would be sure to recognize him. Since they could not grasp his invisible power, he let them see him in a familiar human form so that they could reason to him and contemplate him. For men being what they are could know his Father more quickly and directly through a human form like theirs and by the wonders accomplished through it, recognizing that they are not human acts but the works of God. . . .

The great Greek philosopher Plato says that its Author, seeing the universe tempest-tossed and in danger of descending into chaos, takes his seat at the helm of the soul, rescues it and corrects all its calamities. Therefore, what is so incredible in what we say, that humankind being in error, the Word lighted down upon it and appeared as man so that by his guidance and goodness he might save it?

ST. ATHANASIUS, 297?–373

YOU WILL FIND THE NEXT READING AT LAMENTATIONS 3.

priests ever lack male descendants to stand before me and offer the burnt offering, to burn the cereal offering and offer sacrifice every day." '

¹⁹ The word of Yahweh came to Jeremiah as follows, ²⁰ 'Yahweh says this, "If you could break my covenant with the day and my covenant with the night so that day and night do not come at their due time, ²¹ then my covenant with David my servant might also be broken and he would have no son to reign on his throne, and so also might my covenant with the levitical priests, who are my ministers. ²² As surely as the array of heaven cannot be counted, nor the sand of the sea be measured, so surely shall I increase the heirs of David my servant and the Levites who minister to me." '

²³ The word of Yahweh came to Jeremiah as follows, ²⁴ 'Have you not noticed what these

people say, "The two families which Yahweh chose he has now rejected"? So they despise my people, whom they no longer think of as a nation. 25 Yahweh says this, "If I have not created day and night and fixed the laws governing heaven and earth, 26 why, then I shall reject the descendants of Jacob and of David my servant and cease to choose rulers from his descendants for the heirs of Abraham, Isaac and Jacob! For I shall bring back their captives and take pity on them." '

The fate of Zedekiah

34 The word came to Jeremiah from Yahweh when Nebuchadnezzar king of Babylon and his whole army, with all the kingdoms of the earth under his dominion and all the peoples, were waging war on Jerusalem and all its towns, 2 'Yahweh, God of Israel, says this, "Go and speak to Zedekiah king of Judah and tell him, Yahweh says this: I am going to hand this city over to the power of the king of Babylon, and he will burn it down. 3 And you yourself will not escape his clutches but will certainly be captured and handed over to him. You will see the king of Babylon face to face and speak to him personally. Then you will go to Babylon. 4 Even so, listen to the word of Yahweh, Zedekiah king of Judah! This is what Yahweh says about you: You will not die by the sword; 5 you will die in peace. And as spices were burnt for your ancestors, the kings who in times past preceded you, so spices will be burnt for you and a dirge sung for you: Alas for his highness! I have spoken, Yahweh declares." '

6 The prophet Jeremiah repeated all these words to Zedekiah king of Judah in Jerusalem, 7 while the army of the king of Babylon was attacking Jerusalem and all such towns of Judah as still held out, namely Lachish and Azekah, these being the only fortified towns of Judah remaining.

The episode of the liberated slaves

8 The word came to Jeremiah from Yahweh after King Zedekiah had made a covenant with all the people in Jerusalem to issue a proclamation freeing their slaves: 9 each man was to free his Hebrew slaves, men and women, no one was any longer to keep a brother Judaean in slavery. 10 All the chief men and all the people who had entered into the covenant had agreed that everyone should free his slaves, men or women, and no longer keep them as slaves: they had agreed on this and set them free. 11 Afterwards, however, they changed their minds, recovered the slaves, men and women, whom they had set free, and reduced them to slavery again. 12 The word of Yahweh came then to Jeremiah as follows, 13 'Yahweh, God of Israel, says this, "I made a covenant with your ancestors when I brought them out of Egypt, out of the house of slavery; it said: 14 At the end of seven years each one of you is to free his brother Hebrew who has sold himself to you: he may be your slave for six years, then you must send him away free. But your ancestors did not listen to me and would not pay attention. 15 Now, today you repented and did what pleases me by proclaiming freedom for your neighbour; you made a covenant before me in the Temple that bears my name. 16 And then you changed your minds and, profaning my name, each of you has recovered his slaves, men and women, whom you had sent away free to live their own lives, and has forced them to become your slaves again."

17 'So Yahweh says this: "You have disobeyed me, by failing to grant freedom to brother and neighbour. Very well, I in my turn, Yahweh declares, shall leave sword, famine and plague free to deal with you and I shall make you an object of horror to all the kingdoms of the earth. 18 As for the people who have broken my covenant, who have not observed the terms of the covenant which they made before me, I shall treat them like the calf that people cut in two to pass between its pieces. 19 The chief men of Judah and Jerusalem, the eunuchs, the priests, and all the country people who have passed between the pieces of the calf, 20 I shall hand over to their enemies and those determined to kill them, and their

corpses will be food for the birds of the sky and the animals of earth. ²¹ As for Zedekiah king of Judah and his chief men, I shall hand them to their enemies, to those determined to kill them, and to the army of the king of Babylon which has just withdrawn. ²² Listen, I shall give the order, Yahweh declares, and bring them back to this city to attack it and capture it and burn it down. And I shall make an uninhabited waste of the towns of Judah." '

The example of the Rechabites

35 The word which came to Jeremiah from Yahweh in the days of Jehoiakim son of Josiah, king of Judah, ² 'Go to the clan of the Rechabites and speak to them; bring them into one of the rooms of the Temple of Yahweh and offer them wine to drink.' ³ So I took Jaazaniah son of Jeremiah, son of Habazziniah, with his brothers and all his sons, the whole Rechabite clan, ⁴ and brought them to the Temple of Yahweh into the room of Ben-Johanan son of Igdaliah, a man of God, which was next to that of the chief men, above the room of Maaseiah son of Shallum, guardian of the threshold. ⁵ I then set pitchers full of wine, and some cups, before the members of the Rechabite clan and said, 'Drink some wine.'

⁶ But they replied, 'We do not drink wine, because our ancestor Jonadab son of Rechab gave us this order, "You must not drink wine, neither you nor your sons for ever; ⁷ nor must you build houses, sow seed, plant vineyards or own them, but must live in tents all your lives, so that you may live long on the soil to which you are alien." ⁸ We have punctiliously obeyed the orders of our ancestor, Jonadab son of Rechab, never drinking wine ourselves, nor our wives, our sons or our daughters, ⁹ not building houses to live in, owning neither vineyard nor field nor seed, ¹⁰ living in tents. We have obeyed the orders of our ancestor Jonadab, respecting them in every particular. ¹¹ However, when Nebuchadnezzar king of Babylon invaded this country, we decided, "We must get away! We will go to Jerusalem to escape the armies of the Chaldaeans and Aramaeans." So that is why we are living in Jerusalem.'

¹² Then the word of Yahweh came to Jeremiah as follows, ¹³ 'Yahweh Sabaoth, the God of Israel, says this, "Go and say to the people of Judah and the inhabitants of Jerusalem: Will you never learn the lesson and listen to my words, Yahweh demands? ¹⁴ The words of Jonadab son of Rechab, ordering his sons to drink no wine, have been observed; obedient to their ancestor's command, they drink none even today. But to me, who spoke to you so urgently, so untiringly, you have not listened. ¹⁵ I have urgently and untiringly sent you all my servants the prophets to say: Turn back, each one of you, from your evil behaviour and amend your actions, do not follow other gods to serve them, and you will go on living on the soil I gave to you and your ancestors. But you have not paid attention or listened to me. ¹⁶ Thus the sons of Jonadab son of Rechab have kept the command their ancestor gave them, but this people has not listened to me. ¹⁷ And so, Yahweh, God Sabaoth, God of Israel, says this: Look, on Judah and the citizens of Jerusalem I am going to bring all the disaster which I have decreed for them, because I spoke to them and they would not listen, called to them and they would not answer." '

¹⁸ Then Jeremiah said to the Rechabite clan, 'Yahweh Sabaoth, the God of Israel, says this, "Because you have obeyed the orders of your ancestor Jonadab and observed all his rules and done everything he ordered you to do, ¹⁹ therefore, Yahweh Sabaoth, the God of Israel, says this: Jonadab son of Rechab will never lack a male descendant to stand before me for ever." '

The scroll written in 605–604 BC

36 In the fourth year of Jehoiakim son of Josiah, king of Judah, this word came to Jeremiah from Yahweh, ² 'Take a scroll and on it write all the words I have spoken to you about Israel, Judah and all the nations, from the day I first spoke to you, in the time of Josiah, until today. ³ Perhaps when the House of Judah hears about all the disaster I intend to inflict on them, they will turn, each one of them, from their evil behaviour, so that I can forgive their sinful guilt.' 4 Jeremiah then summoned Baruch son of Neriah, who at his dictation wrote down on the scroll all the words Yahweh had spoken to him.

5 Jeremiah then gave Baruch this order, 'As I am prevented from entering the Temple of Yahweh, 6 you yourself must go and, from the scroll you wrote at my dictation, read all Yahweh's words to the people in his Temple on the day of the fast, and in this way you can read them in the hearing also of all the Judaeans who come in from their towns. 7 Perhaps their prayers will move Yahweh and they will turn one and all from their evil behaviour, for great is the furious anger with which Yahweh has threatened this people.' 8 Baruch son of Neriah duly carried out the order that the prophet Jeremiah had given him, to read all Yahweh's words from the book in his Temple.

9 Now, in the fifth year of Jehoiakim son of Josiah, king of Judah, in the ninth month, all the people of Jerusalem and all the people who could get to Jerusalem from the towns of Judah were summoned to a fast before Yahweh. 10 Baruch then read Jeremiah's words from the book; this happened in the room of Gemariah son of the scribe Shaphan, in the upper court at the entry of the New Gate of the Temple of Yahweh, where all the people could hear.

11 Micaiah son of Gemariah, son of Shaphan, having heard all Yahweh's words read from the book, 12 went down to the royal palace, to the scribe's room. All the chief men were in session: the scribe Elishama, Delaiah son of Shemaiah, Elnathan son of Achbor, Gemariah son of Shaphan, Zedekiah son of Hananiah and all the other chief men; 13 and to them Micaiah reported all the words he heard as Baruch was reading the book aloud to the people. 14 The chief men then by common consent sent Jehudi son of Netaniah to Baruch, with Shelemiah son of Cushi, to say, 'Come, and bring the scroll with you which you have been reading to the people.' 15 Bring-

ing the scroll with him, Baruch son of Neriah appeared before them. 'Sit down,' they said, 'and read it out.' So Baruch read it to them. 16 Having heard all the words they turned to one another in alarm and said to Baruch, 'We must certainly inform the king of this.' 17 They then questioned Baruch, 'Tell us', they said, 'how you came to write all these words.' 18 'Jeremiah dictated them all to me,' Baruch replied, 'and I wrote them down in ink in this book.' 19 The chief men said to Baruch, 'You and Jeremiah had better go into hiding; and do not tell anyone where you are.' 20 Whereupon they went off to the king in the palace court, depositing the scroll in the room of the scribe Elishama. They then informed the king of the whole affair.

21 The king sent Jehudi for the scroll, and he brought it from the room of the scribe Elishama and read it to the king and all the chief men standing round the king. 22 The king was sitting in his winter apartments—it was the ninth month—with a fire burning in a brazier in front of him. 23 Each time Jehudi had read three or four columns, the king cut them off with a scribe's knife and threw them into the fire in the brazier until the whole of the scroll had been burnt in the brazier fire. 24 But in spite of hearing all these words, neither the king nor any of his courtiers took alarm or tore their clothes; 25 and although Elnathan and Delaiah and Gemariah had urged the king not to burn the scroll he would not listen to them, 26 but ordered the king's son Jerahmeel and Seraiah son of Azriel and Shelemiah son of Abdeel to arrest the scribe Baruch and the prophet Jeremiah. But Yahweh had hidden them.

27 Then the word of Yahweh came to Jeremiah, after the king had burnt the scroll containing the words Baruch had written at Jeremiah's dictation, 28 'Take another scroll and write down all the words that were written on the first scroll burnt by Jehoiakim king of Judah. 29 And as regards Jehoiakim king of Judah, you are to say, "Yahweh says this: You have burnt that scroll, saying: Why have you

written down: The king of Babylon will certainly come and lay this country waste and
leave it without human or animal? ³⁰ So, this is
what Yahweh says about Jehoiakim king of
Judah: He will have no one to occupy the
throne of David, and his corpse will be tossed
out to the heat of the day and the frost of the
night. ³¹ I shall punish him, his offspring and
his courtiers for their guilt; on them, on the
citizens of Jerusalem and on the people of
Judah I shall bring the total disaster which I
had decreed for them but to which they have
paid no attention." '

³² Jeremiah then took another scroll and
gave it to the scribe Baruch son of Neriah, who
in it at Jeremiah's dictation wrote all the words
of the book that Jehoiakim king of Judah had
burnt, with many similar words in addition.

A verdict on Zedekiah

37 Zedekiah son of Josiah became king,
succeeding Coniah son of Jehoiakim.
Nebuchadnezzar king of Babylon had made
him king of Judah. ² But neither he nor his
courtiers nor the people of the country paid
any attention to the words Yahweh spoke
through the prophet Jeremiah.

Zedekiah consults Jeremiah during
the respite of 588 BC

³ King Zedekiah sent Jehucal son of Shelemiah and the priest Zephaniah son of Maaseiah to the prophet Jeremiah with this message, 'Intercede for us with Yahweh our God.'
⁴ Now Jeremiah was still moving freely among
the people: he had not yet been put in prison.
⁵ Meanwhile Pharaoh's army was on the move
from Egypt and the Chaldaeans besieging
Jerusalem had raised the siege when they
heard the news.

⁶ Then the word of Yahweh came to the
prophet Jeremiah as follows, ⁷ 'Yahweh, God
of Israel, says this, "To the king of Judah who
sent you to consult me make this reply: Is Pharaoh's army marching to your aid? It will
withdraw to its own country, Egypt. ⁸ The
Chaldaeans will return to attack this city; they

will capture it and burn it down. ⁹ Yahweh
says this: Do not cheer yourselves up by thinking: The Chaldaeans are leaving us for good.
They are not leaving. ¹⁰ Even if you cut to
pieces the whole Chaldaean army now fighting against you until there were only the
wounded left, they would stand up again, each
man in his tent, to burn this city down." '

The arrest of Jeremiah; improvement
in his treatment

¹¹ At the time when the Chaldaean army,
threatened by Pharaoh's army, had raised the
siege of Jerusalem, ¹² Jeremiah set out from
Jerusalem for the territory of Benjamin to see
about a piece of his property among the people
there. ¹³ He was at the Benjamin Gate when
the guard commander there, a certain Irijah
son of Shelemiah, son of Hananiah, arrested
the prophet Jeremiah, shouting, 'You are deserting to the Chaldaeans!' ¹⁴ Jeremiah answered, 'It is a lie! I am not deserting to the
Chaldaeans.' But Irijah would not listen to
Jeremiah and took him under arrest to the
chief men. ¹⁵ And the chief men, furious with
Jeremiah, had him beaten and shut up in the
house of the scribe Jonathan, which had been
turned into a prison. ¹⁶ Thus Jeremiah found
himself in an underground vault. And there
for a long time he stayed.

¹⁷ Later, King Zedekiah had him sent for,
and the king questioned him privately in his
palace. 'Is there any word from Yahweh?' he
asked. 'There is,' Jeremiah answered, and
added, 'you will be handed over to the king of
Babylon.' ¹⁸ Jeremiah then said to King
Zedekiah, 'What wrong have I done you, or
your courtiers or this people, for you to have
put me in prison? ¹⁹ Where are your prophets
now who prophesied, "The king of Babylon
will not attack you or this country"? ²⁰ So now
I beg you to hear me, my lord king! I beg you
to approve my request! Do not have me taken
back to the house of the scribe Jonathan, or I
shall die there.' ²¹ King Zedekiah then gave an
order, and Jeremiah was confined in the Court
of the Guard and given a loaf of bread a day

from the Street of the Bakers as long as there was bread left in the city. So Jeremiah stayed in the Court of the Guard.

Jeremiah is thrown into the storage-well; Ebed-Melech intervenes

38 But Shephatiah son of Mattan, Gedaliah son of Pashhur, Jucal son of Shelemiah and Pashhur son of Malchiah heard the words which Jeremiah was saying to all the people, 2 'Yahweh says this, "Anyone who stays in this city will die by sword, famine or plague; but anyone who leaves it and surrenders to the Chaldaeans will live; he will escape with his life.ª 3 Yahweh says this: This city will certainly be handed over to the army of the king of Babylon, and he will capture it." '

4 The chief men then said to the king, 'You must have this man put to death: he is unquestionably disheartening the remaining soldiers in the city, and all the people too, by talking like this. This man is seeking not the welfare of the people but their ruin.' 5 King Zedekiah answered, 'He is in your hands as you know, for the king is powerless to oppose you.' 6 So they took Jeremiah and put him into the storage-well of the king's son Malchiah in the Court of the Guard, letting him down with ropes. There was no water in the storage-well, only mud, and into the mud Jeremiah sank.

7 But Ebed-Melech the Cushite, a eunuch attached to the palace, heard that Jeremiah had been put into the storage-well. As the king was sitting in the Benjamin Gate, 8 Ebed-Melech came out from the palace and spoke to the king. 9 'My lord king,' he said, 'these men have done a wicked thing by treating the prophet Jeremiah like this: they have thrown him into the storage-well. He will starve to death there, since there is no more food in the city.' 10 At this the king gave Ebed-Melech the Cushite the following order: 'Take thirty men with you from here and pull the prophet Jeremiah out of the storage-well before he dies.' 11 Ebed-Melech took the men with him and went into the palace to the Treasury wardrobe; out of it he took some torn, worn-out rags

which he lowered on ropes to Jeremiah in the storage-well. 12 Ebed-Melech the Cushite then said to Jeremiah, 'These torn, worn-out rags are for you to put under your armpits to pad the ropes.' Jeremiah did this. 13 Then they hauled Jeremiah up with the ropes and pulled him out of the storage-well. And Jeremiah stayed in the Court of the Guard.

The last conversation between Jeremiah and Zedekiah

14 King Zedekiah had the prophet Jeremiah summoned to him at the third entrance to the Temple of Yahweh. 'I want to ask you for a word,' the king said to Jeremiah, 'keep nothing back from me.' 15 Jeremiah answered Zedekiah, 'If I do proclaim it to you, are you not sure to have me put to death? And if I give you advice, you will not listen to me.' 16 King Zedekiah then secretly swore this oath to Jeremiah, 'As Yahweh lives, giver of this life of ours, I will have you neither put to death nor handed over to these men who are determined to kill you.' 17 Jeremiah then said to Zedekiah, 'Yahweh, God Sabaoth, God of Israel, says this, "If you go out and surrender to the king of Babylon's generals, your life will be safe and this city will not be burnt down; you and your family will survive. 18 But if you do not go out and surrender to the king of Babylon's generals, this city will be handed over to the Chaldaeans and they will burn it down; nor will you yourself escape their clutches." ' 19 King Zedekiah then said to Jeremiah, 'I am afraid of the Judaeans who have already gone over to the Chaldaeans: I might be handed over to them and they would ill-treat me.' 20 'You will not be handed over to them,' Jeremiah replied. 'Please listen to Yahweh's voice as I have relayed it to you, and then all will go well with you and your life will be safe. 21 But if you refuse to surrender, this is what Yahweh has shown me: 22 the sight of all the women left in the king of Judah's palace being led off to the king of Babylon's generals and saying:

38a = 21:9.

"They have misled you, they have
        triumphed over you,
those friends of yours!
Your feet have sunk in the mud!
They are up and away!"

²³ 'Yes, all your wives and children will be led
off to the Chaldaeans, and you yourself will
not escape their clutches but will be a prisoner
in the clutches of the king of Babylon. And as
for this city, it will be burnt down.'

²⁴ Zedekiah then said to Jeremiah, 'Do not
let anyone else hear these words or you will
die. ²⁵ If the chief men hear that I have been
talking to you, and come and say, "Tell us
what you said to the king and what the king
said to you; keep nothing back from us, or we
shall put you to death," ²⁶ you must reply, "I
presented this request to the king: that he
would not have me sent back to Jonathan's
house to die." '

²⁷ And in fact all the chief men came to Jeremiah and questioned him. He told them exactly what the king had ordered him to say.
They then left him in peace, since the conversation had not been overheard. ²⁸ And Jeremiah stayed in the Court of the Guard until
the day Jerusalem was captured. And he was
there when Jerusalem actually was captured.

*The fall of Jerusalem and what happened
to Jeremiah*

39 In the ninth year of Zedekiah king of
Judah, in the tenth month, Nebuchadnezzar king of Babylon advanced on Jerusalem with his entire army, and they laid siege to
it. ² In the eleventh year of Zedekiah, in the
fourth month, a breach was made in the city
wall.

³ The king of Babylon's officials, all having
made their entry, took their seats in the Middle Gate: Nergal-Sharezer, Samgar-Nebo,
Sar-Sechim a high dignitary of state, Nergal-
Sharezer the chief astrologer, and all the king
of Babylon's other officials . . .

⁴ On seeing them, Zedekiah king of Judah
and all the fighting men fled, leaving the city

under cover of dark, by way of the king's garden through the gate between the two walls,
and made their way towards the Arabah. ⁵ But
the Chaldaean troops pursued them and
caught up with Zedekiah in the plains of Jericho. They captured him and took him to Nebuchadnezzar king of Babylon at Riblah in the
territory of Hamath, where he passed sentence
on him. ⁶ The king of Babylon had Zedekiah's
sons slaughtered before his eyes at Riblah; the
king of Babylon also had all the leading men
of Judah put to death. ⁷ He then put out
Zedekiah's eyes and, loading him with chains,
carried him off to Babylon. ⁸ The Chaldaeans
burnt down the royal palace and the private
houses, and demolished the walls of Jerusalem. ⁹ Nebuzaradan commander of the guard
deported the remainder of the population left
behind in the city, the deserters who had gone
over to him, and the rest of the artisans to
Babylon. ¹⁰ But Nebuzaradan commander of
the guard left some of the poor people behind
in the country of Judah, those who had nothing, at the same time giving them vineyards
and fields.

¹¹ With regard to Jeremiah, Nebuchadnezzar king of Babylon had given the following
orders to Nebuzaradan, commander of the
guard, ¹² 'Take him, look after him; do him no
harm, but treat him as he may ask you.'

¹³ He entrusted this mission to (Nebuzaradan commander of the guard,) Nebu-
shazban the high dignitary of state, Nergal-
Sharezer the chief astrologer and all the king
of Babylon's other officials.

¹⁴ These despatched men to take Jeremiah
from the Court of the Guard and turned him
over to Gedaliah son of Ahikam, son of
Shaphan for safe conduct home. So he remained among the people.

*A prophecy assuring the safety of
Ebed-Melech*

¹⁵ While Jeremiah was confined in the Court
of the Guard, the word of Yahweh came to
him as follows, ¹⁶ 'Go and say to Ebed-Melech
the Cushite, "Yahweh, God of Israel says this:

Look, I am about to perform my words about this city for its ruin and not for its prosperity. That day they will come true before your eyes. ¹⁷But I shall rescue you that day, Yahweh declares, and you will not be handed over to the hands of the men you fear. ¹⁸Yes, I shall certainly rescue you: you will not fall to the sword; you will escape with your life, because you have put your trust in me, Yahweh declares." '

Further details about the treatment of Jeremiah

40 The word which came to Jeremiah from Yahweh after Nebuzaradan commander of the guard had released him from Ramah, where he had found him in chains with all the other captives from Jerusalem and Judah who were being deported to Babylon: ²The commander of the guard took Jeremiah and said to him, 'Yahweh your God foretold calamity for this country, ³and now he has brought it. He has done what he threatened to do, because you had sinned against Yahweh and would not listen to his voice; so all this has happened to you. ⁴Look, today I am having your hands unchained. If you like to come with me to Babylon, come: I shall look after you. If you do not want to come with me to Babylon, do not. Look, you have the whole country before you: go wherever you think it best and most suitable to go.' ⁵And before Jeremiah retired, he added, 'You can go back to Gedaliah son of Ahikam, son of Shaphan, whom the king of Babylon has appointed governor of the towns of Judah, and stay with him among the people, or go anywhere else you think suitable.' With that, the commander of the guard gave him provisions and a present, and dismissed him. ⁶Jeremiah went to Mizpah, to Gedaliah son of Ahikam and stayed with him, among those people still left in the country.

Gedaliah the governor; his assassination

⁷When the military leaders who with their men were still in the field, all heard that the king of Babylon had appointed Gedaliah son of Ahikam as governor of the country, making him responsible for the men, women and children, and those of the poor country people who had not been deported to Babylon, ⁸they came to Gedaliah at Mizpah: Ishmael son of Nethaniah, Johanan and Jonathan sons of Kareah, Seraiah son of Tanhumeth, the sons of Ephai the Netophathite, Jezaniah son of the Maacathite, they and their men. ⁹To them and to their men Gedaliah son of Ahikam, son of Shaphan, swore an oath. 'Do not be afraid', he said, 'of serving the Chaldaeans, stay in the country, serve the king of Babylon, and all will go well with you. ¹⁰I for my part, as the man answerable to the Chaldaeans when they come to us, shall stay here at Mizpah, whereas you can harvest the wine, summer fruit and oil, fill your storage jars and settle in the towns which you have seized.'

¹¹Similarly, when all the Judaeans living in Moab, with the Ammonites, in Edom and elsewhere, heard that the king of Babylon had left a remnant in Judah and had appointed Gedaliah son of Ahikam, son of Shaphan as their governor, ¹²the Judaeans all came back from wherever they had been driven. On their return to the land of Judah, to Gedaliah at Mizpah, they harvested an immense quantity of wine and summer fruit.

¹³Now Johanan son of Kareah and all the military leaders still in the field, came to Gedaliah at Mizpah ¹⁴and said to him, 'Are you aware that Baalis king of the Ammonites has sent Ishmael son of Nethaniah to assassinate you?' But Gedaliah son of Ahikam would not believe them. ¹⁵Johanan son of Kareah then spoke in secret to Gedaliah at Mizpah, as follows: 'Please let me go and kill Ishmael son of Nethaniah, and no one will be any the wiser. Why should he assassinate you and cause the dispersal of all the Judaeans who have rallied round you. Why should the remnant of Judah perish?' ¹⁶But Gedaliah son of Ahikam replied to Johanan son of Kareah, 'You will do no such thing, for what you say about Ishmael is false.'

41 In the seventh month, however, Ishmael son of Nethaniah son of Elishama, who was of royal descent, came with officers of the king and ten men to Gedaliah son of Ahikam at Mizpah. And as they were taking their meal together, there at Mizpah, ² Ishmael son of Nethaniah stood up with his ten men, and attacking Gedaliah son of Ahikam, son of Shaphan, with their swords, they killed the man whom the king of Babylon had made governor of the country. ³ And all the Judaeans who were with him, that is with Gedaliah at Mizpah, and the Chaldaean soldiers who happened to be there, Ishmael killed too.

⁴ On the day after the murder of Gedaliah, before the news had become known, ⁵ eighty men arrived from Shechem, Shiloh and Samaria, with their beards shaved off, their clothing torn, and covered in self-inflicted gashes; they were bringing cereal offerings and incense with them to present to the Temple of Yahweh. ⁶ Ishmael son of Nethaniah went out of Mizpah to meet them, weeping as he went. When he met them he said, 'Come to Gedaliah son of Ahikam.' ⁷ But once they were well inside the town, Ishmael son of Nethaniah slaughtered them, with the help of his men, and had them thrown into the storage-well. ⁸ There were ten of them, however, who said to Ishmael, 'Do not kill us: we have stocks of wheat and barley, oil and honey, hidden away in the fields.' So he spared them and did not kill them with their brothers. ⁹ The storage-well into which Ishmael threw the corpses of all the men he had killed was a large one, the one which King Asa had built as a precaution against Baasha king of Israel. Ishmael son of Nethaniah filled it with the slaughtered men. ¹⁰ Ishmael then took all the rest of the people prisoner who were at Mizpah, the king's daughters and all the remaining people in Mizpah, whom Nebuzaradan, commander of the guard, had entrusted to Gedaliah son of Ahikam. Ishmael son of Nethaniah took them prisoner and set out, intending to cross over to the Ammonites.

¹¹ When Johanan son of Kareah and all the military leaders who were with him heard about all the crimes committed by Ishmael son of Nethaniah, ¹² they mustered all their men and set out to attack Ishmael son of Nethaniah. They caught up with him at the great Pool of Gibeon. ¹³ At the sight of Johanan son of Kareah and all the military leaders with him, all the people with Ishmael were delighted. ¹⁴ All the people whom Ishmael had taken as prisoners from Mizpah turned about, went back and joined Johanan son of Kareah. ¹⁵ Ishmael son of Nethaniah, however, escaped from Johanan with eight of his men and fled to the Ammonites. ¹⁶ Johanan son of Kareah and all the military leaders with him then rallied all the remaining people whom Ishmael son of Nethaniah had taken as prisoners from Mizpah after killing Gedaliah son of Ahikam: men—fighting men—women, children and eunuchs, whom they brought back from Gibeon. ¹⁷ Setting off, they made a halt at Khan Kimham near Bethlehem, intending to go on to Egypt, ¹⁸ to get away from the Chaldaeans. They were now terrified of them, since Ishmael son of Nethaniah had killed Gedaliah son of Ahikam whom the king of Babylon had made governor of the country.

The flight to Egypt

42 Then all the military leaders, in particular Johanan son of Kareah and Azariah son of Hoshaiah, and all the people from least to greatest, approached ² the prophet Jeremiah and said, 'Please hear our petition and intercede with Yahweh your God for us and for all this remnant—and how few of us are left out of many, your own eyes can see— ³ so that Yahweh your God may show us the way we are to go and what we must do.' ⁴ The prophet Jeremiah replied, 'I hear you; I will indeed pray to Yahweh your God as you ask; and whatever answer Yahweh your God gives you, I will tell you, keeping nothing back from you.' ⁵ They in their turn said to Jeremiah, 'May Yahweh be a true and faithful witness against us, if we do not follow the instructions that Yahweh your God sends us through you.

⁶Whether we like it or not, we shall obey the voice of Yahweh our God to whom we are sending you, so that we may prosper by obeying the voice of Yahweh our God.'

⁷Ten days later the word of Yahweh came to Jeremiah. ⁸He then summoned Johanan son of Kareah and all the military leaders who were with him, and all the people from least to greatest, ⁹and said, 'Yahweh, God of Israel, to whom you deputed me to present your petition says this, ¹⁰"If you will only stay in this country, I shall build you and not overthrow you; I shall plant you and not uproot you, for I am sorry about the disaster I have inflicted on you. ¹¹Do not be afraid of the king of Babylon, whom you fear now; do not fear him, Yahweh declares, for I am with you to save you and rescue you from his clutches. ¹²I shall take pity on you, so that he pities you and lets you return to your native soil. ¹³But if you say: We will not stay in this country; if you disobey the voice of Yahweh your God, ¹⁴and say: No, Egypt is where we shall go, where we shall not see war or hear the trumpet-call or go short of food; that is where we want to live; ¹⁵in that case, remnant of Judah, listen to Yahweh's word: Yahweh Sabaoth, God of Israel, says this: If you are determined to go to Egypt, and if you do go and settle there, ¹⁶the sword you fear will overtake you there in Egypt, and there you will die. ¹⁷Yes, all those who are determined to go to Egypt and settle there, will die by sword, famine and plague: not a single one of them will survive or escape the disaster I shall inflict on them. ¹⁸Yes, Yahweh Sabaoth, the God of Israel, says this: Just as my furious anger was poured out on the inhabitants of Jerusalem, so will my fury be poured out on you if you go to Egypt: you will become an object of execration and horror, a curse, a laughing-stock; and you will never see this place again." ¹⁹Remnant of Judah, Yahweh has told you, "Do not go into Egypt." Understand clearly that today I have given you a solemn warning. ²⁰You were not being sincere when you sent me to Yahweh your God and said, "Intercede for us with Yahweh our God; tell us exactly what Yahweh our God says and we will do it." ²¹Today I have told you, but you have not obeyed the voice of Yahweh your God or any part of the message he sent me to give you. ²²So understand this clearly: you will die by sword, famine and plague in the place where you want to go and settle.'

43 When Jeremiah had finished telling all the people all the words of Yahweh their God, which Yahweh their God had sent him to tell them—all the words quoted above— ²Azariah son of Hoshaiah, and Johanan son of Kareah, and all those arrogant men, said to Jeremiah, 'You are lying. Yahweh our God did not send you to say, "Do not go to Egypt and settle there." ³It was Baruch son of Neriah, who keeps inciting you against us, to hand us over to the Chaldaeans so that they can put us to death or deport us to Babylon.'

⁴So neither Johanan nor any of the military leaders nor any of the people obeyed the voice of Yahweh by staying in the country of Judah. ⁵Instead, Johanan son of Kareah and all the military leaders led off the entire remnant of Judah, those who had come back from all the nations where they had been driven to live in the country of Judah: ⁶men, women, children, the royal princesses too, and every single person that Nebuzaradan commander of the guard had left with Gedaliah son of Ahikam, son of Shaphan, including the prophet Jeremiah and Baruch son of Neriah. ⁷And so, in disobedience to the voice of Yahweh, they reached Egypt and arrived at Tahpanhes.

Jeremiah foretells the invasion of Egypt by Nebuchadnezzar

⁸At Tahpanhes the word of Yahweh was addressed to Jeremiah as follows, ⁹'Take some large stones and bury them in the cement on the terrace outside the entrance of Pharaoh's palace in Tahpanhes, where the Judaeans can see you. ¹⁰Then say to them, "Yahweh, God of Israel, says this: Look, I shall send for my servant Nebuchadnezzar, king of Babylon, and he will place his throne on these stones I have

buried, and spread his canopy above them. ¹¹ When he comes, he will defeat Egypt:

> Those for the plague, to the plague;
> those for captivity, to captivity;
> those for the sword, to the sword! ᵃ

¹² "He will set fire to the temples of the gods of Egypt; he will burn these gods or take them prisoner; like a shepherd wrapping his cloak round him, so he will wrap Egypt round him, and then leave without anyone laying hands on him. ¹³ He will break the obelisks of the temple of the Sun in Egypt, and burn down the temples of the gods of Egypt." '

The last episode of Jeremiah's ministry: the Judaeans in Egypt and the Queen of Heaven

44 The word that came to Jeremiah for all the Judaeans living in Egypt, those, that is, living in Migdol, Tahpanhes, Noph and the territory of Pathros.

² 'Yahweh Sabaoth, God of Israel, says this, "You have seen all the disaster I have brought on Jerusalem and all the towns of Judah; today they lie in ruins and uninhabited. ³ This was because of the wicked deeds they committed to provoke my anger, by going and offering incense and serving other gods whom neither they, nor you, nor your ancestors knew anything about, ⁴ although I urgently and untiringly sent you all my servants the prophets to say: You must not do this loathsome thing, which I hate. ⁵ But they would not listen or pay attention, and turn from their wickedness and stop offering incense to other gods. ⁶ And so my furious anger overflowed, burning down the towns of Judah and the streets of Jerusalem, which were reduced to ruins and wasteland, as they still are today. ⁷ And now, Yahweh, God Sabaoth, God of Israel, says this: Why bring complete disaster on yourselves by cutting yourselves off from Judah—your men, women, children and babes in arms—so as to leave yourselves no remnant, ⁸ by provoking my wrath by your actions, offering incense to

other gods in Egypt where you have come to settle, as though bent on your own destruction and on becoming a curse and a laughing-stock for all the nations of the earth? ⁹ Have you forgotten the wicked deeds of your ancestors, of the kings of Judah and of your princes, your own wicked deeds and those of your wives, committed in the country of Judah and in the streets of Jerusalem? ¹⁰ To this day they have felt neither contrition nor fear; they have not observed my Law or my statutes, which I prescribed for you, as for your ancestors. ¹¹ So, Yahweh Sabaoth, God of Israel, says this: Look, I have determined on disaster and shall destroy Judah completely. ¹² I shall take the remnant of Judah who were determined to come to Egypt and settle there, and in Egypt they will perish; they will fall to the sword or perish of famine, from least to greatest; by sword and famine they will die and be an object of execration and horror, a curse, a laughing-stock. ¹³ I shall punish those who live in Egypt just as I punished Jerusalem: by sword, famine and plague. ¹⁴ Of the remnant of Judah which has come to settle in Egypt, not a single one will escape or survive to return to the country of Judah where they long to return and live. For none of them will return, except a few refugees." '

¹⁵ At this, all the men who knew that their wives offered incense to other gods, and all the women who were standing there, a great crowd (and all the people living in Egypt, in Pathros), answered Jeremiah as follows, ¹⁶ 'We have no intention of listening to the word you have just spoken to us in Yahweh's name, ¹⁷ but intend to go on doing all we have vowed to do: offering incense to the Queen of Heaven and pouring libations in her honour, as we used to do, we and our ancestors, our kings and our chief men, in the towns of Judah and the streets of Jerusalem: we had food in plenty then, we lived well, we suffered no disasters. ¹⁸ But since we gave up offering incense to the Queen of Heaven and pouring libations in her

43a = 15:2.

honour, we have been destitute and have perished either by sword or by famine. ¹⁹Besides, when we offer incense to the Queen of Heaven and pour libations in her honour, do you think we make cakes for her with her features on them, and pour libations to her, without our husbands' knowledge?'

²⁰To all the people, men and women, all those who had made this answer, Jeremiah retorted, ²¹'The incense you offered in the towns of Judah and the streets of Jerusalem, you, your ancestors, your kings, your chief men and the people at large—was this not what Yahweh kept remembering, and found so repellent ²²that Yahweh could not endure your misdeeds and your loathsome practices any longer, with the result that your country has become the uninhabited ruin, the object of horror and cursing it is today? ²³Because you offered incense, because you sinned against Yahweh, refusing to listen to the voice of Yahweh, or to observe his Law, his statutes and his decrees—that is why the present disaster has overtaken you.'

²⁴Further, Jeremiah said to all the people, and particularly to all the women, 'Listen to the word of Yahweh, all you Judaeans in Egypt, ²⁵Yahweh Sabaoth, God of Israel, says this, "You and your wives, what your mouths promised, your hands have indeed performed! You said: We shall punctiliously fulfil the vows we have made and offer incense to the Queen of Heaven and pour libations in her honour. Very well, keep your vows, perform them punctiliously! ²⁶But listen to the word of Yahweh, all you Judaeans living in Egypt: I swear by my great name, Yahweh says, that my name will no longer be uttered by any man of Judah throughout Egypt; no one will say: As Lord Yahweh lives. ²⁷No, I am going to keep my eye on them for disaster, not for prosperity, and all the Judaeans in Egypt will perish either by the sword or by famine until they are wiped out. ²⁸Yet, though few in number, those who escape the sword will return to the country of Judah from Egypt. Then the entire remnant of Judah which has come and settled

in Egypt will know whose word comes true, mine or theirs.

²⁹"And here is the sign for you, Yahweh declares, that I shall punish you in this place: so that you will know that the words with which I threaten you will come true: ³⁰Yahweh says this: Look, I shall hand Pharaoh Hophra, king of Egypt, over to his enemies and to those determined to kill him, just as I handed Zedekiah king of Judah over to his enemy Nebuchadnezzar king of Babylon, who was determined to kill him."'

A prophecy of comfort for Baruch

45 The word that the prophet Jeremiah addressed to Baruch son of Neriah when the latter wrote these words down in a book at Jeremiah's dictation in the fourth year of Jehoiakim son of Josiah, king of Judah, ²'This is what Yahweh God of Israel says about you, Baruch! ³"You have been thinking: what disaster for me, and Yahweh has added further grief to my troubles! I am worn out with groaning, and find no relief!" ⁴Say to him as follows, "Yahweh says this: Now I am knocking down what I have built, am uprooting what I have planted, over the whole country! ⁵And you ask for special treatment! Do not ask, for I am now going to bring disaster on all humanity, Yahweh declares, but you I shall allow to escape with your life, wherever you may go."'

46 The words of Yahweh that were addressed to the prophet Jeremiah against the nations.

Prophecies ᵃ against Egypt; the defeat at Carchemish

²On Egypt.

Against the army of Pharaoh Necho king of Egypt, which was at Carchemish on the River Euphrates when Nebuchadnezzar king

46a The Hebr. text places the prophecies against the nations at the end of the book, chh. 46–51; in Gk they occur after ch. 25.

of Babylon defeated it in the fourth year of Jehoiakim son of Josiah, king of Judah.

3 Buckler and shield at the ready!
  Onward to battle!
4 Harness the horses:
  into the saddle, horsemen!
To your ranks! On with your helmets!
  Sharpen your spears,
  put on your breastplates!
5 Why do I see them
  retreating, panic-stricken?
Their heroes, beaten back,
  are fleeing headlong,
  with not a look behind.
Terror on every side,
  Yahweh declares!
6 No flight for the swift,
  no escape for the strong!
Up in the north on the River Euphrates,
  they have collapsed, have fallen.

7 Who was it rose like the Nile,
  his waters foaming like a torrent?
8 Why, Egypt rose like the Nile,
  his waters foaming like a torrent.
'I shall rise', he said, 'and drown the earth;
  sweep away town and its inhabitants!
9 Charge, horses!
  Forward, chariots!
Let the warriors advance,
  men from Cush and Put with shield in
    hand,
  men from Lud*b* who bend the bow!'
10 For this is the Day of Lord Yahweh
    Sabaoth,
  a day of vengeance when he takes revenge
    on his foes:
the sword will devour until gorged,
  until drunk with their blood,
for Lord Yahweh Sabaoth is holding a
    sacrificial feast
in the land of the north, on the River
    Euphrates.
11 Go up to Gilead and fetch balm,
  virgin daughter of Egypt!
You multiply remedies in vain,

nothing can cure you!
12 The nations have heard of your shame,
  your wailing fills the world,
for warrior has stumbled against warrior,
  and both have fallen together.

The invasion of Egypt

13 The word that came from Yahweh to the prophet Jeremiah when Nebuchadnezzar king of Babylon advanced to attack Egypt.

14 Publish it in Egypt,
  proclaim it in Migdol,
  proclaim it in Noph and Tahpanhes!
Say, 'Stand your ground, be prepared,
  for the sword is devouring all round you!'
15 Why has Apis fled?
  Why has your Mighty One not stood firm?
  Why, Yahweh has overturned him,
16 he has caused many to fall!
  Falling over one another,
they say, 'Up, and back to our own people,
  to the country where we were born,
  away from the devastating sword!'
17 They have given Pharaoh king of Egypt
    the nickname,
  'Much-noise-but-he-lets-the-chance-
    slip-by'!
18 As I live, the King declares,
  whose name is Yahweh Sabaoth,
he is coming, a very Tabor among
    mountains,
  a Carmel high above the sea!

19 Get your bundle ready for exile,
  fair inhabitant of Egypt!
Noph will be reduced to a desert,
  desolate, uninhabited.
20 Egypt was a splendid heifer,
  but a gadfly from the north has settled
    on her.
21 The mercenaries she had with her,
    these too
  were like fattened calves:

46*b* Cush, Put and Lud are perhaps Ethiopia, Lybia and Lydia respectively.

but they too have taken to their heels,
have all run away, not held their ground,
for their day of disaster has overtaken
        them,
    their time for being punished.

²² Hear her hissing like a snake
    as they advance in force
to fall on her with their axes,
    like woodcutters,
²³ they will fell her forest, Yahweh declares,
    however impenetrable it was
for they are more numerous than
        locusts,
    there is no counting them.
²⁴ The daughter of Egypt is put to shame,
    handed over to a people from the north.

²⁵ Yahweh Sabaoth, God of Israel, has said,
'Look, I shall punish Amon of No, Pharaoh,
Egypt, its gods, its kings, Pharaoh and those
who put their trust in him. ²⁶ I shall hand him
over to those who are determined to kill him,
to Nebuchadnezzar king of Babylon, to his
generals. But afterwards, Egypt will be inhabited again as in the past, Yahweh declares.

²⁷ But do not be afraid, my servant Jacob,
    Israel, do not be alarmed:
    for look, I shall rescue you from afar
    and your descendants from the country
            where they are captive.
    Jacob will return and be at peace,
    secure, with no one to trouble him.
²⁸ Do not be afraid, my servant Jacob,
    Yahweh declares, for I am with you:
    I shall make an end of all the nations
    where I have driven you,
    but I shall not make an end of you,
    I shall discipline you only as you
            deserve,
    not leaving you quite unpunished.^c

Prophecy against the Philistines

47 The word of Yahweh that came to Jeremiah about the Philistines before Pharaoh attacked Gaza. ² 'Yahweh says this:

Look, the waters are rising from the
        north
to become an overwhelming flood,
overwhelming the country and all in it,
the town and its inhabitants!
People cry for help, and there is wailing
    from all the country's inhabitants
³ at the thunder of his chargers' hoofs,
    the crash of his chariots, the grinding of
            his wheels.
Fathers forget about their children,
    their hands fall limp
⁴ because the day has come
    for all the Philistines to be destroyed,
    for Tyre and Sidon to be stripped
    to the last of their allies.
Yes, Yahweh is destroying the Philistines,
    the remnant from the Isle of Caphtor.
⁵ Baldness has befallen Gaza,
    Ashkelon has been reduced to silence.
You who remain in the valley,
    how long will you gash yourselves?
⁶ Oh, sword of Yahweh,
    how long before you rest?
Back into your scabbard,
    stop, keep still!
⁷ Yet how can it rest
    when Yahweh has given it an order,
    Ashkelon and the sea coast,
    the targets assigned to it?

Prophecies against Moab

48 On Moab. Yahweh, God of Israel, says
this:

Wretched Nebo, for it has been ravaged,
Kiriathaim has been shamed and taken,
    shame and distraction on the citadel,
² the pride of Moab is no more!
At Heshbon they plotted her downfall,
'Come, let us put an end to her as a
        nation!'
And you too, inhabitants of Madmen, will
        be silenced,
    the sword will be after you.

46c = 30:10–11.

3 A cry of agony goes up from Horonaim,
'Devastation! Dire calamity.
4 Moab has been shattered,'
the agonised cries of her little ones ring
out.
5 Up the slope of Luhith,
weeping they go.
On the road down to Horonaim
is heard the shriek of disaster,*a*
6 'Away! Flee for your lives
like the wild donkey into the desert!'
7 Yes, since you relied on your deeds and
your wealth,
you will be captured too.
Chemosh will go into exile,
with all his priests and princes.
8 The despoiler will descend on every town,
not one will escape;
the Valley will be ravaged, the Plain be
plundered
as Yahweh has said.
9 Give Moab wings
so that she can fly away,
for her towns will be laid in ruins
where no one will ever live again.

10 (Accursed be he who does Yahweh's
work negligently! Accursed be he who deprives his sword of blood!)

11 From his youth Moab lived at ease,
he settled on his lees,
never having been decanted,
never having gone into exile:
and so he kept his own flavour,
his aroma was unchanged.

12 And so the days are coming, Yahweh declares, when I shall send him decanters to de-
cant him; they will empty his pitchers and
break his wine jars to bits. 13 Moab will be
shamed by Chemosh then, as the House of Israel was shamed by Bethel in which they put
their trust.

14 How can you say, 'We are heroes,
sturdy fighting men'?

15 Moab has been ravaged, his cities scaled,
the flower of his youth goes down to the
slaughter,
declares the King, whose name is Yahweh
Sabaoth.
16 Moab's ruin is coming soon,
his downfall comes at top speed.
17 Grieve for him, all you living near him,
all you who knew his name.
Say, 'How shattered it is, that mighty rod,
that splendid sceptre!'

18 Come down from your glory, sit on the
parched ground,
daughter of Dibon,
for the despoiler of Moab has advanced on
you,
he has destroyed your strongholds.
19 Stand by the roadside, keep watch,
daughter of Aroer.
Question fugitive and runaway,
ask, 'What has happened?'
20 'Moab has been shattered and shamed.
Wail and shriek!
Shout along the Arnon,
Moab has been laid waste!'

21 Judgement has also come on the Plain, on
Holon, Jahzah, Mephaath, 22 Dibon, Nebo,
Beth-Diblathaim, 23 Kiriathaim, Beth-Gamul,
Beth-Meon, 24 Kerioth, Bozrah, and all the
towns of Moab, far and near.

25 Moab's horn has been cut off,
his arm is broken, Yahweh declares.

26 Make him drunk! He has set himself up
against Yahweh; let Moab wallow in his vomit
and become a laughing-stock in his turn.
27 Was Israel not a laughing-stock to you? Was
he caught red-handed with the thieves, for
you to shake your head whenever you mention him?

28 Leave the towns, make the rocks your
home,

48a ‖ Is 15:5.

inhabitants of Moab.
Learn from the dove that makes its nest
in the walls of the gaping gorge.

29 We have heard about Moab's pride,
so very proud!
What arrogance! What pride! What
conceit!
What a haughty heart!
30 —I know all about his presumption,
Yahweh declares,
his empty boasting,
those empty deeds of his!
31 —and so I lament for Moab,
for all Moab I raise my cry
and mourn for the people of Kir-Heres.^b
32 More than for Jazer I weep for you,
vineyard of Sibmah:
your shoots stretched beyond the sea,
they reached all the way to Jazer.
On your harvest and vintage
the despoiler has descended.
33 Gladness and joy have vanished
from the orchards of Moab.
I have dried up the wine in the presses,
the treader of grapes treads no more,
the joyful shouting has ceased.

34 The cries of Heshbon and Elealeh can be
heard as far as Jahaz. The shrieks resound
from Zoar to Horonaim and Eglath-Shelishiyah, for even the Waters of Nimrim have
become a wasteland.
35 And in Moab I shall make an end, Yahweh declares, of anyone offering sacrifice on
the high places and anyone offering incense to
his gods.
36 That is why my heart sobs like a flute for
Moab, sobs like a flute for the people of Kir-
Heres, since the wealth he had acquired is lost.
37 Yes, every head is shaved, every beard cut
off, gashes are on every hand, sackcloth round
every waist. 38 On all the housetops of Moab
and in all its squares there is nothing but
lamenting, for I have broken Moab like an un-
wanted pot, Yahweh declares. 39 How shattered he is! Wail! Moab so shamefully in re-

treat! Moab has become a laughing-stock, a
thing of horror to all his neighbours.

40 For Yahweh says this:
(Look, like an eagle, he will hover,
spreading his wings over Moab.)
41 The towns have been captured,
the strongholds seized.
(And the heart of Moab's warriors, that
day,
will be like that of a woman in labour
pains.)
42 Moab will be destroyed, no longer a people,
for setting itself up against Yahweh.
43 Terror, the pit and the snare for you,
inhabitant of Moab,
Yahweh declares.

44 And anyone who escapes from terror
will fall into the pit,
and anyone who climbs out of the pit
will be caught in the snare.^c
Yes, I shall bring all this on Moab
when the year comes for punishing them,
Yahweh declares.
45 In the shelter of Heshbon the fugitives
have paused, exhausted.
But fire will burst from Heshbon,
a flame from the palace of Sihon,
consuming the brows of Moab,
the head of a turbulent brood.
46 Disaster for you, Moab!
The people of Chemosh are lost!
For your sons have been taken into exile
and your daughters into captivity.

47 But I shall bring back Moab's captives
in the final days, Yahweh declares.

Thus far the judgement on Moab.

Prophecy against Ammon

49 To the Ammonites.

Yahweh says this:
Has Israel no sons?

48b ‖ Is 16:6–7.   48c ‖ Is 24:17–18.

Has he no heir?
Why should Milcom have inherited Gad
and his people have settled in its towns?
2 And so the days are coming,
Yahweh declares,
when I shall make the war cry ring out
for Rabbah-of-the-Ammonites.
She will become a desolate mound
and her daughter towns will be burnt
down.
Then Israel will inherit from his heirs,
Yahweh says.
3 Wail, Heshbon, for Ar has been laid
waste!
Shriek, daughters of Rabbah!
Wrap yourself in sackcloth, raise the dirge,
run to and fro among the sheep-pens!
For Milcom is going into exile,
with all his priests and princes.
4 How you used to glory in your Valley,
rebellious daughter,
confident in your resources,
'Who will dare to attack me?'
5 Look, I shall bring terror on you,
Lord Yahweh Sabaoth declares,
from all directions;
you shall be driven away, everyone for
himself,
with no one to rally the fugitives.

6 (But later I shall bring back the captive Ammonites, Yahweh declares.)

Prophecy against Edom[a]

7 To Edom.

Yahweh says this:
Is there no wisdom left in Teman?
Have the shrewd run out of commonsense,
has their wisdom vanished?
8 Away! Take to your heels! Go into hiding,
inhabitants of Dedan,
for I shall bring ruin on Esau
when the time comes for me to punish
him.
9 If grape-pickers were to come to you,
would they not leave a few gleanings?

If robbers came during the night,
would they not steal only as much as they
wanted?
10 But I for my part have stripped Esau,
have laid his hiding places bare:
he can hide no longer.
His race is destroyed,
so are his brothers and neighbours; he is no
more!
11 Leave your orphans, I shall support them,
and let your widows rely on me!

12 For Yahweh says this, 'Look, those who
would not have had to drink the cup will have
to drink it all the same; so why should you go
unpunished? You will not go unpunished, but
will certainly have to drink. 13 For by my
own self I have sworn, Yahweh declares, that
Bozrah will become an object of horror, a
laughing-stock, a desert, a curse, and all its
towns ruins for ever.'

14 I have received a message from Yahweh,
a herald has been sent throughout the
nations,
'Muster! March against this people!
Prepare for battle!'
15 For look, I shall reduce you to the smallest
of nations,
to the most despised of people.
16 Your reputation for ferocity,
your proud heart has misled you.
You whose home is in the crannies of the
Rock,
who cling to the top of the peak!
Though you make your nest as high as the
eagle's,
I shall bring you down from there,
Yahweh declares.

17 Edom will become an object of horror;
everyone going near will be appalled, and
whistle at the sight of all her wounds. 18 As at
the overthrow of Sodom and Gomorrah and
their neighbouring towns, no one will live

49a ‖ Ob 1–6.

[1026]

there any more, Yahweh says, no human being settle there again.*b*

19 Look, like a lion he climbs from the
    thickets of the Jordan
  to the perennial pasture!
  In a flash, I shall make them run away,
  and there appoint someone I shall choose.
  For who is there like me?
  Who can hale me into court?
  Name me the shepherd
  who can stand up to me.
20 So now hear the plan
  that Yahweh has laid against Edom,
  the schemes he has in mind
  against the inhabitants of Teman:
  they will certainly be dragged away
  like the smallest of the flock!
  Their pastures will certainly be sacked
    before their eyes!
21 The earth quakes at the sound of their
    downfall,*c*
  the sound of it echoes to the Sea of Reeds.
22 Look, like an eagle, he will soar and hover,
  spreading his wings over Bozrah.
  And the heart of Edom's warriors,
    that day,
  will be like that of a woman in labour
    pains.

Prophecy against the towns of Syria

23 To Damascus.

  Hamath and Arpad are shamed,
  for they have heard bad news.
  They are convulsed with anxiety
  like the sea that cannot be calmed.
24 Damascus is aghast, she prepares for
    flight,
  she is seized with trembling
  (anguish and sorrow have laid hold on her
    as on a woman in labour).
25 What now! That famous town deserted,
  that city of gaiety?

26 And so in her squares her young men will fall, and all her fighting men will perish, that day, Yahweh Sabaoth declares.*d*

27 I shall light a fire inside the walls of
    Damascus,
  to devour the palaces of Ben-Hadad.

Prophecy against the Arab tribes

28 To Kedar and the kingdoms of Hazor, which were conquered by Nebuchadnezzar king of Babylon. Yahweh says this:

  Up! March on Kedar,
  destroy the sons of the east!
29 Let their tents and their flocks be
    captured,
  their tent-cloths and all their gear;
  let their camels be seized
  and the shout go up, 'Terror on every
    side!'
30 Away! Get into hiding as fast as you can,
  inhabitants of Hazor, Yahweh declares,
  for Nebuchadnezzar king of Babylon has
    made a plan against you,
  he has a scheme in mind against you,
31 Up! March on a nation at its ease,
  living secure, Yahweh declares,
  that has no gates, no bars,
  that lives in a remote place!
32 Their camels will be the plunder,
  their countless sheep the spoil.
  I shall scatter them to the winds,
  those Crop-Heads,
  and bring ruin on them from every side,
  Yahweh declares.
33 Hazor will become the lair of jackals,
  desolate for ever.
  No one will live there any more,
  no human being settle there again.

Prophecy against Elam

34 The word of Yahweh that came to the prophet Jeremiah about Elam, at the beginning of the reign of Zedekiah king of Judah. 35 'Yahweh Sabaoth says this:

  Look, I shall break Elam's bow,
  the source of his might.

49b = 50:40. *49c* = 50:44–46. *49d* = 50:30.

36 I shall bring four winds on Elam
    from the four corners of the sky,
    and I shall scatter them to all these winds:
    there will not be a single nation
    to which people expelled from Elam do
        not go.

37 I shall make the Elamites tremble before
        their enemies,
    before those determined to kill them.
    I shall bring disaster on them,
    my burning anger, Yahweh declares.
    I shall pursue them with the sword
    until I have destroyed them all.
38 I shall set up my throne in Elam,
    uprooting its king and princes,
    Yahweh declares.

39 In the final days, I shall bring Elam's captives back, Yahweh declares.'

Prophecy against Babylon

50 The word that Yahweh spoke against Babylon, against the country of the Chaldaeans, through the prophet Jeremiah.

The fall of Babylon and the liberation of Israel

2 Announce it to the nations, proclaim it,
    hoist a signal and proclaim it,
    making no secret of it, say,
    'Babylon is captured, Bel disgraced,
    Marduk[a] shattered.
    (Her idols are disgraced,
    her Obscenities shattered.)'
3 For a nation is marching on her from the
        north,
    to turn her country into a desert:
    no one will live there any more;
    human and animal have fled and
        gone.

4 In those days and at that time
    the people of Israel will return
    (they and the people of Judah);
    they will come weeping
    in search of Yahweh their God.

5 They will ask the way to Zion
    and turn their faces towards her,
    'Come, let us bind ourselves to Yahweh
    by an everlasting covenant never to be
        forgotten!'

6 Lost sheep, such were my people;
    their shepherds led them astray, the
        mountains misled them;
    from mountain to hill they went,
    forgetful of their fold.
7 Whoever came across them devoured
        them,
    their enemies said, 'We are not to blame,
    since they have sinned against Yahweh, the
        Home of Justice,
    against Yahweh, the Hope of their
        ancestors.'
8 Escape from Babylon,
    leave the country of the Chaldaeans.
    Be like he-goats, leading the sheep!
9 For look, I shall raise a league
    of mighty nations to attack Babylon,
    from the land of the north.
    They will take up position against her;
    by them she will be taken.
    Their arrows, like an experienced soldier's,
    never return in vain.
10 Chaldaea will be plundered,
    all her plunderers will be satisfied,
        Yahweh declares.

11 Rejoice! Have your triumph,
    you plunderers of my heritage!
    Be playful like a heifer let out to grass!
    Neigh like stallions!
12 But your mother is covered with shame,
    disgraced is the woman who bore you;
    she is the least of nations now;
    a desert, a parched land, a wasteland.
13 Because of Yahweh's anger,
    no one will live there any more,
    she will become a total solitude.
    All who pass by Babylon will be appalled
    and whistle at the sight of all her wounds.

50a Bel and Marduk are the chief gods of Babylon.

¹⁴ Take position against Babylon, surround
her,
all you who bend the bow.
Shoot at her! Do not spare your arrows,
for she has sinned against Yahweh!
¹⁵ Raise the war cry against her from all
sides.
She surrenders! Her bastions fall!
Her walls collapse!
This is Yahweh's vengeance! Take revenge
on her.
Treat her as she has treated others.
¹⁶ Deprive Babylon of the man who sows,
of the man who wields the sickle at
harvest.
Away from the devastating sword,
let everyone return to his own people,
let everyone flee to his own country!

¹⁷ Israel was a straying sheep
pursued by lions.

First, the king of Assyria devoured him,
and latterly Nebuchadnezzar king of Babylon
crunched his bones. ¹⁸So Yahweh Sabaoth,
God of Israel, says this: Look, I shall punish
the king of Babylon and his country as I punished the king of Assyria.

¹⁹ I will bring Israel back to his pastures
to browse on Carmel and in Bashan,
on the highlands of Ephraim and in
Gilead,
and he will be satisfied.
²⁰ In those days and at that time, Yahweh
declares,
you may look for Israel's guilt, it will not
be there,
for Judah's sins, you will not find them,
for I shall pardon the remnant that I leave.

The fall of Babylon proclaimed to Jerusalem

²¹ March on the country of Merathaim,
march on it
and on the inhabitants of Pekod;
slaughter and curse with destruction every
last one of them,

Yahweh declares,
carry out my orders to the letter!
²² The din of battle fills the country,
immense destruction.

²³ How utterly shattered
that hammer of the whole world!
What a thing of horror Babylon has
become
throughout the nations!
²⁴ I set a snare for you, Babylon; you were
caught
before you knew it.
You have been found and overpowered
for having defied Yahweh.

²⁵ Yahweh has opened his armoury
and taken out the weapons of his fury.
For Lord Yahweh Sabaoth has work
to do
in the country of the Chaldaeans.
²⁶ Fall on her from every side,
open her granaries,
pile her in heaps, curse her with
destruction,
until nothing is left of her.

²⁷ Slaughter all her bulls,
down to the slaughterhouse with them!
Disaster on them, their day has come,
their time for being punished.

²⁸ Listen! Fugitives and runaways
from the country of Babylon
arrive in Zion and proclaim
the revenge of Yahweh our God,
revenge for his Temple!

The sin of arrogance

²⁹ Call up the archers against Babylon!
All you who bend the bow,
invest her on all sides,
leave her no way of escape.
Repay her as her deeds deserve;
treat her as she has treated others,
for she was arrogant to Yahweh,
to the Holy One of Israel.

30 And so in her squares her young men will fall, and all her fighting men will perish, that day, Yahweh declares.[b]

31 My quarrel is with you, 'Arrogance!'
Lord Yahweh Sabaoth declares,
your day has come,
the time for me to punish you.
32 'Arrogance' will stumble, she will fall,
no one will lift her up:
I shall set fire to her towns
and it will devour all around it.

Yahweh the redeemer of Israel

33 Yahweh Sabaoth says this:
The people of Israel are oppressed
(and the people of Judah too),
all their captors hold them fast,
they will not let them go.
34 But their redeemer is strong:
Yahweh Sabaoth is his name.
He will take up their cause,
to give our country rest
but make the inhabitants of Babylon
tremble.

35 A sword against the Chaldaeans, Yahweh declares,
against the inhabitants of Babylon,
against her princes and her sages!
36 A sword against her diviners: may they lose their wits!
A sword against her warriors: may they panic!
37 A sword against her horses, her chariots
and the conglomeration of people inside her:
may they be like women!
A sword against her treasures: may they be plundered!
38 Drought on her waters: may they dry up!
For it is a country of idols,
and they are mad about those bogeys of theirs!

39 Hence wild cats and jackals will live there,
and ostriches make their home there.

She will never again be inhabited, for ever,
but remain uninhabited age after age.
40 As when God overthrew Sodom and Gomorrah,
and their neighbouring towns,
Yahweh declares,
no one will live there any more,
no human being settle there again.[c]

The enemy from the north and the lion of Jordan

41 Look, a people is coming from the north,
a mighty nation;
from the far ends of the earth
many kings are stirring.
42 They are armed with bow and spear,
they are cruel and pitiless;
their noise is like the roaring of the sea;
they ride horses,
ready as one man to fight you,
daughter of Babylon!
43 The king of Babylon[d] has heard the news,
his hands fall limp,
anguish has seized him,
pain like that of a woman in labour.

44 Look, like a lion he climbs the thickets of the Jordan
to the perennial pasture!
In a flash I shall make them run away
and there appoint someone I shall choose.
For who is there like me?
Who can hale me into court?
Name me the shepherd
who can stand up to me.
45 So now hear the plan
that Yahweh has laid against Babylon,
the schemes he has in mind
against the country of the Chaldaeans:
they will certainly be dragged away
like the smallest in the flock!
Their pastures will certainly be sacked
before their eyes!

50b = 49:26.   50c = 49:18.   50d = 6:22–23.

46 The earth quakes at the sound of
    Babylon's capture,[e]
and the shouting echoes through the
    nations.

Yahweh makes war on Babylon

51 Yahweh says this:
    Against Babylon and the inhabitants
        of Leb-Kamai
I shall rouse a destructive wind.
2 I shall send winnowers to Babylon to
        winnow her
and leave her country bare,
    for she will be beleaguered on all sides,
    on the day of disaster.
3 Let no archer bend his bow!
Let no man swagger in his breastplate!
—No quarter for her young men!
Curse her whole army with destruction!
4 In the country of the Chaldaeans the
        slaughtered will fall,
in the streets of Babylon, those run
        through by the sword.
5 For Israel and Judah have not been bereft
of their God, Yahweh Sabaoth,
although their country was full of sin
against the Holy One of Israel.

6 Escape from Babylon
    (save your lives, each one of you);
do not perish for her guilt,
    for now is the time for Yahweh's
        vengeance:
he will pay her her reward!
7 Babylon was a golden cup in Yahweh's
        hand,
she made the whole world drunk,
    the nations drank her wine
    and then went mad.
8 Babylon has suddenly fallen, is broken:
    wail for her!
Fetch balm for her wounds,
    perhaps she can be cured!
9 —'We tried to cure Babylon; she has got
        no better.
Leave her alone and let us each go to his
        own country.'

—Yes, her sentence reaches to the sky,
    rises to the very clouds.
10 Yahweh has shown the uprightness of our
        cause.
Come, let us tell in Zion
    what Yahweh our God has done.

11 Sharpen the arrows,
    fill the quivers!

Yahweh has roused the spirit of the kings of
the Medes, because he has a plan against Babylon to destroy it; this is Yahweh's revenge, revenge for his Temple.

12 Against the walls of Babylon raise the
        standard!
Strengthen the guard!
Post the sentries!
Take up concealed positions!

For Yahweh has both planned and done
what he promised he would to the inhabitants
of Babylon.

13 Enthroned beside abundant waters,
    rich in treasures,
    you now meet your end,
    the finish of your pillaging.
14 By his own self Yahweh Sabaoth has sworn:
    I shall fill you with men as though with
        grasshoppers,
    and over you they will raise the triumph-
        shout.

15 By his power he made the earth,
    by his wisdom set the world firm,
    by his discernment spread out the heavens.
16 When he thunders
    there is a roaring of waters in heaven;
    he raises clouds from the furthest limits of
        the earth,
    makes the lightning flash for the
        downpour,
    and brings the wind from his storehouse.
17 At this everyone stands stupefied,
        uncomprehending,

50e = 49:19–21.

[1031]

every goldsmith blushes for his idols;
his castings are but delusion,
with no breath in them.
18 They are futile, a laughable production,
when the time comes for them to be
punished, they will vanish.
19 The Heritage of Jacob is not like these,
for he is the maker of everything,
and Israel is the tribe that is his heritage;
His name is Yahweh Sabaoth.ᵃ

Yahweh's hammer and the giant mountain

20 You were my mace,
a weapon of war.
With you I crushed nations,
struck kingdoms down,
21 with you crushed horse and rider,
with you crushed chariot and charioteer,
22 with you crushed man and woman,
with you crushed old man and young,
with you crushed young man and girl,
23 with you crushed shepherd and flock,
with you crushed ploughman and team,
with you crushed governors and
magistrates,

24 and I shall repay Babylon and the inhabitants of Chaldaea, before your eyes, for all the wrongs they have done to Zion, Yahweh declares.

25 I am setting myself against you,
mountain of destruction,
Yahweh declares,
destroyer of the whole world!
I shall reach out my hand for you
and send you tumbling from the crags
and make you a burnt-out mountain.
26 No corner-stone will be taken from you
again
and no foundation-stone,
for you will be a desert for ever,
Yahweh declares.

The end of Babylon is imminent

27 Raise the standard throughout the world,
sound the trumpet among the nations!
Consecrate nations to make war on her;
summon kingdoms against her:
Ararat, Minni, Ashkenaz;
appoint a recruiting-officer for her enemies,
bring up the cavalry, bristling like locusts.

28 Consecrate nations to make war on her: the kings of Media, her governors, all her magistrates and the whole territory under their rule.

29 Then the earth trembled and writhed,
for Yahweh's plan against Babylon was
being executed:
to change the country of Babylon
into an unpopulated desert.

30 The warriors of Babylon have done with
fighting,
they have stayed inside their fortresses;
their courage exhausted,
they are now like women.
Her houses are on fire,
her gates are shattered.
31 Courier follows close on courier,
messenger on messenger,
to tell the king of Babylon
that his city has been taken from all sides,
32 the fords occupied,
the bastions burnt down
and the fighting men seized with panic.
33 For Yahweh Sabaoth, the God of Israel,
says this:
the daughter of Babylon is like a
threshing-floor
when it is being trodden:
a little while, and then the time
for harvesting her will come.

Yahweh's vengeance

34 He devoured me, consumed me,
Nebuchadnezzar king of Babylon,
left me like an empty dish,
like the Dragon he has swallowed me
whole,
filled his belly with my titbits

51a = 10:12–16.

and threw me out.

35 'On Babylon be the wounds I suffered!'
the daughter of Zion will say.
'On the inhabitants of Chaldaea be my
blood!'
Jerusalem will say.

36 So, Yahweh says this:
Look, I am taking up your cause
to make sure you are avenged.
I shall dry her river up,
make her springs run dry.

37 Babylon will become a heap of stones,
the lair of jackals,
a thing of horror and of scorn,
with no one living in it.

38 Like lions they roar together,
they growl like lions' whelps.

39 Are they feverish? I will prepare them a
drink
and make them drink until they are tipsy
and fall into an everlasting sleep,
never to wake again,
Yahweh declares.

40 I will drag them away to the
slaughterhouse like lambs,
like rams and goats.

A dirge for Babylon

41 What! Has Sheshak been taken,
been conquered, the pride of the whole
world?
What a thing of horror Babylon has
become
throughout the nations!

42 The sea has risen over Babylon,
she sinks beneath its boisterous waves.

43 Her towns have been turned into
wasteland,
a parched land, a desert,
a country where no one lives
and where nobody goes.

Yahweh punishes the idols

44 I shall punish Bel in Babylon
and make him disgorge what he has
swallowed.

In future the nations
will stream to him no more.
The very walls of Babylon will fall.

45 Get out of her, my people;
save your lives, each one of you,
from Yahweh's furious anger.

46 But do not be faint-hearted! Do not take
fright at rumours hawked round the country:
one rumour spreads one year, next year another follows; violence rules on earth and one
tyrant succeeds another.

47 So look, the days are coming
when I shall punish the idols of Babylon.
Her entire country will be humbled,
with all her slaughtered lying on
home-soil.

48 The heaven and earth and all within
them
will shout for joy over Babylon,
for the destroyers from the north
are coming to her, Yahweh declares.

49 Babylon in her turn must fall,
you slaughtered ones of Israel,
just as through Babylon there fell
men slaughtered all over the world.

50 You who have escaped her sword,
leave her, do not wait!
Remember Yahweh from afar,
let Jerusalem come into your mind.

51 —'We were ashamed when we heard of
the outrage,
we were covered in confusion
because foreigners had entered
the Temple of Yahweh's holy places.'

52 —So look, the days are coming,
Yahweh declares,
when I shall punish her idols,
and the wounded will groan throughout
her country.

53 Were Babylon to scale the heavens
or reinforce her towering citadel,
destroyers would still come to her on my
orders,
Yahweh declares.

54 The din of shouting from Babylon,
    of immense destruction, from the country
        of the Chaldaeans!
55 Yes, Yahweh is laying Babylon waste
    and silencing her monstrous din,
    whose waves used to roar like the ocean
    and their tumultuous voices rang out.
56 For the destroyer has fallen on Babylon,
    her warriors are captured, their bows are
        broken.
    Yes, Yahweh is a God of retribution,
    he never fails to repay.
57 I shall make her princes and her sages
        drink,
    her governors, her magistrates, her
        warriors;
    they will fall into an everlasting sleep,
    never to wake again,
    declares the King,
    whose name is Yahweh Sabaoth.

Babylon rased to the ground

58 Yahweh Sabaoth says this:
    The walls of Babylon the Great
    will be rased to the ground,
    and her lofty gates
    will be burnt down.
    Thus peoples toil for nothing
    and nations wear themselves out, for the
        flames.

The written prophecy thrown into the Euphrates

59 This is the order that the prophet Jeremiah
gave to Seraiah son of Neriah, son of Mahseiah
when Seraiah left for Babylon with Zedekiah
king of Judah, in the fourth year of his reign.
Seraiah was lord chamberlain. 60 Now, on one
sheet, Jeremiah had written down the entire
disaster that was to befall Babylon, that is, all
these words recorded here against Babylon.
61 Jeremiah then said to Seraiah, 'When you
reach Babylon, see to it that you read all these
words aloud. 62 Then say, "You, Yahweh, have
promised to destroy this place, so that no one
will live here ever again, neither human nor
animal, and it will be desolate for ever."

63 Then, when you have finished reading this
sheet, tie a stone to it and throw it into the middle of the Euphrates, 64 with the words, "So
shall Babylon sink, never to rise again from the
disaster which I am going to bring on her." '
    Thus far the words of Jeremiah.

The destruction of Jerusalem and the pardon of Jehoiachin[a]

52 Zedekiah was twenty-one years old
when he came to the throne, and he
reigned for eleven years in Jerusalem. His
mother's name was Hamital daughter of Jeremiah, of Libnah. 2 He did what is displeasing
to Yahweh, just as Jehoiakim had done. 3 That
this should happen to Jerusalem and Judah
was due to Yahweh's anger, resulting in his
casting them away from his presence.
    Zedekiah rebelled against the king of Bab-
ylon. 4 In the ninth year of his reign, in the
tenth month, on the tenth day of the month,
Nebuchadnezzar king of Babylon advanced
on Jerusalem with his entire army; he pitched
camp in front of the city and threw up earthworks round it. 5 The city lay under siege till
the eleventh year of King Zedekiah. 6 In the
fourth month, on the ninth day of the month,
when famine was raging in the city and there
was no food for the populace, 7 a breach was
made in the city wall. The king and all the
fighting men then fled, leaving the city under
cover of dark, by way of the gate between the
two walls, which is near the king's garden—
the Chaldaeans had surrounded the city—and
made his way towards the Arabah. 8 The Chaldaean troops pursued the king and caught up
with Zedekiah in the plains of Jericho, where
all his troops deserted. 9 But the Chaldaeans
captured the king and took him to the king of
Babylon at Riblah in the territory of Hamath,
where he passed sentence on him. 10 He had
Zedekiah's sons slaughtered before his eyes; he
also had all the chief men of Judah put to death
at Riblah. 11 He then put out Zedekiah's eyes
and, loading him with chains, the king of

52a ‖ 2 K 24:18–25:30.

Babylon carried him off to Babylon where he kept him prisoner until his dying day.

¹² In the fifth month, on the tenth day of the month—it was in the nineteenth year of Nebuchadnezzar king of Babylon—Nebuzaradan commander of the guard, a member of the king of Babylon's staff, entered Jerusalem. ¹³ He burnt down the Temple of Yahweh, the royal palace and all the houses in Jerusalem. ¹⁴ The Chaldaean troops who accompanied the commander of the guard demolished all the walls surrounding Jerusalem.

¹⁵ Nebuzaradan commander of the guard deported (some of the poor people and) the remainder of the population left in the city, the deserters who had gone over to the king of Babylon, and the rest of the artisans. ¹⁶ But Nebuzaradan commander of the guard left some of the poor country-people behind as vineyard workers and ploughmen.

¹⁷ The Chaldaeans broke up the bronze pillars from the Temple of Yahweh, the wheeled stands and the bronze Sea, which were in the Temple of Yahweh, and took all the bronze away to Babylon. ¹⁸ They also took the ash containers, the scoops, the knives, the sprinkling bowls, the incense bowls, and all the bronze furnishings used in worship. ¹⁹ The commander of the guard also took the bowls, the censers, the sprinkling bowls, the ash containers, the lamp-stands, the goblets and the saucers: everything that was made of gold and everything made of silver. ²⁰ As regards the two pillars, the one Sea, the twelve bronze oxen supporting the Sea, and the wheeled stands, which King Solomon had made for the Temple of Yahweh, there was no reckoning the weight of bronze in all these objects. ²¹ As regards the pillars, the height of one pillar was eighteen cubits, its circumference was twelve cubits, it was four fingers thick, and hollow inside; ²² on it stood a capital of bronze, the height of the capital being five cubits; round the capital were filigree and pomegranates, all

in bronze. So also for the second pillar. ²³ There were ninety-six pomegranates round the sides, making a hundred pomegranates round the filigree in all.

²⁴ The commander of the guard took prisoner Seraiah the chief priest, Zephaniah the priest next in rank, and the three guardians of the threshold. ²⁵ In the city he took prisoner an official who was in command of the fighting men, seven of the king's personal friends who were discovered in the city, the secretary to the army commander responsible for military conscription, and sixty men of distinction discovered in the city. ²⁶ Nebuzaradan commander of the guard took these men and brought them to the king of Babylon at Riblah, ²⁷ and at Riblah, in the territory of Hamath, the king of Babylon had them put to death. Thus Judah was deported from its country.

²⁸ The number of people deported by Nebuchadnezzar was as follows. In the seventh year: three thousand and twenty-three Judaeans; ²⁹ in the eighteenth year of Nebuchadnezzar, eight hundred and thirty-two persons were deported from Jerusalem; ³⁰ in the twenty-third year of Nebuchadnezzar, Nebuzaradan commander of the guard deported seven hundred and forty-five Judaeans. In all: four thousand six hundred persons.

³¹ But in the thirty-seventh year of the exile of Jehoiachin king of Judah, in the twelfth month, on the twenty-fifth day of the month, Evil-Merodach king of Babylon, in the year he came to the throne, pardoned Jehoiachin king of Judah and released him from prison. ³² He treated him kindly and allotted him a seat above those of the other kings who were with him in Babylon. ³³ So Jehoiachin laid aside his prisoner's garb and for the rest of his life always ate at the king's table. ³⁴ And his upkeep was permanently ensured by the king, day after day, for the rest of his life until the day he died.

The Book of
LAMENTATIONS

First lamentation

1 ALEPH ¹How deserted she sits,
the city once thronged with people!
Once the greatest of nations,
she is now like a widow.
Once the princess of states,
she is now put to forced labour.

BET ²All night long she is weeping,
tears running down her cheeks.
Not one of all her lovers
remains to comfort her.
Her friends have all betrayed her
and become her enemies.

GIMEL ³Judah has gone into exile
after much pain and toil.
Living among the nations
she finds no respite;
her persecutors all overtake her
where there is no way out.

DALET ⁴The roads to Zion are in mourning;
no one comes to her festivals now.
Her gateways are all deserted;
her priests groan;
her young girls are grief-stricken;
she suffers bitterly.

HE ⁵Her foes now have the upper hand,
her enemies prosper,
for Yahweh has made her suffer
for her many, many crimes;
her children have gone away into captivity
driven in front of the oppressor.

WAW ⁶And from the daughter of Zion
all her splendour has departed.

Her princes were like stags
which could find no pasture,
exhausted, as they flee
before the hunter.

ZAIN ⁷Jerusalem remembers
her days of misery and distress;
when her people fell into the enemy's
clutches
there was no one to help her.
Her enemies looked on
and laughed at her downfall.

HET ⁸Jerusalem has sinned so gravely
that she has become a thing unclean.
All who used to honour her despise her,
having seen her nakedness;
she herself groans aloud
and turns her face away.

TET ⁹Her filth befouls her skirts—
she never thought to end like this,
and hence her astonishing fall
with no one to comfort her.
Yahweh, look at my misery,
for the enemy is triumphant!

YOD ¹⁰The enemy stretched out his hand
for everything she treasured;
she saw the heathen
enter her sanctuary,
whom you had forbidden
to enter your Assembly.

KAPH ¹¹All her people are groaning,
looking for something to eat;
they have bartered their treasures for food,
to keep themselves alive.
Look, Yahweh, and consider
how despised I am!

LAMED ¹²All you who pass this way,
  look and see:
is any sorrow like the sorrow
  inflicted on me,
with which Yahweh struck me
  on the day of his burning anger?

MEM ¹³He sent fire from on high
  deep into my bones;
he stretched a net for my feet,
  he pulled me back;
he left me shattered,
  sick all day long.

NUN ¹⁴He has watched out for my offences,
  with his hand he enmeshes me,
his yoke is on my neck,
  he has deprived me of strength.
The Lord has put me into clutches
  which I am helpless to resist.

SAMEK ¹⁵The Lord has rejected
  all my warriors within my walls,
he has summoned a host against me
  to crush my young men;
in the winepress the Lord trampled
  the young daughter of Judah.

AIN ¹⁶And that is why I weep;
  my eyes stream with water,
since a comforter who could revive me
  is far away.
My children are shattered,
  for the enemy has proved too strong.

PE ¹⁷Zion stretches out her hands,
  with no one to comfort her.
Yahweh has commanded Jacob's enemies
  to surround him;
they treat Jerusalem
  as though she were unclean.

ZADE ¹⁸Yahweh is in the right,
  for I rebelled against his command.
Listen, all you peoples,
  and see my sorrow.
My young girls and my young men
  have gone into captivity.

QOPH ¹⁹I called to my lovers;
  they failed me.
My priests and my elders
  expired in the city,
as they searched for food
  to keep themselves alive.

RESH ²⁰Look, Yahweh. I am in distress!
  My inmost being is in ferment;
my heart turns over inside me—
  how rebellious I have been!
Outside, the sword bereaves;
  inside it is like death.

SHIN ²¹Listen, for I am groaning,
  with no one to comfort me.
All my enemies have heard of my
    disaster,
  they are glad about what you have
    done.
Bring the Day you once foretold,
  so that they may be like me!

TAW ²²Let all their wickedness come before
    you,
and treat them
  as you have treated me
  for all my crimes;
numberless are my groans,
  and I am sick at heart.

Second lamentation

2 ALEPH ¹In his anger, with what darkness
  has the Lord enveloped the daughter
  of Zion!
He has flung the beauty of Israel
  from heaven to the ground,
without regard for his footstool
  on the day of his anger.

BET ²The Lord pitilessly engulfed
  all the homes of Jacob;
in his fury he tore down
  the fortresses of the daughter of
    Judah;
he threw to the ground, he desecrated
  the kingdom and its princes.

GIMEL ³In his burning anger
    he broke all the might of Israel,
withdrew his protecting right hand
    at the coming of the enemy,
and blazed against Jacob like a fire
    that burns up everything near it.

DALET ⁴Like an enemy he bent his bow,
    and his right hand held firm;
like a foe he slaughtered
    all those who were a delight to see;
on the tent of the daughter of Zion
    he poured out his fury like fire.

HE ⁵The Lord behaved like an enemy;
    he engulfed Israel,
he engulfed all its citadels,
    he destroyed its fortresses
and for the daughter of Judah
    multiplied weeping on wailing.

WAW ⁶He wrecked his domain like a garden,
    destroyed his assembly-points,
Yahweh erased the memory
    of festivals and Sabbaths in Zion;
in the heat of his anger he treated
    king and priest with contempt.

ZAIN ⁷The Lord has rejected his altar,
    he has come to loathe his sanctuary
and has given her palace walls
    into the clutches of the enemy;
from the uproar they made in Yahweh's
    temple
    it might have been a festival day!

HET ⁸Yahweh has resolved to destroy
    the walls of the daughter of Zion,
stretching out the line, not staying his
    hand
    until he has engulfed everything,
thus bringing mourning on wall and
    rampart;
    alike they crumbled.

TET ⁹Her gates have sunk into the ground;
    he has broken and shattered their bars.

Her king and her princes are among the
    gentiles,
    there is no instruction,
furthermore her prophets cannot find
    any vision from Yahweh.

YOD ¹⁰Mute, they sit on the ground,
    the elders of the daughter of Zion;
they have put dust on their heads
    and wrapped themselves in sackcloth.
The young girls of Jerusalem bow their
    heads
    to the ground.

KAPH ¹¹My eyes are worn out with weeping,
    my inmost being is in ferment,
my heart plummets
    at the destruction of my young people,
as the children and babies grow faint
    in the streets of the city.

LAMED ¹²They keep saying to their
    mothers,
    'Where is some food?'
as they faint like wounded men
    in the streets of the city,
as they breathe their last
    on their mothers' breasts.

MEM ¹³To what can I compare or liken you,
    daughter of Jerusalem?
Who can rescue and comfort you,
    young daughter of Zion?
For huge as the sea is your ruin:
    who can heal you?

NUN ¹⁴The visions your prophets had for you
    were deceptive whitewash;
they did not lay bare your guilt
    so as to change your fortunes:
the visions they told you
    were deceptive.

SAMEK ¹⁵All who pass your way
    clap their hands at the sight;
they whistle and shake their heads
    over the daughter of Jerusalem,

'Is this the city they call Perfection of
    Beauty,
    the joy of the whole world?'

PE ¹⁶Your enemies open their mouths
    in chorus against you;
they whistle and grind their teeth;
    they say, 'We have swallowed her up.
This is the day we were waiting for;
    at last we have seen it!'

AIN ¹⁷Yahweh has done what he planned,
    has carried out his threat,
as he ordained long ago:
    he has destroyed without pity,
increasing the might of your foes—
    and letting your foes get the credit.

ZADE ¹⁸Cry then to the Lord,
    rampart of the daughter of Zion;
let your tears flow like a torrent,
    day and night;
allow yourself no respite,
    give your eyes no rest!

QOPH ¹⁹Up, cry out in the night-time
    as each watch begins!
Pour your heart out like water
    in Yahweh's presence!
Raise your hands to him
    for the lives of your children
(who faint with hunger
    at the end of every street)!

RESH ²⁰Look, Yahweh, and consider:
    whom have you ever treated like this?
Should women eat their little ones,
    the children they have nursed?
Should priest and prophet be slaughtered
    in the Lord's sanctuary?

SHIN ²¹Children and old people are lying
    on the ground in the streets;
my young men and young girls
    have fallen by the sword;
you have killed them, on the day of your
    anger,
    you have slaughtered them pitilessly.

TAW ²²As though to a festival you called
    together
    terrors from all sides,
so that, on the day of Yahweh's anger,
    none escaped and none survived.
Those whom I had nursed and reared,
    my enemy has annihilated them all.

Third lamentation

3 ALEPH ¹I am the man familiar with
        misery
    under the rod of his fury.
²He has led and guided me
    into darkness, not light.
³Against none but me does he turn his
    hand,
    again and again, all day.

BET ⁴He has wasted my flesh and skin away,
    has broken my bones.
⁵He has besieged me and made hardship
    a circlet round my head.
⁶He has forced me to dwell where all is
    dark,
    like those long-dead in their everlasting
    home.

GIMEL ⁷He has walled me in so that I cannot
        escape;
    he has weighed me down with chains;
⁸even when I shout for help,
    he shuts out my prayer.
⁹He has closed my way with blocks of
    stone,
    he has obstructed my paths.

DALET ¹⁰For me he is a lurking bear,
    a lion in hiding.
¹¹Heading me off, he has torn me apart,
    leaving me shattered.
¹²He has bent his bow and used me
    as a target for his arrows.

HE ¹³He has shot deep into me
    with shafts from his quiver.
¹⁴I have become a joke to all my own people,
    their refrain all day long.

15 He has given me my fill of bitterness,
  he has made me drunk with
    wormwood.

WAW 16 He has broken my teeth with gravel,
  he has fed me on ashes.
17 I have been deprived of peace,
  I have forgotten what happiness is
18 and thought, 'My lasting hope
  in Yahweh is lost.'

ZAIN 19 Bring to mind my misery and
    anguish;
  it is wormwood and gall!
20 My heart dwells on this continually
  and sinks within me.
21 This is what I shall keep in mind
  and so regain some hope:

HET 22 Surely Yahweh's mercies are not over,
  his deeds of faithful love not exhausted;
23 every morning they are renewed;
  great is his faithfulness!
24 'Yahweh is all I have,' I say to myself,
  'and so I shall put my hope in him.'

TET 25 Yahweh is good to those who trust him,
  to all who search for him.
26 It is good to wait in silence
  for Yahweh to save.
27 It is good for someone to bear the yoke
  from a young age,

YOD 28 to sit in solitude and silence
  when it weighs heavy,
29 to lay one's head in the dust—
  maybe there is hope—
30 to offer one's cheek to the striker,
  to have one's fill of disgrace!

KAPH 31 For the Lord will not reject
  anyone for ever.
32 If he brings grief, he will have pity
  out of the fullness of his faithful love,
33 for it is not for his own pleasure
  that he torments and grieves the human
    race.

LAMED 34 When all the prisoners in a
    country
  are crushed underfoot,
35 when human rights are overridden
  in defiance of the Most High,
36 when someone is cheated of justice,
  does not the Lord see it?

MEM 37 Who has only to speak and it is so
    done?
  Who commands, if not the Lord?
38 From where, if not from the mouth of the
    Most High,
  do evil and good come?
39 Why then should anyone complain?
  Better to be bold against one's sins.

NUN 40 Let us examine our path, let us
    ponder it
  and return to Yahweh.
41 Let us raise our hearts and hands
  to God in heaven.
42 We are the ones who have sinned, who
    have rebelled,
  and you have not forgiven.

SAMEK 43 You have enveloped us in anger,
  pursuing us, slaughtering without
    pity.
44 You have wrapped yourself in a cloud
  too thick for prayer to pierce.
45 You have reduced us to rubbish
  and refuse among the nations.

PE 46 Our enemies open their mouths
  in chorus against us.
47 Terror and pitfall have been our lot,
  ravage and ruin.
48 My eyes dissolve in torrents of tears
  at the ruin of my beloved people.

AIN 49 My eyes will weep ceaselessly,
  without relief,
50 until Yahweh looks down
  and sees from heaven.
51 My eyes have grown sore
  over all the daughters of my city.

84 READ LAMENTATIONS 3:19–58.

You are near when I call to you. You said, "Do not be afraid!"—LAMENTATIONS 3:57

HOW TO SUFFER PATIENTLY

Sebastian Valfré, a popular spiritual director in seventeenth-century Turin, Italy, gave this encouragement to an invalid:

Every illness and every trial is permitted by God as the means whereby we can best ensure our salvation and as the material most fitted for our sanctification. Take your illness as a penance given you by God, who knows the extent of your debts to him as well as the best way in which you can discharge them. You should be content to do as he wishes, for he is satisfied with far less than you owe him.

Read into everything God's explicit will. Suffer with our Lord, uniting your sufferings to his. Don't look for sufferings, but do not refuse them. Value them as precious marks of favor that he bestows on you. Don't desire to exchange them for others, but don't torment yourself by adding to them. Don't fix your eyes on the lash that scourges you, but kiss and adore the loving hand and heart wielding it.

God is not content to see you merely suffering with patience. He wants you to be grateful and to approve of what he does. So many of the blessed envy you from heaven and would change places with you if they could.

Feel a more lively gratitude towards those who brace you up and invigorate you in your pain than towards those who merely commiserate with you. An unpitied pain wins greater merit before God. Never say to God: "Enough!" Simply say: "I am ready." When it's over you will regret having suffered so little and suffered that little so badly. Finally, don't give trouble to those who wait on you, and don't be exacting with your nurses.

BL. SEBASTIAN VALFRÉ, 1629–1710

YOU WILL FIND THE NEXT READING AT EZEKIEL 3.

ZADE ⁵²Unprovoked, my enemies
 hunted me down like a bird.
⁵³ They shut me finally in a pit,
 they closed me in with a stone.
⁵⁴ The waters rose over my head;
 I thought, 'I am lost!'

QOPH ⁵⁵Yahweh, I called on your name
 from the deep pit.
⁵⁶ You heard my voice, do not close your ear
 to my prayer, to my cry.
⁵⁷ You are near when I call to you.
 You said, 'Do not be afraid!'

RESH ⁵⁸Lord, you defended my cause,
 you have redeemed my life.
⁵⁹ Yahweh, you have seen the wrong done
 to me,
 grant me redress.
⁶⁰ You have seen their vindictiveness,
 all their plots against me.

SHIN ⁶¹You have heard their insults, Yahweh,
 all their plots against me,
⁶² the whispering and murmuring of my
 enemies
 against me all day long.

63 Look, whether they sit or stand,
   I am their refrain.

TAW 64 Yahweh, repay them
   as their deeds deserve.
65 Lay hardness of heart
   as your curse on them.
66 Angrily pursue them, root them out
   from under your heavens!

Fourth lamentation

4 ALEPH ¹ How the gold has tarnished,
   how the fine gold has changed!
The sacred stones lie scattered
   at the corner of every street.

BET ² The children of Zion,
   as precious as finest gold—
to think that they should now be reckoned
   like crockery made by a potter!

GIMEL ³ The very jackals give the breast,
   and suckle their young:
but the daughter of my people is as cruel
   as the ostriches of the desert.

DALET ⁴ The tongue of the baby at the breast
   sticks to its palate for thirst;
little children ask for bread,
   no one gives them any.

HE ⁵ Those who used to eat only the best,
   now lie dying in the streets;
those who were reared in the purple
   claw at the rubbish heaps,

WAW ⁶ for the wickedness of the daughter of
   my people
   exceeded the sins of Sodom,
which was overthrown in a moment
   without a hand being laid on it.

ZAIN ⁷ Once her young people were brighter
   than snow,
   whiter than milk;
rosier than coral their bodies,
   their hue like sapphire.

HET ⁸ Now their faces are blacker than soot,
   they are not recognised in the streets,
the skin has shrunk over their bones,
   as dry as a stick.

TET ⁹ Happier those killed by the sword
   than those killed by famine:
they waste away, sunken
   for lack of the fruits of the earth.

YOD ¹⁰ With their own hands, kindly women
   cooked their children;
this was their food
   when the daughter of my people was
   ruined.

KAPH ¹¹ Yahweh indulged his fury,
   he vented his fierce anger,
he lit a fire in Zion
   which devoured her foundations.

LAMED ¹² The kings of the earth never
   believed,
   nor did any of the inhabitants of the
   world,
   that foe or enemy would ever penetrate
   the gates of Jerusalem.

MEM ¹³ Owing to the sins of her prophets
   and the crimes of her priests,
who had shed the blood of the upright,
   in the heart of the city,

NUN ¹⁴ they wandered blindly through the
   streets,
   polluted with blood,
so that no one dared
   to touch their clothes.

SAMEK ¹⁵ 'Keep away! Unclean!' people
   shouted,
   'Keep away! Keep away! Don't touch!'
If they left and fled to the nations,
   they were not allowed to stay there
   either.

PE ¹⁶ The face of Yahweh destroyed them,
   he will look on them no more.

There was no respect for the priests,
no deference for the elders.

AIN [17] Continually we were wearing out our
eyes,
watching for help—in vain.
From our towers we watched for a nation
which could not save us anyway.

ZADE [18] Men dogged our steps,
to keep us out of our streets.
Our end was near, our days were done,
our end had come.

QOPH [19] Our pursuers were swifter
than eagles in the sky;
they hounded our steps through the
mountains,
they lay in ambush for us in the wilds.

RESH [20] The breath of our nostrils, Yahweh's
anointed,
was caught in their traps,
he of whom we said, 'In his shadow
we shall live among the nations.'

SHIN [21] Rejoice, exult, daughter of Edom,
you who reside in Uz![a]
To you in turn the cup will pass;
you will get drunk and strip yourself
naked!

TAW [22] Your wickedness is atoned for,
daughter of Zion,
he will never banish you again.
But your wickedness, daughter of Edom,
will he punish,
your sins he will lay bare!

Fifth Lamentation

5 Yahweh, remember what has happened
to us;
consider, and see our degradation.

2 Our heritage has passed to strangers,
our homes to foreigners.

3 We are orphans, we are fatherless;
our mothers are like widows.

4 We have to buy our own water to drink,
our own wood we can get only at a
price.

5 The yoke is on our necks; we are
persecuted;
exhausted we are, allowed no rest.

6 We made a pact with Egypt,
with Assyria, to have plenty of food.

7 Our ancestors sinned; they are no more,
and we bear the weight of their guilt.

8 Slaves rule us;
there is no one to rescue us from their
clutches.

9 At peril of our lives we earn our bread,
by risking the sword of the desert.

10 Our skin is as hot as an oven,
from the scorch of famine.

11 The women in Zion have been raped,
the young girls in the towns of Judah.

12 Princes have been hanged by their
hands;
the face of the old has won no
respect.

13 Youths have been put to the mill,
boys stagger under loads of wood.

14 The elders have deserted the gateway;
the young have given up their
music.

15 Joy has vanished from our hearts;
our dancing has turned to mourning.

16 The crown has fallen from our heads.
Alas that ever we sinned!

4a South of Edom. The neighbouring peoples joined in the
destruction of Jerusalem.

¹⁷ This is why our hearts are sick;
    this is why our eyes are dim:

¹⁸ because Mount Zion is desolate;
    jackals roam to and fro on it.

¹⁹ Yet you, Yahweh, rule from eternity;
    your throne endures from age
        to age.

²⁰ Why do you never remember us?
    Why do you abandon us so long?

²¹ Make us come back to you, Yahweh, and
      we will come back.
    Restore us as we were before!

²² Unless you have utterly rejected us,
    in an anger which knows no limit.

BARUCH

Baruch and the Jews in Babylon

1 This is the text of the book written in Baby-lon by Baruch son of Neraiah, son of Mah-seiah, son of Zedekiah, son of Hasadiah, son of Hilkiah, ²in the fifth year, on the seventh day of the month, at the time when the Chal-daeans had captured Jerusalem and burned it down.

³Baruch read the text of this book aloud to Jeconiah son of Jehoiakim, king of Judah, and to all the people who had come to hear the reading, ⁴to the nobles and the sons of the king, and to the elders; to the whole people, that is, to the least no less than to the greatest, to all who lived in Babylon beside the river Sud. ⁵On hearing it they wept, fasted and prayed before the Lord; ⁶and they collected as much money as each could afford ⁷and sent it to Jerusalem to the priest Jehoiakim son of Hilkiah, son of Shallum, and the other priests, and all the people who were with him in Jeru-salem. ⁸Also on the tenth day of Sivan he was given the utensils of the house of the Lord, which had been removed from the Temple, to take them back to the land of Judah; these were silver utensils which Zedekiah son of Josiah, king of Judah, had had made ⁹after Nebuchadnezzar king of Babylon had de-ported Jeconiah from Jerusalem to Babylon, together with the princes, the metalworkers, the nobles and the common people.

¹⁰Now, they wrote, we are sending you money to pay for burnt offerings, offerings for sin, and incense. Prepare oblations and offer them on the altar of the Lord our God; ¹¹and pray for the long life of Nebuchadnezzar king of Babylon, and of his son Belshazzar, that they may endure on earth as long as the heav-ens endure; ¹²and that the Lord may give us strength and enlighten our eyes, so that we may lead our lives under the protection of Nebuchadnezzar king of Babylon and of his son Belshazzar, and that we may serve them for a long time and win their favour. ¹³Also pray to the Lord our God for us, because we have sinned against him, and the anger, the fury of the Lord, has still not turned away from us. ¹⁴Lastly, you must read the booklet which we are sending you, publicly in the house of the Lord on the feastday and appro-priate days. ¹⁵You must say:

Confession of sins

Saving justice is the Lord's, we have only the look of shame we bear, as is the case today for the people of Judah and the inhabitants of Jerusalem, ¹⁶for our kings and princes, our priests, our prophets, and for our ancestors, ¹⁷because we have sinned before the Lord, ¹⁸have disobeyed him, and have not listened to the voice of the Lord our God telling us to fol-low the commandments which the Lord had ordained for us. ¹⁹From the day when the Lord brought our ancestors out of Egypt until today we have been disobedient to the Lord our God, we have been disloyal, refusing to lis-ten to his voice. ²⁰And we are not free even today of the disasters and the curse which the Lord pronounced through his servant Moses the day he brought our ancestors out of Egypt to give us a land flowing with milk and honey. ²¹We have not listened to the voice of the Lord our God in all the words of those prophets he sent us; ²²but, each following the dictates of our evil heart, we have taken to serving alien gods, and doing what is displeasing to the Lord our God.

2 And so the Lord has carried out the sentence which he passed on us, on our judges who governed Israel, on our kings and leaders and on the people of Israel and of Judah; ²what he did to Jerusalem has never been paralleled under the wide heavens—in conformity with what was written in the Law of Moses; ³we were each reduced to eating the flesh of our own sons and daughters. ⁴Furthermore, he has handed them over into the power of all the kingdoms that surround us, to be the contempt and execration of all the neighbouring peoples among whom the Lord scattered them. ⁵Instead of being masters, they found themselves enslaved, because we had sinned against the Lord our God by not listening to his voice.

⁶Saving justice is the Lord's; we and our ancestors have only the look of shame we bear today. ⁷All those disasters which the Lord pronounced against us have now befallen us. ⁸And yet we have not tried to win the favour of the Lord by each of us renouncing the dictates of our own wicked heart; ⁹so the Lord has been alert to our misdeeds and has brought disaster down on us, since the Lord is upright in everything he had commanded us to do, ¹⁰and we have not listened to his voice so as to follow the commandments which the Lord had ordained for us.

The prayer

¹¹And now, Lord, God of Israel, who brought your people out of Egypt with a mighty hand, with signs and wonders, with great power and with outstretched arm, to win yourself a name such as you have today, ¹²we have sinned, we have committed sacrilege; Lord our God, we have broken all your precepts. ¹³Let your anger turn from us since we are no more than a little remnant among the nations where you have dispersed us. ¹⁴Listen, Lord, to our prayers and our entreaties; deliver us for your own sake and let us win the favour of the people who have deported us, ¹⁵so that the whole world may know that you are the Lord our God, since Israel and his descendants bear your name. ¹⁶Look down, Lord, from your holy dwelling-place and think of us, bow your ear and listen, ¹⁷open your eyes, Lord, and look; the dead down in Sheol, whose breath has been taken from their bodies, are not the ones to give glory and due recognition to the Lord; ¹⁸whoever is overcome with affliction, who goes along bowed down and frail, with failing eyes and hungering soul, that is the one to give you glory and due recognition, Lord.

¹⁹We do not rely on the merits of our ancestors and of our kings to offer you our humble plea, Lord our God. ²⁰No, you have sent down your anger and your fury on us, as you threatened through your servants the prophets when they said, ²¹'The Lord says this: *Bend your necks and serve the king of Babylon,ᵃ* and you will remain in the country which I gave to your ancestors. ²²But if you do not listen to the voice of the Lord and serve the king of Babylon ²³then *I shall silence the shouts of rejoicing and mirth and the voices of bridegroom and bride in the towns of Judah and the streets of Jerusalem, and the whole country will be reduced to desert,ᵇ with no inhabitants.'* ²⁴But we would not listen to your voice and serve the king of Babylon, and so you carried out what you had threatened through your servants the prophets: that the bones of our kings and of our ancestors would be dragged from their resting places. ²⁵They were indeed *tossed out to the heat of the day and the frost of the night.ᶜ* And people died in dreadful agony, from famine, sword and plague. ²⁶And so, because of the wickedness of the House of Israel and the House of Judah, you have made this House, that bears your name, what it is today.

²⁷And yet, Lord our God, you have treated us in a way worthy of all your goodness and boundless tenderness, ²⁸just as you had promised through your servant Moses, the day you told him to write your Law in the presence of the Israelites, and said, ²⁹'If you do not listen to my voice, this great and innumerable multitude will certainly be reduced to a tiny few

2a Jr 27:12.   2b Jr 7:34.   2c Jr 36:30.

among the nations where I shall scatter them— [30] for I knew that, being an obstinate people, they would not listen to me. But in the country of their exile, they will come to themselves [31] and acknowledge that I am the Lord their God. I shall give them a heart and an attentive ear, [32] and they will sing my praises in the country of their exile, they will remember my name; [33] they will stop being obstinate and, remembering what became of their ancestors who sinned before the Lord, will turn from their evil deeds. [34] Then I shall bring them back to the country which I promised on oath to their ancestors Abraham, Isaac and Jacob, and make them masters in it. I shall make their numbers grow; they will not dwindle again. [35] And I shall make an everlasting covenant with them; so that I am their God and they are my people. And never again shall I drive my people Israel out of the country which I have given them.'

3 Almighty Lord, God of Israel, a soul in anguish, a troubled heart now cries to you: [2] Listen and have pity, Lord, for we have sinned before you. [3] You sit enthroned for ever, while we are perishing for ever. [4] Almighty Lord, God of Israel, hear the prayer of the dead of Israel, of the children of those who have sinned against you and have not listened to the voice of the Lord their God; hence the disasters which dog us. [5] Do not call to mind the misdeeds of our ancestors, but remember instead your power and your name. [6] You are indeed the Lord our God and we will praise you, Lord, [7] since you have put respect for you in our hearts to encourage us to call on your name. We long to praise you in our exile, for we have rid our hearts of the wickedness of our ancestors who sinned against you. [8] Look, today we are still in exile where you have scattered us as something contemptible, accursed, condemned, for all the misdeeds of our ancestors who had abandoned the Lord our God.

[9] Listen, Israel, to commands that bring life;
hear, and learn what knowledge means.

[10] Why, Israel, why are you in the country of
your enemies,
growing older and older in an alien land,
[11] defiling yourselves with the dead,
reckoned with those who go to Sheol?
[12] It is because you have forsaken the
fountain of wisdom!
[13] Had you walked in the way of God,
you would be living in peace for ever.
[14] Learn where knowledge is, where
strength,
where understanding, and so learn
where length of days is, where life,
where the light of the eyes and where
peace.

[15] But who has found out where she lives,
who has entered her treasure house?
[16] Where now are the leaders of the nations
and those who ruled even the beasts of
earth,
[17] those who sported with the birds of
heaven,
those who accumulated silver and gold
on which all people rely,
and whose possessions had no end,
[18] those who worked so carefully in silver
—but of whose works no trace is to be
found?
[19] They have vanished, gone down to
Sheol.
Others have risen to their places,
[20] more recent generations have seen
the day
and peopled the earth in their turn,
but the way of knowledge they have not
found;
[21] they have not recognised the paths she
treads.
Nor have their children had any grasp
of her,
remaining far from her way.
[22] Nothing has been heard of her in Canaan,
nothing has been seen of her in Teman;
[23] the children of Hagar in search of worldly
wisdom,
the merchants of Midian and Teman,

the tale-spinners and the philosophers
     have none of them found the way
        to wisdom
or remembered the paths she treads.

24 How great, Israel, is the house of God,
   how wide his domain,
25 immeasurably wide,
   infinitely lofty!
26 In it were born the giants, famous from
       the beginning,
   immensely tall, expert in war;
27 God's choice did not fall on these,
   he did not show them the way of
       knowledge;
28 they perished for lack of wisdom,
   perished by their own folly.
29 Who has ever climbed the sky and seized
       her
   to bring her down from the clouds?
30 Who has ever crossed the ocean and
       found her
   to bring her back in exchange for the
       finest gold?
31 No one can learn the way to her,
   no one can understand the path she
       treads.

32 But the One who knows all discovers her,
   he has grasped her with his own
       intellect,
   he has set the earth firm for evermore
   and filled it with four-footed beasts,
33 he sends the light—and it goes,
   he recalls it—and trembling it obeys;
34 the stars shine joyfully at their posts;
35 when he calls them, they answer, 'Here
       we are';
   they shine to delight their Creator.
36 It is he who is our God,
   no other can compare with him.
37 He has uncovered the whole way of
       knowledge
   and shown it to his servant Jacob,
   to Israel his well-beloved;
38 only then did she appear on earth
   and live among human beings.

4 She is the book of God's commandments,
   the Law that stands for ever;
   those who keep her shall live,
   those who desert her shall die.
2 Turn back, Jacob, seize her,
   in her radiance make your way to light:
3 do not yield your glory to another,
   your privilege to a people not your own.
4 Israel, blessed are we:
   what pleases God has been revealed
       to us!

5 Take courage, my people,
   memorial of Israel!
6 You were sold to the nations,
   but not for extermination.
   You provoked God;
   and so were delivered to your enemies,
7 since you had angered your Creator
   by offering sacrifices to demons, and not to
       God.
8 You had forgotten the eternal God who
       reared you.
   You had also grieved Jerusalem who
       nursed you,
9 for when she saw God's anger
   falling on you, she said:

   Listen, you neighbours of Zion:
   God has sent me great sorrow.
10 I have seen my sons and daughters taken
       into captivity,
   which the Eternal brought down on
       them.
11 I had reared them joyfully;
   in tears, in sorrow, I watched them go
       away.
12 Do not, any of you, exult over me,
   a widow, deserted by so many;
   I am bereaved because of the sins of my
       children,
   who turned away from the Law of God,
13 who did not want to know his precepts
   and would not follow the ways of his
       commandments
   or tread the paths of discipline as his
       justice directed.

¹⁴ Come here, neighbours of Zion!
Remember my sons' and daughters'
captivity,
which the Eternal brought down on them.
¹⁵ How he brought a distant nation down on
them,
a ruthless nation speaking a foreign
language,
they showed neither respect for the aged,
nor pity for the child;
¹⁶ they carried off the widow's cherished sons,
they left her quite alone, bereft of her
daughters.
¹⁷ For my part, how could I help you?
¹⁸ He who brought those disasters down on
you,
is the one to deliver you from your
enemies' clutches.
¹⁹ Go, my children, go your way!
I must stay bereft and lonely;
²⁰ I have taken off the clothes of peace
and put on the sackcloth of entreaty;
all my life I shall cry to the Eternal.

²¹ Take courage, my children, call on God:
he will deliver you from tyranny, from the
clutches of your enemies;
²² for I look to the Eternal for your rescue,
and joy has come to me from the Holy
One
at the mercy soon to reach you
from your Saviour, the Eternal.
²³ In sorrow and tears I watched you go
away,
but God will give you back to me in joy
and gladness for ever.
²⁴ As the neighbours of Zion have now
witnessed your captivity,
so will they soon see your rescue by God,
which will come upon you with great
glory and splendour of the
Eternal.
²⁵ My children, patiently bear the anger
brought on you by God.
Your enemy has persecuted you,
but soon you will witness his destruction
and set your foot on his neck.

²⁶ My favourite children have travelled by
rough roads,
carried off like a flock by a marauding
enemy.
²⁷ Take courage, my children, call on God:
he who brought this on you will remember
you.
²⁸ As by your will you first strayed from
God,
so now turn back and search for him ten
times harder;
²⁹ for as he has been bringing down those
disasters on you,
so will he rescue you and give you eternal
joy.
³⁰ Take courage, Jerusalem:
he who gave you your name will console
you.
³¹ Disaster will come to all who have ill-
treated you
and gloated over your fall.
³² Disaster will come to the cities where your
children were slaves;
disaster to whichever one received your
children,
³³ for just as she rejoiced at your fall
and was happy to see you ruined,
so will she grieve over her own desolation.
³⁴ I shall deprive her of the joy of a populous
city,
and her insolence will turn to mourning;
³⁵ fire from the Eternal will befall her for
many a day,
and demons will dwell in her for ages.
³⁶ Jerusalem, turn your eyes to the east,
see the joy that is coming to you from God.
³⁷ Look, the children you watched go away
are on their way home;
reassembled from east and west, they are
on their way home
at the Holy One's command, rejoicing in
God's glory.

5 Jerusalem, take off your dress of sorrow
and distress,
put on the beauty of God's glory for
evermore,

2 wrap the cloak of God's saving justice
        around you,
    put the diadem of the Eternal One's glory
        on your head,
3 for God means to show your splendour to
        every nation under heaven,
4 and the name God gives you for evermore
        will be,
    'Peace-through-Justice, and Glory-
        through-Devotion'.
5 Arise, Jerusalem, stand on the heights
    and turn your eyes to the east:
    see your children reassembled from west
        and east
    at the Holy One's command, rejoicing
        because God has remembered.
6 Though they left you on foot
    driven by enemies,
    now God brings them back to you,
    carried gloriously, like a royal throne.
7 For God has decreed the flattening
    of each high mountain, of the everlasting
        hills,
    the filling of the valleys to make the
        ground level
    so that Israel can walk safely in God's
        glory.
8 And the forests and every fragrant tree
        will provide shade
    for Israel, at God's command;
9 for God will guide Israel in joy by the light
        of his glory,
    with the mercy and saving justice which
        come from him.

The letter of Jeremiah

*A copy of the letter which Jeremiah sent to those
about to be led captive to Babylon by the king of
the Babylonians, to tell them what he had been
commanded by God:*

6 'Because of the sins which you have committed before God you are to be deported
to Babylon by Nebuchadnezzar king of the
Babylonians. 2 Once you have reached Babylon you will stay there for many years, as long
as seven generations; after which I shall bring

you home in peace. 3 Now in Babylon you will
see gods made of silver, of gold, of wood, being
carried shoulder-high, and filling the gentiles
with fear. 4 Be on your guard! Do not imitate
the foreigners, do not have any fear of their
gods 5 as you see their worshippers prostrating
themselves before and behind them. Instead,
say in your hearts, "Master, it is you that we
must worship." 6 For my angel is with you;
your lives will be in his care.

7 'Overlaid with gold and silver, their
tongues polished smooth by a craftsman, they
are counterfeit and have no power to speak.
8 As though for a girl fond of finery, these people take gold and make crowns for the heads
of their gods. 9 And sometimes, the priests
filch gold and silver from their gods to spend
on themselves, even giving some of it to the
prostitutes on the terrace. 10 They dress up
these gods of silver, gold and wood, in clothes,
like human beings; on their own they cannot
protect themselves from either tarnish or
woodworm; 11 when they have been dressed in
purple cloaks, their faces have to be dusted,
because of the temple dust which settles thick
on them. 12 One holds a sceptre like the governor of a province, yet is powerless to put to
death anyone who offends him; 13 another
holds sword and mace in his right hand, yet is
powerless to defend himself against war or
thieves. 14 From this it is evident that they are
not gods; do not be afraid of them.

15 'Just as a pot in common use becomes useless once it is broken, so are these gods enshrined inside their temples. 16 Their eyes are
full of dust raised by the feet of those who
enter. 17 Just as the doors are locked on all sides
on someone who has offended a king and is
under sentence of death, so the priests secure
the temples of these gods with gates and bolts
and bars for fear of burglary. 18 They light
more lamps for them than they do for themselves, and the gods see none of them. 19 They
are like one of the temple beams, which are
said to be gnawed away from within; the ter-
mites creep out of the ground and eat them
and their clothes too, and they feel nothing.

20 Their faces are blackened by the smoke that rises from the temple. 21 Bats, swallows, birds of every kind perch on their bodies and heads, and so do cats. 22 From this, you can see for yourselves that they are not gods; do not be afraid of them.

23 'The gold with which they are parading their futility before the world is supposed to make them look beautiful, but if someone does not rub off the tarnish, these gods will not be shining much on their own, and even while they were being cast, they felt nothing. 24 However much was paid for them, there is still no breath of life in them. 25 Being unable to walk, they have to be carried on men's shoulders, which shows how futile they are. It is humiliating for their worshippers, too, who have to stand them up again if they fall over. 26 Once they have been stood up, they cannot move on their own; if they tilt askew, they cannot right themselves; offerings made to them might as well be made to the dead. 27 Whatever is sacrificed to them, the priests re-sell and pocket the profit; while their wives salt down part of it, but give nothing to the poor or to the helpless. As to the sacrifices themselves, why, women during their periods and women in childbed are not afraid to touch them! 28 From all this you can tell that they are not gods; do not be afraid of them.

29 'Indeed, how can they even be called gods, when women do the offering to these gods of silver, gold and wood? 30 In their temples, the priests stay sitting down, their garments torn, heads and beard shaved and heads uncovered; 31 they roar and shriek before their gods as people do at funeral feasts. 32 The priests take robes from the gods to clothe their own wives and children. 33 Whether these gods are treated badly or well, they are incapable of paying back either treatment; as incapable too of making or unmaking kings, 34 equally incapable of distributing wealth or money. If anyone fails to honour a vow he has made to them, they cannot call him to account. 35 They can neither save anyone from death nor rescue the weak from the strong, 36 nor re-store sight to the blind, nor save anyone in trouble, 37 nor take pity on a widow, nor be generous to an orphan. 38 These wooden gods overlaid with gold and silver are about as much use as rocks cut out of the mountain side. Their worshippers will be confounded! 39 So how can anyone think or say that they are gods?

40 'The Chaldaeans themselves do them no honour; if they find someone who is dumb and cannot speak, they present him to Bel, entreating him for the gift of speech, as though he could perceive it! 41 And they are incapable of drawing the conclusion and abandoning those gods—such is their lack of perception. 42 Women with strings round their waists sit in the streets, burning bran like incense; 43 when one of these has been picked up by a passer-by and been to bed with him, she then gloats over her neighbour for not having been thought as worthy as herself and for not having had her string broken. 44 Whatever is done for them is spurious. So how can anyone think or say that they are gods?

45 'Made by woodworkers and goldsmiths, they are only what those workmen decide to make them. 46 Their makers have not long to live themselves, so how can the things they make be gods? 47 Their legacy to their descendants is nothing but delusion and dishonour. 48 If war or disasters befall them, the priests discuss where best to hide themselves and these gods; 49 how can anyone fail to realise that they are not gods, if they cannot save themselves from war or from disasters? 50 And since they are only made of wood overlaid with gold or silver, it will later become apparent that they are spurious; it will be obvious to everyone, to nations as to kings, that they are not gods but the work of human hands, and that there is no divine activity in them. 51 Does anyone still need convincing that they are not gods?

52 'They can neither appoint a king over a country, nor give rain to humankind, 53 nor regulate their own affairs, nor rescue anyone who suffers a wrong; they are as helpless as

crows between sky and ground. ⁵⁴If fire falls on the temple of these wooden gods overlaid with gold or silver, their priests fly to safety while they for their part stay there like beams, to be burnt. ⁵⁵They cannot put up any resistance to a king or to enemies. ⁵⁶So how can anyone think or say that they are gods?

⁵⁷'These wooden gods overlaid with gold or silver cannot evade thieves or marauders; strong men may rob them of their gold and silver and make off with the robes they are dressed in; yet they are powerless to help even themselves. ⁵⁸Better to be a king displaying his prowess, a household pot of use to its owner, than to be these counterfeit gods; or merely the door of a house, protecting what is inside, than these counterfeit gods; or a wooden pillar in a palace than these counterfeit gods. ⁵⁹The sun, the moon and the stars, which shine and have been given work to do, are obedient; ⁶⁰similarly, the lightning, as it flashes, is a fine sight; in the same way, the wind blows across every country, ⁶¹the clouds execute the order God gives them to pass over the whole earth, and the fire, sent from above to consume mountain and forest, carries out its orders. ⁶²Now these gods are not their equals, either in beauty or in power. ⁶³So, no one can think or say that they are gods, powerless as they are to administer justice or to do anyone any good. ⁶⁴Therefore, knowing that they are not gods, do not be afraid of them.

⁶⁵'For they can neither curse nor bless kings, ⁶⁶nor produce signs in heaven for the nations, nor shine like the sun, nor shed light like the moon. ⁶⁷The animals are better off than they are, being able to look after themselves by making for cover. ⁶⁸There is not the slightest shred of evidence that they are gods; so do not be afraid of them!

⁶⁹'Their wooden gods overlaid with gold and silver are like a scarecrow in a field of cucumbers—protecting nothing. ⁷⁰Or again, their wooden gods overlaid with gold and silver are like a thorn-bush in a garden—any kind of bird may perch on it—or like a corpse thrown out into the dark. ⁷¹From the purple and linen rotting on their backs you can tell that they are not gods; and in the end, eaten away, they will be the dishonour of the country. ⁷²Better, then, someone upright who has no idols; dishonour will never come near him.'

The Book of

EZEKIEL

1 In the thirtieth year, on the fifth day of the fourth month, as I was among the exiles by the River Chebar, heaven opened and I saw visions from God. 2 On the fifth of the month—it was the fifth year of exile for King Jehoiachin— 3 the word of Yahweh was addressed to the priest Ezekiel son of Buzi, in Chaldaea by the River Chebar. There the hand of Yahweh came on him.

The vision of the Chariot of Yahweh

4 I looked; a stormy wind blew from the north, a great cloud with flashing fire and brilliant light round it, and in the middle, in the heart of the fire, a brilliance like that of amber, 5 and in the middle what seemed to be four living creatures. They looked like this: They were of human form. 6 Each had four faces, each had four wings. 7 Their legs were straight; they had hooves like calves, glittering like polished brass. 8 Below their wings, they had human hands on all four sides corresponding to their four faces and four wings. 9 They touched one another with their wings; they did not turn as they moved; each one moved straight forward. 10 As to the appearance of their faces, all four had a human face, and a lion's face to the right, and all four had a bull's face to the left, and all four had an eagle's face. 11 Their wings were spread upwards, each had one pair touching its neighbour's, and the other pair covering its body. 12 And each one moved straight forward; they went where the spirit urged them, they did not turn as they moved.

13 Between these living creatures were what looked like blazing coals, like torches, darting backwards and forwards between the living creatures; the fire gave a brilliant light, and lightning flashed from the fire, 14 and the living creatures kept disappearing and reappearing like flashes of lightning.

15 Now, as I looked at the living creatures, I saw a wheel touching the ground beside each of the four-faced living creatures. 16 The appearance and structure of the wheels were like glittering chrysolite. All four looked alike, and their appearance and structure were such that each wheel seemed to have another wheel inside it. 17 In whichever of the four directions they moved, they did not need to turn as they moved. 18 Their circumference was of awe-inspiring size, and the rims of all four sparkled all the way round. 19 When the living creatures moved, the wheels moved beside them; and when the living creatures left the ground, the wheels too left the ground. 20 They moved in whichever direction the spirit chose to go, and the wheels rose with them, since the wheels shared the spirit of the animals. 21 When the living creatures moved on, they moved on; when the former halted, the latter halted; when the former left the ground, the wheels too left the ground, since the wheels shared the spirit of the animals. 22 Over the heads of the living creatures was what looked like a solid surface glittering like crystal, spread out over their heads, above them, 23 and under the solid surface, their wings were spread out straight, touching one another, and each had a pair covering its body. 24 I also heard the noise of their wings; when they moved, it was like the noise of flood-waters, like the voice of Shaddai, like the noise of a storm, like the noise of an armed camp; and when they halted, they lowered their wings; 25 there was a noise too.

26 Beyond the solid surface above their heads, there was what seemed like a sapphire, in the form of a throne. High above on the

form of a throne was a form with the appearance of a human being.

27 I saw a brilliance like amber, like fire, radiating from what appeared to be the waist upwards; and from what appeared to be the waist downwards, I saw what looked like fire, giving a brilliant light all round. 28 The radiance of the encircling light was like the radiance of the bow in the clouds on rainy days. The sight was like the glory of Yahweh. I looked and fell to the ground, and I heard the voice of someone speaking to me.

The vision of the scroll

2 He said, 'Son of man, get to your feet; I will speak to you.' 2 As he said these words the spirit came into me and put me on my feet, and I heard him speaking to me. 3 He said, 'Son of man, I am sending you to the Israelites, to the rebels who have rebelled against me. They and their ancestors have been in revolt against me up to the present day. 4 Because they are stubborn and obstinate children, I am sending you to them, to say, "Lord Yahweh says this." 5 Whether they listen or not, this tribe of rebels will know there is a prophet among them. 6 And you, son of man, do not be afraid of them or of what they say, though you find yourself surrounded with brambles and sitting on scorpions. Do not be afraid of their words or alarmed by their looks, for they are a tribe of rebels. 7 You are to deliver my words to them whether they listen or not, for they are a tribe of rebels. 8 But you, son of man, are to listen to what I say to you; do not be a rebel like that rebellious tribe. Open your mouth and eat what I am about to give you.'

9 When I looked, there was a hand stretching out to me, holding a scroll. 10 He unrolled it in front of me; it was written on, front and back; on it was written 'Lamentations, dirges and cries of grief'.

3 He then said, 'Son of man, eat what you see; eat this scroll, then go and speak to the House of Israel.' 2 I opened my mouth; he gave me the scroll to eat 3 and then said, 'Son of man, feed on this scroll which I am giving you and eat your fill.' So I ate it, and it tasted sweet as honey.

4 He then said, 'Son of man, go to the House of Israel and tell them what I have said. 5 You are not being sent to a nation that speaks a difficult foreign language; you are being sent to the House of Israel. 6 Not to big nations that speak difficult foreign languages, and whose words you would not understand—if I sent you to them, they would listen to you; 7 but the House of Israel will not listen to you because it will not listen to me. The whole House of Israel is defiant and obstinate. 8 But now, I am making you as defiant as they are, and as obstinate as they are; 9 I am making your resolution as hard as a diamond, harder than flint. So do not be afraid of them, do not be overawed by them, for they are a tribe of rebels.'

10 Then he said, 'Son of man, take to heart everything I say to you, listen carefully, 11 then go to your exiled countrymen and talk to them. Say to them, "Lord Yahweh says this," whether they listen or not.'

12 The spirit lifted me up, and behind me I heard a great vibrating sound, 'Blessed be the glory of Yahweh in his dwelling-place!' 13 This was the sound of the living creatures' wings beating against each other, and the sound of the wheels beside them: a great vibrating sound. 14 The spirit lifted me up and took me, and I went, bitter and angry, and the hand of Yahweh lay heavy on me. 15 I came to Tel Abib, to the exiles beside the River Chebar where they were living, and there I stayed with them in a stupor for seven days.

The prophet as watchman[a]

16 After seven days the word of Yahweh was addressed to me as follows, 17 'Son of man, I have appointed you as watchman for the House of Israel. When you hear a word from my mouth, warn them from me. 18 If I say to someone wicked, "You will die," and you do not warn this person; if you do not speak to

3a A summary of the fuller version in 33:1–9.

85 READ EZEKIEL 3:16–21.

When you hear a word from my mouth, warn them from me.—EZEKIEL 3:17

THE POWER OF GOOD EXAMPLE

While St. Francis was staying in Siena, he was visited by a doctor of theology from the Order of Preachers, a man who was both humble and sincerely spiritual. When he had discussed the words of our Lord with blessed Francis for some time, this doctor asked him about the passage in Ezekiel: "When I threaten the sinner with doom of death, it is for you to give him word and warn him" (see Ezk 3:18).

And the doctor said, "Good Father, I know many people who are in mortal sin, and do not warn them of their wickedness. Will their souls be required at my hand?" Blessed Francis humbly answered that he was no scholar, so that it would be more profitable for him to receive instruction from his questioner than to offer his own opinion on Scripture. The humble doctor then added, "Brother, although I have heard this passage expounded by various learned men, I would be glad to know how you interpreted it."

So blessed Francis said, "If the passage is to be understood in general terms, I take it to mean that a servant of God should burn and shine in such a way by his own life and holiness that he rebukes all wicked people by the light of his example and the devoutness of his conversation; in this way the brightness of his life and the fragrance of his reputation will make all men aware of their own wickedness."

Greatly edified, the doctor went away, and said to the companions of blessed Francis, "My brothers, this man's theology is grounded on purity and contemplation, and resembles a flying eagle; but our knowledge crawls along the ground on its belly." ST. FRANCIS OF ASSISI, 1181–1226

YOU WILL FIND THE NEXT READING AT EZEKIEL 18.

warn someone wicked to renounce evil and so save his life, it is the wicked person who will die for the guilt, but I shall hold you responsible for that death. [19] If, however, you do warn someone wicked who then fails to renounce wickedness and evil ways, the wicked person will die for the guilt, but you yourself will have saved your life. [20] When someone upright renounces uprightness to do evil and I set a trap for him, it is he who will die; since you failed to warn him, he will die for his guilt, and the uprightness he practised will no longer be remembered; but I shall hold you re-

sponsible for his death. [21] If, however, you warn someone upright not to sin and this person does not sin, such a one will live, thanks to your warning, and you too will have saved your life.'

Ezekiel is struck dumb

[22] While I was there the hand of Yahweh came on me; he said, 'Get up, go out into the valley, and there I shall speak to you.' [23] I got up and went out into the valley; the glory of Yahweh was resting there, like the glory I had seen by the River Chebar, and I fell to the ground.

24 The spirit of Yahweh then entered me and put me on my feet and spoke to me.

He said, 'Go and shut yourself in your house. 25 Son of man, you are about to be tied and bound, and unable to mix with other people. 26 I am going to make your tongue stick to the roof of your mouth; you will be dumb, and no longer able to reprove them, for they are a tribe of rebels. 27 When I speak to you, however, I shall open your mouth and then you will say to them, "Lord Yahweh says this: Let anyone prepared to listen, listen; let anyone who refuses, refuse!"—for they are a tribe of rebels.'

The siege of Jerusalem foretold

4 'For your part, son of man, take a brick and lay it in front of you; on it scratch a city, Jerusalem. 2 You are then to besiege it, trench round it, build earthworks, pitch camps and bring up battering-rams all round. 3 Then take an iron pan and place it as though it were an iron wall between you and the city. Then fix your gaze on it; it is being besieged and you are besieging it. This is a sign for the House of Israel.

4 'Lie down on your left side and take the guilt of the House of Israel on yourself. You will bear their guilt for as many days as you lie on that side. 5 Allowing one day for every year of their guilt, I ordain that you bear it for three hundred and ninety days; this is how you will bear the House of Israel's guilt. 6 And when you have finished doing this, you are to lie down again, on your right side, and bear the guilt of the House of Judah for forty days. I have set the length for you as one day for one year. 7 Then fix your gaze on the siege of Jerusalem, raise your bared arm and prophesy against her. 8 Look, I am going to tie you up and you will not be able to turn over from one side to the other until the period of your seclusion is over.

9 'Now take wheat, barley, beans, lentils, millet and spelt; put them all in the same pot and make them into bread for yourself. You are to eat it for as many days as you are lying

on your side—three hundred and ninety days. 10 Of this food, you are to weigh out a daily portion of twenty shekels and eat it a little piece at a time. 11 And you are to ration the water you drink—a sixth of a *hin*—drinking that a little at a time. 12 You are to eat this in the form of a barley cake baked where they can see you, on human dung.' 13 And Yahweh said, 'This is how the Israelites will have to eat their defiled food, wherever I disperse them among the nations.' 14 I then said, 'Lord Yahweh, my soul is not defiled. From my childhood until now, I have never eaten an animal that has died a natural death or been savaged; no tainted meat has ever entered my mouth.' 15 'Very well,' he said, 'I grant you cow-dung instead of human dung; you are to bake your bread on that.' 16 He then said, 'Son of man, I am going to cut off Jerusalem's food supply; in their extremity, the food they eat will be weighed out; to their horror, the water they drink will be rationed, 17 until there is no food or water left, and they fall into a stupor and waste away because of their guilt.'

5 'Son of man, take a sharp sword, use it like a barber's razor and run it over your head and beard. Then take scales and divide the hair you have cut off. 2 Burn one-third inside the city, while the days of the siege are working themselves out. Then take another third and chop it up with the sword all round the city. The last third you are to scatter to the wind, while I unsheathe the sword behind them. 3 Also take a few hairs and tie them up in the folds of your cloak; 4 and of these again take a few, and throw them on the fire and burn them. From them fire will come on the whole House of Israel.

5 'The Lord Yahweh says this, "This is Jerusalem, which I have placed in the middle of the nations, surrounded with foreign countries. 6 She has rebelled more perversely against my observances than the nations have, and against my laws than the surrounding

countries have; for they have rejected my observances and not kept my laws."

7 'Therefore, the Lord Yahweh says this, "Because your disorders are worse than those of the nations round you, since you do not keep my laws or respect my observances, and since you do not respect even the observances of the surrounding nations, 8 very well, the Lord Yahweh says this: I, too, am against you and shall execute my judgements on you for the nations to see. 9 Because of all your loathsome practices I shall do such things as I have never done before, nor shall ever do again. 10 Those of you who are parents will eat their children, and children will eat their parents. I shall execute judgement on you and disperse what remains of you to the winds. 11 For, as I live—declares Lord Yahweh—as sure as you have defiled my sanctuary with all your horrors and all your loathsome practices, so I too shall reject you without a glance of pity, I shall not spare you. 12 A third of your citizens will die of plague or starve to death inside you; a third will fall by the sword round you; and a third I shall scatter to the winds, unsheathing the sword behind them. 13 I shall sate my anger and bring my fury to rest on them until I am avenged; and when I have sated my fury on them, then they will know that I, Yahweh, spoke out of jealousy for you. 14 Yes, I shall reduce you to a ruin, an object of derision to the surrounding nations, in the eyes of all who pass by. 15 You will be an object of derision and insults, an example, an object of amazement to the surrounding nations, when I execute judgement on you in furious anger and furious punishments. I, Yahweh, have spoken. 16 On them I shall send the deadly arrows of famine, which will destroy you—for I shall send them to destroy you; then I shall make the famine worse and cut off your food supply. 17 I shall send famine and wild animals on you to rob you of your children; plague and bloodshed will sweep through you, and I shall bring the sword down on you. I, Yahweh, have spoken." '

Against the mountains of Israel

6 The word of Yahweh was addressed to me as follows, 2 'Son of man, turn towards the mountains of Israel and prophesy against them. 3 Say, "Mountains of Israel, hear the word of the Lord Yahweh. The Lord Yahweh says this to mountains and hills and ravines and valleys: Look, I am going to summon the sword against you and destroy your high places. 4 Your altars will be wrecked, and your incense burners smashed; I shall fling your butchered inhabitants down in front of your foul idols; 5 I shall lay the corpses of the Israelites in front of their foul idols and scatter their bones all round your altars. 6 Wherever you live, the towns will be destroyed and the high places wrecked, to the ruin and wrecking of your altars, the shattering and abolition of your foul idols, the smashing of your incense burners and the utter destruction of all your works. 7 As the butchered fall about you, you will know that I am Yahweh.

8 "But I shall spare some of you to escape the sword among the nations, when you have been dispersed in their lands; 9 and your survivors will remember me among the nations where they are held captive, since I shall have broken their adulterous hearts for having deserted me, and destroyed their eyes for having turned adulterously towards their foul idols. They will loathe themselves for all the wrong they have caused by their loathsome practices. 10 Then they will know that I am Yahweh and that I was not talking lightly when I said that I would inflict these disasters on them."

The sins of Israel

11 'The Lord Yahweh says this, "Clap your hands, stamp your feet, and say: Alas for all the loathsome sins of the House of Israel, which is about to fall by sword, famine and plague! 12 Far off, they will die by plague; near at hand they will fall by the sword; and any who survive or are spared will die of famine. This is how I shall sate my fury on them. 13 Then you will know that I am Yahweh,

when their butchered corpses lie among their foul idols, all round their altars, on every high hill, on every mountain top, under every green tree, under every leafy oak, wherever they offer a smell pleasing to all their idols. ¹⁴I shall point my finger at them and reduce the country to an empty wasteland from the desert to Riblah, everywhere they live, and they will know that I am Yahweh." '

The end is near

7 The word of Yahweh was addressed to me as follows, ²'Son of man, say, "Lord Yahweh says this to the land of Israel: Finished! The end is coming for the four corners of the country. ³This is the end for you; I shall unleash my anger on you, and judge you as your conduct deserves and call you to account for all your loathsome practices. ⁴I shall show you no pity, I shall not spare you; I shall repay you for your conduct and for the loathsome practices in which you persist. Then you will know that I am Yahweh.

⁵"The Lord Yahweh says this: Disaster, a unique disaster, is coming. ⁶The end is coming, the end is coming, it is on the move towards you, it is coming now. ⁷Now it is your turn, you who dwell in this country. Doom is coming, the day is near; no joy now, only tumult, on the mountains. ⁸Now I shall soon vent my fury on you and sate my anger on you: I shall judge you as your conduct deserves and repay you for all your loathsome practices. ⁹I shall show neither pity nor mercy, but shall repay you for your conduct and the loathsome practices in which you persist. Then you will know that I am Yahweh and that I strike.

¹⁰"Now is the day, your turn has come, it has come, it appears, the sceptre has blossomed, pride is at its peak. ¹¹Violence has risen to become the scourge of wickedness... ¹²Doom is coming, the day is near. Neither should buyer rejoice, nor seller regret, for the fury rests on everyone alike. ¹³The seller will not be able to go back on his bargain; each persists in his sins; they take no defensive measures. ¹⁴The trumpet sounds, all is ready, but no one goes into battle, since my fury rests on all alike.

The sins of Israel

¹⁵"Outside, the sword; inside, plague and famine. Whoever is living in the countryside will die by the sword; whoever is living in the city will be devoured by famine and plague. ¹⁶And those who escape will escape to the mountains and there, like doves of the valleys, I shall slaughter them all, each one for his sin. ¹⁷Every hand will grow limp, every knee turn to water. ¹⁸They will put on sackcloth, each one trembling. Every face will be ashamed and every head be shaved. ¹⁹They will throw their silver away in the streets and their gold they will regard as a pollution; neither their silver nor their gold will be able to save them on the day of Yahweh's fury. Never again will they have enough to eat, never again will they fill their bellies, since that was the occasion for their guilt. ²⁰They used to pride themselves on the beauty of their jewellery, out of which they made their loathsome images, their horrors; so now I have made it pollute them. ²¹I shall hand it over as plunder to foreigners, as loot to the most evil people on earth. They will profane it. ²²I shall turn my face away from them, while my treasure-house is profaned and robbers will force their way in and profane it.

²³"Forge yourself a chain; for the country is full of bloody executions and the city full of deeds of violence, ²⁴so I shall bring the cruellest of the nations to seize their houses. I shall put an end to the pride of their élite, and their sanctuary will be profaned. ²⁵Terror is on the way: they will look for peace and there will be none. ²⁶Disaster will follow on disaster, rumour on rumour; they will pester the prophet for a vision; the priest will be at a loss over the law and the elders on how to advise. ²⁷The king will go into mourning, the prince be plunged in grief, the hands of the country people tremble. I shall treat them as their conduct deserves, and judge them as their own verdicts merit. Then they will know that I am Yahweh!" '

A vision of the sins of Jerusalem[a]

8 In the sixth year, on the fifth day of the sixth month, I was sitting at home and the elders of Judah were sitting with me, when suddenly the hand of the Lord Yahweh fell on me there. [2] I looked, and there was a form with the appearance of a human being. Downwards from what seemed to be the waist there was fire; and upwards from the waist there was a brilliance like the glitter of amber. [3] Something like a hand was stretched out and it took me by a lock of my hair; and the spirit lifted me between heaven and earth and, in visions from God, took me to Jerusalem, to the entrance of the inner north gate, where stands the idol that provokes jealousy. [4] There was the glory of the God of Israel; it looked like what I had seen in the valley. [5] He said, 'Son of man, raise your eyes to the north.' I raised my eyes to the north, and there, to the north of the altar gate, stood this statue of jealousy at the entrance. [6] He said, 'Son of man, do you see what they are doing, the monstrous, loathsome things that the House of Israel is practising here, to drive me out of my sanctuary? And you will see practices more loathsome still.'

[7] He next took me to the entrance to the court. I looked; there was a hole in the wall. [8] He said, 'Son of man, bore through the wall.' I bored through the wall, until I had made an opening. [9] He said, 'Go in and look at the loathsome things they are doing inside.' [10] I went in and looked and there was every kind of reptile and repulsive animal, and all the foul idols of the House of Israel, carved all round the walls. [11] Seventy elders of the House of Israel were worshipping the idols—among them Jaazaniah son of Shaphan—each one with his censer in his hand, from which rose a fragrant cloud of incense. [12] He said, 'Son of man, have you seen what the elders of the House of Israel do in the dark, each in his personal image-shrine? They say, "Yahweh cannot see us; Yahweh has abandoned the coun-

try." ' [13] He said, 'You will see them at practices more loathsome still.'

[14] He next took me to the entrance of the north gate of the Temple of Yahweh where women were sitting, weeping for Tammuz.[b] [15] He said, 'Son of man, do you see that? You will see even more loathsome things than that.'

[16] He then led me to the inner court of the Temple of Yahweh. And there, at the entrance to Yahweh's sanctuary, between the portico and the altar, there were about twenty-five men, with their backs to Yahweh's sanctuary and their faces turned towards the east. They were prostrating themselves to the east, before the rising sun. [17] He said to me, 'Son of man, do you see that? Is it not bad enough for the House of Judah to be doing the loathsome things they are doing here? But they fill the country with violence and provoke my anger further; look at them now putting that branch to their nostrils. [18] And so I shall react in fury; I shall show neither pity nor mercy. They may cry as loudly as they like to me; I will not listen.'

The punishment

9 Then he shouted loudly for me to hear, 'The scourges of the city are approaching, each carrying his weapon of destruction!' [2] Immediately six men advanced from the upper north gate, each holding a deadly weapon. Among them was a man dressed in linen, with a scribe's ink-horn in his belt. They came in and halted in front of the bronze altar. [3] The glory of the God of Israel rose from above the winged creature where it had been, towards the threshold of the Temple. He called to the man dressed in linen with a scribe's ink-horn in his belt [4] and Yahweh said to him, 'Go all through the city, all through Jerusalem, and mark a cross on the foreheads of all who grieve and lament over all the loath-

8a chh. 8–11 are a vision four years before the final siege.

8b A vegetation god whose annual death and rebirth were mourned and greeted.

some practices in it.' ⁵I heard him say to the others, 'Follow him through the city and strike. Not one glance of pity; show no mercy; ⁶old men, young men, girls, children, women, kill and exterminate them all. But do not touch anyone with a cross on his forehead. Begin at my sanctuary.' So they began with the old men who were in the Temple. ⁷He said to them, 'Defile the Temple; fill the courts with corpses; then go out!' They went out and hacked their way through the city.

⁸While they were hacking them down, I was left alone; I fell on my face, crying out, 'Ah, Lord Yahweh, are you going to annihilate all that is left of Israel by venting your fury on Jerusalem?' ⁹He said, 'The guilt of the House of Israel and Judah is immense; the country is full of bloodshed, the city full of perversity, for they say, "Yahweh has abandoned the country, Yahweh cannot see." ¹⁰Then, I too shall neither give one glance of pity nor show any mercy. I shall repay them for what they have done.' ¹¹The man dressed in linen with the scribe's ink-horn in his belt then came back and made his report, 'I have carried out your orders.'

10 Then, in vision I saw that above the solid surface over the heads of the winged creatures there was above them something like sapphire, which seemed to be like a throne. ²He then said to the man dressed in linen, 'Go in between the wheels below the winged creatures; take a handful of burning coal from between the winged creatures and scatter it over the city.' He went in as I watched.

³The winged creatures were on the right of the Temple as the man went in, and the cloud filled the inner court. ⁴The glory of Yahweh rose from above the winged creatures, towards the threshold of the Temple; the Temple was filled by the cloud and the court was full of the brightness of the glory of Yahweh. ⁵The noise of the winged creatures' wings could be heard even in the outer court, like the voice of God Almighty when he speaks.

⁶When he had given the order to the man dressed in linen, 'Take the fire from between the wheels, between the winged creatures,' the man went in and stood by one of the wheels. ⁷One of the winged creatures then reached his hand out towards the fire between the winged creatures, took some of it and put it into the hands of the man dressed in linen, who took it and came out again.

⁸There appeared to be what looked like a human hand under the winged creatures' wings. ⁹And I looked, and there were four wheels beside the winged creatures, one wheel beside each winged creature, and the appearance of the wheels was like the sparkle of chrysolite. ¹⁰In appearance, all four looked alike, as though each wheel had another wheel inside it.

¹¹In whichever of the four directions they moved, they did not need to turn as they moved, but whichever way the head was facing there they followed; they did not turn as they moved, ¹²and their entire bodies, their backs, their hands, their wings, as well as the wheels, had eyes all the way round (the wheels of all four). ¹³In my hearing, these wheels were called 'galgal'. ¹⁴Each had four faces; the first was a winged creature's face, the second a human face, the third a lion's face and the fourth an eagle's face. ¹⁵The winged creatures rose; this was the being I had seen by the River Chebar. ¹⁶When the winged creatures moved, the wheels moved beside them; and when the winged creatures raised their wings to leave the ground, the wheels did not turn beside them. ¹⁷When the former halted the latter halted; when the former rose, the latter rose with them, since they shared the same living spirit.

The glory of Yahweh leaves the Temple

¹⁸The glory of Yahweh then came out over the Temple threshold and paused over the winged creatures. ¹⁹These raised their wings and rose from the ground as I watched, and the wheels were beside them. They paused at the entrance to the east gate of the Temple of Yah-

weh, with the glory of the God of Israel over them, above. ²⁰This was the winged creature I had seen beneath the God of Israel by the River Chebar; I knew that they were winged creatures. ²¹Each had four faces and four wings and what seemed to be human hands under their wings. ²²Their faces were like those I had seen by the River Chebar. Each one moved straight forward.

The sins of Jerusalem (continued)

11 The spirit lifted me up and brought me to the east gate of the Temple of Yahweh, the gate that looks eastwards. There at the entrance to the gate stood twenty-five men, among whom I saw Jaazaniah son of Azzur and Pelatiah son of Benaiah, leaders of the people.

²He said to me, 'Son of man, these are the wicked schemers who are spreading their bad advice through this city. ³They say, "There will be no house-building yet awhile. The city is the cooking pot and we are the meat." ⁴So prophesy against them, prophesy, son of man!' ⁵The spirit of Yahweh fell on me, and he said to me, 'Say, "Yahweh says this: I know what you are saying, House of Israel, I know how insolent you are. ⁶You have filled this city with more and more of your victims; you have strewn its streets with victims. ⁷And so the Lord Yahweh says this: Your victims, whom you have put in it, are the meat, and the city is the cooking pot; but I shall take you out of it. ⁸You are afraid of the sword and I shall bring the sword down on you—declares the Lord Yahweh— ⁹and I shall take you out of it and hand you over to foreigners and bring you to justice; ¹⁰you will fall by the sword on the soil of Israel; I shall execute justice on you, and you will know that I am Yahweh. ¹¹This city will be no cooking pot for you, nor will you be the meat inside; I shall execute justice on you on the soil of Israel; ¹²and you will know that I am Yahweh, whose laws you have not obeyed and whose judgements you have not kept; instead, you have adopted the customs of the nations round you." '

¹³Now as I was prophesying, Pelatiah son of Benaiah dropped dead. I fell to the ground and cried out, 'Ah, Lord Yahweh, are you going to annihilate the remnant of Israel?'

The new covenant promised to the exiles

¹⁴The word of Yahweh was then addressed to me as follows, ¹⁵'Son of man, to your brothers one and all, to your kinsfolk and to the whole House of Israel, the inhabitants of Jerusalem have said, "Keep well away from Yahweh. This country has now been made over to us!" ¹⁶So say, "The Lord Yahweh says this: Yes, I have sent them far away among the nations and I have dispersed them to foreign countries; and for a while I have been a sanctuary for them in the country to which they have gone." ¹⁷So say, "The Lord Yahweh says this: I shall gather you back from the peoples, I shall collect you in from the countries where you have been scattered and give you the land of Israel. ¹⁸When they come back, they will purge it of all its horrors and loathsome practices. ¹⁹I shall give them a single heart and I shall put a new spirit in them; I shall remove the heart of stone from their bodies and give them a heart of flesh, ²⁰so that they can keep my laws and respect my judgements and put them into practice. Then they will be my people and I shall be their God. ²¹But those whose hearts are set on their horrors and loathsome practices I shall repay for their conduct—declares the Lord Yahweh." '

The glory of Yahweh leaves Jerusalem

²²The winged creatures then raised their wings and the wheels moved with them, with the glory of the God of Israel over them, above. ²³And the glory of Yahweh rose from the centre of the city and halted on the mountain to the east of the city.

²⁴Then the spirit lifted me up and took me, in vision, in the spirit of God, to the exiles in Chaldaea, and the vision which I had seen faded. ²⁵I then told the exiles everything that Yahweh had shown me.

The mime of the exile

12 The word of Yahweh was addressed to me as follows, [2] 'Son of man, you are living among a tribe of rebels who have eyes and never see, they have ears and never hear, because they are a tribe of rebels. [3] So, son of man, pack an exile's bundle and set off for exile by daylight while they watch. You will leave your home and go somewhere else while they watch. Then perhaps they will see that they are a tribe of rebels. [4] You will pack your baggage like an exile's bundle, by daylight, while they watch, and leave like an exile in the evening, while they watch. [5] While they watch, make a hole in the wall, and go out through it. [6] While they watch, you will shoulder your pack and go out into the dark; you will cover your face so that you cannot see the ground, since I have made you an omen for the House of Israel.'

[7] I did as I had been told. I packed my baggage like an exile's bundle, by daylight; and in the evening I made a hole through the wall with my hands; then I went out into the dark and shouldered my pack while they watched.

[8] Next morning the word of Yahweh was addressed to me as follows, [9] 'Son of man, did not the House of Israel, did not that tribe of rebels, ask you, "What are you doing?" [10] Say, "The Lord Yahweh says this: This prophecy concerns Jerusalem and the whole House of Israel who live there." [11] Say, "I am an omen for you; as I have done, so will be done to them; they will be deported into exile. [12] Their prince will shoulder his pack in the dark and go out through the wall; a hole will be made to let him out; he will cover his face, so that he cannot see the country. [13] I shall throw my net over him and catch him in my mesh; I shall take him to Babylon,[a] to the land of the Chaldaeans, though he will not see it; and there he will die. [14] And all those in attendance on him, his army and all his troops, I shall scatter to all the winds and unsheathe the sword behind them. [15] Then they will know that I am Yahweh, when I scatter them throughout the nations and disperse them in foreign countries. [16] But I shall let a few of them escape the sword, famine and plague, to describe all their loathsome practices to the peoples among whom they will go, so that these too may know that I am Yahweh." '

[17] The word of Yahweh was addressed to me as follows, [18] 'Son of man, you are to tremble as you eat your food and shudder apprehensively as you drink your water, [19] and you are to say to the people of the country, "The Lord Yahweh says this to the inhabitants of Jerusalem. They will shudder apprehensively as they eat their food, and drink their water in fear, so that the country and its population may be freed from the violence of its inhabitants. [20] When the populous cities have been destroyed and the country has been reduced to desert, then you will know that I am Yahweh." '

Popular proverbs

[21] The word of Yahweh was addressed to me as follows, [22] 'Son of man, what do you understand by the saying pronounced over the land of Israel, "Days go by and visions fade"?

[23] 'Very well, tell them, "The Lord Yahweh says this: I shall put an end to this saying; it will never be used in Israel again." Instead, tell them:

"The days are coming when every vision will come true, [24] for there will be no more futile visions or deceptive prophecy in the House of Israel, [25] since I, Yahweh, shall speak. And what I shall say will come true without delay; for what I shall say, I shall perform in your own lifetime, you tribe of rebels—declares the Lord Yahweh." '

[26] The word of Yahweh was addressed to me as follows, [27] 'Son of man, the House of Israel is now saying, "The vision that this man sees concerns the distant future; he is prophesying for times far ahead." [28] Very well, tell them, "The Lord Yahweh says this: There will be no further delay in the fulfilling of any of

12a = 17:20.

my words. What I have said shall be done now—declares the Lord Yahweh." '

Against the false prophets

13 The word of Yahweh was addressed to me as follows, [2]'Son of man, prophesy against the prophets of Israel; prophesy, and say to those who make up prophecies out of their own heads, "Hear what Yahweh says: [3]The Lord Yahweh says this: Disaster is in store for the foolish prophets who follow their own spirit and have seen nothing! [4]Your prophets, Israel, are like ruin-haunting jackals!

[5]"You have not ventured into the breach; you have not built up the wall round the House of Israel, to hold fast in battle on the Day of Yahweh. [6]Theirs are futile visions and false predictions, who say: A prophecy from Yahweh, when Yahweh has not sent them; yet they expect their words to come true. [7]Have not the visions you see been futile, have not the predictions you make been false, although you say: A prophecy of Yahweh, when I have not spoken?

[8]"Very well, the Lord Yahweh says this: Because of your futile words and false predictions, I am now against you—declares Lord Yahweh. [9]My hand will be against the prophets who have futile visions and give false predictions; they will not be admitted to the council of my people, their names will not be entered in the roll of the House of Israel, they will not set foot on the soil of Israel; and they will know that I am the Lord Yahweh. [10]This is because they have misled my people by saying Peace! when there is no peace. When my people were repairing a wall, these men came and plastered it over! [11]Tell these plasterers: It will rain hard, it will hail, it will blow a gale, [12]and down will come the wall! Will not people ask you: What has become of the plaster you slapped on it? [13]Well then, the Lord Yahweh says this: I am going to unleash a stormy wind in my fury, torrential rain in my anger, hailstones in my destructive fury, [14]and I shall shatter the wall you plastered and knock it

down and lay its foundations bare. It will fall and you will perish under it; then you will know that I am Yahweh."

[15]'When I have sated my anger on the wall and those who plastered it, I shall say to you, "The wall is gone, and so are those who plastered over it, [16]the prophets of Israel who prophesy about Jerusalem and have visions of peace for her when there is no peace—declares the Lord Yahweh."

Against the false prophetesses

[17]'Also, son of man, turn to the women of your people who make up prophecies out of their own heads; prophesy against them. [18]Say, "The Lord Yahweh says this: Disaster is in store for women who sew ribbons round each wrist and make head-cloths for people of all sizes, in their hunt for souls! Are you to hunt the souls of my people and keep your own souls safe? [19]You dishonour me in front of my people for a few handfuls of barley, a few bits of bread, killing those who ought not to die and sparing those who ought not to live, lying to my people who love listening to lies.

[20]"Very well, the Lord Yahweh says this: Look, I am now against your ribbons, with which you hunt souls like birds, and I shall tear them off your arms and free those souls whom you hunt like birds. [21]I shall tear your head-cloths to pieces and rescue my people from your clutches; no longer will they be fair game for you to ensnare. Then you will know that I am Yahweh.

[22]"For having intimidated with lies the heart of the upright whom I had done nothing to alarm, and for having encouraged the wicked not to give up wicked ways and so be saved, [23]very well, you will have no more futile visions and make no more predictions, for I shall rescue my people from your clutches, and you will know that I am Yahweh." '

Against idolatry

14 Next, some elders of Israel visited me and while they were sitting with me, [2]the word of Yahweh was addressed to me as follows, ³'Son of man, these men have enshrined their foul idols in their hearts and placed the cause of their sinning right before their eyes. Why should I let myself be consulted by them? ⁴So speak to them; tell them this, "Lord Yahweh says this: Every member of the House of Israel who enshrines his foul idols in his heart and places the cause of his sinning right before his eyes, and who then approaches the prophet, will get this answer from me, Yahweh, as the multiplicity of his idols deserves, ⁵and in this way I hope to win back the hearts of the House of Israel who have all been estranged from me by their foul idols."

⁶'So say to the House of Israel, "The Lord Yahweh says this: Come back, turn away from your foul idols, turn your backs on all your loathsome practices; ⁷for if any member of the House of Israel—or any foreigner living in Israel—deserts me to enshrine his foul idols in his heart and places the cause of his sinning right before his eyes and then approaches a prophet to consult me through him, he will get his answer from me, Yahweh. ⁸I shall set my face against that person; I shall make him an example and a byword; I shall rid my people of him, and you will know that I am Yahweh. ⁹And if the prophet is seduced into saying something, I, Yahweh, shall have seduced that prophet; I shall point my finger at him and rid my people Israel of him. ¹⁰Both will be punished for their guilt; the prophet's punishment will be the same as that of the person who consults him, ¹¹so that the House of Israel will never stray from me again or defile themselves again with these crimes, but be my people and I their God—declares the Lord Yahweh." '

Individual responsibility ᵃ

¹²The word of Yahweh was addressed to me: ¹³'Son of man, when a country sins against me by being unfaithful and I point my finger at it and destroy its supply of food, inflicting famine on it and denuding it of human and animal, ¹⁴even if the three men, Noah, Danel and Job,ᵇ were living in it, they would save no one but themselves by their uprightness—declares the Lord Yahweh. ¹⁵Were I to unleash wild beasts on that country to rob it of its children and reduce it to a desert which no one would dare to cross because of the animals, ¹⁶even if these three men were living there, as I live—declares the Lord Yahweh—they would not be able to save either son or daughter; they alone would be saved, and the country would become a desert. ¹⁷Were I to bring the sword down on that country and say, "Sword, cross the country!" so as to denude it of human and animal, ¹⁸even if these three men were living there, as I live—declares the Lord Yahweh—they would not be able to save either son or daughter; they alone would be saved. ¹⁹If I were to send the plague on that country and vent my fury on it by bloodshed, so as to denude it of human and animal, ²⁰even if Noah and Danel and Job were living there, as I live—declares the Lord Yahweh—they would be able to save neither son nor daughter, only themselves by their uprightness.

²¹'The Lord Yahweh says this, "Even if I send my four dreadful scourges on Jerusalem—sword, famine, wild beasts and plague—to denude it of human and animal, ²²even so, there will be a remnant left, a few men and women who come through; when they come to you and you see their conduct and actions, you will take comfort in spite of the disaster which I have brought on Jerusalem, in spite of all I have brought on her. ²³They will comfort you, when you see their conduct and actions, and so you will know that I have not done in vain all I have done to her—declares the Lord Yahweh." '

A parable of the vine

15 The word of Yahweh was addressed to me as follows:

14a cf. 18; 33:10–20, and Dt 24; Jr 31 on individual responsibility.

14b Three celebrated heroes of uprightness. Daniel is known from other Near Eastern ancient poetry.

2 Son of man, how is the wood of the vine better
than wood from the branch of a forest tree?
3 Is its wood used for making anything?
Are pegs on which to hang things made from it?
4 There it is, thrown on the fire for fuel.
The fire burns off both ends;
the middle is charred; can it be kept for anything now?
5 While it was intact, you could make nothing with it;
burned and charred, is it any more useful now?

6 So, the Lord Yahweh says this:

As the wood of the vine among the forest trees,
which I have thrown on the fire for fuel,
so shall I treat the inhabitants of Jerusalem.
7 I shall set my face against them.
They have escaped one fire, but fire will devour them yet.
And you will know that I am Yahweh,
when I set my face against them.
8 I shall reduce the country to a desert,
because of their infidelity—
declares the Lord Yahweh.

An allegorical history of Jerusalem[a]

16 The word of Yahweh was addressed to me as follows, 2 'Son of man, confront Jerusalem with her loathsome practices! 3 Say, "The Lord Yahweh says this: By origin and birth you belong to the land of Canaan. Your father was an Amorite and your mother a Hittite. 4 At birth, the very day you were born, there was no one to cut your navel-string, or wash you in water to clean you, or rub you with salt, or wrap you in swaddling clothes. 5 No one looked at you with pity enough to do any of these things out of sympathy for you. You were exposed in the open fields in your own dirt on the day you were born.

6 "I saw you kicking on the ground in your blood as I was passing, and I said to you as you lay in your blood: Live! 7 and I made you grow like the grass of the fields. You developed, you grew, you reached marriageable age. Your breasts became firm and your hair grew richly, but you were stark naked. 8 Then I saw you as I was passing. Your time had come, the time for love. I spread my cloak over you and covered your nakedness; I gave you my oath, I made a covenant with you—declares the Lord Yahweh—and you became mine. 9 I bathed you in water, I washed the blood off you, I anointed you with oil. 10 I gave you embroidered dresses, fine leather shoes, a linen headband and a cloak of silk. 11 I loaded you with jewels, gave you bracelets for your wrists and a necklace for your throat. 12 I gave you nose-ring and earrings; I put a beautiful diadem on your head. 13 You were loaded with gold and silver and dressed in linen and silk and brocade. Your food was the finest flour, honey and oil. You grew more and more beautiful; and you rose to be queen. 14 The fame of your beauty spread through the nations, since it was perfect, because I had clothed you with my own splendour—declares the Lord Yahweh.

15 "But you became infatuated with your own beauty and used your fame to play the whore, lavishing your debauchery on all comers. 16 You took some of your clothes to make for yourself high places bright with colours and there you played the whore. 17 You also took your jewellery, made with my gold and silver which I had given you, and made yourself male images to serve your whorings. 18 You took your embroidered clothes and used these to dress them up, and you offered them my oil and my incense. 19 And the bread I gave you, the finest flour, the oil and honey with which I fed you, you offered them as a pleasing smell.

"What is more—declares the Lord Yahweh— 20 you took the sons and daughters you had borne me and sacrificed them as food to

16a = 23.

the images. Was not your whoring enough in itself, ²¹for you to slaughter my children and hand them over to be burnt in their honour? ²²And in all your loathsome practices and your whorings you never called your early days to mind, when you were stark naked, kicking on the ground in your own blood.

²³"To crown your wickedness—disaster upon you, disaster! declares the Lord Yahweh— ²⁴you built yourself a mound and made yourself a high place in every open space. ²⁵At the entry to every alley you made yourself a high place, defiling your beauty and opening your legs to all comers in countless acts of fornication. ²⁶You have also fornicated with your big-membered neighbours, the Egyptians, provoking my anger with further acts of fornication. ²⁷So now I have raised my hand against you, I have cut down on your food, I have put you at the mercy of your enemies, the Philistine women, who blush at your lewd behaviour. ²⁸Still unsatisfied, you prostituted yourself to the Assyrians; you played the whore with them, but were not satisfied even then. ²⁹You committed further acts of fornication in the country of merchants, with the Chaldaeans, and these did not satisfy you either.

³⁰"How simple-minded you are!—declares the Lord Yahweh—for although you do all the things that a professional prostitute would, ³¹in building a mound and making yourself a high place in every street, you do not act like a proper prostitute because you disdain to take a fee. ³²An adulteress welcomes strangers instead of her husband. ³³All prostitutes accept presents, but you give presents to all your lovers, you bribe them to come from all over the place to fornicate with you! ³⁴In fornicating, you are the opposite of other women, since no one runs after you to fornicate with you; since you give the fee and do not get one, you are the very opposite!

³⁵"Very well, whore, hear the word of Yahweh! ³⁶The Lord Yahweh says this: For having squandered your money and let yourself be seen naked while whoring with your lovers and all the foul idols of your loathsome practices and for giving them your children's blood— ³⁷for all this, I shall assemble all the lovers to whom you have given pleasure, all the ones you liked and also all the ones you disliked; yes, I shall assemble them round you and strip you naked in front of them, and let them see you naked from head to foot. ³⁸I shall pass on you the sentence that adulteresses and murderesses receive; I shall hand you over to their jealous fury; ³⁹I shall hand you over to them; they will destroy your mound and pull down your high place; they will tear off your clothes, take away your jewels and leave you stark naked. ⁴⁰Then they will call an assembly of citizens to deal with you, who will stone you to death and hack you to pieces with their swords, ⁴¹and burn down your premises and execute justice on you, while many other women look on; and I shall put an end to your whoring: no more paid lovers for you! ⁴²Once my fury is exhausted with you, then my jealousy will leave you; I shall be calm and not angry any more. ⁴³Since you never called to mind your early days and have done nothing but provoke me, now I in my turn shall bring your conduct down on your own head—declares the Lord Yahweh!

"Have you not added this lewd behaviour to your other loathsome practices? ⁴⁴So now all dealers in proverbs will apply this one to you: Like mother, like daughter. ⁴⁵Yes; you are a true daughter of your mother, who hated her husband and her children; you are a true sister of your sisters, who hated their husbands and their children. Your mother was a Hittite and your father an Amorite. ⁴⁶Your elder sister is Samaria, who lives to the north of you with her daughters. Your younger sister is Sodom, who lives to the south of you with her daughters. ⁴⁷You never failed to imitate their behaviour and copy their loathsome practices, and soon your behaviour was more corrupt than theirs was. ⁴⁸As I live—declares the Lord Yahweh—your sister Sodom and her daughters never did what you and your daughters have done. ⁴⁹The crime of your sister Sodom was pride, gluttony, calm complacency; such were hers and her daughters' crimes. They never helped the poor and needy; ⁵⁰they were proud, and engaged in loathsome practices before me, and so I swept them away as you have seen. ⁵¹ And yet Samaria never committed half the crimes that you have.

"You have done more loathsome things than they have. By all your loathsome practices you have made your sisters seem innocent, ⁵²and now you bear the shame of which you have freed your sisters; since the sins which you have committed are more revolting than theirs, they are more upright than you are. So now, bear the disgrace and shame of having put your sisters in the right.

⁵³"I shall restore their fortunes, I shall restore Sodom and her daughters, I shall restore Samaria and her daughters, and then I shall restore your fortune with theirs, ⁵⁴so that you can bear your shame and disgrace for all you have done, and so console them. ⁵⁵When your sisters, Sodom and her daughters, are restored to what they were, and Samaria and her daughters are restored to what they were, then you too and your daughters will be restored to what you were. ⁵⁶Did you not gloat over your sister Sodom when you were so proud, ⁵⁷before you were stripped naked? Like her, you are now the laughing-stock of the women of Edom, of all the women round, of the women of Philistia, who pour out their contempt on you. ⁵⁸You have brought this on yourself, with your lewdness and your loathsome practices—declares the Lord Yahweh.

⁵⁹"For the Lord Yahweh says this: I shall treat you as you have deserved for making light of an oath and breaking a covenant, ⁶⁰but I shall remember my covenant with you when you were a girl and shall conclude a covenant with you that will last for ever. ⁶¹ And you for your part will remember your behaviour and feel ashamed of it when you receive your elder and younger sisters and I make them your daughters, although this is not included in my covenant with you. ⁶²I shall renew my covenant with you; and you will know that I am Yahweh, ⁶³and so remember and feel ashamed and in your confusion be reduced to silence, when I forgive you for everything you have done—declares the Lord Yahweh." '

The allegory of the eagle

17 The word of Yahweh was addressed to me as follows, ²'Son of man, put a riddle, propound a parable 'to the House of Israel. ³Say, "The Lord Yahweh says this:

A great eagle with great wings,
long-pinioned,
rich with many-coloured plumage,
came to the Lebanon.
⁴ He took the top of the cedar tree,
he plucked off the top branch,
he carried it off to the country of
        merchants
and set it down in a city of shopkeepers.
⁵ Next, he took one of the country's seeds
and put it in a fertile field;
by the side of a generous stream,
like a willow tree, he placed it.
⁶ It grew and became a fruitful vine
of modest size,
grew up towards the eagle,
its roots grew downwards.
So it became a vine,
branching out and sprouting new shoots.

⁷ But there was another great eagle
with great wings and thick plumage.
And now the vine twisted its roots towards
        him
and stretched its branches towards him,
for him to water it
away from the bed where it was planted.
⁸ It was in a fertile field,
by the side of a wide stream
that the vine had been planted,
to branch out and bear fruit
and become a noble vine."

⁹ Say, "The Lord Yahweh says this:
Will it succeed?
Will the eagle not tear out its roots

and strip off its fruit,
so that all the new leaves it puts out will
     wither,
and no great strength is needed nor many
     people
to pull it up by the roots?
¹⁰ Planted it may be—will it succeed?
Will it not shrivel up when the east wind
     blows?
It will wither in the bed where it was
     growing!" '

¹¹ The word of Yahweh was addressed to me as follows: ¹² 'Say to that tribe of rebels, "Do you not know what this means?" Say this, 'Look, the king of Babylon came to Jerusalem; he carried away the king and the princes, and took them to his home in Babylon. ¹³ He took a member of the royal family and made a treaty with him, forcing him to swear loyalty, having already deported the leading men of the country, ¹⁴ so that the kingdom would remain modest and without ambitions, and would keep and honour his treaty. ¹⁵ But the prince rebelled against him and sent envoys to Egypt to procure himself horses and a large number of troops. Will he succeed? Will a man who has done this go unpunished? Can he break a treaty and go unpunished? ¹⁶ As I live, I swear it—declares the Lord Yahweh—in Babylon, in the country of the king who put him on the throne, whose oath he has disregarded and whose treaty he has broken, there he will die. ¹⁷ Despite the pharaoh's great army and hordes of men, he will not be able to save him by fighting, however many earthworks are raised, however many trenches dug to the loss of many lives. ¹⁸ He has disregarded the oath by breaking the treaty to which he had pledged himself and, having done all this, will not go unpunished. ¹⁹ "So, the Lord Yahweh says this: As I live, I swear it: my oath which he has disregarded, my treaty which he has broken, I shall make them both recoil on his own head. ²⁰ I shall throw my net over him, he will be caught in my mesh; I shall take him to Babylon[a] and punish him there for being unfaithful to me. ²¹ All the pick of all his troops will fall by the sword, and the survivors be scattered to all the winds. And you will know that I, Yahweh, have spoken.

²² "The Lord Yahweh says this:

From the top of the tall cedar tree,
from the highest branch I shall take a
     shoot
and plant it myself on a high and lofty
     mountain.
²³ I shall plant it on the highest mountain in
     Israel.
It will put out branches and bear fruit
and grow into a noble cedar tree.
Every kind of bird will live beneath it,
every kind of winged creature will rest in
     the shade of its branches.
²⁴ And all the trees of the countryside will
     know that I, Yahweh, am
     the one
who lays the tall tree low and raises the
     low tree high,
who makes the green tree wither and
     makes the withered bear fruit.
I, Yahweh, have spoken, and I will
     do it." '

Individual responsibility

18 The word of Yahweh was addressed to me as follows, ² 'Why do you keep repeating this proverb in the land of Israel:

The parents have eaten unripe grapes;
and the children's teeth are set on
     edge?[a]

³ 'As I live—declares the Lord Yahweh—you will have no further cause to repeat this proverb in Israel. ⁴ Look, all life belongs to me; the father's life and the son's life, both alike belong to me. The one who has sinned is the one to die.

17a = 12:13.   18a ∥ Jr 31:29, cf. Ezk 14:12.

5'But if a man is upright, his actions law-abiding and upright, 6and he does not eat on the mountains or raise his eyes to the foul idols of the House of Israel, does not defile his neighbour's wife or touch a woman during her periods, 7oppresses no one, returns the pledge on a debt, does not rob, gives his own food to the hungry, his clothes to those who lack clothing, 8does not lend for profit, does not charge interest, abstains from evil, gives honest judgement between one person and another, 9keeps my laws and sincerely respects my judgements—someone like this is truly upright and will live—declares the Lord Yahweh.

10'But if he has a son prone to violence and bloodshed, who commits one of these misdeeds— 11even though the father never has— a son who dares to eat on the mountains, who defiles his neighbour's wife, 12who oppresses the poor and needy, robs, fails to return pledges, raises his eyes to foul idols, engages in loathsome practices, 13lends for profit, or charges interest, such a person will by no means live; having committed all these appalling crimes he will die, and his blood be on his own head.

14'But if he in turn has a son who, in spite of seeing all the sins that his father has committed, does not imitate him, 15does not eat on the mountains or raise his eyes to the foul idols of the House of Israel, does not defile his neighbour's wife, 16oppresses no one, takes no pledges, does not rob, gives his own food to the hungry, his clothes to those who lack clothing, 17abstains from evil, does not lend for profit or charge interest, respects my judgements and keeps my laws, he will not die for his father's sins: he will most certainly live. 18But his father, because he was violent, robbed others and never did good among his people, will most certainly die in his guilt.

19'Now, you say, "Why doesn't the son bear his father's guilt?" If the son has been law-abiding and upright, has kept all my laws and followed them, most certainly he will live. 20The one who has sinned is the one who must die; a son is not to bear his father's guilt, nor a father his son's guilt. The upright will be credited with his uprightness, and the wicked with his wickedness.

21'If the wicked, however, renounces all the sins he has committed, respects my laws and is law-abiding and upright, he will most certainly live; he will not die. 22None of the crimes he committed will be remembered against him from then on; he will most certainly live*b* because of his upright actions. 23Would I take pleasure in the death of the wicked—declares the Lord Yahweh—and not prefer to see him renounce his wickedness and live?

24'But if the upright abandons uprightness and does wrong by copying all the loathsome practices of the wicked, is he to live? All his upright actions will be forgotten from then on; for the infidelity of which he is guilty and the sin which he has committed, he will most certainly die.

25'Now, you say, "What the Lord does is unjust." Now listen, House of Israel: is what I do unjust? Is it not what you do that is unjust? 26When the upright abandons uprightness and does wrong and dies, he dies because of the wrong which he himself has done. 27Similarly, when the wicked abandons wickedness to become law-abiding and upright, he saves his own life. 28Having chosen to renounce all his previous crimes, he will most certainly live: he will not die. 29And yet the House of Israel says, "What the Lord does is unjust." Is what I do unjust, House of Israel? Is it not what you do that is unjust? 30So in future, House of Israel, I shall judge each of you by what that person does—declares the Lord Yahweh.*c* Repent, renounce all your crimes, avoid all occasions for guilt. 31Shake off all the crimes you have committed, and make yourselves a new heart and a new spirit! Why die, House of Israel? 32I take no pleasure in the death of anyone—declares the Lord Yahweh—so repent and live!'

18b = 33:16.   *18c* = 33:20.

86 READ EZEKIEL 18:21–32.

If the wicked, however, renounces all the sins he has committed, . . . he will most certainly live.—EZEKIEL 18:21

THE GRACE OF MENTAL PRAYER

Many saints and good men have written about the blessings possessed by one who practices prayer— I mean mental prayer. Glory be to God for this! If it were not so, I should not have assurance enough (though I am not very humble) to dare to speak of it. I can say what I know by experience—namely, that no one who has begun this practice, however many sins he may commit, should ever forsake it. For it is the means by which we may amend our lives again, and without it amendment will be very much harder. So let him not be tempted by the devil, as I was, to give it up for reasons of humility. But let him believe that the words cannot fail of Him Who says that, if we truly repent and determine not to offend Him, He will resume His former friendship with us. He will also grant us the favours which He granted aforetime, and sometimes many more, if our repentance merits it. And anyone who has not begun to pray, I beg, for love of the Lord, not to miss so great a blessing. There is no place here for fear, but only desire. For, even if a person fails to make progress, or to strive after perfection, so that he may merit the consolations and favours given to the perfect by God, yet he will gradually gain a knowledge of the road to Heaven. . . . Mental prayer, in my view, is nothing but friendly intercourse, and frequent solitary converse, with Him Who we know loves us.

ST. TERESA OF AVILA, 1515–1582

YOU WILL FIND THE NEXT READING AT EZEKIEL 36.

A lament for the queen-mother and princes of Israel

19 ¹Now, raise a lament for the princes of Israel. ²Say:

What was your mother?
A lioness among lions;
lying among the cubs
she nursed her whelps.
³ She reared one of her whelps:
he grew into a young lion;
he learnt to tear his prey;
he became a man-eater.
⁴ The nations came to hear of him;
he was caught in their pit;
they dragged him away with hooks
to Egypt.ᵃ
⁵ Her expectation thwarted,
and seeing her hope dashed,
she took another of her whelps
and made a young lion of him.
⁶ He prowled among the lions,
he grew into a young lion,
he learnt to tear his prey;
he became a man-eater.
⁷ He tore down their palaces,
he destroyed their cities;
the land and all its inhabitants were
          appalled
by the sound of his roars.

19a King Jehoahaz, the whelp of Israel, was deposed and taken to Egypt.

8 The nations marched out against him
from the surrounding provinces;
they spread their net over him;
he was caught in their pit.
9 They shackled him with hooks,
they took him to the king of Babylon
and threw him into a fortress,
so that his voice could never again be
heard
on the mountains of Israel.

10 Your mother was like a vine
planted beside the water,
fruitful and leafy,
because the water flowed so full.
11 She had stout stems
which became kingly sceptres;
she grew higher and higher,
up into the clouds;
she was admired for her height
and the number of her branches.
12 But she was furiously uprooted
and thrown on the ground;
the east wind dried up her fruit,
she was broken to pieces;
her stout stem dried up,
the fire devoured it.
13 Now she has been transplanted to the
desert,
to a dry and thirsty land.
14 Fire burst out of her stem
devouring her branches and fruit.
No more stout stem for her,
no more kingly sceptre.'

This is a lament; it was used as such.

An account of Israel's infidelities

20 In the seventh year, on the tenth day of
the fifth month, some of the elders of Israel came to consult Yahweh and were sitting
with me, 2 when the word of Yahweh was addressed to me as follows, 3 'Son of man, speak
to the elders of Israel. Say, "The Lord Yahweh
says this: Have you come to consult me? As I
live, I will not be consulted by you—declares
the Lord Yahweh."

4 'Are you ready to judge them? Are you
ready to judge them, son of man? Confront
them with the loathsome practices of their ancestors. 5 Say, "The Lord Yahweh says this: On
the day when I chose Israel, when I pledged
my word to the House of Jacob, I made myself
known to them in Egypt; I pledged my word
to them and said: I am Yahweh your God.
6 That day I pledged them my word that I
would bring them out of Egypt to a country
which I had reconnoitred for them, a country
flowing with milk and honey, and the loveliest
of them all. 7 And I said to them: Each of you
must reject the horrors which attract you; do
not pollute yourselves with the foul idols of
Egypt; I am Yahweh your God. 8 But they rebelled against me and would not listen to me.
Not one of them rejected the horrors which attracted them; they did not give up the foul
idols of Egypt. I then resolved to vent my fury
on them, to sate my anger on them in Egypt.
9 But respect for my own name kept me from
letting it be profaned in the eyes of the nations
among whom they were living, and before
whom I had made myself known to them and
promised to bring them out of Egypt. 10 So I
brought them out of Egypt and led them into
the desert. 11 I gave them my laws and taught
them my judgements, in whose observance
people find life. 12 And I also gave them my
Sabbaths as a sign between me and them, so
that they might know that I, Yahweh, am the
one who sanctifies them. 13 The House of Israel, however, rebelled against me in the
desert; they refused to keep my laws, they
scorned my judgements, in whose observance
people find life, and they grossly profaned my
Sabbaths. I then resolved to vent my fury on
them in the desert and destroy them. 14 But respect for my own name kept me from letting it
be profaned in the eyes of the nations, before
whom I had brought them out. 15 Even so, I
pledged them my word in the desert that I
would not lead them to the country which I
had given them, a country flowing with milk
and honey, and the loveliest of them all,
16 since they had scorned my judgements, had

refused to keep my laws and had profaned my Sabbaths, their hearts being attached to foul idols. ¹⁷In spite of this, I took pity on them; I refrained from destroying them and did not make an end of them in the desert.

¹⁸"I said to their children in the desert: Do not follow the laws of your ancestors, do not practise their judgements, do not defile yourselves with their foul idols. ¹⁹I am Yahweh your God. Keep my laws, respect my judgements and practise them. ²⁰Keep my Sabbaths holy; let them be a sign between me and you, so that people may know that I am Yahweh your God. ²¹Their children, however, rebelled against me; they refused to keep my laws, they did not respect or practise my judgements, which must be practised by all who want to live; they profaned my Sabbaths. I then resolved to vent my fury on them, to sate my anger on them in the desert. ²²But I restrained my hand; respect for my own name kept me from letting it be profaned in the eyes of the nations, before whom I had brought them out. ²³Once again, however, I pledged them my word that I would scatter them throughout the nations and disperse them in foreign countries, ²⁴because they had not followed my judgements but had rejected my laws and profaned my Sabbaths, their eyes being fastened on the foul idols of their ancestors. ²⁵And for this reason I gave them laws that were not good and judgements by which they could never live; ²⁶and I polluted them with their own offerings, making them sacrifice every first-born son in order to fill them with revulsion, so that they would know that I am Yahweh."

²⁷'For this reason, son of man, speak to the House of Israel. Say to them, "The Lord Yahweh says this: Here is another way by which your ancestors outraged me by their infidelity. ²⁸Once I had brought them into the country which I had pledged my word to give them, they then saw all sorts of high hills, all kinds of leafy trees, and there they performed their sacrifices and made offerings that provoked my anger; there they set out their pleasing smell and poured their libations. ²⁹I then said to them: What is this high place where you go? And they gave, and still give it, the name of Bamah."

³⁰'So, say to the House of Israel, "The Lord Yahweh says this: If you are polluting yourselves as your ancestors did by fornicating with their horrors— ³¹for by offering your gifts and by burning your children as sacrifices, you have been polluting yourselves with all your foul idols to this very day—shall I let myself be consulted by you, House of Israel? As I live—declares Lord Yahweh—I shall not let myself be consulted by you. ³²And what you sometimes imagine will never be so, when you say: We shall be like the peoples, the tribes of foreign lands, worshipping wood and stone. ³³As I live I swear it—declares the Lord Yahweh—I am the one who will reign over you, with a strong hand and outstretched arm, once my fury is sated. ³⁴With a strong hand and outstretched arm, once my fury is sated, I shall bring you back from the peoples and gather you again from the countries throughout which you have been scattered. ³⁵I shall lead you into the desert of the nations and there I shall judge you face to face. ³⁶As I judged your ancestors in the desert of Egypt, so will I judge you—declares the Lord Yahweh. ³⁷I shall make you pass under the crook, bring you to respect the covenant ³⁸and rid you of the rebels who have revolted against me; I shall bring them out of the country where they are staying, but they will not enter the country of Israel, and you will know that I am Yahweh. ³⁹House of Israel, Lord Yahweh says this: Go on, all of you, worship your foul idols, but later we shall see if you don't listen to me! Then you will stop profaning my holy name with your offerings and your foul idols. ⁴⁰For on my holy mountain, on the high mountain of Israel—declares the Lord Yahweh—is where the whole House of Israel, everyone in the country, will worship me. There I shall accept and there expect your presents, your choicest offering and all your consecrated gifts. ⁴¹I shall welcome you like a pleasing smell when I bring you back from the peoples and gather

you from the countries throughout which you have been scattered, and through you I shall display my holiness for all the nations to see; ⁴²and you will know that I am Yahweh, when I bring you back to the soil of Israel, to the country which I pledged my word to give to your ancestors. ⁴³There you will remember your past behaviour and all the actions by which you have defiled yourselves, and you will loathe yourselves for all the wrongs which you have committed. ⁴⁴And you will know that I am Yahweh, when I treat you as respect for my own name requires, and not as your wicked behaviour and corrupt actions deserve, House of Israel—declares the Lord Yahweh." '

The sword ᵃ of Yahweh

21 The word of Yahweh was addressed to me as follows, ²'Son of man, turn to the right; utter your word towards the south, prophesy against the forest land of the Negeb. ³Say to the forest of Negeb, "Hear the word of Yahweh! The Lord Yahweh says this: Listen; I am about to kindle a fire in you which will burn up every green tree in you as well as every dry one; it will be an unquenchable blaze and every face will be scorched by it from the Negeb to the north. ⁴All humanity will see that it was I, Yahweh, who kindled it, and it will not be extinguished." ' ⁵I said, 'Lord Yahweh, they say of me, "He does nothing but speak in riddles!" '

⁶Then the word of Yahweh was addressed to me as follows, ⁷'Son of man, turn towards Jerusalem, utter your word towards the sanctuary and prophesy against the land of Israel. ⁸Say to the land of Israel, "Yahweh says this: Now I am against you; I am about to unsheathe my sword and rid you of the upright and the wicked alike. ⁹Since I am going to rid you of upright and wicked alike, I shall unsheathe my sword against everyone alive, from the Negeb to the north, ¹⁰so that everyone alive will know that I, Yahweh, am the one who has unsheathed my sword; it will not go back again."

¹¹'Son of man, groan as though your heart were breaking. Utter your bitter groans where they can see you. ¹²And if they say, "Why these groans?" reply, "Because of the news which is about to come, all hearts will sink, all hands grow weak, all spirits grow faint and all knees turn to water. It is coming now, it is here!—declares Lord Yahweh." '

¹³The word of Yahweh was addressed to me as follows, ¹⁴'Son of man, prophesy. Say, "The Lord says this. Say:

The sword, the sword
has been sharpened and polished,
¹⁵ sharpened for slaughter,
polished to flash like lightning . . .
¹⁶ He has had it polished to be wielded,
this sword sharpened and polished
to put in the slaughterer's hand!
¹⁷ Shout and wail, son of man,
for it will come on my people,
on all the chief men of Israel doomed like
my people to the sword!
So beat your breast, ¹⁸for this will be an
ordeal . . .
declares the Lord Yahweh.
¹⁹ So prophesy, son of man, and clap your
hands!
Let the sword pass three times,
that sword for victims,
that sword for a great victim,
threatening them from every side!
²⁰ To make hearts sink and make sure many
fall,
I have posted the slaughtering sword at
every gate
to flash like lightning, polished for
slaughter.
²¹ Be sharp, on the right, be ready on
the left,
whichever way your blade is needed!
²² I too shall clap my hands
and sate my fury!
I, Yahweh, have spoken." '

21a Four separate sayings (1–12; 13–22; 23–32; 33–37) linked only by this word.

The king of Babylon at the crossroads

23 The word of Yahweh was addressed to me as follows, 24 'Son of man, mark out two roads for the sword of the king of Babylon to come along, making both of them begin from the same country. Then put up a signpost, put it where the road leaves for the city, 25 trace the route which the sword should take for Rabbah-of-the-Ammonites, and for Judah, to the fortress of Jerusalem. 26 For the king of Babylon has halted at the fork where these two roads diverge, to take the omens. He has shaken the arrows, questioned the household gods, inspected the liver. 27 The lot marked 'Jerusalem' is in his right hand: there to set up battering-rams, give the word for slaughter, raise the war cry, level battering-rams against the gates, cast up earthworks, build entrenchments. 28 The inhabitants will believe that these omens are idle, for they have received sworn guarantees, but he will bring their guilt to mind and capture them. 29 And so the Lord Yahweh says this, "Since you have brought your guilt to mind by parading your misdeeds and flaunting your sins in everything you do: because you have drawn attention to yourselves, you will be captured. 30 As for you, impious and wicked prince of Israel, whose doom is approaching to put an end to your crimes, 31 the Lord Yahweh says this: They will take away your diadem and remove your crown. Everything will be changed; the low will be raised and the high brought low! 32 Ruin, ruin, I shall bring such ruin as never was before, until the rightful ruler comes, on whom I shall bestow it."

The punishment of Ammon

33 'Son of man, prophesy and say, "The Lord Yahweh says this: In reply to the Ammonites and their jeers, say: The sword, the sword is drawn for slaughter, polished to devour, to flash like lightning— 34 while you have empty visions and consult lying omens—to cut the throats of the wicked, whose doom is ap-proaching to put an end to their crimes. 35 Put it back in the scabbard. The place where you were created, the land of your origin, will be where I judge you. 36 I shall vent my fury on you, breathe the fire of my rage against you and hand you over to barbarous men whose trade is destruction. 37 You will be fuel for the fire, your blood will flow through the country, you will leave no memory behind you; for I, Yahweh, have spoken!"'

The crimes of Jerusalem

22 The word of Yahweh was addressed to me as follows, 2 'Son of man, are you ready to judge? Are you ready to judge the blood-stained city? Confront her with all her loathsome practices! 3 Say, "The Lord Yahweh says this: City shedding blood inside yourself to hasten your doom, making foul idols on your soil to defile yourself, 4 you have incurred guilt by the blood you have shed, you have defiled yourself with the foul idols you have made, you have shortened your days, you have come to the end of your years. This is why I have made you an object of scorn to the nations and a laughing-stock to every country. 5 From far and near they will taunt you with your infamous disorders.

6 "Look! In you the princes of Israel, one and all, have furthered their own interests at the cost of bloodshed; 7 in you people have despised their fathers and mothers; in you they have ill-treated the settler; in you they have oppressed the widow and orphan. 8 You have treated my sanctuary with contempt, you have profaned my Sabbaths. 9 In you informers incite to bloodshed; in you people eat on the mountains and act licentiously; 10 in you they have sexual intercourse with their fathers; in you they force themselves on women in their periods; 11 in you one man engages in loathsome practices with his neighbour's wife, another lewdly defiles his daughter-in-law, another violates his sister, his own father's daughter. 12 In you people take bribes for shedding blood; you lend for profit and charge interest, you profit from your fellow by extor-

tion and have forgotten about me—declares the Lord Yahweh.

13 "Now I shall clap my hands at your acts of banditry and the blood that flows in you. 14 Will your heart be able to resist, will your hands be steady, the day when I call you to account? I, Yahweh, have spoken and shall act. 15 I shall scatter you among the nations and disperse you in foreign countries, and so put an end to the filthiness now inside you; 16 through your own fault, you will be profaned in the eyes of the nations, and you will know that I am Yahweh!"

17 The word of Yahweh was addressed to me as follows, 18 'Son of man, for me, the House of Israel has become dross: copper, tin, iron, lead, all mixed up together in the melting-pot; they are dross. 19 And so, Lord Yahweh says this, "Since you have all become dross, right! I shall collect you inside Jerusalem. 20 As silver, copper, iron, lead and tin are collected in the melting-pot, and the fire is blown underneath to melt them down, so I shall collect you in my furious anger and have you melted down; 21 I shall collect you and blow up the fire of my rage for you and have you melted down inside the city. 22 As silver is melted in the melting-pot, so you will be melted down inside the city, and you will know that I, Yahweh, have vented my fury on you."'

23 The word of Yahweh was addressed to me as follows, 24 'Son of man, say to her, "You are a land that has not received rain or shower on the day of anger. 25 In you, the princes are like a roaring lion tearing its prey. They have eaten the people, seized wealth and jewels and widowed many inside her. 26 Her priests have violated my law and desecrated my sanctuary; they have made no distinction between sacred and profane, they have not taught people the difference between clean and unclean; they have turned their eyes away from my Sabbaths and I have been dishonoured by them. 27 In her the leaders are wolves tearing their prey, shedding blood and killing people to steal their possessions. 28 Her prophets have plas-

tered these things over with their empty visions and lying prophecies, saying: Yahweh says this, although Yahweh has not spoken. 29 The people of the country have taken to extortion and banditry; they have oppressed the poor and needy and ill-treated the settler in a way that is unjustifiable. 30 I have been looking for someone among them to build a barricade and oppose me in the breach, to defend the country and prevent me from destroying it; but I have found no one. 31 Hence I have vented my fury on them; I have put an end to them in the fire of my rage. I have made their conduct recoil on their own heads—declares the Lord Yahweh."'

An allegorical history of Jerusalem and Samaria [a]

23 The word of Yahweh was addressed to me as follows, 2 'Son of man, there were once two women, daughters of the same mother. 3 They played the whore in Egypt; they played the whore when they were still girls. There their nipples were handled, there their virgin breasts were first fondled. 4 Their names were: Oholah the elder, Oholibah her sister. They belonged to me and bore sons and daughters. As regards their names, Samaria is Oholah, Jerusalem Oholibah. 5 Now Oholah played the whore, although she belonged to me; she lusted after her lovers, her neighbours the Assyrians, 6 dressed in purple, governors and magistrates, all of them young and desirable, and skilful horsemen. 7 She played the whore with all of them, the pick of Assyria, and defiled herself with all the foul idols of all those with whom she was in love, 8 nor did she give up the whoring begun in Egypt, where men had slept with her from her girlhood, fondling her virgin breasts, debauching her over and over again.

9 'That is why I have handed her over to her lovers, to the Assyrians with whom she was in love. 10 They stripped her naked, seized her sons and daughters and put her to the sword.

23a = 16.

She became notorious among women for the justice done on her.

¹¹'Her sister Oholibah saw all this, but she was even more depraved, and her whorings were worse than her sister's. ¹²She fell in love with her neighbours the Assyrians, governors and magistrates, dressed in sumptuous clothes, skilful horsemen, all young and desirable. ¹³Then I saw that she had defiled herself, that both sisters were equally bad. ¹⁴She began whoring worse than ever; no sooner had she seen wall-carvings of men, pictures of Chaldaeans coloured vermilion, ¹⁵men with sashes round their waists and elaborate turbans on their heads, all so lordly of bearing, depicting the Babylonians, natives of Chaldaea, ¹⁶than she fell in love with them at first sight and sent messengers to them in Chaldaea. ¹⁷The Babylonians came to her, shared her love-bed and defiled her with their whoring. Once defiled by them, she withdrew her affection from them. ¹⁸Thus she flaunted her whoring, exposing her body, until I withdrew my affection from her as I had withdrawn it from her sister. ¹⁹But she began whoring worse than ever, remembering her girlhood, when she had played the whore in Egypt, ²⁰when she had been in love with their profligates, big-membered as donkeys, ejaculating as violently as stallions.

²¹'You were hankering for the debauchery of your girlhood, when they used to handle your nipples in Egypt and fondle your young breasts. ²²And so, Oholibah, Lord Yahweh says this, "I shall set all your lovers against you, from whom you have withdrawn your affection, and bring them to assault you from all directions: ²³the Babylonians and all the Chaldaeans, the men of Pekod and Shoa and Koa, and all the Assyrians with them, young and desirable, all governors and magistrates, all famous lords and skilful horsemen. ²⁴From the north, they will advance on you with chariots and wagons and an international army and beset you with shield, buckler and helmet on all sides. I shall charge them to pass sentence on you and they will pass sentence on you as

they think fit. ²⁵I shall direct my jealousy against you; they will treat you with fury; they will cut off your nose and ears, and what is left of your family will fall by the sword; they will seize your sons and daughters, and what is left will be burnt. ²⁶They will strip off your garments and rob you of your jewels. ²⁷I shall put an end to your debauchery and to the whorings you began in Egypt; you will not look to the Egyptians any more, you will never think of them again. ²⁸For the Lord Yahweh says this: Now, I shall hand you over to those you hate, to those for whom you no longer feel affection. ²⁹They will treat you with hatred, they will rob you of the entire fruit of your labours and leave you stark naked. And thus your shameful whorings will be exposed, your debauchery and your whorings. ³⁰This will happen to you because you have played the whore with the nations and have defiled yourself with their foul idols. ³¹Since you have copied your sister's behaviour, I shall put her cup in your hand." ³²The Lord Yahweh says this:

You will drink your sister's cup,
a cup both deep and wide,
leading to laughter and mockery,
so ample the draught it holds.
³³You will be filled with drunkenness and
       sorrow.
Cup of affliction and devastation,
the cup of your sister Samaria,
³⁴you will drink it, you will drain it;
then you will break it in pieces
and lacerate your own breasts.

For I have spoken—declared the Lord Yahweh.

³⁵"And so, the Lord Yahweh says this: Since you have forgotten me and have turned your back on me, you too will have to bear the weight of your debauchery and whorings."' ³⁶And Yahweh said to me, 'Son of man, are you ready to judge Oholah and Oholibah and charge them with their loathsome practices? ³⁷They have been adulteresses, their hands are

dripping with blood, they have committed adultery with their foul idols. As for the children they had borne me, they have offered them as burnt sacrifices to feed them. ³⁸ And here is something else they have done to me: they have defiled my sanctuary today and have profaned my Sabbaths. ³⁹ The same day as sacrificing their children to their idols, they have been to my sanctuary and profaned it. Yes, this is what they have done in my own house.

⁴⁰ 'Worse still, they summoned men from far away, invited by messenger, and they came. For them you bathed, you painted your eyes, put on your jewels ⁴¹ and sat on a sumptuous bed, by which a table was laid out. On this you had put my incense and my oil. ⁴² The noise of the carefree company resounded, made by the crowd of men brought in from the desert; they put bracelets on the women's arms and magnificent crowns on their heads. ⁴³ I thought, "That woman, worn out with adultery! Are they going to fornicate with her too?" ⁴⁴ Yet they visit her like any common prostitute, just as they visited those profligate women Oholah and Oholibah. ⁴⁵ All the same, there are upright men who will judge them as adulteresses and murderesses are judged, since they are adulteresses and their hands are dripping with blood."

⁴⁶ 'The Lord Yahweh says this, "Summon an assembly to deal with them, and hand them over to terror and pillage; ⁴⁷ let the assembly stone them and dispatch them with their swords; let their sons and daughters be slaughtered and their houses set on fire. ⁴⁸ This is how I shall purge the country of debauchery, so that all women will be taught the lesson never to ape your debauchery again. ⁴⁹ Your debauchery will recoil on yourselves, and you will bear the weight of the sins committed with your foul idols and you will know that I am the Lord Yahweh." '

Announcement of the siege of Jerusalem

24 In the ninth year, on the tenth day of the tenth month, the word of Yahweh was addressed to me as follows, ² 'Son of man,

write down today's date, yes, today's, for this very day the king of Babylon began his attack on Jerusalem. ³ So pronounce a parable for this tribe of rebels. Say, "The Lord Yahweh says this:

Put the pot on the fire;
 put it on; pour the water in!
⁴ Now put the cuts of meat all in
    together,
 all the best cuts, leg and shoulder.
 Fill it with the best bones.
⁵ Take the best of the flock,
 then heap wood underneath;
 boil it thoroughly
 until even the bones are cooked.

⁶ "For the Lord Yahweh says this:

Disaster is in store for the bloody city,
 for that rusty cooking pot
 whose rust will not come off!
 Empty it, bit by bit,
 not bothering to draw lots;
⁷ for she is still full of bloodshed,
 she has put blood on the naked rock;
 she did not pour it on the ground
 so as to cover it with dust.
⁸ To make anger rise, to exact vengeance,
 I have put her blood on the naked rock,
 so that it should not be covered:

⁹ "So, the Lord Yahweh says this:

Disaster is in store for the bloody city!
 I too plan to build a great fire.
¹⁰ Heap on the wood, light it,
 cook the meat, prepare the seasoning
 let the bones burn!
¹¹ Put the empty pot on the coals
 to make it hot,
 until the bronze glows,
 the filth inside melts
 and the rust is burnt away!

¹² "But all that rust would not come off in the fire. ¹³ Your filth is infamous. Since I have

tried to purge you and you would not let your-self be purged of your filth, so now you will never be purged of your filth until I have sated my anger on you. ¹⁴I, Yahweh, have spoken; this will happen; I shall act and not relent; I shall show no pity, no compassion. You will be judged as your conduct and actions deserve—declares the Lord Yahweh." '

Ordeals for the prophet

¹⁵The word of Yahweh was addressed to me as follows, ¹⁶'Son of man, at a blow I am about to deprive you of the delight of your eyes. But you are not to lament, not to weep, not to let your tears run down. ¹⁷Groan in silence, do not go into mourning for the dead, knot your turban round your head, put your sandals on your feet, do not cover your beard, do not eat the usual food.' ¹⁸I told this to the people in the morning, and my wife died in the evening, and the next morning I did as I had been or-dered. ¹⁹The people then said to me, 'Will you not explain what meaning these actions have for us?' ²⁰I replied, 'The word of Yahweh has been addressed to me as follows, ²¹"Say to the House of Israel, the Lord Yahweh says this: I am about to profane my sanctuary, the pride of your strength, the delight of your eyes, the joy of your hearts. Your sons and daughters whom you have left behind will fall by the sword. ²²Then you will do as I have done: you will not cover your beards or eat the usual food; ²³you will keep your turbans on your heads and your sandals on your feet; you will not lament or weep but will waste away for your crimes, groaning among yourselves. ²⁴Thus Ezekiel is a sign for you. You will do exactly what he has done. And when this happens, you will know that I am Lord Yah-weh!"

²⁵'And, son of man, the day that I deprive them of their strength, their crowning joy, the delight of their eyes, the joy of their hearts, their sons and daughters, ²⁶that day a survivor will bring you the news. ²⁷That day your mouth will be opened to speak to the survivor; you will speak and no longer be dumb; you

will be a sign for them, and they will know that I am Yahweh.'

PROPHECIES: *Against the Ammonites*

25 The word of Yahweh was addressed to me as follows, ²'Son of man, turn to-wards the Ammonites and prophesy against them. ³Say to the Ammonites, "Hear the word of the Lord Yahweh. The Lord Yahweh says this:

"Since you gloated over my sanctuary when it was profaned, and over the land of Israel when it was ravaged, and over the House of Judah when it went into exile, ⁴I shall let the sons of the East take possession of you; they will pitch their camps inside you, they will make their home in you. They will be the ones to eat your produce and drink your milk. ⁵I shall turn Rabbah into a camel yard and the towns of Ammon into sheepfolds. And so you will know that I am Yahweh.

⁶"The Lord Yahweh says this: Since you have clapped your hands and danced for joy, full of malicious delight at Israel's fate, ⁷my hand will be against you for this; I shall hand you over to be looted by the peoples, obliterate you as a nation and wipe you out as a country. I shall reduce you to nothing, and you will know that I am Yahweh.

Against Moab

⁸"The Lord Yahweh says this:

"Since Moab and Seir have said: Look at the House of Judah; it is no different from any other nation; ⁹very well, I shall expose Moab's heights; its cities will no longer be cities throughout the land—the jewels of the coun-try, Beth-Jeshimoth, Baal-Meon and Kiria-thaim. ¹⁰I shall let the sons of the East and the Ammonites take possession of them, so that they will no longer be remembered by the na-tions. ¹¹I shall bring Moab to justice, and they will know that I am Yahweh.

Against Edom

¹²"The Lord Yahweh says this:

"Since Edom has taken revenge on the

House of Judah and committed great crimes in doing so, ¹³ very well, the Lord Yahweh says this: My hand will be against Edom and denude it of human and animal. I shall lay it waste, from Teman as far as Dedan they will be put to the sword. ¹⁴I shall take vengeance on Edom by means of my people Israel. They will treat Edom as my anger and fury dictate, and they will know this is my vengeance—declares the Lord Yahweh.

Against the Philistines

¹⁵"The Lord Yahweh says this,

"Since the Philistines have acted in revenge and, motivated by malice, have taken revenge, doing their best to destroy because of their long-standing hatred, ¹⁶very well, the Lord Yahweh says this: My hand will be against the Philistines; I shall exterminate the Cherethites and destroy the rest of the coastal peoples. ¹⁷I shall perform frightful acts of vengeance and inflict furious punishments on them; and they will know that I am Yahweh, when I exact my vengeance on them."'

Against Tyre

²⁶In the eleventh year, on the first of the month, the word of Yahweh was addressed to me as follows, ²'Son of man, since Tyre has said of Jerusalem:

"Aha! She is shattered, the Gateway to the Nations;
  she now gives way to me.
  Her riches are ruined!"
³ Very well, the Lord Yahweh says this,
"Now, Tyre, I am against you,
⁴ I shall raise many nations against you
  as the sea raises its waves.
  They will destroy the walls of Tyre,
  they will demolish her towers;
  I shall sweep the dust of her away
  and reduce her to a naked rock.
⁵ She will be a drying-ground out to sea for
  fishing-nets.

For I have spoken—declares Lord Yahweh.
  She will be the prey of the nations.
⁶ As for her daughters on the mainland,
  these will be put to the sword,
  and they will know that I am Yahweh."

⁷'For the Lord Yahweh says this, "From the north, I shall bring Nebuchadnezzar, king of Babylon, king of kings, down on Tyre with horses, chariots, cavalry and an enormous army.

⁸ He will put your daughters
  on the mainland to the sword.
  He will build siege-works against you,
  cast up a siege-ramp against you,
  raise a screen against you;
⁹ he will pound your walls with his
      battering-rams,
  and demolish your towers with his
      siege-engines.
¹⁰ His horses are so many that their dust will
      hide you.
  The noise of his horsemen and his
      chariot-wheels
  will make your walls tremble as he enters
      your gates
  as though storming into a city through the
      breach.
¹¹ With his horses' hoofs he will trample
      through all your streets;
  he will put your people to the sword,
  and throw your massive pillars to the
      ground.
¹² Your wealth will be seized, your
      merchandise looted,
  your walls rased, your luxurious houses
      shattered,
  your stones, your timbers, your very dust,
      thrown into the sea.
¹³ I shall put an end to the sound of your
      songs;
  the sound of your harps will not be heard
      again.
¹⁴ I shall reduce you to a naked rock,

and make you into a drying-ground for
    fishing-nets,
never to be rebuilt;
for I, Yahweh, have spoken
—declares the Lord Yahweh.”

Lament over Tyre

15 'The Lord Yahweh says this to Tyre, “Will
not the islands quake at the sound of your fall,
while the wounded groan and the slaughter
takes place inside you? 16 All the princes of the
sea will leave their thrones, lay aside their
cloaks, take off their embroidered robes.
Dressed in terror they will sit on the ground
trembling incessantly, stunned at your fate.

17 “They will raise the lament for you as follows:

You are destroyed then, vanished from
    the seas,
famous city, former sea-power,
who with her citizens,
used to spread terror
all over the mainland!
18 Now the islands are trembling
on the day of your fall;
the islands of the sea are terrified by
    your end.

19 “For the Lord Yahweh says this:
“When I make you a ruined city like other
deserted cities, when I raise the deep against
you and the ocean covers you, 20 when I fling
you down with those who go down into the
abyss, with the people of long ago, and put you
deep in the underworld, in the ruins of long
ago with those who sink into oblivion, so that
you can never come back or be restored to the
land of the living, 21 I will make you an object
of terror; you will not exist. People will look
for you but never find you again—declares the
Lord Yahweh!”.'

Second lament over the fall of Tyre

27 The word of Yahweh was addressed to
me as follows, 2 'Son of man, raise
the lament for Tyre. 3 Say to Tyre, “City enthroned at the gateway of the sea, agent between the peoples and the many islands, Lord
Yahweh says this:

Tyre, you used to say: I am a ship
perfect in beauty.
4 Your frontiers were far out to sea;
those who built you
made you perfect in beauty.
5 Cypress from Senir they used
for all your planking.
They took a cedar from Lebanon
to make a mast above you.
6 From oaks of Bashan
they made your oars.
They built you a deck of cedar inlaid with
    ivory
from the Kittim isles.
7 Embroidered linen from Egypt was used
    for your sail
and for your flag.
Purple and scarlet from the Elishah islands
formed your deck-tent.
8 The people of Sidon and Arvad
were your oarsmen.
The sages of Tyre were aboard,
serving as sailors.
9 The elders and craftsmen of Gebal were
    there
to caulk your seams.

“Every sea-going ship and crew frequented
you to guarantee your trade. 10 Men from Persia, Lud and Put served as warriors in your
army; hanging up shield and helmet in you,
they displayed your splendour. 11 The sons of
Arvad with their army manned your walls all
round, while the Gammadians manned your
towers; hanging their shields all round your
walls, they completed your beauty. 12 Tarshish
traded with you because of your abundant resources and exchanged your merchandise for
silver, iron, tin and lead. 13 Javan, Tubal and
Meshech traded with you. For your merchandise they traded slaves and bronze artefacts. 14 The people of Beth-Togarmah traded
your horses, chargers, mules. 15 The people of

Dedan traded with you; many islands were your customers and paid you in ivory tusks and ebony. ¹⁶Edom traded with you for the sake of your many manufactured goods, exchanging garnets, purple, embroideries, fine linen, coral and rubies for your goods. ¹⁷Judah and the land of Israel also traded with you, bringing corn from Minnith, *pannag,* honey, oil and balm. ¹⁸Damascus traded with you, for quantities of your manufactured goods and other goods of all kinds, furnishing you with wine from Helbon and wool from Zahar. ¹⁹Dan and Javan, from Uzal onwards, supplied you with wrought iron, cassia and reeds in exchange for your goods. ²⁰Dedan traded with you in saddle-cloths. ²¹Arabia and all the sheikhs of Kedar were your customers; they paid in lambs, rams and he-goats. ²²The merchants of Sheba and Raamah traded with you; they supplied you with the finest spices, precious stones and gold for your merchandise. ²³Haran, Canneh and Eden, the merchants of Sheba, Asshur and Chilmad traded with you. ²⁴They traded rich clothes, embroidered and purple cloaks, multi-coloured materials and strong plaited cords for your markets.

²⁵ Ships of Tarshish sailed on your business;
   you were full and heavily loaded
      far out to sea.
²⁶ Out to the open sea
   your oarsmen rowed you.
   The east wind has wrecked you
      far out to sea.
²⁷ Your riches, your goods, your cargo,
   your seamen, your sailors,
   your caulkers, your commercial agents,
   all the warriors you carry,
   and all the passengers who are aboard
   will founder far out to sea
   on the day of your shipwreck.

²⁸ When they hear the cries of your sailors
   the coasts will tremble.
²⁹ Then the oarsmen will all desert
   their ships.
   The sailors and seafaring people
will stay ashore.
³⁰ They will raise their voices for you
   and weep bitterly.
   They will throw dust on their heads
   and roll in ashes;
³¹ they will shave their heads for you
   and put sackcloth round their waists.
   With heartfelt bitterness they will weep
      for you,
   bitterly wail.
³² Wailing, they will raise the lament for you,
   they will lament over you:

   Who is like Tyre,
   far out to sea?
³³ When you unloaded your goods
   to satisfy so many peoples,
   you enriched the kings of the earth
   with your excess of wealth and goods.
³⁴ Now you have been wrecked by the waves,
   by the depths of the sea.
   Your cargo and all your passengers
   have foundered with you.
³⁵ All those who live in the islands
   will be stunned at your fate.
   Their kings will quake with horror,
   with downcast expressions.
³⁶ The merchants of the nations
   will whistle at your fate.
   You will be an object of terror,
   gone for ever." '

Against the king of Tyre

28 The word of Yahweh was addressed to me as follows, ²'Son of man, say to the ruler of Tyre, "The Lord Yahweh says this:

   Because your heart has grown proud,
   you thought: I am a god;
   I am divinely enthroned
   far out to sea.
   Though you are human, not divine,
   you have allowed yourself to think like
      God.ᵃ

28a Some features of the story of Adam's fall in Eden recur here.

³ So, you are wiser than Danel;
    no sage as wise as you!
⁴ By your wisdom and your intelligence
    you have made yourself a fortune,
    you have put gold and silver
    into your treasuries.
⁵ Such is your skill in trading,
    your fortune has continued to increase,
    and your fortune has made your heart
        grow prouder.

⁶ "And so, the Lord Yahweh says this:

Since you have allowed yourself to think
    like God,
⁷ very well, I am going to bring foreigners
    against you,
    the most barbarous of the nations.
They will draw sword against your fine
    wisdom,
    they will desecrate your splendour,
⁸ they will throw you down into the grave
    and you will die a violent death
    far out to sea.
⁹ Will you still think: I am a god,
    when your slaughterers confront you?
But you will be human, not divine,
    in the clutches of the ones who strike you
        down!
¹⁰ You will die like the uncircumcised
    at the hand of foreigners.

"For I have spoken—declares the Lord Yahweh." '

The fall of the king of Tyre

¹¹ The word of Yahweh was addressed to me
as follows, ¹²'Son of man, raise a lament for
the king of Tyre. Say to him, "The Lord Yahweh says this:

You used to be a model of perfection,
    full of wisdom,
    perfect in beauty;
¹³ you were in Eden, in the garden of God.
All kinds of gem formed your mantle:
    sard, topaz, diamond, chrysolite, onyx,

jasper, sapphire, garnet, emerald,
    and your ear-pendants and spangles were
        made of gold;
    all was ready on the day you were
        created.
¹⁴ I made you a living creature with
        outstretched wings, as guardian,
    you were on the holy mountain of God;
    you walked amid red-hot coals.
¹⁵ Your behaviour was exemplary from the
        day you were created
    until guilt first appeared in you,
¹⁶ because your busy trading
    has filled you with violence and sin.
I have thrown you down from the
        mountain of God
and destroyed you, guardian winged
        creature, amid the coals.
¹⁷ Your heart has grown proud because of
        your beauty,
    your wisdom has been corrupted by your
        splendour.
I have thrown you to the ground;
    I have made you a spectacle for kings.
¹⁸ By the immense number of your crimes,
    by the dishonesty of your trading,
    you have defiled your sanctuary.
So I have brought fire out of you to
        devour you;
I have reduced you to ashes on the
        ground
    before the eyes of all who saw you.
¹⁹ Of the nations, all who know you
    are stunned at your fate.
You are an object of terror;
    gone for ever." '

Against Sidon

²⁰ The word of Yahweh was addressed to me
as follows, ²¹'Son of man, turn towards Sidon
and prophesy against her. ²²Say, "The Lord
Yahweh says this:

I am against you, Sidon,
    I will show my glory in you!
They will know I am Yahweh,
    once I execute sentence on her

and display my holiness in her.
23 For I shall send her the plague,
and there will be blood in her streets,
and in her the dead will fall
under the sword raised against her from
all sides,
and they will know that I am Yahweh.

Israel delivered from the nations

24 "No more, for the House of Israel, shall any of the hostile nations surrounding them be a thorn that wounds or a briar that tears; and they will know that I am Yahweh.

25 "The Lord Yahweh says this: When I gather the House of Israel back from the peoples where they are dispersed, I shall display my glory in them for the nations to see. They will live on the soil which I gave to my servant Jacob. 26 They will live there in confidence, build houses, plant vineyards. They will live in safety, once I inflict punishments on all the hostile nations surrounding them, and they will know that I am Yahweh their God." '

Against Egypt

29 In the tenth year, on the twelfth day of the tenth month, the word of Yahweh was addressed to me as follows, 2 'Son of man, turn towards Pharaoh king of Egypt and prophesy against him and against the whole of Egypt. 3 Speak and say, "The Lord Yahweh says this:

Look, I am against you, Pharaoh king of
Egypt—
the great crocodile wallowing in his
Niles
who thought: My Nile is mine, I made it.
4 I shall put hooks through your jaws,
make your Nile fish stick to your scales,
and pull you out of your Niles
with all your Nile fish sticking to your
scales.
5 I shall drop you in the desert, with all your
Nile fish.
You will fall in the wilds
and not be taken up or buried.

I shall give you as food
to the wild animals and the birds of
heaven,
6 and all the inhabitants of Egypt will know
that I am Yahweh,
for they have given no more support than
a reed to the House of Israel.
7 Wherever they grasped you, you broke in
their hands
and cut their hands all over.
Whenever they leaned on you, you broke,
making all their limbs give way.

8 "So, the Lord Yahweh says this: I shall send the sword against you to denude you of human and animal. 9 Egypt will become a desolate waste, and they will know that I am Yahweh. Because he thought: The Nile is mine, I made it, 10 very well, I am against you and your Niles. I shall make Egypt a waste and a desolation, from Migdol to Syene and beyond to the frontiers of Ethiopia. 11 No human foot will pass through it, no animal foot will pass through it. For forty years it will remain uninhabited. 12 I shall make Egypt the most desolate of countries; for forty years its cities will be the most desolate of wasted cities. And I shall scatter the Egyptians among the nations and disperse them among the countries. 13 The Lord Yahweh, however, says this: After forty years have passed, I shall gather the Egyptians back from the nations where they were dispersed. 14 I shall bring the Egyptian captives back and re-install them in the land of Pathros, in the country of their origin. There they will constitute a modest kingdom. 15 Egypt will be the most modest of kingdoms and no longer dominate other nations; for I shall reduce it, so that it will not rule other nations ever again. 16 It will no longer be anything for the House of Israel to trust in, but will be a reminder of the guilt which lay in turning to it for help. And they will know that I am Lord Yahweh." '

17 In the twenty-seventh year, on the first day of the first month, the word of Yahweh was addressed to me as follows:

¹⁸'Son of man, Nebuchadnezzar king of Babylon has taken his army in a great expedition against Tyre. Their heads have all gone bald, their shoulders are all chafed, but even so he has derived no profit, either for himself or for his army, from the expedition mounted against Tyre. ¹⁹Since this is so, the Lord Yahweh says this, "Look, I shall hand Egypt over to Nebuchadnezzar king of Babylon. He will carry off its riches, loot it, put it to the sack; that will be the wages for his army. ²⁰As wages for the trouble he has taken, I am giving him Egypt instead (for they have been working for me)—declares the Lord Yahweh.

²¹"That day, I shall raise up a new stock for the House of Israel and allow you to open your mouth among them. And they will know that I am Yahweh."'

Against Egypt: the day of Yahweh

30 The word of Yahweh was addressed to me as follows, ²'Son of man, prophesy and say, "The Lord Yahweh says this: Howl: Disaster day! ³For the day is near, the day of Yahweh is near; it will be a day dark with cloud, a time of doom for the nations.

⁴"The sword will come on Egypt, and anguish on the country of Cush when the slaughtered fall in Egypt, when her riches are carried away and her foundations are destroyed. ⁵Cush, Put and Lud, all Arabia, Cub and the children of the country of the covenant will fall by the sword with them.

⁶"Yahweh says this:

"The supports of Egypt will fall; the pride of her strength will crumble; they will fall by the sword from Migdol to Syene—declares the Lord Yahweh.

⁷"They will be the most desolate of desolate countries, and its cities the most ruined of cities. ⁸And they will know that I am Yahweh when I set fire to Egypt and all its supports are shattered.

⁹"That day, I shall send messengers by ship to terrify the carefree Cushites, and anguish will overtake them on the day of Egypt—it is coming now! ¹⁰The Lord Yahweh says this: I

shall destroy the huge population of Egypt at the hand of Nebuchadnezzar king of Babylon. ¹¹He and his people, the most barbarous of nations, will be brought to ravage the country. They will draw the sword against Egypt and fill the country with corpses. ¹²I shall dry up the courses of the Nile and sell the country to the wicked. I shall lay the whole country waste and everything in it, at the hand of foreigners. I, Yahweh, have spoken.

¹³"The Lord Yahweh says this: I shall destroy the foul idols and take the false gods away from Noph. Egypt will be left without a ruler. I shall spread fear through Egypt. ¹⁴I shall lay Pathros waste, set Zoan on fire, inflict my punishments on No. ¹⁵I shall vent my fury on Sin, the bastion of Egypt; I shall wipe out the throngs of No. ¹⁶I shall set fire to Egypt; Sin will be seized with convulsions; a breach will be opened at No and the waters flood out. ¹⁷The young men of On and Pi-Beseth will fall by the sword and the cities themselves go into captivity. ¹⁸At Tahpanhes day will turn to darkness when I shatter the sceptres of Egypt there, when the pride of her strength ceases. A cloud will cover Egypt itself, and its daughters will go into captivity. ¹⁹Such will be the punishments I inflict on Egypt. And they will know that I am Yahweh."'

²⁰In the eleventh year, on the seventh day of the first month, the word of Yahweh was addressed to me as follows, ²¹'Son of man, I have broken the arm of Pharaoh king of Egypt; you can see that no one has dressed his wound by applying remedies to it, by bandaging it and by dressing it, to make it strong enough to wield the sword. ²²This being so, the Lord Yahweh says this, "Look, I am against Pharaoh king of Egypt; I shall break his arms, the sound one and the broken one, and make the sword drop from his hand. ²³I shall scatter Egypt among the nations and disperse it among the countries. ²⁴I shall strengthen the arms of the king of Babylon and put my sword in his hand. I shall break Pharaoh's arms and, confronted with his enemy, he will groan like

a dying man. ²⁵I shall strengthen the arms of the king of Babylon, and the arms of Pharaoh will fall. And they will know that I am Yahweh, when I put my sword into the hands of the king of Babylon and he wields it against Egypt. ²⁶I shall scatter Egypt among the nations and disperse it among the countries; and they will know that I am Yahweh." '

The cedar tree

31 In the eleventh year, on the first day of the third month, the word of Yahweh was addressed to me as follows, ²'Son of man, say to Pharaoh king of Egypt and his throng of subjects:

"What can compare with you for
      greatness?
³ I know: a cedar tree in the Lebanon
with noble branches, dense foliage, lofty
      height.
Its top pierces the clouds.
⁴ The waters have made it grow, the deep
      has made it tall,
pouring its rivers round the place where it
      is planted,
sending rivulets to all the wild trees.
⁵ This is why its height was greater than
      that of other wild trees,
its branches increased in number, its
      boughs stretched wide,
because of the plentiful waters making it
      grow.
⁶ All the birds of heaven nested in its
      branches;
under its boughs all wild animals dropped
      their young;
in its shade sat many, many people.
⁷ It was beautiful in its size, in the span of its
      boughs;
for its roots were in plentiful waters.
⁸ There was no cedar like it in the garden of
      God,
no cypress had branches such as these,
no plane tree could match its boughs,
no tree in the garden of God could rival its
      beauty.

⁹ I had made it so lovely with its many
      branches
that it was the envy of every tree in Eden,
      in the garden of God.

¹⁰"Very well, the Lord Yahweh says this:
"Since it has raised itself to its full height, has lifted its top into the clouds, and has grown arrogant about its height, ¹¹I have handed it over to the prince of the nations, for him to treat as its wickedness deserves; I have rejected it. ¹²Foreigners, the most barbarous of nations, have cut it down and deserted it. On the mountains, in all the valleys, lie its branches; its broken boughs are in every ravine throughout the country; everybody in the country has fled its shade and deserted it. ¹³On its wreckage perch all the birds of heaven; all the wild animals have advanced on its branches.

¹⁴"So in future let no tree rear its height beside the waters, none push its top into the clouds, no watered tree stretch its height towards them. For all of them are doomed to death, to the depths of the underworld, with the common run of humanity, with those who sink into oblivion.

¹⁵"The Lord Yahweh says this: The day it went down to Sheol, I imposed mourning, I closed the deep over it. I stopped its rivers and the plentiful waters dried up; I made Lebanon dark because of it, and all the wild trees wilted because of it. ¹⁶With the noise when it fell I made the nations quake, as I hurled it down to Sheol, with those who sink into oblivion. In the depths of the underworld all the trees of Eden took comfort, the pick of the loveliest trees of the Lebanon, all irrigated by the waters. ¹⁷And its offspring among the nations, once living in its shade, went down to Sheol with it, to those who have been slaughtered by the sword.

¹⁸"Which of the trees of Eden compares with you for glory and greatness? Yet you have been hurled down with the trees of Eden, to the depths of the underworld, among the uncircumcised, and there you lie with those

who have been slaughtered by the sword. So much for Pharaoh and all his throng—declares the Lord Yahweh." '

The crocodile

32 In the twelfth year, on the first day of the twelfth month, the word of Yahweh was addressed to me as follows, 2 'Son of man, raise a lament for Pharaoh king of Egypt. Say to him:

"Young lion of nations, you are destroyed!
Once you were like a crocodile in the
    lagoons;
emerging from your rivers,
you churned up the water with your
    trampling
and fouled their streams.

3 "The Lord Yahweh says this:

I shall throw my net over you in a great
    concourse of nations;
and they will trawl you up in my net.
Then I shall leave you high and dry,
4 I shall throw you out into the wilds
and make all the birds of heaven settle on
    you,
and glut all the beasts of the earth with you.
5 I shall strew your flesh on your mountains
and fill the valleys with your corruption;
6 I shall water the country with what flows
    from you,
with your blood, on the mountainsides,
and you will fill the ravines.
7 When I extinguish you I shall cover the
    skies
and darken the stars.
I shall cover the sun with clouds
and the moon will not give its light.
8 I shall dim every luminary in heaven
    because of you
and cover your country in darkness
    —declares the Lord Yahweh.

9 "I shall grieve the heart of many peoples when I bring about your destruction among the nations, in countries unknown to you. 10 I shall stun many peoples with shock at your fate; their kings will tremble with horror at your fate, when I brandish my sword before their eyes. The day you fall, each will tremble in terror for his life. 11 For the Lord Yahweh says this: The sword of the king of Babylon will overtake you. 12 I shall make your throngs of subjects fall at the swords of my warriors. They are the most barbarous of nations. They will annihilate the pride of Egypt, and all its throngs will be destroyed. 13 I shall also destroy all its cattle beside the plentiful waters. No human foot will churn them, no animal foot will churn them up again; 14 then I shall let their waters settle and make their rivers glide like oil—declares the Lord Yahweh.

15 "When I reduce Egypt to a ruin and the country is stripped of its contents, when I strike all those who live there, they will know that I am Yahweh.

16 "Such is the lament which the daughters of the nations will raise. They will raise it over Egypt and all its throng. This is the lament they will raise—declares the Lord Yahweh." '

Pharaoh goes down to Sheol

17 In the twelfth year, on the fifteenth day of the first month, the word of Yahweh was addressed to me as follows, 18 'Son of man, lament over the throng of Egypt, for down she must go with the daughters of majestic nations to the depths of the underworld with those who sink into oblivion.

19 'Whom do you surpass in beauty? Down with you, make your bed with the uncircumcised, 20 with those who have been slaughtered by the sword. (The sword has been given, it has been drawn.) She and all her throngs have fallen. 21 From the depths of Sheol, the mightiest heroes, her allies, will say to her, "They have come down, they have lain down, uncircumcised, slaughtered by the sword."

22 'Assyria is there and all her hordes, with their graves all round her; all of them slaughtered, fallen by the sword; 23 their graves have been made in the deepest part of the abyss, and

her hordes, with their graves all round her; all of them slaughtered, killed by the sword, who once spread terror through the world of the living.

24 'Elam is there and all her throng round her grave, all of them slaughtered, fallen by the sword; they have gone down uncircumcised to the depths of the underworld, who once spread terror throughout the world of the living. They have borne their shame with those who sink into oblivion. 25 Among the slaughtered, they have put a bed for her, among her throng with their tombs round her, all of them uncircumcised, slaughtered by the sword for having spread terror throughout the world of the living. They have borne their shame with those who sink into oblivion. They have been put among the slaughtered.

26 'Meshech, Tubal are there and all her throng, with their graves round her, all of them uncircumcised, slaughtered by the sword for having spread terror through the world of the living. 27 They do not lie with the heroes who fell long ago, those who went down to Sheol fully armed, who had their swords laid under their heads and their shields put under their bones, since the heroes inspired the world of the living with terror. 28 But you will be broken with the uncircumcised and lie with those slaughtered by the sword.

29 'Edom is there, her kings and all her princes who, despite their valour, have been laid with those slaughtered by the sword. They lie with the uncircumcised, with those who sink into oblivion.

30 'All the princes of the north and all the Sidonians are there, who have gone down with the slaughtered, because of the terror which their power inspired. Ashamed, uncircumcised, they lie among those slaughtered by the sword and bear their shame with those who sink into oblivion.

31 'Pharaoh will see them and take comfort at the sight of all this throng slaughtered by the sword—Pharaoh and all his throng—declares the Lord Yahweh. 32 For having spread terror through the world of the living, he will be laid with the uncircumcised, with those slaughtered by the sword, Pharaoh and all his throng—declares the Lord Yahweh.'

The prophet as watchman

33 The word of Yahweh was addressed to me as follows, 2 'Son of man, speak to the people of your country. Say to them, "When I send the sword against the people of that country, take one of their number and post him as a watchman; 3 if he sees the sword coming against the country, he must sound his horn to warn the people. 4 If someone hears the sound of the horn but pays no attention and the sword overtakes him and destroys him, he will have been responsible for his own death. 5 He has heard the sound of the horn and paid no attention; his death will be his own responsibility. But the life of someone who pays attention will be secure.

6 "If, however, the watchman has seen the sword coming but has not blown his horn, and so the people are not alerted and the sword overtakes them and destroys a single one of them, that person will indeed die for his guilt, but I shall hold the watchman responsible for his death."

7 'Son of man I have appointed you as watchman for the House of Israel. When you hear a word from my mouth, warn them from me. 8 If I say to someone wicked, "Evil-doer, you are to die," and you do not speak to warn the wicked person to renounce such ways, the wicked person will die for this guilt, but I shall hold you responsible for the death. 9 If, however, you do warn someone wicked to renounce such ways and repent, and that person does not repent, then the culprit will die for this guilt, but you yourself will have saved your life.

Conversion and perversity

10 'Son of man, say to the House of Israel, "You are continually saying: Our crimes and sins weigh heavily on us; we are wasting away because of them. How are we to go on living?"

11 Say to them, "As I live—declares the Lord Yahweh—I do not take pleasure in the death of the wicked but in the conversion of the wicked who changes his ways and saves his life. Repent, turn back from your evil ways. Why die, House of Israel?"

12 'Son of man, say to the members of your nation, "The uprightness of an upright person will not save him once he takes to wrong-doing; the wickedness of a wicked person will not ruin him once he renounces his wickedness. No one upright will be able to live on the strength of uprightness, having once taken to sinning. 13 If I say to someone upright: You are to live, and then, trusting in this uprightness, he does wrong, none of the uprightness will be remembered; because of the wrong-doing, he will die. 14 If, however, I say to someone wicked: You are to die, and he turns back from sin and does what is lawful and upright, 15 if he returns pledges, restores what he has stolen, keeps the laws that give life and no longer does wrong, he will live and will not die. 16 None of his previous sins will be remembered against him; having done what is lawful and upright, he will live.*

17 "But the members of your nation say: What the Lord does is unjust. But it is what you do that is unjust. 18 When an upright person gives up being upright and does wrong, he dies for it. 19 And when a wicked person gives up being wicked and does what is lawful and upright, because of this he lives. 20 But you say: What the Lord does is unjust! I shall judge each of you by what you do, House of Israel." ' *b*

The taking of the city

21 In the twelfth year of our captivity, on the fifth day of the tenth month, a fugitive arrived from Jerusalem and said to me, 'The city has been taken.' 22 Now the hand of the Lord had been on me the evening before the fugitive arrived; he had opened my mouth before the fugitive came to me the next morning; my mouth had been opened and I was dumb no longer.

The ravaging of the country

23 The word of Yahweh was then addressed to me as follows, 24 'Son of man, the people living in those ruins on the soil of Israel say this, "Abraham was alone when he was given possession of this country. But we are many; the country has been given us as our heritage."

25 'Very well, tell them, "The Lord Yahweh says this: You eat blood, you raise your eyes to your foul idols, you shed blood; are you to own the country? 26 You rely on your swords, you engage in loathsome practices, each of you defiles his neighbour's wife; are you to own the country?" 27 Tell them this, "The Lord Yahweh says this: As I live, I swear it, those in the ruins will fall to the sword, those in the countryside I shall give to the wild animals for them to eat, and those among the crags and in caves will die of plague. 28 I shall make the country a desolate waste, and the pride of its strength will be at an end. The mountains of Israel will be deserted and no one will pass that way again. 29 Then they will know that I am Yahweh, when I make the country a desolate waste because of all the filthy things they have done."

The results of the preaching

30 'Son of man, the members of your nation are talking about you on the ramparts and in doorways. They keep saying to one another, "Come and hear the word that has come from Yahweh." 31 They throng towards you; my people sit down in front of you and listen to your words, but they do not act on them. What they act on is the lie in their mouths, and their hearts are set on dishonest gain. 32 As far as they are concerned, you are like a love song pleasantly sung to a good musical accompaniment. They listen to your words, but no one acts on them. 33 When the thing takes place—and it is beginning now—they will know that there has been a prophet among them.'

33a = 18:22.   *33b* = 18:29–30.

The shepherds of Israel

34 The word of Yahweh was addressed to me as follows, ²'Son of man, prophesy against the shepherds of Israel; prophesy and say to them, "Shepherds, the Lord Yahweh says this: Disaster is in store for the shepherds of Israel who feed themselves! Are not shepherds meant to feed a flock? ³Yet you have fed on milk, you have dressed yourselves in wool, you have sacrificed the fattest sheep, but failed to feed the flock. ⁴You have failed to make weak sheep strong, or to care for the sick ones, or bandage the injured ones. You have failed to bring back strays or look for the lost. On the contrary, you have ruled them cruelly and harshly. ⁵For lack of a shepherd they have been scattered, to become the prey of all the wild animals; they have been scattered. ⁶My flock is astray on every mountain and on every high hill; my flock has been scattered all over the world; no one bothers about them and no one looks for them.

⁷"Very well, shepherds, hear the word of Yahweh: ⁸As I live, I swear it—declares the Lord Yahweh—since my flock has been pillaged and for lack of a shepherd is now the prey of every wild animal, since my shepherds have ceased to bother about my flock, since my shepherds feed themselves rather than my flock, ⁹very well, shepherds, hear the word of Yahweh: ¹⁰The Lord Yahweh says this: Look, I am against the shepherds. I shall take my flock out of their charge and henceforth not allow them to feed my flock. And the shepherds will stop feeding themselves, because I shall rescue my sheep from their mouths to stop them from being food for them.

¹¹"For the Lord Yahweh says this: Look, I myself shall take care of my flock and look after it. ¹²As a shepherd looks after his flock when he is with his scattered sheep, so shall I look after my sheep. I shall rescue them from wherever they have been scattered on the day of clouds and darkness. ¹³I shall bring them back from the peoples where they are; I shall gather them back from the countries and bring them back to their own land. I shall pasture them on the mountains of Israel, in the ravines and in all the inhabited parts of the country. ¹⁴I shall feed them in good pasturage; the highest mountains of Israel will be their grazing ground. There they will rest in good grazing grounds; they will browse in rich pastures on the mountains of Israel. ¹⁵I myself shall pasture my sheep, I myself shall give them rest—declares the Lord Yahweh. ¹⁶I shall look for the lost one, bring back the stray, bandage the injured and make the sick strong. I shall watch over the fat and healthy. I shall be a true shepherd to them.

¹⁷"As for you, my sheep, the Lord Yahweh says this: I shall judge between sheep and sheep, between rams and he-goats. ¹⁸Not content to drink the clearest of the water, you foul the rest with your feet. ¹⁹And my sheep must graze on what your feet have trampled and drink what your feet have fouled. ²⁰Very well, the Lord Yahweh says this: I myself shall judge between the fat sheep and the thin sheep. ²¹Since you have jostled with flank and shoulder and butted all the ailing sheep with your horns, until you have scattered them outside, ²²I shall come and save my sheep and stop them from being victimised. I shall judge between sheep and sheep.

²³"I shall raise up one shepherd, my servant David, and put him in charge of them to pasture them; he will pasture them and be their shepherd. ²⁴I, Yahweh, shall be their God, and my servant David will be ruler among them. I, Yahweh, have spoken. ²⁵I shall make a covenant of peace with them; I shall rid the country of wild animals. They will be able to live secure in the desert and go to sleep in the woods. ²⁶I shall settle them round my hill; I shall send rain at the proper time; it will be a rain of blessings. ²⁷The trees of the countryside will yield their fruit and the soil will yield its produce; they will be secure on their soil. And they will know that I am Yahweh when I break the bars of their yoke and rescue them from the clutches of their slave-masters. ²⁸No more will they be a prey to the nations, no

more will the wild animals of the country devour them. They will live secure, with no one to frighten them. ²⁹I shall make splendid vegetation grow for them; no more will they suffer from famine in the country; no more will they have to bear the insults of other nations. ³⁰So they will know that I, their God, am with them and that they, the House of Israel, are my people—declares the Lord Yahweh. ³¹And you, my sheep, are the flock of my human pasture, and I am your God—declares the Lord Yahweh." '

Against the mountains of Edom

35 The word of Yahweh was addressed to me as follows, ²'Son of man, turn towards Mount Seir and prophesy against it. ³Say to it, "The Lord Yahweh says this: Look, I am against you, Mount Seir; I shall stretch out my hand against you; I shall make you a desolate waste; ⁴I shall lay your towns in ruins. You will become a waste and you will know that I am Yahweh. ⁵Since, following a long-standing hatred, you betrayed the Israelites to the sword on the day of their distress, on the day when an end came for their guilt, ⁶very well, as I live—declares the Lord Yahweh—I destine you to bloodshed, and bloodshed will pursue you. I swear it; you have incurred guilt by shedding blood, and bloodshed will pursue you. ⁷I shall make Mount Seir a desolate waste and denude it of anyone travelling to and fro. ⁸I shall fill its mountains with its slaughtered; on your hills, in your valleys and in all your ravines, those slaughtered by the sword will fall. ⁹I shall make you a perpetual waste, your towns will never be inhabited again, and you will know that I am Yahweh.

¹⁰"Since you said: The two nations and the two countries will be mine; we are going to take possession of it, although Yahweh was there, ¹¹very well, as I live—declares the Lord Yahweh—I shall act with the same anger and jealousy as you acted in your hatred for them. I shall make myself known for their sake, when I punish you, ¹²and you will know that I, Yahweh, have heard all the blasphemies

which you have uttered against the mountains of Israel, such as: They have been laid waste, they have been given to us for us to devour. ¹³Great was your insolence towards me, many your speeches against me; I have heard! ¹⁴Lord Yahweh says this: To the joy of the whole world, I shall make you a waste. ¹⁵Since you rejoiced because the heritage of the House of Israel had been laid waste, I shall do the same to you, Mount Seir; and you will become a waste, and so will the whole of Edom; and they will know that I am Yahweh.' "

Prophecy about the mountains of Israel

36 'Son of man, prophesy to the mountains of Israel. Say, "Mountains of Israel, hear the word of Yahweh. ²The Lord Yahweh says this: Since the enemy has gloated over you by saying: Aha! These eternal heights are owned by us now, ³very well, prophesy! Say: The Lord Yahweh says this: Since you have been ravaged and seized on from all sides, and have become the property of the rest of the nations, and become the subject of people's talk and gossip, ⁴very well, mountains of Israel, hear the word of the Lord Yahweh! The Lord Yahweh says this to the mountains and hills, to the ravines and valleys, to the devastated ruins and abandoned cities which have been put to the sack and have become a laughing-stock to the rest of the nations all round; ⁵very well, the Lord Yahweh says this: I swear it in the heat of my jealousy; I am speaking to the rest of the nations and to the whole of Edom who so exultantly and contemptuously took possession of my country to despoil its pastureland."

⁶'Because of this, prophesy about the land of Israel. Say to the mountains and hills, to the ravines and valleys, "The Lord Yahweh says this: I am speaking in my jealousy and rage; because you are enduring the insults of the nations, ⁷very well, the Lord Yahweh says this: I raise my hand and I swear that the nations all around you shall have their own insults to bear.

⁸"Mountains of Israel, you will grow branches and bear fruit for my people Israel,

who will soon return. ⁹Yes, I am coming to you, I shall turn to you; you will be tilled and sown. ¹⁰I shall increase your population, the whole House of Israel, yes, all. The cities will be inhabited and the ruins rebuilt. ¹¹I shall increase your population, both human and animal; they will be fertile and reproduce. I shall repopulate you as you were before; I shall make you more prosperous than you were before, and you will know that I am Yahweh. ¹²Thanks to me, men will tread your soil again, my people Israel; they will own you and you will be their heritage, and never again will you rob them of their children.

¹³"The Lord Yahweh says this: Since people have said of you: You are a man-eater, you have robbed your nation of its children, ¹⁴very well, you will eat no more men, never rob your nation of its children again—declares the Lord Yahweh. ¹⁵I shall never again let you hear the insults of the nations, you will never again have to bear the taunts of the peoples, you will never again rob the nation of its children—declares the Lord Yahweh."'

¹⁶The word of Yahweh was addressed to me as follows, ¹⁷'Son of man, the members of the House of Israel used to live in their own territory, but they defiled it by their conduct and actions; to me their conduct was as unclean as a woman's menstruation. ¹⁸I then vented my fury on them because of the blood they shed in the country and the foul idols with which they defiled it. ¹⁹I scattered them among the nations and they were dispersed throughout the countries. I sentenced them as their conduct and actions deserved. ²⁰They have profaned my holy name among the nations where they have gone, so that people say of them, "These are the people of Yahweh; they have been exiled from his land." ²¹But I have been concerned about my holy name, which the House of Israel has profaned among the nations where they have gone. ²²And so, say to the House of Israel, "The Lord Yahweh says this: I am acting not for your sake, House of Israel, but for the sake of my holy name, which you have profaned among the nations where you have gone. ²³I am going to display the holiness of my great name, which has been profaned among the nations, which you have profaned among them. And the nations will know that I am Yahweh—declares the Lord Yahweh—when in you I display my holiness before their eyes. ²⁴For I shall take you from among the nations and gather you back from all the countries, and bring you home to your own country. ²⁵I shall pour clean water over you and you will be cleansed; I shall cleanse you of all your filth and of all your foul idols. ²⁶I shall give you a new heart, and put a new spirit in you; I shall remove the heart of stone from your bodies and give you a heart of flesh instead. ²⁷I shall put my spirit in you, and make you keep my laws, and respect and practise my judgements. ²⁸You will live in the country which I gave your ancestors. You will be my people and I shall be your God. ²⁹I shall save you from everything that defiles you, I shall summon the wheat and make it plentiful and impose no more famines on you. ³⁰I shall increase the yield of tree and field, so that you will never again bear the ignominy of famine among the nations. ³¹Then you will remember your evil conduct and actions. You will loathe yourselves for your guilt and your loathsome practices. ³²I assure you that I am not doing this for your sake—declares the Lord Yahweh. Be ashamed and blush for your conduct, House of Israel.

³³"The Lord Yahweh says this: On the day I cleanse you from all your guilt, I shall repopulate the cities and cause the ruins to be rebuilt. ³⁴Waste land, once desolate for every passer-by to see, will now be farmed again. ³⁵And people will say: This land, so recently a waste, is now like a garden of Eden, and the ruined cities once abandoned and levelled to the ground are now strongholds with people living in them. ³⁶And the nations left round you will know that I, Yahweh, have rebuilt what was levelled and replanted what was ruined. I, Yahweh, have spoken and shall do it.

³⁷"The Lord Yahweh says this: As a further

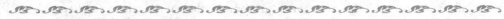

87 READ EZEKIEL 36:22–32.

I shall pour clean water over you and you will be cleansed.—EZEKIEL 36:25

NEW CREATIONS

Because to sin is human . . . the Master did not think it right to leave his creature unaided, or to neglect its danger of separation from himself. But just as he gave existence to that which did not exist, so [in Baptism] he gave a new creation to that which did exist, a diviner creation and a loftier than the first. To those who are beginning life it is a seal and to those who are more mature it is both a gift and a restoration of the divine image that had deteriorated through sin. He renewed us so that we may not, by becoming worse through despair and by falling altogether from good into the depths of evil, end up despising him. But like those who in the course of a long journey take a brief rest at an inn, he enabled us to accomplish the rest of the road fresh and full of courage. Such is the grace and power of Baptism: . . . a purification of the sins of each individual, and a complete cleansing from all the bruises and stains of sin.

And since we are double-made, I mean of body and soul, and the one part is visible, the other invisible, so the cleansing also is twofold, by water and the spirit. The one is received visibly in the body, the other concurring with it invisibly and apart from the body. The one typical, the other real and cleansing the depths. And this that comes to the aid of our first birth, makes us new instead of old, and like God instead of what we now are. It recasts us without fire, and creates us anew without breaking us up. For, to say it all in one word, the virtue of Baptism is to be understood as a *covenant* with God for a second life and a purer conversation.   ST. GREGORY NAZIANZEN, 329?–390

YOU WILL FIND THE NEXT READING AT EZEKIEL 37.

mark of favour, I shall let myself be consulted by the House of Israel; I shall increase their numbers like a human flock, ³⁸ like a flock of sacrificial animals, like the flock in Jerusalem on her solemn feasts. So your ruined cities will be filled with human flocks, and they will know that I am Yahweh." '

The dry bones

37 The hand of Yahweh was on me; he carried me away by the spirit of Yahweh and set me down in the middle of the valley, a valley full of bones. ²He made me walk up and down and all around among them. There were vast quantities of these bones on the floor of the valley; and they were completely dry. ³He said to me, 'Son of man, can these bones live?' I said, 'You know, Lord Yahweh.' ⁴He said, 'Prophesy over these bones. Say, "Dry bones, hear the word of Yahweh. ⁵The Lord Yahweh says this to these bones: I am now going to make breath enter you, and you will live. ⁶I shall put sinews on you, I shall make flesh grow on you, I shall cover you with skin and give you breath, and you will live; and you will know that I am Yahweh." ' ⁷I prophesied as I had been ordered. While I was prophesying, there was a noise, a clattering sound; it was the bones coming together. ⁸And as I looked, they were cov-

88 READ EZEKIEL 37:1–14.

I shall raise you from your graves, my people.—EZEKIEL 37:12

THE RESURRECTION OF THE BODY

The divine Scripture bears witness that there will be a resurrection of the body. God clearly says to Moses: "I am the God of Abraham, the God of Isaac and the God of Jacob" (see Ex 3:6). God is not the God of the dead—those who are dead and will be no more—but of the living. Their souls live in his hand (see Ws 3:1), but their bodies will again come to life through the resurrection.

Here is how David speaks to God about bodies, "[You] take back their breath and they die and revert to dust." Then he adds, "[You] send out your breath and life begins; you renew the face of the earth" (Ps 104:29–30). Further Isaiah says: "Your dead will come back to life, your corpses will rise again" (Is 26:19). It is clear that the souls do not lie in the graves, but the bodies.

And again, the blessed Ezekiel says: "While I was prophesying, there was a noise, a clattering sound; it was the bones coming together. And as I looked, they were covered with sinews; flesh was growing on them." Later he teaches how the spirits came back when they were bidden.

Divine Daniel also says: "At that time Michael will arise—the great Prince, defender of your people. That will be a time of great distress, unparalleled since nations first came into existence. When that time comes, your own people will be spared—all those whose names are found written in the Book. Of those who are sleeping in the Land of Dust, many will awaken, some to everlasting life, some to shame and everlasting disgrace. Those who are wise will shine as brightly as the expanse of the heavens, and those who have instructed many in uprightness, as bright as stars for all eternity" (Dn 12:1–3). The words, "those sleeping in the Land of Dust will awaken" clearly demonstrate that there will be a resurrection of bodies. For surely no one would say that souls sleep in the dust of the earth.   ST. JOHN DAMASCENE, 675?–749?

YOU WILL FIND THE NEXT READING AT DANIEL 2.

ered with sinews; flesh was growing on them and skin was covering them, yet there was no breath in them. [9]He said to me, 'Prophesy to the breath; prophesy, son of man. Say to the breath, "The Lord Yahweh says this: Come from the four winds, breath; breathe on these dead, so that they come to life!" ' [10]I prophesied as he had ordered me, and the breath entered them; they came to life and stood up on their feet, a great, an immense army.

[11]Then he said, 'Son of man, these bones are the whole House of Israel. They keep saying, "Our bones are dry, our hope has gone; we are done for." [12]So, prophesy. Say to them, "The Lord Yahweh says this: I am now going to open your graves; I shall raise you from your graves, my people, and lead you back to the soil of Israel. [13]And you will know that I am Yahweh, when I open your graves and raise you from your graves, my people, [14]and put my spirit in you, and you revive, and I resettle you on your own soil. Then you will know that I, Yahweh, have spoken and done this—declares the Lord Yahweh." '

Judah and Israel in one kingdom

15 The word of Yahweh was addressed to me as follows, 16'Son of man, take a stick and write on it, "Judah and those Israelites loyal to him." Take another stick and write on it, "Joseph (Ephraim's wood) and all the House of Israel loyal to him."

17'Join one to the other to make a single piece of wood, a single stick in your hand. 18 And when the members of your nation say, "Will you not tell us what you mean?" 19 say, "The Lord Yahweh says this: I am taking the stick of Joseph (now in Ephraim's hand) and those tribes of Israel loyal to him and shall join them to the stick of Judah. I shall make one stick out of the two, a single stick in my hand."

20'When the pieces of wood you have written on are in your hand in full sight of them, 21 say, "The Lord Yahweh says this: I shall take the Israelites from the nations where they have gone. I shall gather them together from everywhere and bring them home to their own soil. 22 I shall make them into one nation in the country, on the mountains of Israel, and one king is to be king of them all; they will no longer form two nations, nor be two separate kingdoms. 23 They will no longer defile themselves with their foul idols, their horrors and any of their crimes. I shall save them from the acts of infidelity which they have committed and shall cleanse them; they will be my people and I shall be their God. 24 My servant David will reign over them, one shepherd for all; they will follow my judgements, respect my laws and practise them. 25 They will live in the country which I gave to my servant Jacob, the country in which your ancestors lived. They will live in it, they, their children, their children's children, for ever. David my servant is to be their prince for ever. 26 I shall make a covenant of peace with them, an eternal covenant with them. I shall resettle them and make them grow; I shall set my sanctuary among them for ever. 27 I shall make my home above them; I shall be their God, and they will be my people. 28 And the nations will know

that I am Yahweh the sanctifier of Israel, when my sanctuary is with them for ever." '

Against Gog, king of Magog

38 The word of Yahweh was addressed to me as follows, 2'Son of man, turn towards Gog, to the country of Magog, towards the paramount prince of Meshech and Tubal, and prophesy against him. 3 Say, "The Lord Yahweh says this: I am against you, Gog, paramount prince of Meshech and Tubal. 4 I shall turn you about, I shall fix hooks in your jaws and bring you out with your entire army, horses and horsemen, all perfectly equipped, a huge array armed with shields and bucklers, and all wielding swords. 5 Persia and Cush and Put are with them, all with buckler and helmet; 6 Gomer and all its troops, Beth-Togarmah in the far north and all its troops, and many nations with you. 7 Be ready, be well prepared, you and all your troops and the others rallying to you, and hold yourself at my service.

8"Many days will pass before you are given orders; in the final years you will march on this country, whose inhabitants will have been living in confidence, remote from other peoples, since they escaped the sword and were gathered in from various nations, here in the long-deserted mountains of Israel. 9 Like a storm you will approach, you will advance and cover the country like a cloud, you, all your troops and many nations with you.

10 "The Lord Yahweh says this: That day, a thought will enter your mind and you will form a sinister plan. 11 You will think: I shall attack this undefended country and march on this peaceful nation living secure, all living in towns without walls or bars or gates. 12 You will come to plunder and loot and turn your might against the ruins they live in, against this people gathered back from the nations, these stock-breeders and traders who live at the Navel of the World. 13 Sheba and Dedan, the merchants and all the magnates of Tarshish will ask you: Have you come for plunder? Are you massing your troops with a

view to looting? To make off with gold and silver, seize cattle and goods, and come away with unlimited spoil?"

14 'So, son of man, prophesy. Say to Gog, "The Lord Yahweh says this: Is it not true that you will set out at a time when my people Israel is living secure? 15 You will leave your home in the far north, you and many nations with you, a great army of countless troops all mounted. 16 You will invade Israel, my people. You will be like a cloud covering the country. In the final days, I myself shall bring you to attack my country, so that the nations will know who I am, when I display my holiness to them, by means of you, Gog.

17 "The Lord Yahweh says this: It was of you that I spoke in the past through my servants the prophets of Israel, who prophesied in those days, foretelling your invasion. 18 The day Gog attacks the land of Israel—declares the Lord Yahweh—my furious wrath will boil up. In my anger, 19 in my jealousy, in the heat of my fury I say it: That day, I swear, there will be such a huge earthquake in the land of Israel, 20 that the fish in the sea and the birds of heaven, the wild beasts, all the reptiles creeping along the ground, and all people on the surface of the earth will quake before me. Mountains will fall, cliffs crumble, all walls collapse, and 21 I shall summon every kind of sword against him—declares the Lord Yahweh—and each will turn his sword against his comrade. 22 I shall punish him with plague and bloodshed, and rain down torrential rain, hailstones, fire and brimstone on him, on his troops and on the many nations with him. 23 I shall display my greatness and holiness and bring the many nations to acknowledge me; and they will know that I am Yahweh." '

39 'So, son of man, prophesy against Gog. Say, "The Lord Yahweh says this: Look, I am against you, Gog, paramount prince of Meshech and Tubal. 2 I shall turn you about, lead you on, and bring you from the farthest north against the mountains of Israel. 3 I shall break the bow in your left hand and dash the arrows out of your right. 4 You will fall on the mountains of Israel, you, all your troops and the nations with you. I shall make you food for every kind of bird of prey and wild animals. 5 You will fall in the wilds, for I have spoken—declares the Lord Yahweh. 6 I shall send down fire on Magog and on those living undisturbed in the islands, and they will know that I am Yahweh. 7 I shall see that my holy name is acknowledged by my people Israel, and no longer allow my holy name to be profaned; and the nations will know that I am Yahweh, holy in Israel.

8 "All this is to happen, all this is to take place—declares the Lord Yahweh. This is the day I predicted.

9 "The inhabitants of the towns of Israel will go out and set fire to and burn the weapons, the shields and bucklers, bows and arrows, javelins and spears. They will burn these for seven years 10 and not fetch wood from the countryside or cut it in the forests, since they will be burning the weapons. They will plunder those who plundered them, and despoil those who despoiled them—declares the Lord Yahweh.

11 "That day, I shall give Gog a famous spot in Israel for his grave, the valley of the Obarim, east of the Sea—the valley that halts the traveller—and there Gog and his whole throng will be buried, and it will be called the Valley of Hamon-Gog. 12 The House of Israel will take seven months to bury them and cleanse the country. 13 All the people of the country will dig their graves, thus winning themselves renown, the day when I display my glory—declares the Lord Yahweh. 14 And men will be detailed to the permanent duty of going through the country and burying those left above ground and cleansing it. They will begin their search once the seven months are over, 15 and as they go through the country, if one of them sees any human bones, he will set up a marker beside them until the gravediggers have buried them in the valley of Hamon-Gog 16 (and Hamonah is also the name of a town) and have cleansed the country."

17 'Son of man, the Lord Yahweh says this, "Say to the birds of every kind and to all the wild animals: Muster, come, gather from everywhere around for the sacrifice I am making for you, a great sacrifice on the mountains of Israel, so that you can eat flesh and drink blood. 18 You will eat the flesh of heroes, you will drink the blood of the princes of the world. They are all rams and lambs, goats and fat bulls of Bashan. 19 You will glut yourselves on fat and drink yourselves drunk on blood at this sacrifice I am making for you. 20 You will glut yourselves at my table on horses and chargers, on heroes and every kind of warrior—declares the Lord Yahweh."

Conclusion

21 'I shall display my glory to the nations, and all nations will see my sentence when I inflict it and my hand when I strike them. 22 The House of Israel will know that I am Yahweh their God, from that day forward for ever. 23 The nations too will know that the House of Israel were exiled for their guilt; because they were unfaithful to me, I hid my face from them and put them into the clutches of their enemies, so that they all fell by the sword. 24 I treated them as their loathsome acts of infidelity deserved and hid my face from them.

25 'So, the Lord Yahweh says this, "Now I shall bring Jacob's captives back and take pity on the whole House of Israel and show myself jealous for my holy name. 26 They will forget their disgrace and all the acts of infidelity which they committed against me when they were living safely in their own country, with no one to disturb them. 27 When I bring them home from the peoples, when I gather them back from the countries of their enemies, when I display my holiness in them for many nations to see, 28 they will know that I am Yahweh their God who, having sent them into exile among the nations, have reunited them in their own country, not leaving a single one behind. 29 I shall never hide my face from them again, since I shall pour out my spirit on the House of Israel—declares the Lord Yahweh." '

The future Temple[a]

40 In the twenty-fifth year of our captivity, at the beginning of the year, on the tenth day of the month, fourteen years to the day from the capture of the city, the hand of Yahweh was on me. He carried me away: 2 in divine visions, he carried me away to the land of Israel and put me down on a very high mountain, on the south of which there seemed to be built a city. 3 He took me to it, and there I saw a man, whose appearance was like brass. He had a flax cord and a measuring rod in his hand and was standing in the gateway. 4 The man said to me, 'Son of man, look carefully, listen closely and pay attention to everything I show you, since you have been brought here only for me to show it to you. Tell the House of Israel everything that you see.'

The outer wall

5 Now, the Temple was surrounded on all sides by an outer wall. The man was holding a measuring rod six cubits long, each cubit a forearm and a handsbreadth. He measured the thickness of this construction—one rod; and its height—one rod.

The east gate

6 He went to the east gate, climbed the steps and measured its threshold: one rod deep. 7 Each guardroom one rod by one rod; and the piers between the guardrooms five cubits thick, and the threshold of the gate inwards from the porch of the gate: one rod.[b] 9 He measured the porch of the gate: eight cubits; its piers: two cubits; the porch of the gate was at the inner end. 10 There were three guard-

---

40a This last section, chh. 40–48, is a blueprint for the restored community, alive to the presence of God in his spirit and inspired by the ideal of holiness.

40b v. 8 is omitted: it doubles v. 7.

rooms on each side of the east gate, all three of the same size; the piers between them all of the same thickness each side. ¹¹He measured the width of the entrance: ten cubits; and the width all down the gateway: thirteen cubits. ¹²There was a rail in front of the guardrooms; each rail on either side was one cubit. And the guardrooms on either side were six cubits square. ¹³He measured the width of the gate from the back wall of one guardroom to the back wall of the other; it was twenty-five cubits across, the openings being opposite each other. ¹⁴He measured the porch: twenty cubits; the court surrounded the gate on all sides. ¹⁵From the front of the entrance gate, to the far end of the porch of the inner gate: fifty cubits. ¹⁶All round inside the gate there were trellised windows in the guardrooms and in their piers; similarly, in the porch there were windows all round and palm trees on the piers.

The outer court

¹⁷He then took me to the outer court, which had rooms and a paved terrace going all the way round; there were thirty rooms on this terrace. ¹⁸This terrace, which came up to the sides of the gates and matched their depth, was the Lower Terrace. He measured the width of the court, ¹⁹from the front of the lower gate to the facade of the inner court, outside: a hundred cubits (on the east and on the north).

The north gate

²⁰He measured the length and breadth of the north gate of the outer court. ²¹It had three guardrooms on each side; its piers and porch were of the same size as those of the first gate: fifty cubits long and twenty-five cubits wide. ²²Its windows, its porch and its palm trees were of the same size as those of the east gate. There were seven steps up to it, and its porch was at the inner end. ²³In the inner court there was, opposite the north gate, a gate like the one opposite the east gate. He measured the distance from one gate to the other: a hundred cubits.

The south gate

²⁴He took me to the south side where there was a south gate; he measured its guardrooms, piers and porch; they were of the same size as the others. ²⁵The gateway, as well as its porch, had windows all round, like the windows of the others; it was fifty cubits long and twenty-five cubits wide, ²⁶and it had seven steps up to it; its porch was at the inner end and had palm trees on its piers, one on either side. ²⁷The inner court had a south gate; he measured the distance southwards from one gate to the other: a hundred cubits.

The inner court; the south gate

²⁸He then took me into the inner court by the south gate; he measured the south gate which was of the same size as the others. ²⁹Its guardrooms, piers and porch were of the same size as the others. ³⁰The gateway, as well as its porch, had windows all round; it was fifty cubits long and twenty-five cubits wide. ³¹The porch gave on to the outer court. It had palm trees on its piers and eight steps leading up to it.

The east gate

³²He took me to the eastern part of the inner court and measured the gate. It was of the same size as the others. ³³Its guardrooms, piers and porch were of the same size as the others. The gateway, as well as its porch, had windows all round; it was fifty cubits long and twenty-five cubits wide. ³⁴Its porch gave on to the outer court. There were palm trees on its piers on either side and eight steps leading up to it.

The north gate

³⁵He then took me to the north gate and measured it. ³⁶Its guardrooms, piers and porch were of the same size as the others. The gateway had windows all round; it was fifty cubits long and twenty-five cubits wide. ³⁷Its porch

gave on to the outer court. There were palm trees on its piers on either side and eight steps leading up to it.

Subsidiary buildings at the gate

38 There was a room, the entrance to which was in the porch of the gateway, where they washed the burnt offerings. 39 And inside the porch of the gateway were slabs, two on either side, for slaughtering the burnt offerings, the sacrifice for sin and the sacrifice of reparation. 40 Outside, at the approach to the entrance of the north gate, were two slabs, and on the other side, at the porch end of the gate were two slabs. 41 There were four slabs on one side and four slabs on the other side of the gateway, eight slabs in all, on which the slaughtering was done. 42 There were also four slabs of dressed stone for the burnt offerings, a cubit and a half long, a cubit and a half wide and a cubit high, on which the instruments for slaughtering the burnt offerings and sacrifice were placed; 43 runnels a handsbreadth wide went all round the top, and on these slabs was put the sacrificial flesh.

44 Then he took me into the inner court; there were two rooms in the inner court, one on the side of the north gate, facing south, the other on the side of the south gate, facing north. 45 He told me, 'The room looking south is for the priests responsible for the service of the Temple, 46 and the room looking north is for the priests responsible for the service of the altar. These are the sons of Zadok, those of the sons of Levi who approach Yahweh to serve him.'

The inner court

47 He measured the court; it was a hundred cubits long and a hundred cubits wide, a square with the altar standing in front of the Temple.

The Temple; the Ulam

48 He took me to the Ulam of the Temple and measured the piers of the Ulam: five cubits either side; and the width of the entrance was three cubits either side. 49 The length of the Ulam was twenty cubits and its width twelve cubits. There were ten steps leading up to it, and there were columns by the piers, one on either side.

The Hekal

41 He took me to the Hekal and measured its piers: six cubits wide on the one side, six cubits wide on the other. 2 The width of the entrance was ten cubits, and the returns of the entrance were five cubits on the one side and five cubits on the other. He measured its length: forty cubits; and its width: twenty cubits.

The Debir

3 He then went inside and measured the pier at the entrance: two cubits; then the entrance; six cubits; and the returns of the entrance: seven cubits. 4 He measured its length; twenty cubits; and its width against the Hekal: twenty cubits. He then said to me, 'This is the Holy of Holies.'

The side cells

5 He then measured the wall of the Temple: six cubits. The width of the lateral structure was four cubits, all round the Temple. 6 The cells were one above the other in three tiers of thirty cells each. The cells were recessed into the wall, the wall of the structure comprising the cells, all round, forming offsets; but there were no offsets in the wall of the Temple itself. 7 The width of the cells increased, storey by storey, corresponding to the amount taken in from the wall from one storey to the next, all round the Temple.

8 Then I saw that there was a paved terrace all round the Temple. The height of this, which formed the base of the side cells, was one complete rod of six cubits. 9 The outer wall of the side cells was five cubits thick. There was a passage between the cells of the Temple 10 and the rooms, twenty cubits wide, all round the Temple. 11 As a way in to the lateral cells on the passage there was one entrance on the

north side and one entrance on the south side. The width of the passage was five cubits right round.

The building on the west side

12 The building on the west side of the court was seventy cubits wide, the wall of the building was five cubits thick all round and its length was ninety cubits. 13 He measured the length of the Temple: a hundred cubits. 14 The length of the court plus the building and its walls: a hundred cubits. 15 He measured the length of the building, along the court, at the back, and its galleries on either side: a hundred cubits.

Particulars of the Temple itself

The inside of the Hekal and the porches of the court, 16 the thresholds, the windows, the galleries on three sides, facing the threshold, were panelled with wood all round from floor to windows, and the windows were screened with latticework. 17 From the door to the inner part of the Temple, as well as outside, and on the wall all round, both inside and out, 18 were carved great winged creatures and palm trees, one palm tree between two winged creatures; each winged creature had two faces: 19 a human face turned towards the palm tree on one side and the face of a lion towards the palm tree on the other side, throughout the Temple, all round. 20 Winged creatures and palm trees were carved on the wall from the floor to above the entrance. 21 The doorposts of the Temple were square.

The wooden altar

In front of the sanctuary there was something like 22 a wooden altar, three cubits high and two cubits square. Its corners, base and sides were of wood. He said to me, 'This is the table in the presence of Yahweh.'

The doors

23 The Hekal had double doors and the sanctuary 24 double doors. These doors had two hinged leaves, two leaves for the one door, two leaves for the other. 25 On them (on the doors of the Hekal), were carved great winged creatures and palm trees like those carved on the walls. There was a wooden porch roof on the front of the Ulam on the outside, 26 and windows with flanking palm trees on the sides of the Ulam, the cells to the side of the Temple and the porch-roofs.

Subsidiary buildings of the Temple

42 He then took me out into the outer court on the north side and led me to the room facing the court, that is to say, to the front of the building on the north side. 2 Along the front, it was a hundred cubits long on the north side and fifty cubits wide. 3 Facing the gateways of the inner court and facing the paving of the outer court was a gallery in front of the triple gallery, 4 and in front of the rooms was a walk, ten cubits measured inwards and a hundred cubits long; their doors looked north. 5 The top-floor rooms were narrow because the galleries took up part of the width, being narrower than those on the ground floor or those on the middle floor of the building; 6 these were divided into three storeys and had no columns such as the court had. Hence they were narrower than the ground floor ones or the middle-floor ones (below them). 7 The outer wall parallel to the rooms, facing them and giving onto the outer court, was fifty cubits long, 8 the length of the rooms facing the outer court being fifty cubits, while for those facing the hall of the Temple it was a hundred cubits. 9 Beneath the rooms there was an entrance from the east, leading in from the outer court. 10 In the thickness of the wall of the court, on the south side fronting the court and the building, were rooms. 11 A walk ran in front of them, as with the rooms built on the north side; they were of the same length and breadth, and were of similar design with similar doors in and out. 12 Before the rooms on the south side there was an entrance at the end of each walk, opposite the corresponding wall

on the east side, at their entries. ¹³He said to me, 'The northern and southern rooms giving onto the court are the rooms of the sanctuary, in which the priests who approach Yahweh will eat the most holy things. In them will be placed the most holy things: the oblation, the sacrifice for sin and the sacrifice of reparation, since this is a holy place. ¹⁴Once the priests have entered, they will not go out of the holy place into the outer court without leaving their liturgical vestments there, since these vestments are holy; they will put on other clothes before going near places assigned to the people.'

Measurements of the court

¹⁵When he had finished measuring the inside of the Temple, he took me out to the east gate and measured it right round the sides. ¹⁶He measured the east side with his measuring rod: a total of five hundred cubits by the measuring rod. ¹⁷He then measured the north side: a total of five hundred cubits by the measuring rod. ¹⁸He then measured the south side: five hundred cubits by the measuring rod ¹⁹was the total. On the west side he measured five hundred cubits by the measuring rod. ²⁰He measured the entire enclosing wall on all four sides: length five hundred, breadth five hundred, separating the sacred from the profane.

The return of Yahweh

43 He took me to the gate, the one facing east. ²I saw the glory of the God of Israel approaching from the east. A sound came with him like the sound of the ocean, and the earth shone with his glory. ³This vision was like the one I had seen when I had come for the destruction of the city, and like the one I had seen by the River Chebar. Then I fell to the ground. ⁴The glory of Yahweh arrived at the Temple by the east gate. ⁵The Spirit lifted me up and brought me into the inner court; I saw the glory of Yahweh fill the Temple. ⁶And I heard

someone speaking to me from the Temple while the man stood beside me. ⁷He said, 'Son of man, this is the dais of my throne, the step on which I rest my feet. I shall live here among the Israelites for ever; and the House of Israel, they and their kings, will never again defile my holy name with their whorings and the corpses of their kings, ⁸by putting their threshold beside my threshold and their doorposts beside my doorposts, with a party wall shared by them and me. They used to defile my holy name by their loathsome practices, and this is why I put an end to them in my anger. ⁹From now on they will banish their whorings and the corpses of their kings from my presence and I shall live among them for ever.

¹⁰'Son of man, describe this Temple to the House of Israel, to shame them out of their loathsome practices. (Let them draw up the plan of it.) ¹¹And, if they are ashamed of their behaviour, show them the design and plan of the Temple, its exits and entrances, its shape, how all of it is arranged, the entire design and all its principles. Give them all this in writing so that they can see and take note of its design and the way it is all arranged and carry it out. ¹²This is the charter of the Temple: all the surrounding space on the mountain top is an especially holy area. (Such is the charter of the Temple.)'

The altar

¹³These were the dimensions of the altar, in cubits each of a cubit plus a handsbreadth. The base: one cubit high and one cubit wide; the space by the runnel, all round the edge of the altar, one handsbreadth. ¹⁴From the ground level of the base up to the lower plinth, two cubits high and one cubit wide; from the lesser plinth to the greater plinth, four cubits high and one cubit wide. ¹⁵The altar hearth: four cubits high, with four horns projecting from the hearth, ¹⁶the hearth was four-square: twelve cubits by twelve cubits; ¹⁷and the square plinth: fourteen cubits by fourteen cubits; and the ledge all round: half a cubit; and

the base: one cubit all round. The steps were on the east side.

The consecration of the altar

18 He said to me, 'Son of man, the Lord Yahweh says this, "As regards the altar, this is how things must be done when it has been built for the sacrifice of the burnt offering and for the pouring of blood. 19 To the levitical priests—those of the race of Zadok—who approach me to serve me—declares the Lord Yahweh—you must give a young bull as a sacrifice for sin. 20 You must take some of its blood and put it on the four horns, on the four corners of the plinth and on the surrounding ledge. In this way you will purify it and make expiation on it. 21 Then take the bull of the sacrifice for sin and burn it in that part of the Temple which is cut off from the sanctuary. 22 On the second day, you must offer an unblemished he-goat as the sacrifice for sin, and the altar must be purified again as was done with the bull. 23 When you have finished the purification, you must offer a young, unblemished bull and an unblemished ram from the flock. 24 You must present them before Yahweh, and the priests will sprinkle salt on them and offer them as burnt offerings to Yahweh. 25 As a sacrifice for sin, every day for seven days you must offer a he-goat, a bull and an unblemished ram from the flock. 26 In this way the altar will be expiated and will be purified and inaugurated. 27 At the end of that time, on the eighth day and afterwards, the priest will offer your burnt offerings and your communion sacrifices on the altar, and I shall look favourably on you—declares the Lord Yahweh." '

The use of the east gate

44 He brought me back to the outer east gate of the sanctuary. It was shut. 2 Yahweh said to me, 'This gate will be kept shut. No one may open it or go through it, since Yahweh, God of Israel, has been through it. And so it must be kept shut. 3 The prince himself, however, may sit there to take his meal in the presence of Yahweh. He must enter and leave through the porch of the gate.'

Rules of admission to the Temple

4 He led me through the north gate to the front of the Temple. And then I looked; I saw the glory of Yahweh filling the Temple of Yahweh; and I fell to the ground. 5 Yahweh said to me, 'Son of man, pay attention, look carefully and listen closely to everything I explain; these are all the arrangements of the Temple of Yahweh and all its laws. Be careful about who is admitted to the Temple and who is excluded from the sanctuary. 6 And say to the rebels of the House of Israel, "The Lord Yahweh says this: You have gone beyond all bounds with all your loathsome practices, House of Israel, 7 by admitting aliens, uncircumcised in heart and body, to frequent my sanctuary and profane my Temple, while offering my food, the fat and the blood, and breaking my covenant with all your loathsome practices. 8 Instead of maintaining the service of my holy things, you have deputed someone else to maintain my service in my sanctuary. 9 The Lord Yahweh says this: No alien, uncircumcised in heart and body, may enter my sanctuary, none of the aliens living among the Israelites.

The Levites

10 "As regards the Levites who abandoned me when Israel strayed far from me by following its idols, they must bear the weight of their own sin. 11 They must be servants in my sanctuary, responsible for guarding the Temple gates and serving the Temple. They will kill the burnt offerings and the sacrifice for the people, and hold themselves at the service of the people. 12 Since they used to be at their service in front of their idols and were an occasion of guilt for the House of Israel, very well, I stretch out my hand against them—declares the Lord Yahweh—they will bear the weight of their guilt. 13 They may never approach me again to perform the priestly office in my presence, nor touch my holy things and my most holy things; they must bear the disgrace of

their loathsome practices. ¹⁴I shall give them the responsibility of serving the Temple; I shall make them responsible for serving it and for everything to be done in it.

The priests

¹⁵"As regards the levitical priests, the sons of Zadok, who maintained the service of my sanctuary when the Israelites strayed far from me, they will approach me to serve me; they will stand in my presence to offer me the fat and blood—declares the Lord Yahweh. ¹⁶They will enter my sanctuary and approach my table to serve me; they will maintain my service. ¹⁷Once they enter the gates of the inner court, they must wear linen vestments; they must wear no wool when they serve inside the gates of the inner court and in the Temple. ¹⁸They must wear linen caps on their heads and linen breeches on their loins; they may not wear anything round their waists that makes them sweat. ¹⁹When they go out to the people in the outer court, they must remove the vestments in which they have performed the liturgy and leave them in the rooms of the Holy Place, and put on other clothes, so as not to hallow the people with their vestments. ²⁰They may neither shave their heads nor let their hair grow long, but must cut their hair carefully. ²¹No priest may drink wine on the day he enters the inner court. ²²They may not marry widows or divorced women, but only virgins of the race of Israel; they may, however, marry a widow, if she is the widow of a priest. ²³They must teach my people the difference between what is sacred and what is profane and make them understand the difference between what is clean and what is unclean. ²⁴They must be judges in law-suits; they must judge in the spirit of my judgements; they must follow my laws and ordinances at all my feasts and keep my Sabbaths holy. ²⁵They may not go near a dead person, in case they become unclean, except in these permissible cases, that is, for father, mother, daughter, son, brother or unmarried sister. ²⁶After one of them has been purified, seven days must elapse; ²⁷then, the day he enters the Holy Place in the inner court to minister in the Holy Place, he must offer his sacrifice for sin—declares the Lord Yahweh. ²⁸They may have no heritage; I myself shall be their heritage. You may give them no patrimony in Israel; I myself shall be their patrimony. ²⁹Their food must be the oblation, the sacrifice for sin and the sacrifice of reparation. Everything dedicated by vow in Israel shall be for them. ³⁰The best of all your first-fruits and of all the dues and of everything you offer, must go to the priests; and the best of your dough you must also give to the priests, so that a blessing may rest on your house. ³¹Priests must not eat the flesh of anything that has died a natural death or been savaged, be it bird or animal." '

The division of the country; the portion for Yahweh

45 ¹"When you draw lots to divide the country by heritage, you must set a sacred portion of the country aside for Yahweh: twenty-five thousand cubits long and twenty thousand wide. The whole of this land must be sacred, ²and of this an area five hundred by five hundred cubits must be for the sanctuary, with a boundary fifty cubits wide right round. ³Out of this area you must also measure a section twenty-five thousand by ten thousand cubits, in which will be the sanctuary, the Holy of Holies. ⁴This will be the sacred portion of the country, belonging to the priests who officiate in the sanctuary and approach Yahweh to serve him. It will contain room for their houses and room for the sanctuary. ⁵A portion twenty-five thousand by ten thousand cubits will be owned by the Levites serving the Temple, with towns for them to live in. ⁶You must give the city possession of an area five thousand by twenty-five thousand cubits, near the land belonging to the sanctuary; this must be for the whole House of Israel.

The portion for the prince

⁷"The prince must have a territory either side of the sacred portion and of the property of the

city, adjacent to the sacred portion and the property of the city, stretching westwards from the west and eastwards from the east, its size equal to one of the portions between the west and the east frontiers ⁸of the country. This will be his property in Israel. Then my princes will no longer oppress my people; they must leave the rest of the country for the House of Israel, for its tribes.

⁹"The Lord Yahweh says this: Enough, princes of Israel! Give up your violence and plundering, do what is upright and just, stop crushing my people with taxation—declares the Lord Yahweh. ¹⁰Have fair scales, a fair *ephah*, a fair *bat*. ¹¹Let the *ephah* and *bat* be equal, let the *bat* hold one-tenth of a *homer* and the *ephah* one-tenth of a *homer*. Let the measures be based on the *homer*. ¹²The shekel must be twenty *gerah*. Twenty shekels, twenty-five shekels and fifteen shekels must make one *mina*.

Offerings for worship

¹³"This is the offering that you must levy: the sixth of an *ephah* for every *homer* of wheat, and the sixth of an *ephah* for every *homer* of barley. ¹⁴The dues on oil: one *bat* of oil out of every ten *bat* or out of every *kor* (which is equal to ten *bat* or one *homer*, since ten *bat* equal one *homer*). ¹⁵You must levy one sheep on every flock of two hundred from the pastures of Israel for the oblation, the burnt offerings and the communion sacrifice. This must form your expiation—declares the Lord Yahweh. ¹⁶Let all the people of the country be subject to this due for the prince of Israel. ¹⁷The prince must make himself responsible for providing the burnt offerings, the oblation and the libations for feasts, New Moons, Sabbaths and all the solemn festivals of the House of Israel. He must provide the sacrifice for sin, the oblation, the burnt offerings and the communion sacrifices to make expiation for the House of Israel.

The feast of the Passover

¹⁸"The Lord Yahweh says this: On the first day of the first month, you must take a young

bull without blemish, to purify the sanctuary. ¹⁹The priest must take blood from the sacrifice for sin and put it on the doorposts of the Temple, on the four corners of the altar plinth and on the doorposts of the gates of the inner court. ²⁰You must do the same on the seventh of the month, on behalf of anyone who has sinned through inadvertence or ignorance. This is how you must make expiation for the Temple. ²¹On the fourteenth day of the first month, you must celebrate the feast of the Passover. For seven days everyone must eat unleavened loaves. ²²On that day, the prince must offer a bull as a sacrifice for sin, for himself and all the people of the country. ²³For the seven days of the feast, he must offer Yahweh burnt offerings of seven bulls and seven rams without blemish, daily for a week, and one he-goat daily as a sacrifice for sin, ²⁴and as an oblation, one *ephah* for each bull and one *ephah* for each ram, and a *hin* of oil for every *ephah*.

The feast of Shelters

²⁵"For the feast that falls on the fifteenth day of the seventh month, he must do the same for seven days, offering the sacrifice for sin, the burnt offerings, the oblation and the oil." '

Miscellaneous regulations

46 ' "The Lord Yahweh says this: The east gate of the inner court must be kept shut for the six working days. On the Sabbath day, however, it must be opened, as also on the day of the New Moon; ²and the prince must go in through the porch of the outer gate and take his position by the doorposts of the gate. The priests must then offer his burnt offerings and his communion sacrifice. He must prostrate himself on the threshold of the gate and go out, and the gate must not be shut again until the evening. ³The people of the country must prostrate themselves in the presence of Yahweh at the entrance to the gate on Sabbaths and days of the New Moon. ⁴The burnt offering offered to

Yahweh by the prince on the Sabbath day must consist of six unblemished lambs and one unblemished ram, ⁵with an oblation of one *ephah* for the ram, and such oblation as he pleases for the lambs, and a *hin* of oil for every *ephah*. ⁶On the day of the New Moon it must consist of an unblemished young bull, six unblemished lambs and one unblemished ram, ⁷when he must make an oblation of one *ephah* for the bull and one *ephah* for the ram, and what he pleases for the lambs, and a *hin* of oil for every *ephah*.

⁸"When the prince goes in, he must enter by the porch of the gate, and he must leave by the same way. ⁹When the people of the country come into the presence of Yahweh at the solemn festivals, those who have come in by the north gate to prostrate themselves must go out by the south gate, and those who have come in by the south gate must go out by the north gate; no one must turn back to leave through the gate by which he entered but must go out on the opposite side. ¹⁰The prince will be with them, coming in like them and going out like them.

¹¹"On feast days and solemn festivals the oblation must be one *ephah* for every bull, one *ephah* for every ram, what he pleases for the lambs, and a *hin* of oil for every *ephah*. ¹²When the prince offers Yahweh voluntary burnt offerings or a voluntary communion sacrifice, the east gate must be opened for him, and he must offer his burnt offerings and his communion sacrifice as he does on the Sabbath day; when he has gone out, the gate must be shut after him. ¹³Every day he must offer an unblemished lamb one year old as a burnt offering to Yahweh; he must offer this every morning. ¹⁴Every morning in addition he must offer an oblation of one-sixth of an *ephah* and one-third of a *hin* of oil, for mixing with the flour. This is the oblation to Yahweh, a perpetual decree, fixed for ever. ¹⁵The lamb, the oblation and the oil must be offered morning after morning for ever.

¹⁶"Lord Yahweh says this: If the prince presents part of his hereditary portion to one of his sons, the gift must pass into the ownership of his sons and become their hereditary property. ¹⁷If, however, he presents part of his hereditary portion to one of his slaves, it will belong to the man only until the year of liberation and then must revert to the prince. Only his sons may retain his hereditary portion. ¹⁸The prince may not take any part of the people's hereditary portion, thus robbing them of what is theirs; he must provide the patrimony of his sons out of his own property, so that no member of my people is robbed of what is his!'"

¹⁹He took me through the entrance at the side of the north gate that leads to the rooms of the Holy Place set apart for the priests. And there before us, to the west, was a space at the end. ²⁰He said to me, 'This is where the priests must boil the slaughtered animals for the sacrifice for sin and the sacrifice of reparation, and where they must bake the oblation, without having to carry them into the outer court and so run the risk of hallowing the people.' ²¹He then took me into the outer court and led me to each of its four corners; in each corner of the outer court was a compound; ²²in other words, the four corners of the court contained four small compounds, forty cubits by thirty, all four being the same size. ²³All four were enclosed by a wall, with hearths all round the bottom of the wall. ²⁴He said, 'These are the kitchens where the Temple servants must boil the sacrifices offered by the people.'

The spring in the Temple

47 He brought me back to the entrance of the Temple, where a stream flowed eastwards from under the Temple threshold, for the Temple faced east. The water flowed from under the right side of the Temple, south of the altar. ²He took me out by the north gate and led me right round outside as far as the outer east gate where the water flowed out on the right-hand side. ³The man went off to the east holding his measuring line and measured off a thousand cubits; he then made me wade

across the stream; the water reached my ankles. 4 He measured off another thousand and made me wade across the stream again; the water reached my knees. He measured off another thousand and made me wade across the stream again; the water reached my waist. 5 He measured off another thousand; it was now a river which I could not cross; the stream had swollen and was now deep water, a river impossible to cross. 6 He then said, 'Do you see, son of man?' He then took me and brought me back to the bank of the river. 7 Now, when I reached it, I saw an enormous number of trees on each bank of the river. 8 He said, 'This water flows east down to the Arabah and to the sea; and flowing into the sea it makes its waters wholesome. 9 Wherever the river flows, all living creatures teeming in it will live. Fish will be very plentiful, for wherever the water goes it brings health, and life teems wherever the river flows. 10 There will be fishermen on its banks. Fishing nets will be spread from En-Gedi to En-Eglaim. The species of fish will be the same as the fish of the Great Sea. 11 The marshes and lagoons, however, will not become wholesome, but will remain salt. 12 Along the river, on either bank, will grow every kind of fruit tree with leaves that never wither and fruit that never fails; they will bear new fruit every month, because this water comes from the sanctuary. And their fruit will be good to eat and the leaves medicinal.'

The frontiers of the Holy Land

13 'The Lord Yahweh says this, "This will be the territory which you must distribute among the twelve tribes of Israel, with two portions for Joseph. 14 You will each have a fair share of it, since I swore to your fathers that I would give it to them, and this country now falls to you as your heritage. 15 These will be the frontiers of the country. On the north, from the Great Sea, the road from Hethlon to the Pass of Hamath, Zedad, 16 Berothah, Sibraim lying between the territories of Damascus and Hamath, to Hazer-ha-Tikon on the borders of Hauran; 17 the frontier will extend from the sea to Hazer-Enon, with the territory of Damascus and the territory of Hamath to the north; that will be the northern frontier. 18 On the east, the Jordan will serve as frontier between Hauran and Damascus, between Gilead and Israel, down to the Eastern Sea as far as Tamar; that will be the eastern frontier. 19 On the south, from Tamar southward to the Waters of Meribah in Kadesh, to the Wadi and the Great Sea; that will be the southern frontier. 20 And to the west, the Great Sea will serve as frontier up to the point opposite the Pass of Hamath; that will be the western frontier. 21 You must distribute this country among yourselves, among the tribes of Israel. 22 You must distribute it as a heritage for yourselves and the aliens settled among you who have fathered children among you, since you must treat them as citizens of Israel. They must draw lots for their heritage with you, among the tribes of Israel. 23 You will give the alien his heritage in the tribe where he has settled—declares the Lord Yahweh." '

Distribution of the Holy Land

48 ' "This is the list of the tribes. One portion in the far north by way of Hethlon to the Pass of Hamath, to Hazer-Enon, with the territory of Damascus to the north, and marching with Hamath, from the eastern limit to the western limit: Dan. 2 One portion bordering Dan, from the eastern limit to the western limit: Asher. 3 One portion bordering Asher, from the eastern limit to the western limit: Naphtali. 4 One portion bordering Naphtali, from the eastern limit to the western limit: Manasseh. 5 One portion bordering Manasseh, from the eastern limit to the western limit: Ephraim. 6 One portion bordering Ephraim, from the eastern limit to the western limit: Reuben. 7 One portion bordering Reuben, from the eastern limit to the western limit: Judah. 8 One portion bordering Judah, from the eastern limit to the western limit, is the portion which you must set aside, twenty-five thousand cubits wide, and as long as each

of the other portions from the eastern limit to the western limit. The sanctuary will be in the centre of it.

⁹ "The portion which you must set aside for Yahweh must be twenty-five thousand cubits long and ten thousand cubits wide. ¹⁰ This sacred portion must belong to the priests, being, on the north side, twenty-five thousand cubits; on the west side ten thousand cubits wide, on the east side ten thousand cubits wide and on the south side twenty-five thousand cubits long; the sanctuary of Yahweh will be in the centre of it. ¹¹ This will be for the consecrated priests, those of the sons of Zadok who maintained my liturgy and did not go astray with the straying Israelites, as the Levites went astray. ¹² And so their portion must be taken out of the especially holy portion of the land, near the territory of the Levites. ¹³ The territory of the Levites, like the territory of the priests, must be twenty-five thousand cubits long and ten thousand wide—the whole length being twenty-five thousand and the width ten thousand. ¹⁴ It will be illegal for them to sell or exchange any part of it, and the domain can never be alienated, since it is consecrated to Yahweh. ¹⁵ As regards the remainder, an area of five thousand cubits by twenty-five thousand, this must be for the common use of the city, for houses and pastures. In the middle will be the city. ¹⁶ These will be its dimensions: on the north side, four thousand five hundred cubits; on the south side, four thousand five hundred cubits; on the east side, four thousand five hundred cubits; on the west side, four thousand five hundred cubits. ¹⁷ The pasture land of the city must extend two hundred and fifty cubits to the north, two hundred and fifty to the south, two hundred and fifty to the east, two hundred and fifty to the west. ¹⁸ One strip, contiguous to the sacred portion, must be left over, consisting of ten thousand cubits to eastward and ten thousand to westward, marching with the sacred portion; this will bring in a revenue for feeding the municipal workmen. ¹⁹ And the municipal workmen, drawn from all the tribes of Israel,

will farm it. ²⁰ The portion must have a total area of twenty-five thousand cubits by twenty-five thousand. You must allocate a square area from the sacred portion to constitute the city. ²¹ What is left over will be for the prince, on either side of the sacred portion and of the property of the city, marching with the twenty-five thousand cubits to eastward to the eastern frontier, and marching with the twenty-five thousand cubits to westward to the western frontier—running parallel with the other portions and belonging to the prince. In the centre will be the sacred portion and the sanctuary of the Temple. ²² Thus, apart from the property of the Levites and the property of the city which lie in the middle of the prince's portion, everything between the borders of Judah and the borders of Benjamin must belong to the prince.

²³ "As regards the rest of the tribes: One portion from the eastern limit to the western limit: Benjamin. ²⁴ One portion bordering Benjamin, from the eastern limit to the western limit: Simeon. ²⁵ One portion bordering Simeon, from the eastern limit to the western limit: Issachar. ²⁶ One portion bordering Issachar, from the eastern limit to the western limit: Zebulun. ²⁷ One portion bordering Zebulun, from the eastern limit to the western limit: Gad. ²⁸ On the southern border of Gad, on the south side, the border will run from Tamar to the Waters of Meribah in Kadesh, to the Wadi and the Great Sea. ²⁹ This is how you must distribute the country to the tribes of Israel as their heritage, and these must be their portions—declares the Lord Yahweh.

The gates of Jerusalem

³⁰ "Here are the exits from the city. On the north side, four thousand five hundred cubits are to be measured off. ³¹ The gates of the city are to be named after the tribes of Israel. Three gates to the north: one the gate of Reuben; one the gate of Judah; one the gate of Levi. ³² On the east side, there will be four thousand five hundred cubits and three gates: one the gate of Joseph; one the gate of Ben-

jamin; one the gate of Dan. [33] On the south side, four thousand five hundred cubits are to be measured off, and there are to be three gates: one the gate of Simeon; one the gate of Issachar; one the gate of Zebulun. [34] On the west side, there will be four thousand five hundred cubits and three gates: one the gate of Gad; one the gate of Asher; one the gate of Naphtali. [35] Total perimeter: eighteen thousand cubits.

"The name of the city in future must be: Yahweh-is-there." '[a]

48a Hebr. *yahweh-sham* suggests 'Jerusalem'.

1 In the third year of the reign of Jehoiakim king of Judah, Nebuchadnezzar king of Babylon marched on Jerusalem and besieged it. ²The Lord let Jehoiakim king of Judah fall into his power, as well as some of the vessels belonging to the Temple of God. These he took away to Shinar, putting the vessels into the treasury of his own gods.

³From the Israelites, the king ordered Ashpenaz, his chief eunuch, to bring a certain number of boys of royal or noble descent; ⁴they had to be without any physical defect, of good appearance, versed in every branch of wisdom, well-informed, discerning, suitable for service at the royal court. Ashpenaz was to teach them to speak and write the language of the Chaldaeans. ⁵The king assigned them a daily allowance of food and wine from the royal table. They were to receive an education lasting for three years, after which they would enter the royal service. ⁶Among them were the Judaeans Daniel, Hananiah, Mishael and Azariah. ⁷The chief eunuch gave them other names, calling Daniel Belteshazzar, Hananiah Shadrach, Mishael Meshach, and Azariah Abed-Nego.

⁸Daniel, who was determined not to incur pollution by food and wine from the royal table, begged the chief eunuch to spare him this defilement. ⁹God allowed Daniel to receive faithful love and sympathy from the chief eunuch. ¹⁰But the eunuch warned Daniel, 'I am afraid of my lord the king: he has assigned you food and drink, and if he sees you looking thinner in the face than the other boys of your age, my head will be in danger with the king because of you.' ¹¹To the guard assigned to Daniel, Hananiah, Mishael and Azariah by the chief eunuch, Daniel then said,

¹²'Please allow your servants a ten days' trial, during which we are given only vegetables to eat and water to drink. ¹³You can then compare our looks with those of the boys who eat the king's food; go by what you see, and treat your servants accordingly.' ¹⁴The man agreed to do what they asked and put them on ten days' trial. ¹⁵When the ten days were over, they looked better and fatter than any of the boys who had eaten their allowance from the royal table; ¹⁶so the guard withdrew their allowance of food and the wine they were to drink, and gave them vegetables. ¹⁷To these four boys God gave knowledge and skill in every aspect of literature and learning; Daniel also had the gift of interpreting every kind of vision and dream.

¹⁸When the time stipulated by the king for the boys to be presented to him came round, the chief eunuch presented them to Nebuchadnezzar. ¹⁹The king conversed with them, and among all the boys found none to equal Daniel, Hananiah, Mishael and Azariah. So they became members of the king's court, ²⁰and on whatever point of wisdom or understanding he might question them, he found them ten times better than all the magicians and soothsayers in his entire kingdom. Daniel remained there until the first year of King Cyrus.

The king questions his soothsayers

2 In the second year of his reign, Nebuchadnezzar had a series of dreams; he was perturbed by this and sleep deserted him. ²The king then had magicians and soothsayers, sorcerers and Chaldaeans summoned to tell him what his dreams meant. They arrived and stood in the king's presence. ³The king said to them, 'I have had a dream, and my mind is troubled by a wish to understand it.' [4] The Chaldaeans answered the king:

'May your majesty live for ever! Tell your servants the dream, and we shall reveal its meaning for you.' [5] The king answered the Chaldaeans, 'This is my firm resolve: if you cannot tell me what I dreamt and what it means, I shall have you torn limb from limb and your houses turned into dunghills. [6] If, on the other hand, you can tell me what I dreamt and what it means, I shall give you presents, rewards and high honour. So tell me what I dreamt and what it means.' [7] A second time they said, 'Let the king tell his dream to his servants, and we shall reveal its meaning.' [8] But the king retorted, 'It is plain to me that you are trying to gain time, knowing my proclaimed resolve. [9] If you do not interpret my dream for me, there will be but one sentence passed on you all; you have agreed among yourselves to make me misleading and tortuous speeches while the time goes by. So tell me what my dream was, and then I shall know whether you can interpret it.' [10] The Chaldaeans answered the king, 'Nobody in the world could explain the king's problem; what is more, no other king, governor or chief would think of putting such a question to any magician, soothsayer or Chaldaean. [11] The question the king asks is difficult, and no one can find the king an answer to it, except the gods, whose dwelling is not with mortals.' [12] At this the king flew into a rage and ordered all the Babylonian sages to be put to death. [13] On publication of the decree to have the sages killed, search was made for Daniel and his companions to have them put to death.

Daniel intervenes

[14] Then, with shrewd and cautious words, Daniel approached Arioch, the king's chief executioner, when he was on his way to kill the Babylonian sages. [15] To this royal official Arioch he said, 'Why has the king issued such a harsh decree?' Arioch explained matters to Daniel, [16] and Daniel went off to ask the king for a stay of execution to give him the opportunity of revealing his interpretation to the king. [17] Daniel then went home and told his friends Hananiah, Mishael and Azariah what had happened, [18] urging them to beg the God of heaven to show his mercy and explain the mysterious secret, so that Daniel and his friends might be spared the fate of the other Babylonian sages. [19] The mystery was then revealed to Daniel in a night-vision, and Daniel blessed the God of heaven. [20] This is what Daniel said:

May the name of God
be blessed for ever and ever,
since wisdom and power are his alone.
[21] It is he who controls the procession of
times and seasons,
who makes and unmakes kings,
who confers wisdom on the wise,
and knowledge on those with
discernment,
[22] who uncovers depths and mysteries,
who knows what lies in darkness;
and light dwells with him.
[23] To you, God of my fathers, I give thanks
and praise
for having given me wisdom and strength:
to me you have explained what we asked
you,
to us you have explained the king's
problem.

[24] So Daniel went to see Arioch, whom the king had made responsible for putting the Babylonian sages to death. Going in, he said, 'Do not put the Babylonian sages to death. Take me into the king's presence and I will reveal the meaning to the king.' [25] Arioch lost no time in bringing Daniel to the king. 'Among the exiles from Judah,' he said, 'I have discovered a man who can reveal the meaning to the king.' [26] The king said to Daniel (who had been given the name Belteshazzar), 'Can you tell me what I dreamt and what it means?' [27] Facing the king, Daniel replied, 'None of the sages, soothsayers, magicians or exorcists

89 READ DANIEL 2.

The God of heaven will set up a kingdom which will never be destroyed.—DANIEL 2:44

CHRIST THE KING

Precisely because Daniel had presented himself as the most insignificant of all men, the king established him as prince over all Babylon. This reminds us of Pharaoh's establishing Joseph as ruler over all Egypt. As a matter of fact, Joseph was the only one in Egypt who was able to interpret the Pharaoh's dreams (see Gn 41). Similarly in Babylon no one except Daniel was able to explain the visions of the king. This shows that God in the course of generations raises up for himself holy persons who glorify him in the whole world.

We recognize in those events predicted by Daniel the things that are being accomplished in today's world. The statue that he described for Nebuchadnezzar's benefit represented the empire of the world. In that period of history the Babylonians held sway: they were the statue's golden head. After them the Persians reigned for 245 years, representing the silver part of the statue.

After that the Greeks ruled supreme for 300 years. This began with Alexander and is symbolized by the brass. They were followed by the Romans represented by the iron legs. Then come the toes that point to the future democracies that will be separated from one another. And they are partly iron and partly earthenware.

Then Daniel says: "you saw a stone, untouched by hand, break away from the mountain and reduce iron, bronze, earthenware, silver and gold to powder." When iron becomes mingled with clay, . . . when men no longer will agree among themselves, will any other king remain than Christ? He came from heaven like a stone detached from the mountain to overthrow the earthly kingships, to initiate the heavenly kingdom of the saints "which will never be destroyed." He himself will become the "mountain" and the city of the saints will cover the whole earth.

ST. HIPPOLYTUS, d. 235?

YOU WILL FIND THE NEXT READING AT DANIEL 3.

has been able to tell the king the truth of the mystery which the king has propounded; [28]but there is a God in heaven who reveals mysteries and who has shown King Nebuchadnezzar what is to take place in the final days. These, then, are the dream and the visions that passed through your head as you lay in bed:[a]

[29]'Your Majesty, on your bed your thoughts turned to what would happen in the future, and the Revealer of Mysteries disclosed to you what is to take place. [30]This mystery has been revealed to me, not that I am wiser than anyone else, but for this sole purpose: that the king should learn what it means, and that you should understand your inmost thoughts.

[31]'You have had a vision, Your Majesty; this is what you saw: a statue, a great statue of ex-

2a Under the image of metals these allegories describe successive empires, Babylonian, Median, Persian, Greek, which finally give way to the messianic kingdom.

treme brightness, stood before you, terrible to see. ³²The head of this statue was of fine gold, its chest and arms were of silver, its belly and thighs of bronze, ³³its legs of iron, its feet part iron, part clay. ³⁴While you were gazing, a stone broke away, untouched by any hand, and struck the statue, struck its feet of iron and clay and shattered them. ³⁵Then, iron and clay, bronze, silver and gold, all broke into pieces as fine as chaff on the threshing-floor in summer. The wind blew them away, leaving not a trace behind. And the stone that had struck the statue grew into a great mountain, filling the whole world. ³⁶This was the dream; we shall now explain to the king what it means.

³⁷'You, Your Majesty, king of kings, to whom the God of heaven has given sovereignty, power, strength and honour— ³⁸human beings, wild animals, birds of the air, wherever they live, he has entrusted to your rule, making you king of them all—you are the golden head. ³⁹And, after you, another kingdom will rise, not as great as yours, and then a third, of bronze, which will rule the whole world. ⁴⁰There will be a fourth kingdom, hard as iron, as iron that pulverises and crushes all. Like iron that breaks everything to pieces, it will crush and break all the earlier kingdoms. ⁴¹The feet you saw, part earthenware, part iron, are a kingdom which will be split in two, but which will retain something of the strength of iron, just as you saw the iron and the clay of the earthenware mixed together. ⁴²The feet were part iron, part potter's clay: the kingdom will be partly strong and partly brittle. ⁴³And just as you saw the iron and the clay of the earthenware mixed together, so the two will be mixed together in human seed;*b* but they will not hold together any more than iron will blend with clay. ⁴⁴In the days of those kings, the God of heaven will set up a kingdom which will never be destroyed, and this kingdom will not pass into the hands of another race: it will shatter and absorb all the previous kingdoms and itself last for ever— ⁴⁵just as you saw a stone, un-

touched by hand, break away from the mountain and reduce iron, bronze, earthenware, silver and gold to powder. The Great God has shown the king what is to take place. The dream is true, the interpretation exact.'

The king's profession of faith

⁴⁶At this, King Nebuchadnezzar fell prostrate before Daniel; he gave orders for Daniel to be offered an oblation and a fragrant sacrifice. ⁴⁷The king said to Daniel, 'Your god is indeed the God of gods, the Master of kings, and the Revealer of Mysteries, since you have been able to reveal this mystery.' ⁴⁸The king then conferred high rank on Daniel and gave him many handsome presents. He also made him governor of the whole province of Babylon and head of all the sages of Babylon. ⁴⁹At Daniel's request, the king entrusted the affairs of the province of Babylon to Shadrach, Meshach and Abed-Nego; Daniel himself remained in attendance on the king.

Nebuchadnezzar sets up a golden statue

3 King Nebuchadnezzar had a golden statue made, sixty cubits high and six cubits wide, which he set up on the plain of Dura, in the province of Babylon. ²King Nebuchadnezzar then summoned the satraps, magistrates, governors, counsellors, treasurers, judges, lawyers, and all the provincial authorities to assemble and attend the dedication of the statue set up by King Nebuchadnezzar. ³Satraps, magistrates, governors, counsellors, treasurers, judges, lawyers and all the provincial authorities then assembled for the dedication of the statue set up by King Nebuchadnezzar and stood in front of the statue which King Nebuchadnezzar had set up. ⁴A herald then loudly proclaimed: 'Peoples, nations, languages! Thus are you commanded: ⁵the moment you hear the sound of horn, pipe, lyre, zither, harp, bagpipe and every other kind of instru-

---

2b The short-lived marriage alliance between the Seleucids of Syria and the Ptolemies of Egypt.

ment, you will prostrate yourselves and worship the golden statue set up by King Nebuchadnezzar. ⁶Anyone who does not prostrate himself and worship will immediately be thrown into the burning fiery furnace.' ⁷And so, the instant all the peoples heard the sound of horn, pipe, lyre, zither, harp, bagpipe and all the other instruments, all the peoples, nations and languages prostrated themselves and worshipped the statue set up by King Nebuchadnezzar.

The denunciation and condemnation of the Jews

⁸Some Chaldaeans then came forward and maliciously accused the Jews. ⁹They said to King Nebuchadnezzar, 'May Your Majesty live for ever! ¹⁰You have issued a decree, Your Majesty, to the effect that everyone on hearing the sound of horn, pipe, lyre, zither, harp, bagpipe and every other kind of instrument is to prostrate himself and worship the golden statue; ¹¹and that anyone who does not prostrate himself and worship is to be thrown into the burning fiery furnace. ¹²Now, there are certain Jews to whom you have entrusted the affairs of the province of Babylon: Shadrach, Meshach and Abed-Nego; these men have ignored your command, Your Majesty; they do not serve your gods, and refuse to worship the golden statue you have set up.' ¹³Shaking with fury, Nebuchadnezzar sent for Shadrach, Meshach and Abed-Nego. The men were immediately brought before the king. ¹⁴Nebuchadnezzar addressed them, 'Shadrach, Meshach and Abed-Nego, is it true that you do not serve my gods, and that you refuse to worship the golden statue I have set up? ¹⁵When you hear the sound of horn, pipe, lyre, zither, harp, bagpipe and every other kind of instrument, are you prepared to prostrate yourselves and worship the statue I have made? If you refuse to worship it, you will be thrown forthwith into the burning fiery furnace; then which of the gods could save you from my power?' ¹⁶Shadrach, Meshach and Abed-Nego replied to King Nebuchadnezzar, 'Your question

needs no answer from us: ¹⁷if our God, the one we serve, is able to save us from the burning fiery furnace and from your power, Your Majesty, he will save us; ¹⁸and even if he does not, then you must know, Your Majesty, that we will not serve your god or worship the statue you have set up.' ¹⁹This infuriated King Nebuchadnezzar; his expression was changed now as he looked at Shadrach, Meshach and Abed-Nego. He gave orders for the furnace to be made seven times hotter than usual ²⁰and commanded certain stalwarts from his army to bind Shadrach, Meshach and Abed-Nego and throw them into the burning fiery furnace. ²¹They were then bound in their cloaks, trousers, headgear and other garments, and thrown into the burning fiery furnace. ²²The king's command was so urgent and the heat of the furnace was so fierce, that the men carrying Shadrach, Meshach and Abed-Nego were burnt to death by the flames from the fire; ²³the three men, Shadrach, Meshach and Abed-Nego fell, bound, into the burning fiery furnace.

The song of Azariah in the furnace ᵃ

²⁴*And they walked in the heart of the flames, praising God and blessing the Lord.* ²⁵*Azariah stood in the heart of the fire, praying aloud thus:*

²⁶ *May you be blessed and revered, Lord, God of*
 our ancestors,
   may your name be held glorious for ever.
²⁷ *For you are upright in all that you have*
     done for us,
   all your deeds are true,
   all your ways right,
   all your judgements true.
²⁸ *True is the sentence you have given*
   in all that you have brought down on us
   and on Jerusalem, the holy city of our
     ancestors,
   for you have treated us rightly and
     truly,
   as our sins deserve.

3a The italicised passages are preserved only in Gk.

29 Yes, we have sinned and committed a crime
      by deserting you,
  yes, we have greatly sinned;
  we have not listened to your commandments,
30 we have not observed them,
  we have not done what you commanded us
      to do
  for our own good.
31 Yes, all that you have brought down on us,
  all that you have done to us,
  you have been fully justified in doing.
32 You have handed us over to our enemies,
  to a lawless people, the worst of the godless,
  to an unjust king, the worst in the whole
      world;
33 today we have no right to open our mouths,
  shame and dishonour are the lot
  of those who serve and worship you.

34 Do not abandon us for ever,
  for the sake of your name;
  do not repudiate your covenant,
35 do not withdraw your favour from us,
  for the sake of Abraham, your friend,
  of Isaac, your servant,
  and of Israel, your holy one,
36 to whom you promised to make their
      descendants as many as the stars of
      heaven
  and as the grains of sand on the seashore.
37 Lord, we have become the least of all nations,
  we are put to shame today throughout the
      world,
  because of our sins.

38 We now have no leader, no prophet, no
      prince,
  no burnt offering, no sacrifice, no oblation,
      no incense,
  no place where we can make offerings
      to you
39 and win your favour.
  But may the contrite soul, the humbled spirit,
      be as acceptable to you
40 as burnt offerings of rams and bullocks,
  as thousands of fat lambs:
  such let our sacrifice be to you today,

and may it please you that we follow you
      whole-heartedly,
  since those who trust in you will not be
      shamed.
41 And now we put our whole heart into
      following you,
  into fearing you and seeking your face once
      more.
42 Do not abandon us to shame
  but treat us in accordance with your
      gentleness,
  in accordance with the greatness of your
      mercy.
43 Rescue us in accordance with your wonderful
      deeds
  and win fresh glory for your name, O Lord.
44 Confusion seize all who ill-treat your
      servants:
  may they be covered with shame,
  deprived of all their power,
  and may their strength be broken.
45 Let them learn that you alone are God and
      Lord,
  glorious over the whole world.

46 All this time, the king's servants, who had thrown them into the furnace, had been stoking it with crude oil, pitch, tow and brushwood 47 until the flames rose forty-nine cubits above the furnace 48 and, leaping out, burnt those Chaldaeans to death who were standing round it. 49 But the angel of the Lord came down into the furnace beside Azariah and his companions; he drove the flames of the fire outwards from the furnace 50 and, in the heart of the furnace, wafted a coolness to them as of the breeze and dew, so that the fire did not touch them at all and caused them no pain or distress.

The song of the three young men

51 Then all three in unison began to sing, glorifying and blessing God in the furnace, with the words:

52 May you be blessed, Lord, God of our
      ancestors,
  be praised and extolled for ever.

Blessed be your glorious and holy name,
    praised and extolled for ever.
53 May you be blessed in the Temple of your
        sacred glory,
    exalted and glorified above all for ever:
54 blessed on the throne of your kingdom,
    exalted above all, glorified for ever:
55 blessed are you who fathom the abyss,
        enthroned on the winged creatures,
    praised and exalted above all for ever:
56 blessed in the expanse of the heavens,
    exalted and glorified for ever.

57 Bless the Lord, all the Lord's creation:
    praise and glorify him for ever!
58 Bless the Lord, angels of the Lord,
    praise and glorify him for ever!
59 Bless the Lord, heavens,
    praise and glorify him for ever!
60 Bless the Lord, all the waters above the
        heavens,
    praise and glorify him for ever!
61 Bless the Lord, powers of the Lord,
    praise and glorify him for ever!
62 Bless the Lord, sun and moon,
    praise and glorify him for ever!
63 Bless the Lord, stars of heaven,
    praise and glorify him for ever!

64 Bless the Lord, all rain and dew,
    praise and glorify him for ever!
65 Bless the Lord, every wind,
    praise and glorify him for ever!
66 Bless the Lord, fire and heat,
    praise and glorify him for ever!
67 Bless the Lord, cold and warmth,
    praise and glorify him for ever!
68 Bless the Lord, dew and snow-storm,
    praise and glorify him for ever!
69 Bless the Lord, frost and cold,
    praise and glorify him for ever!
70 Bless the Lord, ice and snow,
    praise and glorify him for ever!
71 Bless the Lord, nights and days,
    praise and glorify him for ever!
72 Bless the Lord, light and darkness,
    praise and glorify him for ever!

73 Bless the Lord, lightning and cloud,
    praise and glorify him for ever!

74 Let the earth bless the Lord:
    praise and glorify him for ever!
75 Bless the Lord, mountains and hills,
    praise and glorify him for ever!
76 Bless the Lord, every plant that grows,
    praise and glorify him for ever!
77 Bless the Lord, springs of water,
    praise and glorify him for ever!
78 Bless the Lord, seas and rivers,
    praise and glorify him for ever!
79 Bless the Lord, whales, and everything that
        moves in the waters,
    praise and glorify him for ever!
80 Bless the Lord, every kind of bird,
    praise and glorify him for ever!
81 Bless the Lord, all animals wild and
        tame,
    praise and glorify him for ever!

82 Bless the Lord, all the human race:
    praise and glorify him for ever!
83 Bless the Lord, O Israel,
    praise and glorify him for ever!
84 Bless the Lord, priests,
    praise and glorify him for ever!
85 Bless the Lord, his servants,
    praise and glorify him for ever!
86 Bless the Lord, spirits and souls of the
        upright,
    praise and glorify him for ever!
87 Bless the Lord, faithful,
    humble-hearted people,
    praise and glorify him for ever!

88 Hananiah, Azariah and Mishael, bless the
        Lord,
    praise and glorify him for ever!—
    For he has rescued us from the Underworld,
    he has saved us from the hand of Death,
    he has snatched us from the burning fiery
        furnace,
    he has drawn us from the heart of the flame!
89 Give thanks to the Lord, for he is good,
    for his love is everlasting.

90   READ DANIEL 3:8–21, 48–90.

Then all three in unison began to sing, glorifying and blessing God in the furnace.

—DANIEL 3:51

UNITY IN PRAYER

The Teacher of peace and Master of unity is unwilling for prayer to be made singly and individually, teaching that he who prays is not to pray for himself alone. For we do not say, *"My* Father who art in heaven," nor "Give *me* this day *my* daily bread." Nor does each one ask that his own trespasses be forgiven, nor does he request that he alone may not be led into temptation and delivered from the evil one. Our prayer is public and common. And when we pray we do not pray for one but for the whole people because we the whole people are one.

    This rule of prayer the three young men observed when shut up in the fiery furnace. Scripture teaches that they prayed in unison and were united in spirit. When the Bible teaches how such persons prayed, it gives us an example that we ought to imitate in our prayers so that we may be like them. "Then all three in unison began to sing," Scripture says, "glorifying and blessing God." They spoke with one mouth, although Christ had not yet taught them to pray. And, therefore, as they prayed their words were beneficial and effective because a quiet, simple, and spiritual prayer pleased the Lord.

    Thus too we find that the Apostles and disciples prayed after the Lord's Ascension: "With one heart all these joined constantly in prayer, together with some women, including Mary the mother of Jesus, and with his brothers" (Ac 1:14). They continued united in prayer, clearly showing by the constancy and unanimity of their prayer that God . . . only admits into the divine and eternal house those among whom prayer is unanimous.   ST. CYPRIAN OF CARTHAGE, 200?–258

YOU WILL FIND THE NEXT READING AT DANIEL 6.

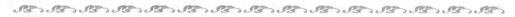

90 Bless the Lord, the God of gods, all who
        fear him,
  give praise and thanks to him,
  for his love is everlasting!

The king acknowledges the miracle [b]

24/91 King Nebuchadnezzar sprang to his feet in amazement. He said to his advisers, 'Did we not have these three men thrown bound into the fire?' They answered the king, 'Certainly, Your Majesty'. 25/92 'But', he went on, 'I can see four men walking free in the heart of the fire and quite unharmed! And the fourth looks like a child of the gods!' 26/93 Nebuchadnezzar

approached the mouth of the burning fiery furnace and said, 'Shadrach, Meshach and Abed-Nego, servants of God Most High, come out, come here!' And from the heart of the fire out came Shadrach, Meshach and Abed-Nego. 27/94 The satraps, magistrates, governors, and advisers of the king crowded round the three men to examine them: the fire had had no effect on their bodies: not a hair of their heads had been singed, their cloaks were not scorched, no smell of burning hung about

3b At this point the Hebr. resumes. The verse numbering is therefore given according to both Hebr. and Gk.

them. Nebuchadnezzar said, ^{28/95}'Blessed be the God of Shadrach, Meshach and Abed-Nego: he has sent his angel to rescue his servants who, putting their trust in him, defied the order of the king, and preferred to forfeit their bodies rather than serve or worship any god but their God. ^{29/96}I therefore decree as follows, "Peoples, nations, and languages! Let any of you speak disrespectfully of the God of Shadrach, Meshach and Abed-Nego, and I shall have him torn limb from limb and his house turned into a dunghill; for there is no other god who can save like this." '

^{30/97}The king then showered favours on Shadrach, Meshach and Abed-Nego in the province of Babylon.

Nebuchadnezzar's proclamation

^{31/98}'King Nebuchadnezzar, to all peoples, nations and languages dwelling throughout the world: may you prosper more and more!

^{32/99}'It is my pleasure to make known the signs and wonders with which the Most High God has favoured me.

^{33/100}How great his signs,
  how mighty his wonders!
His kingdom is an everlasting kingdom,
  his empire endures age after age!'

Nebuchadnezzar describes his dream

4 'I, Nebuchadnezzar, was living comfortably in my house, prosperously in my palace. ²I had a dream; it appalled me. Dread assailed me as I lay in bed; the visions that passed through my head tormented me. ³So I decreed that all the sages of Babylon be summoned to explain to me what the dream meant. ⁴Magicians, soothsayers, Chaldaeans and exorcists came, and I told them what I had dreamt, but they could not interpret it for me. ⁵Daniel, renamed Belteshazzar after my own god, and in whom the spirit of the holy gods resides, then came into my presence. I told him my dream:

⁶' "Belteshazzar, chief of magicians," I said, "I know that the spirit of the holy gods resides

in you and that no mystery puts you at a loss. This is the dream I have had; tell me what it means.

⁷' "The visions that passed through my head as I lay in bed were these:

I saw a tree
in the middle of the world;
it was very tall.
⁸ The tree grew taller and stronger,
  until its top reached the sky
  and it could be seen from the very ends of
      the earth.
⁹ Its foliage was beautiful, its fruit
      abundant,
in it was food for all.
For the wild animals it provided shade,
  the birds of heaven nested in its branches,
  all living creatures found their food on it.

¹⁰' "I watched the visions passing through my head as I lay in bed:

Next, a Watchful One,^a a holy one, came
      down from heaven.
¹¹ At the top of his voice he shouted:
Cut the tree down, lop off its branches,
  strip off its leaves, throw away its fruit;
  let the animals flee from its shelter
  and the birds from its branches.
¹² But leave the stump with its roots in the
      ground,
bound with hoops of iron and bronze,
  in the grass of the countryside.
Let it be drenched by the dew of heaven
  and have its lot with the animals, eating
      grass!
¹³ Let it cease to have a human heart,
  and be given the heart of a beast,
  and seven times shall pass over him!

¹⁴ Such is the sentence proclaimed by the
      Watchers,
  the verdict announced by the holy ones—

4a An angel, one of God's attendants, a term common in extra-biblical contemporary works.

so that every living thing may learn
that the Most High rules over human
    sovereignty;
he confers it on whom he pleases,
and raises the lowest of humankind.

15 ' "This was the dream I had—I, Neb-uchadnezzar the king. Now it is for you, Bel-teshazzar, to pronounce on its meaning, since not one of the sages in my kingdom has been able to interpret it for me; you, however, can do so, since the spirit of the holy gods resides in you." '

Daniel interprets the dream

16 Daniel, known as Belteshazzar, was con-fused for a time and upset.

The king said, 'Belteshazzar, do not be upset at the dream and its meaning.' Belte-shazzar answered, 'My lord, may the dream apply to those who hate you, and its meaning to your foes! 17 The tree you saw, so large and strong and tall that it reached the sky and could be seen throughout the world, 18 the tree with beautiful foliage and abundant fruit, with food for all in it, providing shade for the wild animals, with the birds of heaven nesting in its branches: 19 that tree is yourself, Your Majesty, for you have grown great and strong; your stature is now so great that it reaches the sky, and your empire extends to the ends of the earth.

20 'And the Watchful One seen by the king, the holy one coming down from heaven and saying, "Cut the tree down and destroy it, but leave stump and roots in the ground, bound with hoops of iron and bronze in the grass of the countryside; let it be drenched by the dew and have its lot with the wild animals until seven times have passed over it": 21 the mean-ing of this, Your Majesty, the verdict of the Most High passed on my lord the king, is this:

22 You will be driven from human society
    and will make your home with the wild
        animals,
    you will feed on grass, as oxen do,

you will be drenched by the dew of
    heaven;
seven times will pass over you
until you have learnt
that the Most High rules over human
    sovereignty
and confers it on whom he pleases.

23 'And the order, "Leave the stump and roots of the tree", means that your kingdom will be kept for you until you come to under-stand that Heaven rules all. 24 May it please the king to accept my advice: by upright actions break with your sins, break with your crimes by showing mercy to the poor, and so live long and peacefully.'

The dream comes true

25 This all happened to King Nebuchadnez-zar. 26 At the end of twelve months, while strolling on the roof of the royal palace in Babylon, 27 the king was saying, 'Great Bab-ylon! Was it not built by me as a royal resi-dence, by the force of my might and for the majesty of my glory?' 28 The words were not out of his mouth when a voice came down from heaven:

'Of you, King Nebuchadnezzar, it is
    decreed:
the empire has been taken from you,
29 you will be driven from human society
    and will make your home with the wild
        animals;
you will feed on grass, as oxen do,
and seven times will pass over you
until you have learnt
that the Most High rules over human
    sovereignty
and gives it to whom he pleases.'

30 The words were immediately fulfilled: Nebuchadnezzar was driven from human so-ciety and ate grass as oxen do; he was drenched by the dew of heaven; his hair grew like an eagle's feathers, and his nails became like a bird's talons.

31 'When the time was over, I, Nebuchadnezzar, raised my eyes to heaven: my reason
returned. And I blessed the Most High,

praising and glorifying him who lives for
ever,
for his empire is an everlasting empire,
his kingship endures, age after age.
32 All who dwell on earth count for
nothing;
as he thinks fit, he disposes the army of
heaven
and those who dwell on earth.
No one can arrest his hand
or ask him, "What have you done?"

33 'At that moment my reason returned and,
for the honour of my royal state, my glory and
splendour returned too. My counsellors and
noblemen acclaimed me; I was restored to my
throne, and to my past greatness even more
was added. 34 And now I, Nebuchadnezzar,

praise, extol and glorify the King of
heaven,
all of whose deeds are true,
all of whose ways are right,
and who can humble those who walk in
pride.'

5 King Belshazzar gave a great banquet for
his noblemen, a thousand of them, and, in
the presence of this thousand, he drank his
wine. 2 Having tasted the wine, Belshazzar
gave orders for the gold and silver vessels to be
brought which his father Nebuchadnezzar
had taken from the sanctuary in Jerusalem, so
that the king, his noblemen, his wives and the
women who sang for him could drink out of
them. 3 The gold and silver vessels taken from
the sanctuary of the Temple of God in Jerusalem were brought in, and the king, his noblemen, his wives and the women who sang for
him drank out of them. 4 They drank their
wine and praised their idols of gold and silver,
of bronze and iron, of wood and stone. 5 Suddenly, the fingers of a human hand appeared

and began to write on the plaster of the palace
wall, directly behind the lamp-stand; and the
king could see the hand as it wrote. 6 The king
turned pale with alarm: his hip-joints went
slack and his knees began to knock. 7 He
shouted for his soothsayers, Chaldaeans, and
exorcists. And the king said to the Babylonian
sages, 'Anyone who can read this writing and
tell me what it means shall be dressed in purple, and have a chain of gold put round his
neck, and be one of the three men who govern
the kingdom.' 8 The king's sages all crowded
forward, but they could neither read the writing nor explain to the king what it meant.
9 Greatly alarmed, King Belshazzar turned
even paler, and his noblemen were equally disturbed. 10 Then the queen, attracted by the
noise made by the king and his noblemen,
came into the banqueting hall. 'May Your
Majesty live for ever!' said the queen. 'Do not
be alarmed, do not look so pale. 11 In your
kingdom there is a man in whom lives the
spirit of the holy gods. In your father's days he
was known for a perception, intelligence and
wisdom comparable to that of the gods. King
Nebuchadnezzar, your father, made him head
of the magicians, soothsayers, Chaldaeans and
exorcists. 12 Since this man Daniel, whom the
king had renamed Belteshazzar, is filled with
such a marvellous spirit and such knowledge
and intelligence in interpreting dreams, solv-
ing enigmas and unravelling difficult problems, send for him; he will be able to tell you
what this means.'

13 Daniel was brought into the king's presence; the king said to Daniel, 'Are you the
Daniel who was one of the Judaean exiles
brought by my father the king from Judah?
14 I am told that the spirit of the gods lives in
you, and that you are known for your perception, intelligence and marvellous wisdom.
15 The sages and soothsayers have already been
brought to me to read this writing and tell me
what it means, but they have been unable to
reveal its meaning. 16 I am told that you are
able to give interpretations and to unravel difficult problems, so if you can read the writing

and tell me what it means, you shall be dressed in purple, and have a chain of gold put round your neck, and be one of the three men who govern the kingdom.'

17 Then Daniel spoke up in the presence of the king. 'Keep your gifts for yourself,' he said, 'and give your rewards to others! I can certainly read the writing to the king and tell him what it means. 18 Your Majesty, the Most High God gave Nebuchadnezzar your father sovereignty, greatness, majesty and glory. 19 He made him so great that all peoples, nations and languages shook with dread before him: he killed whom he pleased, spared whom he pleased, promoted whom he pleased, degraded whom he pleased. 20 But because his heart grew swollen with pride, and his spirit stiff with arrogance, he was deposed from his sovereign throne and stripped of his glory. 21 He was driven from human society, his heart was more like an animal's than a man's; he lived with the wild donkeys; he fed on grass like oxen; his body was drenched by the dew of heaven, until he had learnt that the Most High rules over human sovereignty and appoints whom he pleases to rule it. 22 But you, Belshazzar, who are his son, you have not humbled your heart, in spite of knowing all this. 23 You have defied the Lord of heaven, you have had the vessels from his Temple brought to you, and you, your noblemen, your wives and the women singing for you have drunk your wine out of them. You have praised gods of gold and silver, of bronze and iron, of wood and stone, which can neither see, hear nor understand; but you have given no glory to the God in whose hands are your breath itself and all your fortunes. 24 That is why he has sent the hand which has written these words. 25 The writing reads: *mene, mene, teqel* and *parsin*. 26 The meaning of the words is this:^a *mene*: God has *measured* your sovereignty and put an end to it; 27 *teqel*: you have been *weighed* in the balance and found wanting; 28 *parsin*: your kingdom has been *divided* and given to the Medes and the *Persians*.'

29 At Belshazzar's order Daniel was dressed in purple, a chain of gold was put round his neck and he was proclaimed as one of the three men who governed the kingdom.

30 That same night, the Chaldaean king Belshazzar was murdered,

6 and Darius the Mede received the kingdom, at the age of sixty-two.

The satraps resent Daniel's promotion

2 It pleased Darius to appoint a hundred and twenty satraps over his kingdom for the various parts, 3 and over them three presidents— of whom Daniel was one—to whom the satraps were to be responsible. This was to safeguard the king's interests. 4 This Daniel, by virtue of the marvellous spirit residing in him, was so evidently superior to the other presidents and satraps that the king considered appointing him to rule the whole kingdom. 5 The presidents and satraps, in consequence, started hunting for some affair of state by which they could discredit Daniel; but they could find nothing to his discredit, and no case of negligence; he was so punctilious that they could not find a single instance of maladministration or neglect. 6 These men then thought, 'We shall never find a way of discrediting Daniel unless we try something to do with the law of his God.' 7 The presidents and satraps then went in a body to the king. 'King Darius,' they said, 'live for ever! 8 We are all agreed, presidents of the realm, magistrates, satraps, councillors and governors, that the king should issue an edict enforcing the following regulation: Whoever within the next thirty days prays to anyone, divine or human, other than to yourself, Your Majesty, is to be thrown into the lions' den. 9 Your Majesty, ratify the edict at once by signing this document, making it unalterable, as befits the law of the Medes and the Persians, which cannot be revoked.' 10 King Darius accordingly signed the document embodying the edict.

5a The untranslatable play on Aramaic words is shown in the text by italics.

91 READ DANIEL 6.

Three times each day, [Daniel] went down on his knees, praying and giving thanks to God as he had always done.—DANIEL 6:11

THE POWER OF INTEGRITY

Although Daniel had much work to do for the king, he continued to be faithful to daily prayer, rendering to Caesar the things that are Caesar's and to God what belongs to God (see Mt 22:21).

Was it not possible for him to pray to God in the intimacy of his heart during the day? And then at home during the night remain secretly recollected without endangering himself? Of course, he could have acted in that way, but he did not want that kind of conduct. Then the presidents and the satraps might have said: What is the value of the fear of God, since he is afraid of the king's edict? And they would have accused him of infidelity. That would have been hypocrisy, but faith and fear of God do not work that way.

That is why blessed Daniel was saved from the lions by the angel. Had he taken the edict into consideration and remained quiet for thirty days, his faith would not have preserved its purity. "No one can serve two masters" (see Mt 6:24). The wily devil exercises his wits to prevent us from raising holy hands to God in prayer.

The devil knows well that our prayer gives peace to the world and brings chastisement on the wicked. Remember that when Moses raised his hands, Israel overcame, and when he lowered them, Amalek prevailed (see Ex 17:11). This still happens for us today. When we stop praying, the enemy is victorious. And when we persevere in prayer, the evil one's power and energy are fruitless.

ST. HIPPOLYTUS, d. 235?

YOU WILL FIND THE NEXT READING AT HOSEA 14.

Daniel continues to pray

¹¹ When Daniel heard that the document had been signed, he retired to his house. The windows of his upstairs room faced towards Jerusalem. Three times each day, he went down on his knees, praying and giving praise to God as he had always done. ¹² These men came along in a body and found Daniel praying and pleading with God. ¹³ They then went to the king and reminded him of the royal edict, 'Have you not signed an edict forbidding anyone for the next thirty days to pray to anyone, divine or human, other than to yourself, Your Majesty, on pain of being thrown into the lions' den?' 'The decision stands', the king replied, 'as befits the law of the Medes and the Persians, which cannot be revoked.' ¹⁴ They then said to the king, 'Your Majesty, this man Daniel, one of the exiles from Judah, disregards both you and the edict which you have signed: he is at his prayers three times each day.' ¹⁵ When the king heard these words he was deeply distressed and determined to save Daniel; he racked his brains until sunset to find some way to save him. ¹⁶ But the men kept pressing the king, 'Your Majesty, remember that in conformity with the law of the Medes and the Persians, no edict or decree can be altered when once issued by the king.'

Daniel is thrown to the lions

¹⁷ The king then ordered Daniel to be brought and thrown into the lion pit. The king said to Daniel, 'Your God, whom you have served so faithfully, will have to save you.' ¹⁸ A stone was then brought and laid over the mouth of the pit; and the king sealed it with his own signet and with that of his noblemen, so that there could be no going back on the original decision about Daniel. ¹⁹ The king returned to his palace, spent the night in fasting and refused to receive any of his concubines. Sleep eluded him, ²⁰ and at the first sign of dawn he got up and hurried to the lion pit. ²¹ As he approached the pit he called in anguished tones to Daniel, 'Daniel, servant of the living God! Has your God, whom you serve so faithfully, been able to save you from the lions?' ²² Daniel answered the king, 'May Your Majesty live for ever! ²³ My God sent his angel who sealed the lions' jaws; they did me no harm, since in his sight I am blameless; neither have I ever done you any wrong, Your Majesty.' ²⁴ The king was overjoyed and ordered Daniel to be released from the pit. Daniel was released from the pit and found to be quite unhurt, because he had trusted in his God. ²⁵ The king then sent for the men who had accused Daniel and had them thrown into the lion pit, and their wives and children too; and before they reached the floor of the pit the lions had seized them and crushed their bones to pieces.

The king's profession of faith

²⁶ King Darius then wrote to all nations, peoples and languages dwelling throughout the world:

'May you prosper more and more! ²⁷ This is my decree: Throughout every dominion of my realm, let all tremble with fear before the God of Daniel:

He is the living God, he endures for ever,
his kingdom will never be destroyed
and his empire never come to an end.

²⁸ He saves, sets free, and works signs and wonders
in the heavens and on earth;
he has saved Daniel from the power of the lions.'

²⁹ This Daniel flourished in the reign of Darius and the reign of Cyrus the Persian.

The vision of the beasts, the One most venerable and the son of man

7 In the first year of Belshazzar king of Babylon, Daniel had a dream and visions that passed through his head as he lay in bed. He wrote the dream down, and this is how the narrative began: ² Daniel said, 'I have been seeing visions in the night. I saw that the four winds of heaven were stirring up the Great Sea; ³ four great beasts emerged from the sea, each different from the others. ⁴ The first was like a lion with eagle's wings and, as I looked, its wings were torn off, and it was lifted off the ground and set standing on its feet like a human; and it was given a human heart. ⁵ And there before me was a second beast, like a bear, rearing up on one side, with three ribs in its mouth, between its teeth. "Up!" came the command. "Eat quantities of flesh!" ⁶ After this I looked; and there before me was another beast, like a leopard, and with four bird's wings on its flanks; it had four heads and was granted authority. ⁷ Next, in the visions of the night, I saw another vision: there before me was a fourth beast, fearful, terrifying, very strong; it had great iron teeth, and it ate its victims, crushed them, and trampled their remains underfoot. It was different from the previous beasts and had ten horns.ᵃ

⁸ 'While I was looking at these horns, I saw another horn sprouting among them, a little one; three of the original horns were pulled out by the roots to make way for it; and in this horn I saw eyes like human eyes, and a mouth full of boasting.

7a The ten Seleucid kings. The little horn (v. 8) will be Antiochus Epiphanes the persecutor.

9 While I was watching,
  thrones were set in place
  and one most venerable took his seat.
  His robe was white as snow,
  the hair of his head as pure as wool.
  His throne was a blaze of flames,
  its wheels were a burning fire.
10 A stream of fire poured out,
  issuing from his presence.
  A thousand thousand waited on him,
  ten thousand times ten thousand stood
        before him.
  The court was in session
  and the books lay open.

11 'I went on watching: then, because of the
noise made by the boastings of the horn, as I
watched, the beast was put to death, and its
body destroyed and committed to the flames.
12 The other beasts were deprived of their empire, but received a lease of life for a season
and a time.

13 I was gazing into the visions of the night,
  when I saw, coming on the clouds of
        heaven,
  as it were a son of man.[b]
  He came to the One most venerable
  and was led into his presence.
14 On him was conferred rule,
  honour and kingship,
  and all peoples, nations and languages
        became his servants.
  His rule is an everlasting rule
  which will never pass away,
  and his kingship will never come to
        an end.

The interpretation of the vision

15 'I, Daniel, was deeply disturbed and the visions that passed through my head alarmed
me. 16 So I approached one of those who were
standing by and asked him about all this. And
in reply he revealed to me what these things
meant. 17 "These four great beasts are four
kings who will rise up from the earth. 18 Those
who receive royal power are the holy ones of

the Most High, and kingship will be theirs for
ever, for ever and ever." 19 Then I asked about
the fourth beast, different from all the rest,
very terrifying, with iron teeth and bronze
claws; it ate its victims, crushed them, and
trampled their remains underfoot; 20 and
about the ten horns on its head—and why the
other horn sprouted and the three original
horns fell, and why this horn had eyes and a
mouth full of boasting, and why it looked
more impressive than its fellows. 21 This was
the horn I had watched making war on the
holy ones and proving the stronger, 22 until the
coming of the One most venerable who gave
judgement in favour of the holy ones of the
Most High, when the time came for the holy
ones to assume kingship. 23 This is what he
said:

"The fourth beast
  is to be a fourth kingdom on earth,
  different from all other kingdoms.
  It will devour the whole world,
  trample it underfoot and crush it.
24 As for the ten horns: from this kingdom
  will rise ten kings, and another after them;
  this one will be different from the previous
        ones
  and will bring down three kings;
25 he will insult the Most High,
  and torment the holy ones of the Most
        High.
  He will plan to alter the seasons and the
        Law,
  and the Saints will be handed over to him
  for a time, two times, and half a time.
26 But the court will sit, and he will be
        stripped of his royal authority
  which will be finally destroyed and
        reduced to nothing.
27 And kingship and rule
  and the splendours of all the kingdoms
        under heaven

7b This human figure represents the people of God, but may
well bear an individual sense too, as their leader and representative.

will be given to the people of the holy ones
of the Most High,
whose royal power is an eternal power,
whom every empire will serve and obey."

28 'Here the narrative ends.

'I, Daniel, was greatly disturbed in mind,
and I grew pale; but I kept these things to myself.'

Daniel's vision

8 In the third year of King Belshazzar a vision appeared to me, Daniel, after the one
that had originally appeared to me. 2 I gazed at
the vision, and as I gazed I found myself in
Susa, the citadel in the province of Elam; gazing at the vision, I found myself at the Ulai
Gate. 3 I raised my eyes to look, and I saw a
ram standing in front of the gate. It had two
horns; both were tall, but one taller than the
other, and the one that rose the higher was the
second. 4 I saw the ram butting westwards,
northwards and southwards. No animal could
stand up to it, nothing could escape its power.
It did as it pleased and became strong.

5 This is what I observed: a he-goat from the
west, encroaching over the entire surface of
the world though never touching the ground,
and between its eyes the goat had one majestic
horn. 6 It advanced on the two-horned ram,
which I had seen standing in front of the gate,
and charged at it in the full force of its fury. 7 I
saw it reach the ram; it was enraged with the
ram and struck it, breaking both its horns, so
that the ram was not strong enough to hold its
ground; it threw it to the ground and trampled it underfoot; no one was there to rescue
the ram. 8 The he-goat then grew more powerful than ever; but at the height of its strength
the great horn snapped, and in its place
sprouted four majestic horns, pointing to the
four winds of heaven.

9 From one of these, the small one, sprang a
horn which grew to great size towards south
and east and towards the Land of Splendour.
10 It grew right up to the armies of heaven and
flung armies and stars to the ground, and

trampled them underfoot. 11 It even challenged the power of the Prince of the army; it
abolished the perpetual sacrifice and overthrew the foundation of his sanctuary, 12 and
the army too; over the sacrifice it installed iniquity and flung truth to the ground; the horn
was active and successful.

13 I heard a holy one speaking, and another
holy one say to the speaker, 'How long is this
vision to be—of perpetual sacrifice, of horrifying iniquity, of sanctuary and army trampled
underfoot?' 14 The first replied, 'Until two
thousand three hundred evenings and mornings have gone by: then the sanctuary will
have its rights restored.'

The angel Gabriel interprets the vision

15 As I, Daniel, gazed at the vision and tried to
understand it, I saw someone standing in front
of me who looked like a man. 16 I heard a
human voice cry over the Ulai, 'Gabriel, tell
him the meaning of the vision!' 17 He approached the place where I was standing; as he
approached, I was seized with terror and fell
prostrate on the ground. 'Son of man,' he said
to me, 'understand this: the vision shows the
time of the End.' 18 He was still speaking,
when I fainted, face downwards on the
ground. He touched me, however, and raised
me to my feet. 19 'Come,' he said, 'I shall tell
you what is going to happen when the Retribution is over, about the final times. 20 As for
the ram which you saw, its two horns are the
kings of Media and of Persia. 21 The hairy he-
goat is the king of Greece, the large horn between its eyes is the first king. 22 The horn
which snapped and the four horns which
sprouted in its place are four kingdoms rising
from his nation but not having his strength.

23 'And at the end of their reign, when the
measure of their sins is full,
a king will arise, a proud-faced, ingenious-
minded man.
24 His power will grow greater and greater,
though not through any power of his own;
he will plot incredible schemes,

he will succeed in whatever he undertakes,
he will destroy powerful men
and the holy ones, God's people.

25 Such will be his resourcefulness of mind
that all his treacherous activities will
succeed.
He will grow arrogant of heart
and destroy many people by taking them
unawares.
He will challenge the power of the Prince
of princes
but, without any human intervention, he
will be broken.

26 The vision of the evenings and the
mornings which has been revealed
is true,
but you must keep the vision secret, for
there are still many days to go.'

27 At this I, Daniel, lost consciousness; I was
ill for several days. Then I got up to discharge
my duties in the king's service, keeping the vision a secret and still not understanding what
it meant.

Daniel's prayer

9 It was the first year of Darius son of Artaxerxes, a Mede by race who assumed the
throne of Chaldaea. 2 In the first year of his
reign I, Daniel, was studying the scriptures,
counting over the number of years—as revealed by Yahweh to the prophet Jeremiah—
that were to pass before the desolation of Jerusalem would come to an end, namely seventy
years. 3 I turned my face to the Lord God begging for time to pray and to plead, with fasting, sackcloth and ashes. 4 I pleaded with Yahweh my God and made this confession:

'O my Lord, God great and to be feared,
you keep the covenant and show faithful love
towards those who love you and who observe
your commandments: 5 we have sinned, we
have done wrong, we have acted wickedly, we
have betrayed your commandments and rulings and turned away from them. 6 We have
not listened to your servants the prophets, who
spoke in your name to our kings, our chief

men, our ancestors and all people of the country. 7 Saving justice, Lord, is yours; we have
only the look of shame we wear today, we, the
people of Judah, the inhabitants of Jerusalem,
the whole of Israel, near and far away, in every
country to which you have dispersed us because of the treachery we have committed
against you. 8 To us, our kings, our chief men
and our ancestors, belongs the look of shame,
O Yahweh, since we have sinned against you.
9 And it is for the Lord our God to have mercy
and to pardon, since we have betrayed him,
10 and have not listened to the voice of Yahweh
our God nor followed the laws he has given us
through his servants the prophets. 11 The
whole of Israel has flouted your Law and
turned away, unwilling to listen to your voice;
and the curse and imprecation written in the
Law of Moses, the servant of God, have come
pouring down on us, because we have sinned
against him. 12 He has carried out the threats
which he made against us and the chief men
who governed us—that he would bring so
great a disaster down on us that the fate of
Jerusalem would find no parallel under all
heaven. 13 And now, as written in the Law of
Moses, this whole calamity has befallen us;
even so, we have not appeased Yahweh our
God by renouncing our crimes and learning
your truth. 14 Yahweh has watched for the
right moment to bring disaster on us, since
Yahweh our God is just in all his dealings with
us, and we have not listened to his voice.
15 And now, Lord our God, who by your
mighty hand brought us out of Egypt—the
renown you won then endures to this day—
we have sinned, we have done wrong. 16 Lord,
by all your acts of saving justice, turn away
your anger and your fury from Jerusalem,
your city, your holy mountain, for as a result of
our sins and the crimes of our ancestors, Jerusalem and your people are objects of scorn to
all who surround us. 17 And now, our God, listen to the prayer and pleading of your servant.
For your own sake, Lord, let your face smile
again on your desolate sanctuary. 18 Listen, my
God, listen to us; open your eyes and look at

our plight and at the city that bears your name. Relying not on our upright deeds but on your great mercy, we pour out our plea to you. ¹⁹Listen, Lord! Forgive, Lord! Hear, Lord, and act! For your own sake, my God, do not delay—since your city and your people alike bear your name.'

The angel Gabriel explains the prophecy

²⁰I was still speaking, still at prayer, confessing my own sins and the sins of my people Israel, and placing my plea before Yahweh my God for the holy mountain of my God, ²¹still speaking, still at prayer, when Gabriel, the being I had originally seen in vision, swooped on me in full flight at the hour of the evening sacrifice. ²²He came, he spoke, he said to me, 'Now, Daniel; I have come down to teach you how to understand. ²³When your pleading began, a word was uttered, and I have come to tell you. You are a man specially chosen. Grasp the meaning of the word, understand the vision:

²⁴'Seventy weeks are decreed
 for your people and your holy city,
 for putting an end to transgression,
 for placing the seal on sin,
 for expiating crime,
 for introducing everlasting uprightness
 for setting the seal on vision and on
  prophecy,
 for anointing the holy of holies.
²⁵Know this, then, and understand:
 From the time there went out this
  message:
 "Return and rebuild Jerusalem"
 to the coming of an Anointed Prince,
  seven weeks and sixty-two weeks,
 with squares and ramparts restored and
  rebuilt,
 but in a time of trouble.
²⁶And after the sixty-two weeks
 an Anointed One put to death without
  his . . .
 city and sanctuary ruined
 by a prince who is to come.

The end of that prince will be catastrophe
 and, until the end, there will be war
 and all the devastation decreed.
²⁷He will strike a firm alliance with many
  people
 for the space of a week;
 and for the space of one half-week
 he will put a stop to sacrifice and oblation,
 and on the wing of the Temple will be the
  appalling abomination[a]
until the end, until the doom assigned to
  the devastator.'

The vision of the man dressed in linen

10 In the third year of Cyrus king of Persia, a revelation was made to Daniel known as Belteshazzar, a true revelation of a great conflict. He grasped the meaning of the revelation; what it meant was disclosed to him in a vision.

²At that time, I, Daniel, was doing a three-week penance; ³I ate no agreeable food, touched no meat or wine, and did not anoint myself, until these three weeks were over. ⁴On the twenty-fourth day of the first month, as I stood on the bank of that great river, the Tigris, ⁵I raised my eyes to look about me, and this is what I saw:

A man dressed in linen, with a belt of pure
  gold round his waist:
⁶his body was like beryl,
 his face looked like lightning,
 his eyes were like fiery torches,
 his arms and his face had the gleam of
  burnished bronze,
 the sound of his voice was like the roar of a
  multitude.

⁷I, Daniel, alone saw the apparition; the men who were with me did not see the vision, but so great a trembling overtook them that they fled to hide. ⁸I was left alone, gazing on this great vision; I was powerless, my appear-

9a The Hebr. evokes idols of Baal. Antiochus set up a statue of Zeus in the Temple.

ance was changed and contorted; my strength deserted me.

The apparition of the angel

⁹ I heard a voice speaking, and at the sound of the voice I fell fainting, face downwards on the ground. ¹⁰ I felt a hand touching me, setting my knees and my hands trembling. ¹¹ He said, 'Daniel, you are a man specially chosen; understand the words that I am about to say; stand up; I have been sent to you now.' He said this, and I stood up trembling. ¹² He then said, 'Daniel, do not be afraid: from that first day when, the better to understand, you resolved to mortify yourself before God, your words have been heard; and your words are the reason why I have come. ¹³ The Prince of the kingdom of Persia has been resisting me for twenty-one days, but Michael, one of the Chief Princes, came to my assistance. I have left him confronting the kings of Persia ¹⁴ and have come to tell you what will happen to your people in the final days. For here is a new vision about those days.'

¹⁵ When he had said these things to me, I prostrated myself on the ground, without saying a word; ¹⁶ then someone looking like a man touched my lips. I opened my mouth to speak, and I said to the person standing in front of me, 'My lord, anguish overcomes me at this vision, and my strength deserts me. ¹⁷ How can your servant speak to my lord now that I have no strength left and my breath fails me?' ¹⁸ Once again, the person like a man touched me; he gave me strength. ¹⁹ 'Do not be afraid,' he said, 'you are a man specially chosen; peace be with you; play the man, be strong!' And as he spoke to me I felt strong again and said, 'Let my lord speak, you have given me strength.'

The prelude to the prophecy

²⁰ᵃ He then said, 'Do you know why I have come to you? ²¹ᵃ It is to tell you what is written in the Book of Truth. ²⁰ᵇ I must go back to fight the Prince of Persia; when I have overcome him, the Prince of Javan will come next.

²¹ᵇ In all this, there is no one to lend me support except Michael your Prince,

11 on whom I rely to give me support and to reinforce me. ² And now I shall tell you the truth about these things.

Early struggles between Seleucids and Ptolemies

'Three more kings are going to rise in Persia; a fourth will come and be richer than all the others, and when, thanks to his wealth, he has grown powerful, he will make war on all the kingdoms of Greece. ³ A mighty king will rise and govern a vast empire and do whatever he pleases. ⁴ But once he has come to power, his empire will be broken up and parcelled out to the four winds of heaven, though not to his descendants: it will not be ruled as he ruled it, for his sovereignty will be uprooted and will pass to others than his own descendants.

⁵ 'The king of the south will grow powerful, but one of his princes will grow more powerful still, with an empire greater than his own. ⁶ Some years later, these will conclude a treaty and, to ratify the agreement, the daughter of the king of the south will go to the king of the north. Her arm will not, however, retain its strength, nor his posterity endure: she will be handed over, she, her escorts and her child, and he who has had authority over her. In due time ⁷ a sprig from her roots will rise in his place, will march on the defences, force the stronghold of the king of the north, and succeed in overcoming them. ⁸ He will even carry off all their gods, their statues, their precious gold and silver vessels as booty to Egypt. For some years he will leave the king of the north in peace, ⁹ but the latter will invade the kingdom of the king of the south, then retire to his own country. ¹⁰ His sons will next be on the march, mustering a host of powerful forces; and he will advance, deploy, break through and march on the southern stronghold once again. ¹¹ The king of the south will fly into a rage and set out to give battle to the king of the north, who will have an immense army on his side, but this army will be defeated by him. ¹² The

army will be annihilated; he will be triumphant; he will overthrow tens of thousands; yet he will have no enduring strength. ¹³ The king of the north will come back, having recruited an even larger army than before, and finally, after some years, he will advance a second time with a great army and plentiful supplies. ¹⁴ At that time, many will take up arms against the king of the south, and the more violent of your own people will rebel in the hope of realising the vision; but they will fail. ¹⁵ The king of the north will then come and throw up siege-works to capture a strongly fortified city. The forces of the south will not stand their ground; the pick of the people will not be strong enough to resist. ¹⁶ The invader will do as he pleases, no one will be able to resist him: he will take his stand in the Land of Splendour, destruction in his hands. ¹⁷ He will set about conquering his entire kingdom, but will then make a treaty with him and, to overthrow the kingdom, give him a woman's hand; but this will not last or be to his advantage. ¹⁸ He will next turn to the coasts and islands and conquer many of them, but a magistrate will put a stop to his outrages in such a way that he will be unable to repay outrage for outrage.

¹⁹ 'He will then turn on the strongholds of his own country, but will stumble, fall, and never be seen again. ²⁰ In his place there will rise a man who will send an extortioner to despoil the royal splendour; in a few days he will be shattered, though neither publicly nor in battle.

Antiochus Epiphanes

²¹ 'In his place will rise a wretch: royal honours will not be given to him, but rather he will insinuate himself into them at his pleasure and will gain possession of the kingdom by intrigue. ²² Armies will be utterly routed and crushed by him, the Prince of the covenant too. ²³ Through his alliances he will act treacherously and, despite the smallness of his following, grow ever stronger. ²⁴ At his pleasure, he will invade rich provinces, acting as his fathers or his fathers' fathers never acted, distributing among them plunder, spoil and wealth, plotting his stratagems against the fortresses—for a time.

²⁵ 'He will summon up his might and courage against the king of the south with a great army. The king of the south will march to war with a huge and powerful army but will not succeed, since he will be outwitted by trickery. ²⁶ Those who shared his food will ruin him; his army will be swept away, many will fall in the slaughter.

²⁷ 'The two kings, seated at one table, hearts bent on evil, will tell their lies; but they will not have their way, for the appointed time is still to come. ²⁸ Then the wretch will return greatly enriched to his own country, his heart set against the holy covenant; he will take action and then return to his own country. ²⁹ In due time, he will make his way southwards again, but this time the outcome will not be as before. ³⁰ The ships of the Kittim will oppose him, and he will be worsted. He will retire and take furious action against the holy covenant and, as before, will favour those who forsake that holy covenant.

³¹ 'Forces of his will come and profane the Citadel-Sanctuary; they will abolish the perpetual sacrifice and install the appalling abomination there. ³² Those who break the covenant he will seduce by his blandishments, but the people who know their God will stand firm and take action. ³³ Those of the people who are wise leaders will instruct many; for some days, however, they will stumble from sword and flame, captivity and pillage. ³⁴ And thus stumbling, little help will they receive, though many will be scheming in their support. ³⁵ Of the wise leaders some will stumble, and so a number of them will be purged, purified and made clean—until the time of the End, for the appointed time is still to come.

³⁶ 'The king will do as he pleases, growing more and more arrogant, considering himself greater than all the gods; he will utter incredible blasphemies against the God of gods, and he will thrive until the wrath reaches bursting point; for what has been decreed will certainly

be fulfilled. 37 Heedless of his fathers' gods, heedless of the god whom women love, heedless of any god whatever, he will consider himself greatest of all. 38 Instead of them, he will honour the god of fortresses, will honour a god unknown to his ancestors with gold and silver, precious stones and valuable presents. 39 He will use the people of an alien god to defend the fortresses; he will confer great honours on those whom he acknowledges, by giving them wide authority and by parcelling the country out for rent.

The end of the persecutor

40 'When the time comes for the End, the king of the south will try conclusions with him; but the king of the north will come storming down on him with chariots, cavalry, and a large fleet. He will invade countries, overrun them and drive on. 41 He will invade the Land of Splendour, and many will fall; but Edom, Moab, and what remains of the sons of Ammon will escape him.

42 'He will reach out to attack countries: Egypt will not escape him. 43 The gold and silver treasures and all the valuables of Egypt will lie in his power. Libyans and Cushites will be at his feet: 44 but reports coming from the East and the north will worry him, and in great fury he will set out to bring ruin and complete destruction to many. 45 He will pitch the tents of his royal headquarters between the sea and the mountains of the Holy Splendour. Yet he will come to his end—there will be no help for him.'

12 'At that time Michael will arise—the great Prince, defender of your people. That will be a time of great distress, unparalleled since nations first came into existence. When that time comes, your own people will be spared—all those whose names are found written in the Book.

Resurrection and retribution

2 'Of those who are sleeping in the Land of Dust, many will awaken, some to everlasting life, some to shame and everlasting disgrace. 3 Those who are wise will shine as brightly as the expanse of the heavens, and those who have instructed many in uprightness, as bright as stars for all eternity.

4 'But you, Daniel, must keep these words secret and keep the book sealed until the time of the End. Many will roam about, this way and that, and wickedness will continue to increase.'

The sealed prophecy

5 I, Daniel, then looked and saw two other people standing, one on the near bank of the river, the other on the far. 6 One of them said to the man dressed in linen who was standing further up the stream, 'How long until these wonders take place?' 7 I heard the man speak who was dressed in linen, standing further up the stream: he raised his right hand and his left to heaven and swore by him who lives for ever, 'A time and two times, and half a time; and all these things will come true, once the crushing of the holy people's power is over.' 8 I listened but did not understand. I then said, 'My lord, what is to be the outcome?' 9 'Go, Daniel,' he said. 'These words are to remain secret and sealed until the time of the End. 10 Many will be cleansed, made white and purged; the wicked will persist in doing wrong; the wicked will never understand; those who are wise will understand. 11 From the moment that the perpetual sacrifice is abolished and the appalling abomination set up: a thousand two hundred and ninety days. 12 Blessed is he who perseveres and attains a thousand three hundred and thirty-five days. 13 But you, go away and rest; and you will rise for your reward at the end of time.'

Susanna[a] and the judgement of Daniel

13 In Babylon there lived a man named Joakim. 2 He was married to a woman called Susanna daughter of Hilkiah, a woman of great beauty; and she was God-fearing, for

---

13a chh. 13–14 occur in Gk but not in the Hebr. text.

³her parents were worthy people and had instructed their daughter in the Law of Moses. ⁴Joakim was a very rich man and had a garden by his house; he used to be visited by a considerable number of the Jews, since he was held in greater respect than any other man. ⁵Two elderly men had been selected from the people, that year, to act as judges. Of such the Lord had said, 'Wickedness has come to Babylon through the elders and judges posing as guides to the people.' ⁶These men were often at Joakim's house, and all who were engaged in litigation used to come to them. ⁷At midday, when the people had gone away, Susanna would take a walk in her husband's garden. ⁸The two elders, who used to watch her every day as she came in to take her walk, gradually began to desire her. ⁹They threw reason aside, making no effort to turn their eyes to Heaven, and forgetting the demands of virtue. ¹⁰Both were inflamed by passion for her, but they hid their desire from each other, ¹¹for they were ashamed to admit the longing to sleep with her, ¹²but they made sure of watching her every day. ¹³One day, having parted with the words, 'Let us go home, then, it is time for the midday meal,' they went off in different directions, ¹⁴only to retrace their steps and find themselves face to face again. Obliged then to explain, they admitted their desire and agreed to look for an opportunity of surprising her alone. ¹⁵So they waited for a favourable moment; and one day Susanna came as usual, accompanied only by two young maidservants. The day was hot and she wanted to bathe in the garden. ¹⁶There was no one about except the two elders, spying on her from their hiding place. ¹⁷She said to the servants, 'Bring me some oil and balsam and shut the garden door while I bathe.' ¹⁸They did as they were told, shutting the garden door and going back to the house by a side entrance to fetch what she had asked for; they knew nothing about the elders, for they had concealed themselves.

¹⁹Hardly were the maids gone than the two elders sprang up and rushed upon her. ²⁰'Look,' they said, 'the garden door is shut, no one can see us. We want to have you, so give in and let us! ²¹Refuse, and we shall both give evidence that a young man was with you and that this was why you sent your maids away.' ²²Susanna sighed. 'I am trapped,' she said, 'whatever I do. If I agree, it means death for me; if I resist, I cannot get away from you. ²³But I prefer to fall innocent into your power than to sin in the eyes of the Lord.' ²⁴She then cried out as loud as she could. The two elders began shouting too, putting the blame on her, ²⁵and one of them ran to open the garden door. ²⁶The household, hearing the shouting in the garden, rushed out by the side entrance to see what had happened to her. ²⁷Once the elders had told their story, the servants were thoroughly taken aback, since nothing of this sort had ever been said of Susanna.

²⁸Next day a meeting was held at the house of her husband Joakim. The two elders arrived, full of their wicked plea against Susanna, to have her put to death. ²⁹They addressed the company, 'Summon Susanna daughter of Hilkiah and wife of Joakim.' She was sent for, ³⁰and came accompanied by her parents, her children and all her relations. ³¹Susanna was very graceful and beautiful to look at; ³²she was veiled, so the wretches made her unveil in order to feast their eyes on her beauty. ³³All her own people were weeping, and so were all the others who saw her. ³⁴The two elders stood up, with all the people round them, and laid their hands on her head. ³⁵Tearfully she turned her eyes to Heaven, her heart confident in God. ³⁶The elders then spoke, 'While we were walking by ourselves in the garden, this woman arrived with two maids. She shut the garden door and then dismissed the servants. ³⁷A young man, who had been hiding, went over to her and they lay together. ³⁸From the end of the garden where we were, we saw this crime taking place and hurried towards them. ³⁹Though we saw them together, we were unable to catch the man: he was too strong for us; he opened the door and took to his heels. ⁴⁰We did, however, catch this woman and ask her who the young

man was. ⁴¹She refused to tell us. That is our evidence.'

Since they were elders of the people and judges, the assembly accepted their word: Susanna was condemned to death. ⁴²She cried out as loud as she could, 'Eternal God, you know all secrets and everything before it happens; ⁴³you know that they have given false evidence against me. And now I must die, innocent as I am of everything their malice has invented against me!'

⁴⁴The Lord heard her cry ⁴⁵and, as she was being led away to die, he roused the holy spirit residing in a young boy called Daniel ⁴⁶who began to shout, 'I am innocent of this woman's death!' ⁴⁷At this all the people turned to him and asked, 'What do you mean by that?' ⁴⁸Standing in the middle of the crowd, he replied, 'Are you so stupid, children of Israel, as to condemn a daughter of Israel unheard, and without troubling to find out the truth? ⁴⁹Go back to the scene of the trial: these men have given false evidence against her.'

⁵⁰All the people hurried back, and the elders said to Daniel, 'Come and sit with us and tell us what you mean, since God has given you the gifts that elders have.' ⁵¹Daniel said, 'Keep the men well apart from each other, for I want to question them.' ⁵²When the men had been separated, Daniel had one of them brought to him. 'You have grown old in wickedness,' he said, 'and now the sins of your earlier days have overtaken you, ⁵³you with your unjust judgements, your condemnation of the innocent, your acquittal of the guilty, although the Lord has said, "You must not put the innocent and upright to death." ⁵⁴Now then, since you saw her so clearly, tell me what sort of tree you saw them lying under.' He replied, 'Under an acacia tree.' ⁵⁵Daniel said, 'Indeed! Your lie recoils on your own head:^b the angel of God has already received from him your sentence and will cut you in half.' ⁵⁶He dismissed the man, ordered the other to be brought and said to him, 'Son of Canaan, not of Judah, beauty has seduced you, lust has led your heart astray! ⁵⁷This is how you have

been behaving with the daughters of Israel, and they have been too frightened to resist; but here is a daughter of Judah who could not stomach your wickedness! ⁵⁸Now then, tell me what sort of tree you surprised them under.' He replied, 'Under an aspen tree.' ⁵⁹Daniel said, 'Indeed! Your lie recoils on your own head: the angel of God is waiting with a sword to rend you in half, and destroy the pair of you.'

⁶⁰Then the whole assembly shouted, blessing God, the Saviour of those who trust in him. ⁶¹And they turned on the two elders whom Daniel had convicted of false evidence out of their own mouths. ⁶²As the Law of Moses prescribes, they were given the same punishment as they had schemed to inflict on their neighbour. They were put to death. And thus, that day, an innocent life was saved. ⁶³Hilkiah and his wife gave thanks to God for their daughter Susanna, and so did her husband Joakim and all his relations, because she had been acquitted of anything dishonourable.

⁶⁴From that day onwards, Daniel's reputation stood high with the people.

Daniel and the priests of Bel^a

14 When King Astyages joined his ancestors, Cyrus of Persia succeeded him. ²Daniel was very close to the king, who respected him more than any of his other friends. ³Now, in Babylon there was an idol called Bel, to which twelve bushels of the finest flour, forty sheep and six measures of wine were offered every day. ⁴The king venerated this idol and used to go and worship it every day. Daniel, however, worshipped his own God. ⁵'Why do you not worship Bel?' the king asked Daniel. 'I do not worship idols made by human hand,' Daniel replied, 'I worship the living God who made heaven and earth and who is lord over all living creatures.'

13b In Gk, the punishment and the tree in both cases have similar sounds: *shinos/schisei, prinos/kataprisei.*

14a Another name for Marduk, chief god of Babylon.

6 'Do you not believe, then,' said the king, 'that Bel is a living god? Can you not see how much he eats and drinks each day?' 7 Daniel laughed. 'Your Majesty,' he said, 'do not be taken in; he is clay inside, and bronze outside, and has never eaten or drunk anything.' 8 This made the king angry; he summoned his priests, 'Tell me who eats all this food,' he said, 'or die. Prove to me that Bel really eats it, and I will have Daniel put to death for blaspheming him.' 9 Daniel said to the king, 'Let it be as you say.'

10 There were seventy of these priests, to say nothing of their wives and children. The king went to the temple of Bel, taking Daniel with him. 11 The priests of Bel said to him, 'We shall now go out, and you, Your Majesty, will lay out the meal and mix the wine and set it out. Then, lock the door and seal it with your personal seal. If, when you return in the morning, you do not find that everything has been eaten by Bel, let us be put to death; otherwise let Daniel, that slanderer!' 12 They were thinking—hence their confidence—of a secret entrance which they had made under the table, and by which they came in regularly and took the offerings away. 13 When the priests had gone and the king had set out the food for Bel, 14 Daniel made his servants bring ashes and spread them all over the temple floor, with no other witness than the king. They then left the building, shut the door and, sealing it with the king's seal, went away. 15 That night, as usual, the priests came with their wives and children; they ate and drank everything.

16 The king was up very early next morning, and Daniel with him. 17 'Daniel,' said the king, 'are the seals intact?' 'They are intact, Your Majesty,' he replied. 18 The king then opened the door and, taking one look at the table, exclaimed, 'You are great, O Bel! There is no deception in you!' 19 But Daniel laughed; and, restraining the king from going in any further, he said, 'Look at the floor and take note whose footmarks these are!' 20 'I can see the footmarks of men, of women and of children,' said the king, 21 and angrily ordered the priests to

be arrested, with their wives and children. They then showed him the secret door through which they used to come and take what was on the table. 22 The king had them put to death and handed Bel over to Daniel who destroyed both the idol and its temple.

Daniel kills the dragon

23 There was a great dragon which the Babylonians worshipped too. 24 The king said to Daniel, 'Are you going to tell me that this is made of bronze? Look, it is alive; it eats and drinks; you cannot deny that this is a living god; worship it, then.' 25 Daniel replied, 'I will worship the Lord my God; he is the living God. With your permission, Your Majesty, without using either sword or club, I shall kill this dragon.' 26 'You have my permission,' said the king. 27 Whereupon, Daniel took some pitch, some fat and some hair and boiled them up together, rolled the mixture into balls and fed them to the dragon; the dragon swallowed them and burst. Daniel said, 'Now look at the sort of thing you worship!' 28 The Babylonians were furious when they heard about this and rose against the king. 'The king has turned Jew,' they said, 'he has allowed Bel to be overthrown, and the dragon to be killed, and he has put the priests to death.' 29 So they went to the king and said, 'Hand Daniel over to us or else we shall kill you and your family.' 30 They pressed him so hard that the king found himself forced to hand Daniel over to them.

Daniel in the lion pit

31 They threw Daniel into the lion pit, and there he stayed for six days. 32 In the pit were seven lions, which were given two human bodies and two sheep every day; but for this period they were not given anything, to make sure they would eat Daniel.

33 Now, the prophet Habakkuk was in Judaea: he had been making a stew and breaking up bread into a basket. He was on his way to the fields, taking this to the harvesters, 34 when the angel of the Lord spoke to him, 'Take the meal you are carrying to Babylon, and give it

to Daniel in the lion pit.' ³⁵'Lord,' replied Habakkuk, 'I have not even seen Babylon and know nothing about this pit.' ³⁶The angel of the Lord took hold of his head and carried him off by the hair to Babylon where, with a great blast of his breath, he set Habakkuk down on the edge of the pit. ³⁷'Daniel, Daniel,' Habakkuk shouted, 'take the meal that God has sent you.' ³⁸And Daniel said, 'You have kept me in mind, O God; you have not deserted those who love you.' ³⁹Rising to

his feet, he ate the meal, while the angel of God carried Habakkuk back in a moment to his own country.

⁴⁰On the seventh day, the king came to lament over Daniel; on reaching the pit he looked inside, and there sat Daniel. ⁴¹'You are great, O Lord, God of Daniel,' he exclaimed, 'there is no god but you!' ⁴²He then had Daniel released from the pit and the plotters of Daniel's ruin thrown in instead, where they were instantly eaten before his eyes.

1 The word of Yahweh which came to Hosea son of Beeri during the reigns of Uzziah, Jotham, Ahaz and Hezekiah kings of Judah, and of Jeroboam son of Joash, king of Israel.

Hosea's marriage: his three children

² The beginning of what Yahweh said through Hosea:

Yahweh said to Hosea, 'Go, marry a whore, and get children with a whore; for the country itself has become nothing but a whore by abandoning Yahweh.'

³ So he went and married Gomer daughter of Diblaim, who conceived and bore him a son. ⁴ Yahweh then said to him, 'Call him Jezreel, for in a little while I shall punish the House of Jehu for the bloodshed at Jezreel[a] and put an end to the sovereignty of the House of Israel. ⁵ When that day comes, I shall break the bow of Israel in the Valley of Jezreel.'

⁶ She conceived a second time and gave birth to a daughter. Yahweh then said to him, 'Call her Lo-Ruhamah, for I shall show no more pity for the House of Israel, I shall never forgive them again. ⁷ (Instead, I shall take pity on the House of Judah and shall save them, not by bow or sword or force of arms, not by horses or horsemen, but by Yahweh their God.)'

⁸ After weaning Lo-Ruhamah, she conceived and gave birth to a son. ⁹ Yahweh said, 'Call him Lo-Ammi, for you are not my people and I do not exist for you.'

Hope for the future

2 But the Israelites will become as numerous as the sands of the sea, which cannot be measured or counted. In the very place where they were told, 'You are not my people,' they will be told they are 'Children of the living God'.
² The Judaeans and Israelites will be reunited
and will choose themselves a single head,
and will spread far beyond their country,
for great will be the Day of Jezreel!
³ Then call your brothers, 'My people',
and your sisters, 'You have been pitied'.

Yahweh and his unfaithful wife

⁴ To court, take your mother to court!
For she is no longer my wife
nor am I her husband.
She must either remove her whoring ways
from her face
and her adulteries from between her
breasts,
⁵ or I shall strip her and expose her
naked as the day she was born;
I shall make her as bare as the desert,
I shall make her as dry as arid country,
and let her die of thirst.
⁶ And I shall feel no pity for her children
since they are the children of her
whorings.
⁷ Yes, their mother has played the whore,
she who conceived them has disgraced
herself
by saying, 'I shall chase after my lovers;
they will assure me my keep,
my wool, my flax, my oil and my
drinks.'

⁸ This is why I shall block her way with
thorns,
and wall her in to stop her in her tracks;

1a 2 K 9:15–10:14.

9 then if she chases her lovers she will not
      catch them,
   if she looks for them she will not find
      them,
   and then she will say, 'I shall go back to
      my first husband,
   I was better off then than I am now;'
10 she had never realised before
   that I was the one who was giving her
      the grain, new wine and oil,
   giving her more and more silver and
      gold
   which they have spent on Baal!

11 This is why I shall take back my grain
      when it is due
   and my new wine, when the season for it
      comes.
   I shall withdraw my wool and my flax
   which were to cover her naked body,
12 and then display her infamy before her
      lovers' eyes—
   no one will take her from me then!
13 I shall put an end to all her merrymaking,
   her festivals, her New Moons and her
      Sabbaths
   and all her solemn feasts.
14 I shall make her vines and fig trees derelict
   of which she used to say,
   'These are the pay my lovers gave me.'
   I shall turn them into a jungle:
   wild animals will feed on them.
15 I mean to make her pay for the feast-days
   on which she burnt incense to the Baals,
   when she tricked herself out in her
         earrings and necklaces
   to chase after her lovers,
   and forget me!
   —declares Yahweh.

Reconciliation

16 But look, I am going to seduce her
   and lead her into the desert
   and speak to her heart.
17 There I shall give her back her vineyards,
   and make the Vale of Achor[a] a gateway
      of hope.

There she will respond as when she was
      young,
   as on the day when she came up from
      Egypt.

18 When that day comes—declares
      Yahweh—
   you will call me, 'My husband',
   no more will you call me, 'My Baal'.
19 I shall banish the names of the Baals from
      her lips
   and their name will be mentioned no
      more.

20 When that day comes I shall make a treaty
      for them with the wild animals,
   with the birds of heaven and the creeping
      things of the earth;
   I shall break the bow and the sword
   and warfare, and banish them from the
      country,
   and I will let them sleep secure.
21 I shall betroth you to myself for ever,
   I shall betroth you in uprightness and
      justice,
   and faithful love and tenderness.
22 Yes, I shall betroth you to myself in loyalty
   and in the knowledge of Yahweh.
23 When that day comes, I shall respond
   —declares Yahweh—
   I shall respond to the heavens
   and they will respond to the earth
24 and the earth will respond to the grain, the
      new wine and oil,
   and they will respond to Jezreel.
25 I shall sow her in the country to be mine,
   I shall take pity on Lo-Ruhamah,
   I shall tell Lo-Ammi, 'You are my
      people,'
   and he will say, 'You are my God.'

Second account of Hosea's marriage

3 Yahweh said to me, 'Go again, love a
   woman who loves another man, an adulteress, and love her as Yahweh loves the Is-

2a The scene of Achan's sin, Jos 7:24.

raelites although they turn to other gods and love raisin cakes.' ² So I bought her for fifteen shekels of silver, a *homer* of barley and a skin of wine, ³ and I said to her, 'You will have to spend a long time waiting for me without playing the whore and without giving yourself to any man, and I will behave in the same way towards you.'

The explanation

⁴ For the Israelites will have to spend a long time without king or leader, without sacrifice or sacred pillar, without *ephod* or domestic images; ⁵ but after that, the Israelites will return and again seek Yahweh their God and David their king, and turn trembling to Yahweh for his bounty in the final days.

General corruption

4 Israelites, hear what Yahweh says,
for Yahweh indicts the citizens of the
    country:
there is no loyalty, no faithful love,
no knowledge of God in the country,
² only perjury and lying, murder, theft,
adultery and violence,
bloodshed after bloodshed.
³ This is why the country is in mourning
and all its citizens pining away,
the wild animals also and birds of
    the sky,
even the fish in the sea will disappear.

Against the priests

⁴ But let no one denounce, no one rebuke;
it is you, priest, that I denounce.
⁵ Priest, you will stumble in broad daylight,
and the prophet will stumble with you in
    the dark,
and I will make your mother perish.
⁶ My people perish for want of knowledge.
Since you yourself have rejected
    knowledge,
so I shall reject you from my priesthood;
since you have forgotten the teaching of
    your God,
I in my turn shall forget your children.

⁷ The more of them there have been,
the more they have sinned against me;
they have bartered their Glory for
    Shame.ᵃ
⁸ They feed on the sin of my people,
they are greedy for their iniquity.
⁹ But as with the people, so with the
    priest,
I shall punish them for their conduct,
I shall pay them back for their deeds.
¹⁰ They will eat but never be satisfied,
they will play the whore but not grow
    more prolific,
since they have deserted Yahweh
to give themselves up ¹¹ to whoring.

Worship in Israel is idolatrous and debauched

Old wine and new wine addle my people's
    wits,
¹² they consult their block of wood,
and their stick explains what they
    should do.
For an urge to go whoring has led them
    astray
and whoring they go and desert their
    God;
¹³ they offer sacrifice on the mountain tops,
they burn incense on the hills,
under oak and poplar and terebinth,
for pleasant is their shade.
So, although your daughters play the
    whore
and your daughters-in-law commit
    adultery,
¹⁴ I shall not punish your daughters for
    playing the whore
nor your daughters-in-law for committing
    adultery,
when the men themselves are wandering
    off with whores
and offering sacrifice with sacred
    prostitutes,
for a people with no understanding is
    doomed.

4a A contemptuous name for Baal.

[1135]

A warning to Judah and Israel

15 Though you, Israel, play the whore,
    there is no need for Judah to sin too.
  Do not go to Gilgal,
    do not go up to Beth-Aven,[b]
    do not swear oaths 'by Yahweh's life',
16 for Israel is as stubborn
    as a stubborn heifer;
  so is Yahweh likely to pasture him
    like a lamb in a broad meadow?
17 Ephraim has made a pact with idols—let
        him alone!
18 Their drunken orgy over,
    they do nothing but play the whore,
    preferring Shame to their Pride;
19 the wind with its wings will carry them off
    and their sacrifices will bring them
        nothing but disgrace.

Against the priests and royal family

5 Hear this, you priests,
  listen, House of Israel,
  pay attention, royal House,
  for it is you who have justice in your care,
  but you have been a snare at Mizpah
  and a net outspread on Tabor.
2 They have dug the ditch deep at Shittim
  and so I am going to punish them all.

The effects of obduracy

3 Ephraim have I known,
    Israel is not hidden from me;
  and yet, Ephraim, you have played the
        whore,
    Israel is befouled.
4 Their deeds do not allow them to return to
        their God,
  since an urge to play the whore possesses
        them
  and they no longer know Yahweh.
5 Israel's arrogance is his accuser,
  the guilt of Israel and Ephraim is their
        undoing,
  Judah too will be undone with them.
6 Though they go in search of Yahweh with
        their sheep and cattle,

they will not find him;
  he has withdrawn from them.
7 They have betrayed Yahweh
    because they have fathered bastards;
  now the new moon will devour them and
        their fields.

Brother wars against brother

8 Sound the horn in Gibeah,
    the trumpet in Ramah,
  raise the war cry in Beth-Aven,
    'We are behind you, Benjamin!'
9 When the day of punishment comes,
        Ephraim will be a wasteland;
  on the tribes of Israel I have pronounced
        certain doom.
10 The rulers of Judah act like men who
        move the boundary stone;
  I shall pour my wrath out on them like a
        flood.
11 Ephraim is oppressed, crushed by the
        sentence,
  for having deliberately followed a Lie.
12 Because of this, I shall be like ringworm
        for Ephraim
  and like gangrene for the House of
        Judah.

The folly of foreign alliances

13 Once Ephraim realised that he was sick
    and Judah that he had an ulcer,
  Ephraim then went to Assyria,
    he sent messengers to the Great King;
  but he has no power to cure you
    or to heal you of your sore;
14 for I shall be like a lion to Ephraim,
    like a young lion to the House of Judah;
  I myself shall rend them, then go my way,
    shall carry them off, beyond hope of
        rescue.

15 I shall go back to my place
    until they confess their guilt and seek me,
  seek me eagerly in their distress.

4b A nickname (=House of Evil) for the northern national
sanctuary at Bethel (=House of God).

The Israelites reply

6 Come, let us return to Yahweh.
He has rent us and he will heal us;
  he has struck us and he will bind up our
      wounds;

² after two days he will revive us,
  on the third day he will raise us up
  and we shall live in his presence.

³ Let us know, let us strive to know
      Yahweh;
  that he will come is as certain as the
      dawn.
  He will come to us like a shower,
  like the rain of springtime to the earth.

⁴ What am I to do with you, Ephraim?
  What am I to do with you, Judah?
  For your love is like morning mist,
  like the dew that quickly disappears.

⁵ This is why I have hacked them to pieces
      by means of the prophets,
  why I have killed them with words from
      my mouth,
  why my sentence will blaze forth like the
      dawn—

⁶ for faithful love is what pleases me, not
      sacrifice;
  knowledge of God, not burnt offerings.

Disorders in Israel

⁷ But they have broken the covenant at
      Adam,
  there they have betrayed me.

⁸ Gilead is a city of evil-doers,
  full of bloody footprints.

⁹ Like so many robbers in ambush,
  a gang of priests commits murder on the
      road to Shechem—
  what infamous behaviour!

¹⁰ At Bethel I have seen a horrible
      thing;
  there Ephraim plays the whore,
  Israel is befouled.

¹¹ For you too, Judah, a harvest is in
      store,
  when I restore my people's fortunes.

7 Whenever I would heal Israel,
  I am confronted by the guilt of Ephraim
  and the evil-doings of Samaria;
  for deceit is their principle of behaviour;
  the thief breaks into the house,
  marauders raid in the open;

² and they never pause to consider
  that I remember all their wicked deeds;
  and now their own deeds hem them in
  and stare me in the face.

Conspiracy the order of the day in Israel

³ They amuse the king with their
      wickedness
  and the chief men with their lies.

⁴ They are all adulterers, hot as an oven
  which the baker need not stoke
  from the time he has kneaded the dough
      until it rises.

⁵ At the holiday for our king,
  the ministers become inflamed with
      wine,
  while he accepts the homage of people
      ⁶who laugh at him.
  Their hearts are like an oven as they plot,
  all night their passion slumbers,
  then in the morning it bursts into flame;

⁷ yes, all of them as hot as ovens,
  they consume their rulers.
  All their kings have fallen thus,
  not one of them has ever called on me.

Israel ruined by relying on foreign powers

⁸ Ephraim mixes with the nations.
  Ephraim is a half-baked cake.

⁹ Foreigners have eaten his strength away
  but he is unconscious of it;
  even his hair is turning grey
  but he is unconscious of it.

¹⁰ (Israel's arrogance is his own accuser;
  but they do not come back to Yahweh
      their God
  or seek him, despite all this.)

¹¹ Ephraim is like a silly, witless pigeon
  calling on Egypt, turning to Assyria.

¹² Wherever they turn, I shall spread my net
      over them,

I shall bring them down like the birds of
    the sky,
I shall punish them for their perversity.

The ingratitude and punishment of Israel

13 Woe to them for having fled from me!
    Ruin seize them for having wronged me!
    I have rescued them again and again
    and they have only told lies about me.
14 Theirs is no heartfelt cry to me
    when they lament on their beds;
    when they gash themselves over the grain
        and new wine,
    they are still rebelling against me.
15 Though I supported and gave strength to
        their arms,
    they plan how to hurt me.
16 They turn to what does not exist,
    they are like a faulty bow.
    Their leaders will fall by the sword
    because of their arrogant talk;
    how they will be laughed at in Egypt!

An omen

8 Put the trumpet to your lips!
    Like an eagle, disaster is swooping on
        Yahweh's home!
    Because they have violated my covenant
    and been unfaithful to my Law,
2 in vain will they cry, 'My God!'
    In vain, 'We, Israel, know you!'
3 Israel has rejected the good,
    the enemy will pursue them.
4 They have set up kings, but without my
        consent,
    and appointed princes, but without my
        knowledge.
    With their silver and gold, they have made
        themselves idols,
    but only to be destroyed.
5 I spurn your calf,ᵃ Samaria!
    My anger blazes against them!
    How long will it be before they recover
        their innocence?
6 For it is the product of Israel—
    a craftsman made the thing,
    it is no god at all!

The calf of Samaria will be broken to
        pieces!
7 Since they sow the wind, they will reap the
        whirlwind;
    stalk without ear, it will never yield flour—
    or if it does, foreigners will swallow it.

Israel ruined by relying on foreign powers

8 Israel has himself been swallowed;
    now they are lost among the nations
    like something no one wants,
9 for having made approaches to Assyria—
    like a wild donkey, all alone.
    Ephraim has rented lovers
10 and because he has rented them from the
        nations
    I am now going to round them up;
    soon they will feel the weight of the king
        of princes!

Against the outward show of worship

11 Ephraim keeps building altars for his sins,
    these very altars are themselves a sin.
12 However much of my Law I write for him,
    Ephraim regards it as alien to him.
13 They offer sacrifices to me and eat the
        meat,
    they do not win Yahweh's favour.
    On the contrary, he will remember their
        guilt
    and punish their sins;
    they will have to go back to Egypt.
14 Israel has forgotten his Maker
    and has built palaces,
    while Judah keeps on building fortified
        towns;
    but I shall send fire down on his cities
    to devour their citadels.

The sorrows of exile

9 No merrymaking, Israel, for you,
    no rejoicing like other peoples,
    for you have deserted your God to play the
        whore,

8a The golden bull on which the sanctuary at Bethel was
centred.

you have loved the fee of prostitution on
  every threshing-floor.
2 The threshing-floor and wine-press will
  not feed them;
they will be disappointed of new wine.
3 No more will they live in Yahweh's
  country;
Ephraim will have to go back to Egypt,
and eat polluted food in Assyria.
4 No more will they pour libations of wine
  to Yahweh,
and their sacrifices will not win his
  favour
but will be like funeral fare for them:
whoever eats them will be polluted;
for their food will be for themselves
  alone,
not being offered in Yahweh's home.
5 What will you do on the solemn feast-day,
on the day of Yahweh's festival?
6 What a scene of devastation they have
  left!
Egypt will round them up, Memphis will
  bury them,
nettles will inherit their fields
and thorn-bushes invade their homesteads.

Persecution, the prophet's reward for foretelling punishment

7 The days of punishment have come,
the days of retribution are here;
Israel knows it!
'The prophet is mad and the inspired man
  a fool!'
Great has been your guilt—
all the greater then the hostility!
8 The watchman of Ephraim is with my
  God:
it is the prophet—
and a fowler's trap is placed on all his
  paths;
and in the shrine of his God there is
  enmity towards him.
9 They have become deeply corrupt
as in the days of Gibeah;
he will remember their guilt,
he will punish their sins.

Punishment for the crime at Baal-Peor

10 It was like finding grapes in the desert
  when I found Israel,
like seeing early fruit on a fig tree when I
  saw your ancestors;
but when they reached Baal-Peor they
  devoted themselves to Shame[a]
and became as loathsome as the thing they
  loved.
11 The glory of Ephraim will fly away like a
  bird:
no giving birth, no pregnancy, no
  conceiving.
12 If they rear their children, I shall take
  them away
before they grow up!
Woe to them indeed when I leave them!
13 Ephraim looked to me like Tyre, planted
  in a meadow,
so Ephraim will present his children to the
  slaughterer.
14 Give them, Yahweh—what are you to
  give?—
give them wombs that miscarry and
  dried-up breasts.

Gilgal

15 Their wickedness appeared in full at
  Gilgal,
there I came to hate them.
Because of the wickedness of their deeds
I shall drive them from my home,
I shall love them no longer;
all their princes are rebels.
16 Ephraim is blasted,
their root has dried out,
they will bear no more fruit.
And even if they do bear children
I shall slaughter the darlings of their
  womb.
17 Because they have not listened to him, my
  God will cast them off
and they will become wanderers among
  the nations.

9a A nickname for Baal, worshipped at Baal-Peor, Nb 25.

The destruction of Israel's cultic objects

10 Israel was a luxuriant vine
yielding plenty of fruit.
The more his fruit increased,
the more altars he built;
the richer his land became,
the richer he made the sacred pillars.
² Theirs is a divided heart;
now they will have to pay for it.
He himself will hack down their altars
and wreck their sacred pillars.
³ Then they will say,
'We have no king
because we have not feared Yahweh,
but what could the king do for us?'
⁴ Speeches are made, oaths sworn to no
purpose,
agreements concluded,
and so-called justice spreads like a
poisonous weed
along the furrows of the fields!

⁵ Samaria's citizens will tremble
for the calf of Beth-Aven;
the people there will mourn for it,
so will its idol-priests,
as they exult in its glory
once it has been carried away!
⁶ It will be carried off to Assyria
as tribute to the Great King.
Ephraim will reap the shame,
and Israel blush for his intentions.
⁷ Samaria has had her day.
Her king is like a straw drifting on the
water.
⁸ The high places of Aven, the sin of Israel,
will be destroyed;
thorns and thistles will grow over their
altars.
Then they will say to the mountains,
'Cover us!'
and to the hills, 'Fall on us!'

⁹ Since the days of Gibeah, Israel, you have
sinned.
There they have taken their stand,
and will not war overtake the guilty at
Gibeah?
¹⁰ I am coming to punish them;
nations will muster against them
to punish them for their two crimes.

Israel has disappointed Yahweh's hope

¹¹ Ephraim is a well-trained heifer
that loves to tread the grain.
But I have laid a yoke on her fine neck,
I shall put Ephraim into harness,
Judah will have to plough,
Jacob must draw the harrow.

¹² Sow saving justice for yourselves,
reap a harvest of faithful love;
break up your fallow ground:
it is time to seek out Yahweh
until he comes to rain saving justice down
on you.

¹³ You have ploughed wickedness,
you have reaped iniquity,
you have eaten the fruit of falsehood.
Because you have trusted in your chariots,
in your great numbers of warriors,
¹⁴ turmoil is going to break out among your
people,
and all your fortresses will be laid waste.
As Shalman laid Beth-Arbel waste
on the day of battle,
dashing mothers to pieces on their
children,
¹⁵ so it shall be done to you, Bethel,
because of your great wickedness;
at dawn, the king of Israel will be no
more.

God's love despised: his vengeance

11 When Israel was a child I loved him,
and I called my son out of Egypt.
² But the more I called, the further they
went away from me;
they offered sacrifice to Baal
and burnt incense to idols.
³ I myself taught Ephraim to walk,
I myself took them by the arm,

but they did not know that I was the one
    caring for them,
⁴ that I was leading them with human ties,
  with leading-strings of love,
that, with them, I was like someone lifting
    an infant to his cheek,
and that I bent down to feed him.

⁵ He will not have to go back to Egypt,
Assyria will be his king instead!
Since he has refused to come back to me,
⁶ the sword will rage through his cities,
  destroying the bars of his gates,
devouring them because of their plots.

God's love stronger than his vengeance

⁷ My people are bent on disregarding me;
if they are summoned to come up,
  not one of them makes a move.

⁸ Ephraim, how could I part with you?
Israel, how could I give you up?
How could I make you like Admah
  or treat you like Zeboiim?
My heart within me is overwhelmed,
  fever grips my inmost being.
⁹ I will not give rein to my fierce anger,
I will not destroy Ephraim again,
  for I am God, not man,
the Holy One in your midst,
  and I shall not come to you in anger.

The return from exile

¹⁰ They will follow Yahweh;
  he will roar like a lion,
and when he roars,
  his children will come fluttering from the
    west,
¹¹ fluttering like sparrows from Egypt,
  like pigeons from Assyria,
and I shall settle them in their homes
  —declares Yahweh.

Political and religious perversity of Israel

12 Ephraim besieges me with lying,
the House of Israel with duplicity.
(But Judah still is on God's side,

he is faithful to the Holy One.)
² Ephraim feeds himself on wind,
all day he chases the wind from the East,
he heaps up cheating and violence;
  they make a treaty with Assyria,
at the same time sending oil to Egypt.

Against Jacob and Ephraim

³ Yahweh has a case against Judah,
he will punish Jacob as his conduct merits,
he will repay him as his deeds deserve.
⁴ In the very womb he overreached his
    brother,
in maturity he wrestled against God.
⁵ He wrestled with the angel and beat him,
he wept and pleaded with him.
He met him at Bethel
  and there God spoke to us—
⁶ yes, Yahweh, God Sabaoth, Yahweh is his
    title!
⁷ So turn back with God's help,
maintain faithful love and loyalty
and always put your trust in your God.
⁸ Merchants use fraudulent scales.
To defraud is his delight.
⁹ 'How rich I have become!' says Ephraim,
'I have made a fortune.'
But of all his gains he will keep nothing
because of the sin of which he is guilty.

Reconciliation

¹⁰ But I have been Yahweh your God since
    your days in Egypt
and will make you live in tents again
  as in the days of Meeting.
¹¹ I will speak through prophets,
I will give vision after vision
and through the ministry of prophets
  will speak in parables.

New threats

¹² Is Gilead a sink of iniquity?
Yes, they are a worthless lot!
At Gilgal they sacrifice to bulls,
that is why their altars are like heaps of
    stones
in a ploughed field.

¹³ Jacob fled to the countryside of Aram,
Israel slaved to win a wife,
to win a wife he looked after sheep.
¹⁴ By a prophet Yahweh brought Israel out of
Egypt
and by a prophet Israel was preserved.
¹⁵ Ephraim gave bitter provocation—
Yahweh will bring his bloodshed down
on him,
his Lord will repay him for his insult.

Idolatry punished

13 When Ephraim used to speak, all
trembled;
he was a power in Israel;
but once he had incurred guilt with Baal,
he died.
² And now they compound their sins
by casting images for themselves out of
their silver,
idols of their own invention,
the work of craftsmen, all of it!
'Sacrifice to them,' they say!
Men bestow kisses to calves!
³ That is why they will be like morning mist,
like the dew that quickly disappears,
like the chaff whirled from the
threshing-floor,
like smoke escaping through the window.

The punishment for ingratitude

⁴ But I have been Yahweh your God since
your days in Egypt
when you knew no god but me,
since you had no one else to save you.
⁵ I cared for you in the desert,
in the land of dreadful drought.
⁶ I pastured them, and they were satisfied;
once satisfied, their hearts grew proud,
and therefore they forgot me.
⁷ So now I shall be like a lion to them,
like a leopard I shall lurk beside the road,
⁸ like a bear robbed of her cubs I shall meet
them
and rend the membrane of their heart,
and there like a lioness I shall eat them,
like a wild beast tear them to shreds.

The end of the monarchy

⁹ Israel, you have destroyed yourself
though in me lies your help.
¹⁰ Your king, where is he now, to save you,
or the governors in all your cities?—
whom you once pleaded for, saying,
'Give me a king and princes!'
¹¹ In my anger I gave you a king
and in my wrath I have taken him away.

The inevitability of ruin

¹² Ephraim's guilt is packed away,
his sin is locked up.
¹³ Pangs as of childbirth overtake him,
and a stupid child he is;
his time is due, but he does not leave the
womb.
¹⁴ Shall I save them from the clutches of
Sheol?
Shall I buy them back from Death?
Where are your plagues, Death?
Where are your scourges, Sheol?
Compassion will be banished from my
sight!
¹⁵ Though Ephraim bears more fruit than
his brothers,
the wind from the East will come,
Yahweh's breath blowing up from the desert
to dry his spring, to dry up his fountain,
to strip his treasury
of everything worth having.

14 Samaria will pay the penalty
for having rebelled against her God.
They will fall by the sword,
their little children will be dashed to pieces
and their pregnant women
disembowelled.

The sincere conversion of Israel to Yahweh

² Israel, come back to Yahweh your God
your guilt was the cause of your downfall.
³ Provide yourself with words
and come back to Yahweh.
Say to him, 'Take all guilt away
and give us what is good,

92 READ HOSEA 14:2–10.

I shall love them with all my heart, for my anger has turned away from them.
—HOSEA 14:5

OCCASIONS OF GRACE

It is an act of sovereign friendship on the part of our courteous Lord that he tenderly preserves us while we are in sin, and that, furthermore, he touches us most secretly, showing us our sin by the sweet light of mercy and grace. But when we have seen how foul we are, we imagine that God must be angry with us for our sin. Then we are stirred by the Holy Spirit, by means of contrition, to pray and desire to amend our lives, and with all our powers, to lessen God's wrath until such time as we can find rest of soul and relief in confession. Then we hope that God has forgiven us our sins, and that it is true.

Then our courteous Lord shows himself to the soul most merrily and with a glad expression. With a friendly welcome, as if the soul had been in pain and imprisoned, he says sweetly, "My darling, I am glad you have come to me. In all this misery I have ever been with you. Now you see my loving, and we are made one in bliss."

Thus are sins forgiven by mercy and grace, and thus our soul is received with honor, in joy, just as it shall be when it come to heaven—and this as many times as it comes to be forgiven, by the gracious working of the Holy Spirit and the virtue of Christ's passion.

BL. JULIAN OF NORWICH, 1342?–1423?

YOU WILL FIND THE NEXT READING AT JOEL 2.

instead of bulls we will dedicate to you our
    lips.
4 Assyria cannot save us,
  we will not ride horses any more,
  or say, "Our God!" to our own handiwork,
  for you are the one in whom orphans find
    compassion.'

5 I shall cure them of their disloyalty,
  I shall love them with all my heart,
  for my anger has turned away from them.
6 I shall fall like dew on Israel,
  he will bloom like the lily
  and thrust out roots like the cedar of
    Lebanon;
7 he will put out new shoots,
  he will have the beauty of the olive tree

and the fragrance of Lebanon.
8 They will come back to live in my shade;
  they will grow wheat again,
  they will make the vine flourish,
  their wine will be as famous as Lebanon's.
9 What has Ephraim to do with idols any
    more
  when I hear him and watch over him?
  I am like an evergreen cypress,
  you owe your fruitfulness to me.

Concluding admonition

10 Let the wise understand these words,
  let the intelligent grasp their meaning,
  for Yahweh's ways are straight
  and the upright will walk in them,
  but sinners will stumble.

JOEL

1 The word of Yahweh that was addressed to Joel son of Pethuel.

Lament over the ruin of the country

² Listen to this, you elders;
everybody in the country, attend!
Has anything like this ever happened in
your day,
or in your ancestors' days?
³ Tell your children about it
and let your children tell their children,
and their children the next generation!

⁴ What the nibbler has left, the grown locust
has eaten,
what the grown locust has left, the hopper
has eaten,
and what the hopper has left, the shearer
has eaten.

⁵ Wake up, you drunkards, and weep!
All you wine-bibbers, lament
for the new wine: it has been snatched
from your lips.
⁶ For a nation has invaded my country,
mighty and innumerable,
with teeth like a lion's teeth,
with the fangs of a lioness.
⁷ It has reduced my vines to a desolation
and my fig trees to splinters,
stripped them and broken them down,
leaving their branches white.

⁸ Mourn, as a virgin-bride in sackcloth
for the bridegroom of her youth!
⁹ Cereal offering and libation
are lost to Yahweh's Temple.
The priests, the ministers of Yahweh,
are in mourning.

¹⁰ The fields are ruined,
the land is in mourning,
for the grain has been ruined,
the new wine has failed,
of olive oil only a trickle.

¹¹ Stand dismayed, you farmers,
wail, you vinedressers,
for the wheat, for the barley!
The harvest of the fields has been lost!
¹² The vine has withered,
the fig tree wilts away;
pomegranate, palm tree, apple tree,
every tree in the countryside is dry,
and for human beings
joy has run dry too.

A call to repentance and prayer

¹³ Priests, put on sackcloth and lament!
You ministers of the altar, wail!
Come here, lie in sackcloth all night long,
you ministers of my God!
For the Temple of your God has been
deprived
of cereal offering and libation.
¹⁴ Order a fast,
proclaim a solemn assembly;
you elders,
summon everybody in the country
to the Temple of Yahweh your God.
Cry out to Yahweh:
¹⁵ 'Alas for the day!
For the Day of Yahweh is near,
coming as destruction from Shaddai.'

¹⁶ Has not the food disappeared
before our very eyes?
Have not joy and gladness vanished
from the Temple of our God?

¹⁷ The seeds shrivel
  under their clods;
  the granaries are deserted,
  the barns are in ruins,
  because the harvest has dried out.
¹⁸ Loudly the cattle groan!
  The herds of oxen are bewildered
  because they have no pasture.
  The flocks of sheep bear the punishment
      too.

¹⁹ Yahweh, to you I cry:
  for fire has devoured the desert pastures,
  flame has burnt up all the trees in the
      countryside.
²⁰ Even the wild animals pant loudly for you,
  for the watercourses have run dry,
  and fire has devoured the desert
      pastures.

A warning about the Day of Yahweh

2 Blow the ram's-horn in Zion,
  sound the alarm on my holy mountain!
Let everybody in the country tremble,
for the Day of Yahweh is coming,
yes, it is near.

² Day of darkness and gloom,ᵃ
  Day of cloud and blackness.
  Like the dawn, across the mountains
  spreads a vast and mighty people,
  such as has never been before,
  such as will never be again
  to the remotest ages.

The invasion of locusts

³ In their van a fire devours,
  in their rear a flame consumes.
  The country is like a garden of Eden
      ahead of them
  and a desert waste behind them.
  Nothing escapes them.
⁴ They look like horses,
  like chargers they gallop on,
⁵ with a racket like that of chariots
  they spring over the mountain tops,
  with a crackling like a blazing fire

devouring the stubble,
  a mighty army in battle array.

⁶ At the sight of them, people are appalled
  and every face grows pale.
⁷ Like fighting men they press forward,
  like warriors they scale the walls,
  each marching straight ahead,
  not turning from his path;
⁸ they never jostle each other,
  each marches straight ahead:
  arrows fly, they still press forward,
  never breaking ranks.
⁹ They hurl themselves at the city,
  they leap onto the walls,
  swarm up the houses,
  getting in through the windows
  like thieves.

A vision of the Day of Yahweh

¹⁰ As they come on, the earth quakes,
  the skies tremble,
  sun and moon grow dark,
  the stars lose their brilliance.ᵇ
¹¹ Yahweh's voice rings out
  at the head of his troops!
  For mighty indeed is his army,
  strong, the enforcer of his orders,
  for great is the Day of Yahweh,
  and very terrible—who can face it?

A call to repentance

¹² 'But now—declares Yahweh—
  come back to me with all your heart,
  fasting, weeping, mourning.'
¹³ Tear your hearts and not your clothes,
  and come back to Yahweh your God,
  for he is gracious and compassionate,
  slow to anger, rich in faithful love,
  and he relents about inflicting disaster.
¹⁴ Who knows if he will not come back,
      relent
  and leave a blessing behind him,
  a cereal offering and a libation
  to be presented to Yahweh your God?

2a ‖ Zp 1:15.   2b = 4:15.

93 READ JOEL 2:12–18.

Come back to Yahweh your God, for he is gracious and compassionate.—JOEL 2:13

GOD'S PATIENCE

While God is provoked with our frequent and continual offenses, he softens his indignation and patiently waits the day set for retribution. Although vengeance belongs to him, he prefers to be patient for a long time. God mercifully postpones judgment so that we, infected by our faults and sins may at last return to him. As he himself warns, "I do not take pleasure in the death of the wicked but in the conversion of the wicked who changes his ways and saves his life" (Ezk 33:11). And again: "But now—declares Yahweh—come back to me with all your heart, fasting, weeping, mourning.' Tear your hearts and not your clothes, and come back to Yahweh your God, for he is gracious and compassionate, slow to anger, rich in faithful love, and he relents about inflicting disaster" (Jl 2:12–13). God's judgment is just, but it is long delayed so that by the extreme patience of God we may receive the benefit of eternal life. Punishment is only executed on the impious and the sinner when repentance for the sin can no longer help.

Patience is a thing of God, and whoever is gentle, and patient and meek is an imitator of God the Father. As Jesus prescribed in the gospel when he was giving precepts for salvation, "You must therefore be perfect, just as your heavenly Father is perfect" (Mt 5:48). Thus the Lord taught that the children of God, restored by a heavenly birth, would become perfect when the patience of God our Father dwells in us; and when the divine likeness that Adam lost by sin is manifested and shines in our actions. What a glory it is to become like God! What a joy it is to possess such a divine virtue!

ST. CYPRIAN OF CARTHAGE, 200?–258

YOU WILL FIND THE NEXT READING AT AMOS 7.

15 Blow the ram's-horn in Zion!
  Order a fast,
  proclaim a solemn assembly,
16 call the people together,
  summon the community,
  assemble the elders,
  gather the children,
  even infants at the breast!
  Call the bridegroom from his bedroom
  and the bride from her bower!
17 Let the priests, the ministers of Yahweh,
  stand weeping between portico and altar,
  saying, 'Spare your people, Yahweh!
  Do not expose your heritage to the
      contempt,

to the sarcasm of the nations!
Why give the peoples cause to say,
"Where is their God?" '

Yahweh's answer

18 Then, becoming jealous over his country,
  Yahweh took pity on his people.

The plague stops

19 Yahweh said in answer to his people,
  'Now I shall send you
  wheat, wine and olive oil
  until you have enough.
  Never again will I expose you
  to the contempt of the nations.

20 I shall take the northerner far away from
    you
and drive him into an arid, desolate land,
his vanguard to the eastern sea,
his rearguard to the western sea.
He will give off a stench,
he will give off a foul stink
(for what he made bold to do).'

A vision of plenty

21 Land, do not be afraid;
be glad, rejoice,
for Yahweh has done great things.
22 Wild animals, do not be afraid;
the desert pastures are green again,
the trees bear fruit,
vine and fig tree yield their richness.

23 Sons of Zion, be glad,
rejoice in Yahweh your God;
for he has given you
autumn rain as justice demands,
and he will send the rains down for you,
the autumn and spring rain as of old.
24 The threshing-floors will be full of grain,
the vats overflow with wine and oil.

25 'I will make up to you for the years
devoured by grown locust and hopper,
by shearer and young locust,
my great army
which I sent to invade you.

26 'You will eat to your heart's content,
and praise the name of Yahweh your God
who has treated you so wonderfully.
(My people will never be humiliated
    again!)

27 'And you will know that I am among you
in Israel,
I, Yahweh your God, and no one else.
My people will never be humiliated again!'

The outpouring of the spirit

3 'After this
I shall pour out my spirit on all humanity.
Your sons and daughters shall prophesy,
your old people shall dream dreams,
and your young people see visions.
2 Even on the slaves, men and women,
shall I pour out my spirit in those days.
3 I shall show portents in the sky and on
    earth,
blood and fire and columns of smoke.'

4 The sun will be turned into darkness,
and the moon into blood,
before the Day comes,
that great and terrible Day.
5 All who call on the name of Yahweh will
    be saved,
for *on Mount Zion will be those who have
    escaped*,[a]
as Yahweh has said,
and in Jerusalem a remnant whom
    Yahweh is calling.

The judgement of the nations

4 'For in those days and at that time,
when I restore the fortunes of Judah
    and Jerusalem,
2 I shall gather all the nations together
and take them down to the Valley of
    Jehoshaphat;[a]
there I shall put them on trial
because of Israel, my people and my
    heritage,
for having scattered them among the
    nations
and having divided my land among
    themselves.
3 They drew lots for my people,
bartering a boy for a whore
and selling a girl for wine to drink.

Charges against the Phoenicians
and Philistines

4 'And what are you to me, Tyre and
    Sidon
and all you regions of Philistia?
Can you take revenge on me?
If you take revenge on me,

3a Ob 17.   *4a* A symbolic name (= Yahweh judges).

I shall quickly, instantly, make your
    revenge recoil on your own heads
5 for having taken my silver and gold away
and carried off my valuable treasures to
    your temples,
6 and for having sold
the children of Judah and Jerusalem to the
    Ionians,
to be taken far away from their own
    frontiers.
7 Look, I shall rouse them from the places to
    which you have sold them;
I shall make your actions recoil on your
    own heads
8 by selling your sons and daughters
to the sons of Judah,
who in turn will sell them to the Sabaeans,
to a nation far away—
Yahweh has spoken!'

A summons to the nations

9 Proclaim this among the nations.
Prepare for war!
Rouse the champions!
All you troops, advance,
march!
10 Hammer your ploughshares into swords,
your bill-hooks into spears;
let the weakling say, 'I am tough!'
11 Hurry and come,
all the nations around,
and assemble there!
(Yahweh, send down your champions!)
12 'Let the nations rouse themselves and
    march
to the Valley of Jehoshaphat,
for there I shall sit in judgement
on all the nations around.
13 Ply the sickle,
for the harvest is ripe;
come and tread,
for the winepress is full;
the vats are overflowing,
so great is their wickedness!'

14 Multitude on multitude
in the Valley of Decision!

For the Day of Yahweh is near
in the Valley of the Verdict!

The Day of Yahweh

15 Sun and moon grow dark,
the stars lose their brilliance.[b]
16 Yahweh roars from Zion,
he thunders from Jerusalem;[c]
heaven and earth tremble.

But Yahweh will be a shelter for his
    people,
a stronghold for the Israelites.
17 'Then you will know that I am Yahweh
    your God
residing on Zion, my holy mountain.
Jerusalem will then be a sanctuary,
no foreigners will overrun it ever
    again.'

The glorious future of Israel

18 When that Day comes,
the mountains will run with new
    wine
and the hills will flow with milk,
and all the stream-beds of Judah
will run with water.
A fountain will spring from Yahweh's
    Temple
and water the Gorge of the Acacias.
19 Egypt will become a desolation,
and Edom a desert waste
on account of the violence done to the
    children of Judah
whose innocent blood they shed in their
    country.
20 But Judah will be inhabited for ever,
and Jerusalem from generation to
    generation!
21 'I shall avenge their blood and let none
    go unpunished,'
and Yahweh will dwell in Zion.

4b = 2:10.
4c ‖ Am 1:2.

1 Words of Amos one of the shepherds of Tekoa. The visions he had about Israel, in the time of Uzziah king of Judah and Jeroboam son of Joash, king of Israel, two years before the earthquake.
² He said:

Yahweh roars from Zion,
and makes himself heard from Jerusalem;*ª*
the shepherds' pastures mourn,
and the crown of Carmel dries up.

Judgment on: Damascus

³ Yahweh says this:

For the three crimes, the four crimes of
Damascus,
I have made my decree and will not relent:
because they have threshed Gilead with
iron threshing-sledges,
⁴ I shall send fire down on the House of
Hazael
to devour the palaces of Ben-Hadad;
⁵ I shall break the gate-bar of Damascus,
I shall destroy the inhabitant of
Bikath-Aven,
the holder of the sceptre in Beth-Eden,
and the people of Aram will be deported
to Kir,
Yahweh says.

Gaza and Philistia

⁶ Yahweh says this:

For the three crimes, the four crimes of
Gaza,
I have made my decree and will not relent:
because they have deported entire nations
as slaves to Edom,

⁷ I shall send fire down on the walls of
Gaza
to devour its palaces;
⁸ I shall destroy the inhabitant of Ashdod,
the holder of the sceptre in Ashkelon;
I shall turn my hand against Ekron
and the remnant of the Philistines will
perish,
says the Lord Yahweh.

Tyre and Phoenicia

⁹ Yahweh says this:

For the three crimes, the four crimes of
Tyre,
I have made my decree and will not relent:
because they have handed hosts of captives
over to Edom,
heedless of a covenant of brotherhood,
¹⁰ I shall send fire down on the walls of
Tyre
to devour its palaces.

Edom

¹¹ Yahweh says this:

For the three crimes, the four crimes of
Edom,
I have made my decree and will not
relent:
because he has pursued his brother with
the sword,
because he has stifled any sense of pity,
and perpetually nursed his anger
and constantly cherished his rage,
¹² I shall send fire down on Teman
to devour the palaces of Bozrah.

1a ‖ Jr 4:16.

Ammon

13 Yahweh says this:

For the three crimes, the four crimes of the
    Ammonites,
I have made my decree and will not relent:
because they have disembowelled the
    pregnant women of Gilead
in order to extend their own frontiers,
14 I shall light a fire against the walls of
    Rabbah
to devour its palaces
amid war cries on the day of battle,
in a whirlwind on the day of storm,
15 and their king shall go into captivity,
he and his chief men with him,
says Yahweh.

Moab

2 Yahweh says this:

For the three crimes, the four crimes of
    Moab,
I have made my decree and will not relent:
because they have burnt the bones of the
    king of Edom to ash,
2 I shall send fire down into Moab
to devour the palaces of Kerioth,
and Moab will die in the tumult,
amid war cries and the blare of trumpets;
3 I shall destroy the ruler there
and slaughter all the chief men there
    with him,
says Yahweh.

Judah

4 Yahweh says this:

For the three crimes, the four crimes of
    Judah,
I have made my decree and will not relent:
because they have despised Yahweh's law
and not kept his commandments,
since their Falsehoods, which their
    ancestors followed,
have led them astray,

5 I shall send fire down on Judah
to devour the palaces of Jerusalem.

Israel

6 Yahweh says this:

For the three crimes, the four crimes of
    Israel,
I have made my decree and will not
    relent:
because they have sold the upright for
    silver
and the poor for a pair of sandals,[a]
7 because they have crushed the heads of the
    weak into the dust
and thrust the rights of the oppressed to
    one side,
father and son sleeping with the same girl
and thus profaning my holy name,
8 lying down beside every altar
on clothes acquired as pledges,
and drinking the wine of the people they
    have fined
in the house of their god.

9 Yet it was I who destroyed the Amorite
    before them,
he who was as tall as the cedars,
as strong as the oaks;
I who destroyed his fruit above ground
and his roots below.
10 It was I who brought you up from Egypt
and for forty years led you through the
    desert
to take possession of the Amorite's
    country;
11 I who raised up prophets from your sons
and Nazirites from your young men.
Israelites, is this not true?
—declares Yahweh!

12 But you have made the Nazirite drink
    wine
and given orders to the prophets,
'Do not prophesy.'

2a = 8:6.

13 Very well! Like a cart overloaded with
    sheaves
  I shall crush you where you stand;
14 flight will be cut off for the swift,
  the strong will have no chance to exert his
    strength
  nor the warrior be able to save his life;
15 the archer will not stand his ground,
  the swift of foot will not escape,
  nor will the horseman save his life;
16 even the bravest of warriors
  will jettison his arms and run away, that
    day!
  —declares Yahweh!

Election and punishment

3 Listen, Israelites, to this prophecy which
Yahweh pronounces against you, against
the whole family which I brought up from
Egypt:

2 You alone have I intimately known of all
    the families of earth,
  that is why I shall punish you for all your
    wrong-doings.

The prophetic call cannot be resisted

3 Do two people travel together
  unless they have agreed to do so?
4 Does the lion roar in the forest
  if it has no prey?
  Does the young lion growl in his lair
  if it has caught nothing?
5 Does a bird fall on the ground in a net
  unless a trap has been set for it?
  Will the net spring up from the
    ground
  without catching something?
6 Does the trumpet sound in the city
  without the people being alarmed?
  Does misfortune come to a city
  if Yahweh has not caused it?

7 No indeed, Lord Yahweh does nothing
  without revealing his secret to his servants
    the prophets.
8 The lion roars: who is not afraid?

Lord Yahweh has spoken: who will not
    prophesy?

Samaria will perish for her corruption

9 From the palace roofs of Assyria
  and from the palace roofs of Egypt,
  proclaim aloud,
  'Assemble on the hills of Samaria
  and observe the grave disorders inside her
  and the acts of oppression there!'
10 Little they know of right conduct
  —declares Yahweh—
  who cram their palaces with violence and
    extortion.
11 This is why—Lord Yahweh says this—
  an enemy will soon besiege the land,
  he will bring down your strength
  and your palaces will be looted.

12 Yahweh says this:
  As the shepherd rescues two legs or the tip
    of an ear
  from the lion's mouth,
  so will the children of Israel be salvaged
  who now loll in Samaria in the corners of
    their beds, on their divans of
    Damascus.

Against Bethel and domestic luxury

13 Listen and testify against the House of
    Jacob
  —declares the Lord Yahweh, God
    Sabaoth—
14 the day when I punish Israel for his crimes
  I shall also punish the altars of Bethel;
  the horns of the altar will be hacked off
  and will fall to the ground.
15 I shall blast winter house with summer
    house,
  ivory houses will be destroyed
  and many mansions cease to be
  —declares Yahweh.

Against the women of Samaria

4 Listen to this saying, you cows of
    Bashan
  living on the hill of Samaria,

exploiting the weak and ill-treating the
poor,
saying to your husbands, 'Bring us
something to drink!'
2 The Lord God has sworn by his holiness:
Look, the days will soon be on you
when he will use hooks to drag you away
and fish-hooks for the very last of you;
3 through the breaches in the wall you will
leave,
each one straight ahead,
and be herded away towards Hermon
—declares Yahweh.

The self-deception, obstinacy and punishment of Israel

4 Go to Bethel, and sin,
to Gilgal, and sin even harder!
Bring your sacrifices each morning,
your tithes every third day,
5 burn your thank-offering of leaven
and widely publicise your free-will
offerings,
for this, children of Israel, is what makes
you happy
—declares the Lord Yahweh.

6 I even gave you clean teeth in all your
towns
and a shortage of food in all your villages
and still you would not come back to me
—declares Yahweh.

7 I even withheld the rain from you
full three months before harvest-time;
I caused rain to fall in one town
and caused no rain to fall in another;
one field was rained on
and the next for want of rain dried up;
8 two towns, three towns went tottering
to one town for water to drink
but went unsatisfied,
and still you would not come back to me
—declares Yahweh.

9 I struck you with blight and mildew,
I dried up your gardens and vineyards;

the locust devoured your fig trees and
olive trees
and still you would not come back
to me
—declares Yahweh.

10 I sent plague on you like Egypt's plague,
I slaughtered your young men with the
sword
and at the same time your horses were
captured;
I filled your nostrils with the stench of
your camps
and still you would not come back
to me
—declares Yahweh.

11 I overturned you as God overturned
Sodom and Gomorrah;
you were like a brand snatched from the
blaze
and still you would not come back to me
—declares Yahweh.

12 So this, Israel, is what I plan to do to you.
Because I am going to do this to you,
Israel, prepare to meet your God!

Doxology [a]

13 For look, he it is who forges the
mountains, creates the wind,
who reveals his mind to humankind,
changes the dawn into darkness
and strides on the heights of the world:
Yahweh, God Sabaoth, is his name.

Lament for Israel

5 Listen to this word which I utter against
you,
it is a dirge, House of Israel:
2 She has fallen down, never to rise again,
the virgin Israel.
There she lies on her own soil,
with no one to lift her up.

4a A hymnic fragment, probably added later, as 5:8–9 and
9:5–6.

3 For Lord Yahweh says this:
The town which used to put a thousand in
the field
will be left with a hundred,
and the one which used to put a hundred
will be left with ten, to fight for the House
of Israel.

No salvation without repentance

4 For Yahweh says this to the House of
Israel:
Seek me out and you will survive,
5 but do not seek out Bethel,
do not go to Gilgal,
do not journey to Beersheba,
for Gilgal is going into captivity
and Bethel will be brought to nothing.
6 Seek out Yahweh and you will survive,
or else he will sweep like fire upon the
House of Joseph
and burn it down, with no one at Bethel
able to quench the flames.
7 They turn justice into wormwood
and throw uprightness to the ground.

Doxology

8 He it is who makes the Pleiades and
Orion,
who turns shadow dark as death into
morning
and day to darkest night,
who summons the waters of the sea
and pours them over the surface of the
land.
Yahweh is his name.*a*
9 He brings destruction on the strong
and ruin comes on the fortress.

Threats

10 They hate the man who teaches justice at
the city gate
and detest anyone who declares the truth.
11 For trampling on the poor man
and for extorting levies on his wheat:
although you have built houses of dressed
stone,
you will not live in them;

although you have planted pleasant
vineyards,
you will not drink wine from them:
12 for I know how many your crimes are
and how outrageous your sins,
you oppressors of the upright, who hold
people to ransom
and thrust the poor aside at the gates.
13 That is why anyone prudent keeps silent
now,
since the time is evil.

Exhortation

14 Seek good and not evil
so that you may survive,
and Yahweh, God Sabaoth, be with you
as you claim he is.
15 Hate evil, love good,
let justice reign at the city gate:
it may be that Yahweh, God Sabaoth,
will take pity on the remnant of Joseph.

Impending punishment

16 Therefore Yahweh Sabaoth, the Lord, says
this:
In every public square there will be
lamentation,
in every street they will cry out, 'Alas!
Alas!'
The farmer will be called on to mourn,
the professional mourners to lament,
17 and there will be wailing in every
vineyard,
for I mean to pass through among you,
Yahweh says.

The Day*b* of Yahweh

18 Disaster for you who long for the Day of
Yahweh!
What will the Day of Yahweh mean
for you?
It will mean darkness, not light,

5a = 9:6.

5b A day of retribution, punishment of the wicked and vindication of God's faithful people. It figures prominently in all
the prophets.

19 as when someone runs away from a lion,
   only to meet a bear;
   he goes into his house and puts his hand
      on the wall,
   only for a snake to bite him.
20 Will not the Day of Yahweh be darkness,
      not light,
   totally dark, without a ray of light?

Against formalism in religion

21 I hate, I scorn your festivals,
   I take no pleasure in your solemn
      assemblies.
22 When you bring me burnt offerings . . .c
   your oblations, I do not accept them
   and I do not look at your communion
      sacrifices of fat cattle.
23 Spare me the din of your chanting,
   let me hear none of your strumming on
      lyres,
24 but let justice flow like water,
   and uprightness like a never-failing
      stream!
25 Did you bring me sacrifices and oblations
   those forty years in the desert, House of
      Israel?
26 Now you must shoulder Sakkuth your
      king
   and the star of your God, Kaiwan,
   those idols you made for yourselves;
27 for I am about to drive you into captivity
      beyond Damascus,
   Yahweh says—God Sabaoth is his name.

Against the self-indulgent and their false sense of security

6 Disaster for those so comfortable in Zion
  and for those so confident on the hill of
      Samaria,
   the notables of this first of nations,
   those to whom the House of Israel has
      recourse!
2 Travel to Calneh and look,
   go on from there to Hamath the great,
   then go down to Gatha in Philistia.
   Are they more powerful than these
      kingdoms?

   Is their territory larger than yours?
3 Thinking to defer the evil day,
   you are hastening the reign of violence.

4 Lying on ivory beds
   and sprawling on their divans,
   they dine on lambs from the flock,
   and stall-fattened veal;
5 they bawl to the sound of the lyre
   and, like David, they invent musical
      instruments;
6 they drink wine by the bowlful,
   and lard themselves with the finest oils,
   but for the ruin of Joseph they care
      nothing.
7 That is why they will now go into
      captivity,
   heading the column of captives.
   The sprawlers' revelry is over.

The punishment: plague, earthquake, invasion

8 Lord Yahweh has sworn by his own self
   —declares Yahweh, God Sabaoth:
   I detest the pride of Jacob,
   I hate his palaces,
   I shall hand over the city and all in it.
9 If ten people are left in a single house,
   they will die
10 and a few will be left to carry
   the bones from the house,
   and they will say to anyone deep inside the
      house,
   'Any more there?' and he will answer,
      'No.'
   Then he will say, 'Hush!—
   Yahweh's name must not be mentioned.'
11 For look, Yahweh gives the command:
   as he strikes, the great house falls to pieces
   and the small house is in fragments.

12 Can horses gallop over rocks?
   Can the sea be ploughed with oxen?

5c A line seems to be missing here.
6a Calneh, Hamath and Gath were taken by Assyria in 738, 720, 711 BC respectively.

Yet you have changed justice into poison,
and the fruit of uprightness into
wormwood,
13 while rejoicing over Lo-Debar
and saying, 'Wasn't it by our own strength
that we captured Karnaim?'
14 But look, House of Israel, against you
—declares Yahweh, God Sabaoth—
I am raising a nation to oppress you
from the Pass of Hamath to the Gorge of
the Arabah.

First vision: the locusts

7 This is what Lord Yahweh showed me:
there was a swarm of locusts
when the second crop was sprouting,
full-grown locusts, after the king's hay had
been cut.
2 When they had eaten all the grass in the
land,
I said, 'Lord Yahweh, forgive, I beg you.
How can Jacob survive, being so small?'
3 Then Yahweh relented;
'It will not happen,' said Yahweh.

Second vision: the drought

4 This is what Lord Yahweh showed me:
Lord Yahweh summoning fire in
punishment;
it had devoured the great Abyss
and was encroaching on the land,
5 when I said, 'Lord Yahweh, stop, I beg
you.
How can Jacob survive, being so small?'
6 Then Yahweh relented;
'This will not happen either,' said the Lord
Yahweh.

Third vision: the plumb-line

7 This is what he showed me:
the Lord standing by a wall,
with a plumb-line in his hand.
8 'What do you see, Amos?' Yahweh
asked me.
'A plumb-line,' I said.
Then the Lord said,
'Look, I am going to put a plumb-line

in among my people Israel;
never again will I overlook their offences.
9 The high places of Isaac will be ruined
and the sanctuaries of Israel laid waste,
and, sword in hand, I will attack the
House of Jeroboam.'

Amaziah challenges Amos' right to prophesy

10 Amaziah the priest of Bethel then sent word
to Jeroboam king of Israel as follows, 'Amos is
plotting against you in the heart of the House
of Israel; the country cannot tolerate his
speeches. 11 For this is what Amos says, "Jeroboam is going to die by the sword, and Israel
will go into captivity far from its native
land." ' 12 To Amos himself Amaziah said, 'Go
away, seer, take yourself off to Judah, earn
your living there, and there you can prophesy!
13 But never again will you prophesy at Bethel,
for this is a royal sanctuary, a national temple.'
14 'I am not a prophet,' Amos replied to
Amaziah, 'nor do I belong to a prophetic
brotherhood. I am merely a herdsman and
dresser of sycamore-figs. 15 But Yahweh took
me as I followed the flock, and Yahweh said to
me, "Go and prophesy to my people Israel."
16 So now listen to what Yahweh says:

"You say: Do not prophesy against Israel,
do not foretell doom on the House of
Isaac!"
17 Very well, this is what Yahweh says,
"Your wife will become a prostitute in the
streets,
your sons and daughters will fall by the
sword,
your land will be parcelled out by
measuring line,
and you yourself will die on polluted soil
and Israel will go into captivity far from its
own land!" '

Fourth vision: the basket of ripe fruit

8 This is what Lord Yahweh showed me:
A basket of ripe fruit.
2 'What do you see, Amos?' he asked.
'A basket of ripe fruit,' I said.

94 READ AMOS 7.

I am merely a herdsman and dresser of sycamore-figs.—AMOS 7:14

TRANSFORMED BY THE HOLY SPIRIT

The Holy Spirit shares with the Son in working both the Creation and the Resurrection, as this Scripture shows: "By the word of Yahweh the heavens were made, by the breath of his mouth all their array" (Ps 33:6). And also this text: "God's was the spirit that made me, Shaddai's the breath that gave me life" (Jb 33:4). And again, "Send forth your Spirit and they shall be created, and you shall renew the face of the earth" (see Ps 104:30). And he is also the author of spiritual regeneration. Here is your proof: "None can see or enter into the Kingdom, except he be born again of the Spirit" (see Jn 3:3, 5) and be cleansed from the first birth.

Everyone singly is created anew, refashioned by the Light. If this most wise and loving Spirit takes possession of a shepherd, he makes him a psalmist, subduing evil spirits by his song and proclaims him king (see 1 S 16). If he possesses a herdsman and dresser of sycamore-figs, he makes him a prophet. Call to mind David and Amos.

If he takes hold of a good youth, he makes him a judge of elders even beyond his years, as Daniel testifies, who conquered the lions in their den (see Dn 13). If he takes possession of fishermen, he makes them catch the whole world in the nets of Christ, taking them up in the meshes of the Word. Look at Peter and Andrew and the Sons of Thunder, thundering the things of the Spirit. If of publicans, he reaps profits from them for discipleship, and makes them merchants of souls. Witness Matthew, yesterday a publican, today an evangelist. If of zealous persecutors, he redirects the current of their zeal, and makes them Pauls instead of Sauls, and as full of piety as he found them full of wickedness.

ST. GREGORY NAZIANZEN, 329?–390

YOU WILL FIND THE NEXT READING AT JONAH 3.

Then Yahweh said,
'The time is ripe for my people Israel;
I will not continue to overlook their
offences.
³ That day, the palace songs will turn to
howls,
—declares the Lord Yahweh—
the corpses will be many that are thrown
down everywhere.
Keep silent!'

Against swindlers and exploiters

⁴ Listen to this, you who crush the needy
and reduce the oppressed to nothing,

⁵ you who say, 'When will New Moon be
over
so that we can sell our corn,
and Sabbath, so that we can market our
wheat?
Then, we can make the bushel-measure
smaller
and the shekel-weight bigger,
by fraudulently tampering with the
scales.
⁶ We can buy up the weak for silver
and the poor for a pair of sandals,ᵃ

8a = 2:6.

and even get a price for the sweepings of
the wheat.'

7 Yahweh has sworn by the pride of Jacob,
'Never will I forget anything they have
done.'

8 Will not the earth tremble for this
and all who live on it lament,
as it all rises together like the Nile in Egypt,
it swells and then subsides like the
Egyptian Nile?^b

Prediction of punishment: darkness and mourning

9 'On that Day—declares the Lord
Yahweh—
I shall make the sun go down at noon
and darken the earth in broad daylight.

10 I shall turn your festivals into mourning
and all your singing into lamentation;
I shall make you all wear sacking round
your waists
and have all your heads shaved.
I shall make it like the mourning for an
only child,
and it will end like the bitterest of days.

Famine and drought of the word of God

11 'The days are coming—declares the Lord
Yahweh—
when I shall send a famine on the country,
not hunger for food, not thirst for water,
but famine for hearing Yahweh's word.

12 People will stagger from sea to sea,
will wander from the north to the east,
searching for Yahweh's word,
but will not find it.

Fresh prediction of punishment

13 'That Day, fine girls and stalwart youths
will faint from thirst.

14 The people who swear by the Sin^c of
Samaria,
who say, "Long live your god, Dan!"
and "Hurrah for the pilgrimage to
Beersheba!"
will all fall, never to rise again.'

Fifth vision: the fall of the sanctuary

9 I saw the Lord standing by the altar, and
he said,
'Strike the top of the pillar so that the
thresholds shake!
Smash their heads in, one and all!
And I shall put any survivors to the sword;
whoever runs away will not run far,
whoever escapes will not make good his
escape.

2 Should they burrow into Sheol,
my hand will haul them out;
should they climb to heaven,
I shall bring them down.

3 Should they hide on the top of Carmel,
I shall track them down and catch them;
should they hide from me on the sea bed,
I shall order the Serpent there to bite
them;

4 if their enemies herd them into captivity,
I shall order the sword to kill them there,
and I shall fix my eyes on them
for evil and not for good.'

Doxology

5 Lord Yahweh Sabaoth—
he touches the earth and it melts,
and all living things on it lament,
as all rises together like the Nile in Egypt
and then subsides like the Egyptian Nile.^a

6 He who builds his mansions in the
heavens,
supporting his vault on the earth;
who summons the waters of the sea
and pours them over the surface of the
land:
Yahweh is his name.^b

Sinners will all perish

7 Are not you and the Cushites all the same
to me,

8b = 9:5.

8c The Hebr. word is *'ashemah*, a pun on the name of the
goddess Ashimah.

9a = 8:8.　9b = 5:8.

children of Israel?—declares Yahweh.
Did I not bring Israel up from Egypt
and the Philistines from Caphtor, and the
Aramaeans from Kir?

8 Look, Lord Yahweh's eyes are on the
sinful kingdom,
I shall wipe it off the face of the earth,
although I shall not destroy the House of
Jacob completely
—declares Yahweh.

9 For look, I shall give the command
and shall shake out the House of Israel
among all nations
as a sieve is shaken out
without one grain falling on the ground.

10 All the sinners of my people will perish by
the sword, who say,
'Disaster will never approach or
overtake us.'

Prospects of restoration and of idyllic prosperity[c]

11 On that Day, I shall rebuild the tottering
hut of David,
make good the gaps in it, restore its ruins
and rebuild it as it was in the days of old,

12 for them to be master of what is left of
Edom

and of all the nations once called mine
—Yahweh declares, and he will
perform it.

13 The days are coming—declares Yahweh—
when the ploughman will tread on the
heels of the reaper,
and the treader of grapes on the heels of
the sower of seed,
and the mountains will run with new wine
and the hills all flow with it.

14 I shall restore the fortunes of my
people Israel;
they will rebuild the ruined cities and live
in them,
they will plant vineyards and drink
their wine,
they will lay out gardens and eat their
produce.

15 And I shall plant them in their own soil
and they will never be uprooted again
from the country which I have given
them,
declares Yahweh, your God.

9c The only hopeful passage in Amos, perhaps added later.

OBADIAH

Title

Vision of Obadiah: about Edom.

Prologue

1c I have received a message from Yahweh,
   a herald has been sent throughout the
      nations:
   'Up! Let us march against this people.
   Into battle!'

Sentence pronounced on Edom

1b The Lord Yahweh says this:
2 Look, I have reduced you to the smallest
      of nations,
   you are now beneath contempt.

3 Your proud heart has misled you,
   you whose home is in the crannies of the
      Rock,
   who make the heights your dwelling,
   who think to yourself,
   'Who can bring me down to earth?'
4 Though you soar like an eagle,
   though you set your nest among the stars,
   I shall bring you down from there!—
      declares Yahweh.*a*

The annihilation of Edom

5 If thieves were to come to you
   (or robbers during the night)
   surely they would steal only as much as
      they wanted?
   If grape-pickers were to come to you,
   surely they would leave a few gleanings?

   But how you have been pillaged!
6 How Esau has been looted,
   his hidden treasures routed out!*b*

7 Your allies all pursued you right to the
      frontier,
   your confederates kept you in suspense,
      then got the better of you,
   your own guests laid a trap for you,
   'He has quite lost his wits.'

8 When that day comes—declares
      Yahweh—
   shall I not eliminate sages from Edom
   and intelligence from Mount Esau?

9 Your warriors, Teman, will be so
      demoralised
   that the people of Mount Esau will be
      massacred
   to the last one.

The guilt of Edom

For the slaughter, 10 for the violence
   done to your brother Jacob,
   shame will cover you
   and you will be annihilated for ever.

11 On the day, when you stood aloof
   while strangers carried off his riches,
   while foreigners passed through his gate
   and cast lots for Jerusalem,
   you were as bad as the rest of them.

12 Do not feast your eyes on your brother
   on the day of his misfortune.
   Do not gloat over the children of
      Judah
   on the day of their ruin.
   Do not play the braggart
   on the day of distress.

a ‖ Jr 49:14–16.   *b* ‖ Jr 49:9–10.

¹³ Do not enter my people's gate
on their day of calamity.
Do not, you especially, feast your eyes on
their suffering
on their day of calamity.
Do not touch their possessions
on their day of calamity.

¹⁴ Do not wait at the crossroads
to annihilate their fugitives.
Do not hand over their survivors
on the day of distress.
¹⁵ For the Day of Yahweh is near
for all the nations.
As you have done, so will it be done to
you:
your deeds will recoil on your own head.

The Day of Yahweh; Israel revenged on Edom

¹⁶ Just as you have drunk on my holy
mountain,
so will all the nations drink continually,
they will drink, will drink greedily,
but they will be as though they had never
been!

¹⁷ But on Mount Zion will be those who have
escaped
—it will be a sanctuary—
and the House of Jacob will recover
what is rightfully theirs.

¹⁸ Then the House of Jacob will be a fire,
the House of Joseph a flame,
and the House of Esau like stubble.
They will set it alight and burn it up,
and no one of the House of Esau will
survive.
Yahweh has spoken.

The new Israel

¹⁹ People from the Negeb will occupy the
Mount of Esau,
people from the lowlands the country of
the Philistines;
they will occupy Ephraim and Samaria,
and Benjamin will occupy Gilead.
²⁰ The exiles of this army, the sons of
Israel,
will have the Canaanites' land as far as
Zarephthah,
while the exiles from Jerusalem now in
Sepharad
will have the cities of the Negeb.

²¹ Victorious, they will climb Mount
Zion
to rule over Mount Esau,
and sovereignty will be Yahweh's!

Jonah rebels against his mission

1 The word of Yahweh was addressed to Jonah son of Amittai: 2 'Up!' he said, 'Go to Nineveh, the great city, and proclaim to them that their wickedness has forced itself upon me.' 3 Jonah set about running away from Yahweh, and going to Tarshish. He went down to Jaffa and found a ship bound for Tarshish; he paid his fare and boarded it, to go with them to Tarshish, to get away from Yahweh. 4 But Yahweh threw a hurricane at the sea, and there was such a great storm at sea that the ship threatened to break up. 5 The sailors took fright, and each of them called on his own god, and to lighten the ship they threw the cargo overboard. Jonah, however, had gone below, had lain down in the hold and was fast asleep, 6 when the boatswain went up to him and said, 'What do you mean by sleeping? Get up! Call on your god! Perhaps he will spare us a thought and not leave us to die.' 7 Then they said to each other, 'Come on, let us draw lots to find out who is to blame for bringing us this bad luck.' So they cast lots, and the lot pointed to Jonah. 8 Then they said to him, 'Tell us, what is your business? Where do you come from? What is your country? What is your nationality?' 9 He replied, 'I am a Hebrew, and I worship Yahweh, God of Heaven, who made both sea and dry land.' 10 The sailors were seized with terror at this and said, 'Why ever did you do this?' since they knew that he was trying to escape from Yahweh, because he had told them so. 11 They then said, 'What are we to do with you, to make the sea calm down for us?' For the sea was growing rougher and rougher. 12 He replied, 'Take me and throw me into the sea, and then it will calm down for you. I know it is my fault that this great storm has struck you.' 13 The sailors rowed hard in an effort to reach the shore, but in vain, since the sea was growing rougher and rougher. 14 So at last they called on Yahweh and said, 'O, Yahweh, do not let us perish for the sake of this man's life, and do not hold us responsible for causing an innocent man's death; for you, Yahweh, have acted as you saw fit.' 15 And taking hold of Jonah they threw him into the sea; and the sea stopped raging. 16 At this, the men were seized with dread of Yahweh; they offered a sacrifice to Yahweh and made vows to him.

Jonah is saved

2 Now Yahweh ordained that a great fish should swallow Jonah; and Jonah remained in the belly of the fish for three days and three nights. 2 From the belly of the fish, Jonah prayed*a* to Yahweh, his God; he said:

3 Out of my distress I cried to Yahweh
    and he answered me,
from the belly of Sheol I cried
      out;
    you heard my voice!

4 For you threw me into the deep,
    into the heart of the seas,
and the floods closed round me.
All your waves and billows passed
      over me;
5   then I thought, 'I am banished from
      your sight;
how shall I ever see your holy Temple
      again?'

2a The prayer is a later mosaic of psalms.

95 READ JONAH 3.

Let everyone renounce his evil ways.—JONAH 3:8

A PASSION FOR EVANGELIZATION

I tell you quite frankly that whenever I see sinners, I grow restless, I cannot quiet down, I cannot be consoled, my heart goes out to them. To give you an idea of how I feel, I'll draw a comparison. If a loving mother saw her child in danger of falling from a high window or into an open fireplace, wouldn't she run up behind the child and take hold of him and pull him back if she could? My brothers and sisters, you should know that grace is stronger and braver than nature. Well then, if the natural love a mother feels for her child can make her run to him, shout at him, take hold of him, and pull him back from the brink of ruin, that is just what grace does in me.

Charity urges and impels me; it makes me run from town to town shouting, "Sinner, my son, look where you're heading; you're about to fall into hell. Stop! Don't take another step!" I often ask God, as St. Catherine of Siena did: "Lord, let me stand at the gates of hell and stop anyone from entering, by telling each of them, 'Where are you going, poor fool? Turn back! Make a good confession and save your soul. Don't come here, to be lost for all eternity!' "

Another force that drives me to preach and hear confessions is my desire to make my neighbor happy. If there is so much joy in healing the sick, freeing the prisoner, consoling the afflicted, and cheering the sad, then there is far greater joy in bringing one's neighbor to the glory of heaven. It means saving him from every evil and bringing him to the enjoyment of every good—and for all eternity.   ST. ANTHONY MARY CLARET, 1807–1870

YOU WILL FIND THE NEXT READING AT MICAH 6.

6 The waters round me rose to my neck,
   the deep was closing round me,
   seaweed twining round my head.
7 To the roots of the mountains,
   I sank into the underworld,
   and its bars closed round me for ever.

But you raised my life from the Pit,
   Yahweh my God!
8 When my soul was growing ever weaker,
   Yahweh, I remembered you,
and my prayer reached you
   in your holy Temple.

9 Some abandon their faithful love
   by worshipping false gods,

10 but I shall sacrifice to you
   with songs of praise.
The vow I have made I shall fulfil!
   Salvation comes from Yahweh!

11 Yahweh spoke to the fish, which then vomited Jonah onto the dry land.

The conversion of Nineveh and God's pardon

3 The word of Yahweh was addressed to Jonah a second time. 2 'Up!' he said, 'Go to Nineveh, the great city, and preach to it as I shall tell you.' 3 Jonah set out and went to Nineveh in obedience to the word of Yahweh. Now Nineveh was a city great beyond compare; to cross it took three days. 4 Jonah began

by going a day's journey into the city and then proclaimed, 'Only forty days more and Nineveh will be overthrown.' ⁵And the people of Nineveh believed in God; they proclaimed a fast and put on sackcloth, from the greatest to the least. ⁶When the news reached the king of Nineveh, he rose from his throne, took off his robe, put on sackcloth and sat down in ashes. ⁷He then had it proclaimed throughout Nineveh, by decree of the king and his nobles, as follows: 'No person or animal, herd or flock, may eat anything; they may not graze, they may not drink any water. ⁸All must put on sackcloth and call on God with all their might; and let everyone renounce his evil ways and violent behaviour. ⁹Who knows? Perhaps God will change his mind and relent and renounce his burning wrath, so that we shall not perish.' ¹⁰God saw their efforts to renounce their evil ways. And God relented about the disaster which he had threatened to bring on them, and did not bring it.

The grievance of the prophet and God's answer

4 This made Jonah very indignant; he fell into a rage. ²He prayed to Yahweh and said, 'Please, Yahweh, isn't this what I said would happen when I was still in my own country? That was why I first tried to flee to Tarshish, since I knew you were a tender, compassionate God, slow to anger, rich in faithful love, who relents about inflicting disaster. ³So now, Yahweh, please take my life, for I might as well be dead as go on living.' ⁴Yahweh replied, 'Are you right to be angry?'

⁵Jonah then left the city and sat down to the east of the city. There he made himself a shelter and sat under it in the shade, to see what would happen to the city. ⁶Yahweh God then ordained that a castor-oil plant should grow up over Jonah to give shade for his head and soothe his ill-humour; Jonah was delighted with the castor-oil plant. ⁷But at dawn the next day, God ordained that a worm should attack the castor-oil plant—and it withered. ⁸Next, when the sun rose, God ordained that there should be a scorching east wind; the sun beat down so hard on Jonah's head that he was overcome and begged for death, saying, 'I might as well be dead as go on living.' ⁹God said to Jonah, 'Are you right to be angry about the castor-oil plant?' He replied, 'I have every right to be angry, mortally angry!' ¹⁰Yahweh replied, 'You are concerned for the castor-oil plant which has not cost you any effort and which you did not grow, which came up in a night and has perished in a night. ¹¹So why should I not be concerned for Nineveh, the great city, in which there are more than a hundred and twenty thousand people who cannot tell their right hand from their left, to say nothing of all the animals?'

The Book of

MICAH

1 The word of Yahweh which came to Micah
of Moresheth during the reigns of Jotham,
Ahaz and Hezekiah kings of Judah. His visions about Samaria and Jerusalem.

The judgement of Samaria

2 Listen, all you peoples,
 attend, earth and everyone on it!
 Yahweh intends to give evidence against
  you,
 the Lord, from his holy temple.
3 For look, Yahweh is leaving his home,
 down he comes, he treads the heights
  of earth.
4 Beneath him, the mountains melt,
 and valleys are torn open,
 like wax near a fire,
 like water pouring down a slope.

5 All this is because of the crime of
  Jacob,
 the sin of the House of Israel.
 What is the crime of Jacob?
 Is it not Samaria?
 What is the sin of the House of Judah?
 Is it not Jerusalem?
6 So I shall make Samaria a ruin in the
  open country,
 a place for planting vines.
 I shall send her stones rolling into the
  valley,
 until I have laid her foundations bare.
7 All her images will be shattered,
 all her earnings consumed by fire.
 I shall leave all her idols derelict—
 they were amassed out of prostitutes'
  earnings
 and prostitutes' earnings once more they
  will be.

Lament for Jerusalem and the lowland towns

8 This is why I shall howl and wail,
 why I shall go barefoot and naked,
 why I shall howl like the jackals,
 why I shall shriek like the owls;
9 for there is no cure for the wounds that
  Yahweh inflicts:
 the blow falls on Judah,
 it falls on the gateway of my people,
 on Jerusalem itself.
10 *Do not announce it in Gath,*[a]
 in . . .[b] shed no tears!
 In Beth-Leaphrah
 roll in the dust!
11 Sound the horn,
 inhabitant of Shaphir!
 She has not left her city,
 she who lives in Zaanan.
 Beth-Ezel is torn from its foundations,
 from its strong supports.
12 What hope has she of happiness,
 she who lives in Maroth?
 Instead Yahweh sent down disaster
 on the gateway of Jerusalem itself!
13 Harness the horse to the chariot,
 you inhabitant of Lachish!
 That is where the sin of the daughter of
  Zion began;
 the crimes of Israel can be traced to you!
14 And so you must provide a dowry
 for Moresheth-Gath.
 Beth-Achzib will prove a disappointment
 for the kings of Israel.
15 The plunderer will come to you again,

1a 2 S 1:20. The predictions pun on the names of the towns,
e.g. Shaphir and *shophar* = horn.

1b Only one letter is left of this place-name.

[1164]

you citizen of Mareshah!
And into Adullam will vanish
the glory of Israel.

16 Off with your hair, shave your head,
for the children that were your joy.
Make yourselves bald like the vulture,
for they have left you for exile.

Against land-grabbers

2 Disaster for those who plot evil,
who lie in bed planning mischief!
No sooner is it dawn than they do it,
since they have the power to do so.
2 Seizing the fields that they covet,
they take over houses as well,
owner and house they seize alike,
the man himself as well as his inheritance.
3 So Yahweh says this:
Look, I am now plotting
a disaster for this breed
from which you will not extricate your
necks;
you will not hold your heads up then,
for the times will be disastrous indeed.
4 That day they will make a satire on you,
they will strike up a dirge and say,
'We have been stripped of everything;
my people's land has been divided up,
no one else can restore it to them,
our fields have been awarded to our
despoiler.'

5 Because of this, you will have no one
to measure out a share
in Yahweh's community.

The prophet of misfortune

6 'Do not drivel,' they drivel,
'do not drivel like this!
Disgrace will not overtake us!

7 'Can the House of Jacob be accursed?
Has Yahweh grown short-tempered?
Is that his way of going to work?
His prophecies can only be favourable
for his people Israel!'

8 But you are the ones who play the
enemy
to my people.
From the inoffensive man you snatch
his cloak,
on those who feel safe you inflict the
damage of war.
9 My people's women you evict
from the homes they love,
and deprive the children
of my glory for ever,
10 saying, 'Up and off with you! You can't
stay here!'
For a worthless thing you exact
an extortionate pledge.
11 If a man of the spirit came and invented
this lie,
'I prophesy wine and liquor for you,'
he would be the prophet for a people
like this.

Promises of restoration

12 I shall assemble the whole of Jacob,
I shall gather the remnant of Israel,
I shall gather them together like sheep in
an enclosure.
And like a flock within their fold,
they will bleat far away from anyone,
13 their leader will break out first,
then all break out through the gate and
escape,
with their king leading the way
and with Yahweh at their head.

Against the rulers who oppress the people

3 Then I said,
'Kindly listen, you leaders of the House
of Jacob,
you princes of the House of Israel.
Surely you are the ones who ought to
know what is right,
2 and yet you hate what is good and love
what is evil,
skinning people alive, pulling the flesh off
their bones,
3 eating my people's flesh, stripping off their
skin,

breaking up their bones, chopping them
up small
like flesh for the pot, like meat in the
stew-pan?'
4 Then they will call to Yahweh,
but he will not answer them.
When the time comes he will hide his face
from them
because of the crimes they have
committed.

Against venal prophets

5 Yahweh says this against the prophets
who lead my people astray:
So long as they have something to eat
they cry 'Peace'.
But on anyone who puts nothing into
their mouths
they declare war.
6 And so, for you, night will be without
vision
and for you the darkness without
divination.
The sun will set for the prophets,
the daylight will go black above them.
7 Then the seers will be covered with
shame,
the diviners with confusion;
they will all put their hands over their
mouths
because there is no answer from God.
8 Not so with me, I am full of strength
(full of Yahweh's spirit),
of the sense of right, of energy
to accuse Jacob of his crime
and Israel of his sin.

To the rulers: prophecy of the ruin of Zion

9 Kindly listen to this, you leaders of the
House of Jacob,
you princes of the House of Israel,
who detest justice,
wresting it from its honest course,
10 who build Zion with blood,
and Jerusalem with iniquity!
11 Her leaders give verdicts for presents,
her priests take a fee for their rulings,

her prophets divine for money
and yet they rely on Yahweh!
'Isn't Yahweh among us?' they say,
'No disaster is going to overtake us.'
12 That is why, thanks to you,
Zion will become ploughland,
Jerusalem a heap of rubble
and the Temple Mount a wooded
height.

The future reign of Yahweh in Zion[a]

4 But in days to come
Yahweh's Temple Mountain
will tower above the mountains,
rise higher than the hills.
2 Then the peoples will stream to it,
then many nations will come and say,
'Come, we will go up to Yahweh's
mountain,
to the Temple of the God of Jacob,
so that he may teach us his ways
and we may walk in his paths;
for the Law issues from Zion
and Yahweh's word from Jerusalem.'
3 He will judge between many peoples
and arbitrate between mighty
nations.
They will hammer their swords into
ploughshares
and their spears into bill-hooks.
Nation will not lift sword against
nation
or ever again be trained to make war.
4 But each man will sit under his vine
and fig tree
with no one to trouble him.
The mouth of Yahweh Sabaoth has
spoken.

5 For all peoples go forward, each in the
name of its god,
while we go forward in the name of
Yahweh our God
for ever and ever.

4a vv. 1–3 = Is 2:2–4. The universalist theme fits better in
Isaiah.

The scattered flock is gathered to Zion

6 That day—declares Yahweh—
I shall gather in the lame
and bring together the strays
and those whom I have treated harshly.
7 From the footsore I shall make a remnant,
and from the far-flung a mighty nation.
And Yahweh will reign over them on
Mount Zion
thenceforth and for ever.

8 And to you, Tower of the Flock,
Ophel of the daughter of Zion,
to you your former sovereignty will
return,
the royal power of the daughter of
Jerusalem.

The siege, exile and liberation of Zion

9 Why are you crying out now?
Have you no king?
Has your counsellor perished,
for pangs to grip you like those of a
woman in labour?
10 Writhe in pain and cry aloud,
daughter of Zion, like a woman in labour,
for now you must leave the city
and camp in the open country;
to Babylon you must go,
and there you will be rescued;
there Yahweh will ransom you
from the clutches of your enemies.

*Her enemies to be crushed on
the threshing-floor*

11 Now many nations
have mustered against you.
They say, 'Let us desecrate her,
let us gloat over Zion!'
12 But they do not know Yahweh's thoughts,
they do not understand his design:
he has collected them like sheaves on the
threshing-floor.
13 Start your threshing, daughter of Zion,
for I shall make your horn like iron,
I shall make your hooves like bronze,

so that you can crush many peoples.
And you will devote what they have stolen
to Yahweh,
their wealth to the Lord of the whole
earth.

The distress and glory of the Davidic dynasty

14 Now look to your fortifications, Fortress!
They have laid siege to us;
the ruler of Israel will be struck
on the cheek with a rod.

5 But you (Bethlehem) Ephrathah,
the least of the clans of Judah,
from you will come for me
a future ruler of Israel
whose origins go back to the distant past,
to the days of old.
2 Hence Yahweh will abandon them
only until she who is in labour gives birth,
and then those who survive of his race
will be reunited to the Israelites.
3 He will take his stand and he will
shepherd them
with the power of Yahweh,
with the majesty of the name of his God,
and they will be secure, for his greatness
will extend
henceforth to the most distant parts of the
country.

The future conqueror of Assyria

4 He himself will be peace!
Should the Assyrian invade our country,
should he set foot in our land,
we shall raise seven shepherds against him,
eight leaders of men;
5 they will shepherd Assyria with the sword,
the country of Nimrod with naked blade.
He will save us from the Assyrian,
should he invade our country,
should he set foot inside our frontiers.

The future role of the remnant

6 Then what is left of Jacob,
surrounded by many peoples,
will be like a dew from Yahweh,

96   READ MICAH 6:6–8.

With what shall I enter Yahweh's presence and bow down before God All-high?

—MICAH 6:6

PLEASING GOD PERFECTLY

The Gospel sets before us "a rule of perfection," not indeed any sort of perfection but one like to that of the eternal Father. What a wonderful command from the Son of God! "Be perfect, just as your heavenly Father is perfect" (Mt 5:48). That is a high aim, who can reach it? To become perfect as the eternal Father! Nevertheless, that is the standard. . . .

In what does this perfection consist? It consists in making us pleasing in the eyes of God, in possessing sanctifying grace and in possessing it unceasingly. That is what renders all our thoughts, words, and actions pleasing to God. And even what we leave undone, all is pleasing to him. Oh, what happiness! . . .

To labor at acquiring virtues is to labor at rendering oneself pleasing to God. It is essential therefore to labor at it unceasingly, to receive grace unto that end. It is essential to be always advancing *plus ultra* [even higher]. And if, in the morning, we have reached six degrees [of perfection], let us reach seven in the afternoon, by doing all our actions as perfectly as possible. . . .

In a word, what does our perfection consist in? It consists in doing all our actions well; first, as reasonable people, by leading a good life with our fellows and in observing justice toward them; second, as Christians, in practicing those virtues of which our Lord has given us an example; and lastly, as missionaries, in carrying out the works which he did, and in the same Spirit, as far as human weakness allows, which God knows well. . . .

So then . . . we should strive unceasingly after perfection and the proper performance of all our actions that they may be according to the good pleasure of God and that we, by this means, may be made worthy to come to the help of others.　　　St. VINCENT DE PAUL, 1581–1660

YOU WILL FIND THE NEXT READING AT MICAH 7.

like showers on the grass,
　which do not depend on human agency
　and are beyond human control.

7 Then what is left of Jacob,
　surrounded by many peoples,
　will be like a lion among the forest beasts,
　like a fierce lion among flocks of sheep
trampling as he goes,
　mangling his prey which no one takes
　　from him.

Yahweh will destroy all temptations

8 You will be victorious over your foes
　and all your enemies will be torn to
　　pieces.
9 When that day comes—declares
　　Yahweh—
I shall tear your horses away from you,
　I shall destroy your chariots;
10 I shall tear the cities from your country,
　I shall overthrow all your fortresses;

11 I shall tear the spells out of your hands
   and you will have no more soothsayers;
12 I shall tear away your images
   and your sacred pillars from among you,
   and no longer will you worship
   things which your own hands have
      made!
13 I shall uproot your sacred poles
   and shall destroy your cities!

14 In furious anger I shall wreak vengeance
   on the nations who have disobeyed me!

Yahweh's case against Israel

6 Now listen to what Yahweh says:
   'Stand up, state your case to the
      mountains
   and let the hills hear what you have
      to say!'
2 Listen, mountains, to the case as Yahweh
      puts it,
   give ear, you foundations of the earth,
   for Yahweh has a case against his people
   and he will argue it with Israel.
3 'My people, what have I done to you,
   how have I made you tired of me?
      Answer me!
4 For I brought you up from Egypt,
   I ransomed you from the place of
      slave-labour
   and sent Moses, Aaron and Miriam
   to lead you.
5 My people, please remember:
   what was Balak king of Moab's plan
   and how did Balaam son of Beor
      answer him?
   . . .ᵃ from Shittim to Gilgal,
   for you to know Yahweh's saving justice.

6 'With what shall I enter Yahweh's
      presence
   and bow down before God All-high?
   Shall I enter with burnt offerings,
   with calves one year old?
7 Will he be pleased with rams by the
      thousand,
   with ten thousand streams of oil?

Shall I offer my eldest son for my wrong-
      doing,
   the child of my own body for my sin?

8 'You have already been told what is right
   and what Yahweh wants of you.
   Only this, to do what is right,
   to love loyalty
   and to walk humbly with your God.'

Against tricksters in the city

9 Yahweh's voice! He thunders to the city,
   'Listen, tribe of assembled citizens!
10 Can I overlook the false measure,
   that abomination, the short bushel?
11 Can I connive at rigged scales
   and at the bag of fraudulent weights?
12 For the rich there are steeped in violence,
   and the citizens there are habitual liars.

13 'I myself have therefore begun to strike
      you down,
   to bring you to ruin for your sins.
14 You will eat but not be satisfied;
   you will store up but never keep safe;
   what you do keep safe I shall hand over to
      the sword;
15 you will sow but will not reap,
   press the olive but will not rub yourself
      with oil,
   tread the grape but will not drink the
      wine.

The example of Samaria

16 'For you keep the laws of Omri;
   what the House of Ahab did, you have
      done;
   by modelling yourselves on their
      standards,
   you force me to make an appalling
      example of you
   and reduce your citizens to a
      laughing-stock;
   hence you will endure the scorn of other
      peoples.'

6a Some words are missing in the Hebrew text.

97   READ MICAH 7:8–20.

What god can compare with you for pardoning guilt?—MICAH 7:18

CONFESSION — OPENING TO GRACE

Let those who perform works of penance learn from the words of the prophet with what dispositions they must do so, with what zeal, with what spirit, with what purpose, with what inward compunction, with what change of heart: "Look, Yahweh, I am in distress! My inmost being is in ferment; my heart turns over inside me" (Lm 1:20). . . .

So too did the people of Nineveh mourn, and they were spared the destruction of their city (see Jon 3); so great is the remedial efficacy of penance, that God seems to change his decree because of it. It is, therefore, within your power also to escape his punishment. He wants only that you place your hope in him, he wants only that you appeal to his mercy. If you . . . are unwilling to grant pardon to your neighbor unless he asks for it, do you think that, without your asking for forgiveness, God will forgive you?

Let us then mourn for a time, that we may rejoice for eternity. Let us fear the Lord; let us prepare to meet him, confessing our sins; let us correct our failings and make amends for our transgressions, lest of us too it should be said: "The faithful have vanished from the land: there is no one honest left" (Mi 7:2).

Why do you fear to confess your sins to the Lord who is so good? "Confess your sins," he bids you, "so that you may be justified." The grace of justification is offered you, while you are still guilty of sin; for he is justified who voluntarily confesses that he has sinned. . . . The Lord knows all things, but he waits for your confession, not in order to punish but in order to forgive.

ST. AMBROSE, 340?–397

YOU WILL FIND THE NEXT READING AT ZECHARIAH 12

Universal injustice

7 How wretched I am,
  a harvester in summer time,
  like a gleaner at the vintage:
  not a single cluster to eat,
  none of those early figs I love!
2 The faithful have vanished from the
    land:
  there is no one honest left.
  All of them are on the alert for blood,
  every man hunting his brother with a net.
3 Their hands are adept at wrong-doing:

the official makes his demands,
the judge gives judgement for a bribe,
the man in power pronounces as he
    pleases.
4 The best of them is like a briar,
  the most honest of them like a thorn-
    hedge.
  Now from the north their punishment
    approaches!
  That will be when they are confounded!
5 Trust no neighbour,
  put no confidence in a friend;
  do not open your mouth

to the wife who shares your bed.
6 For son insults father,
daughter rebels against mother,
daughter-in-law against mother-in-law;
a person's enemies come from within the
household itself.

7 But I shall look to Yahweh,
my hope is in the God who will save me;
my God will hear me.ᵃ

Zion insulted by enemies

8 Do not gloat over me, my enemy:
though I have fallen, I shall rise;
though I live in darkness,
Yahweh is my light.
9 I must endure Yahweh's anger
for I have sinned against him,
until he takes up my cause
and rights my wrongs;
he will bring me out into the light,
and then I shall contemplate his saving
justice.
10 When my enemy sees this,
she will be covered with shame,
having sneered, 'Where is Yahweh your
God?'
This time, I shall be watching
as she is trampled underfoot
like mud in the streets.

A prophecy of restoration

11 That will be the day for rebuilding your
walls!
The day for expanding your frontiers!
12 The day when others come to you
all the way from Assyria, from Egypt,
from Tyre and all the way from the
Euphrates,
from sea to sea, from the mountains to the
mountains!
13 The earth will become a desert

by reason of its inhabitants, in return for
what they have done.

A prayer for the confusion of Zion's enemies

14 With shepherd's crook lead your people to
pasture,
the flock that is your heritage,
living confined in a forest
with meadow land all round.
Let them graze in Bashan and Gilead
as in the days of old!
15 As in the days when you came out of
Egypt,
grant us to see wonders!
16 The nations will see and be confounded
in spite of all their power;
they will put their hands over their
mouths,
their ears will be deafened.
17 They will lick the dust like snakes,
like reptiles that crawl on the earth.
They will creep trembling out of their
lairs,
in terror before you.

A plea for God's forgiveness

18 What god can compare with you
for pardoning guilt
and for overlooking crime?
He does not harbour anger for ever,
since he delights in showing faithful love.
19 Once more have pity on us,
tread down our faults;
throw all our sins
to the bottom of the sea.
20 Grant Jacob your faithfulness,
and Abraham your faithful love,
as you swore to our ancestors
from the days of long ago.

7a Originally the end of the book. vv. 8–11 are exilic, vv.
14–17 even later, and vv. 18–20 a final psalm.

The Book of

NAHUM

1 Prophecy about Nineveh. Book of the vision of Nahum of Elkosh.

Psalm. The wrath of Yahweh

ALEPH ²Yahweh is a jealous and vengeful
    God,
    Yahweh takes vengeance, he is rich in
      wrath;
    Yahweh takes vengeance on his foes,
    he stores up fury for his enemies.
  ³ Yahweh is slow to anger but great in
      power,
    Yahweh never lets evil go unpunished.
BET In storm and whirlwind he takes his way,
    the clouds are the dust stirred up by his
      feet.
GIMEL ⁴He rebukes the sea, dries it up,
    and makes all the rivers run dry.
DALET ... Bashan and Carmel wither,
    the greenery of the Lebanon withers too.
HE ⁵The mountains tremble before him,
    the hills reel;
WAW the earth collapses before him,
    the world and all who live in it.
ZAIN ⁶His fury—who can withstand it?
    Who can endure his burning wrath?
HET His anger pours out like fire
    and the rocks break apart before him.
TET ⁷Yahweh is better than a fortress
    in time of distress;
YOD he recognises those who trust in him
  ⁸ even when the flood rushes on;
KAPH he will make an end once and for all of
      those who defy him,
    and pursue his foes into darkness.

Prophetic judgement on Judah and Assyria

  ⁹ What are your thoughts about Yahweh?
    He it is who makes a final end:

his adversaries will not rise up a second
    time;
  ¹⁰ like a thicket of tangled brambles,
    like dry straw, they will be burnt up
      completely.

To Assyria
  ¹¹ From you has emerged
    someone plotting evil against
      Yahweh,
    one of Belial's counsellors.ᵃ

To Judah
  ¹² Yahweh says this:
    Unopposed and many though they be,
    they will be cut down and pass away.
    Though I have made you suffer,
    I shall make you suffer no more,
  ¹³ for now I shall break his yoke which
      presses hard on you
    and snap your chains.

To the king of Nineveh
  ¹⁴ As for you, this is Yahweh's decree:
    You will have no heirs to your name,
    from the temple of your gods I shall
      remove
    carved image and cast image,
    and I shall devastate your tomb, for you
      are accursed!

2 *To Judah*
  See on the mountains the feet of the
      herald!
    'Peace!' he proclaims.
    Judah, celebrate your feasts,
    carry out your vows,

1a Belial (= useless) stands for the power of evil.

for Belial will never pass through you
again;
he has been utterly destroyed.

The fall of Nineveh

2 The destroyer has advanced on you,
guarding the siege-works, watching the
road,
bracing himself, mustering great
strength!
3 (For Yahweh has restored the vine
of Jacob,
yes, the vine of Israel,
although the plunderers had plundered
them,
although they had snapped off their
vine-shoots!)
4 The shields of his fighting men
show red,
his warriors are dressed in scarlet;
the metal of the chariots sparkles
as he prepares for battle;
the horsemen are impatient for action;
5 the chariots storm through the streets,
jostling one another in the squares;
they look like blazing flames,
like lightning they dash to and fro.
6 His captains are called out;
stumbling as they go,
they speed towards the wall,
and the mantelet is put in position.
7 The sluices of the River are opened,
and the palace melts in terror.
8 Beauty[a] is taken captive, carried away,
her slave-girls moaning like doves
9 and beating their breasts.
Nineveh is like a lake,
whose waters are draining away.
'Stop! Stop!'
But no one turns back.
10 'Plunder the silver! Plunder the gold!'
There is no end to the treasure,
a mass of everything you could desire!
11 Ravaged, wrecked, ruined!
Heart fails and knees give way,
anguish is in the loins of all,
and every face grows pale!

Sentence passed on the lion of Assyria

12 Where is the lions' den now,
the cave of the lion's whelps,
where the lion and lioness walked with
their cubs
and no one molested them,
13 where the lion would tear up food for his
whelps
and strangle the kill for his mates,
where he filled his caverns with prey
and his lairs with spoil?
14 Look, I am against you!—declares
Yahweh Sabaoth—
I shall send your chariots up in smoke,
and the sword will devour your whelps;
I shall cut short your depredations on
earth,
and the voices of your envoys will be heard
no more.

Sentence passed on Nineveh the harlot

3 Disaster to the city of blood,
packed throughout with lies,
stuffed with booty,
where plundering has no end!
2 The crack of the whip!
The rumble of wheels!
Galloping horse,
jolting chariot,
3 charging cavalry,
flashing swords,
gleaming spears,
a mass of wounded,
hosts of dead,
countless corpses;
they stumble over corpses—
4 because of the countless whorings of the
harlot,
the graceful beauty, the cunning witch,
who enslaved nations by her harlotries
and tribes by her spells.

5 Look, I am against you!—declares
Yahweh Sabaoth—

2a The statue of the goddess Ishtar, a fertility deity.

I shall lift your skirts as high as your face
and show your nakedness to the nations,
your shame to the kingdoms.
6 I shall pelt you with filth,
I shall shame you and put you in the
  pillory.
7 Then all who look at you
will shrink from you and say,
'Nineveh has been ruined!'
Who will mourn for her?
Where would I find people to comfort you?

The lesson of Thebes

8 Are you better off than No-Amon[a]
situated among rivers,
her defences the seas,
her rampart the waters?
9 In Ethiopia and Egypt
lay her strength, and it was boundless;
Put and the Libyans served in her army.
10 But she too went into exile,
into captivity;
her little ones too were dashed to pieces
at every crossroad;
lots were drawn for her nobles,
all her great men were put in chains.

11 You too will become drunk,
you will go into hiding;
you too will have to search
for a refuge from the enemy.

Nineveh's preparations useless

12 Your fortifications are all fig trees,
with early ripening figs:
as soon as they are shaken,
they fall into the mouth of the eater.
13 Look at your people:
you are a nation of women!
The gates of your country
gape open to your enemies;
fire has devoured their bars!
14 Draw yourselves water for the siege,
strengthen your fortifications!
Into the mud with you, puddle the clay,
repair the brick-kiln!
15 There the fire will burn you up,
the sword will cut you down.

The locusts fly away

Make yourselves as numerous as locusts,
make yourselves as numerous as the
  hoppers,
16a let your commercial agents
outnumber the stars of heaven,
17a your garrisons, like locusts,
and your marshals, like swarms of
  hoppers!
They settle on the walls
when the day is cold.
The sun appears,
16b the locusts spread their wings, they fly
  away,
17b away they fly, no one knows where.

A funeral lament

Alas, 18 your shepherds are asleep,
king of Assyria,
your bravest men slumber;
your people are scattered on the
  mountains
with no one to gather them.
19 There is no remedy for your wound,
your injury is past healing.
All who hear the news of you
clap their hands at your downfall.
For who has not felt
your unrelenting cruelty?

3a Thebes in Upper Egypt, taken by Assyria in 633 BC.

The Book of
HABAKKUK

1 The charge that Habakkuk the prophet received in a vision.

First complaint of the prophet:
lawlessness prevails

2 How long, Yahweh, am I to cry for help
while you will not listen;
to cry, 'Violence!' in your ear
while you will not save?

3 Why do you make me see wrong-doing,
why do you countenance oppression?
Plundering and violence confront me,
contention and discord flourish.

4 And so the law loses its grip
and justice never emerges,
since the wicked outwits the upright
and so justice comes out perverted.

First answer: the Chaldaeans as
instrument of God's justice

5 Cast your eyes over the nations, look,
and be amazed, astounded.
For I am doing something in your own
days
which you will not believe if you are told
of it.
6 For look, I am stirring up the Chaldaeans,
that fierce and fiery nation
who march miles across country
to seize the homes of others.
7 They are dreadful and awesome,
a law and authority to themselves.

8 Their horses are swifter than leopards,
fiercer than wolves at night;
their horsemen gallop on,
their horsemen advance from afar,
swooping like an eagle anxious to feed.

9 They are all bent on violence,
their faces scorching like an east wind;
they scoop up prisoners like sand.

10 They scoff at kings,
they despise princes.
They make light of all fortresses:
they heap up earth and take them.

11 Then the wind changes and is gone . . .
Guilty is he who makes his strength
his god.

Second complaint of the prophet:
the tyranny of the conqueror

12 Surely you, Yahweh, are from ancient
times,
my holy God, who never dies!
Yahweh, you have appointed him to
execute judgement;
O Rock, you have set him firm to punish.
13 Your eyes are too pure to rest on evil,
you cannot look on at oppression.
Why do you look on at those who play the
traitor,
why say nothing while the wicked
swallows someone more upright
than himself?
14 Why treat people like fish of the sea,
like gliding creatures who have no leader?
15 They haul them all up on their hook,
they catch them in their net,
they sweep them up in their dragnet
and then make merry and rejoice.

16 And so they offer a sacrifice to their net,
and burn incense to their dragnet,
for by these they get a rich living
and live off the fat of the land.

¹⁷ Are they to go on emptying their net
            unceasingly,
   slaughtering the nations without pity?

*Second answer: the upright will live
through faithfulness*

2 I shall stand at my post,
   I shall station myself on my watch-tower,
   watching to see what he will say to me,
   what answer he will make to my
            complaints.

² Then Yahweh answered me and said,
   'Write the vision down,
   inscribe it on tablets
   to be easily read.
³ For the vision is for its appointed time,
   it hastens towards its end and it will not
            lie;
   although it may take some time, wait
            for it,
   for come it certainly will before too
            long.

⁴ 'You see, anyone whose heart is not
            upright will succumb,
   but the upright will live through
            faithfulness.'ᵃ

Curses on the Oppressor

⁵ Now, surely, wealth is treacherous!
   He is arrogant, for ever on the move,
   with appetite as large as Sheol
   and as insatiable as Death,
   gathering in all the nations,
   and making a harvest of all peoples.
⁶ Are not the peoples all bound to satirise
   and make up cryptic riddles about him?
   As for instance:

Five imprecations

                    I
Disaster to anyone who amasses goods not
            his
   (for how long?)
   and to anyone who weighs himself down
            with goods taken in pledge!

⁷ Will not your creditors suddenly stand up,
   will not those who make you shiver wake
            up,
   and you will fall a prey to them?

⁸ Since you have plundered many nations,
   all the nations that remain will plunder
            you,
   because of the bloodshed and violence
            done to the country,
   to the city and to all who live in it.

                    II
⁹ Disaster to anyone who amasses ill-gotten
            gains for his house,
   so as to fix his nest on high
   and so evade the reach of misfortune!

¹⁰ You have conspired to bring shame on
            your house:
   by overthrowing many peoples
   you have worked your own ruin.

¹¹ For the very stone will protest from the
            wall,
   and the beam will respond from the
            framework.

                    III
¹² Disaster to anyone who builds a town with
            bloodshed
   and founds a city on wrong-doing!

¹³ Is it not thanks to Yahweh Sabaoth
   that the peoples' toil is fuel for the fire,
   and the nations' labour came to nothing?

¹⁴ *But the earth will be full of the knowledge of
            the glory of Yahweh
   as the waters cover the depths of the sea.*ᵇ

                    IV
¹⁵ Disaster to anyone who makes his
            neighbours drink,

2a Paul uses the Gk version 'faith' for the doctrine of justification by faith in Rm 1:17.
2b Is 11:9.

pouring out his poison until they are
    drunk,
so that he can see them naked!
16 You are full of shame, not glory!

Your turn now to drink and show your
    foreskin.
The cup in Yahweh's right hand comes
    round to you,
and disgrace will overshadow your glory.

17 For the violence done to the Lebanon will
    overwhelm you
and the massacre of animals will terrify
    you,
because of the bloodshed and violence
    done to the country,
to the city and to all who live in it.

V

19 c Disaster to anyone who says to the log,
    'Wake up!',
to the dumb stone, 'On your feet!'
(This is the prophecy!)
Look, he is encased in gold and silver,
—but not a breath of life inside it!

18 What use is a sculpted image that a sculptor
    should make it?
—a metal image, a lying instructor!
And why does the image-maker put his
    trust in it,
that he should make dumb idols?
20 But Yahweh is in his holy Temple:
let the whole earth be silent before him.

Plea to Yahweh for deliverance

3 A prayer of the prophet Habakkuk; tone as
  for dirges.

Prayer

2 Yahweh, I have heard of your renown;
    your work, Yahweh, inspires me with
    dread.
Make it live again in our time,
    make it known in our time;
in wrath remember mercy.

Theophany: Yahweh's approach

3 Eloah a comes from Teman,
    and the Holy One from Mount Paran.
                                                    Pause

His majesty covers the heavens,
    and his glory fills the earth.

4 His brightness is like the day,
    rays flash from his hands,
    that is where his power lies hidden.

5 Pestilence goes before him
    and Plague follows close behind.

6 When he stands up, he makes the earth
    tremble,
with his glance he makes the nations
    quake.
And the eternal mountains are dislodged,
the everlasting hills sink down,
his pathway from of old.

7 I saw the tents of Cushan in trouble,
    the tent-curtains of Midian shuddering.

Yahweh's battle

8 Yahweh, are you enraged with the rivers,
    are you angry with the sea,
that you should mount your chargers,
    your rescuing chariots?

9 You uncover your bow,
    and give the string its fill of arrows. *Pause*
You drench the soil with torrents;
10 the mountains see you and tremble,
    great floods sweep by,
    the abyss roars aloud,
    lifting high its waves.

11 Sun and moon stay inside their dwellings,
    they flee at the light of your arrows,
    at the flash of your lightning-spear.

2c vv. 18 and 19 have been transposed.

3a An ancient name for God. Teman is a district, Paran a
mountain in Edom.

12 In rage you stride across the land,
in anger you trample the nations.

13 You marched to save your people,
to save your anointed one;
you wounded the head of the house of the
wicked,
laid bare the foundation to the rock.

Pause

14 With your shafts you pierced the leader of
his warriors
who stormed out with shouts of joy to
scatter us,
as if they meant to devour some poor
wretch in their lair.

15 With your horses you trampled through
the sea,
through the surging abyss!

Conclusion: human fear and faith in God

16 When I heard, I trembled to the core,
my lips quivered at the sound;

my bones became disjointed
and my legs gave way beneath me.

Calmly I await the day of anguish
which is dawning on the people
now attacking us.

17 (For the fig tree is not to blossom,
nor will the vines bear fruit,
the olive crop will disappoint
and the fields will yield no food;
the sheep will vanish from the
fold;
no cattle in the stalls.)

18 But I shall rejoice in Yahweh,
I shall exult in God my Saviour.

19 Yahweh my Lord is my strength,
he will make my feet as light as
a doe's,
and set my steps on the heights.

For the choirmaster; on stringed instruments.

ZEPHANIAH

1 The word of Yahweh which was addressed to Zephaniah son of Cushi, son of Gedaliah, son of Amariah, son of Hezekiah, in the days of Josiah son of Amon king of Judah.

Prelude: judgement on all creation

² I shall sweep away everything
off the face of the earth,
declares Yahweh.
³ I shall sweep away humans and
animals,
the birds of the air and the fish of
the sea,
I shall topple the wicked
and wipe all people off the face of
the earth
—declares Yahweh.

Against the worshippers of alien gods

⁴ I shall raise my hand against Judah
and against all who live in Jerusalem,
and from this place I will wipe out Baal's
remnant,
the very name of his priests,
⁵ and those who prostrate themselves on
the roofs
before the array of heaven,
and those who prostrate themselves
before Yahweh
but swear by Milcom,ᵃ
⁶ and those who have turned their back
on Yahweh,
who do not seek Yahweh
and do not consult him.

⁷ Silence before Lord Yahweh,
for the Day of Yahweh is near!
Yahweh has prepared a sacrifice,
he has consecrated his guests.

Against the courtiers

⁸ On the Day of Yahweh's sacrifice,
I shall punish the courtiers,
the royal princes
and all who dress
in outlandish clothes.
⁹ On that day I shall punish
all who go up the Step
and fill the Temple of their lords,
with violence and deceit.

Against the merchants of Jerusalem

¹⁰ On that Day—declares Yahweh—
uproar will be heard from the Fish
Gate,
wailing from the New Quarter
and a great crash from the hills.
¹¹ Wail, you who live in the Hollow,
for it is all over with the merchants,
all the money-bags have been wiped out!

Against unbelievers

¹² When that time comes
I shall search Jerusalem by lamplight
and punish the men
stagnating over the remains of their
wine,
who say in their hearts,
'Yahweh can do nothing,
either good or bad.'
¹³ For this, their wealth will be looted
and their houses laid in ruins;
they will build houses but not live in
them,
they will plant vineyards but not drink
their wine.

1a A god of Ammon.

[1179]

The Day of Yahweh

¹⁴ The great Day of Yahweh is near,
near, and coming with great speed.
How bitter the sound of the Day of
Yahweh,
the Day when the warrior shouts his cry
of war.
¹⁵ That Day is a day of retribution,
a day of distress and tribulation,
a day of ruin and of devastation,
a day of darkness and gloom,
a day of cloud and thick fog,
¹⁶ a day of trumpet blast and battle cry
against fortified town
and high corner-tower.
¹⁷ I shall bring such distress on humanity
that they will grope their way like the
blind
for having sinned against Yahweh.
Their blood will be poured out
like mud,
yes, their corpses like dung;
¹⁸ nor will their silver or gold
be able to save them.
On the Day of Yahweh's anger,
by the fire of his jealousy,
the whole earth will be consumed.
For he will destroy, yes, annihilate
everyone living on earth.

Conclusion: a call to conversion

2 Gather together, gather together,
nations without shame,
² before you are dispersed like chaff
which disappears in a day;
before Yahweh's burning anger
overtakes you
(before the Day of Yahweh's anger
overtakes you).
³ Seek Yahweh,
all you humble of the earth,
who obey his commands.
Seek uprightness,
seek humility:
you may perhaps find shelter
on the Day of Yahweh's anger.

The enemy to the west: the Philistines

⁴ For Gaza will be abandoned
and Ashkelon reduced to ruins;
Ashdod will be driven out in broad
daylight
and Ekron^a uprooted.
⁵ Disaster to the members of the coastal
league,
to the nation of the Cherethites!
This is the word of Yahweh against you:
I shall subdue you, land of the Philistines,
I shall destroy you till there are no
inhabitants left;
⁶ and the coastal league will be reduced to
pasture land,
to grazing grounds for shepherds
and folds for sheep;
⁷ and the league will belong
to the remnant of the House of Judah;
they will pasture their flocks there,
at night they will rest in the houses of
Ashkelon;
for, when Yahweh their God has punished
them,
he will restore their fortunes.

The enemies to the east: Moab and Ammon

⁸ I have heard the taunt of Moab
and the insults of the Ammonites,
as they taunted my people
and boasted of their own domains.
⁹ For this, as I live—declares Yahweh
Sabaoth,
God of Israel—
Moab will become like Sodom
and the Ammonites like Gomorrah:
a realm of nettles, a heap of salt,
a desolation for ever.
What is left of my people will plunder
them,
the survivors of my nation will take their
heritage.
¹⁰ This will be the price of their pride

2a Four of the five Philistine coastal cities. Gath was already
in ruins.

Saints on Scripture

11 MINDING OUR THOUGHTS WITH SCRIPTURE MEDITATION

ST. JOHN CASSIAN, 360?–433?

Let your minds be filled with everything that is true, everything that is honourable, everything that is upright and pure, everything that we love and admire—with whatever is good and praiseworthy. PHILIPPIANS 4:8

Meditating on Scripture can take several different forms. Sometimes we can reflect on a single text, turning it over in our mind. For example, the early monks used to memorize a verse and repeatedly meditate on it while they worked. This practice, like the repetition of the Hail Mary in the Rosary, drew them close to God in prayer. Sometimes we meditate on a Bible passage in order to figure out how to apply it to our lives. For example, we might reflect this way on the Sunday gospel. This kind of meditation is a mental exercise that precedes prayer and can lead us to it. A third form of meditating on Scripture involves our envisioning a Bible scene and imagining ourselves into it. For example, we might reflect in this way on the parable of the prodigal son, putting ourselves consecutively in the place of the lost son, the father and the dutiful son (see Lk 15:11–31).

In the following excerpt from his *Conferences*, St. John Cassian explains the importance of Scripture meditation in the Christian life:

THOUGHTS CONSTANTLY barrage our minds, but every earnest person possesses the power either to admit them or to reject them. As their instigation does not entirely depend on us, so we have the authority to accept or dismiss them. But just because thoughts bombard us, we must not blame everything on their assault, or on those spirits who strive to instill them into us. Otherwise we would no longer have a free will, nor would we have the power to make efforts for our improvement. But to a great extent we have the ability to improve the character of our thoughts. We can allow either holy and spiritual thoughts or worldly ones to grow up in our hearts.

For this purpose frequently reading Scripture and continually meditating on it will give us opportunities for spiritual recollection. Regularly singing Psalms also arouses constant feelings of compunction in our hearts. And earnestly undertaking vigils, fasts and prayers humbles the mind so that it does not focus on earthly things, but instead contemplates heavenly realities. If we neglect all these practices and allow carelessness to creep up on us, our minds, hardened by the foulness of sin, will surely lean in a carnal direction and eventually fall away.

We can suitably compare this movement of the heart to the operation of a mill wheel, which the headlong rush of water whirls round with revolving impetus, and which can never stop its work so long as the water drives it. However, the person who directs the wheel has the power to decide whether he will have it grind wheat or barley or oats. The wheel can crush only the material that the person in charge puts into it. Similarly, torrents of temptations drive the mind through the trials of this present life. And it cannot be free from the flow of thoughts. But with earnest and diligent effort the person in charge of the mind can determine the character of the thoughts that it should either reject or admit. For if we constantly meditate on Holy Scripture and reflect on Christian realities, the desire for perfection, and the hope of future joy, spiritual thoughts will surely arise in us and cause the mind to dwell on the subjects of our meditation. But if we are overcome by sloth or carelessness and spend our time in idle gossip, or are entangled in the cares of this world and unnecessary anxieties, an evil sort of weed will spring up and damage the fruitfulness of our hearts. As our Lord and Savior says, wherever the treasure of our works or purpose may be, there also our heart is sure to continue (see Mt 6:21).

12 THE BENEFITS OF MEDITATING ON SCRIPTURE

The saints regularly meditated on Bible texts. As a result, God's Word flowed as an undercurrent in their thoughts, giving form and content to their own words. Consider the following three saints to observe how thoroughly Scripture penetrated their thoughts and writings.

ST. VINCENT FERRER, 1350–1419 St. Vincent labored to revive faith in Europe at the turn of the fifteenth century. In this excerpt from his *Treatise on the Spiritual Life* he is reflecting on the verse, the "kingdom of God is within you" (see Lk 17:21).

You must open the interior eyes of your soul on the light, on this heaven within you, a vast horizon stretching far beyond the realm of human activity, an unexplored country to the majority of human beings. The ordinary observer sees in the ocean only the realm of storms, and never guesses that a few feet below the surface its waters are always limpid, and in a scintillating clarity is found vegetation and living creatures of wondrous diversity, marvelous in beauty and structure, mysterious depths where the pearl is formed.

Such is the depth of the soul where God dwells and shows himself to us. And when the soul has seen God, what more can it want? If it possesses him, why and for whom can it ever be moved to abandon him? So at any price, preserve yourself in that calm through which the soul sees the eternal Sun.

ST. CLARE OF ASSISI, 1193–1253 St. Clare founded the women's community that patterned their lives on the Friars Minor of St. Francis. In this letter she is encouraging her friend, Queen Agnes of Bohemia, who has embraced gospel poverty.

You know, I firmly believe that the kingdom of heaven is promised and given by the Lord only to the poor: for he who loves the things of time loses the fruit of charity; and that one cannot serve God and money, for either the one is loved and the other hated, or the one is served and the other despised (see Mt 6:24). You know too that one clothed cannot fight with one naked, because he is more quickly brought to earth who gives his adversary a chance to hold him; that no one can live lordly in this world and rule in heaven with Christ; and that a camel can pass through the eye of a needle more easily than a rich man reach the kingdom of heaven (see Mt 19:24). Therefore you have cast aside your garments—the riches of time—that you may not be overcome by our adversary but through the close way and the narrow gate may enter the kingdom of heaven (see Mt 7:14).

ST. RAYMOND OF PEÑYAFORT, 1175–1275 St. Raymond collected the decrees of popes and councils in the *Decretals*, his book that served as the church's source of canon law for seven centuries. In this excerpt from a letter, he expands on 2 Timothy 3:12: "Anybody who tries to live in devotion to Christ is certain to be persecuted."

The preacher of God's truth has told us that all who want to live righteously in Christ will suffer persecution. The only exception to this general statement is, I think, the person who either neglects, or does not know how, to live justly and righteously in this world.

May you never be numbered among those whose house is peaceful, quiet and free from care; those on whom the Lord's chastisement does not descend; those who live out their days in prosperity, and in the twinkling of an eye will go down to hell.

Your purity of life, your devotion, deserve and call for a reward; because you are acceptable and pleasing to God your purity of life must be made purer still, by frequent buffetings, until you attain perfect sincerity of heart. If from time to time you feel the sword falling on you with double or treble force, you should also see this as sheer joy and the mark of love.

That the saints filled their minds and hearts with Scripture had a lot to do with their sanctity, for they found God in the Bible. Or better, when the saints laid hold of the words of Scripture, the Word himself laid hold of them.

13 MEDITATING ON A SCRIPTURE VERSE

When we fill our minds with Scripture, it influences and shapes our personal prayer, as it penetrated the prayer of Sts. Augustine, John Gabriel Perboyre, and Simeon, the New Theologian.

I have been crucified with Christ and yet I am alive; yet it is no longer I, but Christ living in me. GALATIANS 2:20

ST. AUGUSTINE, 354–430

Lord jesus, let me know myself;
let me know thee,
And desire nothing else but thee.
Let me love myself only if I love thee,
And do all things for thy sake.
Let me humble myself and exalt thee,
And think of nothing else but thee.
Let me die to myself and live in
thee,
And take whatever happens as
coming from thee.
Let me forsake myself and walk after
thee,
And ever desire to follow thee.
Let me flee from myself and turn to
thee,
So that I may merit to be defended by
thee.
Let me fear for myself, let me fear thee,
And ever obey for the love of thee.
Let me cleave to nothing but thee,
And ever be poor because of thee.
Look upon me that I may love thee,
Call me, that I may see thee,
And forever possess thee, for all
eternity.

ST. JOHN GABRIEL PERBOYRE, 1802–1840

O my Divine Savior,
 transform me into yourself,
May my hands be the hands of Jesus.
May my tongue be the tongue of Jesus.
Grant that every faculty of my body
 may serve only to glorify you.
Above all transform my soul and all its
 powers
 that my memory, my will and my
 affections
may be the memory, the will and the
 affections of Jesus.
I pray you to destroy in me all that is
 not of you.
Grant that I may live
 but in you
 and by you
 and for you
that I may truly say with Saint Paul:
"It is no longer I, but Christ living in me."

ST. SIMEON, THE NEW THEOLOGIAN, 949–1022

As the height of heaven is above earth,
so strong is his faithful love for those who fear him.
As the distance of east from west,
so far from us does he put our faults.
As tenderly as a father treats his children,
so Yahweh treats those who fear him;
he knows of what we are made,
he remembers that we are dust. PSALM 103:11–14

Saviour, I know that none other
 Stumbled before Thee as I
 stumbled,
Or did the deeds which I worked.
But this too I know,
That the greatness of my stumblings
And the multitude of my sins
Go not beyond the measure
Of the longsuffering of my God,
Beyond the height of his loving-
 kindness.
These things make me to venture;
These things give me wings, O my
 Christ.
Therefore giving thanks in mind,
Giving thanks in heart,
Giving thanks in the members
Of my soul and of my body,
I worship Thee, I magnify Thee,
I glorify Thee, my God
That art blessed
Now and for evermore.

14 PRAYING WITH SCRIPTURE

ST. BERNARD OF CLAIRVAUX, 1090?–1153

Instead of breaking his legs one of the soldiers pierced his side with a lance; and immediately there came out blood and water. JOHN 19:33–34

The saints immersed themselves in Scripture life-long, setting examples for us. Many prayed daily the Liturgy of the Hours, which consists almost entirely of Psalms and other Scripture readings. All read and studied the Bible. Often when praying, they used words of Scripture that flowed from their hearts. St. Bernard of Clairvaux, for example, filled his praying and preaching with Bible texts, as he does in the following sermon selection. And remember, he was not looking up the verses he quotes—they flooded from his memory into his prayer.

Now that we have once reached the Heart of Jesus, that Heart of exceeding sweetness, and know how that "it is wonderful for us to be here" (Mt 17:4), let us never again allow ourselves to be torn away from him, about whom it is written: "Those who turn from you will be registered in the underworld" (Jr 17:13). But what portion is theirs that draw near to you, you have told us yourself when you said, "Rejoice, because your names are written in heaven" (see Lk 10:20). Therefore let us draw near to you—"you will be our joy and our gladness" (Sg 1:4) when we remember your Heart.

"How good, how delightful it is to live" (Ps 133:1) in this Heart! Yes, let me cast away all things, all my thoughts, and all my feelings, let me cast them all away, and let me "cast all my care" (see 1 P 5:7) upon the Heart of the Lord Jesus and "he shall sustain me" (see Ps 55:22).

Toward this Temple, toward this Holy of Holies, towards this Ark of the Covenant "will I worship and praise your name" (see Ps 138:2). I will say with David, "Your servant has found it in his heart to pray this prayer to you" (see 2 S 7:27). And I have found the Heart of Jesus, the Heart of my king, my brother, and my gentle friend. And am I not to worship? Yes, O most sweet Jesus, now that I have found this Heart, which is both yours and mine, I will worship you, O my God! O, graciously let my prayer enter into that Sanctuary of mercy! Draw me entirely into your Heart! O Jesus, in the perfection of your beauty fairer than the children of men, "wash me clean from my guilt, purify me from my sin" (Ps 51:2); so that purified by you, I may be able to come to you, who are yourself most pure, and that I may be found to "dwell in" your Heart "all the days of my life" (Ps 27:4), to behold you, and to be strong to do your will.

Your side was pierced so that we might find a wide entrance there. Your heart was wounded so that we might be able to dwell in it and in you, hidden "safe in your presence . . . far from human plotting" (Ps 31:20). Your side was also pierced so that behind the physical wound, which we see, we may also perceive that wound of love, which is not physical. And how could he have shown that love more strikingly than by giving not his Body, but his very Heart to be pierced for us? The physical wound reveals the spiritual wound. Is there anyone who would not love that wounded Heart? Is there anyone who would not return love for love to him that has loved so well? Is there anyone who would not embrace him who stands so pure?

Therefore, while we still linger in this body, let us love him and love him again, who has loved us first. Let us embrace that Wounded One, wounded for us . . . (see Mt 21:35–39). Let us stand waiting until he is pleased to tie with the bond and pierce with the spear of his love these hearts of ours that still are so hard and unrepentant.

15 THE PSALMS AND THE CHRISTIAN LIFE

ST. AMBROSE, 339–397

With gratitude in your hearts sing psalms and hymns and inspired songs to God. COLOSSIANS 3:16

ALTHOUGH THE DIVINE Scriptures breathe forth the grace of God, the magnificent Book of Psalms does so in a very special way. . . .

History instructs, the law teaches, prophecy announces, morality exhorts: in the Book of Psalms there is something profitable for all and a kind of medicine for the salvation of mankind. Whoever reads it obtains a special remedy for curing the wounds of his particular ills. Whoever desires to see well—finding in the Psalms various kinds of competitions as in a public training school for souls or a stadium for virtues—let him choose the one most suited to him so that he may more easily obtain the crown (for example, see Pss 116, 139, and 141).

If one applies himself to examining the deeds of the ancients and wishes to imitate them, he finds in a single psalm the entire comprehensive chain of ancestral history, so that by an abridged reading he might obtain a great treasure of ancient memories (for example, see Pss 106, 135, and 136). If one explores the power of the law, which is contained entire in the bond of charity—for "to love the other person is to fulfil the law" (Rm 13:8)—let him read in the Psalms how with such great love a single person [that is, Jesus] exposed himself to grievous dangers in order to remove the reproach against all the people; in this triumph of virtue he will discover the equal glory of charity (for example, see Pss 11, 89, 110, and 132). . . .

In the Psalms Jesus is not only born for us, but he also undergoes that saving bodily passion, dies, rises again, ascends to heaven, and sits at the right hand of the Father. What no man had ever dreamed of saying the Prophet [that is, David] alone has announced in them and then in the gospel the Lord himself publicly manifested it.

THE GOSPEL AND THE CHRISTIAN LIFE ST. JEROME, 341?–420

"Anyone who loves me will keep my word, and my Father will love him, and we shall come to him and make a home in him." JOHN 14:23

THE KINGDOM of heaven is the proclamation of the Gospel and that knowledge of the Scripture that leads to life. . . . This kingdom is like a grain of mustard seed, which a man took and sowed in his field (see Mt 13:4–23). . . . Who is he that sows but our own mind and soul that take the grain from preaching and by nourishing it in the soil cause it to sprout in the field of our own breast? Now understand that the preaching of the gospel is the least of all doctrines [that human beings proclaim]. The one who starts out preaching . . . the stumblingblock of the Cross at first receives very little credit. Compare such teaching with the doctrines of the philosophers with their books, their magnificent eloquence, and their rounded sentences, and you will see how the grain of the Gospel, when it is sown, is the humblest of all seeds.

But when the doctrines of men grow up, there is in them . . . nothing life-giving. The plant is drooping, delicate and soft. We may truly say of some of these that the "grass withers, the flower fades" (Is 40:8). But the grain of the Gospel seed, although when it was sown it seemed to be the least of all seeds, when once it is rooted in the soul of man or in the whole world, grows not into a little plant, but into a tree. And the birds of the air, by which we may understand either the souls of believers or the angelic powers bound to God's service, come and lodge in its branches. I consider that the branches of the Gospel tree, which grows from the grain of mustard seed, are the diverse developments of doctrine, on which these "birds" find resting places.

16 A METHOD OF CONTINUAL PRAYER

ST. JOHN CASSIAN, 360?–433?

Pray constantly. 1 THESSALONIANS 5:17

IN ORDER TO KEEP God always in mind you should frequently pray this verse: "Come to my help, O God. Lord, hurry to my rescue" (see Ps 70:1). With good reason this text has been selected from all of Scripture as a method of continual prayer. It encompasses all the emotions that human beings can experience. We can effectively apply it to any circumstance and use it to resist every temptation. Since the verse appeals to God against all danger, it expresses our humble dependence on him, our anxieties and fears, our admission of our own weakness, and our confidence in answered prayer. And it conveys the assurance of God's present and ever ready help. A person constantly calling on his protector can be sure that he is near. . . .

So we will find this verse useful in all circumstances, whether adverse or prosperous and happy because it confesses our absolute dependence on God: When I am tempted to gluttony, desiring to eat much more than I need, I must immediately pray, "Come to my help, O God. Lord, hurry to my rescue." When a headache or drowsiness interferes with my spiritual reading, I must say, "Come to my help, O God. Lord, hurry to my rescue." When I cannot fall asleep at night, I must sigh and pray, "Come to my help, O God. Lord, hurry to my rescue."

When I am struggling against a sexual temptation and a pleasant feeling draws me to say yes to it, I must cry out, "Come to my help, O God. Lord, hurry to my rescue." When anger or envy threatens to disturb my peacefulness and embitter me, I must force myself to pray, groaning "Come to my help, O God. Lord, hurry to my rescue." When conceit and pride flatter me with the thought that I am more spiritual than other people, I must repent with all my heart and say, "Come to my help, O God. Lord, hurry to my rescue. . . ."

When memories of conversations or of business interrupt my prayer, or when dryness keeps me earthbound and blocks all spiritual thoughts, I can get free from this state of mind only by pleading, "Come to my help, O God. Lord, hurry to my rescue." When the Holy Spirit strengthens my soul, fills me with unspeakable joy and enlightens my mind with new insights, in order to continue enjoying these graces I must pray, "Come to my help, O God. Lord, hurry to my rescue." When diabolical horrors terrify me at night, and I fear that I cannot be saved, I must take refuge in this verse, crying out with all my strength, "Come to my help, O God. Lord, hurry to my rescue." And when the Lord's consolation has restored me and cheered me by his coming to my aid, and I feel as though countless thousands of angels are supporting me, in order to continue to be encouraged in my spiritual battles, I must exclaim, "Come to my help, O God. Lord, hurry to my rescue."

So we must continuously pray this verse both in adversity that we may be delivered, and in prosperity that we may be preserved and not puffed up. Always turn this verse over in your mind. Repeat it when you are working, performing some duty or going on a journey. Meditate on it when you are going to bed, or eating, or taking care of personal needs. This thought may be a saving formula for you, not only protecting you from all the devil's attacks, but also purifying you from your faults and sins, and leading you to . . . that ineffable glow of prayer, which so few experience.

Fall asleep while reflecting on this verse, and when you wake up let it be the first thing to come into your mind. So let it precede all your waking thoughts, and when you get out of bed let it send you down on your knees, then let it send you off to all your work and business, and let it follow you all day long.

17 WHEN GOD SPEAKS TO US IN SCRIPTURE

But you must do what the Word tells you and not just listen to it and deceive yourselves. JAMES 1:22

Sometimes God spoke personally to saints through Scripture in ways that profoundly changed them, as he did to Sts. Anthony, Augustine and Alipius in the following accounts. And they acted on what they heard God say to them with dramatic consequences.

ST. ANTHONY OF EGYPT, 251–356, was born into a well-to-do family near Memphis, Egypt. When Anthony was twenty, his parents died, leaving him responsible for his younger sister. Once he heard this Scripture proclaimed at Mass: "If you wish to be perfect, go and sell your possessions and give the money to the poor, and you will have treasure in heaven; then come, follow me" (Mt 19:21). Anthony felt God was speaking directly to him. So, after setting aside enough money for his sister's care, he donated all his possessions to the poor.

In a short time, Anthony heard another gospel declare, "Do not worry about tomorrow: tomorrow will take care of itself" (Mt 6:34). Again he took the words personally and gave as alms the money he had saved for his sister. He found the little girl a home with a household of nuns. Then Anthony became a hermit, living in a hut outside of town.

Later he went to the desert, where he spent eighty-five years serving God in prayer and helping others who sought his spiritual direction. St. Anthony's choice had a significant effect on the church because by establishing model communities of monks, he became the father of monasticism.

ST. AUGUSTINE, 354–430, took a long, twisted path to Christ. For thirty-two years his restlessness led him into immorality and intellectual confusion. However, in 385 St. Ambrose persuaded him that Christianity was true. But Augustine postponed deciding to follow Christ because he did not feel he was ready for change.

In 386 news that Victorinus, a famous philosopher, had publicly accepted Christianity moved him nearer to conversion. Then one day a friend told Augustine how two men had suddenly turned to serving Christ by reading St. Athanasius' life of St. Anthony.

This conversation plunged Augustine into agitation over his long delay in yielding to God. An audible voice interrupted his emotional turmoil and urged him to open the Bible and read. His eyes fell at once on this text: "Not in orgies and drunkenness, not in promiscuity and licentiousness, not in rivalry and jealousy. But put on the Lord Jesus Christ, and make not provision for the desires of the flesh" (see Rm 13:13–14). Immediately Augustine's resistance and hesitation dissolved, and he decided to embrace Christ and the church—a decision from which he never wavered. For thirty-four years he used his prodigious gifts to pastor and teach the church in North Africa and to protect the faith from the onslaught of heresies.

ST. ALIPIUS, 360?–430, became both a student in Augustine's school in Tagaste, North Africa, and his personal friend. Alipius was weak-willed, fluctuating wildly between strict moral conduct and gross pursuits that were popular in pagan cities. In Carthage he became addicted to watching gladiators slaughter each other in the circus shows—an addiction that he struggled to resist.

When his parents sent Alipius to Rome to study law, he tried to lead a good life. He scrupulously avoided the Roman circus. But one day he gave in to friends who dragged him to watch the bloody sport of the gladiators—and he got hooked again.

Although he applied himself to his studies, he was constantly torn by his spiritual ups and downs.

In Rome, Alipius was reunited with Augustine and later moved with him to Milan. In 386 he witnessed Augustine's miraculous conversion upon his reading a text in Romans 13. Alipius asked to see what Augustine had read, and he was stunned as his eyes fell on Romans 14:1: "Give a welcome to anyone whose faith is not strong." Immediately he saw himself in the text and decided without hesitation to follow his friend to Christ and the church. Together they were baptized at Easter in 387. Later as bishop of Tagaste, he collaborated with Augustine in leading the church of North Africa.

18 USING SCRIPTURE IN DAILY LIFE

All scripture is inspired by God and useful for refuting error, for guiding people's lives and teaching them to be upright. This is how someone who is dedicated to God becomes fully equipped and ready for any good work. 2 TIMOTHY 3:16–17

The saints show us how to apply a text of Scripture to the circumstances of daily life. St. Theresa Margaret, for example, used Psalm 116 as a lever to assist her in humbly serving her sisters. And St. Lutgarde relied on Psalm 70 as a weapon against temptation. We too should be on the lookout for Bible texts that are suited to bring divine grace to bear on our personal lives.

ST. THERESA MARGARET OF THE SACRED HEART, 1747–1770

*What return can I make to Yahweh
for his generosity to me?* PSALM 116:12

IN 1765 AT AGE SEVENTEEN, Anna Maria Redi left her family and entered the Carmelite convent in Florence, Italy. She died five years later. In that brief period, as Sister Theresa Margaret of the Sacred Heart, this young woman spent most of her days in prayer and in caring for her sick sisters. Spirited and unselfish, she became a bright source of encouragement for the other nuns. The saint especially delighted the older sisters, bringing a gentle relief to their lives, which had been hard under the rigors of the Carmelite rule. Once Theresa Margaret found a novice weeping in pain and out of compassion tenderly kissed her cheek. The young sister was tormented with such a severe, chronic toothache that the superiors were hesitant to accept her in the convent permanently. But the moment the saint kissed her she was healed, and later she was able to become a full member of the community.

The nuns who observed Theresa Margaret in prayer frequently heard her whispering repeatedly this line from Psalm 116: "What return can I make to Yahweh for his generosity to me?" Her simple, homey charity flowed from this attitude of thankfulness. She gratefully performed her menial service to the sick. If she ever felt a twinge of impatience or self-concern, her gratitude dissolved it. St. Theresa Margaret's example calls us to cultivate a sense of thankfulnes as an antidote for angry or selfish responses to the inconveniences that pop up in our daily relationships.

ST. LUTGARDE, 1186–1242

Be pleased, God, to rescue me,
*   Yahweh, come quickly and help me!*
Shame and dismay to those
*   who seek my life!*
Back with them! Let them be humiliated
*   who delight in my misfortunes.*
Let them shrink away covered with shame,
*   those who say to me, "Aha, aha!"* PSALM 70:1–3

LUTGARDE COULD NOT MARRY because her father squandered her dowry on a bad business deal. At age twelve she was sent to live at a convent near Liège, Belgium. No one thought this girl had what it took to be a nun, but she surprised everyone. Lutgarde fell in love with Jesus and devoted her life to him. Her prayer life quickly grew into an intimate personal relationship with the Lord. When nuns interrupted her contemplation with tasks, she would say, "Wait here, Lord Jesus, I'll be right back."

Once Lutgarde asked the Lord to give her the miraculous ability to understand Latin, the language which the nuns used for chanting the Psalms. Lutgarde received insight into the meaning of the Psalms, but as the knowledge did not seem to warm her heart with devotion, she asked the Lord to take that gift back too.

Lutgarde, however, had learned how to use the Psalms as a potent weapon against the temptations of the devil. She said that when she reflected on Psalm 70 and other Psalms, in her mind's eye she could see demons dropping their evil suggestions and fleeing in horror. The words of Scripture, she said, had the power to disarm the devil, even if she did not understand them perfectly. So when the tempter called, Lutgarde nipped his seductions in the bud by praying the Psalms for divine assistance.

19 FORMED BY GOD'S WORD

ST. PETER CLAVER, 1580–1654

His words are sweeter than honey, that drips from the comb. Thus your servant is formed by them; observing them brings great reward. PSALM 19:10–11

He has sent me to bring the news to the afflicted, to soothe the broken-hearted, to proclaim liberty to captives. . . . ISAIAH 61:1

This letter from St. Peter Claver to his superior shows how the gospel shaped the life and action of the saints:

YESTERDAY, 30 MAY 1627, the feast of the Most Holy Trinity, a great number of black people who had been seized from along the African rivers were put ashore from one very large vessel. We hurried out with two baskets full of oranges, lemons, sweet biscuits. . . . We had to force our way through the crowds till we reached the sick. There was a great number of them, lying . . . in mud; but someone had formed the idea of making a heap of tiles and broken brick in case the damp should be too much for them. This was all they had for a bed, all the more uncomfortable because they were naked without any covering at all.

We took off our cloaks, went to a store, brought from there all the wood that was available and put it together to make a platform; then, forcing a way through the guards, we eventually managed to carry all the sick on to it. Then we separated them into two groups; one of them my companion addressed with the aid of an interpreter, the other I spoke to myself.

Two of the black slaves were more dead than alive; they were already cold, and we could hardly feel any pulse in their veins. We got together some glowing embers on a tile, placed the dying near them, and then threw aromatic spices on the fire. We had two bags of these spices, and used them all. Then with the help of our cloaks—for the slaves have none of their own, and it would have been a waste of time to ask their masters—we got them to inhale the vapors, which seemed to restore their warmth and vitality. You should have seen the expression of gratitude in their eyes!

In this way we spoke to them, not with words but with deeds. And for people in their situation who were convinced that they had been brought there to be eaten, any other form of address would have been pointless. Then we sat or knelt beside them and washed their faces and bodies with wine. By such acts of kindness we tried to cheer them up and performed for them all the natural services which are calculated to raise the spirits of the sick.

Then we began to instruct them for baptism. We first explained to them the wonderful effects of the sacrament on both body and soul. And when they showed by their answers to our questions that they understood us sufficiently well, we began to teach them at greater length concerning the one God who rewards and punishes each as he deserves, and so on. We urged them to repent and give some indication of sorrow for their sins. Finally, when they seemed to be sufficiently prepared, we explained to them the mysteries of the Trinity, Incarnation and Passion. We showed them a representation of Christ crucified above a baptismal font, into which the blood flowed from his wounds. Then we taught them to repeat the act of contrition in their own language.

20 FROM STUDY TO ACTION

We must study Scripture regularly because we meet God in the Bible. There we hear his voice and learn how to live as he wants us to. However, as these stories about Sts. Jerome and Dominic show, the time comes when we must put what we have learned into action.

ST. JEROME, 341?–420   St. Jerome went to Rome at age eighteen where he mastered Latin and Greek and read the best writers in both languages. The great Roman orator, Cicero, was one of his favorites. By his own admission the allurements of Rome diluted his faith and sullied his behavior. However, at twenty-one he moved to Trier in Germany to further his schooling, and there he experienced a conversion that gave new direction to his life. But it was not until he went to Antioch in 374 that Jerome oriented his life fully on God. There he became very sick with a high fever. While delirious he had a vision of himself before the judgment seat of Christ.

"Who are you?" asked the Lord.

"I am a Christian," said Jerome.

"No, you lie. You are a Ciceronian. For where your treasure is, there also will your heart be."

Shocked into action, Jerome went into the desert where he spent four years in solitude, training himself to obey God through prayer and fasting. From that time he set his heart completely on God, using his gifts to explicate Scripture and perfect the translation of the Bible into Latin. In 385 Jerome moved to Bethlehem, where he founded a monastery and a hospice for visitors to the Holy Land. He continued his study of Scripture—with one significant interruption. After 404, barbarians overran Rome, and many Christians fled to the holy land. To come to their aid, Jerome dropped all of his biblical studies. "Today," he said, "we must translate the words of Scripture into deeds, and instead of speaking saintly words, we must act on them."

ST. DOMINIC, 1170–1221   St. Dominic, the founder of the Friars Preachers, began studying Scripture even as a child. In his late teens as an undergraduate at the University of Palencia in Spain he spent most nights reading the Bible until the wee hours. Dominic had a memory which retained large portions of the Bible for ready reference—a gift that he made great use of as a preacher. At twenty Dominic undertook four years of theological study devoting himself to systematic study of the Bible. He devoured the commentaries of the fathers of the church and attended university lectures on the Scriptures. He owned an expensive sheepskin copy of the Bible, and every evening he religiously recorded in its margins notes on the day's lessons.

In 1195, however, Spain was ravaged by war and famine, and impoverished refugees poured into Palencia. Moved by their plight, Dominic sold all his possessions, even his Bible, in order to contribute to their relief. "I will not study on dead skins," he said, "when living skins are dying of hunger."

How blessed are those whose way is blameless,
who walk in the Law of Yahweh!
Blessed are those who observe his instructions,
who seek him with all their hearts,
and, doing no evil,
who walk in his ways.
You lay down your precepts
to be carefully kept.
May my ways be steady
in doing your will. PSALM 119:1–5

for having taunted and boasted
over the people of Yahweh Sabaoth.
¹¹ Yahweh will be fearsome to them,
for he will scatter all the gods of the earth,
and they will bow down to him,
each from his own place—
all the islands of the nations.

The enemy to the south: Ethiopia

¹² You Ethiopians too
will be run through by my sword.

The enemy to the north: Assyria

¹³ He will raise his hand against the north
and bring Assyria down in ruins;
he will make Nineveh a waste,
as dry as a desert.
¹⁴ Flocks will rest inside there,
so will wild animals;
pelican and porcupine
will nest round her cornices at night;
the owl will hoot at the window
and the raven croak on the doorstep—
for the cedar has been torn down.
¹⁵ This is what the city will be like,
once living happy and carefree
and thinking to itself,
'I have no rival—not I!'
And what will it be now? A ruin,
a lair for wild beasts to rest in,
and everyone who passes by
will whistle and throw up his hands.

Against the rulers of Judah

3 Disaster to the rebellious, the befouled,
the tyrannical city!
² She has not listened to the call,
she has not bowed to correction,
she has not trusted in Yahweh,
she has not drawn near to her God.
³ The rulers she has
are roaring lions,
her judges are wolves of the wastelands
which leave nothing over for the
morning,
⁴ her prophets are braggarts,
impostors,

her priests have profaned what is holy
and violated the Law.

⁵ Yahweh the Upright is in her,
he does no wrong;
morning by morning he gives judgement,
each dawn unfailingly
(but the wrong-doer knows no shame).

The example of the nations

⁶ I have exterminated the nations,
their corner-towers lie in ruins;
I have emptied their streets,
no one walks through them;
their cities have been destroyed
and are now deserted and unpeopled.
⁷ I thought, 'At least you will fear me,
at least you will bow to correction,'
and none of the punishments I brought on
them
will disappear from their view.
But no, it only made them more anxious
to do whatever was corrupt.

⁸ So wait for me—declares Yahweh—
for the day when I rise as accuser,
for I am determined to gather the nations,
to assemble the kingdoms,
and on you to vent my fury,
the whole heat of my anger
(for the whole earth will be devoured
by the fire of my jealousy).

Conversion of the nations

⁹ Yes, then I shall purge
the lips of the peoples,
so that all may invoke the name of
Yahweh
and serve him shoulder to shoulder.
¹⁰ From beyond the rivers of Ethiopia,
my suppliants will bring me tribute.

The humble remnant of Israel

¹¹ When that Day comes
you will never again be ashamed of all the
deeds
with which you once rebelled against me,

for I shall rid you
of those who exult in your pride;
never again will you strut
on my holy mountain.
¹² But in you I shall leave surviving
a humble*a* and lowly people,
¹³ and those who are left in Israel
will take refuge in the name of Yahweh.
They will do no wrong,
will tell no lies;
nor will a deceitful tongue
be found in their mouths.
But they will be able to graze and rest
with no one to alarm them.

Psalms of joy in Zion*b*

¹⁴ Shout for joy, daughter of Zion,
Israel, shout aloud!
Rejoice, exult with all your heart,
daughter of Jerusalem!
¹⁵ Yahweh has repealed your sentence;
he has turned your enemy away.
Yahweh is king among you, Israel,
you have nothing more to fear.
¹⁶ When that Day comes, the message for
Jerusalem will be:
Zion, have no fear,
do not let your hands fall limp.
¹⁷ Yahweh your God is there with you,
the warrior-Saviour.

He will rejoice over you with happy song,
he will renew you by his love,
he will dance with shouts of joy for you,
¹⁸ as on a day of festival.

Return of the exiles

I have taken away your misfortune,
no longer need you bear the disgrace
of it.
¹⁹ I am taking action here and now
against your oppressors.
When that time comes I will rescue the
lame,
and gather the strays,
and I will win them praise and renown
when I restore their fortunes.

²⁰ At that time I shall be your guide,
at the time when I gather you in,
I shall give you praise and renown
among all the peoples of the earth
when I restore your fortunes under your
own eyes,
declares Yahweh.

3a In the prophets the humble and oppressed, specially dependent on Yahweh, are the object of his special care. Here and in the Pss poverty is a spiritual quality, openness to God's love.

3b These two final psalms were probably added later.

The Book of

HAGGAI

The summons to rebuild the Temple

1 In the second year of King Darius, on the first day of the sixth month, the word of Yahweh was addressed through the prophet Haggai to Zerubbabel son of Shealtiel governor of Judah and to Joshua son of Jehozadak the high priest as follows, 2 'Yahweh Sabaoth says this, "This people says: The time has not yet come to rebuild the Temple of Yahweh." ' 3 (And the word of Yahweh was addressed through the prophet Haggai, as follows,) 4 'Is this a time for you to live in your panelled houses, when this House lies in ruins? 5 So now, Yahweh Sabaoth says this, "Think carefully about your behaviour. 6 You have sown much and harvested little; you eat but never have enough, drink but never have your fill, put on clothes but feel no warmth. The wage-earner gets his wages only to put them in a bag with a hole in it." 7 Yahweh Sabaoth says this, "Think carefully about your behaviour. 8 Go up into the hills, fetch timber and rebuild the House; and I shall take pleasure in it and manifest my glory there—Yahweh says. 9 The abundance you expected proved to be little. When you brought the harvest in, I blasted it. And why?—Yahweh Sabaoth declares. Because while my House lies in ruins, each of you is busy with his own house. 10 That is why the sky has withheld the rain and the earth withheld its yield. 11 I have called down drought on land and hills, on grain, on new wine, on olive oil and on all the produce of the ground, on humans and animals and all your labours." '

12 Zerubbabel son of Shealtiel, Joshua son of Jehozadak the high priest and the entire remnant of the people, paid attention to the voice of Yahweh their God and to the words of the prophet Haggai, which Yahweh their God had sent him to deliver. And the people were filled with fear before Yahweh. 13 Haggai, the messenger of Yahweh, then passed on Yahweh's message to the people, 'I am with you—declares Yahweh.' 14 And Yahweh roused the spirit of Zerubbabel son of Shealtiel governor of Judah, the spirit of Joshua son of Jehozadak the high priest and the spirit of the entire remnant of the people; they came and set to work in the Temple of Yahweh Sabaoth, their God. 15 This was on the twenty-fourth day of the sixth month.

The future glory of the Temple

In the second year of King Darius, 2 on the twenty-first day of the seventh month, the word of Yahweh was addressed through the prophet Haggai, as follows, 2 'You are to speak to Zerubbabel son of Shealtiel governor of Judah, to Joshua son of Jehozadak the high priest and to the remnant of the people. Say this, 3 "Is there anyone left among you who saw this Temple in its former glory? And how does it look to you now? Does it not seem as though there is nothing there? 4 But take courage now, Zerubbabel!—Yahweh declares. Courage, Joshua son of Jehozadak high priest! Courage, all you people of the country!—Yahweh declares. To work! I am with you—Yahweh Sabaoth declares— 5 and my spirit is present among you. Do not be afraid! 6 For Yahweh Sabaoth says this: A little while now, and I shall shake the heavens and the earth, the sea and the dry land. 7 I shall shake all the nations, and the treasures of all the nations will flow in, and I shall fill this Temple with glory, says Yahweh Sabaoth. 8 Mine is the silver, mine the gold!—Yahweh Sabaoth declares. [9] The glory of this new Temple will surpass that of the old, says Yahweh Sabaoth, and in this place I shall give peace—Yahweh Sabaoth declares." '

Haggai consults the priests

[10] On the twenty-fourth day of the ninth month, in the second year of Darius, the word of Yahweh was addressed to the prophet Haggai as follows, [11] 'Yahweh Sabaoth says this, "Ask the priests to give a ruling on this: [12] If someone is carrying consecrated meat in the fold of his gown and allows the fold to touch bread, broth, wine, oil or food of any kind, will that become holy?" ' The priests replied, 'No.' [13] Haggai then said, 'If anyone rendered unclean by contact with a corpse touches any of these things, will that become unclean?' The priests replied, 'It will become unclean.' [14] Haggai then spoke out. 'It is the same with this people,' he said, 'the same with this nation, in my view—Yahweh declares—the same with everything they turn their hands to; and whatever they offer here is unclean.

A promise of agricultural prosperity

[15] 'So now think carefully, today and henceforth: before one stone had been laid on another in the sanctuary of Yahweh, [16] what state were you in? You would come to a twenty-measure heap and find only ten; you would come to a vat to draw fifty measures and find only twenty. [17] Everything you turned your hands to, I struck with wind-blast, mildew and hail, and still you would not return to me—Yahweh declares. [18] So think carefully, today and henceforth (from the twenty-fourth day of the ninth month, from the day the foundation of the sanctuary of Yahweh was laid, think carefully) [19] if seed-corn is still short in the barn, and if vine and fig tree, pomegranate and olive tree still bear no fruit.

'From today onwards I intend to bless you.'

The promise to Zerubbabel

[20] On the twenty-fourth day of the month the word of Yahweh was addressed a second time to Haggai, as follows, [21] 'Speak to Zerubbabel governor of Judah. Say this, "I am going to shake the heavens and the earth. [22] I shall overturn the thrones of kingdoms and destroy the power of the kings of the nations. I shall overthrow the chariots and their crews; horses and their riders will fall, every one to the sword of his comrade. [23] When that day comes—Yahweh Sabaoth declares—I shall take you, Zerubbabel son of Shealtiel my servant—Yahweh declares—and make you like a signet ring. For I have chosen you—Yahweh Sabaoth declares." '

ZECHARIAH

A summons to conversion

1 In the second year of Darius, in the eighth month, the word of Yahweh was addressed to the prophet Zechariah (son of Berechiah), son of Iddo, as follows, ²'Yahweh was deeply angry with your ancestors. ³So say this to them, "Yahweh Sabaoth*ᵃ* says this: Return to me—Yahweh Sabaoth declares—and I will return to you, says Yahweh Sabaoth. ⁴Do not be like your ancestors when the prophets in the past cried to them: Yahweh Sabaoth says this: Turn back from your evil ways and evil deeds—they would not listen or pay attention to me—Yahweh declares. ⁵Where are your ancestors now? And the prophets, do they live for ever? ⁶But did not my words and statutes, with which I had charged my servants the prophets, overtake your ancestors just the same?" '

So they repented and said, 'Yahweh Sabaoth has treated us as he resolved to do, and as our ways and deeds deserved.'

First vision: the horsemen

⁷On the twenty-fourth day of the eleventh month (the month of Shebat), in the second year of Darius, the word of Yahweh was addressed to the prophet Zechariah (son of Berechiah), son of Iddo, as follows, ⁸'I had a vision during the night. There was a man riding a red horse standing among the deep-rooted myrtles; behind him were other horses—red, chestnut and white. ⁹I said, "What are these, my lord?" And the angel who was talking to me said, "I will show you what they are." ¹⁰The man standing among the myrtles then replied, "Those are they whom Yahweh has sent to patrol the world."

¹¹They reported to the angel of Yahweh as he stood among the myrtles, "We have been patrolling the world, and indeed the whole world is still and at peace." ¹²The angel of Yahweh then spoke and said, "Yahweh Sabaoth, how long will you wait before taking pity on Jerusalem and the cities of Judah, on which you have inflicted your anger for the past seventy years?" ¹³Yahweh then replied with kind and comforting words to the angel who was talking to me. ¹⁴The angel who was talking to me then said to me, "Make this proclamation: Yahweh Sabaoth says this: I am burning with jealousy for Jerusalem and Zion ¹⁵but am deeply angry with the nations now at ease; before, I was only mildly angry, but they contributed to the disaster. ¹⁶So now Yahweh says this: In compassion I have returned to Jerusalem; my Temple will be rebuilt there— Yahweh Sabaoth declares—and the measuring line will be stretched over Jerusalem. ¹⁷Make this proclamation too: Yahweh Sabaoth says this: My cities are once more to be very prosperous. Yahweh will comfort Zion once again, and again make Jerusalem his choice." '

Second vision: the horns and the smiths

2 Then, raising my eyes, I had a vision. It was this: There were four horns. ²I said to the angel who was talking to me, 'What are these?' He said to me, 'These are the horns which scattered Judah (Israel) and Jerusalem.' ³Yahweh then showed me four smiths. ⁴And I said, 'What are these coming to do?' He said to me, '(Those horns scattered Judah so completely that no one dared to raise his head; but)

1a ‖ Ml 3:7.

these have come to terrify them, to throw down the horns of the nations who raised their horns over the land of Judah to scatter it.'

Third vision: the measurer

⁵ Then, raising my eyes, I had a vision. There was a man with a measuring line in his hand. ⁶ I asked him, 'Where are you going?' He said, 'To measure Jerusalem, to calculate her width and length.' ⁷ And then, while the angel who was talking to me walked away, another angel came out to meet him. ⁸ He said to him, 'Run, and tell that young man this, "Jerusalem is to remain unwalled, because of the great number of men and cattle inside. ⁹ For I—Yahweh declares—shall be a wall of fire all round her and I shall be the Glory within her." '

Two exhortations to the exiles

¹⁰ Look out! Look out! Flee from the land of
    the north
    —Yahweh declares—
    for I have scattered you to the four winds
        of heaven
    —Yahweh declares.
¹¹ Look out! Make your escape, Zion,
    now living with the daughter of Babylon!
¹² For Yahweh Sabaoth says this,
    since the Glory commissioned me,
    about the nations who plundered you,
    'Whoever touches you touches the apple of
        my eye.
¹³ Now look, I shall wave my hand over
        them
    and they will be plundered by those whom
        they have enslaved.'
    Then you will know that Yahweh Sabaoth
        has sent me!

¹⁴ Sing, rejoice, daughter of Zion,
    for now I am coming
    to live among you
    —Yahweh declares!

¹⁵ And on that day many nations
    will be converted to Yahweh.
    Yes, they will become his people,

and they will live among you.
    Then you will know that Yahweh Sabaoth
        has sent me to you!
¹⁶ Yahweh will take possession of Judah,
    his portion in the Holy Land,
    and again make Jerusalem his choice.
¹⁷ Let all people be silent before Yahweh,
    now that he is stirring from his holy
        Dwelling!

Fourth vision: the investiture of Joshua

3 He then showed me the high priest Joshua, standing before the angel of Yahweh, with Satan standing on his right to accuse him. ² The angel of Yahweh said to Satan, 'May Yahweh rebuke you, Satan! May Yahweh rebuke you, since he has made Jerusalem his choice. Is not this man a brand snatched from the fire?' ³ Now Joshua was dressed in dirty clothes as he stood before the angel. ⁴ᵃ The latter then spoke as follows to those who were standing before him, 'Take off his dirty clothes ⁴ᶜ and dress him in splendid robes ⁵ and put a clean turban on his head.' So they put a clean turban on his head and dressed him in clean clothes, while the angel of Yahweh stood by ⁴ᵇ and said, 'You see, I have taken your guilt away.' ⁶ The angel of Yahweh then made this declaration to Joshua, ⁷ 'Yahweh Sabaoth says this, "If you walk in my ways and keep my ordinances, you shall govern my house, you shall watch over my courts, and I will give you free access among those in attendance here. ⁹ᵃ For this is the stone which I have put before Joshua, a stone on which are seven eyes; and I myself shall cut the inscription on it—Yahweh Sabaoth declares."

The coming of the 'Branch'

⁸ 'So listen, High Priest Joshua, you and the colleagues over whom you preside—for they are an omen of things to come—for now I shall bring in my servant the Branch,ᵃ ⁹ᵇ and I shall remove this country's guilt in a single

---

3a A messianic title (*see* Jr 23:5) later applied to Zerubbabel (6:12).

day. ¹⁰On that day—Yahweh Sabaoth declares—invite each other to come under your vine and your fig tree." '

Fifth vision: the lamp-stand and the olive trees

4 The angel who was talking to me came back and roused me as though rousing someone who was asleep. ²And he asked me, 'What do you see?' I replied, 'As I look, there is a lamp-stand entirely of gold with a bowl at the top of it; it holds seven lamps, with seven openings for the lamps on it. ³By it are two olive trees, one to the right and the other to the left.' ⁴I then said to the angel who was talking to me, 'What are those things, my lord?' ⁵The angel who was talking to me replied, 'Do you not know what they are?' I said, 'No, my lord.' ⁶ᵃHe then gave me this answer, ¹⁰ᵇ'These seven are the eyes of Yahweh, which range over the whole world.' ¹¹Then I went on to ask him, 'What is the meaning of these two olive trees, to right and left of the lamp-stand?' ¹²(And I went on to ask him further, 'What is the meaning of the two olive branches discharging oil through the two golden openings?') ¹³He replied, 'Do you not know what they are?' I said, 'No, my lord.' ¹⁴He said, 'These are the two anointed ones in attendance on the Lord of the whole world.'

Three sayings about Zerubbabel

⁶ᵇThis is the word of Yahweh with regard to Zerubbabel, 'Not by might and not by power, but by my spirit'—says Yahweh Sabaoth.

⁷'What are you, great mountain? Beside Zerubbabel you shall become a plain! He will bring out the keystone while it is cheered with Hurrah! Hurrah!'

⁸The word of Yahweh was addressed to me as follows, ⁹'The hands of Zerubbabel have laid the foundation of this Temple; his hands will finish it. (Then you will know that Yahweh Sabaoth has sent me to you.) ¹⁰ᵃA day of little things, no doubt, but who would dare despise it? How they will rejoice when they see the chosen stone in the hands of Zerubbabel!'

Sixth vision: the flying scroll

5 Again raising my eyes, I had a vision. There was a flying scroll. ²The angel who was talking to me said, 'What do you see?' I replied, 'I see a flying scroll; it is twenty cubits long and ten cubits wide.' ³He then said to me, 'This is God's curse sweeping across the face of the whole country; for, according to what it says on one side, every thief will be banished and, according to what it says on the other, everyone who commits perjury in my name will be banished from it. ⁴I am going to release it—Yahweh Sabaoth declares—for it to enter the house of the thief and of anyone who commits perjury in my name, for it to settle deep within his house and consume it, timber, stone and all.'

Seventh vision: the woman in the bushel measure

⁵The angel who was talking to me appeared and said to me, 'Raise your eyes, and see what this is, going along.' ⁶I said, 'What is it?' He said, 'It is a bushel measure going along.' He went on, 'This is their guilt throughout the country.' ⁷At this, a disc of lead was raised, and I saw a woman sitting inside the barrel. ⁸He said, 'This is Wickedness.' And he rammed her back into the barrel and jammed its mouth shut with the mass of lead. ⁹I raised my eyes, and there were two women appearing. The wind caught their wings—they had wings like a stork's; they raised the barrel midway between earth and heaven. ¹⁰I then said to the angel who was talking to me, 'Where are they taking the barrel?' ¹¹He replied, 'To build a temple for it in the land of Shinar ᵃ and make a pedestal on which to put it.'

Eighth vision: the chariots

6 Again I raised my eyes, and this is what I saw: four chariots coming out between two mountains, and the mountains were moun-

5a Babylon, where Wickedness has its temple, leaving the Holy Land pure.

tains of bronze. ²The first chariot had red horses, the second chariot had black horses, ³the third chariot had white horses and the fourth chariot had vigorous, piebald horses. ⁴I asked the angel who was talking to me, 'What are these, my lord?' ⁵The angel replied, 'They are the four winds of heaven now leaving, after attending the Lord of the whole world. ⁶The black horses are leaving for the land of the north; the white are following them, and the piebald are leaving for the land of the south.' ⁷They came out vigorously, eager to patrol the world. He said to them, 'Go and patrol the world.' And they patrolled the world. ⁸He called to me and said, 'Look, the ones going to the land of the north brought my spirit to rest on the land of the north.'

The votive crown

⁹Then the word of Yahweh was addressed to me as follows, ¹⁰'Collect silver and gold from the exiles, from Heldai, Tobijah and Jedaiah, then (you yourself go the same day) go to the house of Josiah son of Zephaniah, who has arrived from Babylon. ¹¹Then, taking the silver and gold, make a crown and place it on the head of the high priest Joshua^a son of Jehozadak. ¹²And say this to him, "Yahweh Sabaoth says this: Here is a man whose name is Branch; where he is, there will be a branching out (and he will rebuild Yahweh's sanctuary). ¹³Yes, he is the one who will rebuild Yahweh's sanctuary; he will wear the royal insignia and sit on his throne and govern, with a priest on his right. Perfect peace will reign between these two. ¹⁴And the crown will serve Heldai, Tobijah, Jedaiah and the son of Zephaniah as a memorial of favour in Yahweh's sanctuary. ¹⁵And those now far away will come and work on the building of Yahweh's sanctuary."

'Then you will know that Yahweh Sabaoth has sent me to you. It will happen if you diligently obey the voice of Yahweh your God.'

A question about fasting

7In the fourth year of King Darius, the word of Yahweh was addressed to Zech-

ariah on the fourth day of the ninth month, the month of Chislev. ²Bethel sent Sharezer with a deputation to entreat Yahweh's favour ³and to ask the priests in the Temple of Yahweh Sabaoth and the prophets, 'Ought I to go on mourning and fasting in the fifth month as I have been doing for so many years past?'

A survey of the nation's past

⁴Then the word of Yahweh Sabaoth was addressed to me as follows, ⁵'Say to all the people of the country and to the priests, "While you have been fasting and mourning in the fifth and seventh months for the past seventy years, have you really been fasting for my sake? ⁶And when you were eating and drinking, were you not eating and drinking for your own sake? ⁷Do you not know the words which Yahweh proclaimed through the prophets in the past, when Jerusalem was inhabited and secure, as were her surrounding towns, and when the Negeb and the lowlands were inhabited?" ' (⁸The word of Yahweh was addressed to Zechariah as follows, ⁹'Yahweh Sabaoth says this.) He said, "Apply the law fairly, and show faithful love and compassion towards one another. ¹⁰Do not oppress the widow and the orphan, the foreigner and the poor, and do not secretly plan evil against one another." ¹¹But they would not listen; they turned a rebellious shoulder; they stopped their ears rather than hear; ¹²they made their hearts adamant rather than listen to the teaching and the words that Yahweh Sabaoth had sent—by his spirit—through the prophets in the past; and consequently the fury of Yahweh Sabaoth overtook them. ¹³And so, since when he called they would not listen, "I would not listen when they called", says Yahweh Sabaoth, ¹⁴"but scattered them among all the nations unknown to them. Hence, after they

6a The original reading must have been 'Zerubbabel'; 'Joshua' was later substituted, when the high priest became the unique head of the community after the disappearance of the royal house.

had gone, the country was deserted, and no one came or went. They had turned a land of delights into a desert." '

A prospect of salvation

8 The word of Yahweh Sabaoth came as follows:

2 Yahweh Sabaoth says this:
I have been burning with jealousy for
 Zion,
with furious jealousy for her sake.

3 Yahweh says this:
I am coming back to Zion
and shall live in the heart of Jerusalem.
Jerusalem will be called Faithful City
and the mountain of Yahweh Sabaoth, the
 Holy Mountain.

4 Yahweh Sabaoth says this:
Aged men and women once again will sit
in the squares of Jerusalem,
each with a stick to lean on
because of their great age.
5 And the squares of the city will be full
of boys and girls
playing there.

6 Yahweh Sabaoth says this:
If this seems a miracle
to the remnant of this people (in those days),
will it seem one to me?
declares Yahweh.

7 Yahweh Sabaoth says this:
Look, I shall rescue my people
from the countries of the east
and from the countries of the west.
8 I shall bring them back
to live in the heart of Jerusalem,
and they will be my people
and I shall be their God,
faithful and just.

9 'Yahweh Sabaoth says this, "Take heart, you who today hear these promises uttered by the prophets since the day when the foundations of the Temple of Yahweh Sabaoth were laid, that the sanctuary would indeed be rebuilt. 10 For up to now, men were not paid their wages and nothing was paid for the animals either; and it has not been safe for anyone to come and go, because of the enemy, since I had set each one against everyone else. 11 But from now on, I shall not treat the remnant of this people as I have treated them in time past—declares Yahweh Sabaoth. 12 Now they will sow in peace; the vine will give its fruit, the soil will give its produce and heaven will give its dew. I shall bestow all these on the remnant of this people. 13 Just as once you were a curse among the nations, House of Judah and House of Israel, so now I shall save you, and you will be a blessing. Do not be afraid. Take heart!"

14 'For Yahweh Sabaoth says this, "Just as I resolved to ill-treat you when your ancestors provoked me to anger and did not relent—says Yahweh Sabaoth— 15 so now I have changed my mind and intend to treat Jerusalem and the House of Judah well. Do not be afraid! 16 "These are the things that you must do. Speak the truth to one another; at your gates, administer fair judgement conducive to peace; 17 do not secretly plot evil against one another; do not love perjury; since I hate all this—Yahweh declares." '

The answer to the question on fasting

18 The word of Yahweh Sabaoth was addressed to me as follows:
19 'Yahweh Sabaoth says this, "The fast of the fourth month, the fast of the fifth, the fast of the seventh and the fast of the tenth are to become glad, joyful, happy festivals for the House of Judah. So love truth and peace!" '

A prospect of salvation

20 'Yahweh Sabaoth says this, "In the future, peoples and citizens of many cities will come; 21 and citizens of one city will go to the next and say: We must certainly go to entreat Yah-

weh's favour and seek out Yahweh Sabaoth; I am going myself. ²² Yes, many peoples and great nations will seek out Yahweh Sabaoth in Jerusalem and entreat Yahweh's favour."

²³ 'Yahweh Sabaoth says this, "In those days, ten men from nations of every language will take a Jew by the sleeve and say: We want to go with you, since we have learnt that God is with you." '

9 A proclamation.

The new promised land

The word of Yahweh is against Hadrach,
it has come to rest on Damascus,
for the source of Aram belongs to Yahweh
no less than all the tribes of Israel;
² on Hamath too, which borders on it,
and on (Tyre and) Sidon, despite her
    acumen.
³ Tyre has built herself a fortress,
has heaped up silver like dust
and gold like the dirt of the streets.
⁴ And now the Lord is going to dispossess
    her;
at sea he will break her power,
and she herself will go up in flames.
⁵ Seeing this, Ashkelon will be terrified,
Gaza too, and writhe with grief,
Ekron too, at the ruin of her prospects;
the king will vanish from Gaza
and Ashkelon be unpeopled,
⁶ while a half-breed will live in Ashdod!
Yes, I shall destroy the pride of the
    Philistine;
⁷ I shall snatch his blood from his mouth,
his abominations from between his teeth.
But his remnant too will belong to our
    God,
becoming like a clan in Judah,
and Ekron will become like a Jebusite.
⁸ I shall stand guard before my home
to defend it against all comers,
and no oppressor will overrun them ever
    again,
for now I am on the alert.

The Royal Saviour

⁹ Rejoice heart and soul, daughter of Zion!
Shout for joy, daughter of Jerusalem!
Look, your king is approaching,
he is vindicated and victorious,
humble and riding on a donkey,
on a colt, the foal of a donkey.
¹⁰ He will banish chariots from Ephraim
and horses from Jerusalem;
the bow of war will be banished.
He will proclaim peace to the nations,
his empire will stretch from sea to sea,
from the River to the limits of the earth.

The restoration of Israel

¹¹ As for you, because of the blood of your
    covenant
I have released your prisoners from the pit
in which there is no water.
¹² Come back to the fortress,
you prisoners waiting in hope.
This very day, I vow,
I shall make it up to you twice over.
¹³ For I have strung Judah as a bow for
    myself,
laid Ephraim on the string as an arrow,
have roused your sons, Zion,
against your sons, Javan,ᵃ
and have made you like a warrior's sword.
¹⁴ Then Yahweh will appear above them
and his arrow will flash out like lightning.
(The Lord) Yahweh will sound the
    trumpet
and advance in the storm-winds of the
    south.
¹⁵ Yahweh Sabaoth will protect them!
They will devour, will trample on the
    sling-stones,
they will drink blood like wine,
awash like bowls, like the corners of the
    altar.
¹⁶ Yahweh their God will give them victory
when that day comes,

9a Greece, now conquering the East under Alexander the Great.

like the sheep who are his people;
yes, the stones of a diadem
will sparkle over his country.
¹⁷ How fine, how splendid that will be,
with wheat to make the young men
flourish,
and new wine the maidens!

Faithfulness to Yahweh

10 Ask Yahweh for rain in autumn
and at the time of the spring rains.
Yahweh is the one to make the
storm-clouds.
He will give them showers of rain;
to each, grass in his field.
² Since the domestic idols have talked
nonsense,
and the diviners have seen false signs,
and dreams have purveyed delusions,
affording empty comfort,
that is why they have strayed like sheep,
in distress for want of a shepherd.

Israel's deliverance and return

³ My anger has been roused by the
shepherds,
and I shall vent it on the he-goats.

When Yahweh Sabaoth comes to visit his
flock,
the House of Judah,
he will make it his royal war-horse.
⁴ From it will emerge Cornerstone and
Tent-peg,
from it, Bow-ready-for-Battle,
from it, every type of leader.
Together ⁵they will be like warriors
trampling the dirt of the streets in
battle;
when they fight, because Yahweh is
with them,
they will put mounted men to rout.
⁶ Then I shall make the House of Judah
mighty
and the House of Joseph victorious.
I shall restore them, because I have taken
pity on them,

and they will be as though I had never cast
them off,
for I am Yahweh their God and shall
answer their prayer.

⁷ Ephraim will be like a warrior.
Their hearts will be cheered as though by
wine.
Their children will see this and rejoice,
their hearts will exult in Yahweh.

⁸ I shall whistle to them and gather them in,
for I have redeemed them;
they will be as numerous as they used to
be.
⁹ I shall scatter them among the peoples
but in distant countries they will
remember me,
they will instruct their children and then
return.
¹⁰ I shall bring them home from Egypt
and gather them back from Assyria;
I shall lead them into Gilead and the
Lebanon,
and even that will not be large enough for
them.
¹¹ They will cross the sea of Egypt
(and the waves of the sea will be struck);
all the depths of the River will be dried up.
The arrogance of Assyria will be cast
down
and the sceptre of Egypt taken away.
¹² I shall make them mighty in Yahweh,
and they will march in my name
—Yahweh declares.

A taunt against enemies

11 Open your gateways, Lebanon,
and the fire shall burn down your
cedar trees!
² Wail, juniper,
for the cedar tree has fallen,
the majestic ones have been ravaged!
Wail, oaks of Bashan,
for the impenetrable forest has been felled!
³ The sound of the wailing of shepherds!

Their majesty has been ravaged.
The sound of the roaring of young lions!
The pride of the Jordan has been ravaged.

The two shepherds

⁴ Yahweh my God says this, 'Pasture the sheep for slaughter, ⁵ whose buyers kill them and go unpunished, whose sellers say of them, "Blessed be Yahweh; now I am rich!" and whose own shepherds show them no pity. ⁶ For I shall show no further pity for the inhabitants of the country—Yahweh declares! Instead, I shall put everyone into the clutches of a neighbour, into the clutches of the king. They will crush the country and I shall not rescue anyone from their clutches.'

⁷ Then I pastured for slaughter the sheep belonging to the sheep-dealers. I took two staves: the one I called 'Goodwill', the other 'Couplers'; and I pastured the sheep myself, ⁸ getting rid of three shepherds in one month. But I lost patience with them, and they equally detested me. ⁹ I then said, 'I am not going to pasture you any more; the one doomed to die can die; the one doomed to perish can perish; and the rest can devour one another.' ¹⁰ I then took my staff, 'Goodwill', and broke it in half, to break my covenant, which I had made with all the peoples. ¹¹ When it was broken, that day the sheep-dealers, who were watching me, realised that this had been a word of Yahweh. ¹² I then said to them, 'If you see fit, give me my wages; if not, never mind.' So they weighed out my wages: thirty shekels of silver. ¹³ Yahweh said to me, 'Throw it to the smelter, this princely sum at which they have valued me!' Taking the thirty shekels of silver, I threw them into the Temple of Yahweh, for the smelter. ¹⁴ I then broke my second staff, 'Couplers,' in half, to rupture the brotherly relationship between Judah and Israel.

¹⁵ Next, Yahweh said to me, 'This time, take the gear of a good-for-nothing shepherd. ¹⁶ For I am now going to raise a shepherd in this country, who will not bother about the lost, who will not go in search of the stray, who will not heal the injured, who will not support

the swollen, but who will eat the meat of the fat ones, tearing off their very hoofs.

¹⁷ Disaster to the shepherd
who deserts his flock!
May the sword attack his arm
and his right eye!
May his arm shrivel completely
and his right eye be totally blinded!'

The deliverance and restoration of Jerusalem

12 A proclamation.
The word of Yahweh about Israel (²ᵇ and also about Judah). Yahweh, who spread out the heaven and founded the earth and formed the human spirit within, declares:
²ᵃ 'Look, I shall make Jerusalem a cup to set all the surrounding peoples reeling. (That will be at the time of the siege of Jerusalem.)

³ 'When that day comes, I shall make Jerusalem a stone too heavy for all the peoples to lift; all those who try to lift it will hurt themselves severely, although all the nations of the world will be massed against her. ⁴ When that day comes—declares Yahweh—I shall strike all the horses with panic and their riders with madness. And I shall strike all the peoples with blindness. (But I shall keep watch over Judah.) ⁵ Then the rulers of Judah will say to themselves, "The strength of the inhabitants of Jerusalem lies in Yahweh Sabaoth their God." ⁶ When that day comes, I shall make the rulers of Judah like a brazier burning in a pile of wood, like a torch flaming in a sheaf; and they will devour all the peoples round them to right and left. And Jerusalem will be full of people as before, where she stands (in Jerusalem). ⁷ Yahweh will first save the tents of Judah, so that the glory of the House of David and the glory of the inhabitants of Jerusalem do not increase at Judah's expense. ⁸ When that day comes, Yahweh will protect the inhabitants of Jerusalem; and the frailest of them will be like David when that day comes, and the House of David will be like God, like the angel of Yahweh, at their head.

⁹ 'When that day comes, I shall set about de-

98 READ ZECHARIAH 12.

They will mourn for the one whom they have pierced as though for an only child.

—ZECHARIAH 12:10

THE SOURCE OF THE SACRAMENTS

That the church might be formed from the side of Christ dead on the cross, and that the words of Scripture might be accomplished that say: "They will mourn for the one whom they have pierced," divine providence allows a soldier to open his most sacred side, piercing it with a lance. Then flowed blood, mingled with water, and the price of our salvation was paid. That price, which issued from the secret of his heart as from a source, gives to the sacraments of the church the power to bestow the life of grace, and becomes, for those who live in Christ, a drink of living water "leaping up to give eternal life" (see Jn 4:14). . . .

Run, then, most eagerly to this source of life and light, whoever you may be. And in your love for God, cry out with all the power of your heart: "You are the inexpressible beauty of the Most High, the most pure splendor of eternal life, the Life that vivifies all life, the brilliancy that enlightens all light and keeps in eternal splendor the diverse stars that shine before the throne of your divinity since the beginning of time!

"You are the eternal and inaccessible flood, limpid and sweet, whose source is hidden to the eyes of all mortals! There is no bottom to your depth, no limit to your height, no end to your width, and nothing troubles your purity. It is from that flows the 'river whose streams brings joy to God's city' (see Ps 46:4) . . . that we might sing hymns of thanksgiving 'among cries of joy and praise' (Ps 42:4), for we know by experience that 'in you is the source of life, [and] by your light we see the light' (see Ps 36:9)." ST. BONAVENTURE, 1218–1274

YOU WILL FIND THE NEXT READING AT MALACHI 1.

stroying all the nations who advance against Jerusalem. ¹⁰ But over the House of David and the inhabitants of Jerusalem I shall pour out a spirit of grace and prayer, and they will look to me. They will mourn for the one whom they have pierced as though for an only child, and weep for him as people weep for a first-born child. ¹¹ When that day comes, the mourning in Jerusalem will be as great as the mourning for Hadad Rimmon in the Plain of Megiddo. ¹² And the country will mourn clan by clan:

The clan of the House of David by itself,
and their women by themselves;

the clan of the House of Nathan by itself,
and their women by themselves;
¹³ the clan of the House of Levi by itself,
and their women by themselves;
the clan of the House of Shimei by itself,
and their women by themselves;
¹⁴ all the rest of the clans, every clan by
itself,
and their women by themselves.'

13 'When that day comes, a fountain will be opened for the House of David and the inhabitants of Jerusalem, to wash sin and impurity away.

2 'When that day comes—Yahweh declares—I shall cut off the names of the idols from the country, and they will never be remembered again; I shall also rid the country of the prophets, and of the spirit of impurity. 3 Then, if anyone still goes on prophesying, his parents, his own father and mother will say to him, "You shall not live, since you utter lies in Yahweh's name." And even while he is prophesying, his parents, his own father and mother will pierce him through. 4 When that day comes, the prophets will all be ashamed to relate their visions when they prophesy and no longer put on their hair cloaks with intent to deceive. 5 Instead, they will say, "I am no prophet. I am a man who tills the soil, for the land has been my living since I was a boy." 6 And if anyone asks him, "What are those gashes on your chest?ᵃ" he will reply, "I got them when I was with my friends."'

Invocation to the sword; the new people

7 Awake, sword, against my shepherd,
against the man who is close to me—
declares Yahweh Sabaoth!
Strike the shepherd, scatter the sheep!
And I shall turn my hand against the
young!
8 So it will be, throughout the country—
declares Yahweh Sabaoth—
two-thirds in it will be cut off (be killed)
and the other third will be left.
9 I shall pass this third through the fire,
refine them as silver is refined,
test them as gold is tested.
He will call on my name
and I shall answer him;
I shall say, 'He is my people,'
and he will say, 'Yahweh is my God!'

The eschatological battle; the splendour of Jerusalem

14 Look, the Day of Yahweh is coming, when the spoils taken from you will be shared out among you. 2 For I shall gather all the nations to Jerusalem for battle. The city will be taken, the houses plundered, the women ravished. Half the city will go into exile, but the rest of the people will not be ejected from the city. 3 Then Yahweh will sally out and fight those nations as once he fought on the day of battle. 4 When that day comes, his feet will rest on the Mount of Olives, which faces Jerusalem on the east, and the Mount of Olives will be split in half from east to west, forming a huge valley; half the Mount will recede northwards, the other half southwards. 5 The valley between the hills will be filled in, yes, it will be blocked as far as Jasol, it will be filled in as it was by the earthquake in the days of Uzziah king of Judah. And Yahweh my God will come, and all the holy ones with him.

6 That Day, there will be no light, but only cold and frost. 7 And it will be one continuous day—Yahweh knows—there will be no more day and night, and it will remain light right into the time of evening. 8 When that Day comes, living waters will issue from Jerusalem, half towards the eastern sea, half towards the western sea; they will flow summer and winter. 9 Then Yahweh will become king of the whole world. When that Day comes, Yahweh will be the one and only and his name the one name. 10 The entire country will be transformed into plain, from Geba to Rimmon in the Negeb, but Jerusalem will stand high in her place and be full of people from the Benjamin Gate to the site of the earlier gate, to the Corner Gate, and from the Tower of Hananel to the king's wine-presses. 11 People will make their homes there. The curse of destruction will be lifted; Jerusalem will be safe to live in.

12 And this is the plague with which Yahweh will strike all the nations who have fought against Jerusalem; their flesh will rot while they are still standing on their feet; their eyes will rot in their sockets; their tongues will rot in their mouths. 15 And the plague afflicting the horses, mules, camels, donkeys and all the other animals in those armies will be the same. 13 When that Day comes, a great terror

13a Such scars were once the hallmark of a prophet (1 K 18:28).

will fall on them from Yahweh; each man will grab his neighbour's hand and they will fall to fighting among themselves. ¹⁴Even Judah will fight against Jerusalem. The wealth of all the surrounding nations will be heaped together: gold, silver, clothing, in vast quantity.

¹⁶After this, all the survivors of all the nations which have attacked Jerusalem will come up year after year to worship the King, Yahweh Sabaoth, and to keep the feast of Shelters. ¹⁷Should one of the races of the world fail to come up to Jerusalem to worship the King, Yahweh Sabaoth, there will be no rain for that one. ¹⁸Should the race of Egypt fail to come up and pay its visit, on it will fall the plague which Yahweh will inflict on each of those nations which fail to come up to keep the feast of Shelters. ¹⁹Such will be the punishment for Egypt and the punishment for all the nations which fail to come up to keep the feast of Shelters.

²⁰When that Day comes, the very bells on the horses will be inscribed with the words, 'Sacred to Yahweh', and the cooking pots of the house of Yahweh will be as holy as the sprinkling bowls before the altar. ²¹Yes, every cooking pot in Jerusalem and in Judah shall be sacred to Yahweh Sabaoth, and all who come to offer sacrifice will help themselves and do their cooking in them, and there will be no more traders in the Temple of Yahweh Sabaoth, when that Day comes.

MALACHI

1 A message.
The word of Yahweh to Israel through
Malachi.

The love of Yahweh for Israel

2 'I have loved you, says Yahweh. But you ask,
"How have you shown your love?" Was not
Esau[a] Jacob's brother? declares Yahweh; even
so, I loved Jacob 3 but I hated Esau. I turned his
mountains into a desert and his heritage into
dwellings in the wastelands. 4 If Edom says,
"We have been struck down but we shall rebuild our ruins," Yahweh Sabaoth says this,
"Let them build, but I shall pull down! They
will be known as Land of Wickedness and
Nation-with-which-Yahweh-is-angry-for-ever.
5 You will see this yourselves and you will
say: Yahweh is mighty beyond the borders of
Israel."

An indictment of the priests

6 'The son honours his father, the slave stands
in awe of his master. But if I am indeed father,
where is the honour due to me? And if I am
indeed master, where is the awe due to me?
says Yahweh Sabaoth to you priests who despise my name. You ask, "How have we despised your name?" 7 By putting polluted food
on my altar. You ask, "How have we polluted
you?" By saying, "The table of Yahweh deserves no respect." 8 When you bring blind animals for sacrifice, is this not wrong? When
you bring the lame and the diseased, is this not
wrong? If you offer them to your governor,
see if he is pleased with them or receives you
graciously, says Yahweh Sabaoth. 9 In that
case, try pleading with God to take pity on us
(that is what you have done), and will he take
any notice? says Yahweh Sabaoth. 10 Why does
one of you not close the doors and so stop the
pointless lighting of fires on my altar? I am not
pleased with you, says Yahweh Sabaoth; from
your hands I find no offerings acceptable.
11 But from farthest east to farthest west my
name is great among the nations, and everywhere incense and a pure gift are offered to
my name, since my name is great among the
nations, says Yahweh Sabaoth.

12 'But you have profaned it by saying, "The
table of the Lord is polluted, hence the food
offered on it deserves no respect." 13 You
say, "How tiresome it all is!" and sniff disdainfully at me, says Yahweh Sabaoth. You bring
a stolen, lame or diseased animal, you bring
that as an offering! Am I to accept this from
you? says Yahweh Sabaoth. 14 Cursed be the
rogue who has a male in his flock but pays
his vow by sacrificing a blemished animal
to me! For I am a great king, says Yahweh
Sabaoth, and among the nations my name inspires awe.'

2 'And now, priests, this commandment is
for you. 2 If you will not listen, if you will
not sincerely resolve to glorify my name, says
Yahweh Sabaoth, I shall certainly lay a curse
on you and I shall curse your blessing. Indeed I
will lay a curse, for none of you makes this resolve. 3 Now, I am going to break your arm and
throw offal in your faces—the offal of your
solemn feasts—and sweep you away with it.
4 Then you will know that I sent this commandment to you, to affirm my intention to
maintain my covenant with Levi, says Yahweh

1a Considered the ancestor of Edom, which is often also
called Esau.

99 READ MALACHI 1:6–11.

Everywhere incense and a pure gift are offered to my name.—MALACHI 1:11

THE EUCHARISTIC SACRIFICE FORETOLD

In the prophet Malachi's condemnation of lax priests of the old covenant, St. Irenaeus saw a foreshadowing of the Eucharistic sacrifice of the new covenant:

Jesus instructed his disciples to offer to God the first fruits of his own created things not because he needed them, but in order that they might themselves be neither unfruitful nor ungrateful. So he took that created thing—bread—and gave thanks, and said, "this is my body" (Mt 26:26). And also the cup, which is part of that creation to which we belong, he confessed to be his blood. He established the new sacrifice of the new covenant that the church received from the apostles. Now the church offers this sacrifice to God throughout the world, to him who sustains us with the first fruits of his own gifts in the New Testament.

The prophet Malachi spoke about this beforehand: "I am not pleased with you, says Yahweh Sabaoth; from your hands I find no offerings acceptable. But from farthest east to farthest west my name is great among the nations, and everywhere incense and a pure gift are offered to my name, since my name is great among the nations, says Yahweh Sabaoth" (verses 10–11). He indicated plainly by these words that the former people [the Jews] shall cease making offerings to God, but that in every place sacrifice shall be offered to him, and that a pure one. And his name is glorified among the nations. ST. IRENAEUS OF LYONS, 130?–200?

YOU WILL FIND THE NEXT READING AT MALACHI 3.

Sabaoth. ⁵My covenant was with him—a covenant of life and peace, and these were what I gave him—a covenant of respect, and he respected me and held my name in awe. ⁶The law of truth was in his mouth and guilt was not found on his lips; he walked in peace and justice with me and he converted many from sinning. ⁷The priest's lips ought to safeguard knowledge; his mouth is where the law should be sought, since he is Yahweh Sabaoth's messenger. ⁸But you yourselves have turned aside from the way; you have caused many to lapse by your teaching. Since you have destroyed the covenant of Levi, says Yahweh Sabaoth, ⁹so I in my turn have made you contemptible and vile to the whole people, for not

having kept my ways and for being partial in applying the law.

Mixed marriage and divorce

¹⁰'Is there not one Father of us all? Did not one God create us? Why, then, do we break faith with one another, profaning the covenant of our ancestors? ¹¹Judah has broken faith; a detestable thing has been done in Israel and in Jerusalem. For Judah has profaned Yahweh's beloved sanctuary; he has married the daughter of an alien god. ¹²May Yahweh deprive such an offender of witness and advocate in the tents of Jacob among those who present offerings to Yahweh Sabaoth! ¹³'And here is something else you do: you

cover the altar of Yahweh with tears, with weeping and wailing, because he now refuses to consider the offering or to accept it from you. ¹⁴ And you ask, "Why?" Because Yahweh stands as witness between you and the wife of your youth, with whom you have broken faith, even though she was your partner and your wife by covenant. ¹⁵ Did he not create a single being, having flesh and the breath of life? And what does this single being seek? God-given offspring! Have respect for your own life then, and do not break faith with the wife of your youth. ¹⁶ For I hate divorce, says Yahweh, God of Israel, and people concealing their cruelty under a cloak, says Yahweh Sabaoth. Have respect for your own life then, and do not break faith.

The Day of Yahweh

¹⁷ 'You have wearied Yahweh with your talk. You ask, "How have we wearied him?" When you say, "Any evil-doer is good as far as Yahweh is concerned; indeed he is delighted with them"; or when you say, "Where is the God of fair judgement now?"

3 'Look, I shall send my messenger to clear a way before me. And suddenly the Lord whom you seek will come to his Temple; yes, the angel of the covenant, for whom you long, is on his way, says Yahweh Sabaoth. ² Who will be able to resist the day of his coming? Who will remain standing when he appears? For he will be like a refiner's fire, like fullers' alkali. ³ He will take his seat as refiner and purifier; he will purify the sons of Levi and refine them like gold and silver, so that they can make the offering to Yahweh with uprightness. ⁴ The offering of Judah and Jerusalem will then be acceptable to Yahweh as in former days, as in the years of old. ⁵ I am coming to put you on trial and I shall be a ready witness against sorcerers, adulterers, perjurers, and against those who oppress the wage-earner, the widow and the orphan, and who rob the foreigner of his rights and do not respect me, says Yahweh Sabaoth.

Temple tithes

⁶ 'No; I, Yahweh, do not change; and you have not ceased to be children of Jacob! ⁷ Ever since the days of your ancestors, you have evaded my statutes and not observed them. Return to me and I will return to you, says Yahweh Sabaoth.ᵃ You ask, "How are we to return? ⁸ Can a human being cheat God?" Yet you try to cheat me! You ask, "How do we try to cheat you?" Over tithes and contributions. ⁹ A curse lies on you because you, this whole nation, try to cheat me. ¹⁰ Bring the tithes in full to the treasury, so that there is food in my house; put me to the test now like this, says Yahweh Sabaoth, and see if I do not open the floodgates of heaven for you and pour out an abundant blessing for you. ¹¹ For your sakes, I shall forbid the locust to destroy the produce of your soil or prevent the vine from bearing fruit in your field, says Yahweh Sabaoth, ¹² and all the nations will call you blessed, for you will be a land of delights, says Yahweh Sabaoth.

The triumph of the upright on the Day of Yahweh

¹³ 'You have said harsh things about me, says Yahweh. And yet you say, "What have we said against you?" ¹⁴ You have said, "It is useless to serve God; what is the good of keeping his commands or of walking mournfully before Yahweh Sabaoth? ¹⁵ In fact, we now call the proud the happy ones; the evil-doers are the ones who prosper; they put God to the test, yet come to no harm!"'

¹⁶ Then those who feared Yahweh talked to one another about this, and Yahweh took note and listened; and a book of remembrance was written in his presence recording those who feared him and kept his name in mind. ¹⁷ 'On the day when I act, says Yahweh Sabaoth, they will be my most prized possession, and I shall spare them in the way a man spares the son who serves him. ¹⁸ Then once again you will see the difference between the upright person

3a ‖ Zc 1:3.

100 READ MALACHI 3:1–5, 13–23.

Suddenly the Lord whom you seek will come to his Temple.—MALACHI 3:1

ANTICIPATING JESUS' SECOND COMING

We preach not one coming only of Christ, but also a second coming, far more glorious than the former. For the first coming gave a view of his patience, but the second coming brings with it the crown of a divine kingdom. . . . In his first coming, he was wrapped in swaddling clothes in the manger; in his second, he is "wearing the light as a robe" (Ps 104:2). In his first coming, "He endured the cross, disregarding the shame of it" (Heb 12:2); in his second, he comes attended by a host of angels, receiving glory.

We rest not then upon his first coming only, but look also for his second. And as at his first coming we said, "Blessed is he who is coming in the name of the Lord" (Mt 21:9), so will we repeat the same at his second coming (see Mt 23:39). . . . The Savior comes, not to be judged again, but to judge them who judged him. . . . Then, he came because of a divine dispensation, teaching men with persuasion. But this time they will of necessity have him for their King, even though they wish it not.

Concerning these two comings, Malachi says, "Suddenly the Lord whom you seek will come to his Temple." This is one coming. And again of the second coming he says, "Yes, the angel of the covenant, for whom you long, is on his way, says Yahweh Sabaoth. Who will be able to resist the day of his coming? Who will remain standing when he appears? For he will be like a refiner's fire, like fullers' alkali. He will take his seat as refiner and purifier." . . .

Thus, our Lord Jesus Christ will come from heaven and he will come at the end of this world on the last day. For this world will have an end, and this created world will be renewed.

ST. CYRIL OF JERUSALEM, 315?–386

YOU WILL FIND THE NEXT READING AT MATTHEW 4.

and the wicked one, between the one who serves God and the one who does not serve him.

¹⁹ 'For look, the Day is coming, glowing like a furnace. All the proud and all the evildoers will be the stubble, and the Day, when it comes, will set them ablaze, says Yahweh Sabaoth, leaving them neither root nor branch. ²⁰ But for you who fear my name, the Sun of justice will rise with healing in his rays, and you will come out leaping like calves from the stall, ²¹ and trample on the wicked, who will be like ashes under the soles of your feet on the day when I act, says Yahweh Sabaoth.

Appendices

²² 'Remember the Law of my servant Moses to whom at Horeb I prescribed decrees and rulings for all Israel.

²³ 'Look, I shall send you the prophet Elijah before the great and awesome Day of Yahweh comes. ²⁴ He will reconcile parents to their children and children to their parents, to forestall my putting the country under the curse of destruction.'

THE NEW TESTAMENT

The Gospel According to

MATTHEW

The ancestry of Jesus

1 Roll of the genealogy of Jesus Christ, son of David, son of Abraham:

2 Abraham fathered Isaac,
Isaac fathered Jacob,
Jacob fathered Judah and his
    brothers,
3 Judah fathered Perez and Zerah,
    whose mother was Tamar,
Perez fathered Hezron,
Hezron fathered Ram,
4 Ram fathered Amminadab,
Amminadab fathered Nahshon,
Nahshon fathered Salmon,
5 Salmon fathered Boaz, whose mother
    was Rahab,
Boaz fathered Obed, whose mother was
    Ruth,
Obed fathered Jesse;
6 and Jesse fathered King David.

David fathered Solomon, whose mother
    had been Uriah's wife,
7 Solomon fathered Rehoboam,
Rehoboam fathered Abijah,
Abijah fathered Asa,
8 Asa fathered Jehoshaphat,
Jehoshaphat fathered Joram,
Joram fathered Uzziah,
9 Uzziah fathered Jotham,
Jotham fathered Ahaz,
Ahaz fathered Hezekiah,
10 Hezekiah fathered Manasseh,
Manasseh fathered Amon,
Amon fathered Josiah;
11 and Josiah fathered Jechoniah and his
    brothers.

Then the deportation to Babylon took place.

12 After the deportation to Babylon:
Jechoniah fathered Shealtiel,
Shealtiel fathered Zerubbabel,
13 Zerubbabel fathered Abiud,
Abiud fathered Eliakim,
Eliakim fathered Azor,
14 Azor fathered Zadok,
Zadok fathered Achim,
Achim fathered Eliud,
15 Eliud fathered Eleazar,
Eleazar fathered Matthan,
Matthan fathered Jacob;
16 and Jacob fathered Joseph the husband of
    Mary;
of her was born Jesus who is called Christ.

17 The sum of generations is therefore: fourteen from Abraham to David; fourteen from David to the Babylonian deportation; and fourteen from the Babylonian deportation to Christ.

Joseph adopts Jesus as his son

18 This is how Jesus Christ came to be born. His mother Mary was betrothed to Joseph; but before they came to live together she was found to be with child through the Holy Spirit. 19 Her husband Joseph, being an upright man and wanting to spare her disgrace, decided to divorce her informally. 20 He had made up his mind to do this when suddenly the angel of the Lord appeared to him in a dream and said, 'Joseph son of David, do not be afraid to take Mary home as your wife, because she has conceived what is in her by the Holy Spirit. 21 She will give birth to a son and

you must name him Jesus, because he is the one who is to save his people from their sins.' 22 Now all this took place to fulfil what the Lord had spoken through the prophet:

23 *Look! the virgin is with child and will give birth to a son whom they will call Immanuel,*[a]

a name which means 'God-is-with-us'. 24 When Joseph woke up he did what the angel of the Lord had told him to do: he took his wife to his home; 25 he had not had intercourse with her when she gave birth to a son; and he named him Jesus.

The visit of the Magi

2 After Jesus had been born at Bethlehem in Judaea during the reign of King Herod, suddenly some wise men came to Jerusalem from the east 2 asking, 'Where is the infant king of the Jews? We saw his star as it rose and have come to do him homage.' 3 When King Herod heard this he was perturbed, and so was the whole of Jerusalem. 4 He called together all the chief priests and the scribes of the people, and enquired of them where the Christ was to be born. 5 They told him, 'At Bethlehem in Judaea, for this is what the prophet wrote:

6 *And you, Bethlehem,* in the land of Judah, you are by no means the *least among the leaders of Judah,* for *from you will come a leader* who will *shepherd* my people Israel.'[a]

7 Then Herod summoned the wise men to see him privately. He asked them the exact date on which the star had appeared 8 and sent them on to Bethlehem with the words, 'Go and find out all about the child, and when you have found him, let me know, so that I too may go and do him homage.' 9 Having listened to what the king had to say, they set out. And suddenly the star they had seen rising went forward and halted over the place where the child was. 10 The sight of the star filled them

with delight, 11 and going into the house they saw the child with his mother Mary, and falling to their knees they did him homage. Then, opening their treasures, they offered him gifts of gold and frankincense and myrrh. 12 But they were given a warning in a dream not to go back to Herod, and returned to their own country by a different way.

The flight into Egypt; the massacre of the Innocents

13 After they had left, suddenly the angel of the Lord appeared to Joseph in a dream and said, 'Get up, take the child and his mother with you, and escape into Egypt, and stay there until I tell you, because Herod intends to search for the child and do away with him.' 14 So Joseph got up and, taking the child and his mother with him, left that night for Egypt, 15 where he stayed until Herod was dead. This was to fulfil what the Lord had spoken through the prophet:

I called my son out of Egypt.[b]

16 Herod was furious on realising that he had been fooled by the wise men, and in Bethlehem and its surrounding district he had all the male children killed who were two years old or less, reckoning by the date he had been careful to ask the wise men. 17 Then were fulfilled the words spoken through the prophet Jeremiah:

18 *A voice is heard in Ramah, lamenting and weeping bitterly: it is Rachel weeping for her children, refusing to be comforted because they are no more.*[c]

From Egypt to Nazareth

19 After Herod's death, suddenly the angel of the Lord appeared in a dream to Joseph in

---

1a Is 7:14.   2a Mi 5:1.   2b Nb 23:22.

2c In Jr 31:15 she weeps for the northern tribes. But traditionally she was buried near Bethlehem.

Egypt [20] and said,[d] 'Get up, take the child and his mother with you and go back to the land of Israel, for those who wanted to kill the child are dead.' [21] So Joseph got up and, taking the child and his mother with him, went back to the land of Israel. [22] But when he learnt that Archelaus had succeeded his father Herod as ruler of Judaea he was afraid to go there, and being warned in a dream he withdrew to the region of Galilee. [23] There he settled in a town called Nazareth. In this way the words spoken through the prophets were to be fulfilled:

> He will be called a Nazarene.

The proclamation of John the Baptist

3 In due course John the Baptist appeared; he proclaimed this message in the desert of Judaea, [2] 'Repent, for the kingdom of Heaven is close at hand.' [3] This was the man spoken of by the prophet Isaiah when he said:

> A voice of one that cries in the desert,
> 'Prepare a way for the Lord,
> make his paths straight.'[a]

[4] This man John wore a garment made of camel-hair with a leather loin-cloth round his waist,[b] and his food was locusts and wild honey. [5] Then Jerusalem and all Judaea and the whole Jordan district made their way to him, [6] and as they were baptised by him in the river Jordan they confessed their sins. [7] But when he saw a number of Pharisees and Sadducees coming for baptism he said to them, 'Brood of vipers, who warned you to flee from the coming retribution? [8] Produce fruit in keeping with repentance, [9] and do not presume to tell yourselves, "We have Abraham as our father," because, I tell you, God can raise children for Abraham from these stones. [10] Even now the axe is being laid to the root of the trees, so that any tree failing to produce good fruit will be cut down and thrown on the fire. [11] I baptise you in water for repentance, but the one who comes after me is more powerful than I, and I am not fit to carry his sandals; he will baptise you with the Holy Spirit

and fire. [12] His winnowing-fan is in his hand; he will clear his threshing-floor and gather his wheat into his barn; but the chaff he will burn in a fire that will never go out.'

Jesus is baptised

[13] Then Jesus appeared: he came from Galilee to the Jordan to be baptised by John. [14] John tried to dissuade him, with the words, 'It is I who need baptism from you, and yet you come to me!' [15] But Jesus replied, 'Leave it like this for the time being; it is fitting that we should, in this way, do all that uprightness demands.' Then John gave in to him.

[16] And when Jesus had been baptised he at once came up from the water, and suddenly the heavens opened and he saw the Spirit of God descending like a dove and coming down on him. [17] And suddenly there was a voice from heaven, 'This is my Son, the Beloved; my favour rests on him.'[c]

Testing in the desert

4 Then Jesus was led by the Spirit out into the desert to be put to the test by the devil. [2] He fasted for forty days and forty nights, after which he was hungry, [3] and the tester came and said to him, 'If you are Son of God, tell these stones to turn into loaves.' [4] But he replied, 'Scripture says:

> Human beings live not on bread alone
> but on every word that comes from the mouth
>   of God.'[a]

[5] The devil then took him to the holy city and set him on the parapet of the Temple. [6] 'If you are Son of God,' he said, 'throw yourself down; for scripture says:

> He has given his angels orders about you,
> and *they will carry you in their arms*
> *in case you trip over a stone.'*[b]

2d cf. Ex. 4:19–20. There are several parallels with the stories of Moses' infancy.

3a Is 40:3.   3b As Elijah, 2 K 1:8.   3c cf. Is 42:1.

4a Dt 8:3.   4b Ps 91:10–12.

101 READ MATTHEW 4:1–11.

He fasted for forty days and forty nights.—MATTHEW 4:2

THE POWER OF FASTING

If anyone should come and say to you, "You should not fast so often because it might injure your health," don't believe them or listen to them. Only tools of the great Enemy would suggest such a thing. . . . Can you see what fasting does? It heals diseases. It strengthens the body by eliminating excess fluids. It frightens away devils. It purges the mind of unclean thoughts. It clarifies the intellect. It purifies the heart. It sanctifies the body. And finally it leads a person to the throne of God. Don't think that this is rash talk. You have evidence for this in the Gospels by the authority of the Savior himself. His disciples asked him why they could not cast out an evil spirit, and he answered, "This is the kind that can be driven out only by prayer [and fasting]" (see Mk 9:28; a variant text adds, "and fasting.").

So if any person is troubled by an unclean spirit and he has recourse to the remedy of fasting, the evil spirit will promptly be compelled to leave him through dread of the power of fasting. Devils take great delight in fullness, and drunkenness, and bodily comfort. Fasting possesses great power and it works glorious things. How do you suppose that some people work wonders and signs and that God gives the sick health through them, unless it comes from their spiritual exercises, the meekness of their souls, and their union with God? To fast is to banquet with angels, and a person that fasts is to be reckoned to some degree among the angelic host.   ST. ATHANASIUS, 297?–373

YOU WILL FIND THE NEXT READING AT MATTHEW 6.

[7] Jesus said to him, 'Scripture also says:

Do not put the Lord your God to the test.' [c]

[8] Next, taking him to a very high mountain, the devil showed him all the kingdoms of the world and their splendour. [9] And he said to him, 'I will give you all these, if you fall at my feet and do me homage.' [10] Then Jesus replied, 'Away with you, Satan! For scripture says:

*The Lord your God is the one to whom you
          must do homage,
him alone you must serve.'* [d]

[11] Then the devil left him, and suddenly angels appeared and looked after him.

Return to Galilee

[12] Hearing that John had been arrested he withdrew to Galilee, [13] and leaving Nazara he went and settled in Capernaum, beside the lake, on the borders of Zebulun and Naphtali. [14] This was to fulfil what was spoken by the prophet Isaiah:

[15] *Land of Zebulun! Land of
          Naphtali!
   Way of the sea beyond Jordan.
   Galilee of the nations!*
[16] *The people that lived in darkness
   have seen a great light;*

4c Dt 6:16.   4d Dt 6:13.

*on those who lived in a country of shadow
dark as death
a light has dawned.*^e

¹⁷ From then onwards Jesus began his proclamation with the message, 'Repent, for the kingdom of Heaven is close at hand.'

The first four disciples are called

¹⁸ As he was walking by the Lake of Galilee he saw two brothers, Simon, who was called Peter, and his brother Andrew; they were making a cast into the lake with their net, for they were fishermen. ¹⁹ And he said to them, 'Come after me and I will make you fishers of people.' ²⁰ And at once they left their nets and followed him.

²¹ Going on from there he saw another pair of brothers, James son of Zebedee and his brother John; they were in their boat with their father Zebedee, mending their nets, and he called them. ²² And at once, leaving the boat and their father, they followed him.

*Jesus proclaims the message and
heals the sick*

²³ He went round the whole of Galilee teaching in their synagogues, proclaiming the good news of the kingdom and curing all kinds of disease and illness among the people. ²⁴ His fame spread throughout Syria, and those who were suffering from diseases and painful complaints of one kind or another, the possessed, epileptics, the paralysed, were all brought to him, and he cured them. ²⁵ Large crowds followed him, coming from Galilee, the Decapolis, Jerusalem, Judaea and Transjordan.

The sermon on the mount

5 Seeing the crowds, he went onto the mountain. And when he was seated his disciples came to him. ² Then he began to speak. This is what he taught them:

The Beatitudes^a

³ How blessed are the poor in spirit:
the kingdom of Heaven is theirs.

⁴ Blessed are *the gentle:*^b
they shall have the earth as inheritance.^c
⁵ Blessed are those who mourn:
they shall be comforted.
⁶ Blessed are those who hunger and thirst
for uprightness:
they shall have their fill.
⁷ Blessed are the merciful:
they shall have mercy shown them.
⁸ Blessed are the pure in heart:
they shall see God.
⁹ Blessed are the peacemakers:
they shall be recognised as children of
God.
¹⁰ Blessed are those who are persecuted in
the cause of uprightness:
the kingdom of Heaven is theirs.

¹¹ 'Blessed are you when people abuse you and persecute you and speak all kinds of calumny against you falsely on my account. ¹² Rejoice and be glad, for your reward will be great in heaven; this is how they persecuted the prophets before you.

Salt for the earth and light for the world

¹³ 'You are salt for the earth. But if salt loses its taste, what can make it salty again? It is good for nothing, and can only be thrown out to be trampled under people's feet.

¹⁴ 'You are light for the world. A city built on a hill-top cannot be hidden. ¹⁵ No one lights a lamp to put it under a tub; they put it on the lamp-stand where it shines for everyone in the house. ¹⁶ In the same way your light must shine in people's sight, so that, seeing your good works, they may give praise to your Father in heaven.

The fulfilment of the Law

¹⁷ 'Do not imagine that I have come to abolish the Law or the Prophets. I have come not to abolish but to complete them. ¹⁸ In truth I tell you, till heaven and earth disappear, not one

4e Is 8:23–9:1.   5a Lk 6:20–23.
5b Ps 37:11.   5c Gn 13:15.

dot, not one little stroke, is to disappear from the Law until all its purpose is achieved. ¹⁹Therefore, anyone who infringes even one of the least of these commandments and teaches others to do the same will be considered the least in the kingdom of Heaven; but the person who keeps them and teaches them will be considered great in the kingdom of Heaven.

The new standard higher than the old

²⁰'For I tell you, if your uprightness does not surpass that of the scribes and Pharisees, you will never get into the kingdom of Heaven.

²¹'You have heard how it was said to our ancestors, *You shall not kill;ᵈ* and if anyone does kill he must answer for it before the court. ²²But I say this to you, anyone who is angry with a brother will answer for it before the court; anyone who calls a brother "Fool" will answer for it before the Sanhedrin; and anyone who calls him "Traitor" will answer for it in hell fire. ²³So then, if you are bringing your offering to the altar and there remember that your brother has something against you, ²⁴leave your offering there before the altar, go and be reconciled with your brother first, and then come back and present your offering. ²⁵Come to terms with your opponent in good time while you are still on the way to the court with him, or he may hand you over to the judge and the judge to the officer, and you will be thrown into prison. ²⁶In truth I tell you, you will not get out till you have paid the last penny.

²⁷'You have heard how it was said, *You shall not commit adultery.ᵉ* ²⁸But I say this to you, if a man looks at a woman lustfully, he has already committed adultery with her in his heart. ²⁹If your right eye should be your downfall, tear it out and throw it away; for it will do you less harm to lose one part of yourself than to have your whole body thrown into hell. ³⁰And if your right hand should be your downfall, cut it off and throw it away; for it will do you less harm to lose one part of yourself than to have your whole body go to hell.

³¹'It has also been said, *Anyone who divorces his wife must give her a writ of dismissal.ᶠ* ³²But I say this to you, everyone who divorces his wife, except for the case of an illicit marriage,ᵍ makes her an adulteress; and anyone who marries a divorced woman commits adultery.

³³'Again, you have heard how it was said to our ancestors, *You must not break your oath, but must fulfil your oaths to the Lord.ʰ* ³⁴But I say this to you, do not swear at all, either by *heaven,* since that is *God's throne;* ³⁵or by *earth,* since that is *his footstool;* or by Jerusalem, since that is *the city of the great King.ⁱ* ³⁶Do not swear by your own head either, since you cannot turn a single hair white or black. ³⁷All you need say is "Yes" if you mean yes, "No" if you mean no; anything more than this comes from the Evil One.

³⁸'You have heard how it was said: *Eye for eye and tooth for tooth.ʲ* ³⁹But I say this to you: offer no resistance to the wicked. On the contrary, if anyone hits you on the right cheek, offer him the other as well; ⁴⁰if someone wishes to go to law with you to get your tunic, let him have your cloak as well. ⁴¹And if anyone requires you to go one mile, go two miles with him. ⁴²Give to anyone who asks you, and if anyone wants to borrow, do not turn away.

⁴³'You have heard how it was said, *You will love your neighbourᵏ* and hate your enemy. ⁴⁴But I say this to you, love your enemies and pray for those who persecute you; ⁴⁵so that you may be children of your Father in heaven, for he causes his sun to rise on the bad as well as the good, and sends down rain to fall on the upright and the wicked alike. ⁴⁶For if you love those who love you, what reward will you get? Do not even the tax collectors do as much? ⁴⁷And if you save your greetings for your brothers, are you doing anything exceptional? ⁴⁸Do not even the gentiles do as much? You

---

5d Ex 20:13.   5e Ex 20:14.   5f Dt 24:1.

5g Marriage within the Jewish forbidden degrees, allowed by the Romans but not in Christianity.

5h Ex 20:7.   5i Ps 48:2.   5j Ex 21:24.

5k Lv 19:18. The rest of the sentence is not from the OT.

must therefore be perfect, just as your heavenly Father is perfect.'

Almsgiving in secret

6 'Be careful not to parade your uprightness in public to attract attention; otherwise you will lose all reward from your Father in heaven. ²So when you give alms, do not have it trumpeted before you; this is what the hypocrites do in the synagogues and in the streets to win human admiration. In truth I tell you, they have had their reward. ³But when you give alms, your left hand must not know what your right is doing; ⁴your almsgiving must be secret, and your Father who sees all that is done in secret will reward you.

Prayer in secret

⁵'And when you pray, do not imitate the hypocrites: they love to say their prayers standing up in the synagogues and at the street corners for people to see them. In truth I tell you, they have had their reward. ⁶But when you pray, *go to your private* room, shut yourself in, and so pray*ᵃ* to your Father who is in that secret place, and your Father who sees all that is done in secret will reward you.

How to pray; the Lord's Prayer

⁷'In your prayers do not babble as the gentiles do, for they think that by using many words they will make themselves heard. ⁸Do not be like them; your Father knows what you need before you ask him. ⁹So you should pray like this:

Our Father in heaven,
may your name be held holy,
¹⁰ your kingdom come,
your will be done,
on earth as in heaven.
¹¹ Give us today our daily bread.
¹² And forgive us our debts,
as we have forgiven those who are in debt
to us.
¹³ And do not put us to the test,
but save us from the Evil One.*ᵇ*

¹⁴'Yes, if you forgive others their failings, your heavenly Father will forgive you yours; ¹⁵but if you do not forgive others, your Father will not forgive your failings either.

Fasting in secret

¹⁶'When you are fasting, do not put on a gloomy look as the hypocrites do: they go about looking unsightly to let people know they are fasting. In truth I tell you, they have had their reward. ¹⁷But when you fast, put scent on your head and wash your face, ¹⁸so that no one will know you are fasting except your Father who sees all that is done in secret; and your Father who sees all that is done in secret will reward you.

True treasures

¹⁹'Do not store up treasures for yourselves on earth, where moth and woodworm destroy them and thieves can break in and steal. ²⁰But store up treasures for yourselves in heaven, where neither moth nor woodworm destroys them and thieves cannot break in and steal. ²¹For wherever your treasure is, there will your heart be too.

The eye, the lamp of the body

²²'The lamp of the body is the eye. It follows that if your eye is clear, your whole body will be filled with light. ²³But if your eye is diseased, your whole body will be darkness. If then, the light inside you is darkened, what darkness that will be!

God and money

²⁴'No one can be the slave of two masters: he will either hate the first and love the second, or be attached to the first and despise the second. You cannot be the slave both of God and of money.

Trust in Providence

²⁵'That is why I am telling you not to worry about your life and what you are to eat, nor

6a Is 26:20.   6b Lk 11:2–4.

102 READ MATTHEW 6:1–14.

When you pray, go to your private room, shut yourself in, and so pray to your Father.

—MATTHEW 6:6

BLESSED DISTRACTIONS

Prayer is the channel that unites our heart to the heart of God. It draws waters from heaven that descend and rise from us to God and from God to us. Prayer is the first act of our faith, and consequently what the apostle says of faith—that it is impossible to please God without it (see Heb 11:6)—we must say of prayer. By it we ask God and Jesus Christ, who is our deliverer, to save us. We feel so despoiled by our weakness that we should perish unless he sustained us every moment with new graces.

When we place ourselves in the presence of his divine goodness to speak to him alone, then our prayer consists in the presence of our spirit before his and of his Spirit before ours. That's the case whether we have good thoughts and good sentiments or not. We need only with all simplicity and without any violent spiritual effort to keep ourselves before him. We should express our love for him and focus our attention on him without entertaining any voluntary distractions.

Then God will view the whole time we are on our knees as prayer. He loves our humbly enduring the vain and involuntary thoughts that attack us as much as the best thoughts we have had at other times. One of the most excellent prayers is the loving desire of our heart towards God, and the suffering of things that displease us. Prayer is then united to patience, which is the premier virtue. And the soul that rises humbly from its distractions may believe that it has prayed as well as if it had not suffered from them at all. ST. JANE DE CHANTAL, 1572–1641

YOU WILL FIND THE NEXT READING AT MATTHEW 7.

about your body and what you are to wear. Surely life is more than food, and the body more than clothing! 26 Look at the birds in the sky. They do not sow or reap or gather into barns; yet your heavenly Father feeds them. Are you not worth much more than they are? 27 Can any of you, however much you worry, add one single cubit to your span of life? 28 And why worry about clothing? Think of the flowers growing in the fields; they never have to work or spin; 29 yet I assure you that not even Solomon in all his royal robes was clothed like one of these. 30 Now if that is how God clothes the wild flowers growing in the field which are there today and thrown into the furnace tomorrow, will he not much more

look after you, you who have so little faith? 31 So do not worry; do not say, "What are we to eat? What are we to drink? What are we to wear?" 32 It is the gentiles who set their hearts on all these things. Your heavenly Father knows you need them all. 33 Set your hearts on his kingdom first, and on God's saving justice, and all these other things will be given you as well. 34 So do not worry about tomorrow: tomorrow will take care of itself. Each day has enough trouble of its own.'

Do not judge

7 'Do not judge, and you will not be judged; 2 because the judgements you give are the judgements you will get, and the standard you

use will be the standard used for you. ³Why do you observe the splinter in your brother's eye and never notice the great log in your own? ⁴And how dare you say to your brother, "Let me take that splinter out of your eye," when, look, there is a great log in your own? ⁵Hypocrite! Take the log out of your own eye first, and then you will see clearly enough to take the splinter out of your brother's eye.

Do not profane sacred things

⁶'Do not give dogs what is holy; and do not throw your pearls in front of pigs, or they may trample them and then turn on you and tear you to pieces.

Effective prayer

⁷'Ask, and it will be given to you; search, and you will find; knock, and the door will be opened to you. ⁸Everyone who asks receives; everyone who searches finds; everyone who knocks will have the door opened. ⁹Is there anyone among you who would hand his son a stone when he asked for bread? ¹⁰Or would hand him a snake when he asked for a fish? ¹¹If you, then, evil as you are, know how to give your children what is good, how much more will your Father in heaven give good things to those who ask him!

The golden rule

¹²'So always treat others as you would like them to treat you; that is the Law and the Prophets.

The two ways

¹³'Enter by the narrow gate, since the road that leads to destruction is wide and spacious, and many take it; ¹⁴but it is a narrow gate and a hard road that leads to life, and only a few find it.

False prophets

¹⁵'Beware of false prophets who come to you disguised as sheep but underneath are ravenous wolves. ¹⁶You will be able to tell them by their fruits. Can people pick grapes from thorns, or figs from thistles? ¹⁷In the same way, a sound tree produces good fruit but a rotten tree bad fruit. ¹⁸A sound tree cannot bear bad fruit, nor a rotten tree bear good fruit. ¹⁹Any tree that does not produce good fruit is cut down and thrown on the fire. ²⁰I repeat, you will be able to tell them by their fruits.

The true disciple

²¹'It is not anyone who says to me, "Lord, Lord," who will enter the kingdom of Heaven, but the person who does the will of my Father in heaven. ²²When the day comes many will say to me, "Lord, Lord, did we not prophesy in your name, drive out demons in your name, work many miracles in your name?" ²³Then I shall tell them to their faces: I have never known you; *away from me, all evil doers!* ᵃ

²⁴'Therefore, everyone who listens to these words of mine and acts on them will be like a sensible man who built his house on rock. ²⁵Rain came down, floods rose, gales blew and hurled themselves against that house, and it did not fall: it was founded on rock. ²⁶But everyone who listens to these words of mine and does not act on them will be like a stupid man who built his house on sand. ²⁷Rain came down, floods rose, gales blew and struck that house, and it fell; and what a fall it had!'

The amazement of the crowds

²⁸Jesus had now finished what he wanted to say, and his teaching made a deep impression on the people ²⁹because he taught them with authority, unlike their own scribes.

Cure of a man with skin-disease

8 After he had come down from the mountain large crowds followed him. ²Suddenly a man with a virulent skin-disease came up and bowed low in front of him, saying, 'Lord, if you are willing, you can cleanse me.' ³Jesus stretched out his hand and touched him say-

7a Ps 6:8.

103 READ MATTHEW 7:21–27.

It is not anyone who says to me, "Lord, Lord," who will enter the kingdom of Heaven.—MATTHEW 7:21

THE TEST OF LOVE

Love certainly gives value to our works, but obedience proves how much our works are worth because they are valuable only so far as they are done with charity and obedience.

I assure you that even though you had the gift of tears to such a degree that you wore yourself out weeping for your neighbor's sins; though you had the gift of prophecy; though you were ravished in ecstasy and saw angels; though you were always recollected and united to God; if you are not obedient and simple, all that I have just said is but a deceit of your enemy, and your love is but an illusion. As our Savior has said, "It is not anyone who says to me, 'Lord, Lord,' " that is, who prays often, "who will enter the kingdom of Heaven, but the person who does the will of my Father. . . ." Notice how he has placed the mark of true love in obedience: "If you love me, keep my commandments" (see Jn 14:21). All these things are truths of Scripture. Recompense is given in proportion to love, and obedience is the proof of true love. You should love supremely this practice of obeying in all things, and do nothing without obedience stamped with the love of Christ.

Don't think that you must do great things to show our Lord that you love him. No, great things are good when God presents them. But let's offer our little things to his goodness with great love and great submissiveness, and the recompense will be in proportion to these two things.

Nowhere in Scripture does the Lord say: My son, my daughter, give me your head, your arms, your life, but only, "My child, give me your heart." Whoever has a person's heart has the whole person. The heart is the seat of love. When I have your heart, I will set my love on it. And I will even make my love dwell in it, and all the rest will follow as a consequence.

ST. JANE DE CHANTAL, 1572–1641

YOU WILL FIND THE NEXT READING AT MATTHEW 8.

ing, 'I am willing. Be cleansed.' And his skin-disease was cleansed at once. ⁴Then Jesus said to him, 'Mind you tell no one, but go and show yourself to the priest and make the offering prescribed by Moses,ᵃ as evidence to them.'

Cure of the centurion's servant

⁵When he went into Capernaum a centurion came up and pleaded with him. ⁶'Sir,' he said, 'my servant is lying at home paralysed and in great pain.' ⁷Jesus said to him, 'I will come myself and cure him.' ⁸The centurion replied, 'Sir, I am not worthy to have you under my roof; just give the word and my servant will be cured. ⁹For I am under authority myself and have soldiers under me; and I say to one man, "Go," and he goes; to another, "Come here," and he comes; to my servant, "Do this," and he does it.' ¹⁰When Jesus heard this he was astonished and said to those following him, 'In

8a Lv 14:1–32.

104 READ MATTHEW 8.

He himself bore our sicknesses away and carried our diseases.—MATTHEW 8:17

FAITH HEALING

As the Lord came down from the mountain, the multitudes met him, because they were unable to ascend to the heights. And the first to meet him was a leper. Because of his leprosy he had been unable to hear the wondrous discourse of the Savior spoken on the mountain. And observe that he was the first to be miraculously cured. . . . Fittingly, after his sermon and instruction, an occasion presents itself for a sign, so that the sermon they had heard might be confirmed by the power of a miracle.

"Lord, if you are willing, you can cleanse me." He who petitions the Lord does not doubt his power. "Jesus stretched out his hand and touched him." Stretching forth his hand, immediately the leprosy disappears. Consider here again how humble and unassuming the answer. The leper had said: "if you are willing." The Lord answers: "I am willing." The leper had already said: "you can cleanse me." The Lord joins both requests and says: "Be cleansed." . . .

Then Jesus said to him, "Mind you tell no one." And indeed what need was there that he should boast by word of mouth of that which his body proclaimed? "But go show yourself to the priest." He bids him, for various reasons, go to the priest. First, out of humility, so that he will be seen to give honor to the priests. For there was a precept of the Law that anyone who was cleansed of leprosy should make an offering to the priests. Again that those seeing the leper now made clean would either believe in the Savior or would not believe. If they believed they would be saved; if they believed not, they would be inexcusable. And lastly, so that he might not seem to infringe the Law, of which they were frequently to accuse him.   ST. JEROME, 341?–420

YOU WILL FIND THE NEXT READING AT MATTHEW 9.

truth I tell you, in no one in Israel have I found faith as great as this. 11 And I tell you that many will come from east and west and sit down with Abraham and Isaac and Jacob at the feast in the kingdom of Heaven; 12 but the children of the kingdom will be thrown out into the darkness outside, where there will be weeping and grinding of teeth.' 13 And to the centurion Jesus said, 'Go back, then; let this be done for you, as your faith demands.' And the servant was cured at that moment.

Cure of Peter's mother-in-law

14 And going into Peter's house Jesus found Peter's mother-in-law in bed and feverish.

15 He touched her hand and the fever left her, and she got up and began to serve him.

A number of cures

16 That evening they brought him many who were possessed by devils. He drove out the spirits with a command and cured all who were sick. 17 This was to fulfil what was spoken by the prophet Isaiah:

> *He himself bore our sicknesses away and carried our diseases.*[b]

8b Is 53:4.

[1213]

Unconditional commitment

18 When Jesus saw the crowd all about him he gave orders to leave for the other side. 19 One of the scribes then came up and said to him, 'Master, I will follow you wherever you go.' 20 Jesus said, 'Foxes have holes and the birds of the air have nests, but the Son of man has nowhere to lay his head.'

21 Another man, one of the disciples, said to him, 'Lord, let me go and bury my father first.' 22 But Jesus said, 'Follow me, and leave the dead to bury their dead.'

The calming of the storm

23 Then he got into the boat followed by his disciples. 24 Suddenly a storm broke over the lake, so violent that the boat was being swamped by the waves. But he was asleep. 25 So they went to him and woke him saying, 'Save us, Lord, we are lost!' 26 And he said to them, 'Why are you so frightened, you who have so little faith?' And then he stood up and rebuked the winds and the sea; and there was a great calm. 27 They were astounded and said, 'Whatever kind of man is this, that even the winds and the sea obey him?'

The demoniacs of Gadara

28 When he reached the territory of the Gadarenes on the other side, two demoniacs came towards him out of the tombs—they were so dangerously violent that nobody could use that path. 29 Suddenly they shouted, 'What do you want with us, Son of God? Have you come here to torture us before the time?' 30 Now some distance away there was a large herd of pigs feeding, 31 and the devils pleaded with Jesus, 'If you drive us out, send us into the herd of pigs.' 32 And he said to them, 'Go then,' and they came out and made for the pigs; and at that the whole herd charged down the cliff into the lake and perished in the water. 33 The herdsmen ran off and made for the city, where they told the whole story, including what had happened to the demoniacs. 34 Suddenly the whole city set out to meet Jesus; and as soon as they saw him they implored him to leave their neighbourhood.

Cure of a paralytic

9 He got back in the boat, crossed the water and came to his home town. 2 And suddenly some people brought him a paralytic stretched out on a bed. Seeing their faith, Jesus said to the paralytic, 'Take comfort, my child, your sins are forgiven.' 3 And now some scribes said to themselves, 'This man is being blasphemous.' 4 Knowing what was in their minds Jesus said, 'Why do you have such wicked thoughts in your hearts? 5 Now, which of these is easier: to say, "Your sins are forgiven," or to say, "Get up and walk"? 6 But to prove to you that the Son of man has authority on earth to forgive sins,'—then he said to the paralytic—'get up, pick up your bed and go off home.' 7 And the man got up and went home. 8 A feeling of awe came over the crowd when they saw this, and they praised God for having given such authority to human beings.

The call of Matthew

9 As Jesus was walking on from there he saw a man named Matthew sitting at the tax office, and he said to him, 'Follow me.' And he got up and followed him.

Eating with sinners

10 Now while he was at table in the house it happened that a number of tax collectors and sinners came to sit at the table with Jesus and his disciples. 11 When the Pharisees saw this, they said to his disciples, 'Why does your master eat with tax collectors and sinners?' 12 When he heard this he replied, 'It is not the healthy who need the doctor, but the sick. 13 Go and learn the meaning of the words: *Mercy is what pleases me, not sacrifice.*[a] And indeed I came to call not the upright, but sinners.'

9a Ho 6:6.

105 READ MATTHEW 9:1–8.

He got back in the boat, crossed the water and came to his home town.—MATTHEW 9:1

THE WEAKNESS OF CHRIST

This day's reading shows us an instance of how Christ, in those things that he did as a human being, worked deep works of God. And how by doing visible things he worked things that were invisible. The Evangelist says, "He got back in the boat, crossed the water and came to his home town." Was not this he who had once parted the waves and made dry ground appear at the bottom of the sea, so that his people Israel passed dry-shod between masses of water standing still as though through a glen in a mountain? Was not this he who made the sea solid under Peter, so that the watery path offered a firm way for human footsteps?

Why then did he deny himself a similar service from the sea, and instead crossed over that narrow lake aboard a ship? Do you wonder, brothers and sisters? Christ came to take our weakness upon himself so that he might make us partakers of his strength; to seek the things of men, that he might give to men the things of God; to receive insults that he might bestow honors; to bear weariness that he might grant rest. The physician who has no frailties does not know how to treat the frailties of others, nor he that is not weak himself, how to make the weak strong.

So if Christ had appeared in his strength he would not really have been like us human beings. If in him flesh had not run the way of all flesh, then it would have been useless for him to have taken flesh at all. The Scripture says "he came to his home town." The Lord, the maker of the world and of all things, choosing for our sakes to imprison himself in our flesh, had a human home and became a citizen of a Jewish city; himself the Father of all, to have parents; and all, so that his love might invite, his charity draw, his tenderness bind, his gentleness persuade them whom his kingdom had scared, his awfulness scattered, and his power terrified out of his dominion.

ST. PETER CHRYSOLOGUS, 406–450?

YOU WILL FIND THE NEXT READING AT MATTHEW 11.

A discussion on fasting

14 Then John's disciples came to him and said, 'Why is it that we and the Pharisees fast, but your disciples do not?' 15 Jesus replied, 'Surely the bridegroom's attendants cannot mourn as long as the bridegroom is still with them? But the time will come when the bridegroom is taken away from them, and then they will fast. 16 No one puts a piece of unshrunken cloth onto an old cloak, because the patch pulls away from the cloak and the tear gets worse. 17 Nor do people put new wine into old wineskins; otherwise, the skins burst, the wine runs out, and the skins are lost. No; they put new wine in fresh skins and both are preserved.'

Cure of the woman with a haemorrhage; the official's daughter raised to life

18 While he was speaking to them, suddenly one of the officials came up, who bowed low in

front of him and said, 'My daughter has just died, but come and lay your hand on her and her life will be saved.' ¹⁹Jesus rose and, with his disciples, followed him.

²⁰Then suddenly from behind him came a woman, who had been suffering from a haemorrhage for twelve years, and she touched the fringe of his cloak, ²¹for she was thinking, 'If only I can touch his cloak I shall be saved.' ²²Jesus turned round and saw her; and he said to her, 'Courage, my daughter, your faith has saved you.' And from that moment the woman was saved.

²³When Jesus reached the official's house and saw the flute-players, with the crowd making a commotion, he said, ²⁴'Get out of here; the little girl is not dead; she is asleep.' And they ridiculed him. ²⁵But when the people had been turned out he went inside and took her by the hand; and she stood up. ²⁶And the news of this spread all round the countryside.

Cure of two blind men

²⁷As Jesus went on his way two blind men followed him shouting, 'Take pity on us, son of David.' ²⁸And when Jesus reached the house the blind men came up to him and he said to them, 'Do you believe I can do this?' They said, 'Lord, we do.' ²⁹Then he touched their eyes saying, 'According to your faith, let it be done to you.' ³⁰And their sight returned. Then Jesus sternly warned them, 'Take care that no one learns about this.' ³¹But when they had gone away, they talked about him all over the countryside.

Cure of a dumb demoniac

³²They had only just left when suddenly a man was brought to him, a dumb demoniac. ³³And when the devil was driven out, the dumb man spoke and the people were amazed and said, 'Nothing like this has ever been seen in Israel.' ³⁴But the Pharisees said, 'It is through the prince of devils that he drives out devils.'

The distress of the crowds

³⁵Jesus made a tour through all the towns and villages, teaching in their synagogues, proclaiming the good news of the kingdom and curing all kinds of disease and all kinds of illness.

³⁶And when he saw the crowds he felt sorry for them because they were harassed and dejected, like sheep without a shepherd. ³⁷Then he said to his disciples, 'The harvest is rich but the labourers are few, so ask the Lord of the harvest to send out labourers to his harvest.'

The mission of the Twelve ᵃ

10He summoned his twelve disciples and gave them authority over unclean spirits with power to drive them out and to cure all kinds of disease and all kinds of illness.

²These are the names of the twelve apostles: first, Simon who is known as Peter, and his brother Andrew; James the son of Zebedee, and his brother John; ³Philip and Bartholomew; Thomas, and Matthew the tax collector; James the son of Alphaeus, and Thaddaeus; ⁴Simon the Zealot and Judas Iscariot, who was also his betrayer. ⁵These twelve Jesus sent out, instructing them as follows:

'Do not make your way to gentile territory, and do not enter any Samaritan town; ⁶go instead to the lost sheep of the House of Israel. ⁷And as you go, proclaim that the kingdom of Heaven is close at hand. ⁸Cure the sick, raise the dead, cleanse those suffering from virulent skin-diseases, drive out devils. You received without charge, give without charge. ⁹Provide yourselves with no gold or silver, not even with coppers for your purses, ¹⁰with no haversack for the journey or spare tunic or footwear or a staff, for the labourer deserves his keep.

¹¹'Whatever town or village you go into, seek out someone worthy and stay with him until you leave. ¹²As you enter his house,

10a Mk 3:14–19; Lk 6:13–16; the order and even some of the names vary in different lists.

salute it, [13]and if the house deserves it, may your peace come upon it; if it does not, may your peace come back to you. [14]And if anyone does not welcome you or listen to what you have to say, as you walk out of the house or town shake the dust from your feet. [15]In truth I tell you, on the Day of Judgement it will be more bearable for Sodom and Gomorrah than for that town. [16]Look, I am sending you out like sheep among wolves; so be cunning as snakes and yet innocent as doves.

Missionaries will be persecuted

[17]'Be prepared for people to hand you over to sanhedrins and scourge you in their synagogues. [18]You will be brought before governors and kings for my sake, as evidence to them and to the gentiles. [19]But when you are handed over, do not worry about how to speak or what to say; what you are to say will be given to you when the time comes, [20]because it is not you who will be speaking; the Spirit of your Father will be speaking in you.

[21]'Brother will betray brother to death, and a father his child; children will come forward against their parents and have them put to death. [22]You will be universally hated on account of my name; but anyone who stands firm to the end will be saved. [23]If they persecute you in one town, take refuge in the next; and if they persecute you in that, take refuge in another. In truth I tell you, you will not have gone the round of the towns of Israel before the Son of man comes.

[24]'Disciple is not superior to teacher, nor slave to master. [25]It is enough for disciple to grow to be like teacher, and slave like master. If they have called the master of the house "Beelzebul", how much more the members of his household?

Open and fearless speech

[26]'So do not be afraid of them. Everything now covered up will be uncovered, and everything now hidden will be made clear. [27]What I say to you in the dark, tell in the daylight; what you hear in whispers, proclaim from the housetops.

[28]'Do not be afraid of those who kill the body but cannot kill the soul; fear him rather who can destroy both body and soul in hell. [29]Can you not buy two sparrows for a penny? And yet not one falls to the ground without your Father knowing. [30]Why, every hair on your head has been counted. [31]So there is no need to be afraid; you are worth more than many sparrows.

[32]'So if anyone declares himself for me in the presence of human beings, I will declare myself for him in the presence of my Father in heaven. [33]But the one who disowns me in the presence of human beings, I will disown in the presence of my Father in heaven.

Jesus, the cause of dissension

[34]'Do not suppose that I have come to bring peace to the earth: it is not peace I have come to bring, but a sword. [35]For I have come to set son against *father, daughter against mother, daughter-in-law against mother-in-law;* [36]*a person's enemies will be the members of his own household.*[b]

Renouncing self to follow Jesus

[37]'No one who prefers father or mother to me is worthy of me. No one who prefers son or daughter to me is worthy of me. [38]Anyone who does not take his cross and follow in my footsteps is not worthy of me. [39]Anyone who finds his life will lose it; anyone who loses his life for my sake will find it.

Conclusion of the Instruction

[40]'Anyone who welcomes you welcomes me; and anyone who welcomes me welcomes the one who sent me.

[41]'Anyone who welcomes a prophet because he is a prophet will have a prophet's reward; and anyone who welcomes an upright person because he is upright will have the reward of an upright person.

10b Mi 7:6.

⁴²'If anyone gives so much as a cup of cold water to one of these little ones because he is a disciple, then in truth I tell you, he will most certainly not go without his reward.'

11 When Jesus had finished instructing his twelve disciples he moved on from there to teach and preach in their towns.

The Baptist's question; Jesus commends him

²Now John had heard in prison what Christ was doing and he sent his disciples to ask him, ³'Are you the one who is to come, or are we to expect someone else?' ⁴Jesus answered, 'Go back and tell John what you hear and see; ⁵the blind see again, and the lame walk, those suffering from virulent skin-diseases are cleansed, and the deaf hear, the dead are raised to life and the good news is proclaimed to the poor;ᵃ ⁶and blessed is anyone who does not find me a cause of falling.'

⁷As the men were leaving, Jesus began to talk to the people about John, 'What did you go out into the desert to see? A reed swaying in the breeze? No? ⁸Then what did you go out to see? A man wearing fine clothes? Look, those who wear fine clothes are to be found in palaces. ⁹Then what did you go out for? To see a prophet? Yes, I tell you, and much more than a prophet: ¹⁰he is the one of whom scripture says:

Look, I am going to send my messenger in front of you
to prepare your way before you.ᵇ

¹¹'In truth I tell you, of all the children born to women, there has never been anyone greater than John the Baptist; yet the least in the kingdom of Heaven is greater than he. ¹²Since John the Baptist came, up to this present time, the kingdom of Heaven has been subjected to violence and the violent are taking it by storm. ¹³Because it was towards John that all the prophecies of the prophets and of the Law were leading; ¹⁴and he, if you will be-lieve me, is the Elijah who was to return. ¹⁵Anyone who has ears should listen!

Jesus condemns his contemporaries

¹⁶'What comparison can I find for this generation? It is like children shouting to each other as they sit in the market place:

¹⁷ We played the pipes for you,
and you wouldn't dance;
we sang dirges,
and you wouldn't be mourners.

¹⁸'For John came, neither eating nor drinking, and they say, "He is possessed." ¹⁹The Son of man came, eating and drinking, and they say, "Look, a glutton and a drunkard, a friend of tax collectors and sinners." Yet wisdom is jus-tified by her deeds.'

Lament over the lake-towns

²⁰Then he began to reproach the towns in which most of his miracles had been worked, because they refused to repent.

²¹'Alas for you, Chorazin! Alas for you, Bethsaida! For if the miracles done in you had been done in Tyre and Sidon, they would have repented long ago in sackcloth and ashes. ²²Still, I tell you that it will be more bearable for Tyre and Sidon on Judgement Day than for you. ²³And as for you, Capernaum, did you want to be *raised as high as heaven? You shall be flung down to hell.ᶜ* For if the miracles done in you had been done in Sodom, it would have been standing yet. ²⁴Still, I tell you that it will be more bearable for Sodom on Judge-ment Day than for you.'

The good news revealed to the simple; the Father and the Son

²⁵At that time Jesus exclaimed, 'I bless you, Father, Lord of heaven and of earth, for hid-ing these things from the learned and the clever and revealing them to little children. ²⁶Yes, Father, for that is what it pleased you to

11a cf. Is 35:5; 61:1. *11b* Ml 3:1. *11c* Is 14:13, 15.

106 READ MATTHEW 11:20–30.

Learn from me, for I am gentle and humble in heart.—MATTHEW 11:29

IMITATING CHRIST'S HUMILITY

Without humility all prayer is vain because after prayer we need humility more than anything. Consider the example of humility Christ gave us in his crucifixion and see its perfection. Look at his life and listen to his teaching that he set forth not only in words but also in actions. . . . Try with all your mind and strength to follow in his steps. He who was in the form of God abandoned his own nature and took the form of a servant, humbling himself and rendering obedience even to death upon the Cross (see Ph 2:6–8). He really offered himself to us as an example of humility, often advising us to imitate him, saying, "Learn from me, for I am gentle and humble in heart."

Reflect now on the depth and profitableness of his teaching. "Learn of me," he said, "and not of the angels or disciples, but of me, whose humility is all the greater because my majesty is more sublime." He did not ask us to learn fasting from him, although he fasted for forty days as an example for us. Neither does he ask us to reject the world and live in poverty, although he embraced poverty and invited his followers to do likewise. Neither does he ask us to learn from him how he made the heavens or performed miracles or other similar things. He only said, "I am gentle and humble in heart," as though he would say, "If by word and deed I have not shown you an example of humility, don't believe me.". . .

This lowliness of heart is mother of all the virtues. From it springs even the exercise of all these virtues, as the trunk and branches of a tree spring from the root. So precious is humility and so firm its foundation upon which is built up the whole perfection of the spiritual life that the Lord did especially desire that we should learn it directly from him.   BL. ANGELA OF FOLIGNO, 1248?–1309

YOU WILL FIND THE NEXT READING AT MATTHEW 12.

do. ²⁷ Everything has been entrusted to me by my Father; and no one knows the Son except the Father, just as no one knows the Father except the Son and those to whom the Son chooses to reveal him.

The gentle mastery of Christ

²⁸ 'Come to me, all you who labour and are overburdened, and I will give you rest. ²⁹ Shoulder my yoke and learn from me, for I am gentle and humble in heart, *and you will find rest for your souls.*ᵈ ³⁰ Yes, my yoke is easy and my burden light.'

Picking corn on the Sabbath

12 At that time Jesus went through the cornfields one Sabbath day. His disciples were hungry and began to pick ears of corn and eat them. ² The Pharisees noticed it and said to him, 'Look, your disciples are doing something that is forbidden on the Sabbath.' ³ But he said to them, 'Have you not read what David did when he and his followers were hungry— ⁴ how he went into the

11d Jr 6:16.

house of God and they ate the loaves of the offering although neither he nor his followers were permitted to eat them, but only the priests? ⁵Or again, have you not read in the Law that on the Sabbath day the Temple priests break the Sabbath without committing any fault? ⁶Now here, I tell you, is something greater than the Temple. ⁷And if you had understood the meaning of the words: *Mercy is what pleases me, not sacrifice,*ᵃ you would not have condemned the blameless. ⁸For the Son of man is master of the Sabbath.'

Cure of the man with a withered hand

⁹He moved on from there and went to their synagogue; ¹⁰now a man was there with a withered hand. They asked him, 'Is it permitted to cure somebody on the Sabbath day?' hoping for something to charge him with. ¹¹But he said to them, 'If any one of you here had only one sheep and it fell down a hole on the Sabbath day, would he not get hold of it and lift it out? ¹²Now a man is far more important than a sheep, so it follows that it is permitted on the Sabbath day to do good.' ¹³Then he said to the man, 'Stretch out your hand.' He stretched it out and his hand was restored, as sound as the other one. ¹⁴At this the Pharisees went out and began to plot against him, discussing how to destroy him.

Jesus the 'servant of Yahweh'

¹⁵Jesus knew this and withdrew from the district. Many followed him and he cured them all ¹⁶but warned them not to make him known. ¹⁷This was to fulfil what was spoken by the prophet Isaiah:

¹⁸ *Look! My servant whom I have chosen,*
my beloved, in whom my soul delights,
I will send my Spirit upon him,
 and he will *present* judgement to the
  nations;
¹⁹ *he will not brawl or cry out,*
his voice is not heard in the streets,
²⁰ *he will not break the crushed reed,*
or snuff the faltering wick,

²¹ *until he has made judgement victorious;*
 *in him the nations will put their hope.*ᵇ

Jesus and Beelzebul

²²Then they brought to him a blind and dumb demoniac; and he cured him, so that the dumb man could speak and see. ²³All the people were astounded and said, 'Can this be the son of David?' ²⁴But when the Pharisees heard this they said, 'The man drives out devils only through Beelzebul, the chief of the devils.'

²⁵Knowing what was in their minds he said to them, 'Every kingdom divided against itself is heading for ruin; and no town, no household divided against itself can last. ²⁶Now if Satan drives out Satan, he is divided against himself; so how can his kingdom last? ²⁷And if it is through Beelzebul that I drive devils out, through whom do your own experts drive them out? They shall be your judges, then. ²⁸But if it is through the Spirit of God that I drive out devils, then be sure that the kingdom of God has caught you unawares.

²⁹'Or again, how can anyone make his way into a strong man's house and plunder his property unless he has first tied up the strong man? Only then can he plunder his house.

³⁰'Anyone who is not with me is against me, and anyone who does not gather in with me throws away. ³¹And so I tell you, every human sin and blasphemy will be forgiven, but blasphemy against the Spirit will not be forgiven. ³²And anyone who says a word against the Son of man will be forgiven; but no one who speaks against the Holy Spirit will be forgiven either in this world or in the next.

Words betray the heart

³³'Make a tree sound and its fruit will be sound; make a tree rotten and its fruit will be rotten. For the tree can be told by its fruit. ³⁴You brood of vipers, how can your speech be good when you are evil? For words flow out of what fills the heart. ³⁵Good people draw good things from their store of goodness; bad

12a Ho 6:6.   12b Is 42:1–4.

107 READ MATTHEW 12:22–32.

If it is through the Spirit of God that I drive out devils, then be sure that the kingdom of God has caught you unawares.—MATTHEW 12:28

JESUS AND THE HOLY SPIRIT

Who will deny that the dispensations made for us by our great God and Savior Jesus Christ were accomplished through the grace of the Spirit? Whether you wish to examine ancient evidence—the blessings of the patriarchs, . . . the prophecies, the valorous feats in war, the signs worked through just men—or the things done in the dispensation of the incarnation of our Lord—all is through the Spirit.

First, as an anointing and an inseparable presence, the Spirit was with the Lord in the flesh, as Scripture says, "The man on whom you see the Spirit come down and rest" (Jn 1:33) is "my Son, the Beloved" (Mt 3:17). . . . After this every operation was worked with the cooperation of the Spirit. He was present when the Lord was being tempted by the devil. For, it is said, "Jesus was led by the Spirit out into the desert to be put to the test by the devil" (Mt 4:1). He was united to him while working his miracles. As Scripture says, "If it is through the Spirit of God that I drive out devils, then be sure that the kingdom of God has caught you unawares."

And he did not leave the Lord when he had risen from the dead. For when renewing humanity by breathing on the face of the disciples and restoring the grace that came of the inbreathing of God, which man had lost, what did the Lord say? "Receive the Holy Spirit. If you forgive anyone's sins, they are forgiven; if you retain anyone's sins, they are retained" (Jn 20:22–23). And is it not plain and incontestable that the ordering of the church is effected through the Spirit? For the Bible says, he gave "in the church, first apostles, secondarily prophets, thirdly teachers, after that miracles, then gifts of healing, helps, governments, diversities of tongues," (see 1 Co 12:28) for this order is ordained in accordance with the division of the gifts that are of the Spirit. ST. BASIL, 329–379

YOU WILL FIND THE NEXT READING AT MATTHEW 13.

people draw bad things from their store of badness. ³⁶ So I tell you this, that for every unfounded word people utter they will answer on Judgement Day, ³⁷ since it is by your words you will be justified, and by your words condemned.'

The sign of Jonah

³⁸ Then some of the scribes and Pharisees spoke up. 'Master,' they said, 'we should like to see a sign from you.' ³⁹ He replied, 'It is an evil and unfaithful generation that asks for a sign! The only sign it will be given is the sign of the prophet Jonah. ⁴⁰ For as Jonah *remained in the belly of the sea-monster for three days and three nights,*ᶜ so will the Son of man be in the heart of the earth for three days and three nights. ⁴¹ On Judgement Day the men of Nineveh will appear against this generation and they will be its condemnation, because when Jonah

12c Jon 2:1.

preached they repented; and look, there is something greater than Jonah here. ⁴²On Judgement Day the Queen of the South will appear against this generation and be its condemnation, because she came from the ends of the earth to hear the wisdom of Solomon; and look, there is something greater than Solomon here.

The return of the unclean spirit

⁴³'When an unclean spirit goes out of someone it wanders through waterless country looking for a place to rest, and cannot find one. ⁴⁴Then it says, "I will return to the home I came from." But on arrival, finding it unoccupied, swept and tidied, ⁴⁵it then goes off and collects seven other spirits more wicked than itself, and they go in and set up house there, and so that person ends up worse off than before. That is what will happen to this wicked generation.'

The true kinsfolk of Jesus

⁴⁶He was still speaking to the crowds when suddenly his mother and his brothersᵈ were standing outside and were anxious to have a word with him. [⁴⁷]ᵉ ⁴⁸But to the man who told him this Jesus replied, 'Who is my mother? Who are my brothers?' ⁴⁹And stretching out his hand towards his disciples he said, 'Here are my mother and my brothers. ⁵⁰Anyone who does the will of my Father in heaven is my brother and sister and mother.'

Introduction to parables

13 That same day, Jesus left the house and sat by the lakeside, ²but such large crowds gathered round him that he got into a boat and sat there. The people all stood on the shore, ³and he told them many things in parables.

Parable of the sower

He said, 'Listen, a sower went out to sow. ⁴As he sowed, some seeds fell on the edge of the path, and the birds came and ate them up. ⁵Others fell on patches of rock where they found little soil and sprang up at once, because there was no depth of earth; ⁶but as soon as the sun came up they were scorched and, not having any roots, they withered away. ⁷Others fell among thorns, and the thorns grew up and choked them. ⁸Others fell on rich soil and produced their crop, some a hundredfold, some sixty, some thirty. ⁹Anyone who has ears should listen!'

Why Jesus speaks in parables

¹⁰Then the disciples went up to him and asked, 'Why do you talk to them in parables?' ¹¹In answer, he said, 'Because to you is granted to understand the mysteries of the kingdom of Heaven, but to them it is not granted. ¹²Anyone who has will be given more and will have more than enough; but anyone who has not will be deprived even of what he has. ¹³The reason I talk to them in parables is that they look without seeing and listen without hearing or understanding. ¹⁴So in their case what was spoken by the prophet Isaiah is being fulfilled:

> *Listen and listen, but never understand!*
> *Look and look, but never perceive!*
> ¹⁵ *This people's heart has grown coarse,*
> *their ears dulled, they have shut their eyes tight*
> *to avoid using their eyes to see, their ears to hear,*
> *their heart to understand,*
> *changing their ways and being healed by me.*ᵃ

¹⁶'But blessed are your eyes because they see, your ears because they hear! ¹⁷In truth I tell you, many prophets and upright people longed to see what you see, and never saw it; to hear what you hear, and never heard it.

12d Not necessarily Mary's children. The Hebr. and Aram. word includes cousins and close relations.

12e v. 47 ('Someone said to him: Your mother and brothers are standing outside and want to speak to you') is omitted by some important textual witnesses. It is probably a restatement of v. 46 modelled on Mk and Lk.

13a Is 6:9–10.

The parable of the sower explained

18 'So pay attention to the parable of the sower. 19 When anyone hears the word of the kingdom without understanding, the Evil One comes and carries off what was sown in his heart: this is the seed sown on the edge of the path. 20 The seed sown on patches of rock is someone who hears the word and welcomes it at once with joy. 21 But such a person has no root deep down and does not last; should some trial come, or some persecution on account of the word, at once he falls away. 22 The seed sown in thorns is someone who hears the word, but the worry of the world and the lure of riches choke the word and so it produces nothing. 23 And the seed sown in rich soil is someone who hears the word and understands it; this is the one who yields a harvest and produces now a hundredfold, now sixty, now thirty.'

Parable of the darnel

24 He put another parable before them, 'The kingdom of Heaven may be compared to a man who sowed good seed in his field. 25 While everybody was asleep his enemy came, sowed darnel all among the wheat, and made off. 26 When the new wheat sprouted and ripened, then the darnel appeared as well. 27 The owner's labourers went to him and said, "Sir, was it not good seed that you sowed in your field? If so, where does the darnel come from?" 28 He said to them, "Some enemy has done this." And the labourers said, "Do you want us to go and weed it out?" 29 But he said, "No, because when you weed out the darnel you might pull up the wheat with it. 30 Let them both grow till the harvest; and at harvest time I shall say to the reapers: First collect the darnel and tie it in bundles to be burnt, then gather the wheat into my barn." '

Parable of the mustard seed

31 He put another parable before them, 'The kingdom of Heaven is like a mustard seed which a man took and sowed in his field. 32 It is the smallest of all the seeds, but when it has grown it is the biggest of shrubs and becomes a tree, so that the birds of the air can come and shelter in its branches.'

Parable of the yeast

33 He told them another parable, 'The kingdom of Heaven is like the yeast a woman took and mixed in with three measures of flour till it was leavened all through.'

The people are taught only in parables

34 In all this Jesus spoke to the crowds in parables; indeed, he would never speak to them except in parables. 35 This was to fulfil what was spoken by the prophet:

I will speak to you in parables,
unfold what has been hidden since the
foundation of the world. [b]

The parable of the darnel explained

36 Then, leaving the crowds, he went to the house; and his disciples came to him and said, 'Explain to us the parable about the darnel in the field.' 37 He said in reply, 'The sower of the good seed is the Son of man. 38 The field is the world; the good seed is the subjects of the kingdom; the darnel, the subjects of the Evil One; 39 the enemy who sowed it, the devil; the harvest is the end of the world; the reapers are the angels. 40 Well then, just as the darnel is gathered up and burnt in the fire, so it will be at the end of time. 41 The Son of man will send his angels and they will gather out of his kingdom all causes of falling and all who do evil, 42 and throw them into the blazing furnace, where there will be weeping and grinding of teeth. 43 Then the upright will shine like the sun in the kingdom of their Father. Anyone who has ears should listen!

Parables of the treasure and of the pearl

44 'The kingdom of Heaven is like treasure hidden in a field which someone has found; he

13b Ps 78:2.

108 READ MATTHEW 13:24–30.

Was it not good seed that you sowed in your field? If so, where does the darnel come from?—MATTHEW 13:27

WHEAT AND DARNEL

How does it happen that evil thoughts come forth from the heart, and defile a man? (see Mt 15:19). Doubtless because the laborers are asleep who should be keeping watch, so as to safeguard and preserve the good seed that is growing up. For unless we have weakened in our vigilance, by gluttony and by sloth defiling the divine image, that is, corrupting the good seed, the sower of darnel would not have found a way to creep up on us. Nor would he have sown within us darnel worthy of the fire; that is, evil thoughts that come forth from the heart and defile a man.

"Do you want us to go and weed it out?" So speak the angels, ever prepared with eager devotion to serve the divine will. . . . But they are forbidden lest they uproot the good wheat together with the darnel. That is, so that the sinner may not be cut off while in his mind there is yet a possibility of repentance; so that innocent children may not be destroyed together with their parents, who though perhaps yet in their parents' loins, nevertheless with God, who sees all things, they already exist. . . .

For God did not cut off the evil doing Esau . . . lest together with him Job might also perish, who from him took descent. . . . Nor did he strike down with death the persecuting Saul, lest the ends of the earth be deprived of salvation.

All [evildoers] that await the time of the harvest, and do not change themselves into fruits of repentance, are being prepared for the great fire. . . . But they whose roots are deep, whose ears of corn are abundant, . . . these Christ orders to be carried by the angels to the heavenly seats, to share their joy, to reign with him, and be sharers of his immortal happiness. . . .

ST. ISIDORE OF PELUSIUM, d. 450?

YOU WILL FIND THE NEXT READING AT MATTHEW 16.

hides it again, goes off in his joy, sells everything he owns and buys the field.

45 'Again, the kingdom of Heaven is like a merchant looking for fine pearls; 46 when he finds one of great value he goes and sells everything he owns and buys it.

Parable of the dragnet

47 'Again, the kingdom of Heaven is like a dragnet that is cast in the sea and brings in a haul of all kinds of fish. 48 When it is full, the fishermen bring it ashore; then, sitting down,

they collect the good ones in baskets and throw away those that are no use. 49 This is how it will be at the end of time: the angels will appear and separate the wicked from the upright, 50 to throw them into the blazing furnace, where there will be weeping and grinding of teeth.

Conclusion

51 'Have you understood all these?' They said, 'Yes.' 52 And he said to them, 'Well then, every scribe who becomes a disciple of the kingdom

of Heaven is like a householder who brings out from his storeroom new things as well as old.'

A visit to Nazareth

53 When Jesus had finished these parables he left the district; 54 and, coming to his home town, he taught the people in their synagogue in such a way that they were astonished and said, 'Where did the man get this wisdom and these miraculous powers? 55 This is the carpenter's son, surely? Is not his mother the woman called Mary, and his brothers James and Joseph and Simon and Jude? 56 His sisters, too, are they not all here with us? So where did the man get it all?' 57 And they would not accept him. But Jesus said to them, 'A prophet is despised only in his own country and in his own house,' 58 and he did not work many miracles there because of their lack of faith.

Herod and Jesus

14 At that time Herod the tetrarch heard about the reputation of Jesus 2 and said to his court, 'This is John the Baptist himself; he has risen from the dead, and that is why miraculous powers are at work in him.'

John the Baptist beheaded

3 Now it was Herod who had arrested John, chained him up and put him in prison because of Herodias, his brother Philip's wife. 4 For John had told him, 'It is against the Law for you to have her.' 5 He had wanted to kill him but was afraid of the people, who regarded John as a prophet. 6 Then, during the celebrations for Herod's birthday, the daughter of Herodias danced before the company and so delighted Herod 7 that he promised on oath to give her anything she asked. 8 Prompted by her mother she said, 'Give me John the Baptist's head, here, on a dish.' 9 The king was distressed but, thinking of the oaths he had sworn and of his guests, he ordered it to be given her, 10 and sent and had John beheaded in the prison. 11 The head was brought in on a dish and given to the girl, who took it to her mother. 12 John's disciples came and took the body and buried it; then they went off to tell Jesus.

First miracle of the loaves[a]

13 When Jesus received this news he withdrew by boat to a lonely place where they could be by themselves. But the crowds heard of this and, leaving the towns, went after him on foot. 14 So as he stepped ashore he saw a large crowd; and he took pity on them and healed their sick.

15 When evening came, the disciples went to him and said, 'This is a lonely place, and time has slipped by; so send the people away, and they can go to the villages to buy themselves some food.' 16 Jesus replied, 'There is no need for them to go: give them something to eat yourselves.' 17 But they answered, 'All we have with us is five loaves and two fish.' 18 So he said, 'Bring them here to me.' 19 He gave orders that the people were to sit down on the grass; then he took the five loaves and the two fish, raised his eyes to heaven and said the blessing. And breaking the loaves he handed them to his disciples, who gave them to the crowds. 20 They all ate as much as they wanted, and they collected the scraps left over, twelve baskets full. 21 Now about five thousand men had eaten, to say nothing of women and children.

Jesus walks on the water and, with him, Peter

22 And at once he made the disciples get into the boat and go on ahead to the other side while he sent the crowds away. 23 After sending the crowds away he went up into the hills by himself to pray. When evening came, he was there alone, 24 while the boat, by now some furlongs from land, was hard pressed by rough waves, for there was a head-wind. 25 In the fourth watch of the night he came towards them, walking on the sea, 26 and when the dis-

14a This and 15:32–39 are probably varying accounts of the same incident. This one echoes 2 K 4:42.

ciples saw him walking on the sea they were terrified. 'It is a ghost,' they said, and cried out in fear. 27 But at once Jesus called out to them, saying, 'Courage! It's me! Don't be afraid.' 28 It was Peter who answered. 'Lord,' he said, 'if it is you, tell me to come to you across the water.' 29 Jesus said, 'Come.' Then Peter got out of the boat and started walking towards Jesus across the water, 30 but then noticing the wind, he took fright and began to sink. 'Lord,' he cried, 'save me!' 31 Jesus put out his hand at once and held him. 'You have so little faith,' he said, 'why did you doubt?' 32 And as they got into the boat the wind dropped. 33 The men in the boat bowed down before him and said, 'Truly, you are the Son of God.'

Cures at Gennesaret

34 Having made the crossing, they came to land at Gennesaret. 35 When the local people recognised him they spread the news through the whole neighbourhood and took all that were sick to him, 36 begging him just to let them touch the fringe of his cloak. And all those who touched it were saved.

The traditions of the Pharisees

15 Then Pharisees and scribes from Jerusalem came to Jesus and said, 2 'Why do your disciples break away from the tradition of the elders? They eat without washing their hands.' 3 He answered, 'And why do you break away from the commandment of God for the sake of your tradition? 4 For God said, "Honour your father and your mother" and "Anyone who curses his father or mother will be put to death."ª 5 But you say, "If anyone says to his father or mother: Anything I might have used to help you is dedicated to God, 6 he is rid of his duty to father or mother." In this way you have made God's word ineffective by means of your tradition. 7 Hypocrites! How rightly Isaiah prophesied about you when he said:

8 *This people honours me only with lip-service, while their hearts are far from me.*

9 *Their reverence of me is worthless; the lessons they teach are nothing but human commandments.*b

On clean and unclean

10 He called the people to him and said, 'Listen, and understand. 11 What goes into the mouth does not make anyone unclean; it is what comes out of the mouth that makes someone unclean.'

12 Then the disciples came to him and said, 'Do you know that the Pharisees were shocked when they heard what you said?' 13 He replied, 'Any plant my heavenly Father has not planted will be pulled up by the roots. 14 Leave them alone. They are blind leaders of the blind; and if one blind person leads another, both will fall into a pit.'

15 At this, Peter said to him, 'Explain the parable for us.' 16 Jesus replied, 'Even you— don't you yet understand? 17 Can't you see that whatever goes into the mouth passes through the stomach and is discharged into the sewer? 18 But whatever comes out of the mouth comes from the heart, and it is this that makes someone unclean. 19 For from the heart come evil intentions: murder, adultery, fornication, theft, perjury, slander. 20 These are the things that make a person unclean. But eating with unwashed hands does not make anyone unclean.'

The daughter of the Canaanite woman healed

21 Jesus left that place and withdrew to the region of Tyre and Sidon. 22 And suddenly out came a Canaanite woman from that district and started shouting, 'Lord, Son of David, take pity on me. My daughter is tormented by a devil.' 23 But he said not a word in answer to her. And his disciples went and pleaded with him, saying, 'Give her what she wants, because she keeps shouting after us.' 24 He said in reply, 'I was sent only to the lost sheep of the

15a Ex 20:12 and 21:17.   15b Is 29:13.

House of Israel.' ²⁵But the woman had come up and was bowing low before him. 'Lord,' she said, 'help me.' ²⁶He replied, 'It is not fair to take the children's food and throw it to little dogs.' ²⁷She retorted, 'Ah yes, Lord; but even little dogs eat the scraps that fall from their masters' table.' ²⁸Then Jesus answered her, 'Woman, you have great faith. Let your desire be granted.' And from that moment her daughter was well again.

Cures near the lake

²⁹Jesus went on from there and reached the shores of the Lake of Galilee, and he went up onto the mountain. He took his seat, ³⁰and large crowds came to him bringing the lame, the crippled, the blind, the dumb and many others; these they put down at his feet, and he cured them. ³¹The crowds were astonished to see the dumb speaking, the cripples whole again, the lame walking and the blind with their sight, and they praised the God of Israel.

Second miracle of the loaves

³²But Jesus called his disciples to him and said, 'I feel sorry for all these people; they have been with me for three days now and have nothing to eat. I do not want to send them off hungry, or they might collapse on the way.' ³³The disciples said to him, 'Where in a deserted place could we get sufficient bread for such a large crowd to have enough to eat?' ³⁴Jesus said to them, 'How many loaves have you?' They said, 'Seven, and a few small fish.' ³⁵Then he instructed the crowd to sit down on the ground, ³⁶and he took the seven loaves and the fish, and after giving thanks he broke them and began handing them to the disciples, who gave them to the crowds. ³⁷They all ate as much as they wanted, and they collected what was left of the scraps, seven baskets full. ³⁸Now four thousand men had eaten, to say nothing of women and children. ³⁹And when he had sent the crowds away he got into the boat and went to the territory of Magadan.

The Pharisees ask for a sign from heaven

16 The Pharisees and Sadducees came, and to put him to the test they asked if he would show them a sign from heaven. ²He replied, 'In the evening you say, "It will be fine; there's a red sky," ³and in the morning, "Stormy weather today; the sky is red and overcast." You know how to read the face of the sky, but you cannot read the signs of the times. ⁴It is an evil and unfaithful generation asking for a sign, and the only sign it will be given is the sign of Jonah.' And he left them and went off.

The yeast of the Pharisees and Sadducees

⁵The disciples, having crossed to the other side, had forgotten to take any food. ⁶Jesus said to them, 'Keep your eyes open, and be on your guard against the yeast of the Pharisees and Sadducees.' ⁷And they said among themselves, 'It is because we have not brought any bread.' ⁸Jesus knew it, and he said, 'You have so little faith, why are you talking among yourselves about having no bread? ⁹Do you still not understand? Do you not remember the five loaves for the five thousand and the number of baskets you collected? ¹⁰Or the seven loaves for the four thousand and the number of baskets you collected? ¹¹How could you fail to understand that I was not talking about bread? What I said was: Beware of the yeast of the Pharisees and Sadducees.' ¹²Then they understood that he was telling them to be on their guard, not against yeast for making bread, but against the teaching of the Pharisees and Sadducees.

Peter's profession of faith; his pre-eminence

¹³When Jesus came to the region of Caesarea Philippi he put this question to his disciples, 'Who do people say the Son of man is?' ¹⁴And they said, 'Some say John the Baptist, some Elijah, and others Jeremiah or one of the prophets.' ¹⁵'But you,' he said, 'who do you say I am?' ¹⁶Then Simon Peter spoke up and said, 'You are the Christ, the Son of the living God.'

109 READ MATTHEW 16:24–28.

What, then, will anyone gain by winning the whole world and forfeiting his life?
—MATTHEW 16:26

FINDING YOUR LIFE

My heart is very sorrowful because like the little girl who wept when she found that her doll was stuffed with sawdust and her drum was hollow, I, too, have made a horrifying discovery. . . . I have ripped both the doll and the drum open and the fact lies plainly and in all its glaring reality before me: All, all, all (there is no exception) is passing away and will pass away.

European travel brings vividly before the mind how cities have risen and fallen, and risen and fallen; and the same of empires and kingdoms and nations. And the billions and billions who lived their common every day life in these nations and kingdoms and empires and cities, where are they? The ashes of the kings and mighty of this earth are mingled with the dust of the meanest slave.

Day succeeds day and, as Byron so beautifully expresses it, when the heavens grow red in the western sky, "The day joins the past eternity." How long will the sun and moon, the stars continue to give forth light? Who can tell? Of one thing alone we are sure. In God's own time—then shall come the Son of Man in great power and majesty to render to each according to his works.

The question alone important, the solution of which depends upon how I have spent my life, is the state of my soul at the moment of death. Infinite misery or infinite happiness! There is no half and half, either one or the other. And this question for me is to be decided at most in seventy years, seventy short years compared with Eternity.

The little girl who found out that her doll was stuffed with sawdust says she does not wish to play with dolls any more. Now, dear Father, that is my case. I am disgusted with the world. God in His mercy has . . . made me see the vile emptiness of this earth. I look to Him, the God of Love, in hope.

ST. KATHARINE DREXEL, 1858–1955

YOU WILL FIND THE NEXT READING AT MATTHEW 17.

17 Jesus replied, 'Simon son of Jonah, you are a blessed man! Because it was no human agency that revealed this to you but my Father in heaven. 18 So I now say to you: You are Peter[a] and on this rock I will build my community. And the gates of the underworld can never overpower it. 19 I will give you the keys of the kingdom of Heaven: whatever you bind on earth will be bound in heaven; whatever you loose on earth will be loosed in heaven.' 20 Then he gave the disciples strict orders not to say to anyone that he was the Christ.

First prophecy of the Passion

21 From then onwards Jesus began to make it clear to his disciples that he was destined to go to Jerusalem and suffer grievously at the hands of the elders and chief priests and scribes and to be put to death and to be raised up on the third day. 22 Then, taking him aside, Peter started to rebuke him. 'Heaven preserve you, Lord,' he said, 'this

16a The name means 'rock'.

must not happen to you.' ²³But he turned and said to Peter, 'Get behind me, Satan! You are an obstacle in my path, because you are thinking not as God thinks but as human beings do.'

The condition of following Christ

²⁴Then Jesus said to his disciples, 'If anyone wants to be a follower of mine, let him renounce himself and take up his cross and follow me. ²⁵Anyone who wants to save his life will lose it; but anyone who loses his life for my sake will find it. ²⁶What, then, will anyone gain by winning the whole world and forfeiting his life? Or what can anyone offer in exchange for his life?

²⁷'For the Son of man is going to come in the glory of his Father with his angels, and then he will reward each one according to his behaviour. ²⁸In truth I tell you, there are some standing here who will not taste death before they see the Son of man coming with his kingdom.'

The transfiguration

17 Six days later, Jesus took with him Peter and James and his brother John and led them up a high mountain by themselves. ²There in their presence he was transfigured: his face shone like the sun and his clothes became as dazzling as light. ³And suddenly Moses and Elijah appeared to them; they were talking with him. ⁴Then Peter spoke to Jesus. 'Lord,' he said, 'it is wonderful for us to be here; if you want me to, I will make three shelters here, one for you, one for Moses and one for Elijah.' ⁵He was still speaking when suddenly a bright cloudᵃ covered them with shadow, and suddenly from the cloud there came a voice which said, 'This is my Son, the Beloved; he enjoys my favour. Listen to him.'ᵇ ⁶When they heard this, the disciples fell on their faces, overcome with fear. ⁷But Jesus came up and touched them, saying, 'Stand up, do not be afraid.' ⁸And when they raised their eyes they saw no one but Jesus.

The question about Elijah

⁹As they came down from the mountain Jesus gave them this order, 'Tell no one about this vision until the Son of man has risen from the dead.' ¹⁰And the disciples put this question to him, 'Why then do the scribes say that Elijah must come first?' ¹¹He replied, 'Elijah is indeed coming, and he will set everything right again; ¹²however, I tell you that Elijah has come already and they did not recognise him but treated him as they pleased; and the Son of man will suffer similarly at their hands.' ¹³Then the disciples understood that he was speaking of John the Baptist.

The epileptic demoniac

¹⁴As they were rejoining the crowd a man came up to him and went down on his knees before him. ¹⁵'Lord,' he said, 'take pity on my son: he is demented and in a wretched state; he is always falling into fire and into water. ¹⁶I took him to your disciples and they were unable to cure him.' ¹⁷In reply, Jesus said, 'Faithless and perverse generation! How much longer must I be with you? How much longer must I put up with you? Bring him here to me.' ¹⁸And when Jesus rebuked it the devil came out of the boy, who was cured from that moment.

¹⁹Then the disciples came privately to Jesus. 'Why were we unable to drive it out?' they asked. ²⁰He answered, 'Because you have so little faith. In truth I tell you, if your faith is the size of a mustard seed you will say to this mountain, "Move from here to there," and it will move; nothing will be impossible for you.'[21]ᶜ

Second prophecy of the Passion

²²When they were together in Galilee, Jesus said to them, 'The Son of man is going to be

---

17a cf. Ex. 13:22.   17b Dt 18:15, 19; Is 42:1.

17c Some authorities add v. 21, 'As for this kind, it is cast out only by prayer and fasting.' cf. Mk 9:29.

110 READ MATTHEW 17:14–20.

If your faith is the size of a mustard seed you will say to this mountain, "Move from here to there," and it will move.—MATTHEW 17:20

FACING TEMPTATION WITH FAITH

When St. Francis was dwelling in the Place of St. Mary he was severely tempted in the spirit for the benefit of his soul. And he was so greatly afflicted by this in both body and soul that he would often withdraw from the company of the friars because he was unable to show his customary cheerfulness. But he mortified himself by abstaining from food and drink and speech, shedding abundant tears, and praying constantly that God might be pleased to deliver him from this affliction.

When he had been thus tormented for more than two years, praying one day in the Church of St. Mary he heard in his spirit the words of the gospel: "If your faith is the size of a mustard seed you will say to this mountain, 'Move from here to there,' and it will move."

Blessed Francis asked, "Lord, what is this mountain?" and it was said to him: "This mountain is your temptation." Then Blessed Francis said, "Lord, be it done to me as you have said." At once he was set perfectly free, so that it seemed to him as if he had never had the temptation.

ST. FRANCIS OF ASSISI, 1181–1226

YOU WILL FIND THE NEXT READING AT MATTHEW 18.

delivered into the power of men; 23 they will put him to death, and on the third day he will be raised up again.' And a great sadness came over them.

The Temple tax paid by Jesus and Peter

24 When they reached Capernaum, the collectors of the half-shekel*d* came to Peter and said, 'Does your master not pay the half-shekel?' 25 'Yes,' he replied, and went into the house. But before he could speak, Jesus said, 'Simon, what is your opinion? From whom do earthly kings take toll or tribute? From their sons or from foreigners?' 26 And when he replied, 'From foreigners,' Jesus said, 'Well then, the sons are exempt. 27 However, so that we shall not be the downfall of others, go to the lake and cast a hook; take the first fish that rises, open its mouth and there you will find a shekel; take it and give it to them for me and for yourself.'

Who is the greatest?

18 At this time the disciples came to Jesus and said, 'Who is the greatest in the kingdom of Heaven?' 2 So he called a little child to him whom he set among them. 3 Then he said, 'In truth I tell you, unless you change and become like little children you will never enter the kingdom of Heaven. 4 And so, the one who makes himself as little as this little child is the greatest in the kingdom of Heaven.

On leading others astray

5 'Anyone who welcomes one little child like this in my name welcomes me. 6 But anyone who is the downfall of one of these little ones who have faith in me would be better drowned in the depths of the sea with a great

17d A yearly tax on all Jews for the upkeep of the Temple.

millstone round his neck. 7 Alas for the world that there should be such causes of falling! Causes of falling indeed there must be, but alas for anyone who provides them!

8 'If your hand or your foot should be your downfall, cut it off and throw it away: it is better for you to enter into life crippled or lame, than to have two hands or two feet and be thrown into eternal fire. 9 And if your eye should be your downfall, tear it out and throw it away: it is better for you to enter into life with one eye, than to have two eyes and be thrown into the hell of fire.

10 'See that you never despise any of these little ones, for I tell you that their angels in heaven are continually in the presence of my Father in heaven.[11]*a*

The lost sheep

12 'Tell me. Suppose a man has a hundred sheep and one of them strays; will he not leave the ninety-nine on the hillside and go in search of the stray? 13 In truth I tell you, if he finds it, it gives him more joy than do the ninety-nine that did not stray at all. 14 Similarly, it is never the will of your Father in heaven that one of these little ones should be lost.

Brotherly correction

15 'If your brother does something wrong, go and have it out with him alone, between your two selves. If he listens to you, you have won back your brother. 16 If he does not listen, take one or two others along with you: *whatever the misdemeanour, the evidence of two or three witnesses is required to sustain the charge.b* 17 But if he refuses to listen to these, report it to the community; and if he refuses to listen to the community, treat him like a gentile or a tax collector.

18 'In truth I tell you, whatever you bind on earth will be bound in heaven; whatever you loose on earth will be loosed in heaven.

Prayer in common

19 'In truth I tell you once again, if two of you on earth agree to ask anything at all, it will be granted to you by my Father in heaven. 20 For where two or three meet in my name, I am there among them.'

Forgiveness of injuries

21 Then Peter went up to him and said, 'Lord, how often must I forgive my brother if he wrongs me? As often as seven times?' 22 Jesus answered, 'Not seven, I tell you, but seventy-seven times.

Parable of the unforgiving debtor

23 'And so the kingdom of Heaven may be compared to a king who decided to settle his accounts with his servants. 24 When the reckoning began, they brought him a man who owed ten thousand talents; 25 he had no means of paying, so his master gave orders that he should be sold, together with his wife and children and all his possessions, to meet the debt. 26 At this, the servant threw himself down at his master's feet, with the words, "Be patient with me and I will pay the whole sum." 27 And the servant's master felt so sorry for him that he let him go and cancelled the debt. 28 Now as this servant went out, he happened to meet a fellow-servant who owed him one hundred denarii;c and he seized him by the throat and began to throttle him, saying, "Pay what you owe me." 29 His fellow-servant fell at his feet and appealed to him, saying, "Be patient with me and I will pay you." 30 But the other would not agree; on the contrary, he had him thrown into prison till he should pay the debt. 31 His fellow-servants were deeply distressed when they saw what had happened, and they went to their master and reported the whole affair to him. 32 Then the master sent for the man and said to him, "You wicked servant, I cancelled all that debt of yours when you appealed to me. 33 Were you not bound, then, to have

18a Some authorities add v. 11, 'For the Son of man has come to save what was lost.' cf. Lk 19:10.

18b Dt 19:15.

18c About $200, contrasted with the other debt of over $60 million.

111 READ MATTHEW 18:23–34.

Were you not bound, then, to have pity on your fellow-servant just as I had pity on you?—MATTHEW 18:33

FORGIVENESS FROM THE HEART

Syrians and Palestinians tend to illustrate their speech with parables so that what their hearers may not be able to catch so easily when spoken plainly, they may be able to grasp by means of analogies and examples. So the Lord, by an allegory about a royal master who forgave a servant a debt of ten thousand talents, taught Peter that he was obliged to forgive his fellow-servants their comparatively trifling offenses. For if that royal master so readily forgave his servant his debt of ten thousand talents, should not his servants all the more forgive the lesser debts owed them by their fellows?

To put this more clearly, let us take a case. If one of us were to commit adultery, or murder, or sacrilege, our sin—great like a debt of ten thousand talents—would be forgiven us in answer to prayer, if we also from our heart forgive our brothers their sins against us. But if we refuse to forgive a slight, and keep up unceasing enmity because of an unkind word, would it not be just that we were punished severely and bring on ourselves by the example of our deeds that our great debt should not be forgiven?

God's awful purpose can be turned and changed. But if we will not forgive our brothers small things, God will not forgive us big things. And if we forgive them, it must be from our hearts. Anyone can say, "I have nothing against so-and-so; he knows what he had done and God will judge him for it. I don't care what he has done; I have forgiven him for it." But the Lord has made his sentence clear and destroys such a mocker of peace as this when he says, "And that is how my heavenly Father will deal with you unless you each forgive your brother from your heart."   ST. JEROME, 341?–420

YOU WILL FIND THE NEXT READING AT MATTHEW 19.

pity on your fellow-servant just as I had pity on you?" ³⁴ And in his anger the master handed him over to the torturers till he should pay all his debt. ³⁵ And that is how my heavenly Father will deal with you unless you each forgive your brother from your heart.'

The question about divorce

19 Jesus had now finished what he wanted to say, and he left Galilee and came into the territory of Judaea on the far side of the Jordan. ² Large crowds followed him and he healed them there.

³ Some Pharisees approached him, and to put him to the test they said, 'Is it against the Law for a man to divorce his wife on any pretext whatever?' ⁴ He answered, 'Have you not read that the Creator from the beginning *made them male and female* ⁵ and that he said: *This is why a man leaves his father and mother and becomes attached to his wife, and the two become one flesh?*ᵃ ⁶ They are no longer two, therefore, but one flesh. So then, what God has united, human beings must not divide.'

⁷ They said to him, 'Then why did Moses command that a writ of dismissal should be

19a Gn 1:17; 2:24.

given in cases of divorce?'[b] [8] He said to them, 'It was because you were so hard-hearted, that Moses allowed you to divorce your wives, but it was not like this from the beginning. [9] Now I say this to you: anyone who divorces his wife— I am not speaking of an illicit marriage—and marries another, is guilty of adultery.'

Continence

[10] The disciples said to him, 'If that is how things are between husband and wife, it is advisable not to marry.' [11] But he replied, 'It is not everyone who can accept what I have said, but only those to whom it is granted. [12] There are eunuchs born so from their mother's womb, there are eunuchs made so by human agency and there are eunuchs who have made themselves so for the sake of the kingdom of Heaven. Let anyone accept this who can.'

Jesus and the children

[13] Then people brought little children to him, for him to lay his hands on them and pray. The disciples scolded them, [14] but Jesus said, 'Let the little children alone, and do not stop them from coming to me; for it is to such as these that the kingdom of Heaven belongs.' [15] Then he laid his hands on them and went on his way.

The rich young man

[16] And now a man came to him and asked, 'Master, what good deed must I do to possess eternal life?' [17] Jesus said to him, 'Why do you ask me about what is good? There is one alone who is good. But if you wish to enter into life, keep the commandments.' [18] He said, 'Which ones?' Jesus replied, 'These: *You shall not kill. You shall not commit adultery. You shall not steal. You shall not give false witness.* [19] *Honour your father and your mother. You shall love your neighbour as yourself.*'[c] [20] The young man said to him, 'I have kept all these. What more do I need to do?' [21] Jesus said, 'If you wish to be perfect, go and sell your possessions and give the money to the poor, and you will have treasure in heaven; then come, follow me.'

[22] But when the young man heard these words he went away sad, for he was a man of great wealth.

The danger of riches

[23] Then Jesus said to his disciples, 'In truth I tell you, it is hard for someone rich to enter the kingdom of Heaven. [24] Yes, I tell you again, it is easier for a camel to pass through the eye of a needle than for someone rich to enter the kingdom of Heaven.' [25] When the disciples heard this they were astonished. 'Who can be saved, then?' they said. [26] Jesus gazed at them. 'By human resources', he told them, 'this is impossible; for God everything is possible.'

The reward of renunciation

[27] Then Peter answered and said, 'Look, we have left everything and followed you. What are we to have, then?' [28] Jesus said to them, 'In truth I tell you, when everything is made new again and the Son of man is seated on his throne of glory, you yourselves will sit on twelve thrones to judge the twelve tribes of Israel. [29] And everyone who has left houses, brothers, sisters, father, mother, children or land for the sake of my name will receive a hundred times as much, and also inherit eternal life.

[30] 'Many who are first will be last, and the last, first.'

Parable of the labourers in the vineyard

20 'Now the kingdom of Heaven is like a landowner going out at daybreak to hire workers for his vineyard. [2] He made an agreement with the workers for one denarius a day and sent them to his vineyard. [3] Going out at about the third hour he saw others standing idle in the market place [4] and said to them, "You go to my vineyard too and I will give you a fair wage." [5] So they went. At about the sixth hour and again at about the ninth hour, he went out and did the same. [6] Then at

19b Dt 24:1. On Mt's exception in v. 9, *see* 5:32.
19c Ex 20:12–16.

112 READ MATTHEW 19:16–22.

If you wish to be perfect, go and sell your possessions and give the money to the poor, and you will have treasure in heaven; then come, follow me.—MATTHEW 19:21

WHAT CAN I DO FOR GOD?

St. Katharine wrote the following excerpts in letters to Bishop James O'Connor, her spiritual director:

This time last year I sat in this same room and wrote to you. . . . I expected that God would have called me from the world and unreality, that he would have called me where I could learn to know him and make it my purpose in life to love him and serve him. Dear Father, as far as I can read my heart, I am not happy in the world. There is a void in my heart that only God can fill. And can God obtain full possession of my heart whilst I live in the world? I wish that these words of the good Master applied to my soul, "Sell all thou hast and come, follow Me." For he that follows Christ "walketh not in darkness." Am I not now walking in darkness? One thing alone consoles me, viz: that if my way is dark I am trying to oppose no obstacle to the rays of the "kindly light" when it is God's will to pour it down upon my soul. Then I shall see the way in which I should walk. . . . I do not ask Our Lord to select my particular state in life for me. I only ask to do His Divine Will and that He will make known to me in His own good time. . . .

The question then, of my state in life resolves itself, it seems to me, into this one. What can I do for God's greater glory and service? . . .

I presume he wishes me to be where I can first save my own soul, secondly, to do as much good as he intends with the means Dear Papa has left me. If Our Lord wishes me to go to a convent, I should be an idiot did I not obey the call. If amongst the temptations of the world, it is His will that I should steer my course to Heaven, *fiat.*   ST. KATHARINE DREXEL, 1858–1955

YOU WILL FIND THE NEXT READING AT MATTHEW 22.

about the eleventh hour he went out and found more men standing around, and he said to them, "Why have you been standing here idle all day?" [7]"Because no one has hired us," they answered. He said to them, "You go into my vineyard too." [8]In the evening, the owner of the vineyard said to his bailiff, "Call the workers and pay them their wages, starting with the last arrivals and ending with the first." [9]So those who were hired at about the eleventh hour came forward and received one denarius each. [10]When the first came, they expected to get more, but they too received one denarius each. [11]They took it, but grumbled at the landowner saying, [12]"The men who came last have done only one hour, and you have treated them the same as us, though we have done a heavy day's work in all the heat." [13]He answered one of them and said, "My friend, I am not being unjust to you; did we not agree on one denarius? [14]Take your earnings and go. I choose to pay the lastcomer as much as I pay you. [15]Have I no right to do what I like with my own? Why should you be envious because I am generous?" [16]Thus the last will be first, and the first, last.'

Third prophecy of the Passion

17 Jesus was going up to Jerusalem, and on the road he took the Twelve aside by themselves and said to them, 18 'Look, we are going up to Jerusalem, and the Son of man is about to be handed over to the chief priests and scribes. They will condemn him to death 19 and will hand him over to the gentiles to be mocked and scourged and crucified; and on the third day he will be raised up again.'

The mother of Zebedee's sons makes her request

20 Then the mother of Zebedee's sons came with her sons to make a request of him, and bowed low; 21 and he said to her, 'What is it you want?' She said to him, 'Promise that these two sons of mine may sit one at your right hand and the other at your left in your kingdom.' 22 Jesus answered, 'You do not know what you are asking. Can you drink the cup that I am going to drink?' They replied, 'We can.' 23 He said to them, 'Very well; you shall drink my cup, but as for seats at my right hand and my left, these are not mine to grant; they belong to those to whom they have been allotted by my Father.'

Leadership with service

24 When the other ten heard this they were indignant with the two brothers. 25 But Jesus called them to him and said, 'You know that among the gentiles the rulers lord it over them, and great men make their authority felt. 26 Among you this is not to happen. No; anyone who wants to become great among you must be your servant, 27 and anyone who wants to be first among you must be your slave, 28 just as the Son of man came not to be served but to serve, and to give his life as a ransom for many.'

The two blind men of Jericho

29 As they left Jericho a large crowd followed him. 30 And now there were two blind men sitting at the side of the road. When they heard that it was Jesus who was passing by, they shouted, 'Lord! Have pity on us, son of David.' 31 And the crowd scolded them and told them to keep quiet, but they only shouted the louder, 'Lord! Have pity on us, son of David.' 32 Jesus stopped, called them over and said, 'What do you want me to do for you?' 33 They said to him, 'Lord, let us have our sight back.' 34 Jesus felt pity for them and touched their eyes, and at once their sight returned and they followed him.

The Messiah enters Jerusalem

21 When they were near Jerusalem and had come to Bethphage on the Mount of Olives, then Jesus sent two disciples, 2 saying to them, 'Go to the village facing you, and you will at once find a tethered donkey and a colt with her. Untie them and bring them to me. 3 If anyone says anything to you, you are to say, "The Master needs them and will send them back at once."' 4 This was to fulfil what was spoken by the prophet:

5 *Say to the daughter of Zion:*
Look, your king is approaching,
humble and riding on a donkey
and on a colt, the foal of a beast of burden.[a]

6 So the disciples went and did as Jesus had told them. 7 They brought the donkey and the colt, then they laid their cloaks on their backs and he took his seat on them. 8 Great crowds of people spread their cloaks on the road, while others were cutting branches from the trees and spreading them in his path. 9 The crowds who went in front of him and those who followed were all shouting:

Hosanna to the son of David!
Blessed is he who is coming in the name
of the Lord![b]
Hosanna in the highest heavens!

10 And when he entered Jerusalem, the whole city was in turmoil as people asked,

21a Zc 9:9.   21b Ps 118:26.

'Who is this?' [11] and the crowds answered, 'This is the prophet Jesus from Nazareth in Galilee.'

The expulsion of the dealers from the Temple

[12] Jesus then went into the Temple and drove out all those who were selling and buying there; he upset the tables of the money-changers and the seats of the dove-sellers. [13] He said to them, 'According to scripture, *my house will be called a house of prayer;* but you are turning it into a *bandits' den.*'[c] [14] There were also blind and lame people who came to him in the Temple, and he cured them. [15] At the sight of the wonderful things he did and of the children shouting, 'Hosanna to the son of David' in the Temple, the chief priests and the scribes were indignant and said to him, [16] 'Do you hear what they are saying?' Jesus answered, 'Yes. Have you never read this:

> *By the mouths of children, babes in arms,*
> *you have made sure of praise?'*[d]

[17] With that he left them and went out of the city to Bethany, where he spent the night.

The barren fig tree withers; faith and prayer

[18] As he was returning to the city in the early morning, he felt hungry. [19] Seeing a fig tree by the road, he went up to it and found nothing on it but leaves. And he said to it, 'May you never bear fruit again,' and instantly the fig tree withered. [20] The disciples were amazed when they saw it and said, 'How is it that the fig tree withered instantly?' [21] Jesus answered, 'In truth I tell you, if you have faith and do not doubt at all, not only will you do what I have done to the fig tree, but even if you say to this mountain, "Be pulled up and thrown into the sea," it will be done. [22] And if you have faith, everything you ask for in prayer, you will receive.'

The authority of Jesus is questioned

[23] He had gone into the Temple and was teaching, when the chief priests and the elders of the people came to him and said, 'What authority have you for acting like this? And who gave you this authority?' [24] In reply Jesus said to them, 'And I will ask you a question, just one; if you tell me the answer to it, then I will tell you my authority for acting like this. [25] John's baptism: what was its origin, heavenly or human?' And they argued this way among themselves, 'If we say heavenly, he will retort to us, "Then why did you refuse to believe him?"; [26] but if we say human, we have the people to fear, for they all hold that John was a prophet.' [27] So their reply to Jesus was, 'We do not know.' And he retorted to them, 'Nor will I tell you my authority for acting like this.'

Parable of the two sons

[28] 'What is your opinion? A man had two sons. He went and said to the first, "My boy, go and work in the vineyard today." [29] He answered, "I will not go," but afterwards thought better of it and went. [30] The man then went and said the same thing to the second who answered, "Certainly, sir," but did not go. [31] Which of the two did the father's will?' They said, 'The first.' Jesus said to them, 'In truth I tell you, tax collectors and prostitutes are making their way into the kingdom of God before you. [32] For John came to you, showing the way of uprightness, but you did not believe him, and yet the tax collectors and prostitutes did. Even after seeing that, you refused to think better of it and believe in him.

Parable of the wicked tenants

[33] 'Listen to another parable. There was a man, a landowner, who planted a vineyard; he fenced it round, dug a winepress in it and built a tower; then he leased it to tenants and went abroad. [34] When vintage time drew near he sent his servants to the tenants to collect his produce. [35] But the tenants seized his servants, thrashed one, killed another and stoned a third. [36] Next he sent some more servants, this

21c Is 56:7; Jr 7:11.   21d Ps 8:2.

time a larger number, and they dealt with them in the same way. 37 Finally he sent his son to them thinking, "They will respect my son." 38 But when the tenants saw the son, they said to each other, "This is the heir. Come on, let us kill him and take over his inheritance." 39 So they seized him and threw him out of the vineyard and killed him. 40 Now when the owner of the vineyard comes, what will he do to those tenants?' 41 They answered, 'He will bring those wretches to a wretched end and lease the vineyard to other tenants who will deliver the produce to him at the proper time.' 42 Jesus said to them, 'Have you never read in the scriptures:

> The stone which the builders rejected
> has become the cornerstone;
> this is the Lord's doing
> and we marvel at it?' [e]

43 'I tell you, then, that the kingdom of God will be taken from you and given to a people who will produce its fruit.' [44] [f]

45 When they heard his parables, the chief priests and the scribes realised he was speaking about them, 46 but though they would have liked to arrest him they were afraid of the crowds, who looked on him as a prophet.

Parable of the wedding feast

22 Jesus began to speak to them in parables once again, 2 'The kingdom of Heaven may be compared to a king who gave a feast for his son's wedding. 3 He sent his servants to call those who had been invited, but they would not come. 4 Next he sent some more servants with the words, "Tell those who have been invited: Look, my banquet is all prepared, my oxen and fattened cattle have been slaughtered, everything is ready. Come to the wedding." 5 But they were not interested: one went off to his farm, another to his business, 6 and the rest seized his servants, maltreated them and killed them. 7 The king was furious. He despatched his troops, destroyed those murderers and burnt their town. 8 Then he said to his servants, "The wedding is ready; but as those who were invited proved to be unworthy, 9 go to the main crossroads and invite everyone you can find to come to the wedding." 10 So these servants went out onto the roads and collected together everyone they could find, bad and good alike; and the wedding hall was filled with guests. 11 When the king came in to look at the guests he noticed one man who was not wearing a wedding garment, 12 and said to him, "How did you get in here, my friend, without a wedding garment?" And the man was silent. 13 Then the king said to the attendants, "Bind him hand and foot and throw him into the darkness outside, where there will be weeping and grinding of teeth." 14 For many are invited but not all are chosen.'

On tribute to Caesar

15 Then the Pharisees went away to work out between them how to trap him in what he said. 16 And they sent their disciples to him, together with some Herodians, to say, 'Master, we know that you are an honest man and teach the way of God in all honesty, and that you are not afraid of anyone, because human rank means nothing to you. 17 Give us your opinion, then. Is it permissible to pay taxes to Caesar or not?' 18 But Jesus was aware of their malice and replied, 'You hypocrites! Why are you putting me to the test? 19 Show me the money you pay the tax with.' They handed him a denarius, 20 and he said, 'Whose portrait is this? Whose title?' 21 They replied, 'Caesar's.' Then he said to them, 'Very well, pay Caesar what belongs to Caesar—and God what belongs to God.' 22 When they heard this they were amazed; they left him alone and went away.

The resurrection of the dead

23 That day some Sadducees—who deny that there is a resurrection—approached him and

---

21e Ps 118:22–23.

21f Some authorities add v. 44, taken from Lk 20:18.

they put this question to him, 24 'Master, Moses said[a] that if a man dies childless, his brother is to marry the widow, his sister-in-law, to raise children for his brother. 25 Now we had a case involving seven brothers; the first married and then died without children, leaving his wife to his brother; 26 the same thing happened with the second and third and so on to the seventh, 27 and then last of all the woman herself died. 28 Now at the resurrection, whose wife among the seven will she be, since she had been married to them all?' 29 Jesus answered them, 'You are wrong, because you understand neither the scriptures nor the power of God. 30 For at the resurrection men and women do not marry; no, they are like the angels in heaven. 31 And as for the resurrection of the dead, have you never read what God himself said to you: 32 *I am the God of Abraham, the God of Isaac and the God of Jacob?*[b] He is God, not of the dead, but of the living.' 33 And his teaching made a deep impression on the people who heard it.

The greatest commandment of all

34 But when the Pharisees heard that he had silenced the Sadducees they got together 35 and, to put him to the test, one of them put a further question, 36 'Master, which is the greatest commandment of the Law?' 37 Jesus said to him, '*You must love the Lord your God with all your heart, with all your soul,* and with all your mind. 38 This is the greatest and the first commandment. 39 The second resembles it: *You must love your neighbour as yourself.*[c] 40 On these two commandments hang the whole Law, and the Prophets too.'

Christ not only son but also Lord of David

41 While the Pharisees were gathered round, Jesus put to them this question, 42 'What is your opinion about the Christ? Whose son is he?' They told him, 'David's.' 43 He said to them, 'Then how is it that David, moved by the Spirit, calls him Lord, where he says:

44 *The Lord declared to my Lord,*
take your seat at my right hand,

till I have made your enemies
your footstool?[d]

45 'If David calls him Lord, how then can he be his son?' 46 No one could think of anything to say in reply, and from that day no one dared to ask him any further questions.

The scribes and Pharisees: their hypocrisy and vanity

23 Then addressing the crowds and his disciples Jesus said, 2 'The scribes and the Pharisees occupy the chair of Moses. 3 You must therefore do and observe what they tell you; but do not be guided by what they do, since they do not practise what they preach. 4 They tie up heavy burdens and lay them on people's shoulders, but will they lift a finger to move them? Not they! 5 Everything they do is done to attract attention, like wearing broader headbands and longer tassels, 6 like wanting to take the place of honour at banquets and the front seats in the synagogues, 7 being greeted respectfully in the market squares and having people call them Rabbi.

8 'You, however, must not allow yourselves to be called Rabbi, since you have only one Master, and you are all brothers. 9 You must call no one on earth your father, since you have only one Father, and he is in heaven. 10 Nor must you allow yourselves to be called teachers, for you have only one Teacher, the Christ. 11 The greatest among you must be your servant. 12 Anyone who raises himself up will be humbled, and anyone who humbles himself will be raised up.

The sevenfold indictment of the scribes and Pharisees

13 'Alas for you, scribes and Pharisees, you hypocrites! You shut up the kingdom of Heaven in people's faces, neither going in

22a Dt 25:5–6.   22b Ex 3:6.
22c Dt 6:5 combined with Lv 19:18.
22d Ps 110:1.

113 READ MATTHEW 22:34–40.

You must love the Lord your God with all your heart, with all your soul, and with all your mind.—MATTHEW 22:37

DESIRES OF THE HEART

The desires of my heart are so great and incomprehensible
That nothing can fill the abyss of my heart.
Even the most beautiful things, gathered from all over the world
Would not for a moment fill your place for me, O God.

With one glance, I penetrated the whole world,
And I found no other love like the love of my heart.
Therefore I looked into the world of eternity—
Because this one is too small for me.
My heart has desired the love of the Immortal One.

My heart has sensed that I am a royal child,
That I have found myself in exile, in a foreign land.
I see that the heavenly palace is my home;
Only there will I feel as in my own fatherland.

You Yourself have drawn my soul to You, O Lord;
O Eternal Word, You Yourself have stooped to me,
Giving my soul a deeper knowledge of Yourself.
Behold the mystery of love for which you have created me!

Pure love has made me strong and brave.
I fear neither the Seraphim nor the Cherubim, standing with sword in hand,
And I pass over with ease where others tremble,
Because there is nothing to fear, there where love is the guide.

And suddenly the eye of my soul came to rest upon You,
O Lord Jesus Christ, stretched upon the Cross.
Here is my Love, with whom I will rest in my grave.
This is my Bridegroom, my incomprehensible Lord and God.

ST. FAUSTINA, 1905–1938

YOU WILL FIND THE NEXT READING AT MATTHEW 25.

yourselves nor allowing others to go in who want to.[14]ᵃ

15 'Alas for you, scribes and Pharisees, you hypocrites! You travel over sea and land to make a single proselyte, and anyone who becomes one you make twice as fit for hell as you are.

16 'Alas for you, blind guides! You say, "If anyone swears by the Temple, it has no force; but anyone who swears by the gold of the Temple is bound." 17 Fools and blind! For which is of greater value, the gold or the Temple that makes the gold sacred? 18 Again, "If anyone swears by the altar it has no force; but anyone who swears by the offering on the altar, is bound." 19 You blind men! For which is of greater worth, the offering or the altar that makes the offering sacred? 20 Therefore, someone who swears by the altar is swearing by that and by everything on it. 21 And someone who swears by the Temple is swearing by that and by the One who dwells in it. 22 And someone who swears by heaven is swearing by the throne of God and by the One who is seated there.

23 'Alas for you, scribes and Pharisees, you hypocrites! You pay your tithe of mint and dill and cummin and have neglected the weightier matters of the Law—justice, mercy, good faith! These you should have practised, those not neglected. 24 You blind guides, straining out gnats and swallowing camels!

25 'Alas for you, scribes and Pharisees, you hypocrites! You clean the outside of cup and dish and leave the inside full of extortion and intemperance. 26 Blind Pharisee! Clean the inside of cup and dish first so that it and the outside are both clean.

27 'Alas for you, scribes and Pharisees, you hypocrites! You are like whitewashed tombs that look handsome on the outside, but inside are full of the bones of the dead and every kind of corruption. 28 In just the same way, from the outside you look upright, but inside you are full of hypocrisy and lawlessness.

29 'Alas for you, scribes and Pharisees, you hypocrites! You build the sepulchres of the prophets and decorate the tombs of the upright, 30 saying, "We would never have joined in shedding the blood of the prophets, had we lived in our ancestors' day." 31 So! Your own evidence tells against you! You are the children of those who murdered the prophets! 32 Very well then, finish off the work that your ancestors began.

Their crimes and approaching punishment

33 'You serpents, brood of vipers, how can you escape being condemned to hell? 34 This is why—look—I am sending you prophets and wise men and scribes; some you will slaughter and crucify, some you will scourge in your synagogues and hunt from town to town; 35 and so you will draw down on yourselves the blood of every upright person that has been shed on earth, from the blood of Abel the holy to the blood of Zechariah son of Barachiah whom you murdered between the sanctuary and the altar. 36 In truth I tell you, it will all recoil on this generation.

Jerusalem admonished

37 'Jerusalem, Jerusalem, you that kill the prophets and stone those who are sent to you! How often have I longed to gather your children together, as a hen gathers her chicks under her wings, and you refused! 38 Look! Your house will be deserted, 39 for, I promise, you shall not see me any more until you are saying:

*Blessed is he who is coming in the name of the Lord!*ᵇ

The end and the second comingᵃ

24 Jesus left the Temple, and as he was going away his disciples came up to draw his attention to the Temple buildings. 2 He said to them in reply, 'You see all these?

23a Some authorities add v. 14, taken from Mk 12:40.

23b Ps 118:26.

24a In this discourse on the future of Christ's community, Mt links the destruction of Jerusalem in AD 70 to the final coming of Christ.

In truth I tell you, not a single stone here will be left on another: everything will be pulled down.' [3] And while he was sitting on the Mount of Olives the disciples came and asked him when they were by themselves, 'Tell us, when is this going to happen, and what sign will there be of your coming and of the end of the world?'

The beginning of sorrows

[4] And Jesus answered them, 'Take care that no one deceives you, [5] because many will come using my name and saying, "I am the Christ," and they will deceive many. [6] You will hear of wars and rumours of wars; see that you are not alarmed, for this is something that must happen, but the end will not be yet. [7] For nation will fight against nation, and kingdom against kingdom. There will be famines and earthquakes in various places. [8] All this is only the beginning of the birthpangs.

[9] 'Then you will be handed over to be tortured and put to death; and you will be hated by all nations on account of my name. [10] And then many will fall away; people will betray one another and hate one another. [11] Many false prophets will arise; they will deceive many, [12] and with the increase of lawlessness, love in most people will grow cold; [13] but anyone who stands firm to the end will be saved. [14] 'This good news of the kingdom will be proclaimed to the whole world as evidence to the nations. And then the end will come.

The great tribulation of Jerusalem

[15] 'So when you see *the appalling abomination,*[b] of which the prophet Daniel spoke, set up in the holy place (let the reader understand), [16] then those in Judaea must escape to the mountains; [17] if anyone is on the housetop, he must not come down to collect his belongings from the house; [18] if anyone is in the fields, he must not turn back to fetch his cloak. [19] Alas for those with child, or with babies at the breast, when those days come! [20] Pray that you will not have to make your escape in winter or on a Sabbath. [21] For then there will be *great dis-*tress, *unparalleled since*[c] the world began, and such as will never be again. [22] And if that time had not been shortened, no human being would have survived; but shortened that time shall be, for the sake of those who are chosen.

[23] 'If anyone says to you then, "Look, here is the Christ," or "Over here," do not believe it; [24] for false Christs and false prophets will arise and provide great signs and portents, enough to deceive even the elect, if that were possible. [25] Look! I have given you warning.

The coming of the Son of man

[26] 'If, then, they say to you, "Look, he is in the desert," do not go there; "Look, he is in some hiding place," do not believe it; [27] because the coming of the Son of man will be like lightning striking in the east and flashing far into the west. [28] Wherever the corpse is, that is where the vultures will gather.

The universal significance of this coming

[29] 'Immediately after the distress of those days the sun will be darkened,[d] the moon will not give its light, the stars will fall from the sky and the powers of the heavens will be shaken. [30] And then the sign of the Son of man will appear in heaven; then, too, all the peoples of the earth will beat their breasts; and they will see the *Son of man coming on the clouds of heaven* with power and great glory.[e] [31] And he will send his angels with a loud trumpet to gather his elect from the four winds, from one end of heaven to the other.

The time of this coming

[32] 'Take the fig tree as a parable: as soon as its twigs grow supple and its leaves come out, you know that summer is near. [33] So with you when you see all these things: know that he is near, right at the gates. [34] In truth I tell you, before this generation has passed away, all these things will have taken place. [35] Sky and earth will pass away, but my words will never pass

24b Dn 9:27; 11:31; 12:11.   24c Dn 12:1.
24d Am 8:9.   24e Dn 7:13–14.

away. ³⁶But as for that day and hour, nobody knows it, neither the angels of heaven, nor the Son, no one but the Father alone.

Be on the alert

³⁷'As it was in Noah's day, so will it be when the Son of man comes. ³⁸For in those days before the Flood people were eating, drinking, taking wives, taking husbands, right up to the day Noah went into the ark,ᶠ ³⁹and they suspected nothing till the Flood came and swept them all away. This is what it will be like when the Son of man comes. ⁴⁰Then of two men in the fields, one is taken, one left; ⁴¹of two women grinding at the mill, one is taken, one left.

⁴²'So stay awake, because you do not know the day when your master is coming. ⁴³You may be quite sure of this, that if the householder had known at what time of the night the burglar would come, he would have stayed awake and would not have allowed anyone to break through the wall of his house. ⁴⁴Therefore, you too must stand ready because the Son of man is coming at an hour you do not expect.

Parable of the conscientious steward

⁴⁵'Who, then, is the wise and trustworthy servant whom the master placed over his household to give them their food at the proper time? ⁴⁶Blessed that servant if his master's arrival finds him doing exactly that. ⁴⁷In truth I tell you, he will put him in charge of everything he owns. ⁴⁸But if the servant is dishonest and says to himself, "My master is taking his time," ⁴⁹and sets about beating his fellow-servants and eating and drinking with drunkards, ⁵⁰his master will come on a day he does not expect and at an hour he does not know. ⁵¹The master will cut him off and send him to the same fate as the hypocrites, where there will be weeping and grinding of teeth.'

Parable of the ten wedding attendants

25'Then the kingdom of Heaven will be like this: Ten wedding attendants took their lamps and went to meet the bridegroom. ²Five of them were foolish and five were sensible: ³the foolish ones, though they took their lamps, took no oil with them, ⁴whereas the sensible ones took flasks of oil as well as their lamps. ⁵The bridegroom was late, and they all grew drowsy and fell asleep. ⁶But at midnight there was a cry, "Look! The bridegroom! Go out and meet him." ⁷Then all those wedding attendants woke up and trimmed their lamps, ⁸and the foolish ones said to the sensible ones, "Give us some of your oil: our lamps are going out." ⁹But they replied, "There may not be enough for us and for you; you had better go to those who sell it and buy some for yourselves." ¹⁰They had gone off to buy it when the bridegroom arrived. Those who were ready went in with him to the wedding hall and the door was closed. ¹¹The other attendants arrived later. "Lord, Lord," they said, "open the door for us." ¹²But he replied, "In truth I tell you, I do not know you." ¹³So stay awake, because you do not know either the day or the hour.

Parable of the talents

¹⁴'It is like a man about to go abroad who summoned his servants and entrusted his property to them. ¹⁵To one he gave five talents, to another two, to a third one, each in proportion to his ability. Then he set out on his journey. ¹⁶The man who had received the five talents promptly went and traded with them and made five more. ¹⁷The man who had received two made two more in the same way. ¹⁸But the man who had received one went off and dug a hole in the ground and hid his master's money. ¹⁹Now a long time afterwards, the master of those servants came back and went through his accounts with them. ²⁰The man who had received the five talents came forward bringing five more. "Sir," he said, "you entrusted me with five talents; here are five more that I have made." ²¹His master said to him, "Well done, good and trustworthy servant; you have shown you are trustworthy in small things; I will trust you with greater;

24f Gn 7:11–23.

come and join in your master's happiness." ²²Next the man with the two talents came forward. "Sir," he said, "you entrusted me with two talents; here are two more that I have made." ²³His master said to him, "Well done, good and trustworthy servant; you have shown you are trustworthy in small things; I will trust you with greater; come and join in your master's happiness." ²⁴Last came forward the man who had the single talent. "Sir," said he, "I had heard you were a hard man, reaping where you had not sown and gathering where you had not scattered; ²⁵so I was afraid, and I went off and hid your talent in the ground. Here it is; it was yours, you have it back." ²⁶But his master answered him, "You wicked and lazy servant! So you knew that I reap where I have not sown and gather where I have not scattered? ²⁷Well then, you should have deposited my money with the bankers, and on my return I would have got my money back with interest. ²⁸So now, take the talent from him and give it to the man who has the ten talents. ²⁹For to everyone who has will be given more, and he will have more than enough; but anyone who has not, will be deprived even of what he has. ³⁰As for this good-for-nothing servant, throw him into the darkness outside, where there will be weeping and grinding of teeth."

The Last Judgement

³¹'When the Son of man comes in his glory, escorted by all the angels, then he will take his seat on his throne of glory. ³²All nations will be assembled before him and he will separate people one from another as the shepherd separates sheep from goats. ³³He will place the sheep on his right hand and the goats on his left. ³⁴Then the King will say to those on his right hand, "Come, you whom my Father has blessed, take as your heritage the kingdom prepared for you since the foundation of the world. ³⁵For I was hungry and you gave me food, I was thirsty and you gave me drink, I was a stranger and you made me welcome, ³⁶lacking clothes and you clothed me, sick and

you visited me, in prison and you came to see me." ³⁷Then the upright will say to him in reply, "Lord, when did we see you hungry and feed you, or thirsty and give you drink? ³⁸When did we see you a stranger and make you welcome, lacking clothes and clothe you? ³⁹When did we find you sick or in prison and go to see you?" ⁴⁰And the King will answer, "In truth I tell you, in so far as you did this to one of the least of these brothers of mine, you did it to me." ⁴¹Then he will say to those on his left hand, "Go away from me, with your curse upon you, to the eternal fire prepared for the devil and his angels. ⁴²For I was hungry and you never gave me food, I was thirsty and you never gave me anything to drink, ⁴³I was a stranger and you never made me welcome, lacking clothes and you never clothed me, sick and in prison and you never visited me." ⁴⁴Then it will be their turn to ask, "Lord, when did we see you hungry or thirsty, a stranger or lacking clothes, sick or in prison, and did not come to your help?" ⁴⁵Then he will answer, "In truth I tell you, in so far as you neglected to do this to one of the least of these, you neglected to do it to me." ⁴⁶And they will go away to eternal punishment, and the upright to eternal life.'

The conspiracy against Jesus

26 Jesus had now finished all he wanted to say, and he told his disciples, ²'It will be Passover, as you know, in two days' time, and the Son of man will be handed over to be crucified.'

³Then the chief priests and the elders of the people assembled in the palace of the high priest, whose name was Caiaphas, ⁴and made plans to arrest Jesus by some trick and have him put to death. ⁵They said, however, 'It must not be during the festivities; there must be no disturbance among the people.'

The anointing at Bethany

⁶Jesus was at Bethany in the house of Simon, a man who had suffered from a virulent skin-disease, when ⁷a woman came to him with an

114 READ MATTHEW 25:31–46.

Come, you whom my Father has blessed, take as your heritage the kingdom prepared for you since the foundation of the world.—MATTHEW 25:34

OUR HEAVENLY HERITAGE

With what joy shall we be filled, if we are directed to the right hand of the King? What must we be like when the Just embrace us there? When . . . they shall embrace you there—Abraham, Isaac, Jacob, Moses, Noah, Job, Daniel, the holy Prophets, the Apostles, the Martyrs, who all were pleasing to God in the days of the flesh? And whomsoever you have heard of, and whose life you have admired, and whom you now wish to look upon, they will come to you and embrace you, rejoicing in your salvation. What manner of people must we then be? Of what kind shall be that unspeakable delight which we are to receive, when the King shall with joyfulness say to those who will be on his right hand: "Come, you whom my Father has blessed, take as your heritage the kingdom prepared for you since the foundation of the world."

Then, my brother, then will you receive the kingdom of beauty, the crown of all your desires, from the hand of the Lord, and reign with Christ for ever. Then you will receive for your inheritance the gifts, "which God has promised to those who love and serve him" (see Jm 1:12). From that time forward you will be secure, no longer filled with anxiety. Be mindful, my brother, of what kind of person it must be, to whom it will be given to reign with Christ in heaven. Reflect upon what it means to dwell forever in the light of his countenance, to possess the source of all light. For "No more will the sun give you daylight, nor moonlight shine on you" (Is 60:19), but Christ will be your unfailing Light, and God your glory. See, my brother, what glory he has laid up for those who fear him, observing his commandments.   ST. EPHREM, 306?–373?

YOU WILL FIND THE NEXT READING AT MATTHEW 26.

alabaster jar of very expensive ointment, and poured it on his head as he was at table. [8] When they saw this, the disciples said indignantly, 'Why this waste? [9] This could have been sold for a high price and the money given the poor.' [10] But Jesus noticed this and said, 'Why are you upsetting the woman? What she has done for me is indeed a good work! [11] You have the poor with you always, but you will not always have me. [12] When she poured this ointment on my body, she did it to prepare me for burial. [13] In truth I tell you, wherever in all the world this gospel is proclaimed, what she has done will be told as well, in remembrance of her.'

Judas betrays Jesus

[14] Then one of the Twelve, the man called Judas Iscariot, went to the chief priests [15] and said, 'What are you prepared to give me if I hand him over to you?' They paid him thirty silver pieces, [16] and from then onwards he began to look for an opportunity to betray him.

Preparations for the Passover supper

[17] Now on the first day of Unleavened Bread the disciples came to Jesus to say, 'Where do you want us to make the preparations for you to eat the Passover?' [18] He said, 'Go to a certain

115 READ MATTHEW 26:26–29.

"Take it and eat," he said, "this is my body."—MATTHEW 26:26

HOW BREAD BECOMES CHRIST'S BODY

Now you ask, how the bread became Christ's body and the wine and water Christ's blood. And I say to you, "The Holy Spirit is present and does those things that surpass reason and thought."

Further, bread and wine are used because God knows our weakness. Since we generally reject anything that we are not accustomed to, God with his usual indulgence performs his supernatural works through familiar objects. For example, in the case of baptism he connected the grace of the Spirit with oil and water and made it the water of regeneration because we wash ourselves with water and anoint ourselves with oil. Similarly, we eat bread and drink water and wine, so he connected his divinity with these and made them his body and blood in order that we may rise to what is supernatural through what is familiar and natural.

. . . The body which was received up into the heavens does not descend, but the bread itself and the wine are changed into God's body and blood. But if you ask how this happens, it is enough for you to learn that it was through the Holy Spirit, just as the Lord took on himself flesh that subsisted in him and was born of the holy Mother of God through the Spirit. And we know nothing further save that the Word of God is true and energizes and is omnipotent, but how this happens cannot be searched out. But we can accurately say that just as in nature the bread by the eating and the wine and the water by the drinking are changed into the body and blood of the eater and drinker, and do not become a different body from the former one, so the bread of the table and the wine and water are supernaturally changed by the invocation and presence of the Holy Spirit into the body and blood of Christ, and are not two but one and the same. ST. JOHN DAMASCENE, 675?–749?

YOU WILL FIND THE NEXT READING AT MATTHEW 27.

man in the city and say to him, "The Master says: My time is near. It is at your house that I am keeping Passover with my disciples."' ¹⁹The disciples did what Jesus told them and prepared the Passover.

The treachery of Judas foretold

²⁰When evening came he was at table with the Twelve. ²¹And while they were eating he said, 'In truth I tell you, one of you is about to betray me.' ²²They were greatly distressed and started asking him in turn, 'Not me, Lord, surely?' ²³He answered, 'Someone who has dipped his hand into the dish with me will betray me. ²⁴The Son of man is going to his fate, as the scriptures say he will, but alas for that man by whom the Son of man is betrayed! Better for that man if he had never been born!' ²⁵Judas, who was to betray him, asked in his turn, 'Not me, Rabbi, surely?' Jesus answered, 'It is you who say it.'

The institution of the Eucharist

²⁶Now as they were eating, Jesus took bread, and when he had said the blessing he broke it and gave it to the disciples. 'Take it and eat,' he said, 'this is my body.' ²⁷Then he took a cup, and when he had given thanks he handed it to them saying, 'Drink from this, all of you, ²⁸for this is my blood, the blood of the

covenant, poured out for many for the forgiveness of sins. [29] From now on, I tell you, I shall never again drink wine until the day I drink the new wine with you in the kingdom of my Father.'

Peter's denial foretold

[30] After the psalms had been sung they left for the Mount of Olives. [31] Then Jesus said to them, 'You will all fall away from me tonight, for the scripture says: *I shall strike the shepherd and the sheep of the flock will be scattered,*[a] [32] but after my resurrection I shall go ahead of you to Galilee.' [33] At this, Peter said to him, 'Even if all fall away from you, I will never fall away.' [34] Jesus answered him, 'In truth I tell you, this very night, before the cock crows, you will have disowned me three times.' [35] Peter said to him, 'Even if I have to die with you, I will never disown you.' And all the disciples said the same.

Gethsemane

[36] Then Jesus came with them to a plot of land called Gethsemane; and he said to his disciples, 'Stay here while I go over there to pray.' [37] He took Peter and the two sons of Zebedee with him. And he began to feel sadness and anguish. [38] Then he said to them, 'My soul is sorrowful to the point of death. Wait here and stay awake with me.' [39] And going on a little further he fell on his face and prayed. 'My Father,' he said, 'if it is possible, let this cup pass me by. Nevertheless, let it be as you, not I, would have it.' [40] He came back to the disciples and found them sleeping, and he said to Peter, 'So you had not the strength to stay awake with me for one hour? [41] Stay awake, and pray not to be put to the test. The spirit is willing enough, but human nature is weak.' [42] Again, a second time, he went away and prayed: 'My Father,' he said, 'if this cup cannot pass by, but I must drink it, your will be done!'[b] [43] And he came back again and found them sleeping, their eyes were so heavy. [44] Leaving them there, he went away again and prayed for the third time, repeating the same words. [45] Then he came back to the disciples and said to them, 'You can sleep on now and have your rest. Look, the hour has come when the Son of man is to be betrayed into the hands of sinners. [46] Get up! Let us go! Look, my betrayer is not far away.'

The arrest

[47] And suddenly while he was still speaking, Judas, one of the Twelve, appeared, and with him a large number of men armed with swords and clubs, sent by the chief priests and elders of the people. [48] Now the traitor had arranged a sign with them saying, 'The one I kiss, he is the man. Arrest him.' [49] So he went up to Jesus at once and said, 'Greetings, Rabbi,' and kissed him. [50] Jesus said to him, 'My friend, do what you are here for.' Then they came forward, seized Jesus and arrested him. [51] And suddenly, one of the followers of Jesus grasped his sword and drew it; he struck the high priest's servant and cut off his ear. [52] Jesus then said, 'Put your sword back, for all who draw the sword will die by the sword. [53] Or do you think that I cannot appeal to my Father, who would promptly send more than twelve legions of angels to my defence? [54] But then, how would the scriptures be fulfilled that say this is the way it must be?' [55] It was at this time that Jesus said to the crowds, 'Am I a bandit, that you had to set out to capture me with swords and clubs? I sat teaching in the Temple day after day and you never laid a hand on me.' [56] Now all this happened to fulfil the prophecies in scripture. Then all the disciples deserted him and ran away.

Jesus before the Sanhedrin[c]

[57] The men who had arrested Jesus led him off to the house of Caiaphas the high priest, where the scribes and the elders were assembled.

26a Zc 13:7. 26b = 6:10.

26c The gospels differ: Lk and Jn mention an interrogation at night and a Sanhedrin session in the morning. Mt and Mk place this morning session in the night.

58 Peter followed him at a distance right to the high priest's palace, and he went in and sat down with the attendants to see what the end would be.

59 The chief priests and the whole Sanhedrin were looking for evidence against Jesus, however false, on which they might have him executed. 60 But they could not find any, though several lying witnesses came forward. Eventually two came forward 61 and made a statement, 'This man said, "I have power to destroy the Temple of God and in three days build it up."' 62 The high priest then rose and said to him, 'Have you no answer to that? What is this evidence these men are bringing against you?' 63 But Jesus was silent. And the high priest said to him, 'I put you on oath by the living God to tell us if you are the Christ, the Son of God.' 64 Jesus answered him, 'It is you who say it. But, I tell you that from this time onward you will see the *Son of man seated at the right hand of the Power* and *coming on the clouds of heaven.'ᵈ* 65 Then the high priest tore his clothes and said, 'He has blasphemed. What need of witnesses have we now? There! You have just heard the blasphemy. 66 What is your opinion?' They answered, 'He deserves to die.'

67 Then they spat in his face and hit him with their fists; others said as they struck him, 68 'Prophesy to us, Christ! Who hit you then?'

Peter's denials

69 Meanwhile Peter was sitting outside in the courtyard, and a servant-girl came up to him saying, 'You, too, were with Jesus the Galilean.' 70 But he denied it in front of them all. 'I do not know what you are talking about,' he said. 71 When he went out to the gateway another servant-girl saw him and said to the people there, 'This man was with Jesus the Nazarene.' 72 And again, with an oath, he denied it, 'I do not know the man.' 73 A little later the bystanders came up and said to Peter, 'You are certainly one of them too! Why, your accentᵉ gives you away.' 74 Then he started cursing and swearing, 'I do

not know the man.' And at once the cock crowed, 75 and Peter remembered what Jesus had said, 'Before the cock crows you will have disowned me three times.' And he went outside and wept bitterly.

Jesus is taken before Pilate

27 When morning came, all the chief priests and the elders of the people met in council to bring about the death of Jesus. 2 They had him bound and led him away to hand him over to Pilate, the governor.

The death of Judas

3 When he found that Jesus had been condemned, then Judas, his betrayer, was filled with remorse and took the thirty silver pieces back to the chief priests and elders 4 saying, 'I have sinned. I have betrayed innocent blood.' They replied, 'What is that to us? That is your concern.' 5 And flinging down the silver pieces in the sanctuary he made off, and went and hanged himself. 6 The chief priests picked up the silver pieces and said, 'It is against the Law to put this into the treasury; it is blood-money.' 7 So they discussed the matter and with it bought the potter's field as a graveyard for foreigners, 8 and this is why the field is still called the Field of Blood. 9 The word spoken through the prophet Jeremiah was then fulfilled: *And they took the thirty silver pieces, the sum at which the precious One was priced by the children of Israel,* 10 *and they gave them for the potter's field, just as the Lord directed me.ᵃ*

Jesus before Pilate

11 Jesus, then, was brought before the governor, and the governor put to him this question, 'Are you the king of the Jews?' Jesus replied, 'It is you who say it.' 12 But when he was accused by the chief priests and the elders he refused to answer at all. 13 Pilate then said to him, 'Do you not hear how many charges they

26d Ps 110:1 and Dn 7:13.

26e Presumably Galileans had a local accent.

27a Zc 11:12–13.

have made against you?' ¹⁴But to the governor's amazement, he offered not a word in answer to any of the charges.

¹⁵At festival time it was the governor's practice to release a prisoner for the people, anyone they chose. ¹⁶Now there was then a notorious prisoner whose name was Barabbas. ¹⁷So when the crowd gathered, Pilate said to them, 'Which do you want me to release for you: Barabbas, or Jesus who is called Christ?' ¹⁸For Pilate knew it was out of jealousy that they had handed him over.

¹⁹Now as he was seated in the chair of judgement, his wife sent him a message, 'Have nothing to do with that upright man; I have been extremely upset today by a dream that I had about him.'

²⁰The chief priests and the elders, however, had persuaded the crowd to demand the release of Barabbas and the execution of Jesus. ²¹So when the governor spoke and asked them, 'Which of the two do you want me to release for you?' they said, 'Barabbas.' ²²Pilate said to them, 'But in that case, what am I to do with Jesus who is called Christ?' They all said, 'Let him be crucified!' ²³He asked, 'But what harm has he done?' But they shouted all the louder, 'Let him be crucified!' ²⁴Then Pilate saw that he was making no impression, that in fact a riot was imminent. So he took some water, washed his hands in front of the crowd and said, 'I am innocent of this man's blood. It is your concern.' ²⁵And the people, every one of them, shouted back, 'Let his blood be on us and on our children!' ²⁶Then he released Barabbas for them. After having Jesus scourged he handed him over to be crucified.

Jesus is crowned with thorns

²⁷Then the governor's soldiers took Jesus with them into the Praetorium and collected the whole cohort round him. ²⁸And they stripped him and put a scarlet cloak round him, ²⁹and having twisted some thorns into a crown they put this on his head and placed a reed in his right hand. To make fun of him they knelt to him saying, 'Hail, king of the Jews!' ³⁰And they spat on him and took the reed and struck him on the head with it. ³¹And when they had finished making fun of him, they took off the cloak and dressed him in his own clothes and led him away to crucifixion.

The crucifixion

³²On their way out, they came across a man from Cyrene, called Simon, and enlisted him to carry his cross. ³³When they had reached a place called Golgotha, that is, the place of the skull, ³⁴they gave him wine to drink mixed with gall,ᵇ which he tasted but refused to drink. ³⁵When they had finished crucifying him they shared out his clothing by casting lots, ³⁶and then sat down and stayed there keeping guard over him.

³⁷Above his head was placed the charge against him; it read: 'This is Jesus, the King of the Jews.' ³⁸Then two bandits were crucified with him, one on the right and one on the left.

The crucified Jesus is mocked

³⁹The passers-by jeered at him; they shook their heads ⁴⁰and said, 'So you would destroy the Temple and in three days rebuild it! Then save yourself if you are God's son and come down from the cross!' ⁴¹The chief priests with the scribes and elders mocked him in the same way, ⁴²with the words, 'He saved others; he cannot save himself. He is the king of Israel; let him come down from the cross now, and we will believe in him. ⁴³He has put his trust in God; now let God rescue him if he wants him. For he did say, "I am God's son."ᶜ ⁴⁴Even the bandits who were crucified with him taunted him in the same way.

The death of Jesus

⁴⁵From the sixth hour there was darkness over all the land until the ninth hour. ⁴⁶And about the ninth hour, Jesus cried out in a loud voice, *'Eli, eli, lama sabachthani?'* that is, *'My God, my God, why have you forsaken me?'*ᵈ

27b cf. Ps 69:21.   27c cf. Ws 2:18–20.   27d Ps 22:1.

116 READ MATTHEW 27:45–56.

But Jesus, again crying out in a loud voice, yielded up his spirit.—MATTHEW 27:50

LAUGHING AT THE DEVIL

Without any words, God allowed me to behold him for a considerable time. . . . And then without voice or any opening of lips, there formed in my soul these words: "Here is how the fiend is overcome." . . .

In this our Lord showed that his blessed passion is the overcoming of the fiend. God showed that the fiend has the same malice now as before the Incarnation; and yet although he labors as hard now, he continually sees all those saved souls escape him, wonderfully by virtue of Christ's precious passion. This is a sorrow to him, an evil reality of which he is ashamed; for all that God allows him to do turns to our joy yet to him it is constant shame and woe. This means that he has as much sorrow when God permits him to work as when he is prevented; and he can never do so much evil as he wishes, for God has taken his power up into his own hands. For as I see it, there can be no wrath with God, for he is our endless Lord, having regard to his own honor as well as the profit of all who will be saved. He withstands these reproved beings with his might and right, while they in their malice and waywardness are busy contriving how they might go against God's will.

Also I saw how our Lord scorns his malice and deadens his might, and he wills us to do the same. And at this sight I laughed so mightily that I made those standing around laugh with me. I thought how much I wanted all my fellow Christians to have seen what I saw, for then could we all have laughed together. And although I did not see Christ laugh, yet I understood that we may rightly laugh, comforting ourselves and finding our joy in God because the devil is overcome.

BL. JULIAN OF NORWICH, 1342?–1423?

YOU WILL FIND THE NEXT READING AT MATTHEW 28.

⁴⁷ When some of those who stood there heard this, they said, 'The man is calling on Elijah,' ⁴⁸ and one of them quickly ran to get a sponge which he filled with vinegar and, putting it on a reed, gave it him to drink. ⁴⁹ But the rest of them said, 'Wait! And see if Elijah will come to save him.' ⁵⁰ But Jesus, again crying out in a loud voice, yielded up his spirit.

⁵¹ And suddenly, the veil of the Sanctuary was torn in two from top to bottom, the earth quaked, the rocks were split, ⁵² the tombs opened and the bodies of many holy people rose from the dead, ⁵³ and these, after his resurrection, came out of the tombs, entered the holy city and appeared to a number of people. ⁵⁴ The centurion, together with the others guarding Jesus, had seen the earthquake and all that was taking place, and they were terrified and said, 'In truth this man was son of God.'

⁵⁵ And many women were there, watching from a distance, the same women who had followed Jesus from Galilee and looked after him. ⁵⁶ Among them were Mary of Magdala, Mary the mother of James and Joseph, and the mother of Zebedee's sons.

117 READ MATTHEW 28:16–20.

Baptise them in the name of the Father and of the Son and of the Holy Spirit.

—MATTHEW 28:19

GOD IS ONE AND THREE

The faith that the holy Patriarchs and Prophets received from God before his Son was made flesh; the faith that the holy Apostles heard from the Lord himself when present in the flesh; the faith that the same Apostles learned by the teaching of the Holy Spirit not only to preach by word of mouth but also to leave behind in their writings for the faithful instruction of all that should come after—that faith teaches that the Trinity, that is, the Father, the Son, and the Holy Spirit, is but one God.

But we could not truly call the Father, the Son, and the Holy Spirit a Trinity, if one and the same person were named Father, Son, and Holy Spirit. For if the being of the Father, the Son, and the Holy Spirit is one being, there would be only one person, and it would not be true to say that God is a Trinity. On the other hand, if the persons of the Father, the Son, and the Holy Spirit are distinguished from one another by that which is proper to each, they would be different by nature, and it would not be true to say that God is One. But since concerning the nature of the one true God, who is a Trinity, it is true to say that God is One, and true to say that God is a Trinity, therefore, the true God is a Trinity in Persons and a Unity in nature.

Through this oneness of nature, all that the Father is is in the Son and the Holy Spirit; and all that the Son is is in the Father and the Holy Spirit; and all that the Holy Spirit is is in the Father and the Son. Of the Father, the Son, and the Holy Spirit, none is without the other, none is before the other, none is mightier than the other.   ST. FULGENTIUS OF RUSPE, 468?–533

YOU WILL FIND THE NEXT READING AT MARK 2.

The burial

⁵⁷ When it was evening, there came a rich man of Arimathaea, called Joseph, who had himself become a disciple of Jesus. ⁵⁸ This man went to Pilate and asked for the body of Jesus. Then Pilate ordered it to be handed over. ⁵⁹ So Joseph took the body, wrapped it in a clean shroud ⁶⁰ and put it in his own new tomb which he had hewn out of the rock. He then rolled a large stone across the entrance of the tomb and went away. ⁶¹ Now Mary of Magdala and the other Mary were there, sitting opposite the sepulchre.

The guard at the tomb

⁶² Next day, that is, when Preparation Day was over, the chief priests and the Pharisees went in a body to Pilate ⁶³ and said to him, 'Your Excellency, we recall that this impostor said, while he was still alive, "After three days I shall rise again." ⁶⁴ Therefore give the order to have the sepulchre kept secure until the third day, for fear his disciples come and steal him away and tell the people, "He has risen from the dead." This last piece of fraud would be worse than what went before.' ⁶⁵ Pilate said to them, 'You may have your guard; go and

make all as secure as you know how.' ⁶⁶ So they went and made the sepulchre secure, putting seals on the stone and mounting a guard.

The empty tomb; the angel's message

28 After the Sabbath, and towards dawn on the first day of the week, Mary of Magdala and the other Mary went to visit the sepulchre. ² And suddenly there was a violent earthquake, for an angel of the Lord, descending from heaven, came and rolled away the stone and sat on it. ³ His face was like lightning, his robe white as snow. ⁴ The guards were so shaken by fear of him that they were like dead men. ⁵ But the angel spoke; and he said to the women, 'There is no need for you to be afraid. I know you are looking for Jesus, who was crucified. ⁶ He is not here, for he has risen, as he said he would. Come and see the place where he lay, ⁷ then go quickly and tell his disciples, "He has risen from the dead and now he is going ahead of you to Galilee; that is where you will see him." Look! I have told you.' ⁸ Filled with awe and great joy the women came quickly away from the tomb and ran to tell his disciples.

Appearance to the women

⁹ And suddenly, coming to meet them, was Jesus. 'Greetings,' he said. And the women came up to him and, clasping his feet, they did him homage. ¹⁰ Then Jesus said to them, 'Do not be afraid; go and tell my brothers that they must leave for Galilee; there they will see me.'

Precautions taken by the leaders of the people

¹¹ Now while they were on their way, some of the guards went off into the city to tell the chief priests all that had happened. ¹² These held a meeting with the elders and, after some discussion, handed a considerable sum of money to the soldiers ¹³ with these instructions, 'This is what you must say, "His disciples came during the night and stole him away while we were asleep." ¹⁴ And should the governor come to hear of this, we undertake to put things right with him ourselves and to see that you do not get into trouble.' ¹⁵ So they took the money and carried out their instructions, and to this day that is the story among the Jews.

Appearance in Galilee; the mission to the world

¹⁶ Meanwhile the eleven disciples set out for Galilee, to the mountain where Jesus had arranged to meet them. ¹⁷ When they saw him they fell down before him, though some hesitated. ¹⁸ Jesus came up and spoke to them. He said, 'All authority in heaven and on earth has been given to me.[a] ¹⁹ Go, therefore, make disciples of all nations; baptise them in the name of the Father and of the Son and of the Holy Spirit, ²⁰ and teach them to observe all the commands I gave you. And look, I am with you always; yes, to the end of time.'

28a cf. Dn 7:14.

MARK

The proclamation of John the Baptist

1 The beginning of the gospel about Jesus Christ, the Son of God. ²It is written in the prophet Isaiah:

> *Look, I am going to send my messenger in*
> *front of you*
> *to prepare your way before you.*ᵃ

> ³*A voice of one that cries in the desert:*
> *Prepare a way for the Lord,*
> *make his paths straight.*

⁴John the Baptist was in the desert, proclaiming a baptism of repentance for the forgiveness of sins. ⁵All Judaea and all the people of Jerusalem made their way to him, and as they were baptised by him in the river Jordan they confessed their sins. ⁶John wore a garment of camel-skin, and he lived on locusts and wild honey. ⁷In the course of his preaching he said, 'After me is coming someone who is more powerful than me, and I am not fit to kneel down and undo the strap of his sandals. ⁸I have baptised you with water, but he will baptise you with the Holy Spirit.'

Jesus is baptised

⁹It was at this time that Jesus came from Nazareth in Galilee and was baptised in the Jordan by John. ¹⁰And at once, as he was coming up out of the water, he saw the heavens torn apart and the Spirit, like a dove, descending on him. ¹¹And a voice came from heaven, 'You are my Son, the Beloved; my favour rests on you.'

Testing in the desert

¹²And at once the Spirit drove him into the desert ¹³and he remained there for forty days, and was put to the test by Satan. He was with the wild animals, and the angels looked after him.

Jesus begins to proclaim the message

¹⁴After John had been arrested, Jesus went into Galilee. There he proclaimed the gospel from God saying, ¹⁵'The time is fulfilled, and the kingdom of God is close at hand. Repent, and believe the gospel.'

The first four disciples are called

¹⁶As he was walking along by the Lake of Galilee he saw Simon and Simon's brother Andrew casting a net in the lake—for they were fishermen. ¹⁷And Jesus said to them, 'Come after me and I will make you into fishers of people.' ¹⁸And at once they left their nets and followed him.

¹⁹Going on a little further, he saw James son of Zebedee and his brother John; they too were in their boat, mending the nets. ²⁰At once he called them and, leaving their father Zebedee in the boat with the men he employed, they went after him.

Jesus teaches in Capernaum and cures a demoniac

²¹They went as far as Capernaum, and at once on the Sabbath he went into the synagogue and began to teach. ²²And his teaching made a

1a Ml 3:1 followed by Is 40:3.

deep impression on them because, unlike the scribes, he taught them with authority.

23 And at once in their synagogue there was a man with an unclean spirit, and he shouted, 24 'What do you want with us, Jesus of Nazareth? Have you come to destroy us? I know who you are: the Holy One of God.' 25 But Jesus rebuked it saying, 'Be quiet! Come out of him!' 26 And the unclean spirit threw the man into convulsions and with a loud cry went out of him. 27 The people were so astonished that they started asking one another what it all meant, saying, 'Here is a teaching that is new, and with authority behind it: he gives orders even to unclean spirits and they obey him.' 28 And his reputation at once spread everywhere, through all the surrounding Galilean countryside.

Cure of Simon's mother-in-law

29 And at once on leaving the synagogue, he went with James and John straight to the house of Simon and Andrew. 30 Now Simon's mother-in-law was in bed and feverish, and at once they told him about her. 31 He went in to her, took her by the hand and helped her up. And the fever left her and she began to serve them.

A number of cures

32 That evening, after sunset, they brought to him all who were sick and those who were possessed by devils. 33 The whole town came crowding round the door, 34 and he cured many who were sick with diseases of one kind or another; he also drove out many devils, but he would not allow them to speak, because they knew who he was.

Jesus quietly leaves Capernaum and travels through Galilee

35 In the morning, long before dawn, he got up and left the house and went off to a lonely place and prayed there. 36 Simon and his companions set out in search of him, 37 and when they found him they said, 'Everybody is looking for you.' 38 He answered, 'Let us go else-where, to the neighbouring country towns, so that I can proclaim the message there too, because that is why I came.' 39 And he went all through Galilee, preaching in their synagogues and driving out devils.

Cure of a man suffering from a virulent skin-disease

40 A man suffering from a virulent skin-disease came to him and pleaded on his knees saying, 'If you are willing, you can cleanse me.' 41 Feeling sorry for him, Jesus stretched out his hand, touched him and said to him, 'I am willing. Be cleansed.' 42 And at once the skin-disease left him and he was cleansed. 43 And at once Jesus sternly sent him away and said to him, 44 'Mind you tell no one anything, but go and show yourself to the priest, and make the offering for your cleansing prescribed by Moses as evidence to them.' 45 The man went away, but then started freely proclaiming and telling the story everywhere, so that Jesus could no longer go openly into any town, but stayed outside in deserted places. Even so, people from all around kept coming to him.

Cure of a paralytic

2 When he returned to Capernaum, some time later word went round that he was in the house; 2 and so many people collected that there was no room left, even in front of the door. He was preaching the word to them 3 when some people came bringing him a paralytic carried by four men, 4 but as they could not get the man to him through the crowd, they stripped the roof over the place where Jesus was; and when they had made an opening, they lowered the stretcher on which the paralytic lay. 5 Seeing their faith, Jesus said to the paralytic, 'My child, your sins are forgiven.' 6 Now some scribes were sitting there, and they thought to themselves, 7 'How can this man talk like that? He is being blasphemous. Who but God can forgive sins?' 8 And at once, Jesus, inwardly aware that this is what they were thinking, said to them, 'Why do you have these thoughts in your hearts? 9 Which of

118   READ MARK 2:1–12.

And the man got up, and at once picked up his stretcher and walked out in front of everyone.—MARK 2:12

THE HEALING POWER OF THE CROSS

Relying on the power of the Cross, St. Mary Magdalen prayed for the healing of a paralyzed woman:

In 1589, Sr. Pace Colombini, a lay sister of the community, suffered a stroke, losing the power of her left side. She did not even feel any pain when the physicians pricked her body with a long pin.

One day the prioress asked Mary Magdalen to pray for the sick sister and bless her. At first out of humility the saint hesitated to pray, but finally out of obedience and charity she made the sign of the Cross over the sister. Immediately, the nun felt that some life was returning to her dead side. Encouraged and hoping for greater improvement, she asked Magdalen to continue to visit and pray for her. As the patient wished, the next day Magdalen visited her and made the sign of the Cross over her. And once again the sister felt a new vigor in her limbs, and she began to move them a little. On the third day when the saint visited and blessed the sister she accomplished the miracle of a perfect cure. "I am healed," declared Sr. Pace, and shortly after got out of her bed, to the amazement of all the nuns and especially the doctor. He had not seen any medical reason to give hope for the sister's recovery nor any human expectation of seeing her whole and returning to her normal housework in the community. And unlike others whose paralysis generally recurs, this lay sister was never more stricken by this illness.   ST. MARY MAGDALEN DEI PAZZI, 1566–1607

YOU WILL FIND THE NEXT READING AT MARK 3.

these is easier: to say to the paralytic, "Your sins are forgiven" or to say, "Get up, pick up your stretcher and walk"? ¹⁰But to prove to you that the Son of man has authority to forgive sins on earth'— ¹¹he said to the paralytic—'I order you: get up, pick up your stretcher, and go off home.' ¹²And the man got up, and at once picked up his stretcher and walked out in front of everyone, so that they were all astonished and praised God saying, 'We have never seen anything like this.'

The call of Levi

¹³He went out again to the shore of the lake; and all the people came to him, and he taught them. ¹⁴As he was walking along he saw Levi the son of Alphaeus sitting at the tax office, and he said to him, 'Follow me.' And he got up and followed him.

Eating with sinners

¹⁵When Jesus was at dinner in his house, a number of tax collectors and sinners were also sitting at table with Jesus and his disciples; for there were many of them among his followers. ¹⁶When the scribes of the Pharisee party saw him eating with sinners and tax collectors, they said to his disciples, 'Why does he eat with tax collectors and sinners?' ¹⁷When Jesus heard this he said to them, 'It is not the healthy who need the doctor, but the sick. I came to call not the upright, but sinners.'

A discussion on fasting

18 John's disciples and the Pharisees were keeping a fast, when some people came to him and said to him, 'Why is it that John's disciples and the disciples of the Pharisees fast, but your disciples do not?' 19 Jesus replied, 'Surely the bridegroom's attendants cannot fast while the bridegroom is still with them? As long as they have the bridegroom with them, they cannot fast. 20 But the time will come when the bridegroom is taken away from them, and then, on that day, they will fast. 21 No one sews a piece of unshrunken cloth on an old cloak; otherwise, the patch pulls away from it, the new from the old, and the tear gets worse. 22 And nobody puts new wine into old wineskins; otherwise, the wine will burst the skins, and the wine is lost and the skins too. No! New wine into fresh skins!'

Picking corn on the Sabbath

23 It happened that one Sabbath day he was taking a walk through the cornfields, and his disciples began to make a path by plucking ears of corn. 24 And the Pharisees said to him, 'Look, why are they doing something on the Sabbath day that is forbidden?' 25 And he replied, 'Have you never read what David did in his time of need when he and his followers were hungry— 26 how he went into the house of God when Abiathar*a* was high priest, and ate the loaves of the offering which only the priests are allowed to eat, and how he also gave some to the men with him?'
27 And he said to them, 'The Sabbath was made for man, not man for the Sabbath; 28 so the Son of man is master even of the Sabbath.'

Cure of the man with a withered hand

3 Another time he went into the synagogue, and there was a man present whose hand was withered. 2 And they were watching him to see if he would cure him on the Sabbath day, hoping for something to charge him with. 3 He said to the man with the withered hand,

'Get up and stand in the middle!' 4 Then he said to them, 'Is it permitted on the Sabbath day to do good, or to do evil; to save life, or to kill?' But they said nothing. 5 Then he looked angrily round at them, grieved to find them so obstinate, and said to the man, 'Stretch out your hand.' He stretched it out and his hand was restored. 6 The Pharisees went out and began at once to plot with the Herodians*a* against him, discussing how to destroy him.

The crowds follow Jesus

7 Jesus withdrew with his disciples to the lakeside, and great crowds from Galilee followed him. From Judaea, 8 and from Jerusalem, and from Idumaea and Transjordan and the region of Tyre and Sidon, great numbers who had heard of all he was doing came to him. 9 And he asked his disciples to have a boat ready for him because of the crowd, to keep him from being crushed. 10 For he had cured so many that all who were afflicted in any way were crowding forward to touch him. 11 And the unclean spirits, whenever they saw him, would fall down before him and shout, 'You are the Son of God!' 12 But he warned them strongly not to make him known.

The appointment of the Twelve

13 He now went up onto the mountain and summoned those he wanted. So they came to him 14 and he appointed twelve; they were to be his companions and to be sent out to proclaim the message, 15 with power to drive out devils. 16 And so he appointed the Twelve, Simon to whom he gave the name Peter, 17 James the son of Zebedee and John the brother of James, to whom he gave the name Boanerges or 'Sons of Thunder'; 18 Andrew, Philip, Bartholomew, Matthew, Thomas, James the son of Alphaeus, Thaddaeus, Simon the Zealot 19 and Judas Iscariot, the man who was to betray him.

2a In fact his father, Ahimelech, was high priest, 1 S 21:1–7.

3a Supporters of the Herodian dynasty, campaigning for the return of all Palestine to their rule.

119 READ MARK 3:22–30.

But no one can make his way into a strong man's house and plunder his property unless he has first tied up the strong man.—MARK 3:27

HOW TO BEAT THE DEVIL

The children of Israel faced the Philistines for forty days (see 1 S 17). These forty days, by reason of the four seasons of the year and of the four continents of the globe are a figure of this present life, during which the Christian world does not cease to be arrayed in battle against the devil and his angels, as against Goliath and the Philistine army. They could not hope to overcome the devil were it not for the true David, Christ with the Cross for his staff. For before Christ came, my dearly beloved brothers and sisters, the devil roamed at large. But when Christ came, he did to the devil what the Gospel says, "No one can make his way into a strong man's house and plunder his property unless he has first tied up the strong man." Christ therefore came and bound the devil.

But some person will ask, "If the devil is bound, why is he still so powerful?" It is quite true that he is very powerful. But his lordship is over the lukewarm and the careless and those who do not truly fear God. The devil is chained up like a dog, and can only bite those who are such suicidal fools as to go within the length of his tether. Consider how stupid a person must be who gets himself bitten by a dog who is chained up. Don't let the desires and lusts of the world draw you within reach of him, and he will not be able to get at you. The devil can bark. He can whine. But he can only bite those who are willing to be bitten. He attacks us not by violence, but by persuasion. He doesn't snatch our consent—he asks for it.   ST. AUGUSTINE, 354–430

YOU WILL FIND THE NEXT READING AT MARK 4.

His family are concerned about Jesus

20 He went home again, and once more such a crowd collected that they could not even have a meal. 21 When his relations heard of this, they set out to take charge of him; they said, 'He is out of his mind.'

Allegations of the scribes

22 The scribes who had come down from Jerusalem were saying, 'Beelzebul is in him,' and, 'It is through the prince of devils that he drives devils out.' 23 So he called them to him and spoke to them in parables, 24 'How can Satan drive out Satan? If a kingdom is divided against itself, that kingdom cannot last. 25 And if a household is divided against itself, that household can never last. 26 Now if Satan has rebelled against himself and is divided, he cannot last either—it is the end of him. 27 But no one can make his way into a strong man's house and plunder his property unless he has first tied up the strong man. Only then can he plunder his house.

28 'In truth I tell you, all human sins will be forgiven, and all the blasphemies ever uttered; 29 but anyone who blasphemes against the Holy Spirit will never be forgiven, but is guilty of an eternal sin.' 30 This was because they were saying, 'There is an unclean spirit in him.'

The true kinsmen of Jesus

31 Now his mother and his brothers arrived and, standing outside, sent in a message asking for him. 32 A crowd was sitting round him at the time the message was passed to him, 'Look, your mother and brothers and sisters are outside asking for you.' 33 He replied, 'Who are my mother and my brothers?' 34 And looking at those sitting in a circle round him, he said, 'Here are my mother and my brothers. 35 Anyone who does the will of God, that person is my brother and sister and mother.'

Parable of the sower

4 Again he began to teach them by the lakeside, but such a huge crowd gathered round him that he got into a boat on the water and sat there. The whole crowd were at the lakeside on land. 2 He taught them many things in parables, and in the course of his teaching he said to them, 3 'Listen! Imagine a sower going out to sow. 4 Now it happened that, as he sowed, some of the seed fell on the edge of the path, and the birds came and ate it up. 5 Some seed fell on rocky ground where it found little soil and at once sprang up, because there was no depth of earth; 6 and when the sun came up it was scorched and, not having any roots, it withered away. 7 Some seed fell into thorns, and the thorns grew up and choked it, and it produced no crop. 8 And some seeds fell into rich soil, grew tall and strong, and produced a good crop; the yield was thirty, sixty, even a hundredfold.' 9 And he said, 'Anyone who has ears for listening should listen!'

Why Jesus spoke in parables

10 When he was alone, the Twelve, together with the others who formed his company, asked what the parables meant. 11 He told them, 'To you is granted the secret of the kingdom of God, but to those who are outside everything comes in parables,

12 so that *they may look and look, but never perceive;*
listen and listen, but never understand;
to avoid changing their ways and being healed.' [a]

The parable of the sower explained

13 He said to them, 'Do you not understand this parable? Then how will you understand any of the parables? 14 What the sower is sowing is the word. 15 Those on the edge of the path where the word is sown are people who have no sooner heard it than Satan at once comes and carries away the word that was sown in them. 16 Similarly, those who are sown on patches of rock are people who, when first they hear the word, welcome it at once with joy. 17 But they have no root deep down and do not last; should some trial come, or some persecution on account of the word, at once they fall away. 18 Then there are others who are sown in thorns. These have heard the word, 19 but the worries of the world, the lure of riches and all the other passions come in to choke the word, and so it produces nothing. 20 And there are those who have been sown in rich soil; they hear the word and accept it and yield a harvest, thirty and sixty and a hundredfold.'

Receiving and handing on the teaching of Jesus

21 He also said to them, 'Is a lamp brought in to be put under a tub or under the bed? Surely to be put on the lamp-stand? 22 For there is nothing hidden, but it must be disclosed, nothing kept secret except to be brought to light. 23 Anyone who has ears for listening should listen!'

Parable of the measure

24 He also said to them, 'Take notice of what you are hearing. The standard you use will be used for you—and you will receive more besides; 25 anyone who has, will be given more;

4a Is 6:9–10.

anyone who has not, will be deprived even of what he has.'

Parable of the seed growing by itself

26 He also said, 'This is what the kingdom of God is like. A man scatters seed on the land. 27 Night and day, while he sleeps, when he is awake, the seed is sprouting and growing; how, he does not know. 28 Of its own accord the land produces first the shoot, then the ear, then the full grain in the ear. 29 And when the crop is ready, at once he starts to reap because the harvest has come.'

Parable of the mustard seed

30 He also said, 'What can we say that the kingdom is like? What parable can we find for it? 31 It is like a mustard seed which, at the time of its sowing, is the smallest of all the seeds on earth. 32 Yet once it is sown it grows into the biggest shrub of them all and puts out big branches so that the birds of the air can shelter in its shade.'

The use of parables

33 Using many parables like these, he spoke the word to them, so far as they were capable of understanding it. 34 He would not speak to them except in parables, but he explained everything to his disciples when they were by themselves.

The calming of the storm

35 With the coming of evening that same day, he said to them, 'Let us cross over to the other side.' 36 And leaving the crowd behind they took him, just as he was, in the boat; and there were other boats with him. 37 Then it began to blow a great gale and the waves were breaking into the boat so that it was almost swamped. 38 But he was in the stern, his head on the cushion, asleep. 39 They woke him and said to him, 'Master, do you not care? We are lost!' And he woke up and rebuked the wind and said to the sea, 'Quiet now! Be calm!' And the wind dropped, and there followed a great calm. 40 Then he said to them, 'Why are you so frightened? Have you still no faith?' 41 They were overcome with awe and said to one another, 'Who can this be? Even the wind and the sea obey him.'

The Gerasene demoniac

5 They reached the territory of the Gerasenes on the other side of the lake, 2 and when he disembarked, a man with an unclean spirit at once came out from the tombs towards him. 3 The man lived in the tombs and no one could secure him any more, even with a chain, 4 because he had often been secured with fetters and chains but had snapped the chains and broken the fetters, and no one had the strength to control him. 5 All night and all day, among the tombs and in the mountains, he would howl and gash himself with stones. 6 Catching sight of Jesus from a distance, he ran up and fell at his feet 7 and shouted at the top of his voice, 'What do you want with me, Jesus, son of the Most High God? In God's name do not torture me!' 8 For Jesus had been saying to him, 'Come out of the man, unclean spirit.' 9 Then he asked, 'What is your name?' He answered, 'My name is Legion, for there are many of us.' 10 And he begged him earnestly not to send them out of the district. 11 Now on the mountainside there was a great herd of pigs feeding, 12 and the unclean spirits begged him, 'Send us to the pigs, let us go into them.' 13 So he gave them leave. With that, the unclean spirits came out and went into the pigs, and the herd of about two thousand pigs charged down the cliff into the lake, and there they were drowned. 14 The men looking after them ran off and told their story in the city and in the country round about; and the people came to see what had really happened. 15 They came to Jesus and saw the demoniac sitting there—the man who had had the legion in him—properly dressed and in his full senses, and they were afraid. 16 And those who had witnessed it reported what had happened to the demoniac and what had become of the pigs. 17 Then they began to implore Jesus to leave their neighbourhood. 18 As he was get-

120 READ MARK 4:35–40.

He . . . said to the sea, "Quiet now! Be calm!" And the wind dropped, and there followed a great calm.—MARK 4:39

CALMING OUR FEARS

At the same moment he calmed the storm, he changed the faith of the holy disciples that had been shaken with their little ship. He changed the ship's wavering into constancy, and he also worked in them a great calm, smoothing the waves of their little faith. . . . He quiets the fear within their souls, chiding them while he teaches them, that the cause of their fears was not the tempest, but their own timidity of soul. For he said: "Where is your faith?" (Lk 8:25). . . .

His manner of acting on this occasion was not that of a suppliant, but of one who rules. This is a great sign, an inspiration to all who hear it. For creation is obedient to every command of Christ. Also, as Mark relates it, the manner in which he reproves the winds is in accord with the divine dignity. For he says that the Lord spoke to the sea: He "rebuked the wind and said to the sea, 'Quiet now! Be calm!'" And as soon as he had spoken there follows that which he commands, and the sea foaming in angry waves hears the Incarnate Word and ceases from its fury. . . .

The sea is for us a figure of the visible world, and the church is the little ship, and the rowers are the just, who because they have received the faith have Christ always present with them. And frequently it is assailed by violent storms of persecutions and trials.

But Christ is among his chosen servants, and while in his holy wisdom he permits that they suffer persecution, he seems to sleep. But when the storm is at is fiercest, and those in the dark can endure no more . . . he will awaken and take away all our fear. He will reprove those that afflict us and change our mourning into joy, unfolding to us a shining and untroubled sky.

ST. CYRIL OF ALEXANDRIA, 376–444

YOU WILL FIND THE NEXT READING AT MARK 7:14.

ting into the boat, the man who had been possessed begged to be allowed to stay with him. ¹⁹Jesus would not let him but said to him, 'Go home to your people and tell them all that the Lord in his mercy has done for you.' ²⁰So the man went off and proceeded to proclaim in the Decapolis all that Jesus had done for him. And everyone was amazed.

Cure of the woman with a haemorrhage; the daughter of Jairus raised to life

²¹When Jesus had crossed again in the boat to the other side, a large crowd gathered round him and he stayed by the lake. ²²Then the president of the synagogue came up, named Jairus, and seeing him, fell at his feet ²³and begged him earnestly, saying, 'My little daughter is desperately sick. Do come and lay your hands on her that she may be saved and may live.' ²⁴Jesus went with him and a large crowd followed him; they were pressing all round him.

²⁵Now there was a woman who had suffered from a haemorrhage for twelve years; ²⁶after long and painful treatment under various doctors, she had spent all she had without

being any the better for it; in fact, she was getting worse. ²⁷ She had heard about Jesus, and she came up through the crowd and touched his cloak from behind, thinking, ²⁸ 'If I can just touch his clothes, I shall be saved.' ²⁹ And at once the source of the bleeding dried up, and she felt in herself that she was cured of her complaint. ³⁰ And at once aware of the power that had gone out from him, Jesus turned round in the crowd and said, 'Who touched my clothes?' ³¹ His disciples said to him, 'You see how the crowd is pressing round you; how can you ask, "Who touched me?" ' ³² But he continued to look all round to see who had done it. ³³ Then the woman came forward, frightened and trembling because she knew what had happened to her, and she fell at his feet and told him the whole truth. ³⁴ 'My daughter,' he said, 'your faith has restored you to health; go in peace and be free of your complaint.'

³⁵ While he was still speaking some people arrived from the house of the president of the synagogue to say, 'Your daughter is dead; why put the Master to any further trouble?' ³⁶ But Jesus overheard what they said and he said to the president of the synagogue, 'Do not be afraid; only have faith.' ³⁷ And he allowed no one to go with him except Peter and James and John the brother of James. ³⁸ So they came to the house of the president of the synagogue, and Jesus noticed all the commotion, with people weeping and wailing unrestrainedly. ³⁹ He went in and said to them, 'Why all this commotion and crying? The child is not dead, but asleep.' ⁴⁰ But they ridiculed him. So he turned them all out and, taking with him the child's father and mother and his own companions, he went into the place where the child lay. ⁴¹ And taking the child by the hand he said to her, *'Talitha kum!'* which means, 'Little girl, I tell you to get up.' ⁴² The little girl got up at once and began to walk about, for she was twelve years old. At once they were overcome with astonishment, ⁴³ and he gave them strict orders not to let anyone know about it, and told them to give her something to eat.

A visit to Nazareth

6 Leaving that district, he went to his home town, and his disciples accompanied him. ² With the coming of the Sabbath he began teaching in the synagogue, and most of them were astonished when they heard him. They said, 'Where did the man get all this? What is this wisdom that has been granted him, and these miracles that are worked through him? ³ This is the carpenter, surely, the son of Mary, the brother of James and Joset and Jude and Simon? His sisters, too, are they not here with us?' And they would not accept him. ⁴ And Jesus said to them, 'A prophet is despised only in his own country, among his own relations and in his own house'; ⁵ and he could work no miracle there, except that he cured a few sick people by laying his hands on them. ⁶ He was amazed at their lack of faith.

The mission of the Twelve

He made a tour round the villages, teaching. ⁷ Then he summoned the Twelve and began to send them out in pairs, giving them authority over unclean spirits. ⁸ And he instructed them to take nothing for the journey except a staff—no bread, no haversack, no coppers for their purses. ⁹ They were to wear sandals but, he added, 'Don't take a spare tunic.' ¹⁰ And he said to them, 'If you enter a house anywhere, stay there until you leave the district. ¹¹ And if any place does not welcome you and people refuse to listen to you, as you walk away shake off the dust under your feet as evidence to them.' ¹² So they set off to proclaim repentance; ¹³ and they cast out many devils, and anointed many sick people with oil and cured them.

Herod and Jesus

¹⁴ King Herod had heard about him, since by now his name was well known. Some were saying, 'John the Baptist has risen from the dead, and that is why miraculous powers are at work in him.' ¹⁵ Others said, 'He is Elijah,' others again, 'He is a prophet, like the

prophets we used to have.' ¹⁶But when Herod heard this he said, 'It is John whose head I cut off; he has risen from the dead.'

John the Baptist beheaded

¹⁷Now it was this same Herod who had sent to have John arrested, and had had him chained up in prison because of Herodias, his brother Philip's wife whom he had married. ¹⁸For John had told Herod, 'It is against the law for you to have your brother's wife.' ¹⁹As for Herodias, she was furious with him and wanted to kill him, but she was not able to do so, ²⁰because Herod was in awe of John, knowing him to be a good and upright man, and gave him his protection. When he had heard him speak he was greatly perplexed, and yet he liked to listen to him.

²¹An opportunity came on Herod's birthday when he gave a banquet for the nobles of his court, for his army officers and for the leading figures in Galilee. ²²When the daughter of this same Herodias came in and danced, she delighted Herod and his guests; so the king said to the girl, 'Ask me anything you like and I will give it you.' ²³And he swore her an oath, 'I will give you anything you ask, even half my kingdom.' ²⁴She went out and said to her mother, 'What shall I ask for?' She replied, 'The head of John the Baptist.' ²⁵The girl at once rushed back to the king and made her request, 'I want you to give me John the Baptist's head, immediately, on a dish.' ²⁶The king was deeply distressed but, thinking of the oaths he had sworn and of his guests, he was reluctant to break his word to her. ²⁷At once the king sent one of the bodyguard with orders to bring John's head. ²⁸The man went off and beheaded him in the prison; then he brought the head on a dish and gave it to the girl, and the girl gave it to her mother. ²⁹When John's disciples heard about this, they came and took his body and laid it in a tomb.

First miracle of the loaves

³⁰The apostles rejoined Jesus and told him all they had done and taught. ³¹And he said to them, 'Come away to some lonely place all by yourselves and rest for a while'; for there were so many coming and going that there was no time for them even to eat. ³²So they went off in the boat to a lonely place where they could be by themselves. ³³But people saw them going, and many recognised them; and from every town they all hurried to the place on foot and reached it before them. ³⁴So as he stepped ashore he saw a large crowd; and he took pity on them because they were like sheep without a shepherd, and he set himself to teach them at some length. ³⁵By now it was getting very late, and his disciples came up to him and said, 'This is a lonely place and it is getting very late, ³⁶so send them away, and they can go to the farms and villages round about, to buy themselves something to eat.' ³⁷He replied, 'Give them something to eat yourselves.' They answered, 'Are we to go and spend two hundred denarii on bread for them to eat?' ³⁸He asked, 'How many loaves have you? Go and see.' And when they had found out they said, 'Five, and two fish.' ³⁹Then he ordered them to get all the people to sit down in groups on the green grass, ⁴⁰and they sat down on the ground in squares of hundreds and fifties. ⁴¹Then he took the five loaves and the two fish, raised his eyes to heaven and said the blessing; then he broke the loaves and began handing them to his disciples to distribute among the people. He also shared out the two fish among them all. ⁴²They all ate as much as they wanted. ⁴³They collected twelve basketfuls of scraps of bread and pieces of fish. ⁴⁴Those who had eaten the loaves numbered five thousand men.

Jesus walks on the water

⁴⁵And at once he made his disciples get into the boat and go on ahead to the other side near Bethsaida, while he himself sent the crowd away. ⁴⁶After saying goodbye to them he went off into the hills to pray. ⁴⁷When evening came, the boat was far out on the sea, and he was alone on the land. ⁴⁸He could see that they were hard pressed in their rowing, for the

wind was against them; and about the fourth watch of the night he came towards them, walking on the sea. He was going to pass them by, ⁴⁹but when they saw him walking on the sea they thought it was a ghost and cried out; ⁵⁰for they had all seen him and were terrified. But at once he spoke to them and said, 'Courage! It's me! Don't be afraid.' ⁵¹Then he got into the boat with them and the wind dropped. They were utterly and completely dumbfounded, ⁵²because they had not seen what the miracle of the loaves meant; their minds were closed.

Cures at Gennesaret

⁵³Having made the crossing, they came to land at Gennesaret and moored there. ⁵⁴When they disembarked people at once recognised him, ⁵⁵and started hurrying all through the countryside and brought the sick on stretchers to wherever they heard he was. ⁵⁶And wherever he went, to village or town or farm, they laid down the sick in the open spaces, begging him to let them touch even the fringe of his cloak. And all those who touched him were saved.

The traditions of the Pharisees

7 The Pharisees and some of the scribes who had come from Jerusalem gathered round him, ²and they noticed that some of his disciples were eating with unclean hands, that is, without washing them. ³For the Pharisees, and all the Jews, keep the tradition of the elders and never eat without washing their arms as far as the elbow; ⁴and on returning from the market place they never eat without first sprinkling themselves. There are also many other observances which have been handed down to them to keep, concerning the washing of cups and pots and bronze dishes. ⁵So the Pharisees and scribes asked him, 'Why do your disciples not respect the tradition of the elders but eat their food with unclean hands?' ⁶He answered, 'How rightly Isaiah prophesied about you hypocrites in the passage of scripture:

This people honours me only with lip-service,
while their hearts are far from me.
⁷ *Their reverence of me is worthless;*
the lessons they teach are nothing but human
*commandments.*ᵃ

⁸You put aside the commandment of God to observe human traditions.' ⁹And he said to them, 'How ingeniously you get round the commandment of God in order to preserve your own tradition! ¹⁰For Moses said: *Honour your father and your mother,* and, *Anyone who curses father or mother must be put to death.*ᵇ ¹¹But you say, "If a man says to his father or mother: Anything I have that I might have used to help you is Korbanᶜ (that is, dedicated to God)," ¹²then he is forbidden from that moment to do anything for his father or mother. ¹³In this way you make God's word ineffective for the sake of your tradition which you have handed down. And you do many other things like this.'

On clean and unclean

¹⁴He called the people to him again and said, 'Listen to me, all of you, and understand. ¹⁵Nothing that goes into someone from outside can make that person unclean; it is the things that come out of someone that make that person unclean. ¹⁶Anyone who has ears for listening should listen!'

¹⁷When he had gone into the house, away from the crowd, his disciples questioned him about the parable. ¹⁸He said to them, 'Even you—don't you understand? Can't you see that nothing that goes into someone from outside can make that person unclean, ¹⁹because it goes not into the heart but into the stomach and passes into the sewer?' (Thus he pronounced all foods clean.) ²⁰And he went on, 'It is what comes out of someone that makes that person unclean. ²¹For it is from within, from the heart, that evil intentions emerge: fornica-

7a Is 29:13.　　7b Ex 20:12; 21:17.

7c Nothing Korban could be used for anyone else—a convenient legal fiction.

121 READ MARK 7:14–23.

All these evil things come from within and make a person unclean.—MARK 7:23

FIGHTING DEPRESSION

We must resist the pangs of gnawing dejection because if this fault has gained possession of our mind, it constantly blocks all insight in divine contemplation and utterly ruins and depresses our mind. Depression does not allow our mind to say its prayers with its usual gladness of heart, nor permit it to rely on the comfort of reading the sacred writings. It makes us impatient and erratic in all the duties of work and devotion. . . . If we are eager to exert ourselves in our spiritual combat, we ought to concentrate on healing this disorder.

The pains of dejection are not caused in us by other people's faults, but rather by our own, as we have stored up in ourselves the causes of offence and the seeds of faults. As soon as a shower of temptation waters our soul these immediately burst forth into shoots and fruits. . . . For another's fault never provokes anyone to sin, unless he has the fuel of evil stored up in his own heart.

And so God commands that we should not give up relating to our brothers and sisters, nor avoid those who we think have been hurt by us, or by whom we have been offended. But he bids us to make peace with them, knowing that perfection of heart is not secured by separating from men so much as by the virtue of patience. When patience is securely held, it can keep us at peace even with those who hate peace. When we are not patient, we may always be at odds with others who are better than we are. Opportunities for disturbance will not be wanting so long as we are living among human beings.

ST. JOHN CASSIAN, 360?–433?

YOU WILL FIND THE NEXT READING AT MARK 7:31.

tion, theft, murder, 22 adultery, avarice, malice, deceit, indecency, envy, slander, pride, folly. 23 All these evil things come from within and make a person unclean.'

Healing the daughter of the Syro-Phoenician woman

24 He left that place and set out for the territory of Tyre. There he went into a house and did not want anyone to know he was there; but he could not pass unrecognised. 25 At once a woman whose little daughter had an unclean spirit heard about him and came and fell at his feet. 26 Now this woman was a gentile, by birth a Syro-Phoenician, and she begged him to drive the devil out of her daughter. 27 And he said to her, 'The children should be fed first, because it is not fair to take the children's food and throw it to little dogs.' 28 But she spoke up, 'Ah yes, sir,' she replied, 'but little dogs under the table eat the scraps from the children.' 29 And he said to her, 'For saying this you may go home happy; the devil has gone out of your daughter.' 30 So she went off home and found the child lying on the bed and the devil gone.

Healing of the deaf man

31 Returning from the territory of Tyre, he went by way of Sidon towards the Lake of Galilee, right through the Decapolis territory. 32 And they brought him a deaf man who had

122 READ MARK 7:31–37.

He . . . put his fingers into the man's ears and touched his tongue with spittle.—MARK 7:33

THE DEEPER MEANING OF A HEALING

What does it signify when God, the Maker of all, heals a deaf and dumb man, as Scripture says, "He put his fingers into the man's ears and touched his tongue with spittle"? What is figured by the fingers of the Redeemer but the gifts of the Holy Spirit? So Luke says that after the Lord cast out an evil spirit, he said, "If it is through the finger of God that I drive devils out, then the kingdom of God has indeed caught you unawares" (Lk 11:20). Matthew renders the same text with these words, "If it is through the Spirit of God that I drive out devils, then be sure that the kingdom of God has caught you unawares" (Mt 12:28). By setting these two passages together we see that the Spirit is called the Finger. For our Lord, then, to put his Fingers into the deaf man's ears was by the gift of the Holy Spirit to enlighten his dark mind unto obedience.

What does it also signify that he "touched his tongue with spittle?" We receive spittle out of the Redeemer's mouth upon our tongues when we receive wisdom to speak God's truth. Spittle is a secretion of the head that flows into the mouth. And so, that wisdom, which is the Lord himself, the great head of his church, as soon as it has touched our tongue, immediately takes the form of preaching.

"Then looking up to heaven, he sighed," not that he had any need to sigh, except that he wanted to teach us to look up and sigh toward him whose throne is in heaven, confessing our need, so that our ears should be opened by the gift of the Holy Spirit, and our tongue loosed by the spittle of our Savior's mouth, that is, by knowledge of his Divine Word, before we can preach it to others.

ST. GREGORY THE GREAT, 540?–604

YOU WILL FIND THE NEXT READING AT MARK 9.

an impediment in his speech; and they asked him to lay his hand on him. ³³ He took him aside to be by themselves, away from the crowd, put his fingers into the man's ears and touched his tongue with spittle. ³⁴ Then looking up to heaven he sighed; and he said to him, *'Ephphatha,'* that is, 'Be opened.' ³⁵ And his ears were opened, and at once the impediment of his tongue was loosened and he spoke clearly. ³⁶ And Jesus ordered them to tell no one about it, but the more he insisted, the more widely they proclaimed it. ³⁷ Their admiration was unbounded, and they said, 'Everything he does is good, he makes the deaf hear and the dumb speak.'

Second miracle of the loaves

8 And now once again a great crowd had gathered, and they had nothing to eat. So he called his disciples to him and said to them, ² 'I feel sorry for all these people; they have been with me for three days now and have nothing to eat. ³ If I send them off home hungry they will collapse on the way; some have come a great distance.' ⁴ His disciples replied, 'Where could anyone get these people enough bread to eat in a deserted place?' ⁵ He asked them, 'How many loaves have you?' And they said to him, 'Seven.' ⁶ Then he instructed the crowd to sit down on the ground, and he took

the seven loaves, and after giving thanks he broke them and began handing them to his disciples to distribute; and they distributed them among the crowd. ⁷They had a few small fishes as well, and over these he said a blessing and ordered them to be distributed too. ⁸They ate as much as they wanted, and they collected seven basketfuls of the scraps left over. ⁹Now there had been about four thousand people. He sent them away ¹⁰and at once, getting into the boat with his disciples, went to the region of Dalmanutha.

The Pharisees ask for a sign from heaven

¹¹The Pharisees came up and started a discussion with him; they demanded of him a sign from heaven, to put him to the test. ¹²And with a profound sigh he said, 'Why does this generation demand a sign? In truth I tell you, no sign shall be given to this generation.' ¹³And, leaving them again, he re-embarked and went away to the other side.

The yeast of the Pharisees and of Herod

¹⁴The disciples had forgotten to take any bread and they had only one loaf with them in the boat. ¹⁵Then he gave them this warning, 'Keep your eyes open; look out for the yeast of the Pharisees and the yeast of Herod.' ¹⁶And they said to one another, 'It is because we have no bread.' ¹⁷And Jesus knew it, and he said to them, 'Why are you talking about having no bread? Do you still not understand, still not realise? Are your minds closed? ¹⁸Have you *eyes and do not see, ears and do not hear?ª* Or do you not remember? ¹⁹When I broke the five loaves for the five thousand, how many baskets full of scraps did you collect?' They answered, 'Twelve.' ²⁰'And when I broke the seven loaves for the four thousand, how many baskets full of scraps did you collect?' And they answered, 'Seven.' ²¹Then he said to them, 'Do you still not realise?'

Cure of a blind man at Bethsaida

²²They came to Bethsaida, and some people brought to him a blind man whom they begged him to touch. ²³He took the blind man by the hand and led him outside the village. Then, putting spittle on his eyes and laying his hands on him, he asked, 'Can you see anything?' ²⁴The man, who was beginning to see, replied, 'I can see people; they look like trees as they walk around.' ²⁵Then he laid his hands on the man's eyes again and he saw clearly; he was cured, and he could see everything plainly and distinctly. ²⁶And Jesus sent him home, saying, 'Do not even go into the village.'

Peter's profession of faith

²⁷Jesus and his disciples left for the villages round Caesarea Philippi. On the way he put this question to his disciples, 'Who do people say I am?' ²⁸And they told him, 'John the Baptist, others Elijah, others again, one of the prophets.' ²⁹'But you,' he asked them, 'who do you say I am?' Peter spoke up and said to him, 'You are the Christ.' ³⁰And he gave them strict orders not to tell anyone about him.

First prophecy of the Passion

³¹Then he began to teach them that the Son of man was destined to suffer grievously, and to be rejected by the elders and the chief priests and the scribes, and to be put to death, and after three days to rise again; ³²and he said all this quite openly. Then, taking him aside, Peter tried to rebuke him. ³³But, turning and seeing his disciples, he rebuked Peter and said to him, 'Get behind me, Satan! You are thinking not as God thinks, but as human beings do.'

The condition of following Christ

³⁴He called the people and his disciples to him and said, 'If anyone wants to be a follower of mine, let him renounce himself and take up his cross and follow me. ³⁵Anyone who wants to save his life will lose it; but anyone who loses his life for my sake, and for the sake of the gospel, will save it. ³⁶What gain, then, is it for anyone to win the whole world and forfeit his

8a Jr 5:21; Ezk 12:2.

life? 37 And indeed what can anyone offer in exchange for his life? 38 For if anyone in this sinful and adulterous generation is ashamed of me and of my words, the Son of man will also be ashamed of him when he comes in the glory of his Father with the holy angels.'

9 And he said to them, 'In truth I tell you, there are some standing here who will not taste death before they see the kingdom of God come with power.'

The Transfiguration

2 Six days later, Jesus took with him Peter and James and John and led them up a high mountain on their own by themselves. There in their presence he was transfigured: 3 his clothes became brilliantly white, whiter than any earthly bleacher could make them. 4 Elijah appeared to them with Moses; and they were talking to Jesus. 5 Then Peter spoke to Jesus, 'Rabbi,' he said, 'it is wonderful for us to be here; so let us make three shelters, one for you, one for Moses and one for Elijah.' 6 He did not know what to say; they were so frightened. 7 And a cloud came, covering them in shadow; and from the cloud there came a voice, 'This is my Son, the Beloved. Listen to him.' 8 Then suddenly, when they looked round, they saw no one with them any more but only Jesus.

The question about Elijah

9 As they were coming down from the mountain he warned them to tell no one what they had seen, until after the Son of man had risen from the dead. 10 They observed the warning faithfully, though among themselves they discussed what 'rising from the dead' could mean. 11 And they put this question to him, 'Why do the scribes say that Elijah must come first?' 12 He said to them, 'Elijah is indeed first coming to set everything right again; yet how is it that the scriptures say about the Son of man that he must suffer grievously and be treated with contempt? 13 But I tell you that Elijah has come and they have treated him as they pleased, just as the scriptures say about him.'

The epileptic demoniac

14 As they were rejoining the disciples they saw a large crowd round them and some scribes arguing with them. 15 At once, when they saw him, the whole crowd were struck with amazement and ran to greet him. 16 And he asked them, 'What are you arguing about with them?' 17 A man answered him from the crowd, 'Master, I have brought my son to you; there is a spirit of dumbness in him, 18 and when it takes hold of him it throws him to the ground, and he foams at the mouth and grinds his teeth and goes rigid. And I asked your disciples to drive it out and they were unable to.' 19 In reply he said to them, 'Faithless generation, how much longer must I be among you? How much longer must I put up with you? Bring him to me.' 20 They brought the boy to him, and at once the spirit of dumbness threw the boy into convulsions, and he fell to the ground and lay writhing there, foaming at the mouth. 21 Jesus asked the father, 'How long has this been happening to him?' 'From childhood,' he said, 22 'and it has often thrown him into fire and into water, in order to destroy him. 23 But if you can do anything, have pity on us and help us.' 24 'If you can?' retorted Jesus. 'Everything is possible for one who has faith.' At once the father of the boy cried out, 'I have faith. Help my lack of faith!' 25 And when Jesus saw that a crowd was gathering, he rebuked the unclean spirit. 'Deaf and dumb spirit,' he said, 'I command you: come out of him and never enter him again.' 26 Then it threw the boy into violent convulsions and came out shouting, and the boy lay there so like a corpse that most of them said, 'He is dead.' 27 But Jesus took him by the hand and helped him up, and he was able to stand. 28 When he had gone indoors, his disciples asked him when they were by themselves, 'Why were we unable to drive it out?' 29 He answered, 'This is the kind that can be driven out only by prayer.'

123 READ MARK 9:14–29.

I command you: come out of him and never enter him again.—MARK 9:25

CROSSING THE DEVIL

By faith in Christ and the power of his Cross, St. Mary Magdalen dei Pazzi freed a girl from the power of the devil:

Catharine, daughter of Carlo Spini, a noble Florentine maiden who was possessed by a wicked spirit, went one day in 1588 with her mother to visit St. Mary Magdalen dei Pazzi, her relative. As the three were visiting at the grate of the parlor, the saint was raised into ecstasy. At the sight of that the devil began greatly to torment the girl, throwing her to the floor, making her throat swell, and causing her to roar and scream with frightful contortions. Moved by tender compassion for the girl, Magdalen sent to the church for her father confessor. As soon as he came to the parlor she begged him to command the evil spirit to depart immediately from the young woman. But the priest, who trusted more in the holiness of St. Mary Magdalen than in himself, said: "I order you under holy obedience that you command him to leave yourself."

Then the saint . . . full of confidence in God said to the spirit: "I command you on the part of God that you depart from this body." Magdalen made the sign of the Cross on the possessed girl, and she was immediately set free and at rest from all trouble, as if she had never suffered it. And never more in her life was she molested by that spirit.　　　　　ST. MARY MAGDALEN DEI PAZZI, 1566–1607

YOU WILL FIND THE NEXT READING AT MARK 10.

Second prophecy of the Passion

30 After leaving that place they made their way through Galilee; and he did not want anyone to know, 31 because he was instructing his disciples; he was telling them, 'The Son of man will be delivered into the power of men; they will put him to death; and three days after he has been put to death he will rise again.' 32 But they did not understand what he said and were afraid to ask him.

Who is the greatest?

33 They came to Capernaum, and when he got into the house he asked them, 'What were you arguing about on the road?' 34 They said nothing, because on the road they had been arguing which of them was the greatest. 35 So he sat down, called the Twelve to him and said, 'If anyone wants to be first, he must make himself last of all and servant of all.' 36 He then took a little child whom he set among them and embraced, and he said to them, 37 'Anyone who welcomes a little child such as this in my name, welcomes me; and anyone who welcomes me, welcomes not me but the one who sent me.'

On using the name of Jesus

38 John said to him, 'Master, we saw someone who is not one of us driving out devils in your name, and because he was not one of us we tried to stop him.' 39 But Jesus said, 'You must not stop him; no one who works a miracle in my name could soon afterwards speak evil of me. 40 Anyone who is not against us is for us.

Generosity shown to Christ's disciples

⁴¹'If anyone gives you a cup of water to drink because you belong to Christ, then in truth I tell you, he will most certainly not lose his reward.

On leading others astray

⁴²'But anyone who is the downfall of one of these little ones who have faith, would be better thrown into the sea with a great millstone hung round his neck. ⁴³And if your hand should be your downfall, cut it off; it is better for you to enter into life crippled, than to have two hands and go to hell, into the fire that can never be put out.[44]ᵃ ⁴⁵And if your foot should be your downfall, cut it off; it is better for you to enter into life lame, than to have two feet and be thrown into hell.[46]ᵇ ⁴⁷And if your eye should be your downfall, tear it out; it is better for you to enter into the kingdom of God with one eye, than to have two eyes and be thrown into hell ⁴⁸where *their worm will never die nor their fire be put out.*ᶜ ⁴⁹For everyone will be salted with fire. ⁵⁰Salt is a good thing, but if salt has become insipid, how can you make it salty again? Have salt in yourselves and be at peace with one another.'

The question about divorce

10After leaving there, he came into the territory of Judaea and Transjordan. And again crowds gathered round him, and again he taught them, as his custom was. ²Some Pharisees approached him and asked, 'Is it lawful for a man to divorce his wife?' They were putting him to the test. ³He answered them, 'What did Moses command you?' ⁴They replied, 'Moses allowed us to draw up a writ of dismissal in cases of divorce.'ᵃ ⁵Then Jesus said to them, 'It was because you were so hard hearted that he wrote this commandment for you. ⁶But from the beginning of creation *he made them male and female.* ⁷This is why a man leaves his father and mother,* ⁸and the two become one flesh.*ᵇ They are no longer two, therefore, but one flesh. ⁹So

then, what God has united, human beings must not divide.' ¹⁰Back in the house the disciples questioned him again about this, ¹¹and he said to them, 'Whoever divorces his wife and marries another is guilty of adultery against her. ¹²And if a woman divorces her husband and marries another she is guilty of adultery too.'

Jesus and the children

¹³People were bringing little children to him, for him to touch them. The disciples scolded them, ¹⁴but when Jesus saw this he was indignant and said to them, 'Let the little children come to me; do not stop them; for it is to such as these that the kingdom of God belongs. ¹⁵In truth I tell you, anyone who does not welcome the kingdom of God like a little child will never enter it.' ¹⁶Then he embraced them, laid his hands on them and gave them his blessing.

The rich young man

¹⁷He was setting out on a journey when a man ran up, knelt before him and put this question to him, 'Good master, what must I do to inherit eternal life?' ¹⁸Jesus said to him, 'Why do you call me good? No one is good but God alone. ¹⁹You know the commandments: *You shall not kill; You shall not commit adultery; You shall not steal; You shall not give false witness; You shall not defraud; Honour your father and mother.'*ᶜ ²⁰And he said to him, 'Master, I have kept all these since my earliest days.' ²¹Jesus looked steadily at him and he was filled with love for him, and he said, 'You need to do one thing more. Go and sell what you own and give the money to the poor, and you will have treasure in heaven; then come, follow me.' ²²But his face fell at these words and he went away sad, for he was a man of great wealth.

9a Omitting, with the best MSS, vv. 44 and 46 (Vulg.), as repetitions of v. 48.

9b See 9a above.

9c Is 66:24. The word for hell is 'Gehenna', the rubbish-dump of Jerusalem, with its perpetual fires.

10a Dt 24:1.   10b Gn 1:27; 2:24.   10c Ex 20:12–16.

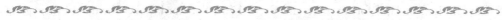

124 READ MARK 10:23–31.

There is no one who has left . . . mother, father . . . for my sake and for the sake of the gospel who will not receive a hundred times as much.—MARK 10:29–30

THE COST OF FOLLOWING CHRIST

Seventeen-year-old St. John Berchmans wrote the following letter to tell his parents of his decision to follow Christ and to join the Jesuits:

For four months now God has been knocking on the door of my heart. . . . I have noticed that during my studies and my relaxation . . . the only thought that kept coming to my mind was to wonder what sort of life I ought to adopt. So after many communions and good works I decided in the end to make a vow to serve God in religious life, provided he helps me with his grace.

I know that friends and parents are always upset by the departure of those they love. But I look at it differently. Supposing that my father and mother were here on the one side, together with my sister and other relatives, and on the other our God and Lord with his, and I hope my, Blessed Mother. And suppose my parents said: "Dear son, we beg you not to leave us; we ask this in return for the labors and cares we have endured for your sake. . . ." And suppose Jesus said: "Follow me. I was born for your sake, scourged for you, crowned with thorns and crucified for you. See the five sacred wounds I suffered for you. Have you forgotten that I have fed your soul with my Body and given it my sacred Blood to drink? Are you not ashamed of your lack of gratitude to me?"

Dear Father and Mother, whenever I think of this my heart is on fire, and I would wish if I could to enter religious life on the spot. My mind and heart have no peace until they find their beloved. I have therefore most willingly decided to offer myself to Christ Jesus and fight his wars in his Society. My only hope is that you will not show yourselves so unreasonable as to set your minds against him. . . .

I ask the Lord to grant me perseverance in my intention . . . , and at the end to grant eternal life to you and to me. ST. JOHN BERCHMANS, 1599–1621

YOU WILL FIND THE NEXT READING AT MARK 11.

The danger of riches

23 Jesus looked round and said to his disciples, 'How hard it is for those who have riches to enter the kingdom of God!' 24 The disciples were astounded by these words, but Jesus insisted, 'My children,' he said to them, 'how hard it is to enter the kingdom of God! 25 It is easier for a camel to pass through the eye of a needle than for someone rich to enter the kingdom of God.' 26 They were more astonished than ever, saying to one another, 'In that case, who can be saved?' 27 Jesus gazed at them and said, 'By human resources it is impossible, but not for God: because for God everything is possible.'

The reward of renunciation

28 Peter took this up. 'Look,' he said to him, 'we have left everything and followed you.' 29 Jesus said, 'In truth I tell you, there is no one who has left house, brothers, sisters, mother,

father, children or land for my sake and for the sake of the gospel ³⁰ who will not receive a hundred times as much, houses, brothers, sisters, mothers, children and land—and persecutions too—now in this present time and, in the world to come, eternal life. ³¹ Many who are first will be last, and the last, first.'

Third prophecy of the Passion

³² They were on the road, going up to Jerusalem; Jesus was walking on ahead of them; they were in a daze, and those who followed were apprehensive. Once more taking the Twelve aside he began to tell them what was going to happen to him, ³³ 'Now we are going up to Jerusalem, and the Son of man is about to be handed over to the chief priests and the scribes. They will condemn him to death and will hand him over to the gentiles, ³⁴ who will mock him and spit at him and scourge him and put him to death; and after three days he will rise again.'

The sons of Zebedee make their request

³⁵ James and John, the sons of Zebedee, approached him. 'Master,' they said to him, 'We want you to do us a favour.' ³⁶ He said to them, 'What is it you want me to do for you?' ³⁷ They said to him, 'Allow us to sit one at your right hand and the other at your left in your glory.' ³⁸ But Jesus said to them, 'You do not know what you are asking. Can you drink the cup that I shall drink, or be baptised with the baptism with which I shall be baptised?' ³⁹ They replied, 'We can.' Jesus said to them, 'The cup that I shall drink you shall drink, and with the baptism with which I shall be baptised you shall be baptised, ⁴⁰ but as for seats at my right hand or my left, these are not mine to grant; they belong to those to whom they have been allotted.'

Leadership with service

⁴¹ When the other ten heard this they began to feel indignant with James and John, ⁴² so Jesus called them to him and said to them, 'You know that among the gentiles those they call

their rulers lord it over them, and their great men make their authority felt. ⁴³ Among you this is not to happen. No; anyone who wants to become great among you must be your servant, ⁴⁴ and anyone who wants to be first among you must be slave to all. ⁴⁵ For the Son of man himself came not to be served but to serve, and to give his life as a ransom for many.'

The blind man of Jericho

⁴⁶ They reached Jericho; and as he left Jericho with his disciples and a great crowd, Bartimaeus—that is, the son of Timaeus—a blind beggar, was sitting at the side of the road. ⁴⁷ When he heard that it was Jesus of Nazareth, he began to shout and cry out, 'Son of David, Jesus, have pity on me.' ⁴⁸ And many of them scolded him and told him to keep quiet, but he only shouted all the louder, 'Son of David, have pity on me.' ⁴⁹ Jesus stopped and said, 'Call him here.' So they called the blind man over. 'Courage,' they said, 'get up; he is calling you.' ⁵⁰ So throwing off his cloak, he jumped up and went to Jesus. ⁵¹ Then Jesus spoke, 'What do you want me to do for you?' The blind man said to him, 'Rabbuni, let me see again.' ⁵² Jesus said to him, 'Go; your faith has saved you.' And at once his sight returned and he followed him along the road.

The Messiah enters Jerusalem

11 When they were approaching Jerusalem, at Bethphage and Bethany, close by the Mount of Olives, he sent two of his disciples ² and said to them, 'Go to the village facing you, and as you enter it you will at once find a tethered colt that no one has yet ridden. Untie it and bring it here. ³ If anyone says to you, "What are you doing?" say, "The Master needs it and will send it back here at once." ' ⁴ They went off and found a colt tethered near a door in the open street. As they untied it, ⁵ some men standing there said, 'What are you doing, untying that colt?' ⁶ They gave the answer Jesus had told them, and the men let them go. ⁷ Then they took the colt to Jesus and threw their cloaks on its back, and he

125 READ MARK 11:1–11.

Those who followed were all shouting, "Hosanna! Blessed is he who is coming in the name of the Lord!"—MARK 11:9

THE DEVIL ENTRAPPED

On Passion Sunday, St. Leo the Great preached this sermon on Christ's royal entry into Jerusalem and the Cross:

Dearly beloved brethren, the jubilant and triumphal day that ushers in the commemoration of the Lord's Passion is come. That day for which we have longed so much, and for whose yearly coming the whole world may well look. Shouts of spiritual exaltation are ringing, and prevent us from keeping silent. . . .

Among all the works of God that frustrate and weary the gaze of humanity's wonder, what at once so ravishes and so exceeds the power of our mind's eye as do the sufferings of the Savior? In order to loose us from the bonds by which we had been bound by the first death-dealing transgression, he brought the power of the divine majesty against the rage of the devil. And he met him with the weakness of our lowly nature.

If our proud and cruel enemy had been able to know the counsel of God's mercy, he would rather have tried to soften the minds of the Jewish leaders into gentleness than to have inflamed them with unrighteous hatred. So he lost the service of his slaves by pursuing for his debtor One that owed him nothing. His own hate dug a pitfall for him. He brought upon the Son of God that death that has become life to all humankind. He shed that innocent Blood that has reconciled the world to God and has become at once the price of our redemption and the cup of our salvation. . . .

The Lord let fall on himself the hands of bloody men. But while they were bent only on their own sin, they were servants ministering to the Redeemer's work. And such was his tenderness even for his murderers that his prayer to his Father from the Cross . . . was not that he might be avenged, but that they might be forgiven. ST. LEO THE GREAT, d. 461

YOU WILL FIND THE NEXT READING AT MARK 12.

mounted it. ⁸Many people spread their cloaks on the road, and others greenery which they had cut in the fields. ⁹And those who went in front and those who followed were all shouting, '*Hosanna! Blessed is he who is coming in the name of the Lord!ᵃ* ¹⁰Blessed is the coming kingdom of David our father!ᵇ *Hosanna* in the highest heavens!' ¹¹He entered Jerusalem and went into the Temple; and when he had sur-

veyed it all, as it was late by now, he went out to Bethany with the Twelve.

The barren fig tree

¹²Next day as they were leaving Bethany, he felt hungry. ¹³Seeing a fig tree in leaf some distance away, he went to see if he could find any

11a Ps 118:25–26. *11b* 2 S 7:16.

fruit on it, but when he came up to it he found nothing but leaves; for it was not the season for figs. ¹⁴And he addressed the fig tree, 'May no one ever eat fruit from you again.' And his disciples heard him say this.

The expulsion of the dealers from the Temple

¹⁵So they reached Jerusalem and he went into the Temple and began driving out the men selling and buying there; he upset the tables of the money changers and the seats of the dove sellers. ¹⁶Nor would he allow anyone to carry anything through the Temple. ¹⁷And he taught them and said, 'Does not scripture say: *My house will be called a house of prayer for all peoples*? But you have turned it into *a bandits' den.*'ᶜ ¹⁸This came to the ears of the chief priests and the scribes, and they tried to find some way of doing away with him; they were afraid of him because the people were carried away by his teaching. ¹⁹And when evening came he went out of the city.

The fig tree withered; faith and prayer

²⁰Next morning, as they passed by, they saw the fig tree withered to the roots. ²¹Peter remembered. 'Look, Rabbi,' he said to Jesus, 'the fig tree that you cursed has withered away.' ²²Jesus answered, 'Have faith in God. ²³In truth I tell you, if anyone says to this mountain, "Be pulled up and thrown into the sea," with no doubt in his heart, but believing that what he says will happen, it will be done for him. ²⁴I tell you, therefore, everything you ask and pray for, believe that you have it already, and it will be yours. ²⁵And when you stand in prayer, forgive whatever you have against anybody, so that your Father in heaven may forgive your failings too.'⁽²⁶⁾ᵈ

The authority of Jesus is questioned

²⁷They came to Jerusalem again, and as Jesus was walking in the Temple, the chief priests and the scribes and the elders came to him, ²⁸and they said to him, 'What authority have you for acting like this? Or who gave you authority to act like this?' ²⁹Jesus said to them,

'And I will ask you a question, just one; answer me and I will tell you my authority for acting like this. ³⁰John's baptism, what was its origin, heavenly or human? Answer me that.' ³¹And they argued this way among themselves, 'If we say heavenly, he will say, "Then why did you refuse to believe him?" ³²But dare we say human?'—they had the people to fear, for everyone held that John had been a real prophet. ³³So their reply to Jesus was, 'We do not know.' And Jesus said to them, 'Nor will I tell you my authority for acting like this.'

Parable of the wicked tenants

12 He went on to speak to them in parables, 'A man planted a vineyard; he fenced it round, dug out a trough for the winepress and built a tower; then he leased it to tenants and went abroad. ²When the time came, he sent a servant to the tenants to collect from them his share of the produce of the vineyard. ³But they seized the man, thrashed him and sent him away empty handed. ⁴Next he sent another servant to them; him they beat about the head and treated shamefully. ⁵And he sent another and him they killed; then a number of others, and they thrashed some and killed the rest. ⁶He had still someone left: his beloved son. He sent him to them last of all, thinking, "They will respect my son." ⁷But those tenants said to each other, "This is the heir. Come on, let us kill him, and the inheritance will be ours." ⁸So they seized him and killed him and threw him out of the vineyard. ⁹Now what will the owner of the vineyard do? He will come and make an end of the tenants and give the vineyard to others. ¹⁰Have you not read this text of scripture:

The stone which the builders rejected
has become the cornerstone;
¹¹ *this is the Lord's doing,*
and we marvel at it?' ᵃ

11c Is 56:7 followed by Jr 7:11.

11d Some authorities add a v. borrowed from Mt 6:15.

12a Ps 118:22–23.

126 READ MARK 12:13–17.

Pay Caesar what belongs to Caesar—and God what belongs to God.—MARK 12:17

GIVING OURSELVES TO GOD

Jesus had often put the Pharisees to confusion, and they could not find any ground to charge him on anything he had said or done. His words and works are necessarily faultless, but still from spite they determined to find some reason to accuse him. He was calling all to turn away from the corruptions of the world and the superstitious devotion invented by men and to fix their hopes on the kingdom of heaven. Therefore, they arranged a question calculated to entrap him into an offense against the civil government, asking "Is it permissible to pay taxes to Caesar or not?"

But Jesus perceived their wickedness, for truly there is nothing hidden in the heart of man that God does not see. And "he said to them, 'Why are you putting me to the test? Hand me a denarius and let me see it.' They handed him one and he said to them, 'Whose portrait is this? Whose title?' They said to him, 'Caesar's.' Jesus said to them, 'Pay Caesar what belongs to Caesar—and God what belongs to God.' " This is a wonderful answer that perfectly prescribes the fulfillment of the divine law. He strikes such a beautiful balance between disdaining the things of the world and the offense of injuring Caesar, that by commanding them to pay Caesar what is Caesar's, he shows the perfect freedom of minds, however devoted to God, to discharge all human cares and duties.

If we have nothing that is Caesar's then we have nothing that we are bound to pay to him. . . . But all of us are always bound to pay to God the things that are God's, that is, our body, soul, and will. These are things we hold from him and of which he is the author and maker. It is therefore simply just that they, who acknowledge that they owe to him their being and creation, should give to him all that they are. ST. HILARY OF POITIERS, 315?–368?

YOU WILL FIND THE NEXT READING AT MARK 14:22.

12 And they would have liked to arrest him, because they realised that the parable was aimed at them, but they were afraid of the crowds. So they left him alone and went away.

On tribute to Caesar

13 Next they sent to him some Pharisees and some Herodians to catch him out in what he said. 14 These came and said to him, 'Master, we know that you are an honest man, that you are not afraid of anyone, because human rank means nothing to you, and that you teach the way of God in all honesty. Is it permissible to pay taxes to Caesar or not? Should we pay or not?' 15 Recognising their hypocrisy he said to them, 'Why are you putting me to the test? Hand me a denarius and let me see it.' 16 They handed him one and he said to them, 'Whose portrait is this? Whose title?' They said to him, 'Caesar's.' 17 Jesus said to them, 'Pay Caesar what belongs to Caesar—and God what belongs to God.' And they were amazed at him.

The resurrection of the dead

18 Then some Sadducees—who deny that there is a resurrection—came to him and they put this question to him, 19 'Master, Moses pre-

scribed for us that if a man's brother dies leaving a wife but no child, the man must marry the widow to raise up children for his brother. ²⁰ Now there were seven brothers; the first married a wife and then died leaving no children. ²¹ The second married the widow, and he too died leaving no children; with the third it was the same, ²² and none of the seven left any children. Last of all the woman herself died. ²³ Now at the resurrection, when they rise again, whose wife will she be, since she had been married to all seven?'

²⁴ Jesus said to them, 'Surely the reason why you are wrong is that you understand neither the scriptures nor the power of God. ²⁵ For when they rise from the dead, men and women do not marry; no, they are like the angels in heaven. ²⁶ Now about the dead rising again, have you never read in the Book of Moses, in the passage about the bush, how God spoke to him and said: *I am the God of Abraham, the God of Isaac and the God of Jacob?* ᵇ ²⁷ He is God, not of the dead, but of the living. You are very much mistaken.'

The greatest commandment of all

²⁸ One of the scribes who had listened to them debating appreciated that Jesus had given a good answer and put a further question to him, 'Which is the first of all the commandments?' ²⁹ Jesus replied, 'This is the first: ᶜ *Listen, Israel, the Lord our God is the one, only Lord,* ³⁰ *and you must love the Lord your God with all your heart, with all your soul,* with all your mind *and with all your strength.* ³¹ The second is this: ᵈ *You must love your neighbour as yourself.* There is no commandment greater than these.' ³² The scribe said to him, 'Well spoken, Master; what you have said is true, that *he is one and there is no other.* ³³ To *love him with all your heart, with all your understanding and strength,* and to *love your neighbour as yourself,* this is far more important than any burnt offering or sacrifice.' ³⁴ Jesus, seeing how wisely he had spoken, said, 'You are not far from the kingdom of God.' And after that no one dared to question him any more.

Jesus not only son but also Lord of David

³⁵ While teaching in the Temple, Jesus said, 'How can the scribes maintain that the Christ is the son of David? ³⁶ David himself, moved by the Holy Spirit, said:

> *The Lord declared to my Lord,*
> *take your seat at my right hand*
> *till I have made your enemies*
> *your footstool.* ᵉ

³⁷ David himself calls him Lord; in what way then can he be his son?' And the great crowd listened to him with delight.

The scribes condemned by Jesus

³⁸ In his teaching he said, 'Beware of the scribes who like to walk about in long robes, to be greeted respectfully in the market squares, ³⁹ to take the front seats in the synagogues and the places of honour at banquets; ⁴⁰ these are the men who devour the property of widows and for show offer long prayers. The more severe will be the sentence they receive.'

The widow's mite

⁴¹ He sat down opposite the treasury and watched the people putting money into the treasury, and many of the rich put in a great deal. ⁴² A poor widow came and put in two small coins, the equivalent of a penny. ⁴³ Then he called his disciples and said to them, 'In truth I tell you, this poor widow has put more in than all who have contributed to the treasury; ⁴⁴ for they have all put in money they could spare, but she in her poverty has put in everything she possessed, all she had to live on.'

The eschatological discourse: Introduction ᵃ

13 As he was leaving the Temple one of his disciples said to him, 'Master, look at the

12b Ex 3:6.   12c Dt 6:4–5.
12d Lv 19:18.   12e Ps 110:1.

13a By contrast with Mt 24–25, Mk's discourse concerns only the destruction of Jerusalem as an act of God delivering his people.

size of those stones! Look at the size of those buildings!' ²And Jesus said to him, 'You see these great buildings? Not a single stone will be left on another; everything will be pulled down.'

³And while he was sitting on the Mount of Olives, facing the Temple, Peter, James, John and Andrew questioned him when they were by themselves, ⁴'Tell us, when is this going to happen, and what sign will there be that it is all about to take place?'

The beginning of sorrows

⁵Then Jesus began to tell them, 'Take care that no one deceives you. ⁶Many will come using my name and saying, "I am he," and they will deceive many. ⁷When you hear of wars and rumours of wars, do not be alarmed; this is something that must happen, but the end will not be yet. ⁸For nation will fight against nation, and kingdom against kingdom. There will be earthquakes in various places; there will be famines. This is the beginning of the birth-pangs.

⁹'Be on your guard: you will be handed over to sanhedrins; you will be beaten in synagogues; and you will be brought before governors and kings for my sake, as evidence to them, ¹⁰since the gospel must first be proclaimed to all nations.

¹¹'And when you are taken to be handed over, do not worry beforehand about what to say; no, say whatever is given to you when the time comes, because it is not you who will be speaking; it is the Holy Spirit. ¹²Brother will betray brother to death, and a father his child; children will come forward against their parents and have them put to death. ¹³You will be universally hated on account of my name; but anyone who stands firm to the end will be saved.

The great tribulation of Jerusalem

¹⁴'When you see *the appalling abomination*ᵇ set up where it ought not to be (let the reader understand), then those in Judaea must escape to the mountains; ¹⁵if a man is on the housetop,

he must not come down or go inside to collect anything from his house; ¹⁶if a man is in the fields, he must not turn back to fetch his cloak. ¹⁷Alas for those with child, or with babies at the breast, when those days come! ¹⁸Pray that this may not be in winter. ¹⁹For in those days there will be *great distress, unparalleled since*ᶜ God created the world, and such as will never be again. ²⁰And if the Lord had not shortened that time, no human being would have survived; but he did shorten the time, for the sake of the elect whom he chose.

²¹'And if anyone says to you then, "Look, here is the Christ" or, "Look, he is there," do not believe it; ²²for false Christs and false prophets will arise and produce signs and portents to deceive the elect, if that were possible. ²³You, therefore, must be on your guard. I have given you full warning.

The coming of the Son of man

²⁴'But in those days, after that time of distress, the sun will be darkened, the moon will not give its light, ²⁵the stars will come falling out of the sky and the powers in the heavens will be shaken. ²⁶And then they will see the *Son of man coming in the clouds* with great power and glory.ᵈ ²⁷And then he will send the angels to gather his elect from the four winds, from the ends of the world to the ends of the sky.ᵉ

The time of this coming

²⁸'Take the fig tree as a parable: as soon as its twigs grow supple and its leaves come out, you know that summer is near. ²⁹So with you when you see these things happening: know that he is near, right at the gates. ³⁰In truth I tell you, before this generation has passed away all these things will have taken place. ³¹Sky and earth will pass away, but my words will not pass away.

³²'But as for that day or hour, nobody

13b Dn 9:27; 11:31; 12:11. 13c Dn 12:1.
13d Dn 7:13–14.
13e Dt 30:4.

knows it, neither the angels in heaven, nor the Son; no one but the Father.

Be on the alert

33'Be on your guard, stay awake, because you never know when the time will come. 34It is like a man travelling abroad: he has gone from his home, and left his servants in charge, each with his own work to do; and he has told the doorkeeper to stay awake. 35So stay awake, because you do not know when the master of the house is coming, evening, midnight, cock-crow or dawn; 36if he comes unexpectedly, he must not find you asleep. 37And what I am saying to you I say to all: Stay awake!'

The conspiracy against Jesus

14 It was two days before the Passover and the feast of Unleavened Bread, and the chief priests and the scribes were looking for a way to arrest Jesus by some trick and have him put to death. 2For they said, 'It must not be during the festivities, or there will be a disturbance among the people.'

The anointing at Bethany

3He was at Bethany in the house of Simon, a man who had suffered from a virulent skin-disease; he was at table when a woman came in with an alabaster jar of very costly ointment, pure nard. She broke the jar and poured the ointment on his head. 4Some who were there said to one another indignantly, 'Why this waste of ointment? 5Ointment like this could have been sold for over three hundred denarii and the money given to the poor'; and they were angry with her. 6But Jesus said, 'Leave her alone. Why are you upsetting her? What she has done for me is a good work. 7You have the poor with you always, and you can be kind to them whenever you wish, but you will not always have me. 8She has done what she could: she has anointed my body beforehand for its burial. 9In truth I tell you, wherever throughout all the world the gospel is proclaimed, what she has done will be told as well, in remembrance of her.'

Judas betrays Jesus

10Judas Iscariot, one of the Twelve, approached the chief priests with an offer to hand Jesus over to them. 11They were delighted to hear it, and promised to give him money; and he began to look for a way of betraying him when the opportunity should occur.

Preparations for the Passover supper

12On the first day of Unleavened Bread, when the Passover lamb was sacrificed, his disciples said to him, 'Where do you want us to go and make the preparations for you to eat the Passover?' 13So he sent two of his disciples, saying to them, 'Go into the city and you will meet a man carrying a pitcher of water. Follow him, 14and say to the owner of the house which he enters, "The Master says: Where is the room for me to eat the Passover with my disciples?" 15He will show you a large upper room furnished with couches, all prepared. Make the preparations for us there.' 16The disciples set out and went to the city and found everything as he had told them, and prepared the Passover.

The treachery of Judas foretold

17When evening came he arrived with the Twelve. 18And while they were at table eating, Jesus said, 'In truth I tell you, one of you is about to betray me, one of you *eating with me.*'[a] 19They were distressed and said to him, one after another, 'Not me, surely?' 20He said to them, 'It is one of the Twelve, one who is dipping into the same dish with me. 21Yes, the Son of man is going to his fate, as the scriptures say he will, but alas for that man by whom the Son of man is betrayed! Better for that man if he had never been born.'

The institution of the Eucharist

22And as they were eating he took bread, and when he had said the blessing he broke it and gave it to them. 'Take it,' he said, 'this is my

14a Ps 41:9.

127 READ MARK 14:22–25.

And he said to them, "This is my blood, the blood of the covenant, poured out for many."
—MARK 14:24

LAST SUPPER, FIRST EUCHARIST

Let old things pass away; let all be fresh and bright;
And welcome we with hearts renewed, this Feast of new delight.

Upon this hallowed eve, Christ with his brethren ate,
Obedient to the ancient Law, the Pasch before him set.

Which done,—himself entire, the true Incarnate God,
Alike on each, alike on all his sacred hands bestowed.

He gave his Flesh; he gave his Precious Blood; and said:
"Receive and drink ye all of this for your salvation shed."

Thus did the Lord appoint this sacrifice sublime,
And made his priests the ministers thorough all the bounds of time.

Farewell to types! Henceforth we feed on angel's food;
The slave—O, wonder!—eats the Flesh of his Incarnate God!

O Blessed Three in One! Visit our hearts, we pray,
And lead us on through thine own paths to thy eternal day. Amen.

ST. THOMAS AQUINAS, 1225?–1275

YOU WILL FIND THE NEXT READING AT MARK 14:32.

body.' 23 Then he took a cup, and when he had given thanks he handed it to them, and all drank from it, 24 and he said to them, 'This is my blood, the blood of the covenant, poured out for many. 25 In truth I tell you, I shall never drink wine any more until the day I drink the new wine in the kingdom of God.'

Peter's denial foretold

26 After the psalms had been sung they left for the Mount of Olives. 27 And Jesus said to them, 'You will all fall away, for the scripture says: *I shall strike the shepherd and the sheep will be scattered;*[b] 28 however, after my resurrection I shall go before you into Galilee.' 29 Peter said, 'Even if all fall away, I will not.' 30 And Jesus said to him, 'In truth I tell you, this day, this very night, before the cock crows twice, you will have disowned me three times.' 31 But he repeated still more earnestly, 'If I have to die with you, I will never disown you.' And they all said the same.

14b Zc 13:7.

128 READ MARK 14:32–42.

Stay awake and pray not to be put to the test.—MARK 14:38

WHOLEHEARTED PRAYER

We must give our hearts wholly to God if we desire to benefit from the fruits of true prayer and not to lose them completely. That our hearts are not entirely given to God is the reason we are tempted during prayer.

Pray, therefore, and pray often. The more often you pray, the more you will be enlightened and the more deeply and clearly and nobly you will perceive the supreme Good and that which is supremely good. And the more deeply and excellently you perceive it, the more you will love it, delight in it and be able to comprehend it.

Jesus Christ has given us an example of this most glorious prayer and of how we should earnestly persevere in it. He taught us by words and actions to pray in a variety of ways. He taught us by words when he said to his disciples, "Stay awake and pray not to be put to the test." Likewise in many other parts of the holy gospel you will find how he instructed us about wholehearted prayer that he indicated he cherished. And we have no excuse: the result of our prayer depends on ourselves because he said, "Ask, and it will be given to you" (Mt 7:7). He also desires that we should pray to him in order that moved and drawn to prayer by his example, we may come to love it above everything else.

The gospel says when Jesus prayed earnestly his sweat ran down upon the ground like drops of blood (see Lk 22:44). So keep this example of prayer always before your eyes and be sure to follow it closely, realizing that he prayed not for himself, but for you.

BL. ANGELA OF FOLIGNO, 1248?–1309

YOU WILL FIND THE NEXT READING AT MARK 15.

Gethsemane

32 They came to a plot of land called Gethsemane, and he said to his disciples, 'Stay here while I pray.' 33 Then he took Peter and James and John with him. 34 And he began to feel terror and anguish. And he said to them, 'My soul is sorrowful to the point of death. Wait here, and stay awake.' 35 And going on a little further he threw himself on the ground and prayed that, if it were possible, this hour might pass him by. 36 'Abba,ᶜ Father!' he said, 'For you everything is possible. Take this cup away from me. But let it be as you, not I, would have it.' 37 He came back and found them sleeping, and he said to Peter, 'Simon, are you asleep? Had you not the strength to stay awake one hour? 38 Stay awake and pray not to be put to the test. The spirit is willing enough, but human nature is weak.' 39 Again he went away and prayed, saying the same words. 40 And once more he came back and found them sleeping, their eyes were so heavy; and they could find no answer for him. 41 He came back a third time and said to them, 'You can sleep on now and have your rest. It is all over. The

14c An affectionate Aramaic word, address of child to father.

hour has come. Now the Son of man is to be betrayed into the hands of sinners. ⁴² Get up! Let us go! My betrayer is not far away.'

The arrest

⁴³ And at once, while he was still speaking, Judas, one of the Twelve, came up and with him a number of men armed with swords and clubs, sent by the chief priests and the scribes and the elders. ⁴⁴ Now the traitor had arranged a signal with them saying, 'The one I kiss, he is the man. Arrest him, and see he is well guarded when you lead him away.' ⁴⁵ So when the traitor came, he went up to Jesus at once and said, 'Rabbi!' and kissed him. ⁴⁶ The others seized him and arrested him. ⁴⁷ Then one of the bystanders drew his sword and struck out at the high priest's servant and cut off his ear.

⁴⁸ Then Jesus spoke. 'Am I a bandit,' he said, 'that you had to set out to capture me with swords and clubs? ⁴⁹ I was among you teaching in the Temple day after day and you never laid a hand on me. But this is to fulfil the scriptures.' ⁵⁰ And they all deserted him and ran away. ⁵¹ A young man followed with nothing on but a linen cloth. They caught hold of him, ⁵² but he left the cloth in their hands and ran away naked.

Jesus before the Sanhedrin

⁵³ They led Jesus off to the high priest; and all the chief priests and the elders and the scribes assembled there. ⁵⁴ Peter had followed him at a distance, right into the high priest's palace, and was sitting with the attendants warming himself at the fire.

⁵⁵ The chief priests and the whole Sanhedrin were looking for evidence against Jesus in order to have him executed. But they could not find any. ⁵⁶ Several, indeed, brought false witness against him, but their evidence was conflicting. ⁵⁷ Some stood up and submitted this false evidence against him, ⁵⁸ 'We heard him say, "I am going to destroy this Temple made by human hands, and in three days build another, not made by human hands." ' ⁵⁹ But even on this point their evidence was conflicting. ⁶⁰ The high priest then rose before the whole assembly and put this question to Jesus, 'Have you no answer to that? What is this evidence these men are bringing against you?' ⁶¹ But he was silent and made no answer at all. The high priest put a second question to him saying, 'Are you the Christ, the Son of the Blessed One?' ⁶² 'I am,' said Jesus, 'and you will see the *Son of man seated at the right hand of the Power and coming with the clouds of heaven.' ^d* ⁶³ The high priest tore his robes and said, 'What need of witnesses have we now? ⁶⁴ You heard the blasphemy. What is your finding?' Their verdict was unanimous: he deserved to die.

⁶⁵ Some of them started spitting at his face, hitting him and saying, 'Play the prophet!' And the attendants struck him too.

Peter's denials

⁶⁶ While Peter was down below in the courtyard, one of the high priest's servant-girls came up. ⁶⁷ She saw Peter warming himself there, looked closely at him and said, 'You too were with Jesus, the man from Nazareth.' ⁶⁸ But he denied it. 'I do not know, I do not understand what you are talking about,' he said. And he went out into the forecourt, and a cock crowed. ⁶⁹ The servant-girl saw him and again started telling the bystanders, 'This man is one of them.' ⁷⁰ But again he denied it. A little later the bystanders themselves said to Peter, 'You are certainly one of them! Why, you are a Galilean.' ⁷¹ But he started cursing and swearing, 'I do not know the man you speak of.' ⁷² And at once the cock crowed for the second time, and Peter recalled what Jesus had said to him, 'Before the cock crows twice, you will have disowned me three times.' And he burst into tears.

Jesus before Pilate

15 First thing in the morning, the chief priests, together with the elders and scribes and the rest of the Sanhedrin, had their

14d Dn 7:13; Ps 110:1.

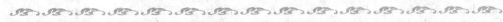

129 READ MARK 15:1–20.

Having Jesus scourged, [Pilate] handed him over to be crucified.—MARK 15:15

THE BLOOD OF CHRIST

In the following vision, Blessed Julian saw the saving power of Christ's blood:

I saw in my beholding that the body seemed to be bleeding plenteously due to the scourging. And this is how it looked: the fair skin was deeply broken into the tender flesh with the sharp beating all across the sweet body; so plenteously did the hot blood run out that there was neither skin nor even wound, but it seemed as if it were all blood. . . . I thought if it had been real and actually happening then it would have soaked the bed in blood and spilled over all around. Then I was reminded how God had made the waters of the earth so plentiful in our service to meet our bodily comfort, all for tender love that he has for us; yet he likes it better that we take his blessed blood quite naturally to wash away sin.

There is no liquid made that he prefers to give us; for it is most plenteous as it is most precious, by virtue of the blessed Godhead. It is our birthright and blissfully flows to us by virtue of his precious love. . . . Behold and see: this precious and plenteous, worthy and dear blood descends down into hell,* bursts forth her bonds, and delivers all there who belong to the court of heaven. The precious plenty of his dear and worthy blood overflows the whole earth and is ready to wash from sin all creatures of good will, both those that have been and those still to come. This same precious plenty of his dear worthy blood goes up into heaven in the blessed body of our Lord Jesus Christ; it is there within him bleeding and praying for us to the Father; and this is and shall be for as long as it is needed. . . .

BL. JULIAN OF NORWICH, 1342?–1423?

* Not the place of eternal doom but a waiting place to which Christ descended after his death.

YOU WILL FIND THE NEXT READING AT MARK 16.

plan ready. They had Jesus bound and took him away and handed him over to Pilate.

²Pilate put to him this question, 'Are you the king of the Jews?' He replied, 'It is you who say it.' ³And the chief priests brought many accusations against him. ⁴Pilate questioned him again, 'Have you no reply at all? See how many accusations they are bringing against you!' ⁵But, to Pilate's surprise, Jesus made no further reply.

⁶At festival time Pilate used to release a prisoner for them, any one they asked for. ⁷Now a man called Barabbas was then in prison with the rebels who had committed murder during the uprising. ⁸When the crowd went up and began to ask Pilate the customary favour, ⁹Pilate answered them, 'Do you want me to release for you the king of the Jews?' ¹⁰For he realised it was out of jealousy that the chief priests had handed Jesus over. ¹¹The chief priests, however, had incited the crowd to demand that he should release Barabbas for them instead. ¹²Then Pilate spoke again, 'But in that case, what am I to do with the man you call king of the Jews?' ¹³They shouted back, 'Crucify him!' ¹⁴Pilate

asked them, 'What harm has he done?' But they shouted all the louder, 'Crucify him!' ¹⁵So Pilate, anxious to placate the crowd, released Barabbas for them and, after having Jesus scourged, he handed him over to be crucified.

Jesus crowned with thorns

¹⁶The soldiers led him away to the inner part of the palace, that is, the Praetorium, and called the whole cohort together. ¹⁷They dressed him up in purple, twisted some thorns into a crown and put it on him. ¹⁸And they began saluting him, 'Hail, king of the Jews!' ¹⁹They struck his head with a reed and spat on him; and they went down on their knees to do him homage. ²⁰And when they had finished making fun of him, they took off the purple and dressed him in his own clothes.

The way of the cross

They led him out to crucify him. ²¹They enlisted a passer-by, Simon of Cyrene, father of Alexander and Rufus,ᵃ who was coming in from the country, to carry his cross. ²²They brought Jesus to the place called Golgotha, which means the place of the skull.

The crucifixion

²³They offered him wine mixed with myrrh, but he refused it. ²⁴Then they crucified him, and shared out his clothing, casting lots to decide what each should get. ²⁵It was the third hour when they crucified him. ²⁶The inscription giving the charge against him read, 'The King of the Jews'. ²⁷And they crucified two bandits with him, one on his right and one on his left.[28]ᵇ

The crucified Jesus is mocked

²⁹The passers-by jeered at him; they shook their heads and said, 'Aha! So you would destroy the Temple and rebuild it in three days! ³⁰Then save yourself; come down from the cross!' ³¹The chief priests and the scribes mocked him among themselves in the same way with the words, 'He saved others, he cannot save himself. ³²Let the Christ, the king of

Israel, come down from the cross now, for us to see it and believe.' Even those who were crucified with him taunted him.

The death of Jesus

³³When the sixth hour came there was darkness over the whole land until the ninth hour. ³⁴And at the ninth hour Jesus cried out in a loud voice, 'Eloi, eloi,ᶜ lama sabachthani?' which means, 'My God, my God, why have you forsaken me?' ³⁵When some of those who stood by heard this, they said, 'Listen, he is calling on Elijah.' ³⁶Someone ran and soaked a sponge in vinegar and, putting it on a reed, gave it to him to drink saying, 'Wait! And see if Elijah will come to take him down.' ³⁷But Jesus gave a loud cry and breathed his last. ³⁸And the veil of the Sanctuary was torn in two from top to bottom. ³⁹The centurion, who was standing in front of him, had seen how he had died, and he said, 'In truth this man was Son of God.'

The women on Calvary

⁴⁰There were some women watching from a distance. Among them were Mary of Magdala, Mary who was the mother of James the younger and Joset, and Salome. ⁴¹These used to follow him and look after him when he was in Galilee. And many other women were there who had come up to Jerusalem with him.

The burial

⁴²It was now evening, and since it was Preparation Day—that is, the day before the Sabbath— ⁴³there came Joseph of Arimathaea, a prominent member of the Council, who himself lived in the hope of seeing the kingdom of God, and he boldly went to Pilate and asked for the body of Jesus. ⁴⁴Pilate, astonished that he should have died so soon, summoned the centurion and enquired if he had been dead for some time. ⁴⁵Having been assured of this

15a cf. Rm 16:13.

15b Some authorities add a verse similar to Lk 22:37.

15c This Aramaic form cf. Ps 22:1, explains the soldiers' pun about Elijah better than Mt's Hebr form eli.

130 READ MARK 16:1–8.

You are looking for Jesus of Nazareth, who was crucified: he has risen, he is not here.

—MARK 16:6

THE ADVANTAGES OF THE RESURRECTION

The resurrection of Jesus Christ is glorious for him because through it his body has received an immortal life, incapable of suffering, which it will enjoy eternally. At the same time it procured immense glory to his Father by repairing the insults sin had offered him. The resurrection is also most advantageous to us, since it is an assurance that we too shall arise. . . .

The resurrection of Jesus is both glorious and advantageous because by it he destroyed sin. For "if we died with Christ, we believe that we shall live with him too because if we have been joined to him by dying a death like his, so we shall be by a resurrection like his" (see Rm 6:8 and 5). Therefore since Jesus Christ in rising from the dead has destroyed sin, let us so act that "sin will not reign in our mortal body" (see Rm 6:12). Let us attach this body with all its regular affections to the cross of Jesus Christ. . . .

The resurrection should also cause us to revive spiritually by making us live the life of grace. That is, we should lead a life entirely new and heavenly. That we may enter into those practices and prove, as St. Paul says, that we are risen with Christ, we must seek the things that are above, and not what is of earth (see Col 3:1–2). . . . Let us therefore discipline our members by stripping ourselves of the old man, and putting on the new (see Col 3:9). . . . Let us correct ourselves of our evil inclinations and arise from the tomb of spiritual sloth, tepidity, and dissipation. We must not only avoid sin, but all that leads to it, so that the angels may say of us as of Jesus: That soul was there, but she is no longer there—that soul was dead through sin, but now she is risen!

ST. JOHN BAPTIST DE LA SALLE, 1651–1719

YOU WILL FIND THE NEXT READING AT LUKE 1.

by the centurion, he granted the corpse to Joseph ⁴⁶who bought a shroud, took Jesus down from the cross, wrapped him in the shroud and laid him in a tomb which had been hewn out of the rock. He then rolled a stone against the entrance to the tomb. ⁴⁷Mary of Magdala and Mary the mother of Joset took note of where he was laid.

The empty tomb; the angel's message

16 When the Sabbath was over, Mary of Magdala, Mary the mother of James, and Salome, bought spices with which to go and anoint him. ²And very early in the morning on the first day of the week they went to the tomb when the sun had risen.

³They had been saying to one another, 'Who will roll away the stone for us from the entrance to the tomb?' ⁴But when they looked they saw that the stone—which was very big—had already been rolled back. ⁵On entering the tomb they saw a young man in a white robe seated on the right-hand side, and they were struck with amazement. ⁶But he said to

them, 'There is no need to be so amazed. You are looking for Jesus of Nazareth, who was crucified: he has risen, he is not here. See, here is the place where they laid him. [7] But you must go and tell his disciples and Peter, "He is going ahead of you to Galilee; that is where you will see him, just as he told you." ' [8] And the women came out and ran away from the tomb because they were frightened out of their wits; and they said nothing to anyone, for they were afraid.[a]

Appearances of the risen Christ

[9] Having risen in the morning on the first day of the week, he appeared first to Mary of Magdala from whom he had cast out seven devils. [10] She then went to those who had been his companions, and who were mourning and in tears, and told them. [11] But they did not believe her when they heard her say that he was alive and that she had seen him.

[12] After this, he showed himself under another form to two of them as they were on their way into the country. [13] These went back and told the others, who did not believe them either.

[14] Lastly, he showed himself to the Eleven themselves while they were at table. He reproached them for their incredulity and obstinacy, because they had refused to believe those who had seen him after he had risen. [15] And he said to them, 'Go out to the whole world; proclaim the gospel to all creation. [16] Whoever believes and is baptised will be saved; whoever does not believe will be condemned. [17] These are the signs that will be associated with believers: in my name they will cast out devils; they will have the gift of tongues; [18] they will pick up snakes in their hands and be unharmed should they drink deadly poison; they will lay their hands on the sick, who will recover.'

[19] And so the Lord Jesus, after he had spoken to them, was taken up into heaven; there at the right hand of God he took his place, [20] while they, going out, preached everywhere, the Lord working with them and confirming the word by the signs that accompanied it.

16a Originally Mk probably ended abruptly on this note of awe and wonder. The next 12 vv., missing in some MSS, are a summary of material gathered from other NT writings.

The Gospel According to

LUKE

Prologue

1 Seeing that many others have undertaken to draw up accounts of the events that have reached their fulfilment among us, ²as these were handed down to us by those who from the outset were eyewitnesses and ministers of the word, ³I in my turn, after carefully going over the whole story from the beginning, have decided to write an ordered account for you, Theophilus,ᵃ ⁴so that your Excellency may learn how well founded the teaching is that you have received.

The birth of John the Baptist foretold

⁵In the days of King Herod of Judaea there lived a priest called Zechariah who belonged to the Abijah section of the priesthood, and he had a wife, Elizabeth by name, who was a descendant of Aaron. ⁶Both were upright in the sight of God and impeccably carried out all the commandments and observances of the Lord. ⁷But they were childless: Elizabeth was barren and they were both advanced in years.

⁸Now it happened that it was the turn of his section to serve, and he was exercising his priestly office before God ⁹when it fell to him by lot, as the priestly custom was, to enter the Lord's sanctuary and burn incense there. ¹⁰And at the hour of incense all the people were outside, praying. ¹¹Then there appeared to him the angel of the Lord, standing on the right of the altar of incense. ¹²The sight disturbed Zechariah and he was overcome with fear. ¹³But the angel said to him, 'Zechariah, do not be afraid, for your prayer has been heard. Your wife Elizabeth is to bear you a son and you shall name him John. ¹⁴He will be your joy and delight

and many will rejoice at his birth, ¹⁵for he will be great in the sight of the Lord; he must drink no wine, no strong drink;ᵇ even from his mother's womb he will be filled with the Holy Spirit, ¹⁶and he will bring back many of the Israelites to the Lord their God. ¹⁷With the spirit and power of Elijah, he will go before him *to reconcile fathers to their children*ᶜ and the disobedient to the good sense of the upright, preparing for the Lord a people fit for him.' ¹⁸Zechariah said to the angel, '*How can I know this?*ᵈ I am an old man and my wife is getting on in years.' ¹⁹The angel replied, 'I am Gabriel, who stand in God's presence, and I have been sent to speak to you and bring you this good news. ²⁰Look! Since you did not believe my words, which will come true at their appointed time, you will be silenced and have no power of speech until this has happened.' ²¹Meanwhile the people were waiting for Zechariah and were surprised that he stayed in the sanctuary so long. ²²When he came out he could not speak to them, and they realised that he had seen a vision in the sanctuary. But he could only make signs to them and remained dumb.

²³When his time of service came to an end he returned home. ²⁴Some time later his wife Elizabeth conceived and for five months she kept to herself, saying, ²⁵'The Lord has done this for me, now that it has pleased him to take away the humiliation I suffered in public.'

The annunciation

²⁶In the sixth month the angel Gabriel was sent by God to a town in Galilee called Naza-

---

1a Theophilus (= 'God-lover') may be real or imaginary.
1b cf. Nb 6:2–3.   *1c* Ml 3:23–24.   *1d* Gn 15:8.

131 READ LUKE 1:26–38.

Look! You are to conceive in your womb and bear a son, and you must name him Jesus.—LUKE 1:31

PURITY OF HEART

Purity is so pleasing to God that his divine Son, having resolved to become man by the operation of the Holy Spirit, wished to be born of a virgin mother. We all know with what an abundance of graces and with what extraordinary purity God was pleased to adorn the body and soul of Mary. Thus he made her a dwelling worthy of the Word who was to become flesh in her chaste womb. So if we wish to induce the Incarnate God to be born spiritually in our souls, we must secure purity of conscience for ourselves. The right way to accomplish this is to banish from our hearts even the smallest faults and cultivate in them all the virtues.

Ah, how great is your goodness, my Jesus! Although I have so deeply offended you, you still wish to clothe yourself with human flesh and to take on yourself all my sins in order to obtain their pardon for me. I deserved to see you sitting in the tribunal of divine justice as a judge angered against one capable of so many failings. And instead I find you in the bosom of Mary, a savior full of indulgence for my sins. O Lamb of God! How efficacious the sweetness of your love should be in softening the hardness of my heart! I detest my sins with all my strength because they are opposed to your infinite goodness. Imprint on my heart such repentance that I may prefer to die rather than ever to offend you again. ST. MARY OF THE ANGELS, 1661–1717

YOU WILL FIND THE NEXT READING AT LUKE 2:1.

reth, 27 to a virgin betrothed to a man named Joseph, of the House of David; and the virgin's name was Mary. 28 He went in and said to her, 'Rejoice, you who enjoy God's favour! The Lord is with you.' 29 She was deeply disturbed by these words and asked herself what this greeting could mean, 30 but the angel said to her, 'Mary, do not be afraid; you have won God's favour. 31 Look! You are to conceive in your womb and bear a son, and you must name him Jesus. 32 He will be great and will be called Son of the Most High. The Lord God will give him the throne of his ancestor David; 33 he will rule over the House of Jacob for ever and his reign will have no end.' e 34 Mary said to the angel, 'But how can this come about, since I have no knowledge of man?' 35 The angel answered, 'The Holy Spirit will come upon you, and the power of the Most High will cover you with its shadow. And so the child will be holy and will be called Son of God. 36 And I tell you this too: your cousin Elizabeth also, in her old age, has conceived a son, and she whom people called barren is now in her sixth month, 37 for nothing is impossible to God.' f 38 Mary said, 'You see before you the Lord's servant, let it happen to me as you have said.' And the angel left her.

The visitation

39 Mary set out at that time and went as quickly as she could into the hill country to a

1e cf. 2 S 7:12–16. 1f Gn 18:14.

town in Judah. ⁴⁰ She went into Zechariah's house and greeted Elizabeth. ⁴¹ Now it happened that as soon as Elizabeth heard Mary's greeting, the child leapt in her womb and Elizabeth was filled with the Holy Spirit. ⁴² She gave a loud cry and said, 'Of all women you are the most blessed, and blessed is the fruit of your womb. ⁴³ Why should I be honoured with a visit from the mother of my Lord? ⁴⁴ Look, the moment your greeting reached my ears, the child in my womb leapt for joy. ⁴⁵ Yes, blessed is she who believed that the promise made her by the Lord would be fulfilled.'

The Magnificat ⁹

⁴⁶ And Mary said:

My soul proclaims the greatness of the
    Lord
⁴⁷ and my spirit *rejoices in God my*
    Saviour;
⁴⁸ because *he has looked upon the*
    humiliation of his servant.
Yes, from now onwards all generations
    will call me blessed,
⁴⁹ for the Almighty has done great things
    for me.
Holy is his name,
⁵⁰ and *his faithful love extends age after age*
    to those who fear him.
⁵¹ He has used the power of his arm,
    he has routed the arrogant of heart.
⁵² *He has pulled down princes* from their
    thrones *and raised high the lowly.*
⁵³ *He has filled the starving with good things,*
    sent the rich away empty.
⁵⁴ *He has come to the help of Israel his*
    servant, mindful of his faithful
    love
⁵⁵ —according to the promise he made to
    our ancestors—
of his mercy to Abraham and to his
    descendants for ever.

⁵⁶ Mary stayed with her some three months and then went home.

The birth of John the Baptist and visit of the neighbours

⁵⁷ The time came for Elizabeth to have her child, and she gave birth to a son; ⁵⁸ and when her neighbours and relations heard that the Lord had lavished on her his faithful love, they shared her joy.

The circumcision of John the Baptist

⁵⁹ Now it happened that on the eighth day they came to circumcise the child; they were going to call him Zechariah after his father, ⁶⁰ but his mother spoke up. 'No,' she said, 'he is to be called John.' ⁶¹ They said to her, 'But no one in your family has that name,' ⁶² and made signs to his father to find out what he wanted him called. ⁶³ The father asked for a writing-tablet and wrote, 'His name is John.' And they were all astonished. ⁶⁴ At that instant his power of speech returned and he spoke and praised God. ⁶⁵ All their neighbours were filled with awe and the whole affair was talked about throughout the hill country of Judaea. ⁶⁶ All those who heard of it treasured it in their hearts. 'What will this child turn out to be?' they wondered. And indeed the hand of the Lord was with him.

The Benedictus ʰ

⁶⁷ His father Zechariah was filled with the Holy Spirit and spoke this prophecy:

⁶⁸ *Blessed be the Lord, the God of Israel,*
    for he has visited his people, he has *set*
        them free,
⁶⁹ and he has established for us a saving
        power
    in the House of his servant David,
⁷⁰ just as he proclaimed,
    by the mouth of his holy prophets from
        ancient times,
⁷¹ that he would save us from our *enemies*

1g Mary's canticle echoes Hannah's 1 S 2:1–10, and also 1 S 1:11; Ps 103:17; 111:9; Jb 5:11; 12:19; Ps 98:2; 107:9; Is 41:8–9.

1h The canticle uses Ps 41:13; 111:9; Lv 26:42; Is 9:1.

and *from the hands of all those who hate us,*

72 and show *faithful love to our ancestors,*
and so *keep in mind his* holy *covenant.*

73 This was the oath he swore
to our father Abraham,

74 that he would grant us, free from fear,
to be delivered from the hands of our
enemies,

75 to serve him in holiness and uprightness
in his presence, all our days.

76 And you, little child,
you shall be called Prophet of the Most
High,
for you will go before *the Lord*
to prepare a way for him,

77 to give his people knowledge of salvation
through the forgiveness of their sins,

78 because of the faithful love of our God
in which the rising Sun has come from on
high to visit us,

79 to give light to *those who live*
in darkness and the shadow dark as death,
and to guide our feet
into *the way of peace.*

The hidden life of John the Baptist

80 Meanwhile the child grew up and his spirit grew strong. And he lived in the desert until the day he appeared openly to Israel.

The birth of Jesus and visit of the shepherds

2 Now it happened that at this time Caesar Augustus issued a decree that a census should be made of the whole inhabited world. 2 This census—the first—took place while Quirinius was governor of Syria, 3 and everyone went to be registered, each to his own town. 4 So Joseph set out from the town of Nazareth in Galilee for Judaea, to David's town called Bethlehem, since he was of David's House and line, 5 in order to be registered together with Mary, his betrothed, who was with child. 6 Now it happened that, while they were there, the time came for her to have her child, 7 and she gave birth to a son, her first-born. She wrapped him in swaddling clothes and laid him in a manger because there was no room for them in the living-space. 8 In the countryside close by there were shepherds out in the fields keeping guard over their sheep during the watches of the night. 9 An angel of the Lord stood over them and the glory of the Lord shone round them. They were terrified, 10 but the angel said, 'Do not be afraid. Look, I bring you news of great joy, a joy to be shared by the whole people. 11 Today in the town of David a Saviour has been born to you; he is Christ the Lord. 12 And here is a sign for you: you will find a baby wrapped in swaddling clothes and lying in a manger.' 13 And all at once with the angel there was a great throng of the hosts of heaven, praising God with the words:

14 Glory to God in the highest heaven,
and on earth peace for those he favours.

15 Now it happened that when the angels had gone from them into heaven, the shepherds said to one another, 'Let us go to Bethlehem and see this event which the Lord has made known to us.' 16 So they hurried away and found Mary and Joseph, and the baby lying in the manger. 17 When they saw the child they repeated what they had been told about him, 18 and everyone who heard it was astonished at what the shepherds said to them. 19 As for Mary, she treasured all these things and pondered them in her heart. 20 And the shepherds went back glorifying and praising God for all they had heard and seen, just as they had been told.

The circumcision of Jesus

21 When the eighth day came and the child was to be circumcised, they gave him the name Jesus, the name the angel had given him before his conception.

Jesus is presented in the Temple

22 And when the day came for them to be purified in keeping with the Law of Moses, they took him up to Jerusalem to present him to the Lord— 23 observing what is written in the

132 READ LUKE 2:1–14.

And she gave birth to a son, her firstborn. She wrapped him in swaddling clothes and laid him in a manger.—LUKE 2:7

BE NOT AFRAID

O man, why are you fearful? Why do you tremble before the face of the Lord because he comes? For he is coming to save the world, not to judge it. Long ago a faithless fellow servant induced you to steal the royal diadem and place it on your head. But you were discovered in the act. You had good reason then to be afraid. You had good reason then to flee from the face of the Lord. . . . Now, however, in a land of exile, you eat your bread by the sweat of your brow, and look, a voice is heard on the earth proclaiming the coming of the Lord. Where shall you go from his Spirit? Or where shall you flee from his face? But don't fear, don't flee. He is not coming now in anger. He seeks you not for punishment but in order to save you. And so that you should not say, "I heard your voice and I hid myself" (see Gn 3:10), look, he has become an infant, a little speechless baby.

His wailing cries should rather move you to compassion than fill you with terror. And even if possibly they are a cause of alarm for some others, surely they are not so for you. He has made himself a little one. His Virgin Mother wraps him in his poor swaddling clothes—and are you still fearful and trembling? This alone should convince you that he comes not to destroy but to save you, to deliver and not to bind you: the fact that he is already fighting against your enemies, that he, as the power and wisdom of God, is already trampling on the necks of the proud and haughty demons.

You, O man, have two enemies, sin and death, that is, the death of the soul and the death of the body. Christ came to conquer both, and from both he will save you. So don't be afraid.

ST. BERNARD OF CLAIRVAUX, 1090?–1153

YOU WILL FIND THE NEXT READING AT LUKE 2:41.

Law of the Lord: *Every first-born male must be consecrated to the Lord*—[a] 24 and also to offer in sacrifice, in accordance with what is prescribed in the Law of the Lord, *a pair of turtle-doves or two young pigeons.*[b] 25 Now in Jerusalem there was a man named Simeon. He was an upright and devout man; he looked forward to the restoration of Israel and the Holy Spirit rested on him. 26 It had been revealed to him by the Holy Spirit that he would not see death until he had set eyes on the Christ of the Lord. 27 Prompted by the Spirit he came to the Temple; and when the parents brought in the child Jesus to do for him what the Law

required, 28 he took him into his arms and blessed God; and he said:

The Nunc Dimittis

29 Now, Master, you are letting your servant
        go in peace
  as you promised;
30 for my eyes have seen the salvation
31 which you have made ready in the sight of
        the nations;
32 a light of revelation for the gentiles
  and glory for your people Israel.

2a Ex 13:2.   *2b* Lv 5:7.

The prophecy of Simeon

³³ As the child's father and mother were wondering at the things that were being said about him, ³⁴ Simeon blessed them and said to Mary his mother, 'Look, he is destined for the fall and for the rise of many in Israel, destined to be a sign that is opposed— ³⁵ and a sword will pierce your soul too—so that the secret thoughts of many may be laid bare.'

The prophecy of Anna

³⁶ There was a prophetess, too, Anna the daughter of Phanuel, of the tribe of Asher. She was well on in years. Her days of girlhood over, she had been married for seven years ³⁷ before becoming a widow. She was now eighty-four years old and never left the Temple, serving God night and day with fasting and prayer. ³⁸ She came up just at that moment and began to praise God; and she spoke of the child to all who looked forward to the deliverance of Jerusalem.

The hidden life of Jesus at Nazareth

³⁹ When they had done everything the Law of the Lord required, they went back to Galilee, to their own town of Nazareth. ⁴⁰ And as the child grew to maturity, he was filled with wisdom; and God's favour was with him.

Jesus among the doctors of the Law

⁴¹ Every year his parents used to go to Jerusalem for the feast of the Passover. ⁴² When he was twelve years old, they went up for the feast as usual. ⁴³ When the days of the feast were over and they set off home, the boy Jesus stayed behind in Jerusalem without his parents knowing it. ⁴⁴ They assumed he was somewhere in the party, and it was only after a day's journey that they went to look for him among their relations and acquaintances. ⁴⁵ When they failed to find him they went back to Jerusalem looking for him everywhere. ⁴⁶ It happened that, three days later, they found him in the Temple, sitting among the teachers, listening to them, and asking them questions; ⁴⁷ and all those who heard him were astounded at his intelligence and his replies. ⁴⁸ They were overcome when they saw him, and his mother said to him, 'My child, why have you done this to us? See how worried your father and I have been, looking for you.' ⁴⁹ He replied, 'Why were you looking for me? Did you not know that I must be in my Father's house?' ⁵⁰ But they did not understand what he meant.

The hidden life at Nazareth resumed

⁵¹ He went down with them then and came to Nazareth and lived under their authority. His mother stored up all these things in her heart. ⁵² And Jesus increased in wisdom, in stature, and in favour with God and with people.

The proclamation of John the Baptist

3 In the fifteenth year of Tiberius Caesar's reign, when Pontius Pilate was governor of Judaea, Herod tetrarch of Galilee, his brother Philip tetrarch of the territories of Ituraea and Trachonitis, Lysanias tetrarch of Abilene, ² and while the high-priesthood was held by Annas and Caiaphas, the word of God came to John the son of Zechariah, in the desert. ³ He went through the whole Jordan area proclaiming a baptism of repentance for the forgiveness of sins, ⁴ as it is written in the book of the sayings of Isaiah the prophet:

> A voice of one that cries in the desert:
> Prepare a way for the Lord,
> make his paths straight!
> ⁵ Let every valley be filled in,
> every mountain and hill be levelled,
> winding ways be straightened
> and rough roads made smooth,
> ⁶ and all humanity will see the salvation
> of God.ᵃ

⁷ He said, therefore, to the crowds who came to be baptised by him, 'Brood of vipers,

3a Is 40:3–5.

133 READ LUKE 2:41–52.

And Jesus increased in wisdom, in stature, and in favour with God and with people.

—LUKE 2:52

ADVANCING IN GRACE

The Lord our God is one God, nor can he change, or be changed. As David declares: "You never alter and your years never end" (Ps 102:27). Therefore, our God—eternal, timeless, unchangeable—became in our nature both changeable and a subject of time; so that for changeable people he might prepare the way to his own eternity, and give us steadfastness, for which he took on our frailty so that in one and the same Savior might be *the way* by which we would ascend; *the life* to which we would come; and *the truth* we would enjoy. As he himself says: "I am the way, the truth, the life" (see Jn 14:6).

The great God abiding in his own nature is born a child according to the flesh, and grows for a certain space of time, and after the manner of the flesh, so that we who are children in mind, and almost without mind, may be spiritually reborn. And that we may grow up according to the grades of the spiritual ages, and advance in wisdom and grace. So his bodily growth is our spiritual growth, and the things that are recorded as done by him in the successive ages are seen as done in us as we advance through the diverse stages of spiritual growth.

So let his corporal birth be our spiritual birth, that is, the beginning of our conversion. Let his persecution, that which he suffered from Herod, be to us a sign of the temptation we suffer from the devil in the beginning of our conversion. Let his growing up in Nazareth express our advancement in perfection.

ST. AELRED OF RIEVAULX, 1110–1167

YOU WILL FIND THE NEXT READING AT LUKE 5.

who warned you to flee from the coming retribution? [8]Produce fruit in keeping with repentance, and do not start telling yourselves, "We have Abraham as our father," because, I tell you, God can raise children for Abraham from these stones. [9]Yes, even now the axe is being laid to the root of the trees, so that any tree failing to produce good fruit will be cut down and thrown on the fire.'

[10]When all the people asked him, 'What must we do, then?' [11]he answered, 'Anyone who has two tunics must share with the one who has none, and anyone with something to eat must do the same.' [12]There were tax collectors, too, who came for baptism, and these said to him, 'Master, what must we do?' [13]He said to them, 'Exact no more than the appointed rate.' [14]Some soldiers asked him in their turn, 'What about us? What must we do?' He said to them, 'No intimidation! No extortion! Be content with your pay!'

[15]A feeling of expectancy had grown among the people, who were beginning to wonder whether John might be the Christ, [16]so John declared before them all, 'I baptise you with water, but someone is coming, who is more powerful than I, and I am not fit to undo the strap of his sandals; he will baptise you with the Holy Spirit and fire. [17]His winnowing-fan is in his hand, to clear his threshing-floor and to gather the wheat into his barn; but the chaff he will burn in a fire

that will never go out.' [18] And he proclaimed the good news to the people with many other exhortations too.

John the Baptist imprisoned

[19] But Herod the tetrarch, censured by John for his relations with his brother's wife Herodias and for all the other crimes he had committed, [20] added a further crime to all the rest by shutting John up in prison.

Jesus is baptised

[21] Now it happened that when all the people had been baptised and while Jesus after his own baptism was at prayer, heaven opened [22] and the Holy Spirit descended on him in a physical form, like a dove. And a voice came from heaven, *You are my Son; today have I fathered you.*' [b]

The ancestry of Jesus

[23] When he began, Jesus was about thirty years old, being the son, as it was thought, of Joseph son of Heli, [24] son of Matthat, son of Levi, son of Melchi, son of Jannai, son of Joseph, [25] son of Mattathias, son of Amos, son of Nahum, son of Esli, son of Naggai, [26] son of Maath, son of Mattathias, son of Semein, son of Josech, son of Joda, [27] son of Joanan, son of Rhesa, son of Zerubbabel, son of Shealtiel, son of Neri, [28] son of Melchi, son of Addi, son of Cosam, son of Elmadam, son of Er, [29] son of Jesus, son of Eliezer, son of Jorim, son of Matthat, son of Levi, [30] son of Symeon, son of Judah, son of Joseph, son of Jonam, son of Eliakim, [31] son of Melea, son of Menna, son of Mattatha, son of Nathan, son of David, [32] son of Jesse, son of Obed, son of Boaz, son of Sala, son of Nahshon, [33] son of Amminadab, son of Admin, son of Arni, son of Hezron, son of Perez, son of Judah, [34] son of Jacob, son of Isaac, son of Abraham, son of Terah, son of Nahor, [35] son of Serug, son of Reu, son of Peleg, son of Eber, son of Shelah, [36] son of Cainan, son of Arphaxad, son of Shem, son of Noah, son of Lamech, [37] son of Methuselah, son of Enoch, son of Jared, son of Mahalaleel, son of Cainan, [38] son of Enos, son of Seth, son of Adam, son of God.

Testing in the desert

4 Filled with the Holy Spirit, Jesus left the Jordan and was led by the Spirit into the desert, [2] for forty days being put to the test by the devil. During that time he ate nothing and at the end he was hungry. [3] Then the devil said to him, 'If you are Son of God, tell this stone to turn into a loaf.' [4] But Jesus replied, 'Scripture says:

Human beings live not on bread alone.' [a]

[5] Then leading him to a height, the devil showed him in a moment of time all the kingdoms of the world [6] and said to him, 'I will give you all this power and their splendour, for it has been handed over to me, for me to give it to anyone I choose. [7] Do homage, then, to me, and it shall all be yours.' [8] But Jesus answered him, 'Scripture says:

You must do homage to the Lord your God, him alone you must serve.' [b]

[9] Then he led him to Jerusalem and set him on the parapet of the Temple. 'If you are Son of God,' he said to him, 'throw yourself down from here, [10] for scripture says:

He has given his angels orders about you, to guard you,

and again:

[11] *They will carry you in their arms in case you trip over a stone.'* [c]

[12] But Jesus answered him, 'Scripture says:

Do not put the Lord your God to the test.' [d]

3b Ps 2:7.   4a Dt 8:3.   4b Dt 6:13.
4c Ps 91:11–12.   4d Dt 6:16.

¹³ Having exhausted every way of putting him to the test, the devil left him, until the opportune moment.

Jesus begins to preach

¹⁴ Jesus, with the power of the Spirit in him, returned to Galilee; and his reputation spread throughout the countryside. ¹⁵ He taught in their synagogues and everyone glorified him.

Jesus at Nazareth

¹⁶ He came to Nazara, where he had been brought up, and went into the synagogue on the Sabbath day as he usually did. He stood up to read, ¹⁷ and they handed him the scroll of the prophet Isaiah. Unrolling the scroll he found the place where it is written:

¹⁸ *The spirit of the Lord is on me,*
* for he has anointed me*
* to bring the good news to the afflicted.*
He has sent me to proclaim liberty to
*   captives,*
* sight to the blind,*
* to let the oppressed go free,*
¹⁹ *to proclaim a year of favour from the*
*   Lord.* ᵉ

²⁰ He then rolled up the scroll, gave it back to the assistant and sat down. And all eyes in the synagogue were fixed on him. ²¹ Then he began to speak to them, 'This text is being fulfilled today even while you are listening.' ²² And he won the approval of all, and they were astonished by the gracious words that came from his lips.

They said, 'This is Joseph's son, surely?' ²³ But he replied, 'No doubt you will quote me the saying, "Physician, heal yourself," and tell me, "We have heard all that happened in Capernaum, do the same here in your own country."' ²⁴ And he went on, 'In truth I tell you, no prophet is ever accepted in his own country.

²⁵ 'There were many widows in Israel, I can assure you, in Elijah's day, when heaven remained shut for three years and six months and a great famine raged throughout the land, ²⁶ but Elijah was not sent to any one of these: he was sent *to a widow at Zarephath, a town in Sidonia.*ᶠ ²⁷ And in the prophet Elisha's time there were many suffering from virulent skin-diseases in Israel, but none of these was cured—only Naaman the Syrian.'ᵍ

²⁸ When they heard this everyone in the synagogue was enraged. ²⁹ They sprang to their feet and hustled him out of the town; and they took him up to the brow of the hill their town was built on, intending to throw him off the cliff, ³⁰ but he passed straight through the crowd and walked away.

Jesus teaches in Capernaum and cures a demoniac

³¹ He went down to Capernaum, a town in Galilee, and taught them on the Sabbath. ³² And his teaching made a deep impression on them because his word carried authority.

³³ In the synagogue there was a man possessed by the spirit of an unclean devil, and he shouted at the top of his voice, ³⁴ 'Ha! What do you want with us, Jesus of Nazareth? Have you come to destroy us? I know who you are: the Holy One of God.' ³⁵ But Jesus rebuked it, saying, 'Be quiet! Come out of him!' And the devil, throwing the man into the middle, went out of him without hurting him at all. ³⁶ Astonishment seized them and they were all saying to one another, 'What is it in his words? He gives orders to unclean spirits with authority and power and they come out.' ³⁷ And the news of him travelled all through the surrounding countryside.

Cure of Simon's mother-in-law

³⁸ Leaving the synagogue he went to Simon's house. Now Simon's mother-in-law was in the grip of a high fever and they asked him to do something for her. ³⁹ Standing over her he rebuked the fever and it left her. And she immediately got up and began to serve them.

4e Is 61:1–2.   4f 1 K 17:9.   4g 2 K 5:14.

A number of cures

⁴⁰ At sunset all those who had friends suffering from diseases of one kind or another brought them to him, and laying his hands on each he cured them. ⁴¹ Devils too came out of many people, shouting, 'You are the Son of God.' But he warned them and would not allow them to speak because they knew that he was the Christ.

Dawn departure from Capernaum and travels through Judaea

⁴² When daylight came he left the house and made his way to a lonely place. The crowds went to look for him, and when they had caught up with him they wanted to prevent him leaving them, ⁴³ but he answered, 'I must proclaim the good news of the kingdom of God to the other towns too, because that is what I was sent to do.' ⁴⁴ And he continued his proclamation in the synagogues of Judaea.

The first four disciples are called

5 Now it happened that he was standing one day by the Lake of Gennesaret, with the crowd pressing round him listening to the word of God, ² when he caught sight of two boats at the water's edge. The fishermen had got out of them and were washing their nets. ³ He got into one of the boats—it was Simon's—and asked him to put out a little from the shore. Then he sat down and taught the crowds from the boat.

⁴ When he had finished speaking he said to Simon, 'Put out into deep water and pay out your nets for a catch.' ⁵ Simon replied, 'Master, we worked hard all night long and caught nothing, but if you say so, I will pay out the nets.' ⁶ And when they had done this they netted such a huge number of fish that their nets began to tear, ⁷ so they signalled to their companions in the other boat to come and help them; when these came, they filled both boats to sinking point.

⁸ When Simon Peter saw this he fell at the knees of Jesus saying, 'Leave me, Lord; I am a sinful man.' ⁹ For he and all his companions were completely awestruck at the catch they had made; ¹⁰ so also were James and John, sons of Zebedee, who were Simon's partners. But Jesus said to Simon, 'Do not be afraid; from now on it is people you will be catching.' ¹¹ Then, bringing their boats back to land they left everything and followed him.

Cure of a man suffering from a virulent skin-disease

¹² Now it happened that Jesus was in one of the towns when suddenly a man appeared, covered with a skin-disease. Seeing Jesus he fell on his face and implored him saying, 'Sir, if you are willing you can cleanse me.' ¹³ He stretched out his hand, and touched him saying, 'I am willing. Be cleansed.' At once the skin-disease left him. ¹⁴ He ordered him to tell no one, 'But go and show yourself to the priest and make the offering for your cleansing just as Moses prescribed, as evidence to them.'

¹⁵ But the news of him kept spreading, and large crowds would gather to hear him and to have their illnesses cured, ¹⁶ but he would go off to some deserted place and pray.

Cure of a paralytic

¹⁷ Now it happened that he was teaching one day, and Pharisees and teachers of the Law, who had come from every village in Galilee, from Judaea and from Jerusalem, were sitting there. And the power of the Lord was there so that he should heal. ¹⁸ And now some men appeared, bringing on a bed a paralysed man whom they were trying to bring in and lay down in front of him. ¹⁹ But as they could find no way of getting the man through the crowd, they went up onto the top of the house and lowered him and his stretcher down through the tiles into the middle of the gathering, in front of Jesus. ²⁰ Seeing their faith he said, 'My friend, your sins are forgiven you.' ²¹ The scribes and the Pharisees began to think this over. 'Who is this man, talking blasphemy?

134 READ LUKE 5:17–26.

Seeing their faith he said, "My friend, your sins are forgiven you."—LUKE 5:20

ADVICE TO THE SICK

The Lord healed this paralytic to set an example for us. . . . Jesus healed many sick people in the presence of the Pharisees and doctors of the law from every town of Galilee, Judea and Jerusalem. However, the gospel specifically describes the healing of this particular paralytic. First of all this instance shows us that every sick person should ask his friends to offer up prayers for his recovery, so that the healing power of the word from heaven may set right the shaky framework of our life.

Therefore we must have advisers who rouse the minds of the sick to higher things because when the body languishes with sickness the mind is apt to follow its example. With the help of such friends a sick person can be brought and laid on the ground before the feet of Jesus, and seem worthy of a glance from the Lord. For the Lord looks upon those who present themselves humbly before him. . . .

"Seeing their faith he said, 'My friend, your sins are forgiven you.'" Great is the Lord, who for the sake of some forgives the sins of others: who tries some and pardons the wanderings of others. . . . O you who judge others, learn to forgive. You who are sick, learn to pray. If you doubt that God forgives your sins because they are grievous, appeal to the church so that she might pray for you. And that the Lord may grant to her petitions what he refuses to yours.

Although we are bound to accept this story of the paralytic as factual and to believe that the Lord healed his body, we must also remember his inward cure because the Lord forgave his sins.

ST. AMBROSE, 339–397

YOU WILL FIND THE NEXT READING AT LUKE 6.

Who but God alone can forgive sins?' ²²But Jesus, aware of their thoughts, made them this reply, 'What are these thoughts you have in your hearts? ²³Which of these is easier: to say, "Your sins are forgiven you," or to say, "Get up and walk"? ²⁴But to prove to you that the Son of man has authority on earth to forgive sins,'—he said to the paralysed man—'I order you: get up, and pick up your stretcher and go home.' ²⁵And immediately before their very eyes he got up, picked up what he had been lying on and went home praising God. ²⁶They were all astounded and praised God and were filled with awe, saying, 'We have seen strange things today.'

The call of Levi

²⁷When he went out after this, he noticed a tax collector, Levi by name, sitting at the tax office, and said to him, 'Follow me.' ²⁸And leaving everything Levi got up and followed him.

Eating with sinners in Levi's house

²⁹In his honour Levi held a great reception in his house, and with them at table was a large gathering of tax collectors and others. ³⁰The Pharisees and their scribes complained to his disciples and said, 'Why do you eat and drink with tax collectors and sinners?' ³¹Jesus said to them in reply, 'It is not those that are well who

need the doctor, but the sick. ³²I have come to call not the upright but sinners to repentance.'

Discussion on fasting

³³They then said to him, 'John's disciples are always fasting and saying prayers, and the disciples of the Pharisees, too, but yours go on eating and drinking.' ³⁴Jesus replied, 'Surely you cannot make the bridegroom's attendants fast while the bridegroom is still with them? ³⁵But the time will come when the bridegroom is taken away from them; then, in those days, they will fast.'

³⁶He also told them a parable, 'No one tears a piece from a new cloak to put it on an old cloak; otherwise, not only will the new one be torn, but the piece taken from the new will not match the old.

³⁷'And nobody puts new wine in old wineskins; otherwise, the new wine will burst the skins and run to waste, and the skins will be ruined. ³⁸No; new wine must be put in fresh skins. ³⁹And nobody who has been drinking old wine wants new. "The old is good," he says.'

Picking corn on the Sabbath

6 It happened that one Sabbath he was walking through the cornfields, and his disciples were picking ears of corn, rubbing them in their hands and eating them. ²Some of the Pharisees said, 'Why are you doing something that is forbidden on the Sabbath day?' ³Jesus answered them, 'So you have not read what David did ᵃ when he and his followers were hungry— ⁴how he went into the house of God and took the loaves of the offering and ate them and gave them to his followers, loaves which the priests alone are allowed to eat?' ⁵And he said to them, 'The Son of man is master of the Sabbath.'

Cure of the man with a withered hand

⁶Now on another Sabbath he went into the synagogue and began to teach, and a man was present, and his right hand was withered. ⁷The scribes and the Pharisees were watching him to see if he would cure somebody on the Sabbath, hoping to find something to charge him with. ⁸But he knew their thoughts; and he said to the man with the withered hand, 'Get up and stand out in the middle!' And he came forward and stood there. ⁹Then Jesus said to them, 'I put it to you: is it permitted on the Sabbath to do good, or to do evil; to save life, or to destroy it?' ¹⁰Then he looked round at them all and said to the man, 'Stretch out your hand.' He did so, and his hand was restored. ¹¹But they were furious and began to discuss the best way of dealing with Jesus.

The choice of the Twelve

¹²Now it happened in those days that he went onto the mountain to pray; and he spent the whole night in prayer to God. ¹³When day came he summoned his disciples and picked out twelve of them; he called them 'apostles': ¹⁴Simon whom he called Peter, and his brother Andrew, James, John, Philip, Bartholomew, ¹⁵Matthew, Thomas, James son of Alphaeus, Simon called the Zealot, ¹⁶Judas son of James, and Judas Iscariot who became a traitor.

The crowds follow Jesus

¹⁷He then came down with them and stopped at a piece of level ground where there was a large gathering of his disciples, with a great crowd of people from all parts of Judaea and Jerusalem and the coastal region of Tyre and Sidon ¹⁸who had come to hear him and to be cured of their diseases. People tormented by unclean spirits were also cured, ¹⁹and everyone in the crowd was trying to touch him because power came out of him that cured them all.

The first sermon; the Beatitudes ᵇ

²⁰Then fixing his eyes on his disciples he said:

> How blessed are you who are poor: the kingdom of God is yours.

6a 1 S 21:2–7.   6b Mt 5:1.

21 Blessed are you who are hungry now: you
shall have your fill.
Blessed are you who are weeping now: you
shall laugh.

22 'Blessed are you when people hate you,
drive you out, abuse you, denounce your name
as criminal, on account of the Son of man.
23 Rejoice when that day comes and dance for
joy, look!—your reward will be great in
heaven. This was the way their ancestors
treated the prophets.

The curses

24 But alas for you who are rich: you are
having your consolation now.
25 Alas for you who have plenty to eat now:
you shall go hungry.
Alas for you who are laughing now: you
shall mourn and weep.

26 'Alas for you when everyone speaks well
of you! This was the way their ancestors
treated the false prophets.

Love of enemies

27 'But I say this to you who are listening: Love
your enemies, do good to those who hate you,
28 bless those who curse you, pray for those
who treat you badly. 29 To anyone who slaps
you on one cheek, present the other cheek as
well; to anyone who takes your cloak from
you, do not refuse your tunic. 30 Give to everyone who asks you, and do not ask for your
property back from someone who takes it.
31 Treat others as you would like people to
treat you. 32 If you love those who love you,
what credit can you expect? Even sinners love
those who love them. 33 And if you do good to
those who do good to you, what credit can you
expect? For even sinners do that much. 34 And
if you lend to those from whom you hope to
get money back, what credit can you expect?
Even sinners lend to sinners to get back the
same amount. 35 Instead, love your enemies
and do good to them, and lend without any
hope of return. You will have a great reward,

and you will be children of the Most High, for
he himself is kind to the ungrateful and the
wicked.

Compassion and generosity

36 'Be compassionate just as your Father is
compassionate. 37 Do not judge, and you will
not be judged; do not condemn, and you will
not be condemned; forgive, and you will be
forgiven. 38 Give, and there will be gifts for
you: a full measure, pressed down, shaken together, and overflowing, will be poured into
your lap; because the standard you use will be
the standard used for you.'

Integrity

39 He also told them a parable, 'Can one blind
person guide another? Surely both will fall
into a pit? 40 Disciple is not superior to teacher;
but fully trained disciple will be like teacher.
41 Why do you observe the splinter in your
brother's eye and never notice the great log in
your own? 42 How can you say to your brother,
"Brother, let me take out that splinter in your
eye," when you cannot see the great log in your
own? Hypocrite! Take the log out of your
own eye first, and then you will see clearly
enough to take out the splinter in your
brother's eye.

43 'There is no sound tree that produces rotten fruit, nor again a rotten tree that produces
sound fruit. 44 Every tree can be told by its own
fruit: people do not pick figs from thorns, nor
gather grapes from brambles. 45 Good people
draw what is good from the store of goodness
in their hearts; bad people draw what is bad
from the store of badness. For the words of the
mouth flow out of what fills the heart.

The true disciple

46 'Why do you call me, "Lord, Lord" and not
do what I say?
47 'Everyone who comes to me and listens to
my words and acts on them—I will show you
what such a person is like. 48 Such a person is
like the man who, when he built a house, dug,
and dug deep, and laid the foundations on

135 READ LUKE 6:27–38.

Forgive, and you will be forgiven. Give, and there will be gifts for you.—LUKE 6:37–38

TWO WORKS OF MERCY

There are two works of mercy that free us. The Lord himself has briefly identified them in the gospel. "Forgive, and you will be forgiven. Give, and there will be gifts for you." "Forgive, and you will be forgiven"—this is the promise of pardon. "Give, and there will be gifts for you"—this is the promise of favor.

Regarding forgiveness, you have offenses that you would like to have forgiven and you have people you have offended that you can forgive. Regarding favor, there are those that beg of you and you are a beggar to God. When we pray, we are all beggars to God, standing at the door of the Great Householder. Yes, we fall down on our knees and earnestly request that he give us something. And that something is God himself. "What does a beggar ask of you? Bread. And what do you ask of God but Christ who says, "I am the living bread which has come down from heaven"? (Jn 6:51).

If you want to be forgiven, forgive. If you want to receive, "give, and there will be gifts for you."

ST. AUGUSTINE, 354–430

YOU WILL FIND THE NEXT READING AT LUKE 7.

rock; when the river was in flood it bore down on that house but could not shake it, it was so well built. ⁴⁹But someone who listens and does nothing is like the man who built a house on soil, with no foundations; as soon as the river bore down on it, it collapsed; and what a ruin that house became!'

Cure of the centurion's servant

7 When he had come to the end of all he wanted the people to hear, he went into Capernaum. ²A centurion there had a servant, a favourite of his, who was sick and near death. ³Having heard about Jesus he sent some Jewish elders to him to ask him to come and heal his servant. ⁴When they came to Jesus they pleaded earnestly with him saying, 'He deserves this of you, ⁵because he is well disposed towards our people; he built us our synagogue himself.' ⁶So Jesus went with them, and was not very far from the house when the centurion sent word to him by some friends to say to him, 'Sir, do not put yourself to any trouble because I am not worthy to have you under my roof; ⁷and that is why I did not presume to come to you myself; let my boy be cured by your giving the word. ⁸For I am under authority myself, and have soldiers under me; and I say to one man, "Go," and he goes; to another, "Come here," and he comes; to my servant, "Do this," and he does it.' ⁹When Jesus heard these words he was astonished at him and, turning round, said to the crowd following him, 'I tell you, not even in Israel have I found faith as great as this.' ¹⁰And when the messengers got back to the house they found the servant in perfect health.

The son of the widow of Nain restored to life

¹¹It happened that soon afterwards he went to a town called Nain, accompanied by his disciples and a great number of people. ¹²Now when he was near the gate of the town there was a dead man being carried out, the only son

136   READ LUKE 7:11–17.

And the dead man sat up and began to talk, and Jesus gave him to his mother.—LUKE 7:15

UNDERSTANDING THE MEANING OF MIRACLES

That her son was called again to life was the joy of that widowed mother; that souls of people are every day called to life is the joy of our mother, the church. He was dead in body; they have been dead in spirit. His death was outward, and was outwardly mourned; their inward death has neither been mourned nor seen. But the Lord sought them, who has seen that they are dead, and he only has seen that they are dead, he who has been able to make them live. If the Lord had not come to raise the dead, the Apostle would not have said, "Wake up sleeper, rise from the dead, and Christ will shine on you" (Ep 5:14).

We find written how the Lord raised from the dead three persons visibly, but thousands invisibly. We do not know how many he raised visibly, for as John says, all the things that Jesus did are not written down because he did so many things the world could not contain the books that would be written (see Jn 21:25). Doubtless he raised many more to life, but it is not meaningless that three are recorded. For our Lord Jesus Christ willed that those things which he did bodily, we should also understand spiritually. He didn't work miracles merely for the sake of working wonders, but that his works might be simultaneously wonderful to those that saw them, and true to those that understand them. . . .

Just as some people can praise the beautiful handwriting on a scroll without understanding a word that is written on it, some people saw Christ's miracles and marveled at them without understanding what they meant. But others saw and marveled at his miracles, and understood them and profited by them. And it is like these latter that we ought to be in the school of Christ.

ST. AUGUSTINE, 354–430

YOU WILL FIND THE NEXT READING AT LUKE 8.

of his mother, and she was a widow. And a considerable number of the townspeople was with her. [13] When the Lord saw her he felt sorry for her and said to her, 'Don't cry.' [14] Then he went up and touched the bier and the bearers stood still, and he said, 'Young man, I tell you: get up.' [15] And the dead man sat up and began to talk, and Jesus *gave him to his mother.*[a] [16] Everyone was filled with awe and glorified God saying, 'A great prophet has risen up among us; God has visited his people.' [17] And this view of him spread throughout Judaea and all over the countryside.

The Baptist's question; Jesus commends him

[18] The disciples of John gave him all this news, and John, summoning two of his disciples, [19] sent them to the Lord to ask, 'Are you the one who is to come, or are we to expect someone else?' [20] When the men reached Jesus they said, 'John the Baptist has sent us to you to ask, "Are you the one who is to come or are we to expect someone else?" ' [21] At that very time he cured many people of diseases and afflictions

7a 1 K 17:23.

and of evil spirits, and gave the gift of sight to many who were blind. ²²Then he gave the messengers their answer, 'Go back and tell John what you have seen and heard: the blind see again, the lame walk, those suffering from virulent skin-diseases are cleansed, and the deaf hear, the dead are raised to life, the good news is proclaimed to the poor; ²³and blessed is anyone who does not find me a cause of falling.'

²⁴When John's messengers had gone he began to talk to the people about John, ²⁵'What did you go out into the desert to see? A reed swaying in the breeze? No! Then what did you go out to see? A man dressed in fine clothes? Look, those who go in magnificent clothes and live luxuriously are to be found at royal courts! ²⁶Then what did you go out to see? A prophet? Yes, I tell you, and much more than a prophet: ²⁷he is the one of whom scripture says:

> Look, I am going to send my messenger in
>   front of you
> to prepare your way before you.[b]

²⁸'I tell you, of all the children born to women, there is no one greater than John; yet the least in the kingdom of God is greater than he.' ²⁹All the people who heard him, and the tax collectors too, acknowledged God's saving justice by accepting baptism from John; ³⁰but by refusing baptism from him the Pharisees and the lawyers thwarted God's plan for them.

Jesus condemns his contemporaries

³¹'What comparison, then, can I find for the people of this generation? What are they like? ³²They are like children shouting to one another while they sit in the market place:

> We played the pipes for you,
>   and you wouldn't dance;
> we sang dirges,
>   and you wouldn't cry.

³³'For John the Baptist has come, not eating bread, not drinking wine, and you say, "He is possessed." ³⁴The Son of man has come, eat-

ing and drinking, and you say, "Look, a glutton and a drunkard, a friend of tax collectors and sinners." ³⁵Yet wisdom is justified by all her children.'

The woman who was a sinner

³⁶One of the Pharisees invited him to a meal. When he arrived at the Pharisee's house and took his place at table, ³⁷suddenly a woman came in, who had a bad name in the town. She had heard he was dining with the Pharisee and had brought with her an alabaster jar of ointment. ³⁸She waited behind him at his feet, weeping, and her tears fell on his feet, and she wiped them away with her hair; then she covered his feet with kisses and anointed them with the ointment.

³⁹When the Pharisee who had invited him saw this, he said to himself, 'If this man were a prophet, he would know who this woman is and what sort of person it is who is touching him and what a bad name she has.' ⁴⁰Then Jesus took him up and said, 'Simon, I have something to say to you.' He replied, 'Say on, Master.' ⁴¹'There was once a creditor who had two men in his debt; one owed him five hundred denarii, the other fifty. ⁴²They were unable to pay, so he let them both off. Which of them will love him more?' ⁴³Simon answered, 'The one who was let off more, I suppose.' Jesus said, 'You are right.'

⁴⁴Then he turned to the woman and said to Simon, 'You see this woman? I came into your house, and you poured no water over my feet, but she has poured out her tears over my feet and wiped them away with her hair. ⁴⁵You gave me no kiss, but she has been covering my feet with kisses ever since I came in. ⁴⁶You did not anoint my head with oil, but she has anointed my feet with ointment. ⁴⁷For this reason I tell you that her sins, many as they are, have been forgiven her, because she has shown such great love.[c] It is someone who is forgiven

---

7b Ml 3:1.

7c In most of the story love wins forgiveness, but in vv. 40–43 and 47a, forgiveness nourishes love.

little who shows little love.' ⁴⁸Then he said to her, 'Your sins are forgiven.' ⁴⁹Those who were with him at table began to say to themselves, 'Who is this man, that even forgives sins?' ⁵⁰But he said to the woman, 'Your faith has saved you; go in peace.'

The women accompanying Jesus

8 Now it happened that after this he made his way through towns and villages preaching and proclaiming the good news of the kingdom of God. With him went the Twelve, ²as well as certain women who had been cured of evil spirits and ailments: Mary surnamed the Magdalene, from whom seven demons had gone out, ³Joanna the wife of Herod's steward Chuza, Susanna, and many others who provided for them out of their own resources.

Parable of the sower

⁴With a large crowd gathering and people from every town finding their way to him, he told this parable:

⁵'A sower went out to sow his seed. Now as he sowed, some fell on the edge of the path and was trampled on; and the birds of the air ate it up. ⁶Some seed fell on rock, and when it came up it withered away, having no moisture. ⁷Some seed fell in the middle of thorns and the thorns grew with it and choked it. ⁸And some seed fell into good soil and grew and produced its crop a hundredfold.' Saying this he cried, 'Anyone who has ears for listening should listen!'

Why Jesus speaks in parables

⁹His disciples asked him what this parable might mean, ¹⁰and he said, 'To you is granted to understand the secrets of the kingdom of God; for the rest it remains in parables, so that

> they may look but not perceive,
> listen but not understand.ᵃ

The parable of the sower explained

¹¹'This, then, is what the parable means: the seed is the word of God. ¹²Those on the edge

of the path are people who have heard it, and then the devil comes and carries away the word from their hearts in case they should believe and be saved. ¹³Those on the rock are people who, when they first hear it, welcome the word with joy. But these have no root; they believe for a while, and in time of trial they give up. ¹⁴As for the part that fell into thorns, this is people who have heard, but as they go on their way they are choked by the worries and riches and pleasures of life and never produce any crops. ¹⁵As for the part in the rich soil, this is people with a noble and generous heart who have heard the word and take it to themselves and yield a harvest through their perseverance.

Parable of the lamp

¹⁶'No one lights a lamp to cover it with a bowl or to put it under a bed. No, it is put on a lampstand so that people may see the light when they come in. ¹⁷For nothing is hidden but it will be made clear, nothing secret but it will be made known and brought to light. ¹⁸So take care how you listen; anyone who has, will be given more; anyone who has not, will be deprived even of what he thinks he has.'

The true family of Jesus

¹⁹His mother and his brothers came looking for him, but they could not get to him because of the crowd. ²⁰He was told, 'Your mother and brothers are standing outside and want to see you.' ²¹But he said in answer, 'My mother and my brothers are those who hear the word of God and put it into practice.'

The calming of the storm

²²It happened that one day he got into a boat with his disciples and said to them, 'Let us cross over to the other side of the lake.' So they set out, ²³and as they sailed he fell asleep. When a squall of wind came down on the lake the boat started shipping water and they found themselves in danger. ²⁴So they went to

8a Is 6:9.

137 READ LUKE 8:4–15.

Saying this he cried, "Anyone who has ears for listening should listen!"—LUKE 8:8

RECEIVING THE WORD

Let's consider why the seed on the edge of the path was seized. A path is almost always hard and unbroken because it is trodden on by the feet of all who pass, and seed is never sown there. Therefore, into whosoever that have minds that are hard and unyielding, no divine or sacred word will enter, by whose aid the joyful fruits of virtue might grow. . . .

Again there are others who carry the faith indifferently within them, a faith that is simply a matter of words. They have a religion that is without root. . . . They readily take part in the sacred mysteries, but they do so from no serious purpose. . . . And when they leave church such people immediately forget the holy teachings. . . .

Let's consider next what the thorns mean, by which the divine seed is choked? What does the Savior say here? For it is he that scatters the seed which, . . . beginning to put forth shoots, is choked by the cares of this world, and as Hosea says "stalk without ear, it will never yield flour" (Hos 8:7). . . . Therefore, that the divine seed may germinate in us, let us first drive forth from our minds all worldly cares.

They are rich and fruitful soil who yield fruit a hundredfold. And good and beautiful are the souls that take deeply into themselves the seeds of the Word, and keep them, and tend them with care. Of these it may be said, as was said by the Lord through the mouth of one of the prophets: "And all the nations will call you blessed, for you will be a land of delights" (Ml 3:12). For when the divine word falls upon a soul purified of the things that afflicted it, then it takes deep root, and comes forth as an ear of corn, and yields fruit abundantly. ST. CYRIL OF ALEXANDRIA, 376–444

YOU WILL FIND THE NEXT READING AT LUKE 9.

rouse him saying, 'Master! Master! We are lost!' Then he woke up and rebuked the wind and the rough water; and they subsided and it was calm again. ²⁵ He said to them, 'Where is your faith?' They were awestruck and astounded and said to one another, 'Who can this be, that gives orders even to winds and waves and they obey him?'

The Gerasene demoniac

²⁶ They came to land in the territory of the Gerasenes, which is opposite Galilee. ²⁷ He was stepping ashore when a man from the city who was possessed by devils came towards him; for a long time the man had been living with no clothes on, not in a house, but in the tombs. ²⁸ Catching sight of Jesus he gave a shout, fell at his feet and cried out at the top of his voice, 'What do you want with me, Jesus, son of the Most High God? I implore you, do not torture me.' ²⁹ For Jesus had been telling the unclean spirit to come out of the man. It had seized on him a great many times, and then they used to secure him with chains and fetters to restrain him, but he would always break the fastenings, and the devil would drive him out into the wilds. ³⁰ Jesus asked him, 'What

is your name?' He said, 'Legion'—because many devils had gone into him. 31 And these begged him not to order them to depart into the Abyss.

32 Now there was a large herd of pigs feeding there on the mountain, and the devils begged him to let them go into these. So he gave them leave. 33 The devils came out of the man and went into the pigs, and the herd charged down the cliff into the lake and was drowned.

34 When the swineherds saw what had happened they ran off and told their story in the city and in the country round about; 35 and the people went out to see what had happened. When they came to Jesus they found the man from whom the devils had gone out sitting at the feet of Jesus, wearing clothes and in his right mind; and they were afraid. 36 Those who had witnessed it told them how the man who had been possessed came to be saved. 37 The entire population of the Gerasene territory was in great fear and asked Jesus to leave them. So he got into the boat and went back.

38 The man from whom the devils had gone out asked to be allowed to stay with him, but he sent him away saying, 39 'Go back home and report all that God has done for you.' So the man went off and proclaimed throughout the city all that Jesus had done for him.

Cure of the woman with a haemorrhage; Jairus' daughter raised to life

40 On his return Jesus was welcomed by the crowd, for they were all there waiting for him. 41 And suddenly there came a man named Jairus, who was president of the synagogue. He fell at Jesus' feet and pleaded with him to come to his house, 42 because he had an only daughter about twelve years old, who was dying. And the crowds were almost stifling Jesus as he went.

43 Now there was a woman suffering from a haemorrhage for the past twelve years, whom no one had been able to cure. 44 She came up behind him and touched the fringe of his cloak; and the haemorrhage stopped at that very moment. 45 Jesus said, 'Who was it that touched me?' When they all denied it, Peter said, 'Master, it is the crowds round you, pushing.' 46 But Jesus said, 'Somebody touched me. I felt that power had gone out from me.' 47 Seeing herself discovered, the woman came forward trembling, and falling at his feet explained in front of all the people why she had touched him and how she had been cured at that very moment. 48 'My daughter,' he said, 'your faith has saved you; go in peace.'

49 While he was still speaking, someone arrived from the house of the president of the synagogue to say, 'Your daughter has died. Do not trouble the Master any further.' 50 But Jesus heard this, and he spoke to the man, 'Do not be afraid, only have faith and she will be saved.' 51 When he came to the house he allowed no one to go in with him except Peter and John and James, and the child's father and mother. 52 They were all crying and mourning for her, but Jesus said, 'Stop crying; she is not dead, but asleep.' 53 But they ridiculed him, knowing she was dead. 54 But taking her by the hand himself he spoke to her, 'Child, get up.' 55 And her spirit returned and she got up at that very moment. Then he told them to give her something to eat. 56 Her parents were astonished, but he ordered them not to tell anyone what had happened.

The mission of the Twelve

9 He called the Twelve together and gave them power and authority over all devils and to cure diseases, 2 and he sent them out to proclaim the kingdom of God and to heal. 3 He said to them, 'Take nothing for the journey: neither staff, nor haversack, nor bread, nor money; and do not have a spare tunic. 4 Whatever house you enter, stay there; and when you leave let your departure be from there. 5 As for those who do not welcome you, when you leave their town shake the dust from your feet as evidence against them.' 6 So they set out and went from village to village proclaiming the good news and healing everywhere.

Herod and Jesus

7 Meanwhile Herod the tetrarch had heard about all that was going on; and he was puzzled, because some people were saying that John had risen from the dead, 8 others that Elijah had reappeared, still others that one of the ancient prophets had come back to life. 9 But Herod said, 'John? I beheaded him. So who is this I hear such reports about?' And he was anxious to see him.

The return of the apostles; miracle of the loaves

10 On their return the apostles gave him an account of all they had done. Then he took them with him and withdrew towards a town called Bethsaida where they could be by themselves. 11 But the crowds got to know and they went after him. He made them welcome and talked to them about the kingdom of God; and he cured those who were in need of healing.

12 It was late afternoon when the Twelve came up to him and said, 'Send the people away, and they can go to the villages and farms round about to find lodging and food; for we are in a lonely place here.' 13 He replied, 'Give them something to eat yourselves.' But they said, 'We have no more than five loaves and two fish, unless we are to go ourselves and buy food for all these people.' 14 For there were about five thousand men. But he said to his disciples, 'Get them to sit down in parties of about fifty.' 15 They did so and made them all sit down. 16 Then he took the five loaves and the two fish, raised his eyes to heaven, and said the blessing over them; then he broke them and handed them to his disciples to distribute among the crowd. 17 They all ate as much as they wanted, and when the scraps left over were collected they filled twelve baskets.

Peter's profession of faith

18 Now it happened that he was praying alone, and his disciples came to him and he put this question to them, 'Who do the crowds say I am?' 19 And they answered, 'Some say John the Baptist; others Elijah; others again one of the ancient prophets come back to life.' 20 'But you,' he said to them, 'who do you say I am?' It was Peter who spoke up. 'The Christ of God,' he said. 21 But he gave them strict orders and charged them not to say this to anyone.

First prophecy of the Passion

22 He said, 'The Son of man is destined to suffer grievously, to be rejected by the elders and chief priests and scribes and to be put to death, and to be raised up on the third day.'

The condition of following Christ

23 Then, speaking to all, he said, 'If anyone wants to be a follower of mine, let him renounce himself and take up his cross every day and follow me. 24 Anyone who wants to save his life will lose it; but anyone who loses his life for my sake, will save it. 25 What benefit is it to anyone to win the whole world and forfeit or lose his very self? 26 For if anyone is ashamed of me and of my words, of him the Son of man will be ashamed when he comes in his own glory and in the glory of the Father and the holy angels.

The kingdom will come soon

27 'I tell you truly, there are some standing here who will not taste death before they see the kingdom of God.'

The transfiguration

28 Now about eight days after this had been said, he took with him Peter, John and James and went up the mountain to pray. 29 And it happened that, as he was praying, the aspect of his face was changed and his clothing became sparkling white. 30 And suddenly there were two men talking to him; they were Moses and Elijah 31 appearing in glory, and they were speaking of his passing which he was to accomplish in Jerusalem. 32 Peter and his companions were heavy with sleep, but they woke up and saw his glory and the two men standing with him. 33 As these were leaving him, Peter said to Jesus, 'Master, it is wonderful for

138 READ LUKE 9:28–36.

And after the voice had spoken, Jesus was found alone.—LUKE 9:36

STRENGTHENED FOR SUFFERING

God, who is pleased to communicate himself freely to such hearts as are pure and have no affection for sin, nevertheless desires that they should not be too much attached to his gifts. For this is a defect that gives him a distaste for the soul that so testifies that it is not God so much as his gifts that they appreciate. God employs this consolation to sustain the soul and to give it time to breathe freely after it has sustained the trial of tribulation. So the soul should accept this comfort as God's good pleasure without becoming dependent on the sensible satisfaction experienced.

The three apostles who accompanied Jesus Christ on Mount Tabor failed to take this precaution. They were as yet but little skilled in the interior life. And they dwelt too much upon the sweetness they tasted in this mystery, instead of contemplating the greatness and goodness of God. . . . The exterior glory of Christ vanished in a moment and disappeared from their sight. In this way God deprives us of the sensible pleasure we experience, when he finds that we are too greatly attached to it and that we relish it with undue complacency.

The short duration of the Transfiguration of our Lord teaches us that the consolations that God gives at times are but a refreshment that he offers holy souls in the midst of their interior desolations. He does it so that they may endure these trials with greater courage and that their affection . . . may increase. Scarcely had Jesus Christ experienced the joys of his Transfiguration when he found himself alone, deprived of all. He had nothing in sight except the picture of what he was to suffer in Jerusalem and about which he had conversed with Moses and Elias (see verse 31). . . . From this we should learn that those passing consolations should only animate and strengthen us in an increased love of sufferings, interior and exterior trials, of which we need never to be relieved in this life.

ST. JOHN BAPTIST DE LA SALLE, 1651–1719

YOU WILL FIND THE NEXT READING AT LUKE 11:1.

us to be here; so let us make three shelters, one for you, one for Moses and one for Elijah.' He did not know what he was saying. ³⁴ As he was saying this, a cloud came and covered them with shadow; and when they went into the cloud the disciples were afraid. ³⁵ And a voice came from the cloud saying, 'This is my Son, the Chosen One. Listen to him.' [a] ³⁶ And after the voice had spoken, Jesus was found alone. The disciples kept silence and, at that time, told no one what they had seen.

The epileptic demoniac

³⁷ Now it happened that on the following day when they were coming down from the mountain a large crowd came to meet him. ³⁸ And suddenly a man in the crowd cried out. 'Master,' he said, 'I implore you to look at my son: he is my only child. ³⁹ A spirit will suddenly take hold of him, and all at once it gives

9a Dt 18:15, 19; Is 42:1.

a sudden cry and throws the boy into convulsions with foaming at the mouth; it is slow to leave him, but when it does, it leaves the boy worn out. [40]I begged your disciples to drive it out, and they could not.' [41]In reply Jesus said, 'Faithless and perverse generation! How much longer must I be among you and put up with you? Bring your son here.' [42]Even while the boy was coming, the devil threw him to the ground in convulsions. But Jesus rebuked the unclean spirit and cured the boy and gave him back to his father, [43]and everyone was awestruck by the greatness of God.

Second prophecy of the Passion

But while everyone was full of admiration for all he did, he said to his disciples, [44]'For your part, you must have these words constantly in mind: The Son of man is going to be delivered into the power of men.' [45]But they did not understand what he said; it was hidden from them so that they should not see the meaning of it, and they were afraid to ask him about it.

Who is the greatest?

[46]An argument started between them about which of them was the greatest. [47]Jesus knew what thoughts were going through their minds, and he took a little child whom he set by his side [48]and then he said to them, 'Anyone who welcomes this little child in my name welcomes me; and anyone who welcomes me, welcomes the one who sent me. The least among you all is the one who is the greatest.'

On using the name of Jesus

[49]John spoke up. 'Master,' he said, 'we saw someone driving out devils in your name, and because he is not with us we tried to stop him.' [50]But Jesus said to him, 'You must not stop him: anyone who is not against you is for you.'

A Samaritan village is inhospitable

[51]Now it happened that as the time drew near for him to be taken up, he resolutely turned his face towards Jerusalem [52]and sent messengers ahead of him. These set out, and they went into a Samaritan village to make preparations for him, [53]but the people would not receive him because he was making for Jerusalem. [54]Seeing this, the disciples James and John said, 'Lord, do you want us to call down fire from heaven to burn them up?' [55]But he turned and rebuked them, [56]and they went on to another village.

Hardships of the apostolic calling

[57]As they travelled along they met a man on the road who said to him, 'I will follow you wherever you go.' [58]Jesus answered, 'Foxes have holes and the birds of the air have nests, but the Son of man has nowhere to lay his head.'

[59]Another to whom he said, 'Follow me,' replied, 'Let me go and bury my father first.' [60]But he answered, 'Leave the dead to bury their dead; your duty is to go and spread the news of the kingdom of God.'

[61]Another said, 'I will follow you, sir, but first let me go and say good-bye to my people at home.' [62]Jesus said to him, 'Once the hand is laid on the plough, no one who looks back is fit for the kingdom of God.'

The mission of the seventy-two disciples

10 After this the Lord appointed seventy-two others and sent them out ahead of him in pairs, to all the towns and places he himself would be visiting. [2]And he said to them, 'The harvest is rich but the labourers are few, so ask the Lord of the harvest to send labourers to do his harvesting. [3]Start off now, but look, I am sending you out like lambs among wolves. [4]Take no purse with you, no haversack, no sandals. Salute no one on the road. [5]Whatever house you enter, let your first words be, "Peace to this house!" [6]And if a man of peace lives there, your peace will go and rest on him; if not, it will come back to you. [7]Stay in the same house, taking what food and drink they have to offer, for the labourer deserves his wages; do not move from house to house. [8]Whenever you go into a town where they

make you welcome, eat what is put before you. ⁹Cure those in it who are sick, and say, "The kingdom of God is very near to you." ¹⁰But whenever you enter a town and they do not make you welcome, go out into its streets and say, ¹¹"We wipe off the very dust of your town that clings to our feet, and leave it with you. Yet be sure of this: the kingdom of God is very near." ¹²I tell you, on the great Day it will be more bearable for Sodom than for that town.

¹³'Alas for you, Chorazin! Alas for you, Bethsaida! For if the miracles done in you had been done in Tyre and Sidon, they would have repented long ago, sitting in sackcloth and ashes. ¹⁴And still, it will be more bearable for Tyre and Sidon at the Judgement than for you. ¹⁵And as for you, Capernaum, did you want to be *raised high as heaven? You shall be flung down to hell.*ᵃ

¹⁶'Anyone who listens to you listens to me; anyone who rejects you rejects me, and those who reject me reject the one who sent me.'

True cause for the apostles to rejoice

¹⁷The seventy-two came back rejoicing. 'Lord,' they said, 'even the devils submit to us when we use your name.' ¹⁸He said to them, 'I watched Satan fall like lightning from heaven. ¹⁹Look, I have given you power to tread down serpents and scorpions and the whole strength of the enemy; nothing shall ever hurt you. ²⁰Yet do not rejoice that the spirits submit to you; rejoice instead that your names are written in heaven.'

The good news revealed to the simple; the Father and the Son

²¹Just at this time, filled with joy by the Holy Spirit, he said, 'I bless you, Father, Lord of heaven and of earth, for hiding these things from the learned and the clever and revealing them to little children. Yes, Father, for that is what it has pleased you to do. ²²Everything has been entrusted to me by my Father; and no one knows who the Son is except the Father, and who the Father is except the Son and those to whom the Son chooses to reveal him.'

The privilege of the disciples

²³Then turning to his disciples he spoke to them by themselves, 'Blessed are the eyes that see what you see, ²⁴for I tell you that many prophets and kings wanted to see what you see, and never saw it; to hear what you hear, and never heard it.'

The great commandment

²⁵And now a lawyer stood up and, to test him, asked, 'Master, what must I do to inherit eternal life?' ²⁶He said to him, 'What is written in the Law? What is your reading of it?' ²⁷He replied, '*You must love the Lord your God with all your heart, with all your soul, with all your strength,* and with all your mind, *and your neighbour as yourself.*'ᵇ ²⁸Jesus said to him, 'You have answered right, do this and life is yours.'

Parable of the good Samaritan

²⁹But the man was anxious to justify himself and said to Jesus, 'And who is my neighbour?' ³⁰In answer Jesus said, 'A man was once on his way down from Jerusalem to Jericho and fell into the hands of bandits; they stripped him, beat him and then made off, leaving him half dead. ³¹Now a priest happened to be travelling down the same road, but when he saw the man, he passed by on the other side. ³²In the same way a Levite who came to the place saw him, and passed by on the other side. ³³But a Samaritan traveller who came on him was moved with compassion when he saw him. ³⁴He went up to him and bandaged his wounds, pouring oil and wine on them. He then lifted him onto his own mount and took him to an inn and looked after him. ³⁵Next day, he took out two denarii and handed them to the innkeeper and said, "Look after him, and on my way back I will make good any extra expense you have." ³⁶Which of these three, do you think, proved himself a neighbour to the man who fell into the bandits'

10a Is 14:13–15.   *10b* Dt 6:5 and Lv 19:18.

hands?' [37] He replied, 'The one who showed pity towards him.' Jesus said to him, 'Go, and do the same yourself.'

Martha and Mary

[38] In the course of their journey he came to a village, and a woman named Martha welcomed him into her house. [39] She had a sister called Mary, who sat down at the Lord's feet and listened to him speaking. [40] Now Martha, who was distracted with all the serving, came to him and said, 'Lord, do you not care that my sister is leaving me to do the serving all by myself? Please tell her to help me.' [41] But the Lord answered, 'Martha, Martha,' he said, 'you worry and fret about so many things, [42] and yet few are needed, indeed only one. It is Mary who has chosen the better part, and it is not to be taken from her.'

The Lord's prayer

11 Now it happened that he was in a certain place praying, and when he had finished, one of his disciples said, 'Lord, teach us to pray, as John taught his disciples.' [2] He said to them, 'When you pray, this is what to say:

Father, may your name be held holy,
 your kingdom come;
[3] give us each day our daily bread,
 and forgive us our sins,
[4] for we ourselves forgive each one who is in
 debt to us.
 And do not put us to the test.' [a]

The importunate friend

[5] He also said to them, 'Suppose one of you has a friend and goes to him in the middle of the night to say, "My friend, lend me three loaves, [6] because a friend of mine on his travels has just arrived at my house and I have nothing to offer him;" [7] and the man answers from inside the house, "Do not bother me. The door is bolted now, and my children are with me in bed; I cannot get up to give it to you." [8] I tell you, if the man does not get up and give it

to him for friendship's sake, persistence will make him get up and give his friend all he wants.

Effective prayer

[9] 'So I say to you: Ask, and it will be given to you; search, and you will find; knock, and the door will be opened to you. [10] For everyone who asks receives; everyone who searches finds; everyone who knocks will have the door opened. [11] What father among you, if his son asked for a fish, would hand him a snake? [12] Or if he asked for an egg, hand him a scorpion? [13] If you then, evil as you are, know how to give your children what is good, how much more will the heavenly Father give the Holy Spirit to those who ask him!'

Jesus and Beelzebul

[14] He was driving out a devil and it was dumb; and it happened that when the devil had gone out the dumb man spoke, and the people were amazed. [15] But some of them said, 'It is through Beelzebul, the prince of devils, that he drives devils out.' [16] Others asked him, as a test, for a sign from heaven; [17] but, knowing what they were thinking, he said to them, 'Any kingdom which is divided against itself is heading for ruin, and house collapses against house. [18] So, too, with Satan: if he is divided against himself, how can his kingdom last?—since you claim that it is through Beelzebul that I drive devils out. [19] Now if it is through Beelzebul that I drive devils out, through whom do your own sons drive them out? They shall be your judges, then. [20] But if it is through the finger of God that I drive devils out, then the kingdom of God has indeed caught you unawares. [21] So long as a strong man fully armed guards his own home, his goods are undisturbed; [22] but when someone stronger than himself attacks and defeats him, the stronger man takes away all the weapons he relied on and shares out his spoil.

11a Mt 6:9–13.

139 READ LUKE 11:1–4.

Give us each day our daily bread.—LUKE 11:3

THE BREAD OF LIFE

We have now reached the conclusion that the good Jesus, being ours, asks his Father to let us have him daily—which appears to mean "for ever." . . . Let us think carefully what this means, so that we may pray rightly, and thank him who is taking such care about teaching us. This bread, then is ours daily . . . because we have him here on earth, since he has remained with us here and we receive him, and, if we profit by his company, we shall also have him in heaven. For the only reason he remains with us is to help and encourage and sustain us so that we shall do that will, which . . . is to be fulfilled in us.

In using the words "each day" he seems to me to be thinking of a day the length of this life. . . . The Son prays the Father that, since this life lasts no more than a day, he will allow him to spend it in our service. As his Majesty has already given his Son to us, by sending him, of his will alone, into the world, so now, of that same will, he is pleased not to abandon us, but to remain here with us for the greater glory of his friends and the discomfiture of his enemies. He prays for nothing more than this "daily" since he has given us this most holy Bread. He has given it to us for ever . . . as the sustenance and manna of humanity. We can have it whenever we please and we shall not die of hunger save through our own fault, for in whatever way the soul desires to partake of food, it will find joy and comfort in the Most Holy Sacrament. There is no need or trial or persecution that cannot be easily borne if we begin to partake and taste of those which he himself bore, and to make them the subject of our meditations. ST. TERESA OF AVILA, 1515–1582

YOU WILL FIND THE NEXT READING AT LUKE 11:33.

No compromise

23 'Anyone who is not with me is against me; and anyone who does not gather in with me throws away.

Return of the unclean spirit

24 'When an unclean spirit goes out of someone it wanders through waterless country looking for a place to rest, and not finding one it says, "I will go back to the home I came from." 25 But on arrival, finding it swept and tidied, 26 it then goes off and brings seven other spirits more wicked than itself, and they go in and set up house there, and so that person ends up worse off than before.'

The truly blessed

27 It happened that as he was speaking, a woman in the crowd raised her voice and said, 'Blessed the womb that bore you and the breasts that fed you!' 28 But he replied, 'More blessed still are those who hear the word of God and keep it!'

The sign of Jonah

29 The crowds got even bigger and he addressed them, 'This is an evil generation; it is asking for a sign. The only sign it will be given is the sign of Jonah. 30 For just as Jonah became a sign to the people of Nineveh, so will the Son of man be a sign to this generation.

31 On Judgement Day the Queen of the South will stand up against the people of this generation and be their condemnation, because she came from the ends of the earth to hear the wisdom of Solomon;*b* and, look, there is something greater than Solomon here. 32 On Judgement Day the men of Nineveh will appear against this generation and be its condemnation, because when Jonah preached they repented; and, look, there is something greater than Jonah here.

The parable of the lamp repeated

33 'No one lights a lamp and puts it in some hidden place or under a tub; they put it on the lamp-stand so that people may see the light when they come in. 34 The lamp of the body is your eye. When your eye is clear, your whole body, too, is filled with light; but when it is diseased your body, too, will be darkened. 35 See to it then that the light inside you is not darkness. 36 If, therefore, your whole body is filled with light, and not darkened at all, it will be light entirely, as when the lamp shines on you with its rays.'

The Pharisees and the lawyers attacked

37 He had just finished speaking when a Pharisee invited him to dine at his house. He went in and sat down at table. 38 The Pharisee saw this and was surprised that he had not first washed before the meal. 39 But the Lord said to him, 'You Pharisees! You clean the outside of cup and plate, while inside yourselves you are filled with extortion and wickedness. 40 Fools! Did not he who made the outside make the inside too? 41 Instead, give alms from what you have and, look, everything will be clean for you. 42 But alas for you Pharisees, because you pay your tithe of mint and rue and all sorts of garden herbs and neglect justice and the love of God! These you should have practised, without neglecting the others. 43 Alas for you Pharisees, because you like to take the seats of honour in the synagogues and to be greeted respectfully in the market squares! 44 Alas for

you, because you are like the unmarked tombs that people walk on without knowing it!'

45 A lawyer then spoke up. 'Master,' he said, 'when you speak like this you insult us too.' 46 But he said, 'Alas for you lawyers as well, because you load on people burdens that are unendurable, burdens that you yourselves do not touch with your fingertips.

47 'Alas for you because you build tombs for the prophets, the people your ancestors killed! 48 In this way you both witness to what your ancestors did and approve it; they did the killing, you do the building.

49 'And that is why the Wisdom of God said, "I will send them prophets and apostles; some they will slaughter and persecute, 50 so that this generation will have to answer for every prophet's blood that has been shed since the foundation of the world, 51 from the blood of Abel to the blood of Zechariah, who perished between the altar and the Temple." Yes, I tell you, this generation will have to answer for it all.

52 'Alas for you lawyers who have taken away the key of knowledge! You have not gone in yourselves and have prevented others from going in who wanted to.'

53 When he left there, the scribes and the Pharisees began a furious attack on him and tried to force answers from him on innumerable questions, 54 lying in wait to catch him out in something he might say.

Open and fearless speech

12 Meanwhile the people had gathered in their thousands so that they were treading on one another. And he began to speak, first of all to his disciples. 'Be on your guard against the yeast of the Pharisees—their hypocrisy. 2 Everything now covered up will be uncovered, and everything now hidden will be made clear. 3 For this reason, whatever you have said in the dark will be heard in the daylight, and what you have whispered in hidden places will be proclaimed from the housetops.

11b 1 K 10:1–10.

140 READ LUKE 11:33–36.

When your eye is clear, your whole body, too, is filled with light.—LUKE 11:34

PRAY SIMPLY

It is a mark of simplicity and even of the love of God to make our requests to him without wishing to constrain him to give us anything, but only so much and so far as it shall please him. The prayer of such a soul—so simple, so humble, so submissive to his will—ravishes him. Then he sees us as we might regard a poor man who asks us for alms, but who is not troubled at our refusal. In fact, however great his persistence, or rather however long he stands before us with downcast eyes, are we not touched when he goes away after the time he has spent in waiting on us?

Of the simplicity of the soul that prays in this way we must say, "When your eye is clear, your whole body, too, is filled with light." That is, following such a prayer, he to whom we have prayed will be very pleased with all the good works we shall do the whole day long. And his invisible and imperceptible divine light will also fill them.

Often it happens that when we think we have light and graces, we don't have them at all. And sometimes when we think we don't have them, we actually have them. Therefore, we trouble ourselves in vain if we seek lights and graces in prayer when we feel that we don't have them. The operation of the Holy Spirit in the soul is wholly interior and often unknown to the soul itself. It is enough, I think, to be present before God and to act as I have said.

When we pray we must be a vessel open and exposed before God that he may drip His grace into it as he wills, drop by drop. And we must be almost as glad to carry this vessel home again empty, as if he had filled it up. For often we think we are going away empty, when we are filled with the Spirit of God, though we know it not. ST. JANE DE CHANTAL, 1572–1641

YOU WILL FIND THE NEXT READING AT LUKE 19.

4 'To you my friends I say: Do not be afraid of those who kill the body and after that can do no more. 5 I will tell you whom to fear: fear him who, after he has killed, has the power to cast into hell. Yes, I tell you, he is the one to fear. 6 Can you not buy five sparrows for two pennies? And yet not one is forgotten in God's sight. 7 Why, every hair on your head has been counted. There is no need to be afraid: you are worth more than many sparrows.

8 'I tell you, if anyone openly declares himself for me in the presence of human beings, the Son of man will declare himself for him in the presence of God's angels. 9 But anyone who disowns me in the presence of human beings will be disowned in the presence of God's angels.

10 'Everyone who says a word against the Son of man will be forgiven, but no one who blasphemes against the Holy Spirit will be forgiven.

11 'When they take you before synagogues and magistrates and authorities, do not worry about how to defend yourselves or what to say, 12 because when the time comes, the Holy Spirit will teach you what you should say.'

On hoarding possessions

13 A man in the crowd said to him, 'Master, tell my brother to give me a share of our inheritance.' 14 He said to him, 'My friend, who appointed me your judge, or the arbitrator of your claims?' 15 Then he said to them, 'Watch, and be on your guard against avarice of any kind, for life does not consist in possessions, even when someone has more than he needs.'

16 Then he told them a parable, 'There was once a rich man who, having had a good harvest from his land, 17 thought to himself, "What am I to do? I have not enough room to store my crops." 18 Then he said, "This is what I will do: I will pull down my barns and build bigger ones, and store all my grain and my goods in them, 19 and I will say to my soul: My soul, you have plenty of good things laid by for many years to come; take things easy, eat, drink, have a good time." 20 But God said to him, "Fool! This very night the demand will be made for your soul; and this hoard of yours, whose will it be then?" 21 So it is when someone stores up treasure for himself instead of becoming rich in the sight of God.'

Trust in Providence

22 Then he said to his disciples, 'That is why I am telling you not to worry about your life and what you are to eat, nor about your body and how you are to clothe it. 23 For life is more than food, and the body more than clothing. 24 Think of the ravens. They do not sow or reap; they have no storehouses and no barns; yet God feeds them. And how much more you are worth than the birds! 25 Can any of you, however much you worry, add a single cubit to your span of life? 26 If a very small thing is beyond your powers, why worry about the rest? 27 Think how the flowers grow; they never have to spin or weave; yet, I assure you, not even Solomon in all his royal robes was clothed like one of them. 28 Now if that is how God clothes a flower which is growing wild today and is thrown into the furnace tomorrow, how much more will he look after you,

who have so little faith! 29 But you must not set your hearts on things to eat and things to drink; nor must you worry. 30 It is the gentiles of this world who set their hearts on all these things. Your Father well knows you need them. 31 No; set your hearts on his kingdom, and these other things will be given you as well.

32 'There is no need to be afraid, little flock, for it has pleased your Father to give you the kingdom.

On almsgiving

33 'Sell your possessions and give to those in need. Get yourselves purses that do not wear out, treasure that will not fail you, in heaven where no thief can reach it and no moth destroy it. 34 For wherever your treasure is, that is where your heart will be too.

On being ready for the Master's return

35 'See that you have your belts done up and your lamps lit. 36 Be like people waiting for their master to return from the wedding feast, ready to open the door as soon as he comes and knocks. 37 Blessed those servants whom the master finds awake when he comes. In truth I tell you, he will do up his belt, sit them down at table and wait on them. 38 It may be in the second watch that he comes, or in the third, but blessed are those servants if he finds them ready. 39 You may be quite sure of this, that if the householder had known at what time the burglar would come, he would not have let anyone break through the wall of his house. 40 You too must stand ready, because the Son of man is coming at an hour you do not expect.'

41 Peter said, 'Lord, do you mean this parable for us, or for everyone?' 42 The Lord replied, 'Who, then, is the wise and trustworthy steward whom the master will place over his household to give them at the proper time their allowance of food? 43 Blessed that servant if his master's arrival finds him doing exactly that. 44 I tell you truly, he will put him in charge of everything that he owns. 45 But if the servant says to himself, "My master is taking

his time coming," and sets about beating the menservants and the servant-girls, and eating and drinking and getting drunk, [46] his master will come on a day he does not expect and at an hour he does not know. The master will cut him off and send him to the same fate as the unfaithful.

[47] 'The servant who knows what his master wants, but has got nothing ready and done nothing in accord with those wishes, will be given a great many strokes of the lash. [48] The one who did not know, but has acted in such a way that he deserves a beating, will be given fewer strokes. When someone is given a great deal, a great deal will be demanded of that person; when someone is entrusted with a great deal, of that person even more will be expected.

Jesus and his Passion

[49] 'I have come to bring fire to the earth, and how I wish it were blazing already! [50] There is a baptism I must still receive, and what constraint I am under until it is completed!

Jesus the cause of dissension

[51] 'Do you suppose that I am here to bring peace on earth? No, I tell you, but rather division. [52] For from now on, a household of five will be divided: three against two and two against three; [53] *father opposed to son,* son to father, mother to daughter, *daughter to mother,* mother-in-law to daughter-in-law, *daughter-in-law to mother-in-law.'* [a]

On reading the signs of the times

[54] He said again to the crowds, 'When you see a cloud looming up in the west you say at once that rain is coming, and so it does. [55] And when the wind is from the south you say it's going to be hot, and it is. [56] Hypocrites! You know how to interpret the face of the earth and the sky. How is it you do not know how to interpret these times?

[57] 'Why not judge for yourselves what is upright? [58] For example: when you are going to court with your opponent, make an effort to settle with him on the way, or he may drag you before the judge and the judge hand you over to the officer and the officer have you thrown into prison. [59] I tell you, you will not get out till you have paid the very last penny.'

Examples inviting repentance

13 It was just about this time that some people arrived and told him about the Galileans whose blood Pilate had mingled with that of their sacrifices. At this he said to them, [2] 'Do you suppose that these Galileans were worse sinners than any others, that this should have happened to them? [3] They were not, I tell you. No; but unless you repent you will all perish as they did. [4] Or those eighteen on whom the tower at Siloam fell, killing them all? Do you suppose that they were more guilty than all the other people living in Jerusalem? [5] They were not, I tell you. No; but unless you repent you will all perish as they did.'

Parable of the barren fig tree

[6] He told this parable, 'A man had a fig tree planted in his vineyard, and he came looking for fruit on it but found none. [7] He said to his vinedresser, "For three years now I have been coming to look for fruit on this fig tree and finding none. Cut it down: why should it be taking up the ground?" [8] "Sir," the man replied, "leave it one more year and give me time to dig round it and manure it: [9] it may bear fruit next year; if not, then you can cut it down."'

Healing of a crippled woman on the Sabbath

[10] One Sabbath day he was teaching in one of the synagogues, [11] and there before him was a woman who for eighteen years had been possessed by a spirit that crippled her; she was bent double and quite unable to stand upright. [12] When Jesus saw her he called her over and said, 'Woman, you are freed from your disability,' [13] and he laid his hands on her. And at once she straightened up, and she glorified God.

12a Mi 7:6.

14 But the president of the synagogue was indignant because Jesus had healed on the Sabbath, and he addressed all those present saying, 'There are six days when work is to be done. Come and be healed on one of those days and not on the Sabbath.' 15 But the Lord answered him and said, 'Hypocrites! Is there one of you who does not untie his ox or his donkey from the manger on the Sabbath and take it out for watering? 16 And this woman, a daughter of Abraham whom Satan has held bound these eighteen years—was it not right to untie this bond on the Sabbath day?' 17 When he said this, all his adversaries were covered with confusion, and all the people were overjoyed at all the wonders he worked.

Parable of the mustard seed

18 He went on to say, 'What is the kingdom of God like? What shall I compare it with? 19 It is like a mustard seed which a man took and threw into his garden: it grew and became a tree, and the birds of the air sheltered in its branches.'

Parable of the yeast

20 Again he said, 'What shall I compare the kingdom of God with? 21 It is like the yeast a woman took and mixed in with three measures of flour till it was leavened all through.'

The narrow door; rejection of the Jews, call of the gentiles

22 Through towns and villages he went teaching, making his way to Jerusalem. 23 Someone said to him, 'Sir, will there be only a few saved?' He said to them, 24 'Try your hardest to enter by the narrow door, because, I tell you, many will try to enter and will not succeed.

25 'Once the master of the house has got up and locked the door, you may find yourself standing outside knocking on the door, saying, "Lord, open to us," but he will answer, "I do not know where you come from." 26 Then you will start saying, "We once ate and drank in your company; you taught in our streets,"

27 but he will reply, "I do not know where you come from; *away from me, all evil doers!*" [a]

28 'Then there will be weeping and grinding of teeth, when you see Abraham and Isaac and Jacob and all the prophets in the kingdom of God, and yourselves thrown out. 29 And people from east and west, from north and south, will come and sit down at the feast in the kingdom of God.

30 'Look, there are those now last who will be first, and those now first who will be last.'

Herod the fox

31 Just at this time some Pharisees came up. 'Go away,' they said. 'Leave this place, because Herod [b] means to kill you.' 32 He replied, 'You may go and give that fox this message: Look! Today and tomorrow I drive out devils and heal, and on the third day I attain my end. 33 But for today and tomorrow and the next day I must go on, since it would not be right for a prophet to die outside Jerusalem.

Jerusalem admonished

34 'Jerusalem, Jerusalem, you that kill the prophets and stone those who are sent to you! How often have I longed to gather your children together, as a hen gathers her brood under her wings, and you refused! 35 Look! Your house will be left to you. Yes, I promise you, you shall not see me till the time comes when you are saying:

> Blessed is he who is coming in the name of the Lord!' [c]

Healing of a dropsical man on the Sabbath

14 Now it happened that on a Sabbath day he had gone to share a meal in the house of one of the leading Pharisees; and they watched him closely. 2 Now there in front of him was a man with dropsy, 3 and Jesus addressed the lawyers and Pharisees with the

13a Ps 6:8.

13b Herod Antipas, son of Herod the Great.

13c Ps 118:26.

words, 'Is it against the law to cure someone on the Sabbath, or not?' ⁴But they remained silent, so he took the man and cured him and sent him away. ⁵Then he said to them, 'Which of you here, if his son falls into a well, or his ox, will not pull him out on a Sabbath day without any hesitation?' ⁶And to this they could find no answer.

On choosing places at table

⁷He then told the guests a parable, because he had noticed how they picked the places of honour. He said this, ⁸'When someone invites you to a wedding feast, do not take your seat in the place of honour. A more distinguished person than you may have been invited, ⁹and the person who invited you both may come and say, "Give up your place to this man." And then, to your embarrassment, you will have to go and take the lowest place. ¹⁰No; when you are a guest, make your way to the lowest place and sit there, so that, when your host comes, he may say, "My friend, move up higher." Then, everyone with you at the table will see you honoured. ¹¹For everyone who raises himself up will be humbled, and the one who humbles himself will be raised up.'

On choosing guests to be invited

¹²Then he said to his host, 'When you give a lunch or a dinner, do not invite your friends or your brothers or your relations or rich neighbours, in case they invite you back and so repay you. ¹³No; when you have a party, invite the poor, the crippled, the lame, the blind; ¹⁴then you will be blessed, for they have no means to repay you and so you will be repaid when the upright rise again.'

The invited guests who made excuses

¹⁵On hearing this, one of those gathered round the table said to him, 'Blessed is anyone who will share the meal in the kingdom of God!' ¹⁶But he said to him, 'There was a man who gave a great banquet, and he invited a large number of people. ¹⁷When the time for the banquet came, he sent his servant to say to those who had been invited, "Come along: everything is ready now." ¹⁸But all alike started to make excuses. The first said, "I have bought a piece of land and must go and see it. Please accept my apologies." ¹⁹Another said, "I have bought five yoke of oxen and am on my way to try them out. Please accept my apologies." ²⁰Yet another said, "I have just got married and so am unable to come."

²¹'The servant returned and reported this to his master. Then the householder, in a rage, said to his servant, "Go out quickly into the streets and alleys of the town and bring in here the poor, the crippled, the blind and the lame." ²²"Sir," said the servant, "your orders have been carried out and there is still room." ²³Then the master said to his servant, "Go to the open roads and the hedgerows and press people to come in, to make sure my house is full; ²⁴because, I tell you, not one of those who were invited shall have a taste of my banquet."'

Renouncing all that one holds dear

²⁵Great crowds accompanied him on his way and he turned and spoke to them. ²⁶'Anyone who comes to me without hating father, mother, wife, children, brothers, sisters, yes and his own life too, cannot be my disciple. ²⁷No one who does not carry his cross and come after me can be my disciple.

Renouncing possessions

²⁸'And indeed, which of you here, intending to build a tower, would not first sit down and work out the cost to see if he had enough to complete it? ²⁹Otherwise, if he laid the foundation and then found himself unable to finish the work, anyone who saw it would start making fun of him and saying, ³⁰"Here is someone who started to build and was unable to finish." ³¹Or again, what king marching to war against another king would not first sit down and consider whether with ten thousand men he could stand up to the other who was ad-

vancing against him with twenty thousand? 32 If not, then while the other king was still a long way off, he would send envoys to sue for peace. 33 So in the same way, none of you can be my disciple without giving up all that he owns.

On loss of enthusiasm in a disciple

34 'Salt is a good thing. But if salt itself loses its taste, what can make it salty again? 35 It is good for neither soil nor manure heap. People throw it away. Anyone who has ears for listening should listen!'

The three parables of God's mercy

15 The tax collectors and sinners, however, were all crowding round to listen to him, 2 and the Pharisees and scribes complained saying, 'This man welcomes sinners and eats with them.' 3 So he told them this parable:

The lost sheep

4 'Which one of you with a hundred sheep, if he lost one, would fail to leave the ninety-nine in the desert and go after the missing one till he found it? 5 And when he found it, would he not joyfully take it on his shoulders 6 and then, when he got home, call together his friends and neighbours, saying to them, "Rejoice with me, I have found my sheep that was lost." 7 In the same way, I tell you, there will be more rejoicing in heaven over one sinner repenting than over ninety-nine upright people who have no need of repentance.

The lost drachma

8 'Or again, what woman with ten drachmas would not, if she lost one, light a lamp and sweep out the house and search thoroughly till she found it? 9 And then, when she had found it, call together her friends and neighbours, saying to them, "Rejoice with me, I have found the drachma I lost." 10 In the same way, I tell you, there is rejoicing among the angels of God over one repentant sinner.'

The lost son (the 'prodigal') and the dutiful son

11 Then he said, 'There was a man who had two sons. 12 The younger one said to his father, "Father, let me have the share of the estate that will come to me." So the father divided the property between them. 13 A few days later, the younger son got together everything he had and left for a distant country where he squandered his money on a life of debauchery.

14 'When he had spent it all, that country experienced a severe famine, and now he began to feel the pinch; 15 so he hired himself out to one of the local inhabitants who put him on his farm to feed the pigs. 16 And he would willingly have filled himself with the husks the pigs were eating but no one would let him have them. 17 Then he came to his senses and said, "How many of my father's hired men have all the food they want and more, and here am I dying of hunger! 18 I will leave this place and go to my father and say: Father, I have sinned against heaven and against you; 19 I no longer deserve to be called your son; treat me as one of your hired men." 20 So he left the place and went back to his father.

'While he was still a long way off, his father saw him and was moved with pity. He ran to the boy, clasped him in his arms and kissed him. 21 Then his son said, "Father, I have sinned against heaven and against you. I no longer deserve to be called your son." 22 But the father said to his servants, "Quick! Bring out the best robe and put it on him; put a ring on his finger and sandals on his feet. 23 Bring the calf we have been fattening, and kill it; we will celebrate by having a feast, 24 because this son of mine was dead and has come back to life; he was lost and is found." And they began to celebrate.

25 'Now the elder son was out in the fields, and on his way back, as he drew near the house, he could hear music and dancing. 26 Calling one of the servants he asked what it was all about. 27 The servant told him, "Your

brother has come, and your father has killed the calf we had been fattening because he has got him back safe and sound." ²⁸He was angry then and refused to go in, and his father came out and began to urge him to come in; ²⁹but he retorted to his father, "All these years I have slaved for you and never once disobeyed any orders of yours, yet you never offered me so much as a kid for me to celebrate with my friends. ³⁰But, for this son of yours, when he comes back after swallowing up your property—he and his loose women—you kill the calf we had been fattening."

³¹'The father said, "My son, you are with me always and all I have is yours. ³²But it was only right we should celebrate and rejoice, because your brother here was dead and has come to life; he was lost and is found." '

The crafty steward

16 He also said to his disciples, 'There was a rich man and he had a steward who was denounced to him for being wasteful with his property. ²He called for the man and said, "What is this I hear about you? Draw me up an account of your stewardship because you are not to be my steward any longer." ³Then the steward said to himself, "Now that my master is taking the stewardship from me, what am I to do? Dig? I am not strong enough. Go begging? I should be too ashamed. ⁴Ah, I know what I will do to make sure that when I am dismissed from office there will be some to welcome me into their homes."

⁵'Then he called his master's debtors one by one. To the first he said, "How much do you owe my master?" ⁶"One hundred measures of oil," he said. The steward said, "Here, take your bond; sit down and quickly write fifty." ⁷To another he said, "And you, sir, how much do you owe?" "One hundred measures of wheat," he said. The steward said, "Here, take your bond and write eighty."

⁸'The master praised the dishonest steward for his astuteness. For the children of this world are more astute in dealing with their own kind than are the children of light.'

The right use of money

⁹'And so I tell you this: use money, tainted as it is, to win you friends, and thus make sure that when it fails you, they will welcome you into eternal dwellings. ¹⁰Anyone who is trustworthy in little things is trustworthy in great; anyone who is dishonest in little things is dishonest in great. ¹¹If then you are not trustworthy with money, that tainted thing, who will trust you with genuine riches? ¹²And if you are not trustworthy with what is not yours, who will give you what is your very own?

¹³'No servant can be the slave of two masters: he will either hate the first and love the second, or be attached to the first and despise the second. You cannot be the slave both of God and of money.'

Against the Pharisees and their love of money

¹⁴The Pharisees, who loved money, heard all this and jeered at him. ¹⁵He said to them, 'You are the very ones who pass yourselves off as upright in people's sight, but God knows your hearts. For what is highly esteemed in human eyes is loathsome in the sight of God.

The kingdom stormed

¹⁶'Up to the time of John it was the Law and the Prophets; from then onwards, the kingdom of God has been preached, and everyone is forcing their way into it.

The Law remains

¹⁷'It is easier for heaven and earth to disappear than for one little stroke to drop out of the Law.

Marriage indissoluble

¹⁸'Everyone who divorces his wife and marries another is guilty of adultery, and the man who marries a woman divorced by her husband commits adultery.

The parable of the rich man and Lazarus

¹⁹'There was a rich man who used to dress in purple and fine linen and feast magnificently

every day. 20 And at his gate there used to lie a poor man called Lazarus, covered with sores, 21 who longed to fill himself with what fell from the rich man's table. Even dogs came and licked his sores. 22 Now it happened that the poor man died and was carried away by the angels into Abraham's embrace. The rich man also died and was buried.

23 'In his torment in Hades he looked up and saw Abraham a long way off with Lazarus in his embrace. 24 So he cried out, "Father Abraham, pity me and send Lazarus to dip the tip of his finger in water and cool my tongue, for I am in agony in these flames." 25 Abraham said, "My son, remember that during your life you had your fill of good things, just as Lazarus his fill of bad. Now he is being comforted here while you are in agony. 26 But that is not all: between us and you a great gulf has been fixed, to prevent those who want to cross from our side to yours or from your side to ours."

27 'So he said, "Father, I beg you then to send Lazarus to my father's house, 28 since I have five brothers, to give them warning so that they do not come to this place of torment too." 29 Abraham said, "They have Moses and the prophets, let them listen to them." 30 The rich man replied, "Ah no, father Abraham, but if someone comes to them from the dead, they will repent." 31 Then Abraham said to him, "If they will not listen either to Moses or to the prophets, they will not be convinced even if someone should rise from the dead."'

On leading others astray

17 He said to his disciples, 'Causes of falling are sure to come, but alas for the one through whom they occur! 2 It would be better for such a person to be thrown into the sea with a millstone round the neck than to be the downfall of a single one of these little ones. 3 Keep watch on yourselves!

Brotherly correction

'If your brother does something wrong, rebuke him and, if he is sorry, forgive him. 4 And if he wrongs you seven times a day and seven times comes back to you and says, "I am sorry," you must forgive him.'

The power of faith

5 The apostles said to the Lord, 'Increase our faith.' 6 The Lord replied, 'If you had faith like a mustard seed you could say to this mulberry tree, "Be uprooted and planted in the sea," and it would obey you.

Humble service

7 'Which of you, with a servant ploughing or minding sheep, would say to him when he returned from the fields, "Come and have your meal at once"? 8 Would he not be more likely to say, "Get my supper ready; fasten your belt and wait on me while I eat and drink. You yourself can eat and drink afterwards"? 9 Must he be grateful to the servant for doing what he was told? 10 So with you: when you have done all you have been told to do, say, "We are useless servants: we have done no more than our duty."'

The ten victims of skin-disease

11 Now it happened that on the way to Jerusalem he was travelling in the borderlands of Samaria and Galilee. 12 As he entered one of the villages, ten men suffering from a virulent skin-disease came to meet him. They stood some way off 13 and called to him, 'Jesus! Master! Take pity on us.' 14 When he saw them he said, 'Go and show yourselves to the priests.' Now as they were going away they were cleansed. 15 Finding himself cured, one of them turned back praising God at the top of his voice 16 and threw himself prostrate at the feet of Jesus and thanked him. The man was a Samaritan. 17 This led Jesus to say, 'Were not all ten made clean? The other nine, where are they? 18 It seems that no one has come back to give praise to God, except this foreigner.' 19 And he said to the man, 'Stand up and go on your way. Your faith has saved you.'

The coming of the kingdom of God

20 Asked by the Pharisees when the kingdom of God was to come, he gave them this answer, 'The coming of the kingdom of God does not admit of observation 21 and there will be no one to say, "Look, it is here! Look, it is there!" For look, the kingdom of God is among you.'

The Day of the Son of man

22 He said to the disciples, 'A time will come when you will long to see one of the days of the Son of man and will not see it. 23 They will say to you, "Look, it is there!" or, "Look, it is here!" Make no move; do not set off in pursuit; 24 for as the lightning flashing from one part of heaven lights up the other, so will be the Son of man when his Day comes. 25 But first he is destined to suffer grievously and be rejected by this generation.

26 'As it was in Noah's day, so will it also be in the days of the Son of man. 27 People were eating and drinking, marrying wives and husbands, right up to the day Noah went into the ark, and the Flood came and destroyed them all. 28 It will be the same as it was in Lot's day: people were eating and drinking, buying and selling, planting and building, 29 but the day Lot left Sodom, it rained fire and brimstone from heaven and it destroyed them all. 30 It will be the same when the day comes for the Son of man to be revealed.

31 'When that Day comes, no one on the housetop, with his possessions in the house, must come down to collect them, nor must anyone in the fields turn back. 32 Remember Lot's wife. 33 Anyone who tries to preserve his life will lose it; and anyone who loses it will keep it safe. 34 I tell you, on that night, when two are in one bed, one will be taken, the other left; 35 when two women are grinding corn together, one will be taken, the other left.' [36] a
37 The disciples spoke up and asked, 'Where, Lord?' He said, 'Where the body is, there too will the vultures gather.'

The unscrupulous judge and the importunate widow

18 Then he told them a parable about the need to pray continually and never lose heart. 2 'There was a judge in a certain town,' he said, 'who had neither fear of God nor respect for anyone. 3 In the same town there was also a widow who kept on coming to him and saying, "I want justice from you against my enemy!" 4 For a long time he refused, but at last he said to himself, "Even though I have neither fear of God nor respect for any human person, 5 I must give this widow her just rights since she keeps pestering me, or she will come and slap me in the face." '

6 And the Lord said, 'You notice what the unjust judge has to say? 7 Now, will not God see justice done to his elect if they keep calling to him day and night even though he still delays to help them? 8 I promise you, he will see justice done to them, and done speedily. But when the Son of man comes, will he find any faith on earth?'

The Pharisee and the tax collector

9 He spoke the following parable to some people who prided themselves on being upright and despised everyone else, 10 'Two men went up to the Temple to pray, one a Pharisee, the other a tax collector. 11 The Pharisee stood there and said this prayer to himself, "I thank you, God, that I am not grasping, unjust, adulterous like everyone else, and particularly that I am not like this tax collector here. 12 I fast twice a week; I pay tithes on all I get." 13 The tax collector stood some distance away, not daring even to raise his eyes to heaven; but he beat his breast and said, "God, be merciful to me, a sinner." 14 This man, I tell you, went home again justified; the other did not. For everyone who raises himself up will be humbled, but anyone who humbles himself will be raised up.'

17a Add. v. 36, 'There will be two men in the fields; one will be taken, the other left.' cf. Mt 24:40.

Jesus and the children

15 People even brought babies to him, for him to touch them; but when the disciples saw this they scolded them. 16 But Jesus called the children to him and said, 'Let the little children come to me, and do not stop them; for it is to such as these that the kingdom of God belongs. 17 In truth I tell you, anyone who does not welcome the kingdom of God like a little child will never enter it.'

The rich aristocrat

18 One of the rulers put this question to him, 'Good Master, what shall I do to inherit eternal life?' 19 Jesus said to him, 'Why do you call me good? No one is good but God alone. 20 You know the commandments: *You shall not commit adultery; You shall not kill; You shall not steal; You shall not give false witness; Honour your father and your mother.'* ᵃ 21 He replied, 'I have kept all these since my earliest days.' 22 And when Jesus heard this he said, 'There is still one thing you lack. Sell everything you own and distribute the money to the poor, and you will have treasure in heaven; then come, follow me.' 23 But when he heard this he was overcome with sadness, for he was very rich.

The danger of riches

24 Jesus looked at him and said, 'How hard it is for those who have riches to make their way into the kingdom of God! 25 Yes, it is easier for a camel to pass through the eye of a needle than for someone rich to enter the kingdom of God.' 26 Those who were listening said, 'In that case, who can be saved?' 27 He replied, 'Things that are impossible by human resources, are possible for God.'

The reward of renunciation

28 But Peter said, 'Look, we left all we had to follow you.' 29 He said to them, 'In truth I tell you, there is no one who has left house, wife, brothers, parents or children for the sake of the kingdom of God 30 who will not receive many times as much in this present age and, in the world to come, eternal life.'

Third prophecy of the Passion

31 Then taking the Twelve aside he said to them, 'Look, we are going up to Jerusalem, and everything that is written by the prophets about the Son of man is to come true. 32 For he will be handed over to the gentiles and will be mocked, maltreated and spat on, 33 and when they have scourged him they will put him to death; and on the third day he will rise again.' 34 But they could make nothing of this; what he said was quite obscure to them, they did not understand what he was telling them.

Entering Jericho: the blind man

35 Now it happened that as he drew near to Jericho there was a blind man sitting at the side of the road begging. 36 When he heard the crowd going past he asked what it was all about, 37 and they told him that Jesus the Nazarene was passing by. 38 So he called out, 'Jesus, Son of David, have pity on me.' 39 The people in front scolded him and told him to keep quiet, but he only shouted all the louder, 'Son of David, have pity on me.' 40 Jesus stopped and ordered them to bring the man to him, and when he came up, asked him, 41 'What do you want me to do for you?' 'Sir,' he replied, 'let me see again.' 42 Jesus said to him, 'Receive your sight. Your faith has saved you.' 43 And instantly his sight returned and he followed him praising God, and all the people who saw it gave praise to God.

Zacchaeus

19 He entered Jericho and was going through the town 2 and suddenly a man whose name was Zacchaeus made his appearance; he was one of the senior tax collectors and a wealthy man. 3 He kept trying to see which Jesus was, but he was too short and could not see him for the crowd; 4 so he ran ahead and climbed a sycamore tree to catch a

18a Ex 20:12–16.

141 READ LUKE 19:1–10.

Zacchaeus, come down. Hurry, because I am to stay at your house today.—LUKE 19:5

MEETING GOD IN DAILY LIFE

For St. John Ruysbroeck, the example of Christ coming to Zacchaeus shows how Christians can meet God in the activity of life:

[The active Christian] must run before the crowd, that is, the multiplicity of created things. These make man so little that he cannot perceive God. Then he must climb up the Tree of Faith that grows from above downwards because its root is in the Godhead. The upper branches reveal the Trinity of persons and the unity of the divine nature. Man must cling to the unity at the tree top because here Jesus will pass by with all his gifts.

Then Jesus comes. He sees man and in the light of faith shows him that by virtue of his divinity he is unlimited, incomprehensible, inaccessible and fathomless. Thus the highest knowledge of God that man can acquire in the active life is to recognize by faith that God is inconceivable and un-knowable.

In this light God says to the desire of man: "Come down. Hurry, because I am to stay at your house today." This is a quick descent by love and desire into the abyss of the Godhead to which no intellect can attain by its created light. When the soul thus leans upon God by intention and love—beyond all her understanding—then she rests in God, and God in her. Stretching by desire towards this incom-prehensible God, she meets Christ and is fulfilled with his gifts. And loving and resting above all things, she dwells in God and God in her. In this way, Christ may be encountered upon the summit of the active life. ST. JOHN RUYSBROECK, 1293–1381

YOU WILL FIND THE NEXT READING AT LUKE 21.

glimpse of Jesus who was to pass that way. ⁵When Jesus reached the spot he looked up and spoke to him, 'Zacchaeus, come down. Hurry, because I am to stay at your house today.' ⁶And he hurried down and welcomed him joyfully. ⁷They all complained when they saw what was happening. 'He has gone to stay at a sinner's house,' they said. ⁸But Zacchaeus stood his ground and said to the Lord, 'Look, sir, I am going to give half my property to the poor, and if I have cheated anybody I will pay him back four times the amount.' ⁹And Jesus said to him, 'Today salvation has come to this house, because this man too is a son of Abra-ham; ¹⁰for the Son of man has come to seek out and save what was lost.'

Parable of the pounds

¹¹While the people were listening to this he went on to tell a parable, because he was near Jerusalem and they thought that the kingdom of God was going to show itself then and there. ¹²Accordingly he said, 'A man of noble birth went to a distant country to be appointed king and then return. ¹³He summoned ten of his servants and gave them ten pounds, telling them, "Trade with these, until I get back." ¹⁴But his compatriots detested him and sent a

delegation to follow him with this message, "We do not want this man to be our king."

15 'Now it happened that on his return, having received his appointment as king, he sent for those servants to whom he had given the money, to find out what profit each had made by trading. 16 The first came in, "Sir," he said, "your one pound has brought in ten." 17 He replied, "Well done, my good servant! Since you have proved yourself trustworthy in a very small thing, you shall have the government of ten cities." 18 Then came the second, "Sir," he said, "your one pound has made five." 19 To this one also he said, "And you shall be in charge of five cities." 20 Next came the other, "Sir," he said, "here is your pound. I put it away safely wrapped up in a cloth 21 because I was afraid of you; for you are an exacting man: you gather in what you have not laid out and reap what you have not sown." 22 He said to him, "You wicked servant! Out of your own mouth I condemn you. So you knew that I was an exacting man, gathering in what I have not laid out and reaping what I have not sown? 23 Then why did you not put my money in the bank? On my return I could have drawn it out with interest." 24 And he said to those standing by, "Take the pound from him and give it to the man who has ten pounds." 25 And they said to him, "But, sir, he has ten pounds . . ." 26 "I tell you, to everyone who has will be given more; but anyone who has not will be deprived even of what he has.

27 "As for my enemies who did not want me for their king, bring them here and execute them in my presence." '

The Messiah enters Jerusalem

28 When he had said this he went on ahead, going up to Jerusalem. 29 Now it happened that when he was near Bethphage and Bethany, close by the Mount of Olives as it is called, he sent two of the disciples, saying, 30 'Go to the village opposite, and as you enter it you will find a tethered colt that no one has ever yet ridden. Untie it and bring it here. 31 If anyone asks you, "Why are you untying it?"

you are to say this, "The Master needs it." ' 32 The messengers went off and found everything just as he had told them. 33 As they were untying the colt, its owners said, 'Why are you untying it?' 34 and they answered, 'The Master needs it.'

35 So they took the colt to Jesus and, throwing their cloaks on its back, they lifted Jesus on to it. 36 As he moved off, they spread their cloaks in the road, 37 and now, as he was approaching the downward slope of the Mount of Olives, the whole group of disciples joyfully began to praise God at the top of their voices for all the miracles they had seen. 38 They cried out:

> Blessed is he who is coming
> as King *in the name of the Lord!*[a]
> Peace in heaven
> and glory in the highest heavens!

Jesus defends his disciples for acclaiming him

39 Some Pharisees in the crowd said to him, 'Master, reprove your disciples,' 40 but he answered, 'I tell you, if these keep silence, the stones will cry out.'

Lament for Jerusalem

41 As he drew near and came in sight of the city he shed tears over it 42 and said, 'If you too had only recognised on this day the way to peace! But in fact it is hidden from your eyes! 43 Yes, a time is coming when your enemies will raise fortifications all round you, when they will encircle you and hem you in on every side; 44 they will dash you and the children inside your walls to the ground; they will leave not one stone standing on another within you, because you did not recognise the moment of your visitation.'

The expulsion of the dealers from the Temple

45 Then he went into the Temple and began driving out those who were busy trading, say-

19a Ps 118:26.

ing to them, [46]'According to scripture, *my house shall be a house of prayer* but you have turned it into *a bandits' den*.'[b]

Jesus teaches in the Temple

[47]He taught in the Temple every day. The chief priests and the scribes, in company with the leading citizens, tried to do away with him, [48]but they could not find a way to carry this out because the whole people hung on his words.

The Jews question the authority of Jesus

20 Now it happened that one day while he was teaching the people in the Temple and proclaiming the good news, the chief priests and the scribes came up, together with the elders, [2]and spoke to him. 'Tell us,' they said, 'what authority have you for acting like this? Or who gives you this authority?' [3]In reply he said to them, 'And I will ask you a question, just one. Tell me: [4]John's baptism: what was its origin, heavenly or human?' [5]And they debated this way among themselves, 'If we say heavenly, he will retort, "Why did you refuse to believe him?"; [6]and if we say human, the whole people will stone us, for they are convinced that John was a prophet.' [7]So their reply was that they did not know where it came from. [8]And Jesus said to them, 'Nor will I tell you my authority for acting like this.'

Parable of the wicked tenants

[9]And he went on to tell the people this parable, 'A man planted a vineyard and leased it to tenants, and went abroad for a long while. [10]When the right time came, he sent a servant to the tenants to get his share of the produce of the vineyard. But the tenants thrashed him, and sent him away empty-handed. [11]But he went on to send a second servant; they thrashed him too and treated him shamefully and sent him away empty-handed. [12]He still went on to send a third; they wounded this one too, and threw him out. [13]Then the owner of the vineyard thought, "What am I to do? I will send them my own beloved son. Perhaps they will respect him." [14]But when the tenants saw him they put their heads together saying, "This is the heir, let us kill him so that the inheritance will be ours." [15]So they threw him out of the vineyard and killed him.

'Now what will the owner of the vineyard do to them? [16]He will come and make an end of these tenants and give the vineyard to others.' Hearing this they said, 'God forbid!' [17]But he looked hard at them and said, 'Then what does this text in the scriptures mean:

The stone which the builders rejected has become the cornerstone?[a]

[18]Anyone who falls on that stone will be dashed to pieces; anyone it falls on will be crushed.'

[19]And the scribes and the chief priests would have liked to lay hands on him that very moment, because they realised that this parable was aimed at them, but they were afraid of the people.

On tribute to Caesar

[20]So they awaited their opportunity and sent agents to pose as upright men, and to catch him out in something he might say and so enable them to hand him over to the jurisdiction and authority of the governor. [21]They put to him this question, 'Master, we know that you say and teach what is right; you favour no one, but teach the way of God in all honesty. [22]Is it permissible for us to pay taxes to Caesar or not?' [23]But he was aware of their cunning and said, [24]'Show me a denarius. Whose portrait and title are on it?' They said, 'Caesar's.' [25]He said to them, 'Well then, pay Caesar what belongs to Caesar—and God what belongs to God.'

[26]They were unable to catch him out in anything he had to say in public; they were amazed at his answer and were silenced.

19b Is 56:7 and Jr 7:11.   *20a* Ps 118:22.

The resurrection of the dead

27 Some Sadducees—those who argue that there is no resurrection—approached him and they put this question to him, 28 'Master, Moses prescribed for us, if a man's married brother dies childless, the man must marry the widow to raise up children for his brother. 29 Well then, there were seven brothers; the first, having married a wife, died childless. 30 The second 31 and then the third married the widow. And the same with all seven, they died leaving no children. 32 Finally the woman herself died. 33 Now, at the resurrection, whose wife will she be, since she had been married to all seven?'

34 Jesus replied, 'The children of this world take wives and husbands, 35 but those who are judged worthy of a place in the other world and in the resurrection from the dead do not marry 36 because they can no longer die, for they are the same as the angels, and being children of the resurrection they are children of God. 37 And Moses himself implies that the dead rise again, in the passage about the bush where he calls the Lord *the God of Abraham, the God of Isaac and the God of Jacob.*[b] 38 Now he is God, not of the dead, but of the living; for to him everyone is alive.'

39 Some scribes then spoke up. They said, 'Well put, Master.' 40 They did not dare to ask him any more questions.

Christ not only son but also Lord of David

41 He then said to them, 'How can people maintain that the Christ is son of David? 42 Why, David himself says in the Book of Psalms:

The Lord declared to my Lord,
take your seat at my right hand,
43 *till I have made your enemies*
your footstool.[c]

44 David here calls him Lord; how then can he be his son?'

The scribes condemned by Jesus

45 While all the people were listening he said to the disciples, 46 'Beware of the scribes who like to walk about in long robes and love to be greeted respectfully in the market squares, to take the front seats in the synagogues and the places of honour at banquets, 47 who devour the property of widows, and for show offer long prayers. The more severe will be the sentence they receive.'

The widow's mite

21 Looking up, he saw rich people putting their offerings into the treasury; 2 and he noticed a poverty-stricken widow putting in two small coins, 3 and he said, 'I tell you truly, this poor widow has put in more than any of them; 4 for these have all put in money they could spare, but she in her poverty has put in all she had to live on.'

Discourse on the destruction of Jerusalem: Introduction

5 When some were talking about the Temple, remarking how it was adorned with fine stonework and votive offerings, he said, 6 'All these things you are staring at now—the time will come when not a single stone will be left on another; everything will be destroyed.' 7 And they put to him this question, 'Master,' they said, 'when will this happen, then, and what sign will there be that it is about to take place?'

The warning signs

8 But he said, 'Take care not to be deceived, because many will come using my name and saying, "I am the one" and "The time is near at hand." Refuse to join them. 9 And when you hear of wars and revolutions, do not be terrified, for this is something that must happen first, but the end will not come at once.' 10 Then he said to them, 'Nation will fight against nation, and kingdom against king-

20b Ex 3:6.   20c Ps 110:1.

dom. ¹¹There will be great earthquakes and plagues and famines in various places; there will be terrifying events and great signs from heaven.

¹²'But before all this happens, you will be seized and persecuted; you will be handed over to the synagogues and to imprisonment, and brought before kings and governors for the sake of my name ¹³—and that will be your opportunity to bear witness. ¹⁴Make up your minds not to prepare your defence, ¹⁵because I myself shall give you an eloquence and a wisdom that none of your opponents will be able to resist or contradict. ¹⁶You will be betrayed even by parents and brothers, relations and friends; and some of you will be put to death. ¹⁷You will be hated universally on account of my name, ¹⁸but not a hair of your head will be lost. ¹⁹Your perseverance will win you your lives.

The siege

²⁰'When you see Jerusalem surrounded by armies, then you must realise that it will soon be laid desolate. ²¹Then those in Judaea must escape to the mountains, those inside the city must leave it, and those in country districts must not take refuge in it. ²²For this is the time of retribution when all that scripture says must be fulfilled. ²³Alas for those with child, or with babies at the breast, when those days come!

The disaster and the age of the gentiles

²⁴'For great misery will descend on the land and retribution on this people. They will fall by the edge of the sword and be led captive to every gentile country; and Jerusalem will be trampled down by the gentiles until their time is complete.

Cosmic disasters and the glorious appearing of the Son of man

²⁵'There will be signs in the sun and moon and stars; on earth nations in agony, bewildered by the turmoil of the ocean and its waves; ²⁶men fainting away with terror and

fear at what menaces the world, for the powers of heaven will be shaken. ²⁷And then they will see the *Son of man coming in a cloud* with power and great glory.^a ²⁸When these things begin to take place, stand erect, hold your heads high, because your liberation is near at hand.'

The time of this coming

²⁹And he told them a parable, 'Look at the fig tree and indeed every tree. ³⁰As soon as you see them bud, you can see for yourselves that summer is now near. ³¹So with you when you see these things happening: know that the kingdom of God is near. ³²In truth I tell you, before this generation has passed away all will have taken place. ³³Sky and earth will pass away, but my words will never pass away.

Be on the alert

³⁴'Watch yourselves, or your hearts will be coarsened by debauchery and drunkenness and the cares of life, and that day will come upon you unexpectedly, ³⁵like a trap. For it will come down on all those living on the face of the earth. ³⁶Stay awake, praying at all times for the strength to survive all that is going to happen, and to hold your ground before the Son of man.'

The last days of Jesus

³⁷All day long he would be in the Temple teaching, but would spend the night in the open on the hill called the Mount of Olives. ³⁸And from early morning the people thronged to him in the Temple to listen to him.

The conspiracy against Jesus:^a Judas betrays him

22 The feast of Unleavened Bread, called the Passover, was now drawing near, ²and the chief priests and the scribes were

21a Dn 7:13–14.

22a For this section Lk has a good deal of information which he does not share with Mt and Mk. It is often close to Jn.

142 READ LUKE 21:25–36.

Stay awake, praying at all times for the strength to survive all that is going to happen.

—LUKE 21:36

GET READY

Keep ever in your mind the fear of the Lord, being mindful at all times of that last and dreadful day, when the heavens shall be consumed by the heat of fire, and the earth and all that is upon it shall perish. When the stars shall fall like leaves, the sun and the moon shall be darkened, nor shall they give forth light. When the Son of man shall appear, and shall descend from heaven upon the earth, the powers of heaven shall be troubled. When the appearance of the angels, and the sound of their trumpets, shall prevail, then fire shall burn before him, and hastening on, it will consume the earth.

Mighty tempests will rise about him, and dreadful lightnings such as have never before been seen, nor will be, until that day; so that the very powers of heaven will be seized with a great trembling. . . .

But what shall we do, I ask you, when God will come down in anger, and dread wrath, and sit on the throne of his glory, and summon to him all the earth . . . so that he may judge his people and render to each according to his works? Oh Woe! Woe! What kind of people shall we be then? In what state of mind shall we be, when naked and fearful we shall appear there, delivered to that dread tribunal? . . . Where now the pride of the flesh? Where now is vain and useless beauty? Where all human delight? Where then, shameless and impudent boldness? Where the delight of sin, sordid and unclean? . . . All these things shall have passed away, and like a little cloud shall have been dissolved. . . . My brother, what shall we be then, and in what state of soul, as we render an account of all things, big and little, that we have done, even to the least?". . .   ST. EPHREM, 306?–373?

YOU WILL FIND THE NEXT READING AT LUKE 22:39.

looking for some way of doing away with him, because they were afraid of the people.

³ Then Satan entered into Judas, surnamed Iscariot, who was one of the Twelve. ⁴ He approached the chief priests and the officers of the guard to discuss some way of handing Jesus over to them. ⁵ They were delighted and agreed to give him money. ⁶ He accepted and began to look for an opportunity to betray him to them without people knowing about it.

Preparation for the Passover supper

⁷ The day of Unleavened Bread came round, on which the Passover had to be sacrificed, ⁸ and he sent Peter and John, saying, 'Go and make the preparations for us to eat the Passover.' ⁹ They asked him, 'Where do you want us to prepare it?' ¹⁰ He said to them, 'Look, as you go into the city you will meet a man carrying a pitcher of water. Follow him into the house he enters ¹¹ and tell the owner of the house, "The Master says this to you: Where is the room for me to eat the Passover with my disciples?" ¹² The man will show you a large upper room furnished with couches. Make the preparations there.' ¹³ They set off and found everything as he had told them and prepared the Passover.

The supper

¹⁴ When the time came he took his place at table, and the apostles with him. ¹⁵ And he said to them, 'I have ardently longed to eat this Passover with you before I suffer; ¹⁶ because, I tell you, I shall not eat it until it is fulfilled in the kingdom of God.'

¹⁷ Then, taking a cup, he gave thanks and said, 'Take this and share it among you, ¹⁸ because from now on, I tell you, I shall never again drink wine until the kingdom of God comes.'

The institution of the Eucharist

¹⁹ Then he took bread, and when he had given thanks, he broke it and gave it to them, saying, 'This is my body given for you; do this in remembrance of me.' ²⁰ He did the same with the cup after supper, and said, 'This cup is the new covenant in my blood poured out for you.

The treachery of Judas foretold

²¹ 'But look, here with me on the table is the hand of the man who is betraying me. ²² The Son of man is indeed on the path which was decreed, but alas for that man by whom he is betrayed!' ²³ And they began to ask one another which of them it could be who was to do this.

Who is the greatest?

²⁴ An argument also began between them about who should be reckoned the greatest; ²⁵ but he said to them, 'Among the gentiles it is the kings who lord it over them, and those who have authority over them are given the title Benefactor. ²⁶ With you this must not happen. No; the greatest among you must behave as if he were the youngest, the leader as if he were the one who serves. ²⁷ For who is the greater: the one at table or the one who serves? The one at table, surely? Yet here am I among you as one who serves!

The reward promised to the apostles

²⁸ 'You are the men who have stood by me faithfully in my trials; ²⁹ and now I confer a kingdom on you, just as my Father conferred one on me: ³⁰ you will eat and drink at my table in my kingdom, and you will sit on thrones to judge the twelve tribes of Israel.

Peter's denial and repentance foretold

³¹ 'Simon, Simon! Look, Satan has got his wish to sift you all like wheat; ³² but I have prayed for you, Simon, that your faith may not fail, and once you have recovered, you in your turn must strengthen your brothers.' ³³ 'Lord,' he answered, 'I would be ready to go to prison with you, and to death.' ³⁴ Jesus replied, 'I tell you, Peter, by the time the cock crows today you will have denied three times that you know me.'

A time of crisis

³⁵ He said to them, 'When I sent you out without purse or haversack or sandals, were you short of anything?' ³⁶ 'No, nothing,' they said. He said to them, 'But now if you have a purse, take it, and the same with a haversack; if you have no sword, sell your cloak and buy one, ³⁷ because I tell you these words of scripture are destined to be fulfilled in me: *He was counted as one of the rebellious.*ᵇ Yes, what it says about me is even now reaching its fulfilment.' ³⁸ They said, 'Lord, here are two swords.' He said to them, 'That is enough!'

The Mount of Olives

³⁹ He then left to make his way as usual to the Mount of Olives, with the disciples following. ⁴⁰ When he reached the place he said to them, 'Pray not to be put to the test.'

⁴¹ Then he withdrew from them, about a stone's throw away, and knelt down and prayed. ⁴² 'Father,' he said, 'if you are willing, take this cup away from me. Nevertheless, let your will be done, not mine.' ⁴³ Then an angel

22b Is 53:12.

143 READ LUKE 22:39–46.

"Father," he said, "if you are willing, take this cup away from me. Nevertheless, let your will be done, not mine."—LUKE 22:42

THE SPIRITUALITY OF JESUS

Jesus did not merely participate in public and prescribed worship services. Perhaps even more often the Gospels tell of solitary prayer in the still of the night, on open mountain tops, in the wilderness far from people (see Mk 1:35). Jesus' public ministry was preceded by forty days and forty nights of prayer (see Mt 4:1–2). Before he chose and commissioned his twelve apostles, he withdrew into the isolation of the mountains (see Lk 6:12). By his hour on the Mount of Olives, he prepared himself for his road to Golgotha. A few short words tell us what he implored of his Father during this most difficult hour of his life, words that are given to us as guiding stars for our own hours on the Mount of Olives. "Father, if you are willing, take this cup away from me. Nevertheless, let your will be done, not mine."

Like lightning, these words for an instant illumine for us the innermost spiritual life of Jesus, the unfathomable mystery of his God-man existence and his dialogue with the Father. Surely, this dialogue was life-long and uninterrupted. Christ prayed interiorly not only when he had withdrawn from the crowd, but also when he was among people. And once he allowed us to look extensively and deeply at this secret dialogue. It was not long before the hour of the Mount of Olives; in fact it was immediately before they set out to go there at the end of the Last Supper, which we recognize as the actual hour of the birth of the church" (see Jn 17).   ST. EDITH STEIN, 1891–1942

YOU WILL FIND THE NEXT READING AT LUKE 23.

appeared to him, coming from heaven to give him strength. ⁴⁴In his anguish he prayed even more earnestly, and his sweat fell to the ground like great drops of blood.

⁴⁵When he rose from prayer he went to the disciples and found them sleeping for sheer grief. ⁴⁶And he said to them, 'Why are you asleep? Get up and pray not to be put to the test.'

The arrest

⁴⁷Suddenly, while he was still speaking, a number of men appeared, and at the head of them the man called Judas, one of the Twelve, who went up to Jesus to kiss him. ⁴⁸Jesus said,

'Judas, are you betraying the Son of man with a kiss?' ⁴⁹His followers, seeing what was about to happen, said, 'Lord, shall we use our swords?' ⁵⁰And one of them struck the high priest's servant and cut off his right ear. ⁵¹But at this Jesus said, 'That is enough.' And touching the man's ear he healed him.

⁵²Then Jesus said to the chief priests and captains of the Temple guard and elders who had come for him, 'Am I a bandit, that you had to set out with swords and clubs? ⁵³When I was among you in the Temple day after day you never made a move to lay hands on me. But this is your hour; this is the reign of darkness.'

Peter's denials

⁵⁴They seized him then and led him away, and they took him to the high priest's house. Peter followed at a distance. ⁵⁵They had lit a fire in the middle of the courtyard and Peter sat down among them, ⁵⁶and as he was sitting there by the blaze a servant-girl saw him, peered at him, and said, 'This man was with him too.' ⁵⁷But he denied it. 'Woman, I do not know him,' he said. ⁵⁸Shortly afterwards someone else saw him and said, 'You are one of them too.' But Peter replied, 'I am not, my friend.' ⁵⁹About an hour later another man insisted, saying, 'This fellow was certainly with him. Why, he is a Galilean.' ⁶⁰Peter said, 'My friend, I do not know what you are talking about.' At that instant, while he was still speaking, the cock crowed, ⁶¹and the Lord turned and looked straight at Peter, and Peter remembered the Lord's words when he had said to him, 'Before the cock crows today, you will have disowned me three times.' ⁶²And he went outside and wept bitterly.

Jesus mocked by the guards

⁶³Meanwhile the men who guarded Jesus were mocking and beating him. ⁶⁴They blindfolded him and questioned him, saying, 'Prophesy! Who hit you then?' ⁶⁵And they heaped many other insults on him.

Jesus before the Sanhedrin

⁶⁶When day broke there was a meeting of the elders of the people, the chief priests and scribes. He was brought before their council, ⁶⁷and they said to him, 'If you are the Christ, tell us.' He replied, 'If I tell you, you will not believe, ⁶⁸and if I question you, you will not answer. ⁶⁹But from now on, the *Son of man will be seated at the* right hand of the Power *of God.'ᶜ* ⁷⁰They all said, 'So you are the Son of God then?' He answered, 'It is you who say I am.' ⁷¹Then they said, 'Why do we need any evidence? We have heard it for ourselves from his own lips.'

23

The whole assembly then rose, and they brought him before Pilate.

Jesus before Pilate

²They began their accusation by saying, 'We found this man inciting our people to revolt, opposing payment of the tribute to Caesar, and claiming to be Christ, a king.' ³Pilate put to him this question, 'Are you the king of the Jews?' He replied, 'It is you who say it.' ⁴Pilate then said to the chief priests and the crowd, 'I find no case against this man.' ⁵But they persisted, 'He is inflaming the people with his teaching all over Judaea and all the way from Galilee, where he started, down to here.' ⁶When Pilate heard this, he asked if the man were a Galilean; ⁷and finding that he came under Herod's jurisdiction, he passed him over to Herod, who was also in Jerusalem at that time.

Jesus before Herod

⁸Herod was delighted to see Jesus; he had heard about him and had been wanting for a long time to set eyes on him; moreover, he was hoping to see some miracle worked by him. ⁹So he questioned him at some length, but without getting any reply. ¹⁰Meanwhile the chief priests and the scribes were there, vigorously pressing their accusations. ¹¹Then Herod, together with his guards, treated him with contempt and made fun of him; he put a rich cloak on him and sent him back to Pilate. ¹²And though Herod and Pilate had been enemies before, they were reconciled that same day.

Jesus before Pilate again

¹³Pilate then summoned the chief priests and the leading men and the people. ¹⁴He said to them, 'You brought this man before me as a popular agitator. Now I have gone into the matter myself in your presence and found no grounds in the man for any of the charges you bring against him. ¹⁵Nor has Herod either, since he has sent him back to us. As you can

22c Ps 110:1.

see, the man has done nothing that deserves death, [16] so I shall have him flogged and then let him go.' [17]*a* [18] But as one man they howled, 'Away with him! Give us Barabbas!' [19] (This man had been thrown into prison because of a riot in the city and murder.)

[20] In his desire to set Jesus free, Pilate addressed them again, [21] but they shouted back, 'Crucify him! Crucify him!' [22] And for the third time he spoke to them, 'But what harm has this man done? I have found no case against him that deserves death, so I shall have him flogged and then let him go.' [23] But they kept on shouting at the top of their voices, demanding that he should be crucified. And their shouts kept growing louder.

[24] Pilate then gave his verdict: their demand was to be granted. [25] He released the man they asked for, who had been imprisoned because of rioting and murder, and handed Jesus over to them to deal with as they pleased.

The way to Calvary

[26] As they were leading him away they seized on a man, Simon from Cyrene, who was coming in from the country, and made him shoulder the cross and carry it behind Jesus. [27] Large numbers of people followed him, and women too, who mourned and lamented for him. [28] But Jesus turned to them and said, 'Daughters of Jerusalem, do not weep for me; weep rather for yourselves and for your children. [29] For look, the days are surely coming when people will say, "Blessed are those who are barren, the wombs that have never borne children, the breasts that have never suckled!" [30] Then they will begin to *say to the mountains, "Fall on us!"; to the hills, "Cover us!"* *b* [31] For if this is what is done to green wood, what will be done when the wood is dry?' [32] Now they were also leading out two others, criminals, to be executed with him.

The crucifixion

[33] When they reached the place called The Skull, there they crucified him and the two criminals, one on his right, the other on his left. [34] Jesus said, 'Father, forgive them; they do not know what they are doing.' Then they cast lots to share out his clothing.

The crucified Christ is mocked

[35] The people stayed there watching. As for the leaders, they jeered at him with the words, 'He saved others, let him save himself if he is the Christ of God, the Chosen One.' [36] The soldiers mocked him too, coming up to him, offering him vinegar, [37] and saying, 'If you are the king of the Jews, save yourself.' [38] Above him there was an inscription: 'This is the King of the Jews'.

The good thief

[39] One of the criminals hanging there abused him: 'Are you not the Christ? Save yourself and us as well.' [40] But the other spoke up and rebuked him. 'Have you no fear of God at all?' he said. 'You got the same sentence as he did, [41] but in our case we deserved it: we are paying for what we did. But this man has done nothing wrong.' [42] Then he said, 'Jesus, remember me when you come into your kingdom.' [43] He answered him, 'In truth I tell you, today you will be with me in paradise.'

The death of Jesus

[44] It was now about the sixth hour and the sun's light failed, so that darkness came over the whole land until the ninth hour. [45] The veil of the Sanctuary was torn right down the middle. [46] Jesus cried out in a loud voice saying, 'Father, *into your hands I commit my spirit.'* *c* With these words he breathed his last.

After the death

[47] When the centurion saw what had taken place, he gave praise to God and said, 'Truly, this was an upright man.' [48] And when all the crowds who had gathered for the spectacle saw what had happened, they went home beating their breasts.

23a Some authorities add v. 17, borrowed from Mt 27:15.
23b Ho 10:8.   23c Ps 31:5.

144 READ LUKE 23:39–43.

In truth I tell you, today you will be with me in paradise.—LUKE 23:43

INFINITE MERCY FOR THE ASKING

Scripture says of the robbers who were crucified with him, he was "counted among the rebellious" (see Is 53:12). Before this both were rebels, but now one was a rebel no longer. But one was a rebel to the end, stubborn against salvation. Though his hands were fastened, he hit Christ with blasphemy by his tongue. He reviled the Lord with the passersby who mocked the Crucified, fulfilling the prophetic psalm that said "they shake their heads at the sight of me" (see Ps 109:25). But the other rebuked the reviler. It was for him the end of his life and the beginning of his restoration, the surrender of his soul, a first share in salvation. After rebuking the other, he says, "Jesus, remember me" (Lk 23:42). Don't remember what I have done because that makes me afraid, but remember me when you come into your kingdom.

What power, O robber, led you to the light? Who taught you to worship that despised Man, your companion on the cross? O Eternal Light that gives light to those that are in darkness! His request reached into a distant time, but grace came quickly. "In truth I tell you, today you will be with me in paradise" (Lk 23:43). "I passed sentence on Adam very quickly, very quickly I pardon you. Adam fell away because of the Tree, and you because of the Tree are brought into paradise."

O mighty and indescribable grace! The faithful Abraham had not yet entered, but the robber enters! Moses and the prophets had not yet entered, and the robber enters, though a breaker of the law. Paul also wondered at this when he said, "however much sin increased, grace was always greater" (Rm 5:20). ST. CYRIL OF JERUSALEM, 315?–386

YOU WILL FIND THE NEXT READING AT JOHN 1.

⁴⁹All his friends stood at a distance; so also did the women who had accompanied him from Galilee and saw all this happen.

The burial

⁵⁰And now a member of the Council arrived, a good and upright man named Joseph. ⁵¹He had not consented to what the others had planned and carried out. He came from Arimathaea, a Jewish town, and he lived in the hope of seeing the kingdom of God. ⁵²This man went to Pilate and asked for the body of Jesus. ⁵³He then took it down, wrapped it in a shroud and put it in a tomb which was hewn in stone and which had never held a body. ⁵⁴It was Preparation day and the Sabbath was beginning to grow light.

⁵⁵Meanwhile the women who had come from Galilee with Jesus were following behind. They took note of the tomb and how the body had been laid.

⁵⁶Then they returned and prepared spices and ointments. And on the Sabbath day they rested, as the Law required.

The empty tomb; the angel's message

24 On the first day of the week, at the first sign of dawn, they went to the tomb

with the spices they had prepared. 2 They found that the stone had been rolled away from the tomb, 3 but on entering they could not find the body of the Lord Jesus. 4 As they stood there puzzled about this, two men in brilliant clothes suddenly appeared at their side. 5 Terrified, the women bowed their heads to the ground. But the two said to them, 'Why look among the dead for someone who is alive? 6 He is not here; he has risen. Remember what he told you when he was still in Galilee: 7 that the Son of man was destined to be handed over into the power of sinful men and be crucified, and rise again on the third day.' 8 And they remembered his words.

The apostles refuse to believe the women

9 And they returned from the tomb and told all this to the Eleven and to all the others. 10 The women were Mary of Magdala, Joanna, and Mary the mother of James. And the other women with them also told the apostles, 11 but this story of theirs seemed pure nonsense, and they did not believe them.

Peter at the tomb

12 Peter, however, went off to the tomb, running. He bent down and looked in and saw the linen cloths but nothing else; he then went back home, amazed at what had happened.

The road to Emmaus

13 Now that very same day, two of them were on their way to a village called Emmaus, seven miles from Jerusalem, 14 and they were talking together about all that had happened. 15 And it happened that as they were talking together and discussing it, Jesus himself came up and walked by their side; 16 but their eyes were prevented from recognising him. 17 He said to them, 'What are all these things that you are discussing as you walk along?' They stopped, their faces downcast.

18 Then one of them, called Cleopas, answered him, 'You must be the only person staying in Jerusalem who does not know the things that have been happening there these last few days.' 19 He asked, 'What things?' They answered, 'All about Jesus of Nazareth, who showed himself a prophet powerful in action and speech before God and the whole people; 20 and how our chief priests and our leaders handed him over to be sentenced to death, and had him crucified. 21 Our own hope had been that he would be the one to set Israel free. And this is not all: two whole days have now gone by since it all happened; 22 and some women from our group have astounded us: they went to the tomb in the early morning, 23 and when they could not find the body, they came back to tell us they had seen a vision of angels who declared he was alive. 24 Some of our friends went to the tomb and found everything exactly as the women had reported, but of him they saw nothing.'

25 Then he said to them, 'You foolish men! So slow to believe all that the prophets have said! 26 Was it not necessary that the Christ should suffer before entering into his glory?' 27 Then, starting with Moses and going through all the prophets, he explained to them the passages throughout the scriptures that were about himself.

28 When they drew near to the village to which they were going, he made as if to go on; 29 but they pressed him to stay with them saying, 'It is nearly evening, and the day is almost over.' So he went in to stay with them. 30 Now while he was with them at table, he took the bread and said the blessing; then he broke it and handed it to them. 31 And their eyes were opened and they recognised him; but he had vanished from their sight. 32 Then they said to each other, 'Did not our hearts burn within us as he talked to us on the road and explained the scriptures to us?'

33 They set out that instant and returned to Jerusalem. There they found the Eleven assembled together with their companions, 34 who said to them, 'The Lord has indeed risen and has appeared to Simon.' 35 Then they told their story of what had happened on the road and how they had recognised him at the breaking of bread.

Jesus appears to the apostles

36 They were still talking about all this when he himself stood among them and said to them, 'Peace be with you!' 37 In a state of alarm and fright, they thought they were seeing a ghost. 38 But he said, 'Why are you so agitated, and why are these doubts stirring in your hearts? 39 See by my hands and my feet that it is I myself. Touch me and see for yourselves; a ghost has no flesh and bones as you can see I have.' 40 And as he said this he showed them his hands and his feet. 41 Their joy was so great that they still could not believe it, as they were dumbfounded; so he said to them, 'Have you anything here to eat?' 42 And they offered him a piece of grilled fish, 43 which he took and ate before their eyes.

Last instructions to the apostles

44 Then he told them, 'This is what I meant when I said, while I was still with you, that everything written about me in the Law of Moses, in the Prophets and in the Psalms, was destined to be fulfilled.' 45 He then opened their minds to understand the scriptures, 46 and he said to them, 'So it is written that the Christ would suffer and on the third day rise from the dead, 47 and that, in his name, repentance for the forgiveness of sins would be preached to all nations, beginning from Jerusalem. 48 You are witnesses to this.

49 'And now I am sending upon you what the Father has promised. Stay in the city, then, until you are clothed with the power from on high.'

The ascension

50 Then he took them out as far as the outskirts of Bethany, and raising his hands he blessed them. 51 Now as he blessed them, he withdrew from them and was carried up to heaven. 52 They worshipped him and then went back to Jerusalem full of joy; 53 and they were continually in the Temple praising God.

Prologue

1 In the beginning was the Word:[a]
the Word was with God
and the Word was God.
² He was with God in the beginning.
³ Through him all things came into being,
not one thing came into being except
through him.
⁴ What has come into being in him was life,
life that was the light of men;
⁵ and light shines in darkness,
and darkness could not overpower it.

⁶ A man came, sent by God.
His name was John.
⁷ He came as a witness,
to bear witness to the light,
so that everyone might believe
through him.
⁸ He was not the light,
he was to bear witness to the light.

⁹ The Word was the real light
that gives light to everyone;
he was coming into the world.
¹⁰ He was in the world
that had come into being through him,
and the world did not recognise him.
¹¹ He came to his own
and his own people did not accept him.
¹² But to those who did accept him
he gave power to become children of God,
to those who believed in his name
¹³ who were[b] born not from human stock
or human desire
or human will
but from God himself.
¹⁴ The Word became flesh,
he lived among us,
and we saw his glory,
the glory that he has from the Father as
only Son of the Father,
full of grace and truth.

¹⁵ John witnesses to him. He proclaims:
'This is the one of whom I said:
He who comes after me
has passed ahead of me
because he existed before me.'

¹⁶ Indeed, from his fullness we have,
all of us, received—
one gift replacing another,
¹⁷ for the Law was given through Moses,
grace and truth have come through Jesus
Christ.
¹⁸ No one has ever seen God;
it is the only Son, who is close to the
Father's heart,
who has made him known.

The witness of John

¹⁹ This was the witness of John, when the Jews
sent to him priests and Levites from Jerusalem
to ask him, 'Who are you?' ²⁰ He declared, he
did not deny but declared, 'I am not the
Christ.' ²¹ So they asked, 'Then are you Elijah?' He replied, 'I am not.' 'Are you the
Prophet?' He answered, 'No.' ²² So they said
to him, 'Who are you? We must take back an
answer to those who sent us. What have you to

1a In the OT the Word or Wisdom of God is present with
God before the world existed and reveals God to the world.
Jn sees this Word-Wisdom in the person of Jesus.

1b Some MSS have the singular 'was', which would refer to
Jesus' divine origin.

145 READ JOHN 1:6–14.

The Word was the real light that gives light to everyone.—JOHN 1:9

ENLIGHTENED BY THE SPIRIT

Once I lay in darkness and in the depths of night and was tossed to and fro in the waves of the turbulent world, uncertain of the correct way to go, ignorant of my true life, and a stranger to the light of truth. At that time and on account of the life I then led, it seemed difficult to believe what divine mercy promised for my salvation, namely, that someone could be born again and to a new life by being immersed in the healing water of Baptism. It was difficult to believe that though I would remain the same man in bodily form, my heart and mind would be transformed.

How was it possible, I thought, that a change could be great enough to strip away in a single moment the innate hardness of our nature? How could the habits acquired over the course of many years disappear, since these are so deeply rooted within us? . . . While temptation still holds us fast we are seduced by wine, inflated with pride, inflamed by anger, troubled by greed, goaded by cruelty, enticed by ambition and cast headlong by lust.

These were my frequent thoughts. For I was held fast by the many sins of my life from which it seemed impossible for me to extricate myself. . . . But after the life-giving water of Baptism came to my rescue and washed away the stain of my former years and poured into my cleansed and purified heart the light which comes from above, and after I had drunk in the heavenly Spirit and was made a new man by the second birth, then amazingly what I had previously doubted became clear to me. What had been hidden was revealed. What had been dark became light. What previously had seemed impossible now seemed possible. What was in me of the guilty flesh now confessed it was earthly. What was made alive in my by the Holy Spirit was now quickened by God.

ST. CYPRIAN OF CARTHAGE, 200?–258

YOU WILL FIND THE NEXT READING AT JOHN 2.

say about yourself?' [23] So he said, 'I am, as Isaiah prophesied:

A voice of one that cries in the desert:
Prepare a way for the Lord.
Make his paths straight!' [c]

[24] Now those who had been sent were Pharisees, [25] and they put this question to him, 'Why are you baptising if you are not the Christ, and not Elijah, and not the Prophet?' [26] John answered them, 'I baptise with water; but standing among you—unknown to you—

[27] is the one who is coming after me; and I am not fit to undo the strap of his sandal.' [28] This happened at Bethany, on the far side of the Jordan, where John was baptising.

[29] The next day, he saw Jesus coming towards him and said, 'Look, there is the lamb of God that takes away the sin of the world. [30] It was of him that I said, "Behind me comes one who has passed ahead of me because he existed before me." [31] I did not know him my-

1c Is 40:3.

self, and yet my purpose in coming to baptise with water was so that he might be revealed to Israel.' [32] And John declared, 'I saw the Spirit come down on him like a dove from heaven and rest on him. [33] I did not know him myself, but he who sent me to baptise with water had said to me, "The man on whom you see the Spirit come down and rest is the one who is to baptise with the Holy Spirit." [34] I have seen and I testify that he is the Chosen One of God.'

The first disciples

[35] The next day as John stood there again with two of his disciples, Jesus went past, [36] and John looked towards him and said, 'Look, there is the lamb of God.' [37] And the two disciples heard what he said and followed Jesus. [38] Jesus turned round, saw them following and said, 'What do you want?' They answered, 'Rabbi'—which means Teacher—'where do you live?' [39] He replied, 'Come and see'; so they went and saw where he lived, and stayed with him that day. It was about the tenth hour.

[40] One of these two who became followers of Jesus after hearing what John had said was Andrew, the brother of Simon Peter. [41] The first thing Andrew did was to find his brother and say to him, 'We have found the Messiah'—which means the Christ— [42] and he took Simon to Jesus. Jesus looked at him and said, 'You are Simon son of John; you are to be called Cephas'—which means Rock.

[43] The next day, after Jesus had decided to leave for Galilee, he met Philip and said, 'Follow me.' [44] Philip came from the same town, Bethsaida, as Andrew and Peter. [45] Philip found Nathanael and said to him, 'We have found him of whom Moses in the Law and the prophets wrote, Jesus son of Joseph, from Nazareth.' [46] Nathanael said to him, 'From Nazareth? Can anything good come from that place?' Philip replied, 'Come and see.' [47] When Jesus saw Nathanael coming he said of him, 'There, truly, is an Israelite in whom there is no deception.' [48] Nathanael asked, 'How do you know me?' Jesus replied, 'Before Philip came to call you, I saw you under the fig tree.'

[49] Nathanael answered, 'Rabbi, you are the Son of God, you are the king of Israel.' [50] Jesus replied, 'You believe that just because I said: I saw you under the fig tree. You are going to see greater things than that.' [51] And then he added, 'In all truth I tell you, you will see heaven open and the angels of God ascending and descending over the Son of man.'

The wedding at Cana

2 On the third day there was a wedding at Cana in Galilee. The mother of Jesus was there, [2] and Jesus and his disciples had also been invited. [3] And they ran out of wine, since the wine provided for the feast had all been used, and the mother of Jesus said to him, 'They have no wine.' [4] Jesus said, 'Woman, what do you want from me? My hour has not come yet.' [5] His mother said to the servants, *Do whatever he tells you.'* [a] [6] There were six stone water jars standing there, meant for the ablutions that are customary among the Jews: each could hold twenty or thirty gallons. [7] Jesus said to the servants, 'Fill the jars with water,' and they filled them to the brim. [8] Then he said to them, 'Draw some out now and take it to the president of the feast.' [9] They did this; the president tasted the water, and it had turned into wine. Having no idea where it came from—though the servants who had drawn the water knew—the president of the feast called the bridegroom [10] and said, 'Everyone serves good wine first and the worse wine when the guests are well wined; but you have kept the best wine till now.'

[11] This was the first of Jesus' signs: it was at Cana in Galilee. He revealed his glory, and his disciples believed in him. [12] After this he went down to Capernaum with his mother and his brothers and his disciples, but they stayed there only a few days.

The cleansing of the Temple

[13] When the time of the Jewish Passover was near Jesus went up to Jerusalem, [14] and in the

2a Gn 41:55.

146 READ JOHN 2:1–11.

On the third day there was a wedding at Cana in Galilee.—JOHN 2:1

MIRACLES AT CANA

Christ came to Cana not so much to partake of the wedding feast, as to perform his miracle. And furthermore that he might sanctify the beginning of human generation. . . . He who was about to restore the nature itself of humanity appropriately gave his blessing for those who were to be born, sanctifying their coming into this world.

And he also came to lift God's curse: "In sorrow shall you bring forth children" (see Gn 3:16). . . . By his presence the Savior sanctified marriage, and he who is the joy and the delight of all human beings has taken away the ancient sadness of childbearing. As Paul says, "For anyone who is in Christ, there is a new creation: the old order is gone and a new being is there" (2 Co 5:17). . . .

Many wondrous things are prefigured at the same time by this singular and earliest sign. For honest nuptials are sanctified, and the curse that was laid on womankind is taken away. . . . And the Savior's glory shines as the light of the sun, and his disciples' faith is confirmed in the wonder of these things.

For the purpose of contemplation another aspect must be considered. . . . The Savior came to the wedding feast, not as one uninvited, but as one besought by the multitude of the voices of the saints. Then . . . the guests ran short of wine. For "the Law could not make anything perfect" (Heb 7:19); the Mosaic code did not suffice for perfect happiness. Neither was that inward guide of natural sobriety equal to the task of conducting us to salvation. And so of us also it can be said: "They have no wine." But the most bountiful God does not despise us who are striving with the hunger for good things. He offers us a wine far better than we had. "For the written letters kill, but the Spirit gives life" (2 Co 3:6).

ST. CYRIL OF ALEXANDRIA, 376–444

YOU WILL FIND THE NEXT READING AT JOHN 3.

Temple he found people selling cattle and sheep and doves, and the money changers sitting there. [15] Making a whip out of cord, he drove them all out of the Temple, sheep and cattle as well, scattered the money changers' coins, knocked their tables over [16] and said to the dove sellers, 'Take all this out of here and stop using my Father's house as a market.' [17] Then his disciples remembered the words of scripture: *I am eaten up with zeal for your house.*[b] [18] The Jews intervened and said, 'What sign can you show us that you should act like this?' [19] Jesus answered, 'Destroy this Temple, and in three days I will raise it up.' [20] The Jews replied, 'It has taken forty-six years to build this Temple:[c] are you going to raise it up again in three days?' [21] But he was speaking of the Temple that was his body, [22] and when Jesus

2b Ps 69:9.

2c Reconstruction work began in 19 BC, so this is Passover AD 28.

rose from the dead, his disciples remembered that he had said this, and they believed the scripture and what he had said.

Jesus in Jerusalem

23 During his stay in Jerusalem for the feast of the Passover many believed in his name when they saw the signs that he did, 24 but Jesus knew all people and did not trust himself to them; 25 he never needed evidence about anyone; he could tell what someone had within.

The conversation with Nicodemus

3 There was one of the Pharisees called Nicodemus, a leader of the Jews, 2 who came to Jesus by night and said, 'Rabbi, we know that you have come from God as a teacher; for no one could perform the signs that you do unless God were with him.' 3 Jesus answered:

In all truth I tell you,
no one can see the kingdom of God
without being born from above.

4 Nicodemus said, 'How can anyone who is already old be born? Is it possible to go back into the womb again and be born?' 5 Jesus replied:

In all truth I tell you,
no one can enter the kingdom of God
without being born through water and
the Spirit;
6 what is born of human nature is human;
what is born of the Spirit is spirit.
7 Do not be surprised when I say:
You must be born from above.
8 The wind blows where it pleases;
you can hear its sound,
but you cannot tell where it comes from
or where it is going.
So it is with everyone who is born of the
Spirit.

9 'How is that possible?' asked Nicodemus. 10 Jesus replied, 'You are the Teacher of Israel, and you do not know these things!

11 'In all truth I tell you,
we speak only about what we know
and witness only to what we have seen
and yet you people reject our evidence.
12 If you do not believe me
when I speak to you about earthly
things,
how will you believe me
when I speak to you about heavenly
things?
13 No one has gone up to heaven
except the one who came down from
heaven,
the Son of man;
14 as Moses lifted up the snake in the
desert,
so must the Son of man be lifted up
15 so that everyone who believes may have
eternal life in him.
16 For this is how God loved the world:
he gave his only Son,
so that everyone who believes in him may
not perish
but may have eternal life.
17 For God sent his Son into the world
not to judge the world,
but so that through him the world might
be saved.
18 No one who believes in him will be
judged;
but whoever does not believe is judged
already,
because that person does not believe
in the Name of God's only Son.
19 And the judgement is this:
though the light has come into the world
people have preferred
darkness to the light
because their deeds were evil.
20 And indeed, everybody who does wrong
hates the light and avoids it,
to prevent his actions from being
shown up;
21 but whoever does the truth
comes out into the light,
so that what he is doing may plainly
appear as done in God.'

147 READ JOHN 3:1–9.

The wind blows where it pleases.... So it is with everyone who is born of the Spirit.

—JOHN 3:8

THE IMPERCEPTIBLE ACTION OF THE SPIRIT

When the Holy Spirit enters us, the way he follows is unknown. As Scripture says, he is like the wind: "You cannot tell where it comes from or where it is going." It is enough to know that we have received him by the effects he produces every day and by feeling ourselves stronger than we were—without knowing how or when this grace came to us. Certainly, it can only have come in prayer and as a result of our frequently offering our heart to God.

We do not see trees or human bodies growing, not even if we were to look at them from morning until evening. But afterwards we are astonished at seeing their increase. It is the same with souls. They advance in the way of God, although they don't perceive it, provided that they faithfully respond to the lights and attractions of grace.

It is the same with the Spirit of God whom we ask for in prayer as it is with the body of Christ that the priest produces by the consecration at Mass. Both are necessary to us, and Jesus Christ, our savior, has promised them to us as nourishment for our souls. Faith teaches us that when we communicate we receive the body of Jesus Christ. But neither the priest nor we can taste or feel it. But we digest the body of Christ by faith, being certain on the Word of God, though we have neither seen, felt nor tasted it, that even so it nourishes our souls. We are sure that it will produce in them effects of light and grace amid the darkness and dryness that it has left in us after we have received it.

ST. JANE DE CHANTAL, 1572–1641

YOU WILL FIND THE NEXT READING AT JOHN 4.

Jesus' ministry in Judaea; John bears witness for the last time

22 After this, Jesus went with his disciples into the Judaean countryside and stayed with them there and baptised. 23 John also was baptising at Aenon near Salim, where there was plenty of water, and people were going there and were being baptised. 24 For John had not yet been put in prison.

25 Now a discussion arose between some of John's disciples and a Jew about purification, 26 so they went to John and said, 'Rabbi, the man who was with you on the far side of the Jordan, the man to whom you bore witness, is baptising now, and everyone is going to him.' 27 John replied:

'No one can have anything
except what is given him from heaven.

28 'You yourselves can bear me out. I said, "I am not the Christ; I am the one who has been sent to go in front of him."

29 'It is the bridegroom who has the bride;
and yet the bridegroom's friend,
who stands there and listens to him,
is filled with joy at the bridegroom's voice.
This is the joy I feel, and it is complete.

30 He must grow greater,
   I must grow less.
31 He who comes from above
   is above all others;
   he who is of the earth
   is earthly himself and speaks in an earthly
        way.
   He who comes from heaven
32 bears witness to the things he has seen and
        heard,
   but his testimony is not accepted by
        anybody;
33 though anyone who does accept his
        testimony
   is attesting that God is true,
34 since he whom God has sent
   speaks God's own words,
   for God gives him the Spirit without
        reserve.
35 The Father loves the Son
   and has entrusted everything to his hands.
36 Anyone who believes in the Son has
        eternal life,
   but anyone who refuses to believe in the
        Son will never see life:
   God's retribution hangs over him.'

Jesus among the Samaritans

4 When Jesus heard that the Pharisees had
found out that he was making and baptising more disciples than John— 2 though in
fact it was his disciples who baptised, not Jesus
himself— 3 he left Judaea and went back to
Galilee. 4 He had to pass through Samaria.
5 On the way he came to the Samaritan town
called Sychar near the land that Jacob gave to
his son Joseph. 6 Jacob's well was there and
Jesus, tired by the journey, sat down by the
well. It was about the sixth hour. 7 When a
Samaritan woman came to draw water, Jesus
said to her, 'Give me something to drink.' 8 His
disciples had gone into the town to buy food.
9 The Samaritan woman said to him, 'You are
a Jew. How is it that you ask me, a Samaritan,
for something to drink?'—Jews, of course, do
not associate with Samaritans. 10 Jesus replied
to her:

If you only knew what God is offering
and who it is that is saying to you,
'Give me something to drink,'
you would have been the one to ask,
and he would have given you living water.

11 'You have no bucket, sir,' she answered,
'and the well is deep: how do you get this living water? 12 Are you a greater man than our
father Jacob, who gave us this well and drank
from it himself with his sons and his cattle?'
13 Jesus replied:

Whoever drinks this water
will be thirsty again;
14 but no one who drinks the water that I
        shall give
will ever be thirsty again:
the water that I shall give
will become a spring of water within,
        welling up for eternal life.

15 'Sir,' said the woman, 'give me some of
that water, so that I may never be thirsty or
come here again to draw water.' 16 'Go and call
your husband,' said Jesus to her, 'and come
back here.' 17 The woman answered, 'I have
no husband.' Jesus said to her, 'You are right to
say, "I have no husband"; 18 for although you
have had five, the one you now have is not
your husband. You spoke the truth there.' 19 'I
see you are a prophet, sir,' said the woman.
20 'Our fathers worshipped on this mountain,*a*
though you say that Jerusalem is the place
where one ought to worship.' 21 Jesus said:

Believe me, woman, the hour is coming
when you will worship the Father
neither on this mountain nor in Jerusalem.
22 You worship what you do not know;
we worship what we do know;
for salvation comes from the Jews.
23 But the hour is coming—indeed is already
        here—

4a Gerizim, where there had been a Temple rivalling Jerusalem's. To Jesus both are provisional.

148 READ JOHN 4:15–24.

God is spirit, and those who worship must worship in spirit and truth.—JOHN 4:24

THE HOLY SPIRIT

Let us now investigate what are our common conceptions concerning the Spirit, as well as those that have been gathered by us from Holy Scripture concerning him. . . . First, who on hearing the titles of the Spirit is not lifted up in soul? . . . He is called "Spirit of God" (Mt 12:28), "Spirit of truth who issues from the Father" (Jn 15:26), "resolute spirit" (Ps 51:10), "a generous spirit" (Ps 51:12). His proper and peculiar title is "Holy Spirit," which is a name especially appropriate to everything that is incorporeal, purely immaterial, and indivisible. So our Lord, when teaching the woman who thought God to be an object of local worship that the incorporeal is incomprehensible, said "God is spirit" (Jn 4:24).

On our hearing, then, of a spirit, it is impossible to form the idea of a nature circumscribed, subject to change and variation, or at all like the creature. We are compelled to advance in our conceptions to the highest, and to think of an intelligent essence, in power infinite, in magnitude unlimited, . . . generous of his good gifts; to whom turn all things needing sanctification . . . as being watered by his inspiration and helped on toward their natural and proper end; perfecting all other things, but himself lacking nothing; . . . in essence simple, in powers various, wholly present in each and being wholly everywhere; . . . shared without loss or ceasing to be entire, after the likeness of the sunbeam, whose kindly light falls on him who enjoys it as though it shone for him alone. Yet it illumines land and sea and mingles with the air. So, too, is the Spirit to every one who receives him, as though given to him alone. And yet he sends forth grace sufficient and full for all humanity, and is enjoyed by all who share him according to the capacity, not of his power, but of their nature.

ST. BASIL, 329–379

YOU WILL FIND THE NEXT READING AT JOHN 6.

when true worshippers will worship the
    Father in spirit and truth:
that is the kind of worshipper
the Father seeks.
²⁴ God is spirit,
  and those who worship
  must worship in spirit and truth.

²⁵ The woman said to him, 'I know that Messiah—that is, Christ—is coming; and when he comes he will explain everything.' ²⁶ Jesus said, 'That is who I am, I who speak to you.'

²⁷ At this point his disciples returned and were surprised to find him speaking to a woman, though none of them asked, 'What do you want from her?' or, 'What are you talking to her about?' ²⁸ The woman put down her water jar and hurried back to the town to tell the people, ²⁹ 'Come and see a man who has told me everything I have done; could this be the Christ?' ³⁰ This brought people out of the town and they made their way towards him.

³¹ Meanwhile, the disciples were urging him, 'Rabbi, do have something to eat'; ³² but

he said, 'I have food to eat that you do not know about.' 33 So the disciples said to one another, 'Has someone brought him food?' 34 But Jesus said:

My food
is to do the will of the one who sent me,
and to complete his work.
35 Do you not have a saying:
Four months and then the harvest?
Well, I tell you,
look around you, look at the fields;
already they are white, ready for harvest!
36 Already the reaper is being paid his wages,
already he is bringing in the grain for
        eternal life,
so that sower and reaper can rejoice
        together.
37 For here the proverb holds true:
one sows, another reaps;
38 I sent you to reap
a harvest you have not laboured for.
Others have laboured for it;
and you have come into the rewards of
        their labour.

39 Many Samaritans of that town believed in him on the strength of the woman's words of testimony, 'He told me everything I have done.' 40 So, when the Samaritans came up to him, they begged him to stay with them. He stayed for two days, and 41 many more came to believe on the strength of the words he spoke to them; 42 and they said to the woman, 'Now we believe no longer because of what you told us; we have heard him ourselves and we know that he is indeed the Saviour of the world.'

Jesus in Galilee

43 When the two days were over Jesus left for Galilee. 44 He himself had declared that a prophet is not honoured in his own home town. 45 On his arrival the Galileans received him well, having seen all that he had done at Jerusalem during the festival which they too had attended.

Second sign at Cana; the cure of a royal official's son

46 He went again to Cana in Galilee, where he had changed the water into wine. And there was a royal official whose son was ill at Capernaum; 47 hearing that Jesus had arrived in Galilee from Judaea, he went and asked him to come and cure his son, as he was at the point of death. 48 Jesus said to him, 'Unless you see signs and portents you will not believe!' 49 'Sir,' answered the official, 'come down before my child dies.' 50 'Go home,' said Jesus, 'your son will live.' The man believed what Jesus had said and went on his way home; 51 and while he was still on the way his servants met him with the news that his boy was alive. 52 He asked them when the boy had begun to recover. They replied, 'The fever left him yesterday at the seventh hour.' 53 The father realised that this was exactly the time when Jesus had said, 'Your son will live'; and he and all his household believed.

54 This new sign, the second, Jesus performed on his return from Judaea to Galilee.

The cure of a sick man at the Pool of Bethesda

5 After this there was a Jewish festival, and Jesus went up to Jerusalem. 2 Now in Jerusalem next to the Sheep Pool there is a pool called Bethesda in Hebrew, which has five porticos; 3 and under these were crowds of sick people, blind, lame, paralysed.ᵃ 5 One man there had an illness which had lasted thirty-eight years, 6 and when Jesus saw him lying there and knew he had been in that condition for a long time, he said, 'Do you want to be well again?' 7 'Sir,' replied the sick man, 'I have no one to put me into the pool when the water is disturbed; and while I am still on the way, someone else gets down there before me.'

5a Some ancient MSS add: 'waiting for the water to move; 4for at intervals the angel of the Lord came down into the pool, and the water was disturbed, and the first person to enter the water after this disturbance was cured of any ailment from which he was suffering'.

⁸Jesus said, 'Get up, pick up your sleeping-mat and walk around.' ⁹The man was cured at once, and he picked up his mat and started to walk around.

Now that day happened to be the Sabbath, ¹⁰so the Jews said to the man who had been cured, 'It is the Sabbath; you are not allowed to carry your sleeping-mat.' ¹¹He replied, 'But the man who cured me told me, "Pick up your sleeping-mat and walk around." ' ¹²They asked, 'Who is the man who said to you, "Pick up your sleeping-mat and walk around"? ' ¹³The man had no idea who it was, since Jesus had disappeared, as the place was crowded. ¹⁴After a while Jesus met him in the Temple and said, 'Now you are well again, do not sin any more, or something worse may happen to you.' ¹⁵The man went back and told the Jews that it was Jesus who had cured him. ¹⁶It was because he did things like this on the Sabbath that the Jews began to harass Jesus. ¹⁷His answer to them was, 'My Father still goes on working, and I am at work, too.' ¹⁸But that only made the Jews even more intent on killing him, because not only was he breaking the Sabbath, but he spoke of God as his own Father and so made himself God's equal.

¹⁹To this Jesus replied:

In all truth I tell you,
by himself the Son can do nothing;
he can do only what he sees the Father
doing:
and whatever the Father does the Son does
too.
²⁰For the Father loves the Son
and shows him everything he himself does,
and he will show him even greater things
than these,
works that will astonish you.
²¹Thus, as the Father raises the dead and
gives them life,
so the Son gives life to anyone he chooses;
²²for the Father judges no one;
he has entrusted all judgement to the Son,
²³so that all may honour the Son
as they honour the Father.

Whoever refuses honour to the Son
refuses honour to the Father who sent
him.
²⁴In all truth I tell you,
whoever listens to my words,
and believes in the one who sent me,
has eternal life;
without being brought to judgement
such a person has passed from death to
life.
²⁵In all truth I tell you,
the hour is coming—indeed it is already
here—
when the dead will hear the voice of the
Son of God,
and all who hear it will live.
²⁶For as the Father has life in himself,
so he has granted the Son also to have life
in himself;
²⁷and, because he is the Son of man,
has granted him power to give
judgement.
²⁸Do not be surprised at this,
for the hour is coming
when the dead will leave their graves
at the sound of his voice:
²⁹those who did good
will come forth to life;
and those who did evil will come forth to
judgement.
³⁰By myself I can do nothing;
I can judge only as I am told to judge,
and my judging is just,
because I seek to do not my own will
but the will of him who sent me.
³¹Were I to testify on my own behalf,
my testimony would not be true;
³²but there is another witness who speaks on
my behalf,
and I know that his testimony is true.
³³You sent messengers to John,
and he gave his testimony to the truth—
³⁴not that I depend on human testimony;
no, it is for your salvation that I mention it.
³⁵John was a lamp lit and shining
and for a time you were content to enjoy
the light that he gave.

36 But my testimony is greater than John's:
the deeds my Father has given me to
        perform,
these same deeds of mine
testify that the Father has sent me.
37 Besides, the Father who sent me
bears witness to me himself.
You have never heard his voice,
you have never seen his shape,
38 and his word finds no home in you
because you do not believe
in the one whom he has sent.

39 You pore over the scriptures,
believing that in them you can find eternal
        life;
it is these scriptures that testify to me,
40 and yet you refuse to come to me to receive
        life!
41 Human glory means nothing to me.
42 Besides, I know you too well:
you have no love of God in you.
43 I have come in the name of my Father
and you refuse to accept me;
if someone else should come in his own
        name
you would accept him.
44 How can you believe,
since you look to each other for glory
and are not concerned
with the glory that comes from the one
        God?
45 Do not imagine that I am going to accuse
        you before the Father:
you have placed your hopes on Moses,
and Moses will be the one who accuses
        you.
46 If you really believed him
you would believe me too,
since it was about me that he was writing;
47 but if you will not believe what he
        wrote,
how can you believe what I say?

The miracle of the loaves

6 After this, Jesus crossed the Sea of Galilee—or of Tiberias— 2 and a large crowd
followed him, impressed by the signs he had
done in curing the sick. 3 Jesus climbed the
hillside and sat down there with his disciples.
4 The time of the Jewish Passover was near.

5 Looking up, Jesus saw the crowds approaching and said to Philip, 'Where can we
buy some bread for these people to eat?' 6 He
said this only to put Philip to the test; he
himself knew exactly what he was going to
do. 7 Philip answered, 'Two hundred denarii
would not buy enough to give them a little
piece each.' 8 One of his disciples, Andrew,
Simon Peter's brother, said, 9 'Here is a small
boy with five barley loaves and two fish; but
what is that among so many?' 10 Jesus said to
them, 'Make the people sit down.' There was
plenty of grass there, and as many as five thousand men sat down. 11 Then Jesus took the
loaves, gave thanks, and distributed them to
those who were sitting there; he then did the
same with the fish, distributing as much as
they wanted. 12 When they had eaten enough
he said to the disciples, 'Pick up the pieces left
over, so that nothing is wasted.' 13 So they
picked them up and filled twelve large baskets
with scraps left over from the meal of five barley loaves. 14 Seeing the sign that he had done,
the people said, 'This is indeed the prophet
who is to come into the world.' 15 Jesus, as he
realised they were about to come and take him
by force and make him king, fled back to the
hills alone.

*Jesus comes to his disciples
walking on the waters*

16 That evening the disciples went down to the
shore of the sea 17 and got into a boat to make
for Capernaum on the other side of the sea. It
was getting dark by now and Jesus had still
not rejoined them. 18 The wind was strong,
and the sea was getting rough. 19 They had
rowed three or four miles when they saw Jesus
walking on the sea and coming towards the
boat. They were afraid, 20 but he said, 'It's me.
Don't be afraid.' 21 They were ready to take
him into the boat, and immediately it reached
the shore at the place they were making for.

The discourse in the synagogue at Capernaum

22 Next day, the crowd that had stayed on the other side saw that only one boat had been there, and that Jesus had not got into the boat with his disciples, but that the disciples had set off by themselves. 23 Other boats, however, had put in from Tiberias, near the place where the bread had been eaten. 24 When the people saw that neither Jesus nor his disciples were there, they got into those boats and crossed to Capernaum to look for Jesus. 25 When they found him on the other side, they said to him, 'Rabbi, when did you come here?' 26 Jesus answered:

In all truth I tell you,
you are looking for me
not because you have seen the signs
but because you had all the bread you
wanted to eat.
27 Do not work for food that goes bad,
but work for food that endures for eternal
life,
which the Son of man will give you,
for on him the Father, God himself, has set
his seal.

28 Then they said to him, 'What must we do if we are to carry out God's work?' 29 Jesus gave them this answer, 'This is carrying out God's work: you must believe in the one he has sent.' 30 So they said, 'What sign will you yourself do, the sight of which will make us believe in you? What work will you do? 31 Our fathers ate manna in the desert; as scripture says: *He gave them bread from heaven to eat.*[a]
32 Jesus answered them:

In all truth I tell you,
it was not Moses who gave you the bread
from heaven,
it is my Father who gives you the bread
from heaven,
the true bread;
33 for the bread of God
is the bread which comes down from
heaven
and gives life to the world.

34 'Sir,' they said, 'give us that bread always.'
35 Jesus answered them:

I am the bread of life.
No one who comes to me will ever hunger;
no one who believes in me will ever thirst.
36 But, as I have told you,
you can see me and still you do not believe.
37 Everyone whom the Father gives me will
come to me;
I will certainly not reject
anyone who comes to me,
38 because I have come from heaven,
not to do my own will,
but to do the will of him who sent me.
39 Now the will of him who sent me
is that I should lose nothing
of all that he has given to me,
but that I should raise it up on the last day.
40 It is my Father's will
that whoever sees the Son and believes
in him
should have eternal life,
and that I should raise that person up on
the last day.

41 Meanwhile the Jews were complaining to each other about him, because he had said, 'I am the bread that has come down from heaven.' 42 They were saying, 'Surely this is Jesus son of Joseph, whose father and mother we know. How can he now say, "I have come down from heaven?" ' 43 Jesus said in reply to them, 'Stop complaining to each other.

44 'No one can come to me
unless drawn by the Father who sent me,
and I will raise that person up on the
last day.
45 It is written in the prophets:

6a Ps 78:24. 'Bread from heaven' is commented vv. 32–48 and 'to eat' vv. 49–58.

They will all be taught by God;[b]
everyone who has listened to the Father,
and learnt from him,
comes to me.

46 Not that anybody has seen the Father,
except him who has his being from God:
he has seen the Father.

47 In all truth I tell you,
everyone who believes has eternal life.

48 I am the bread of life.

49 Your fathers ate manna in the desert
and they are dead;

50 but this is the bread which comes down
from heaven,
so that a person may eat it and not die.

51 I am the living bread which has come
down from heaven.
Anyone who eats this bread will live for
ever;
and the bread that I shall give
is my flesh, for the life of the world.'

52 Then the Jews started arguing among themselves, 'How can this man give us his flesh to eat?' 53 Jesus replied to them:

In all truth I tell you,
if you do not eat the flesh of the Son of man
and drink his blood,
you have no life in you.

54 Anyone who does eat my flesh and drink
my blood
has eternal life,
and I shall raise that person up on the last
day.

55 For my flesh is real food
and my blood is real drink.

56 Whoever eats my flesh and drinks my
blood
lives in me
and I live in that person.

57 As the living Father sent me
and I draw life from the Father,
so whoever eats me will also draw life
from me.

58 This is the bread which has come down
from heaven;

it is not like the bread our ancestors ate:
they are dead,
but anyone who eats this bread will live for
ever.

59 This is what he taught at Capernaum in the synagogue. 60 After hearing it, many of his followers said, 'This is intolerable language. How could anyone accept it?' 61 Jesus was aware that his followers were complaining about it and said, 'Does this disturb you? 62 What if you should see the Son of man ascend to where he was before?

63 'It is the spirit that gives life,
the flesh has nothing to offer.
The words I have spoken to you are spirit
and they are life.

64 'But there are some of you who do not believe.' For Jesus knew from the outset who did not believe and who was to betray him. 65 He went on, 'This is why I told you that no one could come to me except by the gift of the Father.' 66 After this, many of his disciples went away and accompanied him no more.

Peter's profession of faith

67 Then Jesus said to the Twelve, 'What about you, do you want to go away too?' 68 Simon Peter answered, 'Lord, to whom shall we go? You have the message of eternal life, 69 and we believe; we have come to know that you are the Holy One of God.' 70 Jesus replied to them, 'Did I not choose the Twelve of you? Yet one of you is a devil.' 71 He meant Judas son of Simon Iscariot, since this was the man, one of the Twelve, who was to betray him.

Jesus goes up to Jerusalem for the feast and teaches there

7 After this Jesus travelled round Galilee; he could not travel round Judaea, because the Jews were seeking to kill him.

2 As the Jewish feast of Shelters drew near, 3 his brothers said to him, 'Leave this place and

6b Is 54:13.

149 READ JOHN 6:47–58.

Anyone who does eat my flesh and drink my blood has eternal life.—JOHN 6:54

CELEBRATING CHRIST'S BODY AND BLOOD

Of the glorious Body telling, O my tongue, its mystery sing;
And the Blood, all price excelling, which for this world's ransoming
In a noble womb once dwelling, he shed forth, the Gentiles' King.

Given for us, for us descending of a Virgin to proceed,
Man with man in converse blending scattered he the Gospel seed:
Till his sojourn drew to ending which he closed in wondrous deed.

At the Last Great Supper seated, circled by his brethren's band,
All the Law required, completed, in the feast its statutes planned,
To the Twelve himself he provided their food with his own hand.

Word made Flesh, by word he maketh very bread his Flesh to be;
Man for wine Christ's Blood partaketh; and if senses fail to see,
Faith alone the true heart waketh to behold the mystery.

Therefore, we, before it bending, this great sacrament adore;
Types and shadows have their ending in the new rite ever more;
Faith, our outward sense amending, maketh good defects before.

Honor, laud, and praise addressing to the Father and the Son,
Might ascribe we, virtue, blessing, and eternal benediction:
Holy Ghost from both progressing, equal laud to thee be done. Amen.

ST. THOMAS AQUINAS, 1225?–1275

YOU WILL FIND THE NEXT READING AT JOHN 10.

go to Judaea, so that your disciples, too, can see the works you are doing; ⁴no one who wants to be publicly known acts in secret; if this is what you are doing, you should reveal yourself to the world.' ⁵Not even his brothers had faith in him. ⁶Jesus answered, 'For me the right time has not come yet, but for you any time is the right time. ⁷The world cannot hate you, but it does hate me, because I give evidence that its ways are evil. ⁸Go up to the festival yourselves: I am not going to this festival, because for me the time is not ripe yet.' ⁹Having said that, he stayed behind in Galilee.

¹⁰However, after his brothers had left for the festival, he went up as well, not publicly but secretly. ¹¹At the festival the Jews were on the look-out for him: 'Where is he?' they said. ¹²There was a great deal of talk about him in the crowds. Some said, 'He is a good man'; others, 'No, he is leading the people astray.'

13 Yet no one spoke about him openly, for fear of the Jews.

14 When the festival was half over, Jesus went to the Temple and began to teach. 15 The Jews were astonished and said, 'How did he learn to read? He has not been educated.' 16 Jesus answered them:

'My teaching is not from myself:
it comes from the one who sent me;
17 anyone who is prepared to do his will,
will know whether my teaching is
from God
or whether I speak on my own account.
18 When someone speaks on his own
account,
he is seeking honour for himself;
but when he is seeking the honour of the
person who sent him,
then he is true
and altogether without dishonesty.
19 Did not Moses give you the Law?
And yet not one of you keeps the Law!

'Why do you want to kill me?' 20 The crowd replied, 'You are mad! Who wants to kill you?' 21 Jesus answered, 'One work I did, and you are all amazed at it. 22 Moses ordered you to practise circumcision—not that it began with him, it goes back to the patriarchs—and you circumcise on the Sabbath. 23 Now if someone can be circumcised on the Sabbath so that the Law of Moses is not broken, why are you angry with me for making someone completely healthy on a Sabbath? 24 Do not keep judging according to appearances; let your judgement be according to what is right.'

The people discuss the origin of the Messiah

25 Meanwhile some of the people of Jerusalem were saying, 'Isn't this the man they want to kill? 26 And here he is, speaking openly, and they have nothing to say to him! Can it be true the authorities have recognised that he is the Christ? 27 Yet we all know where he comes from, but when the Christ appears no one will know where he comes from.'

28 Then, as Jesus was teaching in the Temple, he cried out:

You know me and you know where I
came from.
Yet I have not come of my own accord:
but he who sent me is true;
You do not know him,
29 but I know him
because I have my being from him
and it was he who sent me.

30 They wanted to arrest him then, but because his hour had not yet come no one laid a hand on him.

Jesus foretells his approaching departure

31 There were many people in the crowds, however, who believed in him; they were saying, 'When the Christ comes, will he give more signs than this man has?' 32 Hearing that talk like this about him was spreading among the people, the Pharisees sent the Temple guards to arrest him.

33 Then Jesus said:

For a short time I am with you still;
then I shall go back to the one who
sent me.
34 You will look for me and will not find me;
Where I am
you cannot come.

35 So the Jews said to one another, 'Where is he intending to go that we shall not be able to find him? Is he intending to go abroad to the people who are dispersed among the Greeks and to teach the Greeks? 36 What does he mean when he says:

"You will look for me and will not
find me;
where I am,
you cannot come?" '

The promise of living water

37 On the last day, the great day of the festival, Jesus stood and cried out:

'Let anyone who is thirsty come to me! ³⁸ Let anyone who believes in me come and
    drink!

As scripture says, "From his heart shall flow streams of living water." '

³⁹ He was speaking of the Spirit which those who believed in him were to receive; for there was no Spirit as yet because Jesus had not yet been glorified.

Fresh discussions on the origin of the Messiah

⁴⁰ Some of the crowd who had been listening said, 'He is indeed the prophet,' ⁴¹ and some said, 'He is the Christ,' but others said, 'Would the Christ come from Galilee? ⁴² Does not scripture say that the Christ must be descended from David and come from Bethlehem, the village where David was?' ⁴³ So the people could not agree about him. ⁴⁴ Some wanted to arrest him, but no one actually laid a hand on him.

⁴⁵ The guards went back to the chief priests and Pharisees who said to them, 'Why haven't you brought him?' ⁴⁶ The guards replied, 'No one has ever spoken like this man.' ⁴⁷ 'So,' the Pharisees answered, 'you, too, have been led astray? ⁴⁸ Have any of the authorities come to believe in him? Any of the Pharisees? ⁴⁹ This rabble knows nothing about the Law—they are damned.' ⁵⁰ One of them, Nicodemus—the same man who had come to Jesus earlier—said to them, ⁵¹ 'But surely our Law does not allow us to pass judgement on anyone without first giving him a hearing and discovering what he is doing?' ⁵² To this they answered, 'Are you a Galilean too? Go into the matter, and see for yourself: prophets do not arise in Galilee.'

The adulterous woman[a]

8 ⁵³ They all went home, and Jesus went to the ¹ Mount of Olives.

² At daybreak he appeared in the Temple again; and as all the people came to him, he sat down and began to teach them.

³ The scribes and Pharisees brought a woman along who had been caught committing adultery; and making her stand there in the middle ⁴ they said to Jesus, 'Master, this woman was caught in the very act of committing adultery, ⁵ and in the Law Moses has ordered us to stone women of this kind. What have you got to say?' ⁶ They asked him this as a test, looking for an accusation to use against him. But Jesus bent down and started writing on the ground with his finger. ⁷ As they persisted with their question, he straightened up and said, 'Let the one among you who is guiltless be the first to throw a stone at her.' ⁸ Then he bent down and continued writing on the ground. ⁹ When they heard this they went away one by one, beginning with the eldest, until the last one had gone and Jesus was left alone with the woman, who remained in the middle. ¹⁰ Jesus again straightened up and said, 'Woman, where are they? Has no one condemned you?' ¹¹ 'No one, sir,' she replied. 'Neither do I condemn you,' said Jesus. 'Go away, and from this moment sin no more.'

Jesus, the light of the world

¹² When Jesus spoke to the people again, he said:

    I am the light of the world;
    anyone who follows me will not be
        walking in the dark,
    but will have the light of life.

A discussion on the testimony of Jesus to himself

¹³ At this the Pharisees said to him, 'You are testifying on your own behalf; your testimony is not true.' ¹⁴ Jesus replied:

    Even though I am testifying on my own
        behalf,
    my testimony is still true,
    because I know
    where I have come from and where I am
        going;

7a Many ancient MSS omit 7:53–8:11.

but you do not know
where I come from or where I am going.
¹⁵ You judge by human standards;
I judge no one,
¹⁶ but if I judge,
my judgement will be true,
because I am not alone:
the one who sent me is with me;
¹⁷ and in your Law it is written
that the testimony of two witnesses
is true.
¹⁸ I testify on my own behalf,
but the Father who sent me testifies on my
behalf, too.

¹⁹ They asked him, 'Where is your Father
then?' Jesus answered:

You do not know me, nor do you know
my Father;
if you did know me, you would know my
Father as well.

²⁰ He spoke these words in the Treasury,
while teaching in the Temple. No one arrested
him, because his hour had not yet come.
²¹ Again he said to them:

I am going away; you will look for me
and you will die in your sin.
Where I am going, you cannot come.

²² So the Jews said to one another, 'Is he going to kill himself, that he says, "Where I am
going, you cannot come?" ' ²³ Jesus went on:

You are from below;
I am from above.
You are of this world;
I am not of this world.
²⁴ I have told you already: You will die in
your sins.
Yes, if you do not believe that I am He,ᵃ
you will die in your sins.

²⁵ So they said to him, 'Who are you?' Jesus
answered:

What I have told you from the outset.
²⁶ About you I have much to say
and much to judge;
but the one who sent me is true,
and what I declare to the world
I have learnt from him.

²⁷ They did not recognise that he was talking to them about the Father. ²⁸ So Jesus said:

When you have lifted up the Son of man,
then you will know that I am He
and that I do nothing of my own accord.
What I say
is what the Father has taught me;
²⁹ he who sent me is with me,
and has not left me to myself,
for I always do what pleases him.

³⁰ As he was saying this, many came to believe in him.

Jesus and Abraham

³¹ To the Jews who believed in him Jesus said:

If you make my word your home
you will indeed be my disciples;
³² you will come to know the truth,
and the truth will set you free.

³³ They answered, 'We are descended from
Abraham and we have never been the slaves of
anyone; what do you mean, "You will be set
free?" ' ³⁴ Jesus replied:

In all truth I tell you,
everyone who commits sin is a slave.
³⁵ Now a slave has no permanent standing in
the household,
but a son belongs to it for ever.
³⁶ So if the Son sets you free,
you will indeed be free.
³⁷ I know that you are descended from
Abraham;

8a Here and in vv. 28, 58 Jesus appropriates the divine name
revealed to Moses in Ex 3:14.

but you want to kill me
because my word finds no place in you.
³⁸ What I speak of
   is what I have seen at my Father's side,
   and you too put into action
   the lessons you have learnt from your
       father.

³⁹ They repeated, 'Our father is Abraham.'
Jesus said to them:

   If you are Abraham's children,
   do as Abraham did.
⁴⁰ As it is, you want to kill me,
   a man who has told you the truth
   as I have learnt it from God;
   that is not what Abraham did.
⁴¹ You are doing your father's work.

They replied, 'We were not born illegitimate, the only father we have is God.' ⁴² Jesus answered:

   If God were your father, you would love
       me,
   since I have my origin in God and have
       come from him;
   I did not come of my own accord,
   but he sent me.
⁴³ Why do you not understand what I say?
   Because you cannot bear to listen to my
       words.
⁴⁴ You are from your father, the devil,
   and you prefer to do
   what your father wants.
   He was a murderer from the start;
   he was never grounded in the truth;
   there is no truth in him at all.
   When he lies
   he is speaking true to his nature,
   because he is a liar, and the father of lies.
⁴⁵ But it is because I speak the truth
   that you do not believe me.
⁴⁶ Can any of you convict me of sin?
   If I speak the truth, why do you not
       believe me?
⁴⁷ Whoever comes from God

listens to the words of God;
   the reason why you do not listen
   is that you are not from God.

⁴⁸ The Jews replied, 'Are we not right in saying that you are a Samaritan and possessed by a devil?' Jesus answered:

⁴⁹ I am not possessed;
   but I honour my Father,
   and you deny me honour.
⁵⁰ I do not seek my own glory;
   there is someone who does seek it and is
       the judge of it.
⁵¹ In all truth I tell you,
   whoever keeps my word
   will never see death.

⁵² The Jews said, 'Now we know that you are possessed. Abraham is dead, and the prophets are dead, and yet you say, "Whoever keeps my word will never know the taste of death." ⁵³ Are you greater than our father Abraham, who is dead? The prophets are dead too. Who are you claiming to be?' ⁵⁴ Jesus answered:

   If I were to seek my own glory
   my glory would be worth nothing;
   in fact, my glory is conferred by the
       Father,
   by the one of whom you say, 'He is our
       God,'
⁵⁵ although you do not know him.
   But I know him,
   and if I were to say, 'I do not know him,'
   I should be a liar, as you yourselves are.
   But I do know him, and I keep his word.
⁵⁶ Your father Abraham rejoiced
   to think that he would see my Day;
   he saw it and was glad.

⁵⁷ The Jews then said, 'You are not fifty yet, and you have seen Abraham!' ⁵⁸ Jesus replied:

   In all truth I tell you,
   before Abraham ever was,
   I am.

59 At this they picked up stones to throw at him; but Jesus hid himself and left the Temple.

The cure of the man born blind

9 As he went along, he saw a man who had been blind from birth. 2 His disciples asked him, 'Rabbi, who sinned, this man or his parents, that he should have been born blind?' 3 'Neither he nor his parents sinned,' Jesus answered, 'he was born blind so that the works of God might be revealed in him.

4 'As long as day lasts
  we must carry out the work of the one
        who sent me;
  the night will soon be here when no one
        can work.
5 As long as I am in the world
  I am the light of the world.'

6 Having said this, he spat on the ground, made a paste with the spittle, put this over the eyes of the blind man, 7 and said to him, 'Go and wash in the Pool of Siloam' (the name means 'one who has been sent'). So he went off and washed and came back able to see.

8 His neighbours and the people who used to see him before (for he was a beggar) said, 'Isn't this the man who used to sit and beg?' 9 Some said, 'Yes, it is the same one.' Others said, 'No, but he looks just like him.' The man himself said, 'Yes, I am the one.' 10 So they said to him, 'Then how is it that your eyes were opened?' 11 He answered, 'The man called Jesus made a paste, daubed my eyes with it and said to me, "Go off and wash at Siloam"; so I went, and when I washed I gained my sight.' 12 They asked, 'Where is he?' He answered, 'I don't know.'

13 They brought to the Pharisees the man who had been blind. 14 It had been a Sabbath day when Jesus made the paste and opened the man's eyes, 15 so when the Pharisees asked him how he had gained his sight, he said, 'He put a paste on my eyes, and I washed, and I can see.' 16 Then some of the Pharisees said, 'That man cannot be from God: he does not keep the Sab-

bath.' Others said, 'How can a sinner produce signs like this?' And there was division among them. 17 So they spoke to the blind man again, 'What have you to say about him yourself, now that he has opened your eyes?' The man answered, 'He is a prophet.'

18 However, the Jews would not believe that the man had been blind without first sending for the parents of the man who had gained his sight and 19 asking them, 'Is this man really the son of yours who you say was born blind? If so, how is it that he is now able to see?' 20 His parents answered, 'We know he is our son and we know he was born blind, 21 but how he can see, we don't know, nor who opened his eyes. Ask him. He is old enough: let him speak for himself.' 22 His parents spoke like this out of fear of the Jews, who had already agreed to ban from the synagogue anyone who should acknowledge Jesus as the Christ. 23 This was why his parents said, 'He is old enough; ask him.'

24 So the Jews sent for the man again and said to him, 'Give glory to God! We are satisfied that this man is a sinner.' 25 The man answered, 'Whether he is a sinner I don't know; all I know is that I was blind and now I can see.' 26 They said to him, 'What did he do to you? How did he open your eyes?' 27 He replied, 'I have told you once and you wouldn't listen. Why do you want to hear it all again? Do you want to become his disciples yourselves?' 28 At this they hurled abuse at him, 'It is you who are his disciple, we are disciples of Moses: 29 we know that God spoke to Moses, but as for this man, we don't know where he comes from.' 30 The man replied, 'That is just what is so amazing! You don't know where he comes from and he has opened my eyes! 31 We know that God doesn't listen to sinners, but God does listen to people who are devout and do his will. 32 Ever since the world began it is unheard of for anyone to open the eyes of someone born blind; 33 if this man were not from God, he wouldn't have been able to do anything.' 34 They retorted, 'Are you trying to teach us, and you a sinner

through and through ever since you were born!' And they ejected him.

³⁵ Jesus heard they had ejected him, and when he found him he said to him, 'Do you believe in the Son of man?' ³⁶ 'Sir,' the man replied, 'tell me who he is so that I may believe in him.' ³⁷ Jesus said, 'You have seen him; he is speaking to you.' ³⁸ The man said, 'Lord, I believe,' and worshipped him.

³⁹ Jesus said:

It is for judgement
that I have come into this world,
so that those without sight may see
and those with sight may become blind.

⁴⁰ Hearing this, some Pharisees who were present said to him, 'So we are blind, are we?' ⁴¹ Jesus replied:

If you were blind,
you would not be guilty,
but since you say, 'We can see,'
your guilt remains.

The good shepherd ᵃ

10 'In all truth I tell you, anyone who does not enter the sheepfold through the gate, but climbs in some other way, is a thief and a bandit. ² He who enters through the gate is the shepherd of the flock; ³ the gatekeeper lets him in, the sheep hear his voice, one by one he calls his own sheep and leads them out. ⁴ When he has brought out all those that are his, he goes ahead of them, and the sheep follow because they know his voice. ⁵ They will never follow a stranger, but will run away from him because they do not recognise the voice of strangers.'

⁶ Jesus told them this parable but they failed to understand what he was saying to them.

⁷ So Jesus spoke to them again:

In all truth I tell you,
I am the gate of the sheepfold.
⁸ All who have come before me
are thieves and bandits,
but the sheep took no notice of them.

⁹ I am the gate.
Anyone who enters through me will be
safe:
such a one will go in and out
and will find pasture.
¹⁰ The thief comes
only to steal and kill and destroy.
I have come
so that they may have life
and have it to the full.
¹¹ I am the good shepherd:
the good shepherd lays down his life for
his sheep.
¹² The hired man, since he is not the
shepherd
and the sheep do not belong to him,
abandons the sheep
as soon as he sees a wolf coming, and runs
away,
and then the wolf attacks and scatters the
sheep;
¹³ he runs away because he is only a
hired man
and has no concern for the sheep.
¹⁴ I am the good shepherd;
I know my own
and my own know me,
¹⁵ just as the Father knows me
and I know the Father;
and I lay down my life for my sheep.
¹⁶ And there are other sheep I have
that are not of this fold,
and I must lead these too.
They too will listen to my voice,
and there will be only one flock,
one shepherd.
¹⁷ The Father loves me,
because I lay down my life
in order to take it up again.
¹⁸ No one takes it from me;
I lay it down of my own free will,
and as I have power to lay it down,
so I have power to take it up again;
and this is the command I have received
from my Father.

10a cf Jr 23; Ezk 34.

150   READ JOHN 10:1–19.

I am the gate. Anyone who enters through me will be safe.—JOHN 10:9

MEDITATING ON CHRIST'S PASSION

The passion of Christ is the gate that opens into the delicious pastures of the soul. Our divine Savior has said: "I am the gate. Anyone who enters through me will be safe."

Imagine yourself seriously indisposed, and that I who love you tenderly come to see you. After saying a few words of sympathy and consolation, I should certainly look at you with compassion and through love of you make your sufferings my own. So when we meditate on the Passion of Christ, seeing him in such affliction, we ought to have compassion for him. And then continue looking upon him in such great torments and through compassionate love make his sufferings our own.

Suppose that you had fallen into a river and that a charitable person threw himself into the water to save you. Moreover, suppose that hardly drawn from the water you had been attacked by assassins, and that your rescuer again risked his life to save you. What would you do in return for such friendship? Certainly you would do all in your power to heal the bruises he received on your account. So ought we to act towards Christ: we must contemplate him engulfed in an ocean of sorrows to save us from the eternal abyss; consider him all covered with wounds and bruises to purchase eternal life for us. Then let us make his pains our own, sympathize with his sorrows and consecrate all our affections to him.

How can you by love make your own the sufferings of our sweet Jesus? God will teach you how when it pleases him, for he alone can do so. The soul inflamed with the love of God, without distraction, in pure and simple faith suddenly finds herself penetrated with the sufferings of Jesus. In a glance of faith she sees them all. For the Passion of our Savior is a labor of love, and the soul thus lost in God, who is all charity, makes herself a fount of love and sorrow.

ST. PAUL OF THE CROSS, 1694–1775

YOU WILL FIND THE NEXT READING AT JOHN 13.

¹⁹ These words caused a fresh division among the Jews. ²⁰ Many said, 'He is possessed, he is raving; why do you listen to him?' ²¹ Others said, 'These are not the words of a man possessed by a devil: could a devil open the eyes of the blind?'

Jesus claims to be the Son of God

²² It was the time of the feast of Dedication in Jerusalem. It was winter, ²³ and Jesus was in the Temple walking up and down in the Portico of Solomon. ²⁴ The Jews gathered round him and said, 'How much longer are you going to keep us in suspense? If you are the Christ, tell us openly.' ²⁵ Jesus replied:

I have told you, but you do not believe.
The works I do in my Father's name are
    my witness;
²⁶ but you do not believe,
because you are no sheep of mine.
²⁷ The sheep that belong to me listen to my
    voice;
I know them and they follow me.

28 I give them eternal life;
  they will never be lost
  and no one will ever steal them from my
    hand.
29 The Father, for what he has given me, is
    greater than anyone,
  and no one can steal anything from the
    Father's hand.
30 The Father and I are one.

31 The Jews fetched stones to stone him,
32 so Jesus said to them, 'I have shown you
many good works from my Father; for which
of these are you stoning me?' 33 The Jews answered him, 'We are stoning you, not for
doing a good work, but for blasphemy; though
you are only a man, you claim to be God.'
34 Jesus answered:

  Is it not written in your Law:
  I said, you are gods? b
35 So it uses the word 'gods'
  of those people to whom the word of God
    was addressed
  —and scripture cannot be set aside.
36 Yet to someone whom the Father has
    consecrated
  and sent into the world you say,
  'You are blaspheming'
  because I said, 'I am Son of God.'
37 If I am not doing my Father's work,
  there is no need to believe me;
38 but if I am doing it,
  then even if you refuse to believe in me,
  at least believe in the work I do;
  then you will know for certain
  that the Father is in me and I am in the
    Father.

39 They again wanted to arrest him then,
but he eluded their clutches.

Jesus withdraws to the other side of the Jordan

40 He went back again to the far side of the Jordan to the district where John had been baptising at first and he stayed there. 41 Many people
who came to him said, 'John gave no signs, but
all he said about this man was true'; 42 and
many of them believed in him.

The resurrection of Lazarus

11 There was a man named Lazarus of
Bethany, the village of Mary and her sister, Martha, and he was ill. 2 It was the same
Mary, the sister of the sick man Lazarus, who
anointed the Lord with ointment and wiped
his feet with her hair. 3 The sisters sent this
message to Jesus, 'Lord, the man you love is
ill.' 4 On receiving the message, Jesus said,
'This sickness will not end in death, but it is
for God's glory so that through it the Son of
God may be glorified.'

5 Jesus loved Martha and her sister and
Lazarus, 6 yet when he heard that he was ill he
stayed where he was for two more days 7 before saying to the disciples, 'Let us go back to
Judaea.' 8 The disciples said, 'Rabbi, it is not
long since the Jews were trying to stone you;
are you going back there again?' 9 Jesus
replied:

  Are there not twelve hours in the day?
  No one who walks in the daytime
    stumbles,
  having the light of this world to see by;
10 anyone who walks around at night
    stumbles,
  having no light as a guide.

11 He said that and then added, 'Our friend
Lazarus is at rest; I am going to wake him.'
12 The disciples said to him, 'Lord, if he is at
rest he will be saved.' 13 Jesus was speaking of
the death of Lazarus, but they thought that by
'rest' he meant 'sleep'; 14 so Jesus put it plainly,
'Lazarus is dead; 15 and for your sake I am glad
I was not there because now you will believe.
But let us go to him.' 16 Then Thomas—
known as the Twin—said to the other disciples, 'Let us also go to die with him.'

17 On arriving, Jesus found that Lazarus

10b Ps 82:6.

had been in the tomb for four days already. [18]Bethany is only about two miles from Jerusalem, [19]and many Jews had come to Martha and Mary to comfort them about their brother. [20]When Martha heard that Jesus was coming she went to meet him. Mary remained sitting in the house. [21]Martha said to Jesus, 'Lord, if you had been here, my brother would not have died, [22]but even now I know that God will grant whatever you ask of him.' [23]Jesus said to her, 'Your brother will rise again.' [24]Martha said, 'I know he will rise again at the resurrection on the last day.' [25]Jesus said:

I am the resurrection.
Anyone who believes in me, even though
      that person dies, will live,
[26] and whoever lives and believes in me
will never die.
Do you believe this?

[27]'Yes, Lord,' she said, 'I believe that you are the Christ, the Son of God, the one who was to come into this world.'
[28]When she had said this, she went and called her sister Mary, saying in a low voice, 'The Master is here and wants to see you.' [29]Hearing this, Mary got up quickly and went to him. [30]Jesus had not yet come into the village; he was still at the place where Martha had met him. [31]When the Jews who were in the house comforting Mary saw her get up so quickly and go out, they followed her, thinking that she was going to the tomb to weep there.
[32]Mary went to Jesus, and as soon as she saw him she threw herself at his feet, saying, 'Lord, if you had been here, my brother would not have died.' [33]At the sight of her tears, and those of the Jews who had come with her, Jesus was greatly distressed, and with a profound sigh he said, [34]'Where have you put him?' They said, 'Lord, come and see.' [35]Jesus wept; [36]and the Jews said, 'See how much he loved him!' [37]But there were some who remarked, 'He opened the eyes of the blind man. Could he not have prevented this man's

death?' [38]Sighing again, Jesus reached the tomb: it was a cave with a stone to close the opening. [39]Jesus said, 'Take the stone away.' Martha, the dead man's sister, said to him, 'Lord, by now he will smell; this is the fourth day since he died.' [40]Jesus replied, 'Have I not told you that if you believe you will see the glory of God?' [41]So they took the stone away. Then Jesus lifted up his eyes and said:

Father, I thank you for hearing my prayer.
[42] I myself knew that you hear me always,
      but I speak
   for the sake of all these who are standing
            around me,
   so that they may believe it was you who
            sent me.

[43]When he had said this, he cried in a loud voice, 'Lazarus, come out!' [44]The dead man came out, his feet and hands bound with strips of material, and a cloth over his face. Jesus said to them, 'Unbind him, let him go free.'

The Jewish leaders decide on the death of Jesus

[45]Many of the Jews who had come to visit Mary, and had seen what he did, believed in him, [46]but some of them went to the Pharisees to tell them what Jesus had done. [47]Then the chief priests and Pharisees called a meeting. 'Here is this man working all these signs,' they said, 'and what action are we taking? [48]If we let him go on in this way everybody will believe in him, and the Romans will come and suppress the Holy Place and our nation.' [49]One of them, Caiaphas, the high priest that year, said, 'You do not seem to have grasped the situation at all; [50]you fail to see that it is to your advantage that one man should die for the people, rather than that the whole nation should perish.' [51]He did not speak in his own person, but as high priest of that year he was prophesying that Jesus was to die for the nation— [52]and not for the nation only, but also to gather together into one the scattered children of God. [53]From that day onwards

they were determined to kill him. ⁵⁴ So Jesus no longer went about openly among the Jews, but left the district for a town called Ephraim, in the country bordering on the desert, and stayed there with his disciples.

The Passover draws near

⁵⁵ The Jewish Passover was drawing near, and many of the country people who had gone up to Jerusalem before the Passover to purify themselves ⁵⁶ were looking out for Jesus, saying to one another as they stood about in the Temple, 'What do you think? Will he come to the festival or not?' ⁵⁷ The chief priests and Pharisees had by now given their orders: anyone who knew where he was must inform them so that they could arrest him.

The anointing at Bethany

12 Six days before the Passover, Jesus went to Bethany, where Lazarus was, whom he had raised from the dead. ² They gave a dinner for him there; Martha waited on them and Lazarus was among those at table. ³ Mary brought in a pound of very costly ointment, pure nard, and with it anointed the feet of Jesus, wiping them with her hair; the house was filled with the scent of the ointment. ⁴ Then Judas Iscariot—one of his disciples, the man who was to betray him—said, ⁵ 'Why was this ointment not sold for three hundred denarii and the money given to the poor?' ⁶ He said this, not because he cared about the poor, but because he was a thief; he was in charge of the common fund and used to help himself to the contents. ⁷ So Jesus said, 'Leave her alone; let her keep it for the day of my burial. ⁸ You have the poor with you always, you will not always have me.'

⁹ Meanwhile a large number of Jews heard that he was there and came not only on account of Jesus but also to see Lazarus whom he had raised from the dead. ¹⁰ Then the chief priests decided to kill Lazarus as well, ¹¹ since it was on his account that many of the Jews were leaving them and believing in Jesus.

The Messiah enters Jerusalem

¹² The next day the great crowd of people who had come up for the festival heard that Jesus was on his way to Jerusalem. ¹³ They took branches of palm and went out to receive him, shouting:

'Hosanna!
Blessed is he who is coming in the name
of the Lord,ᵃ
the king of Israel.'

¹⁴ Jesus found a young donkey and mounted it—as scripture says:

¹⁵ Do not be afraid, daughter of Zion;
look, your king is approaching,
riding on the foal of a donkey.ᵇ

¹⁶ At first his disciples did not understand this, but later, after Jesus had been glorified, they remembered that this had been written about him and that this was what had happened to him. ¹⁷ The crowd who had been with him when he called Lazarus out of the tomb and raised him from the dead kept bearing witness to it; ¹⁸ this was another reason why the crowd came out to receive him: they had heard that he had given this sign. ¹⁹ Then the Pharisees said to one another, 'You see, you are making no progress; look, the whole world has gone after him!'

Jesus foretells his death and subsequent glorification

²⁰ Among those who went up to worship at the festival were some Greeks. ²¹ These approached Philip, who came from Bethsaida in Galilee, and put this request to him, 'Sir, we should like to see Jesus.' ²² Philip went to tell Andrew, and Andrew and Philip together went to tell Jesus.

²³ Jesus replied to them:

12a Ps 118:25–26. 12b Zc 9:9–10.

Now the hour has come
for the Son of man to be glorified.
²⁴ In all truth I tell you,
unless a wheat grain falls into the earth
and dies,
it remains only a single grain;
but if it dies
it yields a rich harvest.
²⁵ Anyone who loves his life loses it;
anyone who hates his life in this world
will keep it for eternal life.
²⁶ Whoever serves me, must follow me,
and my servant will be with me wherever
I am.
If anyone serves me, my Father will
honour him.
²⁷ Now my soul is troubled.
What shall I say:
Father, save me from this hour? ^c
But it is for this very reason that I have
come to this hour.
²⁸ Father, glorify your name!

A voice came from heaven, 'I have glorified
it, and I will again glorify it.'
²⁹ The crowd standing by, who heard this,
said it was a clap of thunder; others said, 'It
was an angel speaking to him.' ³⁰ Jesus answered, 'It was not for my sake that this voice
came, but for yours.

³¹ 'Now sentence is being passed on this
world;
now the prince of this world is to be driven
out.
³² And when I am lifted up from the earth,
I shall draw all people to myself.'

³³ By these words he indicated the kind of
death he would die. ³⁴ The crowd answered,
'The Law has taught us that the Christ will remain for ever. So how can you say, "The Son
of man must be lifted up"? Who is this Son of
man?' ³⁵ Jesus then said:

The light will be with you only a little
longer now.

Go on your way while you have the light,
or darkness will overtake you,
and nobody who walks in the dark knows
where he is going.
³⁶ While you still have the light,
believe in the light
so that you may become children of light.

Having said this, Jesus left them and was
hidden from their sight.

Conclusion: the unbelief of the Jews

³⁷ Though they had been present when he
gave so many signs, they did not believe in
him; ³⁸ this was to fulfil the words of the
prophet Isaiah:

Lord, who has given credence to what they
have heard from us,
and who has seen in it a revelation of the
Lord's arm? ^d

³⁹ Indeed, they were unable to believe be-
cause, as Isaiah says again:
⁴⁰ *He has blinded their eyes,*
he has hardened their heart,
to prevent them from using their eyes to see,
using their heart to understand,
changing their ways and being healed
by me. ^e

⁴¹ Isaiah said this because he saw his glory,
and his words referred to Jesus.
⁴² And yet there were many who did believe
in him, even among the leading men, but they
did not admit it, because of the Pharisees and
for fear of being banned from the synagogue:
⁴³ they put human glory before God's glory.
⁴⁴ Jesus declared publicly:

Whoever believes in me
believes not in me
but in the one who sent me,
⁴⁵ and whoever sees me,
sees the one who sent me.

12c cf. Lk 22:40–46par.   12d Is 53:1.   12e Is 6:10.

46 I have come into the world as light,
to prevent anyone who believes
in me
from staying in the dark any more.
47 If anyone hears my words and does
not keep them faithfully,
it is not I who shall judge such a
person,
since I have come not to judge the
world,
but to save the world:
48 anyone who rejects me and refuses my
words
has his judge already:
the word itself that I have spoken
will be his judge on the last day.
49 For I have not spoken of my own
accord;
but the Father who sent me
commanded me what to say and what to
speak,
50 and I know that his commands mean
eternal life.
And therefore what the Father has
told me
is what I speak.

The washing of feet

13 Before the festival of the Passover, Jesus,
knowing that his hour had come to pass
from this world to the Father, having loved
those who were his in the world, loved them to
the end. 2 They were at supper, and the devil had already put it into the mind of Judas Iscariot son
of Simon, to betray him. 3 Jesus knew that the
Father had put everything into his hands, and
that he had come from God and was returning
to God, 4 and he got up from table, removed
his outer garments and, taking a towel,
wrapped it round his waist; 5 he then poured
water into a basin and began to wash the disciples' feet and to wipe them with the towel he
was wearing. 6 He came to Simon Peter, who said to him,
'Lord, are you going to wash my feet?' 7 Jesus
answered, 'At the moment you do not know

what I am doing, but later you will understand.' 8 'Never!' said Peter. 'You shall never
wash my feet.' Jesus replied, 'If I do not wash
you, you can have no share with me.' Simon
Peter said, 9 'Well then, Lord, not only my feet,
but my hands and my head as well!' 10 Jesus
said, 'No one who has had a bath needs washing, such a person is clean all over. You too are
clean, though not all of you are.' 11 He knew
who was going to betray him, and that was
why he said, 'though not all of you are'.

12 When he had washed their feet and put
on his outer garments again he went back to
the table. 'Do you understand', he said, 'what I
have done to you? 13 You call me Master and
Lord, and rightly; so I am. 14 If I, then, the
Lord and Master, have washed your feet, you
must wash each other's feet. 15 I have given you
an example so that you may copy what I have
done to you.

16 'In all truth I tell you,
no servant is greater than his master,
no messenger is greater than the one
who sent him.

17 'Now that you know this, blessed are you
if you behave accordingly. 18 I am not speaking
about all of you: I know the ones I have chosen; but what scripture says must be fulfilled:

'He who shares my table
takes advantage of me.*a*
19 I tell you this now, before it happens,
so that when it does happen
you may believe that I am He.
20 In all truth I tell you,
whoever welcomes the one I send,
welcomes me,
and whoever welcomes me, welcomes
the one who sent me.'

The treachery of Judas foretold

21 Having said this, Jesus was deeply disturbed
and declared, 'In all truth I tell you, one of you

13a Ps 41:9.

151 READ JOHN 13:31–35.

You must love one another just as I have loved you.—JOHN 13:34

THE MARKS OF REAL LOVE

This selection comes from a talk that St. Jane de Chantal gave to nuns in her religious congregation, but it applies to all Christians:

Our Lord told us that we should love as he loved us. . . . Certainly we can never reach the perfection of this holy love and union with God unless we have this love of neighbor. As St. John wrote, "Anyone who says 'I love God' and hates his brother is a liar, since no one who fails to love the brother whom he can see can love God whom he has not seen" (1 Jn 4:20). If we don't have heartfelt love and holy affection towards our sisters, who represent God's image to us, we must conclude that we don't have true love of God. . . .

Let us see if we're harboring any slight bitterness of heart toward any of our sisters—any jealousy, ambition, dislike. . . . Before God, let's examine ourselves to see if we desire the good of all of our sisters equally, one as much as another. To speak very gently with those for whom we feel a special attraction and liking, to say nothing that downgrades them, to do nothing that puts them out—these are not the marks of perfect charity. Real charity and true virtue require that we speak to all our sisters in the same way—gently, cordially, with humble frankness, . . . and with a good word about all. . . . It is in this that virtue lies, not in our own preferences. And if we happen to find some sisters disagreeable or hostile toward us, remember this: "Do good to those who hate you. Bless your persecutors; never curse them" (Lk 6:27; Rm 12:14).

If we find in ourselves any resentment, aversion, or remembrance of past wrongs, let's immediately pick up the pruning hook of God's holy fear and cut off this evil shoot. . . . In its place let's build up love for this great commandment towards our neighbor . . . "to love one another just as I have loved you."   ST. JANE DE CHANTAL, 1572–1641

YOU WILL FIND THE NEXT READING AT JOHN 14:1.

is going to betray me.' 22 The disciples looked at each other, wondering whom he meant. 23 The disciple Jesus loved was reclining next to Jesus; 24 Simon Peter signed to him and said, 'Ask who it is he means,' 25 so leaning back close to Jesus' chest he said, 'Who is it, Lord?' 26 Jesus answered, 'It is the one to whom I give the piece of bread that I dip in the dish.' And when he had dipped the piece of bread he gave it to Judas son of Simon Iscariot. 27 At that instant, after Judas had taken the bread, Satan entered him. Jesus then said, 'What you are going to do, do quickly.' 28 None of the others at table understood why he said this. 29 Since Judas had charge of the common fund, some of them thought Jesus was telling him, 'Buy what we need for the festival,' or telling him to give something to the poor. 30 As soon as Judas had taken the piece of bread he went out. It was night.

152 READ JOHN 14:1–7.

I am the Way; I am Truth and Life. No one can come to the Father except through me.—JOHN 14:6

LOVING THE TRUTH

This selection is excerpted from a letter St. Catherine wrote to Lorenzo del Pino, a doctor of law:

Dearest brother, I write to you with a desire to see you a lover of truth and a despiser of falsehood. . . . God is the highest and eternal Truth. In whom shall we know him? In sweet Christ Jesus who shows us with his blood the truth of the eternal Father. His truth toward us is this: he created us in his image and likeness to give us eternal life that we might share and enjoy his good. But through our sin this truth was not fulfilled in us. Therefore, God gave us the Word, his Son, and required that he should restore us to grace through much endurance, purging our sin in his own person, and manifesting his truth in his blood.

So we know by the unfathomable love shown to us by the blood of Christ crucified that God wants nothing else but our sanctification. . . . He who knows this truth never resists it but always follows and loves it, walking in the footsteps of Christ crucified. To teach us by example, this sweet loving Word despised the world and all delights, and chose to endure hunger and thirst, shame and reproach, even to the shameful death on the Cross, for the honor of the Father and our salvation. And he who is the lover of the truth . . . must follow this way and these footsteps. . . .

So knowing no other way, I want to see you a lover and follower of truth and a despiser of falsehood; hating the devil, the father of lies, and your own lower nature that follows such a parent; and loving Christ crucified, who is Way, Truth and Life. For he who walks in him reaches the Light, and is clothed in the shining garment of charity in which all virtues are found.

ST. CATHERINE OF SIENA, 1347–1380

YOU WILL FIND THE NEXT READING AT JOHN 14:14.

Farewell discourses[b]

31 When he had gone, Jesus said:

Now has the Son of man been glorified,
and in him God has been glorified.
32 If God has been glorified in him,
God will in turn glorify him in
himself,
and will glorify him very soon.
33 Little children,
I shall be with you only a little longer.

You will look for me,
and, as I told the Jews,
where I am going,
you cannot come.
34 I give you a new commandment:
love one another;
you must love one another
just as I have loved you.

13b These contain teachings given also on other occasions, and perhaps in different versions. Ch. 16 may be another version of ch. 14, and ch. 17 yet another.

35 It is by your love for one another,
  that everyone will recognise you
  as my disciples.

36 Simon Peter said, 'Lord, where are you going?' Jesus replied, 'Now you cannot follow me where I am going, but later you shall follow me.' 37 Peter said to him, 'Why can I not follow you now? I will lay down my life for you.' 38 'Lay down your life for me?' answered Jesus. 'In all truth I tell you, before the cock crows you will have disowned me three times.'

14 Do not let your hearts be troubled.
  You trust in God, trust also in me.
2 In my Father's house there are many
  places to live in;
  otherwise I would have told you.
  I am going now to prepare a place for you,
3 and after I have gone and prepared you
  a place,
  I shall return to take you to myself,
  so that you may be with me
  where I am.
4 You know the way to the place where I
  am going.

5 Thomas said, 'Lord, we do not know where you are going, so how can we know the way?' 6 Jesus said:

I am the Way; I am Truth and Life.
No one can come to the Father except
  through me.
7 If you know me, you will know my Father
  too.
From this moment you know him and
  have seen him.

8 Philip said, 'Lord, show us the Father and then we shall be satisfied.' Jesus said to him, 9 'Have I been with you all this time, Philip, and you still do not know me?

'Anyone who has seen me has seen the
  Father,

so how can you say, "Show us the Father"?
10 Do you not believe
  that I am in the Father and the Father is in
    me?
  What I say to you I do not speak of my
    own accord:
  it is the Father, living in me, who is doing
    his works.
11 You must believe me when I say
  that I am in the Father and the Father is in
    me;
  or at least believe it on the evidence of
    these works.
12 In all truth I tell you,
  whoever believes in me
  will perform the same works as I do
    myself,
  and will perform even greater works,
  because I am going to the Father.
13 Whatever you ask in my name I will do,
  so that the Father may be glorified in the
    Son.
14 If you ask me anything in my name,
  I will do it.
15 If you love me you will keep my
    commandments.
16 I shall ask the Father,
  and he will give you another Paraclete[a]
  to be with you for ever,
17 the Spirit of truth
  whom the world can never accept
  since it neither sees nor knows him;
  but you know him,
  because he is with you, he is in you.
18 I shall not leave you orphans;
  I shall come to you.
19 In a short time the world will no
    longer see me;
  but you will see that I live
  and you also will live.
20 On that day
  you will know that I am in my
    Father
  and you in me and I in you.

14a The Gk word means 'advocate', 'counsellor', 'protector'.

153 READ JOHN 14:14–23.

I shall not leave you orphans; I shall come to you.—JOHN 14:18

PRAYING WITH JESUS

Let us now return to our vocal prayer, so that we may learn to pray in such a way that, without our understanding how, God may give us everything at once: if we do this, as I have said, we shall pray as we ought. As you know, the first things must be an examination of conscience, confession of sin and the signing of yourself with the Cross. Then, . . . as you are alone, you must look for a companion—and who could be a better Companion than the very Master who taught you the prayer that you are about to say?

Imagine that this Lord himself is at your side and see how lovingly and how humbly he is teaching you—and believe me, you should stay with so good a Friend for as long as you can before you leave him. If you become accustomed to having him at your side, and if he sees that you love him to be there and are always trying to please him, you will never be able, as we put it, to send him away, nor will he ever fail you. He will help you in all your trials and you will have him everywhere. Do you think it is a small thing to have such a Friend as that beside you?

. . . Those of you whose minds cannot dwell *upon God* but are *constantly* wandering must at all costs form this habit. I know quite well that you are capable of it—for many years I endured this trial of being unable to concentrate on the subject, and a very sore trial it is. But I know the Lord does not leave us so devoid of help that if we approach him humbly and ask him to be with us he will not grant our request. . . . I am sure we can form this habit and strive to walk at the side of this true Master.

ST. TERESA OF AVILA, 1515–1582

YOU WILL FIND THE NEXT READING AT JOHN 15.

21 Whoever holds to my commandments and
  keeps them
 is the one who loves me;
 and whoever loves me will be loved by my
  Father,
 and I shall love him and reveal myself to
  him.'

22 Judas—not Judas Iscariot—said to him,
'Lord, what has happened, that you intend to
show yourself to us and not to the world?'
23 Jesus replied:

 Anyone who loves me will keep my word,
 and my Father will love him,

and we shall come to him
and make a home in him.
24 Anyone who does not love me does not
  keep my words.
 And the word that you hear is not my
  own:
 it is the word of the Father who sent me.
25 I have said these things to you
 while still with you;
26 but the Paraclete, the Holy Spirit,
 whom the Father will send in my
  name,
 will teach you everything
 and remind you of all I have said
  to you.

27 Peace I bequeath to you,
  my own peace I give you,
  a peace which the world cannot give, this
    is my gift to you.
  Do not let your hearts be troubled or
    afraid.
28 You heard me say:
  I am going away and shall return.
  If you loved me you would be glad that I
    am going to the Father,
  for the Father is greater than I.
29 I have told you this now, before it happens,
  so that when it does happen you may
    believe.
30 I shall not talk to you much longer,
  because the prince of this world is on
    his way.
  He has no power over me,
31 but the world must recognise that I love
    the Father
  and that I act just as the Father
    commanded.
  Come now, let us go.

The true vine^a

15 I am the true vine,
  and my Father is the vinedresser.
2 Every branch in me that bears no fruit
  he cuts away,
  and every branch that does bear fruit he
    prunes
  to make it bear even more.
3 You are clean already,
  by means of the word that I have spoken
    to you.
4 Remain in me, as I in you.
  As a branch cannot bear fruit all by itself,
  unless it remains part of the vine,
  neither can you unless you remain in me.
5 I am the vine,
  you are the branches.
  Whoever remains in me, with me in him,
  bears fruit in plenty;
  for cut off from me you can do nothing.
6 Anyone who does not remain in me
  is thrown away like a branch
  —and withers;

these branches are collected and thrown on
    the fire
  and are burnt.
7 If you remain in me
  and my words remain in you,
  you may ask for whatever you please
  and you will get it.
8 It is to the glory of my Father that you
    should bear much fruit
  and be my disciples.
9 I have loved you
  just as the Father has loved me.
  Remain in my love.
10 If you keep my commandments
  you will remain in my love,
  just as I have kept my Father's
    commandments
  and remain in his love.
11 I have told you this
  so that my own joy may be in you
  and your joy be complete.
12 This is my commandment:
  love one another,
  as I have loved you.
13 No one can have greater love
  than to lay down his life for his
    friends.
14 You are my friends,
  if you do what I command you.
15 I shall no longer call you servants,
  because a servant does not know
  the master's business;
  I call you friends,
  because I have made known to you
  everything I have learnt from my
    Father.
16 You did not choose me,
  no, I chose you;
  and I commissioned you
  to go out and to bear fruit,
  fruit that will last;
  so that the Father will give you
  anything you ask him in my name.
17 My command to you
  is to love one another.

15a cf. Is 5:1–7; Mk 12:1–12.

154   READ JOHN 15:1–17.

No one can have greater love than to lay down his life for his friends.—JOHN 15:13

SACRIFICING YOURSELF FOR OTHERS

Our Divine Master gave up his life not only to heal the sick, to work miracles, and to teach us what we ought to do to be saved or to be pleasing to him. He also spent his entire life even shaping his cross, suffering a thousand persecutions from the very ones to whom he was doing so much good and for whom he laid down his life. We must do the same, says the holy Apostle, that is, we too should shape our cross in suffering for one another as the Savior taught us; in giving our life for those very ones who would take it from us, as he so lovingly did; in spending ourselves for our neighbor, not only in agreeable things, but also in those which are painful and disagreeable such as bearing lovingly those persecutions which might in some fashion cool our hearts towards our brothers.

Some say: "I greatly love my neighbor and would wish, indeed, to render him some service." That is very good, says St. Bernard, but it is not enough . . . "Oh, I love him so much . . . that I would gladly sacrifice all my possessions for him." That is going further and is certainly better, but still it is not enough. "I love him . . . so greatly that I would willingly expend myself for him in whatever he wanted from me." This is certainly a very good sign of your love, but you must go still further; for there is a still higher degree in this love, as St. Paul teaches us, when he wrote, "Take me as your pattern, just as I take Christ for mine" (1 Co 11:1). And in one of his epistles he wrote thus to his most dear children: "I am ready to give my life for you, and give of myself so completely that I make no reservation in proving to you how dearly and tenderly I love you . . ." (see 2 Co 12:14–15). In this he teaches us that to spend ourselves even so far as to give our life for the neighbor is not as much as to allow ourselves to be spent at the will of others, either by them or for them.

ST. FRANCIS DE SALES, 1567–1622

YOU WILL FIND THE NEXT READING AT JOHN 17.

The disciples and the world

18 If the world hates you,
  you must realise that it hated me before it
    hated you.
19 If you belonged to the world,
  the world would love you as its own;
  but because you do not belong to the
    world,
  because my choice of you has drawn you
    out of the world,
  that is why the world hates you.

20 Remember the words I said to you:
  A servant is not greater than his master.
  If they persecuted me,
  they will persecute you too;
  if they kept my word,
  they will keep yours as well.
21 But it will be on my account that they will
    do all this to you,
  because they do not know the one who
    sent me.
22 If I had not come,
  if I had not spoken to them,

[1364]

they would have been blameless;
but as it is they have no excuse for their
    sin.
23 Anyone who hates me hates my Father.
24 If I had not performed such works among
    them
as no one else has ever done,
they would be blameless;
but as it is, in spite of what they have seen,
they hate both me and my Father.
25 But all this was only to fulfil the words
    written in their Law:
They hated me without reason.[b]
26 When the Paraclete comes,
whom I shall send to you from the Father,
the Spirit of truth who issues from the
    Father,
he will be my witness.
27 And you too will be witnesses,
because you have been with me from the
    beginning.

16 I have told you all this
so that you may not fall away.
2 They will expel you from the synagogues,
and indeed the time is coming
when anyone who kills you will think he is
    doing a holy service to God.
3 They will do these things
because they have never known either the
    Father or me.
4 But I have told you all this,
so that when the time for it comes
you may remember that I told you.

The coming of the Paraclete

I did not tell you this from the beginning,
because I was with you;
5 but now I am going to the one who
    sent me.
Not one of you asks, 'Where are you
    going?'
6 Yet you are sad at heart because I have told
    you this.
7 Still, I am telling you the truth:
it is for your own good that I am going,
because unless I go,

the Paraclete will not come to you;
but if I go,
I will send him to you.
8 And when he comes,
he will show the world how wrong it was,
    about sin,
and about who was in the right,
and about judgement:
9 about sin:
in that they refuse to believe in me;
10 about who was in the right:
in that I am going to the Father
and you will see me no more;
11 about judgement:
in that the prince of this world is already
    condemned.
12 I still have many things to say to you
but they would be too much for you to
    bear now.
13 However, when the Spirit of truth comes
he will lead you to the complete truth,
since he will not be speaking of his own
    accord,
but will say only what he has been told;
and he will reveal to you the things to
    come.
14 He will glorify me,
since all he reveals to you
will be taken from what is mine.
15 Everything the Father has is mine;
that is why I said:
all he reveals to you
will be taken from what is mine.

Jesus to return very soon

16 In a short time you will no longer see me,
and then a short time later you will see me
    again.

17 Then some of his disciples said to one
another, 'What does he mean, "In a short
time you will no longer see me, and then
a short time later you will see me again," and,
"I am going to the Father"? 18 What is this
"short time"? We don't know what he means.'

15b Ps 69:4.

19 Jesus knew that they wanted to question him, so he said, 'You are asking one another what I meant by saying, "In a short time you will no longer see me, and then a short time later you will see me again."

20 'In all truth I tell you,
you will be weeping and wailing
while the world will rejoice;
you will be sorrowful,
but your sorrow will turn to joy.
21 A woman in childbirth suffers,
because her time has come;
but when she has given birth to the child
she forgets the suffering
in her joy that a human being has been
born into the world.
22 So it is with you: you are sad now,
but I shall see you again, and your hearts
will be full of joy,
and that joy no one shall take from you.
23 When that day comes,
you will not ask me any questions.
In all truth I tell you,
anything you ask from the Father
he will grant in my name.
24 Until now you have not asked anything in
my name.
Ask and you will receive,
and so your joy will be complete.
25 I have been telling you these things in
veiled language.
The hour is coming
when I shall no longer speak to you in
veiled language
but tell you about the Father in plain words.
26 When that day comes
you will ask in my name;
and I do not say that I shall pray to the
Father for you,
27 because the Father himself loves you
for loving me,
and believing that I came from God.
28 I came from the Father and have come
into the world
and now I am leaving the world to go to
the Father.'

29 His disciples said, 'Now you are speaking plainly and not using veiled language. 30 Now we see that you know everything and need not wait for questions to be put into words; because of this we believe that you came from God.' 31 Jesus answered them:

Do you believe at last?
32 Listen; the time will come—indeed it has
come already—
when you are going to be scattered, each
going his own way
and leaving me alone.
And yet I am not alone,
because the Father is with me.
33 I have told you all this
so that you may find peace in me.
In the world you will have hardship,
but be courageous:
I have conquered the world.

The prayer of Jesus

17 After saying this, Jesus raised his eyes to heaven and said:

Father, the hour has come:
glorify your Son
so that your Son may glorify you;
2 so that, just as you have given him power
over all humanity,
he may give eternal life to all those you
have entrusted to him.
3 And eternal life is this:
to know you,
the only true God,
and Jesus Christ whom you have sent.
4 I have glorified you on earth
by finishing the work
that you gave me to do.
5 Now, Father, glorify me
with that glory I had with you
before ever the world existed.
6 I have revealed your name
to those whom you took from the world
to give me.
They were yours and you gave them
to me,

and they have kept your word.
⁷ Now at last they have recognised
 that all you have given me comes from you
⁸ for I have given them
 the teaching you gave to me,
 and they have indeed accepted it
 and know for certain that I came from
  you,
 and have believed that it was you who
  sent me.
⁹ It is for them that I pray.
 I am not praying for the world
 but for those you have given me,
 because they belong to you.
¹⁰ All I have is yours
 and all you have is mine,
 and in them I am glorified.
¹¹ I am no longer in the world,
 but they are in the world,
 and I am coming to you.
 Holy Father,
 keep those you have given me true to your
  name,
 so that they may be one like us.
¹² While I was with them,
 I kept those you had given me true to your
  name.
 I have watched over them and not one is
  lost
 except one who was destined to be lost,
 and this was to fulfil the scriptures.
¹³ But now I am coming to you
 and I say these things in the world
 to share my joy with them to the full.
¹⁴ I passed your word on to them,
 and the world hated them,
 because they belong to the world
 no more than I belong to the world.
¹⁵ I am not asking you to remove them from
  the world,
 but to protect them from the Evil One.
¹⁶ They do not belong to the world
 any more than I belong to the world.
¹⁷ Consecrate them in the truth;
 your word is truth.
¹⁸ As you sent me into the world,
 I have sent them into the world,

¹⁹ and for their sake I consecrate myself
 so that they too may be consecrated in
  truth.
²⁰ I pray not only for these
 but also for those
 who through their teaching will come to
  believe in me.
²¹ May they all be one,
 just as, Father, you are in me and I am
  in you,
 so that they also may be in us,
 so that the world may believe it was you
  who sent me.
²² I have given them the glory you gave
  to me,
 that they may be one as we are one.
²³ With me in them and you in me,
 may they be so perfected in unity
 that the world will recognise that it was
  you who sent me
 and that you have loved them as you have
  loved me.
²⁴ Father,
 I want those you have given me
 to be with me where I am,
 so that they may always see my glory
 which you have given me
 because you loved me
 before the foundation of the world.
²⁵ Father, Upright One,
 the world has not known you,
 but I have known you,
 and these have known
 that you have sent me.
²⁶ I have made your name known to
  them
 and will continue to make it known,
 so that the love with which you loved
  me may be in them,
 and so that I may be in them.

The arrest of Jesus

18 After he had said all this, Jesus left with his disciples and crossed the Kidron valley where there was a garden into which he went with his disciples. ² Judas the traitor

155   READ JOHN 17.

May they all be one, just as, Father, you are in me and I am in you.—JOHN 17:21

THE TRUE INTERIOR LIFE

The Savior's high priestly prayer unveils the mystery of the inner life: the interrelatedness of the Divine Persons and the indwelling of God in the soul. In these mysterious depths the work of salvation was prepared and accomplished itself in concealment and silence. And so it will continue until the union of all is actually accomplished at the end of time. The decision for the Redemption was conceived in the eternal silence of the inner divine life. The power of the Holy Spirit came over the Virgin praying alone in the hidden, silent room in Nazareth and brought about the Incarnation of the Savior. Congregated around the silently praying Virgin, the emergent church awaited the promised new outpouring of the Holy Spirit that was to quicken it into inner clarity and fruitful outer effectiveness. In the night of blindness that God laid over his eyes, Saul awaited in solitary prayer the Lord's answer to his question, "What do you want me to do?" (see Ac 9). In solitary prayer Peter was prepared for his mission to the Gentiles (see Ac 10). And so it has remained through the centuries. In the silent dialogue with their Lord of souls consecrated to God, the events of church history are prepared that, visible far and wide, renew the face of the earth. The Virgin, who kept every word sent from God in her heart, is the model for such attentive souls in whom Jesus' high priestly prayer comes to life again and again. And women, who like her, were totally self-forgetful because they were steeped in the life and suffering of Christ, were the Lord's preferred choice as instruments to accomplish great things in the church: a St. Bridget, a Catherine of Siena. And when St. Teresa, the powerful reformer of her Order at a time of widespread falling away from the faith, wished to come to the rescue of the church, she saw the renewal of true interior life as the means toward this end.

ST. EDITH STEIN, 1891–1942

YOU WILL FIND THE NEXT READING AT JOHN 19:1.

knew the place also, since Jesus had often met his disciples there, ³so Judas brought the cohort to this place together with guards sent by the chief priests and the Pharisees, all with lanterns and torches and weapons. ⁴Knowing everything that was to happen to him, Jesus came forward and said, 'Who are you looking for?' ⁵They answered, 'Jesus the Nazarene.' He said, 'I am he.' Now Judas the traitor was standing among them. ⁶When Jesus said to them, 'I am he,' they moved back and fell on the ground. ⁷He asked them a second time, 'Who are you looking for?' They said, 'Jesus the Nazarene.' ⁸Jesus replied, 'I have told you that I am he. If I am the one you are looking for, let these others go.' ⁹This was to fulfil the words he had spoken, 'Not one of those you gave me have I lost.'

¹⁰Simon Peter, who had a sword, drew it and struck the high priest's servant, cutting off his right ear. The servant's name was Malchus. ¹¹Jesus said to Peter, 'Put your sword back in its scabbard; am I not to drink the cup that the Father has given me?'

Jesus before Annas and Caiaphas; Peter disowns him

12 The cohort and its tribune and the Jewish guards seized Jesus and bound him. 13 They took him first to Annas, because Annas was the father-in-law of Caiaphas, who was high priest that year. 14 It was Caiaphas who had counselled the Jews, 'It is better for one man to die for the people.'

15 Simon Peter, with another disciple, followed Jesus. This disciple, who was known to the high priest, went with Jesus into the high priest's palace, 16 but Peter stayed outside the door. So the other disciple, the one known to the high priest, went out, spoke to the door-keeper and brought Peter in. 17 The girl on duty at the door said to Peter, 'Aren't you another of that man's disciples?' He answered, 'I am not.' 18 Now it was cold, and the servants and guards had lit a charcoal fire and were standing there warming themselves; so Peter stood there too, warming himself with the others.

19 The high priest questioned Jesus about his disciples and his teaching. 20 Jesus answered, 'I have spoken openly for all the world to hear; I have always taught in the synagogue and in the Temple where all the Jews meet together; I have said nothing in secret. 21 Why ask me? Ask my hearers what I taught; they know what I said.' 22 At these words, one of the guards standing by gave Jesus a slap in the face, saying, 'Is that the way you answer the high priest?' 23 Jesus replied, 'If there is some offence in what I said, point it out; but if not, why do you strike me?' 24 Then Annas sent him, bound, to Caiaphas the high priest.[a]

25 As Simon Peter stood there warming himself, someone said to him, 'Aren't you another of his disciples?' He denied it saying, 'I am not.' 26 One of the high priest's servants, a relation of the man whose ear Peter had cut off, said, 'Didn't I see you in the garden with him?' 27 Again Peter denied it; and at once a cock crowed.

Jesus before Pilate

28 They then led Jesus from the house of Caiaphas to the Praetorium. It was now morning. They did not go into the Praetorium themselves to avoid becoming defiled and unable to eat the Passover. 29 So Pilate came outside to them and said, 'What charge do you bring against this man?' They replied, 30 'If he were not a criminal, we should not have handed him over to you.' 31 Pilate said, 'Take him yourselves, and try him by your own Law.' The Jews answered, 'We are not allowed to put anyone to death.' 32 This was to fulfil the words Jesus had spoken indicating the way he was going to die.

33 So Pilate went back into the Praetorium and called Jesus to him and asked him, 'Are you the king of the Jews?' 34 Jesus replied, 'Do you ask this of your own accord, or have others said it to you about me?' 35 Pilate answered, 'Am I a Jew? It is your own people and the chief priests who have handed you over to me: what have you done?' 36 Jesus replied, 'Mine is not a kingdom of this world; if my kingdom were of this world, my men would have fought to prevent my being surrendered to the Jews. As it is, my kingdom does not belong here.' 37 Pilate said, 'So, then you are a king?' Jesus answered, 'It is you who say that I am a king. I was born for this, I came into the world for this, to bear witness to the truth; and all who are on the side of truth listen to my voice.' 38 'Truth?' said Pilate. 'What is that?' And so saying he went out again to the Jews and said, 'I find no case against him. 39 But according to a custom of yours I should release one prisoner at the Passover; would you like me, then, to release for you the king of the Jews?' 40 At this they shouted, 'Not this man,' they said, 'but Barabbas.' Barabbas was a bandit.

19 Pilate then had Jesus taken away and scourged; 2 and after this, the soldiers

18a Jn has no Sanhedrin session as the other gospels have, only a private interrogation at night.

156 READ JOHN 19:1–30.

Carrying his own cross he went out to the Place of the Skull . . . where they crucified him.—JOHN 19:17–18

RESISTING SIN

We cannot conceive the intensity of the sufferings of Jesus Christ during his Passion. Every portion of his body had its pain, and his soul was so overwhelmed with sadness that, unable to express it, the Lord says it was sufficient to cause his death. . . . Moreover, he was covered with opprobrium and confusion; overwhelmed with injuries, maledictions and calumnies; a seditious thief and murderer is preferred to him. To such a state have our sins reduced our divine Lord, who so merits our esteem, honor, and respect.

Jesus Christ does not suffer less in body than in soul: he is ignominiously bound and dragged by the soldiers. His head is crowned with thorns, which are ruthlessly pierced into his flesh. His tormentors spit in his face and slap him. He is so cruelly scourged that blood flows from all parts of his body. His shoulders are laden with a heavy cross, and he is offered vinegar and gall to drink. He is crucified between two thieves, his hands and feet being pierced with large nails, and his side opened with a lance. . . .

Jesus Christ suffers from all classes of persons: one apostle betrays him, another denies him; the others flee, abandoning him to his enemies; the chief priest's henchmen seize him; soldiers outrage him; the crowd mocks him; a king insults him and sends him away as though he were a fool; a governor condemns him to death; the Jewish leaders regard him as a malefactor, and passersby blaspheme him. Can we contemplate the Man-God in so pitiable a state without conceiving a lively horror for sin and heartfelt sorrow for sins that we have committed? Let us mourn our past faults and firmly resolve never again to commit them. ST. JOHN BAPTIST DE LA SALLE, 1651–1719

YOU WILL FIND THE NEXT READING AT JOHN 19:31.

twisted some thorns into a crown and put it on his head and dressed him in a purple robe. ³They kept coming up to him and saying, 'Hail, king of the Jews!' and slapping him in the face.

⁴Pilate came outside again and said to them, 'Look, I am going to bring him out to you to let you see that I find no case against him.' ⁵Jesus then came out wearing the crown of thorns and the purple robe. Pilate said, 'Here is the man.' ⁶When they saw him, the chief priests and the guards shouted, 'Crucify him! Crucify him!' Pilate said, 'Take him

yourselves and crucify him: I find no case against him.' ⁷The Jews replied, 'We have a Law, and according to that Law he ought to be put to death, because he has claimed to be Son of God.'

⁸When Pilate heard them say this his fears increased. ⁹Re-entering the Praetorium, he said to Jesus, 'Where do you come from?' But Jesus made no answer. ¹⁰Pilate then said to him, 'Are you refusing to speak to me? Surely you know I have power to release you and I have power to crucify you?' ¹¹Jesus replied, 'You would have no power over me at all if it

had not been given you from above; that is why the man who handed me over to you has the greater guilt.'

Jesus is condemned to death

¹²From that moment Pilate was anxious to set him free, but the Jews shouted, 'If you set him free you are no friend of Caesar's; anyone who makes himself king is defying Caesar.' ¹³Hearing these words, Pilate had Jesus brought out, and seated him on the chair of judgement at a place called the Pavement, in Hebrew Gabbatha. ¹⁴It was the Day of Preparation, about the sixth hour. 'Here is your king,' said Pilate to the Jews. ¹⁵But they shouted, 'Away with him, away with him, crucify him.' Pilate said, 'Shall I crucify your king?' The chief priests answered, 'We have no king except Caesar.' ¹⁶So at that Pilate handed him over to them to be crucified.

The crucifixion

They then took charge of Jesus, ¹⁷and carrying his own cross he went out to the Place of the Skull or, as it is called in Hebrew, Golgotha, ¹⁸where they crucified him with two others, one on either side, Jesus being in the middle. ¹⁹Pilate wrote out a notice and had it fixed to the cross; it ran: 'Jesus the Nazarene, King of the Jews'. ²⁰This notice was read by many of the Jews, because the place where Jesus was crucified was near the city, and the writing was in Hebrew, Latin and Greek. ²¹So the Jewish chief priests said to Pilate, 'You should not write "King of the Jews", but that the man said, "I am King of the Jews".' ²²Pilate answered, 'What I have written, I have written.'

Jesus' garments divided

²³When the soldiers had finished crucifying Jesus they took his clothing and divided it into four shares, one for each soldier. His undergarment was seamless, woven in one piece from neck to hem; ²⁴so they said to one another, 'Instead of tearing it, let's throw dice to decide who is to have it.' In this way the words of scripture were fulfilled:

*They divide my garments among them
and cast lots for my clothes.*[a]

That is what the soldiers did.

Jesus and his mother

²⁵Near the cross of Jesus stood his mother and his mother's sister, Mary the wife of Clopas, and Mary of Magdala. ²⁶Seeing his mother and the disciple whom he loved standing near her, Jesus said to his mother, 'Woman, this is your son.' ²⁷Then to the disciple he said, 'This is your mother.' And from that hour the disciple took her into his home.

The death of Jesus

²⁸After this, Jesus knew that everything had now been completed and, so that the scripture should be completely fulfilled, he said:

I am thirsty.[b]

²⁹A jar full of sour wine stood there; so, putting a sponge soaked in the wine on a hyssop stick, they held it up to his mouth. ³⁰After Jesus had taken the wine he said, 'It is fulfilled'; and bowing his head he gave up his spirit.

The pierced Christ

³¹It was the Day of Preparation, and to avoid the bodies' remaining on the cross during the Sabbath—since that Sabbath was a day of special solemnity—the Jews asked Pilate to have the legs broken and the bodies taken away. ³²Consequently the soldiers came and broke the legs of the first man who had been crucified with him and then of the other. ³³When they came to Jesus, they saw he was already dead, and so instead of breaking his legs ³⁴one of the soldiers pierced his side with a lance; and immediately there came out blood and water. ³⁵This is the evidence of one who saw it—true evidence, and he knows that what he says is true—and he gives it so that you may

19a Ps 22:18.　19b Ps 69:21.

157 READ JOHN 19:31–37.

One of the soldiers pierced his side with a lance; and immediately there came out blood and water.—JOHN 19:34

REJOICING IN THE SACRED HEART

In the following vision, Jesus showed Bl. Julian his Sacred Heart:

With joyful face our good Lord looked down at his side and I was invited by his tender gaze to ponder this wound. For there within, he showed a place that was inviting . . . , and large enough . . . to offer refuge for all who will be saved, there to find their rest in peace and love. And with this sweet beholding he brought to mind his most dear blood and the precious water which he let pour from his side, all of his love. And looking with him, I realized that his heart was indeed broken in two. Now with his tender look he revealed something of God's inner bliss, as my soul was led in some measure to know his never-ending love, flowing from before time, to the present and for all eternity. And with this our good Lord gently spoke: "Lo, how I loved you." It was as if he had said, "My darling, behold and see your Lord, and your God, who is your Maker and your endless joy; see what liking and bliss I have in your salvation, and for my love enjoy now with me." To understand to the full these words of his "See how I love you," it was as if he were to say, "Lo, how I loved you. Behold and see that I loved you so much that before ever I died for you, I would die for you; and now I have died for you and willingly suffered all that I may. And now is all my bitter pain and all my hard travail turned into endless joy and bliss to me and to you. How could you pray anything of me that I like that I would not fully grant? For my liking is your holiness and your endless joy and your bliss with me. . . ."

Our good Lord showed us as much to make us glad and merry.

BL. JULIAN OF NORWICH, 1342?–1423?

YOU WILL FIND THE NEXT READING AT JOHN 21.

believe as well. ³⁶Because all this happened to fulfil the words of scripture:

> *Not one bone of his will be broken;*[c]

³⁷and again, in another place scripture says:

> *They will look to the one whom they have pierced.*[d]

The burial

³⁸After this, Joseph of Arimathaea, who was a disciple of Jesus—though a secret one because he was afraid of the Jews—asked Pilate to let him remove the body of Jesus. Pilate gave permission, so they came and took it away. ³⁹Nicodemus came as well—the same one who had first come to Jesus at night-time—and he brought a mixture of myrrh and aloes, weighing about a hundred pounds. ⁴⁰They took the body of Jesus and bound it in linen cloths with the spices, following the Jewish burial custom. ⁴¹At the place where he had

19c Ex 12:46 and Ps 34:20.   *19d* Zc 12:10.

been crucified there was a garden, and in this garden a new tomb in which no one had yet been buried. ⁴²Since it was the Jewish Day of Preparation and the tomb was nearby, they laid Jesus there.

The empty tomb

20 It was very early on the first day of the week and still dark, when Mary of Magdala came to the tomb. She saw that the stone had been moved away from the tomb ²and came running to Simon Peter and the other disciple, the one whom Jesus loved. 'They have taken the Lord out of the tomb,' she said, 'and we don't know where they have put him.'

³So Peter set out with the other disciple to go to the tomb. ⁴They ran together, but the other disciple, running faster than Peter, reached the tomb first; ⁵he bent down and saw the linen cloths lying on the ground, but did not go in. ⁶Simon Peter, following him, also came up, went into the tomb, saw the linen cloths lying on the ground ⁷and also the cloth that had been over his head; this was not with the linen cloths but rolled up in a place by itself. ⁸Then the other disciple who had reached the tomb first also went in; he saw and he believed. ⁹Till this moment they had still not understood the scripture, that he must rise from the dead. ¹⁰The disciples then went back home.

The appearance to Mary of Magdala

¹¹But Mary was standing outside near the tomb, weeping. Then, as she wept, she stooped to look inside, ¹²and saw two angels in white sitting where the body of Jesus had been, one at the head, the other at the feet. ¹³They said, 'Woman, why are you weeping?' 'They have taken my Lord away,' she replied, 'and I don't know where they have put him.' ¹⁴As she said this she turned round and saw Jesus standing there, though she did not realise that it was Jesus. ¹⁵Jesus said to her, 'Woman, why are you weeping? Who are you looking for?' Supposing him to be the gardener, she said, 'Sir, if you have taken him away, tell me where you have put him, and I will go and remove him.' ¹⁶Jesus said, 'Mary!' She turned round then and said to him in Hebrew, 'Rabbuni!'— which means Master. ¹⁷Jesus said to her, 'Do not cling to me, because I have not yet ascended to the Father. But go to the brothers, and tell them: I am ascending to my Father and your Father, to my God and your God.' ¹⁸So Mary of Magdala told the disciples, 'I have seen the Lord,' and that he had said these things to her.

Appearances to the disciples

¹⁹In the evening of that same day, the first day of the week, the doors were closed in the room where the disciples were, for fear of the Jews. Jesus came and stood among them. He said to them, 'Peace be with you,' ²⁰and, after saying this, he showed them his hands and his side. The disciples were filled with joy at seeing the Lord, ²¹and he said to them again, 'Peace be with you.

'As the Father sent me,
so am I sending you.'

²²After saying this he breathed on them and said:

Receive the Holy Spirit.
²³ If you forgive anyone's sins,
they are forgiven;
if you retain anyone's sins,
they are retained.

²⁴Thomas, called the Twin, who was one of the Twelve, was not with them when Jesus came. ²⁵So the other disciples said to him, 'We have seen the Lord,' but he answered, 'Unless I can see the holes that the nails made in his hands and can put my finger into the holes they made, and unless I can put my hand into his side, I refuse to believe.' ²⁶Eight days later the disciples were in the house again and Thomas was with them. The doors were closed, but Jesus came in and stood among

them. 'Peace be with you,' he said. ²⁷Then he spoke to Thomas, 'Put your finger here; look, here are my hands. Give me your hand; put it into my side. Do not be unbelieving any more but believe.' ²⁸Thomas replied, 'My Lord and my God!' ²⁹Jesus said to him:

You believe because you can see me.
Blessed are those who have not seen and
        yet believe.

³⁰There were many other signs that Jesus worked in the sight of the disciples, but they are not recorded in this book. ³¹These are recorded so that you may believe that Jesus is the Christ, the Son of God, and that believing this you may have life through his name.

Epilogue ᵃ

21 Later on, Jesus revealed himself again to the disciples. It was by the Sea of Tiberias, and it happened like this: ²Simon Peter, Thomas called the Twin, Nathanael from Cana in Galilee, the sons of Zebedee and two more of his disciples were together. ³Simon Peter said, 'I'm going fishing.' They replied, 'We'll come with you.' They went out and got into the boat but caught nothing that night.

⁴When it was already light, there stood Jesus on the shore, though the disciples did not realise that it was Jesus. ⁵Jesus called out, 'Haven't you caught anything, friends?' And when they answered, 'No,' ⁶he said, 'Throw the net out to starboard and you'll find something.' So they threw the net out and could not haul it in because of the quantity of fish. ⁷The disciple whom Jesus loved said to Peter, 'It is the Lord.' At these words, 'It is the Lord,' Simon Peter tied his outer garment round him (for he had nothing on) and jumped into the water. ⁸The other disciples came on in the boat, towing the net with the fish; they were only about a hundred yards from land. ⁹As soon as they came ashore they saw that there was some bread there and a charcoal fire with fish cooking on it. ¹⁰Jesus said, 'Bring

some of the fish you have just caught.' ¹¹Simon Peter went aboard and dragged the net ashore, full of big fish, one hundred and fifty-three of them; and in spite of there being so many the net was not broken. ¹²Jesus said to them, 'Come and have breakfast.' None of the disciples was bold enough to ask, 'Who are you?'. They knew quite well it was the Lord. ¹³Jesus then stepped forward, took the bread and gave it to them, and the same with the fish. ¹⁴This was the third time that Jesus revealed himself to the disciples after rising from the dead.

¹⁵When they had eaten, Jesus said to Simon Peter, 'Simon son of John, do you love me more than these others do?' He answered, 'Yes, Lord, you know I love you.' Jesus said to him, 'Feed my lambs.' ¹⁶A second time he said to him, 'Simon son of John, do you love me?' He replied, 'Yes, Lord, you know I love you.' Jesus said to him, 'Look after my sheep.' ¹⁷Then he said to him a third time, 'Simon son of John, do you love me?' Peter was hurt that he asked him a third time, 'Do you love me?' and said, 'Lord, you know everything; you know I love you.' Jesus said to him, 'Feed my sheep.

¹⁸ In all truth I tell you,
    when you were young
    you put on your own belt
    and walked where you liked;
    but when you grow old
    you will stretch out your hands,
    and somebody else will put a belt round
            you
    and take you where you would rather
            not go.'

¹⁹In these words he indicated the kind of death by which Peter would give glory to God. After this he said, 'Follow me.'

²⁰Peter turned and saw the disciple whom Jesus loved ᵇ following them—the one who

21a Added by the evangelist or one of his disciples.
21b The source of Jn's tradition; but his identity is uncertain.

158 READ JOHN 21:1–19

Jesus said to Simon Peter, "Simon son of John, do you love me more than these others do?" He answered, "Yes, Lord. . . ."—JOHN 21:15

A REASON FOR COMPASSION

After his resurrection, Jesus gave Peter three opportunities to express his love as a way of receiving forgiveness for his threefold denial and commissioned him to lead the Christian community. In the following passage, St. Bernardino reflects on the significance of Peter's repentance for the Lord's choosing him as head of the church:

A repentant sinner knows how to be compassionate to people who are leading evil lives. But when a person who has never committed a serious sin sees someone who has fallen, he makes a big deal of it and gives the sinner no peace.

Don't you know why God did not give responsibility for the church to John, who was pure and sinless, but rather to Peter, who among many sins had even denied Christ? God put the church in Peter's hands because he would be able to have compassion on sinners. Before his passion Jesus said to Peter who would deny him, "Peter, I have prayed to my Father that your faith may never fail" (see Lk 22:32). We can almost hear the Lord also say, "Peter, you who have denied me, see that you never drive a repentant sinner away. Comfort him because my Father will pardon freely him just as he pardoned you who have denied me." So the Lord left the faith to Peter rather than to any of the other disciples in order that he might be merciful to those who would fall into sin. Notice how much good God brought out of Peter's sin.

Therefore, because you also have sinned, you should be compassionate to others when they fall.

St. BERNARDINO OF SIENA, 1380–1444

YOU WILL FIND THE NEXT READING AT ACTS 2.

had leant back close to his chest at the supper and had said to him, 'Lord, who is it that will betray you?' 21 Seeing him, Peter said to Jesus, 'What about him, Lord?' 22 Jesus answered, 'If I want him to stay behind till I come, what does it matter to you? You are to follow me.' 23 The rumour then went out among the brothers that this disciple would not die. Yet Jesus had not said to Peter, 'He will not die,' but, 'If I want him to stay behind till I come.'

24 This disciple is the one who vouches for these things and has written them down, and we know that his testimony is true.

25 There was much else that Jesus did; if it were written down in detail, I do not suppose the world itself would hold all the books that would be written.

ACTS

of the Apostles

Prologue

1 In my earlier work, Theophilus, I dealt with everything Jesus had done and taught from the beginning ² until the day he gave his instructions to the apostles he had chosen through the Holy Spirit, and was taken up to heaven. ³ He had shown himself alive to them after his Passion by many demonstrations: for forty days he had continued to appear to them and tell them about the kingdom of God. ⁴ While at table with them, he had told them not to leave Jerusalem, but to wait there for what the Father had promised. 'It is', he had said, 'what you have heard me speak about: ⁵ John baptised with water but, not many days from now, you are going to be baptised with the Holy Spirit.'

The ascension

⁶ Now having met together, they asked him, 'Lord, has the time come for you to restore the kingdom to Israel?' ⁷ He replied, 'It is not for you to know times or dates that the Father has decided by his own authority, ⁸ but you will receive the power of the Holy Spirit which will come on you, and then you will be my witnesses not only in Jerusalem but throughout Judaea and Samaria, and indeed to earth's remotest end.'

⁹ As he said this he was lifted up while they looked on, and a cloud took him from their sight. ¹⁰ They were still staring into the sky as he went, when suddenly two men in white were standing beside them, ¹¹ and they said, 'Why are you Galileans standing here looking into the sky? This Jesus who has been taken up from you into heaven will come back in the same way as you have seen him go to heaven.'

The group of apostles

¹² So from the Mount of Olives, as it is called, they went back to Jerusalem, a short distance away, no more than a Sabbath walk; ¹³ and when they reached the city they went to the upper room where they were staying; there were Peter and John, James and Andrew, Philip and Thomas, Bartholomew and Matthew, James son of Alphaeus and Simon the Zealot, and Jude son of James. ¹⁴ With one heart all these joined constantly in prayer, together with some women, including Mary the mother of Jesus, and with his brothers.

Judas is replaced

¹⁵ One day Peter stood up to speak to the brothers—there were about a hundred and twenty people in the congregation, ¹⁶ 'Brothers,' he said, 'the passage of scripture had to be fulfilled in which the Holy Spirit, speaking through David, foretells the fate of Judas, who acted as guide to the men who arrested Jesus— ¹⁷ after being one of our number and sharing our ministry. ¹⁸ As you know, he bought a plot of land with the money he was paid for his crime. He fell headlong and burst open, and all his entrails poured out.ᵃ ¹⁹ Everybody in Jerusalem heard about it and the plot came to be called "Bloody Acre", in their language Hakeldama. ²⁰ Now in the Book of Psalms it says:

> *Reduce his encampment to ruin*
> *and leave his tent unoccupied.*

And again:

> *Let someone else take over his office.*

1a cf. Ws 4:19. Ps 69:5; 109:8 are also used.

²¹'Out of the men who have been with us the whole time that the Lord Jesus was living with us, ²²from the time when John was baptising until the day when he was taken up from us, one must be appointed to serve with us as a witness to his resurrection.'

²³Having nominated two candidates, Joseph known as Barsabbas, whose surname was Justus, and Matthias, ²⁴they prayed, 'Lord, you can read everyone's heart; show us therefore which of these two you have chosen ²⁵to take over this ministry and apostolate, which Judas abandoned to go to his proper place.' ²⁶They then drew lots for them, and as the lot fell to Matthias, he was listed as one of the twelve apostles.

Pentecost

2 When Pentecost day came round, they had all met together, ²when suddenly there came from heaven a sound as of a violent wind which filled the entire house in which they were sitting; ³and there appeared to them tongues as of fire; these separated and came to rest on the head of each of them. ⁴They were all filled with the Holy Spirit and began to speak different languages as the Spirit gave them power to express themselves.

⁵Now there were devout men living in Jerusalem from every nation under heaven, ⁶and at this sound they all assembled, and each one was bewildered to hear these men speaking his own language. ⁷They were amazed and astonished. 'Surely,' they said, 'all these men speaking are Galileans? ⁸How does it happen that each of us hears them in his own native language? ⁹Parthians, Medes and Elamites; people from Mesopotamia, Judaea and Cappadocia, Pontus and Asia, ¹⁰Phrygia and Pamphylia, Egypt and the parts of Libya round Cyrene; residents of Rome— ¹¹Jews and proselytes alike—Cretans and Arabs, we hear them preaching in our own language about the marvels of God.' ¹²Everyone was amazed and perplexed; they asked one another what it all meant. ¹³Some, however,

laughed it off. 'They have been drinking too much new wine,' they said.

Peter's address to the crowd

¹⁴Then Peter stood up with the Eleven and addressed them in a loud voice:

'Men of Judaea, and all you who live in Jerusalem, make no mistake about this, but listen carefully to what I say. ¹⁵These men are not drunk, as you imagine; why, it is only the third hour of the day. ¹⁶On the contrary, this is what the prophet was saying:

¹⁷ In the last days—the Lord declares—
I shall pour out my Spirit on all humanity.
Your sons and daughters shall prophesy,
your young people shall see visions,
your old people dream dreams.
¹⁸ *Even on the slaves, men and women,*
shall I pour out my Spirit.
¹⁹ *I will show portents in the sky above*
and signs on the earth below.
²⁰ *The sun will be turned into darkness*
and the moon into blood
before the day of the Lord comes,
that great and terrible Day.
²¹ *And all who call on the name of the Lord*
*will be saved.*ᵃ

²²'Men of Israel, listen to what I am going to say: Jesus the Nazarene was a man commended to you by God by the miracles and portents and signs that God worked through him when he was among you, as you know. ²³This man, who was put into your power by the deliberate intention and foreknowledge of God, you took and had crucified and killed by men outside the Law. ²⁴But God raised him to life, freeing him from the pangs of Hades; for it was impossible for him to be held in its power since, ²⁵as David says of him:

I kept the Lord before my sight always,
for with him at my right hand nothing can
shake me.

2a Jl 3:1–5.

159 READ ACTS 2:14–41.

Hearing this, they were cut to the heart and said to Peter and the other apostles, "What are we to do, brothers?"—ACTS 2:37

THE POWER OF GENTLENESS

Do you see how great gentleness is? More than any vehemence, it pricks our hearts, . . . Neither wrath, nor vehement accusation, nor personal abuse softens the heart as gentleness does. . . . If then you want to reprove any delinquent, approach him with all possible mildness. For example, here Peter gently reminds his hearers of the outrages they have committed without comment. He declares the gift of God and speaks of the grace that bore testimony to the event. . . . So they stood in awe of Peter's gentleness, who spoke to them in the character of an affectionate father and teacher. . . .

If, therefore, you wish to convince someone of wrongdoing, beware of accusing him. Instead, plead for him and he will certainly find himself guilty. That's what Peter did. He did not accuse them harshly. But he tried to plead for them, as far as possible. And we know that he penetrated their souls because they say, "What are we to do, brothers?"

Just as a person on the point of shipwreck, upon seeing the pilot would put all into his hands, and follow his directions in everything; so have these also confessed that they are in extreme peril, and destitute of all hope of salvation. They did not say, "How shall we be saved?" but, "What are we to do?" Peter answered, "You must repent . . . and every one of you must be baptised in the name of Jesus Christ." Then he speaks of the gain they would receive in baptism: "For the forgiveness of your sins, and you will receive the gift of the Holy Spirit." . . .

This is the perfection of teaching, comprising something of fear and something of love. "Save yourselves from this perverse generation." Peter says nothing of the future, all is about the present by which indeed people are chiefly swayed. He shows that the gospel releases from present evils. . . .

ST. JOHN CHRYSOSTOM, 347–407

YOU WILL FIND THE NEXT READING AT ACTS 7.

26 *So my heart rejoiced*
   my tongue delighted;
   my body, too, will rest secure,
27 *for you will not abandon me to Hades*
   or allow your holy one to see corruption.
28 *You have taught me the way of life,*
   you will fill me with joy in your presence.[b]

29 'Brothers, no one can deny that the patriarch David himself is dead and buried: his tomb is still with us. 30 But since he was a prophet, and knew that God *had sworn him* an oath *to make one of his descendants succeed him on the throne,* 31 he spoke with foreknowledge about the resurrection of the Christ: he is the one who was *not abandoned to Hades,* and whose body did not *see corruption.* 32 God raised this man Jesus to life, and of that we are all witnesses. 33 Now raised to the heights by God's right hand, he has received from the Fa-

2b Ps 16:8–11 LXX.

ther the Holy Spirit, who was promised, and what you see and hear is the outpouring of that Spirit. 34 For David himself never went up to heaven, but yet he said:

> The Lord declared to my Lord,
> take your seat at my right hand,
> 35 till I have made your enemies
> your footstool.[c]

36 'For this reason the whole House of Israel can be certain that the Lord and Christ whom God has made is this Jesus whom you crucified.'

The first conversions

37 Hearing this, they were cut to the heart and said to Peter and the other apostles, 'What are we to do, brothers?' 38 'You must repent,' Peter answered, 'and every one of you must be baptised in the name of Jesus Christ for the forgiveness of your sins, and you will receive the gift of the Holy Spirit. 39 The promise that was made is for you and your children, and for all *those who are far away, for all those whom the Lord* our God *is calling to himself.'* [d] 40 He spoke to them for a long time using many other arguments, and he urged them, 'Save yourselves from this perverse generation.' 41 They accepted what he said and were baptised. That very day about three thousand were added to their number.

The early Christian community

42 These remained faithful to the teaching of the apostles, to the brotherhood, to the breaking of bread and to the prayers.

43 And everyone was filled with awe; the apostles worked many signs and miracles.

44 And all who shared the faith owned everything in common; 45 they sold their goods and possessions and distributed the proceeds among themselves according to what each one needed.

46 Each day, with one heart, they regularly went to the Temple but met in their houses for the breaking of bread; they shared their food

gladly and generously; 47 they praised God and were looked up to by everyone. Day by day the Lord added to their community those destined to be saved.

The cure of a lame man[a]

3 Once, when Peter and John were going up to the Temple for the prayers at the ninth hour, 2 it happened that there was a man being carried along. He was a cripple from birth; and they used to put him down every day near the Temple entrance called the Beautiful Gate so that he could beg from the people going in. 3 When this man saw Peter and John on their way into the Temple he begged from them. 4 Peter, and John too, looked straight at him and said, 'Look at us.' 5 He turned to them expectantly, hoping to get something from them, 6 but Peter said, 'I have neither silver nor gold, but I will give you what I have: in the name of Jesus Christ the Nazarene, walk!' 7 Then he took him by the right hand and helped him to stand up. Instantly his feet and ankles became firm, 8 he jumped up, stood, and began to walk, and he went with them into the Temple, walking and jumping and praising God. 9 Everyone could see him walking and praising God, 10 and they recognised him as the man who used to sit begging at the Beautiful Gate of the Temple. They were all astonished and perplexed at what had happened to him.

Peter's address to the people

11 Everyone came running towards them in great excitement, to the Portico of Solomon, as it is called, where the man was still clinging to Peter and John. 12 When Peter saw the people he addressed them, 'Men of Israel, why are you so surprised at this? Why are you staring at us as though we had made this man walk by our own power or holiness? 13 It is *the God of Abraham, Isaac and Jacob, the God of our ancestors, who has glorified his servant* [b] Jesus whom you handed over and then disowned in the

2c Ps 110:1.　　2d Ps 57:19.

3a cf. Ac 14:8–10; Lk 8:51.　　3b Ex 3:6 with Is 52:13.

presence of Pilate after he had given his verdict to release him. ¹⁴ It was you who accused the Holy and Upright One, you who demanded that a murderer should be released to you ¹⁵ while you killed the prince of life. God, however, raised him from the dead, and to that fact we are witnesses; ¹⁶ and it is the name of Jesus which, through faith in him, has brought back the strength of this man whom you see here and who is well known to you. It is faith in him that has restored this man to health, as you can all see.

¹⁷ 'Now I know, brothers, that neither you nor your leaders had any idea what you were really doing; ¹⁸ but this was the way God carried out what he had foretold, when he said through all his prophets that his Christ would suffer. ¹⁹ Now you must repent and turn to God, so that your sins may be wiped out, ²⁰ and so that the Lord may send the time of comfort. Then he will send you the Christ he has predestined, that is Jesus, ²¹ whom heaven must keep till the universal restoration comes which God proclaimed, speaking through his holy prophets. ²² Moses, for example, said, *"From among your brothers the Lord God will raise up for you a prophet like me; you will listen to whatever he tells you. ²³ Anyone who refuses to listen to that prophet shall be cut off from the people."* ^c ²⁴ In fact, all the prophets that have ever spoken, from Samuel onwards, have predicted these days.

²⁵ 'You are the heirs of the prophets, the heirs of the covenant God made with your ancestors when he told Abraham, *"All the nations of the earth will be blessed in your descendants".* ^d ²⁶ It was for you in the first place that God raised up his servant and sent him to bless you as every one of you turns from his wicked ways.'

Peter and John before the Sanhedrin

4 While they were still talking to the people the priests came up to them, accompanied by the captain of the Temple and the Sadducees. ² They were extremely annoyed at their teaching the people the resurrection from the dead by proclaiming the resurrection of Jesus. ³ They arrested them, and, as it was already late, they kept them in prison till the next day. ⁴ But many of those who had listened to their message became believers; the total number of men had now risen to something like five thousand.

⁵ It happened that the next day the rulers, elders and scribes held a meeting in Jerusalem ⁶ with Annas the high priest, Caiaphas, Jonathan, Alexander and all the members of the high-priestly families. ⁷ They made the prisoners stand in the middle and began to interrogate them, 'By what power, and by whose name have you men done this?' ⁸ Then Peter, filled with the Holy Spirit, addressed them, 'Rulers of the people, and elders! ⁹ If you are questioning us today about an act of kindness to a cripple and asking us how he was healed, ¹⁰ you must know, all of you, and the whole people of Israel, that it is by the name of Jesus Christ the Nazarene, whom you crucified, and God raised from the dead, by this name and by no other that this man stands before you cured. ¹¹ This is *the stone which* you, *the builders, rejected* but which *has become the cornerstone.* ^a Only in him is there salvation; ¹² for of all the names in the world given to men, this is the only one by which we can be saved.'

¹³ They were astonished at the fearlessness shown by Peter and John, considering that they were uneducated laymen; and they recognised them as associates of Jesus; ¹⁴ but when they saw the man who had been cured standing by their side, they could find no answer. ¹⁵ So they ordered them to stand outside while the Sanhedrin had a private discussion. ¹⁶ 'What are we going to do with these men?' they asked. 'It is obvious to everybody in Jerusalem that a notable miracle has been worked through them, and we cannot deny it. ¹⁷ But to stop the whole thing spreading any further among the people, let us threaten them against ever speaking to anyone in this name again.'

3c Dt 18:15, 19.   3d Gn 22:18.   4a Ps 118:22.

18 So they called them in and gave them a warning on no account to make statements or to teach in the name of Jesus. 19 But Peter and John retorted, 'You must judge whether in God's eyes it is right to listen to you and not to God. 20 We cannot stop proclaiming what we have seen and heard.' 21 The court repeated the threats and then released them; they could not think of any way to punish them, since all the people were giving glory to God for what had happened. 22 The man who had been miraculously cured was over forty years old.

The apostles' prayer under persecution

23 As soon as they were released they went to the community and told them everything the chief priests and elders had said to them. 24 When they heard it they lifted up their voice to God with one heart. 'Master,' they prayed, 'it is you who made sky and earth and sea, and everything in them; 25 it is you who said through the Holy Spirit and speaking through our ancestor David, your servant:

Why this uproar among the nations,
this impotent muttering of the peoples?
26 *Kings on earth take up position,*
princes plot together
against the Lord and his Anointed.[b]

27 'This is what has come true: in this very city Herod and Pontius Pilate *plotted together* with the gentile *nations* and the *peoples* of Israel, against your holy servant Jesus whom you *anointed,* 28 to bring about the very thing that you in your strength and your wisdom had predetermined should happen. 29 And now, Lord, take note of their threats and help your servants to proclaim your message with all fearlessness, 30 by stretching out your hand to heal and to work miracles and marvels through the name of your holy servant Jesus.' 31 As they prayed, the house where they were assembled rocked. From this time they were all filled with the Holy Spirit and began to proclaim the word of God fearlessly.

The early Christian community

32 The whole group of believers was united, heart and soul; no one claimed private ownership of any possessions, as everything they owned was held in common.

33 The apostles continued to testify to the resurrection of the Lord Jesus with great power, and they were all accorded great respect.

34 None of their members was ever in want, as all those who owned land or houses would sell them, and bring the money from the sale of them, 35 to present it to the apostles; it was then distributed to any who might be in need.

The generosity of Barnabas

36 There was a Levite of Cypriot origin called Joseph whom the apostles surnamed Barnabas (which means 'son of encouragement'). 37 He owned a piece of land and he sold it and brought the money and presented it to the apostles.

The fraud of Ananias and Sapphira

5 There was also a man called Ananias. He and his wife, Sapphira, agreed to sell a property; 2 but with his wife's connivance he kept back part of the price and brought the rest and presented it to the apostles. 3 Peter said, 'Ananias, how can Satan have so possessed you that you should lie to the Holy Spirit and keep back part of the price of the land? 4 While you still owned the land, wasn't it yours to keep, and after you had sold it wasn't the money yours to do with as you liked? What put this scheme into your mind? You have been lying not to men, but to God.' 5 When he heard this Ananias fell down dead. And a great fear came upon everyone present. 6 The younger men got up, wrapped up the body, carried it out and buried it.

7 About three hours later his wife came in, not knowing what had taken place. 8 Peter challenged her, 'Tell me, was this the price you

4b Ps 2:1-2.

[1381]

sold the land for?' 'Yes,' she said, 'that was the price.' ⁹Peter then said, 'Why did you and your husband agree to put the Spirit of the Lord to the test? Listen! At the door are the footsteps of those who have buried your husband; they will carry you out, too.' ¹⁰Instantly she dropped dead at his feet. When the young men came in they found she was dead, and they carried her out and buried her by the side of her husband. ¹¹And a great fear came upon the whole church and on all who heard it.

The general situation

¹²The apostles worked many signs and miracles among the people. One in heart, they all used to meet in the Portico of Solomon. ¹³No one else dared to join them, but the people were loud in their praise ¹⁴and the numbers of men and women who came to believe in the Lord increased steadily. Many signs and wonders were worked among the people at the hands of the apostles ¹⁵so that the sick were even taken out into the streets and laid on beds and sleeping-mats in the hope that at least the shadow of Peter might fall across some of them as he went past. ¹⁶People even came crowding in from the towns round about Jerusalem, bringing with them their sick and those tormented by unclean spirits, and all of them were cured.

The apostles' arrest and miraculous deliverance[a]

¹⁷Then the high priest intervened with all his supporters from the party of the Sadducees. Filled with jealousy, ¹⁸they arrested the apostles and had them put in the public gaol.

¹⁹But at night the angel of the Lord opened the prison gates and said as he led them out, ²⁰'Go and take up position in the Temple, and tell the people all about this new Life.' ²¹They did as they were told; they went into the Temple at dawn and began to preach.

A summons to appear before the Sanhedrin

When the high priest arrived, he and his supporters convened the Sanhedrin—this was the full Senate of Israel—and sent to the gaol for them to be brought. ²²But when the officials arrived at the prison they found they were not inside, so they went back and reported, ²³'We found the gaol securely locked and the warders on duty at the gates, but when we unlocked the door we found no one inside.' ²⁴When the captain of the Temple and the chief priests heard this news they wondered what could be happening. ²⁵Then a man arrived with fresh news. 'Look!' he said, 'the men you imprisoned are in the Temple. They are standing there preaching to the people.' ²⁶The captain went with his men and fetched them—though not by force, for they were afraid that the people might stone them.

²⁷When they had brought them in to face the Sanhedrin, the high priest demanded an explanation. ²⁸'We gave you a strong warning', he said, 'not to preach in this name, and what have you done? You have filled Jerusalem with your teaching, and seem determined to fix the guilt for this man's death on us.' ²⁹In reply Peter and the apostles said, 'Obedience to God comes before obedience to men; ³⁰it was the God of our ancestors who raised up Jesus, whom you executed by hanging on a tree. ³¹By his own right hand God has now raised him up to be leader and Saviour, to give repentance and forgiveness of sins through him to Israel. ³²We are witnesses to this, we and the Holy Spirit whom God has given to those who obey him.' ³³This so infuriated them that they wanted to put them to death.

Gamaliel's intervention

³⁴One member of the Sanhedrin, however, a Pharisee called Gamaliel, who was a teacher of the Law respected by the whole people, stood up and asked to have the men taken outside for a time. ³⁵Then he addressed the Sanhedrin, 'Men of Israel, be careful how you deal with these people. ³⁶Some time ago there arose Theudas. He claimed to be someone important, and collected about four hundred fol-

5a cf. 12:6–11; 16:26–27.

lowers; but when he was killed, all his followers scattered and that was the end of them. 37 And then there was Judas the Galilean, at the time of the census, who attracted crowds of supporters; but he was killed too, and all his followers dispersed. 38 What I suggest, therefore, is that you leave these men alone and let them go. If this enterprise, this movement of theirs, is of human origin it will break up of its own accord; 39 but if it does in fact come from God you will be unable to destroy them. Take care not to find yourselves fighting against God.'

His advice was accepted; 40 and they had the apostles called in, gave orders for them to be flogged, warned them not to speak in the name of Jesus and released them. 41 And so they left the presence of the Sanhedrin, glad to have had the honour of suffering humiliation for the sake of the name.

42 Every day they went on ceaselessly teaching and proclaiming the good news of Christ Jesus, both in the temple and in private houses.

The institution of the Seven

6 About this time, when the number of disciples was increasing, the Hellenists[a] made a complaint against the Hebrews: in the daily distribution their own widows were being overlooked. 2 So the Twelve called a full meeting of the disciples and addressed them, 'It would not be right for us to neglect the word of God so as to give out food; 3 you, brothers, must select from among yourselves seven men of good reputation, filled with the Spirit and with wisdom, to whom we can hand over this duty. 4 We ourselves will continue to devote ourselves to prayer and to the service of the word.' 5 The whole assembly approved of this proposal and elected Stephen, a man full of faith and of the Holy Spirit, together with Philip, Prochorus, Nicanor, Timon, Parmenas, and Nicolaus of Antioch, a convert to Judaism. 6 They presented these to the apostles, and after prayer they laid their hands on them.

7 The word of the Lord continued to spread: the number of disciples in Jerusalem was greatly increased, and a large group of priests made their submission to the faith.

Stephen's arrest

8 Stephen was filled with grace and power and began to work miracles and great signs among the people. 9 Then certain people came forward to debate with Stephen, some from Cyrene and Alexandria who were members of the synagogue called the Synagogue of Freedmen, and others from Cilicia and Asia. 10 They found they could not stand up against him because of his wisdom, and the Spirit that prompted what he said. 11 So they procured some men to say, 'We heard him using blasphemous language against Moses and against God.' 12 Having turned the people against him as well as the elders and scribes, they took Stephen by surprise, and arrested him and brought him before the Sanhedrin. 13 There they put up false witnesses to say, 'This man is always making speeches against this Holy Place and the Law. 14 We have heard him say that Jesus, this Nazarene, is going to destroy this Place and alter the traditions that Moses handed down to us.' 15 The members of the Sanhedrin all looked intently at Stephen, and his face appeared to them like the face of an angel.

Stephen's speech[a]

7 The high priest asked, 'Is this true?' 2 He replied, 'My brothers, my fathers, listen to what I have to say. The God of glory appeared to our ancestor Abraham, while he was in Mesopotamia before settling in Haran, 3 and said to him, "Leave your country, your kindred and your father's house for this country which I shall show you." 4 So he left Chaldaea and settled in Haran; and after his father died God made him leave that place and come to this land where you are living today. 5 God did not give him any property in this land or even a foothold, yet he promised to give it to him and

6a Jews from outside Palestine, or Gk-speakers.

7a A survey using chiefly Gn and Ex.

after him to his descendants, *childless* though he was. ⁶The actual words God used when he spoke to him are that *his descendants would be exiles in a land not their own, where they would be enslaved and oppressed for four hundred years.* ⁷*"But I will bring judgement on the nation that enslaves them,"* God said, *"and after this they will leave, and worship me in this place."* ⁸Then he made the *covenant of circumcision* with him: and so when his son Isaac was born Abraham *circumcised him on the eighth day;* similarly Isaac circumcised Jacob, and Jacob the twelve patriarchs.

⁹'The patriarchs were *jealous of Joseph and sold him into slavery in Egypt.* But *God was with him,* ¹⁰and rescued him from all his miseries by making him so wise that he *won the favour* of Pharaoh king of Egypt, who *made him governor of Egypt* and *put him in charge of his household.* ¹¹*Then a famine set in* that caused much suffering *throughout Egypt and Canaan,* and our ancestors could find nothing to eat. ¹²When Jacob *heard that there were supplies in Egypt,* he sent our ancestors there on a first visit; ¹³and on the second *Joseph made himself known to his brothers,* and Pharaoh came to know his origin. ¹⁴Joseph then sent for his father Jacob and his whole family, a total of *seventy-five people.* ¹⁵Jacob went down into Egypt and after he and our ancestors had died there, ¹⁶their bodies were brought back to Shechem and buried in the tomb that Abraham had bought for money from the sons of Hamor, the father of Shechem.

¹⁷'As the time drew near for God to fulfil the promise he had solemnly made to Abraham, our nation in Egypt *became very powerful and numerous,* ¹⁸there came to power in Egypt a new king who had never heard of Joseph. ¹⁹*He took precautions and wore down* our race, forcing our ancestors to expose their babies rather than *letting them live.* ²⁰It was at this time that Moses was born, *a fine child* before God. He was looked after for *three months* in his father's house, ²¹and after he had been exposed, *Pharaoh's daughter adopted* him and brought him up *like a son.* ²²So Moses was taught all the wisdom of the Egyptians and became a man with power both in his speech and in his actions.

²³'At the age of forty he decided to visit *his kinsmen, the Israelites.* ²⁴When he saw one of them being ill-treated he went to his defence and rescued the man by *killing the Egyptian.* ²⁵He thought his brothers would realise that through him God would liberate them, but they did not. ²⁶The next day, when he came across some of them fighting, he tried to reconcile them, and said, "Friends, you are brothers; why are you hurting each other?" ²⁷But *the man who was attacking his kinsman* pushed him aside, saying, *"And who appointed you to be prince over us and judge? ²⁸Do you intend to kill me as you killed the Egyptian yesterday?"* ²⁹Moses fled when he heard this and *he went to dwell in the land of Midian,* where he fathered two sons.

³⁰'When forty years were fulfilled, *in the desert near Mount* Sinai, *an angel appeared to him in a flame blazing from a bush* that was on fire. ³¹Moses was amazed by what he saw. *As he went nearer to look at it, the voice of the Lord was* heard, ³²"I am the God of your ancestors, the God of Abraham, Isaac and Jacob." Moses trembled and *was afraid to look.* ³³The Lord said to him, *"Take off your sandals,* for the place where you are standing is holy ground. ³⁴*I have seen the misery of my people in Egypt, I have heard them crying for help, and I have come down to rescue them. So come here; I am sending you into Egypt."*

³⁵'It was the same Moses that they had disowned when they said, *"Who appointed you to be our leader and judge?"* whom God sent to be both leader and redeemer through the angel who had appeared to him in the bush. ³⁶It was this man who led them out, after performing *miracles and signs in Egypt* and at the Red Sea and *in the desert for forty years.* ³⁷It was this Moses who told the sons of Israel, *"From among your own brothers God will raise up a prophet like me."* ³⁸When they held the assembly in the desert it was he who was with our ancestors and the angel who had spoken to

him on Mount Sinai; it was he who was entrusted with words of life to hand on to us. ³⁹This is the man that our ancestors refused to listen to; they pushed him aside, *went back to Egypt* in their thoughts, ⁴⁰*and said to Aaron, "Make us a god to go at our head; for that Moses, the man who brought us here from Egypt, we do not know what has become of him."* ⁴¹It was then that *they made the statue of a calf and offered sacrifice* to the idol. They were perfectly happy with something they had made for themselves. ⁴²God turned away from them and abandoned them to the worship of the army of heaven, as scripture says in the book of the prophets:

Did you bring me sacrifices and oblations those forty years in the desert, House of Israel?
⁴³*No, you carried the tent of Moloch on your shoulders and the star of the god Rephan, the idols you made for yourselves to adore, and so now I am about to drive you into captivity beyond Babylon.ᵇ*

⁴⁴'While they were in the desert our ancestors possessed the Tent of Testimony that had been constructed according to the instructions God gave Moses, telling him to *work to the design* he had been shown. ⁴⁵It was handed down from one ancestor of ours to another until Joshua brought it into the country that had belonged to the nations which were driven out by God before us. Here it stayed until the time of David. ⁴⁶He won God's favour and asked permission *to find a dwelling for* the House of *Jacob,* ⁴⁷though it was *Solomon* who actually *built a house for God.* ⁴⁸Even so the Most High does not live in a house that human hands have built: for as the prophet says:

⁴⁹*With heaven my throne and earth my footstool, what house could you build me, says the Lord,*
what place for me to rest,
⁵⁰*when all these things were made by me?ᶜ*

⁵¹'You stubborn people, with uncircumcised hearts and ears. You are always resisting the Holy Spirit, just as your ancestors used to do. ⁵²Can you name a single prophet your ancestors never persecuted? They killed those who foretold the coming of the Upright One, and now you have become his betrayers, his murderers. ⁵³In spite of being given the Law through angels, you have not kept it.'

⁵⁴They were infuriated when they heard this, and ground their teeth at him.

The stoning of Stephen; Saul as persecutor

⁵⁵But Stephen, filled with the Holy Spirit, gazed into heaven and saw the glory of God, and Jesus standing at God's right hand. ⁵⁶'Look! I can see heaven thrown open,' he said, 'and the Son of man standing at the right hand of God.' ⁵⁷All the members of the council shouted out and stopped their ears with their hands; then they made a concerted rush at him, ⁵⁸thrust him out of the city and stoned him. The witnesses put down their clothes at the feet of a young man called Saul. ⁵⁹As they were stoning him, Stephen said in invocation, 'Lord Jesus, receive my spirit.' ⁶⁰Then he knelt down and said aloud, 'Lord, do not hold this sin against them.' And with these words he fell asleep.

8 Saul approved of the killing. That day a bitter persecution started against the church in Jerusalem, and everyone except the apostles scattered to the country districts of Judaea and Samaria.

²There were some devout people, however, who buried Stephen and made great mourning for him.

³Saul then began doing great harm to the church; he went from house to house arresting both men and women and sending them to prison.

7b Am 5:25–27. 7c Is 66:1–2.

160 READ ACTS 7:51–60.

But Stephen, filled with the Holy Spirit, gazed into heaven and saw the glory of God.

—ACTS 6:55

A MARTYR'S VICTORY

In this sermon for the feast of St. Stephen, which occurs the day after Christmas, St. Fulgentius compares Stephen's death to Christ's birth:

Yesterday we celebrated the birth in time of our Eternal King; today we celebrate the victory through suffering of one of his soldiers. Yesterday our King, clothed in a robe of flesh, was pleased to come forth from his royal palace of the Virgin's womb to visit the world; today his soldier, laying aside the tabernacle of the body, enters in triumph into the heavenly palaces. The One, preserving unchanged that glory of the Godhead which he had before the world existed, girded himself with the form of a servant and entered the arena of this world to fight sin; the other takes off the garment of this corruptible body and enters into the heavenly mansions where he will reign forever. The One comes down veiled in flesh; the other goes up, clothed in a robe of glory, red with blood. . . .

My brothers, we must consider with what arms Stephen was able to remain more than a conqueror and worthily to attain to so blessed a triumph. In that struggle which brought him to the crown of which his name is a prophecy,* Stephen had for armor the love of God and man, and by it he remained victorious on all sides. The love of God strengthened him against the cruelty of those who stoned him. And the love of his neighbor made him pray for them. Through love he rebuked the wandering so that they might be corrected. Through love he prayed for them that stoned him, that they might not be punished. By the might of his love he overcame Saul his cruel persecutor. And he earned as a comrade in heaven the very man who had done him to death on earth.

ST. FULGENTIUS OF RUSPE, 468?–533

---

* The name *Stephen* comes from a Greek root that means *crown*.

YOU WILL FIND THE NEXT READING AT ACTS 10.

Philip in Samaria

4 Once they had scattered, they went from place to place preaching the good news. 5 And Philip went to a Samaritan town and proclaimed the Christ to them. 6 The people unanimously welcomed the message Philip preached, because they had heard of the miracles he worked and because they saw them for themselves. 7 For unclean spirits came shriek-ing out of many who were possessed, and several paralytics and cripples were cured. 8 As a result there was great rejoicing in that town.

Simon the magician

9 Now a man called Simon had for some time been practising magic arts in the town and astounded the Samaritan people. He had given it out that he was someone momentous, 10 and everyone believed in him; eminent citizens

and ordinary people alike had declared, 'He is the divine power that is called Great.' 11 He had this following because for a considerable period they had been astounded by his wizardry. 12 But when they came to accept Philip's preaching of the good news about the kingdom of God and the name of Jesus Christ, they were baptised, both men and women, 13 and even Simon himself became a believer. After his baptism Simon went round constantly with Philip and was astonished when he saw the wonders and great miracles that took place.

14 When the apostles in Jerusalem heard that Samaria had accepted the word of God, they sent Peter and John to them, 15 and they went down there and prayed for them to receive the Holy Spirit, 16 for as yet he had not come down on any of them: they had only been baptised in the name of the Lord Jesus. 17 Then they laid hands on them, and they received the Holy Spirit.

18 When Simon saw that the Spirit was given through the laying on of the apostles' hands, he offered them money, 19 with the words, 'Give me the same power so that anyone I lay my hands on will receive the Holy Spirit.' 20 Peter answered, 'May your silver be lost for ever, and you with it, for thinking that money could buy what God has given for nothing! 21 You have no share, no part, in this: God can see how your heart is warped. 22 Repent of this wickedness of yours, and pray to the Lord that this scheme of yours may be forgiven; 23 it is plain to me that you are held in the bitterness of gall and the chains of sin.' 24 Simon replied, 'Pray to the Lord for me yourselves so that none of the things you have spoken about may happen to me.'

25 Having given their testimony and proclaimed the word of the Lord, they went back to Jerusalem, preaching the good news to a number of Samaritan villages.

Philip baptises a eunuch

26 The angel of the Lord spoke to Philip saying, 'Set out at noon and go along the road that leads from Jerusalem down to Gaza, the desert road.' 27 So he set off on his journey. Now an Ethiopian had been on pilgrimage to Jerusalem; he was a eunuch and an officer at the court of the kandake, or queen, of Ethiopia; he was her chief treasurer. 28 He was now on his way home; and as he sat in his chariot he was reading the prophet Isaiah. 29 The Spirit said to Philip, 'Go up and join that chariot.' 30 When Philip ran up, he heard him reading Isaiah the prophet and asked, 'Do you understand what you are reading?' 31 He replied, 'How could I, unless I have someone to guide me?' So he urged Philip to get in and sit by his side. 32 Now the passage of scripture he was reading was this:

> Like a lamb led to the slaughter-house,
> like a sheep dumb in front of its shearers,
> he never opens his mouth.
> 33 In his humiliation fair judgement was denied
> him.
> Who will ever talk about his descendants,
> since his life on earth has been cut short? [a]

34 The eunuch addressed Philip and said, 'Tell me, is the prophet referring to himself or someone else?' 35 Starting, therefore, with this text of scripture Philip proceeded to explain the good news of Jesus to him.

36 Further along the road they came to some water, and the eunuch said, 'Look, here is some water; is there anything to prevent my being baptised?' [37] [b] 38 He ordered the chariot to stop, then Philip and the eunuch both went down into the water and he baptised him. 39 But after they had come up out of the water again Philip was taken away by the Spirit of the Lord, and the eunuch never saw him again but went on his way rejoicing. 40 Philip appeared in Azotus and continued his journey, proclaiming the good news in every town as far as Caesarea.

8a Is 53:7–8.

8b v. 37, omitted here, is a very ancient gloss: 'And Philip said, "If you believe with all your heart, you may." And he replied, "I believe that Jesus is the Son of God."'

The conversion of Saul[a]

9 Meanwhile Saul was still breathing threats to slaughter the Lord's disciples. He went to the high priest 2 and asked for letters addressed to the synagogues in Damascus, that would authorise him to arrest and take to Jerusalem any followers of the Way, men or women, that he might find.

3 It happened that while he was travelling to Damascus and approaching the city, suddenly a light from heaven shone all round him. 4 He fell to the ground, and then he heard a voice saying, 'Saul, Saul, why are you persecuting me?' 5 'Who are you, Lord?' he asked, and the answer came, 'I am Jesus, whom you are persecuting. 6 Get up and go into the city, and you will be told what you are to do.' 7 The men travelling with Saul stood there speechless, for though they heard the voice they could see no one. 8 Saul got up from the ground, but when he opened his eyes he could see nothing at all, and they had to lead him into Damascus by the hand. 9 For three days he was without his sight and took neither food nor drink.

10 There was a disciple in Damascus called Ananias, and he had a vision in which the Lord said to him, 'Ananias!' When he replied, 'Here I am, Lord,' 11 the Lord said, 'Get up and go to Straight Street and ask at the house of Judas for someone called Saul, who comes from Tarsus. At this moment he is praying, 12 and has seen a man called Ananias coming in and laying hands on him to give him back his sight.'

13 But in response, Ananias said, 'Lord, I have heard from many people about this man and all the harm he has been doing to your holy people in Jerusalem. 14 He has come here with a warrant from the chief priests to arrest everybody who invokes your name.' 15 The Lord replied, 'Go, for this man is my chosen instrument to bring my name before gentiles and kings and before the people of Israel; 16 I myself will show him how much he must suffer for my name.' 17 Then Ananias went. He entered the house, and laid his hands on Saul and said, 'Brother Saul, I have been sent by the Lord Jesus, who appeared to you on your way here, so that you may recover your sight and be filled with the Holy Spirit.' 18 It was as though scales fell away from his eyes and immediately he was able to see again. So he got up and was baptised, 19 and after taking some food he regained his strength.

Saul's preaching at Damascus

After he had spent only a few days with the disciples in Damascus, 20 he began preaching in the synagogues, 'Jesus is the Son of God.' 21 All his hearers were amazed, and said, 'Surely, this is the man who did such damage in Jerusalem to the people who invoke this name, and who came here for the sole purpose of arresting them to have them tried by the chief priests?' 22 Saul's power increased steadily, and he was able to throw the Jewish colony at Damascus into complete confusion by the way he demonstrated that Jesus was the Christ.

23 Some time passed, and the Jews worked out a plot to kill him, 24 but news of it reached Saul. They were keeping watch at the gates day and night in order to kill him, 25 but the disciples took him by night and let him down from the wall, lowering him in a basket.

Saul's visit to Jerusalem[b]

26 When he got to Jerusalem he tried to join the disciples, but they were all afraid of him: they could not believe he was really a disciple. 27 Barnabas, however, took charge of him, introduced him to the apostles, and explained how the Lord had appeared to him and spoken to him on his journey, and how he had preached fearlessly at Damascus in the name of Jesus. 28 Saul now started to go round with them in Jerusalem, preaching fearlessly in the name of the Lord. 29 But after he had spoken to the Hellenists and argued with them, they became determined to kill him. 30 When the brothers got to know of this, they took

9a = 22; 26; cf. 2 M 3.   9b ‖ Ga 1:18–19?

him to Caesarea and sent him off from there to Tarsus.

A lull

³¹ The churches throughout Judaea, Galilee and Samaria were now left in peace, building themselves up and living in the fear of the Lord; encouraged by the Holy Spirit, they continued to grow.

Peter cures a paralytic at Lydda

³² It happened that Peter visited one place after another and eventually came to God's holy people living down in Lydda. ³³ There he found a man called Aeneas, a paralytic who had been bedridden for eight years. ³⁴ Peter said to him, 'Aeneas, Jesus Christ cures you: get up and make your bed.' Aeneas got up immediately; ³⁵ everybody who lived in Lydda and Sharon saw him, and they were converted to the Lord.

Peter raises a woman to life at Jaffa

³⁶ At Jaffa there was a disciple called Tabitha, or in Greek, Dorcas, who never tired of doing good or giving to those in need. ³⁷ But it happened that at this time she became ill and died, and they washed her and laid her out in an upper room. ³⁸ Lydda is not far from Jaffa, so when the disciples heard that Peter was there, they sent two men to urge him, 'Come to us without delay.'

³⁹ Peter went back with them immediately, and on his arrival they took him to the upper room, where all the widows stood round him in tears, showing him tunics and other clothes Dorcas had made when she was with them. ⁴⁰ Peter sent everyone out of the room and knelt down and prayed. Then he turned to the dead woman and said, 'Tabitha, stand up.' She opened her eyes, looked at Peter and sat up. ⁴¹ Peter helped her to her feet, then he called in the members of the congregation and widows and showed them she was alive. ⁴² The whole of Jaffa heard about it and many believed in the Lord.

⁴³ Peter stayed on some time in Jaffa, lodging with a leather-tanner called Simon.

Peter visits a Roman centurion

10 One of the centurions of the Italica cohort stationed in Caesarea was called Cornelius. ² He and the whole of his household were devout and God-fearing, and he gave generously to Jewish causes and prayed constantly to God.

³ One day at about the ninth hour he had a vision in which he distinctly saw the angel of God come into his house and call out to him, 'Cornelius!' ⁴ He stared at the vision in terror and exclaimed, 'What is it, Lord?' The angel answered, 'Your prayers and charitable gifts have been accepted by God. ⁵ Now you must send some men to Jaffa and fetch a man called Simon, known as Peter, ⁶ who is lodging with Simon the tanner whose house is by the sea.' ⁷ When the angel who said this had gone, Cornelius called two of the slaves and a devout soldier of his staff, ⁸ told them all that had happened, and sent them off to Jaffa.

⁹ Next day, while they were still on their journey and had only a short distance to go before reaching the town, Peter went to the housetop at about the sixth hour to say his prayers. ¹⁰ He felt hungry and was looking forward to his meal, but before it was ready he fell into a trance ¹¹ and saw heaven thrown open and something like a big sheet being let down to earth by its four corners; ¹² it contained every kind of animal, reptile and bird. ¹³ A voice then said to him, 'Now, Peter, kill and eat!' ¹⁴ But Peter answered, 'Certainly not, Lord; I have never yet eaten anything profane or unclean.' ¹⁵ Again, a second time, the voice spoke to him, 'What God has made clean, you have no right to call profane.' ¹⁶ This was repeated three times, and then suddenly the container was drawn up to heaven again.

¹⁷ Peter was still at a loss over the meaning of the vision he had seen, when the men sent by Cornelius arrived. They had asked where Simon's house was and they were now standing at the door, ¹⁸ calling out to know if the

161 READ ACTS 10.

[Cornelius] . . . gave generously to Jewish causes and prayed constantly to God.—ACTS 10:2

STREAMS OF MERCY

In the following sermon excerpt, St. John Chrysostom sees almsgiving to include not only giving material aid, but also the supreme spiritual service of bringing others to Christ:

See how great is the virtue of alms. Here it delivered from eternal death and opened the gates of heaven. Such are the pains taken for the bringing of Cornelius to the faith, that both an angel is sent, and the Spirit works, and the chief of the Apostles is fetched to him, and such a vision is shown, and, in short, nothing is left undone. Great is the virtue of this practice, when the alms is poured forth from pure stores. It is like a limpid and pure stream in a garden, sweet to the sight, sweet to the touch, both light and cool, when given in the noon-day heat. Such is alms.

Beside this fountain flourish, not poplars and pines, nor cypresses, but other lofty plants far better than these: friendship with God, respect from people, worship of God, good-will from all, blotting out of sins, great boldness, contempt of wealth. This is the fountain that nourishes the plant of love. For nothing nourishes love more than acts of mercy. Almsgiving makes love's branches lift themselves on high.

The fountain of mercy is better than the river in Paradise (see Gn 2:10), not dividing into four streams but reaching to heaven itself. It gives birth to the stream that wells up to eternal life (see Jn 4:14). It extinguishes death as it might snuff out a spark. Such are the blessings it causes wherever it flows. This fountain quenches the river of fire as though it were a dying ember and smothers the "worm that will never die" as nothing else can (see Mk 9:48).

A fountain does not give out streams for a while and then run dry, or it would cease to be a fountain. It always gushes. So let our fountain flow copiously with the streams of mercy. If you want God to rain his mercy on you, you must let mercy flow from you as from a fountain.

ST. JOHN CHRYSOSTOM, 347–407

YOU WILL FIND THE NEXT READING AT ACTS 17.

Simon known as Peter was lodging there. [19] While Peter's mind was still on the vision, the Spirit told him, 'Look! Some men have come to see you. [20] Hurry down, and do not hesitate to return with them; it was I who told them to come.' [21] Peter went down and said to them, 'I am the man you are looking for; why have you come?' [22] They said, 'The centurion Cornelius, who is an upright and God-fearing man, highly regarded by the entire Jewish people, was told by God through a holy angel to send for you and bring you to his house and to listen to what you have to say.' [23] So Peter asked them in and gave them lodging.

Next day, he was ready to go off with them, accompanied by some of the brothers from Jaffa. [24] They reached Caesarea the following day, and Cornelius was waiting for them. He had asked his relations and close friends to be there, 25 and as Peter reached the house Cornelius went out to meet him, fell at his feet and did him reverence. 26 But Peter helped him up. 'Stand up,' he said, 'after all, I am only a man!' 27 Talking together they went in to meet all the people assembled there, 28 and Peter said to them, 'You know it is forbidden for Jews to mix with people of another race and visit them; but God has made it clear to me that I must not call anyone profane or unclean. 29 That is why I made no objection to coming when I was sent for; but I should like to know exactly why you sent for me.' 30 Cornelius replied, 'At this time three days ago I was in my house saying the prayers for the ninth hour, when I suddenly saw a man in front of me in shining robes. 31 He said, "Cornelius, your prayer has been heard and your charitable gifts have not been forgotten by God; 32 so now you must send to Jaffa and fetch Simon known as Peter who is lodging in the house of Simon the tanner, by the sea." 33 So I sent for you at once, and you have been kind enough to come. Here we all are, assembled in front of you to hear all the instructions God has given you.'

Peter's address in the house of Cornelius

34 Then Peter addressed them, 'I now really understand', he said, 'that God has no favourites, 35 but that anybody of any nationality who fears him and does what is right is acceptable to him.

36 'God sent his word to the people of Israel, and it was to them that *the good news of peace was brought*[a] by Jesus Christ—he is the Lord of all. 37 You know what happened all over Judaea, how Jesus of Nazareth began in Galilee, after John had been preaching baptism. 38 *God had anointed him with the Holy Spirit* and with power, and because God was with him, Jesus went about doing good and curing all who had fallen into the power of the devil. 39 Now we are witnesses to everything he did throughout the countryside of Judaea and in Jerusalem itself: and they killed him by hanging him on a

tree, 40 yet on the third day God raised him to life and allowed him to be seen, 41 not by the whole people but only by certain witnesses that God had chosen beforehand. Now we are those witnesses—we have eaten and drunk with him after his resurrection from the dead— 42 and he has ordered us to proclaim this to his people and to bear witness that God has appointed him to judge everyone, alive or dead. 43 It is to him that all the prophets bear this witness: that all who believe in Jesus will have their sins forgiven through his name.'

Baptism of the first gentiles

44 While Peter was still speaking the Holy Spirit came down[b] on all the listeners. 45 Jewish believers who had accompanied Peter were all astonished that the gift of the Holy Spirit should be poured out on gentiles too, 46 since they could hear them speaking strange languages and proclaiming the greatness of God. Peter himself then said, 47 'Could anyone refuse the water of baptism to these people, now they have received the Holy Spirit just as we have?' 48 He then gave orders for them to be baptised in the name of Jesus Christ. Afterwards they begged him to stay on for some days.

Jerusalem: Peter justifies his conduct

11 The apostles and the brothers in Judaea heard that gentiles too had accepted the word of God, 2 and when Peter came up to Jerusalem the circumcised believers protested to him 3 and said, 'So you have been visiting the uncircumcised and eating with them!' 4 Peter in reply gave them the details point by point, 5 'One day, when I was in the town of Jaffa,' he began, 'I fell into a trance as I was praying and had a vision of something like a big sheet being let down from heaven by its four corners. This sheet came right down beside me. 6 I looked carefully into it and saw four-footed animals of the earth, wild beasts, reptiles, and birds of heaven. 7 Then I heard a

10a Is 52:7 and in v. 38 Is 61:1. 10b cf. 2:3–4.

voice that said to me, "Now, Peter, kill and eat!" 8 But I answered, "Certainly not, Lord; nothing profane or unclean has ever crossed my lips." 9 And a second time the voice spoke from heaven, "What God has made clean, you have no right to call profane." 10 This was repeated three times, before the whole of it was drawn up to heaven again.

11 'Just at that moment, three men stopped outside the house where we were staying; they had been sent from Caesarea to fetch me, 12 and the Spirit told me to have no hesitation about going back with them. The six brothers here came with me as well, and we entered the man's house. 13 He told us he had seen an angel standing in his house who said, "Send to Jaffa and fetch Simon known as Peter; 14 he has a message for you that will save you and your entire household."

15 'I had scarcely begun to speak when the Holy Spirit came down on them in the same way as it came on us at the beginning, 16 and I remembered that the Lord had said, "John baptised with water, but you will be baptised with the Holy Spirit." 17 I realised then that God was giving them the identical gift he gave to us when we believed in the Lord Jesus Christ; and who was I to stand in God's way?'

18 This account satisfied them, and they gave glory to God, saying, 'God has clearly granted to the gentiles too the repentance that leads to life.'

Foundation of the church of Antioch

19 Those who had scattered because of the persecution that arose over Stephen travelled as far as Phoenicia and Cyprus and Antioch, but they proclaimed the message only to Jews. 20 Some of them, however, who came from Cyprus and Cyrene, went to Antioch where they started preaching also to the Greeks, proclaiming the good news of the Lord Jesus to them. 21 The Lord helped them, and a great number believed and were converted to the Lord.

22 The news of them came to the ears of the church in Jerusalem and they sent Barnabas out to Antioch. 23 There he was glad to see for himself that God had given grace, and he urged them all to remain faithful to the Lord with heartfelt devotion; 24 for he was a good man, filled with the Holy Spirit and with faith. And a large number of people were won over to the Lord.

25 Barnabas then left for Tarsus to look for Saul, 26 and when he found him he brought him to Antioch. And it happened that they stayed together in that church a whole year, instructing a large number of people. It was at Antioch that the disciples were first called 'Christians'.

Barnabas and Saul sent as deputies to Jerusalem

27 While they were there some prophets came down to Antioch from Jerusalem, 28 and one of them whose name was Agabus, seized by the Spirit, stood up and predicted that a severe and universal famine was going to happen. This in fact happened while Claudius was emperor. 29 The disciples decided to send relief, each to contribute what he could afford, to the brothers living in Judaea. 30 They did this and delivered their contributions to the elders through the agency of Barnabas and Saul.

Peter's arrest and miraculous deliverance

12 It was about this time that King Herod started persecuting certain members of the church. 2 He had James the brother of John beheaded, 3 and when he saw that this pleased the Jews he went on to arrest Peter as well. 4 As it was during the days of Unleavened Bread that he had arrested him, he put him in prison, assigning four sections of four soldiers each to guard him, meaning to try him in public after the Passover. 5 All the time Peter was under guard the church prayed to God for him unremittingly.

6 On the night before Herod was to try him, Peter was sleeping between two soldiers, fastened with two chains, while guards kept watch at the main entrance to the prison.

7 Then suddenly an angel of the Lord stood there, and the cell was filled with light. He tapped Peter on the side and woke him. 'Get up!' he said, 'Hurry!'—and the chains fell from his hands. 8 The angel then said, 'Put on your belt and sandals.' After he had done this, the angel next said, 'Wrap your cloak round you and follow me.' 9 He followed him out, but had no idea that what the angel did was all happening in reality; he thought he was seeing a vision. 10 They passed through the first guard post and then the second and reached the iron gate leading to the city. This opened of its own accord; they went through it and had walked the whole length of one street when suddenly the angel left him. 11 It was only then that Peter came to himself. And he said, 'Now I know it is all true. The Lord really did send his angel and save me from Herod and from all that the Jewish people were expecting.'

12 As soon as he realised this he went straight to the house of Mary the mother of John Mark, where a number of people had assembled and were praying. 13 He knocked at the outside door and a servant called Rhoda came to answer it. 14 She recognised Peter's voice and was so overcome with joy that, instead of opening the door, she ran inside with the news that Peter was standing at the main entrance. 15 They said to her, 'You are out of your mind,' but she insisted that it was true. Then they said, 'It must be his angel!' 16 Peter, meanwhile, was still knocking. When they opened the door, they were amazed to see that it really was Peter himself. 17 He raised his hand for silence and described to them how the Lord had led him out of prison. He added, 'Tell James and the brothers.' Then he left and went elsewhere.

18 When daylight came there was a great commotion among the soldiers, who could not imagine what had become of Peter. 19 Herod put out an unsuccessful search for him; he had the guards questioned, and before leaving Judaea to take up residence in Caesarea he gave orders for their execution.

The death of the persecutor[a]

20 Now Herod was on bad terms with the Tyrians and Sidonians. Yet they sent a joint deputation which managed to enlist the support of Blastus, the king's chamberlain, and through him negotiated a treaty, since their country depended for its food supply on the king's territory. 21 A day was fixed, and Herod, wearing his robes of state and seated on a throne, began to make a speech to them. 22 The people acclaimed him with, 'It is a god speaking, not a man!' 23 and at that moment the angel of the Lord struck him down, because he had not given the glory to God. He was eaten away by worms and died.

Barnabas and Saul return to Antioch

24 The word of God continued to spread and to gain followers.

25 Barnabas and Saul completed their task at Jerusalem and came back, bringing John Mark with them.

The mission sent out

13 In the church at Antioch the following were prophets and teachers: Barnabas, Simeon called Niger, and Lucius of Cyrene, Manaen, who had been brought up with Herod the tetrarch, and Saul. 2 One day while they were offering worship to the Lord and keeping a fast, the Holy Spirit said, 'I want Barnabas and Saul set apart for the work to which I have called them.' 3 So it was that after fasting and prayer they laid their hands on them and sent them off.

Cyprus: the magician Elymas

4 So these two, sent on their mission by the Holy Spirit, went down to Seleucia and from there set sail for Cyprus. 5 They landed at Salamis and proclaimed the word of God in the synagogues of the Jews; John acted as their assistant.

6 They travelled the whole length of the is-

12a cf. 2 M 9:5–28.

[1393]

land, and at Paphos they came in contact with a Jewish magician and false prophet called Bar-Jesus. [7] He was one of the attendants of the proconsul Sergius Paulus, who was an extremely intelligent man. The proconsul summoned Barnabas and Saul and asked to hear the word of God, [8] but Elymas the magician (this is what his name means in Greek) tried to stop them so as to prevent the proconsul's conversion to the faith. [9] Then Saul, whose other name is Paul, filled with the Holy Spirit, looked at him intently [10] and said, 'You utter fraud, you impostor, you son of the devil, you enemy of all uprightness, will you not stop twisting the straightforward ways of the Lord? [11] Now watch how the hand of the Lord will strike you: you will be blind, and for a time you will not see the sun.' That instant, everything went misty and dark for him, and he groped about to find someone to lead him by the hand. [12] The proconsul, who had watched everything, became a believer, being much struck by what he had learnt about the Lord.

They arrive at Antioch in Pisidia

[13] Paul and his companions went by sea from Paphos to Perga in Pamphylia where John left them to go back to Jerusalem. [14] The others carried on from Perga till they reached Antioch in Pisidia. Here they went to synagogue on the Sabbath and took their seats. [15] After the passages from the Law and the Prophets had been read, the presidents of the synagogue sent them a message, 'Brothers, if you would like to address some words of encouragement to the congregation, please do so.' [16] Paul stood up, raised his hand for silence and began to speak:

Paul's preaching before the Jews[a]

'Men of Israel, and fearers of God, listen! [17] The God of our nation Israel chose our ancestors and made our people great when they were living in Egypt, a land not their own; then by divine power he led them out [18] and for about forty years *took care of* them in the

desert. [19] *When he had destroyed seven nations in Canaan, he put them in possession* of their land [20] for about four hundred and fifty years. After this he gave them judges, down to the prophet Samuel. [21] Then they demanded a king, and God gave them Saul son of Kish, a man of the tribe of Benjamin. After forty years, [22] he deposed him and raised up David to be king, whom he attested in these words, *"I have found David* son of Jesse, *a man after my own heart, who will perform my entire will."* [23] To keep his promise, God has raised up for Israel one of David's descendants, Jesus, as Saviour, [24] whose coming was heralded by John when he proclaimed a baptism of repentance for the whole people of Israel. [25] Before John ended his course he said, "I am not the one you imagine me to be; there is someone coming after me whose sandal I am not fit to undo."

[26] 'My brothers, sons of Abraham's race, and all you godfearers, this message of salvation is meant for you. [27] What the people of Jerusalem and their rulers did, though they did not realise it, was in fact to fulfil the prophecies read on every Sabbath. [28] Though they found nothing to justify his execution, they condemned him and asked Pilate to have him put to death. [29] When they had carried out everything that scripture foretells about him they took him down from the tree and buried him in a tomb. [30] But God raised him from the dead, [31] and for many days he appeared to those who had accompanied him from Galilee to Jerusalem: and it is these same companions of his who are now his witnesses before our people.

[32] 'We have come here to tell you the good news that the promise made to our ancestors has come about. [33] God has fulfilled it to their children by raising Jesus from the dead. As scripture says in the psalms: *You are my son: today I have fathered you.* [34] The fact that God raised him from the dead, never to return to corruption, is no more than what he had de-

13a Paul uses Dt 1:31; 7:1; Ps 89:14; 2:7; Is 55:3; Ps 16:9; Hab 1:5.

clared: *To you I shall give the holy things promised to David which can be relied upon.* 35 This is
also why it says in another text: *You will not
allow your Holy One to see corruption.* 36 Now
when David in his own time had served God's
purposes he died; he was buried with his ancestors and has certainly *seen corruption.* 37 The
one whom God has raised up, however, has
not *seen corruption.*

38 'My brothers, I want you to realise that it
is through him that forgiveness of sins is being
proclaimed to you. Through him justification
from all sins from which the Law of Moses
was unable to justify 39 is being offered to
every believer.

40 'So be careful—or what the prophets say
will happen to you.

41 *Cast your eyes around you, mockers;
be amazed, and perish!
For I am doing something in your own days
that you would never believe if you were told
of it.'*

42 As they left they were urged to continue
this preaching the following Sabbath. 43 When
the meeting broke up many Jews and devout
converts followed Paul and Barnabas, and in
their talks with them Paul and Barnabas
urged them to remain faithful to the grace
God had given them.

Paul and Barnabas preach to the gentiles

44 The next Sabbath almost the whole town assembled to hear the word of God. 45 When
they saw the crowds, the Jews, filled with jealousy, used blasphemies to contradict everything Paul said. 46 Then Paul and Barnabas
spoke out fearlessly. 'We had to proclaim the
word of God to you first, but since you have
rejected it, since you do not think yourselves
worthy of eternal life, here and now we turn to
the gentiles. 47 For this is what the Lord commanded us to do when he said:

*I have made you a light to the nations,
so that my salvation may reach the remotest
parts of the earth.'* [b]

48 It made the gentiles very happy to hear
this and they gave thanks to the Lord for his
message; all who were destined for eternal life
became believers. 49 Thus the word of the
Lord spread through the whole countryside.

50 But the Jews worked on some of the devout women of the upper classes and the leading men of the city; they stirred up a persecution against Paul and Barnabas and expelled
them from their territory. 51 So they shook the
dust from their feet in protest against them
and went off to Iconium; but the converts
were filled with joy and the Holy Spirit.

Iconium evangelised

14 It happened that at Iconium they went
to the Jewish synagogue, in the same
way, and they spoke so effectively that a great
many Jews and Greeks became believers. 2 (However, the Jews who refused to believe
stirred up the gentiles against the brothers and
set them in opposition.) 3 Accordingly Paul and Barnabas stayed on
for some time, preaching fearlessly in the
Lord; and he attested all they said about his
gift of grace, allowing signs and wonders to be
performed by them. 4 The people in the city were divided; some
supported the Jews, others the apostles, 5 but
eventually with the connivance of the authorities a move was made by gentiles as well as
Jews to make attacks on them and to stone
them. 6 When they came to hear of this, they
went off for safety to Lycaonia where, in the
towns of Lystra and Derbe and in the surrounding country, 7 they preached the good
news.

Healing of a cripple

8 There was a man sitting there who had never
walked in his life, because his feet were crippled from birth; 9 he was listening to Paul
preaching, and Paul looked at him intently
and saw that he had the faith to be cured. 10 Paul said in a loud voice, 'Get to your feet—

13b Is 49:6; cf. 18:6; 28:25.

stand up,' and the cripple jumped up and began to walk.

[11] When the crowds saw what Paul had done they shouted in the language of Lycaonia, 'The gods have come down to us in human form.' [12] They addressed Barnabas as Zeus, and since Paul was the principal speaker they called him Hermes. [13] The priests of Zeus-outside-the-Gate, proposing that all the people should offer sacrifice with them, brought garlanded oxen to the gates. [14] When the apostles Barnabas and Paul heard what was happening they tore their clothes, and rushed into the crowd, shouting, [15] 'Friends, what do you think you are doing? We are only human beings, mortal like yourselves. We have come with good news to make you turn from these empty idols to the living God who made sky and earth and the sea and all that these hold. [16] In the past he allowed all the nations to go their own way; [17] but even then he did not leave you without evidence of himself in the good things he does for you: he sends you rain from heaven and seasons of fruitfulness; he fills you with food and your hearts with merriment.' [18] With this speech they just managed to prevent the crowd from offering them sacrifice.

End of the mission

[19] Then some Jews arrived from Antioch and Iconium and turned the people against them. They stoned Paul and dragged him outside the town, thinking he was dead. [20] The disciples came crowding round him but, as they did so, he stood up and went back to the town. The next day he and Barnabas left for Derbe.

[21] Having preached the good news in that town and made a considerable number of disciples, they went back through Lystra, Iconium and Antioch. [22] They put fresh heart into the disciples, encouraging them to persevere in the faith, saying, 'We must all experience many hardships before we enter the kingdom of God.' [23] In each of these churches they appointed elders, and with prayer and fasting they commended them to the Lord in whom they had come to believe.

[24] They passed through Pisidia and reached Pamphylia. [25] Then after proclaiming the word at Perga they went down to Attalia [26] and from there sailed for Antioch, where they had originally been commended to the grace of God for the work they had now completed.

[27] On their arrival they assembled the church and gave an account of all that God had done with them, and how he had opened the door of faith to the gentiles. [28] They stayed there with the disciples for some time.

Controversy at Antioch

15 Then some men came down from Judaea and taught the brothers, 'Unless you have yourselves circumcised in the tradition of Moses you cannot be saved.' [2] This led to disagreement, and after Paul and Barnabas had had a long argument with these men it was decided that Paul and Barnabas and others of the church should go up to Jerusalem and discuss the question with the apostles and elders.

[3] The members of the church saw them off, and as they passed through Phoenicia and Samaria they told how the gentiles had been converted, and this news was received with the greatest satisfaction by all the brothers. [4] When they arrived in Jerusalem they were welcomed by the church and by the apostles and elders, and gave an account of all that God had done through them.

Controversy at Jerusalem

[5] But certain members of the Pharisees' party who had become believers objected, insisting that gentiles should be circumcised and instructed to keep the Law of Moses. [6] The apostles and elders met[a] to look into the matter, [7] and after a long discussion, Peter stood up and addressed them.

15a Two disputes are combined: Peter's speech concerns obligations of gentiles to keep the Jewish Law, James' concerns social contact.

Peter's speech

'My brothers,' he said, 'you know perfectly well that in the early days God made his choice among you: the gentiles were to learn the good news from me and so become believers. [8] And God, who can read everyone's heart, showed his approval of them by giving the Holy Spirit to them just as he had to us. [9] God made no distinction between them and us, since he purified their hearts by faith. [10] Why do you put God to the test now by imposing on the disciples the very burden that neither our ancestors nor we ourselves were strong enough to support? [11] But we believe that we are saved in the same way as they are: through the grace of the Lord Jesus.'

[12] The entire assembly fell silent, and they listened to Barnabas and Paul describing all the signs and wonders God had worked through them among the gentiles.

James' speech

[13] When they had finished it was James who spoke. 'My brothers,' he said, 'listen to me. [14] Simeon has described how God first arranged to enlist a people for his name out of the gentiles. [15] This is entirely in harmony with the words of the prophets, since the scriptures say:

[16] *After that I shall return*
and rebuild the fallen hut of David;
I shall make good the gaps in it
and restore it.
[17] *Then the rest of humanity,*
and of all the nations once called mine,
will look for the Lord,
says the Lord who made this [18] known so
long ago.*b*

[19] 'My verdict is, then, that instead of making things more difficult for gentiles who turn to God, [20] we should send them a letter telling them merely to abstain from anything polluted by idols, from illicit marriages, from the meat of strangled animals and from blood.

[21] For Moses has always had his preachers in every town and is read aloud in the synagogues every Sabbath.'

The apostolic letter

[22] Then the apostles and elders, with the whole church, decided to choose delegates from among themselves to send to Antioch with Paul and Barnabas. They chose Judas, known as Barsabbas, and Silas, both leading men in the brotherhood, [23] and gave them this letter to take with them:

'The apostles and elders, your brothers, send greetings to the brothers of gentile birth in Antioch, Syria and Cilicia. [24] We hear that some people coming from here, but acting without any authority from ourselves, have disturbed you with their demands and have unsettled your minds; [25] and so we have decided unanimously to elect delegates and to send them to you with our well-beloved Barnabas and Paul, [26] who have committed their lives to the name of our Lord Jesus Christ. [27] Accordingly we are sending you Judas and Silas, who will confirm by word of mouth what we have written. [28] It has been decided by the Holy Spirit and by ourselves not to impose on you any burden beyond these essentials: [29] you are to abstain from food sacrificed to idols, from blood, from the meat of strangled animals and from illicit marriages. Avoid these, and you will do what is right. Farewell.'

The delegates at Antioch

[30] The party left and went down to Antioch, where they summoned the whole community and delivered the letter. [31] The community read it and were delighted with the encouragement it gave them. [32] Judas and Silas, being themselves prophets, spoke for a long time, encouraging and strengthening the brothers. [33] These two spent some time there, and then

15b Am 9:11–12.

the brothers wished them peace and they went back to those who had sent them.[34]c 35 Paul and Barnabas, however, stayed on in Antioch, and there with many others they taught and proclaimed the good news, the word of the Lord.

Paul separates from Barnabas and recruits Silas

36 On a later occasion Paul said to Barnabas, 'Let us go back and visit the brothers in all the towns where we preached the word of the Lord, so that we can see how they are doing.' 37 Barnabas suggested taking John Mark, 38 but Paul was not in favour of taking along the man who had deserted them in Pamphylia and had refused to share in their work.

39 There was sharp disagreement so that they parted company, and Barnabas sailed off with Mark to Cyprus. 40 Before Paul left, he chose Silas to accompany him and was commended by the brothers to the grace of God.

Lycaonia: Paul recruits Timothy

41 He travelled through Syria and Cilicia, consolidating the churches.

16 From there he went to Derbe, and then on to Lystra, where there was a disciple called Timothy, whose mother was Jewish and had become a believer; but his father was a Greek. 2 The brothers at Lystra and Iconium spoke well of him, 3 and Paul, who wanted to have him as a travelling companion, had him circumcised. This was on account of the Jews in the locality where everyone knew his father was a Greek.

4 As they visited one town after another, they passed on the decisions reached by the apostles and elders in Jerusalem, with instructions to observe them.

5 So the churches grew strong in the faith, as well as growing daily in numbers.

The crossing into Asia Minor

6 They travelled through Phrygia and the Galatian country, because they had been told by the Holy Spirit not to preach the word in Asia. 7 When they reached the frontier of Mysia they tried to go into Bithynia, but as the Spirit of Jesus would not allow them, 8 they went through Mysia and came down to Troas.

9 One night Paul had a vision: a Macedonian appeared and kept urging him in these words, 'Come across to Macedonia and help us.' 10 Once he had seen this vision we lost no time in arranging a passage to Macedonia, convinced that God had called us to bring them the good news.

Arrival at Philippi

11 Sailing from Troas we made a straight run for Samothrace; the next day for Neapolis, 12 and from there for Philippi, a Roman colony and the principal city of that district of Macedonia. 13 After a few days in this city we went outside the gates beside a river as it was the Sabbath and this was a customary place for prayer. We sat down and preached to the women who had come to the meeting. 14 One of these women was called Lydia, a woman from the town of Thyatira who was in the purple-dye trade, and who revered God. She listened to us, and the Lord opened her heart to accept what Paul was saying. 15 After she and her household had been baptised she kept urging us, 'If you judge me a true believer in the Lord,' she said, 'come and stay with us.' And she would take no refusal.

Imprisonment of Paul and Silas

16 It happened one day that as we were going to prayer, we were met by a slave-girl who was a soothsayer and made a lot of money for her masters by foretelling the future. 17 This girl started following Paul and the rest of us and shouting, 'Here are the servants of the Most High God; they have come to tell you how to be saved!' 18 She did this day after day until Paul was exasperated and turned round and said to the spirit, 'I order you in the name of

15c Some MSS add v. 34 'But Silas decided to stay there'.

Jesus Christ to leave that woman.' The spirit went out of her then and there.

¹⁹ When her masters saw that there was no hope of making any more money out of her, they seized Paul and Silas and dragged them into the market place before the authorities. ²⁰ Taking them before the magistrates they said, 'These people are causing a disturbance in our city. They are Jews ²¹ and are advocating practices which it is unlawful for us as Romans to accept or follow.' ²² The crowd joined in and showed its hostility to them, so the magistrates had them stripped and ordered them to be flogged. ²³ They were given many lashes and then thrown into prison, and the gaoler was told to keep a close watch on them. ²⁴ So, following such instructions, he threw them into the inner prison and fastened their feet in the stocks.

The miraculous deliverance of Paul and Silas

²⁵ In the middle of the night Paul and Silas were praying and singing God's praises, while the other prisoners listened. ²⁶ Suddenly there was an earthquake that shook the prison to its foundations. All the doors flew open and the chains fell from all the prisoners. ²⁷ When the gaoler woke and saw the doors wide open he drew his sword and was about to commit suicide, presuming that the prisoners had escaped. ²⁸ But Paul shouted at the top of his voice, 'Do yourself no harm; we are all here.'

²⁹ He called for lights, then rushed in, threw himself trembling at the feet of Paul and Silas, ³⁰ and escorted them out, saying, 'Sirs, what must I do to be saved?' ³¹ They told him, 'Become a believer in the Lord Jesus, and you will be saved, and your household too.' ³² Then they preached the word of the Lord to him and to all his household. ³³ Late as it was, he took them to wash their wounds, and was baptised then and there with all his household. ³⁴ Afterwards he took them into his house and gave them a meal, and the whole household celebrated their conversion to belief in God.

³⁵ When it was daylight the magistrates sent the lictors with the order: 'Release those men.' ³⁶ The gaoler reported the message to Paul, 'The magistrates have sent an order for your release; you can go now and be on your way.' ³⁷ 'What!' Paul replied. 'Without trial they gave us a public flogging, though we are Roman citizens, and threw us into prison, and now they want to send us away on the quiet! Oh no! They must come and escort us out themselves.'

³⁸ The lictors reported this to the magistrates, who were terrified when they heard they were Roman citizens. ³⁹ They came and urged them to leave the town. ⁴⁰ From the prison they went to Lydia's house where they saw all the brothers and gave them some encouragement; then they left.

Thessalonica: difficulties with the Jews

17 Passing through Amphipolis and Apollonia, they eventually reached Thessalonica, where there was a Jewish synagogue. ² Paul as usual went in and for three consecutive Sabbaths developed the arguments from scripture for them, ³ explaining and proving how it was ordained that the Christ should suffer and rise from the dead. 'And the Christ', he said, 'is this Jesus whom I am proclaiming to you.' ⁴ Some of them were convinced and joined Paul and Silas, and so did a great many godfearing people and Greeks, as well as a number of the leading women.

⁵ The Jews, full of resentment, enlisted the help of a gang from the market place, stirred up a crowd, and soon had the whole city in an uproar. They made for Jason's house, hoping to bring them before the People's Assembly; ⁶ however, they found only Jason and some of the brothers, and these they dragged before the city council, shouting, 'The people who have been turning the whole world upside down have come here now; ⁷ they have been staying at Jason's. They have broken Caesar's edicts by claiming that there is another king, Jesus.' ⁸ Hearing this, the citizens and the city councillors were alarmed, ⁹ and they made

Jason and the rest give security before setting them free.

Fresh difficulties at Beroea

¹⁰ When it was dark the brothers immediately sent Paul and Silas away to Beroea, where they went to the Jewish synagogue as soon as they arrived. ¹¹ Here the Jews were more noble-minded than those in Thessalonica, and they welcomed the word very readily; every day they studied the scriptures to check whether it was true. ¹² Many of them became believers, and so did many Greek women of high standing and a number of the men.

¹³ When the Jews of Thessalonica came to learn that the word of God was being preached by Paul in Beroea as well, they went there to make trouble and stir up the people. ¹⁴ So the brothers arranged for Paul to go immediately as far as the coast, leaving Silas and Timothy behind. ¹⁵ Paul's escort took him as far as Athens, and went back with instructions for Silas and Timothy to rejoin Paul as soon as they could.

Paul in Athens

¹⁶ Paul waited for them in Athens and there his whole soul was revolted at the sight of a city given over to idolatry. ¹⁷ In the synagogue he debated with the Jews and the godfearing, and in the market place he debated every day with anyone whom he met. ¹⁸ Even a few Epicurean and Stoic philosophers argued with him. Some said, 'What can this parrot mean?' And, because he was preaching about Jesus and Resurrection, others said, 'He seems to be a propagandist for some outlandish gods.'

¹⁹ They got him to accompany them to the Areopagus, where they said to him, 'Can we know what this new doctrine is that you are teaching? ²⁰ Some of the things you say seemed startling to us and we would like to find out what they mean.' ²¹ The one amusement the Athenians and the foreigners living there seem to have is to discuss and listen to the latest ideas.

²² So Paul stood before the whole council of the Areopagus and made this speech:

Paul's speech before the council of the Areopagus

'Men of Athens, I have seen for myself how extremely scrupulous you are in all religious matters, ²³ because, as I strolled round looking at your sacred monuments, I noticed among other things an altar inscribed: To An Unknown God. In fact, the unknown God you revere is the one I proclaim to you.

²⁴ 'Since the God who made the world and everything in it is himself Lord of heaven and earth, he does not make his home in shrines made by human hands. ²⁵ Nor is he in need of anything, that he should be served by human hands; on the contrary, it is he who gives everything—including life and breath—to everyone. ²⁶ From one single principle he not only created the whole human race so that they could occupy the entire earth, but he decreed the times and limits of their habitation. ²⁷ And he did this so that they might seek the deity and, by feeling their way towards him, succeed in finding him; and indeed he is not far from any of us, ²⁸ since it is in him that we live, and move, and exist,ᵃ as indeed some of your own writers have said:

We are all his children.ᵇ

²⁹ 'Since we are the children of God, we have no excuse for thinking that the deity looks like anything in gold, silver or stone that has been carved and designed by a man.

³⁰ 'But now, overlooking the times of ignorance, God is telling everyone everywhere that they must repent, ³¹ because he has fixed a day when the whole world will be judged in uprightness by a man he has appointed. And God has publicly proved this by raising him from the dead.'

³² At this mention of rising from the dead,

17a From the Gk poet Epimenides.
17b The Gk philosopher Aratus.

162 READ ACTS 17:16–34.

It is in him that we live, and move, and exist.—ACTS 17:28

PRACTICING THE PRESENCE OF GOD

A short, simple method of mental prayer "consists in two points: (1) place yourself in the presence of God, and (2) invoke his assistance. To help you place yourself in God's presence, I propose four principal means that you can use. . . .

The first consists of a lively, attentive realization of God's absolute presence, that is, that God is in all things and all places. . . . Just as wherever birds fly they always encounter the air, so also wherever we go or wherever we are we find God present. . . .

The second way to place yourself in God's holy presence is to remember that . . . he is present in a most particular manner in your heart and in the very center of your spirit. . . . Just as the soul is diffused throughout the entire body . . . but resides in a special manner in the heart, so also God is present in all things but always resides in our spirit. For this reason David calls him "the God of his heart" (see Ps 73:26) and St. Paul says that "in him we live, and move, and exist."

A third way is to consider how our Savior in his humanity gazes from heaven on all mankind and particularly on Christians, who are his children, and most especially on those who are at prayer. . . . At the time of his martyrdom, St. Stephen saw him in this way (see Ac 7:55–57). . . .

A fourth method consists in use of simple imagination when we represent to ourselves the Savior in his sacred humanity as if he were near us, just as we sometimes imagine a friend to be present and say, "I imagine that I see such a one who is doing this or that. . . ." If the most Blessed Sacrament of the Altar is present, then Christ's presence is real and not purely imaginary. The species and appearance of bread are like a tapestry behind which our Lord is really present and sees and observes us, although we do not see him in his own form. ST. FRANCIS DE SALES, 1567–1622

YOU WILL FIND THE NEXT READING AT ROMANS 6.

some of them burst out laughing; others said, 'We would like to hear you talk about this another time.' ³³ After that Paul left them, ³⁴ but there were some who attached themselves to him and became believers, among them Dionysius the Aeropagite and a woman called Damaris, and others besides.

Foundation of the church of Corinth

18 After this Paul left Athens and went to Corinth, ² where he met a Jew called Aquila whose family came from Pontus. He and his wife Priscilla had recently left Italy because an edict of Claudius had expelled all the Jews from Rome. Paul went to visit them, ³ and when he found they were tentmakers, of the same trade as himself, he lodged with them, and they worked together. ⁴ Every Sabbath he used to hold debates in the synagogues, trying to convert Jews as well as Greeks.

⁵ After Silas and Timothy had arrived from Macedonia, Paul devoted all his time to preaching, declaring to the Jews that Jesus was the Christ. ⁶ When they turned against him

and started to insult him, he took his cloak and shook it out in front of them,[a] saying, 'Your blood be on your own heads; from now on I will go to the gentiles with a clear conscience.' [7] Then he left the synagogue and moved to the house next door that belonged to a worshipper of God called Justus. [8] Crispus, president of the synagogue, and his whole household, all became believers in the Lord. Many Corinthians when they heard this became believers and were baptised. [9] One night the Lord spoke to Paul in a vision, 'Be fearless; speak out and do not keep silence: [10] I am with you. I have so many people that belong to me in this city that no one will attempt to hurt you.' [11] So Paul stayed there preaching the word of God among them for eighteen months.

The Jews take Paul to court

[12] But while Gallio was proconsul of Achaia, the Jews made a concerted attack on Paul and brought him before the tribunal, saying, [13] 'We accuse this man of persuading people to worship God in a way that breaks the Law.' [14] Before Paul could open his mouth, Gallio said to the Jews, 'Listen, you Jews. If this were a misdemeanour or a crime, it would be in order for me to listen to your plea; [15] but if it is only quibbles about words and names, and about your own Law, then you must deal with it yourselves—I have no intention of making legal decisions about these things.' [16] Then he began to hustle them out of the court, [17] and at once they all turned on Sosthenes, the synagogue president, and beat him in front of the tribunal. Gallio refused to take any notice at all.

Return to Antioch and departure for the third journey

[18] After staying on for some time, Paul took leave of the brothers and sailed for Syria, accompanied by Priscilla and Aquila. At Cenchreae he had his hair cut off, because of a vow he had made. [19] When they reached Ephesus, he left them, but first he went alone to the synagogue to debate with the Jews. [20] They asked him to stay longer, but he declined, [21] though when he took his leave he said, 'I will come back another time, God willing.' Then he sailed from Ephesus.

[22] He landed at Caesarea and went up to greet the church. Then he came down to Antioch [23] where he spent a short time before continuing his journey through the Galatian country and then through Phrygia, encouraging all the followers.

Apollos

[24] An Alexandrian Jew named Apollos[b] now arrived in Ephesus. He was an eloquent man, with a sound knowledge of the scriptures, and yet, [25] though he had been given instruction in the Way of the Lord and preached with great spiritual fervour and was accurate in all the details he taught about Jesus, he had experienced only the baptism of John. [26] He began to teach fearlessly in the synagogue and, when Priscilla and Aquila heard him, they attached themselves to him and gave him more detailed instruction about the Way.

[27] When Apollos thought of crossing over to Achaia, the brothers encouraged him and wrote asking the disciples to welcome him. When he arrived there he was able by God's grace to help the believers considerably [28] by the energetic way he refuted the Jews in public, demonstrating from the scriptures that Jesus was the Christ.

The disciples of John at Ephesus

19 It happened that while Apollos was in Corinth, Paul made his way overland as far as Ephesus, where he found a number of disciples. [2] When he asked, 'Did you receive the Holy Spirit when you became believers?' they answered, 'No, we were never even told there was such a thing as a Holy Spirit.' [3] He asked, 'Then how were you baptised?' They replied, 'With John's baptism.' [4] Paul said, 'John's baptism was a baptism of repentance; but he insisted that the people should believe

18a cf. 13:47; 28:25.   18b cf. 1 Co 1:12; 3:4–11.

in the one who was to come after him—namely Jesus.' ⁵When they heard this, they were baptised in the name of the Lord Jesus, ⁶and the moment Paul had laid hands on them the Holy Spirit came down on them, and they began to speak with tongues and to prophesy. ⁷There were about twelve of these men in all.

Foundation of the church of Ephesus

⁸He began by going to the synagogue, where he spoke out fearlessly and argued persuasively about the kingdom of God. He did this for three months, ⁹till the attitude of some of the congregation hardened into unbelief. As soon as they began attacking the Way in public, he broke with them and took his disciples apart to hold daily discussions in the lecture room of Tyrannus. ¹⁰This went on for two years, with the result that all the inhabitants of Asia, both Jews and Greeks, were able to hear the word of the Lord.

The Jewish exorcists

¹¹So remarkable were the miracles worked by God at Paul's hands ¹²that handkerchiefs or aprons which had touched him were taken to the sick, and they were cured of their illnesses, and the evil spirits came out of them.

¹³But some itinerant Jewish exorcists too tried pronouncing the name of the Lord Jesus over people who were possessed by evil spirits; they used to say, 'I adjure you by the Jesus whose spokesman is Paul.' ¹⁴Among those who did this were seven sons of Sceva, a Jewish chief priest. ¹⁵The evil spirit replied, 'Jesus I recognise, and Paul I know, but who are you?' ¹⁶and the man with the evil spirit hurled himself at them and overpowered first one and then another, and handled them so violently that they fled from that house stripped of clothing and badly mauled. ¹⁷Everybody in Ephesus, both Jews and Greeks, heard about this episode; everyone was filled with awe, and the name of the Lord Jesus came to be held in great honour.

¹⁸Some believers, too, came forward to admit in detail how they had used spells ¹⁹and a number of them who had practised magic collected their books and made a bonfire of them in public. The value of these was calculated to be fifty thousand silver pieces.

²⁰In this powerful way the word of the Lord spread more and more widely and successfully.

Paul's plans

²¹When all this was over Paul made up his mind to go back to Jerusalem through Macedonia and Achaia. 'After I have been there,' he said, 'I must go on to see Rome as well.' ²²So he sent two of his helpers, Timothy and Erastus, ahead of him to Macedonia, while he remained for a time in Asia.

Ephesus: the silversmiths' riot

²³It was during this time that a serious disturbance broke out in connection with the Way. ²⁴A silversmith called Demetrius, who provided work for a large number of craftsmen making silver shrines of Diana, ²⁵called a general meeting of them with others in the same trade. 'As you know,' he said, 'it is on this industry that we depend for our prosperity. ²⁶Now you must have seen and heard how, not just in Ephesus but nearly everywhere in Asia, this man Paul has persuaded and converted a great number of people with his argument that gods made by hand are not gods at all. ²⁷This threatens not only to discredit our trade, but also to reduce the sanctuary of the great goddess Diana to unimportance. It could end up by taking away the prestige of a goddess venerated all over Asia, and indeed all over the world.' ²⁸This speech roused them to fury, and they started to shout, 'Great is Diana of the Ephesians!' ²⁹The whole town was filled with the uproar and the mob made a concerted rush to the theatre, dragging along two of Paul's Macedonian travelling companions, Gaius and Aristarchus. ³⁰Paul wanted to make an appeal to the people, but the disciples refused to let him; ³¹in fact, some of the Asiarchs, who were friends of his, sent mes-

sages urging him not to take the risk of going into the theatre.

[32] By now everybody was shouting different things, till the assembly itself had no idea what was going on; most of them did not even know why they had gathered together. [33] Some of the crowd prevailed upon Alexander, whom the Jews pushed forward; he raised his hand for silence with the intention of explaining things to the people. [34] As soon as they realised he was a Jew, they all started shouting in unison, 'Great is Diana of the Ephesians!' and they kept this up for two hours. [35] When the town clerk eventually succeeded in calming the crowd, he said, 'Citizens of Ephesus! Is there anybody who does not know that the city of the Ephesians is the guardian of the temple of great Diana and of her statue that fell from heaven? [36] Nobody can contradict this and there is no need for you to get excited or do anything rash. [37] These men you have brought here are not guilty of any sacrilege or blasphemy against our goddess. [38] If Demetrius and the craftsmen he has with him want to complain about anyone, there are the assizes and the proconsuls; let them take the case to court. [39] And if you want to ask any more questions you must raise them in the regular assembly. [40] We could easily be charged with rioting for today's happenings: there is no ground for it all, and we can give no justification for this gathering.' When he had finished this speech he dismissed the assembly.

Paul leaves Ephesus

20 When the disturbance was over, Paul sent for the disciples and, after speaking words of encouragement to them, said goodbye and set out for Macedonia. [2] On his way through those areas he said many words of encouragement to them and then made his way into Greece, [3] where he spent three months. He was leaving by ship for Syria when a plot organised against him by the Jews made him decide to go back by way of Macedonia. [4] He was accompanied by Sopater, son of Pyrrhus, who came from Beroea; Aristarchus and Se-

cundus who came from Thessalonica; Gaius from Derbe, and Timothy, as well as Tychicus and Trophimus who were from Asia. [5] They all went on to Troas where they waited for us. [6] We ourselves left Philippi by ship after the days of Unleavened Bread and joined them five days later at Troas, where we stayed for a week.

Troas: Paul raises a dead man to life

[7] On the first day of the week we met for the breaking of bread. Paul was due to leave the next day, and he preached a sermon that went on till the middle of the night. [8] A number of lamps were lit in the upstairs room where we were assembled, [9] and as Paul went on and on, a young man called Eutychus who was sitting on the window-sill grew drowsy and was overcome by sleep and fell to the ground three floors below. He was picked up dead. [10] Paul went down and stooped to clasp the boy to him, saying, 'There is no need to worry, there is still life in him.' [11] Then he went back upstairs where he broke the bread and ate and carried on talking till he left at daybreak. [12] They took the boy away alive, and were greatly encouraged.

From Troas to Miletus

[13] We were now to go on ahead by sea, so we set sail for Assos, where we were to take Paul on board; this was what he had arranged, for he wanted to go overland. [14] When he rejoined us at Assos we took him aboard and went on to Mitylene. [15] The next day we sailed from there and arrived opposite Chios. The second day we touched at Samos and, after stopping at Trogyllium, made Miletus the next day. [16] Paul had decided to pass wide of Ephesus so as to avoid spending time in Asia, since he was anxious to be in Jerusalem, if possible, for the day of Pentecost.

Farewell to the elders of Ephesus

[17] From Miletus he sent for the elders of the church of Ephesus. [18] When they arrived he addressed these words to them:

'You know what my way of life has been ever since the first day I set foot among you in Asia, [19] how I have served the Lord in all humility, with all the sorrows and trials that came to me through the plots of the Jews. [20] I have not hesitated to do anything that would be helpful to you; I have preached to you and instructed you both in public and in your homes, [21] urging both Jews and Greeks to turn to God and to believe in our Lord Jesus.

[22] 'And now you see me on my way to Jerusalem in captivity to the Spirit; I have no idea what will happen to me there, [23] except that the Holy Spirit, in town after town, has made it clear to me that imprisonment and persecution await me. [24] But I do not place any value on my own life, provided that I complete the mission the Lord Jesus gave me—to bear witness to the good news of God's grace.

[25] 'I now feel sure that none of you among whom I have gone about proclaiming the kingdom will ever see my face again. [26] And so on this very day I swear that my conscience is clear as far as all of you are concerned, [27] for I have without faltering put before you the whole of God's purpose.

[28] 'Be on your guard for yourselves and for all the flock of which the Holy Spirit has made you the guardians, to feed the Church of God which he bought with the blood of his own Son.

[29] 'I know quite well that when I have gone fierce wolves will invade you and will have no mercy on the flock. [30] Even from your own ranks there will be men coming forward with a travesty of the truth on their lips to induce the disciples to follow them. [31] So be on your guard, remembering how night and day for three years I never slackened in counselling each one of you with tears. [32] And now I commend you to God and to the word of his grace that has power to build you up and to give you your inheritance among all the sanctified.

[33] 'I have never asked anyone for money or clothes; [34] you know for yourselves that these hands of mine earned enough to meet my needs and those of my companions. [35] By every means I have shown you that we must exert ourselves in this way to support the weak, remembering the words of the Lord Jesus, who himself said, "There is more happiness in giving than in receiving." '[a]

[36] When he had finished speaking he knelt down with them all and prayed. [37] By now they were all in tears; they put their arms round Paul's neck and kissed him; [38] what saddened them most was his saying they would never see his face again. Then they escorted him to the ship.

The journey to Jerusalem

21 When we had at last torn ourselves away from them and put to sea, we set a straight course and arrived at Cos; the next day we reached Rhodes, and from there went on to Patara. [2] Here we found a ship bound for Phoenicia, so we went on board and sailed in her. [3] After sighting Cyprus and leaving it to port, we sailed to Syria and put in at Tyre, since the ship was to unload her cargo there. [4] We sought out the disciples and stayed there a week. Speaking in the Spirit, they kept telling Paul not to go on to Jerusalem, [5] but when our time was up we set off. Together with the women and children they all escorted us on our way till we were out of the town. When we reached the beach, we knelt down and prayed; [6] then, after saying good-bye to each other, we went aboard and they returned home.

[7] The end of our voyage from Tyre came when we landed at Ptolemais, where we greeted the brothers and stayed one day with them. [8] The next day we left and came to Caesarea. Here we called on Philip the evangelist, one of the Seven, and stayed with him. [9] He had four unmarried daughters who were prophets. [10] When we had been there several days a prophet called Agabus arrived from Judaea. [11] He came up to us, took Paul's belt and tied up his own feet and hands, and said, 'This is what the Holy Spirit says, "The man to

20a This saying does not occur in the gospels.

whom this girdle belongs will be tied up like this by the Jews in Jerusalem and handed over to the gentiles." ' ¹²When we heard this, we and all the local people urged Paul not to go on to Jerusalem. ¹³To this he replied, 'What are you doing, weeping and breaking my heart? For my part, I am ready not only to be bound but even to die in Jerusalem for the name of the Lord Jesus.' ¹⁴And so, as he would not be persuaded, we gave up the attempt, saying, 'The Lord's will be done.'

Paul's arrival in Jerusalem

¹⁵After this we made our preparations and went on up to Jerusalem. ¹⁶Some of the disciples from Caesarea accompanied us and took us to the house of a Cypriot with whom we were to lodge; he was called Mnason and had been one of the earliest disciples.

¹⁷On our arrival in Jerusalem the brothers gave us a very warm welcome. ¹⁸The next day Paul went with us to visit James, and all the elders were present. ¹⁹After greeting them he gave a detailed account of all that God had done among the gentiles through his ministry. ²⁰They gave glory to God when they heard this. Then they said, 'You see, brother, how thousands of Jews have now become believers, all of them staunch upholders of the Law; ²¹and what they have heard about you is that you instruct all Jews living among the gentiles to break away from Moses, authorising them not to circumcise their children or to follow the customary practices. ²²What is to be done? A crowd is sure to gather, for they will hear that you have come. ²³So this is what we suggest that you should do; we have four men here who are under a vow; ²⁴take these men along and be purified with them and pay all the expenses connected with the shaving of their heads. This will let everyone know there is no truth in the reports they have heard about you, and that you too observe the Law by your way of life. ²⁵About the gentiles who have become believers, we have written giving them our decision that they must abstain from things sacrificed to idols, from blood, from the meat of strangled animals and from illicit marriages.'

²⁶So the next day Paul took the men along and was purified with them, and he visited the Temple to give notice of the time when the period of purification would be over and the offering would have to be presented on behalf of each of them.

Paul's arrest

²⁷The seven days were nearly over when some Jews from Asia caught sight of him in the Temple and stirred up the crowd and seized him, ²⁸shouting, 'Men of Israel, help! This is the man who preaches to everyone everywhere against our people, against the Law and against this place. He has even profaned this Holy Place by bringing Greeks into the Temple.' ²⁹They had, in fact, previously seen Trophimus the Ephesian in the city with him and thought that Paul had brought him into the Temple.

³⁰This roused the whole city; people came running from all sides; they seized Paul and dragged him out of the Temple, and the gates were closed behind them. ³¹While they were setting about killing him, word reached the tribune of the cohort that there was tumult all over Jerusalem. ³²He immediately called out soldiers and centurions and charged down on the crowd, who stopped beating Paul when they saw the tribune and the soldiers. ³³When the tribune came up he took Paul into custody, had him bound with two chains and enquired who he was and what he had done. ³⁴People in the crowd called out different things, and since the noise made it impossible for him to get any positive information, the tribune ordered Paul to be taken into the fortress. ³⁵When Paul reached the steps, the crowd became so violent that he had to be carried by the soldiers; ³⁶and indeed the whole mob was after them, shouting, 'Do away with him!'

³⁷Just as Paul was being taken into the fortress, he asked the tribune if he could have a word with him. The tribune said, 'You speak Greek, then? ³⁸Aren't you the Egyptian who

started the recent revolt and led those four thousand cut-throats out into the desert?' ³⁹'I?' said Paul, 'I am a Jew and a citizen of the well-known city of Tarsus in Cilicia. Please give me permission to speak to the people.' ⁴⁰The man gave his consent and Paul, standing at the top of the steps, raised his hand to the people for silence. A profound silence followed, and he started speaking to them in Hebrew.

Paul's address to the Jews of Jerusalem

22 'My brothers, my fathers, listen to what I have to say to you in my defence.' ²When they realised he was speaking in Hebrew, the silence was even greater than before. ³'I am a Jew', Paul said, 'and was born at Tarsus in Cilicia. I was brought up here in this city. It was under Gamaliel that I studied and was taught the exact observance of the Law of our ancestors. In fact, I was as full of duty towards God as you all are today. ⁴I even persecuted this Way to the death and sent women as well as men to prison in chains ⁵as the high priest and the whole council of elders can testify. I even received letters from them to the brothers in Damascus, which I took with me when I set off to bring prisoners back from there to Jerusalem for punishment.

⁶'It happened^a that I was on that journey and nearly at Damascus when in the middle of the day a bright light from heaven suddenly shone round me. ⁷I fell to the ground and heard a voice saying, "Saul, Saul, why are you persecuting me?" ⁸I answered, "Who are you, Lord?" and he said to me, "I am Jesus the Nazarene, whom you are persecuting." ⁹The people with me saw the light but did not hear the voice which spoke to me. ¹⁰I said, "What am I to do, Lord?" The Lord answered, "Get up and go into Damascus, and there you will be told what you have been appointed to do." ¹¹Since the light had been so dazzling that I was blind, I got to Damascus only because my companions led me by the hand.

¹²'Someone called Ananias, a devout follower of the Law and highly thought of by all the Jews living there, ¹³came to see me; he stood beside me and said, "Brother Saul, receive your sight." Instantly my sight came back and I was able to see him. ¹⁴Then he said, "The God of our ancestors has chosen you to know his will, to see the Upright One and hear his own voice speaking, ¹⁵because you are to be his witness before all humanity, testifying to what you have seen and heard. ¹⁶And now why delay? Hurry and be baptised and wash away your sins, calling on his name."

¹⁷'It happened that, when I got back to Jerusalem, and was praying in the Temple, I fell into a trance ¹⁸and then I saw him. "Hurry," he said, "leave Jerusalem at once; they will not accept the testimony you are giving about me." ¹⁹"Lord," I answered, "they know that I used to go from synagogue to synagogue, imprisoning and flogging those who believed in you; ²⁰and that when the blood of your witness Stephen was being shed, I, too, was standing by, in full agreement with his murderers, and in charge of their clothes." ²¹Then he said to me, "Go! I am sending you out to the gentiles far away." '

Paul the Roman citizen

²²So far they had listened to him, but at these words they began to shout, 'Rid the earth of the man! He is not fit to live!' ²³They were yelling, waving their cloaks and throwing dust into the air, ²⁴and so the tribune had him brought into the fortress and ordered him to be examined under the lash, to find out the reason for the outcry against him. ²⁵But when they had strapped him down Paul said to the centurion on duty, 'Is it legal for you to flog a man who is a Roman citizen and has not been brought to trial?' ²⁶When he heard this the centurion went and told the tribune; 'Do you realise what you are doing?' he said. 'This man is a Roman citizen.' ²⁷So the tribune came and asked him, 'Tell me, are you a Roman citizen?' Paul answered 'Yes'. ²⁸To this the tribune replied, 'It cost me a large sum

22a = 9; 26.

to acquire this citizenship.' 'But I was born to it,' said Paul. ²⁹ Then those who were about to examine him hurriedly withdrew, and the tribune himself was alarmed when he realised that he had put a Roman citizen in chains.

His appearance before the Sanhedrin

³⁰ The next day, since he wanted to know for sure what charge the Jews were bringing, he freed Paul and gave orders for a meeting of the chief priests and the entire Sanhedrin; then he brought Paul down and set him in front of them.

23 Paul looked steadily at the Sanhedrin and began to speak, 'My brothers, to this day I have conducted myself before God with a perfectly clear conscience.' ² At this the high priest Ananias ordered his attendants to strike him on the mouth. ³ Then Paul said to him, 'God will surely strike you, you white-washed wall! How can you sit there to judge me according to the Law, and then break the Law by ordering a man to strike me?' ⁴ The attendants said, 'Are you insulting the high priest of God?' ⁵ Paul answered, 'Brothers, I did not realise it was the high priest; certainly scripture says, *"You will not curse your people's leader."* '[a]

⁶ Now Paul was well aware that one party was made up of Sadducees and the other of Pharisees, so he called out in the Sanhedrin, 'Brothers, I am a Pharisee and the son of Pharisees. It is for our hope in the resurrection of the dead that I am on trial.' ⁷ As soon as he said this, a dispute broke out between the Pharisees and Sadducees, and the assembly was split between the two parties. ⁸ For the Sadducees say there is neither resurrection, nor angel, nor spirit, while the Pharisees accept all three. ⁹ The shouting grew louder, and some of the scribes from the Pharisees' party stood up and protested strongly, 'We find nothing wrong with this man. Suppose a spirit has spoken to him, or an angel?' ¹⁰ Feeling was running high, and the tribune, afraid that they would tear Paul to pieces, ordered his troops to go

down and haul him out and bring him into the fortress.

¹¹ Next night, the Lord appeared to him and said, 'Courage! You have borne witness for me in Jerusalem, now you must do the same in Rome.'

The conspiracy of the Jews against Paul

¹² When it was day, the Jews held a secret meeting at which they made a vow not to eat or drink until they had killed Paul. ¹³ More than forty of them entered this pact, ¹⁴ and they went to the chief priests and elders and told them, 'We have made a solemn vow to let nothing pass our lips until we have killed Paul. ¹⁵ Now it is up to you and the Sanhedrin together to apply to the tribune to bring him down to you, as though you meant to examine his case more closely; we, on our side, are prepared to dispose of him before he reaches you.'

¹⁶ But the son of Paul's sister heard of the ambush they were laying and made his way into the fortress and told Paul, ¹⁷ who called one of the centurions and said, 'Take this young man to the tribune; he has something to tell him.' ¹⁸ So the man took him to the tribune, and reported, 'The prisoner Paul summoned me and requested me to bring this young man to you; he has something to tell you.' ¹⁹ Then the tribune took him by the hand and drew him aside and questioned him in private, 'What is it you have to tell me?' ²⁰ He replied, 'The Jews have made a plan to ask you to take Paul down to the Sanhedrin tomorrow, as though they meant to enquire more closely into his case. ²¹ Do not believe them. There are more than forty of them lying in wait for him, and they have vowed not to eat or drink until they have got rid of him. They are ready now and only waiting for your order to be given.' ²² The tribune let the young man go with this order, 'Tell no one that you have given me this information.'

23a Ex 22:27. Ananias became high priest in AD 47.

Paul transferred to Caesarea

23 Then he summoned two of the centurions and said, 'Get two hundred soldiers ready to leave for Caesarea by the third hour of the night with seventy cavalry and two hundred auxiliaries; 24 provide horses for Paul, and deliver him unharmed to Felix the governor.' 25 He also wrote a letter in these terms:

26 'Claudius Lysias to his Excellency the governor Felix, greetings. 27 This man had been seized by the Jews and would have been murdered by them; but I came on the scene with my troops and got him away, having discovered that he was a Roman citizen. 28 Wanting to find out what charge they were making against him, I brought him before their Sanhedrin. 29 I found that the accusation concerned disputed points of their Law, but that there was no charge deserving death or imprisonment. 30 Acting on information that there was a conspiracy against the man, I hasten to send him to you, and have notified his accusers that they must state their case against him in your presence.'

31 The soldiers carried out their orders; they took Paul and escorted him by night to Antipatris. 32 Next day they left the mounted escort to go on with him and returned to the fortress. 33 On arriving at Caesarea the escort delivered the letter to the governor and handed Paul over to him. 34 When he had read it, he asked Paul what province he came from. Learning that he was from Cilicia he said, 35 'I will hear your case as soon as your accusers are here too.' Then he ordered him to be held in Herod's praetorium.

The case before Felix

24 Five days later the high priest Ananias came down with some of the elders and an advocate named Tertullus, and they laid information against Paul before the governor. 2 Paul was called, and Tertullus opened for the prosecution, 'Your Excellency, Felix, the unbroken peace we enjoy and the reforms this nation owes to your foresight 3 are matters we accept, always and everywhere, with all gratitude. 4 I do not want to take up too much of your time, but I urge you in your graciousness to give us a brief hearing. 5 We have found this man a perfect pest; he stirs up trouble among Jews the world over and is a ringleader of the Nazarene sect. 6 He has even attempted to profane the Temple. We placed him under arrest.ᵃ[7] 8 If you ask him you can find out for yourself the truth of all our accusations against this man.' 9 The Jews supported him, asserting that these were the facts.

10 When the governor motioned him to speak, Paul answered:

Paul's speech before the Roman governor

'I know that you have administered justice over this nation for many years, and I can therefore speak with confidence in my defence. 11 As you can verify for yourself, it is no more than twelve days since I went up to Jerusalem on pilgrimage, 12 and it is not true that they ever found me arguing with anyone or stirring up the mob, either in the Temple, in the synagogues, or about the town; 13 neither can they give you any proof of the accusations they are making against me now.

14 'What I do admit to you is this: it is according to the Way, which they describe as a sect, that I worship the God of my ancestors, retaining my belief in all points of the Law and in what is written in the prophets; 15 and I hold the same hope in God as they do that there will be a resurrection of the upright and the wicked alike. 16 In these things, I, as much as they, do my best to keep a clear conscience at all times before God and everyone.

17 'After several years I came to bring relief-money to my nationᵇ and to make offerings;

24a Several witnesses add 'intending to judge him according to our Law, [7] but the tribune Lysias intervened and took him out of our hands by force, [8] ordering the accusers to appear before you'.

24b cf. 1 Co 16:1.

18it was in connection with these that they found me in the Temple; I had been purified, and there was no crowd involved, and no disturbance. 19But some Jews from Asia—these are the ones who should have appeared before you and accused me of whatever they had against me. 20At least let those who are present say what crime they held against me when I stood before the Sanhedrin, 21unless it were to do with this single claim, when I stood up among them and called out, "It is about the resurrection of the dead that I am on trial before you today."'

Paul's captivity at Caesarea

22At this, Felix, who was fairly well informed about the Way, adjourned the case, saying, 'When Lysias the tribune comes down I will give judgement about your case.' 23He then gave orders to the centurion that Paul should be kept under arrest but free from restriction, and that none of his own people should be prevented from seeing to his needs.

24Some days later Felix came with his wife Drusilla who was a Jewess. He sent for Paul and gave him a hearing on the subject of faith in Christ Jesus. 25But when Paul began to treat of uprightness, self-control and the coming Judgement, Felix took fright and said, 'You may go for the present; I will send for you when I find it convenient.' 26At the same time he had hopes of receiving money from Paul, and for this reason he sent for him frequently and had talks with him.

27When two years came to an end, Felix was succeeded by Porcius Festus and, being anxious to gain favour with the Jews, Felix left Paul in custody.

Paul appeals to Caesar

25 Three days after his arrival in the province, Festus went up to Jerusalem from Caesarea. 2The chief priests and leaders of the Jews informed him of the case against Paul, 3urgently asking him to support them against him, and to have him transferred to Jerusalem. They were preparing an ambush to murder him on the way. 4But Festus replied that Paul was in custody in Caesarea, and that he would be going back there shortly himself. 5He said, 'Let your authorities come down with me, and if there is anything wrong about the man, they can bring a charge against him.'

6After staying with them for eight or ten days at the most, he went down to Caesarea and the next day he took his seat on the tribunal and had Paul brought in. 7As soon as Paul appeared, the Jews who had come down from Jerusalem surrounded him, making many serious accusations which they were unable to substantiate. 8Paul's defence was this, 'I have committed no offence whatever against either Jewish law, or the Temple, or Caesar.' 9Festus was anxious to gain favour with the Jews, so he said to Paul, 'Are you willing to go up to Jerusalem and be tried on these charges before me there?' 10But Paul replied, 'I am standing before the tribunal of Caesar and this is where I should be tried. I have done the Jews no wrong, as you very well know. 11If I am guilty of committing any capital crime, I do not ask to be spared the death penalty. But if there is no substance in the accusations these persons bring against me, no one has a right to surrender me to them. I appeal to Caesar.' 12Then Festus conferred with his advisers and replied, 'You have appealed to Caesar; to Caesar you shall go.'

Paul appears before King Agrippa

13Some days later King Agrippa and Bernice arrived in Caesarea and paid their respects to Festus. 14Their visit lasted several days, and Festus put Paul's case before the king, saying, 'There is a man here whom Felix left behind in custody, 15and while I was in Jerusalem the chief priests and elders of the Jews laid information against him, demanding his condemnation. 16But I told them that Romans are not in the habit of surrendering any man, until the accused confronts his accusers and is given an opportunity to defend himself against the charge. 17So they came here with me, and I wasted no time but took my seat on the tribunal the very next day and had the man brought in. [18] When confronted with him, his accusers did not charge him with any of the crimes I had expected; [19] but they had some argument or other with him about their own religion and about a dead man called Jesus whom Paul alleged to be alive. [20] Not feeling qualified to deal with questions of this sort, I asked him if he would be willing to go to Jerusalem to be tried there on this issue. [21] But Paul put in an appeal for his case to be reserved for the judgement of the emperor, so I ordered him to be remanded until I could send him to Caesar.' [22] Agrippa said to Festus, 'I should like to hear the man myself.' He answered, 'Tomorrow you shall hear him.'

[23] So the next day Agrippa and Bernice arrived in great state and entered the audience chamber attended by the tribunes and the city notables; and Festus ordered Paul to be brought in. [24] Then Festus said, 'King Agrippa, and all here present with us, you see before you the man about whom the whole Jewish community has petitioned me, both in Jerusalem and here, loudly protesting that he ought not to be allowed to remain alive. [25] For my own part I am satisfied that he has committed no capital crime, but when he himself appealed to the emperor I decided to send him. [26] But I have nothing definite that I can write to his Imperial Majesty about him; that is why I have produced him before you all, and before you in particular, King Agrippa, so that after the examination I may have something to write. [27] It seems to me pointless to send a prisoner without indicating the charges against him.'

26 Then Agrippa said to Paul, 'You have leave to speak on your own behalf.' And Paul held up his hand and began his defence:

Paul's speech before King Agrippa

[2] 'I consider myself fortunate, King Agrippa, in that it is before you I am to answer today all the charges made against me by the Jews, [3] the more so because you are an expert in matters of custom and controversy among the Jews. So I beg you to listen to me patiently.

[4] 'My manner of life from my youth, a life spent from the beginning among my own people and in Jerusalem, is common knowledge among the Jews. [5] They have known me for a long time and could testify, if they would, that I followed the strictest party in our religion and lived as a Pharisee. [6] And now it is for my hope in the promise made by God to our ancestors that I am on trial, [7] the promise that our twelve tribes, constant in worship night and day, hope to attain. For that hope, Your Majesty, I am actually put on trial by Jews! [8] Why does it seem incredible to you that God should raise the dead?

[9] 'As for me, I once thought it was my duty to use every means to oppose the name of Jesus the Nazarene. [10] This I did in Jerusalem; I myself threw many of God's holy people into prison, acting on authority from the chief priests, and when they were being sentenced to death I cast my vote against them. [11] I often went round the synagogues inflicting penalties, trying in this way to force them to renounce their faith; my fury against them was so extreme that I even pursued them into foreign cities.

[12] 'On such an expedition I was going to Damascus, armed with full powers and a commission from the chief priests,[a] [13] and in the middle of the day as I was on my way, Your Majesty, I saw a light from heaven shining more brilliantly than the sun round me and my fellow-travellers. [14] We all fell to the ground, and I heard a voice saying to me in Hebrew, "Saul, Saul, why are you persecuting me? It is hard for you, kicking against the goad." [15] Then I said, "Who are you, Lord?" And the Lord answered, "I am Jesus, whom you are persecuting. [16] But get up and stand on your feet, for I have appeared to you for this reason: to appoint you as my servant and as witness of this vision in which you have seen

26a = 9; 22.

me, and of others in which I shall appear to you. [17] *I shall rescue you* from the people and from *the nations to whom I send you* [18] *to open their eyes,* so that they may turn *from darkness to light,*[b] from the dominion of Satan to God, and receive, through faith in me, forgiveness of their sins and a share in the inheritance of the sanctified."

[19] 'After that, King Agrippa, I could not disobey the heavenly vision. [20] On the contrary I started preaching, first to the people of Damascus, then to those of Jerusalem and all Judaean territory, and also to the gentiles, urging them to repent and turn to God, proving their change of heart by their deeds. [21] This was why the Jews laid hands on me in the Temple and tried to do away with me. [22] But I was blessed with God's help, and so I have stood firm to this day, testifying to great and small alike, saying nothing more than what the prophets and Moses himself said would happen: [23] that the Christ was to suffer and that, as the first to rise from the dead, he was to proclaim a light for our people and for the gentiles.'

His hearers' reactions

[24] He had reached this point in his defence when Festus shouted out, 'Paul, you are out of your mind; all that learning of yours is driving you mad.' [25] But Paul answered, 'Festus, your Excellency, I am not mad: I am speaking words of sober truth and good sense. [26] The king understands these matters, and to him I now speak fearlessly. I am confident that nothing of all this comes as a surprise to him; after all, these things were not done in a corner. [27] King Agrippa, do you believe in the prophets? I know you do.' [28] At this Agrippa said to Paul, 'A little more, and your arguments would make a Christian of me.' [29] Paul replied, 'Little or much, I wish before God that not only you but all who are listening to me today would come to be as I am—except for these chains.'

[30] At this the king rose to his feet, with the governor and Bernice and those who sat there with them. [31] When they had retired they talked together and agreed, 'This man is doing nothing that deserves death or imprisonment.' [32] And Agrippa remarked to Festus, 'The man could have been set free if he had not appealed to Caesar.'

The departure for Rome

27 When it had been decided that we should sail to Italy, Paul and some other prisoners were handed over to a centurion called Julius, of the Augustan cohort. [2] We boarded a vessel from Adramyttium bound for ports on the Asiatic coast and put to sea; we had Aristarchus with us, a Macedonian of Thessalonica. [3] Next day we put in at Sidon, and Julius was considerate enough to allow Paul to go to his friends to be looked after.

[4] From there we put to sea again, but as the winds were against us we sailed under the lee of Cyprus, [5] then across the open sea off Cilicia and Pamphylia, taking a fortnight to reach Myra in Lycia. [6] There the centurion found an Alexandrian ship leaving for Italy and put us aboard.

[7] For some days we made little headway, and we had difficulty in making Cnidus. The wind would not allow us to touch there, so we sailed under the lee of Crete off Cape Salmone [8] and struggled along the coast until we came to a place called Fair Havens, near the town of Lasea.

Storm and shipwreck

[9] A great deal of time had been lost, and navigation was already hazardous, since it was now well after the time of the Fast, so Paul gave them this warning, [10] 'Friends, I can see this voyage will be dangerous and that we will run considerable risk of losing not only the cargo and the ship but also our lives as well.' [11] But the centurion took more notice of the captain and the ship's owner than of what Paul was saying; [12] and since the harbour was un-

26b Jr 1:5–8 followed by Is 42:16.

suitable for wintering, the majority were for putting out from there in the hope of wintering at Phoenix—a harbour in Crete, facing south-west and north-west.

¹³ A southerly breeze sprang up and, thinking their objective as good as reached, they weighed anchor and began to sail past Crete, close inshore. ¹⁴ But it was not long before a hurricane, the 'north-easter' as they call it, burst on them from across the island. ¹⁵ The ship was caught and could not keep head to wind, so we had to give way to the wind and let ourselves be driven. ¹⁶ We ran under the lee of a small island called Cauda and managed with some difficulty to bring the ship's boat under control. ¹⁷ Having hauled it up they used it to undergird the ship; then, afraid of running aground on the Syrtis banks, they floated out the sea-anchor and so let themselves drift. ¹⁸ As we were thoroughly storm-bound, the next day they began to jettison the cargo, ¹⁹ and the third day they threw the ship's gear overboard with their own hands. ²⁰ For a number of days both the sun and the stars were invisible and the storm raged unabated until at last we gave up all hope of surviving.

²¹ Then, when they had been without food for a long time, Paul stood up among the men. 'Friends,' he said, 'you should have listened to me and not put out from Crete. You would have spared yourselves all this damage and loss. ²² But now I ask you not to give way to despair. There will be no loss of life at all, only of the ship. ²³ Last night there appeared beside me an angel of the God to whom I belong and whom I serve, ²⁴ and he said, "Do not be afraid, Paul. You are destined to appear before Caesar, and God grants you the safety of all who are sailing with you." ²⁵ So take courage, friends; I trust in God that things will turn out just as I was told; ²⁶ but we are to be stranded on some island.'

²⁷ On the fourteenth night we were being driven one way and another in the Adriatic, when about midnight the crew sensed that land of some sort was near. ²⁸ They took soundings and found twenty fathoms; after a short interval they sounded again and found fifteen fathoms. ²⁹ Then, afraid that we might run aground somewhere on a reef, they dropped four anchors from the stern and prayed for daylight. ³⁰ When the crew tried to escape from the ship and lowered the ship's boat into the sea as though they meant to lay out anchors from the bows, Paul said to the centurion and his men, ³¹ 'Unless those men stay on board you cannot hope to be saved.' ³² So the soldiers cut the boat's ropes and let it drop away.

³³ Just before daybreak Paul urged them all to have something to eat. 'For fourteen days', he said, 'you have been in suspense, going hungry and eating nothing. ³⁴ I urge you to have something to eat; your safety depends on it. Not a hair of any of your heads will be lost.' ³⁵ With these words he took some bread, gave thanks to God in view of them all, broke it and began to eat. ³⁶ They all plucked up courage and took something to eat themselves. ³⁷ In all we were two hundred and seventy-six souls on board that ship. ³⁸ When they had eaten what they wanted they lightened the ship by throwing the corn overboard into the sea.

³⁹ When day came they did not recognise the land, but they could make out a bay with a beach; they planned to run the ship aground on this if they could. ⁴⁰ They slipped the anchors and let them fall into the sea, and at the same time loosened the lashings of the rudders; then, hoisting the foresail to the wind, they headed for the beach. ⁴¹ But the cross-currents carried them into a shoal and the vessel ran aground. The bows were wedged in and stuck fast, while the stern began to break up with the pounding of the waves.

⁴² The soldiers planned to kill the prisoners for fear that any should swim off and escape. ⁴³ But the centurion was determined to bring Paul safely through and would not let them carry out their plan. He gave orders that those who could swim should jump overboard first and so get ashore, ⁴⁴ and the rest follow either on planks or on pieces of wreckage. In this

way it happened that all came safe and sound to land.

Waiting in Malta

28 Once we had come safely through, we discovered that the island was called Malta. ²The inhabitants treated us with unusual kindness. They made us all welcome by lighting a huge fire because it had started to rain and the weather was cold. ³Paul had collected a bundle of sticks and was putting them on the fire when a viper brought out by the heat attached itself to his hand. ⁴When the inhabitants saw the creature hanging from his hand they said to one another, 'That man must be a murderer; he may have escaped the sea, but divine justice would not let him live.' ⁵However, he shook the creature off into the fire and came to no harm, ⁶although they were expecting him at any moment to swell up or drop dead on the spot. After they had waited a long time without seeing anything out of the ordinary happen to him, they changed their minds and began to say he was a god.

⁷In that neighbourhood there were estates belonging to the chief man of the island, whose name was Publius. He received us and entertained us hospitably for three days. ⁸It happened that Publius' father was in bed, suffering from fever and dysentery. Paul went in to see him, and after a prayer he laid his hands on the man and healed him. ⁹When this happened, the other sick people on the island also came and were cured; ¹⁰they honoured us with many marks of respect, and when we sailed they put on board the provisions we needed.

From Malta to Rome

¹¹At the end of three months we set sail in a ship that had wintered in the island; she came from Alexandria and her figurehead was the Twins. ¹²We put in at Syracuse and spent three days there; ¹³from there we followed the coast up to Rhegium. After one day there a south wind sprang up and on the second day we made Puteoli, ¹⁴where we found some brothers and had the great encouragement of staying a week with them. And so we came to Rome.

¹⁵When the brothers there heard about us they came to meet us, as far as the Forum of Appius and the Three Taverns. When Paul saw them he thanked God and took courage. ¹⁶On our arrival in Rome Paul was allowed to stay in lodgings of his own with the soldier who guarded him.

Paul makes contact with the Roman Jews

¹⁷After three days he called together the leading Jews. When they had assembled, he said to them, 'Brothers, although I have done nothing against our people or the customs of our ancestors, I was arrested in Jerusalem and handed over to the Romans. ¹⁸They examined me and would have set me free, since they found me guilty of nothing involving the death penalty; ¹⁹but the Jews lodged an objection, and I was forced to appeal to Caesar, though not because I had any accusation to make against my own nation. ²⁰That is why I have urged you to see me and have a discussion with me, for it is on account of the hope of Israel that I wear this chain.'

²¹They answered, 'We have received no letters from Judaea about you, nor has any of the brothers arrived here with any report or story of anything to your discredit. ²²We think it would be as well to hear your own account of your position; all we know about this sect is that it encounters opposition everywhere.'

Paul's declaration to the Roman Jews

²³So they arranged a day with him and a large number of them visited him at his lodgings. He put his case to them, testifying to the kingdom of God and trying to persuade them about Jesus, arguing from the Law of Moses and the prophets from early morning until evening; ²⁴and some were convinced by what he said, while the rest were sceptical. ²⁵So they disagreed among themselves and, as they

went away, Paul had one last thing to say to them, 'How aptly the Holy Spirit spoke when he told your ancestors through the prophet Isaiah:

26 *Go and say to this people:*
Listen and listen but never understand!
Look and look but never perceive!
27 *This people's heart is torpid,*
their ears dulled, they have shut their
eyes tight,
to avoid using their eyes to see, their ears
to hear,
using their heart to understand,
changing their ways and being healed
by me.[a]

28 'You must realise, then, that this salvation of God has been sent to the gentiles; and they will listen to it.' [29][b]

Epilogue

30 He spent the whole of the two years in his own rented lodging. He welcomed all who came to visit him, 31 proclaiming the kingdom of God and teaching the truth about the Lord Jesus Christ with complete fearlessness and without any hindrance from anyone.

28a Is 6:9–10; cf. 13:47; 18:6.

28b Some MSS add v. 29 'And when he had said this, the Jews left, arguing hotly among themselves.'

ROMANS

Address

1 From Paul, a servant of Christ Jesus, called to be an apostle, [2] set apart for the service of the gospel that God promised long ago through his prophets in the holy scriptures.

[3] This is the gospel concerning his Son who, in terms of human nature [4] was born a descendant of David and who, in terms of the Spirit and of holiness, was designated Son of God in power by resurrection from the dead: Jesus Christ, our Lord, [5] through whom we have received grace and our apostolic mission of winning the obedience of faith among all the nations for the honour of his name. [6] You are among these, and by his call you belong to Jesus Christ. [7] To you all, God's beloved in Rome, called to be his holy people. Grace and peace from God our Father and the Lord Jesus Christ.

Thanksgiving and prayer

[8] First I give thanks to my God through Jesus Christ for all of you because your faith is talked of all over the world. [9] God, whom I serve with my spirit in preaching the gospel of his Son, is my witness that I continually mention you in my prayers, [10] asking always that by some means I may at long last be enabled to visit you, if it is God's will. [11] For I am longing to see you so that I can convey to you some spiritual gift that will be a lasting strength, [12] or rather that we may be strengthened together through our mutual faith, yours and mine. [13] I want you to be quite certain too, brothers, that I have often planned to visit you—though up to the present I have always been prevented—in the hope that I might work as fruitfully among you as I have among

the gentiles elsewhere. [14] I have an obligation to Greeks as well as barbarians, to the educated as well as the ignorant, [15] and hence the eagerness on my part to preach the gospel to you in Rome too.

The theme stated

[16] For I see no reason to be ashamed of the gospel; it is God's power for the salvation of everyone who has faith—Jews first, but Greeks as well— [17] for in it is revealed the saving justice of God: a justice based on faith and addressed to faith. As it says in scripture: *Anyone who is upright through faith will live.*[a]

God's retribution against the gentiles

[18] The retribution of God from heaven is being revealed against the ungodliness and injustice of human beings who in their injustice hold back the truth. [19] For what can be known about God is perfectly plain to them, since God has made it plain to them: [20] ever since the creation of the world, the invisible existence of God and his everlasting power have been clearly seen by the mind's understanding of created things. And so these people have no excuse: [21] they knew God and yet they did not honour him as God or give thanks to him, but their arguments became futile and their uncomprehending minds were darkened. [22] While they claimed to be wise, in fact they were growing so stupid [23] that *they exchanged the glory* of the immortal God *for an imitation,*[b] for the image of a mortal human being, or of birds, or animals, or crawling things.

[24] That is why God abandoned them in their inmost cravings to filthy practices of dis-

1a Hab 2:4 LXX.   *1b* Jr 2:11.

honouring their own bodies— 25because they *exchanged God's truth* for a lie and have worshipped and served the creature instead of the Creator, who is blessed for ever. Amen.

26That is why God abandoned them to degrading passions: 27why their women have exchanged natural intercourse for unnatural practices; and the men, in a similar fashion, too, giving up normal relations with women, are consumed with passion for each other, men doing shameful things with men and receiving in themselves due reward for their perversion.

28In other words, since they would not consent to acknowledge God, God abandoned them to their unacceptable thoughts and indecent behaviour. 29And so now they are steeped in all sorts of injustice, rottenness, greed and malice; full of envy, murder, wrangling, treachery and spite, 30libellers, slanderers, enemies of God, rude, arrogant and boastful, enterprising in evil, rebellious to parents, 31without brains, honour, love or pity. 32They are well aware of God's ordinance: that those who behave like this deserve to die—yet they not only do it, but even applaud others who do the same.

The Jews are not exempt from the retribution of God

2 So no matter who you are, if you pass judgement you have no excuse. It is yourself that you condemn when you judge others, since you behave in the same way as those you are condemning. 2We are well aware that people who behave like that are justly condemned by God. 3But you—when you judge those who behave like this while you are doing the same yourself—do you think you will escape God's condemnation? 4Or are you not disregarding his abundant goodness, tolerance and patience, failing to realise that this generosity of God is meant to bring you to repentance? 5Your stubborn refusal to repent is only storing up retribution for yourself on that Day of retribution when God's just verdicts will be made known. 6*He will repay everyone as their deeds deserve.*[a] 7For those who aimed for glory and honour and immortality by persevering in doing good, there will be eternal life; 8but for those who out of jealousy have taken for their guide not truth but injustice, there will be the fury of retribution. 9Trouble and distress will come to every human being who does evil— Jews first, but Greeks as well; 10glory and honour and peace will come to everyone who does good—Jews first, but Greeks as well. 11*There is no favouritism with God.*[b]

The Law will not save them

12All those who have sinned without the Law will perish without the Law; and those under the Law who have sinned will be judged by the Law. 13For the ones that God will justify are not those who have heard the Law but those who have kept the Law. 14So, when gentiles, not having the Law, still through their own innate sense behave as the Law commands, then, even though they have no Law, they are a law for themselves. 15They can demonstrate the effect of the Law engraved on their hearts, to which their own conscience bears witness; since they are aware of various considerations, some of which accuse them, while others provide them with a defence . . . on the day when, 16according to the gospel that I preach, God, through Jesus Christ, judges all human secrets.

17If you can call yourself a Jew, and you really trust in the Law, and are proud of your God, 18and know his will, and tell right from wrong because you have been taught by the Law; 19if you are confident that you are a guide to the blind and a beacon to those in the dark, 20that you can teach the ignorant and instruct the unlearned because the Law embodies all knowledge and all truth— 21so then, in teaching others, do you teach yourself as well? You preach that there is to be no stealing, but do you steal? 22You say that adultery is forbidden, but do you commit adultery? You detest the worship of objects, but do you desecrate

2a Ps 62:12.   *2b* Dt 10:17.

holy things yourself? ²³If, while you are boasting of the Law, you disobey it, then you are bringing God into contempt. ²⁴As scripture says: *It is your fault that the name of God is held in contempt among the nations.*^c

Circumcision will not save them

²⁵Circumcision has its value if you keep the Law; but if you go on breaking the Law, you are no more circumcised than the uncircumcised. ²⁶And if an uncircumcised man keeps the commands of the Law, will not his uncircumcised state count as circumcision? ²⁷More, the man who, in his native uncircumcised state, keeps the Law, is a condemnation of you, who, by your concentration on the letter and on circumcision, actually break the Law. ²⁸Being a Jew is not only having the outward appearance of a Jew, and circumcision is not only a visible physical operation. ²⁹The real Jew is the one who is inwardly a Jew, and real circumcision is in the heart, a thing not of the letter but of the spirit. He may not be praised by any human being, but he will be praised by God.

God's promises will not save them

3 Is there any benefit, then, in being a Jew? Is there any advantage in being circumcised? ²A great deal, in every way. First of all, it was to the Jews that the message of God was entrusted. ³What if some of them were unfaithful? Do you think their lack of faith could cancel God's faithfulness? ⁴Out of the question! God will always be true even if *no human being can be relied on.*^a As scripture says: *That you may show your saving justice when you pass sentence and your victory may appear when you give judgement.* ⁵But if our injustice serves to bring God's saving justice into view, can we say that God is unjust when—to use human terms—he brings his retribution down on us? ⁶Out of the question! It would mean that God could not be the judge of the world. ⁷You might as well say that if my untruthfulness makes God demonstrate his truthfulness, to his greater glory, then I should not be judged to be a sinner at all. ⁸In this case, the slanderous report some people are spreading would be true, that we teach that one should do evil that good may come of it. In fact such people are justly condemned.

All are guilty

⁹Well: are we any better off? Not at all: we have already indicted Jews and Greeks as being all alike under the dominion of sin. ¹⁰As scripture says:

Not one of them is upright, not a single one,
¹¹ *not a single one is wise,*
not a single one seeks God.
¹² *All have turned away, all alike turned sour,*
not one of them does right, not a single one.
¹³ *Their throats are wide-open graves,*
their tongues seductive.
Viper's venom behind their lips;
¹⁴ *their speech is full of cursing and bitterness.*
¹⁵ *Their feet quick to shed innocent blood,*
¹⁶ *wherever they go there is havoc and ruin.*
¹⁷ *They do not know the way of peace,*
¹⁸ *there is no fear of God before their eyes.*

¹⁹Now we are well aware that whatever the Law says is said for those who are subject to the Law, so that every mouth may be silenced, and the whole world brought under the judgement of God. ²⁰So then, *no human being can be found upright at the tribunal* of God by keeping the Law; all that the Law does is to tell us what is sinful.

The revelation of God's judgement

²¹God's saving justice was witnessed by the Law and the Prophets, but now it has been revealed altogether apart from law: ²²God's saving justice given through faith in Jesus Christ to all who believe. ²³No distinction is made: all have sinned and lack God's glory, ²⁴and all are justified by the free gift of his grace through

2c Ezk 36:20.

3a In vv. 4–20 Paul uses numerous quotations from the Pss and Is 59:7–8.

being set free in Christ Jesus. ²⁵God appointed him as a sacrifice for reconciliation, through faith, by the shedding of his blood, and so showed his justness; first for the past, when sins went unpunished because he held his hand; ²⁶and now again for the present age, to show how he is just and justifies everyone who has faith in Jesus.

What faith does

²⁷So what becomes of our boasts? There is no room for them. On what principle—that only actions count? No; that faith is what counts, ²⁸since, as we see it, a person is justified by faith and not by doing what the Law tells him to do. ²⁹Do you think God is the God only of the Jews, and not of gentiles too? Most certainly of gentiles too, ³⁰since there is only one God; he will justify the circumcised by their faith, and he will justify the uncircumcised through their faith. ³¹Are we saying that the Law has been made pointless by faith? Out of the question; we are placing the Law on its true footing.

Abraham justified by faith

4 Then what do we say about Abraham, the ancestor from whom we are descended physically? ²If Abraham had been justified because of what he had done, then he would have had something to boast about. But not before God: ³does not scripture say: *Abraham put his faith in God and this was reckoned to him as uprightness?*ᵃ ⁴Now, when someone works, the wages for this are not considered as a favour but as due; ⁵however, when someone, without working, puts faith in the one who justifies the godless, it is this faith that is reckoned as uprightness. ⁶David, too, says the same: he calls someone blessed if God attributes uprightness to that person, apart from any action undertaken:

⁷ *How blessed are those whose offence is forgiven,*
whose sin is blotted out.

⁸ *How blessed are those to whom the Lord imputes no guilt.*ᵇ

Justified before circumcision

⁹Is this blessing only for the circumcised, or is it said of the uncircumcised as well? Well, we said of Abraham that *his faith was reckoned to him as uprightness.* ¹⁰Now how did this come about? When he was already circumcised, or before he had been circumcised? Not when he had been circumcised, but while he was still uncircumcised; ¹¹and *circumcision*ᶜ was given to him later, *as a sign* and a guarantee that the faith which he had while still uncircumcised was reckoned to him as uprightness. In this way, Abraham was to be the ancestor of all believers who are uncircumcised, so that they might be reckoned as upright; ¹²as well as the ancestor of those of the circumcision who not only have their circumcision but who also follow our ancestor Abraham along the path of faith that he trod before he was circumcised.

Not justified by obedience to the Law

¹³For the promise to Abraham and his descendants that he should inherit the world was not through the Law, but through the uprightness of faith. ¹⁴For if it is those who live by the Law who will gain the inheritance, faith is worthless and the promise is without force; ¹⁵for the Law produces nothing but God's retribution, and it is only where there is no Law that it is possible to live without breaking the Law. ¹⁶That is why the promise is to faith, so that it comes as a free gift and is secure for all the descendants, not only those who rely on the Law but all those others who rely on the faith of Abraham, the ancestor of us all ¹⁷(as scripture says: *I have made you the father of many nations*). Abraham is our father in the eyes of God, in whom he put his faith, and who brings the dead to life and calls into existence what does not yet exist.

4a Gn 15:6.   4b Ps 32:1–2.

4c Quotations about Abraham from Gn (17:10; 17:5; 15:5; 17:17).

Abraham's faith a model of Christian faith

18 Though there seemed no hope, he hoped and believed that he was to become *father of many nations* in fulfilment of the promise: *Just so will your descendants be.* 19 Even the thought that his body was as good as dead—he was about a hundred years old—and that Sarah's womb was dead too did not shake his faith. 20 Counting on the promise of God, he did not doubt or disbelieve, but drew strength from faith and gave glory to God, 21 fully convinced that whatever God promised he has the power to perform. 22 This is the faith that was *reckoned to him as uprightness.* 23 And the word 'reckoned' in scripture applies not only to him; 24 it is there for our sake too—our faith, too, will be 'reckoned' 25 because we believe in him who raised from the dead our Lord Jesus who was *handed over to death for our sins*ᵈ and raised to life for our justification.

Faith guarantees salvation

5 So then, now that we have been justified by faith, we are at peace with God through our Lord Jesus Christ; 2 it is through him, by faith, that we have been admitted into God's favour in which we are living, and look forward exultantly to God's glory. 3 Not only that; let us exult, too, in our hardships, understanding that hardship develops perseverance, 4 and perseverance develops a tested character, something that gives us hope, 5 and a hope which will not let us down, because the love of God has been poured into our hearts by the Holy Spirit which has been given to us. 6 When we were still helpless, at the appointed time, Christ died for the godless. 7 You could hardly find anyone ready to die even for someone upright; though it is just possible that, for a really good person, someone might undertake to die. 8 So it is proof of God's own love for us, that Christ died for us while we were still sinners. 9 How much more can we be sure, therefore, that, now that we have been justified by his death, we shall be saved through him from the retribution of God. 10 For if, while we were enemies, we were reconciled to God through the death of his Son, how much more can we be sure that, being now reconciled, we shall be saved by his life. 11 What is more, we are filled with exultant trust in God, through our Lord Jesus Christ, through whom we have already gained our reconciliation.

Adam and Jesus Christ

12 Well then; it was through one man that sin *came into the world,*ᵃ and through sin death, and thus death has spread through the whole human race because everyone has sinned. 13 Sin already existed in the world before there was any law, even though sin is not reckoned when there is no law. 14 Nonetheless death reigned over all from Adam to Moses, even over those whose sin was not the breaking of a commandment, as Adam's was. He prefigured the One who was to come . . .

15 There is no comparison between the free gift and the offence. If death came to many through the offence of one man, how much greater an effect the grace of God has had, coming to so many and so plentifully as a free gift through the one man Jesus Christ! 16 Again, there is no comparison between the gift and the offence of one man. One single offence brought condemnation, but now, after many offences, have come the free gift and so acquittal! 17 It was by one man's offence that death came to reign over all, but how much greater the reign in life of those who receive the fullness of grace and the gift of saving justice, through the one man, Jesus Christ. 18 One man's offence brought condemnation on all humanity; and one man's good act has brought justification and life to all humanity. 19 Just as by one man's disobedience many were made sinners, so by one man's obedience are many to be made upright. 20 When law came on the scene, it was to multiply the offences. But however much sin increased, grace was always greater; 21 so that as sin's reign brought death, so grace was to rule through saving jus-

4d Is 53:6. 5a Ws 2:24.

tice that leads to eternal life through Jesus Christ our Lord.

Baptism

6 What should we say then? Should we remain in sin so that grace may be given the more fully? ²Out of the question! We have died to sin; how could we go on living in it? ³You cannot have forgotten that all of us, when we were baptised into Christ Jesus, were baptised into his death. ⁴So by our baptism into his death we were buried with him, so that as Christ was raised from the dead by the Father's glorious power, we too should begin living a new life. ⁵If we have been joined to him by dying a death like his, so we shall be by a resurrection like his; ⁶realising that our former self was crucified with him, so that the self which belonged to sin should be destroyed and we should be freed from the slavery of sin. ⁷Someone who has died, of course, no longer has to answer for sin.

⁸But we believe that, if we died with Christ, then we shall live with him too. ⁹We know that Christ has been raised from the dead and will never die again. Death has no power over him any more. ¹⁰For by dying, he is dead to sin once and for all, and now the life that he lives is life with God. ¹¹In the same way, you must see yourselves as being dead to sin but alive for God in Christ Jesus.

Holiness, not sin, to be the master

¹²That is why you must not allow sin to reign over your mortal bodies and make you obey their desires; ¹³or give any parts of your bodies over to sin to be used as instruments of evil. Instead, give yourselves to God, as people brought to life from the dead, and give every part of your bodies to God to be instruments of uprightness; ¹⁴and then sin will no longer have any power over you—you are living not under law, but under grace.

The Christian is freed from the slavery of sin

¹⁵What is the implication? That we are free to sin, now that we are not under law but under grace? Out of the question! ¹⁶You know well that if you undertake to be somebody's slave and obey him, you are the slave of him you obey: you can be the slave either of sin which leads to death, or of obedience which leads to saving justice. ¹⁷Once you were slaves of sin, but thank God you have given whole-hearted obedience to the pattern of teaching to which you were introduced; ¹⁸and so, being freed from serving sin, you took uprightness as your master. ¹⁹I am putting it in human terms because you are still weak human beings: as once you surrendered yourselves as servants to immorality and to a lawlessness which results in more lawlessness, now you have to surrender yourselves to uprightness which is to result in sanctification.

The reward of sin and the reward of uprightness

²⁰When you were the servants of sin, you felt no obligation to uprightness, ²¹and what did you gain from living like that? Experiences of which you are now ashamed, for that sort of behaviour ends in death. ²²But, now you are set free from sin and bound to the service of God, your gain will be sanctification and the end will be eternal life. ²³For the wage paid by sin is death; the gift freely given by God is eternal life in Christ Jesus our Lord.

The Christian is freed from slavery to the Law

7 As people who are familiar with the Law, brothers, you cannot have forgotten that the law can control a person only during that person's lifetime. ²A married woman, for instance, is bound to her husband by law, as long as he lives, but when her husband dies all her legal obligation to him as husband is ended. ³So if she were to have relations with another man while her husband was still alive, she would be termed an adulteress; but if her husband dies, her legal obligation comes to an end and if she then has relations with another man, that does not make her an adulteress. ⁴In the same way you, my brothers, through the

163 READ ROMANS 6:1–14.

Someone who has died, of course, no longer has to answer for sin.—ROMANS 6:7

FREE NOT TO SIN

After the dignity of our adoption the devil plots more vehemently against us, pining away with envy, when he sees the beauty of the new-born person, earnestly tending towards that heavenly city, from which he fell. And he raises up against us fiery temptations, seeking eagerly to despoil us. But when we are aware of his attacks, we ought to repeat to ourselves the apostolic words, "All of us, when we were baptised into Christ Jesus, were baptised into his death" (Rm 6:3). Now if we have been conformed to his death, sin in us is surely now a corpse, pierced through by the javelin of baptism, as that fornicator was thrust through by the zealous Phinehas (see Nb 25:7–8).

Flee therefore from us, ill-omened one! For you seek to despoil a corpse, one long ago joined to you, but one who long since lost his senses for pleasures. A corpse is not enamored of bodies, a corpse is not captivated by wealth, a corpse slanders not, a corpse lies not, snatches not at what is not its own, reviles not those who encounter it. My way of living is oriented to another life. I have learned to despise worldly things—to pass by the things of earth, to hasten to things of heaven—even as Paul expressly testifies, that the world is crucified to him, and he to the world (see Ga 6:14).

These are the words of a soul truly regenerated. These are the utterances of the newly-baptized person, who remembers his own profession, which he made to God, when the sacrament was administered to him, promising that he would despise for the sake of love towards God all torment and all pleasure alike.   ST. GREGORY OF NYSSA, 330?–395?

YOU WILL FIND THE NEXT READING AT ROMANS 8.

body of Christ have become dead to the Law and so you are able to belong to someone else, that is, to him who was raised from the dead to make us live fruitfully for God. ⁵While we were still living by our natural inclinations, the sinful passions aroused by the Law were working in all parts of our bodies to make us live lives which were fruitful only for death. ⁶But now we are released from the Law, having died to what was binding us, and so we are in a new service, that of the spirit, and not in the old service of a written code.

The function of the Law

⁷What should we say, then? That the Law itself is sin? Out of the question! All the same, if it had not been for the Law, I should not have known what sin was; for instance, I should not have known what it meant to covet if the Law had not said: *You are not to covet.*ᵃ ⁸But, once it found the opportunity through that commandment, sin produced in me all kinds of covetousness; as long as there is no Law, sin is dead.

⁹Once, when there was no Law, I used to be alive; but when the commandment came, sin came to life ¹⁰and I died. The commandment was meant to bring life but I found it brought death, ¹¹because sin, finding its opportunity by means of the commandment, *beguiled*ᵇ me and, by means of it, killed me.

¹²So then, the Law is holy, and what it com-

7a Ex 20:17.   7b Gn 3:13.

mands is holy and upright and good. ¹³Does that mean that something good resulted in my dying? Out of the question! But sin, in order to be identified as sin, caused my death through that good thing, and so it is by means of the commandment that sin shows its unbounded sinful power.

The inward struggle

¹⁴We are well aware that the Law is spiritual: but I am a creature of flesh and blood sold as a slave to sin. ¹⁵I do not understand my own behaviour; I do not act as I mean to, but I do things that I hate. ¹⁶While I am acting as I do not want to, I still acknowledge the Law as good, ¹⁷so it is not myself acting, but the sin which lives in me. ¹⁸And really, I know of nothing good living in me—in my natural self, that is—for though the will to do what is good is in me, the power to do it is not: ¹⁹the good thing I want to do, I never do; the evil thing which I do not want—that is what I do. ²⁰But every time I do what I do not want to, then it is not myself acting, but the sin that lives in me.

²¹So I find this rule: that for me, where I want to do nothing but good, evil is close at my side. ²²In my inmost self I dearly love God's law, ²³but I see that acting on my body there is a different law which battles against the law in my mind. So I am brought to be a prisoner of that law of sin which lives inside my body.

²⁴What a wretched man I am! Who will rescue me from this body doomed to death? ²⁵God—thanks be to him—through Jesus Christ our Lord.

So it is that I myself with my mind obey the law of God, but in my disordered nature I obey the law of sin.

The life of the spirit

8 Thus, condemnation will never come to those who are in Christ Jesus, ²because the law of the Spirit which gives life in Christ Jesus has set you free from the law of sin and death. ³What the Law could not do because of the weakness of human nature, God did, sending his own Son in the same human nature as any sinner to be a sacrifice for sin, and condemning sin in that human nature. ⁴This was so that the Law's requirements might be fully satisfied in us as we direct our lives not by our natural inclinations but by the Spirit. ⁵Those who are living by their natural inclinations have their minds on the things human nature desires; those who live in the Spirit have their minds on spiritual things. ⁶And human nature has nothing to look forward to but death, while the Spirit looks forward to life and peace, ⁷because the outlook of disordered human nature is opposed to God, since it does not submit to God's Law, and indeed it cannot, ⁸and those who live by their natural inclinations can never be pleasing to God. ⁹You, however, live not by your natural inclinations, but by the Spirit, since the Spirit of God has made a home in you. Indeed, anyone who does not have the Spirit of Christ does not belong to him. ¹⁰But when Christ is in you, the body is dead because of sin but the spirit is alive because you have been justified; ¹¹and if the Spirit of him who raised Jesus from the dead has made his home in you, then he who raised Christ Jesus from the dead will give life to your own mortal bodies through his Spirit living in you.

¹²So then, my brothers, we have no obligation to human nature to be dominated by it. ¹³If you do live in that way, you are doomed to die; but if by the Spirit you put to death the habits originating in the body, you will have life.

Children of God

¹⁴All who are guided by the Spirit of God are sons of God; ¹⁵for what you received was not the spirit of slavery to bring you back into fear; you received the Spirit of adoption, enabling us to cry out, 'Abba, Father!' ¹⁶The Spirit himself joins with our spirit to bear witness that we are children of God. ¹⁷And if we are children, then we are heirs, heirs of God and joint-

164 READ ROMANS 8:1–13.

Those who live by their natural inclinations can never be pleasing to God.—ROMANS 8:8

UPROOTING EVIL DESIRES

Let us learn self-control while we have time. Why do we neglect ourselves? . . . God knows I am frightened by our imperviousness. We who can be saved, and do not even desire it. For we can cut off our unruly desires when they are newly born and we don't think about it; we allow them to grow up and harden against us, so that we make the last evil greater than the first. . . .

   One of the great old men was at recreation with his disciples in a place where there were cypresses of different shapes and sizes, some large, some small. And he said to one of his disciples, "Pull up that cypress over there." It was a very small one and immediately the disciple pulled it up with one hand. Then the old man showed him another one, larger than the first, and he said, "Pull up that one." Working it backwards and forwards with both hands, he pulled it up. . . . Then he showed him an even larger one and with much more labor, straining backwards and forwards and sweating profusely, he finally lifted that one too. The old man showed him a still larger one, but for all his energy and sweating he could not pull it up. . . . Then the old man said to all the brothers, "So it is with our evil desires: insofar as they are small to start with, we can, if we want to, cut them off with ease. If we neglect them as mere trifles they harden, and the more they harden, the more labor is needed to get rid of them. But if they grow to any degree of maturity inside us, we shall no longer be able to remove them from ourselves no matter how we labor unless we have the help of the saints interceding for us with God." St. Dorotheos of Gaza, Sixth Century

YOU WILL FIND THE NEXT READING AT ROMANS 12:1.

heirs with Christ, provided that we share his suffering, so as to share his glory.

Glory as our destiny

18 In my estimation, all that we suffer in the present time is nothing in comparison with the glory which is destined to be disclosed for us, 19 for the whole creation is waiting with eagerness for the children of God to be revealed. 20 It was not for its own purposes that creation had frustration imposed on it, but for the purposes of him who imposed it— 21 with the intention that the whole creation itself might be freed from its slavery to corruption and brought into the same glorious freedom as the children of God. 22 We are well aware that the whole creation, until this time, has been groaning in labour pains. 23 And not only that: we too, who have the first-fruits of the Spirit, even we are groaning inside ourselves, waiting with eagerness for our bodies to be set free. 24 In hope, we already have salvation; in hope, not visibly present, or we should not be hoping—nobody goes on hoping for something which is already visible. 25 But having this hope for what we cannot yet see, we are able to wait for it with persevering confidence.

   26 And as well as this, the Spirit too comes to help us in our weakness, for, when we do not know how to pray properly, then the Spirit personally makes our petitions for us in groans

that cannot be put into words; 27 and he who can see into all hearts knows what the Spirit means because the prayers that the Spirit makes for God's holy people are always in accordance with the mind of God.

God has called us to share his glory

28 We are well aware that God works with those who love him, those who have been called in accordance with his purpose, and turns everything to their good. 29 He decided beforehand who were the ones destined to be moulded to the pattern of his Son, so that he should be the eldest of many brothers; 30 it was those so destined that he called; those that he called, he justified, and those that he has justified he has brought into glory.

A hymn to God's love

31 After saying this, what can we add? If God is for us, who can be against us? 32 Since he did not spare his own Son, but gave him up for the sake of all of us, then can we not expect that with him he will freely give us all his gifts? 33 Who can bring any accusation against those that God has chosen? *When God grants saving justice* 34 *who can condemn?*ᵃ Are we not sure that it is Christ Jesus, who died—yes and more, who was raised from the dead and is at God's right hand—and who is adding his plea for us? 35 Can anything cut us off from the love of Christ—can hardships or distress, or persecution, or lack of food and clothing, or threats or violence; 36 as scripture says:

> For your sake we are being massacred all
>   day long,
>   treated as sheep to be slaughtered?ᵇ

37 No; we come through all these things triumphantly victorious, by the power of him who loved us. 38 For I am certain of this: neither death nor life, nor angels, nor principalities, nothing already in existence and nothing still to come, nor any power, 39 nor the heights nor the depths, nor any created thing whatever, will be able to come between us and the love of God, known to us in Christ Jesus our Lord.

The privileges of Israelᵃ

9 This is the truth and I am speaking in Christ, without pretence, as my conscience testifies for me in the Holy Spirit; 2 there is great sorrow and unremitting agony in my heart: 3 I could pray that I myself might be accursed and cut off from Christ, if this could benefit the brothers who are my own flesh and blood. 4 They are Israelites; it was they who were adopted as children, the glory was theirs and the covenants; to them were given the Law and the worship of God and the promises. 5 To them belong the fathers and out of them, so far as physical descent is concerned, came Christ who is above all, God, blessed for ever. Amen.

God has kept his promise

6 It is not that God's promise has failed. Not all born Israelites belong to Israel, 7 and not all the descendants of Abraham count as his children, for

> Isaac is the one through whom your Name
>   will be carried on.

8 That is, it is not by being children through physical descent that people become children of God; it is the children of the promise that are counted as the heirs. 9 The actual words of the promise were: *I shall come back to you at this season, and Sarah will have a son.* 10 Even more to the point is what was said to Rebecca when she was pregnant by our ancestor, Isaac, 11 before her children were born, so that neither had yet done anything either good or bad, but in order that it should be God's choice which prevailed 12 —not human merit, but his call—she was told: *the elder one will serve the younger.* 13 Or as scripture says elsewhere: *I loved Jacob but hated Esau.*

8a Is 50:8.   8b Ps 44:22.

9a The quotations in chh. 9–11 are too frequent to be placed.

God is not unjust

14 What should we say, then? That God is unjust? Out of the question! 15 For speaking to Moses, he said: *I am gracious to those to whom I am gracious and I take pity on those on whom I take pity.* 16 So it is not a matter of what any person wants or what any person does, but only of God having mercy. 17 Scripture says to Pharaoh: *I raised you up for this reason,* to display my power in you and to have my name talked of throughout the world. 18 In other words, if God wants to show mercy on someone, he does so, and if he wants to harden someone's heart, he does so.

19 Then you will ask me, 'How then can he ever blame anyone, since no one can oppose his will?' 20 But you—who do you think you, a human being, are, to answer back to God? *Something that was made, can it say to its maker: why did you make me* this shape? 21 A potter surely has the right over his clay to make out of the same lump either a pot for special use or one for ordinary use.

22 But suppose that God, although all the time he wanted to reveal his retribution and demonstrate his power, has with great patience gone on putting up with those who are the instruments of his retribution and designed to be destroyed; 23 so that he may make known the glorious riches ready for the people who are the instruments of his faithful love and were long ago prepared for that glory. 24 We are that people, called by him not only out of the Jews but out of the gentiles too.

All has been foretold in the Old Testament

25 Just as he says in the book of Hosea: *I shall tell those who were not my people, 'You are my people,' and I shall take pity on those on whom I had no pity.* 26 *And in the very place where they were told, 'You are not my people,' they will be told that they are 'children of the living God'.* 27 And about Israel, this is what Isaiah cried out: *Though the people of Israel are like the sand of the sea, only a remnant will be saved;* 28 *for without hesitation or delay the Lord will execute his sentence on the earth.* 29 As Isaiah foretold: *Had the Lord Sabaoth not left us a few survivors, we should be like Sodom, we should be the same as Gomorrah.*

30 What should we say, then? That the gentiles, although they were not looking for saving justice, found it, and this was the saving justice that comes of faith; 31 while Israel, looking for saving justice by law-keeping, did not succeed in fulfilling the Law. 32 And why? Because they were trying to find it in actions and not in faith, and so they stumbled over the *stumbling-stone*— 33 as it says in scripture: *Now I am laying in Zion a stumbling-stone, a rock to trip people up; but he who relies on this will not be brought to disgrace.*

Israel fails to see that it is God who makes us holy

10 Brothers, my dearest wish and my prayer to God is for them, that they may be saved. 2 I readily testify to their fervour for God, but it is misguided. 3 Not recognising God's saving justice they have tried to establish their own, instead of submitting to the saving justice of God. 4 But the Law has found its fulfilment in Christ so that all who have faith will be justified.

The testimony of Moses

5 Moses writes of the saving justice that comes by the Law and says that *whoever complies with it will find life in it.* 6 But the saving justice of faith says this: *Do not think in your heart, 'Who will go up to heaven?'* — 7 that is to bring Christ down; or *'Who will go down to the depths?'* — that is to bring Christ back from the dead. 8 What does it say, then? *The word is very near to you; it is in your mouth and in your heart,* that is, the word of faith, the faith which we preach, 9 that if you declare with your mouth that Jesus is Lord, and if you believe with your heart that God raised him from the dead, then you will be saved. 10 It is by believing with the heart that you are justified, and by making the declaration with your lips that you are saved. 11 When scripture says: *No one who relies on*

this will be brought to disgrace, ¹²it makes no distinction between Jew and Greek: the same Lord is the Lord of all, and his generosity is offered to all who appeal to him, ¹³for *all who call on the name of the Lord will be saved.*

Israel has no excuse

¹⁴How then are they to call on him if they have not come to believe in him? And how can they believe in him if they have never heard of him? And how will they hear of him unless there is a preacher for them? ¹⁵And how will there be preachers if they are not sent? As scripture says: *How beautiful are the feet of the messenger of good news.*

¹⁶But in fact they have not all responded to the good news. As Isaiah says: *Lord, who has given credence to what they have heard from us?* ¹⁷But it is in that way faith comes, from hearing, and that means hearing the word of Christ.

¹⁸Well then, I say, is it possible that they have not heard? Indeed they have: *in the entire earth their voice stands out, their message reaches the whole world.* ¹⁹Well, another question, then: is it possible that Israel did not understand? In the first place Moses said: *I shall rouse you to jealousy with a non-people, I shall exasperate you with a stupid nation.* ²⁰And Isaiah is even bold enough to say: *I have let myself be found by those who did not seek me; I have let myself be seen by those who did not consult me;* ²¹and referring to Israel, he says: *All day long I have been stretching out my hands to a disobedient and rebellious people.*

The remnant of Israel

11 What I am saying is this: is it possible that *God abandoned his people?* Out of the question! I too am an Israelite, descended from Abraham, of the tribe of Benjamin. ²God never abandoned his own people to whom, ages ago, he had given recognition. Do you not remember what scripture says about Elijah and how he made a complaint to God against Israel: ³*Lord, they have put your prophets to the sword, torn down your altars. I am*

the only one left, and now they want to kill me? ⁴And what was the prophetic answer given? *I have spared* for myself *seven thousand men that have not bent the knee to Baal.* ⁵In the same way, then, in our own time, there is a remnant, set aside by grace. ⁶And since it is by grace, it cannot now be by good actions, or grace would not be grace at all!

⁷What follows? Israel failed to find what it was seeking; only those who were chosen found it and the rest had their minds hardened; ⁸just as it says in scripture: *God has infused them with a spirit of lethargy; until today they have not eyes to see or ears to hear.* ⁹David too says: *May their own table prove a trap for them,* a pitfall and *a snare; let that be their retribution.* ¹⁰*May their eyes grow so dim they cannot see, and their backs be bent for ever.*

The Jews to be restored in the future

¹¹What I am saying is this: Was this stumbling to lead to their final downfall? Out of the question! On the contrary, their failure has brought salvation for the gentiles, in order to stir them to envy. ¹²And if their fall has proved a great gain to the world, and their loss has proved a great gain to the gentiles—how much greater a gain will come when all is restored to them!

¹³Let me say then to you gentiles that, as far as I am an apostle to the gentiles, I take pride in this work of service; ¹⁴and I want it to be the means of rousing to envy the people who are my own blood-relations and so of saving some of them. ¹⁵Since their rejection meant the reconciliation of the world, do you know what their re-acceptance will mean? Nothing less than life from the dead!

The Jews are still the chosen people

¹⁶When the first-fruits are made holy, so is the whole batch; and if the root is holy, so are the branches. ¹⁷Now suppose that some branches were broken off, and you are wild olive, grafted among the rest to share with the others the rich sap of the olive tree; ¹⁸then it is not for you to consider yourself superior to the other

branches; and if you start feeling proud, think: it is not you that sustain the root, but the root that sustains you. ¹⁹You will say, 'Branches were broken off on purpose for me to be grafted in.' True; ²⁰they through their unbelief were broken off, and you are established through your faith. So it is not pride that you should have, but fear: ²¹if God did not spare the natural branches, he might not spare you either. ²²Remember God's severity as well as his goodness: his severity to those who fell, and his goodness to you as long as you persevere in it; if not, you too will be cut off. ²³And they, if they do not persevere in their unbelief, will be grafted in; for it is within the power of God to graft them back again. ²⁴After all, if you, cut off from what was by nature a wild olive, could then be grafted unnaturally on to a cultivated olive, how much easier will it be for them, the branches that naturally belong there, to be grafted on to the olive tree which is their own.

The conversion of the Jews

²⁵I want you to be quite certain, brothers, of this mystery, to save you from *congratulating yourselves on your own good sense:* part of Israel had its mind hardened, but only until the gentiles have wholly come in; ²⁶and this is how all Israel will be saved. As scripture says:

> *From Zion will come the Redeemer,*
> *he will remove godlessness from Jacob.*
> ²⁷ *And this will be my covenant with them,*
> *when I take their sins away.*

²⁸As regards the gospel, they are enemies, but for your sake; but as regards those who are God's choice, they are still well loved for the sake of their ancestors. ²⁹There is no change of mind on God's part about the gifts he has made or of his choice.

³⁰Just as you were in the past disobedient to God but now you have been shown mercy, through their disobedience; ³¹so in the same way they are disobedient now, so that through the mercy shown to you they too will receive mercy. ³²God has imprisoned all human beings in their own disobedience only to show mercy to them all.

A hymn to God's mercy and wisdom

³³How rich and deep are the wisdom and the knowledge of God! We cannot reach to the root of his decisions or his ways. ³⁴*Who has ever known the mind of the Lord? Who has ever been his adviser?* ³⁵*Who has given anything to him, so that his presents come only as a debt returned?* ³⁶Everything there is comes from him and is caused by him and exists for him. To him be glory for ever! Amen.

Spiritual worship

12 I urge you, then, brothers, remembering the mercies of God, to offer your bodies as a living sacrifice, dedicated and acceptable to God; that is the kind of worship for you, as sensible people. ²Do not model your behaviour on the contemporary world, but let the renewing of your minds transform you, so that you may discern for yourselves what is the will of God—what is good and acceptable and mature.

Humility and charity

³And through the grace that I have been given, I say this to every one of you: never pride yourself on being better than you really are, but think of yourself dispassionately, recognising that God has given to each one his measure of faith. ⁴Just as each of us has various parts in one body, and the parts do not all have the same function: ⁵in the same way, all of us, though there are so many of us, make up one body in Christ, and as different parts we are all joined to one another. ⁶Then since the gifts that we have differ according to the grace that was given to each of us: if it is a gift of prophecy, we should prophesy as much as our faith tells us; ⁷if it is a gift of practical service, let us devote ourselves to serving; if it is teaching, to teaching; ⁸if it is encouraging, to encouraging. When you give, you should give generously from the heart; if you are put in

165 READ ROMANS 12:1–2.

Offer your bodies as a living sacrifice, dedicated and acceptable to God.—ROMANS 12:1

SACRIFICING OURSELVES TO GOD

Reason teaches that we should condemn this present world with our whole souls and offer to God the daily sacrifice of his Body and Blood. For the Eucharistic sacrifice, which in mystery renews for us the death of the Son of God, saves our souls from everlasting damnation. When we participate at Mass we should also sacrifice ourselves to almighty God with heartfelt contrition. For when we celebrate the mystery of our Lord's passion, we ought to imitate it. If we also offer ourselves to him in sacrifice, then the Eucharist shall truly be a sacrifice to God for us.

After we have spent some time in prayer—as much as we can by God's grace—we must be careful that we keep our mind fixed on him. We must not let any idle thoughts lead us astray, nor any foolishness captivate our hearts. We don't want any such passing thoughts to rob our souls of all that our contrition has gained for us. Remember that Hannah deserved to obtain what she craved at God's hands because after her tears she continued to pray conscientiously. Scripture says of her: "And her looks were not any more directed to divers things" (see 1 S 1:18). Because Hannah did not forget what she desired, she was not deprived of the gift she requested.   ST. GREGORY THE GREAT, 540?–604

YOU WILL FIND THE NEXT READING AT ROMANS 12:3.

charge, you must be conscientious; if you do works of mercy, let it be because you enjoy doing them. ⁹Let love be without any pretence. Avoid what is evil; stick to what is good. ¹⁰In brotherly love let your feelings of deep affection for one another come to expression and regard others as more important than yourself. ¹¹In the service of the Lord, work not halfheartedly but with conscientiousness and an eager spirit. ¹²Be joyful in hope, persevere in hardship; keep praying regularly; ¹³share with any of God's holy people who are in need; look for opportunities to be hospitable.

Charity to everyone, including enemies

¹⁴Bless your persecutors; never curse them, bless them. ¹⁵Rejoice with others when they rejoice, and be sad with those in sorrow. ¹⁶Give the same consideration to all others alike. Pay no regard to social standing, but meet humble people on their own terms. *Do*

not congratulate yourself on your own wisdom.[a] ¹⁷Never pay back evil with evil, but *bear in mind the ideals that all regard with respect.* ¹⁸As much as possible, and to the utmost of your ability, be at peace with everyone. ¹⁹Never try to get revenge: leave that, my dear friends, to the Retribution. As scripture says: *Vengeance is mine—I will pay them back,* the Lord promises. ²⁰And more: *If your enemy is hungry, give him something to eat; if thirsty, something to drink. By this, you will be heaping red-hot coals on his head.* ²¹Do not be mastered by evil, but master evil with good.

Submission to civil authority

13 Everyone is to obey the governing authorities, because there is no authority except from God and so whatever authorities exist have been appointed by God. ²So anyone

12a Pr 3:7, followed by Lv 19:18; Pr 25:21–22.

166 READ ROMANS 12:3–13.

If you do works of mercy, let it be because you enjoy doing them.—ROMANS 12:8

A HEART FOR MERCY

O Most Holy Trinity! As many times as I breathe, as many times as my heart beats, as many times as my blood pulsates through my body, so many thousand times do I want to glorify your mercy.

I want to be completely transformed into your mercy and to be your living reflection, O Lord. May the greatest of all divine attributes, that of your unfathomable mercy, pass through my heart and soul to my neighbor.

Help me, O Lord, that my eyes may be merciful, so that I may never suspect or judge from appearances, but look for what is beautiful in my neighbor's souls and come to their rescue.

Help me, that my ears may be merciful, so that I may give heed to my neighbors' needs and not be indifferent to their pains and moanings.

Help me, O Lord, that my tongue may be merciful, so that I should never speak negatively of my neighbor, but have a word of comfort and forgiveness for all.

Help me, O Lord, that my hands may be merciful and filled with good deeds, so that I may do only good to my neighbor and take upon myself the more difficult and toilsome tasks.

Help me, that my feet may be merciful, so that I may hurry to assist my neighbor, overcoming my own fatigue and weariness. My true rest is in the service of my neighbor.

Help me, O Lord, that my heart may be merciful so that I myself may feel all the sufferings of my neighbor. I will refuse my heart to no one. I will be sincere even with those who, I know, will abuse my kindness. And I will lock myself up in the most merciful heart of Jesus. I will bear my own suffering in silence. May Your mercy, O Lord, rest upon us. ST. FAUSTINA, 1905–1938

YOU WILL FIND THE NEXT READING AT ROMANS 13:8.

who disobeys an authority is rebelling against God's ordinance; and rebels must expect to receive the condemnation they deserve. ³ Magistrates bring fear not to those who do good, but to those who do evil. So if you want to live with no fear of authority, live honestly and you will have its approval; ⁴ it is there to serve God for you and for your good. But if you do wrong, then you may well be afraid; because it is not for nothing that the symbol of authority is the sword: it is there to serve God, too, as his avenger, to bring retribution to wrongdoers. ⁵ You must be obedient, therefore, not only because of this retribution, but also for conscience's sake. ⁶ And this is why you should pay taxes, too, because the authorities are all serving God as his agents, even while they are busily occupied with that particular task. ⁷ Pay to each one what is due to each: taxes to the one to whom tax is due, tolls to the one to whom tolls are due, respect to the one to whom respect is due, honour to the one to whom honour is due.

Love and Law

⁸ The only thing you should owe to anyone is love for one another, for to love the other person is to fulfil the law. ⁹ All these: *You shall not*

167 READ ROMANS 13:8–14.

Love can cause no harm to your neighbour, and so love is the fulfilment of the Law.
—ROMANS 13:10

LOVE YOUR NEIGHBOR

In this selection the Lord teaches St. Catherine the importance of loving our neighbor:

"You are obliged to love your neighbor as yourself (see Mt 22:39). And loving him, you ought to help him by praying for him, counseling him, and assisting him both spiritually and temporally. You ought to serve his needs at least with your goodwill if you have nothing else. Therefore, a person who fails to love his neighbor does not help him and so does himself an injury. He cuts himself off from grace. And he injures his neighbor by depriving him of the benefit of the prayers and of the sweet desires that he is bound to offer to me for him.

"Every act of help that a person performs should proceed from the charity that he has through loving me. Also, every evil a person does comes through his neighbor because if he does not love me he cannot have charity toward others. So all evils derive from the soul's failing to love me and her neighbor.

"Since a person who fails to love others does no good, it follows that he must do evil. First of all he harms himself, and then he damages his neighbor. He does not harm me because no evil can touch me except as I count as done to me the evil he does to himself. He injures himself with sin that deprives him of grace. . . . He hurts his neighbor by not paying him the debt of that he owes him. Love should cause him to help his neighbor by means of prayer and holy desire offered to me for him.

"This assistance is owed generally to every rational creature, but particularly to those nearest to you that you see all the time. You are all obliged to help one another by word, teaching, the example of good works, and in every other respect in which you see your neighbor to be in need."

ST. CATHERINE OF SIENA, 1347–1380

YOU WILL FIND THE NEXT READING AT ROMANS 14.

commit adultery, You shall not kill, You shall not steal, You shall not covet, and all the other commandments that there are, are summed up in this single phrase: *You must love your neighbour as yourself.*[a] [10] Love can cause no harm to your neighbour, and so love is the fulfilment of the Law.

Children of the light

[11] Besides, you know the time has come; the moment is here for you to stop sleeping and wake up, because by now our salvation is nearer than when we first began to believe. [12] The night is nearly over, daylight is on the way; so let us throw off everything that belongs to the darkness and equip ourselves for the light. [13] Let us live decently, as in the light of day; with no orgies or drunkenness, no promiscuity or licentiousness, and no wrangling or jealousy. [14] Let your armour be the

13a Ex 20:13–17 summed up in Lv 19:18.

168 READ ROMANS 14:1–13.

Let each of them be fully convinced in his own mind.—ROMANS 14:5

AGAINST MORAL RELATIVISM

Some think that what the Apostle says, *Let each one abound in his own sense,* was said in such a way as if he meant to say: "It suffices unto righteousness for each one to do those things that appear best to himself." But it is by no means to be understood in this way. For what if there is a heretic who thinks himself to be Catholic, if there is someone living wickedly who supposes that he is walking in the right way of truth? Will labor or faith of that sort suffice for him as a work of righteousness through which he may come to salvation, especially since the Apostle does not say in the indicative mood, "He abounds" but in the imperative, *Let each one abound in his own sense?* Therefore, he was commanding that if we cannot grasp the more sublime secrets of the divine mysteries, we should nevertheless humbly and devoutly serve the Lord in those things that we understand and perceive to be truly believed and confessed. In this way what he commanded will be fulfilled—that each one should abound in his own sense—when we take care to persevere abundantly by good works in those things which we have learned from the great teachers ought to be believed or done, in order that by performing those things that we have come to understand, we may also merit to apprehend sublimer things that we have not yet come to understand.

Hence, he properly adds: *If you discern something otherwise, this also God will reveal to you* (see Ph 3:15), that is: "If through charity you put into operation the good things that you know, then should you discern something in a way that is other than seemly, divine grace will eventually grant you a right understanding of this as well."   ST. BEDE, THE VENERABLE, 673–735

YOU WILL FIND THE NEXT READING AT 1 CORINTHIANS 2.

Lord Jesus Christ, and stop worrying about how your disordered natural inclinations may be fulfilled.

Charity towards the scrupulous

14 Give a welcome to anyone whose faith is not strong, but do not get into arguments about doubtful points. ²One person may have faith enough to eat any kind of food; another, less strong, will eat only vegetables. ³Those who feel free to eat freely are not to condemn those who are unwilling to eat freely; nor must the person who does not eat freely pass judgement on the one who does— because God has welcomed him. ⁴And who are you, to sit in judgement over somebody else's servant? Whether he deserves to be upheld or to fall is for his own master to decide; and he shall be upheld, for the Lord has power to uphold him. ⁵One person thinks that some days are holier than others, and another thinks them all equal. Let each of them be fully convinced in his own mind. ⁶The one who makes special observance of a particular day observes it in honour of the Lord. So the one who eats freely, eats in honour of the Lord, making his thanksgiving to God; and the one who does not, abstains from eating in honour of the Lord and makes his thanksgiving to God. ⁷For none of us lives for himself and none of

us dies for himself; [8] while we are alive, we are living for the Lord, and when we die, we die for the Lord: and so, alive or dead, we belong to the Lord. [9] It was for this purpose that Christ both died and came to life again: so that he might be Lord of both the dead and the living. [10] Why, then, does one of you make himself judge over his brother, and why does another among you despise his brother? All of us will have to stand in front of the judgement-seat of God: [11] as scripture says: *By my own life says the Lord, every knee shall bow before me, every tongue shall give glory to God.*[a] [12] It is to God, then, that each of us will have to give an account of himself.

[13] Let us each stop passing judgement, therefore, on one another and decide instead that none of us will place obstacles in any brother's way, or anything that can bring him down. [14] I am sure, and quite convinced in the Lord Jesus, that no food is unclean in itself; it is only if someone classifies any kind of food as unclean, then for him it is unclean. [15] And indeed, if through any kind of food you are causing offence to a brother, then you are no longer being guided by love. You are not to let the food that you eat cause the ruin of anyone for whom Christ died. [16] A privilege of yours must not be allowed to give rise to harmful talk; [17] for it is not eating and drinking that make the kingdom of God, but the saving justice, the peace and the joy brought by the Holy Spirit. [18] It is the person who serves Christ in these things that will be approved by God and respected by everyone. [19] So then, let us be always seeking the ways which lead to peace and the ways in which we can support one another. [20] Do not wreck God's work for the sake of food. Certainly all foods are clean; but all the same, any kind can be evil for someone to whom it is an offence to eat it. [21] It is best to abstain from eating any meat, or drinking any wine, or from any other activity which might cause a brother to fall away, or to be scandalised, or to weaken.

[22] Within yourself, before God, hold on to what you already believe. Blessed is the person whose principles do not condemn his practice. [23] But anyone who eats with qualms of conscience is condemned, because this eating does not spring from faith—and every action which does not spring from faith is sin.

15 It is for us who are strong to bear with the susceptibilities of the weaker ones, and not please ourselves. [2] Each of us must consider his neighbour's good, so that we support one another. [3] Christ did not indulge his own feelings, either; indeed, as scripture says: *The insults of those who insult you fall on me.*[a] [4] And all these things which were written so long ago were written so that we, learning perseverance and the encouragement which the scriptures give, should have hope. [5] Now the God of perseverance and encouragement give you all the same purpose, following the example of Christ Jesus, [6] so that you may together give glory to the God and Father of our Lord Jesus Christ with one heart.

[7] Accept one another, then, for the sake of God's glory, as Christ accepted you. [8] I tell you that Christ's work was to serve the circumcised, fulfilling the truthfulness of God by carrying out the promises made to the fathers, [9] and his work was also for the gentiles, so that they should give glory to God for his faithful love; as scripture says: *For this I shall praise you among the nations and sing praise to your name.*[b] [10] And in another place it says: *Nations, rejoice, with his people,* [11] and in another place again: *Praise the Lord, all nations, extol him, all peoples.* [12] And in Isaiah, it says: *The root of Jesse will appear, he who rises up to rule the nations, and in him the nations will put their hope.*

[13] May the God of hope fill you with all joy and peace in your faith, so that in the power of the Holy Spirit you may be rich in hope.

Paul's ministry

[14] My brothers, I am quite sure that you, in particular, are full of goodness, fully in-

14a Is 45:23.   *15a* Ps 69:9.

15b Ps 18:49, followed by Dt 32:43; Ps 117:1; Is 11:10.

structed and capable of correcting each other. [15] But I have special confidence in writing on some points to you, to refresh your memories, because of the grace that was given to me by God. [16] I was given grace to be a minister of Christ Jesus to the gentiles, dedicated to offer them the gospel of God, so that gentiles might become an acceptable offering, sanctified by the Holy Spirit.

[17] So I can be proud, in Christ Jesus, of what I have done for God. [18] Of course I can dare to speak only of the things which Christ has done through me to win the allegiance of the gentiles, using what I have said and done, [19] by the power of signs and wonders, by the power of the Spirit of God. In this way, from Jerusalem and all round, even as far as Illyricum, I have fully carried out the preaching of the gospel of Christ; [20] and what is more, it has been my rule to preach the gospel only where the name of Christ has not already been heard, for I do not build on another's foundations; [21] in accordance with scripture: *Those who have never been told about him will see him, and those who have never heard about him will understand.*[c]

Paul's plans[d]

[22] That is why I have been so often prevented from coming to see you; [23] now, however, as there is nothing more to keep me in these parts, I hope, after longing for many years past to visit you, to see you when I am on the way to Spain— [24] and after enjoying at least something of your company, to be sent on my way with your support. [25] But now I have undertaken to go to Jerusalem in the service of the holy people of God there, [26] since Macedonia and Achaia have chosen to make a generous contribution to the poor among God's holy people at Jerusalem.

[27] Yes, they chose to; not that they did not owe it to them. For if the gentiles have been given a share in their spiritual possessions, then in return to give them help with material possessions is repaying a debt to them. [28] So when I have done this, and given this harvest into their possession, I shall visit you on the way to Spain. [29] I am sure that, when I do come to you, I shall come with the fullest blessing of Christ.

[30] Meanwhile I urge you, brothers, by our Lord Jesus Christ and by the love of the Spirit, that in your prayers to God for me you exert yourselves to help me; [31] praying that I may escape the unbelievers in Judaea, and that the aid I am carrying to Jerusalem will be acceptable to God's holy people. [32] Then I shall come to you, if God wills, for a happy time of relaxation in your company. [33] The God of peace be with you all. Amen.

Greetings and good wishes[a]

16 I commend to you our sister Phoebe, a deaconess of the church at Cenchreae; [2] give her, in the Lord, a welcome worthy of God's holy people, and help her with whatever she needs from you—she herself has come to the help of many people, including myself.

[3] My greetings to Prisca and Aquila, my fellow-workers in Christ Jesus, [4] who risked their own necks to save my life; to them, thanks not only from me, but from all the churches among the gentiles; [5] and my greetings to the church at their house.

Greetings to my dear friend Epaenetus, the first of Asia's offerings to Christ. [6] Greetings to Mary, who worked so hard for you. [7] Greetings to those outstanding apostles, Andronicus and Junias, my kinsmen and fellow-prisoners, who were in Christ before me. [8] Greetings to Ampliatus, my dear friend in the Lord. [9] Greetings to Urban, my fellow-worker in Christ, and to my dear friend Stachys. [10] Greetings to Apelles, proved servant of Christ. Greetings to all the household of Aristobulus. [11] Greetings to my kinsman, Herodion, and greetings to those who belong to the Lord in the household of Narcissus. [12] Greetings to Tryphaena and Tryphosa who work hard in the Lord; greetings to my dear friend

15c Is 52:15.

15d We do not know whether Paul completed this journey.

16a vv. 1–23 possibly formed no part of the original letter.

Persis, also a very hard worker in the Lord. [13]Greetings to Rufus, chosen servant of the Lord, and to his mother—a mother to me too. [14]Greetings to Asyncritus, Phlegon, Hermes, Patrobas, Hermas, and the brothers who are with them. [15]Greetings to Philologus and Julia, Nereus and his sister, and Olympas and all God's holy people who are with them. [16]Greet each other with the holy kiss. All the churches of Christ send their greetings.

A warning and first postscript

[17]I urge you, brothers, be on your guard against the people who are out to stir up disagreements and bring up difficulties against the teaching which you learnt. Avoid them. [18]People of that sort are servants not of our Lord Christ, but of their own greed; and with talk that sounds smooth and reasonable they deceive the minds of the unwary. [19]Your obedience has become known to everyone, and I am very pleased with you for it; but I should want you to be learned only in what is good, and unsophisticated about all that is evil. [20]The God of peace will soon crush Satan under your feet. The grace of our Lord Jesus Christ be with you.

Last greetings and second postscript

[21]Timothy, who is working with me, sends greetings to you, and so do my kinsmen Lucius, Jason and Sosipater. [22]I, Tertius, who am writing this letter, greet you in the Lord. [23]Greetings to you from Gaius, my host here, and host of the whole church. Erastus, the city treasurer, sends greetings to you, and our brother Quartus.[24]b

Doxology c

[25] And now to him who can make you
    strong
  in accordance with the gospel that I
    preach
  and the proclamation of Jesus Christ,
  in accordance with that mystery
  which for endless ages was kept
    secret
[26] but now (as the prophets wrote) is
    revealed,
  as the eternal God commanded,
  to be made known to all the
    nations,
  so that they obey in faith:
[27] to him, the only wise God,
  give glory through Jesus Christ
  for ever and ever. Amen.

16b Some authorities add v. 24, 'The grace . . . with you' as in v. 20.

16c A solemn summary, placed by some authorities after 15:33.

The First Letter to the

CORINTHIANS

Address and greetings

1 Paul, called by the will of God to be an apostle of Christ Jesus, and Sosthenes, our brother, ²to the church of God in Corinth, to those who have been consecrated in Christ Jesus and called to be God's holy people, with all those everywhere who call on the name of our Lord Jesus Christ, their Lord as well as ours. ³Grace to you and peace from God our Father and the Lord Jesus Christ.

⁴I am continually thanking God about you, for the grace of God which you have been given in Christ Jesus; ⁵in him you have been richly endowed in every kind of utterance and knowledge; ⁶so firmly has witness to Christ taken root in you. ⁷And so you are not lacking in any gift as you wait for our Lord Jesus Christ to be revealed; ⁸he will continue to give you strength till the very end, so that you will be irreproachable on the Day of our Lord Jesus Christ. ⁹You can rely on God, who has called you to be partners with his Son Jesus Christ our Lord.

Dissensions among the faithful

¹⁰Brothers, I urge you, in the name of our Lord Jesus Christ, not to have factions among yourselves but all to be in agreement in what you profess; so that you are perfectly united in your beliefs and judgements. ¹¹From what Chloe's people have been telling me about you, brothers, it is clear that there are serious differences among you. ¹²What I mean is this: every one of you is declaring, 'I belong to Paul,' or 'I belong to Apollos,' or 'I belong to Cephas,'ᵃ or 'I belong to Christ.' ¹³Has Christ been split up? Was it Paul that was crucified for you, or was it in Paul's name that you were

baptised? ¹⁴I am thankful I did not baptise any of you, except Crispus and Gaius, ¹⁵so that no one can say that you were baptised in my name. ¹⁶Yes, I did baptise the family of Stephanas, too; but besides these I do not think I baptised anyone.

The true wisdom and the false

¹⁷After all, Christ sent me not to baptise, but to preach the gospel; and not by means of wisdom of language, wise words which would make the cross of Christ pointless. ¹⁸The message of the cross is folly for those who are on the way to ruin, but for those of us who are on the road to salvation it is the power of God. ¹⁹As scripture says: *I am going to destroy the wisdom of the wise and bring to nothing the understanding of any who understand.* ²⁰*Where are the philosophers? Where are the experts?*ᵇ And where are the debaters of this age? Do you not see how God has shown up human wisdom as folly? ²¹Since in the wisdom of God the world was unable to recognise God through wisdom, it was God's own pleasure to save believers through the folly of the gospel. ²²While the Jews demand miracles and the Greeks look for wisdom, ²³we are preaching a crucified Christ: to the Jews an obstacle they cannot get over, to the gentiles foolishness, ²⁴but to those who have been called, whether they are Jews or Greeks, a Christ who is both the power of God and the wisdom of God. ²⁵God's folly is wiser than human wisdom, and God's weakness is stronger than human strength. ²⁶Consider, brothers, how you were called; not many

1a Cephas is the Aramaic word for 'Peter'. For Apollos *see* Ac 18:24.

1b Is 29:14; 19:12.

of you are wise by human standards, not many influential, not many from noble families. ²⁷No, God chose those who by human standards are fools to shame the wise; he chose those who by human standards are weak to shame the strong, ²⁸those who by human standards are common and contemptible—indeed those who count for nothing—to reduce to nothing all those that do count for something, ²⁹so that no human being might feel boastful before God. ³⁰It is by him that you exist in Christ Jesus, who for us was made wisdom from God, and saving justice and holiness and redemption. ³¹As scripture says: *If anyone wants to boast, let him boast of the Lord.*ᶜ

2 Now when I came to you, brothers, I did not come with any brilliance of oratory or wise argument to announce to you the mystery of God. ²I was resolved that the only knowledge I would have while I was with you was knowledge of Jesus, and of him as the crucified Christ. ³I came among you in weakness, in fear and great trembling ⁴and what I spoke and proclaimed was not meant to convince by philosophical argument, but to demonstrate the convincing power of the Spirit, ⁵so that your faith should depend not on human wisdom but on the power of God.

⁶But still, to those who have reached maturity, we do talk of a wisdom, not, it is true, a philosophy of this age or of the rulers of this age, who will not last long now. ⁷It is of the mysterious wisdom of God that we talk, the wisdom that was hidden, which God predestined to be for our glory before the ages began. ⁸None of the rulers of the age recognised it; for if they had recognised it, they would not have crucified the Lord of glory; ⁹but it is as scripture says: *What no eye has seen and no ear has heard, what the mind of man cannot visualise; all that God has prepared for those who love him;*ᵃ ¹⁰to us, though, God has given revelation through the Spirit, for the Spirit explores the depths of everything, even the depths of God. ¹¹After all, is there anyone who knows the qualities of anyone except his own spirit,

within him; and in the same way, nobody knows the qualities of God except the Spirit of God. ¹²Now, the Spirit we have received is not the spirit of the world but God's own Spirit, so that we may understand the lavish gifts God has given us. ¹³And these are what we speak of, not in the terms learnt from human philosophy, but in terms learnt from the Spirit, fitting spiritual language to spiritual things. ¹⁴The natural person has no room for the gifts of God's Spirit; to him they are folly; he cannot recognise them, because their value can be assessed only in the Spirit. ¹⁵The spiritual person, on the other hand, can assess the value of everything, and that person's value cannot be assessed by anybody else. ¹⁶For: *who has ever known the mind of the Lord? Who has ever been his adviser?*ᵇ But we are those who have the mind of Christ.

3 And so, brothers, I was not able to talk to you as spiritual people; I had to talk to you as people still living by your natural inclinations, still infants in Christ; ²I fed you with milk and not solid food, for you were not yet able to take it—and even now, you are still not able to, ³for you are still living by your natural inclinations. As long as there are jealousy and rivalry among you, that surely means that you are still living by your natural inclinations and by merely human principles. ⁴While there is one that says, 'I belong to Paul' and another that says, 'I belong to Apollos' are you not being only too human?

The place of the Christian preacher

⁵For what is Apollos and what is Paul? The servants through whom you came to believe, and each has only what the Lord has given him. ⁶I did the planting, Apollos did the watering, but God gave growth. ⁷In this, neither the planter nor the waterer counts for anything; only God, who gives growth. ⁸It is all

1c cf. Jr 9:22–23.

2a A free combination of Is 64:3 and Jr 3:16.

2b Is 40:13.

169 READ 1 CORINTHIANS 2:1–10.

What no eye has seen and no ear has heard . . . ; all that God has prepared for those who love him.—1 CORINTHIANS 2:9

HEAVEN AND HELL

The joys of the Kingdom of God no one can tell, nor even conceive or understand, while he is yet clothed in the flesh. For they are greater and more wondrous than they are imagined or conceived to be. So it is written: *"What no eye has seen and no ear has heard, what the mind of man cannot visualise; all that God has prepared for those who love him."* For the Kingdom of God is greater than all report, better than all praise of it, more manifold than all knowledge, more perfect than every conceivable glory. The miseries of hell, as they truly are, no tongue can tell; no mind conceive; for in their reality they are far more dreadful than they are thought to be.

And likewise the Kingdom of God is so full of light, and peace, and charity, and wisdom, and glory, and honesty, and sweetness, and loving kindness, and every unspeakable and unutterable good, that it can neither be described nor envisioned by the mind. But the abode of hell is so full of darkness, of discord, of hate, of folly, of unhappiness, of pain, of burning heat, of thirst, of inextinguishable fire, of sadness, of unending punishment, and of every indescribable evil that neither can it be told nor yet conceived by man. . . .

In the Kingdom of God every good abounds and there is nothing of evil; in the prison of hell every evil abounds and there is nothing of good. In the Kingdom of Heaven no one who is unworthy is received; but no one worthy, no just one, is brought down to hell. In the eternal Kingdom there shall be life without death, truth without falsehood, and happiness without shadow of unrest or change, in Christ Jesus Our Lord, who lives and reigns world without end, Amen.   ST. PATRICK, 389–461

YOU WILL FIND THE NEXT READING AT 1 CORINTHIANS 10.

one who does the planting and who does the watering, and each will have the proper pay for the work that he has done. 9After all, we do share in God's work; you are God's farm, God's building.

10By the grace of God which was given to me, I laid the foundations like a trained master-builder, and someone else is building on them. Now each one must be careful how he does the building. 11For nobody can lay down any other foundation than the one which is there already, namely Jesus Christ. 12On this foundation, different people may build in gold, silver, jewels, wood, hay or straw 13but each person's handiwork will be shown for what it is. The Day which dawns in fire will make it clear and the fire itself will test the quality of each person's work. 14The one whose work stands up to it will be given his wages; 15the one whose work is burnt down will suffer the loss of it, though he himself will be saved; he will be saved as someone might expect to be saved from a fire.

16Do you not realise that you are a temple of God with the Spirit of God living in you? 17If anybody should destroy the temple of God, God will destroy that person, because God's temple is holy; and you are that temple.

Conclusions

18 There is no room for self-delusion. Any one of you who thinks he is wise by worldly standards must learn to be a fool in order to be really wise. 19 For the wisdom of the world is folly to God. As scripture says: *He traps the crafty in the snare of their own cunning* 20 and again: *The Lord knows the plans of the wise and how insipid they are.*[a] 21 So there is to be no boasting about human beings: everything belongs to you, 22 whether it is Paul, or Apollos, or Cephas, the world, life or death, the present or the future—all belong to you; 23 but you belong to Christ and Christ belongs to God.

4 People should think of us as Christ's servants, stewards entrusted with the mysteries of God. 2 In such a matter, what is expected of stewards is that each one should be found trustworthy. 3 It is of no importance to me how you or any other human court may judge me: I will not even be the judge of my own self. 4 It is true that my conscience does not reproach me, but that is not enough to justify me: it is the Lord who is my judge. 5 For that reason, do not judge anything before the due time, until the Lord comes; he will bring to light everything that is hidden in darkness and reveal the designs of all hearts. Then everyone will receive from God the appropriate commendation.

6 I have applied all this to myself and Apollos for your sakes, so that you can learn how the saying, 'Nothing beyond what is written' is true of us: no individual among you must become filled with his own importance and make comparisons, to another's detriment. 7 Who made you so important? What have you got that was not given to you? And if it was given to you, why are you boasting as though it were your own? 8 You already have everything—you are rich already—you have come into your kingdom, without any help from us! Well, I wish you were kings and we could be kings with you! 9 For it seems to me that God has put us apostles on show right at the end, like men condemned to death: we have been exhibited as a spectacle to the whole universe, both angelic and human. 10 Here we are, fools for Christ's sake, while you are the clever ones in Christ; we are weak, while you are strong; you are honoured, while we are disgraced. 11 To this day, we go short of food and drink and clothes, we are beaten up and we have no homes; 12 we earn our living by labouring with our own hands; when we are cursed, we answer with a blessing; when we are hounded, we endure it passively; 13 when we are insulted, we give a courteous answer. We are treated even now as the dregs of the world, the very lowest scum.

An appeal

14 I am writing all this not to make you ashamed but simply to remind you, as my dear children; 15 for even though you might have ten thousand slaves to look after you in Christ, you still have no more than one father, and it was I who fathered you in Christ Jesus, by the gospel. 16 That is why I urge you to take me as your pattern 17 and why I have sent you Timothy, a dear and faithful son to me in the Lord, who will remind you of my principles of conduct in Christ, as I teach them everywhere in every church.

18 On the assumption that I was not coming to you, some of you have become filled with your own self-importance; 19 but I shall be coming to you soon, the Lord willing, and then I shall find out not what these self-important people say, but what power they have. 20 For the kingdom of God consists not in spoken words but in power. 21 What do you want then? Am I to come to you with a stick in my hand or in love, and with a spirit of gentleness?

Incest in Corinth

5 It is widely reported that there is sexual immorality among you, immorality of a kind that is not found even among gentiles: that one

3a Jb 5:13 followed by Ps 94:11.

of you is living with his stepmother.ᵃ ²And you so filled with your own self importance! It would have been better if you had been grieving bitterly, so that the man who has done this thing were turned out of the community. ³For my part, however distant I am physically, I am present in spirit and have already condemned the man who behaved in this way, just as though I were present in person. ⁴When you have gathered together in the name of our Lord Jesus, with the presence of my spirit, and in the power of our Lord Jesus, ⁵hand such a man over to Satan, to be destroyed as far as natural life is concerned, so that on the Day of the Lord his spirit may be saved.

⁶Your self-satisfaction is ill founded. Do you not realise that only a little yeast leavens the whole batch of dough? ⁷Throw out the old yeast so that you can be the fresh dough, unleavened as you are. For our Passover has been sacrificed, that is, Christ; ⁸let us keep the feast, then, with none of the old yeast and no leavening of evil and wickedness, but only the unleavened bread of sincerity and truth.

⁹In my letter, I wrote to you that you should have nothing to do with people living immoral lives. ¹⁰I was not including everybody in this present world who is sexually immoral, or everybody who is greedy, or dishonest or worships false gods—that would mean you would have to cut yourselves off completely from the world. ¹¹In fact what I meant was that you were not to have anything to do with anyone going by the name of brother who is sexually immoral, or is greedy, or worships false gods, or is a slanderer or a drunkard or dishonest; never even have a meal with anybody of that kind. ¹²It is no concern of mine to judge outsiders. It is for you to judge those who are inside, is it not? ¹³But outsiders are for God to judge.

*You must banish this evil-doer from among you.*ᵇ

Recourse to the gentile courts

6 Is one of you with a complaint against another so brazen as to seek judgement from sinners and not from God's holy people? ²Do you not realise that the holy people of God are to be the judges of the world? And if the world is to be judged by you, are you not competent for petty cases? ³Do you not realise that we shall be the judges of angels?—then quite certainly over matters of this life. ⁴But when you have matters of this life to be judged, you bring them before those who are of no account in the Church! ⁵I say this to make you ashamed of yourselves. Can it really be that it is impossible to find in the community one sensible person capable of deciding questions between brothers, ⁶and that this is why brother goes to law against brother, and that before unbelievers? ⁷No; it is a fault in you, by itself, that one of you should go to law against another at all: why do you not prefer to suffer injustice, why not prefer to be defrauded? ⁸And here you are, doing the injustice and the defrauding, and to your own brothers.

⁹Do you not realise that people who do evil will never inherit the kingdom of God? Make no mistake—the sexually immoral, idolaters, adulterers, the self-indulgent, sodomites, ¹⁰thieves, misers, drunkards, slanderers and swindlers, none of these will inherit the kingdom of God. ¹¹Some of you used to be of that kind: but you have been washed clean, you have been sanctified, and you have been justified in the name of the Lord Jesus Christ and through the Spirit of our God.

Sexual immorality

¹²'For me everything is permissible';ᵃ maybe, but not everything does good. True, for me everything is permissible, but I am determined not to be dominated by anything. ¹³Foods are for the stomach, and the stomach is for foods; and God will destroy them both.

5a Against OT and Roman law, but seemingly not Corinthian law, it was forbidden by the Jerusalem decision (Ac 15:20).

5b Dt 13:6.

6a Perhaps a saying of Paul now (and 10:23) quoted against him.

But the body is not for sexual immorality; [14] it is for the Lord, and the Lord is for the body. God raised up the Lord and he will raise us up too by his power. [15] Do you not realise that your bodies are members of Christ's body; do you think one can take parts of Christ's body and join them to the body of a prostitute? Out of the question! [16] Or do you not realise that anyone who attaches himself to a prostitute is one body with her, since *the two,* as it is said, *become one flesh.*[b] [17] But anyone who attaches himself to the Lord is one spirit with him.

[18] Keep away from sexual immorality. All other sins that people may commit are done outside the body; but the sexually immoral person sins against his own body. [19] Do you not realise that your body is the temple of the Holy Spirit, who is in you and whom you received from God? [20] You are not your own property, then; you have been bought at a price. So use your body for the glory of God.

Marriage and virginity

7 Now for the questions about which you wrote. Yes, it is a good thing for a man not to touch a woman; [2] yet to avoid immorality every man should have his own wife and every woman her own husband. [3] The husband must give to his wife what she has a right to expect, and so too the wife to her husband. [4] The wife does not have authority over her own body, but the husband does; and in the same way, the husband does not have authority over his own body, but the wife does. [5] You must not deprive each other, except by mutual consent for a limited time, to leave yourselves free for prayer, and to come together again afterwards; otherwise Satan may take advantage of any lack of self-control to put you to the test. [6] I am telling you this as a concession, not an order. [7] I should still like everyone to be as I am myself; but everyone has his own gift from God, one this kind and the next something different.

[8] To the unmarried and to widows I say: it is good for them to stay as they are, like me. [9] But if they cannot exercise self-control, let them marry, since it is better to be married than to be burnt up.

[10] To the married I give this ruling, and this is not mine but the Lord's: a wife must not be separated from her husband— [11] or if she has already left him, she must remain unmarried or else be reconciled to her husband—and a husband must not divorce his wife.

[12] For other cases these instructions are my own, not the Lord's. If one of the brothers has a wife who is not a believer, and she is willing to stay with him, he should not divorce her; [13] and if a woman has a husband who is not a believer and he is willing to stay with her, she should not divorce her husband. [14] You see, the unbelieving husband is sanctified through his wife and the unbelieving wife is sanctified through the brother. If this were not so, your children would be unclean, whereas in fact they are holy. [15] But if the unbeliever chooses to leave, then let the separation take place: in these circumstances, the brother or sister is no longer tied. But God has called you to live in peace: [16] as a wife, how can you tell whether you are to be the salvation of your husband; as a husband, how can you tell whether you are to be the salvation of your wife?

[17] Anyway let everyone continue in the part which the Lord has allotted to him, as he was when God called him. This is the rule that I give to all the churches. [18] If a man who is called has already been circumcised, then he must stay circumcised; when an uncircumcised man is called, he may not be circumcised. [19] To be circumcised is of no importance, and to be uncircumcised is of no importance; what is important is the keeping of God's commandments. [20] Everyone should stay in whatever state he was in when he was called. [21] So, if when you were called, you were a slave, do not think it matters—even if you have a chance of freedom, you should prefer to make full use of your condition as a slave. [22] You see, anyone who was called in the Lord while a slave, is a freeman of the Lord; and in the same

6b Gn 2:24.

way, anyone who was free when called, is a slave of Christ. 23 You have been bought at a price; do not be slaves now to any human being. 24 Each one of you, brothers, is to stay before God in the state in which you were called.

25 About people remaining virgin, I have no directions from the Lord, but I give my own opinion as a person who has been granted the Lord's mercy to be faithful. 26 Well then, because of the stress which is weighing upon us, the right thing seems to be this: it is good for people to stay as they are. 27 If you are joined to a wife, do not seek to be released; if you are freed of a wife, do not look for a wife. 28 However, if you do get married, that is not a sin, and it is not sinful for a virgin to enter upon marriage. But such people will have the hardships consequent on human nature, and I would like you to be without that.

29 What I mean, brothers, is that the time has become limited, and from now on, those who have spouses should live as though they had none; 30 and those who mourn as though they were not mourning; those who enjoy life as though they did not enjoy it; those who have been buying property as though they had no possessions; 31 and those who are involved with the world as though they were people not engrossed in it. Because this world as we know it is passing away.

32 I should like you to have your minds free from all worry. The unmarried man gives his mind to the Lord's affairs and to how he can please the Lord; 33 but the man who is married gives his mind to the affairs of this world and to how he can please his wife, and he is divided in mind. 34 So, too, the unmarried woman, and the virgin, gives her mind to the Lord's affairs and to being holy in body and spirit; but the married woman gives her mind to the affairs of this world and to how she can please her husband. 35 I am saying this only to help you, not to put a bridle on you, but so that everything is as it should be, and you are able to give your undivided attention to the Lord.

36 If someone with strong passions thinks that he is behaving badly towards his fiancee and that things should take their due course, he should follow his desires. There is no sin in it; they should marry. 37 But if he stands firm in his resolution, without any compulsion but with full control of his own will, and decides to let her remain as his fiancee, then he is acting well. 38 In other words, he who marries his fiancee is doing well, and he who does not, better still.

39 A wife is tied as long as her husband is alive. But if the husband dies, she is free to marry anybody she likes, only it must be in the Lord. 40 She would be happier if she stayed as she is, to my way of thinking—and I believe that I too have the Spirit of God.

Food offered to false gods

8 Now about food which has been dedicated to false gods.*a* We are well aware that all of us have knowledge; but while knowledge puffs up, love is what builds up. 2 Someone may think that he has full knowledge of something and yet not know it as well as he should; 3 but someone who loves God is known by God. 4 On the subject of eating foods dedicated to false gods, we are well aware that none of the false gods exists in reality and that there is no God other than the One. 5 Though there are so-called gods, in the heavens or on earth— and there are plenty of gods and plenty of lords— 6 yet for us there is only one God, the Father from whom all things come and for whom we exist, and one Lord, Jesus Christ, through whom all things come and through whom we exist.

The claims of knowledge

7 However, not everybody has this knowledge. There are some in whose consciences false gods still play such a part that they take the food as though it had been dedicated to a god; then their conscience, being vulnerable, is defiled. 8 But of course food cannot make us ac-

---

8a Food, especially meat, left over from sacrifices, was offered for sale cheap in the markets.

ceptable to God; we lose nothing by not eating it, we gain nothing by eating it. ⁹Only be careful that this freedom of yours does not in any way turn into an obstacle to trip those who are vulnerable. ¹⁰Suppose someone sees you, who have the knowledge, sitting eating in the temple of some false god, do you not think that his conscience, vulnerable as it is, may be encouraged to eat foods dedicated to false gods? ¹¹And then it would be through your knowledge that this brother for whom Christ died, vulnerable as he is, has been lost. ¹²So, sinning against your brothers and wounding their vulnerable consciences, you would be sinning against Christ. ¹³That is why, if food can be the cause of a brother's downfall, I will never eat meat any more, rather than cause my brother's downfall.

Paul invokes his own example

9 Am I not free? Am I not an apostle? Have I not seen Jesus our Lord? Are you not my work in the Lord? ²Even if to others I am not an apostle, to you at any rate I am, for you are the seal of my apostolate in the Lord. ³To those who want to interrogate me, this is my answer. ⁴Have we not every right to eat and drink? ⁵And every right to be accompanied by a Christian wife, like the other apostles, like the brothers of the Lord, and like Cephas? ⁶Are Barnabas and I the only ones who have no right to stop working? ⁷What soldier would ever serve in the army at his own expense? And who is there who would plant a vineyard and never eat the fruit from it; or would keep a flock and not feed on the milk from his flock? ⁸Do not think that this is merely worldly wisdom. Does not the Law say exactly the same? It is written in the Law of Moses: ⁹*You must not muzzle an ox when it is treading out the corn.*ᵃ Is it about oxen that God is concerned here, ¹⁰or is it not said entirely for our sake? Clearly it was written for our sake, because it is right that whoever ploughs should plough with the expectation of having his share, and whoever threshes should thresh with the expectation of having his share. ¹¹If

we have sown the seed of spiritual things in you, is it too much to ask that we should receive from you a crop of material things? ¹²Others have been given such rights over you and do we not deserve more? In fact, we have never exercised this right; on the contrary, we have put up with anything rather than obstruct the gospel of Christ in any way. ¹³Do you not realise that the ministers in the Temple get their food from the Temple, and those who serve at the altar can claim their share from the altar? ¹⁴In the same way, the Lord gave the instruction that those who preach the gospel should get their living from the gospel.

¹⁵However, I have never availed myself of any rights of this kind; and I have not written this to secure such treatment for myself; I would rather die than that . . . No one shall take from me this ground of boasting. ¹⁶In fact, preaching the gospel gives me nothing to boast of, for I am under compulsion and I should be in trouble if I failed to do it. ¹⁷If I did it on my own initiative I would deserve a reward; but if I do it under compulsion I am simply accepting a task entrusted to me. ¹⁸What reward do I have, then? That in my preaching I offer the gospel free of charge to avoid using the rights which the gospel allows me.

¹⁹So though I was not a slave to any human being, I put myself in slavery to all people, to win as many as I could. ²⁰To the Jews I made myself as a Jew, to win the Jews; to those under the Law as one under the Law (though I am not), in order to win those under the Law; ²¹to those outside the Law as one outside the Law, though I am not outside the Law but under Christ's law, to win those outside the Law. ²²To the weak, I made myself weak, to win the weak. I accommodated myself to people in all kinds of different situations, so that by all possible means I might bring some to salvation. ²³All this I do for the sake of the gospel, that I may share its benefits with others.

²⁴Do you not realise that, though all the runners in the stadium take part in the race,

9a Dt 25:4.

only one of them gets the prize? Run like that—to win. ²⁵Every athlete concentrates completely on training, and this is to win a wreath that will wither, whereas ours will never wither. ²⁶So that is how I run, not without a clear goal; and how I box, not wasting blows on air. ²⁷I punish my body and bring it under control, to avoid any risk that, having acted as herald for others, I myself may be disqualified.

A warning and the lessons of Israel's history

10 I want you to be quite certain, brothers, that our ancestors all had the cloud over them and all passed through the sea. ²In the cloud and in the sea they were all baptised into Moses; ³all ate the same spiritual food ⁴and all drank the same spiritual drink, since they drank from the spiritual rock which followed them,ᵃ and that rock was Christ. ⁵In spite of this, God was not pleased with most of them, and their corpses *were scattered over the desert.*ᵇ ⁶Now these happenings were examples, for our benefit, so that we should never set our hearts, as they did, on evil things; ⁷nor are you to worship false gods, as some of them did, as it says in scripture: *The people sat down to eat and drink, and afterwards got up to amuse themselves.*ᶜ ⁸Nor, again, are we to fall into sexual immorality; some of them did this, and twenty-three thousand met their downfall in one day. ⁹And we are not to put the Lord to the test; some of them put him to the test, and they were killed by snakes. ¹⁰Never complain; some of them complained, and they were killed by the Destroyer. ¹¹Now all these things happened to them by way of example, and they were described in writing to be a lesson for us, to whom it has fallen to live in the last days of the ages. ¹²Everyone, no matter how firmly he thinks he is standing, must be careful he does not fall. ¹³None of the trials which have come upon you is more than a human being can stand. You can trust that God will not let you be put to the test beyond your strength, but with any trial will also provide a way out by enabling you to put up with it.

Sacrificial feasts; no compromise with idolatry

¹⁴For that reason, my dear friends, have nothing to do with the worship of false gods. ¹⁵I am talking to you as sensible people; weigh up for yourselves what I have to say. ¹⁶The blessing-cup, which we bless, is it not a sharing in the blood of Christ; and the loaf of bread which we break, is it not a sharing in the body of Christ? ¹⁷And as there is one loaf, so we, although there are many of us, are one single body, for we all share in the one loaf. ¹⁸Now compare the natural people of Israel: is it not true that those who eat the sacrifices share the altar? ¹⁹What does this mean? That the dedication of food to false gods amounts to anything? Or that false gods themselves amount to anything? ²⁰No, it does not; simply that when pagans sacrifice, *what is sacrificed by them is sacrificed to demons who are not God.*ᵈ I do not want you to share with demons. ²¹You cannot drink the cup of the Lord and the cup of demons as well; you cannot have a share at the Lord's table and the demons' table as well. ²²Do we really want to arouse the Lord's jealousy; are we stronger than he is?

Food sacrificed to idols; practical solutions

²³'Everything is permissible'; maybe so, but not everything does good. True, everything is permissible, but not everything builds people up. ²⁴Nobody should be looking for selfish advantage, but everybody for someone else's. ²⁵Eat anything that is sold in butchers' shops; there is no need to ask questions for conscience's sake, ²⁶since *To the Lord belong the earth and all it contains.*ᵉ ²⁷If an unbeliever invites you to a meal, go if you want to, and eat whatever is put before you; you need not ask questions of conscience first. ²⁸But if someone says to you, 'This food has been offered in sacrifice,' do not eat it, out of consideration

10a In rabbinic tradition the rock of Nb 20:8 followed them.
10b Nb 14:16. 10c Ex 32:6.
10d Dt 32:17. 10e Ps 24:1.

170 READ 1 CORINTHIANS 10:14–22.

We, although there are many of us, are one single body.—1 CORINTHIANS 10:17

APPLYING THE POWER OF THE EUCHARIST

Dearly beloved brothers and sisters, it's to our benefit to understand the miracle of the Eucharist—what the Gift is, why it was given, what is its use. "We, although there are many of us, are one single body," says the Apostle Paul. . . . This union may happen not only by love of others, but truly we ought to mingle our own flesh with his Flesh. And we do this by eating that Food that he has given to us because he wanted to show the exceedingly great love he has for us. For this reason he has mingled himself with us and infused his Body into our bodies so that we may be one together, just as the limbs of a human being and his head are united in one body.

When we come back from that Table, we ought to be like so many lions breathing fire, dreadful to the devil. Our thoughts ought to be concentrated on our great Head and the love that he shows us. . . . I feed you with my own Flesh, says the Lord, and join myself to you, desiring that you should all be children of noble blood now and giving you a noble hope of what you shall be hereafter. . . .

Therefore, as the bearers of such a great mercy, let's watch our behavior. When any foul word springs to our lips, or we feel anger taking possession of us, or the sting of any other sinful passion, let's recall of what we have been counted worthy and let that remembrance restrain the unruly emotion. As often as we eat that Body, as often as we taste that Blood, let us remember that we are feeding on him who is sitting on high, adored by angels, at the right hand of the Eternal Power. Ah me, how many a way is open to us by which we may be saved! He has made us his own—he has given us his Body to us—and we still are not turned away from evil! ST. JOHN CHRYSOSTOM, 347–407

YOU WILL FIND THE NEXT READING AT 1 CORINTHIANS 11:23.

for the person that told you, for conscience's sake— ²⁹ not your own conscience, I mean, but the other person's. Why should my freedom be governed by somebody else's conscience? ³⁰ Provided that I accept it with gratitude, why should I be blamed for eating food for which I give thanks? ³¹ Whatever you eat, then, or drink, and whatever else you do, do it all for the glory of God. ³² Never be a cause of offence, either to Jews or to Greeks or to the Church of God, ³³ just as I try to accommodate everybody in everything, not looking for my own advantage, but for the advantage of everybody else, so that they may be saved.

11 Take me as your pattern, just as I take Christ for mine.

Women's behaviour at services

² I congratulate you for remembering me so consistently and for maintaining the traditions exactly as I passed them on to you. ³ But I should like you to understand that the head of every man is Christ, the head of woman is man, and the head of Christ is God. ⁴ For any man to pray or to prophesy with his head covered shows disrespect for his head. ⁵ And for a woman to pray or prophesy with her head uncovered shows disrespect for her head; it is ex-

actly the same as if she had her hair shaved off. [6] Indeed, if a woman does go without a veil, she should have her hair cut off too; but if it is a shameful thing for a woman to have her hair cut off or shaved off, then she should wear a veil.

[7] But for a man it is not right to have his head covered, since he is the image of God and reflects God's glory; but woman is the reflection of man's glory. [8] For man did not come from woman; no, woman came from man; [9] nor was man created for the sake of woman, but woman for the sake of man: [10] and this is why it is right for a woman to wear on her head a sign of the authority over her, because of the angels. [11] However, in the Lord, though woman is nothing without man, man is nothing without woman; [12] and though woman came from man, so does every man come from a woman, and everything comes from God.

[13] Decide for yourselves: does it seem fitting that a woman should pray to God without a veil? [14] Does not nature itself teach you that if a man has long hair, it is a disgrace to him, [15] but when a woman has long hair, it is her glory? After all, her hair was given to her to be a covering.

[16] If anyone wants to be contentious, I say that we have no such custom, nor do any of the churches of God.

The Lord's Supper

[17] Now that I am on the subject of instructions, I cannot congratulate you on the meetings you hold; they do more harm than good. [18] In the first place, I hear that when you all come together in your assembly, there are separate factions among you, and to some extent I believe it. [19] It is no bad thing, either, that there should be differing groups among you so that those who are to be trusted among you can be clearly recognised. [20] So, when you meet together, it is not the Lord's Supper that you eat; [21] for when the eating begins, each one of you has his own supper first, and there is one going hungry while another is getting drunk. [22] Surely you have homes for doing your eating and drink-

ing in? Or have you such disregard for God's assembly that you can put to shame those who have nothing? What am I to say to you? Congratulate you? On this I cannot congratulate you.

[23] For the tradition I received[a] from the Lord and also handed on to you is that on the night he was betrayed, the Lord Jesus took some bread, [24] and after he had given thanks, he broke it, and he said, 'This is my body, which is for you; do this in remembrance of me.' [25] And in the same way, with the cup after supper, saying, 'This cup is the new covenant in my blood. Whenever you drink it, do this as a memorial of me.' [26] Whenever you eat this bread, then, and drink this cup, you are proclaiming the Lord's death until he comes. [27] Therefore anyone who eats the bread or drinks the cup of the Lord unworthily is answerable for the body and blood of the Lord.

[28] Everyone is to examine himself and only then eat of the bread or drink from the cup; [29] because a person who eats and drinks without recognising the body is eating and drinking his own condemnation. [30] That is why many of you are weak and ill and a good number have died. [31] If we were critical of ourselves we would not be condemned, [32] but when we are judged by the Lord, we are corrected by the Lord to save us from being condemned along with the world.

[33] So then, my brothers, when you meet for the Meal, wait for each other; [34] anyone who is hungry should eat at home. Then your meeting will not bring your condemnation. The other matters I shall arrange when I come.

Spiritual gifts

12 About the gifts of the Spirit, brothers, I want you to be quite certain. [2] You remember that, when you were pagans, you were irresistibly drawn to inarticulate heathen gods. [3] Because of that, I want to make it quite clear to you that no one who says 'A curse on Jesus' can be speaking in the Spirit of God, and

11a cf. 15:3.

171   READ 1 CORINTHIANS 11:23–27.

This is my body, which is for you; do this in remembrance of me.—1 CORINTHIANS 11:24

FOOD FOR THE SOUL

O how precious a thing, how marvelous, how health-giving, how delicious is the Supper of the Lord! Can anything be more precious than his Supper? There is put before us as food, not the flesh of bulls and goats as in the past, but Christ himself, our very God. Can anything be more marvelous than this sacrament? There bread and wine are bread and wine no more, but instead there is the Body and the Blood of Christ. Christ himself, perfect God and perfect man, Christ himself is there under the appearance of a little bread and wine. . . .

All that the senses can reach in this sacrament—see, taste, feel, smell—tell of bread and wine, but the thing is not bread and wine. And so room is left for faith. Christ who has a form that can be seen is here taken and received not only unseen but seeming to be bread and wine. . . .

Can anything be more health-giving than this sacrament? By it sins are purged away, strength renewed, and the soul fed upon the fatness of spiritual gifts. This Supper is offered up in the church for the living and the dead. It was ordained to the health of all, all get the good of it.

Can anything be more delicious than this sacrament? Its glorious sweetness is of such a truth that no one can fully tell it. There spiritual comfort is sucked from its very wellspring. In this sacrament a memorial is made of that exceeding great love that Christ showed in time of his sufferings. It was in order that the boundless goodness of his love might be driven home into the hearts of his faithful ones . . . that he instituted this sacrament. This sacrament, the everlasting proclamation of his death until he comes. . . . This sacrament, the greatest miracle that he ever worked, and the one mighty joy of them that now have sorrow till he shall come again. . . .   ST. THOMAS AQUINAS, 1225?–1275

YOU WILL FIND THE NEXT READING AT 1 CORINTHIANS 13.

nobody is able to say, 'Jesus is Lord' except in the Holy Spirit.

The variety and the unity of gifts

⁴There are many different gifts, but it is always the same Spirit; ⁵there are many different ways of serving, but it is always the same Lord. ⁶There are many different forms of activity, but in everybody it is the same God who is at work in them all. ⁷The particular manifestation of the Spirit granted to each one is to be used for the general good. ⁸To one is given from the Spirit the gift of utterance expressing wisdom; to another the gift of utterance ex-

pressing knowledge, in accordance with the same Spirit; ⁹to another, faith, from the same Spirit; and to another, the gifts of healing, through this one Spirit; ¹⁰to another, the working of miracles; to another, prophecy; to another, the power of distinguishing spirits; to one, the gift of different tongues and to another, the interpretation of tongues. ¹¹But at work in all these is one and the same Spirit, distributing them at will to each individual.

The analogy of the body

¹²For as with the human body which is a unity although it has many parts—all the parts of

the body, though many, still making up one single body—so it is with Christ. ¹³We were baptised into one body in a single Spirit, Jews as well as Greeks, slaves as well as free men, and we were all given the same Spirit to drink. ¹⁴And indeed the body consists not of one member but of many. ¹⁵If the foot were to say, 'I am not a hand and so I do not belong to the body,' it does not belong to the body any the less for that. ¹⁶Or if the ear were to say, 'I am not an eye, and so I do not belong to the body,' that would not stop its belonging to the body. ¹⁷If the whole body were just an eye, how would there be any hearing? If the whole body were hearing, how would there be any smelling?

¹⁸As it is, God has put all the separate parts into the body as he chose. ¹⁹If they were all the same part, how could it be a body? ²⁰As it is, the parts are many but the body is one. ²¹The eye cannot say to the hand, 'I have no need of you,' and nor can the head say to the feet, 'I have no need of you.'

²²What is more, it is precisely the parts of the body that seem to be the weakest which are the indispensable ones. ²³It is the parts of the body which we consider least dignified that we surround with the greatest dignity; and our less presentable parts are given greater presentability ²⁴which our presentable parts do not need. God has composed the body so that greater dignity is given to the parts which were without it, ²⁵and so that there may not be disagreements inside the body but each part may be equally concerned for all the others. ²⁶If one part is hurt, all the parts share its pain. And if one part is honoured, all the parts share its joy.

²⁷Now Christ's body is yourselves, each of you with a part to play in the whole. ²⁸And those whom God has appointed in the Church are, first apostles, secondly prophets, thirdly teachers; after them, miraculous powers, then gifts of healing, helpful acts, guidance, various kinds of tongues. ²⁹Are all of them apostles? Or all prophets? Or all teachers? Or all mira-cle-workers? ³⁰Do all have the gifts of heal-ing? Do all of them speak in tongues and all interpret them?

The order of importance in spiritual gifts; hymn to Love

³¹Set your mind on the higher gifts. And now I am going to put before you the best way of all.

13 Though I command languages both human and angelic—if I speak without love, I am no more than a gong booming or a cymbal clashing. ²And though I have the power of prophecy, to penetrate all mysteries and knowledge, and though I have all the faith necessary to move mountains—if I am without love, I am nothing. ³Though I should give away to the poor all that I possess, and even give up my body to be burned—if I am without love, it will do me no good what-ever.

⁴Love is always patient and kind; love is never jealous; love is not boastful or conceited, ⁵it is never rude and never seeks its own ad-vantage, it does not take offence or store up grievances. ⁶Love does not rejoice at wrong-doing, but finds its joy in the truth. ⁷It is al-ways ready to make allowances, to trust, to hope and to endure whatever comes.

⁸Love never comes to an end. But if there are prophecies, they will be done away with; if tongues, they will fall silent; and if knowledge, it will be done away with. ⁹For we know only imperfectly, and we prophesy imperfectly; ¹⁰but once perfection comes, all imperfect things will be done away with. ¹¹When I was a child, I used to talk like a child, and see things as a child does, and think like a child; but now that I have become an adult, I have finished with all childish ways. ¹²Now we see only reflections in a mirror, mere riddles, but then we shall be seeing face to face. Now I can know only imperfectly; but then I shall know just as fully as I am myself known.

¹³As it is, these remain: faith, hope and love, the three of them; and the greatest of them is love.

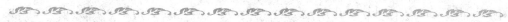

172 READ 1 CORINTHIANS 13.

If I am without love, I am nothing.—1 CORINTHIANS 13:2

DO EVERYTHING WITH LOVE

We must not prefer anything whatsoever before the possession of charity. And let us have nothing against one another, nor render evil for evil, nor let the sun go down on our anger. But let us forgive everything that has been done against us, and let us procure for ourselves that love that covers a multitude of sins (see 1 P 4:8).

For what does it profit us . . . to possess all things, and to be without this life-giving and saving love? It would be just as if you had prepared a great feast, and had invited kings and great persons, and had omitted nothing that was wanted to the feast; but there was not salt: could anyone be pleased with a meal of that kind? Far from it. And what is more you will have suffered loss because of it: for you lose not only your toil and trouble, but you also have been shamed in the presence of those whom you invited.

And this is how it is here. For all your labor is in vain and without profit, if you do not have charity, without which whatever the good work or deed you do remains unsanctified. Even though the one who does them may lay claim to virginity, even though he fasts, or keeps watch in the night, though he gives shelter to the poor, though he is seen to offer gifts to God, to tithe, or to do good works, even though he should build a church, or do any other kind of good work—without possessing love, God will regard all these things as nothing. For without love there is nothing in them that is pleasing to the Lord. ST. EPHREM, 306?–373?

YOU WILL FIND THE NEXT READING AT 1 CORINTHIANS 15.

Spiritual gifts: their respective importance in the community

14 Make love your aim; but be eager, too, for spiritual gifts, and especially for prophesying. ²Those who speak in a tongue speak to God, but not to other people, because nobody understands them; they are speaking in the Spirit and the meaning is hidden. ³On the other hand, someone who prophesies speaks to other people, building them up and giving them encouragement and reassurance. ⁴Those who speak in a tongue may build themselves up, but those who prophesy build up the community. ⁵While I should like you all to speak in tongues, I would much rather

you could prophesy; since those who prophesy are of greater importance than those who speak in tongues, unless they can interpret what they say so that the church is built up by it.

⁶Now suppose, brothers, I come to you and speak in tongues, what good shall I do you if my speaking provides no revelation or knowledge or prophecy or instruction? ⁷It is the same with an inanimate musical instrument. If it does not make any distinction between notes, how can one recognise what is being played on flute or lyre? ⁸If the trumpet sounds a call which is unrecognisable, who is going to get ready for the attack? ⁹It is the same with you: if you do not use your tongue to produce

speech that can be readily understood, how can anyone know what you are saying? You will be talking to the air. ¹⁰However many the languages used in the world, all of them use sound; ¹¹but if I do not understand the meaning of the sound, I am a barbarian ᵃ to the person who is speaking, and the speaker is a barbarian to me. ¹²So with you, as you are eager to have spiritual powers, aim to be rich in those which build up the community.

¹³That is why anybody who speaks in a tongue must pray that he may be given the interpretation. ¹⁴For if I pray in a tongue, my spirit may be praying but my mind derives no fruit from it. ¹⁵What then? I shall pray with the spirit, but I shall pray with the mind as well: I shall sing praises with the spirit and I shall sing praises with the mind as well. ¹⁶Otherwise, if you say your blessing only with the spirit, how is the uninitiated person going to answer 'Amen' to your thanksgiving, without understanding what you are saying? ¹⁷You may be making your thanksgiving well, but the other person is not built up at all. ¹⁸I thank God that I speak with tongues more than any of you; ¹⁹all the same, when I am in the assembly I would rather say five words with my mind, to instruct others as well, than ten thousand words in a tongue.

²⁰Brothers, do not remain children in your thinking; infants in wickedness—agreed, but in your thinking grown-ups. ²¹It says in the written Law: *In strange tongues and in a foreign language I will talk to this nation, and even so they will refuse to listen,*ᵇ says the Lord. ²²So then, strange languages are significant not for believers, but for unbelievers; whereas on the other hand, prophesying is not for unbelievers, but for believers. ²³Suppose that, if the whole congregation were meeting and all of them speaking in tongues, and some uninitiated people or unbelievers were to come in, don't you think they would say that you were all raving? ²⁴But if you were all prophesying when an unbeliever or someone uninitiated came in, he would find himself put to the test by all and judged by all ²⁵and the secrets of his heart revealed; and so he would fall down on his face and worship God, declaring that *God is indeed among you.*ᶜ

Regulating spiritual gifts

²⁶Then what should it be like, brothers? When you come together each of you brings a psalm or some instruction or a revelation, or speaks in a tongue or gives an interpretation. Let all these things be done in a way that will build up the community. ²⁷If there are to be any people speaking in a tongue, then let there be only two, or at the most three, and those one at a time, and let one of these interpret. ²⁸If there is no interpreter, then let each of them be quiet in the assembly, and speak only to himself and God. ²⁹Let two prophets, or three, speak while the rest weigh their words; ³⁰and if a revelation comes to someone else who is sitting by, the speaker should stop speaking. ³¹You can all prophesy, but one at a time, then all will learn something and all receive encouragement. ³²The prophetic spirit is to be under the prophets' control, ³³for God is a God not of disorder but of peace.

As in all the churches of God's holy people, ³⁴women are to remain quiet in the assemblies, since they have no permission to speak: theirs is a subordinate part, as the Law itself says. ³⁵If there is anything they want to know, they should ask their husbands at home: it is shameful for a woman to speak in the assembly.

³⁶Do you really think that you are the source of the word of God? Or that you are the only people to whom it has come? ³⁷Anyone who claims to be a prophet, or to have any spiritual powers must recognise that what I am writing to you is a commandment from the Lord. ³⁸If anyone does not recognise this, it is because that person is not recognised himself.

³⁹So, my brothers, be eager to prophesy, and do not suppress the gift of speaking in

14a i.e. someone who does not understand Gk.

14b Is 28:11–12.   14c Is 45:14.

tongues. 40 But make sure that everything is done in a proper and orderly fashion.

The fact of the resurrection

15 I want to make quite clear to you, brothers, what the message of the gospel that I preached to you is; you accepted it and took your stand on it, 2 and you are saved by it, if you keep to the message I preached to you; otherwise your coming to believe was in vain. 3 The tradition I handed on to you in the first place, a tradition which I had myself received,[a] was that Christ died for our sins, in accordance with the scriptures, 4 and that he was buried; and that on the third day, he was raised to life, in accordance with the scriptures; 5 and that he appeared to Cephas; and later to the Twelve; 6 and next he appeared to more than five hundred of the brothers at the same time, most of whom are still with us, though some have fallen asleep; 7 then he appeared to James, and then to all the apostles. 8 Last of all he appeared to me too, as though I was a child born abnormally.

9 For I am the least of the apostles and am not really fit to be called an apostle, because I had been persecuting the Church of God; 10 but what I am now, I am through the grace of God, and the grace which was given to me has not been wasted. Indeed, I have worked harder than all the others—not I, but the grace of God which is with me. 11 Anyway, whether it was they or I, this is what we preach and what you believed.

12 Now if Christ is proclaimed as raised from the dead, how can some of you be saying that there is no resurrection of the dead? 13 If there is no resurrection of the dead, then Christ cannot have been raised either, 14 and if Christ has not been raised, then our preaching is without substance, and so is your faith. 15 What is more, we have proved to be false witnesses to God, for testifying against God that he raised Christ to life when he did not raise him—if it is true that the dead are not raised. 16 For, if the dead are not raised, neither is Christ; 17 and if Christ has not been raised,

your faith is pointless and you have not, after all, been released from your sins. 18 In addition, those who have fallen asleep in Christ are utterly lost. 19 If our hope in Christ has been for this life only, we are of all people the most pitiable.

20 In fact, however, Christ has been raised from the dead, as the first-fruits of all who have fallen asleep. 21 As it was by one man that death came, so through one man has come the resurrection of the dead. 22 Just as all die in Adam, so in Christ all will be brought to life; 23 but all of them in their proper order: Christ the first-fruits, and next, at his coming, those who belong to him. 24 After that will come the end, when he will hand over the kingdom to God the Father, having abolished every principality, every ruling force and power. 25 For he is to be king *until he has made* his enemies his footstool, 26 and the last of the enemies to be done away with is death, for *he has put all things under his feet*.[b] 27 But when it is said everything is subjected, this obviously cannot include the One who subjected everything to him. 28 When everything has been subjected to him, then the Son himself will be subjected to the One who has subjected everything to him, so that God may be all in all.

29 Otherwise, what are people up to who have themselves baptised on behalf of the dead? If the dead are not raised at all, what is the point of being baptised on their behalf? 30 And what about us? Why should we endanger ourselves every hour of our lives? 31 I swear by the pride that I take in you, in Christ Jesus our Lord, that I face death every day. 32 If I fought wild animals at Ephesus in a purely human perspective, what had I to gain by it? 33 If the dead are not going to be raised, then *Let us eat and drink, for tomorrow we shall be dead.*[c] 34 So do not let anyone lead you astray, 'Bad company corrupts good ways.'[d] Wake up from your stupor as you should and leave sin

15a cf. 11:23.   15b Ps 110:1.   15c Is 22:13.
15d A proverb found also in Menander's *Thais*.

173 READ 1 CORINTHIANS 15:20–34.

I face death every day.—1 CORINTHIANS 15:31

PUTTING SIN TO DEATH

Let's continue to be strenuous in pursuing virtue. Let's not grow tired of seeking it, for our Lord has become a guide for us and for every person who has a desire for the virtues. And so that it might not be tedious for us, St. Paul became our example when he said, "I face death every day." Now, if we were to think each day that we had to die that day, we would never sin at all. This is the explanation of Paul's saying. If in the morning we imagined that we would never last till evening, and if at evening we thought that we would never see morning, we would never sin.

If we were to keep the imminence of our death in mind, we would never be overcome by sin: lust which is fleeting would not reign over us; we would never harbor anger against another human being; we would not love the possessions which pass away; and we would forgive every person who offended us. Therefore, beloved, let's be zealous in carrying out the work we have committed ourselves to, and let's travel to the end on the road on which we have begun our journey.

ST. ATHANASIUS, 297?–373

YOU WILL FIND THE NEXT READING AT 2 CORINTHIANS 5:1.

alone; some of you have no understanding of God; I tell you this to instil some shame in you.

The manner of the resurrection

35 Someone may ask: How are dead people raised, and what sort of body do they have when they come? 36 How foolish! What you sow must die before it is given new life; 37 and what you sow is not the body that is to be, but only a bare grain, of wheat I dare say, or some other kind; 38 it is God who gives it the sort of body that he has chosen for it, and for each kind of seed its own kind of body.

39 Not all flesh is the same flesh: there is human flesh; animals have another kind of flesh, birds another and fish yet another. 40 Then there are heavenly bodies and earthly bodies; the heavenly have a splendour of their own, and the earthly a different splendour. 41 The sun has its own splendour, the moon another splendour, and the stars yet another splendour; and the stars differ among them

selves in splendour. 42 It is the same too with the resurrection of the dead: what is sown is perishable, but what is raised is imperishable; 43 what is sown is contemptible but what is raised is glorious; what is sown is weak, but what is raised is powerful; 44 what is sown is a natural body, and what is raised is a spiritual body.

If there is a natural body, there is a spiritual body too. 45 So the first *man,* Adam, as scripture says, *became a living soul;*[e] and the last Adam has become a life-giving spirit. 46 But first came the natural body, not the spiritual one; that came only afterwards. 47 The first man, being made of earth, is earthly by nature; the second man is from heaven. 48 The earthly man is the pattern for earthly people, the heavenly man for heavenly ones. 49 And as we have borne the likeness of the earthly man, so we shall bear the likeness of the heavenly one.

15e Gn 2:7.

⁵⁰What I am saying, brothers, is that mere human nature cannot inherit the kingdom of God: what is perishable cannot inherit what is imperishable. ⁵¹Now I am going to tell you a mystery: we are not all going to fall asleep, ⁵²but we are all going to be changed, instantly, in the twinkling of an eye, when the last trumpet sounds. The trumpet is going to sound, and then the dead will be raised imperishable, and we shall be changed, ⁵³because this perishable nature of ours must put on imperishability, this mortal nature must put on immortality.

A hymn of triumph; conclusion

⁵⁴And after this perishable nature has put on imperishability and this mortal nature has put on immortality, then will the words of scripture come true: *Death is swallowed up in victory.* ⁵⁵*Death, where is your victory? Death, where is your sting?*[f] ⁵⁶The sting of death is sin, and the power of sin comes from the Law. ⁵⁷Thank God, then, for giving us the victory through Jesus Christ our Lord.

⁵⁸So, my dear brothers, keep firm and immovable, always abounding in energy for the Lord's work, being sure that in the Lord none of your labours is wasted.

Commendations; greetings

16 Now about the collection for God's holy people;[a] you are to do the same as I prescribed for the churches in Galatia. ²On the first day of the week, each of you should put aside and reserve as much as each can spare; do not delay the collection till I arrive. ³When I come, I will send to Jerusalem with letters of introduction those people you approve to deliver your gift; ⁴if it is worth my going too, they can travel with me.

⁵In any case, I shall be coming to you after I have passed through Macedonia, as I have to go through Macedonia; ⁶and I may be staying some time with you, perhaps wintering, so that you can start me on my next journey, wherever I may be going. ⁷I do not want to make only a passing visit to you, and I am hoping to spend quite a time with you, the Lord permitting. ⁸But I shall remain at Ephesus until Pentecost, ⁹for a very promising door is standing wide open to me and there are many against us.

¹⁰If Timothy comes, make sure that he has nothing to fear from you; he is doing the Lord's work, just as I am, ¹¹and nobody is to underrate him. Start him off in peace on his journey to come on to me: the brothers and I are waiting for him. ¹²As for our brother Apollos, I urged him earnestly to come to you with the brothers, but he was quite firm that he did not want to go yet, and he will come when he finds an opportunity.

¹³Be vigilant, stay firm in the faith, be brave and strong. ¹⁴Let everything you do be done in love.

¹⁵There is something else I must urge you to do, brothers. You know how Stephanas' family have been the first-fruits of Achaia and have devoted themselves to the service of God's holy people; ¹⁶I ask you in turn to put yourselves at the service of people like this and all that work with them in this arduous task. ¹⁷I am delighted that Stephanas and Fortunatus and Achaicus have arrived; they have made up for your not being here. ¹⁸They have set my mind at rest, just as they did yours; you should appreciate people like them.

¹⁹The churches of Asia send their greetings. Aquila and Prisca send their best wishes in the Lord, together with the church that meets in their house. ²⁰All the brothers send their greetings. Greet one another with the holy kiss.

²¹This greeting is in my own hand—PAUL.

²²If there is anyone who does not love the Lord, a curse on such a one. *Maranatha.*[b]

²³The grace of the Lord Jesus Christ be with you.

²⁴My love is with you all in Christ Jesus.

15f A free version of Is 25:8 and Hos 13:14.

16a cf. Ac 24:17; 2 Co 8–9.

16b Aram. 'The Lord is coming' (or perhaps 'Lord, come').

Address and greetings

1 Paul, by the will of God an apostle of Christ Jesus, and Timothy, our brother, to the church of God in Corinth and to all God's holy people in the whole of Achaia. ²Grace to you and peace from God our Father and the Lord Jesus Christ.

³Blessed be the God and Father of our Lord Jesus Christ, the merciful Father and the God who gives every possible encouragement; ⁴he supports us in every hardship, so that we are able to come to the support of others, in every hardship of theirs because of the encouragement that we ourselves receive from God. ⁵For just as the sufferings of Christ overflow into our lives; so too does the encouragement we receive through Christ. ⁶So if we have hardships to undergo, this will contribute to your encouragement and your salvation; if we receive encouragement, this is to gain for you the encouragement which enables you to bear with perseverance the same sufferings as we do. ⁷So our hope for you is secure in the knowledge that you share the encouragement we receive, no less than the sufferings we bear.

⁸So in the hardships we underwent in Asia, we want you to be quite certain, brothers, that we were under extraordinary pressure, beyond our powers of endurance, so that we gave up all hope even of surviving. ⁹In fact we were carrying the sentence of death within our own selves, so that we should be forced to trust not in ourselves but in God, who raises the dead. ¹⁰He did save us from such a death and will save us—we are relying on him to do so. ¹¹Your prayer for us will contribute to this, so that, for God's favour shown to us as the result

of the prayers of so many, thanks too may be given by many on our behalf.

Why Paul changed his plans

¹²There is one thing that we are proud of, namely our conscientious conviction that we have always behaved towards everyone, and especially towards you, with that unalloyed holiness that comes from God, relying not on human reasoning but on the grace of God. ¹³In our writing, there is nothing that you cannot read clearly and understand; ¹⁴and it is my hope that, just as you have already understood us partially, so you will understand fully that you can be as proud of us as we shall be of you when the Day of our Lord Jesus comes.

¹⁵It was with this assurance that I had been meaning to come to you first, so that you would benefit doubly; ¹⁶both to visit you on my way to Macedonia, and then to return to you again from Macedonia, so that you could set me on my way to Judaea. ¹⁷Since that was my purpose, do you think I lightly changed my mind? Or that my plans are based on ordinary human promptings and I have in my mind Yes, yes*ᵃ* at the same time as No, no? ¹⁸As surely as God is trustworthy, what we say to you is not both Yes and No. ¹⁹The Son of God, Jesus Christ, who was proclaimed to you by us, that is, by me and by Silvanus and Timothy, was never Yes-and-No; his nature is all Yes. ²⁰For in him is found the Yes to all God's promises and therefore it is 'through him' that we answer 'Amen' to give praise to God. ²¹It is God who gives us, with you, a sure place in Christ ²²and has both anointed us and marked

---

1a The argument is based on the Hebr. word *Amen* = Yes. The root meaning is 'faithful', 'solid'.

us with his seal, giving us as pledge the Spirit in our hearts.

²³ By my life I call on God to be my witness that it was only to spare you that I did not come to Corinth again.ᵇ ²⁴ We have no wish to lord it over your faith, but to work with you for your joy; for your stand in the faith is firm.

2 I made up my mind, then, that my next visit to you would not be a painful one, ² for if I cause you distress I am causing distress to my only possible source of joy. ³ Indeed, I wrote as I did precisely to spare myself distress when I visited you, from the very people who should have given me joy, in the conviction that for all of you my joy was yours too. ⁴ I wrote to you in agony of mind, not meaning to cause you distress but to show you how very much love I have for you.

⁵ If anyone did cause distress, he caused it not to me, but—not to exaggerate—in some degree to all of you. ⁶ The punishment already imposed by the majority was quite enough for such a person; ⁷ and now by contrast you should forgive and encourage him all the more, or he may be overwhelmed by the extent of his distress. ⁸ That is why I urge you to give your love towards him definite expression. ⁹ This was in fact my reason for writing, to test your quality and whether you are completely obedient. ¹⁰ But if you forgive anybody, then I too forgive that person; and whatever I have forgiven, if there is anything I have forgiven, I have done it for your sake in Christ's presence, ¹¹ to avoid being outwitted by Satan, whose scheming we know only too well.

From Troas to Macedonia; the apostolate: its importance

¹² When I came to Troas for the sake of the gospel of Christ and a door was opened for me there in the Lord, ¹³ I had no relief from anxiety, not finding my brother Titus there, and I said goodbye to them and went on to Macedonia. ¹⁴ But, thanks be to God who always gives us in Christ a part in his triumphal procession, and through us is spreading everywhere the fragrance of the knowledge of himself. ¹⁵ To God we are the fragrance of Christ, both among those who are being saved and among those who are on the way to destruction; ¹⁶ for these last, the smell of death leading to death, but for the first, the smell of life leading to life. Who is equal to such a task? ¹⁷ At least we do not adulterate the word of God, as so many do, but it is in all purity, as envoys of God and in God's presence, that we speak in Christ.

3 Are we beginning to commend ourselves to you afresh—as though we needed, like some others, to have letters of commendation either to you or from you? ² You yourselves are our letter, written in our hearts, that everyone can read and understand; ³ and it is plain that you are a letter from Christ, entrusted to our care, written not with ink but with the Spirit of the living God; not on stone tablets but on the tablets of human hearts.

⁴ Such is the confidence we have through Christ in facing God; ⁵ it is not that we are so competent that we can claim any credit for ourselves; all our competence comes from God. ⁶ He has given us the competence to be ministers of a new covenant, a covenant which is not of written letters, but of the Spirit; for the written letters kill, but the Spirit gives life. ⁷ Now if the administering of death, engraved in letters on stone, occurred in such glory that the Israelites could not look Moses steadily in the face,ᵃ because of its glory, transitory though this glory was, ⁸ how much more will the ministry of the Spirit occur in glory! ⁹ For if it is glorious to administer condemnation, to administer saving justice is far richer in glory. ¹⁰ Indeed, what was once considered glorious has lost all claim to glory, by contrast with the glory which transcends it. ¹¹ For if what was

1b After writing 1 Co Paul *1* paid a brief, stern visit to Corinth and promised to return, *2* sent a messenger who was insulted, *3* sent a severe reprimand which was effective, and *4* wrote this letter.

3a cf. Ex 34:29–35.

transitory had any glory, how much greater is the glory of that which lasts for ever.

¹²With a hope like this, we can speak with complete fearlessness; ¹³not like Moses who put a veil over his face so that the Israelites should not watch the end of what was transitory. ¹⁴But their minds were closed; indeed, until this very day, the same veil remains over the reading of the Old Testament: it is not lifted, for only in Christ is it done away with. ¹⁵As it is, to this day, whenever Moses is read, their hearts are covered with a veil, ¹⁶and this veil will not be taken away till they turn to the Lord. ¹⁷Now this Lord is the Spirit and where the Spirit of the Lord is, there is freedom. ¹⁸And all of us, with our unveiled faces like mirrors reflecting the glory of the Lord, are being transformed into the image that we reflect in brighter and brighter glory; this is the working of the Lord who is the Spirit.

4 Such by God's mercy is our ministry, and therefore we do not waver ²but have renounced all shameful secrecy. It is not our way to be devious, or to falsify the word of God; instead, in God's sight we commend ourselves to every human being with a conscience by showing the truth openly. ³If our gospel seems to be veiled at all, it is so to those who are on the way to destruction, ⁴the unbelievers whose minds have been blinded by the god of this world, so that they cannot see shining the light of the gospel of the glory of Christ, who is the image of God. ⁵It is not ourselves that we are proclaiming, but Christ Jesus as the Lord, and ourselves as your servants for Jesus' sake. ⁶It is God who said, 'Let light shine out of darkness,' that has shone into our hearts to enlighten them with the knowledge of God's glory, the glory on the face of Christ.

The hardships and hopes of the apostolate

⁷But we hold this treasure in pots of earthenware, so that the immensity of the power is God's and not our own. ⁸We are subjected to every kind of hardship, but never distressed; we see no way out but we never despair; ⁹we

are pursued but never cut off; knocked down, but still have some life in us; ¹⁰always we carry with us in our body the death of Jesus so that the life of Jesus, too, may be visible in our body. ¹¹Indeed, while we are still alive, we are continually being handed over to death, for the sake of Jesus, so that the life of Jesus, too, may be visible in our mortal flesh. ¹²In us, then, death is at work; in you, life.

¹³But as we have the same spirit of faith as is described in scripture—*I believed and therefore I spoke*ᵃ—we, too, believe and therefore we, too, speak, ¹⁴realising that he who raised up the Lord Jesus will raise us up with Jesus in our turn, and bring us to himself—and you as well. ¹⁵You see, everything is for your benefit, so that as grace spreads, so, to the glory of God, thanksgiving may also overflow among more and more people.

¹⁶That is why we do not waver; indeed, though this outer human nature of ours may be falling into decay, at the same time our inner human nature is renewed day by day. ¹⁷The temporary, light burden of our hardships is earning us for ever an utterly incomparable, eternal weight of glory, ¹⁸since what we aim for is not visible but invisible. Visible things are transitory, but invisible things eternal.

5 For we are well aware that when the tent that houses us on earth is folded up, there is a house for us from God, not made by human hands but everlasting, in the heavens. ²And in this earthly state we do indeed groan, ³longing to put on our heavenly home over the present one; if indeed we are to be found clothed rather than stripped bare. ⁴Yes, indeed, in this present tent, we groan under the burden, not that we want to be stripped of our covering, but because we want to be covered with a second garment on top, so that what is mortal in us may be swallowed up by life. ⁵It is God who designed us for this very purpose, and he has given us the Spirit as a pledge.

⁶We are always full of confidence, then,

4a Ps 116:10.

174 READ 2 CORINTHIANS 5:1–10.

We want to be covered with a second garment on top, so that what is mortal in us may be swallowed up by life.—2 CORINTHIANS 5:4

DIVINIZED HUMANITY

Do not devote your attention to the fallacies of artificial discourses, nor to the vain promises of heretics, but to the venerable simplicity of unassuming truth. By means of this knowledge you shall escape the approaching threat of the fire of judgment, and the rayless scenery of gloomy Tartarus, where never shines a beam from the irradiating voice of the Word!

You shall escape the boiling flood of hell's eternal lake of fire and the menacing glare of fallen angels chained in Tartarus as punishment for their sins. And you shall escape the worm that ceaselessly coils for food around the body whose scum has bred it. You shall avoid such punishments by being instructed in a knowledge of the true God.

You shall possess an immortal body, one placed beyond the possibility of corruption, just like the soul. And you who in this life knew the celestial king shall receive the kingdom of heaven. You shall be a companion of the deity and a co-heir with Christ, no longer enslaved by lusts or passions and never again wasted by disease. For you have "become" God: for God has promised to bestow on you whatever is consistent with God to impart, for you have been deified and begotten unto immortality. This constitutes the import of the proverb, "Know yourself," that is, discover God within yourself, for he has formed you after his own image.   ST. HIPPOLYTUS, d. 235?

YOU WILL FIND THE NEXT READING AT 2 CORINTHIANS 5:11.

realising that as long as we are at home in the body we are exiled from the Lord, 7 guided by faith and not yet by sight; 8 we are full of confidence, then, and long instead to be exiled from the body and to be at home with the Lord. 9 And so whether at home or exiled, we make it our ambition to please him. 10 For at the judgement seat of Christ we are all to be seen for what we are, so that each of us may receive what he has deserved in the body, matched to whatever he has done, good or bad.

The apostolate in action

11 And so it is with the fear of the Lord always in mind that we try to win people over. But God sees us for what we are, and I hope your consciences do too. 12 Again we are saying this not to commend ourselves to you, but simply to give you the opportunity to take pride in us, so that you may have an answer for those who take pride in appearances and not inner reality. 13 If we have been unreasonable, it was for God; if reasonable, for you. 14 For the love of Christ overwhelms us when we consider that if one man died for all, then all have died; 15 his purpose in dying for all humanity was that those who live should live not any more for themselves, but for him who died and was raised to life for them.

16 From now onwards, then, we will not consider anyone by human standards: even if we were once familiar with Christ according to human standards, we do not know him in

175 READ 2 CORINTHIANS 5:11-21.

In the name of Christ we appeal to you to be reconciled to God.—2 CORINTHIANS 5:20

PASS IT ON

In the Tabernacle of the Lord there were not only golden drinking goblets, but, at the command of the Lord, there also were made ladles, or spoons for filling the drinking vessels. For the goblets here understand fullness of holy doctrine, for the ladles a small and restricted acquaintance with doctrine....

You ... who live in the Tabernacle of the Lord, that is, in the Holy Church, if you cannot fill up the goblets with the teachings of holy wisdom, as well then as you can, as far as the divine bounty has endowed you, give to your neighbors spoonfuls of the good word.

And when you consider that you have yourself made some little progress, draw others along with you. Seek to make comrades on the road to God. Should one among you ... stroll out towards the forum or the baths, he will invite a friend whom he thinks is not busy to keep him company. This simple action of our ordinary life is pleasant to you, and if it be that you are going towards God, give a thought not to journey alone. So Scripture says: "Let everyone who listens answer, 'Come!' " (Rv 22:17). So let him who has heard in his heart the invitation of divine love, pass on to his neighbors around about him, the message of the invitation. And though a person may not have even bread to give as alms to the hungry; yet, what is still more precious, he is able to give who possesses but a tongue. For it is a greater thing to strengthen with the nourishment of a word that will feed the mind forever, than to fill with earthly bread a stomach of perishable flesh.

Do not, my dearest brethren, withhold from your brother the charity of a word.

ST. GREGORY THE GREAT, 540?–604

YOU WILL FIND THE NEXT READING AT 2 CORINTHIANS 11.

that way any longer. ¹⁷So for anyone who is in Christ, there is a new creation: the old order is gone and a new being is there to see. ¹⁸It is all God's work; he reconciled us to himself through Christ and he gave us the ministry of reconciliation. ¹⁹I mean, God was in Christ reconciling the world to himself, not holding anyone's faults against them, but entrusting to us the message of reconciliation.

²⁰So we are ambassadors for Christ; it is as though God were urging you through us, and in the name of Christ we appeal to you to be reconciled to God. ²¹For our sake he made the sinless one a victim for sin, so that in him we might become the uprightness of God.

6 As his fellow-workers, we urge you not to let your acceptance of his grace come to nothing. ² As he said, *'At the time of my favour I have answered you; on the day of salvation I have helped you;'*ᵃ well, now is the real time of favour, now the day of salvation is here. ³ We avoid putting obstacles in anyone's way, so that no blame may attach to our work of service;

6a Is 49:8.

4but in everything we prove ourselves authentic servants of God; by resolute perseverance in times of hardships, difficulties and distress; 5when we are flogged or sent to prison or mobbed; labouring, sleepless, starving; 6in purity, in knowledge, in patience, in kindness; in the Holy Spirit, in a love free of affectation; 7in the word of truth and in the power of God; by using the weapons of uprightness for attack and for defence: 8in times of honour or disgrace, blame or praise; taken for impostors and yet we are genuine; 9unknown and yet we are acknowledged; dying, and yet here we are, alive; scourged but not executed; 10in pain yet always full of joy; poor and yet making many people rich; having nothing, and yet owning everything.

A warning

11People of Corinth, we have spoken frankly and opened our heart to you. 12Any distress you feel is not on our side; the distress is in your own selves. 13In fair exchange—I speak as though to children of mine—you must open your hearts too.

14Do*b* not harness yourselves in an uneven team with unbelievers; how can uprightness and law-breaking be partners, or what can light and darkness have in common? 15How can Christ come to an agreement with Beliar and what sharing can there be between a believer and an unbeliever? 16The temple of God cannot compromise with false gods, and that is what we are—the temple of the living God. We have God's word for it: *I shall fix my home among them and live among them; I will be their God and they will be my people.* 17*Get away from them, purify yourselves,* says the Lord. *Do not touch anything unclean,* and then *I shall welcome you.* 18*I shall be father to you, and* you *will be sons* and daughters *to me,c* says the almighty Lord.

7 Since these promises have been made to us, my dear friends, we should wash ourselves clean of everything that pollutes either body or spirit, bringing our sanctification to completion in the fear of God.

2Keep a place for us in your hearts. We have not injured anyone, or ruined anyone, or taken advantage of anyone. 3I am not saying this to condemn anybody; as I have already told you, you are in our hearts—so that together we live and together we die. 4I can speak with the greatest frankness to you; and I can speak with the greatest pride about you: in all our hardship, I am filled with encouragement and overflowing with joy.

Paul in Macedonia; he is joined by Titus

5Even after we had come to Macedonia, there was no rest for this body of ours. Far from it; we were beset by hardship on all sides, there were quarrels all around us and misgivings within us. 6But God, who encourages all those who are distressed, encouraged us through the arrival of Titus; 7and not simply by his arrival only, but also by means of the encouragement that you had given him, as he told us of your desire to see us, how sorry you were and how concerned for us; so that I was all the more joyful.

8So now, though I did distress you with my letter, I do not regret it. Even if I did regret it—and I realise that the letter distressed you, even though not for long— 9I am glad now, not because you were made to feel distress, but because the distress that you were caused led to repentance; your distress was the kind that God approves and so you have come to no kind of harm through us. 10For to be distressed in a way that God approves leads to repentance and then to salvation with no regrets; it is the world's kind of distress that ends in death. 11Just look at this present case: at what the result has been of your being made to feel distress in the way that God approves—what concern, what defence, what indignation and what alarm; what yearning, and what enthusi-

6*b* 6:14–7:1 may be a fragment on its own, a warning against infiltration of gentile ways.

6*c* Lv 26:11–12; Is 52:11; 2 S 7:14.

asm, and what justice done. In every way you have cleared yourselves of blame in this matter. [12] So although I wrote a letter to you, it was not for the sake of the offender, nor for the one offended, but only so that you yourselves should fully realise in the sight of God what concern you have for us. [13] That is what I have found encouraging.

In addition to all this to encourage us, we were made all the more joyful by Titus' joy, now that his spirit has been refreshed by you all. [14] And if I boasted about you to him in any way, then I have not been made to look foolish; indeed, our boast to Titus has been proved to be as true as anything we said to you. [15] His personal affection for you is all the stronger when he remembers how obedient you have all been, and how you welcomed him with fear and trembling. [16] I am glad that I have every confidence in you.

Why the Corinthians should be generous

8 Next, brothers, we will tell you of the grace of God which has been granted to the churches of Macedonia, [2] and how, throughout continual ordeals of hardship, their unfailing joy and their intense poverty have overflowed in a wealth of generosity on their part. [3] I can testify that it was of their own accord that they made their gift, which was not merely as far as their resources would allow, but well beyond their resources; [4] and they had kept imploring us most insistently for the privilege of a share in the fellowship of service to God's holy people— [5] it was not something that we expected of them, but it began by their offering themselves to the Lord and to us at the prompting of the will of God. [6] In the end we urged Titus, since he had already made a beginning, also to bring this work of generosity to completion among you. [7] More, as you are rich in everything—faith, eloquence, understanding, concern for everything, and love for us too—then make sure that you excel in this work of generosity too. [8] I am not saying this as an order, but testing the genuineness of your love against the concern of others. [9] You

are well aware of the generosity which our Lord Jesus Christ had, that, although he was rich, he became poor for your sake, so that you should become rich through his poverty. [10] I will give you my considered opinion in the matter; this will be the right course for you as you were the first, a year ago, not only to take any action but also even to conceive the project. [11] Now, then, complete the action as well, so that the fulfilment may—so far as your resources permit—be proportionate to your enthusiasm for the project. [12] As long as the enthusiasm is there, the basis on which it is acceptable is what someone has, not what someone does not have. [13] It is not that you ought to relieve other people's needs and leave yourselves in hardship; but there should be a fair balance— [14] your surplus at present may fill their deficit, and another time their surplus may fill your deficit. So there may be a fair balance; [15] as scripture says: *No one who had collected more had too much, no one who collected less had too little.*[a]

The delegates recommended to the Corinthians

[16] Thank God for putting into Titus' heart the same sincere concern for you. [17] He certainly took our urging to heart; but greater still was his own enthusiasm, and he went off to you of his own accord. [18] We have sent with him the brother who is praised as an evangelist in all the churches [19] and who, what is more, was elected by the churches to be our travelling companion in this work of generosity, a work to be administered by us for the glory of the Lord and our complete satisfaction. [20] We arranged it this way so that no one should be able to make any accusation against us about this large sum we are administering. [21] And so *we have been careful to do right* not only *in the sight of the Lord* but also *in the sight of people.*[b] [22] Along with these, we have sent a brother of ours whose eagerness we have tested over and over again in many ways and who is now all

8a Ex 16:18.   8b Pr 3:4 LXX.

the more eager because he has so much faith in you. 23 If Titus is in question—he is my own partner and fellow-worker in your interests; and if our brothers—they are the emissaries of the churches and the glory of Christ. 24 So then, in full view of all the churches, give proof that you love them, and that we were right to boast of you to them.

9 About the help to God's holy people, there is really no need for me to write to you;[a] 2 for I am well aware of your enthusiasm, and I have been boasting of it to the Macedonians that 'Achaia has been ready for a year'; your enthusiasm has been a spur to many others. 3 All the same, I have sent the brothers, to make sure that our boast about you may not prove hollow in this respect and that you may be ready, as I said you would be; 4 so that if by chance some of the Macedonians came with me and found you unprepared we—to say nothing of yourselves—would not be put to shame by our confidence in you. 5 So I have thought it necessary to encourage the brothers to go to you ahead of us and make sure in advance of the gift that you have already promised, so that it is all at hand as a real gift and not an imposition.

Blessings to be expected from the collection

6 But remember: anyone who sows sparsely will reap sparsely as well—and anyone who sows generously will reap generously as well. 7 Each one should give as much as he has decided on his own initiative, not reluctantly or under compulsion, for *God loves a cheerful giver.*[b] 8 God is perfectly able to enrich you with every grace, so that you always have enough for every conceivable need, and your resources overflow in all kinds of good work. 9 As scripture says: *To the needy he gave without stint, his uprightness stands firm for ever.*[c] 10 The one who so freely provides *seed for the sower and food to eat*[d] will provide you with ample store of seed for sowing and make *the harvest of your uprightness*[e] a bigger one: 11 you will be rich enough in every way for every

kind of generosity that makes people thank God for what we have done. 12 For the help provided by this contribution not only satisfies the needs of God's holy people, but also overflows into widespread thanksgiving to God; 13 because when you have proved your quality by this help, they will give glory to God for the obedience which you show in professing the gospel of Christ, as well as for the generosity of your fellowship towards them and towards all. 14 At the same time, their prayer for you will express the affection they feel for you because of the unbounded grace God has given you. 15 Thanks be to God for his gift that is beyond all telling!

Paul's reply to accusations of weakness

10 I urge you by the gentleness and forbearance of Christ—this is Paul now speaking personally—I, the one who is so humble when he is facing you but full of boldness at a distance. 2 Yes, my appeal to you is that I should not have to be bold when I am actually with you, or show the same self-assurance as I reckon to use when I am challenging those who reckon that we are guided by human motives. 3 For although we are human, it is not by human methods that we do battle. 4 The weapons with which we do battle are not those of human nature, but they have the power, in God's cause, to demolish fortresses. It is ideas that we demolish, 5 every presumptuous notion that is set up against the knowledge of God, and we bring every thought into captivity and obedience to Christ; 6 once you have given your complete obedience, we are prepared to punish any disobedience. 7 Look at the evidence of your eyes. Anybody who is convinced that he belongs to Christ should go on to reflect that we belong to Christ no less than he does. 8 Maybe I have taken rather too much pride in our authority, but the Lord

9a As he has just done so, this chapter may be a separate note.

9b Pr 22:8 LXX.   9c Ps 112:9.

9d Is 55:10.   9e Ho 12:12.

gave us that for building you up, not for knocking you down, and I am not going to be shamed [9]into letting you think that I can put fear into you only by letter. [10]Someone said, 'His letters are weighty enough, and full of strength, but when you see him in person, he makes no impression and his powers of speaking are negligible.' [11]I should like that sort of person to take note that our deeds when we are present will show the same qualities as our letters when we were at a distance.

His reply to the accusation of ambition

[12]We are not venturing to rank ourselves, or even to compare ourselves with certain people who provide their own commendations. By measuring themselves by themselves and comparing themselves to themselves, they only show their folly. [13]By contrast we do not intend to boast beyond measure, but will measure ourselves by the standard which God laid down for us, namely that of having come all the way to you. [14]We are not overreaching ourselves as we would be if we had not come all the way to you; in fact we were the first to come as far as you with the good news of Christ. [15]So we are not boasting beyond measure, about other men's work; in fact, we hope, as your faith increases, to grow greater and greater by this standard of ours, [16]by preaching the gospel to regions beyond you, rather than boasting about work already done in someone else's province. [17]*Let anyone who wants to boast, boast of the Lord.*[a] [18]For it is not through self-commendation that recognition is won, but through commendation.

Paul is driven to sound his own praises

11 I wish you would put up with a little foolishness from me—not that you don't do this already. [2]The jealousy that I feel for you is, you see, God's own jealousy: I gave you all in marriage to a single husband, a virgin pure for presentation to Christ. [3]But I am afraid that, just as the snake with his cunning seduced Eve, your minds may be led astray from single-minded devotion to Christ. [4]Be-cause any chance comer has only to preach a Jesus other than the one we preached, or you have only to receive a spirit different from the one you received, or a gospel different from the one you accepted—and you put up with that only too willingly. [5]Now, I consider that I am not in the least inferior to the super-apos-tles. [6]Even if there is something lacking in my public speaking, this is not the case with my knowledge, as we have openly shown to you at all times and before everyone.

[7]Have I done wrong, then, humbling my-self so that you might be raised up, by preach-ing the gospel of God to you for nothing? [8]I was robbing other churches, taking wages from them in order to work for you. [9]When I was with you and needed money, I was no burden to anybody, for the brothers from Macedonia brought me as much as I needed when they came; I have always been careful not to let myself be a burden to you in any way, and I shall continue to be so. [10]And as Christ's truth is in me, this boast of mine is not going to be silenced in the regions of Achaia. [11]Why should it be? Because I do not love you? God knows that I do. [12]I will go on acting as I do at present, to cut the ground from under the feet of those who are looking for a chance to be proved my equals in grounds for boasting. [13]These people are counterfeit apostles, dis-honest workers disguising themselves as apos-tles of Christ. [14]There is nothing astonishing in this; even Satan disguises himself as an angel of light. [15]It is nothing extraordinary, then, when his servants disguise themselves as the servants of uprightness. They will come to the end appropriate to what they have done.

[16]To repeat: let no one take me for a fool, but if you do, then treat me as a fool, so that I, too, can do a little boasting. [17]I shall not be fol-lowing the Lord's way in what I say now, but will be speaking out of foolishness in the con-viction that I have something to boast about. [18]So many people boast on merely human grounds that I shall too. [19]I know how happy

10a Jr 9:22–23.

176 READ 2 CORINTHIANS 11:16–33.

There is, day in day out, the pressure on me of my anxiety for all the churches.

—2 CORINTHIANS 11:28

THE COST OF EVANGELIZATION

In this letter St. John de Brébeuf invited fellow Jesuits to serve in the North American mission. Like St. Paul, he celebrated the hardships that accompany dedicated evangelization:

When you reach the land of the Hurons, you will find us full of love. We will receive you in a hut so miserable that there is none in France to compare it to. Completely exhausted as you will be, we shall be able to give you nothing but a mat for a bed. Besides you will arrive in the season when ubiquitous fleas will prevent you from closing an eye all night long. "You may have been a famous professor, but here you will be merely a student and with what students—savages who will constantly ridicule you. The Huron language will be your St. Thomas and your Aristotle, and—clever and glib man that you are—you must decide to be mute for a long time among these barbarians.

You will spend the winter in almost continuous discomforts—excessive cold, smoke, the annoying habits of the savages, who crowd around our fireplace all day expecting to be fed.

For the rest—well, so far life has been a bed of roses. We have Christians in almost every village, so must plan on making rounds at all seasons. And our lives hang by a thread. Our straw cabin may catch fire at any moment. The malice of the savages causes perpetual fear. Some malcontent may cleave open your head because he believes you are the cause of droughts.

Here we have nothing to incite us toward good, living among people who are astonished when you speak to them of God.

St. JOHN DE BRÉBEUF, 1593–1649

YOU WILL FIND THE NEXT READING AT 2 CORINTHIANS 12.

you are to put up with fools, being so wise yourselves; 20 and how you will still go on putting up with a man who enslaves you, eats up all you possess, keeps you under his orders and sets himself above you, or even slaps you in the face. 21 I say it to your shame; perhaps we have been too weak.

Whatever bold claims anyone makes— now I am talking as a fool—I can make them too. 22 Are they Hebrews? So am I. Are they Israelites? So am I. Are they descendants of Abraham? So am I. 23 Are they servants of Christ? I speak in utter folly—I am too, and more than they are: I have done more work, I have been in prison more, I have been flogged more severely, many times exposed to death. 24 Five times I have been given the thirty-nine lashes by the Jews; 25 three times I have been beaten with sticks; once I was stoned; three times I have been shipwrecked, and once I have been in the open sea for a night and a day; 26 continually travelling, I have been in danger from rivers, in danger from brigands, in danger from my own people and in danger from the gentiles, in danger in the towns and in danger in the open country, in danger at sea and in danger from people masquerading as brothers; 27 I have worked with unsparing energy, for many nights without sleep; I have been hungry and thirsty, and often altogether without food or drink; I have been cold and lacked clothing. 28 And, besides all the external things, there is, day in day out, the pressure on me of my anxiety for all the churches. 29 If anyone weakens, I am weakened as well; and when anyone is made to fall, I burn in agony myself.

30 If I have to boast, I will boast of all the ways in which I am weak. 31 The God and Father of the Lord Jesus—who is for ever to be blessed—knows that I am not lying. 32 When I was in Damascus, the governor who was under King Aretas put guards round Damascus city to catch me, 33 and I was let down in a basket through a window in the wall, and that was how I escaped from his hands.

12 I am boasting because I have to. Not that it does any good, but I will move on to visions and revelations from the Lord. 2 I know a man in Christ who fourteen years ago—still in the body? I do not know; or out of the body? I do not know: God knows—was caught up right into the third heaven. 3 And I know that this man—still in the body? or outside the body? I do not know, God knows— 4 was caught up into Paradise and heard words said that cannot and may not be spoken by any human being. 5 On behalf of someone like that I am willing to boast, but I am not going to boast on my own behalf except of my weaknesses; 6 and then, if I do choose to boast I shall not be talking like a fool because I shall be speaking the truth. But I will not go on in case anybody should rate me higher than he sees and hears me to be, because of the exceptional greatness of the revelations.

7 Wherefore, so that I should not get above myself, I was given a thorn in the flesh, a messenger from Satan to batter me and prevent me from getting above myself. 8 About this, I have three times pleaded with the Lord that it might leave me; 9 but he has answered me, 'My grace is enough for you: for power is at full stretch in weakness.' It is, then, about my

weaknesses that I am happiest of all to boast, so that the power of Christ may rest upon me; 10 and that is why I am glad of weaknesses, insults, constraints, persecutions and distress for Christ's sake. For it is when I am weak that I am strong.

11 I have turned into a fool, but you forced me to it. It is you that should have been commending me; those super-apostles had no advantage over me, even if I am nothing at all. 12 All the marks characteristic of a true apostle have been at work among you: complete perseverance, signs, marvels, demonstrations of power. 13 Is there any way in which you have been given less than the rest of the churches, except that I did not make myself a burden to you? Forgive me for this unfairness!

14 Here I am, ready to come to you for the third time and I am not going to be a burden on you: it is not your possessions that I want, but yourselves. Children are not expected to save up for their parents, but parents for their children, 15 and I am more than glad to spend what I have and to be spent for the sake of your souls. Is it because I love you so much more, that I am loved the less?

16 All right, then; I did not make myself a burden to you, but, trickster that I am, I caught you by trickery. 17 Have I taken advantage of you through any of the people I have sent to you? 18 Titus came at my urging, and I sent his companion with him. Did Titus take advantage of you? Can you deny that he and I were following the guidance of the same Spirit and were on the same tracks?

Paul's fears and anxieties

19 All this time you have been thinking that we have been pleading our own cause before you; no, we have been speaking in Christ and in the presence of God—and all, dear friends, to build you up. 20 I am afraid that in one way or another, when I come, I may find you different from what I should like you to be, and you may find me what you would not like me to be; so that in one way or the other there will be rivalry, jealousy, bad temper, quarrels, slan-

177 READ 2 CORINTHIANS 12:1–6.

I know a man in Christ who fourteen years ago . . . was caught up right into the third heaven.—2 CORINTHIANS 12:2

EXTRAORDINARY EXPERIENCES OF GOD'S PRESENCE

Sometimes God comes into the soul when it has neither called, prayed, or summoned him. And he instills into the soul an uncommon fire and love and sweetness in which it delights and rejoices greatly. The soul believes that the presence of God himself has caused this consolation, but this is not certain. But then the soul perceives that God is within itself—although it cannot see him inwardly—because it does sense and take delight in that his grace is present. Yet even this is not certain.

But then the soul further perceives that God speaks to it with most sweet words that it delights in still more. And it rejoices because it feels God's presence. Yet some doubts still remain, but only a few. For as yet the soul possesses no perfect certainty that God is truly within it because other spirits can produce such conversation and feelings. So it still may be in doubt. It seems to me that this comes either from the soul's own wickedness and sinfulness, or else by the will of God, who does not want the soul to feel certain and secure.

But when the soul senses the presence of God more deeply than usual, then it assures itself of his inward presence. The soul feels his presence with an understanding so marvelous and so profound and with such great love and divine fire that it loses all love for itself and for the body. It speaks and knows and understands things that it has never heard from any human being. And it understands with such great illumination that it can scarcely hold its peace. If it does hold its peace, it does so out of the abundance of its zeal so that it may not displease God its Lover, nor cause offence, and likewise by reason of its humility. It does not want to speak of things so exceedingly high in order that it may not draw attention to itself.

BL. ANGELA OF FOLIGNO, 1248?–1309

YOU WILL FIND THE NEXT READING AT GALATIANS 2.

der, gossip, arrogance and disorders; ²¹ and when I come again, my God may humiliate me in front of you and I shall be grieved by all those who sinned in the past and have still not repented of the impurities and sexual immorality and debauchery that they have committed.

13 This will be the third time I have confronted you. *Whatever the misdemeanour, the evidence of two or three witnesses is required to sustain a charge.*ᵃ ²I gave you notice once, and now, though I am not with you, I give notice again, just as when I was with you for a second time, to those who sinned before, and to all others; and it is to this effect, that when I do come next time, I shall have no mercy. ³Since you are asking for a proof that it is Christ who speaks in me; he is not weak with you but his power is at work among you; ⁴for, though it was out of weakness that he was crucified, he is alive now with the power

13a Dt 19:15.

of God. We, too, are weak in him, but with regard to you we shall live with him by the power of God.

⁵ Put yourselves to the test to make sure you are in the faith. Examine yourselves. Do you not recognise yourselves as people in whom Jesus Christ is present?—unless, that is, you fail the test. ⁶ But we, as I hope you will come to recognise, do not fail the test. ⁷ It is our prayer to God that you may do nothing wrong—not so that we have the credit of passing a test, but because you will be doing what is right, even if we do not pass the test. ⁸ We have no power to resist the truth; only to further the truth; ⁹ and we are delighted to be weak if only you are strong. What we ask in our prayers is that you should be made perfect.

¹⁰ That is why I am writing this while still far away, so that when I am with you I shall not have to be harsh, with the authority that the Lord has given me, an authority that is for building up and not for breaking down.

Recommendations, greetings, final good wishes

¹¹ To end then, brothers, we wish you joy; try to grow perfect; encourage one another; have a common mind and live in peace, and the God of love and peace will be with you.

¹² Greet one another with the holy kiss. All God's holy people send you their greetings.

¹³ The grace of the Lord Jesus Christ, the love of God and the fellowship of the Holy Spirit be with you all.

GALATIANS

Address[a]

1 From Paul, an apostle appointed not by human beings nor through any human being but by Jesus Christ and God the Father who raised him from the dead, 2and all the brothers who are with me, to the churches of Galatia. 3Grace and peace from God the Father and our Lord Jesus Christ 4who gave himself for our sins to liberate us from this present wicked world, in accordance with the will of our God and Father, 5to whom be glory for ever and ever. Amen.

A warning

6I am astonished that you are so promptly turning away from the one who called you in the grace of Christ and are going over to a different gospel— 7not that it is another gospel; except that there are trouble-makers among you who are seeking to pervert the gospel of Christ. 8But even if we ourselves or an angel from heaven preaches to you a gospel other than the one we preached to you, let God's curse be on him. 9I repeat again what we declared before: anyone who preaches to you a gospel other than the one you were first given is to be under God's curse. 10Whom am I trying to convince now, human beings or God? Am I trying to please human beings? If I were still doing that I should not be a servant of Christ.

God's call

11Now I want to make it quite clear to you, brothers, about the gospel that was preached by me, that it was no human message. 12It was not from any human being that I received it, and I was not taught it, but it came to me through a revelation of Jesus Christ. 13You have surely heard how I lived in the past, within Judaism, and how there was simply no limit to the way I persecuted the Church of God in my attempts to destroy it; 14and how, in Judaism, I outstripped most of my Jewish contemporaries in my limitless enthusiasm for the traditions of my ancestors. 15But when God, who had set me apart from the time when I was *in my mother's womb, called*[b] me through his grace and chose 16to reveal his Son in me, so that I should preach him to the gentiles, I was in no hurry to confer with any human being, 17or to go up to Jerusalem to see those who were already apostles before me. Instead, I went off to Arabia, and later I came back to Damascus. 18Only after three years did I go up to Jerusalem to meet Cephas. I stayed fifteen days with him 19but did not set eyes on any of the rest of the apostles, only James, the Lord's brother. 20I swear before God that what I have written is the truth. 21After that I went to places in Syria and Cilicia; 22and was still unknown by sight to the churches of Judaea which are in Christ, 23they simply kept hearing it said, 'The man once so eager to persecute us is now preaching the faith that he used to try to destroy,' 24and they gave glory to God for me.

The meeting at Jerusalem

2 It was not until fourteen years had gone by that I travelled up to Jerusalem again, with Barnabas, and I took Titus with me too. 2My journey was inspired by a revelation and there,

1a Unusually, there are no thanks or praise in this address.
1b Jr 1:5.

178 READ GALATIANS 2:15–21.

I have been crucified with Christ and yet I am alive; yet it is no longer I, but Christ living in me.—GALATIANS 2:20

LOSING YOURSELF IN GOD

To live no more in yourself but lost in God is the most sublime perfection the soul can reach. We should all aim for this, losing ourselves again and again a thousand times in the ocean of this infinite greatness. . . .

Now, some of us want to lose ourselves, but we also want it not to hurt too much. We do indeed tell our Lord that we're surrendering ourselves into his divine arms, but don't do it in the right way. We want to retain some degree of control—not so much in temporal matters as in spiritual ones. Self-love, with its subtle tricks, always tries to persuade us that things won't go the way they should unless we remain somewhat involved in them. But people who are completely lost in God don't want to have any virtue or perfection except what God wants. They work faithfully because God wishes it, but they let God take concern for their work. They don't go looking for new methods of achieving perfection but simply concentrate on making good use of the ones that providence supplies and offers in every situation.

It's true that even once we've given ourselves to God completely, we tend to take back the gift. What else is there to do, in that case, but humble ourselves, acknowledge the incompleteness of our surrender, . . . and follow this act of deep humility by . . . throwing ourselves back into God like a little drop of water falling into the sea—losing ourselves in the ocean of divine Goodness, never to find ourselves again. Repeat this process constantly, and if you faithfully persevere in it, I dare promise you that you will lose yourself at last and never find yourself again. Such a happy loss!

ST. JANE DE CHANTAL, 1572–1641

YOU WILL FIND THE NEXT READING AT GALATIANS 5.

in a private session with the recognised leaders, I expounded the whole gospel that I preach to the gentiles, to make quite sure that the efforts I was making and had already made should not be fruitless. ³Even then, and although Titus, a Greek, was with me, there was no demand that he should be circumcised; ⁴but because of some false brothers who had secretly insinuated themselves to spy on the freedom that we have in Christ Jesus, intending to reduce us to slavery— ⁵people we did not defer to for one moment, or the truth of the gospel preached to you might have been compromised . . . ⁶but those who were recognised as important people—whether they actually were important or not: *There is no favouritism with God*ᵃ—those recognised leaders, I am saying, had nothing to add to my message. ⁷On the contrary, once they saw that the gospel for the uncircumcised had been entrusted to me, just as to Peter the gospel for the circumcised ⁸(for he who empowered Peter's

2a Dt 10:17.

apostolate to the circumcision also empowered mine to the gentiles), [9] and when they acknowledged the grace that had been given to me, then James and Cephas and John, who were the ones recognised as pillars, offered their right hands to Barnabas and to me as a sign of partnership: we were to go to the gentiles and they to the circumcised. [10] They asked nothing more than that we should remember to help the poor, as indeed I was anxious to do in any case.

Peter and Paul at Antioch[b]

[11] However, when Cephas came to Antioch, then I did oppose him to his face since he was manifestly in the wrong. [12] Before certain people from James came, he used to eat with gentiles; but as soon as these came, he backed out and kept apart from them, out of fear of the circumcised. [13] And the rest of the Jews put on the same act as he did, so that even Barnabas was carried away by their insincerity.

[14] When I saw, though, that their behaviour was not true to the gospel, I said to Cephas in front of all of them, 'Since you, though you are a Jew, live like the gentiles and not like the Jews, how can you compel the gentiles to live like the Jews?'

The gospel as preached by Paul

[15] We who were born Jews and not gentile sinners [16] have nevertheless learnt that someone is reckoned as upright not by practising the Law but by faith in Jesus Christ; and we too came to believe in Christ Jesus so as to be reckoned as upright by faith in Christ and not by practising the Law: since no human being *can be found upright*[c] by keeping the Law. [17] Now if we too are found to be sinners on the grounds that we seek our justification in Christ, it would surely follow that Christ was at the service of sin. Out of the question! [18] If I now rebuild everything I once demolished, I prove that I was wrong before. [19] In fact, through the Law I am dead to the Law so that I can be alive to God. [20] I have been crucified with Christ and yet I am alive; yet it is no longer I, but Christ living in me. The life that I am now living, subject to the limitation of human nature, I am living in faith, faith in the Son of God who loved me and gave himself for me. [21] I am not setting aside God's grace as of no value; it is merely that if saving justice comes through the Law, Christ died needlessly.

The Christian experience

3 You stupid people in Galatia! After you have had a clear picture of Jesus Christ crucified, right in front of your eyes, who has put a spell on you? [2] There is only one thing I should like you to tell me: How was it that you received the Spirit—was it by the practice of the Law, or by believing in the message you heard? [3] Having begun in the Spirit, can you be so stupid as to end in the flesh? [4] Can all the favours you have received have had no effect at all—if there really has been no effect? [5] Would you say, then, that he who so lavishly sends the Spirit to you, and causes the miracles among you, is doing this through your practice of the Law or because you believed the message you heard?

Witness of scripture: faith and the Law

[6] *Abraham,* you remember, *put his faith in God,*[a] and this was reckoned to him as uprightness. [7] Be sure, then, that it is people of faith who are the children of Abraham. [8] And it was because scripture foresaw that God would give saving justice to the gentiles through faith, that it announced the future gospel to Abraham in the words: *All nations will be blessed in you.*[b] [9] So it is people of faith who receive the same blessing as Abraham, the man of faith.

The curse brought by the Law

[10] On the other hand, all those who depend on the works of the Law are under a curse, since scripture says: *Accursed be he who does not make*

2b cf. Ac 15:19–29.   2c Ps 143:2.
3a Gn 15:6.   3b Gn 12:3.

what is written in the book of the Law effective, by putting it into practice.[c] 11 Now it is obvious that nobody is reckoned as upright in God's sight by the Law, since *the upright will live through faith;* 12 and the Law is based not on faith but on the principle, *whoever complies with it will find life in it.* 13 Christ redeemed us from the curse of the Law by being cursed for our sake since scripture says: *Anyone hanged is accursed,* 14 so that the blessing of Abraham might come to the gentiles in Christ Jesus, and so that we might receive the promised Spirit through faith.

The Law did not cancel the promise

15 To put it in human terms, my brothers: even when a will is only a human one, once it has been ratified nobody can cancel it or add more provisions to it. 16 Now the promises were addressed to Abraham *and to his progeny.* The words were not *and to his progenies* in the plural, but in the singular; *and to your progeny,* which means Christ. 17 What I am saying is this: once a will had been long ago ratified by God, the Law, coming four hundred and thirty years later, could not abolish it and so nullify its promise. 18 You see, if the inheritance comes by the Law, it no longer comes through a promise; but it was by a promise that God made his gift to Abraham.

The purpose of the Law

19 Then what is the purpose of the Law? It was added to deal with crimes until the *'progeny'* to whom the promise had been made should come; and it was promulgated through angels,[d] by the agency of an intermediary. 20 Now there can be an intermediary only between two parties, yet God is one. 21 Is the Law contrary, then, to God's promises? Out of the question! If the Law that was given had been capable of giving life, then certainly saving justice would have come from the Law. 22 As it is, scripture makes no exception when it says that sin is master everywhere; so the promise can be given only by faith in Jesus Christ to those who have this faith.

The coming of faith

23 But before faith came, we were kept under guard by the Law, locked up to wait for the faith which would eventually be revealed to us. 24 So the Law was serving as a slave to look after us, to lead us to Christ, so that we could be justified by faith. 25 But now that faith has come we are no longer under a slave looking after us; 26 for all of you are the children of God, through faith, in Christ Jesus, 27 since every one of you that has been baptised has been clothed in Christ. 28 There can be neither Jew nor Greek, there can be neither slave nor freeman, there can be neither male nor female—for you are all one in Christ Jesus. 29 And simply by being Christ's, you are that *progeny* of Abraham, the heirs named in the promise.

Sons of God

4 What I am saying is this: an heir, during the time while he is still under age, is no different from a slave, even though he is the owner of all the property; 2 he is under the control of guardians and administrators until the time fixed by his father. 3 So too with us, as long as we were still under age, we were enslaved to the elemental principles of this world; 4 but when the completion of the time came, God sent his Son, born of a woman, born a subject of the Law, 5 to redeem the subjects of the Law, so that we could receive adoption as sons. 6 As you are sons, God has sent into our hearts the Spirit of his Son crying, *'Abba,* Father';[a] 7 and so you are no longer a slave, but a son; and if a son, then an heir, by God's own act.

8 But formerly when you did not know God, you were kept in slavery to things which are not really gods at all, 9 whereas now that you have come to recognise God—or rather, be recognised by God—how can you now

3c Dt 27:26; Hab 2:4; Lv 18:5; Dt 21:23.

3d A rabbinic tradition. The intermediary is Moses.

4a cf. Rom 8:15.

turn back again to those powerless and bankrupt elements whose slaves you now want to be all over again? [10] You are keeping special days, and months, and seasons and years— [11] I am beginning to be afraid that I may, after all, have wasted my efforts on you.

A personal appeal

[12] I urge you, brothers,—be like me, as I have become like you. You have never been unfair to me; [13] indeed you remember that it was an illness that first gave me the opportunity to preach the gospel to you, [14] but though my illness was a trial to you, you did not show any distaste or revulsion; instead, you welcomed me as a messenger of God, as if I were Christ Jesus himself. [15] What has happened to the utter contentment you had then? For I can testify to you that you would have plucked your eyes out, were that possible, and given them to me. [16] Then have I turned into your enemy simply by being truthful with you? [17] Their devotion to you has no praiseworthy motive; they simply want to cut you off from me, so that you may centre your devotion on them. [18] Devotion to a praiseworthy cause is praiseworthy at any time, not only when I am there with you. [19] My children, I am going through the pain of giving birth to you all over again, until Christ is formed in you; [20] and how I wish I could be there with you at this moment and find the right way of talking to you: I am quite at a loss with you.

The two covenants: Hagar and Sarah

[21] Tell me then, you are so eager to be subject to the Law, have you listened to what the Law says? [22] Scripture says that Abraham had two sons, one by the slave girl and one by the free-woman. [23] The son of the slave girl came to be born in the way of human nature; but the son of the freewoman came to be born through a promise. [24] There is an allegory here: these women stand for the two covenants. The one given on Mount Sinai—that is Hagar, whose children are born into slavery; [25] now Sinai is a mountain in Arabia and represents Jerusalem in its present state, for she is in slavery together with her children. [26] But the Jerusalem above is free, and that is the one that is our mother; [27] as scripture says: *Shout for joy, you barren woman who has borne no children! Break into shouts of joy, you who were never in labour. For the sons of the forsaken one are more in number than the sons of the wedded wife.*[b] [28] Now you, brothers, are like Isaac, children of the promise; [29] just as at that time, the child born in the way of human nature persecuted the child born through the Spirit, so now. [30] But what is it that scripture says? *Drive away that slave girl and her son; the slave girl's son is not to share the inheritance with the son*[c] *of the freewoman.* [31] So, brothers, we are the children not of the slave girl but of the freewoman.

Christian liberty

5 Christ set us free, so that we should remain free. Stand firm, then, and do not let yourselves be fastened again to the yoke of slavery.

[2] I, Paul, give you my word that if you accept circumcision, Christ will be of no benefit to you at all. [3] I give my assurance once again to every man who accepts circumcision that he is under obligation to keep the whole Law; [4] once you seek to be reckoned as upright through the Law, then you have separated yourself from Christ, you have fallen away from grace. [5] We are led by the Spirit to wait in the confident hope of saving justice through faith, [6] since in Christ Jesus it is not being circumcised or being uncircumcised that can effect anything—only faith working through love.

[7] You began your race well; who came to obstruct you and stop you obeying the truth? [8] It was certainly not any prompting from him who called you! [9] A pinch of yeast ferments the whole batch. [10] But I feel sure that, united in the Lord, you will not be led astray, and that anyone who makes trouble with you will be condemned, no matter who he is. [11] And I, brothers—if I were still preaching circumci-

4b Is 54:1.   4c Gn 21:10.

179 READ GALATIANS 5:13–25.

Be guided by the Spirit, and you will no longer yield to self-indulgence.—GALATIANS 5:16

OVERCOMING EVIL TENDENCIES

In this letter St. Jane de Chantal teaches a close associate how to correct evil inclinations with good behaviors—the fruit of the Holy Spirit:

My dearest daughter, may the good God inspire me to say what is for his glory and your consolation. In my judgment all the repugnancies of which you speak, all your feelings, aversions, difficulties, are for your greater good. And you are bound not to yield to them. You should keep making resolutions every day to fight and resist them. Yet when you fall—say as many as fifty times a day—never on any account be astonished or uneasy. But quite gently reproach yourself and take up again the practice of the contrary virtue. All the while speak words of love and confidence to our Lord. Speak them just as much after you have fallen into a thousand faults as if you had only fallen into one.

Do not forget all that we have said to you on this subject. Practice it for the love of God, assured that God will draw his glory and your perfection out of this weakness. Never have a doubt on this point, and bear up bravely and sweetly whatever happens. If sometimes you feel weak, cowardly, with no confidence in God, compel your lips to utter words the very opposite of your feelings, and say them firmly: My Savior, my all, despite my miseries and my distrust, I trust you completely. You are the strength of the weak, the refuge of the miserable, the wealth of the poor. In a word, you are my Savior, who has always loved the sinner.

Now these and similar words, my dearest daughter, you can say—perhaps not with devotion or tears, but with set purpose. Then pass on to divert your mind in some way, for the Almighty will not let you escape from his hand that has so securely captured you. Don't you see how his sweet goodness comes to your aid in such a striking and beneficial way? ST. JANE DE CHANTAL, 1572–1641

YOU WILL FIND THE NEXT READING AT EPHESIANS 2.

sion, why should I still be persecuted? For then the obstacle which is the cross would have no point any more. ¹²I could wish that those who are unsettling you would go further and mutilate themselves.ᵃ

Liberty and love

¹³After all, brothers, you were called to be free; do not use your freedom as an opening for self-indulgence, but be servants to one another in love, ¹⁴since the whole of the Law is summarised in the one commandment: *You must love your neighbour as yourself.*ᵇ ¹⁵If you go snapping at one another and tearing one another to pieces, take care: you will be eaten up by one another.

¹⁶Instead, I tell you, be guided by the Spirit, and you will no longer yield to self-indul-

5a Perhaps a reference to the castration practised by the priests of Cybele.

5b Lv 19:18.

gence. [17] The desires of self-indulgence are always in opposition to the Spirit, and the desires of the Spirit are in opposition to self-indulgence: they are opposites, one against the other; that is how you are prevented from doing the things that you want to. [18] But when you are led by the Spirit, you are not under the Law. [19] When self-indulgence is at work the results are obvious: sexual vice, impurity, and sensuality, [20] the worship of false gods and sorcery; antagonisms and rivalry, jealousy, bad temper and quarrels, disagreements, [21] factions and malice, drunkenness, orgies and all such things. And about these, I tell you now as I have told you in the past, that people who behave in these ways will not inherit the kingdom of God. [22] On the other hand the fruit of the Spirit is love, joy, peace, patience, kindness, goodness, trustfulness, [23] gentleness and self-control; no law can touch such things as these. [24] All who belong to Christ Jesus have crucified self with all its passions and its desires.

[25] Since we are living by the Spirit, let our behaviour be guided by the Spirit [26] and let us not be conceited or provocative and envious of one another.

On kindness and perseverance

6 Brothers, even if one of you is caught doing something wrong, those of you who are spiritual should set that person right in a spirit of gentleness; and watch yourselves that you are not put to the test in the same way. [2] Carry each other's burdens; that is how to keep the law of Christ. [3] Someone who thinks himself important, when he is not, only deceives himself; [4] but everyone is to examine his own achievements, and then he will confine his boasting to his own achievements, not comparing them with anybody else's. [5] Each one has his own load to carry.

[6] When someone is under instruction in doctrine, he should give his teacher a share in all his possessions. [7] Don't delude yourself: God is not to be fooled; whatever someone sows, that is what he will reap. [8] If his sowing is in the field of self-indulgence, then his harvest from it will be corruption; if his sowing is in the Spirit, then his harvest from the Spirit will be eternal life. [9] And let us never slacken in doing good; for if we do not give up, we shall have our harvest in due time. [10] So then, as long as we have the opportunity let all our actions be for the good of everybody, and especially of those who belong to the household of the faith.

Postscript

[11] Notice what large letters I have used in writing to you with my own hand. [12] It is those who want to cut a figure by human standards who force circumcision on you, simply so that they will not be persecuted for the cross of Christ. [13] Even though they are circumcised they still do not keep the Law themselves; they want you to be circumcised only so that they can boast of your outward appearance. [14] But as for me, it is out of the question that I should boast at all, except of the cross of our Lord Jesus Christ, through whom the world has been crucified to me, and I to the world. [15] It is not being circumcised or uncircumcised that matters; but what matters is a new creation. [16] Peace and mercy to all who follow this as their rule and to the Israel of God.

[17] After this, let no one trouble me; I carry branded on my body the marks of Jesus.

[18] The grace of our Lord Jesus Christ be with your spirit, my brothers. Amen.

The Letter to the

EPHESIANS
</>

Address and greetings

1 Paul, by the will of God an apostle of Christ Jesus, to God's holy people,[a] faithful in Christ Jesus. 2 Grace and peace to you from God our Father and from the Lord Jesus Christ.

God's plan of salvation

3 Blessed be God the Father of our Lord
  Jesus Christ,
who has blessed us with all the spiritual
  blessings of heaven in Christ.
4 Thus he chose us in Christ before the
  world was made
to be holy and faultless before him
  in love,
5 marking us out for himself beforehand, to
  be adopted sons, through Jesus
  Christ.
Such was his purpose and good pleasure,
6 to the praise of the glory of his grace,
his free gift to us in the Beloved,
7 in whom, through his blood, we gain our
  freedom, the forgiveness of our
  sins.
Such is the richness of the grace
8 which he has showered on us
in all wisdom and insight.
9 He has let us know the mystery of his
  purpose,
according to his good pleasure which he
  determined beforehand in Christ,
10 for him to act upon when the times had
  run their course:
that he would bring everything together
  under Christ, as head,
everything in the heavens and everything
  on earth.

11 And it is in him that we have received our
  heritage,
marked out beforehand as we were,
under the plan of the One who guides all
  things
as he decides by his own will,
12 chosen to be,
for the praise of his glory,
the people who would put their hopes in
  Christ before he came.
13 Now you too, in him,
have heard the message of the truth and
  the gospel of your salvation,
and having put your trust in it
you have been stamped with the seal of the
  Holy Spirit of the Promise,
14 who is the pledge of our inheritance,
for the freedom of the people whom God
  has taken for his own,
for the praise of his glory.

The triumph and the supremacy of Christ

15 That is why I, having once heard about your faith in the Lord Jesus, and your love for all God's holy people, 16 have never failed to thank God for you and to remember you in my prayers. 17 May the God of our Lord Jesus Christ, the Father of glory, give you a spirit of wisdom and perception of what is revealed, to bring you to full knowledge of him. 18 May he enlighten the eyes of your mind so that you can see what hope his call holds for you, how rich is the glory of the heritage he offers among his holy people, 19 and how extraordinarily great is the power that he has exercised for us believers; this accords with the strength

1a Some authorities add 'who are at Ephesus' or 'who are . . .', leaving a gap for a place-name to be filled in.

of his power [20]at work in Christ, the power which he exercised in raising him from the dead and enthroning him at his right hand, in heaven, [21]far above every principality, ruling force, power or sovereignty,[b] or any other name that can be named, not only in this age but also in the age to come. [22]*He has put all things under his feet,*[c] and made him, as he is above all things, the head of the Church; [23]which is his Body, the fullness of him who is filled, all in all.

Salvation in Christ a free gift

2 And you were dead, through the crimes and the sins [2]which used to make up your way of life when you were living by the principles of this world, obeying the ruler who dominates the air, the spirit who is at work in those who rebel. [3]We too were all among them once, living only by our natural inclinations, obeying the demands of human self-indulgence and our own whim; our nature made us no less liable to God's retribution than the rest of the world. [4]But God, being rich in faithful love, through the great love with which he loved us, [5]even when we were dead in our sins, brought us to life with Christ—it is through grace that you have been saved— [6]and raised us up with him and gave us a place with him in heaven, in Christ Jesus.

[7]This was to show for all ages to come, through his goodness towards us in Christ Jesus, how extraordinarily rich he is in grace. [8]Because it is by grace that you have been saved, through faith; not by anything of your own, but by a gift from God; [9]not by anything that you have done, so that nobody can claim the credit. [10]We are God's work of art, created in Christ Jesus for the good works which God has already designated to make up our way of life.

Reconciliation of the Jews and the gentiles with each other and with God

[11]Do not forget, then, that there was a time when you who were gentiles by physical descent, termed the uncircumcised by those who speak of themselves as the circumcised by reason of a physical operation, [12]do not forget, I say, that you were at that time separate from Christ and excluded from membership of Israel, aliens with no part in the covenants of the Promise, limited to this world, without hope and without God. [13]But now in Christ Jesus, you that used to be so far off have been brought close, by the blood of Christ. [14]For he is the peace between us, and has made the two into one entity and broken down the barrier which used to keep them apart, by destroying in his own person the hostility, [15]that is, the Law of commandments with its decrees. His purpose in this was, by restoring peace, to create a single New Man out of the two of them, [16]and through the cross, to reconcile them both to God in one Body; in his own person he killed the hostility. [17]He came to bring the good news of *peace to you who were far off and peace to those who were near.*[a] [18]Through him, then, we both in the one Spirit have free access to the Father.

[19]So you are no longer aliens or foreign visitors; you are fellow-citizens with the holy people of God and part of God's household. [20]You are built upon the foundations of the apostles and prophets, and Christ Jesus himself is the cornerstone. [21]Every structure knit together in him grows into a holy temple in the Lord; [22]and you too, in him, are being built up into a dwelling-place of God in the Spirit.

Paul, a servant of the mystery

3 It is because of this that I, Paul, a prisoner of the Lord Jesus on behalf of you gentiles ... [2]You have surely heard the way in which God entrusted me with the grace he gave me for your sake; [3]he made known to me by a revelation the mystery I have just described briefly— [4]a reading of it will enable you to perceive my understanding of the mystery of Christ. [5]This mystery, as it is now revealed in the Spirit to his holy apostles and

1b Names for cosmic powers.   1c Ps 8:6.   2a Is 57:19.

180 READ EPHESIANS 2:1–14.

[God] raised us up with him and gave us a place with him in heaven, in Christ Jesus.

—EPHESIANS 2:6

CHRIST'S TENDER MERCY

In her Revelations, *St. Gertrude gave this moving account of her adult conversion to Christ:*

You attracted my heart and my eyes by the infinite light of your glory. Then with tenderness you said to me, "Your salvation is near. Why are you consumed with grief?" Although I knew I was standing bodily in our dormitory, it seemed to me that I was in the corner of the choir where I usually offered up my tepid prayers. There I seemed to hear these words: "I will save you. I will deliver you. Don't be afraid." Afterward I saw you place your right hand in mine, as if to ratify your promise.

Then I heard you say, "You have licked the dust with my enemies, and you have sucked honey from thorns. But return now to me—I will receive you and my divine delights will be like wine for you."

My soul melted within me, and I wanted to approach you. But I saw between you and me a hedge that seemed to have no end. The top of it appeared to be covered with thorns, so that I could find no way to return to you. I paused to weep over my sins that the hedge doubtlessly represented. In my weakness you mercifully took me by the hand and instantly placed me beside you without any difficulty. Then in that hand which you had extended to me as a pledge of your promises, I recognized your radiant wounds that have wiped out the record of the debt that was against us (see Col 2:14).

ST. GERTRUDE THE GREAT, 1256–1302

YOU WILL FIND THE NEXT READING AT EPHESIANS 4.

prophets, was unknown to humanity in previous generations: 6 that the gentiles now have the same inheritance and form the same Body and enjoy the same promise in Christ Jesus through the gospel. 7 I have been made the servant of that gospel by a gift of grace from God who gave it to me by the workings of his power. 8 I, who am less than the least of all God's holy people, have been entrusted with this special grace, of proclaiming to the gentiles the unfathomable treasure of Christ 9 and of throwing light on the inner workings of the mystery kept hidden through all the ages in God, the Creator of everything. 10 The purpose of this was, that now, through the Church, the principalities and ruling forces should learn how many-sided God's wisdom is, 11 according to the plan which he had formed from all eternity in Christ Jesus our Lord. 12 In him we are bold enough to approach God in complete confidence, through our faith in him; 13 so, I beg you, do not let the hardships I go through on your account make you waver; they are your glory.

Paul's prayer

14 This, then, is what I pray, kneeling before the Father, 15 from whom every fatherhood, in heaven or on earth, takes its name. 16 In the abundance of his glory may he, through his

Spirit, enable you to grow firm in power with regard to your inner self, ¹⁷ so that Christ may live in your hearts through faith, and then, planted in love and built on love, ¹⁸ with all God's holy people you will have the strength to grasp the breadth and the length, the height and the depth; ¹⁹ so that, knowing the love of Christ, which is beyond knowledge, you may be filled with the utter fullness of God.

²⁰ Glory be to him whose power, working in us, can do infinitely more than we can ask or imagine; ²¹ glory be to him from generation to generation in the Church and in Christ Jesus for ever and ever. Amen.

A call to unity

4 I, the prisoner in the Lord, urge you therefore to lead a life worthy of the vocation to which you were called. ² With all humility and gentleness, and with patience, support each other in love. ³ Take every care to preserve the unity of the Spirit by the peace that binds you together. ⁴ There is one Body, one Spirit, just as one hope is the goal of your calling by God. ⁵ There is one Lord, one faith, one baptism, ⁶ and one God and Father of all, over all, through all and within all.

⁷ On each one of us God's favour has been bestowed in whatever way Christ allotted it. ⁸ That is why it says:

He went up to the heights, took captives, he gave gifts to humanity.ᵃ

⁹ When it says, 'he went up', it must mean that he had gone down to the deepest levels of the earth. ¹⁰ The one who went down is none other than the one who went up above all the heavens to fill all things. ¹¹ And to some, his 'gift' was that they should be apostles; to some prophets; to some, evangelists; to some, pastors and teachers; ¹² to knit God's holy people together for the work of service to build up the Body of Christ, ¹³ until we all reach unity in faith and knowledge of the Son of God and form the perfect Man, fully mature with the fullness of Christ himself.

¹⁴ Then we shall no longer be children, or tossed one way and another, and carried hither and thither by every new gust of teaching, at the mercy of all the tricks people play and their unscrupulousness in deliberate deception. ¹⁵ If we live by the truth and in love, we shall grow completely into Christ, who is the head ¹⁶ by whom the whole Body is fitted and joined together, every joint adding its own strength, for each individual part to work according to its function. So the body grows until it has built itself up in love.

The new life in Christ

¹⁷ So this I say to you and attest to you in the Lord, do not go on living the empty-headed life that the gentiles live. ¹⁸ Intellectually they are in the dark, and they are estranged from the life of God, because of the ignorance which is the consequence of closed minds. ¹⁹ Their sense of right and wrong once dulled, they have abandoned all self-control and pursue to excess every kind of uncleanness. ²⁰ Now that is hardly the way you have learnt Christ, ²¹ unless you failed to hear him properly when you were taught what the truth is in Jesus. ²² You were to put aside your old self, which belongs to your old way of life and is corrupted by following illusory desires. ²³ Your mind was to be renewed in spirit ²⁴ so that you could put on the New Man that has been created on God's principles, in the uprightness and holiness of the truth.

²⁵ So from now on, there must be no more lies. *Speak the truth to one another,*ᵇ since we are all parts of one another. ²⁶ *Even if you are angry, do not sin:*ᶜ never let the sun set on your anger ²⁷ or else you will give the devil a foothold. ²⁸ Anyone who was a thief must stop stealing; instead he should exert himself at some honest job with his own hands so that he may have something to share with those in need. ²⁹ No foul word should ever cross your lips; let your words be for the improvement of others, as occasion offers, and do good to your listeners; ³⁰ do not grieve the Holy Spirit of God who

4a Ps 68:18.   4b Zc 8:16.   4c Ps 4:4.

181 READ EPHESIANS 4:17–24.

Your mind was to be renewed in spirit so that you could put on the New Man.

—EPHESIANS 4:23–24

THE WORK OF THE HOLY SPIRIT

Now the Holy Spirit is not brought into intimate association with the soul by physical nearness. Indeed, how could there be a corporeal approach to the incorporeal? Intimacy with the Spirit results from the withdrawal of the passions . . . that have alienated the soul from its close relationship with God. Only after a person is purified from the shame whose stain he took through his wickedness, and has come back again to his natural beauty, cleaning the Royal Image and restoring its ancient form, only in this way is it possible for him to draw near to the Paraclete.

And the Spirit, like the sun, will by the aid of your purified eye show you in himself the image of the invisible, and in the blessed vision of the image you shall behold the unspeakable beauty of the archetype. Through the Spirit's aid hearts are lifted up, the weak are held by the hand, and they who are advancing are brought to perfection.

Shining upon those that are cleansed from every spot, the Holy Spirit makes them spiritual by fellowship with himself. Just as when a sunbeam falls on bright and transparent bodies, they themselves become brilliant too, and shed forth a fresh brightness from themselves, so souls in which the Spirit dwells, illuminated by the Spirit, themselves become spiritual, and send forth their grace to others. From this comes foreknowledge of the future, understanding of mysteries, apprehension of what is hidden, distribution of good gifts, the heavenly citizenship, a place in the chorus of angels, joy without end, abiding in God, the being made like to God, and, highest of all, the incorporation into God. Such, then, to instance a few out of many, are the conceptions concerning the Holy Spirit that we have been taught to hold concerning his greatness, his dignity, and his operations, by the oracles of the Spirit themselves.

ST. BASIL, 329–379

YOU WILL FIND THE NEXT READING AT EPHESIANS 5.

has marked you with his seal, ready for the day when we shall be set free. ³¹ Any bitterness or bad temper or anger or shouting or abuse must be far removed from you—as must every kind of malice. ³² Be generous to one another, sympathetic, forgiving each other as readily as God forgave you in Christ.

5 As God's dear children, then, take him as your pattern, ² and follow Christ by loving as he loved you, giving himself up for us *as an offering and a sweet-smelling sacrifice to God.*ᵃ

³ Among you there must be not even a mention of sexual vice or impurity in any of its forms, or greed: this would scarcely become the holy people of God! ⁴ There must be no foul or salacious talk or coarse jokes—all this is wrong for you; there should rather be thanksgiving. ⁵ For you can be quite certain that nobody who indulges in sexual immorality or impurity or greed—which is worshipping a false god—can inherit the kingdom of

5a Ex 29:18.

182 READ EPHESIANS 5:8–20.

Wake up, sleeper, rise from the dead, and Christ will shine on you.—EPHESIANS 5:14

LIFE IN THE LIGHT

Don't consider what you are, but what you will be. What you are only lasts a moment, what you will be is eternal. Don't indulge yourself in laziness, but rather acquire in a short time what you will possess forever. Overcome your dislike for exertion in the present by thinking of the reward to come. If the world lures you, remember that your pursuit of it is vain. What does it profit you to gaze at a shadow reflected in the water? How do you benefit from joy and happiness tasted in a dream? All dreams, no matter how long they last, are short-lived. And life's joys are like dreams in a dark night.

Awake, therefore, out of the night and seek the light so that you may see and be seen. Your life is a wheel that is ever turning and never waits for you. You must keep up with it. You have nothing on earth. And you will die as naked as you were when you were born. You have only the prospect of heaven, your inheritance, provided you do not forfeit it.

But if you have lost it already, sell yourself to regain it. What do I mean by "sell yourself"? Sell your vices and buy life. Do you want to know what those vices are? Above all, sell pride, the root-vice, and buy humility. Then you will be like Christ who says, "Learn from me, for I am gentle and humble in heart" (Mt 11:29). ST. COLUMBAN, 542?–615

YOU WILL FIND THE NEXT READING AT EPHESIANS 6.

God. ⁶Do not let anyone deceive you with empty arguments: it is such behaviour that draws down God's retribution on those who rebel against him. ⁷Make sure that you do not throw in your lot with them. ⁸You were darkness once, but now you are light in the Lord; behave as children of light, ⁹for the effects of the light are seen in complete goodness and uprightness and truth. ¹⁰Try to discover what the Lord wants of you, ¹¹take no part in the futile works of darkness but, on the contrary, show them up for what they are. ¹²The things which are done in secret are shameful even to speak of; ¹³but anything shown up by the light will be illuminated ¹⁴and anything illuminated is itself a light. That is why it is said:

Wake up, sleeper,
rise from the dead,
and Christ will shine on you.

¹⁵So be very careful about the sort of lives you lead, like intelligent and not like senseless people. ¹⁶Make the best of the present time, for it is a wicked age. ¹⁷This is why you must not be thoughtless but must recognise what is the will of the Lord. ¹⁸*Do not get drunk with wine;*[b] this is simply dissipation; be filled with the Spirit. ¹⁹Sing psalms and hymns and inspired songs among yourselves, singing and chanting to the Lord in your hearts, ²⁰always and everywhere giving thanks to God who is our Father in the name of our Lord Jesus Christ.

The morals of the home

²¹Be subject to one another out of reverence for Christ. ²²Wives should be subject to their husbands as to the Lord, ²³since, as Christ is head of the Church and saves the whole body,

5b Pr 23:31.

183 READ EPHESIANS 6:10–20.

Put on the full armour of God so as to be able to resist the devil's tactics.—EPHESIANS 6:11

SPIRITUAL SELF-DEFENSE

Hear Paul saying: "whatever someone sows, that is what he will reap"; sow in the spirit so that you shall reap life everlasting. For "if his sowing is in the field of self-indulgence, then his harvest from it shall be corruption" (Ga 6:7–8). . . .

Get ready to go forth to your work, and gird yourself to cultivate your field. Your field is your present life, and for a hoe take with you the Old Testament together with the New Testament. Put a hedge of thorns about your field and your soil, by prayer and fasting together with instruction. If you are protected by this enclosure, the wild beast shall not invade you, by which I mean the devil. Tend your soul after the manner of a beautiful vineyard. And as the guardians of the vineyard strike at the thieves with their fists, and keep them at a distance with stones, so you cry out in prayer, and shout with the song of psalmody, and put to flight the thieving fox, that is, the devil, of whom the Scripture says: "Catch the foxes for us, the little foxes that make havoc of the vineyards" (Sg 2:15).

Be watchful of the enemy, lest he pierce your heart with some obstinate and unfitting desire. If he seeks to possess your soul as a field, and places there his unclean thoughts, resist and oppose him with the shield of faith. Put on the helmet of hope. Draw the sword of the spirit, which is the word of God. And so armed against the enemy, stand fast, and be not unwatchful in the battle, but show yourself sober and vigilant in all things. For we are not ignorant of his designs. "Rejoice always in the Lord," as it is written. "Let your modesty be known to all men" (see Ph 4:4–5). Let the fear of the Lord have place in your heart. But be not a timid soldier, nor a slothful, lazy workman.

ST. EPHREM, 306?–373?

YOU WILL FIND THE NEXT READING AT PHILIPPIANS 1.

so is a husband the head of his wife; ²⁴and as the Church is subject to Christ, so should wives be to their husbands, in everything. ²⁵Husbands should love their wives, just as Christ loved the Church and sacrificed himself for her ²⁶to make her holy by washing her in cleansing water with a form of words, ²⁷so that when he took the Church to himself she would be glorious, with no speck or wrinkle or anything like that, but holy and faultless. ²⁸In the same way, husbands must love their wives as they love their own bodies; for a man to love his wife is for him to love himself. ²⁹A man never hates his own body, but he feeds it and looks after it; and that is the way Christ treats the Church, ³⁰because we are parts of his Body. ³¹*This is why a man leaves his father and mother and becomes attached to his wife, and the two become one flesh.*[c] ³²This mystery has great significance, but I am applying it to Christ and the Church. ³³To sum up: you also, each one of you, must love his wife as he loves himself; and let every wife respect her husband.

6Children, be obedient to your parents in the Lord—that is what uprightness de-

5c Gn 2:24.

mands. ²The first commandment that has a promise attached to it is: *Honour your father and your mother,* ³and the promise is: *so that you may have long life and prosper in the land.*^a ⁴And parents, never drive your children to resentment but bring them up with correction and advice inspired by the Lord.

⁵Slaves, be obedient to those who are, according to human reckoning, your masters, with deep respect and sincere loyalty, as you are obedient to Christ: ⁶not only when you are under their eye, as if you had only to please human beings, but as slaves of Christ who wholeheartedly do the will of God. ⁷Work willingly for the sake of the Lord and not for the sake of human beings. ⁸Never forget that everyone, whether a slave or a free man, will be rewarded by the Lord for whatever work he has done well. ⁹And those of you who are employers, treat your slaves in the same spirit; do without threats, and never forget that they and you have the same Master in heaven and there is no favouritism with him.

The spiritual war

¹⁰Finally, grow strong in the Lord, with the strength of his power. ¹¹Put on the full armour of God so as to be able to resist the devil's tactics. ¹²For it is not against human enemies that we have to struggle, but against the principalities and the ruling forces who are masters of the darkness in this world, the spirits of evil in the heavens. ¹³That is why you must take up all God's armour, or you will not be able to put up any resistance on the evil day, or stand your ground even though you exert yourselves to the full.

¹⁴So stand your ground, with *truth a belt round your waist,* and *uprightness a breastplate,* ¹⁵wearing for shoes on your feet *the eagerness to spread the gospel of peace*^b ¹⁶and always carrying the shield of faith so that you can use it to quench the burning arrows of the Evil One. ¹⁷And then you must take *salvation as your helmet* and the sword of the Spirit, that is, the word of God.

¹⁸In all your prayer and entreaty keep praying in the Spirit on every possible occasion. Never get tired of staying awake to pray for all God's holy people, ¹⁹and pray for me to be given an opportunity to open my mouth and fearlessly make known the mystery of the gospel ²⁰of which I am an ambassador in chains; pray that in proclaiming it I may speak as fearlessly as I ought to.

Personal news and final salutation

²¹So that you know, as well, what is happening to me and what I am doing, my dear friend Tychicus, my trustworthy helper in the Lord, will tell you everything. ²²I am sending him to you precisely for this purpose, to give you news about us and encourage you thoroughly.

²³May God the Father and the Lord Jesus Christ grant peace, love and faith to all the brothers. ²⁴May grace be with all who love our Lord Jesus Christ, in life imperishable.

6a Ex 20:12. *6b* Is 59:17; 40:9.

Address

1 Paul and Timothy, servants of Christ Jesus, to all God's holy people in Christ Jesus at Philippi, together with their presiding elders and the deacons. ²Grace and peace to you from God our Father and the Lord Jesus Christ.

Thanksgiving and prayer

³I thank my God whenever I think of you, ⁴and every time I pray for you all, I always pray with joy ⁵for your partnership in the gospel from the very first day up to the present. ⁶I am quite confident that the One who began a good work in you will go on completing it until the Day of Jesus Christ comes. ⁷It is only right that I should feel like this towards you all, because you have a place in my heart, since you have all shared together in the grace that has been mine, both my chains and my work defending and establishing the gospel. ⁸For God will testify for me how much I long for you all with the warm longing of Christ Jesus; ⁹it is my prayer that your love for one another may grow more and more with the knowledge and complete understanding ¹⁰that will help you to come to true discernment, so that you will be innocent and free of any trace of guilt when the Day of Christ comes, ¹¹entirely filled with the fruits of uprightness through Jesus Christ, for the glory and praise of God.

Paul's own circumstances

¹²Now I want you to realise, brothers, that the circumstances of my present life are helping rather than hindering the advance of the gospel. ¹³My chains in Christ have become well known not only to all the Praetorium,ᵃ but to everybody else, ¹⁴and so most of the brothers in the Lord have gained confidence from my chains and are getting more and more daring in announcing the Message without any fear. ¹⁵It is true that some of them are preaching Christ out of malice and rivalry; but there are many as well whose intentions are good; ¹⁶some are doing it out of love, knowing that I remain firm in my defence of the gospel. ¹⁷There are others who are proclaiming Christ out of jealousy, not in sincerity but meaning to add to the weight of my chains. ¹⁸But what does it matter? Only that in both ways, whether with false motives or true, Christ is proclaimed, and for that I am happy; ¹⁹and I shall go on being happy, too, because I know that *this is what will save me,ᵇ* with your prayers and with the support of the Spirit of Jesus Christ; ²⁰all in accordance with my most confident hope and trust that I shall never have to admit defeat, but with complete fearlessness I shall go on, so that now, as always, Christ will be glorified in my body, whether by my life or my death. ²¹Life to me, of course, is Christ, but then death would be a positive gain. ²²On the other hand again, if to be alive in the body gives me an opportunity for fruitful work, I do not know which I should choose. ²³I am caught in this dilemma: I want to be gone and to be with Christ, and this is by far the stronger desire— ²⁴and yet for your sake to stay alive in this body is a more urgent need. ²⁵This much I know for certain, that I shall stay and stand by you all, to encourage

---

1a The headquarters of the Praetorian guard wherever Paul is captive (Ephesus, Caesarea, Rome?).

1b Jb 13:16.

184 READ PHILIPPIANS 1:12–26.

Life to me, of course, is Christ, but then death would be a positive gain.—PHILIPPIANS 1:21

PRAYING FOR HEAVEN

While in prison and awaiting execution, St. Thomas More wrote this letter to his beloved daughter Margaret Roper:

Your daughterly loving letter . . . was and is, I faithfully assure you, much more inward comfort to me than my pen can express well to you. I marked some things in it. But most especially that God in his high goodness gives you the grace to consider the incomparable difference between the wretched condition of this present life and the rich state of the life to come for them that die in God. . . . It does me good here to rehearse your own words: "Of his tender pity so firmly to rest our love in him, with little regard of this world, and so to flee sin and embrace virtue, that we may say with St. Paul, 'Life to me, of course, is Christ, but then death would be a positive gain . . . I want to be gone and to be with Christ.' "

I ask our Lord . . . that it may please him to give your father the grace daily to remember and pray this wholesome prayer, which he has put in your mind. And also to yourself as you have written it, even so daily devoutly to kneel and pray it. For surely if God gives us that, he gives us and will give us all we can ever wish.

And therefore, good Margaret, when you pray it, pray it for us both. And I on my part shall do the same, in such manner as it shall please our Lord to give me, poor wretch, the grace . . . that likewise as in this wretched world I have been very glad of your company and you of mine, and yet would if it might be . . . so we may rejoice and enjoy each other's company with our other kinsfolk, allies, and friends everlastingly in the glorious bliss of heaven. And in the meantime with good counsel and prayer, each help the other on the way there.   ST. THOMAS MORE, 1477–1535

YOU WILL FIND THE NEXT READING AT PHILIPPIANS 2.

your advance and your joy in the faith, ²⁶ so that my return to be among you may increase to overflowing your pride in Jesus Christ on my account.

Fight for the faith

²⁷ But you must always behave in a way that is worthy of the gospel of Christ, so that whether I come to you and see for myself or whether I only hear all about you from a distance, I shall find that you are standing firm and united in spirit, battling, as a team with a single aim, for the faith of the gospel, ²⁸ undismayed by any of your opponents. This will be a clear sign, for them that they are to be lost, and for you that you are to be saved. ²⁹ This comes from God, for you have been granted the privilege for Christ's sake not only of believing in him but of suffering for him as well; ³⁰ you are fighting the same battle which you saw me fighting for him and which you hear I am fighting still.

Preserve unity in humility

2 So if in Christ there is anything that will move you, any incentive in love, any fellowship in the Spirit, any warmth or sympathy—I appeal to you, ² make my joy complete by being of a single mind, one in love, one in heart and one in mind. ³ Nothing is to be done out of jealousy or vanity; instead, out of humility of mind everyone should give preference to others, ⁴ everyone pursuing not selfish interests but those of others. ⁵ Make your own the mind of Christ Jesus:

⁶ Who, being in the form of God,
   did not count equality with God
   something to be grasped.

⁷ But he emptied himself,
   taking the form of a slave,
   becoming as human beings are;
   and being in every way like a human
       being,
⁸ he was humbler yet,
   even to accepting death, death on a cross.

⁹ And for this God raised him high,
   and gave him the name
   which is above all other names;

¹⁰ so that *all beings*
   in the heavens, on earth and in the
       underworld,
   should bend the knee at the name of Jesus

¹¹ and that *every tongue should acknowledge*ª
   Jesus Christ as Lord,
   to the glory of God the Father.

Work for salvation

¹² So, my dear friends, you have always been obedient; your obedience must not be limited to times when I am present. Now that I am absent it must be more in evidence, so work out your salvation in fear and trembling. ¹³ It is God who, for his own generous purpose, gives you the intention and the powers to act. ¹⁴ Let your behaviour be free of murmuring and complaining ¹⁵ so that you remain faultless and pure, *unspoilt children of God* surrounded by *a deceitful and underhand brood,*ᵇ shining out among them like bright stars in the world, ¹⁶ proffering to it the Word of life. Then I shall have reason to be proud on the Day of Christ, for it will not be for nothing that I have run the race and toiled so hard. ¹⁷ Indeed, even if my blood has to be poured as a libation over your sacrifice and the offering of your faith, then I shall be glad and join in your rejoicing— ¹⁸ and in the same way, you must be glad and join in my rejoicing.

The mission of Timothy and Epaphroditus

¹⁹ I hope, in the Lord Jesus, to send Timothy to you soon, so that my mind may be set at rest when I hear how you are. ²⁰ There is nobody else that I can send who is like him and cares as sincerely for your well-being; ²¹ they all want to work for themselves, not for Jesus Christ. ²² But you know what sort of person he has proved himself, working with me for the sake of the gospel like a son with his father. ²³ That is the man, then, that I am hoping to send to you immediately I can make out what is going to happen to me; ²⁴ but I am confident in the Lord that I shall come myself, too, before long. ²⁵ Nevertheless I thought it essential to send to you Epaphroditus, my brother and fellow-worker and companion-in-arms since he came as your representative to look after my needs; ²⁶ because he was missing you all and was worrying because you had heard that he was ill. ²⁷ Indeed he was seriously ill and nearly died; but God took pity on him—and not only on him but also on me, to spare me one grief on top of another. ²⁸ So I am sending him back as promptly as I can so that you will have the joy of seeing him again, and that will be some comfort to me in my distress. ²⁹ Welcome him in the Lord, then, with all joy; hold people like him in honour, ³⁰ because it was for Christ's work that he came so near to dying, risking his

2a Is 45:23.   *2b* Dt 32:5.

185 READ PHILIPPIANS 2:1–11.

But he emptied himself, taking the form of a slave, becoming as human beings are.
—PHILIPPIANS 2:7

GOD INCARNATE

Without detriment to the properties of the divine and the human that came together in one person, majesty took on humility, strength weakness, eternity mortality.

Then the Son of God entered the lower parts of the world—descending from his heavenly home and yet not quitting his Father's glory, begotten in a new order by a new birthing. Invisible in his own nature, he became visible in ours. And he whom nothing could contain was content to be contained.

Abiding before all time, he began to be in time. The Lord of all things, he obscured his immeasurable majesty and took on the form of a servant. Being God who cannot suffer, he did not disdain to be man that can suffer and, immortal as he is, to subject himself to the laws of death.

The Lord assumed his mother's nature without faultiness. Nor does the marvel of his birth make his nature unlike ours. For he who is true God is also true man. In this union there is no deceit, since the humility of humanness and the loftiness of the Godhead both meet there.

To be hungry and thirsty, to be weary and to sleep is clearly human. But to satisfy five thousand men with five loaves, to walk on the surface of the water with feet that do not sink and to quell the risings of the waves by rebuking the winds is without any doubt divine. For as God is not changed by the showing of pity, so man is not swallowed up in the dignity of the divine.

ST. LEO THE GREAT, d. 461

YOU WILL FIND THE NEXT READING AT PHILIPPIANS 3:7.

life to do the duty to me which you could not do yourselves.

3 Finally, brothers, I wish you joy in the Lord.

The true way of Christian salvation

To write to you what I have already written before is no trouble to me and to you will be a protection. ² Beware of dogs! Beware of evil workmen! Beware of self-mutilators! ³ We are the true people of the circumcision since we worship by the Spirit of God and make Christ Jesus our only boast, not relying on physical qualifications, ⁴ although, I myself could rely on these too. If anyone does claim to rely on

them, my claim is better. ⁵ Circumcised on the eighth day of my life, I was born of the race of Israel, of the tribe of Benjamin, a Hebrew born of Hebrew parents. In the matter of the Law, I was a Pharisee; ⁶ as for religious fervour, I was a persecutor of the Church; as for the uprightness embodied in the Law, I was faultless. ⁷ But what were once my assets I now through Christ Jesus count as losses. ⁸ Yes, I will go further: because of the supreme advantage of knowing Christ Jesus my Lord, I count everything else as loss. For him I have accepted the loss of all other things, and look on them all as filth if only I can gain Christ ⁹ and be given a place in him, with the uprightness I have gained not from the Law, but through

186 READ PHILIPPIANS 3:7–21.

Let us go forward from the point we have each attained.—PHILIPPIANS 3:16

LIVING ON PURPOSE

He who enters into the secret place of his own soul passes beyond himself and truly ascends to God.

Therefore, banish from your heart the distractions of earth. Turn your eyes to spiritual joys so that you may learn at last to rest in the light of the contemplation of God. Indeed, the soul's true life and repose are to abide in God, held fast by love and refreshed by divine consolations.

In your spiritual ascent and your search for a closer union with God, you must allow yourself no rest, no slipping back. You must go forward till you have obtained the object of your desires. Follow the example of mountain climbers. If your desires turn aside after objects that pass below, you will lose yourself in byways and your mind will be drawn in all directions. Your progress will be uncertain. You will not reach your goal. And you will not find rest after your labors.

But if your heart and mind, led by love and desire, withdraw from the distractions of the world, you will grow strong. Your recollection will deepen the higher you rise on the wings of knowledge and desire. Little by little as you abandon baser things to rest in the one true and unchangeable Good, you will dwell there, held fast by the bonds of love.   ST. ALBERT THE GREAT, 1206–1280

YOU WILL FIND THE NEXT READING AT COLOSSIANS 2.

faith in Christ, an uprightness from God, based on faith, ¹⁰that I may come to know him and the power of his resurrection, and partake of his sufferings by being moulded to the pattern of his death, ¹¹striving towards the goal of resurrection from the dead. ¹²Not that I have secured it already, nor yet reached my goal, but I am still pursuing it in the attempt to take hold of the prize for which Christ Jesus took hold of me. ¹³Brothers, I do not reckon myself as having taken hold of it; I can only say that forgetting all that lies behind me, and straining forward to what lies in front, ¹⁴I am racing towards the finishing-point to win the prize of God's heavenly call in Christ Jesus. ¹⁵So this is the way in which all of us who are mature should be thinking, and if you are still thinking differently in any way, then God has yet to make this matter clear to you. ¹⁶Meanwhile, let us go forward from the point we have each attained.

¹⁷Brothers, be united in imitating me. Keep your eyes fixed on those who act according to the example you have from me. ¹⁸For there are so many people of whom I have often warned you, and now I warn you again with tears in my eyes, who behave like the enemies of Christ's cross. ¹⁹They are destined to be lost; their god is the stomach; they glory in what they should think shameful, since their minds are set on earthly things. ²⁰But our homeland is in heaven and it is from there that we are expecting a Saviour, the Lord Jesus Christ, ²¹who will transfigure the wretched body of ours into the mould of his glorious body, through the working of the power which he has, even to bring all things under his mastery.

4 So then, my brothers and dear friends whom I miss so much, my joy and my crown, hold firm in the Lord, dear friends.

Last advice

2 I urge Euodia, and I urge Syntyche to come to agreement with each other in the Lord; 3 and I ask you, Syzygus, really to be a 'partner' *a* and help them. These women have struggled hard for the gospel with me, along with Clement and all my other fellow-workers, whose names are written in the book of life.

4 Always be joyful, then, in the Lord; I repeat, be joyful. 5 Let your good sense be obvious to everybody. The Lord is near. 6 Never worry about anything; but tell God all your desires of every kind in prayer and petition shot through with gratitude, 7 and the peace of God which is beyond our understanding will guard your hearts and your thoughts in Christ Jesus. 8 Finally, brothers, let your minds be filled with everything that is true, everything that is honourable, everything that is upright and pure, everything that we love and admire—with whatever is good and praiseworthy. 9 Keep doing everything you learnt from me and were told by me and have heard or seen me doing. Then the God of peace will be with you.

Thanks for help received

10 As for me, I am full of joy in the Lord, now that at last your consideration for me has blossomed again; though I recognise that you really did have consideration before, but had no opportunity to show it. 11 I do not say this because I have lacked anything; I have learnt to manage with whatever I have. 12 I know how to live modestly, and I know how to live luxu- riously too: in every way now I have mastered the secret of all conditions: full stomach and empty stomach, plenty and poverty. 13 There is nothing I cannot do in the One who strengthens me. 14 All the same, it was good of you to share with me in my hardships. 15 In the early days of the gospel, as you of Philippi well know, when I left Macedonia, no church other than yourselves made common account with me in the matter of expenditure and receipts. You were the only ones; 16 and what is more, you have twice sent me what I needed in Thessalonica. 17 It is not the gift that I value most; what I value is the interest that is mounting up in your account. 18 I have all that I need and more: I am fully provided, now that I have received from Epaphroditus the offering that you sent, *a pleasing smell,* *b* the sacrifice which is acceptable and pleasing to God. 19 And my God will fulfil all your needs out of the riches of his glory in Christ Jesus. 20 And so glory be to God our Father, for ever and ever. Amen.

Greetings and final wish

21 My greetings to every one of God's holy people in Christ Jesus. The brothers who are with me send you their greetings. 22 All God's holy people send you their greetings, especially those of Caesar's household.

23 May the grace of the Lord Jesus Christ be with your spirit.

4a Syzygus means 'yoke-fellow' or 'partner'.
4b Gn 8:21.

The Letter to the

COLOSSIANS

Address

1 From Paul, by the will of God an apostle of Christ Jesus, and from our brother Timothy ²to God's holy people in Colossae, our faithful brothers in Christ. Grace and peace to you from God our Father.

Thanksgiving and prayer

³We give thanks for you to God, the Father of our Lord Jesus Christ, continually in our prayers, ⁴ever since we heard about your faith in Christ Jesus and the love that you show towards all God's holy people ⁵because of the hope which is stored up for you in heaven. News of this hope reached you not long ago through the word of truth, the gospel ⁶that came to you in the same way as it is bearing fruit and growing throughout the world. It has had the same effect among you, ever since you heard about the grace of God and recognised it for what it truly is. ⁷This you learnt from Epaphras, our very dear fellow-worker and a trustworthy deputy for us as Christ's servant, ⁸and it was he who also told us all about your love in the Spirit.

⁹That is why, ever since the day he told us, we have never failed to remember you in our prayers and ask that through perfect wisdom and spiritual understanding you should reach the fullest knowledge of his will ¹⁰and so be able to lead a life worthy of the Lord, a life acceptable to him in all its aspects, bearing fruit in every kind of good work and growing in knowledge of God, ¹¹fortified, in accordance with his glorious strength, with all power always to persevere and endure, ¹²giving thanks with joy to the Father who has made you able

to share the lot of God's holy people and with them to inherit the light.

¹³Because that is what he has done. It is he who has rescued us from the ruling force of darkness and transferred us to the kingdom of the Son that he loves, ¹⁴and in him we enjoy our freedom, the forgiveness of sin.

Christ is the head of all creation ᵃ

¹⁵ He is the image of the unseen God,
　the first-born of all creation,
¹⁶ for in him were created all things
　in heaven and on earth:
　everything visible and everything
　　invisible,
　thrones, ruling forces, sovereignties,
　　powers—
　all things were created through him
　　and for him.
¹⁷ He exists before all things
　and in him all things hold together,
¹⁸ and he is the Head of the Body,
　that is, the Church.

　He is the Beginning,
　the first-born from the dead,
　so that he should be supreme in
　　every way;
¹⁹ because God wanted all fullness to
　　be found in him
²⁰ and through him to reconcile all things
　　to him,
　everything in heaven and everything on
　　earth,
　by making peace through his death on
　　the cross.

1a cf. Ws 7:26.

[1488]

The Colossians have their share in salvation

21 You were once estranged and of hostile intent through your evil behaviour; 22 now he has reconciled you, by his death and in that mortal body, to bring you before himself holy, faultless and irreproachable— 23 as long as you persevere and stand firm on the solid base of the faith, never letting yourselves drift away from the hope promised by the gospel, which you have heard, which has been preached to every creature under heaven, and of which I, Paul, have become the servant.

Paul's labours in the service of the gentiles

24 It makes me happy to be suffering for you now, and in my own body to make up all the hardships that still have to be undergone by Christ for the sake of his body, the Church, 25 of which I was made a servant with the responsibility towards you that God gave to me, that of completing God's message, 26 the message which was a mystery hidden for generations and centuries and has now been revealed to his holy people. 27 It was God's purpose to reveal to them how rich is the glory of this mystery among the gentiles; it is Christ among you, your hope of glory: 28 this is the Christ we are proclaiming, admonishing and instructing everyone in all wisdom, to make everyone perfect in Christ. 29 And it is for this reason that I labour, striving with his energy which works in me mightily.

Paul's concern for the Colossians' faith

2 I want you to know, then, what a struggle I am having on your behalf and on behalf of those in Laodicea, and on behalf of so many others who have never seen me face to face. 2 It is all to bind them together in love and to encourage their resolution until they are rich in the assurance of their complete understanding and have knowledge of the mystery of God 3 in which all the jewels of wisdom and knowledge are hidden.

4 I say this to make sure that no one deceives you with specious arguments. 5 I may be ab-

sent in body, but in spirit I am there among you, delighted to find how well-ordered you are and to see how firm your faith in Christ is.

Live according to the true faith in Christ, not according to false teaching

6 So then, as you received Jesus as Lord and Christ, now live your lives in him, 7 be rooted in him and built up on him, held firm by the faith you have been taught, and overflowing with thanksgiving.

8 Make sure that no one captivates you with the empty lure of a 'philosophy' of the kind that human beings hand on, based on the principles of this world and not on Christ.

Christ alone is the true head of all humanity and the angels

9 In him, in bodily form, lives divinity in all its fullness, 10 and in him you too find your own fulfilment, in the one who is the head of every sovereignty and ruling force.

11 In him you have been circumcised, with a circumcision performed, not by human hand, but by the complete stripping of your natural self. This is circumcision according to Christ. 12 You have been buried with him by your baptism; by which, too, you have been raised up with him through your belief in the power of God who raised him from the dead. 13 You were dead, because you were sinners and uncircumcised in body: he has brought you to life with him, he has forgiven us every one of our sins.

14 He has wiped out the record of our debt to the Law, which stood against us; he has destroyed it by nailing it to the cross; 15 and he has stripped the sovereignties and the ruling forces, and paraded them in public, behind him in his triumphal procession.

Against the false asceticism based on the 'principles of this world'

16 Then never let anyone criticise you for what you eat or drink, or about observance of annual festivals, New Moons or Sabbaths. 17 These are only a shadow of what was com-

187 READ COLOSSIANS 2:6–14.

He has brought you to life with him, he has forgiven us every one of our sins.
—COLOSSIANS 2:13

FROM DEATH TO LIFE

The dispensation of our God and Savior concerning man is a recall from the fall and a return from the alienation caused by disobedience to close communion with God. This is the reason for the sojourn of Christ in the flesh, the pattern life described in the gospels, the sufferings, the cross, the tomb, the descent into hell, the resurrection.... For perfection of life the imitation of Christ is necessary, not only in his example of gentleness, lowliness, and long suffering, but also of his actual death.... We are made in the likeness of his death in that we were buried with him by baptism....

It is necessary that the continuity of the old life be cut. And this is impossible unless a person be born again, according to the Lord's word. For the regeneration, as indeed the name shows, is a beginning of a second life. So before beginning the second, it is necessary to put an end to the first. For just as in the case of runners who turn and take the second course, a pause intervenes between the movements in the opposite direction, so also in making a change in lives it seemed necessary for death to come as mediator between the two, ending all that goes before, and beginning all that comes after.

How then do we achieve the descent into hell? By imitating, through baptism, the burial of Christ. For the bodies of the baptized are, as it were, buried in the water. Baptism then symbolically signifies the putting off of the works of the flesh; as the apostle says, you were "circumcised, with a circumcision performed, not by human hand, but by the complete stripping of your natural self. This is circumcision according to Christ. You have been buried with him by your baptism" (verses 11–12).

And there is a cleansing of the soul from the filth that has grown on it from the carnal mind, as it is written, "Wash me till I am whiter than snow" (Ps 51:7).   ST. BASIL, 329–379

YOU WILL FIND THE NEXT READING AT COLOSSIANS 3.

ing: the reality is the body of Christ. ¹⁸Do not be cheated of your prize by anyone who chooses to grovel to angels and worship them, pinning every hope on visions received, vainly puffed up by a human way of thinking; ¹⁹such a person has no connection to the Head, by which the whole body, given all that it needs and held together by its joints and sinews, grows with the growth given by God.

²⁰If you have really died with Christ to the principles of this world, why do you still let rules dictate to you, as though you were still living in the world? ²¹—'Do not pick up this, do not eat that, do not touch the other,' ²²and all about things which perish even while they are being used—according to merely *human commandments and doctrines!*ᵃ ²³In these rules you can indeed find what seems to be good sense—the cultivation of the will, and a humility which takes no account of the body; but in fact they have no value against self-indulgence.

2a Is 29:13.

188 READ COLOSSIANS 3:1–15.

And may the peace of Christ reign in your hearts.—COLOSSIANS 3:15

KEEPING CHRIST'S PEACE

We are not to be imprints of a foreign image. . . . And in order to avoid introducing in us the image of pride, we must let Christ imprint his image in us. He has imprinted it in us already when he said: "Peace is my farewell to you, my peace is my gift to you" (see Jn 14:27). But what use to us is the knowledge that this peace is good if we do not watch for it? Anything that is very good is customarily very fragile. And precious goods call for greater care and vigilance. His peace is very fragile and can be lost by a careless word or a slight hurt inflicted on a friend.

Now people like nothing more than to speak impertinently and to occupy themselves with what does not concern them, to carry on vain conversations and criticize those who are absent. From now on may those keep silent who cannot say, "Lord Yahweh has given me a disciple's tongue, for me to know how to give a word of comfort to the weary" (Is 50:4). Or if they say anything let it be a word of peace. . . .

"To love the other person is to fulfill the law" (Rm 13:8). May our good Lord and Savior Jesus Christ, the author of peace and the God of love, inspire this in us.　　　ST. COLUMBAN, 542?–615

YOU WILL FIND THE NEXT READING AT 1 THESSALONIANS 5.

Life-giving union with the glorified Christ

3 Since you have been raised up to be with Christ, you must look for the things that are above, where Christ is, sitting at God's right hand. ²Let your thoughts be on things above, not on the things that are on the earth, ³because you have died, and now the life you have is hidden with Christ in God. ⁴But when Christ is revealed—and he is your life—you, too, will be revealed with him in glory.

General rules of Christian behaviour

⁵That is why you must kill everything in you that is earthly: sexual vice, impurity, uncontrolled passion, evil desires and especially greed, which is the same thing as worshipping a false god; ⁶it is precisely these things which draw God's retribution upon those who resist. ⁷And these things made up your way of life when you were living among such people, ⁸but now you also must give up all these things: human anger, hot temper, malice, abusive language and dirty talk; ⁹and do not lie to each other. You have stripped off your old behaviour with your old self, ¹⁰and you have put on a new self which will progress towards true knowledge the more it is renewed in the image of its Creator; ¹¹and in that image there is no room for distinction between Greek and Jew, between the circumcised and uncircumcised, or between barbarian and Scythian, slave and free. There is only Christ: he is everything and he is in everything.

¹²As the chosen of God, then, the holy people whom he loves, you are to be clothed in heartfelt compassion, in generosity and humility, gentleness and patience. ¹³Bear with one another; forgive each other if one of you has a complaint against another. The Lord has forgiven you; now you must do the same. ¹⁴Over all these clothes, put on love, the perfect bond. ¹⁵And may the peace of Christ reign in your hearts, because it is for this that

you were called together in one body. Always be thankful.

¹⁶Let the Word of Christ, in all its richness, find a home with you. Teach each other, and advise each other, in all wisdom. With gratitude in your hearts sing psalms and hymns and inspired songs to God; ¹⁷and whatever you say or do, let it be in the name of the Lord Jesus, in thanksgiving to God the Father through him.

The morals of the home and household

¹⁸Wives, be subject to your husbands, as you should in the Lord. ¹⁹Husbands, love your wives and do not be sharp with them. ²⁰Children, be obedient to your parents always, because that is what will please the Lord. ²¹Parents, do not irritate your children or they will lose heart.

²²Slaves, be obedient in every way to the people who, according to human reckoning, are your masters; not only when you are under their eye, as if you had only to please human beings, but wholeheartedly, out of respect for the Master. ²³Whatever your work is, put your heart into it as done for the Lord and not for human beings, ²⁴knowing that the Lord will repay you by making you his heirs. It is Christ the Lord that you are serving. ²⁵Anyone who does wrong will be repaid in kind. For there is no favouritism.

4 Masters, make sure that your slaves are given what is upright and fair, knowing that you too have a Master in heaven.

The apostolic spirit

²Be persevering in your prayers and be thankful as you stay awake to pray. ³Pray for us especially, asking God to throw open a door for us to announce the message and proclaim the mystery of Christ, for the sake of which I am in chains; ⁴pray that I may proclaim it as clearly as I ought.

⁵Act wisely with outsiders, making the best of the present time. ⁶Always talk pleasantly and with a flavour of wit but be sensitive to the kind of answer each one requires.

Personal news

⁷Tychicus will tell you all the news about me. He is a very dear brother, and a trustworthy helper and companion in the service of the Lord. ⁸I am sending him to you precisely for this purpose: to give you news about us and to encourage you thoroughly. ⁹With him I am sending Onesimus,ᵃ that dear and trustworthy brother who is a fellow-citizen of yours. They will tell you everything that is happening here.

Greetings and final wishes

¹⁰Aristarchus, who is here in prison with me, sends his greetings, and so does Mark, the cousin of Barnabas—you were sent some instructions about him; if he comes to you, give him a warm welcome— ¹¹and Jesus Justus adds his greetings. Of all those who have come over from the circumcision, these are the only ones actually working with me for the kingdom of God. They have been a great comfort to me. ¹²Epaphras, your fellow-citizen, sends his greetings; this servant of Christ Jesus never stops battling for you, praying that you will never lapse but always hold perfectly and securely to the will of God. ¹³I can testify for him that he works hard for you, as well as for those at Laodicea and Hierapolis. ¹⁴Greetings from my dear friend Luke, the doctor, and also from Demas.

¹⁵Please give my greetings to the brothers at Laodicea and to Nympha and the church which meets in her house. ¹⁶After this letter has been read among you, send it on to be read in the church of the Laodiceans; and get the letter from Laodiceaᵇ for you to read yourselves. ¹⁷Give Archippus this message, 'Remember the service that the Lord assigned to you, and try to carry it out.'

¹⁸This greeting is in my own hand—PAUL. Remember the chains I wear. Grace be with you.

4a cf. Phm 10.   4b Possibly this letter is Ep.

THESSALONIANS

Address

1 Paul, Silvanus and Timothy, to the Church in Thessalonica which is in God the Father and the Lord Jesus Christ. Grace to you and peace.

Thanksgiving and congratulations

2 We always thank God for you all, mentioning you in our prayers continually. 3 We remember before our God and Father how active is the faith, how unsparing the love, how persevering the hope which you have from our Lord Jesus Christ.

4 We know, brothers loved by God, that you have been chosen, 5 because our gospel came to you not only in words, but also in power and in the Holy Spirit and with great effect. And you observed the sort of life we lived when we were with you, which was for your sake. 6 You took us and the Lord as your model, welcoming the word with the joy of the Holy Spirit in spite of great hardship. 7 And so you became an example to all believers in Macedonia and Achaia 8 since it was from you that the word of the Lord rang out—and not only throughout Macedonia and Achaia, for your faith in God has spread everywhere. We do not need to tell other people about it: 9 other people tell us how we started the work among you, how you broke with the worship of false gods when you were converted to God and became servants of the living and true God; 10 and how you are now waiting for Jesus, his Son, whom he raised from the dead, to come from heaven. It is he who saves us from the Retribution which is coming.

Paul's example in Thessalonica

2 You know yourselves, my brothers, that our visit to you has not been pointless. 2 Although, as you know, we had received rough treatment and insults at Philippi, God gave us the courage to speak his gospel to you fearlessly, in spite of great opposition. 3 Our encouragement to you does not come from any delusion or impure motives or trickery. 4 No, God has approved us to be entrusted with the gospel, and this is how we preach, seeking to please not human beings but God who *tests our hearts.*[a] 5 Indeed, we have never acted with the thought of flattering anyone, as you know, nor as an excuse for greed, God is our witness; 6 nor have we ever looked for honour from human beings, either from you or anybody else, 7 when we could have imposed ourselves on you with full weight, as apostles of Christ.

Instead, we lived unassumingly among you. Like a mother feeding and looking after her children, 8 we felt so devoted to you, that we would have been happy to share with you not only the gospel of God, but also our own lives, so dear had you become. 9 You remember, brothers, with what unsparing energy we used to work, slaving night and day so as not to be a burden on any one of you while we were proclaiming the gospel of God to you. 10 You are witnesses, and so is God, that our treatment of you, since you believed, has been impeccably fair and upright. 11 As you know, we treated every one of you as a father treats his children, 12 urging you, encouraging you and appealing to you to live a life worthy of

2a Jr 11:20.

God, who calls you into his kingdom and his glory.

The faith and the patience of the Thessalonians

13 Another reason why we continually thank God for you is that as soon as you heard the word that we brought you as God's message, you welcomed it for what it really is, not the word of any human being, but God's word, a power that is working among you believers. 14 For you, my brothers, have modelled yourselves on the churches of God in Christ Jesus which are in Judaea, in that you have suffered the same treatment from your own countrymen as they have had from the Jews, 15 who put the Lord Jesus to death, and the prophets too, and persecuted us also. Their conduct does not please God, and makes them the enemies of the whole human race, 16 because they are hindering us from preaching to gentiles to save them. Thus all the time they are *reaching the full extent of* their *iniquity,b* but retribution has finally overtaken them.

Paul's anxiety

17 Although we had been deprived of you for only a short time in body but never in affection, brothers, we had an especially strong desire and longing to see you face to face again, 18 and we tried hard to come and visit you; I, Paul, tried more than once, but Satan prevented us. 19 What do you think is our hope and our joy, and what *our crown of honourc* in the presence of our Lord Jesus when he comes? 20 You are, for you are our pride and joy.

Timothy's mission to Thessalonica

3 When we could not bear it any longer, we decided it would be best to be left without a companion at Athens, 2 and sent our brother Timothy, who is God's helper in spreading the gospel of Christ, to keep you firm and encourage you about your faith 3 and prevent any of you from being unsettled by the present hardships. As you know, these are bound to come our way: 4 indeed, when we were with you, we warned you that we are certain to have hardships to bear, and that is what has happened now, as you have found out. 5 That is why, when I could not bear it any longer, I sent to assure myself of your faith: I was afraid the Tester might have put you to the test, and all our work might have been pointless.

Paul thanks God for good reports of the Thessalonians

6 However, Timothy has returned from you and has given us good news of your faith and your love, telling us that you always remember us with pleasure and want to see us quite as much as we want to see you. 7 And so, brothers, your faith has been a great encouragement to us in the middle of our own distress and hardship; 8 now we can breathe again, as you are holding firm in the Lord. 9 How can we thank God enough for you, for all the joy we feel before our God on your account? 10 We are earnestly praying night and day to be able to see you face to face again and make up any shortcomings in your faith.

11 May God our Father himself, and our Lord Jesus, ease our path to you. 12 May the Lord increase and enrich your love for each other and for all, so that it matches ours for you. 13 And may he so confirm your hearts in holiness that you may be blameless in the sight of our God and Father when our Lord Jesus comes *with all his holy ones.a*

Live in holiness and charity

4 Finally, brothers, we urge you and appeal to you in the Lord Jesus; we instructed you how to live in the way that pleases God, and you are so living; but make more progress still. 2 You are well aware of the instructions we gave you on the authority of the Lord Jesus.

3 God wills you all to be holy. He wants you to keep away from sexual immorality, 4 and each one of you to know how to control his body in a way that is holy and honourable, 5 not giving way to selfish lust like *the nations*

2b Gn 15:16.   2c Pr 16:31.   3a Zc 14:5.

189 READ 1 THESSALONIANS 5:4–19.

Pray constantly.—1 THESSALONIANS 5:17

A WAY TO PRAY ALWAYS

St. Angela Merici instructed her sisters that praying constantly meant building liturgical, vocal, and mental prayer into their daily life:

Each one of the sisters should be solicitous about prayer, mental as well as vocal, that is a companion to fasting. For Scripture says prayer is good with fasting. As by fasting we mortify the carnal appetites and the senses, so by prayer we beg God for the true grace of spiritual life. Thus, from the great need we have of divine aid, we must pray always with mind and heart, as it is written, "Pray constantly." To all we counsel frequent vocal prayer that prepares the mind by exercising the bodily senses. So each one of you, every day will say with devotion and attention at least the Office of the Blessed Virgin and the seven penitential psalms (Pss 6, 32, 38, 51, 102, 130 and 143) because in saying the office we are speaking with God.

To afford matter and some method in mental prayer, we exhort each one to raise her mind to God and to exercise herself in it every day. And so in the secret of her heart, let her say:

"My Savior, illumine the darkness of my heart, and grant me grace rather to die than to offend your Divine Majesty any more. Guard, O Lord my affections and my senses, that they may not stray, nor lead me away from the light of your face, the satisfaction of every afflicted heart.

"I ask you, Lord, to receive all my self-will that by the infection of sin is unable to distinguish good from evil. Receive, O Lord, all my thoughts, words, and deeds, interior and exterior, that I lay at the feet of your Divine Majesty. Although I am utterly unworthy, I beseech you to accept all my being."

ST. ANGELA MERICI, 1470?–1540

YOU WILL FIND THE NEXT READING AT 1 TIMOTHY 2.

who do not acknowledge God.*ᵃ* ⁶He wants nobody at all ever to sin by taking advantage of a brother in these matters; the Lord always *pays back*ᵇ sins of that sort, as we told you before emphatically. ⁷God called us to be holy, not to be immoral; ⁸in other words, anyone who rejects this is rejecting not human authority, but God, *who gives you his Holy Spirit.*ᶜ

⁹As for brotherly love, there is no need to write to you about that, since you have yourselves learnt from God to love one another, ¹⁰and in fact this is how you treat all the brothers throughout the whole of Macedonia.

However, we do urge you, brothers, to go on making even greater progress ¹¹and to make a point of living quietly, attending to your own business and earning your living, just as we told you to, ¹²so that you may earn the respect of outsiders and not be dependent on anyone.

The dead and the living at the time of the Lord's coming

¹³We want you to be quite certain, brothers, about those who have fallen asleep, to make

4a Ps 79:6.   *4b* Dt 32:35.   *4c* Ezk 37:14.

sure that you do not grieve for them, as others do who have no hope. ¹⁴We believe that Jesus died and rose again, and that in the same way God will bring with him those who have fallen asleep in Jesus. ¹⁵We can tell you this from the Lord's own teaching, that we who are still alive for the Lord's coming will not have any advantage over those who have fallen asleep. ¹⁶At the signal given by the voice of the Archangel and the trumpet of God, the Lord himself will come down from heaven; those who have died in Christ will be the first to rise, ¹⁷and only after that shall we who remain alive be taken up in the clouds, together with them, to meet the Lord in the air. This is the way we shall be with the Lord for ever. ¹⁸With such thoughts as these, then, you should encourage one another.

Watchfulness while awaiting the coming of the Lord

5 About times and dates, brothers, there is no need to write to you ²for you are well aware in any case that the Day of the Lord is going to come like a thief in the night. ³It is when people are saying, 'How quiet and peaceful it is' that sudden destruction falls on them, as suddenly as labour pains come on a pregnant woman; and there is no escape.

⁴But you, brothers, do not live in the dark, that the Day should take you unawares like a thief. ⁵No, you are all children of light and children of the day: we do not belong to the night or to darkness, ⁶so we should not go on sleeping, as everyone else does, but stay wide awake and sober. ⁷Night is the time for sleepers to sleep and night the time for drunkards to be drunk, ⁸but we belong to the day and we should be sober; let us put on faith and love for a *breastplate,* and the hope of *salvation* for a *helmet.*ᵃ ⁹God destined us not for his retribution, but to win salvation through our Lord Jesus Christ, ¹⁰who died for us so that, awake or asleep, we should still live united to him. ¹¹So give encouragement to each other, and keep strengthening one another, as you do already.

¹²We appeal to you, my brothers, to be considerate to those who work so hard among you as your leaders in the Lord and those who admonish you. ¹³Have the greatest respect and affection for them because of their work.

Be at peace among yourselves. ¹⁴We urge you, brothers, to admonish those who are undisciplined, encourage the apprehensive, support the weak and be patient with everyone. ¹⁵Make sure that people do not try to repay evil for evil; always aim at what is best for each other and for everyone. ¹⁶Always be joyful; ¹⁷pray constantly; ¹⁸and for all things give thanks; this is the will of God for you in Christ Jesus.

¹⁹Do not stifle the Spirit ²⁰or despise the gift of prophecy with contempt; ²¹test everything and hold on to what is good ²²and *shun every* form of *evil.*ᵇ

Closing prayer and farewell

²³May the God of peace make you perfect and holy; and may your spirit, life and body be kept blameless for the coming of our Lord Jesus Christ. ²⁴He who has called you is trustworthy and will carry it out.

²⁵Pray for us, my brothers.

²⁶Greet all the brothers with a holy kiss. ²⁷My orders, in the Lord's name, are that this letter is to be read to all the brothers.

²⁸The grace of our Lord Jesus Christ be with you.

5a Is 59:17.   5b Jb 1:8.

The Second Letter to the

THESSALONIANS

Address

1 Paul, Silvanus and Timothy, to the Church in Thessalonica which is in God our Father and the Lord Jesus Christ. ²Grace to you and peace from God the Father and the Lord Jesus Christ.

Thanksgiving and encouragement; the Last Judgement

³We must always thank God for you, brothers; quite rightly, because your faith is growing so wonderfully and the mutual love that each one of you has for all never stops increasing. ⁴Among the churches of God we take special pride in you for your perseverance and faith under all the persecutions and hardships you have to bear. ⁵It all shows that God's judgement is just, so that you may be found worthy of the kingdom of God; it is for the sake of this that you are suffering now.

⁶For God's justice will surely mean hardship being inflicted on those who are now inflicting hardship on you, ⁷and for you who are now suffering hardship, relief with us, when the Lord Jesus appears from heaven with the angels of his power. ⁸He will come *amid flaming fire; he will impose a penalty*[a] on those who *do not acknowledge God* and *refuse to accept* the gospel of our Lord Jesus. ⁹Their punishment is to be lost eternally, excluded *from the presence of the Lord and from the glory of his strength* ¹⁰*on that day* when he comes *to be glorified among his holy ones* and *marvelled at* by all who believe in him; and you are among those who believed our witness.

¹¹In view of this we also pray continually that our God will make you worthy of his call, and by his power fulfil all your desires for

goodness, and complete all that you have been doing through faith; ¹²so that the *name* of our Lord Jesus Christ *may be glorified* in you and you in him, by the grace of our God and the Lord Jesus Christ.

The coming of the Lord and the prelude to it

2 About the coming of our Lord Jesus Christ, brothers, and our being gathered to him: ²please do not be too easily thrown into confusion or alarmed by any manifestation of the Spirit or any statement or any letter claiming to come from us, suggesting that the Day of the Lord has already arrived. ³Never let anyone deceive you in any way.

It cannot happen until the Great Revolt[a] has taken place and there has appeared the wicked One, the lost One, ⁴the Enemy, who *raises himself above every* so-called *God* or object of worship to *enthrone himself in God's* sanctuary and flaunts the claim that he is God. ⁵Surely you remember my telling you about this when I was with you? ⁶And you know, too, what is still holding him back from appearing before his appointed time. ⁷The mystery of wickedness is already at work, but let him who is restraining it once be removed, ⁸and the wicked One will appear openly. The Lord *will destroy him with the breath of his mouth* and will annihilate him with his glorious appearance at his coming.

⁹But the coming of the wicked One will be marked by Satan being at work in all kinds of counterfeit miracles and signs and

1a This threatening imagery of the Day of the Lord uses Is 66:15; Jr 10:25; Is 2:10–17; 49:3; 66:5.

2a Paul uses biblical symbolism: Is 11:4; 14:13; Ezk 28:2; Ps 33:6.

wonders, [10] and every wicked deception aimed at those who are on the way to destruction because they would not accept the love of the truth and so be saved. [11] And therefore God sends on them a power that deludes people so that they believe what is false, [12] and so that those who do not believe the truth and take their pleasure in wickedness may all be condemned.

Encouragement to persevere

[13] But we must always thank God for you, brothers whom the Lord loves, because God chose you from the beginning to be saved by the Spirit who makes us holy and by faith in the truth. [14] Through our gospel he called you to this so that you should claim as your own the glory of our Lord Jesus Christ. [15] Stand firm, then, brothers, and keep the traditions that we taught you, whether by word of mouth or by letter. [16] May our Lord Jesus Christ himself, and God our Father who has given us his love and, through his grace, such ceaseless encouragement and such sure hope, [17] encourage you and strengthen you in every good word and deed.

3 Finally, brothers, pray for us that the Lord's message may spread quickly, and be received with honour as it was among you; [2] and pray that we may be preserved from bigoted and evil people, for not everyone has faith. [3] You can rely on the Lord, who will give you strength and guard you from the evil One, [4] and we, in the Lord, have every confidence in you, that you are doing and will go on doing all that we tell you. [5] May the Lord turn your hearts towards the love of God and the perseverance of Christ.

Against idleness and disunity

[6] In the name of the Lord Jesus Christ, we urge you, brothers, to keep away from any of the brothers who lives an undisciplined life, not in accordance with the tradition you received from us.

[7] You know how you should take us as your model: we were not undisciplined when we were with you, [8] nor did we ever accept food from anyone without paying for it; no, we worked with unsparing energy, night and day, so as not to be a burden on any of you. [9] This was not because we had no right to be, but in order to make ourselves a model for you to imitate.

[10] We urged you when we were with you not to let anyone eat who refused to work. [11] Now we hear that there are some of you who are living lives without any discipline, doing no work themselves but interfering with other people's. [12] In the Lord Jesus Christ, we urge and call on people of this kind to go on quietly working and earning the food that they eat.

[13] My brothers, never slacken in doing what is right. [14] If anyone refuses to obey what I have written in this letter, take note of him and have nothing to do with him, so that he will be ashamed of himself, [15] though you are not to treat him as an enemy, but to correct him as a brother.

Prayer and farewell wishes

[16] May the Lord of peace himself give you peace at all times and in every way. The Lord be with you all.

[17] This greeting is in my own hand—PAUL. It is the mark of genuineness in every letter; this is my own writing. [18] May the grace of our Lord Jesus Christ be with you all.

TIMOTHY

Address

1 Paul, apostle of Christ Jesus appointed by the command of God our Saviour and of Christ Jesus our hope, ² to Timothy, true child of mine in the faith. Grace, mercy and peace from God the Father and from Christ Jesus our Lord.

Suppress the false teachers

³ When I was setting out for Macedonia I urged you to stay on in Ephesus to instruct certain people not to spread wrong teaching ⁴ or to give attention to myths and unending genealogies; these things only foster doubts instead of furthering God's plan which is founded on faith. ⁵ The final goal at which this instruction aims is love, issuing from a pure heart, a clear conscience and a sincere faith. ⁶ Some people have missed the way to these things and turned to empty speculation, ⁷ trying to be teachers of the Law; but they understand neither the words they use nor the matters about which they make such strong assertions.

The purpose of the Law

⁸ We are well aware that the Law is good, but only provided it is used legitimately, ⁹ on the understanding that laws are not framed for people who are upright. On the contrary, they are for criminals and the insubordinate, for the irreligious and the wicked, for the sacrilegious and the godless; they are for people who kill their fathers or mothers and for murderers, ¹⁰ for the promiscuous, homosexuals, kidnappers, for liars and for perjurers—and for everything else that is contrary to the sound teaching ¹¹ that accords with the gospel of the glory of the blessed God, the gospel that was entrusted to me.

Paul on his own calling

¹² I thank Christ Jesus our Lord, who has given me strength. By calling me into his service he has judged me trustworthy, ¹³ even though I used to be a blasphemer and a persecutor and contemptuous. Mercy, however, was shown me, because while I lacked faith I acted in ignorance; ¹⁴ but the grace of our Lord filled me with faith and with the love that is in Christ Jesus. ¹⁵ Here is a saying that you can rely on and nobody should doubt: that Christ Jesus came into the world to save sinners. I myself am the greatest of them; ¹⁶ and if mercy has been shown to me, it is because Jesus Christ meant to make me the leading example of his inexhaustible patience for all the other people who were later to trust in him for eternal life. ¹⁷ To the eternal King, the undying, invisible and only God, be honour and glory for ever and ever. Amen.

Timothy's responsibility

¹⁸ Timothy, my son, these are the instructions that I am giving you, in accordance with the words once spoken over you by the prophets, so that in their light you may fight like a good soldier ¹⁹ with faith and a good conscience for your weapons. Some people have put conscience aside and wrecked their faith in consequence. ²⁰ I mean men like Hymenaeus and Alexander, whom I have handed over to Satan so that they may learn not to be blasphemous.

Liturgical prayer

2 I urge then, first of all that petitions, prayers, intercessions and thanksgiving

190 READ 1 TIMOTHY 2:1–8.

There is only one mediator between God and humanity, himself a human being, Christ Jesus.—1 TIMOTHY 2:5

PRAYING THROUGH CHRIST

"Through him, with him and in him in the unity of the Holy Spirit, all honor and glory is yours, Almighty Father, for ever and ever." With these solemn words, the priest ends the Eucharistic prayer at the center of which is the mysterious event of the consecration. These words at the same time encapsulate the prayer of the church: honor and glory to the triune God through, with, and in Christ. Although the words are directed to the Father, all glorification of the Father is at the same time glorification of the Son and of the Holy Spirit. Indeed, the prayer extols the majesty that the Father imparts to the Son and that both impart to the Holy Spirit from eternity to eternity.

All praise of God is *through, with,* and *in* Christ. *Through* him, because only through Christ does humanity have access to the Father and because his existence as God-man and his work of salvation are the fullest glorification of the Father; *with* him, because all authentic prayer is the fruit of union with Christ and at the same time buttresses this union, and because in honoring the Son one honors the Father and vice versa; *in* him, because the praying church is Christ himself, with every individual praying member as a part of his Mystical Body, and because the Father is in the Son and the Son the reflection of the Father, who makes his majesty visible. The dual meanings of *through, with,* and *in* clearly express the God-man's mediation.   ST. EDITH STEIN, 1891–1942

YOU WILL FIND THE NEXT READING AT 2 TIMOTHY 2.

should be offered for everyone, ²for kings and others in authority, so that we may be able to live peaceful and quiet lives with all devotion and propriety. ³To do this is right, and acceptable to God our Saviour: ⁴he wants everyone to be saved and reach full knowledge of the truth. ⁵For there is only one God, and there is only one mediator between God and humanity, himself a human being, Christ Jesus, ⁶who offered himself as a ransom for all. This was the witness given at the appointed time, ⁷of which I was appointed herald and apostle and—I am telling the truth and no lie—a teacher of the gentiles in faith and truth.

⁸In every place, then, I want the men to lift their hands up reverently in prayer, with no anger or argument.

Women in the assembly

⁹Similarly, women are to wear suitable clothes and to be dressed quietly and modestly, without braided hair or gold and jewellery or expensive clothes; ¹⁰their adornment is to do the good works that are proper for women who claim to be religious. ¹¹During instruction, a woman should be quiet and respectful. ¹²I give no permission for a woman to teach or to have authority over a man. A woman ought to be quiet, ¹³because Adam was formed first and Eve afterwards, ¹⁴and it was not Adam who was led astray but the woman who was led astray and fell into sin. ¹⁵Nevertheless, she will be saved by child-bearing, provided she lives a sensible life and is constant in faith and love and holiness.

The elder-in-charge

3 Here is a saying that you can rely on: to want to be a presiding elder is to desire a noble task. ²That is why the presiding elder must have an impeccable character. Husband of one wife, he must be temperate, discreet and courteous, hospitable and a good teacher; ³not a heavy drinker, nor hot-tempered, but gentle and peaceable, not avaricious, ⁴a man who manages his own household well and brings his children up to obey him and be well-behaved: ⁵how can any man who does not understand how to manage his own household take care of the Church of God? ⁶He should not be a new convert, in case pride should turn his head and he incur the same condemnation as the devil. ⁷It is also necessary that he be held in good repute by outsiders, so that he never falls into disrepute and into the devil's trap.

Deacons

⁸Similarly, deacons must be respectable, not double-tongued, moderate in the amount of wine they drink and with no squalid greed for money. ⁹They must hold to the mystery of the faith with a clear conscience. ¹⁰They are first to be examined, and admitted to serve as deacons only if there is nothing against them. ¹¹Similarly, women must be respectable, not gossips, but sober and wholly reliable. ¹²Deacons must be husbands of one wife and must be people who manage their children and households well. ¹³Those of them who carry out their duties well as deacons will earn a high standing for themselves and an authoritative voice in matters concerning faith in Christ Jesus.

The Church and the mystery of the spiritual life

¹⁴I write this to you in the hope that I may be able to come to you soon; ¹⁵but in case I should be delayed, I want you to know how people ought to behave in God's household—that is, in the Church of the living God, pillar and support of the truth. ¹⁶Without any doubt, the mystery of our religion is very deep indeed:

He was made visible in the flesh,
justified in the Spirit,
seen by angels,
proclaimed to the gentiles,
believed in throughout the world,
taken up in glory.

False teachers

4 The Spirit has explicitly said that during the last times some will desert the faith and pay attention to deceitful spirits and doctrines that come from devils, ²seduced by the hypocrisy of liars whose consciences are branded as though with a red-hot iron: ³they forbid marriage and prohibit foods which God created to be accepted with thanksgiving by all who believe and who know the truth. ⁴Everything God has created is good, and no food is to be rejected, provided it is received with thanksgiving: ⁵the word of God and prayer make it holy. ⁶If you put all this to the brothers, you will be a good servant of Christ Jesus and show that you have really digested the teaching of the faith and the good doctrine which you have always followed. ⁷Have nothing to do with godless myths and old wives' tales. Train yourself for religion. ⁸Physical exercise is useful enough, but the usefulness of religion is unlimited, since it holds out promise both for life here and now and for the life to come; ⁹that is a saying that you can rely on and nobody should doubt it. ¹⁰I mean that the point of all our toiling and battling is that we have put our trust in the living God and he is the Saviour of the whole human race but particularly of all believers. ¹¹This is what you are to instruct and teach.

¹²Let no one disregard you because you are young, but be an example to all the believers in the way you speak and behave, and in your love, your faith and your purity. ¹³Until I arrive, devote yourself to reading to the people, encouraging and teaching. ¹⁴You have in you a spiritual gift which was given to you when

the prophets spoke and the body of elders laid their hands on you; do not neglect it. ¹⁵Let this be your care and your occupation, and everyone will be able to see your progress. ¹⁶Be conscientious about what you do and what you teach; persevere in this, and in this way you will save both yourself and those who listen to you.

Pastoral practice

5 Never speak sharply to a man older than yourself, but appeal to him as you would to your own father; treat younger men as brothers, ²older women as mothers and young women as sisters with all propriety.

Widows

³Be considerate to widows—if they really are widowed. ⁴If a widow has children or grandchildren, they are to learn first of all to do their duty to their own families and repay their debt to their parents, because this is what pleases God. ⁵But a woman who is really widowed and left on her own has set her hope on God and perseveres night and day in petitions and prayer. ⁶The one who thinks only of pleasure is already dead while she is still alive: ⁷instruct them in this, too, so that their lives may be blameless. ⁸Anyone who does not look after his own relations, especially if they are living with him, has rejected the faith and is worse than an unbeliever.

⁹Enrolment as a widow is permissible only for a woman at least sixty years old who has had only one husband. ¹⁰She must be a woman known for her good works—whether she has brought up her children, been hospitable to strangers and washed the feet of God's holy people, helped people in hardship or been active in all kinds of good work. ¹¹Do not accept young widows because if their natural desires distract them from Christ, they want to marry again, ¹²and then people condemn them for being unfaithful to their original promise. ¹³Besides, they learn how to be idle and go round from house to house; and then, not merely idle, they learn to be gossips

and meddlers in other people's affairs and to say what should remain unsaid. ¹⁴I think it is best for young widows to marry again and have children and a household to look after, and not give the enemy any chance to raise a scandal about them; ¹⁵there are already some who have turned aside to follow Satan. ¹⁶If a woman believer has widowed relatives, she should support them and not make the Church bear the expense but enable it to support those who are really widowed.

The elders

¹⁷Elders who do their work well while they are in charge earn double reward, especially those who work hard at preaching and teaching. ¹⁸As scripture says: *You must not muzzle an ox when it is treading out the corn;*[a] and again: *The worker deserves his wages.* ¹⁹Never accept any accusation brought against an elder unless it is supported *by two or three witnesses.* ²⁰If anyone is at fault, reprimand him publicly, as a warning to the rest. ²¹Before God, and before Jesus Christ and the angels he has chosen, I charge you to keep these rules impartially and never to be influenced by favouritism. ²²Do not be too quick to lay hands on anyone, and never make yourself an accomplice in anybody else's sin; keep yourself pure.

²³You should give up drinking only water and have a little wine for the sake of your digestion and the frequent bouts of illness that you have.

²⁴The faults of some people are obvious long before they come to the reckoning, while others have faults that are not discovered until later. ²⁵Similarly, the good that people do can be obvious; but even when it is not, it cannot remain hidden.

Slaves

6 All those under the yoke of slavery must have unqualified respect for their masters, so that the name of God and our teaching are not brought into disrepute. ²Those whose

5a Dt 25:4 followed by Lk 10:7; Dt 19:15.

masters are believers are not to respect them less because they are brothers; on the contrary, they should serve them all the better, since those who have the benefit of their services are believers and dear to God.

The true teacher and the false teacher

This is what you are to teach and urge. ³ Anyone who teaches anything different and does not keep to the sound teaching which is that of our Lord Jesus Christ, the doctrine which is in accordance with true religion, ⁴ is proud and has no understanding, but rather a weakness for questioning everything and arguing about words. All that can come of this is jealousy, contention, abuse and evil mistrust; ⁵ and unending disputes by people who are depraved in mind and deprived of truth, and imagine that religion is a way of making a profit. ⁶ Religion, of course, does bring large profits, but only to those who are content with what they have. ⁷ We brought nothing into the world, and we can take nothing out of it; ⁸ but as long as we have food and clothing, we shall be content with that. ⁹ People who long to be rich are a prey to trial; they get trapped into all sorts of foolish and harmful ambitions which plunge people into ruin and destruction. ¹⁰ 'The love of money is the root of all evils' and there are some who, pursuing it, have wandered away from the faith and so given their souls any number of fatal wounds.

Timothy's vocation recalled

¹¹ But, as someone dedicated to God, avoid all that. You must aim to be upright and religious, filled with faith and love, perseverance and gentleness. ¹² Fight the good fight of faith and win the eternal life to which you were called and for which you made your noble profession of faith before many witnesses. ¹³ Now, before God, the source of all life, and before Jesus Christ, who witnessed to his noble profession of faith before Pontius Pilate, I charge you ¹⁴ to do all that you have been told, with no faults or failures, until the appearing of our Lord Jesus Christ,

¹⁵ who at the due time will be revealed
by God, the blessed and only Ruler of all,
the King of kings and the Lord of lords,
¹⁶ who alone is immortal,
whose home is in inaccessible light,
whom no human being has seen or is able
to see:
to him be honour and everlasting power.
Amen.

Rich Christians

¹⁷ Instruct those who are rich in this world's goods that they should not be proud and should set their hopes not on money, which is untrustworthy, but on God who gives us richly all that we need for our happiness. ¹⁸ They are to do good and be rich in good works, generous in giving and always ready to share— ¹⁹ this is the way they can amass a good capital sum for the future if they want to possess the only life that is real.

Final warning and conclusion

²⁰ My dear Timothy, take great care of all that has been entrusted to you. Turn away from godless philosophical discussions and the contradictions of the 'knowledge' which is not knowledge at all; ²¹ by adopting this, some have missed the goal of faith. Grace be with you.

[1503]

TIMOTHY

Greeting and thanksgiving

1 From Paul, apostle of Christ Jesus through the will of God in accordance with his promise of life in Christ Jesus, ²to Timothy, dear son of mine. Grace, mercy and peace from God the Father and from Christ Jesus our Lord.

³Night and day I thank God whom I serve with a pure conscience as my ancestors did. I remember you in my prayers constantly night and day; ⁴I remember your tears and long to see you again to complete my joy. ⁵I also remember your sincere faith, a faith which first dwelt in your grandmother Lois, and your mother Eunice, and I am sure dwells also in you.

The gifts that Timothy has received

⁶That is why I am reminding you now to fan into a flame the gift of God that you possess through the laying on of my hands. ⁷God did not give us a spirit of timidity, but the Spirit of power and love and self-control. ⁸So you are never to be ashamed of witnessing to our Lord, or ashamed of me for being his prisoner; but share in my hardships for the sake of the gospel, relying on the power of God ⁹who has saved us and called us to be holy—not because of anything we ourselves had done but for his own purpose and by his own grace. This grace had already been granted to us, in Christ Jesus, before the beginning of time, ¹⁰but it has been revealed only by the appearing of our Saviour Christ Jesus. He has abolished death, and he has brought to light immortality and life through the gospel, ¹¹in whose service I have been made herald, apostle and teacher.

¹²That is why I am experiencing my present sufferings; but I am not ashamed, because I know in whom I have put my trust, and I have no doubt at all that he is able to safeguard until that Day what I have entrusted to him.

¹³Keep as your pattern the sound teaching you have heard from me, in the faith and love that are in Christ Jesus. ¹⁴With the help of the Holy Spirit who dwells in us, look after that precious thing given in trust.

¹⁵As you know, Phygelus and Hermogenes and all the others in Asia have deserted me. ¹⁶I hope the Lord will be kind to all the family of Onesiphorus, because he has often been a comfort to me and has never been ashamed of my chains. ¹⁷On the contrary, as soon as he reached Rome, he searched hard for me and found me. ¹⁸May the Lord grant him to find the Lord's mercy on that Day. You know better than anyone else how much he helped me at Ephesus.

How Timothy should face hardships

2 As for you, my dear son, take strength from the grace which is in Christ Jesus. ²Pass on to reliable people what you have heard from me through many witnesses so that they in turn will be able to teach others.

³Bear with your share of difficulties, like a good soldier of Christ Jesus. ⁴No one on active service involves himself in the affairs of civilian life, because he must win the approval of the man who enlisted him; ⁵or again someone who enters an athletic contest wins only by competing in the sports—a prize can be won only by competing according to the rules; ⁶and again, it is the farmer who works hard that has the first claim on any crop that is harvested. ⁷Think over what I have said, and the Lord will give you full understanding.

191 READ 2 TIMOTHY 2:8–13.

I persevere for the sake of those who are chosen, so that they, too, may obtain the salvation that is in Christ Jesus with eternal glory.—2 TIMOTHY 2:10

SUFFERING IN ACTION

I know all that suffering means, the fine and mysterious power it possesses, what it obtains and what it accomplishes. After all, our activity is of little importance. When Providence prefers to work by means of suffering, we should not complain too much. Then we can be sure that the work will be well done and not mixed up with all the misery of egotism and pride which sometimes spoil so much of our outward activity. I know by experience that in hours of trial certain graces are obtained for others which all our efforts had not previously obtained. I have thus concluded that suffering is the higher form of action, the best expression in the wonderful communion of saints. In suffering one is sure not to make mistakes, sure to be useful to others and to the great causes one longs to serve.

The Stoics said, "Suffering is nothing." They were wrong. Illuminated by a clearer light we Christians say, "Suffering is everything!" It demands, it obtains, everything. Through it God consents to accomplish everything. Suffering helps Christ to save the world and souls. When I am overwhelmed by the immensity of my desires for those I love, . . . it is toward suffering that I turn. It is through suffering that I ask to be allowed to serve as an intermediary between God and souls. It is the perfect form of prayer, the only infallible form of action. . . . Through the Cross to the Light.

ELIZABETH LESEUR, 1866–1914

YOU WILL FIND THE NEXT READING AT HEBREWS 12.

8 Remember the gospel that I carry, 'Jesus Christ risen from the dead, sprung from the race of David'; 9 it is on account of this that I have to put up with suffering, even to being chained like a criminal. But God's message cannot be chained up. 10 So I persevere for the sake of those who are chosen, so that they, too, may obtain the salvation that is in Christ Jesus with eternal glory.

11 Here is a saying that you can rely on:

If we have died with him, then we shall
　　live with him.
12 If we persevere, then we shall reign with
　　him.
If we disown him, then he will
　　disown us.

13 If we are faithless, he is faithful still,
　　for he cannot disown his own self.

The struggle against the immediate danger from false teachers

14 Remind them of this; and tell them in the name of God that there must be no wrangling about words: all that this ever achieves is the destruction of those who are listening. 15 Make every effort to present yourself before God as a proven worker who has no need to be ashamed, but who keeps the message of truth on a straight path. 16 Have nothing to do with godless philosophical discussions—they only lead further and further away from true religion. 17 Talk of this kind spreads corruption like gangrene, as in the case of Hymenaeus

and Philetus, [18] the men who have gone astray from the truth, claiming that the resurrection has already taken place. They are upsetting some people's faith.

[19] However, God's solid foundation-stone stands firm, and this is the seal on it: 'The Lord knows those who are his own' and 'All who call on the name of the Lord[a] must avoid evil.'

[20] Not all the dishes in a large house are made of gold and silver; some are made of wood or earthenware: the former are held in honour, the latter held cheap. [21] If someone holds himself aloof from these faults I speak of, he will be a vessel held in honour, dedicated and fit for the Master, ready for any good work.

[22] Turn away from the passions of youth, concentrate on uprightness, faith, love and peace, in union with all those who call on the Lord with a pure heart. [23] Avoid these foolish and undisciplined speculations, understanding that they only give rise to quarrels; [24] and a servant of the Lord must not engage in quarrels, but must be kind to everyone, a good teacher, and patient. [25] He must be gentle when he corrects people who oppose him, in the hope that God may give them a change of mind so that they recognise the truth [26] and come to their senses, escaping the trap of the devil who made them his captives and subjected them to his will.

The dangers of the last days

3 You may be quite sure that in the last days there will be some difficult times. [2] People will be self-centred and avaricious, boastful, arrogant and rude; disobedient to their parents, ungrateful, irreligious; [3] heartless and intractable; they will be slanderers, profligates, savages and enemies of everything that is good; [4] they will be treacherous and reckless and demented by pride, preferring their own pleasure to God. [5] They will keep up the outward appearance of religion but will have rejected the inner power of it. Keep away from people like that.

[6] Of the same kind, too, are those men who insinuate themselves into families in order to get influence over silly women who are obsessed with their sins and follow one craze after another, [7] always seeking learning, but unable ever to come to knowledge of the truth. [8] Just as Jannes and Jambres defied Moses,[a] so these men defy the truth, their minds corrupt and their faith spurious. [9] But they will not be able to go on much longer: their folly, like that of the other two, must become obvious to everybody.

[10] You, though, have followed my teaching, my way of life, my aims, my faith, my patience and my love, my perseverance [11] and the persecutions and sufferings that came to me in places like Antioch, Iconium and Lystra—all the persecutions I have endured; and the Lord has rescued me from every one of them. [12] But anybody who tries to live in devotion to Christ is certain to be persecuted; [13] while these wicked impostors will go from bad to worse, deceiving others, and themselves deceived.

[14] You must keep to what you have been taught and know to be true; remember who your teachers were, [15] and how, ever since you were a child, you have known the holy scriptures[b]—from these you can learn the wisdom that leads to salvation through faith in Christ Jesus. [16] All scripture is inspired by God and useful for refuting error, for guiding people's lives and teaching them to be upright. [17] This is how someone who is dedicated to God becomes fully equipped and ready for any good work.

A solemn charge

4 Before God and before Christ Jesus who is to be judge of the living and the dead, I charge you, in the name of his appearing and of his kingdom: [2] proclaim the message and, welcome or unwelcome, insist on it. Refute

2a Nb 16:5; Is 26:13.

3a In Jewish tradition (but not the Bible) the leaders of the Egyptian magicians, cf. Ex 7:11.

3b Probably the OT. There is no sign that the NT writings were yet set on the same level.

falsehood, correct error, give encouragement—but do all with patience and with care to instruct. ³The time is sure to come when people will not accept sound teaching, but their ears will be itching for anything new and they will collect themselves a whole series of teachers according to their own tastes; ⁴and then they will shut their ears to the truth and will turn to myths. ⁵But you must keep steady all the time; put up with suffering; do the work of preaching the gospel; fulfil the service asked of you.

Paul in the evening of his life

⁶As for me, my life is already being poured away as a libation, and the time has come for me to depart. ⁷I have fought the good fight to the end; I have run the race to the finish; I have kept the faith; ⁸all there is to come for me now is the crown of uprightness which the Lord, the upright judge, will give to me on that Day; and not only to me but to all those who have longed for his appearing.

Final advice

⁹Make every effort to come and see me as soon as you can. ¹⁰As it is, Demas has deserted me for love of this life and gone to Thessalonica, Crescens has gone to Galatia and Titus to Dalmatia; ¹¹only Luke is with me. Bring Mark with you; I find him a useful helper in my work. ¹²I have sent Tychicus to Ephesus.

¹³When you come, bring the cloak I left with Carpus in Troas, and the scrolls, especially the parchment ones. ¹⁴Alexander the coppersmith has done me a lot of harm; *the Lord will repay him as his deeds deserve.*[a] ¹⁵Be on your guard against him yourself, because he has been bitterly contesting everything that we say.

¹⁶The first time I had to present my defence, no one came into court to support me. Every one of them deserted me—may they not be held accountable for it. ¹⁷But the Lord stood by me and gave me power, so that through me the message might be fully proclaimed for all the gentiles to hear; and so I was *saved from the lion's mouth.*[b] ¹⁸The Lord will rescue me from all evil attempts on me, and bring me safely to his heavenly kingdom. To him be glory for ever and ever. Amen.

Farewells and final good wishes

¹⁹Greetings to Prisca and Aquila, and the family of Onesiphorus. ²⁰Erastus stayed behind at Corinth, and I left Trophimus ill at Miletus. ²¹Make every effort to come before the winter.

Greetings to you from Eubulus, Pudens, Linus, Claudia and all the brothers.

²²The Lord be with your spirit. Grace be with you.

4a Ps 28:4.   4b Ps 22:21.

The Letter to

TITUS

Address

1 From Paul, servant of God, an apostle of Jesus Christ to bring those whom God has chosen to faith and to the knowledge of the truth that leads to true religion, ² and to give them the hope of the eternal life that was promised so long ago by God. He does not lie ³ and so, in due time, he made known his message by a proclamation which was entrusted to me by the command of God our Saviour. ⁴ To Titus, true child of mine in the faith that we share. Grace and peace from God the Father and from Christ Jesus our Saviour.

The appointment of elders

⁵ The reason I left you behind in Crete was for you to organise everything that still had to be done and appoint elders in every town, in the way that I told you, ⁶ that is, each of them must be a man of irreproachable character, husband of one wife, and his children must be believers and not liable to be charged with disorderly conduct or insubordination. ⁷ The presiding elder has to be irreproachable since he is God's representative: never arrogant or hot-tempered, nor a heavy drinker or violent, nor avaricious; ⁸ but hospitable and a lover of goodness; sensible, upright, devout and self-controlled; ⁹ and he must have a firm grasp of the unchanging message of the tradition, so that he can be counted on both for giving encouragement in sound doctrine and for refuting those who argue against it.

Opposing the false teachers

¹⁰ And in fact there are many people who are insubordinate, who talk nonsense and try to make others believe it, particularly among those of the circumcision. ¹¹ They must be silenced: people of this kind upset whole families, by teaching things that they ought not to, and doing it for the sake of sordid gain. ¹² It was one of themselves, one of their own prophets, who said,ᵃ 'Cretans were never anything but liars, dangerous animals, all greed and laziness'; ¹³ and that is a true statement. So be severe in correcting them, and make them sound in the faith ¹⁴ so that they stop taking notice of Jewish myths and the orders of people who turn away from the truth.

¹⁵ To those who are pure themselves, everything is pure; but to those who have been corrupted and lack faith, nothing can be pure—the corruption is both in their minds and in their consciences. ¹⁶ They claim to know God but by their works they deny him; they are outrageously rebellious and quite untrustworthy for any good work.

Some specific moral instruction

2 It is for you, then, to preach the behaviour which goes with healthy doctrine. ² Older men should be reserved, dignified, moderate, sound in faith and love and perseverance. ³ Similarly, older women should behave as befits religious people, with no scandal-mongering and no addiction to wine—they must be the teachers of right behaviour ⁴ and show younger women how they should love their husbands and love their children, ⁵ how they must be sensible and chaste, and how to work in their homes, and be gentle, and obey their husbands, so that the message of God is not disgraced. ⁶ Similarly, urge younger men to be moderate in everything that they do, ⁷ and you

---

1a Attributed to the Cretan poet Epimenides.

yourself set an example of good works, by sincerity and earnestness, when you are teaching, and by a message sound and irreproachable [8] so that any opponent will be at a loss, with no accusation to make against us. [9] Slaves must be obedient to their masters in everything, and do what is wanted without argument; [10] and there must be no pilfering—they must show complete honesty at all times, so that they are in every way a credit to the teaching of God our Saviour.

The basis of the Christian moral life

[11] You see, God's grace has been revealed to save the whole human race; [12] it has taught us that we should give up everything contrary to true religion and all our worldly passions; we must be self-restrained and live upright and religious lives in this present world, [13] waiting in hope for the blessing which will come with the appearing of the glory of our great God and Saviour Christ Jesus. [14] He offered himself for us in order to ransom us from all our *faults* and *to purify a people to be his very own*[a] and eager to do good.

[15] This is what you must say, encouraging or arguing with full authority; no one should despise you.

General instruction for believers

3 Remind them to be obedient to the officials in authority; to be ready to do good at every opportunity; [2] not to go slandering other people but to be peaceable and gentle, and always polite to people of all kinds. [3] There was a time when we too were ignorant, disobedient and misled and enslaved by different passions and dissipations; we lived then in wickedness and malice, hating each other and hateful ourselves.

[4] But when the kindness and love of God our Saviour for humanity were revealed, [5] it was not because of any upright actions we had done ourselves; it was for no reason except his own faithful love that he saved us, by means of the cleansing water of rebirth and renewal in the Holy Spirit [6] which he has so generously poured over us through Jesus Christ our Saviour; [7] so that, justified by his grace, we should become heirs in hope of eternal life. [8] This is doctrine that you can rely on.

Personal advice to Titus

I want you to be quite uncompromising in teaching all this, so that those who now believe in God may keep their minds constantly occupied in doing good works. All this is good, and useful for everybody. [9] But avoid foolish speculations, and those genealogies, and the quibbles and disputes about the Law—they are useless and futile. [10] If someone disputes what you teach, then after a first and a second warning, have no more to do with him: [11] you will know that anyone of that sort is warped and is self-condemned as a sinner.

Practical recommendations, farewells and good wishes

[12] As soon as I have sent Artemas or Tychicus to you, do your best to join me at Nicopolis, where I have decided to spend the winter. [13] Help eagerly on their way Zenas the lawyer and Apollos, and make sure they have everything they need. [14] All our people must also learn to occupy themselves in doing good works for their practical needs, and not to be unproductive.

[15] All those who are with me send their greetings. Greetings to those who love us in the faith. Grace be with you all.

2a Ex 19:5.

PHILEMON

Address

From Paul, a prisoner of Christ Jesus and from our brother Timothy; to our dear fellow worker Philemon, 2 our sister Apphia, our fellow soldier Archippus and the church that meets in your house. 3 Grace and the peace of God our Father and the Lord Jesus Christ.

Thanksgiving and prayer

4 I always thank my God, mentioning you in my prayers, 5 because I hear of the love and the faith which you have for the Lord Jesus and for all God's holy people. 6 I pray that your fellowship in faith may come to expression in full knowledge of all the good we can do for Christ. 7 I have received much joy and encouragement by your love; you have set the hearts of God's holy people at rest.

The request about Onesimus

8 Therefore, although in Christ I have no hesitations about telling you what your duty is, 9 I am rather appealing to your love, being what I am, Paul, an old man, and now also a prisoner of Christ Jesus. 10 I am appealing to you for a child of mine, whose father I became while wearing these chains: I mean Onesimus.*a* 11 He was of no use to you before, but now he is useful both to you and to me. 12 I am sending him back to you—that is to say, sending you my own heart. 13 I should have liked to keep him with me; he could have been a substitute for you, to help me while I am in the chains that the gospel has brought me. 14 However, I did not want to do anything without your consent; it would have been forcing your act of kindness, which should be spontaneous. 15 I suppose you have been deprived of Onesimus for a time, merely so that you could have him back for ever, 16 no longer as a slave, but something much better than a slave, a dear brother; especially dear to me, but how much more to you, both on the natural plane and in the Lord. 17 So if you grant me any fellowship with yourself, welcome him as you would me; 18 if he has wronged you in any way or owes you anything, put it down to my account. 19 I am writing this in my own hand: I, Paul, shall pay it back—I make no mention of a further debt, that you owe your very self to me! 20 Well then, brother, I am counting on you, in the Lord; set my heart at rest, in Christ. 21 I am writing with complete confidence in your compliance, sure that you will do even more than I ask.

A personal request; good wishes

22 There is another thing: will you get a place ready for me to stay in? I am hoping through your prayers to be restored to you.

23 Epaphras, a prisoner with me in Christ Jesus, sends his greetings; 24 so do my fellow-workers Mark, Aristarchus, Demas and Luke.

25 May the grace of our Lord Jesus Christ be with your spirit.

a A pun: Onesimus means 'useful'.

HEBREWS

The greatness of the incarnate Son of God

1 At many moments in the past and by many means, God spoke to our ancestors through the prophets; but ²in our time, the final days, he has spoken to us in the person of his Son, whom he appointed heir of all things and through whom he made the ages. ³He is the reflection of God's glory and bears the impress of God's own being,ᵃ sustaining all things by his powerful command; and now that he has purged sins away, he has taken his seat at the right hand of the divine Majesty on high. ⁴So he is now as far above the angels as the title which he has inherited is higher than their own name.

Proof from the scriptures ᵇ

⁵To which of the angels, then, has God ever said:

You are my Son, today I have fathered you,

or:

I shall be a father to him and he a son to me?

⁶Again, when he brings the First-born into the world, he says:

Let all the angels of God pay him homage.

⁷To the angels, he says:

appointing the winds his messengers and
flames of fire his servants,

⁸but to the Son he says:

Your throne, God, is for ever and ever;

and:

the *sceptre of* his *kingdom* is *a sceptre of*
justice;
⁹*you love uprightness and detest evil.*
This is why God, your God, has anointed you
with the oil of gladness, as none of your rivals.

¹⁰And again:

Long ago, Lord, you laid earth's foundations,
the heavens are the work of your hands.
¹¹*They pass away but you remain,*
they all wear out like a garment.
¹²*Like a cloak you will roll them up, like a*
garment,
and they will be changed.
But you never alter and your years are
unending.

¹³To which of the angels has God ever said:

Take your seat at my right hand
till I have made your enemies your footstool?

¹⁴Are they not all ministering spirits, sent to serve for the sake of those who are to inherit salvation?

An exhortation

2 We ought, then, to turn our minds more attentively than before to what we have been taught, so that we do not drift away. ²If a message that was spoken through angels proved to be so reliable that every infringement and disobedience brought its own proper punish-

---

1a cf. Ws 7:25–26.

1b Texts used: Ps 2:7; 2 S 7:14; Ps 97:7; 104:4; 45:6–7; 102:25–27; 110:1.

ment, ³then we shall certainly not go unpunished if we neglect such a great salvation. It was first announced by the Lord himself, and is guaranteed to us by those who heard him; ⁴God himself confirmed their witness with signs and marvels and miracles of all kinds, and by distributing the gifts of the Holy Spirit in the various ways he wills.

Redemption brought by Christ, not by angels

⁵It was not under angels that he put the world to come, about which we are speaking. ⁶Someone witnesses to this somewhere with the words:

> *What are human beings that you spare a*
> *thought for them,*
> *a child of Adam that you care for him?*
> ⁷ *For a short while you have made him less*
> *than the angels;*
> *you have crowned him with glory and*
> *honour,*
> ⁸ *put all things under his feet.*ᵃ

For in *putting all things under* him he made no exceptions. At present, it is true, we are not able to see that *all things are under him,* ⁹but we do see Jesus, who was *for a short while made less than the angels,* now *crowned with glory and honour* because he submitted to death; so that by God's grace his experience of death should benefit all humanity.
¹⁰It was fitting that God, for whom and through whom everything exists, should, in bringing many sons to glory, make perfect through suffering the leader of their salvation. ¹¹For consecrator and consecrated are all of the same stock; that is why he is not ashamed to call them *brothers* ¹²in the text: *I shall proclaim your name to my brothers, praise you in full assembly;* or in the text: ¹³*I shall put my hope in him;* followed by *Look, I and the children whom God has given me.*ᵇ
¹⁴Since all the *children* share the same human nature, he too shared equally in it, so that by his death he could set aside him who held the power of death, namely the devil,

¹⁵and set free all those who had been held in slavery all their lives by the fear of death. ¹⁶For it was not the angels that he took to himself; he took to himself *the line of Abraham.* ¹⁷It was essential that he should in this way be made completely like his brothers so that he could become a compassionate and trustworthy high priest for their relationship to God, able to expiate the sins of the people. ¹⁸For the suffering he himself passed through while being put to the test enables him to help others when they are being put to the test.

Christ higher than Moses

3 That is why all you who are holy brothers and share the same heavenly call should turn your minds to Jesus, the apostle and the high priest of our profession of faith. ²He was *trustworthy* to the one who appointed him, just like *Moses,* who remained trustworthy *in all his household;*ᵃ ³but he deserves a greater glory than Moses, just as the builder of a house is more honoured than the house itself. ⁴Every house is built by someone, of course; but God built everything that exists. ⁵It is true that Moses was *trustworthy in the household* of God, as a *servant* is, acting as witness to the things which were yet to be revealed, ⁶but Christ is trustworthy as a son is, over his household. And we are his household, as long as we fearlessly maintain the hope in which we glory.

How to reach God's land of restᵇ

⁷That is why, as the Holy Spirit says:

> *If only you would listen to him today!*
> ⁸ *Do not harden your hearts, as at the*
> *rebellion,*
> *as at the time of testing in the desert,*
> ⁹ *when your ancestors challenged me,*
> *and put me to the test, and saw what I*
> *could do*
> ¹⁰ *for forty years.*

2a Ps 8:4–6. 2b Ps 22:22; Is 8:17, 18.
3a Nb 12:7. 3b An elaboration on Ps 95:7–11.

That was why

> that generation sickened me
> and I said, 'Always fickle hearts,
> that cannot grasp my ways!'
> [11] And then in my anger I swore
> that they would never enter my place of rest.

[12] Take care, brothers, that none of you ever has a wicked heart, so unbelieving as to turn away from the living God. [13] Every day, as long as this *today* lasts, keep encouraging one another so that none of you is *hardened* by the lure of sin, [14] because we have been granted a share with Christ only if we keep the grasp of our first confidence firm to the end. [15] In this saying: *If only you would listen to him today; do not harden your hearts, as at the Rebellion,* [16] who was it who *listened* and then *rebelled*? Surely all those whom Moses led out of Egypt. [17] And with whom was he *angry for forty years*? Surely with those who sinned and whose *dead bodies fell in the desert.* [18] To whom did he *swear they would never enter his place of rest*? Surely those who would not believe. [19] So we see that it was their refusal to believe which prevented them from entering.

4 Let us beware, then: since the promise never lapses, none of you must think that he has come too late for the promise of *entering his place of rest.* [2] We received the gospel exactly as they did; but hearing the message did them no good because they did not share the faith of those who did listen. [3] We, however, who have faith, are *entering a place of rest,* as in the text: *And then in my anger I swore that they would never enter my place of rest.* Now God's work was all finished at the beginning of the world; [4] as one text says, referring to the seventh day: *And God rested on the seventh day after all the work he had been doing.* [5] And, again, the passage above says: *They will never reach my place of rest.* [6] It remains the case, then, that there would be some people who would reach it, and since those who first heard the good news were prevented from entering by their refusal to believe, [7] God fixed another day, a *Today,* when he said through David in the text already quoted: *If only you would listen to him today; do not harden your hearts.* [8] If Joshua had led them into this place of rest, God would not later have spoken of another day. [9] There must still be, therefore, a seventh-day rest reserved for God's people, [10] since to *enter the place of rest* is to *rest after your work,* as God did after his. [11] Let us, then, press forward to *enter this place of rest,* or some of you might copy this example of refusal to believe and be lost.

[12] The word of God is something alive and active: it cuts more incisively than any two-edged sword: it can seek out the place where soul is divided from spirit, or joints from marrow; it can pass judgement on secret emotions and thoughts. [13] No created thing is hidden from him; everything is uncovered and stretched fully open to the eyes of the one to whom we must give account of ourselves.

Jesus the compassionate high priest

[14] Since in Jesus, the Son of God, we have the supreme high priest who has gone through to the highest heaven, we must hold firm to our profession of faith. [15] For the high priest we have is not incapable of feeling our weaknesses with us, but has been put to the test in exactly the same way as ourselves, apart from sin. [16] Let us, then, have no fear in approaching the throne of grace to receive mercy and to find grace when we are in need of help.

5 Every high priest is taken from among human beings and is appointed to act on their behalf in relationships with God, to offer gifts and sacrifices for sins; [2] he can sympathise with those who are ignorant or who have gone astray, because he too is subject to the limitations of weakness. [3] That is why he has to make sin offerings for himself as well as for the people. [4] No one takes this honour on himself; it needs a call from God, as in Aaron's case. [5] And so it was not Christ who gave himself the glory of becoming high priest, but the

one who said to him: *You are my Son, today I have fathered you,* [a] [6] and in another text: *You are a priest for ever, of the order of Melchizedek.* [7] During his life on earth, he offered up prayer and entreaty, with loud cries and with tears, to the one who had the power to save him from death, and, winning a hearing by his reverence, [8] he learnt obedience, Son though he was, through his sufferings; [9] when he had been perfected, he became for all who obey him the source of eternal salvation [10] and was acclaimed by God with the title of high *priest of the order of Melchizedek.*

Christian life and theology

[11] On this subject we have many things to say, and they are difficult to explain because you have grown so slow at understanding. [12] Indeed, when you should by this time have become masters, you need someone to teach you all over again the elements of the principles of God's sayings; you have gone back to needing milk, and not solid food. [13] Truly, no one who is still living on milk can digest the doctrine of saving justice, being still a baby. [14] Solid food is for adults with minds trained by practice to distinguish between good and bad.

The author explains his intention

6 Let us leave behind us then all the elementary teaching about Christ and go on to its completion, without going over the fundamental doctrines again: the turning away from dead actions, faith in God, [2] the teaching about baptisms and the laying-on of hands, about the resurrection of the dead and eternal judgement. [3] This, God willing, is what we propose to do.

[4] As for those people who were once brought into the light, and tasted the gift from heaven, and received a share of the Holy Spirit, [5] and tasted the goodness of God's message and the powers of the world to come [6] and yet in spite of this have fallen away—it is impossible for them to be brought to the freshness of repentance a second time, since they are crucifying the Son of God again for themselves, and making a public exhibition of him. [7] A field that drinks up the rain that has fallen frequently on it, and yields the crops that are wanted by the owners who grew them, receives God's blessing; [8] but one that grows brambles and thistles is worthless, and near to being cursed. It will end by being burnt.

Words of hope and encouragement

[9] But you, my dear friends—in spite of what we have just said, we are sure you are in a better state and on the way to salvation. [10] God would not be so unjust as to forget all you have done, the love that you have for his name or the services you have done, and are still doing, for the holy people of God. [11] Our desire is that every one of you should go on showing the same enthusiasm till the ultimate fulfilment of your hope, [12] never growing careless, but taking as your model those who by their faith and perseverance are heirs of the promises.

[13] When God made the promise to Abraham, he *swore by his own self,* since there was no one greater he could swear by: [14] *I will shower blessings on you and give you many descendants.* [a] [15] Because of that, Abraham persevered and received fulfilment of the promise. [16] Human beings, of course, swear an oath by something greater than themselves, and between them, confirmation by an oath puts an end to all dispute. [17] In the same way, when God wanted to show the heirs of the promise even more clearly how unalterable his plan was, he conveyed it by an oath [18] so that through two unalterable factors in which God could not be lying, we who have fled to him might have a vigorous encouragement to grasp the hope held out to us. [19] This is the anchor our souls have, as sure as it is firm, and reaching right through *inside the curtain* [20] where Jesus has entered as a forerunner on our behalf, having become a high *priest for ever, of the order of Melchizedek.*

5a Ps 2:7 followed by Ps 110:4.   6a Gn 22:16.

Melchizedek[a]

7 ¹Melchizedek, king of Salem, a priest of God Most High, came to meet Abraham when he returned from defeating the kings, and blessed him; ²and Abraham gave him a tenth of everything. By the interpretation of his name, he is, first, 'king of saving justice' and also king of Salem, that is, 'king of peace'; ³he has no father, mother or ancestry, and his life has no beginning or ending; he is like the Son of God. He remains a priest for ever.

Melchizedek accepted tithes from Abraham

⁴Now think how great this man must have been, if the patriarch Abraham gave him a tenth of the finest plunder. ⁵We know that any of the descendants of Levi who are admitted to the priesthood are obliged by the Law to take tithes from the people, that is, from their own brothers although they too are descended from Abraham. ⁶But this man, who was not of the same descent, took his tithe from Abraham, and he gave his blessing to the holder of the promises. ⁷Now it is indisputable that a blessing is given by a superior to an inferior. ⁸Further, in the normal case it is ordinary mortal men who receive the tithes, whereas in that case it was one who is attested as being alive. ⁹It could be said that Levi himself, who receives tithes, actually paid tithes, in the person of Abraham, ¹⁰because he was still in the loins of his ancestor when Melchizedek came to meet him.

From levitical priesthood to the priesthood of Melchizedek

¹¹Now if perfection had been reached through the levitical priesthood—and this was the basis of the Law given to the people—why was it necessary for a different kind of priest to arise, spoken of as being of the order of Melchizedek rather than of the order of Aaron? ¹²Any change in the priesthood must mean a change in the Law as well.

¹³So our Lord, of whom these things were said, belonged to a different tribe, the members of which have never done service at the altar; ¹⁴everyone knows he came from Judah, a tribe which Moses did not mention at all when dealing with priests.

The abrogation of the old law

¹⁵This becomes even more clearly evident if another priest, of the type of Melchizedek, arises who is a priest ¹⁶not in virtue of a law of physical descent, but in virtue of the power of an indestructible life. ¹⁷For he is attested by the prophecy: You are a priest for ever of the order of Melchizedek. ¹⁸The earlier commandment is thus abolished, because of its weakness and ineffectiveness ¹⁹since the Law could not make anything perfect; but now this commandment is replaced by something better— the hope that brings us close to God.

Christ's priesthood is unchanging

²⁰Now the former priests became priests without any oath being sworn, ²¹but this one with the swearing of an oath by him who said to him, The Lord has sworn an oath he will never retract: you are a priest for ever; ²²the very fact that it occurred with the swearing of an oath makes the covenant of which Jesus is the guarantee all the greater. ²³Further, the former priests were many in number, because death put an end to each one of them; ²⁴but this one, because he remains for ever, has a perpetual priesthood. ²⁵It follows, then, that his power to save those who come to God through him is absolute, since he lives for ever to intercede for them.

The perfection of the heavenly high priest

²⁶Such is the high priest that met our need, holy, innocent and uncontaminated, set apart from sinners, and raised up above the heavens; ²⁷he has no need to offer sacrifices every day, as the high priests do, first for their own sins and only then for those of the people; this he did once and for all by offering himself. ²⁸The Law appoints high priests who are men sub-

7a A commentary on Gn 14:17–20.

ject to weakness; but the promise on oath, which came after the Law, appointed the Son who is made perfect *for ever.*

The new priesthood and the new sanctuary

8 The principal point of all that we have said is that we have a high priest of exactly this kind. He *has taken his seat at the right*[a] of the throne of divine Majesty in the heavens, [2]and he is the minister of the sanctuary and of the true *Tent* which *the Lord,* and not any man, *set up.*[b] [3]Every high priest is constituted to offer gifts and sacrifices, and so this one too must have something to offer. [4]In fact, if he were on earth, he would not be a priest at all, since there are others who make the offerings laid down by the Law, [5]though these maintain the service only of a model or a reflection of the heavenly realities; just as Moses, when he had the Tent to build, was warned by God who said: *See that you work to the design that was shown you on the mountain.*[c]

Christ is the mediator of a greater covenant

[6]As it is, he has been given a ministry as far superior as is the covenant of which he is the mediator, which is founded on better promises. [7]If that first covenant had been faultless, there would have been no room for a second one to replace it. [8]And in fact God does find fault with them; he says:

Look, the days are coming, the Lord declares,
when I will make a new covenant
with the House of Israel and the House of Judah,
[9]but not a covenant like the one I made with their ancestors,
the day I took them by the hand to bring them out of Egypt,
which covenant of mine they broke,
and I too abandoned them, the Lord declares.
[10]No, this is the covenant I will make with the House of Israel,
when those days have come, the Lord declares:

In their minds I shall plant my laws
writing them on their hearts.
Then I shall be their God,
and they shall be my people.
[11]There will be no further need for each to teach his neighbour,
and each his brother, saying 'Learn to know the Lord!'
No, they will all know me,
from the least to the greatest,
[12]since I shall forgive their guilt
and never more call their sins to mind.[d]

[13]By speaking of a *new* covenant, he implies that the first one is old. And anything old and ageing is ready to disappear.

Christ enters the heavenly sanctuary

9 The first covenant also had its laws governing worship and its sanctuary, a sanctuary on this earth. [2]There was a tent which comprised two compartments: the first, in which the lamp-stand, the table and the loaves of permanent offering were kept, was called the Holy Place; [3]then beyond the second veil, a second compartment which was called the Holy of Holies [4]to which belonged the gold altar of incense, and the ark of the covenant, plated all over with gold. In this were kept the gold jar containing the manna, Aaron's branch that grew the buds, and the tables of the covenant. [5]On top of it were the glorious winged creatures, overshadowing the throne of mercy. This is not the time to go into detail about this.

[6]Under these provisions, priests go regularly into the outer tent to carry out their acts of worship, [7]but the second tent is entered only once a year, and then only by the high priest who takes in the blood to make an offering for his own and the people's faults of inadvertence. [8]By this, the Holy Spirit means us to see that as long as the old tent stands, the way into the holy place is not opened up; [9]it is a

8a Ps 110:1. 8b Nb 24:6.
8c Ex 25:40. 8d Jr 31:31–34.

symbol for this present time. None of the gifts and sacrifices offered under these regulations can possibly bring any worshipper to perfection in his conscience; ¹⁰they are rules about outward life, connected with food and drink and washing at various times, which are in force only until the time comes to set things right.

¹¹But now Christ has come, as the high priest of all the blessings which were to come. He has passed through the greater, the more perfect tent, not made by human hands, that is, not of this created order; ¹²and he has entered the sanctuary once and for all, taking with him not the blood of goats and bull calves, but his own blood, having won an eternal redemption. ¹³The blood of goats and bulls and the ashes of a heifer, sprinkled on those who have incurred defilement, may restore their bodily purity. ¹⁴How much more will the blood of Christ, who offered himself, blameless as he was, to God through the eternal Spirit, purify our conscience from dead actions so that we can worship the living God.

Christ seals the new covenant with his blood

¹⁵This makes him the mediator of a new covenant, so that, now that a death has occurred to redeem the sins committed under an earlier covenant, those who have been called to an eternal inheritance may receive the promise. ¹⁶Now wherever a will is in question, the death of the testator must be established; ¹⁷a testament comes into effect only after a death, since it has no force while the testator is still alive. ¹⁸That is why even the earlier covenant was inaugurated with blood, ¹⁹and why, after Moses had promulgated all the commandments of the Law to the people, he took the calves' blood, the goats' blood and some water, and with these he sprinkled the book itself and all the people, using scarlet wool and hyssop; ²⁰saying as he did so: *This is the blood of the covenant that God has made with you.*[a] ²¹And he sprinkled both the tent and all the liturgical vessels with blood in the same way. ²²In fact, according to the Law, practi-cally every purification takes place by means of blood; and if there is no shedding of blood, there is no remission. ²³Only the copies of heavenly things are purified in this way; the heavenly things themselves have to be purified by a higher sort of sacrifice than this. ²⁴It is not as though Christ had entered a man-made sanctuary which was merely a model of the real one; he entered heaven itself, so that he now appears in the presence of God on our behalf. ²⁵And he does not have to offer himself again and again, as the high priest goes into the sanctuary year after year with the blood that is not his own, ²⁶or else he would have had to suffer over and over again since the world began. As it is, he has made his appearance once and for all, at the end of the last age, to do away with sin by sacrificing himself. ²⁷Since human beings die only once, after which comes judgement, ²⁸so Christ too, having offered himself only once *to bear the sin of many,*[b] will manifest himself a second time, sin being no more, to those who are waiting for him, to bring them salvation.

The old sacrifices ineffective

10 So, since the Law contains no more than a reflection of the good things which were still to come, and no true image of them, it is quite incapable of bringing the worshippers to perfection, by means of the same sacrifices repeatedly offered year after year. ²Otherwise, surely the offering of them would have stopped, because the worshippers, when they had been purified once, would have no awareness of sins. ³But in fact the sins are recalled year after year in the sacrifices. ⁴Bulls' blood and goats' blood are incapable of taking away sins, ⁵and that is why he said, on coming into the world:

> *You wanted no sacrifice or cereal offering,*
> *but you gave me a body.*
> ⁶ *You took no pleasure in burnt offering or*
> *sacrifice for sin;*

9a Ex 24:8. 9b Is 53:12.

7 then I said, 'Here I am, I am coming,'
in the scroll of the book it is written of me,
to do your will, God.[a]

8 He says first *You did not want* what the Law lays down as the things to be offered, that is: *the sacrifices, the cereal offerings, the burnt offerings and the sacrifices for sin,* and *you took no pleasure* in them; 9 and then he says: *Here I am! I am coming to do your will.* He is abolishing the first sort to establish the second. 10 And this *will* was for us to be made holy by the *offering* of the *body* of Jesus Christ made once and for all.

The efficacy of Christ's sacrifice

11 Every priest stands at his duties every day, offering over and over again the same sacrifices which are quite incapable of taking away sins. 12 He, on the other hand, has offered one single sacrifice for sins, and then *taken his seat for ever, at the right hand of God,* 13 where he is now waiting *till his enemies are made his footstool.*[b] 14 By virtue of that one single offering, he has achieved the eternal perfection of all who are sanctified. 15 The Holy Spirit attests this to us, for after saying:

16 *No, this is the covenant I will make with them,*
when those days have come.

the Lord says:

In their minds I will plant my Laws
writing them on their hearts,
17 *and I shall never more call their sins to mind,*[c]
or their offences.

18 When these have been forgiven, there can be no more sin offerings.

The Christian opportunity

19 We have then, brothers, complete confidence through the blood of Jesus in entering the sanctuary, 20 by a new way which he has opened for us, a living opening through the curtain, that is to say, his flesh. 21 And we have the *high priest* over all *the sanctuary of God.*[d] 22 So as we go in, let us be sincere in heart and filled with faith, our hearts sprinkled and free from any trace of bad conscience, and our bodies washed with pure water. 23 Let us keep firm in the hope we profess, because the one who made the promise is trustworthy. 24 Let us be concerned for each other, to stir a response in love and good works. 25 Do not absent yourself from your own assemblies, as some do, but encourage each other; the more so as you see the Day drawing near.

The danger of apostasy

26 If, after we have been given knowledge of the truth, we should deliberately commit any sins, then there is no longer any sacrifice for them. 27 There is left only the dreadful prospect of judgement and of *the fiery wrath* that is to *devour your enemies.*[e] 28 Anyone who disregards the Law of Moses is ruthlessly *put to death on the word of two witnesses or three;*[f] 29 and you may be sure that anyone who tramples on the Son of God, and who treats *the blood of the covenant* which sanctified him as if it were not holy, and who insults the Spirit of grace, will be condemned to a far severer punishment. 30 We are all aware who it was that said: *Vengeance is mine; I will pay them back.*[g] And again: *The Lord will vindicate his people.* 31 It is a dreadful thing to fall into the hands of the living God.

Motives for perseverance

32 Remember the great challenge of the sufferings that you had to meet after you received the light, in earlier days; 33 sometimes by being yourselves publicly exposed to humiliations and violence, and sometimes as associates of others who were treated in the same way. 34 For you not only shared in the sufferings of those who were in prison, but you accepted

10a Ps 40:6–8.   10b Ps 110:1.   10c Jr 31:33–34.
10d Zc 6:11–12.   10e Is 26:11.
10f Dt 17:6.   10g Dt 32:35–36.

with joy being stripped of your belongings, knowing that you owned something that was better and lasting. ³⁵ Do not lose your fearlessness now, then, since the reward is so great. ³⁶ You will need perseverance if you are to do God's will and gain what he has promised.

³⁷ Only *a little while now, a very little while,*
   *for come he certainly will before too long.*ʰ
³⁸ *My upright person will live through faith*
   but if he draws back, my soul will take no
      *pleasure in him.*ⁱ

³⁹ We are not the sort of people who *draw back,* and are lost by it; we are the sort who keep *faith* until our souls are saved.

The exemplary faith of our ancestors

11 Only faith can guarantee the blessings that we hope for, or prove the existence of realities that are unseen. ² It is for their faith that our ancestors are acknowledged.

³ It is by faith that we understand that the ages were created by a word from God, so that from the invisible the visible world came to be.

⁴ It was because of his faith that Abel offered God a better sacrifice than Cain, and for that he was acknowledged as upright when *God* himself made acknowledgement of *his offerings.* Though he is dead, he still speaks by faith.

⁵ It was because of his faith that Enoch was taken up and did not experience death: *he was no more, because God took him;*ᵃ because before his assumption he was acknowledged to *have pleased God.* ⁶ Now it is impossible to please God without faith, since anyone who comes to him must believe that he exists and rewards those who seek him.

⁷ It was through his faith that Noah, when he had been warned by God of something that had never been seen before, took care to build an ark to save his family. His faith was a judgement on the world, and he was able to claim the uprightness which comes from faith.

⁸ It was by faith that Abraham obeyed the call to *set out* for a country that was the inheritance given to him and his descendants, and that *he set out* without knowing where he was going. ⁹ By faith he *sojourned* in the Promised Land as though it were not his, living in tents with Isaac and Jacob, who were heirs with him of the same promise. ¹⁰ He looked forward to the well-founded city, designed and built by God.

¹¹ It was equally by faith that Sarah, in spite of being past the age, was made able to conceive, because she believed that he who had made the promise was faithful to it. ¹² Because of this, there came from one man, and one who already had the mark of death on him, descendants *as numerous as the stars of heaven and the grains of sand on the seashore which cannot be counted.*ᵇ

¹³ All these died in faith, before receiving any of the things that had been promised, but they saw them in the far distance and welcomed them, recognising that they were only *strangers and nomads on earth.* ¹⁴ People who use such terms about themselves make it quite plain that they are in search of a homeland. ¹⁵ If they had meant the country they came from, they would have had the opportunity to return to it; ¹⁶ but in fact they were longing for a better homeland, their heavenly homeland. That is why God is not ashamed to be called their God, since he has founded the city for them.

¹⁷ It was by faith that Abraham, *when put to the test, offered up Isaac.*ᶜ He offered to sacrifice *his only son* even though he had yet to receive what had been promised, ¹⁸ and he had been told: *Isaac is the one through whom your name will be carried on.*ᵈ ¹⁹ He was confident that God had the power even to raise the dead; and so, figuratively speaking, he was given back Isaac from the dead.

²⁰ It was by faith that this same Isaac gave his blessing to Jacob and Esau for the still distant future. ²¹ By faith Jacob, when he was dying, blessed each of Joseph's sons, *bowed in*

10h Is 26:20.   10i Hab 2:3–4.   11a Gn 5:24.
11b Gn 22:17.   11c Gn 22:1–14.   11d Gn 21:12.

reverence, as he leant on his staff.[e] 22 It was by faith that, when he was about to die, Joseph mentioned the Exodus of the Israelites and gave instructions about his own remains.

23 It was by faith that Moses, when he was born, *was kept hidden by his parents for three months;*[f] because they *saw* that he was a *fine* child; they were not afraid of the royal edict. 24 It was by faith that, *when he was grown up,* Moses refused to be known as the son of Pharaoh's daughter 25 and chose to be ill-treated in company with God's people rather than to enjoy the transitory pleasures of sin. 26 He considered that the humiliations offered to the Anointed were something more precious than all the treasures of Egypt, because he had his eyes fixed on the reward. 27 It was by faith that he left Egypt without fear of the king's anger; he held to his purpose like someone who could see the Invisible. 28 It was by faith that he kept *the Passover* and sprinkled *the blood* to prevent *the Destroyer* from touching any of their firstborn sons. 29 It was by faith they crossed the Red Sea as easily as dry land, while the Egyptians, trying to do the same, were drowned.

30 It was through faith that the walls of Jericho fell down when the people had marched round them for seven days. 31 It was by faith that Rahab the prostitute welcomed the spies and so was not killed with the unbelievers.

32 What more shall I say? There is not time for me to give an account of Gideon, Barak, Samson, Jephthah, or of David, Samuel and the prophets. 33 These were men who through faith conquered kingdoms, did what was upright and earned the promises. They could keep a lion's mouth shut, 34 put out blazing fires and emerge unscathed from battle. They were weak people who were given strength to be brave in war and drive back foreign invaders. 35 Some returned to their wives from the dead by resurrection; and others submitted to torture, refusing release so that they would rise again to a better life. 36 Some had to bear being pilloried and flogged, or even chained up in prison. 37 They were stoned, or sawn in half,[g] or killed by the sword; they were home-less, and wore only the skins of sheep and goats; they were in want and hardship, and maltreated. 38 They were too good for the world and they wandered in deserts and mountains and in caves and ravines. 39 These all won acknowledgement through their faith, but they did not receive what was promised, 40 since God had made provision for us to have something better, and they were not to reach perfection except with us.

The example of Jesus Christ

12 With so many witnesses in a great cloud all around us, we too, then, should throw off everything that weighs us down and the sin that clings so closely, and with perseverance keep running in the race which lies ahead of us. 2 Let us keep our eyes fixed on Jesus, who leads us in our faith and brings it to perfection: for the sake of the joy which lay ahead of him, he endured the cross, disregarding the shame of it, and *has taken his seat at the right* of God's throne. 3 Think of the way he persevered against such opposition from sinners and then you will not lose heart and come to grief. 4 In the fight against sin, you have not yet had to keep fighting to the point of bloodshed.

God's fatherly instruction

5 Have you forgotten that encouraging text in which you are addressed as sons?

My son, do not scorn correction from the Lord,
do not resent his training,
6 *for the Lord trains those he loves,*
and chastises every son he accepts.[a]

7 Perseverance is part of your *training;* God is treating you as his *sons.* Has there ever been any *son* whose father did not *train* him? 8 If

11e Gn 47:31. *11f* Ex 2:2, 11.

11g Some apocryphal texts say that Isaiah was executed in this way by King Manasseh.

12a Pr 3:11–12.

192 READ HEBREWS 12:1–13.

In those who have undergone [discipline], it bears fruit in peace and uprightness.
—HEBREWS 12:11

GOD'S TENDER DISCIPLINE

Our good Lord showed me the enmity of the fiend, by which I understood that all that is opposed to love and to peace is from the fiend and his party. And through our feebleness and folly we must fall yet, through the mercy and grace of the Holy Spirit, we are able to rise up again with even more joy. And if our enemy wins anything from our falling, for such is his liking, he loses far more when we rise up again by love and meekness. And this glorious rising causes him great sorrow and pain, for the hatred he has for our soul makes him burn continually with envy. And all this sorrow that he would make us have turns back upon himself. That is why our Lord scorned him; and it made me laugh mightily.

This, then, is the remedy: that we be aware of our wretchedness and flee to our Lord; for the greater be our need, the more speedily must we come near him. And we could sum up our state in these words: "I know well that I have a sharp pain, but our Lord is almighty and is able to punish me mightily, and he is all wise and knows how to punish me skillfully, and he is all goodness and loves me with every tenderness." And we need to stay awhile and behold this; for it is loving meekness in a sinful soul, brought about by mercy and grace in the Holy Spirit, when we gladly and willingly accept the scourge and chastisement that our Lord himself decides to give us. And it will be very tender and most easy, if we will only hold ourselves content with him and all that he does. For the kind of penance that we take upon ourselves was not shown to me. . . . But it was shown clearly, and shown with a look of gladdest love, that we shall meekly and patiently bear and suffer the penance that God himself gives us, remembering his own blessed passion.

BL. JULIAN OF NORWICH, 1342?–1423?

YOU WILL FIND THE NEXT READING AT JAMES 1.

you were not getting this training, as all of you are, then you would be not *sons* but bastards. [9] Besides, we have all had our human fathers who punished us, and we respected them for it; all the more readily ought we to submit to the Father of spirits, and so earn life. [10] Our human fathers were training us for a short life and according to their own lights; but he does it all for our own good, so that we may share his own holiness. [11] Of course, any discipline is at the time a matter for grief, not joy; but later, in those who have undergone it, it bears fruit in peace and uprightness. [12] So *steady all weary hands and trembling knees*[b] [13] and make your crooked paths straight; then the injured limb will not be maimed, it will get better instead.

Unfaithfulness is punished

[14] *Seek peace*[c] with all people, and the holiness without which no one can ever see the Lord.

12b Is 35:3. *12c* Ps 34:14.

15 Be careful that no one is deprived of the grace of God and that no *root of bitterness should begin to grow and make trouble;*[d] this can poison a large number. 16 And be careful that there is no immoral person, or anyone worldly minded like Esau, *who sold his birthright*[e] for one single meal. 17 As you know, when he wanted to obtain the blessing afterwards, he was rejected and, though he pleaded for it with tears, he could find no way of reversing the decision.

The two covenants

18 What you have come to is nothing known to the senses: not a *blazing fire,*[f] or *gloom* or *total darkness,* or a *storm;* 19 or *trumpet-blast* or the *sound of a voice speaking* which made everyone that heard it beg that no more should be said to them. 20 They could not bear the order that was given: *If even a beast touches the mountain, it must be stoned.*[g] 21 The whole scene was so terrible that Moses said, 'I am afraid and trembling.' 22 But what you have come to is Mount Zion and the city of the living God, the heavenly Jerusalem where the millions of angels have gathered for the festival, 23 with the whole Church of first-born sons, enrolled as citizens of heaven. You have come to God himself, the supreme Judge, and to the spirits of the upright who have been made perfect; 24 and to Jesus, the mediator of a new covenant, and to purifying blood which pleads more insistently than Abel's. 25 Make sure that you never refuse to listen when he speaks. If the people who on earth refused to listen to a warning could not escape their punishment, how shall we possibly escape if we turn away from a voice that warns us from heaven? 26 That time his voice made the earth shake, but now he has given us this promise: *I am going to shake the earth once more and* not only the earth but *heaven as well.*[h] 27 The words *once more* indicate the removal of what is shaken, since these are created things, so that what is not shaken remains. 28 We have been given possession of an unshakeable kingdom. Let us therefore be grateful and use our gratitude to worship God in the way that pleases him, in reverence and fear. 29 For our *God is a consuming fire.*[i]

Final recommendations

13 Continue to love each other like brothers, 2 and remember always to welcome strangers, for by doing this, some people have entertained angels without knowing it. 3 Keep in mind those who are in prison, as though you were in prison with them; and those who are being badly treated, since you too are in the body. 4 Marriage must be honoured by all, and marriages must be kept undefiled, because the sexually immoral and adulterers will come under God's judgement. 5 Put avarice out of your lives and be content with whatever you have; God himself has said: *I shall not fail you or desert you,*[a] 6 and so we can say with confidence: *With the Lord on my side, I fear nothing: what can human beings do to me?*[b]

Faithfulness

7 Remember your leaders, who preached the word of God to you, and as you reflect on the outcome of their lives, take their faith as your model. 8 Jesus Christ is the same today as he was yesterday and as he will be for ever. 9 Do not be led astray by all sorts of strange doctrines: it is better to rely on grace for inner strength than on food, which has done no good to those who concentrate on it. 10 We have our own altar from which those who serve the Tent have no right to eat. 11 The bodies of the animals *whose blood is taken into the sanctuary* by the high priest *for the rite of expiation are burnt outside the camp,*[c] 12 and so Jesus too suffered outside the gate to sanctify the people with his own blood. 13 Let us go to

12d Dt 29:17.   12e Gn 25:33.

12f Ex 19–20, followed by Dt 9:19; Hg 2:6; Dt 4:24.

12g Ex 19:12seq.   12h Hg 2:6.

12i Dt 4:24.   13a Dt 31:6.

13b Ps 118:6.   13c Lv 16:27.

him, then, *outside the camp,* and bear his humiliation. ¹⁴There is no permanent city for us here; we are looking for the one which is yet to be. ¹⁵Through him, *let us offer God* an unending *sacrifice* of praise, the fruit of the lips of those who acknowledge his name. ¹⁶Keep doing good works and sharing your resources, for these are the kinds of sacrifice that please God.

Obedience to religious leaders

¹⁷Obey your leaders and give way to them; they watch over your souls because they must give an account of them; make this a joy for them to do, and not a grief—you yourselves would be the losers. ¹⁸Pray for us; we are sure that our own conscience is clear and we are certainly determined to behave honourably in everything we do. ¹⁹I ask you very particularly to pray that I may come back to you all the sooner.

News, good wishes and greetings

²⁰I pray that the God of peace, *who brought back* from the dead our Lord Jesus, the great *Shepherd of the sheep, by the blood that sealed an eternal covenant,^d* ²¹may prepare you to do his will in every kind of good action; effecting in us all whatever is acceptable to himself through Jesus Christ, to whom be glory for ever and ever. Amen.

²²I urge you, brothers, to take these words of encouragement kindly; that is why I have written to you briefly.

²³I want you to know that our brother Timothy has been set free. If he arrives in time, he will be with me when I see you. ²⁴Greetings to all your leaders and to all God's holy people. God's holy people in Italy send you greetings. ²⁵Grace be with you all.

13d A combination of Is 63:11 with Ezk 34:23; 37:26.

The Letter of

JAMES

Address and greetings

1 From James, servant of God and of the Lord Jesus Christ. Greetings to the twelve tribes of the Dispersion.[a]

Trials a privilege

[2] My brothers, consider it a great joy when trials of many kinds come upon you, [3] for you well know that the testing of your faith produces perseverance, and [4] perseverance must complete its work so that you will become fully developed, complete, not deficient in any way.

Prayer with confidence

[5] Any of you who lacks wisdom must ask God, who gives to all generously and without scolding; it will be given. [6] But the prayer must be made with faith, and no trace of doubt, because a person who has doubts is like the waves thrown up in the sea by the buffeting of the wind. [7] That sort of person, in two minds, [8] inconsistent in every activity, must not expect to receive anything from the Lord.

The lot of the rich

[9] It is right that the brother in humble circumstances should glory in being lifted up, [10] and the rich in being brought low. For the rich will last no longer than *the wild flower;* [11] the scorching sun comes up, and the *grass withers,* its *flower falls,*[b] its beauty is lost. It is the same with the rich: in the middle of a busy life, the rich will wither.

Temptation

[12] *Blessed is anyone who perseveres*[c] when trials come. Such a person is of proven worth and will win the prize of life, the crown that the Lord has promised to those who love him.

[13] Never, when you are being put to the test, say, 'God is tempting me'; God cannot be tempted by evil, and he does not put anybody to the test. [14] Everyone is put to the test by being attracted and seduced by that person's own wrong desire. [15] Then the desire conceives and gives birth to sin, and when sin reaches full growth, it gives birth to death.

Receiving the Word and putting it into practice

[16] Make no mistake about this, my dear brothers: [17] all that is good, all that is perfect, is given us from above; it comes down from the Father of all light; with him there is no such thing as alteration, no shadow caused by change.

[18] By his own choice he gave birth to us by the message of the truth so that we should be a sort of first-fruits of all his creation.

True religion

[19] Remember this, my dear brothers: everyone should be *quick to listen*[d] but *slow* to speak and slow to human anger; [20] God's saving justice is never served by human anger; [21] so do away with all impurities and remnants of evil. Humbly welcome the Word which has been planted in you and can save your souls.

[22] But you must do what the Word tells you and not just listen to it and deceive yourselves. [23] Anyone who listens to the Word and takes no action is like someone who looks at his own features in a mirror and, [24] once he has

---

1a Properly, Jews scattered in the gentile world, successors of the twelve tribes.

1b Is 40:6–7.   1c Dn 12:2.   1d Si 5:11.

[1524]

193 READ JAMES 1:12–15.

The testing of your faith produces perseverance.—JAMES 1:3

FACING TEMPTATION PATIENTLY

God does not allow us to be burdened with anything beyond our power of endurance, and therefore, when difficulties come upon us, we do not sin unless we are unwilling to endure a little tribulation or to suffer anything unforeseen. As the Apostle says, "You can trust that God will not let you be put to the test beyond your strength" (1 Co 10:13). But we . . . have no patience and no desire for a little labor and [no desire] to brace ourselves to accept anything with humility. Therefore we are crushed [by our difficulties]. The more we run away from temptations, the more they weigh us down and the less we are able to drive them away.

Suppose a man for some reason dives into the sea: if he knows the art of swimming, what does he do when a great wave comes along? He ducks under it until it goes past and then he goes on swimming unharmed. But if he is determined to set himself against it, it pushes him away and hurls him back a great distance, and when he begins to swim forward, another wave comes upon him, and if again he tries to swim against it, again it forces him back, and he only tires himself out and makes no headway. But if he ducks his head and lowers himself under the wave, . . . no harm comes to him and he continues to swim as long as he likes. Those who go on doing their work this way when they are in trouble, putting up with their temptations with patience and humility, come through unharmed. But if they get distressed and downcast, seeking the reasons for everything, tormenting themselves and being annoyed with themselves instead of helping themselves, they do themselves harm.

ST. DOROTHEOS OF GAZA, SIXTH CENTURY

YOU WILL FIND THE NEXT READING AT 1 PETER 1.

seen what he looks like, goes off and immediately forgets it. ²⁵But anyone who looks steadily at the perfect law of freedom and keeps to it—not listening and forgetting, but putting it into practice—will be blessed in every undertaking.

²⁶Nobody who fails to keep a tight rein on the tongue can claim to be religious; this is mere self-deception; that person's religion is worthless. ²⁷Pure, unspoilt religion, in the eyes of God our Father, is this: coming to the help of orphans and widows in their hardships, and keeping oneself uncontaminated by the world.

Respect for the poor

2 My brothers, do not let class distinction enter into your faith in Jesus Christ, our glorified Lord. ²Now suppose a man comes into your synagogue, well-dressed and with a gold ring on, and at the same time a poor man comes in, in shabby clothes, ³and you take notice of the well-dressed man, and say, 'Come this way to the best seats'; then you tell the poor man, 'Stand over there' or 'You can sit on the floor by my foot-rest.' ⁴In making this distinction among yourselves have you not used a corrupt standard?

⁵Listen, my dear brothers: it was those who were poor according to the world that God chose, to be rich in faith and to be the heirs to the kingdom which he promised to those who love him. ⁶You, on the other hand, have dishonoured the poor. Is it not the rich who lord it over you? ⁷Are not they the ones who drag you into court, who insult the honourable name which has been pronounced over you? ⁸Well, the right thing to do is to keep the supreme Law of scripture: *you will love your neighbour as yourself;* ⁹ but as soon as you make class distinctions, you are committing sin and under condemnation for breaking the Law.

¹⁰You see, anyone who keeps the whole of the Law but trips up on a single point, is still guilty of breaking it all. ¹¹He who said, *'You must not commit adultery'* said also, *'You must not kill.'* ᵇ Now if you commit murder, you need not commit adultery as well to become a breaker of the Law. ¹²Talk and behave like people who are going to be judged by the law of freedom. ¹³Whoever acts without mercy will be judged without mercy but mercy can afford to laugh at judgement.

Faith and good deeds

¹⁴How does it help, my brothers, when someone who has never done a single good act claims to have faith? Will that faith bring salvation? ¹⁵If one of the brothers or one of the sisters is in need of clothes and has not enough food to live on, ¹⁶and one of you says to them, 'I wish you well; keep yourself warm and eat plenty,' without giving them these bare necessities of life, then what good is that? ¹⁷In the same way faith, if good deeds do not go with it, is quite dead.

¹⁸But someone may say: So you have faith and I have good deeds? Show me this faith of yours without deeds, then! It is by my deeds that I will show you my faith. ¹⁹You believe in the one God—that is creditable enough, but even the demons have the same belief, and they tremble with fear. ²⁰Fool! Would you not like to know that faith without deeds is useless? ²¹Was not Abraham our father justified by his deed, because he *offered his son Isaac on the altar?* ᶜ ²²So you can see that his faith was working together with his deeds; his faith became perfect by what he did. ²³In this way the scripture was fulfilled: *Abraham put his faith in God, and this was considered as making him upright;* ᵈ and he received the name 'friend of God'.

²⁴You see now that it is by deeds, and not only by believing, that someone is justified. ²⁵There is another example of the same kind: Rahab the prostitute,ᵉ was she not justified by her deeds because she welcomed the messengers and showed them a different way to leave? ²⁶As a body without a spirit is dead, so is faith without deeds.

Uncontrolled language

3 Only a few of you, my brothers, should be teachers, bearing in mind that we shall receive a stricter judgement. ²For we all trip up in many ways.

Someone who does not trip up in speech has reached perfection and is able to keep the whole body on a tight rein. ³Once we put a bit in the horse's mouth, to make it do what we want, we have the whole animal under our control. ⁴Or think of ships: no matter how big they are, even if a gale is driving them, they are directed by a tiny rudder wherever the whim of the helmsman decides. ⁵So the tongue is only a tiny part of the body, but its boasts are great. Think how small a flame can set fire to a huge forest; ⁶The tongue is a flame too. Among all the parts of the body, the tongue is a whole wicked world: it infects the whole body; catching fire itself from hell, it sets fire to the whole wheel of creation. ⁷Wild animals and birds, reptiles and fish of every kind can all be tamed, and have been tamed, by humans; ⁸but nobody can tame the tongue—it is a pest that will not keep still, full of deadly poison. ⁹We use it to bless the Lord and Father,

2a Lv 19:18.   2b Ex 20:3, 14.   2c Gn 22:9.

2d Gn 15:6.   2e Jos 2:1seq.

but we also use it to curse people who are made in God's image: [10]the blessing and curse come out of the same mouth. My brothers, this must be wrong— [11]does any water supply give a flow of fresh water and salt water out of the same pipe? [12]Can a fig tree yield olives, my brothers, or a vine yield figs? No more can sea water yield fresh water.

Real wisdom and its opposite

[13]Anyone who is wise or understanding among you should from a good life give evidence of deeds done in the gentleness of wisdom. [14]But if at heart you have the bitterness of jealousy, or selfish ambition, do not be boastful or hide the truth with lies; [15]this is not the wisdom that comes from above, but earthly, human and devilish. [16]Wherever there are jealousy and ambition, there are also disharmony and wickedness of every kind; [17]whereas the wisdom that comes down from above is essentially something pure; it is also peaceable, kindly and considerate; it is full of mercy and shows itself by doing good; nor is there any trace of partiality or hypocrisy in it. [18]The peace sown by peacemakers brings a harvest of justice.

Disunity among Christians

4 Where do these wars and battles between yourselves first start? Is it not precisely in the desires fighting inside your own selves? [2]You want something and you lack it; so you kill. You have an ambition that you cannot satisfy; so you fight to get your way by force. It is because you do not pray that you do not receive; [3]when you do pray and do not receive, it is because you prayed wrongly, wanting to indulge your passions.

[4]Adulterers! Do you not realise that love for the world is hatred for God? Anyone who chooses the world for a friend is constituted an enemy of God. [5]Can you not see the point of the saying in scripture, 'The longing of the spirit he sent to dwell in us is a jealous longing.'? [6]But he has given us an even greater grace, as scripture says:[a] *God opposes the proud*

but he accords his favour to the humble. [7]Give in to God, then; resist the devil, and he will run away from you. [8]The nearer you go to God, the nearer God will come to you. Clean your hands, you sinners, and clear your minds, you waverers. [9]Appreciate your wretchedness, and weep for it in misery. Your laughter must be turned to grief, your happiness to gloom. [10]Humble yourselves before the Lord and he will lift you up.

[11]Brothers, do not slander one another. Anyone who slanders a brother, or condemns one, is speaking against the Law and condemning the Law. But if you condemn the Law, you have ceased to be subject to it and become a judge over it.

[12]There is only one lawgiver and he is the only judge and has the power to save or to destroy. Who are you to give a verdict on your neighbour?

A warning for the rich and self-confident

[13]Well now, you who say, 'Today or tomorrow, we are off to this or that town; we are going to spend a year there, trading, and make some money.' [14]You never know what will happen tomorrow: you are no more than a mist that appears for a little while and then disappears. [15]Instead of this, you should say, 'If it is the Lord's will, we shall still be alive to do this or that.' [16]But as it is, how boastful and loud-mouthed you are! Boasting of this kind is always wrong. [17]Everyone who knows what is the right thing to do and does not do it commits a sin.

5 Well now, you rich! Lament, weep for the miseries that are coming to you. [2]Your wealth is rotting, your clothes are all motheaten. [3]All your gold and your silver are corroding away, and the same corrosion will be a witness against you and eat into your body. It is like a fire which you have stored up for the final days. [4]Can you hear crying out against

4a Pr 3:34. The saying in v. 5 is not in the OT.

you the wages which you kept back from the labourers mowing your fields? The cries of the reapers have reached the ears of the Lord Sabaoth. [5]On earth you have had a life of comfort and luxury; in the time of slaughter you went on eating to your heart's content. [6]It was you who condemned the upright and killed them; they offered you no resistance.

The coming of the Lord

[7]Now be patient, brothers, until the Lord's coming. Think of a farmer: how patiently he waits for the precious fruit of the ground until it has had the autumn rains and the spring rains! [8]You too must be patient; do not lose heart, because the Lord's coming will be soon. [9]Do not make complaints against one another, brothers, so as not to be brought to judgement yourselves; the Judge is already to be seen waiting at the gates. [10]For your example, brothers, in patiently putting up with persecution, take the prophets who spoke in the Lord's name; [11]remember it is those who had perseverance that we say are the blessed ones. You have heard of the perseverance of Job and understood the Lord's purpose, realising that *the Lord is kind and compassionate.*[a]

[12]Above all, my brothers, do not swear by heaven or by the earth or use any oaths at all. If you mean 'yes', you must say 'yes'; if you mean 'no', say 'no'. Otherwise you make yourselves liable to judgement.

[13]Any one of you who is in trouble should pray; anyone in good spirits should sing a psalm. [14]Any one of you who is ill should send for the elders of the church, and they must anoint the sick person with oil in the name of the Lord and pray over him. [15]The prayer of faith will save the sick person and the Lord will raise him up again; and if he has committed any sins, he will be forgiven. [16]So confess your sins to one another, and pray for one another to be cured; the heartfelt prayer of someone upright works very powerfully. [17]Elijah was a human being as frail as ourselves—he prayed earnestly for it not to rain, and no rain fell for three and a half years; [18]then he prayed again and the sky gave rain and the earth gave crops.

[19]My brothers, if one of you strays away from the truth, and another brings him back to it, [20]he may be sure that anyone who can bring back a sinner from his erring ways will be saving his soul from death and *covering over many a sin.*[b]

5a Ps 103:8.

5b Pr 10:12; Tb 12:9.

PETER

Address and greetings

1 Peter, apostle of Jesus Christ, to all those living as aliens in the Dispersion[a] of Pontus, Galatia, Cappadocia, Asia and Bithynia, who have been chosen, [2] in the foresight of God the Father, to be made holy by the Spirit, obedient to Jesus Christ and sprinkled with his blood: Grace and peace be yours in abundance.

Introduction; the inheritance of Christians

[3] Blessed be God the Father of our Lord Jesus Christ, who in his great mercy has given us a new birth into a living hope through the resurrection of Jesus Christ from the dead [4] and into a heritage that can never be spoilt or soiled and never fade away. It is reserved in heaven for you [5] who are being kept safe by God's power through faith until the salvation which has been prepared is revealed at the final point of time.

Faithfulness to Christ and love of Christ

[6] This is a great joy to you, even though for a short time yet you must bear all sorts of trials; [7] so that the worth of your faith, more valuable than gold, which is perishable even if it has been tested by fire, may be proved—to your praise and glory and honour when Jesus Christ is revealed. [8] You have not seen him, yet you love him; and still without seeing him you believe in him and so are already filled with a joy so glorious that it cannot be described; [9] and you are sure of the goal of your faith, that is, the salvation of your souls.

The hope of the prophets

[10] This salvation was the subject of the search and investigation of the prophets who spoke of the grace you were to receive, [11] searching out the time and circumstances for which the Spirit of Christ, bearing witness in them, was revealing the sufferings of Christ and the glories to follow them. [12] It was revealed to them that it was for your sake and not their own that they were acting as servants delivering the message which has now been announced to you by those who preached to you the gospel through the Holy Spirit sent from heaven. Even the angels long to catch a glimpse of these things.

The demands of the new life; holiness of the newly baptised

[13] Your minds, then, must be sober and ready for action; put all your hope in the grace brought to you by the revelation of Jesus Christ. [14] Do not allow yourselves to be shaped by the passions of your old ignorance, [15] but as obedient children, be yourselves holy in all your activity, after the model of the Holy One who calls us, [16] since scripture says, 'Be holy, for I am holy.'[b] [17] And if you address as Father him who judges without favouritism according to each individual's deeds, live out the time of your exile here in reverent awe. [18] For you know that the price of your ransom from the futile way of life handed down from your ancestors was paid, not in anything perishable like silver or gold,[c] [19] but in precious blood as of a blameless and spotless lamb, Christ. [20] He was marked out before the world was made, and was revealed at the final point of time for your sake. [21] Through him you now have faith in God, who raised him from the dead and gave him

1a See Jm 1a note.   *1b* Lv 19:2.   *1c* Is 52:3.

194   READ 1 PETER 1:3–9.

For a short time yet you must bear all sorts of trials.—1 PETER 1:6

TAKING COMFORT IN TRIALS

Comfort in tribulation can be secured only on the sure ground of faith holding as true the words of Scripture and the teaching of the Catholic Church. With this conviction we shall consider tribulation as a gracious gift of God given to his friends and highly praised in Scripture. The contrary, where long continued, is perilous. If God does not send tribulation, then we must put it on ourselves by undertaking penance—a purgation from past sins and a preservative from future sins otherwise inevitable; a thing detaching us from the world, drawing us towards God; diminishing our purgatory, increasing our reward in heaven; the means by which our Savior entered his kingdom and the apostles followed him there; to which our Savior exhorted all people; the one thing necessary to be his disciple and for winning heaven.

Whoever thinks on and remembers well these things shall in tribulation neither murmur nor be resentful. But first by patience take his pain as valuable, and then he shall grow in goodness and think of himself as worthy. Then shall he consider that God sends it for his well-being, and so shall he be moved to thank God for it. He shall increase in grace. God will comfort him if he considers that God is always near to him when he is in trouble; that his joy [in God's nearness] shall diminish much of his pain. And he shall not seek for vain comfort elsewhere, but specially trust in God, and seek for help of him, submitting his own will wholly to God's pleasure. . . .

If we do this, I boldly say that we shall never live here less than half an hour, but shall find our hearts lightened with comfort and the grief of our tribulation lessened. . . .

ST. THOMAS MORE, 1477–1535

YOU WILL FIND THE NEXT READING AT 1 PETER 2.

glory for this very purpose—that your faith and hope should be in God.

Regeneration by the Word

22 Since by your obedience to the truth you have purified yourselves so that you can experience the genuine love of brothers, love each other intensely from the heart; 23 for your new birth was not from any perishable seed but from imperishable seed, the living and enduring Word of God. 24 For *all humanity is grass, and all its beauty like the wild flower's. As grass withers, the flower fades,* 25 *but the Word of the Lord remains for ever.*[d] And this Word is the Good News that has been brought to you.

2 Rid yourselves, then, of all spite, deceit, hypocrisy, envy and carping criticism. 2 Like new-born babies all your longing should be for milk—the unadulterated spiritual milk—which will help you to grow up to salvation, 3 at any rate if *you have tasted that the Lord is good*[a].

1d Is 40:6–8.   2a Ps 34:8.

195 READ 1 PETER 2:1–10.

Set yourselves close to him so that you, too, may be living stones making a spiritual house. . . . —1 PETER 2:4–5

LIVING STONES

If you live the same life as Jesus Christ, your thorn-crowned head, you must expect only thorns, scourgings, nails—you must look only for the Cross. For the disciple must be treated as his master, and the member as its head. And if God offered for your choice, as he offered to St. Catherine of Siena, a crown of thorns or a crown of roses, without hesitating choose with her the crown of thorns and press it down upon your head that you may resemble Jesus Christ.

You know that you are the living temple of the Holy Spirit. You are to be placed as so many living stones by the God of love in the building of the heavenly Jerusalem. You must expect then to be hewn and cut and chiseled with the hammer and chisel of the Cross. Otherwise you will remain as rough stones that are good for nothing but to be despised and thrown away.

Don't wince under the hammer that strikes you. Have an eye to the chisel that cuts you and to the hand that shapes you. The skillful and loving Architect may wish to make of you the chief stones of his eternal edifice and the fairest statues in his kingdom. Then let him do it. He loves you. He knows what he is doing. He has had experience. All his blows are skillful and straight and loving. He never misses, unless you cause him to by your impatience. ST. LOUIS DE MONTFORT, 1673–1716

YOU WILL FIND THE NEXT READING AT 1 PETER 3.

The new priesthood

⁴He is the living stone, rejected by human beings but chosen by God and precious to him; set yourselves close to him ⁵so that you, too, may be living stones making a spiritual house as a holy priesthood to offer the spiritual sacrifices made acceptable to God through Jesus Christ. ⁶As scripture says: *Now I am laying a stone in Zion, a chosen, precious cornerstone and no one who relies on this will be brought to disgrace.*ᵇ ⁷To you believers it brings honour. But for unbelievers, it is rather a *stone which the builders rejected that became a cornerstone,*ᶜ ⁸*a stumbling stone, a rock to trip people up.*ᵈ They stumble over it because they do not believe in the Word; it was the fate in store for them.

⁹But you are *a chosen race, a kingdom of priests, a holy nation, a people to be a personal possession*ᵉ to sing the praises of God who called you out of the darkness into his wonderful light. ¹⁰Once you were *a non-people* and now you are the People of God; once you were *outside his pity;* now you *have received pity.*ᶠ

The obligations of Christians: towards unbelievers

¹¹I urge you, my dear friends, as *strangers and nomads,*ᵍ to keep yourselves free from the disordered natural inclinations that attack the soul. ¹²Always behave honourably among gentiles so that they can see for themselves what moral lives you lead, and when the day

2b Is 28:16. 2c Ps 118:22. 2d Is 8:14. 2e Is 43:20–21.
2f Ho 1:9 and allusions to Ho 2. 2g Ps 39:12.

of reckoning comes, give thanks to God for the things which now make them denounce you as criminals.

Towards civil authority

¹³For the sake of the Lord, accept the authority of every human institution: the emperor, as the supreme authority, ¹⁴and the governors as commissioned by him to punish criminals and praise those who do good. ¹⁵It is God's will that by your good deeds you should silence the ignorant talk of fools. ¹⁶You are slaves of no one except God, so behave like free people, and never use your freedom as a cover for wickedness. ¹⁷Have respect for everyone and love for your fellow-believers; fear God and honour the emperor.

Towards masters

¹⁸Slaves, you should obey your masters respectfully, not only those who are kind and reasonable but also those who are difficult to please. ¹⁹You see, there is merit if, in awareness of God, you put up with the pains of undeserved punishment; ²⁰but what glory is there in putting up with a beating after you have done something wrong? The merit in the sight of God is in putting up with it patiently when you are punished for doing your duty.

²¹This, in fact, is what you were called to do, because Christ suffered for you and left an example for you to follow in his steps. ²²He had done nothing wrong, and *had spoken no deceit.*ʰ ²³He was insulted and did not retaliate with insults; when he was suffering he made no threats but put his trust in the upright judge. ²⁴He was *bearing our sins* in his own body on the cross, so that we might die to our sins and live for uprightness; *through his bruises you have been healed.* ²⁵You had *gone astray like sheep* but now you have returned to the shepherd and guardian of your souls.

In marriage

3 In the same way, you wives should be obedient to your husbands. Then if there are some husbands who do not believe the Word,

they may find themselves won over, without a word spoken, by the way their wives behave, ²when they see the reverence and purity of your way of life. ³Your adornment should be not an exterior one, consisting of braided hair or gold jewellery or fine clothing, ⁴but the interior disposition of the heart, consisting in the imperishable quality of a gentle and peaceful spirit, so precious in the sight of God. ⁵That was how the holy women of the past dressed themselves attractively—they hoped in God and were submissive to their husbands; ⁶like Sarah, who was obedient to Abraham, and called him her *lord.*ᵃ You are now her children, as long as you live good lives free from fear and worry.

⁷In the same way, husbands must always treat their wives with consideration in their life together, respecting a woman as one who, though she may be the weaker partner, is equally an heir to the generous gift of life. This will prevent anything from coming in the way of your prayers.

Love the brothers

⁸Finally: you should all agree among yourselves and be sympathetic; love the brothers, have compassion and be self-effacing. ⁹Never repay one wrong with another, or one abusive word with another; instead, repay with a blessing. That is what you are called to do, so that you inherit a blessing. ¹⁰For

Who among you delights in life,
longs for time to enjoy prosperity?
Guard your tongue from evil,
your lips from any breath of deceit.
¹¹ *Turn away from evil and do good, seek*
peace and pursue it.
¹² *For the eyes of the Lord are on the*
upright,
his ear turned to their cry.
But the Lord's face is set against those who
*do evil.*ᵇ

2h Several quotations from Is 53:5–9.

3a Gn 18:12.   3b Ps 34:12–16.

In persecution

13 No one can hurt you if you are determined to do only what is right; 14 and blessed are you if you have to suffer for being upright. *Have no dread of them; have no fear.*[c] 15 Simply *proclaim the Lord* Christ *holy* in your hearts, and always have your answer ready for people who ask you the reason for the hope that you have. 16 But give it with courtesy and respect and with a clear conscience, so that those who slander your good behaviour in Christ may be ashamed of their accusations. 17 And if it is the will of God that you should suffer, it is better to suffer for doing right than for doing wrong.

The resurrection and the descent into hell

18 Christ himself died once and for all for sins, the upright for the sake of the guilty, to lead us to God. In the body he was put to death, in the spirit he was raised to life, 19 and, in the spirit, he went to preach to the spirits in prison. 20 They refused to believe long ago, while God patiently waited to receive them, in Noah's time when the ark was being built. In it only a few, that is eight souls, were saved through water. 21 It is the baptism corresponding to this water which saves you now—not the washing off of physical dirt but the pledge of a good conscience given to God through the resurrection of Jesus Christ, 22 who has entered heaven and is at God's right hand, with angels, ruling forces and powers subject to him.

The break with sin

4 As Christ has undergone bodily suffering, you too should arm yourselves with the same conviction, that anyone who has undergone bodily suffering has broken with sin, 2 because for the rest of life on earth that person is ruled not by human passions but only by the will of God. 3 You spent quite long enough in the past living the sort of life that gentiles choose to live, behaving in a debauched way, giving way to your passions, drinking to excess, having wild parties and drunken orgies and sacrilegiously worshipping false gods. 4 So people are taken aback that you no longer hurry off with them to join this flood which is rushing down to ruin, and then abuse you for it. 5 They will have to answer for it before the judge who is to judge the living and the dead. 6 And this was why the gospel was brought to the dead as well, so that, though in their bodies they had undergone the judgement that faces all humanity, in their spirit they might enjoy the life of God.

The revelation of Christ is close

7 The end of all things is near, so keep your minds calm and sober for prayer. 8 Above all preserve an intense love for each other, since *love covers over many a sin.*[a] 9 Welcome each other into your houses without grumbling. 10 Each one of you has received a special grace, so, like good stewards responsible for all these varied graces of God, put it at the service of others. 11 If anyone is a speaker, let it be as the words of God, if anyone serves, let it be as in strength granted by God; so that in everything God may receive the glory, through Jesus Christ, since to him alone belong all glory and power for ever and ever. Amen.

Suffering for Christ

12 My dear friends, do not be taken aback at the testing by fire which is taking place among you, as though something strange were happening to you; 13 but in so far as you share in the sufferings of Christ, be glad, so that you may enjoy a much greater gladness when his glory is revealed. 14 If you are insulted for bearing Christ's name, blessed are you, for *on you rests the Spirit of God,*[b] the Spirit of glory. 15 None of you should ever deserve to suffer for being a murderer, a thief, a criminal or an informer; 16 but if any one of you should suffer for being a Christian, then there must be no shame but thanksgiving to God for bearing this name. 17 The time has come for the judge-

3c Is 8:12–13.   4a Pr 10:12; Tb 12:9.   4b Is 11:2.

196 READ 1 PETER 3:13–4:2.

Blessed are you if you have to suffer for being upright.—1 PETER 3:14

PREPARED FOR SUFFERING

Give me thy grace, good Lord
To set the world at nought,
To set my mind fast upon you,
And not to hang upon the blast of men's
    mouths.
To be content to be solitary.
Not to long for worldly company.
Little and little utterly to cast off the world,
And rid my mind of all of its business.
Not to long to hear of any worldly things,
But that the hearing of worldly fantasies
    may be to me unpleasant.
Gladly to be thinking of God,
Piteously to call for his help,
To lean on the comfort of God.
Busily to labor to love him.
To know my own vileness and wretchedness,
To humble and lower myself under the
    mighty hand of God,
To bewail my past sins,
For the purging of them, patiently to suffer
    adversity.
Gladly to bear my purgatory here,
To be joyful of tribulations,
To walk the narrow way that leads to life,
To bear the cross with Christ,
To have the last thing in remembrance,

To have ever before my eye my death that is
    ever at hand,
To make death no stranger to me
To foresee and consider the everlasting fire
    of hell,
To pray for pardon before the judge come.
To have continually in mind the passion that
    Christ suffered for me,
For his benefits unceasingly to give him
    thanks.
To buy the time again that I before have lost.
To abstain from vain discussions,
To eschew light foolish mirth and gladness,
Recreations not necessary to cut off.
Of worldly substance, friends, liberty, life and
    all, to set the loss at nothing for the
    winning of Christ.
To think my most enemies my best friends.
For the brothers of Joseph could never have
    done him so much good, with their love
    and favor as they did him with their
    malice and hatred.
These minds are more to be desired of every
    man than all the treasure of all the princes
    and kings, Christian and heathen, were it
    gathered and laid together all upon one
    heap.

ST. THOMAS MORE, 1477–1535

YOU WILL FIND THE NEXT READING AT 2 PETER 1.

ment to begin at the household of God; and if it begins with us, what will be the end for those who refuse to believe God's gospel? [18]*If it is hard for the upright to be saved, what will happen to the wicked and to sinners?*[c] [19]So even those whom God allows to suffer should commit themselves to a Creator who is trustworthy, and go on doing good.

Instructions: to the elders

5 I urge the elders among you, as a fellow-elder myself and a witness to the sufferings of Christ, and as one who is to have a share in the glory that is to be revealed: [2]give a shep-

4c Pr 11:31 LXX.

herd's care to the flock of God that is entrusted to you: watch over it, not simply as a duty but gladly, as God wants; not for sordid money, but because you are eager to do it. ³Do not lord it over the group which is in your charge, but be an example for the flock. ⁴When the chief shepherd appears, you will be given the unfading crown of glory.

To the faithful

⁵In the same way, younger people, be subject to the elders. Humility towards one another must be the garment you all wear constantly, because *God opposes the proud but accords his favour to the humble.*ᵃ ⁶Bow down, then, before the power of God now, so that he may raise you up in due time; ⁷*unload all your burden on to him,*ᵇ since he is concerned about you. ⁸Keep sober and alert, because your enemy the devil is on the prowl like a *roaring lion,*ᶜ looking for someone to devour. ⁹Stand up to him, strong in faith and in the knowledge that it is the same kind of suffering that the community of your brothers throughout the world is undergoing. ¹⁰You will have to suffer only for a little while: the God of all grace who called you to eternal glory in Christ will restore you, he will confirm, strengthen and support you. ¹¹His power lasts for ever and ever. Amen.

Last words. Greetings

¹²I write these few words to you through Silvanus, who is a trustworthy brother, to encourage you and attest that this is the true grace of God. Stand firm in it!

¹³Your sister in Babylon, who is with you among the chosen, sends you greetings; so does my son, Mark.

¹⁴Greet one another with a kiss of love. Peace to you all who are in Christ.

5a Pr 3:34 LXX. 5b Ps 55:22. 5c Ps 22:13.

PETER

Greetings

1 Simon Peter, servant and apostle of Jesus Christ, to those who have received a faith as precious as our own, given through the saving justice of our God and Saviour Jesus Christ. ²Grace and peace be yours in abundance through the knowledge of our Lord.

The generosity of God

³By his divine power, he has lavished on us all the things we need for life and for true devotion, through the knowledge of him who has called us by his own glory and goodness. ⁴Through these, the greatest and priceless promises have been lavished on us, that through them you should share the divine nature and escape the corruption rife in the world through disordered passion. ⁵With this in view, do your utmost to support your faith with goodness, goodness with understanding, ⁶understanding with self-control, self-control with perseverance, perseverance with devotion, ⁷devotion with kindness to the brothers, and kindness to the brothers with love. ⁸The possession and growth of these qualities will prevent your knowledge of our Lord Jesus Christ from being ineffectual or unproductive. ⁹But without them, a person is blind or short-sighted, forgetting how the sins of the past were washed away. ¹⁰Instead of this, brothers, never allow your choice or calling to waver; then there will be no danger of your stumbling, ¹¹for in this way you will be given the generous gift of entry to the eternal kingdom of our Lord and Saviour Jesus Christ.

The apostolic witness

¹²That is why I will always go on recalling the same truths to you, even though you already know them and are firmly fixed in these truths. ¹³I am sure it is my duty, as long as I am in this tent, to keep stirring you up with reminders, ¹⁴since I know the time for me to lay aside this tent is coming soon, as our Lord Jesus Christ made clear to me. ¹⁵And I shall take great care that after my own departure you will still have a means to recall these things to mind.

¹⁶When we told you about the power and the coming of our Lord Jesus Christ, we were not slavishly repeating cleverly invented myths; no, we had seen his majesty with our own eyes. ¹⁷He was honoured and glorified by God the Father, when a voice came to him from the transcendent Glory, *This is my Son, the Beloved; he enjoys my favour.ᵃ* ¹⁸We ourselves heard this voice from heaven, when we were with him on the holy mountain.

The value of prophecy

¹⁹So we have confirmation of the words of the prophets; and you will be right to pay attention to it as to a lamp for lighting a way through the dark, until the dawn comes and the morning star rises in your minds. ²⁰At the same time, we must recognise that the interpretation of scriptural prophecy is never a matter for the individual. ²¹For no prophecy ever came from human initiative. When people spoke for God it was the Holy Spirit that moved them.

1a Mt 17:5par.

197 READ 2 PETER 1:3–11.

By his divine power, he has lavished on us all the things we need for life and for true devotion.—2 PETER 1:3

TRUE HUMAN DIGNITY

The immeasurable benefits that the goodness of God has bestowed on Christian people have also conferred on them a dignity beyond all price. "And indeed, what great nation has its gods as near as Yahweh our God is to us whenever we call to him?" (Dt 4:7). The Only-begotten Son of God was pleased to give us a share in the divine nature, becoming a man himself so that he might make us gods. And all, as much of our nature as he took, he applied to our salvation.

On the altar of the Cross he offered up his body to God the Father as a sacrifice for our reconciliation. He shed his blood as the price by which he redeemed us from wretchedness and bondage, and as the washing by which he cleansed us from all sin.

And for a noble and abiding memorial of that so great work of his goodness, he has left for his faithful ones his very same Body for food and his very same Blood for drink, to be fed upon under the appearance of bread and wine.　　　　　　　　　　　　　　ST. THOMAS AQUINAS, 1225?–1275

YOU WILL FIND THE NEXT READING AT 1 JOHN 4.

False teachers

2 As there were false prophets in the past history of our people, so you too will have your false teachers, who will insinuate their own disruptive views and, by disowning the Lord who bought them freedom, will bring upon themselves speedy destruction. ²Many will copy their debauched behaviour, and the Way of Truth will be brought into disrepute on their account. ³In their greed they will try to make a profit out of you with untrue tales. But the judgement made upon them long ago is not idle, and the destruction awaiting them is for ever on the watch.

Lessons of the past

⁴When angels sinned, God did not spare them: he sent them down into the underworld and consigned them to the dark abyss to be held there until the Judgement. ⁵He did not spare the world in ancient times: he saved only Noah, the preacher of uprightness, along with seven others, when he sent the Flood over a world of sinners. ⁶He condemned the cities of Sodom and Gomorrah by reducing them to ashes as a warning to future sinners; ⁷but rescued Lot, an upright man who had been sickened by the debauched way in which these vile people behaved— ⁸for that upright man, living among them, was outraged in his upright soul by the crimes that he saw and heard every day. ⁹All this shows that the Lord is well able to rescue the good from their trials, and hold the wicked for their punishment until the Day of Judgement, ¹⁰especially those who follow the desires of their corrupt human nature and have no respect for the Lord's authority.

The punishment to come

Such self-willed people with no reverence are not afraid of offending against the glorious ones, [11] but the angels in their greater strength and power make no complaint or accusation against them in the Lord's presence. [12] But these people speak evil of what they do not understand; they are like brute beasts, born only to be caught and killed, and like beasts they will be destroyed, being injured in return for the injuries they have inflicted. [13] Debauchery even by day they make their pleasure; they are unsightly blots, and amuse themselves by their trickery even when they are sharing your table; [14] with their eyes always looking for adultery, people with an insatiable capacity for sinning, they will seduce any but the most stable soul. Where greed is concerned they are at their peak of fitness. They are under a curse. [15] They have left the right path and wandered off to follow the path of Balaam son of Bosor, who set his heart on a dishonest reward, but soon had his fault pointed out to him: [16] a dumb beast of burden, speaking with a human voice, put a stop to the madness of the prophet.

[17] People like this are dried-up springs, fogs swirling in the wind, and the gloom of darkness is stored up for them. [18] With their high-sounding but empty talk they tempt back people who have scarcely escaped from those who live in error, by playing on the disordered desires of their human nature and by debaucheries. [19] They may promise freedom but are themselves slaves to corruption; because if anyone lets himself be dominated by anything, then he is a slave to it; [20] and anyone who has escaped the pollution of the world by coming to know our Lord and Saviour Jesus Christ, and who then allows himself to be entangled and mastered by it a second time, ends up by being worse than he was before. [21] It would have been better for them never to have learnt the way of uprightness, than to learn it and then desert the holy commandment that was entrusted to them. [22] What they have done is exactly as the proverb rightly says: *The dog goes back to its vomit*[a] and: As soon as the sow has been washed, it wallows in the mud.

The Day of the Lord; the prophets and the apostles

3 My dear friends, this is the second letter I have written to you, trying to awaken in you by my reminders an unclouded understanding. [2] Remember what was said in the past by the holy prophets and the command of the Lord and Saviour given by your apostles.

False teachers

[3] First of all, do not forget that in the final days there will come sarcastic scoffers whose life is ruled by their passions. [4] 'What has happened to the promise of his coming?' they will say, 'Since our Fathers died everything has gone on just as it has since the beginning of creation!' [5] They deliberately ignore the fact that long ago there were the heavens and the earth, formed out of water and through water by the Word of God, [6] and that it was through these same factors that the world of those days was destroyed by the floodwaters. [7] It is the same Word which is reserving the present heavens and earth for fire, keeping them till the Day of Judgement and of the destruction of sinners.

[8] But there is one thing, my dear friends, that you must never forget: that with the Lord, a day is like a thousand years, and *a thousand years are like a day.*[a] [9] The Lord is not being slow in carrying out his promises, as some people think he is; rather is he being patient with you, wanting nobody to be lost and everybody to be brought to repentance. [10] The Day of the Lord will come like a thief, and then with a roar the sky will vanish, the elements will catch fire and melt away, the earth and all that it contains will be burned up.

Fresh call to holiness; doxology

[11] Since everything is coming to an end like this, what holy and saintly lives you should be living [12] while you wait for the Day of God to come, and try to hasten its coming: on that

2a Pr 26:11.
3a Ps 90:4.

Day the sky will dissolve in flames and the elements melt in the heat. [13] What we are waiting for, relying on his promises, is the new heavens and new earth, where uprightness will be at home. [14] So then, my dear friends, while you are waiting, do your best to live blameless and unsullied lives so that he will find you at peace. [15] Think of our Lord's patience as your opportunity to be saved; our brother Paul, who is so dear to us, told you this when he wrote to you with the wisdom that he was given. [16] He makes this point too in his letters as a whole wherever he touches on these things. In all his letters there are of course some passages which are hard to understand, and these are the ones that uneducated and unbalanced people distort, in the same way as they distort the rest of scripture[b]—to their own destruction. [17] Since you have been forewarned about this, my dear friends, be careful that you do not come to the point of losing the firm ground that you are standing on, carried away by the errors of unprincipled people. [18] Instead, continue to grow in the grace and in the knowledge of our Lord and Saviour Jesus Christ. To him be glory, in time and eternity. Amen.

3b Paul's letters seemingly already exist as a collection, and are put on the same level as the OT.

The First Letter of

JOHN

*The Incarnate Word and sharing with
the Father and the Son*

1 Something which has existed since the
beginning,
which we have heard,
which we have seen with our own
eyes,
which we have watched
and touched with our own hands,
the Word of life—
this is our theme.
² That life was made visible;
we saw it and are giving our testimony,
declaring to you the eternal life,
which was present to the Father
and has been revealed to us.
³ We are declaring to you
what we have seen and heard,
so that you too may share our life.
Our life is shared with the Father
and with his Son Jesus Christ.
⁴ We are writing this to you so that our
joy may be complete.

To walk in the light

⁵ This is what we have heard from him
and are declaring to you:
God is light, and there is no darkness in
him at all.
⁶ If we say that we share in God's life
while we are living in darkness,
we are lying, because we are not living
the truth.
⁷ But if we live in light,
as he is in light,
we have a share in one another's life,
and the blood of Jesus, his Son,
cleanses us from all sin.

First condition: to break with sin

⁸ If we say, 'We have no sin,'
we are deceiving ourselves,
and truth has no place in us;
⁹ if we acknowledge our sins,
he is trustworthy and upright,
so that he will forgive our sins
and will cleanse us from all evil.
¹⁰ If we say, 'We have never sinned,'
we make him a liar,
and his word has no place in us.

2 My children, I am writing this to prevent
you from sinning;
but if anyone does sin,
we have an advocate with the Father,
Jesus Christ, the upright.
² He is the sacrifice to expiate our sins,
and not only ours,
but also those of the whole world.

*Second condition: to keep the
commandments, especially that of love*

³ In this way we know
that we have come to know him,
if we keep his commandments.
⁴ Whoever says, 'I know him'
without keeping his commandments,
is a liar,
and truth has no place in him.
⁵ But anyone who does keep his word,
in such a one God's love truly reaches its
perfection.
This is the proof
that we are in God.
⁶ Whoever claims to remain in him
must act as he acted.
⁷ My dear friends,

[1540]

this is not a new commandment I am
    writing for you,
but an old commandment
that you have had from the beginning;
the old commandment is the message you
    have heard.
8 Yet in another way, I am writing a new
    commandment for you
—and this is true for you, just as much as
    for him—
for darkness is passing away
and the true light is already shining.
9 Whoever claims to be in light
but hates his brother
is still in darkness.
10 Anyone who loves his brother remains in
    light
and there is in him nothing to make him
    fall away.
11 But whoever hates his brother is in
    darkness
and is walking about in darkness
not knowing where he is going,
because darkness has blinded him.

Third condition: detachment from the world

12 I am writing to you, children,
because your sins have been forgiven
    through his name.
13 I am writing to you, fathers,
because you have come to know the One
    who has existed since the
    beginning.
I am writing to you, young people,
because you have overcome the Evil One.
14 I have written to you, children,
because you have come to know the
    Father.
I have written to you, parents,
because you have come to know the One
    who has existed since the
    beginning.
I have written to you, young people,
because you are strong,
and God's word remains in you,
and you have overcome the Evil One.
15 Do not love the world

or what is in the world.
If anyone does love the world,
the love of the Father finds no place in
    him,
16 because everything there is in the world—
disordered bodily desires,
disordered desires of the eyes,
pride in possession—
is not from the Father
but is from the world.
17 And the world, with all its disordered
    desires,
is passing away.
But whoever does the will of God
remains for ever.

*Fourth condition: to be on guard
against Antichrists*

18 Children, this is the final hour;
you have heard that the Antichrist[a] is
    coming,
and now many Antichrists have already
    come;
from this we know that it is the final hour.
19 They have gone from among us,
but they never really belonged to us;
if they had belonged to us, they would
    have stayed with us.
But this was to prove
that not one of them belonged to us.
20 But you have been anointed by the
    Holy One,
and have all received knowledge.
21 I have written to you
not because you are ignorant of the truth,
but because you are well aware of it,
and because no lie can come from the
    truth.
22 Who is the liar,
if not one who claims that Jesus is not the
    Christ?
This is the Antichrist,
who denies both the Father and the Son.
23 Whoever denies the Son cannot have the
    Father either;

2a cf. 2 Th 2:3–4.

whoever acknowledges the Son has the
 Father too.

24 Let what you heard in the beginning
 remain in you;
as long as what you heard in the beginning
 remains in you,
you will remain in the Son
and in the Father.

25 And the promise he made you himself
is eternal life.

26 So much have I written to you
about those who are trying to lead you
 astray.

27 But as for you, the anointing you received
 from him
remains in you,
and you do not need anyone to teach you;
since the anointing he gave you teaches
 you everything,
and since it is true, not false,
remain in him just as he has taught you.

28 Therefore remain in him now, children,
so that when he appears we may be
 fearless,
and not shrink from him in shame
at his coming.

To live as God's children

29 If you know that he is upright
you must recognise that everyone whose
 life is upright
is a child of his.

3 You must see what great love the Father
 has lavished on us
by letting us be called God's children—
which is what we are!
The reason why the world does not
 acknowledge us
is that it did not acknowledge him.

2 My dear friends, we are already God's
 children,
but what we shall be in the future has not
 yet been revealed.
We are well aware that when he appears
we shall be like him,
because we shall see him as he really is.

First condition: to break with sin

3 Whoever treasures this hope of him
purifies himself, to be as pure as he is.

4 Whoever sins, acts wickedly,
because all sin is wickedness.

5 Now you are well aware that he has
 appeared in order to take sins
 away,
and that in him there is no sin.

6 No one who remains in him sins,
and whoever sins
has neither seen him nor recognised him.

7 Children, do not let anyone lead you
 astray.
Whoever acts uprightly is upright,
just as he is upright.

8 Whoever lives sinfully belongs to the
 devil,
since the devil has been a sinner from the
 beginning.
This was the purpose of the appearing of
 the Son of God,
to undo the work of the devil.

9 No one who is a child of God sins
because God's seed remains in him.
Nor can he sin, because he is a child
 of God.

10 This is what distinguishes
the children of God from the children of
 the devil:
whoever does not live uprightly
and does not love his brother
is not from God.

Second condition: to keep the commandments, especially that of love

11 This is the message
which you heard from the beginning,
that we must love one another,

12 not to be like Cain, who was from the
 Evil One
and murdered his brother.
And why did he murder his brother?
Because his own actions were evil and his
 brother's upright.

13 Do not be surprised, brothers,

if the world hates you.

14 We are well aware that we have passed
over from death to life
because we love our brothers.
Whoever does not love, remains in
death.

15 Anyone who hates his brother is a
murderer,
and you are well aware that no
murderer
has eternal life remaining in him.

16 This is the proof of love,
that he laid down his life for us,
and we too ought to lay down our lives for
our brothers.

17 If anyone is well-off in worldly possessions
and sees his brother in need
but closes his heart to him,
how can the love of God be remaining
in him?

18 Children,
our love must be not just words or mere
talk,
but something active and genuine.

19 This will be the proof that we belong to
the truth,
and it will convince us in his presence,

20 even if our own feelings condemn us,
that God is greater than our feelings and
knows all things.

21 My dear friends,
if our own feelings do not condemn us,
we can be fearless before God,

22 and whatever we ask
we shall receive from him,
because we keep his commandments
and do what is acceptable to him.

23 His commandment is this,
that we should believe in the name of
his Son Jesus Christ
and that we should love one another
as he commanded us.

24 Whoever keeps his commandments
remains in God, and God in him.
And this is the proof that he remains
in us:
the Spirit that he has given us.

Third condition: to be on guard against Antichrists and against the world

4 My dear friends,
not every spirit is to be trusted,
but test the spirits to see whether they are
from God,
for many false prophets are at large in the
world.

2 This is the proof of the spirit of God:
any spirit which acknowledges Jesus
Christ, come in human nature,
is from God,

3 and no spirit which fails to acknowledge
Jesus
is from God;
it is the spirit of Antichrist,
whose coming you have heard of;
he is already at large in the world.

4 Children, you are from God
and have overcome them,
because he who is in you
is greater than he who is in the world.

5 They are from the world,
and therefore the world inspires what
they say,
and listens to them.

6 We are from God;
whoever recognises God listens to us;
anyone who is not from God refuses to
listen to us.
This is how we can distinguish
the spirit of truth from the spirit of
falsehood.

The source of love

7 My dear friends,
let us love one another,
since love is from God
and everyone who loves is a child of God
and knows God.

8 Whoever fails to love does not know God,
because God is love.

9 This is the revelation of God's love
for us,
that God sent his only Son into the world
that we might have life through him.

198 READ 1 JOHN 4.

It is not we who loved God, but God loved us and sent his Son to expiate our sins.

—1 JOHN 4:10

FIRST LOVE

In this vision of St. Hildegard of Bingen, the voice of God interrupts the narration:

The Trinity is not able to be divided, but remains always inviolable without any change. The Father is declared through the Son, and the Son through the birth of creatures, and the Holy Spirit through the same Son Incarnate.

How? It is the Father who before all ages begat the Son, the Son, through whom all things were made in the beginning of creatures, by the Father, and the Holy Spirit who appeared in the form of a dove in the baptism of the Son of God at the end of the ages.

"So never let humankind forget to invoke me as one God in three Persons. These things are shown to them so that they may burn more ardently in my love. For love of them I sent my own Son into the world, as my beloved John testified, saying: 'This is the revelation of God's love for us, that God sent his only Son into the world that we might have life through him. Love consists in this: it is not we who loved God, but God loved us and sent his Son to expiate our sins.' . . ."

Why so? Because through that fountain of life, [the Son,] came the paternal love of the embrace of God that led us into life, and in our dangers was our help, and is the deepest and beautiful light teaching us repentance. . . .

This salvation of love did not spring from us because we neither knew nor were able to love God unto salvation; but because he the Creator and Lord of all so loved the world that he sent his Son for its salvation, the Prince and Savior of the faithful, who washed and dried our wounds. From him also came that sweet medicine from which all the good things of salvation flow.

ST. HILDEGARD OF BINGEN, 1098–1179

YOU WILL FIND THE NEXT READING AT REVELATION 3.

¹⁰ Love consists in this:
it is not we who loved God,
but God loved us and sent his Son
to expiate our sins.
¹¹ My dear friends,
if God loved us so much,
we too should love one another.
¹² No one has ever seen God,
but as long as we love one another
God remains in us

and his love comes to its perfection in us.
¹³ This is the proof that we remain in him
and he in us,
that he has given us a share in his
Spirit.
¹⁴ We ourselves have seen and testify
that the Father sent his Son
as Saviour of the world.
¹⁵ Anyone who acknowledges that Jesus is
the Son of God,

God remains in him and he in God.

¹⁶ We have recognised for ourselves,
and put our faith in, the love God has
for us.
God is love,
and whoever remains in love remains
in God
and God in him.

¹⁷ Love comes to its perfection in us
when we can face the Day of Judgement
fearlessly,
because even in this world
we have become as he is.

¹⁸ In love there is no room for fear,
but perfect love drives out fear,
because fear implies punishment
and no one who is afraid has come to
perfection in love.

¹⁹ Let us love, then,
because he first loved us.

²⁰ Anyone who says 'I love God'
and hates his brother,
is a liar,
since no one who fails to love the brother
whom he can see
can love God whom he has not seen.

²¹ Indeed this is the commandment we have
received from him,
that whoever loves God, must also love his
brother.

5 Whoever believes that Jesus is the Christ
is a child of God,
and whoever loves the father
loves the son.

² In this way we know that we love God's
children,
when we love God and keep his
commandments.

³ This is what the love of God is:
keeping his commandments.
Nor are his commandments burdensome,

⁴ because every child of God
overcomes the world.
And this is the victory that has overcome
the world—
our faith.

The source of faith

⁵ Who can overcome the world
but the one who believes that Jesus is the
Son of God?

⁶ He it is who came by water and blood,ᵃ
Jesus Christ,
not with water alone
but with water and blood,
and it is the Spirit that bears witness,
for the Spirit is Truth.

⁷ So there are three witnesses,

⁸ the Spirit, water and blood;
and the three of them coincide.

⁹ If we accept the testimony of human
witnesses,
God's testimony is greater,
for this is God's testimony
which he gave about his Son.

¹⁰ Whoever believes in the Son of God
has this testimony within him,
and whoever does not believe
is making God a liar,
because he has not believed
the testimony God has given about
his Son.

¹¹ This is the testimony:
God has given us eternal life,
and this life is in his Son.

¹² Whoever has the Son has life,
and whoever has not the Son of God has
not life.

¹³ I have written this to you
who believe in the name of the Son of God
so that you may know that you have
eternal life.

Prayer for sinners

¹⁴ Our fearlessness towards him consists in
this,
that if we ask anything in accordance with
his will
he hears us.

¹⁵ And if we know that he listens to
whatever we ask him,

5a cf. Jn 19:34.

we know that we already possess whatever
    we have asked of him.

16 If anyone sees his brother commit a sin
    that is not a deadly sin,
    he has only to pray, and God will give life
        to this brother
    —provided that it is not a deadly sin.
    There is sin that leads to death
    and I am not saying you must pray about
        that.

17 Every kind of wickedness is sin,
    but not all sin leads to death.

Summary of the letter

18 We are well aware that no one who is a
        child of God sins,
    because he who was born from God
        protects him,
    and the Evil One has no hold over him.

19 We are well aware that we are from God,
    and the whole world is in the power of the
        Evil One.

20 We are well aware also that the Son of
        God has come,
    and has given us understanding
    so that we may know the One who is true.
    We are in the One who is true
    as we are in his Son, Jesus Christ.
    He is the true God
    and this is eternal life.
    Children, be on your guard against
        false gods.

Greetings

From the Elder:[a] my greetings to the Lady, the chosen one,[b] and to her children, whom I love in truth—and I am not the only one, for so do all who have come to know the Truth— 2 because of the truth that remains in us and will be with us for ever. 3 In our life of truth and love, we shall have grace, faithful love and peace from God the Father and from Jesus Christ, the Son of the Father.

The law of love

4 It has given me great joy to find that children of yours have been living the life of truth as we were commanded by the Father. 5 And now I am asking you—dear lady, not as though I were writing you a new commandment, but only the one which we have had from the beginning—that we should love one another.

6 To love is to live according to his commandments: this is the commandment which you have heard since the beginning, to live a life of love.

The enemies of Christ

7 There are many deceivers at large in the world, refusing to acknowledge Jesus Christ as coming in human nature. They are the Deceiver; they are the Antichrist. 8 Watch yourselves, or all our work will be lost and you will forfeit your full reward. 9 If anybody does not remain in the teaching of Christ but goes beyond it, he does not have God with him: only those who remain in what he taught can have the Father and the Son with them. 10 If anyone comes to you bringing a different doctrine, you must not receive him into your house or even give him a greeting. 11 Whoever greets him has a share in his wicked activities.

12 There are several things I have to tell you, but I have thought it best not to trust them to paper and ink. I hope instead to visit you and talk to you in person, so that our joy may be complete.

13 Greetings to you from the children of your sister,[c] the chosen one.

a The elders were the leaders in each community; *'the* Elder' must indicate a special leadership.

b i.e. one of the local churches.

c A neighbouring church.

The Third Letter of

JOHN

Greetings

From the Elder: greetings to my dear friend Gaius, whom I love in truth. ²My dear friend, I hope everything is going happily with you and that you are as well physically as you are spiritually. ³It was a great joy to me when some brothers came and told of your faithfulness to the truth, and of your life in the truth. ⁴It is always my greatest joy to hear that my children are living according to the truth.

⁵My dear friend, you have done loyal work in helping these brothers, even though they were strangers to you. ⁶They are a proof to the whole Church of your love and it would be a kindness if you could help them on their journey as God would approve. ⁷It was entirely for the sake of the name that they set out, without depending on the non-believers for anything: ⁸it is our duty to welcome people of this sort and contribute our share to their work for the truth.

Beware of the example of Diotrephes

⁹I have written a note for the members of the church, but Diotrephes, who enjoys being in charge of it, refuses to accept us. ¹⁰So if I come, I shall tell everyone how he has behaved, and about the wicked accusations he has been circulating against us. As if that were not enough, he not only refuses to welcome our brothers, but prevents from doing so other people who would have liked to, and expels them from the church. ¹¹My dear friend, never follow a bad example, but keep following the good one; whoever does what is right is from God, but no one who does what is wrong has ever seen God.

Commendation of Demetrius

¹²Demetrius has been approved by everyone, and indeed by Truth itself. We too will vouch for him and you know that our testimony is true.

Epilogue

¹³There were several things I had to tell you but I would rather not trust them to pen and ink. ¹⁴However, I hope to see you soon and talk to you in person. ¹⁵Peace be with you; greetings from your friends; greet each of our friends by name.

The Letter of

JUDE

Address

From Jude, servant of Jesus Christ and brother of James; to those who are called, to those who are dear to God the Father and kept safe for Jesus Christ, ²mercy, peace and love be yours in abundance.

The reason for this letter

³My dear friends, at a time when I was eagerly looking forward to writing to you about the salvation that we all share, I felt that I must write to you encouraging you to fight hard for the faith which has been once and for all entrusted to God's holy people. ⁴Certain people have infiltrated among you, who were long ago marked down for condemnation on this account; without any reverence they pervert the grace of our God to debauchery and deny all religion, rejecting our only Master and Lord, Jesus Christ.

The false teachers: the certainty of punishment

⁵I should like to remind you—though you have already learnt it once and for all—that the Lord rescued the nation from Egypt, but afterwards he still destroyed the people who refused to believe him; ⁶and the angels who did not keep to the authority they had, but left their appointed sphere,ᵃ he has kept in darkness in eternal bonds until the judgement of the great Day. ⁷Sodom and Gomorrah, too, and the neighbouring towns, who with the same sexual immorality pursued unnatural lusts,ᵇ are put before us as an example since they are paying the penalty of eternal fire.

Their violent language

⁸Nevertheless, these people are doing the same: in their delusions they not only defile their bodies and disregard Authority, but abuse the Glories as well. ⁹Not even the archangel Michael, when he was engaged in argument with the devil about the corpse of Moses,ᶜ dared to denounce him in the language of abuse; all he said was, 'May the Lord rebuke you.'ᵈ ¹⁰But these people abuse anything they do not understand; and the only things they do understand—merely by nature like unreasoning animals—will turn out to be fatal to them.

Their vicious behaviour

¹¹Alas for them, because they have followed Cain;ᵉ they have thrown themselves into the same delusion as Balaamᶠ for a reward; they have been ruined by the same rebellion as Korahᵍ—and share the same fate. ¹²They are a dangerous hazard at your community meals, coming for the food and quite shamelessly only looking after themselves. They are like the clouds blown about by the winds and bringing no rain, or like autumn trees, barren and uprooted and so twice dead; ¹³like wild sea waves with their own shame for foam; or

a Gn 6:1–2, elaborated in *The Book of Enoch*.

b Gn 19:1–11, elaborated in *The Testament of the Twelve Patriarchs*.

c *See* the apocryphal *Assumption of Moses*.

d Zc 3:2.

e Gn 4:8.

f Nb 22:2.

g Nb 16.

like wandering stars for whom the gloom of darkness is stored up for ever. ¹⁴It was with them in mind that Enoch, the seventh patriarch from Adam, made his prophecy when he said, 'I tell you, the Lord will come with his holy ones in their tens of thousands, ¹⁵to pronounce judgement on all humanity and to sentence the godless for all the godless things they have done, and for all the defiant things said against him by godless sinners.'ʰ ¹⁶They are mischief-makers, grumblers governed only by their own desires, with *mouths full of boastful talk,*ⁱ ready to flatter others for gain.

A warning

¹⁷But remember, my dear friends, what the apostles of our Lord Jesus Christ foretold. ¹⁸'At the final point of time', they told you, 'there will be mockers who follow nothing but their own godless desires.' ¹⁹It is they who cause division, who live according to nature and do not possess the Spirit.

The duties of love

²⁰But you, my dear friends, must build yourselves up on the foundation of your most holy faith, praying in the Holy Spirit; ²¹keep yourselves within the love of God and wait for the mercy of our Lord Jesus Christ to give you eternal life. ²²To some you must be compassionate because they are wavering; ²³others you must save by snatching them from the fire; to others again you must be compassionate but wary, hating even the tunic stained by their bodies.

Doxology

²⁴To him who can keep you from falling and bring you safe to his glorious presence, innocent and joyful, ²⁵to the only God, our Saviour, through Jesus Christ our Lord, be glory, majesty, authority and power, before all ages, now and for ever. Amen.

h Enoch 1:9.   *i* Lv 19:15.

THE REVELATION

to John

Prologue

1 A revelation of Jesus Christ, which God gave him so that he could tell his servants *what is* now *to take place*[a] very soon; he sent his angel to make it known to his servant John, [2] and John has borne witness to the Word of God and to the witness of Jesus Christ, everything that he saw. [3] Blessed is anyone who reads the words of this prophecy, and blessed those who hear them, if they treasure the content, because the Time is near.

Address and greeting[b]

[4] John, to the seven churches of Asia: grace and peace to you from him who is, who was, and who is to come, from the seven spirits who are before his throne, [5] and from Jesus Christ, *the faithful witness, the First-born* from the dead, *the highest of earthly kings.* He loves us and has washed away our sins with his blood, [6] and made us a *Kingdom of Priests* to serve his God and Father; to him, then, be glory and power for ever and ever. Amen. [7] Look, he *is coming on the clouds;* everyone will see him, even *those who pierced him,* and *all the races of the earth will mourn over him.* Indeed this shall be so. Amen. [8] 'I am the Alpha and the Omega,' says the Lord God, who is, who was, and who is to come, the Almighty.

Preliminary vision

[9] I, John, your brother and partner in hardships, in the kingdom and in perseverance in Jesus, was on the island of Patmos on account of the Word of God and of witness to Jesus; [10] it was the Lord's Day and I was in ecstasy, and I heard a loud voice behind me, like the sound of a trumpet, saying, [11] 'Write down in a book all that you see, and send it to the seven churches of Ephesus, Smyrna, Pergamum, Thyatira, Sardis, Philadelphia and Laodicea.' [12] I turned round to see who was speaking to me, and when I turned I saw seven golden lamp-stands [13] and, in the middle of them, one *like a Son of man,*[c] dressed in a long robe tied at the waist with a *belt of gold.* [14] *His head and his hair were white with the whiteness of wool, like snow, his eyes* like a *burning* flame, [15] *his feet like burnished bronze* when it has been refined in a furnace, and *his voice like the sound of the ocean.* [16] In his right hand he was holding seven stars, out of his mouth came a sharp sword, double-edged, and his face was like the sun shining with all its force.

[17] When I saw him, I fell at his feet as though dead, but he laid his right hand on me and said, 'Do not be afraid; it is I, *the First* and *the Last;* I am the Living One, [18] I was dead and look—I am alive for ever and ever, and I hold the keys of death and of Hades. [19] Now write down all that you see of present happenings and *what is still to come.*[d] [20] The secret of the seven stars you have seen in my right hand, and of the seven golden lamp-stands, is this: the seven stars are the angels of the seven churches, and the seven lamp-stands are the seven churches themselves.'

1 Ephesus

2 'Write to the angel of the church in Ephesus and say, "Here is the message of the one who holds the seven stars in his right hand

---

1a Dn 2:28.

1b The quotations point to the glorious Messiah: Ps 89:37, 27; Is 55:4; Ex 19:6; Dn 7:13; Zc 12:10, 44.

1c Allusions to Dn 7 and 10 and Ezk 43:2.   *1d* Dn 2:28.

and who lives among the seven golden lamp-stands: ²I know your activities, your hard work and your perseverance. I know you cannot stand wicked people, and how you put to the test those who were self-styled apostles, and found them false. ³I know too that you have perseverance, and have suffered for my name without growing tired. ⁴Nevertheless, I have this complaint to make: you have less love now than formerly. ⁵Think where you were before you fell; repent, and behave as you did at first, or else, if you will not repent, I shall come to you and take your lamp-stand from its place. ⁶It is in your favour, nevertheless, that you loathe as I do the way the Nicolaitans are behaving. ⁷Let anyone who can hear, listen to what the Spirit is saying to the churches: those who prove victorious I will feed *from the tree of life* set *in* God's *paradise."* ᵃ

2 Smyrna

⁸'Write to the angel of the church in Smyrna and say, "Here is the message of *the First* and *the Last,* who was dead and has come to life again: ⁹I know your hardships and your poverty, and—though you are rich—the slander of the people who falsely claim to be Jews but are really members of the synagogue of Satan. ¹⁰Do not be afraid of the sufferings that are coming to you. Look, the devil will send some of you to prison *to put you to the test,* and you must face hardship for *ten days.* ᵇ Even if you have to die, keep faithful, and I will give you the crown of life for your prize. ¹¹Let anyone who can hear, listen to what the Spirit is saying to the churches: for those who prove victorious will come to no harm from the second death."

3 Pergamum

¹²'Write to the angel of the church in Pergamum and say, "Here is the message of the one who has the sharp sword, double-edged: ¹³I know where you live, in the place where Satan is enthroned, and that you still hold firmly to my name, and did not disown your faith in me

even when my faithful witness, Antipas, was killed among you, where Satan lives.

¹⁴"Nevertheless, I have one or two charges against you: some of you are followers of Balaam, who taught Balak to set a trap for the Israelites so that they committed adultery by eating food that had been sacrificed to idols; ¹⁵and among you too there are some also who follow the teaching of the Nicolaitans. ¹⁶So repent, or I shall soon come to you and attack these people with the sword out of my mouth. ¹⁷Let anyone who can hear, listen to what the Spirit is saying to the churches: to those who prove victorious I will give some hidden manna and a white stone, with *a new name* written on it, known only to the person who receives it."

4 Thyatira

¹⁸'Write to the angel of the church in Thyatira and say, "Here is the message of the Son of God who has eyes like a burning flame and feet like burnished bronze: ¹⁹I know your activities, your love, your faith, your service and your perseverance, and I know how you are still making progress. ²⁰Nevertheless, I have a complaint to make: you tolerate the woman Jezebel ᶜ who claims to be a prophetess, and by her teaching she is luring my servants away to commit the adultery of eating food which has been sacrificed to idols. ²¹I have given her time to repent but she is not willing to repent of her adulterous life. ²²Look, I am consigning her to a bed of pain, and all her partners in adultery to great hardship, unless they repent of their practices; ²³and I will see that her children die, so that all the churches realise that it is I who *test motives and thoughts and repay* you *as your deeds deserve.* ᵈ ²⁴But on the rest of you in Thyatira, all of you who have not accepted this teaching or learnt the deep secrets of Satan, as they are called, I am not laying any other burden; ²⁵but hold on firmly to what you already have until I come. ²⁶To anyone

2a Gn 2:9.   2b Dn 1:12.

2c cf. 2 K 9:22.   2d Jr 11:20; 17:10.

who proves victorious, and keeps working for me until the end, *I will give* the authority over *the nations* 27 which I myself have been given by my Father, *to rule them with an iron sceptre and shatter them like so many pots.*[e] 28 And I will give such a person the Morning Star. 29 Let anyone who can hear, listen to what the Spirit is saying to the churches."

5 Sardis

3 'Write to the angel of the church in Sardis and say, "Here is the message of the one who holds the seven spirits of God and the seven stars: I know about your behaviour: how you are reputed to be alive and yet are dead. 2 Wake up; put some resolve into what little vigour you have left: it is dying fast. So far I have failed to notice anything in your behaviour that my God could possibly call perfect; 3 remember how you first heard the message. Hold on to that. Repent! If you do not wake up, I shall come to you like a thief, and you will have no idea at what hour I shall come upon you. 4 There are a few in Sardis, it is true, who have kept their robes unstained, and they are fit to come with me, dressed in white. 5 Anyone who proves victorious will be dressed, like these, in white robes; I shall not blot that name out of the book of life, but acknowledge it in the presence of my Father and his angels. 6 Let anyone who can hear, listen to what the Spirit is saying to the churches."

6 Philadelphia

7 'Write to the angel of the church in Philadelphia and say, "Here is the message of the holy and true one who *has the key of David,* so that *when he opens, no one will close, and when he closes, no one will open:*[a] 8 I know about your activities. Look, I have opened in front of you a door that no one will be able to close—and I know that though you are not very strong, you have kept my commandments and not disowned my name. 9 Look, I am going to make the synagogue of Satan—those who falsely claim to be Jews, but are liars, because they are no such thing—I will make them *come and fall*

at your feet and recognize that *I have loved you.*[b] 10 Because you have kept my commandment to persevere, I will keep you safe in the time of trial which is coming for the whole world, to put the people of the world to the test. 11 I am coming soon: hold firmly to what you already have, and let no one take your victor's crown away from you. 12 Anyone who proves victorious I will make into a pillar in the sanctuary of my God, and it will stay there for ever; I will inscribe on it the name of my God and the name of the city of my God, the new Jerusalem which is coming down from my God in heaven, and my own new name as well. 13 Let anyone who can hear, listen to what the Spirit is saying to the churches."

7 Laodicea

14 'Write to the angel of the church in Laodicea and say, "Here is the message of the Amen,[c] the trustworthy, the true witness, the Principle of God's creation: 15 I know about your activities: how you are neither cold nor hot. I wish you were one or the other, 16 but since you are neither hot nor cold, but only lukewarm, I will spit you out of my mouth. 17 You say to yourself: I am rich, I have made a fortune and have everything I want, never realising that you are wretchedly and pitiably poor, and blind and naked too. 18 I warn you, buy from me the gold that has been tested in the fire to make you truly rich, and white robes to clothe you and hide your shameful nakedness, and ointment to put on your eyes to enable you to see. 19 I *reprove* and *train those whom I love:*[d] so repent in real earnest. 20 Look, I am standing at the door, knocking. If one of you hears me calling and opens the door, I will come in to share a meal at that person's side. 21 Anyone who proves victorious I will allow to share my throne, just as I have myself overcome and have taken my seat with my Father on his throne. 22 Let anyone who can hear, listen to what the Spirit is saying to the churches." '

2e Ps 2:8–9.   3a Is 22:22.   3b Is 43:3.
3c *Amen* is Hebr. for truth, firmness.   3d Pr 3:12.

199 READ REVELATION 3:20–22.

If one of you hears me calling and opens the door, I will come in to share a meal at that person's side.—REVELATION 3:20

THE HUMBLE HEART

Four things cause the present coming of Christ our Bridegroom that takes place daily within our souls: God's mercy and our destitution, God's generosity and our desire. These four things produce the growth of virtue and nobleness.

Consider that when the sun sends its radiance into a deep valley between two high mountains, and yet standing in the zenith can shine upon the bottom of the valley, then three things happen: the valley becomes full of light by reflection from the mountains, it receives more heat, and becomes more fruitful than the level country. Likewise when a good man takes his stand upon his own littleness and . . . confesses his poverty and his helplessness, then he makes a valley of humility.

And when he is thus humble, and needy, and knows his own need, he lays his distress . . . before the bounty and mercy of God. So he marks the sublimity of God and his own lowliness; and thus he becomes a deep valley. And Christ is a Sun of righteousness and also of mercy, who stands in the highest part of the firmament, that is on the right hand of the Father, and from there he shines into the bottom of the humble heart. For Christ is always moved by helplessness, whenever a person complains of it and lays it before him with humility. Then there arise two mountains, that is, two desires. One to serve God and praise him with reverence, the other to attain noble virtues. Those two mountains are higher than the heavens for these longings touch God without intermediary and crave his ungrudging generosity. And then that generosity cannot withhold itself, it must flow forth. For then the soul is ready to receive more gifts.

Then this valley, the humble heart receives three things: it becomes more radiant and enlightened by grace. It becomes more ardent in charity. And it becomes more fruitful in perfect virtues and good works. —ST. JOHN RUYSBROECK, 1293–1381

YOU WILL FIND THE NEXT READING AT REVELATION 19.

God entrusts the future of the world to the Lamb[a]

4 Then, in my vision, I saw a door open in heaven and heard the same voice speaking to me, the voice like a trumpet, saying, 'Come up here: I will show you *what is to take place* in the future.' [2] With that, I fell into ecstasy and I saw a throne standing in heaven, and the *One* who was *sitting on the throne,* [3] and the One sitting there looked like a diamond and a ruby. There was a rainbow encircling the throne, and this looked like an emerald. [4] Round the throne in a circle were twenty-four thrones, and on them twenty-four elders sitting, dressed in white robes with golden crowns on their heads. [5] Flashes of lightning were coming from the throne, and the sound of peals of

4a The scene draws on Ezk 1; 10 and Is 6.

thunder, and in front of the throne there were seven flaming lamps burning, the seven Spirits of God. ⁶ In front of the throne was a sea as transparent as crystal. *In the middle* of the throne and around it, were *four living creatures all studded with eyes,* in front and behind. ⁷ *The first* living creature was like *a lion, the second* like *a bull, the third* living creature had a *human face,* and *the fourth* living creature was like a flying *eagle.* ⁸ *Each* of the four living creatures had *six wings* and *was studded with eyes all the way round* as well as inside; and day and night they never stopped singing:

> *Holy, Holy, Holy*
> *is the Lord God, the Almighty;*
> *who was, and is and is to come.'*

⁹ Every time the living creatures glorified and honoured and gave thanks to the One sitting on the throne, *who lives for ever and ever,* ¹⁰ the twenty-four elders prostrated themselves before him to worship the One *who lives for ever and ever,* and threw down their crowns in front of the throne, saying:

> ¹¹ You are worthy, our Lord and God,
> to receive glory and honour and power,
> for you made the whole universe;
> by your will, when it did not exist, it was created.

5 I saw that in the right hand of the One sitting on the throne there was *a scroll that was written on back and front*[a] and was sealed with seven seals. ² Then I saw a powerful angel who called with a loud voice, 'Who is worthy to open the scroll and break its seals?' ³ But there was no one, in heaven or on the earth or under the earth, who was able to open the scroll and read it. ⁴ I wept bitterly because nobody could be found to open the scroll and read it, ⁵ but one of the elders said to me, 'Do not weep. Look, *the Lion* of the tribe *of Judah, the Root*[b] of David, has triumphed, and so he will open the scroll and its seven seals.'

⁶ Then I saw, in the middle of the throne with its four living creatures and the circle of the elders, a Lamb standing that seemed to have been sacrificed; it had seven horns, and it had seven eyes, which are the seven Spirits that God has *sent out over the whole world.*[c] ⁷ The Lamb came forward to take the scroll from the right hand of the One sitting on the throne, ⁸ and when he took it, the four living creatures prostrated themselves before him and with them the twenty-four elders; each one of them was holding a harp and had a golden bowl full of incense which are the prayers of the saints. ⁹ They sang a new hymn:

> You are worthy to take the scroll
> and to break its seals,
> because you were sacrificed, and with your blood
> you bought people for God
> of every race, language, people and nation
> ¹⁰ and made them *a line of kings and priests*[d]
> for God,
> to rule the world.

¹¹ In my vision, I heard the sound of an immense number of angels gathered round the throne and the living creatures and the elders; there were *ten thousand times ten thousand of them* and *thousands upon thousands,*[e] ¹² loudly chanting:

> Worthy is the Lamb that was sacrificed
> to receive power, riches, wisdom,
> strength, honour, glory and blessing.

¹³ Then I heard all the living things in creation—everything that lives in heaven, and on earth, and under the earth, and in the sea, crying:

> To the One seated on the throne and to the Lamb,
> be all praise, honour, glory and power,
> for ever and ever.

5a Ezk 2:9. 5b Gn 49:9; Is 11:10. 5c Zc 4:10.
5d Is 61:6. 5e Dn 7:10.

¹⁴ And the four living creatures said, 'Amen'; and the elders prostrated themselves to worship.

The Lamb breaks the seven seals

6 Then, in my vision, I saw the Lamb break one of the seven seals, and I heard one of the four living creatures shout in a voice like thunder, 'Come!' ² Immediately I saw a white horse*ᵃ* appear, and its rider was holding a bow; he was given a victor's crown and he went away, to go from victory to victory.

³ When he broke the second seal, I heard the second living creature shout, 'Come!' ⁴ And out came another horse, bright red, and its rider was given this duty: to take away peace from the earth and set people killing each other. He was given a huge sword.

⁵ When he broke the third seal, I heard the third living creature shout, 'Come!' Immediately I saw a black horse appear, and its rider was holding a pair of scales; ⁶ and I seemed to hear a voice shout from among the four living creatures and say, 'A day's wages for a quart of corn, and a day's wages for three quarts of barley, but do not tamper with the oil or the wine.'

⁷ When he broke the fourth seal, I heard the voice of the fourth living creature shout, 'Come!' ⁸ Immediately I saw another horse appear, deathly pale, and its rider was called Death, and Hades followed at its heels.

They were given authority over a quarter of the earth, *to kill by the sword, by famine, by plague and through wild beasts.ᵇ*

⁹ When he broke the fifth seal, I saw underneath the altar the souls of all the people who had been killed on account of the Word of God, for witnessing to it. ¹⁰ They shouted in a loud voice, 'Holy, true Master, how much longer will you wait before you pass sentence and take vengeance for our death on the inhabitants of the earth?' ¹¹ Each of them was given a white robe, and they were told to be patient a little longer, until the roll was completed of their fellow-servants and brothers who were still to be killed as they had been.

¹² In my vision, when he broke the sixth seal, there was a violent earthquake and the sun went as black as coarse sackcloth; the moon turned red as blood all over, ¹³ and *the stars of the sky fellᶜ* onto the earth *like figs* dropping from a fig tree when a high wind shakes it; ¹⁴ the *sky disappeared like a scroll rolling up* and all the mountains and islands were shaken from their places. ¹⁵ Then all the kings of the earth, the governors and the commanders, the rich people and the men of influence, the whole population, slaves and citizens, *hid in caverns and among the rocks of the mountains.ᵈ* ¹⁶ *They said to the mountainsᵉ* and the rocks, *'Fall on us* and hide us away from the One who sits on the throne and from the retribution of the Lamb. ¹⁷ For *the Great Day of his retribution* has come, *and who can face it?'ᶠ*

God's servants will be preservedᵃ

7 Next I saw four angels, standing at *the four corners of the earth,ᵇ* holding back the four winds of the world to keep them from blowing over the land or the sea or any tree. ² Then I saw another angel rising where the sun rises, carrying the seal of the living God; he called in a powerful voice to the four angels whose duty was to devastate land and sea, ³ 'Wait before you do any damage on land or at sea or to the trees, until we have put the *seal on the foreheadsᶜ* of the servants of our God.' ⁴ And I heard how many had been sealed: a hundred and forty-four thousand,ᵈ out of all the tribes of Israel.

⁵ From the tribe of Judah,
 twelve thousand had been sealed;
 from the tribe of Reuben, twelve thousand;
 from the tribe of Gad, twelve thousand;
⁶ from the tribe of Asher, twelve thousand;
 from the tribe of Naphtali, twelve
 thousand;

6a The horsemen echo Zc 1:8–10; 6:1–3. 6b Ezk 14:21.
6c Is 34:4. 6d Ho 10:8. 6e Is 2:10, 18, 19.
6f Jl 2:11; 3:4. 7a = 14:1–5. 7b Ezk 7:2. 7c Ezk 9:4.
7d The sacred number 12 squared and multiplied by 1000 indicates the totality of the saved.

from the tribe of Manasseh, twelve thousand;

[7] from the tribe of Simeon, twelve thousand; from the tribe of Levi, twelve thousand; from the tribe of Issachar, twelve thousand;

[8] from the tribe of Zebulun, twelve thousand; from the tribe of Joseph, twelve thousand; and from the tribe of Benjamin, twelve thousand had been sealed.

The rewarding of the saints[e]

[9] After that I saw that there was a huge number, impossible for anyone to count, of people from every nation, race, tribe and language; they were standing in front of the throne and in front of the Lamb, dressed in white robes and holding palms in their hands. They shouted in a loud voice, [10] 'Salvation to our God, who sits on the throne, and to the Lamb!' [11] And all the angels who were standing in a circle round the throne, surrounding the elders and the four living creatures, prostrated themselves before the throne, and touched the ground with their foreheads, worshipping God [12] with these words:

Amen. Praise and glory and wisdom,
thanksgiving and honour and power and
        strength
to our God for ever and ever. Amen.

[13] One of the elders then spoke and asked me, 'Who are these people, dressed in white robes, and where have they come from?' [14] I answered him, 'You can tell me, sir.' Then he said, 'These are the people who have been through the great trial; they have washed their robes white again in the blood of the Lamb. [15] That is why they are standing in front of God's throne and serving him day and night in his sanctuary; and the One who sits on the throne will spread his tent over them. [16] *They will never hunger or thirst again; sun and scorching wind will never plague them,* [17] because the Lamb who is at the heart of the throne *will be*

their shepherd and will guide them to springs of living water;[f] and God will wipe away all tears from their eyes.'[g]

The seventh seal

[8] The Lamb then broke the seventh seal, and there was silence in heaven for about half an hour.

The prayers of the saints bring the coming of the Great Day nearer

[2] Next I saw seven trumpets being given to the seven angels who stand in the presence of God. [3] Another angel, who had a golden censer, came and stood at the altar. A large quantity of incense was given to him to offer with the prayers of all the saints on the golden altar that stood in front of the throne; [4] and so from the angel's hand the smoke of the incense went up in the presence of God and with it the prayers of the saints. [5] Then the angel took the censer and *filled it from the fire of the altar,[a]* which he then hurled down onto the earth; immediately there came peals of thunder and flashes of lightning, and the earth shook.

The first four trumpets[b]

[6] The seven angels that had the seven trumpets now made ready to sound them. [7] The first blew his trumpet and, with that, hail and fire, mixed with blood, were hurled on the earth: a third of the earth was burnt up, and a third of all trees, and every blade of grass was burnt. [8] The second angel blew his trumpet, and it was as though a great mountain blazing with fire was hurled into the sea: a third of the sea turned into blood, [9] a third of all the living things in the sea were killed, and a third of all ships were destroyed. [10] The third angel blew his trumpet, and a huge star fell from the sky, burning like a ball of fire, and it fell on a third of all rivers and on the springs of water; [11] this was the star called Wormwood, and a third of

7e = 15:2–5.   7f Is 49:10.   7g = 21:4; Is 25:8.
8a Lv 16:12; Ezk 10:2.   8b = 16:1–9.

all water turned to wormwood, so that many people died; the water had become so bitter. ¹²The fourth angel blew his trumpet, and a third of the sun and a third of the moon and a third of the stars were blasted, so that the light went out of a third of them and the day lost a third of its illumination, and likewise the night.

¹³In my vision, I heard an eagle, calling aloud as it flew high overhead, 'Disaster, disaster, disaster, on all the people on earth at the sound of the other three trumpets which the three angels have yet to blow!'

The fifth trumpet

9 Then the fifth angel blew his trumpet, and I saw a star that had fallen from heaven onto the earth, and the angel was given the key to the shaft leading down to the Abyss. ²When he unlocked the shaft of the Abyss, *smoke rose out of the Abyss like the smoke from a* huge *furnace*[a] so that the sun and the sky were darkened by the smoke from the Abyss, ³and out of the smoke dropped locusts onto the earth: they were given the powers that scorpions have on the earth: ⁴they were forbidden to harm any fields or crops or trees and told to attack only those people who were without God's seal on their foreheads. ⁵They were not to kill them, but to give them anguish for five months, and the anguish was to be the anguish of a scorpion's sting. ⁶When this happens, *people will long for death and not find it anywhere;*[b] they will want to die and death will evade them.

⁷These locusts *looked like horses*[c] armoured *for battle;* they had what looked like gold crowns on their heads, and their faces looked human, ⁸and their hair was like women's hair, and *teeth like lion's teeth.* ⁹They had body-armour like iron breastplates, and the noise of their wings sounded like *the racket of chariots with many horses charging.* ¹⁰Their tails were like scorpions' tails, with stings, and with their tails they were able to torture people for five months. ¹¹As their leader they had their emperor, the angel of the Abyss, whose name in Hebrew is Abaddon, and in Greek Apollyon.[d]

¹²That was the first of the disasters; there are still two more to come.

The sixth trumpet

¹³The sixth angel blew his trumpet, and I heard a single voice issuing from the four horns of the golden altar in God's presence. ¹⁴It spoke to the sixth angel with the trumpet, and said, 'Release the four angels that are chained up at the great river Euphrates.' ¹⁵These four angels had been ready for this hour of this day of this month of this year, and ready to destroy a third of the human race. ¹⁶I learnt how many there were in their army: twice ten thousand times ten thousand mounted men. ¹⁷In my vision I saw the horses, and the riders with their breastplates of flame colour, hyacinth-blue and sulphur-yellow; the horses had lions' heads, and fire, smoke and sulphur were coming from their mouths. ¹⁸It was by these three plagues, the fire, the smoke and the sulphur coming from their mouths, that the one third of the human race was killed. ¹⁹All the horses' power was in their mouths and their tails: their tails were like snakes, and had heads which inflicted wounds. ²⁰But the rest of the human race, who escaped death by these plagues, refused either to abandon *their own handiwork*[e] or to stop worshipping devils, the *idols made of gold, silver, bronze, stone and wood*[f] that can neither see nor hear nor move. ²¹Nor did they give up their murdering, or witchcraft, or fornication or stealing.

The imminence of the last punishment

10 Then I saw another powerful angel coming down from heaven, wrapped in cloud, with a rainbow over his head; his face was like the sun, and his legs were pillars of fire. ²In his hand he had a small scroll, unrolled; he put his right foot in the sea and his

9a Ex 19:18.   9b Jb 3:21.

9c The details of vv. 7–9 echo Jl 1 and 2.

9d Both names mean 'Destroyer'.

9e Is 17:8.   9f Dn 5:4.

left foot on the land ³ and he shouted so loud, it was *like a lion roaring.*[a] At this, the seven claps of thunder made themselves heard ⁴ and when the seven thunderclaps had sounded, I was preparing to write, when I heard a voice from heaven say to me, 'Keep the words of the seven thunderclaps secret and do not write them down.' ⁵ Then the angel that I had seen, standing on the sea and the land, *raised his right hand to heaven,*[b] ⁶ and *swore by him who lives for ever and ever, and made heaven and all that it contains,*[c] and *earth and all it contains,* and *the sea and all it contains,* 'The time of waiting is over; ⁷ at the time when the seventh angel is heard sounding his trumpet, the mystery of God will be fulfilled, just as he announced in the gospel to *his servants the prophets.*'

The seer eats the small scroll

⁸ Then I heard the voice I had heard from heaven speaking to me again. 'Go', it said, 'and take that open scroll from the hand of the angel standing on sea and land.' ⁹ I went to the angel and asked him to give me the small scroll, and he said, 'Take it and eat it; it will turn your stomach sour, but it will taste as sweet as honey.' ¹⁰ So I took it out of the angel's hand, and *I ate it and it tasted sweet as honey,*[d] but when I had eaten it my stomach turned sour. ¹¹ Then I was told, 'You are to prophesy again, this time against many different nations and countries and languages and kings.'

The two witnesses

11 Then I was given a long cane like a measuring rod, and I was told, 'Get up and measure God's sanctuary, and the altar, and the people who worship there; ² but exclude the outer court and do not measure it, because it has been handed over to gentiles— they will trample on the holy city for forty-two months.[a] ³ But I shall send my two witnesses to prophesy for twelve hundred and sixty days, wearing sackcloth. ⁴ These are the *two olive trees*[b] and the two lamps *in attendance on the Lord of the world.*[c] ⁵ Fire comes from their mouths and consumes their enemies if anyone

tries to harm them; and anyone who tries to harm them will certainly be killed in this way. ⁶ They have the power to lock up the sky so that it does not rain as long as they are prophesying; they have the power to turn water into blood and strike the whole world with any plague as often as they like. ⁷ When they have completed their witnessing, the beast that comes out of the Abyss *is going to make war on them and overcome them*[d] and kill them. ⁸ Their corpses lie in the main street of the great city[e] known by the symbolic names Sodom and Egypt, in which their Lord was crucified. ⁹ People of every race, tribe, language and nation stare at their corpses, for three-and-a-half days, not letting them be buried, ¹⁰ and the people of the world are glad about it and celebrate the event by giving presents to each other, because these two prophets have been a plague to the people of the world.'

¹¹ After the three-and-a-half days, *God breathed life into them and they stood up on their feet,*[f] and everybody who saw it happen was terrified; ¹² then I heard a loud voice from heaven say to them, 'Come up here,' and while their enemies were watching, they went up to heaven in a cloud. ¹³ Immediately, there was a violent earthquake, and a tenth of the city collapsed; seven thousand persons were killed in the earthquake, and the survivors, overcome with fear, could only praise the God of heaven.

¹⁴ That was the second of the disasters; the third is to come quickly after it.

The seventh trumpet

¹⁵ Then the seventh angel blew his trumpet, and voices could be heard shouting in heaven, calling, 'The kingdom of the world has be-

10a Am 1:2; 3:8. 10b Dt 32:40.

10c Ne 9:6. 10d Ezk 3:1–13.

11a cf. Dn 7:25. Half seven years, so the opposite of completion, a short and incomplete time of persecution.

11b Zc 4:3, 14. 11c 2 K 1:10. 11d Dn 7:21.

11e Also called Babylon. It is the centre of evil and persecution, possibly Rome.

11f Ezk 37:5, 10.

come the kingdom of our Lord and his Christ, and he will reign for ever and ever.' ¹⁶ The twenty-four elders, enthroned in the presence of God, prostrated themselves and touched the ground with their foreheads worshipping God ¹⁷ with these words, 'We give thanks to you, Almighty Lord God, He who is, He who was, for assuming your great power and beginning your reign. ¹⁸ *The nations were in uproar* ᵍ and now the time has come for your retribution, and for the dead to be judged, and for *your servants the prophets,* for the saints and for *those who fear* your name, *small and great alike,* to be rewarded. The time has come to destroy those who are destroying the earth.'

¹⁹ Then the sanctuary of God in heaven opened, and the ark of the covenant could be seen inside it. Then came flashes of lightning, peals of thunder and an earthquake and violent hail.

The vision of the woman and the dragon

12 Now a great sign appeared in heaven: a woman, robed with the sun, standing on the moon, and on her head a crown of twelve stars. ² She was pregnant, and in labour, crying aloud in the pangs of childbirth. ³ Then a second sign appeared in the sky: there was a huge red dragon with seven heads and ten horns, and each of the seven heads crowned with a coronet. ⁴ Its tail swept a third of *the stars from the sky and hurled them to the ground,* ᵃ and the dragon stopped in front of the woman as she was at the point of giving birth, so that it could eat the child as soon as it was born. ⁵ The woman *was delivered of a boy,* ᵇ the son who was *to rule all the nations with an iron sceptre,* and the child was taken straight up to God and to his throne, ⁶ while the woman escaped into the desert, where God had prepared a place for her to be looked after for twelve hundred and sixty days.

⁷ And now war broke out in heaven, when *Michael* ᶜ with his angels attacked the dragon. The dragon fought back with his angels, ⁸ but they were defeated and driven out of heaven. ⁹ The great dragon, the primeval serpent, known as the devil or Satan, who had led all the world astray, was hurled down to the earth and his angels were hurled down with him. ¹⁰ Then I heard a voice shout from heaven, 'Salvation and power and empire for ever have been won by our God, and all authority for his Christ, now that the accuser, who accused our brothers day and night before our God, has been brought down. ¹¹ They have triumphed over him by the blood of the Lamb and by the word to which they bore witness, because even in the face of death they did not cling to life. ¹² So let the heavens rejoice and all who live there; but for you, earth and sea, disaster is coming—because the devil has gone down to you in a rage, knowing that he has little time left.'

¹³ As soon as the dragon found himself hurled down to the earth, he sprang in pursuit of the woman, the mother of the male child, ¹⁴ but she was given a pair of the great eagle's wings to fly away from the serpent into the desert, to the place where she was to be looked after for *a time, two times and half a time.* ᵈ ¹⁵ So the serpent vomited water from his mouth, like a river, after the woman, to sweep her away in the current, ¹⁶ but the earth came to her rescue; it opened its mouth and swallowed the river spewed from the dragon's mouth. ¹⁷ Then the dragon was enraged with the woman and went away to make war on the rest of her children, who obey God's commandments and have in themselves the witness of Jesus.

The dragon delegates his power to the beast

¹⁸ And I took my stand on the seashore.

13 Then I saw *a beast* ᵃ *emerge from the sea:* it had seven heads and ten horns, with a coronet on each of its ten horns, and its heads

---

11g Ps 2:1, 5, followed by Am 3:7; Ps 115:13. *12a* Dn 8:10.

12b Is 66:7, followed by Ps 2:9. The woman is the people of God, and the boy is the Messiah.

12c God's champion in Dn 10:13; 12:1. *12d* See 11a note.

13a The vision draws on Dn 7.

were marked with blasphemous titles. ²I saw that the beast *was like a leopard,* with paws like *a bear* and a mouth like *a lion;* the dragon had handed over to it his own power and his throne and his immense authority. ³I saw that one of its heads seemed to have had a fatal wound but that this deadly injury had healed and the whole world had marvelled and followed the beast. ⁴They prostrated themselves in front of the dragon because he had given the beast his authority; and they prostrated themselves in front of the beast, saying, 'Who can compare with the beast? Who can fight against it?' ⁵The beast was allowed *to mouth its boasts* and blasphemies and to be active for forty-two months; ⁶and it mouthed its blasphemies against God, against his name, his heavenly Tent and all those who are sheltered there. ⁷It was allowed *to make war against the saints and conquer them, and given power* over every race, people, language and nation; ⁸and all people of the world will worship it, that is, everybody whose name has not been written down since the foundation of the world in the sacrificial Lamb's book of life. ⁹Let anyone who can hear, listen: ¹⁰*Those for captivity to captivity; those for* death by *the sword to* death by *the sword.*ᵇ This is why the saints must have perseverance and faith.

The false prophet as the slave of the beast

¹¹Then I saw a second beast, emerging from the ground; it had two horns like a lamb, but made a noise like a dragon. ¹²This second beast exercised all the power of the first beast, on its behalf making the world and all its people worship the first beast, whose deadly injury had healed. ¹³And it worked great miracles, even to calling down fire from heaven onto the earth while people watched. ¹⁴Through the miracles which it was allowed to do on behalf of the first beast, it was able to lead astray the people of the world and persuade them to put up a statue in honour of the beast that had been wounded by the sword and still lived. ¹⁵It was allowed to breathe life into this statue, so that the statue of the beast

was able to speak, and to have *anyone who refused to worship the statue*ᶜ of the beast put to death. ¹⁶It compelled everyone—small and great alike, rich and poor, slave and citizen—to be branded on the right hand or on the forehead, ¹⁷and made it illegal for anyone to buy or sell anything unless he had been branded with the name of the beast or with the number of its name.

¹⁸There is need for shrewdness here: anyone clever may interpret the number of the beast: it is the number of a human being, the number 666.ᵈ

The companions of the Lambª

14 Next in my vision I saw Mount Zion, and standing on it the Lamb who had with him a hundred and forty-four thousand people, all with his name and his Father's name written on their foreheads. ²I heard a sound coming out of heaven like the sound of the ocean or the roar of thunder; it was like the sound of harpists playing their harps. ³There before the throne they were singing a new hymn in the presence of the four living creatures and the elders, a hymn that could be learnt only by the hundred and forty-four thousand who had been redeemed from the world. ⁴These are the ones who have kept their virginity and not been defiled with women; they *follow* the Lamb wherever he goes; they, out of all people, have been redeemed to be *the first-fruits for God*ᵇ and for the Lamb. ⁵*No lie*ᶜ was found in their mouths and no fault can be found in them.

Angels announce the Day of Judgement

⁶Then I saw another angel, flying high overhead, sent to announce the gospel of eternity to all who live on the earth, every nation, race, language and tribe. ⁷He was calling, 'Fear God and glorify him, because the time has

13b Jr 15:2.   *13c* Dn 3:5–7, 15.

13d 6 = 7–1, so 666 = triple imperfection. It may also symbolise a name.

14a = 7:1–8.   *14b* Jr 2:2–3.   *14c* Zp 3:13.

come for him to sit in judgement; worship *the maker of heaven and earth and sea*[d] and the springs of water.'

[8] A second angel followed him, calling, '*Babylon has fallen, Babylon the Great has fallen,* Babylon which gave the whole world *the wine of retribution* to drink.'[e]

[9] A third angel followed, shouting aloud, 'All those who worship the beast and his statue, or have had themselves branded on the hand or forehead, [10] will be made to drink the wine of God's fury which is ready, undiluted, in his cup of retribution; in *fire and brimstone*[f] they will be tortured in the presence of the holy angels and the Lamb [11] and *the smoke* of their torture will *rise for ever and ever.*[g] There will be no respite, *night or day,* for those who worship the beast or its statue or accept branding with its name.' [12] This is why there must be perseverance in the saints who keep the commandments of God and faith in Jesus. [13] Then I heard a voice from heaven say to me, 'Write down: Blessed are those who die in the Lord! Blessed indeed, the Spirit says; now they can rest for ever after their work, since their good deeds go with them.'

The harvest and vintage of the gentiles[h]

[14] Now in my vision I saw a white *cloud* and, *sitting on it, one like a son of man* with a gold crown on his head and a sharp sickle in his hand. [15] Then another angel came out of the sanctuary and shouted at the top of his voice to the one sitting on the cloud, '*Ply your sickle* and reap: harvest time has come and *the harvest* of the earth *is ripe.*' [16] Then the one sitting on the cloud set his sickle to work on the earth, and the harvest of earth was reaped.

[17] Another angel, who also carried a sharp sickle, came out of the temple in heaven, [18] and the angel in charge of the fire left the altar and shouted at the top of his voice to the one with the sharp sickle, 'Put your sickle in, and harvest the bunches from the vine of the earth; all its grapes are ripe.' [19] So the angel set his sickle to work on the earth and harvested the whole vintage of the earth and put it into a huge winepress, the winepress of God's anger, [20] outside the city, where it was trodden until the blood that came out of the winepress was up to the horses' bridles as far away as sixteen hundred furlongs.

The hymn of Moses and the Lamb[a]

15 And I saw in heaven another sign, great and wonderful: seven angels were bringing the seven plagues that are the last of all, because they exhaust the anger of God. [2] I seemed to be looking at a sea of crystal suffused with fire, and standing by the lake of glass, those who had fought against the beast and won, and against his statue and the number which is his name. They all had harps from God, [3] and they were singing the hymn of Moses,[b] the servant of God, and the hymn of the Lamb:

How great and wonderful are all your
works,
Lord God Almighty;
upright and true are all your ways,
King of nations.
[4] *Who does not revere* and *glorify your name,*
O Lord?
For you alone are holy,
and all nations will come and adore you
for the many acts of saving justice you
have shown.

The seven bowls of plagues

[5] After this, in my vision, the sanctuary, the tent of the Testimony, opened in heaven, [6] and out came the seven angels with the seven plagues, wearing pure white linen, fastened round their waists with belts of gold. [7] One of the four living creatures gave the seven angels seven golden bowls filled with the anger of God who lives for ever and ever. [8] *The smoke from the glory* and the power *of God filled* the

14d Ex 20:11.   14e = 18:2–3; cf. Is 21:9; 51:17.

14f Gn 19:24.   14g Is 34:9–10.   14h Dn 7:13; Jl 4:12–13.

15a = 7:1–8.

15b Ex 15; in fact the hymn uses Jr 10:7; Ps 86:9.

temple^c so that no one could go into it until the seven plagues of the seven angels were completed.

16 Then I heard a loud voice^a from the sanctuary calling to the seven angels, 'Go, and empty the seven bowls of God's anger over the earth.'

² The first angel went and emptied his bowl over the earth; at once, on all the people who had been branded with the mark of the beast and had worshipped its statue, there came disgusting and virulent sores.

³ The second angel emptied his bowl over the sea, and it turned to blood, like the blood of a corpse, and every living creature in the sea died.

⁴ The third angel emptied his bowl into the rivers and springs of water and they turned into blood. ⁵ Then I heard the angel of water say, 'You are the Upright One, He who is, He who was, the Holy One, for giving this verdict: ⁶ they spilt the blood of the saints and the prophets, and blood is what you have given them to drink; it is what they deserve.' ⁷ And I heard the altar itself say, 'Truly, Lord God Almighty, the punishments you give are true and just.'

⁸ The fourth angel emptied his bowl over the sun and it was made to scorch people with its flames; ⁹ but though people were scorched by the fierce heat of it, they cursed the name of God who had the power to cause such plagues, and they would not repent and glorify him.

¹⁰ The fifth angel emptied his bowl over the throne of the beast and its whole empire was plunged into darkness. People were biting their tongues for pain, ¹¹ but instead of repenting for what they had done, they cursed the God of heaven because of their pains and sores.

¹² The sixth angel emptied his bowl over the great river Euphrates; all the water dried up so that a way was made for the kings of the East to come in. ¹³ Then from the jaws of dragon and beast and false prophet I saw three foul spirits come; they looked like frogs ¹⁴ and in fact were demon spirits, able to work miracles, going out to all the kings of the world to call them together for the war of the Great Day of God the Almighty.— ¹⁵ Look, I shall come like a thief. Blessed is anyone who has kept watch, and has kept his clothes on, so that he does not go out naked and expose his shame.— ¹⁶ They called the kings together at the place called, in Hebrew, Armageddon.^b

¹⁷ The seventh angel emptied his bowl into the air, and a great voice boomed out from the sanctuary, 'The end has come.' ¹⁸ Then there were flashes of lightning and peals of thunder and a violent earthquake, *unparalleled since* humanity *first came into existence.*^c ¹⁹ The Great City was split into three parts and the cities of the world collapsed; Babylon the Great was not forgotten: God made her drink the full winecup of his retribution. ²⁰ Every island vanished and the mountains disappeared; ²¹ and hail, with great hailstones weighing a talent each, fell from the sky on the people. They cursed God for sending a plague of hail; it was the most terrible plague.

The punishment of Babylon

17 One of the seven angels that had the seven bowls came to speak to me, and said, 'Come here and I will show you the punishment of the great prostitute *who is enthroned beside abundant waters,*^a ² with whom all the kings of the earth have prostituted themselves, and who has made all the population of the world drunk with the wine of her adultery.' ³ He took me in spirit to a desert, and there I saw a woman riding a scarlet beast which had seven heads and ten horns and had blasphemous titles written all over it. ⁴ The woman was dressed in purple and scarlet and glittered with gold and jewels and pearls, and she was holding a gold winecup filled with the disgusting filth of her prostitution; ⁵ on her

---

15c 1 K 8:10.   16a = 8:6–12.

16b i.e. the mountains of Megiddo, symbol of disaster since King Josiah was killed there, 2 K 23:29.

16c Dn 12:1.

17a Jr 51:13. The seven heads are the seven hills of Rome.

forehead was written a name, a cryptic name: 'Babylon the Great, the mother of all the prostitutes and all the filthy practices on the earth.' 6 I saw that she was drunk, drunk with the blood of the saints, and the blood of the martyrs of Jesus; and when I saw her, I was completely mystified. 7 The angel said to me, 'Do you not understand? I will tell you the meaning of this woman, and of the beast she is riding, with the seven heads and the ten horns.

The symbolism of the beast and the prostitute

8 'The beast you have seen was once alive and is alive no longer; it is yet to come up from the Abyss, but only to go to its destruction. And the people of the world, whose names have not been written since the beginning of the world in the book of life, will be astonished when they see how the beast was once alive and is alive no longer, and is still to come.

9 'This calls for shrewdness. The seven heads are the seven hills, on which the woman is sitting. 10 The seven heads are also seven emperors. Five of them have already gone, one is here now, and one is yet to come; once here, he must stay for a short while. 11 The beast, who was alive and is alive no longer, is at the same time the eighth and one of the seven, and he is going to his destruction.

12 'The ten horns which you saw are ten kings b who have not yet been given their royal power but will have royal authority only for a single hour and in association with the beast. 13 They are all of one mind in putting their strength and their powers at the beast's disposal, 14 and they will go to war against the Lamb; but because the Lamb is Lord of lords and King of kings, c he will defeat them, he and his followers, the called, the chosen, the trustworthy.'

15 The angel continued, 'The waters you saw, beside which the prostitute was sitting, are all the peoples, the populations, the nations and the languages. 16 But the ten horns and the beast will turn against the prostitute, and tear off her clothes and leave her stark naked; d then they will eat her flesh and burn the remains in

the fire. 17 In fact, God has influenced their minds to do what he intends, to agree together to put their royal powers at the beast's disposal until the time when God's words shall be fulfilled. 18 The woman you saw is the great city which has authority over all the rulers on earth.'

An angel announces the fall of Babylon a

18 After this, I saw another angel come down from heaven, with great authority given to him; the earth shone with his glory. 2 At the top of his voice he shouted, b 'Babylon has fallen, Babylon the Great has fallen, and has become the haunt of devils and a lodging for every foul spirit and dirty, loathsome bird. 3 All the nations have drunk deep of the wine of her prostitution; every king on the earth has prostituted himself with her, and every merchant grown rich through her debauchery.'

The people of God summoned to flee

4 Another voice spoke from heaven; I heard it say, 'Come out, my people, away from her, so that you do not share in her crimes and have the same plagues to bear. 5 Her sins have reached up to the sky, and God has her crimes in mind: treat her as she has treated others. 6 She must be paid double the amount she exacted. She is to have a doubly strong cup of her own mixture. 7 Every one of her pomps and orgies is to be matched by a torture or an agony. I am enthroned as queen, she thinks; I am no widow and will never know bereavement. 8 For that, in one day, the plagues will fall on her: disease and mourning and famine. She will be burned to the ground. The Lord God who has condemned her is mighty.'

The people of the world mourn for Babylon.

9 'There will be mourning and weeping for her by the kings of the earth who have prosti-

17b Dn 7:24.   17c Dn 10:17.   17d Ezk 16:39.

18a These songs of doom draw on OT threats to a proud city, especially Jr 50–51; Ezk 26–28; Is 47.

18b = 14:8.

tuted themselves with her and held orgies with her. They see the smoke as she burns, ¹⁰while they keep at a safe distance through fear of her anguish. They will say:

Mourn, mourn for this great city,
Babylon, so powerful a city,
in one short hour your doom has come
    upon you.

¹¹'There will be weeping and distress over her among all the traders of the earth when no one is left to buy their cargoes of goods; ¹²their stocks of gold and silver, jewels and pearls, linen and purple and silks and scarlet; all the sandalwood, every piece in ivory or fine wood, in bronze or iron or marble; ¹³the cinnamon and spices, the myrrh and ointment and incense; wine, oil, flour and corn; their stocks of cattle, sheep, horses and chariots, their slaves and their human cargo.

¹⁴'All the fruits you had set your hearts on have failed you; gone for ever, never to return again, is your life of magnificence and ease.

¹⁵'The traders who had made a fortune out of her will be standing at a safe distance through fear of her anguish, mourning and weeping. ¹⁶They will be saying:

Mourn, mourn for this great city;
for all the linen and purple and scarlet that
    you wore,
for all your finery of gold and jewels and
    pearls;
¹⁷your huge riches are all destroyed within a
    single hour.'

All the captains and seafaring men, sailors and all those who make a living from the sea kept a safe distance, ¹⁸watching the smoke as she burned, and crying out, 'Has there ever been a city as great as this!' ¹⁹They threw dust on their heads and said, with tears and groans:

'Mourn, mourn for this great city
whose lavish living has made a fortune
for every owner of a sea-going ship,
ruined within a single hour.

²⁰'Now heaven, celebrate her downfall, and all you saints, apostles and prophets: God has given judgement for you against her.'

²¹Then a powerful angel picked up a boulder like a great millstone, and as he hurled it into the sea, he said, 'That is how the great city of Babylon is going to be hurled down, never to be seen again.

²²Never again in you
will be heard the song of harpists and
    minstrels,
the music of flute and trumpet;
never again will craftsmen of every skill be
    found in you
or *the sound of the handmill*ᶜ be heard;
²³never again will shine *the light of the lamp*
    in you,
never again will be heard in you
the voices of bridegroom and bride.
Your traders were the princes of the earth,
all the nations were led astray by your
    sorcery.

²⁴In her was found the blood of prophets and saints, and all the blood that was ever shed on earth.'

Songs of victory in heaven

19 After this I heard what seemed to be the great sound of a huge crowd in heaven, singing, 'Alleluia! Salvation and glory and power to our God! ²He judges fairly, he punishes justly, and he has condemned the great prostitute who corrupted the earth with her prostitution; he has avenged the blood of his servants which she shed.' ³And again they sang, 'Alleluia! *The smoke* of her *will rise for ever and ever.*'ᵃ ⁴Then the twenty-four elders and the four living creatures threw themselves down and worshipped God seated on his throne, and they cried, 'Amen, Alleluia.'

⁵Then a voice came from the throne; it said, 'Praise our God, you servants of his and *those*

18c Jr 25:10, followed by Jr 7:34; Is 23:8.
19a Is 34:10.

200 READ REVELATION 19:1–10.

His bride is ready, and she has been able to dress herself in dazzling white linen, because her linen is made of the good deeds of the saints.—REVELATION 19:8

LONGING FOR GOD

With longing I gave into the starlit sky,
Into the sapphire of fathomless firmaments.
There the pure heart leaps out to find You, O God,
And yearns to be freed of the bonds of the flesh.

With great longing, I gaze upon you, my homeland,
When will this, my exile, come to an end?
O Jesus, such is the call of Your bride
Who suffers agony in her thirst for You.

With longing, I gaze at the footprints of the saints
Who crossed this wilderness on their way to the fatherland.
They left me the example of their virtue and their counsels,
And they say to me, "Patience, Sister, soon the fetters will break."

But my longing soul hears not these words.
Ardently it yearns for its Lord and its God,
And it understands not human language,
Because it is enamored of him alone.

My longing soul, wounded with love,
Forces its way through all created things
And unites itself with infinite eternity,
With the Lord whom my heart has espoused.

Allow my longing soul, O God,
To be drowned in Your Divine Three-fold Essence.
Fulfill my desires, for which I humbly beg You,
With a heart brimming with love's fire.

ST. FAUSTINA, 1905–1938

who fear him, small and great alike.'[b] 6 And I heard what seemed to be the voices of a huge crowd, like the sound of the ocean or the great roar of thunder, answering, 'Alleluia! The reign of the Lord our God Almighty has begun; 7 let us be glad and joyful and give glory to God, because this is the time for the marriage of the Lamb. 8 His bride is ready, and

19b Ps 115:13.

she has been able to dress herself in dazzling white linen, because her linen is made of the good deeds of the saints.' ⁹The angel said, 'Write this, "Blessed are those who are invited to the wedding feast of the Lamb," ' and he added, 'These words of God are true.' ¹⁰Then I knelt at his feet to worship him, but he said to me, 'Never do that: I am your fellow-servant and the fellow-servant of all your brothers who have in themselves the witness of Jesus. God alone you must worship.' The witness of Jesus is the spirit of prophecy.

The first eschatological battle^c

¹¹And now I saw heaven open, and a white horse appear; its rider was called Trustworthy and True; *in uprightness he judges* and makes war. ¹²His eyes were flames of fire, and he was crowned with many coronets; the name written on him was known only to himself, ¹³*his cloak was soaked in blood.* He is known by the name, The Word of God. ¹⁴Behind him, dressed in linen of dazzling white, rode the armies of heaven on white horses. ¹⁵From his mouth came a sharp sword with which to strike the unbelievers; he is the one *who will rule them with an iron sceptre,* and tread out the wine of Almighty God's fierce retribution. ¹⁶On his cloak and on his thigh a name was written: *King of kings* and *Lord of lords.*

¹⁷I saw an angel standing in the sun, and he shouted aloud to all the birds that were flying high overhead in the sky, 'Come here. *Gather together at* God's *great feast.* ¹⁸*You will eat the flesh of kings,* and the flesh of great generals and heroes, the flesh of horses and their riders and of all kinds of people, citizens and slaves, small and great alike.'

¹⁹Then I saw the beast, with all the kings of the earth and their armies, gathered together to fight the Rider and his army. ²⁰But the beast was taken prisoner, together with the false prophet who had worked miracles on the beast's behalf and by them had deceived those who had accepted branding with the mark of the beast and those who had worshipped his statue. These two were hurled alive into the fiery lake of burning sulphur. ²¹All the rest were killed by the sword of the Rider, which came out of his mouth, and *all the birds glutted themselves with their flesh.*

The reign of a thousand years

20 Then I saw an angel come down from heaven with the key of the Abyss in his hand and an enormous chain. ²He overpowered the dragon, that primeval serpent which is the devil and Satan, and chained him up for a thousand years. ³He hurled him into the Abyss and shut the entrance and sealed it over him, to make sure he would not lead the nations astray again until the thousand years had passed. At the end of that time he must be released, but only for a short while.

⁴Then I saw thrones, where they took their seats, and *on them was conferred the power to give judgement.*^a I saw the souls of all who had been beheaded for having witnessed for Jesus and for having preached God's word, and those who refused to worship the beast or his statue and would not accept the brand-mark on their foreheads or hands; they came to life, and reigned with Christ for a thousand years.^b ⁵The rest of the dead did not come to life until the thousand years were over; this is the first resurrection. ⁶Blessed and holy are those who share in the first resurrection; the second death has no power over them but they will be priests of God and of Christ and reign with him for a thousand years.

⁷When the thousand years are over,^c Satan will be released from his prison ⁸and will come out to lead astray all the nations in the four quarters of the earth, *Gog and Magog,*^d and mobilise them for war, his armies being as many as the sands of the sea. ⁹They came swarming over the entire country and be-

19c = 20:7–10. The OT allusions show this avenger to be the Messiah: Is 11:4; 63:1; Ps 2:9; Ezk 39:17, 20.

20a Dn 7:22.

20b The time of the Church after the end of the persecution, not a reign of a returned Christ.

20c = 19:11–21.   20d Ezk 38:2.

sieged the camp of the saints, which is the beloved City. *But fire rained down on them from heaven*[e] and consumed them. [10] Then the devil, who led them astray, was hurled into the lake of fire and sulphur, where the beast and the false prophet are, and their torture will not come to an end, day or night, for ever and ever.

The Last Judgement

[11] Then I saw a great white throne and the One who was sitting on it. In his presence, earth and sky vanished, leaving no trace. [12] I saw the dead, great and small alike, standing in front of his throne while *the books lay open.*[f] And another book was opened, which is the book of life, and the dead were judged from what was written in the books, as their deeds deserved.

[13] The sea gave up all the dead who were in it; [14] Death and Hades were emptied of the dead that were in them; and every one was judged as his deeds deserved. Then Death and Hades were hurled into the burning lake. This burning lake is the second death; [15] and anybody whose name could not be found written in the book of life was hurled into the burning lake.

The heavenly Jerusalem

21 Then I saw *a new heaven and a new earth;*[a] the first heaven and the first earth had disappeared now, and there was no longer any sea. [2] I saw the holy city, the new Jerusalem, coming down out of heaven from God, prepared as a bride dressed for her husband. [3] Then I heard a loud voice call from the throne, 'Look, here God lives among human beings. He will make *his home among them; they will be his people,*[b] and he will be their God, *God-with-them.* [4] *He will wipe* away all *tears from their eyes;*[c] there will be no more death, and no more mourning or sadness or pain. The world of the past has gone.'

[5] Then the One sitting on the throne spoke. 'Look, I am making the whole of creation new. Write this, "What I am saying is trust-

worthy and will come true." ' [6] Then he said to me, 'It has already happened. I am the Alpha and the Omega, the Beginning and the End. I will give water from the well of life free to anybody who is thirsty; [7] anyone who proves victorious will inherit these things; and *I will be his* God and *he will be my son.*[d] [8] But the legacy for cowards, for those who break their word, or worship obscenities, for murderers and the sexually immoral, and for sorcerers, worshippers of false gods or any other sort of liars, is the second death in the burning lake of sulphur.'

The messianic Jerusalem

[9] One of the seven angels that had the seven bowls full of the seven final plagues came to speak to me and said, 'Come here and I will show you the bride that the Lamb has married.' [10] *In the spirit, he carried me to the top of a very high mountain,*[e] and showed me Jerusalem, the holy city, coming down out of heaven from God. [11] It had *all the glory of God*[f] and glittered like some precious jewel of crystal-clear diamond. [12] Its wall was of a great height and had twelve gates; at each of the twelve gates there was an angel, and over the gates were written the names *of the twelve tribes of Israel;* [13] *on the east there were three gates, on the north three gates, on the south three gates, and on the west three gates.*[g] [14] The city walls stood on twelve foundation stones, each one of which bore the name of one of the twelve apostles of the Lamb.

[15] The angel that was speaking to me was carrying a gold measuring rod to measure the city and its gates and wall. [16] The plan of the city is perfectly square, its length the same as its breadth. He measured the city with his rod and it was twelve thousand furlongs, equal in

20e Ezk 38:22.

20f Dn 7:10. A register of human deeds and a list of the pre-destined.

21a Is 65:17.   21b Ezk 37:27.   21c Is 8:8; 25:8.
21d 2 S 7:14.   21e Ezk 40:2.
21f Is 60:1–2.   21g Ezk 48:31–35.

length and in breadth, and equal in height. [17]He measured its wall, and this was a hundred and forty-four cubits high—by human measurements. [18]The wall was built of diamond, and the city of pure gold, like clear glass. [19]The foundations of the city wall were faced with all kinds of precious stone: the first with diamond, the second lapis lazuli, the third turquoise, the fourth crystal, [20]the fifth agate, the sixth ruby, the seventh gold quartz, the eighth malachite, the ninth topaz, the tenth emerald, the eleventh sapphire and the twelfth amethyst. [21]The twelve gates were twelve pearls, each gate being made of a single pearl, and the main street of the city was pure gold, transparent as glass. [22]I could not see any temple in the city since the Lord God Almighty and the Lamb were themselves the temple, [23]and the city did not need the sun or the moon for light, since it was lit by the radiant glory of God, and the Lamb was a lighted torch for it. [24]*The nations will come to its light*[h] and the kings of the earth will bring it their treasures. [25]Its *gates will never be closed by day*—and there will be no night there— [26]and *the nations will come, bringing their treasure* and their wealth. [27]Nothing unclean may come into it: no one who does what is loathsome or false, but only those who are listed in the Lamb's book of life.

22 Then the angel showed me the river of life, rising from the throne of God and of the Lamb and flowing crystal-clear. [2]Down the middle of the city street, *on either bank of the river were the trees of life, which bear twelve crops of fruit in a year, one in each month, and the leaves of which are the cure for the nations.*[a]

[3]*The curse of destruction will be abolished.*[b] The throne of God and of the Lamb will be in the city; his servants will worship him, [4]they will see him face to face, and his name will be written on their foreheads. [5]And night will be abolished; they will not need lamplight or sunlight, because the Lord God will be shining on them. They will reign for ever and ever.

[6]The angel said to me, 'All that you have written is sure and will come true: the Lord God who inspires the prophets has sent his angel to reveal to his servants *what is soon to take place.* [7]I am coming soon!' Blessed are those who keep the prophetic message of this book.

[8]I, John, am the one who heard and saw these things. When I had heard and seen them all, I knelt at the feet of the angel who had shown them to me, to worship him; [9]but he said, 'Do no such thing: I am your fellow-servant and the fellow-servant of your brothers the prophets and those who keep the message of this book. God alone you must worship.'

[10]This, too, he said to me, 'Do not keep the prophecies in this book a secret, because the Time is close. [11]Meanwhile let the sinner continue sinning, and the unclean continue to be unclean; let the upright continue in his uprightness, and those who are holy continue to be holy. [12]*Look, I am coming* soon, and my *reward is with* me, *to repay everyone as their deeds deserve.*[c] [13]I am the Alpha and the Omega, *the First and the Last,* the Beginning and the End. [14]Blessed are those who will have washed their robes clean, so that they will have the right to feed on the tree of life and can come through the gates into the city. [15]Others must stay outside: dogs, fortune-tellers, and the sexually immoral, murderers, idolaters, and everyone of false speech and false life.'

Epilogue

[16]I, Jesus, have sent my angel to attest these things to you for the sake of the churches. I am the sprig from the root of David and the bright star of the morning.

[17]The Spirit and the Bride say, 'Come!' Let everyone who listens answer, 'Come!' Then *let all who are thirsty come:*[d] all who want it may *have the water* of life, and have it *free.*

[18]This is my solemn attestation to all who hear the prophecies in this book: if anyone adds anything to them, God will add to him

---

21h Is 60:3.   22a Ezk 47:12.   22b Zc 14:11.
22c Ps 62:12.   22d Is 55:1.

every plague mentioned in the book; 19 if anyone cuts anything out of the prophecies in this
book, God will cut off his share of the tree of
life and of the holy city, which are described in
the book.

20 The one who attests these things says: I
am indeed coming soon.

Amen; come, Lord Jesus.

21 May the grace of the Lord Jesus be with
you all. Amen.

ABOUT THE SAINTS

INDEXES OF SELECTIONS

SOURCES

Biographical Sketches of the Saints
and Index of Their Readings

In brackets at the end of each saint's life sketch, you will find the chapters at which his or her selections appear.

St. Aelred of Rievaulx, born in 1110 at Hexham, England, and died in 1167 at Rievaulx in Yorkshire, England. From 1147 to 1167 Aelred governed 150 choir monks and 500 lay brothers at the Cistercian abbey at Rievaulx. Although constantly suffering from kidney stones, he visited many other abbeys, extending his gentle influence throughout western monasticism. Encouraged by St. Bernard of Clairvaux, he wrote numerous books, including *The Mirror of Charity* and *On Spiritual Friendship*. Feast: January 12. [Ruth 2; Ecclesiasticus 6; Luke 2:41.]

St. Albert the Great, born in 1206 at Lauingen, Swabia, Germany, and died in 1280 at Cologne. St. Albert became a Dominican friar at age sixteen, and after completing his schooling, he taught for twenty years at various German universities and in Paris. He is regarded as a founder of medieval scholastic philosophy, but he also wrote extensively about natural science. From 1254 to 1262 Albert held various church offices, serving as a Dominican provincial, theologian to the pope, and bishop of Regensberg. He spent the autumn of his life teaching at Cologne. In 1277 he went to Paris to defend the work of his student, Thomas Aquinas, who had died in 1275, but he was not able to prevent his friend's condemnation. Albert seems to have succumbed to Alzheimer's disease in 1278 and died two years later. Feast: November 15. [Philippians 3.]

St. Alipius, born around 360 at Tagaste, North Africa, and died there in 430. His biographical sketch appears in Saints on Scripture 17, following page 1180.

Bl. Alphonsus de Orozco, born in 1500 at Oropesa, Avila, Spain, and died at Madrid in 1591. A mystic and spiritual writer sometimes compared to Teresa of Avila, Bl. Alphonsus wrote extensively on prayer and the Christian life. Although he preferred a life of solitude, his gifts required him to serve both his religious community and the state. After 1538 he led four Augustinian houses as prior, and in 1554 he assumed responsibility for the community in Valladolid, where King Philip II noticed him. In 1556 the king took him to Madrid as court chaplain, where for thirty-five years people flocked to his sermons and queued up at his confessional. Feast: September 19. [Saints on Scripture 2, following page 364.]

St. Alphonsus Liguori, born near Naples, Italy, in 1696, and died at Nocera, Italy, in 1787. In 1732 Alphonsus Liguori founded the Redemptorists, to do parish mission work. For thirteen years after 1752 he served as the reforming bishop of Sant' Agata dei Goti. He preached hundreds of sermons, wrote extensively on theological, moral, and ascetical topics and is best known for his *Moral Theology*. Feast: August 1. [Wisdom 11–12.]

St. Ambrose, born at Trier, Germany around 339 and died at Milan in 397. In 374, while Ambrose was a Roman governor in north Italy and only a catechumen, the church of Milan acclaimed him bishop. After his ordination, he immersed himself in Scripture and the fathers, soon becoming the most eloquent preacher of his day and the most formidable opponent of the Arian heresy in the West. His leadership and writing significantly contributed to the rise of Christianity in western Europe. Feast: December 7. [Genesis 45; Exodus 15; 2 Samuel 12; 2 Kings 6; Job 21; Micah 7; Luke 5; Saints on Scripture 15, following page 1180.]

St. Angela Merici, born at Desenzano, Lombardy around 1470, and died at Brescia in 1540. A leader of the Catholic Reformation in north Italy, St. Angela Merici established groups of dedicated single women that she organized into the Ursulines after 1535. The Ursulines consecrated themselves to God, but they lived at home with their families and looked for ways to serve their neighbors. St. Angela gave the Ursulines a military structure, dividing towns into districts governed by mature Christian women. This design allowed the community to support members in daily Christian living and protect them from spiritually unhealthy influences. Over the years, the Ursulines have flourished as the oldest and one of the most respected of the church's teaching orders. Feast: January 27. [1 Thessalonians 5.]

Bl. Angela of Foligno, born about 1248 at Foligno, Italy, and died there in 1309. In 1285 Angela turned from a life of sensuality and luxury to embrace a life of gospel simplicity and repentance. Her mother, husband, and sons died of a plague in 1288, freeing Angela to concentrate on her pursuit of holiness. She modeled herself after St. Francis of Assisi and joined the Franciscan Third Order in 1291. Angela of Foligno was a visionary who at the drop of a hat might fall into a trance. From 1292 to 1296 she dictated her revelations to Brother Arnold, her confessor. Angela recorded thirty steps of her tortured spiritual journey, which always seemed to blend awareness and absence of God, certitude and doubt, and joy and agony. Feast: February 28. [Psalm 63; Matthew 11; Mark 14:32; 2 Corinthians 12.]

St. Anthony Mary Claret, born at Sallent, Spain, in 1807, and died at Rome in 1870. As a young priest St. Anthony spent the dozen years from 1837 to 1849 preaching missions and retreats in Catalonia and the Canary Islands. Then he founded a community dedicated to conducting missions, now called the Claretians. He served as the reforming bishop of Santiago, Cuba, from 1850 to 1857. He returned to Spain in 1858 as confessor to Queen Isabella II. For the rest of his life at court he invested himself in directing the evangelistic activities of his community. He also founded a scientific laboratory, music and language schools, and a museum. Feast: October 24. [Jonah 3.]

St. Anthony of Egypt, born in 251 near Memphis, Egypt, and died at Mount Kolzim in 356. At age twenty Anthony made a radical response to God's call to him, which he heard in the proclamation of the gospel at Mass. He divested himself of all of his property and went to live as a hermit outside of Memphis. Then he went into the desert to live a solitary life, becoming one of the first monks. At fifty-five he founded a community of monks, who lived as hermits, but who came together for worship and teaching. He maintained contact with the church in Alexandria, visiting the city on occasion to use his influence against heretics. St. Athanasius wrote his biography, which communicated the ideals of Egyptian monasticism to the West. Feast: January 17. [Saints on Scripture 17, following page 1180.]

St. Aphraates of Persia, born in Syria on the Persian border, date unknown, and died around 345. After his conversion to Christ, St. Aphraates became a hermit in Edessa, Mesopotamia. He dwelt in a cell outside the city, giving himself over to penance, fasting, and contemplation. Later he moved to a hut at a monastery near Antioch, and there he gradually began to interrupt his solitude to counsel visitors and to give public support to the opponents of Arianism. Many historians believe this saint is the Aphraates who wrote the twenty-three *Demonstrations* that are the earliest documents of the Syrian church. Feast: April 7. [Jeremiah 4.]

St. Athanasius, born around 297 at Alexandria, Egypt, and died there in 373. As bishop of Alexandria, Athanasius cared for the churches of Egypt and Ethiopia and for the burgeoning monastic communities in the North African desert. His main work was his defense of Christianity against the Arian heresy, which denied Christ's divinity. He led the Council of Nicea in 325 that condemned the heresy and built the orthodox party that ultimately conquered it by the end of the fourth century. Feast: May 2. [Numbers 24; Jeremiah 33; Matthew 4; 1 Corinthians 15.]

St. Augustine, born in 354 at Tagaste in North Africa, and died at Hippo in 430. After his conversion in 386 at Milan, Italy, Augustine returned to Africa where he was ordained a priest at Hippo in 391 and became bishop in 396. Augustine led the North African church for four decades. He built monastic communities and marshaled the church's defense against numerous heresies. His apologetical books written in the midst of these controversies laid a foundation for Christian philosophy and theology through the middle ages, the Reformation, and down to the present. Feast: August 28. [Leviticus 26; 1 Samuel 26; Wisdom 3; Ecclesiasticus 10; Mark 3; Luke 6; Luke 7; Saints on Scripture 7, 13, and 17, following pages 364, 1180.]

St. Basil, born in 329 at Caesarea, Cappadocia, Asia Minor, and died there in 379. Influenced by his sister, St. Macrina, St. Basil abandoned a promising secular career to follow Christ. He established a monastic community on his family estate in Pontus. He gave his brothers a communitarian *Rule* that helped shape monasticism throughout the entire church. As the gritty bishop of Caesarea, Basil successfully resisted the attempts of the emperor to control the state. With his close friend, St. Gregory Nazianzen, Basil also actively opposed Arianism. His treatise *On the Holy Spirit* has become recognized as a classic work of Catholic theology. Feast: January 2. [Matthew 12; John 4; Ephesians 4; Colossians 2.]

St. Bede, the Venerable, born in 673 near Sunderland, England, and died at Jarrow in 735. For his education his family entrusted seven-year-old Bede to St. Benedict Biscop at Wearmouth Abbey. Then he was placed under the tutelage of Ceolfrith at Jarrow, where he spent the rest of his life as a monk. Bede lived a routine and uneventful life. His long years in the monastery unfolded daily at praying the hours in church and studying Scripture in his cell. However, without leaving his cell, Bede exerted a wide, missionary influence. His teaching equipped Anglo-Saxon monks and nuns to carry the Christian faith to the people of England and Germany. Today we still read with profit his Bible commentaries, but we value even more his *History of the English Church and People.* Feast: May 25. [Romans 14; Saints on Scripture 3 and 6, following page 364.]

St. Bernard of Clairvaux, born around 1090 at Fontaines de Dijon, near Dijon, Burgundy, and died at Clairvaux in 1153. Bernard became a monk at the reformed Benedictine abbey of Cîteaux in 1113. Three

years later the abbot sent him with twelve monks to start a new monastery at Clairvaux in Champagne. Under his leadership Clairvaux founded or reformed sixty-eight monasteries, generating a spiritual renewal throughout western Europe. In 1145 he preached the disastrous Second Crusade, which he said that he had launched for a divine cause and that the sins of the armies had ruined. Feast: August 20. [Job 7; Psalm 116; Proverbs 16; Jeremiah 17; Luke 2; Saints on Scripture 14, following page 1180.]

St. Bernardino of Siena, born in 1380 at Massa Marittima in Siena, Italy, and died at Aquiela, Italy, in 1444. Bernardino became a Franciscan Friar of the Strict Observance in 1403. He spent fourteen unnoticed years in Fiesole, Italy, until the prophecy of a novice sent him to Milan where he found his true vocation as a preacher. Thousands came to hear this entertaining friar who used his personable humor and wisdom to penetrate their souls with truth. For nearly a quarter of a century he crisscrossed Italy on foot, calling people to repentance. Feast: May 20. [Ecclesiasticus 31; Jeremiah 8; John 21.]

St. Bonaventure, born about 1218 at Bagnorea, near Viterbo, Italy, and died at Lyons, France, in 1274. Bonaventure became a Franciscan in 1238. From 1248 to 1257 he taught Scripture and theology at the Franciscan school in Paris, establishing himself as a leading scholastic theologian. After 1257 Bonaventure served as Master General of the Franciscans. He reorganized the community and defended it against the ongoing opposition of the secular clergy. He became cardinal archbishop of Albano in 1273. A year later he died during the Council of Lyons, where he had led an unsuccessful effort to reunite the churches of the West and East. Feast: July 15. [Wisdom 7–8; Zechariah 12; Saints on Scripture 3, following page 364.]

St. Bridget of Sweden, born in 1303 in the province of Upland, Sweden, and died at Rome in 1373. Bridget lived as a married woman for twenty-eight years and bore eight children. After her husband died in 1344 she founded a monastery for women and men at Vadstena, Sweden, that evolved into the religious order now called the Brigettines. At a time when the church suffered from confusion and moral decay, Bridget used her gift of prophetic preaching to call laity and clergy alike to repentance. For two decades after 1350, she unsuccessfully campaigned with three popes to return from their refuge in Avignon to Rome. Feast: July 23. [Ecclesiasticus 18.]

St. Caesarius of Arles, born in 470 at Châlons in Burgundy, and died at Arles in France in 543. As bishop of Arles for forty years after 503, St. Caesarius called his people to a high standard of Christian living. He adapted the Liturgy of the Hours for laypeople and had them celebrated publicly every day so that their worship might flow into their daily lives. Perhaps the first popular preacher in the western church, Caesarius frequently addressed the local church, admirably never speaking longer than fifteen minutes. He had his sermons copied and disseminated widely throughout Western Europe, possibly making him one of the earliest Christian publishers and best-selling authors. Feast: August 27. [Deuteronomy 15; Deuteronomy 30.]

St. Camillus de Lellis, born in 1550 at Bocchianico, Italy, and died at Rome in 1614. After his conversion to Christ and deliverance from an addiction to gambling, Camillus became a Capuchin novice. However, he could not become professed because of a chronically diseased leg, so he devoted himself to caring for the sick. Encouraged by St. Philip Neri, Camillus founded the Ministers of the Sick, an order of men who served the sick in hospitals throughout Italy. In 1591 and 1607, Camillus and his brothers cared for wounded soldiers in Croatia and Hungary, the first recorded field medical unit. Feast: July 14. [Saints on Scripture 10, following page 364.]

St. Catherine of Siena, born in 1347 at Siena, Italy, and died at Rome in 1380. St. Catherine was a member of the Dominican Third Order, a lay person and not a nun. She gathered a family of disciples who lived in poverty and served the material and spiritual needs of the people of Siena. She evangelized many people including hardened criminals. God spoke to Catherine when she was rapt in prayer, and secretaries recorded *The Dialogue* that she dictated while in a state of ecstasy. During the Avignon Papacy and scandalous Great Western Schism, Catherine advised the pope at

Rome. The divided condition of the church grieved her enormously and she offered her final suffering as a sacrifice for its renewal. Feast: April 29. [John 14; Romans 13.]

St. Clare of Assisi, born in 1193 at Assisi, Italy, and died there in 1253. St.Francis invited Clare to lead a community of women who would live like his friars. On Palm Sunday, 1212, Clare met him and his brothers at a chapel where she committed herself to live by the gospel in poverty and chastity. Francis gave Clare a house near the church of San Damiano outside the walls of Assisi. There she and her sisters happily followed a severe pattern of life. The women wore rough habits, went barefoot, fasted often, slept on the floor, abstained from meat entirely, and spoke only when necessary. Within a few years, convents of Clare's followers popped up in Italy, France, and Bohemia. Clare seems to have had a gift of healing which blessed her sisters and neighbors, but she herself was ill for twenty-seven years before she died in 1253. Feast: August 11. [Saints on Scripture 8 and 12, following pages 364, 1180.]

St. Clement of Rome, birth date and place unknown, died around 100, probably at Rome. We know only a little for sure about St. Clement. Clement probably associated directly with the apostles. St. Irenaeus placed him with the apostles as a student of their teachings, and Origen called him "a disciple of the apostles." No doubt he succeeded St. Peter as his third successor. And Clement was possibly the co-worker St. Paul mentioned to the Philippians (Ph 4:3). He wrote an important letter to the Christians at Corinth that the early church esteemed so highly that it was sometimes regarded as Scripture. Feast: November 23. [Isaiah 1; Joshua 2.]

St. Columban, born at West Leinster, Ireland, around 542, and died in 615 at the monastery of Bobbio near Milan, Italy. After a quiet life in the Irish monastery of Bangor, in 590 Columban and twelve companions went as missionaries to Gaul, now modern France. He established several monasteries in Europe that became centers of evangelization and learning, most notably the monastery of Bobbio in northern Italy. Feast: November 23. [Genesis 1–2; Ephesians 5; Colossians 3.]

St. Cyprian of Carthage, born at Carthage in North Africa around 200, and was beheaded there during the persecution of Emperor Valerian in 258. A prominent pagan lawyer, Cyprian converted to Christ in 245 and transferred his skills to study of Scripture and the fathers of the church. He became bishop of Carthage in 248 during an age of intense persecution. His numerous treatises on Scripture, the church, the sacraments, and Christian service have won him recognition as a pioneer of Christian Latin literature. Feast: September 16. [Tobit 12; Ecclesiasticus 3–4; Daniel 3; Joel 2; John 1.]

St. Cyril of Alexandria, born in 376 at Alexandria, Egypt, and died there in 444. As the patriarch of Alexandria from 412 to 444, St. Cyril focused on caring for his church and on defending the faith against Nestorianism, which denied the humanity of Christ. In 431 he presided at the Council of Ephesus that condemned the teaching of Nestorius, then the patriarch of Constantinople, and excommunicated him. Some historians praise Cyril for his unbending orthodoxy and flinty leadership. Others criticize him for his inflexibility and intransigence. Feast: June 27. [Mark 4; Luke 8; John 2.]

St. Cyril of Jerusalem, born around 315, probably at Jerusalem, and died there in 386. St. Cyril served as bishop of Jerusalem in the heyday of the Arian heresy, which denied the divinity of Christ. Exiled three times by Arian opponents, Cyril spent sixteen of his thirty-seven years as bishop away from his see. But in 381 he participated at the Council of Constantinople that pulled down the final curtain on Arianism. Chief among St. Cyril's surviving writings are his twenty-four *Catechetical Lectures,* nineteen of which prepared catechumens for baptism and the rest instructed the newly baptized in basic Christian living. Feast: March 18. [Genesis 4; Isaiah 53; Malachi 3; Luke 23.]

St. Dominic, born in 1170 at Calaruega, Spain, and died at Bologna, Italy, in 1221. In 1204 St. Dominic accompanied his bishop on a mission to evangelize the Albigensians in Languedoc in Southern France. There he used his gift of preaching to convert some of these heretics, who taught a dualism between good and evil. He also decided that the best way to combat the Albigensians was to develop communities of men and women who devoted themselves to living the Christian ideal. So in 1206 he founded a community of women dedicated to educating and evangelizing young women. And he gathered about himself a group of men that he formed into a new religious order. By 1216 the church recognized Dominic's Friars Preachers and by his death in 1221 he had sixty friaries dispersed throughout Europe. Feast: August 8. [Saints on Scripture 20, following page 1180.]

St. Dorotheos of Gaza lived in the sixth century. A disciple of the great desert father Barsanuphios, Dorotheos founded a monastery near Gaza in Palestine around 540. He wrote a series of instructions on the ascetic life for his followers. He taught that humility was the highest of the virtues, even ranking it above love. His instructions are an important source for the teachings of earlier ascetical writers on whose works he frequently drew. [Romans 8; James 1.]

St. Edith Stein, born in 1891 at Breslau, Germany, and died at Auschwitz in 1942. In 1916 Edith Stein completed a Ph.D. in philosophy at Freiburg University and became an assistant to the renowned philosopher, Edmund Husserl. A secularized Jew from her youth, Edith became a convert in 1921 after reading Teresa of Avila's *Autobiography.* She entered the Carmelite community at Cologne in 1932, taking the name Sister Teresa Benedicta of the Cross. In 1938 the Nazi threat compelled Edith to seek refuge at the Carmelite convent in Echt, Holland. But when the Dutch bishops denounced the Nazis in 1942, they retaliated by rounding up Catholics of Jewish descent. They arrested Edith in July, 1942, and she was executed in the gas chambers at Auschwitz a month later. Feast: August 10. [Exodus 12; Leviticus 16; Luke 22; John 17; 1 Timothy 2.]

St. Elizabeth Ann Seton, born in 1774 in New York, and died at Emmitsburg, Maryland, in 1821. Before the death of her husband in 1803, Elizabeth Ann Seton had been married nine years and bore five children. She became a Catholic in 1805 and three years later opened a school for girls in Baltimore, Maryland. A group of like-minded women joined her, and in 1809 they formed a religious community at Emmitsburg that became the Sisters of Charity. St. Elizabeth and her sisters set up schools and orphanages along the East Coast. They are credited with launching the parochial school system, which became a mainstay of Catholicism in the United States. Feast: January 4. [Psalm 139.]

Elizabeth Leseur, born in 1866, and died in 1914 at Paris. Elizabeth experienced a spiritual awakening in 1899 when her husband Felix, a doctor and an atheist, persuaded her to read Renan's *Life of Jesus.* From that time she kept a *Journal* in which she recorded her progress in making her life a purer and better instrument for serving God and others. Sick all her life with hepatitis, Elizabeth's condition worsened after 1908. And in 1911 she was diagnosed with cancer. She calmly accepted the disease's intense pain and understood it as a form of prayer. After her death her husband was profoundly touched by discovering that she had offered her suffering for him. He became a Dominican priest and spread Elizabeth's spiritual message in his preaching. The Congregation for the Causes of Saints has initiated the process of considering her for canonization. Feast: May 3. [2 Timothy 2.]

St. Ephrem, born about the year 306 in Nisibia in Mesopotamia, and died around 373 at Edessa, Syria. For a quarter of a century after 325, Ephrem headed up a theological school at Nisidis, Syria. In 350 he fled a Persian invasion and moved to a cave in Edessa where he lived the rest of his life. Ephrem was a prolific writer of apologetics, theology, and commentaries on Scripture, for which he has been recognized as a doctor of the church. He also wrote many beautiful hymns, and is credited with the extensive introduction of hymns into the church's public worship and their use as tools for Christian teaching. Feast: June 18. [Matthew 25; Luke 21; 1 Corinthians 13; Ephesians 6; Saints on Scripture 4, following page 364.]

St. Faustina, born at Glogowiec, Poland, in 1905, and died in 1938 at Lagiewniki. In 1925, Helena Kowalska entered the Congregation of Sisters of Our Lady of Mercy at Warsaw, Poland. She took the name Faustina and was assigned to domestic service which she performed throughout her life as a nun. In a series of visions, Jesus appeared to Faustina and directed her

to establish a devotion to the Divine Mercy. The saint overcame much resistance to her efforts, but by the time of her canonization in 2000, the devotion had spread throughout the church. Feast: October 5. [Matthew 22; Romans 12; Revelation 19.]

St. Francis de Sales, born at Thorens, Savoy, in 1567, and died at Lyons, France, in 1622. As missionary, bishop, founder, and writer, St. Francis de Sales was a dynamic leader of the Counter Reformation. Ordained in 1593, he spent five years evangelizing the people of Chablais, winning many people to the Catholic Church. He became bishop of Geneva in 1602 and proved himself to be an able pastor, administrator, and educator. He was also the spiritual director for other saints, including St. Jane de Chantal. With her he founded the Order of the Visitation in 1610. Two of his books, *Introduction to the Devout Life* and *Treatise on the Love of God,* have become classics of spiritual reading. Feast: January 24. [Genesis 19; Genesis 28; Ruth 3; Psalm 51; Matthew 7; John 15; Acts 17.]

St. Francis of Assisi, born at Assisi, Italy, in 1181, and died there in 1226. Converted as a young man to a radical obedience of the gospel, Francis embraced poverty and became an itinerant evangelist in central Italy. His charism attracted many disciples that he organized into the Friars Minor. With his friend St. Clare he also founded a religious community for women. In 1224, while on retreat at Mt. Alvernia, Francis received the stigmata, the imprint, and experience in his body of Christ's wounds. His simplicity and faithfulness have caused him to become one of the most popular and honored saints of all time. Feast: October 4. [Ezekiel 3; Matthew 17.]

Bl. Frederic Ozanam, born at Milan, Italy, in 1813, and died at Marseilles, France, in 1853. In the 1830s as a student at the Sorbonne in Paris, Frederic Ozanam defended the Catholic faith against all public attacks. He also began to visit the poor, providing them fuel, food, and clothing out of his own resources. Seven other students joined him, and he organized them into a group that became first conference of the St. Vincent de Paul Society. By 1837 Ozanam's little association had mushroomed into a national movement with 2,000 members. Just before his marriage in 1841, Ozanam was appointed professor of literature at the Sorbonne. With his prestige and through his writing, he exerted considerable influence on French public affairs in the tempestuous 1840s. After 1846 he was constantly ill, and he died in 1853 at the age of forty. Feast: September 8. [1 Kings 17.]

St. Fulgentius of Ruspe, born around 468 at Carthage, and died at Ruspe in North Africa in 533. At age twenty-two, Fulgentius entered a monastery at Carthage. He made Augustine his ideal, and like him, Fulgentius defended the faith against heresy, fostered monastic communities, and became a model bishop. He was appointed bishop of Ruspe in 508. However, an Arian king exiled him and sixty other bishops to Sardinia. There he founded a monastery, became the spokesman for the persecuted bishops, and wrote treatises against Arianism. Upon the king's death in 523, Fulgentius returned to his flock at Ruspe, where he devoted himself to renewing the spiritual life of his people. Feast: January 1. [Matthew 28; Acts 6.]

St. Gertrude the Great, born in 1256, birthplace unknown, and died at Helfta, Saxony, in 1302. At age five, Gertrude came as an orphan to the monastery at Helfta. By age twenty-five, she had taken her vows as a nun and had become a proficient student of Latin literature. Gertrude had a profound conversion at age twenty-six that initiated her life-long career as a mystic and visionary. She left a record of her intimate relationship with the Lord in the book commonly called the *Revelations of St. Gertrude.* Feast: November 16. [Song of Songs 3; Ephesians 2.]

St. Gregory Nazianzen, born around 329 at Nazianzus, Cappadocia (present-day Turkey), and died there in 390. As a young man, Gregory spent two years living as a monk with his friend, St. Basil. Then he spent fifteen years serving as coadjutor bishop of Nazianzus with his father, who was the bishop. In 380 he became the patriarch of Constantinople and in 381 he presided over the Council of Constantinople, which condemned the Arian heresy that denied the divinity of Christ. Feast: January 2. [Genesis 3; 2 Maccabees 7; Proverbs 4; Ezekiel 36; Amos 7.]

St. Gregory of Nyssa, born about 331 at Caesarea, Cappadocia, and died around 395, possibly at Nyssa. In 372, St. Basil appointed his brother Gregory bishop of Nyssa, expecting him to counteract the influence of Arian heretics, who denied the divinity of Christ. But he was unskilled in diplomacy, and Gregory failed to curb the heretics. They trumped up charges against him and drove him into exile until 378. However, in 381 he played a significant role at the Council of Constantinople, which ended the Arian controversy. The church of Gregory's day esteemed him as an apologist, honoring him as "the Father of the Fathers." His major writings include a catechetical discourse, Bible commentaries, and ascetical treatises. Feast: March 9. [Joshua 3; 1 Samuel 17; Ecclesiastes 3; Romans 6.]

St. Gregory the Great, born around 540 in Rome, and died there in 604. After serving as a civic leader in Rome, Gregory launched a significant spiritual career from 574 till his death, first as a monk, then as deacon, papal diplomat, abbot, and finally as pope. As pope he assumed the leadership of Rome, which had been devastated by barbarian invasions, virtually establishing the political power of the medieval papacy. His achievements included a general reform of the church, the promotion of Benedictine monasticism, the conversion of the English to Christianity, and the creation of the "Gregorian" chant. Feast: September 3. [Job 1; Job 12; Ecclesiasticus 1; Mark 7:31; Romans 12; 2 Corinthians 5:11; Saints on Scripture 8, following page 364.]

St. Hilary of Poitiers, born about 315 at Poitiers, France, and died there around 368. A wealthy and gifted pagan rhetorician, St. Hilary reasoned himself to faith in the 350s. Although he was a married man with a daughter, he was acclaimed bishop of Poitiers in 353. Hilary administered his diocese well and emerged as the chief opponent of Arianism in the West. In 356 he was exiled for three years because he refused to sign a document that deposed Athanasius, his counterpart in the East. During that time he wrote *On the Trinity,* his major treatise against the Arian heresy. Feast: January 13. [Wisdom 13; Mark 12.]

St. Hildegard of Bingen, born in 1098 at Bokelheim in present-day West Germany, and died in 1179 at Rupertsburg, near Bingen. From childhood Hildegard lived in a small community of nuns near Speyer, Germany, and became their prioress in 1136. Five years later a divine light illumined her with an understanding of all salvation history. Aided by a monk named Volmar, from 1141 to 1151 Hildegard recorded her visions in a book of twenty-six revelations that she called the *Scivias,* or *Know God's Ways.* In 1147 Hildegard founded a monastery at Rupertsburg, near Bingen. From 1152 to 1162 the abbess preached reform to lax churches and monasteries throughout the Rhineland. Indefatigably creative, Hildegard also wrote liturgical hymns and two books of medicine and natural history. Feast: September 17. [1 John 4.]

St. Hippolytus, birth date and place unknown; died around 235 in exile on the island of Sardinia. A priest at Rome and possibly a disciple of St. Irenaeus, Hippolytus was a major theologian and opponent of heresies in the early church. His most important book was *A Refutation of All Heresies.* He denounced four popes for their leniency in dealing with heresies, even allowing himself to be elected an antipope. During a persecution in 235, Hippolytus was banished to Sardinia with Pope Pontian, who reconciled him to the church. Feast: August 13. [Daniel 2; Daniel 6; 2 Corinthians 5.]

Bl. Humbert of Romans, born around 1200 at Romans, near Valence in France, and died there in 1277. When Humbert became the fifth master-general of St. Dominic's Order of Preachers in 1254, he faced the massive task of consolidating a very diverse community that had spread throughout the world. A lawyer by training and a man marked by kindness, over a period of twenty-five years he accomplished an effective and gracious structural reform of the order. Much of his time was also spent defending the Dominicans from the attacks of jealous secular clergy. Because of his leadership, Humbert is sometimes called the second founder of the Order of Preachers. Feast: July 14. [Saints on Scripture 1, following page 364.]

St. Irenaeus, born around 130, probably at Smyrna in Asia Minor, and died around 200 at Lyons, in present-day France. A disciple of St. Polycarp, Irenaeus is regarded as the first theologian of the early church. Polycarp sent him to Gaul, where he became bishop of Lyons in 178. Irenaeus aggressively opposed the Gnostic heresy that denied Christ's humanity. He refuted Gnosticism in his five-volume treatise *Against All Heresies.* Feast: June 28. [Deuteronomy 6; Malachi 1.]

St. Isidore of Pelusium, born probably at Alexandria, Egypt, and died around 450 at Pelusium. Isidore served as abbot of a monastery near Pelusium, Egypt, and his contemporaries admired him as a model of holiness. An adviser to St. Cyril of Alexandria, he was also a great letter writer. More than 2,000 of his letters survive, containing excellent instruction in the spiritual life. Feast: February 4. [Matthew 13:24.]

St. Jane de Chantal, born in 1572 at Dijon, France, and died at Moulins in 1641. At twenty, Jane Frances Frémyot married Baron Christopher de Chantal and by his death nine years later the happy couple had borne seven children. In 1610, guided by her spiritual director, St. Francis de Sales, she founded the Congregation of the Visitation. The two saints designed the community for women who wanted to live a dedicated Christian life, but who were unable to undertake the extreme austerities that typified religious orders of the day. Feast: December 12. [Psalm 22; Matthew 6; Luke 11; John 3; John 13; Galatians 2; Galatians 5.]

St. Jerome, born around 341 at Strido, Dalmatia, and died in 420 at Bethlehem. He was baptized at Rome in 360, and for more than a decade lived as a monk and scholar. Jerome experienced a profound conversion in 374 and then spent five years of solitude in the desert. Afterwards Jerome undertook biblical studies with St. Gregory Nazianzen at Constantinople. Then over several decades he translated afresh most of the Old Testament and corrected the text of the New Testament. His edition of Scripture, called the Vulgate, for fifteen centuries was the benchmark translation of the Bible in the western church. In 385 he moved from Rome to Bethlehem, where he established a monastery and a hospice for pilgrims to the Holy Land. Feast: September 30. [Matthew 8; Matthew 18; Saints on Scripture 4, 15 and 20, following pages 364, 1180.]

St. Joan Delanoue, born in Samur, Anjou, France, in 1666, and died at Fencet in 1736. Prompted by a vision and a word from a prophetess, Joan closed her family's religious goods store and devoted herself to caring for the poor, the sick, and the abandoned. In 1704 she founded the Sisters of St. Anne of Providence of Samur. Feast: August 17. [Saints on Scripture 10, following page 364.]

St. John Baptist de La Salle, born in 1651 at Reims in northern France, and died in 1719 at St. Yon, in Rouen. John Baptist de La Salle was a Christian educational reformer—a pioneer in education for the working classes, in the training of teachers, and in the rehabilitation of delinquents. In the 1680s he opened four schools and training colleges for teachers at Reims, Paris, and Saint-Denis. From these groups, he drew men into a religious community devoted to education, the Brothers of the Christian Schools. To maintain focus on teaching and to prevent distinctions among the brothers, the saint decided that none would ever become a priest. By the turn of the eighteenth century, over the opposition of secular school masters and Jansenists, the Christian Brothers had established schools throughout France. Feast: April 7. [Mark 16; Luke 9; John 19:1.]

St. John Berchmans, born in 1599 at Brabant, Belgium, and died in 1621 at Rome. As a boy John Berchmans determined to become a priest and a saint. His father, a master shoemaker in Brabant, Belgium, could not afford to send him to school, but instead placed him under the tutelage of a priest at a local abbey. At seventeen, John decided to become a Jesuit, a move his parents resisted. But he overcame their opposition and entered the Jesuit novitiate in 1617. Four years later he graduated from the Roman College and was poised for a great career as a scholar priest. But in the summer of 1621 the young saint was afflicted with a mysterious disease, and he died at the young age of twenty-two. Feast: August 13. [Mark 10.]

St. John Cassian, born about 360 in Romania, and died at Marseilles, France, around 433. Around 380, John Cassian became a monk at Bethlehem. After 385 he wandered the Egyptian desert, where he absorbed the teachings of the desert fathers. Later he founded two monasteries in Marseilles, France, one for men and another for women. To instruct his monks and nuns,

Cassian wrote two significant books, the *Institutes* and the *Conferences,* which presented eastern monasticism's wisdom and pattern of life to the western church. Through their influence Cassian shaped the practice of monasticism in the West through the middle ages and even into the present. Feast: February 29. [Exodus 33; Judges 3; Mark 7; Saints on Scripture 11 and 16, following page 1180.]

St. John Chrysostom, born around 347 at Antioch in Syria, and died in 407 at Pontus in modern-day Turkey. He became a Christian at age twenty, was ordained a priest in 385, and was named patriarch of Constantinople in 397. John came to be nicknamed "the golden mouthed" because of his marvelous preaching gift. Many of his sermons survive, and history regards him as one of the church's greatest preachers, pastors, and expositors of the faith. John's effort to bring moral reform to the imperial court made him many enemies, who conspired to have him exiled. He died of exhaustion in 407, while being marched in bad weather to a remote spot on the Black Sea. Feast: September 13. [1 Kings 21; Ecclesiastes 1; Acts 2; Acts 10; 1 Corinthians 10; Saints on Scripture 2, following page 364.]

St. John Damascene, born about 675 at Damascus, and died at the Mar Saba, near Jerusalem, around 749. In 716 John resigned his post as chief financial officer under the Muslim caliph of Damascus and became a monk at the Mar Saba near Jerusalem. There he wrote three major treatises against Iconoclasm, which denounced the veneration of images, and thus became a chief opponent of that heresy. He also wrote *An Exact Exposition of the Orthodox Faith,* a significant treatise that summed up the teaching of the Greek fathers of the church. Feast: December 4. [Exodus 14; Numbers 20; 1 Kings 18; Ezekiel 37; Matthew 26.]

St. John de Brébeuf, born at Condé-sur-Vire, Normandy, France, in 1593, and died at Ste. Marie, Canada, in 1649. Even though weakened by tuberculosis, Jesuit St. John de Brébeuf joined the Canada mission in 1625. For a quarter of a century with only a four-year interlude, he evangelized the Hurons in Quebec. He lived with them, embraced their customs, mastered their language, and wrote a catechism for them. In 1649 the Iroquois attacked the Huron village where John was living. They brutally martyred him, Gabriel Lalement, his companion, and their converts. Their suffering was indescribable: bludgeoned, burned with red hot hatchets, baptized with boiling water, mutilated, flesh stripped off and eaten, hearts plucked out and devoured. St. John de Brébeuf traded his life for the 7,000 souls he had converted and baptized. Feast: October 19. [2 Corinthians 11.]

St. John Eudes, born in 1601 at Ri, Normandy, France, and died in 1680 at Caen, France. In 1623, St. John entered the French Oratory and spent the next six decades generating spiritual renewal throughout France by his preaching, counsel, and service to the poor and sick. Over the years he presented 110 missions, helping to establish that modern form of parish renewal. Twice he interrupted his preaching to care for plague victims, and he also opened a refuge for reformed prostitutes. John left the Oratory in 1643 to found the Community of Jesus and Mary, an association of secular priests committed to work for the renewal of the priesthood. Toward the end of his life he helped promulgate devotion to the Sacred Heart by providing a doctrinal basis for it. Feast: August 19. [Isaiah 49.]

St. John Gabriel Perboyre, born in 1802 at LePeuch, Cahors, France, and died at Wuchangfu, China, in 1840. St. John Gabriel, a Lazarist priest, was sent as a missionary to China in 1835. Four years later he was arrested during a persecution, and for a year he endured brutal torture because he refused to inform on his associates and to stomp on a crucifix. Finally, in 1840 he was strangled to death. Feast: September 11. [Saints on Scripture 13, following page 1180.]

Ven. John Henry Newman, born in 1801 at London, England, and died at Birmingham in 1890. Newman was raised as an Evangelical in the Anglican Church and in his twenties became a fellow at Oxford. After 1833 he acted as the spiritual leader of the Oxford Movement that advocated a return of the church to the catholic elements of the early Christian centuries. In 1845 Newman became a Roman Catholic. For the next half century he devoted himself to prayer and writing. His books, like *An Essay on the Development of Christian Doctrine* and *A Grammar of Assent,* helped shape modern Catholic theology. In 1879 Pope Leo XIII made him a cardinal. Feast: August 11. [1 Samuel 3.]

St. John Ruysbroeck, born in 1293 at Ruysbroeck near Brussels in present-day Belgium, and died at Groenendael in 1381. St. John Ruysbroeck was a leader of the *Devotio Moderna,* a fourteenth-century renewal movement that brought people to a personal commitment to follow Christ and to a deeper life in the Holy Spirit. Between 1317 and 1343 he devoted himself to prayer and publishing several books on the spiritual life. In 1349, Ruysbroeck co-founded a monastery at Groenendael in present-day Belgium. Under his leadership the monastery became a renewal center for the *Devotio Moderna,* where hundreds came to hear him and obtain his advice. Feast: December 2. [Luke 19; Revelation 3.]

Bl. Julian of Norwich, born around 1342, birthplace unknown, and died around 1423, probably at Norwich, England. We don't know much about this fourteenth-century recluse because she deliberately hid herself. We don't even know her name, so we identify her with the Church of St. Julian in Norwich, where she had attached her hut. In 1373, Julian received sixteen revelations that were mainly concerned with aspects of Christ's passion. She meditated on these for the rest of her life and recorded her reflections in the *Revelations of Divine Love,* which has become a most influential piece of spiritual writing. Feast: May 13. [Hosea 14; Matthew 27; Mark 15; John 19; Hebrews 12.]

St. Justin, born around A.D. 100 at Flavia Neapolis, Italy, and died a martyr at Rome in 165. A Greek philosopher, Justin converted to Christianity around 135. As a Christian layperson, Justin continued to teach philosophy, addressing himself in particular to pagans and Jews. He was convinced that a well-developed presentation of theology would win all thinking persons to Christ. In 150 he moved to Rome where he opened a school of philosophy and wrote many books explaining the reasonableness of Christianity. Justin's aggressive presentation of the faith made many enemies at Rome and ultimately cost him his life. He was beheaded for refusing to worship the Roman gods. Feast: June 1. [Exodus 20; Jeremiah 10; Jeremiah 31.]

St. Katharine Drexel, born at Philadelphia in 1858, and died there in 1955. In 1885 St. Katharine and her sisters inherited the annual income from a 14-million-dollar estate, and she immediately donated thousands of dollars to the church for schools for Native American children, which became her life's passion. In 1891, Katharine founded the Sisters of the Blessed Sacrament to serve Native Americans and African-Americans. By 1904, 104 sisters had joined her. Katharine established 145 Catholic missions and 12 schools for Native Americans and 50 schools for African-Americans. During her lifetime she gave away about twenty million dollars, mostly for these causes. In 1935, Katharine suffered a severe heart attack. Two years later she retired and was able to spend eighteen years of quiet contemplation before her death. Feast: March 3. [Matthew 16; Matthew 19.]

St. Leo the Great, born probably at Rome, date unknown, and died there in 461. As pope from 440 to his death, he exercised his authority more widely than any predecessor, taking a concern, for example, for the church in Africa, France, and Spain. He definitively shaped the papacy by developing the belief that, as the heir of Peter, the bishop of Rome exercised a supreme and universal authority over the church and a primacy over all other bishops. Feast: November 10. [Isaiah 42; Isaiah 60; Mark 11; Philippians 2.]

St. Leonard of Port Maurice, born in 1676 at Port Maurice on the Italian Riviera, and died at Rome in 1751. At age twenty-one Leonard joined a strict branch of Franciscans called the Riformella and quickly became a leader in the community. From his bases in Rome and Florence he preached throughout northern Italy, his words gently turning thousands to God. The churches could not hold the crowds that gathered for Leonard's parish missions. So, like that other great eighteenth-century evangelist, John Wesley, he often held open-air meetings. He used the Stations of the Cross as illustrations in his talks and pop-

ularized the devotion by installing 571 sets of stations throughout Italy. Feast: November 26. [Proverbs 6.]

St. Louis de Montfort, born in 1673 at Montfort, France, and died at Saint-Laurent-sur-Sèvre in 1716. A poor man himself, St. Louis devoted his life to evangelizing the poor in his native Brittany. His unconventional and emotional missions to the poor made many of the upper crust uncomfortable. But the poor loved him. They crowded to hear him preach, watch his mini-dramas, sing his hymns, learn to pray the rosary, and—at his urging—to reform their lives. Today, people still use his book, *True Devotion to the Blessed Virgin* that was popular in his own time. And near the end of his life he organized a few associates who shared his devotion to the virgin into *The Company of Mary.* Feast: April 28. [1 Peter 2.]

St. Lutgarde, born at Tongres, Brabant, in 1186, and died in 1242 at Aywières, Belgium. At twelve, Lutgarde's parents placed her at the convent of St. Catherine's near Liège, Belgium. There she experienced a profound conversion and became a nun. In 1205, Lutgarde was elected prioress of St. Catherine's, a job she abhorred because it interfered with her prayer. So a year later she moved to a French-speaking Cistercian convent at Aywières, near Brussels. Since the saint spoke only Flemish, she figured she had little chance of being chosen for offices in that community. Lutgarde devoted the rest of her life to interceding for Christ's concerns. Feast: June 16. [Saints on Scripture 18, following page 1180.]

St. Mary Magdalen dei Pazzi, born in 1566 at Florence, Italy, and died there in 1607. A strikingly beautiful and wealthy woman, Mary Magdalen gave up everything to become a Carmelite nun in 1584. She became a leader in the convent, holding the offices of novice mistress and subprioress. In her extraordinary spiritual life, the saint experienced ecstasies and visions. At these times, Mary Magdalen sometimes had conversations with Christ and the saints; her sisters recorded her locutions in seven volumes. She suffered severe physical illnesses and spiritual temptations that she regarded as sharing in Christ's suffering. As a sign of her holiness, St. Mary Magdalen's body remains in-corrupt at St. Maria degl'Angeli, Florence. Feast: May 25. [Mark 2; Mark 9.]

St. Mary of the Angels, born in 1661 at Baldinero near Turin, Italy, and died in 1717 at Turin. St. Mary became a Carmelite at the convent of St Cristina in Turin, Italy. During her early years as a nun she suffered from doubt and other spiritual trials, and later she imposed on herself unusual and excessive penances in an attempt to imitate Christ's passion. At age thirty she was chosen novice mistress and three years later she became the prioress. She governed the convent competently and despite her own severity directed her sisters' spirituality with balance. Feast: December 16. [Luke 1.]

St. Maximus of Turin, born at Vercelli, Italy, around 380 and died at Turin in 467. Not much is know about Maximus, except what we can derive from the 106 sermons he has left us. He became bishop of Turin, and for twenty years preached nearly every Sunday to his rural community. Prominent among his themes were his efforts to uproot all traces of paganism and to train his flock in the spiritual disciplines. Feast: June 25. [Psalm 103.]

St. Norbert, born around 1080 at Xanten, in the duchy of Cleves, Prussia, and died at Magdeburg, Saxony, in 1134. As a canon of the cathedral at Xanten, St. Norbert lived a life of pleasure until he experienced a dramatic conversion in 1115. Then he was ordained a priest and began to live as a monk. In 1120, with thirteen followers, Norbert founded the Canons Regular of Prémontré, now called Premonstratensians. In 1126 he was appointed Archbishop of Magdeburg, where he served until his death. Feast: June 6. [Saints on Scripture 8, following page 364.]

St. Pachomius, born around 292 near Thebes, Egypt, and died of plague, probably at Pabau, near Thebes in 346. After a stint in the Roman army, Pachomius became a Christian and a hermit. Around 320 he gathered monks into a community at Tabennesi, a desert wasteland along the Nile. He gave his associates a simple rule of life, remarkable for its balance. Thus we remember Pachomius as the founder of community monasticism. By the time of his death, approximately

three thousand monks and nuns lived in the nine monasteries and two convents that he governed. Feast: May 9. [Ecclesiasticus 17.]

St. Patrick, born around 389 somewhere in Roman Britain, and died around 461, probably at Saul on Strangford Lough in Downpatrick, Ireland. As a youth Patrick was carried off as a slave from Roman Britain to Northern Ireland. He escaped after six years and returned to his family. However, Patrick became convinced that he had a divine commission to establish the church in Ireland, and in 432 he returned to Ireland as a bishop. After winning protection from local rulers, Patrick traversed the island, making thousands of converts. Everywhere he equipped his new Christian communities with church buildings and liturgical vessels. Patrick also founded monasteries that became centers of learning and sources of a native Irish clergy. In twenty-nine years he had transformed Ireland, replacing an ancient paganism with a vibrant Christian church. Feast: March 17. [2 Samuel 7; Jeremiah 16; 1 Corinthians 2.]

St. Paul of the Cross, born in 1694 at Ovada, Italy, and died at Rome in 1775. In 1727, with his brother and best friend, John Battista, St. Paul was ordained a priest and founded a new religious order, now called the Passionists. He viewed his brothers as monk activists who obligated themselves both to extreme personal austerities and to preaching to the poor. The Passionists became known for their parish missions and soon were in high demand throughout central Italy. Paul himself became famous as an outstanding preacher, exciting crowds with his words about the Cross. People regarded him as a living saint because of his austerity and spiritual gifts of healing, prophecy, and reading consciences. Feast: October 19. [John 10.]

St. Peter Chrysologus, born in 406 at Imola, Italy, and died there around 450. The little information we have tells us that Peter Chrysologus became archbishop of Ravenna in 433 and worked hard to extirpate the lingering traces of paganism from his diocese. Renowned for his practical sermons, Peter became known as "golden-worded," perhaps because he preached simply so that all members of the community could benefit from his teaching. Peter's sermons so impressed the empress that she supported him in an extensive building program, and his sermons caused Pope Benedict XIII to name him a Doctor of the Church in 1729. Feast: July 30. [Psalm 80; Matthew 9.]

St. Peter Claver, born in 1580 at Verdu near Barcelona, Spain, and died at Cartagena in present-day Colombia in 1654. In 1610 Jesuit St. Peter Claver was sent to Cartagena, the center of the slave trade in South America, where thousands of slaves arrived every year from West Africa. Deeply moved by their unimaginable misery, Peter Claver vowed that he would be "the slave of the enslaved Africans forever." For forty years he gave personal care to them, feeding, clothing, and nursing them. With the aid of native interpreters, he also evangelized and indoctrinated them in the faith. He estimated that he baptized more than 300,000 people, an average of two a day. And he heard as many as 5,000 confessions in a year. Feast: September 9. [Saints on Scripture 19, following page 1180.]

St. Raymond of Peñyafort, born in 1175 at Peñyafort, Catalonia, and died at Barcelona, Spain, in 1275. As a lawyer, priest and preacher, Raymond made a significant mark on the history of Spain and the church. His preaching helped re-Christianize Spain after the Moors were overthrown. He collected all the decrees of popes and councils since 1150 in his book, the *Decretals,* which became the main source of canon law for seven centuries. He was elected the third general of the Friars Preachers, but he retired in 1240. But he continued to work 35 more years, focusing on bringing Jews and Moors to Christ. Feast: January 7. [Saints on Scripture 12, following page 1180.]

St. Robert Southwell, born in 1561 at Horsham Saint Faith, Norfolk, England, and died a martyr at London in 1595. The Jesuits ordained Robert Southwell in 1584 and two years later sent him as an underground priest to serve beleaguered Catholics in Queen Elizabeth's England. He devoted himself to encouraging Catholics incarcerated in London's prisons, serving openly and avoiding all intrigue. However, in 1592, Robert was betrayed to the authorities and tortured mercilessly. Then he was locked in solitary confinement in the Tower until he was condemned to death

as a traitor and executed in 1595. St. Robert was an accomplished poet and in his verse he declared the radical love for God that animated his entire life. Feast: February 21. [Genesis 1; Psalm 19; Isaiah 5.]

St. Sebastian Valfré, born in 1629 at Verduno, Piedmont, Italy, and died at Turin in 1710. Sebastian Valfré joined the Oratory at Turin in 1651, where he quickly rose to leadership. For nearly sixty years he preached missions, evangelized youth, heard confessions, and gave spiritual direction, sparking spiritual renewal for many people in Turin and the surrounding communities. Sebastian's innate cheerfulness and friendly disposition made his ministry especially effective. *Butler's Lives of the Saints* describes him as an ideal inner city pastor. Feast: January 30. [Lamentations 3.]

St. Simeon, The New Theologian, born in 949 at Paphlagonia in Asia Minor, and died in 1022 at Paloutikon on the Asiatic side of the Bosporus. At fourteen St. Simeon decided to be a monk, but he was not allowed to enter the Studion in Constantinople until he was twenty-seven. The other monks forced him to leave because of his radicalism. So he joined the monastery at St. Mamas, where he became the abbot and conducted a reform. However, in 1009, opponents had him exiled. Although the ban on him was lifted, Simeon preferred to live in voluntary exile until his death. He is called the New Theologian because by his writing and leadership he spawned a renewal of the church in the East. Feast: March 12. [Saints on Scripture 13, following page 1180.]

St. Syncletica, lived during the fourth century near Alexandria, Egypt, and died there around 400. As the daughter of wealthy Macedonian parents, marriage into a high-society family was Syncletica's expected course. But as a young girl she had pointed her life in a different direction by promising to live single for Christ. When Syncletica's parents died, she inherited their fortune and responsibility for her blind sister. She distributed her wealth to the poor and abandoned the seductions of the world. Together with her sister she went to live in an unused burial chamber on a relative's estate. Regarded as a "desert mother," for more than half a century Syncletica led and advised women who wanted to live a dedicated Christian life. Feast: January 5. [Psalm 118.]

St. Teresa of Avila, born at Avila, Castile, Spain, in 1515, and died at Alba de Tormes, Spain, in 1582. St. Teresa joined the Carmelite order at Avila in 1536. Touched by God in profound ways around age forty, she dedicated her life to bringing reform to Carmelite convents throughout Spain. She influenced her friend St. John of the Cross to launch a reform of Carmelite monasteries. While traveling throughout Spain, Teresa wrote books now regarded as spiritual classics, including her *Autobiography, The Way of Perfection,* and *Interior Castle.* Pope Paul VI declared her a Doctor of the Church in 1970. Feast: October 15. [Proverbs 8; Ezekiel 18; Luke 11:1; John 14:14.]

St. Theresa Margaret of the Sacred Heart, born in 1747 at Arezzo, Italy, and died in 1770 at Florence. In 1764, at age seventeen, Anna Maria Redi entered St. Teresa of Avila's convent at Florence, Italy. As Sister Theresa Margaret of the Sacred Heart, she invaded the convent, refreshing the nuns with her friendliness, service and purposefulness. Even when she was ill herself, she tenderly cared for her sick and elderly sisters. Her heart's desire was to imitate the famous foundress, and she got her wish. She seems to have received the same mystical experiences as St. Teresa of Avila, who says her heart was divinely wounded and set afire by his love. Feast: March 11. [Saints on Scripture 18, following page 1180.]

St. Thérèse of Lisieux, born at Alençon, France, in 1873, and died at Lisieux, France, in 1897. In 1890 Marie Françoise Martin became a Carmelite at Lisieux, taking the name Thérèse of the Child Jesus. Afflicted with tuberculosis, during her short life the saint learned how to serve others, doing everything out of love, which she called her "little way." Her superiors directed her to write about her childhood and life in the convent. These autobiographical writings were gathered into *The Story of a Soul,* which has become one of the most popular spiritual books of modern times. Pope John Paul II named Thérèse a Doctor of the Church in 1998. Feast: October 1. [Psalm 50; Song of Songs 1; Saints on Scripture 9, following page 364.]

St. Thomas Aquinas, born around 1225 at Aquino, Italy, and died in 1275 at Fossanova. In 1245 St. Thomas became a Dominican priest. After he studied philosophy and theology with St. Albert the Great, he spent two decades teaching and writing prodigiously. Between 1259 and 1264 he developed the *Summa Contra Gentes* in order to give a rational explanation of Christianity to Jews, Muslims, and pagans. In 1266, Thomas began to write his most important work, the *Summa Theologica,* a systematic statement of his mature thought on all Christian doctrine. But he left the work incomplete because a profound experience of God in 1273 drew him to devote himself to prayer instead of writing. Feast: January 28. [Mark 14:22; John 6; 1 Corinthians 11; 2 Peter 1.]

St. Thomas More, born at London in 1477, and died a martyr there in 1535. A family man, happily married with four children, St. Thomas More served as a barrister, a member of parliament, an officer in local government, and finally after 1529, Lord Chancellor of England. He is also recognized as a leader of the Renaissance. His best remembered work, *Utopia,* appeared in 1516. When King Henry VIII decided to divorce his wife and declare himself head of the church in England, More opposed him, but he scrupulously obeyed the law, never speaking of "the King's great matter." However, because More refused to take the oath supporting Henry, the king had him arrested and ultimately executed. Feast: June 22. [Philippians 1; 1 Peter 1; 1 Peter 3.]

St. Thomas of Villanova, born at Fuentellana, Castile, Spain, in 1488, and died at Valencia in 1555. From 1518 to 1533 St. Thomas of Villanova held many leadership offices among the Spanish Augustinian friars. In 1533 he sent the first Augustinian missionaries to Mexico. Then after serving as chaplain to the Emperor Charles V, he became the archbishop of Valencia in 1544 where for eleven years he was much beloved for his kindness and simplicity. Feast: September 22. [Psalm 72.]

St. Vincent de Paul, born in 1581 at Pouy, France, and died at Paris in 1660. In 1625 St. Vincent founded the Congregation of the Mission, a community of priests with a threefold commitment. Members obligated themselves to pattern their lives on Christ, to take the gospel to the rural poor, and to help educate priests in their practical duties. The priests mainly conducted parish missions, preaching and hearing confessions. With the collaboration of St. Louise de Marillac, in 1633 Vincent founded the Sisters of Charity, the first community of "unenclosed" women dedicated to the care of the sick and the poor. In his last years Vincent was confined to an armchair with swollen and ulcerous legs, but he remained cheerful, directing his charitable works by writing hundreds of letters. Feast: September 27. [Psalm 84; Micah 6.]

St. Vincent Ferrer, born at Valencia, Spain, in 1350, and died at Vannes, Brittany, in 1419. Dominican Vincent Ferrer's life spanned the Great Western Schism, when popes rivaled each other at Rome and at Avignon, France. He was loyal to the Avignon popes, but he pressured them to cooperate with efforts to restore unity. For twenty years after 1399, Vincent crisscrossed Europe four times on foot to revive the church's faith that the schism had weakened. Everywhere, large crowds gathered to hear his message. In response to his ministry thousands revolutionized their lives. Thousands also were miraculously healed during his missionary visits. Feast: April 5. [Saints on Scripture 12, following page 1180.]

St. Vincent of Lérins, birth date and place unknown; died at Lérins, France, around 450. St. Vincent was a native of Gaul, possibly the brother of St. Loup, Bishop of Troyes. We don't know much about his life, except that after a career as a soldier he became a monk and priest at the monastery of Lérins on an island opposite Cannes, France. From his works we know that he was an excellent scholar and teacher. His most influential book, the *Commonitory,* dealt with the relationship of Scripture and Tradition. Feast: May 24. [Saints on Scripture 5, following page 364.]

Themes

Almsgiving
Deuteronomy 15
Ecclesiasticus 3–4
1Kings 17
Tobit 12
Acts 10

Baptism
Exodus 15
Joshua 3
1 Kings 18
Ezekiel 36
Jeremiah 4
Colossians 2
John 1

Chastity
Proverbs 6
Luke 1

Christian Living
Genesis 28
Exodus 20
Joshua 3
1 Samuel 17
Job 12
Psalm 139
Ecclesiastes 3
Ecclesiasticus 18
Micah 6
Luke 19
1 Corinthians 10
1 Corinthians 13
Revelation 3

The Church
Daniel 2
John 17

Confession
2 Samuel 12
Micah 7

Contemplation
Genesis 3
Exodus 33

Conversion
Acts 2

The Cross
Exodus 14
Numbers 20
Mark 11
John 10
John 19–21
1 Peter 2

Death
Ecclesiastes 3
Ecclesiasticus 17
Ecclesiasticus 18
Philippians 1
1 Peter 3

Depression
Mark 7:14

The Devil
Matthew 27
Mark 3

Discipleship
1 Samuel 3
Matthew 16
Matthew 19
Mark 10

Discipline
Wisdom 7–8

The End Times
Luke 21

Envy
Genesis 45

Eternal Perspective
Wisdom 13
Ecclesiasticus 1
Daniel 2
Matthew 16
Philippians 1
1 Peter 3

The Eucharist
Exodus 12
2 Kings 6
Malachi 1
Matthew 26
Mark 14:22
Luke 11:1
John 3
John 6
Romans 12:1
1 Corinthians 10
1 Corinthians 11
1 Timothy 2

Evangelization
2 Samuel 7
Isaiah 60
Jeremiah 16
Jonah 3
2 Corinthians 5:11
2 Corinthians 11

Example
Ezekiel 3

Faith
Deuteronomy 6
Deuteronomy 30
Wisdom 13
Matthew 8
Matthew 17

Fasting
Tobit 12
Matthew 4

Forgiveness
Genesis 4
Genesis 45
Deuternonomy 15
Hosea 14
Matthew 18
Luke 5
Luke 6

Friendship
Ruth 2
Ecclesiasticus 6
2 Corinthians 5:11

The Fruit of the Holy Spirit
Acts 2
Galatians 5

Gentleness
Acts 2

Generosity
Luke 6
John 15

Grace
Isaiah 1
Jeremiah 10
2 Peter 1

Gratitude
2 Samuel 7
Psalm 116
Proverbs 8

Healing
Matthew 8
Mark 2
Mark 7:31
Luke 5

Heaven
Leviticus 26
Matthew 25
1 Corinthians 2

Hell
Matthew 13:24
1 Corinthians 2

The Holy Spirit
1 Kings 18
Amos 7
Matthew 12
Mark 7:31
John 3
John 4
Ephesians 4

Humility
Ruth 3
Matthew 11

Image of God
Genesis 1–2
Isaiah 42
Ephesians 4

The Incarnation
Numbers 24
Jeremiah 33
Luke 2

Luke 2:41
Philippians 2

Integrity
Daniel 6
Job 12

Intercession
Luke 5
Romans 13
2 Timothy 2

Jesus Christ
Leviticus 16
1 Samuel 17
Psalm 72
Psalm 103
Isaiah 53
Isaiah 60
Jeremiah 31
Daniel 2
Malachi 3
Matthew 9
Matthew 12
Mark 4
Luke 22
John 14
Philippians 2
1 Timothy 2

Judgment
Wisdom 3
Matthew 16
Matthew 25
Luke 21

Justice
Mark 12

Kindness
Joshua 2
Ruth 2

Love
Genesis 1
Genesis 1–2
Genesis 28

Psalm 19
Psalm 63
Psalm 50
Isaiah 49

Love of God
Psalm 80
Micah 6
Matthew 7
Matthew 22
John 19–31
Galatians 2
1 John 4
Revelation 19

Love of Others
Joshua 2
1 Samuel 26
Ecclesiasticus 6
John 13
John 15
Romans 12:3
Romans 13
1 Corinthians 13

Marriage
John 2

Martyrdom
2 Maccabees 7
Acts 6

Mary
Luke 1
John 17

Mass
Romans 12:1

Mental Prayer
Acts 17

Mercy
Genesis 4
Deuteronomy 15
1 Samuel 26
Psalm 72

Proverbs 8
Wisdom 11–12
Hosea 14
Joel 2
Matthew 18
Luke 1
Luke 23
Acts 10
Romans 12:3

Miracles
Matthew 8
Mark 4
Luke 7
John 2

New Covenant
Jeremiah 4
Jeremiah 31
Ezekiel 36
John 2

Obedience
Exodus 20
Deuteronomy 6
Job 7
Proverbs 16
Wisdom 7–8
Jeremiah 17
Matthew 7
Luke 8
Galatians 2

The Passion of Christ
Mark 11
Mark 15
John 10
John 19–21

Patience
Job 1
Wisdom 11–12
Lamentations 3
Joel 2
Matthew 6
Mark 7:14
Hebrews 12

James 1
1 Peter 1

Penance
Hebrews 12

Perfection
Genesis 1–2
Psalm 51
Proverbs 4
John 13

Perseverance
Deuteronomy 6
Psalm 22
Psalm 84
Psalm 118
Jeremiah 8
Philippians 3
James 1

The Poor
1 Kings 17

Possessions
Ecclesiastes 1
Ecclesiasticus 1
Ecclesiasticus 31

Prayer
Genesis 28
Exodus 33
Tobit 12
Psalm 22
Song of Songs 1
Song of Songs 3
Ezekiel 18
Daniel 3
Daniel 6
Matthew 6
Mark 14–32
Luke 9
Luke 11:33
Luke 19
Luke 22
John 14:14

2 Corinthians 12
1 Thessalonians 5

Pride
Ecclesiasticus 10

Purpose
Philippians 3

Real Presence
Proverbs 8
Acts 17

Relativism
Romans 14

Repentance
Genesis 19
Deuteronomy 30
2 Samuel 12
Psalm 51
Wisdom 11–12
Ecclesiasticus 3–4
Isaiah 1
Jeremiah 8
Ezekiel 18
Jonah 3
Micah 7
Matthew 13:24
Luke 23
John 19–21

The Resurrection
Mark 16

Resurrection of the Body
Ezekiel 37
2 Corinthians 5

The Sacred Heart
Zechariah 12
John 19–21

Sacraments
1 Kings 18
Zechariah 12

Matthew 26
Luke 11:1
1 Corinthians 11

Salvation
Exodus 14
Leviticus 16
Numbers 20
Psalm 103
Ecclesiastes 3
Isaiah 53
Jeremiah 31
Jonah 3
Matthew 27
Mark 15
Luke 2
Luke 7
John 14
2 Peter 1

The Second Coming
Malachi 3

Self-Indulgence
Job 7
Ecclesiastes 1
Ecclesiasticus 31

Service
Romans 13

Sickness
Psalm 118
Luke 5

The Sign of the Cross
Mark 2
Mark 9

Simplicity
Job 12
Luke 11:33

Sin
Genesis 3
Genesis 4
Genesis 19

2 Samuel 12
1 Kings 21
Psalm 139
Ecclesiasticus 10
Isaiah 1
Ezekiel 3
Mark 16
Romans 6
Romans 8

Spiritual Life
Psalm 84
Proverbs 4
Jeremiah 17
Mark 16
Luke 2:41
Luke 7
Luke 22
John 3
John 17
2 Corinthians 12

Spiritual Warfare
Psalm 51
Matthew 4
Matthew 27
Mark 3
Mark 9
Mark 11
Romans 6
Hebrews 12

Suffering
Job 1
Job 21
Psalm 22
Psalm 118
Wisdom 3
Lamentations 3
Mark 4
Luke 9
John 10
2 Corinthians 11
Hebrews 12
2 Timothy 2
1 Peter 2
1 Peter 3

THEMES

Temptation
Proverbs 6
Matthew 17
Romans 8
Galatians 5
James 1

Transformation
Psalm 116
Proverbs 4
Proverbs 16
Isaiah 42
Ezekiel 36
Amos 7
John 1
Galatians 5

Trials
Luke 9
1 Peter 1
1 Peter 2

The Trinity
Matthew 28
1 John 4

Trust
Isaiah 49

Truth
Deuteronomy 6
John 14
Romans 14

Union with God
Leviticus 26
Psalm 63
Psalm 80
Psalm 139
Song of Songs 1
Song of Songs 3
Isaiah 49
Jeremiah 4

John 14:14
2 Corinthians 5
Philippians 3
Revelation 3
Revelation 19

Unity
Daniel 3

Vocation
Judges 3
1 Samuel 3
Matthew 19
Mark 10

Wisdom
Wisdom 7–8

The Word of God
Luke 8

Works of Mercy
Luke 6

The World
Mark 12

Worship
Psalm 19
Ecclesiasticus 17
Isaiah 5
Jeremiah 10
Daniel 3
Romans 12:1
1 Timothy 2

A Calendar of Saints

Based on the Sacramentary and the Liturgy of the Hours of the Roman Catholic Church, this calendar features saints whose feasts are universally celebrated throughout the church as well as those of special interest to the English-speaking world.

January
1   Mary, Mother of God; St. Fulgentius of Ruspe
2   St. Basil and St. Gregory Nazianzen
4   St. Elizabeth Ann Seton
5   St. John Neumann; St. Syncletica
6   Bl. André Bessette
7   St. Raymond of Peñyafort
12 St. Aelred of Rievauly
13 St. Hilary of Poitiers
17 St. Anthony of Egypt
20 St. Fabian and St. Sebastian
21 St. Agnes
22 St. Vincent of Saragossa
24 St. Francis de Sales
25 Conversion of St. Paul
26 St. Timothy and St. Titus
27 St. Angela Merici
28 St. Thomas Aquinas
30 St. Sebastian Valfré
31 St. John Bosco

February
3   St Blaise or St. Ansgar
4   St. Isidore of Pelusium
5   St. Agatha
6   St. Paul Miki and Companions
8   St. Jerome Emiliani
10 St. Scholastica
11 Our Lady of Lourdes
14 St. Cyril and St. Methodius
17 Seven Founders of the Servite Order
21 St. Peter Damian; St. Robert Southwell
22 Chair of St. Peter
23 St. Polycarp

28 Bl. Angela of Foligno
29 St. John Cassian

March
3   St. Katharine Drexel
4   St. Casimir
7   St. Perpetua and St. Felicity
8   St. John of God
9   St. Frances of Rome; St. Gregory of Nyssa
12 St. Simeon, The New Theologian
17 St. Patrick
18 St. Cyril of Jerusalem
19 St. Joseph
24 St. Turibius of Mongrovejo

April
2   St. Francis of Paola
4   St. Isidore of Seville
5   St. Vincent Ferrer
7   St. John Baptist de La Salle; St. Aphraates of Persia
11 St. Stanislaus
13 St. Martin I
21 St. Anselm
23 St. George
24 St. Fidelis of Sigmaringen
25 St. Mark
28 St. Peter Chanel; St. Louis de Montfort
29 St. Catherine of Siena
30 St. Pius V

May
1   St. Joseph the Worker
2   St. Athanasius
3   St. Philip and St. James; Elizabeth Leseur

9   St. Pachomius
12 St. Nereus and St. Achilleus; St. Pancras
13 Bl. Julian of Norwich
14 St. Matthias
15 St. Isidore
18 St. John 1
20 St. Bernardino of Siena
24 St. Vincent of Lérins
25 St. Bede, the Venerable; St. Gregory VII;
    St. Mary Magdalen dei Pazzi
26 St. Philip Neri
27 St. Augustine of Canterbury
31 Visitation of the Blessed Virgin Mary

June
1   St. Justin
2   St. Marcellinus and St. Peter
3   St. Charles Lwanga and Companions
5   St. Boniface
6   St. Norbert
9   St. Ephrem
11 St. Barnabas
13 St. Anthony of Padua
16 St. Lutgarde
18 St. Ephrem
19 St. Romuald
21 St. Aloysius Gonzaga
22 St. Paulinus of Nola; St. John Fisher and
    St. Thomas More
24 Birth of St. John the Baptist
25 St. Maximus of Turin
27 St. Cyril of Alexandria
28 St. Irenaeus
29 St. Peter and St. Paul
30 First Martyrs of the Church of Rome

July
1   Bl. Junipéro Serra
3   St. Thomas
4   St. Elizabeth of Portugal
5   St. Anthony Zaccaria
6   St.Maria Goretti
11 St. Benedict
13 St. Henry
14 Bl. Kateri Tekawitha; St. Camillus de Lellis;
    Bl. Humbert of Romans
15 St. Bonaventure

16 Our Lady of Mt. Carmel
21 St. Lawrence of Brindisi
22 St. Mary Magdalene
23 St. Bridget of Sweden
25 St. James
26 St. Joachim and St. Ann
29 St. Martha
30 St. Peter Chrysologus
31 St. Ignatius Loyola

August
1   St. Alphonsus Liguori
2   St. Eusebius of Vercelli
4   St. John Vianney
5   Dedication of the Basilica of St. Mary Major
7   St. Sixtus and Companions; St. Cajetan
8   St. Dominic
10 St. Lawrence; St. Edith Stein
11 St. Clare of Assisi; Ven John Henry Newman
13 St. Pontian and St. Hippolytus;
    St. John Berchmans
14 St. Maximilian Kolbe
15 Assumption of the Blessed Virgin Mary
16 St. Stephen of Hungary
17 St. Joan Delanoue
19 St. John Eudes
20 St. Bernard of Clairvaux
21 St. Pius X
22 Queenship of Mary
23 St. Rose of Lima
24 St. Bartholomew
25 St. Louis; St. Joseph Calasanz
27 St. Monica; St. Caesarius of Arles
28 St. Augustine of Hippo
29 Beheading of St. John the Baptist

September
3   St. Gregory the Great
8   Birth of the Blessed Virgin Mary;
    Bl. Frederic Ozanam
9   St. Peter Claver
11 St. John Gabriel Perboyre
13 St. John Chrysostom
15 Our Lady of Sorrows
16 St. Cornelius and St. Cyprian
17 St. Robert Bellarmine; St. Hildegard of Bingen
19 St. Januarius; Bl. Alphonsus de Orzoco

20 St. Andrew Kim Taegon, St Paul; Chong Hasang and Companions
21 St. Matthew
22 St. Thomas of Villanova
26 St. Cosmas and Damian
27 St. Vincent de Paul
28 St. Lawrence Ruiz and Companions
29 St. Michael, St. Gabriel and St. Raphael
30 St. Jerome

October
1 St. Thérèse of Lisieux
2 Guardian Angels
4 St. Francis of Assisi
5 St. Faustina
6 St. Bruno; Bl. Marie Rose Durocher
7 Our Lady of the Rosary
9 St. Denis and Companions; St. John Leonardi
14 St. Callistus
15 St. Teresa of Avila
16 St. Hedwig; St. Margaret Mary Alacoque
17 St. Ignatius of Antioch
18 St. Luke
19 St. Isaac Jogues, St. John de Brébeuf and Companions; St. Paul of the Cross
23 St. John of Capistrano
24 St. Anthony Mary Claret
28 St. Simon and St. Jude

November
1 All Saints
2 All Souls
3 St. Martin de Porres
4 St. Charles Borromeo
9 Dedication of St. John Lateran Basilica
10 St. Leo the Great

11 St. Martin of Tours
12 St. Josaphat
13 St. Frances Xavier Cabrini
15 St. Albert the Great
16 St. Margaret of Scotland; St.Gertrude the Great
17 St. Elizabeth of Hungary
18 Dedication of the Churches of St. Peter and St. Paul; St. Rose Philippine Duchesne
21 Presentation of the Blessed Virgin Mary
22 St. Cecelia
23 St. Clement of Rome; St. Columban; Bl. Miguel Agustin Pro
24 St. Andrew Dung-Lac and Companions
26 St. Leonard of Port Maurice
30 St. Andrew

December
2 St. John Ruysbroeck
3 St. Francis Xavier
4 St. John Damascene
6 St. Nicholas
7 St. Ambrose
8 Immaculate Conception of the Blessed Virgin Mary
11 St. Damasus
12 Our Lady of Guadalupe; St. Jane de Chantal
13 St. Lucy
14 St. John of the Cross
16 St. Mary of the Angels
21 St. Peter Canisius
23 St. John of Kanty
26 St. Stephen
28 Holy Innocents
29 St.Thomas Becket
31 St. Sylvester

Patron Saints

The church has named some saints as patrons for occupations, vocations, personal needs, countries, and other special concerns. In this role these saints serve us in three ways—as intercessors, exemplars, and protectors. So we may invite them to pray for us, which is our most common practice. But we should also look to them as examples and expect them as sisters and brothers to help us and guide us.

OCCUPATIONS AND VOCATIONS

Accountants: Matthew
Actors: Genesius
Actresses: Pelagia
Advertising: Bernardino of Siena
Air travelers: Joseph of Cupertino
Anesthetists: René Goupil
Apologists: Justin Martyr
Architects: Barbara; Thomas the
    Apostle
Artists: Luke
Astronomers: Dominic
Athletes: Sebastian
Authors: Francis de Sales

Bakers: Elizabeth of Hungary
Bankers: Matthew
Barbers: Cosmas and Damian
Bookkeepers: Matthew
Booksellers: John of God
Bricklayers: Stephen
Brides: Nicholas of Myra
Builders: Vincent Ferrer
Businesswomen: Margaret
    Clitherow
Butchers: Anthony of Egypt

Cab drivers: Fiacre
Carpenters: Joseph
Catechists: Charles Borromeo;
    Robert Bellarmine

Communications personnel:
    Bernardino of Siena
Construction workers: Thomas
Cooks: Lawrence

Dairy workers: Brigid
Dancers: Vitus
Deacons: Stephen
Dentists: Apollonia
Dieticians: Martha

Ecologists: Francis of Assisi
Editors: John Bosco
Engineers: Ferdinand III

Farmers: Isidore the Farmer
Fathers: Joseph
Firemen: Florian
Fishermen: Andrew
Florists: Thérèse of Lisieux
Foresters: John Gualbert
Funeral directors: Joseph of
    Arimathea; Dismas

Gardeners: Adelard; Dorothy
Grocers: Michael the Archangel

Hairdressers: Martin de Porres
Hospital administrators: Basil;
    Frances Xavier Cabrini
Hospital workers: Camillus de
    Lellis
Housewives: Anne
Hunters: Eustachius; Hubert

Infantrymen: Maurice

Jewelers: Dunstan; Eligius
Journalists: Francis de Sales
Jurists: John of Capistrano

Laborers: Isidore the Farmer;
    John Bosco
Lawyers: Thomas More
Lectors: Pollio; Sabas
Librarians: Jerome
Linguists: Gottshalk
Locksmiths: Dunstan

Magistrates: Nicholas of Flue
Maids: Zita
Mariners: Michael; Nicholas of
    Tolentino
Medical technicians: Albert the
    Great
Merchants: Francis of Assisi
Midwives: Margaret of Cortona
Monks: Benedict of Nursia
Mothers: Monica
Motorists: Christopher; Frances
    of Rome
Musicians: Cecilia; Gregory the
    Great

Nuns: Brigid
Nurses: Agatha; Camillus de
    Lellis

Orators: John Chrysostom

Pharmacists: Cosmas and Damian
Philosophers: Justin Martyr
Physicians: Cosmas; Damian;
Luke
Pilots: Joseph of Cupertino
Plumbers: Vincent Ferrer
Poets: Cecilia
Policemen: Michael the
Archangel
Postal workers: Gabriel
Preachers: John Chrysostom
Priests: John Vianney
Printers: Augustine of Hippo;
John of God
Public relations: Bernardino of
Siena
Publishers: John of God

Radiologists: Michael the
Archangel

Sailors: Brendan; Cuthbert
Scholars: Brigid
Scientists: Albert the Great
Sculptors: Castorius
Secretaries: Genesius
Seminarians: Charles Borromeo
Singers: Cecilia; Gregory the
Great
Skaters: Lydwine of Shiedem
Skiers: Bernard of Montjoux
Social workers: Louise de
Marillac
Soldiers: George; Ignatius of
Loyola
Students: Joseph Calasanz;
Thomas Aquinas

Tailors: Homobonus
Teachers: Gregory the Great;
John Baptist de la Salle
Telecommunications workers:
Gabriel
Television workers: Gabriel

Theologians: Alphonsus Liguori;
Augustine of Hippo

Workingmen: Joseph
Writers: Francis de Sales

PERSONAL NEEDS

Abandoned: Flora
Abandoned children: Jerome
Emiliani
Abuse victims: Fabiola; Monica
Alcoholism: Monica

Blindness: Odilia; Raphael

Cancer sufferers: Peregrine
Laziosi
Child abuse victims: Alodia;
Germaine Cousin
Childbirth: Gerard Majella
Childless: Anne Line; Catherine
of Genoa
Convulsive children: Scholastica

Deafness: Francis de Sales
Death of children: Clotilde;
Elizabeth of Hungary
Desperate situations: Jude
Difficult marriages: Catherine
of Genoa
Divorced: Fabiola
Drug addiction: Maximilian
Kolbe
Dying: Joseph

Emigration: Frances Xavier
Cabrini
Epilepsy: Vitus
Expectant mothers: Gerard
Majella
Eye disease: Lucy

Falsely accused: Blandina;
Dominic

Handicapped: Alphais; Gerard of
Aurillac
Headache suffers: Teresa of Avila
Heart patients: John of God
Homeless: Benedict Joseph Labre;
Elizabeth of Hungary

Invalids: Roch

Kidnap victims: Arthelais;
William of Norwich

Lost items: Anthony of Padua

Mental illnesses: Benedict Joseph
Labre; Dymphna

Orphans: Frances Xavier Cabrini;
Jerome Emiliani

Poverty: Julia; Macrina the
Elder
Prisoners: Joseph Cafasso; Louis
IX

Rape victims: Agatha; Agnes;
Maria Goretti
Runaways: Eulalia of Merida

Sickness: Camillus de Lellis; John
of God; Syncletica

Throat disease: Blaise

Women in labor: Anne

COUNTRIES

Americas: Rose of Lima
Argentina: Our Lady of Lujan
Australia: Our Lady Help of
Christians
Austria: Severino

Belgium: Joseph
Bohemia: Ludmilla

Bolivia: Our Lady of Copacabana
Brazil: Immaculate Conception; Peter of Alcántara

Canada: Anne; Joseph
Chile: Our Lady of Mt. Carmel; James
China: Joseph
Colombia: Peter Claver
Czechoslovakia: John Nepomucene

Denmark: Ansgar; Canute
Dominican Republic: Our Lady of High Grace; Dominic

East Indies: Francis Xavier; Thomas
Ecuador: Sacred Heart
El Salvador: Our Lady of Peace
England: Augustine of Canterbury; George; Gregory the Great
Ethiopia: Frumentius
Europe: Benedict of Nursia; Cyril; Methodius

Finland: Henry of Uppsala
France: Our Lady of the Assumption; Denis; Joan of Arc; Martin of Tours Remigius; Thérèse of Lisieux

Germany: Boniface; Michael; Peter Canisius
Greece: Andrew; Nicholas of Myra

Holland: Willibrord
Hungary: Stephen

India: Our Lady of the Assumption
Ireland: Brigid; Columba; Patrick

Italy: Bernardino of Siena; Catherine of Siena; Francis of Assisi

Japan: Francis Xavier; Peter Baptist

Korea: Mary

Lithuania: Casimir; John Cantius

Mexico: Our Lady of Guadalupe

New Zealand: Our Lady Help of Christians
North America: Isaac Jogues and Companions
Norway: Olaf

Paraguay: Our Lady of the Assumption
Peru: Joseph
Philippines: Sacred Heart of Mary
Poland: Casimir; Our Lady of Czestochowa; Stanislaus
Portugal: Francis Borgia; George; Immaculate Conception

Romania: Nicetas
Russia: Andrew; Nicholas of Myra

Scandinavia: Ansgar
Scotland: Andrew; Columba; Margaret of Scotland
Silesia: Hedwig
South Africa: Our Lady of the Assumption
Spain: Teresa of Avila
Sri Lanka: Lawrence
Sweden: Bridget
Switzerland: Gall

Tanzania: Immaculate Conception

Uganda: Mary, Queen of Africa
United States: Immaculate Conception

Vietnam: Our Lady of La Vang

Wales: David
West Indies: Gertrude

SPECIAL CONCERNS

Animals: Francis of Assisi

Babies: The Holy Innocents
Blended families: Adelaide; Thomas More

Catholic Press: Francis de Sales
Charities: Vincent de Paul
Children: Nicholas of Myra
Converts: Helena; Flora; Vladimir

Internet: Isidore of Seville

Retreats: Ignatius Loyola

Schools: Joseph Calasanz; Thomas Aquinas
Second marriages: Adelaide; Matilda
Single women: Agatha; Flora; Syncletica

Television: Clare of Assisi

Widows: Angela of Foligno; Clotilde; Elizabeth of Hungary

Youth: Aloysius Gonzaga; Gabriel Possenti; John Berchmans

Sources

ABBREVIATIONS

ANF   *Ante-Nicene Fathers: The Writings of the Fathers Down to A. D. 325;* Christian Classics Ethereal Library at Calvin College (www.ccel.org).

CR   *Christian Readings* (New York: Catholic Book Publishing Company, 1972).

CWS   *The Classics of Western Spirituality* (New York: Paulist Press).

NPNF   *Nicene and Post-Nicene Fathers;* Christian Classics Ethereal Library at Calvin College (www.ccel.org).

OR   *The Office of Readings According to the Roman Rite* (Boston: Daughters of St. Paul, 1983).

RB   *The Roman Breviary;* tr. John, Marquess of Bute, K. T. (Edinburgh and London: William Blackwood and Sons, 1908) 4 vols.

Toal   M. F. Toal, tr. and ed., *The Sunday Sermons of the Great Fathers* (Swedesboro, New Jersey: Preservation Press, 1996).

SAINTS ON SCRIPTURE

1. **Experiencing the Power of God's Word (Bl. Humbert of Romans):** *Early Dominicans: Selected Writings. CWS* (1999), 201–3.

2. **Reading Scripture: Essential for Christian Living (St. John Chrysostom):** Sermon on Lazarus, 3; tr. by Kevin Perrotta in Benedict Groeschel and Kevin Perrotta, *The Journey Toward God* (Servant Publications, 2000), 195–96; used by permission of the translator.
   Pursuing God in Scripture: Practical Advice on Reading the Bible (St. Alphonsus de Orozco: *The Mount of Contemplation, 7,* in Kathleen Pond, *The Spirit of the Spanish Mystics* (London: Burns & Oates, 1958), 51–52.

3. **Scripture Leads Us to Eternal Life; Understanding Scripture through Faith in Christ (St. Bonaventure):** *Breviloquim Prologue,* 2–5 *CR* 1 (Year 2), 217; *The Hodder Book of Christian Prayers;* ed. Tony Castle (London: Hodder and Stoughton, 1986), 40–41.

4. **The Inexhaustible Richness of God's Word (St. Ephrem):** Diatessaron, 1, 18–19; *CR* 2 (Year 2), 203.
   We Need a Guide to the Bible (St. Jerome): *Letter 13, To Paulinus. (NPNF* Series 2, Vol. 6, No. 3).

5. **Scripture and Tradition (St. Vincent of Lérins):** *The Commonitory of St. Vincent of Lérins;* tr. T. Herbert Bindley (London: SPCK, 1914), 22–24.

6. **Understanding the Spiritual Sense of Scripture (St. Bede, the Venerable):** *The Venerable Bede,* ed. Benedicta Ward, S.L.G. (Harrisburg, Pennsylvania: Morehouse Publishing, 1990), 49–50; Bede, *A History of the English Church and People;* tr. Leo Sherley-Price (Baltimore, Maryland: Penguin Books, 1970), 338.

7. **Putting God's Word into Practice (St. Augustine):** *Sermon 179; CR* 2 (Year 3), 141.

8. **Scripture as a Mirror of the Soul (St. Gregory the Great):** *Book of Moral Reflections on Job,* 2, 1; *RB,* 4, 214–15. **(St. Norbert):** Cornelius J. Kirkfleet,

O. Praem., *History of St. Norbert* (St. Louis, Missouri: B. Herder, 1916) 222–23. **(St. Clare of Assisi):** *The Legend and Writings of Saint Clare of Assisi* (St. Bonaventure, New York: The Franciscan Institute, 1953), 97–98.

9. **Finding Her Way in Scripture (St. Thérèse of Lisieux):** *The Autobiography of St. Thérèse of Lisieux;* tr. John Beevers (New York: Doubleday Image, 1989), 113–14; 153–55; 126–27.

10. **Patterning Their Lives on Scripture (St. Joan Delanoue):** *Butler's Lives of the Saints;* ed. Herbert Thurston, S. J., and Donald Attwater (London: Burns & Oates, 1956), Vol. 3, 342–45. **(St. Camillus de Lellis):** Bert Ghezzi, *Voices of the Saints* (New York: Doubleday, 2000), 112–13.

11. **Minding Our Thoughts with Scripture Meditation (St. John Cassian):** *The Conferences of John Cassian,* 1 (*NPNF* Series 2, Vol. 11).

12. **The Benefits of Meditating on Scripture (St. Vincent Ferrer):** S[ister] M[ary] C[atherine], *Angel of the Judgment: a Life of Vincent Ferrer* (Notre Dame, Indiana: Ave Maria Press, 1954); **(St. Clare of Assisi):** *The Legend and Writings of Saint Clare of Assisi* (St. Bonaventure, New York: The Franciscan Institute, 1953); **(St. Raymond of Peñyafort):** *OR,* 1305.

13. **Meditating on a Scripture Verse (St. Augustine):** *The Hodder Book of Christian Prayers;* ed. Tony Castle (London: Hodder and Stoughton, 1986), 41; **(St. John Gabriel Perboyre):** G. de Montgesty, *Two Vincentian Martyrs;* adapted by Florence Gilmore (Maryknoll, New York: Catholic Foreign Mission Society of America, 1925), 127; **(St. Simeon, the New Theologian):** *The Hodder Book of Christian Prayers;* ed. Tony Castle (London: Hodder and Stoughton, 1986), 36.

14. **Praying with Scripture (St. Bernard of Clairvaux):** *Third Sermon on the Lord's Passion; RB,* 3, 261–62.

15. **The Psalms and the Christian Life (St. Ambrose):** *Discourses on the Psalms,* 1, 4, 7–8; *CR* 4 (Year 1), 137.
The Gospel and the Christian Life (St. Jerome): Book 2, *Commentary on Matthew 13; RB,* 4, 343–44.

16. **A Method of Continual Prayer (St. John Cassian):** *Conferences of John Cassian,* 10, (*NPNF* Series 2, Vol. 11).

17. **When God Speaks to Us in Scripture (St. Anthony):** St. Athanasius, *Life of St. Anthony* in *The Paradise or Garden of the Holy Fathers* (Seattle, Washington: Saint Nectarios Press, 1978); **(Sts. Augustine and Alipius):** *The Confessions of St. Augustin* (*NPNF* Vol. 1).

18. **Using Scripture in Daily Life (St. Theresa Margaret of the Sacred Heart):** James F. Newcomb, *St. Theresa Margaret of the Sacred Heart* (New York: Benziger Brothers, 1934); **(St. Lutgarde):** Thomas de Cantimpré. *The Life of Lutgard of Aywières* (Saskatoon: Peregrina, 1987).

19. **Formed by God's Word (St. Peter Claver):** *Letter to his superior, 31 May 1627;* ed. A. Valtierra, S.J., *San Pedro Claver,* Cartagena, 1964, pp. 140–41 in the *Supplement to the Divine Office* for the Society of Jesus (Rome: Society of Jesus, 1974). 51–53.

20. **From Study to Action (St. Jerome):** *Butler's Lives of the Saints;* ed. Herbert Thurston, S. J., and Donald Attwater (London: Burns & Oates, 1956), Vol. 3, 686–93; **(St. Dominic):** *Butler's Lives of the Saints,* Vol. 3, 258–64.

THE HEBREW SCRIPTURES

Amos 7: *Oration 41, On Pentecost* (*NPNF* Series 2, Vol. 7).

Daniel 2: *CR* 2 (Year 2), 241.
Daniel 3: T. Herbert Bindley, *St. Cyprian on the Lord's Prayer* (London: SPCK, 1914), 32–34.
Daniel 6: *CR* 2 (Year 2), 249.
Deuteronomy 6: *St. Irenaios' The Preaching of the*

Apostles (Brookline, Massachusetts: Holy Cross Orthodox Press).

Deuteronomy 15: *CR* 2 (Year 2), 159.

Deuteronomy 30: *CR* 2 (Year 2), 119.

Ecclesiastes 1: *RB,* 3, 342–43.

Ecclesiastes 3: *CR* 2 (Year 2), 53.

Ecclesiasticus 1: *RB,* 3, 356.

Ecclesiasticus 3–4: *Treatise on Works and Almsgiving; CR* 4 (Year 1), 189.

Ecclesiasticus 6: Aelred of Rievaulx, *Spiritual Friendship;* tr. Mary Eugenia Laker, SSND (Kalamazoo, Michigan: Cistercian Publications, 1977), 71–73.

Ecclesiasticus 10: St. Augustine, *The City of God;* ed. Vernon J. Bourke (New York: Doubleday Image, 1958), 308–9.

Ecclesiasticus 17: *The Paradise or Garden of the Holy Fathers* (Seattle, Washington: Saint Nectarios Press, 1978), Vol. 1, 297–98.

Ecclesiasticus 18: *Select Revelations of St. Bridget* (London: Art and Book Company, 1892), 107–8.

Ecclesiasticus 31: Saint Bernardine of Siena, *Sermons* (Siena: Tipografia Sociale, 1920), 222–23.

Exodus 12: Edith Stein, *The Hidden Life* (Washington, D. C.: ICS Publications, 1992), 7–8.

Exodus 14: *An Exact Exposition of the Orthodox Faith,* 4, 4 (*NPNF* Series 2, Vol. 9).

Exodus 15: *The Book Concerning the Mysteries,* 3, 10–12; (*NPNF* Series 2, Vol. 10).

Exodus 20: *Dialogue of Justin,* 93 (*ANF,* vol. 1).

Exodus 33: *The Conferences of John Cassian,* 1, 15 (*NPNF* Series 2, Vol. 11).

Ezekiel 3: *The Mirror of Perfection;* tr. Constance, Countess de la Warr (London: Burns & Oates, 1902).

Ezekiel 18: *The Life of Teresa of Jesus;* tr. E. Allison Peers (New York: Doubleday, 1991), 110.

Ezekiel 36: *Oration 40, On Holy Baptism,* 7–8; (*NPNF* Series 2, Vol. 7).

Ezekiel 37: *An Exact Exposition of the Orthodox Faith,* 4, 27 (*NPNF* Series 2, Vol. 9).

Genesis 1: Robert Southwell, *A Hundred Meditations on the Love of God* (London: Burns & Oates, 1873), 1–2.

Genesis 1–2: *CR* 1 (Year 2), 153.

Genesis 3: *Oration 45, Second Oration on Easter,* 8; (*NPNF* Series 2, Vol. 7).

Genesis 4: *Catechetical Lectures,* 2, 6–7 (*NPNF* Series 2, Vol. 7).

Genesis 19: St. Francis de Sales, *Introduction to the Devout Life;* tr. John K. Ryan (New York: Doubleday, 1989), 50–51.

Genesis 28: St. Francis de Sales, *Introduction to the Devout Life;* tr. John K. Ryan (New York: Doubleday, 1989), 42–43.

Genesis 45: *RB,* 2, 276–77.

Hosea 14: Juliana of Norwich, *Revelations of Divine Love* (Garden City, New York: Doubleday Image, 1977), 143–44.

Isaiah 1: *The First Epistle of Clement to the Corinthians,* 7–8 (*ANF,* vol. 1).

Isaiah 5: Robert Southwell, *A Hundred Meditations on the Love of God* (London: Burns & Oates, 1873), 5–8.

Isaiah 42: *RB,* 1, 257–58.

Isaiah 49: St. John Eudes, *Selections from His Writings* (London: Burns, Oates & Washbourne, 1925), 41–42.

Isaiah 53: *Catechetical Lectures,* 13, 3 (*NPNF* Series 2, Vol. 7).

Isaiah 60: *RB,* 1, 334–35.

Jeremiah 4: *OR,* 362–64.

Jeremiah 8: Saint Bernardine of Siena, *Sermons* (Siena: Tipografia Sociale, 1920), 236–37.

Jeremiah 10: *The First Apology of Justin,* 9–10 (*ANF,* vol. 1).

Jeremiah 16: *The Confession of St. Patrick and Letter to Coroticus;* tr. John Skinner (New York: Doubleday, 1998), 57–59.

Jeremiah 17: *Sermon 5 "de diversisis"; CR* 1 (Year 2), 139.

Jeremiah 31: *Dialogue of Justin,* 11 (*ANF,* vol. 1).

Jeremiah 33: *On the Incarnation of the Word,* 43 (*NPNF* Series 2, Vol. 4).

Job 1: *CR* 1 (Year 2), 171.

Job 7: St. Bernard of Clairvaux, *On Loving God,* 5, 14; *Treatises II;* tr. Robert Walton, O.S.B. (Kalamazoo, Michigan: Cistercian Publications, 1980), 127–28.

Job 12: *CR* 2 (Year 2), 19.

Job 21: *The Principal Works of St. Ambrose (NPNF* Series 2, Vol. 10).

Joel 2: Treatise 9: *On the Advantage of Patience,* 4–5 (*ANF,* vol. 5).

Jonah 3: St. Anthony Mary Claret, *Autobiography;* ed. José Marian Viñas, C.M.F. (Chicago: Claretian Publications, 1976), 77–78.

Joshua 2: *Epistle to the Corinthians,* 12–13; *CR* 4 (Year 1), 129.

Joshua 3: *Treatise on Baptism; CR* 4 (Year 1), 125.

Judges 3: *The Conferences of John Cassian,* 3, 4 (*NPNF* Series 2, Vol. 11).

1 Kings 17: Kathleen O'Meara (Grace Ramsay), *Frederic Ozanam* (New York: Catholic School Book Company, n.d.), 176–77.

1 Kings 18: *An Exact Exposition of the Orthodox Faith,* 4, 9 (*NPNF* Series 2, Vol. 9).

1 Kings 21: *RB,* 3, 318–19.

2 Kings 6: *The Book Concerning the Mysteries,* 9, 50–52, 54 (*NPNF* Series 2, Vol. 10).

Lamentations 3: Lady Amabel Kerr, *The Life of Blessed Sebastian Valfré* (London: Catholic Truth Society, 1896), 141–43.

Leviticus 16: Edith Stein, *The Hidden Life* (Washington, D. C.: ICS Publications, 1992), 12.

Leviticus 26: St. Augustine, *The City of God;* ed. Vernon J. Bourke (New York: Doubleday Image, 1958), 540–41.

2 Maccabees 7: *RB,* 4, 278–79.

Malachi 1: *Irenaeus Against Heresies,* 4, 17, 5 (*ANF,* Vol. 1).

Malachi 3: *Catechetical Lectures,* 15, 1–3 (*NPNF* Series 2, Vol. 7).

Micah 6: "Conferences of Vincent de Paul to the Congregation of the Mission," *Vincent de Paul and Louise de Marillax. CWS* (1995), 138–39.

Micah 7: *Treatise on Penance; CR* 4 (Year 1), 201.

Numbers 20: *An Exact Exposition of the Orthodox Faith,* 4, 11 (*NPNF* Series 2, Vol. 9).

Numbers 24: *On the Incarnation of the Word,* 33 (*NPNF* Series 2, Vol. 4).

Proverbs 4: *Oration 39, On the Holy Lights,* 8–10 (*NPNF* Series 2, Vol. 7).

Proverbs 6: Dominic Devas, O.F.M., *Life of St. Leonard of Port-Maurice, O.F.M.* (London: Burns, Oates & Warhbourne, 1920).

Proverbs 8: *The Life of Teresa of Jesus;* tr. E. Allison Peers (New York: Doubleday, 1991), 153.

Proverbs 16: St. Bernard of Clairvaux, *On Loving God,* 5, 14; *Treatises II;* tr. Robert Walton, O.S.B. (Kalamazoo, Michigan: Cistercian Publications, 1980), 120–21.

Psalm 19: Robert Southwell, *A Hundred Meditations on the Love of God* (London: Burns & Oates, 1873), 3–4.

Psalm 22: *Selected Letters of Saint Jane Frances de Chantal;* tr. The Sisters of the Visitation (London: R. & T. Washbourne, Ltd., 1918), 9–10.

Psalm 50: *The Autobiography of Saint Thérèse of Lisieux;* tr. John Beevers (New York: Doubleday, 1989), 150–51.

Psalm 51: St. Francis de Sales, *Introduction to the Devout Life;* tr. John K. Ryan (New York: Doubleday, 1989), 48–49.

Psalm 63: *The Book of the Visions of Blessed Angela of Foligno* (Leamington: Art and Book Co., 1888), 204–6.

Psalm 72: *Sermons,* Part 1: Advent; *The Works of Saint Thomas of Villanova; The Augustinian Series,* Vol. 20 (Villanova, Pennsylvania: Augustinian Press, 1994), 56–57.

Psalm 80: *CR* 3 (Year 1), 59.

Psalm 84: *Some Counsels of S. Vincent de Paul;* tr. E. K. Sanders (St. Louis, Missouri: B. Herder, 1914), 56–57.

Psalm 103: *RB,* 2, 482–83.

Psalm 116: St. Bernard of Clairvaux, *On Loving God,* 5, 14; *Treatises II;* tr. Robert Walton, O.S.B. (Kalamazoo, Michigan: Cistercian Publications, 1980), 107–8.

Psalm 118: *The Sayings of the Desert Fathers: The Alphabetical Collection;* tr. Benedicta Ward, S.L.G. (Kalamazoo, Michigan: Cistercian Publications, 1975), 194.

Psalm 139: *Elizabeth Ann Seton: A Woman of Prayer;* ed. Sister Mary Celeste, S.C. (New York: Alba House, 1993), 69–70.

Ruth 2: Aelred of Rievaulx, *Spiritual Friendship;* tr. Mary Eugenia Laker, SSND (Kalamazoo, Michigan: Cistercian Publications, 1977), 118–19.

Ruth 3: St. Francis de Sales, *Introduction to the Devout Life;* tr. John K. Ryan (New York: Doubleday, 1989), 126–27.

1 Samuel 3: *Parochial and Plain Sermons,* vol. 8; *CR* 4 (Year 1), 163.

1 Samuel 17: *OR,* 812–13.

1 Samuel 26: *Against Adimantus,* 17; *CR* 4 (Year 1), 191.

2 Samuel 7: *The Confession of St. Patrick and Letter to Coroticus;* tr. John Skinner (New York: Doubleday, 1998), 53–54.

2 Samuel 12: *Treatise in Defense of the Prophet David; CR* 4 (Year 1), 207.

The Song of Songs 1: *The Autobiography of Saint Thérèse of Lisieux;* tr. John Beevers (New York: Doubleday, 1989), 147–48.

The Song of Songs 3: *The Life and Revelations of St. Gertrude* (London: Burns, Lambert & Oates, 1865), 149–51.

Tobit 12: (*ANF,* vol. 5).

Wisdom 3: St. Augustine, *The City of God;* ed. Vernon J. Bourke (New York: Doubleday Image, 1958), 484–86.

Wisdom 7: *CR* 2 (Year 2), 173.

Wisdom 11: *Sermons for All the Sundays in the Year* by St. Alphonsus Liguori (Dublin: James Duffy, Sons & Co., 1874) 238–39.

Wisdom 13: *On the Trinity,* 1 (*NPNF* Series 2, Vol. 9).

Zechariah 12: Bonaventure, *The Tree of Life; CR* 4 (Year 1), 109.

THE NEW TESTAMENT

Acts 2: Homily 7; *Homilies on the Acts of the Apostles* (*NPNF* Vol. 11).

Acts 6: *RB,* 2282–83.

Acts 10: Homily 22; *Homilies on the Acts of the Apostles* (*NPNF* Vol. 11).

Acts 17: St. Francis de Sales, *Introduction to the Devout Life;* tr. John K. Ryan (New York: Doubleday, 1989), 84–85.

Colossians 2: *The Book of Saint Basil on the Spirit,* 15, 35 (*NPNF* Series 2, Vol. 8).

Colossians 3: *CR* 1, (Year 2), 153.

1 Corinthians 2: *Book of the Three Habitations;* Toal (Vol. 1), 44–45.

1 Corinthians 10: *RB,* 3, 240.

1 Corinthians 11: *RB* 3, 230–31.

1 Corinthians 13: Toal (Vol. 3), 234.

1 Corinthians 15: St. Athanasius, *Life of St. Anthony* in *The Paradise or Garden of the Holy Fathers* (Seattle, Washington: Saint Nectarios Press, 1978).

2 Corinthians 5: *The Writings of the Fathers Down to a. d. 325* (*ANF,* vol. 5).

2 Corinthians 5:11: *Sermon given at the Basilica of S. S. Marcellinus and Peter;* Toal (Vol. 1), 48–49.

2 Corinthians 11: *The Jesuit Relations and Allied Documents: Travels and Explorations of the Jesuit Missionaries in New France, 1610–1791,* Vol. 10; ed. Reuben Gold Thwaites (Cleveland, Ohio: The Burrows Brothers, 1897).

2 Corinthians 12: *The Book of Divine Consolation of the Blessed Angela of Foligno,* Treatise 2, 1; tr. Mary G. Steegmann (New York: Duffield & Co., 1909), 24–25.

Ephesians 2: *The Life and Revelations of St. Gertrude* (London: Burns, Lambert & Oates, 1865), 71–72.

Ephesians 4: *The Book of Saint Basil on the Spirit,* 9, 23 (*NPNF* Series 2, Vol. 8).

Ephesians 5: George Metlake, *The Life and Writings of Saint Columban* (Philadelphia: The Dolphin Press, 1914).

Ephesians 6: *Sermon on Patience, the Second Coming and the Last Judgment,* Toal (Vol. 1), 10–11.

Galatians 2: St. Jane de Chantal, *Her Exhortations, Conferences and Instructions* in *Love Jesus!,* ed. Louise Perrotta (Ijamsville, Maryland: The Word Among Us, 2000), 133–34.

Galatians 5: *Selected Letters of Saint Jane Frances de Chantal;* tr. The Sisters of the Visitation (London: R. & T. Washbourne, Ltd., 1918), 27–28.

Hebrews 12: Julian of Norwich, *Revelation of Love;* tr. John Skinner (New York: Doubleday Image, 1997), 167–68.

James 1: *Dorotheos of Gaza: Discourses and Sayings;* ed. Eric P. Wheeler (Kalamazoo, Michigan: Cistercian Publications, 1977).

1 John 4: Francesca Maria Steele, *The Life and Visions of St. Hildegard* (St. Louis, Missouri: B. Herder, 1915), 156–59.

John 1: From *Born to New Life—Cyprian of Carthage;* tr. Tim Witherow; ed. Oliver Davies (London: New City Press, 1991; New Rochelle, New York: New City Press, 1992).

John 2: Toal (Vol. 1), 275–78.

John 3: Saint Jane Frances Frémyot de Chantal, Conference 30, "On the Excellence of Prayer," *Her Exhortations, Conferences, Instructions and Retreat* (Clifton: E. Austin & Sons, 1888), 206–7.

John 4: *The Book of Saint Basil on the Spirit,* 9, 22 (*NPNF* Series 2, Vol. 8).

John 6: *RB,* 3, 227.

John 10: *Flowers of the Passion: Thoughts of St. Paul of the Cross;* tr. Ella A Mulligan (New York: Benziger Brothers, 1893), 7–8.

John 13: St. Jane de Chantal, *Her Exhortations, Conferences and Instructions* in *Love Jesus!,* ed. Louise Perrotta (Ijamsville, Maryland: The Word Among Us, 2000), 120–21.

John 14: *Saint Catherine of Siena as Seen in Her Letters;* tr. Vida D. Scudder (London: J. M. Dent & Co., 1905), 218 and 221.

John 14:14: Teresa of Avila, *The Way of Perfection,* 26: tr. E. Allison Peers (New York: Doubleday Image, 1964 and 1991), 172–73.

John 15: *The Sermons of St. Francis de Sales for Lent,* vol. 3; tr. Nuns of the Visitation; ed. Lewis S. Fiorelli, O.S.F.S. (Rockford, Ill.: Tan Books and Publishers, 1987), 93–94.

John 17: Edith Stein, *The Hidden Life* (Washington, D. C.: ICS Publications, 1992), 12–13.

John 19:1: John B. de La Salle, *Meditations for Sundays and Festivals* (West Chester, New York: The New York Catholic Protectory, 1882) I, 120–22.

John 19:31: Julian of Norwich, *Revelation of Love;* tr. John Skinner (New York: Doubleday Image, 1997), 50–51.

John 21: Saint Bernardine of Siena, *Sermons* (Siena: Tipografia Sociale, 1920), 238–39.

Luke 1: George O'Neill, S. J., *Blessed Mary of the Angels* (London: R. & T. Washbourne, Ltd., 1901).

Luke 2: First Sermon for Christmas Day, *St. Bernard's Sermons* (Dublin: Browne and Nolan, Ltd., 1921), 383–84.

Luke 2:41: *Jesus Twelve Years Old;* Toal (Vol. 1), 252–53.

Luke 5: *RB,* 2, 510–11.

Luke 6: *RB,* 3, 218.

Luke 7: *RB,* 4, 328.

Luke 8: Toal (Vol. 1), 397–99.

Luke 9: John B. de La Salle, *Meditations for Sundays and Festivals* (West Chester, New York: The New York Catholic Protectory, 1882) I, 88–89.

Luke 11:1: Teresa of Avila, *The Way of Perfection,* 34: tr. E. Allison Peers (New York: Doubleday Image, 1964 and 1991), 222–24.

Luke 11:33: Saint Jane Frances Frémyot de Chantal, Conference 30, "On the Excellence of Prayer," *Her Exhortations, Conferences, Instructions and Retreat* (Clifton: E. Austin & Sons, 1888), 205–6.

Luke 19: Evelyn Underhill, *Ruysbroeck* (London: G. Bell and Sons, Ltd.), 111–13.

Luke 21: *Sermon on Patience, the Second Coming and the Last Judgment,* Toal (Vol. 1), 11–13.

Luke 22: Edith Stein, *The Hidden Life* (Washington, D. C.: ICS Publications, 1992), 11.

Luke 23: *Catechetical Lectures,* 13, 30–31 (*NPNF* Series 2, Vol. 7).

Mark 2: Antonio Isoleri, *St. Mary Magdalen dei Pazzi* (Philadelphia: H. McGrath, 1884), 67–68.

Mark 3, *RB,* 3, 276–77.

Mark 4: Toal (Vol. 1), 325–27.

Mark 7:14 *The Twelve Books on the Institutes of the Coenobia* 9 (*NPNF* Series 2, Vol. 11).

Mark 7:31: *RB,* 4, 323–24.

Mark 9: Antonio Isoleri, *St. Mary Magdalen dei Pazzi* (Philadelphia: H. McGrath, 1884), 64–65.

Mark 10: Albert S. Foley, S.J., *A Modern Galahad: St. John Berchmans* (Milwaukee, Wisconsin: The Bruce Publishing Company, 1937), 65.

Mark 11: *RB,* 2, 352–53.

Mark 12: *RB,* 4, 336–37.

Mark 14:22: *RB,* 2, 1033.

Mark 14:32: *The Book of Divine Consolation of the Blessed Angela of Foligno,* 21; tr. Mary G. Steegmann (New York: Duffield & Co., 1909), 101–3.

Mark 15: Julian of Norwich, *Revelation of Love;* tr. John Skinner (New York: Doubleday Image, 1997), 28–29.

Mark 16: John B. de La Salle, *Meditations for Sundays and Festivals* (West Chester, New York: The New York Catholic Protectory, 1882) 1, 127–29.

Matthew 4: *RB,* 4, 302–3.

Matthew 6: Saint Jane Frances Frémyot de Chantal, Conference 30, "On the Excellence of Prayer," *Her Exhortations, Conferences, Instructions and Retreat* (Clifton: E. Austin & Sons, 1888), 205.

Matthew 7: Saint Jane Frances Frémyot de Chantal, Instruction 20, *Her Exhortations, Conferences, Instructions and Retreat* (Clifton: E. Austin & Sons, 1888), 410.

Matthew 8: Toal (Vol. 1), 303–4.

Matthew 9: *RB,* 4, 331–32.

Mattthew 11: *The Book of Divine Consolation of the Blessed Angela of Foligno,* 24; tr. Mary G. Steegmann (New York: Duffield & Co., 1909), 108–11.

Matthew 12: *The Book of Saint Basil on the Spirit,* 9, 39 (*NPNF* Series 2, Vol. 8).

Matthew 13: Toal (Vol. 1), 339–40.

Matthew 16: Sr. Consuela Marie Duffy, S.B.S., *Katharine Drexel: A Biography* (Cornwells Heights, Pennsylvania: Sisters of the Blessed Sacrament, 1966), 121–22.

Matthew 17: *The Mirror of Perfection;* tr. Constance, Countess de la Warr (London: Burns & Oates, 1902), 144–45.

Matthew 18: *RB,* 334–35.

Matthew 19: Sr. Consuela Marie Duffy, S.B.S., *Katharine Drexel: A Biography* (Cornwells Heights, Pennsylvania: Sisters of the Blessed Sacrament, 1966), 125–26.

Matthew 22: *The Diary of Sr. Faustina Kowalska: Divine Mercy in My Soul (Diary,* 1632). (Stockbridge, Massachusetts: Congregation of Marians of the Immaculate Conception, 1987).

Matthew 25: *Sermon on Patience, the Second Coming and the Last Judgment,* Toal (Vol. 1), 13.

Matthew 26: *An Exact Exposition of the Orthodox Faith,* 4, 13 (*NPNF* Series 2, Vol. 9).

Matthew 27: Julian of Norwich, *Revelation of Love;* tr. John Skinner (New York: Doubleday Image, 1997), 30–31.

Matthew 28: *RB,* 3, 215–16.

1 Peter 1: *Crumbs of Comfort from the Dialogue of Comfort Under Tribulation by Blessed Thomas More;* ed. Henry Sebastian Bowden (London: Burns & Oates, 1915) 67–69.

1 Peter 2: *Life and Select Writings of Louis-Marie Grignon de Montfort* (London: Thomas Richardson and Son, 1870).

1 Peter 3: Thomas More, "A Prayer Facing Death: From the Tower of London," cited in Benedict Groeschel CFR, *The Journey Toward God* (Ann Arbor, Michigan: Servant Publications, 2000), 86–87.

2 Peter 1: *RB* 3, 230.

Philippians 1: *The Last Letters of Blessed Thomas More,* 13; ed. W. E. Campbell (London: The Manresa Press, 1924), 97–98.

Philippians 2: *The Letters and Sermons of Leo the Great;* (*NPNF* Series 2, Vol. 12).

Philippians 3: Albert the Great, *On Union With God,* 7 (Flelinfach: Llanerch Publishers, 1915).

Revelation 3: John of Ruysbroeck, *The Adornment of the Spiritual Marriage;* tr. C. A. Wynschenk (London: John M. Watkins, 1951), 17–19.

Revelation 19: *The Diary of Sr. Faustina Kowalska: Divine Mercy in My Soul (Diary,* 1304). Stockbridge, Massachusetts: Congregation of Marians of the Immaculate Conception, 1987.

Romans 6: *Select Writings and Letters of Gregory, Bishop of Nyssa* (*NPNF* Vol. 5).

Romans 8: *Dorotheos of Gaza: Discourses and Sayings;* ed. Eric P. Wheeler (Kalamazoo, Michigan: Cistercian Publications, 1977).

Romans 12:1 *The Dialogues of St. Gregory the Great;* tr. Henry James Coleridge (London: Burns & Oates, 1874), 305.

Romans 12:3 *The Diary of Sr. Faustina Kowalska: Divine Mercy in My Soul (Diary,* 163). Stockbridge, Massachusetts: Congregation of Marians of the Immaculate Conception, 1987.

Romans 13: *The Dialogue of the Seraphic Virgin Catherine of Siena;* tr. Algar Thorold (London: Kegan, Paul, Trench, Truebner & Co., 1907), 39–40.

Romans 14: "On Eight Questions," in *Bede: A Biblical Miscellany;* tr. W. Trent Foley and Arthur G. Holder (Liverpool: Liverpool University Press, 1999), 154–55.

1 Thessalonians 5: Sr. M. Monica, *Angela Merici and Her Teaching Idea* (New York: Longmans, Green & Co., 1927).

1 Timothy 2: Edith Stein, *The Hidden Life* (Washington, D. C.: ICS Publications, 1992), 7.

2 Timothy 2: Lucy Menzies, *Mirrors of the Holy* (London: A. R. Mowbray & Co., 1928).

Copyright Acknowledgments

The editor and the publisher are grateful to the publishers and individuals listed below for permission to reprint excerpts from books for which they hold the copyright. If we failed to obtain permission for an excerpt where it was required, we regret the oversight and will gladly secure the necessary permission for future printings.

Alba House: *Elizabeth Ann Seton: A Woman of Prayer;* edited by Sister Mary Celeste, S.C. (New York, 1993), 69–70.

Augustinian Press: *Sermons,* Part 1: Advent; *The Works of Saint Thomas of Villanova; The Augustinian Series,* Vol. 20 (Villanova, Pennsylvania, 1994), 56–57.

Ave Maria Press: S[ister] M[ary] C[atherine], *Angel of the Judgment: A Life of Vincent Ferrer.* Copyright © 1954 by Ave Maria Press, Notre Dame, Indiana 46556. Used with permission of the publisher.

Catholic Book Publishing Company: Christian Readings, Vols. 1–4. New York, 1972.

The Catholic University of America Press: St. Augustine, *The City of God; The Fathers of the Church,* (Washington, D.C.), Vol. 14, 380–81; Vol. 24, 251–53; 505–6. Used by permission of the publisher. [Excerpted from St. Augustine, *The City of God;* ed. Vernon J. Bourke (New York: Doubleday Image, 1958), 308–9; 484–86; 540–41.]

Cistercian Publications: *The Sayings of the Desert Fathers: The Alphabetical Collection;* tr. Benedicta Ward, S.L.G., 194. Copyright © 1975 by Cistercian Publications, Kalamazoo, Michigan. Aelred of Rievaulx, *Spiritual Friendship;* tr. Mary Eugenia Laker, S.S.N.D., 118–19. Copyright © 1977 by Cistercian Publications, Kalamazoo, Michigan. *Dorotheos of Gaza: Discourses and Sayings;* ed. Eric P. Wheeler, O.S.B. Copyright © 1977 by Cistercian Publications, Kalamazoo, Michigan; St. Bernard of Clairvaux, *On Loving God,* V, 14; *Treatises II;* tr. Robert Walton, O.S.B., 127–28. Copyright © 1980 by Cistercian Publications, Kalamazoo, Michigan. Used by permission of the publisher.

Claretian Publications: St. Anthony Mary Claret, *Autobiography;* ed. José Marian Viñas, C.M.F. (Chicago, 1976), 77–78. Reprinted with permission of Claretian Publications, www.claretianpubs.com; 800-328-6515.

Congregation of Marians of the Immaculate Conception: *The Diary of Sr. Faustina Kowalska: Divine Mercy in My Soul* (Stockbridge, Massachusetts, © 1987), *Diary,* 163, 1304, and 1632.

The Franciscan Institute: *The Legend and Writings of Saint Clare of Assisi* (St. Bonaventure, New York, 1953), 97–98.

The Franciscan Press, Quincy University: St. Bonaventure, *Breviloquium, Works of Bonaventure,* Vol. II, and *Collations on the Six Days, Works of Bonaventure,* Vol. V, both originally published at Paterson, New Jersey, by St. Anthony Guild Press. Excerpted from *Christian Readings* (New York: Catholic Book Publishing Company, 1972), Vol. 1, 217, and Vol. 2, 173.

Hodder & Stoughton Publishers: *The Hodder Book of Christian Prayers;* ed. Tony Castle (London: Hodder and Stoughton, 1986), 36 and 40–41.

Holy Cross Orthodox Press: St. *Irenaios' The Preaching of the Apostles* (Brookline, Massachusetts), 26–27.

International Comission on English in the Liturgy: Excerpts from the English translation of the nonbiblical readings from the Office of Readings from *The Liturgy of the Hours.* Copyright © 1974, International Committee on English in the Liturgy, Inc. All rights reserved. Quoted from *The Office of Readings According to the Roman Rite* (Boston: Daughters of St. Paul, 1983), 362–64 and 812–13.